| DATE | | | |
|---|---|---|---|
| | | | |
| | | | |
| | | | |
| | | | |
| | | | |
| | | | |
| | | | |
| | | | |
| | | | |
| | | | |
| | | | |
| | | | |

© THE BAKER & TAYLOR CO.

# CHEERS FOR THE COMPLETE BOOK OF THE OLYMPICS

1992 Edition

# THE COMPLETE BOOK OF THE OLYMPICS

## DAVID WALLECHINSKY

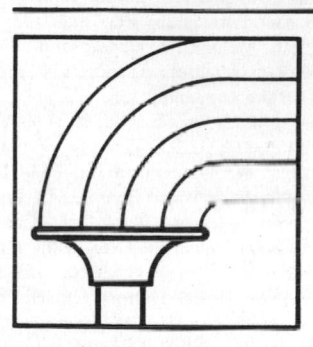

Little, Brown and Company

Boston   Toronto   London

# TO ELIJAH AND AARON

*First Edition*

HC: 10  9  8  7  6  5  4  3  2  1

PB: 10  9  8  7  6  5  4  3  2  1

FG

Published simultaneously in Canada
by Little, Brown & Company (Canada) Limited

*Printed in the United States of America*

*Library of Congress Cataloging-in-Publication Data*

Wallechinsky, David, 1948-
    The complete book of the Olympics / by David Wallechinsky.
—1992 ed.
        p.    cm.
    ISBN 0-316-92054-1 (hc)
    ISBN 0-316-92053-3 (pb)
    1. Olympics—History.  2. Olympics—Records.  I. Title.
GV721.5.W25  1992
796.48 — dc20                                                        91-13275

# PHOTO CREDITS

Photo Number 1, U.S.O.C.; 3, U.S.O.C.; 4, Popperfoto; 6, U.S.O.C.; 7, Brown Brothers; 8, U.S.O.C.; 9, Popperfoto; 10, Reportagebild; 11, AP; 12, Inter-Sport Publications; 13, Swiss Timing; 14, U.S.O.C.; 15, U.S.O.C.; 16, Pressebild-Agentur Schirner; 17, U.S.O.C.; 19, U.S.O.C.; 20, *Herald and Weekly Times,* Ltd., Melbourne picture; 21, AP; 22, AP; 23, Popperfoto; 24, U.S.O.C.; 25, U.S.O.C.; 26, U.S.O.C.; 27, Popperfoto; 29, U.S.O.C.; 31, UPI; 33, Missouri Historical Society; 34, Missouri Historical Society; 35, Missouri Historical Society; 37, U.S.O.C.; 39, Mark Shearman; 41, UPI; 43, U.S.O.C.; 44, U.S.O.C.; 45, Popperfoto; 46, Pelham Books; 47, Popperfoto; 48, Reportagebild; 49, Reportagebild; 50, Pressen Bild; 51, Pressen Bild; 52, Pressen Bild; 53, U.S.O.C.; 54, U.S.O.C.; 55, J. Fairfax & Sons, Ltd.; 56, AP/Wide World Photos; 59, Pelham Books; 60, Toni Nett; 61, Toni Nett; 62, Toni Nett; 63, Toni Nett; 64, U.S.O.C.; 65, Reportagebild; 66, University of Michigan Archives; 68, UPI; 69, U.S.O.C.; 70, Courtesy of Erich Kamper; 71, Progress Publishers, Moscow; 72, U.S.O.C.; 73, U.S.O.C.; 77, U.S.O.C.; 78, U.S.O.C.; 79, Courtesy of Bob Mathias; 81, Pressebild-Agentur Schirner; 82, Pressen Bild; 83, Pressen Bild; 85, U.S.O.C.; 89, U.S.O.C.; 90, U.S.O.C.; 92, Pressen Bild; 93, AP/Wide World Photos; 94, Rich Clarkson/*Sports Illustrated* © Time Inc.,; 95, Rich Clarkson/*Sports Illustrated* © Time Inc.; 96, Szwarc Photo-Sport; 97, Rich Clarkson/*Sports Illustrated* © Time Inc.; 98, Paul Chinn/*L.A. Herald Examiner;* 99, © Andrew Kent 85; 101, Canada's Sports Hall of Fame; 102, U.S.O.C.; 103, Lia Manoliu; 104, U.S.O.C.; 105, U.S.O.C.; 106, Frederick Fliegner, Publ.; 107, U.S.O.C.; 108, U.S.O.C.; 110, U.S.O.C.; 111, Olympische Sports Bibliotek; 112, U.S.O.C.; 113, AP; 114, AP/Wide World Photos; 115, U.S.O.C.; 117, Hungarian Olympic Committee; 118, David Wallechinsky; 120, AP; 121, U.S.O.C.; 122, U.S.O.C.; 123, Gerry Cranham of Sporting Colour Library; 124, VMS Publications; 125, Michael Porte; 126, Reportagebild; 128, Erik Betting/Pressehusel; 130, Melbourne *Herald and Weekly Times;* 132, Popperfoto; 133, Novosti Press Agency; 134, Proteus Books, Ltd.; 135, © Photo Kishimoto, Japan; 136, U.S.O.C.; 138, Canada's Sports Hall of Fame; 140, The Academy of Motion Picture Arts and Sciences; 142, UPI; 143, U.S.O.C.; 144, Fizkultura Isdalesvo, Moscow; 145, Hungarian Olympic Committee; 146, Con Keyes/© *Los Angeles Times;* 147, Wide World Photos; 148, Pressen Bild; 149, Reprinted by permission of Coward, McCann & Geoghegan, Inc., from *The Miracle Machine,* by Doug Gilbert, copyright © 1980 by P.L.T. Consultants, Ltd.; 150, U.S.O.C.; 152, Mike Gosman; 153, AP/Wide World Photos; 155, Hulton-Deutsch Collection; 156, from the David Webster Collection; 157, Xinhua Photo; 158, David Woo/*Dallas Morning News;* 160, U.S.O.C.; 162, from the David Webster Collection; 163, Progress Publishers; 164, Frederick Fliegner; 167, NYT Pictures; 168, Wide World Photos; 170, Athanassios Tarassouleas; 174, U.S.O.C.; 175, Barton Silverman/*The New York Times;* 177, City of Calgary Archives; 178, Klaus Schlage; 179, U.S.O.C.; 180, Pressen Bild; 181, U.S.O.C.; 184, U.S.O.C.; 186, ADN; 187, AP; 188, Frederick Fliegner; 190, Sportverlag Berlin; 191, Sportverlag Berlin; 193, U.S.O.C.; 196, U.S.O.C.; 197, U.S.O.C.; 198, U.S.O.C.; 199, Keystone Press Agency; 200, U.S.O.C.; 202, U.S.O.C.; 203, Bill Hickey, reprinted with permission from the book *The Rings of Destiny,* © 1968, published by David McKay Co. Inc.; 205, Pressen Bild; 207, U.S.O.C.; 208, Pressebild-Agentur Schirner; 209, Pressen Bild.

# CONTENTS

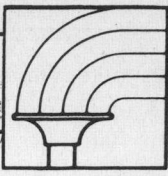

# SUMMER GAMES

# WINTER GAMES

*Photographs follow pages 143, 399, 521, and 669.*

# THE OLYMPIC GAMES

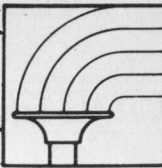

## SUMMER

| | | | | COMPETITORS | | NATIONS |
| | | | | Men | Women | REPRESENTED |
|---|---|---|---|---|---|---|
| I | 1896 | ATHENS, GREECE | April 6–15 | 311 | 0 | 13 |
| II | 1900 | PARIS, FRANCE | May 20–October 28 | 1319 | 11 | 22 |
| III | 1904 | ST. LOUIS, U.S.A. | July 1–November 23 | 681 | 6 | 12 |
| — | 1906 | ATHENS, GREECE | April 22–May 2 | 877 | 7 | 20 |
| IV | 1908 | LONDON, GREAT BRITAIN | April 27–October 31 | 1999 | 36 | 23 |
| V | 1912 | STOCKHOLM, SWEDEN | May 5–July 22 | 2490 | 57 | 28 |
| VI | 1916 | BERLIN, GERMANY | Cancelled because of war | — | — | — |
| VII | 1920 | ANTWERP, BELGIUM | April 20–September 12 | 2543 | 64 | 29 |
| VIII | 1924 | PARIS, FRANCE | May 4–July 27 | 2956 | 136 | 44 |
| IX | 1928 | AMSTERDAM, HOLLAND | May17–August 12 | 2724 | 290 | 46 |
| X | 1932 | LOS ANGELES, U.S.A. | July 30–August 14 | 1281 | 127 | 37 |
| XI | 1936 | BERLIN, GERMANY | August 1–16 | 3738 | 328 | 49 |
| XII | 1940 | TOKYO, JAPAN; HELSINKI, FINLAND | Cancelled because of war | — | — | — |
| XIII | 1944 | LONDON, GREAT BRITAIN | Cancelled because of war | — | — | — |
| XIV | 1948 | LONDON, GREAT BRITAIN | July 29–August 14 | 3714 | 385 | 59 |
| XV | 1952 | HELSINKI, FINLAND | July 19–August 3 | 4407 | 518 | 69 |
| XVI | 1956 | MELBOURNE, AUSTRALIA* | November 22–December 8 | 2958 | 384 | 67 |
| XVII | 1960 | ROME, ITALY | August 25–September 11 | 4738 | 610 | 83 |
| XVIII | 1964 | TOKYO, JAPAN | October 10–24 | 4457 | 683 | 93 |
| XIX | 1968 | MEXICO CITY, MEXICO | October 12–27 | 4750 | 781 | 112 |
| XX | 1972 | MUNICH, GERMANY | August 26–September 10 | 5848 | 1299 | 122 |
| XXI | 1976 | MONTREAL, CANADA | July 17–August 1 | 4834 | 1251 | 92† |
| XXII | 1980 | MOSCOW, U.S.S.R. | July 19–August 3 | 4265 | 1088 | 81 |
| XXIII | 1984 | LOS ANGELES, U.S.A. | July 28–August 12 | 5458 | 1620 | 141 |
| XXIV | 1988 | SEOUL, SOUTH KOREA | September 17–October 2 | 6983 | 2438 | 159‡ |
| XXV | 1992 | BARCELONA, SPAIN | July 25–August 9 | | | |
| XXVI | 1996 | ATLANTA, USA | July 20–August 4 | | | |

*The equestrian events were held in Stockholm, Sweden, June 10–17, 1956.
†Most sources list this figure as 88. Cameroon, Egypt, Morocco, and Tunisia all boycotted the 1976 Olympics; however, athletes from each of these countries had already competed before the boycott was officially announced.
‡Most sources list this figure as 160. However, the delegation from Brunei, which marched in the Opening Ceremonies, included one official, but no athletes.

# *WINTER*

| | | | | COMPETITORS | | NATIONS |
| | | | | Men | Women | REPRESENTED |
|---|---|---|---|---|---|---|
| I | 1924 | CHAMONIX, FRANCE | January 25–February 4 | 281 | 13 | 16 |
| II | 1928 | ST. MORITZ, SWITZERLAND | February 11–19 | 468 | 27 | 25 |
| III | 1932 | LAKE PLACID, U.S.A. | February 4–15 | 274 | 32 | 17 |
| IV | 1936 | GARMISCH-PARTENKIRCHEN, GERMANY | February 6–16 | 675 | 80 | 28 |
| — | 1940 | SAPPORO, JAPAN; ST. MORITZ, SWITZERLAND; GARMISCH-PARTENKIRCHEN, GERMANY | Cancelled because of war | — | — | — |
| — | 1944 | CORTINA D'AMPEZZO, ITALY | Cancelled because of war | — | — | — |
| V | 1948 | ST. MORITZ, SWITZERLAND | January 30–February 8 | 636 | 77 | 28 |
| VI | 1952 | OSLO, NORWAY | February 14–25 | 623 | 109 | 30 |
| VII | 1956 | CORTINA D'AMPEZZO, ITALY | January 26–February 5 | 686 | 132 | 32 |
| VIII | 1960 | SQUAW VALLEY, U.S.A. | February 18–28 | 521 | 144 | 30 |
| IX | 1964 | INNSBRUCK, AUSTRIA | January 29–February 9 | 986 | 200 | 36 |
| X | 1968 | GRENOBLE, FRANCE | February 6–18 | 1081 | 212 | 37 |
| XI | 1972 | SAPPORO, JAPAN | February 3–13 | 1015 | 217 | 35 |
| XII | 1976 | INNSBRUCK, AUSTRIA | February 4–15 | 900 | 228 | 37 |
| XIII | 1980 | LAKE PLACID, U.S.A. | February 14–23 | 833 | 234 | 37 |
| XIV | 1984 | SARAJEVO, YUGOSLAVIA | February 7–19 | 1002 | 276 | 49 |
| XV | 1988 | CALGARY, CANADA | February 13–28 | 1270 | 364 | 57 |
| XVI | 1992 | ALBERTVILLE, FRANCE | February 8–23 | | | |
| XVII | 1994 | LILLEHAMMER, NORWAY | February 12–27 | | | |
| XVIII | 1998 | NAGANO, JAPAN | | | | |

# NATIONAL MEDAL TOTALS IN EACH OLYMPICS

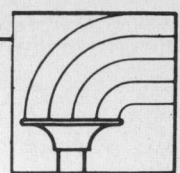

## SUMMER

### 1896 Athens

|     | G  | S  | B* |
|-----|----|----|----|
| USA | 11 | 6  | 2  |
| GRE | 10 | 19 | 18 |
| GER | 7  | 5  | 3  |
| FRA | 5  | 4  | 2  |
| GBR | 3  | 3  | 1  |
| HUN | 2  | 1  | 3  |
| AUT | 2  | 0  | 3  |
| AUS | 2  | 0  | 0  |
| DEN | 1  | 2  | 4  |
| SWI | 1  | 2  | 0  |

### 1900 Paris

|     | G  | S  | B  |
|-----|----|----|----|
| FRA | 29 | 41 | 32 |
| USA | 20 | 14 | 19 |
| GBR | 17 | 8  | 10 |
| BEL | 8  | 7  | 5  |
| SWI | 6  | 2  | 1  |
| AUS | 4  | 0  | 4  |
| GER | 3  | 2  | 2  |
| DEN | 2  | 3  | 2  |
| ITA | 2  | 2  | 0  |
| HUN | 1  | 3  | 2  |
| HOL | 1  | 1  | 3  |
| CUB | 1  | 1  | 0  |
| CAN | 1  | 0  | 1  |
| SWE | 1  | 0  | 1  |
| AUT | 0  | 3  | 3  |
| NOR | 0  | 2  | 3  |
| IND | 0  | 2  | 0  |
| BOH | 0  | 1  | 0  |
| SPA | 0  | 1  | 0  |

### 1904 St. Louis

|     | G  | S  | B  |
|-----|----|----|----|
| USA | 80 | 86 | 72 |
| GER | 5  | 4  | 6  |
| CUB | 5  | 3  | 3  |
| CAN | 4  | 1  | 1  |
| HUN | 2  | 1  | 1  |
| AUT | 1  | 1  | 1  |
| GRE | 1  | 0  | 1  |
| SWI | 1  | 0  | 1  |
| IRL | 1  | 0  | 0  |
| GBR | 0  | 1  | 1  |

### 1906 Athens

|     | G  | S  | B  |
|-----|----|----|----|
| FRA | 15 | 9  | 16 |
| USA | 12 | 6  | 5  |
| GRE | 8  | 13 | 13 |
| GBR | 8  | 11 | 6  |
| ITA | 7  | 6  | 3  |
| SWI | 5  | 4  | 2  |
| GER | 4  | 6  | 4  |
| NOR | 4  | 1  | 0  |
| AUT | 3  | 3  | 2  |
| SWE | 2  | 5  | 7  |
| HUN | 2  | 5  | 3  |
| BEL | 2  | 2  | 3  |
| DEN | 2  | 2  | 1  |
| FIN | 2  | 0  | 1  |
| CAN | 1  | 1  | 0  |
| HOL | 0  | 1  | 2  |
| AUS | 0  | 0  | 3  |
| CZE | 0  | 0  | 2  |
| SAF | 0  | 0  | 1  |

### 1908 London

|     | G  | S  | B  |
|-----|----|----|----|
| GBR | 56 | 50 | 39 |
| USA | 23 | 12 | 12 |
| SWE | 8  | 6  | 11 |
| FRA | 5  | 5  | 9  |
| GER | 3  | 5  | 5  |
| HUN | 3  | 4  | 2  |
| CAN | 3  | 3  | 10 |
| NOR | 2  | 3  | 3  |
| ITA | 2  | 2  | 0  |
| BEL | 1  | 5  | 2  |
| AUS | 1  | 2  | 2  |
| RUS | 1  | 2  | 0  |
| FIN | 1  | 1  | 3  |
| SAF | 1  | 1  | 0  |
| GRE | 0  | 3  | 1  |
| DEN | 0  | 2  | 3  |
| BOH | 0  | 0  | 2  |
| HOL | 0  | 0  | 2  |
| AUT | 0  | 0  | 1  |

### 1912 Stockholm

|     | G  | S  | B  |
|-----|----|----|----|
| SWE | 24 | 24 | 17 |
| USA | 23 | 19 | 19 |
| GBR | 10 | 15 | 16 |
| FIN | 9  | 8  | 9  |
| FRA | 7  | 4  | 3  |
| GER | 5  | 13 | 7  |
| SAF | 4  | 2  | 0  |
| NOR | 4  | 1  | 5  |
| CAN | 3  | 2  | 3  |
| HUN | 3  | 2  | 3  |
| ITA | 3  | 1  | 2  |
| AUS | 2  | 2  | 3  |
| BEL | 2  | 1  | 3  |
| DEN | 1  | 6  | 5  |

### 1920 Antwerp

|     | G  | S  | B  |
|-----|----|----|----|
| GRE | 1  | 0  | 1  |
| RUS | 0  | 2  | 3  |
| AUT | 0  | 2  | 2  |
| HOL | 0  | 0  | 3  |

### 1920 Antwerp

|     | G  | S  | B  |
|-----|----|----|----|
| USA | 41 | 27 | 28 |
| SWE | 19 | 20 | 24 |
| GBR | 15 | 15 | 13 |
| FIN | 15 | 10 | 9  |
| BEL | 14 | 11 | 10 |
| NOR | 13 | 7  | 8  |
| ITA | 13 | 5  | 5  |
| FRA | 9  | 19 | 13 |
| HOL | 4  | 2  | 5  |
| DEN | 3  | 9  | 1  |
| SAF | 3  | 4  | 3  |
| CAN | 3  | 3  | 3  |
| SWI | 2  | 2  | 7  |
| EST | 1  | 2  | 0  |
| BRA | 1  | 1  | 1  |
| AUS | 0  | 2  | 1  |
| JPN | 0  | 2  | 0  |
| SPA | 0  | 2  | 0  |
| GRE | 0  | 1  | 0  |
| LUX | 0  | 1  | 0  |
| CZE | 0  | 0  | 2  |
| NZE | 0  | 0  | 1  |

### 1924 Paris

|     | G  | S  | B  |
|-----|----|----|----|
| USA | 45 | 27 | 27 |
| FIN | 14 | 13 | 10 |
| FRA | 13 | 15 | 10 |
| GBR | 9  | 13 | 12 |
| ITA | 9  | 3  | 5  |
| SWI | 7  | 8  | 10 |

*G = gold, S = silver, B = bronze.

| | G | S | B |
|---|---|---|---|
| NOR | 5 | 2 | 3 |
| SWE | 4 | 13 | 12 |
| HOL | 4 | 1 | 5 |
| AUS | 3 | 1 | 2 |
| DEN | 2 | 5 | 2 |
| HUN | 2 | 3 | 4 |
| YUG | 2 | 0 | 0 |
| CZE | 1 | 4 | 5 |
| ARG | 1 | 3 | 2 |
| EST | 1 | 1 | 4 |
| SAF | 1 | 1 | 1 |
| URU | 1 | 0 | 0 |
| AUT | 0 | 3 | 1 |
| CAN | 0 | 3 | 1 |
| POL | 0 | 1 | 1 |
| HAI | 0 | 0 | 1 |
| JPN | 0 | 0 | 1 |
| NZE | 0 | 0 | 1 |
| POR | 0 | 0 | 1 |
| ROM | 0 | 0 | 1 |

## 1928 Amsterdam

| | G | S | B |
|---|---|---|---|
| USA | 22 | 18 | 16 |
| GER | 10 | 7 | 14 |
| FIN | 8 | 8 | 9 |
| SWE | 7 | 6 | 12 |
| ITA | 7 | 5 | 7 |
| SWI | 7 | 4 | 4 |
| FRA | 6 | 10 | 5 |
| HOL | 6 | 9 | 4 |
| HUN | 4 | 5 | 0 |
| CAN | 4 | 4 | 7 |
| GBR | 3 | 10 | 7 |
| ARG | 3 | 3 | 1 |
| DEN | 3 | 1 | 2 |
| CZE | 2 | 5 | 2 |
| JPN | 2 | 2 | 1 |
| EST | 2 | 1 | 2 |
| EGY | 2 | 1 | 1 |
| AUT | 2 | 0 | 1 |
| AUS | 1 | 2 | 1 |
| NOR | 1 | 2 | 1 |
| POL | 1 | 1 | 3 |
| YUG | 1 | 1 | 3 |
| SAF | 1 | 0 | 2 |
| IND | 1 | 0 | 0 |

| | G | S | B |
|---|---|---|---|
| IRL | 1 | 0 | 0 |
| NZE | 1 | 0 | 0 |
| SPA | 1 | 0 | 0 |
| URU | 1 | 0 | 0 |
| BEL | 0 | 1 | 2 |
| CHI | 0 | 1 | 0 |
| HAI | 0 | 1 | 0 |
| PHI | 0 | 0 | 1 |
| POR | 0 | 0 | 1 |

## 1932 Los Angeles

| | G | S | B |
|---|---|---|---|
| USA | 41 | 32 | 31 |
| ITA | 12 | 12 | 12 |
| FRA | 10 | 5 | 4 |
| SWE | 9 | 5 | 9 |
| JPN | 7 | 7 | 4 |
| HUN | 6 | 4 | 5 |
| FIN | 5 | 8 | 12 |
| GER | 4 | 12 | 5 |
| GBR | 4 | 7 | 5 |
| AUS | 3 | 1 | 1 |
| ARG | 3 | 1 | 0 |
| CAN | 2 | 5 | 8 |
| HOL | 2 | 5 | 0 |
| POL | 2 | 1 | 4 |
| SAF | 2 | 0 | 3 |
| IRL | 2 | 0 | 0 |
| CZE | 1 | 2 | 1 |
| AUT | 1 | 1 | 3 |
| IND | 1 | 0 | 0 |
| DEN | 0 | 3 | 3 |
| MEX | 0 | 2 | 0 |
| LAT | 0 | 1 | 0 |
| NZE | 0 | 1 | 0 |
| SWI | 0 | 1 | 0 |
| PHI | 0 | 0 | 3 |
| SPA | 0 | 0 | 1 |
| URU | 0 | 0 | 1 |

## 1936 Berlin

| | G | S | B |
|---|---|---|---|
| GER | 33 | 26 | 30 |
| USA | 24 | 20 | 12 |
| HUN | 10 | 1 | 5 |
| ITA | 8 | 9 | 5 |
| FIN | 7 | 6 | 6 |

| | | | |
|---|---|---|---|
| FRA | 7 | 6 | 6 |
| SWE | 6 | 5 | 9 |
| HOL | 6 | 4 | 7 |
| JPN | 5 | 4 | 7 |
| GBR | 4 | 7 | 3 |
| AUT | 4 | 6 | 3 |
| CZE | 3 | 5 | 0 |
| ARG | 2 | 2 | 3 |
| EST | 2 | 2 | 3 |
| EGY | 2 | 1 | 2 |
| SWI | 1 | 9 | 5 |
| CAN | 1 | 3 | 5 |
| NOR | 1 | 3 | 2 |
| KOR | 1 | 0 | 1 |
| TUR | 1 | 0 | 1 |
| IND | 1 | 0 | 0 |
| NZE | 1 | 0 | 0 |
| POL | 0 | 3 | 3 |
| DEN | 0 | 2 | 3 |
| LAT | 0 | 1 | 1 |
| ROM | 0 | 1 | 0 |
| SAF | 0 | 1 | 0 |
| YUG | 0 | 1 | 0 |
| MEX | 0 | 0 | 3 |
| BEL | 0 | 0 | 2 |
| AUS | 0 | 0 | 1 |
| PHI | 0 | 0 | 1 |
| POR | 0 | 0 | 1 |

## 1948 London

| | G | S | B |
|---|---|---|---|
| USA | 38 | 27 | 19 |
| SWE | 16 | 11 | 17 |
| FRA | 10 | 6 | 13 |
| HUN | 10 | 5 | 12 |
| ITA | 8 | 12 | 9 |
| FIN | 8 | 7 | 5 |
| TUR | 6 | 4 | 2 |
| CZE | 6 | 2 | 3 |
| SWI | 5 | 10 | 5 |
| DEN | 5 | 7 | 8 |
| HOL | 5 | 2 | 9 |
| GBR | 3 | 14 | 6 |
| ARG | 3 | 3 | 1 |
| AUS | 2 | 6 | 5 |
| BEL | 2 | 2 | 3 |
| EGY | 2 | 2 | 1 |

| | | | |
|---|---|---|---|
| MEX | 2 | 1 | 2 |
| SAF | 2 | 1 | 1 |
| NOR | 1 | 3 | 3 |
| JAM | 1 | 2 | 0 |
| AUT | 1 | 0 | 3 |
| IND | 1 | 0 | 0 |
| PER | 1 | 0 | 0 |
| YUG | 0 | 2 | 0 |
| CAN | 0 | 1 | 2 |
| POR | 0 | 1 | 1 |
| URU | 0 | 1 | 1 |
| CUB | 0 | 1 | 0 |
| SPA | 0 | 1 | 0 |
| TRI | 0 | 1 | 0 |
| SRL | 0 | 1 | 0 |
| KOR | 0 | 0 | 2 |
| PAN | 0 | 0 | 2 |
| BRA | 0 | 0 | 1 |
| IRN | 0 | 0 | 1 |
| POL | 0 | 0 | 1 |
| PUR | 0 | 0 | 1 |

## 1952 Helsinki

| | G | S | B |
|---|---|---|---|
| USA | 40 | 19 | 17 |
| SOV | 22 | 30 | 19 |
| HUN | 16 | 10 | 16 |
| SWE | 12 | 13 | 10 |
| ITA | 8 | 9 | 4 |
| CZE | 7 | 3 | 3 |
| FRA | 6 | 6 | 6 |
| FIN | 6 | 3 | 13 |
| AUS | 6 | 2 | 3 |
| NOR | 3 | 2 | 0 |
| SWI | 2 | 6 | 6 |
| SAF | 2 | 4 | 4 |
| JAM | 2 | 3 | 0 |
| BEL | 2 | 2 | 0 |
| DEN | 2 | 1 | 3 |
| TUR | 2 | 0 | 1 |
| JPN | 1 | 6 | 2 |
| GBR | 1 | 2 | 8 |
| ARG | 1 | 2 | 2 |
| POL | 1 | 2 | 1 |
| CAN | 1 | 2 | 0 |
| YUG | 1 | 2 | 0 |
| ROM | 1 | 1 | 2 |
| BRA | 1 | 0 | 2 |

|     | G | S | B |
| --- | --- | --- | --- |
| NZE | 1 | 0 | 2 |
| IND | 1 | 0 | 1 |
| LUX | 1 | 0 | 0 |
| GER | 0 | 7 | 17 |
| HOL | 0 | 5 | 0 |
| IRN | 0 | 3 | 4 |
| CHI | 0 | 2 | 0 |
| AUT | 0 | 1 | 1 |
| LEB | 0 | 1 | 1 |
| IRL | 0 | 1 | 0 |
| MEX | 0 | 1 | 0 |
| SPA | 0 | 1 | 0 |
| KOR | 0 | 0 | 2 |
| URU | 0 | 0 | 2 |
| TRI | 0 | 0 | 2 |
| BUL | 0 | 0 | 1 |
| EGY | 0 | 0 | 1 |
| POR | 0 | 0 | 1 |
| VEN | 0 | 0 | 1 |

## 1956 Melbourne

|     | G | S | B |
| --- | --- | --- | --- |
| SOV | 37 | 20 | 32 |
| USA | 32 | 25 | 17 |
| AUS | 13 | 8 | 14 |
| HUN | 9 | 10 | 7 |
| ITA | 8 | 8 | 9 |
| SWE | 8 | 5 | 6 |
| GBR | 6 | 7 | 11 |
| GER | 5 | 9 | 6 |
| ROM | 5 | 3 | 5 |
| JAP | 4 | 10 | 5 |
| FRA | 4 | 4 | 6 |
| TUR | 3 | 2 | 2 |
| FIN | 3 | 1 | 11 |
| IRN | 2 | 2 | 1 |
| CAN | 2 | 1 | 3 |
| NZE | 2 | 0 | 0 |
| POL | 1 | 4 | 4 |
| GDR | 1 | 4 | 2 |
| CZE | 1 | 4 | 1 |
| BUL | 1 | 3 | 1 |
| DEN | 1 | 2 | 1 |
| IRL | 1 | 1 | 3 |
| NOR | 1 | 0 | 2 |
| MEX | 1 | 0 | 1 |
| BRA | 1 | 0 | 0 |

|     | G | S | B |
| --- | --- | --- | --- |
| IND | 1 | 0 | 0 |
| YUG | 0 | 3 | 0 |
| CHI | 0 | 2 | 2 |
| BEL | 0 | 2 | 0 |
| ARG | 0 | 1 | 1 |
| KOR | 0 | 1 | 1 |
| ICE | 0 | 1 | 0 |
| PAK | 0 | 1 | 0 |
| SAF | 0 | 0 | 4 |
| AUT | 0 | 0 | 2 |
| BAH | 0 | 0 | 1 |
| GRE | 0 | 0 | 1 |
| SWI | 0 | 0 | 1 |
| URU | 0 | 0 | 1 |

## 1960 Rome

|     | G | S | B |
| --- | --- | --- | --- |
| SOV | 43 | 29 | 31 |
| USA | 34 | 21 | 16 |
| ITA | 13 | 10 | 13 |
| GER | 10 | 10 | 6 |
| AUS | 8 | 8 | 6 |
| TUR | 7 | 2 | 0 |
| HUN | 6 | 8 | 7 |
| JPN | 4 | 7 | 7 |
| POL | 4 | 6 | 11 |
| GDR | 3 | 9 | 7 |
| CZE | 3 | 2 | 3 |
| ROM | 3 | 1 | 6 |
| GBR | 2 | 6 | 12 |
| DEN | 2 | 3 | 1 |
| NZE | 2 | 0 | 1 |
| BUL | 1 | 3 | 3 |
| SWE | 1 | 2 | 3 |
| FIN | 1 | 1 | 3 |
| AUT | 1 | 1 | 0 |
| YUG | 1 | 1 | 0 |
| PAK | 1 | 0 | 1 |
| ETH | 1 | 0 | 0 |
| GRE | 1 | 0 | 0 |
| NOR | 1 | 0 | 0 |
| SWI | 0 | 3 | 3 |
| FRA | 0 | 2 | 3 |
| BEL | 0 | 2 | 2 |
| IRN | 0 | 1 | 3 |
| HOL | 0 | 1 | 2 |
| SAF | 0 | 1 | 2 |

|     | G | S | B |
| --- | --- | --- | --- |
| ARG | 0 | 1 | 1 |
| UAR | 0 | 1 | 1 |
| CAN | 0 | 1 | 0 |
| GHA | 0 | 1 | 0 |
| IND | 0 | 1 | 0 |
| MOR | 0 | 1 | 0 |
| POR | 0 | 1 | 0 |
| SIN | 0 | 1 | 0 |
| TAI | 0 | 1 | 0 |
| BRA | 0 | 0 | 2 |
| BWI | 0 | 0 | 2 |
| IRQ | 0 | 0 | 1 |
| MEX | 0 | 0 | 1 |
| SPA | 0 | 0 | 1 |
| VEN | 0 | 0 | 1 |

## 1964 Tokyo

|     | G | S | B |
| --- | --- | --- | --- |
| USA | 36 | 26 | 28 |
| SOV | 30 | 31 | 25 |
| JPN | 16 | 5 | 8 |
| ITA | 10 | 10 | 7 |
| HUN | 10 | 7 | 5 |
| GER | 7 | 14 | 14 |
| POL | 7 | 6 | 10 |
| AUS | 6 | 2 | 10 |
| CZE | 5 | 6 | 3 |
| GBR | 4 | 12 | 2 |
| GDR | 3 | 11 | 5 |
| BUL | 3 | 5 | 2 |
| FIN | 3 | 0 | 2 |
| NZE | 3 | 0 | 2 |
| ROM | 2 | 4 | 6 |
| HOL | 2 | 4 | 4 |
| TUR | 2 | 3 | 1 |
| SWE | 2 | 2 | 4 |
| DEN | 2 | 1 | 3 |
| YUG | 2 | 1 | 2 |
| BEL | 2 | 0 | 1 |
| FRA | 1 | 8 | 6 |
| CAN | 1 | 2 | 1 |
| SWI | 1 | 2 | 1 |
| BAH | 1 | 0 | 0 |
| ETH | 1 | 0 | 0 |
| IND | 1 | 0 | 0 |
| KOR | 0 | 2 | 1 |
| TRI | 0 | 1 | 2 |

|     | G | S | B |
| --- | --- | --- | --- |
| TUN | 0 | 1 | 1 |
| ARG | 0 | 1 | 0 |
| CUB | 0 | 1 | 0 |
| PAK | 0 | 1 | 0 |
| PHI | 0 | 1 | 0 |
| IRN | 0 | 0 | 2 |
| BRA | 0 | 0 | 1 |
| GHA | 0 | 0 | 1 |
| IRL | 0 | 0 | 1 |
| KEN | 0 | 0 | 1 |
| MEX | 0 | 0 | 1 |
| NGR | 0 | 0 | 1 |
| URU | 0 | 0 | 1 |

## 1968 Mexico City

|     | G | S | B |
| --- | --- | --- | --- |
| USA | 45 | 28 | 34 |
| SOV | 29 | 32 | 30 |
| JPN | 11 | 7 | 7 |
| HUN | 10 | 10 | 12 |
| GDR | 9 | 9 | 7 |
| FRA | 7 | 3 | 5 |
| CZE | 7 | 2 | 4 |
| GER | 5 | 11 | 10 |
| AUS | 5 | 7 | 5 |
| GBR | 5 | 5 | 3 |
| POL | 5 | 2 | 11 |
| ROM | 4 | 6 | 5 |
| ITA | 3 | 4 | 9 |
| KEN | 3 | 4 | 2 |
| MEX | 3 | 3 | 3 |
| YUG | 3 | 3 | 2 |
| HOL | 3 | 3 | 1 |
| BUL | 2 | 4 | 3 |
| IRN | 2 | 1 | 2 |
| SWE | 2 | 1 | 1 |
| TUR | 2 | 0 | 0 |
| DEN | 1 | 4 | 3 |
| CAN | 1 | 3 | 1 |
| FIN | 1 | 2 | 1 |
| ETH | 1 | 1 | 0 |
| NOR | 1 | 1 | 0 |
| NZE | 1 | 0 | 2 |
| TUN | 1 | 0 | 1 |
| PAK | 1 | 0 | 0 |
| VEN | 1 | 0 | 0 |
| CUB | 0 | 4 | 0 |

|     | G | S | B |
|-----|---|---|---|
| AUT | 0 | 2 | 2 |
| SWI | 0 | 1 | 4 |
| MON | 0 | 1 | 3 |
| BRA | 0 | 1 | 2 |
| KOR | 0 | 1 | 1 |
| UGA | 0 | 1 | 1 |
| CAM | 0 | 1 | 0 |
| JAM | 0 | 1 | 0 |
| ARG | 0 | 0 | 2 |
| GRE | 0 | 0 | 1 |
| IND | 0 | 0 | 1 |
| TAI | 0 | 0 | 1 |

## 1972 Munich

|     | G | S | B |
|-----|----|----|----|
| SOV | 50 | 27 | 22 |
| USA | 33 | 31 | 30 |
| GDR | 20 | 23 | 23 |
| GER | 13 | 11 | 16 |
| JPN | 13 | 8 | 8 |
| AUS | 8 | 7 | 2 |
| POL | 7 | 5 | 9 |
| HUN | 6 | 13 | 16 |
| BUL | 6 | 10 | 5 |
| ITA | 5 | 3 | 10 |
| SWE | 4 | 6 | 6 |
| GBR | 4 | 5 | 9 |
| ROM | 3 | 6 | 7 |
| FIN | 3 | 1 | 4 |
| CUB | 3 | 1 | 4 |
| HOL | 3 | 1 | 1 |
| FRA | 2 | 4 | 7 |
| CZE | 2 | 4 | 2 |
| KEN | 2 | 3 | 4 |
| YUG | 2 | 1 | 2 |
| NOR | 2 | 1 | 1 |
| PRK | 1 | 1 | 3 |
| NZE | 1 | 1 | 1 |
| UGA | 1 | 1 | 0 |
| DEN | 1 | 0 | 0 |
| SWI | 0 | 3 | 0 |
| CAN | 0 | 2 | 3 |
| IRN | 0 | 2 | 1 |
| BEL | 0 | 2 | 0 |
| GRE | 0 | 2 | 0 |
| AUT | 0 | 1 | 2 |
| COL | 0 | 1 | 2 |

|     |   |   |   |
|-----|---|---|---|
| ARG | 0 | 1 | 0 |
| KOR | 0 | 1 | 0 |
| LEB | 0 | 1 | 0 |
| MEX | 0 | 1 | 0 |
| MON | 0 | 1 | 0 |
| PAK | 0 | 1 | 0 |
| TUN | 0 | 1 | 0 |
| TUR | 0 | 1 | 0 |
| BRA | 0 | 0 | 2 |
| ETH | 0 | 0 | 2 |
| GHA | 0 | 0 | 1 |
| IND | 0 | 0 | 1 |
| JAM | 0 | 0 | 1 |
| NIG | 0 | 0 | 1 |
| NGR | 0 | 0 | 1 |
| SPA | 0 | 0 | 1 |

## 1976 Montreal

|     | G | S | B |
|-----|----|----|----|
| SOV | 49 | 41 | 35 |
| GDR | 40 | 25 | 25 |
| USA | 34 | 35 | 25 |
| GER | 10 | 12 | 17 |
| JPN | 9 | 6 | 10 |
| POL | 7 | 6 | 13 |
| BUL | 6 | 9 | 7 |
| CUB | 6 | 4 | 3 |
| ROM | 4 | 9 | 14 |
| HUN | 4 | 5 | 13 |
| FIN | 4 | 2 | 0 |
| SWE | 4 | 1 | 0 |
| GBR | 3 | 5 | 5 |
| ITA | 2 | 7 | 4 |
| FRA | 2 | 3 | 4 |
| YUG | 2 | 3 | 3 |
| CZE | 2 | 2 | 4 |
| NZE | 2 | 1 | 1 |
| KOR | 1 | 1 | 4 |
| SWI | 1 | 1 | 2 |
| JAM | 1 | 1 | 0 |
| NOR | 1 | 1 | 0 |
| PRK | 1 | 1 | 0 |
| DEN | 1 | 0 | 2 |
| MEX | 1 | 0 | 1 |
| TRI | 1 | 0 | 0 |
| CAN | 0 | 5 | 6 |
| BEL | 0 | 3 | 3 |

|     |   |   |   |
|-----|---|---|---|
| HOL | 0 | 2 | 3 |
| POR | 0 | 2 | 0 |
| SPA | 0 | 2 | 0 |
| AUS | 0 | 1 | 4 |
| IRN | 0 | 1 | 1 |
| MON | 0 | 1 | 0 |
| VEN | 0 | 1 | 0 |
| BRA | 0 | 0 | 2 |
| AUT | 0 | 0 | 1 |
| BER | 0 | 0 | 1 |
| PAK | 0 | 0 | 1 |
| PUR | 0 | 0 | 1 |
| THA | 0 | 0 | 1 |

## 1980 Moscow

|     | G | S | B |
|-----|----|----|----|
| SOV | 80 | 69 | 46 |
| GDR | 47 | 37 | 42 |
| BUL | 8 | 16 | 17 |
| CUB | 8 | 7 | 5 |
| ITA | 8 | 3 | 4 |
| HUN | 7 | 10 | 15 |
| ROM | 6 | 6 | 13 |
| FRA | 6 | 5 | 3 |
| GBR | 5 | 7 | 9 |
| POL | 3 | 14 | 15 |
| SWE | 3 | 3 | 6 |
| FIN | 3 | 1 | 4 |
| CZE | 2 | 3 | 9 |
| YUG | 2 | 3 | 4 |
| AUS | 2 | 2 | 5 |
| DEN | 2 | 1 | 2 |
| BRA | 2 | 0 | 2 |
| ETH | 2 | 0 | 2 |
| SWI | 2 | 0 | 0 |
| SPA | 1 | 3 | 2 |
| AUT | 1 | 2 | 1 |
| GRE | 1 | 0 | 2 |
| BEL | 1 | 0 | 0 |
| IND | 1 | 0 | 0 |
| ZIM | 1 | 0 | 0 |
| PRK | 0 | 3 | 2 |
| MON | 0 | 2 | 2 |
| TAN | 0 | 2 | 0 |
| MEX | 0 | 1 | 3 |
| HOL | 0 | 1 | 2 |
| IRL | 0 | 1 | 1 |

|     |   |   |   |
|-----|---|---|---|
| UGA | 0 | 1 | 0 |
| VEN | 0 | 1 | 0 |
| JAM | 0 | 0 | 3 |
| GUY | 0 | 0 | 1 |
| LEB | 0 | 0 | 1 |

## 1984 Los Angeles

|     | G | S | B |
|-----|----|----|----|
| USA | 83 | 61 | 30 |
| ROM | 20 | 16 | 17 |
| GER | 17 | 19 | 23 |
| CHN | 15 | 8 | 9 |
| ITA | 14 | 6 | 12 |
| CAN | 10 | 18 | 16 |
| JPN | 10 | 8 | 14 |
| NZE | 8 | 1 | 2 |
| YUG | 7 | 4 | 7 |
| KOR | 6 | 6 | 7 |
| GBR | 5 | 10 | 22 |
| FRA | 5 | 7 | 16 |
| HOL | 5 | 2 | 6 |
| AUS | 4 | 8 | 12 |
| FIN | 4 | 2 | 6 |
| SWE | 2 | 11 | 6 |
| MEX | 2 | 3 | 1 |
| MOR | 2 | 0 | 0 |
| BRA | 1 | 5 | 2 |
| SPA | 1 | 2 | 2 |
| BEL | 1 | 1 | 2 |
| AUT | 1 | 1 | 1 |
| KEN | 1 | 0 | 2 |
| POR | 1 | 0 | 2 |
| PAK | 1 | 0 | 0 |
| SWI | 0 | 4 | 4 |
| DEN | 0 | 3 | 3 |
| JAM | 0 | 1 | 2 |
| NOR | 0 | 1 | 2 |
| GRE | 0 | 1 | 1 |
| NGR | 0 | 1 | 1 |
| PUR | 0 | 1 | 1 |
| COL | 0 | 1 | 0 |
| EGY | 0 | 1 | 0 |
| IRL | 0 | 1 | 0 |
| IVC | 0 | 1 | 0 |
| PER | 0 | 1 | 0 |
| SYR | 0 | 1 | 0 |
| THA | 0 | 1 | 0 |

|     | G | S | B |
|-----|---|---|---|
| TUR | 0 | 0 | 3 |
| VEN | 0 | 0 | 3 |
| ALG | 0 | 0 | 2 |
| CAM | 0 | 0 | 1 |
| DOM | 0 | 0 | 1 |
| ICE | 0 | 0 | 1 |
| TAI | 0 | 0 | 1 |
| ZAM | 0 | 0 | 1 |

## 1988 Seoul

|     | G | S | B |
|-----|----|----|----|
| SOV | 55 | 31 | 46 |
| GDR | 37 | 35 | 30 |
| USA | 36 | 31 | 27 |
| KOR | 12 | 10 | 11 |
| GER | 11 | 14 | 15 |
| HUN | 11 | 6 | 6 |
| BUL | 10 | 12 | 13 |
| ROM | 7 | 11 | 6 |
| FRA | 6 | 4 | 6 |
| ITA | 6 | 4 | 4 |
| CHN | 5 | 11 | 12 |
| GBR | 5 | 10 | 9 |
| KEN | 5 | 2 | 2 |
| JPN | 4 | 3 | 7 |
| AUS | 3 | 6 | 5 |
| YUG | 3 | 4 | 5 |
| CZE | 3 | 3 | 2 |
| NZE | 3 | 2 | 8 |
| CAN | 3 | 2 | 5 |
| POL | 2 | 5 | 9 |
| NOR | 2 | 3 | 0 |
| HOL | 2 | 2 | 5 |
| DEN | 2 | 1 | 1 |
| BRA | 1 | 2 | 3 |
| FIN | 1 | 1 | 2 |
| SPA | 1 | 1 | 2 |
| TUR | 1 | 1 | 0 |
| MOR | 1 | 0 | 2 |
| AUT | 1 | 0 | 0 |
| POR | 1 | 0 | 0 |
| SUR | 1 | 0 | 0 |
| SWE | 0 | 4 | 7 |
| SWI | 0 | 2 | 2 |
| JAM | 0 | 2 | 0 |
| ARG | 0 | 1 | 1 |
| CHI | 0 | 1 | 0 |

| CRC | 0 | 1 | 0 |
|-----|---|---|---|
| INA | 0 | 1 | 0 |
| IRN | 0 | 1 | 0 |
| NLA | 0 | 1 | 0 |
| PER | 0 | 1 | 0 |
| SEN | 0 | 1 | 0 |
| VIR | 0 | 1 | 0 |
| BEL | 0 | 0 | 2 |
| MEX | 0 | 0 | 2 |
| COL | 0 | 0 | 1 |
| DJI | 0 | 0 | 1 |
| GRE | 0 | 0 | 1 |
| MON | 0 | 0 | 1 |
| PAK | 0 | 0 | 1 |
| PHI | 0 | 0 | 1 |
| THA | 0 | 0 | 1 |

# WINTER

## 1924 Chamonix

|     | G | S | B |
|-----|---|---|---|
| NOR | 4 | 7 | 6 |
| FIN | 4 | 3 | 3 |
| AUT | 2 | 1 | 0 |
| USA | 1 | 2 | 1 |
| SWI | 1 | 0 | 1 |
| CAN | 1 | 0 | 0 |
| SWE | 1 | 0 | 0 |
| GBR | 0 | 1 | 2 |
| BEL | 0 | 0 | 1 |
| FRA | 0 | 0 | 1 |

## 1928 St. Moritz

|     | G | S | B |
|-----|---|---|---|
| NOR | 6 | 4 | 5 |
| USA | 2 | 2 | 2 |
| SWE | 2 | 2 | 1 |
| FIN | 2 | 1 | 1 |
| CAN | 1 | 0 | 0 |
| FRA | 1 | 0 | 0 |
| AUT | 0 | 3 | 1 |
| BEL | 0 | 0 | 1 |
| CZE | 0 | 0 | 1 |
| GBR | 0 | 0 | 1 |
| GER | 0 | 0 | 1 |
| SWI | 0 | 0 | 1 |

## 1932 Lake Placid

|     | G | S | B |
|-----|---|---|---|
| USA | 6 | 4 | 2 |
| NOR | 3 | 4 | 3 |
| SWE | 1 | 2 | 0 |
| CAN | 1 | 1 | 5 |
| FIN | 1 | 1 | 1 |
| AUT | 1 | 1 | 0 |
| FRA | 1 | 0 | 0 |
| SWI | 0 | 1 | 0 |
| GER | 0 | 0 | 2 |
| HUN | 0 | 0 | 1 |

## 1936 Garmisch-Partenkirchen

|     | G | S | B |
|-----|---|---|---|
| NOR | 7 | 5 | 3 |
| GER | 3 | 3 | 0 |
| SWE | 2 | 2 | 3 |
| FIN | 1 | 2 | 3 |
| SWI | 1 | 2 | 0 |
| AUT | 1 | 1 | 2 |
| GBR | 1 | 1 | 1 |
| USA | 1 | 0 | 3 |
| CAN | 0 | 1 | 0 |
| FRA | 0 | 0 | 1 |
| HUN | 0 | 0 | 1 |

## 1948 St. Moritz

|     | G | S | B |
|-----|---|---|---|
| NOR | 4 | 3 | 3 |
| SWE | 4 | 3 | 3 |
| SWI | 3 | 4 | 3 |
| USA | 3 | 4 | 2 |
| FRA | 2 | 1 | 2 |
| CAN | 2 | 0 | 1 |
| AUT | 1 | 3 | 4 |
| FIN | 1 | 3 | 2 |
| BEL | 1 | 1 | 0 |
| ITA | 1 | 0 | 0 |
| CZE | 0 | 1 | 0 |
| HUN | 0 | 1 | 0 |
| GBR | 0 | 0 | 2 |

## 1952 Oslo

|     | G | S | B |
|-----|---|---|---|
| NOR | 7 | 3 | 6 |
| USA | 4 | 6 | 1 |
| FIN | 3 | 4 | 2 |
| GER | 3 | 2 | 2 |
| AUT | 2 | 4 | 2 |
| CAN | 1 | 0 | 1 |
| ITA | 1 | 0 | 1 |
| GBR | 1 | 0 | 0 |
| HOL | 0 | 3 | 0 |
| SWE | 0 | 0 | 4 |
| SWI | 0 | 0 | 2 |
| FRA | 0 | 0 | 1 |
| HUN | 0 | 0 | 1 |

## 1956 Cortina d'Ampezzo

|     | G | S | B |
|-----|---|---|---|
| SOV | 7 | 3 | 6 |
| AUT | 4 | 3 | 4 |
| FIN | 3 | 3 | 1 |
| SWI | 3 | 2 | 1 |
| SWE | 2 | 4 | 4 |
| USA | 2 | 3 | 2 |
| NOR | 2 | 1 | 1 |
| ITA | 1 | 2 | 0 |
| GER | 1 | 0 | 0 |
| CAN | 0 | 1 | 2 |
| JPN | 0 | 1 | 0 |
| GDR | 0 | 0 | 1 |
| HUN | 0 | 0 | 1 |
| POL | 0 | 0 | 1 |

## 1960 Squaw Valley

|     | G | S | B |
|-----|---|---|---|
| SOV | 7 | 5 | 9 |
| USA | 3 | 4 | 3 |
| NOR | 3 | 3 | 0 |
| SWE | 3 | 2 | 2 |
| FIN | 2 | 3 | 3 |
| GER | 2 | 2 | 1 |
| CAN | 2 | 1 | 1 |
| GDR | 2 | 1 | 0 |
| SWI | 2 | 0 | 0 |
| AUT | 1 | 2 | 3 |
| FRA | 1 | 0 | 2 |
| HOL | 0 | 1 | 1 |
| POL | 0 | 1 | 1 |
| CZE | 0 | 1 | 0 |
| ITA | 0 | 0 | 1 |

**1964 Innsbruck**

|     | G  | S | B |
| --- | -- | - | - |
| SOV | 11 | 8 | 6 |
| AUT | 4  | 5 | 3 |
| NOR | 3  | 6 | 6 |
| FIN | 3  | 4 | 3 |
| FRA | 3  | 4 | 0 |
| SWE | 3  | 3 | 1 |
| GDR | 2  | 2 | 0 |
| USA | 1  | 2 | 3 |
| HOL | 1  | 1 | 0 |
| GER | 1  | 0 | 3 |
| CAN | 1  | 0 | 2 |
| GBR | 1  | 0 | 0 |
| ITA | 0  | 1 | 3 |
| PRK | 0  | 1 | 0 |
| CZE | 0  | 0 | 1 |

**1968 Grenoble**

|     | G | S | B |
| --- | - | - | - |
| NOR | 6 | 6 | 2 |
| SOV | 5 | 5 | 3 |
| FRA | 4 | 3 | 2 |
| ITA | 4 | 0 | 0 |
| AUT | 3 | 4 | 4 |
| HOL | 3 | 3 | 3 |
| SWE | 3 | 2 | 3 |
| GER | 2 | 2 | 3 |
| USA | 1 | 5 | 1 |
| FIN | 1 | 2 | 2 |
| GDR | 1 | 2 | 2 |
| CZE | 1 | 2 | 1 |
| CAN | 1 | 1 | 1 |
| SWI | 0 | 2 | 4 |
| ROM | 0 | 0 | 1 |

**1972 Sapporo**

|     | G | S | B |
| --- | - | - | - |
| SOV | 8 | 5 | 3 |
| GDR | 4 | 3 | 7 |
| SWI | 4 | 3 | 3 |
| HOL | 4 | 3 | 2 |
| USA | 3 | 2 | 3 |
| GER | 3 | 1 | 1 |
| NOR | 2 | 5 | 5 |
| ITA | 2 | 2 | 1 |
| AUT | 1 | 2 | 2 |
| SWE | 1 | 1 | 2 |
| JPN | 1 | 1 | 1 |
| CZE | 1 | 0 | 2 |
| POL | 1 | 0 | 0 |
| SPA | 1 | 0 | 0 |
| FIN | 0 | 4 | 1 |
| FRA | 0 | 1 | 2 |
| CAN | 0 | 1 | 0 |

**1976 Innsbruck**

|     | G  | S | B |
| --- | -- | - | - |
| SOV | 13 | 6 | 8 |
| GDR | 7  | 5 | 7 |
| USA | 3  | 3 | 4 |
| NOR | 3  | 3 | 1 |
| GER | 2  | 5 | 3 |
| FIN | 2  | 4 | 1 |
| AUT | 2  | 2 | 2 |
| SWI | 1  | 3 | 1 |
| HOL | 1  | 2 | 3 |
| ITA | 1  | 2 | 1 |
| CAN | 1  | 1 | 1 |
| GBR | 1  | 0 | 0 |
| CZE | 0  | 1 | 0 |
| LIE | 0  | 0 | 2 |
| SWE | 0  | 0 | 2 |
| FRA | 0  | 0 | 1 |

**1980 Lake Placid**

|     | G  | S | B |
| --- | -- | - | - |
| SOV | 10 | 6 | 6 |
| GDR | 9  | 7 | 7 |
| USA | 6  | 4 | 2 |
| AUT | 3  | 2 | 2 |
| SWE | 3  | 0 | 1 |
| LIE | 2  | 2 | 0 |
| FIN | 1  | 5 | 3 |
| NOR | 1  | 3 | 6 |
| HOL | 1  | 2 | 1 |
| SWI | 1  | 1 | 3 |
| GBR | 1  | 0 | 0 |
| GER | 0  | 2 | 3 |
| ITA | 0  | 2 | 0 |
| CAN | 0  | 1 | 1 |
| HUN | 0  | 1 | 0 |
| JPN | 0  | 1 | 0 |
| BUL | 0  | 0 | 1 |
| CZE | 0  | 0 | 1 |
| FRA | 0  | 0 | 1 |

**1984 Sarajevo**

|     | G | S  | B |
| --- | - | -- | - |
| GDR | 9 | 9  | 6 |
| SOV | 6 | 10 | 9 |
| USA | 4 | 4  | 0 |

| FIN | 4 | 3 | 6 |
| --- | - | - | - |
| SWE | 4 | 2 | 2 |
| NOR | 3 | 2 | 4 |
| SWI | 2 | 2 | 1 |
| CAN | 2 | 1 | 1 |
| GER | 2 | 1 | 1 |
| ITA | 2 | 0 | 0 |
| GBR | 1 | 0 | 0 |
| CZE | 0 | 2 | 4 |
| FRA | 0 | 1 | 2 |
| JPN | 0 | 1 | 0 |
| YUG | 0 | 1 | 0 |
| LIE | 0 | 0 | 2 |
| AUT | 0 | 0 | 1 |

**1988 Calgary**

|     | G  | S  | B |
| --- | -- | -- | - |
| SOV | 11 | 9  | 9 |
| GDR | 9  | 10 | 6 |
| SWI | 5  | 5  | 5 |
| FIN | 4  | 1  | 2 |
| SWE | 4  | 0  | 2 |
| AUT | 3  | 5  | 2 |
| HOL | 3  | 2  | 2 |
| GER | 2  | 4  | 2 |
| USA | 2  | 1  | 3 |
| ITA | 2  | 1  | 2 |
| FRA | 1  | 0  | 0 |
| NOR | 0  | 3  | 2 |
| CAN | 0  | 2  | 3 |
| YUG | 0  | 2  | 1 |
| CZE | 0  | 1  | 2 |
| JPN | 0  | 0  | 1 |
| LIE | 0  | 0  | 1 |

# A BRIEF HISTORY OF THE MODERN OLYMPICS

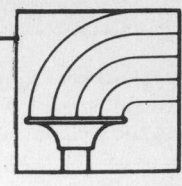

The ancient Olympic games were held in Olympia, Greece, every four years from at least 776 B.C., until they were banned by Emperor Theodosius in 393 A.D. Originally there was only one race, a sprint, and the prize for the winner was an olive wreath. As time went on, other races were added, as were other sports, including boxing and wrestling. Prizes became more elaborate, and there were even cases of bribery, corruption and boycotts.

Inspired by the original, uncorrupted Olympics, Baron Pierre de Coubertin of France conceived the modern Olympic Games. He proposed the idea publicly for the first time in 1892 and then spent the next three and a half years drumming up support. Interest was strongest in Greece, so it was decided to hold the first Olympics in Athens.

The **1896** Athens Games were funded by a gift from wealthy architect Georgios Averoff of one million drachma, and by the sale of souvenir stamps and medals. Although the quality of the athletes' performances was only mediocre, the Games were a huge success. The enthusiasm and good sportsmanship of the Greek spectators were rewarded when the highlight event, the marathon, was won by a Greek peasant, Spiridon Louis.

The second Olympic Games were held in de Coubertin's hometown of Paris in **1900,** but they turned out to be a failure. Reduced to a mere appendage to the World Exhibition of that year, the events of the Olympics were spread out over five months. Poor organization and poor attendance made things worse; some of the athletes were actually unaware that the meet they had taken part in was the Olympics.

De Coubertin had high hopes for the **1904** Games, which were scheduled for Chicago because Americans had shown such great enthusiasm for the first two Olympics. However, a dispute broke out between Chicago and St. Louis, which wanted the Games to be held as part of the Louisiana Purchase Exhibition. President Theodore Roosevelt eventually sided with St. Louis, and the Games were moved. This change proved to be an awful mistake, as the St. Louis organizers turned out to be even less competent than the Paris organizers. Most European nations skipped the Games, and not even Baron de Coubertin bothered to attend. Events were spread out

over four and a half months, and some included only U.S. athletes.

After two straight disasters the Olympic movement might have died had it not been for the Intercalated (or Interim) Games of **1906.** After the success of the 1896 Games, the Greeks had hoped to hold their own international games every four years between Olympics. However the proposed Games of 1898 had to be cancelled because of political and economic upheaval, and the 1902 Games weren't even considered. By 1906, though, the Greeks were ready to try again. Although de Coubertin opposed the Intercalated Games, they were quite successful and actually helped save the Olympic movement. These Games are considered unofficial by the International Olympic Committee (I.O.C.).

The **1908** Games had been planned for Rome, but the Italians backed out for financial reasons, and the Games were then awarded to London. Most of the events were held in Shepherd's Bush Stadium, which included a cycle track, a running track, a soccer field, a swimming pool, and a platform for wrestling and gymnastics. The London Games were basically well organized and produced the first comprehensive Official Report. There were, however, numerous disputes. The Russians tried to prevent the Finns from displaying the Finnish flag, and the English did the same to the Irish. The competitions were run entirely by the British, which led to protests over the rules by representatives of France, Canada, Italy, Sweden, and, especially, the United States. The bickering between Great Britain and its cheeky former colony was so acute that it almost put an end to the Olympics.

Fortunately, the **1912** Olympics were held in Stockholm. Well-organized, the Stockholm Games saw the first use of electronic timing devices and a public address system. The Swedes refused to allow boxing matches to be held in their country, which led the I.O.C. to pass a rule limiting the power of local organizing committees in future Olympics. The success of the 1912 Games helped the Olympic movement survive the interruption that came to be known as World War I. In ancient times, all wars were suspended during the period of the Olympics. In modern times, the reverse has been true. Scheduled for Berlin, the **1916** Olympics were cancelled.

The **1920** Games were awarded to Antwerp, Belgium, as compensation for all the grief that had been inflicted on the Belgians during the war. The losers of World War I, Austria, Bulgaria, Germany, Hungary, and Turkey, were not allowed to participate. With little money available to run the Games, the 1920 Olympics were not very impressive and were not well documented. An Official Report does not exist for 1920—only a typed manuscript containing an incomplete listing of the results.

Much to the delight of Baron de Coubertin, Paris was given a second chance to host the Olympics in **1924,** which also saw the staging of the first Winter Olympics in Chamonix, France. The second Paris Games were well attended, with athletes from 44 nations taking part, as opposed to the previous record of 29. Competition was of a very high standard. However, the fanaticism of Parisian sports fans led to several outrages, including booing during the playing of national anthems of other countries and numerous incidents during the boxing and fencing tournaments. The French, who never had a very high opinion of their neighbors, were particularly irritated by the Americans, since the U.S. government had only recently criticized the French occupation of the Rühr. During a rugby match between France and the United States, an American art student was severely caned by an incensed French spectator who had become annoyed by the loud U.S. "rooting."

In Europe and North America countless editorials were written calling for an end to the Olympics, but the next Games were held on schedule in Amsterdam in **1928,** with Germany taking part for the first time since 1912. The boxing tournament was once again disrupted by protests, but for the most part, the Amsterdam Games were a success. For the first time track and field events for women were included in the program, although women had previously taken part in tennis, golf, archery, figure skating, yachting, swimming, and fencing.

The **1932** Los Angeles Olympics faced two major obstacles: the Depression and the geographical isolation of California. Participation was the lowest since 1906, although the level of competition was excellent. Only three teams took part in the field hockey tournament, and football (soccer) had to be dropped completely. All of the male athletes lived in a makeshift Olympic Village in Baldwin Hills, while the women stayed in a hotel on Wilshire Boulevard. Although the United States was in the midst of Prohibition, an exception was made for the French, who claimed that wine was an essential component of their diet. The 1932 Olympics saw the introduction of automatic timing and the photo-finish camera.

In 1931, when Berlin was chosen as the site for the **1936** Olympics, few people suspected that a mere five years would see the rise to power of Adolf Hitler and the Nazi Party. Jews in various countries asked for a boycott of the Berlin Olympics, and in the United States a boycott proposal was only narrowly defeated. An alternative People's Olympics was scheduled to take place in Barcelona, Spain, but it was cancelled at the last minute when the Spanish Civil War broke out the day before competition was set to begin. The 1936 Olympics are best remembered by Hitler's failed attempt to use them to prove his theories of Aryan superiority, but they are also noteworthy because they saw the introduction of the torch relay, in which a lighted torch is carried from Olympia to the site of the current Games. The 1936 Olympics were also the first to be shown on television. Twenty-five large TV screens were set up in theaters throughout Berlin, allowing locals to see the Games for free.

The **1940** Olympics were awarded to Japan—the Winter Games to Sapporo and the Summer Games to Tokyo—but when Japan invaded China and became caught up in a major war, the Olympics were taken away from the Japanese. The Winter Games, rescheduled for Garmisch-Partenkirchen, site of the 1936 Games, were cancelled less than five months before the planned starting date, when Germany invaded Poland to kick off World War II. The Summer Games, reawarded to Helsinki, were cancelled when Soviet troops invaded Finland.

After the war ended, London took on the unenviable task of staging the **1948** Olympics, the first in 12 years. There was much grumbling in England that the project was a waste of money, considering that Britain was still recovering from the war. However, the Games went off well, and interest among Londoners increased rapidly as the competitions progressed. Following the precedent set after World War I, the World War II losers, Germany and Japan, were not invited to participate. A minor incident developed when two swimmers from Northern Ireland were refused permission to compete for the team from Eire (Ireland). The 1948 Olympics also saw the first participation by Communist countries and, with this, the first defections of participants.

The U.S.S.R. joined the Olympics for the first time in Helsinki in **1952.** In the United Nations, the Ukraine and Byelorussia are both treated as independent nations, with full voting privileges. In the Olympics, on the other hand, the Ukraine and Byelorussia are considered part of the U.S.S.R., and Ukrainian and Byelorussian athletes were forced to represent the Soviet Union. Despite fears of a Cold War showdown, Soviet and American athletes in Helsinki were on their best behavior and actually got along quite well. In fact, the 1952 Games were so well run that some observers suggested that the Olympics be held permanently in Scandinavia.

In **1956** the Olympics were staged in the southern hemisphere for the first and only time. Melbourne, Australia, was so remote from most parts of the world that the number of competitors was the smallest since 1932. Australian quarantine laws caused the equestrian events to be held separately, in Stockholm. The Melbourne Games were stung by two boycotts. Egypt, Iraq, and Lebanon withdrew to protest the Israeli-led takeover of the Suez Canal, and Holland, Spain, and Switzerland boycotted to protest the Soviet invasion of Hungary. Actually, public pressure in Switzerland was so great that the Swiss Olympic Committee changed its mind and voted to participate after all, but by then it was too late to get the entire Swiss team to Australia in time. The I.O.C. scored a political coup by forcing West and East Germany to enter a combined team. This practice continued for the next two Olympics. The 1956 Olympics were also highlighted by an innovation in the closing ceremonies. Following a suggestion by John Ian Wing, an Australian-born Chinese carpenter's apprentice, it was decided to let all the athletes march together instead of by nation, as a symbol of global unity.

The **1960** Olympics, held beneath the blazing summer sun of Rome, went off without major incident. Like Londoners in 1948, the Romans were fairly blasé at first, but got caught up in the excitement once the games got going. Even the Pope became a spectator, as he watched the canoeing semifinals from a window of his summer residence. The Rome Olympics were the last in which South Africa was allowed to take part, as the I.O.C. bowed to international pressure to punish the South African government for its racist policies.

In 1962 Indonesia hosted the Asian Games in Jakarta. When the Indonesian government refused to allow athletes from Israel and Taiwan to take part, the I.O.C. suspended the Indonesian Olympic Committee until it agreed to abide by the rules of the I.O.C. Indonesia withdrew its team from the **1964** Tokyo Olympics, as did North Korea. With that problem out of the way, the 1964 Olympics proceeded smoothly and efficiently.

The **1968** Mexico City Olympics are best known for the Black Power protests of the U.S. runners Tommie Smith and John Carlos, which are discussed at greater length in the following section, "Issues: Olympic Politics." The year 1968 was a highly politicized one. China was in the throes of the Cultural Revolution, Czechoslovakia's burst of freedom was crushed by Soviet troops, the government of France was almost overthrown by student-led demonstrations, and civil rights and antiwar demonstrations were spreading across the United States. Mexico was by no means immune to such revolutionary activity. As the Olympics approached, 300,000 Mexican students and teachers were on strike. Ten days before the Olympics were scheduled to begin, government troops opened fire on several thousand unarmed students holding a rally in the Plaza de las Tres Culturas. Hundreds of young people were killed. The I.O.C. refused to take a stand on this, declaring that the incident was "an internal affair" which was "under control." Yet exactly two weeks later, when two black men made a silent, nonviolent protest, the I.O.C. was up in arms, condemning Smith and Carlos for their shocking, disrespectful behavior.

Two other controversies of 1968 were the introduction of sex tests for women athletes (first used at the Winter Games in Grenoble) and the altitude of Mexico City (7347 feet). The rarefied air led to numerous world records in races of short distances, but was disastrous to

competitors engaged in endurance events, except those who had trained at high altitudes.

In **1972** the West Germans, hoping to erase embarrassing memories of the Nazi Games of 1936, staged the biggest Olympics yet in Munich. However, the Olympic movement was permanently scarred on the morning of September 5, when eight Palestinian terrorists broke into the Olympic Village and made their way to the dormitory of the Israeli team. Two Israelis were killed immediately and another nine were taken hostage. The terrorists demanded the release of 200 prisoners from Israeli jails and safe passage for themselves out of Germany. They got as far as the airport, where West German sharpshooters killed three of the terrorists. The battle that ensued left all nine Israeli hostages dead, as well as two more terrorists and one policeman. The Olympics were suspended for 34 hours, and a memorial service was held in the main stadium.

The **1976** Olympics, held in Montreal, were hit by a boycott of African nations led by Tanzania. The Africans had demanded expulsion of New Zealand because a rugby team from that nation had made a tour of South Africa. The I.O.C. claimed that controlling the travel of rugby teams was outside its authority since rugby isn't an Olympic sport, but the Africans, joined by Iraq and Guyana, held firm. Of the boycotting nations, only Tanzania stayed home completely, while the others traveled to Canada and didn't make their final decision until the last minute. Despite the absence of the Africans, the 1976 Olympics were filled with excellent competitions. However, poor planning and corruption caused the city of Montreal to suffer a major financial loss.

The **1980** Moscow Olympics were disrupted by another boycott, this one led by U.S. President Jimmy Carter, part of a package of actions to protest the Soviet invasion of Afghanistan. With his eyes on the upcoming presidential election and his pride on the line, Carter engaged in extensive arm-twisting to get other nations to support the boycott. Some governments, such as those of Great Britain and Australia, supported the boycott, but allowed the athletes to decide for themselves if they wanted to go to Moscow. No such freedom of choice was allowed U.S. athletes, as Carter threatened to revoke the passport of any athlete who tried to travel to the U.S.S.R.

Certain sports, such as yachting, equestrian events, field hockey, and men's swimming were hit particularly hard by the boycott. Yet the Games proceeded with much pomp and more world records than had been set in 1976. Security precautions were paranoiacally thorough, with track and field winners physically prevented from taking victory laps. Meanwhile, the Soviet spectators gave the worst impression of any host city since the Paris Olympics of 1924. With traditional Olympic powers West Germany, Japan, and the United States missing, some Soviet fans took out their aggressions by booing and heckling the Poles and East Germans.

Not surprisingly, with the **1984** Olympics being held in

Los Angeles, the government of the U.S.S.R. responded with a revenge boycott. Although the Soviets were noticeably unsuccessful in convincing other nations to join their action—more countries attended than ever before—those nations that did stay home accounted for 58% of the gold medals in 1976. Among the sports which lost most of their medal contenders were weightlifting, wrestling, gymnastics, women's swimming, football, handball, modern pentathlon and women's track and field. Nevertheless, the 1984 Games, the first since 1896 to be staged without government financing, were very successful. Good feelings prevailed to such an extent that at the Opening Ceremonies the athletes broke ranks to join in spontaneous dancing, such celebration usually being reserved for the Closing Ceremonies.

When the **1988** Olympics were awarded to Seoul, South Korea, grave concerns were raised about the ability of the organizers to run the Games in a nation which was not only ruled by an unpopular dictatorship but was in a state of permanent hostility with North Korea. The first half of the problem was solved when the South Korean government bowed to international pressure and held democratic elections. Attempts were made to appease the North Koreans by allowing them to stage several events, but in the end they boycotted the Olympics, taking Cuba, Ethiopia, and Nicaragua with them. Madagascar and the Seychelles also stayed away for reasons which are unclear, while Albania, acting independently, declared its fourth consecutive boycott—an Olympic record.

Although tainted by steroid scandals and the assault on a referee by South Korean boxing officials, the Seoul Games were efficiently staged and the people of South Korea received high marks for their hospitality.

# ISSUES

## OLYMPIC POLITICS

There are only two places today where people from all parts of the world gather: the United Nations and the Olympics. The trouble with the United Nations is that two-thirds of the governments represented are ruled by dictators, royal families, and single parties that permit no opposition. Consequently, the people who represent these countries at the United Nations, far from being typical citizens, are generally the worst the country has to offer. Even those nations that aspire to democracy are represented by a most unrepresentative group: wealthy men and women, mostly men, who have gone to the right schools and know the right people.

Unlike U.N. delegates, Olympic athletes represent an almost complete economic cross-section of the world's population. In this book you will meet carpenters, farmers, housewives, teachers, psychiatrists, accountants, nurses, secretaries, and cartoonists, as well as the usual hordes of students, soldiers, and state-supported athletes. Some Olympians have been unemployed. Others came from families of sharecroppers, or from no families at all. Even lawyers, businessmen, and royalty have taken part in the Olympics.

This is not to say that the Olympics are any less political than the United Nations. However, contrary to popular belief, the politicization of the Olympics is not a recent phenomenon. From the very beginning the Olympics were exploited by the ruling classes of the nations in which they were held. In 1896 and 1906 the Greek royal family was highly visible at the Games, placing its box at the finish line and inserting itself into the festivities at the most exciting parts—the moment of victory and the award ceremonies. The British royal family did the same thing in 1908. In 1912 awards were handed out not only by King Gustav of Sweden, but by Czar Nicholas of Russia as well.

Staging the Olympics also helped the ruling classes by providing a distraction from serious political and economic problems. During the 1906 Intercalated Games in Athens, British and American tourists were shocked when a riot broke out in front of their hotel. Government troops attacked a political demonstration, killing three people and injuring 57. Meanwhile the Greek royal family was busy entertaining the English royal family at Olympic-related functions, including the competitions themselves.

Despite this history, it is often stated that the "intrusion" of politics into the Olympics began in a serious manner with the black-gloved, clenched-fist salutes of U.S. sprinters Tommie Smith and John Carlos in Mexico City in 1968. Smith and Carlos staged their Black Power protest while "The Star-Spangled Banner" was being played during the medal ceremony for the 200-meter dash. They were immediately suspended by the I.O.C. and ordered to leave the Olympic Village by the U.S.O.C. Yet they were hardly the first to make political gestures on the victory platform. During the 1936 Berlin Games, all German winners and several foreigners as well raised their right arms in the Nazi salute. Countless American athletes have placed their right hands over their hearts during the playing of their national anthem. Needless to say, none of these athletes was punished the way Smith and Carlos were.

The question then arises: If it was acceptable in 1936 to raise your right arm in the air with the open palm face down, and today it is acceptable to put your right hand over your heart, why was it *not* acceptable in 1968 to bow your head and raise your arm into the air with your gloved fist closed?

From the point of view of the I.O.C., the "crime" committed by Smith and Carlos was not that they had made a political statement, but that they had made the *wrong* political statement. Although Olympic *athletes* may be a representative group, I.O.C. members and other Olympic leaders are not. They are, in fact, very much like U.N. delegates. They have definite political beliefs. They support nationalism, and they support the ruling elites of the various nations of the world, no matter if they are Communist or capitalist. Thus it was perfectly all right in 1936 for German athletes to give the Nazi salute, because that salute was approved by the German government. And it is quite within the rules for

U.S. athletes to put their hands over their hearts because that is a patriotic gesture which shows support for nationalism and the status quo.

It was *not* acceptable to the I.O.C. to have Smith and Carlos raise clenched fists because their gesture, rather than showing support for a recognized nation-state, showed support for an unrecognized political entity—black Americans.

The Olympics have always reflected the politics of the world, from which they provide a temporary respite, and they always will.

# AMATEURISM

Contrary to popular belief, the Ancient Greek athletes were not amateurs. Not only were they fully supported throughout their training, but even though a winner received only an olive wreath at the Games, back home he was amply rewarded and could become quite rich.

The concept of amateurism actually developed in nineteenth-century England as a means of preventing the working classes from competing against the aristocracy. The wealthy could take part in sports without worrying about having to make a living, and thus could pursue the ideal of amateurism. Everyone else had to give up training time in order to earn a living, or else take money for sports performances and become a professional, ineligible for competitions such as the Olympics.

Baron de Coubertin, although a member of the French aristocracy, was well aware of the inequities of the amateur system. His solution was to have wealthy people come forward as "patrons" to support worthy working-class athletes.

The qualifications for being an amateur have varied from decade to decade and from sport to sport. In the 1920s British sportsmen accused the Americans of circumventing the rules of amateurism by the awarding of athletic scholarships to universities (although even the ancient Greek medical colleges recruited athletes). As late as the 1930s physical education teachers and recreation directors were considered professional athletes and thus ineligible for the Olympics.

These restrictions seem archaic today, but don't be surprised a few decades from now if our present-day restrictions seem just as silly. I believe that the code of amateurism will eventually be discarded and that the Olympics will be declared open to all qualified athletes. If the constant bickering over the definition of amateurism doesn't bring about the change, then the absurd advantage given to Communist countries will. Because the Communist nations claim that they have no professional athletes, they are able to field the best possible teams in every sport. Non-Communist countries are handicapped in any sport popular enough to support professionals, such as basketball, boxing, cycling, and football (soccer).

I appreciate the arguments of those who believe the Olympics would be made gaudy and commercial if they were opened to professionals, but I believe it is more important to eliminate the unfair advantages that the rules of amateurism provide for the rich and the Communists.

# DRUGS

Although the subject received unprecedented attention in 1988, the use of performance-enhancing drugs and concoctions by Olympic athletes was nothing new. The winner of the 1904 marathon, Thomas Hicks, was administered multiple doses of strychnine and brandy *during* the race. Just before the running of the 1920 men's 100 meters, the U.S. sprint coach gave his soon-to-be-victorious team members a mixture of sherry and raw egg. In 1960, Danish cyclist Knut Jensen died during the Olympic road race as a result of ingesting amphetamines and nicotinyl tartrate.

It was not until 1967 that the Medical Commission of the International Olympic Committee began outlawing drugs. The following year, Hans-Gunnar Liljenvall, of the Swedish modern pentathlon team, was disqualified for using alcohol. Full-scale drug testing began in 1972. By this time the use of stimulants, sedatives, hormones, and steroids was so common that doctors and coaches were already coming up with masking agents to beat the tests and studying how close to competition an athlete could continue his drug program without risking a positive test result.

Although fewer athletes tested positive for drugs in 1988 than in 1984, it was in Seoul that the issue came to a head because one of those caught was Ben Johnson, the most visible hero of the Games (see p. 12). The subsequent investigation by the Canadian government into the use of banned substances by its athletes, as well as the revelations by athletes from East Germany and Czechoslovakia following the collapse of Communism in Eastern Europe, revealed that the use of steroids was widespread and extremely sophisticated.

There are those who say that all performance-enhancing drugs should be legalized, that the drug users will always stay one step ahead of the testers. Although it often does seem to be a losing battle, the harmful side effects of banned substances, steroids in particular, would seem to justify continued vigilance.

# ACKNOWLEDGMENTS

First of all I would like to thank my father, Irving Wallace, who introduced me to the world of the Olympics. In the course of my research I have encountered numerous people who have graciously helped me on my way, starting with C. Robert Paul, who made available to me the archives of the United States Olympic Committee, including the Official Reports of the Organizing Committees of the various Olympic Games, which form the basis of the statistics in this book. Mr. Paul was also kind enough to review my manuscript in light of his long experience with the Olympic movement. I would also like to acknowledge the aid of David Kelly at the Library of Congress, Jan Foulstich and other members of the staff of Representative Anthony Beilenson, the staff of the Library of Notre Dame University, Maynard Brichford and others at the University of Illinois, Champaign-Urbana, which houses the Avery Brundage Collection, the staff of the Amateur Athletic Foundation library in Los Angeles, and Sandy Duncan of the British Olympic Association.

I am indebted to John Lucas, Bill Mallon, Harvey Abrams, and Peter Diamond, who allowed me to enjoy and make use of their personal libraries. I would also like to thank the following people for their help in the research process: Vicki Baker, Gail Hammer, C. Frank Zarnowsky, Wally Wolf, and Dr. Jae Yoon Ryoo, as well as the numerous people who read the 1988 edition of this book and sent in corrections, updates and new information, particularly Joel Jeffries, Malcolm R. Heyworth, and Eric Aldin.

Special acknowledgments are due to my wife, Flora Chavez, who helped when I needed it most; to my agent, Ed Victor, for his support and encouragement; and to my editor, Irv Goodman.

The author of this book may be reached by writing to:

Olympics
P.O. Box 49328
Los Angeles, California 90049

I would particularly appreciate hearing from former Olympians willing to share their recollections.

# THE CHARTS

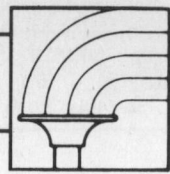

## SOURCES

Although the primary sources for the information included in the charts are the Official Reports of the various Olympics, these reports are often incomplete or incorrect. The man who has done the most to correct these inadequacies is Erich Kamper of Austria, author of *Enzyklopädie der Olympischen Spiele,* which lists the top six places in each event of the Summer Games from 1896 to 1968, and *Lexikon der 14,000 Olympioniken,* which gives basic biographical information for all medal winners through 1980. My search for correct spellings and accent marks also led me to *Die Olympischen Spiele von 1896 bis 1980* by Volker Kluge of East Germany; *Starozytne i Nowozytne Igrazyska Olimpyskie* by Zbigniew Porada of Poland; *Meet the Bulgarian Olympians* by Kostadinov, Georgiev, and Kambourov; *Az Olimpiajátékokon Indult Magyar Versenyzök Névsora 1896–1980; Die Deutschen Sportler der Olympischen Spiele 1896 bis 1968;* and *Sveriges Deltagare i de Olympiska Spelen 1896–1952.* For the early games (1896–1904) I am particularly indebted to Bill Mallon of the United States, author of *A Statistical Summary of the 1904 Olympic Games* and *The Olympic Record Book,* and co-author, with Ian Buchanan, of *Quest For Gold: The Encyclopedia of American Olympians.* Many of the 1896 statistics are based on the research of Ture Widlund, who is also the author of *Weightlifting in the Olympic Games 1896–1988.*

Numbers in the charts indicate times unless otherwise noted. A dash symbol in the numbers column means that the information was not taken or is otherwise unavailable.

Whenever possible I have included an athlete's first and last names. If the first name was unavailable, I have included the first initial. If that was unavailable I have just included the surname. If a female athlete competed under her maiden name, then got married and took part in a second Olympics using her married name, I have included her maiden name in parentheses.

## HOW TO READ THEM

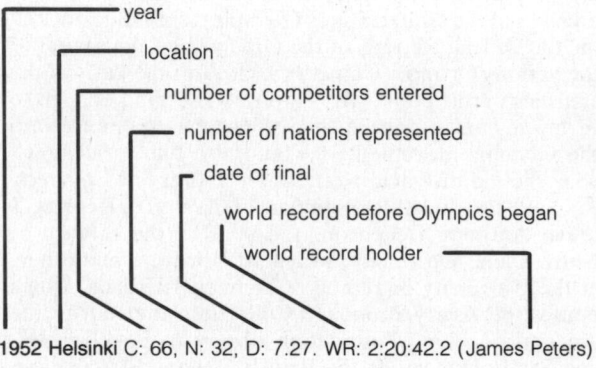

1952 Helsinki C: 66, N: 32, D: 7.27. WR: 2:20:42.2 (James Peters)

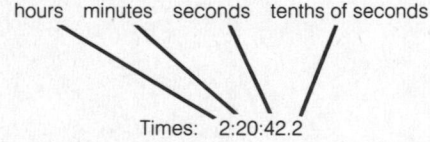

Times:    2:20:42.2

The 1906 Intercalated Games are considered unofficial by the I.O.C., but I have included them because of their historical importance.

In 1956, 1960, and 1964, West Germany (GER) and East Germany (GDR) entered combined teams. Nevertheless I have indicated which athletes were actually from each country because I thought it was interesting.

# KEY TO ABBREVIATIONS

## NATIONS

| | |
|---|---|
| AFG | Afghanistan |
| ALG | Algeria |
| ARG | Argentina |
| AUS | Australia |
| AUT | Austria |
| BAH | Bahamas |
| BEL | Belgium |
| BER | Bermuda |
| BOH | Bohemia |
| BRA | Brazil |
| BUL | Bulgaria |
| BWI | British West Indies (Jamaica and Trinidad) |
| CAM | Cameroon |
| CAN | Canada |
| CHI | Chile |
| CHN | China |
| COL | Colombia |
| CON | Congo |
| CRC | Costa Rica |
| CUB | Cuba |
| CZE | Czechoslovakia |
| DEN | Denmark |
| DJI | Djibouti |
| DOM | Dominican Republic |
| EGY | Egypt |
| EST | Estonia |
| ETH | Ethiopia |
| FIN | Finland |
| FRA | France |
| GBR | Great Britain and Northern Ireland |
| GDR | East Germany (German Democratic Republic, 1956–1988) |
| GER | Germany (1896–1936), West Germany (Federal Republic of Germany, 1952–1988) |
| GHA | Ghana |
| GRE | Greece |
| GUA | Guatemala |
| GUY | Guyana |
| HAI | Haiti |
| HOL | Holland (Netherlands) |
| HUN | Hungary |
| ICE | Iceland |
| INA | Indonesia |
| IND | India |
| INT | International team |
| IRL | Ireland (Eire) |
| IRN | Iran |
| IRQ | Iraq |
| ISR | Israel |
| ITA | Italy |
| IVC | Ivory Coast |
| JAM | Jamaica |
| JPN | Japan |
| KEN | Kenya |
| KOR | South Korea |
| KUW | Kuwait |
| LAT | Latvia |
| LEB | Lebanon |
| LIE | Liechtenstein |
| LIT | Lithuania |
| LUX | Luxembourg |
| MAD | Madagascar |
| MAL | Malaysia |
| MEX | Mexico |
| MLW | Malawi |
| MON | Mongolia |
| MOR | Morocco |
| MYA | Myanmar (Burma) |
| NGR | Nigeria |
| NIG | Niger |
| NLA | Netherland Antilles |
| NOR | Norway |
| NZE | New Zealand |
| OMA | Oman |
| PAK | Pakistan |
| PAN | Panama |
| PER | Peru |
| PHI | Philippines |
| POL | Poland |
| POR | Portugal |
| PRK | North Korea (People's Republic of Korea) |

| | | | | |
|---|---|---|---|---|
| PUR | Puerto Rico | | DNC | Did not compete in final |
| ROM | Romania | | DNF | Did not finish |
| RUS | Russia (1908–1912) | | DNS | Did not start in final |
| SAA | Saar | | e | Estimated |
| SAF | South Africa | | elim. | Eliminated |
| SEN | Senegal | | EOR | Equaled Olympic record |
| SIN | Singapore | | EWR | Equaled world record |
| SLE | Sierra Leone | | F.I.N.A. | International Amateur Swimming Federation |
| SMR | San Marino | | FT. | Feet |
| SOV | Soviet Union | | GA | Goals against |
| SPA | Spain | | GF | Goals for |
| SRL | Sri Lanka (Ceylon) | | GRW | Greco-Roman wrestling |
| SUD | Sudan | | H | Hurdles |
| SUR | Surinam | | HAM | Hammer throw |
| SWE | Sweden | | HJ | High jump |
| SWI | Switzerland | | I.A.A.F. | International Amateur Athletic Federation |
| SYR | Syria | | IN. | Inches |
| TAI | Taiwan | | I.O.C. | International Olympic Committee |
| TAN | Tanzania | | JAV | Javelin throw |
| THA | Thailand | | kg | Kilograms |
| TOG | Togo | | km | Kilometers |
| TON | Tonga | | KO | Knockout |
| TRI | Trinidad and Tobago | | L | Lost |
| TUN | Tunisia | | LBS. | Pounds |
| TUR | Turkey | | LJ | Long jump (broad jump) |
| UAR | United Arab Republic (Egypt and Syria) | | M | Meters |
| UGA | Uganda | | m.p.s. | Meters per second |
| URU | Uruguay | | N: | Number of nations represented |
| USA | United States of America | | OR | Olympic record |
| VEN | Venezuela | | PA | Points against |
| VIR | U.S. Virgin Islands | | PF | Points for |
| YUG | Yugoslavia | | PTS. | Points |
| ZAM | Zambia | | PV | Pole vault |
| ZIM | Zimbabwe | | Ret | Retired |
| | | | RSC | Referee stopped contest |
| | | | SLJ | Standing long jump |
| | | | SP | Shot put |

# TERMS

| | | | | |
|---|---|---|---|---|
| | | | T: | Number of teams entered |
| | | | T | Tied |
| | | | TG | Touches given |
| | | | TR | Touches received |
| A.A.A. | Amateur Athletic Association | | W | Won |
| A.A.U. | Amateur Athletic Union | | w | Wind-aided |
| AC | Also competed | | with | Withdrawn |
| C: | Number of competitors entered | | WB | World best |
| D: | Date of final | | WO | Walkover |
| Dec. | Won by judges' decision | | WR | World record |
| DISC | Discus throw | | YDS | Yards |
| DISQ | Disqualified | | | |

*THE COMPLETE BOOK OF THE OLYMPICS*

David Wallechinsky was introduced to the joys of the Olympics by his father, Irving Wallace, who took him to the Summer Games at Rome in 1960. Mr. Wallechinsky lives in Santa Monica, California, with his wife and their two sons.

# SUMMER GAMES

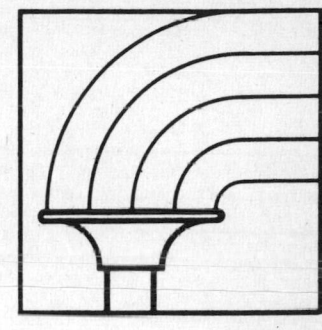

# TRACK AND FIELD

**MEN**

| | | | | |
|---|---|---|---|---|
| 100 Meters | 5000 Meters | 3000-Meter Steeplechase | High Jump | Discus Throw |
| 200 Meters | 10,000 Meters | 4 × 100-Meter Relay | Pole Vault | Hammer Throw |
| 400 Meters | Marathon | 4 × 400-Meter Relay | Long Jump | Javelin Throw |
| 800 Meters | 110-Meter Hurdles | 20,000-Meter Walk | Triple Jump | Decathlon |
| 1500 Meters | 400-Meter Hurdles | 50,000-Meter Walk | Shot Put | Discontinued Events |

## MEN

### 100 METERS

**1896 Athens** C: 15, N: 8, D: 4.10. WR: 10.8 (Luther Cary)

| | | |
|---|---|---|
| 1. Thomas Burke | USA | 12.0 |
| 2. Fritz Hofmann | GER | 12.2e |
| 3. Alajos Szokolyi | HUN | 12.6e |
| 4. Francis Lane | USA | 12.6e |
| 5. Alexandros Chalkokondilis | GRE | 12.6e |

DNS: Thomas Curtis (USA)

The very first race of the modern Olympics was the opening heat of the 100-meter dash. It was won by Francis Lane of Princeton in the time of 12⅕ seconds. The European crowd was fascinated by the "crouch" start of the Americans, as Thomas Curtis and Thomas Burke, both of Boston, won the other two qualifying heats. The first two finishers in each of the heats qualified for the final four days later, but Curtis chose not to start, preferring to save himself for the 110-meter hurdles, which was the next race. Burke, who had registered the fastest time (12.0) in the heats, equaled his time in the final and defeated Hofmann by two meters. The other runners were bunched four meters further back. Although Hofmann was a champion sprinter, his athletic specialty was actually rope climbing. Thomas Burke, the first Olympic 100 meters champion, later became a lawyer and also wrote part-time for the *Boston Journal* and the *Boston Post*. He died on Valentine's Day, 1929, at the age of 53.

**1900 Paris** C: 20, N: 9, D: 7.14. WR: 10.8 (Luther Cary)

| | | |
|---|---|---|
| 1. Frank Jarvis | USA | 11.0 |
| 2. John Walter Tewksbury | USA | 11.1 |
| 3. Stanley Rowley | AUS | 11.2 |

DNF: Arthur Duffey (USA)

The American runners had never competed before on a grass track, however this didn't prevent Jarvis of Princeton and Tewksbury of Pennsylvania from equaling the world record of 10.8 in the heats and semifinals, respectively. Despite these performances, the clear favorite was 5-foot 7-inch Arthur Duffey of Georgetown University,

who had defeated both Jarvis and Tewksbury in London the previous week. As expected, Duffey burst into the lead and seemed well on his way to victory when he suddenly began to wobble and fell to the ground at the 50-meter mark, the victim of a strained tendon in his left leg. Jarvis went on to win by about two feet. Duffey later told the press, "I do not know why my leg gave way. I felt a peculiar twitching after going twenty yards. I then seemed to lose control of it, and suddenly it gave out, throwing me on my face. But that is one of the fortunes of sport, and I cannot complain." In 1902 Duffey ran 100 yards in 9.6 seconds, setting a world record which stayed in the books for 24 years. Later he became a columnist for the *Boston Post*.

**1904 St. Louis** C: 13, N: 2, D: 9.3. WR: 10.8 (Luther Cary, Frank Jarvis, John Walter Tewksbury)

| | | |
|---|---|---|
| 1. Archibald Hahn | USA | 11.0 |
| 2. Nathaniel Cartmell | USA | 11.2 |
| 3. William Hogenson | USA | 11.2 |
| 4. Fay Moulton | USA | — |
| 5. Frederick Heckwolf | USA | — |
| 6. Lawson Robertson | USA | — |

Archie Hahn, "The Milwaukee Meteor," had already won the 60-meter and 200 meter dashes when he settled down for the final of the 100. Running into a heavy wind, he shot out to a fast start, had a one yard lead by the 20-meter mark, and held off the fast-finishing Louisville sprinter Nate Cartmell to win by almost two yards.

**1906 Athens** C: 42, N: 13, D: 4.27. WR: 10.8 (Luther Cary, Frank Jarvis, John Walter Tewksbury)

| | | |
|---|---|---|
| 1. Archibald Hahn | USA | 11.2 |
| 2. Fay Moulton | USA | 11.3 |
| 3. Nigel Barker | AUS | 11.3 |
| 4. William Eaton | USA | — |
| 5. Lawson Robertson | USA | — |
| 6. Knut Lindberg | SWE | — |

William Eaton of Boston recorded the fastest time in the semifinals (11.2), but in the final Hahn, with a quick start, led the whole way and won by a yard. Back in the United States, Hahn studied law at Michigan, but never practiced his profession. Instead he devoted his life to coaching younger runners. His book *How to Sprint* is still considered a classic text.

**1908 London** C: 57, N: 16, D: 7.22. WR: 10.6 (Knut Lindberg)

| | | | |
|---|---|---|---|
| 1. Reginald Walker | SAF | 10.8 | EOR |
| 2. James Rector | USA | 10.9 | |
| 3. Robert Kerr | CAN | 11.0 | |
| 4. Nathaniel Cartmell | USA | 11.2 | |

In 1908 the excitement surrounding the 100-meter race rivaled that of the marathon. The tension was heightened by the fact that only the winner of each heat advanced to the next round. The favorites, James Rector, a University of Virginia student from Hot Springs, Arkansas, and Bobbie Kerr, the Irish-born Canadian champion, did not disappoint their supporters in the opening heats. Rector was particularly impressive, tying the Olympic record of 10.8 seconds. He equaled this time in the semifinals, but so did Reggie Walker, a 19-year-old clerk from Durban. Walker had not been chosen for the South African team, but was sent to London as an afterthought by his fans in Natal. Arriving three weeks before the Olympics, he lost to Kerr in the final of the British A.A.A. Championship. Nevertheless he caught the eye of the famous coach Sam Mussabini, who took the young man under his wing and spent the next couple of weeks working with him on his start. This last-minute training worked wonders. Running on the inside lane, Walker stormed into an early lead, gave way to Rector at the halfway point, and then was able to pull ahead once again to win by a "long yard," with Rector holding on to second by mere inches. The 5-foot 7-inch, 130-pound Walker, who had been previously unknown to the general public, became an instant hero, as the crowd of 49,000 cheered wildly and threw their hats and programs into the air, while friends and officials competed for the right to carry him on their shoulders. In the words of one U.S. newspaper, "The Englishmen were gratified to see the monotonous succession of American victories broken by a Britisher, even if he was a colonist."

**1912 Stockholm** C: 68, N: 22, D: 7.7. WR: 10.5 (Richard Rau)

| | | |
|---|---|---|
| 1. Ralph Craig | USA | 10.8 |
| 2. Alvah Meyer | USA | 10.9 |
| 3. Donald Lippincott | USA | 10.9 |
| 4. George Patching | SAF | 11.0 |
| 5. Frank Belote | USA | — |

DNS: Howard Drew (USA)

Ralph Craig of the University of Michigan was considered the pre-Olympic favorite until he was beaten in the U.S trials by Howard Drew, a strong black student from Springfield, Massachusetts. In the first round in Stockholm, Donald Lippincott, the star of the University of Pennsylvania track team, set an Olympic record by winning his heat in 10.6 seconds. The semifinals were run with only the winner of each race advancing to the final. The Americans showed their strength by winning all five

of the heats in which they were entered. Unfortunately, Drew strained a tendon just before the finish of his heat and, despite qualifying, was unable to start in the final.

The final was marred by seven false starts, the first three by Craig. At the eighth try a clean break was made, with Patching taking the early lead. Craig caught him at the 60-meter mark and went on to win by two feet. Thirty-six years later, Craig, by then a wealthy 59-year-old industrial engineer, reappeared at the London Olympics as an alternate on the U.S. yachting team.

**1920 Antwerp** C: 59, N: 23, D: 8.16. WR: 10.5 (Richard Rau)

| | | |
|---|---|---|
| 1. Charles Paddock | USA | 10.8 |
| 2. Morris Kirksey | USA | 10.8 |
| 3. Harry Edward | GBR | 11.0 |
| 4. Jackson Scholz | USA | 11.0 |
| 5. Emile Ali Khan | FRA | 11.1 |
| 6. Loren Murchison | USA | — |

Charley Paddock was born in Gainesville, Texas, on August 11, 1900. A sickly child, he weighed only 7½ pounds at the age of 7 months. His parents moved to Southern California for his health, eventually settling in Pasadena. The change of climate must have done the trick, because by age 15, Charley was a barrel-chested 170-pounder with big strong legs and a sprinter's body. He loved to run long distances, but his father convinced him to concentrate on the 100 yards and the 220 yards. Paddock came to international attention in 1919 when he won both metric sprints at the Inter-Allied Games in Paris, with times of 10.8 and 21.6. Charley was a great crowd-pleaser, who delighted photographers with a flying finish in which he would leap at the tape from about 12 feet out, with his arms flung wide.

The semifinals of the Olympic championship were held in the early morning on Monday, August 16. The first heat was won by Guyanese-born Harry Edward and the second by Charley Paddock, both in 10.8. Scholz and Murchison had also run 10.8 in the earlier rounds. All four Americans qualified for the final and spent the next few hours together, waiting anxiously for their late afternoon race. The blond-haired Murchison kept muttering, half to himself, "I'm going to win. I've known it all along. . . . I can trim any sprinter who ever lived." The others tried to ignore him. Just before it was time to take the field, the four runners were approached by coach Lawson Robertson, who said, "What you fellows need to warm up is a glass of sherry and a raw egg." Murchison, Scholz, and Paddock were horrified by the suggestion, but when Stanford's Morris Kirksey agreed to try the drink, the others feared it would give him a psychological advantage to be the only one to follow the coach's advice, so they guzzled down the strange concoction as well.

Like many athletes, Charley Paddock followed a set of good luck rituals. On the way to the starting line he would knock on "a friendly piece of wood." When called to his mark, he would put his hands far across the starting line and then draw them slowly back before the second call of "get set." Paddock was the last to stoop to his mark at the starting line of the 1920 100-meter final. The assistant starter, unaware of Charley's ritual, ordered him in French to pull back his hands, which he was actually already in the process of doing. The starter then called out "*prêt*," the French equivalent of "get set." Murchison misinterpreted the exchange and thought the runners had been ordered to stand up, so he was just beginning to relax and rise when the gun went off. He was left 10 yards behind. Kirksey took the early lead, but at the halfway mark Scholz had a two-foot advantage, with Edward in second. Then Kirksey surged ahead again, with Paddock at his shoulder. In the words of Charley Paddock: "Then I saw the thin white string stretched to the breaking point in front of me. I drove my spikes into the soft cinders and felt my foot give way as I sprang forward in a final jump for the tape. . . . There was nothing more I could do. My eyes closed as my chest hit the string and when I opened them, my feet were on the ground again and I was yards ahead of the field. I did not know if I had been in front when the string was broken. I dared not ask." In fact, Charley Paddock had won the race by 12 inches. "My dream had come true," he later wrote, "and I thrilled to the greatest moment I felt that I should ever know. . . . The real pleasure had been in the anticipation and in that single moment of glorious realization."

**1924 Paris** C: 82, N: 34, D: 7.7. WR: 10.2 (Charles Paddock)
1. Harold Abrahams  GBR  10.6  EOR
2. Jackson Scholz  USA  10.7
3. Arthur Porritt  NZE  10.8
4. Chester Bowman  USA  10.9
5. Charles Paddock  USA  10.9
6. Loren Murchison  USA  11.0

The story of Harold Abrahams' victory in Paris in 1924 is well told in the beautiful film *Chariots of Fire*. Unfortunately, despite its claim of being "A true story," the film contains several factual distortions. Abrahams did not race around the great courtyard of Trinity College at Cambridge. (It was Lord Burghley who did that.) He did not look at the 100-meter contest as a chance to redeem himself after his failure in the 200, since the running of the 100 actually preceded the 200 in real life. Although Abrahams did feel himself an outsider because he was Jewish, a much more important motivating factor in his quest for victory was a desire to do better than his two older brothers, both of whom were well-known athletes and one of whom had represented Great Britain at the 1912 Olympics in Stockholm. Abrahams himself had competed in the 100 and 200 meters in Antwerp in 1920, but had been eliminated in the quarterfinals. In the year preceding the Paris Olympics, Abrahams came under the direction of Sam Mussabini, who had successfully coached Reggie Walker to victory in 1908. Among other things, Mussabini stressed to Abrahams the importance

of the length and number of his strides. During practice sessions Abrahams would place pieces of paper on the track, to indicate where each stride should end. Then he would try to pick them up on his spikes as he ran. He always carried with him a piece of string the length of his first stride. Before a race he would pull out the string, measure forward from the starting line, and make a mark on the track where his first step should land.

Abrahams was also a proficient long-jumper. One month before the Olympics he leaped 24 feet 2½ inches (7.38 meters) to set an English record which lasted until 1956. For this reason he was chosen to represent Great Britain in the long jump as well as the 100, 200 and 4 × 100 relay. When an anonymous letter appeared in the *Daily Express,* criticizing the decision to enter Abrahams in the long jump, few people knew that the letter had been written by Harold Abrahams himself. He made his point and was excused from that event.

Despite his great feats, the 6-foot ½-inch 175-pound Abrahams was considered a long shot in comparison to the U.S. team, which included defending champion Charley Paddock as well as Antwerp finalists Jackson Scholz and Loren Murchison. On June 18, 1921, Paddock had stunned the track world by running 110 yards (which is actually longer than 100 meters) in the unheard-of time of 10.2 seconds, a record that remained unbeaten for 29 years. Although the Americans were the favorites, it was Harold Abrahams, running faster than he had ever run before, who registered the fastest times in the early heats, tying the Olympic record (10.6) twice, in the quarterfinals and the semifinals, where he overcame an awful start. For the first time Abrahams realized that he had a chance to win the Olympic gold, and for the first time he lost his carefree attitude and began to feel the pressure. For the next 3¾ hours, as he waited for the final, he "felt like a condemned man feels just before going to the scaffold." As he went to his mark at 7:05 p.m. on July 7, Abrahams recalled Sam Mussabini's final words of advice: "Only think of two things—the report of the pistol and the tape. When you hear the one, just run like hell till you break the other." After a perfect start, the runners ran almost even for the first 40 or 50 meters, but than Abrahams began to move ahead, gaining with each stride until he crossed the tape with a two-foot victory.

Harold Abrahams is a perfect example of an athlete who peaks at exactly the right moment. After that day at the Stade Colombes in Paris, he never raced well again. The following year he injured his thigh while long-jumping and retired from competition forever. He once wrote, "I wonder if, in a sense, that was not another piece of good bad-luck. How many people find it almost impossible to retire at the right time. Would I have gone downhill, and tried to go on? That was the decision I never had to make; it was made for me. Rather painfully, but it was made." Abrahams went on to great success as a radio commentator, lawyer, writer, statistician and as president of the British Amateur Athletic Association.

Arthur Porritt, who took the bronze medal even though he failed to win a single heat, had an even more distinguished career, culminating in a five-year term as Governor-General of New Zealand and 35 years as Surgeon to the British royal family. Until Abrahams's death in 1978, he and Porritt and their wives had dinner every year at 7:00 p.m. on July 7—the day and the hour of the 1924 100-meter-final. As for Charley Paddock, he died in a plane crash in 1943 while a captain in the U.S. Marine Corps and had a ship named after him.

**1928 Amsterdam** C: 81, N: 33, D: 7.30. WR: 10.2 (Charles Paddock)

| | | |
|---|---|---|
| 1. Percy Williams | CAN | 10.8 |
| 2. Jack London | GBR | 10.9 |
| 3. Georg Lammers | GER | 10.9 |
| 4. Frank Wykoff | USA | 11.0 |
| 5. Wilfred Legg | SAF | 11.0 |
| 6. Robert McAllister | USA | 11.0 |

Percy Williams was one of the most popular winners of the Amsterdam Games. Not considered a serious threat by the experts, the slim, almost frail-looking 20-year-old from Vancouver, British Columbia, caught the fancy of the crowd in the second round, when he tied the Olympic record of 10.6. This time was matched in both semifinals, first by Bob McAllister, "The Flying Cop" of New York City, who barely held off a slow-starting Williams, and then by Jack London, a Guyanese-born university student who was the first Briton to use starting blocks. As the six finalists lined up for the deciding race, the 126-pound Williams seemed an unlikely bet to become Olympic champion, particularly as he was standing beside the muscular 6-foot 2-inch, 200-pound London. After two false starts, by Legg and Wykoff (who had gained 10 pounds on the boat ride from the United States), the runners were off. Williams took the lead immediately and kept it the entire way, holding off late rushes by London and Lammers to win by two feet. McAllister pulled a tendon 20 meters from the tape and finished last.

Upon his return to Canada, Williams, who also won the 200 meters, was greeted with an enthusiasm reminiscent of the ancient Greek Olympics. Crossing the continent by train with his mother, he stopped in Montreal, where he was presented with a gold watch. In Hamilton he received a silver tea service and in Winnipeg a bronze statue and a silver cup. When he finally reached Vancouver, he was met by tens of thousands of cheering fans and was given a blue Graham-Paige sports car as well as $14,500 for his education.

**1932 Los Angeles** C: 32, N: 17, D: 8.1. WR: 10.2 (Charles Paddock, Ralph Metcalfe)

| | | | |
|---|---|---|---|
| 1. Thomas "Eddie" Tolan | USA | 10.3 | OR |
| 2. Ralph Metcalfe | USA | 10.3 | |
| 3. Arthur Jonath | GER | 10.4 | |
| 4. George Simpson | USA | 10.5 | |
| 5. Daniel Joubert | SAF | 10.6 | |
| 6. Takayoshi Yoshioka | JPN | 10.8 | |

Eddie Tolan was the third University of Michigan athlete to win the Olympic 100 meters gold medal, following in the tradition of Archie Hahn and Ralph Craig. The 5-foot 7-inch Tolan dominated U.S. sprinting from 1929 to 1931, but he was dethroned by Ralph Metcalfe of Marquette University in Milwaukee, who breezed undefeated through the 1932 season. At the U.S. Olympic trials Metcalfe beat Tolan in both sprints and went to Los Angeles as the favorite. But in the second round it was Tolan who set an Olympic record of 10.4. In the final Yoshioka, an excellent starter, took the lead from the first step and held it for 40 meters, when he was caught by Tolan. Yoshioka faded at 60 meters, while Metcalfe began his famous finishing spurt. He pulled even with Tolan at 80 meters and the two ran neck and neck for the rest of the race, crossing the finish line in a near dead heat. Most of the spectators felt that there had been a tie or that Metcalfe had won. Several hours later, seven judges viewed a film of the race and determined that Tolan had *crossed* the line two inches ahead of Metcalfe. Current rules state that the first runner to *reach* the finish line is the winner. So close was the race that if the current rules had been in effect in 1932, Metcalfe would have been the winner.

After the games Tolan tried his hand at the vaudeville circuit, joining forces with the famous dancer Bill "Bojangles" Robinson. He was more successful as a professional runner, and was especially popular in Australia. There were also two also-rans who provoked interest in 1932. The first was Daniel Joubert, a white South African who spoke seven African dialects. Joubert arrived in Los Angeles in a somewhat weakened condition, having traveled 38 days to get there. Considering his ordeal, it was quite an achievement that he even made the final. The other was Liu Changchun, who marched in the opening day ceremony as the one and only representative of the 400,000,000 people of China. Liu finished last in his first round heat in both the 100 and 200. He also competed in both events at the Berlin Olympics four years later.

**1936 Berlin** C: 63, N: 30, D: 8.3. WR: 10.2 (Charles Paddock, Ralph Metcalfe, James "Jesse" Owens)

| | | |
|---|---|---|
| 1. James "Jesse" Owens | USA | 10.3 |
| 2. Ralph Metcalfe | USA | 10.4 |
| 3. Martinus Osendarp | HOL | 10.5 |
| 4. Frank Wykoff | USA | 10.6 |
| 5. Erich Borchmeyer | GER | 10.7 |
| 6. Lennart Strandberg | SWE | 10.9 |

Jesse Owens assured himself a permanent place in sports history on May 25, 1935, when, while competing at the Big Ten championships at Ann Arbor, Michigan, he broke five world records and equaled a sixth in the space of 45 minutes. At 3:15 p.m. he won the 100-yard dash by five yards in 9.4 seconds to tie the world record. At 3:25 he long-jumped 26 feet 8¼ inches, breaking the existing world record by six inches. It was his only jump of the day, but it wasn't beaten for 25 years. At 3:45 he scored a ten-yard victory in the 220-yard dash, clocking 20.3 seconds and bettering the listed record by three-tenths of a second. He was also given credit for lowering the world record in the shorter 200-meter dash. At 4:00 p.m. he flew over the 220-yard low hurdles in 22.6, the first man to beat 23 seconds. En route he also established a record for the 200-meter hurdles. Despite these and other sensational performances, in the following year Owens lost three times to the great Alabama-born sprinter Eulace Peacock. And it wasn't until one week before the Olympic trials that Jesse was able to defeat Ralph Metcalfe. But he peaked when he needed to, winning the 100, 200, and long jump at the trials, and he went to Berlin as the favorite in all three events.

Owens had little trouble living up to expectations. In the first round of the 100 meters he tied the Olympic record of 10.3. In the second round he ran a wind-aided 10.2. Jesse took it easy in the semifinals, winning his heat in 10.4 while Metcalfe won the other in 10.5. The final saw Owens take the lead from the first stride and pull out to a five-foot lead by the halfway mark. As usual Metcalfe started slowly and came on strong in the last 25 meters. He closed the gap, but was still a yard back when Owens broke the tape. Metcalfe, who was elected to the U.S. Congress 34 years later, picked up his second straight 100 meters silver medal, while Osendarp became the first Dutchman to win an individual track and field medal. Strandberg appeared to be a sure medalist, but he strained a tendon at the 80-meter mark and limped home in last place. Before the week was out, Jesse Owens had earned three more gold medals.

Nazi propaganda had portrayed Negroes as inferior, taunting the United States for relying on "black auxiliaries." Evidently, though, the message had little effect on the German masses, who considered Owens the hero of Berlin. Everywhere he went around town he was mobbed by fans seeking his autograph or photograph. They even shoved autograph books through his bedroom window in the Olympic Village while he tried to sleep.

Jesse Owens was born September 12, 1913, in Danville, Alabama, the son of sharecroppers and the grandson of slaves. By the age of 7 he was expected to pick 100 pounds of cotton a day. When he was 9 his family moved north to Cleveland, where Jesse pumped gas and delivered groceries. After he set national high school records in the broad jump, the 100-yard dash, and the 220, he was recruited by 28 colleges, but chose to stay close to home at Ohio State. While a student there he worked as an elevator operator and, later, as a page in the state legislature. There is a famous myth that after Jesse won the 100 meters in Berlin he was snubbed by Adolf Hitler, who refused to meet Owens after he had personally congratulated three earlier gold medal winners. Actually, if such a snub did occur, the recipient was not Jesse Owens, but Cornelius Johnson and David Albritton, black Americans who had finished one-two in the high jump the previous day.

Owens *was* snubbed by a different world leader— Franklin Delano Roosevelt. Although Jesse received tickertape parades in New York City and Cleveland, the President not only failed to invite him to the White House, he never even sent a letter of congratulations. Owens was also snubbed by the Amateur Athletic Union, which suspended him for refusing to run in a Swedish meet which he had never agreed to enter. The A.A.U. also bypassed him for the Sullivan award, which was presented to the best U.S. amateur athlete of the year. In 1935, the year that Jesse Owens set six world records, the award was given to a golfer named Lawson Little. In 1936, the year of Owens' four gold medals, the award went to Glenn Morris, the Olympic decathlon champion.

After the Olympics Jesse worked as a paid campaigner for presidential candidate Alf Landon. When Landon lost to Roosevelt in a landslide, Owens took a $130-a-month job as a playground instructor in Cleveland. In an attempt to make ends meet, the hero of Berlin, "The Ebony Antelope," allowed promoters to stage exhibitions in which he raced against horses, dogs, and motorcycles. Tiring of this, he returned to his job as a playground instructor. Then he lent his name to a chain of cleaning stores which went bankrupt, leaving Jesse $114,000 in debt. In the 1950s he finally achieved financial security when he opened a public relations firm and became a public speaker on behalf of various corporate sponsors. He developed a repertoire of five basic speeches including ones on religion, patriotism, and marketing for salesmen. In the words of writer William Oscar Johnson, Jesse Owens had become "a professional good example."

In 1968 Owens took the side of the U.S. Olympic Committee in its struggle with militant black athletes and two years later he wrote a book called *Blackthink*, which criticized racial militancy. However in 1972 he published another book, *I Have Changed*, retracting his earlier criticisms. After 35 years of pack-a-day cigarette smoking, Jesse Owens died of lung cancer in Tucson, Arizona, on March 31, 1980. Four years later a street in Berlin was renamed in his honor.

Would-be Olympic sprint champions might be interested to know the secret of Owens' success. In 1936 he told one London reporter, "I let my feet spend as little time on the ground as possible. From the air, fast down, and from the ground, fast up. My foot is only a fraction of the time on the track."

**1948 London** C: 66, N: 34, D: 7.31. WR: 10.2 (Charles Paddock, Ralph Metcalfe, James "Jesse" Owens, Harold Davis, Lloyd LaBeach, H. Norwood "Barney" Ewell)

| | | | |
|---|---|---|---|
| 1. Harrison Dillard | USA | 10.3 | EOR |
| 2. H. Norwood "Barney" Ewell | USA | 10.4 | |
| 3. Lloyd LaBeach | PAN | 10.4 | |
| 4. Alistair McCorquodale | GBR | 10.4 | |
| 5. Melvin Patton | USA | 10.5 | |
| 6. Emmanuel McDonald Bailey | GBR | 10.6 | |

Harrison Dillard was a 13-year-old schoolboy in Cleveland when he attended the huge parade in 1936 in honor of Jesse Owens. Later he met Owens, who took a liking to the young man and presented him with his first pair of running shoes. Dillard put those shoes to good use. By 1952 he had matched his hero's total of four Olympic victories. From May 31, 1947, through June 26, 1948, "Bones" Dillard, running mostly the hurdles, ran up an unprecedented string of 82 consecutive victories. The streak finally came to an end at the A.A.U. meet in Milwaukee when he tried to run four races in 67 minutes. First he lost the 100 meters to Barney Ewell and then he lost the 110-meter hurdles to Bill Porter. Nevertheless, when the Olympics trials were held the following week in Evanston, Illinois, there seemed no surer gold medal bet than Harrison Dillard, the world record holder in the 110-meters hurdles. However, in the final he uncharacteristically hit the first hurdle, lost his stride, hit two more hurdles, and stopped at the seventh hurdle as the others raced ahead. Dillard's Olympic hopes seemed over. Fortunately he had qualified the day before as third man in the 100 meters. But Dillard would face stiff competition in London. First there was the prerace favorite, U.S.C.'s Mel Patton, who held the world record of 9.3 in the 100 yards. Then there was 30-year-old Barney Ewell, who had beaten Patton at the U.S. trials in the world record time of 10.2. And there was Patton's arch rival from U.C.L.A., Lloyd LaBeach, who had also run 100 meters in 10.2 and who went to London as the sole representative of his native country, Panama.

The three favorites and Dillard were joined in the Olympic final by two representatives of Great Britain, Mac Bailey of Trinidad who, like Dillard, had been inspired by the feats of Jesse Owens, and Alistair McCorquodale, a burly Scot who had taken up running only a year earlier and who actually preferred rugby and cricket to track. After one false start, Dillard flashed into the lead and held it the entire way. Ewell caught him at the tape and, thinking he had won, danced around the field joyfully and embraced his opponents. When the photo-finish had been studied and it was announced that Dillard had won, Ewell happily congratulated him on his good fortune, greatly impressing the crowd of 82,000 with his sportsmanship. LaBeach is the only Panamanian ever to have won an Olympic medal.

**1952 Helsinki** C: 72, N: 33, D: 7.21. WR: 10.1 (Lloyd LaBeach)
1. Lindy Remigino       USA   10.4
2. Herbert McKenley      JAM   10.4
3. Emmanuel McDonald Bailey   GBR   10.4
4. F. Dean Smith         USA   10.4
5. Vladimir Sukharyev     SOV   10.5
6. John Treloar          AUS   10.5

The 1952 100-meter final produced the closest finish in Olympic history and also one of the biggest sprint upsets. The title seemed pretty much up for grabs, particularly after the U.S. college champion, Jim Golliday, was in-

jured and unable to participate in the Olympics. The position of favorite shifted to 31-year-old Mac Bailey and Arthur Bragg of Morgan State College. But Bragg pulled a muscle in the semifinals, which were won by Bailey and 30-year-old Herb McKenley, the 400-meter world record holder who had also entered the 100 as a means of practicing his start. The surviving U.S. representatives were Texan Dean Smith, who later became a stuntman in hundreds of television shows and films including *Stagecoach* and *True Grit,* and Lindy Remigino, a modest Manhattan College student from Hartford, Connecticut. Remigino must have been amazed to find himself a finalist in the Olympics. He had barely qualified for the U.S. Olympic tryouts by finishing fifth in the N.C.A.A. championship. Smith showed in front first, but Remigino had a clear lead at the halfway mark. He held on gamely for 90 meters, but was passed by McKenley just as they reached the tape.

"I was sure I had lost the race," said Remigino afterward. "I started my lean too early . . . and I saw Herb McKenley shoot past me. I was heartsick. I figured I had blown it." Lindy walked over to the delighted Jamaican and offered his congratulations. But a photo-finish showed that Remigino's right shoulder had reached the finish line an inch ahead of McKenley's chest, and the judges ruled him the winner. When someone told Remigino the results before they had been flashed on the scoreboard, he was incredulous and was sure there had been a mistake. Finally he turned to McKenley and is reputed to have said, "Gosh, Herb, it looks as though I won the darn thing." The closeness of the finish is shown by the fact that Dean Smith was only 14 inches behind the winner, yet placed only fourth.

**1956 Melbourne** C: 65, N: 31, D: 11.24. WR: 10.1 (Lloyd LaBeach, Willie Williams, Ira Murchison, Leamon King)
1. Bobby Joe Morrow   USA   10.5
2. W. Thane Baker     USA   10.5
3. Hector Hogan       AUS   10.6
4. Ira Murchison      USA   10.6
5. Manfred Germar    GER   10.7
6. Michael Agostini    TRI   10.7

The Olympic record was tied in the second round by the favorites, 6-foot 1½-inch Bobby Morrow and 5-foot 4½-inch Ira Murchison. The same pair won the two semifinal heats with Morrow again running 10.3. The final was run into a 9 m.p.h. wind, which accounts for the slow times. Hec Hogan, the five-time Australian 100-yard champion from Queensland, took the early lead, but Morrow passed him after 50 meters and stormed to a decisive victory. Baker and Murchison caught Hogan with 25 yards to go, but Hogan churned out a final burst, and only a desperate lunge by Baker kept the Aussie from a silver medal. Morrow, a devout Christian from Harlingen, Texas, never tried to anticipate the starters' gun with a rolling start because he considered it unsportsmanlike. A cotton and carrot farmer, he relied on getting 11 hours' sleep a night to keep up his strength. "Whatever success I have had," he said, "is due to being so perfectly relaxed that I can feel my jaw muscles wiggle." Bronze medalist Hogan died of leukemia at the age of 29 on September 2, 1960, the day after the 100-meter final at Rome.

**1960 Rome** C: 61, N: 45, D: 9.1. WR: 10.0 (Armin Hary, Harry Jerome)

| | | | |
|---|---|---|---|
| 1. Armin Hary | GER | 10.2 | OR |
| 2. David Sime | USA | 10.2 | |
| 3. Peter Radford | GBR | 10.3 | |
| 4. Enrique Figuerola Camue | CUB | 10.3 | |
| 5. Francis "Frank" Budd | USA | 10.3 | |
| 6. O. Ray Norton | USA | 10.4 | |

On June 21, 1960, Armin Hary, a controversial, self-coached office worker from Frankfurt, became the first man to be credited with 10.0 in the 100 meters. Running in Zurich, this fast-starting son of a coal miner in Quierschied, Saarland, actually achieved the time twice in one day. On the first occasion he was accused of "taking a flyer," or beating the gun, a tactic for which he was notorious. When the starter ordered the race rerun, Hary protested, but went ahead and ran another 10.0. Three and a half weeks later, on July 15, the son of a Pullman coach attendant, 19-year-old Harry Jerome of Vancouver, recorded the second official 10.0 at the Canadian Olympic trials at Saskatoon.

Despite the achievements of Hary and Jerome, most track aficionados were predicting victory for Ray Norton, who had swept both sprints at the U.S.A.-U.S.S.R. meet, the 1959 Pan American Games, and the 1960 U.S. Olympic trials. Another contender was Dave Sime, a medical student from Fair Lawn, New Jersey. Sime set a rather unusual world record when he ran 100 yards in 9.8 seconds while dressed in a baseball uniform. The previous record had been set by Jesse Owens in 1936.

In the second round in Rome, Armin Hary beat Dave Sime by a yard and set an Olympic record of 10.2. The first semifinal was won by Peter Radford, a Walsall schoolteacher who had spent three childhood years in a wheelchair because of a kidney disease. Harry Jerome had been in the lead when he pulled a muscle and couldn't finish. The second semi saw Armin Hary beat both Sime and Norton, who was running unusually tightly.

The start of the final was a tense affair. First Hary and Sime broke without a gun, but neither was penalized. The next try for a start was halted when Figuerola needed his starting block repaired. Then Hary beat the gun and was penalized. One more false start and he would be disqualified. But the usually volatile Hary kept his poise and at the next attempt got off to a fair and perfect start. By the end of the first stride he was already in the lead, and at the five-meter mark he led by a full

meter. In the second half of the race, Sime stormed back from last place to make up over three meters, but Hary held on to win by a "long foot." Not only was Armin Hary the first winner of the Olympic 100 meters to come from a non-English-speaking country, he was also the first German male to win an Olympic gold medal in a track event.

In the end Hary proved that his amazing "blitz start" was legitimate. He contended, however, that there was more to it than quick reflexes. "More important to me," he said, "is the fact that I have learned, through relaxation, how to achieve full stride and smooth forward action very early in the race." He did, however, employ one "trick." Whenever the starter called "set," Hary would stay down until all the other runners were hanging heavily in the set position. Only then would he rise. Unsuspecting starters would invariably wait for him and then pull the trigger for the start, allowing Hary, in effect, to control the beginning of the race. Hary's competitive career came to an abrupt halt shortly after the Olympics, when his knee was severely injured in an auto accident. In 1981 his name reappeared in the news when he was convicted of diverting Roman Catholic Church funds for use in a personal investment.

**1964 Tokyo** C: 73, N: 49, D: 10.15. WR: 10.0 (Armin Hary, Harry Jerome, Horacio Estevez)

| | | | |
|---|---|---|---|
| 1. Robert Hayes | USA | 10.0 | EWR |
| 2. Enrique Figuerola Camue | CUB | 10.2 | |
| 3. Harry Jerome | CAN | 10.2 | |
| 4. Wieslaw Maniak | POL | 10.4 | |
| 5. Heinz Schumann | GER | 10.4 | |
| 6. Gaoussou Kone | IVC | 10.4 | |
| 6. Melvin Pender | USA | 10.4 | |
| 8. Thomas Robinson | BAH | 10.5 | |

This was one 100-meter final that was run exactly to form. Any doubts that Hayes had not recovered from a June leg injury were quickly dispelled when the burly, pigeon-toed Florida speedster demolished the field in the first semifinal in a wind-aided 9.9. Harry Jerome won the second semi, ahead of Kone, Figuerola, and Pender. Pender led most of the way but tore a rib muscle and had to be carried off the field on a stretcher. Advised by doctors to withdraw from the final, he ran anyway and spent the next three days in the hospital as a result. Hayes, who was the first person to run 100 yards in 9.1 and the first person to break 6.0 for 60 yards, entered the Olympics with a record of 48 straight finals victories at 100 yards and 100 meters. The start was delayed 10 minutes while the curb lane, Hayes' lane, was raked after having been chewed up by the start of the 20-kilometer walk. The big three, Hayes, Figuerola and Jerome, had pulled away from the others by the 10-meter mark. Then Hayes unleashed his power, took a one-meter lead halfway, and pulled away to an awesome seven-foot victory. Both Figuerola, who became the first Cuban to win an

Olympic track and field medal, and Jerome called it the best race they had run all year and had nothing but praise for the winner. After the Olympics, Bob Hayes became a professional football player and was twice chosen All-Pro as a wide receiver for the Dallas Cowboys.

**1968 Mexico City** C: 64, N: 42, D: 10.14. WR: 9.9 (James Hines, Ronnie Ray Smith, Charles Greene)

| | | | |
|---|---|---|---|
| 1. James Hines | USA | 9.95 | WR |
| 2. Lennox Miller | JAM | 10.04 | |
| 3. Charles Greene | USA | 10.07 | |
| 4. Pablo Montes | CUB | 10.14 | |
| 5. Roger Bambuck | FRA | 10.15 | |
| 6. Melvin Pender | USA | 10.17 | |
| 7. Harry Jerome | CAN | 10.20 | |
| 8. Jean-Louis Ravelomanatsoa | MAD | 10.27 | |

The first accredited time of 9.9 seconds for 100 meters was registered at the A.A.U. Championships in Sacramento, California, on June 20, 1968, by Jim Hines, the son of an Oakland construction worker. Hines had run a wind-aided 9.8 in a heat, then followed with his history-making run in the semifinal. However, in the final he was beaten by Charlie Greene, a graduate of the University of Nebraska. Previous to the Olympics, Hines and Greene had met in 12 finals, with Greene winning eight of them. However two of Hines' four victories had been the last two times they met, at the U.S. Olympic trials.

Competition was stiff in Mexico City. In the second round Heinz Erbstösser of East Germany had the distinction of being the first person to run 10.2 and not qualify for the semifinals. Greene clocked 10.0 in his first two heats, while Hines matched the time in the semis. Hermes Ramirez of Cuba also ran 10.0 in the second round, but was eliminated in the semis. The 1968 100 meters saw the first all-black final in Olympic history. Hines got off to what he later said was the best start of his career. However it was U.S. Army captain Mel Pender, now 30, who took the early lead. By 50 meters Hines and Greene had pulled even, and at 70 meters Hines shifted gears and pulled away to win by a meter. Greene, discouraged and suffering a cramp, was nipped at the tape by Lennox Miller, who represented U.S.C. in U.S. collegiate competition. Hines' electronically timed 9.95 was considered faster than the hand-timed world record of 9.9. Four days after his Olympic victory, Hines signed a contract with the Miami Dolphins football team. Another man who went into professional sports was Japan's Hideo Iijima, who made it to the semifinals in 1964 and 1968. As the fastest sprinter in Japanese history, Iijima attracted the attention of the Lotte Orions baseball team, who hired him to become a pinch-runner and base-stealer. The club insured Iijima's legs for 50 million yen. Unfortunately Iijima, though fast, hadn't played baseball since he was 12 and had no aptitude for getting a jump on a pitch or for sliding. After two years, during which he was caught stealing 17 of 40 times, he was finally dropped from the team.

**1972 Munich** C: 84, N: 55, D: 9.1. WR: 9.95 (James Hines)

| | | |
|---|---|---|
| 1. Valery Borzov | SOV | 10.14 |
| 2. Robert Taylor | USA | 10.24 |
| 3. Lennox Miller | JAM | 10.33 |
| 4. Aleksandr Kornelyuk | SOV | 10.36 |
| 5. Michael Fray | JAM | 10.40 |
| 6. Jobst Hirscht | GER | 10.40 |
| 7. Zenon Nowosz | POL | 10.46 |

DNF: Hasely Crawford (TRI)

Valery Borzov was the clear favorite in 1972. The blond-haired, blue-eyed Ukrainian was extremely consistent and had not been beaten in almost two years. However, Eddie Hart of Pittsburg, California, and Rey Robinson of Lakeland, Florida, had both been timed at 9.9 in the U.S. Olympic trials. Hart was considered the number-one threat to Borzov. The first round of 12 heats began at 11:09 a.m. on August 31. Borzov, Hart, and Robinson each won their heats. Vassilios Papageorgopoulous of Greece recorded the fastest time of the round, 10.24, a time that might have earned him a silver medal had he not suffered a groin injury that forced him to withdraw from the semifinals. The second round, the quarterfinals, was scheduled to commence at 4:15 p.m. As that time drew nearer, 1968 400-meter gold medalist Lee Evans noticed that Hart, Robinson and the third U.S. sprinter, Robert Taylor, had not yet arrived at the stadium. When he couldn't find them at the warm-up track, Evans began to worry. Scheduled to run in the 4 × 400-meter relay later in the week, he raced at top speed from the stadium to the Olympic Village three quarters of a mile away in search of the missing Americans. But it was too late.

Two minutes earlier, Hart, Robinson, and Taylor, thinking the quarterfinals didn't begin until 7 p.m., had casually left their quarters to return to the stadium. Accompanied by their coach, Stan Wright, who had been working from an outdated 18-month-old preliminary schedule, the trio made their way to the bus stop at the Village gate. While waiting for the track stadium bus, they wandered into the doorway of the ABC-TV headquarters and began watching the television monitor. What they saw on the screen was several 100-meter runners lining up at the starting line. Robinson asked if this was a rerun of the first round. Told that it was a live transmission, Robinson realized with horror that he was watching the very heat in which he had been scheduled to run. Hart was entered in the second heat and Taylor in the third. The three athletes and their coach were pushed into a car and driven at breakneck speed to the stadium by ABC employee Bill Norris. It was too late for Robinson and Hart, but Taylor who, like Jim Hines, had studied at Texas Southern, arrived just in time to slip off his sweats, put on his shoes, do a couple knee-bends, and settle into the starting blocks. He finished second in the heat, a yard behind Borzov, which is exactly where he ended up 25 hours later, in the final. In that race, Borzov took the lead after 30 meters and was never headed. He even eased up at the end, throwing his arms wide in exultation five meters from the finish. A last-chance dive gained dental student Lennox Miller third place over Aleksandr Kornelyuk, the 5-foot 5-inch surprise from Azerbaijan.

Following the race, Borzov told reporters (in English) that he owed his success, "First and foremost to my country, secondly to my coach, Valentin Petrovsky, thirdly to all the people who helped me develop, and fourthly to myself." Borzov wasn't just toeing the party line. Listen to Petrovsky explain what went on at the Kiev Institute of Physical Culture, where Borzov was a graduate student: "We began with a search for the most up-to-date model of sprinting. We studied slow-motion films of leading world sprinters of past and present, figured out the push-off angle and the body incline at the breakaway and went deeply into a whole number of minor details. . . . For Borzov to be able to clock 10 seconds flat over 100 meters, a whole team of scientists conducted research resembling the work of, say, car or aircraft designers. . . . When the mathematical equivalent of a runner was worked out and given a scientific basis, we began testing our calculations in practice. It was subtle work, which could be compared to the training of a ballerina." Such statements give the impression that Borzov was just a machine, but he was quite human. He once said, "I very often have the following urge: I suddenly feel on the street that I have to run. I absolutely have to run, dressed in a suit, wearing my hat and tie, not paying any attention to the passers-by. . . . Then convention gets the upper hand and I restrain myself." Borzov eventually married the famous gymnast Lyudmila Turischeva, who won even more gold medals than he did.

**1976 Montreal** C: 63, N: 40, D: 7.24. WR: 9.95 (James Hines)

| | | |
|---|---|---|
| 1. Hasely Crawford | TRI | 10.06 |
| 2. Donald Quarrie | JAM | 10.08 |
| 3. Valery Borzov | SOV | 10.14 |
| 4. Harvey Glance | USA | 10.19 |
| 5. Guy Abrahams | PAN | 10.25 |
| 6. John Jones | USA | 10.27 |
| 7. Klaus-Dieter Kurrat | GDR | 10.31 |
| 8. Peter Petrov | BUL | 10.35 |

Several runners were given a strong chance to win, but the leading choices of track experts were Donald Quarrie, Silvio Leonard of Cienfuegos, Cuba, and Valery Borzov, who was aiming to become the first man to win two 100 meters gold medals (not counting Archie Hahn, whose second victory was in the Intercalated Games of 1906). In fact, Borzov was the first gold medalist even to attempt the feat since Percy Williams had been eliminated in the semifinals in 1932. The first of the leading contenders to fall by the wayside was the accident-prone Cuban Silvio Leonard. Leonard had won the 100 meters at the 1975 Pan American Games in Mexico City, but had pulled a muscle as he crossed the finish line. Hobbling forward in pain, he was unable to stop himself and fell into the 10-foot moat that surrounded the track. Seriously injured, Leonard nonetheless regained his form in time for the Olympics. Ten days before the Games, however, he stepped on a cologne bottle during a bit of horseplay and cut his foot. He was eliminated in the quarterfinals.

Meanwhile, 6-foot 2¾-inch Hasely Crawford, a gear machinist from San Fernando, Trinidad, was breezing through his heats. In the quarterfinals he beat Borzov, and in the semis he defeated Quarrie. Crawford had been a finalist in Munich four years earlier but had stopped running after four or five strides, the victim of a hamstring pull and nervousness. He was still fighting his nerves in Montreal, but he wasn't the only one. In the staging room before the final he looked over at Glance and Jones, who were only 19 and 18 respectively, and their "eyes showed they were already defeated." Crawford later told reporters, "At the line I knew I could beat Borzov. I feared Don Quarrie." At the starting line, Crawford "shook a little bit," but got a good start anyway. Glance took the early lead. Quarrie caught him after 60 meters and passed him at 75 meters. Then Crawford flew past on the curb lane. He stumbled just before the finish, but held off the lunging Quarrie to win. Crawford kept running for another 150 meters, then stopped suddenly, as if the realization of his accomplishment had just hit him.

As Trinidad's first Olympic champion, Crawford received more than his share of honors. He was awarded the Trinity Cross Gold, his picture appeared on two postage stamps, an airplane was named after him, and six different Calypso songs were written in his honor.

**1980 Moscow** C: 65, N: 40, D: 7.25. WR: 9.95 (James Hines)

| | | |
|---|---|---|
| 1. Allan Wells | GBR | 10.25 |
| 2. Silvio Leonard Tartabull | CUB | 10.25 |
| 3. Peter Petrov | BUL | 10.39 |
| 4. Aleksandr Aksinin | SOV | 10.42 |
| 5. Osvaldo Lara Cañizares | CUB | 10.43 |
| 6. Vladimir Muravyov | SOV | 10.44 |
| 7. Marian Woronin | POL | 10.46 |
| 8. Hermann Panzo | FRA | 10.49 |

Stanley Floyd of Albany, Georgia, won the U.S. Olympic trials and also recorded the best time of the year (10.07). But with U.S. athletes boycotted out of the Olympics the mantle of favorite fell to Silvio Leonard, who had successfully managed to steer clear of moats and cologne bottles. His most serious challengers were considered to be Marian Woronin, who predicted that he would win the gold medal in a time of 10.10, and Eugen Ray of East Germany. Aleksandr Aksinin recorded the fastest time of the first round—10.26. When the draw was announced for the second round, many eyebrows were raised. Of the nine first-round winners, four were thrown into the first heat, as was defending champion Hasely Crawford. On the other hand, heat number three saw Aksinin unburdened by competition from other first-round winners. Aksinin won that heat in 10.29, a time which would have placed him seventh in the first heat. Heat number one was won by Allan Wells, a marine engineer from Edinburgh. His time of 10.11 pushed him to cofavorite with Leonard.

The final took place during the last round of the triple jump, an event of great interest to the Soviet crowd. Just as the starter called "set," a great roar went up for a jump made by local favorite Viktor Saneyev. The starter held the runners in their crouch, then shot the gun. Aksinin and Lara were off the fastest, with Leonard and Wells close behind. By 60 meters Lara had faded, and by 80 meters the race was between Leonard on the inside and Wells on the outside. Wells edged ahead, but Leonard drew even again. With seven meters to go the stocky Scot began an extreme lean which allowed his shoulder to cross the finish line two or three inches before Leonard's chest. Allan Wells had become Great Britain's first 100 meters winner since Harold Abrahams and Scotland's first track gold medalist since Eric Liddell. At 28 he was also the oldest winner of the 100 meters in Olympic history. As a youngster Wells had enrolled in a Charles Atlas correspondence course in bodybuilding. His father was a blacksmith and his mother sewed nets for fishermen and worked as a hospital cleaner. Coached by his wife, Wells did not use starting blocks until 1980, when the International Amateur Athletic Federation (I.A.A.F.) required their use in international competitions.

**1984 Los Angeles** C: 82, N: 59, D: 8.4. WR: 9.93 (Calvin Smith)
1. F. Carlton Lewis       USA   9.99
2. Sam Graddy             USA   10.19
3. Benjamin Johnson       CAN   10.22
4. Ron Brown              USA   10.26
5. Michael McFarlane      GBR   10.27
6. Raymond Stewart        JAM   10.29
7. Donovan Reid           GBR   10.33
8. Tony Sharpe            CAN   10.35

The third son of two track coaches, Carl Lewis was born in Birmingham, Alabama, and raised in Willingboro, New Jersey. Small for his age and shy, Lewis began to grow so rapidly at the age of 15, that he had to walk with crutches for three weeks while his body adjusted. Previously thought to be the least athletic member of his talented family, Lewis' achievements began to outstrip all around him. By 1981 he was ranked number one in the world in the 100-meter dash and in the long jump. In June of 1983, he won the 100, the 200 and the long jump at the U.S. national championships, the first person to do so since Malcolm Ford in 1886. Two months later, he earned three gold medals at the Helsinki world championships. The following year he qualified for four events at the Los Angeles Olympics, giving him the opportunity to match Jesse Owens' four gold medal feat of 1936.

Lewis' first stop was the 100 meters, the event at which he was considered most vulnerable. As it turned out, he dominated the field. His second-round time of 10.04 was

the best ever at a low-altitude Olympics. In the final, Graddy and Johnson were out fastest. Graddy still led at the 80-meter mark. "I thought, 'Hey, I'm going to win a gold medal,' " Graddy would later say. "Then I saw him out of the corner of my eye." Lewis, who was clocked at 28 miles per hour at the finish, pulled away so strongly that his winning margin was a remarkable eight feet—the widest in Olympic history. Carl Lewis had won the first of his four gold medals.

**1988 Seoul** C: 102, N: 69, D: 9.24. WR: 9.83 (Benjamin Johnson)
1. F. Carlton Lewis       USA   9.92   OR
2. Linford Christie       GBR   9.97
3. Calvin Smith           USA   9.99
4. Dennis Mitchell        USA   10.04
5. Robson Caetano da Silva   BRA   10.11
6. Desai Williams         CAN   10.11
7. Raymond Stewart        JAM   12.26
DISQ (Drugs): Benjamin Johnson (CAN) 9.79

Ben Johnson was born in Falmouth, Jamaica, on December 30, 1961. Small and shy, he began to stutter at the age of 12 as a result of constantly mimicking his older brother's stammer. When he was 14 he moved to Toronto with his mother and three of his five siblings. Like his future rival, Carl Lewis, Johnson experienced a rapid growth spurt when he was 15 years old. It was also at this time that Johnson came under the tutelage of sprint coach Charlie Francis, the man who would guide his running career for the next 11 years.

On August 29, 1980, Johnson took part in the Pan-American Junior Championships in Sudbury, Ontario, finishing sixth with a time of 10.86. This seemingly unimportant race would, in retrospect, earn significance as the first encounter between Johnson and Lewis, who won the contest in 10.43. Johnson scored his first major international success two years later when he finished second at the 1982 Commonwealth Games. Two years after that he qualified for the 100-meter final at the Los Angeles Olympics. After purposely false-starting in an unsuccessful attempt to rattle Lewis, Johnson surprised track fans by earning the bronze medal behind Lewis and Sam Graddy.

In 1985, after seven consecutive losses, Johnson finally defeated Lewis. By 1986 there was no question that "Big Ben" had wrested the title of Fastest Man on Earth from "King Carl." By the time of their classic confrontation at the 1987 world championships in Rome, it was Johnson who had won their last four encounters. By that time, also, Johnson had developed a reputation as an incredibly fast starter who appeared to leap out of the blocks like a panther going after a kill or a guard dog attacking an intruder. In the Rome final he burst off the line with so much power that he almost fell over. After 10 meters he was already in front by a full meter, a lead he would hold all the way to the finish line, which he reached in a mere 9.83 seconds, breaking the world record by a full tenth of a second. In less than 10 seconds Ben Johnson had become an international celebrity. He would soon sign commercial endorsement contracts worth millions of dollars.

Meanwhile, Carl Lewis, who had equaled the world record of 9.93 only to finish second, was livid. Although he refused to name names, he made it clear that he thought Johnson was taking illegal, performance-enhancing drugs. Although many dismissed Lewis' charges as sour grapes, he was not alone in his suspicions. On the track circuit, Johnson's highly sculptured muscles and yellow-tinged eyes, two indications of steroid use, had earned Johnson the nickname "Benoid." However, as his coach, Charlie Francis, was quick to point out, Johnson had passed innumerable drug tests. In 1985 Johnson himself told Canada's *Athletics* magazine, "Drugs are both demeaning and despicable and when people are caught they should be thrown out of the sport for good. . . . I want to be the best on my own natural ability and no drugs will pass into my body."

As 1988 began, Johnson seemed to have a lock on the Olympic gold medal. But then disaster struck. In February, he pulled a hamstring muscle. In May, he reinjured his leg. In June, he broke away from Charlie Francis for the first time. However, a few weeks later they reconciled and Johnson returned to competition in time to win the Canadian Olympic trials. On August 17 in Zurich, the site of Johnson's first victory over Lewis three years earlier, the two met again for the first time since the Rome world championships. As usual, Johnson broke in front, but this time Lewis mowed him down to win with a time of 9.93 seconds. Calvin Smith was second at 9.97 and Johnson third at 10.00. Five days later in Cologne, Johnson was again beaten into third place, this time by Smith and Dennis Mitchell.

While Johnson retreated to Canada for a final month of training, Lewis was installed as the overwhelming favorite to become the first male sprinter to retain his Olympic title. Johnson dismissed this growing consensus. "When the gun go off," he said, "the race be over."

In Seoul, Lewis appeared to be in perfect form. He registered the fastest time in each of the first two rounds: 10.14 and 9.99. Johnson, meanwhile, caused a minor sensation in the second round. The rules stated that the top two finishers in each of the six heats would advance to the semifinals, as would the four fastest of the remaining runners. Johnson, apparently believing that the top *three* from each heat qualified automatically, eased up at the end and dropped to third behind Linford Christie and Dennis Mitchell. Fortunately, Johnson's 10.17 allowed him to advance anyway.

The semifinals were held the following day, Saturday, at noon. Lewis won the first heat in 9.97. In the second, Johnson was called for a false start, a ruling that infuriated him. Still, he managed to control his anger and win the race in 10.03 despite running into a 1.2-meters-per-second head wind.

Less than an hour and a half later, the eight finalists met at the starting line. Carl Lewis was in lane 3, Ben Johnson in lane 6. They were separated by Linford Christie and Calvin Smith. By now Johnson's muscles were so highly developed that, as he waited for the sound of the starter's pistol, they seemed to be separate beings on the verge of exploding out of his skin. As expected, Johnson charged into the lead immediately.

On May 5, 1987, Carl Lewis' father had died of cancer. At the funeral, Carl had reached into his pocket and pulled out the gold medal he had earned for winning the 100 meters in 1984. He placed the medal in his father's hands and said, "I want you to have this because it was your favorite event." Noting his mother's surprise, he added, "Don't worry, I'll get another one."

Now, halfway through the 1988 final, he glanced to his right, saw Ben Johnson 5 feet ahead of him, and was convinced that he could catch him. At the 80-meter mark Lewis looked over again and discovered that he was still 5 feet behind. This time he knew the race was lost. "Damn," he thought. "Ben did it again. The bastard got away with it again. It's over, Dad." Just before the finish line, Johnson stared back at Lewis and thrust his right arm into the air, his index finger pointed to the sky. His time was an amazing 9.79.

Lewis, convinced that Johnson was on steroids, wanted to protest, but held his tongue. As he later wrote in his autobiography, *Inside Track,* "I didn't have the medal to replace the one I had given [my father], and that hurt. But I could still give something to my father by acting the way he had always wanted me to act, with class and dignity." He shook Johnson's hand and walked away, ignoring the taunts of a group of Canadian fans who chanted, "When the gun go off, the race be over."

Johnson accepted the accolades of the crowd, appeared live on Canadian television, and then went off to doping control where he required one and a half hours and several beers to produce a urine sample. Afterward he spent over an hour in a sauna, then celebrated by eating half of a cream cake given to him by his mother, dining with friends at an Italian restaurant, and visiting a disco.

Back in Canada, the population was in ecstasy. In the 12 Olympics prior to the boycotted Games of 1980 and 1984, Canada had averaged one gold medal per Olympics. Its last track-and-field gold had come in 1932. The headline in the *Toronto Star* summed up the mood of the nation: "Ben Johnson—a national treasure."

Meanwhile, Johnson's urine sample was delivered to the Olympic Doping Control Center, numbered, and divided into two parts labeled "A" and "B." On Sunday, the testing center, not knowing whose urine they were examining, discovered that the "A" sample contained steroids. This information was passed on to Prince Alexandre de Merode of Belgium, the chairman of the I.O.C.'s medical commission. He matched the sample to a list of athletes' numbers and became the first person to learn that the guilty party was Ben Johnson. De Merode wrote a letter to the Canadian team, which was delivered at 1:45 a.m., Monday. At 7:00 a.m., Carol Anne Letheren, the Canadian *chef de mission* informed Johnson of the positive test. Three hours later, with Canadian representatives in attendance, the "B" sample was tested and it too registered positive.

At 3:30 Tuesday morning, Letheren revisited Johnson to collect his gold medal. "We love you," she told him, "but you're guilty."

At 10:00 a.m., the I.O.C. called a press conference and issued the following statement: "The urine sample of Ben Johnson (Canada—Athletics—100 meters) collected on Saturday, 24th September 1988 was found to contain the metabolites of a banned substance namely stanozolol (anabolic steroid). . . . The I.O.C. Medical Commission recommends the following sanction: disqualification of this competitor from the Games of the XXIV Olympiad in Seoul. Of course, the gold medal has been withdrawn by the I.O.C."

Although Johnson was the 39th Olympic athlete to be disqualified because of drugs since testing began in 1968, he was the first "big fish" to be caught. His disgrace was front-page news all over the world. Initially, Johnson denied having taken steroids. Charlie Francis claimed that Johnson was a victim of sabotage, that he had been given a spiked drink. Francis even hinted that agents of Carl Lewis had been responsible.

The Canadian government, to its great credit, wasted no time in ordering an investigation into the use of banned substances by Canadian athletes, including several of Johnson's sprinting teammates and a number of weightlifters who tested positive before the Games and were not allowed to travel to Seoul. The investigation, much of which was televised live, became known as the Dubin Inquiry in honor of the man in charge of the hearings, Charles Dubin, an associate chief justice of the Ontario Supreme Court.

Testifying before the Dubin Commission, Charlie Francis and Johnson's doctor, George (Jamie) Astaphan, revealed that the sprinter began taking steroids in November 1981 because Francis convinced him that everyone else was taking them and that if he didn't, he would be left behind. Over the next seven years, Johnson took the anabolic steroids Dianabol, stanozolol, and furazabol, as well as testosterone, diuretics, which he used as masking agents, and human growth hormone, which is made from human cadavers. Although Astaphan had once labeled a bottle of steroids "Do Not Take Within 28 Days of Competition," he apparently gave Johnson an injection only 26 days before the Olympic final. The Dubin Commission concluded that this injection contained Winstrol-V, a stanozolol compound used to fatten cattle before they are sent to market.

On June 12, 1989, Johnson himself appeared before the Dubin Commission. He admitted taking steroids and lying to the public when he said he hadn't. The following day, he was asked if he had any message for young athletes who had considered him their idol. With tears in his eyes, he replied, "I want to tell them to be honest and don't take drugs. It happened to me. I've been there. I know what it's like to cheat."

Three months later, the I.A.A.F., in a controversial decision, retroactively rescinded Johnson's 1987 world record even though he had passed the drug test in Rome. Johnson served out his standard two-year suspension and returned to competition in 1991.

The gold medal which Johnson lost did go to Carl Lewis after all, giving Lewis a career total of six golds and one silver.

## 200 METERS

**1896** not held

**1900 Paris** C: 15?, N: 7?, D: 7.22. WR(220 yards): 21.2 (Bernie Wefers)

| | | |
|---|---|---|
| 1. John Walter Tewksbury | USA | 22.2 |
| 2. Norman Pritchard | IND | 22.8 |
| 3. Stanley Rowley | AUS | 22.9 |
| 4. William Joseph Holland | USA | — |

With this victory Tewksbury earned his fifth medal of the games. He had already won the 400-meter hurdles, finished second in the 60-meter and 100-meter sprints, and third in the 200-meter hurdles.

**1904 St. Louis** C: 7, L: 2, D: 8.31. WR(220 yards): 21.2 (Bernie Wefers)

| | | | |
|---|---|---|---|
| 1. Archie Hahn | USA | 21.6 | OR |
| 2. Nathaniel Cartmell | USA | 21.9 | |
| 3. William Hogenson | USA | — | |
| 4. Fay Moulton | USA | — | |

Cartmell, Hogenson, and Moulton each false started once which, according to the rules at that time, resulted in their being penalized two yards. Hahn took good advantage of his head start and led the entire way. Cartmell closed within one yard, but Hahn pulled away again and won by three yards. Commented Cartmell, "He's little, but he certainly can run."

**1906** not held

**1908 London** C: 43, N: 14, D: 7.23. WR(220 yards): 21.2 (Bernie Wefers, Dan Kelly)

| | | |
|---|---|---|
| 1. Robert Kerr | CAN | 22.6 |
| 2. Robert Cloughen | USA | 22.6 |
| 3. Nathaniel Cartmell | USA | 22.7 |
| 4. George Hawkins | GBR | — |

Bobby Kerr was born in Enniskillen, Ireland. When he was 7 years old his family moved to Canada, settling in Hamilton, Ontario. As a teenager Kerr joined the International Harvester Fire Brigade, which prided itself on the speed of its members. Kerr represented Canada at the St. Louis Olympics in 1904 and had hoped to compete at Athens in 1906, but not enough money could be raised to pay his passage. He did make it to London, where, ten days before the Olympics, he swept both sprints at the British A.A.A. championships. At the 1908 Olympics he rebounded from the disappointment of finishing third in the 100 meters to win the 200 meters by less than a foot. The following year Kerr returned to Ireland and fulfilled his dream of representing the nation of his birth in an international meet. In 1928 he was the captain of the Canadian Olympic team, and in 1932 he was manager of the track and field division. Cloughen, the silver medalist, did not qualify for the U.S. team and was only able to compete because his parents paid his way.

**1912 Stockholm** C: 60, N: 19, D: 7.11. WR(220 yards): 21.2 (Bernie Wefers, Dan Kelly, Ralph Craig)

| | | |
|---|---|---|
| 1. Ralph Craig | USA | 21.7 |
| 2. Donald Lippincott | USA | 21.8 |
| 3. William Applegarth | GBR | 22.0 |
| 4. Richard Rau | GER | 22.2 |
| 5. Charles Reidpath | USA | 22.3 |
| 6. Donnell Young | USA | 22.3 |

**1920 Antwerp** C: 45, D: 17, D: 8.20. WR(220 yards): 21.2 (Bernie Wefers, Dan Kelly, Ralph Craig, Howard Drew, William Applegarth)

| | | |
|---|---|---|
| 1. Allen Woodring | USA | 22.0 |
| 2. Charles Paddock | USA | 22.1 |
| 3. Harry Edward | GBR | 22.2 |
| 4. Loren Murchison | USA | — |
| 5. George Davidson | NZE | — |
| 6. Jack Oosterlaak | SAF | — |

Allen Woodring of Syracuse University had qualified for the U.S. team only as an alternate, but when George Massengale of Missouri was stiffened by an attack of rheumatism, Woodring was allowed to compete. In the final Paddock led from the start, but Woodring caught him at the 180-meter mark. Just as Paddock began the takeoff of his flying finish, Woodring flashed by him to steal the victory. The young New Yorker couldn't believe he had won and was sure that Paddock had graciously allowed him to finish first. Paddock finally convinced him that he had given his all and that the victory was legitimate.

**1924 Paris** C: 62, N: 32, D: 7.9. WR: 21.0 (Charles Paddock)

| | | |
|---|---|---|
| 1. Jackson Scholz | USA | 21.6 |
| 2. Charles Paddock | USA | 21.7 |
| 3. Eric Liddell | GBR | 21.9 |
| 4. George Hill | USA | 22.0 |
| 5. Bayes Norton | USA | 22.0 |
| 6. Harold Abrahams | GBR | 22.3 |

The day before the semifinals and final, Charley Paddock was convinced that he was over the hill and could never succeed the following day. His friend Douglas Fairbanks took him home, and together they dined and joked with Mary Pickford and Maurice Chevalier, who entertained them with imitations of Paavo Nurmi and Harold Abrahams, who had already won the 100 meters and who had beaten Charley in the first round of the 200 earlier that day. After dinner Fairbanks and Chevalier went for a walk while Mary Pickford gave Paddock an inspirational pep talk. She told him that his fate rested in his own hands. "If you believe in yourself," she said, "you will win tomorrow."

Paddock took her advice to heart, slept well, and awoke the next day refreshed and relaxed. He won his semifinal heat with ease, with Scholz winning the other semi. In the final Abrahams fell behind quickly while the others ran almost evenly. By the 120-meter mark Paddock had opened up a two-foot lead, but Scholz came on strong, reaching Paddock's shoulder with ten yards to go. In the final stride he moved ahead and won by less than a foot. Paddock pulled a ligament in his thigh in his final leap and collapsed to the ground beyond the finish line.

Scholz, who was born in St. Louis, later made his living as an author of "pulp" fiction, publishing 31 sports novels. Interest in Scholz was renewed with the release of the film *Chariots of Fire,* which took great liberties in its portrayal of him. There is one scene in the film in which Scholz, just before the start of the 400 meters, approaches Eric Liddell and hands him a piece of paper inscribed with a religious message. Scholz actually did no such thing—he wasn't even religious. This put him in a difficult situation. When *Chariots of Fire* became a hit, the 84-year-old Scholz, now living in Delray Beach, Florida, was inundated with mail from people requesting spiritual inspiration. "I'm afraid," he told reporters, "that my religious background was rather casual."

**1928 Amsterdam** C: 62, N: 30, D: 8.1. WR (track with curve): 20.6 (Roland Locke)

| | | |
|---|---|---|
| 1. Percy Williams | CAN | 21.8 |
| 2. Walter Rangeley | GBR | 21.9 |
| 3. Helmuth Körnig | GER | 21.9 |
| 4. Jackson Scholz | USA | 21.9 |
| 5. John Fitzpatrick | CAN | 22.1 |
| 6. Jakob Schuller | GER | 22.2 |

The early rounds saw unusually stiff competition. In the quarterfinals Helmuth Körnig, pressed by Walter Rangeley of Salford, Lancashire, and Charlie Borah, the U.S. champion, equaled the Olympic record of 21.6. Since only two from each heat advanced to the semifinals, Borah was eliminated. The first semi saw the fall of Charley Paddock, who finished fifth behind Williams and Rangeley. The second semi was won by Körnig, with defending champion Scholz second. In the final Körnig led coming out of the turn, but with 50 meters to go he was passed by Williams and Rangeley. Williams, running his eighth race in four days, pulled away and won by almost a yard. A dead heat was declared for third place between Körnig and Scholz, and a rerun between the two was ordered. However, by the time this decision had been reached, Scholz had already broken training, so he forfeited the runoff. Subsequent examination of the photo-finish revealed that Körnig had actually won third place anyway.

**1932 Los Angeles** C: 25, N: 13, D: 8.3. WR: 20.6 (Roland Locke, James Carlton)
1. Thomas "Eddie" Tolan   USA  21.2  OR
2. George Simpson   USA  21.4
3. Ralph Metcalfe   USA  21.5
4. Arthur Jonath   GER  21.6
5. Carlos Bianchi Luti   ARG  21.7
6. William Walters   SAF  21.9

One man who did not compete in the 1932 Olympics was James Carlton of Lismore, New South Wales, who had beaten George Simpson twice. On January 16, 1932, Carlton shocked the world by winning the Australian 220-yard championship in 20.6, around the curve of an oval track. Speculation on Carlton's chance for an Olympic gold medal was cut short when the 24-year-old became a monk and retired to a monastery. In the quarterfinals at Los Angeles the Olympic record of 21.6, which had first been set by Archie Hahn back in 1904, was broken in each of the four heats. In the first two heats it was lowered to 21.5 by Metcalfe, who had won the U.S. trials, and by Tolan, who had edged Metcalfe to win the 100 meters gold medal the day before. In the third heat Luti broke the record again, at 21.4, and in the fourth heat his time was matched by sportswriter Arthur Jonath. The following day the first heat of the semifinals was won by Metcalfe, with Simpson beside him. In the second semi, won by Jonath, Tolan was almost eliminated. Content to qualify for the final with a third-place finish, Tolan almost failed to notice the closing rush of Canadian Harold Wright, who closed within a foot but fell short.

Luti had the quickest start in the final, but as they came out of the turn Simpson of Ohio State was leading by almost a yard. Tolan, who chewed gum while he ran, surged ahead with 50 meters to go, stumbled just before the finish, and held on to win by five or six feet. When films of the race were viewed, it was discovered that Metcalfe had inadvertently been forced to dig his starting holes three or four feet behind the spot where they should have been, which deprived him of a silver medal. Metcalfe was offered a rerun by race officials, but he didn't want to jeopardize the U.S. medal sweep and so declined.

**1936 Berlin** C: 44, N: 22, D: 8.5. WR: 20.6 (Roland Locke, James Carlton)
1. James "Jesse" Owens   USA  20.7  OR
2. Matthew "Mack" Robinson   USA  21.1
3. Martinus Osendarp   HOL  21.3
4. Paul Hänni   SWI  21.6
5. Lee Orr   CAN  21.6
6. Wijnand van Beveren   HOL  21.9

In the first round Jesse Owens set an Olympic record of 21.1 seconds, a time that he repeated in the second round and which was matched by Mack Robinson of Pasadena, California, in the semifinals. The final was run in a light rain, but this didn't prevent Owens from sprinting away from the field in record time. He led by almost two yards entering the straightaway and won by four yards to gain his third gold medal of the Berlin games. Silver medalist Robinson was something of a surprise. In high school coaches did not consider him athletic material and made his mother sign a statement absolving them of blame if his heart was damaged. Local businessmen paid his way to the U.S. Olympic trials. His younger brother, Jackie Robinson, gained fame with the Brooklyn Dodgers as the first black major league player in modern baseball history.

**1948 London** C: 50, N: 26, D: 8.3. WR: 20.6 (Roland Locke, James Carlton)
1. Melvin Patton   USA  21.1
2. H. Norwood "Barney" Ewell   USA  21.1
3. Lloyd LaBeach   PAN  21.2
4. Herbert McKenley   JAM  —
5. Clifford Bourland   USA  —
6. Leslie Laing   JAM  —

McKenley and Bourland looked strongest in the preliminaries, both of them clocking 21.3 in each of the first two rounds. They also won their respective semifinal heats. In the final, however, it was the favorites who came through fastest. Patton, intent on making up for his disappointing fifth place finish in the 100, pulled away coming out of the turn and led by almost two meters. Ewell closed fast, but Patton held him off with a final spurt to win by two feet.

**1952 Helsinki** C: 71, N: 35, D: 7.23. WR: 20.6 (Roland Locke, James Carlton, Andrew Stanfield)
1. Andrew Stanfield   USA  20.7
2. W. Thane Baker   USA  20.8
3. James Gathers   USA  20.8
4. Emmanuel McDonald Bailey   GBR  21.0
5. Leslie Laing   JAM  21.2
6. Gerardo Bönnhoff   ARG  21.3

Stanfield, a 6-foot 1-inch 24-year-old from Jersey City, New Jersey, was the unanimous favorite. As expected, he and Mac Bailey won the semifinals. Bailey ran well on the turn in the final, and as they hit the straightaway he was almost even with Stanfield, but Stanfield pulled away with ease and won by a yard and a half. The official times appear to be incorrect, since Bailey actually finished quite close to Gathers. The electronic times for the first four were 20.81, 20.97, 21.08, and 21.14.

**1956 Melbourne** C: 67, N: 32, D: 11.27. WR: 20.6 (Roland Locke, James Carlton, Andrew Stanfield, Bobby Joe Morrow, W. Thane Baker)
1. Bobby Joe Morrow   USA  20.6  OR
2. Andrew Stanfield   USA  20.7
3. W. Thane Baker   USA  20.9
4. Michael Agostini   TRI  21.1
5. Boris Tokaryev   SOV  21.2
6. José Telles da Conceição   BRA  21.3

Bobby Morrow, the winner of the 100, was the favorite to win the 200 and become the first man since Jesse Owens to achieve a double in the Olympic sprints. He appeared for the first round with his left thigh bandaged, having suffered a slight groin pull in the final of the 100. Fortunately he was able to breeze through the early heats with little competition while allowing his muscle to heal. Abdul Khaliq of Pakistan ran 21.1 in both of the first two rounds, but wore himself out and was eliminated in the semifinals, which were won by Baker (21.1) and Stanfield (21.2). One unexpected finalist was Telles da Conceição, who had won the bronze medal in the high jump at Helsinki four years earlier. Baker was so upset at receiving the outside lane in the final, just as he had at Helsinki, that he put his starting blocks in backwards, necessitating a delay while he readjusted them. At the halfway mark Stanfield led Morrow by a foot, but 20 meters later Morrow swept past the defending champion and won going away, with Stanfield and Baker completing the second straight sweep of the 200 for the United States. Of the 15 medals awarded between 1932 and 1956, 13 were won by the United States, which took the first two places in five straight Olympics.

**1960 Rome** C: 62, N: 47, D: 9.3. WR: 20.5 (Peter Radford, Stonewall Johnson, O. Ray Norton)

| | | | |
|---|---|---|---|
| 1. Livio Berruti | ITA | 20.5 | EWR |
| 2. Lester Carney | USA | 20.6 | |
| 3. Abdoulaye Seye | FRA/SEN | 20.7 | |
| 4. Marian Foik | POL | 20.8 | |
| 5. Stonewall Johnson | USA | 20.8 | |
| 6. O. Ray Norton | USA | 20.9 | |

On May 28, 1960, Peter Radford set a world record of 20.5. His record was matched five weeks later at the U.S. Olympic trials in Los Angeles by Stone Johnson of Dallas, Texas, and Ray Norton. In Rome, the first semifinal was won by Seye in 20.8. The second semi saw some bad seeding as the three world record holders were thrown together with local favorite Livio Berruti, with only three to qualify for the final. It was Radford who was left out, with Berruti, a chemistry student at the University of Padua, finishing first in the world record time of 20.5. The second semi was so hotly contested that last-place finisher, Paul Genevay of France, ran 21.0, good enough to take second place in the first semi.

The final saw one false start by Berruti and Johnson, although neither was charged. Berruti, always strong on the curve, hit the straight with a one-yard lead, which he held until the finish. Norton was placed second with 80 meters to go, but he faded. After crossing the line, both Berruti, who ran with dark glasses, and Carney (of Akron, Ohio) fell to the ground. Berruti's victory was met with enthusiastic cheering that went on for five minutes, and after the medal ceremony he was led to the V.I.P. box, where each Italian dignitary kissed him on both cheeks. Berruti was the first non-North American to win the 200 meters.

**1964 Tokyo** C: 57, N: 42, D: 10.17. WR: 20.2 (Henry Carr)

| | | | |
|---|---|---|---|
| 1. Henry Carr | USA | 20.3 | OR |
| 2. O. Paul Drayton | USA | 20.5 | |
| 3. Edwin Roberts | TRI | 20.6 | |
| 4. Harry Jerome | CAN | 20.8 | |
| 5. Livio Berruti | ITA | 20.8 | |
| 6. Marian Foik | POL | 20.8 | |
| 7. Richard Stebbins | USA | 20.8 | |
| 8. Sergio Ottolina | ITA | 20.9 | |

This event went according to form. Drayton, a 25-year-old Army private, recorded the best series in the preliminaries (20.7, 20.9, and 20.5), but Carr, the world record holder, had paced himself well and turned it on in the final. Carr overtook Drayton quickly, led by a yard entering the stretch, and was able to extend his lead to win by over four feet.

**1968 Mexico City** C: 49, N: 36, D: 10.16. WR: 19.92 (John Carlos)

| | | | |
|---|---|---|---|
| 1. Tommie Smith | USA | 19.83 | WR |
| 2. Peter Norman | AUS | 20.06 | |
| 3. John Carlos | USA | 20.10 | |
| 4. Edwin Roberts | TRI | 20.34 | |
| 5. Roger Bambuck | FRA | 20.51 | |
| 6. Larry Questad | USA | 20.62 | |
| 7. Michael Fray | JAM | 20.63 | |
| 8. Joachim Eigenherr | GER | 20.66 | |

There seemed little question that the battle for the gold medal would be between Tommie Smith and John Carlos, both students at San Jose State College in California and both members of the Olympic Project for Human Rights, a group of athletes organized to protest the treatment of blacks in the United States. The 6-foot 3-inch, 180-pound Smith was an extraordinary runner who held 11 world records indoors and outdoors at distances up to 440 yards. He had also long-jumped 25 feet 11 inches (7.90 meters). Carlos, who grew up in Harlem, beat Smith for the first time (by three yards) at the U.S. Olympic trials and clocked a world record time of 19.7 seconds. His record was never officially recognized because he was wearing multipronged "brush spike" shoes which, at the time, were considered illegal. At 6 feet 4 inches and 198 pounds, Carlos was the largest competitor in the 1968 200 meters, 90 pounds heavier than José Astacio, who represented El Salvador.

In Mexico City Smith set the stage in the first round by tying the Olympic record of 20.3. But four heats later a surprise occurred when Peter Norman ran 20.2 to break the Olympic record. Norman, a 26-year-old physical education teacher and Salvation Army officer, had never beaten 20.5 until he arrived in Mexico. In the first heat of the second round Carlos slipped on the bend, but he regained his balance and won in 20.6. In the third heat Smith equaled Norman's earlier mark of 20.2. The semis were won by Carlos and Smith in 20.1, but Smith pulled an abductor muscle in his groin and limped off the field. "I was 80 percent certain I was out," he said, but he made it to the starting line of the final anyway. Coming out of the turn Carlos led by 1½ yards, but then Smith turned on his "Tommie-jets," in a stunning display of speed reminiscent of Bob Hayes' 4 × 100-meter relay anchor leg in Tokyo. He passed his teammate with 60 meters to go and won so decisively that he was able to raise his arms in victory 10 yards from the tape and smile and wave as he crossed the finish line. Carlos turned his head to watch Smith go by, allowing Norman, who had been in only sixth place entering the straight, to slip by on the other side and take the silver medal with a final lunge.

Smith's victory caused a sensation, but it was nothing compared to the sensation that he and Carlos caused at the victory ceremony. Mounting the dais barefooted, they wore civil rights buttons, as did Norman. When "The Star-Spangled Banner" was played, Smith and Carlos bowed their heads and each raised one black-gloved hand in the black-power salute. They later explained that their clenched fists symbolized black strength and unity and that their bare feet were a reminder of black poverty in the United States. They bowed their heads to express their belief that the words of freedom in the U.S. national anthem only applied to Americans with white skin. Carlos told reporters, "White America will only give us credit for an Olympic victory. They'll say I'm an American, but if I did something bad, they'd say I was a Negro." Olympic officials were outraged. The International Olympic Committee made it known that Smith and Carlos should be punished, and the U.S. Olympic Committee responded quickly, suspending the two athletes and ordering them to leave the Olympic village.

The international response to the demonstration by Smith and Carlos was generally sympathetic, but back in the United States they were not so well received. Chicago sports columnist Brent Musberger spoke for the Establishment when he called them "black-skinned storm troopers." The two Olympic medalists found it difficult to make a living, and both their marriages broke up. Carlos' wife committed suicide. In 1972 Smith finally got a position as track coach at Oberlin College in Ohio. Six years later he moved to Santa Monica College in California. Carlos had an even tougher time—hustling, gambling, taking menial jobs. In 1977 he founded the John Carlos Youth Development Program in Los Angeles, which encourages ghetto youth to become well educated. In February 1982, Carlos' Olympic experiences came full circle when he was hired by the Los Angeles Olympic Organizing Committee to promote the 1984 games and act as liaison with the black ghetto.

In retrospect, Smith and Carlos' gestures on the victory platform in Mexico City appear as eloquent expressions of nonviolent protest, while the reactions of the I.O.C. and the U.S.O.C. come off as knee-jerk traditionalism. Smith and Carlos made their point without interfering with anyone's free will. The same cannot be said of government-inspired boycotts or of the Black September guerrillas, whose attempt to stop the games was accompanied by murder. John Carlos responded to criticisms that his political protest had tainted the games by pointing out that the Olympic movement was already highly political. "Why do you have to wear the uniform of your country?" he asked. "Why do they play national anthems? Why do we have to beat the Russians? Why do the East Germans want to beat the West Germans? Why can't everyone wear the same colors but wear numbers to tell them apart? What happened to the Olympic ideal of man against man?"

**1972 Munich** C: 57, N: 42, D: 9.4. WR: 19.83 (Tommie Smith)

| | | | |
|---|---|---|---|
| 1. | Valery Borzov | SOV | 20.00 |
| 2. | Larry Black | USA | 20.19 |
| 3. | Pietro Mennea | ITA | 20.30 |
| 4. | Lawrence Burton | USA | 20.37 |
| 5. | Charles Smith | USA | 20.55 |
| 6. | Siegfried Schenke | GDR | 20.56 |
| 7. | Martin Jellinghaus | GER | 20.65 |
| 8. | Hans-Joachim Zenk | GDR | 21.05 |

Borzov completely dominated the opposition to become the first non-North American to win the Olympic sprint double. He won his first two heats in 20.64 and 20.30 despite the fact that he turned around several times to check the position of the other runners. In the first heat of the semifinals he turned and spoke to Larry Burton as he passed him with 50 meters to go. Burton was a 6-foot 2-inch Purdue football player who had run in his first track meet only eight months earlier, and had competed in his first 220-yard race a mere four and a half months before the Olympics. The winner of the second semi was Larry Black, a Florida-born student of North Carolina Central. In the final, Black came out of the turn with a slight lead, but with 70 meters to go Borzov appeared to shift into overdrive, rocketing ahead to a clear two-meter lead. With five meters left, Borzov turned back for a final look at Black and the others, then crossed the line with arms flung high. Mennea edged past Burton at the 175-meter mark to take third. During the second round Mennea had entertained the crowd by stripping down to his jock strap while changing into his running shorts. Borzov refused to participate in the postrace interview, stating, with some justification, that he had been treated in an insulting manner by U.S. journalists after his victory in the 100.

**1976 Montreal** C: 45, N: 33, D: 7.26. WR: 19.83 (Tommie Smith)

| | | | |
|---|---|---|---|
| 1. | Donald Quarrie | JAM | 20.23 |
| 2. | Millard Hampton | USA | 20.29 |
| 3. | Dwayne Evans | USA | 20.43 |
| 4. | Pietro Mennea | ITA | 20.54 |
| 5. | Ruy da Silva | BRA | 20.84 |
| 6. | Bogdan Grzejszczak | POL | 20.91 |
| 7. | Colin Bradford | JAM | 21.17 |
| 8. | Hasely Crawford | TRI | 1:19.60 |

Donald Quarrie's Olympic career began back in 1968 when he was 17 years old. He made it to Mexico City but injured himself during training and was unable to compete. In 1971 he won the Pan American Games in 19.86, the second fastest electronically timed 200 on record, but at the Olympics in Munich he pulled a hamstring muscle in the semifinals and had to be carried off the field on a stretcher. At Montreal he had already finished second to Hasely Crawford in the 100 and was now the odds-on favorite to take the gold in the 200.

His challengers included one man who wanted to run but wasn't allowed to and another who didn't want to run but was forced to. James Gilkes of Guyana was the victor in the 1975 Pan American Games, but his government decided to boycott the Olympics. Gilkes appealed to the I.O.C. to let him compete under the Olympic flag, but his request was denied. Pietro Mennea, on the other hand, was so disappointed with his performance at the Italian championships in July that he decided not to compete in Montreal. Public reaction to his decision was so strong that he changed his mind. Also in the running were Millard Hampton of San Jose and 17-year-old Dwayne Evans of Phoenix, the first high school student to represent the United States in an Olympic running event since 1964.

Quarrie had the lead coming out of the turn. Hampton made a run at him, but Quarrie held on to win by two feet. His long quest for an Olympic gold medal finally achieved, Don Quarrie is now honored by a statue in his hometown of Kingston, Jamaica.

The three medalists took the slowest victory lap on record. Forced to stop when they encountered the victory ceremony for the javelin, it was ten minutes before they completed their circuit of the track.

Hasely Crawford, whom the official report lists as not finishing, suffered a cramp after 50 meters and ended up on the ground, but a California track fan named Pitch Johnson noted that Crawford never actually left his lane until after he had jogged past the finish line, so he did finish the race, albeit in a rather unusual time.

**1980 Moscow** C: 57, N: 37, D: 7.28. WR: 19.72 (Pietro Mennea)

| | | |
|---|---|---|
| 1. Pietro Mennea | ITA | 20.19 |
| 2. Allan Wells | GBR | 20.21 |
| 3. Donald Quarrie | JAM | 20.29 |
| 4. Silvio Leonard Tartabull | CUB | 20.30 |
| 5. Bernhard Hoff | GDR | 20.50 |
| 6. Leszek Dunecki | POL | 20.68 |
| 7. Marian Woronin | POL | 20.81 |
| 8. Osvaldo Lara Cañizares | CUB | 21.19 |

Like Donald Quarrie before him, Pietro Mennea of Barletta, Italy, had to wait until his third try to gain an Olympic gold medal. In 1979 at the World Student Games in Mexico City, Mennea had run 19.72 to break Tommie Smith's 11-year-old world record. But that same year, before a hometown crowd at the European Cup in Torino, Mennea had lost to Allan Wells. For this insult, the otherwise blameless Wells had become known as "The Beast" in Mennea's household. For the final of the

1980 Olympics, Mennea drew the outside lane, with "The Beast" just behind him in Lane 7. At the sound of the gun Wells tore out of the blocks at full speed and had made up the stagger after only 50 meters. Coming out of the turn he had a two-meter lead over Leonard, with Quarrie and Mennea close behind. But Mennea, as usual, shifted gears in the straight, closing the gap with each stride until he moved ahead of Wells with less than ten meters to go. At the last moment Wells attempted the same final dip which had brought him victory in the 100, but this time he fell short. Quarrie's third-place finish, impressive as it was, was all the more remarkable considering he had been injured in an auto accident the previous year. Mennea, employed by the public relations department of Fiat, had received his doctorate in political science two weeks before the Olympics. He had been a candidate for local office for the Social Democratic Party, which supported the Moscow boycott, but 15 years of training and his belief in the Olympic ideal proved more important than the party line, and he decided to enter anyway.

**1984 Los Angeles** C: 76, N: 58, D: 8.8. WR: 19.72 (Pietro Mennea)

| | | | |
|---|---|---|---|
| 1. F. Carlton Lewis | USA | 19.80 | OR |
| 2. Kirk Baptiste | USA | 19.96 | |
| 3. Thomas Jefferson | USA | 20.26 | |
| 4. João Batista da Silva | BRA | 20.30 | |
| 5. Ralf Lübke | GER | 20.51 | |
| 6. Jean-Jacques Boussemart | FRA | 20.55 | |
| 7. Pietro Mennea | ITA | 20.55 | |
| 8. Adeoye Mafe | GBR | 20.85 | |

Carl Lewis, holder of the low-altitude world record with a 1983 time of 19.75, won his third gold medal by getting off to an unusually fast start. He came out of the curve with a two-meter lead and then held off the fast-finishing Kirk Baptiste to win by 1½ meters. Considering that the race was run into the wind, Lewis' time was more impressive than Mennea's high-altitude world record of 19.72 or his own 19.75. Pietro Mennea, in seventh place, became the first runner to qualify for the final of the same event in four straight Olympics.

**1988 Seoul** C: 72, N: 59, D: 9.28. WR: 19.72 (Pietro Mennea)

| | | | |
|---|---|---|---|
| 1. Joseph DeLoach | USA | 19.75 | OR |
| 2. F. Carlton Lewis | USA | 19.79 | |
| 3. Robson Caetano da Silva | BRA | 20.04 | |
| 4. Linford Christie | GBR | 20.09 | |
| 5. Atlee Mahorn | CAN | 20.39 | |
| 6. Gilles Quénéhervé | FRA | 20.40 | |
| 7. Michael Rosswess | GBR | 20.51 | |
| 8. Bruno Marie-Rose | FRA | 20.58 | |

Carl Lewis suffered his first 200-meter defeat in two years when he was beaten 19.96-20.01 at the U.S. Olympic trials by his training partner, 21-year-old Joe DeLoach of Bay City, Texas. The two had first met when DeLoach, the youngest of 13 children, had asked Lewis for his autograph. In Seoul, Lewis led coming out of the turn. DeLoach drew even after 150 meters, then surged ahead 30 meters from the finish.

## 400 METERS

**1896 Athens** C: 7, N: 4, D: 4.7. WR(440 yards): 48.5 (Henry Tindall, Edgar Bredin)
1. Thomas Burke        USA   54.2
2. Herbert Jamison     USA   —
3. Charles Gmelin      GBR   —
4. Fritz Hofmann       GER   —

The slow time was a result of the quality of the track rather than the quality of the contestants. The turns were so sharp that the runners had to slow down drastically to keep from falling. Burke, who won by over 13 meters, had previously beaten the world record holder Edgar Bredin. In 1896 Bredin, in the words of former 440 champion Montague Shearman, "voluntarily joined the professional ranks, a step which was received with great surprise, as he was a gentleman by birth and education."

**1900 Paris** C: 16, N: 7, D: 7.15. WR(440 yards): 48.5 (Henry Tindall, Edgar Bredin)
1. Maxwell "Maxey" Long   USA   49.4   OR
2. William Holland         USA   49.6
3. Ernst Schultz           DEN   —
DNS: Dixon Boardman (USA), Harry Lee (USA), William Moloney (USA)

Long was cheered heartily by the French spectators, who mistook his light-blue-and-white Columbia University uniform for that of the Racing Club of Paris. Boardman, Lee, and Moloney refused to compete in the final for religious reasons, since the race was run on a Sunday.

**1904 St. Louis** C: 13, N: 3, D: 8.29. WR(440 yards): 47.8 (Maxwell "Maxey" Long)
1. Harry Hillman      USA   49.2   OR
2. Frank Waller       USA   49.9
3. Herman Groman      USA   50.0
4. Joseph Fleming     USA   —
5. Meyer Prinstein    USA   —
6. George Poage       USA   —

One can only imagine the chaos of this race, which the 13 entrants ran without lanes even though the course was only 1¼ laps long. Poage of Milwaukee was one of the first two black athletes to compete in the Olympics.

**1906 Athens** C: 25, N: 8, D: 4.29. WR(440 yards): 47.8 (Maxwell "Maxey" Long)
1. Paul Pilgrim        USA   53.2
2. Wyndham Halswelle   GBR   53.8
3. Nigel Barker        AUS   54.1
4. Harry Hillman       USA   —
5. Charles Bacon       USA   —
6. Fay Moulton         USA   —

7. William Anderson    GBR   —
8. M. Bellin du Coteau  FRA   —

The victory of Pilgrim came as a complete surprise. This was the first time that the United States sent an official team. Pilgrim, a member of the New York Athletic Club, didn't make the team, but he paid his own way to Athens and was allowed to compete.

**1908 London** C: 36, N: 11, D: 7.25. WR(440 yards): 47.8 (Maxwell "Maxey" Long)
1. Wyndham Halswelle   GBR   50.0
DNS: William Robbins (USA), John Taylor (USA)
DISQ: John Carpenter (USA)

Few events in Olympic history have caused as much controversy as the final of the 1908 400 meters in London. The favorite was Lieutenant Wyndham Halswelle, a 26-year-old London-born Scot who had served in the Boer War. Halswelle was joined in the final by three Americans—John Taylor, William Robbins, and John Carpenter of Cornell. The British, afraid that the Americans would use team tactics, stationed officials every 20 yards around the track. Robbins charged to the front and built up a 12-yard lead by the halfway mark. Coming into the homestretch he was passed by Carpenter and Halswelle. Halswelle then attempted to go by Carpenter on the outside, but the American ran wide and kept Halswelle from taking the lead. British officials yelled "foul" and "no race" and broke the tape before Carpenter reached it. Taylor was physically pulled off the track by officials. British and American partisans argued and yelled at each other for a half hour before the track could be cleared. Carpenter was disqualified and the race was ordered rerun without him two days later, this time with strings laid out to divide the lanes. Robbins and Taylor refused to participate, however, and Halswelle was left to run the race alone. Halswelle had set an Olympic record of 48.4 in the semifinals.

**1912 Stockholm** C: 49, N: 16, D: 7.13. WR(440 yards): 47.8 (Maxwell "Maxey" Long)
1. Charles Reidpath      USA   48.2   OR
2. Hanns Braun           GER   48.3
3. Edward Lindberg       USA   48.4
4. James "Ted" Meredith  USA   49.2
5. Carroll Haff          USA   49.5

The 400 meters was again the subject of controversy, this time occasioned by an incident at the beginning of the last heat of the semifinal round. Donnell Young of the United States jumped into the lead, but before the first curve the German champion, Hanns Braun, tried to cut in front of him. Young refused to allow this and rammed into Braun, throwing him to the outside. Young went on to win, but was disqualified. Young deserved to be disqualified; however, Braun's move was uncalled for and might have resulted in *his* disqualification had not Young responded so violently. The Swedish officials wisely decided that the final should be run in lanes. Braun took the lead at the halfway mark, but Charlie Reidpath of Syracuse passed him with 15 meters to go and won by two feet.

**1920 Antwerp** C: 37, N: 14, D: 8.20. WR(440 yards): 47.4 (James "Ted" Meredith, Jesse Binga Dismond)
| | | |
|---|---|---|
| 1. Bevil Rudd | SAF | 49.6 |
| 2. Guy Butler | GBR | 49.9 |
| 3. Nils Engdahl | SWE | 50.0 |
| 4. Frank Shea | USA | — |
| 5. John Ainsworth-Davis | GBR | — |
| 6. Harry Davel | SAF | — |

Born in South Africa and educated at Oxford, Bevil Gordon D'Urban Rudd was an extremely popular winner who looked at running as a joyful experience. He was often seen smoking a pipe and drinking beer while watching the other athletes go through their strenuous exercises.

**1924 Paris** C: 60, N: 27, D: 7.11. WR(440 yards): 47.4 (James "Ted" Meredith, Jesse Binga Dismond)
| | | | |
|---|---|---|---|
| 1. Eric Liddell | GBR | 47.6 | OR |
| 2. Horatio Fitch | USA | 48.4 | |
| 3. Guy Butler | GBR | 48.6 | |
| 4. David Johnson | CAN | 48.8 | |
| 5. John Coard Taylor | USA | — | |
DNF: Josef Imbach (SWI)

Eric Liddell was born on January 16, 1902, in Tientsin, China, where his father was a missionary. He grew up in Scotland from the age of 5. His favorite sport was rugby, but he gave up a promising career in it in order to concentrate on running. He gained national attention in 1923 when he won both sprints at the A.A.A. championships. The following week his reputation was enhanced when he was knocked to the ground during a 440-yard race against England and Ireland. By the time he had regained his feet, Liddell was 20 yards behind the field. Yet he was able to overtake every runner and win the race. Afterward he repeated his oft-spoken dictum, "I do not like to be beaten."

In the film *Chariots of Fire* Eric Liddell is portrayed as a devout Christian who learns, as he is boarding a ship en route to the Paris Olympics, that the heats of the 100-meter dash, his specialty, will be run on a Sunday. Because of his respect for the Sabbath, he refuses to run. Finally another member of the British team, a cinematic version of Lord Burghley, offers Liddell his spot in the 400 meters. This highly dramatized rendition of Liddell's Olympic experience bears only a slight resemblance to reality.

Liddell was in fact a devout Christian, and it is true that he withdrew from the 100 because he wouldn't run on a Sunday. He dropped out of the relays for the same reason. However, he did *not* find out the Olympic schedule at the last minute. In real life Liddell learned the schedule over six months in advance and, once he had made his decision not to enter the 100, he was able to

concentrate his training on the 200 and 400. As for Lord Burghley, he wasn't even entered in the 400 meters. Liddell did spend the Sunday of the 100-meter heats giving a sermon at a Scottish church in Paris, but he had doubts about his decision right up to the end, particularly as a result of criticism he received from certain quarters that he was being unpatriotic, since Scotland had few opportunities to win Olympic championships.

On July 9, Liddell finished third in the 200 meters, behind Jackson Scholz and Charley Paddock. The first two rounds of the 400 were held the next day, and Liddell qualified in respectable, but unspectacular times. The fastest race of the day was won by Imbach in 48.0. The first semifinal, held the morning of July 11, was won by Fitch in 47.8 and the second by Liddell in 48.2, an impressive performance by the "Flying Scot" considering that he had never before beaten the 49-second mark. The final, contested later in the day, was won by Liddell in an unorthodox and electrifying manner. Racing in the outside lane, Liddell took off as if he were running a short dash and passed the halfway mark in an extraordinary 22.2 seconds, only 0.3 seconds slower than he had run in the 200-meter final. Track experts considered this to be tactical foolishness, but Liddell was a man inspired. He actually increased his lead during the second half of the race and won by over five meters. His pace was so fast that two of his opponents, Imbach and Taylor, fell while trying to keep up. Taylor crawled and scrambled the last few yards to the finish line.

Eric Liddell returned to Scotland a hero of heroes and was paraded through the streets of Edinburgh. A year after his Olympic triumph, he returned to China to join his father in missionary work. Liddell made two more trips to Scotland, but he was back in China during World War II. He died of a brain tumor in a Japanese internment camp, on February 21, 1945.

**1928 Amsterdam** C: 51, N: 20, D: 8.3. WR: 47.0 (Emerson Spencer)
| | | |
|---|---|---|
| 1. Raymond Barbuti | USA | 47.8 |
| 2. James Ball | CAN | 48.0 |
| 3. Joachim Büchner | GER | 48.2 |
| 4. John Rinkel | GBR | 48.4 |
| 5. Werner "Harry" Storz | GER | 48.8 |
| 6. Herman Phillips | USA | 49.0 |

On May 12, 1928, Emerson Spencer set a world record of 47.0. But he failed to qualify for the Olympics except as a member of the relay team, because of a major misunderstanding at the U.S. Final Olympic Tryouts. Thinking he was running in a heat, he finished only fast enough to qualify for what he thought was the next round. Actually the race had been to decide the final places on the U.S. team and Spencer lost out.

The semifinals in Amsterdam were won by Ball and Büchner in 48.6. In the final Barbuti, a former captain of the Syracuse football team, started his finishing kick at the 300-meter mark even though he had been instructed to wait an extra 30 meters. Fortunately for Barbuti, James Ball of Winnipeg made the opposite mistake. Unaccustomed to running in lanes, Ball misjudged his position until the final straightaway and then unleashed a great finishing kick. As they approached the finish line, Ball had closed within a foot of Barbuti, but he turned to see where his opponent was just as Barbuti lunged for the tape. The plucky New Yorker fell to the ground, scraping his arm, leg, and side, but he had gained the victory. Afterward he told reporters, "I never noticed the other runners after the start. I heard them, but all I kept thinking was 'run, kid, run.' I don't remember anything of the last 100 meters except a mad desire to get to that tape."

**1932 Los Angeles** C: 27, N: 15, D: 8.5. WR(440 yards): 46.4 (Benjamin Eastman)

| | | | |
|---|---|---|---|
| 1. | William Carr | USA | 46.2 WR |
| 2. | Benjamin Eastman | USA | 46.4 |
| 3. | Alexander Wilson | CAN | 47.4 |
| 4. | William Walters | SAF | 48.2 |
| 5. | James Gordon | USA | 48.2 |
| 6. | George Golding | AUS | 48.8 |

Ben Eastman of Stanford University was considered king of the world at 400 and 800 meters, particularly after March 26, 1932, when he lowered his own world record at 440 yards (402.3 meters) by a full second in running the extraordinary time of 46.4. He ran 46.5 two months later and appeared to be a sure bet to win either the 400 or 800 at the Los Angeles Olympics. Then, seemingly from out of nowhere, came a new contender, University of Pennsylvania junior Bill Carr of Pine Bluff, Arkansas. At the U.S. intercollegiate championships at Berkeley on July 2, Carr came from behind to gain a shocking 440 victory over Eastman, 47.0 to 47.2. Two weeks later at the U.S. Olympic tryouts on Eastman's home track in Palo Alto, California, Carr again came from behind to defeat Eastman, 46.9 to 47.1.

Unfortunately, Eastman got caught up in a rivalry between his own coach, Dink Templeton of Stanford, and Carr's coach, Lawson Robertson of Pennsylvania, who had been chosen to coach the U.S. Olympic team. Obsessed with beating Robertson, Templeton convinced Eastman to skip the Olympic 800 meters, which was actually his best event, and concentrate on beating Carr at 400 meters.

At the 1932 Olympics Carr posted the fastest time in each of the first two rounds. Then he won the first semifinal in 47.2. Eastman won the second in 47.6. In the final Eastman held a slight edge through most of the race. Carr drew even with 80 meters to go and gradually pulled away to win by two yards. Whatever Dink Templeton thought of the race, Ben Eastman himself was an amiable loser. "Bill's just too fast for me," he said. "You don't need to sympathize. I know when I'm licked by a better runner." Unfortunately, Bill Carr's running career came to an abrupt halt on March 17, 1933, when he broke both ankles and fractured his pelvis in an automobile accident.

**1936 Berlin** C: 42, N: 25, D: 8.7. WR: 46.1 (Archie Williams)

| | | | |
|---|---|---|---|
| 1. | Archie Williams | USA | 46.5 |
| 2. | Arthur Godfrey Brown | GBR | 46.7 |
| 3. | James LuValle | USA | 46.8 |
| 4. | William Roberts | GBR | 46.8 |
| 5. | William Fritz | CAN | 47.8 |
| 6. | John Loaring | CAN | 48.2 |

Prior to the 1936 season, Archie Williams of Oakland, California had never run a quarter-mile faster than 49 seconds. However, in April, 1936, he ran 47.4, in May 46.8, and on June 19, at the N.C.A.A. championships in Chicago, he clocked 46.5 for 440 yards around one turn, passing the 400-meter mark in 46.1 to break Bill Carr's world record. In the Olympic final Williams and fellow Californian James LuValle led the field entering the homestretch. But Godfrey Brown, three yards behind with 100 meters to go, staged a thrilling stretch drive, passed LuValle 40 meters from the tape, and closed in on the exhausted Williams. Brown had pulled within seven inches and was still coming strong when Williams breasted the tape before Brown could get any closer. The official times appear to have been inaccurate; the photo-finish camera yielded the following, more reliable results: Williams 46.66, Brown 46.68, LuValle 46.84, and Roberts 46.87. The day after Godfrey Brown won the 400 meters silver medal, his sister Audrey earned a silver medal of her own in the women's 4 × 100-meter relay. Godfrey added a gold medal to the family haul in the men's 4 × 400-meter relay.

**1948 London** C: 53, N: 28, D: 8.5. WR: 45.9 (Herbert McKenley) WR(440 yards): 46:0 (Rudolf Harbig, Grover Klemmer, Herbert McKenley)

| | | | |
|---|---|---|---|
| 1. | Arthur Wint | JAM | 46.2 |
| 2. | Herbert McKenley | JAM | 46.4 |
| 3. | Malvin Whitfield | USA | 46.9 |
| 4. | David Bolen | USA | 47.2 |
| 5. | Morris Curotta | AUS | 47.9 |
| 6. | George Guida | USA | 50.2 |

Jesse Abramson of the New York *Herald Tribune* had called Herb McKenley "the surest sure thing of the Games," but whenever anyone asked McKenley about it, he told them that his older teammate, 6-foot 4½-inch Arthur Wint, was really the man to beat. McKenley may not have actually believed that himself at the time, but it turned out that he was absolutely correct. Wint, a minister's son whose mother was a Scot, had joined the Royal Air Force during World War II. Staying on in England after the war, Wint was a 28-year-old medical student at the University of London at the time of the 1948 Olympics. Consequently, he was quite a local favorite among London sports fans.

Disappointed at having lost to Mal Whitfield at 800 meters, Wint was determined to finish ahead of the American at 400 meters. Although Wint had never lost to McKenley at 400 meters, he was prepared to settle for a silver medal behind his friend and rival, who seemed to be in prime condition. McKenley's usual tactics, or lack of them, consisted of running as fast as he could as soon as the starter's gun went off. Normally he could keep up his all-out pace for 350 meters and then coast through the final 50 meters.

True to form, McKenley went away at breakneck speed in the London final. Coming out of the final curve he was four yards ahead of Whitfield. But, McKenley, uncharacteristically, broke stride about 25 meters early and began to fade. Noticing the plight of his fellow Jamaican, Wint took off after him, closed the gap, caught McKenley with about 20 yards to go, and went on to win by two and a half yards.

Dave Bolen, who finished fourth, was later appointed U.S. ambassador to Botswana, Lesotho, and Swaziland, as well as East Germany.

**1952 Helsinki** C: 71, N: 35, D: 7.25. WR: 45.8 (V. George Rhoden)

| | | | |
|---|---|---|---|
| 1. | V. George Rhoden | JAM | 45.9 OR |
| 2. | Herbert McKenley | JAM | 45.9 |
| 3. | Ollie Matson | USA | 46.8 |
| 4. | Karl-Friedrich Haas | GER | 47.0 |
| 5. | Arthur Wint | JAM | 47.0 |
| 6. | Malvin Whitfield | USA | 47.1 |

In 1952 the track world had different expectations of Herb McKenley. The 30-year-old McKenley was considered a sure finalist but an unlikely medal winner. The favorite was George Rhoden, a 25-year-old from Kingston who had just graduated from Morgan State College in Baltimore. In the 1948 Olympics he had been eliminated in the semifinals, but by August of 1950 he had broken the 400-meter world record in 45.8.

Rhoden and McKenley were joined in the 1952 final by fellow Olympic veterans Arthur Wint and Mal Whitfield, who had already won the 800 meters, but was now fighting off a cold with benzedrine. The other starters were University of San Francisco football star Ollie Matson, who later achieved success as a five-time All-Pro back in the National Football League, and Kaaro Haas, the only white finalist. McKenley had the sympathy of much of the crowd as a result of his photo-finish loss in the 100-meter final four days earlier.

The amazing thing about the 1952 400-meter final was that Wint and McKenley completely reversed the tactics that they had used in the 1948 final. McKenley, having learned from his experience four years earlier, began cautiously and saved his strength for the finish. Wint, on the other hand, for some reason unknown even to himself, took off at full speed and led by three yards at the 200-meter mark in 21.7—0.2 second faster than he had ever run the distance. Not surprisingly, Wint ran out of steam early and was passed by Rhoden, who entered the long final straightaway with a four-yard lead over McKenley. But then McKenley began to close the gap, pulling closer with every stride until he almost drew even. Rhoden recalled the moment after the race: "About 20 meters from

home I heard the roar of the crowd and with split vision saw someone coming up. From someplace I summoned the necessary strength and held him off. I surely was glad to see that tape." Rhoden's margin of victory was about 18 inches.

**1956 Melbourne** C: 42, N: 23, D: 11.29. WR: 45.2 (Louis Jones)

| | | | |
|---|---|---|---|
| 1. | Charles Jenkins | USA | 46.7 |
| 2. | Karl-Friedrich Haas | GER | 46.8 |
| 3. | Voitto Hellsten | FIN | 47.0 |
| 3. | Ardalion Ignatyev | SOV | 47.0 |
| 5. | Louis Jones | USA | 48.1 |
| 6. | Malcolm Spence | SAF | 48.3 |

Lou Jones set a world record of 45.2 at the U.S. Olympic tryouts and went to Melbourne as the clear favorite. Ignatyev won the first semifinal in 46.8, with Jones coasting in third place to qualify for the final. The second semi was a hard-fought affair, won by the third-string U.S. runner, Charley Jenkins of Cambridge, Massachusetts. Jenkins had barely made the semifinal round by finishing third in his first- and second-round heats. The second semifinal was so fast that Kevan Gosper of Australia was eliminated even though he finished in 46.2 seconds.

Jones led the final for the first 300 meters. Coming out of the final turn he had expected to have a three- or four-meter lead and was psychologically unprepared when he realized that Ignatyev was right behind him. The Soviet runner took the lead with 60 yards to go, but then Jenkins launched a finishing kick, passed Ignatyev 25 yards from the finish, and broke the tape just ahead of Haas, who came from last place to second in the final 100 meters. The photo-finish was unable to separate Hellsten and Ignatyev, so they were both awarded third place. After the race Jenkins modestly told reporters, "Jones is still the champ. That 45.2 is it."

**1960 Rome** C: 54, N: 41, D: 9.6. WR: 45.2 (Louis Jones)

| | | | |
|---|---|---|---|
| 1. | Otis Davis | USA | 44.9 WR |
| 2. | Carl Kaufmann | GER | 44.9 WR |
| 3. | Malcolm Spence | SAF | 45.5 |
| 4. | Milkha Singh | IND | 45.6 |
| 5. | Manfred Kinder | GER | 45.9 |
| 6. | Earl Young | USA | 45.9 |

This was the first time since 1912 that the final was held on a different day than the semifinals. The improvement in times spoke well for the new procedure. Spence took the early lead and was still in front at 200 meters, followed by Kaufmann, Milkha Singh, and Davis. Then Davis accelerated dramatically, covering the next 100 meters in 10.8 seconds and entering the final straight with a four-yard lead over Brooklyn-born Carl Kaufmann. Next it was Kaufmann's turn to stage a sensational sprint. He almost caught Davis, but the American leaned forward just in time, crossing the finish line ahead of the flying Kaufmann, who ended up sprawled on the track from exhaustion. The electronic timer gave Davis a victory of .02 seconds, both men being credited with a new world record.

Otis Davis was born in Tuscaloosa, Alabama. A basketball player at the University of Oregon, he didn't start running until he was 26 years old, two years before the Olympics. Like Charley Jenkins before him, Davis finished only third at the U.S. Olympic tryouts. Carl Kaufmann went on to become an operetta singer and actor.

**1964 Tokyo** C: 50, N: 33, D: 10.19. WR: 44.9 (Otis Davis, Carl Kaufmann, Adolph Plummer, Michael Larrabee)
1. Michael Larrabee      USA   45.1
2. Wendell Mottley       TRI   45.2
3. Andrzej Badeński      POL   45.6
4. Robbie Brightwell     GBR   45.7
5. Ulis Williams         USA   46.0
6. Timothy Graham        GBR   46.0
7. Peter Vassella        AUS   46.3
8. Edwin Skinner         TRI   46.8

His students laughed when Los Angeles high school mathematics teacher Mike Larrabee told them he was going to try out for the Olympics, but their laughter turned to excitement when they saw the times he was producing on the school track and at local meets. Larrabee had been a major contender in 1960, until he injured a tendon. Most observers thought Larrabee's track career was finished, but he returned in 1964 and qualified for the U.S. team at the age of 30. Sixth at the halfway mark of the final and fifth coming out of the final curve, Larrabee unleashed his patented finishing kick and churned past one runner after another. At last he caught Wendell Mottley of Yale ten meters from the finish and won by two feet. During a record-setting two-hour press conference following his victory, Larrabee told reporters, "I kept a copy of one story written about me that said I was too old. It's still on my wall. I think I'll take it down now." Larrabee was the first white winner of the 400 meters in 32 years.

**1968 Mexico City** C: 54, N: 35, D: 10.18. WR: 44.0 (Lee Evans)
1. Lee Evans             USA   43.86   WR
2. Larry James           USA   43.97
3. Ronald Freeman        USA   44.41
4. Amadou Gakou          SEN   45.01
5. Martin Jellinghaus    GER   45.32
6. Tegegne Bezabeh       ETH   45.42
7. Andrzej Badeński      POL   45.42
8. Amos Omolo            UGA   47.6

A U.S. sweep seemed inevitable, considering that the top 12 400-meter runners in the world were all Americans. With each nation limited to only three entrants per event, several first-class U.S. runners had to be left behind. The big surprise was the success of the Africans, particularly Amadou Gakou of Senegal, who lowered his personal best from 46.7 to 45.0 and became the first black to hold the African 400-meter record.

Initially Lee Evans announced his intention to withdraw from the final after his friends John Carlos and Tommie Smith were expelled from the Olympic Village after their Black Power protest at the 200-meter victory ceremony. But Carlos and Smith personally convinced him to run and to win. Evans expected to have a five-yard lead when he reached the final straightaway. Instead he realized that Larry James was right behind him. "I felt faint. . . . Three steps from the finish, Larry dropped his head. I knew I had it then. . . . Larry ran three hundred ninety-five meters. I ran four hundred and one. That was the difference."

The first seven finishers all bettered their pre-Olympic best times. When asked his theory as to why U.S. blacks were such good runners, Evans replied, "Maybe a white boy can get an education because his parents can pay for it, but I wouldn't be going to school right now if I hadn't got an athletic scholarship. That's my theory—others may have a different one." However Evans was quick to thank his white friends as well as his black friends for all the help they had given him.

**1972 Munich** C: 64, N: 49, D: 9.7. WR: 43.86 (Lee Evans)
1. Vincent Matthews        USA   44.66
2. Wayne Collett           USA   44.80
3. Julius Sang             KEN   44.92
4. Charles Asati           KEN   45.13
5. Horst-Rüdiger Schlöske  GER   45.31
6. Markku Kukkoaho         FIN   45.59
7. Karl Honz               GER   45.68
DNF: John Smith (USA)

Another U.S. sweep seemed to be a distinct possibility even though defending champion Lee Evans, hampered by a hamstring pull, had finished fourth at the U.S. Olympics trials and only qualified as a member of the 4 × 400 relay team. In his place was Vince Matthews, a New York City social worker who had just missed making the U.S. entry in 1968. U.S. officials and coaches were clearly disappointed that Evans hadn't qualified for the 400, and made Matthews feel extremely unwanted. The pre-Olympics favorites were Californians John Smith and Wayne Collett. In the final, Smith, running with an injured leg, pulled up lame after only 80 meters, but Collett and Matthews drove on. Matthews was somewhat shocked to find himself in the lead entering the final straight and still feeling strong. He held off Collett the rest of the way and won by four feet.

At the medal ceremony, Matthews and Collett showed little respect for the proceedings, talking and fidgeting during the playing of "The Star-Spangled Banner" rather than standing quietly at attention. The West German crowd booed them, and the International Olympic Committee, ignoring the U.S. Olympic Committee, banned the two runners from further competition. Matthews and Collett denied that their actions had constituted an organized protest. "If we did have any ideas about a demonstration," Matthews said, "we could have done a better job than that." Collett added, "I couldn't stand there and sing the words [to the national anthem] because I don't believe they're true. I wish they were. I think we have the potential to have a beautiful country, but I don't think we do."

Stepping down from the victory platform, Matthews had taken off his gold medal and twirled it around his finger, leading some people to believe that the medal meant little to him. In an article in *The New York Times,* Matthews responded to this criticism: "I took it off to tell them this was my medal. A lot of people had forgotten about me and given up on me. . . . Twenty years from now, I can look at this medal and say, 'I was the best quarter-miler in the world that day.' If you don't think that's important, you don't know what's inside an athlete's soul."

John Smith, the frustrated favorite, finally achieved Olympic satisfaction when he coached Steve Lewis and Danny Everett to gold and bronze in 1988. Lewis, who wasn't certain he had won until he and Smith watched a replay of the race on the stadium scoreboard, then turned to Smith and said, "That one is for you, Coach."

**1976 Montreal** C: 44, N: 29, D: 7.29. WR: 43.86 (Lee Evans)
1. Alberto Juantorena Danger    CUB    44.26
2. Frederick Newhouse    USA    44.40
3. Herman Frazier    USA    44.95
4. Alfons Brijdenbach    BEL    45.04
5. Maxie Parks    USA    45.24
6. Richard Mitchell    AUS    45.40
7. David Jenkins    GBR    45.57
8. Jan Werner    POL    45.63

In 1972 Alberto Juantorena had been narrowly eliminated in the Olympic semifinals. He was unbeaten in 1973 and 1974, but before the 1975 season he underwent two operations on his foot. By the time of the Montreal Olympics he had emerged as the clear favorite at 400 meters. When he scored a surprising victory at 800 meters, it appeared that he had an excellent chance to become the first runner to score a 400/800 double since Paul Pilgrim in the Intercalated Games of 1906. Juantorena waltzed through the first two rounds, content to qualify without extending himself. After finishing his second-round heat, he kept on running, continuing through the tunnel and into the locker room without stopping. In the semifinals, Juantorena started poorly, then accelerated into first place and jogged home in 45.10, looking back at the other runners seven times on his way to the tape. Fred Newhouse, winner of the second semifinal in 44.89, sprinted into the lead in the final and was sure he was about to win the gold medal when Juantorena, the man with the nine-foot stride, appeared at his shoulder with 20 meters to go and moved right by him. Juantorena's winning time was a half-second faster than he had ever run before. The 6-foot 2-inch Cuban hero became the first man from a non-English-speaking country to win the 400 meters, although Juantorena himself actually spoke English quite well. Before the 1976 Olympics were over, Alberto Juantorena had run nine races and lost 11 pounds.

**1980 Moscow** C: 50, N: 32, D: 7.30. WR: 43.86 (Lee Evans)
1. Viktor Markin    SOV    44.60
2. Richard Mitchell    AUS    44.84
3. Frank Schaffer    GDR    44.87
4. Alberto Juantorena Danger    CUB    45.09
5. Alfons Brijdenbach    BEL    45.10
6. Michael Solomon    TRI    45.55
7. David Jenkins    GBR    45.56
8. Joseph Coombs    TRI    46.33

For the third straight time the 400 meters was won by the runner in Lane 2. This time, though, the man in Lane 2 was a complete outsider: a 23-year-old Siberian-born medical student named Viktor Markin, who wasn't even listed in the 300-page U.S.S.R. Olympic Candidate book. Markin gained the lead from Schaffer with 80 meters to go. Mitchell also finished strongly, moving from last to second in the final 100 meters. Although Juantorena was only a shadow of his former self, his fourth-place finish was actually quite an achievement considering that he was still recovering from an Achilles tendon operation. Markin's time, 0.73 seconds faster than his previous best, was the fastest 400 meters to be run in over two years. "I don't know my own limits," he said afterward. "Everything came to me so quickly in the final. . . . I finished like I was in a dream."

**1984 Los Angeles** C: 80, N: 57, D: 8.8. WR: 43.86 (Lee Evans)
1. Alonzo Babers    USA    44.27
2. Gabriel Tiacoh    IVC    44.54
3. Antonio McKay    USA    44.71
4. Darren Clark    AUS    44.75
5. Sunder Nix    USA    44.75
6. Sunday Uti    NGR    44.93
7. Innocent Egbunike    NGR    45.35
DNS: Bertland Cameron (JAM)

The battle on the track for the 400-meters title was preceded by a war of words between world champion Bert Cameron and U.S. Olympic Trials winner Antonio McKay. Cameron had stated that the gold medal already had his name written on it. McKay responded by vowing, "I'm going to destroy Cameron." Cameron seemed unconcerned about McKay, for whom the Olympics would be his first international meet. But he was worried about Air Force second lieutenant Alonzo Babers who had handed Cameron his only two defeats of the past two years. "He is so relaxed when he's running," Cameron would say of Babers on the eve of the Games. "Maybe McKay should be watching him instead of me."

The first round included one bizarre occurrence. Innocent Egbunike, one of the secondary favorites, thought he had prepared for any eventuality. But shortly after the start of the third heat, Egbunike, running in the inside lane, found himself cut off by Secundino Borabota of the small, impoverished West African nation of Equatorial Guinea. After yelling at Borabota for 100 meters, Egbunike finally squeezed by on the inside and went on to win the heat. After the race, Borabota, evidently unaware that 400-meter runners are supposed to stay in the same lane from start to finish, explained rather cryptically that an injury led him to switch lanes temporarily. "Lane one is a good lane," he added.

The quarterfinals saw some surprisingly fast times. McKay led 18-year-old Darren Clark 44.72 to 44.77 in the first heat, and Babers recorded 44.75 in the third. The following day, the first semifinal was won by Egbunike over Babers 45.16 to 45.17. But the real drama began in the second semi which pitted Cameron against McKay for the first time. After 100 meters Cameron was charging down the backstretch when he suddenly leaped into the air and grabbed his left thigh, the victim of a pulled hamstring muscle. Cameron's Olympics seemed over, but, remarkably, he took off again, having lost a good eight to ten meters to the field. Last at the halfway point and seventh with 100 meters to go, Cameron caught up in the homestretch, finishing fourth and earning a place in the final. Cameron's phenomenal performance overshadowed a great race by Gabriel Tiacoh, who set an African record of 44.64, with Sunday Uti placing second in 44.83 and McKay third at 44.92.

Of the eight finalists, all but Clark were U.S. collegians. Unfortunately, two days' rest did not heal Cameron's leg and he was forced to scratch from the final. Clark went out strongly and led the race all the way into the final straightaway. He thought the victory was his, but about 50 meters from the finish line, Tiacoh and Babers blew by him with Babers pulling away to win by 2½ meters. McKay just nipped Clark at the end for the bronze in what turned out to be the first 400-meter race in which six runners finished under 45 seconds. Babers' time of 44.27 was only one-hundredth of a second off Alberto Juantorena's sea-level best and was the fastest 400 meters in the world since Juantorena set that record at the 1976 Olympics. It was also .71 second better than Babers' pre-Olympic personal record. Tiacoh, who improved his own pre-Olympic best by .70 second, became the first representative of the Ivory Coast to win an Olympic medal.

**1988 Seoul** C: 75, N: 55, D: 9.26. WR: 43.29 (Harry "Butch" Reynolds)

| | | |
|---|---|---|
| 1. Steven Lewis | USA | 43.87 |
| 2. Harry "Butch" Reynolds | USA | 43.93 |
| 3. Danny Everett | USA | 44.09 |
| 4. Darren Clark | AUS | 44.55 |
| 5. Innocent Egbunike | NGR | 44.72 |
| 6. Bertland Cameron | JAM | 44.94 |
| 7. Ian Morris | TRI | 44.95 |
| 8. Mohamed Al Malky | OMA | 45.03 |

The U.S. Olympic trials were won by 24-year-old Butch Reynolds in a time of 43.93, with Danny Everett close behind in 43.98. It was the first time that the 44-second barrier had been broken since the 1968 Olympics. The third U.S. qualifier was Everett's U.C.L.A. teammate, 19-year-old Steve Lewis. As recently as May 1988, Lewis' personal record had been only 45.68, but in the semifi-

nals of the trials he dropped it to 44.11. Four weeks later, on August 17, at the Weltklasse meet in Zurich, Reynolds shattered Lee Evans' 19-year-old world record, stopping the clock at 43.29 seconds.

Reynolds entered the Olympics as the overwhelming favorite, but Lewis recorded the fastest times in both of the first two rounds: 45.31 and 44.41. Lewis won the first semifinal in 44.35 and Reynolds the second in 44.33. The latter race saw the elimination of world champion Thomas Schönlebe of East Germany.

Everett led at the halfway point in the final, followed closely by Lewis. Reynolds, renowned for his powerful finishing kick, was sixth. With 100 meters to go, Lewis took the lead. Reynolds was still in only fifth place, a good 6 meters back. Then the world record holder made his move. But it was too late. He passed Everett 20 meters from the finish and had just caught Lewis when Lewis executed a perfect lean to snatch the victory. Lewis was the youngest male runner to win an individual gold medal since Reggie Walker took the 100 meters in 1908. Lewis was four days older than Walker had been.

Following a meet on August 12, 1990, Butch Reynolds tested positive for steroids and received a two-year suspension.

## 800 METERS

**1896 Athens** C: 9, N: 6, D: 4.9. WR(880 yards): 1:53.4 (Charles Kirkpatrick)

| | | |
|---|---|---|
| 1. Edwin Flack | AUS | 2:11.0 |
| 2. Nándor Dáni | HUN | 2:11.8e |
| 3. Demitrios Golemis | GRE | — |
| DNS: Albin Lermusiaux (FRA) | | |

Teddy Flack was a 22-year-old accountant who took a month's holiday from his job with Price, Waterhouse and Company in London to travel to Athens and take part in the Olympics.

**1900 Paris** C: 18, N: 8, D: 7.16. WR(880 yards): 1:53.4 (Charles Kirkpatrick)

| | | |
|---|---|---|
| 1. Alfred Tysoe | GBR | 2:01.2 |
| 2. John Cregan | USA | 2:03.0 |
| 3. David Hall | USA | — |
| 4. Henri Deloge | FRA | — |
| 5. Zoltán Speidl | HUN | — |
| 6. John Bray | USA | — |

David Hall won the first qualifying heat in 1:59.0, but was unable to repeat his time in the final, which was won by Tysoe, who ran the last lap in 56.2 seconds.

**1904 St. Louis** C: 13, N: 3, D: 9.1. WR(880 yards): 1:53.4 (Charles Kirkpatrick)

| | | |
|---|---|---|
| 1. James Lightbody | USA | 1:56.0 OR |
| 2. Howard Valentine | USA | 1:56.3 |
| 3. Emil Breitkreutz | USA | 1:56.4 |
| 4. George Underwood | USA | — |
| 5. Johannes Runge | GER | — |
| 6. William Frank Verner | USA | — |

Lightbody ran most of the race in fifth place, then moved to the outside and passed the leaders to win by one and a half yards. Runge had the misfortune of being misdirected by incompetent officials into a minor handicap race, which he won easily. He then learned that the race he was supposed to be in—the Olympic championship—was about to begin. Runge still managed to place fifth.

**1906 Athens** C: 23, N: 7, D: 4.30. WR(880 yards): 1:53.4 (Charles Kirkpatrick)

| | | |
|---|---|---|
| 1. Paul Pilgrim | USA | 2:01.5 |
| 2. James Lightbody | USA | 2:01.6 |
| 3. Wyndham Halswelle | GBR | 2:03.0 |
| 4. Reginald Percy Crabbe | GBR | — |
| 5. Kristian Hellström | SWE | — |
| 6. Charles Bacon | USA | — |
| 7. Eli Burton Parsons | USA | — |

DNF: Johannes Runge (GER)

Coming down the homestretch, Lightbody looked over his left shoulder to check the position of the other runners. Just then, Paul Pilgrim, the upset winner of the 400 meters the previous day, sped past him on the right to win by about two feet. Pilgrim never won a major race before or after the 1906 Games.

**1908 London** C: 39, N: 10, D: 7.21. WR(880 yards): 1:53.4 (Charles Kirkpatrick)

| | | | |
|---|---|---|---|
| 1. Melvin Sheppard | USA | 1:52.8 | WR |
| 2. Emilio Lunghi | ITA | 1:54.2 | |
| 3. Hanns Braun | GER | 1:55.2 | |
| 4. Ödön Bodor | HUN | 1:55.4 | |
| 5. Theodore Just | GBR | — | |
| 6. John Halstead | USA | | |

DNF: Clarke Beard (USA), Ian Fairbairn-Crawford (GBR)

Fairbairn-Crawford raced into the lead and set a blistering pace, in the hope of wearing out 1500-meter winner Mel Sheppard for the benefit of Britain's number-one runner, Theodore Just. Fairbairn-Crawford opened a 15-yard gap after 200 meters and finished the first lap in 53 seconds. The British strategy failed, as Sheppard kept to his own pace, moved into the lead after 500 meters, and won by ten yards over the surprising Emilio Lunghi. A second tape had been set up 5 yards 4 inches after the finish so that the winner's time could be measured at 880 yards. Sheppard slowed down so much that he needed 2.2 seconds to cover the extra distance, and thus missed breaking Kirkpatrick's 13-year-old half-mile world record.

**1912 Stockholm** C: 48, N: 15, D: 7.8. WR: 1:52.8 (Melvin Sheppard)

| | | | |
|---|---|---|---|
| 1. James "Ted" Meredith | USA | 1:51.9 | WR |
| 2. Melvin Sheppard | USA | 1:52.0 | |
| 3. Ira Davenport | USA | 1:52.0 | |
| 4. Melville Brock | CAN | 1:52.7 | |
| 5. Daniel Caldwell | USA | 1:52.8 | |
| 6. Hanns Braun | GER | 1:53.1 | |
| 7. Clarence Edmundson | USA | — | |
| 8. Herbert Putnam | USA | — | |

Sheppard led from the start, passing the halfway mark in 52.5. Ted Meredith edged ahead in the final straightaway and won by about 18 inches, with the first four runners all breaking the world record. Meredith continued on to set a new 880-yard record of 1:52.5. According to *The New York Times,* "The excitement during the race was terrific, and was made more so by the terrible noise caused by thousands of throats yelling injunctions in every language to those in front to 'sit down.' "

**1920 Antwerp** C: 39, N: 18, D: 8.17. WR: 1:51.9 (James "Ted" Meredith)

| | | |
|---|---|---|
| 1. Albert Hill | GBR | 1:53.4 |
| 2. Earl Eby | USA | 1:53.6 |
| 3. Bevil Rudd | SAF | 1:54.0 |
| 4. Edgar Mountain | GBR | — |
| 5. Donald Scott | USA | — |
| 6. Albert Sprott | USA | — |
| 7. Esparbès | FRA | — |
| 8. Adriaan Paulen | HOL | 1:56.4 |

Albert Hill, a 31-year-old World War I veteran, won an exciting race in which the lead changed hands numerous times. A notable instance of gentlemanly good sportsmanship was related by bronze medalist Bevil Rudd. When one of the American runners accidentally bumped into Rudd in the midst of the race, he turned to the South African and said, "Sorry, Bevil."

**1924 Paris** C: 41, N: 21, D: 7.8. WR: 1:51.9 (James "Ted" Meredith)

| | | |
|---|---|---|
| 1. Douglas Lowe | GBR | 1:52.4 |
| 2. Paul Martin | SWI | 1:52.6 |
| 3. Schuyler Enck | USA | 1:53.0 |
| 4. Henry Stallard | GBR | 1:53.0 |
| 5. William Richardson | USA | 1:53.8 |
| 6. Ray Dodge | USA | 1:54.2 |
| 7. John Watters | USA | — |
| 8. Charles Hoff | NOR | — |

The favorite, Henry Stallard, was suffering from an injured foot, but this didn't stop him from giving his all in the final and leading for the first 700 meters. Finally he was passed by Lowe and Martin, who engaged in a frantic battle, which Lowe won by about a yard. The final took place on Lowe's 22nd birthday. Charles Hoff, who finished in eighth place, was the reigning world record holder in the pole vault.

**1928 Amsterdam** C: 54, N: 26, D: 7.31. WR: 1:50.6 (Séraphin Martin)

| | | | |
|---|---|---|---|
| 1. Douglas Lowe | GBR | 1:51.8 | OR |
| 2. Erik Byléhn | SWE | 1:52.8 | |
| 3. Hermann Engelhard | GER | 1:53.2 | |
| 4. Philip Edwards | CAN | 1:54.0 | |
| 5. Lloyd Hahn | USA | 1:54.2 | |
| 6. Séraphin Martin | FRA | 1:54.6 | |
| 7. Earl Fuller | USA | 1:55.0 | |
| 8. Jean Keller | FRA | — | |

The 1928 800 meters was an anxiously awaited contest among Germany's Dr. Otto Peltzer, who had broken Ted Meredith's 14-year-old world record in a classic showdown with Douglas Lowe in 1926, Lloyd Hahn, who had broken Peltzer's record, and Séra Martin, who had broken Hahn's record. Unfortunately, Peltzer became ill and was eliminated in the semifinals. As it turned out, the big confrontation was actually a rout, as defending champion Douglas Lowe swept past Hahn in the final curve and won by about eight yards.

**1932 Los Angeles** C: 19, N: 10, D: 8.2. WR: 1:50.6 (Séraphin Martin)

| | | | |
|---|---|---|---|
| 1. Thomas Hampson | GBR | 1:49.7 | WR |
| 2. Alexander Wilson | CAN | 1:49.9 | |
| 3. Philip Edwards | CAN | 1:51.5 | |
| 4. Edwin Genung | USA | 1:51.7 | |
| 5. Edwin Turner | USA | 1:52.5 | |
| 6. Charles Hornbostel | USA | 1:52.7 | |
| 7. John Powell | GBR | 1:53.0 | |
| 8. Séraphin Martin | FRA | 1:53.6 | |

Missing from the competition was Ben Eastman, who had recorded 1:50.0 for 800 meters earlier in the year on his way to a time of 1:50.9 for 880 yards. Eastman had decided to concentrate on the 400 meters. Guyanese-born medical student Phil Edwards sprinted into the lead, covering the first lap in 52.8 seconds. Inevitably, he faded and was passed, first by Alex Wilson and then by 24-year-old schoolteacher Tommy Hampson, who had never before run faster than 1:52.4. Wilson and Hampson dueled stride for stride over the last 50 yards with Hampson just edging ahead to win by a foot.

Two days after his victory, Hampson recorded in his diary his impressions during the last half-lap of the race: "Oh God help me—I'm tired. Oh Winnie [his fiancée], my darling, I cannot manage it. Yes I can, though, I beat Wilson two years ago. I beat Edwards twice two years ago. Oh damn this run—round the bend I can't see what's happening.

"We're in the straight. Oh God, let me get there—musn't disappoint Winnie. Ah, goodbye Phil; now for Wilson. Wonder how far from the tape. I can't see. Caught him now for it. Harder, harder, harder—shall I do it? Yes, I will. Help me now, darling. I can't drop him; damn the man. At last, just in front—my shadow just ahead. Oh where is that tape? My legs won't take me there. What a row the crowd are making too! Ah, thank God, I felt it break, it must have been. Yes, here's Wilson, patting me: 'Well run Tommy.' "

Hampson credited his victory to his love for his future wife. "I can truly say that but for her I would never have got where I am. A runner perhaps, for they can be made by diligence and hard work; a racer possibly, for they are born of experience in running; but a world beater must, like a great artist, be inspired—and what greater inspiration can anyone have than the love of such a beautiful, kind, gentle, sweet, good creature."

**1936 Berlin** C: 43, N: 24, D: 8.4. WR: 1:49.7 (Thomas Hampson)

| | | |
|---|---|---|
| 1. John Woodruff | USA | 1:52.9 |
| 2. Mario Lanzi | ITA | 1:53.3 |
| 3. Philip Edwards | CAN | 1:53.6 |
| 4. Kazimierz Kucharski | POL | 1:53.8 |
| 5. Charles Hornbostel | USA | 1:54.6 |
| 6. Harry Williamson | USA | 1:55.8 |
| 7. Juan Carlos Anderson | ARG | — |
| 8. Gerald Backhouse | AUS | — |

John Woodruff was a 21-year-old University of Pittsburgh freshman who came from a poor black family in South Connellsville, Pennsylvania. His time of 1:52.7 was the fastest of the qualifying rounds. As usual, Phil Edwards, now a doctor, stormed into the lead and led the field around the first lap. Meanwhile Woodruff was executing one of the most unusual tactics ever seen in the Olympics. Finding himself boxed in after 300 meters, Woodruff slowed down to the pace of a brisk walk and let all the other runners pass him. Then he moved way to the outside and sprinted past his opponents one by one until he found himself in the lead with one lap to go. Edwards regained the lead on the backstretch, but Woodruff took over again in the last curve. Mario Lanzi staged a great finishing drive, but Woodruff used his loping ten-foot stride to stave off the challenge and win by two yards. Phil Edwards won his fifth Olympic bronze medal.

**1948 London** C: 41, N: 24, D: 8.2. WR: 1:46.6 (Rudolf Harbig)

| | | | |
|---|---|---|---|
| 1. Malvin Whitfield | USA | 1:49.2 | OR |
| 2. Arthur Wint | JAM | 1:49.5 | |
| 3. Marcel Hansenne | FRA | 1:49.8 | |
| 4. Herbert Barten | USA | 1:50.1 | |
| 5. Ingvar Bengtsson | SWE | 1:50.5 | |
| 6. Robert Chambers | USA | 1:52.1 | |
| 7. Robert Chef d'Hôtel | FRA | 1:53.0 | |
| 8. Niels Holst-Sörensen | DEN | 1:53.4 | |

Chef d'Hôtel held the early lead, but at the end of the first lap 23-year-old Air Force sergeant Mal Whitfield jumped the field and pulled away. Arthur Wint made a late charge, but Whitfield held on to win by three yards. Between 1948 and 1954 Whitfield won 66 of 69 half-mile races.

**1952 Helsinki** C: 50, N: 32, D: 7.22. WR: 1:46.6 (Rudolf Harbig)

| | | | |
|---|---|---|---|
| 1. Malvin Whitfield | USA | 1:49.2 | EOR |
| 2. Arthur Wint | JAM | 1:49.4 | |
| 3. Heinz Ulzheimer | GER | 1:49.7 | |
| 4. Gunnar Nielsen | DEN | 1:49.7 | |
| 5. Albert Webster | GBR | 1:50.2 | |
| 6. Günter Steines | GER | 1:50.6 | |
| 7. Reginald Pearman | USA | 1:52.1 | |
| 8. Lars-Eric Wolfbrandt | SWE | 1:52.1 | |

Between Olympics Mal Whitfield had worked as a tail-gunner during the Korean War. But on July 22, 1952, he was back in the final of the Olympic 800 meters run, once again facing the challenge of Arthur Wint. The 32-year-old Wint led the field around the first lap, reaching 400 meters with Ulzheimer second and Whitfield third. On the backstretch, with 250 meters to go, Whitfield made his move and entered the final curve in first place. Coming into the homestretch, Wint made a move of his own and gradually drew up to Whitfield's shoulder. But Whitfield had kept some extra strength in reserve and was able to pull away to a two-yard victory. Whitfield's time was exactly what it had been four years earlier, but Wint finished one yard closer.

**1956 Melbourne** C: 38, N: 24, D: 11.26. WR: 1:45.7 (Roger Moens)

| | | | |
|---|---|---|---|
| 1. Thomas Courtney | USA | 1:47.7 | OR |
| 2. Derek Johnson | GBR | 1:47.8 | |
| 3. Audun Boysen | NOR | 1:48.1 | |
| 4 Arnold Sowell | USA | 1:48.3 | |
| 5. Michael Farrell | GBR | 1:49.2 | |
| 6. Lonnie Spurrier | USA | 1:49.3 | |
| 7. Emile Leva | BEL | 1:51.8 | |
| 8. Bill Butchart | AUS | — | |

On August 3, 1955, Roger Moens of Belgium ran 1:45.7 to break finally Rudolf Harbig's 1939 world record. Unfortunately, Moens sustained a leg injury late in the 1956 season and was unable to compete in the Olympics. Nevertheless, the 800 meters final turned out to be the most dramatic race of the Melbourne Olympics. With Moens gone, the race shaped up to be the climactic chapter in the ongoing rivalry between Arnie Sowell of Pittsburgh and Tom Courtney of Livingston, New Jersey.

Sure enough, Courtney took the early lead, but Sowell quickly passed him and led the pack through the first lap and into the second. Toward the end of the backstretch, Courtney tried to pass Sowell, and the two ran shoulder to shoulder around the final curve. Emerging into the homestretch, the runners found themselves confronted by a stiff wind. Courtney moved ahead and then shifted to the third lane in order to avoid the chewed up inner lane. Noticing the sudden opening between the two Americans, Derek Johnson dashed between them and, with 60 yards to go, pushed into first place. It looked like a major upset in the making, but Courtney was not about to give up. Courtney later recalled, "I looked at the tape just 40 yards away and realized this was the only chance I would ever have to win the Olympics." Ignoring the pain throughout his body, Courtney fashioned one last sprint out of nothing but determination. Step by step he gained on Johnson and lunged across the finish line. In a delirium, he turned to Johnson and asked who had won. "Why you did, Tom," came the reply.

"It was a new kind of agony for me," Courtney recalled. "I had never run myself into such a state. My head was exploding, my stomach ripping and even the tips of my fingers ached. The only thing I could think was, 'If I live, I will never run again!'" The victory ceremony had to be delayed for an hour until he recovered.

Twenty years later, Tom Courtney wrote about his years of competitive running: "It is a world that is gone now, but I still enjoy going out to a local track and taking a run and, with a half lap to go, I kind of savor the idea that I am re-running the last half lap of the best part of my life."

**1960 Rome** C: 51, N: 35, D: 9.2. WR: 1:45.7 (Roger Moens)

| | | | |
|---|---|---|---|
| 1. Peter Snell | NZE | 1:46.3 | OR |
| 2. Roger Moens | BEL | 1:46.5 | |
| 3. George Kerr | JAM | 1:47.1 | |
| 4. Paul Schmidt | GER | 1:47.6 | |
| 5. Christian Wägli | SWI | 1:48.1 | |
| 6. Manfred Matuschewski | GDR | 1:52.0 | |

The 1960 800 meters was expected to be a great duel between 30-year-old world record holder Roger Moens and George Kerr of Jamaica. Kerr won the first semifinal, but the second semi produced a surprise when Moens was beaten by a little-known New Zealander named Peter Snell, whose pre-Olympic best had been 1:49.2 for 880 yards. However Moens had not really extended himself, so Snell was still not taken seriously. As expected, Christian Wägli took the lead in the final and held on for 700 meters, at which point Moens moved ahead. In the homestretch he looked back three times to check the position of the other runners, particularly George Kerr. Moens was still ahead 25 yards from the tape when Snell, realizing for the first time that he actually had a chance to win, charged ahead on the inside. "All I remember from that point is hurling every ounce of effort into the finish, and flinging myself forward," Snell wrote in his autobiography, *No Bugles, No Drums*. Like Tom Courtney four years earlier, Peter Snell had no idea in which place he had finished. Then a dejected Roger Moens approached him with congratulations. "Who won?" asked Snell. "You did," replied Moens.

"It was a strange moment," Snell recalled. "What should I do now? Flashingly, I recalled films of past Olympics, and of champions who cavorted round the track, presumably letting their happy emotions run riot. But I felt in a semi-daze, partly from fatigue, partly from disbelief that this had actually happened to me." Snell did not take a victory lap. Instead he channeled his emotions into rooting for fellow New Zealander Murray Halberg, who won the next race on the schedule, the 5000 meters.

A word about one runner who never even made it to the starting line. Wym Essajas was the first person to represent the South American nation of Surinam at the Olympics. Unfortunately he was mistakenly told that the 800-meter heats would be held in the afternoon, so he spent the morning resting. When Essajas arrived at the stadium the heats were over, and he was forced to return to Surinam without having competed. It was eight years before Surinam sent another athlete to the Olympics.

**1964 Tokyo** C: 47, N: 32, D: 10.16. WR: 1:44.3 (Peter Snell)

| | | | |
|---|---|---|---|
| 1. Peter Snell | NZE | 1:45.1 | OR |
| 2. William Crothers | CAN | 1:45.6 | |
| 3. Wilson Kiprugut Chuma | KEN | 1:45.9 | |
| 4. George Kerr | JAM | 1:45.9 | |
| 5. Thomas Farrell | USA | 1:46.6 | |
| 6. Jerome Siebert | USA | 1:47.0 | |
| 7. Dieter Bogatzki | GER | 1:47.2 | |
| 8. Jacques Pennewaert | BEL | 1:50.5 | |

When Peter Snell arrived in Rome in 1960, no one had paid any attention, but four years later in Tokyo it was a completely different story. In one week in 1962 Snell had set world records of 3:54.4 for the mile and 1:44.3 for 800 meters. Now he was the favorite in both the 800 and 1500, although he didn't make his final decision to enter the 800 until the last minute. In the first round, Francis Chatelet of France had the unfortunate experience of recording the fifth fastest time of the round, and yet being eliminated because he finished fifth in his heat, with only the top four from each heat advancing to the semifinals. The final saw stocky Wilson Kiprugut lead the field for 550 meters. Then Snell swung outside, stormed around the leaders into first place, and pulled away to win by four yards. Kiprugut tripped on George Kerr's heel 50 yards from the finish, but still managed to gain a bronze medal, the first Olympic medal ever won by a Kenyan. Snell's winning time was the best on record since his own world record performance.

**1968 Mexico City** C: 41, N: 31, D: 10.15. WR: 1:44.3 (Peter Snell)

| | | | |
|---|---|---|---|
| 1. Ralph Doubell | AUS | 1:44.3 | EWR |
| 2. Wilson Kiprugut Chuma | KEN | 1:44.5 | |
| 3. Thomas Farrell | USA | 1:45.4 | |
| 4. Walter Adams | GER | 1:45.8 | |
| 5. Josef Plachy | CZE | 1:45.9 | |
| 6. Dieter Fromm | GDR | 1:46.2 | |
| 7. Thomas Saisi | KEN | 1:47.5 | |
| 8. Benedict Cayenne | TRI | 1:54.3 | |

Following the usual Kenyan tactics, Kiprugut led the field from the start and still had a six-yard lead after 600 meters. Unheralded Ralph Doubell, who had nipped Kiprugut in the second semifinal, repeated his come-from-behind performance in the final. He passed Kiprugut 50 yards from the finish and won by a long yard.

**1972 Munich** C: 61, N: 46, D: 9.2. WR: 1:44.3 (Peter Snell, Ralph Doubell, David Wottle)

| | | |
|---|---|---|
| 1. David Wottle | USA | 1:45.9 |
| 2. Yevgeny Arzhanov | SOV | 1:45.9 |
| 3. Michael Boit | KEN | 1:46.0 |
| 4. Franz-Josef Kemper | GER | 1:46.5 |
| 5. Robert Ouko | KEN | 1:46.5 |
| 6. Andrew Carter | GBR | 1:46.6 |
| 7. Andrzej Kupczyk | POL | 1:47.1 |
| 8. Dieter Fromm | GDR | 1:48.0 |

At the U.S. Olympic tryouts, Dave Wottle of Canton, Ohio, had equaled the world record of 1:44.3, three seconds faster than he had ever run before. However, because of his lack of international experience and because he had suffered a recent attack of tendinitis, Wottle was not the favorite in Munich. This role fell rather naturally to Yevgeny Arzhanov, who had not lost an 800-meter final in four years. As expected, the two Kenyans, Ouko and Boit, rushed into the early lead in the Olympic final, while Wottle ran in sixth place. Coming into the homestretch it looked like Arzhanov's race, and even Wottle, who had now begun his finishing kick, was only hoping for a medal. As the Kenyans faded, Wottle, who always wore an old golf cap while he ran, saw his chance for second place. Then, 20 yards from the finish, he realized that Arzhanov had run out of steam and that the gold medal was still a possibility. Drawing on his last reserve of energy, Wottle caught and passed Arzhanov, who stumbled two meters short of the tape and fell onto the synthetic track. "It is very disappointing," Arzhanov later told the press, "to lose in the very last stride by the length of your nose."

Wottle was so shocked by his victory that he forgot to take off his cap during the playing of "The Star-Spangled Banner" at the medal ceremony. He didn't realize what he had done until a reporter asked him if he had been staging a protest. Although nobody back in the United States actually held it against him, Wottle, a member of the Air Force ROTC at Bowling Green University, was embarrassed to the point of tears and felt obliged to make a formal apology to the American people.

**1976 Montreal** C: 42, N: 31, D: 7.25. WR: 1:43.7 (Marcello Fiasconaro)

| | | | |
|---|---|---|---|
| 1. Alberto Juantorena Danger | CUB | 1:43.50 | WR |
| 2. Ivo van Damme | BEL | 1:43.86 | |
| 3. Richard Wohlhuter | USA | 1:44.12 | |
| 4. Willi Wülbeck | GER | 1:45.26 | |
| 5. Steven Ovett | GBR | 1:45.44 | |
| 6. Luciano Susanj | YUG | 1:45.75 | |
| 7. Sriram Singh | IND | 1:45.77 | |
| 8. Carlo Grippo | ITA | 1:48.39 | |

Alberto Juantorena went to the Montreal Olympics as the favorite at 400 meters, but somewhat of an unknown quantity at 800 meters. Although he had recorded 1:44.9 in April, the second fastest time of the year (to Rick Wohlhuter's 1:44.8), Juantorena had very little experience at the distance. In fact, his coach had tricked him into entering 800-meter races by telling him they would build his endurance for the 400. Wohlhuter himself dismissed the Cuban as a noncontender, assuming that he would not have the stamina to make it through three rounds of metric half-mile races. Wohlhuter could not have been more wrong. In the final, Juantorena moved ahead as the runners broke to the inside after running the first 300 meters in lanes. He passed the halfway mark in 50.9 seconds. Sriram Singh took the lead briefly, but Juantorena fought him off, easily beat back a challenge from Wohlhuter, and won decisively, to become the first 800 meters gold medalist from a non-English-speaking country. Conspicuously missing from the competition was Mike Boit of Kenya, who was forced to watch the meet from the stands after his nation's government joined the African boycott. Four weeks later Boit ran 1:43.90 and 1:43.57, leaving track fans to wonder what might have been. Silver medalist Ivo van Damme died in a car crash on December 29, 1976. He was only 22 years old.

Olympic history, of course, is not just made up of medalists, and some mention should be made of Wilnor Joseph of the notorious Haitian track and field team. Joseph finished the second heat of the first round in 2:15.26, a time so slow that it would not have qualified him for the 800 meters final in 1900, much less 1976.

**1980 Moscow** C: 41, N: 28, D: 7.26. WR: 1:42.33 (Sebastian Coe)

| | | |
|---|---|---|
| 1. Steven Ovett | GBR | 1:45.4 |
| 2. Sebastian Coe | GBR | 1:45.9 |
| 3. Nikolai Kirov | SOV | 1:46.0 |
| 4. Agberto Guimaraes | BRA | 1:46.2 |
| 5. Andreas Busse | GDR | 1:46.9 |
| 6. Detlef Wagenknecht | GDR | 1:47.0 |
| 7. Jose Marajo | FRA | 1:47.3 |
| 8. David Warren | GBR | 1:49.3 |

The final of the 1980 800 meters race was one of the most eagerly anticipated confrontations in Olympic history. Although there were six other runners in the race, the entire focus of sports fans around the world was on the two English world record holders, Sebastian Coe and Steve Ovett. The last time the two had met was at the 1978 European championships, where Ovett had beaten Coe at 800 meters, but both had lost to Olaf Beyer of East Germany. Since then Ovett and Coe had avoided each other like the plague, preferring to heat up their rivalry with increasingly faster times.

In 1979 Coe set the track world on its heels by breaking three world records in 41 days. On July 5 he ran 800 meters in 1:42.33 to lower Alberto Juantorena's world record by a full second. On July 17 Coe became the first person since Peter Snell to hold the records for both the 800 and the mile, when he ran the classic distance in 3:48.95. Then, on August 15, he covered 1500 meters in 3:32.03, to break Filbert Bayi's five-year-old mark.

The following year it was Steve Ovett's turn to enter the record books. On July 1, 1980, less than an hour after Coe set a new record for 1000 meters, Ovett gained great satisfaction by running a 3:48.8 mile to snatch the world record away from his rival. On July 15, nine days before the heats of the Olympic 800, Ovett beat a distinguished field of Olympic boycotters to win a 1500-meter race in 3:32.09, a time that rounded up to 3:32.1, the same as Coe's 3:32.03. The stage was definitely set for fireworks in the Olympics.

When Coe arrived in Moscow with the rest of the British team, he was met by an army of no less than 400 journalists, who assaulted him with a barrage of inane questions,

such as, "Do you think you will win?" "How do you feel as a human being?" (this one from the representative of Tass, the Soviet news agency), and "How do you like Moscow?" (he had been there only a few hours). Ovett, on the other hand, slipped in two days before he was due to run and, following his usual procedure, refused to talk to the press, a wise decision considering Coe's experience.

The consensus of track experts was that Coe was the favorite at 800 meters, but that the 1500 was a toss-up. Ovett, on the other hand, had issued a public statement that the 800 was a toss-up, but that he was 90 percent sure he would win the 1500. The two did not meet in the heats and semifinals of the 800 meters, the first middle-distance race to be contested.

The first round was run without incident, but the semifinals saw the surprise elimination of Olaf Beyer. The three semifinal heats were won by Ovett, Nikolai Kirov, and Coe.

The final, run at 7:25 p.m. on July 26, turned out to be a strange, almost sluggish race. The first lap was covered in the unusually slow time of 54.3 with Guimaraes in the lead, Ovett badly boxed in, in sixth place, and Coe running last. Dave Warren jumped into the lead, but in the backstretch Kirov moved in front by three meters, while Ovett pushed his way into second place, throwing so many elbows that he verged on disqualification. Meanwhile Coe was floundering, wasting his time in outside lanes and evidently unsure of what tactics to follow. By the time he finally made his move, it was too late. Ovett shot past Kirov 70 meters from the finish and won by over three meters. Ironically, Ovett's winning time was exactly the same as his fifth-place time in Montreal four years earlier. Coe outsprinted Kirov for the silver medal, a prize that would earn a place of honor in most homes, but which for Sebastian Coe was a symbol of failure.

As usual, Ovett declined to attend the postrace press conference. However Coe did not. Sorrowfully, he told the world, "I chose this day of all days to run the worst race of my life. I cannot explain why. I suppose I must have compounded more cardinal sins of middle-distance running in 1½ minutes than I've done in a lifetime. What a race to choose." Fortunately for Coe, he still had a chance to redeem himself six days later. "I've got to come back and climb the mountain again," he said. "The 1500 was going to be a hard event anyway, but now it's going to be the big race of my life. I must win it."

**1984 Los Angeles** C: 69, N: 55, D: 8.6. WR: 1:41.73 (Sebastian Coe)

| | | | |
|---|---|---|---|
| 1. Joaquim Cruz | BRA | 1:43.00 | OR |
| 2. Sebastian Coe | GBR | 1:43.64 | |
| 3. Earl Jones | USA | 1:43.83 | |
| 4. Billy Konchellah | KEN | 1:44.03 | |
| 5. Donato Sabia | ITA | 1:44.53 | |
| 6. Edwin Koech | KEN | 1:44.86 | |
| 7. Johnny Gray | USA | 1:47.89 | |
| 8. Steve Ovett | GBR | 1:52.28 | |

Joaquim Cruz grew up in a poor neighborhood in Taguatinga, Brazil. Although his father worked from morning until night to support his wife and five children, it took a month's pay to produce enough extra to buy a pair of shoes for his only son. A few months after his father died in 1981, the 18-year-old Cruz, a reluctantly converted basketball player, set a world junior record of 1:44.3. His coach, Luiz de Oliveira, decided that if Cruz's potential was to be fulfilled, he would have to move north to the United States. So Cruz, de Oliveira and de Oliveira's family went to live in Utah and then in Eugene, Oregon. By 1983 Cruz was ranked second in the world. The following year he entered the Olympics as a slight favorite over the veteran Sebastian Coe.

The young Brazilian was clearly in top form in Los Angeles. He won his first round heat in 1:45.66, his quarterfinal heat in 1:44.84 and his semifinal in a personal best of 1:43.82. The other semi was won by Coe. In the final, Cruz positioned himself in second place and let Edwin Koech do the front-running, while Coe stayed right behind them. Coming out of the final turn, Cruz did a double-take at Coe behind him and then burst away from the other runners. Coe and Jones took off after him, but they never had a chance. Cruz's winning margin of five meters was the event's largest since 1928.

Sebastian Coe's silver medal was ample reward for a remarkable comeback. Only twelve months earlier, worn out by a prolonged debilitating illness, Coe had declared, "As far as the 800 meters goes, the game is up. . . . I have been obliged to walk away from an event which I did not believe I had fully explored." As for defending Olympic champion Steve Ovett, he had struggled to qualify for the final, lunging across the line to gain the last spot ahead of Omar Khalifa of Sudan. Ovett's semifinal time of 1:44.81 was his fastest 800 in six years. After the final, Ovett, who had been battling bronchitis, collapsed twice in the tunnel leading away from the track. Taken away on a stretcher, he spent the next two nights in a hospital, suffering from broncho-spasms, which he attributed to the legendary Los Angeles smog. Courageously, or, as he would later say, foolishly, Ovett returned to the track to compete in the 1500 meters.

**1988 Seoul** C: 70, N: 53, D: 9.26. WR: 1:41.73 (Sebastian Coe)

| | | | |
|---|---|---|---|
| 1. | Paul Ereng | KEN | 1:43.45 |
| 2. | Joaquim Cruz | BRA | 1:43.90 |
| 3. | Said Aouita | MOR | 1:44.06 |
| 4. | Peter Elliott | GBR | 1:44.12 |
| 5. | Johnny Gray | USA | 1:44.80 |
| 6. | José Luiz Barbosa | BRA | 1:46.39 |
| 7. | Donato Sabia | ITA | 1:48.03 |
| 8. | Nixon Kiprotich | KEN | 1:49.55 |

In 1988 the 800 meters was blessed with a talent-rich field led by Said Aouita, who hadn't lost a flat race at any distance between 800 and 10,000 meters in over three years. Challenging the multitalented Moroccan were Commonwealth champion Steve Cram, the man who had

beaten Aouita at 1500 meters more than 50 races ago on July 16, 1985, and Joaquim Cruz, the defending Olympic champion. The big three were expected to be pressed by the world championship silver and bronze medalists, Peter Elliott, a carpenter at a steelworks in Rotherham, South Yorkshire, and José Luiz Barbosa, who grew up in Três Lagoas in the jungles of western Brazil, and by Johnny Gray, who had recorded the fastest time of the year, 1:42.65, just one month before the Olympics. No one paid any attention to Paul Ereng. And why should they?

A converted quartermiler, the 21-year-old Ereng did not begin competing at 800 meters until 1988. Running for the University of Virginia, he won the N.C.A.A. title, then ran ten races in Europe, finishing first in only one. He was invited to the Kenyan Olympic trials only after someone sent Kenyan officials a newspaper article about Ereng's N.C.A.A. victory. In the absence of world champion Billy Konchellah, who was suffering a relapse of tuberculosis, the Kenyan trials were won by Nixon Kiprotich. Ereng, who led for most of the race, died at the end and barely held on for third place. He was the first member of the Turkana tribe to qualify for the Olympics.

Ereng still was not given serious consideration, even when he ran the fastest time of the opening round in Seoul (1:46.14). The quarterfinals saw the surprising elimination of Steve Cram. The semifinals were won by Ereng, in a personal record of 1:44.55, and Kiprotich in 1:44.71.

With two men in the final, the Brazilians planned a team race. Their strategy was to have Barbosa take out the first lap with a fast pace of between 49 and 50 seconds and try to disrupt Aouita by surging between 300 and 400 meters and 500 and 600, which was when they expected the Moroccan to accelerate. Then Cruz would take over in the backstretch and race to the tape.

The Kenyans had a similar plan, but with a twist. Kiprotich suggested that he set the early pace. Because he was better known, he reasoned, the others would not be expecting such a tactic and would be caught by surprise when Ereng made his move. Kiprotich did set a fast early pace (23.0 for 200 meters), so fast in fact that Ereng was horrified and almost yelled at him to stop. Barbosa moved ahead and led at the bell in 49.54, with Kiprotich second and Cruz third. Aouita was holding back in sixth place and Ereng in seventh.

The real scramble began in the backstraight. First Kiprotich regained the lead from Barbosa. Then Cruz shot by both of them with Elliott and Aouita close behind. Elliott tried to take the lead entering the final turn, but Cruz fought him off and reached the final straight looking like a winner. Meanwhile, though, Ereng was weaving his way between runners. While Elliott and Aouita engaged in a tough battle for second behind Cruz, Ereng slipped by both of them on the inside, then passed a shocked Cruz to win by 2 meters.

# 1500 METERS

**1896 Athens** C: 8, N: 6, D: 4.7. WR(1 mile): 4:12.8 (Walter George)

| | | |
|---|---|---|
| 1. Edwin Flack | AUS | 4:33.2 |
| 2. Arthur Blake | USA | 4:33.6e |
| 3. Albin Lermusiaux | FRA | 4.36.0e |
| 4. Karl Galle | GER | 4.39.0e |
| 5. Angelos Phetsis | GRE | — |
| 6. Demitrios Golemis | GRE | — |

Flack outsprinted Blake in the final straightaway to win by about two meters. Two days later Flack also won the 800 meters race.

**1900 Paris** C: 9, N: 6, D: 7.15. WR: 4:10.4 (Albin Lermusiaux)

| | | | |
|---|---|---|---|
| 1. Charles Bennett | GBR | 4:06.2 | WR |
| 2. Henri Deloge | FRA | 4:06.6 | |
| 3. John Bray | USA | 4:07.2 | |
| 4. Christian Christensen | DEN | — | |
| 5. David Hall | USA | — | |
| 6. Hermann Wraschtil | AUT | — | |

Two of the leading contenders, John Cregan and Alex Grant of the United States, withdrew because the race was held on a Sunday.

**1904 St. Louis** C: 9, N: 3, D: 9.3. WR: 4:06.2 (Charles Bennett)

| | | | |
|---|---|---|---|
| 1. James Lightbody | USA | 4:05.4 | WR |
| 2. William Frank Verner | USA | 4.06.8 | |
| 3. Lacey Hearn | USA | — | |
| 4. David Munson | USA | — | |
| 5. Johannes Runge | GER | — | |
| 6. Peter Deer | CAN | — | |
| 7. Howard Valentine | USA | — | |
| 8. Harvey Cohn | USA | — | |

Lightbody moved into the lead at the end of the back stretch and won by six yards. The first three finishers were all members of the Chicago Athletic Association.

**1906 Athens** C: 20, N: 8, D: 4.30. WR: 4:05.4 (James Lightbody)

| | | |
|---|---|---|
| 1. James Lightbody | USA | 4:12.0 |
| 2. John McGough | GBR/IRL | 4:12.6 |
| 3. Kristian Hellström | SWE | 4:13.4 |
| 4. George Wheatley | AUS | — |
| 5. James Sullivan | USA | — |
| 6. George Bonhag | USA | — |

AC: Reginald Percy Crabbe (GBR), Harvey Cohn (USA)

**1908 London** C: 43, N: 15, D: 7.14. WR: 3:59.8 (Harold Wilson)

| | | | |
|---|---|---|---|
| 1. Melvin Sheppard | USA | 4:03.4 | OR |
| 2. Harold Wilson | GBR | 4:03.6 | |
| 3. Norman Hallows | GBR | 4:04.0 | |
| 4. John Tait | CAN | — | |
| 5. Ian Fairbairn-Crawford | GBR | — | |
| 6. Joseph Deakin | GBR | — | |

AC: James Sullivan (USA), E.V. Loney (GBR)

Unfortunately, British officials decided to divide the 43 entrants into eight heats and allow only the winner of each heat to advance to the final. Because the runners were not seeded, this caused the elimination of several major contenders, most notably Emilio Lunghi, who clocked the second fastest time (4:03.8), but lost his heat to Norman Hallows, who ran 4:03.4. The final looked like a victory for the 5-foot 4-inch, 115-pound world record holder, Harold Wilson, until Mel Sheppard launched a sprint 100 yards from the tape, passed Wilson with 15 yards to go, and won by a yard and a half. For Sheppard, it was the first of his four Olympic gold medals. Ironically, Sheppard had applied to become a New York City policeman, but was rejected because he had a "weak heart."

**1912 Stockholm** C: 46, N: 14, D: 7.10. WR: 3:55.8 (Abel Kiviat)

| | | | |
|---|---|---|---|
| 1. Arnold Jackson | GBR | 3:56.8 | OR |
| 2. Abel Kiviat | USA | 3:56.9 | |
| 3. Norman Taber | USA | 3:56.9 | |
| 4. John Paul Jones | USA | 3:57.2 | |
| 5. Ernst Wide | SWE | 3:57.6 | |
| 6. Philip Baker | GBR | 4:01.0c | |
| 7. John Zander | SWE | 4:02.0e | |
| 8. Henri Arnaud | FRA | 4:02.2e | |

The United States entered a powerful team, including defending champion Mel Sheppard, 1500-meter world record holder Abel Kiviat, and mile world record holder John Paul Jones. Kiviat took the lead entering the final lap, followed by Taber and Jones, with Jackson and Sheppard close behind. Sheppard faded first. Entering the final straight it still looked like an American sweep, as Kiviat, Taber and Jones raced almost shoulder to shoulder. Thirty meters from the finish Kiviat seemed assured of victory, when suddenly Arnold Jackson of Great Britain burst by on the outside and won by almost two yards. The winner later gained greater fame as Arnold Nugent Strode-Jackson following his participation in World War I, during which he was wounded three times. In 1918, at the age of 27, he became the youngest acting brigadier general in the British army. As an athlete, Jackson was rather casual in his training, preferring golf, walking, and massages to the more vigorous and acceptable techniques of keeping in shape. As for Kiviat, 72 years later, at the age of 91, he participated in the 1984 torch relay, carrying the flame for one kilometer in New York City.

**1920 Antwerp** C: 26, N: 11, D: 8.19. WR: 3:54.7 (John Zander)

| | | |
|---|---|---|
| 1. Albert Hill | GBR | 4:01.8 |
| 2. Philip Baker | GBR | 4:02.4 |
| 3. Lawrence Shields | USA | 4:03.1 |
| 4. Václav Vohralik | CZE | — |
| 5. Sven Lundgren | SWE | — |
| 6. André Audinet | FRA | — |
| 7. Arturo Porro | ITA | — |
| 8. Joie Ray | USA | — |

The 31-year-old Hill completed his 800/1500 double with the help of Baker, who ran beside him for most of the final lap in order to "protect him from attacks." Baker later adopted his wife's maiden name and changed his name to Philip Noel-Baker. He served as a member of Parliament for 36 years and was awarded the 1959 Nobel Peace Prize in honor of his work in the pursuit of disarmament.

**1924 Paris** C: 40, N: 22, D: 7.10. WR: 3:52.6 (Paavo Nurmi)

| | | | |
|---|---|---|---|
| 1. Paavo Nurmi | FIN | 3:53.6 | OR |
| 2. Wilhelm Schärer | SWI | 3:55.0 | |
| 3. Henry Stallard | GBR | 3:55.6 | |
| 4. Douglas Lowe | GBR | 3:57.0 | |
| 5. Raymond Buker | USA | 3:58.6 | |
| 6. Lloyd Hahn | USA | 3:59.0 | |
| 7. Raymond Watson | USA | 4:00.0 | |
| 8. Frej. Liewendahl | FIN | 4:00.4 | |

The crowd at the Stade Colombes Stadium rose to their feet to watch the thrilling race to the finish line, as Willy Schärer moved ahead in the last few strides to defeat the desperately struggling Henry Stallard, who collapsed to the ground and remained unconscious for a half hour. It had been an exciting battle—for second place. The race for first place had been no race at all, due to the presence of "The Phantom Finn," Paavo Nurmi.

Finnish Olympic officials had been extremely upset when the track and field schedule was announced and they learned that the final of the 1500 meters and the final of the 5000 meters would be separated by only a half hour, giving negligible time for recuperation to Nurmi, their star entrant in both events. A protest was filed, and the French organizers grudgingly agreed to expand the interval to 55 minutes. It still seemed an impossible feat to attempt, particularly after Nurmi injured both legs in training. But the challenge simply made Nurmi more determined to succeed. On June 19, three weeks before the day of the two Olympic finals, Nurmi decided to simulate the task ahead of him. First he ran a 1500-meter race, setting a world record of 3:52.6. After a one-hour rest he returned to the track and ran 5000 meters, setting another world record of 14:28.2.

Needless to say, when the other runners lined up for the start of the Olympic 1500 final in Paris, they had little hope for the gold medal. Nurmi took off, stopwatch in hand, as usual, covering the first 400 meters in a blistering 58.0 designed to kill off the opposition. Ray Watson made the mistake of trying to keep up with the Finnish running machine, and paid for his folly by fading to a disappointing seventh place. As soon as Watson had dropped away, Nurmi consulted his stopwatch one last time, tossed it onto the infield, and sprinted away to a 40-meter lead. In order to save his strength for the 5000, he coasted the final 300 meters, picking up speed briefly just before the end to make sure the others didn't catch up. After he crossed the finish line, he ignored the cheers of the crowd, picked up his sweater, and disappeared into the dressing room to rest up for his next race.

**1928 Amsterdam** C: 54, N: 26, D: 8.2. WR: 3:51.0 (Otto Peltzer)

| | | | |
|---|---|---|---|
| 1. Harry Larva | FIN | 3:53.2 | OR |
| 2. Jules Ladoumègue | FRA | 3:53.8 | |
| 3. Eino Purje-Borg | FIN | 3:56.4 | |
| 4. Hans-Georg Wichmann | GER | 3:56.8 | |
| 5. Cyril Ellis | GBR | 3:57.6 | |
| 6. Paul Martin | SWI | 3:58.4 | |
| 7. Helmut Krause | GER | 3:59.0 | |
| 8. William Whyte | AUS | 4:00.0 | |

Two hundred meters from the finish, Ladoumègue took the lead from Purje and appeared to be headed for victory. However he was passed 20 meters from the tape by "Harri" Larva, a goldsmith's engraver, who won by four yards. Larva was born to Swedish parents who lived in Turku, the hometown of Paavo Nurmi. He began training as a runner in 1924 after attending a post-Olympic race between Nurmi and Ritola.

**1932 Los Angeles** C: 27, N: 15, D: 8.4. WR: 3:49.2 (Jules Ladoumègue)

| | | | |
|---|---|---|---|
| 1. Luigi Beccali | ITA | 3:51.2 | OR |
| 2. John Cornes | GBR | 3:52.6 | |
| 3. Philip Edwards | CAN | 3:52.8 | |
| 4. Glenn Cunningham | USA | 3:53.4 | |
| 5. Eric Ny | SWE | 3:54.6 | |
| 6. Norwood Hallowell | USA | 3:55.0 | |
| 7. John Lovelock | NZE | 3:57.8 | |
| 8. Frank Crowley | USA | — | |

World record holder Jules Ladoumègue was banned from competition by the French Federation after being charged with accepting pay for running in certain meets. The heated protests of French sports fans were to no avail. Still, the 1932 Olympic final was packed with splendid runners. The lead changed hands several times in the early going. Then, as the second lap came to a close, Glenn Cunningham, who was suffering a bad case of tonsilitis, burst ahead, followed by Phil Edwards. By the time the bell had rung to signal the final lap, Cunningham and Edwards had opened a 15-meter gap over the rest of the field. With 300 meters to go, John Cornes and 5-foot 6½-inch Luigi Beccali gave chase. In the backstretch Edwards passed Cunningham and took a five-yard lead. Beccali caught Cunningham at the head of the homestretch and then passed Edwards 100 yards from the finish. The young man from Milan won by six yards, breaking the tape by grabbing it in his hands and tearing it apart. At the medal ceremony Beccali gave the Fascist salute and became a national hero overnight. As a matter of fact, when he emerged from his cottage in the Olympic Village the next morning, he discovered that his Italian teammates had covered the walk from his bungalow with rugs from their own rooms and lined the path with wicker chairs adorned with flowers. Standing behind the chairs were his teammates, chanting, "Luigi, Luigi, Luigi." Beccali, choked with emotion, was speechless. He later emigrated to New York and went into the wine business.

**1936 Berlin** C: 44, N: 27, D: 8.6. WR: 3:48.8 (William Bonthron)

| | | | |
|---|---|---|---|
| 1. | John Lovelock | NZE | 3:47.8 | WR |
| 2. | Glenn Cunningham | USA | 3:48.4 |
| 3. | Luigi Beccali | ITA | 3:49.2. |
| 4. | Archie San Romani | USA | 3:50.0 |
| 5. | Philip Edwards | CAN | 3:50.4 |
| 6. | John Cornes | GBR | 3:51.4 |
| 7. | Miklós Szabó | HUN | 3:53.0 |
| 8. | Robert Goix | FRA | 3:53.8 |

The 1936 1500-meter final promised to be one of the great races of all time and, unlike many athletic contests with great expectations, it lived up to its advance billing. Among the starters were six of the top seven finishers from the 1932 Olympics. The favorites were defending champion Luigi Beccali, one mile world record holder Glenn Cunningham of Elkhart, Kansas, whose leg had been severely burned in a fire when he was 8 years old, and Jack Lovelock of New Zealand, who had beaten Cunningham in "The Mile of the Century" at Princeton in 1935. Lovelock, a former Rhodes scholar at Oxford, was now a medical student who ran numerous tests on himself in order to determine the conditions necessary to achieve an optimum performance. He was particularly interested in learning how long he could sustain a final sprint, and this led to his development of a secret strategy to win at the Berlin Olympics.

When the great race finally began at 4:18 p.m., there was a good deal of jockeying for position. Cunningham took the lead at 400 meters, followed by Lovelock, who later dropped back to fourth place. Just before the bell, Eric Ny passed Cunningham. Then, 300 yards from the tape, Lovelock passed Cunningham and reached Ny's shoulder. Cunningham followed him. Then Lovelock paused and so did Cunningham, thinking the move had been a false alarm. But one second later Lovelock was off again, beginning the unusually long sprint that he had planned so carefully. Cunningham raced after him, but Lovelock was able to open up a lead of six yards. Cunningham tried to close the gap, but he could get no closer than four yards. Lovelock ran the final 400 meters in 56.8 seconds and the last 200 meters in 27.2, even though he slowed up in the last 20 yards, realizing that his victory was assured. Lovelock didn't believe in setting records, only in winning, but he broke the world record by a full second because that was what was required to defeat Cunningham.

In 1940 Jack Lovelock was thrown from a horse during a hunt and lay unconscious for an hour before he was discovered. He recovered, but suffered double vision and occasional dizziness for the rest of his life. He and his wife moved to New York, where Lovelock obtained a position as assistant director of physical medicine at the Hospital for Special Surgery. On December 28, 1949, eight days before his 40th birthday, Lovelock began having dizzy spells and telephoned his wife that he would be coming home early. He was standing on the southbound platform of the Church Street subway station in Brooklyn when he suddenly pitched forward onto the tracks. He was struck by an oncoming train and died instantly.

**1948 London** C: 37, N: 22, D: 8.6. WR: 3:43.0 (Günder Hägg, Lennart Strand)

| | | | |
|---|---|---|---|
| 1. | Henry Eriksson | SWE | 3:49.8 |
| 2. | Lennart Strand | SWE | 3:50.4 |
| 3. | Willem Slijkhuis | HOL | 3:50.4 |
| 4. | Václav Čevona | CZE | 3:51.2 |
| 5. | Gösta Bergkvist | SWE | 3:52.2 |
| 6. | William Nankeville | GBR | 3:52.6 |
| 7. | Sándor Garay | HUN | 3:52.8 |
| 8. | Erik Jörgensen | DEN | — |

The 1948 final was run on a rain-soaked track in the middle of a downpour. The two great Swedish runners Günder Hägg and Arne Andersson had been banned as professionals, but the Swedes still fielded the strongest team in Lennart Strand, Henry Eriksson, and Gösta Bergkvist. Marcel Hansenne of France led for 1000 meters, at which point the three Swedes, led by Eriksson, made their move. Coming out of the final turn, Eriksson, who had never beaten Strand, held a three-yard lead. Strand closed up to his shoulder and ran even for another 20 yards, but with 50 yards to go he realized that he couldn't pass his teammate. Looking behind him he saw Slijkhuis coming with a great rush on the inside. Determined to preserve second place, Strand veered to his left and bumped the Dutch runner off the track long enough to prevent him from passing. Eriksson was a fireman, Strand a linotype operator and pianist.

**1952 Helsinki** C: 52, N: 26, D: 7.26. WR: 3:43.0 (Günder Hägg, Lennart Strand, Werner Lueg)

| | | | |
|---|---|---|---|
| 1. | Josef "Josy" Barthel | LUX | 3:45.1 | OR |
| 2. | Robert McMillen | USA | 3:45.2 |
| 3. | Werner Lueg | GER | 3:45.4 |
| 4. | Roger Bannister | GBR | 3:46.0 |
| 5. | Patrick El Mabrouk | FRA | 3:46.0 |
| 6. | Rolf Lamers | GER | 3:46.8 |
| 7. | Olle Åberg | SWE | 3:47.0 |
| 8. | Ingvar Ericsson | SWE | 3:47.6 |

The 1952 1500 meters was up for grabs. If there were favorites they were probably Werner Lueg, who had tied the world record at the German championships on June 29, and Roger Bannister, whose greatest fame was yet to come. Bannister, a medical intern, had prepared himself very carefully for a competition that would include a heat and than a final two days later. Unfortunately, I.A.A.F. officials decided to add a semifinal round, which meant that the finalists would run three races in three days. This change of schedule greatly upset Bannister's plans. The semifinals were won by local favorite Denis Johansson in 3:49.8 and lightly regarded Josy Barthel, a small man from the small nation of Luxembourg, who finished in 3:50.4.

Audun Boysen of Norway was the first in front in the final, but he was soon passed by Rolf Lamers, who held the lead until the third lap, when he surrendered it to his teammate Werner Lueg. Coming into the backstretch, the action became frantic. Lueg fought off challenges from Olle Åberg, Patrick El Mabrouk, and Bannister. Lueg opened up a three-yard lead and held it around the final turn. However, almost unnoticed, two outsiders, Josy Barthel and Bob McMillen, had sprinted up from the very back of the field to within striking distance.

Fifty yards from the finish, Lueg began to tie up. With the crowd screaming wildly, first Barthel and then McMillen passed the German. Barthel could feel McMillen literally breathing down his back as the American inched closer with every stride until he was only one and a half feet behind. Let Josy Barthel tell the rest of the story: "Five meters to run, the victory is mine, and, just as I had always dreamed in secret, I raised my arms, I smiled and I crossed the finish line.

"Afterward, I didn't appreciate right away that I had won. For me, as for the public, it was a surprise. I sat down, without being excited, on a bench in the middle of the infield. Then, no longer able to contain my joy, I cried. My friend Audun Boysen asked me, '*Eh bien,* Josy, why are you crying? Are you ill?' It was only then that I truly understood. 'No,' I replied, 'I am crying because I won.' "

Six of the 12 finalists had run their best time ever, including Barthel, whose previous best had been 3:48.4, and McMillen, who had never bettered 3:49.3. On the victory platform, as he listened to the national anthem of Luxembourg being played for the first and only time in Olympic history, Josy Barthel cried again. Roger Bannister recalled, "He raised his hand to wipe away a tear. His great strength was overcome by the tide of joy. Then he turned the movement into a wave of gratitude to the crowd. . . . In the great joy of that single moment the agony of the previous week was quite forgotten. I had found new meaning in the Olympic words that the important thing was not the winning but the taking part—not the conquering but the fighting well."

**1956 Melbourne** C: 37, N: 22, D: 12.1. WR: 3:40.6 (István Rózsavölgyi)

| | | | |
|---|---|---|---|
| 1. Ron Delany | IRL | 3:41.2 | OR |
| 2. Klaus Richtzenhain | GDR | 3:42.0 | |
| 3. John Landy | AUS | 3:42.0 | |
| 4. László Tábori | HUN | 3:42.4 | |
| 5. Brian Hewson | GBR | 3:42.6 | |
| 6. Stanislav Jungwirth | CZE | 3:42.6 | |
| 7. Neville Scott | NZE | 3:42.8 | |
| 8. Ian Boyd | GBR | 3:43.0 | |

May 6, 1954, stands as probably the greatest day in track and field history. Running in Oxford with the help of pace-setters Chris Brasher and Chris Chataway, Roger Bannister attempted to break the barrier of barriers— the four-minute mile. In his autobiography, appropriately entitled *The Four-Minute Mile,* Bannister recalled the final lap of that race: "I felt that the moment of a

lifetime had come. . . . The world seemed to stand still, or did not exist. The only reality was the next two hundred yards of track under my feet. . . .

"I felt at that moment that it was my chance to do one thing supremely well. I drove on, impelled by a combination of fear and pride. The air I breathed filled me with the spirit of the track where I had run my first race. The noise in my ears was that of the faithful Oxford crowd. Their hope and encouragement gave me greater strength. I had now turned the last bend and there were only fifty yards more. . . .

"Those last few seconds seemed never-ending. The faint line of the finishing tape stood ahead as a haven of peace, after the struggle. The arms of the world were waiting to receive me if only I reached the tape without slackening my speed. If I faltered, there would be no arms to hold me and the world would be a cold, forbidding place, because I had been so close. I leapt at the tape like a man taking his last spring to save himself from the chasm that threatens to engulf him."

The track announcer that day was none other than Norris McWhirter, who later became world famous as the compiler, along with his brother Ross, of *The Guinness Book of World Records.* McWhirter milked the dramatic moment for all it was worth. "Ladies and gentlemen," he began, "here is the result of event number nine, the one mile. First, number forty-one, R. G. Bannister of the Amateur Athletic Association and formerly of Exeter and Merton Colleges, with a time which is a new meeting and track record and which, subject to ratification, will be a new English Native, British National, British All-Comers', European, British Empire and World's record. The time is THREE . . ." The rest of the announcement was lost in the roar of the crowd. In fact, Bannister's time was 3:59.4.

In the two and a half years between that day in Oxford and the Melbourne Olympics, Bannister had retired from competition, but nine other runners had broken the four-minute barrier. All ten were present in Melbourne for the running of the 1500 meters—six on the track (John Landy, Brian Hewson, László Tábori, Ron Delany, Gunnar Nielsen, and István Rózsavölgyi) and four in the stands (Bannister, Jim Bailey, Chris Chataway, and Derek Ibbotson). Bannister presented to each of his successors a black silk tie with a monogram of a silver "4" and two gold "M"s within a gold laurel wreath.

The very first heat saw the elimination of several great runners, including Josy Barthel, István Rózsavölgyi, who had broken training during the Hungarian uprising against the U.S.S.R., Michel Jazy, who was to win a silver medal four years later in Rome, and an obscure Ethiopian named Mamo Wolde, who would gain fame *12* years later when he won the 1968 Olympic marathon.

The final turned out to be just as great a contest as had been expected. Before the race, the great sportsman John Landy, who once stopped in the middle of a race to help a fallen runner, gave a pep talk to Ron Delany, the youngest of the four-minute milers, and told him, "I think you can win this one, Ron." The twelve finalists were so well matched that when they began the final lap, less than eight yards separated the leader from the man in last place. The official in charge of signaling the beginning of the final lap was so excited that he forgot to ring the bell. Hewson and Merv Lincoln of Australia were in the lead, but Lincoln, feeling a pain in his leg, began to fall back quickly. Meanwhile, Ron Delany was boxed in at tenth place. His coach at Villanova University, Jumbo Elliott, had always told him that if he was ever in a box just to relax. So Delany relaxed, even though there were only 300 yards left in the race.

Just then the runner in front of Delany, Gunnar Nielsen, realizing that he himself couldn't win the race, turned around and motioned Delany to pass him on the inside. Gradually Delany moved up; then, 120 meters from the finish, he burst out with all he had. The power of his sprint demoralized the other runners, and he was home free. He ran the last lap in 53.8, the last 200 meters in 25.6, and the final 100 meters in 12.9. He flew past the tiring Hewson and won by almost six yards, breasting the tape with his arms spread wide and a huge grin on his face. After crossing the finish, Delany fell to his knees. John Landy, thinking Delany was ill or injured, rushed up to help him, only to discover that the new Olympic champion was actually deep in prayer.

**1960 Rome** C:39, N: 25, D: 9.6. WR: 3:36.0 (Herbert Elliot)
1. Herbert Elliott     AUS   3:35.6   WR
2. Michel Jazy     FRA   3:38.4
3. István Rózsavölgyi   HUN   3:39.2
4. Dan Waern     SWE   3:40.0
5. Zoltan Vamos     ROM   3:40.8
6. Dyrol Burleson     USA   3:40.9
7. Michel Bernard     FRA   3:41.5
8. James Grelle     USA   3:45.0

World record holder Herb Elliott of Perth was the clear favorite in 1960. After 950 meters he passed Michel Bernard and took off like a "scared bunny." To his opponents and to the 90,000 people in the stadium, Elliott appeared to be a sure winner, but Elliott himself refused to look behind him. Unaware that he had opened up an insurmountable 15-meter lead, he was sure that someone was close on his heels. When he reached the backstretch he saw his coach, Percy Cerutty, standing by the side of the track waving a white towel, which meant that a world record was achievable and that Elliott should give it all he had. Actually, the 66-year-old Cerutty had raced out of the stands and dashed across the protective moat that surrounded the track in order to signal his pupil. He was quickly grabbed by the police and hauled away, but his effort had been worth it. Elliott, still refusing to turn around and still thinking he might lose the gold medal, strained to the finish line and won by the amazing margin of 20 yards. His time of 3:35.6 was a new world record. Elliott, whose diet usually consisted of raw, natural

foods, celebrated by going out drinking. His most difficult concern for the remainder of the Olympics was protecting his kangaroo-hide track shoes, which were almost stolen on three separate occasions. Between 1954 and 1960, Herb Elliott won 44 consecutive races at 1500 meters or one mile before retiring from competition at that distance.

**1964 Tokyo** C: 43, N: 34, D: 10.21. WR: 3:35.6 (Herbert Elliott)
1. Peter Snell     NZE   3:38.1
2. Josef Odložil     CZE   3:39.6
3. John Davies     NZE   3:39.6
4. Alan Simpson     GBR   3:39.7
5. Dyrol Burleson     USA   3:40.0
6. Witold Baran     POL   3:40.3
7. Michel Bernard     FRA   3:41.2
8. John Whetton     GBR   3:42.4

Before the Tokyo Olympics, Peter Snell had never run a race at 1500 meters, although he had competed in many one-mile contests. Running his sixth race in eight days, Snell was boxed in at the bell when John Whetton stepped aside and let him through. Snell ran away from the field in the backstretch and won by 12 yards, to gain his third Olympic gold medal.

**1968 Mexico City** C:54, N: 37, D: 10.20. WR: 3:33.1 (James Ryun)
1. H. Kipchoge Keino     KEN   3:34.9   OR
2. James Ryun     USA   3:37.8
3. Bodo Tümmler     GER   3:39.0
4. Harald Norpoth     GER   3:42.5
5. John Whetton     GBR   3:43.8
6. Jacques Boxberger     FRA   3:46.6
7. Henryk Szordykowski   POL   3:46.6
8. Josef Odložil     CZE   3:48.6

Jim Ryun of Wichita, Kansas, went to the 1968 Olympics as the world record holder at 880 yards, 1500 meters, and the mile. He had not been beaten at 1500 or the mile in over three years. Yet his status as favorite was threatened by an attack of mononucleosis in June and by the fact that the Olympics were being held in the high altitude of Mexico City. For this reason, 28-year-old Kip Keino, an uncoached Nandi tribesman who had never defeated Ryun, was considered a serious contender. However Keino was having problems of his own. Recently he had been suffering violent stomach pains, which later turned out to be the result of a severe gall bladder infection. Ignoring the advice of doctors, Keino went ahead and entered not only the 1500, but also the 5000 and the 10,000. The 10,000 came first and Keino was running with the leaders with only two laps to go, when he suddenly doubled up in pain and fell onto the infield. When the stretcher-bearers came to get him, he jumped back onto the track and, even though he had been disqualified, he finished the race. Four days later he took second place in the 5000 meters.

As if he hadn't run enough already, the day of the 1500

meters final he got caught in a traffic jam and jogged the last mile to the stadium. Keino was well aware that Jim Ryun possessed a devasting finishing kick, so he decided to try a dangerous gamble, hoping to neutralize Ryun's sprint by building up a huge lead. After fellow Kenyan Ben Jipcho set a torrid pace of 56.0 for the first 400 meters, Keino took over and pulled away from the pack, passing the 800-meter mark in a seemingly suicidal 1:55.3. Everyone waited for Keino to run out of steam but, remarkably, he never did. Ryun's famous kick was impressive, but he was unable to close within 12 yards of Keino and finally eased up in pain, as the Kenyan went on to win by 20 meters, the largest margin of victory in Olympic 1500 meters history. Keino improved his personal best by 1.8 seconds and lowered his own high-altitude world record by a phenomenal five seconds. That same day, back in Kenya, Kip Keino's wife gave birth to their third daughter, who was named Milka Olympia Chelagat in honor of her father's achievement.

**1972 Munich** C: 66, N: 46, D: 9.10. WR: 3:33.1 (James Ryun)

| | | | |
|---|---|---|---|
| 1. | Pekka Vasala | FIN | 3:36.3 |
| 2. | H. Kipchoge Keino | KEN | 3:36.8 |
| 3. | Rodney Dixon | NZE | 3:37.5 |
| 4. | Michael Boit | KEN | 3:38.4 |
| 5. | Brendan Foster | GBR | 3:39.0 |
| 6. | Herman Mignon | BEL | 3:39.1 |
| 7. | Paul-Heinz Wellmann | GER | 3:40.1 |
| 8. | Vladimir Pantelei | SOV | 3:40.2 |

Track aficionados awaited another showdown between defending champion Kip Keino and Jim Ryun, who had retired, returned to competition, had his ups and downs, and was now in top form once again. What no one expected was that their last confrontation as amateurs would come not in the Olympic final, but in the opening round. Entrants in the Olympics are seeded according to their previous times, so that leading contenders are separated in the opening heats. U.S. officials had submitted Ryun's superb time of 3:52.8 for the mile. However, somewhere along the line, this time was interpreted as being for 1500 meters, so the computer in charge of seeding treated Ryun as just another mediocre runner. Consequently, Ryun was thrown into the same first round heat as top-seeded Kip Keino.

The fateful fourth heat, won easily by Keino, was to prove the end of Jim Ryun's amateur career. Caught in a box 550 meters from the finish, Ryun tried to squeeze his way between runners rather than pass on the outside. As early leader Mohamed Younis of Pakistan faded on the inside lane, Vitus Ashaba of Uganda stepped to the outside to avoid him, and moved right into the space that Ryun was trying to fill. Ryun tripped on Ashaba's heel and fell back on Billy Fordjour of Ghana, sending both of them crashing to the ground. Ryun landed on the curb and Fordjour landed on Ryun, who came away with a bruised hip, a scraped knee, a sprained left ankle, and a contusion of his Adam's apple. Stunned, Ryun lay on the

track for eight seconds before he got up and began chasing after the field. The sympathetic German crowd rooted him on, but he had lost at least 75 meters and it proved impossible for him to catch up. Ryun was in shock. "All I know is everything was going well," he said, "and I felt good, and the next thing I knew I was trying to figure out what happened."

Two days later, in the final, Kip Keino faced the challenge of Pekka Vasala, by no means an outsider, even though he was known in Finland as "Mr. Unpredictable." Vasala had competed in the Mexico City Games, but, struck down by "Montezuma's Revenge," he had finished last in his heat. Nevertheless, he had been quite moved by the opening ceremonies and vowed to himself that "someday, somewhere, I would accomplish something great."

In Munich, Keino made his move after 600 meters and Vasala followed close behind, dogging the former goat-herder all the way until the homestretch, when he moved ahead to win by about three meters. Vasala had run the last 800 meters in the amazing time of 1:49.0. The surprise bronze medalist was Rod Dixon of New Zealand, who began sobbing when he realized that his dream of an Olympic medal had come true. Still weeping, he was ushered backstage for the urine test. After producing a meager sample, Dixon sheepishly asked the German official if it was enough. "For the gold medal, no," was the reply, "but for the bronze medal, it will do."

Dixon was not the only one to be moved to tears. Pekka Vasala recalled, "When I walked into the dressing room after the race . . . I realized in a second I had won. Somehow I had not fully understood it on the track. All became misty and I was crying uncontrollably. I had completely lost control of myself. I was still confused on the victory stand. It was not until I put the gold medal into my pocket and grabbed it in my fingers that I finally woke up."

**1976 Montreal** C: 42, N: 28, D: 7.31. WR: 3:32.2 (Filbert Bayi)

| | | | |
|---|---|---|---|
| 1. | John Walker | NZE | 3:39.17 |
| 2. | Ivo van Damme | BEL | 3:39.27 |
| 3. | Paul-Heinz Wellmann | GER | 3:39.33 |
| 4. | Eamonn Coghlan | IRL | 3:39.51 |
| 5. | Frank Clement | GBR | 3:39.65 |
| 6. | Richard Wohlhuter | USA | 3:40.64 |
| 7. | David Moorcroft | GBR | 3:40.94 |
| 8. | Graham Crouch | AUS | 3:41.80 |

In 1976, black African nations boycotted the Olympics because a rugby team from New Zealand had played a team from South Africa. Ironically, this prevented Tanzanian world record holder Filbert Bayi from competing, and handed over an almost sure gold medal to New Zealand, which was represented by John Walker, who held the world record for the mile. It was Walker who had pushed Bayi to his 1500 meters record at the 1974 Commonwealth Games, and the two friends had been looking forward to their Olympics showdown ever since. Without

Bayi and Kenyan Mike Boit to set the pace, the Olympic final was a slow, almost dull race that came down to the final sprint. Walker passed Eamonn Coghlan in the backstretch and won by a meter. His winning time was the slowest in 20 years. When asked why he hadn't tried for a record even with Bayi missing, Walker replied, "Every record set in Montreal will eventually be broken and forgotten. The gold medal is the thing they can never take away from you." On February 17, 1985, running on his home track at Mount Smart Stadium in Auckland, John Walker became the first person to run 100 sub-four-minute miles, beating out Steve Scott of the United States by barely three months. Walker had first broken the four-minute barrier 11½ years earlier.

**1980 Moscow** C: 40, N: 29, D: 8.1. WR: 3:32.1 (Sebastian Coe, Steven Ovett)

| | | |
|---|---|---|
| 1. Sebastian Coe | GBR | 3:38.4 |
| 2. Jürgen Straub | GDR | 3:38.8 |
| 3. Steven Ovett | GBR | 3:39.0 |
| 4. Andreas Busse | GDR | 3:40.2 |
| 5. Vittorio Fontanella | ITA | 3:40.4 |
| 6. Josef Plachy | CZE | 3:40.7 |
| 7. José Marajo | FRA | 3:41.5 |
| 8. Stephen Cram | GBR | 3:42.0 |

It certainly seemed to most observers that Steve Ovett entered the 1500 meters final with a tremendous advantage. Not only had he defeated Sebastian Coe at Coe's best distance, the 800, but Ovett had won 42 consecutive races at 1500 meters and one mile, going back to May 1977. In the semifinals Ovett had been so relaxed and in control that he actually gave a victory wave to the crowd before he had even taken the lead. Coe, on the other hand, had struggled through his first round heat and had been hounded and mercilessly criticized by the British press during the six days since the 800 meters final. As it turned out, however, Ovett's gold medal had taken away his competitive edge ever so slightly, while Coe had conquered his disappointment and depression, and couldn't wait to get out on the track to prove that he was a winner and not just a record-setter.

The withdrawal of Filbert Bayi, who had decided to concentrate on the 3000 meters steeplechase, left the race without a pace-setter, but before the first lap had ended it became clear that this was not going to be just a two-man race. Jürgen Straub took the lead at 400 meters, followed by Coe, who was determined to stay near the front and avoid the tactical errors he had committed in the 800. With 780 meters to go, Straub stepped up the pace, with Coe and Ovett close behind. It was just what Coe had hoped for: a long, open run to the finish.

With 200 meters to go, Straub was four meters ahead of Coe and six meters ahead of Ovett. Coming into the final curve, Coe unleashed his finishing kick, unaware that Ovett had chosen the exact same moment to make *his* move. Straub was not about to give in, but by the time they had hit the homestretch, Coe had taken the lead. A

quick glance to each side to check the position of his opponents, and then, 80 meters from the finish line, Coe increased his speed again, crossing the finish line with a look of ecstatic relief that spoke far more than a thousand words. Straub, four meters back, held off Ovett for second place. Coe dropped to his knees and touched his forehead to the ground, seemingly unaware of the hearty congratulations being offered by Straub and Ovett. Coe had run the last lap in 52.2 seconds and the final 100 meters in 12.1.

Afterward, Coe and Ovett, who had been constantly portrayed by the press as bitter rivals, discussed the relief that they both felt and agreed to have a couple drinks together. Ovett let it be known that he was just as proud of his bronze medal as he was of his gold, because he had given his best. On the victory stand, Coe looked up to the sky. When asked why he had done this, Coe replied, "Perhaps somebody, somewhere, loves me after all."

**1984 Los Angeles** C: 59, N: 40, D: 8.11. WR: 3:30.77 (Steven Ovett)

| | | | |
|---|---|---|---|
| 1. Sebastian Coe | GBR | 3:32.53 | OR |
| 2. Steve Cram | GBR | 3:33.40 | |
| 3. José Abascal | SPA | 3:34.30 | |
| 4. Joseph Chesire | KEN | 3:34.52 | |
| 5. Jim Spivey | USA | 3:36.07 | |
| 6. Peter Wirz | SWI | 3:36.97 | |
| 7. Andrés Vera | SPA | 3:37.02 | |
| 8. Omar Khalifa | SUD | 3:37.11 | |

Following his Olympic victory in 1980, Sebastian Coe had been forced to call it quits for the rest of the season because of a back injury. He came back with a vengeance in 1981 and set four world records—in the 800, the 1000, and twice in the mile. However his 1982 season was a disappointing one, due apparently to an attack of glandular fever. Early in 1983 he seemed to have recovered, but as the season progressed, he found himself losing race after race. Finally, after withdrawing from the world championships, he checked into a hospital, where he underwent surgery for removal of a lymph node. It was discovered that Coe had been suffering from toxoplasmosis, a rare, sometimes fatal, protozoan infection. It looked like his championship days were over. As noted track writer Bob Hersh put it in an early Olympic preview article for *The Runner* magazine: "Based on 1983, I'd write Coe off completely."

It was to prove a premature obituary. After months of treatments and much time spent lying in hospital beds, Coe was released to resume training in December, 1983. In the meantime his throne had been usurped by Steve Cram who had gone undefeated at 1500 meters in 1983 and had beaten Steve Scott, Said Aouita and Steve Ovett in a tactical race at the world championships. Coe's comeback was treated with scorn by much of the British press, particularly after he was selected for the 1500 meters Olympic event even though he lost to Peter Elliott at the British Amateur Athletic Association championships in

June in what had been billed as a showdown for the final spot on the team.

The Olympic 1500 developed into a battle of survivors. Said Aouita withdrew to concentrate on the less competitive 5000 meters. Former world record holder Sydney Maree withdrew due to a hamstring tear that failed to heal. World championship finalist Dragon Zdravković was sent home by Yugoslav officials for refusing to wear Adidas shoes. World record holder Steve Ovett had collapsed after the 800-meter final and spent two nights in the hospital. Yet there he was the next day on the starting line of heat 3 of the opening round. Ovett won the heat, but right behind him yet another contender fell by the wayside. Ten meters from the finish line, world championship finalist Pierre Delézè of Switzerland tripped on Ovett's heel and sprawled on the ground just short of his goal. The fourth heat was won by 800-meter gold medalist Joaquim Cruz, but the next day he pulled out of the semifinals because of a head cold.

Still, when the twelve finalists gathered barely 24 hours after the semifinals, the four leading favorites, Cram, Scott, Ovett and Coe, were right there on the starting line. Ovett did seem doubtful, having required medical attention following the semifinals, and, although Coe had looked strong in winning the 800 silver, he, like Ovett, was about to run his seventh race in nine days.

Coe broke to the front, but quickly relinquished the lead to Omar Khalifa. Less than 600 meters from the start came the big surprise. For many years 1500-meter races in major championships had been run as kickers' races: three slow laps, followed by a final sprint. Steve Scott had decided to turn the 1984 Olympic final into "a true miler's race." In the backstretch of the second lap, he tore into the lead and forced the pace, testing the strength of the other runners. He passed the 800-meter mark in 1:56.81, followed more closely than he had hoped by Coe, Abascal, Khalifa, Cram and Ovett.

The next runner to make a move was José Abascal. Knowing that he too would lose a kicker's finish, Abascal took the lead with about a lap and a quarter to go. Coe and Cram chased after him while Scott began to fade to an eventual tenth-place finish. Three hundred and fifty yards from the finish, Steve Ovett, running in fourth place, was overcome by the same chest pains he had experienced four days earlier. He stepped off the track and was taken away on a stretcher. Abascal sprinted down the backstretch, but he couldn't shake Coe and Cram. Coming into the final curve, Cram made his move, pulling up to Coe's shoulder. Coe glanced up quickly to see who was there, then began his own kick. They both sped by Abascal, racing hard around the turn. Coe entered the final straight with a four-foot lead which he extended to a six-meter winning margin.

Coe crossed the finish line with a smile on his face. Then he turned in the direction of the British press, made a defiant gesture, and shouted, "Who says I'm finished?!" He had run the final 200 meters in 26.1 seconds

and the last 100 meters in 13.04. At the age of 27, Sebastian Coe had become the first male repeat winner of the Olympic 1500 meters (excepting James Lightbody's victory in the 1906 Intercalated Games).

**1988 Seoul** C: 59, N: 46, D: 10.1. WR: 3:29.46 (Said Aouita)

| | | |
|---|---|---|
| 1. Peter Rono | KEN | 3:35.96 |
| 2. Peter Elliott | GBR | 3:36.15 |
| 3. Jens-Peter Herold | GDR | 3:36.21 |
| 4. Steve Cram | GBR | 3:36.24 |
| 5. Steve Scott | USA | 3:36.99 |
| 6. Han Kulker | HOL | 3:37.08 |
| 7. S. Kipkoech Cheruiyot | KEN | 3:37.94 |
| 8. Marcus O'Sullivan | IRL | 3:38.39 |

On the eve of the Olympics, the favorites were world record holder Said Aouita; Steve Cram, who had recorded the fastest time of the year, 3:30.95, on August 19; and world champion Abdi Bile of Somalia. But Bile was forced to withdraw after suffering a tibial stress fracture and Aouita, also the victim of a leg injury, dropped out before the semifinals. Joaquim Cruz, the 800-meter silver medalist, also failed to appear for his semifinal heat. The finalists set out at a sluggish pace. With two laps to go, 5-foot 5¾-inch, 117-pound Peter Rono decided he had had enough. "The other guys were holding me up," he would later explain. He rushed into the lead. "I thought some of the fellows behind would follow me, but they didn't."

Most likely, the other fellows didn't take Rono seriously. After all, the undersized economics student at Mount St. Mary's College in Emmitsburg, Maryland, had no major victories to his credit. Besides, they were too busy watching Steve Cram. With half a lap to go, Rono led by 2 meters over Elliott, with Cram and Herold close behind. Elliott tried desperately to close the gap but could make little headway. Rono, who looked back 13 times in the final 200 meters, ran the last 800 meters in 1 minute 50 seconds. Afterward, Rono seemed as surprised as anyone by the result. "It was tougher to win the Kenyan trials," he said. At 21 years of age, he was the youngest 1500-meter medalist in Olympic history.

# 5000 METERS

**1896–1908** not held

**1912 Stockholm** C: 31, N: 11, D: 7.10. WR: 15:01.2 (Arthur Robinson)

| | | | |
|---|---|---|---|
| 1. Johan "Hannes" Kolehmainen | FIN | 14:36.6 | WR |
| 2. Jean Bouin | FRA | 14:36.7 | |
| 3. George Hutson | GBR | 15:07.6 | |
| 4. George Bonhag | USA | 15:09.8 | |
| 5. Tel Berna | USA | 15:10.0 | |
| 6. Mauritz Karlsson | SWE | 15:18.6 | |
| 7. Henry Scott | USA | — | |
| 8. Alex Decoteau | CAN | — | |

Hannes Kolehmainen, a vegetarian bricklayer from a running family, had already won the 10,000 meters two days earlier, and was taking part in his fourth long-distance race in four days. He and Jean Bouin pulled away from the other eight finalists after a couple of laps and ran the rest of the race with Bouin in front and Kolehmainen right behind him. Every time Kolehmainen tried to pass, Bouin would resist his challenge. On the final curve of the final lap, Kolehmainen tried again. Bouin swung wide, forcing the Finn back in line. When they reached the homestretch, Kolehmainen tried once more, finally reaching Bouin's shoulder 20 meters from the tape. Bouin veered into Kolehmainen, but his legs began to buckle, and "Hannes the Mighty," as he became known, was able to win by a yard. Silver medalist Bouin and bronze medalist George Hutson were both killed in action in 1914. Kolehmainen, on the other hand, moved to the United States and reappeared in Antwerp to win the 1920 marathon.

**1920 Antwerp** C: 31, N: 11, D: 8.17. WR: 14:36.6 (Johan "Hannes" Kolehmainen)

| | | |
|---|---|---|
| 1. Joseph Guillemot | FRA | 14:55.6 |
| 2. Paavo Nurmi | FIN | 15:00.0 |
| 3. Erik Backman | SWE | 15:13.0 |
| 4. Teodor Koskenniemi | FIN | 15:17.0 |
| 5. Charles Blewitt | GBR | — |
| 6. William Seagrove | GBR | — |
| 7. Carlo Speroni | ITA | — |
| 8. Alfred Nichols | GBR | — |

This race, the first Olympic appearance by Paavo Nurmi, proved to be sweet, though temporary, revenge by the French for Kolehmainen's defeat of Bouin eight years earlier. Nurmi took the lead during the third lap and the 5-foot 3-inch Guillemot, whose heart was on the right side of his chest, followed him around until the final straightaway, at which point Guillemot sprinted away to win by 30 yards.

**1924 Paris** C: 39, N: 22, D: 7.10. WR: 14:28.2 (Paavo Nurmi)

| | | |
|---|---|---|
| 1. Paavo Nurmi | FIN | 14:31.2 OR |
| 2. Vilho "Ville" Ritola | FIN | 14:31.4 |
| 3. Edvin Wide | SWE | 15:01.8 |
| 4. John Romig | USA | 15:12.4 |
| 5. Eino Seppälä | FIN | 15:18.4 |
| 6. Charles Clibbon | GBR | 15:29.0 |
| 7. Lucien Dolques | FRA | 15:33.0 |
| 8. Axel Eriksson | SWE | 15:38.0 |

Paavo Nurmi had hoped to defend his 10,000 meters championship in Paris and was very resentful when Ville Ritola returned from four years in the United States to break Nurmi's world record and bump him from the Finnish 10,000 meters entry. On July 6, Ritola had proved his worth by winning the 10,000 in world record time. Nurmi got his chance to face Ritola four days later in the 5000, a race that began less than an hour after Nurmi had won the 1500 meters. Taking advantage of Paavo's lack

of rest, his opponents set a torrid pace, passing the 1000-meter mark in 2:46.4, the same pace as the 1972 Olympic final 48 years later. Unruffled, Nurmi stayed close and then took the lead at the halfway mark, followed by Ritola. For the last eight laps, Nurmi, refusing to look behind him, stayed two yards ahead of his rival. With 500 meters to go he checked his watch for the last time, threw it to the grass, and picked up the pace. Twenty yards from the tape Ritola tried to pass, but Nurmi increased his speed and won—by two yards.

**1928 Amsterdam** C: 36, N: 17, D: 8.3. WR: 14:28.2 (Paavo Nurmi)

| | | |
|---|---|---|
| 1. Vilho "Ville" Ritola | FIN | 14:38.0 |
| 2. Paavo Nurmi | FIN | 14:40.0 |
| 3. Edvin Wide | SWE | 14:41.2 |
| 4. Leo Lermond | USA | 14:50.0 |
| 5. Ragnar Magnusson | SWE | 14:59.6 |
| 6. Armas Kinnunen | FIN | 15:02.0 |
| 7. S. Patkevics | LAT | — |
| 8. Harold Johnston | GBR | — |

By 1928 it was a familiar sight to see Nurmi and Ritola pull away from the field, with only Edvin Wide able to keep close. This time Ritola drew clear of Nurmi in the final curve and won by over 12 yards. Wide picked up his fourth bronze medal to go with his one silver. Ritola finished his Olympic career with five gold medals and three silver medals.

**1932 Los Angeles** C: 19, N: 12, D: 8.5. WR: 14:17.0 (Lauri Lehtinen)

| | | |
|---|---|---|
| 1. Lauri Lehtinen | FIN | 14:30.0 OR |
| 2. Ralph Hill | USA | 14:30.0 |
| 3. Lauri Virtanen | FIN | 14:44.0 |
| 4. John Savidan | NZE | 14:49.6 |
| 5. Jean-Gunnar Lindgren | SWE | 14:54.8 |
| 6. Max Syring | GER | 14:59.0 |
| 7. James Burns | GBR | — |
| 8. Erik Pettersson | SWE | 15:13.4 |

This race produced the ugliest incident of the 1932 Olympics. Running in last place for the first mile, Ralph Hill of Oregon gradually moved his way up to third place behind the Finnish favorites, Lehtinen and Virtanen. Then, with the surprised American crowd wild with excitement, Hill passed Virtanen, who faded back. Over the last two laps Lehtinen tried desperately to shake the pesky Hill, but couldn't. Fifty yards from the finish, Hill moved to pass Lehtinen on the outside, but the world record holder swerved out to the third lane and blocked his path. Hill broke stride, dropped back, and attempted to pass on the inside. Lehtinen swerved back into lane one, again impeding Hill's progress. Forced to break stride again, Hill made one more move, but Lehtinen was able to beat him to the tape by about three inches. After a moment of stunned silence, the audience broke into a loud chorus of boos, which didn't end until announcer Bill Henry got on the public address system and said, "Please remember, folks, that these people are our guests." Although films of the race clearly showed that Lehtinen had interfered with Hill, U.S. officials declined to lodge a protest. At the victory ceremony, a chagrined Lehtinen attempted to lift Hill onto the first-place platform, but Hill refused.

**1936 Berlin** C: 41, N: 23, D: 8.7. WR: 14:17.0 (Lauri Lehtinen)

| | | | |
|---|---|---|---|
| 1. Gunnar Höckert | FIN | 14:22.2 | OR |
| 2. Lauri Lehtinen | FIN | 14:25.8 | |
| 3. Henry Jonsson | SWE | 14:29.0 | |
| 4. Kohei Murakoso | JPN | 14:30.0 | |
| 5. Józef Noji | POL | 14:33.4 | |
| 6. Ilmari Salminen | FIN | 14:39.8 | |
| 7. Umberto Cerati | ITA | 14:44.4 | |
| 8. Louis Zamperini | USA | 14:46.8 | |

The 10,000 meters champion, Ilmari Salminen, lost his chance for a second medal when he tripped on Lehtinen with two laps to go and fell. At the same moment, Höckert made his move into the lead. Ahead by two yards at the bell, he sprinted away and won by 20 yards.

**1948 London** C: 33, N: 20, D: 8.2. WR: 13:58.2 (Günder Hägg)

| | | | |
|---|---|---|---|
| 1. Gaston Reiff | BEL | 14:17.6 | OR |
| 2. Emil Zátopek | CZE | 14:17.8 | |
| 3. Willem Slijkhuis | HOL | 14:26.8 | |
| 4. Erik Ahldén | SWE | 14:28.6 | |
| 5. Bertil Albertsson | SWE | 14:39.0 | |
| 6. Curtis Stone | USA | 14:39.4 | |
| 7. Vaino Koskela | FIN | 14:41.0 | |
| 8. Vaino Makela | FIN | 14:43.0 | |

Zátopek was perhaps a bit too tired from winning the 10,000 meters three days earlier, particularly after he had unnecessarily sprinted at the end of his 5000 heat. Trailing Reiff by 50 meters at the bell in the final, Zátopek thrilled the crowd by sprinting around the rain-soaked track and pulling closer and closer. Reiff thought that the applause he heard was for him, until someone on the infield called his attention to Zátopek's unexpected spurt. Reiff was able to pick up his own speed just enough to reach the finish one and a half meters ahead of the charging Czech. Reiff was the first Belgian to win a track and field gold medal.

**1952 Helsinki** C: 45, N: 24, D: 7.24. WR: 13:58.2 (Günder Hägg)

| | | | |
|---|---|---|---|
| 1. Emil Zátopek | CZE | 14:06.6 | OR |
| 2. Alain Mimoun O'Kacha | FRA | 14:07.4 | |
| 3. Herbert Schade | GER | 14:08.6 | |
| 4. Gordon Pirie | GBR | 14:18.0 | |
| 5. Christopher Chataway | GBR | 14:18.0 | |
| 6. Leslie Perry | AUS | 14:23.6 | |
| 7. Ernö Béres | HUN | 14:24.8 | |
| 8. Åke Andersson | SWE | 14:26.0 | |

After he had won the 10,000 meters for the second time, Emil Zátopek was asked if it was true that he would also contest the 5000. "The marathon contest won't be for a long time yet, so I simply must do something until then," he replied. With five runners in each of the three heats

qualifying for the final, Zátopek decided to enjoy himself during his heat. As the laps piled up, the multilingual Czech chatted amiably with the other runners, particularly after it had become clear who the five qualifiers would be. As they approached the bell lap, Zátopek, in the lead, slowed down, waited for Aleksandr Anoufriev of the U.S.S.R., and motioned for him to pass, acting like a traffic cop clearing an intersection. As he rounded the final turn, Zátopek noticed Bertil Albertsson of Sweden sprinting for the finish. Slowing down again, he hailed Albertsson as if he were hitching a ride and engaged him in conversation. The two ran the last straight together, with Zátopek giving way just before the finish. He also took a liking to fourth-place finisher Les Perry of Australia and later presented him with a gift of his training suit.

The final was, of course, a more serious affair. Yet Zátopek still took the time to speak to Herbert Schade before the start, advising him to hold back for the first 2000 meters and not waste his energy setting the pace. Schade ignored this advice and paid the price. The race itself was full of action, with the lead changing hands numerous times. As the laps wound down, it appeared that any of five runners could win: Zátopek, Schade, Mimoun, Chataway, or Pirie. At the bell, Zátopek was in first place, hard-pressed by Schade. In the backstretch, Chris Chataway, who later paced Roger Bannister and John Landy to the first two sub-four-minute miles, dashed into the lead, followed by Mimoun and Schade, leaving Zátopek in fourth place. Entering the final curve, Zátopek made his move, swinging wide into Lane 3. Halfway through the bend, he was already in front again and pulling away. Entering the home straightaway, Chataway, exhausted, stepped on the curb and fell. He was able to regain his feet and stagger home, but by that time Zátopek had already gained a five-yard victory over Mimoun, who finished second to Zátopek for the third time in an Olympic final and improved his personal best by over 14 seconds.

Later in the afternoon, Emil Zátopek learned that his wife, Dana, had won a gold medal in the javelin throw. When asked if it was true that he was going to try for another win in the marathon, Zátopek replied, "At present, the score of the contest in the Zátopek family is 2–1. This result is too close. To restore some prestige I will try to improve on it—in the marathon race."

**1956 Melbourne** C: 23, N: 13, D: 11.28. WR: 13:36.8 (Gordon Pirie)

| | | | |
|---|---|---|---|
| 1. Vladimir Kuts | SOV | 13:39.6 | OR |
| 2. Gordon Pirie | GBR | 13:50.6 | |
| 3. Derek Ibbotson | GBR | 13:54.4 | |
| 4. Miklos Szabo II | HUN | 14:03.4 | |
| 5. Albert Thomas | AUS | 14:04.6 | |
| 6. László Tábori | HUN | 14:09.8 | |
| 7. Maiyoro Nyandika | KEN | 14:19.0 | |
| 8. Thyge Tögersen | DEN | 14:21.0 | |

After Kuts' decisive victory in the 10,000 five days earlier, it seemed a long shot that anyone would beat him in the 5000, although Gordon Pirie had defeated Kuts at this distance in world record time on June 9. In the Olympic final, Kuts went to the front immediately and was never headed, finishing 75 yards in front of Pirie and Ibbotson. Unfortunately for Kuts, the experimental training program which the Soviet coaches had imposed on him apparently took its toll. By 1960 he had suffered his first heart attack. His fourth heart attack killed him, on August 17, 1975, at the age of 48.

**1960 Rome** C: 48, N: 31, D: 9.2. WR: 13:35.0 (Vladimir Kuts)

| | | |
|---|---|---|
| 1. Murray Halberg | NZE | 13:43.4 |
| 2. Hans Grodotzki | GDR | 13:44.6 |
| 3. Kazimierz Zimny | POL | 13:44.8 |
| 4. Friedrich Janke | GDR | 13:46.8 |
| 5. David Power | AUS | 13:51.8 |
| 6. Maiyoro Nyandika | KEN | 13:52.8 |
| 7. Michel Bernard | FRA | 14:04.2 |
| 8. Horst Flossbach | GER | 14:06.6 |

When he was 17 years old, Murray Halberg was hit from behind in a crash tackle during a rugby match. He was left with a dislocated shoulder, ruptured veins and arteries, blood clots, and a paralyzed left arm. After two months in the hospital and two operations, he was released with a withered arm and shoulder. He had to relearn how to walk, run, dress himself, and feed himself. Prevented from competing in contact sports, Halberg concentrated on running. Six years after his accident, he represented New Zealand at the Melbourne Olympics and two years after that he broke the four-minute mile.

Back in the Olympics in 1960, Halberg and his coach, Arthur Lydiard, devised a radical strategy to win the 5000 meters. With three laps to go, at the stage in the race when runners usually gather their strength for the last lap sprint, Halberg suddenly pushed to the front of the pack and then darted away as if the finish line was just around the next curve. The tactic worked perfectly. His startled opponents were confused, and before Grodotzki was able to respond, Halberg had covered the tenth lap in 61.1 seconds and opened up a lead of 25 yards. He also ran the next lap as fast as he could, preventing Grodotzki from closing any ground. Then Halberg faced the grim task of completing the final lap even though he was totally exhausted. Checking behind himself frequently, he watched as Grodotzki gradually whittled his lead down to 15 yards, 12 yards, 10 yards. But then Halberg reached the finish line with eight yards to spare. He collapsed on his back on the infield, still holding the tape between his fingers. In his autobiography, *A Clean Pair of Heels,* Halberg recalled, "I had always imagined an Olympic champion was something more than a mere mortal, in fact, a god. Now I knew he was just a human being."

**1964 Tokyo** C: 48, N: 29, D: 10.18. WR: 13:35.0 (Vladimir Kuts)

| | | |
|---|---|---|
| 1. Robert Schul | USA | 13:48.8 |
| 2. Harald Norpoth | GER | 13:49.6 |
| 3. William Dellinger | USA | 13:49.8 |
| 4. Michel Jazy | FRA | 13:49.8 |
| 5. H. Kipchoge Keino | KEN | 13:50.4 |
| 6. William Baillie | NZE | 13:51.0 |
| 7. Nikolai Dutov | SOV | 13:53.8 |
| 8. Thor Helland | NOR | 13:57.0 |

Ron Clarke of Australia led the way for most of the race, but gave up the lead to Michel Jazy shortly before the 4000-meter mark. With one and a half laps to go, Bill Dellinger moved ahead, but just after the bell Jazy regained the lead and pulled ahead by ten yards, with Norpoth second and the favorite, Bob Schul, third. Schul, known for his finishing kick, began sprinting in the backstretch. By the final curve he had cut Jazy's lead to five yards. Coming out of the turn, Schul saw Jazy look back and noticed his shoulders tighten. "I smiled inwardly," said Schul. "I knew I had him." He passed the discouraged Frenchman 50 meters from the tape. Schul had run the last 300 meters in 38.7 seconds. Jazy was so disappointed that he wasn't even able to hold on to third place.

**1968 Mexico City** C: 37, N: 25, D: 10.17. WR: 13:16.6 (Ronald Clarke)

| | | |
|---|---|---|
| 1. Mohamed Gammoudi | TUN | 14:05.0 |
| 2. H. Kipohogo Keino | KEN | 14:05.2 |
| 3. Naftali Temu | KEN | 14:06.4 |
| 4. Juan Martinez | MEX | 14:10.8 |
| 5. Ronald Clarke | AUS | 14:12.4 |
| 6. Wohib Masresha | ETH | 14:17.6 |
| 7. Nikolai Sviridov | SOV | 14:18.4 |
| 8. Fikru Deguefu | ETH | 14:19.0 |

Mohamed Gammoudi, a 29-year-old soldier, moved in front with two laps to go and, with great grit and determination, held off alternating challenges from Keino and Temu, finally winning by about four feet after running the last lap in 54.8 seconds. A Tunisian biography of Gammoudi claimed that a typical day's diet for the Olympic champion consisted of five yogurts, ten pieces of fruit, four cups of tea, two coffees, two pastries, large quantities of meat, fish, milk, and cheese, and as much parsley as he could eat. Gammoudi weighed 135 pounds.

**1972 Munich** C: 61, N: 35, D: 9.10. WR: 13:16.6 (Ronald Clarke)

| | | | |
|---|---|---|---|
| 1. Lasse Viren | FIN | 13:26.4 | OR |
| 2. Mohamed Gammoudi | TUN | 13:27.4 | |
| 3. Ian Stewart | GBR | 13:27.6 | |
| 4. Steve Prefontaine | USA | 13:28.4 | |
| 5. Emiel Puttemans | BEL | 13:30.8 | |
| 6. Harald Norpoth | GER | 13:32.6 | |
| 7. Per Halle | NOR | 13:34.4 | |
| 8. Nikolai Sviridov | SOV | 13:39.4 | |

Before the competition, Steve Prefontaine had boldly warned that he would run the final mile in less than four minutes. Right on cue, Prefontaine took the lead with four laps to go and picked up the pace. Most of the field fell behind, but Viren and Gammoudi would not be shaken and were still shooting for the gold medal when the bell rang to signal the final lap. Viren led the way into the backstretch, was headed briefly by Gammoudi, but was back in the lead before the homestretch and couldn't be caught. Prefontaine faded and lost the bronze medal to the fast-finishing Ian Stewart. The last mile had been run in 4:01.2. Lasse Viren became the fourth runner to achieve a 5000/10,000 double, joining the ranks of Hannes Kolehmainen, Emil Zátopek, and Vladimir Kuts. On May 30, 1975, Steve Prefontaine lost control of his sports car and was killed in a crash, at the age of 24.

**1976 Montreal** C: 36, N: 23, D: 7.30. WR: 13:13.0 (Emiel Puttemans)

| | | | |
|---|---|---|---|
| 1. Lasse Viren | FIN | 13:24.76 |
| 2. Dick Quax | NZE | 13:25.16 |
| 3. Klaus-Peter Hildenbrand | GER | 13:25.38 |
| 4. Rodney Dixon | NZE | 13:25.50 |
| 5. Brendan Foster | GBR | 13:26.19 |
| 6. Willy Polleunis | BEL | 13:26.99 |
| 7. Ian Stewart | GBR | 13:27.65 |
| 8. Aniceto Silva Simoes | POR | 13:29.38 |

Following his victory in the 10,000 meters, Lasse Viren was subjected to a double inquisition. First, members of the press grilled him about the practice of blood boosting. This unnatural, but not illegal, procedure involves the extraction of a quart or more of blood from a runner before a major competition. This blood is frozen, while the runner's body rebuilds its blood to a normal level. Then, just before the race, the extracted blood is unfrozen and reinjected into the runner, increasing the body's hemoglobin level and oxygen-carrying capability, and thus providing the runner with greater endurance. Viren was accused of blood boosting because the procedure was first experimented with in Scandinavia, and because Viren only recorded his best performances in major competitions, particularly the Olympics. Viren always denied that he engaged in blood boosting and claimed that his training schedule was organized to peak at the Olympics, because only the Olympics really mattered to him.

The day before the 5000 meters final, Viren was called before the Technical Committee of the International Olympic Committee and asked to explain why he had carried his running shoes aloft while taking his victory lap following the 10,000 meters final. Accused of commercialism, the soft-spoken policeman said that he had removed his shoes because he had a blister. This seemed to satisfy the committee, which allowed him to continue competing.

The most notable performers in the 5000 heats were Brendan Foster, who set an Olympic record of 13:20.34 and Dieudonne Lamothe of Haiti, who led after the first lap, but finished five minutes after the other runners in his heat. His time, 18:50.07, was the slowest ever recorded in the Olympics.

In the final, most of the pace-setting was done by Viren and Foster, although the fourth kilometer saw Quax and Hildenbrand take their turns in front. With three laps to go, Viren picked up the pace, but at the start of the final lap there were still only five meters separating the first six runners. "At the bell," said Viren later, "I gave just one quick glance behind me and took in the situation in all its ghastliness. The wall at my heels was thick. . . . I had put in a couple of sixty-second laps and almost everybody was still chasing me, damn it! I was the fugitive now, and I realized I had to flee as if my life depended on it. . . . In the far turn I had the most frightening experience of my career. Some guy in black was forcing himself past me. It was Quax, whom I really hadn't reckoned very seriously. . . . I found my last gear, and it was just enough. The black shadow glided away from my eyes. The holy sanctuary of the finish line engulfed me—I had won!" Lasse Viren had earned his fourth gold medal and had become the first repeat winner of the 5000.

**1980 Moscow** C: 35, N: 22, D: 8.1. WR: 13:08.4 (Henry Rono)

| | | | |
|---|---|---|---|
| 1. Miruts Yifter | ETH | 13:21.0 |
| 2. Suleiman Nyambui | TAN | 13:21.6 |
| 3. Kaarlo Maaninka | FIN | 13:22.0 |
| 4. Eamonn Coghlan | IRL | 13:22.8 |
| 5. Markus Ryffel | SWI | 13:23.1 |
| 6. Dietmar Millonig | AUT | 13:23.3 |
| 7. John Treacy | IRL | 13:23.7 |
| 8. Aleksandr Fedotkin | SOV | 13:24.1 |

Miruts Yifter's quest for a gold medal at 5000 meters is a frustrating eight-year saga with a happy ending. Yifter first gained international attention in 1971 at a U.S.-Africa meet in North Carolina, when he sprinted to an apparent victory over Steve Prefontaine in the 5000 meters race, only to discover that he had miscounted the laps and quit running one lap too soon. The next day he made up for his mistake by defeating Frank Shorter at 10,000 meters. At the Munich Olympics in 1972, Yifter gained a bronze medal at 10,000 meters, but missed the start of his heat in the 5000 meters race. Typical of the mystery surrounding Yifter is the fact that there are three explanations for his failure to appear at the starting line. The first is that he was directed to the wrong check-in gate at the stadium and was refused admittance by German guards. The second is that he spent too long in the toilet before the race, and the third is that he left the bathroom in time but got lost on the way to the track. In 1976 he was prevented from competing when Ethiopia boycotted the Olympics.

In Moscow, the 5-foot 4-inch, 117-pound father of six faced no such problems. For some strange reason, a semifinal round was added to the 5000 meters competition, despite the fact that the field of 35 was the smallest in 24 years. This didn't bother Yifter, who won his opening heat and finished second to teammate Yohannes Mohammed in the semifinals.

After 4000 meters of the final, the 12 finalists were still bunched within 12 meters. Ninety-nine-pound Mohammed Kedir led at the bell, as everyone waited for the infamous Yifter kick that had already brought victory in the 10,000 meters. However, in the backstretch Yifter was completely caught in a box, with Kedir in front of him, Eamonn Coghlan beside Kedir, and the pack behind him. Then, with less than 300 meters to go, Kedir turned around and asked Yifter if he was ready. A wave of the hand from the master and the selfless Kedir stepped aside. Yifter shot through on the inside as Coghlan watched in amazement. The rest was academic. Yifter ran the last 200 meters in 27.2 seconds to gain his long-awaited 5000 meters gold medal. Kedir got tripped up by the pack, lost his shoe, and finished last. Coghlan lost the bronze medal to Kaarlo Maaninka, who came from a family of 23 children in Lapland.

Part of the mystery of Miruts Yifter is the question of his age, which was variously reported as 33, 35, 36, 37, or 42. When asked for a definitive answer, Yifter would only reply, "I don't count the years. Men may steal my chickens, men may steal my sheep. But no man can steal my age."

**1984 Los Angeles** C: 56, N: 40, D: 8.11. WR: 13:00.41 (David Moorcroft)

| | | | |
|---|---|---|---|
| 1. Said Aouita | MOR | 13:05.59 | OR |
| 2. Markus Ryffel | SWI | 13:07.54 | |
| 3. Antonio Leitão | POR | 13:09.20 | |
| 4. Timothy Hutchings | GBR | 13:11.50 | |
| 5. Paul Kipkoech | KEN | 13:14.40 | |
| 6. Charles Cheruiyot | KEN | 13:18.41 | |
| 7. Doug Padilla | USA | 13:23.56 | |
| 8. John Walker | NZE | 13:24.46 | |

Despite the fact that the 5000 meters field was decimated by injuries, illness, boycott and drug disqualification, the 1984 Olympic final was the fastest mass race ever at that distance. The favorite was Said Aouita by virtue of his June 13th performance of 13:04.78, second only to Dave Moorcroft's world record. Aouita did not disappoint, although it was the Portuguese runners Ezequiel Canario and Antonio Leitão who created the pace. Canario led for the first 1000 meters. When he couldn't push any harder, Leitão took over. One by one he burned away the other runners with successive 64-second laps until, with 500 meters to go, only Aouita and Markus Ryffel remained. With one-half lap left, Aouita sprinted ahead. Ryffel tried to keep up, but gave up in the final turn and concentrated on protecting second place. Aouita ran the final lap in 55.08 despite taking time to wave to the crowd during the last 50 yards. Ryffel, Hutchings, Kipkoech and Cheruiyot all bettered their personal records by at least five seconds. To celebrate the victory, King Hassan II of Morocco gave Aouita a villa in Casablanca. The Rabat-to-Casablanca express train was also renamed in his honor.

**1988 Seoul** C: 56, N: 39, D: 10.1. WR: 12:58.39 (Said Aouita)

| | | |
|---|---|---|
| 1. John Ngugi | KEN | 13:11.70 |
| 2. Dieter Baumann | GER | 13:15.52 |
| 3. Hansjörg Kunze | GDR | 13:15.73 |
| 4. Domingos Castro | POR | 13:16.09 |
| 5. Sydney Maree | USA | 13:23.69 |
| 6. Jack Buckner | GBR | 13:23.85 |
| 7. Stefano Mei | ITA | 13:26.17 |
| 8. Yevgeny Ignatov | BUL | 13:26.41 |

Just before the 1000-meter mark, three-time world cross-country champion John Ngugi, aware that he could not match the finishing kicks of the other runners, suddenly burst into the lead and ran away from the pack. Covering the next 800 meters in a startling 2:00.25, he opened up a huge gap of almost 50 meters. With four laps to go it became clear that Ngugi was not going to fall apart, so Domingos Castro reluctantly gave chase. He managed to close within about 25 meters, 1000 meters from the finish, but Ngugi, constantly looking back to check for challengers, loped steadily onward to win by 30 meters. The unfortunate Castro, who was passed by Baumann and Kunze in the last 50 meters and left without a medal, spent the next half hour sobbing inconsolably.

## 10,000 METERS

**1896–1908** not held

**1912 Stockholm** C: 30, N: 13, D: 7.8, WR: 30:58.8 (Jean Bouin)

| | | |
|---|---|---|
| 1. Johan "Hannes" Kolehmainen | FIN | 31:20.8 |
| 2. Louis Tewanima | USA | 32:06.6 |
| 3. Albin Stenroos | FIN | 32:21.8 |
| 4. Joseph Keeper | CAN | 32:36.2 |
| 5. Alfonso Orlando | ITA | 33:31.2 |

Fifteen men qualified for the final but only 11 started. The hot sun and hard pace cut the field down further and only five finished. Twenty-two-year-old Hannes Kolehmainen took the lead in the first lap and won the first of his four Olympic gold medals without being challenged. Silver medalist Louis Tewanima was a Hopi Indian.

**1920 Antwerp** C: 37, N: 17, D: 8.20. WR: 30:58.8 (Jean Bouin)

| | | |
|---|---|---|
| 1. Paavo Nurmi | FIN | 31:45.8 |
| 2. Joseph Guillemot | FRA | 31:47.2 |
| 3. James Wilson | GBR | 31:50.8 |
| 4. Augusto Maccario | ITA | 32:02.0 |
| 5. James Hatton | GBR | 32:14.0 |
| 6. Jean Manhès | FRA | 32:26.0 |
| 7. Heikki Liimatainen | FIN | 32:28.0 |
| 8. Frederick Faller | USA | 32:38.0 |

Paavo Nurmi was born in Turku, Finland, on June 13, 1897, the son of a carpenter who died when Paavo was 12. He first gained athletic renown in Finland while serving in the army in the early summer of 1919. He entered a 20-kilometer march with full equipment. Running was allowed, so Nurmi ran the entire distance. Carrying a rifle, a cartridge belt, and an 11-pound sack of sand, he finished the course so quickly that some officials thought he must have discovered a shortcut.

In Antwerp Nurmi lost his first final, the 5000 meters, to Joseph Guillemot, but sought revenge three days later in the 10,000. This time he let James Wilson of Scotland do most of the pace-setting. Nurmi took the lead with two laps to go. Guillemot passed him in the backstretch of the final lap, but Nurmi sprinted back into the lead almost immediately and won by eight yards.

Although Paavo Nurmi's first Olympic victory was not his most difficult, it *was* his most unpleasant, since Guillemot vomited on him as soon as he crossed the finish line. The source of Guillemot's distress was a last-minute change in the starting time of the race. Guillemot had just finished a large lunch when he was informed that the race had been moved up from 5:30 p.m. to 2:15 p.m. at the request of the king of Belgium, leaving the Frenchman no time to digest his food.

**1924 Paris** C: 43, N: 17, D: 7.6. WR: 30:35.4 (Vilho "Ville" Ritola)

| | | | |
|---|---|---|---|
| 1. Vilho "Ville" Ritola | FIN | 30:23.2 | WR |
| 2. Edvin Wide | SWE | 30:55.2 | |
| 3. Eero Berg | FIN | 31:43.0 | |
| 4. Väinö Sipilä | FIN | 31:50.2 | |
| 5. Ernest Harper | GBR | 31:58.0 | |
| 6. Halland Britton | GBR | 32:06.0 | |
| 7. Guillaume Tell | FRA | 32:12.0 | |
| 8. Earl Johnson | USA | 32:17.0 | |

For the first time, the 10,000 meters was run without heats. Ritola and Wide pulled away from the other 41 contestants after only two laps, but even Wide couldn't keep up with Ritola, who won by a half lap and broke his own world record by over 12 seconds. He continued on for another quarter lap before the officials were able to convince him that the race was over. Paavo Nurmi had been prevented from entering this race by Finnish officials, who felt he was entering too many events. Back in Finland after the games, Nurmi made his point by setting a world record of 30:06.2 that was to last for almost 13 years.

**1928 Amsterdam** C: 24, N: 12, D: 7.29. WR: 30:06.2 (Paavo Nurmi)

| | | | |
|---|---|---|---|
| 1. Paavo Nurmi | FIN | 30:18.8 | OR |
| 2. Vilho "Ville" Ritola | FIN | 30:19.4 | |
| 3. Edvin Wide | SWE | 31:00.8 | |
| 4. Jean-Gunnar Lindgren | SWE | 31:26.0 | |
| 5. Anthony Muggridge | GBR | 31:31.8 | |
| 6. Ragnar Magnusson | SWE | 31:37.2 | |
| 7. Toivo Loukola | FIN | 31:39.0 | |
| 8. Kalle Matilainen | FIN | 31:45.0 | |

Paavo Nurmi earned his ninth and last gold medal in the 10,000 meters flat race, the same event in which he had won his first gold medal. After nine laps only Ritola, Nurmi and Wide were still in contention. During the 18th lap the Swede dropped back. Nurmi dogged Ritola for the remainder of the race, then passed him about 50 yards from the tape and won by two or three meters. Nurmi refused to be congratulated or photographed, and simply picked up his sweatsuit and walked off the track without a smile. The following week he gained two silver medals in the 5000 and the steeplechase.

Nurmi had planned to enter the 10,000 and the marathon in the 1932 Olympics, but was declared a professional by the International Amateur Athletic Federation and banned from competition. For a time Nurmi ran a construction business and then a men's clothing store, eventually gaining considerable financial security as a result of wise real estate investments. His last appearance on a track was a dramatic one. When the 1952 Olympics were held in Helsinki, Finland, the opening ceremonies were staged in the Olympic Stadium, which was graced with a bronze statue of Nurmi in the front. After the athletes had paraded around the track and onto the infield, the audience awaited the arrival of the Olympic torch. When the final runner, whose name had not been announced, appeared from out of the tunnel bearing the torch aloft, the Finnish spectators broke into thunderous applause as they recognized the runner as none other than Paavo Nurmi, whose stride was unmistakable even though he was 55 years old. The athletes of the world broke rank and dashed to the side of the track to catch a glimpse of the legendary "Flying Finn," who bounded up the steps and passed the torch to 62-year-old Hannes Kolehmainen, who lit the Olympic flame.

Paavo Nurmi, who set 29 world records at distances ranging from 1500 meters to 20,000 meters, died on October 2, 1974. Six Finnish gold medal winners served as pallbearers at his funeral. Nurmi left the bulk of his estate to help the cause of heart research.

**1932 Los Angeles** C: 16, N: 11, D: 7.31. WR: 30:06.2 (Paavo Nurmi)

| | | | |
|---|---|---|---|
| 1. Janusz Kusociński | POL | 30:11.4 | OR |
| 2. Volmari Iso-Hollo | FIN | 30:12.6 | |
| 3. Lauri Virtanen | FIN | 30:35.0 | |
| 4. John Savidan | NZE | 31:09.0 | |
| 5. Max Syring | GER | 31:35.0 | |
| 6. Jean-Gunnar Lindgren | SWE | 31:37.0 | |

Kusociński and Iso-Hollo dueled at close quarters for 24 of 25 laps. Iso-Hollo led by one yard entering the final lap, but then Kusociński sprinted away to a big lead, before slowing to a jog and finishing with ten yards to spare. Among the unplaced entrants were Juan Rodriguez, a Yaqui Indian from Mexico who ran barefooted, and Adalberto Cardoso of Brazil, who got stranded in San Francisco and didn't arrive in Los Angeles until the day of the race.

**1936 Berlin** C: 30, N: 18, D: 8.2. WR: 30:06.2 (Paavo Nurmi)

| | | |
|---|---|---|
| 1. Ilmari Salminen | FIN | 30:15.4 |
| 2. Arvo Askola | FIN | 30:15.6 |
| 3. Volmari Iso-Hollo | FIN | 30:20.2 |
| 4. Kohei Murakoso | JPN | 30:25.0 |
| 5. James Burns | GBR | 30:58.2 |
| 6. Juan Carlos Zabala | ARG | 31:22.0 |
| 7. Max Gebhardt | GER | 31:29.6 |
| 8. Donald Lash | USA | 31:39.4 |

Murakoso fought valiantly against the three Finns, who ran a team race that included a good deal of jostling every time one of them passed him. However Murakoso finally had to give in with one lap to go. Salminen, a 33-year-old army sergeant, jumped the others at the start of the last lap, but Askola regained the lead in the backstretch. Salminen caught him again coming out of the final turn and gradually inched ahead for a narrow victory.

**1948 London** C: 27, N: 15, D: 7.30. WR: 29:35.8 (Viljo Heino)

| | | | |
|---|---|---|---|
| 1. Emil Zátopek | CZE | 29:59.6 | OR |
| 2. Alain Mimoun O'Kacha | FRA | 30:47.4 | |
| 3. Bertil Albertsson | SWE | 30:53.6 | |
| 4. Martin Stokken | NOR | 30:58.6 | |
| 5. Severt Dennolf | SWE | 31:05.0 | |
| 6. Abdallah ben Said | FRA | 31:07.8 | |
| 7. Stanley Cox | GBR | 31:08.0 | |
| 8. James Peters | GBR | 31:16.0 | |

World record holder Viljo Heino was expected to receive a stiff challenge from Czech army lieutenant Emil Zátopek. As it turned out, it was the challenger who controlled the race. Moving in front during the tenth lap, Zátopek ground out the laps at a steady pace until both Heino and his teammate, Heinstrom, were forced to drop out from exhaustion. Eventually Zátopek lapped all but two runners and won by over 300 meters. The incompetent officials in charge of the race became confused by Zátopek's performance and announced the start of the final circuit one lap too soon. Fortunately Zátopek knew better, although others didn't. When the race was over, it was announced that Dennolf of Sweden had finished fourth and Stokken of Norway fifth. The Norwegians protested, but the matter was settled quickly when Dennolf himself supported their case. Sixth place was awarded to Robert Everaert of Belgium, who had actually dropped out of the race over five laps before the finish. Everaert pointed out the mistake, but the judges refused to change their decision until a Belgian official intervened.

**1952 Helsinki** C: 33, N: 21, D: 7.20. WR: 20:02.6 (Emil Zátopek)

| | | | |
|---|---|---|---|
| 1. Emil Zátopek | CZE | 29:17.0 | OR |
| 2. Alain Mimoun O'Kacha | FRA | 29:32.8 | |
| 3. Aleksandr Anufriev | SOV | 29:48.2 | |
| 4. Hannu Posti | FIN | 29:51.4 | |
| 5. Frank Sando | GBR | 29:51.8 | |

| | | | |
|---|---|---|---|
| 6. Valter Nyström | SWE | 29:52.8 | |
| 7. Gordon Pirie | GBR | 30:09.5 | |
| 8. Fred Norris | GBR | 30:09.8 | |

The result was never in doubt as Zátopek wore out his opponents one by one, with Mimoun the last to go, four and a half laps from the finish. Zátopek won by about 100 yards to gain the first part of his unprecedented long-distance triple. Between 1948 and 1954 Emil Zátopek won 38 consecutive races at 10,000 meters. Many years later, Zátopek presented his 1952 10,000-meter gold medal to the great Australian runner Ron Clarke, who had never won one.

**1956 Melbourne** C: 25, N: 15, D: 11.23. WR: 28:30.4 (Vladimir Kuts)

| | | | |
|---|---|---|---|
| 1. Vladimir Kuts | SOV | 28:45.6 | OR |
| 2. József Kovács | HUN | 28:52.4 | |
| 3. Allan Lawrence | AUS | 28:53.6 | |
| 4. Zdzislaw Kryszkowlak | POL | 29:05.0 | |
| 5. Kenneth Norris | GBR | 29:21.6 | |
| 6. Ivan Chernyavsky | SOV | 29:31.6 | |
| 7. David Power | AUS | 29:49.2 | |
| 8. Gordon Pirie | GBR | 29:49.6 | |

Vladimir Kuts was a teenager when the Germans invaded his Ukrainian village in 1943. After the war, he joined the U.S.S.R. navy, and it was only then that he attracted the attention of Soviet coaches, who introduced him to competitive running at the age of 23.

Two months before the Melbourne Olympics, while running in Moscow, Kuts broke the world 10,000 meters record by over 12 seconds. By virtue of this performance, he was considered the favorite. But there were those who remembered that two months before that, Kuts had been beaten in England by Gordon Pirie, and although he had never run the 10,000 faster than 29:17.2, Pirie was also given a good shot at the gold medal.

Kuts took off like a flash and completed the first of 25 laps in only 61.2 seconds. Slowing down only slightly, he had outdistanced everyone but Pirie by the seventh lap. Kuts ran the first half of the race so quickly that he passed the 5000-meter mark at 14:07.0, which almost equaled Emil Zátopek's Olympic record for that distance. And he still had another 5000 meters to run. Between laps 8 and 20, Kuts tried a variety of tactics to rid himself of the stubborn Pirie. Several times he sprinted out at a seemingly insane pace, only to have Pirie catch up each time. Alternatively, Kuts would slow down, move to the outside, and wave Pirie past him. But Pirie refused to bite, preferring to remain at Kuts' shoulder.

Suddenly, at the end of the 20th lap, Kuts stopped so abruptly that Pirie was forced to take the lead. Relieved of the pressure of having Pirie on his heels, Kuts rested for a half lap while he studied his adversary in front of him. Then, just as suddenly as he had slowed, Kuts burst past Pirie to take the lead for good. Pirie struggled to keep pace, but with four laps to go, he gave up, eventually dropping back to eighth place. Kovács and Lawrence finished strongly, but Kuts' victory was never in doubt.

**1960 Rome** C: 32, N: 20, D: 9.8. WR: 28:30.4 (Vladimir Kuts)

| | | | |
|---|---|---|---|
| 1. Pyotr Bolotnikov | SOV | 28:32.2 | OR |
| 2. Hans Grodotzki | GDR | 28:37.0 | |
| 3. David Power | AUS | 28:38.2 | |
| 4. Aleksei Desyachikov | SOV | 28:39.6 | |
| 5. Murray Halberg | NZE | 28:48.6 | |
| 6. Max Truex | USA | 28:50.2 | |
| 7. Zdzislaw Krzyszkowiak | POL | 28:52.4 | |
| 8. John Merriman | GBR | 28:52.6 | |

Dave Power tried to pull away with seven laps to go, but Bolotnikov, Grodotzki and Desyachikov were able to stay with him. Seven hundred meters from the finish, Bolotnikov, a 30-year-old pupil of Vladimir Kuts, left the others behind, running the last lap in 57.4 seconds and winning by 30 yards. Nine of the first 10 finishers achieved personal records, including Power, who bettered his previous best time by 53.8 seconds.

**1964 Tokyo** C: 29, N: 17, D: 10.14. WR: 28:15.6 (Ronald Clarke)

| | | | |
|---|---|---|---|
| 1. William Mills | USA | 28:24.4 | OR |
| 2. Mohamed Gammoudi | TUN | 28:24.8 | |
| 3. Ronald Clarke | AUS | 28:25.8 | |
| 4. Mamo Wolde | ETH | 28:31.8 | |
| 5. Leonid Ivanov | SOV | 28:53.2 | |
| 6. Kokichi Tsuburaya | JPN | 28:59.4 | |
| 7. Murray Halberg | NZE | 29:10.8 | |
| 8. Anthony Cook | AUS | 29:15.8 | |

The 1964 10,000 meters produced one of the most electrifying upsets in Olympic history. Pregame predictions had the race as a tough battle among defending 5000-meter champion Murray Halberg, defending 10,000 meters champion Pyotr Bolotnikov and the main favorite, world record holder Ron Clarke. By the halfway mark, Clarke, following a strategy of surging every other lap, had managed to eliminate from contention all but four runners: Mohamed Gammoudi and Mamo Wolde, who would both win gold medals four years later in Mexico City, local favorite Kokichi Tsuburaya, and Billy Mills, who had finished second at the U.S. Olympic trials. Tsuburaya was the first to lose contact; then, with two and a half laps to go, Wolde dropped away.

At this point, Ron Clarke appeared assured of victory, since neither Gammoudi nor Mills had ever broken 29 minutes. It was surely just a matter of time before Clarke would break away. They reached the final lap with Clarke and Mills running abreast and Gammoudi right behind. The track was cluttered with stragglers, and the three leaders were forced to thread their way through the congestion. It was "like a dash for a train in a peak-hour crowd," Clarke would later recall. In the backstretch Clarke found himself faced with a problem. In front of him was a straggler who wouldn't move aside to be passed. To his right was Mills. Clarke tapped Mills a

couple times, but he wouldn't step aside either. So Clarke gave him a shove that sent the American unknown careening to the outside. Seeing his chance, Gammoudi, putting one hand on Clarke and the other on Mills, pushed his way to the front and opened a sudden ten-yard lead. Clarke took off after the Tunisian, while Mills appeared to be out of the running. By this time, the audience was already going wild with excitement.

Clarke gradually closed the gap, finally passing Gammoudi at the beginning of the homestretch. But Gammoudi wasn't finished. With a major upset within his grasp, he pulled up to Clarke's shoulder once again. Then came one of those rare moments that sports fans never forget. Billy Mills, fighting his way through still more stragglers, let loose a final sprint that sent Clarke and Gammoudi into shock and carried him across the finish line with a three-yard victory that left the crowd of 75,000 as exhausted as the runners. Mills was immediately surrounded by Japanese officials, one of whom asked him, "Who are you?"

During the two weeks that he had spent in the Olympic Village prior to the opening of the games, not one reporter had asked Billy Mills a single question. Now he was besieged by journalists from all over the world, all asking the same question: "Who is Billy Mills?" Humble and calm (after crying on the victory platform), Mills explained that he was 7/16 Sioux Indian, and had been born in Pine Ridge, South Dakota. Orphaned at 12, he had been sent to Haskell Institute, a school for Native Americans in Lawrence, Kansas. He had taken up running as training to become a boxer, but after losing a couple of fights, he had decided to stick to running. After attending the University of Kansas, he had joined the Marines and was now a motor pool officer at Camp Pendleton in California. His winning time in Tokyo was 46 seconds faster than his previous best (Gammoudi had improved his own personal record by 47 seconds). "I'm flabbergasted," said Mills. "I can't believe it. I suppose I was the only person who thought I had a chance."

In 1965 Billy Mills proved that his Olympic victory was no fluke by bettering Ron Clarke's six-mile world record by six seconds. That same year, he received an award that was to prove more meaningful to him than his gold medal—a ring made from Black Hills gold that was presented to him by the elders of the Oglala Sioux tribe. They also gave him warrior status, which he didn't have because he was a half-breed, and an Indian name: Loves His Country.

But there was one thing missing from Billy Mills' Olympic experience: because there were so many runners still finishing the race, he was not allowed to take a victory lap. Twenty years later, on a rainy day in 1984, Mills returned to the National Stadium in Tokyo along with his wife, Pat, U.S. filmmaker Bud Greenspan, and a film crew. Mills described what followed in the book *Tales of Gold*, by Lewis Carlson and John Fogarty: "I knew what

I wanted, and Pat knew what I was going to do. I went down onto the track and . . . went on around, taking that victory lap I so desperately needed. At the same time, in my mind, I was reliving the race. I could feel Clarke push me, and I could sense people in the stadium. Toward the end of my lap, I heard one person clapping; it was Pat, clapping for me. I started to cry. I needed that victory lap so badly, I started crying, and rather than let the group see me cry, I lifted my face up to the rain, walked up the track a way to get my composure, then finished my lap."

**1968 Mexico City** C: 37, N: 23, D: 10.13. WR: 27:39.4 (Ronald Clarke)

| | | | |
|---|---|---|---|
| 1. | Naftali Temu | KEN | 29:27.4 |
| 2. | Mamo Wolde | ETH | 29:28.0 |
| 3. | Mohamed Gammoudi | TUN | 29:34.2 |
| 4. | Juan Martinez | MEX | 29:35.0 |
| 5. | Nikolai Sviridov | SOV | 29:43.2 |
| 6. | Ronald Clarke | AUS | 29:44.8 |
| 7. | Ronald Hill | GBR | 29:53.2 |
| 8. | Wohib Masresha | ETH | 29:57.0 |

When the International Olympic Committee first announced that the 1968 Olympics would be held in Mexico City, there was much criticism that the competitions would be adversely affected by the high altitude. The I.O.C. denied that the altitude would make a difference, but they couldn't have been more wrong.

The 10,000 meters was the first track and field event to be decided. With six laps to go, two runners were carried away on stretchers. The first surprise came after 8900 meters, when Kip Keino dropped out, suffering stomach cramps as a result of a gall bladder infection. Although 11 different men had led over the first 8000 meters, with 800 meters left, the only runners still in contention were Wolde, Clarke, Temu, and Gammoudi. One and a half laps from the finish, Clarke finally lost contact. A 64.4-second 24th lap by Temu got rid of Gammoudi, but just after the bell Wolde shot past Temu and opened up a five yard gap. However Temu had the most strength left. He caught Wolde 50 meters from the finish line and won by four yards. The first five finishers were all from high-altitude countries or had lived in high-altitude areas of their nations. The first non-high-altitude runner to finish was Ron Clarke, who collapsed and was unconscious for ten minutes.

Temu, a 23-year-old Kisii tribesman, was resentful, as well he should have been, when he learned that his victory was being belittled because of the altitude. In 1966 he had attracted attention by finishing first at the Commonwealth Games in Jamaica. "Now tell me," he said after his win in Mexico City, "I beat that Clarke they were talking about in Jamaica, and tell me . . . were there mountains in Kingston?" Temu was the first Kenyan to earn an Olympic gold medal. The 1968 10,000 meters marked the first time that all three medals in an Olympic event had been won by Africans.

**1972 Munich** C: 50, N: 34, D: 8.31. WR: 27:39.4 (Ronald Clarke)

| | | | | |
|---|---|---|---|---|
| 1. | Lasse Viren | FIN | 27:38.4 | WR |
| 2. | Emiel Puttemans | BEL | 27:39.6 | |
| 3. | Miruts Yifter | ETH | 27:41.0 | |
| 4. | Mariano Haro Cisneros | SPA | 27:48.2 | |
| 5. | Frank Shorter | USA | 27:51.4 | |
| 6. | David Bedford | GBR | 28:05.4 | |
| 7. | Daniel Korica | YUG | 28:15.2 | |
| 8. | Abdelkader Zaddem | TUN | 28:18.2 | |

With 50 runners entered, qualifying heats were reinstituted for the first time since 1920. In the first heat, Dave Bedford and Emiel Puttemans pulled away from the field. After reaching 8000 meters in 22:16.2, Bedford turned to Puttemans and asked him if they should go for the world record. Puttemans declined. "But we're so close to the mark," said Bedford. Finally Puttemans convinced him that they should save themselves for the final, not to mention the 5000. The second heat saw the Olympic debut of Lasse Viren, a 23-year-old Finnish policeman from the small village of Myrskyla. Two and a half weeks earlier Viren had defeated Puttemans and Bedford in Stockholm, setting a two-mile world record of 8:14.0.

The third and last heat was highlighted by the appearance of Anilus Joseph of Haiti, who had evidently never taken part in a 10,000 meters race before. Joseph took off as if he was two laps from the finish line. He covered the first lap in 59.6 seconds, opening up a lead of 50 meters. He was still in first place after 800 meters, but then he ran out of steam, and by the 1000-meter mark he was in last place. By the eighth lap he had been lapped by all the other runners and by the twelfth he had been lapped again. When the bell rang to signal the final lap for the leaders, Joseph thought that it meant that he too only had one more lap to go, so he began sprinting again. Informed by an official that even though all the other runners had finished, he still had another mile to run, Joseph finally dropped out. He wasn't seen again in the Olympics, but his performance was only a prelude to the unusual feats that would be accomplished by the Haitian track team four years later in Montreal.

The final, two days later, was a more serious race. Although Bedford set a pace not unlike that of Joseph's, he was able to sustain it for much longer. He was still in the lead after 4600 meters, when a surprising incident occurred behind him.

Running in fifth place, Lasse Viren, without being interfered with, stumbled and fell. Mohamed Gammoudi tripped on Viren and crashed to the ground. Gammoudi, stunned, was forced to give up a couple laps later, but Viren rose quickly and moved up to second place after only 230 meters.

Viren passed Bedford at the 6000-meter mark and Bedford began to fade soon after. Only Yifter, Haro, Puttemans, and Shorter were still in the hunt. The lead changed hands several times during the next few laps. Six hundred meters from the finish, Viren poured it on.

Shorter fell back immediately, and Haro lost contact 100 meters later. Yifter fell away in the final backstretch. Puttemans tried desperately to keep up, but Viren had too much strength left and was able to pull away in the final straight to win by about six or seven yards. Viren's times for the last two laps were a remarkable 60.0 and 56.4. Lasse Viren had broken Ron Clarke's seven-year-old world record and won the first of his four gold medals.

**1976 Montreal** C: 41, N: 26, D: 7.26. WR: 27:30.8 (David Bedford)

| | | |
|---|---|---|
| 1. Lasse Viren | FIN | 27:40.38 |
| 2. Carlos Lopes | POR | 27:45.17 |
| 3. Brendan Foster | GBR | 27:54.92 |
| 4. Anthony Simmons | GBR | 27:56.26 |
| 5. Ilie Floroiu | ROM | 27:59.93 |
| 6. Mariano Haro Cisneros | SPA | 28:00.28 |
| 7. Marc Smet | BEL | 28:02.80 |
| 8. Bernard Ford | GBR | 28:17.78 |

The final was a relatively simple race. Lopes took the lead after 3200 meters and eventually drew away from everyone but Viren, who passed him 450 meters from the finish and won easily by 30 meters.

However, the 1976 10,000 meters competition should not be left without making mention of Olmeus Charles of Haiti, whose performance in the opening heat was the ultimate expression of the Olympic ideal that what counts is not the winning, but the taking part. Charles completed the course in 42:00.11, the slowest time ever recorded in the Olympics, almost 14 minutes slower than Carlos Lopes, who won the heat, and over 8½ minutes slower than Chris McCubbins of Canada, who placed next to last. The entire schedule had to be held up while Charles plodded the final six laps alone. In 1972 and 1976 Haitian runners consistently finished in last place. At first reflection, one might feel sympathy for the Haitians. After all, Haiti is the poorest country in the Western Hemisphere, and malnutrition is widespread. However, there is no evidence that tryouts were actually held to determine the nation's best runners. Instead, "Baby Doc" Duvalier, the dictator of Haiti, simply chose his friends and other trusted soldiers, and rewarded them with a free trip to Canada. Unfortunately, none of them were athletes.

**1980 Moscow** C: 40, N: 26, D: 7.27. WR: 27:22.5 (Henry Rono)

| | | |
|---|---|---|
| 1. Miruts Yifter | ETH | 27:42.7 |
| 2. Kaarlo Maaninka | FIN | 27:44.3 |
| 3. Mohammed Kedir | ETH | 27:44.7 |
| 4. Tolossa Kofu | ETH | 27:46.5 |
| 5. Lasse Viren | FIN | 27:50.5 |
| 6. Jörg Peter | GDR | 28:05.6 |
| 7. Werner Schildhauer | GDR | 28:11.0 |
| 8. Enn Sellik | SOV | 28:13.8 |

The final resembled a dual meet between Ethiopia and Finland more than an international contest. The Ethiopians dominated the proceedings, changing the pace and the lead every few hundred meters. After lulling the pack into confusion for the first 5000 meters, they set off at a torrid clip until only Viren and Maaninka were left to challenge. In the 22nd lap Maaninka broke ahead, only to be passed by Kedir and Yifter. Then Viren took the lead, but Kedir moved ahead again just before the bell. Finally, the inevitable took place. With 300 meters left in the race, Miruts Yifter sprinted into the lead, covered the last 200 meters in 26.8 seconds, and won by ten meters. Viren faded to fifth, but Maaninka, who later admitted to blood boosting before the Olympics, finished strongly to prevent an Ethiopian sweep.

**1984 Los Angeles** C: 45, N: 33, D: 8.6. WR: 27:13.81 (Fernando Mamede)

| | | |
|---|---|---|
| 1. Alberto Cova | ITA | 27:47.54 |
| 2. Michael McLeod | GBR | 28:06.22 |
| 3. Mike Musyoki | KEN | 28:06.46 |
| 4. Salvatore Antibo | ITA | 28:06.50 |
| 5. Christoph Herle | GER | 28:08.21 |
| 6. Sosthenes Bitok | KEN | 28:09.01 |
| 7. Yutaka Kanai | JPN | 28:27.06 |
| 8. Steve Jones | GBR | 28:28.08 |

DISQ (Drugs): Martti Vainio (FIN) 27:51:10

In 1982, Alberto Cova won the European championships by outsprinting Werner Schildhauer of East Germany. In 1983, Cova won the world championships by outsprinting Schildhauer. In 1984, with Schildhauer missing because of the Soviet-bloc boycott, Cova's only competition was thought to be world record holder Fernando Mamede. But even Mamede was considered a doubtful challenger because of his long record of becoming overcome by nerves at important meets. True to form, Mamede, after winning his qualifying heat, raced off the track halfway through the final.

While Mamede was disappearing into the tunnel, Nick Rose was making the first significant move of an otherwise slow race. He opened a ten-meter lead, but was quickly hauled in by Martti Vainio and Cova. Vainio then ran away from the field—except for Cova, who tracked him relentlessly for 2½ miles. The result seemed inevitable. With 200 meters to go, Cova shot past the tall Finn and pulled away to a 25-meter victory. The second 5000 meters of the race had been run in 13:27.71. Vainio was subsequently disqualified when his drug test turned up traces of an anabolic steroid.

One admirable characteristic of the audience at the 1984 track events was their tendency to vigorously applaud last-place finishers. One such also-ran was Basil Kilani of Jordan, who finished the first preliminary heat in 30 minutes and 43.54 seconds, almost 2½ minutes behind Fernando Mamede. The crowd probably would have given Kilani an even bigger ovation had they realized that their support had helped Kilani improve his personal record by a surprising 2 minutes and 50 seconds.

**1988 Seoul** C: 52, N: 35, D: 9.26. WR: 27:13.81 (Fernando Mamede)

| | | | |
|---|---|---|---|
| 1. Moulay Brahim Boutaib | MOR | 27:21.46 | OR |
| 2. Salvatore Antibo | ITA | 27:23.55 | |
| 3. Kipkemboi Kimeli | KEN | 27:25.16 | |
| 4. Jean-Louis Prianon | FRA | 27:36.43 | |
| 5. Arturo Barrios | MEX | 27:39.32 | |
| 6. Hansjörg Kunze | GDR | 27:39.35 | |
| 7. Paul Arpin | FRA | 27:39.36 | |
| 8. Moses Tanui | KEN | 27:47.23 | |

Sicilian Salvatore Antibo rattled the field by running the first 800 meters in 2:07.4. Moses Tanui surged into the lead at the 2000-meter mark, carrying Kipkemboi Kimeli and Antibo with him. They were joined, three laps later, by Brahim Boutaib, a former protege of Said Aouita, who had broken away from his mentor only a month before the Olympics. The rest of the runners were already out of the race, 40 meters back. Kimeli reached the halfway point in world record pace: 13:35.32. Boutaib was on his heels. Tanui trailed by 10 meters with Antibo another 10 meters behind. One lap later Boutaib made his move. By the end of the next lap he had opened up a 10-meter lead, which he gradually expanded to 40 meters by the bell. He slowed to a walk before the end, stopping completely just after the finish line in order to embrace Antibo, who passed Kimeli in the final straight to take the silver. At 21 years of age, Boutaib was the youngest winner in the event's history. When asked "Where do you go from here?" he replied, "What can you ask a flower that is just blooming?"

# MARATHON
## (42,195 Meters—26 Miles 385 Yards)

**1896 Athens** C: 17, N: 5, D: 4.10.
**(40,000 Meters)**

| | | |
|---|---|---|
| 1. Spiridon Louis | GRE | 2:58:50 |
| 2. Charilaos Vasilakos | GRE | 3:06:03 |
| 3. Gyula Kellner | HUN | 3:06:35 |
| 4. Ioannis Vrettos | GRE | — |
| 5. Elevtherios Papasimeon | GRE | — |
| 6. Demetrios Deligannis | GRE | — |
| 7. Evangelos Gerakakis | GRE | — |
| 8. Stamatios Massouris | GRE | — |

The idea for a marathon race was inspired by the legend of Pheidippides, a professional runner who allegedly carried the news of the Greek victory over the Persians at the Battle of Marathon in 490 B.C. Upon his arrival in Athens, he called out, "Be joyful, we win!" and then dropped dead of exhaustion. Actually there is no evidence that this dramatic incident ever took place. The fifth century B.C. historian Herodotus, who thrived on such juicy tidbits, wrote about the Battle of Marathon, but made no mention of Pheidippides' feat. The story didn't appear in print until the second century A.D.— over 600 years after it was alleged to have occurred. The longest race to be included in the ancient Greek Olympics was only 4800 meters.

However, when meetings began to be held in 1894 to organize an international revival of the Olympics, Michel Bréal, a French linguist and historian, proposed that a long-distance race be included. He even offered to present a silver cup to the winner. Invoking the legend of Pheidippides, Bréal and Baron Pierre de Coubertin presented the idea to the Organizing Committee of the Athens Olympics. The Greeks, moved by the presumed historical importance associated with such a race, agreed immediately. Georgious Averoff, designer of the refurbished Pananthenaic Stadium and the primary financial supporter of the Games, added an antique vase to the offer of Bréal's silver cup.

Before long, the marathon race had come to be considered the most important event of the upcoming games, and two preliminary races for Greeks were held along the proposed route from the Marathon Bridge to the stadium in Athens. The first race, on March 10, was won by Charilaos Vasilakos in 3:18:00. He was followed by Spiridon Belokas and Demetrios Deligannis. The second race was officially designated an Olympic trial and was contested by 38 runners. The winner was Ioannis Lavrentis, in 3:11:27. In fifth place was a young man of 24 years, from the village of Amarousion, named Spiridon Louis.

On the afternoon of Thursday, April 9, 17 runners were transported from Athens to an inn near the starting point of the race in Marathon. Among them were four foreigners, including the first three finishers in the 1500 meters: Edwin Flack, the London-based Australian accountant, who had won the 800 meters only a couple of hours earlier, Arthur Blake, and Albin Lermusiaux.

The next afternoon, the 17 entrants gathered on the Marathon Bridge and endured a preliminary speech by the starter, Major Papadiamantopoulos, who finally fired a gun to begin the race. There was much excitement among the Greek populace, and all along the route the runners were cheered by curious and enthusiastic peasants. Of the foreigners, only the Hungarian, Gyula Kellner, had ever run a race of such length, having qualified for the trip to Athens by winning a 40-kilometer trial in Budapest. The other three set off relatively quickly and eventually paid for their inexperience. Lermusiaux set the early pace and soon built up a huge lead, which he carried past the halfway mark. At the village of Palini (Kharvati), the local people had built a triumphal arch. When Lermusiaux approached in first place, the villagers crowned him with a floral victor's wreath. By this time, Blake and four of the Greeks had already dropped out.

Shortly after Palini, there was an incline, and Lermusiaux began to stagger from exhaustion. A French companion, riding beside him on a bicycle, revived his countryman with an alcohol rubdown, but this delay allowed Flack to pass him and take the lead. Lermusiaux continued for some distance, but finally collapsed. Flack, who had never before run more than ten miles, had over-extended himself in his attempt to catch Lermusiaux, and he too began to weave and sway four kilometers short of the stadium. Flack's companion, an Englishman, asked a nearby Greek to keep the Australian from falling over while he rushed off to get a wrap. The delirious Flack, thinking that he was being attacked, smashed the helpful Greek with his fist and knocked him to the ground. Flack was loaded into a carriage and driven to the dressing room at the stadium, where he was tended to by Prince Nicholas himself, and revived with a drink of egg and brandy.

As the race progressed, messengers were sent to the stadium on horseback and bicycle to convey the identity of the leaders. The last news that the 100,000 spectators in and around the stadium heard was that Flack was in front, and their disappointment was great. Then Major Papadiamantopoulos entered the stadium on horseback and rushed to the royal box, where the King and Queen and the rest of the royal family were anxiously awaiting the latest news. The word spread "with the rapidity of lightning," according to the Official Report of the Games. Shouts of "*Elleen! Elleen!*" ("A Greek! A Greek!") announced the joyous news that a Greek was in the lead. Then the Commissioner of Police appeared and formally announced what the growing roar of the crowd in the streets had already implied: the winner had arrived. At last, a small, dusty runner, Spiridon Louis, appeared at the marble entrance to the stadium. Prince George and Crown Prince Constantine rushed down to greet him and, one on each side, ran with him the rest of the way to the finish line, where Louis summoned enough energy to bow to the delighted King George. Louis was kissed and hugged and hauled off to the dressing room upon the shoulders of his admirers, while a collective ectasy spread from the stadium throughout the city.

Seven minutes later, a second Greek, Charilaos Vasilakos, crossed the finish to be followed shortly by a third Greek, Spiridon Belokas. However, the fourth-place finisher, Gyula Kellner, raised a protest that Belokas had ridden part of the way in a carriage. Belokas admitted his deception, and was stripped of his awards, as well as his shirt, and thoroughly ostracized.

The story of Spiridon Louis is one of which legends are made. In fact, so many legends developed about Louis that it is difficult to sort out the truth. Was he a poor shepherd, a well-to-do farmer, a soldier, a post office messenger? Probably he was a shepherd who served in the army and became a messenger. A modest man, he appeared in the stadium the day after the race to accept his prize, but then returned quickly to his village, allowing journalists to invent whatever details they saw fit. Typical of the rumors that spread was that he had entered the race in hopes of convincing the king to grant clemency to his imprisoned brother—a romantic story that was deflated when it was learned that Louis didn't

even have a brother. It is true that merchants throughout Athens tried to shower him with gifts, including watches, jewelry, wine, free haircuts, free clothing for life, free meals, free coffee for a year, monthly stipends, a shotgun, and a Singer sewing machine. Evidently, Louis graciously turned down all the offers except a horse and cart, which were needed to help transport water to his village.

Amazingly, Spiridon Louis managed to return to a relatively normal life. In 1936, however, he was rediscovered by the German Olympic Organizing Committee, which brought him to Berlin. There he presented a laurel wreath from the sacred grove at Olympia to Adolf Hitler. Louis died on March 27, 1940, but his name entered the Greek language in the expression "*egine Louis*": "became Louis," or ran quickly. More than any single event, the victory of Spiridon Louis served as an inspiration to keep the Olympics going through the hard times that the movement faced over the next 12 years.

**1900 Paris** C: 13?, N: 5, D: 7.19.
**(40,260 Meters)**

| | | |
|---|---|---|
| 1. Michel Théato | FRA | 2:59:45 |
| 2. Emile Champion | FRA | 3:04:17 |
| 3. Ernst Fast | SWE | 3:37:14 |
| 4. Eugene Bessemar | FRA | 4:00:43 |
| 5. Arthur Newton | USA | 4:04:12 |
| 6. Richard Grant | USA | — |
| 7. Ronald MacDonald | CAN | — |

This unfortunate event was held in 102 degrees Fahrenheit (39 degrees Centigrade) heat. The course began in the Bois de Boulogne, followed the old city wall, and ended up back in the Bois. Only 7 of the runners were able to finish. Michel Théato, a 23-year-old baker's deliveryman, took the lead shortly after the halfway point and never relinquished it.

**1904 St. Louis** C: 32, N: 5, D: 8.30.
**(40,000 Meters)**

| | | |
|---|---|---|
| 1. Thomas Hicks | USA | 3:28:53 |
| 2. Albert Corey | FRA | 3:34:52 |
| 3. Arthur Newton | USA | 3:47:33 |
| 4. Félix Carvajal | CUB | — |
| 5. Demetrios Velouis | GRE | — |
| 6. David Kneeland | USA | — |
| 7. Henry Brawley | USA | — |
| 8. Sidney Hatch | USA | — |

The 1904 marathon ranks very high on the list of bizarre events in Olympic history. Among the more unusual entrants in the race was 5-foot-tall Félix Carvajal, a Cuban mail carrier, who raised the money for his trip to St. Louis by staging exhibitions in Havana. He took a boat to the United States and got as far as New Orleans, where he lost the rest of his savings in a crap game. After hitchhiking to St. Louis, he arrived on the starting line wearing heavy street shoes, long trousers, a long-sleeved shirt, and a beret. The start of the race was delayed while

Martin Sheridan, the discus thrower, cut off Carvajal's pants at the knees. Also entered were the first two black Africans to participate in the Olympics: Lentauw and Yamasani, Zulu tribesmen who were in St. Louis as part of the Boer War exhibit at the Louisiana Purchase Exposition. Another foreign contestant was Albert Corey, a professional strikebreaker, who had arrived in Chicago in 1903 during a butchers' strike and stayed around, since there was never a shortage of business for him in the Windy City.

Among the American entrants were Sam Mellor, winner of the 1902 Boston Marathon; John Lordon, winner of the 1903 Boston Marathon; Michael Spring, winner of the 1904 Boston Marathon; Thomas Hicks, who had finished second at Boston in 1904; and Arthur Newton, who had finished fifth in Paris in 1900.

Unfortunately, the organizers of the race knew almost nothing about staging such an event. The course included seven hills and was run on dusty roads, made dustier by the many automobiles which the judges, doctors, and journalists used to follow—and lead—the runners. The brutal nature of the contest was made worse by the fact that it was scheduled for the middle of the afternoon in 90 degrees Fahrenheit (32 degrees Centigrade) heat. In addition, the only water available to the runners was from a well located 12 miles from the stadium, where the race began and ended.

With all these obstacles in their path, it is not surprising that only 14 of the 32 starters made it back to the finish line. John Lordon, for example, began vomiting after ten miles and had to withdraw. William Garcia of San Francisco was discovered lying unconscious by the side of the road. Sam Mellor, the leader at the halfway mark, finally gave up after 16 miles. Meanwhile, Lentauw lost a great deal of valuable time when he was chased off the course and through a cornfield by two large dogs. He still managed to finish ninth. The only runner who didn't seem bothered by all these catastrophes was Félix Carvajal, who stopped a number of times to chat with bystanders, discuss the progress of the race, and practice his English. He also quenched his thirst by snatching a couple of peaches from an official in one of the cars, and by raiding a farmer's orchard of some green apples. The latter detour caused him an attack of stomach cramps.

Back in the stadium, the spectators were unaware of all that had transpired, although the more knowledgeable sports fans may have wondered why three hours had passed without any of the runners showing up. Finally, after 3 hours and 13 minutes, Fred Lorz of New York appeared, and was immediately hailed as the winner. He had already been photographed with Alice Roosevelt, the daughter of the President of the United States, and was about to be awarded the gold medal, when it was discovered that he had actually stopped running after 9 miles, hitched a ride in a car for 11 miles, and then started running again. Lorz readily admitted his practical

joke, but A.A.U. officials were not amused, and he was slapped with a lifetime ban. However, he was reinstated well before the ban ran out and managed to win the Boston Marathon of 1905.

The real winner of the 1904 Olympic marathon was Thomas Hicks, an English-born brass worker from Cambridge, Massachusetts. If present-day rules had been enforced, however, he would have been disqualified. Second at the halfway point, Hicks found himself in front after Sam Mellor collapsed. Ten miles from the finish Hicks begged to be allowed to lie down, but his handlers wouldn't allow it, even though he had a lead of one and a half miles. Instead they administered to him an oral dose of strychnine sulfate mixed with raw egg white. A few miles later he was given more strychnine, as well as some brandy. He was also bathed with water made warm by being kept next to the boiler of the steam-powered automobile that accompanied him.

Hicks was forced to slow to a walk when faced with a final, steep hill two miles from the stadium, but a couple more doses of strychnine and brandy revived him enough to win the race by six minutes. Needless to say, Hicks was in something of a stupor afterward. He had lost ten pounds during the afternoon, and gladly announced his retirement. When he had finally recovered, he told reporters, "I would rather have won this race than be President of the United States." The athletes who suffered through the 1904 marathon may have received some satisfaction when they learned that two of the officials in charge of patrolling the course were badly injured as well, when their brand-new car swerved to avoid one of the runners and careened down an embankment.

**1906 Athens** C: 53, N: 15, D: 5.1.
**(41,860 Meters)**

| | | | |
|---|---|---|---|
| 1. | William Sherring | CAN | 2:51:23.6 |
| 2. | John Svanberg | SWE | 2:58:20.8 |
| 3. | William Frank | USA | 3:00:46.8 |
| 4. | Gustaf Törnros | SWE | 3:01:00.0 |
| 5. | John Alepous | GRE | 3:09:25.4 |
| 6. | George Blake | AUS | 3:09:35.0 |
| 7. | Constantinos Karvelas | GRE | 3:15:54.0 |
| 8. | André Roffi | FRA | 3:17:49.8 |

There was great excitement in Athens when it was learned that another Olympic-style marathon would be held. Local merchants offered the winner a statue of Hermes, a loaf of bread every day for a year, three coffees a day for a year, free shaves for life, and a free lunch for six every Sunday for a year—but only if the winner was a Greek.

Billy Sherring of Hamilton, Ontario, had other ideas. Convinced he could win, he gathered his savings from his job as a railway brakeman, but they weren't enough to pay his way to Greece. A local athletic club raised an extra $75, but it still wasn't enough. In desperation, Sherring turned over the $75 to a friendly bartender, who bet the money on a horse named Cicely, who won and paid 6-1 odds. At last Billy Sherring was able to travel to Athens. He arrived two months early and took a job as a railway station porter, training every other day. On March 17, the Greeks staged a trial run that was won in 3:04:29.6. Sherring watched with pleasure, knowing that he had covered the same course, in secret, 20 minutes faster.

When the big day finally came, George Blake of Australia took the early lead. After four miles he was passed by William Frank of New York, who led for three miles before Blake regained the lead. Blake faded, however, and after 15 miles he was passed by Sherring and Frank. The two ran together for three more miles, at which point Sherring turned to Frank and said, "Well, goodbye, Billy." Then he took off and built up such a large lead that he was able to walk part of the way to the finish.

There was great disappointment in the Olympic Stadium when the news spread that the leader was not a Greek. However, when Sherring passed through the marble entrance, he was met by Prince George, who applauded him and ran with him around the track to the finish line, where Sherring bowed to the king, just as Spiridon Louis had done ten years earlier. Billy Sherring had weighed 135 pounds when he left Canada. By the morning of the race he was down to 112, and by the end of the race he had evaporated to 98 pounds. Sherring didn't receive all the goodies that had been offered a Greek winner, but he was presented with a three-foot statue of Athena and a young lamb. Back in Canada he did much better. The city of Hamilton gave him a purse of $5,000, while the city of Toronto chipped in $400.

One runner who was overlooked in 1906 was a 20-year-old Italian who developed stomach problems and dropped out after 24 kilometers. His name was Dorando Pietri. Before the decade was out, he would become a living legend.

**1908 London** C: 56, N: 16, D: 7.24.

| | | | |
|---|---|---|---|
| 1. John Hayes | USA | 2:55:18.4 | OR |
| 2. Charles Hefferon | SAF | 2:56:06.0 | |
| 3. Joseph Forshaw | USA | 2:57:10.4 | |
| 4. Alton Welton | USA | 2:59:44.4 | |
| 5. William Wood | CAN | 3:01:44.0 | |
| 6. Frederick Simpson | CAN | 3:04:28.2 | |
| 7. Harry Lawson | CAN | 3:06:47.2 | |
| 8. John Svanberg | SWE | 3:07:50.8 | |

DISQ: Dorando Pietri (ITA) 2:54:46.4

July 24, 1908, dawned hot (by English standards) and muggy. The talk of the town was the bitter hostilities that had erupted between the British and the Americans following the controversial running of the 400 meters final the previous day. People had been looking forward to the marathon race with great anticipation, and a large crowd lined the 26-mile route from Windsor Castle to the Olympic Stadium in Shepherd's Bush. The race was scheduled to conclude with 385 yards around the stadium track, so that the finish line would be directly in front of the royal box of Queen Alexandra. As it happened, this random distance of 26 miles and 385 yards would later become the standardized length for marathon races.

The first 26 miles of the 1908 marathon were actually quite exciting, although they were quickly forgotten as a result of the extraordinary incidents which occurred during the final 385 yards. The British runners, under great pressure to perform well, started off at far too fast a clip and later paid the price of their folly. T. Jack of Scotland led for the first five miles, but quickly exhausted himself. Fred Lord and Jack Price took his place in front. Lord began to fade after ten miles. At the halfway mark at Ruislip, Price led by 200 yards. Charles Hefferon had moved into second place, followed by Lord and Dorando Pietri. The American entrants, at this point, were calmly running their own race, unruffled by the fast pace of the leaders.

Shortly after the 14-mile mark, Hefferon passed Price, who dropped out not long after. Lord also began to fade, eventually finishing 15th. The well-known Onondaga Indian Tom Longboat, of Toronto, who had been one of the favorites, came up to challenge, but he too fell back, slowing to a walk and then retiring completely.

By the 18-mile mark, it appeared that only Hefferon and Pietri (or Dorando, as he became better known) had a chance for the gold medal. Hefferon led by 3:18. By 20 miles he had built up a lead of 3 minutes 52 seconds, but then Dorando began to close the gap. Two miles from the stadium, the exhausted Hefferon made a crucial mistake. He accepted a drink of champagne and, within a mile, he had developed stomach cramps and become dizzy. Dorando also committed a major tactical blunder. Urged on by the well-meaning but overzealous crowd, he picked up his pace too early. Meanwhile, Americans John Hayes, Joseph Forshaw, and Alton Welton were drawing closer.

The spectators lining the route, having inadvertently damaged Dorando's chances for victory, now did the same to Hefferon. Hoping to boost his spirits, they slapped him on the back so many times that they sapped him of what little energy he had left. A half-mile from the entrance to the stadium, he was passed by Dorando.

The last report that had been received inside the stadium was that South Africa and Italy were in the lead. All eyes were on the entrance as Dorando Pietri, a small man from the small town of Carpi, near Mòdena, made his appearance. However, it immediately became obvious that something was wrong. Dorando appeared dazed and headed off in the wrong direction. Track officials rushed to his aid and pointed him the right way. But after going only a few yards, he collapsed on the track. The audience, which had never before seen or heard of Dorando, immediately became sympathetic. While many people screamed for the officials to help him, others, knowing that such aid would automatically disqualify the plucky Italian, called out to leave him alone. However, in the words of the official report, "It was impossible to leave him there, for it looked as if he might die in the very presence of the Queen . . ." Doctors and officials rushed to help him, and Dorando managed to struggle to his feet and plod on, only to fall again. And again and again. By this time, a second runner had arrived on the track. However, much to the horror of the spectators, he was not Charles Hefferon, a good man of the Empire, but an American, 5-foot 4-inch John Hayes, who had breezed past Hefferon 20 yards before the stadium grounds.

This was too much for the British officials. When Dorando started to collapse for a fifth time, just short of the finish, Jack Andrew, the head organizer of the race, caught him and carried him across the line. The Italian flag was immediately run up the victory pole, even as Hayes, still in good shape, crossed the finish himself. The Americans wasted no time in lodging a protest, and while Dorando, who had been carried away on a stretcher, lay seemingly on the verge of death, the protest was allowed and Hayes was declared the winner.

Remarkably, Dorando was back on his feet the next day, complaining that the British officials should have left him alone and that he could have finished without their assistance. However, photos of the incident make it quite clear that this was highly unlikely, and that the stretcher probably should have been called for the first time he fell. At any rate, Dorando showed up at the stadium the day after the race and was presented with a special gold cup by the Queen. Overnight he became an international celebrity. Even in the United States, songs were written about him, including one by Irving Berlin. Unfortunately, Berlin completely missed the point of what had happened, entitling his song, "Dorando He'sa Gooda for Not," and portraying the courageous Italian as a "bigga de flop."

Somewhat lost in the excitement was the actual winner, John Hayes, a 22-year-old clerk at Bloomingdale's department store in New York City. Hayes, who had prepared for the big race by resting in bed for two days, had finished fifth in the 1906 Boston Marathon and third in 1907, before winning the 1907 Yonkers Marathon on Thanksgiving Day. Mr. Bloomingdale himself had taken a liking to Hayes, and ordered the construction of a cinder path on the roof of his store so that Hayes could train during his breaks. When Hayes was chosen for the Olympic team, Bloomingdale gave him a full vacation with pay, and when he won the gold medal, Hayes was promoted to manager of the sporting goods department.

But this job was not to last long. Dorando's sensational effort in London had set off a marathon craze that swept around the world. He and Hayes were offered very good money to turn professional. Both of them did, and they each built up a good deal of capital running scores of races over the next couple of years, far more than Hayes could have earned at Bloomingdale's or than Dorando could have earned back in Capri. The most notable contests were two match races between Hayes and Dorando

held in New York City on November 25, 1908, and March 15, 1909, both of which were won by the Italian. Dorando, whose opportunistic brother ran off with his fortune, lived out his life driving a taxi in Italy. He also received a stipend from the Italian government for scouting promising marathon runners.

**1912 Stockholm** C: 68, N: 19, D: 7.14. WB: 2:42:31.0 (Frederick "Harry" Barrett)
**(40,200 Meters)**

| | | | |
|---|---|---|---|
| 1. Kenneth McArthur | SAF | 2:36:54.8 | |
| 2. Christian Gitsham | SAF | 2:37:52.0 | |
| 3. Gaston Strobino | USA | 2:38:42.4 | |
| 4. Andrew Sockalexis | USA | 2:42:07.9 | |
| 5. James Duffy | CAN | 2:42:18.8 | |
| 6. Sigfrid "Sigge" Jacobsson | SWE | 2:43:24.9 | |
| 7. John Gallagher | USA | 2:44:19.4 | |
| 8. Joseph Erxleben | USA | 2:45:47.4 | |

Once again, the Olympic marathon was held on an oppressively hot day that caused half of the runners to retire before the finish. Tatu Kolehmainen, the older brother of Hannes, took the lead before three miles had been covered, and held it until just before the turnaround point, when he was passed by Gitsham. McArthur was third, followed by Fred Lord. After 17 miles, Gitsham and Kolehmainen were running together, with McArthur only a meter or two behind. Two or three miles later, Kolehmainen was forced to retire, and the two South Africans went on alone. Two miles from the stadium they reached a refreshment stand, and Gitsham stopped to take a drink of water. McArthur had said he would wait for his teammate, but instead he kept on going, opening up a lead that Gitsham was unable to close. McArthur was a 30-year-old policeman who had emigrated from Ireland seven years earlier.

The 1912 marathon was marred by a sad note. The 21-year-old Portuguese runner Francisco Lazaro collapsed from sunstroke and heart trouble toward the end of the race and was taken to a hospital, where he died the following day. He was the first of only two athletes to die as a result of their participation in the Olympics.

**1920 Antwerp** C: 48, N: 17, D: 8.22. WB: 2:36:06:6 (Alexis Ahlgren)
**(42,750 Meters)**

| | | | |
|---|---|---|---|
| 1. Johan "Hannes" Kolehmainen | FIN | 2:32:35.8 | WB |
| 2. Jüri Lossmann | EST | 2:32:48.6 | |
| 3. Valerio Arri | ITA | 2:36:32.8 | |
| 4. Auguste Broos | BEL | 2:39:25.8 | |
| 5. Jaako Tuomikoski | FIN | 2:40:10.8 | |
| 6. Sofus Rose | DEN | 2:41:18.0 | |
| 7. Joseph Organ | USA | 2:41:30.8 | |
| 8. Rudolf Hansen | DEN | 2:41:40.9 | |

At last the Olympic marathon was contested on a cool day, and the runners responded with excellent times, particularly considering that the course was longer than ever before. Christian Gitsham took the early lead, but after 15 kilometers he was joined by Hannes Kolehmainen, who had returned from Brooklyn to compete for Finland. They reached the turnaround together, but after 27 kilometers, Kolehmainen moved ahead and began to draw away. Gitsham, suffering from foot trouble after one of his shoes tore open, retired after 35 kilometers. Meanwhile, Jüri Lossmann of Estonia closed the gap that separated him from the famous Finn, but Kolehmainen managed to hold on to his lead and win by 70 yards—the closest marathon finish in Olympic history.

In direct contrast to previous marathons, the runners finished in good health. Valerio Arri, the Italian champion, even celebrated his bronze medal by performing three cartwheels as soon as he crossed the finish line.

**1924 Paris** C: 58, N: 20, D: 7.13. WB: 2:32:35.8 (Johan "Hannes" Kolehmainen)

| | | | |
|---|---|---|---|
| 1. Albin Stenroos | FIN | 2:41:22.6 |
| 2. Romeo Bertini | ITA | 2:47:19.6 |
| 3. Clarence DeMar | USA | 2:48:14.0 |
| 4. Lauri Halonen | FIN | 2:49:47.4 |
| 5. Samuel Ferris | GBR | 2:52:26.0 |
| 6. Miguel Plaza Reyes | CHI | 2:52:54.0 |
| 7. Boughèra El Ouafi | FRA | 2:54:19.6 |
| 8. Gustav Kinn | SWE | 2:54:33.4 |

Albin Stenroos, a 35-year-old woodworker, had won a bronze medal in the 1912 10,000 meters race. However he did not run a single marathon between 1909 and May 18, 1924, when he placed second in the Finnish Olympic trial. In Paris, he passed G. Verger of France after 19½ kilometers, and steadily drew away to a huge lead, winning by almost six minutes. Silver medalist Romeo Bertini was 31 years old, while bronze medalist Clarence DeMar was 36. In 1930 DeMar won his seventh Boston Marathon at the age of 42. In the 1924 Olympics, 28 of the 58 starters failed to finish the course.

**1928 Amsterdam** C: 68, N: 23, D: 8.5. WB: 2:29:01.8 (Albert Michelsen)

| | | | |
|---|---|---|---|
| 1. Boughèra El Ouafi | FRA | 2:32:57 |
| 2. Miguel Plaza Reyes | CHI | 2:33:23 |
| 3. Martti Marttelin | FIN | 2:35:02 |
| 4. Kanematsu Yamada | JPN | 2:35:29 |
| 5. Joie Ray | USA | 2:36:04 |
| 6. Seiichiro Tsuda | JPN | 2:36:20 |
| 7. Yrjo Korholin-Koski | FIN | 2:36:40 |
| 8. Samuel Ferris | GBR | 2:37:41 |

The lead changed several times during the first half of the race, with Joie Ray in first place at the turnaround. Shortly thereafter he was passed by Yamada and Tsuda. These three remained in front past 30 kilometers. By this time two outsiders, Algerian-born Boughèra El Ouafi and Miguel Plaza of Chile, had moved up to challenge. Plaza had evidently decided to run the race on El Ouafi's shoulder, just as he had four years earlier. Three kilometers short of the finish they had taken over second and third place, finally wearing down Yamada during the ap-

proach to the stadium. Both El Ouafi and Plaza finished strongly, with El Ouafi winning by about 150 meters. The victor was a former member of the French Colonial Army who had settled in Paris and was employed as an automobile mechanic. Twenty-eight years later, when another French-Arab, Alain Mimoun, won the Olympic marathon, journalists sought out El Ouafi and discovered him unemployed and living in poverty in Paris. French sportsmen got together a fund to help the forgotten hero of Amsterdam. However, three years later, on October 18, 1959, El Ouafi was shot to death while sitting in a café. He was 60 years old.

**1932 Los Angeles** C: 29, N: 15, D: 8.7. WB: 2:29:01.8 (Albert Michelsen)

| | | | |
|---|---|---|---|
| 1. Juan Carlos Zabala | ARG | 2:31:36 | OR |
| 2. Samuel Ferris | GBR | 2:31:55 | |
| 3. Armas Toivonen | FIN | 2:32:12 | |
| 4. Duncan McLeod Wright | GBR | 2:32:41 | |
| 5. Seiichiro Tsuda | JPN | 2:35:42 | |
| 6. Kim Eun-bae | KOR | 2:37:28 | |
| 7. Albert Michelsen | USA | 2:39:38 | |
| 8. Oskar Heks | CZE | 2:41:35 | |

Paavo Nurmi had been considered the favorite to win the 1932 marathon, until he was suspended by the I.A.A.F. one week before the race for accepting payments in excess of his expenses during an exhibition tour. Juan Carlos Zabala, a 20-year-old Argentinian, had set a world record at 30,000 meters in 1931. On June 25, 1932, the *Los Angeles Times* sponsored a marathon race over the Olympic course. Zabala built up an eight-and-a-half-minute lead in that race, but developed foot problems and was ordered to withdraw by his trainer. Albert Michelsen went on to win.

Zabala took the early lead in the Olympics. He was passed briefly by Margarito Baños of Mexico, but regained the lead and held it for over 30 kilometers. At the 31-kilometer mark, Lauri Virtanen, who had already finished third in the 10,000 and 5000, sprinted ahead suddenly and opened up a 300-meter gap. This shook up the field, and there was much jockeying for position. Duncan Wright, following a well-laid-out British plan, forged to the front after 20 miles (35.5 kilometers), and as Virtanen faded, he moved a full minute ahead of Zabala, with Toivonen another half-minute further back. By 37 kilometers, Virtanen had dropped out and Wright had begun to fade. Zabala moved back into the lead, and Sam Ferris, taking over second place, took off after him. But he had waited too long. Zabala entered the Coliseum with a one-minute lead and was almost three quarters of the way around the track when Ferris appeared, followed closely by Toivonen and Wright. Thus, the crowd was treated to the rare spectacle of the first four finishers of the marathon being on the track at the same time. Zabala struggled across the finish line and then collapsed, whereas Ferris was still full of strength and probably would have won had the race continued for an extra half lap.

**1936 Berlin** C: 56, N: 27, D: 8.9. WB: 2:26:42.0 (Sohn Kee-chung)
1. Sohn Kee-chung     KOR    2:29:19.2    OR
2. Ernest Harper     GBR    2:31:23.2
3. Nam Seung-yong     KOR    2:31:42.0
4. Erkki Tamila     FIN    2:32:45.0
5. Väinö Muinonen     FIN    2:33:46.0
6. Johannes Coleman     SAF    2:36:17.0
7. Donald Robertson     GBR    2:37:06.2
8. Henry Gibson     SAF    2:38:04.0

On November 3, 1935, Sohn Kee-chung of Korea set a world marathon record of 2:26:42.0. Because Korea was, at the time, occupied by Japanese forces, Sohn's hopes for competing in the Olympics depended on his ability to qualify for the Japanese team. This he accomplished, as did fellow Korean Nam Seung-yong. Both young men were forced to endure the further insult of adopting Japanese names. Sohn, a fervent nationalist, always signed his Korean name in Berlin, and whenever he was asked where he was from, he made it a point to explain that Korea was a separate nation which was currently a victim of Japanese imperialism.

Defending champion Juan Carlos Zabala had arrived in Berlin months in advance, and during his period of extended training had become a local favorite, particularly in the absence of a serious German threat in the marathon. As usual, Zabala tore into the lead and was 30 seconds in front at the four-kilometer mark. After 15 kilometers he was ahead by 1 minute and 40 seconds. He let the margin slip to 50 seconds at the turnaround, but pumped it back up to 90 seconds after 25 kilometers. For quite some time, Zabala had been followed by Sohn and 34-year-old Ernest Harper, who had been running together since the beginning. However, it came as a shock to Zabala when, after 28 kilometers, he was suddenly passed, first by Sohn and, ten meters later, by Harper. Zabala fell, got up, struggled on for four more kilometers, and then retired. Meanwhile, Sohn pulled away and won by over two minutes. Harper finished heroically, holding off the fast-closing Nam despite a bad blister that had filled one of his shoes with blood.

At the medal ceremony Sohn was forced to endure the humiliation of having his victory celebrated by the raising of the Japanese flag and by the playing of the Japanese national anthem. Both Sohn and Nam registered a silent protest by bowing their heads. Interviewed by the press afterwards, Sohn used the opportunity to educate the world about the plight of his nation. Few reporters were interested, and most seemed relieved when he turned to the race itself. "The human body can do so much," he said. "Then the heart and spirit must take over."

Back in Korea, however, Sohn was a national hero. One newspaper, *Dong-a-Ilbo,* published a wire-service photograph of Sohn on the victory platform—but with one alteration: they painted over the Japanese flag on his sweatshirt. The Japanese colonial government responded by jailing eight people connected with the paper and suspending its publication for nine months.

In 1948 Sohn was given the honor of carrying the South Korean flag in the Opening Ceremonies of the London Olympics, the first to be attended by an independent Korea. Forty years later, in a moment that brought tears to an entire nation, Sohn Kee-chung entered the Seoul Olympic Stadium bearing the Olympic torch. The 76-year-old Sohn bounded around the track, leaping for joy and bursting with pride for himself and for his country.

**1948 London** C: 41, N: 21, D: 8.7. WB: 2:25:39.0 (Suh Yun-bok)
1. Delfo Cabrera     ARG    2:34:51.6
2. Thomas Richards     GBR    2:35:07.6
3. Etienne Gailly     BEL    2:35:33.6
4. Johannes Coleman     SAF    2:36:06.0
5. Eusebio Guinez     ARG    2:36:36.0
6. Thomas Sidney Luyt     SAF    2:38:11.0
7. Gustav Ostling     SWE    2:38:40.6
8. John Systad     NOR    2:38:41.0

Twenty-five-year-old Etienne Gailly, running his first race longer than 32.5 kilometers, was in the lead by the ten-kilometer post and had opened up a 41-second gap by 25 kilometers, at which point he was followed by Guinez, Ostling, and Cabrera. The field then began to close in on him, and after 32.5 kilometers he was passed by Choi Yoon-chil of Korea. At 35 kilometers, Choi led by 28 seconds, with Delfo Cabrera, a 29-year-old fireman also running his first marathon, in second place. Gailly was third and Guinez fourth.

But Choi had used up all his energy and soon retired. Five thousand meters from Wembley Stadium, Cabrera led Gailly by five seconds. Tom Richards, a 38-year-old Welsh nurse, had moved into third place. Gailly gathered his strength and regained the lead. A half mile from the stadium, he led Cabrera by 50 yards and Richards by 100. The exhausted Belgian was the first to enter the stadium, but by now he was barely running. Spectators were immediately reminded of the ordeal endured by Dorando Pietri the last time the Olympics had been held in London. Gailly managed to stay on his feet, but before he had covered 100 yards of the track, he was passed by Cabrera and then by Richards. Gailly staggered on, almost collapsing 60 yards short of his goal. But he did finally cross the finish line and gain a well-earned bronze medal, much to the relief of the sympathetic crowd. In fourth place was 38-year-old Johannes Coleman, who had finished sixth in the last Olympics 12 years earlier.

**1952 Helsinki** C: 66, N: 32, D: 7.27. WB: 2:20:42.2 (James Peters)
1. Emil Zátopek     CZE    2:23:03.2    OR
2. Reinaldo Gorno     ARG    2:25:35.0
3. Gustav Jansson     SWE    2:26:07.0
4. Choi Yoon-chil     KOR    2:26:36.0
5. Veikko Karvonen     FIN    2:26:41.8
6. Delfo Cabrera     ARG    2:26:42.4
7. József Dobronyi     HUN    2:28:04.8
8. Erkki Puolakka     FIN    2:29:35.0

Emil Zátopek was born in Koprivnice, Northern Moravia, on September 19, 1922, the exact same day that his wife, Dana, was born. He made his first appearance in the Olympics in 1948, finishing first in the 10,000 meters and second at 5000. Whenever he ran, his face was always contorted by a grimace, and his shoulders and body looked hunched with pain. Observers, on first viewing Zátopek, were sure that he was on the verge of collapse, but it turned out that that was just his style. Years later Zátopek was asked about this idiosyncrasy. He replied, "I was not talented enough to run and smile at the same time."

In 1952 Zátopek became the first runner since Hannes Kolehmainen to win both the 5000- and 10,000-meter races. But that wasn't enough for Zátopek. He decided to attempt an unprecedented triple by also competing in the marathon. The fact that he had never run a marathon before bothered him only slightly. He wasn't concerned about coming up with the necessary endurance, but it did worry him a bit that there might be pacing strategies with which he was not familiar. With this in mind, Zátopek decided to run along with the man whom he considered to be the favorite in the race—Jim Peters of Great Britain, who had run the fastest marathon in history only six weeks earlier. Zátopek took note of Peters' running number in the newspaper, and the next day he located Peters on the starting line and introduced himself.

Peters took off at what seemed to be an outlandish pace, but Zátopek, as well as Gustaf Jansson, kept contact with him. After 15 kilometers Zátopek and Jansson caught up with Peters, and the three ran together for a couple of miles. Then Zátopek turned to Peters and said, in English, "The pace? Is it good enough?" Peters, who had exhausted himself with his early running, pretended that he was still fresh, and replied, "Pace too slow." Zátopek mulled this over for a few moments and then said, "You say, 'too slow.' Are you sure the pace is too slow?" "Yes," came the reply. They continued on in silence for a short while, and then Zátopek zipped by Peters, taking Jansson with him.

They passed the turnaround together, with Peters ten seconds behind. Now Zátopek had to deal with Jansson. "He stopped at one feeding station," Zátopek later recalled, "and picked up a slice of lemon to suck. I was not so sure. I had never taken anything before in racing or training. But I thought, 'If he runs well, at the next feeding station I will take *two* lemons.' " Instead, Jansson began to fade. After 20 miles Peters developed a leg cramp and dropped out. By this time Zátopek had shaken off Jansson completely, and he was able to continue alone, chatting amiably with policemen, spectators, and cyclists along the route. He entered the stadium far ahead of the other runners. The huge crowd greeted him as the hero of the 1952 Games, chanting "Zá-to-pek, Zá-to-pek," as he completed the final lap. The Jamaican 4 × 400-meter relay team hoisted him on their shoulders and carried him around the field. Zátopek was already sign-

ing autographs by the time the next runner, the surprising Reinaldo Gorno, arrived. Zátopek greeted him at the finish line with a slice of orange.

Despite his convincing victory, Zátopek later said, "I was unable to walk for a whole week after that, so much did the race take out of me. But it was the most pleasant exhaustion I have ever known."

Emil Zátopek also entered the Olympic marathon in 1956. But six weeks before the Games he had developed a hernia while trying to train with his wife on his shoulders. His doctors told him not to run for two months after his operation, but instead he resumed training the day after he left the hospital. Under the circumstances, his sixth-place finish could hardly be considered a failure.

Zátopek had been a member of the Czech army since 1944. His athletic successes gained him promotion to the rank of lieutenant-colonel, as well as a prominent position in the Communist Party. However, Emil Zátopek was not really a party man. In 1968 he signed the *2000 Words Manifesto,* which supported the establishment of freedom in Czechoslovakia. When Soviet tanks moved in and crushed the growing democratic movement in Czechoslovakia, Zátopek was expelled from both the army and the Communist Party. The only work he could find was a construction job, digging ditches and hauling sacks of cement for a geological survey team. Seven years later, the Ministry of Sport, taking advantage of his facility with languages, hired him as a "sports spy," translating sports periodicals in a search for tips from foreign coaches. He served in this capacity until his retirement in 1982.

Emil Zátopek has left an indelible impression on the world of sports that goes beyond his four gold medals and 18 world records. Unlike his predecessor Paavo Nurmi, Zátopek was greatly loved by his fellow competitors, as well as by all those who have had the good fortune to meet him personally.

**1956 Melbourne** C: 46, N: 23, D: 12.1. WB: 2:17:39.4 (James Peters)

| | | | |
|---|---|---|---|
| 1. | Alain Mimoun O'Kacha | FRA | 2:25:00 |
| 2. | Franjo Mihalič | YUG | 2:26:32 |
| 3. | Veikko Karvonen | FIN | 2:27:47 |
| 4. | Lee Chang-hoon | KOR | 2:28:45 |
| 5. | Yoshiaki Kawashima | JPN | 2:29:19 |
| 6. | Emil Zátopek | CZE | 2:29:34 |
| 7. | Ivan Filin | SOV | 2:30:27 |
| 8. | Evert Nyberg | SWE | 2:31:12 |

Thirty-five-year-old Algerian-born Alain Mimoun had made a habit of finishing second to Emil Zátopek—three times in the Olympics and twice in the European championships. But he was sure that December 1, 1956, would be his lucky day. Frenchmen had won the Olympic marathon in 1900, and then 28 years later in 1928. Now, 28 more years had passed. In addition, Mimoun was wearing what he considered to be the lucky number 13. As if these weren't enough good omens, he had just learned that he had become a father.

For the first time in Olympic history, there was a false start in the marathon. Mimoun stayed with the leading group for the first half of the race. Then he surged forward during an uphill segment before the turnaround. By the 25-kilometer mark he had opened a 50-second gap, and no one came close to him again. For the third time in a row, the Olympic marathon had been won by a converted track star competing in his first marathon.

At the finish line Mimoun waited for his old friend Emil Zátopek, who trotted home in a trance four and a half minutes later. "Emil," he asked, "why don't you congratulate me? I am an Olympic champion. It was I who won." Zátopek snapped out of his trance, took off his cap, saluted Mimoun, and then embraced him. "For me," Mimoun recalled, "that was better than the medal."

Surprisingly, Mimoun's marathon career had only just begun. He proceeded to win the French championship six times, the last in 1966, when he was 42 years old. At the age of 51, Mimoun completed the 26-mile, 385-yard race in a time of 2:34:36.2.

**1960 Rome** C: 69, N: 35, D: 9.10. WB: 2:15:17.0 (Sergei Popov)

| | | | | |
|---|---|---|---|---|
| 1. | Abebe Bikila | ETH | 2:15:16.2 | WB |
| 2. | Rhadi Ben Abdesselem | MOR | 2:15:41.6 | |
| 3. | Barry Magee | NZE | 2:17:18.2 | |
| 4. | Konstantin Vorobyev | SOV | 2:19:09.6 | |
| 5. | Sergei Popov | SOV | 2:19:18.8 | |
| 6. | Thyge Törgersen | DEN | 2:21:03.4 | |
| 7. | Abebe Wakgira | ETH | 2:21:10.0 | |
| 8. | Bakir Benaissa | MOR | 2:21:22.0 | |

The 1960 Olympic marathon was the first to be run at night, the first to start and end outside the stadium, and, as it turned out, the first to be won by a black African. After 18 kilometers, two men pulled away from the field: Rhadi Ben Abdesselem, who was one of the favorites, and barefooted Abebe Bikila, who was not. A member of the Ethiopian Imperial Bodyguard, the 28-year-old Abebe was running in his third marathon. The two ran side by side, mile after mile, never looking at each other, along a course lit by torches held by Italian soldiers, and lined by thousands of spectators who had to be restrained from interfering with the runners.

Reconnoitering the route some days earlier, Abebe and his Swedish coach, Onni Niskanen, had noticed that less than a mile from the finish line at the Arch of Constantine was the obelisk of Axum, which had been plundered from Ethiopia by Italian troops and hauled off to Rome. It seemed appropriate that the slight incline that followed the obelisk would be the proper place for Abebe to make his final move. Although none of the experts had even considered that the Ethiopian would still be in contention by that point, Abebe was sure that he would be. Right on schedule he pulled away from Rhadi, and his lead had increased to almost 200 yards by the time he breasted the tape. His final obstacle was a typical Roman driver, who had lurched his motor scooter onto the course 60 yards from the end.

**1964 Tokyo** C: 68, N: 35, D: 10.21. WB: 2:13:55.0 (Basil Heatley)

| | | | | |
|---|---|---|---|---|
| 1. | Abebe Bikila | ETH | 2:12:11.2 | WB |
| 2. | Basil Heatley | GBR | 2:16:19.2 | |
| 3. | Kokichi Tsuburaya | JPN | 2:16:22.8 | |
| 4. | Brian Kilby | GBR | 2:17:02.4 | |
| 5. | József Sütö | HUN | 2:17:55.8 | |
| 6. | Leonard "Buddy" Edelen | USA | 2:18:12.4 | |
| 7. | Aurele Vandendriessche | BEL | 2:18:42.6 | |
| 8. | Kenji Kimihara | JPN | 2:19:49.0 | |

There was no clear-cut favorite in the 1964 marathon, with at least 15 runners in serious contention for the gold medal. Defending champion Abebe Bikila had undergone an appendectomy only 40 days before the race. The Australian Ron Clarke, running his fourth race in a week, rushed to an early lead, followed closely by Jim Hogan of Ireland. Abebe, running this time with shoes and socks, joined them before the seven-kilometer mark, and the three ran together for about half an hour. After 15 kilometers, Abebe, attempting to become the first person in history to win two Olympic marathons, began to apply pressure. By the turning point—Tobitakyumachi, in Chofu city—Clarke had fallen behind and Abebe was five seconds ahead of Hogan. From 25 kilometers on, Abebe moved ahead steadily until, ten kilometers later, he led Hogan by two and a half minutes. Hogan slowed to a walk and then dropped out, leaving Kokichi Tsuburaya, who was running only the fourth marathon of his career, in second place.

When Abebe Bikila entered the stadium, he was greeted by 75,000 waving and cheering spectators. After crossing the finish line in the fastest marathon time ever recorded, Abebe entertained the crowd by doing stretching and bicycling exercises and generally looking like he was sorry the race had been so short. He told the press that he could have kept up the pace for another ten kilometers. At the medal ceremony later in the day, none of the Japanese officials knew the Ethiopian national anthem, so the band took the opportunity to play the Japanese anthem instead.

Tsuburaya was the second man to enter the stadium, followed ten yards later by Heatley. Despite the encouragement of the hometown crowd, Tsuburaya was exhausted, and when Heatley moved past him before the final curve, he was unable to respond. However, Tsuburaya's third-place finish brought him Japan's first track and field medal in 28 years, and he became a national hero.

Unfortunately, Kokichi Tsuburaya met a tragic end. A member of the Training School of the Japanese Ground Self-Defense Force, after the 1964 race he was ordered to stop seeing his fiancée and to begin training immediately for the 1968 Olympics. But in 1967 he suffered two injuries and was forced to spend three months in the hospital. The doctors declared him completely recovered, but when Tsuburaya started running again, he realized that his body had been irreversibly weakened and that he could not possibly win the next Olympic marathon. On January 9, 1968, two months after his release from the hospital and nine months before the Mexico Olympics, Kokichi Tsuburaya ended his own life by cutting his right carotid artery with a razor blade. Beside him was a piece of paper on which he had written a single phrase: "Cannot run anymore."

Abebe Bikila also came up against tragedy. He entered the 1968 marathon, but had to withdraw after 17 kilometers because of a bone fracture in his leg. The following year he was driving his Volkswagen, a gift from the government following his second gold medal, when he crashed. He suffered a broken neck and a spinal cord injury that left him paralyzed below the waist. Confined to a wheelchair for the rest of his life, he died of a brain hemorrhage on October 25, 1973, at the age of 41.

**1968 Mexico City** C: 74, N: 41, D: 10.20. WB: 2:09:36.4 (Derek Clayton)

| | | | |
|---|---|---|---|
| 1. | Mamo Wolde | ETH | 2:20:26.4 |
| 2. | Kenji Kimihara | JPN | 2:23:31.0 |
| 3. | Michael Ryan | NZE | 2:23:45.0 |
| 4. | Ismail Akcay | TUR | 2:25:18.8 |
| 5. | William Adcocks | GBR | 2:25:33.0 |
| 6. | Merawi Gebru | ETH | 2:27:16.8 |
| 7. | Derek Clayton | AUS | 2:27:23.8 |
| 8. | Timothy Johnston | GBR | 2:28:04.4 |

Mamo Wolde had a long and unusual involvement in the Olympics. His first appearance was in Melbourne in 1956, where he had entered the 800 and 1500, and finished last in his heat in both events. He also ran the third leg for the Ethiopian 4 × 400 relay team, which finished last in its heat. He did not compete in 1960, but he was back in 1964. He failed to complete the marathon, but placed fourth in the 10,000. In 1968 he finished a close second to Naftali Temu in the 10,000, a week before the marathon. In the later race, Wolde and Temu let others set the pace without allowing the leaders to get too far ahead. Then, about the halfway mark, they picked up the pace considerably and left the others behind. Shortly after 30 kilometers Temu ran out of steam and began to drift back, eventually finishing 19th. This left Wolde with almost a two-minute lead at 35 kilometers. He went on to win as easily as Abebe Bikila had four years earlier. At the age of 36, he had finally come out from the shadow of his famous teammate and won an Olympic gold medal.

**1972 Munich** C: 69, N: 35, D: 9.10. WB: 2:08:33.6 (Derek Clayton)

| | | | |
|---|---|---|---|
| 1. | Frank Shorter | USA | 2:12:19.8 |
| 2. | Karel Lismont | BEL | 2:14:31.8 |
| 3. | Mamo Wolde | ETH | 2:15:08.4 |
| 4. | Kenneth Moore | USA | 2:15:39.8 |
| 5. | Kenji Kimihara | JPN | 2:16:27.0 |
| 6. | Ronald Hill | GBR | 2:16:30.6 |
| 7. | Donald Macgregor | GBR | 2:16:34.4 |
| 8. | Jack Foster | NZE | 2:16:56.2 |

Munich-born Yale graduate Frank Shorter, annoyed by the slow pace, took the lead before the fifteen-kilometer mark and pulled away steadily as the race progressed. He was never challenged. Quite naturally, he entered the stadium expecting to be greeted by cheers and applause. Instead, all he heard was whistling and booing, and he wondered what he had done wrong. Unbeknownst to Shorter, a hoaxer had appeared on the track a couple of minutes before him and run a full lap before being hustled away by security guards. The sounds of derision had been aimed at the hoaxer, not at Shorter. The silver medal went to previously undefeated Karel Lismont, and the bronze to Mamo Wolde, who ran his fastest marathon ever at the age of 40. Eighth-place finisher Jack Foster was also 40 years old. After the race, Shorter went back to his room and celebrated his victory by drinking three gins in the bathtub.

**1976 Montreal** C: 67, N: 35, D: 7.31. WB: 2:08:33.6 (Derek Clayton)

| | | | | |
|---|---|---|---|---|
| 1. | Waldemar Cierpinski | GDR | 2:09:55.0 | OR |
| 2. | Frank Shorter | USA | 2:10:45.8 | |
| 3. | Karel Lismont | BEL | 2:11:12.6 | |
| 4. | Donald Kardong | USA | 2:11:15.8 | |
| 5. | Lasse Viren | FIN | 2:13:10.8 | |
| 6. | Jerome Drayton | CAN | 2:13:30.0 | |
| 7. | Leonid Moseyev | SOV | 2:13:33.4 | |
| 8. | Franco Fava | ITA | 2:14:24.6 | |

Defending champion Frank Shorter looked like the man to beat in 1976, although Lasse Viren was an unknown quantity. Viren had already run 30,000 meters during the last seven days, including victories in the 10,000 and, 24 hours before the marathon, in the 5,000. This was his first marathon race. Bill Rodgers of the United States, who eventually finished 40th, guided the leading pack through the first ten kilometers, but the real action didn't begin until just before the 25-kilometer mark, when Shorter surged through the rain, leaving the others behind. Viren tried to keep up for 200 meters, but fell back. About four minutes later, Waldemar Cierpinski, a relatively unknown converted steeplechaser from East Germany, who had entered his first marathon on a whim in 1974, decided that Shorter wasn't really running so fast after all, and caught up with him.

"It was a wonderful feeling when I came alongside," Cierpinski later recalled. "I glanced at Shorter as I did so, and looked right into the eyes of the man who was my idol as a marathon runner. I knew all about him. And yet I could tell by the return glance that he didn't know much, if anything, about me. The psychological advantage was mine." In fact, for the entire race, Shorter thought Cierpinski was actually Carlos Lopes of Portugal. Cierpinski's coaches had told him to annoy Shorter by getting as close to his body as possible. This he did, until a couple shoves separated them. Shorter made periodic surges, but each time Cierpinski caught him. Then, after 34 kilometers, they disappeared from the sight of the crowds and the cameras during a short stretch through the campus of McGill University. When they emerged again, Cierpinski had taken the lead and begun to draw away. Shorter tried to close the gap, but couldn't.

Cierpinski entered the stadium just as the band had finished playing the East German national anthem to celebrate the victory of the women's 4 × 400-meter relay team. When he reached the finish line, Cierpinski noticed that the lap indicator read "1." Confused, he continued running for another lap and was surprised, when he crossed the finish again, to find Frank Shorter waiting to congratulate him.

Cierpinski's victory came as a shock even to his fellow countrymen. Back in the Olympic Village, the East German soccer team watched the race on television while waiting for their final match against Poland. Goalie Jürgen Croy later recalled, "We just sat there staring at each other, thinking that if this living example of mediocrity can lift himself up and win the marathon, and we don't beat Poland, we are never going to hear the end of it." They won.

**1980 Moscow** C: 74, N: 40, D: 8.1. WB: 2:08:33.6 (Derek Clayton)

| 1. | Waldemar Cierpinski | GDR | 2:11:03 |
|----|---------------------|-----|---------|
| 2. | Gerard Nijboer | HOL | 2:11:20 |
| 3. | Satymkul Dzhumanazarov | SOV | 2:11:35 |
| 4. | Vladimir Kotov | SOV | 2:12:05 |
| 5. | Leonid Moseyev | SOV | 2:12:14 |
| 6. | Rodolfo Gomez | MEX | 2:12:39 |
| 7. | Dereje Nedi | ETH | 2:12:44 |
| 8. | Massimo Magnani | ITA | 2:13:12 |

Vladimir Kotov led for the first half of the race. After 24 kilometers, Lasse Viren, who had been running with the leaders, suddenly rushed off into the bushes with diarrhea. He dropped out three kilometers later. Rodolfo Gomez took advantage of Viren's indisposition to jump into the lead, quickly opening a 100-meter gap. At the 30-kilometer mark, he led by 23 seconds. However, five and a half kilometers later he was passed by Gerard Nijboer. Six hundred meters further along, Cierpinski passed them both, and was never headed. He ran the last 200 meters in 33.4 seconds and won by about 80 meters. As he crossed the finish line, there were five runners on the track, an Olympic record. Although he was only two days shy of his 30th birthday, Waldemar Cierpinski was still described by East German sources as a "sports student." After becoming the only person besides Abebe Bikila to win two Olympic marathons, he was elevated to "sports teacher."

**1984 Los Angeles** C: 107, N: 60, D: 8.12. WB: 2:08.18 (F. Robert de Castella)

| 1. | Carlos Lopes | POR | 2:09:21 | OR |
|----|--------------|-----|---------|----|
| 2. | John Treacy | IRL | 2:09:56 | |
| 3. | Charles Spedding | GBR | 2:09:58 | |
| 4. | Takeshi So | JPN | 2:10:55 | |
| 5. | F. Robert de Castella | AUS | 2:11:09 | |
| 6. | Juma Ikangaa | TAN | 2:11:10 | |
| 7. | Joseph Nzau | KEN | 2:11:28 | |
| 8. | Djama Robleh | DJI | 2:11:39 | |

The 1984 men's marathon was an eagerly awaited race with a talent-packed field that included seven different runners who had clocked times under 2 hours and 9 minutes. The leading favorites were world champion Rob de Castella, who had won all four marathons he had run in the last 3½ years, and the reclusive Japanese star, Toshihiko Seko, whose last loss in 1979 had been followed by five victories. Among the other highly regarded entrants was Carlos Lopes, the 1976 Olympic silver medalist at 10,000 meters. Lopes had completed only one of three marathons he had attempted, but that was a two-second loss to de Castella in 1983, in which he had pushed de Castella to his best time ever.

Not surprisingly, the Olympic marathon was closely fought for the first half of the race. By the 25-kilometer mark, Juma Ikangaa, one of the sub-2:09 men, was heading a lead pack that still contained twelve runners. At the 20-mile mark, de Castella slowed down to grab a cup of water and looked up to discover himself 50 meters behind the pack. He was never able to close the gap. The lead pack was down to seven. A mile later, Seko lost contact. Then Charlie Spedding, a dark horse despite having won the Houston and London Marathons earlier in the year, forced the pace. The only ones who were able to stay with him were the 37-year old Lopes and John Treacy, who was running his first marathon. Treacy had placed ninth in the 10,000-meter run six days earlier.

Then Lopes turned on the pressure, running the next five kilometers in 14 minutes 33 seconds, a remarkable achievement, considering he had just run 21½ hot and humid miles against the best marathon field ever assembled. Spedding and Treacy had no choice but to let him go. Lopes breezed ahead to win the gold medal. Treacy ran a 67-second last lap to earn the silver, while Spedding, whose dedication was so great that he had foresworn alc for an entire week before the race, happily settled for the bronze. De Castella finished fifth and Seko fourteenth.

World-class athletes often face unexpected obstacles on their way to the Olympics. Lopes, for example, was hit by a Mercedes-Benz while training only fifteen days before the Olympic marathon. "There goes the Olympics," Lopes thought, as he rolled over the hood and watched his elbow crash through the windshield. As luck would have it, his injuries were minor. The same could not be said of the unfortunate Richard Mbewa, the Tanzanian marathon alternate, who was shot to death while jogging on a golf course by a policeman who mistook him for a thief. And then there is the story of the 78th and last man to cross the finish line in the 1984 Olympic marathon: Dieudonne Lamothe of Haiti. When last heard from, Lamothe had competed in the 1976 5000-meter race, recording the slowest time in Olympic history, but insisting on finishing. While in Los Angeles in 1984, Lamothe did not speak to the press. However, after the fall of Haitian dictator Baby Doc Duvalier, Lamothe revealed that Haitian Olympic officials had threatened to kill him if he failed to finish. He did make it across the finish line—in 2 hours 52 minutes and 18 seconds, a much more respectable time than his 1976 performance. In 1988, under considerably less pressure, Lamothe placed 20th in 2:16:15.

**1988 Seoul** C: 118, N: 66, D: 10.2. WB: 2:06:50 (Belayneh Densimo)

| | | | |
|---|---|---|---|
| 1. | Gelindo Bordin | ITA | 2:10:32 |
| 2. | Douglas Wakiihuri | KEN | 2:10:47 |
| 3. | Ahmed Saleh | DJI | 2:10:59 |
| 4. | Takeyuki Nakayama | JPN | 2:11:05 |
| 5. | Stephen Moneghetti | AUS | 2:11:49 |
| 6. | Charles Spedding | GBR | 2:12:19 |
| 7. | Juma Ikangaa | TAN | 2:13:06 |
| 8. | F. Robert de Castella | AUS | 2:13:07 |

The 1988 men's marathon was run in humid weather along a route lined with 36,000 policemen. By the 25-kilometer mark Juma Ikangaa was leading a pack of 13. Four kilometers later the pace was forced by the 1986 European champion, Gelindo Bordin, who, back in April 1981, had been presumed dead after being hit from behind by a car while training in Verona.

By 30 kilometers the lead pack was down to Bordin; Nakayama, who had won two marathons on the Seoul course in 1985 and 1986; world champion Douglas Wakiihuri; the favorite, Ahmed Saleh, who had also triumphed on the Seoul course at the 1987 World Cup; Ikangaa; Charlie Spedding; and Toshihiko Seko, whose disappointing performance at the 1984 Olympics remained his only loss in 9 years. After 31 kilometers Nakayama surged, causing Spedding and Seko to fall behind, the latter eventually finishing ninth. Spedding fought his way back over the next few kilometers, but 400 meters past the 35-kilometer mark, Saleh and Nakayama increased the pace, and Spedding and Ikangaa lost contact for good. Just short of 37 kilometers, Nakayama fell back as well.

With 3 miles left, the medals were to be decided among Saleh, Wakiihuri, and Bordin, the same three who had medaled at the 1987 world championships in Rome. In that race the then unknown Wakiihuri had run away from Saleh just before the 38-kilometer mark, while Bordin had come from behind to snatch the bronze from Steve Moneghetti.

Now, 13 months later, it was Saleh who broke away at 38 kilometers, gradually opening a lead of about 25 meters over Wakiihuri. Bordin, exhausted and suffering leg cramps, resigned himself to third place. In order to distract himself from worrying about Nakayama behind him, Bordin focused his attention on Wakiihuri's back. One and a half miles from the finish, Bordin suddenly

realized, to his great surprise, that he was gaining on the Kenyan. At 40 kilometers he passed him and set his sights on Saleh, who was now in pain and looking back frequently. At 40.5 kilometers Saleh glanced over his left shoulder and didn't see Bordin. He looked over his right shoulder and there he was, with a smile on his face, only 3 meters behind.

Fifty meters later Bordin drove past Saleh and, another 250 meters on, so did Wakiihuri. Bordin went on to win the closest Olympic marathon in 68 years. As soon as he crossed the finish line he crossed himself, then knelt down and kissed the track. Approached by reporters, he described the last two kilometers as "a war" and commented that he was "too tired even to be happy."

## 110-METER HURDLES

Contestants must clear ten hurdles, each of which is 3 feet 6 inches high. The United States has dominated this event. Competing in 21 Olympics (including 1906), U.S. hurdlers have won eighteen gold medals, fourteen silver, and fifteen bronze.

**1896 Athens** C: 7, N: 6, D: 4.10. WR(120 yards): 15.4 (Stephen Chase)

| | | | |
|---|---|---|---|
| 1. | Thomas Curtis | USA | 17.6 |
| 2. | Grantley Goulding | GBR | 17.6e |

DNS: William Hoyt (USA) and Frantz Reichel (FRA)

Curtis won by about two inches.

**1900 Paris** C: 10, N: 4, D: 7.14. WR(120 yards): 15.2 (Alvin Kraenzlein)

| | | | | |
|---|---|---|---|---|
| 1. | Alvin Kraenzlein | USA | 15.4 | OR |
| 2. | John McLean | USA | 15.5 | |
| 3. | Frederick Moloney | USA | — | |
| 4. | Jean Lécuyer | FRA | — | |
| 5. | Norman Pritchard | IND | — | |

Alvin Kraenzlein won the first of his four gold medals at the 1900 Games. Kraenzlein was responsible for introducing the leg-extended style to hurdling.

**1904 St. Louis** C: 8, N: 2, D: 9.3. WR(120 yards): 15.2 (Alvin Kraenzlein)

| | | | |
|---|---|---|---|
| 1. | Frederick Schule | USA | 16.0 |
| 2. | Thaddeus Shideler | USA | 16.3 |
| 3. | Lesley Ashburner | USA | 16.4 |
| 4. | Frank Castleman | USA | — |

**1906 Athens** C: 15, N: 8, D: 5.1. WR(120 yards): 15.2 (Alvin Kraenzlein)

| | | | |
|---|---|---|---|
| 1. | Robert Leavitt | USA | 16.2 |
| 2. | Alfred Healey | GBR | 16.2 |
| 3. | Vincent Duncker | SAF | 16.3 |
| 4. | Hugo Friend | USA | 16.4 |
| 5. | Henri Molinié | FRA | — |
| 6. | G. Issidonis | GRE | — |

**1908 London** C: 25, N: 10, D: 7.25. WR(120 yards): 15.2 (Alvin Kraenzlein)
1. Forrest Smithson   USA   15.0   WR
2. John Garrels   USA   15.7
3. Arthur Shaw   USA   —
4. William Rand   USA   —

Smithson, of Portland, Oregon, shot into the lead before the first hurdle and won by five yards. There is an enduring anecdote that Smithson, while running the final, carried a Bible in one hand as a protest against Sunday competition. There is no evidence to support this otherwise admirable story. It is not mentioned in any contemporary newspaper accounts and none of Smithson's races were held on a Sunday. A much-reprinted photograph of Smithson clearing a hurdle while holding a Bible is clearly a posed shot not taken during competition.

**1912 Stockholm** C: 21, N: 9, D: 7.12. WR: 15.0 (Forrest Smithson)
1. Frederick Kelly   USA   15.1
2. James Wendell   USA   15.2
3. Martin Hawkins   USA   15.3
4. John Case   USA   15.3
5. Kenneth Powell   GBR   15.5
DNF: John Nicholson (USA)

**1920 Antwerp** C: 21, N: 13, D: 8.18. WR(120 yards): 14.4 (Earl Thomson)
1. Earl Thomson   CAN   14.8   WR
2. Harold Barron   USA   15.1
3. Frederick Murray   USA   15.2
4. Harry Wilson   NZE   15.3
5. Walker Smith   USA   —
6. Carl-Axel Christiernsson   SWE   —

Thomson was born in Saskatchewan, but grew up in Southern California from the age of 8. He represented Dartmouth in intercollegiate competition, but because he was still a Canadian citizen, he competed for Canada in the Olympics. Thomson, who survived a near-fatal rifle accident in 1914, took his hurdling very seriously, going so far as to tie his legs to the foot of his bed so that he wouldn't curl up and risk cramping. Thomson spent most of his life as a track coach, including 37 years as head coach of the Navy team at Annapolis. His Olympic time of 14.8 seconds was accepted as a world record even though his 14.4 for the slightly shorter distance of 120 yards was much more impressive.

**1924 Paris** C: 27, N: 15, D: 7.9. WR(120 yards): 14.4 (Earl Thomson)
1. Daniel Kinsey   USA   15.0
2. Sydney Atkinson   SAF   15.0
3. Sten Pettersson   SWE   15.4
4. Carl-Axel Christiernsson   SWE   15.5
5. Karl Anderson   USA   —
DISQ: George Guthrie (USA)

Atkinson was in the lead as he and Kinsey rose to clear the last hurdle. However, the South African clipped the barrier with his rear foot and stumbled. He recovered well, but lost by inches. Guthrie finished third, but was disqualified for knocking over three hurdles.

**1928 Amsterdam** C: 41, N: 24, D: 8.1. WR(120 yards): 14.4 (Earl Thomson)
1. Sydney Atkinson   SAF   14.8
2. Stephen Anderson   USA   14.8
3. John Collier   USA   14.9
4. Leighton Dye   USA   14.9
5. George Weightman-Smith   SAF   15.0
6. Frederick Gaby   GBR   15.2

In the semifinals, Weightman-Smith set a metric world record of 14.6 seconds. The finalists awaited the draw for lanes with great apprehension, as the inside lane had been severely chewed up by rain and overuse. It was Syd Atkinson, who had come so close to victory four years earlier, who drew the unwanted lane. However, Weightman-Smith walked over to his bitterly disappointed teammate and offered to switch lanes. Atkinson refused, but Weightman-Smith insisted, and the change was made. Taking full advantage of his reprieve, Atkinson finished first, while Weightman-Smith sloshed home in fifth place.

**1932 Los Angeles** C: 17, N: 10, D: 8.3. WR(120 yards): 14.2 (Percy Beard)
1. George Saling   USA   14.6
2. Percy Beard   USA   14.7
3. Donald Finlay   GBR   14.8
4. Jack Keller   USA   14.8
5. David Burghley   GBR   14.8
DISQ: Willi Welscher (GER)

Jack Keller won the first semifinal in 14.5 and George Saling the second in 14.4. In the final, Keller showed in front first, but hit the fifth hurdle, allowing Beard to move ahead. However, Beard hit the sixth hurdle. Saling then caught up and took the lead. He tripped on the ninth hurdle, but held on to win by a yard. Welscher finished fourth, but was disqualified for knocking over four hurdles, a prohibition that is no longer in the rules. For the first time in Olympic history, the results of a final were changed after a film of the race had been viewed. Originally Keller had been placed third and awarded the bronze medal. When the revised results were announced, Keller sought out Finlay in the Olympic Village and handed over the medal.

**1936 Berlin** C: 31, N: 20, D: 8.6. WR: 14.1 (Forrest Towns)
1. Forrest Towns   USA   14.2
2. Donald Finlay   GBR   14.4
3. Frederick Pollard   USA   14.4
4. Håkan Lidman   SWE   14.4
5. John Thornton   GBR   14.7
6. Lawrence O'Connor   CAN   15.0

Forrest "Spec" Towns of Georgia equaled his own world record of 14.1 in the semifinals and then skimmed to a two-yard victory in the final.

**1948 London** C: 28, N: 18, D: 8.4. WR(120 yards): 13.6 (Harrison Dillard)
1. William Porter     USA   13.9   OR
2. Clyde Scott        USA   14.1
3. Craig Dixon        USA   14.1
4. Alberto Triulzi    ARG   14.6
5. Peter Gardner      AUS   —
6. Håkan Lidman       SWE   —

The absence of world record holder Harrison Dillard, eliminated at the U.S. trials, did not prevent the U.S. from sweeping the medals so decisively that the final appeared to be two separate races.

**1952 Helsinki** C: 30, N: 20, D: 7.24. WR: 13.5 (Richard Attlesey)
1. Harrison Dillard      USA   13.7   OR
2. Jack Davis            USA   13.7
3. Arthur Barnard        USA   14.1
4. Yevgeny Bulanchik     SOV   14.5
5. Kenneth Doubleday     AUS   14.7
6. Raymond Weinberg      AUS   14.8

In 1948 Harrison Dillard was the unquestioned world champion of the high hurdles. However, he lost his stride in the U.S. Olympic trials and failed to finish. He did qualify in the 100-meter dash and went on to win the gold medal. Despite this unexpected triumph, he still wanted to earn an Olympic victory in the hurdles. Four years later, at the age of 29, Dillard got his chance. He was hard-pressed by Jack Davis, who knocked down the ninth hurdle, allowing Dillard to achieve the victory "on which I had set my heart." The usually calm Dillard jumped for joy and exclaimed, "Good things come to those who wait."

**1956 Melbourne** C: 24, N: 15, D: 11.26. WR: 13.4 (Jack Davis)
1. Lee Calhoun       USA   13.5   OR
2. Jack Davis        USA   13.5
3. Joel Shankle      USA   14.1
4. Martin Lauer      GER   14.5
5. Stanko Lorger     YUG   14.5
6. Boris Stolyarov   SOV   14.6

Once again, if each nation had not been limited to three entrants, the final would probably have been an all-American affair. Running into a 1.9 meters per second wind, Calhoun and Davis were even by the eighth hurdle. Using a lunge that he had learned from Davis, Calhoun got his shoulder across the finish line inches ahead. For the second straight time, Jack Davis had recorded the same time as the winner yet had been forced to settle for a silver medal.

**1960 Rome** C: 36, N: 21, D: 9.5. WR: 13.2 (Martin Lauer, Lee Calhoun)
1. Lee Calhoun          USA   13.8
2. Willie May           USA   13.8
3. Hayes Jones          USA   14.0
4. Martin Lauer         GER   14.0
5. Keith Gardner        JAM   14.4
6. Valentin Chistyakov  SOV   14.6

Lee Calhoun had to sit out the 1958 season after being suspended for receiving gifts on the television game show *Bride and Groom*. He was back in uniform in 1960, winning his second gold medal with the same lunge that he had used to win four years earlier, and United States hurdlers achieved their fourth consecutive sweep.

**1964 Tokyo** C: 37, N: 23, D: 10.18. WR: 13.2 (Martin Lauer, Lee Calhoun)
1. Hayes Jones                 USA   13.6
2. H. Blaine Lindgren          USA   13.7
3. Anatoly Mikhailov           SOV   13.7
4. Eddy Ottoz                  ITA   13.8
5. Gurbachan Randhawa Singh    IND   14.0
6. Marcel Duriez               FRA   14.0
7. Giovanni Cornacchia         ITA   14.1
8. Giorgio Mazza               ITA   14.1

A U.S. sweep was prevented when Willie Davenport, the surprise winner of the U.S. Olympic trials, succumbed to a leg injury and was eliminated in the semifinals. Jones and Lindgren ran evenly for almost the entire race, but Lindgren started his lean too early and was nipped at the tape.

**1968 Mexico City** C: 33, N: 23, D: 10.17. WR: 13.2 (Martin Lauer, Lee Calhoun, Earl McCullouch)
1. Willie Davenport   USA   13.33   OR
2. Ervin Hall         USA   13.42
3. Eddy Ottoz         ITA   13.46
4. Leon Coleman       USA   13.67
5. Werner Trzmiel     GER   13.68
6. Bo Forssander      SWE   13.73
7. Marcel Duriez      FRA   13.77
8. Pierre Schoebel    FRA   14.01

In 1968, 19 of the world's top 25 high hurdlers were from the United States. Since 1964, Willie Davenport had struggled through four years of injuries to gain another chance at an Olympic gold medal. He was so nervous before the start of the final that he almost fell while taking off his sweat pants, and he never even heard the starter say, "set." Yet "from the first step, the gun," he said, "I knew I had won the race. It was perhaps the only race I ever ran that way, but that first step was so perfect—right on the money. I coasted over the last three hurdles thinking, 'It's over, it's over.' " His official time of 13.3 equaled the Olympic record set by Erv Hall in the semifinals.

**1972 Munich** C: 39, N: 27, D: 9.7. WR: 13.2 (Martin Lauer, Lee Calhoun, Earl McCullouch, Willie Davenport); WR (120 yards): 13.0 (Rodney Milburn)

| | | | |
|---|---|---|---|
| 1. Rodney Milburn | USA | 13.24 | EWR |
| 2. Guy Drut | FRA | 13.34 | |
| 3. Thomas Hill | USA | 13.48 | |
| 4. Willie Davenport | USA | 13.50 | |
| 5. Frank Siebeck | GBR | 13.71 | |
| 6. Leszek Wodzyński | POL | 13.72 | |
| 7. Lubomir Nadenicek | CZE | 13.76 | |
| 8. Petr Cech | CZE | 13.86 | |

Rod Milburn almost pulled a Harrison Dillard in 1972. After going undefeated in 1971 and winning 27 consecutive finals, he hit two hurdles in the U.S. Olympic trials and barely qualified in third place. However, in Munich his superiority was absolute. He was first over the first hurdle and almost two meters in front by the sixth hurdle, winning by one meter over fast-closing Guy Drut.

**1976 Montreal** C: 23, N: 17, D: 7.28. WR: 13.0 (Guy Drut)

| | | |
|---|---|---|
| 1. Guy Drut | FRA | 13.30 |
| 2. Alejandro Casañas Ramirez | CUB | 13.33 |
| 3. Willie Davenport | USA | 13.38 |
| 4. Charles Foster | USA | 13.41 |
| 5. Thomas Munkelt | GDR | 13.44 |
| 6. James Owens | USA | 13.73 |
| 7. Vyacheslav Kulebyakin | SOV | 13.93 |
| 8. Victor Myasnikov | SOV | 13.94 |

Early in 1975 Guy Drut predicted that he would win the Olympics in a time of 13.28. By 1976 he was under so much pressure from French sports fans that he was forced to train in secret. The son of a French father and an English mother, he was born in Oignies, on the same street as France's last male track and field medalist, Michel Jazy. Drut got off to a good start, took a slight lead after the third hurdle and held it the rest of the way. He was the first person from a non-English-speaking country to win the high hurdles. Drut was an excellent all-around athlete, whose other feats included pole-vaulting 17 feet ¾ inch, long-jumping 24 feet ½ inch, and high-jumping 6 feet 7 inches.

Thirty-three-year-old bronze medalist Willie Davenport was competing in his fourth Olympics. In 1980 he also took part in the Winter Olympics, in the four-man bobsled event.

**1980 Moscow** C: 22, N: 16, D: 7.27. WR: 13.00 (Renaldo Nehemiah)

| | | |
|---|---|---|
| 1. Thomas Munkelt | GDR | 13.39 |
| 2. Alejandro Casañas Ramirez | CUB | 13.40 |
| 3. Aleksandr Puchkov | SOV | 13.44 |
| 4. Andrei Prokofiev | SOV | 13.49 |
| 5. Jan Pusty | POL | 13.68 |
| 6. Arto Bryggare | FIN | 13.76 |
| 7. Javier Moracho | SPA | 13.78 |
| 8. Yuri Chervanyev | SOV | 15.80 |

Renaldo Nehemiah, Dedy Cooper, and Greg Foster of the United States would have been favorites to finish at least first and second. Without them, the winning time was the slowest since 1964. Thomas Munkelt, a good-humored 27-year-old dental student, commented before the final, "I will drill through my opposition." He ended up winning by the skin of his teeth. Alejandro Casañas, having lost in 1976 by 0.03 second, experienced the frustration of coming even closer in 1980—0.01 second.

**1984 Los Angeles** C: 26, N: 17, D: 8.6. WR: 12.93 (Renaldo Nehemiah)

| | | | |
|---|---|---|---|
| 1. Roger Kingdom | USA | 13.20 | OR |
| 2. Gregory Foster | USA | 13.23 | |
| 3. Arto Bryggare | FIN | 13.40 | |
| 4. Mark McKoy | CAN | 13.45 | |
| 5. Anthony Campbell | USA | 13.55 | |
| 6. Stephane Caristan | FRA | 13.71 | |
| 7. Carlos Sala | SPA | 13.80 | |
| 8. Jeff Glass | CAN | 14.15 | |

When world-record holder Renaldo Nehemiah gave up his eligibility to become a professional football player, the title of World's Best High Hurdler passed to Greg Foster. In the opening round, Foster equaled Rod Milburn's 12-year-old Olympic record of 13.24. In the first semifinal, the record was tied again, this time by fast-improving newcomer Roger Kingdom. Ten minutes later, Foster, running into the wind, clocked yet another 13.24.

In the final, Foster hesitated slightly after the gun, thinking he had false-started. But he recovered quickly and moved into the lead by the second hurdle. About four meters from the finish, Foster, in lane one, glanced to his right as Kingdom, in lane eight, pulled even and lunged for the tape. Kingdom thought he had finished second and didn't believe he had won until he watched a slow-motion replay of the finish on the huge video screen at the end of the stadium. Only then did he begin leaping up and down with joy.

**1988 Seoul** C: 41, N: 31, D: 9.28. WR: 12.93 (Renaldo Nehemiah)

| | | | |
|---|---|---|---|
| 1. Roger Kingdom | USA | 12.98 | OR |
| 2. Colin Jackson | GBR | 13.28 | |
| 3. Anthony Campbell | USA | 13.38 | |
| 4. Vladimir Shishkin | SOV | 13.51 | |
| 5. Jonathan Ridgeon | GBR | 13.52 | |
| 6. Tony Jarrett | GBR | 13.54 | |
| 7. Mark McKoy | CAN | 13.61 | |
| 8. Arthur Blake | USA | 13.96 | |

On July 16, 1985, Roger Kingdom pulled his left hamstring muscle. As it was his first major injury, he did not take it seriously enough and it failed to heal properly. The following year he injured it again. By 1987 he was no longer competing. When Greg Foster won the Rome world championships, Kingdom watched the race on television. He even had to listen to one of the TV commentators refer to him as "the forgotten man of the hurdles."

However, when the 1988 season began, Kingdom was fully healed. He entered the Olympics undefeated with victories in 16 straight meets. Arthur Blake caught a flyer in the final. Kingdom started in third place, took the lead after the fourth hurdle, and powered to an impressive 3-meter victory.

## 400-METER HURDLES

Contestants in this event must clear ten 3-foot hurdles.

**1896** not held

**1900 Paris** C: 5, N: 4, D: 7.15. WR(440 yards): 57.2 (Godfrey Shaw)
1. John Walter Tewksbury   USA   57.6
2. Henri Tauzin   FRA   58.3
3. George Orton   CAN/USA   —
4. William Lewis   USA   —

The results were a great disappointment to the French, since this event was unfamiliar to the Americans. This didn't prevent Tewksbury from easily defeating the previously unbeaten Tauzin. The "hurdles" were actually 30-foot-long telephone poles. A water jump was added just before the finish.

**1904 St. Louis** C: 4, N: 1, D: 8.31. WR(440 yards): 57.2 (Godfrey Shaw)
1. Harry Hillman   USA   53.0
2. Frank Waller   USA   53.2
3. George Poage   USA   —
4. George Varnell   USA   —

An oddity in the world of U.S. athletics, Harry Hillman was a 22-year-old bank teller who had never attended college. Writing in the September 1905 issue of *Physical Culture* magazine, Hillman advised aspiring hurdlers to avoid candy, pastries, tobacco and meat, although he did recommend swallowing whole raw eggs, which he claimed were "excellent for the wind and stomach." He concluded by advising young men in the business world to take up athletics because it "gives one the needed virility demanded by modern business life." Hillman's time was not allowed as a world record because he tipped over one hurdle, and because the hurdles were only 2 feet 6 inches high anyway. George Poage was the first black runner to win an Olympic medal. On April 24, 1909, Harry Hillman and Lawson Robertson set a world record of 11.0 seconds in the 100-yard three-legged race.

**1906** not held

**1908 London** C: 15, N: 6, D: 7.22. WR(440 yards): 57.2 (Godfrey Shaw)
1. Charles Bacon   USA   55.0   WR
2. Harry Hillman   USA   55.3
3. Leonard Tremeer   GBR   57.0
DNF: Leslie Burton (GBR)

Bacon won a close and exciting contest despite the fact that he went over a hurdle in the wrong lane midway through the race. When the judges measured the course he had taken, they discovered that he had actually run farther than if he had stayed in his own lane, so he was saved from disqualification.

**1912** not held

**1920 Antwerp** C: 21, N: 10, D: 8.16. WR(440 yards): 54.2 (John Norton)
1. Frank Loomis   USA   54.0   WR
2. John Norton   USA   54.3
3. August Desch   USA   54.5
4. Georges "Géo" André   FRA   54.6
5. Carl-Axel Christiernsson   SWE   54.9
6. Charles Daggs   USA   —

Fourth-place finisher Géo André had won a silver medal in the high jump in 1908.

**1924 Paris** C: 23, N: 13, D: 7.7. WR: 54.0 (Frank Loomis)
1. F. Morgan Taylor   USA   52.6
2. Erik Vilén   FIN   53.8   OR
3. Ivan Riley   USA   54.2
4. Georges "Géo" André   FRA   56.2
DISQ: Charles Brookins (USA), F. J. Blackett (GBR)

Taylor's world record time was not allowed because he knocked down one hurdle, thus violating the rules of that time. Brookins finished second, but was disqualified for running out of his lane and clearing a hurdle improperly. Consequently, it was Erik Vilén who was credited with an Olympic record, even though he finished only third.

**1928 Amsterdam** C: 27, N: 16, D: 7.30. WR: 52.0 (F. Morgan Taylor)
1. David Burghley   GBR   53.4   OR
2. Frank Cuhel   USA   53.6
3. F. Morgan Taylor   USA   53.6
4. Sten Pettersson   SWE   53.8
5. Thomas Livingstone-Learmonth   GBR   54.2
6. Luigi Facelli   ITA   55.8

Lord David George Brownlow Cecil Burghley was one of the most popular winners of the 1928 Games. Heir to the Marquess of Exeter, he first appeared in the Olympics in 1924, when he was elminated in the first round of the 110-meter hurdles. In 1927, during his last year at Cambridge, he caused a sensation by running around the Great Court at Trinity College in the time it took the Trinity Clock to toll 12 o'clock. A completely distorted version of this event was presented in the film *Chariots of Fire*, in which the feat is credited to Harold Abrahams. For this reason, Lord Burghley, who was then 76 years old, reportedly refused to view the film. Actually, Lord Burghley was not the first person to accomplish the Great Court run. It had been done in the 1890s by Sir Walter Borley Fletcher, but in Sir Walter's time the clock took five more seconds to complete its toll.

Burghley was an extremely colorful character, who once set another unusual record by racing around the upper promenade deck of the ocean liner *Queen Mary* in 57 seconds, dressed in street clothes. Once he showed up for a meet in Antwerp, but was denied admission at the main gate, and told to circle the stadium and enter by the competitors' gate. Burghley took a few steps back, tightened his bowler hat on his head, got a firm grip on his attaché case, hurdled the four-foot fence, and dashed off before the astonished guards could react. He was elected to Parliament in 1931, but was granted a leave of absence to compete in the 1932 Olympics in Los Angeles. He later served as governor of Bermuda for three years, as well as president of the International Amateur Athletic Federation for 30 years. He was also chairman of the Organizing Committee of the 1948 Olympics.

**1932 Los Angeles** C: 18, N: 13, D: 8.1. WR: 52.0 (F. Morgan Taylor)

| | | | |
|---|---|---|---|
| 1. Robert Tisdall | IRL | 51.7 | |
| 2. Glenn Hardin | USA | 51.9 | WR |
| 3. F. Morgan Taylor | USA | 52.0 | |
| 4. David Burghley | GBR | 52.2 | |
| 5. Luigi Facelli | ITA | 53.0 | |
| 6. Johan Kjell Areskoug | SWE | 54.6 | |

Bob Tisdall, a well-known athlete while a student at Cambridge, had run the 400-meter hurdles only once when, in March 1932, he decided to try out for the Irish Olympic team. He quit his job in London and, with his wife, moved into a converted railway carriage in an orchard in Sussex, where he spent the next three months training, although he had no hurdles to practice with. He won a match race in early June and then, on June 18, finished first in the All-Ireland Championships in a time of 54.2 seconds. Less than a month later he was on his way to Los Angeles with the rest of the Irish team. Weakened by the two-week journey, he stayed in bed for 15 hours a day until the morning of his first-round heat. Full of energy, he qualified easily. In the semifinals, he surprised even himself by winning in 52.8, equaling the Olympic record that had been set by Glenn Hardin in the first semi. The final was only Tisdall's seventh race at the distance, and he faced not only Hardin, but former champions Morgan Taylor and Lord Burghley as well. Completely relaxed, Tisdall took the lead early and approached the last hurdle five yards ahead of the others.

"At that moment," Tisdall recalled, "I experienced a strange feeling of loneliness. . . . Everything was strangely quiet. . . . I began to wonder if the rest of the field had fallen over." He mistimed his leap, knocked over the barrier, and stumbled for five or six yards before regaining his balance. Hardin and Taylor closed fast, but Tisdall beat them to the tape in world record time. According to the rules of the day, which were not changed until 1938, his record was disallowed because he had failed to clear the final barrier. So Glenn Hardin

entered the record books as world record holder even though he only finished second.

**1936 Berlin** C: 32, N: 20, D: 8.4. WR: 50.6 (Glenn Hardin)

| | | |
|---|---|---|
| 1. Glenn Hardin | USA | 52.4 |
| 2. John Loaring | CAN | 52.7 |
| 3. Miguel White | PHI | 52.8 |
| 4. Joseph Patterson | USA | 53.0 |
| 5. Sylvio de Magalhäes Padilha | BRA | 54.0 |
| 6. Christos Mantikas | GRE | 54.2 |

On July 26, 1934, while running in Stockholm, Glenn Hardin of Louisiana took a full second off the existing world record. His time of 50.6 was not beaten for more than 19 years. Following his second-place finish in the 1932 Olympics, Hardin never lost another race. In Berlin, he caught the fading Joe Patterson in the stretch and won by four yards.

**1948 London** C: 25, N: 17, D: 7.31. WR: 50.6 (Glenn Hardin)

| | | | |
|---|---|---|---|
| 1. Roy Cochran | USA | 51.1 | OR |
| 2. Duncan White | SRL | 51.8 | |
| 3. Rune Larsson | SWE | 52.2 | |
| 4. Richard Ault | USA | 52.4 | |
| 5. Yves Cros | FRA | 53.3 | |
| 6. Ottavio Missoni | ITA | 54.0 | |

**1952 Helsinki** C: 40, N: 24, D: 7.21. WR: 50.6 (Glenn Hardin)

| | | | |
|---|---|---|---|
| 1. Charles Moore | USA | 50.0 | OR |
| 2. Yuri Lituyev | SOV | 51.3 | |
| 3. John Holland | NZE | 52.2 | |
| 4. Anatoly Yulin | SOV | 52.8 | |
| 5. Harry Whittle | GBR | 53.1 | |
| 6. Armando Filiput | ITA | 54.4 | |

Remarkably, the six finalists cleared the first five hurdles in unison. Then Moore, whose father had been an alternate on the 1924 U.S. Olympic team, pulled ahead. Lituyev drew even by the eighth hurdle, but Moore moved ahead again and won by four yards. Moore's near-world record time was quite extraordinary considering that the track had been soaked by rain. He also ran 50.8 in the second round.

**1956 Melbourne** C: 28, N: 13, D: 11.24. WR: 49.5 (Glenn Davis)

| | | | |
|---|---|---|---|
| 1. Glenn Davis | USA | 50.1 | EOR |
| 2. Silas "Eddie" Southern | USA | 50.8 | |
| 3. Joshua Culbreath | USA | 51.6 | |
| 4. Yuri Lituyev | SOV | 51.7 | |
| 5. David Lean | AUS | 51.8 | |
| 6. Gerhardus Potgieter | SAF | 56.0 | |

On June 29, at the U.S. Olympic trials, Glenn Davis set a world record of 49.5, pressed by Eddie Southern, who ran 49.7. In Melbourne Southern set an Olympic record of 50.1 in the semifinals, then set the pace in the final. Davis caught him midway and surged ahead at the seventh hurdle to win decisively.

**1960 Rome** C: 34, N: 23, D: 9.2. WR: 49.2 (Glenn Davis)

| | | | |
|---|---|---|---|
| 1. Glenn Davis | USA | 49.3 | OR |
| 2. Clifton Cushman | USA | 49.6 | |
| 3. Richard Howard | USA | 49.7 | |
| 4. Helmut Janz | GER | 49.9 | |
| 5. Jussi Rintamäki | FIN | 50.8 | |
| 6. Bruno Galliker | SWI | 51.0 | |

"Running scared," Glenn Davis ran off stride until the seventh hurdle, when he regained his poise, passed Janz at the ninth hurdle and Howard at the tenth, to win by two meters. Silver medalist Cliff Cushman was lost in action in Vietnam in 1966. Bronze medalist Dick Howard died of a heroin overdose in 1967. They were 28 and 32 years old, respectively.

**1964 Tokyo** C: 39, N: 25, D: 10.16. WR: 49.1 (Warren "Rex" Cawley)

| | | |
|---|---|---|
| 1. Warren "Rex" Cawley | USA | 49.6 |
| 2. John Cooper | GBR | 50.1 |
| 3. Salvatore Morale | ITA | 50.1 |
| 4. Gary Knoke | AUS | 50.4 |
| 5. James Luck | USA | 50.5 |
| 6. Roberto Frinolli | ITA | 50.7 |
| 7. Vasily Anisimov | SOV | 51.1 |
| 8. Wilfried Geeroms | BEL | 51.4 |

Rex Cawley ran off stride until the sixth hurdle, and was still three yards behind Frinolli at the eighth hurdle. Then the world record holder turned on his speed and pulled away to a clear victory. Silver medalist John Cooper was one of the 346 people who died in the famous Turkish Air Lines plane crash over France on March 3, 1974. He was 33 years old.

**1968 Mexico City** C: 30, N: 24, D: 10.15. WR: 48.8 (Geoffrey Vanderstock)

| | | | |
|---|---|---|---|
| 1. David Hemery | GBR | 48.12 | WR |
| 2. Gerhard Hennige | GER | 49.02 | |
| 3. John Sherwood | GBR | 49.03 | |
| 4. Geoffrey Vanderstock | USA | 49.06 | |
| 5. Vyacheslav Skomorokhov | SOV | 49.12 | |
| 6. Ronald Whitney | USA | 49.26 | |
| 7. Rainer Schubert | GER | 49.29 | |
| 8. Roberto Frinolli | ITA | 50.13 | |

The 1968 final had all the makings of a spectacular race. The favorites were world record holder Geoff Vanderstock, fellow American Ron Whitney, and David Hemery, who had beaten Vanderstock at the N.C.A.A. championships. Hemery, although born in England, had spent 10 of his 24 years in the United States. Other finalists included John Sherwood, whose wife, Sheila, had won a silver medal in the long jump the day before, Vyacheslav Skomorokhov, who was deaf, and 1964 finalist Roberto Frinolli, who had stripped down to his bikini-style black jock strap before the race, unaware that he was being shown live on U.S. television. Hemery was in Lane 6, just inside Ron Whitney, the man he most feared because of his strong finishing kick.

Frinolli and Vanderstock were off quickest, but Hemery had taken the lead by the third hurdle. He passed the halfway mark in 23.3 and demoralized the rest of the field with an awesome display of speed in which he gained at least a yard between and over each of the next five hurdles. He crossed the finish line with an eight-yard lead, the largest winning margin since 1924. While millions of people around the world marveled at his extraordinary performance, Hemery himself wasn't even sure he had won. He had looked to his right at the end to check for Ron Whitney, but had failed to look to his left. It wasn't until he was approached by a BBC camera crew that his uncertainty was erased. At the victory ceremony, Hemery received his gold medal from David Burghley, who had won the same event 40 years earlier.

Final mention should be made of U.S. hurdler Boyd Gittins, who was eliminated at the U.S. Olympic semitrials when a pigeon dropping hit him in the eye and dislodged his contact lens just before the first hurdle. Fortunately, he won a runoff to qualify for the final Olympic trials, and then made the team. Unfortunately, a leg injury forced him to withdraw from his first-round heat.

**1972 Munich** C: 37, N: 25, D: 9.2. WR: 48.12 (David Hemery)

| | | | |
|---|---|---|---|
| 1. John Akii-Bua | UGA | 47.82 | WR |
| 2. Ralph Mann | USA | 48.51 | |
| 3. David Hemery | GBR | 48.52 | |
| 4. James Seymour | USA | 48.64 | |
| 5. Rainer Schubert | GER | 49.65 | |
| 6. Yevgeny Gavrilenko | SOV | 49.66 | |
| 7. Stavros Tziortzis | GRE | 49.66 | |
| 8. Yuri Zorin | SOV | 50.25 | |

The second semifinal was filled with misfortune. James Seymour and Australia's Gary Knoke, running in the two outside lanes, mistook the echo of the starter's gun for a second shot and thought a false start had been declared. Seymour, in Lane 7, realized his mistake quickly enough to avoid disaster and win the heat anyway, but Knoke, in Lane 8, was unable to recover, and finished last. As the runners cleared the tenth hurdle, East Germany's Christian Rudolph, in Lane 1, stumbled and fell heavily into Lane 2, right into the path of Dieter-Wolfgang Büther of West Germany, who also fell. Neither man was able to finish. The judges decided not to order a rerun, since Büther was only in fifth place at the time of the mishap.

In the final David Hemery actually set an even faster pace than he had in Mexico City, covering the first 200 meters in 22.8 seconds. Thus it came as quite a shock when he discovered that John Akii-Bua, running in Lane 1, was right beside him with 100 meters to go. Akii-Bua surged ahead between the eighth and ninth hurdles and won by six meters. Despite the fact that he had just set a world record, Uganda's first gold medalist kept right on going over the next two flights of hurdles. Akii-Bua, who was also Uganda's decathlon champion, said that he was "scared to death" when he learned that he had drawn Lane 1. "When you are in Lane 1," he said, "you are always the loser. I couldn't sleep that night." Akii-Bua's father had eight wives and 43 children, 29 of whom were still alive in 1972. A police instructor, John Akii-Bua fled Uganda in 1979, following the overthrow of Idi Amin, and spent a month in a Kenyan jail before he was recognized and released. He eventually returned and in 1987 was arrested again for illegal possession of a submachine gun.

**1976 Montreal** C: 22, N: 16, D: 7.25. WR: 47.82 (John Akii-Bua)

| | | | |
|---|---|---|---|
| 1. Edwin Moses | USA | 47.64 | WR |
| 2. Michael Shine | USA | 48.69 | |
| 3. Yevgeny Gavrilenko | SOV | 49.45 | |
| 4. Quentin Wheeler | USA | 49.86 | |
| 5. José Carvalho | POR | 49.94 | |
| 6. Yanko Bratanov | BUL | 50.03 | |
| 7. Damaso Alfonso | CUB | 50.19 | |
| 8. Alan Pascoe | GBR | 51.29 | |

The African boycott prevented a potentially historic showdown. No matter how sympathetic one is to the movement to bring self-determination for blacks in South Africa, it is difficult to not be cynical when you realize that John Akii-Bua was not allowed to compete in Montreal because the leader of his nation's government, Idi Amin, was offended by human rights violations in another country.

With Akii-Bua gone and Alan Pascoe still recovering from a leg injury, the competition turned into a one-man show. Edwin Moses was a 20-year-old engineering and physics major at Atlanta's Moorhouse College, a school without a track and which he had entered with an academic rather than an athletic scholarship. Basically self-coached, Moses had entered only one 400-meter hurdles race before March 27, 1976. The Olympics was his first international meet. Moses wore down his last challenger, Yevgeny Gavrilenko, by the seventh hurdle and won by eight meters, the largest winning margin in the history of the event. Afterward, Moses said that his major regret was that training for the Olympics had interfered with his studies, allowing his grade-point average to dip to 3.57.

**1980 Moscow** C: 22, N: 19, D: 7.26. WR: 47.13 (Edwin Moses)

| | | |
|---|---|---|
| 1. Volker Beck | GDR | 48.70 |
| 2. Vassily Arkhipenko | SOV | 48.86 |
| 3. Gary Oakes | GBR | 49.11 |
| 4. Nicolai Vassilev | SOV | 49.34 |
| 5. Rok Kopitar | YUG | 49.67 |
| 6. Horia Toboc | ROM | 49.84 |
| 7. Franz Meier | SWI | 50.00 |
| 8. Yanko Bratanov | BUL | 56.35 |

The year 1980 saw a severely devalued competition as a result of the Jimmy Carter boycott. The preboycott favorite, Edwin Moses, set a world record of 47.13 on July 3, three weeks before the Olympics. The silver medal had been expected to be a toss-up among Harald Schmid of West Germany and James Walker and David Lee of the United States. In their absence, Volker Beck passed

Arkhipenko on the run-in to win the closest 400-meter hurdles final in Olympic history. His winning time was the slowest since 1964.

**1984 Los Angeles** C: 45, N: 30, D: 8.5. WR: 47.02 (Edwin Moses)

| | | |
|---|---|---|
| 1. Edwin Moses | USA | 47.75 |
| 2. Danny Harris | USA | 48.13 |
| 3. Harald Schmid | GER | 48.19 |
| 4. Sven Nylander | SWE | 48.97 |
| 5. Amadou Ba | SEN | 49.28 |
| 6. Tranel Hawkins | USA | 49.42 |
| 7. Michel Zimmerman | BEL | 50.69 |
| 8. Henry Amike | NGR | 53.78 |

On August 26, 1977, Edwin Moses lost a race to Harald Schmid in Berlin. One week later in Düsseldorf he beat Schmid by 15 yards to begin an incredible winning streak that took him through 22 countries and extended, by the time of the 1984 Olympics, to 102 races including 89 finals. By this time the 48-second barrier had been broken 32 times: once by John Akii-Bua, once by Andre Phillips, three times by Harald Schmid, and 27 times by Edwin Moses, who also owned the nine fastest times ever recorded. Needless to say, Moses was a prohibitive favorite to win what should have been his third gold medal.

After being distracted at the starting line by the hundreds of cameras clicking away at him, Moses got off to a quick start and was never headed. Second place went to 18-year-old Danny Harris, who had not run his first 400-meter hurdle race until March 17, 1984. On June 4, 1987, it was Harris who finally ended Moses' finals winning streak at 107 by defeating him 47.56 to 47.69 in a race in Madrid. The streak had lasted 9 years, 9 months, and 9 days.

**1988 Seoul** C: 37, N: 28, D: 9.25. WR: 47.02 (Edwin Moses)

| | | | |
|---|---|---|---|
| 1. Andre Phillips | USA | 47.19 | OR |
| 2. Amadou Ba | SEN | 47.23 | |
| 3. Edwin Moses | USA | 47.56 | |
| 4. Kevin Young | USA | 47.94 | |
| 5. Winthrop Graham | JAM | 48.04 | |
| 6. Kriss Akabusi | GBR | 48.69 | |
| 7. Harald Schmid | GER | 48.76 | |
| 8. Edgar Itt | GER | 48.78 | |

Following Danny Harris' defeat of Edwin Moses in Madrid, the next big 400-meter hurdles race came at the world championships in Rome on September 1, 1987. Moses won that contest, leaning across the finish line in 47.46 to beat Harris and Harald Schmid by a mere 6 inches.

At the 1988 U.S. Olympic trials, Moses won again, clocking 47.37 in the first race in which five runners went under 48 seconds. Andre Phillips was second in 47.58, with Danny Harris beaten back into fifth.

In Seoul the 29-year-old Phillips, who had lost over 20 times to the 33-year-old Moses without a single victory, chose a strategy which mirrored Moses' usual tactics— racing as hard as possible through three hurdles, then surging again at the seventh hurdle. Phillips reacted quickly to the gun and led by almost 2 meters after the third hurdle. Moses gradually closed the gap, then inched ahead as they reached the seventh barrier. Between the seventh and ninth hurdles, Phillips, following his plan perfectly, regained a clear lead. Moses faded, while Amadou Ba came on with a rush, passing Moses and almost catching Phillips. Phillips' first thought after he realized he had won was not that he was the Olympic champion, but that he had beaten Moses. Both Phillips and Ba ran the race of their lives, the former improving his personal record by .32, the latter by .80. Phillips' margin of victory was provided by the seven hundredths of a second he gained over Ba between the gun and his first stride. Ba earned Senegal's first Olympic medal, although in 1960, Abdoulaye Seye, another Senegalese, had won a bronze in the 200 meters while competing for France.

## 3000-METER STEEPLECHASE

In the steeplechase, runners must negotiate a course of 28 hurdles and 7 water jumps. The hurdles are 3 feet high and are solid, so that they cannot be knocked over. The tops of the hurdles are 5 inches wide, allowing the contestants to step on them. The water jump, which is preceded by a hedge, is 12 feet long, with a maximum depth of 2 feet 3½ inches. The steeplechase event appears to have been introduced in Edinburgh in 1828, although the distance was not standardized at 3000 meters until 1920.

**1896** not held

**1900 Paris** C: 6, N: 6, D: 7.15.
**(2500 Meters)**

| | | |
|---|---|---|
| 1. George Orton | CAN | 7:34.4 |
| 2. Sidney Robinson | GBR | 7:38.0 |
| 3. Jacques Chastanié | FRA | — |
| 4. Arthur Newton | USA | — |
| 5. Hermann Wraschtil | AUT | — |
| 6. Franz Duhne | GER | — |

**1904 St. Louis** C: 7, N: 2, D: 8.29.
**(2590 Meters)**

| | | |
|---|---|---|
| 1. James Lightbody | USA | 7:39.6 |
| 2. John Daly | IRL | 7:40.6 |
| 3. Arthur Newton | USA | — |
| 4. W. Frank Verner | USA | — |

Lightbody came from behind to win the first of his three gold medals at St. Louis.

**1906** not held

**1908 London** C: 24, N: 6, D: 7.18.
**(3200 Meters)**

| | | |
|---|---|---|
| 1. Arthur Russell | GBR | 10:47.8 |
| 2. Archie Robertson | GBR | 10:48.4 |
| 3. John Eisele | USA | — |
| 4. C. Guy Holdaway | GBR | — |
| 5. Harold Sewell | GBR | — |
| 6. William Galbraith | CAN | — |

A rather unusual controversy developed during the heats, when some of the American runners showed up wearing white shorts, which were prohibited by A.A.A. rules. They were finally allowed to compete after they had been provided with dark shorts. Russell and Robertson cleared the last hurdle together in the final, but Russell won by two yards in the run-in.

**1912** not held

**1920 Antwerp** C: 16, N: 6, D: 8.20. WR: 9.49.8 (Josef Ternström)

| | | |
|---|---|---|
| 1. Percy Hodge | GBR | 10:00.4 OR |
| 2. Patrick Flynn | USA | — |
| 3. Ernesto Ambrosini | ITA | — |
| 4. Gustaf Mattsson | SWE | — |
| 5. Michael Devaney | USA | — |
| 6. Albert Hulsebosch | USA | — |
| 7. Lars Hedvall | SWE | — |
| 8. Raymond Watson | USA | — |

The 29-year-old Hodge won easily by 100 yards. Earlier in the year he had entered the A.A.A. steeplechase championship. In the second lap of that race, he was spiked and lost the heel of his shoe. Hodge stopped running, took off his shoe, readjusted and relaced it, and then took off again. He won by 60 yards.

**1924 Paris** C: 21, N: 9, D: 7.9. WR: 9:33.4 (Paul Bontemps)

| | | |
|---|---|---|
| 1. Vilho "Ville" Ritola | FIN | 9:33.6 OR |
| 2. Elias Katz | FIN | 9:44.0 |
| 3. Paul Bontemps | FRA | 9:45.2 |
| 4. E. Marvin Rick | USA | 9:56.4 |
| 5. Karl Ebb | FIN | 9:57.6 |
| 6. Evelyn Montague | GBR | — |
| 7. Michael Devaney | USA | — |
| 8. Albert Isola | FRA | 10:14.9 |

Paul Bontemps had run a 9:33.4 on June 9, 1924, but was unable to repeat his performance one month later at the Olympics, as Ville Ritola won by 75 meters. Sixth-place finisher Evelyn Aubrey Montague is introduced in the film *Chariots of Fire* as a good friend of Harold Abrahams, whose acquaintance he makes when they both arrive at Cambridge as freshmen. In reality, Abrahams and Montague were rivals, since Montague attended not Cambridge, but Oxford.

**1928 Amsterdam** C: 22, N: 10, D: 8.4. WR: 9.33.4 (Paul Bontemps)

| | | |
|---|---|---|
| 1. Toivo Loukola | FIN | 9:21.8 WR |
| 2. Paavo Nurmi | FIN | 9:31.2 |
| 3. Ove Andersen | FIN | 9:35.6 |
| 4. Nils Eklöf | SWE | 9:38.0 |
| 5. Henri Dartigues | FRA | 9:40.0 |
| 6. Lucien Duquesne | FRA | 9:40.6 |
| 7. Melvin Dalton | USA | — |
| 8. William Spencer | USA | — |

In the second heat of the qualifying round, Paavo Nurmi fell head over heels into the first water jump and had to be fished out by Lucien Duquesne. Nurmi repaid Duquesne's kindness by pacing him for the rest of the race, the two finishing together. The final marked the last Olympic appearances of Nurmi and Ville Ritola, both of whom were exhausted from their duel in the 5000 meters final the previous day. Ritola dropped out 600 yards short of the finish, but Nurmi held on grimly and placed second, 60 yards behind Toivo Loukola. Five years earlier Loukola had been declared unfit for military service because he had tuberculosis. He had then returned home and taken up running to restore his health.

**1932 Los Angeles** C: 15, N: 8, D: 8.6. WR: 9:08.4 (George Lermond)
**(3460 Meters)**

| | | |
|---|---|---|
| 1. Volmari Iso-Hollo | FIN | 10:33.4 |
| 2. Thomas Evenson | GBR | 10:46.0 |
| 3. Joseph McCluskey | USA | 10:46.2 |
| 4. Martti Matilainen | FIN | 10:52.4 |
| 5. George Bailey | GBR | 10:53.2 |
| 6. Glen Dawson | USA | — |
| 7. Giuseppe Lippi | ITA | — |
| 8. Walter Pritchard | USA | — |

Volmari Iso-Hollo, a 25-year-old typesetter, crossed the finish line with a 40 yard lead, only to discover that there was no tape awaiting him and that the lap counter still read "1." He continued on for an extra lap and won by 75 yards. It was later determined that the lap checker, a substitute for the regular man, who was ill, had forgotten to change the lap count the first time the runners passed by. It didn't make any difference to Iso-Hollo, but the blunder had a profound effect on who won the silver medal. At the end of the regulation distance, McCluskey was in second place and Evenson in third. But during the extra lap Evenson passed McCluskey and beat him to the finish by two yards. When McCluskey pointed out to track officials what had happened, he was offered the opportunity of having the race re-run the next day. Quite exhausted, McCluskey declined, stating that anyway "a race has only one finish line."

**1936 Berlin** C: 28, N: 13, D: 8.8. WR: 9:08.2 (Harold Manning)

| | | | |
|---|---|---|---|
| 1. Volmari Iso-Hollo | FIN | 9:03.8 | WR |
| 2. Kaarlo Tuominen | FIN | 9:06.8 | |
| 3. Alfred Dompert | GER | 9:07.2 | |
| 4. Martii Matilainen | FIN | 9:09.0 | |
| 5. Harold Manning | USA | 9:11.2 | |
| 6. Lars Larsson | SWE | 9:16.6 | |
| 7. Woldemars Wihtols | LAT | 9:18.8 | |
| 8. Glen Dawson | USA | 9:21.2 | |

**1948 London** C: 26, N: 12, D: 8.5. WR: 8:59.6 (Erik Elmsater)

| | | |
|---|---|---|
| 1. Thore Sjöstrand | SWE | 9:04.6 |
| 2. Erik Elmsäter | SWE | 9:08.2 |
| 3. Göte Hagström | SWE | 9:11.3 |
| 4. Alex Guyodo | FRA | 9:13.6 |

| | | |
|---|---|---|
| 5. Pentti Siltaloppi | FIN | 9:19.6 |
| 6. Petar Šegedin | YUG | 9:20.4 |
| 7. H. Browning Ross | USA | 9:23.2 |
| 8. Constantino Miranda Justo | SPA | 9:25.0 |

The only runner given a chance of defeating the Swedes was the European champion, Raphael Pujazon of France. However, Pujazon developed a stomach cramp midway through the final and was forced to retire.

**1952 Helsinki** C: 35, N: 12, D: 7.25. WR: 8:48.6 (Vladimir Kazantsev)

| | | | |
|---|---|---|---|
| 1. Horace Ashenfelter | USA | 8:45.4 | WR |
| 2. Vladimir Kazantsev | SOV | 8:51.6 | |
| 3. John Disley | GBR | 8:51.8 | |
| 4. Olavi Rinteenpää | FIN | 8:55.2 | |
| 5. Curt Söderberg | SWE | 8:55.6 | |
| 6. Günther Hesselmann | GER | 8:55.8 | |
| 7. Mikhail Saltykov | SOV | 8:56.2 | |
| 8. Helmut Gude | GER | 9:01.4 | |

Twenty-seven-year-old F.B.I. agent Horace Ashenfelter of Glen Ridge, New Jersey, caused something of a stir when he won his preliminary heat in 8:51.0. Not only was it the fastest time of the round, but Ashenfelter's previous best had been an undistinguished 9:06.4. Still, it seemed unlikely that Ashenfelter, who had trained at night, using park benches as hurdles, could seriously challenge world record holder Vladimir Kazantsev. Mikhail Saltykov was the early leader in the final, but before the third lap had ended, Ashenfelter had moved ahead, followed closely by Kazantsev. They continued running together until the final lap. With half a lap to go, Kazantsev forged ahead, and it looked like the race was his. But Kazantsev stumbled slightly at the final water jump, while Ashenfelter breezed through without even breaking stride. Kazantsev had run out of energy, and Ashenfelter pulled away dramatically over the last 150 meters to win by almost 30 yards. Gleeful American sportswriters had a field day—it was the first time that an F.B.I. man had allowed himself to be followed by a Russian.

**1956 Melbourne** C: 23, N: 13, D: 11.29. WR: 8:35.6 (Semyon Rzhischin)

| | | | |
|---|---|---|---|
| 1. Christopher Brasher | GBR | 8:41.2 | OR |
| 2. Sándor Rozsnyói | HUN | 8:43.6 | |
| 3. Ernst Larsen | NOR | 8:44.0 | |
| 4. Heinz Laufer | GER | 8:44.4 | |
| 5. Semyon Rzhischin | SOV | 8:44.6 | |
| 6. John Disley | GBR | 8:44.6 | |
| 7. Neil Robbins | AUS | 8:50.0 | |
| 8. Eric Shirley | GBR | 8:57.0 | |

Larsen led until two laps from the finish, after which Rzhischin surged ahead. Entering the final curve, Rozsnyói made his move, with Larsen at his shoulder. As they approached the fourth-to-last hurdle, Rozsnyói swung wide to give himself room to clear. Chris Brasher, a 28-year-old oil company executive, saw his chance, elbowed his way between the two leaders, and sprinted away to an unexpected 15-yard victory. Twelve minutes later came an announcement that Brasher had been disqualified for interfering with Larsen. However, Larsen made it clear that although he had been bumped, he considered the incident insignificant, and not worthy of disqualification. Rozsnyói, who was considerably more concerned about the fact that he hadn't heard from his wife or children since Soviet troops had invaded Hungary, also supported Brasher. Three hours later, the Jury of Appeal voted unanimously to rescind the disqualification, giving Great Britain its first track and field gold medal since 1936.

**1960 Rome** C: 32, N: 20, D: 9.3. WR: 8.31.4 (Zdzislaw Krzyszkowiak)

| | | | |
|---|---|---|---|
| 1. Zdzislaw Krzyszkowiak | POL | 8:34.2 | OR |
| 2. Nikolai Sokolov | SOV | 8:36.4 | |
| 3. Semyon Rzhischin | SOV | 8:42.2 | |
| 4. Gaston Roelants | BEL | 8:47.6 | |
| 5. Gunnar Tjörnebo | SWE | 8:58.6 | |
| 6. Ludwig Müller | GER | 9:01.6 | |
| 7. Charles "Deacon" Jones | USA | 9:18.2 | |
| 8. Aleksei Konov | SOV | 9:18.2 | |

The three Soviet runners ran a team race, hoping to wear down Krzyszkowiak. It didn't work. The 31-year-old Polish world record holder glided past Sokolov on the final backstretch and won by 15 yards.

**1964 Tokyo** C: 29, N: 19, D: 10.17. WR: 8:29.6 (Gaston Roelants)

| | | | |
|---|---|---|---|
| 1. Gaston Roelants | BEL | 8:30.8 | OR |
| 2. Maurice Herriott | GBR | 8:32.4 | |
| 3. Yvan Belyayev | SOV | 8:33.8 | |
| 4. Manuel de Oliveira | POR | 8:36.2 | |
| 5. George Young | USA | 8:38.2 | |
| 6. Guy Texereau | FRA | 8:38.6 | |
| 7. Adolfas Alekseunas | SOV | 8:39.0 | |
| 8. Lars-Erik Gustafsson | SWE | 8:41.8 | |

Ahead by five yards after the first lap, Gaston Roelants broke away from the field and led by 50 yards at the start of the bell lap. Maurice Herriott closed the gap rapidly, but fell 10 yards short. Between 1961 and 1966 Roelants won 45 straight steeplechase finals. In 1977, at the age of 40, he was clocked in 8:41.5.

**1968 Mexico City** C: 37, N: 26, D: 10.16. WR: 8:24.2 (Jouko Kuha)

| | | |
|---|---|---|
| 1. Amos Biwott | KEN | 8:51.0 |
| 2. Benjamin Kogo | KEN | 8:51.6 |
| 3. George Young | USA | 8:51.8 |
| 4. Kerry O'Brien | AUS | 8:52.0 |
| 5. Aleksandr Morozov | SOV | 8:55.8 |
| 6. Mikhail Chelev | BUL | 8:58.4 |
| 7. Gaston Roelants | BEL | 8:59.4 |
| 8. Arne Risa | NOR | 9:09.0 |

No one except the most fanatic track fans had ever heard of Amos Biwott before the 1968 Olympics. But the 20-year-old Kenyan literally leaped to prominence in the third and final elimination heat. Either unaware of or disdainful of accepted racing tactics and steeplechase techniques, Biwott sprinted to a 30-yard lead in the first half lap and led by 70 yards before the first lap had been completed. But what really made the crowd go wild was Biwott's bizarre method of clearing the water jump. Contradicting the teachings of every coach in the world, he would jump onto the hedge and then hop over the water, triple-jump-style, landing on dry ground with the same foot he used to take off. His hurdle style was also unique: he jumped over the barriers with his feet together. In the words of Joe Henderson of *Track and Field News*, "He cleared the hurdles like he feared they had spikes imbedded on the top and leaped the water hazard as if he thought crocodiles were swimming in it." Despite his unorthodox approach, Biwott won his heat by 11.6 seconds.

Naturally, there was a great deal of curiosity as to how well Biwott would stand up in the final two days later against favorites Ben Kogo, Victor Kudinsky, and George Young. Surprisingly, Biwott started slowly, letting Kogo do most of the pace-setting. Unfortunately, Kudinsky withdrew with a hip injury during the second lap. With two laps to go, Gaston Roelants took the lead, while Biwott lingered in ninth place. By the start of the last lap, Kogo was back in the lead. Then, with 300 meters left, Young made his move, passing Kogo on the backstretch. Kogo fought him off, but out of nowhere came Amos Biwott. Kogo was still in front as they cleared the last hurdle, 60 meters from the finish, but Biwott loped right by him and won by three yards.

**1972 Munich** C: 49, N: 29, D: 9.4. WR: 8:22.0 (Kerry O'Brien)

| | | | |
|---|---|---|---|
| 1. H. Kipchoge Keino | KEN | 8:23.6 | OR |
| 2. Benjamin Jipcho | KEN | 8:24.6 | |
| 3. Tapio Kantanen | FIN | 8:24.8 | |
| 4. Bronislaw Malinowski | POL | 8:28.0 | |
| 5. Dušan Moravčik | CZE | 8:29.2 | |
| 6. Amos Biwott | KEN | 8:33.6 | |
| 7. Romualdas Bite | SOV | 8:34.6 | |
| 8. Pekka Paivarinta | FIN | 8:37.2 | |

The second preliminary heat seemed to be cursed. Sergei Skrypka of the Soviet Union lost a shoe with six laps to go, but managed to stay with the leaders until the final water jump, when he slipped and fell headlong into the pond. World record holder Kerry O'Brien had similar bad luck, losing a shoe 200 meters from the finish and smashing into the water jump barrier. In the fourth heat, Amos Biwott set an Olympic record of 8:23.8.

The final was won by Kip Keino, who outkicked his teammate Ben Jipcho. Keino had little steeplechase experience, having entered the race as a challenge. "I had a lot of fun jumping the hurdles," he said, although his lack of experience caused him to jump "like an animal. My style is not good."

**1976 Montreal** C: 24, N: 16, D: 7.28. WR: 8:09.7 (Anders Gärderud)
1. Anders Gärderud SWE 8:08.2 WR
2. Bronislaw Malinowski POL 8:09.2
3. Frank Baumgartl GDR 8:10.4
4. Tapio Kantanen FIN 8:12.6
5. Michael Karst GER 8:20.1
6. Euan Robertson NZE 8:21.1
7. Dan Glans SWE 8:21.5
8. Antonio Campos SPA 8:22.7

The 1976 final was one of the greatest steeplechase races of all time. Antonio Campos led for almost half the race. Then Bronislaw Malinowski, who had issued a warning that he planned to run away from the field in order to make it difficult for "followers" like Anders Gärderud, took over and tried to pull away. But Gärderud and Frank Baumgartl stayed with him. With 300 meters to go, Gärderud, who previously had had trouble living up to expectations in major competitions, flew by Malinowski, with Baumgartl right behind him. Gärderud cleared the final water jump beautifully and opened a five-yard lead. However, the surprising Baumgartl closed the gap as they approached the final hurdle. Gärderud cleared perfectly again, but Baumgartl clipped the barrier with his trail knee and sprawled to the ground. Malinowski jumped over the human hurdle and beat the world record, but he couldn't catch Gärderud. Baumgartl, recalling Lasse Viren's fall in the 1972 10,000 meters, leaped to his feet and salvaged the bronze medal, improving his personal best by 7.2 seconds, despite his mishap.

**1980 Moscow** C: 31, N: 18, D: 7.31. WR: 8:05.4 (Henry Rono)
1. Bronislaw Malinowski POL 8:09.7
2. Filbert Bayi TAN 8:12.5
3. Eshetu Tura ETH 8:13.0
4. Domingo Ramón SPA 8:15.8
5. Francisco Sanchez SPA 8:18.0
6. Giuseppe Gerbi ITA 8:18.5
7. Boguslaw Mamiński POL 8:19.5
8. Anatoly Dimov SOV 8:19.8

No longer contemptuous of those who only follow during the early going, Bronislaw Malinowski was quite content to let Filbert Bayi set the pace in Moscow. Bayi, an air force mechanic from the Mbulu tribe, had little steeplechase experience, whereas Malinowski had been concentrating on the event for 13 years. The offspring of a Polish father and a Scottish mother, Malinowski had finished fourth in 1972 and second in 1976.

Bayi drove into the lead immediately and led by 35 meters with two laps to go, but about a half lap later he suddenly began to tire. Malinowski caught him on the backstretch and won easily, finally achieving his goal of

an Olympic gold medal. When asked why he had followed such a suicidal race plan, Bayi replied, "Because it's fun. . . . It is fun to run as fast as one can until you are dead-tired." He was the first Tanzanian ever to win an Olympic medal. Unfortunately, Bronislaw Malinowski was killed in a car crash on September 26, 1981, near his hometown of Grudziadz. He was 30 years old.

**1984 Los Angeles** C: 35, N: 25, D: 8.10. WR: 8:05.4 (Henry Rono)
1. Julius Korir KEN 8:11.80
2. Joseph Mahmoud FRA 8:13.31
3. Brian Diemer USA 8:14.06
4. Henry Marsh USA 8:14.25
5. Colin Reitz GBR 8:15.48
6. Domingo Ramón SPA 8:17.27
7. Julius Kariuki KEN 8:17.47
8. Pascal Debacker FRA 8:21.51

After a slow first lap, Peter Renner of New Zealand moved to the front and set a hard pace for the first 2000 meters. With 500 meters to go, Washington St. student Julius Korir took the lead. The pre-race favorite, Henry Marsh, moved into second shortly after the bell, positioning himself well for his famous finishing kick. But 220 meters from the finish line, Korir pulled away and scored a decisive victory. Mahmoud and Diemer passed Marsh in the stretch to gain the other medals. Marsh, suffering from a lingering virus, collapsed after the race and was taken away on a stretcher. Of the eight top finishers, all but Marsh and Ramón bettered their pre-Olympic personal records.

**1988 Seoul** C: 32, N: 24, D: 9.30. WR: 8:05.4 (Henry Rono)
1. Julius Kariuki KEN 8:05.51 OR
2. Peter Koech KEN 8:06.79
3. Mark Rowland GBR 8:07.96
4. Alessandro Lambruschini ITA 8:12.17
5. William Van Dijck BEL 8:13.99
6. Henry Marsh USA 8:14.39
7. Patrick Sang KEN 8:15.22
8. Boguslaw Mamiński POL 8:15.97

Francesco Panetta of Italy won the 1987 world championship with an inspired piece of frontrunning. He tried the same strategy at the Olympics, but with considerably less success. Panetta held a slight lead for the first 2000 meters, but then began to struggle. Kariuki, finding himself in front, turned back toward Koech and asked him to take over. Koech whipped into the lead, taking his teammate with him. Panetta faded to a ninth-place finish. With 600 meters to go, Kariuki moved past Koech and opened a 10-meter lead. He eased up at the finish, unaware that he was so close to breaking Henry Rono's 10-year-old world record. Kariuki seemed unconcerned. At the post-race press conference he asked, "What did you say the time was? 8:05.51? Ah, truly not bad." On July 3, 1989, Rono's record finally was beaten: by Peter Koech in 8:05.35.

# 4 × 100-METER RELAY

This event has been dominated by the United States, which has won it 13 of 17 times. The only U.S. losses have been the result of disqualification (1912, 1960, and 1988) and boycott (1980).

**1896–1908** not held

**1912 Stockholm** T: 8, N: 8, D: 7.9
1. GBR (David Jacobs, Harold Macintosh, Victor d'Arcy, William Applegarth) 42.4
2. SWE (Ivan Möller, Charles Luther, Ture Persson, Knut Lindberg) 42.6
DISQ: GER (Otto Röhr, Max Herrmann, Erwin Kern, Richard Rau)

The U.S. team of Courtney, Belote, Wilson, and Cooke won the first semifinal in a time of 42.2, but was disqualified for passing out of the zone. The third semifinal was won by the German team, in 42.3; however they too were disqualified for passing out of the zone in the final, in which they finished second.

**1920 Antwerp** T: 13, N: 13, D: 8.22. WR: 42.3 (GER—Röhr, Herrmann, Kern, Rau)
1. USA (Charles Paddock, Jackson Scholz, Loren Murchison, Morris Kirksey) 42.2 WR
2. FRA (René Tirard, René Lorain, René Mourlon, Emile Ali Khan) 42.6
3. SWE (Agne Holmström, William Petersson [Björneman], Sven Malm, Nils Sandström) 42.9
4. GBR (William Hill, Harold Abrahams, Victor d'Arcy, Harry Edward) —
5. DEN (Henri Thorsen, Fritjoff Andersen, August Sörensen, Marinus Sörensen) —
6. LUX (Jean Colbach, Paul Hammer, Jean Proess, Alex Servais) —

**1924 Paris** T: 15, N: 15, D: 7.13. WR: 42.2 (USA—Paddock, Scholz, Murchison, Kirksey)
1. USA (Francis Hussey, Louis Clarke, Loren Murchison, Alfred Leconey) 41.0 EWR
2. GBR (Harold Abrahams, Walter Rangeley, Lancelot Royle, William Nichol) 41.2
3. HOL (Jacob Boot, Henricus Broos, Jan de Vries, Marinus van den Berge) 41.8
4. HUN (Ferenc Gerö, Lajos Kurunczy, László Muskát, Gusztáv Rózsahegyi) 42.0
5. FRA (Maurice Degrelle, Albert Heise, René Mourlon, André Mourlon) 42.2
DISQ: SWI (Karl Borner, Heinz Hemmi, Joseph Imbach, David Moriaud)

A wholesale assault on the world record began in the first heat of the first round, when Great Britain clocked 42.0. The Dutch team equaled this time in the next heat, but in the sixth heat the Americans ran away in 41.2. In the semifinal, the United States recorded a time of 41.0, and repeated this performance in the final. The most surprising aspect of the final was that the U.S. leadoff runner, Francis Hussey of Stuyvesant High School in New York City, beat 100-meter gold medalist Harold Abrahams by two yards.

**1928 Amsterdam** T: 13, N: 13, D: 8.5. WR: 41.0 (USA—Hussey, Clarke, Murchison, Leconey; Newark Athletic Club, USA—Bowman, Currie, Pappas, Cumming; Sports Club Eintracht, GER—Geerling, Wichmann, Metzner, Salz)
1. USA (Frank Wykoff, James Quinn, Charles Borah, Henry Russell) 41.0 EWR
2. GER (Georg Lammers, Richard Corts, Hubert Houben, Helmut Körnig) 41.2
3. GBR (Cyril Gill, Edward Smouha, Walter Rangeley, Jack London) 41.8
4. FRA (André Cerbonney, Gilbert Auvergne, Pierre Dufau, André Mourlon) 42.0
5. SWI (Emmanuel Goldsmith, Willy Weibel, Willy Tschopp, Hans Niggl) 42.6
DISQ: CAN (Ralph Adams, John Fitzpatrick, George Hester, Percy Williams)

**1932 Los Angeles** T: 8, N: 8, D: 8.7. WR: 40.8 (GER—Jonath, Corts, Houben, Körnig; Sports Club Charlottenburg, GER—Körnig, Grosser, Natan, Schloske; University of Southern California, USA—Delby, Mauer, Guyer, Wykoff)
1. USA (Robert Kiesel, Emmett Toppino, Hector Dyer, Frank Wykoff) 40.0 WR
2. GER (Helmut Körnig, Friedrich Hendrix, Erich Borchmeyer, Arthur Jonath) 40.9
3. ITA (Giuseppe Castelli, Ruggero Maregatti, Gabriele Salviati, Edgardo Toetti) 41.2
4. CAN (Percy Williams, James Brown, Harold Wright, Birchall Pearson) 41.3
5. JPN (Takayoshi Yoshioka, Chuhei Nambu, Izuo Anno, Itaro Nakajima) 41.3
6. GBR (Donald Finlay, Stanley Fuller, Stanley Englehart, Ernest Page) 41.4

The U.S. team set world records of 40.6 in the preliminaries and 40.0 in the final without having to use their leading sprinters, Eddie Tolan, Ralph Metcalfe, and George Simpson.

**1936 Berlin** T: 15, N: 15, D: 8.9. WR: 40.0 (USA—Kiesel, Toppino, Dyer, Wykoff)
1. USA (James "Jesse" Owens, Ralph Metcalfe, Foy Draper, Frank Wykoff) 39.8 WR
2. ITA (Orazio Mariani, Gianni Caldana, Elio Ragni, Tullio Gonnelli) 41.1
3. GER (Wilhelm Leichum, Erich Borchmeyer, Erwin Gillmeister, Gerd Hornberger) 41.2
4. ARG (Juan Lavenas, Antonio Sande, Carlos Hofmeister, Tomas Clifford Beswick) 42.2
5. CAN (Samuel Richardson, Arthur Bruce Humber, Lee Orr, Howard McPhee) 42.7
DISQ: HOL (Tjeerd Boersma, Wijnand van Beveren, Christiaan Berger, Martinus Osendarp)

The 4 × 100-meter relay was the focus of one of the uglier incidents of the 1936 Games, one that caused great embarrassment to the United States. For weeks it had been assumed that the U.S. team would consist of Sam Stoller, Marty Glickman, Frank Wykoff, and Foy Draper, and the foursome spent a good deal of time practicing their baton passing. On August 5, three days before the qualifying heats, Jesse Owens won the 200-meter dash, gaining his third gold medal. When asked if Owens would be added to the relay quartet, coach Lawson Robertson replied, "Owens has had enough glory and collected enough gold medals and oak trees to last him a while. We want to give the other boys a chance to enjoy the 'cérémonie protocolaire.' Marty Glickman, Sam Stoller, and Frank Wykoff are assured places on the relay team. The fourth choice rests between Foy Draper and Ralph Metcalfe."

Two days later, however, Robertson announced that Owens would probably replace Glickman. Then, on the morning of the heats, the U.S. coaches informed both Glickman and Stoller that they were being dropped from the team and replaced by Owens and Metcalfe. What made the situation ugly was that Stoller and Glickman were the only Jews on the U.S. track team, and they returned to the United States as the only members of the squad who didn't compete. Robertson's excuse was that he feared the speed of the Dutch and German teams, and wanted to field the fastest foursome possible. Robertson's fears turned out to be unfounded. If he had really been concerned about fielding the best teams possible, he should have paid more attention to the 4 × 400-meter relay team. In that event, Robertson bypassed medal winners Archie Williams, James LuValle, and Glenn Hardin, and stuck with the original foursome, who promptly lost to the British by over 12 yards.

At any rate, the U.S. 4 × 100 team won easily by 15 yards, setting a world record that would last for 20 years. Frank Wykoff, running the anchor leg, won his third straight relay gold medal, setting a world record each time.

**1948 London** T: 15, N: 15, D: 8.7. WR: 39.8 (USA—Owens, Metcalfe, Draper, Wykoff)
1. USA (Norwood "Barney" Ewell, Lorenzo Wright, Harrison Dillard, Melvin Patton) 40.6
2. GBR (John Archer, John Gregory, Alistair McCorquodale, Kenneth Jones) 41.3
3. ITA (Michele Tito, Enrico Perucconi, Antonio Siddi, Carlo Monti) 41.5
4. HUN (Ferenc Tima, László Bartha, György Csányi, Béla Goldoványi) 41.6
5. CAN (Don McFarlane, James O'Brien, Donald Pettie, Edward Haggis) 41.9
6. HOL (Jan Lammers, Johannes Meyer, Gabe Scholten, Jan Zwaan) 41.9

The U.S. team crossed the finish line six yards ahead of the British, but were disqualified when a judge claimed that the first pass, between Barney Ewell and Lorenzo Wright, had taken place beyond the legal zone. The Americans were dumbfounded and immediately lodged a formal protest. The medal ceremony was held anyway, but three days later a Jury of Appeal viewed films of the race and discovered that the pass had been perfectly legal, and that the track official had been in error. The disqualification was therefore rescinded.

**1952 Helsinki** T: 22, N: 22, D: 7.27. WR: 39.8 (USA—Owens, Metcalfe, Draper, Wykoff)
1. USA (F. Dean Smith, Harrison Dillard, Lindy Remigino, Andrew Stanfield) 40.1
2. SOV (Boris Tokaryev, Levan Kalyayev, Levan Sanadze, Vladimir Sukharyev) 40.3
3. HUN (László Zarándi, Géza Varasdi, György Csányi Bela Goldoványi) 40.5
4. GBR (Emmanuel McDonald Bailey, William Jack, John Gregory, Brian Shenton) 40.6
5. FRA (Alain Porthault, Etienne Bally, Yves Camus, René Bonino) 40.9
6. CZE (František Brož, Jiři David, Miroslav Horčic, Zdenek Pospišil) 41.2

The United States and the U.S.S.R. were almost even after three legs, but Stanfield drew away from Sukharyev to win by two yards.

**1956 Melbourne** T: 18, N: 18, D: 12.1. WR: 39.8 (USA—Owens, Metcalfe, Draper, Wykoff)
1. USA (Ira Murchison, Leamon King, W. Thane Baker, Bobby Joe Morrow) 39.5 WR
2. SOV (Boris Tokaryev, Vladimir Sukharyev, Leonid Bartenyev, Yuri Konovalov) 39.8
3. GER (Lothar Knörzer, Leonhard Pohl, Heinz Fütterer, Manfred Germar) 40.3
4. ITA (Franco Galbiati, Giovanni Ghiselli, Luigi Gnocchi, Vincenzo Lombardo) 40.3
5. GBR (Kenneth Box, Roy Sandstrom, Brian Shenton, David Segal) 40.6
6. POL (Marian Foik, Janusz Jarzembowski, Edward Schmidt, Zenon Baranowski) 40.6

**1960 Rome** T: 19, N: 19, D: 9.8. WR: 39.5 (USA—Baker, King, Morrow, Murchison; GER—Steinbach, Lauer, Fütterer, Germar)
1. GER (Bernd Cullmann, Armin Hary, Walter Mahlendorf, Martin Lauer) 39.5 EWR
2. SOV (Gusman Kosanov, Leonid Bartenyev, Yuri Konovalov, Edvins Ozoliņs) 40.1
3. GBR (Peter Radford, David Jones, David Segal, Neville Whitehead) 40.2
4. ITA (Armando Sardi, Pier Giorgio Cazzola, Salvatore Giannone, Livio Berruti) 40.2
5. VEN (S. Clive Bonas, Lloyd Murad, Emilio Romero, Rafael Romero) 40.7
DISQ: USA (Frank Budd, O. Ray Norton, Stonewall Johnson, David Sime)

The United States had won eight straight 4 × 100-meter relays, but in the opening round the West Germans served notice that they would be serious contenders when they equaled the world record of 39.5. Disaster struck the Americans in the final. Ray Norton, anxious to make up for his disappointing sixth place finishes in the 100 and 200, took off too quickly on his second leg. Leadoff runner Frank Budd yelled at Norton, who came to almost a complete halt. But it was too late. He was already three yards beyond the twenty-meter passing zone. Norton didn't realize it at the time, and ran a strong leg anyway, moving the United States from fourth to second. Dave Sime's come-from-behind anchor leg brought the United States through the tape in first place, in world record time, but the disqualification gave the victory to the Germans, who equaled the world record again in the final.

**1964 Tokyo** T: 21, N: 21, D: 10.21. WR: 39.1 (USA—Jones, Budd, Frazier, Drayton)

| | | | |
|---|---|---|---|
| 1. USA | (O. Paul Drayton, Gerald Ashworth, Richard Stebbins, Robert Hayes) | 39.0 | WR |
| 2. POL | (Andrzej Zieliński, Wieslaw Maniak, Marian Foik, Marian Dudziak) | 39.3 | |
| 3. FRA | (Paul Genevay, Bernard Laidebeur, Claude Piquemal, Jocelyn Delecour) | 39.3 | |
| 4. JAM | (Pablo McNeil, Patrick Robinson, Lynworth Headley, Dennis Johnson) | 39.4 | |
| 5. SOV | (Edvin Ozolin, Boris Zubov, Gusman Kosanov, Boris Savchuk) | 39.4 | |
| 6. VEN | (Arquimedes Herrera, Lloyd Murad, Rafael Romero, Hortensio Herrera Fucil) | 39.5 | |
| 7. ITA | (Livio Berruti, Ennio Preatoni, Sergio Ottolina, Pasquale Giannattasio) | 39.5 | |
| 8. GBR | (Peter Radford, Ronald Jones, Walter Campbell, Lynn Davies) | 39.6 | |

Poor baton passing put the United States in fifth place, three meters behind France, when Bob Hayes took over for the anchor leg. Hayes then unleashed one of the most awesome and breathtaking displays of sprinting ever seen. He swept into the lead after only 30 yards and crossed the finish line with a three-meter margin of victory. Observers disagreed as to Hayes' time for his flying-start 100-meter leg, but the slowest estimate was 8.9 seconds.

**1968 Mexico City** T: 19, N: 19, D: 10.20. WR: 38.6 (University of Southern California, USA/JAM—McCulloch, Kuller, Simpson, Miller)

| | | | |
|---|---|---|---|
| 1. USA | (Charles Greene, Melvin Pender, Ronnie Ray Smith, James Hines) | 38.23 | WR |
| 2. CUB | (Hermes Ramirez, Juan Morales, Pablo Montes, Enrique Figuerola Camue) | 38.39 | |
| 3. FRA | (Gérard Fénouil, Jocelyn Delecour, Claude Piquemal, Roger Bambuck) | 38.42 | |
| 4. JAM | (Errol Stewart, Michael Fray, Clifton Forbes, Lennox Miller) | 38.46 | |
| 5. GDR | (Heinz Erbstösser, Hartmut Schelter, Peter Hasse, Harald Eggers) | 38.66 | |
| 6. GER | (Karl-Peter Schmidtke, Gerhard | 38.76 | |

Wucherer, Gert Metz, Joachim Eigenherr)

| | | | |
|---|---|---|---|
| 7. ITA | (Sergio Ottolina, Ennio Preatoni, Angelo Sguazzero, Livio Berruti) | 39.21 | |
| 8. POL | (Wieslaw Maniak, Edward Romanowski, Zenon Nowosz, Marian Dudziak) | 39.22 | |

With Charlie Greene running with heavily bandaged legs, the United States was beaten to the tape by Cuba in both the opening round and the semifinals. Although Greene ran the final as if uninjured, mediocre baton passing left the United States in only third place when Jim Hines took over for the anchor leg. Five feet behind Enrique Figuerola at the exchange, Hines ripped into the lead after 30 yards and won by a yard. The Cubans mailed their silver medals to activist Stokely Carmichael as a symbol of support for U.S. blacks.

**1972 Munich** T: 27, N: 27, D: 9.10. WR: 38.23 (USA—Greene, Pender, R. R. Smith, Hines)

| | | | |
|---|---|---|---|
| 1. USA | (Larry Black, Robert Taylor, Gerald Tinker, Edward Hart) | 38.19 | WR |
| 2. SOV | (Aleksandr Kornelyuk, Vladimir Lovetski, Juris Silovs, Valery Borzov) | 38.50 | |
| 3. GER | (Jobst Hirscht, Karlheinz Klotz, Gerhard Wucherer, Klaus Ehl) | 38.79 | |
| 4. CZE | (Jaroslav Matoušek, Juraj Demeč, Jiři Kynos, Ludvik Bohman) | 38.82 | |
| 5. GDR | (Manfred Kokot, Bernd Borth, Hans-Jürgen Bombach, Siegfried Schenke) | 38.90 | |
| 6. POL | (Stanislaw Wagner, Tadeusz Cuch, Jerzy Czerbniak, Zenon Nowosz) | 39.03 | |
| 7. FRA | (Patrick Bourbeillon, Jean-Pierre Gres, Gerard Fenouil, Bruno Cherrier) | 39.14 | |
| 8. ITA | (Vincenzo Guerini, Ennio Preatoni, Luigi Benedetti, Pietro Mennea) | 39.41 | |

For the first time since 1932, the 4 × 100-meter relay was won by a team that did not include the 100-meter gold medalist. Eddie Hart, running the anchor leg for the United States, gained some degree of satisfaction after missing the start of his 100-meter quarterfinal heat.

**1976 Montreal** T: 20, N: 20, D: 7.31. WR: 38.19 (USA—Black, Taylor, Tinker, Hart)

| | | | |
|---|---|---|---|
| 1. USA | (Harvey Glance, John Wesley Jones, Millard Hampton, Steven Riddick) | 38.33 | |
| 2. GDR | (Manfred Kokot, Jörg Pfeifer, Klaus-Dieter Kurrat, Alexander Thieme) | 38.66 | |
| 3. SOV | (Alexander Aksinin, Nikolai Kolesnikov, Juris Silovs, Valery Borzov) | 38.78 | |
| 4. POL | (Andrzej Świerczyński, Marian Woronin, Bogdan Grzejszczak, Zenon Licznerski) | 38.83 | |
| 5. CUB | (Francisco Gomez, Alejandro Casañas Ramirez, Hermes Ramirez, Silvio Leonard Tartabull) | 39.01 | |
| 6. ITA | (Vincenzo Guerini, Luciano Caravani, Luigi Benedetti, Pietro Mennea) | 39.08 | |
| 7. FRA | (Claude Amoureux, Joseph Arame, Lucien Sainte-Rose, Dominique Chauvelot) | 39.16 | |

8. CAN   (Hugh Spooner, Marvin Nash, Albin Dukowski,   39.47
          Hugh Fraser)

**1980 Moscow** T: 16, N: 16, D: 9.1. WR: 38.03 (USA—Collins, Riddick, Wiley, Williams)
1. SOV   (Vladimir Muravyov, Nikolai Sidorov, Aleksandr   38.26
          Aksinin, Andrei Prokofiev)
2. POL   Krzysztof Zwoliński, Zenon Licznerski, Leszek   38.33
          Dunecki, Marian Woronin)
3. FRA   (Antoine Richard, Pascal Barré, Patrick Barré,   38.53
          Hermann Panzo)
4. GBR   (Michael McFarlane, Allan Wells, Cameron   38.62
          Sharp, Andrew McMaster)
5. GDR   (Sören Schlegel, Eugen Ray, Bernhard Hoff,   38.73
          Thomas Munkelt)
6. BUL   (Pavel Pavlov, Vladimir Ivanov, Ivailo   38.99
          Karaniotov, Peter Petrov)
7. NGR   (Hammed Adio, Kayode Elegbede, Samson   39.12
          Oyeledun, Peter Okodogbe)
8. BRA   (Milton Costa de Castro, Nelson Rocha Dos   39.54
          Santos, Katsuiko Nakaia, Altevir Araujo Filho)

The French team included 21-year-old twins, Pascal and Patrick Barré.

**1984 Los Angeles** T: 20, N: 20, D: 8.11. WR: 37.86 (USA—King, Gault, C. Smith, Lewis)
1. USA   (Sam Graddy, Ron Brown, Calvin Smith,   37.83   WR
          F. Carlton Lewis)
2. JAM   (Albert Lawrence, Gregory Meghoo, Don-   38.62
          ald Quarrie, Raymond Stewart)
3. CAN   (Benjamin Johnson, Tony Sharpe, Desai   38.70
          Williams, Sterling Hinds)
4. ITA   (Antonio Ullo, Giovanni Bongiorni, Ste-   38.87
          fano Tilli, Pietro Mennea)
5. GER   (Jürgen Koffler, Peter Klein, Jürgen   38.99
          Evers, Ralf Lübke)
6. FRA   (Antoine Richard, Jean-Jacques Bousse-   39.10
          mart, Marc Gasparoni, Bruno Marie-
          Rose)
7. GBR   (Daley Thompson, Donovan Reid, Mi-   39.13
          chael McFarlane, Allan Wells)
8. BRA   (Arnaldo da Silva, Nelson Rocha Dos   39.40
          Santos, Katsuiko Nakaia, Paulo Correia)

Running an 8.94 anchor leg, Carl Lewis won his fourth gold medal, as the U.S. team set the only track and field world record of the Los Angeles Games. The second-place Jamaican squad included 33-year-old Donald Quarrie, who brought his three-Olympic medal total to one gold, two silver and one bronze.

**1988 Seoul** T: 30, N: 30, D: 10.1. WR: 37.83 (USA—Graddy, Brown, Smith, Lewis)
1. SOV   (Victor Bryzgin, Vladimir Krylov, Vladimir   38.19
          Muravyov, Vitaly Savin)
2. GBR   (Elliott Bunney, John Regis, Michael   38.28
          McFarlane, Linford Christie)
3. FRA   (Bruno Marie-Rose, Daniel Sangouma,   38.40
          Gilles Quénéhervé, Max Morinière)

4. JAM   (Christopher Faulknor, Gregory Meghoo,   38.47
          Clive Wright, John Mair)
5. ITA   (Ezio Madonia, Sandro Floris,   38.54
          Pierfrancesco Pavoni, Stefano Tilli)
6. GER   (Fritz Heer, Christian Haas, Peter Klein,   38.55
          Dirk Schweisfurth)
7. CAN   (Desai Williams, Atlee Mahorn, Cyprian   38.93
          Enweani, Brian Morrison)
8. HUN   (György Bakos, László Karaffa, István   39.19
          Tatár, Attila Kovács)

The favored U.S. team was disqualified in the opening round when Lee McNeill, who had finished eighth at the U.S. Olympic trials, failed to receive the pass from Calvin Smith until he was over 5 meters beyond the passing zone.

# 4 × 400-METER RELAY

**1896–1906** not held

**1908 London** T: 7, N: 7, D: 7.25.
*(Medley Relay: 200, 200, 400, 800)*
1. USA   (William Hamilton, Nathaniel Cartmell, John   3:29.4
          Taylor, Melvin Sheppard)
2. GER   (Arthur Hoffman, Hans Eicke, Otto Trieloff,   3:32.4
          Hanns Braun)
3. HUN   (Pal Simon, Frigyes Mezey-Wiesner, József   3:32.5
          Nagy, Ödön Bodor)

The U.S. team clocked 3:27.2 in the first round, but eased up in the final, winning by 25 yards. John Taylor, who ran the third leg, was the first black athlete to win an Olympic gold medal. He was just about to open up practice as a doctor, when he died of typhoid on December 2, 1908, at the age of 24.

**1912 Stockholm** T: 7, N: 7, D: 7.15. WR: 3.18.2 (USA—Schaaf, Sheppard, Gissing, Rosenberger)
1. USA   (Melvin Sheppard, Edward Lindberg,   3:16.6   WR
          James "Ted" Meredith, Charles Reid-
          path)
2. FRA   (Charles Lelong, Robert Schurrer, Pierre   3:20.7
          Failliot, Charles Poulenard)
3. GBR   (George Nicol, Ernest Henley, James   3:23.2
          Tindal Soutter, Cyril Seedhouse)

**1920 Antwerp** T: 6, N: 6, D: 8.23. WR: 3:16.6 (USA—Sheppard, Lindberg, Meredith, Reidpath)
1. GBR   (Cecil Griffiths, Robert Lindsay, John Ainsworth-   3:22.2
          Davis, Guy Butler)
2. SAF   (Harry Davel, Clarence Oldfield, Jack Ooster-   3:24.2
          laak, Bevil Rudd)
3. FRA   (Georges "Géo" André, Gaston Féry, Maurice   3:24.8
          Delvart, Jean Devaux)
4. USA   (James "Ted" Meredith, Frank Shea, George   3:25.2
          Bretnall, George Schiller)
5. SWE   (Sven Krokström, Sven Malm, Erik Sundblad,   —
          Nils Engdahl)
6. BEL   (Jules Migeot, Auguste Corteyn, Omer Smet,   —
          François Morren)

**1924 Paris** T: 7, N: 7, D: 7.13. WR: 3:16.4 (American Legion, Pennsylvania, USA—Rodgers, Eby, Brown, Maxam)

1. USA    Commodore Cochrane, Alan Helffrich, J.    3:16.0    WR
         Oliver MacDonald, William Stevenson)
2. SWE    (Artur Svensson, Erik Byléhn, Gustaf    3:17.0
         Wejnarth, Nils Engdahl)
3. GBR    (Edward Toms, George Renwick, Rich-    3:17.4
         ard Ripley, Guy Butler)
4. CAN    (Horace Aylwin, Allan Christie, David    3:22.8
         Johnson, William Maynes)
5. FRA    (Raymond Fritz, Gaston Féry, Francis    3:23.4
         Galtier, Barthélémy Favaudon)
6. ITA    (Guido Cominotto, Alfredo Gargiullo,    3:28.0
         Ennio Maffiolini, Luigi Facelli)

The British team was hampered by the absence of Eric Liddell, who was off preaching a sermon, it being a Sunday.

**1928 Amsterdam** T: 16, N: 16, D: 8.5. WR: 3:16.0 (USA—Cochran, Helffrich, McDonald, Stevenson)

1. USA    (George Baird, Emerson "Bud" Spencer,    3:14.2    WR
         Frederick Alderman, Raymond Barbuti)
2. GER    (Otto Neumann, Richard Krebs, Werner    3:14.8
         "Harry" Storz, Hermann Engelhard)
3. CAN    (Alexander Wilson, Philip Edwards, Stan-    3:15.4
         ley Glover, James Ball)
4. SWE    (Björn Kugelberg, Bertil von Wachen-    3:15.8
         feldt, Erik Byléhn, Sten Pettersson)
5. GBR    (Roger Leigh-Wood, William Craner,    3:16.4
         John Rinkel, Douglas Lowe)
6. FRA    (Georges Krotoff, Joseph Jackson,    3:19.4
         Georges Dupont, René Féger)

**1932 Los Angeles** T: 7, N: 7, D: 8.7. WR: 3:12.6 (Stanford University, USA—Shore, A. Hables, L. Hables, Eastman)

1. USA    (Ivan Fuqua, Edgar Ablowich, Karl    3:08.2    WR
         Warner, William Carr)
2. GBR    (Crew Stoneley, Thomas Hampson, Da-    3:11.2
         vid Burghley, Godfrey Rampling)
3. CAN    (Raymond Lewis, James Ball, Philip Ed-    3:12.8
         wards, Alexander Wilson)
4. GER    (Joachim Büchner, Walter Nehb, Adolf    3:14.4
         Metzner, Otto Peltzer)
5. JPN    (Itaro Nakajima, Iwao Masuda, Seikan    3:14.6
         Oki, Teiichi Nishi)
6. ITA    (Giacomo Carlini, Giovanni Turba, Mario    3:17.8
         De Negri, Luigi Facelli)

The U.S. team set a world record of 3:11.8 in the opening heat. In the final Bill Carr took off with a 12-yard lead. Godfrey Rampling closed the gap to six yards, at which point Carr pulled away and won by over 20 yards.

**1936 Berlin** T: 12, N: 12, D: 8.9. WR: 3:08.2 (USA—Fuqua, Ablowich, Warner, Carr)

1. GBR    (Frederick Wolff, Godfrey Rampling, William    3:09.0
         Roberts, Arthur Godfrey Brown)
2. USA    (Harold Cagle, Robert Young, Edward O'Brien,    3:11.0
         Alfred Fitch)
3. GER    (Helmut Hamann, Friedrich von Stülpnagel,    3:11.8
         Harry Voigt, Rudolf Harbig)

4. CAN    (Marshall Limon, Philip Edwards, William Fritz,    3:11.8
         John Loaring)
5. SWE    (Sven Strömberg, Per Edfeldt, Olle Danielsson,    3:13.0
         Bertil von Wachenfeldt)
6. HUN    (Tibor Ribényi, Zoltán Zsitavi, József Vadas,    3:14.8
         József Kovacs)

This race marked the only Olympic appearance of the great German runner Rudolf Harbig. Between August 1938 and September 1940, Harbig won 55 consecutive races at distances ranging from 50 meters to 1000 meters. On July 15, 1939, he ran 800 meters in 1:46.6, setting a world record that would last for 16 years. On August 12, he set a 400-meter world record of 46.0 that wasn't bettered until 1948. Harbig was killed fighting the Russians in World War II, on March 5, 1944.

**1948 London** T: 15, N: 15, D: 8.7. WR: 3:08.2 (USA—Fuqua, Ablowich, Warner, Carr)

1. USA    (Arthur Harnden, Clifford Bourland, Roy Coch-    3:10.4
         ran, Malvin Whitfield)
2. FRA    (Jean Kerebel, François Schewetta, Robert    3:14.8
         Chef d'Hotel, Jacques Lunis)
3. SWE    (Kurt Lundkvist, Lars Wolfbrandt, Folke Alnevik,    3:16.0
         Rune Larsson)
4. FIN    (Tauno Suvanto, Olli Talja, Runar Holmberg,    3:24.8
         Bertil Storskrubb)
DNF: JAM (V. George Rhoden, Leslie Laing, Arthur Wint, Herbert McKenley), ITA (Giovanni Rocca, Ottavio Missoni, Luigi Paterlini, Antonio Siddi)

**1952 Helsinki** T: 18, N: 18, D: 7.27. WR: 3:08.2 (USA—Fuqua, Ablowich, Warner, Carr)

1. JAM    (Arthur Wint, Leslie Laing, Herbert    3:03.9    WR
         McKenley, V. George Rhoden)
2. USA    (Ollie Matson, Gerald Cole, Charles    3:04.0
         Moore, Malvin Whitfield)
3. GER    (Hans Geister, Günther Steines, Heinz    3:06.6
         Ulzheimer, Karl-Friedrich Haas)
4. CAN    (Douglas Clement, John Hutchins, John    3:09.3
         Carroll, James Lavery)
5. GBR    (Leslie Lewis, Alan Dick, Terence Hig-    3:10.0
         gins, Nicholas Stacey)
6. FRA    (Jean-Pierre Goudeau, Robert Bart,    3:10.1
         Jacques Degats, Jean-Paul Martin du
         Gard)

In 1948, the Jamaican relay team had wanted more than anything to defeat the United States and win the gold medal. But Arthur Wint, running the third leg, had pulled a muscle and hobbled off the track in pain and anguish. Four years later the same four Jamaicans were back on the track, ready for another shot at their goal. Before the final began, Wint, Laing, McKenley, and Rhoden locked arms in a circle and said a prayer.

Wint ran the first leg and gave up a slight lead to Ollie Matson. Gerald Cole ran a tremendous second lap for the United States. When Herb McKenley took over for Jamaica, he was 12 yards behind 400-meter hurdles' champion Charley Moore. McKenley, competing in his fifth

Olympic final without ever having won a gold medal, ran like a man inspired. Incredibly, he closed the gap and passed Moore in the last second, running a phenomenal 44.6 to Moore's far from shabby 46.3, and allowing 400-meter gold medalist George Rhoden to take off with a one-yard lead. Victory now seemed assured for the Jamaicans, since Mal Whitfield, the U.S. anchor man, had run a disappointing sixth in the 400-meter final. But Whitfield didn't give in, refusing to yield an inch the entire way. However, Rhoden, wearing the same vest that Wint had worn to run the first leg, also refused to let up, and managed to break the tape exactly one yard ahead of Whitfield. The 20-year-old world record, set at the Los Angeles Games, had been demolished by 4.3 seconds. That night, the Jamaican foursome celebrated in their quarters by drinking whisky with the Duke of Edinburgh, out of the only available vessel—a toothbrush tumbler.

**1956 Melbourne** T: 15, N: 15, D: 12.1. WR: 3:03.9 (JAM—Wint, Laing, McKenley, Rhoden)
1. USA (Louis Jones, Jesse Mashburn, Charles Jenkins, Thomas Courtney) 3:04.8
2. AUS (Leon Gregory, David Lean, Graham Gipson, Kevan Gosper) 3:06.2
3. GBR (John Salisbury, Michael Wheeler, F. Peter Higgins, Derek Johnson) 3:07.2
4. GER (Jürgen Kühl, Walter Oberste, Manfred Pörschke, Karl-Friedrich Haas) 3:08.2
5. CAN (Laird Sloan, Murray Cockburn, Douglas Clement, Terry Tobacco) 3:10.2
DISQ: JAM (Keith Gardner, George Kerr, Malcolm Spence, Melville Spence)

**1960 Rome** T: 19, N: 19, D: 9.8. WR: 3:03.9 (JAM—Wint, Laing, McKenley, Rhoden)
1. USA (Jack Yerman, Earl Young, Glenn Davis, Otis Davis) 3:02.2 WR
2. GER (Hans-Joachim Reske, Manfred Kinder, Johannes Kaiser, Carl Kaufmann) 3:02.7
3. DWI (Malcolm Spence, James Wedderburn, Keith Gardner, George Kerr) 3:04.0
4. SAF (Edward Jefferys, Edgar Davis, Gordon Day, Malcolm Spence) 3:05.0
5. GBR (Malcolm Yardley, Barry Jackson, John Wrighton, Robbie Brightwell) 3:08.3
6. SWI (René Weber, Ernst Zaugg, Hansrüdi Bruder, Christian Wägli) 3:09.4

Otis Davis began the anchor leg six yards ahead of Carl Kaufmann. Kaufmann closed the gap to one yard, but in the middle of the final curve, Davis accelerated and pulled away to win by four yards.

**1964 Tokyo** T: 17, N: 17, D: 10.21. WR: 3:02.2 (USA—Yerman, Young, G. Davis, O. Davis)
1. USA (Ollan Cassell, Michael Larrabee, Ulis Williams, Henry Carr) 3:00.7 WR
2. GBR (Timothy Graham, Adrian Metcalfe, John Cooper, Robbie Brightwell) 3:01.6

3. TRI (Edwin Skinner, Kent Bernard, Edwin Roberts, Wendell Mottley) 3:01.7
4. JAM (Lawrence Kahn, Malcolm Spence, Melville Spence, George Kerr) 3:02.3
5. GER/GDR (Jörg Jüttner, Hans-Ullrich Schulz, Johannes Schmitt, Manfred Kinder) 3:04.3
6. POL (Marian Filipiuk, Ireneusz Kluczek, Stanislaw Swatowski, Andrzej Badeński) 3:05.3
7. SOV (Grigory Sverbetov, Victor Bychkov, Vasily Anisimov, Vadim Arkhipchuk) 3:05.9
8. FRA (Michel Hiblot, Bernard Martin, Germain Nelzy, Jean Pierre Boccardo) 3:07.4

**1968 Mexico City** T: 16, N: 16, D: 10.20. WR: 2:59.6 (USA—Frey, Evans, Smith, Lewis)
1. USA (Vincent Matthews, Ronald Freeman, Larry James, Lee Evans) 2:56.16 WR
2. KEN (Daniel Rudisha, Matesi Munyoro Nyamau, Naftali Bon, Charles Asati) 2:59.6
3. GER (Helmar Müller, Manfred Kinder, Gerhard Hennige, Martin Jellinghaus) 3:00.5
4. POL (Jan Balachowski, Stanislaw Grędziński, Jan Werner, Andrzej Badeński) 3:00.5
5. GBR (Martin Winbolt Lewis, Colin Campbell, David Hemery, John Sherwood) 3:01.2
6. TRI (George Simon, Euric Bobb, Benedict Cayenne, Edwin Roberts) 3:04.5
7. ITA (Sergio Ottolina, Giacomo Puosi, Furlo Fusi, Sergio Bello) 3:04.6
8. FRA (Jean Nallet, Jacques Carette, Gilles Bertould, Jean Boccardo) 3:07.5

The final was really two separate races: the United States fighting for a world record and the other teams battling it out for second through eighth places. It was Ron Freeman's remarkable second leg that really did the trick for the Americans. His unofficial time of 43.2 is the fastest leg ever recorded in a 4 × 400-meter relay. Anchor man Lee Evans crossed the finish line 30 yards ahead of Charles Asati in second place.

**1972 Munich** T: 21, N: 21, D: 9.10. WR: 2:56.16 (USA—Matthews, Freeman, James, Evans)
1. KEN (Charles Asati, Hezakiah Nyamau, Robert Ouko, Julius Sang) 2:59.8
2. GBR (Martin Reynolds, Alan Pascoe, David Hemery, David Jenkins) 3:00.5
3. FRA (Gilles Bertould, Daniel Velasques, Francis Kerbiriou, Jacques Carette) 3:00.7
4. GER (Bernd Herrmann, Horst-Rüdiger Schlöske, Hermann Köhler, Karl Honz) 3:00.9
5. POL (Jan Werner, Jan Balachowski, Zbigniew Jaremski, Andrzej Badeński) 3:01.1
6. FIN (Stig Lönnqvist, Ari Salin, Ossi Karttunen, Markku Kukkoaho) 3:01.1
7. SWE (Eric Carlgren, Anders Faager, Kenth Oehman, Ulf Roenner) 3:02.6
8. TRI (Arthur Cooper, Pat Marshall, Charles Joseph, Edwin Roberts) 3:03.6

Ten days before the heats, each nation submitted a list of six names from which a team of four could be chosen. The names submitted by the United States were Vince Matthews, Wayne Collett, Lee Evans, John Smith, Maurice Peoples, and Tommie Turner. Unfortunately, Matthews and Collett were banned from further competition because of their behavior on the victory platform following the 400-meter final. Meanwhile, Smith had pulled a hamstring muscle and was unable to run. This left the United States without a full team, so they were forced to withdraw.

The final was an exciting race, with the hometown West Germans in first place most of the way. But Julius Sang, running a 43.5 anchor leg, passed the fading Karl Honz 75 meters from the finish and went on to give Kenya a three-meter victory.

The British anchor, David Jenkins, was sent to prison in 1987 after pleading guilty to charges related to the manufacture and smuggling of anabolic steroids.

**1976 Montreal** T: 16, N: 16, D: 7.31. WR: 2:56.16 (USA—Matthews, Freeman, James, Evans)

| 1. | USA | (Herman Frazier, Benjamin Brown, Frederick Newhouse, Maxie Parks) | 2:58.65 |
| 2. | POL | (Ryszard Podlas, Jan Werner, Zbigniew Jaremski, Jerzy Pietrzyk) | 3:01.43 |
| 3. | GER | (Franz-Peter Hofmeister, Lothar Krieg, Harald Schmid, Bernd Herrmann) | 3:01.98 |
| 4. | CAN | (Ian Seale, Don Domansky, Leighton Hope, Brian Saunders) | 3:02.64 |
| 5. | JAM | (Leighton Priestley, Donald Quarrie, Colin Bradford, Seymour Newman) | 3:02.84 |
| 6. | TRI | (Michael Solomon, Horace Tuitt, Joseph Coombs, Charles Joseph) | 3:03.46 |
| 7. | CUB | (Eddy Gutierrez, Damaso Alfonso, Carlos Alvarez, Alberto Juantorena Danger) | 3:03.81 |
| 8. | FIN | (Hannu Makela, Ossi Karttunen, Stig Lonnqvist, Markku Kukkoaho) | 3:06.51 |

With the defending champions from Kenya boycotted out of the Olympics, the Americans were left unchallenged. The final was run during a hard rain.

**1980 Moscow** T: 24, N: 24, D: 8.1. WR: 2:56.16 (USA—Matthews. Freeman, James, Evans)

| 1. | SOV | (Remigijus Valiulis, Mikhail Linge, Nikolai Chernetsky, Viktor Markin) | 3:01.1 |
| 2. | GDR | (Klaus Thiele, Andreas Knebel, Frank Schaffer, Volker Beck) | 3:01.3 |
| 3. | ITA | (Stefano Malinverni, Mauro Zuliani, Roberto Tozzi, Pietro Mennea) | 3:04.3 |
| 4. | FRA | (Jacques Fellice, Robert Froissart, Didier Dubois, Francis Demarthon) | 3:04.8 |
| 5. | BRA | (Paulo Roberto Correia, Antonio Dias Ferreira, Agberto Conceição Guimaraes, Geraldo José Pegado) | 3:05.9 |
| 6. | TRI | (Joseph Coombs, Charles Joseph, Rafee Mohammed, Michael Solomon) | 3:06.6 |

| 7. | CZE | (Josef Lomicky, Dusan Malovec, Frantisek Brecka, Karel Kolar) | 3:07.0 |
| DNF: | GBR | (Alan Bell, Terry Whitehead, Roderic Milne, Glendon Cohen) | |

With the top three teams—the United States, West Germany and Kenya—absent because of the anti-Soviet boycott, this was a severely devalued contest. The Soviets, desperate for a victory, rested 400-meter champion Viktor Markin in the opening heat, then claimed that his replacement, Victor Burakov, had been injured, and brought Markin back for the final. They used the same trick to circumvent the anti-replacement rules in the women's 4 × 400 relay. The rejuvenated Markin fought off a surprisingly strong challenge from 400-meter hurdle gold medalist Volker Beck to gain a victory-at-any-cost for the U.S.S.R. The winning time was the slowest in 20 years. The slowest losing time since 1956 (3:25.0) was recorded by Sierra Leone.

**1984 Los Angeles** T: 25, N: 25, D: 8.11. WR: 2:56.16 (USA—Matthews, Freeman, James, Evans)

| 1. | USA | (Sunder Nix, Ray Armstead, Alonzo Babers, Antonio McKay) | 2:57.91 |
| 2. | GBR | (Kriss Akabusi, Garry Cook, Todd Bennett, Philip Brown) | 2:59.13 |
| 3. | NGR | (Sunday Uti, Moses Ugbusien, Rotimi Peters, Innocent Egbunike) | 2:59.32 |
| 4. | AUS | (Bruce Frayne, Darren Clark, Gary Minihan, Rick Mitchell) | 2:59.70 |
| 5. | ITA | (Roberto Tozzi, Ernesto Nocco, Roberto Ribaud, Pietro Mennea) | 3:01.44 |
| 6. | BAR | (Richard Louis, David Peltier, Clyde Edwards, Elvis Forde) | 3:01.60 |
| 7. | UGA | (John Govile, Moses Kyeswa, Peter Rwamuhanda, Mike Okot) | 3:02.09 |
| 8. | CAN | (Michael Sokolowski, Doug Hinds, Bryan Saunders, Tim Bethune) | 3:02.82 |

The United States almost lost this one in the semifinals, when Walter McCoy took five steps in the wrong lane. A formal protest was rejected because his violation was unintentional and had not impeded the progress of any other runners.

The final was hotly contested and marked the first time that four teams had broken three minutes in a single race. Sunday Uti gave Nigeria the first lap lead, while Darren Clark's 43.86 leg put Australia ahead at the midway point. Then Alonzo Babers ran a 43.75 lap to put the U.S. in first place to stay.

**1988 Seoul** T: 22, N: 22, D: 10.1. WR: 2:56.16 (USA—Matthews, Freeman, James, Evans)

| 1. | USA | (Danny Everett, Steven Lewis, Kevin Robinzine, Harry "Butch" Reynolds) | 2:56.16 | EWR |
| 2. | JAM | (Howard Davis, Devon Morris, Winthrop Graham, Bertland Cameron) | 3:00.30 | |
| 3. | GER | (Norbert Dobeleit, Edgar Itt, Jörg Vaihinger, Ralf Lübke) | 3:00.56 | |

| 4. GDR | (Jens Carlowitz, Mathias Schersing, Frank Möller, Thomas Schönlebe) | | 3:01.13 |
| 5. GBR | (Brian Whittle, Kriss Akabusi, Todd Bennett, Philip Brown) | | 3:02.00 |
| 6. AUS | (Robert Ballard, Mark Garner, Miles Murphy, Darren Clark) | | 3:02.49 |
| 7. NGR | (Sunday Uti, Moses Ugbisie, Henry Amike, Innocent Egbunike) | | 3:02.50 |
| 8. KEN | (Tito Sawe, Lucas Sang, Paul Ereng, Simon Kipkemboi) | | 3:04.69 |

The U.S. team found that their real race was not against the other teams, but against the world record set in the 1968 Olympics. When Butch Reynolds crossed the finish line 40 meters clear of the rest of the field, the scoreboard clock stopped at 2:56.17, a frustrating one one-hundredth of a second short of the record. However, the official time turned out to be 2:56.16.

# 20,000-METER WALK

In walking races, the contestants must keep at least one foot in contact with the ground at all times. If a walker loses contact with the ground, he receives a caution for "lifting." A third infraction results in disqualification. Another rule requires walkers to straighten the leg at each step.

Official world records can only be set in walking races contested on a track. Since Olympic walking events are held on the road, winning times are not eligible for world record consideration.

**1896–1952** not held

**1956 Melbourne** C: 21, N: 10, D: 11.28. WR: 1:27:58.2 (Mikhail Lavrov)

| 1. Leonid Spirin | SOV | 1:31:27.4 |
| 2. Antanas Mikėnas | SOV | 1:32:03.0 |
| 3. Bruno Junk | SOV | 1:32:12.0 |
| 4. John Ljunggren | SWE | 1:32:24.0 |
| 5. Stanley Vickers | GBR | 1:32:34.2 |
| 6. Donald Keane | AUS | 1:00:52.0 |
| 7. George Coleman | GBR | 1:34:01.8 |
| 8. Roland Hardy | GBR | 1:34:40.4 |

So many disputes had developed over the judging of the comparatively fast-paced 10,000-meter walk that it was replaced by the less controversial 20,000-meter event. Mikenas, leading after 15 kilometers, received a warning, and resigned himself to second place, urging on Spirin, who had only been placed tenth at the halfway mark.

**1960 Rome** C: 36, N: 18, D: 9.2. WR: 1:27.05.0 (Vladimir Golubnichiy)

| 1. Vladimir Golubnichiy | SOV | 1:34:07.2 |
| 2. Noel Freeman | AUS | 1:34:16.4 |
| 3. Stanley Vickers | GDR | 1:34:56.4 |
| 4. Dieter Lindner | GER | 1:35:33.8 |

| 5. Norman Read | NZE | 1:36:59.0 |
| 6. Lennart Back | SWE | 1:37:17.0 |
| 7. John Ljunggren | SWE | 1:37:59.0 |
| 8. Ladislav Moc | CZE | 1:38:32.4 |

Golubnichiy, a 24-year-old Ukrainian who eventually competed in five Olympics, won the first of his four medals. Freeman, who apparently had not gone over the course beforehand, misjudged his closing surge and fell 50 yards short of victory. In 1968 Freeman became something of a cause célèbre in Australia when he was omitted from the national Olympic team despite the submission of a 41,000-signature petition to the Australian Olympic Federation.

**1964 Tokyo** C: 30, N: 15, D: 10.15. WR: 1:27:05.0 (Vladimir Golubnichiy)

| 1. Kenneth Matthews | GBR | 1:29:34.0 | OR |
| 2. Dieter Lindner | GDR | 1:31:13.2 | |
| 3. Vladimir Golubnichiy | SOV | 1:31:59.4 | |
| 4. Noel Freeman | AUS | 1:32:06.8 | |
| 5. Gennady Solodov | SOV | 1:32:33.0 | |
| 6. Ronald Zinn | USA | 1:32:43.0 | |
| 7. Boris Khrolovich | SOV | 1:32:45.4 | |
| 8. John Edgington | GBR | 1:32:46.0 | |

Ken Matthews, an electrician at a power station near his hometown of Sutton Coldfield, had collapsed and failed to finish in 1960 after leading for eight kilometers. In 1964 he knew he would have a better chance of winning if his wife, Sheila, could join him in Tokyo. His mates agreed and collected £742 to send her along. Sure enough, Matthews crossed the finish line far ahead of the others. Sheila broke through stadium security, rushed onto the track, and gave her hubby what was probably the longest victory kiss in Olympic history. At the postrace interview, Matthews said, "My legs hurt me at the end of the race. They still do. But I wouldn't mind going dancing now."

Sixth-place finisher Ron Zinn died in the Vietnam War less than nine months later. He was 26 years old.

**1968 Mexico City** C: 33, N: 20, D: 10.14. WR: 1:27:05.0 (Vladimir Golubnichiy)

| 1. Vladimir Golubnichiy | SOV | 1:33:58.4 |
| 2. José Pedraza Zuniga | MEX | 1:34:00.0 |
| 3. Nikolai Smaga | SOV | 1:34:03.4 |
| 4. Rudolph Haluza | USA | 1:35:00.2 |
| 5. Gerhard Sperling | GDR | 1:35:27.2 |
| 6. Otto Bartsch | SOV | 1:36:16.8 |
| 7. Hans Reimann | GDR | 1:36:31.4 |
| 8. Stefan Ingvarsson | SWE | 1:36:43.4 |

After 85 minutes of hard walking, Vladimir Golubnichiy entered the stadium in first place, followed closely by teammate Nikolai Smaga. Then the 60,000-plus spectators went wild as a third walker appeared—José Pedraza, a 31-year-old Mexican soldier. Two hundred meters from the finish, Pedraza passed Smaga and set his sights on

Golubnichiy. Pedraza's style seemed far from legal, but it would have taken a suicidal judge to disqualify the determined Pedraza while the stadium echoed with chants of "May-hee-co" and "Pay-drah-zah." An international incident was avoided when Golubnichiy drew away slightly in the homestretch to win by a mere three yards.

**1972 Munich** C: 24, N: 12, D: 8.31. WR: 1:25:19.4 (Peter Frenkel, Hans Reimann)

| | | | |
|---|---|---|---|
| 1. Peter Frenkel | GDR | 1:26:42.4 | OR |
| 2. Vladimir Golubnichiy | SOV | 1:26:55.2 | |
| 3. Hans Reimann | GDR | 1:27:16.6 | |
| 4. Gerhard Sperling | GDR | 1:27:55.0 | |
| 5. Nikolai Smaga | SOV | 1:28:16.6 | |
| 6. Paul Nihill | GBR | 1:28:44.4 | |
| 7. Jan Ornoch | POL | 1:32:01.6 | |
| 8. Vittorio Visino | ITA | 1:32:30.0 | |

Frenkel, Reimann, and Golubnichiy were even after 15 kilometers, with the deaf walker, Gerhard Sperling, six seconds behind. Approaching the stadium, Golubnichiy moved ahead, but Frenkel had the strongest finishing kick and was able to enter the stadium with a small but growing lead. Frenkel was described in East German press handouts as a "color designer and decorator."

**1976 Montreal** C: 38, N: 21, D: 7.23. WR: 1:24:45.0 (Bernd Kannenberg)

| | | | |
|---|---|---|---|
| 1. Daniel Bautista Rocha | MEX | 1:24:40.6 | OR |
| 2. Hans-Georg Reimann | GDR | 1:25:13.8 | |
| 3. Peter Frenkel | GDR | 1:25:29.4 | |
| 4. Karl-Heinz Stadtmüller | GDR | 1:26:50.6 | |
| 5. Raúl González | MEX | 1:28:18.2 | |
| 6. Armando Zambaldo | ITA | 1:28.25.2 | |
| 7. Vladimir Golubnichiy | SOV | 1:29:24.6 | |
| 8. Vittorio Visini | ITA | 1:29:31.6 | |

The contestants in the 1976 20-kilometer walk covered one of the widest age ranges in the Olympics. Eighteen-year-old Bengt Simonsen of Sweden finished 26th, while 48-year-old Alex Oakley of Canada placed 35th. The winner, Daniel Bautista, brought Mexico its first-ever track and field gold medal. He was so dehydrated at the end that he had to drink 10 cans of soft drinks before he could produce enough urine for the drug test. Bautista's time was not accepted as a world record because it was set on the road rather than on a track.

**1980 Moscow** C: 34, N: 20, D: 7.24. WR: 1:20:06.8 (Daniel Bautista)

| | | | |
|---|---|---|---|
| 1. Maurizio Damilano | ITA | 1:23:35.5 | OR |
| 2. Pyotr Pochinchuk | SOV | 1:24:45.4 | |
| 3. Roland Wieser | GDR | 1:25:58.2 | |
| 4. Yevgeny Yevsyukov | SOV | 1:26:28.3 | |
| 5. José Marin | SPA | 1:26:45.6 | |
| 6. Raúl González | MEX | 1:27:48.6 | |
| 7. Bohdan Bulakowski | POL | 1:28:36.3 | |
| 8. Karl-Heinz Stadtmüller | GDR | 1:29:21.7 | |

In 1976 walk officials had been embarrassed by the publication of photographs which clearly showed gold medal winner Daniel Bautista with both feet off the ground during his final lap. In 1980 the officials decided to get tough. With less than 2500 meters to go, Bautista was in first place when he was suddenly disqualified and ordered off the course. This left Anatoly Solomin of the U.S.S.R. in front, but a few hundred meters later he too was disqualified. By the end of the race seven walkers had been ordered off by the judges, including three of the six leaders at the 15-kilometer mark. These crackdowns allowed Maurizio Damilano to win a surprise gold medal. His twin brother, Giorgio, finished 11th. Thipsamay Chanthaphone of Laos, celebrating his 19th birthday, crossed the finish line in 2:20:22.0—over a half hour after the other walkers, and 21½ minutes slower than any contestant since the event began in 1952. But, unlike Bautista and Solomin, he *did* finish.

**1984 Los Angeles** C: 38, N: 22, D: 8.3. WR: 1:18:39.9 (Ernesto Canto)

| | | | |
|---|---|---|---|
| 1. Ernesto Canto | MEX | 1:23:13 | OR |
| 2. Raúl González | MEX | 1:23:20 | |
| 3. Maurizio Damilano | ITA | 1:23:26 | |
| 4. Guillaume Leblanc | CAN | 1:24:29 | |
| 5. Carlo Mattioli | ITA | 1:25:07 | |
| 6. José Marin | SPA | 1:25:32 | |
| 7. Marco Evoniuk | USA | 1:25:42 | |
| 8. Erling Andersen | NOR | 1:25:54 | |

The Mexican population of Los Angeles is second only to that of Mexico City and it was out in force for the 20-kilometer walk, most of which was held on the streets surrounding the stadium. Guillaume Leblanc opened up an early lead, but by the halfway point, he had been passed by defending Olympic champion Maurizio Damilano and by world champion and world record holder Ernesto Canto. Damilano moved ahead by almost 40 meters in the next five kilometers, but was overhauled by Canto and González, who were enthusiastically rooted on by the home away from hometown crowd. The two Mexicans entered the stadium to tumultuous applause with Canto prevailing by 40 meters. For the first time in Olympic history, not one walker was disqualified for improper technique.

**1988 Seoul** C: 53, N: 28, D: 9.23. WR: 1:18:39.9 (Ernesto Canto)

| | | | |
|---|---|---|---|
| 1. Jozef Pribilinec | CZE | 1:19:57 | OR |
| 2. Ronald Weigel | GDR | 1:20:00 | |
| 3. Maurizio Damilano | ITA | 1:20:14 | |
| 4. José Marin | SPA | 1:20:34 | |
| 5. Roman Mrázek | CZE | 1:20:43 | |
| 6. Mikhail Shchennikov | SOV | 1:20:47 | |
| 7. Carlos Mercenario | MEX | 1:20:53 | |
| 8. Axel Noack | GDR | 1:21:14 | |

After 15 kilometers, Pribilinec, 50-kilometer world champion Weigel, and defending Olympic champion Ernesto

Canto were 8 seconds clear of the rest of the field. But then Canto was disqualified, just as he had been at the 1987 world championships. Pribilinec entered the stadium less than 10 meters ahead of Weigel but managed to extend his lead slightly on the track. After the finish, Pribilinec collapsed on his back. Weigel knelt over him and tried to extend his congratulations. But the Czechoslovak winner was so exhausted that he was unable to respond. Silently, Weigel kissed Pribilinec and walked away.

## 50,000-METER WALK

**1896–1928** not held

**1932 Los Angeles** C: 15, N: 10, D: 8.3. WR: 4:34:03.0 (Paul Sievert)
1. Thomas Green     GBR    4:50:10
2. Jánis Dalinch    LAT    4:57:20
3. Ugo Frigerio     ITA    4:59:06
4. Karl Hähnel      GER    5:06:06
5. Ettore Rivolta   ITA    5:07:39
6. Paul Sievert     GER    5:16:41
7. Henri Quintric   FRA    5:27:25
8. Ernest Crosbie   USA    5:28:02

Thomas Green, a 38-year-old railway worker, took the lead seven miles from the finish and won easily. Ugo Frigerio added a bronze medal to the three golds he had won in 1920 and 1924.

**1936 Berlin** C: 33, N: 16, D: 8.5. WR: 4:34:03.0 (Paul Sievert)
1. H. Harold Whitlock   GBR    4:30:41.4   OR
2. Arthur Schwab        SWI    4:32:09.2
3. Adalberts Bubenko    LAT    4:32:42.2
4. Jaroslav Štork       CZE    4:34:00.2
5. Edgar Bruun          NOR    4:34:50.2
6. Fritz Bleiweiss      GER    4:36:48.4
7. Karl Reiniger        SWI    4:40:45.0
8. Etienne Laisne       FRA    4:41:40.0

Harold Whitlock, a 32-year-old auto mechanic, moved into first place after 33 kilometers. However, at the 38-kilometer mark, he began to vomit. His sickness continued for five kilometers, but he kept walking, recovered, and won by a wide margin.

**1948 London** C: 23, N: 11, D: 7.31. WR: 4:34:03.0 (Paul Sievert)
1. John Ljunggren       SWE    4:41:52
2. Godel Gaston         SWI    4:48:17
3. Tebbs Lloyd-Johnson  GBR    4:48:31
4. Edgar Bruun          NOR    4:53:18
5. Harry Martineau      GBR    4:53:58
6. Rune Bjurström       SWE    4:56:43
7. Pierre Mazille       FRA    5:01:40
8. Claude Hubert        FRA    5:03:12

Ljunggren led from start to finish and won easily. Bronze medalist Tebbs Lloyd-Johnson was 48 years old, the oldest person ever to win an Olympic track and field medal.

**1952 Helsinki** C: 31, N: 16, D: 7.21. WR: 4:31:21.6 (Antal Roka)
1. Giuseppe Dordoni       ITA    4:28:07.8   OR
2. Josef Doležal          CZE    4:30:17.8
3. Antal Róka             HUN    4:31:27.2
4. George Whitlock        GBR    4:32:21.0
5. Sergei Lobastov        SOV    4:32:34.2
6. Vladimir Ukhov         SOV    4:32:51.6
7. Dumitru Paraschivescu  ROM    4:41:05.2
8. Ionescu Baboie         ROM    4:41:52.8

**1956 Melbourne** C: 21, N: 10, D: 11.24. WR: 4:21:07.0 (Ladislav Moc)
1. Norman Read         NZE    4:30:42.8
2. Yevgeny Maskinskov  SOV    4:32:57.0
3. John Ljunggren      SWE    4:35:02.0
4. Abdon Pamich        ITA    4:39:00.0
5. Antal Róka          HUN    4:50:09.0
6. Raymond Smith       AUS    4:56:08.0
7. Adolf Weinacker     USA    5:00:16.0
8. Albert Johnson      GBR    5:02:19.0

Norman Read moved from England to New Zealand in 1954. As the Melbourne Olympics approached, he wrote to the British A.A.A. asking for permission to represent Great Britain as a walker. He was rejected. At first he was rejected in New Zealand as well, but a strong showing in races in Australia and New Zealand paved the way for him. He got his naturalization papers and was ready to fulfill his dream. On the day of the 50,000-meter race Read got lost in the corridors of the stadium and didn't find his way to the track until the other runners were already standing on the starting line. Maskinskov led over most of the course, with Read two and a half minutes back after 30 kilometers. At 42 kilometers, however, Read caught the tiring Soviet walker and pulled away to a decisive victory. His unexpected win caused wild cheering in the stadium, and a whole section of the New Zealand contingent had to be restrained from streaming onto the track.

**1960 Rome** C: 39, N: 20, D: 9.7. WR: 4:16:08.6 (Sergei Lobastov)
1. Donald Thompson      GBR    4:25:30.0   OR
2. John Ljunggren       SWE    4:25:47.0
3. Abdon Pamich         ITA    4:27:55.4
4. Aleksandr Stcherbina SOV    4:31:44.0
5. Thomas Misson        GBR    4:33:03.0
6. Alexander Oakley     CAN    4:33:08.6
7. Giuseppe Dordoni     ITA    4:33:28.8
8. Zora Singh           IND    4:37:45.0

In 1956, Don Thompson had been in fifth place with only 5000 meters to go, when he collapsed and failed to finish. With this bad memory in mind, he decided to acclimatize himself well in advance. But it is not easy to simulate a hot and humid September day in Rome when you live in

Cranford, Middlesex. Fortunately, Don Thompson was quite a resourceful person. Several times each week, the 5-foot 5½-inch fire insurance clerk hauled heaters, hot water, and boiling kettles into his bathroom, sealed the doors and windows, and did his exercises in steaming 100-degree Fahrenheit (38-degree Centigrade) heat.

Sure enough, the race began in 87-degree Fahrenheit (30.5-degree Centigrade) weather, but Don Thompson was ready. At the halfway point, he found himself in first place, following the disqualification of two of the leaders and the early overexertions of several others. Surprisingly, his only challenger was 1948 gold medalist John Ljunggren, who was two days shy of his 41st birthday. With 5000 meters to go, the two men were only one second apart. But then Thompson managed to pull away by 18 seconds over the next two kilometers, a lead that he was able to maintain the rest of the way.

**1964 Tokyo** C: 34, N: 19, D: 10.18. WR: 4:14:02.4 (Abdon Pamich)
1. Abdon Pamich        ITA    4:11:12.4   OR
2. Paul Nihill         GBR    4:11:31.2
3. Ingvar Pettersson   SWE    4:14:17.4
4. Burkhard Leuschke   GDR    4:15:26.8
5. Robert Gardiner     AUS    4:17:06.8
6. Christoph Höhne     GDR    4:17:41.6
7. Anatoly Vedyakov    SOV    4:19:56.0
8. Kurt Sakowski       GDR    4:20:31.0

The race resolved into a two-man battle between Pamich and Nihill. At the 38-kilometer mark, Pamich was overcome by nausea and forced to take a 15-second vomit break. He regained the lead quickly, however, and fought off Nihill's challenges for the remainder of the race.

**1968 Mexico City** C: 36, N: 18, D: 10.17. WR: 4:10:41.8 (Christoph Höhne)
1. Christoph Höhne     GDR    4:20:13.6
2. Antal Kiss          HUN    4:30:17.0
3. Larry Young         USA    4:31:55.4
4. Peter Selzer        GDR    4:33:09.8
5. Stig-Erik Lindberg  SWE    4:34:05.0
6. Vittorio Visini     ITA    4:36:33.2
7. Bryan Eley          GBR    4:37:33.0
8. José Pedraza Zuniga MEX    4:37:52.0

Favorite Christoph Höhne drew away after passing the halfway mark, and won by an incredible ten-minute margin. Paul Nihill, who collapsed after 44 kilometers, suffered his only defeat in 86 races between December 1967 and June 1970. He finished ninth at the 1972 Olympics.

**1972 Munich** C: 36, N: 18, D: 9.3. WR: 3:52:44.6 (Bernd Kannenberg)
1. Bernd Kannenberg    GER    3:56:11.6   OR
2. Veniamin Soldatenko SOV    3:58:24.0
3. Larry Young         USA    4:00:46.0
4. Otto Barch          SOV    4:01:35.4
5. Peter Selzer        GDR    4:04:05.4

6. Gerhard Weidner     GER    4:06:26.0
7. Vittorio Visini     ITA    4:08:31.4
8. Gabriel Hernandez   MEX    4:12:09.0

Kannenberg and Soldatenko walked together for 35 kilometers. Kannenberg, who had dropped out in the middle of the 20-kilometer race, noticed that Soldatenko was slow in taking his refreshments at the 35-kilometer food and drink stand, so he decided to pick up the pace. Soldatenko, worried because he had already received a warning, was unable to respond.

**1976** not held

**1980 Moscow** C: 27, N: 14, D: 7.30. WR: 3:41:38.4 (Raúl González)
1. Hartwig Gauder      GDR    3:49:24     OR
2. Jorge Llopart       SPA    3:51:25
3. Yevgeny Ivchenko    SOV    3:56:32
4. Bengt Simonsen      SWE    3:57:08
5. Vyacheslav Fursov   SOV    3:58:32
6. José Marin          SPA    4:03:08
7. Stanislaw Rola      POL    4:07:07
8. Willi Sawall        AUS    4:08:25

Gold medalist Hartwig Gauder was born in West Germany, but his family moved to East Germany in 1960. Forty-two-year-old bronze medalist Yevgeny Ivchenko had been credited with a controversial time of 3:37:36.0 on the Olympic course on May 23, 1980.

**1984 Los Angeles** C: 31, N: 16, D: 8.11. WR: 3:41:38.4 (Raúl González)
1. Raúl González       MEX    3:47:26     OR
2. Bo Gustafsson       SWE    3:53:19
3. Alessandro Bellucci ITA    3:53:45
4. Reima Salonen       FIN    3:58:30
5. Raffaello Ducceschi ITA    3:59:26
6. Carl Schueler       USA    3:59:46
7. Jorge Llopart       SPA    4:03:09
8. José Pinto          POR    4:04:42

The popular 32-year-old veteran Raúl González, competing in his fourth Olympics, pushed the other walkers through a brutal early pace until the hot sun had worn out all of the leading challengers. Maurizio Damilano was the last to go, staying with González for 35 kilometers, before losing contact and then dropping out seven kilometers from the finish. Of the 31 starters, five were disqualified and nine more failed to complete the course.

**1988 Seoul** C: 42, N: 22, D: 9.30. WR: 3:41:38.4 (Raúl González)
1. Vyacheslav Ivanenko SOV    3:38:29     OR
2. Ronald Weigel       GDR    3:38:56
3. Hartwig Gauder      GDR    3:39:45
4. Aleksandr Potasov   SOV    3:41:00
5. José Marin          SPA    3:43:03
6. Simon Baker         AUS    3:44:07
7. Bo Gustafsson       SWE    3:44:49
8. Raffaello Ducceschi ITA    3:45:43

Vyacheslav Ivanenko was a 22-year-old machine repairman at a textile factory when he watched a television program that said that walking was good therapy for a bad back. The 5-foot 4½-inch Ivanenko began walking the two and a half miles to work. Because he lived in Siberia, he walked fast. One day he was noticed by a coach, who began training him in earnest.

At the 20-kilometer mark in the Olympic contest, Hernan Andrade of Mexico led teammate Martin Bermudez by 14 seconds; the rest of the walkers were at least 32 seconds farther back. Ten minutes later Andrade was disqualified. Bermudez held a 1-minute lead at the halfway point, but a group of five caught him in the 32nd kilometer and Bermudez eventually faded to fifteenth. The favorites, Gauder, Weigel, and Ivanenko, pulled away from Marin and Potasov, with Ivanenko holding a 3-second lead after 40 kilometers. Ivanenko then pressed the pace, dropping first Gauder and then Weigel, who resigned himself to protecting second place after receiving his second warning for lifting.

## HIGH JUMP

In high-jump competitions, a contestant may pass at any height. Three successive misses results in elimination, even if the misses are at different heights. Current rules decide ties in the following manner:

1. The competitor with the fewest misses at the last cleared height wins. If there is still a tie, then:
2. The competitor with the fewest total misses wins. If there is still a tie, then:
3. The competitor who has taken the fewest attempts, successful or unsuccessful, wins. If there is still a tie, it is recorded as such, unless the tie is for first place. In which case:
4. Each competitor is given one extra jump. If there is still a tie, then the bar is raised or lowered until the tie is broken.

High-jumpers must take off from one foot. In April 1954, U.S. tumbler Dick Browning reportedly somersaulted over a bar set at 7 feet 6 inches (2.28 meters). In 1962 Gary Chamberlain did a back handspring with a back flip over a bar set at 7 feet 4 inches (2.23 meters). He landed on his feet.

**1896 Athens** C: 5, N: 3, D: 4.10. WR: 1.97, 6-5 ⅝ (Michael Sweeney)

| | | | FT.- | |
| | | | M | IN. |
|---|---|---|---|---|
| 1. | Ellery Clark | USA | 1.81 | 5-11¼ |
| 2. | James Connolly | USA | 1.65 | 5-5 |
| 2. | Robert Garrett | USA | 1.65 | 5-5 |
| 4. | Henrik Sjöberg | SWE | 1.60 | 5-3 |
| 5. | Fritz Hofmann | GER | 1.55 | 5-1 |

Ellery Clark was a 22-year-old Harvard undergraduate who was granted a leave of absence for the Olympics because of his high grade-average.

**1900 Paris** C: 11, N: 7, D: 7.15. WR: 1.97, 6-5 ⅝ (Michael Sweeney)

| | | | FT.- | | |
| | | | M | IN. | |
|---|---|---|---|---|---|
| 1. | Irving Baxter | USA | 1.90 | 6-2¾ | OR |
| 2. | Patrick Leahy | GBR/IRL | 1.78 | 5-10 | |
| 3. | Lajos Gönczy | HUN | 1.75 | 5-8¾ | |
| 4. | Carl-Albert Andersen | NOR | 1.70 | 5-7 | |
| 5. | Eric Lemming | SWE | 1.70 | 5-7 | |
| 6. | Waldemar Steffen | GER | 1.70 | 5-7 | |
| 7. | Louis Monnier | FRA | 1.60 | 5-3 | |
| 8. | Tore Blom | SWE | 1.50 | 4-11 | |

Two Americans, William Remington and Walter Carroll, refused to take part in the final because it was held on a Sunday. Silver medalist Pat Leahy had reportedly cleared 6 feet 4 inches at least six times back in Ireland, but in Paris he missed three times at 6 feet.

**1904 St. Louis** C: 6, N: 3, D: 8.29. WR: 1.97, 6-5 ⅝ (Michael Sweeney)

| | | | FT.- | |
| | | | M | IN. |
|---|---|---|---|---|
| 1. | Samuel Jones | USA | 1.80 | 5-11 |
| 2. | Garrett Serviss | USA | 1.77 | 5-9¾ |
| 3. | Paul Weinstein | GER | 1.77 | 5-9¾ |
| 4. | Lajos Gönczy | HUN | 1.75 | 5-9 |
| 5. | Emil Freymark | USA | — | — |
| 6. | Ervin Barker | USA | 1.70 | 5-7 |

Lajos Gönczy had brought with him to the United States several bottles of potent Hungarian wine, which were confiscated by Hungarian team officials prior to the competition. Unable to clear even 5 feet 9¾ inches, Gönczy finished a disappointing fourth. Several days later, Gönczy took part in an unofficial handicap event and successfully cleared 6 feet 2 inches. When the other Hungarians rushed up to congratulate him, they smelled his breath and discovered that he had found the hidden bottles of wine.

**1906 Athens** C: 24, N: 10, D: 5.1. WR: 1.97, 6-5 ⅝ (Michael Sweeney)

| | | | FT.- | |
| | | | M | IN. |
|---|---|---|---|---|
| 1. | Cornelius Leahy | GBR/IRL | 1.775 | 5-10 |
| 2. | Lajos Gönczy | HUN | 1.75 | 5-8¾ |
| 3. | Themistoklis Diakidis | GRE | 1.725 | 5-8 |
| 3. | Herbert Kerrigan | USA | 1.725 | 5-8 |
| 5. | Gunnar Rönström | SWE | 1.70 | 5-7 |

Herbert Kerrigan had been the favorite, but he was injured when a huge wave hit the ship that carried the U.S. team to Athens.

**1908 London** C: 20, N: 10, D: 7.21. WR: 1.97, 6-5 ⅝ (Michael Sweeney)

| | | | FT.- | |
| --- | --- | --- | --- | --- |
| | | | M | IN. |
| 1. Harry Porter | USA | 1.905 | 6-3 | OR |
| 2. Georges "Géo" André | FRA | 1.88 | 6-2 | |
| 2. Cornelius Leahy | GBR/IRL | 1.88 | 6-2 | |
| 2. István Somodi | HUN | 1.88 | 6-2 | |
| 5. Herbert Gidney | USA | 1.853 | 6-1 | |
| 5. Thomas Moffitt | USA | 1.853 | 6-1 | |
| 7. John Neil Patterson | USA | 1.83 | 6-0 | |

DNC: Axel Hedenlund (SWE)

**1912 Stockholm** C: 26, N: 9, D: 7.8. WR: 2.005, 6-7 (George Horine)

| | | | FT.- | |
| --- | --- | --- | --- | --- |
| | | | M | IN. |
| 1. Alma Richards | USA | 1.93 | 6-4 | OR |
| 2. Hans Liesche | GER | 1.91 | 6-3¼ | |
| 3. George Horine | USA | 1.89 | 6-2¼ | |
| 4. Egon Erickson | USA | 1.87 | 6-1½ | |
| 4. James Thorpe | USA | 1.87 | 6-1½ | |
| 6. Harry Grumpelt | USA | 1.85 | 6-0¾ | |
| 6. John Johnstone | USA | 1.85 | 6-0¾ | |
| 8. Karl-Axel Kullerstrand | SWE | 1.83 | 6-0 | |

Alma Richards was a tall, awkward-looking 22-year-old Mormon from Parowan, Utah. On the ship from New York to Stockholm, he became the butt of countless "country boob" jokes made by the other members of the U.S. team. In the final Olympic competition, Richards seemed to have quite a bit of trouble, missing as many jumps as he made. Yet when the bar was raised to 6 feet 3¼ inches, the only jumpers left were Richards, Hans Liesche of Germany, and the favorite, George Horine, inventor of what came to be known as the "western-roll" style of high-jumping. Liesche cleared smoothly on the first try, but Horine missed three times and was eliminated. Richards, however, cleared the bar on his third and final attempt.

The bar was then put up to 6 feet 4 inches. Alma Richards, scheduled to jump first, walked away from the high jump area to be by himself. He closed his eyes and bowed his head, and made a deal with God. "I told the Lord," he later wrote, "that if He would help me to win the high jump in the Olympic Games at Stockholm, I would do my best to be a good boy and set a good example." Without further hesitation, Richards, who had never before come close to jumping 6 feet 4 inches, dashed toward the bar and sailed over with almost two inches to spare. Liesche was completely unnerved. He failed twice. Then, just as he had composed himself for his final attempt, a gun went off to signal the start of a race. Liesche waited for the race to end and then composed himself once more. This time the band began to play. After nine minutes, a Swedish official approached him and asked him to hurry up. This was the final blow.

Liesche ran at the bar, but missed completely. Alma Richards, transformed from a country bumpkin into a hero in the eyes of his teammates, went on to be a good boy for the rest of his life.

**1920 Antwerp** C: 22, N: 8, D: 8.17. WR: 2.01, 6-7¼ (Edward Beeson)

| | | | FT.- | |
| --- | --- | --- | --- | --- |
| | | | M | IN. |
| 1. Richmond Landon | USA | 1.935 | 6-4 | EOR |
| 2. Harold Muller | USA | 1.90 | 6-2¾ | |
| 3. Bo Ekelund | SWE | 1.90 | 6-2¾ | |
| 4. Walter Whalen | USA | 1.85 | 6-0¾ | |
| 5. John Murphy | USA | 1.85 | 6-0¾ | |
| 6. B. Howard Baker | GBR | 1.85 | 6-0¾ | |
| 7. Pierre Lewden | FRA | 1.80 | 5-10¾ | |
| 7. Einar Thulin | SWE | 1.80 | 5-10¾ | |

**1924 Paris** C: 21, N: 15, D: 7.7. WR: 2.03, 6-8¼ (Harold Osborn)

| | | | FT.- | |
| --- | --- | --- | --- | --- |
| | | | M | IN. |
| 1. Harold Osborn | USA | 1.98 | 6-6 | OR |
| 2. Leroy Brown | USA | 1.95 | 6-4¾ | |
| 3. Pierre Lewden | FRA | 1.92 | 6-3½ | |
| 4. Thomas Poor | USA | 1.88 | 6-2 | |
| 5. Jenö Gáspár | HUN | 1.88 | 6-2 | |
| 6. Helge Jansson | SWE | 1.85 | 6-0¾ | |
| 7. Pierre Guilloux | FRA | 1.85 | 6-0¾ | |
| 8. Sverre Helgesen | NOR | 1.83 | 6-0 | |
| 8. L. Roberts | SAF | 1.83 | 6-0 | |

Harold Osborn cleared every height on his first attempt. Five days later he earned a second gold medal in the decathlon.

**1928 Amsterdam** C: 35, N: 17, D: 7.29. WR: 2.03, 6-8¼ (Harold Osborn)

| | | | FT.- | |
| --- | --- | --- | --- | --- |
| | | | M | IN. |
| 1. Robert King | USA | 1.94 | 6-4½ | |
| 2. Benjamin Hedges | USA | 1.91 | 6-3¼ | |
| 3. Claude Ménard | FRA | 1.91 | 6-3¼ | |
| 4. Simeon Toribio | PHI | 1.91 | 6-3¼ | |
| 5. Harold Osborn | USA | 1.91 | 6-3¼ | |
| 6. Kazuo Kimura | JPN | 1.88 | 6-2 | |
| 7. A. Cherrier (FRA), Pierre Lewden (FRA), Charles McGinnis (USA), Mikio Oda (JPN) | | 1.88 | 6-2 | |

Places two through five were decided by a jump-off.

**1932 Los Angeles** C: 14, N: 10, D: 7.31. WR: 2.03, 6-8¼ (Harold Osborn)

| | | | FT.- | |
| --- | --- | --- | --- | --- |
| | | | M | IN. |
| 1. Duncan McNaughton | CAN | 1.97 | 6-5½ | |
| 2. Robert Van Osdel | USA | 1.97 | 6-5½ | |
| 3. Simeon Toribio | PHI | 1.97 | 6-5½ | |

| | | | FT.- |
|---|---|---|---|
| 4. Cornelius Johnson | USA | 1.97 | 6-5½ |
| 5. Ilmari Reinikka | FIN | 1.94 | 6-4¼ |
| 6. Kazuo Kimura | JPN | 1.94 | 6-4¼ |
| 7. Misao Ono | JPN | 1.90 | 6-2¾ |
| 7. Jerzy Plawczyk | POL | 1.90 | 6-2¾ |

Bob Van Osdel and Duncan McNaughton were good friends and fellow students at the University of Southern California in Los Angeles. Van Osdel had qualified for the U.S. team, as expected, by clearing 6 feet 6⅝ inches at the U.S. trials. McNaughton, on the other hand, had to wage a one-man campaign to convince the Canadian Olympic Association to let him compete. Undeterred by their constant refusals, McNaughton waited until the Canadian team arrived in Los Angeles, and then badgered them in person until they finally relented.

Van Osdel, McNaughton, Toribio, and 18-year-old Los Angeles High School student Cornelius Johnson all cleared 6 feet 5½ inches, but they all missed at 6 feet 6¾ inches. Following the rules in force at the time, the bar was then raised, lowered, raised and lowered until the contest was decided. After Johnson and Toribio had been eliminated, Van Osdel, who had been informally coaching McNaughton ever since he had first arrived in Los Angeles from Vancouver two years earlier, approached his Canadian friend and advised him on improving his technique. He concluded, "Get your kick working and you will be over." That piece of advice and encouragement did the trick. McNaughton cleared the bar while Van Osdel missed.

If current tie-breaking rules had been used back in 1932, Van Osdel would have won the gold medal, Johnson the silver, and McNaughton the bronze.

**1936 Berlin** C: 40, N: 24, D: 8.2. WR: 2.07, 6-9¾ (Cornelius Johnson, David Albritton)

| | | | FT.- | |
|---|---|---|---|---|
| | | | M | IN. |
| 1. Cornelius Johnson | USA | 2.03 | 6-8 | OR |
| 2. David Albritton | USA | 2.00 | 6-6¾ | |
| 3. Delos Thurber | USA | 2.00 | 6-6¾ | |
| 4. Kalevi Kotkas | FIN | 2.00 | 6-6¾ | |
| 5. Kimio Yada | JPN | 1.97 | 6-5½ | |
| 6. Yoshiro Asakuma | JPN | 1.94 | 6-4¼ | |
| 6. Lauri Kalima | FIN | 1.94 | 6-4¼ | |
| 6. Hiroshi Tanaka | JPN | 1.94 | 6-4¼ | |
| 6. Gustav Weinkötz | GER | 1.94 | 6-4¼ | |

Johnson won the gold medal without a miss and didn't even take off his sweatsuit until the bar had reached 6 feet 6¾ inches. Places 2 through 4 were decided by a jump-off. Adolf Hitler had personally congratulated the winners of the first two events of the day, Germans and Finns, but he left the stadium before the ceremony honoring the three Americans. Both Johnson and Albritton were black. Fourth-place finisher Kotkas had finished seventh in the discus throw four years earlier.

**1948 London** C: 26, N: 16, D: 7.30. WR: 2.11, 6-11 (Lester Steers)

| | | | FT.- | |
|---|---|---|---|---|
| | | | M | IN. |
| 1. John Winter | AUS | 1.98 | 6-6 | |
| 2. Björn Paulson | NOR | 1.95 | 6-4¾ | |
| 3. George Stanich | USA | 1.95 | 6-4¾ | |
| 4. Dwight Eddleman | USA | 1.95 | 6-4¾ | |
| 5. Georges Damitio | FRA | 1.95 | 6-4¾ | |
| 6. Arthur Jackes | CAN | 1.90 | 6-2¾ | |
| 7. Alan Paterson | GBR | 1.90 | 6-2¾ | |
| 7. Hans Wähli | SWI | 1.90 | 6-2¾ | |

John Winter, a 23-year-old bank clerk from Perth, injured his back when he cleared 6 feet 4¾ inches. He decided to try one more height anyway, and made 6 feet 6 inches on his first attempt. Then he watched in surprise as the remaining four jumpers, including two Americans who had had to clear 6 feet 7¼ inches just to make the team, failed three times each. For the first time in the Olympics, ties were decided according to fewer misses.

**1952 Helsinki** C: 36, N: 24, D: 7.20. WR: 2.11, 6-11 (Lester Steers)

| | | | FT.- | |
|---|---|---|---|---|
| | | | M | IN. |
| 1. Walter Davis | USA | 2.04 | 6-8½ | OR |
| 2. Kenneth Wiesner | USA | 2.01 | 6-7 | |
| 3. José Telles da Conceição | BRA | 1.98 | 6-6 | |
| 4. Gösta Svensson | SWE | 1.98 | 6-6 | |
| 5. Ronald Pavitt | GBR | 1.95 | 6-4¾ | |
| 6. Ion Soter | ROM | 1.95 | 6-4¾ | |
| 7. Arnold Betton | USA | 1.95 | 6-4¾ | |
| 8. Björn Gundersen | NOR | 1.90 | 6-2¾ | |

The 6-foot 8-inch, 206-pound Davis was an All-American basketball player from Texas A. & M. Stricken by polio at the age of 8, he had been unable to walk for three years.

**1956 Melbourne** C: 28, N: 19, D: 11.23. WR: 2.15, 7-0½ (Charles Dumas)

| | | | FT.- | |
|---|---|---|---|---|
| | | | M | IN. |
| 1. Charles Dumas | USA | 2.12 | 6-11½ | OR |
| 2. Charles Porter | AUS | 2.10 | 6-10¾ | |
| 3. Igor Kashkarov | SOV | 2.08 | 6-9¾ | |
| 4. Stig Pettersson | SWE | 2.06 | 6-9 | |
| 5. Kenneth Money | CAN | 2.03 | 6-8 | |
| 6. Vladimir Sitkin | SOV | 2.00 | 6-6¾ | |
| 7. Phil Reavis | USA | 2.00 | 6-6¾ | |
| 7. Colin Ridgeway | AUS | 2.00 | 6-6¾ | |

When Les Steers jumped 6 feet 11 inches on June 14, 1941, it seemed that the magic 7-foot barrier would be cleared at any time. But it was 12 years before Walt Davis bettered Steer's record with a leap of 6 feet 11½ inches, and even he was unable to go that extra half-inch. It was as if the 7-foot mark was guarded by a protective aura. It is true that 7-foot jumps had been claimed, most notably by Davis in an exhibition, but the first official, in-competition 7-foot jump wasn't achieved until June 29, 1956, when 19-year-old Charley Dumas glided over at the U.S. Olympic trials. There was great interest in Dumas when he arrived in Melbourne, but some of that interest turned to hostility when it turned out that Dumas didn't believe in practicing or even training, other than a few stretching exercises each morning.

However, Dumas knew what he was up to. He won the gold medal with relative ease, despite the spirited challenge of local favorite Chilla Porter, who improved his personal best by two inches.

Ken Money, who finished fifth, later became a space scientist and astronaut.

**1960 Rome** C: 32, N: 23, D: 9.1. WR: 2.23, 7-3¾ (John Thomas)

|  |  | M | FT.-IN. |  |
|---|---|---|---|---|
| 1. Robert Shavlakadze | SOV | 2.16 | 7-1 | OR |
| 2. Valery Brumel | SOV | 2.16 | 7-1 |  |
| 3. John Thomas | USA | 2.14 | 7-0¼ |  |
| 4. Viktor Bolshov | SOV | 2.14 | 7-0¼ |  |
| 5. Stig Pettersson | SWE | 2.09 | 6-10¼ |  |
| 6. Charles Dumas | USA | 2.03 | 6-8 |  |
| 7. Jiři Lansky | CZE | 2.03 | 6-8 |  |
| 7. Kjell-Ake Nilsson | SWE | 2.03 | 6-8 |  |
| 7. Theo Püll | GER | 2.03 | 6-8 |  |

American sportswriters boasted that the high jump was one gold medal that was "in the bag" for the United States. The U.S. team consisted of 17-year-old Joe Faust, who had cleared 7 feet, defending champion Charley Dumas, and the 6-foot 5-inch world record holder John Thomas, who had jumped 7 feet over 30 times and hadn't been defeated in two years. But Faust, hampered by an ankle injury, was unable to clear 6 feet 6¾ inches. And Dumas, plagued by a knee injury that American officials had tried to convince him was imaginary, bowed out at 6 feet 10¼ inches. This left Thomas to battle it out with three jumpers from the U.S.S.R.: Soviet champion Viktor Bolshov, 18-year-old Siberian-born Valery Brumel, who had suddenly improved three and a half inches in August to 7 feet 1½ inches, and Robert Shavlakadze, a mustachioed 27-year-old from Tbilisi, Georgia.

At 6 feet 11½ inches Thomas passed. Bolshov and Shavlakadze went over the bar on their first attempts, while Brumel missed twice before clearing. This height also saw the departure of Stig Pettersson. The bar was raised to 7 feet ¼ inch. Brumel and Bolshov missed, but Shavlakadze cleared with his first try, the first time he had ever jumped over 7 feet in competition. Thomas missed, but the second time around, he and the other two Soviet jumpers all cleared the bar.

The next height was 7 feet 1 inch. The only one to clear on the first attempt was Shavlakadze, who had now made seven straight successful jumps since missing his first try of the afternoon at 6 feet 6¾ inches. Brumel cleared on his second try, but Bolshov and Thomas missed all three

times. For Robert Shavlakadze, this was the greatest day of his career. For Valery Brumel, it was just the beginning. As for John Thomas, he was disappointed, but proud that he had earned an Olympic medal. Consequently, it came as a shock to the mild-mannered teenager when the very same sportswriters and fans who had been singing his praises only a few days earlier turned on him and accused him of getting carried away with all the publicity that they themselves had spread.

"That was the first time I learned people didn't like me," Thomas later recalled. "They only like winners. They don't give credit to a man for trying. I was called a quitter, a man with no heart. It left me sick." Thomas had nightmares for months until he finally came to accept that American sports fans were fickle. "American spectators are frustrated athletes," he concluded. "In the champion, they see what they'd like to be. In the loser, they see what they actually are, and they treat him with scorn."

**1964 Tokyo** C: 29, N: 20, D: 10.21. WR: 2.28, 7-5¾ (Valery Brumel)

|  |  | M | FT.-IN. |  |
|---|---|---|---|---|
| 1. Valery Brumel | SOV | 2.18 | 7-1¾ | OR |
| 2. John Thomas | USA | 2.18 | 7-1¾ | OR |
| 3. John Rambo | USA | 2.16 | 7-1 |  |
| 4. Stig Pettersson | SWE | 2.14 | 7-0¼ |  |
| 5. Robert Shavlakadze | SOV | 2.14 | 7-0¼ |  |
| 6. Ralf Drecoll | GER | 2.09 | 6-10¼ |  |
| 6. Kjell-Åke Nilsson | SWE | 2.09 | 6-10¼ |  |
| 8. Edward Caruthers | USA | 2.09 | 6-10¼ |  |

By 1964 the situation had become easier for John Thomas, since he was no longer the favorite. Instead, the pressure of great expectations had shifted to Valery Brumel, the current world record holder. And Brumel definitely felt that pressure. He lost to Shavlakadze at the 1964 U.S.S.R. championships, and arrived in Tokyo in somewhat of a crisis. Well below form, he worked out in secret so that his image of invincibility wouldn't be tarnished. When he cleared 6 feet 9¾ inches in practice, his coach lied to him and told him the bar had actually been two inches higher.

The Olympic qualifying round was held on October 20. Brumel missed twice at 6 feet 8 inches and was on the verge of not even making it to the final, when he got himself together and cleared the bar successfully, thus preventing a complete disaster.

The next day, for the final, Brumel was more composed. He made it through 6 feet 11½ inches without a miss, a feat matched only by Robert Shavlakadze. Pettersson, Rambo, and Thomas each cleared 6 feet 11½ inches with their second try. At 7 feet ¼ inch, only Rambo went over the first time, and only Pettersson made it the second time. The three medalists from 1960 were now each one miss from elimination. But all three literally rose to the challenge and sailed over without dislodging the bar. This seemed to be a turning point for

Valery Brumel. With renewed confidence, he cleared 7 feet 1 inch on his first attempt. Thomas made it the second time around, and Rambo the third, while Pettersson and Shavlakadze failed at all three attempts. Rambo bowed out at 7 feet 1¾ inches, while Brumel and Thomas both succeeded with their first tries. However, neither man, by now good friends after four years of competition, was able to make it over 7 feet 2½ inches. Brumel and Thomas were both credited with the Olympic record, but Brumel was awarded first place because he had committed fewer misses.

On October 4, 1965, Valery Brumel was riding on the back of a motorcycle being driven by female motorcycle racing champion Tamara Golikova, when they skidded out of control. Although Golikova was unhurt, Brumel was smashed into a concrete pillar and suffered multiple fractures to his right leg. His right foot was hanging limply, barely connected to the rest of his body.

When Brumel had traveled to the United States to compete in a series of competitions against John Thomas, he had been shocked by the behavior of American crowds, which booed Thomas when he missed a jump or, worst of all, when he committed the sin of finishing second. But now that his own sporting career had come to a sudden end, Brumel learned that Soviet fans could be just as harsh. The newspapers lost interest in him, most of his friends drifted away, his wife, perhaps wondering what he had been doing whizzing around on the back of a motorcycle with Tamara Golikova in the first place, divorced him.

After his accident, Brumel had received a telegram that read, "Sometimes a twist of fate seems to have been put there to test a man's strength of character. Don't admit defeat. I sincerely hope you come back to jump again." It was signed "John Thomas." Remarkably, Valery Brumel did jump again. Although he never made it back to international competition, in 1970 he actually cleared 6 feet 11¾ inches. He was also able to channel his energy into other directions, earning a doctorate in sports psychology and publishing a novel.

**1968 Mexico City** C: 39, N: 25, D: 10.20. WR: 2.28, 7-5¾ (Valery Brumel)

|  |  |  | M | FT.-IN. |  |
|---|---|---|---|---|---|
| 1. | Richard Fosbury | USA | 2.24 | 7-4¼ | OR |
| 2. | Edward Caruthers | USA | 2.22 | 7-3¼ |  |
| 3. | Valentin Gavrilov | SOV | 2.20 | 7-2½ |  |
| 4. | Valery Skvortsov | SOV | 2.16 | 7-1 |  |
| 5. | Reynaldo Brown | USA | 2.14 | 7-0¼ |  |
| 6. | Giacomo Crosa | ITA | 2.14 | 7-0¼ |  |
| 7. | Gunther Spielvogel | GER | 2.14 | 7-0¼ |  |
| 8. | Lawrie Peckham | AUS | 2.12 | 6-11½ |  |

The 1968 Olympics marked the international debut of Dick Fosbury and his celebrated "Fosbury Flop," which would soon revolutionize high-jumping. Fosbury's technique began by racing up to the bar at great speed and taking off with his left foot. But instead of swinging his right foot up and over the bar, as everyone else did, Fosbury would pivot his right leg back and approach head first with his back to the bar. While the coaches of the world, already exasperated by the steeplechase style of Amos Biwott, shook their heads in disbelief, the Mexico City audience was absolutely captivated by Fosbury. Fosbury cleared every height through 7 feet 3¼ inches without a miss and then achieved a personal record of 7 feet 4¼ inches to win the gold medal. By 1980, 13 of the 16 Olympic finalists were using the Fosbury Flop.

**1972 Munich** C: 40, N:29, D: 9.10. WR: 2.29, 7-6 (Ni Chihchin, Patrick Matzdorf)

|  |  |  | M | FT.-IN. |
|---|---|---|---|---|
| 1. | Jüri Tarmak | SOV | 2.23 | 7-3¾ |
| 2. | Stefan Junge | GDR | 2.21 | 7-3 |
| 3. | Dwight Stones | USA | 2.21 | 7-3 |
| 4. | Hermann Magerl | GER | 2.18 | 7-1¾ |
| 5. | Ádám Szepesi | HUN | 2.18 | 7-1¾ |
| 6. | John Beers | CAN | 2.15 | 7-0½ |
| 6. | István Major | HUN | 2.15 | 7-0½ |
| 8. | Rustam Akhmyetov | SOV | 2.15 | 7-0½ |

**1976 Montreal** C: 36, N: 23, D: 7.31. WR: 2.31, 7-7 (Dwight Stones)

|  |  |  | M | FT.-IN. |  |
|---|---|---|---|---|---|
| 1. | Jacek Wszola | POL | 2.25 | 7-4½ | OR |
| 2. | Gregory Joy | CAN | 2.23 | 7-3¾ |  |
| 3. | Dwight Stones | USA | 2.21 | 7-3 |  |
| 4. | Sergei Budalov | SOV | 2.21 | 7-3 |  |
| 5. | Sergei Senyukov | SOV | 2.18 | 7-1¾ |  |
| 6. | Rodolfo Bergamo | ITA | 2.18 | 7-1¾ |  |
| 7. | Rolf Beilschmidt | GDR | 2.18 | 7-1¾ |  |
| 8. | Jesper Torring | DEN | 2.18 | 7-1¾ |  |

In 1972 Dwight Stones had been one of the darlings of the Munich Games. A mere 18 years old, he had delighted the crowd with his exuberance. Four years later in Montreal, it was a completely different story. Now he was the world record holder and heavy favorite. But several days before the competition began, Stones had launched a verbal attack against the French-Canadian organizers of the Games for failing to complete the stadium as planned. Of particular concern to Stones was the nonappearance of a retractable roof, which would have kept out the rain. Fear of rain was an obsession with Stones because his approach to the bar was unusually fast and sharp. Stones called the Olympic organizers "rude" for forcing the athletes to compete in an unfinished stadium. But by the time that his remarks had been translated into the local papers, he was being accused of calling all French-Canadians "rude."

When Stones appeared on the track for the qualifying round, he was loudly booed. Whenever his name was announced, he was booed; whenever he began a jump he was booed; whenever he missed or made a jump he was booed. The situation degenerated rather badly when U.S. fans in the stadium retaliated by booing a French-Canadian high-jumper, Claude Ferragne.

The next day, Stones tried to make peace with the local crowd by wearing a shirt that bore on the back the slogan "I love French Canadians." Track officials made him take it off. Underneath he had on a 1972 Olympic shirt, which he was wearing because it had been made by a company with whom he had a financial relationship. The officials made him take that one off too. By the time the bar had been raised to 7 feet 1¾ inches, a light rain had begun to fall. At 7 feet 3 inches, the rain had become heavy. Huge puddles formed in the high jump area. Stones, exasperated by the ineffectual attempts of the officials to clear the area, grabbed a squeegee and started mopping up the area himself. Other jumpers joined him, including surprise local favorite Greg Joy. For Stones it was a hopeless cause. Even the eventual winner, 19-year-old Jacek Wszola, when asked later at what point he knew he would win, replied, "When it started to rain."

Four days later, in Philadelphia, Dwight Stones broke his own world record with a leap of 7 feet 7¼ inches.

**1980 Moscow** C: 30, N: 19, D: 8.1. WR: 2.35, 7-8½ (Jacek Wszola, Dietmar Mögenburg)

|  |  | | FT.- | |
| --- | --- | --- | --- | --- |
|  |  | M | IN. | |
| 1. Gerd Wessig | GDR | 2.36 | 7-8¾ | WR |
| 2. Jacek Wszola | POL | 2.31 | 7-7 | |
| 3. Jörg Freimuth | GDR | 2.31 | 7-7 | |
| 4. Henry Lauterbach | GDR | 2.29 | 7-6 | |
| 5. Roland Dalhäuser | SWI | 2.24 | 7-4¼ | |
| 6. Vaso Komnenić | YUG | 2.24 | 7-4¼ | |
| 7. Adrian Proteasa | ROM | 2.21 | 7-3 | |
| 8. Aleksandr Grigoriev | SOV | 2.21 | 7-3 | |

The anticipated showdown between co-world record holders Jacek Wszola and Dietmar Mogenburg was spoiled when West Germany joined the anti-Soviet boycott. As it turned out, however, neither of them held the world record anymore once the competition was over. Gerd Wessig, a 6-foot 5-inch 21-year-old cook from Schwerin, was one of the big surprises of the 1980 Olympics. He had only qualified for the East German team two weeks earlier when he won the national championship with what was then his personal record of 7 feet 6½ inches. In Moscow he improved by over two inches to become the first man to set a world record in the high jump in the Olympics. Oddly enough, Wessig was also the first jumper since 1896 to make a successful jump beyond the height that had won him the gold medal.

**1984 Los Angeles** C: 30, N: 20, D: 8.11. WR: 2.39, 7-10 (Zhu Jianhua)

|  |  | | FT.- | |
| --- | --- | --- | --- | --- |
|  |  | M | IN. | |
| 1. Dietmar Mögenburg | GER | 2.35 | 7-8½ | |
| 2. Patrik Sjöberg | SWE | 2.33 | 7-7¾ | |
| 3. Zhu Jianhua | CHN | 2.31 | 7-7 | |
| 4. Dwight Stones | USA | 2.31 | 7-7 | |
| 5. Doug Nordquist | USA | 2.29 | 7-6¼ | |
| 6. Milton Ottey | CAN | 2.29 | 7-6¼ | |
| 7. Liu Yunpeng | CHN | 2.29 | 7-6¼ | |
| 8. Cai Shu | CHN | 2.27 | 7-5¼ | |

While the experts predicted the gold medal would go to world-record holder Zhu Jianhua, with two-time bronze medalist Dwight Stones fighting it out for second place with Dietmar Mögenburg, *the* expert on the high jump knew better. That expert, loquacious Dwight Stones himself, picked the 6-foot, 7-inch Mögenburg for the gold, Zhu for the silver and himself for the bronze. Had not 19-year-old Patrik Sjöberg equaled his personal record to take second, Stones's soothsaying would have been right on the mark. The most important factor, as Stones well knew, was that Mögenburg had a history of rising to the occasion at important meets, while Zhu seemed to falter when the going got rough.

Two months earlier Zhu had defeated Mögenburg in West Germany by setting a world record of 7 feet 10 inches, but in Los Angeles Zhu's concentration was broken by an unexpected occurrence. After recording his first miss at 7-7¾, Zhu was just about to try again when 1500-meter finalist Steve Ovett walked off the track and collapsed on the apron of the high jump area. Startled officials prevented Zhu from going ahead with his jump until Ovett had been tended to. By this time Zhu had changed his mind and decided to pass. His final two attempts were taken at 7-8½ and he missed both. Meanwhile, Mögenburg cleared every height on the first try and gained the gold medal without a miss.

**1988 Seoul** C: 27, N: 18, D: 9.25. WR: 2.42, 7-11½ (Javier Sotomayor Sanabria)

|  |  | | FT.- | |
| --- | --- | --- | --- | --- |
|  |  | M | IN. | |
| 1. Gennady Avdeyenko | SOV | 2.38 | 7-9¾ | OR |
| 2. Hollis Conway | USA | 2.36 | 7-8¾ | |
| 3. Rudolf Povarnitsyn | SOV | 2.36 | 7-8¾ | |
| 3. Patrik Sjöberg | SWE | 2.36 | 7-8¾ | |
| 5. Clarence Saunders | BER | 2.34 | 7-8 | |
| 6. Dietmar Mögenburg | GER | 2.34 | 7-8 | |
| 7. Dalton Grant | GBR | 2.31 | 7-7 | |
| 7. Igor Paklin | SOV | 2.31 | 7-7 | |
| 7. Carlo Thränhardt | GER | 2.31 | 7-7 | |

The 1988 high jump field included five former world record holders: Mögenburg, Zhu Jianhua (who failed to qualify for the final), Povarnitsyn, Paklin, and Sjöberg. None of them placed higher than third. Instead, the winner was 6-foot 7½-inch Gennady Avdeyenko, who made all five jumps he attempted through 7 feet 8¾ inches, and then cleared 7 feet 9¾ inches on his second try. Second place went to unheralded Hollis Conway, who, at 6 feet ¼ inch, was unusually short for a successful high jumper. Javier Sotomayor, kept out of the Olympics by the Cuban boycott, set a world record of 7 feet 11½ inches only

17 days before the Seoul final. On July 29, 1989, Sotomayor became the first person to clear 8 feet.

## POLE VAULT

The tie-breaking rules for the pole vault are the same as those for the high jump.

**1896 Athens** C: 5, N: 2, D: 4.10. WR: 3.49, 11-5 ⅜ (Walter Rodenbaugh)

| | | M | FT.-IN. |
|---|---|---|---|
| 1. | William Welles Hoyt | USA | 3.30 | 10-10 |
| 2. | Albert Tyler | USA | 3.20 | 10-6 |
| 3. | Evangelos Damaskos | GRE | 2.60 | 8-6¼ |
| 3. | Ioannis Theodoropoulos | GRE | 2.60 | 8-6¼ |
| 3. | Vasilios Xydas | GRE | 2.60 | 8-6¼ |

**1900 Paris** C: 8, N: 5, D: 7.15. WR: 3.62, 11-10½ (Raymond Clapp)

| | | M | FT.-IN. |
|---|---|---|---|
| 1. | Irving Baxter | USA | 3.30 | 10-10 |
| 2. | Michael Colket | USA | 3.25 | 10-8 |
| 3. | Carl-Albert Andersen | NOR | 3.20 | 10-6 |
| 4. | Eric Lemming | SWE | 3.10 | 10-2 |
| 4. | Jakab Kauser | HUN | 3.10 | 10-2 |
| 4. | Louis Gontier | FRA | 3.10 | 10-2 |
| 7 | Karl Gustaf Staaf | SWE | 2.80 | 9-2¼ |
| 8. | August Nilsson | SWE | 2.60 | 8-6¼ |

This event was marred by indecision on the part of the officials in charge. Three of the leading American entrants, Bascom Johnson, Charles Dvorak, and Daniel Horton, objected to the scheduling of the pole vault on a Sunday. Johnson and Dvorak showed up anyway, but were told that the event would be rescheduled, so they left. Then the officials changed their minds and went ahead with the contest without Johnson and Dvorak. In their absence, the pole vault was won by Irving Baxter, who was still on the field after winning the high jump. The next day Baxter finished second to Ray Ewry in the three standing jump events. A few days later, in order "to appease the indignant visitors from across the seas," a second pole vault contest was staged. This was won by Horton at 11 feet 3¾ inches with Dvorak second at 11 feet 1¾ inches.

**1904 St. Louis** C: 7, N: 2, D: 9.3. WR: 3.69, 12-1½ (Norman Dole)

| | | M | FT.-IN. |
|---|---|---|---|
| 1. | Charles Dvorak | USA | 3.50 | 11-5¾ |
| 2. | Leroy Samse | USA | 3.43 | 11-3 |
| 3. | Louis Wilkins | USA | 3.43 | 11-3 |
| 4. | Ward McLanahan | USA | 3.35 | 10-11¾ |
| 5. | Claude Allen | USA | 3.35 | 10-11¾ |
| 6. | Walter Dray | USA | — | — |
| 7. | Paul Weinstein | GER | — | — |

**1906 Athens** C: 11, N: 8, D: 4.25. WR: 3.74, 12-3¼ (Fernand Gonder)

| | | M | FT.-IN. |
|---|---|---|---|
| 1. | Fernand Gonder | FRA | 3.50 | 11-5¾ |
| 2. | Bruno Söderström | SWE | 3.40 | 11-1¾ |
| 3. | Edward Glover | USA | 3.35 | 10-11¾ |
| 4. | Theodoris Makris | GRE | 3.25 | 10-8 |
| 5. | Heikki Ahlmann (Pennola) (FIN), Georgios Banikas (GRE), Otto Haug (NOR), I. Kiss (HUN), Stefanos Koudouriotis (GRE) | | 3.00 | 9-10 |

Gonder won first place by clearing 11 feet 5¾ inches with ease. When Glover attempted to clear the same height, an official crossed his path. Glover lost his balance and was injured. The Canadian vaulter, Ed Archibald, also had a tough time. His pole disappeared on a train ride through Italy. Olympic officials gave him some local models when he arrived in Athens, but when one of them broke and almost impaled him, he lost confidence and was unable to perform at his usual level.

**1908 London** C: 14, N: 7, D: 7.24. WR: 3.90, 12-9½ (Walter Dray)

| | | M | FT.-IN. | |
|---|---|---|---|---|
| 1. | Edward Cooke | USA | 3.71 | 12-2 | OR |
| 1. | Alfred Gilbert | USA | 3.71 | 12-2 | OR |
| 3. | Ed Archibald | CAN | 3.58 | 11-9 | |
| 3. | Charles Jacobs | USA | 3.58 | 11-9 | |
| 3. | Bruno Söderström | SWE | 3.58 | 11-9 | |
| 6. | Georgios Banikas | GRE | 3.50 | 11-6 | |
| 6. | Sam Bellah | USA | 3.50 | 11-6 | |
| 8. | Károly Szathmáry | HUN | 3.35 | 11-0 | |

Competition in the pole vault was severely disrupted by the sensational incidents surrounding the finish of the marathon. Gold medalist Alfred Gilbert worked his way through Yale as a magician. He is best known today as the inventor of the Erector Set, one of the most popular toys of all time.

**1912 Stockholm** C: 24, N: 11, D: 7.11. WR: 4.02, 13-2¼ (Marcus Wright)

| | | M | FT.-IN. | |
|---|---|---|---|---|
| 1. | Harry Babcock | USA | 3.95 | 12-11½ | OR |
| 2. | Frank Nelson | USA | 3.85 | 12-7½ | |
| 3. | Marcus Wright | USA | 3.85 | 12-7½ | |
| 4. | William Hapenny | CAN | 3.80 | 12-5½ | |
| 4. | Frank Murphy | USA | 3.80 | 12-5½ | |
| 4. | Bertil Uggla | SWE | 3.80 | 12-5½ | |
| 7. | Samuel Bellah | USA | 3.75 | 12-3½ | |
| 8. | Frank Coyle (USA), Gordon Dukes (USA), Bill Fritz (USA) | | 3.65 | 11-11¾ | |

**1920 Antwerp** C: 14, N: 6, D: 8.20. WR: 4.02, 13-2¼ (Marcus Wright)

| | | M | FT.-IN. | |
|---|---|---|---|---|
| 1. Frank Foss | USA | 4.09 | 13-5 | WR |
| 2. Henry Petersen | DEN | 3.70 | 12-1½ | |
| 3. Edwin Myers | USA | 3.60 | 11-9¾ | |
| 4. Edward Knourek | USA | 3.60 | 11-9¾ | |
| 5. Ernfrid Rydberg | SWE | 3.60 | 11-9¾ | |
| 6. Lauritz Jörgensen | DEN | 3.60 | 11-9¾ | |
| 7. Eldon Jenne | USA | 3.60 | 11-9¾ | |

Foss' world record leap, made in the midst of wind and rain, excited the crowd more than any other event in the 1920 Games. His 15½ inch margin of victory was by far the largest in Olympic history.

**1924 Paris** C: 20, N: 13, D: 7.10. WR: 4.21, 13-9¾ (Charles Hoff)

| | | M | FT.-IN. |
|---|---|---|---|
| 1. Lee Barnes | USA | 3.95 | 12-11½ |
| 2. Glenn Graham | USA | 3.95 | 12-11½ |
| 3. James Brooker | USA | 3.90 | 12-9½ |
| 4. Henry Petersen | DEN | 3.90 | 12-9½ |
| 5. Victor Pickard | CAN | 3.80 | 12-5½ |
| 6. Ralph Spearow | USA | 3.70 | 12-1½ |
| 7. Maurice Henrijean | BEL | 3.66 | 12-0 |

Charles Hoff, the Norwegian world record holder, withdrew because of an injury. He did, however, take part in the 400- and 800-meter runs, finishing eighth in the latter. In Hoff's absence, the pole vault was won by 17-year-old Lee Barnes, a student at Hollywood High School in Los Angeles. In 1927 Barnes appeared in the film *College,* as a stand-in for Buster Keaton in a scene that required him to pole vault into a second-story window.

**1928 Amsterdam** C: 20, N: 13, D: 8.1. WR: 4.31, 14-1¾ (Lee Barnes)

| | | M | FT.-IN. | |
|---|---|---|---|---|
| 1. Sabin Carr | USA | 4.20 | 13-9¼ | OR |
| 2. William Droegemuller | USA | 4.10 | 13-5¼ | |
| 3. Charles McGinnis | USA | 3.95 | 12-11½ | |
| 4. Victor Pickard | CAN | 3.95 | 12-11½ | |
| 5. Lee Barnes | USA | 3.95 | 12-11½ | |
| 6. Yonataro Nakazawa | JPN | 3.90 | 12-9½ | |
| 7. Henry Lindblad | SWE | 3.90 | 12-9½ | |
| 8. János Karlovits | HUN | 3.80 | 12-5½ | |

Sabin Carr of Yale had become the first vaulter to clear 14 feet on May 27, 1927.

**1932 Los Angeles** C: 8, N: 4, D: 8.3. WR: 4.37, 14-4¼ (William Graber)

| | | M | FT.-IN. | |
|---|---|---|---|---|
| 1. William Miller | USA | 4.31 | 14-1¾ | OR |
| 2. Shuhei Nishida | JPN | 4.30 | 14-1¼ | |
| 3. George Jefferson | USA | 4.20 | 13-9½ | |
| 4. William Graber | USA | 4.15 | 13-7½ | |
| 5. Shizuo Mochizuki | JPN | 4.00 | 13-1½ | |
| 6. Lucio de Castro | BRA | 3.90 | 12-9½ | |
| 7. Peter Chlentzos | GRE | 3.75 | 12-3½ | |

The 1932 competition was expected to provide a clean sweep for the United States, but no one had counted on the unexpected determination of Japan's Shuhei Nishida, who gained the support of the previously partisan crowd with his great performance and sportsmanship. Nevertheless, most of the 80,000 American spectators breathed a sigh of relief when Bill Miller avoided a vault-off by clearing 14 feet 1¾ inches on his third attempt.

**1936 Berlin** C: 30, N: 21, D: 8.5. WR: 4.43, 14-6½ (George Varoff)

| | | M | FT.-IN. | |
|---|---|---|---|---|
| 1. Earle Meadows | USA | 4.35 | 14-3¼ | OR |
| 2. Shuhei Nishida | JPN | 4.25 | 13-11¼ | |
| 3. Sueo Oe | JPN | 4.25 | 13-11¼ | |
| 4. William Sefton | USA | 4.25 | 13-11¼ | |
| 5. William Graber | USA | 4.15 | 13-7¼ | |
| 6. Kiyoshi Adachi (JPN), Sylvanus Apps (CAN), Péter Bácsalmási (HUN), Josef Haunzwickel (AUT), Danilo Innocenti (ITA), Jan Korejs (CZE), Bo Ljungberg (SWE), Alfred Proksch (AUT), Wilhelm Sznajder (POL), Frederick Webster (GBR), Viktor Zsuffka (HUN) | | 4.00 | 13-1½ | |

On July 4, 1936, George Varoff, a 22-year-old janitor from San Francisco, rose from obscurity to set a world record of 14 feet 6½ inches at the A.A.U. championships in Princeton, New Jersey. Sportswriters rushed in to get his story. They learned that he came from a poor family of Ukrainian immigrants; that he was a music major at Oregon University who played the string fiddle; that he hoped to land a good job in order to help his family. VAROFF TYPIFIES SPIRIT OF AMERICA read a typical headline. But the following week at the U.S. Olympic trials, Varoff bowed out at 14 feet 3 inches and failed to make the U.S. team. The press moved on to other stories.

The 1936 Olympic final was another dramatic duel between the Americans and the Japanese that lasted into the night and finished in the eerie glow of floodlights. After it had been determined that Meadows had finished first and Sefton fourth, Nishida and Oe refused to vault-off for second and third. Instead they decided by lot that Nishida would be placed second and Oe third. Back home in Japan, they brought their medals to a jeweler and had them cut in half lengthwise. Then they were fused back together so that each man had a medal that was half silver and half bronze.

**1948 London** C: 19, N: 10, D: 8.2. WR: 4.77, 15-7¾ (Cornelius Warmerdam)

|    |                  |     | M    | FT.-IN. |
|----|------------------|-----|------|---------|
| 1. | O. Guinn Smith   | USA | 4.30 | 14-1¼   |
| 2. | Erkki Kataja     | FIN | 4.20 | 13-9¼   |
| 3. | Robert Richards  | USA | 4.20 | 13-9¼   |
| 4. | Erling Kaas      | NOR | 4.10 | 13-5¼   |
| 5. | Ragnar Lundberg  | SWE | 4.10 | 13-5¼   |
| 6. | Richmond Morcom  | USA | 3.95 | 12-11½  |
| 7. | Hugo Göllors     | SWE | 3.95 | 12-11½  |
| 7. | Valto Olenius    | FIN | 3.95 | 12-11½  |

The period between the 1936 and 1948 Olympics was dominated by Cornelius "Dutch" Warmerdam, the first person to vault 15 feet. Between 1940 and his retirement in 1944, Warmerdam cleared 15 feet 43 times. No one else accomplished the height until 1951. In fact, when he retired, Warmerdam's best vault was nine inches higher than anyone else's. His world record of 15 feet 7¾ inches, set on May 23, 1942, wasn't broken until April 1957.

The 1948 Olympic final was concluded during a downpour. With ties now decided on the basis of fewer misses, Erkki Kataja was poised for victory if no one could clear 14 feet 1¼ inches. But Guinn Smith made it on his final try, and the U.S. pole vault winning streak was kept alive.

**1952 Helsinki** C: 25, N: 17, D: 7.22. WR: 4.77, 15-7¾ (Cornelius Warmerdam)

|    |                   |     | M    | FT.-IN. |    |
|----|-------------------|-----|------|---------|----|
| 1. | Robert Richards   | USA | 4.55 | 14-11   | OR |
| 2. | Donald Laz        | USA | 4.50 | 14-9    |    |
| 3. | Ragnar Lundberg   | SWE | 4.40 | 14-5¼   |    |
| 4. | Pyotr Denisenko   | SOV | 4.40 | 14-5¼   |    |
| 5. | Valto Olenius     | FIN | 4.30 | 14-1¼   |    |
| 6. | Bunkichi Sawada   | JPN | 4.20 | 13-9¼   |    |
| 7. | Vladimir Bražnik  | SOV | 4.20 | 13-9¼   |    |
| 8. | Viktor Knyazev    | SOV | 4.20 | 13-9¼   |    |

The competition came down to a duel between Don Laz and "The Vaulting Vicar," Reverend Bob Richards, a theology professor in California. They both missed for the first time at 14 feet 9 inches and then cleared with their second attempts. When they both missed twice at 14 feet 11 inches, discussions began as to how a vault-off would be conducted. But Richards solved the problem quickly by clearing the bar on his third attempt. The year 1952 was the first time that the U.S.S.R. competed in the Olympics, and many politicians, journalists, and athletes looked at the Olympics as a front-line battle in the Cold War. Bob Richards thought otherwise and was a major force in encouraging interaction and friendship between athletes from the United States and the U.S.S.R.

**1956 Melbourne** C: 19, N: 12, D: 11.26. WR: 4.77, 15-7¾ (Cornelius Warmerdam)

|    |                    |     | M    | FT.-IN. |    |
|----|--------------------|-----|------|---------|----|
| 1. | Robert Richards    | USA | 4.56 | 14-11½  | OR |
| 2. | Robert Gutowski    | USA | 4.53 | 14-10¼  |    |
| 3. | Georgios Roubanis  | GRE | 4.50 | 14-9    |    |
| 4. | George Mattos      | USA | 4.35 | 14-3¼   |    |
| 5. | Ragnar Lundberg    | SWE | 4.25 | 13-11¼  |    |
| 6. | Zenon Wazny        | POL | 4.25 | 13-11¼  |    |
| 7. | Eeles Landström    | FIN | 4.25 | 13-11¼  |    |
| 8. | Manfred Preussger  | GDR | 4.25 | 13-11¼  |    |

The qualifying round almost saw a major upset when Bob Richards missed twice at the shockingly low height of 13 feet 1½ inches. He cleared on his third attempt and was in control for the rest of the contest. Gusty winds and a patchy runway hampered the quality of performance in the final. As it happened though, the wind actually helped Richards on his winning vault. After missing once at 14 feet 11½ inches, he hit the bar on his second attempt. Richards lay on his back for 30 seconds watching the bar bounce and quiver. "I was scared to change my position in the pit in case the slightest vibration brought it down," he explained. But the wind kept the bar in place and Richards became the only person to win two gold medals and three total medals in the pole vault.

It was silver medalist Bob Gutowski who finally broke Cornelius Warmerdam's world record with a vault of 15 feet 8¼ inches on April 27, 1957. Richards had predicted that Gutowski would someday be the first vaulter to break the 16-foot barrier. However, Bob Gutowski was killed in a car crash at the age of 25 on August 2, 1960.

The 1956 competition was also noteworthy because it saw the first appearance in the pole vault competition of the fiberglass pole, which would revolutionize pole vaulting. It was used by bronze medalist Georgios Roubanis, who improved his personal best by three and a half inches. The first Olympic athlete to use a fiberglass pole was Bob Mathias in the 1952 decathlon.

**1960 Rome** C: 30, N: 20, D: 9.7. WR: 4.80, 15-9¼ (Donald Bragg)

|    |                  |     | M    | FT.-IN. |    |
|----|------------------|-----|------|---------|----|
| 1. | Donald Bragg     | USA | 4.70 | 15-5    | OR |
| 2. | Ronald Morris    | USA | 4.60 | 15-1    |    |
| 3. | Eeles Landström  | FIN | 4.55 | 14-11   |    |
| 4. | Rolando Cruz     | PUR | 4.55 | 14-11   |    |
| 5. | Günter Malcher   | GDR | 4.50 | 14-9    |    |
| 6. | Igor Petrenko    | SOV | 4.50 | 14-9    |    |
| 6. | Matti Sutinen    | FIN | 4.50 | 14-9    |    |
| 8. | Rudolf Tomášek   | CZE | 4.50 | 14-9    |    |

Don "Tarzan" Bragg began the final competition cautiously, but gained confidence with each leap and finished strongly. After he had won, Bragg, whose dream it was to play Tarzan in the movies, delighted the crowd by celebrating with a Tarzan yell.

Silver medalist Ron Morris had failed to clear the qualifying height of 14 feet 5¼ inches. However, Olympic rules state that at least 12 men must compete in the final. Since only 10 had made the required height, the three vaulters with the next best records were added to the final. One of them was Morris. Bragg, by the way, never did get to play Tarzan, although he did come close. Shooting had already begun for *Tarzan and the Jewels of Opar* in 1964, and Bragg was in front of the cameras, happily swinging from vines, when a court order halted the production because of copyright infringement. Forced to become a salesman of drug supplies, Bragg later opened a boys' camp in New Jersey.

**1964 Tokyo** C: 32, N: 20, D: 10.17. WR: 5.28, 17-4 (Frederick Hansen)

| | | | FT.- | |
|---|---|---|---|---|
| | | M | IN. | |
| 1. Frederick Hansen | USA | 5.10 | 16-8¾ | OR |
| 2. Wolfgang Reinhardt | GER | 5.05 | 16-6¾ | |
| 3. Klaus Lehnertz | GER | 5.00 | 16-4¾ | |
| 4. Manfred Preussger | GDR | 5.00 | 16-4¾ | |
| 5. Gennady Bliznyetsov | SOV | 4.95 | 16-2¾ | |
| 6. Rudolf Tomášek | CZE | 4.90 | 16-0¾ | |
| 7. Pentti Nikula | FIN | 4.90 | 16-0¾ | |
| 8. Billy Pemelton | USA | 4.80 | 15-9 | |

The pole vault world record was broken 17 times between the Rome Olympics and the Tokyo Olympics, the last two times by Fred Hansen of Cuero, Texas. The 1964 final was a long, drawn-out competition that ended up lasting 8¾ hours. For the first eight hours, Hansen attempted only four vaults, all of them successful. When the bar was raised to 16 feet 6¾ inches, Hansen gambled by passing. Tomášek, Bliznyetsov, Preussger and Lehnertz all bowed out, but Wolfgang Reinhardt, who had beaten Hansen earlier in the year, cleared on his first try. The bar was moved up to 16 feet 8¾ inches and suddenly, after hours of boredom, the pole vault had become a dramatic contest. Hansen and Reinhardt both missed twice. If Hansen missed again, the gold medal would go to Reinhardt and the United States would lose the pole vault for the first time ever (not including the 1906 Intercalated Games). "Please don't think I'm corny," Hansen later said, "but I was thinking what I could do for my country, not for myself." Hansen had the uprights moved back eight inches. Then he prepared himself at great length, raced down the runway, and cleared the bar by half a foot. Reinhardt had one more attempt, but he missed, and the competition was finally over.

**1968 Mexico City** C: 23, N: 15, D: 10.16. WR: 5.41, 17-9 (Robert Seagren)

| | | | FT.- | |
|---|---|---|---|---|
| | | M | IN. | |
| 1. Robert Seagren | USA | 5.40 | 17-8½ | OR |
| 2. Claus Schiprowski | GER | 5.40 | 17-8½ | OR |
| 3. Wolfgang Nordwig | GDR | 5.40 | 17-8½ | OR |
| 4. Christos Papanicolaou | GRE | 5.35 | 17-6½ | |
| 5. John Pennel | USA | 5.35 | 17-6½ | |
| 6. Gennady Bliznyetsov | SOV | 5.30 | 17-4½ | |
| 7. Herve D'Encausse | FRA | 5.25 | 17-2¾ | |
| 8. Heinfried Engel | GER | 5.20 | 17-0¾ | |

Bob Seagren had set a world record of 17 feet 9 inches at the U.S. Olympic Trials five weeks before the Olympics, but no one expected him to have an easy time of it in Mexico City, as the field was thick with great vaulters. Ignacio Sola of Spain cleared 17 feet 0¾ inch and only placed ninth. Herve D'Encausse cleared 17 feet 2¾ inches. This put him in first place, so he elected to pass the next height of 17 feet 4½ inches. He then watched in horror as the remaining six vaulters all made the height, dropping D'Encausse to seventh, which is where he finished.

At 17 feet 6½ inches, Seagren passed. This was thought to be a dangerous but shrewd gamble, comparable to Fred Hansen's pass four years earlier. Actually it was an error due to Seagren's unfamiliarity with the metric system. "If I'd known the metric system better," he later revealed, "I wouldn't have passed that high—5.35 meters doesn't sound as high as 17 feet 6½ inches." Ironically, Seagren's mistake may have won him the gold medal. At any rate, it was now Seagren's turn to sit on the sidelines and watch as the remaining four competitors all cleared the bar, dropping Seagren from first to fifth.

Next the bar was raised to 17 feet 8½ inches, only one half-inch below Seagren's new world record. Papanicolaou, Nordwig, Seagren, Pennel, and Schiprowski all missed their first attempts. If they continued to miss, the victory would go to Nordwig, since he had only missed once at lower heights. The second time around, Papanicolaou and Nordwig missed again, but Seagren cleared, to move into the lead again. Then John Pennel made a successful clearance, but his pole passed under the bar. The I.A.A.F. had just voted a new rule making such an occurrence legal, but they had also decreed that the rule wouldn't take effect until the following May. Too late for Pennel, who lost out on at least a bronze medal. Schiprowski, whose pre-Olympic best was only 17 feet, then cleared 17 feet 8½ inches, bettering his previous record for the fifth time in one day. Papanicolaou, who would later become the first person to vault 18 feet, and Pennel failed one last time, but Nordwig made it.

The bar then went up to 17 feet 10½ inches, but before Nordwig, Seagren and Schiprowski could start vaulting, the competition was delayed while the victory ceremony for the 200 meters took place. This turned out to be a sensational event, as Tommie Smith and John Carlos staged their now famous black power protest, which was greeted by booing and whistling. This may have disturbed the concentration of the vaulters, but it didn't prevent each of them from making superb efforts at the world record height. None of them succeeded, however, so the medals were decided on the basis of fewer misses.

Personal records had been set by five of the top six vaulters and eight of the top 11.

**1972 Munich** C: 21, N: 12, D: 9.2. WR: 5.63, 18-5¾ (Robert Seagren)

| | | M | FT.-IN. | |
|---|---|---|---|---|
| 1. | Wolfgang Nordwig | GDR | 5.50 | 18-0½ | OR |
| 2. | Robert Seagren | USA | 5.40 | 17-8½ |
| 3. | Jan Johnson | USA | 5.35 | 17-6½ |
| 4. | Reinhard Kuretzky | GER | 5.30 | 17-4½ |
| 5. | Bruce Simpson | CAN | 5.20 | 17-0¾ |
| 6. | Volker Ohl | GER | 5.20 | 17-0¾ |
| 7. | Hans Lagerqvist | SWE | 5.20 | 17-0¾ |
| 8. | Francois Tracanelli | FRA | 5.10 | 16-8¾ |

The U.S. monopoly of the pole vault was finally broken in 1972, but only after a series of disruptive and disturbing events. On July 25, the Technical Committee of the International Amateur Athletic Federation announced that it was banning the new model of Cata-Poles, which was being used by most of the leading vaulters, including Olympic favorites Bob Seagren, Kjell Isaksson of Sweden, and Steve Smith of the United States. The original complaint, lodged by East Germany, was that the poles contained carbon fiber. Manufacturers of the poles pointed out that they didn't contain carbon fiber at all, while the vaulters referred to I.A.A.F. rules, which said that poles could be made of any material, anyway. The I.A.A.F. refused to withdraw the ban on the grounds that the new Cata-Poles "had not been available through normal supply channels" for at least 12 months prior to the Olympics. Once again it was pointed out that the I.A.A.F. rule book made no mention of such a requirement.

On August 27, four days before the competition was to begin, the I.A.A.F. reversed itself and lifted the ban. Relieved vaulters returned to practicing with their usual poles. Then, on August 30, the ban was reimposed. The night before the qualifying round, I.A.A.F. officials went to the athletes' rooms, confiscated all their poles, and brought them off for inspection. Those vaulters who were found to be in possession of the now illegal poles were handed new ones, or rather, new old ones.

The qualifying round turned out to be a pretty sad affair. Only ten men were able to clear the qualifying height of 16 feet 8¾ inches, so four more who had only cleared 16 feet 4¾ inches were added for the final.

The vaulter who had benefited most by the ban of the new model Cata-Pole was Wolfgang Nordwig of East Germany, who had not adapted well to the new Cata-Pole and still used an old model. Nordwig, who kept out the noise of the stadium by stuffing his ears, missed once at 17 feet 4½ inches before clearing, which put him behind Seagren, who reached 17 feet 8½ inches without a miss. Nordwig made that height with his second attempt, while Seagren needed a third. This reversed their positions. At 17 feet 10½ inches, Nordwig went over the

first time, but Seagren missed all three of his attempts. After his final miss, Seagren approached Adriaan Paulen, the I.A.A.F. official who had taken responsibility for the Cata-Pole ban, and thrust his pole into Paulen's lap. Seagren stated that Paulen had given him the unwanted pole and now he was returning it. Nordwig, a 29-year-old precision engineer, had the bar raised once more, and cleared 18 feet for the first time in his life.

**1976 Montreal** C: 27, N: 13, D: 7.26. WR: 5.70, 18-8¼ (David Roberts)

| | | M | FT.-IN. | |
|---|---|---|---|---|
| 1. | Tadeusz Ślusarski | POL | 5.50 | 18-0½ | EOR |
| 2. | Antti Kalliomäki | FIN | 5.50 | 18-0½ | EOR |
| 3. | David Roberts | USA | 5.50 | 18-0½ | EOR |
| 4. | Patrick Abada | FRA | 5.45 | 17-10½ |
| 5. | Wojciech Buciarski | POL | 5.45 | 17-10½ |
| 6. | Earl Bell | USA | 5.45 | 17-10½ |
| 7. | Jean-Michel Bellot | FRA | 5.45 | 17-10½ |
| 8. | Itsuo Takanezawa | JPN | 5.40 | 17-8½ |

Pre-Olympic prognostications had the battle for the gold medal among Earl Bell, who had set a world record of 18 feet 7¼ inches on May 29, Dave Roberts, who had broken Bell's record on June 22, and Wladyslaw Kozakiewicz, known for his strong performances in important meets. Surprisingly, Kozakiewicz, hampered by injury, was unable to clear 17 feet 10½ inches. Since he had passed the previous three heights, he ended up in 11th place. Roberts, too, was playing a passing game. He didn't even start jumping until 17 feet 6¾ inches. He missed his first attempt, a miss that would later prove crucial, but cleared the second time. Then he passed the next two heights before sailing over 18 feet ½ inch with his first try.

When the bar was raised to 18 feet 2½ inches, there were still six vaulters left in the competition. Roberts, following a strategy he had prepared a month earlier, passed. His reasoning was that the contest would go on for quite some time and that fewer misses and fewer attempts might become crucial. He was absolutely right about that. But then two things happened that were unexpected. All five of the other remaining vaulters missed every one of their attempts at 18 feet 2½ inches, leaving Roberts alone with the bar at 18 feet 4½ inches, and facing the other unexpected element—a strong and unpredictable headwind. He missed all three attempts and ended up in third place.

The silver medal went to surprising Antti Kalliomäki and the gold to Kozakiewicz's Polish teammate Tadeusz Ślusarski. Ślusarski had the same number of misses as Kalliomäki, but had made fewer attempts. As it turned out, if Dave Roberts hadn't missed his initial attempt at 17 feet 6¾ inches, he would have finished in first place.

**1980 Moscow** C: 19, N: 10, D: 7.30. WR: 5.77, 18-11 (Philippe Houvion)

|   |   |   | FT.- | |   |
|---|---|---|---|---|---|
|   |   |   | M | IN. |   |
| 1. | Wladyslaw Kozakiewicz | POL | 5.78 | 18-11½ | WR |
| 2. | Tadeusz Ślusarski | POL | 5.65 | 18-6½ |   |
| 2. | Konstantin Volkov | SOV | 5.65 | 18-6½ |   |
| 4. | Philippe Houvion | FRA | 5.65 | 18-6½ |   |
| 5. | Jean-Michel Bellot | FRA | 5.60 | 18-4½ |   |
| 6. | Mariusz Klimczyk | POL | 5.55 | 18-2½ |   |
| 7. | Thierry Vigneron | FRA | 5.45 | 17-10½ |   |
| 8. | Sergei Kulibaba | SOV | 5.45 | 17-10½ |   |

The year 1980 was a banner one for pole vaulting. For the first time ever, three different men set world records in the same season. Wladyslaw Kozakiewicz began the onslaught on May 11 when his jump of 18 feet 9¼ inches broke Dave Roberts' 1976 record. Three weeks later, on June 1, Thierry Vigneron vaulted 18 feet 10¼ inches. On June 29, he repeated this feat. On July 17, less than two weeks before the Olympic competition, Philippe Houvion set a new record of 18 feet 11 inches. The stage was set for a classic showdown, particularly with the addition of defending champion Tadeusz Ślusarski and local favorite, Konstantin Volkov.

Unfortunately, the competition was marred by the incredibly boorish behavior of many of the Soviet fans, who whistled and jeered at the foreign vaulters, particularly the Poles. The 3000 Poles in the audience responded in kind whenever Volkov vaulted. Through it all, Wladyslaw Kozakiewicz seemed unperturbed. Indeed, he seemed to gain strength from the hostility of the Russians. He won the gold medal without a miss and punctuated his winning leap with an obscene gesture to the crowd. Then he had the bar raised, and set a world record on his second attempt, the first pole vault world record to be set in the Olympics since Frank Foss' in 1920. Afterward, Kozakiewicz ran into the stands and shook hands with his compatriots, while the Poles, surrounded by Soviet soldiers, sang "Poland Is Not Beaten. . . ." Subsequently, Kozakiewicz defected to West Germany.

**1984 Los Angeles** C: 19, N: 13, D: 8.8. WR: 5.90, 19-4¼ (Sergei Bubka)

|   |   |   | FT.- | |
|---|---|---|---|---|
|   |   |   | M | IN. |
| 1. | Pierre Quinon | FRA | 5.75 | 18-10¼ |
| 2. | Mike Tully | USA | 5.65 | 18-6½ |
| 3. | Earl Bell | USA | 5.60 | 18-4½ |
| 3. | Thierry Vigneron | FRA | 5.60 | 18-4½ |
| 5. | Kimmo Pallonen | FIN | 5.45 | 17-10½ |
| 6. | Doug Lytle | USA | 5.40 | 17-8½ |
| 7. | Felix Böhni | SWI | 5.30 | 17-4½ |
| 8. | Mauro Barella | ITA | 5.30 | 17-4½ |

The pre-boycott favorite, Ukrainian Sergei Bubka, set a world record of 19 feet 4¼ inches two weeks before the Olympics began. Nine days after the Olympic final Bubka was beaten at the Friendship Games by Soviet teammate Konstantin Volkov, but two weeks after that he set another world record of 19 feet 5¾ inches.

In the absence of the Soviets, the Los Angeles competition became a French-American confrontation with both teams fielding two 19-foot vaulters. By the time the bar reached 18 feet 4½ inches, only the four favorites remained, although none of the them had taken more than two vaults. At this point, Bell and Vigneron cleared on their first attempts, while Quinon and Tully passed. The bar was raised two inches and, while Bell and Vigneron watched, Quinon and Tully each missed. Quinon then elected to pass again, while Tully, after one more miss, cleared 18-6½ on his final attempt to take the lead. At the next height, 18-8¾, Tully passed, Quinon cleared immediately, and Bell and Vigneron missed all three attempts, finishing in a tie for third.

With Quinon vaulting first, the bar was raised to 18-10¼. The young Frenchman with a reputation for inconsistency cleared on his first try. Although a clearance at this height would have put Tully in a tie for first, he elected to pass. Neither man was successful at 19-0¼ and the competition was over.

**1988 Seoul** C: 21, N: 13, D: 9.28. WR: 6.06, 19-10½ (Sergei Bubka)

|   |   |   | FT.- | |   |
|---|---|---|---|---|---|
|   |   |   | M | IN. |   |
| 1. | Sergei Bubka | SOV | 5.90 | 19-4¼ | OR |
| 2. | Rodion Gataullin | SOV | 5.85 | 19-2¼ |   |
| 3. | Grigory Yegorov | SOV | 5.80 | 19-0¼ |   |
| 4. | Earl Bell | USA | 5.70 | 18-8¼ |   |
| 5. | Philippe Collet | FRA | 5.70 | 18-8¼ |   |
| 5. | Thierry Vigneron | FRA | 5.70 | 18-8¼ |   |
| 7. | István Bagyula | HUN | 5.60 | 18-4½ |   |
| 8. | Philippe D'Encausse | FRA | 5.60 | 18-4½ |   |

Sergei Bubka was the sort of child who makes parents grow old fast. When he was 3 years old he tried to run away from home. When he was 4 he almost drowned in a barrel of water used for salting cabbage. He also fell out of a tree and was only saved from serious injury when his suspenders caught on a branch. When he finally started flying through the air at the end of a pole, it was almost a relief.

Bubka burst on the international scene when, as a 19-year-old, he won an upset victory at the 1983 world championships. He completely dominated the event for the next five years, setting nine outdoor world records and winning another world championship in 1987 with only two vaults.

A minor revolt developed during the Olympic qualifying round. The leading vaulters objected to the fact that the bar used by the contestants in Group A was being raised at a rate different from the bar in Group B. The vaulters refused to continue the competition and the officials were forced to advance 15 of the 21 competitors into the final.

Bubka and his main rival, medical student Rodion

Gataullin, did not begin vaulting in the final until the bar reached 18 feet 8¼ inches. Gataullin cleared on his first attempt, but Bubka needed two tries, and even then he grazed the bar on the way down. Yegorov cleared 19 feet ¼ inch, while Bubka and Gataullin passed. Then Gataullin cleared 19 feet 2¼ inches on his third attempt to take the lead, dropping Yegorov to second and Bubka to fourth behind Bell, who had already missed three times at 18 feet 10¼ inches. Yegorov went out at 19 feet 4¼ inches. Meanwhile Bubka missed twice at the same height. Suddenly, one of the surest favorites of the 1988 Games was one miss away from finishing out of the medals. Desperately nervous, Bubka sprinted down the runway, hurled himself into the air and cleared the bar by a huge margin—perhaps 7 or 8 inches. Gataullin made three attempts at 19 feet 6¼ inches, but was never close.

# LONG JUMP

A valid jump must be made from behind the far edge of the take-off board, which is eight inches wide and level to the ground. Jumps are measured from the nearest impression made in the sand by any part of the jumper's body or limbs. Current competitions begin with a qualifying round, the results of which are not carried over to the final. In the final, each contestant is allowed three jumps. Then the first eight are allowed three more jumps. The long jump has been dominated by U.S. athletes, who have won 19 of 22 times. The only U.S. losses have been by two and a quarter inches, one and a half inches, and one boycott.

**1896 Athens** C: 9, N: 5, D: 4.7. WR: 7.21, 23-8 (J. J. Mooney)

| | | | FT.- | |
| | | | M | IN. |
|---|---|---|---|---|
| 1. Ellery Clark | USA | 6.35 | 20-10 |
| 2. Robert Garrett | USA | 6.00 | 19-8¼ |
| 3. James Connolly | USA | 5.84 | 19-2 |
| 4. Alexandros Chalkokondilis | GRE | 5.74 | 18-10 |

Each man was allowed three jumps. Clark fouled the first two times. "It was little short of agony," he later wrote. "I shall never forget my feelings as I stood at the end of the path for my third—and last—try. Five thousand miles, I reflected, I had come; and was it to end in this? Three fouls, and then five thousand miles back again, with that for my memory of the games." Fortunately, his last jump was not only valid, but good enough to win.

**1900 Paris.** C: 12, N: 6, D: 7.15. WR: 7.50, 24-7¼ (Meyer Prinstein)

| | | | FT.- | | |
| | | | M | IN. | |
|---|---|---|---|---|---|
| 1. Alvin Kraenzlein | USA | 7.18 | 23-6¾ | OR |
| 2. Meyer Prinstein | USA | 7.17 | 23-6¼ | |
| 3. Patrick Leahy | GBR/IRL | 6.95 | 22-9¾ | |
| 4. William Remington | USA | 6.82 | 22-4½ | |
| 5. Albert Delannoy | FRA | 6.75 | 22-1¾ | |
| 6. John McLean | USA | 6.65 | 21-10 | |

| 7. Thaddeus McClain | USA | 6.43 | 21-1¼ |
| 8. Waldemar Steffen | GER | 6.30 | 20-8 |

Prinstein achieved his 23-foot 6¼-inch jump in the qualifying round, which, according to the rules of the time, counted in the final placings. The final was held on the next day, which was a Sunday. The official in charge of the Syracuse team prohibited Prinstein from competing on a Sunday even though Prinstein was Jewish. Kraenzlein did take part in the final and bettered Prinstein's mark by one centimeter. Peter O'Connor of Ireland was entered, but did not compete. The following month he broke Prinstein's world record with a leap of 24 feet 7¾ inches. On August 5, 1901, he jumped 24 feet 11¾ inches to set a record that would last 20 years. In fact, O'Connor's jump remained an Irish national record until Carlos O'Connell broke it on June 2, 1990!

**1904 St. Louis** C: 10, N: 3, D: 9.1. WR: 7.61, 24-11¾ (Peter O'Connor)

| | | | FT.- | | |
| | | | M | IN. | |
|---|---|---|---|---|---|
| 1. Meyer Prinstein | USA | 7.34 | 24-1 | OR |
| 2. Daniel Frank | USA | 6.89 | 22-7¼ | |
| 3. Robert Stangland | USA | 6.88 | 22-7 | |
| 4. Fred Englehardt | USA | 6.63 | 21-9 | |
| 5. George Van Cleaf | USA | — | | |
| 6. John Hagerman | USA | — | — | |

Prinstein earned his well-deserved Olympic long-jump championship after a four year wait.

**1906 Athens** C: 27, N: 10, D: 4.27. WR: 7.61, 24-11¾ (Peter O'Connor)

| | | | FT.- | |
| | | | M | IN. |
|---|---|---|---|---|
| 1. Meyer Prinstein | USA | 7.20 | 23-7½ |
| 2. Peter O'Connor | GBR/IRL | 7.02 | 23-0½ |
| 3. Hugo Friend | USA | 6.96 | 22-10 |
| 4. Hjalmar Mellander | SWE | 6.58 | 21-7¼ |
| 5. Sidney Abrahams | GBR | 6.21 | 20-4½ |
| 6. Thomas Cronan | USA | 6.18 | 20-3½ |
| 7. Gunnar Rönström | SWE | 6.15 | 20-2¼ |
| 8. István Somodi | HUN | 6.05 | 19-10 |

Including the Intercalated Games of 1906, Meyer Prinstein won four gold medals and one silver in the long jump and triple jump.

**1908 London** C: 30, N: 9, D: 7.22. WR: 7.61, 24-11¾ (Peter O'Connor)

| | | | FT.- | | |
| | | | M | IN. | |
|---|---|---|---|---|---|
| 1. Francis "Frank" Irons | USA | 7.48 | 24-6½ | OR |
| 2. Daniel Kelly | USA | 7.09 | 23-3¼ | |
| 3. Calvin Bricker | CAN | 7.08 | 23-3 | |
| 4. Edward Cooke | USA | 6.97 | 22-10½ | |
| 5. John Brennan | USA | 6.86 | 22-6¼ | |
| 6. Frank Mount Pleasant | USA | 6.82 | 22-4½ | |
| 7. Albert Weinstein | GER | 6.77 | 22-2¾ | |
| 8. Timothy Ahearne | GBR/IRL | 6.72 | 22-0¾ | |

The victory of 5-foot 5½-inch Frank Irons came as quite a surprise since his pre-Olympic best was only 22 feet 7½ inches. Many British sports enthusiasts were disgusted by the exuberant displays of the Americans whenever a U.S. athlete won an event. One London paper described the American response to Irons' victory: "They were entertained then from the American stand by the singing of 'There'll be a hot time in the old town tonight,' by the fluttering of United States flags, and by the blowing of a new squeaking instrument of torture such as is employed at country fairs [probably a kazoo]. The Americans made themselves a nuisance and behaved in a manner which is happily quite foreign to the athletic grounds of England."

**1912 Stockholm** C: 32, N: 12, D: 7.13. WR: 7.61, 24-11¾ (Peter O'Connor)

| | | M | FT.-IN. | |
|---|---|---|---|---|
| 1. Albert Gutterson | USA | 7.60 | 24-11¼ | OR |
| 2. Calvin Bricker | CAN | 7.21 | 23-8 | |
| 3. Georg Åberg | SWE | 7.18 | 23-6¾ | |
| 4. Harry Worthington | USA | 7.03 | 23-0¾ | |
| 5. Eugene Leroy Mercer | USA | 6.97 | 22-10½ | |
| 6. Fred Allen | USA | 6.94 | 22-9¼ | |
| 7. James Thorpe | USA | 6.89 | 22-7¼ | |
| 8. Robert Pasemann | GER | 6.82 | 22-4½ | |

Gutterson, of Andover, Vermont, settled the competition with his first jump, which was the best in the world since Peter O'Connor's record of 1901.

**1920 Antwerp** C: 29, N: 11, D: 8.18. WR: 7.61, 24-11¾ (Peter O'Connor)

| | | M | FT.-IN. |
|---|---|---|---|
| 1. William Petersson (Björneman) | SWE | 7.15 | 23-5½ |
| 2. Carl Johnson | USA | 7.09 | 23-3¼ |
| 3. Erik Abrahamsson | SWE | 7.08 | 23-2¾ |
| 4. Robert "Dink" Templeton | USA | 6.95 | 22-9¾ |
| 5. Erling Aastad | NOR | 6.88 | 22-7 |
| 6. Rolf Franksson | SWE | 6.73 | 22-1 |
| 7. Sol Butler | USA | 6.60 | 21-8 |
| 8. Einar Raeder | NOR | 6.58 | 21-7¼ |

William Petersson, who later changed his last name to Björneman, was preparing to take his first jump when he noticed a silver coin lying on the runway. He picked it up and discovered that it was an American quarter. He put it in his left shoe for good luck and went on to win the gold medal. The favorite, Sol Butler, pulled a tendon on his first jump and had to withdraw. Fourth-place finisher Dink Templeton later became a famous track coach at Stanford University.

**1924 Paris** C: 34, N: 21, D: 7.8. WR: 7.69, 25-3 (Edward Gourdin)

| | | M | FT.-IN. |
|---|---|---|---|
| 1. William De Hart Hubbard | USA | 7.44 | 24-5 |
| 2. Edward Gourdin | USA | 7.27 | 23-10¼ |

| | | M | FT.-IN. |
|---|---|---|---|
| 3. Sverre Hansen | NOR | 7.26 | 23-10 |
| 4. Vilho Tuulos | FIN | 7.07 | 23-2½ |
| 5. Louis Wilhelme | FRA | 6.99 | 22-11¼ |
| 6. Christopher Macintosh | GBR | 6.92 | 22-8½ |
| 7. Virgilio Tommasi | ITA | 6.89 | 22-7¼ |
| 8. Jacob Boot | HOL | 6.86 | 22-6¼ |

De Hart Hubbard was the first black athlete to win an individual Olympic gold medal. His performance, however, was overshadowed by that of Robert LeGendre the day before. LeGendre, who had failed to make the U.S. long jump team, set a world record of 25 feet 5¾ inches while competing in the pentathlon.

**1928 Amsterdam** C: 41, N: 23, D: 7.31. WR: 7.90, 25-11 (Edward Hamm)

| | | M | FT.-IN. | |
|---|---|---|---|---|
| 1. Edward Hamm | USA | 7.73 | 25-4½ | OR |
| 2. Silvio Cator | HAI | 7.58 | 24-10½ | |
| 3. Alfred Bates | USA | 7.40 | 24-3½ | |
| 4. Willi Meier | GER | 7.39 | 24-3 | |
| 5. Erich Köchermann | GER | 7.35 | 24-1½ | |
| 6. Hannes de Boer | HOL | 7.32 | 24-0¼ | |
| 7. Edward Gordon | USA | 7.32 | 24-0¼ | |
| 8. Erik Svensson | SWE | 7.29 | 23-11 | |

Six weeks after the Olympic competition, silver medalist Silvio Cator became the first man to break the 26-foot barrier with a jump of 26 feet ¼ inch. Cator was also the captain of the Haitian soccer team. As it turned out, five different past and future gold medal winners took part in the 1928 long jump. In addition to Hamm, 1924 winner De Hart Hubbard finished 11th, 1932 winner Ed Gordon placed seventh, 1928 triple jump winner Mikio Oda tied with Hubbard for 11th, and 1932 triple jump winner Chuhei Nambu finished ninth.

**1932 Los Angeles** C: 12, N: 9, D: 8.2. WR: 7.98, 26-2¼ (Chuhei Nambu)

| | | M | FT.-IN. |
|---|---|---|---|
| 1. Edward Gordon | USA | 7.64 | 25-0¾ |
| 2. Charles Lambert Redd | USA | 7.60 | 24-11¼ |
| 3. Chuhei Nambu | JPN | 7.45 | 24-5½ |
| 4. Erik Svensson | SWE | 7.41 | 24-3¾ |
| 5. Richard Barber | USA | 7.39 | 24-3 |
| 6. Naoto Tajima | JPN | 7.15 | 23-5½ |
| 7. Hector Berra | ARG | 6.66 | 21-10¼ |
| 8. Clovis de Figueiredo Raposo | BRA | 6.43 | 21-1¼ |

**1936 Berlin** C: 43, N: 27, D: 8.4. WR: 8.13, 26-8¼ (James "Jesse" Owens)

| | | M | FT.-IN. | |
|---|---|---|---|---|
| 1. James "Jesse" Owens | USA | 8.06 | 26-5½ | OR |
| 2. Luz Long | GER | 7.87 | 25-10 | |
| 3. Naoto Tajima | JPN | 7.74 | 25-4¾ | |

| | | | | |
|---|---|---|---|---|
| 4. Wilhelm Leichum | GER | 7.73 | 25-4½ |
| 4. Arturo Maffei | ITA | 7.73 | 25-4½ |
| 6. Robert Clark | USA | 7.67 | 25-2 |
| 7. John Brooks | USA | 7.41 | 24-3¾ |
| 8. Robert Paul | FRA | 7.34 | 24-1 |

On May 25, 1935, Jesse Owens had jumped 26 feet 8¼ inches, setting a world record that would last for 25 years and 79 days. He seemed a sure bet to win the Olympic gold medal. But when he walked over to the long jump area, he was surprised to see a tall, blue-eyed, blond German taking practice jumps in the 26-foot range. Owens was fully aware of the Nazis' desire to prove their theory of "Aryan superiority" and he was also fully aware that Hitler and his followers had a par-ticular distaste for Negroes. With this in mind, Jesse, still in his sweatsuit, took a practice run down the run-way and into the pit. To his surprise, the officials in charge counted this as his first attempt of the qualifying round. Somewhat rattled, he fouled his second attempt. He was now one foul away from being eliminated from his best event.

At this point, Owens was approached by the tall, blue-eyed, blond German, who introduced himself, in En-glish, as Luz Long.

"Glad to meet you," said Owens tentatively. "How are you?"

"I'm fine," replied Long. "The question is: How are *you*?"

"What do you mean?" asked Owens.

"Something must be *eating* you," said Long, proud to display his knowledge of American slang. "You should be able to qualify with your eyes closed." For the next few minutes the black son of sharecroppers and the white model of Nazi manhood chatted. It turned out that Luz Long didn't believe in the theory of Aryan superiority and the two joked about the fact that he looked the part anyway. Then Long made a suggestion. Since the qualify-ing distance was only 23 feet 5½ inches, why didn't Ow-ens make a mark several inches before the takeoff board and jump from there to play it safe. Owens did just that, and qualified easily.

The final was held that afternoon. Jesse Owens opened with an Olympic record of 25 feet 5½ inches and then followed with 25 feet 10 inches. In the fifth of six rounds, Luz Long brought the German crowd to life by matching Owens' jump exactly. Inspired by the chal-lenge, Owens leaped 26 feet 3¾ inches. Then, with his final jump, he hit 26 feet 5½ inches, to clinch his second of four gold medals. The first person to congratulate Owens, in full view of Adolf Hitler, was Luz Long. "You can melt down all the medals and cups I have," Jesse Owens later wrote, "and they wouldn't be a plat-ing on the 24-carat friendship I felt for Luz Long at that moment." Long was killed in the Battle of St. Pietro on July 14, 1943, but Owens continued to correspond with his family.

**1948 London** C: 21, N: 17, D: 7.31. WR: 8.13, 26-8¼ (James "Jesse" Owens)

| | | | FT.- | |
|---|---|---|---|---|
| | | M | IN. |
| 1. Willie Steele | USA | 7.82 | 25-8 |
| 2. Theodore Bruce | AUS | 7.55 | 24-9¼ |
| 3. Herbert Douglas | USA | 7.54 | 24-9 |
| 4. Lorenzo Wright | USA | 7.45 | 24-5½ |
| 5. Adegboyega Folaranmi Adedoyin | GBR/NGR | 7.27 | 23-10¼ |
| 6. Georges Damitio | FRA | 7.07 | 23-2½ |
| 7. Harry Whittle | GBR | 7.03 | 23-0¾ |
| 8. Felix Wurth | AUS | 7.00 | 22-11¾ |

Fifth-place finisher Prince Adegboyega Folaranmi Adedoyin was a member of the royal family of the king-dom of Ijabu-Remo in Nigeria. A medical student at Queen's University in Belfast, he represented Great Brit-ain, since Nigeria was not yet considered an independent nation.

**1952 Helsinki** C: 27, N: 19, D: 7.21. WR: 8.13, 26-8¼ (James "Jesse" Owens)

| | | | FT.- | |
|---|---|---|---|---|
| | | M | IN. |
| 1. Jerome Biffle | USA | 7.57 | 24-10 |
| 2. Meredith Gourdine | USA | 7.53 | 24-8½ |
| 3. Ödön Földessy | HUN | 7.30 | 23-11½ |
| 4. Ary Facanha de Sá | BRA | 7.23 | 23-8¾ |
| 5. Jorma Valtonen | FIN | 7.16 | 23-6 |
| 6. Leonid Grigoryev | SOV | 7.14 | 23-5¼ |
| 7. Karl-Erik Israelsson | SWE | 7.10 | 23-3½ |
| 8. Paul Faucher | FRA | 7.02 | 23-0½ |

George Brown of U.C.L.A. had won 41 straight competi-tions before placing third at the U.S. Olympic trials. Yet he was still the heavy favorite to win in Helsinki. In the final, however, he fouled three times in a row and was eliminated. Gold medalist Jerome Biffle was an Army private who came out of two years retirement to com-pete. Neville Price of South Africa jumped 24 feet 1¾ inches in the qualifying round, but was unable to take part in the final because of an injury.

**1956 Melbourne** C: 32, N: 21, D: 11.24. WR: 8.13, 26-8¼ (James "Jesse" Owens)

| | | | FT.- | |
|---|---|---|---|---|
| | | M | IN. |
| 1. Gregory Bell | USA | 7.83 | 25-8¼ |
| 2. John Bennett | USA | 7.68 | 25-2½ |
| 3. Jorma Valkama | FIN | 7.48 | 24-6½ |
| 4. Dmitri Bondarenko | SOV | 7.44 | 24-5 |
| 5. Karim Olowu | NGR | 7.36 | 24-1¾ |
| 6. Kazimierz Kropidlowski | POL | 7.30 | 23-11½ |
| 7. Neville Price | SAF | 7.28 | 23-10¾ |
| 8. Oleg Fyedoseyev | SOV | 7.27 | 23-10¼ |

A short, loose runway and a strong fluctuating wind caused all entrants to perform well below their normal standards.

**1960 Rome** C: 49, N: 34, D: 9.2. WR: 8.21, 26-11¼ (Ralph Boston)

| | | M | FT.-IN. | |
|---|---|---|---|---|
| 1. | Ralph Boston | USA | 8.12 | 26-7¾ | OR |
| 2. | Irvin "Bo" Roberson | USA | 8.11 | 26-7¼ | |
| 3. | Igor Ter-Ovanesyan | SOV | 8.04 | 26-4½ | |
| 4. | Manfred Steinbach | GER | 8.00 | 26-3 | |
| 5. | Jorma Valkama | FIN | 7.69 | 25-2¾ | |
| 6. | Christian Collardot | FRA | 7.68 | 25-2½ | |
| 7. | Henk Visser | HOL | 7.66 | 25-1¾ | |
| 8. | Dmitri Bondarenko | SOV | 7.58 | 24-10½ | |

On August 12, 1960, two weeks before the opening of the Rome Olympics, Ralph Boston finally broke Jesse Owens' 25-year-old world record with a leap of 26 feet 11¼ inches. He was expected to receive his stiffest challenge from Armenian Igor Ter-Ovanesyan, who had fouled out of the 1956 final, and who would eventually go on to take part in five Olympics. Ter-Ovanesyan led at 25 feet 11 inches after the first round of the final. Bo Roberson, whose pre-Olympic best had been 26 feet 0 inches, jumped 26 feet 4¼ inches in the second round to take the lead. However, the third round saw Boston's big jump of 26 feet 7¾ inches. There were no changes in position during the next two rounds, but the competition was far from over. With his last attempt, Ter-Ovanesyan leaped 26 feet 4½ inches to edge into second place. An exhausted Bo Roberson had considered passing, but now he had to give it one last try. He zoomed seven inches beyond his pre-Olympic record, but landed one centimeter short of a gold medal. This was the first meet in which four different men jumped over 26 feet.

**1964 Tokyo** C: 32, N: 23, D: 10.18. WR: 8.34, 27-4¼ (Ralph Boston)

| | | M | FT.-IN. |
|---|---|---|---|
| 1. | Lynn Davies | GBR | 8.07 | 26-5¾ |
| 2. | Ralph Boston | USA | 8.03 | 26-4¼ |
| 3. | Igor Ter-Ovanesyan | SOV | 7.99 | 26-2¾ |
| 4. | Wariboko West | NGR | 7.60 | 24-11¼ |
| 5. | Jean Cochard | FRA | 7.44 | 24-5 |
| 6. | Luis Felipe Areta | SPA | 7.34 | 24-1 |
| 7. | Mike Ahey | GHA | 7.30 | 23-11½ |
| 8. | Andrzej Stalmach | POL | 7.26 | 23-10 |

Lynn Davies, a physical education teacher from Nantymoel, Glamorganshire, in Wales, wasn't on anyone's list of potential winners in 1964. In fact, he barely made it into the final, qualifying with his last attempt. But the weather, cold, windy, and raining, was much more familiar to Davies than it was to the favorites, Ralph Boston and Igor Ter-Ovanesyan. The American and Soviet champions tried to convince the officials to reverse the running of the event, so that they would be jumping with the wind behind them instead of against them, but to no avail.

Ter-Ovanesyan took the first round lead at 25 feet 6¼ inches. Boston moved ahead in the second round with a jump of 25 feet 9¼ inches. In the fourth round, he improved to 25 feet 10¼ inches. Entering the fifth round, Lynn Davies was in third place. "I remember thinking, this is it," he recalled. "I glanced up at the flag at the top of the stadium. Boston told me about this in New York, six months previously. 'If the flag drops,' he had said, 'it's a good indication that the wind is about to fade inside the stadium.' And as I looked up at it, it dropped dead." Davies took off down the runway immediately and hit the best jump of his career—26 feet 5¾ inches.

Ter-Ovanesyan followed with 26 feet 2¾ inches to move back into second place. The competition came down to Ralph Boston's final leap. Davies covered his face and peeked through his fingers. Boston's jump was long and Davies prepared himself for disappointment. But the measurement showed Boston had missed by four centimeters, and Lynn Davies had become the first Welshman ever to win an Olympic gold medal.

**1968 Mexico City** C: 35, N: 22, D: 10.18. WR: 8.35, 27-4¾ (Ralph Boston, Igor Ter-Ovanesyan)

| | | M | FT.-IN. | |
|---|---|---|---|---|
| 1. | Robert Beamon | USA | 8.90 | 29-2½ | WR |
| 2. | Klaus Beer | GDR | 8.19 | 26-10½ | |
| 3. | Ralph Boston | USA | 8.16 | 26-9¼ | |
| 4. | Igor Ter-Ovanesyan | SOV | 8.12 | 26-7¾ | |
| 5. | Tonu Lepik | SOV | 8.09 | 26-6½ | |
| 6. | Allen Crawley | AUS | 8.02 | 26-3¾ | |
| 7. | Jacques Pani | FRA | 7.97 | 26-1¾ | |
| 8. | Andrzej Stelmach | POL | 7.94 | 26-0¾ | |

All three medalists from 1964, Lynn Davies, Ralph Boston, and Igor Ter-Ovanesyan, were back in 1968, and all three were in good enough shape to win the gold medal. However, none of them was the favorite. That distinction fell to Bob Beamon, a 6-foot 3-inch 22-year-old from South Jamaica in New York. In 1968 Beamon had won 22 of 23 meets, losing only once indoors. But Beamon was by no means a sure bet. Unlike the other leading contenders, he made no checkmarks on the side of the runway to help him with his stride, so he was unusually prone to fouling. In addition, he had been without the benefit of a regular coach since mid-April, when he had been suspended from the track team at the University of Texas at El Paso for refusing to compete against Brigham Young University, as a protest against the racial policies of the Mormon Church.

Beamon almost met disaster in the qualifying round. His first jump took off a full foot after the board and his second jump was also a foul. He was now one foul away from elimination. Remembering the Jesse Owens-Luz Long incident of 1936, Ralph Boston, who had been informally coaching Beamon, walked up to the nervous favorite and had a few words with him. He told Beamon to relax and to take off from a mark a few inches before the takeoff board. Like Jesse Owens 32 years earlier, Bob Beamon made a mark one foot up the runway, then raced down the path and qualified easily.

According to Dick Schaap's biography, *The Perfect Jump,* that night, the night before the most important final of his career, Bob Beamon did something he had never done before: he engaged in sexual intercourse the night before a major competition. At the moment of orgasm, he was suddenly overcome with the horrible feeling that he had blown it, that his chances for a gold medal and for the world record he had boldly predicted he would achieve had been thrown away right there in bed.

The following day was gloomy, with occasional rain, the kind of day that supposedly favored Lynn Davies. There were 17 finalists ready to begin the competition at 3:40 p.m. Beamon's jumping order was fourth, Davies' 12th, Ter-Ovanesyan's 13th, and Ralph Boston's 17th. The first three jumpers fouled. Then it was Bob Beamon's turn. Boston called out to him, "Come on, make it a good one." For 20 seconds Beamon stood at the beginning of the runway, gathering his strength and telling himself, "Don't foul, don't foul." Then he tore down the runway (he was a 9.5 sprinter at 100 yards), hit the takeoff board perfectly, and sailed through the air at what seemed to be an uncommon elevation, estimated by observers to be between five and a half and six feet. He hit the sand so powerfully that he bounced back up and landed outside the pit.

"That's over 28 feet," Ralph Boston said to Lynn Davies. "With his first jump?" replied Davies. "No, it can't be." They trotted over to the pit to get a better look. Officials slid the marker of the sophisticated optical measuring device down its rail to the point where Beamon's feet had hit the sand. But before it got there, the marker fell off the end of the rail. An official turned to Beamon and murmured, "Fantastic. Fantastic." An old-fashioned steel tape was called for. A couple measurements were taken and then the result was flashed on the electronic scoreboard: 8.90 meters. Beamon knew he had set a record, but being unfamiliar with the metric system, he didn't really understand how far he had jumped. He ran up to Ralph Boston, the man who had helped him so much, and embraced him. Boston then told Beamon, "Bob, you jumped 29 feet."

Beamon was stunned. "What do I do now?" he asked. "Ralph, I know you're gonna kick my ass."

"No, no," said Boston. "It's over for me. I can't jump that far."

"What about the Great Britain dude?" asked Beamon. "And what about the Russian?"

"The Russian," Igor Ter-Ovanesyan, had turned to Lynn Davies and said, "Compared to this jump, we are as children." Davies told Boston, "I can't go on. What is the point? We'll all look silly." Then he turned to Beamon and said, "You have destroyed this event."

By this time, Beamon's jump had been officially converted to 29 feet 2½ inches. Suddenly, Beamon realized what he had done. His legs gave in and he sank to the ground, experiencing what doctors would later describe as a "cataplectic seizure," an "atonic state of the somatic muscles which develops suddenly on the heels of emotional excitement." He was overcome with nausea and tears, and was helped to his feet by Boston and U.S. teammate Charlie Mays, who supported him until he recovered from his dizziness.

The contest continued, but just as Ter-Ovanesyan began his first jump, the skies began pouring rain. Beamon took one more jump of 26 feet 4½ inches but then passed his last four opportunities. Boston, Ter-Ovanesyan and Davies (who finished ninth), who had waited four years for another chance at Olympic victory, were dazed and unable to perform up to par. Klaus Beer of East Germany, on the other hand, had had no such grand expectations, and was able to take the silver medal by bettering his personal best by four inches. Lepik and Crawley also had their best jumps ever.

Beamon's 29-foot 2½-inch jump was hailed as the greatest athletic achievement of all time, although detractors criticized the suspicious Mexican wind readings which measured the exact legal maximum of 2.0 m.p.s. In the 33 years since Jesse Owens' 1935 jump of 26 feet 8¼ inches, the world record had progressed eight and a half inches. In a matter of seconds, Beamon had added another 21¾ inches. Ironically—since Beamon completely bypassed the 28-foot barrier—the first 28-foot jump didn't take place until the 1980 Olympics.

**1972 Munich** C: 36, N: 25, D: 9.9. WR: 8.90, 29-2½ (Robert Beamon)

| | | | FT.- | |
| | | M | IN. | |
|---|---|---|---|---|
| 1. Randy Williams | USA | 8.24 | 27-0½ |
| 2. Hans Baumgartner | GER | 8.18 | 26-10 |
| 3. Arnie Robinson | USA | 8.03 | 26-4¼ |
| 4. Joshua Owusu | GHA | 8.01 | 26-3½ |
| 5. Preston Carrington | USA | 7.99 | 26-2¾ |
| 6. Max Klauss | GDR | 7.96 | 26-1½ |
| 7. Alan Lerwill | GBR | 7.91 | 25-11½ |
| 8. Leonid Barkovsky | SOV | 7.75 | 25-5¼ |

Nineteen-year-old Randy Williams, the youngest entrant, led the qualifying round with a jump of 27 feet 4¼ inches—over a foot farther than his pre-Olympic, non-wind-aided best. He was followed by Preston Carrington at 26 feet 11¾ inches, 7¾ inches better than *his* pre-Olympic record. Neither American was able to do as well in the final. Williams, who kept a good-luck teddy bear with him at all times, injured his leg warming up before the final, and wisely decided to put all his effort into his first leap, which turned out to be good enough for the gold medal.

**1976 Montreal** C: 33, N: 25, D: 7.29. WR: 8.90, 29-2½ (Robert Beamon)

|  |  | M | FT.-IN. |
|---|---|---|---|
| 1. Arnie Robinson | USA | 8.35 | 27-4¾ |
| 2. Randy Williams | USA | 8.11 | 26-7¼ |
| 3. Frank Wartenberg | GDR | 8.02 | 26-3¾ |
| 4. Jacques Rousseau | FRA | 8.00 | 26-3 |
| 5. João Carlos de Olivera | BRA | 8.00 | 26-3 |
| 6. Nenad Stekić | YUG | 7.89 | 25-10¾ |
| 7. Valery Podluzhniy | SOV | 7.88 | 25-10¼ |
| 8. Hans Baumgartner | GER | 7.82 | 25-8 |

For the third straight time, the long jump was won with a first round leap, and for the tenth time in 12 Olympics, it was won by a black American.

**1980 Moscow** C: 32, N: 24, D: 7.28. WR: 8.90, 29-2½ (Robert Beamon)

|  |  | M | FT.-IN. |
|---|---|---|---|
| 1. Lutz Dombrowski | GDR | 8.54 | 28-0¼ |
| 2. Frank Paschek | GDR | 8.21 | 26-11¼ |
| 3. Valery Podluzhniy | SOV | 8.18 | 26-10 |
| 4. László Szalma | HUN | 8.13 | 26-8¼ |
| 5. Stanislaw Jaskulka | POL | 8.13 | 26-8¼ |
| 6. Viktor Belsky | SOV | 8.10 | 26-7 |
| 7. Antonio Corgos | SPA | 8.09 | 26-6½ |
| 8. Yordan Yanev | BUL | 8.02 | 26-3¾ |

Before the Moscow Olympics, the longest jump other than Bob Beamon's had been 27 feet 11½ inches, by Larry Myricks of the United States. Myricks had qualified for the 1976 final, but fractured a bone in his foot and had to withdraw. In 1980, he was kept out again, this time by the Jimmy Carter boycott. Without him, the long jump competition was dominated by Lutz Dombrowski, who put together a tremendous series that averaged 27 feet 3¼ inches. His fifth round jump of 28 feet ¼ inch was the first ever in the 28-foot range. Something of a rebel, Dombrowski kept running away from the schools to which he had been assigned by the East German government, in order to return home to his family, his girl friend, and his soccer team. When he broke his left leg playing soccer in 1979, he finally gave in to the East German coaches, although he continued to insist that he preferred the triple jump to the long jump.

**1984 Los Angeles** C: 31, N: 25, D: 8.6. WR: 8.90, 29-2½ (Robert Beamon)

|  |  | M | FT.-IN. |
|---|---|---|---|
| 1. F. Carlton Lewis | USA | 8.54 | 28-0¼ |
| 2. Gary Honey | AUS | 8.24 | 27-0½ |
| 3. Giovanni Evangelisti | ITA | 8.24 | 27-0½ |
| 4. Larry Myricks | USA | 8.16 | 26-9¼ |
| 5. Liu Yuhuang | CHN | 7.99 | 26-2¾ |
| 6. Joey Wells | BAH | 7.97 | 26-1¾ |
| 7. Junichi Usui | JPN | 7.87 | 25-10 |
| 8. Kim Jong-il | KOR | 7.81 | 25-7½ |

When Carl Lewis was seven years old his parents began a track club. Carl and his five-year-old sister, Carol, used the landing area in the long jump pit to build sand castles. As they grew older, Carl and Carol used the pit for more conventional purposes. By 1981, Carl Lewis was the world's leading long-jumper. After losing an indoor meet to Larry Myricks on February 28, 1981, Lewis won 36 straight competitions leading up to the Olympics, including 16 meets in which he leaped over 28 feet. Twice he reached 28 feet 10¼ inches, both times at low-altitude. Once, in 1982, he landed about thirty feet from the take-off board, but the jump was ruled a foul after a controversial judge's decision.

At the Los Angeles Olympics, Lewis secured the gold medal with a first round leap into the wind that once again surpassed 28 feet. He took one more jump and then, with six races behind him and five more to go, he passed the last four rounds.

Meanwhile, the battle for second place continued hot and heavy. Giovanni Evangelisti took the first round non-Lewis lead at 26 feet 6½ inches. In the third round he was passed by Gary Honey's personal record of 26 feet 10 inches. Evangelisti led off the final round with his first-ever jump over 27 feet. But Honey, next down the runway, matched him to the centimeter and won the silver medal by virtue of a better second jump.

Unfortunately, Carl Lewis' performance was met by boos by many in the crowd who resented his refusal to challenge Bob Beamon's record by taking four more jumps. These boorish "fans" seemed unappreciative of Lewis' exacting Olympic schedule, and unaware that he had never taken a full complement of jumps at a meet in which he also competed in the sprints. It is also worth noting that the legendary Jesse Owens, to whom Lewis was often compared, took only one jump on the day he set his 1935 world record that would last for 25 years and, during his entire career, only twice did Owens take a full set of jumps.

At the 1984 Olympics, Carl Lewis' sister, Carol, placed ninth in the women's long jump.

**1988 Seoul** C: 41, N: 31, D: 9.26. WR: 8.90, 29-2½ (Robert Beamon)

|  |  | M | FT.-IN. |
|---|---|---|---|
| 1. F. Carlton Lewis | USA | 8.72 | 28-7¼ |
| 2. Michael Powell | USA | 8.49 | 27-10¼ |
| 3. Larry Myricks | USA | 8.27 | 27-1½ |
| 4. Giovanni Evangelisti | ITA | 8.08w | 26-6 |
| 5. Antonio Corgos | SPA | 8.03 | 26-4¼ |
| 6. László Szalma | HUN | 8.00 | 26-3 |
| 7. Norbert Brige | FRA | 7.97 | 26-1¾ |
| 8. Leonid Voloshin | SOV | 7.89 | 25-10¾ |

Carl Lewis went to the Olympics with a winning streak of 55 meets over 7½ years. His latest victory came in a dramatic seesaw battle with longtime rival Larry Myricks at the U.S. Olympic trials. Lewis won that one 28 feet 9 inches (8.76 meters) to 28 feet 8¼ inches (8.74 meters). In Seoul, however, Lewis faced a tough assignment: the long jump final began only 55 minutes after he finished competing in the preliminaries of the 200-meter dash. Drawn to jump in the first position, Lewis appealed to the officials in charge of the event and was allowed to jump twelfth and last instead. He took the first-round lead with a leap of 27 feet 7 inches, then lengthened his lead with a wind-aided second jump of 28 feet.

After the third round, a new official arrived on the scene and ordered Lewis to begin jumping first instead of last. Lewis argued that if he had to comply, he should at least be allowed a 10-minute break. The Korean official refused, but then the long jump clock malfunctioned and Lewis got his break anyway. He responded with his winning leap of 28 feet 7¼ inches. Lewis, who registered the four longest jumps of the competition, became the first repeat winner in the history of the event (not including Meyer Prinstein's victory at the 1906 Intercalated Games).

## TRIPLE JUMP

This used to be known as the hop, step, and jump, which accurately describes the event. The contestants land on the same foot with which they take off, take one step onto the other foot, and then jump. If their trailing foot touches the ground, the jump is ruled a foul. Other rules are the same as those for the long jump.

**1896 Athens** C: 7, N: 5, D: 4.6. WR: 15.25, 50-0½ (Daniel Shanahan)

|   |   |   | FT.- |
|---|---|---|---|
|   |   | M | IN. |
| 1. James Connolly | USA | 13.71 | 44-11¾ |
| 2. Alexandre Tuffère | FRA | 12.70 | 41-8 |
| 3. Ioannis Persakis | GRE | 12.565 | 41-3 |
| 4. Alajos Szokolyi | HUN | 11.26 | 36-11½ |
| 5. Karl Schumann | GER | — |   |

James Brendan Connolly came from a poor Irish-American family in South Boston, Massachusetts. He was a 27-year-old, self-educated undergraduate at Harvard when he read about the revival of the Olympic Games. As the national triple jump champion, he decided to go to Athens and take part. He asked permission for a leave of absence. When his dean refused, he dropped out and went anyway. Ten American athletes and one trainer spent 16½ days on a ship to Naples, where Connolly's wallet was stolen. Then they took the train to Athens, arriving at nine p.m. on April 5. At 4 a.m. the following morning, they were awakened by a brass band and discovered, to their shock, that the competition was to begin that day rather than twelve days hence as they had expected. Apparently the Americans had forgotten that the Greek calendar differed from the American one.

At 2 p.m., the first modern Olympic Games were officially opened. Connolly was the last to jump in the triple-jump competition. After his second try he turned to the Englishman raking the pit and said, "They ought to tell how far each man jumps. Then a fellow won't be breaking his back when there's no need of it." The pit raker replied, "As far as the measurements go, there's nobody within a yard of you." James Connolly had become the first Olympic champion since the boxer Barasdates of Armenia in 369 A.D. Actually, Connolly had performed two hops and a jump rather than a hop, step, and jump, which followed the rules of the competition at the time.

Connolly later became a noted journalist and war correspondent, and also authored 25 novels and 200 short stories. He was once offered an honorary degree from Harvard, but refused it. Connolly died on January 20, 1957, at the age of 87.

**1900 Paris** C: 13, N: 6, D: 7.16. WR: 15.25, 50-0½ (Daniel Shanahan)

|   |   |   | FT.- |   |
|---|---|---|---|---|
|   |   | M | IN. |   |
| 1. Meyer Prinstein | USA | 14.47 | 47-5¾ | OR |
| 2. James Connolly | USA | 13.97 | 45-10 |   |
| 3. Lewis Sheldon | USA | 13.64 | 44-9 |   |
| 4. Patrick Leahy | GBR/IRL | — | — |   |
| 5. Albert Delannoy | FRA | — | — |   |
| 6. Alexandre Tuffère | FRA | — | — |   |

Prinstein made up for his disappointment at not being allowed to take part in the previous day's long jump final.

**1904 St. Louis** C: 7, N: 1, D: 9.1. WR: 5.25, 50-0½ (Daniel Shanahan)

|   |   |   | FT.- |
|---|---|---|---|
|   |   | M | IN. |
| 1. Meyer Prinstein | USA | 14.35 | 47-1 |
| 2. Fred Englehardt | USA | 13.90 | 45-7¼ |
| 3. Robert Stangland | USA | 13.36 | 43-10 |
| 4. John Fuhler | USA | 12.91 | 42-4½ |
| 5. George Van Cleaf | USA | — | — |
| 6. John Hagerman | USA | — | — |
| 7. Samuel Jones | USA | — | — |

Prinstein won with his sixth and final jump.

**1906 Athens** C: 21, N: 8, D: 4.30. WR: 15.25, 50-0½ (Daniel Shanahan)

|   |   |   | FT.- |
|---|---|---|---|
|   |   | M | IN. |
| 1. Peter O'Connor | GBR/IRL | 14.075 | 46-2¼ |
| 2. Cornelius Leahy | GBR/IRL | 13.98 | 45-10½ |
| 3. Thomas Cronan | USA | 13.70 | 44-11½ |
| 4. Oscar Guttormsen | NOR | 13.34 | 43-9¼ |
| 5. Dimitrios Müller | GRE | 13.125 | 43-0¾ |
| 6. Francis Connolly | USA | 12.75 | 41-10 |
| 7. Vasilios Stournares | GRE | 12.725 | 41-9 |
| 8. Carl Pedersen | NOR | 12.68 | 41-7¼ |

After his victory, O'Connor, who won with his final attempt, climbed the flagpole, pulled down the Union Jack of Great Britain, and replaced it with the green flag of Ireland.

**1908 London** C: 19, N: 7, D: 7.25. WR: 15.25, 50-0½ (Daniel Shanahan)

| | | | FT.- | |
|---|---|---|---|---|
| | | M | IN. | |
| 1. Timothy Ahearne | GBR/IRL | 14.92 | 48-11¼ | OR |
| 2. J. Garfield MacDonald | CAN | 14.76 | 48-5¼ | |
| 3. Edvard Larsen | NOR | 14.39 | 47-2¾ | |
| 4. Calvin Bricker | CAN | 14.10 | 46-3 | |
| 5. Platt Adams | USA | 14.07 | 46-2 | |
| 6. Frank Mount Pleasant | USA | 13.97 | 45-10 | |

**1912 Stockholm** C: 22, N: 9, D: 7.15. WR: 15.52, 50-11 (Daniel Ahearn)

| | | | FT.- | |
|---|---|---|---|---|
| | | M | IN. | |
| 1. Gustaf Lindblom | SWE | 14.76 | 48-5¼ | |
| 2. Georg Åberg | SWE | 14.51 | 47-7¼ | |
| 3. Erik Almlöf | SWE | 14.17 | 46-6 | |
| 4. Erling Vinne | NOR | 14.14 | 46-4¾ | |
| 5. Platt Adams | USA | 14.09 | 46-2¾ | |
| 6. Edvard Larsen | NOR | 14.06 | 46-1½ | |
| 7. Hjalmar Olsson | SWE | 14.01 | 45-11¾ | |
| 8. Nils Fiksdal | NOR | 13.96 | 45-9¾ | |

**1920 Antwerp** C: 19, N: 7, D: 8.21. WR: 15.52, 50-11 (Daniel Ahearn)

| | | | FT.- | |
|---|---|---|---|---|
| | | M | IN. | |
| 1. Vilho Tuulos | FIN | 14.50 | 47-7 | |
| 2. Folke Jansson | SWE | 14.48 | 47-6 | |
| 3. Erik Almlöf | SWE | 14.27 | 46-9¾ | |
| 4. Ivar Sahlin | SWE | 14.17 | 46-6 | |
| 5. Sherman Landers | USA | 14.17 | 46-6 | |
| 6. Daniel Ahearn | USA | 14.08 | 46-2¼ | |
| 7. Ossian Nylund | FIN | 13.74 | 45-0½ | |
| 8. Benjamin Howard Baker | GBR | 13.67 | 44-10 | |

**1924 Paris** C: 20, N: 12, D: 7.12. WR: 15.52, 50-11 (Daniel Ahearn)

| | | | FT.- | |
|---|---|---|---|---|
| | | M | IN. | |
| 1. Anthony Winter | AUS | 15.525 | 50-11¼ | WR |
| 2. Luis Brunetto | ARG | 15.42 | 50-7¼ | |
| 3. Vilho Tuulos | FIN | 15.37 | 50-5 | |
| 4. Väinö Rainio | FIN | 15.01 | 49-3 | |
| 5. Folke Jansson | SWE | 14.97 | 49-1½ | |
| 6. Mikio Oda | JPN | 14.35 | 47-1 | |
| 7. R. Earle Wilson | USA | 14.235 | 46-8 | |
| 8. Ivar Sahlin | SWE | 14.16 | 46-5½ | |

In setting a world record, Nick Winter improved on his pre-Olympic best by 14½ inches.

**1928 Amsterdam** C: 24, N: 13, D: 8.2. WR: 15.525, 50-11¼ (Anthony Winter)

| | | | FT.- | |
|---|---|---|---|---|
| | | M | IN. | |
| 1. Mikio Oda | JPN | 15.21 | 49-11 | |
| 2. Levi Casey | USA | 15.17 | 49-9¼ | |
| 3. Vilho Tuulos | FIN | 15.11 | 49-7 | |
| 4. Chuhei Nambu | JPN | 15.01 | 49-3 | |
| 5. Toimi Tulikoura | FIN | 14.70 | 48-2¾ | |
| 6. Erkki Järvinen | FIN | 14.65 | 48-0¾ | |
| 7. Willem Peters | HOL | 14.55 | 47-9 | |
| 8. Väinö Rainio | FIN | 14.41 | 47-3½ | |

Mikio Oda of Japan was the first Asian to win an Olympic gold medal.

**1932 Los Angeles** C: 16, N: 12, D: 8.4. WR: 15.58, 51-1½ (Mikio Oda)

| | | | FT.- | |
|---|---|---|---|---|
| | | M | IN. | |
| 1. Chuhei Nambu | JPN | 15.72 | 51-7 | WR |
| 2. Eric Svensson | SWE | 15.32 | 50-3¼ | |
| 3. Kenkichi Oshima | JPN | 15.12 | 49-7¼ | |
| 4. Eamon Fitzgerald | IRL | 15.01 | 49-3 | |
| 5. Willem Peters | HOL | 14.93 | 48-11¾ | |
| 6. Sol Furth | USA | 14.88 | 48-10 | |
| 7. Sidney Bowman | USA | 14.87 | 48-9½ | |
| 8. Rolland Romero | USA | 14.85 | 48-8¾ | |

Chuhei Nambu was the world record holder in the long jump, but a leg injury prevented him from placing better than third in Los Angeles. Two days later he entered the triple jump and finished first, achieving the rare distinction of holding the world record in both horizontal jump events.

**1936 Berlin** C: 31, N: 19, D: 8.6. WR: 15.78, 51-9¼ (Jim Metcalfe)

| | | | FT.- | |
|---|---|---|---|---|
| | | M | IN. | |
| 1. Naoto Tajima | JPN | 16.00 | 52-6 | WR |
| 2. Masao Harada | JPN | 15.66 | 51-4½ | |
| 3. Jim Metcalfe | AUS | 15.50 | 50-10¼ | |
| 4. Heinz Wöllner | GER | 15.27 | 50-1¼ | |
| 5. Rolland Romero | USA | 15.08 | 49-5¾ | |
| 6. Kenkichi Oshima | JPN | 15.07 | 49-5½ | |
| 7. Erich Joch | GER | 14.88 | 48-10 | |
| 8. Dudley Wilkins | USA | 14.83 | 48-8 | |

Tajima duplicated Nambu's feat of winning the triple jump gold medal two days after he had earned a bronze medal in the long jump. Long jump silver medalist Luz Long placed tenth in the triple jump.

**1948 London** C: 29, N: 18, D: 8.3. WR: 16.00, 52-6 (Naoto Tajima)

| | | | FT.- | |
|---|---|---|---|---|
| | | M | IN. | |
| 1. Arne Åhman | SWE | 15.40 | 50-6¼ | |
| 2. George Avery | AUS | 15.36 | 50-4¾ | |
| 3. Ruhi Sarialp | TUR | 15.02 | 49-3½ | |
| 4. Preben Larsen | DEN | 14.83 | 48-8 | |

| | | | FT.- | |
|---|---|---|---|---|
| 5. Geraldo de Oliveira | BRA | 14.82 | 48-7½ | |
| 6. Valdemar Rautio | FIN | 14.70 | 48-2¾ | |
| 7. Les McKeand | AUS | 14.53 | 47-8 | |
| 8. Helio Coutinho de Silva | BRA | 14.49 | 47-6½ | |

**1952 Helsinki** C: 35, N: 23, D: 7.23. WR: 16.01, 52-6½ (Adhemar Ferreira da Silva)

| | | | FT.- | |
|---|---|---|---|---|
| | | M | IN. | |
| 1. Adhemar Ferreira da Silva | BRA | 16.22 | 53-2¾ | WR |
| 2. Leonid Sherbakov | SOV | 15.98 | 52-5¼ | |
| 3. Arnoldo Devonish | VEN | 15.52 | 50-11 | |
| 4. Walter Ashbaugh | USA | 15.39 | 50-6 | |
| 5. Rune Nilsen | NOR | 15.13 | 49-7¾ | |
| 6. Yoshio Iimuro | JPN | 14.99 | 49-2¼ | |
| 7. Geraldo de Oliveira | BRA | 14.95 | 49-0¾ | |
| 8. Roger Norman | SWE | 14.89 | 48-10¼ | |

Da Silva put on an incredible show, breaking his old world record four times in six attempts in the final. Arnoldo Devonish was the first Venezuelan to win an Olympic medal.

**1956 Melbourne** C: 32, N: 20, D: 11.27. WR: 16.56, 54-4 (Adhemar Ferreira da Silva)

| | | | FT.- | |
|---|---|---|---|---|
| | | M | IN. | |
| 1. Adhemar Ferreira da Silva | BRA | 16.35 | 53-7¾ | OR |
| 2. Vilhjálmur Einarsson | ICE | 16.26 | 53-4¼ | |
| 3. Vitold Kreyer | SOV | 16.02 | 52-6¾ | |
| 4. William Sharpe | USA | 15.88 | 52-1¼ | |
| 5. Martin Rehák | CZE | 15.85 | 52-0 | |
| 6. Leonid Sherbakov | SOV | 15.80 | 51-10 | |
| 7. Koji Sakurai | JPN | 15.73 | 51-7¼ | |
| 8. Teruji Kogake | JPN | 15.64 | 51-3¾ | |

The second round of the final produced a tremendous shock, when a completely unknown Icelander, 22-year-old Vilhjálmur Einarsson, took the lead with a jump of 53 feet 4¼ inches, improving his personal record by 17 inches. Nevertheless, defending champion da Silva regained the lead in the fourth round and won his second gold medal. Afterward, reporters searched frantically to find an Icelandic interpreter, only to have Einarsson save them the trouble by explaining that he spoke English quite well, since he had just graduated from Dartmouth University, in New Hampshire. Einarsson was Iceland's first Olympic medal winner.

In 1958 Adhemar Ferreira da Silva acted in the internationally acclaimed film *Black Orpheus.*

**1960 Rome** C: 39, N: 24, D: 9.6. WR: 17.03, 55-10½ (Józef Schmidt)

| | | | FT.- | |
|---|---|---|---|---|
| | | M | IN. | |
| 1. Józef Schmidt | POL | 16.81 | 55-2 | |
| 2. Vladimir Goryayev | SOV | 16.63 | 54-6¾ | |
| 3. Vitold Kreyer | SOV | 16.43 | 53-11 | |
| 4. Ira Davis | USA | 16.41 | 53-10¼ | |
| 5. Vilhjálmur Einarsson | ICE | 16.37 | 53-8½ | |
| 6. Ryszard Malcherczyk | POL | 16.01 | 52-6½ | |
| 7. Manfred Hinze | GDR | 15.93 | 52-3¼ | |
| 8. Kari Rahkamo | FIN | 15.84 | 51-11¾ | |

On August 5, 1960, Józef Schmidt had jumped 55 feet 10½ inches to become the first person to break both the 55-foot barrier and the 17-meter barrier, bettering the world record by 13 inches. In Rome, he won easily.

**1964 Tokyo** C: 34, N: 21, D: 10.16. WR: 17.03, 55-10½ (Józef Schmidt)

| | | | FT.- | |
|---|---|---|---|---|
| | | M | IN. | |
| 1. Józef Schmidt | POL | 16.85 | 55-3½ | OR |
| 2. Oleg Fyedoseyev | SOV | 16.58 | 54-4¾ | |
| 3. Viktor Kravchenko | SOV | 16.57 | 54-4½ | |
| 4. Frederick Alsop | GBR | 16.46 | 54-0 | |
| 5. Șerban Ciochină | ROM | 16.23 | 53-3 | |
| 6. Manfred Hinze | GDR | 16.15 | 53-0 | |
| 7. Georgi Stoikovski | BUL | 16.10 | 52-10 | |
| 8. Hans-Jürgen Rückborn | GDR | 16.09 | 52-9½ | |

Józef Schmidt had dominated the triple jump for six years. However, he underwent an operation to his knee less than two months before the Tokyo Games, and his condition was still in doubt. Competing in pain, needing an injection of novocaine, Schmidt jumped 54 feet 7½ inches in the second round of the final, and then set an Olympic record of 55 feet 3½ inches with his last attempt.

**1968 Mexico City** C:34, N:24, D: 10.17. WR: 17.03, 55-10½ (Józef Schmidt)

| | | | FT.- | |
|---|---|---|---|---|
| | | M | IN. | |
| 1. Viktor Saneyev | SOV | 17.39 | 57-0¾ | WR |
| 2. Nelson Prudencio | BRA | 17.27 | 56-8 | |
| 3. Giuseppe Gentile | ITA | 17.22 | 56-6 | |
| 4. Arthur Walker | USA | 17.12 | 56-2 | |
| 5. Nikolai Dudkin | SOV | 17.09 | 56-1 | |
| 6. Phillip May | AUS | 17.02 | 55-10¼ | |
| 7. Józef Schmidt | POL | 16.89 | 55-5 | |
| 8. Mamadou Mansour-Dia | SEN | 16.73 | 54-10¾ | |

Giuseppe Gentile, a bearded 25-year-old law student who later played opposite Maria Callas in the film version of *Medea,* produced a stunning performance in the qualifying round when he leaped 56 feet 1¼ inches to break Józef Schmidt's eight-year-old world record. But this was just a prelude to the extraordinary events of the following day's final.

In the very first round, Gentile hit a whopping 56 feet 6 inches, 19 inches farther than his pre-Olympic best, and it seemed that he had surely put a lock on the gold medal. But in the second round, Nelson Prudencio, who had never jumped beyond 53 feet 5¾ inches before Mexico City, leaped an ominous 55 feet 11¼ inches. In the third round it was the turn of Viktor Saneyev, a graduate of the Georgian Sub-Tropical Plant Cultivation Institute.

The pre-Olympic favorite, Saneyev reached 56 feet 6½ inches, to move ahead of Gentile by one centimeter.

In the fifth round, Nikolai Dudkin moved into third place with 56 feet 1 inch. Two jumps later, Prudencio exploded with another world record of 56 feet 8 inches. With his last jump, Prudencio again broke Schmidt's old record with a jump of 56 feet 3¼ inches. Saneyev, Art Walker, and Gentile each had one jump remaining. It was Saneyev who came up with the clutch performance, extending to 57 feet ¾ inch for yet another world record. Walker jumped 56 feet 2 inches, leaving Nikolai Dudkin in fifth place even though he had bettered the pre-Olympic world record. Gentile closed the amazing competition with his fourth foul in five jumps, and had to settle for a bronze medal after twice setting a world record. The best jumps of Saneyev and Prudencio were both accompanied by suspicious wind readings of exactly 2.0 m.p.s., which didn't affect the competition, but did affect their validity as world records, since 2.0 m.p.s. happened to be the maximum allowable wind speed.

**1972 Munich** C: 36, N: 28, D: 9.4. WR: 17.40, 57-1 (Pedro Perez Dueñas)

| | | | FT.- |
|---|---|---|---|
| | | M | IN. |
| 1. Viktor Saneyev | SOV | 17.35 | 56-11¼ |
| 2. Jörg Drehmel | GDR | 17.31 | 56-9½ |
| 3. Nelson Prudencio | BRA | 17.05 | 55-11¼ |
| 4. Carol Corbu | ROM | 16.85 | 55-3½ |
| 5. John Craft | USA | 16.83 | 55-2¾ |
| 6. Mamadou Mansour-Dia | SEN | 16.83 | 55-2¾ |
| 7. Michal Joachimowski | POL | 16.69 | 54-9¼ |
| 8. Kristen Flogstad | NOR | 16.44 | 53-11¼ |

This was expected to be a dramatic showdown between defending champion Viktor Saneyev and his rival Jörg Drehmel, who had twice beaten Saneyev in important meets. But Saneyev belted out the third best jump of all time in the first round of the final, and Drehmel was unable to even come close until the fifth round. World record holder Pedro Perez withdrew in the middle of the qualifying round because of injury. Nelson Prudencio's final jump was his best since the 1968 Olympic final.

**1976 Montreal** C: 25, N: 18, D: 7.30. WR: 17.89, 58-8½ (João Carlos de Oliveira)

| | | | FT.- |
|---|---|---|---|
| | | M | IN. |
| 1. Viktor Saneyev | SOV | 17.29 | 56-8¾ |
| 2. James Butts | USA | 17.18 | 56-4½ |
| 3. João Carlos de Oliveira | BRA | 16.90 | 55-5½ |
| 4. Pedro Perez Dueñas | CUB | 16.81 | 55-2 |
| 5. Tommy Haynes | USA | 16.78 | 55-0¾ |
| 6. Wolfgang Kolmsee | GER | 16.68 | 54-8¾ |
| 7. Eugeniusz Biskupski | POL | 16.49 | 54-1¼ |
| 8. Carol Corbu | ROM | 16.43 | 53-11 |

On October 15, 1975, João Carlos de Oliveira, competing at the Pan American Games in Mexico City, triple-jumped 58 feet 8½ inches to better Viktor Saneyev's world record by an incredible 17¾ inches. At the Montreal Olympics, de Oliveira led the qualifying round with a reserved jump of 55 feet 2 inches, followed by Saneyev at 55 feet ¼ inch. In the final, Perez took the first round lead at 55 feet 2 inches, but Saneyev moved ahead in the third round with a jump of 55 feet 11¾ inches. In the fourth round, James Butts, aiming to become the first U.S. triple jump medalist in 48 years, leaped into the lead at 56 feet 4½ inches. However, Saneyev, ever the clutch performer, rebounded in the fifth round with a jump of 56 feet 8¾ inches and that settled the issue. He joined standing jumper Ray Ewry, hammer thrower John Flanagan, and discus champion Al Oerter as the only track and field athletes to win three or more individual gold medals in the same event.

**1980 Moscow** C: 23, N: 19, D: 7.25. WR: 17.89, 58-8½ (João Carlos de Oliveira)

| | | | FT.- |
|---|---|---|---|
| | | M | IN. |
| 1. Jaak Uudmäe | SOV | 17.35 | 56-11¼ |
| 2. Viktor Saneyev | SOV | 17.24 | 56-6¾ |
| 3. João Carlos de Oliveira | BRA | 17.22 | 56-6 |
| 4. Keith Connor | GBR | 16.87 | 55-4¼ |
| 5. Ian Campbell | AUS | 16.72 | 54-10¼ |
| 6. Atanas Chochev | BUL | 16.56 | 54-4 |
| 7. Béla Bakosi | HUN | 16.47 | 54-0½ |
| 8. Kenneth Lorraway | AUS | 16.44 | 53-11¼ |

Unfortunately, this event was marred by ugly scenes: Soviet spectators whistling while de Oliveira jumped, and controversial officiating which caused leading non-Soviet contenders de Oliveira and Ian Campbell to be charged with nine fouls in 12 jumps. In the third round Campbell received a no-jump after allegedly dragging his trail leg during the step stage. He argued his case, but the pit was raked before impartial observers could arrive. The very next jump was the gold medal winner for 25-year-old Estonian Jaak Uudmäe. The final round was highlighted by a near world record by de Oliveira that was ruled a foul, and by 34-year-old Viktor Saneyev's noble attempt to match Al Oerter's feat of four consecutive gold medals. He landed four and a half inches short, but did manage to edge past de Oliveira for the silver medal. In January 1982, João Carlos de Oliveira was badly injured in an auto accident. After a nine-month battle to salvage his athletic career, his right leg was finally amputated below the knee.

**1984 Los Angeles** C: 28, N: 21, D: 8.4. WR: 17.89, 58-8½ (João Carlos de Oliveira)

| | | | FT.- |
|---|---|---|---|
| | | M | IN. |
| 1. Alfrederick Joyner | USA | 17.26 | 56-7½ |
| 2. Michael Conley | USA | 17.18 | 56-4½ |
| 3. Keith Connor | GBR | 16.87 | 55-4¼ |
| 4. Zou Zhenxian | CHN | 16.83 | 55-2¾ |
| 5. Peter Bouschen | GER | 16.77 | 55-0¼ |

| | | | | |
|---|---|---|---|---|
| 6. William Banks | USA | 16.75 | 54-11½ | |
| 7. Ajayi Agbebaku | NGR | 16.67 | 54-8¼ | |
| 8. Eric McCalla | GBR | 16.66 | 54-8 | |

Mike Conley solidified his role of favorite by leading the qualifying round with a near Olympic record jump of 56 feet 11½ inches. The next morning, Conley's teammate, Al Joyner, was watching a television preview of the day's events when he saw pictures of Conley and the third U.S. triple-jumper, Willie Banks, come on the screen. "I thought they would show me too," Joyner would later recall, "but they didn't. So I wanted to go out and let everybody know who I was."

Joyner's first round jump, aided by the only significant tailwind of the day, held up for the gold medal. He also recorded three of the four next best jumps as well. The first seven places were decided by the second round, although Conley almost pulled it out with a huge last round leap that turned out to be a foul.

Joyner, of East St. Louis, Illinois, competed at the same time that his younger sister, Jackie, was taking part in the heptathlon. In fact, he passed his fourth round turn in order to root her on during the last lap of the 800-meter run, On the way to the triple jump award ceremony he ran into Jackie coming off the platform after receiving her silver medal. Several days after the competition, while other athletes were nursing injured leg muscles, upset winner Al Joyner confided that he was suffering from sore *cheek* muscles—from smiling so much.

**1988 Seoul** C: 43, N: 31, D: 9.24. WR: 17.97, 58-11½ (William Banks)

| | | | FT.- | |
|---|---|---|---|---|
| | | M | IN. | |
| 1. Khristo Markov | BUL | 17.61 | 57-9¼ | OR |
| 2. Igor Lapshin | SOV | 17.52 | 57-5¾ | |
| 3. Aleksandr Kovalenko | SOV | 17.42 | 57-1¾ | |
| 4. Oleg Protsenko | SOV | 17.38 | 57-0¼ | |
| 5. Charlie Simpkins | USA | 17.29 | 56-8¾ | |
| 6. William Banks | USA | 17.03 | 55-10½ | |
| 7. Ivan Slanař | CZE | 16.75 | 54-11½ | |
| 8. Jacek Pastusiński | POL | 16.72 | 54-10¼ | |

Markov's first-round attempt held up for the gold medal, but Lapshin gained the silver with his final try.

# SHOT PUT

A shot is a 16-pound ball made of iron or brass. It must be put rather than thrown and must not drop below the level of the contestant's shoulder.

**1896 Athens** C: 7, N: 4, D: 4.7. WR: 14.32, 47-0 (George Gray)

| | | | FT.- | |
|---|---|---|---|---|
| | | M | IN. | |
| 1. Robert Garrett | USA | 11.22 | 36-9¾ | |
| 2. Miltiades Gouskos | GRE | 11.20 | 36-9 | |
| 3. Georgios Papasideris | GRE | 10.36 | 34-0 | |
| 4. Karl Schumann | GER | — | — | |

Garrett, who had placed first in the discus the day before, won the shot put with his first attempt.

**1900 Paris** C: 10, N: 6, D: 7.15. WR: 14.68, 48-2 (Dennis Horgan)

| | | | FT.- | |
|---|---|---|---|---|
| | | M | IN. | |
| 1. Richard Sheldon | USA | 14.10 | 46-3¼ | OR |
| 2. Josiah McCracken | USA | 12.85 | 42-2 | |
| 3. Robert Garrett | USA | 12.37 | 40-7 | |
| 4. Rezsö Crettier | HUN | 12.05 | 39-6½ | |
| 5. Panagiotis Paraskevopoulos | GRE | 11.52 | 37-9½ | |
| 6. Gustaf Söderström | SWE | 11.18 | 36-8¼ | |

**1904 St. Louis** C: 8, N: 2, D: 8.31. WR: 14.68, 48-2 (Dennis Horgan)

| | | | FT.- | |
|---|---|---|---|---|
| | | M | IN. | |
| 1. Ralph Rose | USA | 14.81 | 48-7 | WR |
| 2. William Coe | USA | 14.40 | 47-3 | |
| 3. Leon Feuerbach | USA | 13.37 | 43-10½ | |
| 4. Martin Sheridan | USA | 12.39 | 40-8 | |
| 5. Charles Chadwick | USA | — | — | |
| 6. Albert Johnson | USA | — | — | |
| 7. John Guiney | USA | — | — | |

Ralph Rose was a 6-foot 6-inch, 235-pound giant from California. Before his Olympic career was over, he had won three gold medals, two silver, and one bronze. He died on October 16, 1913, at the age of 29. Nicolaos Georgantas of Greece was also entered in this event, but after his first two attempts were disallowed for throwing, he withdrew in disgust.

**1906 Athens** C: 18, N: 10, D: 4.27. WR: 15.09, 49-6 (Wesley Coe)

| | | | FT.- | |
|---|---|---|---|---|
| | | M | IN. | |
| 1. Martin Sheridan | USA | 12.325 | 40-6¼ | |
| 2. Mihály Dávid | HUN | 11.83 | 38-9¾ | |
| 3. Eric Lemming | SWE | 11.26 | 36-11½ | |
| 4. André Tison | FRA | 11.02 | 36-2 | |

Martin Sheridan was the star of the Intercalated Games, winning two gold medals and three silver medals. In 1908 he added two gold and a silver.

**1908 London** C: 26, N: 8, D: 7.16. WR: 15.12, 49-7½ (Ralph Rose)

| | | | FT.- | |
|---|---|---|---|---|
| | | M | IN. | |
| 1. Ralph Rose | USA | 14.21 | 46-7½ | |
| 2. Dennis Horgan | GBR/IRL | 13.62 | 44-8¼ | |
| 3. John Garrels | USA | 13.18 | 43-3 | |
| 4. William Coe | USA | 13.07 | 42-10½ | |
| 5. Edmond Barrett | GBR | 12.89 | 42-3½ | |
| 6. Marquis Horr | USA | 12.82 | 42-1 | |
| 7. Jalmari Sauli | FIN | 12.58 | 41-3¼ | |
| 8. Lee Talbott | USA | 11.63 | 38-1¾ | |

Dennis Horgan was 37 years old and past his prime. His second-place performance was particularly noteworthy considering that he had almost been killed the year before. On duty as a New York City policeman, Horgan tried to break up a brawl and was severely attacked with sticks and shovels. After his surprising recovery, he was given a pension and allowed to return to Ireland.

**1912 Stockholm** C: 22, N: 14, D: 7.10. WR: 15.545, 51-0 (Ralph Rose)

| | | | FT.- | |
|---|---|---|---|---|
| | | M | IN. | |
| 1. Patrick McDonald | USA | 15.34 | 50-4 | OR |
| 2. Ralph Rose | USA | 15.25 | 50-0½ | |
| 3. Lawrence Whitney | USA | 13.93 | 45-8½ | |
| 4. Elmer Niklander | FIN | 13.65 | 44-9½ | |
| 5. George Philbrook | USA | 13.13 | 43-1 | |
| 6. Imre Mudin | HUN | 12.81 | 42-0½ | |
| 7. Einar Nilsson | SWE | 12.62 | 41-5 | |
| 8. Patrick Quinn | GBR | 12.53 | 41-1½ | |

McDonald, another New York City policeman, surprised Rose, in the fourth round of six, by achieving the best put of his career.

**1920 Antwerp** C: 20, N: 10, D: 8:18. WR: 15.545, 51-0 (Ralph Rose)

| | | | FT.- | |
|---|---|---|---|---|
| | | M | IN. | |
| 1. Frans "Ville" Pörhölä | FIN | 14.81 | 48-7¼ | |
| 2. Elmer Niklander | FIN | 14.155 | 46-5¼ | |
| 3. Harry Liversedge | USA | 14.15 | 46-5¼ | |
| 4. Patrick McDonald | USA | 14.08 | 46-2½ | |
| 5. Einar Nilsson | SWE | 13.87 | 45-6¼ | |
| 6. Harald Tammer | EST | 13.605 | 44-7½ | |
| 7. George Bihlman | USA | 13.575 | 44-6½ | |
| 8. Howard Cann | USA | 13.52 | 44-4¼ | |

**1924 Paris** C: 28, N: 15, D: 7.8. WR: 15.545, 51-0 (Ralph Rose)

| | | | FT.- | |
|---|---|---|---|---|
| | | M | IN. | |
| 1. L. Clarence "Bud" Houser | USA | 14.99 | 49-2¼ | |
| 2. Glenn Hartranft | USA | 14.89 | 48-10¼ | |
| 3. Ralph Hills | USA | 14.64 | 48-0½ | |
| 4. Hannes Torpo | FIN | 14.45 | 47-5 | |
| 5. Norman Anderson | USA | 14.29 | 46-10¾ | |
| 6. Elmer Niklander | FIN | 14.26 | 49-9½ | |
| 7. Frans "Ville" Pörhölä | FIN | 14.10 | 46-3¼ | |
| 8. Bertil Jansson | SWE | 13.76 | 45-1¾ | |

**1928 Amsterdam** C: 22, N: 14, D: 7.29. WR: 15.79, 51-9¾ (Emil Hirschfeld)

| | | | FT.- | |
|---|---|---|---|---|
| | | M | IN. | |
| 1. John Kuck | USA | 15.87 | 52-0¾ | WR |
| 2. Herman Brix | USA | 15.75 | 51-8¼ | |
| 3. Emil Hirschfeld | GER | 15.72 | 51-7 | |
| 4. Eric Krenz | USA | 14.99 | 49-2¼ | |
| 5. Armas Wahlstedt | FIN | 14.69 | 48-2½ | |
| 6. Wilhelm Uebler | GER | 14.69 | 48-2½ | |
| 7. Harlow Rothert | USA | 14.68 | 48-2 | |
| 8. József Darányi | HUN | 14.35 | 47-1 | |

On May 6, 1928, Emil Hirschfeld finally broke Ralph Rose's 1909 world record. He was in good form in Amsterdam, but Kuck and Brix were superb. Kuck started his road to shot put gold when, at the age of 4, he discovered a 3-pound agate sphere and began throwing it around his yard. His practice shot turned out to be a 20,000-year-old Native American relic. Brix later changed his name to Bruce Bennett and became a well-known movie actor. Among his early roles was Tarzan in *The New Adventures of Tarzan* (1935).

**1932 Los Angeles** C: 15, N: 10, D: 7.31. WR: 16.05, 52-8 (Zygmont Heljasz)

| | | | FT.- | |
|---|---|---|---|---|
| | | M | IN. | |
| 1. Leo Sexton | USA | 16.00 | 52-6 | OR |
| 2. Harlow Rothert | USA | 15.67 | 51-5 | |
| 3. František Douda | CZE | 15.61 | 51-2¾ | |
| 4. Emil Hirschfeld | GER | 15.56 | 51-0¾ | |
| 5. Nelson Gray | USA | 15.47 | 50-9¼ | |
| 6. Hans-Heinrich Sievert | GER | 15.07 | 49-5½ | |
| 7. József Darányi | HUN | 14.67 | 48-1¾ | |
| 8. Jules Noël | FRA | 14.53 | 47-8 | |

Leo Sexton was a 6-foot 4-inch insurance broker from New York. World record holder Zygmont Heljasz of Poland was able to place only ninth.

**1936 Berlin** C: 22, N: 14, D: 8.2. WR: 17.40, 57-1 (Jack Torrance)

| | | | FT.- | |
|---|---|---|---|---|
| | | M | IN. | |
| 1. Hans Woellke | GER | 16.20 | 53-1¾ | OR |
| 2. Sulo Bärlund | FIN | 16.12 | 52-10¾ | |
| 3. Gerhard Stöck | GER | 15.66 | 51-4½ | |
| 4. Samuel Francis | USA | 15.45 | 50-8¼ | |
| 5. Jack Torrance | USA | 15.38 | 50-5½ | |
| 6. Dimitri Zaitz | USA | 15.32 | 50-3¼ | |
| 7. František Douda | CZE | 15.28 | 50-1¾ | |
| 8. Arnold Viiding | EST | 15.23 | 49-11¾ | |

Hans Woellke, a 25-year-old policeman, was the first German to win a track and field gold medal. Another policeman, 304-pound world record holder Jack Torrance of Baton Rouge, Louisiana, was out of shape and finished a disappointing fifth.

**1948 London** C: 24, N: 14, D: 8.3. WR: 17.68, 58-0⅜ (Charles Fonville)

| | | | FT.- | |
|---|---|---|---|---|
| | | M | IN. | |
| 1. Wilbur Thompson | USA | 17.12 | 56-2 | OR |
| 2. F. James Delaney | USA | 16.68 | 54-8¾ | |
| 3. James Fuchs | USA | 16.42 | 53-10½ | |
| 4. Mieczyslaw Lomowski | POL | 15.43 | 50-7½ | |
| 5. Gösta Arvidsson | SWE | 15.37 | 50-5¼ | |
| 6. Yrjö Lehtilä | FIN | 15.05 | 49-4½ | |
| 7. Pentti Jouppila | FIN | 14.59 | 47-10½ | |
| 8. Cestmir Kalina | CZE | 14.55 | 47-9 | |

The American putters were so strong that world record holder Charles Fonville failed to make the U.S. team. At

London the Americans outdistanced the rest of the world by over three feet.

**1952 Helsinki** C: 20, N: 14, D: 7.21. WR: 17.95, 58-10½ (James Fuchs)

| | | FT.- M | FT.- IN. | |
|---|---|---|---|---|
| 1. W. Parry O'Brien | USA | 17.41 | 57-1½ | OR |
| 2. C. Darrow Hooper | USA | 17.39 | 57-0¾ | |
| 3. James Fuchs | USA | 17.06 | 55-11¾ | |
| 4. Otto Grigalka | SOV | 16.78 | 55-0¾ | |
| 5. Roland Nilsson | SWE | 16.55 | 53-3¾ | |
| 6. John Savidge | GBR | 16.19 | 53-1½ | |
| 7. Georgi Fyodorov | SOV | 16.06 | 52-8¼ | |
| 8. Per Stavem | NOR | 16.02 | 52-6¾ | |

World record holder Jim Fuchs had won 88 consecutive meets when he was beaten at the 1951 A.A.U. championships by Parry O'Brien. At the 1952 U.S. Olympic trials, O'Brien was beaten by Darrow Hooper. It was his last loss for four years, during which time he won 116 straight meets. O'Brien and Hooper were almost the exact same size and weight. Their similarity also extended to their performances in the Olympics. O'Brien, who was two days older than Hooper, outputted him by only two centimeters. Parry O'Brien, a student at the University of Southern California, practiced at the Los Angeles Memorial Coliseum, site of the 1932 and 1984 Olympics, by sneaking over a fence late at night while no one was there. He revolutionized shot putting by introducing a new style in which he began with his back to the front of the throwing circle and then used every bit of momentum he could gather before he let go of the shot.

**1956 Melbourne** C: 14, N: 10, D: 11.28. WR: 19.25, 63-2 (W. Parry O'Brien)

| | | FT.- M | FT.- IN. | |
|---|---|---|---|---|
| 1. W. Parry O'Brien | USA | 18.57 | 60-11¼ | OR |
| 2. William Nieder | USA | 18.18 | 59-7¾ | |
| 3. Jiří Skobla | CZE | 17.65 | 57-11 | |
| 4. Kenneth Bantum | USA | 17.48 | 57-4¼ | |
| 5. Boris Balyayev | SOV | 16.96 | 55-7¾ | |
| 6. Erik Uddebom | SWE | 16.65 | 54-7½ | |
| 7. Karlheinz Wegmann | GER | 16.63 | 54-6¾ | |
| 8. Georgios Tsakanikas | GRE | 16.56 | 54-4 | |

On May 8, 1954, two days after Roger Bannister broke the four-minute mile, Parry O'Brien became the first person to put the shot more than 60 feet, with a toss of 60 feet 5¼ inches. In Melbourne, at the 1956 Olympics, O'Brien overwhelmed the field, recording the five best puts of the competition. Even his worst put was beaten only by Bill Nieder's best. Parry O'Brien became the first reigning world record holder to win the shot put at the Olympics since 1908. Bronze medalist Jiří Skobla was the son of Jaroslav Skobla, who won the heavyweight weightlifting gold medal in 1932.

**1960 Rome** C: 24, N: 16, D: 8.31. WR: 20.06, 65-10 (William Nieder)

| | | FT.- M | FT.- IN. | |
|---|---|---|---|---|
| 1. William Nieder | USA | 19.68 | 64-6¾ | OR |
| 2. W. Parry O'Brien | USA | 19.11 | 62-8½ | |
| 3. Dallas Long | USA | 19.01 | 62-4½ | |
| 4. Viktor Lipsnis | SOV | 17.90 | 58-8¾ | |
| 5. Michael Lindsay | GBR | 17.80 | 58-4¾ | |
| 6. Alfred Sosgórnik | POL | 17.57 | 57-7¾ | |
| 7. Dieter Urbach | GER | 17.47 | 57-3¾ | |
| 8. Martyn Lucking | GBR | 17.43 | 57-2¼ | |

Bill Nieder had failed to qualify for the U.S. team after finishing fourth in the Olympic trials. But a wrist injury suffered by Dave Davis, and a world record put by Nieder, convinced U.S. officials to make a rare replacement. In Rome, Nieder showed that they had made the right decision. Parry O'Brien led after four rounds, but in the fifth round, Nieder, recalling O'Brien's disparaging remark that he was a "cow pasture performer" who choked in important meets, let loose a monster toss that was almost two feet better than anything the defending champion was able to produce.

**1964 Tokyo** C: 22, N: 13, D: 10.17. WR: 20.68, 67-10 (Dallas Long)

| | | FT.- M | FT.- IN. | |
|---|---|---|---|---|
| 1. Dallas Long | USA | 20.33 | 66-8½ | OR |
| 2. James Randel Matson | USA | 20.20 | 66-3¼ | |
| 3. Vilmos Varju | HUN | 19.39 | 63-7½ | |
| 4. W. Parry O'Brien | USA | 19.20 | 63-0 | |
| 5. Zsigmond Nagy | HUN | 18.88 | 61-11½ | |
| 6. Nikolai Karasyov | SOV | 18.86 | 61-10½ | |
| 7. Leslie Mills | NZE | 18.52 | 60-9¼ | |
| 8. Adolfas Varanauskas | SOV | 18.41 | 60-4¾ | |

Twenty-four-year-old Dallas Long, a 6-foot 4-inch, 260-pound dentist from Los Angeles, took the lead with a first round toss of 64 feet 4 inches. In the third round, 19-year-old Randy Matson of Pampa, Texas, moved ahead at 65 feet 2¾ inches. With his next throw he improved to 66 feet 3¼ inches, a new Olympic record. However, his record was short-lived. Two minutes later, Long countered with a put of 66 feet 8½ inches that held up for first place.

**1968 Mexico City** C: 19, N: 14, D: 10.14. WR: 21.78, 71-5½ (James Randel Matson)

| | | FT.- M | FT.- IN. | |
|---|---|---|---|---|
| 1. James Randel Matson | USA | 20.54 | 67-4¾ | |
| 2. George Woods | USA | 20.12 | 66-0¼ | |
| 3. Eduard Gushchin | SOV | 20.09 | 65-11 | |
| 4. Dieter Hoffmann | GDR | 20.00 | 65-7½ | |
| 5. David Maggard | USA | 19.43 | 63-9 | |
| 6. Wladyslaw Komar | POL | 19.28 | 63-3¼ | |
| 7. Uwe Grabe | GDR | 19.03 | 62-5¼ | |
| 8. Heinfried Birlenbach | GER | 18.80 | 61-8¼ | |

Although he only placed third at the U.S. Olympic trials, 6-foot 6½-inch, 265-pound Randy Matson was still the overwhelming favorite by virtue of the fact that he had completely dominated the event over the previous four years. On May 8, 1965, he had demolished the world record with a put of 70 feet 7¼ inches, bettering the previous record by 2 feet 9¼ inches. By the time of the Mexico City Olympics, Matson had registered 23 of the 25 longest puts in history. He led the qualifying round with an Olympic record of 67 feet 10¼ inches. His first toss of the final was 67 feet 4¾ inches. No one else came close to that for the rest of the competition. U.S. shot putters finished first and second for the fifth straight time. Like many athletes during the Vietnam War period, Randy Matson was declared unfit for military service because of knee problems.

**1972 Munich** C: 29, N: 19, D: 9.9. WR: 21.78, 71-5½ (James Randel Matson)

| | | M | FT.-IN. | |
|---|---|---|---|---|
| 1. Wladyslaw Komar | POL | 21.18 | 69-6 | OR |
| 2. George Woods | USA | 21.17 | 69-5½ | |
| 3. Hartmut Briesenick | GDR | 21.14 | 69-4¼ | |
| 4. Hans-Peter Gies | GDR | 21.14 | 69-4¼ | |
| 5. Allan Feuerbach | USA | 21.01 | 68-11¼ | |
| 6. Brian Oldfield | USA | 20.91 | 68-7¼ | |
| 7. Heinfried Birlenbach | GER | 20.37 | 66-10 | |
| 8. Vilmos Varjú | HUN | 20.10 | 65-11½ | |

The 6-foot 5¼ inch, 276-pound Wladyslaw Komar had twice been kicked off the Polish team for "misbehavior," including once when he received a "life ban." However, he was back again in Munich for his third Olympics. Ninth in 1964, sixth in 1968, the 32-year-old Komar connected with the greatest put of his career in the first round of the 1972 final, bettering his previous best by seven and a quarter inches. Woods, Briesenick, and Gies all came very, very close, but each fell short by inches. George Woods' last toss caused much controversy since it hit the marker which indicated Komar's best put. Many observers were quite surprised when it was measured at only 69 feet ¾ inch, and Woods himself believed that at the very least he deserved an extra put. But the officials in charge ruled it a valid toss and called an end to the competition. Films of the incident were inconclusive.

**1976 Montreal** C: 23, N: 18, D: 7.24. WR: 22.00, 72-2¼ (Aleksandr Baryshnikov)

| | | M | FT.-IN. |
|---|---|---|---|
| 1. Udo Beyer | GDR | 21.05 | 69-0¾ |
| 2. Yevgeny Mironov | SOV | 21.03 | 69-0 |
| 3. Aleksandr Baryshnikov | SOV | 21.00 | 68-10¾ |
| 4. Allan Feuerbach | USA | 20.55 | 67-5¼ |
| 5. Hans-Peter Gies | GDR | 20.47 | 67-2 |
| 6. Geoffrey Capes | GBR | 20.36 | 66-9¾ |

| | | M | FT.-IN. |
|---|---|---|---|
| 7. George Woods | USA | 20.26 | 66-5¾ |
| 8. Hans Hoglund | SWE | 20.17 | 66-2¼ |

Missing from the Olympics was the number-one shot putter in the world, Brian Oldfield, who owned the four longest unofficial puts in history, including one of 75 feet. Oldfield was a professional and thus ineligible to compete. The amateur record of 72 feet 2¼ inches, was set by Aleksandr Baryshnikov on July 10. Baryshnikov looked good as gold when his one put of the qualifying round sailed 69 feet 11½ inches to break the Olympic record. Baryshnikov also took the lead in the first round of the final with a toss of 67 feet 4¼ inches. In the second round he was passed by Al Feuerbach's 67 feet 5 inches. Baryshnikov boomed back in front with a third-round 68 feet 10¾ inches. Then, in the fifth round, 20-year-old Udo Beyer, the youngest man in the competition, unleashed a put of 69 feet ¾ inch. Beyer had only been added to the East German team one week before the Olympics began. Yevgeny Mironov, who had been mired inconspicuously in sixth place, followed a few minutes later with 69 feet 0 inches and the medals were decided. Most of the leading contenders fell several feet short of their best performances. Although the pressure of the Olympics may have been a contributing factor, most observers felt that the institution of steroid testing played a more important role.

**1980 Moscow** C: 16, N: 11, D: 7.30. WR: 22.15, 72-8 (Udo Beyer)

| | | M | FT.-IN. | |
|---|---|---|---|---|
| 1. Vladimir Kiselyov | SOV | 21.35 | 70-0½ | OR |
| 2. Aleksandr Baryshnikov | SOV | 21.08 | 69-2 | |
| 3. Udo Beyer | GDR | 21.06 | 69-1¼ | |
| 4. Reijo Ståhlberg | FIN | 20.82 | 68-3¾ | |
| 5. Geoffrey Capes | GBR | 20.50 | 67-3¼ | |
| 6. Hans-Jürgen Jacobi | GDR | 20.32 | 66-8 | |
| 7. Jaromir Vlk | CZE | 20.24 | 66-5 | |
| 8. Vladimir Milic | YUG | 20.07 | 65-10¼ | |

Vladimir Kiselyov was the only shot putter to achieve a personal best, ending Udo Beyer's string of 34 consecutive victories.

**1984 Los Angeles** C: 19, N: 13, D: 8.11. WR: 22.22, 72-10¾ (Udo Beyer)

| | | M | FT.-IN. |
|---|---|---|---|
| 1. Alessandro Andrei | ITA | 21.26 | 69-9 |
| 2. Michael Carter | USA | 21.09 | 69-2½ |
| 3. Dave Laut | USA | 20.97 | 68-9¾ |
| 4. Augie Wolf | USA | 20.93 | 68-8 |
| 5. Werner Günthör | SWI | 20.28 | 66-6½ |
| 6. Marco Montelatici | ITA | 19.98 | 65-6¾ |
| 7. Sören Tallhem | SWE | 19.81 | 65-0 |
| 8. Erik de Bruin | HOL | 19.65 | 64-5¾ |

The quality of the 1984 shot put competition, already lessened by the Soviet-bloc boycott, was further diminished when the final was interrupted by no less than six medal award ceremonies. Michael Carter took the first-round lead with a put of 67 feet 8¼ inches. But 25-year-old Florence policeman Alessandro Andrei moved ahead with a second-round toss of 68 feet 9¾ inches. He improved by almost a foot with his next attempt. Carter improved as well, but still had to settle for the silver. Six days after the Olympic final, Carter was playing in his first professional football pre-season game, and six months later, he was taking part in the San Francisco 49ers' Super Bowl victory.

**1988 Seoul** C: 21, N: 17, D: 9.23. WR: 23.06, 75-8 (Ulf Timmermann)

| | | M | FT.-IN. | |
|---|---|---|---|---|
| 1. Ulf Timmermann | GDR | 22.47 | 73-8¾ | OR |
| 2. E. Randolph Barnes | USA | 22.39 | 73-5½ | |
| 3. Werner Günthör | SWI | 21.99 | 72-1¾ | |
| 4. Udo Beyer | GDR | 21.40 | 70-2½ | |
| 5. Remigius Machura | CZE | 20.57 | 67-5¾ | |
| 6. Gert Weil | CHI | 20.38 | 66-10¼ | |
| 7. Alessandro Andrei | ITA | 20.36 | 66-9½ | |
| 8. Sergei Smirnov | SOV | 20.36 | 66-9½ | |

World champion Werner Günthör set an Olympic record with an opening put of 70 feet 4½ inches. Later in the first round, Ulf Timmermann, who had broken the world record on May 22, took the lead at 72 feet 3 inches. Timmermann improved to 72 feet 8½ inches in the third round and to 73 feet 1½ inches in the fifth round. People began congratulating the East German, but Timmermann wisely noted that it was too early for a victory celebration. He breathed a little easier after Günthör failed to improve on his fifth-round best of 72 feet 1¾ inches. Then 22-year-old Randy Barnes, who was languishing in fourth place, uncorked a toss of 73 feet 5½ inches and suddenly the shot put circle was the site of high drama. Two throwers later, Timmermann stepped up for the last put of the competition. Concentrating intensely, he shut out the outside world. "It was like I went into a tunnel," he later told *Track and Field News.* "Time became just a blur, a haze; throwing was just a reflex . . . I knew inside that this was my big chance; I could make my place in Olympic history." Timmermann heaved with everything he had—and managed to out-distance Barnes by a mere 3¼ inches.

On May 20, 1990, Randy Barnes broke Timmermann's world record, but two and a half months later he tested positive for anabolic steroids and was subsequently slapped with a two-year suspension.

## DISCUS THROW

The men's discus weighs 2 kilograms (4 pounds 6.55 ounces). The discus throw is the only track and field event in which a world record has never been set in the Olympics.

**1896 Athens** C: 9, N: 6, D: 4.6.

| | | M | FT.-IN. |
|---|---|---|---|
| 1. Robert Garrett | USA | 29.15 | 95-7½ |
| 2. Panagiotis Paraskevopoulos | GRE | 28.955 | 95-0 |
| 3. Sotirios Versis | GRE | 27.78 | 91-1¾ |

Twenty-year-old Robert Garrett came from a wealthy Baltimore banking family. While a student at Princeton, he was shown a drawing of an ancient Greek discus. He ordered a facsimile made and tried practicing with it, but it proved too heavy and unwieldy and so he lost interest quickly. However, while strolling on the field in Athens, he chanced upon a similar object and was told that this was a real discus, which turned out to be much lighter than his American version. Encouraged, yet risking what he feared would be great embarrassment, he entered the Olympic discus contest. To the disappointment of the Greeks, he won the event with his final throw. Before the games were over, Garrett had won two events, placed second in two more, and third in yet another two.

**1900 Paris** C: 20, N: 8. D: 7.15. WR: 36.20, 118-9 (Charles Henneman)

| | | M | FT.-IN. | |
|---|---|---|---|---|
| 1. Rudolf (Rezsö) Bauer | HUN | 36.04 | 118-3 | OR |
| 2. František Janda-Suk | BOH | 35.25 | 115-7 | |
| 3. Richard Sheldon | USA | 34.60 | 113-6 | |
| 4. Panagiotis Paraskevopoulos | GRE | 34.04 | 111-8 | |
| 5. Rozsö Crottier | HUN | 33.65 | 110-4 | |
| 6. Gustaf Söderström | SWE | 33.30 | 109-3 | |
| 7. Robert Garrett | USA | 33.07 | 108-5 | |
| 8. Eric Lemming | SWE | 32.50 | 106-7 | |
| 8. Carl Winckler | DEN | 32.50 | 106-7 | |

**1904 St. Louis** C: 6, N: 2, D: 9.3. WR: 40.71, 133-6½ (Martin Sheridan)

| | | M | FT.-IN. | |
|---|---|---|---|---|
| 1. Martin Sheridan | USA | 39.28 | 128-10½ | OR |
| 2. Ralph Rose | USA | 39.28 | 128-10½ | |
| 3. Nicolaos Georgantas | GRE | 37.68 | 123-7½ | |
| 4. John Flanagan | USA | 36.14 | 118-7 | |
| 5. John Biller | USA | — | — | |
| 6. James Mitchell | USA | — | — | |

Sheridan and Rose finished in a tie, so, for the only time in Olympic history, a throw-off was held to determine first place. Each man was given three throws. Sheridan won by about five feet.

**1906 Athens** C: 21, N: 9. D: 4.25. WR: 42.14, 138-3 (Martin Sheridan)

| | | M | FT.-IN. |
|---|---|---|---|
| 1. Martin Sheridan | USA | 41.46 | 136-0 |
| 2. Nicolaos Georgantas | GRE | 38.06 | 124-10 |
| 3. Werner Järvinen | FIN | 36.82 | 120-9 |
| 4. Eric Lemming | SWE | 35.62 | 116-10 |
| 5. André Tison | FRA | 34.81 | 114-2 |

**1908 London** C: 41, N: 11, D: 7.16. WR: 42.63, 139-10½ (Martin Sheridan)

|   |   |   | M | FT.-IN. |   |
|---|---|---|---|---|---|
| 1. | Martin Sheridan | USA | 40.89 | 134-2 | OR |
| 2. | Merritt Giffin | USA | 40.70 | 133-6 |   |
| 3. | Marquis Horr | USA | 39.44 | 129-5 |   |
| 4. | Werner Järvinen | FIN | 39.42 | 129-4 |   |
| 5. | Arthur Dearborn | USA | 38.52 | 126-4 |   |
| 6. | György Luntzer | HUN | 38.34 | 125-9 |   |
| 7. | André Tison | FRA | 38.30 | 125-8 |   |
| 8. | Wilbur Burroughs | USA | 37.42 | 122-9 |   |

Competing in the 1904, 1906, and 1908 Games, Irish-born policeman Martin Sheridan won five gold medals and four silver. He died of pneumonia on March 27, 1918, at the age of 37.

**1912 Stockholm** C: 40, N: 15, D: 7.12. WR: 47.58, 156-1 (James Duncan)

|   |   |   | M | FT.-IN. |   |
|---|---|---|---|---|---|
| 1. | Armas Taipale | FIN | 45.21 | 148-3 | OR |
| 2. | Richard Byrd | USA | 42.32 | 138-10 |   |
| 3. | James Duncan | USA | 42.28 | 138-8 |   |
| 4. | Elmer Niklander | FIN | 42.09 | 138-1 |   |
| 5. | Hans Tronner | AUS | 41.24 | 135-4 |   |
| 6. | Arlie Mucks | USA | 40.93 | 134-3 |   |
| 7. | George Philbrook | USA | 40.92 | 134-2½ |   |
| 8. | Emil Magnusson | SWE | 39.91 | 130-11 |   |

**1920 Antwerp** C: 28, N: 12, D: 8.22. WR: 47.58, 156-1 (James Duncan)

|   |   |   | M | FT.-IN. |
|---|---|---|---|---|
| 1. | Elmer Niklander | FIN | 44.685 | 146-7 |
| 2. | Armas Taipale | FIN | 44.19 | 145-0 |
| 3. | Augustus Pope | USA | 42.13 | 138-2 |
| 4. | Otto Zallhagen | SWE | 41.07 | 134-9 |
| 5. | William Bartlett | USA | 40.875 | 134-1 |
| 6. | Allan Eriksson | SWE | 39.41 | 129-3 |
| 7. | Walther Jensen | DEN | 38.23 | 125-5 |
| 8. | André Tison | FRA | 37.35 | 122-6 |

**1924 Paris** C: 32, N: 18, D: 7.13. WR: 47.58, 156-1 (James Duncan)

|   |   |   | M | FT.-IN. |   |
|---|---|---|---|---|---|
| 1. | L. Clarence "Bud" Houser | USA | 46.15 | 151-4 | OR |
| 2. | Vilho Niittymaa | FIN | 44.95 | 147-5 |   |
| 3. | Thomas Lieb | USA | 44.83 | 147-0 |   |
| 4. | Augustus Pope | USA | 44.42 | 145-9 |   |
| 5. | Ketil Askildt | NOR | 43.40 | 142-5 |   |
| 6. | Glenn Hartranft | USA | 42.49 | 139-4 |   |
| 7. | Elmer Niklander | FIN | 42.09 | 138-1 |   |
| 8. | Heikki Malmivirta | FIN | 41.16 | 135-0 |   |

Bud Houser also won the shot put five days later. He is the last athlete to achieve such a double in the Olympics.

**1928 Amsterdam** C: 34, N: 19, D: 8.1. WR: 48.20, 158-2 (L. Clarence "Bud" Houser)

|   |   |   | M | FT.-IN. |   |
|---|---|---|---|---|---|
| 1. | L. Clarence "Bud" Houser | USA | 47.32 | 155-3 | OR |
| 2. | L. Antero Kivi | FIN | 47.23 | 154-11 |   |
| 3. | James Corson | USA | 47.10 | 154-6 |   |
| 4. | Harald Stenerud | NOR | 45.80 | 150-3 |   |
| 5. | John Anderson | USA | 44.87 | 147-2 |   |
| 6. | Eino Kenttä | FIN | 44.17 | 144-10 |   |
| 7. | Ernst Paulus | GER | 44.15 | 144-9 |   |
| 8. | Johan Trandem | NOR | 43.97 | 144-3 |   |

**1932 Los Angeles** C: 18, N: 11, D: 8.3. WR: 51.73, 169-9 (Paul Jessup)

|   |   |   | M | FT.-IN. |   |
|---|---|---|---|---|---|
| 1. | John Anderson | USA | 49.49 | 162-4 | OR |
| 2. | Henri Jean Laborde | USA | 48.47 | 159-0 |   |
| 3. | Paul Winter | FRA | 47.85 | 156-11 |   |
| 4. | Jules Noël | FRA | 47.74 | 156-7 |   |
| 5. | István Donogán | HUN | 47.08 | 154-5 |   |
| 6. | Endre Madarász | HUN | 46.52 | 152-7 |   |
| 7. | Kalevi Kotkas | FIN | 45.87 | 150-5 |   |
| 8. | Paul Jessup | USA | 45.25 | 148-5 |   |

Two of the favorites, József Remecz of Hungary and Paul Jessup, the 6-foot 7-inch world record holder, failed to qualify for the final round of six. But the final competition was still hotly contested, as Anderson and Laborde traded the lead, with Anderson breaking the previous Olympic record four times in six throws. The Americans may have won the medals, but it was the fourth-place finisher, Jules Noël, who made the news. Because the 1932 Olympics were held in the United States during Prohibition, the French team had to receive special permission to import several thousand bottles of wine into the United States. The French successfully argued that although alcohol might be illegal in the United States, it was an essential part of the diet of many of the French athletes.

Evidently, Jules Noël was one of those athletes, as he caused the American track and field officials great consternation during the competition by making periodic visits to the dark tunnel which joined the field to the locker rooms. There he swigged champagne with his compatriots.

On his fourth attempt, Noël lofted a great throw that appeared to land just beyond the flag that marked Anderson's first-place effort. Unfortunately, every one of the officials in charge of the discus was, at that moment, distracted by the tense proceedings of the pole vault, taking place nearby, so none of them saw where Noël's discus had landed. Embarrassed by this blunder, they awarded Noël an extra throw in addition to the two that he still had coming. However, the Frenchman was unable to come up with another big throw, and he was forced to return home without a medal.

**1936 Berlin** C: 31, N: 17, D: 8.5. WR: 53.10, 174-2 (Willy Schröder)

|  |  | FT.- | |  |
|  |  | M | IN. |  |
| 1. W. Kenneth Carpenter | USA | 50.48 | 165-7 | OR |
| 2. Gordon Dunn | USA | 49.36 | 161-11 |  |
| 3. Giorgio Oberweger | ITA | 49.23 | 161-6 |  |
| 4. Reidar Sörlie | NOR | 48.77 | 160-0 |  |
| 5. Willy Schröder | GER | 47.93 | 157-3 |  |
| 6. Nicolaos Syllas | GRE | 47.75 | 156-7 |  |
| 7. Gunnar Bergh | SWE | 47:22 | 154-11 |  |
| 8. Åke Hedvall | SWE | 46.20 | 151-7 |  |

The two favorites, Harald Andersson of Sweden and Willy Schröder of Germany, were unable to rise to the occasion. Andersson, hampered by injury, failed to qualify for the semifinals, while Schröder only made it to the final group of six by winning a throw-off against Bergh. Carpenter overhauled Dunn and Oberweger with his next to last attempt.

**1948 London** C: 28, N: 18, D: 8.2. WR: 54.93, 180-3 (Robert Fitch)

|  |  | FT.- | |  |
|  |  | M | IN. |  |
| 1. Adolfo Consolini | ITA | 52.78 | 173-2 | OR |
| 2. Giuseppe Tosi | ITA | 51.78 | 169-10 |  |
| 3. Fortune Gordien | USA | 50.77 | 166-6 |  |
| 4. Ivar Ramstad | NOR | 49.21 | 161-5 |  |
| 5. Ferenc Klics | HUN | 48.21 | 158-2 |  |
| 6. Veikko Nyqvist | FIN | 47.33 | 155-3 |  |
| 7. Nicolaos Syllas | GRE | 47.25 | 155-0 |  |
| 8. Stein Johnson | NOR | 46.54 | 152-8 |  |

Adolfo Consolini held the world record from October 1941 until June 1948. Two months after earning the Olympic gold medal, he regained the world record.

**1952 Helsinki** C: 32, N: 20, D: 7.22. WR: 56.97, 186-11 (Fortune Gordien)

|  |  | FT.- | |  |
|  |  | M | IN. |  |
| 1. Sim Iness | USA | 55.03 | 180-6 | OR |
| 2. Adolfo Consolini | ITA | 53.78 | 176-5 |  |
| 3. James Dillion | USA | 53.28 | 174-10 |  |
| 4. Fortune Gordien | USA | 52.66 | 172-9 |  |
| 5. Ferenc Klics | HUN | 51.13 | 167-9 |  |
| 6. Otto Grigalka | SOV | 50.71 | 166-4 |  |
| 7. Roland Nilsson | SWE | 50.06 | 164-3 |  |
| 8. Giuseppe Tosi | ITA | 49.03 | 160-10 |  |

Sim Iness of Tulare, California bettered Consolini's Olympic record with all six of his throws in the final. Nicolaos Syllas of Greece, who had finished sixth in 1936, was still able to place ninth 16 years later.

**1956 Melbourne** C: 20, N: 15, D: 11.27. WR: 59.28, 194-6 (Fortune Gordien)

|  |  | FT.- | |  |
|  |  | M | IN. |  |
| 1. Alfred Oerter | USA | 56.36 | 184-11 | OR |
| 2. Fortune Gordien | USA | 54.81 | 179-9 |  |
| 3. Desmond Koch | USA | 54.40 | 178-6 |  |
| 4. Mark Pharaoh | GBR | 54.27 | 178-0 |  |
| 5. Otto Grigalka | SOV | 52.37 | 171-9 |  |
| 6. Adolfo Consolini | ITA | 52.21 | 171-3 |  |
| 7. Ferenc Kics | HUN | 51.82 | 170-0 |  |
| 8. Dako Radosević | YUG | 51.69 | 169-7 |  |

Twenty-year-old Al Oerter of West Babylon, New York, watched the favorites, Adolfo Consolini and Fortune Gordien, make their first round throws. When his turn came, he felt "keyed up" and "inspired" and let loose the best throw of his career—184 feet 11 inches. No one else came within five feet as Oerter ended up with the three longest throws of the competition. On the victory rostrum he suddenly realized that he had actually won. His knees buckled and he almost fell. As it turned out, in the years to come Al Oerter would have plenty of opportunities to get used to standing on the gold medal platform at Olympic medal ceremonies.

**1960 Rome** C: 35, N: 22, D: 9.7. WR: 59.91, 196-6 (Edmund Piątkowski, Richard "Rink" Babka)

|  |  | FT.- | |  |
|  |  | M | IN. |  |
| 1. Alfred Oerter | USA | 59.18 | 194-2 | OR |
| 2. Richard "Rink" Babka | USA | 58.02 | 190-4 |  |
| 3. Richard Cochran | USA | 57.16 | 187-6 |  |
| 4. József Szécsényi | HUN | 55.79 | 183-0 |  |
| 5. Edmund Piątkowski | POL | 55.12 | 180-10 |  |
| 6. Viktor Kompanyeyets | SOV | 55.06 | 180-8 |  |
| 7. Carmelo Rado | ITA | 54.00 | 177-2 |  |
| 8. Kim Bukhantsev | SOV | 53.61 | 175-10 |  |

In 1957 Al Oerter was involved in a near-fatal car crash, but he recovered fully and was back in shape before long. Then, at the U.S. Olympic trials, he suffered his first defeat in over two years when he lost to giant Rink Babka. Oerter was still considered a slight favorite at the Olympics, but he was definitely under great pressure. While warming up for the qualifying round, he casually threw the discus beyond the world record marker, and then qualified with an Olympic record of 191 feet 8 inches. But the day of the final he was "so tense I could barely throw." Babka led off with a toss of 190 feet 4 inches. Oerter followed with 189 feet 1 inch, but couldn't get closer over the next three rounds. As Oerter prepared for his fifth throw, Babka told him that he seemed to be carrying his left arm too low as he spun. Oerter made the necessary adjustment and threw his discus 194 feet 2 inches—a personal record. He thanked Babka and wished him luck on his last throw, but Babka fell short and settled for the silver medal.

**1964 Tokyo** C: 28, N: 21, D: 10.15. WR: 64.54, 211-9 (Ludvik Daněk)

|  |  |  | FT.- |  |
|---|---|---|---|---|
|  |  | M | IN. |  |
| 1. Alfred Oerter | USA | 61.00 | 200-1 | OR |
| 2. Ludvik Daněk | CZE | 60.52 | 198-7 |  |
| 3. David Weill | USA | 59.49 | 195-2 |  |
| 4. L. Jay Silvester | USA | 59.09 | 193-10 |  |
| 5. József Szécsényi | HUN | 57.23 | 187-9 |  |
| 6. Zenon Begier | POL | 57.06 | 187-2 |  |
| 7. Edmund Piątkowski | POL | 55.81 | 183-1 |  |
| 8. Vladimir Trusenyov | SOV | 54.78 | 179-9 |  |

On May 18, 1962, Al Oerter became the first discus thrower to break officially the 200-foot barrier, with a throw of 200 feet 5 inches. Surprisingly, it was his first world record. It lasted only 17 days, when it was broken by Vladimir Trusenyov. But 27 days later Oerter had the record back again.

In 1964, however, Oerter knew that he would be in for a real struggle if he wanted to win a third gold medal. Not only did he have to face current world record holder Ludvik Daněk, who had won 45 straight competitions, but he had also been suffering for quite some time from a chronic cervical disc injury, which caused him to wear a neck harness. As if that wasn't trouble enough, Oerter tore the cartilage in his lower ribs while practicing in Tokyo less than a week before the competition. Doctors advised him to rest for six weeks, but the day of the preliminary round, he showed up anyway, shot up with novocaine and wrapped with ice packs and tape to prevent internal bleeding. With his first throw Oerter set an Olympic record of 198 feet 8 inches.

Ludvik Daněk opened the final at 195 feet 11 inches. Before the competition, Al Oerter had told a fellow athlete, "If I don't do it on the first throw, I won't be able to do it at all." But his first attempt only went 189 feet 1 inch. After four rounds Oerter was in third place behind Daněk and David Weill. Then, with his fifth throw, Oerter gave it everything he had. While he doubled over in pain, his discus sailed 200 feet 1 inch to set another Olympic record and earn Oerter a third gold medal.

**1968 Mexico City** C: 27, N: 19, D: 10.15. WR: 68.40, 224-5 (L. Jay Silvester)

|  |  |  | FT.- |  |
|---|---|---|---|---|
|  |  | M | IN. |  |
| 1. Alfred Oerter | USA | 64.78 | 212-6 | OR |
| 2. Lothar Milde | GDR | 63.08 | 206-11 |  |
| 3. Ludvik Daněk | CZE | 62.92 | 206-5 |  |
| 4. Hartmut Losch | GDR | 62.12 | 203-10 |  |
| 5. L. Jay Silvester | USA | 61.78 | 202-8 |  |
| 6. Gary Carlsen | USA | 59.46 | 195-1 |  |
| 7. Edmund Piątkowski | POL | 59.40 | 194-10 |  |
| 8. Björn Rickard Bruch | SWE | 59.28 | 194-6 |  |

Jay Silvester, the 31-year-old world record holder, was the favorite in Mexico City. And yet, one couldn't help but wonder if Al Oerter might pull off one more miracle.

Silvester dampened such speculations in the qualifying round by opening up with an Olympic record of 207 feet 10 inches, 16½ feet less than his own best, but several inches better than anything Oerter had ever done.

The final was delayed an hour because of rain and this seemed to upset Silvester in particular. Lothar Milde took the first round lead with a throw of 204 feet 10 inches, and then improved to 206 feet 11 inches with his second attempt. The third round began with Oerter in fourth place, behind Milde, Losch, and Silvester. But, as if out of a fairy tale, the incomparable Oerter uncorked a throw of 212 feet 6 inches—five feet farther than he had ever thrown before. The rest of the finalists were demoralized, particularly Silvester, who fouled three times in a row. Oerter, meanwhile, added throws of 212 feet 5 inches and 210 feet 1 inch. Al Oerter had become the first track and field athlete to win four gold medals in the same event.

Oerter, after throwing the discus 33,000 times, didn't take part in the 1972 or 1976 Olympics, but then he came out of retirement to try out for the 1980 U.S. team. At the age of 43, he finished fourth at the U.S. Olympic trials, which were held after the anti-Soviet boycott had been declared. But who knows, if the top three had really been assured of going to Moscow instead of settling for symbolic honors, Al Oerter, the ultimate clutch performer, just might have qualified after all.

**1972 Munich** C: 29, N: 19, D: 9.2. WR: 68.40, 224-5 (L. Jay Silvester, Björn Rickard Bruch)

|  |  |  | FT.- |
|---|---|---|---|
|  |  | M | IN. |
| 1. Ludvik Daněk | CZE | 64.40 | 211-3 |
| 2. L. Jay Silvester | USA | 63.50 | 208-4 |
| 3. Björn Rickard Bruch | SWE | 63.40 | 208-0 |
| 4. John Powell | USA | 62.82 | 206-1 |
| 5. Géza Fejér | HUN | 62.62 | 205-5 |
| 6. Detlef Thorith | GDR | 62.42 | 204-9 |
| 7. Ferenc Tégla | HUN | 60.60 | 198-10 |
| 8. Tim Vollmer | USA | 60.24 | 197-8 |

With Al Oerter gone, Ludvik Daněk and Jay Silvester, both 35 years old, could finally relax and get down to the business of winning a gold medal. They had previously met 24 times, with Daněk finishing ahead 12 times and Silvester 12 times. In Munich they also had to contend with high-strung, but increasingly consistent Ricky Bruch.

Daněk led the qualifying round with an impressive throw of 211 feet. In the final, Géza Fejér took the first round lead at 205 feet 1 inch. John Powell moved ahead in the second round at 206 feet 1 inch, and then Silvester took over at the halfway mark with 208 feet 4 inches. With one round to go, the order was Silvester, Bruch, Powell, Fejér, and Daněk, who hadn't come within five feet of his qualifying toss. Since no Olympic discus contest had been won in the final round since 1896, it seemed a good bet that Jay Silvester was on the verge of victory.

But Daněk, who had enlisted the aid of a psychologist to help him prepare for just such last-ditch situations, broke tradition and won with a final throw of 211 feet 3 inches.

**1976 Montreal** C: 30, N: 20, D: 7.25. WR: 70.86, 232-6 (Maurice "Mac" Wilkins)

|  |  | | FT.- |
| --- | --- | --- | --- |
|  |  | M | IN. |
| 1. Maurice "Mac" Wilkins | USA | 67.50 | 221-5 |
| 2. Wolfgang Schmidt | GDR | 66.22 | 217-3 |
| 3. John Powell | USA | 65.70 | 215-7 |
| 4. Norbert Thiede | GDR | 64.30 | 210-11 |
| 5. Siegfried Pachale | GDR | 64.24 | 210-9 |
| 6. Pentti Kahma | FIN | 63.12 | 207-1 |
| 7. Knut Hjeltnes | NOR | 63.06 | 206-11 |
| 8. L. Jay Silvester | USA | 61.98 | 203-4 |

With his first and only throw of the preliminary round, Mac Wilkins, a 25-year-old schoolteacher from Oregon, set an Olympic record of 224 feet. The next day, his second round throw of 221 feet 5 inch put a quick end to any doubt as to who would win the final. Wilkins was sharply criticized by the U.S. press for congratulating East German silver medalist Wolfgang Schmidt, with whom he had become quite friendly, while ignoring American bronze medalist John Powell, with whom he did not get along. The criticism seemed ironic in view of the concern which was simultaneously being expressed about excessive nationalism in the Olympics.

Beginning in 1982, Schmidt was imprisoned for fifteen months for "antisocial behavior" because of his opposition to Communism and his friendships with Western athletes. He was unable to return to competition until 1988, after he was given permission to emigrate to West Germany.

**1980 Moscow** C: 18, N: 12, D: 7.28. WR: 71.16, 233-5 (Wolfgang Schmidt)

|  |  | | FT.- |
| --- | --- | --- | --- |
|  |  | M | IN. |
| 1. Viktor Rashchupkin | SOV | 66.64 | 218-8 |
| 2. Imrich Bugár | CZE | 66.38 | 217-9 |
| 3. Luis Delis Fournier | CUB | 66.32 | 217-7 |
| 4. Wolfgang Schmidt | GDR | 65.64 | 215-4 |
| 5. Yuri Dumchev | SOV | 65.58 | 215-2 |
| 6. Igor Duginets | SOV | 64.04 | 210-1 |
| 7. Emil Vladimirov | BUL | 63.18 | 207-3 |
| 8. Velko Velev | BUL | 63.04 | 206-10 |

Conspicuously missing because of the anti-Soviet boycott were Knut Hjeltnes of Norway, and Mac Wilkins, John Powell, and Ben Plucknett, each of whom had to throw over 223 feet just to make the U.S. team. With these leading contenders absent, Wolfgang Schmidt seemed a sure bet for the gold medal, but a foot injury upset his performance and he had to settle for fourth place. The first round lead in the final went to Imrich Bugár at 213 feet 8 inches. The lead changed hands four more times before Rashchupkin moved from fourth place to first

with his gold-medal-winning fourth round throw. His pre-Olympic best had only been 216 feet 6 inches. The contest ended in controversy, as many observers felt that Luis Delis' final throw had been marked about a foot short, keeping him from a silver medal or maybe even a gold.

**1984 Los Angeles** C: 20, N: 14, D: 8.10. WR: 71.86, 235-9 (Yuri Dumchev)

|  |  | | FT.- |
| --- | --- | --- | --- |
|  |  | M | IN. |
| 1. Rolf Danneberg | GER | 66.60 | 218-6 |
| 2. Maurice "Mac" Wilkins | USA | 66.30 | 217-6 |
| 3. John Powell | USA | 65.46 | 214-9 |
| 4. Knut Hjeltnes | NOR | 65.28 | 214-2 |
| 5. Arthur Burns | USA | 64.98 | 213-2 |
| 6. Alwin Wagner | GER | 64.72 | 212-4 |
| 7. Luciano Zerbini | ITA | 63.50 | 208-4 |
| 8. Stefan Fernholm | SWE | 63.22 | 207-5 |

With pre-boycott favorites Luis Delis and Imrich Bugár among the missing, a U.S. sweep seemed a distinct possibility. Olympic record holder Mac Wilkins took the early lead at 216 feet 5 inches, but in the fourth round, unheralded Rolf Danneberg, a bearded, 6-foot 6-inch unemployed schoolteacher, unleashed a toss of 218 feet 6 inches. Wilkins improved by a foot in the fifth round, but could come no closer. The 31-year-old Danneberg, who wore dark glasses while competing, was the least-expected track and field winner of the 1984 Olympics.

**1988 Seoul** C: 29, N: 20, D: 10.1. WR: 74.08, 243-0 (Jürgen Schult)

|  |  | | FT.- | |
| --- | --- | --- | --- | --- |
|  |  | M | IN. | |
| 1. Jürgen Schult | GDR | 68.82 | 225-9 | OR |
| 2. Romas Ubartas | SOV | 67.48 | 221-5 | |
| 3. Rolf Danneberg | GER | 67.38 | 221-1 | |
| 4. Yuri Dumchev | SOV | 66.42 | 217-11 | |
| 5. Maurice "Mac" Wilkins | USA | 65.90 | 216-2 | |
| 6. Gejza Valent | CZE | 65.80 | 215-10 | |
| 7. Knut Hjeltnes | NOR | 64.94 | 213-1 | |
| 8. Alois Hannecker | GER | 63.28 | 207-7 | |

World champion and world record holder Jürgen Schult earned the gold medal with his first throw. He also recorded the three next best throws of the competition. Dumchev held second place until the fifth round, when he was passed by Danneberg. But it was Lithuanian Ubartas who grabbed the silver medal with his final attempt.

## HAMMER THROW

The hammer is a 16-pound metal sphere attached to a grip by means of a spring steel wire not longer than 3 feet 11¾ inches (121.5 centimeters). This potentially dangerous sport appears to have had it origins in the practice of sledge-hammer throwing in fifteenth- and sixteenth-century England and Scotland.

**1896** not held

**1900 Paris** C: 5, N: 2, D: 7.16. WR: 51.105, 167-8 (John Flanagan)

| | | M | FT.-<br>IN. | |
|---|---|---|---|---|
| 1. | John Flanagan | USA | 49.73 | 163-1 |
| 2. | Thomas Truxtun Hare | USA | 49.13 | 161-2 |
| 3. | Josiah McCracken | USA | 42.46 | 139-4 |
| 4. | Eric Lemming | SWE | — | — |
| 5. | Karl Gustaf Staaf | SWE | — | — |

Irish-born John Flanagan emigrated to the United States in 1896 and became a policeman in New York City. Truxtun Hare was a four-time All-American football selection from the University of Pennsylvania.

**1904 St. Louis** C: 6, N: 1, D: 8.29. WR: 52.705, 172-11 (John Flanagan)

| | | M | FT.-<br>IN. | |
|---|---|---|---|---|
| 1. | John Flanagan | USA | 51.23 | 168-1 OR |
| 2. | John DeWitt | USA | 50.26 | 164-11 |
| 3. | Ralph Rose | USA | 45.73 | 150-0 |
| 4. | Charles Chadwick | USA | 42.78 | 140-4 |
| 5. | James Mitchell | USA | — | — |
| 6. | Albert Johnson | USA | — | — |

**1906** not held

**1908 London** C: 18, N: 8, D: 7.14. WR: 53.35, 175-0 (Matthew McGrath)

| | | M | FT.-<br>IN. | |
|---|---|---|---|---|
| 1. | John Flanagan | USA | 51.92 | 170-4 OR |
| 2. | Matthew McGrath | USA | 51.18 | 167-11 |
| 3. | Cornelius Walsh | USA | 48.51 | 159-1 |
| 4. | Thomas Nicolson | GBR | 48.09 | 157-9 |
| 5. | Lee James Talbott | USA | 47.86 | 157-0 |
| 6. | Marquis Horr | USA | 46.94 | 154-0 |
| 7. | Simon Gillis | USA | 45.58 | 149-6 |
| 8. | Eric Lemming | SWE | 43.06 | 141-3 |

With his last attempt, Flanagan won his third straight hammer throw gold medal. On July 24, 1909, Flanagan threw the hammer 184 feet 4 inches to become the oldest world record breaker in the history of track and field. He was 41 years, 196 days old. He returned to Ireland in 1911 and lived there until his death in 1938.

**1912 Stockholm** C: 14, N: 4, D: 7.14. WR: 57.10, 187-4 (Matthew McGrath)

| | | M | FT.-<br>IN. | |
|---|---|---|---|---|
| 1. | Matthew McGrath | USA | 54.74 | 179-7 OR |
| 2. | Duncan Gillis | CAN | 48.39 | 158-9 |
| 3. | Clarence Childs | USA | 48.17 | 158-0 |
| 4. | Robert Olsson | SWE | 46.50 | 152-7 |
| 5. | Carl Johan Lind | SWE | 45.61 | 149-7 |

| | | M | FT.-<br>IN. | |
|---|---|---|---|---|
| 6. | Denis Carey | GBR | 43.78 | 143-8 |
| 7. | Nils Linde | SWE | 43.32 | 142-1 |
| 8. | Carl Jahnzon | SWE | 42.58 | 139-8 |

Irish-American policeman Matt McGrath was truly in a class by himself in Stockholm. The *shortest* of his six throws—173 feet 4 inches—was almost 15 feet longer than anyone else's *longest* throw. McGrath's Olympic record held up for 24 years.

**1920 Antwerp** C: 12, N: 5, D: 8.18. WR: 57.77, 189-6 (Patrick Ryan)

| | | M | FT.-<br>IN. | |
|---|---|---|---|---|
| 1. | Patrick Ryan | USA | 52.875 | 173-5 |
| 2. | Carl Johan Lind | SWE | 48.43 | 158-10 |
| 3. | Basil Bennet | USA | 48.25 | 158-3 |
| 4. | Malcom Svensson | SWE | 47.29 | 155-1 |
| 5. | Matthew McGrath | USA | 46.67 | 153-1 |
| 6. | Thomas Nicolson | GBR | 45.70 | 149-11 |
| 7. | Nils Linde | SWE | 44.88 | 147-3 |
| 8. | James McEachern | USA | 44.70 | 146-8 |

Pat Ryan emigrated from Ireland to New York in 1910. On August 17, 1913, he set a world record of 189 feet 6 inches that would last for 25 years. It remained as a U.S. record until 1953. In Antwerp Ryan was unchallenged, particularly after Matt McGrath injured his knee and was forced to withdraw after only two throws.

**1924 Paris** C: 15, N: 10, D: 7.10. WR: 57.77, 189-6 (Patrick Ryan)

| | | M | FT.-<br>IN. | |
|---|---|---|---|---|
| 1. | Frederick Tootell | USA | 53.295 | 174-10 |
| 2. | Matthew McGrath | USA | 50.84 | 166-9 |
| 3. | Malcolm Nokes | GBR | 48.875 | 160-4 |
| 4. | Erik Eriksson | FIN | 48.74 | 159-11 |
| 5. | Ossian Skiöld | SWE | 45.285 | 148-7 |
| 6. | James McEachern | USA | 45.225 | 148-4 |
| 7. | Carl Johan Lind | SWE | 44.785 | 146-11 |
| 8. | John Murdock | CAN | 42.48 | 139-4 |

Fred Tootell was the first American-born winner of the hammer throw. Silver medalist Matt McGrath was 45 years old.

**1928 Amsterdam** C: 16, N: 11, D: 7.30. WR: 57.77, 189-6 (Patrick Ryan)

| | | M | FT.-<br>IN. | |
|---|---|---|---|---|
| 1. | Patrick O'Callaghan | IRL | 51.39 | 168-7 |
| 2. | Ossian Skiöld | SWE | 51.29 | 168-3 |
| 3. | Edmund Black | USA | 49.03 | 160-10 |
| 4. | Armando Poggioli | ITA | 48.37 | 158.8 |
| 5. | Donald Gwinn | USA | 47.15 | 154-8 |
| 6. | Frank Connor | USA | 46.75 | 153-4 |
| 7. | Federico Kleger | ARG | 46.60 | 152-11 |
| 8. | Ricardo Bayer | CHI | 46.34 | 152-0 |

Pat O'Callaghan, of Derrygallon in North Cork, had only been competing for 13 months when he won an Olympic gold medal with his next-to-last throw, improving his personal best by 20 inches.

**1932 Los Angeles** C: 14, N: 9, D: 8.1. WR: 57.77, 189-6 (Patrick Ryan)

| | | | FT.- |
|---|---|---|---|
| | | M | IN. |
| 1. Patrick O'Callaghan | IRL | 53.92 | 176-11 |
| 2. Frans "Ville" Pörhölä | FIN | 52.27 | 171-6 |
| 3. Peter Zaremba | USA | 50.33 | 165-1 |
| 4. Ossian Skiöld | SWE | 49.24 | 161-6 |
| 5. Grant McDougall | USA | 49.12 | 161-2 |
| 6. Federico Kleger | ARG | 48.33 | 158-7 |
| 7. Gunnar Jansson | SWE | 47.79 | 156-9 |
| 8. Armando Poggioli | ITA | 46.90 | 153-10 |

Ville Pörhölä, who had won the shot put gold medal 12 years earlier in Antwerp, led after five rounds. However, defending champion Dr. Pat O'Callaghan, who spent every free moment between throws filing down the spikes on his shoes, came through with a dramatic victory on his final attempt.

**1936 Berlin** C: 27, N: 16, D: 8.3, WR: 57.77, 189-6 (Patrick Ryan)

| | | | FT.- | |
|---|---|---|---|---|
| | | M | IN. | |
| 1. Karl Hein | GER | 56.49 | 185-4 | OR |
| 2. Erwin Blask | GER | 55.04 | 180-7 | |
| 3. O. Fred Warngård | SWE | 54.83 | 179-10 | |
| 4. Gustaf Alfons Koutonen | FIN | 51.90 | 170-3 | |
| 5. William Rowe | USA | 51.66 | 169-6 | |
| 6. Donald Favor | USA | 51.01 | 167-4 | |
| 7. Bernhard Greulich | GER | 50.61 | 166-0 | |
| 8. Koit Annamaa | EST | 50.46 | 165-7 | |

Hein, a 28-year-old Hamburg carpenter, scored an upset victory with his final throw. All three medalists achieved personal records.

**1948 London** C: 24, N: 16, D: 7.31. WR: 59.02, 193-8 (Imre Németh)

| | | | FT.- |
|---|---|---|---|
| | | M | IN. |
| 1. Imre Németh | HUN | 56.07 | 183-11 |
| 2. Ivan Gubijan | YUG | 54.27 | 178-0 |
| 3. Robert Bennett | USA | 53.73 | 176-3 |
| 4. Samuel Felton | USA | 53.66 | 176-0 |
| 5. Lauri Tamminen | FIN | 53.08 | 174-2 |
| 6. Bo Ericson | SWE | 52.98 | 173-10 |
| 7. Teseo Taddia | ITA | 51.74 | 169-9 |
| 8. Einar Söderqvist | SWE | 51.48 | 168-11 |

Imre Németh, who broke Erwin Blask's ten-year-old world record two weeks before the Olympics began, weighed a mere 184 pounds.

**1952 Helsinki** C: 33, N: 18, D: 7.24. WR: 59.88, 196-5 (Imre Németh)

| | | | FT.- | |
|---|---|---|---|---|
| | | M | IN. | |
| 1. József Csérmák | HUN | 60.34 | 197-11 | WR |
| 2. Karl Storch | GER | 58.86 | 193-1 | |
| 3. Imre Németh | HUN | 57.74 | 189-5 | |
| 4. Jiří Dadák | CZE | 56.80 | 186-4 | |
| 5. Nikolai Redkin | SOV | 56.55 | 185-6 | |
| 6. Karl Wolf | GER | 56.49 | 185-4 | |
| 7. Sverre Strandli | NOR | 56.36 | 184-11 | |
| 8. Georgi Dybenko | SOV | 55.03 | 180-6 | |

Twenty-year-old József Csérmák, a pupil of defending champion Imre Németh, broke the 60-meter barrier for the first time with his third throw. Silver medalist Karl Storch, who had first cleared 190 feet in 1939, was 38 years old.

**1956 Melbourne** C: 22, N: 14, D: 11.24. WR: 68.54, 224-10 (Harold Connolly)

| | | | FT.- | |
|---|---|---|---|---|
| | | M | IN. | |
| 1. Harold Connolly | USA | 63.19 | 207-3 | OR |
| 2. Mikhail Krivonosov | SOV | 63.03 | 206-9 | |
| 3. Anatoly Samotsvetov | SOV | 62.56 | 205-3 | |
| 4. Albert Hall | USA | 61.96 | 203-3 | |
| 5. József Csérmák | HUN | 60.70 | 199-2 | |
| 6. Krešimir Račić | YUG | 60.36 | 198-0 | |
| 7. Dmitri Yegorov | SOV | 60.22 | 197-7 | |
| 8. Sverre Strandli | NOR | 59.21 | 194-3 | |

For several months, Harold Connolly and Mikhail Krivonosov had been carrying on a long-distance duel between Boston and Minsk, breaking each other's most recent records. Krivonosov was a Byelorussian who attracted the attention of athletic coaches during a hand-grenade throwing contest. In 1952 he had hoped to go to the Helsinki Olympics as a discus thrower, but finished only fourth in the U.S.S.R. trials and failed to make the team. Two days later he qualified in the hammer throw instead. In Helsinki he fouled twice, fell once, and failed to register a valid throw. Concentrating on the hammer from then on, Krivonosov set his first world record in 1954. His sixth record, 220 feet 10 inches, was made on October 22, 1956. Eleven days later, Harold Connolly, whose left arm was withered as a result of an accident at birth, broke Krivonosov's record by four feet. Three weeks later the two rivals met at the Melbourne Olympics.

The first-round lead went to Siberia's Anatoly Samotsvetov at 203 feet 9 inches. Krivonosov moved ahead in the second round with a throw of 206 feet 8 inches. His last three attempts were all fouls. Hal Connolly, wearing ballet shoes to improve his footing, finally won the contest with a fifth round heave of 207 feet 3 inches.

What gained Connolly international attention was not his gold medal but his Olympic Village romance with Czechoslovakian discus champion Olga Fikotová. After a great deal of pressure, the Iron Curtain was drawn open long enough for Olga and Harold to wed. Forty thousand well-wishers attended their civil ceremony in Prague, which was followed by two more services, one Catholic and one Protestant. The couple then settled in the United States. Harold eventually took part in four Olympics and Olga in five. After they divorced in 1973, Harold married three-time Olympian Pat Daniels.

**1960 Rome** C: 28, N: 18, D: 9.3. WR: 70.33, 230-9 (Harold Connolly)

| | | M | FT.-IN. | |
|---|---|---|---|---|
| 1. Vasily Rudenkov | SOV | 67.10 | 220-2 | OR |
| 2. Gyula Zsivótzky | HUN | 65.79 | 215-10 | |
| 3. Tadeusz Rut | POL | 65.64 | 215-4 | |
| 4. John Lawlor | IRL | 64.95 | 213-1 | |
| 5. Olgierd Cieply | POL | 64.57 | 211-10 | |
| 6. Zvonko Bezjak | YUG | 64.21 | 210-7 | |
| 7. Anatoly Samotsvetov | SOV | 63.60 | 208-8 | |
| 8. Harold Connolly | USA | 63.58 | 208-7 | |

Harold Connolly broke his own world record only two weeks before the Olympics began, but was troubled by injury and finished a disappointing eighth in Rome. Meanwhile, metal worker Vasily Rudenkov set an Olympic record of 219 feet 10 inches in the qualifying round and then led the final from start to finish.

**1964 Tokyo** C: 24, N: 13, D: 10.18. WR: 70.66, 231-10 (Harold Connolly)

| | | M | FT.-IN. | |
|---|---|---|---|---|
| 1. Romuald Klim | SOV | 69.74 | 228-10 | OR |
| 2. Gyula Zsivótzky | HUN | 69.09 | 226-8 | |
| 3. Uwe Beyer | GER | 68.09 | 223-4 | |
| 4. Yuri Nikulin | SOV | 67.69 | 222-1 | |
| 5. Yuri Bakarinov | SOV | 66.72 | 218-11 | |
| 6. Harold Connolly | USA | 66.65 | 218-8 | |
| 7. Edward Burke | USA | 65.66 | 215-5 | |
| 8. Olgierd Cieply | POL | 64.82 | 212-8 | |

Romuald Klim, a 31-year-old from Byelorussia, won with his fourth throw.

**1968 Mexico City** C: 22, N: 12, D: 10.17. WR: 73.76, 242-0 (Gyula Zsivótsky)

| | | M | FT.-IN. | |
|---|---|---|---|---|
| 1. Gyula Zsivótzky | HUN | 73.36 | 240-8 | OR |
| 2. Romuald Klim | SOV | 73.28 | 240-5 | |
| 3. Lázár Lovász | HUN | 69.78 | 228-11 | |
| 4. Takeo Sugawara | JPN | 69.78 | 228-11 | |
| 5. Sándor Eckschmidt | HUN | 69.46 | 227-11 | |
| 6. Gennady Kondrashov | SOV | 69.08 | 226-8 | |
| 7. Reinhard Theimer | GDR | 68.84 | 225-10 | |
| 8. Helmut Baumann | GDR | 68.26 | 223-11 | |

On September 4, 1965, Gyula Zsivótzky threw the hammer 241 feet 11 inches to better the world record by a

shocking 8 feet 2 inches. Three years later he bumped the record up an extra inch, but at the Olympics he was not the favorite. Romuald Klim, unbeaten in three years, had defeated Zsivótzky nine straight times. Zsivótzky seemed to be held back by a psychological barrier whenever he faced Klim, but he received a big boost when he threw 247 feet 1 inch in practice one week before the competition began.

Klim's first throw of the final was 237 feet, but Zsivótzky, throwing immediately after Klim, gained further confidence by recording 237 feet 9 inches with his second throw. However, the third round saw Klim take the lead at 238 feet 11 inches, while Zsivótzky could only respond with 238 feet, two inches less than the Olympic record he had set in the qualifying round the previous day. In the fourth round of the final, Klim reached 240 feet 5 inches, while Zsivótzky fouled. However, the Hungarian put it together with his next-to-last throw and won with 240 feet 8 inches.

Takeo Sugawara, the smallest man in the competition at 5 feet 8½ inches and 185 pounds, tied with Lázár Lovász, but Lovász was awarded the bronze medal because his second best throw was one foot longer than Sugawara's.

**1972 Munich** C: 31, N: 18, D: 9.7. WR: 76.40, 250-8 (Walter Schmidt)

| | | M | FT.-IN. | |
|---|---|---|---|---|
| 1. Anatoly Bondarchuk | SOV | 75.50 | 247-8 | OR |
| 2. Jochen Sachse | GDR | 74.96 | 245-11 | |
| 3. Vasily Khmelevski | SOV | 74.04 | 242.11 | |
| 4. Uwe Beyer | GER | 71.52 | 234-8 | |
| 5. Gyula Zsivótzky | HUN | 71.38 | 234-2 | |
| 6. Sándor Eckschmidt | HUN | 71.20 | 233-7 | |
| 7. Edwin Klein | GER | 71.14 | 233-5 | |
| 8. Shigenobu Murofushi | JPN | 70.88 | 232-6 | |

The favorite, 32-year-old Anatoly Bondarchuk, settled matters early in the final with an opening throw of 247 feet 8 inches. He claimed to have thrown the hammer 100,000 times in the previous 13 years.

**1976 Montreal** C: 20, N: 13, D: 7.28. WR: 79.30, 260-2 (Walter Schmidt)

| | | M | FT.-IN. | |
|---|---|---|---|---|
| 1. Yuri Sedykh | SOV | 77.52 | 254-4 | OR |
| 2. Aleksei Spiridonov | SOV | 76.08 | 249-7 | |
| 3. Anatoly Bondarchuk | SOV | 75.48 | 247-8 | |
| 4. Karl-Hans Riehm | GER | 75.46 | 247-7 | |
| 5. Walter Schmidt | GER | 74.72 | 245-2 | |
| 6. Jochen Sachse | GDR | 74.30 | 243-9 | |
| 7. Chris Black | GBR | 73.18 | 240-1 | |
| 8. Edwin Klein | GER | 71.34 | 234-1 | |

On May 19, 1975, Karl-Hans Riehm had a truly remarkable day. Competing at Rehlingen, he bettered the previous world record with all six of his throws, his best of the day being 257 feet 6 inches. Three months later, he lost the record to Walter Schmidt, who was famous for achieving his best performances at minor meets. In Montreal, Riehm led the qualifying round at 244 feet 3 inches, but in the final, he and Schmidt had to take a back seat to the Soviet trio. Yuri Sedykh, a 21-year-old student of Anatoly Bondarchuk, won the competition with his second throw. Sedykh was introduced to the sport that would become his specialty in an unusual way. When he was 12 years old he chased a soccer ball onto a field, not realizing that hammer throwers were practicing nearby. He came very close to being decapitated by a flying hammer. He lingered—at a respectful distance—long enough to become fascinated, then returned every day until he was allowed to join in.

**1980 Moscow** C: 17, N: 12, D: 7.31. WR: 81.66, 267-11 (Sergei Litvinov)

|   |   |     | FT.- | |   |
|---|---|-----|------|-----|---|
|   |   |     | M    | IN. |   |
| 1. | Yuri Sedykh | SOV | 81.80 | 268-4 | WR |
| 2. | Sergei Litvinov | SOV | 80.64 | 264-7 | |
| 3. | Jüri Tamm | SOV | 78.96 | 259-1 | |
| 4. | Roland Steuk | GDR | 77.54 | 254-5 | |
| 5. | Detlef Gerstenberg | GDR | 74.60 | 244-9 | |
| 6. | Emannouil Dulgherov | BUL | 74.04 | 242-11 | |
| 7. | Gianpaulo Urlando | ITA | 73.90 | 242-5 | |
| 8. | Ireneusz Golda | POL | 73.74 | 241-11 | |

Unfortunately missing because of the anti-Soviet boycott was Karl-Hans Riehm, who threw 265 feet 1 inch the day before the Olympic final. Riehm was the only man capable of threatening the Soviets, who dominated hammer throwing so thoroughly that three of their team members set world records during one nine-day period. On May 16, 1980, Sedykh took the record away from Riehm with a throw of 263 feet 8 inches. Then Yuri Tamm entered the circle and threw 263 feet 9 inches. Not to be outdone, Sedykh countered with 264 feet 7 inches. Eight days later, Sergei Litvinov beat them both with a new record of 267 feet 11 inches.

In Moscow Sedykh opened the Olympic final with a world record of 268 feet 4 inches. Litvinov's first throw gained him the silver medal. He followed with five straight fouls.

**1984 Los Angeles** C: 23, N: 13, D: 8.6. WR: 86.34, 283-3 (Yuri Sedykh)

|   |   |     | FT.- | |
|---|---|-----|------|-----|
|   |   |     | M    | IN. |
| 1. | Juha Tiainen | FIN | 78.08 | 256-2 |
| 2. | Karl-Hans Riehm | GER | 77.98 | 255-10 |
| 3. | Klaus Ploghaus | GER | 76.68 | 251-7 |
| 4. | Orlando Bianchini | ITA | 75.94 | 249-2 |
| 5. | Bill Green | USA | 75.60 | 248-0 |
| 6. | Harri Huhtala | FIN | 75.28 | 247-0 |
| 7. | Walter Ciofani | FRA | 73.46 | 241-0 |
| 8. | Bob Weir | GBR | 72.62 | 238-3 |

DISQ (Drugs): Giampaolo Urlando (ITA) 75.96 249-3

On July 3, 1984, Yuri Sedykh added 7 feet 3 inches to Sergei Litvinov's world record. Sadly, the Soviet boycott prevented these two great champions from battling it out at the Olympics. Juha Tiainen, the only one of the top twelve ranked hammer throwers present in Los Angeles, won with his third round throw. Fourth-place finisher Urlando was disqualified when his doping test registered positive for testosterone.

**1988 Seoul** C: 30, N: 16, D: 9.26. WR: 86.74, 284-7 (Yuri Sedykh)

|   |   |     | FT.- | |   |
|---|---|-----|------|-----|---|
|   |   |     | M    | IN. |   |
| 1. | Sergei Litvinov | SOV | 84.80 | 278-2 | OR |
| 2. | Yuri Sedykh | SOV | 83.76 | 274-10 | |
| 3. | Jüri Tamm | SOV | 81.16 | 266-3 | |
| 4. | Ralf Haber | GDR | 80.44 | 263-11 | |
| 5. | Heinz Weis | GER | 79.16 | 259-8 | |
| 6. | Tibor Gécsek | HUN | 78.36 | 257-1 | |
| 7. | Imre Szitás | HUN | 77.04 | 252-9 | |
| 8. | Ivan Tanev | BUL | 76.08 | 249-7 | |

The three medalists from 1980 returned to the victory platform in 1988. Two-time world champion Sergei Litvinov settled the competition with a first-round heave of 278 feet 1 inch, then added a slightly longer throw in the fifth round.

## JAVELIN THROW

A javelin must weigh a minimum of 800 grams (1 pound 12¼ ounces) and measure between 2.60 meters (8 feet 6¼ inches) and 2.70 meters (8 feet 10¼ inches). The shaft may be either wood or metal. In 1986, the balance point and grip of the men's javelin was moved up 10 cm. and the tail was made more narrow. These modifications were instituted in response to the increased frequency of dangerously long throws. For a throw to be considered valid the pointed metal head must break the turf. The javelin is thrown on the run and must be released above the shoulder. Spinning around before throwing is illegal, since this technique could seriously discourage spectators from coming anywhere near the part of the stadium where the javelin competition is taking place.

**1896–1906** not held

**1908 London** C: 16, N: 6, D: 7.17. WR: 54.40, 178-6 (Eric Lemming)

|   |   |     | FT.- | |   |
|---|---|-----|------|-----|---|
|   |   |     | M    | IN. |   |
| 1. | Eric Lemming | SWE | 54.825 | 179-10 | WR |
| 2. | Arne Halse | NOR | 50.57 | 165-11 | |
| 3. | Otto Nilsson | SWE | 47.105 | 154-6 | |
| 4. | Aarne Salovaara | FIN | 45.89 | 150-6 | |
| 5. | Armas Pesonen | FIN | 45.18 | 148-3 | |
| 6. | Juho Halme | FIN | 44.96 | 147-6 | |
| 7. | Jalmari Sauli | FIN | — | — | |

Eric Lemming, a 6-foot 3-inch, 26-year-old Stockholm policeman, had dominated javelin throwing since 1899.

**1912 Stockholm** C: 25, N: 7, D: 7.6. WR: 58.27, 191-2 (Eric Lemming)

| | | | FT.- | |
|---|---|---|---|---|
| | | M | IN. | |
| 1. Eric Lemming | SWE | 60.64 | 198-11 | WR |
| 2. Julius Juho Saaristo | FIN | 58.66 | 192-5 | |
| 3. Mór Kóczán | HUN | 55.50 | 182-1 | |
| 4. Juho Halme | FIN | 54.65 | 179-3 | |
| 5. Väinö Siikaniemi | FIN | 52.43 | 172-0 | |
| 6. Richard Åbrink | SWE | 52.20 | 171-3 | |
| 7. Arne Halse | NOR | 51.98 | 170-6 | |
| 8. Jonni Myyrä | FIN | 51.32 | 168-4 | |

Lemming received a standing ovation from the home-town crowd after he made the world's first 60-meter throw. Three days later, while competing in the now discontinued combined left- and right-hand event, Juho Saaristo set a world record of 200 feet 1 inch using his right hand.

**1920 Antwerp** C: 30, N: 13, D: 8.15. WR: 66.10, 216-10 (Jonni Myyrä)

| | | | FT.- | |
|---|---|---|---|---|
| | | M | IN. | |
| 1. Jonni Myyrä | FIN | 65.78 | 215-10 | OR |
| 2. Urho Peltonen | FIN | 63.50 | 208-4 | |
| 3. Paavo Jaale-Johansson | FIN | 63.095 | 207-0 | |
| 4. Julius Juho Saaristo | FIN | 62.395 | 204-9 | |
| 5. Alexander Klumberg | EST | 62.39 | 204-8 | |
| 6. Gunnar Lindström | SWE | 60.52 | 198-7 | |
| 7. Milton Angier | USA | 59.26 | 194-5 | |
| 8. Erik Blomqvist | SWE | 58.18 | 190-10 | |

**1924 Paris** C: 30, N: 13, D: 8.15. WR: 66.10, 216-10 (Jonni Myyrä)

| | | | FT.- |
|---|---|---|---|
| | | M | IN. |
| 1. Jonni Myyrä | FIN | 62.96 | 206-7 |
| 2. Gunnar Lindström | SWE | 60.92 | 199-10 |
| 3. Eugene Oberst | USA | 58.35 | 191-5 |
| 4. Yrjö Ekqvist | FIN | 57.56 | 188-10 |
| 5. William Neufeld | USA | 56.96 | 186-10 |
| 6. Erik Blomqvist | SWE | 56.85 | 186-6 |
| 7. Urho Peltonen | FIN | 55.66 | 182-7 |
| 8. Paavo Jaale-Johansson | FIN | 55.10 | 180-9 |

The 32-year-old Myyrä successfully defended his title. However he lost his world record two months later, when Lindström threw 218 feet 7 inches.

**1928 Amsterdam** C: 28, N: 18, D: 8.2. WR: 69.88, 229-3 (Eino Penttilä)

| | | | FT.- | |
|---|---|---|---|---|
| | | M | IN. | |
| 1. Erik Lundkvist | SWE | 66.60 | 218-6 | OR |
| 2. Béla Szepes | HUN | 65.26 | 214-1 | |
| 3. Olav Sunde | NOR | 63.97 | 209-10 | |

| 4. Paavo Liettu | FIN | 63.86 | 209-6 |
|---|---|---|---|
| 5. W. Bruno Schlokat | GER | 63.40 | 208-0 |
| 6. Eino Penttilä | FIN | 63.20 | 207-4 |
| 7. Stanley Lay | NZE | 62.89 | 206-3 |
| 8. Johan Meimer | EST | 61.46 | 201-8 |

On October 8, 1927, Eino Penttilä recorded a throw of 229 feet 3 inches to improve the world record by an impressive 10 feet 8 inches. In Amsterdam, however, Penttilä suffered from overtraining, the pressure of high expectations, and a sore foot, and was only able to finish sixth. The winner, sign painter Erik Lundkvist, went on to set a world record of 232 feet 11 inches two weeks later.

**1932 Los Angeles** C: 13, N: 7, D: 8.4. WR: 74.02, 242-10 (Matti Järvinen)

| | | | FT.- | |
|---|---|---|---|---|
| | | M | IN. | |
| 1. Matti Järvinen | FIN | 72.71 | 238-6 | OR |
| 2. Matti Sippala | FIN | 69.80 | 229-0 | |
| 3. Eino Penttilä | FIN | 68.70 | 225-5 | |
| 4. Gottfried Weimann | GER | 68.18 | 223-8 | |
| 5. Lee Bartlett | USA | 64.46 | 211-6 | |
| 6. Kenneth Churchill | USA | 63.24 | 207-6 | |
| 7. Malcolm Metcalf | USA | 61.89 | 203-0 | |
| 8. Kohsaku Sumiyoshi | JPN | 61.14 | 200-7 | |

Three sons of Finland's first gold medal winner, Verner Järvinen, took part in the 1932 Olympics, but only the youngest, Matti, won a gold medal. Matti's first five throws were the best of the competition, and all of them bettered the previous Olympic record. Matti didn't bother to take off the trousers of his track suit until the contest was over and it was time for photographs to be taken. Between 1930 and 1936 Matti Järvinen broke the javelin world record ten times and became known as "Mr. Javelin."

**1936 Berlin** C: 28, N: 19, D: 8.6. WR: 77.23, 253-4 (Matti Järvinen)

| | | | FT.- |
|---|---|---|---|
| | | M | IN. |
| 1. Gerhard Stöck | GER | 71.84 | 235-8 |
| 2. Yrjö Nikkanen | FIN | 70.77 | 232-2 |
| 3. Kaarlo Kalervo Toivonen | FIN | 70.72 | 232-0 |
| 4. Lennart Attervall | SWE | 69.20 | 227-0 |
| 5. Matti Järvinen | FIN | 69.18 | 227-0 |
| 6. Alton Terry | USA | 67.15 | 220-4 |
| 7. Eugeniusz Lokajski | POL | 66.39 | 217-9 |
| 8. József Várszegi | HUN | 65.30 | 214-3 |

Gerhard Stöck, who had finished third in the shot put four days earlier, was in fifth place after four rounds. It was then that Adolf Hitler arrived in the stadium. With the crowd chanting, "Stöck, Stöck, don't be a 'wet blanket,' go ahead and finally throw 70 meters," Stöck unleashed a throw of almost 72 meters that turned out to be sufficient for the gold medal. Matti Järvinen, suffering from a back injury, was only able to place fifth.

**1948 London** C: 22, N: 15, D: 8.4. WR: 78.70, 258-2 (Yrjö Nikkanen)

| | | M | FT.-IN. | |
|---|---|---|---|---|
| 1. Kai Tapio Rautavaara | FIN | 69.77 | 228-10 | |
| 2. Steve Seymour | USA | 67.56 | 221-8 | |
| 3. József Várszegi | HUN | 67.03 | 219-11 | |
| 4. Pauli Vesterinen | FIN | 65.89 | 216-2 | |
| 5. Odd Maehlum | NOR | 65.32 | 214-3 | |
| 6. Martin Biles | USA | 65.17 | 213-9 | |
| 7. Mirko Vujacic | YUG | 64.89 | 212-10 | |
| 8. Robert Likens | USA | 64.51 | 211-7 | |

Marty Biles led the qualifying round with a throw of 222 feet, which would have been good enough for a silver medal if he had been able to repeat it in the final. Gold medal winner Tapio Rautavaara later became a successful archer, folk singer, and actor. While posing for a photograph, he fell and hit his head on a concrete floor; he died on September 25, 1979, at the age of 64.

**1952 Helsinki** C: 26, N: 16, D: 7.23. WR: 78.70, 258-2 (Yrjö Nikkanen)

| | | M | FT.-IN. | |
|---|---|---|---|---|
| 1. Cyrus Young | USA | 73.78 | 242-1 | OR |
| 2. William Miller | USA | 72.46 | 237-9 | |
| 3. Tolvo Hyytiäinen | FIN | 71.89 | 235-10 | |
| 4. Viktor Tsibulenko | SOV | 71.72 | 234-4 | |
| 5. Branko Dangubić | YUG | 70.55 | 231-5 | |
| 6. Vladimir Kuznetsov | SOV | 70.37 | 230-10 | |
| 7. Ragnar Ericzon | SWE | 69.04 | 226-6 | |
| 8. Soini Nikkinen | FIN | 68.80 | 225-9 | |

The two American medalists presented an unusual contrast. Cy Young, who celebrated his 24th birthday by winning the gold medal, was 6 feet 5 inches, while Bill Miller was only 5 feet 9 inches. When a third American, ninth-place finisher Bud Held, broke Yrjö Nikkanen's 15-year-old world record in 1953, it looked like the United States had found itself another specialty. However, the expected U.S. dominance did not materialize.

**1956 Melbourne** C: 21, N: 12, D: 26.11. WR: 83.66, 274-6 (Janusz Sidlo)

| | | M | FT.-IN. | |
|---|---|---|---|---|
| 1. Egil Danielson | NOR | 85.71 | 281-2 | WR |
| 2. Janusz Sidlo | POL | 79.98 | 262-5 | |
| 3. Viktor Tsibulenko | SOV | 79.50 | 260-10 | |
| 4. Herbert Koschel | GER | 74.68 | 245-0 | |
| 5. Jan Kopyto | POL | 74.28 | 243-8 | |
| 6. Giovanni Lievore | ITA | 72.88 | 239-1 | |
| 7. Michel Macquet | FRA | 71.84 | 235-8 | |
| 8. Aleksandr Gorshkov | SOV | 70.32 | 230-8 | |

Cy Young led the qualifying round with a throw of 245 feet 3 inches. After three rounds of the final, Sidlo was in

first place, followed by Tsibulenko and Koschel. For his fourth throw, Tsibulenko abandoned the wooden javelin he had been using and picked up a steel one which had been made in Sweden. He immediately improved his standing by almost 15 feet. Egil Danielsen, who had won 36 consecutive meets but was only in sixth place, asked Tsibulenko if he could borrow his steel javelin. He then let loose an enormous throw that broke the world record and almost landed on the runway of the pole vault. Danielsen danced around, hugging and kissing everyone in the area of the javelin competition, while Tsibulenko was left to laugh, shake his head, and marvel at the result of his good sportsmanship.

**1960 Rome** C: 28, N: 18, D: 9.8. WR: 86.04, 282-3 (Albert Cantello)

| | | M | FT.-IN. |
|---|---|---|---|
| 1. Viktor Tsibulenko | SOV | 84.64 | 277-8 |
| 2. Walter Krüger | GDR | 79.36 | 260-4 |
| 3. Gergely Kulcsár | HUN | 78.57 | 257-9 |
| 4. Väinö Kuisma | FIN | 78.40 | 257-3 |
| 5. Willy Rasmussen | NOR | 78.36 | 257-1 |
| 6. Knut Fredriksson | SWE | 78.33 | 256-11 |
| 7. Zbigniew Radziwonowicz | POL | 77.30 | 253-7 |
| 8. Janusz Sidlo | POL | 76.46 | 250-10 |

In 1960 the javelin throw turned out to be a strange contest. The preliminary round was led by Janusz Sidlo at 279 feet 4 inches and Al Cantello at 261 feet 6 inches. If Sidlo and Cantello had been able to reproduce their form in the final, they would have finished first and third. Instead, they ended up eighth and tenth. The preliminary round also saw the elimination of defending champion Egil Danielsen and Bill Alley of the United States, who had a pending (and subsequently never ratified) world record of 283 feet 8 inches. The final was settled early with Viktor Tsibulenko's first-round throw of 277 feet 8 inches. Gusty winds and rain disrupted the competition from the second round on, and no one, Tsibulenko included, was able to do better than 257 feet 1 inch after that.

**1964 Tokyo** C: 25, L: 15, D: 10.14. WR: 91.72, 300-11 (Terje Pedersen)

| | | M | FT.-IN. |
|---|---|---|---|
| 1. Pauli Nevala | FIN | 82.66 | 271-2 |
| 2. Gergely Kulcsár | HUN | 82.32 | 270-1 |
| 3. Jānis Lūsis | SOV | 80.57 | 264-4 |
| 4. Janusz Sidlo | POL | 80.17 | 263-0 |
| 5. Urs von Wartburg | SWI | 78.72 | 258-3 |
| 6. Jorma Kinnunen | FIN | 76.94 | 252-5 |
| 7. Rolf Herings | GER | 74.72 | 245-2 |
| 8. Vladimir Kuznetsov | SOV | 74.26 | 243-8 |

On September 2, 1964, Terje Pedersen shocked the track and field world with a monster throw of 300 feet 11 inches that bettered his own world record by 15 feet 1 inch. Yet six weeks later in Tokyo, he could do no better than 236 feet 6 inches, and failed to qualify for the final. The 1964 Olympic competition, like the one in 1960, was marred by wind and rain. Janusz Sidlo had the best throw of the first round of the final at 263 feet. Jānis Lūsis took the lead in the second round with a throw of 264 feet 4 inches. But the real action took place in the fourth round. Ever-consistent Gergely Kulcsár reached 270 feet 1 inch, only to be topped by unheralded Pauli Nevala at 271 feet 2 inches. Von Wartburg's final throw appeared good enough for a silver medal, but was declared invalid on the grounds that it landed incorrectly, a ruling that raised many eyebrows.

Finnish Olympic officials had been criticized for wasting their money sending Nevala to Tokyo, particularly after he had failed to win the national championship. "Even if I'm not the Finnish champion," Nevala commented, "at least I've won the Olympics."

**1968 Mexico City** C: 27, N: 18, D: 10.16. WR: 91.98, 301-9 (Jānis Lūsis)

|   |   |   | FT.- |   |
|---|---|---|---|---|
|   |   | M | IN. |   |
| 1. Jānis Lūsis | SOV | 90.10 | 295-7 | OR |
| 2. Jorma Kinnunen | FIN | 88.58 | 290-7 |   |
| 3. Gergely Kulcsár | HUN | 87.06 | 285-7 |   |
| 4. Wladislaw Nikiciuk | POL | 85.70 | 281-2 |   |
| 5. Manfred Stolle | GDR | 84.42 | 277-0 |   |
| 6. Åke Nilsson | SWE | 83.48 | 273-11 |   |
| 7. Janusz Sidlo | POL | 80.58 | 264-4 |   |
| 8. Urs von Wartburg | SWI | 80.56 | 264-4 |   |

A surprising thing happened in the 1968 javelin competition. For the first time since 1932, it was won by the favorite. The first-round lead went to 5-foot 9-inch, 165-pound Jorma Kinnunen. Popular Jānis Lūsis of Latvia, who was married to Elvira Ozolina, winner of the 1960 women's javelin, edged ahead by four centimeters in the second round. In the fourth round, Gergely Kulcsár moved in front with a personal and Olympic record of 285 feet 7 inches. And so the situation stood with one round remaining: Kulcsár in first, followed by Lūsis and Kinnunen. Lūsis calmly took his spear in hand and made his last attempt his best—295 feet 7 inches. He had one more moment of concern when Kinnunen also came up with a clutch performance, 290 feet 7 inches, but the Finn had to be content with second place. Janusz Sidlo, competing in his fifth Olympics, finished a creditable seventh.

**1972 Munich** C: 23, N: 15, D: 9.3. WR: 93.80, 307-9 (Jānis Lūsis)

|   |   |   | FT.- |   |
|---|---|---|---|---|
|   |   | M | IN. |   |
| 1. Klaus Wolfermann | GER | 90.48 | 296-10 | OR |
| 2. Jānis Lūsis | SOV | 90.46 | 296-9 |   |
| 3. William Schmidt | USA | 84.42 | 277-0 |   |
| 4. Hannu Siitonen | FIN | 84.32 | 276-8 |   |
| 5. Björn Grimnes | NOR | 83.08 | 272-7 |   |
| 6. Jorma Kinnunen | FIN | 82.08 | 269-3 |   |
| 7. Miklos Németh | HUN | 81.98 | 268-11 |   |
| 8. Fredrick Luke | USA | 80.06 | 262-8 |   |

Jānis Lūsis dominated javelin throwing between Olympics. In 1972 no one came within 17 feet of his performance of the year until one week before the Munich Games, when Klaus Wolfermann hit 296 feet 7 inches. In the Olympic final, Lūsis had the first big throw—291 feet 7 inches in the first round. He improved to 293 feet 9 inches with his third attempt. Wolfermann, cheered on by the German crowd, picked up steam in the fourth round with a throw of 290 feet. Then, in the fifth round, he caused the spectators to roar with excitement when he exploded for a personal best of 296 feet 10 inches. However, Jānis Lūsis still had one attempt left, and many remembered his dramatic last-round victory four years earlier. Sure enough, Lūsis let loose a big one. Wolfermann and his supporters waited anxiously for the measurement. And then it came—296 feet 9 inches. The two-centimeter difference is the smallest unit of measurement used in javelin competitions. One more inch and Lūsis would have won on the basis of a longer second throw.

When Jānis Lūsis was a little boy, he had been forced to watch the execution of his father by German soldiers. Yet as a grown man, he bore no grudge against the German people, and later became good friends with Klaus Wolfermann, even vacationing with him in Bavaria.

**1976 Montreal** C: 23, N: 15, D: 7.25. WR: 94.08, 308-8 (Klaus Wolfermann)

|   |   |   | FT.- |   |
|---|---|---|---|---|
|   |   | M | IN. |   |
| 1. Miklos Németh | HUN | 94.58 | 310-4 | WR |
| 2. Hannu Siitonen | FIN | 87.92 | 288-5 |   |
| 3. Gheorghe Megelea | ROM | 87.16 | 285-11 |   |
| 4. Pyotr Bielczyk | POL | 86.50 | 283-9 |   |
| 5. Sam Colson | USA | 86.16 | 282-8 |   |
| 6. Vasily Yershov | SOV | 85.26 | 279-9 |   |
| 7. Seppo Hovinen | FIN | 84.26 | 276-5 |   |
| 8. Jānis Lūsis | SOV | 80.26 | 263-4 |   |

Miklos Németh was less than two years old when his father, Imre, won the gold medal for the hammer throw at the 1948 Olympics in London. His father pressed him to take up the hammer, but Miklos preferred the javelin, and by 1967 he was ranked second in the world. But he never performed well in major championships. In the 1968 Olympics an elbow injury kept Miklos from qualifying for the final. In 1972 he was one of the favorites, but finished a disappointing seventh. His father said he was too gentle. His critics said he was a choker. Miklos himself said, "It is not an easy thing in my country to be the son of an Olympic champion."

Then came Montreal. Now 29 years old and no longer a favorite, Miklos Németh was almost ignored as interest centered on the leading contenders, Hovinen, Siitonen, and Bielczyk. Németh was the tenth man up in the final, and with his first attempt he uncorked a beauty. He tried not to watch it, but kept looking back as the spear sailed on and on until it finally landed 310 feet 4 inches away from the throwing area. It was ten and a half feet farther than Németh had ever thrown before. It was also a new world record.

While Németh jumped for joy, the rest of the javelin throwers were absolutely demoralized. The remaining medals, it turned out, were also decided by first-round throws. Hovinen, who had led the qualifiers at 294 feet 6 inches, could do no better than 276 feet 5 inches. Nineteen-year-old Phil Olson of Canada, who had qualified with a throw of 287 feet 11 inches, finished 11th at 254 feet 11 inches. Németh was so excited that he had to pass the next two rounds. His winning margin was the widest in any field event in Olympic history (excluding the Intercalated Games of 1906). Imre and Miklos Németh are the only father-and-son combination ever to win track and field gold medals at the Olympics.

**1980 Moscow** C: 18, N: 11, D: 7.27. WR: 96.72, 317-4 (Ferenc Paragi)

|   |   |     | M | FT.-IN. |
|---|---|-----|---|-----|
| 1. | Dainis Kūla | SOV | 91.20 | 299-2 |
| 2. | Aleksandr Makarov | SOV | 89.64 | 294-1 |
| 3. | Wolfgang Hanisch | GDR | 86.72 | 284-6 |
| 4. | Heino Puuste | SOV | 86.10 | 282-6 |
| 5. | Antero Puranen | FIN | 85.12 | 279-3 |
| 6. | Pentti Sinersaari | FIN | 84.34 | 276-8 |
| 7. | Detlef Fuhrmann | GDR | 83.50 | 273-11 |
| 8. | Miklos Németh | HUN | 82.40 | 270-4 |

Only once since World War II has the leader of the qualifying round in the javelin gone on to victory, the exception being Klaus Wolfermann in 1972. Unfortunately for world record holder Ferenc Paragi, the jinx continued. After a preliminary throw of 291 feet 2 inches, his best in the final was only 260 feet 11 inches and he placed tenth. After two rounds, the leader was Wolfgang Hanisch, followed by Heino Puuste. The decisive moment came at the end of the third round. The last man to throw was Dainis Kūla, a 21-year-old Latvian. Having fouled on his first two attempts, Kūla needed not only a valid throw, but a big one, just to qualify for the extra three attempts accorded the top eight. To most observers, Kūla's third try appeared to land tail first and then bounce, which should have led to his immediate elimination. Instead, Soviet officials rushed out to measure it and announced a valid throw of 291 feet 7 inches. Taking advantage of his questionable reprieve, Kūla followed with an excellent, and perfectly legal, throw of 299 feet 2 inches that held up for the gold medal.

The U.S. team trials had been won by Rod Ewaliko at 291 feet, but Bruce Kennedy, who finished second, set what must be an Olympic record—and a most unfortunate one. A citizen of Zimbabwe, then known as Rhodesia, Kennedy had gone to Munich in 1972 as part of his nation's Olympic team. However, pressure from black African nations opposed to Rhodesia's white minority government prevented the Rhodesians from competing. In 1976 Kennedy was again selected to compete in the Olympics, but again Rhodesia was excluded. Meanwhile, Kennedy had moved to the United States and married an American. In 1977 he became a U.S. citizen. In 1980 he qualified for the U.S. team, but, for the third time, he was prevented from competing in the Olympics because of politics. Ironically, Zimbabwe, now ruled by its black majority, was readmitted into the Olympic movement and allowed to take part in the Moscow Games. In 1984 Bruce Kennedy, who by this time had earned a master's degree from Stanford University, finally made it inside an Olympic stadium—as an usher.

**1984 Los Angeles** C: 28, N: 19, D: 8.5. WR: 104.80, 343-10 (Uwe Hohn)

|   |   |     | M | FT.-IN. |
|---|---|-----|---|-----|
| 1. | Arto Härkönen | FIN | 86.76 | 284-8 |
| 2. | David Ottley | GBR | 85.74 | 281-3 |
| 3. | Kenth Eldebrink | SWE | 83.72 | 274-8 |
| 4. | Wolfram Gambke | GER | 82.46 | 270-6 |
| 5. | Masami Yoshida | JPN | 81.98 | 268-11 |
| 6. | Einar Vihjalmsson | ICE | 81.58 | 267-8 |
| 7. | Roald Bradstock | GBR | 81.22 | 266-6 |
| 8. | Laslo Babits | CAN | 80.68 | 264-8 |

On May 15, 1983, Tom Petranoff of the United States broke Ferenc Paragi's three-year-old world record by almost ten feet with a throw of 327 feet 2 inches (99.72 meters). At the world championships three months later, Petranoff was beaten by East Germany's Detlef Michel, with 1980 Olympic champion Dainis Kūla in third place. It seemed just a matter of time before Petranoff or Michel broke through the 100-meter barrier. However, on July 20, 1984, it was another East German, 22-year-old Uwe Hohn, who accomplished the feat. And Hohn, who also held the East German national record for throwing a 21-ounce grenade (328 feet 2 inches), did it in grand style with a massive throw of 343 feet 10 inches (104.80 meters)—the greatest world record improvement in javelin history.

With Hohn, Michel and Kūla among the boycott missing, Petranoff found himself in the unusual and uncomfortable position of being the favorite in the most important meet of his career, the 1984 Olympics. Petranoff led the qualifying round with a throw of 282 feet, but like Ferenc Paragi four years earlier, he could do no better than tenth place in the final. David Ottley took the surprise early lead with a near-personal best of 281 feet 3 inches. But in the fourth round, Arto Härkönen, whose father was the coach of women's silver medalist Tiina Lillak, launched a throw of 284 feet 8 inches, to bring Finland its first javelin gold medal in twenty years.

**1988 Seoul** C: 38, N: 22, D: 9.25. WR: 87.66, 287-7 (Jan Železný)

| | | M | IN. |
|---|---|---|---|
| | | | FT.- |
| 1. Tapio Korjus | FIN | 84.28 | 276-6 |
| 2. Jan Železný | CZE | 84.12 | 276-0 |
| 3. Seppo Räty | FIN | 83.26 | 273-2 |
| 4. Klaus Tafelmeier | GER | 82.72 | 271-5 |
| 5. Viktor Yevsyukov | SOV | 82.32 | 270-1 |
| 6. Gerald Weiss | GDR | 81.30 | 266-9 |
| 7. Vladimir Ovchinnikov | SOV | 79.12 | 259-7 |
| 8. Dag Wennlund | SWE | 78.30 | 256-11 |

World record holder Jan Železný recorded the longest throw of the qualifying round at 281 feet 10 inches. In the final, Tapio Korjus took the first round lead with a throw of 271 feet 5 inches. The second round was highlighted by throws of 270 feet 1 inch by both Železný and Viktor Yevsyukov. Seppo Räty, practically unknown when he won the 1987 world championship, moved ahead in the third round with a throw of 273 feet 2 inches. Meanwhile, Korjus passed his next two opportunities because of a cramp in his left leg. In his absence, Železný regained the lead by 8 inches. Korjus returned for the fifth round, but fouled. In the sixth and final round, Železný reached 276 feet to lengthen his lead. Korjus, in third place, was the final thrower of the competition. "This is all or nothing," he thought. "It was a good throw," he said of his last attempt. "You know it when you see only a dot against the sky." It landed 6 inches beyond Železný's mark to give Finland its seventh javelin gold.

## DECATHLON

The decathlon consists of ten events held over a two-day period. On the first day, the athletes take part in the 100-meter dash, long jump, shot put, high jump, and 400-meter run. On the second day they compete in the 110-meter hurdles, discus throw, pole vault, javelin throw and 1500-meter run. Points are scored according to a set of tables approved by the International Amateur Athletic Federation. The tables currently in use were devised in 1962 and revised in 1971 and 1977 to take into account the advent of automatic electronic timing, with accuracy to $1/100$ second. They were further adjusted in 1985. The 1985 equivalent of each athlete's performance is included here for the purpose of historical comparison.

Decathletes tend to show up later as movie actors. Jim Thorpe was an extra in several Westerns, Glenn Morris played Tarzan, Floyd Simmons was in *South Pacific,* Bob Mathias acted with Jayne Mansfield in *It Happened in Athens.* Rafer Johnson and C.K. Yang also appeared in movies. The 1976 gold medalist Bruce Jenner made his screen debut in *Can't Stop the Music,* one of the worst films ever made. Dennis Weaver, who became famous for his roles in the television series *Gunsmoke* and *McCloud,* placed sixth in the 1948 U.S. Olympic trials.

### KEY TO ABBREVIATIONS

DISC = Discus throw
H = Hurdles
HAM = Hammer throw
HJ = High jump
JAV = Javelin throw
LJ = Long jump
M = Meters
PV = Pole vault
SP = Shot put

**1896–1900** not held.

**1904 St. Louis** C: 7, N: 2, D: 7.4.

| | | 100 YDS | SP | HJ | 800-YD WALK | HAM | PV | 120-YD. H | 56-LB. THROW | LJ | MILE | TOTAL POINTS |
|---|---|---|---|---|---|---|---|---|---|---|---|---|
| 1. Thomas Kiely | IRL | 11.2 | 10.82 | 1.52 | 3:59.0 | 36.76 | 2.74 | 17.8 | 8.91 | 5.94 | 5:51.0 | 6036 |
| 2. Adam Gunn | USA | 11.2e | 12.21 | 1.65 | 4:13.0 | 31.40 | 2.97 | 17.9 | 7.22 | 5.53 | 5:45.0 | 5907 |
| 3. Thomas Truxtun Hare | USA | 10.8 | 12.09 | 1.52 | 4:20.0 | 36.28 | 2.44 | 18.27 | 7.59 | 6.07 | 5:40.0 | 5813 |
| 4. John Holloway | IRL | 10.9e | 10.01 | 1.68 | 3:59.0 | 27.51 | 2.89 | 18.33 | 5.98 | 5.53 | 5:40.0 | 5273 |
| 5. Ellery Clark | USA | 11.0 | 10.26 | 1.62 | 4:11.0 | 29.11 | DNF | | | | | 2778 |
| 6. John Grieb | USA | 11.2e | 10.54 | 1.62 | 4:49.0 | DNF | | | | | | 2199 |

This competition was known as the "All-Around Championship" and was noteworthy because all ten events were held on the same day. Offered a free trip if he would compete for Great Britain, 35-year-old Tom Kiely refused, paid his own way, and competed for Ireland.

**1906–1908** not held

**1912 Stockholm** C: 29, N: 12, D: 7.13-15. WR: 7414 (James Austin Menaul)

| | | 100 M | LJ | SP | HJ | 400 M | DISC | 110 H | PV | JAV | 1500 M | TOTAL POINTS | | 1985 TABLES |
|---|---|---|---|---|---|---|---|---|---|---|---|---|---|---|
| 1. | James Thorpe | USA | 11.2 | 6.79 | 12.89 | 1.87 | 52.2 | 36.98 | 15.6 | 3.25 | 45.70 | 4:40.1 | 8412 | WR | 6564 |
| 2. | Hugo Wieslander | SWE | 11.8 | 6.42 | 12.14 | 1.75 | 53.6 | 36.29 | 17.2 | 3.10 | 50.40 | 4:45.0 | 7724 | | 5965 |
| 3. | Charles Lomberg | SWE | 11.8 | 6.87 | 11.67 | 1.80 | 55.0 | 35.35 | 17.6 | 3.25 | 41.83 | 5:12.2 | 7414 | | 5721 |
| 4. | Gösta Holmér | SWE | 11.4 | 5.98 | 10.98 | 1.70 | 53.2 | 31.78 | 17.0 | 3.20 | 46.28 | 4:41.9 | 7348 | | 5748 |
| 5. | James Donahue | USA | 11.8 | 6.48 | 9.67 | 1.65 | 51.6 | 29.95 | 16.2 | 3.40 | 37.09 | 4:44.0 | 7083 | | 5701 |
| 6. | Eugene Leroy Mercer | USA | 11.0 | 6.84 | 9.76 | 1.65 | 49.9 | 21.95 | 16.4 | 3.60 | 32.32 | 4:46.3 | 7075 | | 5825 |
| 7. | Woldemar Wickholm | FIN | 11.5 | 5.95 | 11.09 | 1.60 | 52.3 | 29.78 | 17.0 | 3.25 | 42.58 | 4:33.9 | 7059 | | 5676 |
| 8. | Erik Kugelberg | SWE | 12.3 | 6.20 | 9.99 | 1.65 | 55.7 | 31.48 | 17.2 | 3.00 | 45.67 | 4:43.5 | 6758 | | 5346 |

James Francis Thorpe was born on May 28, 1888, on a farm near the town of Prague in what was then known as the Oklahoma Territory. His father was part Irish, part Sac and Fox Indian. His mother, who was part Potawatomie and Kickapoo Indian and part French, gave him the Indian name Wa-Tho-Huck, or "Bright Path." Jim's twin brother, Charles, died of pneumonia at the age of 10. His mother died when he was 12 and his father when he was 15. Educated at the government-run Indian schools of Haskell and Carlisle, Jim Thorpe did not become a noteworthy athlete until 1907. In the spring of that year he walked past the track area where the high jumpers were trying—and failing—to clear 5 feet 9 inches. Thorpe, dressed in work clothes, went over the bar on his first attempt, setting a school record.

He first came to national prominence as a football player. In 1911, tiny Carlisle upset Harvard 18-15, with Thorpe scoring all of Carlisle's points on four field goals and a touchdown. The following year against Army, he ran 92 yards for a touchdown, only to have the score nullified because of a penalty. On the next play, he ran 97 yards for a touchdown. Thorpe was chosen as an All-American halfback in both 1911 and 1912. An all-around athlete, he earned varsity letters in 11 different sports, and even won the 1912 intercollegiate ballroom dancing championship. He so excelled at track and field that he was chosen to represent the United States at the 1912 Olympics.

In Stockholm, Thorpe began by winning the pentathlon. The next day, while the other pentathletes were recuperating, Thorpe was back on the field taking fourth place in the high jump. He also finished seventh in the long jump. Finally, he took part in the decathlon, which was spread over three days because of the large number of entrants. Although he had never before competed in a decathlon, and had never thrown a javelin until two months earlier, he won easily. His performance was so impressive that it would have earned him a silver medal in the *1948* Olympics.

Besides his gold medals, Thorpe was awarded a jewel-encrusted chalice by Czar Nicholas of Russia, in honor of his victory in the decathlon, and a bronze bust of King Gustav V of Sweden for winning the pentathlon. When Gustav handed Jim the bust, he said, "Sir, you are the greatest athlete in the world." To which Thorpe replied shyly, "Thanks, King."

Back in the United States, Jim Thorpe had become a national hero. Honored with a ticker tape parade down Broadway in New York City, Jim marveled at the experience. "I heard people yelling my name—and I couldn't realize how one fellow could have so many friends," he recalled.

But in January 1913, Thorpe received a hard blow. It was revealed that in 1909 and 1910 he had earned $25 a week playing minor league baseball in North Carolina. Thus, by the strictest definition of the word, he had been a professional athlete and therefore ineligible to compete in the Olympics. Thorpe wrote a letter to James E. Sullivan, chairman of the Amateur Athletic Union, admitting what he had done but asking for leniency.

"I hope I will be partly excused by the fact that I was simply an Indian schoolboy and did not know all about such things," he wrote. "In fact, I did not know that I was doing wrong because I was doing what I knew several other college men had done except that they did not use their own names . . .

"I have received offers amounting to thousands of dollars since my victories last summer, but I have turned them all down because I did not care to make money from my athletic skill . . . I hope the Amateur Athletic Union and the people will not be too hard in judging me."

The "people" were not hard in judging Jim Thorpe, and generally rallied to his side. The A.A.U., on the other hand, was very hard in judging him. He was publicly vilified and his name was stricken from all record books. The American Olympic Committee issued a formal apology to the International Olympic Committee, which asked for the return of Thorpe's medals and trophies. The one bright spot in the whole unfortunate affair was that both Hugo Wieslander, who had finished second in the decathlon, and Ferdinand Bie, who had been runner-up in the pentathlon, refused to accept the trophies which the I.O.C. forwarded to them.

As soon as he had been declared a professional, Thorpe received offers to play major-league baseball. He signed with the New York Giants first, and played as well for the Cincinnati Reds until 1919. He also played professional football between 1915 and 1928. During the Depression, Jim Thorpe drifted from job to job. He was discovered wielding a pick and shovel at a construction site in Los Angeles, and when the 1932 Olympics came to town he was invited to sit with U.S. Vice-President Charles Curtis, who was also part-Indian. Such high spots were few, however. He worked as an extra in Hollywood, mostly playing Indian chiefs, gave lectures, joined the Merchant Marine in 1945, and took a job as a bouncer in 1949.

In February 1950, a poll of sportswriters taken by the Associated Press voted Thorpe the greatest athlete of the first half of the century. The following year *Jim Thorpe—All-American,* a film based on his life and starring Burt Lancaster, was released. Yet two months later, when Jim was hospitalized with cancer of the lip, he was admitted as a charity case because he had no money. He had sold the film rights to his life to MGM in 1931 for $1500. When MGM sold the rights to Warner Bros., Thorpe thought he would be paid again, but he had failed to read the fine print. He died of a heart attack in Lomita, California on March 28, 1953. Thorpe was buried in Mauch Chunk, Pennsylvania, a small town which agreed to change its name to Jim Thorpe in return for the right to have his body.

The movement to reinstate Jim Thorpe's records and trophies began in 1943, but met with no success during his lifetime. "Rules are like steam rollers," he once wrote. "There is nothing they won't do to flatten the man who stands in their way." It is interesting to note that Avery Brundage, who was President of the International Olympic Committee from 1952 to 1972, and who did nothing to help Jim Thorpe's cause, also took part in the 1912 pentathlon and decathlon, placing sixth in the former and failing to finish the latter. Not until October 13, 1982, did the I.O.C. finally lift the ban against Thorpe and allow his name to be returned to the record books. On January 18, 1983, his gold medals were presented to his children.

**1920 Antwerp** C: 23, N: 12, D: 8.20-21. WR: 7751 (James Thorpe)

| | | | 100 M | LJ | SP | HJ | 400 M | 110 H | DISC | PV | JAV | 1500 M | TOTAL POINTS | 1985 TABLES |
|---|---|---|---|---|---|---|---|---|---|---|---|---|---|---|
| 1. | Helge Lövland | NOR | 12.0 | 6.28 | 11.19 | 1.65 | 54.8 | 16.2 | 37.34 | 3.20 | 48.01 | 4:48.4 | 6803 | 5803 |
| 2. | Brutus Hamilton | USA | 11.4 | 6.325 | 11.61 | 1.60 | 55.0 | 17.3 | 36.14 | 3.30 | 48.08 | 4:57.8 | 6771 | 5739 |
| 3. | Bertil Ohlson | SWE | 12.0 | 6.435 | 11.07 | 1.65 | 55.0 | 17.0 | 37.78 | 3.30 | 39.89 | 4:50.6 | 6580 | 5639 |
| 4. | Gösta Holmér | SWE | 11.8 | 5.92 | 11.06 | 1.70 | 56.5 | 16.6 | 34.82 | 3.20 | 47.62 | 5:01.6 | 6532 | 5551 |
| 5. | Everett Nilsson | SWE | 12.2 | 5.67 | 11.39 | 1.75 | 55.7 | 20.0 | 34.77 | 3.40 | 49.28 | 4:45.6 | 6433 | 5371 |
| 6. | Woldemar Wickholm | FIN | 11.6 | 6.12 | 11.44 | 1.60 | 52.8 | 16.8 | 32.30 | 3.00 | 42.76 | 4:45.6 | 6405 | 5630 |
| 7. | Gene Vidal | USA | 12.0 | 6.13 | 11.16 | 1.65 | 55.7 | 17.1 | 37.30 | 3.30 | 35.32 | 4:46.6 | 6358 | 5489 |
| 8. | Axel-Erik Gyllenstolpe | SWE | 12.0 | 6.35 | 10.69 | 1.65 | 55.4 | 16.8 | 33.65 | 2.90 | 49.31 | 5:01.4 | 6331 | 5482 |

Lövland passed Hamilton in the last event. His margin of victory was the equivalent of six seconds in the 1500 meters. In 1952 Brutus Hamilton served as coach of the U.S. Olympic track team.

**1924 Paris** C: 36, N: 22, D: 7.11-12. WR: 7482 (Aleksandr Klumberg-Kolmpere)

| | | | 100 M | LJ | SP | HJ | 400 M | 110 H | DISC | PV | JAV | 1500 M | TOTAL POINTS | | 1985 TABLES |
|---|---|---|---|---|---|---|---|---|---|---|---|---|---|---|---|
| 1. | Harold Osborn | USA | 11.2 | 6.92 | 11.435 | 1.97 | 53.2 | 16.0 | 34.51 | 3.50 | 46.69 | 4:50.0 | 7711 | WR | 6476 |
| 2. | Emerson Norton | USA | 11.6 | 6.92 | 13.04 | 1.92 | 53.0 | 16.6 | 33.11 | 3.80 | 42.09 | 5:38.0 | 7351 | | 6117 |
| 3. | Aleksandr Klumberg-Kolmpere | EST | 11.6 | 6.96 | 12.27 | 1.75 | 54.4 | 17.6 | 36.795 | 3.30 | 57.70 | 5:16.0 | 7329 | | 6056 |
| 4. | Anton Huusari | FIN | 12.0 | 6.16 | 12.025 | 1.70 | 53.4 | 16.6 | 33.15 | 3.20 | 53.65 | 4:37.2 | 7005 | | 5952 |
| 5. | Edward Sutherland | SAF | 11.6 | 6.67 | 10.865 | 1.80 | 56.0 | 16.6 | 30.83 | 3.30 | 51.015 | 5:19.0 | 6794 | | 5928 |
| 6. | Ernst Gerspach | SWI | 11.4 | 6.46 | 10.355 | 1.70 | 53.4 | 16.8 | 33.91 | 3.40 | 44.82 | 5:08.2 | 6744 | | 5765 |
| 7. | Helge Jansson | SWE | 11.6 | 6.32 | 12.22 | 1.83 | 54.2 | 17.8 | 32.08 | 3.10 | 47.20 | 5:22.0 | 6656 | | 5633 |
| 8. | Harry Frieda | USA | 11.6 | 5.94 | 11.01 | 1.60 | 54.0 | 19.0 | 35.095 | 3.40 | 54.90 | 5:02.6 | 6618 | | 5541 |

Norton led after eight events, but fell off badly in the javelin, and barely finished the 1500 meters. Osborn, having already won a gold medal in the high jump on July 7, achieved a unique double.

**1928 Amsterdam** C: 38, N: 19, D: 8.3-4. WR: 7995 (Paavo Yrjölä)

| | | | 100 M | LJ | SP | HJ | 400 M | 110 H | DISC | PV | JAV | 1500 M | TOTAL POINTS | | 1985 TABLES |
|---|---|---|---|---|---|---|---|---|---|---|---|---|---|---|---|
| 1. | Paavo Yrjölä | FIN | 11.8 | 6.72 | 14.11 | 1.87 | 53.2 | 16.6 | 42.09 | 3.30 | 55.70 | 4:44.0 | 8053 | WR | 6607 |
| 2. | Akilles Järvinen | FIN | 11.2 | 6.87 | 13.64 | 1.75 | 51.4 | 15.6 | 36.95 | 3.30 | 55.58 | 4:52.4 | 7932 | | 6645 |
| 3. | John Kenneth Doherty | USA | 11.6 | 6.61 | 11.85 | 1.80 | 52.0 | 15.8 | 38.72 | 3.30 | 56.56 | 4:54.0 | 7707 | | 6428 |
| 4. | James Stewart | USA | 11.2 | 6.61 | 13.04 | 1.87 | 52.8 | 16.6 | 40.90 | 3.30 | 48.07 | 5:17.0 | 7624 | | 6310 |
| 5. | Thomas Churchill | USA | 11.6 | 6.32 | 12.28 | 1.70 | 52.2 | 16.8 | 38.19 | 3.60 | 50.93 | 4:55.0 | 7417 | | 6165 |
| 6. | Helge Jansson | SWE | 11.4 | 6.85 | 13.59 | 1.87 | 53.2 | 16.6 | 36.83 | 3.30 | 41.73 | 5:27.0 | 7286 | | 6111 |
| 7. | Ludwig Vesely | AUT | 11.6 | 6.73 | 12.58 | 1.70 | 52.2 | 15.8 | 35.46 | 3.20 | 47.44 | 4:47.0 | 7274 | | 6224 |
| 8. | Albert Andersson | SWE | 12.0 | 6.30 | 12.19 | 1.75 | 54.0 | 15.8 | 36.64 | 3.30 | 45.81 | 4:44.2 | 7109 | | 6031 |

Yrjölä lived on a farm and trained alone, using equipment he fashioned himself out of local lumber.

**1932 Los Angeles** C. 14, N: 9, D: 8.5-6. WR: 8255 (Akilles Järvinen)

| | | | 100 M | LJ | SP | HJ | 400 M | 110 H | DISC | PV | JAV | 1500 M | TOTAL POINTS | | 1985 TABLES |
|---|---|---|---|---|---|---|---|---|---|---|---|---|---|---|---|
| 1. | James Bausch | USA | 11.7 | 6.95 | 15.32 | 1.70 | 54.2 | 16.2 | 44.58 | 4.00 | 61.91 | 5:17.0 | 8462 | WR | 6735 |
| 2. | Akilles Järvinen | FIN | 11.1 | 7.00 | 13.11 | 1.75 | 50.6 | 15.7 | 36.80 | 3.60 | 61.00 | 4:47.0 | 8292 | | 6879 |
| 3. | Wolrad Eberle | GER | 11.4 | 6.77 | 13.22 | 1.65 | 50.8 | 16.7 | 41.34 | 3.50 | 57.49 | 4:34.4 | 8031 | | 6661 |
| 4. | Wilson Charles | USA | 11.2 | 7.24 | 12.56 | 1.85 | 51.2 | 16.2 | 38.71 | 3.40 | 47.72 | 4:39.8 | 7985 | | 6716 |
| 5. | Hans-Heinrich Sievert | GER | 11.4 | 6.97 | 14.50 | 1.78 | 53.6 | 16.1 | 44.54 | 3.20 | 53.91 | 5:18.0 | 7941 | | 6515 |
| 6. | Paavo Yrjölä | FIN | 11.8 | 6.59 | 13.68 | 1.75 | 52.6 | 17.0 | 40.77 | 3.10 | 56.12 | 4:37.4 | 7688 | | 6385 |
| 7. | Clyde Clifford Coffman | USA | 11.3 | 6.77 | 11.86 | 1.70 | 51.8 | 17.8 | 34.40 | 4.00 | 48.88 | 4:48.0 | 7534 | | 6265 |
| 8. | Robert Tisdall | IRL | 11.3 | 6.60 | 12.58 | 1.65 | 49.0 | 15.5 | 33.31 | 3.20 | 45.26 | 4:34.4 | 7327 | | 6398 |

Akilles Järvinen, older brother of javelin gold medalist Matti Järvinen, was the heavy favorite to win the decathlon. He did in fact break his own world record, but he was only able to place second. The upset winner was ex-University of Kansas football star Jim Bausch, whose entire decathlon career lasted less than 16 months. Fifth after the first day's events, Bausch took advantage of splendid performances in the discus and pole vault to build an insurmountable lead. Although Järvinen did win his second silver medal, had the 1985 tables been in use at the time he would have finished first in both 1928 and 1932.

**1936 Berlin** C: 28, N: 17, D: 8.7-8. WR: 7880 (Glenn Morris)

| | | | 100 M | LJ | SP | HJ | 400 M | 110 H | DISC | PV | JAV | 1500 M | TOTAL POINTS | | 1985 TABLES |
|---|---|---|---|---|---|---|---|---|---|---|---|---|---|---|---|
| 1. | Glenn Morris | USA | 11.1 | 6.97 | 14.10 | 1.85 | 49.4 | 14.9 | 43.02 | 3.50 | 54.52 | 4:33.2 | 7900 | WR | 7254 |
| 2. | Robert Clark | USA | 10.9 | 7.62 | 12.68 | 1.80 | 50.0 | 15.7 | 39.39 | 3.70 | 51.12 | 4:44.4 | 7601 | | 7063 |
| 3. | Jack Parker | USA | 11.4 | 7.35 | 13.52 | 1.80 | 53.3 | 15.0 | 39.11 | 3.50 | 56.46 | 5:07.8 | 7275 | | 6760 |
| 4. | Erwin Huber | GER | 11.5 | 6.89 | 12.70 | 1.70 | 52.3 | 15.8 | 35.46 | 3.80 | 56.45 | 4:35.2 | 7087 | | 6588 |
| 5. | Reindert Brasser | HOL | 11.6 | 6.69 | 13.49 | 1.90 | 51.5 | 16.2 | 39.45 | 3.40 | 55.75 | 5:06.0 | 7046 | | 6570 |
| 6. | Armin Guhl | SWI | 11.3 | 7.04 | 12.30 | 1.80 | 52.3 | 15.6 | 40.97 | 3.30 | 51.20 | 4:49.2 | 7033 | | 6618 |
| 7. | Olle Bexell | SWE | 11.6 | 6.68 | 13.54 | 1.75 | 54.9 | 16.0 | 38.83 | 3.70 | 57.07 | 4:40.4 | 7024 | | 6558 |
| 8. | Helmut Bonnet | GER | 11.6 | 6.66 | 13.45 | 1.75 | 53.7 | 16.2 | 39.16 | 3.60 | 58.15 | 4:54.0 | 6939 | | 6489 |

A new set of tables were instituted in 1934, which accounts for the lower scores. Just before the running of the 1500 meters, it was announced that Glenn Morris, a 24-year-old automobile salesman from Colorado, needed to run 4:32.0 in order to set a new world record. This was 16 seconds faster than Morris, who was only competing in his third decathlon, had ever run. When he crossed the finish line in 4:33.2, there was much disappointment. But then it was discovered that an error had been made in computing his score, and that he had in fact broken the record after all. Morris's victory earned him an invitation to Hollywood, where he appeared in two bad films, *Tarzan's Revenge* and *Hold That Co-Ed*.

**1948 London** C: 35, N: 20, D: 8.5-6. WR: 7900 (Glenn Morris)

| | | 100 M | LJ | SP | HJ | 400 M | 110 H | DISC | PV | JAV | 1500 M | TOTAL POINTS | 1985 TABLES |
|---|---|---|---|---|---|---|---|---|---|---|---|---|---|
| 1. Robert Mathias | USA | 11.2 | 6.615 | 13.04 | 1.86 | 51.7 | 15.7 | 44.00 | 3.50 | 50.32 | 5:11.0 | 7139 | 6628 |
| 2. Ignace Heinrich | FRA | 11.3 | 6.895 | 12.85 | 1.86 | 51.6 | 15.6 | 40.94 | 3.20 | 40.98 | 4:43.8 | 6974 | 6559 |
| 3. Floyd Simmons | USA | 11.2 | 6.725 | 12.80 | 1.86 | 51.9 | 15.2 | 32.73 | 3.40 | 51.99 | 4:58.0 | 6950 | 6531 |
| 4. C. Enrique Kistenmacher | ARG | 10.9 | 7.08 | 12.67 | 1.70 | 50.5 | 16.3 | 41.11 | 3.20 | 45.06 | 4:49.6 | 6929 | 6542 |
| 5. Erik Peter Andersson | SWE | 11.6 | 6.595 | 12.66 | 1.75 | 52.0 | 15.9 | 36.07 | 3.60 | 51.04 | 4:34.0 | 6877 | 6486 |
| 6. Peter Mullins | AUS | 11.2 | 6.645 | 12.75 | 1.83 | 53.2 | 15.2 | 33.94 | 3.40 | 51.32 | 5:17.6 | 6739 | 6334 |
| 7. Per Axel Eriksson | SWE | 11.9 | 6.80 | 11.96 | 1.80 | 52.5 | 16.2 | 34.91 | 3.30 | 56.70 | 4:35.8 | 6731 | 6382 |
| 8. Irving Mondschein | USA | 11.3 | 6.810 | 12.74 | 1.83 | 51.6 | 16.6 | 38.74 | 3.50 | 36.81 | 4:49.8 | 6715 | 6357 |

Bob Mathias was only 17 years old when his track coach at Tulare High School in Central California suggested that he take up the decathlon. Mathias learned quickly, and less than three months later he had qualified for the U.S. Olympic team and was on his way to London. His inexperience led to one setback in the shot put. After lofting the 16-pound ball over 45 feet, he was surprised when an official raised the red flag that indicated a foul. The perplexed teenager was informed that he had left the throwing circle from the front, which was against the rules. Nobody had ever told Mathias about this particular rule, but there was nothing he could do about it. His best throw after that was only 42 feet 9¼ inches.

The next event was the high jump, and here Mathias almost met disaster, as he missed twice at the mediocre height of 5 feet 9 inches. Faced with virtual elimination, he ignored formal technique and threw himself over the bar with a jump that was clumsy, but successful. He went on to clear 6 feet 1¼ inches. After the first day's events, Mathias was in third place behind Enrique Kistenmacher and Ignace Heinrich.

The second day's competition began at 10 a.m., but bad weather and general confusion caused it to drag on into the night. The discus was Bob Mathias' specialty, and he connected with a good throw of about 145 feet. Unfortunately, the marker for his throw got knocked over. After a half hour search in the rain and gloom for the hole left by his discus, officials gave him credit for 144 feet 4 inches. Mathias' older brother, Gene, who had gained access to the field by flashing a bogus press pass, raced up to Bob and urged him to press the search. But Bob felt guilty about the delay he was causing, and so accepted his fate. The throw was good enough, however, to put him into first place. Because there were no infield lights, before the javelin throw began, cars were driven into the stadium and their headlights were turned on to illuminate the foul line. By the time he staggered across the finish line at the end of the 1500 meters, it was 10:35 p.m. and Bob Mathias had become the youngest winner of a men's track and field event in the history of the Olympics. In the dressing room afterward, the exhausted teenager was asked how he intended to celebrate his victory. He replied, "I'll start shaving, I guess." In fact, he was so drained that he went right to sleep and had to be awakened to take part in the victory ceremony the next day.

Back home in Tulare, a small farming town of 12,000, the entire population had been on pins and needles waiting for the results from London. When the news came over the radio that Mathias had won, the town went wild. Factory whistles and fire sirens blared for 45 minutes, businesses closed down, and a spontaneous three-hour parade of cars clogged the downtown area and the nearby interstate highway. The local telegraph office had to stay open into the night as friends stood in line to send their congratulations to the hometown boy who had made good. When Mathias finally returned three weeks later, the excitement was so great that the airplane he was on had to delay its landing until the crowd could be cleared from around the runway.

**1952 Helsinki** C: 28, N: 16, D: 7.25-26. WR: 7825 (Robert Mathias)

| | | 100 M | LJ | SP | HJ | 400 M | 110 H | DISC | PV | JAV | 1500 M | TOTAL POINTS | | 1985 TABLES |
|---|---|---|---|---|---|---|---|---|---|---|---|---|---|---|
| 1. Robert Mathias | USA | 10.9 | 6.98 | 15.30 | 1.90 | 50.2 | 14.7 | 46.89 | 4.00 | 59.21 | 4:50.8 | 7887 | WR | 7580 |
| 2. Milton Campbell | USA | 10.7 | 6.74 | 13.89 | 1.85 | 50.9 | 14.5 | 40.50 | 3.30 | 54.54 | 5:07.2 | 6975 | | 6948 |
| 3. Floyd Simmons | USA | 11.5 | 7.06 | 13.18 | 1.92 | 51.1 | 15.0 | 37.77 | 3.60 | 54.69 | 4:53.4 | 6788 | | 6903 |
| 4. Vladimir Volkov | SOV | 11.4 | 7.09 | 12.62 | 1.75 | 51.2 | 15.8 | 38.04 | 3.80 | 56.68 | 4:33.2 | 6674 | | 6868 |
| 5. Josef Hipp | GER | 11.4 | 6.85 | 13.26 | 1.75 | 51.3 | 16.1 | 45.84 | 3.50 | 54.14 | 4:57.2 | 6449 | | 6705 |
| 6. Göran Widenfeldt | SWE | 11.4 | 6.76 | 11.61 | 1.94 | 51.3 | 16.1 | 39.53 | 3.50 | 49.36 | 4:38.6 | 6388 | | 6661 |
| 7. Kjell Tånnander | SWE | 11.4 | 6.90 | 12.97 | 1.85 | 52.6 | 15.8 | 39.30 | 3.50 | 52.79 | 4:57.2 | 6308 | | 6607 |
| 8. Friedel Schirmer | GER | 11.7 | 6.37 | 12.69 | 1.80 | 50.5 | 16.0 | 37.01 | 3.50 | 54.00 | 4:47.6 | 6118 | | 6464 |

World records for this period get very confusing, since yet another new set of tables was devised in 1950 and revised a few days before the Olympics. It made little difference to Bob Mathias, who won by the largest margin in Olympic history. His only problem developed in the javelin, when his first two throws fell far short of his capabilities. Up in the stands, Jack Weiershauser, Mathias' track coach at Stanford, convinced a bunch of American rooters to chant, "Oh Bob, hey you, don't forget to follow through." Bob got the message, and followed through with a throw of 194 feet 3 inches.

**1956 Melbourne** C: 15, N: 8, D: 11.29-30. WR: 7985 (Rafer Johnson)

| | | 100 M | LJ | SP | HJ | 400 M | 110 H | DISC | PV | JAV | 1500 M | TOTAL POINTS | | 1985 TABLES |
|---|---|---|---|---|---|---|---|---|---|---|---|---|---|---|
| 1. Milton Campbell | USA | 10.8 | 7.33 | 14.76 | 1.89 | 48.8 | 14.0 | 44.98 | 3.40 | 57.08 | 4:50.6 | 7937 | OR | 7565 |
| 2. Rafer Johnson | USA | 10.9 | 7.34 | 14.48 | 1.83 | 49.3 | 15.1 | 42.17 | 3.90 | 60.27 | 4:54.2 | 7587 | | 7422 |
| 3. Vassily Kuznyetsov | SOV | 11.2 | 7.04 | 14.49 | 1.75 | 50.2 | 14.9 | 44.33 | 3.95 | 65.13 | 4:53.8 | 7465 | | 7330 |
| 4. Uno Palu | SOV | 11.5 | 6.65 | 13.39 | 1.89 | 50.8 | 15.4 | 40.38 | 3.60 | 61.59 | 4:35.6 | 6930 | | 7028 |
| 5. Martin Lauer | GER | 11.1 | 6.83 | 12.86 | 1.83 | 48.2 | 14.7 | 39.38 | 3.10 | 50.66 | 4:43.8 | 6853 | | 6910 |
| 6. Walter Meier | GDR | 11.3 | 6.80 | 12.99 | 1.86 | 49.3 | 16.1 | 37.59 | 3.70 | 47.97 | 4:20.6 | 6773 | | 6910 |
| 7. Torbjörn Lassenius | FIN | 11.8 | 6.62 | 13.45 | 1.70 | 50.8 | 15.9 | 41.36 | 3.80 | 59.33 | 4:36.2 | 6565 | | 6782 |
| 8. Yang Chuan-kwang | TAI | 11.2 | 6.90 | 11.56 | 1.95 | 51.3 | 15.0 | 33.92 | 3.30 | 57.88 | 5:00.8 | 6521 | | 6697 |

World record holder Rafer Johnson was hampered by injury, but even in full health he probably couldn't have beaten Milt Campbell in Melbourne. Campbell, a 22-year-old sailor from Plainfield, New Jersey, had hoped to qualify for the U.S. Olympic team as a hurdler, but only finished fourth in the final tryouts. "I was stunned," he said. "But then God seemed to reach into my heart and tell me he didn't want me to compete in the hurdles, but in the decathlon."

In the Olympics he led from start to finish. A time of 14.0 in the hurdles earned him 1124 points and assured him the victory. He lost his shot at a world record when he could do no better than 11 feet 1¾ inches in the pole vault, almost 20 inches below his best performance. But, paced and urged on by 11th-place finisher Ian Bruce of Australia, he ran the 1500 meters in 4:50.6 to gain the Olympic record.

**1960 Rome** C: 30, N: 20, D: 9.5-6. WR: 8683 (Rafer Johnson)

| | | 100 M | LJ | SP | HJ | 400 M | 110 H | DISC | PV | JAV | 1500 M | TOTAL POINTS | | 1985 TABLES |
|---|---|---|---|---|---|---|---|---|---|---|---|---|---|---|
| 1. Rafer Johnson | USA | 10.9 | 7.35 | 15.82 | 1.85 | 48.3 | 15.3 | 48.49 | 4.10 | 69.76 | 4:49.7 | 8392 | OR | 7901 |
| 2. Yang Chuan-kwang | TAI | 10.7 | 7.46 | 13.33 | 1.90 | 48.1 | 14.6 | 39.83 | 4.30 | 68.22 | 4:48.5 | 8334 | | 7820 |
| 3. Vassily Kuznyetsov | SOV | 11.1 | 6.96 | 14.46 | 1.75 | 50.2 | 15.0 | 50.52 | 3.90 | 71.20 | 4:53.8 | 7809 | | 7527 |
| 4. Yuri Kutyenko | SOV | 11.4 | 6.93 | 13.97 | 1.80 | 51.1 | 15.6 | 45.63 | 4.20 | 71.44 | 4:44.2 | 7567 | | 7401 |
| 5. Evert Kamerbeek | HOL | 11.3 | 7.21 | 13.76 | 1.80 | 51.1 | 14.9 | 44.31 | 3.80 | 57.49 | 4:43.6 | 7236 | | 7212 |
| 6. Franco Sar | ITA | 11.4 | 6.69 | 13.89 | 1.80 | 51.3 | 14.7 | 49.58 | 3.80 | 55.74 | 4:49.2 | 7195 | | 7140 |
| 7. Markus Kahma | FIN | 11.5 | 6.93 | 14.55 | 1.75 | 50.5 | 15.9 | 44.93 | 3.60 | 60.50 | 4:22.8 | 7112 | | 7161 |
| 8. Klaus Grogorenz | GDR | 10.8 | 6.93 | 12.42 | 1.73 | 48.0 | 16.9 | 40.12 | 3.70 | 60.81 | 4:27.0 | 7032 | | 7078 |

Rafer Johnson and Yang Chuan-kwang grew up in very different circumstances, yet they came together as fellow students at U.C.L.A., and then as friendly rivals at the Rome Olympics. Johnson was born in Hillsboro, Texas. In 1945, when Rafer was 11, his family moved to the small town of Kingsburg, California, less than 25 miles from Bob Mathias' hometown of Tulare. There they lived in a boxcar for a year until things started looking up. Yang was a member of the Takasago ethnic group, which inhabited the island of Formosa long before the Chinese arrived. He visited the United States for a couple of months and decided to stay. At U.C.L.A. Johnson and Yang, now known as C.K. Yang, trained together, but in Rome Johnson represented the United States and Yang, Taiwan.

The first day of competition, interrupted by an 80-minute thunder shower, didn't end until 11 p.m. After five events, Johnson led Yang by only 55 points. They were back on the track again at 9 a.m. for the sixth event, the 110-meter hurdles, which was one of Johnson's specialties. But the poorly rested American hit the first hurdle badly and took 15.3 seconds to reach the finish line, far slower than his best of 13.9. He made up the lost points in the pole vault by achieving a personal record of 13 feet 5½ inches.

With only the 1500 meters left to run, Johnson led Yang by 67 points. This meant that if Yang, whose best time for the distance was 4:36.0, could beat Johnson by ten seconds, he would become Taiwan's first-ever gold medalist. Johnson's 1500 best was the 4:54.2 that he had recorded at the 1956 Olympics. The two very tired rivals took off at 9:15 p.m., with Yang in front and Johnson dogging him the entire way. Yang tried desperately to pull away in the final lap, but Johnson stuck close and earned the gold medal by finishing only six yards behind, in a career best of 4:49.7. Johnson and Yang wobbled on for a few yards and then fell against each other for support, while Italian fans chanted, "Give them both the gold medal." Yang was the first Taiwanese athlete to gain an Olympic medal.

Rafer Johnson later became an actor and television sportscaster before becoming involved in politics. On June 5, 1968, Johnson was walking through the kitchen in the Ambassador Hotel in Los Angeles with Robert Kennedy, when the Presidential candidate was shot and killed. In 1984, it was Johnson who was chosen to light the torch at the Opening Ceremonies of the Los Angeles Olympics.

**1964 Tokyo** C: 22, N: 14, D: 10.19-20. WR: 8089 (Yang Chuan-kwang)

| | | 100 M | LJ | SP | HJ | 400 M | 110 H | DISC | PV | JAV | 1500 M | TOTAL POINTS | 1985 TABLES |
|---|---|---|---|---|---|---|---|---|---|---|---|---|---|
| 1. Willi Holdorf | GER | 10.7 | 7.00 | 14.95 | 1.84 | 48.2 | 15.0 | 46.05 | 4.20 | 57.37 | 4:34.3 | 7887 | 7726 |
| 2. Rein Aun | SOV | 10.9 | 7.22 | 13.82 | 1.93 | 48.8 | 15.9 | 44.19 | 4.20 | 59.06 | 4:22.3 | 7842 | 7677 |
| 3. Hans-Joachim Walde | GER | 11.0 | 7.21 | 14.45 | 1.96 | 49.5 | 15.3 | 43.15 | 4.10 | 62.90 | 4:37.0 | 7809 | 7666 |
| 4. Paul Herman | USA | 11.2 | 6.97 | 13.89 | 1.87 | 49.2 | 15.2 | 44.15 | 4.35 | 63.35 | 4:25.4 | 7787 | 7651 |
| 5. Yang Chuan-kwang | TAI | 11.0 | 6.80 | 13.23 | 1.81 | 49.0 | 14.7 | 39.59 | 4.60 | 68.15 | 4:48.4 | 7650 | 7539 |
| 6. Horst Beyer | GER | 11.2 | 7.02 | 14.32 | 1.90 | 49.8 | 15.2 | 45.17 | 3.80 | 58.17 | 4:23.6 | 7647 | 7488 |
| 7. Vassily Kuznyetsov | SOV | 10.9 | 6.98 | 14.06 | 1.70 | 49.5 | 14.9 | 43.81 | 4.40 | 67.87 | 5:02.5 | 7569 | 7454 |
| 8. Mikhail Storozhenko | SOV | 11.0 | 7.22 | 16.37 | 1.84 | 53.6 | 15.0 | 43.20 | 4.00 | 59.10 | 5:00.7 | 7464 | 7307 |

On April 28, 1963, Yang Chuan-kwang had severely disrupted the scoring of the decathlon by pole-vaulting 15 feet 10½ inches, which put him above the maximum height accounted for by the charts then in use. The new charts, known as the 1962 tables, were not released until August, 1964. They tended to equalize the ten events, and were particularly damaging to Yang, whose pole-vault best was suddenly worth 501 points less than it had been. Using the old tables, Yang's best total of 1964 had been 485 points higher than anyone else's. With the new tables, he trailed both Holdorf and Beyer.

At the end of the first day in Tokyo, Holdorf led with 4090 points. He was followed by Walde with 4074 and Aun with 4067. After nine events, Holdorf led Walde by 60 points and Aun by 137. The 1500, however, was one

of Aun's strong points. To win, Holdorf had to finish within 17 seconds of Aun, but his best time of the year was more than 30 seconds slower than Aun's. Holdorf's coach, Friedel Schirmer, purposely misled him, telling Holdorf that he had only 12 seconds to spare.

Aun finished in 4:22.3, while Holdorf pushed himself as hard as he could. Forty yards from the finish, he began to weave and appeared on the verge of collapse. But he struggled on until the end, crossing the finish with a time of 4:34.3—exactly 12 seconds slower than Aun. Then he collapsed. Aun tried to congratulate his fallen conqueror, but Holdorf was too dazed to comprehend. Eventually he was revived and shown the scoreboard that displayed his winning score.

**1968 Mexico City** C: 33, N: 20, D: 10.18-19. WR: 8319 (Kurt Bendlin)

|   |   |   | 100 M | LJ | SP | HJ | 400 M | 110 H | DISC | PV | JAV | 1500 M | TOTAL POINTS |   | 1985 TABLES |
|---|---|---|-------|-----|------|------|-------|-------|-------|------|-------|--------|--------------|---|-------------|
| 1. | William Toomey | USA | 10.4 | 7.87 | 13.75 | 1.95 | 45.6 | 14.9 | 43.68 | 4.20 | 62.80 | 4:57.1 | 8193 | OR | 8158 |
| 2. | Hans-Joachim Walde | GER | 10.9 | 7.64 | 15.13 | 2.01 | 49.0 | 14.8 | 43.54 | 4.30 | 71.62 | 4:58.5 | 8111 |   | 8120 |
| 3. | Kurt Bendlin | GER | 10.7 | 7.56 | 14.74 | 1.80 | 48.3 | 15.0 | 46.78 | 4.60 | 75.42 | 5:09.8 | 8064 |   | 8096 |
| 4. | Nikolai Avilov | SOV | 10.9 | 7.64 | 13.41 | 2.07 | 49.9 | 14.5 | 46.64 | 4.10 | 60.12 | 5:00.8 | 7909 |   | 7884 |
| 5. | Joachim Kirst | GDR | 10.5 | 7.61 | 16.43 | 1.98 | 50.2 | 15.6 | 46.89 | 4.15 | 57.02 | 5:20.1 | 7861 |   | 7791 |
| 6. | Thomas Waddell | USA | 11.3 | 7.47 | 14.45 | 2.01 | 51.2 | 15.3 | 43.73 | 4.50 | 63.70 | 5:04.5 | 7719 |   | 7694 |
| 7. | Rick Sloan | USA | 11.2 | 6.72 | 14.07 | 2.10 | 51.0 | 15.5 | 45.58 | 4.85 | 49.90 | 4:44.0 | 7692 |   | 7553 |
| 8. | Steen Smidt-Jensen | DEN | 10.9 | 7.17 | 13.03 | 1.95 | 50.2 | 14.9 | 41.07 | 4.85 | 46.80 | 4:41.3 | 7648 |   | 7507 |

"Behind every good decathlon man, there's a good doctor," Bill Toomey once declared, and he was an expert on the subject. Aside from the usual array of illnesses and pulled muscles, Toomey had suffered through hepatitis, mononucleosis, and a shattered kneecap on his way to an Olympic gold medal. A 29-year-old English teacher from California, Toomey faced his moment of truth in the pole vault. Leading after seven events, he suddenly found himself one miss away from elimination at the opening height of 11 feet 9¼ inches.

"I had done so many things wrong on my first two jumps," he later recalled, "I couldn't figure out how to correct anything. . . . Everything was closing in on me—the people in that huge arena, the people watching on televi-

sion back home, my whole life, all those years of working and waiting for this moment. If I missed, it would be like dying." Fortunately, Toomey didn't miss. "All the technique I had learned and practiced . . . had been forgotten in the fear and frustration I felt. I was like a beginner, clumsy and uncertain. But I had made that jump on sheer determination. I'm not even sure I needed my pole."

Toomey went on to clear 13 feet 9½ inches, his best ever in competition, and then managed to stave off the competition through the final two events.

Tom Waddell, who placed sixth, became a gay activist who organized the Gay Games to highlight the accomplishments of homosexual athletes. He died of AIDS on July 11, 1987, at the age of 49.

**1972 Munich** C: 33, N: 19, D: 9.7-8. WR: 8417 (William Toomey)

|   |   |   | 100 M | LJ | SP | HJ | 400 M | 110 H | DISC | PV | JAV | 1500 M | TOTAL POINTS |   | 1985 TABLES |
|---|---|---|-------|-----|------|------|-------|-------|-------|------|-------|--------|--------------|---|-------------|
| 1. | Nikolai Avilov | SOV | 11.00 | 7.68 | 14.36 | 2.12 | 48.45 | 14.31 | 46.98 | 4.55 | 61.66 | 4:22.8 | 8454 | WR | 8466 |
| 2. | Leonid Litvinenko | SOV | 11.13 | 6.81 | 14.18 | 1.89 | 48.40 | 15.03 | 47.84 | 4.40 | 58.94 | 4:05.9 | 8035 |   | 7970 |
| 3. | Ryszard Katus | POL | 10.89 | 7.09 | 14.39 | 1.92 | 49.11 | 14.41 | 43.00 | 4.50 | 59.96 | 4:31.9 | 7984 |   | 7936 |
| 4. | Jefferson Bennett | USA | 10.73 | 7.26 | 12.82 | 1.86 | 46.25 | 15.58 | 36.58 | 4.80 | 57.48 | 4:12.2 | 7974 |   | 7920 |
| 5. | Stefan Schreyer | GDR | 10.82 | 7.44 | 15.02 | 1.92 | 49.51 | 15.00 | 45.08 | 4.40 | 50.42 | 4:48.2 | 7950 |   | 7907 |
| 6. | Freddy Herbrand | BEL | 11.00 | 7.30 | 13.91 | 2.04 | 49.78 | 14.87 | 47.12 | 4.40 | 50.42 | 4:27.1 | 7947 |   | 7897 |
| 7. | Steen Smidt-Jensen | DEN | 11.07 | 6.95 | 13.35 | 2.01 | 50.10 | 14.65 | 44.80 | 4.80 | 55.24 | 4:24.7 | 7947 |   | 7908 |
| 8. | Tadeusz Janczenko | POL | 10.64 | 7.28 | 14.45 | 2.04 | 49.10 | 16.89 | 45.26 | 4.50 | 63.80 | 5:01.5 | 7861 |   | 7791 |

The 1972 decathlon looked to be a wide-open affair, with at least four men considered leading contenders: two-time European champion Joachim Kirst of East Germany, Jeff Bannister of the United States, veteran Lennart Hedmark of Sweden, and the fast-improving Ukrainian Jew, Nikolai Avilov of the U.S.S.R. Unfortunately, Hedmark, troubled by an injured foot, was forced to withdraw after three events. After five events, Kirst was in first place with 4364 points, followed by Avilov with 4345, and Tadeusz Janczenko and Ryszard Skowronek of Poland with 4266 and 4240, respectively.

The turning point came shortly after 9 a.m. the following morning, in the second heat of the high hurdles. Kirst hit the first hurdle, fell heavily at the next and pulled a muscle. Bannister, in the next lane, was thrown off stride, fell after the fourth hurdle, pushed over the next

one, and was disqualified. Janczenko, forced to add the fallen Bannister to the obstacles in his path, was slowed down so much that it may have cost him a medal. Meanwhile, Avilov, unaware of the chaos behind him, finished first with a time of 14.31. In addition to all this, Skowronek had pulled a muscle in his heat and had to retire in the middle of the next event.

Avilov, who suddenly found himself with a huge lead, finished the day brilliantly, eventually recording personal records in seven of the ten decathlon events, and equaling his best in an eighth. A strong finish in the 1500 earned him a world record. Fellow Ukrainian Leonid Litvinenko ran an even better 1500-meter race, enabling him to move from eighth place after nine events to second after ten.

The first to congratulate Avilov was the man whose

record he had broken, Bill Toomey, on hand as a television commentator. Both Toomey and Avilov married Olympic medalists. Toomey wed 1964 long-jump champion Mary Rand, and Avilov married Valentina Kozyr, winner of the bronze medal in the 1968 high jump.

**1976 Montreal** C: 28, N: 17, D: 7.29-30. WR: 8538 (Bruce Jenner)

| | | 100 M | LJ | SP | HJ | 400 M | 110 H | DISC | PV | JAV | 1500 M | TOTAL POINTS | | 1985 TABLES |
|---|---|---|---|---|---|---|---|---|---|---|---|---|---|---|
| 1. Bruce Jenner | USA | 10.94 | 7.22 | 15.35 | 2.03 | 47.51 | 14.84 | 50.04 | 4.80 | 68.52 | 4:12.6 | 8617 | WR | 8634 |
| 2. Guido Kratschmer | GER | 10.66 | 7.39 | 14.74 | 2.03 | 48.19 | 14.58 | 45.70 | 4.60 | 66.32 | 4:29.1 | 8411 | | 8416 |
| 3. Nikolai Avilov | SOV | 11.23 | 7.52 | 14.81 | 2.14 | 48.16 | 14.20 | 45.60 | 4.45 | 62.28 | 4:26.3 | 8369 | | 8403 |
| 4. Raimo Pihl | SWE | 10.93 | 6.99 | 15.55 | 2.00 | 47.97 | 15.81 | 44.30 | 4.40 | 77.34 | 4:28.8 | 8218 | | 8216 |
| 5. Ryszard Skowronek | POL | 11.02 | 7.26 | 13.74 | 1.91 | 47.91 | 14.75 | 45.34 | 4.80 | 62.22 | 4:29.9 | 8113 | | 8099 |
| 6. Siegfried Stark | GDR | 11.35 | 6.98 | 15.08 | 1.91 | 49.14 | 15.65 | 45.48 | 4.65 | 74.18 | 4:24.9 | 8048 | | 8051 |
| 7. Leonid Litvinenko | SOV | 11.12 | 6.92 | 14.20 | 1.91 | 48.44 | 14.71 | 46.26 | 4.60 | 53.66 | 4:11.4 | 8025 | | 7963 |
| 8. Lennart Hedmark | SWE | 11.36 | 7.09 | 15.00 | 1.91 | 49.80 | 14.79 | 46.42 | 4.30 | 78.58 | 4:44.2 | 7974 | | 8002 |

The 1976 decathlon was looked forward to as a classic duel between Nikolai Avilov, the defending champion and holder of the automatically timed world record, and Bruce Jenner, tenth in Munich, but now the holder of the official, albeit hand-timed, world record. From the very first event, however, it was Jenner who was in control. Hoping to be within 200 points of the leaders, Kratschmer and Avilov, at the end of the first day, Jenner found himself only 35 points behind Kratschmer and 17 points behind Avilov. He went to bed completely confident of victory since the second day's events were his best.

By the time eight events had been completed, Jenner's victory was assured, and he began to cry as he realized that his goal was about to be achieved, and that his athletic career was about to come to an end. Encouraged by his wife, Chrystie, who had supported the young couple with her job as an air hostess, Jenner had totally immersed himself in the world of the decathlon. At night, he dreamed about the different events so often that Chrystie could tell which one he was unconsciously practicing. As Jenner rested on the infield in Montreal, his reverie was broken by Leonid Litvinenko, who patted him on the shoulder and said, "Bruce, you going to be Olympic champion."

"Thanks," said Jenner.

Litvinenko stared at Jenner for a few seconds, and then asked, "Bruce, you going to be a millionaire?"

Jenner just laughed.

Unlike most decathletes, who dread the 1500 meters, Jenner actually looked forward to it, and ran his final race full of strength, leaning forward as he crossed the finish line. The North American crowd roared with delight, but eventually Bruce made his way through the adulation, found Chrystie, and told her, "Congratulations. We did it together." When he left the stadium, he didn't even bother to take his vaulting poles with him, because he knew he wouldn't need them where he was going.

Bruce Jenner did become rich and famous, just as Litvinenko had wondered, but his marriage didn't last. Since the media had constantly portrayed Bruce and Chrystie as the All-American couple, their divorce was a difficult one. Jenner later married Linda Thompson, former girlfriend of Elvis Presley.

**1980 Moscow** C: 21, N: 12, D: 7.25-26. WR: 8649 (Guido Kratschmer)

| | | 100 M | LJ | SP | HJ | 400 M | 110 H | DISC | PV | JAV | 1500 M | TOTAL POINTS | 1985 TABLES |
|---|---|---|---|---|---|---|---|---|---|---|---|---|---|
| 1. Francis "Daley" Thompson | GBR | 10.62 | 8.00 | 15.18 | 2.08 | 48.01 | 14.47 | 42.24 | 4.70 | 64.16 | 4:39.9 | 8495 | 8522 |
| 2. Yuri Kutsenko | SOV | 11.19 | 7.74 | 14.50 | 2.08 | 48.67 | 15.04 | 39.86 | 4.90 | 68.08 | 4:22.6 | 8331 | 8369 |
| 3. Sergei Zhelanov | SOV | 11.40 | 7.60 | 14.17 | 2.18 | 49.27 | 14.83 | 42.80 | 4.60 | 57.30 | 4:27.5 | 8315 | 8135 |
| 4. Georg Werthner | AUT | 11.44 | 7.27 | 13.45 | 2.03 | 49.26 | 15.08 | 38.14 | 4.85 | 73.66 | 4:23.4 | 8050 | 8084 |
| 5. Josef Zeilbauer | AUT | 11.29 | 7.14 | 15.31 | 2.03 | 50.91 | 14.80 | 44.00 | 4.50 | 64.86 | 4:30.6 | 8007 | 7989 |
| 6. Dariusz Ludwig | POL | 11.35 | 7.51 | 13.32 | 2.08 | 50.55 | 15.38 | 45.82 | 4.80 | 58.38 | 4:29.7 | 7978 | 7972 |
| 7. Atanas Andonov | BUL | 11.38 | 6.86 | 15.59 | 2.00 | 50.36 | 14.83 | 47.62 | 4.70 | 53.54 | 4:29.2 | 7927 | 7887 |
| 8. Steffen Grummt | GDR | 11.35 | 6.86 | 16.15 | 1.94 | 49.39 | 14.82 | 48.56 | 4.30 | 55.24 | 4:30.2 | 7892 | 7840 |

In Montreal Daley Thompson had been the youngest entrant in the decathlon, finishing 18th at the age of 18. Four years later this gregarious offspring of a Nigerian father and a Scottish mother was expected to face a tough battle for the gold medal against Guido Kratschmer of West Germany. When West Germany joined the Jimmy Carter boycott, Thompson broke training, so that he could compete against Kratschmer. He beat his rival in May, and set a world record of 8622 in the process. Kratschmer responded with another world record of 8649 in June, but he would have been hard-pressed to beat Thompson in Moscow.

At the Olympics, Thompson was not seriously challenged. His nearest rival, Valery Kachanov of the U.S.S.R., pulled a calf muscle during the pole vault and had to withdraw while in second place. Thompson's world record pace was thwarted by rain on the second day, but the Soviet fans, who had been none too friendly to foreign athletes, gave Thompson a standing ovation anyway when he finished the 1500 meters.

**1984 Los Angeles** C: 26, N: 18, D: 8.8-9. WR: 8798 (Jürgen Hingsen)

| | | 100 M | LJ | SP | HJ | 400 M | 110 H | DISC | PV | JAV | 1500 M | TOTAL POINTS | | 1985 TABLES |
|---|---|---|---|---|---|---|---|---|---|---|---|---|---|---|
| 1. Francis "Daley" Thompson | GBR | 10.44 | 8.01 | 15.72 | 2.03 | 46.97 | 14.33 | 46.56 | 5.00 | 65.24 | 4:35.00 | 8798 | EWR | 8847 |
| 2. Jürgen Hingsen | GER | 10.91 | 7.80 | 15.87 | 2.12 | 47.69 | 14.29 | 50.82 | 4.50 | 60.44 | 4:22.60 | 8673 | | 8695 |
| 3. Siegfried Wentz | GER | 10.99 | 7.11 | 15.87 | 2.09 | 47.78 | 14.35 | 46.60 | 4.50 | 67.68 | 4:33.96 | 8412 | | 8416 |
| 4. Guido Kratschmer | GER | 10.80 | 7.40 | 15.93 | 1.94 | 49.25 | 14.66 | 47.28 | 4.90 | 69.40 | 4:47.99 | 8326 | | 8357 |
| 5. William Motti | FRA | 11.28 | 7.45 | 14.42 | 2.06 | 48.13 | 14.71 | 50.92 | 4.50 | 63.76 | 4:35.15 | 8266 | | 8278 |
| 6. John Crist | USA | 11.33 | 6.98 | 14.05 | 2.06 | 48.45 | 15.01 | 46.18 | 4.80 | 61.88 | 4:23.78 | 8130 | | 8115 |
| 7. Jim Wooding | USA | 11.04 | 7.01 | 13.90 | 1.97 | 47.62 | 14.57 | 47.38 | 4.60 | 57.20 | 4:28.31 | 8091 | | 8054 |
| 8. David Steen | CAN | 11.20 | 7.41 | 12.57 | 2.03 | 48.09 | 15.39 | 44.04 | 4.80 | 56.92 | 4:17.70 | 8047 | | 8034 |

In 1982, Jürgen Hingsen entered the European championships as the world-record holder. Daley Thompson beat him. In 1983, Jürgen Hingsen entered the world championships as the world-record holder. Daley Thompson beat him. In 1984, Jürgen Hingsen entered the Olympics as the world-record holder. Guess what?

This time the crucial moment in the meet came in the seventh event, the discus throw. While Thompson was flubbing his first two attempts, Hingsen hit a strong 166 feet 9 inches. If the defending Olympic champion couldn't improve with his final attempt, Hingsen would take the lead for the first time. Thompson, who relished moments such as these, threw 152 feet 9 inches to pick up 100 points and put himself back in front. During the next event, the pole vault, Hingsen became ill, performed well below standard, and the rest of the contest was a mere formality. Except that Daley Thompson still had a shot at Hingsen's world record. He needed to run the 1500 meters in 4:34.98, much slower than his personal best. However, the irreverent champion exasperated the crowd by easing off at the tape and finishing in 4:35.00. He then took a victory lap wearing a sweat shirt which read on the front: "THANKS AMERICA FOR A GOOD GAMES AND A GREAT TIME." On the back was another message: "BUT WHAT ABOUT THE TV COVERAGE," a reference to the myopic nationalism displayed by the U.S. television network which covered the Games.

In 1986, the I.A.A.F. announced that close examination of the electric phototimer revealed that Thompson had actually completed the 110-meter hurdles in 14.33 seconds rather than 14.34 seconds. One more point was added to his Olympic total, and he was given a belated share of the world record despite himself.

**1988 Seoul** C: 39, N: 26, D: 9.28-29. WR: 8847 (Francis "Daley" Thompson)

| | | 100 M | LJ | SP | HJ | 400 M | 110 H | DISC | PV | JAV | 1500 M | TOTAL POINTS |
|---|---|---|---|---|---|---|---|---|---|---|---|---|
| 1. Christian Schenk | GDR | 11.25 | 7.43 | 15.48 | 2.27 | 48.90 | 15.13 | 49.28 | 4.70 | 61.32 | 4:28.95 | 8488 |
| 2. Torsten Voss | GDR | 10.87 | 7.45 | 14.97 | 1.97 | 47.71 | 14.46 | 44.36 | 5.10 | 61.76 | 4:33.02 | 8399 |
| 3. David Steen | CAN | 11.18 | 7.44 | 14.20 | 1.97 | 48.29 | 14.81 | 43.66 | 5.20 | 64.16 | 4:23.20 | 8328 |
| 4. Francis "Daley" Thompson | GBR | 10.62 | 7.38 | 15.02 | 2.03 | 49.06 | 14.72 | 44.80 | 4.90 | 64.04 | 4:45.11 | 8306 |
| 5. Christian Plaziat | FRA | 10.83 | 7.62 | 13.58 | 2.12 | 48.34 | 14.18 | 43.06 | 4.90 | 52.18 | 4:34.07 | 8272 |
| 6. Alain Blondel | FRA | 11.02 | 7.43 | 12.92 | 1.97 | 47.44 | 14.40 | 41.20 | 5.20 | 57.46 | 4:16.64 | 8268 |
| 7. Timothy Bright | USA | 11.18 | 7.05 | 14.12 | 2.06 | 49.34 | 14.39 | 41.68 | 5.70 | 61.60 | 4:51.20 | 8216 |
| 8. Robert de Wit | HOL | 11.05 | 6.95 | 15.34 | 2.00 | 48.21 | 14.36 | 41.32 | 4.80 | 63.00 | 4:25.86 | 8189 |

The competition began on a startling note when, in the first heat of the 100 meters, Jürgen Hingsen was disqualified for committing three false starts. Christian Schenk, a 6-foot 7-inch medical student from Rostock, moved into the lead when he high jumped 7 feet 5¼ inches, using the archaic straddle technique. At the end of the first day, Schenk was in first place with 4470 points, Plaziat was second at 4375, Thompson third at 4332, and Voss fourth at 4299. Schenk's lead shrank to 25 points after the pole vault, but when Plaziat blew his javelin throw, Schenk found himself a solid 62 points ahead of Voss and 78 ahead of Thompson. The 23-year-old Schenk, who had won only one previous decathlon, had no trouble maintaining his lead in the final event. Dave Steen, in only eighth place after nine events, ran a strong 1500 meters to snatch the bronze medal from Thompson.

# Discontinued Events

## 60 METERS

**1900 Paris** C: 10, N: 6, D: 7.15.
1. Alvin Kraenzlein     USA.     7.0     WR
2. John Walter Tewksbury     USA     7.1
3. Stanley Rowley     AUS     7.2
4. Edmund Minahan     USA     7.2

**1904 St. Louis** C: 15, N: 3, D: 8.29. WR: 7.0 (Alvin Kraenzlein)
1. Archie Hahn     USA     7.0     EWR
2. William Hogenson     USA     7.2
3. Fay Moulton     USA     7.2
4. Clyde Blair     USA     7.2
5. Meyer Prinstein     USA     —
6. Frank Castleman     USA     —

Hahn won the first of his three gold medals at the St. Louis Games.

## 5 MILES (8047 METERS)

**1906 Athens** C: 28, N: 12, D: 4.25. WR: 24:33.4 (Alfred Shrubb)
1. Henry Hawtrey     GBR     26:11.8
2. John Svanberg     SWE     26:19.4
3. Edward Dahl     SWE     26:26.2
4. George Bonhag     USA     —
5. Pericle Pagliani     ITA     —
6. George Blake     AUS     —

John Daly of Ireland finished third, but was disqualified for staggering in front of Dahl and impeding his progress.

**1908 London** C: 35, N: 14, D: 7.18. WR: 24:33.4 (Alfred Shrubb)
1. Emil Voigt     GBR     25:11.2
2. Edward Owen     GBR     25:24.0
3. John Svanberg     SWE     25:37.2
4. Charles Hefferon     SAF     25:44.0
5. Archie Robertson     GBR     26:13.0
6. Frederick Meadows     CAN     —
7. J. F. Fitzgerald     CAN     —
8. Frederick Bellars     USA     —

Voigt, a 5-foot 5-inch vegetarian from Manchester, sprinted away in the final lap and won by 50 yards.

## CROSS-COUNTRY, INDIVIDUAL

**1912 Stockholm** C: 46, N: 10, D: 7.15.
**(ca. 12,000 Meters)**
1. Johan "Hannes" Kolehmainen     FIN     45:11.6
2. Hjalmar Andersson     SWE     45:44.8
3. John Eke     SWE     46:37.6
4. Jalmari Eskola     FIN     46:54.8
5. Josef Ternström     SWE     47:07.1
6. Albin Stenroos     FIN     47:23.4
7. William Kyronen     FIN     47:32.0
8. Leonard Richardson     SAF     47:33.5

Hannes Kolehmainen won his third gold medal of the Stockholm Games, having already triumphed in the 5000 meters and 10,000 meters.

**1920 Antwerp** C: 42, N: 10, D: 8.23.
*(ca. 8000 Meters)*

| | | | |
|---|---|---|---|
| 1. | Paavo Nurmi | FIN | 27:15.0 |
| 2. | Erik Backman | SWE | 27:17.6 |
| 3. | Heikki Liimatainen | FIN | 27:37.4 |
| 4. | James Wilson | GBR | 27:45.2 |
| 5. | Frank Hegarty | GBR | 27:57.0 |
| 6. | Teudor Koskenniemi | FIN | 27:57.2 |
| 7. | Julien van Campenhout | BEL | 28:00.0 |
| 8. | Gaston Heuet | FRA | 28:10.0 |

Nurmi and Joseph Guillemot had split the 5000 and 10,000. The cross-country was to be the tie-breaker, but three kilometers from the finish Guillemot stepped in a hole, injured his ankle, and had to withdraw.

**1924 Paris** C: 38, N: 10, D: 7.12.
*(ca. 10,000 Meters)*

| | | | |
|---|---|---|---|
| 1. | Paavo Nurmi | FIN | 32:54.8 |
| 2. | Vilho "Ville" Ritola | FIN | 34:19.4 |
| 3. | Earl Johnson | USA | 35:21.0 |
| 4. | Ernest Harper | GBR | 35:45.4 |
| 5. | Henri Lauvaux | FRA | 36:44.8 |
| 6. | Arthur Studenroth | USA | 36:45.4 |
| 7. | Carlo Martinenghi | ITA | 37:01.0 |
| 8. | August Fager | USA | 37:40.6 |

This event proved to be an almost total disaster, which put an end to cross country races in the Olympics. Thirty-eight runners started off in the afternoon of one of the hottest days in Parisian history. Only fifteen finished. The course was unusually difficult, including stone paths that were covered in knee-high thistles and weeds. The race was also run too close to an energy plant that was belching out poisonous fumes. The first man to enter the stadium and cross the finish line was Paavo Nurmi. He appeared so fresh and untroubled that the spectators had no reason to suspect that anything was wrong. But as soon as the other runners started to arrive, the horrible situation began to unfold. One after another, strong athletes staggered onto the track. Aguilar of Spain collapsed, hit his head on a marker, and began bleeding. Sewell of Great Britain headed the wrong way. Pointed in the right direction, he collided with another runner. Both of them fell and failed to finish. Out on the roads there had been worse scenes of carnage, as various contestants were overcome by sunstroke and vomiting. Hours later, the Red Cross and Olympic officials were still searching the sides of the road for missing runners.

When the full extent of the tragedy became known, the remarkable performance of Paavo Nurmi was seen as even more impressive. Not only had the race taken place only two days after Nurmi had won the 1500 meters and the 5000 meters on the same day, but the very next day after the catastrophe, while most of the other cross-country runners were recuperating in bed or in the hospital, Nurmi was back again, winning another gold medal in the 3000 meters team race.

# 3000-METER TEAM RACE

**1912 Stockholm** T: 5, N: 5, D: 7.13.

| | | TEAM TOTALS | |
|---|---|---|---|
| 1. | USA | 9 | (1—Tel Berna 8:44.6, 3—Norman Taber 8:45.2, 5—George Bonhag 8:46.6) |
| 2. | SWE | 13 | (2—Thorild Ohlsson 8:44.6, 4—Ernst Wide 8:46.2, 7—Bror Fock 8:47.1) |
| 3. | GBR | 23 | (6—William Cottrill 8:46.8, 8—George Hutson 8:47.2, 9—Cyril Porter 8:48.0) |

Finland was eliminated in the first-round heat by the well-balanced U.S. team, despite the fact that Hannes Kolehmainen set a world record of 8:36.9.

**1920 Antwerp** T: 6, N: 6, D: 8.22.

| | | TEAM TOTALS | |
|---|---|---|---|
| 1. | USA | 10 | (1—Horace Brown 8:45.4, 3—Arlie Schardt, 6—Ivan Dresser) |
| 2. | GBR | 20 | (5—Charles Blewitt, 7—Albert Hill, 9—William Seagrove) |
| 3. | SWE | 24 | (2—Erik Backman, 13—Sven Lundgren, 15—Edvin Wide) |
| 4. | FRA | 30 | (4—Armand Burtin, Gaston Heuet, Edmond Brossard) |
| 5. | ITA | 34 | (11—Ernesto Ambrosini, Augusto Maccario, Carlo Speroni) |

For the team race, only the placings for the first three finishers from each country were counted. This explains why the team totals were less than the combined totals of the individual runners.

**1924 Paris** T: 9, N: 9, D: 7.13.

| | | TEAM TOTALS | |
|---|---|---|---|
| 1. | FIN | 8 | (1—Paavo Nurmi 8:32.0, 2—Vilho "Ville" Ritola 8:40.6, 5—Elias Katz 8:45.4) |
| 2. | GBR | 14 | (3—Bernard McDonald 8:44.0, 4—Harry Johnston, 7—George Webber) |
| 3. | USA | 25 | (6—Edward Kirby 8:53.0, 8—William Cox, 11—Willard Tibbets) |
| 4. | FRA | 31 | (9—Paul Bontemps, 10—Armand Burtin, 12—Léonard Mascaux) |

Paavo Nurmi, running his seventh race in six days, won his fifth gold medal.

# 3-MILE TEAM RACE (4828 METERS)

**1908 London** T: 6, N: 6, D: 7.15.

| | | TEAM TOTALS | |
|---|---|---|---|
| 1. | GBR | 6 | (1—Joseph Deakin 14:39.6, 2—Archie Robertson, 14:41.0, 3—Wilfred Coales 14:41.6) |
| 2. | USA | 19 | (4—John Eisele 14:41.8, 6—George Bonhag 15:05.0, 9—Herbert Trube 15:11.0) |
| 3. | FRA | 32 | (8—Louis de Fleurac 15:08.4, 11—Joseph Dreher 15:40.0, 13—Paul Lizandier 16:03.0) |

## 5000-METER TEAM RACE

**1900 Paris** T: 2, N: 3, D: 7.22.

|  |  | TEAM TOTALS |  |
|---|---|---|---|
| 1. | GBR/AUS | 26 | (1—Charles Bennett 15:20.0, 2—John Rimmer, 6—Sidney Robinson, 7—Alfred Tysoe, 10—Stanley Rowley AUS) |
| 2. | FRA | 29 | (3—Henri Deloge, 4—Gaston Ragueneau, 5—Jacques Chastanié, 8—André Castanet, 9—Michel Champoudry) |

## 4-MILE TEAM RACE (6437 METERS)

**1904 St. Louis** T: 2, N: 2, D: 9.3.

|  |  | TEAM TOTALS |  |
|---|---|---|---|
| 1. | New York A.C. | 27 | (1—Arthur Newton 21:17.8, 5—George Underwood, 6—Paul Pilgrim, 7—Howard Valentine, 8—David Munson) |
| 2. | Chicago A.A. | 28 | (2—James Lightbody, 3—William Frank Verner, 4—Lacey Hearn, 9—Albert Corey [FRA], 10—Sidney Hatch) |

## CROSS-COUNTRY TEAM RACE

**1912 Stockholm** T: 6, N: 6, D: 7.15.
*(ca. 12,000 Meters)*

|  |  | TEAM TOTALS |  |
|---|---|---|---|
| 1. | SWE | 10 | (2—Hjalmar Andersson 45:44.8, 3—John Eke 46:37.6, 5—Josef Ternström 47:07.1) |
| 2. | FIN | 11 | (1—Johan "Hannes" Kolehmainen 45:11.6, 4—Jalmari Eskola 46:54.8, 6—Albin Stenroos 47:23.4) |
| 3. | GBR | 49 | (15—Frederick Hibbins 49:18.2, 16—Ernest Glover 49:53.7, 18—Thomas Humphreys 50:28.0) |
| 4. | NOR | 61 | (19—Olav Hovdenak 50:40.8, 20—Parelius Finnerud 51:16.2, 22—Johannes Andersen 51:47.4) |
| 5. | DEN | 63 | (14—Lauritz Christiansen, 49:06.4, 23—Viggo Pedersen 53:00.8, 26—Carl Alfred Holmberg 54:24.9) |

**1920 Antwerp** T: 7, N: 7, D: 8.23.
*(ca. 8000 Meters)*

|  |  | TEAM TOTALS |  |
|---|---|---|---|
| 1. | FIN | 10 | (1—Paavo Nurmi 27:15.0, 3—Heikki Liimatainen 27:37.00, 6—Teudor Koskenniemi 27:57.2) |
| 2. | GBR | 21 | (4—James Wilson 27:45.2, 5—Frank Hegarty 27:57.0, 12—Arthur Nichols) |
| 3. | SWE | 23 | (2—Erik Backman 27:15.6, 10—Gustaf Mattsson 28:16.0, 11—Hilding Ekman 28:17.0) |

|  |  |  |  |
|---|---|---|---|
| 4. | USA | 36 | (9—Patrick Flynn 28:12.0, 15—Frederick Faller, 16—Max Bohland) |
| 5. | FRA | 40 | (8—Gaston Heuet 28:10.0, 17—Gustave Lauvaux, 21—Joseph Servella) |
| 6. | BEL | 48 | (7—Julien van Campenhout 28:00.0, 33—Henri Smets, 36—Aimée Proot) |
| 7. | DEN | 53 | — |

**1924 Paris** T: 7, N: 7, D: 7.12.
*(ca. 10,000 Meters)*

|  |  | TEAM TOTALS |  |
|---|---|---|---|
| 1. | FIN | 11 | (1—Paavo Nurmi 32:54.8, 2—Vilho "Ville" Ritola 34:19.4, 8—Heikki Liimatainen 38:12.0) |
| 2. | USA | 14 | (3—Earl Johnson 35:21.0, 5—Arthur Studenroth 36:45.44, 6—August Fager 37:40.2) |
| 3. | FRA | 20 | (4—Henri Lauvaux 36:44.8, 7—Gaston Heuet 37:52.0, 9—Maurice Norland 41:38.6) |

The same horrible race that was the individual cross-country also counted as the team race. In order for Finland to win, at least three men had to cross the finish line. Nurmi and Ritola finished easily, but Liimatainen, staggering along in the oppressive heat, halted 30 meters short of his goal. Delirious, he turned around and began staggering back the way he had come. The crowd shouted at him and he stopped. After standing for a while with his back to the finish line, he finally regained control of his senses, turned around, and walked across the finish. The British, Italian, Spanish, and Swedish teams failed to complete the course.

## 200-METER HURDLES

**1900 Paris** C: 8, N: 5, D: 7:16. WR: 23.6 (Alvin Kraenzlein)

| 1. | Alvin Kraenzlein | USA | 25.4 |
|---|---|---|---|
| 2. | Norman Pritchard | IND | 26.6 |
| 3. | John Walter Tewksbury | USA | — |
| 4. | Eugene Choisel | FRA | — |

Kraenzlein won his fourth gold medal of the Paris Games.

**1904 St. Louis** C: 5, N: 1, D: 9.1. WR: 23.6 (Alvin Kraenzlein)

| 1. | Harry Hillman | USA | 24.6 | OR |
|---|---|---|---|---|
| 2. | Frank Castleman | USA | 24.9 | |
| 3. | George Poage | USA | — | |
| 4. | George Varnell | USA | — | |
| 5. | Frederick Schule | USA | — | |

## 4000-METER STEEPLECHASE

**1900 Paris** C: 8, N: 5, D: 7.16.

| 1. | John Thomas Rimmer | GBR | 12:58.4 |
|---|---|---|---|
| 2. | Charles Bennett | GBR | 12:58.6 |
| 3. | Sidney Robinson | GBR | 12:58.8 |
| 4. | Jacques Chastanié | FRA | — |

5. George Orton    CAN    —
6. Franz Duhne    GER    —
AC: Alexander Grant (CAN), Thaddeus McClain (USA)

## 1500-METER WALK

**1906 Athens** C: 9, N: 6, D: 4:30.
1. George Bonhag    USA    7:12.6
2. Donald Linden    CAN    7:19.8
3. Konstantin Spetsiotis    GRE    7:24.0
4. Georgios Saridakis    GRE    —
5. Charilaos Vasilakos    GRE    —
6. Alexandros Kouris    GRE    —
7. György Sztantics    HUN    —
DISQ: Richard Wilkinson (GBR), Eugen Spiegler (AUT)

Wilkinson and Spiegler finished first and second, but were disqualified for illegal technique. This left Bonhag with first place, although he too was disqualified by two of the four judges. The deciding vote in favor of Bonhag was cast by the president of the jury, Prince George. Bonhag had actually never entered a walking race before. Disappointed by his showings in the 5-mile run and the 1500-meter run in which he had finished fourth and sixth, Bonhag entered the 1500-meter walk hoping to make up for his previous failures. Vasilakos, who placed fifth, had finished second in the 1896 marathon.

## 3000-METER WALK

**1906 Athens** C: 8, N: 5, D: 5.1.
1. György Sztantics    HUN    15:13.2
2. Hermann Müller    GER    15:20.0
3. Georgios Saridakis    GRE    15:33.0
4. Pandelis Ektoros    GRE    —
5. I. Panagoulopoulos    GRE    —
DISQ: Richard Wilkinson (GBR), Eugen Spiegler (AUT), Konstantin Spetsiotis (GRE)

The day after the controversial 1500-meter walk, a second contest was held at 3000 meters. Once again Wilkinson and Spiegler moved to the front. Fifty meters from the finish, they both began to run and were again disqualified.

**1908–1912** not held

**1920 Antwerp** C: 22, N: 12, D: 8.21. WR: 12:53.8 (Gunnar Rasmussen)
1. Ugo Frigerio    ITA    13:14.2    OR
2. George Parker    AUS    13:20.6
3. Richard Remer    USA    13:23.6
4. Cecil McMaster    SAF    13:25.2
5. Thomas Maroney    USA    13:26.8
6. Charles Dowson    GBR    13:30.0
7. William Hehir    GBR    —
8. William Roelker    USA    —

Ugo Frigerio was such a colorful character that his flamboyance often obscured the fact that he was a superb athlete who combined great speed with perfect style. While other walkers became nervous or annoyed when a judge got down on his hands and knees to scrutinize their style Frigerio seemed to enjoy the attention, and always made it a point to thank the judge when he was finished. Frigerio also enjoyed the attentions of the crowd, sometimes taking the time to exchange remarks with spectators, and even leading cheers for himself.

Just before the beginning of the 3000-meter walk, Frigerio approached the conductor of the band in the middle of the field and handed him several pages of sheet music which he requested to be played during the course of the race. Accompanied by the proper background music, Frigerio moved quickly to the front and led the entire race pausing only once toward the end to admonish the band for not playing at the correct tempo. He won easily by 20 meters.

## 3500-METER WALK

**1908 London** C: 24, N: 9, D: 7.14.
1. George Larner    GBR    14:55.0
2. Ernest Webb    GBR    15:07.4
3. Harry Kerr    AUS/NZE    15:43.4
4. George Goulding    CAN    15:49.8
5. Edward Rowland    AUS/NZE    16:07.0
6. Charles Westergaard    DEN    17:21.8
7. Einar Rothman    SWE    17:50.0

Larner, a 33-year-old Brighton policeman, came out of retirement to take part in the Olympics. He won by 45 yards.

## 10,000-METER WALK

**1912 Stockholm** C: 22, N: 11, D: 7.11. WR: 45:15.6 (Ernest Webb)
1. George Goulding    CAN    46:28.4
2. Ernest Webb    GBR    46:50.4
3. Fernando Altimani    ITA    47:37.6
4. Aage Rasmussen    DEN    48:00.0

George Goulding, an English-born Canadian, had competed in the 1908 Olympics as both a walker and a runner, placing fourth in the 3500-meter walk and 22nd in the marathon. In 1912 he kept up such a rapid pace in the 10,000-meter walk that three of the ten finalists dropped out and another three were disqualified for lifting. After his victory, the laconic Canadian sent a telegram to his wife which read simply, "Won—George." Ernest Webb, who earned his third Olympic silver medal, was 40 years old.

**1920 Antwerp** C: 23, N: 13, D: 8.18. WR: 45:26.4 (Gunnar Rasmussen)
1. Ugo Frigerio     ITA    48:06.2
2. Joseph Pearman     USA    49:40.8 e
3. Charles Gunn     GBR    49:44.4 e
4. Cecil McMaster     SAF    50:02.8 e
5. William Hehir     GBR    50:13.0 e
6. Thomas Maroney     USA    50:20.6 e
7. Joseph Seghers.     BEL    —
8. Albert Doyen     BEL    —

Frigerio, as boisterous as ever, won by 250 meters to gain the first of his three gold medals.

**1924 Paris** C: 23, N: 13, D: 7:13. WR: 45:26.4 (Gunnar Rasmussen)
1. Ugo Frigerio     ITA    47:49.0
2. George Goodwin     GBR    48:37.9
3. Cecil McMaster     SAF    49:08.0
4. Donato Pavesi     ITA    49:17.0
5. Arthur Tell Schwab     SWI    49:50.0
6. Ernest Clarke     GBR    49:59.2 e
7. Armando Valente     ITA    —
8. Luigi Besatra     ITA    —

Frigerio's final gold medal was won by 200 meters.

**1928–1936** not held

**1948 London** C: 19, N: 10, D: 8.7. WR: 42:39.6 (Verner Hardmo)
1. John Mikaelsson     SWE    45:13.2
2. Ingemar Johansson     SWE    45:43.8
3. Fritz Schwab     SWI    46:00.2
4. Charles Morris     GBR    46:04.0
5. Harry Churcher     GBR    46:28.0
6. Emile Maggi     FRA    47:02.8
7. Richard West     GBR    —
8. Giuseppe Dordoni     ITA    —

Mikaelsson set an Olympic record of 45:03.0 in the first round. The final saw the disqualification of the great Verner Hardmo, who set 29 ratified and unratified world records between 1943 and 1945, at distances ranging from 3000 meters to 10 miles.

**1952 Helsinki** C: 23, N: 12, D: 7.27. WR: 42:39.6 (Verner Hardmo)
1. John Mikaelsson     SWE    45:02.8    OR
2. Fritz Schwab     SWI    45:41.0
3. Bruno Junk     SOV    45:41.0
4. Louis Chevalier     FRA    45:50.4
5. George Coleman     GBR    46:06.8
6. Yvan Yarmysch     SOV    46:07.0
7. Emile Maggi     FRA    46:08.0
8. Bruno Fait     ITA    46:25.6

Mikaelsson was 38 years old when he won his second gold medal. Silver medalist Fritz Schwab was the son of Arthur Schwab, who won the 50-kilometer silver medal in 1936. Both Schwab and Junk began running 30 yards from the finish, making the judges, who had disqualified seven men in the heats and final, look foolish. The contro-

versies which resulted from this race led Olympic officials to drop the 10,000 meters event and replace it with a 20,000 meters contest in 1956.

## 10-MILE WALK (16,093 METERS)

**1908 London** C: 25, N: 8, D: 7.17. WR: 1:14:45.0 (J. W. Raby)
1. George Larner     GBR    1:15:57.4
2. Ernest Webb     GBR    1:17:31.0
3. Edward Spencer     GBR    1:21:20.2
4. Frank Carter     GBR    1:21:20.2
5. Ernest Larner     GBR    1:24:26.2
DNF: William Palmer (GBR), Richard Harrison (GBR), Harry Kerr (NZE)

Larner broke the 11-year-old world's amateur record of 1:17:38.4 in winning his second gold medal in four days.

## STANDING HIGH JUMP

**1900 Paris** C: 6, N: 3, D: 7.16. WR: 1.63, 5-4¼ (Raymond Ewry)

|  |  | FT.- | |  |
|---|---|---|---|---|
|  |  | M | IN. | |
| 1. Raymond Ewry | USA | 1.65 | 5-5 | WR |
| 2. Irving Baxter | USA | 1.525 | 5-0 | |
| 3. Lewis Sheldon | USA | 1.50 | 4-11 | |

Ray Ewry won eight Olympic gold medals in 1900, 1904, and 1908, and added two more in the Intercalated Games of 1906. Yet he is almost unknown today because his unprecedented feats were performed in events that are no longer held. Born on October 18, 1873, in Lafayette, Indiana, Ewry contracted polio as a small boy. Confined to a wheelchair, it was thought that he might be paralyzed for life. However he began exercising on his own, and not only regained the use of his legs, but eventually grew up to be a superb athlete who specialized in the standing jumps. On July 16, 1900, Ewry won three gold medals in Paris, sweeping the standing high jump, the standing long jump, and the standing triple jump. He repeated his sweep in 1904. With the triple jump eliminated from the Games, he had to settle for double victories in 1906 and 1908. The standing jumps were dropped from the Olympics after 1912. Ewry also held the amateur record for the backward standing long jump—9 feet 3 inches. He died on September 27, 1937, at the age of 63.

**1904 St. Louis** C: 4, N: 1, D: 8.31. WR: 1.65, 5-5 (Raymond Ewry)

|  |  | FT.- | |
|---|---|---|---|
|  |  | M | IN. |
| 1. Raymond Ewry | USA | 1.60 | 5-3 |
| 2. Joseph Stadler | USA | 1.45 | 4-9 |
| 3. Lawson Robertson | USA | 1.45 | 4-9 |
| 4. John Biller | USA | 1.42 | 4-8 |

Joseph Stadler was the first black athlete to win an Olympic medal in a field event. He was awarded second place after a jump-off.

**1906 Athens** C: 10, N: 6, D: 5.1. WR: 1.65, 5-5 (Raymond Ewry)

| | | M | FT.-IN. |
|---|---|---|---|
| 1. Raymond Ewry | USA | 1.56 | 5-1¼ |
| 2. Léon Dupont | BEL | 1.40 | 4-7 |
| 2. Lawson Robertson | USA | 1.40 | 4-7 |
| 2. Martin Sheridan | USA | 1.40 | 4-7 |
| 5. Lajos Gönczy | HUN | 1.35 | 4-5 |
| 6. Constantin Tsiklitiras | GRE | 1.30 | 4-3¼ |
| 7. Themistoklis Diakidis | GRE | 1.25 | 4-1¼ |
| 7. Paul Weinstein | GER | 1.25 | 4-1¼ |

**1908 London** C: 22, N: 11, D: 7.23. WR: 1.65, 5-5 (Raymond Ewry)

| | | M | FT.-IN. |
|---|---|---|---|
| 1. Raymond Ewry | USA | 1.575 | 5-2 |
| 2. John Biller | USA | 1.55 | 5-1 |
| 2. Constantin Tsiklitiras | GRE | 1.55 | 5-1 |
| 4. F. Leroy Holmes | USA | 1.525 | 5-0 |
| 5. Platt Adams | USA | 1.47 | 4-10 |
| 5. Georges "Géo" André | FRA | 1.47 | 4-10 |
| 5. Alfred Motté | FRA | 1.47 | 4-10 |

**1912 Stockholm** C: 16, N: 8, D: 7.13. WR: 1.65, 5-5 (Raymond Ewry)

| | | M | FT.-IN. |
|---|---|---|---|
| 1. Platt Adams | USA | 1.63 | 5-4¼ |
| 2. Benjamin Adams | USA | 1.60 | 5-3 |
| 3. Constantin Tsiklitiras | GRE | 1.55 | 5-1 |
| 4. Richard Byrd | USA | 1.50 | 4-11 |
| 4. Leo Goehring | USA | 1.50 | 4-11 |
| 4. Evald Möller | SWE | 1.50 | 4-11 |

Platt Adams was 27 years old. His brother Ben was 22. In 1980, Rune Almen of Sweden cleared 6 feet 2¾ inches in the standing high jump to set the current record in the event.

## STANDING LONG JUMP

**1900 Paris** C: 7, N: 4, D: 7.16.

| | | M | FT.-IN. |
|---|---|---|---|
| 1. Raymond Ewry | USA | 3.21 | 10-6¼ |
| 2. Irving Baxter | USA | 3.135 | 10-3¼ |
| 3. Emile Torcheboeuf | FRA | 3.03 | 9-11¼ |
| 4. Lewis Sheldon | USA | 3.02 | 9-10¾ |

**1904 St. Louis** C: 4, N: 1, D: 8.29.

| | | M | FT.-IN. | |
|---|---|---|---|---|
| 1. Raymond Ewry | USA | 3.476 | 11-4⅞ | WR |
| 2. Charles King | USA | 3.28 | 10-9 | |
| 3. John Biller | USA | 3.26 | 10-8¼ | |
| 4. Henry Field | USA | 3.19 | 10-5½ | |

**1906 Athens** C: 30, N: 10, D: 4.27.

| | | M | FT.-IN. |
|---|---|---|---|
| 1. Raymond Ewry | USA | 3.30 | 10-10 |
| 2. Martin Sheridan | USA | 3.095 | 10-1¾ |
| 3. Lawson Robertson | USA | 3.05 | 10-0 |
| 4. Léon Dupont | BEL | 2.975 | 9-9 |
| 5. Axel Ljung | SWE | 2.955 | 9-8¼ |
| 6. Istzán Somodi | HUN | 2.86 | 9-4½ |
| 7. Constantin Tsiklitiras | GRE | 2.84 | 9-3¾ |
| 8. Henri Jardin | FRA | 2.83 | 9-3¼ |
| 8. Herbert Kerrigan | USA | 2.83 | 9-3¼ |

**1908 London** C: 25, N: 11, D: 7.20.

| | | M | FT.-IN. |
|---|---|---|---|
| 1. Raymond Ewry | USA | 3.335 | 10-11¼ |
| 2. Constantin Tsiklitiras | GRE | 3.235 | 10-7¼ |
| 3. Martin Sheridan | USA | 3.23 | 10-7 |
| 4. John Biller | USA | 3.215 | 10-6½ |
| 5. Raghar Ekberg | SWE | 3.195 | 10-5¾ |
| 6. Platt Adams | USA | 3.11 | 10-2½ |
| 6. F. LeRoy Holmes | USA | 3.11 | 10-2½ |

**1912 Stockholm** C: 19, N: 8, D: 7.8.

| | | M | FT.-IN. |
|---|---|---|---|
| 1. Constantin Tsiklitiras | GRE | 3.37 | 11-0¾ |
| 2. Platt Adams | USA | 3.36 | 11-0¼ |
| 3. Benjamin Adams | USA | 3.28 | 10-9 |
| 4. Gustaf Malmsten | SWE | 3.20 | 10-6 |
| 5. Leo Goehring | USA | 3.14 | 10-3½ |
| 6. Evald Möller | SWE | 3.14 | 10-3½ |
| 7. András Baronyi | HUN | 3.13 | 10-3¼ |
| 8. Richard Byrd | USA | 3.12 | 10-2¾ |

In 1962 Johann Evandt of Norway performed a standing long jump of 11 feet 11¾ inches. The claims of professional jumpers are difficult to substantiate. Joe Darby of Great Britain was said to have jumped 12 feet 1½ inches on May 28, 1890, and W. Barker was reputed to have leaped 12 feet 6½ inches in May 1904.

## STANDING TRIPLE JUMP

**1900 Paris** C: 10, N: 4, D: 7.16.

| | | M | FT.-IN. |
|---|---|---|---|
| 1. Raymond Ewry | USA | 10.58 | 34-8½ |
| 2. Irving Baxter | USA | 9.95 | 32-7¾ |
| 3. Robert Garrett | USA | 9.50 | 31-2 |
| 4. Lewis Sheldon | USA | 9.45 | 31-0 |

**1904 St. Louis** C: 4, N: 1, D: 9.3.

| | | M | FT.-IN. |
|---|---|---|---|
| 1. Raymond Ewry | USA | 10.54 | 34-7¼ |
| 2. Charles King | USA | 10.16 | 33-4 |
| 3. Joseph Stadler | USA | 9.60 | 31-6 |
| 4. Garrett Serviss | USA | 9.53 | 31-3¼ |

## STONE THROW
(6.40 kg—14.08 lbs.)

**1906 Athens** C: 15, N: 8, D: 4.27.

|   |   | M | FT.-IN. |
|---|---|---|---|
| 1. | Nicolaos Georgantas | GRE | 19.925 | 65-4½ |
| 2. | Martin Sheridan | USA | 19.035 | 62-5½ |
| 3. | Michel Dorizas | GRE | 18.585 | 60-11¾ |
| 4. | Eric Lemming | SWE | 18.21 | 59-9 |

The American favorite, James Mitchell, was unable to compete because he had suffered a dislocated shoulder when the ship carrying the U.S. team to Europe was hit by a large wave.

## SHOT PUT (BOTH HANDS)

**1912 Stockholm** C: 7, N: 4, D: 7.11.

|   |   |   | M | TWO HANDS | FT.-IN. |
|---|---|---|---|---|---|
| 1. | Ralph Rose | USA | 27.70 | (15.23 + 12.47) | 90-10½ |
| 2. | Patrick McDonald | USA | 27.53 | (15.08 + 12.45) | 90-4 |
| 3. | Elmer Niklander | FIN | 27.14 | (14.71 + 12.43) | 89-0½ |
| 4. | Lawrence Whitney | USA | 24.09 | (13.48 + 10.61) | 79-0½ |
| 5. | Einar Nilsson | SWE | 23.37 | (12.52 + 10.85) | 76-8¼ |
| 6. | Paavo Aho | FIN | 23.30 | (12.72 + 10.58) | 76-5½ |
| 7. | Megerdich Megherian | TUR | 19.78 | (10.85 + 8.93) | 64-10¾ |

The current world record for this event is 121 feet 6¼ inches, set by Al Feuerbach on August 24, 1974. He put 70 feet 1¾ inches with his right hand and 51 feet 5 inches with his left.

## 56-POUND WEIGHT THROW
(25.4 kg)

**1904 St. Louis** C: 6, N: 2, D: 9.1.

|   |   |   | M | FT.-IN. |
|---|---|---|---|---|
| 1. | Etienne Desmarteau | CAN | 10.46 | 34-4 |
| 2. | John Flanagan | USA | 10.16 | 33-4 |
| 3. | James Mitchel | USA | 10.13 | 33-3 |
| 4. | Charles Henneman | USA | 9.18 | 30-1½ |
| 5. | Charles Chadwick | USA | — | — |
| 6. | Ralph Rose | USA | 8.53 | 28-0 e |

Refused a leave of absence from his job as a Montreal policeman to compete in the St. Louis Games, Étienne Desmarteau went anyway and was fired. When it was learned that he had won a gold medal, his dismissal notice was conveniently lost. Unfortunately, Desmarteau, who was the first individual Olympic champion to represent Canada, died of typhoid the following year at the age of 32. A park was named in his honor.

**1906–1912** not held

**1920 Antwerp** C: 6, N: 4, D: 8.21. WR: 12.36, 40-6¾ (Matthew McGrath)

|   |   |   | M | FT.-IN. |   |
|---|---|---|---|---|---|
| 1. | Patrick McDonald | USA | 11.265 | 36-11½ | OR |
| 2. | Patrick Ryan | USA | 10.965 | 35-11½ |   |
| 3. | Carl Johan Lind | SWE | 10.25 | 33-7½ |   |
| 4. | Archie McDiarmid | CAN | 10.12 | 33-2½ |   |
| 5. | Malcolm Svensson | SWE | 9.45 | 31-0 |   |
| 6. | Petter Pettersson | FIN | 9.37 | 30-9 |   |

McDonald is the oldest person ever to win an Olympic track and field gold medal. He was 42 years and 26 days old.

## DISCUS (GREEK-STYLE)

**1906 Athens** C: 21, N: 9, D: 5.1.

|   |   |   | M | FT.-IN. |
|---|---|---|---|---|
| 1. | Verner Järvinen | FIN | 35.17 | 115-4½ |
| 2. | Nicolaos Georgantas | GRE | 32.80 | 107-7 |
| 3. | István Mudin | HUN | 31.91 | 104-8½ |
| 4. | Martin Sheridan | USA | — | — |

Contestants threw the discus from a pedestal that sloped forward, and they were required to follow a restricted set of movements. The discus had to be released from a standing position, with no spinning allowed. Verner Järvinen had four sons, three of whom competed in the 1932 Olympics.

**1908 London** C: 24, N: 9, D: 7.18.

|   |   |   | M | FT.-IN. |   |
|---|---|---|---|---|---|
| 1. | Martin Sheridan | USA | 38.00 | 124-8 | OR |
| 2. | Marquis Horr | USA | 37.33 | 122-5½ |   |
| 3. | Verner Järvinen | FIN | 36.48 | 119-8¼ |   |
| 4. | Arthur Dearborn | USA | 35.65 | 116-11½ |   |
| 5. | Michel Dorizas | GRE | 33.35 | 109-4½ |   |
| 6. | Nicolaos Georgantas | GRE | 33.20 | 108-11¼ |   |
| 7. | István Mudin | HUN | 33.11 | 108-7½ |   |
| 8. | W. G. Burroughs | USA | 32.73 | 107-4¾ |   |

## DISCUS (BOTH HANDS)

**1912 Stockholm** C: 20, N: 6, D: 7.13.

|   |   |   | M | TWO HANDS | FT-IN. |
|---|---|---|---|---|---|
| 1. | Armas Taipale | FIN | 82.86 | (44.68 + 38.18) | 271-10 |
| 2. | Elmer Niklander | FIN | 77.96 | (40.28 + 37.68) | 255-9 |
| 3. | Emil Magnusson | SWE | 77.37 | (40.58 + 36.79) | 253-10 |
| 4. | Einar Nilsson | SWE | 71.40 | (40.99 + 30.41) | 234-3 |
| 5. | James Duncan | USA | 71.13 | (39.78 + 31.35) | 233-4½ |
| 6. | Emil Muller | USA | 69.56 | (39.83 + 29.73) | 229-2 |
| 7. | Folke Fleetwood | SWE | 68.22 | (34.20 + 33.82) | 223-10 |
| 8. | Carl Johan Lind | SWE | 68.02 | (34.98 + 32.12) | 223-2 |

The current record for this event, 324 feet 6 inches (178-0 + 146-6) was set by Hank Kraychir on March 24, 1984. This broke Fortune Gordien's 30-year-old record of 305 feet 10 inches.

# JAVELIN (FREESTYLE)

**1906 Athens** C: 22, N: 7, D: 7.27. WR: 53.79, 176-5 (Eric Lemming)

|  |  | M | FT-IN. |  |
|---|---|---|---|---|
| 1. Eric Lemming | SWE | 53.90 | 176-10 | WR |
| 2. Knut Lindberg | SWE | 45.17 | 148-2 | |
| 3. Bruno Söderström | SWE | 44.92 | 147-4 | |
| 4. Hjalmar Mellander | SWE | 44.30 | 145-4 | |
| 5. Verner Järvinen | FIN | 44.25 | 145-2 | |

**1908 London** C: 31, N: 9, D: 7.15. WR: 54.92, 180-2 (Eric Lemming)

|  |  | M | FT-IN. |
|---|---|---|---|
| 1. Eric Lemming | SWE | 54.45 | 178-7½ |
| 2. Michel Dorizas | GRE | 51.36 | 168-6 |
| 3. Arne Halse | NOR | 49.73 | 163-1¾ |
| 4. Charalambos Zouras | GRE | 48.61 | 159-5¾ |
| 5. Hugo Wieslander | SWE | 47.55 | 156-0 |
| 6. Armas Pesonen | FIN | 46.04 | 151-0½ |
| 7. Imre Mudin | HUN | 45.95 | 150-9 |
| 8. Jalmari Sauli | FIN | 43.31 | 142-1 |

Since all of the successful throwers held the javelin in the middle, just as they did in the regular javelin event, the freestyle javelin was dropped from the Olympics.

# JAVELIN (BOTH HANDS)

**1912 Stockholm** C: 14, N: 4, D: 7.9.

|  |  | M | TWO HANDS | FT-IN. |
|---|---|---|---|---|
| 1. Juho Julius Saaristo | FIN | 109.42 | (61.00 WR + 48.42) | 359-0 |
| 2. Väino Siikaniemi | FIN | 101.13 | (54.09 + 47.04) | 331-9½ |
| 3. Urho Peltonen | FIN | 100.24 | (53.58 + 46.66) | 328-10 |
| 4. Eric Lemming | SWE | 98.59 | (58.33 + 40.26) | 323-5½ |
| 5. Arne Halse | NOR | 96.92 | (55.05 + 41.87) | 318-0 |
| 6. Richard Åbrink | SWE | 93.12 | (50.04 + 43.08) | 305-6 |
| 7. Daniel Johanson | NOR | 92.82 | (48.78 + 44.04) | 304-6 |
| 8. Otto Nilsson | SWE | 88.90 | (50.21 + 38.69) | 291-8 |

When Finnish team officials realized that all three finalists were from Finland, they asked that the final round be canceled and that the preliminary results be allowed to stand. Swedish Olympic officials agreed with the request.

# TRIATHLON

**1904 St. Louis** C: 118, N: 4, D: 7.1-2.

|  |  | PTS. | LJ | SP | 100 YARDS |
|---|---|---|---|---|---|
| 1. Max Emmerich | USA | 35.7 | 21-7 | 32-2¼ | 10.6 |
| 2. John Grieb | USA | 34.0 | 20-2¼ | 33-7 | 11.0 |
| 3. William Merz | USA | 32.95 | 19-10¾ | 31-1 | 10.8 |
| 4. George Mayer | USA | 32.4 | 18-1 | 36-7 | 11.4 |
| 5. John Bissinger | USA | 30.8 | 18-4¾ | 32-9½ | 11.4 |
| 6. Phillip Kassel | USA | 30.1 | 19-2¼ | 28-9½ | 11.2 |
| 7. Christian Busch | GER | 30.05 | 18-10¾ | 31-3½ | 11.6 |
| 8. Fred Schmind | USA | 30.0 | 19-4¾ | 30-2¼ | 11.6 |

This event was part of a combined gymnastics and track and field competition known as "turning" or "turnverein gymnastics."

# PENTATHLON

Unlike the decathlon, the pentathlon was decided according to placement points. After the first three events, all but the top 12 athletes were eliminated. After the fourth event, only the top six could continue. Oddly enough, despite these rules, seven men competed in the final event in 1912, 1920, and 1924. In 1912, this was the result of a tie; in 1920, it was due to a controversy concerning the eligibility of Hugo Lahtinen; and in 1924 it was because of a mistake in computing the point total of Göran Unger. Ties in the final places were decided according to the decathlon tables.

**1006 Athens** C: 26, N: 10, D: 4.27
*(Standing Long Jump, Greek-Style Discus, Javelin, 192-Meter Race, Greco-Roman Wrestling)*

|  |  | SLJ | DISC | JAV | 192M | GRW | PTS. |
|---|---|---|---|---|---|---|---|
| 1. Hjalmar Mellander | SWE | 7 | 5 | 5 | 4 | 3 | 24 |
| 2. István Mudin | HUN | 6 | 1 | 9 | 8 | 1 | 25 |
| 3. Erik Lemming | SWE | 15 | 2 | 1 | 7 | 4 | 29 |
| 4. Uno Häggman (Tuomela) | FIN | 18 | 9 | 2 | 3 | 2 | 34 |
| 5. Lawson Robertson | USA | 1 | 17 | 11 | 1 | 6 | 36 |
| 6. Knut Lindberg | SWE | 16 | 11 | 3 | 2 | 5 | 37 |
| 7. Edward Archibald | CAN | 10 | 13 | 4 | 6 | — | — |
| 8. Julius Wagner | GER | 8 | 6 | 18 | 5 | — | — |

The events of the 1906 pentathlon were the same as those of the ancient Greek pentathlon.

**1908** not held

**1912 Stockholm** C: 26, N: 11, D: 7.7.

|  |  | LJ | JAV | 200M | DISC | 1500M | TOTAL PTS. |
|---|---|---|---|---|---|---|---|
| 1. James Thorpe | USA | 7.07 (1) | 46.71 (3) | 22.9 (1) | 35.75 (1) | 4:44.8 (1) | 7 |
| 2. Ferdinand Bie | NOR | 6.85 (2) | 46.45 (4) | 23.5 (5) | 31.79 (4) | 5:07.8 (6) | 21 |
| 3. James Donahue | USA | 6.83 (3) | 38.28 (10) | 23.0 (2) | 29.64 (11) | 4:51.0 (3) | 29 |
| 4. Frank Lukeman | CAN | 6.45 (6) | 36.02 (11) | 23.2 (4) | 33.76 (3) | 5:00.2 (5) | 29 |
| 5. James Austin Menaul | USA | 6.40 (8) | 35.85 (12) | 23.0 (2) | 31.38 (6) | 4:49.6 (2) | 30 |
| 6. Avery Brundage | USA | 6.58 (4) | 42.85 (7) | 24.2 (11) | 34.72 (2) | DNF (7) | 31 |
| 7. Hugo Wieslander | SWE | 6.27 (10) | 49.56 (1) | 24.1 (10) | 30.74 (7) | 4:51.1 (4) | 32 |
| 8. Inge Lindholm | SWE | 6.32 (12) | 41.94 (12) | 23.5 (7) | 30.47 (8) | — |  |

**1920 Antwerp** C: 19, N: 8, D: 8.6.

|  |  | LJ | JAV | 200M | DISC | 1500M | TOTAL PTS. |
|---|---|---|---|---|---|---|---|
| 1. Eero Lehtonen | FIN | 6.635 (2) | 54.67 (2) | 23.0 (1) | 34.64 (7) | 4:40.2 (2) | 14 |
| 2. Everett Bradley | USA | 6.61 (3) | 49.16 (8) | 23.0 (1) | 36.78 (6) | 5:10.0 (6) | 24 |
| 3. Hugo Lahtinen | FIN | 6.59 (4) | 54.25 (3) | 23.6 (5) | 31.12 (13) | 4:36.0 (1) | 26 |
| 4. Robert LeGendre | USA | 6.505 (5) | 44.60 (11) | 23.0 (1) | 37.39 (4) | 4:46.0 (5) | 26 |
| 5. Helge Lövland | NOR | 6.32 (7) | 53.13 (4) | 24.0 (10) | 39.51 (2) | 4:45.8 (4) | 27 |
| 6. Brutus Hamilton | USA | 6.86 (1) | 48.36 (10) | 23.4 (4) | 37.13 (5) | 5:12.8 (7) | 27 |
| 7. Robert Olsson | SWE | 6.27 (9) | 43.68 (12) | 23.6 (5) | 39.80 (1) | 4:42.8 (3) | 30 |
| 8. Aleksandr Klumberg-Kolmpere | EST | 6.25 (10) | 60.76 (1) | 25.3 (15) | 38.62 (3) | — | — |

**1924 Paris** C: 30, N: 17, D: 7.7.

|  |  | LJ | JAV | 200M | DISC | 1500M | TOTAL PTS. |
|---|---|---|---|---|---|---|---|
| 1. Eero Lehtonen | FIN | 6.68 (7) | 50.93 (4) | 23.0 (1) | 40.44 (1) | 4:47.1 (1) | 14 |
| 2. Elemér Somfay | HUN | 6.77 (5) | 52.07 (2) | 23.4 (5) | 37.76 (2) | 4:48.4 (2) | 16 |
| 3. Robert LeGendre | USA | 7.765 (1) | 48.04 (9) | 23.0 (1) | 36.76 (4) | 4:52.6 (3) | 18 |
| 4. Leo Leino | FIN | 6.72 (6) | 54.12 (1) | 23.2 (4) | 33.62 (8) | 4:55.4 (4) | 23 |
| 5. Morton Kaer | USA | 6.96 (2) | 50.20 (5) | 23.0 (1) | 32.70 (10) | 5:38.6 (6) | 24 |
| 6. Hugo Lahtinen | FIN | 6.895 (3) | 48.66 (7) | 23.6 (7) | 36.08 (5) | 4:55.6 (5) | 27 |
| 7. Brutus Hamilton | USA | 6.83 (4) | 48.96 (8) | 24.4 (18) | 37.70 (3) | — | — |
| 8. Göran Unger | SWE | 6.55 (8) | 48.45 (10) | 23.8 (8) | 35.11 (6) | — | — |

The highlight of this competition was the surprising world record of 25 feet 5¾ inches set in the long jump by Robert LeGendre of Georgetown University. First place was not decided until Lehtonen edged Somfay in the 1500 meters.

# TRACK AND FIELD

## WOMEN

### 100 METERS

**1896–1924** not held

**1928 Amsterdam** C: 31, N: 13, D: 7.31. WR: 12.2 (Elizabeth Robinson)
1. Elizabeth Robinson    USA    12.2    EWR
2. Fanny Rosenfeld       CAN    12.3
3. Ethel Smith           CAN    12.3
4. Erna Steinberg        GER    12.4
DISQ: Myrtle Cook (CAN), Helene "Leni" Schmidt (GER)

This was the first women's track event to be contested in the Olympics, so the entrants were unusually nervous, as was the primarily male audience. The men found it particularly unsettling when the three Canadian finalists hugged and kissed each other before the race. First Cook and then Schmidt were disqualified for false-starting twice. The winner, Betty Robinson, was a 16-year-old high school student from Riverdale, Illinois. Robinson didn't know that she was a fast runner until one of her teachers saw her running for a bus and asked if he could time her running down the school corridor. The Olympics was only her fourth track meet of any kind. Three years after her victory she was badly injured in a plane crash, suffering a concussion, a broken leg, a crushed arm, and a severe cut across her forehead and eyelid. She was unconscious for seven weeks and was unable to walk normally for two years. However, she regained the use of her leg and returned to competitive running. Because she could not bend her leg fully at the knee, she could not assume the crouched starting position of a sprinter. She could, however, run in relays. In 1936, Betty Robinson won a second gold medal as a member of the U.S. 4 × 100-meter relay team.

**1932 Los Angeles** C: 20, N: 10, D. 8.2. WR: 11.9 (Tollien Schuurman)
1. Stanislawa Walasiewicz    POL    11.9    EWR
2. Hilde Strike              CAN    11.9
3. Wilhelmina Von Bremen     USA    12.0
4. Marie Dollinger           GER    12.2
5. Eileen Hiscock            GBR    12.3
6. Elizabeth Wilde           USA    —

Stanislawa Walasiewicz was born in Rypin, Poland, on April 3, 1911. When she was still an infant her family moved to the United States and settled in Cleveland, Ohio, where she grew up and became known as Stella Walsh. On May 30, 1930, she became the first woman to break the 11-second barrier for 100 yards. By 1932 U.S. track enthusiasts were looking forward to a gold medal from her in the Olympics. But Stella Walsh had a problem: as a result of the worldwide depression, her job with the New York Central Railroad had been eliminated. She was offered a position with the Cleveland Recreation Department, but taking it would have made her ineligible for the Olympics, since Olympic regulations at the time disqualified athletes who made their living from physical education or recreation. With no help forthcoming from her adopted country, Stella Walsh made a major decision in her life. Twenty-four hours before she was scheduled to take out U.S. naturalization papers, she accepted a job offer from the Polish consulate in New York and decided to compete for Poland.

Stella Walsh's performance in Los Angeles was no disappointment. Running with what the Canadian official report called "long man-like strides," Stella Walsh equaled Tollien Schuurman's two-month-old world record in every one of her three races. In the final she was hard-pressed by Hilde Strike, but managed to win by half a yard. While some U.S. observers pointed to the loss of Walsh to Poland as an example of the consequences of the lack of support for women's athletics in the U.S., there were also those who held a grudge against Walsh

# TRACK AND FIELD

1. *Charley Paddock wins the 1920 100 meters with his famous "flying finish." Morris Kirksey* (right) *placed second and Jackson Scholz* (left) *fourth.*

2. (Left to right) *Charley Paddock, Jackson Scholz, Loren Murchison, and Morris Kirksey spent anxious hours together before the final of the 100-meter dash in 1920. Six days later they teamed up to win the 4 x 100-meter relay.*

# CHARIOTS OF FIRE

3. *The real Harold Abrahams. Despite the film* Chariots of Fire, *Abrahams did not run around the courtyard at Trinity College, Cambridge. He did, however, win the 100-meter dash at the 1924 Olympics in Paris.*

4. Chariots of Fire *portrayed Eric Liddell as learning at the last minute that the final of his specialty, the 100-meter dash, would be held on a Sunday. Actually Liddell was informed of the schedule six months in advance and had plenty of time to adjust his training for the 200 and 400.*

# JESSE OWENS

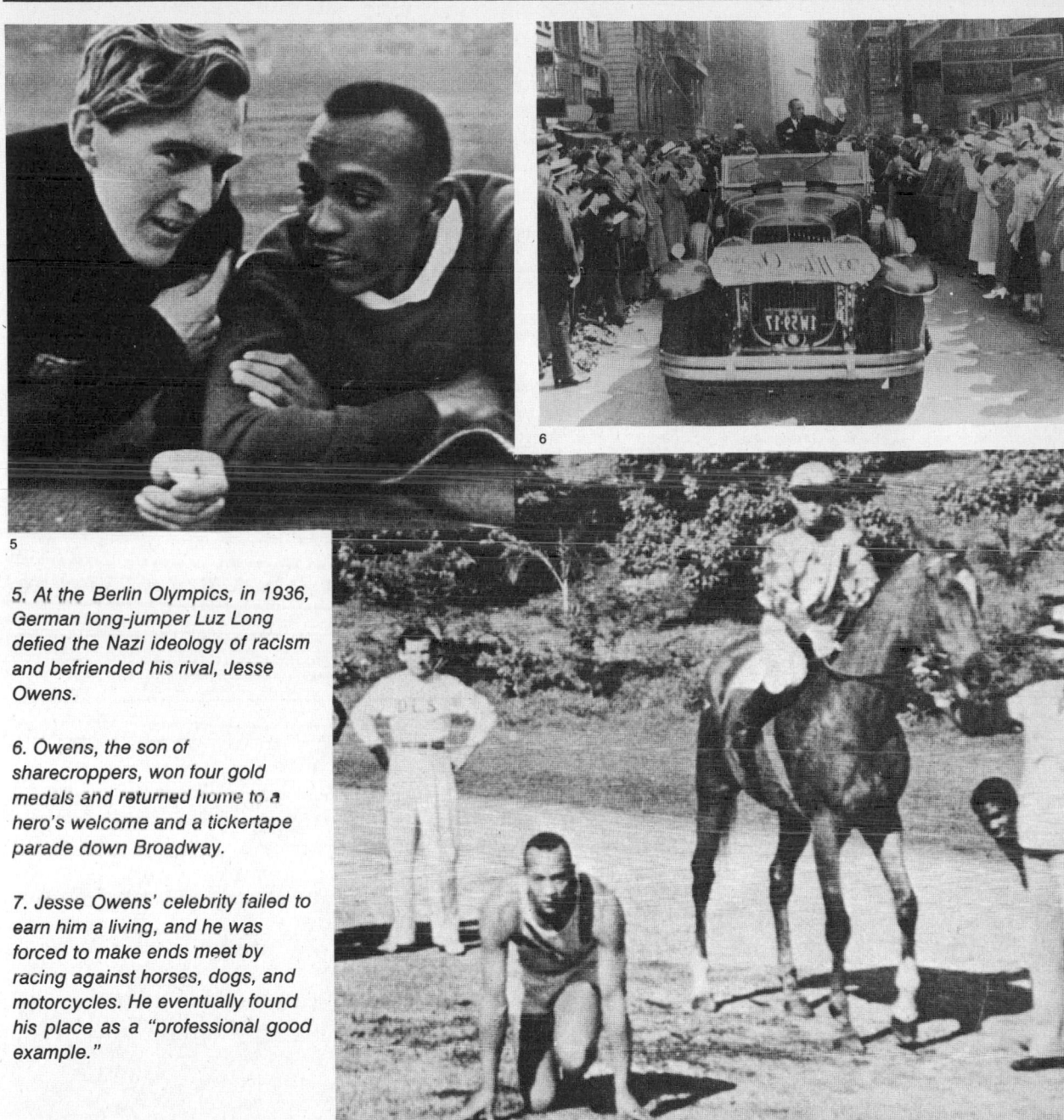

5. At the Berlin Olympics, in 1936, German long-jumper Luz Long defied the Nazi ideology of racism and befriended his rival, Jesse Owens.

6. Owens, the son of sharecroppers, won four gold medals and returned home to a hero's welcome and a tickertape parade down Broadway.

7. Jesse Owens' celebrity failed to earn him a living, and he was forced to make ends meet by racing against horses, dogs, and motorcycles. He eventually found his place as a "professional good example."

8. The controversial finish of the 1952 100-meter dash. The straight white line down the middle is not the finish line, but a flash from a photographer's bulb. To see if Herb McKenley (Lane 2 from top) beat Lindy Remigino (Lane 3), take a piece of transparent lined paper and match one of the lines with the black line below the words "Omega Timer." Slowly move the paper to the left until it reaches one of the runners. Arms and legs don't count; only shoulders and torso.

9. An ecstatic Pietro Mennea pulls ahead of "The Beast" to win the 1980 200 meters.

# TOMMIE SMITH

10. Tommie Smith won the 1968 200 meters in world record time. When he raised two clenched fists at the finish line to celebrate his victory he was hailed as a hero . . .

11. . . . but when he raised one clenched fist on the victory platform he was denounced by the I.O.C., suspended by the U.S. Olympic Committee, and ordered to leave Mexico within 48 hours.

12. Hasely Crawford, Henry Ngoawe, and Michael McFarlane all divert their attention from the finish line as Carl Lewis (right) breezes past them to win the opening heat of the 1984 100 meters. Lewis went on to match Jesse Owens' four gold medals of 1936. Four years later, in Seoul, he became the first man to win the 100 meters twice.

13. The finish of the 1988 100-meter dash—without Ben Johnson.

14. Unknown Paul Pilgrim scored an upset victory in the 1906 400 meters. The next day he also won the 800 meters. He never again won a major race. Wyndham Halswelle (right), seen here finishing second, was the beneficiary two years later in the famous 400 meters controversy of 1908.

15. James Ball (left) loses the 1928 400 meters to Ray Barbuti by committing the classic mistake of turning his head to check his position.

16. (Left to right) *George Rhoden, Leslie Laing, Arthur Wint, and Herb McKenley failed to finish the 4 x 400-meter relay in 1948, when Wint pulled a muscle during the third leg. Four years later the same foursome fought back the challenge of the U.S. team to win the gold medal by one tenth of a second.*

17. *Tom Courtney (153) edges Derek Johnson (137) in the 800 meters final of 1956, the most dramatic race of the Melbourne Olympics. Courtney exhausted himself so thoroughly that the award ceremony had to be delayed an extra hour until he recovered.*

18. *Peter Snell (right) scores a surprise victory over world record holder Roger Moens in the 1960 800 meters.*

# 1500 METERS

19

20

19. *Josy Barthel of Luxembourg wins the 1500 meters in 1952. "Just as I had always dreamed in secret," he later recalled, "I raised my arms, I smiled, and I crossed the finish line."*

20. *Ron Delany leads the great mass finish of the 1956 1500 meters.*

21

22

21. *After the race, John Landy goes to the aid of Delany, whom he assumes to be doubled over in pain. Instead he discovers that Delany is deep in prayer.*

22. *Mexico City, 1968: Kip Keino of Kenya scores the most decisive 1500 meters victory in Olympic history.*

23. *Sebastian Coe winning the 1500 meters in 1980 after his disappointing second-place finish in the 800.*

23

# GREAT MOMENTS IN LONG - DISTANCE

24

25

26

24. Hannes Kolehmainen (left) passes Jean Bouin just before the finish of the 1912 5000 meters.

25. Paavo Nurmi checks his watch during the running of the 1924 5000 meters. He is followed by fellow Finn Ville Ritola.

26. Emil Zátopek enters the homestretch of the 1952 5000 meters, followed by Alain Mimoun and Herbert Schade. An exhausted Chris Chataway has fallen after stepping on the curb.

27. Gordon Pirie and Vladimir Kuts, still friendly despite their intense rivalry. In 1956 Kuts defeated Pirie in both the 10,000 meters and the 5000 meters.

27

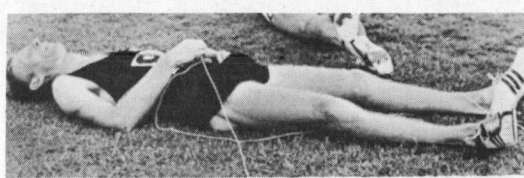

28

29

30

28. Murray Halberg, winner of the 5000 meters in 1960, collapses in the infield, still holding the tape that marked his victory.

29. The varied emotions of the finish of the 1964 5000 meters. The joy of the winner, Bob Schul (center), the surprised thrill of silver medalist Harald Norpoth (left) and the agony and disappointment of Michel Jazy (third from left), who was in first place only 50 meters from the tape, but finished only fourth.

30. Mohamed Gammoudi (second from left) pushes his way past Billy Mills (left) and Ron Clarke (right) during the spectacular last lap of the 1964 10,000 meters.

31

32

31. Lasse Viren, having fallen halfway through the final of the 1972 10,000 meters, briefly contemplates his fate before regaining his feet. Viren went on to win the first of his four gold medals and set a world record as well.

32. Miruts Yifter celebrates the culmination of his eight-year quest for a gold medal in the 5000 meters. In 1972 he spent too long in the toilet and missed the start of his heat. In 1976 Ethiopia boycotted the Olympics. In 1980 he won at last.

# THE 1904 MARATHON

33. *Lentauw and Yamasani, the first black Africans to compete in the Olympics. They happened to be in St. Louis as part of the Boer War exhibit at the World's Fair and decided to enter the marathon race.*

34. *The one and only Félix Carvajal. Financing his own trip from Cuba, he lost all his money in a crap game in New Orleans. He hitchhiked to St Louis and arrived at the starting line wearing long pants and heavy boots. The start of the race was delayed while a sympathetic U.S. athlete cut off Carvajal's pants at the knees.*

35. *Thomas Hicks, the winner of the St. Louis marathon, visibly under the influence of the strychnine and brandy that was administered to him during the course of the race.*

33

34

35

# MARATHON WINNERS

36. *Spiridon Louis, 1896.*
37. *Boughèra El Ouafi, 1928.*

38. *Delfo Cabrera, 1948.*
39. *Waldemar Cierpinski, 1976 and 1980.*

# THE LAST LAP—MARATHON

40. *Dorando Pietri collapses within sight of the finish of the 1908 marathon. This photo puts to rest Dorando's contention that he could have completed the course unaided if meddlesome British officials had not interfered with him.*

41. *A perplexed Frank Shorter wonders why the spectators are booing as he circles the stadium on his way to victory in the 1972 Munich marathon.*

42                 43               44

42. *Alvin Kraenzlein won four gold medals in three days at the 1900 Paris Olympics. His wins came in the 60-meter dash, the long jump, and the 110- and 200-meter hurdles.*

43. *Harrison Dillard, the king of the high hurdles, failed to qualify in that event for the 1948 Olympics, but won the 100-meter dash instead. Four years later, in Helsinki, he finally earned his high hurdles gold medal.*

44. *Lord Burghley* (center), *winner of the 1928 400-meter hurdles, clears a barrier in classic style during a preliminary heat.*

45. *David Hemery* (center), *the 1968 gold medalist, and John Akii-Bua* (right), *the 1972 gold medalist, in a heat of the 1972 400-meter hurdles.*

46. *FBI agent Horace Ashenfelter surges past favorite Vladimir Kazantsev at the final water jump of the 1952 steeplechase.*

47. *Amos Biwott, defying accepted technique, soars over the water barrier in the 1968 steeplechase.*

45

46                                                                                      47

# THE 1976 STEEPLECHASE

48. Frank Baumgartl (384) and Anders Gärderud (812) negotiate the final hurdle of the 1976 steeplechase, followed closely by Bronislaw Malinowski (724).

49. Gärderud makes a successful clearance, but Baumgartl clips the barrier with his knee and falls.

50. Gärderud takes off for the finish line, while Malinowski is forced to add a human hurdle to the obstacles in his path.

51. Gärderud holds off Malinowski for the victory, while Baumgartl gets up to salvage the bronze medal.

# WALKS

52

53

54

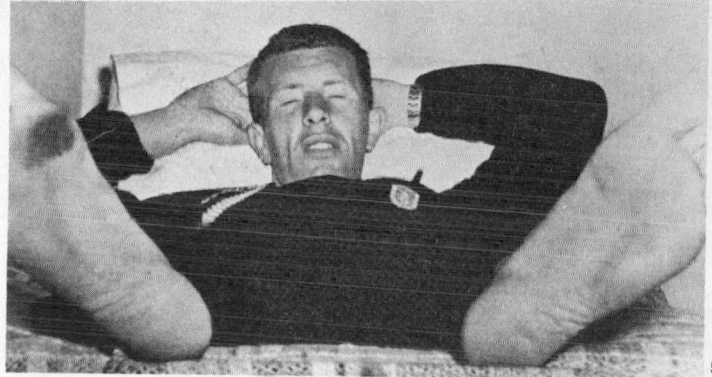

55

52. Vladimir Golubnichiy holds off a frantic finish of dubious legality by local favorite José Pedraza to win the 20,000-meter walk in Mexico City in 1968.

53. Musically minded crowd-pleaser Ugo Frigerio won a total of three walking gold medals in 1920 and 1924.

54. Ken Matthews celebrates his victory in the 1964 20,000-meter walk with his wife, Sheila.

55. Norman Read celebrates his victory in the 1956 50,000-meter walk by resting his feet.

56

56. *Jozef Pribilinec (bottom) defeated Ronald Weigel by three seconds in the 1988 20,000-meter walk. When Pribilinec proved too exhausted to respond to Weigel's congratulations, Weigel kissed his conqueror and silently walked away.*

# HIGH-JUMPERS

57. Duncan McNaughton pestered the Canadian Olympic Association into letting him compete in the 1932 Olympics, since he lived in Los Angeles anyway. He went on to win the gold medal in the high jump.

58. John Thomas (left) congratulates Robert Shavlakadze after the latter's upset victory in the 1960 high jump.

59. The ecstasy of victory: Valery Brumel wins the 1964 high jump.

57

58

59

60

61

62

63

60–63. Dick Fosbury introduces the Fosbury Flop at the 1968 Olympics.

64

65

66

67

64. *With his final attempt, Fred Hansen clears 16 feet 8¾ inches to win the 1964 pole vault in Tokyo.*

65. *Wladyslaw Kozakiewicz of Poland, winner of the 1980 Moscow pole vault, expresses his opinion of the Soviet crowd.*

66. *William DeHart Hubbard became the first black athlete to win an Olympic gold medal in an individual event when he won the 1924 long jump in Paris.*

67. *The three medalists in the 1960 long jump: (left to right) Bo Roberson, Ralph Boston, and Igor Ter-Ovanesyan.*

# BOB BEAMON

68. Bob Beamon stunned the sports world when he bettered the world long jump record by 21¾ inches, with a leap of 29 feet 2½ inches, in 1968.

69. When he realized what he had accomplished, Beamon suffered a cataplectic seizure and fell to the ground in shock.

68

70

71

70. James Connolly of Boston became tho first Olympic champion in 1527 years when he won the triple jump in 1896. He later became a well-known writer.

71. Viktor Saneyev won three gold medals in the triple jump, in 1968, 1972, and 1976, and came within 4½ inches of winning a fourth in 1980.

72. The winners of the 1912 shot put: (left to right) Patrick McDonald (gold), Lawrence Whitney (bronze), and Ralph Rose (silver). Rose also won gold medals in 1904 and 1908.

72

73

74

73. Al Oerter, the only athlete ever to win the same Olympic track and field event four straight times. He earned four gold medals in the discus throw, in 1956, 1960, 1964, and 1968.

74. Eric Lemming of Sweden dominated the javelin throw from 1899 until 1912.

75. Matti Järvinen pretending to throw the javelin following his victory in 1932. He competed with his sweat pants on and only took them off to pose for photographers.

75

# DECATHLON

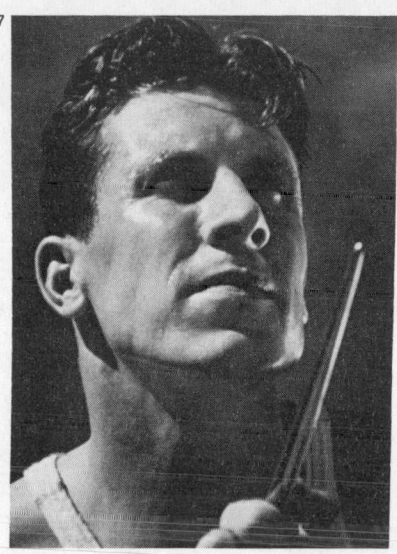

76. Jim Thorpe led a tickertape parade in New York City following his victories in the decathlon and pentathlon in 1912. "I heard people yelling my name," he recalled, "and I couldn't realize how one fellow could have so many friends."

77. Glenn Morris was an automobile salesman when he won the Olympic decathlon in Berlin in 1936.

78. Seventeen-year-old Bob Mathias was the youngest winner of a men's track and field gold medal in Olympic history.

80. U.C.L.A. teammates Rafer Johnson (USA) and Yang Chuan-Kwang (Taiwan) collapse against each other after completing the final event of the 1960 decathlon.

79. After his victory in the 1948 decathlon, Mathias returned home to Tulare, California, for the small-town equivalent of a tickertape parade.

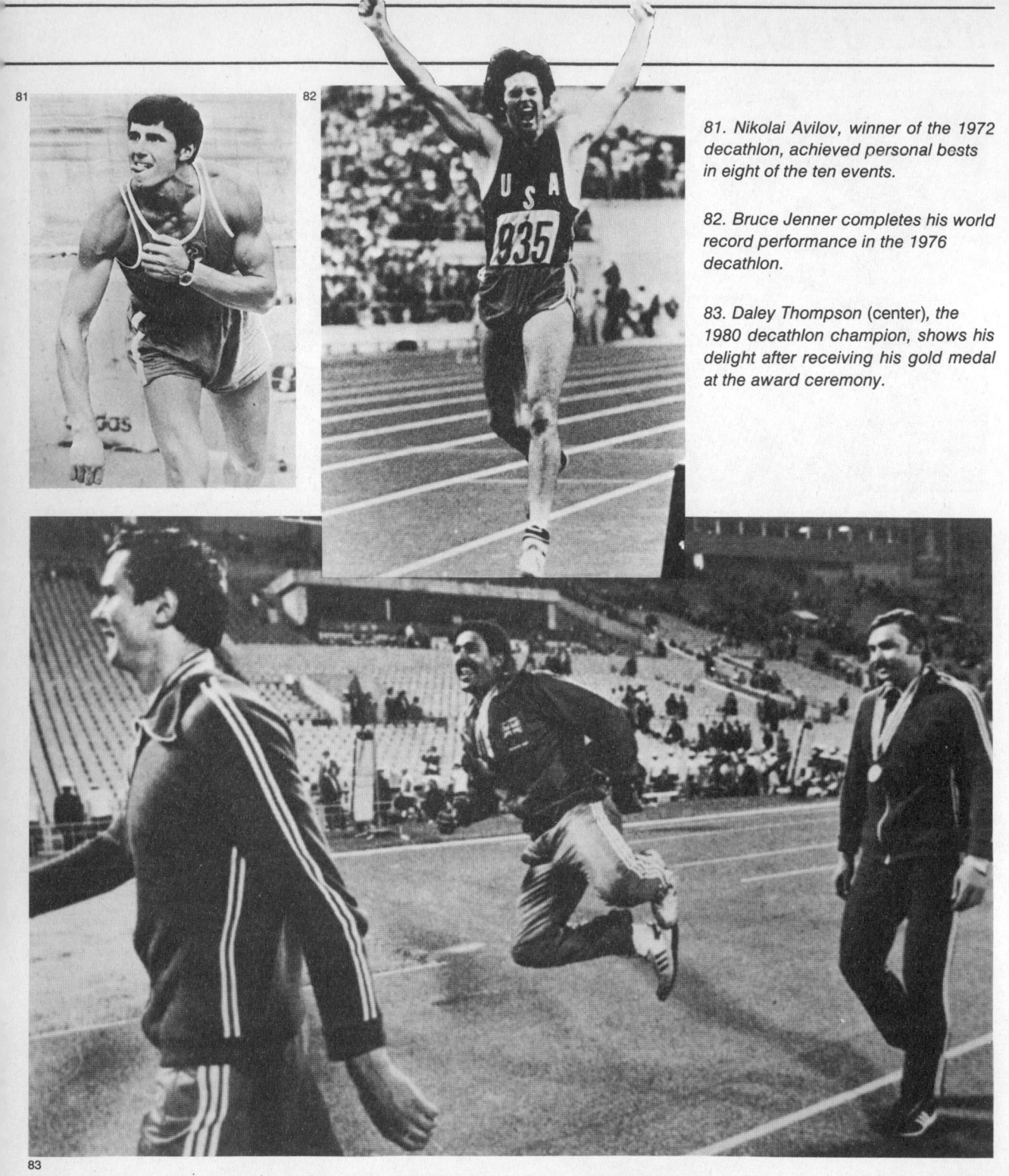

81. *Nikolai Avilov, winner of the 1972 decathlon, achieved personal bests in eight of the ten events.*

82. *Bruce Jenner completes his world record performance in the 1976 decathlon.*

83. *Daley Thompson (center), the 1980 decathlon champion, shows his delight after receiving his gold medal at the award ceremony.*

84

84. Paavo Nurmi leads the field during the running of the murderous 1924 cross-country race that put an end to cross-country as an Olympic event.

85

85. Ray Ewry, a victim of childhood polio, won eight gold medals in the standing jump events of 1900, 1904, and 1908, and two more in the Intercalated Games of 1906. He is seen here taking off in the standing high jump.

86. Martin Sheridan earned five gold medals and four silver medals in 1904, 1906, and 1908. In this photo he is standing on the pedestal that was used for the Greek-style discus throw of 1908. Sheridan is also credited with shortening Félix Carvajal's pants at the starting line of the 1904 marathon.

# WOMEN'S TRACK AND FIELD

87

88

87. What deep, dark secret prevented Stella Walsh from smiling even after she had won the gold medal in the 1932 100-meter dash?

88. Adolph Hitler made advances to Helen Stephens after her victory in the 1936 100 meters, but she turned him down.

89. In 1948 Fanny Blankers-Koen won four of the nine women's track and field events.

89

90

91

90. *As a child in rural Tennessee, Wilma Rudolph suffered through polio, double pneumonia, and scarlet fever. Yet she grew up to win three gold medals in 1960, in the 100- and 200-meter dashes and the 4 x 100-meter relay.*

91. *In 1968 Wyomia Tyus became the only woman to win the 100-meter dash twice.*

92

93

92. *Between 1964 and 1976 Irena Szewińska won seven medals in five different events. Here she acknowledges the applause of the crowd after winning the 400 meters in 1976.*

93. *Florence Griffith Joyner won three gold medals and one silver in 1988 to go with the silver she won in 1984.*

94

95

*94. Disaster strikes the 1984 women's 3000-meter run as gold-medal favorite Mary Decker steps on the barefooted heel of Zola Budd.*

*95. Decker falls to the ground as Budd tries to regain her balance, and the eventual winner, Maricica Puică (behind Budd), sidesteps Decker.*

96

96. Zola Budd looks back to see her idol hit the infield in pain.

97. Mary Decker, too injured to continue, writhes in agony as the race goes on without her.

97

98. Joan Benoit, first across the finish line in the 1984 inaugural women's marathon.

99. Gabriele Andersen-Scheiss, who gained unsought celebrity as a result of her staggering 5-minute 44-second final lap in the 1984 women's marathon.

100. The 1952 Australian 4 x 100-meter relay team set a world record in their qualifying heat and were on their way to victory in the final when Winsome Cripps and Marjorie Jackson dropped the baton during the final changeover.

# WOMEN'S TRACK AND FIELD

101

101. Ethel Catherwood, "The Saskatoon Lily," won the 1928 high jump in Amsterdam.

102. The medalists in the 1956 shot put: (left to right) Marianne Werner, Tamara Tyshkevich, and Galina Zybina.

102

103

103. Lia Manoliu, the first track and field athlete to take part in six Olympics, finally won a gold medal on her fifth attempt, in the 1968 discus throw

104

105

104. Babe Didriksen qualified for all five individual women's track and field events in 1932, but was allowed to compete in only three of them. She won the javelin throw and the 80-meter hurdles and set a world record in the high jump, despite being placed second. She was later voted the greatest female athlete of the first half of the twentieth century.

105. Elvira Ozolina, winner of the 1960 javelin throw, was so humiliated at finishing only fifth in 1964 that she shaved off all her hair and refused to wear a scarf to hide her shame.

106. The medalists in the 1972 pentathlon: (left to right) Heidemarie Rosendahl (silver), Mary Peters (gold), and Burglinde Pollak (bronze).

106

# DOMINANT WOMEN

107. *Iolanda Balaş completely dominated the high jump between 1957 and 1967, setting fourteen world records and winning two Olympic gold medals.*

108. *Tamara Press overwhelmed the opposition in the 1960 and 1964 shot put but disappeared from international competition when sex tests were introduced.*

107

108

herself, and she was not granted her naturalization papers until 1947.

**1936 Berlin** C: 30, N: 15, D: 8.4. WR: 11.6 (Helen Stephens)

| | | |
|---|---|---|
| 1. Helen Stephens | USA | 11.5w |
| 2. Stanislawa Walasiewicz | POL | 11.7 |
| 3. Käthe Krauss | GER | 11.9 |
| 4. Marie Dollinger | GER | 12.0 |
| 5. Annette Rogers | USA | 12.2 |
| 6. Emmy Albus | GER | 12.3 |

Helen Stephens was a 6-foot farm girl from Calloway County, Missouri, who loved to run. When she entered Fulton High School she was routinely timed in the 50-yard dash. Coach Burton Moore was astounded to discover that Stephens had run the race in 5.8 seconds, equaling the existing world record held by Betty Robinson. Moore taught Stephens the various events of track and field and then entered her in the 1935 national A.A.U. meet, which was being held in St. Louis. Wearing a borrowed sweatshirt and shoes, she won the shot put, set a world record in the 200 meters, and set another world record in the standing long jump. But the real sensation came when she beat Stella Walsh in the 50-yard dash, this time officially tying the world record. Walsh was outraged by such impudence and referred to Stephens as a "greenie from the sticks." When Stephens and Walsh met again in the Olympics in Berlin there was never any question as to who would take the gold medal. In the opening round Helen Stephens ran a wind-aided 11.4 to win her heat by ten yards. She ran wind-aided 11.5s in the semifinals and final, finishing the latter two yards ahead of Stella Walsh. After the race, Stephens was taken to meet Adolf Hitler in his private glass-enclosed box. "Hitler comes in and gives me the Nazi salute," she later recalled. "I gave him a good old Missouri handshake. Immediately Hitler goes for the jugular vein. He gets ahold of my fanny, and he begins to squeeze and pinch and hug me up, and he said, 'You're a true Aryan type. You should be running for Germany.' So after he gave me the once-over and a full massage, he asked me if I'd like to spend the weekend in Berchtesgoden." She declined.

After only two and a half years of competition, Helen Stephens retired from amateur athletics with an undefeated record in running events. For a while she made a living playing basketball and softball and then served as a marine during World War II. Later she worked until retirement for the Defense Mapping Agency Aerospace Center in St. Louis.

The rivalry between Helen Stephens and Stella Walsh had an ironic and long-delayed ending. After Stephens' victory in Berlin, a Polish journalist accused her of actually being a man, and German officials were forced to issue a statement that they had given her a sex check and that she had passed. Forty-four years later, on December 4, 1980, Stella Walsh went to a discount store in Cleveland to buy streamers for a reception for the Polish na-

tional basketball team. In the parking lot she got caught in the middle of a robbery attempt and was shot to death. When an autopsy was performed afterward, it turned out that although Helen Stephens may not have had male sexual organs, Stella Walsh did. All the while that Walsh had been setting 11 world records, winning 41 A.A.U. titles and two Olympic medals, she was, in fact, a man.

**1948 London** C: 38, N: 21, D: 8.2. WR: 11.5 (Helen Stephens)

| | | |
|---|---|---|
| 1. Francina "Fanny" Blankers-Koen | HOL | 11.9 |
| 2. Dorothy Manley | GBR | 12.2 |
| 3. Shirley Strickland | AUS | 12.2 |
| 4. Viola Myers | CAN | — |
| 5. Patricia Jones | CAN | — |
| 6. Cynthia Thompson | JAM | — |

Fanny Koen was 18 years old when she was chosen to join the Dutch team for the 1936 Olympics in Berlin. She tied for sixth place in the high jump and was part of the 4 × 100-meter relay team that finished fifth. The highlight of the games for her was when she got Jesse Owens' autograph. When the Olympics resumed after a 12-year break, Fanny was the holder of six world records—in the 100 yards, the 80-meter hurdles, the high jump, the long jump, and in two relays. In the interim she had also married her coach, Jan Blankers, and given birth to two children. At 30 years of age she was thought by some to be too old to win the Olympic sprints, despite her string of records. She quieted her critics almost immediately by recording the best time of the opening round (12.0), in the 100-meter dash. She went on to win the final in the mud by three yards. Later in the week she also won gold medals in the 80-meter hurdles, the 200 meters, and the 4 × 100-meter relay. Of the nine women's track and field events included in the 1948 Olympics, Fanny Blankers-Koen won four of them. If she had entered the long jump she probably would have won that too, considering that the winning jump was 20 inches shorter than Fanny's world record. When she returned to Amsterdam she was driven through the crowded streets in an open carriage drawn by four gray horses. Her neighbors gave her a bicycle, "so she won't have to run so much."

**1952 Helsinki** C: 56, N: 27, D: 7.22. WR: 11.5 (Helen Stephens, Francina "Fanny" Blankers-Koen)

| | | | |
|---|---|---|---|
| 1. Marjorie Jackson | AUS | 11.5 | EWR |
| 2. Daphne Hasenjager (Robb) | SAF | 11.8 | |
| 3. Shirley Strickland | AUS | 11.9 | |
| 4. Winsome Cripps | AUS | 11.9 | |
| 5. Maria Sander | GER | 12.0 | |
| 6. Mae Faggs | USA | 12.1 | |

British fans, who had been looking forward to the playing of "God Save the Queen" following the victory of Marjorie Jackson, whom they considered a British subject, were stunned when what they heard instead was "Advance Australia Fair." Back home in Australia, the residents of Jackson's hometown of Lithgow welcomed her with a 250-pound cake to help her break training.

**1956 Melbourne** C: 34, N: 16, D: 11.26. WR: 11.3 (Shirley Strickland)

| | | |
|---|---|---|
| 1. Betty Cuthbert | AUS | 11.5 |
| 2. Christa Stubnick | GDR | 11.7 |
| 3. Marlene Matthews | AUS | 11.7 |
| 4. Isabelle Daniels | USA | 11.8 |
| 5. Giuseppina Leone | ITA | 11.9 |
| 6. Heather Armitage | GBR | 12.0 |

Eighteen-year-old Betty Cuthbert broke the Olympic record in the first round with an 11.4. In the semifinals she was beaten by Stubnick, but in the final she led from start to finish to win by five feet. Betty Cuthbert was as unassuming a heroine as one could hope for. In her autobiography, *Golden Girl,* she wrote, "I broke the tape in 11.5s just like in any other race and there seemed nothing special about it. I couldn't realize then just what I had done and even later, when the telegrams, letters, honours, victory functions and the like started, I was too shy and self-conscious fully to appreciate it. . . . However, at the time, Mum must have realized what I had done because I looked up in the crowd just after the race was over and saw her crying her eyes out." Four days later Cuthbert won the 200-meter dash and then earned another gold medal as part of the Australian 4 × 100-meter relay team.

**1960 Rome** C: 31, N: 18, D: 9.2. WR: 11.3 (Shirley Strickland, Vyera Krepkina)

| | | |
|---|---|---|
| 1. Wilma Rudolph | USA | 11.0w |
| 2. Dorothy Hyman | GBR | 11.3 |
| 3. Giuseppina Leone | ITA | 11.3 |
| 4. Maria Itkina | SOV | 11.4 |
| 5. Catherine Capdeville | FRA | 11.5 |
| 6. Jennifer Smart | GBR | 12.0 |

Wilma Rudolph was born in rural Tennessee on June 23, 1940, the 20th of her father's 22 children. She was born prematurely and weighed only 4½ pounds at birth. She suffered through polio, double pneumonia, and scarlet fever, which caused her to lose the use of her left leg. From the age of 6 she wore a brace. Her mother learned from doctors that rubbing her daughter's leg might help, so each day Wilma received four leg rubs from her brothers, sisters, and mother. Eventually she graduated from a brace to an orthopedic shoe and she joined her brothers playing basketball whenever she could. When Wilma was 11, her mother returned home one day to find her daughter playing basketball barefooted, having thrown away her corrective shoes. By the time she was 16, Rudolph had developed into a star runner and had qualified for the U.S. Olympic team. In Melbourne in 1956 she was eliminated in the first round of the 200 meters, but earned a bronze medal running the third leg of the U.S. 4 × 100-meter relay team. The same day that she returned from Australia to her hometown of Clarksville, Tennessee, she played for her high school's basketball team.

Four years later, the 5-foot 11-inch Rudolph, now a mother and a member of the Tennessee State University "Tigerbelles," went to the Rome Olympics as the favorite to succeed Betty Cuthbert as the world's fastest woman. She dominated the competition from the beginning. She actually fell asleep while waiting for her semifinal heat. Well-rested, she swept to a three-yard victory, equaling the world record of 11.3. She won the final by the same wide margin and was clocked in 11.0. However her time was not accepted as a world record because the wind was 2.752 meters per second—above the acceptable limit of 2 meters per second. She went on to match Betty Cuthbert's triple gold by winning the 200 meters and the 4 × 100-meter relay.

**1964 Tokyo** C: 44, N: 27, D: 10.16. WR: 11.2 (Wilma Rudolph)

| | | |
|---|---|---|
| 1. Wyomia Tyus | USA | 11.4 |
| 2. Edith McGuire | USA | 11.6 |
| 3. Ewa Klobukowska | POL | 11.6 |
| 4. Marilyn White | USA | 11.6 |
| 5. Miguelina Cobián | CUB | 11.7 |
| 6. Marilyn Black | AUS | 11.7 |
| 7. Halina Górecka | POL | 11.8 |
| 8. Dorothy Hyman | GBR | 11.9 |

Until the Olympics, 19-year-old Wyomia Tyus of Griffin, Georgia, had been overshadowed by her Tennessee State teammate Edith McGuire, whom she had never beaten. But in Tokyo, Tyus improved her personal best from 11.5 to 11.2 to equal Wilma Rudolph's world record in the second round. She won the final handily by two yards. Bronze medalist Klobukowska was later the subject of much controversy. On September 15, 1967, she was barred from international competition after she failed a sex chromosome test. Although she passed a visual examination she was subsequently stripped of all her records.

**1968 Mexico City** C: 41, N: 20, D: 10.15. WR: 11.1 (Irena Szewińska [Kirszenstein], Wyomia Tyus, Barbara Ferrell, Lyudmila Samotyosova, Margaret Bailes)

| | | | |
|---|---|---|---|
| 1. Wyomia Tyus | USA | 11.08 | WR |
| 2. Barbara Ferrell | USA | 11.15 | |
| 3. Irena Szewińska (Kirszenstein) | POL | 11.19 | |
| 4. Raelene Boyle | AUS | 11.19 | |
| 5. Margaret Bailes | USA | 11.3 | |
| 6. Dianne Burge | AUS | 11.4 | |
| 7. Chi Cheng | TAI | 11.5 | |
| 8. Miguelina Cobián | CUB | 11.6 | |

Competition was particularly stiff in 1968. In the first round, all three Americans, Tyus, Bailes, and Ferrell, equaled the Olympic record of 11.2. The second round saw Ferrell and Szewińska tie the world record of 11.1, while Wyomia Tyus ran a wind-aided 11.0. The semifinals, run in the rain, were won by Szewińska and Tyus, as co-world record holder Lyudmila Samotyosova was eliminated. The final matched four of the five world record holders. After false-starting, Tyus won a clear victory to become the first runner, male or female, to win an Olympic sprint title twice in a row.

**1972 Munich** C: 47, N: 33, D: 9.2. WR: 11.08 (Wyomia Tyus)

| | | | |
|---|---|---|---|
| 1. Renate Stecher | GDR | 11.07 | WR |
| 2. Raelene Boyle | AUS | 11.23 | |
| 3. Silvia Chibás | CUB | 11.24 | |
| 4. Iris Davis | USA | 11.32 | |
| 5. Annegret Richter | GER | 11.38 | |
| 6. Alice Annum | GHA | 11.41 | |
| 7. Barbara Ferrell | USA | 11.45 | |
| 8. Eva Gleskova | CZE | 12.48 | |

Although 17-year-old Silvia Chibás recorded the fastest times of the first two rounds (11.18 and 11.22), there was never any doubt that Stecher would win the gold.

**1976 Montreal** C: 39, N: 22, D: 7.25. WR: 10.8 (Renate Stecher, Annegret Richter); 11.04 (Inge Helten)

| | | |
|---|---|---|
| 1. Annegret Richter | GER | 11.08 |
| 2. Renate Stecher | GDR | 11.13 |
| 3. Inge Helten | GER | 11.17 |
| 4. Raelene Boyle | AUS | 11.23 |
| 5. Evelyn Ashford | USA | 11.24 |
| 6. Chandra Cheeseborough | USA | 11.31 |
| 7. Andrea Lynch | GBR | 11.32 |
| 8. Marlies Oelsner | GDR | 11.34 |

Richter defeated Stecher 11.19 to 11.21 in heat number 6 of the first round. In the second round she ran an impressive 11.05. The next day she set a world record of 11.01 in the semifinals, before leading a German sweep in the final. Less than a yard separated the three medalists at the finish.

**1980 Moscow** C: 40, N: 25, D: 7.26. WR: 10.88 (Marlies Göhr [Oelsner])

| | | |
|---|---|---|
| 1. Lyudmila Kondratyeva | SOV | 11.06 |
| 2. Marlies Göhr (Oelsner) | GDR | 11.07 |
| 3. Ingrid Auerswald | GDR | 11.14 |
| 4. Linda Haglund | SWE | 11.16 |
| 5. Romy Müller | GDR | 11.16 |
| 6. Kathryn Smallwood | GBR | 11.28 |
| 7. Chantal Rega | FRA | 11.32 |
| 8. Heather Hunte | GBR | 11.34 |

Haglund led at the halfway mark, but Kondratyeva and Göhr stormed by her after 60 meters. Göhr edged ahead with a few meters to go, but Kondratyeva came back and, despite pulling a hamstring muscle at the finish, won by the smallest margin imaginable.

**1984 Los Angeles** C: 46, N: 33, D: 8.5. WR: 10.79 (Evelyn Ashford)

| | | | |
|---|---|---|---|
| 1. Evelyn Ashford | USA | 10.97 | OR |
| 2. Alice Brown | USA | 11.13 | |
| 3. Merlene Ottey-Page | JAM | 11.16 | |
| 4. Jeannette Bolden | USA | 11.25 | |
| 5. Grace Jackson | JAM | 11.39 | |
| 6. Angela Bailey | CAN | 11.40 | |
| 7. Heather Oakes | GBR | 11.43 | |
| 8. Angella Taylor | CAN | 11.62 | |

In 1976, 19-year-old Evelyn Ashford competed at the Montreal Olympics, finishing fifth in the 100 meters. Three years later, back in Montreal, she gained international acclaim at the World Cup meet by defeating East German world record holder Marita Koch in the 200, 21.83 to 22.02 and then beating the 100-meter world record holder, Marlies Göhr, 11.06 to 11.17. Ashford seemed right on track to fulfill her dreams of Olympic glory—until Jimmy Carter announced that U.S. athletes would not be allowed to go to Moscow. When the boycott was made official, Ashford was competing in Canada. She and her coach and a teammate went to a bar, where Evelyn, completely out of character, "got sloppy drunk," stood up and fell on her face.

Ashford reset her goals for the 1983 inaugural world championships in Helsinki and for the 1984 Olympics. In June of 1983 she was beaten by Göhr in Los Angeles 11.39 to 11.53, but one week later, competing in Colorado, she set a world record of 10.79. Annoyed that her record was not properly respected because it was set at high-altitude, Ashford vowed to prove herself by defeating Göhr in Helsinki. She recorded the fastest time in each of the three preliminary rounds, but in the final she pulled a hamstring muscle and fell to the ground while Göhr sped on to victory, followed closely by Marita Koch.

For all of her frustrations, Ashford still had the Los Angeles Olympics to look forward to. But as she warmed up for her semifinal heat at the U.S. trials on June 18, 1984, Ashford felt a twinge in her right hamstring muscle. Running very carefully, she qualified for the Olympic team, but, although she had hoped to win three gold medals at the Olympics, she withdrew from the 200 meters to protect her leg.

With Göhr boycotted out of the Olympics, only the very real threat of injury stood between Evelyn Ashford and her long-awaited goal of an Olympic title. In Los Angeles, her leg held up as she again recorded the fastest time in each of the three preliminary rounds. In the final, she took command at the midway point and won going away.

Over the years Evelyn Ashford had earned a reputation as a shy, somewhat unfriendly loner, who shunned the media and rarely expressed her emotions. "They should be bottled up inside," she would say. "You want it to come out on the track." But after crossing the finish line and hearing the track announcer say that she had broken the Olympic record, the years of frustration and anguish gave way to tearful relief. After collapsing into the arms of teammate Jeannette Bolden, she cried her way through her victory lap while she received a standing ovation.

"When I caught my first glimpse of the gold medal while I waited on the victory stand," she would later recall, "I was emotionally overcome. I couldn't believe it was over. I couldn't stop crying."

Actually it wasn't all over. Not quite. Evelyn Ashford

was now the world record holder and the Olympic champion, but one more challenge remained: she wanted to beat Marlies Göhr. In fact, on August 16, Göhr won the Friendship Games meet with a time of 10.95, faster than Ashford's Olympic record. But the next day, in Berlin, Ashford clocked 10.92 and 10.94. Then, on August 22, the two met head-to-head in Zurich. Ashford overcame Göhr's fast start and final surge to gain the victory—and set a new world record of 10.76 in the process. When the time was announced, Göhr and East German teammate Ingrid Auerswald, gracious in defeat, each took one of Ashford's hands and raised it in the air. Finally, ten years after she had begun competing for the *boys'* track team at Roseville High School in California, Evelyn Ashford had proved that she was the fastest woman in the world.

**1988 Seoul** C. 64, N: 42, D: 9.25. WR: 10.49 (Florence Griffith Joyner)

| 1. | Florence Griffith Joyner | USA | 10.54w |
|----|--------------------------|-----|--------|
| 2. | Evelyn Ashford | USA | 10.83 |
| 3. | Heike Drechsler (Daute) | GDR | 10.85 |
| 4. | Grace Jackson | JAM | 10.97 |
| 5. | Gwen Torrence | USA | 10.97 |
| 6. | Natalya Pomoshchnikova | SOV | 11.00 |
| 7. | Juliet Cuthbert | JAM | 11.26 |
| 8. | Anelia Vechernikova | BUL | 11.49 |

Florence Griffith was born December 21, 1959. The seventh of eleven children, she grew up in Watts, a neighborhood in Los Angeles best known as the site of a black uprising in 1965. Griffith was always a bit eccentric. Once she was asked to leave a local shopping mall because she was wearing her pet boa constrictor like a muffler. But what really set her apart from her peers was her speed. She began racing at age 7 and continued to compete until 1979 when she was forced to drop out of college in order to help support her family.

Sprint coach Bob Kersee found Griffith working as a bank teller and helped her get financial aid so that she could attend U.C.L.A. Griffith first gained serious international attention when she placed fourth in the 200 meters at the 1983 world championships. The following year she earned a silver medal in the 200 at the Los Angeles Olympics, although her six-inch, wildly painted fingernails gained her more press than her running.

By 1986, Griffith, seemingly a perennial runner-up, was in semi-retirement, working in a bank again and also as a beautician. She returned to serious training in 1987 and finished second to Silke Gladisch of East Germany in that year's world championship 200. Her marriage to 1984 triple jump Olympic champion Al Joyner and her loss to Gladisch marked a turning point in her career. Now known as Florence Griffith Joyner, she became determined to end her string of second places. She obtained a videotape of Ben Johnson's explosive start in the world championship 100-meter final and watched it every day. After consulting with Johnson, she embarked on a vigorous weight-lifting program. She also incorporated endurance runs into her training and, along with her studies of Ben Johnson's start, she watched tapes of Carl Lewis to analyze his form and his ability to run in a relaxed manner.

Griffith Joyner was still considered a 200-meter specialist, but on June 25, 1988, she ran a 10.89 100 in San Diego. Then, at the U.S. Olympic trials, exactly three weeks later, she achieved a stunning breakthrough. Running in a quarterfinal heat, she crossed the finish line in 10.49 seconds, obliterating Evelyn Ashford's 1984 world record of 10.76. In fact her time was faster than the automatically timed *men's* record in a wide range of nations, including Ireland, New Zealand, Norway, Iran, and Turkey. Griffith Joyner's shocking performance was not without controversy. Although the wind gauge next to the triple jump runway 30 feet away registered an unacceptable 4.3 meters per second, the gauge at the track registered exactly 0.0. Because gusty winds were sweeping through the stadium, it was assumed that the instrument had malfunctioned. But Omega Electronics defended their measuring device. In an official memo to the I.A.A.F., the company explained that a wind of 2.80 meters per second had blown across the track, but in a direction of 91 degrees perpendicular to the track. Griffith Joyner's record stood. The next day she won the final in 10.61 with a legal wind of 1.2 meters per second.

Her spectacular times, coupled with her outrageous running suits, which she changed for each race, brought Florence Griffith Joyner overnight celebrity. She acquired yet another name: Flojo. Because of the wind controversy and because her record had been set at a domestic meet, the European sports press was still skeptical of Griffith Joyner's abilities. In Seoul, she put their doubts to rest. In the opening round she set an Olympic record of 10.88. Evelyn Ashford matched that time in the second round, but one heat later, Flojo ran a 10.62. She followed that with a wind-aided 10.70 in the semifinals.

In the final Griffith Joyner showed that her obsessive study of Ben Johnson's start was not wanted. Her reaction time of 0.131 seconds was not only the best in the race, it was faster than that of Johnson himself. Halfway through the race a smile began to spread across her face, and by the time she flashed across the finish line in a wind-aided 10.54, she was positively beaming. Behind her, Ashford edged Heike Drechsler for second place to become, at age 31, the oldest sprint medalist in Olympic history. Anelia Vechernikova was even with Ashford at 80 meters, but pulled a muscle and hobbled in in last place.

Florence Griffith Joyner went on to win two more gold medals and one silver. Unfortunately, the disqualification of Ben Johnson left a cloud of suspicion over Flojo's performances as well. Skeptics pointed to her sudden improvement and her bulging muscles as evidence that she might be using steroids or human growth hormones. Griffith Joyner fueled this speculation by announcing her retirement on February 25, 1989, on the eve of the institution of mandatory random drug testing. However, the record clearly shows that Florence Griffith Joyner passed every drug test she ever took.

## 200 METERS

**1896–1936** not held

**1948 London** C: 33, N: 17, D: 8.6. WR: 23.6 (Stanislawa Walasiewicz)
1. Francina "Fanny" Blankers-Koen   HOL   24.4
2. Audrey Williamson   GBR   25.1
3. Audrey Patterson   USA   25.2
4. Shirley Strickland   AUS   25.2e
5. Margaret Walker   GBR   —
6. Daphne Robb   SAF   —

Fanny Blankers-Koen had already won two gold medals in the 100-meter dash and the 80-meter hurdles. Far from being exuberant about these accomplishments, she felt tremendous pressure to win a third gold medal and was close to a mental breakdown. Prior to the semifinals of the 200 meters she told her husband, Jan, that she wanted to withdraw. Jan tried to calm her down and gave her words of encouragement, but to no avail. In desperation he evoked memories of her parents and her two children, and she burst into tears. When she finally came out of her cry, she had recovered and was once again eager to run. She went out and won her heat by six yards, establishing an Olympic record of 24.3 seconds. The next day, running on a muddy track, she won the final by seven yards, the largest margin ever recorded in the women's 200 meters. In 1975, the photo finish of this race was discovered. It revealed that Strickland had actually finished ahead of Patterson.

**1952 Helsinki** C: 38, N: 21, D: 7.26. WR: 23.6 (Stanislawa Walasiewicz)
1. Marjorie Jackson   AUS   23.7
2. Bertha Brouwer   HOL   24.2
3. Nadezhda Khnykina   SOV   24.2
4. Winsome Cripps   AUS   24.2
5. Helga Klein   GER   24.6
6. Daphne Hasenjager (Robb)   SAF   24.6

The longest-lasting women's track and field world record ever was set by Stanislawa Walasiewicz on August 15, 1935, when she/he ran the 200 meters in 23.6 seconds. Almost 17 years later, Marjorie Jackson tied that record in the first round of the 1952 Helsinki Olympics, and in the first semifinal she ran a 23.4 to finally break it. In the final she reached the tape four yards ahead of her nearest rival.

**1956 Melbourne** C: 27, N: 12, D: 11.30. WR: 23.2 (Betty Cuthbert)
1. Betty Cuthbert   AUS   23.4   EOR
2. Christa Stubnick   GDR   23.7
3. Marlene Matthews   AUS   23.8
4. Norma Croker   AUS   24.0

5. June Paul (Foulds)   GBR   24.3
6. Gisela Köhler   GDR   24.3

For the first and only time in Olympic history, the medalists in the two sprints (100 and 200 meters) finished in the exact same order.

**1960 Rome** C: 29, N: 17, D: 9.5. WR: 22.9 (Wilma Rudolph)
1. Wilma Rudolph   USA   24.0
2. Jutta Heine   GER   24.4
3. Dorothy Hyman   GBR   24.7
4. Maria Itkina   SOV   24.7
5. Barbara Janiszewska   POL   24.8
6. Giuseppina Leone   ITA   24.9

Wilma Rudolph dominated the event, setting an Olympic record of 23.2 in her opening heat. Silver medalist Jutta Heine was the daughter of a millionaire, while the father of bronze medalist Dorothy Hyman was a Yorkshire miner.

**1964 Tokyo** C: 29, N: 21, D: 10.19. WR: 22.9 (Wilma Rudolph, Margaret Burvill)
1. Edith McGuire   USA   23.0   OR
2. Irena Kirszenstein   POL   23.1
3. Marilyn Black   AUS   23.1
4. Una Morris   JAM   23.5
5. Lyudmila Samotyosova   SOV   23.5
6. Barbara Sobotta (Janiszewska)   POL   23.9
7. Janet Simpson   GBR   23.9
8. Daphne Arden   GBR   24.0

**1968 Mexico City** C: 36, N: 21, D: 10.18. WR: 22.7 (Irena Szewińska [Kirszenstein])
1. Irena Szewińska (Kirszenstein)   POL   22.58   WR
2. Raelene Boyle   AUS   22.73
3. Jennifer Lamy   AUS   22.88
4. Barbara Ferrell   USA   22.92
5. Nicole Montandon   FRA   23.08
6. Wyomia Tyus   USA   23.08
7. Margaret Bailes   USA   23.18
8. Jutta Stöck   GER   23.24

Irena Kirszenstein was born in Leningrad to Jewish parents from Poland on May 24, 1946. Beginning in 1964 she competed in five Olympics, winning seven medals in five different events. As an 18-year-old at the 1964 Tokyo Olympics she finished second in the long jump and the 200 meters and ran the second leg on the Polish 4 × 100-meter relay team, which scored an upset victory. In 1967 she culminated a five-year courtship by marrying Janusz Szewińsk, and when she arrived in Mexico City for the 1968 Olympics she was running under the name Irena Szewińska. She was disappointed in her first two events, failing to qualify for the final of the long jump and finishing third in the 100 meters, but in the final of the 200 meters she overcame a slow start to win in world record time.

Most people attribute the plethora of world records which were set in Mexico City to the altitude, but another factor was the unusual method that the Mexicans used for determining wind conditions. With the acceptable limit for world records set at a wind speed of 2 meters per second, the measurement during the women's 200 meters was exactly 2 m.p.s. The same recording of exactly 2.0 m.p.s. was registered when Bob Beamon made his famous 29-foot 2½-inch leap and when Nelson Prudencio and Viktor Saneyev set world records in the triple jump.

Eighth-place finisher Jutta Stöck was the daughter of 1936 javelin gold-medalist Gerhard Stöck.

**1972 Munich** C: 37, N: 27, D: 9.7. WR: 22.4 (Chi Cheng)

| | | | | |
|---|---|---|---|---|
| 1. | Renate Stecher | GDR | 22.40 | EWR |
| 2. | Raelene Boyle | AUS | 22.45 | |
| 3. | Irena Szewińska (Kirszenstein) | POL | 22.74 | |
| 4. | Ellen Stropahl | GDR | 22.75 | |
| 5. | Christina Heinich | GDR | 22.89 | |
| 6. | Annegret Kroniger | GER | 22.89 | |
| 7. | Alice Annum | GHA | 22.99 | |
| 8. | Rosie Allwood | JAM | 23.11 | |

Between August 1970 and June 1974, Renate Stecher won 90 straight outdoor races at 100 meters and 200 meters.

**1976 Montreal** C: 36, N: 21, D: 7.28. WR: 22.21 (Irena Szewińska [Kirszenstein])

| | | | | |
|---|---|---|---|---|
| 1. | Bärbel Eckert | GDR | 22.37 | OR |
| 2. | Annegret Richter | GER | 22.39 | |
| 3. | Renate Stecher | GDR | 22.47 | |
| 4. | Carla Bodendorf | GDR | 22.64 | |
| 5. | Inge Helten | GER | 22.68 | |
| 6. | Tatyana Prorochenko | GBR | 23.03 | |
| 7. | Denise Robertson | AUS | 23.05 | |
| 8. | Chantal Rega | FRA | 23.09 | |

The first shock came in the semifinals, when five-time sprint finalist Raelene Boyle was disqualified for false-starting twice. Boyle was furious and protested unsuccessfully. The electronic starting device had registered a clean start the first time, but the recall judge claimed that Boyle's head and shoulders had been moving. Unaware that she had actually been charged with a false start rather than a mere warning, Boyle was stunned when she was disqualified after her next false start. The real surprise was 21-year-old Bärbel Eckert, East Germany's third-string sprinter. In the quarterfinals she equaled her personal best of 22.85. She won her semifinal heat in 22.71 and then set an Olympic record to win the final.

**1980 Moscow** C: 35, N: 25, D: 7.30. WR: 21.71 (Marita Koch)

| | | | | |
|---|---|---|---|---|
| 1. | Bärbel Wöckel (Eckert) | GDR | 22.03 | OR |
| 2. | Natalya Bochina | SOV | 22.19 | |
| 3. | Merlene Ottey | JAM | 22.20 | |
| 4. | Romy Müller | GDR | 22.47 | |
| 5. | Kathryn Smallwood | GBR | 22.61 | |
| 6. | Beverley Goddard | GBR | 22.72 | |
| 7. | Denise Boyd (Robertson) | AUS | 22.76 | |
| 8. | Sonia Lannaman | GBR | 22.80 | |

Defending champion Bärbel Eckert of Leipzig, now married, a mother, and renamed Wöckel, made it through to the final without winning a single heat. She finished second each time, once to Lyudmila Maslakova of the U.S.S.R., and twice to Merlene Ottey. Meanwhile, 18-year-old Natalya Bochina ran a 22.26 in the second round to break Wöckel's Olympic record. In the final, however, it was Wöckel who took the lead coming out of the turn and won going away. Missing from the competition were the two women who had clocked the fastest times in the world: Marita Koch, who chose to concentrate on the 400 meters, and Evelyn Ashford, who suffered the double blow of injury and boycott.

**1984 Los Angeles** C: 37, N: 28, D: 8.9. WR: 21.71 (Marita Koch)

| | | | | |
|---|---|---|---|---|
| 1. | Valerie Brisco-Hooks | USA | 21.81 | OR |
| 2. | Florence Griffith | USA | 22.04 | |
| 3. | Merlene Ottey-Page | JAM | 22.09 | |
| 4. | Kathryn Cook (Smallwood) | GBR | 22.10 | |
| 5. | Grace Jackson | JAM | 22.20 | |
| 6. | Randy Givens | USA | 22.36 | |
| 7. | Rose-Aimée Bacoul | FRA | 22.78 | |
| 8. | Liliane Gaschet | FRA | 22.86 | |

In 1982, Valerie Brisco-Hooks was a retired runner, forty pounds overweight after giving birth to a baby boy. Encouraged by her family and her coach, she returned to the track the following year and found that childbirth and motherhood had actually increased her strength. In 1984, she seemed to come out of nowhere to make the U.S. team. Three days after winning the 400 meters, Brisco-Hooks, aided by the absence of East Germans Marita Koch and Marlies Göhr, overcame a mediocre start to become the first person to record a 200-400 double win in the Olympics.

**1988 Seoul** C: 59, N: 42, D: 9.29. WR: 21.71 (Marita Koch, Heike Drechsler)

| | | | | |
|---|---|---|---|---|
| 1. | Florence Griffith Joyner | USA | 21.34 | WR |
| 2. | Grace Jackson | JAM | 21.72 | |
| 3. | Heike Drechsler (Daute) | GDR | 21.95 | |
| 4. | Merlene Ottey | JAM | 21.99 | |
| 5. | Silke Möller [Gladisch] | GDR | 22.09 | |
| 6. | Gwen Torrence | USA | 22.17 | |
| 7. | Maia Azarashvili | SOV | 22.33 | |
| 8. | Galina Malchugina | SOV | 22.42 | |

Florence Griffith Joyner set an Olympic record of 21.76 in the quarterfinals. In the semifinals she ran a 21.56 to break the nine-year-old world record. The final, run 100 minutes later, was more of the same: Griffith Joyner pulled away in the second half of the race and leaped joyously across the finish line, stopping the clock in an almost unbelievable 21.34. Grace Jackson took almost a half second off her pre-Olympic best and came within one one-hundredth of a second of the pre-Olympic world record, yet found herself 4 meters behind Griffith Joyner at the finish.

# 400 METERS

**1896–1960** not held

**1964 Tokyo** C: 23, N: 17, D: 10.17. WR: 51.4 (Dan Shin-geum)
| | | | |
|---|---|---|---|
| 1. Betty Cuthbert | AUS | 52.0 | OR |
| 2. Ann Packer | GBR | 52.2 | |
| 3. Judith Amoore | AUS | 53.4 | |
| 4. Antonia Munkácsi | HUN | 54.4 | |
| 5. Maria Itkina | SOV | 54.6 | |
| 6. Mathilda "Tilly" van der Zwaard | HOL | 55.2 | |
| 7. Gertrud Schmidt | GDR | 55.4 | |
| 8. Evelyne Lebret | FRA | 55.5 | |

World record holder Dan Shin-geum of North Korea was barred from participating in the Olympics because of a dispute between the I.O.C. and the North Korean government. In her absence, the inaugural Olympic 400 meters was won by Betty Cuthbert, the remarkable Australian who had earned three gold medals eight years earlier in Melbourne. At the Rome Olympics in 1960 she was suffering from a hamstring pull and was forced to withdraw from competition after only one race. In Tokyo she coasted through the opening round and the semifinals, satisfied to qualify for the final. Then, on October 16, she ran what she later called "the only perfect race I have ever run" to finish a long yard ahead of Ann Packer.

**1968 Mexico City** C: 29, N: 21. D: 10.16. WR: 51.2 (Dan Shin-geum)
| | | | |
|---|---|---|---|
| 1. Colette Besson | FRA | 52.03 | EOR |
| 2. Lillian Board | GBR | 52.12 | |
| 3. Natalya Pechenkina | SOV | 52.25 | |
| 4. Janet Simpson | GBR | 52.57 | |
| 5. Aurelia Penton | CUB | 52.7 | |
| 6. Jarvis Scott | USA | 52.7 | |
| 7. Helga Henning | GER | 52.8 | |
| 8. Hermina Van Der Hoeven | HOL | 53.0 | |

The victory of Colette Besson, a 22-year-old physical education teacher from Bordeaux, came as a complete surprise. Her best time previous to the Olympics was 53.8, but she was able to improve by 1.8 seconds when it counted. She passed the favorite, Lillian Board, just before the finish line and won by almost two feet. Although the harsher members of the British sports press were critical of Board for missing the gold medal, she was only 19 years old and seemed a good bet for the 1972 Olympics in Munich. She did make it to Munich, but the circumstances were tragic. In 1970 she developed cancer, complicated by peritonitis. She died in a Munich clinic 13 days after her 22nd birthday.

**1972 Munich** C: 49, N: 29, D: 9.7. WR: 51.0 (Marilyn Neufville, Monika Zehrt)
| | | | |
|---|---|---|---|
| 1. Monika Zehrt | GDR | 51.08 | OR |
| 2. Rita Wilden | GER | 51.21 | |
| 3. Kathy Hammond | USA | 51.64 | |
| 4. Helga Seidler | GDR | 51.86 | |
| 5. Mable Fergerson | USA | 51.96 | |
| 6. Charlene Rendina | AUS | 51.99 | |
| 7. Dagmar Käsling | GDR | 52.19 | |
| 8. Györgyi Balogh | HUN | 52.39 | |

Despite the absence of injured co-world record holder Marilyn Neufville of Jamaica, the competition was excellent. The Olympic record was broken by five different women before the final was run. However 19-year-old Monika Zehrt of Berlin seemed unaffected by the pressure of her opponents or by her role as favorite. She had taken the lead by the halfway mark and held off a late challenge by local favorite Rita Wilden to win by a meter.

**1976 Montreal** C: 38, N: 19, D: 7:29. WR: 49.75 (Irena Szewińska [Kirszenstein])
| | | | |
|---|---|---|---|
| 1. Irena Szewińska (Kirszenstein) | POL | 49.29 | WR |
| 2. Christina Brehmer | GDR | 50.51 | |
| 3. Ellen Streidt | GDR | 50.55 | |
| 4. Pirjo Häggman | FIN | 50.56 | |
| 5. Rosalyn Bryant | USA | 50.65 | |
| 6. Sheila Ingram | USA | 50.90 | |
| 7. Riita Salin | FIN | 50.98 | |
| 8. Debra Sapenter | USA | 51.66 | |

The amazing Irena Szewińska had already won Olympic medals in the 100 meters, 200 meters, long jump, and 4 × 100-meter relay when she switched to the 400 meters in 1973. The following year she became the first woman to break 50 seconds in what was only the second 400 meters race of her career. Early in 1976 her world record was broken by Christina Brehmer. But later in the year Szewińska regained the record, and an Olympic showdown between the 18-year-old Brehmer and the 30-year-old Szewińska was eagerly awaited. Irena coasted through the first two rounds and then set an Olympic record of 50.48 in the semifinals. For the first 300 meters, the final was a close race, but then Szewińska pulled away dramatically to win by almost ten meters. Her total of seven medals (three gold, two silver, and two bronze) ranks her along with Shirley Strickland as one of the most successful female track and field athletes in Olympic history. Between 1974 and 1978 she won 34 straight 400-meter finals, until she was finally beaten by Marita Koch at the European championships. In 1980 Szewińska took part in the Moscow Olympics, but was eliminated in the semifinals when she pulled a muscle.

Pirjo Häggman, who finished fourth in Montreal, later became the first woman to be elected to the I.O.C.

**1980 Moscow** C: 38, N: 22, D: 7.28. WR: 48.60 (Marita Koch)
| | | | |
|---|---|---|---|
| 1. Marita Koch | GDR | 48.88 | OR |
| 2. Jarmila Kratochvilová | CZE | 49.46 | |
| 3. Christina Lathan (Brehmer) | GDR | 49.66 | |
| 4. Irina Nazarova | SOV | 50.07 | |
| 5. Nina Zyuskova | SOV | 50.17 | |
| 6. Gabriele Löwe | GDR | 51.33 | |
| 7. Pirjo Häggman | FIN | 51.35 | |
| 8. Linsey MacDonald | GBR | 52.40 | |

Marita Koch had been one of the favorites in 1976, but was forced to withdraw from her semifinal heat because of injury. In 1979 she became the first woman to break 22 seconds for 200 meters as well as the first woman to beat 49 seconds for 400 meters. In Moscow, using the same spikes she had used four years earlier in Montreal, Koch won a clear victory over Kratochvilová and Lathan, both of whom recorded personal bests. The race was the first in history in which three women broke the 50-second barrier.

**1984 Los Angeles** C: 28, N: 18, D: 8.6. WR: 47.99 (Jarmila Kratochvilová)

| 1. | Valerie Brisco-Hooks | USA | 48.83 | OR |
|----|----------------------|-----|-------|----|
| 2. | Chandra Cheeseborough | USA | 49.05 | |
| 3. | Kathryn Cook (Smallwood) | GBR | 49.42 | |
| 4 | Marita Payne | CAN | 49.91 | |
| 5. | Lillie Leatherwood | USA | 50.25 | |
| 6. | Ute Thimm | GER | 50.37 | |
| 7. | Charmaine Crooks | CAN | 50.45 | |
| 8. | Ruth Waithera | KEN | 51.56 | |

At the U.S. trials, Cheeseborough had come from behind to defeat Brisco-Hooks, but in the Olympic final, competing only three miles from where her older brother had been shot to death by a stray bullet ten years earlier while jogging on a high school track, Brisco-Hooks held off Cheeseborough's finishing kick to win the first of her three gold medals.

Of the 28 women who took part in the 400-meter competition in 1984, the slowest was Zeina Mina who finished last in her heat with a time of 59.56. However, it is worth bearing in mind the difficulties which Mina faced training in her hometown—Beirut. Lebanon's leading heptathlete, Mina was unable to train for her specialty because shelling prevented her from reaching the stadium. So she ran on the beach, in the subway, anywhere she could find. For a year she didn't run on a track, until two weeks before the Olympics. Her performance in Los Angeles did not bother her. "It is wonderful here," she said, "away from the bombs."

**1988 Seoul** C: 46, N: 33, D: 9.26. WR: 47.60 (Marita Koch)

| 1. | Olga Bryzgina | SOV | 48.65 | OR |
|----|---------------|-----|-------|----|
| 2. | Petra Müller | GDR | 49.45 | |
| 3. | Olga Nazarova | SOV | 49.90 | |
| 4. | Valerie Brisco | USA | 50.16 | |
| 5. | Diane Dixon | USA | 50.72 | |
| 6. | Denean Howard | USA | 51.12 | |
| 7. | Helga Arendt | GER | 51.17 | |
| 8. | Maree Holland | AUS | 51.25 | |

Defending champion Valerie Brisco took the early lead. World champion Olga Bryzgina, fifth at the halfway mark, caught Brisco after 300 meters, opened up an 8-meter lead and won by 6 meters. Her husband, Viktor Bryzgin, also won a gold medal in the 4 × 100-meter relay. With the exception of Bryzgina and Müller, the times in the final were surprisingly slow. In the semis all three Americans had broken 50 seconds, while Olga Nazarova had clocked a 49.11. Unlike the men's 400-meter runners, the women were not allowed a day off between the semifinals and the final.

## 800 METERS

**1896–1924** not held

**1928 Amsterdam** C: 25, N: 13, D: 8.2. WR: 2:19.6 (Lina Radke)

| 1. | Lina Radke | GER | 2:16.8 | WR |
|----|------------|-----|--------|----|
| 2. | Kinue Hitomi | JPN | 2:17.6 | |
| 3. | Inga Gentzel | SWE | 2:17.8 | |
| 4. | Jenny Thompson | CAN | 2:21.6 | |
| 5. | Fanny Rosenfield | CAN | 2:22.4 | |
| 6. | Florence McDonald | USA | 2:22.6 | |
| 7. | Marie Dollinger | GER | 2:23.0 | |
| 8. | Gertruda Kilos | POL | 2:28.0 | |

The 1928 women's 800-meter race touched off a major controversy in the athletic world. The competition itself was exciting enough. The three German finalists, Lina Radke, Marie Dollinger, and Elfriede Wever, ran a team race, with Dollinger and Wever wearing down the opposition and keeping a steady pace for Radke, who pulled away in the final 300 meters. Radke's winning time was a world record that lasted for sixteen years. After the race, several of the women collapsed in exhaustion and some had to be given aid. Antifeminists in the press and in the International Amateur Athletic Federation (I.A.A.F.) seized on their condition as evidence that women should be banned from running races of more than 200 meters. The London *Daily Mail* quoted doctors who said that women who took part in races of 800 meters and other such "feats of endurance" would "become old too soon." The president of the International Olympic Committee, Comte de Baillet-Latour, spoke out in favor of eliminating all women's sports from the Olympics and returning to the ancient Greek custom of an all-male competition. But there were those who supported women's athletics, and they pointed out that men frequently fainted after races just as women did. In fact, male rowers were *expected* to be nearly comatose at the finish of important races, such as those between Oxford and Cambridge or Harvard and Yale. In retrospect, of course, the arguments of the antiwomen forces seem foolish and ridiculous, particularly in light of the inclusion of a women's marathon in the 1984 Olympics. What makes the story more of a tragedy than a comedy, however, is that the executive committee of the I.A.A.F. actually *did* ban races longer than 200 meters, and no women's race longer than ½ lap was run at the Olympics for another 32 years.

Some of the early women athletes were extremely versatile. Fifth-place finisher Fanny Rosenfield, who worked in a Toronto chocolate factory, also took second in the 100 meters and first in the 4 × 100-meter relay. Silver medalist Kinue Hitomi was the world record holder in the 200 meters and the long jump. Since neither event was included in the Olympics program, she took part instead in the 100 meters and the 800 meters. At the third Women's World Games, held in Prague in 1930, Hitomi delighted the crowd by winning four medals: a gold in the long jump, a silver in the triathlon, and bronzes in the 60-meter dash and the discus. The following year Kinue Hitomi died of tuberculosis at the age of 23.

**1932–1956** not held

**1960 Rome** C: 27, N: 15, D: 9.7. WR: 2:04.3 (Lyudmila Shevtsova)
1. Lyudmila Shevtsova SOV 2:04.3 EWR
2. Brenda Jones AUS 2:04.4
3. Ursula Donath GDR 2:05.6
4. Vera Kummerfeldt GER 2:05.9
5. Antje Gleichfeld GER 2:06.5
6. Joyce Jordan GBR 2:07.8
7. Gizella Csoka HUN 2:08.0
8. Beata Zbikowska POL 2:11.8

Dixie Willis of Australia led the field for most of the race, but, with 150 meters to go, she suddenly threw her arms into the air and staggered off the track. Brenda Jones took the lead, but was passed by world record holder Lyudmila Shevtsova just before the finish.

**1964 Tokyo** C: 23, N: 15, D: 10.20. WR: 1:58.0 (Dan Shin-geum)
1. Ann Packer GBR 2:01.1 OR
2. Maryvonne Dupureur FRA 2:01.9
3. M. Ann Marise Chamberlain NZE 2:02.8
4. Zsuzsa Szabó HUN 2:03.5
5. Antje Gleichfeld GER 2:03.9
6. Laine Erik SOV 2:05.1
7. Gerarda Kraan HOL 2:05.8
8. Anne Smith GBR 2:05.8

With unofficial world record holder Dan Shin-geum out because of politics and official world record holder (2:01.2) Dixie Willis out because of illness, the 800 meters looked like an open race. In the semifinals, Maryvonne Dupureur, a housewife and physical education teacher from Lille, set an Olympic record of 2:04.1. In the final Dupureur had a five-yard lead entering the last straightaway, but Britain's Ann Packer, who had already won a silver medal in the 400 meters, turned on a fantastic finishing kick, passed Dupureur with 70 yards to go, and won by five yards. The 800 meters was not really Packer's race. She had finished fifth in her opening heat and third in her semifinal heat. She had considered skipping the final and going shopping instead, but when her fiancé, Robbie Brightwell, finished a disappointing fourth in the men's 400 meters, she decided to go all-out in his honor. "It was so easy, I could not believe I had won," she told reporters afterward. "I was thinking about him and not about myself, and so I wasn't nervous."

**1968 Mexico City** C: 24, N: 16, D: 10.19. WR: 1:58.0 (Dan Shin-geum)
1. Madeline Manning USA 2:00.9 OR
2. Ileana Silai ROM 2:02.5
3. Maria Gommers HOL 2:02.6
4. Sheila Taylor GBR 2:03.8
5. Doris Brown USA 2:03.9
6. Patricia Lowe GBR 2:04.2
7. Abigail Hoffman CAN 2:06.8
8. Maryvonne Dupureur FRA 2:08.2

The most shocking incident of the 1968 women's events occurred in the first semifinal heat, when the 20-year-old favorite, and official world record holder (2:00.5) Vera Nikolić of Yugoslavia, overcome by the pressure of being her nation's only hope for a track and field medal, dropped out after 300 meters and left the stadium. Rumors quickly spread that she had gone straight to a nearby bridge and was only prevented from committing suicide by her coach, who had followed her. That race was won by 20-year-old Madeline Manning, a Tennessee State "Tigerbelle" from Cleveland. Two days later, in the final, Manning took the early lead, then, spurred on by the garlicky perspiration of one of the other runners, she pulled away in the backstretch of the final lap and won by over ten meters.

**1972 Munich** C: 38, N: 26, D: 9.3. WR: 1:58.0 (Dan Shin-geum)
1. Hildegard Falck GER 1:58.55 OR
2. Nijolė Sabaitė SOV 1:58.65
3. Gunhild Hoffmeister GDR 1:59.19
4. Svetla Zlateva BUL 1:59.72
5. Vera Nikolić YUG 1:59.98
6. Ileana Silai ROM 2:00.04
7. Rosemary Stirling GBR 2:00.15
8. Abigail Hoffman CAN 2:00.17

The fireworks started in the second heat of the first round, when Svetla Zlateva slashed three seconds off her personal best to set an Olympic record of 1:58.9. Vera Nikolić finished close behind her in 1:59.6. Previous to this race, the only women to better two minutes had been Dan Shin-geum, Hildegard Falck, and Vasilena Amzina of Bulgaria, who had run a 1:59.9 a week before the Olympics began. In the fourth heat of the first round Amzina collided with Raisa Ruus of the U.S.S.R. and fell to the ground. She got up and finished the race with blood on her face, but she failed to qualify for the next round. The first semifinal was won by Lithuanian Nijolė Sabaitė and the second by local favorite Hildegard Falck, a 23-year-old schoolteacher. In the second semi, defending champion Madeline Manning was eliminated when she misjudged the finish line and was passed just before the real line by Rosemary Stirling. The final was a thrilling race. Falck, urged on by the partisan crowd, pulled away coming out of the last curve and held off a final burst by Sabaitė.

**1976 Montreal** C: 35, N: 20, D: 7.26. WR: 1:56.0 (Valentina Gerassimova)

| | | | |
|---|---|---|---|
| 1. Tatyana Kazankina | SOV | 1:54.94 | WR |
| 2. Nikolina Shtereva | BUL | 1:55.42 | |
| 3. Elfi Zinn | GDR | 1:55.60 | |
| 4. Anita Weiss | GDR | 1:55.74 | |
| 5. Svetlana Styrkina | SOV | 1:56.44 | |
| 6. Svetla Zlateva | BUL | 1:57.21 | |
| 7. Doris Gluth | GDR | 1:58.99 | |
| 8. Mariana Suman | ROM | 2:02.21 | |

The level of the competition was so high that world record holder Valentina Gerassimova, European champion Liliana Tomova of Bulgaria, Commonwealth champion Charlene Rendina of Australia, and 1968 Olympic champion Madeline Jackson (Manning) were all eliminated in the semifinals. Anita Weiss, who lowered the Olympic record by two seconds with a 1:56.53 in her semifinal heat, broke the world record in the final, but didn't even win a medal. Kazankina, a 1500-meter specialist who had been entered in the 800 meters as well on the final day for entries, moved from fifth place to first in the last 50 meters and slashed the world record by over a second.

**1980 Moscow** C: 28, N: 17, D: 7.27. WR: 1:54.8 (Nadezhda Olizarenko)

| | | | |
|---|---|---|---|
| 1. Nadezhda Olizarenko | SOV | 1:53.42 | WR |
| 2. Olga Minoyova | SOV | 1:54.9 | |
| 3. Tatyana Providokhina | SOV | 1:55.5 | |
| 4. Martina Kämpfert | GDR | 1:56.3 | |
| 5. Hildegard Ullrich | GDR | 1:57.2 | |
| 6. Jolanta Januchta | POL | 1:58.3 | |
| 7. Nikolina Shtereva | BUL | 1:58.8 | |
| 8. Gabriella Dorio | ITA | 1:59.2 | |

For the first time in Olympic history, all three medals in a women's track event were won by athletes from the same nation. Olizarenko, a 26-year-old military office worker from Odessa, ran a spectacular race, leading from start to finish (a rarity at 800 meters) and clipping almost one and a half seconds from her own world record, set only six weeks earlier.

**1984 Los Angeles** C: 25, N: 20, D: 8.6. WR: 1:53.28 (Jarmila Kratochvílová)

| | | |
|---|---|---|
| 1. Doina Melinte | ROM | 1:57.60 |
| 2. Kimberly Gallagher | USA | 1:58.63 |
| 3. Rafira Fita Lovin | ROM | 1:58.83 |
| 4. Gabriella Dorio | ITA | 1:59.05 |
| 5. Lorraine Baker | GBR | 2:00.03 |
| 6. Ruth Wysocki | USA | 2:00.34 |
| 7. Margrit Klinger | GER | 2:00.65 |
| 8. Caroline O'Shea | IRL | 2:00.77 |

Melinte, known for her fast times, but disappointing performances in important meets, took the lead from Dorio with about 225 meters to go and won by over five meters. Conspicuously missing because of the Soviet-bloc boycott was Czech world record holder Jarmila Kratochvílová, who had caused a sensation at the 1983 world

championships by winning the 400- and 800-meter races, a most unusual double.

**1988 Seoul** C: 29, N: 20, D: 9.26. WR: 1:53.28 (Jarmila Kratochvílová)

| | | |
|---|---|---|
| 1. Sigrun Wodars | GDR | 1:56.10 |
| 2. Christine Wachtel | GDR | 1:56.64 |
| 3. Kimberly Gallagher | USA | 1:56.91 |
| 4. Slobodanka Čolović | YUG | 1:57.50 |
| 5. Delisa Floyd | USA | 1:57.80 |
| 6. Inna Yevseyeva | SOV | 1:59.37 |
| 7. Teresa Zuniga | SPA | 1:59.82 |
| 8. Diane Edwards | GBR | 2:00.77 |

The two Ws, Wodars and Wachtel, had a lot in common. They were both born in 1965, they were both 5 feet 5¼ inches tall, they ran for the same club and trained under the same coach, and they both liked champagne, ice cream, and chocolate. Most important of all, they were both experts at running 800 meters. In 1987, Wachtel defeated Wodars four straight times, but in the biggest meet of the year, the world championships in Rome, Wodars came out on top.

In 1988, Wachtel was again dominant, finishing ahead of Wodars seven of eight times in the run-up to the Olympics. In Seoul, the two Ws took turns setting the pace. Wodars forged ahead in the final straightaway and went on to win by 5 meters. Unfortunately, the Cuban boycott prevented the participation of Ana Quirot, who had won all 13 of her 800-meter races in 1988, including victories over both Wodars and Wachtel. The entire Romanian squad also missed the Games; they were victims of blundering team officials who forgot to file their entry forms.

## 1500 METERS

**1896–1968** not held

**1972 Munich** C: 36, N: 21, D: 9.9. WR: 4:06.9 (Lyudmila Bragina)

| | | | |
|---|---|---|---|
| 1. Lyudmila Bragina | SOV | 4:01.4 | WR |
| 2. Gunhild Hoffmeister | GDR | 4:02.8 | |
| 3. Paola Cacchi | ITA | 4:02.9 | |
| 4. Karin Burneleit | GDR | 4:04.1 | |
| 5. Sheila Carey | GBR | 4:04.8 | |
| 6. Ilja Keizer | HOL | 4:05.1 | |
| 7. Tamara Pangelova | SOV | 4:06.5 | |
| 8. Jennifer Orr | AUS | 4:12.2 | |

Twenty-nine-year-old Lyudmila Bragina exploded onto the international scene six weeks before the Olympics when she chopped 2.7 seconds off Karin Burneleit's world record by running a 4:06.9 in a *heat* of the Soviet championships. A few weeks later she ran 3000 meters in 8:53.0, to better the world record at that distance by over 16 seconds. In the first heat of the first round of the 1500 meters at Munich, Bragina led from start to finish and broke her own world record in 4:06.47, carrying 17-year-old Glenda Reiser of Canada with her in 4:06.71. Three days later Bragina again broke the world record with a 4:05.07 in her semifinal heat. The semifinals saw 13 women better the pre-Olympic world record. In the final, Bragina moved to the front after two laps and pulled away to a 12-meter lead, which she held for the entire last lap. In a postrace interview, Bragina told reporters, "We shall be running 3 minutes 56 seconds before the next Olympics." She hit it right on the button, as 3:56.0 was exactly the world record at the time of the 1976 Olympics.

**1976 Montreal** C: 36, N: 19, D: 7.30. WR: 3:56.0 (Tatyana Kazankina)
1. Tatyana Kazankina       SOV   4:05.48
2. Gunhild Hoffmeister     GDR   4:06.02
3. Ulrike Klapezynski      GDR   4:06.09
4. Nikolina Shtereva       BUL   4:06.57
5. Lyudmila Bragina        SOV   4:07.20
6. Gabriella Dorio         ITA   4:07.27
7. Ellen Wellmann          GER   4:07.91
8. Janice Merrill          USA   4:08.54

Bragina's Munich world record went unbeaten until one month before the next Olympics, when Kazankina lowered it by 5.4 seconds. Track fans who had hoped for a new record in the Olympic final were disappointed, as the race turned into a tactical affair. With one lap to go, Bragina took the lead, but 200 meters later, with elbows flying, she was passed by the two East German training mates, Hoffmeister on the inside and Klapezynski on the outside. Meanwhile, Kazankina, who had already won the 800 meters gold medal, steered clear of the elbowing and moved up on the outside to take the lead with 50 meters to go. She won by three meters. Defending champion Lyudmila Bragina had to settle for fifth place, but her career was hardly over. A few days later, at a U.S.A. vs. U.S.S.R. meet, she ran the 3000 meters in 8:27.2, 18.3 seconds faster than the previous world record. This put her only 50 years behind the men's pace, something of a record in women's track events.

**1980 Moscow** C: 24, N: 14, D: 8.1. WR: 3:55.0 (Tatyana Kazankina)
1. Tatyana Kazankina       SOV   3:56.6   OR
2. Christiane Wartenberg   GDR   3:57.8
3. Nadezhda Olizarenko     SOV   3:59.6
4. Gabriella Dorio         ITA   4:00.3
5. Ulrike Bruns            GDR   4:00.7
6. Lyubov Smolka           SOV   4:01.3
7. Maricica Puică          ROM   4:01.3
8. Ileana Silai            ROM   4:03.0

Covering the final 800 meters in 1:59.0, Kazankina took the lead with 600 meters to go and had left the other runners 20 meters behind by the time she reached the last curve. Twelve days later she lowered the world record to 3:52.47 and became the first woman to run 1500 meters faster than Paavo Nurmi. In September, 1984, Kazankina received an 18-month suspension for refusing to sub-

mit to a test for drugs following a 5000-meter race in Paris.

**1984 Los Angeles** C: 22, N: 15, D: 8.11. WR: 3:52.47 (Tatyana Kazankina)
1. Gabriella Dorio         ITA   4:03.25
2. Doina Melinte           ROM   4:03.76
3. Maricica Puică          ROM   4:04.15
4. Roswitha Gerdes         GER   4:04.41
5. Christine Benning       GBR   4:04.70
6. Christina Boxer         GBR   4:05.53
7. Brit McRoberts          CAN   4:05.98
8. Ruth Wysocki            USA   4:08.92

At the 1983 world championships, the first five places had gone to Mary Decker, three Soviet runners, and Wendy Sly of Great Britain. With all five absent, the roles of favorites went to the two Romanians, Maricica Puică, who had won the 3000-meter gold 24 hours earlier, and Doina Melinte, who had been victorious in the 800 meters five days before the final of the 1500. But Gabriella Dorio had other ideas. Having suffered from taking the early lead in the 800, she held back in the 1500, allowing Chris Boxer to set a slow pace. Then, with 1½ laps to go, Dorio moved to the front, followed closely by Melinte. Melinte took the lead on the final lap and it looked like a repeat of the 800. But this time Dorio had saved an extra charge of energy for the finish. She regained the lead coming into the homestretch and could not be caught. Puică, who waited too long to make her final sprint, finished strongly to take the bronze. Among the many rewards that came Dorio's way as a result of her victory was an unusual one: her husband had promised her that if she won a gold medal he would give her a bath—in wine.

**1988 Seoul** C: 28, N: 19, D: 10.1. WR: 3:52.47 (Tatyana Kazankina)
1. Paula Ivan              ROM   3:53.96   OR
2. Laimutė Baikauskaite    SOV   4:00.24
3. Tatyana Samolenko       SOV   4:00.30
4. Christina Cahill (Boxer) GBR  4:00.64
5. Lynn Williams           CAN   4:00.86
6. Andrea Hahmann          GDR   4:00.96
7. Shireen Bailey          GBR   4:02.32
8. Mary Slaney (Decker)    USA   4:02.49

Until 1988, the career of 25-year-old Paula Ivan had been decent but undistinguished. Beginning in July of the Olympic year, she suddenly showed rapid and spectacular improvement. On August 17, she ran 3:56.22 for her third personal best in 6 weeks. Only Mary Slaney's 3:58.92 at the U.S. Olympic trials came within 4 seconds of Ivan's pre-Olympic time. In Seoul, 6 days before the 1500-meter final, Ivan thought she was about to win the gold medal at 3000 meters, when Tatyana Samolenko sprinted by her to steal the victory.

In order to neutralize Samolenko's kick, Ivan decided

to try to run away from the field early in the 1500. Her strategy worked perfectly. She led by 3 meters after 400 meters, 10 meters after 800, and then seemed to increase her lead with each step for the remainder of the race, until she crossed the finish line with an unprecedented margin of victory of 40 meters. The battle for second was won by Lithuanian Laimutė Baikauskaite, who came from last place at the halfway mark to nip Samolenko in a photo finish.

# 3000 METERS

**1896–1980** not held.

**1984 Los Angeles** C: 31, N: 21, D: 8.10. WR: 8:26.78 (Svetlana Ulmasova)

| | | | |
|---|---|---|---|
| 1. Maricica Puică | ROM | 8:35.96 | OR |
| 2. Wendy Sly | GBR | 8:39.47 | |
| 3. Lynn Williams | CAN | 8:42.14 | |
| 4. Cindy Bremser | USA | 8:42.78 | |
| 5. Cornelia Bürki | SWI | 8:45.20 | |
| 6. Aurora Cunha | POR | 8:46.37 | |
| 7. Zola Budd | GBR | 8:48.80 | |
| 8. Joan Hansen | USA | 8:51.53 | |

They called her "Little Mary Decker" when she first attracted international attention in 1973 by upsetting Olympic 800-meter silver medalist Nijolė Sabaitė at a U.S.A.-U.S.S.R. dual meet in Minsk. And why not? Five feet tall and weighing 86 pounds, the fawn-like Decker was only 14 years old at the time. She had discovered running at age 11, during a period when her life was in turmoil. Her family had just moved from New Jersey to California and her parents were on the road to divorce. Mary Decker threw herself into her new pursuit. During one seven-day period when she was 12 years old, she competed in a marathon (finishing with a time of 3:09), a 440, an 880, a mile race and a two-mile. The next day she was hospitalized for an emergency appendectomy.

In 1974, Decker again caused a minor sensation at a U.S.A.-U.S.S.R. dual meet, this time in Moscow. Running the anchor leg in a 4 × 800-meter relay, she was shoved off the indoor track by Latvian Sarmite Shtula. Decker responded by throwing her relay baton at Shtula. She retrieved the baton and continued the race, but at the finish line Decker again threw the baton at Shtula. Both teams were disqualified, and Decker was admonished for her unsportsmanlike behavior. However, no one in the United States has ever been condemned for responding violently to blatant Soviet aggression, so she was quickly forgiven. Besides, she was still only 15 years old.

At this point, Mary Decker's career took a drastic downward turn. Her intense, some would say obsessive, devotion to running began to take its toll on her still-growing body. Her legs, in particular, began to give in to the strain, and for the next three years she went from doctor to doctor and treatment to treatment desperately trying to relieve her pain. In tears she watched the 1976 Olympics on television, as runners she had beaten two years earlier collected medals that should have been hers.

Then in 1977, she chanced to meet 1976 10,000-meter silver medalist Dick Quax, who immediately recognized her physical problems as Compartment Syndrome in which the sheaths of tissues surrounding muscles fail to expand with the muscles' growth. An operation on her calf relieved the pain. After surviving two automobile accidents and then another operation, her times began improving again.

In 1980 she set her first world record, running the mile in 4:21.7. She qualified easily for the U.S. Olympic team, but the anti-Soviet boycott prevented her from competing. Again she watched the Olympics on television. Then she flew to Europe where she was beaten at 1500 meters by Olympic champion Tatyana Kazankina and by Gabriella Dorio, who became the first Western woman to run the 1500 in less than four minutes. Despite increasing pain in her legs, Decker kept running until finally she had to be operated on to repair a partial tear of her Achilles' tendon. In 1981 she underwent a third operation on her shins and was forced to sit out the year.

The following year was her best yet. In June she set a 5000-meter world record of 15:08.26. On July 9, in Paris, she broke the mile record again with a time of 4:18.08. On the 14th, in Lausanne, she ran the 800 in 1:58.33. Two days later, after flying back to Eugene, Oregon, she set a 10,000-meter world record with a time of 31:35.3. 1983 would see further improvements. Until this time Decker was still considered unproven, because she had not beaten the Eastern Europeans who dominated women's middle-distance running. But then came Mary Decker's masterpieces. At the inaugural world championships in Helsinki she scored a thrilling start to finish victory in the 3000 meters, stunning 3-time Olympic champion Tatyana Kazankina, as well as world record holder Svetlana Ulmasova. Four days later, in the 1500 meters, she again led from the beginning. Entering the final curve she was passed and cut off by Zamira Zaitseva. Decker lost her momentum, but in the homestretch she came roaring back. After a heart-stopping stretch run she nipped Zaitseva at the finish to complete a spectacular double victory. Immediately, Decker became the early favorite for the 1984 Olympics, which would take place in her former hometown, Los Angeles.

Mary Decker returned to the United States as a national hero. Beautiful and strong, she had defeated the Soviets. She seemed to symbolize all that was good about the American character. Of course, track aficionados were all too aware of the dark side of Decker's personality. For example, there was the ugly incident that took place at the 1983 Millrose Games in New York. When Angelita Lind, a Puerto Rican runner about to be lapped, failed to move to the outside to let Decker pass, America's sweetheart shoved her to the ground and forged ahead. Decker's belated sensitivity to this incident would have tragic consequences 18 months later at the Olympics. In the meantime, all over the nation, all over the world in fact, young girls dreamed of becoming like Mary Decker.

One such hero-worshiper, half a world away, was a slight, shy South African teenager named Zola Budd, who kept a poster of Decker on the wall beside her bed. Like Decker, Budd was a precocious talent. When she first told her father that she was winning races at school, he thought that was nice, but when he watched her win one such race by a lap—in a three-lap race—he realized that he should take the situation more seriously and find her a coach. As Budd's times improved, word of her accomplishments began to trickle out to the outside world. In 1983, at the age of 17, the 5-foot, 82-pound Budd was ranked number one in the world at 5000 meters by *Track and Field News*. On January 5, 1984, Budd, who always competed barefooted, ran the distance in 15:01.83 to break Mary Decker's world record by over six seconds. Clearly Zola Budd was ready for international competition. However, South Africa had been banned by the I.A.A.F. in 1976 and had not been allowed in the Olympics since 1960. As long as Budd remained a South African citizen, her running career had no future.

But for Zola Budd, there was a loophole. Because her paternal grandfather was British, she could move to Great Britain and change her citizenship. On March 24, with all expenses paid by the *Daily Mail* newspaper, Zola and her parents arrived in England and set up residency in Guildford, Surrey. Less than two weeks later Zola Budd was granted British citizenship. The next four months would be enormously traumatic for the shy young girl. Accustomed to the quiet life on her farm in Bloemfontein in Orange Free State, she suddenly found herself the object of intense hostility—from other British runners, from the *Daily Mail*'s rivals and from the many opponents of South Africa's racial policies. She ran her first race in England on April 14, then withdrew from another to avoid confrontations with the left-wing local government. On April 25, she won a 1500-meter race, but crossed the finish line in tears after being taunted throughout the race by blacks displaying signs that read, "WHITE TRASH GO HOME." Amidst all this turmoil, she also had to qualify for the British team. This she did, by winning every race that she was required to. After one race, teammate Jane Furniss, who had initially harshly criticized Budd, hugged her and gave her a kiss. At last, it seemed, Zola Budd would be allowed to get on with her running.

Back in the United States, Mary Decker had come up against another setback. In Helsinki she had been able to achieve her 1500/3000 double because the heats for the 1500 hadn't begun until after the final of the 3000. The Olympic schedule was different. The two events overlapped, making a double more difficult. The U.S. trials

were set up with the same schedule as the Olympics, giving Decker an opportunity to try it out. She won the 3000, but was upset by Ruth Wysocki in the 1500. On July 11, 2½ weeks before the Games would begin, Decker announced that she would withdraw from the 1500 and compete only in the 3000, the same race that Zola Budd would be entering.

The scheduled Decker-Budd confrontation encouraged the U.S. media to indulge in an absolute orgy of pre-Olympic hype, much to the annoyance of both parties concerned. The problem was that all track fans knew that Budd was not really ready to compete at Decker's level, especially since Budd specialized at longer distances which were not yet a part of the Olympic program. Decker's real threat came not from Zola Budd, but from 34-year-old Maricica Puică. Although Puică had missed the Helsinki championships because of an injury sustained while playing basketball, her credentials were solid. Not only had she previously competed in the 1976 and 1980 Olympics, but she was the current world record holder in the mile and the reigning world cross-country champion. She had also recorded the fastest 3000-meter time of the pre-Olympic season: 8:33.57.

The qualifying heats of the Olympic 3000 were held on August 8. The first heat was won by Mary Decker, the second by Brigitte Kraus of West Germany, who placed second behind Decker in the world championship 3000. In the third heat Budd led from the start but was passed in the run-in by Puică and Cindy Bremser. "It's unusual to run with a pack of people," commented Budd afterwards. "I'm happy to be running here, it's very nice."

The final was held two days later. The intense midday heat had cooled to a pleasant 75° Fahrenheit (24° Centigrade) by race time. Decker took the early lead and set a fast pace, followed closely by Budd, Puică and Wendy Sly, although all of the runners were tightly packed. At the 1400-meter mark Joan Hansen tripped on Aurora Cunha's heel and fell. She recovered quickly and continued running. At 1600 meters, Sly moved up to challenge Decker along the backstretch, but Budd moved between them and took the lead entering the turn. As the pace accelerated, Budd, Decker, Sly and Puică began to pull away from the others.

Coming out of the turn Budd was in front, running on the outside edge of lane one. Decker, on the inside of the lane, maintained her position and pace. At about the 1700-meter mark, Decker hit one of Budd's legs, throwing Budd off balance just a bit. Five strides later, they bumped again. This time Budd landed awkwardly, her left leg shooting out in search of balance. Decker, running straight and hard, tripped on Budd's right leg, her spikes cutting deeply into Budd's heel. Decker lost her balance and pitched forward onto the infield. Puică, running directly behind Decker, hurdled over her leg. Budd looked back to see her idol falling to the ground. As the runners zipped by, Mary Decker attempted to rise. But her hard landing had caused her to suffer a pulled left hip stabilizer muscle. "It was like I was tied to the ground," she would later explain. As the race continued, Decker was left writhing in agony, weeping in frustration.

The partisan crowd of over 85,000 was stunned. At first the stadium went silent. Then the booing began. Fifty-two years earlier, in the same stadium, a similar incident had occurred between a U.S. athlete and a foreign athlete during the running of the men's 5000-meter final at the 1932 Olympics. That time the track announcer, Bill Henry, had silenced the crowd by reminding them that "these people are our guests." In 1984 there was no Bill Henry to intervene. As the race continued, Zola Budd was met by booing at every turn. Bleeding, and in tears because of the crowd's reaction, she kept running, but her spirit was gone.

Five hundred meters from the finish, Sly and Puică passed Budd, entering the final lap with Sly in the lead. With 250 meters to go, Puică moved effortlessly ahead of Sly and went on to win by over fifteen meters. Budd, still in third only 200 meters from the finish, slowed to a jog and finished seventh.

In the tunnel leading away from the track, Mary Decker was being comforted by her fiancé, discus thrower Richard Slaney. As the other runners filed by, they offered their condolences. Budd approached Decker and said, "I'm sorry. I'm sorry. I'm sorry."

"Don't bother," replied Decker, "I don't want to talk to you."

As Budd stood crying, fifth place finisher Cornelia Bürki, a Swiss runner who was born in South Africa, came to Budd's defense. "It wasn't Zola's fault, Mary!" she said. "Not her fault."

"Yes, it was," Decker shot back. "I know it was. It was!"

Initially Budd was disqualified on the testimony of two track officials, both Americans. But upon reviewing videotapes of the incident from various angles, a jury of appeal voted unanimously to reinstate her. Decker, however, would never budge from her position that Zola Budd was at fault for cutting in before she had established a clear lead.

The controversy raged across the Atlantic Ocean. At first the U.S. media supported Decker, while the British press took Budd's side. The issue was so emotional that the comments of Maricica Puică, who was the closest witness to the incident, were quoted completely differently in the U.S. and Great Britain. American newspapers, without exception, limited their coverage of Puică's remarks to "It was tough for me to decide [who was at fault]. I'm sorry for what happened to Mary. She is a fine competitor." In Great Britain, and the rest of the world, Puică was quoted as saying that Decker was at fault because Budd was in the lead and Decker tried to pass her on the inside, an assertion which Decker flatly denied.

As the public viewed repeated replays of the race, opinions on both sides of the Atlantic began to soften and almost everyone apologized. The truth is that neither Budd nor Decker was actually *at fault,* although both made mistakes. Budd should not have cut in so sharply. However such moves are not uncommon and are never cause for disqualification. Decker, for her part, should have known better than to bull forward like a tailgating commuter rushing home on a Friday evening. She could have given Budd a slight push, perhaps not quite as hard as the one she gave Angelita Lind at the Millrose Games. It is true that reaction to the Millrose incident might have haunted Decker. At her post-race press conference in Los Angeles, she said, "Looking back, I should have pushed her, but the headlines tomorrow would have read 'DECKER PUSHES ZOLA.' " Decker's other alternative was to do what she had done in Helsinki when she was cut off by Zaitseva in the last lap of the 1500: slow down and pass on the outside. In Los Angeles she even had the luxury of 1300 meters left in the race rather than 200.

Mary Decker did not run again in 1984. However, by 1985 she had recovered from her injuries and had a brilliant season, which she completed undefeated. Amongst her victories was a sensational mile race in Zurich in which she defeated both Puică and Budd, and stripped Puică of her world record to boot. Decker returned to the Olympics in 1988, placing tenth in the 3000 and eighth in the 1500.

If Decker's performance in Seoul was disappointing, at least she was able to compete. Zola Budd was not so lucky. She won the world cross-country championship in 1985 and 1986, then was forced to take time off because of injury. She returned to competition, but in April 1988, the I.A.A.F. recommended that the British Amateur Athletic Board suspend her from international athletics for at least twelve months because she *attended* a cross-country event in Brakpan, South Africa, even though she didn't compete in it. On the verge of emotional collapse, Budd gave up her Olympic dreams and returned to her family in South Africa. During her tumultuous four years in Great Britain, Zola Budd had steadfastly refused to comment on South Africa's racial policies, even though a simple statement against apartheid would have helped her personal cause immensely. Instead, she waited until 1989, when her racing career appeared to be finished, to issue an unequivocal denouncement of apartheid.

**1988 Seoul** C: 35, N: 24, D: 9.25. WR: 8:22.62 (Tatyana Kazankina)

| | | | |
|---|---|---|---|
| 1. Tatyana Samolenko | SOV | 8:26.53 | OR |
| 2. Paula Ivan | ROM | 8:27.15 | |
| 3. Yvonne Murray | GBR | 8:29.02 | |
| 4. Yelena Romanova | SOV | 8:30.45 | |
| 5. Natalya Artemova | SOV | 8:31.67 | |
| 6. Vicki Huber | USA | 8:37.25 | |
| 7. Wendy Sly | GBR | 8:37.70 | |
| 8. Lynn Williams | CAN | 8:38.43 | |

Mary Slaney (Decker) rushed into the lead, taking the pack through a torrid world record pace for the first 1000 meters. She was still in front at the halfway mark, but, much to her disappointment, nine other runners were close behind her. Shortly before the 2000-meter mark, Vicki Huber swept by Slaney with Yvonne Murray, Paula Ivan, and the 27-year-old world champion, Tatyana Samolenko, right on her heels. With 450 meters to go, Murray made her move. Ivan and Samolenko followed easily. On the backstretch, about 200 meters from the finish, Ivan took the lead and tried to pull away. But Samolenko was not to be denied. Running a 59.4 last lap, she edged past a surprised Ivan 50 meters from the finish. Thanks in part to the pacesetting Americans, the final times were excellent. Samolenko, Ivan, Romanova, and Huber each improved their personal bests by over 9 seconds, Murray by over 8 seconds and Artemova by 7½.

On the darker side is the story of the South Korean record holder, Lim Chun-ae. A complete unknown from a poor rural family, Lim became a national hero in 1986 when, at the age of 17, she won three gold medals at the Asian Games. In June of 1987, word leaked out that Lim had been hospitalized for two weeks with a broken eardrum after her coach, Kim Pon-il, beat her as punishment for performing poorly in training. Kim was not punished, while Lim publicly accepted blame for her "accident." When the Olympics came to Seoul, Lim Chun-ae was chosen to be the final bearer of the Olympic torch. As the whole world watched, it was Lim who carried the torch around the track in the main stadium and handed it to the cauldron lighters. Six days later, Lim took part in her only individual event: the 3000 meters. Unfortunately, she finished fifteenth and last in her qualifying heat, crossing the finish line over fourteen seconds after the other runners were done. She immediately fell to the ground, buried her head between her legs, and wept. The following year, she retired from competition.

## 10,000-METERS

**1896-1984** not held

**1988 Seoul** C: 34, N: 20, D: 9.30. WR: 30:13.74 (Ingrid Kristiansen)

| | | | |
|---|---|---|---|
| 1. Olga Bondarenko | SOV | 31:05.21 | OR |
| 2. Elizabeth McColgan | GBR | 31:08.44 | |
| 3. Yelena Zhupiyeva | SOV | 31:19.82 | |
| 4. Kathrin Ullrich | GDR | 31:29.27 | |
| 5. Frances Larrieu Smith | USA | 31:35.52 | |
| 6. Lynn Jennings | USA | 31:39.93 | |
| 7. Wang Xiuting | CHN | 31:40.23 | |
| 8. Susan Lee | CAN | 31:50.51 | |

Ingrid Kristiansen of Norway had dominated this event since 1985 when she set her first world record at 10,000 meters at the Bislett Games in Oslo. The following year,

at the next Bislett Games, she ran a 30:13.74 to take an amazing 45.72 seconds off her own record. She also won the 1986 European championship and the 1987 world championship. But at the 1988 Bislett Games on July 2, she suffered her first defeat at 10,000 meters. At the 9000-meter mark Kristiansen experienced such a severe stomach cramp that she stopped running. She still managed to finish second, behind Scotland's Liz McColgan. A few days later, Kristiansen, who did not know that she was pregnant, suffered a miscarriage.

In Seoul, Kristiansen won the first qualifying heat, McColgan the second. The final began uneventfully. The early pace was set by Ludmila Matveyeva of the Soviet Union and Lynn Nelson of the United States. Kristiansen moved in front after six laps, but then, at the end of the seventh lap, she suddenly stepped off the track—she had badly bruised the sole of her right foot in the preliminary round.

While Kristiansen was carried away on a stretcher, Kathrin Ullrich unexpectedly found herself in first place with a lead of 10 meters. She eventually increased the gap to 30 meters. McColgan finally hauled her in after 4800 meters, with Zhupiyeva and Bondarenko close behind. Ullrich lost contact with the leaders after 7600 meters and Zhupiyeva fell back after 8800. That left only McColgan and Bondarenko in contention with three laps to go. The 5-foot ¾-inch, 91-pound Bondarenko patiently tracked McColgan until the middle of the last lap. Then she shot past her on the back straightaway, ran the final 200 meters in 31.2 seconds, and won by 20 meters. Bondarenko was one of the pioneers of the women's 10,000-meter run, having set world records at the distance in 1981 and 1984.

## MARATHON

**1896–1980** not held

**1984 Los Angeles** C: 50, N: 28, D: 8.5. WB: 2:22:43 (Joan Benoit)

| | | |
|---|---|---|
| 1. Joan Benoit | USA | 2:24:52 |
| 2. Grete Waitz | NOR | 2:26:18 |
| 3. Rosa Mota | POR | 2:26:57 |
| 4. Ingrid Kristiansen | NOR | 2:27:34 |
| 5. Lorraine Moller | NZE | 2:28:34 |
| 6. Priscilla Welch | GBR | 2:28:54 |
| 7. Lisa Martin | AUS | 2:29:03 |
| 8. Sylvie Ruegger | CAN | 2:29:09 |

The first woman to be officially timed in a marathon run was Violet Piercy of Great Britain who, on October 3, 1926, completed the Chiswick course in three hours forty minutes and twenty-two seconds. Her "record" stood, completely unchallenged, for 37 years until Merry Lepper of the U.S. ran a 3:37:07 on December 16, 1963. The three-hour barrier was first broken, and well-broken at that, on August 31, 1971, when Australia's Adrienne

Beames clocked a 2:46:30. By 1981, Allison Roe of New Zealand had taken the record down to 2:25:29. Then, on April 18, 1983, Joan Benoit of Freeport, Maine, smashed Roe's record, finishing the Boston Marathon in 2:22:43.

Although Benoit did not compete in another marathon until the U.S. Olympic trials 13 months later, her Boston feat qualified her as co-favorite with the popular Norwegian runner, Grete Waitz. Waitz, a two-time Olympian at 1500 meters and a former marathon world record holder, was undefeated in the seven marathons she had completed and had beaten Benoit at various distances 10 of the 11 times they had met. She was also the victor at the 1983 world championships, finishing a full 3 minutes ahead of Marianne Dickerson in second place.

Favorites though they were, both Benoit and Waitz considered themselves blessed to make it to the Olympic starting line at all. Benoit had undergone arthroscopic surgery on her right knee only seventeen days before the U.S. Olympic trials, which she won anyway. Waitz woke up the morning before the Olympic marathon with a sore back that left her unable to run or even stand up straight. She spent the day crying with disappointment, but by racetime the next day the pain had disappeared.

As an event, the inaugural women's Olympic marathon was charged with emotion. The long struggle to achieve recognition for women's long-distance running had finally reached fruition and many spectators along the route were moved to tears as the women dashed by. As a race, however, there wasn't much to it. Benoit, wearing a white painter's cap with the flap in back, moved ahead after only 14 minutes and pulled away at will, amazed that no one went with her.

As Waitz watched her disappear in the distance, she was convinced that Benoit had taken a reckless gamble and would eventually fade back to the pack. She never did. At 15 km., Benoit's lead was 51 seconds, by 25 km. it was 1 minute and 51 seconds. Waitz began to reel her in after 30 km., but by then it was too late. Meanwhile, Benoit had simply ploughed ahead, smiling only once when she spotted a banner of Bowdoin College, her alma mater. When she reached the Marina Freeway, a three-mile stretch where no spectators were allowed, Benoit chuckled to herself at the irony that this hunk of concrete had provided her with the peace and quiet she was used to during her training runs back home in Maine. "The one thing I'll tell my grandchildren," she later mused, "is that one time I ran alone on an L.A. freeway." One half mile from the stadium, she passed an enormous wall mural depicting her crossing of the finish line at the Boston Marathon.

As she approached the tunnel leading to the Coliseum track, she heard the crowd erupt and sensed the audience rise to its feet. In the tunnel, Benoit, a very private person, not comfortable with celebrity, told herself, "When you come out from underneath the tunnel, you're going to be a different person. Do you want to come out of the tunnel?" It was too late to turn back. "When I came into the stadium," she later recalled, "and saw all the colors and everything, I told myself, 'Listen, just look straight ahead, because if you don't you're probably going to faint.'" She ended up finishing 400 meters ahead of silver medalist Grete Waitz.

The race for the medals may have lacked suspense, but there was still high drama ahead. Twenty minutes after Joan Benoit entered the stadium, a ghostly figure emerged from the tunnel. It was 39-year-old Gabriele Andersen-Scheiss, an Idaho ski instructor, who had taken advantage of her dual citizenship to represent Switzerland. Suffering from heat prostration (but fortunately not heatstroke), she staggered forward, her left arm hanging limply, her right leg stiffened. It was as if Dorando Pietri had reappeared after 76 years. The audience gasped in horror, but when medical officers approached her, Andersen-Scheiss waved them off. As with Pietri in 1908, the crowd alternately cheered her on and begged for her to be stopped. Doctors accompanying her around the track noted that she was sweating profusely, a good sign, and let her proceed. For 5 minutes and 44 seconds she lurched along, occasionally stopping, blacking out on her feet, holding her head. Finally she fell across the finish line into the waiting arms of three medics. The records will show that Gabriele Andersen-Scheiss placed 37th.

Remarkably, she recovered rapidly and was released by medical personnel only two hours later to return to the Olympic Village and grab a bite to eat. Ten hours after her ordeal, Andersen-Scheiss was being interviewed on television. Two weeks later she was finishing fifth in a Utah "ride and tie" competition in which she ran twenty miles and rode a horse for eighteen. As a result of the controversy surrounding her condition during that final lap, the I.A.A.F. passed the "Scheiss rule," which allows athletes ro receive a hands-on medical examination without being subject to disqualification.

The travails of Gaby Andersen-Scheiss received a great deal of attention, but those of another runner received too little. Anne Audain of New Zealand, one of the secondary favorites, became ill after the 18th mile and began asking people the location of the nearest aid station. No one seemed to know, so she staggered on until she collapsed, as luck would have it, in front of two Los Angeles Fire Department paramedics who had stopped to watch the race. They carried her to their ambulance and drove her to a nearby hospital where she was treated for dehydration.

One more contestant worth noting was a late entrant, Leda Diaz de Cano of Honduras. De Cano fell behind immediately, trailing all of the other runners by 6½ minutes after only five kilometers. She was 27½ minutes behind at the 20-kilometer mark. Shortly thereafter, race officials, concerned less with the Olympic credo of taking part being more important than winning than they were with not interrupting the day's schedule at the track, convinced de Cano to leave the course and allow vehicular traffic to recapture the streets of Los Angeles.

**1988 Seoul** C: 69, N: 39, D: 9.23. WB: 2:21:06 (Ingrid Kristiansen)
| | | |
|---|---|---|
| 1. Rosa Mota | POR | 2:25:40 |
| 2. Lisa Martin | AUS | 2:25:53 |
| 3. Kathrin Dörre | GDR | 2:26:21 |
| 4. Tatyana Polovinskaya | SOV | 2:27:05 |
| 5. Zhao Youfeng | CHN | 2:27:06 |
| 6. Laura Fogli | ITA | 2:27:49 |
| 7. Daniele Kaber | LUX | 2:29:23 |
| 8. Maria Curatolo | ITA | 2:30:14 |

In 1982, Rosa Mota was a 24-year-old middle-distance runner who was enjoying her sport, but whose career was going nowhere. At the European championships in Athens that year she finished twelfth at 3000 meters and then decided to enter the marathon as an experiment. Previously, she had never run more than 20 kilometers, even in practice. To everyone's surprise, including her own, she won. Two years later, she placed third in Los Angeles to become the first Portuguese woman ever to earn an Olympic medal.

By 1986, the 5-foot 1¾-inch, 97-pound Mota was not only winning every marathon she entered, she was winning big. She took the European championship by 4 minutes 14 seconds and the Tokyo marathon by 4 minutes 39 seconds. In 1987, she won the Boston marathon by 4 minutes 29 seconds and the world championship by a stunning 7 minutes 11 seconds. She tuned up for the Olympics by repeating at Boston in 1988, this time by 4 minutes 54 seconds.

Mota arrived in Seoul as the overwhelming favorite. She did not disappoint her fans. By the 30-kilometer mark the lead group had dwindled to Mota in front, with Martin, Dörre, and Polovinskaya close behind. At 32 kilometers, Mota motioned for the others to take their turn in the lead, but found no takers. Four kilometers later, Polovinskaya faded and the medal winners were decided, although who got what was still in doubt. About 2½ miles from the finish, Mota's coach and lover, José Pedroza, appeared on his bicycle and asked how she was feeling. When she replied that she was feeling fine, he advised her to follow their original plan: to take off when she reached the next hill, one of only a few bumps in an unusually flat course. Immediately, Mota made her move. Martin, mesmerized and feeling "inert," failed to respond until it was too late. She pulled away from Dörre, but was unable to catch Mota, who went on to win by about 75 meters.

# 100-METER HURDLES

**1896–1928** not held

**1932 Los Angeles** C: 9, N: 6, D: 8.4. WR: 11.8 (Marjorie Clark)
**(80 Meters)**
| | | | |
|---|---|---|---|
| 1. Mildred Didriksen | USA | 11.7 | WR |
| 2. Evelyne Hall | USA | 11.7 | |
| 3. Marjorie Clark | SAF | 11.8 | |
| 4. Simone Schaller | USA | 11.9 | |
| 5. Violet Webb | GBR | 11.9 | |
| 6. Alda Wilson | CAN | 12.0 | |

Babe Didriksen had already won a gold medal in the javelin throw when she began competition in the 80-meter hurdles. In her opening heat she tied the world record of 11.8 seconds. In the final she committed one false start and then broke the record, beating Evelyne Hall of Chicago by a mere two inches. Fourth-place finisher Simone Schaller of Pasadena, California, had taken up hurdling only three months earlier.

**1936 Berlin** C: 22, N: 11, D: 8.6. WR: 11.6 (Ruth Engelhard)
**(80 Meters)**
| | | |
|---|---|---|
| 1. Trebisonda Valla | ITA | 11.7 |
| 2. Anni Steuer | GER | 11.7 |
| 3. Elizabeth Taylor | CAN | 11.7 |
| 4. Claudia Testoni | ITA | 11.7 |
| 5. Catharina ter Braake | HOL | 11.8 |
| 6. Doris Eckert | GER | 12.0 |

The finish was so close that the judges spent 30 minutes studying the photo-finish before they were able to sort out the places and announce the results. In the semifinals, Valla had run a wind-aided 11.6, which was recognized as an Olympic record but not a world record.

**1948 London** C: 21, N: 12, D: 8.4. WR: 11.0 (Francina "Fanny" Blankers-Koen)
**(80 Meters)**
| | | | |
|---|---|---|---|
| 1. Francina "Fanny" Blankers-Koen | HOL | 11.2 | OR |
| 2. Maureen Gardner | GBR | 11.2 | |
| 3. Shirley Strickland | AUS | 11.4 | |
| 4. Yvette Monginou | FRA | — | |
| 5. Maria Oberbreyer | AUS | — | |
| 6. Libuše Lomská | CZE | — | |

Fanny Blankers-Koen had already won the 100-meter dash, but she was quite nervous about 19-year-old Maureen Gardner in the hurdles. She didn't meet her rival until the day of the opening heats, when Gardner showed up at the warmup track with her own set of hurdles. In the semifinals Gardner hit a hurdle and stumbled, barely qualifying in third place. But in the final it was Blankers-Koen who had a tough race. Left behind at the start, she caught Gardner at the fifth barrier, but hit the hurdle and lurched clumsily to the finish line. It was unclear who had won, and the first three finishers waited impatiently for the results. Suddenly the band struck up "God Save the King" and Fanny thought that meant she had lost. Actually the band was playing not because Maureen Gardner had won, but because the British royal family had just arrived at the stadium. Then the results appeared on the scoreboard, and Fanny Blankers-Koen had gained her second gold medal. The fact that she was a devoted mother and housewife and that Maureen Gardner was a ballet instructor did much to counter the pre-World War

II masculine image of women athletes that had been established by Stella Walsh, Babe Didriksen, and Helen Stephens. Bronze medalist Shirley Strickland also finished third in the 100 meters, fourth in the 200, and second in the relay. Her official time of 11.4 is undoubtedly a mistake, since she was less than a meter behind the winner.

**1952 Helsinki** C: 33, N: 21, D: 7.24. WR: 11.0 (Francina "Fanny" Blankers-Koen)
*(80 Meters)*
1. Shirley Strickland    AUS   10.9   WR
2. Maria Golubnichaya    SOV   11.1
3. Maria Sander    GER   11.1
4. Anneliese Seonbuchner    GER   11.2
5. Jean Desforges    GBR   11.6
DNF: Francina "Fanny" Blankers-Koen (HOL)

Shirley Strickland, a 27-year-old teacher from Western Australia, equaled Fanny Blankers-Koen's world record in the first heat. The Dutch defending champion, suffering from a carbuncle on her leg, ran 11.2 and 11.3 to qualify for the final, while Strickland ran a wind-aided 10.8 in the semifinals. In the final, Blankers-Koen hit the first two hurdles and stopped running. Meanwhile, Shirley Strickland streaked to victory in world record time.

**1956 Melbourne** C: 22, N: 11, D: 11.28. WR: 10.6 (Zenta Gastl)
*(80 Meters)*
1. Shirley Strickland    AUS   10.7   OR
2. Gisela Köhler    GDR   10.9
3. Norma Thrower    AUS   11.0
4. Galina Bystrova    SOV   11.0
5. Maria Golubnichaya    SOV   11.3
6. Gloria Cooke    AUS   11.4

By 1956 Shirley Strickland had become a wife, a mother, and an assistant lecturer in physics and mathematics at Perth Technical College. Her decisive two-yard victory in the 80-meter hurdles and her gold medal in the relay gave her a total of seven Olympic medals: three gold, one silver, three bronze.

**1960 Rome** C: 28, N: 17, D: 9.1. WR: 10.5 (Gisela Birkemeyer [Köhler])
*(80 Meters)*
1. Irina Press    SOV   10.8
2. Carole Quinton    GBR   10.9
3. Gisela Birkemeyer (Köhler)    GDR   11.0
4. Mary Bignal    GBR   11.1
5. Galina Bystrova    SOV   11.2
6. Rimma Koschelyova    SOV   11.2

Irina Press, the younger sister of shot put and discus champion Tamara Press, set an Olympic record of 10.6 in the semifinals before winning a clear start-to-finish victory in the final.

**1964 Tokyo** C: 27, N: 19, D: 10.19. WR: 10.5 (Gisela Birkemeyer [Köhler], Betty Moore, Karin Balzer, Irina Press, Draga Stamejčić)
*(80 Meters)*
1. Karin Balzer    GDR   10.5w
2. Teresa Ciepla-Wieczorek    POL   10.5
3. Pamela Kilborn    AUS   10.5
4. Irina Press    SOV   10.6
5. Ikuko Yoda    JPN   10.7
6. Maria Piatkowska    POL   10.7
7. Draga Stamejčić    YUG   10.8
8. Rosie Bonds    USA   10.8

Hometown favorite Ikuko Yoda delighted the crowd with her unusual prerace routine, which included sweeping her lane up to the first hurdle, sucking a lemon, and dabbing cream behind her ears. She led until the third hurdle, but couldn't hold off the favorites. The three medalists finished within 12 inches of one another. Their world record time was disallowed because of a 2.23 meters per second wind. The competition was marred in the opening round when Canadian Marion Snider crashed into a hurdle and was carried away, unconscious, on a stretcher.

**1968 Mexico City** C: 32, N: 23, D: 10.18. WR: 10.2 (Vyera Korsakova)
*(80 Meters)*
1. Maureen Caird    AUS   10.3   OR
2. Pamela Kilborn    AUS   10.4
3. Chi Cheng    TAI   10.4
4. Patricia Van Wolvelaere    USA   10.5
5. Karin Balzer    GDR   10.6
6. Danuta Straszyńska    POL   10.6
7. Elżbieta Zebrowska    POL   10.6
8. Tatyana Talysheva    SOV   10.7

When word spread from the U.S.S.R. that unknown Vyera Korsakova had broken Irina Press's world record, many eyebrows were raised. Cynics doubted her time of 10.2 and said that it was just the Soviets' way of removing from the record books the names of the Press sisters, who had disappeared from competition following the institution of sex tests. Sure enough, Korsakova was eliminated in the semifinals after clocking only 10.6 and 10.8. Pam Kilborn had been undefeated since the Tokyo Olympics, but she suffered a slow start in the final and was unable to catch her 17-year-old teammate Maureen Caird. Chi Cheng, the first Asian woman in 40 years to win an Olympic track and field medal, was elected to the Taiwan parliament in 1981.

**1972 Munich** C: 25, N: 15, D: 9.8. WR: 12.5 (Annelie Ehrhardt, Pamela Ryan [Kilborn])
1. Annelie Ehrhardt    GDR   12.59   WR
2. Valeria Bufanu    ROM   12.84
3. Karin Balzer    GDR   12.90
4. Pamela Ryan (Kilborn)    AUS   12.98
5. Teresa Nowak    POL   13.17
6. Danuta Straszyńska    POL   13.18
7. Annerose Krumpholz    GDR   13.27
8. Grażyna Rabsztyn    POL   13.44

Esther Shakhamorov had the potential of becoming Israel's first Olympic finalist, but she withdrew following the terrorist murder of Israeli athletes, including her coach, Amitzur Shapira. Annelie Ehrhardt was never seriously challenged. The final was noteworthy for the success of the "older women," including 34-year-old Karin Balzer and 33-year-old Pam Ryan.

**1976 Montreal** C: 27, N: 15, D: 7.29. WR: 12.59 (Annelie Ehrhardt)

| | | |
|---|---|---|
| 1. Johanna Schaller | GDR | 12.77 |
| 2. Tatiana Anisimova | SOV | 12.78 |
| 3. Natalya Lebedeva | SOV | 12.80 |
| 4. Gudrun Behrend | GDR | 12.82 |
| 5. Grażyna Rabsztyn | POL | 12.96 |
| 6. Esther Rot (Shakhamorov) | ISR | 13.04 |
| 7. Valeria Stefanescu | ROM | 13.35 |
| 8. Ileana Ongar | ITA | 13.51 |

The semifinals saw an unusual incident. In the second heat, Lyubov Kononova of the U.S.S.R. stumbled and smashed into Valeria Stefanescu in the next lane. At first both women were disqualified, but fair play prevailed. Stefanescu was reinstated, and a rerun was ordered for the next day, 75 minutes before the final. This rerun allowed Stefanescu to replace injured defending champion Ehrhardt as the eighth finalist. The final was so close that only one and a half feet separated Schaller from fourth-place finisher Behrend. Esther Shakhamorov, now married and living in Tarzana, California, at last succeeded in becoming Israel's first finalist.

**1980 Moscow** C: 20, N: 11, D: 7.28. WR: 12.36 (Grażyna Rabsztyn)

| | | | |
|---|---|---|---|
| 1. Vera Komisova | SOV | 12.56 | OR |
| 2. Johanna Klier (Schaller) | GDR | 12.63 | |
| 3. Lucyna Langer | POL | 12.65 | |
| 4. Kerstin Claus | GDR | 12.66 | |
| 5. Grażyna Rabsztyn | POL | 12.74 | |
| 6. Irina Litovchenko | SOV | 12.84 | |
| 7. Bettine Gärtz | GDR | 12.93 | |
| 8. Zofia Bielczyk | POL | 13.08 | |

Twenty-seven-year-old Vera Komisova was one of the surprise winners of the Moscow Games, as she improved her pre-Olympic best by .28 seconds, even greater than Schaller's 1976 Olympic improvement of .22.

**1984 Los Angeles** C: 22, N: 14, D: 8.10. WR: 12.36 (Grażyna Rabsztyn)

| | | |
|---|---|---|
| 1. Benita Fitzgerald-Brown | USA | 12.84 |
| 2. Shirley Strong | GBR | 12.88 |
| 3. Michele Chardonnet | FRA | 13.06 |
| 3. Kim Turner | USA | 13.06 |
| 5. Glynis Nunn | AUS | 13.20 |
| 6. Marie Noëlle-Savigny | FRA | 13.28 |
| 7. Ulrike Denk | GER | 13.32 |
| 8. Pamela Page | USA | 13.40 |

In 1984 all of the leading contenders in the 100-meter hurdles came from boycotting nations, including the twelve women who registered the fastest times of the year.

Originally a dead-heat was announced for third place, but after viewing films of the race for 50 minutes, a jury of appeal awarded sole possession to Turner. Unfortunately, Chardonnet was not informed of this decision until she was standing in the award ceremony area. When her name was not announced, she was led away in tears. Three and a half months later, the I.A.A.F. reversed the decision of the jury of appeal and Chardonnet was awarded her bronze medal.

**1988 Seoul** C: 36, N: 24, D: 9.30. WR: 12.21 (Yordanka Donkova)

| | | | |
|---|---|---|---|
| 1. Yordanka Donkova | BUL | 12.38 | OR |
| 2. Gloria Siebert | GDR | 12.61 | |
| 3. Claudia Zackiewicz | GER | 12.75 | |
| 4. Natalya Grigoryeva | SOV | 12.79 | |
| 5. Florence Colle | FRA | 12.98 | |
| 6. Julie Rocheleau | CAN | 12.99 | |
| 7. Monique Ewanje-Épée | FRA | 13.14 | |
| 8. Cornelia Oschkenat | GDR | 13.73 | |

In 1986, Yordanka Donkova broke the world record four times in 27 days. The following year she lost the record to teammate Ginka Zagorcheva and finished a disappointing fourth at the world championship in Rome. However, in 1988 she continued her pattern of excelling in even-numbered years. She regained the world record on August 20th and won all 15 finals that she entered, including the Olympics, which she led from start to finish. Her chief rivals both bowed out to injuries in Seoul—Zagorcheva failed to complete her opening-round heat and Oschkenat pulled a hamstring in the final while running in third place.

## 400-METER HURDLES

**1896–1980** not held

**1984 Los Angeles** C: 26, N: 20, D: 8.8. WR: 53.58 (Margarita Ponomaryeva)

| | | | |
|---|---|---|---|
| 1. Nawal El Moutawakel | MOR | 54.61 | OR |
| 2. Judi Brown | USA | 55.20 | |
| 3. Cristina Cojocaru | ROM | 55.41 | |
| 4. Pilavullakandi "P.T." Usha | IND | 55.42 | |
| 5. Ann-Louise Skoglund | SWE | 55.43 | |
| 6. Debra Flintoff | AUS | 56.21 | |
| 7. Tuija Helander | FIN | 56.55 | |
| 8. Sandra Farmer | JAM | 57.15 | |

Nawal El Moutawakel, who led from start to finish and improved her personal best by .76 seconds, was the first woman from an Islamic nation to win an Olympic medal. She was also the first ever gold-medal winner from Morocco, a fact which did not go unnoticed in her hometown of Casablanca, where the 400-meter hurdle final was televised live at 2 a.m. After she crossed the finish line in first place and took her victory lap carrying a huge Moroccan flag, people poured into the streets of Casablanca to celebrate.

**1988 Seoul** C: 35, N: 25, D: 9.28. WR: 52.94 (Marina Stepanova)
1. Debra Flintoff-King AUS 53.17 OR
2. Tatyana Ledovskaya SOV 53.18
3. Ellen Fiedler GDR 53.63
4. Sabine Busch GDR 53.69
5. Sally Gunnell GBR 54.03
6. Gudrun Abt GER 54.04
7. Tatyana Kurochkina SOV 54.39
8. LaTanya Sheffield USA 55.32

On the day that she and the rest of the Australian team left for Seoul, Debbie Flintoff-King attended the funeral of her sister, who had died of a heart attack three days earlier. In the semifinals, Flintoff-King edged Tatyana Ledovskaya 54.00 to 54.01. Halfway through the final she was in fifth place behind Ledovskaya, Fiedler, Kurochkina, and world champion Sabine Busch. By the eighth hurdle Fiedler was slightly in front of Ledovskaya, Busch had passed Kurochkina, and Flintoff-King was still fifth. Ledovskaya moved decisively into the lead over the ninth hurdle. As they cleared the tenth and final barrier, Flintoff-King caught Busch, but still trailed Fiedler and Ledovskaya, the latter by 0.24. She sprinted past the East German. Then, at the finish line, Ledovskaya failed to lean and Flintoff-King nipped her in the final stride.

# 4 × 100-METER RELAY

**1896–1924** not held

**1928 Amsterdam** T: 8, N: 8, D: 8.5. WR (440 yards): 49.8 (GBR — Scovler, Haynes, Edwards, Thompson)
1. CAN (Fanny Rosenfeld, Ethel Smith, Florence 48.4 WR
   Bell, Myrtle Cook)
2. USA (Mary Washburn, Jessie Cross, Loretta 48.8
   McNeil, Elizabeth Robinson)
3. GER (Rosa Kellner, Helene "Leni" Schmidt, 49.0
   Anni Holdmann, Helene "Leni" Junker)
4. FRA (Georgette Gagneux, Yvonne Plancke, 49.6
   Marguerite Radideau, Lucienne Velu)
5. HOL (Mechelina Aengenendt, Marla Briejer, 49.8
   Jeannette Hendrika Grooss, Elisabeth ter
   Horst)
6. ITA (Luisa Bonfanti, Giannina Marchini, 53.6
   Derna Polazzo, Vittorina Vivenza)

The relay victory was sweet revenge for the Canadian team, particularly for Fanny Rosenfeld, who had lost first place in the 100 meters on a disputed judges' decision, and for Myrtle Cook, who had cried by the side of the track for a half hour after being disqualified in the 100 meters final. Myrtle Cook and Fanny Rosenfeld both became sports editors for Canadian newspapers.

**1932 Los Angeles** T: 6, N: 6, D: 8.7. WR: 48.4 (CAN—Rosenfeld, Smith, Bell, Cook)
1. USA (Mary Carew, Evelyn Furtsch, Annette 46.9 WR
   Rogers, Wilhelmina Von Bremen)
2. CAN (Mildred Frizzel, Lilian Palmer, Mary 47.0
   Frizzel, Hilda Strike)
3. GBR (Eileen Hiscock, Gwendoline Porter, Vio- 47.6
   let Webb, Nellie Halstead)
4. HOL (Johanna Dalmolen, Cornelia Aalten, —
   Elisabeth du Mee, Tollien Schurrman)
5. JPN (Mie Muraoka, Michi Nakanishi, Asa —
   Dogura, Sumiko Watanabe)
6. GER (Grete Heublein, Ellen Braumüller, Tilly —
   Fleischer, Marie Dollinger)

**1936 Berlin** T: 8, N: 8, D: 8.9. WR: 46.5 (GER—Albus, Krauss, Dollinger, Dörffeldt)
1. USA (Harriet Bland, Annette Rogers, Elizabeth 46.9
   Robinson, Helen Stephens)
2. GBR (Eileen Hiscock, Violet Olney, Audrey 47.6
   Brown, Barbara Burke)
3. CAN (Dorothy Brookshaw, Mildred Dolson, 47.8
   Hilda Cameron, Aileen Meagher)
4. ITA (Lydia Bongiovanni, Trebisonda Valla, 48.7
   Fernanda Bullano, Claudia Testoni)
5. HOL (Catharina ter Braake, Francina "Fanny" 48.8
   Koen, Alida de Vries, Elisabeth Koning)
DISQ: GER (Emmy Albus, Käthe Krauss, Marie Dollinger, Ilse
   Dörffeldt)

In the opening round the German team set a world record of 46.4 that was to remain unbroken for sixteen years. In the final they led by eight meters as Marie Dollinger prepared to make the final pass to Ilse Dörffeldt. However, as Adolf Hitler, King Boris of Bulgaria, and 100,000 others watched, Ilse Dörffeldt dropped the baton. The U.S. team, anchored by the heroic 1928 100 meters winner Betty Robinson and the 1936 100 meters winner Helen Stephens, took advantage of the German catastrophe and won by eight yards. Hitler was so moved by the sight of Dörffeldt sobbing after the race that he called the four German women to his booth and comforted them.

**1948 London** T: 10, N: 10, D: 8.7. WR: 46.4 (GER—Albus, Krauss, Dollinger, Dörffeldt)
1. HOL (Xenia Stad-de Jong, Jeanette Witziers-Timmer, 47.5
   Gerda van der Kade-Koudijs, Francina "Fanny"
   Blankers-Koen)
2. AUS (Shirley Strickland, June Maston, Elizabeth 47.6
   McKinnon, Joyce King)
3. CAN (Viola Myers, Nancy MacKay, Diane Foster, 47.8
   Patricia Jones)
4. GBR (Dorothy Manley, Muriel Pletts, Margaret 48.0
   Walker, Maureen Gardner)
5. DEN (Grete Lövsöe [Nielsen], Bente Bergendorff, 48.2
   Birte Nielsen, Hildegard Nissen)
6. AUT (Grete Jenny, Elfi Steurer, Grete Pavlousek, 49.2
   Maria Oberbreyer)

Fanny Blankers-Koen took over in fourth place, but was able to race through the field and catch Joyce King just before the finish. She thus became the only woman to win four track and field gold medals.

**1952 Helsinki** T: 15, N: 15, D: 7.27. WR: 46.4 (GER—Albus, Krauss, Dollinger, Dörffeldt)

1. USA (Mae Faggs, Barbara Jones, Janet   45.9  WR
Moreau, Catherine Hardy)
2. GER (Ursula Knab, Maria Sander, Helga Klein,   45.9  WR
Marga Petersen)
3. GBR (Sylvia Cheeseman, June Foulds, Jean   46.2
Desforges, Heather Armitage)
4. SOV (Irina Turova, Yevgenya Setshenova,   46.3
Nadezhda Khnykina, Vyera Kalashni-
kova)
5. AUS (Shirley Strickland, Verna Johnson, Win-   46.6
some Cripps, Marjorie Jackson)
6. HOL (Grietje de Jongh, Bertha Brouwer,   47.8
Neeltje Büch, Wilhelmina Lust)

The Australians set a world record of 46.1 in the very first heat. They led by one meter in the final at the last changeover. Winsome Cripps made a clean pass to Marjorie Jackson, winner of both sprints, but as Jackson took off, her hand hit Cripps's knee and the baton was jarred loose. Jackson caught it on a bounce and raced on, but the delay proved decisive. One of the four black women who made up the U.S. team was 15-year-old Barbara Jones of Chicago, who is the youngest person in Olympic history to win a gold medal in track and field.

**1956 Melbourne** T: 9, N: 9, D: 12.1. WR: 45.2 (SOV—Krepkina, Itkina, Kocheleva, Botchkaryova)

1. AUS (Shirley Strickland, Norma Croker,   44.5  WR
Fleur Mellor, Betty Cuthbert)
2. GBR (Anne Pashley, Jean Scrivens, June   44.7
Paul [Foulds], Heather Armitage)
3. USA (Mae Faggs, Margaret Matthews,   44.9
Wilma Rudolph, Isabelle Daniels)
4. SOV (Vyera Krepkina, Galina Reschikova,   45.6
Maria Itkina, Irina Botchkaryova)
5. ITA (Maria Musso, Letizia Bertoni, Maria   45.7
Greppi, Giuseppina Leone)
6. GDR/GER (Maria Sander, Christa Stubnick,   47.2
Gisela Köhler, Barbara Mayer)

Pressed by the Germans, the Australian team set a world record of 44.9 in the opening heat. In the final, though, it was the British women who put on the pressure. Heather Armitage finished only half a yard behind Betty Cuthbert (a closer margin than indicated by Great Britain's time of 44.7). Anne Pashley, who ran the opening leg for the British team, later gained renown as a mezzo-soprano.

**1960 Rome** T: 10, N: 10, D: 9.8. WR: 44.5 (AUS—Strickland, Croker, Meltor, Cuthbert)

1. USA (Martha Hudson, Lucinda Williams, Barbara   44.5
Jones, Wilma Rudolph)

2. GER (Martha Langbein, Annie Biechl, Brunhilde   44.8
Hendrix, Jutta Heine)
3. POL (Teresa Wieczorek, Barbara Janiszewska,   45.0
Celina Jesionowska, Halina Richter)
4. SOV (Vyera Krepkina, Valentina Maslovskaya, Maria   45.2
Itkina, Irina Press)
5. ITA (Letizia Bertoni, Sandra Valenti, Piera Tizzoni,   45.6
Giuseppina Leone)
DNF: GBR (Carole Quinton, Dorothy Hyman, Jennifer Smart, Mary Bignal)

Marie Dollinger was one of the two unfortunate German women who dropped their baton in 1936, during the changeover from the third runner to the fourth. Twenty-four years later she sat in the stands in Rome and watched tensely as her daughter, Brunhilde Hendrix, the third runner on the German team, prepared to pass the baton to Jutta Heine. Fortunately all went well, and the 1960 German team finished impressively in second place. The U.S. team from Tennessee State had a two-yard lead that was lost in a sloppy final pass. However Wilma Rudolph was able to regain the lead and cross the tape in first place for the ninth time in the Rome Games. The U.S. women had set a world record of 44.4 in the semifinals.

**1964 Tokyo** T: 15, N: 15, D: 10.21. WR: 44.3 (USA—White, Pollards, Brown, Rudolph)

1. POL (Teresa Ciepla [Wieczorek], Irena Kirszenstein,   43.6
Halina Górecka [Richter], Ewa Klobukowska)
2. USA (Willye White, Wyomia Tyus, Marilyn White,   43.9
Edith McGuire)
3. GBR (Janet Simpson, Mary Rand [Bignal], Daphne   44.0
Arden, Dorothy Hyman)
4. SOV (Galina Gaide, Renata Latse, Lyudmila Samo-   44.4
tyosova, Galina Popova)
5. GER (Karin Frisch, Erika Pollmann, Martha Pens-   44.7
berger [Langbein], Jutta Heine)
6. AUS (Dianne Bowering, Marilyn Black, Margaret   45.0
Burvill, Joyce Bennett)
7. HUN (Erzsébet Bartos Heldt, Margit Nemesházi   45.2
Markó, Antónia Munkácsi, Ida Such)
8. FRA (Marlene Canguio, Daniele Gueneau, Michele   46.1
Lurot, Denise Guenard)

The Polish team was originally credited with a world record, but their names were later struck from the record books when Ewa Klobukowska became the first athlete to fail a sex test.

**1968 Mexico City** T: 14, N: 14, D: 10.20. WR: 43.6 (SOV — Zharkova, Bukharina, Popkova, Samotysova)

1. USA (Barbara Ferrell, Margaret Bailes, Mil-   42.87  WR
drette Netter, Wyomia Tyus)
2. CUB (Marlene Elejarde, Fulgencia Romay, Vio-   43.35
letta Quesada, Miguelina Cobián)
3. SOV (Lyudmila Zharkova, Galina Bukharina,   43.41
Vyera Popkova, Lyudmila Samotysova)
4. HOL (Geertruida Hennipman, Mieke Sterk,   43.44
Cornelia Bakker, Wilhelmina van den Berg)

5. AUS (Jennifer Lamy, Joyce Bennett, Raelene 43.50
Boyle, Dianne Burge)
6. GER (Renate Meyer, Jutta Stöck, Rita Jahn, 43.70
Ingrid Becker)
7. GBR (Anita Neil, Maureen Tranter, Janet Simp- 43.7
son, Lillian Board)
8. FRA (Michele Alayrangues, Gabrielle Meyer, 44.2
Nicole Montandon, Silviane Telliez)

The American women set a world record of 43.4 in the first heat. This time was equaled, surprisingly, in the second heat by the unheralded Dutch team. In the final the U.S. team overcame mediocre baton-passing with rare speed to win by five yards and establish a new world record.

**1972 Munich** T: 15, N: 15, D: 9.10. WR: 42.87 (USA—Ferrell, Balles, Netter, Tyus)
1. GER (Christiane Krause, Ingrid Mickler 42.81 WR
[Becker], Annegret Richter, Heidemarie
Rosendahl)
2. GDR (Evelyn Kaufer, Christina Heinich, Bärbel 42.95
Struppert, Renate Stecher)
3. CUB (Marlene Elejarde, Carmen Valdes, 43.36
Fulgencia Romay, Silvia Chibás)
4. USA (Martha Watson, Mattline Render, 43.39
Mildrette Netter, Iris Davis)
5. SOV (Marina Sidorova, Galina Bukharina, 43.59
Lyudmila Zharkova, Nadozhda Besfamil-
naya)
6. AUS (Maureen Caird, Raelene Boyle, Marion 43.61
Hoffman, Penelope Gillies)
7. GBR (Andrea Lynch, Della Pascoe, Judith 43.71
Vernon, Anita Neil)
8. POL (Helena Fliśnik, Barbara Bakulin, Urszula 44.20
Jóźwik, Danuta Jędrejek)

The East Germans had edged the West Germans in the European championships. Rematched in a poorly seeded opening heat, the East Germans again finished ahead, 42.88 to 42.97. In the final, however, long jump gold medalist Heide Rosendahl began the anchor leg with a one-meter advantage and raced flat-out to hold off Renate Stecher, who had won both the 100 meters and 200 meters earlier in the games.

**1976 Montreal** T: 10, N: 10, D: 7.31. WR: 42.51 (GDR—Maletzki, Stecher, Heinich, Eckert)
1. GDR (Marlies Oelsner, Renate Stecher, Carla 42.55 OR
Bodendorf, Bärbel Eckert)
2. GER (Elvira Possekel, Inge Helten, Annegret 42.59
Richter, Annegret Kroniger)
3. SOV (Tatyana Prorochenko, Lyudmila 43.09
Maslakova [Zharkova], Nadezhda Besfa-
milnaya, Vera Anisimova)
4. CAN (Margaret Howe, Patty Loverock, Joanne 43.17
McTaggart, Marjorie Bailey)
5. AUS (Barbara Wilson, Deborah Wells, Denise 43.18
Robertson, Raelene Boyle)

6. JAM (Leleith Hodges, Rose Allwood, Carol 43.24
Cummings, Jacqueline Pusey)
7. USA (Martha Watson, Evelyn Ashford, Debra 43.35
Armstrong, Chandra Cheeseborough)
8. GBR (Wendy Clarke, Denise Ramsden, 43.79
Sharon Colyear, Andrea Lynch)

The 200 meters champion, Bärbel Eckert, made up a one-meter deficit on the anchor leg to win by a foot. The East German victory brought Renate Stecher's Olympic medal total to six: three gold, two silver, and one bronze.

**1980 Moscow** T:8, N: 8, D: 8.1. WR: 41.85 (GDR—Müller, Wöckel [Eckert], Auerswald, Göhr [Oelsner])
1. GDR (Romy Müller, Bärbel Wöckel [Eckert], 41.60 WR
Ingrid Auerswald, Marlies Göhr
[Oelsner])
2. SOV (Vera Komisova, Lyudmila Maslakova 42.10
[Zharkova], Vera Anisimova, Natalya
Bochina)
3. GBR (Heather Hunte, Kathryn Smallwood, Bev- 42.43
erley Goddard, Sonia Lannaman)
4. BUL (Sofka Popova, Liliana Panayotova, Ma- 42.67
ria Shishkova, Galina Encheva)
5. FRA (Veronique Grandrieux, Chantal Rega, 42.84
Raymonde Naigre, Emma Sulter)
6. JAM (Leleith Hodges, Jacqueline Pusey, 43.19
Rosie Allwood, Merlene Ottey)
7. POL (Lucyna Langer, Elżbieta Stachurska, 43.59
Zofia Bielczyk, Grażyna Rabsztyn)
DNF: SWE (Linda Haglund, Lena Moller, Ann-Louise Skoglund, Helena Pihl)

Unusually poor baton passing failed to prevent the East Germans from winning by five meters and breaking their own world record.

**1984 Los Angeles** T: 11, N: 11, D: 8.11. WR: 41.53 (GDR—Gladisch, Koch, Auerswald, Göhr [Oelsner])
1. USA (Alice Brown, Jeanette Bolden, Chandra 41.65
Cheeseborough, Evelyn Ashford)
2. CAN (Angela Bailey, Marita Payne, Angella 42.77
Taylor, France Gareau)
3. GBR (Simone Jacobs, Kathryn Cook [Small- 43.11
wood], Beverley Callender, Heather
Oakes)
4. FRA (Rose-Aimee Bacoul, Liliane Gaschet, 43.15
Marie France Loval, Raymonde Naigre)
5. GER (Edith Oker, Michaela Schabinger, 43.57
Heide-Elke Gaugel, Ute Thimm)
6. BAH (Eldece Clarke, Pauline Davis, Debbie 44.18
Greene, Oralee Fowler)
7. TRI (Janice Bernard, Gillian Forde, Ester 44.23
Hope-Washington, Angela Williams)
8. JAM (Juliette Cuthbert, Grace Jackson, Veron- 53.54
ica Findlay, Merlene Ottey-Page)

**1988 Seoul** T: 19, N: 19, D: 10.1. WR: 41.37 (GDR—Gladisch, Reiger, Auerswald, Göhr [Oelsner])

| | | | |
|---|---|---|---|
| 1. | USA | (Alice Brown, Sheila Echols, Florence Griffith Joyner, Evelyn Ashford) | 41.98 |
| 2. | GDR | (Silke Möller [Gladisch], Kerstin Behrendt, Ingrid Lange [Auerswald], Marlies Göhr [Oelsner]) | 42.09 |
| 3. | SOV | (Lyudmila Kondratyeva, Galina Malchugina, Marina Zhirova, Natalya Pomoshchnikova) | 42.75 |
| 4. | GER | (Sabine Richter, Ulrike Sarvari, Andrea Thomas, Ute Thimm) | 42.76 |
| 5. | BUL | (Tzvetanka Ilieva, Valia Demireva, Nadezhda Georgieva, Yordanka Donkova) | 43.02 |
| 6. | POL | (Joanna Smolarek, Jolanta Janota, Ewa Pisiewicz, Agnieszka Siwek) | 43.93 |
| 7. | FRA | (Françoise Leroux, Muriel Leroy, Laurence Bily, Patricia Girard) | 44.02 |

DNS: JAM (Ethlyn Tate, Grace Jackson, Juliet Cuthbert, Merlene Ottey)

In the semifinals, Evelyn Ashford, running the anchor leg, almost took off too quickly to receive the baton from Florence Griffith Joyner. In the final, Ashford overcompensated. Although Griffith Joyner reached her in first place, by the time Ashford achieved a tenuous grip on the baton, she trailed her rival of 12 years, Marlies Göhr, as well as Natalya Pomoshchnikova. Pomoshchnikova passed Göhr but then pulled a hamstring muscle 40 meters from the finish. She still managed to hobble across the line in third place. Meanwhile, Ashford was tearing up the track. She passed Göhr 20 meters before the finish and won by 1 meter to gain her third Olympic gold medal.

The Jamaican team qualified for the final but was forced to withdraw because of an injury to Merlene Ottey.

# 4 × 400-METER RELAY

**1896–1968** not held

**1972 Munich** T: 14, N: 14, D: 9.10. WR: 3:28.8 (GDR—Käsling, Seidler, Zehrt, Rohde)

| | | | |
|---|---|---|---|
| 1. | GDR | (Dagmar Käsling, Rita Kühne, Helga Seidler, Monika Zehrt) | 3:23.0 WR |
| 2. | USA | (Mable Fergerson, Madeline Manning, Cheryl Toussaint, Kathy Hammond) | 3:25.2 |
| 3. | GER | (Anette Rückes, Inge Bödding, Hildegard Falck, Rita Wilden) | 3:26.5 |
| 4. | FRA | (Martine Duvivier, Colette Besson, Bernadette Martin, Nicole Duclos) | 3:27.5 |
| 5. | GBR | (Verona Bernard, Janet Simpson, Jannette Roscoe, Rosemary Stirling) | 3:28.7 |
| 6. | AUS | (Alison Rose-Edwards, Raelene Boyle, Cheryl Peasley, Charlene Rendina) | 3:28.8 |
| 7. | FIN | (Marika Eklund, Pirjo Wilmi, Tuula Rautanen, Mona-Lisa Strandvall) | 3:29.4 |
| 8. | SOV | (Lyubov Runtso, Olga Syrovatskaya, Natalya Chistiakova, Nadezhda Kolesnikova) | 3:31.9 |

**1976 Montreal** T: 11, D: 7.31. WR: 3:23.0 (GDR—Käsling, Kühne, Seidler, Zehrt)

| | | | |
|---|---|---|---|
| 1. | GDR | (Doris Maletzki, Brigitte Rohde, Ellen Streidt, Christina Brehmer) | 3:19.23 WR |
| 2. | USA | (Debra Sapenter, Sheila Ingram, Pamela Jiles, Rosalyn Bryant) | 3:22.81 |
| 3. | SOV | (Inta Klimoviča, Lyudmila Aksenova, Natalya Sokolova, Nadezhda Ilyina) | 3:24.24 |
| 4. | AUS | (Judith Canty, Verna Burnard, Charlene Rendina, Bethanie Nail) | 3:25.56 |
| 5. | GER | (Claudia Steger, Dagmar Fuhrmann, Elke Barth, Rita Wilden) | 3:25.71 |
| 6. | FIN | (Marika Lindholm, Pirjo Häggman [Wilmi], Mona-Lisa Pursiainen [Strandvall], Riita Salin) | 3:25.87 |
| 7. | GBR | (Elizabeth Barnes, Gladys Taylor, Verona Elder [Bernard], Donna Murray) | 3:28.01 |
| 8. | CAN | (Margaret Stride, Joyce Yakubowich, Rachelle Campbell, Yvonne Saunders) | 3:28.91 |

The remarkable East German women won by almost 30 meters.

**1980 Moscow** T: 11, N: 11, D: 8.1. WR: 3:19.23 (GDR—Maletzki, Rohde, Streidt, Brehmer)

| | | | |
|---|---|---|---|
| 1. | SOV | (Tatyana Prorochenko, Tatyana Goistchik, Nina Zyuskova, Irina Nazarova) | 3:20.2 |
| 2. | GDR | (Gabriele Löwe, Barbara Krug, Christina Lathan [Brehmer], Marita Koch) | 3:20.4 |
| 3. | GBR | (Linsey MacDonald, Michelle Probert, Joslyn Hoyte-Smith, Janine Macgregor) | 3:27.5 |
| 4. | ROM | (Iboia Korodi, Niculina Lazarciuc, Maria Samungi, Elena Tarita) | 3:27.7 |
| 5. | HUN | (Irén Orosz, Judit Forgacs, Éva Toth, Ilona Pal) | 3:27.9 |
| 6. | POL | (Grażyna Oliszewska, Elżbieta Katolik-Skowrońska, Jolanta Januchta, Malgorzata Dunecka) | 3:27.9 |
| 7. | BEL | (Lea Alaerts, Regine Berg, Anne Michel, Rosine Wallez) | 3:31.6 |

DNF: BUL (Svobodka Damianova, Rossitza Stamenova, Milena Andonova, Bonka Dimova)

The defeat of the East German 4 × 400-meter relay team was a major upset, but it took an unusual set of circumstances to produce the result. Olympic rules at the time stated that the same athletes who ran in the heats had to run in the final, unless official certificates could be produced proving that they were medically unfit to run. The U.S.S.R. came up with two such certificates to replace Olga Mineyeva and Lyudmila Chernova with two fresh runners—Nina Zyuskova and Irina Nazarova, who had finished fifth and fourth respectively in the individual 400 meters event. At the beginning of the third leg, East Germany's Christine Lathan shot ahead of Zyuskova, but the Soviet runner pushed back in front as Lathan stepped on the curb and lost her rhythm. Nazarova took over with a lead of about 10 meters, but 400 meters champion Marita Koch slowly but surely closed the gap. As they entered the final straight it looked as if Koch would move ahead. However Nazarova, inspired by the wildly cheering hometown crowd of 100,000, managed to hold off Koch's challenge and win by one meter.

**1984 Los Angeles** T: 10, N: 10, D: 8.11. WR: 3:15.92 (GDR—Walther, Busch, Rubsam, Koch)

| | | | | |
|---|---|---|---|---|
| 1. | USA | (Lillie Leatherwood, Sherri Howard, Valerie Brisco-Hooks, Chandra Cheeseborough) | 3:18.29 | OR |
| 2. | CAN | (Charmaine Crooks, Jillian Richardson, Molly Killingbeck, Marita Payne) | 3:21.21 | |
| 3. | GER | (Heike Schulte-Mattler, Ute Thimm, Heide-Elke Gaugel, Gaby Bussmann) | 3:22.98 | |
| 4. | GBR | (Michelle Scutt, Helen Barnett, Gladys Taylor, Joslyn Hoyte-Smith) | 3:25.51 | |
| 5. | JAM | (Ilrey Oliver, Cynthia Green, Cathy Rattray, Grace Jackson) | 3:27.51 | |
| 6. | ITA | (Patrizia Lombardo, Cosetta Compana, Marisa Masullo, Erica Rossi) | 3:30.82 | |
| 7. | IND | (M.D. Valsamma, Vandana Rao, Shiny Abraham, Pilavullakandi "P.T." Usha) | 3:32.49 | |

DNS: PUR (Evelyn Mathieu, Madeline de Jesus, Angelita Lind, Marie Lande Mathieu)

Valerie Brisco-Hooks earned her third gold medal of the Los Angeles Games, while Chandra Cheeseborough won two gold medals in one hour, becoming the first woman to win golds in both Olympic relays. The Puerto Rican coach refused to let his team take part in the final when he discovered that the woman who ran the second leg for the Puerto Ricans in their qualifying heat was not team member Madeline de Jesus, but her twin sister Margaret. After being injured in the long jump, Madeline had asked her sister, who was in Los Angeles as a spectator, to take her place in the relay.

**1988 Seoul** T: 13, N: 13, D: 10.1. WR: 3:15.92 (GDR—Walther, Busch, Rübsam, Koch)

| | | | |
|---|---|---|---|
| 1. | SOV | (Tatyana Ledovskaya, Olga Nazarova, Maria Pinigina, Olga Bryzgina) | 3:15.18 WR |
| 2. | USA | (Denean Howard, Diane Dixon, Valerie Brisco, Florence Griffith Joyner) | 3:15.51 |
| 3. | GDR | (Dagmar Neubauer [Rübsam], Kirsten Emmelmann, Sabine Busch, Petra Müller) | 3:18.29 |
| 4. | GER | (Ute Thimm, Helga Arendt, Andrea Thomas, Gudrun Abt) | 3:22.49 |
| 5. | JAM | (Sandie Richards, Andrea Thomas, Cathy Rattray-Williams, Sharon Powell) | 3:23.13 |
| 6. | GBR | (Linda Keough, Jennifer Stoute, Angela Piggford, Sally Gunnell) | 3:26.89 |
| 7. | FRA | (Fabienne Ficher, Nathalie Simon, Nadine Debois, Evelyne Elien) | 3:29.37 |

DNF: CAN (Charmaine Crooks, Molly Killingbeck, Marita Payne-Wiggins, Jillian Richardson)

Running the third leg, Valerie Brisco of the United States cut a Soviet lead of about 8 meters down to 2. The anchor leg pitted 400-meter gold medalist Olga Bryzgina against Florence Griffith Joyner, who had won her third gold medal only 40 minutes earlier in the 4 × 100-meter relay. Griffith Joyner, who had never before run a 4 × 400-meter relay in an international meet, tucked in behind Bryzgina and chased the Soviet champion around the track. Although Griffith Joyner ran the fastest split of any of the U.S. runners, Bryzgina maintained her 2-meter lead all the way to the finish line.

## 10,000-METER WALK

This event will be held for the first time in 1992.

## HIGH JUMP

**1896–1924** not held

**1928 Amsterdam** C: 20, N: 9, D: 8.5. WR: 1.61, 5-3¼ (Carolina Gisolf)

| | | | M | FT.-IN. |
|---|---|---|---|---|
| 1. | Ethel Catherwood | CAN | 1.59 | 5-2½ |
| 2. | Carolina Gisolf | HOL | 1.56 | 5-1¼ |
| 3. | Mildred Wiley | USA | 1.56 | 5-1¼ |
| 4. | Joan Shiloy | USA | 1.51 | 4-11½ |
| 5. | Marjorie Clark | SAF | 1.48 | 4-10¼ |
| 6. | Helma Notte | GER | 1.48 | 4-10¼ |
| 7. | Inge Braumüller | GER | 1.48 | 4-10¼ |
| 8. | Catherine Maguire | USA | 1.48 | 4-10¼ |

Ethel Catherwood, "The Saskatoon Lily," was a beautiful 18-year-old who became a favorite of the spectators and the photographers. During the three-hour competition she kept herself wrapped up in a big red blanket and didn't even take off her sweatsuit until the five-foot mark had been reached. Before each jump she would face the bar, smile and then go over. Her return to Saskatoon caused the largest celebration since the signing of the 1918 Armistice. She was presented with a $3000 education trust fund to be used to continue her piano studies. When asked about rumors that she had received offers to go to Hollywood, Catherwood replied, "I'd rather gulp poison than try my hand at motion pictures." However, she did move to the United States the following year, eventually settling in San Francisco.

**1932 Los Angeles** C: 10, N: 6, D: 8.7. WR: 1.62, 5-3¾ (Carolina Gisolf)

| | | | M | FT.-IN. | |
|---|---|---|---|---|---|
| 1. | Jean Shiley | USA | 1.657 | 5-5¼ | WR |
| 2. | Mildred Didriksen | USA | 1.657 | 5-5¼ | WR |
| 3. | Eva Dawes | CAN | 1.60 | 5-3 | |
| 4. | Carolina Gisolf | HOL | 1.58 | 5-2¼ | |
| 5. | Marjorie Clark | SAF | 1.58 | 5-2¼ | |
| 6. | Annette Rogers | USA | 1.58 | 5-2¼ | |
| 7. | Helman Notte | GER | 1.55 | 5-1 | |
| 8. | Yuriko Hirohashi | JPN | 1.49 | 4-10½ | |

Jean Shiley and Babe Didriksen had tied for first place in the U.S. Olympic trials and they tied again in Los Angeles. Both women cleared 5 feet 5¼ inches but failed at

5 feet 6 inches. A jump-off was ordered, and both cleared a world record height of 5 feet 5¾ inches. At this point the judges intervened and declared that Didriksen's western-roll style caused her head to clear the bar before her body. This was deemed "diving" and ruled illegal. Deprived of her third gold medal, Babe was nonetheless given a share of the world record. Her jumping style was legalized not long afterward. Shiley wanted to try out for the U.S. team in 1936, but was declared ineligible because she had once worked as a swimming instructor.

**1936 Berlin** C: 17, N: 12, D: 8.7. WR: 1.67, 5-5¾ (Jean Shiley, Mildred Didriksen)

| | | M | FT.-IN. |
|---|---|---|---|
| 1. Ibolya Csák | HUN | 1.60 | 5-3 |
| 2. Dorothy Odam | GBR | 1.60 | 5-3 |
| 3. Elfriede Kaun | GER | 1.60 | 5-3 |
| 4. Dora Ratjen | GER | 1.58 | 5-2¼ |
| 5. Marguerite Nicolas | FRA | 1.58 | 5-2¼ |
| 6. Doris Carter | AUS | 1.55 | 5-1 |
| 6. Francina "Fanny" Blankers-Koen | HOL | 1.55 | 5-1 |
| 6. Annette Rogers | USA | 1.55 | 5-1 |

Csák was awarded first place after clearing 1.62 meters in a jump-off. If the current tie-breaking rules had been in force, 16-year-old Dorothy Odam would have won the gold medal. Fourth-place finisher Dora Ratjen was barred from competition in 1938, when it was discovered that she was a hermaphrodite, a rare sexual group for which international athletics has made no provisions.

**1948 London** C: 19, N: 10, D: 8.7. WR: 1.71, 5-7¼ (Francina "Fanny" Blankers-Koen)

| | | M | FT.-IN. | |
|---|---|---|---|---|
| 1. Alice Coachman | USA | 1.68 | 5-6 | OR |
| 2. Dorothy Tyler (Odam) | GBR | 1.68 | 5-6 | OR |
| 3. Micheline Ostermeyer | FRA | 1.61 | 5-3¼ | |
| 4. Vinton Beckett | CAN | 1.58 | 5-2¼ | |
| 4. Doreen Dredge | CAN | 1.58 | 5-2¼ | |
| 6. Bertha Crowther | GBR | 1.58 | 5-2¼ | |
| 7. Ilse Steinegger | AUT | 1.55 | 5-1 | |
| 8. Dorothy Gardner | GBR | 1.55 | 5-1 | |

Once again, Dorothy Odam, now Dorothy Tyler, lost a tie despite having fewer misses than the winner. This time Alice Coachman was awarded first place because she cleared the final height on her first try, while Tyler required a second attempt. Coachman was the first black woman to win an Olympic gold medal. Bronze medalist Micheline Ostermeyer had already won the shot put and discus.

**1952 Helsinki** C: 17, N: 10, D: 7.27. WR: 1.72, 5-7¾ (Sheila Lerwill)

| | | M | FT.-IN. |
|---|---|---|---|
| 1. Esther Brand | SAF | 1.67 | 5-5¾ |
| 2. Sheila Lerwill | GBR | 1.65 | 5-5 |
| 3. Aleksandra Chudina | SOV | 1.63 | 5-4¼ |

| | | | |
|---|---|---|---|
| 4. Thelma Hopkins | GBR | 1.58 | 5-2¼ |
| 5. Olga Modrachová | CZE | 1.58 | 5-2¼ |
| 6. Theodora Schenk-Solms | AUT | 1.58 | 5-2¼ |
| 7. Nina Kossova | SOV | 1.58 | 5-2¼ |
| 7. Dorothy Tyler (Odam) | GBR | 1.58 | 5-2¼ |

**1956 Melbourne** C: 19, N: 12, D: 12.1. WR: 1.75, 5-8¾ (Iolanda Balaş)

| | | M | FT.-IN. | |
|---|---|---|---|---|
| 1. Mildred McDaniel | USA | 1.76 | 5-9¼ | WR |
| 2. Thelma Hopkins | GBR | 1.67 | 5-5¾ | |
| 2. Maria Pissaryeva | SOV | 1.67 | 5-5¾ | |
| 4. Gunhild Larking | SWE | 1.67 | 5-5¾ | |
| 5. Iolanda Balaş | ROM | 1.67 | 5-5¾ | |
| 6. Michele Mason | AUS | 1.67 | 5-5¾ | |
| 7. Mary Donaghy | NZE | 1.67 | 5-5¾ | |
| 8. Hermina Geyser | SAF | 1.64 | 5-4¼ | |
| 8. Jirina Voborilova | CZE | 1.64 | 5-4½ | |

**1960 Rome** C: 23, N: 15, D: 9.8. WR: 1.86, 6-1¼ (Iolanda Balaş)

| | | M | FT.-IN. | |
|---|---|---|---|---|
| 1. Iolanda Balaş | ROM | 1.85 | 6-0¾ | OR |
| 2. Jaroslawa Jóźwiakowska | POL | 1.71 | 5-7¼ | |
| 2. Dorothy Shirley | GBR | 1.71 | 5-7¼ | |
| 4. Galina Dolya | SOV | 1.71 | 5-7¼ | |
| 5. Taisiya Chenchik | SOV | 1.68 | 5-6 | |
| 6. Helen Frith | AUS | 1.65 | 5-5 | |
| 6. Inga-Britt Lorentzon | SWE | 1.65 | 5-5 | |
| 6. Frances Slaap | GBR | 1.65 | 5-5 | |

Few people have dominated an event as completely as Iolanda Balaş dominated the women's high jump. Following her fifth-place finish at the Melbourne Olympics, she won an incredible 140 consecutive competitions over the next ten and a half years. She set 14 world records and was the first woman to high-jump 6 feet. By the time a second woman, Michele Brown of Australia, had cleared that barrier, Balaş had done it in 46 different meets. On July 16, 1961, the 6-foot Balaş jumped 6 feet 3¼ inches, a height that wasn't beaten until September 4, 1971.

**1964 Tokyo** C: 27, N: 18, D: 10.15. WR: 1.91, 6-3¼ (Iolanda Balaş)

| | | M | FT.-IN. | |
|---|---|---|---|---|
| 1. Iolanda Balaş | ROM | 1.90 | 6-2¾ | OR |
| 2. Michele Brown (Mason) | AUS | 1.80 | 5-11 | |
| 3. Taisiya Chenchik | SOV | 1.78 | 5-10 | |
| 4. Aida Dos Santos | BRA | 1.74 | 5-8½ | |
| 5. Dianne Gerace | CAN | 1.71 | 5-7¼ | |
| 6. Frances Slaap | GBR | 1.71 | 5-7¼ | |
| 7. Olga Pluic | YUG | 1.71 | 5-7¼ | |
| 8. Eleanor Montgomery | USA | 1.71 | 5-7¼ | |

**1968 Mexico City** C: 24, N: 14, D: 10.17. WR: 1.91, 6-3¼ (Iolanda Balaş)

| | | M | FT.-IN. |
|---|---|---|---|
| 1. Miloslava Režková | CZE | 1.82 | 5-11½ |
| 2. Antonina Okorokova | SOV | 1.80 | 5-10¾ |
| 3. Valentina Kozyr | SOV | 1.80 | 5-10¾ |

| | | M | FT.-IN. | |
|---|---|---|---|---|
| 4. Jaroslava Valentová | CZE | 1.78 | 5-10 | |
| 5. Rita Schmidt | GDR | 1.78 | 5-10 | |
| 6. Maria Faithová | CZE | 1.78 | 5-10 | |
| 7. Karin Schulze | GDR | 1.76 | 5-9¼ | |
| 8. Ilona Gusenbauer | AUT | 1.76 | 5-9¼ | |

Eighteen-year-old Milena Režková was a popular winner. Not only was she a complete outsider who had improved her personal best by 6 inches since the beginning of the year and who jumped 5 inches over her own height, but she was a Czech who won a dramatic showdown against two women from the U.S.S.R. Her victory was gained on her third and final try at 5 feet 11½ inches. Had Režková missed, Okorokova would have won on the basis of fewer misses.

**1972 Munich** C: 40, N: 22, D: 9.4. WR: 1.92, 6-3½ (Ilona Gusenbauer)

| | | M | FT.-IN. | |
|---|---|---|---|---|
| 1. Ulrike Meyfarth | GER | 1.92 | 6-3½ | EWR |
| 2. Yordanka Blagoyeva | BUL | 1.88 | 6-2 | |
| 3. Ilona Gusenbauer | AUT | 1.88 | 6-2 | |
| 4. Barbara Inkpen | GBR | 1.85 | 6-0¾ | |
| 5. Rita Schmidt | GDR | 1.85 | 6-0¾ | |
| 6. Sara Simeoni | ITA | 1.85 | 6-0¾ | |
| 7. Rosemarie Witschas | GDR | 1.85 | 6-0¾ | |
| 8. Deborah Brill | CAN | 1.82 | 5-11½ | |

If Režková's win in Mexico City was considered an upset, then the victory of 16-year-old Ulrike Meyfarth in Munich was more like a fairy tale. The 6-foot ½-inch Köln-Rodenkirchen schoolgirl, who had only finished third in the West German trials, jumped 2¾ inches higher than her pre-Olympic best. Blagoyeva appeared to have cleared the bar on her last attempt at 6 feet 2¾ inches and was already starting to put her sweatsuit back on, when the bar fell and the judges ruled a miss. The admirably neutral German audience jeered the decision, which was, however, entirely in keeping with the rules of the competition. Gusenbauer looked the other way as Meyfarth equaled the world record that the Austrian had set exactly one year earlier to the day. Three weeks later, Blagoyeva raised the world record to 6 feet 4½ inches. Ulrike Meyfarth is the youngest person of either sex to win an individual track and field gold medal in the Olympics.

**1976 Montreal** C: 35, N: 23, D: 7.28. WR: 1.96, 6-5¼ (Rosemarie Ackermann [Witschas])

| | | M | FT.-IN. | |
|---|---|---|---|---|
| 1. Rosemarie Ackermann (Witschas) | GDR | 1.93 | 6-4 | OR |
| 2. Sara Simeoni | ITA | 1.91 | 6-3¼ | |
| 3. Yordanka Blagoyeva | BUL | 1.91 | 6-3¼ | |
| 4. Mária Mrachnová | CZE | 1.89 | 6-2½ | |
| 5. Joni Huntley | USA | 1.89 | 6-2½ | |
| 6. Tatyana Shlyakhto | SOV | 1.87 | 6-1½ | |
| 7. Annette Tannander | SWE | 1.87 | 6-1½ | |
| 8. Cornelia Popa | ROM | 1.87 | 6-1½ | |

The qualifying rounds saw the surprising early elimination of Ulrike Meyfarth, Rita Kirst (Schmidt), Debbie Brill of Canada, and Vera Bradacová of Czechoslovakia, all of whom had cleared 6 feet 3 inches previously. Although the competition was won by the favorite, Rosemarie Ackermann, the field had such depth that 18 women cleared 6 feet and 13 were still in the running after three hours. On August 26, 1977, Ackermann, a shop clerk from Cottbus, became the first woman to jump two meters—9½ inches over her own head.

**1980 Moscow** C: 20, N: 13, D: 7.26. WR: 2.01, 6-7 (Sara Simeoni)

| | | M | FT.-IN. | |
|---|---|---|---|---|
| 1. Sara Simeoni | ITA | 1.97 | 6-5½ | OR |
| 2. Urszula Kielan | POL | 1.94 | 6-4¼ | |
| 3. Jutta Kirst | GDR | 1.94 | 6-4¼ | |
| 4. Rosemarie Ackermann (Witschas) | GDR | 1.91 | 6-3¼ | |
| 5. Marina Sysoyeva | SOV | 1.91 | 6-3¼ | |
| 6. Christine Stanton | AUS | 1.91 | 6-3¼ | |
| 7. Andrea Reichstein | GDR | 1.91 | 6-3¼ | |
| 8. Cornelia Popa | ROM | 1.88 | 6-2 | |

The ever-popular Sara Simeoni had switched to high-jumping at the age of 12 after being told that she couldn't be a ballet dancer because she was too tall and her feet were too big. She lost six out of seven meets to Rosemarie Ackermann between 1973 and 1977. Then she beat her in a dramatic showdown at the European championships in Prague in August 1978, and the tide turned. In Moscow Simeoni recorded her first miss at 1.94, but cleared on her second attempt to earn the gold medal. Fifth-place finisher Marina Sysoyeva jumped 6 feet 4 inches earlier in the year to set a women's world record for jumping higher than one's own height—10¼ inches.

**1984 Los Angeles** C: 29, N: 18, D: 8.10. WR: 2.07, 6-9½ (Lyudmila Andanova)

| | | M | FT.-IN. | |
|---|---|---|---|---|
| 1. Ulrike Meyfarth | GER | 2.02 | 6-7½ | OR |
| 2. Sara Simeoni | ITA | 2.00 | 6-6¾ | |
| 3. Joni Huntley | USA | 1.97 | 6-5½ | |
| 4. Maryse Ewanje-Épée | FRA | 1.94 | 6-4¼ | |
| 5. Deborah Brill | CAN | 1.94 | 6-4¼ | |
| 6. Vanessa Browne | AUS | 1.94 | 6-4¼ | |
| 7. Zheng Dazhen | CHN | 1.91 | 6-3¼ | |
| 8. D. Louise Ritter | USA | 1.91 | 6-3¼ | |

Twelve years after becoming the youngest Olympic track and field champion ever, Ulrike Meyfarth earned her second gold medal to become the *oldest* person to win an Olympic high jump competition. The largest woman in the field, at 6 feet 2 inches and 154 pounds, Meyfarth also became the only track and field athlete besides Al Oerter and Irena Szewińska to win gold medals twelve years apart. Three of the top five places in 1984 belonged to women who had been finalists in Munich in 1972.

**1988 Seoul** C : 24, N: 15, D: 9.30. WR: 2.09, 6-10¼ ( Stefka Kostadinova)

| | | M | FT.-IN. | |
|---|---|---|---|---|
| 1. D. Louise Ritter | USA | 2.03 | 6-8 | OR |
| 2. Stefka Kostadinova | BUL | 2.01 | 6-7¼ | |
| 3. Tamara Bykova | SOV | 1.99 | 6-6¼ | |
| 4. Olga Turchak | SOV | 1.96 | 6-5¼ | |
| 5. Lyudmila Andonova | BUL | 1.93 | 6-4 | |
| 5. Galina Astafei | ROM | 1.93 | 6-4 | |
| 7. Christine Stanton | AUS | 1.93 | 6-4 | |
| 8. Diana Davies | GBR | 1.90 | 6-2¾ | |
| 8. Kim Hee-sun | KOR | 1.90 | 6-2¾ | |

Between 1985 and 1987 Stefka Kostadinova of Plovdiv, Bulgaria, won 73 of 77 meets and set three world records, the last at the 1987 world championships. By the time of the Seoul Olympics, she had cleared 6 feet 8 inches at 29 different meets, compared to 10 times for all other jumpers combined. She also owned 11 of the top 12 jumps in history. Although she had lost twice in late June, she had also won 19 meets in 1988, so she entered the Olympic competition as the prohibitive favorite.

' Favored for second place was 30-year-old Louise Ritter, who grew up in the tiny Texas town of Red Oak. Ritter's injury-riddled career had seen many disappointments, including eighth-place finishes at the 1984 Olympics and the 1987 world championships. However she had also earned a bronze medal at the 1983 world championships and handed Kostadinova two of her three defeats in 1987.

Kostadinova and Ritter both cleared seven heights without a miss to knock out the rest of their opponents. But then they both missed all three attempts at 6 feet 8 inches, forcing a sudden-death jump-off. Kostadinova missed a fourth time at 6–8 and it was Ritter's turn. The lanky Texan realized that this was probably her last chance for victory. "My hamstrings were about to fall off my legs," she would later explain in her thick drawl. Besides, she knew that Kostadinova was too good a competitor to miss again.

Ritter moved the start of her run-up back 1 foot, raced down the runway and leapt for all she was worth. She grazed the bar with her right thigh, but not hard enough to dislodge it, and the victory was hers.

## LONG JUMP

**1896–1936** not held

**1948 London** C: 26, N: 13, D: 8.4. WR: 6.25, 20-6¼ (Francina "Fanny" Blankers-Koen)

| | | M | FT.-IN. |
|---|---|---|---|
| 1. Olga Gyarmati | HUN | 5.695 | 18-8¼ |
| 2. Noëmi Simonetto De Portela | ARG | 5.60 | 18-4½ |
| 3. Ann-Britt Leyman | SWE | 5.575 | 18-3¼ |
| 4. Gerda van der Kade-Koudijs | HOL | 5.57 | 18-3¼ |
| 5. Neeltje Karelse | HOL | 5.545 | 18-2¼ |
| 6. Kathleen Russell | JAM | 5.495 | 18-0¼ |
| 7. Judy Canty | AUS | 5.38 | 17-7¾ |
| 8. Yvonne Curtet-Chabot | FRA | 5.35 | 17-6½ |

The importance of this competition was somewhat muted by the absence of world record holder Fanny Blankers-Koen, who was busy winning gold medals in four other events.

**1952 Helsinki** C: 34, N: 22, D: 7.23. WR: 6.25, 20-6¼ (Francina "Fanny" Blankers-Koen)

| | | M | FT.-IN. | |
|---|---|---|---|---|
| 1. Yvette Williams | NZE | 6.24 | 20-5¾ | OR |
| 2. Aleksandra Chudina | SOV | 6.14 | 20-1¾ | |
| 3. Shirley Cawley | GBR | 5.92 | 19-5¼ | |
| 4. Irmgard Schmelzer | GER | 5.90 | 19-4¼ | |
| 5. Wilhelmina Lust | HOL | 5.81 | 19-0¾ | |
| 6. Nina Tyurkina | SOV | 5.81 | 19-0¾ | |
| 7. Mabel Landry | USA | 5.75 | 18-10½ | |
| 8. Verna Johnson | AUS | 5.74 | 18-10 | |

Twenty-three-year-old Yvette Williams led the qualifying rounds with a jump of 6.16 meters (20 feet 2½ inches). She faulted twice in the final and was one jump away from elimination. However, her third jump of 5.90 meters (19 feet 4¼ inches) was good enough to put her in the top six who qualified for three more jumps. Her fourth attempt was the winning one, and none of the leaders was able to improve after that. Williams also finished sixth in the shot put. However, the real award for versatility in field events went to Chudina, who took second in the long jump, second in the javelin, and third in the high jump.

**1956 Melbourne** C: 19, N: 11, D: 11.27. WR: 6.35, 20-10 (Elżbieta Krzesińska)

| | | M | FT.-IN. | |
|---|---|---|---|---|
| 1. Elżbieta Krzesińska | POL | 6.35 | 20-10 | EWR |
| 2. Willye White | USA | 6.09 | 19-11¾ | |
| 3. Nadezhda Dvalischvili (Khnykina) | SOV | 6.07 | 19-11 | |
| 4. Erika Fisch | GER | 5.89 | 19-4 | |
| 5. Marthe Lambert | FRA | 5.88 | 19-3½ | |
| 6. Valentina Schaprunova | SOV | 5.85 | 19-2¼ | |
| 7. Beverly Weigel | NZE | 5.85 | 19-2¼ | |
| 8. Nancy Borwick | AUS | 5.82 | 19-1¼ | |

Krzesińska, a 21-year-old medical student, was in a class by herself. Seventeen-year-old Willye White, who was born in Money, Mississippi, was a surprise silver medalist. She read the New Testament between jumps and won second place with her final leap. She also competed in the next four Olympics, earning another silver medal as a member of the 1964 U.S. 4 × 100-meter relay team.

**1960 Rome** C: 30, N: 18, D: 8.31. WR: 6.40, 21-0 (Hildrun Claus)

| | | M | FT.-IN. | |
|---|---|---|---|---|
| 1. Vyera Krepkina | SOV | 6.37 | 20-10¾ | OR |
| 2. Elżbieta Krzesińska | POL | 6.27 | 20-7 | |
| 3. Hildrun Claus | GDR | 6.21 | 20-4½ | |
| 4. Renate Junker | GER | 6.19 | 20-3¾ | |
| 5. Lyudmila Radchenko | SOV | 6.16 | 20-2½ | |
| 6. Helga Hoffmann | GER | 6.11 | 20-0½ | |
| 7. Johanna Bijleveld | HOL | 6.11 | 20-0½ | |
| 8. Valentina Schaprunova | SOV | 6.01 | 19-8¾ | |

Krepkina's victory came as a complete surprise, since she was better known as a sprinter. In fact, she was co-holder of the world record for the 100 meters.

**1964 Tokyo** C: 31, N: 20, D: 10.14. WR: 6.70, 21-11¾ (Tatyana Schelkanova)

| | | M | FT.-IN. | |
|---|---|---|---|---|
| 1. Mary Rand (Bignal) | GBR | 6.76 | 22-2¼ | WR |
| 2. Irena Kirszenstein | POL | 6.60 | 21-8 | |
| 3. Tatyana Schelkanova | SOV | 6.42 | 21-0¾ | |
| 4. Ingrid Becker | GER | 6.40 | 21-0 | |
| 5. Viorica Viscopoleanu | ROM | 6.35 | 20-10 | |
| 6. Diana Yorgova | BUL | 6.24 | 20-5¾ | |
| 7. Hildrun Laufer (Claus) | GDR | 6.24 | 20-5¾ | |
| 8. Helga Hoffmann | GER | 6.23 | 20-5¼ | |

In 1960 Mary Rand (then Mary Bignal) had been considered the favorite in the long jump, particularly after she had led the qualifying round with a personal best of 20 feet 9¼ inches. That jump would have won her a silver medal if she had been able to repeat it in the final. Instead she ran through twice and had to settle for ninth place with her third jump. She also finished fourth in the 80-meter hurdles the following day. Four years later in Tokyo, Mary Rand again had the best jump of the qualifying round—21 feet 4¾ inches. This time, though, everything went right in the final. Four of her six jumps were her best ever, and her whole series was so consistent that her worst leap would have earned her a silver medal. Her fifth jump registered 6.76 meters. Unfamiliar with the metric system, she raced back to her bag, pulled out the program, and learned that she had broken the world record. And this despite the fact that she had jumped into a 1.69 meters per second wind. Mary Rand was the first British woman to win an Olympic gold medal in track and field. Later in the week she also won a silver medal in the pentathlon and a bronze in the 4 × 100-meter relay. In 1967 she went to Mexico City and met her future second husband, the U.S. decathlon champion Bill Toomey.

The woman who finished sixth in 1964, Bulgarian Diana Yorgova, made the news several days later when she and Bulgarian gymnast Nikolai Prodanov held the first-ever Olympic wedding. The ceremony took place in the International Club of the Olympic Village in front of a huge Olympic flag and a photo of the Olympic flame. The couple honeymooned in Kyoto, but returned to Tokyo in time for the closing ceremonies.

**1968 Mexico City** C: 27, N: 19, D: 10.14. WR: 6.76, 22-2¼ (Mary Rand [Bignal])

| | | M | FT.-IN. | |
|---|---|---|---|---|
| 1. Viorica Viscopoleanu | ROM | 6.82 | 22-4½ | WR |
| 2. Sheila Sherwood | GBR | 6.68 | 21-11 | |
| 3. Tatyana Talisheva | SOV | 6.66 | 21-10¼ | |
| 4. Burghild Wieczorek | GDR | 6.48 | 21-3¼ | |
| 5. Miroslawa Sarna | POL | 6.47 | 21-2¾ | |
| 6. Ingrid Becker | GER | 6.43 | 21-1¼ | |
| 7. Berit Berthelsen | NOR | 6.40 | 21-0 | |
| 8. Heidemarie Rosendahl | GER | 6.40 | 21-0 | |

Viscopoleanu recorded her winning jump on her first attempt of the final. The 29-year-old Romanian improved on her pre-Olympic personal best by no less than nine inches.

**1972 Munich** C: 33, N: 19, D: 8.31. WR: 6.84, 22-5¼ (Heidemarie Rosendahl)

| | | M | FT.-IN. |
|---|---|---|---|
| 1. Heidemarie Rosendahl | GER | 6.78 | 22-3 |
| 2. Diana Yorgova | BUL | 6.77 | 22-2½ |
| 3. Eva Suranová | CZE | 6.67 | 21-10¾ |
| 4. Marcia Garbey | CUB | 6.52 | 21-4¾ |
| 5. Heidi Schüller | GER | 6.51 | 21-4¼ |
| 6. Meta Antenen | SWI | 6.49 | 21-3½ |
| 7. Viorica Viscopoleanu | ROM | 6.48 | 21-3¼ |
| 8. Margrit Olfert | GDR | 6.46 | 21-2½ |

Heidemarie Rosendahl brought great joy to the crowd by becoming the first West German gold medal winner of the Munich Games. Her first leap of 6.78 meters appeared to be good enough for first place until the fourth round, when Diana Yorgova, the first Bulgarian to win a track and field medal, hit the best jump of her career. But it was one centimeter too short. Yorgova's last jump was also a long one, but was disallowed because her foot went over the board. Later in the Games Rosendahl picked up a silver medal in the pentathlon and another gold in the 4 × 100-meter relay.

**1976 Montreal** C: 30, N: 19, D: 7.23. WR: 6.99, 22-11¼ (Siegrun Siegl)

| | | M | FT.-IN. |
|---|---|---|---|
| 1. Angela Voigt | GDR | 6.72 | 22-0¾ |
| 2. Kathy McMillan | USA | 6.66 | 21-10¼ |
| 3. Lidia Alfeyeva | SOV | 6.60 | 21-8 |
| 4. Siegrun Siegl | GDR | 6.59 | 21-7½ |
| 5. Ildikó Szabo | HUN | 6.59 | 21-7½ |
| 6. Jarmila Nygrýnová | CZE | 6.54 | 21-5½ |
| 7. Heidemarie Wycisk | GDR | 6.39 | 20-11¾ |
| 8. Elena Vintila | ROM | 6.38 | 20-11¼ |

For the third straight time the women's long jump was won on a first-round jump. Angela Voigt had held the world record for ten days earlier in the year, but she had a reputation for doing poorly in important meets. The last jumper of the competition, 18-year-old Kathy McMillan of Raeford, North Carolina, finished with the longest leap of the day; however she had stepped an inch or so over the board, and a no-jump was declared.

**1980 Moscow** C: 19, N: 11, D: 7.31. WR: 7.09, 23-3¼ (Vilma Bardauskiene)

| | | M | FT.-IN. | |
|---|---|---|---|---|
| 1. Tatyana Kolpakova | SOV | 7.06 | 23-2 | OR |
| 2. Brigitte Wujak | GDR | 7.04 | 23-1¼ | |
| 3. Tatyana Skachko | SOV | 7.01 | 23-0 | |
| 4. Anna Wlodarczyk | POL | 6.95 | 22-9¾ | |
| 5. Siegrun Siegl | GDR | 6.87 | 22-6½ | |
| 6. Jarmila Nygrýnová | CZE | 6.83 | 22-5 | |
| 7. Siegrid Heimann | GDR | 6.71 | 22-0¼ | |
| 8. Lidiya Alfeyeva | SOV | 6.71 | 22-0¼ | |

This was, without question, the most exciting women's Olympic long-jump contest ever. In 1978 Vilma Bardauskiene had become the first woman to break the 7-meter barrier, but two years later, hampered by injuries, she was unable to make the Soviet team. With one round to go Skachko was in first place as a result of her third round leap of 7.01 meters. She was followed by Wujak and Wlodarczyk, with 6.88 each, and Kolpakova with 6.87. Wlodarczyk's final jump of 6.95 put her into second place and had her crying for joy, but she and Skachko watched in horror as the situation changed dramatically in the next two minutes. First Kolpakova, third string on the U.S.S.R. team, jumped into first place with a 7.06—nine inches further than her pre-Olympic best. Then Wujak improved her personal best by 5½ inches to take the silver medal. Skachko, who had been in front for two hours, was forced to settle for a bronze medal, and Wlodarczyk was left without any medal at all. At the postrace press conference, Kolpakova, a shy 20-year-old from Frunze in the Kirghiz Soviet Socialist Republic, summed up the competition by saying, "I think that one should always fight until the end, and my last attempt confirmed it."

**1984 Los Angeles** C: 23, N: 17, D: 8.9. WR: 7.43, 24-4½ (Anişoara Cuşmir-Stanciu)

| | | M | FT.-IN. |
|---|---|---|---|
| 1. Anişoara Cuşmir-Stanciu | ROM | 6.96 | 22-10 |
| 2. Valeria Ionescu | ROM | 6.81 | 22-4¼ |
| 3. Susan Hearnshaw | GBR | 6.80 | 22-3¾ |
| 4. Angela Thacker | USA | 6.78 | 22-3 |
| 5. Jacqueline Joyner | USA | 6.77 | 22-2½ |
| 6. Robyn Lorraway | AUS | 6.67 | 21-10¾ |
| 7. Glynis Nunn | AUS | 6.53 | 21-5¼ |
| 8. Shonel Ferguson | BAH | 6.44 | 21-1½ |

The Soviet bloc boycott prevented the anticipated showdown between world record holder Anişoara Cuşmir-Stanciu and the rising East German star Heike Daute, who had upset Stanciu at the Helsinki world championships. At the Olympics Stanciu went ahead on her own, taking a first-round lead of 6.80 and sealing the victory in the fourth round.

**1988 Seoul** C: 30, N: 20, D: 9.29. WR: 7.52, 24-8 (Galina Chistyakova)

| | | M | FT.-IN. | |
|---|---|---|---|---|
| 1. Jacqueline Joyner-Kersee | USA | 7.40 | 24-3¼ | OR |
| 2. Heike Drechsler (Daute) | GDR | 7.22 | 23-8¼ | |
| 3. Galina Chistyakova | SOV | 7.11 | 23-4 | |
| 4. Yelena Belevskaya | SOV | 7.04 | 23-1¼ | |
| 5. Nicole Boegman | AUS | 6.73 | 22-1 | |
| 6. Fiona May | GBR | 6.62 | 21-8¾ | |
| 7. Agata Karczmarek | POL | 6.60 | 21-7¾ | |
| 8. Sabine John | GDR | 6.55 | 21-5¾ | |

This event pitted world record holder Galina Chistyakova against former world record holders Heike Drechsler and Jackie Joyner-Kersee. Drechsler, then

known by her maiden name, Heike Daute, had won the 1983 world championship at the tender age of 18. She was ranked number one in the world four years in a row. Then her 27-meet winning streak was broken when she finished third at the 1987 world championships after injuring her knee on her fourth jump. The winner of that competition was Jackie Joyner-Kersee with a jump of 24 feet 1¾ inches (7.36 meters).

Five days before the Olympic final, Joyner-Kersee won a gold medal in the heptathlon, setting an Olympic long jump record of 23 feet 10½ inches (7.27 meters) in the process.

Chistyakova took the first-round lead with a leap of 7.11, but, hampered by injury, she was unable to improve after that. In the second round, Yelena Belevskaya jumped 7.04 and Drechsler followed with a 7.06. She improved to 7.18 with her next jump, while Joyner-Kersee moved into second at 7.16. In the fourth round, Drechsler improved again, this time to 7.22, while Joyner-Kersee fouled. As she prepared for her fifth jump, Joyner-Kersee noticed that her opponents were tiring and decided to go for one big one. Her husband and coach, Bob Kersee, called out to her, "You have a 7.40 in you." Concentrating on keeping her knees high and staying in the air as long as possible, Joyner-Kersee then won the competition with a jump of exactly 7.40 meters.

## SHOT PUT

The women's shot weighs 4 kilograms (8 pounds 13 ounces).

**1896–1936** not held

**1948 London** C: 19, N: 12, D: 8.4. WR: 14.89, 48-10¼ (Tatyana Sevryukova)

| | | M | FT.-IN. |
|---|---|---|---|
| 1. Micheline Ostermeyer | FRA | 13.75 | 45-1½ |
| 2. Amelia Piccinini | ITA | 13.09 | 42-11½ |
| 3. Ine Schäffer | AUT | 13.08 | 42-11 |
| 4. Paulette Veste | FRA | 12.985 | 42-7¼ |
| 5. Jaroslava Komárková | CZE | 12.92 | 42-4¾ |
| 6. Anni Bruk | AUT | 12.50 | 42-0¼ |
| 7. Maria Radosaljevic | YUG | 12.355 | 40-6½ |
| 8. Bevis Reid | GBR | 12.17 | 39-11¼ |

Three months before the Olympics, pianist Micheline Ostermeyer had graduated with high honors from the Paris Conservatory of Music. In London she used the hands that so delicately played the piano to win gold medals in both the shot put and discus. She also placed third in the high jump. Her success in track and field actually hurt her reputation as a concert pianist, and for a long time she was afraid to play Liszt because he was too *"sportif."*

**1952 Helsinki** C: 20, N: 13, D: 7.26. WR: 15.19, 49-10 (Galina Zybina)

| | | M | FT.-IN. | |
|---|---|---|---|---|
| 1. Galina Zybina | SOV | 15.28 | 50-1¾ | WR |
| 2. Marianne Werner | GER | 14.57 | 47-9¾ | |
| 3. Klaudia Tochenova | SOV | 14.50 | 47-7 | |
| 4. Tamara Tyshkevich | SOV | 14.42 | 47-3¾ | |
| 5. Gertrud Kille | GER | 13.84 | 45-5 | |
| 6. Yvette Williams | NZE | 13.35 | 43-9¾ | |
| 7. Maria Radosaljevic | YUG | 13.30 | 43-7¾ | |
| 8. Meeri Saari | FIN | 13.02 | 42-8¾ | |

As a ten-year-old child, Galina Zybina had watched her mother and brother die of cold and starvation during World War II. She barely survived herself and entered adolescence thin and sickly. However, ten years after her ordeal, she proved to be one of the strongest women in the world. In Helsinki Zybina had the three longest throws of the competition and had already secured first place when she broke the world record on her final attempt. Werner moved from fourth to second on her final throw to prevent a Soviet sweep.

**1956 Melbourne** C: 18, N: 9, D: 11.30. WR: 16.76, 55-0 (Galina Zybina)

| | | M | FT.-IN. | |
|---|---|---|---|---|
| 1. Tamara Tyshkevich | SOV | 16.59 | 54-5 | OR |
| 2. Galina Zybina | SOV | 16.53 | 54-2¾ | |
| 3. Marianne Werner | GER | 15.61 | 51-2¾ | |
| 4. Zinaida Doynikova | SOV | 15.54 | 51-0 | |
| 5. Valerie Sloper | NZE | 15.34 | 50-4 | |
| 6. Earlene Brown | USA | 15.12 | 49-7¼ | |
| 7. Regina Branner | AUS | 14.60 | 47-10¾ | |
| 8. Nadya Kotlusek | YUG | 14.56 | 47-9¼ | |

Zybina took the lead in the first round and appeared to be headed for a second gold medal. However, in the final round her 231-pound teammate, Tamara Tyshkevich, scored a dramatic victory by heaving the shot 2¼ inches further than Zybina's best. Los Angeles housewife Earlene Brown made a great impression on the Australians and became a local favorite. Arriving in Melbourne early, she took part in a regional meet and won. When a fan informed her that she had just broken the Victoria state record, Brown replied, "I'm sorry, honey, If I'd known I was going to do that I wouldn't have thrown it so far."

**1960 Rome** C: 18, N: 12, D: 9.2. WR: 17.78, 58-4 (Tamara Press)

| | | M | FT.-IN. | |
|---|---|---|---|---|
| 1. Tamara Press | SOV | 17.32 | 56-10 | OR |
| 2. Johanna Lüttge | GDR | 16.61 | 54-6 | |
| 3. Earlene Brown | USA | 16.42 | 53-10½ | |
| 4. Valerie Sloper | NZE | 16.39 | 53-9¼ | |
| 5. Zinaida Doynikova | SOV | 16.13 | 52-11 | |
| 6. Renate Garisch | GDR | 15.94 | 52-3¾ | |
| 7. Galina Zybina | SOV | 15.56 | 51-0¾ | |
| 8. Wilfriede Hoffmann | GDR | 15.14 | 49-8¼ | |

Between them, Tamara Press and her younger sister Irina set 26 world records and won five Olympic gold medals and one silver. Unfortunately, when sex tests were instituted at international competitions, the careers of both Press sisters came to a sudden halt.

**1964 Tokyo** C: 16, N: 11, D: 10.20. WR: 18.55, 60-10½ (Tamara Press)

| | | M | FT.-IN. | |
|---|---|---|---|---|
| 1. Tamara Press | SOV | 18.14 | 59-6¼ | OR |
| 2. Renate Garisch-Culmberger | GDR | 17.61 | 57-9½ | |
| 3. Galina Zybina | SOV | 17.45 | 57-3 | |
| 4. Valerie Young-Sloper | NZE | 17.26 | 56-7½ | |
| 5. Margitta Helmboldt | GDR | 16.91 | 55-5¾ | |
| 6. Irina Press | SOV | 16.71 | 54-10 | |
| 7. Nancy McCredie | CAN | 15.89 | 52-1¾ | |
| 8. Ana Salagean | ROM | 15.83 | 51-11¼ | |

Tamara Press won the discus gold the day before the shot put. Zybina's bronze gave her a complete set of Olympic medals.

**1968 Mexico City** C: 14, N: 10, D: 10.20. WR: 18.87, 61-11 (Margitta Gummel [Helmboldt])

| | | M | FT.-IN. | |
|---|---|---|---|---|
| 1. Margitta Gummel (Helmboldt) | GDR | 19.61 | 64-4 | WR |
| 2. Marita Lange | GDR | 18.78 | 61-7½ | |
| 3. Nadezhda Chizhova | SOV | 18.19 | 59-8¼ | |
| 4. Judit Bognar | HUN | 17.78 | 58-4 | |
| 5. Renate Boy (Garisch-Culmberger) | GDR | 17.72 | 58-1¾ | |
| 6. Ivanka Hristova | BUL | 17.25 | 56-7¼ | |
| 7. Marlene Fuchs | GER | 17.11 | 56-1¾ | |
| 8. Els Van Noorduyn | HOL | 16.23 | 53-3 | |

In the very first round Marita Lange heaved the shot 61 feet 7½ inches to improve her personal best by over a yard. Gummel broke the world record in the third round and then unleashed an amazing fifth-round toss of 64 feet 4 inches to better her own pre-Olympic world record by 29 inches.

**1972 Munich** C: 18, N: 11, D: 9.7. WR: 20.63, 67-8¼ (Nadezhda Chizhova)

| | | M | FT.-IN. | |
|---|---|---|---|---|
| 1. Nadezhda Chizhova | SOV | 21.03 | 69-0 | WR |
| 2. Margitta Gummel (Helmboldt) | GDR | 20.22 | 66-4¼ | |
| 3. Ivanka Hristova | BUL | 19.35 | 63-6 | |
| 4. Esfir Dolzhenko | SOV | 19.24 | 63-1½ | |
| 5. Marianne Adam | GDR | 18.94 | 62-1¾ | |
| 6. Marita Lange | GDR | 18.85 | 61-10¼ | |
| 7. Helena Fibingerová | CZE | 18.81 | 61-8½ | |
| 8. Yelena Stoyanova | BUL | 18.34 | 60-2 | |

Siberian-born Nadezhda Chizhova put the championship out of reach on her first attempt with a world record of 69 feet.

**1976 Montreal** C: 13, N: 8, D: 7.31. WR: 21.89, 71-10 (Ivanka Hristova)

| | | M | FT.-IN. | |
|---|---|---|---|---|
| 1. Ivanka Hristova | BUL | 21.16 | 69-5¼ | OR |
| 2. Nadezhda Chizhova | SOV | 20.96 | 68-9¼ | |
| 3. Helena Fibingerová | CZE | 20.67 | 67-9¾ | |
| 4. Marianne Adam | GDR | 20.55 | 67-5¼ | |
| 5. Ilona Schoknecht | GDR | 20.54 | 67-4¾ | |
| 6. Margitta Droese | GDR | 19.79 | 64-11¼ | |
| 7. Eva Wilms | GER | 19.29 | 63-3½ | |
| 8. Yelena Stoyanova | BUL | 18.89 | 61-11¾ | |

The 1976 shot put competition matched the world record holder against three former world record holders. Defending champion Chizhova led after the first round with a throw of 68 feet 4½ inches. In the second round Hristova hit 68 feet 6 inches, but Chizhova responded with 68 feet 9¼ inches. However, Chizhova slipped and injured her leg and was unable to come up with another serious throw. Her lead held up until the fifth round, when Hristova secured the victory with a new Olympic record of 69 feet 5¼ inches. Hristova's win culminated a steady rise in her career. In the 1964 Olympics she finished tenth. In 1968 she was sixth, and in 1972 she was third. Finally, at the age of 34, she won a gold medal, the first ever by a Bulgarian track and field athlete. Chizhova matched Galina Zybina's feat of earning a complete set of medals.

**1980 Moscow** C: 14, N: 8, D: 7.24. WR: 22.45, 73-8 (Ilona Slupianek [Schoknecht])

| | | M | FT.-IN. |
|---|---|---|---|
| 1. Ilona Slupianek (Schoknecht) | GDR | 22.41 | 73-6¼ |
| 2. Svetlana Krachevskaya (Esfir Dolzhenko) | SOV | 21.42 | 70-3½ |
| 3. Margitta Pufe (Droese) | GDR | 21.20 | 69-6¾ |
| 4. Nunu Abashidze | SOV | 21.15 | 69-4¾ |
| 5. Verginia Vesselinova | BUL | 20.72 | 67-11¾ |
| 6. Elena Stoyanova | BUL | 20.22 | 66-4¼ |
| 7. Natalya Akhrimenko | SOV | 19.74 | 64-9¼ |
| 8. Ines Reichenbach | GDR | 19.66 | 64-6 |

Slupianek was forced to sit out the 1978 season when she was caught taking steroids. In Moscow she put on an extraordinary performance, outclassing the opposition. The last to throw, she broke the Olympic record on her first attempt and then went over 70 feet on each of her five remaining throws. Her *worst* put, 70 feet 3½ inches, was equal to the *best* put of silver medalist Svetlana Krachevskaya.

**1984 Los Angeles** C: 13, N: 8, D: 8.3. WR: 22.53, 73-11 (Natalya Lisovskaya)

| | | M | FT.-IN. |
|---|---|---|---|
| 1. Claudia Losch | GER | 20.48 | 67-2¼ |
| 2. Mihaela Loghin | ROM | 20.47 | 67-2 |
| 3. Gael Martin | AUS | 19.19 | 62-11½ |
| 4. Judith Oakes | GBR | 18.14 | 59-6¼ |
| 5. Li Meisu | CHN | 17.96 | 58-11¼ |
| 6. Venissa Head | GBR | 17.90 | 58-8¾ |
| 7. Carol Cady | USA | 17.23 | 56-6½ |
| 8. Florenta Craciunescu | ROM | 17.23 | 56-6½ |

Claudia Losch, a 24-year-old Bavarian optician, defeated a severely depleted field by edging Mihaela Loghin with her final throw.

**1988 Seoul** C: 25, N: 14, D: 10.1. WR: 22.63, 74-3 (Natalya Lisovskaya)

| | | M | FT.-IN. |
|---|---|---|---|
| 1. Natalya Lisovskaya | SOV | 22.24 | 72-11¾ |
| 2. Kathrin Neimke | GDR | 21.07 | 69-1½ |
| 3. Li Meisu | CHN | 21.06 | 69-1¼ |
| 4. Ines Müller | GDR | 20.37 | 66-10 |
| 5. Claudia Losch | GER | 20.27 | 66-6 |
| 6. Heike Hartwig | GDR | 20.20 | 66-3¼ |
| 7. Natalya Akhrimenko | SOV | 20.13 | 66-0½ |
| 8. Huang Zhihong | CHN | 19.82 | 65-0¼ |

The 6-foot 2-inch, 218-pound Lisovskaya so dominated the competition that *any* of her six throws would have won the gold medal. The battle for the silver, on the other hand, was extremely close, as Neimke came from behind to edge Li by 1 centimeter with her final throw.

## DISCUS THROW

The women's discus weighs 1 kilogram (2 pounds 3.27 ounces).

**1896–1924** not held

**1928 Amsterdam** C: 21, N: 12, D: 7.31. WR: 39.18, 128-6 (Halina Konopacka)

| | | M | FT.-IN. | |
|---|---|---|---|---|
| 1. Halina Konopacka | POL | 39.62 | 129-11¾ | WR |
| 2. Lillian Copeland | USA | 37.08 | 121-8 | |
| 3. Ruth Svedberg | SWE | 35.92 | 117-10 | |
| 4. Emilie "Milly" Reuter | GER | 35.86 | 117-8 | |
| 5. Grete Heublein | GER | 35.56 | 116-8 | |
| 6. Liesl Perkaus | AUT | 33.54 | 110-0½ | |
| 7. Maybelle Reichardt | USA | 33.52 | 110-0 | |
| 8. Genowefa Kobielska | POL | 32.72 | 107-4 | |

This was the first women's track and field event to be decided in the history of the Olympics.

**1932 Los Angeles** C: 9, N: 4, D: 8.2. WR: 42.43, 139-2½ (Jadwiga Wajs)

| | | M | FT.-IN. | |
|---|---|---|---|---|
| 1. Lillian Copeland | USA | 40.58 | 133-2 | OR |
| 2. Ruth Osburn | USA | 40.12 | 131-7 | |
| 3. Jadwiga Wajs | POL | 38.74 | 127-1 | |
| 4. Tilly Fleischer | GER | 36.12 | 118-6 | |
| 5. Grete Heublein | GER | 34.66 | 113-8 | |
| 6. Stanislawa Walasiewicz | POL | 33.60 | 110-3 | |
| 7. Mitsue Ishizu | JPN | 33.52 | 110-0 | |
| 8. Ellen Braümuller | GER | 33.15 | 108-9 | |

Twenty-seven-year-old Lillian Copeland, a student at the nearby University of Southern California, won the contest on her final throw. She told reporters, "The only thing I could think of as I stood there waiting for my last throw of the day was Dr. O'Callaghan, who won the hammer throw [the previous day] on *his* last throw of the day."

**1936 Berlin** C: 19, N: 11, D: 8.4. WR: 48.31, 158-6 (Gisela Mauermayer)

| | | M | FT.-IN. | |
|---|---|---|---|---|
| 1. Gisela Mauermayer | GER | 47.63 | 156-3 | OR |
| 2. Jadwiga Wajs | POL | 46.22 | 151-8 | |
| 3. Paula Mollenhauer | GER | 39.80 | 130-7 | |
| 4. Ko Nakamura | JPN | 38.24 | 125-5 | |
| 5. Hide Mineshima | JPN | 37.35 | 122-6 | |
| 6. Birgit Lundström | SWE | 35.92 | 117-10 | |
| 7. Anna Niesink | HOL | 35.21 | 115-6 | |
| 8. Gertrude Wilhemsen | USA | 34.43 | 112-11½ | |

Three weeks before the games began, Gisela Mauermayer heaved the discus 158 feet 6 inches to set a world record that would last for twelve years. Mauermayer was a modest 22-year-old, a 6-foot blonde, who was hailed in Germany as the perfect example of Aryan womanhood. She gave the Nazi salute on the victory stand and became a top-ranking member of the Nazi women's organization. During World War II she was a teacher in Munich. After the war she lost her job because of her high-profile Nazi involvement. Starting over at the Zoological Institute of Munich University she gained a doctor's degree by studying the social behavior of ants. Like Helen Stephens, another star of the 1936 games, Mauermayer eventually settled down as a librarian.

**1948 London** C: 21, N: 11, D: 7.30. WR: 48.31, 158-6 (Gisela Mauermayer)

| | | M | FT.-IN. |
|---|---|---|---|
| 1. Micheline Ostermeyer | FRA | 41.92 | 137-6 |
| 2. Edera Cordiale Gentile | ITA | 41.17 | 135-0 |
| 3. Jacqueline Mazeas | FRA | 40.47 | 132-9 |
| 4. Jadwiga Wajs-Marcinkiewicz | POL | 39.30 | 128-11 |
| 5. Charlotte "Lotte" Haidegger | AUT | 38.81 | 127-3 |
| 6. Anna Panhorst Niesink | HOL | 38.74 | 127-1 |
| 7. Majken Åberg | SWE | 36.40 | 126-0 |
| 8. Ingeborg Mello | ARG | 38.44 | 126-1 |

**1952 Helsinki** C: 20, N: 16, D: 7.20. WR: 53.37, 175-1 (Nina Dumbadze)

| | | M | FT.-IN. | |
|---|---|---|---|---|
| 1. Nina Romaschkova | SOV | 51.42 | 168-8 | OR |
| 2. Yelisaveta Bagryantseva | SOV | 47.08 | 154-5 | |
| 3. Nina Dumbadze | SOV | 46.29 | 151-10 | |
| 4. Toyoko Yoshino | JPN | 43.81 | 143-8 | |
| 5. Charlotte "Lotte" Haidegger | AUT | 43.49 | 142-8 | |
| 6. Lia Manoliu | ROM | 42.65 | 139-11 | |
| 7. Ingeborg Pfuller (Mello) | ARG | 41.73 | 136-11 | |
| 8. Ilona Jozsa | HUN | 41.61 | 136-6 | |

Romaschkova was well known to British fans as a result of an incident in London in which she had been arrested for shoplifting five hats. Her margin of victory in Helsinki was extraordinary, particularly considering the presence of world record holder Nina Dumbadze. The follow-ing month Romaschkova broke Dumbadze's record, but on October 18, Dumbadze threw the discus 187 feet 1½ inches to set a world record that would last for almost eight years. Olympic silver medalist Yelisaveta Bagryantseva was the mother of Irina Bagryantseva, who, under her married name, Nazarova, won a gold medal in the 4 × 400-meter relay in 1980.

**1956 Melbourne** C: 22, N: 12, D: 11.23. WR: 57.04, 187-1½ (Nina Dumbadze)

| | | M | FT.-IN. | |
|---|---|---|---|---|
| 1. Olga Fikotová | CZE | 53.69 | 176-1 | OR |
| 2. Irina Beglyakova | SOV | 52.54 | 174-4 | |
| 3. Nina Ponomaryeva (Romaschkova) | SOV | 52.02 | 170-8 | |
| 4. Earlene Brown | USA | 51.35 | 168-5 | |
| 5. Albina Yelkina | SOV | 48.20 | 158-2 | |
| 6. Isabel Ercilia Avellán | ARG | 46.73 | 153-3 | |
| 7. Jiřina Voborilova | CZE | 45.84 | 150-5 | |
| 8. Stepanka Mertová | CZE | 45.78 | 150-2 | |

A former member of the Czechoslovakian national hand-ball team, Fikotová was taught by her first discus coach to regard the event as a dance step and was allowed to practice to the sounds of "The Blue Danube." In 1956, she gained great fame as a result of her Cold War–thawing romance with and marriage to U.S. hammer thrower Harold Connolly. The couple eventually settled in California, although they divorced in 1973. Olga took part in four more Olympics, finishing seventh in 1960, twelfth in 1964, sixth in 1968, and sixteenth in 1972.

**1960 Rome** C: 24, N: 15, D: 9.5, WR: 57.04, 187-1½ (Nina Dumbadze)

| | | M | FT.-IN. | |
|---|---|---|---|---|
| 1. Nina Ponomaryeva (Romaschkova) | SOV | 55.10 | 180-9 | OR |
| 2. Tamara Press | SOV | 52.59 | 172-4 | |
| 3. Lia Manoliu | ROM | 52.36 | 171-9 | |
| 4. Krimhild Hausmann | GER | 51.47 | 168-10 | |
| 5. Yevgenya Kuznyetsova | SOV | 51.43 | 168-8 | |
| 6. Earlene Brown | USA | 51.29 | 168-3 | |
| 7. Olga Connolly (Fikotová) | USA | 50.95 | 167-2 | |
| 8. Jiřina Nemcova (Voborilova) | CZE | 50.12 | 164-5 | |

The 1960 discus competition matched two former gold medal winners and two future gold medal winners. Ponomaryeva took the lead in the second round and won with the contest's three longest throws. A week later, Tamara Press set a world record of 57.15 meters (187 feet 6 inches).

**1964 Tokyo** C: 21, N: 15, D: 10.19. WR: 59.28, 194-5¾ (Tamara Press)

| | | M | FT.-IN. | |
|---|---|---|---|---|
| 1. Tamara Press | SOV | 57.27 | 187-10 | OR |
| 2. Ingrid Lotz | GDR | 57.21 | 187-8 | |
| 3. Lia Manoliu | ROM | 56.97 | 186-10 | |
| 4. Virzhinia Mikhailova | BUL | 56.70 | 186-0 | |
| 5. Yevgenya Kuznyetsova | SOV | 55.17 | 181-0 | |
| 6. Jolán Kleiber | HUN | 54.87 | 180-0 | |
| 7. Krimhild Limberg (Hausmann) | GER | 53.81 | 176-6 | |
| 8. Olimpia Catarama | ROM | 53.08 | 173-11 | |

After four rounds, world record holder Tamara Press was only in fourth place. Her fifth attempt, however, stretched two inches beyond Ingrid Lotz's first-round mark and gave Press the closest victory in Olympic discus history.

**1968 Mexico City** C: 15, N: 8, D: 10.18. WR: 62.54, 205-2¼ (Liesel Westermann)

| | | M | FT.-IN. | |
|---|---|---|---|---|
| 1. Lia Manoliu | ROM | 58.28 | 191-2 | OR |
| 2. Liesel Westermann | GER | 57.76 | 189-6 | |
| 3. Jolán Kleiber | HUN | 54.90 | 180-1 | |
| 4. Anita Otto | GDR | 54.40 | 178-6 | |
| 5. Antonina Popova | SOV | 53.42 | 175-3 | |
| 6. Olga Connolly (Fikotová) | USA | 52.96 | 173-9 | |
| 7. Christine Speilberg | GDR | 52.86 | 173-5 | |
| 8. Brigitte Berendonk | GER | 52.80 | 173-3 | |

On November 5, 1967, while competing in Brazil, Liesel Westermann became the first woman to throw the discus over 200 feet, with a heave of 201 feet (61.26 meters). In Mexico City she was one of the three favorites, along with the East German Christine Speilberg and the Romanian Lia Manoliu, who was taking part in her fifth Olympics. In 1952 Manoliu had finished sixth, in 1956 ninth, in 1960 third, and in 1964 third again. Manoliu entered the competition in 1968 with a sore elbow, so she decided to put everything she had into her first throw. It went 191 feet 2 inches, good enough to take the lead after the first round. After that she fouled three times, passed once, and got off one poor throw. However, a rainstorm arrived during the second round, and the rest of the competition was severely impaired as the throwing circle became wetter and wetter. It turned out that Lia Manoliu's first toss held up to take first place, and the 36-year-old Manoliu became the oldest woman in Olympic history to win a track and field gold medal. She took part in one more Olympics in 1972, finishing ninth. No other female track and field athlete has taken part in six different Olympic Games.

**1972 Munich** C: 17, N: 10, D: 9.10. WR: 66.76, 219-0¼ (Faina Melnik)

| | | M | FT.-IN. | |
|---|---|---|---|---|
| 1. Faina Melnik | SOV | 66.62 | 218-7 | OR |
| 2. Argentina Menis | ROM | 65.06 | 213-5 | |
| 3. Vassilka Stoeva | BUL | 64.34 | 211-1 | |
| 4. Tamara Danilova | SOV | 62.86 | 206.3 | |
| 5. Liesel Westermann | GER | 62.18 | 204-0 | |
| 6. Gabriele Hinzmann | GDR | 61.72 | 202-6 | |
| 7. Carmen Ionescu | ROM | 60.42 | 198-3 | |
| 8. Lyudmila Muraviova | SOV | 59.00 | 193-7 | |

Argentina Menis, who wore makeup and false eyelashes while competing, led after three rounds, with world champion Faina Melnik struggling in fifth place. However, Melnik, who yelled at the top of her lungs with each throw, came within 5½ inches of her best ever on her fourth attempt. Menis gave one last mighty effort on her final try, nearly decapitating a marker judge with a throw of 212 feet 11 inches. Less than two weeks later Menis set a world record of 220 feet 10 inches.

**1976 Montreal** C: 15, N: 9, D: 7.29. WR: 70.50, 231-3½ (Faina Melnik)

| | | M | FT.-IN. | |
|---|---|---|---|---|
| 1. Evelin Schlaak | GDR | 69.00 | 226-4 | OR |
| 2. Maria Vergova | BUL | 67.30 | 220-9 | |
| 3. Gabriele Hinzmann | GDR | 66.84 | 219-3 | |
| 4. Faina Melnik | SOV | 66.40 | 217-10 | |
| 5. Sabine Engel | GDR | 65.88 | 216-2 | |
| 6. Argentina Menis | ROM | 65.38 | 214-6 | |
| 7. Maria Betancourt | CUB | 63.86 | 209-6 | |
| 8. Natalya Gorbachova | SOV | 63.46 | 208-2 | |

Twenty-year-old Schlaak shocked the opposition with a 69-meter first throw that held up for the victory. It was originally announced that Faina Melnik had taken second place by virtue of her fifth-round toss of 225 feet 1 inch. However, the throw was later ruled illegal because Melnik had stepped in front of the circle twice before taking her shot. Danuta Rosani of Poland qualified for the final, but was disqualified after failing the test for anabolic steroids. She was the first Olympic track and field athlete to be disqualified for taking drugs.

**1980 Moscow** C: 17, N: 10, D: 8.1. WR: 71.80, 235-7 (Maria Petkova [Vergova])

| | | M | FT.-IN. | |
|---|---|---|---|---|
| 1. Evelin Jahl (Schlaak) | GDR | 69.96 | 229.6 | OR |
| 2. Maria Petkova (Vergova) | BUL | 67.90 | 222-9 | |
| 3. Tatyana Lesovaya | SOV | 67.40 | 221-1 | |
| 4. Gisela Beyer | GDR | 67.08 | 220-1 | |
| 5. Margitta Pufe (Droese) | GDR | 66.12 | 216-1 | |
| 6. Florenţa Ţacu | ROM | 64.38 | 211-2 | |
| 7. Galina Murashova | SOV | 63.84 | 209-5 | |
| 8. Svetla Gunleva | BUL | 63.14 | 207-1 | |

Now married and a first lieutenant in the army, Jahl had lost her world record to Petkova a few weeks before the games. However, in Moscow she posted the four longest throws of the competition after Petkova had taken the opening-round lead.

**1984 Los Angeles** C: 17, N: 14, D: 8.11. WR: 73.26, 240-4¼ (Galina Savinkova)

| | | M | FT.-IN. | |
|---|---|---|---|---|
| 1. Ria Stalman | HOL | 65.36 | 214-5 | |
| 2. Leslie Deniz | USA | 64.86 | 212-9 | |
| 3. Florenţa Craciunescu (Ţacu) | ROM | 63.64 | 208-9 | |
| 4. Ulla Lundholm | FIN | 62.84 | 206-2 | |
| 5. Meg Ritchie | GBR | 62.58 | 205-4 | |
| 6. Ingra Manecke | GER | 58.56 | 192-1 | |
| 7. Venissa Head | GBR | 58.18 | 190-10 | |
| 8. Gael Martin | AUS | 55.88 | 183-4 | |

In a competition severely depleted by the Soviet-bloc boycott, Ria Stalman won a dramatic victory over her former Arizona State U. roommate, Leslie Deniz.

Stalman took the lead with her first throw of 64.50, but was passed in the fifth round by Deniz's 64.86. But the 32-year-old Stalman was able to secure the gold medal with a final toss of 65.36.

**1988 Seoul** C: 22, N: 13, D: 9.29. WR: 76.80, 252-0 (Gabriele Reinsch)

| | | | M | FT.-IN. | |
|---|---|---|---|---|---|
| 1. | Martina Hellmann | GDR | 72.30 | 237-2½ | OR |
| 2. | Diana Gansky | GDR | 71.88 | 235-10 | |
| 3. | Tzvetanka Hristova | BUL | 69.74 | 228-10 | |
| 4. | Svetla Mitkova | BUL | 69.14 | 226-10 | |
| 5. | Yellina Zvereva | SOV | 68.94 | 226-2 | |
| 6. | Zdeňka Šilhavá | CZE | 67.84 | 222-7 | |
| 7. | Gabriele Reinsch | GDR | 67.26 | 220-8 | |
| 8. | Hou Xuemei | CHN | 65.94 | 216-4 | |

Gabriele Reinsch, whose pre-1988 best was 220 feet 5 inches (67.18 meters), added over 7 feet to Zdeňka Šilhavá's 1984 world record with a throw of 252 feet on July 9, 1988. At the Olympics two and a half months later, she needed all three attempts to make it out of the preliminary round, then placed a disappointing seventh in the final. Meanwhile, her teammate, two-time world champion Martina Hellmann, hit a 71.84 in the first round and extended to 72.30 with her fourth throw, to outdistance the third East German, Diana Gansky, whose fifth-round throw earned her the silver.

## JAVELIN THROW

The women's javelin must weigh a minimum of 600 grams (26.16 ounces) and measure between 2.20 meters (7 feet 2⅔ inches) and 2.30 meters (7 feet 6½ inches).

**1896–1928** not held

**1932 Los Angeles** C: 8, N: 4, D: 7.31. WR: 46.75, 153-4½ (Nan Gindele)

| | | | M | FT.-IN. | |
|---|---|---|---|---|---|
| 1. | Mildred Didriksen | USA | 43.68 | 143-4 | OR |
| 2. | Ellen Braumüller | GER | 43.49 | 142-8 | |
| 3. | Tilly Fleischer | GER | 43.00 | 141-1 | |
| 4. | Masako Shimpo | JPN | 39.07 | 128-2 | |
| 5. | Nan Gindele | USA | 37.95 | 124-6 | |
| 6. | Gloria Russell | USA | 36.73 | 120-6 | |
| 7. | Maria Uribe Jasso | MEX | 33.66 | 110-5 | |
| 8. | Mitsue Ishizu | JPN | 30.81 | 101-1 | |

Born in Port Arthur, Texas, and raised in nearby Beaumont, Mildred "Babe" Didriksen* was already an all-American basketball player when she gained sudden and dramatic national attention as a track and field star. On July 4, 1932, the women's A.A.U. championships, which also served as the Olympic trials, were held in Evanston, Illinois, on the campus of Northwestern University. Babe caused a sensation at the opening parade when she ap-

*Preferred family spelling

peared as the entire team representing the Employers Casualty Insurance Company of Dallas, for whom she worked as an 85 w.p.m. typist. In the next three hours she took part in eight of the ten events and won six of them. She set world records in the 80-meter hurdles, the javelin, and the high jump, in which she tied with Jean Shiley. She also won the shot put, long jump, and baseball throw, and finished fourth in the discus. When the point totals were tallied, it was announced that Babe Didriksen had won the team title with 30 points. In second place with 22 points was the University of Illinois, which had sent a 22-woman contingent.

Olympic rules limited Babe to only three events, even though she had qualified for five, so she chose the three at which she had set world records. On the train across the country to the Los Angeles Olympics, the 21-year-old Babe irritated her fellow teammates by playing the harmonica, exercising in the aisles, and bragging about her numerous feats, which included earning a blue ribbon for sewing at the Texas State Fair. The same qualities that annoyed the athletes delighted reporters. Upon arrival in California, she told them, "I am out to beat everybody in sight, and that's just what I'm going to do." Her first event was the javelin, in which her first throw of 143 feet 4 inches was good enough for the gold medal even though the javelin slipped out of her hand. Before the Olympics were over she had recorded new world marks in the 80 meter hurdles and the high jump.

Overnight Babe Didriksen became a celebrity. But before the year was out she had been barred from amateur competition because she had allowed a photo of herself and an interview to be used in an automobile ad campaign. She tried her hand on the vaudeville circuit, telling jokes, shotputting, playing harmonica, and performing various athletic feats. For a time she toured as the only female and only nonbearded member of the House of David baseball team. She even pitched an inning against the Philadelphia Athletics during an exhibition game with the St. Louis Cardinals. After loading the bases with no outs, she got out of the inning on a double play and a fly ball to the outfield. Eventually she turned to golf, and it was there that she gained her greatest success. Encouraged by her 285-pound husband, wrestler George Zaharias, she became the greatest woman golfer in the world. During one 12-month period from 1946 to 1947, she won 14 straight tournaments and became the first American woman to win the British Amateur Open.

In 1953 Babe learned that she had cancer and was forced to undergo an emergency colostomy. Three and a half months after the surgery she was back on the circuit, finishing third in a minor tournament. The following year she won the U.S. Open by 12 strokes. But the cancer returned, and on September 17, 1956, Babe Didriksen, who had been voted the greatest female athlete of the half-century in an Associated Press poll, died at the age of 45.

**1936 Berlin** C: 14, N: 10, D: 8.2. WR: 46.75, 153-4½ (Nan Gindele)

|   |   |   | M | FT.-IN. |   |
|---|---|---|---|---|---|
| 1. | Tilly Fleischer | GER | 45.18 | 148-3 | OR |
| 2. | Luise Krüger | GER | 43.29 | 142-8 |   |
| 3. | Maria Kwaśniewska | POL | 41.80 | 137-2 |   |
| 4. | Hermine "Herma" Bauma | AUT | 41.66 | 136-8 |   |
| 5. | Sadako Yamamoto | JPN | 41.45 | 135-11 |   |
| 6. | Lydia Eberhardt | GER | 41.37 | 135-8 |   |
| 7. | Gertrude Wilhelmsen | USA | 37.35 | 122-6 |   |
| 8. | Gerda de Kock | HOL | 36.93 | 121-2 |   |

**1948 London** C: 15, N: 10, D: 7.31. WR: 50.32, 165-1 (Klavdia Mayuchaya)

|   |   |   | M | FT.-IN. |
|---|---|---|---|---|
| 1. | Hermine "Herma" Bauma | AUT | 45.57 | 149-6 |
| 2. | Kaisa Parviainen | FIN | 43.79 | 143-8 |
| 3. | Lily Carlstedt | DEN | 42.08 | 138-1 |
| 4. | Dorothy Dodson | USA | 41.96 | 137-8 |
| 5. | Johanna Tenunissen Waalboer | HOL | 40.92 | 134-3 |
| 6. | Johanna Koning | HOL | 40.33 | 132-3 |
| 7. | Dana Ingrova | CZE | 39.64 | 130-0 |
| 8. | Elly Dammers | HOL | 38.23 | 125-5 |

**1952 Helsinki** C: 19, N: 13, D: 7.24. WR: 53.41, 175-2¾ (Nina Smirnitskaya)

|   |   |   | M | FT.-IN. |
|---|---|---|---|---|
| 1. | Dana Zátopková (Ingrova) | CZE | 50.47 | 165-7 |
| 2. | Aleksandra Chudina | SOV | 50.01 | 164-0 |
| 3. | Yelena Gorchakova | SOV | 49.76 | 163-3 |
| 4. | Galina Zybina | SOV | 48.35 | 158-7 |
| 5. | Lily Kelsby-Carlstedt | DEN | 46.23 | 151-8 |
| 6. | Marlies Müller | GER | 44.37 | 145-6 |
| 7. | Maria Ciach | POL | 44.31 | 145-4½ |
| 8. | Jutta Kruger | GER | 44.30 | 145.4 |

Shortly before the competition began, Dana Zátopková's husband, Emil Zátopek, was awarded a gold medal for winning the 5000 meters. After the ceremony, she rushed up to him and said, "You've won! Splendid! Show me that medal." After examining it, she added, "I'll take it with me for luck." She put it in her bag and left. On her first throw she set an Olympic record and earned a gold medal of her own. That evening Emil claimed that he deserved partial credit for his wife's gold medal because he had inspired her. Naturally, Dana was quite offended and replied, "What? All right, go and inspire some other girl and see if she throws a javelin fifty meters."

**1956 Melbourne** C: 19, N: 12, D: 11.28. WR: 55.48, 182-0 (Nadezhda Konyayeva)

|   |   |   | M | FT.-IN. |
|---|---|---|---|---|
| 1. | Ineze Jaunzeme | SOV | 53.86 | 176-8 |
| 2. | Marlene Ahrens | CHI | 50.38 | 165-3 |
| 3. | Nadezhda Konyayeva | SOV | 50.28 | 164-11½ |
| 4. | Dana Zátopková (Ingrova) | CZE | 49.83 | 163-5½ |
| 5. | Ingrid Almqvist | SWE | 49.74 | 163-2 |
| 6. | Urszula Figwer | POL | 48.16 | 158-0 |
| 7. | Erszébeth Vig | HUN | 48.07 | 157-8½ |
| 8. | Karen Anderson | USA | 48.00 | 157-5½ |

**1960 Rome** C: 20, N: 14, D: 9.1. WR: 59.54, 195-4 (Elvira Ozolina)

|   |   |   | M | FT.-IN. |   |
|---|---|---|---|---|---|
| 1. | Elvira Ozolina | SOV | 55.98 | 183-8 | OR |
| 2. | Dana Zátopková (Ingrova) | CZE | 53.78 | 176-5 |   |
| 3. | Birutė Kalėdienė | SOV | 53.45 | 175-4 |   |
| 4. | Vlasta Pesková | CZE | 52.56 | 172-5 |   |
| 5. | Urszula Figwer | POL | 52.33 | 171-8 |   |
| 6. | Anna Pazera | AUS | 51.15 | 167-9 |   |
| 7. | Susan Platt | GBR | 51.01 | 167-4 |   |
| 8. | Alevtina Shastitko | SOV | 50.92 | 167-1 |   |

Ozolina unleashed her winning throw at her first attempt. Zátopková was 18 days shy of her 38th birthday when she won her second Olympic medal. Not only was she the oldest woman in Olympic history to win a track and field medal, but two years earlier she had thrown the javelin 182 feet 10 inches to become the oldest female world record breaker.

In the third round, Susan Platt of Great Britain threw past the 177-foot mark. However she was so excited that she stepped over the line on her way to see where the spear had fallen. The judge immediately ruled a foul and Platt had to settle for seventh place.

**1964 Tokyo** C: 16, N: 10, D: 10.16. WR: 61.38, 201-4½ (Elvira Ozolina)

|   |   |   | M | FT.-IN. |
|---|---|---|---|---|
| 1. | Mihaela Peneş | ROM | 60.54 | 198-7 |
| 2. | Márta Rudas | HUN | 58.27 | 191-2 |
| 3. | Yelena Gorchakova | SOV | 57.06 | 187-2 |
| 4. | Birute Kalediene | SOV | 56.31 | 184-8 |
| 5. | Elvira Ozolina | SOV | 54.81 | 179-9 |
| 6. | Maria Diaconescu | ROM | 53.71 | 176-2 |
| 7. | Hiroko Sato | JPN | 52.48 | 172-2 |
| 8. | Anneliese Gerhards | GER | 52.37 | 171-10 |

The 1964 javelin competition was full of surprises. On the very first throw of the qualification round, 31-year-old Yelena Gorchakova set a world record of 62.40 meters (204 feet 9 inches). This boosted her up to co-favorite along with defending champion Elvira Ozolina. However, when the final began a few hours later, it was 17-year-old high school student Mihaela Peneş of Bucharest who stunned the crowd with a throw of 198 feet 7 inches—17 feet further than she had ever thrown before. No one came close to her for the rest of the competition. Ozolina fouled on her last four attempts and had to settle for fifth place. She was so distressed by her performance that she went straight to the hairdresser at the Olympic Village and asked to have her head shaved. When the Japanese hairdresser refused, Ozolina took the clippers herself and removed a chunk of her long tresses. The hairdresser finished the job and Ozolina left the parlor bald, refusing a scarf to hide her shame. Ozolina was not the first Olympic athlete to react to defeat by having her head shaved, although she was the first woman. Four years earlier, in Rome, the entire Japanese wrestling team had had their heads shaved after an all-around poor showing.

**1968 Mexico City** C: 16, N: 11, D: 10.14. WR: 62.40, 204-8¾ (Yelena Gorchakova)

| | | M | FT.-IN. |
|---|---|---|---|
| 1. Angéla Németh | HUN | 60.36 | 198-0 |
| 2. Mihaela Peneş | ROM | 59.92 | 196-7 |
| 3. Eva Janko | AUT | 58.04 | 190-5 |
| 4. Márta Rudas | HUN | 56.38 | 185-0 |
| 5. Daniela Jaworska | POL | 56.06 | 183-11 |
| 6. Nataša Urbančič | YUG | 55.42 | 181-10 |
| 7. Ameli Koloska | GER | 55.20 | 181-1 |
| 8. Kaisa Launela | FIN | 53.96 | 177-0 |

**1972 Munich** C: 19, N: 10, D: 9.1. WR: 65.06, 213-5½ (Ruth Fuchs)

| | | M | FT.-IN. | |
|---|---|---|---|---|
| 1. Ruth Fuchs | GDR | 63.88 | 209-7 | OR |
| 2. Jacqueline Todten | GDR | 62.54 | 205-2 | |
| 3. Kathryn Schmidt | USA | 59.94 | 196-8 | |
| 4. Liutvian Mollova | BUL | 59.36 | 194-9 | |
| 5. Nataša Urbančič | YUG | 59.06 | 193-9 | |
| 6. Eva Janko | AUT | 58.56 | 192-1 | |
| 7. Ewa Gryziecka | POL | 57.00 | 187-0 | |
| 8. Svetlana Korolyova | SOV | 56.36 | 184-11 | |

Yelena Gorchakova's 1964 qualifying toss of 204 feet 8¾ inches had been in the books as a world record for over seven and a half years when it was suddenly beaten twice in one day. On June 11, 1972, Ewa Gryziecka, competing in Bucharest, threw the javelin 205 feet 8 inches (62.70 meters). One half hour later, in Potsdam, East Germany, Ruth Fuchs began her domination of women's javelin with a throw of 213 feet 5½ inches (65.06 meters). Two and a half months later, at the Munich Olympics, Fuchs took the lead from Kate Schmidt in the second round, improved in the fourth round, and broke the Olympic record in the fifth round. The competition ended on an exciting note when Urbančič's final throw almost skewered a wandering photographer.

**1976 Montreal** C: 15, N: 10, D: 7.24. WR: 69.12, 226-9¼ (Ruth Fuchs)

| | | M | FT.-IN. | |
|---|---|---|---|---|
| 1. Ruth Fuchs | GDR | 65.94 | 216-4 | OR |
| 2. Marion Becker | GER | 64.70 | 212-3 | |
| 3. Kathryn Schmidt | USA | 63.96 | 209-10 | |
| 4. Jacqueline Hein (Todten) | GDR | 63.84 | 209-5 | |
| 5. Sabine Sebrowski | GDR | 63.08 | 206-11 | |
| 6. Svetlana Babich (Korolyova) | SOV | 59.42 | 194-11 | |
| 7. Nadezhda Yakubovich | SOV | 59.16 | 194-1 | |
| 8. Karin Smith | USA | 57.50 | 188-8 | |

Marion Becker reached the victory platform in Montreal after an unusual odyssey. Born in Hamburg in West Germany in 1950, she was nonetheless raised in East Germany. After marrying, she moved to Romania and represented Romania at the 1972 Olympics in Munich, finishing seventeenth. After the games, she stayed behind in West Germany and four years later competed for the nation of her birth in the 1976 Olympics. In the qualifying round she broke the Olympic record with a throw of 213 feet 8 inches (65.14 meters). However, in the competition proper, Ruth Fuchs knocked out her opposition with an opening throw of 216 feet 4 inches (65.94 meters).

**1980 Moscow** C: 21, N: 14, D: 7.25. WR: 70.08, 229-10 (Tatyana Biryulina)

| | | M | FT.-IN. | |
|---|---|---|---|---|
| 1. Maria Colon Rueñes | CUB | 68.40 | 224-5 | OR |
| 2. Saida Gunba | SOV | 67.76 | 222-2 | |
| 3. Ute Hommola | GDR | 66.56 | 218-4 | |
| 4. Ute Richter | GDR | 66.54 | 218-4 | |
| 5. Ivanka Vancheva | BUL | 66.38 | 217-9 | |
| 6. Tatyana Biryulina | SOV | 65.08 | 213-6 | |
| 7. Eva Raduly-Zorgo | ROM | 64.08 | 210-3 | |
| 8. Ruth Fuchs | GDR | 63.94 | 209-9 | |

Ruth Fuchs continued to be the queen of javelin throwing all the way into 1980. On April 29 she set a world record of 69.96 meters (229 feet 6 inches) and she looked poised to become the first woman to break the 70-meter barrier. However, on July 12 a complete unknown, Tatyana Biryulina, improved her personal best by 27½ feet with a throw of 70.08. Less than two weeks later, at the Olympics, Biryulina could do no better than 65.08 and sixth place. In fact, the women with the four best pre-Olympic records all had disappointing performances. Fuchs, competing with a back injury, finished eighth, Raduly was seventh, and Tessa Sanderson, who had thrown 69.70, failed to qualify for the final. It was left to Maria Colon to win the competition on her first throw. She was the first Cuban woman to win an Olympic gold medal. Fuchs needn't have felt ashamed by her loss. From 1970 through 1980 she took part in 129 meets and won 113 of them, including 30 straight from 1972 to 1974.

**1984 Los Angeles** C: 24, N: 16, D: 8.6. WR: 74.73, 245-3 (Ilse "Tiina" Lillak)

| | | M | FT.-IN. | |
|---|---|---|---|---|
| 1. Theresa "Tessa" Sanderson | GBR | 69.56 | 228-2 | OR |
| 2. Ilse "Tiina" Lillak | FIN | 69.00 | 226-4 | |
| 3. Fatima Whitbread | GBR | 67.14 | 220-3 | |
| 4. Tuula Laaksalo | FIN | 66.40 | 217-10 | |
| 5. Trine Solberg | NOR | 64.52 | 211-8 | |
| 6. Ingrid Thyssen | GER | 63.26 | 207-6 | |
| 7. Beate Peters | GER | 62.34 | 204-6 | |
| 8. Karin Smith | USA | 62.06 | 203-7 | |

Jamaican-born Tessa Sanderson, competing in her third Olympics, broke the Olympic record with her first throw. World record holder Tiina Lillak had won the 1983 world championship with a dramatic last round throw in front of an adoring hometown crowd. In Los Angeles her second round effort came within two feet of Sanderson's best, but she was forced to pass her last four chances because of a stress fracture of her right foot. Sanderson's record held up for the gold medal, while Fatima Whitbread, who had beaten Sanderson three times in a row after losing 21 of their first 22 confrontations, overhauled Laaksalo in the fifth round to secure the bronze. Sanderson was the first Briton and the first black athlete to win an Olympic throwing event.

**1988 Seoul** C: 29, N: 18, D: 9.26. WR: 80.00, 262-6 (Petra Felke)

|   |   |   | M | FT.-IN. |   |
|---|---|---|---|---------|---|
| 1. | Petra Felke | GDR | 74.68 | 245-0 | OR |
| 2. | Fatima Whitbread | GBR | 70.32 | 230-8½ |   |
| 3. | Beate Koch | GDR | 67.30 | 220-10 |   |
| 4. | Irina Kostyuchenkova | SOV | 67.00 | 219-10 |   |
| 5. | Silke Renk | GDR | 66.38 | 217-9 |   |
| 6. | Natalya Yermolovich | SOV | 64.84 | 212-9 |   |
| 7. | Donna Mayhew | USA | 61.78 | 202-8 |   |
| 8. | Ingrid Thyssen | GER | 60.76 | 199-4 |   |

Between 1984 and the opening of the 1988 Olympics, Petra Felke won 69 of 76 meets. Her last three losses were all to Fatima Whitbread, who defeated her at the two most important meets—the 1986 European championships and the 1987 world championships. Eight days before the opening of the Seoul Games, Felke served notice that she was finally ready to win the big one when she became the first woman to throw a javelin 80 meters. In Seoul she delivered the three longest throws of the competitions. Whitbread secured the silver medal despite the fact that in the 12 preceding months she had suffered a trapped nerve in her throwing shoulder, a foot injury, a mouth infection, an abscess in her back, hamstring problems, glandular fever, and a car crash.

## HEPTATHLON/PENTATHLON

In 1984 the five-event pentathlon was replaced by the seven-event heptathlon. Points are scored according to a set of tables approved by the International Amateur Athletic Federation.

**1896–1960** not held

**1964 Tokyo** C: 20, N: 15, D: 10.16–17. WR: 5194 (Irina Press)

|   |   |   | 80M H | SP | HJ | LJ | 200M | TOTAL |   |
|---|---|---|-------|-----|-----|-----|------|-------|---|
| 1. | Irina Press | SOV | 10.7 | 17.16 | 1.63 | 6.24 | 24.7 | 5246 | WR |
| 2. | Mary Rand | GBR | 10.9 | 11.05 | 1.72 | 6.55 | 24.2 | 5035 |   |
| 3. | Galina Bystrova | SOV | 10.7 | 14.47 | 1.60 | 6.11 | 25.2 | 4956 |   |
| 4. | Mary Peters | GBR | 11.0 | 14.48 | 1.60 | 5.60 | 25.4 | 4797 |   |
| 5. | Draga Stamejčič | YUG | 10.9 | 12.73 | 1.54 | 6.19 | 25.2 | 4790 |   |
| 6. | Helga Hoffman | GER | 11.2 | 10.67 | 1.60 | 6.44 | 25.0 | 4737 |   |
| 7. | Patricia Winslow | USA | 12.0 | 13.04 | 1.63 | 5.90 | 24.6 | 4724 |   |
| 8. | Ingrid Becker | GER | 11.6 | 11.62 | 1.60 | 6.17 | 24.6 | 4717 |   |

Press's margin of victory was provided in the shot put, where she outpointed Rand 1173 to 789 with a throw of 56 feet 2½ inches, which was 16½ inches farther than she was able to throw in the shot put competition three days later.

**1968 Mexico City** C: 33, N: 24, D: 10.15–16. WR: 5246 (Irina Press)

|   |   |   | 80M H | SP | HJ | LJ | 200M | TOTAL |
|---|---|---|-------|-----|-----|-----|------|-------|
| 1. | Ingrid Becker | GER | 10.9 | 11.48 | 1.71 | 6.43 | 23.5 | 5098 |
| 2. | Elisabeth "Liese" Prokop | AUT | 11.2 | 14.61 | 1.68 | 5.97 | 25.1 | 4966 |
| 3. | Annamária Tóth | HUN | 10.9 | 12.68 | 1.59 | 6.12 | 23.8 | 4959 |
| 4. | Valentina Tikhomirova | SOV | 11.2 | 14.12 | 1.65 | 5.99 | 24.9 | 4927 |
| 5. | Manon Bornholdt | GER | 11.0 | 12.37 | 1.59 | 6.42 | 24.8 | 4890 |
| 6. | Patricia Winslow | USA | 11.4 | 13.33 | 1.65 | 5.97 | 24.5 | 4877 |
| 7. | Ingeborg Bauer | GDR | 11.4 | 13.00 | 1.59 | 6.22 | 24.5 | 4849 |
| 8. | Meta Antenen | SWI | 10.7 | 11.06 | 1.62 | 6.30 | 24.9 | 4848 |

Heidemarie Rosendahl of West Germany was considered the pre-Games favorite, but she pulled a muscle while warming up and was unable to compete. Liese Prokop was the surprise leader after four events, but Ingrid Becker, competing in her third Olympics, ran the fastest 200 meters of the competition to take the gold medal.

**1972 Munich** C: 28, N: 18, D: 9.2–3. WR: 4775 (Burglinde Pollack)

|   | | | 100M H | SP | HJ | LJ | 200M | TOTAL | |
|---|---|---|---|---|---|---|---|---|---|
| 1. | Mary Peters | GBR | 13.29 | 16.29 | 1.82 | 5.98 | 24.08 | 4801 | WR |
| 2. | Heidemarie Rosendahl | GER | 13.34 | 13.86 | 1.65 | 6.83 | 22.96 | 4791 | |
| 3. | Burglinde Pollak | GDR | 13.53 | 16.04 | 1.76 | 6.21 | 23.93 | 4768 | |
| 4. | Christine Bodner | GDR | 13.25 | 12.51 | 1.76 | 6.40 | 23.66 | 4671 | |
| 5. | Valentina Tikhomirova | SOV | 13.77 | 14.64 | 1.74 | 6.15 | 24.25 | 4597 | |
| 6. | Nedialka Angelova | BUL | 13.84 | 13.96 | 1.68 | 6.32 | 24.58 | 4496 | |
| 7. | Karen Mack | GER | 14.45 | 14.10 | 1.76 | 6.11 | 24.72 | 4449 | |
| 8. | Ilona Bruzsenyák | HUN | 13.65 | 12.48 | 1.65 | 6.29 | 24.35 | 4419 | |

In 1971, the 80-meter hurdles was replaced by the 100-meter hurdles, necessitating a change in the scoring tables and a reevaluation of the world record. Mary Peters, a 33-year-old English-born secretary from Belfast, Northern Ireland, finished fourth at Tokyo in 1964 and ninth in Mexico City in 1968. During the first day of competition in Munich she recorded personal bests in two of the three events—the 100-meter hurdles and the high jump. The high jump was a particularly magical moment for her, as the German crowd rooted her on and chanted her name despite the fact that she was competing against local favorite Heide Rosendahl, who had won the long jump two days earlier. At the end of the first day, Peters was 97 points ahead of Pollak and 301 points ahead of Rosendahl, who was in fifth place. But the two events of the second day, the long jump and the 200 meters, were Rosendahl's best and Peters' worst. Sure enough, Rosendahl jumped 22 feet 5 inches, 1 centimeter short of her world record. The 200 meters saw both women achieve personal bests. If Mary Peters had run one-tenth of a second slower she would have lost the gold medal. Afterward she told the press that she had become so exhausted in the last 50 meters of the 200 that her legs felt like jelly. In her autobiography, *Mary P.,* she revised her description and wrote that her legs felt like lead.

**1976 Montreal** C: 20, N: 13, D: 7.28–26. WR: 4932 (Burglinde Pollack)

|   | | | 100M H | SP | HJ | LJ | 200M | TOTAL |
|---|---|---|---|---|---|---|---|---|
| 1. | Siegrun Siegl | GDR | 13.31 | 12.92 | 1.74 | 6.49 | 23.09 | 4745 |
| 2. | Christine Laser (Bodner) | GDR | 13.55 | 14.29 | 1.78 | 6.27 | 23.48 | 4745 |
| 3. | Burglinde Pollak | GDR | 13.30 | 16.25 | 1.64 | 6.30 | 23.64 | 4740 |
| 4. | Lyudmila Popovskaya | SOV | 13.33 | 15.02 | 1.74 | 6.19 | 24.10 | 4700 |
| 5. | Nadezhda Tkachenko | SOV | 13.41 | 14.90 | 1.80 | 6.08 | 24.61 | 4669 |
| 6. | Diane Jones | CAN | 13.79 | 14.58 | 1.80 | 6.29 | 25.33 | 4582 |
| 7. | Jane Frederick | USA | 13.54 | 14.55 | 1.76 | 5.99 | 24.70 | 4566 |
| 8. | Margit Papp | HUN | 14.14 | 14.80 | 1.78 | 6.35 | 25.43 | 4535 |

Anyone who enjoys close finishes need look no further than the 1976 pentathlon. With four events finished and only the 200 meters to be run, the standings were as follows:

| | | | | | |
|---|---|---|---|---|---|
| 1. | Tkachenko | 3788 | 5. | Laser | 3757 |
| 2. | Popovskaya | 3772 | 6. | Papp | 3726 |
| 3. | Pollak | 3768 | 7. | Siegl | 3718 |
| 4. | Jones | 3764 | 8. | Frederick | 3693 |

All the leaders were matched against one another in the final heat. When the dust cleared 26 seconds later, officials and fans hurriedly consulted their scoring tables. It was discovered that Siegl, the world record holder in the long jump, and Laser, who had achieved personal records in the high jump and 200, had finished with the exact same point total, while Pollak was only five points behind. Siegl was finally awarded first place on the basis of having beaten Laser in three of the five events. Had Pollak run six one-hundredths of a second faster she would have won the gold medal. Instead she had to settle for her second straight bronze. While Siegl jumped from seventh to first in one event, Tkachenko had the misfortune of dropping from first to fifth in less than 25 seconds.

**1980 Moscow** C: 19, N: 12, D: 7.23-24. WR (with 800m): 4856 (Olga Kuragina)

| | | | 100M H | SP | HJ | LJ | 800M | TOTAL | |
|---|---|---|---|---|---|---|---|---|---|
| 1. | Nadezhda Tkachenko | SOV | 13.29 | 16.84 | 1.84 | 6.73 | 2:05.2 | 5083 | WR |
| 2. | Olga Rukavishnikova | SOV | 13.66 | 14.09 | 1.88 | 6.79 | 2:04.8 | 4937 | |
| 3. | Olga Kuragina | SOV | 13.26 | 12.49 | 1.84 | 6.77 | 2:03.6 | 4875 | |
| 4. | Ramona Neubert | GDR | 13.93 | 13.68 | 1.77 | 6.63 | 2:07.7 | 4698 | |
| 5. | Margit Papp | HUN | 13.96 | 14.94 | 1.74 | 6.35 | 2:15.8 | 4562 | |
| 6. | Burglinde Pollak | GDR | 13.74 | 16.67 | 1.68 | 5.93 | 2:14.4 | 4553 | |
| 7. | Valentina Dimitrova | BUL | 14.39 | 15.65 | 1.74 | 5.91 | 2:15.5 | 4458 | |
| 8. | Emilia Kounova | BUL | 13.73 | 11.98 | 1.74 | 6.10 | 2:11.1 | 4431 | |

The 1980 pentathlon saw tremendous performances by all three Soviet athletes, each of whom broke the existing world record. Thirty-one-year-old Nadezhda Tkachenko followed a long road to her gold medal. Ninth in Munich, fifth in Montreal, she won the European title in 1978 only to lose it after failing a test for anabolic steroids. Handed an 18-month suspension by the I.A.A.F., she was back in time for the 1980 Olympics. In Moscow she achieved personal bests in four of the five events and fell only three-quarters of an inch short of her lifetime record in the shot put. Rukavishnikova has the unusual distinction of setting the shortest-lived world record in history—two-fifths of a second. When she crossed the finish line of the 800 meters she became the world record holder in the pentathlon. But when Tkachenko finished right behind her, a new record was set.

**1984 Los Angeles** C: 23, N: 13, D: 8.3–4. WR: 6867 (Sabine Paetz)

| | | | 100M H | HJ | SP | 200M | LJ | JT | 800M | TOTAL | |
|---|---|---|---|---|---|---|---|---|---|---|---|
| 1. | Glynis Nunn | AUS | 13.02 | 1.80 | 12.82 | 24.06 | 6.66 | 35.58 | 2:10.57 | 6390 | OR |
| 2. | Jacqueline Joyner | USA | 13.63 | 1.80 | 14.39 | 24.05 | 6.11 | 44.52 | 2:13.03 | 6385 | |
| 3. | Sabine Everts | GER | 13.54 | 1.89 | 12.49 | 24.05 | 6.71 | 32.62 | 2:09.05 | 6363 | |
| 4. | Cindy Greiner | USA | 13.71 | 1.83 | 13.36 | 24.40 | 6.15 | 40.86 | 2:11.75 | 6281 | |
| 5. | Judy Simpson | GBR | 13.07 | 1.86 | 13.86 | 24.95 | 6.33 | 33.64 | 2:13.01 | 6280 | |
| 6. | Sabine Braun | GER | 13.61 | 1.80 | 12.09 | 24.22 | 6.10 | 44.14 | 2:12.48 | 6236 | |
| 7. | Tineke Hidding | HOL | 13.70 | 1.74 | 13.48 | 24.12 | 6.35 | 33.94 | 2:12.84 | 6147 | |
| 8. | Kim Hagger | GBR | 13.39 | 1.86 | 12.29 | 24.72 | 6.37 | 35.42 | 2:18.44 | 6127 | |

With all of the leading medal contenders among the boycott missing, the first Olympic heptathlon became an open competition. After the four events of the first day, Simpson led with 3759 points. She was followed closely by Joyner at 3739, Nunn with 3731 and Everts with 3721. The first event of the second day, the long jump, turned out to be the turning point. This was Joyner's specialty. But after fouling her first two tries, she played it safe with her final jump, taking off over a foot before the takeoff board and registering only 20 feet ½ inch, 26 inches less than she would achieve in placing fifth in the long jump competition five days later. Meanwhile, Everts moved into first place, one point ahead of Nunn. However, Joyner took the lead for the first time following the javelin throw.

As Jackie Joyner struggled through the 800-meter run, she was rooted on by her brother Al, who was in the midst of winning the triple jump. When the race was over, coaches and officials rushed to their scoring tables booklets to compute the results. Initially, Glynis Nunn, a 24-year-old schoolteacher, thought she had lost by 3 points. In fact, she had improved her personal record by 108 points and won by 5 points. If Joyner had long-jumped 3 centimeters further or finished the 800 0.33 seconds faster, the victory would have been hers. Later in the Olympics Nunn placed seventh in the long jump and fifth in the 100-meter hurdles.

**1988 Seoul** C: 20, N: 10, D: 9.23-24. WR: 7215 (Jacqueline Joyner-Kersee)

| | | | 100M H | HJ | SP | 200M | LJ | JT | 800M | TOTAL | |
|---|---|---|---|---|---|---|---|---|---|---|---|
| 1. | USA | Jacqueline Joyner-Kersee | 12.69 | 1.86 | 15.80 | 22.56 | 7.27 | 45.66 | 2:08.51 | 7291 | WR |
| 2. | GDR | Sabine John | 12.85 | 1.80 | 16.23 | 23.65 | 6.71 | 42.56 | 2:06.14 | 6897 | |
| 3. | GDR | Anke Behmer | 13.20 | 1.83 | 14.20 | 23.10 | 6.68 | 44.54 | 2:04.20 | 6858 | |
| 4. | SOV | Natalya Shubenkova | 13.51 | 1.74 | 14.76 | 23.93 | 6.32 | 47.46 | 2:07.90 | 6540 | |
| 5. | SOV | Remigia Sablovskaitė | 13.61 | 1.80 | 15.23 | 23.92 | 6.25 | 42.78 | 2:12.24 | 6456 | |
| 6. | GDR | Ines Schulz | 13.75 | 1.83 | 13.50 | 24.65 | 6.33 | 42.82 | 2:05.79 | 6411 | |
| 7. | AUS | Jane Flemming | 13.38 | 1.80 | 12.88 | 23.59 | 6.37 | 40.28 | 2:12.54 | 6351 | |
| 8. | USA | Cindy Greiner | 13.55 | 1.80 | 14.13 | 24.48 | 6.47 | 38.00 | 2:13.65 | 6297 | |

The baby girl born into the Joyner family on March 3, 1962, was named Jacqueline after the wife of U.S. President John Kennedy because, in the words of her grandmother, "Someday this girl will be the First Lady of something." How right she was. After finishing second in the 1984 Olympics, Jackie Joyner won all nine heptathlons that she entered over the next four years. She also married her coach, Bob Kersee, who told her that she couldn't use his name until she broke a world record. She became Jackie Joyner-Kersee in Moscow on July 7, 1986, when she became the first woman to break the 7000-point mark with a score of 7148. She set another world record 26 days later and another one at the U.S. Olympic trials in 1988.

By that time, Joyner-Kersee was so much better than all the other heptathletes that her husband had to create a new opponent for her: Wilhelmina World Record. In Seoul, Joyner-Kersee beat Wilhelmina again. Five days after the heptathlon, Joyner-Kersee earned a second gold medal in long jump.

# ARCHERY

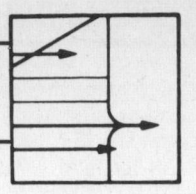

| MEN | WOMEN |
|-----|-------|
| Individual | Individual |
| Team | Team |
| Discontinued Events | Discontinued Events |

## MEN

Competitors in men's Olympic archery begin by shooting one F.I.T.A. round. An F.I.T.A. round consists of 36 arrows at each of four distances: 90, 70, 50, and 30 meters. The target is divided into ten rings. The inner ring is worth ten points and the outer ring one point. Thus, a perfect score for an F.I.T.A. round would be 1440 points. Before 1988, Olympic competition consisted of two F.I.T.A. rounds. The leading archers still shoot a total of 288 arrows, but under a different format known as Grand F.I.T.A. All competitors take part in the initial open round. The top twenty-four move on to the eighth final where they shoot nine arrows at each distance. The top eighteen in this round advance to the quarterfinal. The top twelve scorers in the quarterfinal advance to the semifinal. The top eight in that round take part in the final. Scores are not cumulative. In the semifinal and final rounds, the distances are reversed: 30, 50, 70, and 90 meters. Modern bows are incredibly complicated and are augmented by bowsights, bowmarks, foresights, and stabilizers.

### INDIVIDUAL

**1896–1968** not held

**1972 Munich** C: 55, N: 24, D: 9.10. WR: 2445 (John Williams)

| | | | 1st ROUND | | 2nd ROUND | TOTAL POINTS | |
|---|---|---|---|---|---|---|---|
| 1. | John Williams | USA | 1268 | WR | 1260 | 2528 | WR |
| 2. | Gunnar Jarvil | SWE | 1229 | | 1252 | 2481 | |
| 3. | Kyösti Laasonen | FIN | 1213 | | 1254 | 2467 | |
| 4. | Robert Cogniaux | BEL | 1205 | | 1240 | 2445 | |
| 5. | Edwin Eliason | USA | 1193 | | 1245 | 2438 | |
| 6. | Donald Jackson | CAN | 1225 | | 1212 | 2437 | |
| 7. | Victor Sidorouk | SOV | 1205 | | 1222 | 2427 | |
| 8. | Arne Jacobsen | DEN | 1188 | | 1235 | 2423 | |

The reigning world champion, John Williams, was an 18-year-old army private from Cranesville, Pennsylvania, who spent 42 hours a week in training. In the first F.I.T.A. round he broke Arne Jacobsen's single round world record despite missing the target completely with one arrow.

**1976 Montreal** C: 37, N: 23, D: 7.30. WR: 2570 (Darrell Pace)

| | | | 1st ROUND | 2nd ROUND | TOTAL POINTS | |
|---|---|---|---|---|---|---|
| 1. | Darrell Pace | USA | 1264 | 1307 | 2571 | WR |
| 2. | Hiroshi Michinaga | JPN | 1226 | 1276 | 2502 | |
| 3. | Giancarlo Ferrari | ITA | 1220 | 1275 | 2495 | |
| 4. | Richard McKinney | USA | 1230 | 1241 | 2471 | |
| 5. | Vladimir Chendarov | SOV | 1217 | 1250 | 2467 | |
| 6. | Willi Gabriel | GER | 1203 | 1232 | 2435 | |
| 7. | Dave Mann | CAN | 1190 | 1241 | 2431 | |
| 8. | Takanobu Nishi | JPN | 1191 | 1231 | 2422 | |

**1980 Moscow** C: 38, N: 25, D: 8.2. WR (single round): 1341 (Darrell Pace)

| | | | 1st ROUND | 2nd ROUND | TOTAL POINTS |
|---|---|---|---|---|---|
| 1. | Tomi Poikolainen | FIN | 1220 | 1235 | 2455 |
| 2. | Boris Isachenko | SOV | 1217 | 1235 | 2452 |
| 3. | Giancarlo Ferrari | ITA | 1215 | 1234 | 2449 |
| 4. | Mark Blenkarne | GBR | 1224 | 1222 | 2446 |
| 5. | Béla Nagy | HUN | 1225 | 1221 | 2446 |
| 6. | Vladimir Yesheyev | SOV | 1222 | 1210 | 2432 |
| 7. | Kyösti Laasonen | FIN | 1212 | 1207 | 2419 |
| 8. | Tiny Reniers | HOL | 1205 | 1213 | 2418 |

**1984 Los Angeles-Long Beach** C: 62, N: 25, D: 8.11. WR: 1341 (Darrell Pace)

| | | | 1st ROUND | 2nd ROUND | TOTAL POINTS | |
|---|---|---|---|---|---|---|
| 1. | Darrell Pace | USA | 1317 | 1299 | 2616 | OR |
| 2. | Richard McKinney | USA | 1295 | 1269 | 2564 | |
| 3. | Hiroshi Yamamoto | JPN | 1276 | 1287 | 2563 | |
| 4. | Takayoshi Matsushita | JPN | 1264 | 1288 | 2552 | |
| 5. | Tomi Poikolainen | FIN | 1275 | 1263 | 2538 | |
| 6. | Göran Bjerendal | SWE | 1275 | 1247 | 2522 | |
| 7. | Marnix Vervinck | BEL | 1260 | 1259 | 2519 | |
| 8. | Koo Ja-chung | KOR | 1226 | 1274 | 2500 | |

Darrell Pace and Rick McKinney grew up 85 miles apart in Reading, Ohio, and Muncie, Indiana. Their rivalry began in 1973 when both were teenagers and Pace, at 16, won a place on the U.S. world championship team by finishing one point ahead of McKinney at the trials. In 1975, Pace won the next world championship and the following year added an Olympic victory. A discouraged McKinney decided to give himself one more year before retiring from competition. Relaxed and unpressured,

McKinney won the 1977 world championship, with Pace slipping to fourth. However, Pace regained the title in 1979.

Pace and McKinney's most dramatic confrontation came at the 1983 world championship held at the Olympic site in Long Beach. Pace needed to fire all tens with his final three arrows to clinch another world championship. His first two arrows were bull's-eyes. But his final shot was so perfect that the arrow struck the nock of one of the first two arrows and glanced off into the nine ring.

McKinney, firing two targets away, heard Pace's arrow hit the nock and knew that if *he* could hit the ten ring with his final shot *he* would be the world champion. After many moments of quiet tension, McKinney released his bow and achieved his ten.

Ten months later, at the Los Angeles Olympics, there was no such drama, at least not for the gold medal. Pace took a 13-point lead after the first of four days and steadily widened the gap to win easily. McKinney, however, needed to fire a ten with his final arrow to secure second place. He did and the silver medal was his.

**1988 Seoul** C: 84, N: 34, D: 9.30. WR: 1341 (Darrell Pace)

|   |   |   | OPEN ROUND | 8th FINAL | QUART. FINAL | SEMI- FINAL | GRAND FINAL | GRAND TOTAL |
|---|---|---|---|---|---|---|---|---|
| 1. | Jay Barrs | USA | 1294 (3) | 313 (10) | 326 (4) | 334 (2) | 338 (1) | 2605 |
| 2. | Park Sung-soo | KOR | 1300 (2) | 322 (4) | 324 (5) | 329 (4) | 336 (2) | 2614 |
| 3. | Vladimir Yesheev | SOV | 1304 (1) | 313 (14) | 320 (9) | 328 (5) | 335 (3) | 2600 |
| 4. | Chun In-soo | KOR | 1284 (6) | 326 (2) | 323 (6) | 334 (1) | 331 (4) | 2598 |
| 5. | Martinus Reniers | HOL | 1286 (5) | 328 (1) | 328 (2) | 324 (8) | 327 (5) | 2593 |
| 6. | Richard McKinney | USA | 1288 (4) | 321 (6) | 327 (3) | 332 (3) | 324 (6) | 2592 |
| 7. | Pentti Vikström | FIN | 1273 (13) | 312 (15) | 320 (10) | 324 (7) | 323 (7) | 2552 |
| 8. | Hiroshi Yamamoto | JPN | 1271 (14) | 316 (7) | 318 (12) | 324 (6) | 321 (8) | 2550 |

Twenty-six-year-old Jay Barrs, who listened to heavy metal music between rounds, gained his victory by picking up 2 points on Park during the final 18 arrows. Defending champion Darrell Pace finished ninth. In last place was Derrick Tenai, a security guard from the Solomon Islands, who had never seen a modern bow until he arrived in Seoul. In the open round, Tenai hit the target 89 times and missed 55 times. None of the other 83 contestants missed the target more than 5 times and 65 of them had no misses at all.

# TEAM

Scores from the individual open round are used to determine the 12 teams which are allowed to advance to the semifinal round. The top 8 in the semifinal go on to the final. In the semifinal the order of shooting is 30, 50, 70, and 90 meters. In the final it is reversed.

**1896–1984** not held

**1988 Seoul** T: 22, N: 22, D: 10.1. WR: 3948 (USA—McKinney, Barrs, Pace)

| | | OPEN ROUND | SEMI-FINAL | GRAND FINAL |
|---|---|---|---|---|
| 1. KOR | (Chun In-soo, Lee Han-sup, Park Sung-soo) | 3862 (1) | 960 (6) | 986 (1) |
| 2. USA | (Jay Barrs, Richard McKinney, Darrell Pace) | 3839 (2) | 992 (1) | 972 (2) |
| 3. GBR | (Steven Hallard, Richard Priestman, Leroy Watson) | 3733 (8) | 965 (4) | 968 (3) |
| 4. FIN | (Ismo Falck, Tomi Poikolainen, Pentti Vikström) | 3797 (4) | 960 (7) | 956 (4) |
| 5. SOV | (Konstantin Shkolny, Vladimir Yesheev, Yuri Leontyev) | 3799 (3) | 976 (2) | 949 (5) |
| 6. JPN | (Terushi Furuhashi, Takayoshi Matsushita, Hiroshi Yamamoto) | 3766 (5) | 958 (8) | 948 (6) |
| 7. TAI | (Chiu Ping-kun, Hu Pei-wen, Yen Man-sung) | 3693 (11) | 968 (3) | 937 (7) |
| 8. SWE | (Gert Bjerendal, Göran Bjerendal, Mats Nordlander) | 3759 (6) | 964 (5) | 925 (8) |

The Koreans trailed the U.S. team by two points before surging ahead at the final distance of 90 meters.

# Discontinued Events

**1900 Paris** C: 68, N: 2, D: 5.28.
*Au cordon doré—50 Meters*

| | | PTS. |
|---|---|---|
| 1. Henri Herouin | FRA | 31 |
| 2. Hubert van Innis | BEL | 29 |
| 3. Emile Fisseux | FRA | 28 |

*Au chapelet—50 Meters*

| | | |
|---|---|---|
| 1. Eugène Mougin | FRA | — |
| 2. Henri Helle | FRA | — |
| 3. Emile Mercier | FRA | — |

*Au cordon doré—33 Meters*

| | | |
|---|---|---|
| 1. Hubert van Innis | BEL | — |
| 2. Victor Thibaud | FRA | — |
| 3. Charles Frédéric Petit | FRA | — |

*Au chapelet—33 Meters*

| | | |
|---|---|---|
| 1. Hubert van Innis | BEL | — |
| 2. Victor Thibaud | FRA | — |
| 3. Charles Frédéric Petit | FRA | — |

*Sur la perche à la herse*

| | | |
|---|---|---|
| 1. Emmanuel Foulon | FRA | — |
| 2. Serrurier | FRA | — |
| 3. Druart, Jr. | BEL | — |

*Sur la perche à la pyramide*

| | | |
|---|---|---|
| 1. Emile Grumiaux | FRA | — |
| 2. Louis Glineux | BEL | — |

**1904 St. Louis** C: 16, N: 1, D: 9.20.
*Double York Round (100 Yards—80 Yards—60 Yards)*

| | | PTS. |
|---|---|---|
| 1. George Phillip Bryant | USA | 820 |
| 2. Robert Williams | USA | 819 |
| 3. William Thompson | USA | 816 |
| 4. Wallace Bryant | USA | 618 |
| 5. Benjamin Keys | USA | 532 |
| 6. Ernest Frentz | USA | 528 |
| 7. Homer Taylor | USA | 506 |
| 8. C. S. Woodruff | USA | 487 |

**1904 St. Louis** C: 22, N: 1, D: 9.19.
*Double American Round (60 Yards—50 Yards—40 Yards)*

| | | PTS. |
|---|---|---|
| 1. George Phillip Bryant | USA | 1048 |
| 2. Robert Williams | USA | 991 |
| 3. William Thompson | USA | 949 |
| 4. C. S. Woodruff | USA | 907 |
| 5. William Clark | USA | 880 |
| 6. Benjamin Keys | USA | 840 |
| 7. Wallace Bryant | USA | 818 |
| 8. Cyrus Dallin | USA | 816 |

**1904 St. Louis** T: 4, N: 1, D: 9.21.
*Team Round (60 Yards)*

| | PTS. |
|---|---|
| 1. (Potomac Archers, Washington D.C.—William Thompson, Robert Williams, Louis Maxson, Galen Spencer) | 1344 |
| 2. (Cincinnati Archers—C.S. Woodruff, William Clark, Charles Hubbard, Samuel Duvall) | 1341 |
| 3. (Boston Archers—George Phillip Bryant, Wallace Bryant, Cyrus Dallin, Henry Richardson) | 1268 |
| 4. (Chicago Archers—Benjamin Keys, Homer Taylor, Edward Weston, Edward Bruce) | 942 |

**1908 London** C: 27, N: 3, D: 7.18.
*York Round (100 Yards—80 Yards—60 Yards)*

| | | PTS. |
|---|---|---|
| 1. William Dod | GBR | 815 |
| 2. R. B. Brooks-King | GBR | 768 |
| 3. Henry Richardson | USA | 760 |
| 4. John Penrose | GBR | 709 |
| 5. John Bridges | GBR | 687 |
| 6. H. V. James | GBR | 652 |
| 7. T. Robinson | GBR | 647 |
| 8. H. P. Nesham | GBR | 643 |

Dod had the distinction of being part of the first brother-sister Olympic medalists. His sister, Lottie, a former golf and tennis champion, won the silver medal in the women's national round.

**1908 London** C: 17, N: 2, D: 7.20.
*Continental Style (50 Meters)*

|  |  | PTS. |
|---|---|---|
| 1. E.G. Grisot | FRA | 263 |
| 2. Louis Vernet | FRA | 256 |
| 3. Gustave Cabaret | FRA | 255 |
| 4. C. Aubras | FRA | 231 |
| 5. C. Querviel | FRA | 223 |
| 6. A. Dauchez | FRA | 222 |
| 7. Salingre | FRA | 215 |
| 8. Berton | FRA | 212 |

An unofficial entrant, R.O. Backhouse of Great Britain, finished second with a score of 260 and was awarded a certificate for special merit.

**1920 Antwerp** C: 30, N: 3, D: 8.3-8, 8.22-29.
*Fixed Bird Target*

|  |  | PTS. |
|---|---|---|
| 1. Edmond van Moer | BEL | 11 |
| 2. Louis van de Perck | BEL | 8 |
| 3. Joseph Hermans | BEL | 6 |

*Large Birds*

|  |  | PTS. |
|---|---|---|
| 1. Edouard Cloetens | BEL | 13 |
| 2. Louis van de Perck | BEL | 11 |
| 3. Firmin Flamand | BEL | 7 |

*Moving Bird Target*
28 Meters:

|  |  | PTS. |
|---|---|---|
| 1. Hubert van Innis | BEL | 144 |
| 2. Léonce Quentin | FRA | 115 |

33 Meters:

|  |  | PTS. |
|---|---|---|
| 1. Hubert van Innis | BEL | 139 |
| 2. Julien Brulé | FRA | 94 |

50 Meters:

|  |  | PTS. |
|---|---|---|
| 1. Julien Brulé | FRA | 134 |
| 2. Hubert van Innis | BEL | 106 |

*Teams*
28 Meters:

|  | PTS. |
|---|---|
| 1. HOL | 3087 |

(Adrianus Theeuwes, Hendrikus van Bussel, Jan Packbiers, Adrianus van Merrienboer, Jan Babtiest, Josef van Gestel, Theodorus Willems, Petrus de Brouwer, Johannes van Gastel)

| 2. BEL | 2924 |
|---|---|

(Hubert van Innis, Alphonse Allaert, Edmond de Knibber, Louis Delcon, Jérome de Mayer, Louis van Beeck, Pierre van Thielt, Louis Fierens)

| 3. FRA | 2328 |
|---|---|

(Léonce Quentin, Julien Brulé, Pascal Fauvel, E. G. Grisot, Eugène Richez, Leroy, Mabellon, Epin)

33 Meters:

| 1. BEL | PTS. 2958 |
|---|---|

(Hubert van Innis, Alphonse Allaert, Edmond de Knibber, Louis Delcon, Jérome de Mayer, Louis van Beeck, Pierre van Thielt, Louis Fierens)

| 2. FRA | 2586 |
|---|---|

(Léonce Quentin, Julien Brulé, Pascal Fauvel, E. G. Grisot, Eugene Richez, Leroy, Mabellon, Epin)

50 Meters:

| 1. BEL | PTS. 2701 |
|---|---|

(Hubert van Innis, Alphonse Allaert, Edmond de Knibber, Louis Delcon, Jérome de Mayer, Louis van Beeck, Pierre van Thielt, Louis Fierens)

| 2. FRA | 2493 |
|---|---|

(Léonce Quentin, Julien Brulé, Pascal Fauvel, E. G. Grisot, Eugene Richez, Leroy, Mabellon, Epin)

# WOMEN

Women's Olympic archery rules differ from men's only in that the distances are 70, 60, 50, and 30 meters.

## INDIVIDUAL

**1896–1968** not held

**1972 Munich** C: 40, N: 21, D: 9.10. WR: 2380 (Emma Gaptchenko)

|  |  | 1st ROUND | 2nd ROUND | TOTAL POINTS |  |
|---|---|---|---|---|---|
| 1. Doreen Wilber | USA | 1198 | 1226 | 2424 | WR |
| 2. Irena Szydlowska | POL | 1224 | 1183 | 2407 | |
| 3. Emma Gaptchenko | SOV | 1201 | 1202 | 2403 | |
| 4. Keto Lossaberidze | SOV | 1195 | 1207 | 2402 | |
| 5. Linda Myers | USA | 1200 | 1185 | 2385 | |
| 6. Maria Maczyńska | POL | 1173 | 1198 | 2371 | |
| 7. Kim Ho-gu | PRK | 1195 | 1174 | 2369 | |
| 8. Alla Peounova | SOV | 1180 | 1184 | 2364 | |

Wilber was a 42-year-old housewife from Jefferson, Iowa.

**1976 Montreal** C: 27, N: 16, D: 7.30. WR: 2465 (Zebiniso Rustamova)

|  |  | 1st ROUND | 2nd ROUND | TOTAL POINTS |  |
|---|---|---|---|---|---|
| 1. Luann Ryon | USA | 1217 | 1282 | 2499 | WR |
| 2. Valentina Kovpan | SOV | 1182 | 1278 | 2460 | |
| 3. Zebiniso Rustamova | SOV | 1202 | 1205 | 2407 | |
| 4. Jang Sun-yong | PRK | 1200 | 1205 | 2405 | |
| 5. Lucille Lemay | CAN | 1181 | 1220 | 2401 | |
| 6. Jadwiga Wilejto | POL | 1200 | 1195 | 2395 | |
| 7. Linda Myers | USA | 1180 | 1213 | 2393 | |
| 8. Maria Urban | GER | 1216 | 1160 | 2376 | |

Ryon, a 23-year-old student from Riverside, California, had never before competed in an international tournament.

**1980 Moscow** C: 29, N: 19, D: 8.2. WR (Single Round): 1321 (Natalya Butuzova)

|  |  | 1st ROUND | 2nd ROUND | TOTAL POINTS |
|---|---|---|---|---|
| 1. Keto Losaberidze | SOV | 1257 | 1234 | 2491 |
| 2. Natalya Butuzova | SOV | 1251 | 1226 | 2477 |
| 3. Päivi Meriluoto | FIN | 1217 | 1232 | 2449 |
| 4. Ždenka Padevetova | CZE | 1206 | 1199 | 2405 |
| 5. O Gwang-sun | PRK | 1195 | 1206 | 2401 |
| 6. Catherina Floris | HOL | 1186 | 1196 | 2382 |
| 7. Maria Szeliga | POL | 1190 | 1175 | 2365 |
| 8. Lotti Tschanz | SWI | 1184 | 1162 | 2346 |

**1984 Los Angeles-Long Beach** C: 47, N: 24, D: 8.11. WR: 1325 (Lyudmila Arzhanikova)

|  |  | 1st ROUND | 2nd ROUND | TOTAL POINTS |  |
|---|---|---|---|---|---|
| 1. Seo Hyang-soon | KOR | 1275 | 1293 | 2568 | OR |
| 2. Li Lingjuan | CHN | 1279 | 1280 | 2559 |  |

| 3. Kim Jin-ho | KOR | 1276 | 1279 | 2555 |
| 4. Hiroko Ishizu | JPN | 1263 | 1261 | 2524 |
| 5. Päivi Meriluoto | FIN | 1259 | 1250 | 2509 |
| 6. Manuela Dachner | GER | 1260 | 1248 | 2508 |
| 6. Katrina King | USA | 1265 | 1243 | 2508 |
| 8. Wu Yanan | CHN | 1240 | 1253 | 2493 |

Two-time world champion Kim Jin-ho was upset by 18-year-old Li Lingjuan and 17-year-old Seo Hyang-soon, the latter coming from behind to win on the final day of competition.

Finishing in 35th place was New Zealand's Neroli Fairhall, the first paraplegic athlete to take part in the Olympics. Paralyzed from the waist down following a motorbike accident, she competed while seated in a wheelchair.

**1988 Seoul** C: 62, N: 30, D: 9.30. WR: 1338 (Kim Soo-nyung)

|  |  | OPEN ROUND | | 8th FINAL | | QUART. FINAL | | SEMI-FINAL | GRAND FINAL | GRAND TOTAL |
|---|---|---|---|---|---|---|---|---|---|---|
| 1. Kim Soo-nyung | KOR | 1331 | (1) | 331 | (2) | 337 | (1) | 340 (1) | 344 (1) | 2683 |
| 2. Wang Hee-kyung | KOR | 1298 | (2) | 320 | (5) | 330 | (2) | 332 (2) | 332 (2) | 2612 |
| 3. Yun Young-sook | KOR | 1296 | (3) | 328 | (3) | 326 | (5) | 326 (7) | 327 (3) | 2593 |
| 4. Lyudmila Arzhanikova | SOV | 1279 | (6) | 332 | (1) | 326 | (6) | 329 (5) | 327 (4) | 2593 |
| 5. Jenny Sjöwall | SWE | 1294 | (4) | 305 | (16) | 327 | (4) | 330 (3) | 325 (5) | 2581 |
| 6. Claudia Kriz | GER | 1250 | (17) | 311 | (11) | 322 | (8) | 326 (8) | 318 (6) | 2527 |
| 7. Joanne Franks | GBR | 1281 | (5) | 301 | (18) | 327 | (3) | 330 (4) | 318 (7) | 2557 |
| 8. Tatyana Muntyan | SOV | 1272 | (7) | 319 | (6) | 316 | (12) | 328 (6) | 314 (8) | 2549 |

The three Korean medalists were 17, 18, and 17 years old, respectively.

# TEAM

The rules for the women's team competition are the same as those for the men, with the exception that the women shoot at distances of 70, 60, 50, and 30 meters.

**1896–1984** not held

**1988 Seoul** T: 15, N: 15, D: 10.1. WR: 3981 (KOR—Lee H.Y., Kim K.W., Kim S.N.)

|  |  |  | OPEN ROUND | | SEMI-FINAL | | GRAND FINAL | |
|---|---|---|---|---|---|---|---|---|
| 1. KOR | (Kim Soo-nyung, Wang Hee-kyung, Yun Young-sook ) | 3925 | (1) | 1000 | (1) | 982 | (1) |
| 2. INA | (Lilies Handayani, Nurfitriyana Saiman, Kusuma Wardhani) | 3720 | (5) | 975 | (4) | 952 | (2) |
| 3. USA | (Debra Ochs, Denise Parker, Melanie Skillman) | 3742 | (4) | 988 | (2) | 952 | (3) |
| 4. SOV | (Lyudmila Arzhanikova, Natalya Butuzova, Tatyana Muntyan) | 3818 | (2) | 978 | (3) | 951 | (4) |
| 5. GBR | (Pauline Edwards, Joanne Franks, Cheryl Sutton) | 3692 | (7) | 962 | (5) | 933 | (5) |
| 6. FRG | (Doris Haas, Claudia Kriz, Christa Öckl) | 3702 | (6) | 953 | (6) | 931 | (6) |
| 7. SWE | (Liselotte Andersson, Carina Jonsson, Jenny Sjöwall) | 3662 | (10) | 949 | (8) | 930 | (7) |
| 8. FRA | (Marie-Josée Bazin, Nathalie Hibon, Catherine Pellen) | 3653 | (11) | 950 | (7) | 898 | (8) |

The unheralded Indonesian team earned their nation's first-ever Olympic medals by defeating the U.S. in a shoot-out, 72-67. Said the Indonesian coach, Donald Pandiangan, "It is a silver, but for us it is more than one hundred gold medals, it is more than even a gold mine."

# Discontinued Events

**1904 St. Louis** C: 6, N: 1, D: 9.19.
*Double Columbia Round (50 Yards—40 Yards—30 Yards)*

|   |   |   | PTS. |
|---|---|---|------|
| 1. | Lida Howell | USA | 867 |
| 2. | Emma Cooke | USA | 630 |
| 3. | Jessie Pollock | USA | 630 |
| 4. | Laura Woodruff | USA | 547 |
| 5. | Mabel Taylor | USA | 243 |
| 6. | Louise Taylor | USA | 229 |

**1904 St. Louis** C: 6, N: 1, D: 9.20.
*Double National Round (60 Yards—50 Yards)*

|   |   |   | PTS. |
|---|---|---|------|
| 1. | Lida Howell | USA | 620 |
| 2. | Emma Cooke | USA | 419 |

|   |   |   |     |
|---|---|---|-----|
| 3. | Jessie Pollock | USA | 419 |
| 4. | Laura Woodruff | USA | 234 |
| 5. | Mabel Taylor | USA | 160 |
| 6. | Louise Taylor | USA | 159 |

**1908 London** C: 25, N: 1, D: 7.20.
*National Round (60 Yards—50 Yards)*

|   |   |   | PTS. |
|---|---|---|------|
| 1. | Sybil "Queenie" Newall | GBR | 688 |
| 2. | Charlotte "Lottie" Dod | GBR | 642 |
| 3. | A. Hill-Lowe | GBR | 618 |
| 4. | Wadworth | GBR | 605 |
| 5. | Honnywill | GBR | 587 |
| 6. | Armitage | GBR | 582 |
| 7. | Foster | GBR | 553 |
| 8. | Wilson | GBR | 534 |

Silver medalist "Lottie" Dod was an exceptional athlete. In 1887, at the age of 15, she won the first of five Wimbledon tennis championships. She was also a champion golfer and field hockey player. In 1894 she became one of the first women to attempt the Cresta Run at St. Moritz. She was also a fine skater who once played a cricket match on ice skates.

# *BADMINTON*

## MEN

### SINGLES

This event will be held for the first time in 1992.

### DOUBLES

This event will be held for the first time in 1992.

## WOMEN

### SINGLES

This event will be held for the first time in 1992.

### DOUBLES

This event will be held for the first time in 1992.

# BASEBALL

Although it has been included as a demonstration sport eight times since 1912, baseball will make its first appearance as an official medal sport in 1992.

# BASKETBALL

## MEN

**1896–1932** not held

**1936 Berlin** T: 21, N: 21, D: 8.14.

| | | W | L | PF | PA |
|---|---|---|---|---|---|
| 1. USA | (Ralph Bishop, Joe Fortenberry, Carl Knowles, Jack Ragland, Carl Shy, William Wheatley, Francis Johnson, Samuel Balter, John Gibbons, Frank Lubin, Arthur Mollner, Donald Piper, Duane Swanson, Willard Schmidt) | 4 | 0 | 152 | 69 |
| 2. CAN | (Gordon Aitchison, Jan Allison, Arthur Chapman, Charles Chapman, Douglas Peden, James Stewart, Malcolm Wiseman, Edward John Dawson, Irving Meretsky) | 5 | 1 | 176 | 104 |
| 3. MEX | (Carlos Borja Morca, Victor Hugo Borja Morca, Raúl Fernández Robert, Francisco Martinez Cordero, Jesus Olmos Moreni, Greer Skousen Spilsbury, Luis Ignacio de la Vega Leija, Rodolfo Choperno Irizarri, José Pamplona Lecuanda, Andrés Gómez Dominguez, Silvio Hernandez del Valle) | 4 | 2 | 160 | 115 |
| 4. POL | (Zdzislaw Filipkiewicz, Florian Grzechowiak, Jakub Kopowski, Edwaryst Lój, Andrzej Pluciński, Zenon Rózycki, Edward Szostak, Zdzislaw Kasprzak, Janusz Patrzykont, Pavel Stok) | 1 | 4 | 119 | 180 |
| 5. PHI | (Charles Bork, Jacinto Cruz Ciria, Franco Marquicias, Primitivo Martinez, Jesús Marzan, Amador Obordo, Ambrosio Padilla, Bibiano Ouano, Fortunato Yamboa) | 4 | 1 | 159 | 145 |
| 6. URU | (Gregorio Agos, Rodolfo Braseili, Leandro Gomez Harley, Alejo Gonzalez Roig, Victor Lato Jaimeu, Prudencio de Pena, Tabaré Quintans, Humberto Bernasconi, Carlos Gabin) | 2 | 3 | 125 | 136 |
| 7. ITA | (Enrico Castelli, Galeazzo Dondi, Livio Franeschini, Emilio Giasetti, Gian Carlo Marinelli, Sergio Paganella, Egidio Premiani, Gino Basso) | 3 | 2 | 160 | 129 |

Final: USA 19—8 CAN

3rd Place: MEX 26—12 POL
5th Place: PHI 33—23 URU

The first official Olympic basketball tournament was held outdoors in a tennis stadium on courts of clay and sand. Half the U.S. squad was made up of members of the winner of the U.S. trials—the team from Universal Studios. During the tournament, the International Basketball Federation passed a rule that banned all players who were taller than 6 feet 3 inches. The United States, which would have lost three of its players, objected, and the rule was withdrawn. The day of the final saw heavy rain, which turned the courts into mud. The players found it quite difficult to dribble on wet sand, which undoubtedly contributed to the low score. The United States led 15–4 at the half. Six-foot 8-inch center Joe Fortenberry of McPherson, Kansas, scored eight points to match the score of the entire Canadian team.

**1948 London** T: 23, N: 23, D: 8.13.

| | | W | L | PF | PA |
|---|---|---|---|---|---|
| 1. USA | (Clifford Barker, Donald Barksdale, Ralph Beard, Lewis Beck, Vincent Boryla, Gordon Carpenter, Alexander Groza, Wallace Jones, Robert Kurland, Raymond Lumpp, Robert Pitts, Jesse Renick, Robert Robinson, Kenneth Rollins) | 8 | 0 | 524 | 256 |
| 2. FRA | (André Barrais, Michel Bonnevie, André Buffière, René Chocat, René Dérency, Maurice Desaymonnet, André Even, Maurice Girardot, Fernand Guillou, Raymond Offner, Jacques Perrier, Yvan Quénin, Lucien Rebuffic, Pierre Thiolon) | 5 | 2 | 331 | 281 |
| 3. BRA | (Zenny de Azevedo, João Francisco Bráz, Marcus Vinicius Dias, Alfonso Azevedo Evora, Ruy de Freitas, Alexandre Gemignani, Alberto Marson, Alfredo Rodrigues da Motta, Nilton Pacheco de Oliveira, Massinet Sorcinelli) | 7 | 1 | 374 | 263 |
| 4. MEX | (Angel Acuna Lizaña, Isaac Alfaro Loza, Alberto Bienvenu Barajas, José de la Cruz Cabrera Gándara, Jorge Cardiel Gaitán, Rodolfo Diaz Mercado, Francisco Galinda Chávez, Jorge Gudiño Goya, Héctor Guerrero Delgado, Emilio López Enriquez, Ignacio Romo Porches, José Rojas Herrera, Fernando | 5 | 2 | 314 | 264 |

Rojas Herrera, José Santos de León)

5. URU (Martin Acosta y Lara, Néstor Anton, Victorio Cieslinskas, Nelson Demarco, Miguel Diab, Abraham Eidlin, Eduardo Folle, Héctor Garcia Otero, Eduardo Gordon, Adesio Lombardo, Roberto Lovera, Gustavo Margariños, Carlos Rosselló, Héctor Ruiz)    5   3   369   301

6. CHI (Eduardo Cordero Fernandez, Exequiel Figueroa Reyes, Juan Gallo Chinchilla, R. Hammer Casadio, E. Kapstein Suckel, M. Ledesma Barraies, Victor Mahana Badrie, G. L. Marmentini, A. Mitrovic Guic, A. Moreno Rodillo, E. Parra Rojas, H. Raffo Abarca, Marcos Sanchez Carmona, G. Yanez Verdugo)    4   4   391   301

7 CZE (J. Belohradsky, C. Benacek, Z. Chlup, J. Drvota, J. Ezr, J. Kalina, J. Kozak, V. Krasa, Z. Krenicky, J. Krepela, I. Mrazek, J. Seigel, J. Toms, L. Trpkos)    5   3   315   294

8. KOR (B. Ahn, W. Bang, Chang Chin-ri, Chyo Joon-deuk, Kang Hyunbong, Kim Shin-chung, Lee Yungchoon, Lee Hoon-sang, Oh Chulsoo)    3   5   364   279

Final: USA 65—21 FRA
3rd Place: BRA 52—47 MEX

The 1948 tournament had some unusual highlights: A British referee was knocked unconscious during a preliminary game between Chile and Iraq. A Chinese player dribbled between the legs of the 7-foot U.S. center, Bob Kurland, and followed through by scoring a basket. In the fiercely contested match for third place, da Motta of Brazil lost his pants and had to retire to the dressing room. Iraq lost by 100 points twice—to Korea and China (which finished eighteenth), and gave up an average of 104 points per game while scoring only 23.5. Ireland's offense was even less effective, averaging only 17 points a game. Meanwhile, the U.S. team survived an early 59–57 scare against Argentina and then breezed through the rest of its games. The halftime score in the final was 28–9. J. Llanusa Gobel of the Cuban team went on to become Minister of Education under Fidel Castro.

**1952 Helsinki** T: 23, N: 23, D:8.2.

|  |  | W | L | PF | PA |
|---|---|---|---|---|---|
| 1. USA | (Charles Hoag, William Hougland, Melvin Dean Kelley, Robert Kenney, Clyde Lovellette, Marcus Freiberger, Victor Wayne Glasgow, Frank McCabe, Daniel Pippin, Howard Williams, Ronald Bontemps, Robert Kurland, William Lienhard, John Keller) | 8 | 0 | 562 | 406 |
| 2. SOV | (Viktor Vlassov, Stepas Butautas, Joann Lõssov, Kazys Petkevičius, Nodar Dshordshikiya, Anatoly Konyev, Otar Korkiya, Ilmar Kullam, Yuri Ozerov, Aleksandr Moiseyev, Heino Kruus, Justinas Lagunavičius, Maigonis Valdmanis, Stasys Stonkus) | 6 | 2 | 468 | 431 |
| 3. URU | (Martin Acosta y Lara, Enrique Baliño, Victorio Cieslinskas, Héctor Costa, Nelson Demarco, Héctor Garcia Otero, Roberto Lovera, Adesio Lombardo, Tabaré Larre Borges, Sergio Matto, Wilfredo Pelaez, Carlos Rosselló) | 5 | 3 | 486 | 471 |
| 4. ARG | (Ruben Francisco Menini, Hugo Oscar del Vecchio, Leopoldo Contarbio, Raúl Perez Varela, Juan Gazso, Roberto Viau, Ricardo Primitiva Gonzalez, Juan Carlos Uder, Omar Monza, Ruben Pagliari, Rafael Liedo, Oscar Alberto Furlong, Alberto Lopez, Ignacio Poletti) | 5 | 3 | 600 | 523 |
| 5. CHI | (Juan Gallo Chinchilla, Victor Mahana Badrie, Exequiel Figueroa Reyes, Eduardo Cordero Fernandez, Rufino Bernedo Zorzano, Alvaro Salvadores Salvi, Eric Maehn Godoy, Herman Ramos Muñoz, Hugo Fernandez Díaz, Orlando Silva Infante, Hernan Raffo Abarca, Pedro Araya Zabala, Juan Ostoic) | 4 | 4 | 447 | 508 |
| 6. BRA | (Zenny de Azevedo, Sebastião Gimenez, Ruy de Freitas, Mayr Facci, Raymundo Carvalho dos Santos, Angelo Bonfietti, João Francisco Bráz, Alfredo Rodrigues da Motta, Almir Nelson de Almeida, Mario Jorge da Fonseca Hermes, Thales Monteiro, José Luiz Santos Azevedo, Helio Marquez Pereira) | 4 | 4 | 469 | 436 |
| 7. BUL | (Kiril Semov, Hristo Donchev, Vasil Manchenko, Peter Shishkov, Georgi Panov, Konstantin Totev, Anton Kuzov, Gencho Rashkov, Ivan Nikolov, Veselin Penkov, Konstantin Georgiev, Vladimir Slavov) | 4 | 4 | 451 | 506 |
| 8. FRA | (Bernard Planque, Robert Monclar, René Chocat, Jean Perniceni, Louis Devoti, Robert Guillin, Robert Crost, Jacques Dessemme, André Buffière, André Vacheresse, André Chavet, Jean-Paul Beugnot, | 4 | 4 | 468 | 460 |

Roger Haudegand, Jean-Pierre Salignon)

|  | W | L | PF | PA |
|---|---|---|---|---|

Final: USA 36—25 SOV
3rd Place: URU 68—59 ARG
5th Place: CHI 58—49 BRA
7th Place: BUL 58—44 FRA

Having been crushed by the United States 86–58, in the semifinal round, the Soviet team decided to freeze the ball in the final match. After ten minutes, the United States led 4–2. At halftime the score was still only 17–15. With five minutes to play, Clyde Lovellette scored a basket to give the United States a lead of 31–25. The next time the Americans got the ball, it was their turn to stall. One Soviet player became so exasperated that he sat down on the floor until his coach ordered him to stand up.

The tournament was enlivened by the participation of Uruguay. In the semifinal round, France had a 66–64 lead over the team from South America, which had been reduced to three players due to excessive fouling. With one minute to play, Uruguay tied the score, whereupon the American referee, Vincent Farrell, whistled a foul against Uruguay. The Uruguayan team rushed off the bench and abused Farrell for five minutes until he was finally able to communicate that the foul had occurred *after* the basket and that the 2 points had not been disallowed. France took the ball out of bounds and worked the ball to Jacques Dessemme, who scored an easy layup to win the game. At this point Uruguayan players and spectators attacked Farrell again. This time he was kicked in the groin and had to be carried from the court. Two Uruguayan players were banned from further competition. Three days later it was the U.S.S.R.'s turn to face the volatile Uruguayans. In the second half, three Soviet players had to receive first aid. The following day, the now exhausted Uruguayans faced their bitter rival, Argentina, in the match for third place. They mustered up enough energy for one more brawl with 25 people involved. So many fouls were called that Uruguay finished the game with only four players and Argentina with only three.

**1956 Melbourne** T: 15, N: 15, D: 12.1.

|  |  |  | W | L | PF | PA |
|---|---|---|---|---|---|---|
| 1. | USA | (Carl Cain, William Hougland, K.C. Jones, William Russell, James Walsh, William Evans, Burdette Haldorson, Ronald Tomsic, Richard Boushka, Gilbert Ford, Robert Jeangerard, Charles Darling) | 8 | 0 | 793 | 365 |
| 2. | SOV | (Valdis Muižnieks, Maigonis Valdmanis, Vladimir Torban, Stasys Stonkus, Kazys Petkevičius, Arkady Bochkaryov, Janis Krumiņš, Mikhail Semyonov, Algirdas Lauritenas, Yuri Ozerov, Viktor Zubkov, Mikhail Studenetsky) | 5 | 3 | 574 | 524 |
| 3. | URU | (Carlos Blixen, Ramiro Cortes, Héctor Costa, Nelson Chelle, Nelson Demarco, Héctor Garcia Otero, Carlos González, Sergio Matto, Oscar Moglia, Raúl Merá, Ariel Olascoaga, Milton Scarón) | 6 | 2 | 568 | 559 |
| 4. | FRA | (Roger Haudegand, Christian Baltzer, Robert Monclar, Roger Veyron, Gérard Sturla, Henri Rey, Roger Antoine, Henri Grange, Yves Gominon, Maurice Buffière, André Schlupp, Jean-Paul Beugnot) | 5 | 3 | 542 | 497 |
| 5. | BUL | (Atanas Atanasov, Vladimir Slavov, Ilia Mirchev, Victor Radev, Georgi Kunev, Vasil Manchenko, Georgi Panov, Konstantin Totev, Tsviatko Slavov, Lyubomir Panov, Nikola Ilov) | 5 | 3 | 568 | 545 |
| 6. | BRA | (Zenny de Azevedo, Noel Marques Lisboa, Wlamir Marques, Angelo Bonfietti, Jamil Gedeão, Wilson Bombarda, Jorge Dortas Olivieri, Mayr Facci, Edson Bispo dos Santos, José Luiz Santos Azevedo, Fausto Sucena Rasga Filho, Amaury Antônio Pasos) | 3 | 4 | 500 | 535 |
| 7. | PHI | (Ramon Manulat, Ramon Campos, Carlos Badion, Loreto Carbonel, Martin Urra, Rafael Barretto, Leonardo Marquicias, Antonio Villamor, Mariano Tolentino, Carlos Loyzaga, Antonio Genato, Eduardo Lim) | 4 | 4 | 534 | 599 |
| 8. | CHI | (Luis Salvadores, Juan Ostoic, Maximiliano Garafulic, Pedro Araya, Rufino Bernedo, Victor Mahana, Orlando Silva, Raul Urra, Hernán Raffo, Orlando Etcheverregaray, J. Arrendondo, Rolando Etchepare) | 2 | 5 | 490 | 518 |

Final: USA 89—55 SOV
3rd Place: URU 71—62 FRA
5th Place: BUL 64—52 BRA
7th Place: PHI 75—68 CHI

Led by Bill Russell and K.C. Jones, who later became great professional stars with the Boston Celtics, the United States won all eight of their games by at least 30 points and scored over 100 points four times. Their average score was 99–46.

**1960 Rome** T: 16, N: 16, D: 9.10.

|  |  |  | W | L | PF | PA |
|---|---|---|---|---|---|---|
| 1. | USA | (Jay Arnette, Walter Bellamy, Robert Boozer, Terry Dischinger, Jerry Lucas, Oscar Robertson, Adrian Smith, Burdette Haldorson, Darrall Imhoff, Allen Kelley, Lester Lane, Jerry West) | 8 | 0 | 815 | 476 |

2. SOV (Yuri Korneyev, Janis Kruminš, Guram Minaschvill, Valdis Muiž-nieks, Cesars Ozers, Aleksandr Petrov, Mikhail Semyonov, Vladimir Ugrekhelidze, Maigonis Valdmanis, Albert Valtin, Gennady Volnov, Viktor Zubkov)  6 2 596 497

3. BRA (Edson Bispo dos Santos, Moyses Blas, Waldemar Blatkauskas, Zenny de Azevedo, Carmo de Souza, Carlos Domingos Massoni, Waldyr Geraldo Boccardo, Wlamir Marques, Amaury Antônio Pasos, Fernando Pereira de Freitas, Antônio Salvador Sucar, Jatyr Eduardo Schall)  6 2 568 573

4. ITA (Augusto Giomo, Gabriele Vianello, Alessandro Riminucci, Gianfranco Lombardi, Gianfranco Pieri, Alessandro Gamba, Mario Alesini, Achille Canna, Antonio Calebotta, Paolo Vittori, Giovanni Gavagnin, Gianfranco Sardagna)  4 4 603 653

5. CZE (Jaroslav Tetiva, Josef Kinský, Zdeněk Bobrovský, Boris Lukašik, František Konvička, Zdeněk Konečný, Dušan Lukašik, Bohuslav Rylich, Jiři Baumruk, Vladimir Pištělák, Jiři Štastný, Bohumil Tomášek)  5 3 632 594

6. YUG (Slobodan Gordič, Ivo Daneu, Sreten Dragojlovič, Josip Djerdja, Nemanja Djurič, Marjan Kandus, Radivoje Korač, Boris Kristančič, Miha Lokar, Miodrag Nikolič, Zvonimir Petricevič, Radovan Radovič)  4 4 582 603

7. POL (Jerzy Piskun, Janusz Wichowski, Andrzej Pstrokoński, Andrzej Nartowski, Jerzy Mlynarczyk, Ryszard Olszewski, Krzysztof Sitkowski, Mieczyslaw Lopatka, Zbigniew Dregier, Bogdan Przywarski, Tadeusz Pacula, Dariusz Świerczewski)  4 4 582 653

8. URU (Sergio Matto, Raul Mera, Nelson Chelle, Waldemar Rial, Washington Poyet, Carlos Blixen, Milton Scaron, Aldofo Lubnicki, Hector Costa, Danilo Coito, Edison Ciavattone, Manuel Gadea)  2 6 548 678

Final Round: USA 81—57 SOV
BRA 78—75 ITA
USA 112—81 ITA
SOV 64—62 BRA
SOV 78—70 ITA
USA 90—63 BRA

The 1960 U.S. squad was the greatest Olympic team ever assembled. Ten members of the team went on to play professionally in the National Basketball Association. The team was so strong that future Boston Celtic star John Havlicek qualified only as an alternate. Led by Jerry Lucas and Oscar Robertson, both of whom averaged 17 points a game, the Americans won every game by at least 24 points despite a much improved international field. The U.S. team averaged 102 points per game while giving up only 59.5. In the final match against Brazil, the United States built up a 41–14 lead after only 14 minutes and coasted for the rest of the game.

**1964 Tokyo** T: 16, N: 16, D: 10.23.

| | | | W | L | PF | PA |
|---|---|---|---|---|---|---|
| 1. | USA | (James Barnes, William Bradley, Lawrence Brown, Joseph Caldwell, Mel Counts, Richard Davies, Walter Hazzard, Lucius Jackson, John McCaffrey, Jeffrey Mullins, Jerry Shipp, George Wilson) | 9 | 0 | 704 | 434 |
| 2. | SOV | (Valdis Muižnieks, Nikolai Bagley, Armenak Alachachyan, Aleksandr Travin, Vyacheslav Khrynin, Janis Kruminš, Levan Mosechvili, Yuri Korneyev, Aleksandr Petrov, Gennady Volnov, Jaak Lipso, Juris Kalninš) | 8 | 1 | 674 | 544 |
| 3. | BRA | (Amaury Antônio Pasos, Wlamir Marques, Ubiratan Pereira Maciel, Carlos Domingos Massoni, Friedrich Wilhelm Braun, Carmo de Souza, Jatyr Eduardo Schall, Edson Bispo dos Santos, Antônio Salvador Sucar, Victor Mirshawka, Sergio de Toledo Machado, José Edvar Simões) | 6 | 3 | 596 | 565 |
| 4. | PUR | (William McCadney, Evelio Droz Ramos, Ruben Adorno Melendez, Teofilo Cruz Downs, Juan Vicens Sastre, Alberto Zamot Bula, Martin Anza Ortiz, Jaime Frontera Colley, Juan Ramon Baez Marino, Angel Garcia Lucas, Angel Cancel Acevedo, Thomas Gutierrez Ferrer) | 5 | 4 | 595 | 592 |
| 5. | ITA | (Augusto Giomo, Giusto Pellanera, Gianfranco Lombardi, Gianfranco Pieri, Gianfranco Bertini, Paolo Vittori, Gianfranco Sardagna, Ottorino Flaborea, Massimo Masini, Sauro Bufalini, Gabriele Vianello, Giovanni Gavagnin) | 6 | 3 | 649 | 602 |
| 6. | POL | (Janusz Wichowski, Andrzej Pstrokonski, Tadeusz Blauth, Andrzej Perka, Stanislaw Olejniczak, Krystian Czernichowski, Zbigniew Dregier, Kazimierz Frelkiewicz, Bogdan Liszko, Mieczyslaw Lopatka, Jerzy Piskun, Krzysztof Sitkowski) | 5 | 4 | 608 | 596 |
| 7. | YUG | (Slobodan Gordic, Radivoje Korač, Trajko Rajkovič, Dragan Kovacic, Josip Djerdja, Dragoslav | 6 | 3 | 670 | 583 |

| | | W | L | PF | PA |
|---|---|---|---|---|---|

Ražnatuvič, Ivo Daneu, Zvonko Petricevic, Vital Eiselt, Vladimir Cvetkovič, Menamja Djuric, Miodrag Nikolic)

| | | | W | L | PF | PA |
|---|---|---|---|---|---|---|
| 8. | URU | (Washington Poyet, Walter Marquez, Julio Cesar Gomez, Luis Eduardo Koster, Edison Ciavattone, Alvaro Eduardo Roca, Sergio Pisano, Luis Agustin Garcia, Manuel Roberto Gadea, Ramiro Eduardo de Leon, Waldemar Jose Rial, Jorge Maya) | 4 | 5 | 596 | 642 |

Final: USA 73—59 SOV
3rd Place: BRA 76—60 PUR
5th Place: ITA 79—59 POL
7th Place: YUG 78—55 URU

Once again the Americans went through the tournament undefeated. They were pressed only by the Yugoslavs, whom they beat 69–61. In the final, the U.S.S.R. led 16–13 after the first ten minutes, but the United States went on an 18–4 spurt and were never headed again. The Peruvian team sported four brothers, Ricardo, Enrique, Raul, and Luis Duarte.

**1968 Mexico City** T: 16, N: 16, D: 10.25.

| | | | W | L | PF | PA |
|---|---|---|---|---|---|---|
| 1. | USA | (John Clawson, Kenneth Spain, Joseph "Jo-Jo" White, Michael Barrett, Spencer Haywood, Charles Scott, William Hosket, Calvin Fowler, Michael Silliman, Glynn Saulters, James King, Donald Dee) | 9 | 0 | 739 | 505 |
| 2. | YUG | (Aljoša Žorga, Radivoje Korač, Zoran Maroevič, Trajko Rajkovič, Vladimir Cvetkovič, Dragoslav Ražnatovič, Ivo Daneu, Krešimir Čošić, Damir Šolman, Nikola Plečas, Dragutin Čermak, Petar Skansi) | 7 | 2 | 705 | 638 |
| 3. | SOV | (Anatoli Krikun, Modestas Paulauskas, Zurab Sakandelidze, Vadim Kapranov, Yuri Selikhov, Anatoly Polivoda, Sergei Belov, Priit Tomson, Sergei Kovalenko, Gennady Volnov, Jaak Lipso, Vladimir Andreyev) | 8 | 1 | 774 | 524 |
| 4. | BRA | (Sergio de Toledo Machado, Wlamir Marques, Ubiratan Pereira Maciel, Celso Luiz Scarpini, Helio Rubens Garcia, Carmo de Souza, José Aparecido dos Santos, Luiz Claudio Menon, Antônio Salvador Sucar, José Edvar Simões, José Geraldo de Castro, Carlos Domingos Massoni) | 6 | 3 | 677 | 563 |
| 5. | MEX | (Rafael Heredia Estrella, Arturo Guerrero, Fernando Tiscareño, Miguel Arellano, Antonio Ayala, Oscar Asiain, Luis Grajeda, Alejandro Guzman, Carlos Quintanar, Ricardo Pontvianne, John Hatch, Mañuel Raga) | 7 | 2 | 641 | 580 |
| 6. | POL | (Grzegorz Korcz, Wlodzimierz Trams, Czeslaw Malec, Henryk Cegielski, Andrzej Kasprzak, Edward Jurkiewicz, Adam Niemiec, Bogdan Lilsszo, Mieczyslaw Lopatka, Kazimierz Frelkiewicz, Boleslaw Kwiatkowski, Andrzej Pasiorowski) | 5 | 4 | 604 | 631 |
| 7. | SPA | (Juan Martinez, Vicente Ramos, Luis Santiago, Jesus Codina, Enrique Margall, Antonio Nava, Emiliano Rodriguez, Clifford Luyk, José Vela Sagi, Francisco Buscato, Lorenzo Alocen, Alfonso Martinez) | 5 | 4 | 717 | 693 |
| 8. | ITA | (Carlo Recalcati, Giusto Pellanera, Gianfranco Lombardi, Enrico Bovone, Massimo Masini, Paolo Vittori, Gabriele Vianello, Guido Gatti, Ottorino Flaborea, Sauro Fufalini, Massimo Cosmelli, Gianluigi Jessi) | 5 | 4 | 686 | 693 |

Final: USA 65—50 YUG
3rd Place: SOV 70—53 BRA
5th Place: MEX 76—65 POL
7th Place: SPA 88—72 ITA

The best of the U.S. college players stayed away from the Olympic trials for various reasons. Notable absentees included Elvin Hayes, who had signed a professional contract, and Lew Alcindor (Kareem Abdul-Jabbar), who gave two reasons: not wanting to take time off from his studies and support for the threatened black boycott of the Olympics. But the U.S. team, although held to a 5-point victory by Puerto Rico, made it to the final by beating Brazil 75–63. In the other semifinal, Yugoslavia's captain, Ivo Daneu, sank two free throws with four seconds to play to upset the U.S.S.R. 63–62. At the end of the first half of the final, the Yugoslavs trailed the United States by only three points, 32–29. But at the beginning of the second half Spencer Haywood and Jo-Jo White went on a rampage, as the U.S. outscored Yugoslavia 22–3 to put the game out of reach. The vocal Mexican crowd, which had been rooting for the underdog Yugoslavs, was so impressed by the display of Haywood and White that they switched allegiance. The only incident of the tournament occurred when some photographers attempted to shoot pictures of the weeping Cuban team, which had just lost to Mexico by one point. The Cubans took out their frustrations by chasing the photographers across the court. There were no injuries.

**1972 Munich** T: 16, N: 16, D: 9.10.

| | | W | L | PF | PA |
|---|---|---|---|---|---|
| 1. SOV | (Anatoly Polivoda, Modestas Paulauskas, Zurab Sakandelidze, Alshan Sharmukhamedov, Aleksandr Boloshev, Ivan Edeshko, Sergei Belov, Mishako Korkia, Ivan Dvorni, Gennady Volnov, Aleksandr Belov, Sergei Kovalenko) | 9 | 0 | 757 | 590 |
| 2. USA | (Kenneth Davis, Douglas Collins, Thomas Henderson, Michael Bantom, Robert Jones, Dwight Jones, James Forbes, James Brewer, Tommy Burleson, Thomas McMillen, Kevin Joyce, Ed Ratleff) | 8 | 1 | 660 | 401 |
| 3. CUB | (Juan Domecq, Ruperto Herrera, Juan Roca, Pedro Chappé, José Miguel Alvarez Pozo, Rafael Canizares, Conrado Perez, Miguel Calderon, Tomas Herrea, Oscar Varona, Alejandro Urgelles, Franklin Standard) | 7 | 2 | 687 | 577 |
| 4. ITA | Ottorino Flaborea, Giuseppe Brumatti, Giorgio Giomo, Mauro Cerioni, Massimo Masini, Renzo Bariviera, Marino Zanatta, Dino Meneghin, Pierluigi Marzorati, Luigi Serafini, Ivan Bisson, Giulio Jellini) | 5 | 4 | 650 | 605 |
| 5. YUG | (Ratko Tvrdić, Ljubodrag Simonović, Vinko Jelovać, Žarko Knezevič, Miroljub Damnjanovič, Dragan Kapicić, Blagoje Georgievski, Krešimir Čošić, Damir Solman, Nikola Plecas, Dragutin Cermak, Milun Marovič) | 7 | 2 | 734 | 617 |
| 6. PUR | (Joe Hatton, Neftali Rivera, James Thordsen, Ruben Rodriguez, Eric William Baum, Hector Blondet, Earl Brown, Mariano Ortiz, Teofilo Cruz Downa, Raymond Dalmau, Ricardo Calzada) | 6 | 3 | 743 | 683 |
| 7. BRA | (Joseph Washington, Radvilas Gorauskas, Maciel Pereira Ubiratan, Sergio Francisco Garcia, Rubens Helio Garcia, Abdalla Marcos Leite, José Aparecido dos Santos, Luiz Claudio Menon, Adilson de Nascimento, José Edivar Simões, José Geraldo de Castro, Carlos Domingos Massoni) | 3 | 5 | 625 | 642 |
| 8. CZE | (Petr Noviky, Zdenek Dousa, Jiři Konopasek, Jiři Pospisil, Zdenek Kos, Jiři Balastik, Jiři Zidek, Jiři Zednicek, Jan Bobrovsky, Kamil Brabenec, Jan Blazek, Jiři Ruzicka) | 4 | 5 | 625 | 642 |

Final: SOV 51—50 USA
3rd Place: CUB 66—65 ITA

5th Place: YUG 86—70 PUR
7th Place: BRA 87—69 CZE

One of the greatest controversies in the history of international sports took place in Munich in the early morning hours of Sunday, September 10. The United States entered the final match with a record of 62 wins and no losses in Olympic basketball competition. The game began at 11:45 p.m., in order to accommodate U.S. television. The U.S.S.R. scored first, led 26–21 at the half, and was ahead by eight points with 6:07 to play. The United States closed the gap, but still trailed by one point with six seconds left. Then the Soviet star Sasha Belov inadvertently threw the ball toward Doug Collins of Illinois State. With three seconds left, Collins was fouled intentionally by Sako Sakandelidze. Collins calmly sank two free throws to give the United States its first lead of the game, 50–49. The Soviet team in-bounded the ball, but two seconds later head referee Renato Righetto of Brazil noted a disturbance at the scorer's table and called an administrative time out. The U.S.S.R. coach, Vladimir Kondrashkin, claimed that he had called a time out after Collins' first shot. Indeed, the time out horn had gone off just as Collins released his second free throw attempt. Both Righetto and André Chopard, who was the timekeeper, thought that one second remained. But at this point Great Britain's R. William Jones, the Secretary-General of the International Amateur Basketball Federation (F.I.B.A.), intervened and ordered the clock set back to three seconds. Technically, Jones had no right to make any decisions, but he ruled F.I.B.A. with an iron hand, and hardly anyone dared to question his authority. Kondrashkin brought in Ivan Yedeshko, who threw a long pass to Sasha Belov. Belov caught the pass perfectly, pushed past two defenders, and scored the winning basket. The United States filed a protest, which was heard by a five-man Jury of Appeal. Jones appointed Terence Hepp of Hungary to be chairman of the committee, and Hepp provided the deciding vote in favor of the U.S.S.R. He was joined by representatives of Poland and Cuba, while representatives of Italy and Puerto Rico voted to disallow Belov's basket. The U.S. team voted unanimously to refuse their silver medals. Coach Hank Iba felt doubly robbed. At two a.m., while he was signing the official protest, his pocket was picked and he lost $370.

**1976 Montreal** T: 12, N: 12, D: 7.27.

| | | W | L | PF | PA |
|---|---|---|---|---|---|
| 1. USA | (Phil Ford, Steve Sheppard, Adrian Dantley, Walter Davis, William "Quinn" Buckner, Ernie Grunfeld, Kenneth Carr, Scott May, Michel Armstrong, Thomas La Garde, Philip Hubbard, Mitchell Kupchak) | 7 | 0 | 584 | 500 |
| 2. YUG | (Blagoje Georgievski, Dragan Kicanović, Vinko Jelovać, Rajko | 5 | 2 | 527 | 522 |

## UNITED STATES' BASKETBALL WINNING STREAK

**1936**

| USA | 52—28 | EST |
|-----|-------|-----|
| USA | 56—23 | PHI |
| USA | 25—10 | MEX |
| USA | 19— 8 | CAN |

**1948**

| USA | 86—21 | SWI |
|-----|-------|-----|
| USA | 53—28 | CZE |
| USA | 59—57 | ARG |
| USA | 66—28 | EGY |
| USA | 61—33 | PER |
| USA | 63—28 | URU |
| USA | 71—40 | MEX |
| USA | 65—21 | FRA |

**1952**

| USA | 66—48 | HUN |
|-----|-------|-----|
| USA | 72—47 | CZE |
| USA | 57—44 | URU |
| USA | 86—58 | SOV |
| USA | 103—55 | CHI |
| USA | 57—53 | BRA |
| USA | 85—76 | ARG |
| USA | 36—25 | SOV |

**1956**

| USA | 98—40 | JPN |
|-----|-------|-----|
| USA | 101—29 | THA |
| USA | 121—53 | PHI |
| USA | 84—44 | BUL |
| USA | 113—51 | BRA |
| USA | 85—55 | SOV |
| USA | 101—38 | URU |
| USA | 89—55 | SOV |

**1960**

| USA | 88—54 | ITA |
|-----|-------|-----|
| USA | 125—66 | JPN |
| USA | 107—63 | HUN |
| USA | 104—42 | YUG |
| USA | 108—50 | URU |
| USA | 81—57 | SOV |
| USA | 112—81 | ITA |
| USA | 90—63 | BRA |

**1964**

| USA | 78—45 | AUS |
|-----|-------|-----|
| USA | 77—51 | FIN |
| USA | 60—45 | PER |
| USA | 83—28 | URU |
| USA | 69—61 | YUG |
| USA | 86—53 | BRA |
| USA | 116—50 | KOR |
| USA | 62—42 | PUR |
| USA | 73—59 | SOV |

**1968**

| USA | 81—46 | SPA |
|-----|-------|-----|
| USA | 93—36 | SEN |
| USA | 96—75 | PHI |
| USA | 73—58 | YUG |
| USA | 95—50 | PAN |
| USA | 100—61 | ITA |
| USA | 61—56 | PUR |
| USA | 75—63 | BRA |
| USA | 65—50 | YUG |

**1972**

| USA | 65—35 | CZE |
|-----|-------|-----|
| USA | 81—55 | AUS |
| USA | 67—48 | CUB |
| USA | 61—54 | BRA |
| USA | 96—31 | EGY |
| USA | 72—56 | SPA |
| USA | 99—33 | JPN |
| USA | 68—38 | ITA |

| | | | W | L | PF | PA |
|---|---|---|---|---|---|---|
| | Žižić, Željko Jerkov, Andro Knego, Zoran Slavnić, Krešimir Čošić, Damir Solman, Žarko Varajić, Dražen Dalipagić, Mirza Delibašić) | | | | | |
| 3. SOV | (Vladimir Arzamaskov, Aleksandr Salnikov, Valery Miloserdov, Alshan Sharmukhamedov, Andrei Makeev, Ivan Edeshko, Sergei Belov, Vladimir Tkachenko, Anatoly Myshkin, Mikhail Korkiya, Aleksandr Belov, Vladimir Zhigily) | | 6 | 1 | 732 | 535 |
| 4. CAN | (Alexander Devlin, Martin Riley, Bill Robinson, John Cassidy, Derek Sankey, Robert Sharpe, Cameron Hall, James Russell, Robert Town, Romel Raffin, Lars Hansen, Phillip Tollestrup) | | 4 | 3 | 595 | 611 |
| 5. ITA | (Giulio Jellini, Carlo Recalcati, Luciano Vendemini, Fabrizio Della Fiori, Renzo Bariviera, Marino Zanatta, Dino Meneghin, Pierluigi Marzorati, Luigi Serafini, Ivan Bisson, Gianni Bertolotti) | | 5 | 2 | 526 | 491 |
| 6. CZE | (Vladimir Ptaček, Petr Vojtech, Jiři Konopašek, Justin Sedlak, Stanislav Kropilak, Jaroslav Kanturek, Zedenek Kos, Jiři Pospišil, Vladimir Padrta, Kamil Brabeneč, Zdenek Douša, Gustav Hraška) | | 3 | 4 | 584 | 580 |
| 7. CUB | (Juan Domecq, Ruperto Herrera, Juan Roca, Pedro Alejandro Ortiz, Rafael Canizares, Daniel Scott, Angel Padron, Tomas Herrera, Oscar Varona, Alejandro Urgelles, Felix Morales) | | 4 | 3 | 616 | 574 |
| 8. AUS | (Andrew Campbell, Ian Watson, Robert Cadee, Anthony Barnett, Edward Palubinskas, Andris Blicavs, Michael Tucker, Perry Crosswhite, Russell Simon, Peter Walsh, John Maddock, Ray Tomlinson) | | 2 | 5 | 625 | 652 |

Final: USA 95—74 YUG
3rd Place: SOV 100—72 CAN
5th Place: ITA 98—75 CZE
7th Place: CUB 92—81 AUS

For four years the United States waited to gain revenge for their loss to the U.S.S.R., but their train was almost derailed by a young man from New York who also had something to prove. Butch Lee of Marquette University had been prevented from trying out for the U.S. team when his college coach, Al McGuire, sent another player to the tryouts instead. Lee returned to his birthplace of Puerto Rico and made the team there. Puerto Rico faced the United States in the second game of the Olympic tournament: Lee shot 15 of 18 from the field and scored 35 points, while his teammate Neftali Rivera added 26. But the gutsy Puerto Ricans fell one point short and lost 95–94. However, the U.S.–U.S.S.R. showdown was not to be. In the semifinals, an inspired Yugoslav team upset the Soviets 89–84. The final was no contest, as the Americans took an 8–0 lead and never looked back. High scorer in the tournament for the United States was Adrian Dantley of Notre Dame, who averaged 19.3 points a game.

**1980 Moscow** T: 12, N: 12, D: 7.30.

| | | W | L | PF | PA |
|---|---|---|---|---|---|
| 1. YUG | (Andro Knego, Dragan Kicanović, Rajko Žižić, Mihovil Nakić-Vojnovic, Zeljko Jerkov, Branko Skroce, Zoran Slavnić, Krešimir Čošić, Ratko Radovanović, Duje Krstulović, Dražen Dalipagić, Mirze Delibašić) | 9 | 0 | 920 | 768 |
| 2. ITA | (Romeo Sacchetti, Roberto Brunamonti, Michael Sylvester, Enrico Gilardi, Fabrizio Della Fiori, Marco Solfrini, Marco Bonamico, Dino Meneghin, Renato Villalta, Renzo Vecchiato, Pier Luigi Marzorati, Pietro Generali) | 5 | 4 | 744 | 757 |
| 3. SOV | (Stanislav Eremin, Valery Miloserdov, Sergei Tarakanov, Aleksandr Salnikov, Andrei Lopatov, Nikolai Deruguin, Sergei Belov, Vladimir Tkachenko, Anatoly Myshkin, Sergejus Jovaiša, Aleksandr Belostenny, Vladimir Zhigily) | 7 | 2 | 943 | 797 |
| 4. SPA | (Wayne Brabender, José Luis Llorente, Candido-Antonio Sibilio, José Maria Margall, Manuel Flores, Fernando Roman, Luis-Miguel Santillana, Juan-Antonio Corbalan, Ignacio Solozabal, Juan-Domingo Delacruz, Juan Lopeziturriaga, Juan Antonio San Epifanio) | 4 | 5 | 871 | 843 |
| 5. BRA | (André Ernesto Stoffel, Luiz Gustavo de Lage, José Carlos Saiani, Milton Setrini, Wagner Machado da Silva, Marcos Abdalla Leite, Gilson Trindade de Jesus, Marcel Ramon de Souza, Adilson de Nascimento, Marcelo Vido, Oscar Daniel Schmidt, Ricardo Cardoso Guimaraes) | 4 | 4 | 745 | 712 |
| 6. CUB | (Jorge Moro Rojas, Ruperto Herrera Tabio, Alejandro Ortiz Herrara, Noangel Luaces Rodriguez, Generoso Marquez Saes, Raul Dubois Cumbath, Pedro Abreu Pascual, Miguel Calderon Gomez, Tomas Herrera Martinez, Daniel Scott Brice, Alejandro Urgelles Guibot, Felix Morales Alphonso) | 2 | 6 | 660 | 704 |
| 7. POL | (Dariusz Zelig, Leszek Doliński, Wojciech Rosinski, Eugeniusz Kijewski, Jerzy Bińkowski, Andrzej Michalski, Ireneusz Mulak, Justyn Weglorz, Mieczyslaw Mylarski, Zdzislaw Myrda, Ryszard Prostak, Kryzstof Fikiel) | 5 | 3 | 709 | 656 |
| 8. AUS | (Melvyn Dalgleish, Gordon McLeod, Philip Smyth, Larry Seng- | 6 | 2 | 641 | 596 |

stock, Peter Ali, Michael Tucker, Stephan Berheny, Les Riddle, Ian Davies, Peter Walsh, Danny Morseu, Perry Crosswhite)

Final: YUG 86—77 ITA
3rd Place: SOV 117—94 SPA

The Yugoslavs were led by Dalipagić and Kicanović, who averaged 24.4 and 23.6 points per game respectively. The team from India brought back memories of the 1948 Iraqi squad, losing their eight matches by an average score of 65.5 to 116.

**1984 Los Angeles-Inglewood** T: 12, N: 12, D: 8.10.

| | | W | L | PF | PA |
|---|---|---|---|---|---|
| 1. USA | (Steve Alford, Leon Wood, Patrick Ewing, Vern Fleming, Alvin Robertson, Michael Jordan, Joseph Kleine, Jon Koncak, Wayman Tisdale, Chris Mullin, Samuel Perkins, Jeffrey Turner) | 8 | 0 | 763 | 506 |
| 2. SPA | (José Manuel Beiran, José Luis Llorente, Fernando Arcega, José Maria Margall, Andres Jimenez, Fernando Romay, Fernando Martin, Juan Antonio Corbalan, Ignacio Solozabal, Juan Domingo de la Cruz, Juan Maria Lopez, Juan Antonio San Epifanio) | 6 | 2 | 697 | 688 |
| 3. YUG | (Dražen Petrović, Aleksandar Petrović, Nebojsa Zorkić, Rajko Žižić, Ivan Sunara, Emir Mutapcić, Saabit Hadžić, Andro Knego, Ratko Radovanović, Mihovil Nakić-Vojnovic, Dražen Dalipagić, Branko Vukicević) | 7 | 1 | 716 | 604 |
| 4. CAN | (Howard Kelsey, Tony Simms, Eli Pasquale, Karl Tilleman, Gerald Kazanowski, Jay Triano, John Hatch, Gord Herbert, Bill Wennington, Romel Raffin, Greg Wiltier, Dan Meagher) | 4 | 4 | 681 | 639 |
| 5. ITA | (Carlo Caglieris, Roberto Premier, Marco Bonamico, Enrico Gilardi, Walter Magnifico, Roberto Brunamonti, Renato Villata, Dino Meneghin, Antonello Riva, Renzo Vecchiato, Pierluigi Marzorati, Romeo Sacchetti) | 6 | 2 | 718 | 614 |
| 6. URU | (Horacio Lopez, Luis Larrosa, Luis Pierri Barros, Hebert Nuñez Gonzalez, Wilfredo Ruiz Bruno, Horacio Perdomo Shaban, Carlos Peinado Stagnero, Julio Pereyra Mele, Alvaro Tito Moreno, Juan Mignone Crisera, Victor Frattini Bononi) | 3 | 5 | 688 | 776 |
| 7. AUS | (Andrew Campbell, Damian Keogh, Philip Smyth, Larry Sengstock, Mark Dalton, Wayne Carroll, Melvyn Dalgleish, Andrew Gaze, | 4 | 4 | 654 | 683 |

|  |  | W | L | PF | PA |
|---|---|---|---|---|---|
| | Ian Davies, Daniel Morseu, Bradley Dalton, Raymond Borner) | | | | |
| 8. GER | (Christoph Korner, Vladimir Kadlec, Uwe Brauer, Uwe Sauer, Ulrich Peters, Klaus Zander, Michael Pappert, Armin Sowa, Detlef Schrempf, Uwe Blab, Ingo Mendel, Christian Welp) | 2 | 6 | 600 | 635 |

Final: USA 96—65 SPA
3rd Place: YUG 88—82 CAN
5th Place: ITA 111—102 URU
7th Place: AUS 83—78 GER

The powerful U.S. team breezed through the tournament, winning by an average of 32 points per game. Their only weak game was a 78–67 quarterfinal victory over West Germany. The well-balanced American squad included Michael Jordan, who averaged 17.1 points per game, Wayman Tisdale, who led the team in rebounding, Patrick Ewing, the tournament blocked-shot leader with 18, Leon Wood, the tournament assist leader with 63, and Alvin Robertson, who shot 65% from the field and registered 17 steals.

**1988 Seoul** T: 12, N: 12, D: 9.30.

|  |  | W | L | PF | PA |
|---|---|---|---|---|---|
| 1. SOV | (Aleksandr Volkov, Tiit Sokk, Sergei Tarakanov, Šarunas Marčulonis, Igors Miglinieks, Vadim Tikhonenko, Rimas Kurtinaitis, Arvydas Sabonis, Victor Pankracskin, Valdemaras Chomičius, Aleksandr Belostennyi, Valery Goborov) | 7 | 1 | 728 | 637 |
| 2. YUG | (Dražen Petrović, Zdravko Radulović, Zoran Čutura, Toni Kukoč, Žarko Paspalj, Zelimir Obradović, Jurij Zdovc, Stojan Vranković, Vlade Divac, Franjo Arapović, Dino Radja, Danko Cvjetićanin) | 6 | 2 | 717 | 603 |
| 3. USA | (Mitchell Richmond, Charles D. Smith, Vernell Coles, Hersey Hawkins, Jeffrey Grayer, Charles E. Smith, Willie Anderson, Stacey Augmon, Daniel Majerle, Danny Manning, Herman Reid, David Robinson) | 7 | 1 | 733 | 490 |
| 4. AUS | (Darryl Pearce, Philip Smyth, Larry Sengstock, Damian Keogh, Wayne Carroll, Lucien Longley, Andrew Gaze, Mark Bradtke, Bradley Dalton, Andrew Vlahov, Raymond Borner) | 4 | 4 | 625 | 651 |
| 5. BRA | (Paulo Almeida, Jorge Guerra, Gerson Victalino, João Vianna, Rolando Ferreira, Richardo Guimaraes, Maury Souza, Marcel Souza, Luiz Azevedo, Paulo Silva, Oscar Schmidt, Israel Andrade) | 5 | 3 | 905 | 808 |
| 6. CAN | (Norman Clarke, David Turcotte, Ilario Enrico Pasquale, Karl Tilleman, Alan Kristmanson, James Triano, Dwight Walton, John Hatch, Barry Mungar, Romel Raffin, Wayne Yearwood, Gerald François Kazanowski) | 3 | 5 | 738 | 747 |
| 7. PUR | (José Ortiz Rijos, Federico López, Raymond Gause, Vicente Ithier, Jerome Mincy, Roberto Rioos, Angel Cruz, Ramon Rivas, Mario Morales, Edgar Leon, Francisco Leon, Ramon Ramos) | 4 | 4 | 618 | 677 |
| 8. SPA | (Jordi Villacampa, José Luis Llorente, José Biryukov, José Maria Margall, Andres Jiménez, Enrique Andreu, José António Montero, Fernando Arcega, Ignacio Solozabal, Ferran Martinez, António Martin, Juan António San Epifanio) | 4 | 4 | 741 | 701 |

Final: SOV 76–63 YUG
3rd Place: USA 78–49 AUS
5th Place: BRA 106–90 CAN
7th Place: PUR 93–92 SPA

The long-awaited Olympic rematch between the U.S. and the U.S.S.R. finally took place in the semifinal round at Seoul, 16 years after the controversial 1972 Munich final. This time the Soviets took a 10-point halftime lead, beat back every American challenge, and won 82–76. With this bit of history out of the way, the Soviets faced their arch rivals, the Yugoslavs, in the final, in what would be the sixth match between the two teams in six months.

Although the Yugoslavs had won four of the five previous encounters, including a 92–79 victory in the tournament's opening round, they had to have been haunted by memories of two earlier losses. In the semifinals of the 1986 world championships, Yugoslavia led by 9 points with 47 seconds left in the game. The Soviets then hit three straight three-point shots and went on to win by 1 point in overtime. In the 1988 European Olympic qualifying tournament, the Soviets overcame a 15-point second-half deficit to defeat the Yugoslavs 86–83.

In the Olympic final, Yugoslavia took a 24–12 lead. However the Soviets, led by Lithuanians Marčulonis, Sabonis, and Kurtinaitis, went on a 19–2 run and were never headed again.

In a preliminary-round loss to Spain, Brazil's Oscar Schmidt scored an Olympic record 55 points. Schmidt also *averaged* 42¼ points per game for the entire tournament.

# WOMEN

**1896–1972** not held

**1976 Montreal** T: 6, N: 6, D: 7.27.

| | | W | L | PF | PA |
|---|---|---|---|---|---|
| 1. SOV | (Angelė Rupšienė, Tatyana Zakharova, Raisa Kurvyakova, Olga Barisheva, Tatyana Ovechkina, Nadezhda Shubaeva, Uljana Semjonova, Nadezhda Zakharova, Nelly Feriabnikova, Olga Sukharnova, Tamara Davinene-Kaljagina, Natalya Klimova) | 5 | 0 | 504 | 346 |
| 2. USA | (Cindy Brogdon, Susan Rojcewicz, Ann Meyers, Lusia Harris, Nancy Dunkle, Charlotte Lewis, Nancy Lieberman, Gail Marquis, Patricia Roberts, Mary Anne O'Connor, Patricia Head, Julienne Simpson) | 3 | 2 | 415 | 417 |
| 3. BUL | (Nadka Golcheva, Penka Motodieva, Petkana Makaveeva, Snezhana Mihailova, Krassima Gyurova, Krassimira Bogdanova, Todorka Yordanova, Diana Dilova, Margarita Shturkelova, Maria Stoyanova, Girgina Skerlatova, Penka Stoyanova) | 3 | 2 | 365 | 377 |
| 4. CZE | (Ludmila Kralíková, Dana Ptáčková, Pavla Davidová, Ludmila Chmeliková, Martina Balaštiková, Ivana Korinková, Marta Pechová, Hana Doušová, Božena Miklošovičová) | 2 | 3 | 351 | 359 |
| 5. JPN | (Kazuko Kadoya, Kimi Wakitashiro, Mieko Fukui, Miyako Otsuka, Miho Matsuoka, Kazuyo Hayashida, Teruko Miyamoto, Keiko Namai, Reiko Aonuma, Sachiyo Yamamoto, Misako Satake) | 2 | 3 | 405 | 400 |
| 6. CAN | (Joyce Douthwright, Joanne Sargent, Anne Hurley, Christine Critelli, Beverly Bland, Coleen Dufresne, Sheila Strike, Sylvia Sweeney, Carol Turney, Donna Hobin, Angela Johnson, Beverly Barnes) | 0 | 5 | 336 | 477 |

The Soviet women's basketball team had not lost a game for five years and was undefeated in international tournament competition since 1958. Not surprisingly, they won the Olympic gold medal with ease. High scorer for the Soviets was 6-foot 10½-inch, 284-pound Uljana Semjonova of Riga, who averaged 19.4 points and 12.4 rebounds a game, despite the fact that she spent more than half the time on the bench. The United States was awarded second place by virtue of its 95–79 victory over Bulgaria.

Ten years after the Montreal Olympics, silver medalist Nancy Lieberman became the first woman to play in a men's professional league when she took the court for the Springfield, Mass., Fame of the United States Basketball League.

**1980 Moscow** T: 6, N: 6, D: 7.30.

| | | W | L | PF | PA |
|---|---|---|---|---|---|
| 1. SOV | (Angelė Rupšienė, Lyubov Sharmay, Vida Beselienė, Olga Korosteleva, Tatiana Ovechkina, Nadezhda Olkhova, Uljana Semjonova, Lyudmila Rogozina, Nelly Feriabnikova, Olga Sukharnova, Tatyana Nadyrova, Tatyana Ivinskaya) | 6 | 0 | 657 | 389 |
| 2. BUL | (Nadka Golcheva, Penka Metodieva, Petkana Makaveeva, Snezhana Mihailova, Vania Dermandzhieva, Krassimira Bogdanova, Angelina Mihailova, Diana Brainova, Evladia Zakatanova, Kostadinka Radkova, Silvia Germanova, Penka Stoyanova) | 4 | 2 | 513 | 509 |
| 3. YUG | (Vera Djurasković, Mersada Becirspahić, Jelica Komnenović, Mira Bjedov, Vukica Mitić, Sanja Ozegović, Sofija Pekić, Marija Tonković, Zorica Djurković, Vesna Despotović, Biljana Majstorović, Jasmina Perazić) | 4 | 2 | 424 | 429 |
| 4. HUN | (Éva Gulyás, Ágnes Németh, Ilona Kovács, Györgyi Vertetics, Zsuzsa Boksay, Ilona Lörincz, Katalin Szuchy, Magda Gulyás, Ildikó Gulyás, Judit Medgyesi, Lenke Kiss, Erzsébet Szentesi) | 2 | 4 | 409 | 475 |
| 5. CUB | (Leonor Borrell Hernandez, Nancy Aties Sanchez, Barbara Becquer Rivero, Maria Moret Hernandez, Inocenta Corbea Aguirre, Caridad Despaigne Savig, Matilde Charro Mendoza, Maria de Los Santos Iglesias, Sonia de La Paz Galan, Virginia Perez Viart, Margarita Skeet Quiñones, Vicenta Salom Smith) | 1 | 4 | 346 | 403 |
| 6. ITA | (Chiara Guzzonato, Nunziata Serradimigni, Roberta Faccin, Lidia Gorlin, Emanuela Silimbani, Wanda Sandon, Bianca Rossi, Antonietta Baistrocchi, Marinella Draghetti, Rosanna Vergnano, Mariangela Piancastelli, Orietta Grossi) | 0 | 5 | 308 | 452 |

Final: SOV 104—73 BUL
3rd Place: YUG 68—65 HUN

The U.S.S.R. had an even easier time than they had had in 1976, winning all their games by 31 points or more.

Their average score was 109.5 to 65. Semjonova, now 27 years old, was high scorer in the tournament, with 21.8 points a game. She also averaged 12.5 rebounds. In fact, Semjonova and her 6-foot 3-inch teammate Olga Sukharnova pulled down more rebounds than the entire 12-woman Italian team.

**1984 Los Angeles-Inglewood** T: 6, N: 6, D: 8.7.

| | | | W | L | PF | PA |
|---|---|---|---|---|---|---|
| 1. | USA | (Teresa Edwards, Lea Henry, Lynette Woodard, Anne Donovan, Cathy Boswell, Cheryl Miller, Janice Lawrence, Cindy Noble, Kim Mulkey, Denise Curry, Pamela McGee, Carol Menken-Schaudt) | 6 | 0 | 516 | 320 |
| 2. | KOR | (Choi Aei-young, Kim Eun-sook, Lee Hyung-sook, Choi Kyung-hee, Lee Mi-ja, Moon Kyung-ja, Kim Hwa-soon, Jeong Myung-hee, Kim Young-hee, Sung Jung-a, Park Chan-sook) | 4 | 2 | 347 | 387 |
| 3. | CHN | (Chen Yuefang, Li Xiaoqin, Ba Yan, Song Xiaobo, Qui Chen, Wang Jun, Xiu Lijuan, Zheng Haixia, Cong Xuedi, Zhang Hui, Liu Qing, Zhang Yueqin) | 3 | 3 | 381 | 405 |
| 4. | CAN | (Lynn Polson, Tracie McAra, Anna Pendergast, Debbie Huband, Carol Jane Sealey, Alison Lang, Bev Smith, Sylvia Sweeney, Candi Clarkson-Lohr, Toni Kordic, Andrea Blackwell, Misty Thomas) | 2 | 4 | 370 | 398 |
| 5. | AUS | (Robyn Maher, Bronwyn Marshall, Jennifer Cheesman, Patricia Cockrem, Donna Quinn, Patricia Mickan, Julie Nykiel, Kathryn Foster, Marina Moffa, Karen Dalton, Wendy Laidlaw, Susanna Geh) | 1 | 4 | 267 | 317 |
| 5. | YUG | (Sanja Ozegović, Slavica Suka, Jelica Komnenović, Zagorka Poceković, Stojna Vangelovska, Slavica Pecikoza, Sladjana Golić, Polona Dornik, Biljana Majstorović, Jasmina Perazić, Gvetana Dekleva, Marija Uzelać) | 1 | 4 | 293 | 347 |

Final: USA 85—55 KOR
3rd Place: CHN 63—57 CAN

In 1982 the Soviet women's 24-year winning streak was finally broken by a U.S. team that beat them 85–83 in Budapest. The following year the Soviets came back to score a two-point victory of their own in the final of the world championships. The eagerly anticipated Olympic showdown between the two squads was prevented by the Soviet boycott.

The U.S. team cruised through the Olympic tournament, winning all of their games by 28 points or more. Cheryl Miller, averaging 16.5 points and 7 rebounds per game, led the team in scoring, rebounding, steals

and assists. Another U.S. star, Lynette Woodard, later became the first female member of the Harlem Globetrotters.

As for the big U.S.–U.S.S.R. showdown, it finally took place two years later in Moscow, when the American women crushed the Soviets 83–60 in the finals of the Goodwill Games. Five weeks later, again in Moscow, the two teams met in the title match of the world championships, and again the U.S. won easily, 108–88.

**1988 Seoul** T: 8, N: 8, D: 9.29.

| | | | W | L | PF | PA |
|---|---|---|---|---|---|---|
| 1. | USA | (Teresa Edwards, Mary Ethridge, Cynthia Brown, Anne Donovan, Teresa Weatherspoon, Bridgette Gordon, Vitora Bullett, Andrea Lloyd, Katrina McClain, Jennifer Gillom, Cynthia Cooper, Suzanne McConnell) | 5 | 0 | 461 | 392 |
| 2. | YUG | (Stojna Vangelovska, Mara Lakić, Žana Lelas, Eleonora Vild, Kornelija Kvesić, Danira Nakić, Sladjana Golić, Polona Dornik, Razija Mujanović, Vesna Bajkuša, Andjelija Arbutina, Bojana Milošević) | 3 | 2 | 326 | 344 |
| 3. | SOV | (Olga Yevkova, Irina Gerlits, Olesya Barel, Irina Sumnikova, Olga Buryakina, Olga Yakovleva, Irina Minkh, Aleksandra Leonova, Yelena Khudashova, Vitalija Tuomaite, Galina Savitskaya) | 3 | 2 | 364 | 343 |
| 4. | AUS | (Robyn Maher, Jennifer Cheesman, Michele Timms, Donna Brown, Patricia Mickan, Julie Nykiel, Debra Slimmon, Marina Moffa, Karen Dalton, Shelley Gorman, Maree White) | 2 | 3 | 287 | 321 |
| 5. | BUL | (Nina Khadzhiyankova, Larissa Spasova, Mariana Naydenova, Tzonka Vaysilova, Vania Dermendzhieva, Sonia Dragomirova, Radmila Vasileva, Kostadinka Radkova, Yevladiya Stefanova, Madlen Staneva, Polina Tzekova, Mariana Chobanova) | 3 | 2 | 400 | 393 |
| 6. | CHN | (Han Qingling, Ling Guang, Li Xiaoqin, Zhao Wei, Peng Ping, Zheng Haixia, Cong Xuedi, Xue Cuilan, Liu Qing, Xu Chunmei) | 2 | 3 | 371 | 411 |
| 7. | KOR | (Lee Keum-jin, Kim Mal-lyun, Choi Kyung-hee, Lee Hyung-sook, Park Chan-mi, Woo Eun-kyung, Chung Mi-kyung, Kim Hwa-soon, Kim Hye-youn, Park Chan-sook, Sung Jung-a, Cho Mun-joo) | 2 | 3 | 416 | 375 |
| 8. | CZE | (Svatava Kysilková, Alena Kašová, Eva Kaluzáková, Ivana Nováková, Zuzana Hájková, Anna Janošti- | 0 | 5 | 339 | 382 |

nová, Zora Brziaková, Hana Za-
revúcka, Erika Dobrovičová, Eva
Křížová, Irma Valová, Eva Ber-
ková)
Final: USA 77–70 YUG
3rd Place: SOV 68–53 AUS
5th Place: BUL 102–74 CHN
7th Place: KOR 77–59 CZE

The victorious U.S. team was led by playmaker Teresa Edwards, who averaged 16.6 points a game, and her former University of Georgia teammate, Katrina McClain, who led the Americans in scoring (17.6 points a game) and rebounding (10.4 per game).

# BOXING

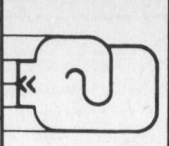

| | |
|---|---|
| Light Flyweight | Welterweight |
| Flyweight | Light Middleweight |
| Bantamweight | Middleweight |
| Featherweight | Light Heavyweight |
| Lightweight | Heavyweight |
| Light Welterweight | Super Heavyweight |

Amateur boxing matches consist of three 3-minute rounds. Defeated quarterfinalists are listed as tied for fifth place. Beginning in 1952, third-place matches were no longer held, and defeated semifinalists were both awarded bronze medals. Competitors must be no younger than 17 and no older than 37. Boxing is the only Olympic sport with a maximum age limit.

## LIGHT FLYWEIGHT
### (48 kg–106 lbs)

**1896–1964** not held

**1968 Mexico City** C: 24, N: 24, D: 10.26.

| | | | FINAL MATCH |
|---|---|---|---|
| 1. | Francisco Rodriguez | VEN | Dec 3–2 |
| 2. | Jee Yong-ju | KOR | |
| 3. | Harlan Marbley | USA | |
| 3. | Hubert Skrzypczak | POL | |
| 5. | Joseph Donovan (AUS), Hatha Karunaratne (SRL), Alberto Morales (MEX), Gabriel Ogun (NGR) | | |

After Rodriguez's victory was announced, few in the crowd could fail to be moved by the sight of the 23-year-old Venezuelan joyfully weeping into the national flag that his seconds had draped over his shoulders. Rodriguez is the only Venezuelan gold-medalist in Olympic history.

**1972 Munich** C: 31, N: 31, D: 9.10.

| | | | FINAL MATCH |
|---|---|---|---|
| 1. | György Gedó | HUN | Dec 5–0 |
| 2. | U-Gil Kim | PRK | |
| 3. | Ralph Evans | GBR | |
| 4. | Enrique Rodriguez | SPA | |
| 5. | Rafael Carbonell (CUB), Chanyalew Haile (ETH), Vladimir Ivanov (SOV), James Odwori (UGA) | | |

**1976 Montreal** C: 27, N: 27, D: 7.31.

| | | | FINAL MATCH |
|---|---|---|---|
| 1. | Jorge Hernandez | CUB | Dec 4–1 |
| 2. | Li Byong-uk | PRK | |
| 3. | Orlando Maldonado | PUR | |
| 3. | Payao Pooltarat | THA | |
| 5. | György Gedó (HUN), Armando Guevara (VEN), Park Chan-lee (KOR), Hector Patri (ARG) | | |

Hernandez was the reigning world amateur and Pan-American champion. Eighteen-year-old bronze medalist Payao Pooltarat from Prachub Khirikhan was the first Thai athlete to win an Olympic medal. He accomplished this by outpointing defending champion Gedó in the quarterfinals.

**1980 Moscow** C: 22, N: 22, D: 8.2.

| | | | FINAL MATCH |
|---|---|---|---|
| 1. | Shamil Sabyrov | SOV | Dec 3–2 |
| 2. | Hipólito Ramos | CUB | |
| 3. | Ismail Hjuseinov | BUL | |
| 3. | Li Byong-uk | PRK | |
| 5. | György Gedó (HUN), Dietmar Geilich (GDR), Dumitru Schiopu (ROM), Ahmed Siad (ALG) | | |

**1984 Los Angeles** C: 24, N: 24, D: 8.11.

| | | | FINAL MATCH |
|---|---|---|---|
| 1. | Paul Gonzales | USA | Default |
| 2. | Salvatore Todisco | ITA | |
| 3. | José Marcelino Bolivar | VEN | |
| 3. | Keith Mwila | ZAM | |
| 5. | Mamoru Kuroiwa (JPN), John Lyon (GBR), Carlos Motta-Taracena (GUA), Rafael Ramos (PUR) | | |

It was less than four miles from Paul Gonzales' home in the Aliso Village housing project to the gold medal platform at the 1984 Olympics, but so rocky was the road he traveled to get there that they might as well have been a continent apart.

Growing up in what he called "a ghetto's ghetto," Gonzales saw his father walk out when he was 7, leaving his mother to raise 8 children on her own. By the time he was nine years old, Paul Gonzales had joined Primera Flats, one of 13 "major" gangs operating in his area. When he was 12 years old, he and his buddies were out cruising one night, when their '64 Chevy Impala stalled in an area controlled by a rival gang. Shots were fired through the car window and Gonzales was hit in the side of the head. Following a well-known local procedure, he washed his head in a lake at a nearby park and then had his cousin remove the remaining pieces of shot and glass with a pair of tweezers.

When he was 15, Gonzales was arrested on a murder charge. Fortunately he had a perfect alibi—he was boxing at the time—and his coach was a policeman. That policeman, Al Stankie, had convinced Gonzales to try his hands at boxing after seeing the 10-year-old in a street fight. At first Gonzales climbed into the gym through a back window, since it was located in the basement of the police station and he didn't want his fellow gang members to think he was a snitch.

As he began to take boxing more seriously, his friends would mock him because he stopped drinking, went home each night at 9 o'clock, and was up at 5 in the morning, running. But as he achieved more and more success, his friends became protective, making sure that he didn't stay out late or break training.

When he was 17, Gonzales missed 11 months of competition because of surgery to remove a bone spur from the back of his right hand. His first bout after the layoff was an upset victory over defending Olympic champion Shamil Sabyrov.

At the Los Angeles Olympics, Gonzales blocked out the pressure and expectations of the wildly enthusiastic local crowd by imagining, as he entered the ring for each bout, that he was fighting in his opponent's home town. His performances were impressive enough to earn him the Val Barker award for the best boxer at the Olympics.

He won his final match in a walkover, when his opponent, Salvatore Todisco, showed up with his hand in a cast, having broken his thumb in his semifinal bout. Ironically, Gonzales himself, had sustained a hairline stress fracture above his right wrist during his first round fight, requiring post-Olympic surgery and a cast of his own.

When he mounted the gold-medal platform, Paul Gonzales carried with him a United States flag in one hand and a Mexican flag in the other. He also carried with him the hopes and dreams of many disadvantaged youths, to whom he sent a message: "I won this gold medal, not just for myself or my mom or my coach, but for the kids like me who are always told, 'You're nothing.' The only way you're going to make it come true is by dreaming it, and when you dream something, you've got to turn it into reality. Because if you don't, you just die with your dreams."

**1988 Seoul** C: 34, N: 34, D: 10.1.

|   |   |   | FINAL MATCH |
|---|---|---|---|
| 1. | Ivailo Hristov [Ismail Hjuseinov] | BUL | Dec 5–0 |
| 2. | Michael Carbajal | USA | |
| 3. | Róbert Isaszegi | HUN | |
| 4. | Leopoldo Serantes | PHI | |
| 5. | Aleksandr Makhmutov (SOV), Mahjoub M'Jirih (MOR), Robert Olson (CAN), Chatchai Sasakul (THA) | | |

Ivailo Hristov, a 28-year-old sailor, used a quick left jab and clever counterpunching to earn his gold medal. However, he was aided by a secret weapon: his frequent changes of name. Few ringside observers in Seoul were aware that Hristov was the same fighter who won an Olympic bronze medal in 1980 using the name Ismail Hjuseinov, a world championship in 1982 as Ismail Mustafov, and a silver medal at the 1985 European championship as Ivajlo Marinov. The name changes were not meant to cause confusion or to put his opponents off their guard—Hristov, a member of Bulgaria's Turkish minority, was forced to change his name because of the Bulgarian government's attempt to crush all remnants of Turkish ethnic identity.

# FLYWEIGHT
## (51 kg–112½ lbs)

**1896–1900** not held

**1904 St. Louis** C: 2, N: 1, D: 9.22.
*(47.63 kg–105 lbs)*

|   |   |   | FINAL MATCH |
|---|---|---|---|
| 1. | George Finnegan | USA | RSC 1 |
| 2. | Miles Burke | USA | |

For some unknown reason Burke was allowed to compete even though he was almost three pounds over the weight limit.

**1906–1912** not held

**1920 Antwerp** C: 12, N: 7, D: 8.26.
*(50.80 kg–112 lbs)*

|   |   |   | FINAL MATCH |
|---|---|---|---|
| 1. | Frank Di Gennara | USA | Dec |
| 2. | Anders Petersen | DEN | |
| 3. | William Cuthbertson | GBR | |
| 4. | J. Albert | FRA | |
| 5. | Rampignon (FRA), Zegwaard (HOL), Peter Zivic (USA) | | |

Seven and a half years later, Di Gennara, fighting under the name Frankie Genaro, won the World Flyweight title by defeating Frenchy Belanger in Toronto.

**1924 Paris** C: 19, N: 13, D: 7.20.
**(50.80 kg–112 lbs)**

|   |   |   | FINAL MATCH |
|---|---|---|---|
| 1. | Fidel LaBarba | USA | Dec |
| 2. | James McKenzie | GBR | |
| 3. | Raymond Fee | USA | |
| 4. | Rinaldo Castellenghi | ITA | |
| 5. | Oscar Bergström (SWE), R. Biete-Berdes (SPA), John Mac-Gregor (CAN), S. Rennie (CAN) | | |

LaBarba, an 18-year-old Los Angeles high school student, went on to a successful professional career. In 1925 he defeated Frankie Genaro for the American Flyweight title, and in 1927 he won the vacant World Flyweight title. He later worked as a screenwriter in Hollywood.

**1928 Amsterdam** C: 19, N: 19, D: 8.11.
**(50.80 kg–112 lbs)**

|   |   |   | FINAL MATCH |
|---|---|---|---|
| 1. | Antal Kocsis | HUN | Dec |
| 2. | Armand Appell | FRA | |
| 3. | Carlo Cavagnoli | ITA | |
| 4. | B. "Buddy" Lebanon | SAF | |
| 5. | Hubert Ausböck (GER), B. Bril (HOL), Alfred Gaona (MEX), Cuthbert Taylor (GBR) | | |

In the first contest of the tournament, 16-year-old Hyman Miller of California appeared to have easily defeated Marcel Santos of Belgium. When the decision was announced in Santos' favor, Miller's confident smile turned to convulsive sobbing. The U.S. boxing team was so outraged that they requested permission to withdraw all their boxers from the Olympics. However the president of the U.S. Olympic Committee, Major-General Douglas MacArthur, refused permission, stating, "Americans never quit." The eventual winner, Antal Kocsis, was Hungary's first Olympic gold medalist in boxing. The following year he turned professional and emigrated to the United States.

**1932 Los Angeles** C: 12, N: 12, D: 8.13.
**(50.80 kg–112 lbs)**

|   |   |   | FINAL MATCH |
|---|---|---|---|
| 1. | István Énekes | HUN | Dec |
| 2. | Francisco Cabañas | MEX | |
| 3. | Louis Salica | USA | |
| 4. | Thomas Pardoe | GBR | |
| 5. | Isaac Duke (SAF), Kiyonobu Murakami (JPN), Edelweis Rodriguez (ITA), Werner Spannagel (GER) | | |

**1936 Berlin** C: 25, N: 25, D: 8.15.
**(50.80 kg–112 lbs)**

|   |   |   | FINAL MATCH |
|---|---|---|---|
| 1. | Willi Kaiser | GER | Dec |
| 2. | Gavino Matta | ITA | |

| 3. | Louis Daniel Laurie | USA | |
| 4. | Alfredo Carlomagno | ARG | |
| 5. | Raoul Degryse (BEL), William Passmore (SAF), Edmund Sobkowiak (POL), Fidel Tricanico (URU) | | |

**1948 London** C: 26, N: 26, D: 8.13.

|   |   |   | FINAL MATCH |
|---|---|---|---|
| 1. | Pascual Perez | ARG | Dec |
| 2. | Spartaco Bandinelli | ITA | |
| 3. | Soo-Ann Han | KOR | |
| 4. | František Majdloch | CZE | |
| 5. | Alex Bollaert (BEL), H.A.H. Corman (HOL), Luis Martinez Zapata (SPA), Frank Sodano (USA) | | |

Pascual Perez, a 22-year-old clerk in the Chamber of Deputies in Buenos Aires, faced his most difficult challenge *before* the fighting began. Perez was unexpectedly disqualified for being overweight. However, it was later discovered that officials had confused him with his bantamweight teammate Arnoldo *Pares*.

**1952 Helsinki** C: 28, N: 28, D: 8.2.

|   |   |   | FINAL MATCH |
|---|---|---|---|
| 1. | Nathan Brooks | USA | Dec 3–0 |
| 2. | Edgar Basel | GER | |
| 3. | Anatoly Bulakov | SOV | |
| 3. | William Toweel | SAF | |
| 5. | Thorbjorn Clausen (NOR), David Dower (GBR), Mircea Dobrescu (ROM), Soo-Ann Han (KOR) | | |

**1956 Melbourne** C: 19, N: 19, D: 12.1.

|   |   |   | FINAL MATCH |
|---|---|---|---|
| 1. | Terence Spinks | GBR | Dec |
| 2. | Mircea Dobrescu | ROM | |
| 3. | John Caldwell | IRL | |
| 3. | René Libeer | FRA | |
| 5. | Warner Batchelor (AUS), Ray Perez (USA), Vladimir Stolnikov (SOV), Kenji Yonekura (JPN) | | |

**1960 Rome** C: 33, N: 33, D: 9.5.

|   |   |   | FINAL MATCH |
|---|---|---|---|
| 1. | Gyula Török | HUN | Dec 3–2 |
| 2. | Sergey Sivko | SOV | |
| 3. | Abdelmoneim Elguindi | UAR | |
| 3. | Kiyoshi Tanabe | JPN | |
| 5. | Humberto Barrera (USA), Miguel Botta (ARG), Mircea Dobrescu (ROM), Manfred Homberg (GER) | | |

**1964 Tokyo** C: 28, N: 28, D: 10.23.

|   |   |   | FINAL MATCH |
|---|---|---|---|
| 1. | Fernando Atzori | ITA | Dec 4–1 |
| 2. | Artur Olech | POL | |
| 3. | Robert Carmody | USA | |
| 3. | Stanislav Sorokin | SOV | |

5. Otto Babiasch (GER), Choh Dong-kih (KOR), Constantin Ciuca (ROM), John McCafferty (IRL)

After one minute and six seconds of the first round of his quarterfinal bout against Stanislaw Sorokin, Korean boxer Choh Dong-kih was disqualified for holding his head too low. Unable to accept this verdict, Choh sat down in the middle of the ring and refused to leave. His sitdown strike continued for 51 minutes, until officials persuaded him to leave. Ironically, Sorokin was forced to withdraw before his next fight because of a cut that wasn't healing. The winner, Sardinian house-painter Fernando Atzori, fought the final with a black eye.

**1968 Mexico City** C: 26, N: 26, D: 10.26.

| | | FINAL MATCH |
|---|---|---|
| 1. Ricardo Delgado | MEX | Dec 5–0 |
| 2. Artur Olech | POL | |
| 3. Servilio Oliveira | BRA | |
| 3. Leo Rwabwogo | UGA | |

5. Tibor Badari (HUN), Joseph Destimo (GHA), Tetsuaki Nakamura (JPN), Nicolai Novikov (SOV)

Heriberto Cintron of Puerto Rico was standing in the ring waiting for his first-round bout with Polish policeman Artur Olech when he was suddenly disqualified for being younger than the minimum age of 17 years. He was, in fact, 16 years and one month old.

**1972 Munich** C: 37, N: 37, D: 9.10.

| | | FINAL MATCH |
|---|---|---|
| 1. Georgi Kostadinov | BUL | Dec 5–0 |
| 2. Leo Rwabwogo | UGA | |
| 3. Leszek Blazyński | POL | |
| 3. Douglas Rodriguez | CUB | |

5. Neil McLaughlin (IRL), Calixto Perez (COL), You Chong-man (KOR), Boris Zoriktuev (SOV)

Most Olympic boxers who went on to become world champions were also Olympic champions, or at least medalists. But there is one boxing star who made little impression in his Olympic debut. As an underage 15-year-old representative of Puerto Rico, Wilfredo Gomez lost a 4–1 decision in the first round to Mohamed Selin of Egypt, who was in turn knocked out in his next fight. Less than five years later, on May 21, 1977, Gomez won the World Super Bantamweight championship and on March 9, 1979, he won the Junior Featherweight title.

**1976 Montreal** C: 26, N: 26, D: 7.31.

| | | FINAL MATCH |
|---|---|---|
| 1. Leo Randolph | USA | Dec 3–2 |
| 2. Ramon Duvalon | CUB | |
| 3. Leszek Blazyński | POL | |
| 3. David Torosyan | SOV | |

5. Ian Clyde (CAN), Jong Jo-ung (PRK), David Larmour (IRL), Alfrede Perez (VEN)

Leo Randolph, an 18-year-old high school student from Tacoma, Washington, called his surprise victory "the best thing that happened to me since I became a Christian in 1969."

**1980 Moscow** C: 20, N: 20, D: 8.2.

| | | FINAL MATCH | |
|---|---|---|---|
| 1. Peter Lessov | BUL | RSC 2 | 2:08 |
| 2. Viktor Miroshnichenko | SOV | | |
| 3. Hugh Russell | IRL | | |
| 3. János Váradi | HUN | | |

5. Roman Gilberto (MEX), Daniel Radu (ROM), Henryk Średnicki (POL), Yo Ryon-sik (PRK)

**1984 Los Angeles** C: 31, N: 31, D: 8.11.

| | | FINAL MATCH |
|---|---|---|
| 1. Steven McCrory | USA | Dec 4–1 |
| 2. Redzep Redzepovski | YUG | |
| 3. Ibrahim Bilali | KEN | |
| 3. Eyup Can | TUR | |

5. Peter Ayesu (MLW), Jeffrey Fenech (AUS), Heo Yong-mo (KOR), Laureano Ramirez (DOM)

Detroit's Steve McCrory, the younger brother of World Welterweight champion Milton McCrory, won a close decision over veteran Redzep Redzepovski, who complained, "As long as an American is standing on his feet for three rounds it is hard to get a decision over him."

**1988 Seoul** C: 44, N: 44, D: 10.2.

| | | FINAL MATCH |
|---|---|---|
| 1. Kim Kwang-sun | KOR | Dec 4–1 |
| 2. Andreas Tews | GDR | |
| 3. Mario González | MEX | |
| 4. Timofei Skriabin | SOV | |

5. Benaissa Abed (ALG), Melvin Deleon (DOM), Alfred Amon Kotey (GHA), Serafim Todorov (BUL)

In 1984, Kim Kwang-sun was favored to win the light flyweight division in Los Angeles. However, he was upset in his first-round bout by eventual gold-medal winner Paul Gonzales. Deeply depressed, Kim vowed that he would return to the Olympics and win a gold medal himself. For four years his mother went to a Buddhist temple every day and prayed for her son. In 1988, Kim, by then a flyweight, blasted his way through four opponents and into the final. There he faced European champion Andreas Tews, who had beaten him 3-2 at the 1987 World Cup. This time Kim dominated the last two rounds, bringing great joy to the highly partisan crowd.

# BANTAMWEIGHT
(54 kg–119½ lbs)

**1896–1900** not held

**1904 St. Louis** C: 2, N: 1, D: 9.22.
*(52.16 kg–115 lbs)*

| | | FINAL MATCH |
|---|---|---|
| 1. Oliver Kirk | USA | RSC 3 |
| 2. George Finnegan | USA | |

**1906** not held

**1908 London** C: 6, N: 2, D: 10.27.
*(52.62 kg–116 lbs)*

| | | FINAL MATCH |
|---|---|---|
| 1. A. Henry Thomas | GBR | Dec |
| 2. John Condon | GBR | |
| 3. W. Webb | GBR | |
| 4. P. Mazior (FRA), F. McGurk (GBR), H. Perry (GBR) | | |

**1912** not held

**1920 Antwerp** C: 8, N: 8, D: 8.26.
*(53.52 kg–118 lbs)*

| | | FINAL MATCH |
|---|---|---|
| 1. Clarence Walker | SAF | Dec |
| 2. Chris Graham | CAN | |
| 3. James McKenzie | GBR | |
| 4. Henri Hebrants | BEL | |
| 5. Edward Earl Hartman (USA), Maurice Herschman (USA), Ricard (FRA), Voss (NOR) | | |

**1924 Paris** C: 21, N: 15, D: 7.20.
*(53.52 kg–118 lbs)*

| | | FINAL MATCH |
|---|---|---|
| 1. William Smith | SAF | Dec |
| 2. Salvatore Tripoli | USA | |
| 3. Jean Ces | FRA | |
| 4. Oscar Andrén | SWE | |
| 5. Alfred Barber (GBR), A. Sanchez Dietz (SPA), J. Lemouton (FRA), Benjamin Pertuzzo (ARG) | | |

Joe Lazarus of Cornell University had the unusual misfortune of knocking out his opponent, Oscar Andrén of Sweden, and yet being declared the loser. As Andrén was being revived, the referee announced that Lazarus was disqualified for hitting during a clinch a few seconds before the knockout punch. Swedish officials were so embarrassed by the ruling that they offered to have the bout refought, but Olympic officials wouldn't allow it.

**1928 Amsterdam** C: 18, N: 18, D: 8.11.
*(53.52 kg–118 lbs)*

| | | FINAL MATCH |
|---|---|---|
| 1. Vittorio Tamagnini | ITA | Dec |
| 2. John Daley | USA | |
| 3. Harry Isaacs | SAF | |
| 4. Edward Traynor | IRL | |

5. John Garland (GBR), Vincent Glionna (CAN), Carmelo Robledo (ARG), János Széles (HUN)

Controversy developed when Harry Isaacs was announced the winner of his semifinal bout with John Daley. In what the U.S. Official Report would refer to as "a demonstration never equalled in Olympic history," American supporters stormed the judges' table demanding that the decision be reversed. After several minutes, it was announced that one of the judges had transposed his figures for the two fighters. Daley was declared the victor. He moved on to the final while Isaacs went home certain that he had been robbed. It was, in the words of the London *Daily Express,* "an example of vacillation unprecedented in the history of a meeting of such worldwide scope."

In the final, Daley, perhaps rattled by his earlier experience, fought below his usual standard and Tamagnini was given a narrow victory. Again the Americans howled their disapproval. Complained one British reporter, "For more than two hours, there was little else save din and clatter, screeching and raving, and several skirmishes with the police. . . ." This time it was to no avail: the decision stood.

**1932 Los Angeles** C: 10, N: 10, D: 8.13.

| | | FINAL MATCH |
|---|---|---|
| 1. Horace Gwynne | CAN | Dec |
| 2. Hans Ziglarski | GER | |
| 3. José Villanueva | PHI | |
| 4. Joseph Lang | USA | |
| 5. Vito Melis (ITA), Akira Nakao (JPN), Paul Nicolas (FRA), Carlos Alberto Pereyra (ARG) | | |

Although he made his living as a jockey, Toronto's Lefty Gwynne started boxing when he was 4 years old. He and his 6-year-old brother put on exhibitions for British army troops in Wales. In Los Angeles Gwynne made no attempt to study the other fighters and didn't even bother to learn who his next opponent would be until he arrived at the arena. When Gwynne, now 19, returned to Toronto after winning the Olympic gold medal, the city honored him with a reception and a gold watch. Gwynne, well aware of the realities of the Depression, immediately asked the mayor for a job. Although he did fight professionally until 1939, there was little money for bantamweights and he was forced to supplement his income by working in an auto plant.

**1936 Berlin** C: 24, N: 24, D: 8.15.
*(53.52 kg–118 lbs)*

| | | FINAL MATCH |
|---|---|---|
| 1. Ulderico Sergo | ITA | Dec |
| 2. Jack Wilson | USA | |
| 3. Fidel Ortiz | MEX | |
| 4. Stig Cederberg | SWE | |
| 5. Joseph Cornelis (BEL), Oscar Larrazabal (PHI), Alexander Hannan (SAF), Shunpei Haskioka (JPN) | | |

**1948 London** C: 30, N: 30, D: 8.13.

|   | | FINAL<br>MATCH |
|---|---|---|
| 1. Tibor Csik | HUN | Dec |
| 2. Giovanni Battista Zuddas | ITA | |
| 3. Juan Venegas | PUR | |
| 4. Alvaro Vicente Domenech | SPA | |
| 5. James Carruthers (AUS), Celestine Gonzalez Henriquez (CHI), Willie Lenihan (IRL), Albert Perera (SRL) | | |

Argentina's Arnoldo Pares, although innocent of any wrongdoing, was the center of much confusion and controversy. At the weigh-in he was found to be overweight. In a panic, his supporters cut off his hair, rubbed him down with a towel, scrubbed the soles of his feet, and blew the dust off the scales. He even wept for a few minutes which further reduced his weight. It was no use: he still couldn't make the limit. The Argentinians filed a protest, and weights and measures experts were sent for. Sure enough, it turned out that the scales were inaccurate, and Pares was allowed to compete. In his first match the nearly bald Pares won a disputed decision over Vic Toweel of South Africa. Toweel didn't let this setback hurt his career. He turned professional and, less than two years later, won the World Bantamweight title, which he held for two and a half years before losing to Jimmy Carruthers of Australia, who happened to have been Arnoldo Pares' second opponent at the 1948 Olympics. Carruthers won that fight but sustained an eye injury that forced him to withdraw from his quarterfinal bout with Tibor Csik. The unusually lucky Csik was thus able to move on to the semifinals even though he had fought only one regular fight. (His first-round opponent had been disqualified.)

**1952 Helsinki** C: 23, N: 23, D: 8.2.

|   | | FINAL<br>MATCH |
|---|---|---|
| 1. Pentti Hämäläinen | FIN | Dec 2–1 |
| 2. John McNally | IRL | |
| 3. Gennady Garbuzov | SOV | |
| 3. Kang Joon-ho | KOR | |
| 5. Vincenzo Dall'osso (ITA), František Majdloch (CZE), David Moore (USA), Helmuth Von Gravenitz (SAF) | | |

The victory of Hämäläinen, a 23-year-old typewriter mechanic from Kotka, was greeted with great enthusiasm by the local Finnish crowd, although the Irish felt they had gotten a raw deal. Nevertheless, Belfast's John McNally was the first Irishman to win an Olympic boxing medal.

**1956 Melbourne** C: 18, N: 18, D: 12.1.

|   | | FINAL<br>MATCH |
|---|---|---|
| 1. Wolfgang Behrendt | GDR | Dec |
| 2. Song Soon-chun | KOR | |
| 3. Claudio Barrientos | CHI | |
| 3. Frederick Gilroy | IRL | |
| 5. Eder Jofre (BRA), Owen Reilly (GBR), Mario Sitri (ITA), Carmelo Adolfo Tomaselli (ARG) | | |

Twenty-year-old Berlin machine-fitter Wolfgang Behrendt was the first Olympic champion from the German Democratic Republic (East Germany).

**1960 Rome** C: 33, N: 33, D: 9.5.

|   | | FINAL<br>MATCH |
|---|---|---|
| 1. Oleg Grigoryev | SOV | Dec |
| 2. Primo Zamparini | ITA | |
| 3. Brunon Bendig | POL | |
| 3. Oliver Taylor | AUS | |
| 5. Jerry Armstrong (USA), Fernandez Alfred Carbajo (SPA), Horst Rascher (GER), Myint Thein (BUR) | | |

In the third round of competition, Oleg Grigoryev won a much-disputed split decision over 17-year-old Frankie Taylor of Great Britain. Although a British protest was rejected, all three judges who voted for Grigoryev were fired, as were no less than half of the 30 referees and judges involved in the Olympic tournament.

**1964 Tokyo** C: 32, N: 32, D: 10.23.

|   | | FINAL<br>MATCH | |
|---|---|---|---|
| 1. Takao Sakurai | JPN | RSC 2 | 1:18 |
| 2. Chung Shin-cho | KOR | | |
| 3. Juan Fabila Mendoza | MEX | | |
| 3. Washington Rodriguez | URU | | |
| 5. Fermin Espinosa (CUB), Oleg Grigoryev (SOV), Nicolae Puiu (ROM), Karimu Young (NGR) | | | |

The final contest was stopped after Sakurai had knocked down Chung four times in less than four and a half minutes. After a brief career as a professional, Sakurai opened a coffee shop in Tokyo called "The Medalist."

**1968 Mexico City** C: 39, N: 39, D: 10.26.

|   | | FINAL<br>MATCH | |
|---|---|---|---|
| 1. Valery Sokolov | SOV | RSC 2 | 2:15 |
| 2. Eridari Mukwanga | UGA | | |
| 3. Chang Kyou-chull | KOR | | |
| 3. Eiji Morioka | JPN | | |
| 5. Roberto Cervantes (MEX), Michael Dowling (IRL), Samuel Mbugua (KEN), Horst Rascher (GER) | | | |

**1972 Munich** C: 38, N: 38, D: 9.10.

|   | | FINAL<br>MATCH |
|---|---|---|
| 1. Orlando Martinez | CUB | Dec 5–0 |
| 2. Alfonso Zamora | MEX | |
| 3. Ricardo Carreras | USA | |
| 3. George Turpin | GBR | |
| 5. Ferry Egberty Moniaga (INA), John Mwaura Nderu (KEN), Juan Francisco Rodriguez (SPA), Vassily Solomin (SOV) | | |

Martinez was the first Cuban to win an Olympic gold medal since Ramón Fonst, the fencer, in 1904.

**1976 Montreal** C: 24, N: 24, D: 7.31.

|   |   |   | FINAL MATCH |
|---|---|---|---|
| 1. | Gu Yong-ju | PRK | Dec 5–0 |
| 2. | Charles Mooney | USA |   |
| 3. | Patrick Cowdell | GBR |   |
| 3. | Victor Rybakov | SOV |   |

5. Stefan Förster (GDR), Reynaldo Fortaleza (PHI), Hwang Chul-soon (KOR), Veerachat Saturngrum (THA)

**1980 Moscow** C: 33, N: 33, D: 8.2.

|   |   |   | FINAL MATCH |
|---|---|---|---|
| 1. | Juan Hernandez | CUB | Dec 5–0 |
| 2. | Bernardo José Pinango | VEN |   |
| 3. | Michael Anthony | GUY |   |
| 3. | Dumitru Cipere | ROM |   |

5. Geral Issaick (TAN), Samson Khachatrian (SOV), John Sirakibbe (UGA), Daniel Zaragoza (MEX)

Seventeen-year-old Hernandez was the second youngest boxer at the Moscow Olympics. He stopped two African boxers before the fights had gone the distance, and he defeated his other three opponents with clear-cut decisions.

**1984 Los Angeles** C: 35, N: 35, D: 8.11.

|   |   |   | FINAL MATCH |
|---|---|---|---|
| 1. | Maurizio Stecca | ITA | Dec 4–1 |
| 2. | Hector Lopez | MEX |   |
| 3. | Pedro Nolasco | DOM |   |
| 3. | Dale Walters | CAN |   |

5. Pedro Ruben Decima (ARG), Ndaba Dube (ZIM), Moon Sung-kil (KOR), Robinson Pitalua Tamara (COL)

**1988 Seoul** C: 48, N: 48, D: 10.1.

|   |   |   | FINAL MATCH |
|---|---|---|---|
| 1. | Kennedy McKinney | USA | Dec 5–0 |
| 2. | Alexander Hristov | BUL |   |
| 3. | Phajol Moolsan | THA |   |
| 3. | Jorge Julio Rocha | COL |   |

5. Nyamaa Altankhuyag (MON), Aleksandr Artemyev (SOV), Katsuyuki Matsushima (JPN), Stephen Mwema (KEN)

Since 1924, Olympic boxing tournaments have been plagued by riots and demonstrations of varying magnitude. In 1988, however, a new twist was added to the ringside ugliness when a referee was attacked, not by spectators, but by Korean boxing officials and security guards.

The incident was rooted in the 1984 Los Angeles Olympics, when the Korean team became upset by what they perceived as biased judging against their boxers. They were particularly incensed by the dubious victory of light welterweight Jerry Page of the U.S. over Kim Dong-kil. Four years later the wound was reopened when Korean light flyweight favorite Oh Kwang-soo was narrowly upset by Michael Carbajal of the U.S.

The day after the Carbajal-Oh fight, Korean bantamweight Byun Jong-il faced one of the division favorites, Alexander Hristov of Bulgaria. The fight was not a pretty one. There was much pushing, shoving, grabbing, and general brawling. Referee Keith Walker of New Zealand tried to control the bout, cautioning both boxers, but he focused his reprimands on Byun. After warning Byun three times to stop using his head as a battering ram, Walker ordered the judges to deduct a point from the Korean's score. Another head butt in the final round led to the deduction of a second point. As it turned out, those two points decided the outcome of the fight. Without the penalties Byun would have won the decision; instead, he lost 4–1.

As soon as the verdict was announced, Korean boxing trainer Lee Heung-soo charged into the ring and struck Keith Walker on the back. Other Koreans, apparently under the mistaken assumption that Walker had also refereed the Carbajal-Oh fight, followed suit. Within seconds the ring was filled with angry Koreans pummeling Walker. Walker's fellow referees came to his aid and held off his attackers until security personnel could escort him out of the arena. Unfortunately, some of the security guards also took part in the riot, one of them aiming a kick at Walker's head as he fled. Another guard, Yoon S. L., who took off his uniform jacket before going after Walker, was quoted as saying, "I acted instinctively for the love of my fatherland."

Walker went straight from the arena to his hotel, checked out and took the next flight to New Zealand. Ironically, earlier in the tournament, Walker had been criticized by Irish officials for *not* penalizing Korean welterweight Song Kyung-sup when he engaged in head butting.

Another victim of the Koreans' fury was Emil Jetchev, the Bulgarian president of the Referees' Committee of the International Amateur Boxing Association. When a Korean coach attempted to smash Jetchev on the head with a plastic box, a U.S. judge, Stan Hamilton, reached out and blunted the blow. Hamilton had to be treated for a badly cut hand.

After the ring was cleared of unauthorized personnel and miscellaneous debris, Byun sat down in the middle of the ring and staged a silent protest. After 35 minutes he was given a chair. He finally left after 67 minutes, breaking the Olympic sit-in record of 51 minutes set in 1964 by Byun's countryman, flyweight Choh Dong-kih. Before leaving the arena, Byun returned to the ring and bowed to the remaining spectators.

Eventually, five Korean boxing officials were suspended, the president of the Korean Olympic Committee resigned, and the Korean government apologized to the government of New Zealand. Three days after the incident, Lee Heung-soo, the supposedly suspended trainer who had led the charge on Walker, was back in the arena shouting orders to his boxers from a ringside seat.

Hristov, who had slipped out of the stadium without harm, squeaked into the final by winning agonizingly close 3-2 decisions over Aleksandr Artemyev and Jorge Julio Rocha. The latter verdict led to bitter protests from the Colombian corner.

In the final, Hristov ran out of luck. Kennedy Mc-Kinney of Killeen, Texas, floored him with a left hook only 11 seconds into the fight. Although Hristov rose and completed the bout without going down again, Mc-Kinney was the clear winner.

One final note about a boxer who never made it to the starting gate: Eduard Paululum was scheduled to be the first-ever Olympic competitor from the small Pacific island nation of Vanuatu. Unfortunately, Paululum ate a large breakfast *before* the weigh-in and was disqualified for being 1 pound overweight.

## FEATHERWEIGHT
### (57 kg–126 lbs)

**1896–1900** not held

**1904 St. Louis** C: 3, N: 1, D: 9.22.
*(56.70 kg–125 lbs)*

|   |   | FINAL MATCH |
|---|---|---|
| 1. Oliver Kirk | USA | Dec |
| 2. Frank Haller | USA | |
| 3. Fred Gilmore | USA | |

Kirk is the only person to win two boxing titles at a single Olympics. The importance of his achievement is certainly muted by the fact that he fought only one bout in each division (Bantamweight and Featherweight).

**1906** not held

**1908 London** C: 8, N: 2, D: 10.27.
*(57.15 kg–126 lbs)*

|   |   | FINAL MATCH |
|---|---|---|
| 1. Richard Gunn | GBR | Dec |
| 2. Charles Morris | GBR | |
| 3. Hugh Roddin | GBR | |
| 4. T. Ringer | GBR | |

At 37, Gunn was the oldest fighter ever to win an Olympic championship. He had been British amateur champion from 1894 to 1896. Unfortunately, his superiority over other British featherweights was so pronounced that his entry in a tournament caused others to drop out. Consequently, Gunn, the true sportsman, retired from competition. He came out of retirement for the London Olympics and defeated one Frenchman and two Englishmen to win the gold medal. Then he retired again, having lost only one fight in 15 years.

**1912** not held

**1920 Antwerp** C: 15, N: 9, D: 8.26.
*(57.15 kg–126 lbs)*

|   |   | FINAL MATCH |
|---|---|---|
| 1. Paul Fritsch | FRA | Dec |
| 2. Jean Gachet | FRA | |
| 3. Edoardo Garzena | ITA | |
| 4. Jack Zivic | USA | |
| 5. Philippe Bovy (BEL), J. Cater (GBR), Nicoloj Clausen (DEN), Paul Erdahl (NOR) | | |

**1924 Paris** C: 24, N: 17, D: 7.20.
*(57.15 kg–126 lbs)*

|   |   | FINAL MATCH |
|---|---|---|
| 1. John Fields | USA | Dec |
| 2. Joseph Salas | USA | |
| 3. Pedro Quartucci | ARG | |
| 4. Jean Devergnies | BEL | |
| 5. C. Abarca-Gonzalez (CHI), M. Depont (FRA), H. Dingley (GBR), Bruno Petrarca (ITA) | | |

Jackie Fields and Joe Salas were best friends back home in Los Angeles. At 16, Fields, whose real name was Jacob Finkelstein, was the youngest boxer at the Paris Olympics. Salas later recalled, "We had to dress in the same room. When they knocked on the door to call us to the fight, we looked up at each other and started to cry and hugged. Ten minutes later we were beating the hell out of each other." After his victory over Salas in the final, Fields was so upset at having defeated his buddy that he went back to the dressing room and cried again. In 1929 Fields won the World Welterweight title. Fields and Salas died eight days apart in June 1987.

**1928 Amsterdam** C: 18, N: 18, D: 8.11.
*(57.15 kg–126 lbs)*

|   |   | FINAL MATCH |
|---|---|---|
| 1. Lambertus van Klaveren | HOL | Dec |
| 2. Victor Peralta | ARG | |
| 3. Harold Devine | USA | |
| 4. Lucien Biquet | BEL | |
| 5. George Boireau (FRA), Jan Górny (POL), Frederick Perry (GBR), Olavi Vakeva (FIN) | | |

There seemed little question in anyone's mind that Peralta had outclassed van Klaveren. Anyone, that is, except the judges who awarded the decision to the Dutch fighter. "It was as plain as a pike-staff which was the master," wrote the reporter for the London *Daily Telegraph*. A battle ensued between Argentinian spectators and Dutch police, and the commotion was still bubbling when the decision of the next match, the Lightweight championship, set off outrage among the Americans in the crowd.

**1932 Los Angeles** C: 10, N: 10, D: 8.13.
*(57.15 kg–126 lbs)*

|  |  |  | FINAL MATCH |
|---|---|---|---|
| 1. | Carmelo Robledo | ARG | Dec |
| 2. | Josef Schleinkofer | GER |  |
| 3. | Carl Carlsson | SWE |  |
| 4. | Gaspare Alessandri | ITA |  |
| 5. | John Hines (USA), John Keller (CAN), Ernest Smith (IRL) | | |

**1936 Berlin** C: 25, N: 25, D: 8.15.
*(57.15 kg–126 lbs)*

|  |  |  | FINAL MATCH |
|---|---|---|---|
| 1. | Oscar Casanovas | ARG | Dec |
| 2. | Charles Catterall | SAF |  |
| 3. | Josef Miner | GER |  |
| 4. | Dezsö Frigyes | HUN |  |
| 5. | Theodore Ernst Kara (USA), William Marquart (CAN), Aleksander Polus (POL), John Treadaway (GBR) | | |

**1948 London** C: 30, N: 30, D: 8.13.
*(58 kg–128 lbs)*

|  |  |  | FINAL MATCH |
|---|---|---|---|
| 1. | Ernesto Formenti | ITA | Dec |
| 2. | Dennis Shephard | SAF |  |
| 3. | Aleksy Antkiewicz | POL |  |
| 4. | Francisco Núñez | ARG |  |
| 5. | Edward Johnson (USA), Edward Kerschbaumer (AUT), Armand Savoie (CAN), Su Bung-nan (KOR) | | |

A new style in Olympic boxing protests was created following the announcement that American Eddie Johnson had been declared the winner over 33-year-old Basilio Alves of Uruguay in their second-round match. While the crowd booed for more than fifteen minutes, Alves' supporters hoisted him on their shoulders and stormed the table of the Jury of Appeal. In the semifinals, it was the turn of the Argentinians to protest. Upset over the loss of Núñez to Shephard, they grabbed Núñez, who had refused to leave the ring, lifted him to their shoulders, and attempted a Uruguayan charge toward the Jurors' table. Repulsed by a phalanx of twelve attendants, the Argentinians listened to speeches by two of their officials and were finally convinced to end their protest by an Argentinian member of the Jury of Appeal, Señor Oriani. The final saw Shephard enter the ring with six stitches over his right eye, the result of a cut that had been opened in four of his five preliminary bouts. He fought gamely but was finally worn down by Formenti in the final minute and a half.

**1952 Helsinki** C: 30, N: 30, D: 8.2.

|  |  |  | FINAL MATCH |
|---|---|---|---|
| 1. | Jan Zachara | CZE | Dec 2–1 |
| 2. | Sergio Caprari | ITA |  |
| 3. | Leonard Leisching | SAF |  |

|  |  |  |
|---|---|---|
| 3. | Joseph Ventaja | FRA |
| 5. | Edson Brown (USA), Leszek Drogosz (POL), János Erdei (HUN), Leonard Walters (CAN) | |

**1956 Melbourne** C: 18, N: 18, D: 12.1.

|  |  |  | FINAL MATCH |
|---|---|---|---|
| 1. | Vladimir Safronov | SOV | Dec |
| 2. | Thomas Nicholls | GBR |  |
| 3. | Pentti Hämäläinen | FIN |  |
| 3. | Henryk Niedźwiedzki | POL |  |
| 5. | Andre De Sousa (FRA), Tristan Octavio Falfan (ARG), Shinetsu Suzuki (JPN), Jan Zachara (CZE) | | |

Safronov, an artist from Siberia, gained the U.S.S.R.'s first Olympic boxing title. He was added to the team at the last minute when Soviet champion Aleksandr Zasukhin injured his hand in training.

**1960 Rome** C: 31, N: 31, D: 9.5.

|  |  |  | FINAL MATCH |
|---|---|---|---|
| 1. | Francesco Musso | ITA | Dec 4–1 |
| 2. | Jerzy Adamski | POL |  |
| 3. | Jorma Limmonen | FIN |  |
| 3. | William Meyers | SAF |  |
| 5. | Abel Bekker (ZIM), Ernest Chervet (SWI), Constantin Gheorghiu (ROM), Boris Nikanorov (SOV) | | |

In the first round of the tournament, Boris Nikanorov outpointed Nick Spanakos to become the first Soviet boxer ever to defeat an American.

**1964 Tokyo** C: 32, N: 32, D: 10.23.

|  |  |  | FINAL MATCH |
|---|---|---|---|
| 1. | Stanislav Stepashkin | SOV | Dec 3–2 |
| 2. | Anthony Villanueva | PHI |  |
| 3. | Charles Brown | USA |  |
| 3. | Heinz Schulz | GDR |  |
| 5. | Constantin Crudu (ROM), José Duran Aguirre (MEX), Piotr Gutman (POL), Tun Tin (BUR) | | |

After all the hoopla and uproar that had gone on as a result of unpopular decisions in Olympic boxing, it was left to Spanish featherweight Valentin Loren to register the ultimate protest. Disqualified for repeated holding and open-glove hitting in the second round of his first fight, Loren turned on the Hungarian referee, György Sermer, and punched him in the face. This unfortunate indiscretion caused the Saragoza southpaw to receive a lifetime ban from international amateur boxing. Silver medalist Anthony Villanueva was the son of José "Cely" Villanueva, who had won the Bantamweight bronze medal at the 1932 Olympics in Los Angeles. Anthony tried a brief career as a movie actor and then turned professional boxer. Stepashkin won his first four fights by knockout and technical knockout before gaining a split decision over Villanueva.

**1968 Mexico City** C: 28, N: 28, D: 10.26.

|   |   |   | FINAL MATCH |
|---|---|---|---|
| 1. | Antonio Roldan | MEX | DISQ 2 |
| 2. | Albert Robinson | USA | |
| 3. | Ivan Mihailov | BUL | |
| 3. | Philip Waruinge | KEN | |
| 5. | Miguel Garcia (ARG), Abdel Khallaf (UAR), Valery Plotnikov (SOV), Seyfi Tatar (TUR) | | |

The final match came to a sudden end when Robinson was disqualified for butting. Although the Mexican crowd was delighted with the victory, Roldan himself seemed apologetic. As the first disqualified finalist since Ingemar Johansson in 1952, Robinson was prevented from receiving his silver medal. After a protest by American officials, Robinson was finally awarded the medal after his return to the United States. In 1971 Robinson was injured while training and lapsed into a coma in which he remained until his death three years later.

**1972 Munich** C: 45, N: 45, D: 9.10.

|   |   |   | FINAL MATCH |
|---|---|---|---|
| 1. | Boris Kousnetsov | SOV | Dec 3–2 |
| 2. | Philip Waruinge | KEN | |
| 3. | András Botos | HUN | |
| 3. | Clemente Rojas | COL | |
| 5. | Kazuo Kobayashi (JPN), Jouko Lindberg (FIN), Gabriel Pometcu (ROM), Antonio Rubio (SPA) | | |

**1976 Montreal** C: 26, N: 26, D: 7.31.

|   |   |   | FINAL MATCH |
|---|---|---|---|
| 1. | Angel Herrera | CUB | KO 2  2:18 |
| 2. | Richard Nowakowski | GDR | |
| 3. | Leszek Kosedowski | POL | |
| 3. | Juan Paredes | MEX | |
| 5. | Davey Armstrong (USA), Choi Choon-gil (KOR), Gheorghe Ciochina (ROM), Bratislav Ristic (YUG) | | |

**1980 Moscow** C: 35, N: 35, D: 8.2.

|   |   |   | FINAL MATCH |
|---|---|---|---|
| 1. | Rudi Fink | GDR | Dec 4–1 |
| 2. | Adolfo Horta | CUB | |
| 3. | Krzysztof Kosedowski | POL | |
| 3. | Viktor Rybakov | SOV | |
| 5. | Tzacho Andreikovski (BUL), Sidnei Dalrovere (BRA), Winfred Kabunda (ZAM), Luis Pizarro (PUR) | | |

**1984 Los Angeles** C: 36, N: 36, D: 8.11.

|   |   |   | FINAL MATCH |
|---|---|---|---|
| 1. | Meldrick Taylor | USA | Dec 5–0 |
| 2. | Peter Konyegwachie | NGR | |
| 3. | Targut Aykac | TUR | |
| 3. | Omar Catari Peraza | VEN | |
| 5. | Mohamed Hegazy (EGY), Charles Lubulwa (UGA), Park Hyeong-oc (KOR), John Wanjau (KEN) | | |

**1988 Seoul** C: 48, N: 48, D: 10.2.

|   |   |   | FINAL MATCH |
|---|---|---|---|
| 1. | Giovanni Parisi | ITA | RSC 1  1:41 |
| 2. | Daniel Dumitrescu | ROM | |
| 3. | Abdelhak Achik | MOR | |
| 3. | Lee Jae-hyuk | KOR | |
| 5. | Liu Dong (CHN), Tomasz Nowak (POL), Jacov Shmuel (ISR), Regilio Tuur (HOL) | | |

An unusual incident occurred during the first-round match between Jamie Pagendam of Canada and Tserendorj Awarjargal of Mongolia. Pagendam, a 22-year-old crane operator from St. Catharines, Ontario, registered three knockdowns in the second round (including one standing eight-count). According to amateur rules, Pagendam should automatically have been declared the winner after the third knockdown. However, the referee, Marius Guiramo Lougbo of the Ivory Coast, lost count of the knockdowns and allowed the bout to continue. When Pagendam was himself floored in the third round, Lougbo stopped the fight and gave the victory to Awarjargal. A protest was filed and the decision was in fact overturned. However, because Pagendam's final knockdown was the result of a blow to his head, he received a 30-day medical suspension and was not allowed to advance in the tournament. Neither was Lougbo—he was suspended for the remainder of the Olympics.

# LIGHTWEIGHT
(60 kg–132 lbs)

**1890–1900** not held

**1904 St. Louis** C: 8, N: 1, D: 9.22.
*(61.24 kg–135½ lbs)*

|   |   |   | FINAL MATCH |
|---|---|---|---|
| 1. | Harry Spanger | USA | Dec |
| 2. | James Eagan | USA | |
| 3. | Russell Van Horn | USA | |
| 4. | Peter Sturholdt | USA | |

A well-known local boxer, Carroll Burton, entered the tournament and won his first match. However, it was then discovered that the victor was not Burton at all, but a man named Bollinger posing as Burton. Bollinger was disqualified and his opponent, Sturholdt, was advanced to the next round.

**1906** not held

**1908 London** C: 12, N: 3, D: 10.27.
*(63.50 kg–140 lbs)*

|   |   |   | FINAL MATCH |
|---|---|---|---|
| 1. | Frederick Grace | GBR | Dec |
| 2. | Frederick Spiller | GBR | |
| 3. | H.H. Johnson | GBR | |
| 4. | Harold Holmes (GBR), G. Jessup (GBR), Matthew Wells (GBR) | | |

Early in the second round, the two finalists swung hard at each other. Both missed and fell on their faces.

**1912** not held

**1920 Antwerp** C: 12, N: 12, D: 8.26.
*(61.24 kg–135½ lbs)*

|   |   |   | FINAL MATCH |
|---|---|---|---|
| 1. | Samuel Mosberg | USA | Dec |
| 2. | Gotfred Johansen | DEN | |
| 3. | Clarence Newton | CAN | |
| 4. | Richard Beland | SAF | |
| 5. | Frederick Grace (GBR), Julian van Muyzen (BEL), Johan Saeterhang (NOR) | | |

**1924 Paris** C: 30, N: 22, D: 7.20.
*(61.24 kg–135½ lbs)*

|   |   |   | FINAL MATCH |
|---|---|---|---|
| 1. | Hans Nielsen | DEN | Dec |
| 2. | Alfredo Copello | ARG | |
| 3. | Frederick Boylstein | USA | |
| 4. | Jean Tholey | FRA | |
| 5. | Richard Beland (SAF), Alfred Genon (BEL), Haakon Hansen (NOR), Ben Rothwell (USA) | | |

**1928 Amsterdam** C: 24, N: 24, D: 8.11.
*(61.24 kg–135½ lbs)*

|   |   |   | FINAL MATCH |
|---|---|---|---|
| 1. | Carlo Orlandi | ITA | Dec |
| 2. | Stephen Michael Halaiko | USA | |
| 3. | Gunnar Berggren | SWE | |
| 4. | Hans Nielsen | DEN | |
| 5. | Dirk Baan (HOL), Cecil Bissett (ZIM), Pascual Bonfiglio (ARG), Jorge Diaz Hernandez (CHI) | | |

**1932 Los Angeles** C: 13, N: 13, D: 8.13.
*(61.24 kg–135½ lbs)*

|   |   |   | FINAL MATCH |
|---|---|---|---|
| 1. | Lawrence Stevens | SAF | Dec |
| 2. | Thure Ahlqvist | SWE | |
| 3. | Nathan Bor | USA | |
| 4. | Mario Bianchini | ITA | |
| 5. | Frank Genovese (CAN), Franz Kartz (GER), Gaston Mayor (FRA) | | |

**1936 Berlin** C: 26, N: 26, D: 8.15.
*(61.24 kg–135½ lbs)*

|   |   |   | FINAL MATCH |
|---|---|---|---|
| 1. | Imre Harangi | HUN | Dec |
| 2. | Nikolai Stepulov | EST | |
| 3. | Erik Ågren | SWE | |
| 4. | Poul Kops | DEN | |
| 5. | Carlos Lillo (CHI), Lidoro Oliver (ARG), José Padilla (PHI), Andrew Scrivani (USA) | | |

Prior to the Olympics, Harangi was urged by doctors to retire from boxing and undergo an operation on his nose, which had been badly injured in previous fights. Harangi refused and went on to win the gold medal in Berlin. One unfortunate competitor was Thomas Hamilton-Brown of South Africa. In his opening-round match, he lost a split decision to Carlos Lillo of Chile. However, it was later discovered that one of the judges had mistakenly reversed his scores for the two boxers and that Hamilton-Brown was in fact the winner and thus eligible to move on to the next round. Unfortunately, Hamilton-Brown, who had had trouble making the weight limit, had softened the disappointment of his loss by going on an eating binge. By the time the South African manager found him it was after midnight and the boxer had already put on nearly five pounds. Desperately his trainer tried to boil him down, but it was no use. The next day Hamilton-Brown, still over the weight limit, was disqualified and Lillo was allowed to advance in his place.

**1948 London** C: 28, N: 28, D: 8.13.
*(62 kg–135½ lbs)*

|   |   |   | FINAL MATCH |
|---|---|---|---|
| 1. | Gerald Dreyer | SAF | Dec |
| 2. | Joseph Vissers | BEL | |
| 3. | Svend Wad | DEN | |
| 4. | Wallace Smith | USA | |
| 5. | Oeivind Breiby (NOR), Edward Haddad (CAN), Maxie McCullagh (IRL), Ralf Benedito Zumbano (BRA) | | |

**1952 Helsinki** C: 27, N: 27, D: 8.2.

|   |   |   | FINAL MATCH |
|---|---|---|---|
| 1. | Aureliano Bolognesi | ITA | Dec 2–1 |
| 2. | Aleksy Antkiewicz | POL | |
| 3. | Gheorghe Fiat | ROM | |
| 3. | Erkki Pakkanen | FIN | |
| 5. | Americo Bonetti (ARG), István Juhász (HUN), Vincente Matute (VEN), Frederick Reardon (GBR) | | |

**1956 Melbourne** C: 18, N: 18, D: 12.1.

|   |   |   | FINAL MATCH |
|---|---|---|---|
| 1. | Richard McTaggart | GBR | Dec |
| 2. | Harry Kurschat | GER | |
| 3. | Anthony Byrne | IRL | |
| 3. | Anatoly Lagetko | SOV | |

5. Edward Beattie (CAN), Zygmunt Milewski (POL), Louis Molina (USA), André Vairolatto (FRA)

**1960 Rome** C: 34, N: 34, D: 9.5.

|   |   |   | FINAL MATCH |
| --- | --- | --- | --- |
| 1. | Kazimierz Paździor | POL | Dec 4–1 |
| 2. | Sandro Lopopolo | ITA | |
| 3. | Abel Laudonio | ARG | |
| 3. | Richard McTaggart | GBR | |
| 5. | Velikton Barannikov (SOV), Harry Campbell (USA), Ferenc Kellner (HUN), Salah Shokweir (UAR) | | |

Paździor, a 25-year-old blacksmith from Radom, used his experience of 175 fights to outpoint five straight opponents, although he had a tough time with McTaggart in the semifinals.

**1964 Tokyo** C: 34, N: 34, D: 10.23.

|   |   |   | FINAL MATCH |
| --- | --- | --- | --- |
| 1. | Józef Grudzień | POL | Dec |
| 2. | Velikton Barannikov | SOV | |
| 3. | Ronald Allan Harris | USA | |
| 3. | James McCourt | IRL | |
| 5. | Rodolfo Arpon (PHI), Domingo Barrera (SPA), János Kajdi (HUN), Stoyan Pilichev (BUL) | | |

**1968 Mexico City** C: 37, N: 37, D: 10.26.

|   |   |   | FINAL MATCH |
| --- | --- | --- | --- |
| 1. | Ronald W. Harris | USA | Dec 5–0 |
| 2. | Józef Grudzień | POL | |
| 3. | Calistrat Cutov | ROM | |
| 3. | Zvonimir Vujin | YUG | |
| 5. | Luis Minami (PER), Mohamed Muruli (UGA), Enzo Petriglia (ITA), Stoyan Pilichev (BUL) | | |

**1972 Munich** C: 37, N: 37, D: 9.10.

|   |   |   | FINAL MATCH |
| --- | --- | --- | --- |
| 1. | Jan Szczepański | POL | Dec 5–0 |
| 2. | László Orbán | HUN | |
| 3. | Samuel Mbugua | KEN | |
| 3. | Alfonso Pérez | COL | |
| 5. | Eraslan Doruk (TUR), Kim Tai-ho (KOR), Charles Nash (IRL), Sven Erik Paulsen (NOR) | | |

The 32-year-old European champion, Szczepański, was almost upset in the third round when he won the closest of split decisions over Chaidau Altankhuiag of Mongolia. He won his next two fights on a disqualification and a walkover. Then he took a close but unanimous decision from Orbán, the 1969 European champion.

**1976 Montreal** C: 23, N: 23, D: 7.31.

|   |   |   | FINAL MATCH |
| --- | --- | --- | --- |
| 1. | Howard Davis | USA | Dec 5–0 |
| 2. | Simion Cutov | ROM | |

3. Ace Rusevski   YUG
3. Vassily Solomin   SOV
5. András Botos (HUN), Yves Jeudy (HAI), Ove Lundby (SWE), Tsvetan Tsvetkov (BUL)

The year 1976 was a full one for Howard "John John" Davis. The father of a 2-year-old boy, Davis played guitar in a rock and soul group, having previously played drums for James Brown. In January he graduated from Glen Cove High School on Long Island. In February he turned 20. In July he went to Montreal with the intention of beating the favorite, European champion Simion Cutov. Two days before the start of the Olympics, Davis' mother, Catherine, died of a heart attack. Davis, deciding to honor his mother by winning the gold medal, was voted the Val Barker Award for most outstanding boxer of the Olympics. Two of his five fights were stopped in the first round and the other three were won by unanimous decision.

**1980 Moscow** C: 29, N: 29, D: 8.2.

|   |   |   | FINAL MATCH | |
| --- | --- | --- | --- | --- |
| 1. | Angel Herrera | CUB | RSC 3 | 0:13 |
| 2. | Viktor Demianenko | SOV | | |
| 3. | Kazimierz Adach | POL | | |
| 3. | Richard Nowakowski | GDR | | |
| 5. | Galsandorj Batbileg (MON), George Gilbody (GBR), Yordan Lessov (BUL), Florian Livadaru (ROM) | | | |

Herrera, who had won the 1976 Olympic Featherweight title, moved up successfully to Lightweight four years later, winning four unanimous decisions on his way to the final.

**1984 Los Angeles** C: 40, N: 40, D: 8.11.

|   |   |   | FINAL MATCH | |
| --- | --- | --- | --- | --- |
| 1. | Pernell Whitaker | USA | Ref 2 | 2:57 |
| 2. | Luis Ortiz | PUR | | |
| 3. | Chun Chil-sung | KOR | | |
| 3. | Martin Ndongo Ebanga | CAM | | |
| 5. | Leopoldo Cantancio (PHI), Reiner Gies (GER), José Antonio Hernando (SPA), Fahri Sumer (TUR) | | | |

Whitaker, of Norfolk, Va., like Herrera four years earlier, won four unanimous decisions on his way to the final. Ortiz's semifinal split decision victory over Ndongo Ebanga was roundly booed. In the final, Ortiz's handlers stopped the fight following a standing eight-count three seconds before the end of the second round. Whitaker went on to win the lightweight title of all three international professional federations, unifying the division in 1990 for the first time in 8 years. However, he said that winning these championships did not compare to winning an Olympic gold medal, which he described as, "the most exciting thing that's ever happened to me."

**1988 Seoul** C: 39, N: 39, D: 10.1.

|   |   |   | FINAL MATCH |
|---|---|---|---|
| 1. | Andreas Zuelow | GDR | Dec 5–0 |
| 2. | George Cramne | SWE | |
| 3. | Romallis Ellis | USA | |
| 3. | Nerguy Enkhbat | MON | |
| 5. | Mohamed Hegazy (EGY), Charles Kane (GBR), Kamal Marjonane (MOR), Emil Chuprenski (BUL) | | |

The key matchup of the tournament took place in the round of 16 when Andreas Zuelow, a technically pure boxer, faced Konstantin Tszu of the Soviet Union, who had knocked out his first two opponents in the first round. Two judges gave Zuelow the nod, two more gave the edge to Tszu, while the fifth judge, Abdul Hani of Iraq, scored the bout a draw. Olympic rules require each judge to designate a winner. Hani leaned toward Zuelow, who went on to win the gold medal with three straight unanimous decisions.

George Cramne, who fought for Sweden, was born in Liberia.

# LIGHT WELTERWEIGHT
## (63.5 kg—140 lbs)

**1896–1948** not held

**1952 Helsinki** C: 28, N: 28, D: 8.2.

|   |   |   | FINAL MATCH |
|---|---|---|---|
| 1. | Charles Adkins | USA | Dec 2–1 |
| 2. | Viktor Mednov | SOV | |
| 3. | Erkki Mallenius | FIN | |
| 3. | Bruno Visintin | ITA | |
| 5. | Terence Milligan (IRL), Jean Paternotte (BEL), Alexander Webster (SAF), René Weismann (FRA) | | |

The final saw the first-ever boxing match between fighters from the United States and the U.S.S.R. Adkins, a 20-year-old police administration student from Gary, Indiana, had had no trouble with his preliminary fights. Mednov, on the other hand, entered the ring with stitches over both eyes, the result of a brutal second-round fight with Ambrus of Romania, which was finally stopped by a doctor due to injuries to both men. Fortunately for Mednov, his semifinal opponent, Erkki Mallenius, injured his hand and had to withdraw, allowing the Soviet boxer an extra day to heal. In the final bout Mednov fought gallantly, but was no match for Adkins' powerful two-handed hooking.

**1956 Melbourne** C: 22, N: 22, D: 12.1.

|   |   |   | FINAL MATCH |
|---|---|---|---|
| 1. | Vladimir Yengibaryan | SOV | Dec |
| 2. | Franco Nenci | ITA | |

| 3. | Constantin Dumitrescu | ROM |
|---|---|---|
| 3. | Henry Loubscher | SAF |
| 5. | Hwang Ei-kyung (KOR), Antonio Salvador Marcilla (ARG), Claude Saluden (FRA), Joseph Shaw (USA) | |

**1960 Rome** C: 34, N: 34, D: 9.5.

|   |   |   | FINAL MATCH |
|---|---|---|---|
| 1. | Bohumil Nemeček | CZE | Dec 5–0 |
| 2. | Clement "Ike" Quartey | GHA | |
| 3. | Quincey Daniels | USA | |
| 3. | Marian Kasprzyk | POL | |
| 5. | Piero Brandi (ITA), Sayed Elnahas (UAR), Kim Duck-bong (KOR), Vladimir Yengibaryan (SOV) | | |

The final matched two underdogs and was won by Bohumil Nemeček, a 22-year-old railway worker from Decin. Ike Quartey, however, gained distinction by becoming the first black African to win an Olympic medal.

**1964 Tokyo** C: 35, N: 35, D: 10.23.

|   |   |   | FINAL MATCH |
|---|---|---|---|
| 1. | Jerzy Kulej | POL | Dec 5–0 |
| 2. | Yevgeny Frolov | SOV | |
| 3. | Eddie Blay | GHA | |
| 3. | Habib Galhia | TUN | |
| 5. | Felix Betancourt (CUB), Joao Henrique da Silva (BRA), Vladimir Kucera (CZE), Iosif Mihalic (ROM) | | |

**1968 Mexico City** C: 35, N: 35, D: 10.26.

|   |   |   | FINAL MATCH |
|---|---|---|---|
| 1. | Jerzy Kulej | POL | Dec 3–2 |
| 2. | Enrique Regueiferos | CUB | |
| 3. | Arto Nilsson | FIN | |
| 3. | James Wallington | USA | |
| 5. | Yevgeny Frolov (SOV), Kim Sa-yong (KOR), Peter Stoichev (BUL), Peter Tiepold (GDR) | | |

Policeman Jerzy Kulej beat Enrique Requeiferos, a strong puncher eight years his junior, to win a rare repeat Olympic boxing title.

**1972 Munich** C: 32, N: 32, D: 9.10.

|   |   |   | FINAL MATCH |
|---|---|---|---|
| 1. | Ray Seales | USA | Dec 3–2 |
| 2. | Angel Angelov | BUL | |
| 3. | Issaka Daborg | NIG | |
| 3. | Zvonimir Vujin | YUG | |
| 5. | Srisook Bantow (THA), Andres Molina (CUB), Graham Moughton (GBR), Kyoji Shinohara (JPN) | | |

The final between Angel Angelov and "Sugar Ray" Seales of Tacoma, Washington, was a surprisingly dull affair. Many observers felt that Sugar Ray's mother, who rooted him on enthusiastically from ringside, had shadow boxed a better fight than her son's. Seales turned professional and was reasonably successful until his career was ended by encroaching blindness.

**1976 Montreal** C: 32, N: 32, D: 7.31.

|   |   |   | FINAL<br>MATCH |
|---|---|---|---|
| 1. | Ray Leonard | USA | Dec 5–0 |
| 2. | Andrés Aldama | CUB | |
| 3. | Vladimir Kolev | BUL | |
| 3. | Kazimierz Szczerba | POL | |
| 5. | Ulrich Beyer (GDR), Calistrat Cutov (ROM), József Nagy (HUN), Luis Portillo (ARG) | | |

Ray Leonard, of Palmer Park, Maryland, made it two in a row for light welterweights nicknamed "Sugar Ray." He faced a tough customer in Andrés Aldama, who had stopped his first three opponents in the second round and knocked out Kolev in the semifinals. But Sugar Ray, wearing a photo of his girlfriend and their 2-year-old son on his shoes, won a clear victory. He turned professional a few months later and won the World Welterweight championship on November 30, 1979. He lost the title to Roberto Duran on June 20, 1980, but regained it later in the year. In 1982 he retired as a result of an eye injury. However, he returned to the ring in 1987 and scored a controversial victory over Marvin Hagler in a fight for the World Middleweight championship.

**1980 Moscow** C: 30, N: 30, D: 8.2.

|   |   |   | FINAL<br>MATCH |
|---|---|---|---|
| 1. | Patrizio Oliva | ITA | Dec 4–1 |
| 2. | Serik Konakbaev | SOV | |
| 3. | José Aguilar | CUB | |
| 3. | Anthony Willis | GBR | |
| 5. | Farouk Chanchoun Jawad (IRQ), William Lyimo (TAN), José Angel Molina (PUR), Ace Rusevski (YUG) | | |

Bronze medalist Tony Willis followed in the great British tradition of middleweight Chris Finnegan and hurdler David Hemery when he required three hours, an orangeade, and a glass of water to produce enough urine to be used for a drug test. He passed.

**1984 Los Angeles** C: 32, N: 32, D: 8.11.

|   |   |   | FINAL<br>MATCH |
|---|---|---|---|
| 1. | Jerry Page | USA | Dec 5–0 |
| 2. | Dhawee Umponmaha | THA | |
| 3. | Mircea Fulger | ROM | |
| 3. | Mirko Puzović | YUG | |
| 5. | Lotfi Belkhir (TUN), Kim Dong-kil (KOR), Jorge Maisonet (PUR), Jean Pierre Mbereke (CAM) | | |

The light welterweight division was disrupted by controversy in 1984. In a preliminary bout, Jorge Maisonet of Puerto Rico was declared a split decision winner over Nigeria's Charles Nwokolo. While the crowd chanted references to animal excrement, Colonel J. Whyte Ukor, the president of the Nigerian Boxing Association, rushed towards the jury waving his walking stick. After striking at least one boxing official, he was restrained by his coaches and removed from the arena.

Two days later, eventual gold medal winner Jerry Page was awarded a 4–1 quarterfinal victory over South Korean medal favorite Kim Dong-kil, in a match that most ringside observers thought Page had lost. The Korean delegation was so enraged that they threatened to withdraw from the tournament, but they later admitted that the threat was primarily an attempt to call attention to a string of controversial pro-U.S. jury decisions.

Umponmaha's silver medal was the highest placing ever by a Thai Olympic athlete.

**1988 Seoul** C: 45, N: 45, D: 10.2.

|   |   |   | FINAL<br>MATCH |
|---|---|---|---|
| 1. | Vyacheslav Yanovsky | SOV | Dec 5–0 |
| 2. | Grahame Cheney | AUS | |
| 3. | Reiner Gies | GER | |
| 3. | Lars Myrberg | SWE | |
| 5. | Sodnomdar Jaa Altansukh (MON), Todd Foster (USA), Antony Mwamba (ZAM), Humberto Rodriguez (MEX) | | |

Because there were so many entrants in the 1988 boxing tournament, two rings were used simultaneously until the quarterfinals. To avoid confusion, the end of a round was announced by a bell in ring A and a buzzer in ring B. The system did not work perfectly, leading to a bizarre incident in the round of 16 during the bout between Todd Foster of Great Falls, Montana, and Chun Jin-chul of South Korea.

The match was held in ring B. Just before the fight began, Foster's coaches reminded him to ignore the bell and listen only for "the horn." With 17 seconds left in round one, the bell sounded in ring A. In ring B Foster, Chun, and the Hungarian referee, Sandor Pajar, hesitated for a moment. Chun dropped his hands and took a step toward his corner. The referee called "Stop." Foster, realizing that Chun and the referee had made a mistake, blasted Chun with a left hook that caught the Korean in his eye. Chun looked to his corner, then collapsed to the canvas, pretending to be knocked down in an attempt to have Foster disqualified for a late blow. Pajar began to count Chun out, but stopped at four and walked over to the judges for a consultation. Jury president Emil Jetchev called the bout a no-contest and ordered a rematch for the following day. An hour and a half later, Foster was sitting in the stands waiting to watch another American fight when he was told that, as a result of a U.S. protest, the rematch would take place in 45 minutes. Foster opened the second bout by charging after Chun and knocking him to the canvas only 6 seconds into the fight. In the final minute of the first round Chun pounded Foster's nose, splattering blood on both boxers. Round two began with the spilling of more Foster blood, but the American took charge, knocking out Chun with a left hook to the chin.

In his next bout, Foster lost a split decision to Grahame Cheney, who later became Australia's first-ever Olympic boxing finalist. In the final, Cheney fought gamely, but was no match for the experienced 31-year-old Yanovsky.

# WELTERWEIGHT
## (67 kg–148 lbs)

**1896–1900** not held

**1904 St. Louis** C: 4, N: 1, D: 9.22.
*(65.77 kg–145 lbs)*

|   |   |   | FINAL MATCH |
|---|---|---|---|
| 1. | Albert Young | USA | Dec |
| 2. | Harry Spanger | USA |   |
| 3. | Jack Eagan | USA |   |
| 3. | Joseph Lydon | USA |   |

**1906–1912** not held

**1920 Antwerp** C: 15, N: 10, D: 8.26.
*(66.68 kg–147 lbs)*

|   |   |   | FINAL MATCH |
|---|---|---|---|
| 1. | Albert Schneider | CAN | Dec |
| 2. | Alexander Ireland | GBR |   |
| 3. | Frederick Colberg | USA |   |
| 4. | William Clark | USA |   |
| 5. | Gillet (FRA), Aage Steen (NOR), Trygve Stokstad (NOR), Suhr (DEN) | | |

Bert Schneider of Canada was acutally a U.S. citizen. Born in Cleveland, his family moved to Montreal when he was 9 years old. Unaware that boxing was an Olympic sport, Schneider learned that he had been chosen for the Canadian team when he read it in a newspaper. His final bout with Ireland ended in a draw, so the referee ordered the two exhausted fighters to square off for an extra round. Schneider had the most energy left and earned the gold medal.

**1924 Paris** C: 29, N: 18, D: 7.20.
*(66.68 kg–147 lbs)*

|   |   |   | FINAL MATCH |
|---|---|---|---|
| 1. | Jean Delarge | BEL | Dec |
| 2. | Héctor Méndez | ARG |   |
| 3. | Douglas Lewis | CAN |   |
| 4. | Patrick Dwyer | IRL |   |
| 5. | Hugh Haggerty (USA), Roy Ingram (SAF), Al Mello (USA), T. Stauffer (SWI) | | |

The first two rounds of the final match were all Delarge's, as Méndez tried unsuccessfully to land his notorious knockout right. He finally caught the Belgian in the third round and pummeled him around the ring. But it was too late. Delarge wouldn't go down, and he had already built up a big enough lead to secure the victory. When the verdict was announced, pandemonium broke loose as thousands of Argentinians began chanting, "Méndez! Méndez! Méndez!" A furious Belgian rushed in among them and unfurled a Belgian flag, which led to

further chaos. The demonstration went on for over fifteen minutes before order was restored. This incident was actually a mere anticlimax to what had occurred following a preliminary match three days earlier. On that day an English referee, T.H. Walker, disqualified an Italian boxer named Giusseppi Oldani for persistent holding of his opponent. Oldani fell to the floor, sobbing, while his supporters pelted Walker with sticks, coins, and walking stick knobs. This went on for almost an hour, until Walker was finally escorted from the arena by a contingent of British, American, and South African boxers, headed by the 265-pound wrestler Con O'Kelly.

**1928 Amsterdam** C: 22, N: 22, D: 8.11.
*(66.68 kg–147 lbs)*

|   |   |   | FINAL MATCH |
|---|---|---|---|
| 1. | Edward Morgan | NZE | Dec |
| 2. | Raúl Landini | ARG |   |
| 3. | Raymond Smillie | CAN |   |
| 4. | R. Galataud | FRA |   |
| 5. | C.F.J. Blommers (HOL), R. Caneva (ITA), Johan Hellstrom (FIN), Kintaro Usuda (JPN) | | |

**1932 Los Angeles** C: 16, N: 16, D: 8.13.
*(66.68 kg–147 lbs)*

|   |   |   | FINAL MATCH |
|---|---|---|---|
| 1. | Edward Flynn | USA | Dec |
| 2. | Erich Campe | GER |   |
| 3. | Bruno Ahlberg | FIN |   |
| 4. | David McCleave | GBR |   |
| 5. | Robert Barton (SAF), Luciano Fabbroni (ITA), Lucien Laplace (FRA), Carl Jensen (DEN) | | |

After the Olympics Flynn turned professional and fought just long enough to finance his way through dental school, eventually setting up practice in New Orleans.

**1936 Berlin** C: 25, N: 25, D: 8.15.
*(66.68 kg–147 lbs)*

|   |   |   | FINAL MATCH |
|---|---|---|---|
| 1. | Sten Suvio | FIN | Dec |
| 2. | Michael Murach | GER |   |
| 3. | Gerhard Petersen | DEN |   |
| 4. | Roger Tritz | FRA |   |
| 5. | Simplicio de Castro (PHI), Heinrich Dekkers (HOL), Imre Mándi (HUN), Raul Rodriguez (ARG) | | |

**1948 London** C: 26, N: 26, D: 8.13.

|   |   |   | FINAL MATCH |
|---|---|---|---|
| 1. | Julius Torma | CZE | Dec |
| 2. | Horace Herring | USA |   |
| 3. | Alessandro D'Ottavio | ITA |   |
| 4. | Douglas Du Preez | SAF |   |
| 5. | William Boyce (AUS), Zygmunt Chychla (POL), Aurelio Cadabeda Diaz (SPA), Eladio Herrera (ARG) | | |

Before his second-round bout with C.G. Blackburn of Canada, Julius Torma of Czechoslovakia attempted to shake hands with his opponent in the dressing room. When Blackburn refused, Torma became angry and decided to give the Canadian a lesson in the ring. This he did, with the referee stopping the fight in the second round. However, Torma's final left hook fractured a bone in his hand and it looked as if he might have to withdraw. Instead the 26-year-old Hungarian-born store clerk was able to hide his injury from his next three opponents, winning with careful defense and judicious use of his right hand.

**1952 Helsinki** C: 29, N: 29, D: 8.2.

| | | FINAL MATCH |
|---|---|---|
| 1. Zygmunt Chychla | POL | Dec 3–0 |
| 2. Sergei Scherbakov | SOV | |
| 3. Günther Heidemann | GER | |
| 3. Victor Jörgensen | DEN | |
| 5. Nicholaas Linneman (HOL), Ron Norris (IND), Julius Torma (CZE), Franco Vescovi (ITA) | | |

**1956 Melbourne** C: 16, N: 16, D: 12.1.

| | | FINAL MATCH |
|---|---|---|
| 1. Nicolae Linca | ROM | Dec 3–2 |
| 2. Frederick Tiedt | IRL | |
| 3. Nicholas Gargano | GBR | |
| 3. Kevin John Hogarth | AUS | |
| 5. Nicholas André (SAF), András Döri (HUN), Francisco Gelabert (ARG), Pearce Allen Lane (USA) | | |

Tiedt actually received more total points than Linca, but the Romanian was given the nod by three of the five judges.

**1960 Rome** C: 33, N: 33, D: 9.5.

| | | FINAL MATCH |
|---|---|---|
| 1. Giovanni Benvenuti | ITA | Dec 4–1 |
| 2. Yuri Radonyak | SOV | |
| 3. Leszek Drogosz | POL | |
| 3. James Lloyd | GBR | |
| 5. A. Phil Baldwin (USA), Henry Loubscher (SAF), Shishman Mitsev (BUL), Andres Moreno Navarro (SPA) | | |

The European amateur Light Middleweight champion, Benvenuti dropped down in weight class for the Olympics. He floored Radonyak toward the end of the first round, but the Soviet boxer came back strongly and was the aggressor in the final round. Benvenuti turned professional in 1961 and won the World Junior Middleweight title in 1965. On April 17, 1967, he defeated Emile Griffith for the World Middleweight championship, a title which he held for three of the next three and a half years.

**1964 Tokyo** C: 30, N: 30, D: 10.23.

| | | FINAL MATCH |
|---|---|---|
| 1. Marian Kasprzyk | POL | Dec 4–1 |
| 2. Ričardas Tamulis | SOV | |

| | |
|---|---|
| 3. Silvano Bertini | ITA |
| 3. Pertti Purhonen | FIN |
| 5. Issaka Daborg (NIG), Kichijiro Hamada (JPN), Ernest Powell Mabwa (UGA), Michael Varley (GBR) | |

**1968 Mexico City** C: 33, N: 33, D: 10.26.

| | | FINAL MATCH |
|---|---|---|
| 1. Manfred Wolke | GDR | Dec 4–1 |
| 2. Joseph Bessala | CAM | |
| 3. Mario Guilloti | ARG | |
| 3. Vladimir Mussalimov | SOV | |
| 5. Armando Muniz (USA), Alfonso Ramirez Gutierrez (MEX), Celal Sandal (TUR), Victor Zilberman (ROM) | | |

**1972 Munich** C: 37, N: 37, D: 9.10.

| | | FINAL MATCH |
|---|---|---|
| 1. Emilio Correa | CUB | Dec 5–0 |
| 2. János Kajdi | HUN | |
| 3. Dick Tiger Murunga | KEN | |
| 3. Jesse Valdez | USA | |
| 5. Maurice Hope (GBR), Anatoly Khohlov (SOV), Sergio Lozano (MEX), Günter Meier (GER) | | |

The final matched the 19-year-old Pan American champion, Emilio Correa, and the 32-year-old European titleholder, János Kajdi. The Cuban won a close but unanimous decision.

**1976 Montreal** C: 31, N: 31, D: 7.31.

| | | FINAL MATCH |
|---|---|---|
| 1. Jochen Bachfeld | GDR | Dec 3–2 |
| 2. Pedro Gamarro | VEN | |
| 3. Reinhard Skricek | GER | |
| 3. Victor Zilberman | ROM | |
| 5. Clinton Jackson (USA), Michael McCallum (JAM), Carmen Rinke (CAN), Carlos Santos (PUR) | | |

Silver medalist Pedro Gamarro was the surprise of the tournament. In his third bout he stopped defending Olympic and world amateur champion Correa, and in the quarterfinals he defeated favorite Clinton Jackson on a split decision. The 21-year-old Venezuelan almost went all the way, but he lost a close split decision in the title match to 24-year-old Jochen Bachfeld.

**1980 Moscow** C: 29, N: 29, D: 8.2.

| | | FINAL MATCH |
|---|---|---|
| 1. Andrés Aldama | CUB | Dec 4–1 |
| 2. John Mugabi | UGA | |
| 3. Karl-Heinz Krüger | GDR | |
| 3. Kazimierz Szczerba | POL | |
| 5. Memet Bogujević (YUG), Ionel Budusan (ROM), Joseph Frost (GBR), Plamen Yankov (BUL) | | |

John Mugabi needed a total of only nine minutes to knock out his first three opponents. He got by Kazimierz

Szczerba on a split decision but was defeated by Andrés Aldama, who had won the Light Welterweight silver medal four years earlier.

**1984 Los Angeles** C: 36, N: 36, D: 8.11.

|  |  | FINAL MATCH |
|---|---|---|
| 1. Mark Breland | USA | Dec 5–0 |
| 2. An Young-su | KOR |  |
| 3. Luciano Bruno | ITA |  |
| 3. Joni Nyman | FIN |  |
| 5. Dwight Frazer (JAM), Vesa Koskela (SWE), Alexander Künzler (GER), Genaro Leon (MEX) | | |

At 6 feet 2 inches, Brooklyn's Mark Breland, the most ballyhooed boxer at the Los Angeles Olympics, towered over his fellow welterweights. He also sported a 78-inch reach. Entering the tournament, Breland was the overwhelming favorite, having won the 1982 world amateur championship and having beaten everyone in his division including those from boycotting nations. His pre-Olympic record was 104 wins and 1 loss. As if all this wasn't intimidating enough to his opponents, Breland, who sparred with Tommy Hearns and with a professional karate champion, also received pre-fight advice from Muhammad Ali, Sugar Ray Robinson and Sugar Ray Leonard. A well-composed student of yoga, the 20-year-old Breland had already gained fame outside the world of boxing by starring in the 1983 film *The Lords of Discipline.*

**1988 Seoul** C: 44, N: 44, D: 10.1.

|  |  | FINAL MATCH |  |
|---|---|---|---|
| 1. Robert Wangila | KEN | KO 2 | 0:44 |
| 2. Laurent Boudouani | FRA |  |  |
| 3. Jan Dydak | POL |  |  |
| 3. Kenneth Gould | USA |  |  |
| 5. Adewale Adegbusi (NGR), Hristo Furnigov (BUL), Joni Nyman (FIN), Song Kyung-sup (KOR) | | | |

Wangila was the first black African boxer to win an Olympic championship. This was also the first welterweight final to be decided by a knockout after 16 consecutive decisions.

# LIGHT MIDDLEWEIGHT
## (71 kg–156 lbs)

**1896–1948** not held

**1952 Helsinki** C: 23, N: 23, D: 8.2.

|  |  | FINAL MATCH |
|---|---|---|
| 1. László Papp | HUN | Dec 3–0 |
| 2. Theunis van Schalkwyk | SAF |  |
| 3. Eladio Herrera | ARG |  |
| 3. Boris Tischin | SOV |  |

5. Paulo de Jesus Cavalheiro (BRA), Guido Mazzinghi (ITA), Erich Schöppner (GER), Peter Stankov (BUL)

Papp had a tough time with van Schalkwyk until the final round of their bout, when a right hook dropped the South African to his knees for an eight-count.

**1956 Melbourne** C: 14, N: 14, D: 12.1.

|  |  | FINAL MATCH |
|---|---|---|
| 1. László Papp | HUN | Dec |
| 2. José Torres | USA |  |
| 3. John McCormack | GBR |  |
| 3. Zbigniew Pietrzykowski | POL |  |
| 5. Ulrich Kienast (GER), Boris Georgiev (BUL), Alberto Manuel Saenz (ARG), Franco Scisciani (ITA) | | |

In defeating Torres, the 30-year-old Papp became the first boxer to win three Olympic gold medals (he had won the Middleweight title in 1948). In 1965 Torres won the World Light Heavyweight professional title by knocking out Willie Pastrano.

**1960 Rome** C: 23, N: 23, D: 9.5.

|  |  | FINAL MATCH |
|---|---|---|
| 1. Wilbert McClure | USA | Dec 4–1 |
| 2. Carmelo Bossi | ITA |  |
| 3. William Fisher | GBR |  |
| 3. Boris Lagutin | SOV |  |
| 5. John Bukowski (AUS), Henryk Dempc (POL), Souleymane Diallo (FRA), Celedonio Lima (ARG) | | |

"Skeeter" McClure of Toledo, Ohio, survived two very close split decisions over Lima and Lagutin to qualify for the final. Against Bossi, he used his strong in-fighting abilities to wear down the aggressive Italian. McClure later became a professor at Northeastern University in Boston.

**1964 Tokyo** C: 25, N: 25, D: 10.23.

|  |  | FINAL MATCH |
|---|---|---|
| 1. Boris Lagutin | SOV | Dec 4–1 |
| 2. Joseph Gonzales | FRA |  |
| 3. Józef Grzesiak | POL |  |
| 3. Nojim Maiyegun | NGR |  |
| 5. Anthony Barber (AUS), Tom Bogs (DEN), Eddie Davies (GHA), Vasile Mirza (ROM) | | |

Boris Lagutin's path to the final included a victory by disqualification over José Chirino of Argentina, who was penalized for punching the referee, and a walkover in the quarterfinals. After two rounds with Gonzales, Lagutin had matters well in hand. But in the third round he decided to mix it up and received for his efforts a cut eye and a warning for pulling Gonzales. Maiyegun was the first Nigerian to win an Olympic medal.

**1968 Mexico City** C: 27, N: 27, D: 10.26.

| | | FINAL MATCH |
|---|---|---|
| 1. Boris Lagutin | SOV | Dec 5–0 |
| 2. Rolando Garbey | CUB | |
| 3. John Baldwin | USA | |
| 3. Günther Meier | GER | |
| 5. Mario Benitez (URU), Eric Blake (GBR), David Jackson (UGA), Ianos Kovacs (ROM) | | |

The 30-year-old Lagutin outclassed all of his opponents to win his third straight medal. His final match with Garbey was an ugly, brawling contest, which led the crowd to boo and throw coins and burning newspapers at the Korean referee for failing to take action.

**1972 Munich** C: 33, N: 33, D: 9.10.

| | | FINAL MATCH |
|---|---|---|
| 1. Dieter Kottysch | GER | Dec 3–2 |
| 2. Wieslaw Rudkowski | POL | |
| 3. Alan Minter | GBR | |
| 3. Peter Tiepold | GDR | |
| 5. Rolando Garbey (CUB), Loucif Hamani (ALG), Mohamed Majeri (TUN), Emeterio Villanueva (MEX) | | |

Kottysch eked out controversial split decisions over Minter and Rudkowski to take the gold medal. However, the most disputed verdict came in the opening round of the tournament when a battered and bleeding Valery Tregubov of the U.S.S.R. was declared the winner against Reggie Jones of the United States. The announcement was met by a quarter-hour of international catcalls, which continued throughout the next bout.

**1976 Montreal** C: 23, N: 23, D: 7.31.

| | | FINAL MATCH |
|---|---|---|
| 1. Jerzy Rybicki | POL | Dec 5–0 |
| 2. Tadija Kacar | YUG | |
| 3. Rolando Garbey | CUB | |
| 3. Victor Savchenko | SOV | |
| 5. Vasile Didea (ROM), Wilfredo Guzman (PUR), Kalevi Kosunen (FIN), Alfredo Lemus (VEN) | | |

**1980 Moscow** C: 23, N: 23, D: 8.2.

| | | FINAL MATCH |
|---|---|---|
| 1. Armando Martinez | CUB | Dec 4–1 |
| 2. Aleksandr Koshkin | SOV | |
| 3. Ján Franek | CZE | |
| 3. Detlef Kästner | GDR | |
| 5. Francisco Carlos Jesus (BRA), Wilson Kaoma (ZAM), Leonidas Njunwa (TAN), Nicholas Colin Wilshire (GBR) | | |

**1984 Los Angeles** C: 34, N: 34, D: 8.11.

| | | FINAL MATCH |
|---|---|---|
| 1. Frank Tate | USA | Dec 5–0 |
| 2. Shawn O'Sullivan | CAN | |

| | | |
|---|---|---|
| 3. Christophe Tiozzo | FRA | |
| 3. Manfred Zielonka | GER | |
| 5. Israel Cole (SLE), Roderick Douglas (GBR), Christopher Kapopo (ZAM), Gnohere Sery (IVC) | | |

As expected, the final matched Frank Tate and Shawn O'Sullivan, who had split two previous fights with each other. What was not expected was that both boxers would reach the final as a result of unpopular decisions. Tate's came in his first bout against Lotfi Ayed, a Tunisian-born Swede. Despite being staggered and outpunched, Tate won a unanimous verdict.

Even more controversial was O'Sullivan's semifinal victory over Christophe Tiozzo. The judges voted 3–2 in Tiozzo's favor. However, new rules instituted before the 1984 Games required that all 3–2 decisions be submitted to a 5-man jury. If the jury voted 4–1 or 5–0 for the loser of the split decision, then the decision was reversed. The jury gave the nod to O'Sullivan, 4–1.

In the second round of the championship bout, Tate was twice given a standing eight-count. Nevertheless, four of the five judges awarded him the round. The announcement of Tate's victory by unanimous decision was met by a chorus of boos, but O'Sullivan, who was raised with the teachings of Henry David Thoreau, was philosophical. "It was an unfortunate decision," he told reporters. "I dearly wish things had gone different, but they didn't, and there's no gain in crying over spilled milk."

**1988 Seoul** C: 36, N: 36, D: 10.2.

| | | FINAL MATCH |
|---|---|---|
| 1. Park Si-hun | KOR | Dec 3–2 |
| 2. Roy Jones | USA | |
| 3. Raymond Downey | CAN | |
| 3. Richard Woodhall | GBR | |
| 5. Martin Kitel (SWE), Vincenzo Nardiello (ITA), Rey Rivera (PUR), Yevgeny Zaitsev (SOV) | | |

Probably no gold medalist in Olympic history has been less deserving of his prize than Park Si-hun, who benefited from five "hometown" decisions. Park's first bout, against Abdalla Ramadan of Sudan, was halted in the second round with Ramadan doubled over in pain and unable to continue following two illegal blows to the hip and kidney. The Australian referee, Ronald Mark Gregor, undoubtedly haunted by the attack on referee Keith Walker five days earlier, was hesitant to disqualify Park. Instead, he consulted the five judges, one of whom, Elmo Adolph of the U.S., told him that because Gregor had failed to caution Park after the low blows and because the fouls were not "flagrant," disqualification was inappropriate. Gregor ruled that the injured Ramadan had "retired" and declared Park the winner.

Park's second opponent was one of the favorites, Torsten Schmitz of East Germany. Most observers thought Schmitz had won the fight; however, Park was judged the victor in a narrow but unanimous decision.

While the East Germans vented their fury, Park moved on to the quarterfinals and a bout with Vincenzo Nardiello of Acilia, Italy. Once again, it appeared to most observers that Park had been defeated. In fact, Nardiello was ahead on the cards of all five judges after the first two rounds. Two of the judges gave Nardiello the final round as well. However, the other three judges decided that Park had won the round by such a wide margin that they gave him the fight. When the verdict was announced, Nardiello fell to his knees and pounded the canvas. Then he charged out of the ring and began screaming at the jury. Italian team officials dragged him off to the dressing room. He raced back into the arena crying and screaming, only to be hauled back to his room.

In the semifinals, Park won another narrow but unanimous victory, defeating Ray Downey by the same margin by which he had beaten Schmitz. He was becoming known as "the unbeatable Park Si-hun." Now all that stood between Park and a gold medal was 19-year-old Roy Jones, Jr., of Pensacola, Florida. Jones had already alienated local fight fans and many others as well with his arrogant demeanor and showboating style. In the ring he emulated the theatrical ways of Muhammad Ali and Sugar Ray Leonard, dropping his guard and taunting his opponents, doing the Ali shuffle. Outside the ring, he gracelessly referred to one defeated opponent as "a bum." Nevertheless, Jones had also shown that he was a skillful boxer with unusually quick hands. He made it to the final without being seriously challenged. Three days before the gold-medal bout, Jones told reporters, "I know how tough it is to get a decision against a South Korean, but it doesn't matter. If they cheat me, that's OK. I'll know if I really won it." Still, to be on the safe side, Jones announced that he would be going for a knockout.

He didn't get the knockout, but he did pummel Park, dominating all three rounds. Compubox, a private company that kept track of punches thrown and connected for NBC, the U.S. television network, registered 86 hits for Jones and only 32 for Park. Incredibly, three of the five judges gave the victory to the Korean. Veteran ring observers of all nationalities, reporters, referees and fans agreed that it was the worst decision they had ever seen. The French sports newspaper *L'Equipe* summed up the consensus in blunt terms: "Scandalous. To vomit." The decision was so bad that Korean fans were embarrassed, telephoning local newspapers and television stations to complain. Even Park himself apologized to Jones, telling him, through an interpreter, "I am sorry. I lost the fight. I feel very bad." On the victory stand, Park raised Jones' arm in triumph.

So how could such an unjust decision have been made? There were accusations that officials of the Korea Amateur Boxing Federation had bribed or otherwise persuaded some of the judges as a payback for pro-U.S. decisions at the 1984 Olympics. *Sports Illustrated* reported that one judge, Hiouad Larbi of Morocco, told angry journalists, "The American won easily; so easily, in fact, that I was positive my four fellow judges would score the fight for the American by a wide margin. So I voted for the Korean to make the score only 4–1 for the American and not embarrass the host country." Unfortunately, the judges from Uruguay and Uganda did the same thing.

The Park-Jones affair, as well as numerous other dubious decisions, forced the International Boxing Federation to institute radical changes in scoring in 1989. Ringside computers are now used to allow the judges to push a button whenever a scoring punch is made. If a majority of the judges push the button simultaneously, a point is recorded on a scoreboard visible to all in the arena. The winner is known the instant a bout is over.

# MIDDLEWEIGHT
## (75 kg–165½ lbs)

**1896–1900** not held

**1904 St. Louis** C: 2, N: 1, D: 9.22.
*(71.67 kg–158 lbs)*

| | | FINAL MATCH | |
|---|---|---|---|
| 1. Charles Mayer | USA | RSC 3 | 1:40 |
| 2. Benjamin Spradley | USA | | |

**1906** not held

**1908 London** C: 10, N: 3, D: 10.27.
*(71.67 kg–158 lbs)*

| | | FINAL MATCH |
|---|---|---|
| 1. John Douglas | GBR | Dec |
| 2. Reginald Baker | AUS | |
| 3. W. Philo | GBR | |
| 4. Ruben Warnes | GBR | |
| 5. W. Childs | GBR | |

Douglas was a well-known cricketer, known as "Johnny Won't Hit Today" Douglas because of his defensive batting. Silver medalist Reginald "Snowy" Baker also took part in the springboard diving competition and 4 × 200-meter freestyle relay at the 1908 Olympics. In fact, Baker was probably the greatest all-around athlete ever produced by Australia. He competed in twenty-nine different sports. He also knocked out Douglas in a rematch a few days after the Olympics. In later years, Baker starred in several silent films, most notably *The Fighting Breed* (1921), moved to Hollywood, and taught fencing, riding, and swimming to stars such as Greta Garbo and Douglas Fairbanks.

**1912** not held

**1920 Antwerp** C: 15, N: 8, D: 8.26.
*(72.57 kg–160 lbs)*

|   |   |   | FINAL MATCH |
|---|---|---|---|
| 1. | Harry Mallin | GBR | Dec |
| 2. | Georges Prudhomme | CAN | |
| 3. | Montgomery "Moe" Herscovitch | CAN | |
| 4. | Hjalmar Strömme | NOR | |
| 5. | W. Bradley (SAF), Samuel Lagonia (USA), Martin Olsen (DEN), Pegoliet (FRA) | | |

**1924 Paris** C: 23, N: 14, D: 7.20.
*(72.57 kg–160 lbs)*

|   |   |   | FINAL MATCH |
|---|---|---|---|
| 1. | Harry Mallin | GBR | Dec |
| 2. | John Elliott | GBR | |
| 3. | Joseph Beecken | BEL | |
| 4. | Leslie Black | CAN | |
| 5. | Roger Brousse (FRA), Daney (FRA), T. Harry Henning (CAN), James Murphy (IRL) | | |

Olympic boxing has a long and glorious history of protests, demonstrations, and general outrages. But of all the incidents and controversies, the real gold medal winner was the Brousse-Mallin Affair, which occurred in Paris in 1924. Mallin, the defending champion, was a 32-year-old London policeman. In the quarterfinals he faced 23-year-old Roger Brousse of France. As soon as the fight ended, Mallin approached the Belgian referee and displayed several well-defined teeth marks on his chest. The referee ignored him and proceeded to read out the verdict. Although most ringside observers gave the fight to Mallin, it was Brousse who won the decision, 2–1. The Italian judge and the Belgian referee voted for Brousse, while the South African judge sided with Mallin. Mallin, who had never lost a fight, left the ring without further comment. However, a protest was lodged by Mr. Söderland, a Swedish member of the International Boxing Association, and an inquiry was held. Examination of Mallin's chest revealed that he had most definitely been bitten, and quite robustly at that. In fact, in his previous bout Brousse had also been accused of biting his opponent, Gallardo of Argentina. Brousse's supporters claimed that he had an odd habit of snapping his jaw whenever he threw a punch. What had happened, they said, was that Mallin had ducked one of Brousse's punches and, coming back up, bumped his chest against Brousse's snapping mouth. The Jury of Appeal ruled that Brousse's bite had been unintentional, but disqualified him anyway. When this decision was announced at the Vélodrome d'Hiver the following evening, Brousse leapt to his feet and burst into tears. Immediately the hall became a scene of turmoil. Brousse was hoisted upon the shoulders of his loyal fans and paraded about the arena. Hundreds of demonstrators hooted and hollered and attempted to enter the ring. They were repulsed by the police. After about a half hour the commotion died

down, but Brousse's supporters continued to launch attacks against the judges and referees for the rest of the evening.

The boxing finals were held the following night. The evening began with the announcement that two Italian boxers, flyweight Rinaldo Castellenghi and light heavyweight Carlo Saraudi, had withdrawn from the tournament to protest the poor officiating. After the Mendez-Delarge welterweight final the arena was in an uproar, with hundreds of Argentinians expressing their outrage and anger vociferously. The confusion was added to when Mallin and Elliot entered the ring, for the mere sight of Mallin set off the French spectators in their own chorus of catcalls. Not surprisingly, the two English middleweights had a hard time concentrating on their contest, which Mallin won in an uncharacteristically uninspired manner. The official report of the British Olympic Association included this account of the bout: "Mallin eventually won a close fight, but we are unable to give a more detailed description, owing to the fact that we were seated in the centre of a group of excited and gesticulating Frenchmen, who, not content with making themselves ridiculous . . . also refused to allow anyone in their proximity to get a view of the fight." The British press had a field day with the affair. "It was found necessary," said the *Daily Sketch*, "to substitute for a mere boxer a man eating expert named Brousse, whose passion for raw meat led him to attempt to bite off portions of his opponents' anatomies." Another reporter wrote, "Having got his teeth into a piece of Argentine meat during one of the earlier contests, M. Brousse decided to vary the menu by sampling some of the unroasted human beef of Old England." Less light-hearted observers called for an end to boxing, an end to the Olympics, and, at the very least, an end to the French. However, life did go on and so did boxing and so did the Olympics and so did the French.

**1928 Amsterdam** C: 17, N: 17, D: 8.11.
*(72.57 kg–160 lbs)*

|   |   |   | FINAL MATCH |
|---|---|---|---|
| 1. | Piero Toscani | ITA | Dec |
| 2. | Jan Heřmánek | CZE | |
| 3. | Leonard Steyaert | BEL | |
| 4. | Fred Mallin | GBR | |
| 5. | John Chase (IRL), Humberto Curi (ARG), Harry Henderson (USA), Oscar Kjällander (SWE) | | |

Wild scenes and alleged injustice hit the Middleweight division again in Amsterdam. In the final Heřmánek appeared to be the winner, but Toscani was awarded the gold medal. Heřmánek was hoisted on the shoulders of his countrymen and dumped at the feet of the judges, where he argued his case while the demonstration spread, erupting into violence in the back of the hall. While the light heavyweight finalists, Avendano and Pistulla, prepared for their bout, Heřmánek's seconds tried to push him back into the ring. Finally the police intervened, and action *inside* the ring resumed.

**1932 Los Angeles** C: 10, N: 10, D: 8.13.
*(72.57 kg–160 lbs)*

|   |   |   | FINAL MATCH |
|---|---|---|---|
| 1. | Carmen Barth | USA | Dec |
| 2. | Amado Azar | ARG | |
| 3. | Ernest Pierce | SAF | |
| 4. | Roger Michelot | FRA | |
| 5. | Hans Bernlöhr (GER) | | |

**1936 Berlin** C: 19, N: 19, D: 8.15.
*(72.57 kg–160 lbs)*

|   |   |   | FINAL MATCH |
|---|---|---|---|
| 1. | Jean Despeaux | FRA | Dec |
| 2. | Henry Tiller | NOR | |
| 3. | Raúl Villareal | ARG | |
| 4. | Henryk Chmielewski | POL | |
| 5. | Adolf Baumgarten (GER), James Atkinson (USA), Gerardus Dekkers (HOL), Josef Hrubes (CZE) | | |

**1948 London** C: 25, N: 25, D: 8.13.
*(73 kg–161 lbs)*

|   |   |   | FINAL MATCH |
|---|---|---|---|
| 1. | László Papp | HUN | Dec |
| 2. | John Wright | GBR | |
| 3. | Ivano Fontana | ITA | |
| 4. | Michael McKeon | IRL | |
| 5. | August Cavignac (BEL), Aime-Joseph Escudie (FRA), Dogomar Martinez (URU), Jan Schubart (HOL) | | |

This was the first milestone in László Papp's illustrious career. In 1952 he would go on to win the Light Middleweight gold medal and in 1956 he would successfully defend his title. The following year, at the age of 31, Papp gained permission from the Hungarian government to become the first boxer from a Communist country to fight professionally. He won the European Middleweight championship, but the Hungarian government refused to let him challenge for the world championship. He retired undefeated in 1965 and became a coach for the Hungarian Olympic team.

**1952 Helsinki** C: 23, N: 23, D: 8.2.

|   |   |   | FINAL MATCH |   |
|---|---|---|---|---|
| 1. | Floyd Patterson | USA | KO 1 | 1:14 |
| 2. | Vasile Țiță | ROM | | |
| 3. | Boris Georgiev | BUL | | |
| 3. | Stig Sjölin | SWE | | |
| 5. | Leonardus Jansen (HOL), Anthony Madigan (AUS), Walter Sentimenti (ITA), Dieter Wemhöner (GER) | | | |

Seventeen-year-old Floyd Patterson of Brooklyn breezed through his four bouts in the easiest manner imaginable. When the bell sounded at the start of the final, Patterson spun around in a circle, which earned him a warning from the Polish referee. A tremendous uppercut to Țiță's chin ended the contest after 74 seconds. Four years later Patterson knocked out Archie Moore to win the vacant World Heavyweight title. In 1959 he lost the title to Ingemar Johansson; then, in 1960, he defeated Johansson to become the first boxer to regain the heavyweight championship.

**1956 Melbourne** C: 14, N: 14, D: 12.1.

|   |   |   | FINAL MATCH |
|---|---|---|---|
| 1. | Gennady Schatkov | SOV | KO 1 |
| 2. | Rámon Tapia | CHI | |
| 3. | Gilbert Chapron | FRA | |
| 3. | Victor Zalazar | ARG | |
| 5. | Giulio Rinaldi (ITA), Roger Rouse (USA), Julius Torma (CZE), Dieter Wemhöner (GER) | | |

**1960 Rome** C: 25, N: 25, 9.5.

|   |   |   | FINAL MATCH |
|---|---|---|---|
| 1. | Edward Crook | USA | Dec 3–2 |
| 2. | Tadeusz Walasek | POL | |
| 3. | Evgeny Feofanov | SOV | |
| 3. | Ion Monea | ROM | |
| 5. | Hans Buechi (SWI), Chang Lo-Pu (TAI), Luigi Napoleoni (ITA) Frederik Van Rooyen (SAF) | | |

The announcement of Crook's victory over Walasek was greeted by prolonged booing and whistling, which caused a delay in the awards ceremony.

**1964 Tokyo** C: 20, N: 20, D: 10.23.

|   |   |   | FINAL MATCH |   |
|---|---|---|---|---|
| 1. | Valery Popenchenko | SOV | RSC 1 | 2:05 |
| 2. | Emil Schulz | GER | | |
| 3. | Franco Valle | ITA | | |
| 3. | Tadeusz Walasek | POL | | |
| 5. | Joe Darkey (GHA), Ahmed Hassan (UAR), Ion Monea (ROM), Guillermo Slinas (CHI) | | | |

**1968 Mexico City** C: 22, N: 22, D: 10.26.

|   |   |   | FINAL MATCH |
|---|---|---|---|
| 1. | Christopher Finnegan | GBR | Dec 3–2 |
| 2. | Aleksei Kisselyov | SOV | |
| 3. | Alfred Jones | USA | |
| 3. | Agustin Zaragoza | MEX | |
| 5. | Simeon Georgiev (BUL), Jan Hejdik (CZE), Mate Parlov (YUG), Wieslaw Rudkowski (POL) | | |

Chris Finnegan, a 24-year-old bricklayer from Iver, Buckinghamshire, won his semifinal bout by gaining an unpopular 4–1 decision over Al Jones of Detroit. In the final he faced Aleksei Kisselyov who had won the Light Heavyweight silver medal four years earlier. Kisselyov started strong, but was already tiring by the second round. The fight was close, but Finnegan thought he had won. "Then we were called to the centre of the ring for the announcement," he recalled in his autobiography *Finnegan: Self-Portrait of a Fighting Man.* "At first I couldn't cotton on to the jabber, but all of a sudden I heard the magic word which sounds the same in any language—FINNEGAN!" Three judges had voted 59–58 for Finnegan and two had voted 59–58 for Kisselyov. "I shall never be able to properly describe my feelings as I climbed up on that rostrum for the medal presentation," he went on. "The nearest I've felt to it was when walking down the aisle with my old woman after our wedding. . . . Only there was no gold medal at the end of that—only the golden rivet."

But Finnegan's most difficult challenge was still ahead: the urine test for drugs. As Finnegan put it: "Now if there's one thing I've never been able to do, it's have a piss while someone's watching me. I can never stand at those long urinals you get in gents' bogs, with all the other blokes having a quick squint." Sure enough, he was unable to produce. People turned on water faucets, whistled, whispered encouragement. He drank several glasses of water. Still nothing. Then he downed three or four pints of beer, but still without the desired result. After giving a television interview, Finnegan was hauled off to a local restaurant for a victory meal. Two Olympic officials tagged along with the necessary collection equipment. Finally, at 1:40 a.m., Finnegan jumped up and shouted, "Who wants some piss?" The officials followed him to the men's room, secured their sample, and returned to the lab. The test, of course, proved negative.

**1972 Munich** C: 22, N: 22, D: 9.10.

| | | | FINAL MATCH | |
|---|---|---|---|---|
| 1. Vyacheslav Lemechev | SOV | KO 1 | 2:17 |
| 2. Reima Virtanen | FIN | | |
| 3. Prince Amartey | GHA | | |
| 3. Marvin Johnson | USA | | |
| 5. Poul Knudsen (DEN), Nazif Kuran (TUR), Alejandro Montoya (CUB), Witold Stachurski (POL) | | | |

Lemechev's performance was so impressive that only one of his five opponents lasted the full three rounds. In the semifinals he stopped Marvin Johnson in the second round to avenge an earlier loss in the Soviet Union. In the final, Lemechev, a great counterpuncher, scored a sharp right cross over Virtanen's left lead that put the Finnish boxer out cold for a minute.

**1976 Montreal** C: 19, N: 19, D: 7.31.

| | | | FINAL MATCH | |
|---|---|---|---|---|
| 1. Michael Spinks | USA | RSC 3 | 1:54 |
| 2. Rufat Riskiev | SOV | | |
| 3. Luis Martinez | CUB | | |
| 3. Alec Nastac | ROM | | |
| 5. Siraj Din (PAK), Fernando Martins (BRA), Ryszard Pasiewicz (POL), Dragomir Vujkovic (YUG) | | | |

Twenty-year-old Michael Spinks of St. Louis won the gold medal even though he fought only two fights—his path to the title included one bye and two forfeits. Six months earlier Spinks had been beaten by Riskiev in Tashkent, but in the third round of the final in Montreal, Spinks landed a tremendous blow to the Russian's stomach, causing Riskiev to double up in pain and the referee to stop the contest. Spinks went on to great success as a professional boxer, gaining the WBA light heavyweight championship in 1981 and adding the WBC title in 1983. In 1985, he defeated Larry Holmes for the World Heavyweight championship.

**1980 Moscow** C: 19, N: 19, D. 8.2.

| | | | FINAL MATCH | |
|---|---|---|---|---|
| 1. José Gomez | CUB | Dec 4–1 | |
| 2. Viktor Savchenko | SOV | | |
| 3. Jerzy Rybicki | POL | | |
| 3. Valentin Silaghi | ROM | | |
| 5. Jang Bong-mun (PRK), Mark Kaylor (GBR), Peter Odhiambo (UGA), Manfred Trauten (GDR) | | | |

Savchenko won his first four fights by technical knockouts, but Gomez, the favorite, was too much for him in the final.

**1984 Los Angeles** C: 27, N: 27, D: 8.11.

| | | | FINAL MATCH | |
|---|---|---|---|---|
| 1. Shin Joon-sup | KOR | Dec 3–2 | |
| 2. Virgil Hill | USA | | |
| 3. Aristides Gonzalez | PUR | | |
| 3. Mohamed Zaoui | ALG | | |
| 5. Moses Mwaba (ZAM), Jeremiah Okorodudu (NGR), Damir Škaro (YUG), Pedro van Raamsdonk (HOL) | | | |

Of the 38 fights involving U.S. boxers at the Los Angeles Olympics that went the full three rounds, 37 of them were decided in favor of the Americans. The only exception was the middleweight final in which Virgil Hill of North Dakota lost a very close decision to 23-year-old Shin Joon-sup, providing a cathartic happy ending for an otherwise frustrated and embittered Korean boxing squad. Four of Shin's five victories were by split decision.

**1988 Seoul** C: 33, N: 33, D: 10.1.

| | | | FINAL MATCH | |
|---|---|---|---|---|
| 1. Henry Maske | GDR | Dec 5–0 | |
| 2. Egerton Marcus | CAN | | |
| 3. Chris Sande | KEN | | |
| 3. Hussain Shah Syed | PAK | | |
| 5. Zoltán Füzesy (HUN), Michele Mastrodonato (ITA), Sven Ottke (GER), Franco Wanyama (UGA) | | | |

The most respected boxer in the middleweight division, Angel Espinoza of Cuba, was unable to compete because his government boycotted the Seoul Games. This put 6-foot 3½-inch Henry Maske into the role of favorite. Maske did not disappoint, registering unanimous decisions in each of his four fights.

Maske's last victim, Guyana-born Egerton Marcus, fought the final with an injured right hand. Marcus' uncle, Charlie Arnos, represented Guyana in the 1968 Olympics. His mother was a boxer as well.

In a repeat of the 1972 men's 100-meter sprint snafu, the U.S. entrant, Anthony Hembrick, failed to show up on time for his opening bout when his coaches misread the day's schedule.

# LIGHT HEAVYWEIGHT
## (81 kg–179 lbs)

**1896–1912** not held

**1920 Antwerp** C: 8, N: 6, D: 8.26.
*(79.38 kg–175 lbs)*

|   |   |   | FINAL MATCH |
|---|---|---|---|
| 1. | Edward Eagan | USA | Dec |
| 2. | Sverre Sörsdal | NOR | |
| 3. | H. Franks | GBR | |
| 4. | Hugh Brown | GBR | |
| 5. | Andersen (DEN), Thomas Hohstock (SAF), Prachelle (FRA), Edwin Schell (USA) | | |

A Yale graduate who later attended Oxford as a Rhodes scholar, Eagan was a member of the four-man bobsled team that won a gold medal at the Lake Placid Olympics in 1932.

**1924 Paris** C: 21, N: 15, D: 7.20.
*(79.38 kg–175 lbs)*

|   |   |   | FINAL MATCH |
|---|---|---|---|
| 1. | Harry Mitchell | GBR | Dec |
| 2. | Thyge Petersen | DEN | |
| 3. | Sverre Sörsdal | NOR | |
| 4. | Carlo Saraudi | ITA | |
| 5. | J. Courtis (GBR), Thomas Kirby (USA), George Mulholland (USA), Rossignon (FRA). | | |

**1928 Amsterdam** C: 16, N: 16, D: 8.11.
*(79.38 kg–175 lbs)*

|   |   |   | FINAL MATCH |
|---|---|---|---|
| 1. | Victor Avendaño | ARG | Dec |
| 2. | Ernst Pistulla | GER | |
| 3. | Karl Leendert Miljon | HOL | |
| 4. | Donald McCorkindale | SAF | |
| 5. | Donald Carrick (CAN), Alfred Jackson (GBR), Juozas Vinca (LIT), William Murphy (IRL) | | |

**1932 Los Angeles** C: 8, N: 8, D: 8.13.
*(79.38 kg–175 lbs)*

|   |   |   | FINAL MATCH |
|---|---|---|---|
| 1. | David Carstens | SAF | Dec |
| 2. | Gino Rossi | ITA | |
| 3. | Peter Jörgensen | DEN | |
| 4. | James Murphy | IRL | |
| 5. | Hans Berger (GER), Rafael Lang (ARG), Nikolaos Mastoridis (GRE), John Miler (USA) | | |

**1936 Berlin** C: 22, N: 22, D: 8.15.
*(79.38 kg–175 lbs)*

|   |   |   | FINAL MATCH |
|---|---|---|---|
| 1. | Roger Michelot | FRA | Dec |
| 2. | Richard Vogt | GER | |
| 3. | Francisco Risiglione | ARG | |
| 4. | Sydney Leibbrandt | SAF | |
| 5. | Thomas Griffin (GBR), František Havelka (CZE), Borge Holm (DEN), Johannes Koivunen (FIN) | | |

**1948 London** C: 24, N: 24, D: 8.13.
*(80 kg–177 lbs)*

|   |   |   | FINAL MATCH |
|---|---|---|---|
| 1. | George Hunter | SAF | Dec |
| 2. | Donald Scott | GBR | |
| 3. | Maurio Cia | ARG | |
| 4. | Adrian Holmes | AUS | |
| 5. | Giacomo Di Segni (ITA), Hugh O'Hagan (IRL), Harri Siljander (FIN), Franciszek Szymura (POL) | | |

Before the match for third place, Maurio Cia had his broken right hand shot up with cocaine, then used it to knock down Adrian Holmes, who broke his ankle when he fell. Gold medalist George Hunter, a 21-year-old boilermaker, was awarded the Val Barker trophy for the best boxer of the Olympics.

**1952 Helsinki** C: 18, N: 18, D: 8.2.

|   |   |   | FINAL MATCH |
|---|---|---|---|
| 1. | Norvel Lee | USA | Dec 3–0 |
| 2. | Antonio Pacenza | ARG | |
| 3. | Anatoly Perov | SOV | |
| 3. | Harri Siljander | FIN | |
| 5. | Giovanni Battista Alfonsetti (ITA), Lucio Grotone (BRA), Tadeusz Grzelak (POL), Karl Kistner (GER) | | |

Norvel Lee went to Helsinki as a reserve heavyweight. Informed that he could compete as a light heavyweight if he made the weight limit, he lost twelve pounds and won the gold medal. An exception among boxers, Lee already had a master's degree, from Howard University. In 1948 Lee had been arrested in his hometown of Covington, Kentucky, for being one of the first blacks to sit in the all-white front section of a local bus.

**1956 Melbourne** C: 11, N: 11, D: 12.1.

| | | FINAL MATCH |
|---|---|---|
| 1. James Boyd | USA | Dec |
| 2. Gheorghe Negrea | ROM | |
| 3. Carlos Lucas | CHI | |
| 3. Romualdas Murauskas | SOV | |
| 5. Rodolfo Luciano Diaz (ARG), Anthony Madigan (AUS), Ottavio Panunzi (ITA), Andrzej Wojciechowski (POL) | | |

**1960 Rome** C: 19, N: 19, D: 9.5.

| | | FINAL MATCH |
|---|---|---|
| 1. Cassius Clay | USA | Dec 5–0 |
| 2. Zbigniew Pietrzykowski | POL | |
| 3. Anthony Madigan | AUS | |
| 3. Giulio Saraudi | ITA | |
| 5. Gennady Schatkov (SOV), Rafael Gargiulo (ARG), Gheorghe Negrea (ROM), Peter Stankov (BUL) | | |

Long before Muhammad Ali became one of the most famous people in the world, he was Cassius Marcellus Clay, a brash and friendly 18-year-old who traveled to Rome from his hometown of Louisville, Kentucky, with hopes of winning a gold medal. Clay thrived in the atmosphere of the Olympic Village, garrulously introducing himself to people of all countries, joking with them, having his picture taken with them.

In the ring he was equally in his element. After stopping Yan Becaus of Belgium in the second round, he defeated the 1956 Olympic Middleweight champion, Gennady Schatkov, and the Australian Tony Madigan, by unanimous decisions. In the final he met the three-time European champion, Zbigniew Pietrzykowski who was a veteran of 231 fights. Clay spent the first two rounds nimbly avoiding everything Pietrzykowski threw at him. Then in the last round he overwhelmed the Pole to earn a clear, unanimous decision.

At a press conference after the fight, a Soviet journalist asked Clay how he, as a Negro, felt about the fact that he wasn't allowed to eat at certain restaurants back home. Sensing an attempt to exploit him, Clay shot back, "Russian, we got qualified men working on that problem. We got the biggest and the prettiest cars. We get all the food we can eat. America is the greatest country in the world, and as far as places I can't eat goes, I got lots of places I can eat—more places I can than I can't."

And so Cassius Marcellus Clay achieved his goal of winning a gold medal. But the story of what happened to that medal tells volumes about the state of race relations in America at the beginning of the 1960s. Clay loved his medal. He slept with it, he ate with it, he wore it all the time. He wore it so much in fact that the gold began to wear off, revealing a common lead base. He returned to a hero's welcome in Louisville. The porch of his house was decorated with American flags, and his father had painted the steps red, white and blue. Cassius posed for

photographers with his father —and his medal—while his father sang "The Star-Spangled Banner."

It wasn't long before Cassius turned professional and signed a contract with ten white Louisville millionaires, who agreed to sponsor his career. The millionaires gave him a slip of paper with all their phone numbers on it in case he ever needed help.

One day the mayor of Louisville asked Clay to come to his office so he could show off the gold medal to some visiting dignitaries. The mayor boasted to his visitors about the response Cassius had given to the Soviet reporter about the status of Negroes in the United States. The mayor told them, "Why, Cassius stood up tall, 'Look here, Commie . . . I'd rather live here in Louisville than in Africa cause at least I ain't fightin' off no snakes and alligators and livin' in mud huts.' He sho' told 'em! He's our own boy, Cassius, our next world champion."

By now Clay was sorry he had responded to the Soviet journalist the way he had. On the way home, he and a friend, Ronnie King, stopped at a whites-only restaurant and attempted to order two hamburgers and two vanilla milk shakes. They were refused service. "Miss," Clay told the waitress, "I'm Cassius Clay, the Olympic champion," and he showed off his gold medal with its red, white, and blue ribbons. The waitress turned to the owner of the restaurant who boomed out, "I don't give a damn who he is! I done told you, we don't serve no niggers!" Several members of a white motorcycle gang happened to be in the restaurant and they rose and joined the owner by the counter. Ronnie King pulled out the paper with the names and numbers of Clay's millionaire sponsors and urged his friend to call them up for help. But Cassius just couldn't ask. In his book, *The Greatest,* Ali wrote, "I had earned my Gold Medal without their permission. It should mean something without their permission. I wanted that medallion to mean that I owned myself. And to call seemed to me to be exchanging one Owner for the Other."

Clay and Ronnie King left the restaurant. "Whatever illusions I'd built up in Rome as the All-American Boy were gone. My Olympic honeymoon was over." In the parking lot Clay was approached by one of the gang members, who ordered him to hand over his gold medal. Instead, he and Ronnie King raced off on their motor bikes, well aware that this gang had already seriously beaten several blacks who had been caught in white neighborhoods. Two of the gang leaders caught up with Clay and King at the Jefferson County Bridge on the Indiana border. A violent confrontation followed, which left the gang members bleeding and badly injured. When they left, Clay and King walked down to the river to wash the blood off their bodies and clothes. Ronnie King took the gold medal, cleaned it carefully, and hung it over his neck. It was the first time the medal had been away from Clay's chest. "For the first time," he wrote, "I saw it as it was. Ordinary, just an object." King put the gold medal back around Clay's neck, and the two friends walked back to the bridge. When they got to the middle of the bridge, Cassius Clay walked over to the side, pulled the gold medal off his chest, and threw it into the Ohio River. Later Ali wrote, "The medal was gone, but . . . I felt calmly relaxed, confident. My holiday as a White Hope was over. I felt a new, secret strength."

**1964 Tokyo** C: 19, N: 19, D: 10.23.

|   |   |   | FINAL MATCH |
|---|---|---|---|
| 1. | Cosimo Pinto | ITA | Dec 3–2 |
| 2. | Aleksei Kisselyov | SOV | |
| 3. | Alexander Nikolov | BUL | |
| 3. | Zbigniew Pietrzykowski | POL | |
| 5. | Rafael Luis Gargiulo (ARG), Sayed Mersal (UAR), František Polacek (CZE), Jürgen Schlegel (GDR) | | |

**1968 Mexico City** C: 18, N: 18, D: 10.26.

|   |   |   | FINAL MATCH |
|---|---|---|---|
| 1. | Dan Poznjak | SOV | Default |
| 2. | Ion Monea | ROM | |
| 3. | Stanislaw Dragan | POL | |
| 3. | Georgi Stankov | BUL | |
| 5. | Fatai Ayinia (NGR), Walter Facchinetti (ITA), Bernard Malherbe (FRA), Jürgen Schlegel (GDR) | | |

Monea suffered a broken nose in his semifinal victory over Dragan and was unable to compete in the final.

**1972 Munich** C: 28, N: 28, D: 9.10.

|   |   |   | FINAL MATCH |
|---|---|---|---|
| 1. | Mate Parlov | YUG | RSC 2  2:39 |
| 2. | Gilberto Carrillo | CUB | |
| 3. | Janusz Gortat | POL | |
| 3. | Isaac Ikhouria | NGR | |
| 5. | Nikolai Anfimov (SOV), Miguel Angel Cuello (ARG), Rudi Hornig (GER), Harald Skog (NOR) | | |

Parlov blasted his way through the tournament, winning one walkover and stopping three of his other four opponents in the second round. Parlov turned professional in 1975 and three years later won the World Light Heavyweight title.

**1976 Montreal** C: 18, N: 18, D: 7.31.

|   |   |   | FINAL MATCH |
|---|---|---|---|
| 1. | Leon Spinks | USA | RSC 3  1:09 |
| 2. | Sixto Soria | CUB | |
| 3. | Costica Dafinoiu | ROM | |
| 3. | Janusz Gortat | POL | |
| 5. | Robert Burgess (BER), Wolfgang Gruber (GER), Ottomar Sachse (GDR), Juan Suarez (ARG) | | |

Marine Corps Lance Corporal Leon Spinks stepped into the ring for his Olympic final immediately after his younger brother, Michael, had won the Middleweight championship. He faced knockout artist Sixto Soria, who had required only 9 minutes and 5 seconds to dispose of his first three opponents. However, the Cuban met his match in Spinks, who knocked him down in the first round and continued to batter him until the referee stopped the fight. A year and a half later Spinks defeated Muhammad Ali to win the World Heavyweight championship.

**1980 Moscow** C: 15, N: 15, D: 8.2.

|   |   |   | FINAL MATCH |
|---|---|---|---|
| 1. | Slobodan Kacar | YUG | Dec 4–1 |
| 2. | Pawel Skrzeck | POL | |
| 3. | Herbert Bauch | GDR | |
| 3. | Ricardo Rojas | CUB | |
| 5. | Georgica Donici (ROM), David Kvachadze (SOV), Michael Madsen (DEN), Geoffrey Pike (AUS) | | |

**1984 Los Angeles** C: 24, N: 24, D: 8.11.

|   |   |   | FINAL MATCH |
|---|---|---|---|
| 1. | Anton Josipović | YUG | Default |
| 2. | Kevin Barry | NZE | |
| 3. | Evander Holyfield | USA | |
| 3. | Mustapha Moussa | ALG | |
| 5. | Georgica Donici (ROM), Jean Paul Nanga (CAM), Syivaus Okello (KEN), Anthony Wilson (GBR) | | |

Despite all of the uproar about pro-American judging at the Los Angeles Olympics, it was a U.S. boxer who was the victim of the most controversial decision of all. Evander Holyfield, who had defeated world amateur champion Ricky Womack to qualify for the U.S. team, had stopped his first three opponents and was on the verge of knocking out a fourth, when an unusual incident occurred. A few seconds before the end of the second round of his semifinal bout with Kevin Barry, Holyfield lashed out a right to the ribs and followed with a left hook that floored Barry for good. The referee, Gligorije Novicić of Yugoslavia, motioned Holyfield to a neutral corner, counted out Barry, then turned to Holyfield and disqualified him for throwing the left hook after Novicić had yelled, "Stop." Subsequent viewing of the videotapes of the fight confirmed the late hit, but also showed that Barry and Holyfield had previously thrown four late blows each.

When the decision was announced, Barry turned to Holyfield and said, "You won the fight fair and square." Then he took the American's hand and raised it in the air. The crowd went berserk, raining abuse and refuse on the Yugoslavian referee. The police had to be brought in to escort Novicić from the arena. Novicić had been scheduled to work one of the final bouts three days later, but was relieved of his obligation for security reasons.

What made the incident all the more shocking was the subsequent ruling that because Barry had been declared a knockout victim, amateur boxing regulations prevented him from fighting again for 28 days. This meant that the gold medal was awarded by default to the other semifinal winner, Anton Josipović, who, like referee Novicić, happened to hail from Yugoslavia.

At the medal ceremony, Josipović, a handsome 22-year-old literature student from Bosnia, endured loud booing. But after the playing of the Yugoslav national anthem, he reached down and pulled up a surprised Holyfield to join him on the gold-medal platform. Afterwards, he told reporters, "It is a great honor to win the gold medal in this city of light and sun. I would have liked to fight Holyfield, to show what I am capable of doing and to win the medal that way. I am a bit disappointed that the audience doesn't realize that this is not the way I wanted it. I took the opportunity to have Holyfield join me on the top step because I believe the Olympics are the spirit of friendliness and goodwill."

**1988 Seoul** C: 26, N: 26, D: 10.2.

|   |   |   | FINAL MATCH |
|---|---|---|---|
| 1. | Andrew Maynard | USA | Dec 5–0 |
| 2. | Nuramgomed Shanavazov | SOV | |
| 3. | Henryk Petrich | POL | |
| 3. | Damir Škaro | YUG | |
| 5. | Joseph Akhasamba (KEN), Ahmed Elnagar (EGY), Lajos Erös (HUN), Andrea Magi (ITA) | | |

The 12th of 14 children, Andrew Maynard grew up on the streets of Cheverly, Maryland. His mother died when he was 3 years old; his father, a truck driver, was frequently on the road. Maynard, who was once a marijuana dealer, was in and out of juvenile court for such charges as assault and breaking and entering. Finally, a judge told him that he would have to go to college, join the Army or go to jail. Maynard chose the Army. In the armed service, he became a cook and a boxer. He also married, became a father, and generally turned his life around. The Olympic final, a turgid affair that resembled two bears dancing, was not a fair representation of either boxer's talents. Bronze medalist Damir Škaro set a curious record by losing to the eventual silver-medal winner for the third straight Olympics. In 1980 and 1984 he had competed as a middleweight.

# HEAVYWEIGHT
(91 kg–200½ lbs)

**1896–1980** not held

**1984 Los Angeles** C: 15, N: 15, D: 8.11.

|   |   |   | FINAL MATCH |
|---|---|---|---|
| 1. | Henry Tillman | USA | Dec 5–0 |
| 2. | William deWit | CAN | |
| 3. | Angelo Musone | ITA | |
| 3. | Arnold Vanderlijde | HOL | |
| 5. | Håkan Brock (SWE), Dodovic Owiny (UGA), George Stefanopoulos (GRE), Tevita Taufoou (TON) | | |

Tillman, who learned to box while serving time for armed robbery, qualified for the U.S. team by twice defeating future World Heavyweight champion Mike Tyson. Tillman's semifinal victory was a controversial jury reversal decision over Angelo Musone, a decision that the Italian newspapers referred to as "hallucinatory" and "scandalous." In the final, Tillman upset deWit, who had beaten the American in their two previous encounters.

**1988 Seoul** C: 18, N: 18, D: 10.1.

|   |   |   | FINAL MATCH | |
|---|---|---|---|---|
| 1. | Raymond Mercer | USA | KO 1 | 2:16 |
| 2. | Baik Hyan-man | KOR | | |
| 3. | Andrzej Golota | POL | | |
| 3. | Arnold Vanderlijde | HOL | | |
| 5. | Gyula Alvics (HUN), Luigi Gaudiano (ITA), Maik Heydeck (GDR), Harold Obunga (KEN) | | | |

World champion Felix Savon was conspicuously missing from the tournament because of Cuba's boycott of the Seoul Games. In Savon's absence, 27-year-old infantryman Ray Mercer blasted his way through the tournament. His four opponents, none of whom survived the full three rounds, lasted a total of 17 minutes 6 seconds. An oddity among boxers, Mercer did not take up the sport until he was 22, and only then because being a sparring partner for the camp champion meant that he wouldn't have to take part in a 30-day winter survival field exercise.

# SUPER HEAVYWEIGHT
(Over 91 kg–200 ½ lbs)

This division, which is the unlimited weight class, was known as Heavyweight from 1904 to 1980.

**1896–1900** not held

**1904 St. Louis** C: 2, N: 1, D: 9.22.
*(Over 71.67 kg–158 lbs)*

|   |   |   | FINAL MATCH |
|---|---|---|---|
| 1. | Samuel Berger | USA | Dec |
| 2. | Charles Mayer | USA | |
| 3. | William Michaels | USA | |

**1906** not held

**1908 London** C: 6, N: 1, D: 10.27.
*(Over 71.67 kg–158 lbs)*

|   |   |   | FINAL MATCH | |
|---|---|---|---|---|
| 1. | Albert Oldham | GBR | KO 1 | 2:00 |
| 2. | S.C.H. Evans | GBR | | |
| 3. | Frederick Parks | GBR | | |
| 4. | H. Brewer (GBR), Albert Ireton (GBR), I. Myrams (GBR) | | | |

**1912** not held

**1920 Antwerp** C: 8, N: 6, D: 8.26.
*(Over 79.38 kg–175 lbs)*

|   |   |   | FINAL MATCH |
|---|---|---|---|
| 1. | Ronald Rawson | GBR | Dec |
| 2. | Sören Petersen | DEN | |
| 3. | Xavier Eluere | FRA | |
| 4. | William Spengler | USA | |
| 5. | Creusen (BEL), F. S. Dove (GBR), Sigurd Hoel (NOR), Samuel Steward (USA) | | | |

**1924 Paris** C: 15, N: 10, D: 7.20.
*(Over 79.38 kg–175 lbs)*

|   |   |   | FINAL MATCH |
|---|---|---|---|
| 1. | Otto von Porat | NOR | Dec |
| 2. | Sören Petersen | DEN | |
| 3. | Alfredo Porzio | ARG | |
| 4. | Henk de Best | HOL | |
| 5. | Bertazzolo (ITA), A. J. Clifton (GBR), H. G. Greathouse (USA), Larsen (DEN) | | | |

The final was a popular battle that saw Petersen almost knocked out in the first round and von Porat almost put away in the second. The Norwegian rebounded in the final round to earn the victory.

**1928 Amsterdam** C: 10, N: 10, D: 8.11.
*(Over 79.38 kg–175 lbs)*

|   |   |   | FINAL MATCH |
|---|---|---|---|
| 1. | Arturo Rodriguez Jurado | ARG | RSC 1 |
| 2. | Nils Ramm | SWE | |
| 3. | M. Jacob Michaelsen | DEN | |
| 4. | Sverre Sörsdal | NOR | |
| 5. | Georges Gardebois (FRA), Alexander Kaletchetz (USA), Sam Oliji (NZE), Hans Schönrath (GER) | | | |

**1932 Los Angeles** C: 6, N: 6, D: 8.13.
*(Over 79.38 kg–175 lbs)*

|   |   |   | FINAL MATCH |
|---|---|---|---|
| 1. | Santiago Lovell | ARG | Dec |
| 2. | Luigi Rovati | ITA | |
| 3. | Frederick Feary | USA | |
| 4. | George Maughan | CAN | |
| 5. | Gunnar Barlund (FIN), Heinz Kohlhaas (GER) | | | |

**1936 Berlin** C: 17, N: 17, D: 8.15.
*(Over 79.38 kg–175 lbs)*

|   |   |   | FINAL MATCH |
|---|---|---|---|
| 1. | Herbert Runge | GER | Dec |
| 2. | Guillermo Lovell | ARG | |
| 3. | Erling Nilsen | NOR | |
| 4. | Ferenc Nagy | HUN | |
| 5. | Jose Feans (URU), Vincent Stuart (GBR), Olle Tandberg (SWE), Ernest Toussaint (LUX) | | | |

**1948 London** C: 17, N: 17, D: 8.13.
*(Over 80 kg–176½ lbs)*

|   |   |   | FINAL MATCH |
|---|---|---|---|
| 1. | Rafael Iglesias | ARG | KO 2 |
| 2. | Gunnar Nilsson | SWE | |
| 3. | John Arthur | SAF | |
| 4. | Hans Müller | SWI | |
| 5. | Uber Baccilieri (ITA), Adam Faul (CAN), Jack Gardner (GBR), E. Jay Lambert (USA), | | | |

**1952 Helsinki** C: 22, N: 22, D: 8.2.
*(Over 81 kg–179 lbs)*

|   |   |   | FINAL MATCH |
|---|---|---|---|
| 1. | H. Edward Sanders | USA | DISQ 2 |
| 2. | Ingemar Johansson | SWE | |
| 3. | Ilkka Koski | FIN | |
| 3. | Andries Nieman | SAF | |
| 5. | Giacomo Di Segni (ITA), Edgar Hearn (GBR), Tomislav Krizmanic (YUG), Algirdas Schocikas (SOV) | | | |

Evidently the punishment that Sanders inflicted on his first three opponents made a great impression on Ingemar Johansson, because the Swede spent all his time in the ring back-pedaling, without throwing a single punch. After receiving several warnings from the referee, he was finally disqualified for not "giving of his best." Because of the disqualification, he was not awarded his silver medal. Ironically, it was not Sanders but Johansson who went on to a successful professional career, knocking out Floyd Patterson in 1959 to win the World Heavyweight championship. He was finally awarded his silver medal in 1982. Sanders died of a brain hemorrhage on December 12, 1954, after being knocked out in his ninth professional bout.

**1956 Melbourne** C: 11, N: 11, D: 12.1.
*(Over 81 kg–179 lbs)*

|   |   |   | FINAL MATCH | |
|---|---|---|---|---|
| 1. | T. Peter Rademacher | USA | RSC 1 | 2.27 |
| 2. | Lev Mukhin | SOV | | |
| 3. | Daniel Bekker | SAF | | |
| 3. | Giacomo Bozzano | ITA | | |
| 5. | Thorner Åhsman (SWE) | | | |

The final looked as if it would be a classic. Mukhin had beaten all three of his opponents by knockout or technical knockout, coming off the floor himself in two of the fights. Rademacher, a soldier from Yakima, Washington, never gave Mukhin a chance to make a third comeback. He knocked down the Soviet boxer in the first 50 seconds. Mukhin got up, but Rademacher flattened him twice more in the next 80 seconds, and the referee finally stopped the fight. Eight and a half months later, Rademacher became the first boxer to fight for the Heavyweight title in his first professional contest. Rademacher, who had never gone more than three rounds, sent champion Floyd Patterson to the canvas in the second round, but Patterson came back to win in round 6.

**1960 Rome** C: 17, N: 17, D: 9.5.
*(Over 81 kg–179 lbs)*

| | | FINAL MATCH | |
|---|---|---|---|
| 1. Franco De Piccoli | ITA | KO 1 | 1:30 |
| 2. Daniel Bekker | SAF | | |
| 3. Josef Nemec | CZE | | |
| 3. Günter Siegmund | GDR | | |

5. Andrey Abramov (SOV), Vasile Mariutan (ROM), Percy Price (USA), Obrad Sretenovic (YUG)

**1964 Tokyo** C: 14, N: 14, D: 10.23.
*(Over 81 kg–179 lbs)*

| | | FINAL MATCH | |
|---|---|---|---|
| 1. Joseph Frazier | USA | Dec 3–2 | |
| 2. Hans Huber | GER | | |
| 3. Giuseppe Ros | ITA | | |
| 3. Vadim Yemelyanov | SOV | | |

5. Santiago Alberto Lovell (ARG), Vasile Mariutan (ROM), Athol McQueen (AUS)

Philadelphia butcher's apprentice Joe Frazier was a last-minute substitute for 293-pound Buster Mathis, who had broken his knuckle. Frazier demolished his first three opponents and then won a much tamer split decision over Regensburg bus driver Hans Huber in the final, which Frazier fought with a broken right hand. In 1970 Frazier won the World Heavyweight championship, and in 1980 he was elected to the Boxing Hall of Fame.

**1968 Mexico City** C: 14, N: 14, D: 10.23.
*(Over 81 kg–179 lbs)*

| | | FINAL MATCH | |
|---|---|---|---|
| 1. George Foreman | USA | RSC 2 | |
| 2. Jonas Čepulis | SOV | | |
| 3. Giorgio Bambini | ITA | | |
| 3. Joaquin Rocha | MEX | | |

5. Ion Alexe (ROM), Bernd Anders (GDR), Rudolfus Lubbers (HOL), Kiril Pandov (BUL)

The relatively inexperienced Foreman, who had fought only 18 times before the Olympics, had little trouble winning the gold medal. After his final victory he paraded around the ring holding aloft a small U.S. flag. On January 22, 1973, Foreman knocked out Joe Frazier to win the World Heavyweight title.

**1972 Munich** C: 14, N: 14, D: 9.10.
*(Over 81 kg–179 lbs)*

| | | FINAL MATCH |
|---|---|---|
| 1. Teófilo Stevenson | CUB | Default |
| 2. Ion Alexe | ROM | |

3. Peter Hussing   GER
3. Hasse Thomsén   SWE
5. Duane Bobick (USA), Jürgen Fanghänel (GDR), Carroll Morgan (CAN)

Teófilo Stevenson, a handsome Jamaican-born 6-foot 3½-inch Cuban from Las Tunas, Oriente, was the most impressive Olympic boxer since Cassius Clay. After disposing of Poland's Ludwik Denderys in one round, he faced Duane Bobick of the U.S. Navy. In 1971 Bobick had beaten Stevenson in the semifinals of the Pan-American Games. Now, at the Munich Olympics, Bobick wasn't too worried about Stevenson. "I know he's tall and strong," he told reporters, "but the last time all he had was a good jab—no right hand." Unbeknownst to Bobick, the Cuban had spent twelve months working on just that problem. Using a stinging left jab and a now powerful right hand, Stevenson plastered Bobick until the fight was stopped in the third round.

Stevenson's semifinal opponent was Peter Hussing of Germany. He lasted 4 minutes and 3 seconds. "I have never been hit so hard in all my 212 bouts," said the good-natured Hussing. "You just don't see his right hand. All of a sudden it is there—on your chin." The other semifinal matched Alexe of Romania and Thomsén of Sweden, both of whom had been knocked out by Stevenson in previous tournaments. Some observers suggested that the *loser* should be forced to face Stevenson in the final.

In fact, neither of them did. Alexe won a unanimous decision over Thomsén, but showed up for the final with his hand in plaster, the result of a broken thumb. Although capitalist fight promoters drooled at the prospect, Stevenson refused to turn professional, stating that he was more interested in his studies and in revolution than he was in making a million dollars. In fact, he turned down an offer of $2,000,000. "Professional boxing treats a fighter like a commodity to be bought and sold and discarded when he is no longer of use," he said. "I wouldn't exchange my piece of Cuba for all the money they could give me."

**1976 Montreal** C: 15, N: 15, D: 7.31.
*(Over 81 kg–179 lbs)*

| | | FINAL MATCH | |
|---|---|---|---|
| 1. Teófilo Stevenson | CUB | KO 3 | 2:35 |
| 2. Mircea Simon | ROM | | |
| 3. Clarence Hill | BER | | |
| 3. Johnny Tate | USA | | |

5. Peter Hussing (GER), Atanas Souvandzhiev (BUL)

In the four years since the Munich Olympics, Stevenson had lost two fights—both to Igor Vysotsky of the U.S.S.R., who had knocked out the Cuban in Minsk three months before the 1976 Olympics. However, Vysotsky was unable to compete in Montreal because of eye injuries, and the road seemed clear for Stevenson to defend his title. He demolished his first three opponents in a record 7 minutes and 22 seconds. His last victim was Mircea Simon, who avoided Stevenson completely for the first two rounds. Although this same tactic had earned Ingemar Johansson a disqualification 24 years earlier, it seemed quite understandable in Simon's case. When Stevenson finally hit Simon in the third round, the Romanian's seconds immediately threw in the towel. Simon later defected to the United States. Clarence Hill's bronze made Bermuda (pop. 53,500) the smallest country ever to win a Summer Olympics medal.

**1980 Moscow** C: 14, N: 14, D: 8.2.
*(Over 81 kg–179 lbs)*

|   |   |   | FINAL MATCH |
|---|---|---|---|
| 1. | Teófilo Stevenson | CUB | Dec 4–1 |
| 2. | Pyotr Zaev | SOV | |
| 3. | Jürgen Fanghänel | GDR | |
| 3. | István Levai | HUN | |
| 5. | Francesco Damiani (ITA), Grzegorz Skrzecz (POL), Peter Stoimenov (BUL) | | |

In the semifinals, Levai ran around the ring for three rounds, becoming the first Olympic boxer to go the distance against Stevenson. Stevenson, in turn, became the first boxer to win three Olympic gold medals in the same division. As late as 1986, he proved that he was still the best amateur boxer in the world by winning the world championship at age 34.

**1984 Los Angeles** C: 11, N: 11, D: 8.11.

|   |   |   | FINAL MATCH |
|---|---|---|---|
| 1. | Tyrell Biggs | USA | Dec 4–1 |
| 2. | Francesco Damiani | ITA | |
| 3. | Salihu Azis | YUG | |
| 3. | Robert Wells | GBR | |
| 5. | Peter Hussing (GER), Lennox Lewis (CAN) | | |

**1988 Seoul** C: 17, N: 17, D: 10.2.

|   |   |   | FINAL MATCH |   |
|---|---|---|---|---|
| 1. | Lennox Lewis | CAN | RSC 2 | 0:43 |
| 2. | Riddick Bowe | USA | | |
| 3. | Aleksandr Miroshnichenko | SOV | | |
| 3. | Janusz Zarenkiewicz | POL | | |
| 5. | Petr Hrivnak (CZE), Ulli Kaden (GDR), Kim Yoo-hyun (KOR), Andreas Schneiders (GER) | | | |

Lennox Lewis of Kitchener, Ontario, needed only 10 minutes 16 seconds to dispatch his three opponents. Most startling was his 34-second knockout of World Cup champion Ulli Kaden in the quarterfinals. One unfortunate boxer was Mohamed Hammad of Sudan. When the bell rang to begin his opening round bout with South Korean Kim Yoo-hyun, Hammad took three steps forward and discovered that the fight was over and he was the loser. His coach, Abdellatif Mohamed Abbas, had literally thrown in the towel as a protest against an earlier decision in which South Korean light middleweight Park Si-hun had been declared the winner over Sudan's Abdallah Ramadan. Park had incapacitated Ramadan with an illegal kidney punch.

Another unusual highlight was the appearance of 5-foot 11-inch, 260-pound Ali Albaluchi of Kuwait. Clearly outclassed by the more athletically shaped Aleksandr Miroshnichenko, the good-natured Albaluchi took advantage of his moment in the spotlight to imitate Muhammad Ali. While Kuwaiti supporters chanted, "Ali, Ali," Albaluchi performed the rope-a-dope and the Ali Shuffle. He dropped his gloves, stuck out his chin and dared Miroshnichenko to hit him. Miroshnichenko won the fight easily, but it was Albaluchi who received the only standing ovation of the entire 429-match Seoul tournament.

## THE VAL BARKER CUP

The Val Barker Cup, named in honor of the first General-Secretary of the International Amateur Boxing Association, is awarded to the boxer who displays the best style and technique.

| 1936 | Louis Laurie | USA | flyweight | bronze |
|---|---|---|---|---|
| 1948 | George Hunter | SAF | light heavyweight | gold |
| 1952 | Norvel Lee | USA | light heavyweight | gold |
| 1956 | Richard McTaggart | GBR | lightweight | gold |
| 1960 | Giovanni Benevenuti | ITA | welterweight | gold |
| 1964 | Valery Popenchenko | SOV | middleweight | gold |
| 1968 | Philip Waruingi | KEN | featherweight | bronze |
| 1972 | Teofilo Stevenson | CUB | heavyweight | gold |
| 1976 | Howard Davis | USA | lightweight | gold |
| 1980 | Patrizio Oliva | ITA | light welterweight | gold |
| 1984 | Paul Gonzales | USA | light flyweight | gold |
| 1988 | Roy Jones | USA | light middleweight | silver |

# CANOEING

**MEN**
Kayak Singles 500 Meters
Kayak Singles 1000 Meters
Kayak Pairs 500 Meters
Kayak Pairs 1000 Meters
Kayak Fours 1000 Meters
Canadian Singles 500 Meters
Canadian Singles 1000 Meters
Canadian Pairs 500 Meters
Canadian Pairs 1000 Meters
Kayak Slalom Singles
Canadian Slalom Singles
Canadian Slalom Pairs
Discontinued Events

**WOMEN**
Kayak Singles 500 Meters
Kayak Pairs 500 Meters
Kayak Fours 500 Meters
Kayak Slalom Singles

## MEN

Olympic canoeing events are divided into two types, depending on the kind of paddle that is used. In *kayak* events, a paddle with a blade on each end is used. The canoeist alternatively paddles one blade on the left side and the other on the right side. The paddle in *Canadian* canoeing has only one blade. The canoeist sits in a half-kneeling position, switching the blade from side to side.

Canoeing contests begin with qualifying heats. The three winners of each heat advance directly to the semifinals, while the rest take part in a repêchage, or second-chance round (repêchage being the French word for "fishing again"). The four fastest participants in each repêchage race join the semifinals. Until 1984 the top six semifinalists took part in the final, while the other six took part in a *petit final* to determine seventh through twelfth places. In 1984 the final was expanded to nine participants and the *petit final* was eliminated.

## KAYAK SINGLES 500 METERS

**1896–1972** not held

**1976 Montreal** C: 18, N: 18, D: 7.30
| | | |
|---|---|---|
| 1. Vasile Diba | ROM | 1:46.41 |
| 2. Zoltán Sztanity | HUN | 1:46.95 |
| 3. Rüdiger Helm | GDR | 1:48.30 |
| 4. Herminio Menendez | SPA | 1:48.40 |
| 5. Grzegorz Śledziewski | POL | 1:48.49 |
| 6. Sergei Lizunov | SOV | 1:49.21 |
| 7. Oreste Perri | ITA | 1:50.27 |
| 8. Douglas Parnham | GBR | 1:50.33 |

**1980 Moscow** C: 17, N: 17, D: 8.1
| | | |
|---|---|---|
| 1. Vladimir Parfenovich | SOV | 1:43.43 |
| 2. John Sumegi | AUS | 1:44.12 |
| 3. Vasile Diba | ROM | 1:44.90 |
| 4. Milan Janic | YUG | 1:45.63 |
| 5. Frank-Peter Bischof | GDR | 1:45.97 |
| 6. Anders Andersson | SWE | 1:46.32 |
| 7. Ian Ferguson | NZE | 1:47.36 |
| 8. Felix Masar | CZE | 1:48.18 |

Parvenovich, a 21-year-old physical education instructor from Minsk, won three gold medals at the Moscow Olympics.

**1984 Los Angeles-Lake Casitas** C: 19, N: 19, D: 8.10
| | | |
|---|---|---|
| 1. Ian Ferguson | NZE | 1:47.84 |
| 2. Lars-Erik Moberg | SWE | 1:48.18 |
| 3. Bernard Bregeon | FRA | 1:48.41 |
| 4. Vasile Diba | ROM | 1:48.77 |
| 5. David Upson | GBR | 1:49.32 |
| 6. Daniele Scarpa | ITA | 1:49.60 |
| 7. Guillermo Del Riego | SPA | 1:49.71 |
| 8. Reiner Scholl | GER | 1:49.89 |

A trained accountant, Ian Ferguson retired from kayaking after the Moscow Olympics and opened a business in Auckland repairing and distributing video-game machines. But when the New Zealand Sports Federation offered increased financial support to kayakers, Ferguson returned to the sport and won a silver medal at the 1983 world championships. The following year, at age 32, he won three gold medals at the Los Angeles Olympics.

**1988 Seoul** C: 18, N: 18, D: 9.30.
| | | |
|---|---|---|
| 1. Zsolt Gyulay | HUN | 1:44.82 |
| 2. Andreas Stähle | GDR | 1:46.38 |
| 3. Paul MacDonald | NZE | 1:46.46 |
| 4. Michael Herbert | USA | 1:46.73 |
| 5. Karl Axel Sundqvist | SWE | 1:46.76 |
| 6. Attila Szabó | CZE | 1:47.38 |
| 7. Martin Hunter | AUS | 1:47.66 |
| 8. Dirk Joestel | GER | 1:47.91 |

## KAYAK SINGLES 1000 METERS

**1896–1904** not held

**1906 Athens** C: 2, N: 1.
| | | |
|---|---|---|
| 1. Delaplane | FRA | 5:53.4 |
| 2. Larran | FRA | 6:07.2 |

**1908–1932** not held

**1936 Berlin** C: 15, N: 15, D: 8.8.
| | | |
|---|---|---|
| 1. Gregor Hradetzky | AUT | 4:22.9 |
| 2. Helmut Cämmerer | GER | 4:25.6 |
| 3. Jacobus Kraaier | HOL | 4:35.1 |
| 4. Ernest Riedel | USA | 4:38.1 |
| 5. Joel Rahmqvist | SWE | 4:39.5 |
| 6. Henri Eberhardt | FRA | 4:41.2 |
| 7. Birger Johansson | FIN | 4:42.2 |
| 8. Iversen | NOR | 4:44.2 |

**1948 London** C: 15, N: 15, D: 8.12.
| | | |
|---|---|---|
| 1. Gert Fredriksson | SWE | 4:33.2 |
| 2. Johan Frederik Kobberup | DEN | 4:39.9 |
| 3. Henri Eberhardt | FRA | 4:41.4 |
| 4. Hans Martin Gulbrandsen | NOR | 4:41.7 |
| 5. Willem Frederik van der Kroft | HOL | 4:43.5 |
| 6. Harry Åkerfelt | FIN | 4:44.2 |
| 7. Lubomir Vambera | CZE | 4:44.3 |
| 8. Walter Piemann | AUT | 4:50.3 |

In the first heat Fredricksson showed his superiority by casually lying in fourth place for the first 950 meters and then sprinting at the end to take first. The final was no contest, as Fredriksson attained the longest winning margin in any Olympic kayak final other than 10,000 meters.

**1952 Helsinki** C: 20, N: 20, D: 7.28.
| | | |
|---|---|---|
| 1. Gert Fredriksson | SWE | 4:07.9 |
| 2. Thorvald Strömberg | FIN | 4:09.7 |
| 3. Louis Gantois | FRA | 4:20.1 |
| 4. Willem Frederik van der Kroft | HOL | 4:20.8 |
| 5. Meinrad Miltenberger | GER | 4:21.6 |
| 6. Lubomir Vambera | CZE | 4:24.0 |
| 7. Hendrik Verbrugghe | BEL | 4:25.0 |
| 8. Lev Nikitin | SOV | 4:26.2 |

Fredriksson started a long, sustained sprint from the halfway mark, which wore down his opponents and allowed him to turn the tables on Strömberg, who had beaten him the previous evening in the 10,000 meters.

**1956 Melbourne** C: 13, N: 13, D: 12.1.
| | | |
|---|---|---|
| 1. Gert Fredriksson | SWE | 4:12.8 |
| 2. Igor Pissaryev | SOV | 4:15.3 |
| 3. Lajos Kiss | HUN | 4:16.2 |
| 4. Stefan Kaplaniak | POL | 4:19.8 |
| 5. Louis Gantois | FRA | 4:22.1 |
| 6. Ladislav Čepčianský | CZE | 4:23.2 |
| 7. Villy Christiansen | DEN | 4:25.2 |
| 8. Ernst Steinhauer | GER | 4:25.5 |

Fredriksson earned his fifth individual Olympic gold medal.

**1960 Rome** C: 22, N: 22, D: 8.29.
| | | |
|---|---|---|
| 1. Erik Hansen | DEN | 3:53.00 |
| 2. Imre Szöllösi | HUN | 3:54.02 |
| 3. Gert Fredriksson | SWE | 3:55.89 |
| 4. Ibragim Khasanov | SOV | 3:56.38 |
| 5. Ronald Rhodes | GBR | 4:01.15 |
| 6. Rolf Olsen | NOR | 4:02.31 |
| 7. Wolfgang Lange | GDR | 4:03.05 |
| 8. Simo Kusimanen | FIN | 4:03.66 |

**1964 Tokyo** C: 15, N: 15, D: 10.22.
| | | |
|---|---|---|
| 1. Rolf Peterson | SWE | 3:57.13 |
| 2. Mihály Hesz | HUN | 3:57.28 |
| 3. Aurel Vernescu | ROM | 4:00.77 |
| 4. Erich Suhrbier | GER | 4:01.62 |
| 5. Günther Pfaff | AUT | 4:03.56 |
| 6. Antonius Geurts | HOL | 4:04.48 |
| 7. Erik Hansen | DEN | 4:04.72 |
| 8. Alistair Wilson | GBR | 4:05.80 |

Mihály Hesz and Aurel Vernescu, the reigning world champion, were the favorites, but were upset by Rolf Peterson, a 22-year-old student from Halmstead.

**1968 Mexico City** C: 20, N: 20, D: 10.25.
| | | |
|---|---|---|
| 1. Mihály Hesz | HUN | 4:02.63 |
| 2. Aleksandr Shaparenko | SOV | 4:03.58 |
| 3. Erik Hansen | DEN | 4:04.39 |
| 4. Wladyslaw Szuszkiewicz | POL | 4:06.36 |
| 5. Rolf Peterson | SWE | 4:07.86 |
| 6. Václav Mára | CZE | 4:09.35 |
| 7. Andrei Contolenco | ROM | 4:09.96 |
| 8. Wolfgang Lange | GDR | 4:10.03 |

Lying fifth at the halfway mark, Hesz waited to make his move until there were only 200 meters to go. In the last 100 meters he passed Hansen, the 1960 Olympic champion, and Shaparenko, the reigning world champion.

**1972 Munich** C: 24, N: 24, D: 9.9.
| | | |
|---|---|---|
| 1. Aleksandr Shaparenko | SOV | 3:48.06 |
| 2. Rolf Peterson | SWE | 3:49.38 |
| 3. Géza Csapó | HUN | 3:49.38 |
| 4. Jean-Pierre Burny | BEL | 3:50.29 |
| 5. Ladislav Souček | CZE | 3:51.05 |
| 6. Joachim Mattern | GDR | 3:51.94 |
| 7. Erik Hansen | DEN | 3:52.15 |
| 8. Grzegorz Śledziewski | POL | 3:53.22 |

**1976 Montreal** C: 19, N: 19, D: 7.31.
1. Rüdiger Helm          GDR   3:48.20
2. Géza Csapó            HUN   3:48.84
3. Vasile Diba           ROM   3:49.65
4. Oreste Perri          ITA   3:51.13
5. Aleksandr Shaparenko  SOV   3:51.45
6. Berndt Andersson      SWE   3:52.46
7. Douglas Parnham       GBR   3:52.64
8. Grzegorz Śledziewski  POL   3:54.29

In the opening heats Oreste Perri, the world champion, and Vasile Diba were disqualified for using underweight boats. However, the decision was reversed when the judges announced that the super sensitive electronic scales had responded to a change in atmospheric pressure. Helm made his move in the last quarter of the race, passed Csapó, and shouted with joy as he stormed across the finish line. At 19, he was the youngest competitor in the event.

**1980 Moscow** C: 20, N: 20, D: 8.2.
1. Rüdiger Helm      GDR   3:48.77
2. Alain Lebas       FRA   3:50.20
3. Ion Birladeanu    ROM   3:50.49
4. John Sumegi       AUS   3:50.63
5. Oreste Perri      ITA   3:51.95
6. Felix Masár       CZE   3:52.19
7. Milan Janic       YUG   3:53.50
8. Ian Ferguson      NZE   3:53.78

Two hours after this race, Helm joined his teammates in winning the Kayak Fours, to bring his Olympic medal total to five: three gold and two bronze.

**1984 Los Angeles-Lake Casitas** C: 19, N: 19, D: 8.11.
1. Alan Thompson      NZE   3:45.73
2. Milan Janić        YUG   3:46.88
3. Greg Barton        USA   3:47.38
4. Kalle Sundqvist    SWE   3:48.69
5. Peter Genders      AUS   3:49.11
6. Philippe Boccara   FRA   3:49.38
7. Vasile Diba        ROM   3:51.61
8. Stephen Jackson    GBR   3:52.25

**1988 Seoul** C: 19, N: 19, D: 10.1.
1. Gregory Barton     USA   3:55.27
2. Grant Davies       AUS   3:55.28
3. André Wohllebe     GDR   3:55.55
4. Dmitri Bankovsky   SOV   3:56.49
5. Gunnar Olsson      SWE   3:56.84
6. Alan Thompson      NZE   3:56.91
7. Attila Szabó       CZE   3:57.52
8. Morten Ivarsen     NOR   3:59.18

Greg Barton was a mechanical engineer who grew up in Homer, Michigan, a small town with more pigs than human beings. He was born with two club feet, a condition that was only aggravated by four operations. In Seoul, Barton and Davies crossed the finish line in a near dead heat. Barton was told by Korean officials that he had won. Then the scoreboard flashed the news that Davies was the victor. While the Australians celebrated and Barton prepared for the final of the 1000-meter pairs, the jury of the International Canoe Federation examined the finish line photo. A few minutes later they announced that Barton had won by .005 seconds—less than 1 centimeter. Greg Barton had become the first U.S. kayaker to win an Olympic gold medal. Davies was stoic. "If that's the biggest disappointment in my life," he said, "I can handle it."

## KAYAK PAIRS 500 METERS

**1896–1972** not held

**1976 Montreal** T: 21, N: 21, D: 7.28.
1. Joachim Mattern, Bernd Olbricht         GDR   1:35.87
2. Sergei Nagorny, Vladimir Romanovsky     SOV   1:36.81
3. Larion Serghei, Policarp Malihin        ROM   1:37.43
4. José Seguin, Guiller Del Riego          SPA   1:38.50
5. József Deme, János Rátkai               HUN   1:38.81
6. Hannu Kojo, Kari Markkanen              FIN   1:39.59
7. Anders Andersson, Lars Andersson        SWE   1:39.63
8. John Southwood, John Sumegi             AUS   1:39.77

**1980 Moscow** T: 18, N: 18, D: 8.1.
1. Vladimir Parfenovich, Sergei Chukhrai   SOV   1:32.38
2. Herminio Menendez, Guillermo Del Riego  SPA   1:33.65
3. Rüdiger Helm, Bernd Olbricht            GDR   1:34.00
4. Francis Hervieu, Alain Lebas            FRA   1:36.22
5. Barry Kelly, Robert Lee                 AUS   1:36.45
6. Alexandru Giura, Ion Birladeanu         ROM   1:36.96
7. Waldemar Merk, Zdzislaw Szubski         POL   1:37.20
8. László Szabó, Zoltán Romhányi           HUN   1:37.66

**1984 Los Angeles-Lake Casitas** T: 21, N: 21, D: 8.10.
1. Ian Ferguson, Paul MacDonald            NZE   1:34.21
2. Per-Inge Bengtsson, Lars-Erik Moberg    SWE   1:35.26
3. Hugh Fisher, Alwyn Morris               CAN   1:35.41
4. Daniele Scarpa, Francesco Uberti        ITA   1:35.50
5. Nicolae Fedosei, Angelin Velea          ROM   1:35.60
6. Francis Hervieu, Daniel Legras          FRA   1:36.40
7. Matthias Seack, Oliver Seack            GER   1:36.51
8. Andrew Sheriff, Jeremy West             GBR   1:36.73

**1988 Seoul** T: 22, N: 22, D: 9.30.
1. Ian Ferguson, Paul MacDonald            NZE   1:33.98
2. Igor Nagayev, Viktor Denisov            SOV   1:34.15
3. Attila Ábrahám, Ferenc Csipes           HUN   1:34.32
4. Reiner Scholl, Thomas Pfrang            GER   1:34.40
5. Daniel Stoian, Angelin Velea            ROM   1:35.96
6. Maciej Frejmut, Wojciech Kurpiewski     POL   1:36.22
7. Kay Bluhm, André Wohllebe               GDR   1:36.49
8. Olney Kent, Terry White                 USA   1:36.62

Ferguson and MacDonald opened a big lead and managed to lunge across the finish line before the field could catch them.

# KAYAK PAIRS 1000 METERS

**1896–1932** not held

**1936 Berlin** T: 12, N: 12, D: 8.8.
1. Adolf Kainz, Alfons Dorfner — AUT — 4:03.8
2. Ewald Tilker, Fritz Bondroit — GER — 4:08.9
3. Nicolaas Tates, Willem Frederik van der Kroft — HOL — 4:12.2
4. František Brzák-Felix, Josef Dusil — CZE — 4:15.2
5. Rudolf Vilim, Werner Klingelfuss — SWI — 4:22.8
6. Edward Deir, Francis Willis — CAN — 4:24.5
7. Werner Lovgreen, Axel Svendsen — DEN — 4:26.6
DISQ: Sixten Jansson, Gunnar Lundqvist (SWE)

**1948 London** T: 16, T: 16, D: 8.12.
1. Hans Berglund, Lennart Klingström — SWE — 4:07.3
2. Ejvind Hansen, Bernhard Jensen — DEN — 4:07.5
3. Thor Axelsson, Nils Björklof — FIN — 4:08.7
4. Ivar Mathisen, Knut Östbye — NOR — 4:09.1
5. Otto Kroutil, Miloš Pech — CZE — 4:09.8
6. Cornelis Gravesteyn, Willem Pool — HOL — 4:15.8
7. Gerald Covey, Henry Harper — CAN — 4:56.8
DISQ: János Toldi, Gyula Andrási (HUN)

Toldi and Andrási were disqualified for "hanging" in the wake of another canoe. It was thought by many that the ruling was a harsh one.

**1952 Helsinki** T: 19, N: 19, D: 7.28.
1. Kurt Wires, Yrjö Hietanen — FIN — 3:51.1
2. Lars Glassér, Ingemar Hedberg — SWE — 3:51.1
3. Max Raub, Herbert Wiedermann — AUT — 3:51.4
4. Gustav Schmidt, Helmut Noller — GER — 3:51.8
5. Ivar Mathisen, Knut Östbye — NOR — 3:54.7
6. Maurice Graffen, Marcel Renaud — FRA — 3:55.1
7. István Granek, János Kulcsár — HUN — 3:55.1
8. Cornelis Koch, Abraham Klingers — HOL — 3:55.8

Wires and Hietanen, who had already won the 10,000 meter pairs, were awarded a second set of gold medals only after a photo-finish had been studied.

**1956 Melbourne** T:15, N: 15, D: 7.28.
1. Michael Scheuer, Meinrad Miltenberger — GER — 3:49.6
2. Mikhail Kaaleste, Anatoly Demitkov — SOV — 3:51.4
3. Maximilian Raub, Herbert Wiedermann — AUT — 3:55.8
4. Mircea Anastasescu, Stavru Teodorov — ROM — 3:56.1
5. Maurice Graffen, Michel Meyer — FRA — 3:58.3
6. Henri Verbrugghe, Germain van de Moere — BEL — 3:58.7
7. Walter Brown, Dennis Green — AUS — 3:59.1
8. Miroslav Jemelka, Rudolph Klabouch — CZE — 4:01.4

**1960 Rome** T: 23, N: 23, D: 8.29.
1. Gert Fredriksson, Sven-Olov Sjödelius — SWE — 3:34.73
2. György Mészáros, András Szente — HUN — 3:34.91
3. Stefan Kaplaniak, Wladislaw Zielinski — POL — 3:37.34
4. Nikolas Rudzinskas, Ivan Golovachev — SOV — 3:37.48
5. Kaj Schmidt, Vagn Schmidt — DEN — 3:39.06
6. František Riha, František Vršovsky — CZE — 3:40.78

7. Rudolf Knuppe, Antonius Geurts — HOL — 3:41.01
8. Wolfgang Lange, Dieter Krause — GDR — 3:41.46

Fredriksson completed his Olympic career with six gold medals, one silver medal, and one bronze medal. Four years later in Tokyo he was the coach of the Swedish team.

**1964 Tokyo** T: 14, N: 14, D: 10.22.
1. Sven-Olov Sjödelius, Nils Gunnar Utterberg — SWE — 3:38.54
2. Antonius Geurts, Paul Hoekstra — HOL — 3:39.30
3. Heinz Büker, Holger Zander — GER — 3:40.69
4. Haralambie Ivanov, Vasile Nicoară — ROM — 3:41.12
5. György Mészáros, Imre Szöllösi — HUN — 3:41.39
6. Cesare Beltrami, Cesare Zilioli — ITA — 3:43.55
7. Erik Kalugin, Ibragim Khasanov — SOV — 3:44.19
8. Gordan Jeffery, Adrian Powell — AUS — 3:44.52

**1968 Mexico City** T: 20, N: 20, D: 10.25.
1. Aleksandr Shaparenko, Vladimir Morozov — SOV — 3:37.54
2. Csaba Giczi, István Timár — HUN — 3:38.44
3. Gerhard Seibold, Günther Pfaff — AUT — 3:40.71
4. Paul Hoekstra, Antonius Geurts — HOL — 3:41.36
5. Lars Andersson, Nils Gunnar Utterberg — SWE — 3:41.99
6. Atanase Sciotnic, Aurel Vernescu — ROM — 3:45.18
7. Jean-Pierre Burny, Herman Naegels — BEL — 3:45.21
8. Cesare Beltrami, Cesare Zilioli — ITA — 3:46.08

**1972 Munich** T: 25, N: 25, D: 9.9.
1. Nikolai Gorbachev, Viktor Kratassyuk — SOV — 3:31.23
2. József Deme, János Rátkai — HUN — 3:32.00
3. Wladyslaw Szuszkiewicz, Rafal Piszcz — POL — 3:33.83
4. Reiner Kurth, Alexander Slatnow — GDR — 3:34.16
5. Costel Coşniţă, Vasile Simiocenco — ROM — 3:35.66
6. Jean-Pierre Cordebois, Didier Niquet — FRA — 3:36.51
7. Günther Pfaff, Helmut Hediger — AUT — 3:36.61
8. Hans-Jürgen Riemenschneider, Horst Mattern — GER — 3:38.67

**1976 Montreal** T: 24, N: 24, D: 7.31.
1. Sergei Nagorny, Vladimir Romanovsky — SOV — 3:29.01
2. Joachim Mattern, Bernd Olbricht — GDR — 3:29.33
3. Zoltán Bakó, István Szabó — HUN — 3:30.36
4. Jean-Paul Hanquier, Alain Lebas — FRA — 3:33.05
5. Guillermo Del Riego, José Seguin — SPA — 3:33.16
6. Jean-Pierre Burny, Paul Hoekstra — BEL — 3:33.86
7. Policarp Malihin, Larion Serghei — ROM — 3:34.27
8. Steve King, Denis Barre — CAN — 3:34.46

**1980 Moscow** T: 16, N: 16, D: 8.2.
1. Vladimir Parfenovich, Sergei Chukhrai — SOV — 3:26.72
2. István Szabó, István Joós — HUN — 3:28.49
3. Luis Ramos-Misione, Herminio Menendez — SPA — 3:28.66
4. Alexandru Giura, Nicolae Ticu — ROM — 3:28.94
5. Peter Hempel, Harry Nolte — GDR — 3:31.02
6. José Marrero Rodriguez, Reynaldo Cunill Infante — CUB — 3:31.12
7. Ron Stevens, Gert Lebbink — HOL — 3:33.18
8. Alan Thompson, Geoffrey Walker — NZE — 3:33.83

**1984 Los Angeles-Lake Casitas** T: 17, N: 17, D: 8.11.

| | | | |
|---|---|---|---|
| 1. | Hugh Fisher, Alwyn Morris | CAN | 3:24.22 |
| 2. | Bernard Bregeon, Patrick Lefoulon | FRA | 3:25.97 |
| 3. | Barry Kelly, Grant Kenny | AUS | 3:26.80 |
| 4. | Olney Kent, Terry White | USA | 3:27.01 |
| 5. | Matthias Seack, Oliver Seack | GER | 3:27.28 |
| 6. | Daniele Scarpa, Francesco Uberti | ITA | 3:27.46 |
| 7. | Hermino Menendez, Guillermo Del Riego | SPA | 3:27.53 |
| 8. | Bengt Andersson, Kalle Sundqvist | SWE | 3:29.39 |

Alwyn Morris, a Mohawk Indian from the Caughawaga Reserve in Quebec, carried with him to the medal ceremony a decorated eagle feather to symbolize the sharing of his victory with the native people of North America. The feather had been presented to him by a California Indian group.

**1988 Seoul** T: 20, N: 20, D: 10.1.

| | | | |
|---|---|---|---|
| 1. | Gregory Barton, Norman Bellingham | USA | 3:32.42 |
| 2. | Ian Ferguson, Paul MacDonald | NZE | 3:32.71 |
| 3. | Peter Foster, Kelvin Graham | AUS | 3:33.76 |
| 4. | Niels Ellwanger, Carsten Lömker | GER | 3:34.63 |
| 5. | Guido Behling, Torsten Krentz | GDR | 3:35.44 |
| 6. | Daniel Stoian, Angelin Velea | ROM | 3:35.75 |
| 7. | Anders Ohlsén, Hans Olsson | SWE | 3:36.13 |
| 8. | Svein Egil Solvang, Harald Amundsen | NOR | 3:38.16 |

Pre-Olympic favorites Philippe Boccara and Pascal Boucherit of France were disqualified in the semifinals when they failed to make it to the starting line on time. Barton, the son of a pig farmer, and Bellingham, the son of a CIA agent, came from behind in the last 250 meters to nip Ferguson and MacDonald, who happened to have been Bellingham's mentors.

# KAYAK FOURS 1000 METERS

**1896–1960** not held

**1964 Tokyo** T: 14, N: 14, D: 10.22.

| | | | |
|---|---|---|---|
| 1. | SOV | (Nikolai Chuzhikov, Anatoly Grischin, Vyacheslav Ionov, Vladimir Morozov) | 3:14.67 |
| 2. | GER | (Günther Perleberg, Bernhard Schulze, Friedhelm Wentzke, Holger Zander) | 3:15.39 |
| 3. | ROM | (Simion Cuciuc, Atanase Sciotnic, Mihai Turcaş, Aurel Vernescu) | 3:15.51 |
| 4. | HUN | (Imre Kemecsey, György Mészáros, András Szente, Imre Szöllösi) | 3:16.24 |
| 5. | SWE | (Rolf Peterson, Sven-Olov Sjödelius, Nils Gunnar Utterberg, Carl von Gerber) | 3:17.47 |
| 6. | ITA | (Claudio Agnisetta, Cesare Beltrami, Angelo Pedroni, Cesare Zilioli) | 3:19.32 |
| 7. | HOL | (Paul Hoekstra, Theodorus van Halteren, Guillaume Weijzen, Jan Wittenberg) | 3:19.36 |
| 8. | YUG | (Dragan Desancić, Vladimir Ignjatijević, Aleksandar Kercov, Stanisa Radmanović | 3:19.79 |

**1968 Mexico City** T: 19, N: 19, D: 10.25.

| | | | |
|---|---|---|---|
| 1. | NOR | (Steinar Admundsen, Egil Söby, Tore Berger, Jan Johansen) | 3:14.38 |
| 2. | ROM | (Anton Calenic, Dimitrie Ivanov, Haralambie Ivanov, Mihai Turcaş) | 3:14.81 |
| 3. | HUN | (Csaba Giczi, Istvan Timár, Imre Szöllösi, István Csizmadia) | 3:15.10 |
| 4. | SWE | (Per Larsson, Hans Nilsson, Tord Sahlén, Åke Sandin) | 3:16.68 |
| 5. | FIN | (Karl-Gustav von Alfthan, Heikki Mäkelä, Jorma Lehtosalo, Ilkka Nummisto) | 3:17.28 |
| 6. | GDR | (Joachim Wenzke, Klaus-Uwe Will, Erhard Riedrich, Klaus-Peter Ebeling) | 3:18.03 |
| 7. | AUS | (Helmut Hediger, Kurt Lindlgruber, Günther Pfaff, Gerhard Seibold) | 3:18.95 |
| 8. | POL | (Ewald Janusz, Ryszard Marchlik, Rafal Piszcz, Wladyslaw Zieliński) | 3:22.10 |

Much credit for the Norwegians' upset victory went to their trainer, Stein Johnson, who had successfully coached track and field, skiing, and speed skating before trying his hand at canoeing. Johnson himself placed eighth in the 1948 discus throw.

**1972 Munich** T: 20, N: 20, D: 9.9.

| | | | |
|---|---|---|---|
| 1. | SOV | (Yuri Filatov, Yuri Stezenko, Vladimir Morozov, Valery Didenko) | 3:14.02 |
| 2. | ROM | (Aurel Vernescu, Mihai Zafiu, Roman Vartolomeu, Atanase Sciotnic) | 3:15.07 |
| 3. | NOR | (Egil Söby, Steinar Amundsen, Tore Berger, Jan Johansen) | 3:15.27 |
| 4. | ITA | (Alberto Ughi, Pier Angelo Congiu, Mario Pedretti, Oreste Perri) | 3:15.60 |
| 5. | GER | (Rudolf Blass, Eberhard Fischer, Rainer Hennes, Hans-Erich Pasch) | 3:16.63 |
| 6. | HUN | (István Szabó, Peter Várhelyi, Zoltán Bakó, Csongor Vargha) | 3:16.88 |
| 7. | FIN | (Kari Markkanen, Heikki Mäkelä, Ilkka Nummisto, Jorma Lehtosalo) | 3:16.92 |
| 8. | SWE | (Lars Andersson, Nils Gunnar Utterberg, Per Larsson, Hans Nilsson) | 3:17.39 |

**1976 Montreal** T: 20, N: 20, D: 7.31.

| | | | |
|---|---|---|---|
| 1. | SOV | (Sergei Chuhrai, Aleksandr Degtiarev, Yuri Filatov, Vladimir Morozov) | 3:08.69 |
| 2. | SPA | (José Celorrio, José Diaz-Flor, Herminio Menendez, Luis Ramos Misione) | 3:08.95 |
| 3. | GDR | (Peter Bischof, Bernd Duvigneau, Rüdiger Helm, Jürgen Lehnert) | 3:10.76 |
| 4. | ROM | (Nicusor Eseanu, Vasile Simioncenco, Neculai Simioncenco, Mihai Zafiu) | 3:11.35 |
| 5. | POL | (Henryk Budzicz, Kazimierz Górecki, Grzegorz Koltan, Ryszard Oborski) | 3:12.17 |
| 6. | NOR | (Morten Moerland, Einar Rasmussen, Olaf Soeyland, Jostein Stiege) | 3:12.28 |
| 7. | BUL | (Ivan Manev, Bojidar Milenkov, Nikolai Nachev, Vasil Chilingirov) | 3:12.94 |
| 8. | HUN | (József Deme, Csaba Giczi, János Rátkai, Zoltán Romhányi) | 3:14.67 |

The Soviet team came from third place in the last 250 meters to nose out Spain, which had been the surprise winner of the 1975 world championship.

**1980 Moscow** T: 12, N; 12, D: 8.2.
1. GDR  (Rüdiger Helm, Bernd Olbricht, Harald Marg, Bernd Duvigneau)  3:13.76
2. ROM  (Mihai Zafiu, Vasile Diba, Ion Geanta, Nicusor Esanu)  3:15.35
3. BUL  (Borislav Borissov, Bozhidar Milenkov, Lazar Hristov, Ivan Manev)  3:15.46
4. POL  (Ryszard Oborski, Grzegorz Koltan, Daniel Welna, Grzegorz Śledziewski)  3:16.33
5. HUN  (József Deme, János Rátkai, József Kosztyán, Zoltán Sztaniti)  3:17.27
6. FRA  (François Barouh, Patrick Berard, Philippe Boccara, Patrick Lefoulon)  3:17.60
7. SOV  (Gennady Makhnev, Sergei Nagornyi, Aleksandr Avdyev, Vladimir Tainikov)  3:19.83
8. AUS  (Barry Kelly, Robert Lee, Ken Vidler, Crosbie Baulch)  3:19.87

**1984 Los Angeles-Lake Casitas** T: 15, N: 15, D: 8.11.
1. NZE  (Grant Bramwell, Ian Ferguson, Paul MacDonald, Alan Thompson)  3:02.28
2. SWE  (Per-Inge Bengtsson, Tommy Karls, Lars-Erik Moberg, Thomas Ohlsson)  3:02.81
3. FRA  (François Barouh, Philippe Boccara, Pascal Boucherit, Didier Vavasseur)  3:03.94
4. ROM  (Ionel Constantin, Nicolae Fedosei, Ionel Letcaie, Angelin Velea)  3:04.39
5. GBR  (Grayson Bourne, Andrew Sheriff, Kevin Smith, Jeremy West)  3:04.59
6. SPA  (Ivan Gonzalez, Luis Gregorio Ramos-Misione, Juan José Roman, Juan Manuel Sanchez)  3:04.71
7. AUS  (John Doak, Robert Doak, Raymond Martin, Scott Wooden)  3:06.02
8. GER  (Bernd Hessel, Oliver Kegel, Deiter Schmidt, Reiner Scholl)  3:06.47

**1988 Seoul** T: 18, N: 18, D: 10.1.
1. HUN  (Zsolt Gyulay, Ferenc Csipes, Sándor Hódosi, Attila Ábrahám)  3:00.20
2. SOV  (Aleksandr Motuzenko, Sergei Kirsanov, Igor Nagayev, Viktor Denisov)  3:01.40
3. GDR  (Kay Bluhm, André Wohllebe, Andreas Stähle, Hans-Jörg Bliesener)  3:02.37
4. AUS  (Bryan Thomas, Steven Wood, Grant Kenny, Paul Gilmour)  3:03.70
5. POL  Maciej Frejmut, Wojciech Kurpiewski, Grzegorz Krawców, Kazimierz Krzyżański)  3:04.73
6. GER  (Gilbert Schneider, Reiner Scholl, Dirk Joestel, Thomas Reineck)  3:05.43
7. ITA  (Beniamino Bonomi, Daniele Scarpa, Alessandro Pieri, Francesco Mandragona)  3:05.97
8. SWE  (Per-Inge Bengtsson, Lars-Erik Moberg, Karl Axel Sundkvist, Bengt Andersson)  3:06.03

The Hungarians, seventh at the halfway point, blew away the field in the third quarter.

## CANADIAN SINGLES 500 METERS

**1896–1972** not held

**1976 Montreal** C: 15, N: 15, D: 7.30.
1. Aleksandr Rogov  SOV  1:59.23
2. John Wood  CAN  1:59.58
3. Matija Ljubek  YUG  1:59.60
4. Borislav Ananiev  BUL  1:59.92
5. Wilfried Stephan  GDR  2:00.54
6. Károly Szegedi  HUN  2:01.12
7. Ivan Patzaichin  ROM  2:01.40
8. Ulrich Eicke  GER  2:02.30

John Wood thrilled the Canadian crowd of 5000 by leading from the start until the last few strokes, when he was overtaken by the favorite, Aleksandr Rogov.

**1980 Moscow** C: 11, N: 11, D: 8.1.
1. Sergei Postrekhin  SOV  1:53.37
2. Lyubomir Lyubenov  BUL  1:53.49
3. Olaf Heukrodt  GDR  1:54.38
4. Tamás Wichmann  HUN  1:54.58
5. Marek Lbik  POL  1:55.90
6. Timo Grönlund  FIN  1:55.94
7. Lipat Varabiev  ROM  1:56.80
8. Radomir Blazik  CZE  1:56.83

**1984 Los Angeles-Lake Casitas** C: 13, N: 13, D: 8.10.
1. Larry Cain  CAN  1:57.01
2. Henning Jakobsen  DEN  1:58.45
3. Costica Olaru  ROM  1:59.86
4. Philippe Renaud  FRA  1:59.95
5. Timo Grönlund  FIN  2:01.00
6. Kiyoto Inoue  JPN  2:01.79
7. Hartmut Faust  GER  2:01.86
8. Robert Rozanski  NOR  2:02.12

**1988 Seoul** C: 18, N: 18, D: 9.30.
1. Olaf Heukrodt  GDR  1:56.42
2. Mikhail Slivinsky  SOV  1:57.26
3. Martin Marinov  BUL  1:57.27
4. Attila Szabó  HUN  1:59.87
5. Jan Pinczura  POL  1:59.90
6. Aurel Macarencu  ROM  2:00.98
7. Narciso Suárez  SPA  2:01.33
8. Petr Procházka  CZE  2:01.36

Five-time world champion Olaf Heukrodt of Magdeburg moved up from last place at the halfway mark. Heukrodt, who was married to world champion swimmer Birgit Meinecke, would have been the clear favorite four years earlier in Los Angeles had not East Germany boycotted the 1984 Games.

## CANADIAN SINGLES 1000 METERS

**1896–1932** not held

**1936 Berlin** C: 6, N: 6, D: 8.8.
1. Francis Amyot          CAN    5:32.1
2. Bohuslav Karlik        CZE    5:36.9
3. Erich Koschik          GER    5:39.0
4. Otto Neumüller         AUT    5:47.0
5. Joseph Hasenfus        USA    6:02.6
6. Joe Treinen            LUX    7:39.5

Amyot, who once saved three Ottawa Rough Riders football players from drowning, took an early lead but was passed by Karlik at the 750-meter mark. A 31-year-old veteran, Amyot refused to be rattled and continued stroking smoothly, until he had burst past Karlik with 50 meters to go. Amyot was Canada's only gold medal winner at the Berlin Olympics, thus embarrassing the Canadian Olympic Committee, which had refused to pay his way.

**1948 London** C: 6, N: 6, D: 8.12.
1. Josef Holeček          CZE    5:42.0
2. Douglas Bennett        CAN    5:53.3
3. Robert Boutigny        FRA    5:55.9
4. Ingemar Andersson      SWE    6:08.0
5. Frank Havens           USA    6:14.3
6. H. E. Maidment         GBR    6:37.0

**1952 Helsinki** C: 10, N: 10, D: 7.28.
1. Josef Holeček          CZE    4:56.3
2. János Parti            HUN    5:03.6
3. Olavi Ojanperä         FIN    5:08.5
4. Frank Havens           USA    5:13:7
5. Ingemar Andersson      SWE    5:15.0
6. Ralf Berckhan          GER    5:22.8
7. Jean Molle             FRA    5:24.1
8. Vladimir Kotyrev       SOV    5:24.5

**1956 Melbourne** C: 9, N: 9, D: 12.1.
1. Leon Rotman            ROM    5:05.3
2. István Hernek          HUN    5:06.2
3. Gennady Bukharin       SOV    5:12.7
4. Karel Hradil           CZE    5:15.9
5. Franz Johannsen        GER    5:18.6
6. Verner Wettersten      SWE    5:28.0
7. Bryan Harper           AUS    5:37.6
8. George Bossy           CAN    5:39.4

**1960 Rome** C: 13, N: 13, D: 8.29.
1. János Parti            HUN    4:33.93
2. Aleksandr Silayev      SOV    4:34.41
3. Leon Rotman            ROM    4:35.87
4. Ove Emanuelsson        SWE    4:36.46
5. Tibor Polakovič        CZE    4:39.28
6. Detlef Lewe            GER    4:39.72
7. Don Stringer           CAN    4:40.65
8. Bogdan Ivanov          BUL    4:42.52

**1964 Tokyo** C: 11, N: 11, D: 10.22.
1. Jürgen Eschert         GDR    4:35.14
2. Andrei Igorov          ROM    4:37.89
3. Yevgeny Penyayev       SOV    4:38.31
4. András Törö            HUN    4:39.95
5. Ove Emanuelsson        SWE    4:42.70

6. Bogdan Ivanov          BUL    4:44.76
7. Paul Stahl             CAN    5:04.79
8. Dennis Van Valkenburgh USA    5:12.55

**1968 Mexico City** C: 12, N: 12, D: 10.25.
1. Tibor Tatai            HUN    4:36.14
2. Detlef Lewe            GER    4:38.31
3. Vitaly Galkov          SOV    4:40.42
4. Jiří Čtvrtečka         CZE    4:40.74
5. Boris Lyubenov         BUL    4:43.43
6. Ove Emanuelsson        SWE    4:45.80
7. Ivan Patzaichin        ROM    4:49.32
8. Andreas Weigand        USA    4:50.42

Tibor Tatai made the Hungarian team only as a reserve, but he drove the other finalists to exhaustion and won decisively.

**1972 Munich** C: 13, N: 13, D: 9.9.
1. Ivan Patzaichin        ROM    4:08.94
2. Tamás Wichmann         HUN    4:12.42
3. Detlef Lewe            GER    4:13.63
4. Dirk Weise             GDR    4:14.38
5. Vassili Yurchenko      SOV    4:14.43
6. Boris Lyubenov         BUL    4:14.65
7. Jiří Čtvrtečka         CZE    4:14.98
8. Roberto Altamirano     MEX    4:20.39

**1976 Montreal** C: 15, N: 15, D: 7.31.
1. Matija Ljubek          YUG    4:09.51
2. Vassily Urchenko       SOV    4:12.57
3. Tamás Wichmann         HUN    4:14.11
4. Borislav Ananiev       BUL    4:14.41
5. Ivan Patzaichin        ROM    4:15.08
6. Roland Iche            FRA    4:18.23
7. Wilfried Stephan       GDR    4:22.43
8. Ulrich Eicke           GER    4:22.77

Ljubek, a carpenter from Belisce, was the only finalist to paddle the second half of the race faster than the first. He was fourth at the halfway mark but won going away.

**1980 Moscow** C: 12, N: 12, D: 8.2.
1. Lyubomir Lyubenov      BUL    4:12.38
2. Sergei Postrekhin      SOV    4:13.53
3. Eckhard Leue           GDR    4:15.02
4. Libor Dvořák           CZE    4:15.25
5. Lipat Varabiev         ROM    4:16.68
6. Timo Grönlund          FIN    4:17.37
7. Thomas Falk            SWE    4:20.66
8. Matija Ljubek          YUG    4:22.40

**1984 Los Angeles-Lake Casitas** C: 11, N: 11, D: 8.11.
1. Ulrich Eicke           GER    4:06.32
2. Larry Cain             CAN    4:08.67
3. Henning Jakobsen       DEN    4:09.51
4. Timo Grönlund          FIN    4:15.58
5. Costica Olaru          ROM    4:16.39
6. Stephen Train          GBR    4:16.64
7. Bruce Merritt          USA    4:18.17
8. Kiyoto Inoue           JPN    4:18.72

**1988 Seoul** C: 15, N: 15, D: 10.1.

| | | | |
|---|---|---|---|
| 1. | Ivan Klementyev | SOV | 4:12.78 |
| 2. | Jörg Schmidt | GDR | 4:15.83 |
| 3. | Nikolai Bukhalov | BUL | 4:18.94 |
| 4. | Larry Cain | CAN | 4:20.70 |
| 5. | Aurel Macarencu | ROM | 4:21.72 |
| 6. | Imre Pulai | HUN | 4:21.86 |
| 7. | Petr Pales | CZE | 4:22.14 |
| 8. | Ivan Šabjan | YUG | 4:24.67 |

## CANADIAN PAIRS 500 METERS

**1896–1972** not held

**1976 Montreal** T: 15, N: 15, D: 7.30.

| | | | |
|---|---|---|---|
| 1. | Sergei Petrenko, Aleksandr Vinogradov | SOV | 1:45.81 |
| 2. | Andrzej Gronowicz, Jerzy Opara | POL | 1:47.77 |
| 3. | Tamás Buday, Oszkár Frey | HUN | 1:48.35 |
| 4. | Gheorghe Danilov, Gheorghe Simionov | ROM | 1:48.84 |
| 5. | Gerald Delacroix, Jean-François Millot | FRA | 1:49.74 |
| 6. | Ivan Burchin, Krasimir Hristov | BUL | 1:50.43 |
| 7. | Gregory Smith, John Wood | CAN | 1:50.74 |
| 8. | Jiři Čtvrtecka, Tomáš Sach | CZE | 1:50.85 |

**1980 Moscow** T: 10, N: 10, D: 8.1.

| | | | |
|---|---|---|---|
| 1. | László Foltán, István Vaskuti | HUN | 1:43.39 |
| 2. | Petre Capusta, Ivan Patzaichin | ROM | 1:44.12 |
| 3. | Borislav Ananiev, Nikolai Ilkov | BUL | 1:44.83 |
| 4. | Jerzy Dunajski, Marek Wisla | POL | 1:45.10 |
| 5. | Petr Kubiček, Jiři Vrdlovec | CZE | 1:46.48 |
| 6. | Sergei Petrenko, Aleksandr Vinogradov | SOV | 1:46.95 |
| 7. | Santos Magaz, Narciso Suárez | SPA | 1:48.18 |
| 8. | Bernt Lindelof, Erik Zeidlitz | SWE | 1:48.69 |

**1984 Los Angeles-Lake Casitas** T: 11, N: 11, D: 8.10.

| | | | |
|---|---|---|---|
| 1. | Matija Ljubek, Mirko Nišović | YUG | 1:43.67 |
| 2. | Ivan Patzaichin, Toma Simionov | ROM | 1:45.68 |
| 3. | Enrique Miguez, Narciso Suárez | SPA | 1:47.71 |
| 4. | Didier Hoyer, Eric Renaud | FRA | 1:47.72 |
| 5. | Steve Botting, Eric Smith | CAN | 1:48.81 |
| 6. | Wolfram Faust, Ralf Wienand | GER | 1:48.97 |
| 7. | Eric Jamieson, Andrew Train | GBR | 1:49.59 |
| 8. | Shusei Fukuzato, Hiroyuki Izumi | JPN | 1:50.22 |

Ljubek and Nišović won the gold with a devastating closing spurt that pushed them past the Romanians after 400 meters.

**1988 Seoul** T: 17, N: 17, D: 9.30.

| | | | |
|---|---|---|---|
| 1. | Viktor Reneisky, Nikolai Zhuravsky | SOV | 1:41.77 |
| 2. | Marek Dopierala, Marek Lbik | POL | 1:43.61 |
| 3. | Philippe Renaud, Joël Bettin | FRA | 1:43.81 |
| 4. | Deyan Bonev, Petar Bozhilov | BUL | 1:44.32 |
| 5. | Alexander Schuck, Thomas Zereske | GDR | 1:44.36 |
| 6. | János Kis Sarusi, István Vaskuti | HUN | 1:44.85 |
| 7. | Grigore Obreja, Gheorghe Andriev | ROM | 1:45.84 |
| 8. | Christian Frederiksen, Arne Nielsson | DEN | 1:45.90 |

Third-place finisher Philippe Renaud was the third member of his family to win a canoeing medal. His father, Marcel, earned a silver in the 10,000-meter Canadian pairs in 1956. In 1984, Philippe's brother, Eric, took a bronze in the 1000-meter Canadian pairs. In addition, his uncle, also named Marcel, placed fourth in the 1924 team pursuit cycling race.

## CANADIAN PAIRS 1000 METERS

**1896–1932** not held

**1936 Berlin** T: 5, N: 5, D: 8.8.

| | | | |
|---|---|---|---|
| 1. | Vladimir Syrovátka, Jan Brzák-Felix | CZE | 4:50.1 |
| 2. | Rupert Weinstabl, Karl Proisl | AUT | 4:53.8 |
| 3. | Frank Saker, Harvey Charters | CAN | 4:56.7 |
| 4. | Hans Wedemann, Heinrich Sack | GER | 5:00.2 |
| 5. | Clarence McNutt, Robert Graf | USA | 5:14.0 |

**1948 London** T: 8, N: 8, D: 8.12.

| | | | |
|---|---|---|---|
| 1. | Jan Brzák-Felix, Bohumil Kudrna | CZE | 5:07.1 |
| 2. | Stephen Lysak, Stephan Macknowski | USA | 5:08.2 |
| 3. | Georges Dransart, Georges Gandil | FRA | 5:15.2 |
| 4. | Douglas Bennett, Harry Poulton | CAN | 5:20.7 |
| 5. | Karl Molnar, Viktor Salmhofer | AUT | 5:37.3 |
| 6. | Gunnar Johansson, Verner Wettersten | SWE | 5:44.9 |
| 7. | J. Symons, H. Van Zwanenberg | GBR | 5:50.8 |

DNF: H. Coomans, J. Dubois (BEL), man overboard

Jan Brzák was one of the few gold medal winners at the Berlin Olympics who was able to retain his championship 12 years later in London. In 1955, when he was 43 years old, Brzák teamed with 46-year-old Bohuslav Karlik to paddle the 118 miles from Ceske Budejovice to Prague in 20 hours.

**1952 Helsinki** T: 11, N: 11, D: 7.28.

| | | | |
|---|---|---|---|
| 1. | Bent Peder Rasch, Finn Haunstoft | DEN | 4:38.3 |
| 2. | Jan Brzák-Felix, Bohumil Kudrna | CZE | 4:42.9 |
| 3. | Egon Drews, Wilfried Soltau | GER | 4:48.3 |
| 4. | Georges Dransart, Armand Loreau | FRA | 4:48.6 |
| 5. | István Bodor, József Tuza | HUN | 4:51.9 |
| 6. | Kurt Liebhart, Englebert Lulla | AUT | 4:55.8 |
| 7. | John Haas, Frank Krick | USA | 4:59.0 |
| 8. | Arthur Johnson, Thomas Hodgson | CAN | 5:01.4 |

**1956 Melbourne** T: 10, N: 10, D: 12.1.

| | | | |
|---|---|---|---|
| 1. | Alexe Dumitru, Simion Ismailciuc | ROM | 4:47.4 |
| 2. | Pavel Kharine, Gratsian Botev | SOV | 4:48.6 |
| 3. | Károly Wieland, Ferenc Mohácsi | HUN | 4:54.3 |
| 4. | Georges Dransart, Marcel Renaud | FRA | 4:57.7 |
| 5. | William Jones, Thomas Ohman | AUS | 5:03.0 |
| 6. | Otto Schindler, Walter Waldner | AUT | 5:04.4 |
| 7. | William Collins, Bert Oldershaw | CAN | 5:11.0 |

DISQ: Kai Sylvan, Gerner Christiansen (DEN)

**1960 Rome** T: 11, N: 11, D: 8.29.

| | | | |
|---|---|---|---|
| 1. | Leonid Geischtor, Sergei Makarenko | SOV | 4:17.94 |
| 2. | Aldo Dezi, Francesco La Macchia | ITA | 4:20.77 |
| 3. | Imre Farkas, András Törö | HUN | 4:20.89 |
| 4. | Igor Lipalit, Alexe Dumitru | ROM | 4:22.36 |
| 5. | Jiři Kodeš, Václav Vokal | CZE | 4:27.66 |
| 6. | Marin Gopov, Toma Sokolov | BUL | 4:31.52 |
| 7. | Willi Mehlberg, Werner Ulrich | GDR | 4:31.68 |
| 8. | Georges Turlier, Michel Picard | FRA | 4:35.48 |

**1964 Tokyo** T: 12, N: 12, D: 10.22.

| | | | |
|---|---|---|---|
| 1. | Andrey Khimich, Stepan Oschepkov | SOV | 4:04.64 |
| 2. | Jean Boudehen, Michel Chapuis | FRA | 4:06.52 |
| 3. | Peer Norrbohm Nielsen, John Sörensen | DEN | 4:07.48 |
| 4. | Antal Hajba, Árpád Soltesz | HUN | 4:08.97 |
| 5. | Igor Lipalit, Achim Sidorov | ROM | 4:09.88 |
| 6. | Klaus Böhle, Detlef Lewe | GER | 4:13.18 |
| 7. | Andor Ebert, Fred Heese | CAN | 4:21.99 |
| 8. | Miloslav Houzim, Rudolf Penkava | CZE | 4:22.89 |

**1968 Mexico City** T: 12, N: 12, D: 10.25.

| | | | |
|---|---|---|---|
| 1. | Ivan Patzaichin, Serghei Covaliov | ROM | 4:07.18 |
| 2. | Tamás Wichmann, Gyula Petrikovics | HUN | 4:08.77 |
| 3. | Naum Prokupets, Mikhail Zamotin | SOV | 4:11.30 |
| 4. | Juan Martinoz, Felix Altamirano | MEX | 4:15.24 |
| 5. | Bernt Lindelöf, Erik Zeidlitz | SWE | 4:16.60 |
| 6. | Jürgen Harpke, Helmut Wagner | GDR | 4:22.53 |
| 7. | Roland Kapf, Klaus Lewandowsky | GER | 4:26.36 |
| 8. | Ivan Vulov, Alexander Damianov | BUL | 4:26.74 |

Ivan Patzaichin and Serghei Covaliov were fishermen from the village of Crisan-Mila, in the Danube delta. Silver medalist Tamás Wichmann was a chef.

**1972 Munich** T: 16, N: 16, D: 9.9.

| | | | |
|---|---|---|---|
| 1. | Vladislavas Česiunas, Yuri Lobanov | SOV | 3:52.60 |
| 2. | Ivan Patzaichin, Serghei Covaliov | ROM | 3:52.63 |
| 3. | Fedia Damianov, Ivan Burchin | BUL | 3:58.10 |
| 4. | Hans Peter Hoffmann, Hermann Glaser | GER | 3:59.24 |
| 5. | Miklós Darvas, Péter Povázsay | HUN | 4:00.42 |
| 6. | Roland Mullen, Andreas Weigand | USA | 4,01.28 |
| 7. | Dirk Weiso, Dieter Lichtenberg | GDR | 4:01.50 |
| 8. | Berndt Lindelöf, Eric Zeidlitz | SWE | 4:01.60 |

Česiunas and Lobanov took an early lead, but at the 700-meter mark Patzaichin and Covaliov mounted a furious challenge that brought them to the finish line only three one-hundredths of a second too late.

**1976 Montreal** T: 15, N: 15, D: 7.31.

| | | | |
|---|---|---|---|
| 1. | Sergei Petrenko, Aleksandr Vinogradov | SOV | 3:52.76 |
| 2. | Gheorghe Danielov, Gheorghe Simionov | ROM | 3:54.28 |
| 3. | Tamás Buday, Oszkár Frey | HUN | 3:55.66 |
| 4. | Jerzy Opara, Andrzej Gronowicz | POL | 3:59.56 |
| 5. | Detlef Bothe, Hans-Jürgen Tode | GDR | 4:00.37 |
| 6. | Jiři Čtvrtečka, Tomáš Sach | CZE | 4:01.48 |
| 7. | Ivan Burchin, Krasimir Hristov | BUL | 4:02.44 |
| 8. | Hermann Glaser, Heinz Lucke | GER | 4:03.86 |

**1980 Moscow** T: 11, N: 11, D: 8.2.

| | | | |
|---|---|---|---|
| 1. | Ivan Patzaichin, Toma Simionov | ROM | 3:47.65 |
| 2. | Olaf Heukrodt, Uwe Madeja | GDR | 3:49.93 |
| 3. | Vassily Yurchenko, Yuri Lobanov | SOV | 3:51.28 |
| 4. | Matija Ljubek, Mirko Nišović | YUG | 3:51.30 |
| 5. | Jiři Vrdlovec, Petr Kubiček | CZE | 3:52.50 |
| 6. | Marek Dopiérala, Jan Pinczura | POL | 3:53.01 |
| 7. | Raiko Kurmadzhiev, Kamen Koutzev | BUL | 3:53.89 |
| 8. | Tamás Buday, Oszkár Frey | HUN | 3:54.31 |

**1984 Los Angeles-Lake Casitas** T: 10, N: 10, D: 8.11.

| | | | |
|---|---|---|---|
| 1. | Ivan Patzaichin, Toma Simionov | ROM | 3:40.60 |
| 2. | Matija Ljubek, Mirko Nišović | YUG | 3:41.56 |
| 3. | Didier Hoyer, Eric Renaud | FRA | 3:48.01 |
| 4. | Wolfram Faust, Ralf Wienand | GER | 3:52.69 |
| 5. | John Plankenhorn, Rodney McClain | USA | 3:52.72 |
| 6. | Enrique Miguez, Narciso Suárez | SPA | 3:56.92 |
| 7. | Steve Botting, Eric Smith | CAN | 3:56.99 |
| 8. | Arturo Ferrer, Victor Velasco | MEX | 3:57.49 |

Thirty-four-year-old Ivan Patzaichin closed out his Olympic career with four gold medals and three silvers.

**1988 Seoul** T: 17, N: 17, D: 10.1

| | | | |
|---|---|---|---|
| 1. | Victor Reneisky, Nikolai Zhuravsky | SOV | 3:48.36 |
| 2. | Olaf Heukrodt, Ingo Spelly | GDR | 3:51.44 |
| 3. | Marek Dopierala, Marek Lbik | POL | 3:54.33 |
| 4. | Christian Frederiksen, Arne Nielsson | DEN | 3:54.94 |
| 5. | Hartmut Faust, Wolfram Faust | GER | 3:55.62 |
| 6. | Grigore Obreja, Gheorghe Andriev | ROM | 3:56.56 |
| 7. | Gábor Takács, Gusztáv Leikep | HUN | 4:04.18 |
| 8. | Pascal Sylvoz, Didier Hoyer | FRA | 4:04.75 |

# KAYAK SLALOM SINGLES

This unusual event, also known as white water canoeing, requires the canoeist to paddle down an obstacle course in much the same manner as the slalom races in skiing. Each competitor runs the course twice, with only the better run, as defined by both time and penalty points, counting.

**1896–1968** not held

**1972 Munich** C: 37, N: 15, D: 8.28.

| | | | PTS |
|---|---|---|---|
| 1. | Siegbert Horn | GDR | 268.56 |
| 2. | Norbert Sattler | AUT | 270.76 |
| 3. | Harald Gimpel | GDR | 277.95 |
| 4. | Ulrich Peters | GER | 282.82 |
| 5. | Alfred Baum | GER | 288.01 |
| 6. | Marian Havliček | CZE | 289.56 |
| 7. | Eric Evans | USA | 296.34 |
| 8. | Jürgen Bremer | GDR | 303.15 |

The West Germans spent 17 million marks ($4 million) constructing an artificial river at Augsburg for the competition, and they hoped to gain several medals at the Olympics. However, a year before the Munich games, the East Germans came over, studied the facilities at Augsburg, and built an exact replica back home. In 1972 East Germany won all four canoe slalom events. Their first winner was Siegbert Horn, a 22-year-old army sergeant from Leipzig. Horn keeled over in the first run and finished 17th. But the second time he paddled a smooth race and, although his time was only the eighth best, he picked up so few penalty points that he won anyway.

**1976–1988** not held

This event will be reinstated in 1992.

## CANADIAN SLALOM SINGLES

**1896–1968** not held

**1972 Munich** C: 22, N: 9, D: 7.28.

|  |  | PTS |
|---|---|---|
| 1. Reinhard Eiben | GDR | 315.84 |
| 2. Reinhold Kauder | GER | 327.89 |
| 3. Jamie McEwan | USA | 335.95 |
| 4. Jochen Förster | GDR | 354.42 |
| 5. Wolfgang Peters | GER | 356.25 |
| 6. Jürgen Köhler | GDR | 372.88 |
| 7. Karel Tresnak | CZE | 385.07 |
| 8. Petr Sodomka | CZE | 391.11 |

The victory of Reinhard Eiben, a 20-year-old industrial blacksmith from Zwickau, came as a complete surprise. He had placed 13th at the 1971 world championships and only sixth in the East German championships. However, at the Olympics he recorded the best time in both rounds to finish well ahead of the favorite, Reinhold Kauder.

**1976–1988** not held

This event will be reinstated in 1992.

## CANADIAN SLALOM PAIRS

**1896–1968** not held

**1972 Munich** T: 20, N: 9, D: 8.30.

|  |  | PTS |
|---|---|---|
| 1. Walter Hofmann, Rolf-Dieter Amend | GDR | 310.68 |
| 2. Hans Otto Schumacher, Wilhelm Baues | GER | 311.90 |
| 3. Jean-Louis Olry, Jean-Claude Olry | FRA | 315.10 |
| 4. Jürgen Kretschmer, Klaus Trummer | GDR | 329.57 |
| 5. Jan Frączek, Ryszard Seruga | POL | 366.21 |
| 6. Janez Andrijasić, Peter Guzelj | YUG | 368.01 |
| 7. Michael Reimann, Olaf Fricke | GER | 371.86 |
| 8. Heimo Müllneritsch, Helmar Steindl | AUT | 375.14 |

**1976–1988** not held

This event will be reinstated in 1992.

# Discontinued Events

## KAYAK SINGLES 10,000 METERS

**1936 Berlin** C: 15, N: 15, D: 8.7.

| 1. Ernst Krebs | GER | 46:01.6 |
|---|---|---|
| 2. Fritz Landertinger | AUT | 46:17.7 |
| 3. Ernest Riedl | USA | 47.23.9 |
| 4. Jacobus van Tongeren | HOL | 47:31.0 |
| 5. Evert Johansson | FIN | 47:35.5 |
| 6. František Brzák-Felix | CZE | 47:36.8 |
| 7. Bruno Lips | SWI | 48:01.2 |
| 8. Sasso Sant | ITA | 49:20.0 |

**1948 London** C: 13, N: 13, D: 8.11.

| 1. Gert Fredriksson | SWE | 50:47.7 |
|---|---|---|
| 2. Kurt Wires | FIN | 51:18.2 |
| 3. Eivind Skabo | NOR | 51:35.4 |
| 4. Knud Ditlevsen | DEN | 51:54.2 |
| 5. Henri Eberhardt | FRA | 52:09.0 |
| 6. Jochem Bobeldijk | HOL | 52:13.2 |
| 7. Czeslaw Sobieraj | POL | 52:51.0 |
| 8. A. Cobiaux | BEL | 53:23.5 |

**1952 Helsinki** C: 17, N: 17, D: 7.27.

| 1. Thorvald Strömberg | FIN | 47:22.8 |
|---|---|---|
| 2. Gert Fredriksson | SWE | 47:34.1 |
| 3. Michael Scheuer | GER | 47:54.4 |
| 4. Ejvind Hansen | DEN | 47:58.8 |
| 5. Hans Martin Gulbrandsen | NOR | 48:12.9 |
| 6. Miloš Pech | CZE | 48:25.8 |
| 7. Ivan Sotnikov | SOV | 48:36.8 |
| 8. Jochem Bobeldijk | HOL | 49:36.2 |

Fredriksson spent most of the race hanging in the wake of Strömberg's bow, but when he finally made his move, the 21-year-old Finnish fisherman had saved enough for a spurt of his own and pulled away to victory.

**1956 Melbourne** C: 11, N: 11, D: 11.30.

| 1. Gert Fredriksson | SWE | 47:43.4 |
|---|---|---|
| 2. Ferenc Hatlaczky | HUN | 47:53.3 |
| 3. Michael Scheuer | GER | 48:00.3 |
| 4. Thorvald Strömberg | FIN | 48:15.8 |
| 5. Igor Pissaryev | SOV | 49:58.2 |
| 6. Ladislav Čepciansky | CZE | 50:08.2 |
| 7. Svend Fromming | DEN | 50:10.0 |
| 8. Knut Östbye | NOR | 51:28.2 |

---

**1976–1988** not held

This event will be reinstated in 1992.

## FOLDING KAYAK SINGLES
## 10,000 METERS

**1936 Berlin** C: 13, N: 13, D: 8.7.
1. Gregor Hradetzky     AUT  50:01.2
2. Henri Eberhardt      FRA  50:04.2
3. Xaver Hörmann        GER  50:06.5
4. Lennart Dozzi        SWE  51:23.8
5. František Svoboda     CZE  51:52.5
6. Hans Mooser          SWE  52:43.8
7. Frans Nordberg       FIN  52:45.8
8. George Lawton        GBR  52:50.0

## KAYAK PAIRS 10,000 METERS

**1936 Berlin** T: 12, N: 12, D: 8.7.
1. Paul Wevers, Ludwig Landen          GER  41:45.0
2. Viktor Kalisch, Karl Steinhuber     AUT  42:05.4
3. Tage Falhborg, Helge Larsson        SWE  43:06.1
4. Werner Lövgreen, Axel Svendsen      DEN  44:39.8
5. Hendrik Starreveld, Gerardus Siderius  HOL  45:12.5
6. Werner Zimmermann, Othmar Bach      SWI  45:14.6
7. William Gaehler, William Lofgren    USA  45:15.4
8. Zdenek Cernicky, Jaroslav Humpal    CZE  46:05.4

**1948 London** T: 15, N: 15, D: 8.11.
1. Gunnar Åkerlund, Hans Wetterström   SWE  46:09.4
2. Ivar Mathisen, Knut Östbye          NOR  46:44.8
3. Thor Axelsson, Nils Björklof        FIN  46:48.2
4. Alfred Christensen, Finn Rasmussen  DEN  47:17.5
5. Gyula Andrási, János Urányi         HUN  47:33.1
6. Cornelius Koch, Hendrik Stroo       HOL  47:35.6
7. Ludvik Klima, K. Lomecky            CZE  48:14.9
8. Hilaire Deprez, J. Massy            BEL  48.23.1

**1952 Helsinki** T: 18, N: 18, D: 7.27.
1. Kurt Wires, Yrjö Hietanen          FIN  44:21.3
2. Gunnar Åkerlund, Hans Wetterström   SWE  44:21.7
3. Ferenc Varga, József Gurovits       HUN  44:26.6
4. Max Raub, Herbert Wiedermann        AUT  44:29.1
5. Ivar Mathiesen, Knut Östbye         NOR  45:04.7
6. Karl-Heinz Schäfer, Meinrad Miltenberger  GER  45:15.2
7. Rudolf Klabouch, Bedřich Dvořák     CZE  45:39.6
8. Ingvard Norregaard, Svend Fromming  DEN  45:59.6

Although Wires and Hietanen led from start to finish, they won by only half a meter.

**1956 Melbourne** T:12, N: 12, D: 11.30.
1. János Urányi, László Fábián         HUN  43:37.0
2. Fritz Briel, Theo Kleine            GER  43:40.6
3. Dennis Green, Walter Brown          AUS  43:43.2
4. Hans Wetterström, Carl-Axel Sundin  SWE  44:06.7
5. Yevgeny Yatsynyenki, Sergei Klimov  SOV  45:49.3
6. Miloslav Jemelka, Rudolf Klabouch   CZE  46:13.1
7. Yrjö Hietanen, Simo Kuismanen       FIN  46:40.4
8. Brian Bullivant, Raymond Blick      GBR  47:03.7

## FOLDING KAYAK PAIRS
## 10,000 METERS

**1936 Berlin** T: 13, N: 13, D: 8.7.
1. Sven Johansson, Eric Bladström      SWE  45:48.9
2. Willi Horn, Erich Hanisch           GER  45:49.2
3. Pieter Wijdekop, Cornelis Wijdekop  HOL  46:12.4
4. Adolf Kainz, Alfons Dorfner         AUT  46:26.1
5. Otokar Kouba, Ludvik Klima          CZE  47:46.2
6. Eugen Knoblauch, Emil Bottlang      SWI  47:54.4
7. John Lysak, James O'Rourke          USA  49:46.0
8. Armand Pagnoulle, Charles Pasquier  BEL  49:57.1

## KAYAK SINGLES
## RELAY 4 × 500 METERS

**1960 Rome** T: 18, N: 18, D: 8.29.
1. GDR/GER (Paul Lange, Günter Perleberg, Friedhelm Wentzke, Dieter Krause) 7:39.43
2. HUN (Imre Szöllösi, Imre Kemecsey, András Szente, György Mészáros) 7:44.02
3. DEN (Helmuth Sörensen, Arne Höyer, Erling Jessen, Erik Hansen) 7:46.09
4. POL (Stefan Kaplaniak, Wladislaw Zieliński, Ryszard Skwarski, Ryszard Marchlik) 7:49.93
5. SOV (Igor Pissaryev, Anatoly Kononyenko, Fyodor Lyakhovsky, Vladimir Natalukha) 7.50.72
6. ROM (Mircea Anastasescu, Aurel Vernescu, Ion Siderl, Stavru Teodorov) 7:53.00

## CANADIAN SINGLES 10,000 METERS

**1948 London** C: 5, N: 5, D: 8.11.
1. František Čapek       CZE  1:02:05.2
2. Frank Havens         USA  1:02:40.4
3. Norman Lane          CAN  1:04:35.3
4. Raymond Argentin     FRA  1:06:44.2
5. Ingemar Andersson    SWE  1.07.27.1

Čapek, a 33-year-old bank clerk from Prague, used a "crooked" canoe which curved at the keel, allowing him to paddle on one side and not waste energy maintaining a straight course.

**1952 Helsinki** C: 10, N: 10, D: 7.27.
1. Frank Havens         USA  57:41.1
2. Gábor Novák          HUN  57:49.2
3. Alfréd Jindra        CZE  57:53.1
4. Bengt Backlund       SWE  59:02.8
5. Norman Lane          CAN  59:26.4
6. Jarl Fagerström      FIN  59:45.9
7. Franz Johannsen      GER  1:00.26.5
8. Robert Boutigny      FRA  1:01.15.2

Jindra led most of the way, but Havens, a 28-year-old auto insurance adjuster from Arlington, Virginia, overtook him on the home stretch of the last lap and won by about 18 yards.

**1956 Melbourne** C: 9, N: 9, D: 11.30.

| | | |
|---|---|---|
| 1. Leon Rotman | ROM | 56:41.0 |
| 2. János Parti | HUN | 57:11.0 |
| 3. Gennady Bukharin | SOV | 57:14.5 |
| 4. Jiři Vokněr | CZE | 57:44.5 |
| 5. Franz Johannsen | GER | 58:50.1 |
| 6. Verner Wettersten | SWE | 59:24.7 |
| 7. Donald Stringer | CAN | 59:57.5 |
| 8. Frank Havens | USA | 1:01:23.6 |

## CANADIAN PAIRS 10,000 METERS

**1936 Berlin** T: 5, N: 5, D: 8.7.

| | | |
|---|---|---|
| 1. Václav Mottl, Ždenek Škrdlant | CZE | 50:35.5 |
| 2. Frank Saker, Harvey Charters | CAN | 51:15.8 |
| 3. Rupert Weinstabl, Karl Proisl | AUT | 51:28.0 |
| 4. Walter Schuur, Christian Holzenberg | GER | 52:35.6 |
| 5. Joseph Hasenfus, Walter Hasenfus | USA | 57:06.2 |

**1948 London** T: 6, N: 6, D: 8.11.

| | | |
|---|---|---|
| 1. Stephen Lysak, Stephan Macknowski | USA | 55:55.4 |
| 2. Václav Havel, Jiři Pecka | CZE | 57:38.5 |
| 3. Georges Dransart, Georges Gandil | FRA | 58:00.8 |
| 4. Karl Molnar, Viktor Salmhofer | AUT | 58:59.3 |
| 5. Bert Oldershaw, William Stevenson | CAN | 59:48.4 |
| 6. Gunnar Johansson, Verner Wettersten | SWE | 1:03:34.4 |

Stephen Lysak, age 26, and Stephen Macknowski, age 33, of Yonkers, New York, using a homemade mahogany canoe, took the lead after only five strokes and went on to win by an enormous margin.

**1952 Helsinki** T: 9, N: 9. D: 7.27.

| | | |
|---|---|---|
| 1. Georges Turlier, Jean Laudet | FRA | 54:08.3 |
| 2. Kenneth Lane, Donald Hawgood | CAN | 54:09.9 |
| 3. Egon Drews, Wilfried Soltau | GER | 54:28.1 |
| 4. Valentin Orischenko, Nikolai Perevozchikov | SOV | 54:36.6 |
| 5. John Haas, Frank Krick | USA | 54:42.5 |
| 6. Bohuslav Karlík, Oldřich Lomecky | CZE | 55:10.9 |
| 7. Ernö Söptei, Róbert Söptei | HUN | 55:35.3 |
| 8. Rune Blomqvist, Harry Lindbeck | SWE | 55:41.3 |

**1956 Melbourne** T: 10, N: 10, D: 11.30.

| | | |
|---|---|---|
| 1. Pavel Kharin, Gratsian Botev | SOV | 54:02.4 |
| 2. Georges Dransart, Marcel Renaud | FRA | 54:48.3 |
| 3. Imre Farkas, József Hunics | HUN | 55:15.6 |
| 4. Egon Drews, Wilfried Soltau | GER | 55:21.1 |
| 5. Alexe Dumitru, Simion Ismailciuc | ROM | 55:51.1 |
| 6. Aksel Dunn, Finn Haunstoft | DEN | 55:54.3 |
| 7. William Jones, Thomas Ohman | AUS | 56:18.6 |
| 8. Otto Schindler, Walter Waldner | AUT | 56:48.7 |

# WOMEN
## KAYAK SINGLES 500 METERS

**1896–1936** not held

**1948 London** C: 10, N: 10, D: 8.12.

| | | |
|---|---|---|
| 1. Karen Hoff | DEN | 2:31.9 |
| 2. Alida van der Anker-Doedens | HOL | 2:32.8 |
| 3. Fritzi Schwingl | AUT | 2:32.9 |
| 4. Klára Bánfalvi | HUN | 2:33.8 |
| 5. Ružena Koštalová | CZE | 2:38.2 |
| 6. Sylvi Saimo | FIN | 2:38.4 |
| 7. A. Van Marcke | BEL | 2:43.4 |
| 8. C. Vautrin | FRA | 2:44.4 |

**1952 Helsinki** C: 13, N: 13, D: 7.28.

| | | |
|---|---|---|
| 1. Sylvi Saimo | FIN | 2:18.4 |
| 2. Gertrude Liebhart | AUT | 2:18.8 |
| 3. Nina Savina | SOV | 2:21.6 |
| 4. Alida van der Anker-Doedens | HOL | 2:22.3 |
| 5. Bodil Svendsen | DEN | 2:22.7 |
| 6. Cecília Hartmann | HUN | 2:23.0 |
| 7. Marta Kroutilová | CZE | 2:23.8 |
| 8. Josefa Köster | GER | 2:25.9 |

**1956 Melbourne** C: 10, N: 10, D: 12.1.

| | | |
|---|---|---|
| 1. Yelisaveta Dementyeva | SOV | 2:18.9 |
| 2. Therese Zenz | GER | 2:19.6 |
| 3. Tove Soby | DEN | 2:22.3 |
| 4. Cecília Berkes (Hartmann) | HUN | 2:23.5 |
| 5. Edith Cochrane | AUS | 2:23.8 |
| 6. Daniela Walkowiak | POL | 2:24.1 |
| 7. Patricia Moody | GBR | 2:25.3 |
| 8. Eva Marion | FRA | 2:27.9 |

Dementyeva false-started once, then spurted into the lead and held on to win by six feet. Zenz had competed at the 1952 Helsinki Olympics as a representative of the then independent nation of Saar.

**1960 Rome** C: 13, N: 13, D: 8.29.

| | | |
|---|---|---|
| 1. Antonina Seredina | SOV | 2:08.08 |
| 2. Therese Zenz | GER | 2:08.22 |
| 3. Daniela Walkowiak | POL | 2:10.46 |
| 4. Annemarie Werner-Hansen | DEN | 2:13.88 |
| 5. Klára Fried-Bánfalvi | HUN | 2:14.02 |
| 6. Else Marie Lindmark | SWE | 2:14.17 |
| 7. Alberta Zanardi | ITA | 2:14.31 |
| 8. Eva Kutova | CZE | 2:15.30 |

**1964 Tokyo** C: 13, N: 13, D: 10.22.

| | | |
|---|---|---|
| 1. Lyudmila Khvedosyuk | SOV | 2:12.87 |
| 2. Hilde Lauer | ROM | 2:15.35 |
| 3. Marcia Jones | USA | 2:15.68 |
| 4. Elke Felten | GER | 2:15.94 |
| 5. Else Marie Ljungdahl (Lindmark) | SWE | 2:16.00 |
| 6. Hanneliese Spitz | AUT | 2:16.11 |

| | | | |
|---|---|---|---|
| 7. | Daniela Pilecka | POL | 2:17.52 |
| 8. | Mária Roka | HUN | 2:17.85 |

**1968 Mexico City** C: 13, N: 13, D: 10.25.

| | | | |
|---|---|---|---|
| 1. | Lyudmila Pinayeva (Khvedosyuk) | SOV | 2:11.09 |
| 2. | Renate Breuer | GER | 2:12.71 |
| 3. | Victoria Dumitru | ROM | 2:13.22 |
| 4. | Marcia Smoke (Jones) | USA | 2:14.68 |
| 5. | Ivona Vávrová | CZE | 2:14.78 |
| 6. | Anita Nüssner | GDR | 2:16.02 |
| 7. | Ingmårie Svensson | SWE | 2:16.04 |
| 8. | Mieke Jaapies | HOL | 2:18.38 |

In the middle of the race the ninth finalist, Anna Pfeffer of Hungary, spun over in the water and was rescued by a special emergency craft following the kayakists. One and a half hours later she was back in action, winning a silver medal in the kayak pairs.

**1972 Munich** C: 15, N: 15, D: 9.5.

| | | | |
|---|---|---|---|
| 1. | Yulia Ryabchinskaya | SOV | 2:03.17 |
| 2. | Mieke Jaapies | HOL | 2:04.03 |
| 3. | Anna Pfeffer | HUN | 2:05.50 |
| 4. | Irene Pepinghege | GER | 2:06.55 |
| 5. | Bettina Müller | GDR | 2:06.85 |
| 6. | Maria Nichiforov | ROM | 2:07.13 |
| 7. | Kate Olsen | DEN | 2:07.16 |
| 8. | Ingmårie Svensson | SWE | 2:07.61 |

Four months after winning her gold medal, Ryabchinskaya, exhausted and flushed after a winter training session, fell into the cold water of Lake Paleostomi in Soviet Georgia and died as a result of abrupt cooling. Every spring, in Moscow, an international competition is held in her honor.

**1976 Montreal** C: 15, N: 15, D: 7.30.

| | | | |
|---|---|---|---|
| 1. | Carola Zirzow | GDR | 2:01.05 |
| 2. | Tatiana Korshunova | SOV | 2:03.07 |
| 3. | Klára Rajnai | HUN | 2:05.01 |
| 4. | Ewa Kamińska | POL | 2:05.16 |
| 5. | Maria Mihoreanu | ROM | 2:05.40 |
| 6. | Anastazie Hajná | CZE | 2:06.72 |
| 7. | Julie Leach | USA | 2:06.92 |
| 8. | Irene Peppinghege | GER | 2:07.80 |

East German boat designers spent a month in Montreal studying the layout of the Olympic course. Then they went home and constructed special fiberglass canoes and kayaks that curved inward when placed in the water, becoming longer and faster. Using one of these kayaks, Carola Zirzow, a 5-foot 10-inch, 21-year-old student of physiotherapy, overcame a poor start to take first place.

**1980 Moscow** C: 11, N: 11, D: 8.1.

| | | | |
|---|---|---|---|
| 1. | Birgit Fischer | GDR | 1:57.96 |
| 2. | Vania Gesheva | BUL | 1:59.48 |
| 3. | Antonina Melnikova | SOV | 1:59.66 |
| 4. | Maria Stefan | ROM | 2:00.90 |
| 5. | Ewa Eichler | POL | 2:01.23 |
| 6. | Agneta Andersson | SWE | 2:01.33 |

| | | | |
|---|---|---|---|
| 7. | Katalin Povázsán | HUN | 2:01.52 |
| 8. | Beatrice Knopf | FRA | 2:02.91 |

**1984 Los Angeles-Lake Casitas** C: 11, N: 11, D: 8.10.

| | | | |
|---|---|---|---|
| 1. | Agneta Andersson | SWE | 1:58.72 |
| 2. | Barbara Schüttpelz | GER | 1:59.93 |
| 3. | Annemiek Derckx | HOL | 2:00.11 |
| 4. | Tecla Marinescu | ROM | 2:00.12 |
| 5. | Beatrice Basson | FRA | 2:01.21 |
| 6. | Sheila Conover | USA | 2:02.38 |
| 7. | Lucie Guay | CAN | 2:02.49 |
| 8. | Elizabeth Blencowe | AUS | 2:02.63 |

**1988 Seoul** C: 15, N: 15, D: 9.30.

| | | | |
|---|---|---|---|
| 1. | Vania Gesheva | BUL | 1:55.19 |
| 2. | Birgit Schmidt (Fischer) | GDR | 1:55.31 |
| 3. | Izabela Dylewska | POL | 1:57.38 |
| 4. | Rita Köbán | HUN | 1:57.58 |
| 5. | Yvonne Brandstrup Knudsen | DEN | 1:58.80 |
| 6. | Traci Phillips | USA | 2:00.81 |
| 7. | Galina Savenko | SOV | 2:00.88 |
| 8. | Agneta Andersson | SWE | 2:01.00 |

In 1980, Birgit Schmidt, then 18 years old, defeated Vania Gesheva to become the youngest-ever winner of an Olympic canoeing event. If East Germany had not boycotted the 1984 Games, she would have been favored to win all three women's kayak events, just as she did in the world championships of 1981, 1982, 1983, 1985, and 1987. She took off 1986 to have a baby. Schmidt was the overwhelming favorite again in Seoul but was upset in the final by the fast-finishing Gesheva.

## KAYAK PAIRS 500 METERS

**1896–1956** not held

**1960 Rome** T: 11, N: 11, D: 8.29.

| | | | |
|---|---|---|---|
| 1. | Maria Chubina, Antonina Seredina | SOV | 1:54.76 |
| 2. | Therese Zenz, Ingrid Hartmann | GER | 1:56.66 |
| 3. | Klára Fried-Bánfalvi, Vilma Egresi | HUN | 1:58.22 |
| 4. | Daniela Walkowiak, Janina Mondalska | POL | 1:59.03 |
| 5. | Annemarie Werner-Hansen, Birgit Jensen | DEN | 2:01.36 |
| 6. | Maria Szekeli, Elena Lipalit | ROM | 2:01.68 |
| 7. | Gabriella Cotta Ramusino, Luciana Guindani | ITA | 2:02.47 |
| 8. | Eva Kutova, Eva Kolinska | CZE | 2:02.76 |

**1964 Tokyo** T: 10, N: 10, D: 10.22.

| | | | |
|---|---|---|---|
| 1. | Roswitha Esser, Annemarie Zimmermann | GER | 1:56.95 |
| 2. | Francine Fox, Gloriane Perrier | USA | 1:59.16 |
| 3. | Hilde Lauer, Cornelia Sideri | ROM | 2:00.25 |
| 4. | Nina Gruzintseva, Antonina Seredina | SOV | 2:00.69 |
| 5. | Birthe Hansen, Annemarie Werner-Hansen | DEN | 2:00.88 |
| 6. | Else-Marie Ljungdahl (Lindmark), Eva-Britt Sisth | SWE | 2:02.24 |
| 7. | Katalin Benkö, Mária Roka | HUN | 2:03.67 |
| 8. | Izabella Antonowicz, Daniela Pilecka | POL | 2:04.31 |

Silver medalist Francine Fox was only 15 years old, while her partner, Glorianne Perrier, was 20 years older.

**1968 Mexico City** T: 11, N: 11, D: 10.25.

| | | | |
|---|---|---|---|
| 1. | Roswitha Esser, Annemarie Zimmermann | GER | 1:56.44 |
| 2. | Anna Pfeffer, Katalin Rozsnyói | HUN | 1:58.60 |
| 3. | Lyudmila Pinayeva (Khvedosyuk), Antonina Seredina | SOV | 1:58.61 |
| 4. | Valentina Serghei, Viorica Dumitru | ROM | 1:59.17 |
| 5. | Anita Kobuss, Karin Haftenberger | GDR | 2:00.18 |
| 6. | Mieke Jaapies, Tjeertje Bergers-Duif | HOL | 2:02.02 |
| 7. | Sperry Rademaker, Marcia Smoke (Jones) | USA | 2:02.97 |
| 8. | Lesley Oliver, Barbara Mean | GBR | 2:03.70 |

**1972 Munich** T: 12, N: 12, D: 9.9.

| | | | |
|---|---|---|---|
| 1. | Lyudmila Pinayeva (Khvedosyuk), Ekaterina Kuryshko | SOV | 1:53.50 |
| 2. | Ilse Kaschube, Petra Grabowski | GDR | 1:54.30 |
| 3. | Maria Nichiforov, Victoria Dumitru | ROM | 1:55.01 |
| 4. | Anna Pfeffer, Katalin Hollósy | HUN | 1:55.12 |
| 5. | Roswitha Esser, Renate Breuer | GER | 1:55.64 |
| 6. | Izabella Antonowicz-Szuszkiewicz, Ewa Grajkowska | POL | 1:57.45 |
| 7. | Mieke Jaapies, Maria van der Holst | HOL | 1:58.11 |
| 8. | Natasha Petrova, Petrana Koleva | BUL | 1:59.40 |

**1976 Montreal** T: 14, N: 14, D: 7.30.

| | | | |
|---|---|---|---|
| 1. | Nina Gopova, Galina Kreft | SOV | 1:51.15 |
| 2. | Anna Pfeffer, Klára Rajnai | HUN | 1:51.69 |
| 3. | Bärbel Köster, Carola Zirzow | GDR | 1:51.81 |
| 4. | Nastasia Nichitov, Agafia Orlov | ROM | 1:53.77 |
| 5. | Barbara Lewe-Pohlmann, Heiderose Wallbaum | GER | 1:53.86 |
| 6. | Maria Kazanecka, Katarzyna Kulczak | POL | 1:55.05 |
| 7. | Maria Mincheva, Natasha Yanakieva | BUL | 1:55.95 |
| 8. | Anne Dodge, Susan Holloway | CAN | 1:56.75 |

**1980 Moscow** T: 12, N: 12, D: 8.1.

| | | | |
|---|---|---|---|
| 1. | Carsta Genäuss, Martina Bischof | GDR | 1:43.88 |
| 2. | Galina Alexeyeva, Nina Trofimova | SOV | 1:46.91 |
| 3. | Éva Rakusz, Mária Zakariás | HUN | 1:47.95 |
| 4. | Elisabeta Babeanu, Agafia Buhaev | ROM | 1:48.04 |
| 5. | Agneta Andersson, Karin Olsson | SWE | 1:49.27 |
| 6. | Anne-Marie Loriot, Valerie Leclerc | FRA | 1:49.48 |
| 7. | Ewa Eichler, Ewa Wojtaszek | POL | 1:51.31 |
| 8. | Frances Wetherall, Lesley Smither | GBR | 1:52.76 |

Genäuss and Bischof achieved the most decisive victory ever in women's Olympic canoeing.

**1984 Los Angeles-Lake Casitas** T: 10, N: 10, D: 8.10.

| | | | |
|---|---|---|---|
| 1. | Agneta Andersson, Anna Olsson | SWE | 1:45.25 |
| 2. | Alexandra Barre, Susan Holloway | CAN | 1:47.13 |
| 3. | Josefa Idem, Barbara Schüttpelz | GER | 1:47.32 |
| 4. | Agafia Constantin, Nastasia Ionescu | ROM | 1:47.56 |
| 5. | Shirley Dery, Leslie Klein | USA | 1:49.51 |
| 6. | Bernadette Hettich, Cathérine Mathevon | FRA | 1:51.40 |
| 7. | Kari Ofstad, Anne Wahl | NOR | 1:51.61 |
| 8. | Lucy Perrett, Lesley Smither | GBR | 1:51.73 |

Silver medalist Sue Holloway had represented Canada in nordic skiing in 1976.

**1988 Seoul** T: 15, N: 15, D: 9.30.

| | | | |
|---|---|---|---|
| 1. | Birgit Schmidt (Fischer), Anke Nothnagel | GDR | 1:43.46 |
| 2. | Vania Gesheva, Diana Paliiska | BUL | 1:44.06 |
| 3. | Annemiek Derckx, Annemarie Cox | HOL | 1:46.00 |
| 4. | Erika Mészáros, Éva Rakusz | HUN | 1:46.58 |
| 5. | Irina Salomykova, Irina Khmelevskaya | SOV | 1:47.68 |
| 6. | Anna Olsson, Agneta Andersson | SWE | 1:48.39 |
| 7. | Sheila Conover, Cathy Marino-Geers | USA | 1:50.33 |
| 8. | Barbara Olmsted, Sheila Taylor | CAN | 1:51.03 |

One and a half hours after being upset in the singles final, Birgit Schmidt teamed with Anke Nothnagel to win a gold medal in the pairs.

## KAYAK FOURS 500 METERS

**1896–1980** not held

**1984 Los Angeles-Lake Casitas** T: 7, N: 7, D: 8.11.

| | | | |
|---|---|---|---|
| 1. | ROM | (Agafia Constantin, Nastasia Ionescu, Tecla Marinescu, Maria Stefan) | 1:38.34 |
| 2. | SWE | (Agneta Andersson, Anna Olsson, Eva Karlsson, Susanne Wiberg) | 1:38.87 |
| 3. | CAN | (Alexandra Barre, Lucie Guay, Susan Holloway, Barbara Olmsted) | 1:39.40 |
| 4. | USA | (Sheila Conover, Shirley Dery, Leslie Klein, Ann Turner) | 1:40.49 |
| 5. | GER | (Josefa Idem, Regina Schmidt, Barbara Schüttpelz, Judith Skolnik) | 1:42.68 |
| 6. | NOR | (Wenche Legraid, Kari Ofstad, Ingeborg Rasmussen, Anne Wahl) | 1:42.97 |
| 7. | GBR | (Janine Lawler, Lucy Perrett, Lesley Smither, Deborah Watson) | 1:46.30 |

**1988 Seoul** T: 13, N: 13, D: 10.1.

| | | | |
|---|---|---|---|
| 1. | GDR | (Birgit Schmidt [Fischer], Anke Nothnagel, Ramona Portwich, Heike Singer) | 1:40.78 |
| 2. | HUN | (Erika Géczi, Erika Mészáros, Éva Rakusz, Rita Kóbán) | 1:41.88 |
| 3. | BUL | (Vania Gesheva, Diana Paliiska, Ogniana Petkova, Borislava Ivanova) | 1:42.63 |
| 4. | SOV | (Irina Salomykova, Irina Khmelevskaya, Alexandra Apanovich, Nadezhda Kovalevich) | 1:44.26 |
| 5. | GER | (Josefa Idem, Claudia Österheld, Andrea Martin, Ruth Domgörgen) | 1:45.62 |
| 6. | SWE | (Anna Olsson, Agneta Andersson, Susanne Wiberg, Liselotte Olsson) | 1:45.67 |
| 7. | DEN | (Yvonne Brandstrup Knudsen, Susanne Sanggaard Petersen, Jeanette Brandstrup Knudsen, Birgitte Lynning Froberg) | 1:47.10 |
| 8. | POL | (Bozena Ksiazek, Jolanta Lukaszewicz, Elżbieta Urbanczyk, Katarzyna Weiss) | 1:47.40 |

## KAYAK SLALOM SINGLES

**1896–1968** not held

**1972 Munich** C: 22, N: 10, D: 8.30.

|  | | | PTS |
|---|---|---|---|
| 1. | Angelika Bahmann | GDR | 364.50 |
| 2. | Gisela Grothaus | GER | 398.15 |
| 3. | Magdalena Wunderlich | GER | 400.50 |
| 4. | Maria Ćwiertniewicz | POL | 432.30 |
| 5. | Kunegunda Godawska | POL | 441.05 |
| 6. | Victoria Brown | GBR | 443.71 |
| 7. | Ulrike Deppe | GER | 456.44 |
| 8. | Bohumila Kapplova | CZE | 460.16 |

**1976–1988** not held

This event will be reinstated in 1992.

# CYCLING

**MEN**
1000-Meter Sprint (Scratch)
1000-Meter Time Trial
4000-Meter Individual Pursuit
4000-Meter Team Pursuit
50-Kilometer Points Race
Road Race
Team Time Trial
Discontinued Events

**WOMEN**
1000-Meter Sprint (Scratch)
4000-Meter Individual Pursuit
Road Race

## MEN

### 1000-METER SPRINT (SCRATCH)

The individual sprint, or scratch, is a tactical, and some-times violent, race. For the first 800 meters the cyclists circle the track, carefully maneuvering for position, usu-ally trying to avoid taking the lead so that they can take advantage of the slipstream created by the leader. Then they sprint for the finish line. Times are usually taken only for the final 200 meters.

Since 1928 separate races have been held to determine first place and third place. Since 1976 all four defeated quarterfinalists have raced off for places 5 through 8.

**1896 Athens** C: 4, N: 3, D: 4.11.
**(2000 Meters)**

| | | |
|---|---|---|
| 1. Paul Masson | FRA | 4:58.2 |
| 2. Stamatios Nikolopoulos | GRE | 5:00.2 |
| 3. Léon Flameng | FRA | — |
| 4. Joseph Rosemeyer | GER | — |

**1900 Paris** C: 26, N: 5, D: 9.13.
**(2000 Meters)**

| | | |
|---|---|---|
| 1. Georges Taillandier | FRA | 2:52.0 (last 200 meters 13.0) |
| 2. Fernand Sanz | FRA | — |
| 3. John Henry Lake | USA | — |

**1904** not held

**1906 Athens** C: 26, N: 9, D: 4.23.

| | | |
|---|---|---|
| 1. Francesco Verri | ITA | 1:42.2 |
| 2. H.C. Bouffler | GBR | — |
| 3. Eugène Debougnie | BEL | — |

**1908 London** C: 40, N: 9, D: 7.16.

The final was declared void because the time limit was exceeded. The finalists were: 1. Maurice Schilles (FRA), 2. Ben Jones (GBR). DNF: Victor Johnson (GBR) and Charles Kingsbury (GBR).

Johnson suffered a punctured tire shortly after the start. The other three crawled around the track, carefully jockeying for position. At the beginning of the last bank, Kingsbury also punctured. Then the remaining two raced to the finish line, with Schilles winning by inches. How-ever, the time limit of 1 minute 45 seconds had been exceeded, so the race was declared void. Much to the surprise of most of those present, the judges of the Na-tional Cyclists' Union refused to allow the race to be rerun.

**1912** not held

**1920 Antwerp** C: 37, N: 11, D: 8.12.

| | | |
|---|---|---|
| 1. Maurice Peeters | HOL | 1:38.3 |
| 2. Thomas Johnson | GBR | — |
| 3. Harry Ryan | GBR | — |
| 4. Gerald Halpin (AUS), Lanusse (FRA), Fred Taylor (USA), Thurs-field (SAF), James Walker (SAF), Albert White (GBR) | | |

**1924 Paris** C: 31, N: 17, D: 7.27.

| | | |
|---|---|---|
| 1. Lucien Michard | FRA | 12.8 (last 200 meters) |
| 2. Jacob Meijer | HOL | — |
| 3. Jean Cugnot | FRA | — |

**1928 Amsterdam** C: 18, N: 18, D: 8.7.

| | | |
|---|---|---|
| 1. Roger Beaufrand | FRA | 13.2 (last 200 meters) |
| 2. Antoine Mazairac | HOL | — |
| 3. Willy Falck-Hansen | DEN | — |
| 4. Hans Bernhardt | GER | — |
| 5. Jerzy Koszutski (POL), A. Malvassi (ARG), Jack Standen (AUS), Yves van Massenhove (BEL) | | |

**1932 Los Angeles** C: 9, N: 9, D: 8.3.

| | | 1ST RACE | 2ND RACE | 3RD RACE |
|---|---|---|---|---|
| 1. Jacobus van Egmond | HOL | — | 12.6 | 12.6 |
| 2. Louis Chaillot | FRA | 12.5 | — | — |
| 3. Bruno Pellizzari | ITA | | | |
| 4. Edgar Gray | AUS | | | |
| 5. Ernest Henry Chambers (GBR), Willy Gervin (DEN), Leo Marchiori (CAN), Robert Thomas (USA) | | | | |

Beginning in 1932, it was necessary to win two out of three races. Louis Chaillot won the first race of the final by inches. But Jacobus van Egmond set the pace in the second, leading all the way to the finish. He then won the tie-breaker by a foot.

**1936 Berlin** C: 20, N: 20, D: 8.7.

|   |   |   | 1ST RACE | 2ND RACE |
|---|---|---|---|---|
| 1. | Toni Merkens | GER | 11.8 | 11.8 |
| 2. | Arie van Vliet | HOL | — | — |
| 3. | Louis Chaillot | FRA | | |
| 4. | Benedetto Pola | ITA | | |
| 5. | Henri Collard (BEL), Edgar Gray (AUS), Carl Magnussen (DEN), Werner Wagelin (SWI) | | | | |

As Arie van Vliet began to overtake Toni Merkens in the first race of the final, the German swerved to his right and blatantly interfered with his rival. No foul was called, and a disconcerted Van Vliet lost the second race as well. The Dutch team protested. In a bizarre twist, cycling officials decided not to disqualify Merkens, but to fine him 100 marks instead. The next day, Van Vliet returned to win the 1000-meter time trial. Merkens died toward the end of World War II after being wounded while fighting the Russians.

**1948 London** C: 23, N: 23, D: 8.9.

|   |   |   | 1ST RACE | 2ND RACE |
|---|---|---|---|---|
| 1. | Mario Ghella | ITA | 12.2 | 12.0 |
| 2. | Reginald Harris | GBR | — | — |
| 3. | Axel Schandorff | DEN | | |
| 4. | Charles Bazzano | AUS | | |
| 5. | John Heid (USA), M. Masanes Gimeno (CHI), L. Rocca (URU), E. Van de Velde (BEL) | | | | |

Reg Harris, the reigning world sprint champion, was struck from the British team a few days before the Olympics because he insisted on staying in his hometown of Manchester instead of training with the rest of the team in London. After a public outcry, Harris was reinstated, but not until he had won a ride-off against his tandem partner, Alan Bannister. In the final he faced 20-year-old Mario Ghella, a student from Turin. In the first race, Ghella caught Harris in a moment of inattention with 350 meters to go, slipped inside of him, and won easily. In the second race, Ghella fought off three challenges from Harris to earn a dramatic and emotional victory.

**1952 Helsinki** C: 27, N: 27, D: 7.31.

| 1. | Enzo Sacchi | ITA | 12.0 |
|---|---|---|---|
| 2. | Lionel Cox | AUS | — |
| 3. | Werner Potzernheim | GER | |
| 4. | Cyril Peacock (GBR), Raymond Robinson (SAF), Béla Szekeres (HUN) | | | |

**1956 Melbourne** C: 19, N: 19, D: 12.6. WR: 11.0 (Arie van Vliet)

|   |   |   | 1ST RACE | 2ND RACE |
|---|---|---|---|---|
| 1. | Michel Rousseau | FRA | 11.4 | 11.4 |
| 2. | Guglielmo Presenti | ITA | — | — |
| 3. | Richard Ploog | AUS | | |
| 4. | Warren Johnston | NZE | | |
| 5. | Jack Disney (USA), Ladislav Fouček (CZE), Boris Romanov (SOV), Thomas Shardelow (SAF) | | | | |

**1960 Rome** C: 30, N: 18, D: 8.29. WR: 10.8 (Antonio Maspes)

|   |   |   | 1ST RACE | 2ND RACE |
|---|---|---|---|---|
| 1. | Sante Gaiardoni | ITA | 11.1 | 11.5 |
| 2. | Leo Sterckx | BEL | — | — |
| 3. | Valentino Gasparella | ITA | | |
| 4. | Ronald Baensch | AUS | | |
| 5. | Anesio Argenton (BRA), Lloyd Binch (GBR), Antoine Pellegrina (FRA), August Rieke (GER) | | | | |

For the third straight time, the Olympic sprint championship was won by the reigning world champion. The 5-foot 6-inch 174-pound Gaiardoni had already won the 1000-meter time trial when he swept through the sprint competition without being seriously challenged.

**1964 Tokyo** C: 39, N: 22, D: 10.19. WR: 10.8 (Antonio Maspes)

|   |   |   | 1ST RACE | 2ND RACE |
|---|---|---|---|---|
| 1. | Giovanni Pettenella | ITA | 13.85 | 13.69 |
| 2. | Sergio Bianchetto | ITA | — | — |
| 3. | Daniel Morelon | FRA | | |
| 4. | Pierre Trentin | FRA | | |
| 5. | Willi Fuggerer (GER), Patrick Sercú (BEL), Mario Vanegas Jimenez (COL), Zbyslaw Zając (POL) | | | | |

In the semifinals Pettenella and Trentin set an Olympic record by standing still for 21 minutes 57 seconds.

**1968 Mexico City** C: 46, N: 27, D: 19.10. WR: 10.61 (Omari Phakadze)

|   |   |   | 1ST RACE | 2ND RACE |
|---|---|---|---|---|
| 1. | Daniel Morelon | FRA | 11.27 | 10.68 |
| 2. | Giordano Turrini | ITA | — | — |
| 3. | Pierre Trentin | FRA | | |
| 4. | Omari Phakadze | SOV | | |
| 5. | Jürgen Barth (GER), Johannes Jansen (HOL), Leijn Loevesijn (HOL), Dino Verzini (ITA) | | | | |

The tactical highlight of the competition came in the first race of the quarterfinal contest between Dino Verzini and Omari Phakadze. The first time out they stood and watched each other until a restart was ordered. The second attempt saw them both stop again, with Pkhakadze slipping off the banking and causing both of them to slide into the infield. The next restart, the two cyclists stopped for 4 minutes 47 seconds before continuing. This time they made it all the way to the finish with Verzini in the lead. However, Phakadze won the next two races and advanced to the semifinals, where he lost two out of three to Daniel Morelon, the eventual gold medalist. Morelon was a police officer from Bourg-en-Bresse, northeast of Lyon.

**1972 Munich** C: 51, N: 29, D: 9.2. WR: 10.61 (Omari Phakadze)

| | | 1ST RACE | 2ND RACE |
|---|---|---|---|
| 1. Daniel Morelon | FRA | 11.69 | 11.25 |
| 2. John Nicholson | AUS | — | |
| 3. Omari Phakadze | SOV | | |
| 4. Klaas Balk | HOL | | |
| 5. Niels Fredborg (DEN), Hans-Jürgen Geschke (GDR), Massimo Marino (ITA), Peter van Doorn (HOL) | | | |

**1976 Montreal** C: 25, N: 25, D: 7.24. WR: 10.61 (Omari Phakadze)

| | | 1ST RACE | 2ND RACE | 3RD RACE |
|---|---|---|---|---|
| 1. Anton Tkáč | CZE | 10.78 | — | 11.17 |
| 2. Daniel Morelon | FRA | — | 11.58 | — |
| 3. Hans-Jürgen Geschke | GDR | | | |
| 4. Dieter Berkmann | GER | | | |
| 5. Sergei Kravtsov | SOV | | | |
| 6. Yoshika Cho | JPN | | | |
| 7. Niels Fredborg | DEN | | | |
| 8. Giorgio Rossi | ITA | | | |

This was the first time that Olympic cycling events were held indoors. The Czech team got off to a bad start at the Montreal Olympics when all of their wheels and spare tires were inadvertently picked up by garbage collectors and fed into a trash compactor. The final was held the day before the 32nd birthday of Daniel Morelon, the sentimental as well as the betting favorite. But Anton Tkáč, a pipe fitter from Bratislava, jumped early in the tie-breaker, took a five-length lead, and was too strong to be caught. In the first race Tkáč had crossed the finish line at almost 42 miles per hour. Morelon's second-place finish earned him his fifth Olympic medal: two golds, one silver, and one bronze in the sprint, and one more gold in the tandem.

**1980 Moscow** C: 15, N: 15, D: 7.26. WR: 10.61 (Omari Phakadze)

| | | 1ST RACE | 2ND RACE | 3RD RACE |
|---|---|---|---|---|
| 1. Lutz Hesslich | GDR | 11.40 | — | 12.01 |
| 2. Yave Cahard | FRA | — | 10.86 | — |
| 3. Sergei Kopylov | SOV | | | |
| 4. Anton Tkáč | CZE | | | |
| 5. Henrik Salee | DEN | | | |
| 6. Heinz Isler | SWI | | | |
| 7. Kenrick Tucker | AUS | | | |
| 8. Octavio Dazzan | ITA | | | |

**1984 Los Angeles-Carson** C: 33, N: 25, D: 8.3. WR: 10.249 (Sergei Kopylov)

| | | 1ST RACE | 2ND RACE |
|---|---|---|---|
| 1. Mark Gorski | USA | 10.49 | 10.95 |
| 2. Nelson Vails | USA | — | — |

| 3. Tsutomu Sakamoto | JPN |
|---|---|
| 4. Philippe Vernet | FRA |
| 5. Gerhard Scheller | GER |
| 6. Marcelo Alexandre | ARG |
| 7. Kenrick Tucker | AUS |
| 8. Fredy Schmidtke | GER |

With the winners of the last four world championships, Lutz Hesslich and Sergei Kopylov, boycotted out of the Olympics, the final became an all-American contest.

In 1981, Nelson Vails, the youngest of ten children and a father himself since age 15, was living in Harlem, working eight hours a day as a bicycle messenger in Manhattan and training two hours a night in New York City's Central Park. In 1981, Mark Gorski had given up on cycling following a bad spill that left him with a broken collarbone and a severe concussion. Gorski returned to racing and, in 1983, defeated Kopylov three times. He had also defeated the fast-improving Vails three times before their Olympic encounter. After making it four in a row for the gold medal, Gorski took his 13-month-old son, Alexander, along with him on his victory lap.

**1988 Seoul** C: 25, N: 25, D: 9.24. WR: 10.118 (Michael Hübner)

| | | 1ST RACE | 2ND RACE |
|---|---|---|---|
| 1. Lutz Hesslich | GDR | 13.98 | 11.82 |
| 2. Nikolai Kovsh | SOV | — | |
| 3. Gary Neiwand | AUS | | |
| 4. Edward Alexander | GBR | | |
| 5. Vratislav Šuster | CZE | | |
| 6. Erik Schoefs | BEL | | |
| 7. Frank Weber | GER | | |
| 8. Maxwell Cheesman | TRI | | |

In the last three world championships, all three medals had gone to East Germans. In the Olympics, however, each nation is allowed only one entrant. Thus it came as no surprise that Hesslich, having defeated his friend and rival Michael Hübner to qualify for the East German team, was not seriously challenged in Seoul.

## 1000-METER TIME TRIAL

In the time trial, the competitors take turns racing against the clock.

**1896–1924** not held

**1928 Amsterdam** C: 14, N: 14, D: 8.7.

| 1. Willy Flack Hansen | DEN | 1:14.4 |
|---|---|---|
| 2. Gerard Bosch van Drakestein | HOL | 1:15.2 |
| 3. Edgar Gray | AUS | 1:15.6 |
| 4. Octave Dayen | FRA | 1:16.0 |
| 5. Kurt Einsiedel | GER | 1:17.2 |
| 6. E.J. Kerridge | GBR | 1:18.0 |
| 6. Józef Lange | POL | 1:18.0 |
| 8. Jean Aerts | BEL | 1:18.6 |

**1932 Los Angeles** C: 9, N: 9, D: 8.1.
1. Edgar Gray               AUS   1:13.0   OR
2. Jacobus van Egmond       HOL   1:13.3
3. Charles Rampelberg       FRA   1:13.4
4. Luigi Consonni           ITA   1:14.7
4. William Harvell          GBR   1:14.7
6. Lewis Rush               CAN   1:15.6
7. Harald Christensen       DEN   1:16.0
8. Bernard Mammes           USA   1:18.0

**1936 Berlin** C: 19, N: 19, D: 8.8.
1. Arie van Vliet           HOL   1:12.0   OR
2. Pierre Georget           FRA   1:12.8
3. Rudolf Karsch            GER   1:13.2
4. Benedetto Pola           ITA   1:13.6
5. László Orczán            HUN   1:14.0
5. Arne Pedersen            DEN   1:14.0
7. Raymond Hicks            GBR   1:14.8
8. George Giles             NZE   1:15.0

**1948 London** C: 21, N: 21, D: 8.11. WR: 1:10.0 (F. Battesini)
1. Jacques Dupont           FRA   1:13.5
2. Pierre Nihant            BEL   1:14.5
3. Thomas Godwin            GBR   1:15.0
4. Hans Fluckiger           SWI   1:15.3
5. Axel Schandorff          DEN   1:15.5
6. Sidney Patterson         AUS   1:15.7
6. John Heid                USA   1:16.2
8. Walter Freitag           AUT   1:16.8

**1952 Helsinki** C: 27, N: 27, D: 7.31. WR: 1:09.8 (Reginald Harris)
1. Russell Mockridge        AUS   1:11.1   OR
2. Marino Morettini         ITA   1:12.7
3. Raymond Robinson         SAF   1:13.0
4. Clodomiro Cortoni        ARG   1:13.2
5. Donald McKellow          GBR   1:13.3
6. Ib Vagn Hansen           DEN   1:14.4
7. Ion Ioniță               ROM   1:14.4
8. Johannes Hijzelendoorn   HOL   1:14.5

Russell Mockridge believed that cycling was somewhat boring, but he felt compelled to keep returning to it because it was clearly something that he was very good at. Mockridge worked as a journalist but quit his job. He studied art but dropped out. After competing in the road race at the 1948 London Olympics and winning two gold medals at the 1950 British Empire Games, Mockridge told the press, "I feel there is a lot more to this life than riding a bicycle," and announced that he was giving up cycling to become a minister in the Church of England. A few months later he changed his mind again and returned to competitive cycling.

Mockridge seemed assured a place on the 1952 Australian Olympic team until he refused to sign a statement that he would refrain from turning professional for two years. While the controversy over his participation was reaching the floor of Parliament, Mockridge was racing in Europe. A month before the Olympics he became the first amateur to win the Paris Open Grand Prix. Back in Australia, Mockridge's hometown of Geelong worked out a face-saving compromise with the Australian Olympic Federation by which the agreement was limited to one year.

Mockridge arrived in Helsinki four days before he was scheduled to compete. On July 31 he won the gold medal for the time trial and then teamed with Lionel Cox to win a second gold medal in the tandem. Six years later Mockridge was in Melbourne, competing in the 140-mile Tour of Gippsland. Three miles after the start, Mockridge and five other cyclists, followed in a car by Mockridge's wife and 3-year-old daughter, were crossing an intersection when a bus came up on the right and struck Mockridge, killing him instantly. He was 30 years old.

**1956 Melbourne** C: 22, N: 22, D: 12.6. WR: 1:08.6 (Reginald Harris)
1. Leandro Faggin           ITA   1:09.8   OR
2. Ladislav Fouček          CZE   1:11.4
3. Alfred Swift             SAF   1:11.6
4. Warren Scarfe            AUS   1:12.1
5. Alan Danson              GBR   1:12.3
5. Boris Savostin           SOV   1:12.3
5. Louis Serra              URU   1:12.3
8. Warwick Dalton           NZE   1:12.6

**1960 Rome** C: 25, N: 25, D: 8.26. WR: 1:07.5 (Sante Gaiardoni)
1. Sante Gaiardoni          ITA   1:07.27   WR
2. Dieter Gieseler          GER   1:08.75
3. Rostislav Vargashkin     SOV   1:08.86
4. Pieter van der Touw      HOL   1:09.20
5. Ian Chapman              AUS   1:09.55
6. Anesio Argenton          BRA   1:09.96
7. Jean Govaerts            BEL   1:10.23
8. Josef Helbling           SWI   1:10.42

**1964 Tokyo** C: 27, N: 27, D: 10.16. WR: 1:07.27 (Sante Gaiardoni)
1. Patrick Sercu            BEL   1:09.59
2. Giovanni Pettenella      ITA   1:10.00
3. Pierre Trentin           FRA   1:10.42
4. Pieter van der Touw      HOL   1:10.68
5. Jiří Pecka               CZE   1:10.70
6. Lothar Claesges          GER   1:10.86
7. Waclaw Latocha           POL   1:11.12
8. Roger Gibbon             TRI   1:11.19

**1968 Mexico City** C: 32, N: 32, D: 10.17. WR: 1:04.61 (Gianni Sartori)
1. Pierre Trentin           FRA   1:03.91   WR
2. Niels Fredborg           DEN   1:04.61
3. Janusz Kierzkowski       POL   1:04.63
4. Gianni Sartori           ITA   1:04.65
5. Roger Gibbon             TRI   1:04.66
6. Leijn Loevesijn          HOL   1:04.84
7. Jocelyn Lovell           CAN   1:05.18
8. Sergei Kravtsov          SOV   1:05.21

Trentin won three medals in Mexico City: a gold in the time trial, a gold in the tandem, and a bronze in the sprint.

**1972 Munich** C: 32, N: 32, D: 8.31. WR: 1:03.91 (Pierre Trentin)
| | | |
|---|---|---|
| 1. Niels Fredborg | DEN | 1:06.44 |
| 2. Daniel Clark | AUS | 1:06.87 |
| 3. Jürgen Schütze | GDR | 1:07.02 |
| 4. Karl Köther | GER | 1:07.21 |
| 5. Janusz Kierzkowski | POL | 1:07.22 |
| 6. Dimo Angelov | BUL | 1:07.55 |
| 7. Christian Brunner | SWI | 1:07.71 |
| 8. Eduard Rapp | SOV | 1:07.73 |

**1976 Montreal** C: 30, N: 30, D: 7.20. WR: 1:03.91 (Pierre Trentin)
| | | |
|---|---|---|
| 1. Klaus-Jürgen Grünke | GDR | 1:05.927 |
| 2. Michel Vaarten | BEL | 1:07.516 |
| 3. Niels Fredborg | DEN | 1:07.617 |
| 4. Janusz Kierzkowski | POL | 1:07.660 |
| 5. Eric Vermeulen | FRA | 1:07.846 |
| 6. Hans Michalsky | GER | 1:07.878 |
| 7. Harald Bundli | NOR | 1:08.093 |
| 8. Walter Baeni | SWE | 1:08.112 |

One of the favorites, Eduard Rapp of the U.S.S.R. was eliminated due to an unfortunate incident. He started before the gun and, assuming he would be ordered to restart, he stopped racing. But the officials ruled his start to be legal, and he was disqualified for stopping.

**1980 Moscow** C: 18, N: 18, D: 7.22. WR: 1:04.225 (José Ruchansky)
| | | | |
|---|---|---|---|
| 1. Lothar Thoms | GDR | 1:02.955 | WR |
| 2. Aleksandr Panfilov | SOV | 1:04.845 | |
| 3. David Weller | JAM | 1:05.241 | |
| 4. Guido Bontempi | ITA | 1:05.478 | |
| 5. Yave Cahard | FRA | 1:05.584 | |
| 6. Heinz Isler | SWI | 1:06.273 | |
| 7. Petr Kocek | CZE | 1:06.368 | |
| 8. Bjarne Carl Sorensen | DEN | 1:07.422 | |

**1984 Los Angeles-Carson** C: 25, N: 25, D: 7.30. WR: 1:02.547 (Maik Malchow)
| | | |
|---|---|---|
| 1. Fredy Schmidtke | GER | 1:06.10 |
| 2. Curtis Harnett | CAN | 1:06.44 |
| 3. Fabrice Colas | FRA | 1:06.65 |
| 4. Gene Samuel | TRI | 1:06.69 |
| 5. Craig Adair | NZE | 1:06.96 |
| 6. David Weller | JAM | 1:07.24 |
| 7. Marcelo Alexandre | ARG | 1:07.29 |
| 8. Rory O'Reilly | USA | 1:07.39 |

**1988 Seoul** C: 30, N: 30, D: 9.20. WR: 1:02.091 (Maic Malchow)
| | | |
|---|---|---|
| 1. Aleksandr Kirichenko | SOV | 1:04.499 |
| 2. Martin Vinnicombe | AUS | 1:04.784 |
| 3. Robert Lechner | GER | 1:05.114 |
| 4. Kurt Kenneth Ropke | DEN | 1:05.168 |
| 5. Bernardo Gonzalez | SPA | 1:05.281 |
| 6. Maic Malchow | GDR | 1:05.393 |

| | | |
|---|---|---|
| 7. Anthony Graham | NZE | 1:05.744 |
| 8. Frédéric Magné | FRA | 1:06.142 |

Kirichenko's rear tire began to deflate with one lap to go. By the time he crossed the finish line, half the air was gone. According to the rules of the competition, Kirichenko could have demanded a restart, but his coach, Boris Vasilyev (a bronze medalist in the 1960 tandem), refused, reasoning that Kirichenko would be too exhausted to improve his time. Soviet team officials were furious and let it be known that Vasilyev could begin looking for a new job. When the last rider, the favorite, Martin Vinnicombe, crossed the finish line without bettering Kirichenko's time, Vasilyev tearfully embraced Kirichenko and thanked him for saving his job.

## 4000-METER INDIVIDUAL PURSUIT

In pursuit races, two cyclists or teams of cyclists start off on opposite sides of the track. If one cyclist, or team, catches the other, the race is over. Otherwise, the winner is the first one to cross the finish line. Two cyclists or teams take part in the race for first place and two in the race for third. For this reason, the times for third through eighth place are often faster than those for first and second.

**1896–1960** not held

**1964 Tokyo** C: 24, N: 24, D: 10.17. WR: 4:51.20 (Van Looy)
| | | |
|---|---|---|
| 1. Jiři Daler | CZE | 5:04.75 |
| 2. Giorgio Ursi | ITA | 5:05.96 |
| 3. Preben Isaksson | DEN | 5:01.90 |
| 4. Tiemen Groen | HOL | 5:04.21 |
| 5. Lucjan Józefowicz (POL), Stanislav Moskvin (SOV), Hugh Porter (GBR), Lothar Spiegelberg (GER) | | |

**1968 Mexico City** C: 28, N: 28, D: 10.18. WR: 4:45.94 (Jiři Daler)
| | | |
|---|---|---|
| 1. Daniel Rebillard | FRA | 4:41.71 |
| 2. Mogens Frey Jensen | DEN | 4:42.43 |
| 3. Xaver Kurmann | SWI | 4:39.42 |
| 4. John Bylsma | AUS | 4:41.60 |
| 5. Cipriano Chamello (ITA), Paul Crapez (BEL), Rupert Kratzer (GER), Radamés Treviño (MEX) | | |

Jensen set a world record of 4:37.54 in the quarterfinals to defeat the favorite, Chamello.

**1972 Munich** C: 28, N: 28, D: 9.1. WR: 4:37.54 (Mogens Frey Jensen)
| | | |
|---|---|---|
| 1. Knut Knudsen | NOR | 4:45.74 |
| 2. Xaver Kurmann | SWI | 4:51.96 |
| 3. Hans Lutz | GER | 4:50.80 |
| 4. John Christopher Bylsma | AUS | 4:54.93 |
| 5. Carlos Miguel Alvarez (ARG), Luciano Borgognoi (ITA), Luis Diaz (COL), Roy Schuiten (HOL) | | |

Knut Knudsen was such an outsider that he didn't even get nervous until the final. Using wheels lent to him by the Danish team, the 21-year-old welder from Levanger took the lead from Kurmann after the fourth of 14 laps and pulled away to win comfortably.

**1976 Montreal** C: 28, N: 28, D: 7.22. WR: 4:37.54 (Mogens Frey Jensen)
1. Gregor Braun       GER   4:47.61
2. Herman Ponsteen    HOL   4:49.72
3. Thomas Huschke     GDR   4:52.71
4. Vladimir Osokin    SOV   4:57.34
5. Jan Iversen (NOR), Michal Klasa (CZE), Orfeo Pizzoferrato (ITA), Garry Sutton (AUS)

The crucial match-up occurred in the semifinals, when the 20-year-old Braun upset Osokin by 0.17 seconds, as both men recorded personal bests.

**1980 Moscow** C: 14, N: 14, D: 7.24. WR: 4:34.66 (Uwe Unterwalder)
1. Robert Dill-Bundi      SWI   4:35.66
2. Alain Bondue           FRA   4:42.96
3. Hans-Henrik Örsted     DEN   4:36.54
4. Harald Wolf            GDR   4:37.58
5. Pierangelo Bincoletto (ITA), Vladimir Osokin (SOV), Martin Penc (CZE), Sean Yates (GBR)

In the semifinals Robert Dill-Bundi set a world record of 4:32.29. After his victory in the final he got off his bike and kissed the track.

**1984 Los Angeles-Carson** C: 33, N: 21, D: 8.1. WR: 4:32.29 (Robert Dill-Bundi)
1. Steve Hegg             USA   4:39.35
2. Rolf Gölz              GER   4:43.82
3. Leonard Harvey Nitz    USA   4:44.03
4. Dean Woods             AUS   4:44.08
5. Jörgen Pedersen        DEN
6. Jelle Nijdam           HOL
7. Robert Pascal          FRA
8. Michael Grenda         AUS

Former U.S. downhill ski champion Steve Hegg stunned his fellow cyclists by posting an opening round qualifying time that was almost 11 seconds faster than that of any of the other 32 riders. Considered a dark horse for a medal, the 20-year-old Hegg powered his way into the final against the more experienced Gölz. The night before the gold medal race, Hegg, who began cycling after reading that his hero, Jean-Claude Killy, cycled, dreamt that he had skiied the greatest run of his life. The next day he scored a decisive victory when Gölz, unnerved by the enthusiastic pro-U.S. crowd and by the bizarre space-age bicycles being used by the U.S. team, pushed the pace too quickly and was unable to withstand Hegg's finishing rush. After the race, Gölz bitterly told Hegg, "You wouldn't have beaten me in Germany." To which Hegg replied, "I really don't care—this is Los Angeles."

As it turned out, it wasn't just the hometown crowd and the advanced technology that gave Hegg an extra edge. Less than a week before the competition, Hegg, bronze medalist Leonard Harvey Nitz, and six other members of the U.S. cycling team, encouraged by their coach, Eddie Borysewicz, had taken advantage of the dubious practice called blood boosting.

Blood boosting, which first became an Olympic issue as a result of long-distance runner Lasse Viren's successes in 1976 (see p. 40), is a procedure whereby blood is extracted from an athlete's body and frozen while the athlete's blood returns to a normal level. Then, before an important competition, it is reinjected, increasing the athlete's hemoglobin level and endurance. Borysewicz, who had also experimented with giving his cyclists caffeine suppositories, seemed to approach the issue with the same nonchalance that allowed U.S. track coach Lawson Robertson to suggest to his sprinters that they drink warm sherry and a raw egg before the 1920 100-meter final (see p. 4).

Ethically questionable to begin with, blood boosting was given an uglier twist by the U.S. cyclists. Because it was too late to remove and freeze their own blood, the eight U.S. team members went to a nearby motel and injected other people's blood, some of them relatives, some of them not. The two U.S. points racers, Mark Whitehead and Danny Van Haute, both became ill. Match sprinter Nelson Vails seemed to think the procedure was required of team members and was standing in line waiting for his transfusion when team doctor Thomas Dickson informed him that it was optional and discouraged him from going ahead with it. A relieved Vails left immediately. Blood boosting was finally banned in 1985.

In 1988, Steve Hegg was chosen to represent the U.S. in the team pursuit. However, one week before the Games began, he was kicked off the team when he tested positive for excessive caffeine.

**1988 Seoul** C: 22, N: 22, D: 9.22. WR: 4.31.16 (Gintautas Umaras)
1. Gintautas Umaras     SOV   4:32.00
2. Dean Woods           AUS   4:35.00
3. Bernd Dittert        GDR   4:34.17
4. Colin Sturgess       GBR   4:34.90
5. Ryszard Dawidowicz   POL   4:39.44
6. Peter Clausen        DEN   4:42.62
7. Gary Anderson        NZE   4:42.82
8. Ivan Beltrami        ITA   Overtaken

In the final, Woods rushed out to an early lead. However, Umaras, the 25-year-old world champion from Klaipeda, Lithuania, caught him just after the halfway point and went on to an easy victory.

# 4000-METER TEAM PURSUIT

The official time is that of the third rider on each team.

**1896–1906** not held

**1908 London** T:5, N: 5, D: 7.17.
*(1810.5 Meters)*
1. GBR  (Leonard Meredith, Benjamin Jones, Ernest   2:18.6
        Payne, Charles Kingsbury)
2. GER  (Hermann Martens, Bruno Götze, Karl Neumer,   2:28.6
        Richard Katzer)
3. CAN  (William Morton, Walter Andrews, Frederick   2:29.6
        McCarthy, William Anderson)
4. HOL  (Johannes van Spengen, Antonie Gerrits,   2:44.0
        Dorotheus Nijland, Gerard Bosch van
        Drakestein)

**1912** not held

**1920 Antwerp** T: 8, N: 8, D: 8.12.
1. ITA  (Franco Giorgetti, Ruggero Ferrario, Arnaldo   5:20.0
        Carli, Primo Magnani)
2. GBR  (Albert White, H. Thomas Johnson, William
        Stewart, Cyril Albert Alden)
3. SAF  (James Walker, William Smith, Henry Justaves
        Kaltenbrun, Harry Goosen)
4. BEL  (Albert de Buinne, Charles van Doorselaer,
        Gustave Deschryver, Jean Janssens)

The British team actually finished first, but a protest of
interference was allowed and Italy was awarded first
place.

**1924 Paris** T: 10, N: 10, D: 7.27.
1. ITA  (Angelo De Martino, Alfredo Dinale, Aleardo   5:15.0
        Menegazzi, Francesco Zucchetti)
2. POL  (Józef Lange, Jan Lazarski, Tomasz   —
        Stankiewicz, Franciszek Szymczyk)
3. BEL  (Léonard Daghelinckx, Henri Hoevenaers, Fer-   —
        nand Saive, Jean van den Bosch)
4. FRA  (Lucien Choury, Joseph Vuillemin, R. Hournon,   —
        Marcel Renaud)

The French team set an Olympic record of 5:11.4 in the
heats.

**1928 Amsterdam** T: 12, N: 12, D: 8.7.
1. ITA  (Luigi Tasselli, Giacomo Gaioni, Cesare   5:01.8
        Facciani, Mario Lusiani)
2. HOL  (Adriaan Braspenninx, Jacobus Maas, Jo-   5:06.2
        hannes Pijnenburg, Piet van der Horst)
3. GBR  (Frank Wyld, Leonard Wyld, Percy Wyld, M.   —
        George Southall)
4. FRA  (André Aumerle, Octave Dayen, René Brossy,   —
        André Trantoul)
5. BEL (August Meuleman, Yves van Massenhove, A. Muylle, Jean
   van Buggenhout, CAN (L.R. Elder, J. Davies, A. Houting, William Peden), GER (Josef Steger, Anton Joksch, Kurt Einsiedel,
   Hans Dornebach), POL (Józef Lange, Artur Reul, Jan Zybert,
   Józef Oksiutycz)

The British team set an Olympic record of 5:11.2 in the
quarter finals. Three of the four British riders were the
Wyld brothers from Derby: Frank, Leonard, and Percy.

**1932 Los Angeles** T: 5, N: 5, D: 8.3.
1. ITA  (Marco Cimatti, Paolo Pedretti, Alberto Ghilardi,   4:53.0
        Nino Bosari)
2. FRA  (Amédée Fournier, René Legrèves, Henri   4:55.7
        Mouillefarine, Paul Chocque)
3. GBR  (Ernest Johnson, William Harvell, Frank South-   4:56.0
        all, Charles Holland)
4. CAN  (Lewis Rush, Glen Robbins, Russell Hunt,   6:04.0
        Francis Elliott)

The Italian team set an Olympic record of 4:52.9 in the
heats.

**1936 Berlin** T: 13, N: 13, D: 8.8.
1. FRA  (Robert Charpentier, Jean Goujan, Guy   4:45.0
        Lapébie, Roger Le Nizerhy)
2. ITA  (Bianco Bianchi, Mario Gentili, Armando Latini,   4:51.0
        Severino Rigoni)
3. GBR  (Harry Hill, Ernest Johnson, Charles King,   4:53.6
        Ernest Mills)
4. GER  (Erich Arndt, Heinz Hasselberg, Heiner Hoff-   4:55.0
        man, Karl Klockner)

The French team set an Olympic record of 4:41.8 in the
heats.

**1948 London** T: 15, N: 15, D: 8.9.
1. FRA  (Charles Coste, Serge Blusson, Ferdinand   4:57.8
        Decanali, Pierre Adam)
2. ITA  (Arnaldo Benfenati, Guido Bernardi, Anselmo   5:36.7
        Citterio, Rino Pucci)
3. GBR  (Alan Geldard, Thomas Godwin, David Ricketts,   4:55.8
        Wilfred Waters)
4. URU  (Atilio François, Juan De Armas, Luis De Los   5:04.4
        Santos, W. Bernatsky)
5. AUS (Sidney Patterson, Jim Nestor, Jack Hoobin, Russell
   Mockridge), BEL (Joseph DeBeukelaere, Maurice Blomme, Lionel van Brabant, Raphael Glorieux), DEN (Max Jorgensen,
   Borge Gissel, Borge Mortensen, Benny Schnoor), SWI (W.
   Bucher, G. Gerosa, E. Kamber, Hans Pfenninger)

**1952 Helsinki** T: 22, N: 22, D: 7.29.
1. ITA  (Marino Morettini, Guido Messina, Mino De   4:46.1
        Rossi, Loris Campana)
2. SAF  (Thomas Shardelow, Alfred Swift, Robert   4:53.6
        Fowler, George Estman)
3. GBR  (Ronald Stretton, Alan Newton, George New-   4:51.5
        berry, Donald Burgess)
4. FRA  (Henri Andrieux, Pierre Michel, Jean-Marie   4:51.9
        Joubert, Claude Brugerolles)
5. BEL (Gabriel Glorieux, José Pauwels, Robert Raymond, Paul de
   Paepe), DEN (Knud Andersen, Edvard Preben Lundgren-
   Kristensen, J. Hansen, Bent Jorgensen), HOL (Johannes
   Plantaz, Adrianus Voorting, Daniël de Groot, Jules Maenen),
   SWI (Hans Pfenninger, Heini Müller, Max Wirth, Oscar von
   Büren)

**1956 Melbourne** T: 16, N: 16, D: 12.4.
1. ITA  (Leandro Faggin, Valentino Gasparella, Antonio   4:37.4
        Domenicali, Franco Gandini)

2. FRA (Michel Vermeulin, Jean-Claude Lecante, René 4:39.4
Bianchi, Jean Graczyk)
3. GBR (Donald Burgess, Michael Gambrill, John 4:42.4
Geddes, Thomas Simpson)
4. SAF (Alfred Swift, Robert Fowler, Charles Jonker, 4:43.8
Anne-Jan Hettema)
5. BEL (André Bar, Gustave de Smet, François de Wagheneire,
Guillaume Van Tongerloo), CZE (Jaroslav Cihlar, Jiří Opavsky,
Jiří Nouza, Františhek Jursa), NZE (Warwick Dalton, Donald Ea-
gle, Leonard Kent, Neil Ritchie), SOV (Victor Iline, Vladimir
Mitine, Rodislav Tchijikov, Edouard Goussev)

Great Britain won its sixth straight bronze medal in the
team pursuit. One member of the British team, Thomas
Simpson, later became the only cyclist to die during the
Tour de France.

**1960 Rome** T: 19, N: 19, D: 8.29.
1. ITA (Luigi Arienti, Franco Testa, Mario Vallotto, 4:30.90
Marino Vigna)
2. GDR (Siegfried Köhler, Peter Gröning, Manfred 4:35.78
Klleme, Bernd Barleben)
3. SOV (Stanislav Moskvin, Viktor Romanov, Leonid 4:34.05
Kolumbet, Arnold Belgardt)
4. FRA (Marcel Delattre, Jacques Suire, Guy Claud, 4:35.72
Michel Nedelec)
5. ARG (Alberto Trillo, Ernesto Contreras, Hector Agosta, Juan
Brotto), CZE (Slavoy Cerny, Ferdinand Duchon, Jan Chlistovsky,
Josef Volf), DEN (John Lundgren, Leif Larsen, Jens Sorensen,
Kurt Stein), HOL (Jacob Oudkerk, Theodorus Nikkessen,
Hendrix Nijdam, Petrus van der Lans)

The Italian team set an Olympic record of 4:28.88 in the
semifinals.

**1964 Tokyo** T: 18, N: 18, D: 10.21. WR: 4:26.60 (West Germany)
1. GER (Lothar Claesges, Karlheinz Henrichs, Karl 4:35.67
Link, Ernst Streng)
2. ITA (Luigi Roncaglia, Vincenzo Mantovani, Carlo 4:35.74
Rancati, Franco Testa)
3. HOL (Gerard Koel, Hendrik Cornelissen, Jacob 4:38.99
Oudkerk, Cornelis Schuuring)
4. AUS (Kevin Brislin, Robert Baird, Victor Browne, 4:39.42
Hendrikus Vogels)
5. ARG (Carlos Alvarez, Ernesto Contreras, Juan Alberto Merlos,
Alberto Trillo), CZE (Jiří Daller, Antonin Kritz, Jiří Pecka,
Františhek Rezac), DEN (Bent Kurt Hansen, Preben Isaksson, Alf
Johansen, Kurt Vid Stein), SOV (Zintars Latsis, Leonid
Kolumbet, Stanislav Moskvin, Sergei Terechenkov)

The world champion German team broke the Italian pursuit monopoly in dramatic fashion. The two teams raced
evenly for the last quarter of the contest. The finish was
so close that it took ten minutes to determine the winner,
despite the use of electronic timing devices.

**1968 Mexico City** T: 20, N: 20, D: 10.21. WR: 4:20.64 (Italy)
1. DEN (Gunnar Asmussen, Per Pedersen Lyngemark, 4:22.44
Reno Olsen, Mogens Frey Jensen)
2. GER (Udo Hempel, Karl Link, Karlheinz Henrichs, 4:18.94
Jürgen Kissner)

3. ITA (Lorenzo Bosisio, Cipriano Chemello, Luigi 4:18.35
Roncaglia, Giorgio Morbiato)
4. SOV (Zintars Latsis, Stanislav Moskvin, Vladimir 4:33.39
Kuznyetsov, Mikhail Kolyuschev)
5. BEL (Ernest Bens, Ronny Vanmarcke, Willy Debosscher, Paul
Crapez), CZE (Jiří Daler, Pavel Kondr, Milan Puzrla, Františhek
Rezac), FRA (Bernard Darmet, Daniel Rebillard, Jack Mourioux,
Alain Van Lancker), POL (Wojciech Matusiak, Janusz
Kierzkowski, Waclaw Latocha, Rajmund Zieliński)

In the qualifying round the West Germans set a world
record of 4:19.90, which was broken quickly by the Italians at 4:16.10. In the first semifinal the Germans took
back the record by beating the Italians 4:15.76 to 4:16.21.
The final saw the exhausted West Germans hold on to
finish first. But with one lap to go, Jürgen Kissner touched his teammate Karlheinz Henrichs on the back. East
German officials, bitter because West German team
member Kissner was a defector from the east, protested
that the "touch" had been an illegal shove. Their protest
was upheld, and West Germany was disqualified. At first
it was announced that Italy would receive the silver
medal and the U.S.S.R. the bronze, but a post-Olympic
decision allowed the West Germans to retain second
place.

**1972 Munich** T: 22, N: 22, D: 9.4.
1. GER (Jürgen Colombo, Günter Haritz, Udo 4:22.14
Hempel, Günther Schumacher)
2. GDR (Thomas Huschke, Heinz Richter, Herbert 4:25.25
Richter, Uwe Unterwalder)
3. GBR (Michael Bennett, Ian Hallam, Ronald Keeble, 4:23.78
William Moore)
4. POL (Bernard Kreçzyński, Pawel Kaczorowski, Ja- 4:26.06
nusz Kierzkowski, Mieczyslaw Nowicki)
5. BUL (Nikifor Petrov, Plamen Timchev, Dimo Angelov, Ivan
Stanoev), HOL (Ad Dekkers, Gerard Kamper, Herman
Ponsteen, Roy Schuiten), SOV (Viktor Bykov, Vladimir
Kuznyetsov, Anatoly Stepanenko, Aleksandr Yudin), SWI (Martin
Steger, Xaver Kurmann, René Savary, Christian Brunner)

The dramatic confrontation between the two German
teams turned out to be a one-sided affair, as the West
Germans took an early lead and were up by 3.82 seconds
with 1000 meters to go.

**1976 Montreal** T:16, N: 16, D: 7.24.
1. GER (Gregor Braun, Hans Lutz, Günther 4:21.06
Schumacher, Peter Vonhof)
2. SOV (Vladimir Osokin, Aleksandr Perov, Vitaly Pe- 4:27.15
trakov, Victor Sokolov)
3. GBR (Ian Banbury, Michael Bennett, Robin Croker, 4:22.41
Ian Hallam)
4. GDR (Norbert Dürpisch, Thomas Huschke, Uwe 4:22.75
Unterwalder, Matthias Wiegand)
5. CZE (Ždenek Dohnal, Michal Klasa, Petr Koček, Jiří Pokorny),
HOL (Gerrit Mohlmann, Peter Nieuwenhuis, Herman Ponsteen,
Gerrit Slot), ITA (Sandro Callari, Cesare Cipollini, Rino de Can-
dido, Giuseppe Saronni), POL (Jan Jankiewicz, Czeslaw Lang,
Krzysztof Sujka, Zbigniew Szczepkowski)

The world champion West German team filled their tires with helium instead of air because it was lighter. They also arrived in Montreal with one-piece silk racing suits, which they were not allowed to use because of the unfair aerodynamic advantage it would have given them.

**1980 Moscow** C: 13, N: 13, D: 7.26.
1. SOV (Viktor Manakov, Valery Movchan, Vladimir 4:15.70 Osokin, Vitaly Petrakov)
2. GDR (Gerald Mortag, Uwe Unterwalder, Matthias 4:19.67 Wiegand, Volker Winkler)
3. CZE (Teodor Černý, Martin Penc, Jiři Pokorný, Igor Over Sláma) took
4. ITA (Pierangelo Bincoletto, Guido Bontempi, Ivano Maffei, Silvestro Milani)
5. AUS (Colin Fitzgerald, Kevin Nichols, Kelvin Poole, Garry Sutton), FRA (Alain Bondue, Philippe Chevalier, Pascal Poisson, Jean-Marc Rebiere), GBR (Anthony Doyle, Malcolm Elliott, Glen Mitchell, Sean Yates), SWI (Robert Dill-Bundi, Urs Freuler, Hans Kaenel, Hans Ledermann)

The Soviet team set a world record of 4:14.64 in the quarterfinals, achieving a speed of 56.55 kilometers per hour.

**1984 Los Angeles-Carson** C: 14, N: 14, D: 8.3.
1. AUS (Michael Grenda, Kevin Nichols, Michael 4:25.99 Turtur, Dean Woods)
2. USA (David Grylls, Steve Hegg, R. Patrick 4:29.85 McDonough, Leonard Harvey Nitz)
3. GER (Reinhard Alber, Rolf Gölz, Roland Günther, 4:25.60 Michael Marx)
4. ITA (Roberto Amadio, Massimo Brunelli, Maurizio 4:26.90 Colombo, Silvio Martinello)
5. DEN (Dan Frost, Michael Marcussen, Jörgen 4:25.16 Pedersen, Brian Holm Sörensen)
6. FRA (Didier Garcia, Eric Louvel, Pascal Potie, 4:30.28 Robert Pascal)
7. SWI (Daniel Huwyler, Hans Ledermann, Hansrüdi 4:30.47 Märki, Jörg Müller)
8. BEL (Rudi Ceyssens, Roger Ilegems, Peter Roes, 4:31.53 Joseph Smeets)

In the final, the toe strap of U.S. team member Dave Grylls came loose almost immediately, forcing the Americans to complete the race with only three riders. The Australians took an early lead, allowed the Americans to pull close by the halfway mark, and then drew away for a clear victory.

**1988 Seoul** T: 19, N: 19, D: 9.24. WR: 4:17.71 (CZE—Soukup, Buchta, Cerny, Trčka)
1. SOV (Vyacheslav Ekimov, Artūras Kasputis, 4:13.31 WR Dmitri Nelyubin, Gintautas Umaras)
2. GDR (Steffen Blochwitz, Roland Hennig, Dirk 4:14.09 Meier, Carsten Wolf)
3. AUS (Brett Dutton, Wayne McCarney, Ste- 4:16.02 phen McGlede, Dean Woods)

4. FRA (Hervé Dagorne, Pascal Lino, Didier 4:22.23 Pasgrimaud, Pascal Potie)
5. CZE (Svatopluk Buchta, Zbynek Fiala, Pavel 4:19.05 Soukup, Aleš Trčka)
6. ITA (Ivan Beltrami, Gianpaolo Grisandi, Da- 4:20.90 vid Solari, Fabrizio Trezzi)
7. POL (Ryszard Dawidowicz, Joachim 4:22.50 Halupczok, Andrzej Sikorski, Marian Turowski)
8. DEN (Peter Clausen, Dan Frost, Jimmi 4:25.30 Madsen, Lars Olsen)

Four different teams broke the world record in the qualifying round, with the Soviets leading the way in 4:16.10. In the quarterfinals they lowered their time to 4:14.22, then set a third record in the final. The East Germans almost edged the Soviets for the gold. They trailed by only three tenths of a second with half a lap to go and were closing fast when two of their riders, Wolf and Hennig, misjudged the finish line and sat up in their seats.

## 50-KILOMETER POINTS RACE

In the 50-kilometer points race, the riders complete 150 laps of the track with points being scored for sprints which take place every five laps. Double points are awarded for the 75-lap sprint and the final sprint.

**1896–1980** not held

**1984 Los Angeles-Carson** C: 43, N: 25, D: 8.3.

| | | | LAPS DOWN | POINTS |
|---|---|---|---|---|
| 1. | Roger Ilegems | BEL | 0 | 37 |
| 2. | Uwe Messerschmidt | GER | 0 | 15 |
| 3. | José Manuel Youshimatz | MEX | 1 | 29 |
| 4. | Jörg Müller | SWI | 1 | 23 |
| 5. | Juan Esteban Curuchet | ARG | 1 | 20 |
| 6. | Glenn Clarke | AUS | 1 | 13 |
| 7. | Brian Fowler | NZE | 1 | 12 |
| 8. | Derk van Egmond | HOL | 2 | 56 |

Roger Ilegems, Belgium's only gold-medal winner of the Los Angeles Games, moved into the lead after 110 laps. World champion and heavy favorite Michael Marcussen of Denmark was relegated to ninth place.

**1988 Seoul** C: 34, N: 34, D: 9.24.

| | | | LAPS DOWN | POINTS |
|---|---|---|---|---|
| 1. | Dan Frost | DEN | 0 | 38 |
| 2. | Leo Peelen | HOL | 0 | 26 |
| 3. | Marat Ganeev | SOV | 1 | 46 |

| 4. | Robert Burns | AUS | 1 | 20 |
|---|---|---|---|---|
| 5. | Juan Esteban Curuchet | ARG | 1 | 18 |
| 6. | Uwe Messerschmidt | GER | 2 | 28 |
| 7. | Pascal Lino | FRA | 2 | 21 |
| 8. | Frankie Andreu | USA | 2 | 21 |

## ROAD RACE

**1896 Athens** C: 7, N: 3, D: 4.12.
*87 KM*

| 1. | Aristidis Konstantinidis | GRE | 3:21:10. |
|---|---|---|---|
| 2. | August Goedrich | GER | 3:31:14. |
| 3. | E. Battel | GBR | — |

The cyclists raced from Athens to Marathon, where they signed their names, and then rode back again on the same road.

**1900–1904** not held

**1906 Athens** C: 24, N: 9, D: 5.1.
*84 KM*

| 1. | Fernand Vast | FRA | 2:41:28.0 |
|---|---|---|---|
| 2. | Maurice Bardonneau | FRA | 2:41:28.4 |
| 3. | Edmond Luguet | FRA | 2:41:28.6 |
| 4. | Prospère Verschelden-Romeo | BEL | — |
| 5. | Ad. Böhm | GER | — |
| 6. | I. Petritsas | GRE | — |
| 7. | Carl Andreasen | DEN | — |
| 8. | Hans Holly | AUT | — |

**1908** not held

**1912 Stockholm** C: 123, N: 16, D: 7.7.
*320 KM*

| 1. | Rudolph "Okey" Lewis | SAF | 10:42:39.0 |
|---|---|---|---|
| 2. | Frederick Grubb | GBR | 10:51:24.2 |
| 3. | Carl Schutte | USA | 10:52:38.8 |
| 4. | Leonard Meredith | GBR | 11:00:02.6 |
| 5. | Frank Brown | CAN | 11:01:00.0 |
| 6. | Antti Raita | FIN | 11:02:20.3 |
| 7. | Eric Friborg | SWE | 11:04:17.0 |
| 8. | Ragnar Malm | SWE | 11:08:14.5 |

This grueling 199-mile race around Lake Mälar was begun at 2:00 a.m. The competitors were sent out on the course at two-minute intervals over the next four hours. "Okey" Lewis of South Africa began at an unusually fast pace and held an 11½-minute lead at the 120 km control station. He increased this lead to 17 minutes at 200 km and held on for the last 4¼ hours to win by 8¾ minutes. While racing in Germany, Lewis got caught up in World War I. He was wounded several times and incarcerated in prison camps. He returned to Johannesburg after the war in very poor health, but survived until 1933.

There was one terrible accident at the beginning of the race. A few hundred meters after the start, Karl Landsberg of Sweden was hit by a motor-wagon and dragged along for some distance before the wagon stopped.

**1920 Antwerp** C: 46, N: 13, D: 8.9.-12?.
*175 KM*

| 1. | Harry Stenqvist | SWE | 4:40:01.8 |
|---|---|---|---|
| 2. | Henry Kaltenbrun | SAF | 4:41:26.6 |
| 3. | Fernand Canteloube | FRA | 4:42:54.4 |
| 4. | Jean Janssens | BEL | 4:44:20.6 |
| 5. | Albert de Buinne | BEL | 4:45:23.4 |
| 6. | Georges Detreille | FRA | 4:46:13.4 |
| 7. | Ragnar Malm | SWE | — |
| 8. | Piet Ikelaar | HOL | — |

The course was intersected by six railway crossings which might be closed at any time. Timekeepers were posted at each crossing to record any delays. At first it appeared that Kaltenbrun had won, and his victory was acknowledged by triumphant music in the stadium. However, it was later learned that Stenqvist had been held up for four minutes at a railway crossing, and the subtraction from his time put him into first place.

**1924 Paris** C: 72, N: 22, D: 7.23.
*188 KM*

| 1. | Armand Blanchonnet | FRA | 6:20:48.0 |
|---|---|---|---|
| 2. | Henri Hoevenaers | BEL | 6:30.27.0 |
| 3. | René Hamel | FRA | 6:30:51.6 |
| 4. | Gunnar Sköld | SWE | 6:33:36.2 |
| 5. | Albert Blattmann | SWE | 6:34:09.0 |
| 6. | Alphonse Pardondry | BEL | 6:35:57.0 |
| 7. | Eric Bohlin | SWE | 6:36:12.4 |
| 8. | Georges Wambst | FRA | 6:38:34.4 |

**1928 Amsterdam** C: 63, N: 21, D: 8.7.
*168 KM*

| 1. | Henry Hansen | DEN | 4.47.10 |
|---|---|---|---|
| 2. | Frank Southall | GBR | 4:55:06 |
| 3. | Gösta Carlsson | SWE | 5:00:17 |
| 4. | Allegro Grandi | ITA | 5:02.05 |
| 5. | Jack Lauterwasser | GBR | 5:02:57 |
| 6. | Gottlieb Amstein | SWI | 5:04:48 |
| 7. | Leo Nielsen | DEN | 5:05:37 |
| 8. | A. Aumerle | FRA | 5:07:12 |

**1932 Los Angeles** C: 33, N: 11, D: 8.4.
*100 KM*

| 1. | Attilio Pavesi | ITA | 2:28:05.6 |
|---|---|---|---|
| 2. | Guglielmo Segato | ITA | 2:29:21.4 |
| 3. | Bernhard Britz | SWE | 2:29:45.2 |
| 4. | Giuseppe Olmo | ITA | 2:29:48.2 |
| 5. | Frode Sörensen | DEN | 2:30:11.2. |
| 6. | Frank Southall | GBR | 2:30:16.2 |
| 7. | Giovanni Cazzulani | ITA | 2:31:07.2 |
| 8. | Sven Hoglund | SWE | 2:31:29.4 |

258 / THE COMPLETE BOOK OF THE OLYMPICS

**1936 Berlin** C: 100, N: 29, D: 8.10.
**100 KM**

| | | | |
|---|---|---|---|
| 1. | Robert Charpentier | FRA | 2:33:05.0 |
| 2. | Guy Lapébie | FRA | 2:33:05.2 |
| 3. | Ernst Nievergelt | SWI | 2:33.05.8 |
| 4. | Fritz Scheller | GER | 2:33:06.0 |
| 4. | Charles Holland | GBR | 2:33:06.0 |
| 4. | Robert Dorgebray | FRA | 2:33:06.0 |
| 7. | Pierino Favalli | ITA | 2:33:06.2 |
| 8. | Auguste Garrebeek | BEL | 2:33:06.6 |
| 8. | Armand Putzeys | BEL | 2:33:06.6 |
| 8. | Tuncalp | TUR | 2:33:06.6 |

For the first time, all the competitors started together rather than at intervals. This, coupled with the narrow road, caused numerous accidents and injuries during the last five kilometers. Charpentier had already won a gold medal in the team pursuit two days earlier.

**1948 London** C: 101, N: 29, D: 8.13.
**194.63 KM**

| | | | |
|---|---|---|---|
| 1. | José Beyaert | FRA | 5:18:12.6 |
| 2. | Gerardus Petrus Voorting | HOL | 5:18:16.2 |
| 3. | Lode Wouters | BEL | 5:18:16.2 |
| 4. | Léon Delathouwer | BEL | 5:18:16.2 |
| 5. | Nils Johansson | SWE | 5:18:16.2 |
| 6. | Robert Maitland | GBR | 5:18:16.2 |
| 7. | Jack Hoobin | AUS | 5:18:18.2 |
| 8. | Gordon Thomas | GBR | 5:18:18.2 |

Beyaert, a 22-year-old shoemaker from Lens, sprinted ahead with half a mile to go and won by 8 lengths.

**1952 Helsinki** C: 112, N: 30, D: 8.2.
**190.4 KM**

| | | | |
|---|---|---|---|
| 1. | André Noyelle | BEL | 5:06:03.4 |
| 2. | Robert Grondelaers | BEL | 5:06:51.2 |
| 3. | Edi Ziegler | GER | 5:07:47.5 |
| 4. | Lucien Victor | BEL | 5:07:52.0 |
| 5. | Dino Bruni | ITA | 5:10:54.0 |
| 6. | Vincenzo Zucconelli | ITA | 5:11:16.5 |
| 7. | Gianni Ghidini | ITA | 5:11:16.8 |
| 8. | Oscar Zeissner | GER | 5:11:18.5 |

**1956 Melbourne** C: 88, N: 28, D: 12.7.
**187.73 KM**

| | | | |
|---|---|---|---|
| 1. | Ercole Baldini | ITA | 5:21:17 |
| 2. | Arnaud Geyre | FRA | 5:23:16 |
| 3. | Alan Jackson | GBR | 5:23:16 |
| 4. | Horst Tüller | GDR | 5:23:16 |
| 5. | Gustav-Adolf Schur | GDR | 5:23:16 |
| 6. | A. Stanley Brittain | GBR | 5:23:40 |
| 7. | Arnaldo Pambianco | ITA | 5:23:40 |
| 8. | Maurice Moucheraud | FRA | 5:23:40 |

The year 1956 was known as "Baldini's Year," because the 23-year-old Italian won the world championship in the 4000-meter pursuit, set a world record for the one-hour time trial, and won the Olympic road race by a full mile. His victory was protested by the French and British, who charged that in the later stages of the race he had been pro-tected from the hot sun by the Olympic film unit van that rode alongside him. The protest was rejected. The start of the race was delayed fifteen minutes when it was discovered that two "unauthorized" Irish bicyclists, butcher Tom Gerrard and carpenter Paul Fitzgerald, were in the middle of the 88 starters. After they were removed, they joined 200 supporters in passing out Irish nationalist literature.

**1960 Rome** C: 148, N: 42, D: 8.30.
**175.38 KM**

| | | | |
|---|---|---|---|
| 1. | Viktor Kapitonov | SOV | 4:20:37 |
| 2. | Livio Trapé | ITA | 4:20:37 |
| 3. | Willy van den Berghen | BEL | 4:20:57 |
| 4. | Yuri Melikhov | SOV | 4:20:57 |
| 5. | Ion Cosma | ROM | 4:20:57 |
| 6. | Stanislaw Gazda | POL | 4:20:57 |
| 7. | Benoni Beheyt | BEL | 4:20:57 |
| 8. | Janez Zirovnık | YUG | 4:20:57 |

Kapitonov sprinted to the finish line to defeat Trapé by inches, only to discover that he still had one more 14½-km lap to go. Twenty-four-minutes later, the scene was repeated but this time Kapitonov's victory was official. Kapitonov later joined the editorial board of *Theory and Practice of Physical Culture* magazine and became the manager of the U.S.S.R. cycling team.

The race, which was run in 93-degree heat, was marred by the death of Danish cyclist Knut Jensen, who collapsed from sunstroke and suffered a fractured skull. It was later determined that before the race Jensen had taken Ronicol, a blood circulation stimulant. Jensen was the first person to die in Olympic competition since the 1912 marathon.

**1964 Tokyo** C: 132, N: 35, D: 10.22.
**194.83 KM**

| | | | |
|---|---|---|---|
| 1. | Mario Zanin | ITA | 4:39:51.63 |
| 2. | Kjell Åkerström Rodian | DEN | 4:39:51.65 |
| 3. | Walter Godefroot | BEL | 4:39:51.74 |
| 4. | Raymond Bilney | AUS | 4:39:51.74 |
| 5. | José Lopez Rodriguez | SPA | 4:39:51.74 |
| 6. | Wilfried Peffgen | GER | 4:39:51.74 |
| 7. | Gösta Pettersson | SWE | 4:39:51.74 |
| 8. | Delmo Delmastro | ARG | 4:39:51.74 |

A spectacular finish saw Zanin, a mechanic from Treviso, emerge from the pack with 20 meters to go and win by a wheel. Sture Pettersson of Sweden finished only sixteen-hundredths of a second behind Zanin, yet he ended up in 51st place.

**1968 Mexico City** C: 144, N: 44, D: 10.23.
**196.2 KM**

| | | | |
|---|---|---|---|
| 1. | Pierfranco Vianelli | ITA | 4:41:25.24 |
| 2. | Leif Mortensen | DEN | 4:42:49.71 |
| 3. | Gösta Pettersson | SWE | 4:43:15.24 |
| 4. | Stephan Abrahamian | FRA | 4:43:36.54 |
| 5. | Marinus Pijnen | HOL | 4:43:36.81 |
| 6. | Jean-Pierre Monsère | BEL | 4:43:51.77 |
| 7. | Tomas Pettersson | SWE | 4:43:58.11 |
| 8. | Giovanni Bramucci | ITA | 4:43:58.19 |

**1972 Munich** C: 163, N: 48, D: 9.7.
*182.4 KM*

| | | | |
|---|---|---|---|
| 1. | Hennie Kuiper | HOL | 4:14.37 |
| 2. | Keven Clyde Sefton | AUS | 4:15:04 |
| 3. | Bruce Biddle | NZE | 4:15:04 |
| 4. | Philip Bayton | GBR | 4:15:07 |
| 5. | Philip Edwards | GBR | 4:15.13 |
| 6. | Wilfried Trott | GER | 4:15:13 |
| 7. | Francesco Moser | ITA | 4:15:13 |
| 8. | Miguel Samaca | COL | 4:15:21 |

DISQ (Drugs): Jaime Huelamo (SPA) 4:15.04

The four Dutch contestants rode a team race with Cees Priem and Fedor den Hertog protecting Kuiper and fighting off challengers. Freddy Maertens was so frustrated by Priem's dogged persistance in sticking to his wheel that he tried to hit Priem in the face. Said Priem, "We worked for Hennie because he is one of the nicest blokes around." Four Irish Republican Army cyclists joined the race to protest the fact that the Irish Cycling Federation competed against cyclists from Northern Ireland. One of them tried to run Irish Olympian Noel Taggart into a ditch. The 4 IRA cyclists were arrested but later released without charge.

Third-place finisher Jaime Huelamo was disqualified after he failed a test for drugs.

**1976 Montreal** C: 134, N: 40, D: 7.26.
*175 KM*

| | | | |
|---|---|---|---|
| 1. | Bernt Johansson | SWE | 4:46:52 |
| 2. | Giuseppe Martinelli | ITA | 4.47.23 |
| 3. | Mieczyslaw Nowicki | POL | 4:47:23 |
| 4. | Alfons de Wolf | BEL | 4:47:23 |
| 5. | Nikolai Gorelov | SOV | 4:17:23 |
| 6. | George Mount | USA | 4:47:23 |
| 7. | Jean René Bernaudeau | FRA | 4:47:23 |
| 8. | Vittorio Algeri | ITA | 4:47:23 |

Peter Thaler of Germany crossed the finish line in second place, but was demoted to ninth because he had interfered with Martinelli in the final sprint.

**1980 Moscow** C: 112, N: 32, D: 7.28.
*189 KM*

| | | | |
|---|---|---|---|
| 1. | Sergei Sukhoruchenkov | SOV | 4:48:28.9 |
| 2. | Czeslaw Lang | POL | 4:51:26.9 |
| 3. | Yuri Barinov | SOV | 4:51:29.9 |
| 4. | Thomas Barth | GDR | 4:56:12.9 |
| 5. | Tadeusz Wojtas | POL | 4:56:12.9 |
| 6. | Anatoly Yarkin | SOV | 4:56:54.9 |
| 7. | Adri van der Poel | HOL | 4:56:54.9 |
| 8. | Christian Faure | FRA | 4:56:54.9 |

Sukhoruchenkov pulled away with 20 miles to go to win by the largest Olympics margin since 1928.

**1984 Los Angeles-Mission Viejo** C: 135, N: 43, D: 7.29.
*190.2 KM*

| | | | |
|---|---|---|---|
| 1. | Alexi Grewal | USA | 4:59:57 |
| 2. | Steve Bauer | CAN | 4:59:57 |
| 3. | Dag Otto Lauritzen | NOR | 5:00:18 |
| 4. | Morten Saether | NOR | 5:00:18 |
| 5. | Davis Phinney | USA | 5:01:16 |
| 6. | Thurlow Rogers | USA | 5:01:16 |
| 7. | Bojan Ropret | YUG | 5:01:16 |
| 8. | Nestor Mora | COL | 5:01:16 |

The son of a Sikh father from India and a British mother of German descent, Alexi Grewal was considered too temperamental and too much of a loner to be an effective member of the U.S. team. Two places on the team were to be decided by the combined results of three trials; the other two were to be filled by the team coaches. Since U.S. head coach Eddie Borysewicz was definitely *not* a fan of Grewal's, the 23-year-old naturalized U.S. citizen had no choice but to make it as one of the two automatic qualifiers. He succeeded, but his troubles were not yet over. Ten days before the Olympic road race, Grewal won a 92-mile contest in Colorado, but his post-race doping test turned up positive for phenyethylamine, apparently caused by a Chinese herbal tablet which he had casually popped before the race. The U.S. Cycling Federation immediately slapped him with a 30-day suspension and dropped him from the Olympic team.

Grewal appealed the ruling by pointing out that he regularly took albuterol, a legal drug, for asthma, and that the doping test had not been sophisticated enough to distinguish between the asthma drug and the herbal pill. On the Monday before the Sunday Olympic race, Grewal was reinstated.

In Los Angeles, with a crowd of 300,000 lining the route, Grewal broke away from the pack 20 kilometers from the finish and opened up a 24-second lead after 11 of 12 laps. With 10 kilometers to go he appeared exhausted and began to wobble and weave. Steve Bauer of Fenwick, Ontario, passed him. Grewal faced a moment of panic and confusion, then regained his self-control and caught Bauer. The two raced the final lap together. After almost 5 hours of riding, the gold medal was to be decided by a sprint, which was Bauer's specialty. Bauer made his jump 100 meters from the finish, but Grewal zipped by with less than 50 meters to go and won by little more than a bike length.

Bronze medalist Dag Otto Lauritzen took up cycling in 1981 to rehabilitate his knee after suffering an injury while parachute jumping.

**1988 Seoul** C: 136, N: 54, D: 9.27.
*196.8 KM*

| | | | |
|---|---|---|---|
| 1. | Olaf Ludwig | GDR | 4:32:22 |
| 2. | Bernd Gröne | GER | 4:32:25 |
| 3. | Christian Henn | GER | 4:32:46 |
| 4. | Robert Mionske | USA | 4:32:46 |
| 5. | Djamolidin Abdoujaparov | SOV | 4:32:46 |
| 6. | Edward Salas | AUS | 4:32:46 |
| 7. | Roberto Pelliconi | ITA | 4:32:46 |
| 8. | Graeme Miller | NZE | 4:32:46 |

The unusually flat course laid out by the Seoul organizers was good news for talented sprinter Olaf Ludwig of Gera-

Thieschity. Eight years earlier, in Moscow, Ludwig had taken a silver in the team time trial and finished thirty-second in the road race. In Seoul he placed fourteenth in the points race three days before winning the road race.

A sidelight of note: by finishing ninth, 21-year-old Emili Perez became the highest placed athlete in Olympic history in any sport from the minuscule European nation of Andorra (pop. 50,000).

## TEAM TIME TRIAL

Until 1960 the results of the individual road race were used to determine the team winner. However, starting with the 1960 Rome Olympics a separate team event was held in which four cyclists from each team race against the clock, riding together in a line and periodically changing positions as in the team pursuit. The official time is that of the third rider for each team.

**1896–1908** not held

**1912 Stockholm** T: 15, N: 15, D: 7.7.
*320 KM*

| | | COMBINED TIME |
|---|---|---|
| 1. SWE | (Eric Friborg, Ragnar Malm, Axel Persson, Algot Lönn) | 44:35:33.6 |
| 2. GBR/England | (Frederick Grubb, Leonard Meredith, Charles Moss, Victor Hammond) | 44:44:39.2 |
| 3. USA | (Carl Schutte, Alvin Loftes, Albert Krushel, Walter Martin) | 44:47:55.5 |
| 4. GBR/Scotland | (John Wilson, Robert Thompson, John Miller, D.M. Stevensen) | 46:29:55.1 |
| 5. FIN | (Antti Raita, Vilho Tilkanen, Johan Kankonnen, Hjalmar Väre) | 46:34:03.5 |
| 6. GER | (Franz Lemnitz, Rudolf Baier, Oswald Rathmann, Georg Warsow) | 46:35:16.1 |
| 7. AUT | (Robert Rammer, Adolf Kofler, Rudolf Kramer, Josef Hellensteiner) | 46:57:26.4 |
| 8. DEN | (Olaf Meyland Smith, Charles Hansen, Johannes Reinwald, Hans Olsen) | 47:16:07.0 |

**1920 Antwerp** T:11, N: 11, D: 8.9.
*175 KM*

| | | COMBINED TIME |
|---|---|---|
| 1. FRA | (Fernand Canteloube, Georges Detreille, Achille Souchard, Marcel Gobillot) | 19:16:43.2 |
| 2. SWE | (Harry Stenqvist, Ragnar Malm, Axel Persson, Sigfrid Lundberg) | 19:23:10.0 |
| 3. BEL | (Jean Janssens, Albert de Buinne, André Vercruysse, Albert Wyckmans) | 19:28:44.4 |
| 4. DEN | (Christian Johansen, Arnold Lundgren, Christian Frisch, Ahrensberg Clausen) | 19:52:35.0 |
| 5. ITA | (Federico Gay, Pietro Bestetti, Camillo Arduino, Dante Guindani) | 20:24:44.0 |
| 6. HOL | (Petrus Ikelaar, Nico de Jong, Arie Gerrit van der Stel, Pieter Kloppenburg) | 20:28:39.2 |

| | | |
|---|---|---|
| 7. USA | (James Freeman, Ernest Kockler, August Nogara, John Otto) | 21:32:36.6 |
| 8. NOR | (Flately, Hanrickson, Nijgaard, Strycken) | 21:40:16.8 |

**1924 Paris** T: 16, N: 16, D: 7.23.
*188 KM*

| | | COMBINED TIME |
|---|---|---|
| 1. FRA | (Armand Blanchonnet, René Hamel, Georges Wambst) | 19:30:14.0 |
| 2. BEL | (Henri Hoevenaers, Alphonse Parfondry, Jean van den Bosch) | 19:46:55.4 |
| 3. SWE | (Gunnar Sköld, Erik Bohlin, Ragnar Malm) | 19:59:41.6 |
| 4. SWI | (Albert Blattmann, Otto Lehner, Georg Antenen) | 20:11:15.0 |
| 5. ITA | (Ardito Bresciani, Antonio Negrini, Nello Ciaccheri) | 20:19:59.2 |
| 6. HOL | (C. Heeren, Jan Maas, Phillippus Hendrik Innemee) | 20:37:27.8 |

**1928 Amsterdam** T: 15, N: 15, D: 8.7.
*168 KM*

| | | COMBINED TIME |
|---|---|---|
| 1. DEN | (Henry Hansen, Leo Nielsen, Orla Jörgensen) | 15:09:14.0 |
| 2. GBR | (Frank Southall, Jack Lauterwasser, John Middleton) | 15:14:49.0 |
| 3. SWE | (Gösta Carlsson, Erik Jansson, E. Georg Johnsson) | 15:27:49.0 |
| 4. ITA | (Allegro Grandi, Michele Orecchia, Ambrogio Beretta) | 15:33:12.0 |
| 5. BEL | (Jean Aerts, Pierre Houdé, Joseph Lowagie) | 15:33:50.0 |
| 6. SWI | (Gottlieb Amstein, Jakob Caironi, Tütel Wanzenried) | 15:35:21.0 |
| 7. FRA | (A. Aumerle, L. Bessiere, O. Dayen) | 15:38:20.0 |
| 8. ARG | (C. Saavedra, F. Bonvehi, J. Lopez) | 15:42:55.0 |

**1932 Los Angeles** T: 8, N: 8, D: 8.4.
*100 KM*

| | | COMBINED TIME |
|---|---|---|
| 1. ITA | (Attilio Pavesi, Guglielmo Segato, Giuseppe Olmo) | 7:27:15.2 |
| 2. DEN | (Frode Sörensen, Leo Nielsen, Henry Hansen) | 7:38:50.2 |
| 3. SWE | (Bernhard Britz, Sven Höglund, A. Arne Berg) | 7:39:12.6 |
| 4. GBR | (Frank Southall, Charles Holland, Stanley Butler) | 7:44:53.0 |
| 5. FRA | (Paul Chocque, Amédée Fournier, Henri Mouillefarine) | 7:46:31.8 |
| 6. USA | (Henry O'Brien, Frank Connell, Otto Luedeke) | 7:51:55.6 |
| 7. CAN | (Frances Elliott, James Jackson, Francis Robbins) | 8:01:38.0 |
| 8. GER | (Hubert Ebner, W. Lange-Wittich, Julius Maus) | 8:21:21.2 |

**1936 Berlin** T:22, N: 22, D: 8.10.
**100 KM**

| | | | COMBINED TIME |
|---|---|---|---|
| 1. | FRA | (Robert Charpentier, Guy Lapébie, Robert Dorgebray) | 7:39:16.2 |
| 2. | SWI | (Ernst Nievergelt, Edgar Buchwalder, Kurt Ott) | 7:39:20.4 |
| 3. | BEL | (Auguste Garrebeek, Armand Putzeys, Francois Vandermette) | 7:39:21.0 |
| 4. | ITA | (Pierino Favalli, Glauco Servadei, Corrado Ardizzoni) | 7:39:22.0 |
| 5. | AUT | (Virgilius Altmann, Hans Höfner, Hans Schnalek) | 7:39:24.0 |

**1948 London** T: 25, N: 25, D: 8.13.
**194.63 KM**

| | | | COMBINED TIME |
|---|---|---|---|
| 1. | BEL | (Lode Wouters, Léon Delathouwer, Eugène van Roosbroeck) | 15:58:17.4 |
| 2. | GBR | (Robert Maitland, Gordon Thomas, C.S. Ian Scott) | 16:03:31.6 |
| 3. | FRA | (José Beyaert, Alain Moineau, Jacques Dupont) | 16:08:19.4 |
| 4. | ITA | (Alfo Ferrari, Silvio Pedroni, Franco Fanti) | 16:13:05.2 |
| 5. | SWE | (Nils Johansson, Harry Snell, Åke Olivestedt) | 16:20:26.6 |
| 6. | SWI | (Jakob Schenk, Jean Brun, Walter Reiser) | 16:23:04.2 |
| 7 | ARG | (C. Perone, D. Benvenuti, M. Sevillano) | 16:39:46.2 |

**1952 Helsinki** T: 27, N: 27, D: 8.2.
**190.4 KM**

| | | | COMBINED TIME |
|---|---|---|---|
| 1. | BEL | (André Noyelle, Robert Grondelaers, Lucien Victor) | 15:20:46.6 |
| 2. | ITA | (Dino Bruni, Vincenzo Zucconelli, Gianni Ghidini) | 15:33:27.3 |
| 3. | FRA | (Jacques Anquetil, Alfred Tonello, Claude Rover) | 15:38:58.1 |
| 4. | SWE | (Yngve Lundh, Stig Mårtensson, Allan Carlsson) | 15:41:34.3 |
| 5. | GER | (Edi Ziegler, Oskar Zeissner, Paul Maue) | 15:43:50.5 |
| 6. | DEN | (Hans Andersen, Jörgen Rasmussen, Poul Östergaard) | 15:48:02.0 |
| 7. | LUX | (André Moes, Roger Ludwig, Nicolas Morn) | 15:49:04.0 |
| 8. | HOL | (Arend Van't Hof, Johannes Planatz, Adrianus Voorting) | 15:52:22.7 |

Jacques Anquetil of the French team went on to win the Tour de France five times.

**1956 Melbourne** T: 20, N: 20, D: 12.7.
**187.73 KM**

| | | | PTS. |
|---|---|---|---|
| 1. | FRA | (2—Arnaud Geyre, 8—Maurice Moucheraud, 12—Michel Vermeulin) | 22 |
| 2. | GBR | (3—Alan Jackson, 6—Arthur Stanley Brittain, 14—William Holmes) | 23 |
| 3. | GDR/GER | (4—Horst Tüller, 5—Gustav-Adolf Schur, 18—Reinhold Pommer) | 27 |
| 4. | ITA | (1—Ercole Baldini, 7—Arnaldo Pambianco, 28—Dino Bruni) | 36 |
| 5. | SWE | (10—Lars Nordwall, 17—Karl-Ivan Andersson, 20—Roland Ströhm) | 47 |
| 6. | SOV | (15—Anatoly Cherepovich, 16—Nikolai Kolumbet, 32—Viktor Kapitonov) | 63 |
| 7. | BEL | (23—Norbert Verougstraete, 24—Gustave De Smet, 42—François van den Bosch) | 89 |
| 8. | COL | (13—Ramon Hoyos Vallejo, 39—Pablo Hurtada Castañeda 40—Jaime Villegas) | 92 |

In 1956 the placings in the team road race were determined not by combined times, but by adding together the individual placings of the team members. Great Britain lost its chances for a gold medal when Billy Holmes crashed into a photographer who had stepped onto the course. Holmes was injured, but worse still, was delayed two and a half minutes while he changed a wheel. Holmes caught up with the leaders eleven miles later, but had he finished one second earlier, Britain would have taken first place.

**1960 Rome** T: 32, N: 32, D: 8.26.
**100 KM**

| | | | |
|---|---|---|---|
| 1. | ITA | (Antonio Bailetti, Ottavio Cogilati, Giacomo Fornoni, Livio Trapé) | 2:14:33.53 |
| 2. | GDR | (Gustav-Adolf Schur, Egon Adler, Erich Hagen, Günter Lörke) | 2:16:56.31 |
| 3. | SOV | (Viktor Kapitonov, Yevgeny Klevzov, Yuri Melikhov, Aleksei Petrov) | 2:18:41:67 |
| 4. | HOL | (Johannes Hugens, Cornelis Lotz, Albert Sluis, Pieter van Kreuningen) | 2:19:15.71 |
| 5. | SWE | (Owe Adamson, Gunnar Göransson, Oswald Johansson, Gösta Pettersson) | 2:19:36.37 |
| 6. | ROM | (Ion Cosma, Gabriel Moiceanu, Aurel Selaru, Ludovic Zanoni) | 2:20:18.91 |
| 7. | FRA | (Henri Duez, François Hamon, Roland Lacombe, Jacques Simon) | 2:20:36.38 |
| 8. | SPA | (Ignacio Astigarraga Uriarte, Juan Sanchez Camero, José Momene Campo, Ramon Saez Marzo) | 2:21:34:59 |

**1964 Tokyo** T:33, N: 33, D: 10.14.
**109.89 KM**

| | | | |
|---|---|---|---|
| 1. | HOL | (Evert Dolman, Gerben Karstens, Johannes Pieterse, Hubertus Zoet) | 2:26:31.19 |
| 2. | ITA | (Severino Andreoli, Luciano Dalla Bona, Pietro Guerra, Ferrucio Manza) | 2:26:55.39 |
| 3. | SWE | (Sven Hamrin, Erik Pettersson, Gösta Pettersson, Sture Pettersson) | 2:27:11.52 |
| 4. | ARG | (Hector Acosta, Roberto Breppe, Delmo Delmastro, Ruben Placanica) | 2:27:58.55 |
| 5. | SOV | (Yuri Melikhov, Anatoly Olizarenko, Aleksei Petrov, Gaynan Saidkhuschin) | 2:28:26.48 |
| 6. | FRA | (Marcel-Ernest Bidault, Georges Chappe, André Desvages, Jean-Claude Wuillemin) | 2:28:52.74 |
| 7. | DEN | (Flemming Hansen, Henning Petersen, Ole Pedersen, Ole Ritter) | 2:29:10.33 |

8. SPA    (José Goyeneche, José Lopez, Mariano    2:30:55.26
          Diaz, Luis Santamarina)

**1968 Mexico City** T: 30, N: 30, D: 10.15.
*104 KM*
1. HOL    (Fedor den Hertog, Jan Krekels, Marinus    2:07:49.06
          Pijnen, Gerardes Zoetemelk)
2. SWE    (Erik Pettersson, Gösta Pettersson, Sture    2:09:26.60
          Pettersson, Tomas Pettersson)
3. ITA    (Giovanni Bramucci, Vittorio Marcelli,    2:10:18.74
          Mauro Simonetti, Pierfranco Vianelli)
4. DEN    (Verner Blaudzun, Jörgen Emil Hansen,    2:12:41.41
          Ole Hojlund Pederson, Leif Martensen)
5. NOR    (Thorleif Andresen, Ornulf Andresen, Tore    2:14:32.85
          Milsett, Leif Yli)
6. POL    (Jan Magiera, Zenon Czechowski, Marian    2:14:40.98
          Kegel, Andrzej Blawdzin)
7. ARG    (Juan Merlos, Carlos Alvarez, Roberto    2:15:34.24
          Breppe, Ernesto Contreras)
8. GER    (Burkhard Ebert, Jürgen Tschan, Ortwin    2:15:37.25
          Czarnowski, Dieter Koslar)

The four Swedish silver medalists were all brothers. All
four of them subsequently changed their last names from
Pettersson to that of their home village, Fåglum.

**1972 Munich** T:35, N: 35, D: 9.6.
*100 KM*
1. SOV    (Boris Chouhov, Valery Iardy, Gennady    2:11:17.8
          Komnatov, Valery Likhachev)
2. POL    (Lucjan Lis, Edward Barcik, Stanislaw    2:11:47.5
          Szozda, Ryszard Szurkowski)
3. BEL    (Ludo Delcroix, Gustaaf Hermans,    2:12:36.7
          Gustaaf Van Cauter, Louis Verreydt)
4. NOR    (Thorleif Andresen, Arve Haugen, Knut    2:13:20.7
          Knudsen, Magne Orre)
5. SWE    (Lennart Fagerlund, Tord Filipsson, Leif    2:13:36.9
          Hansson, Sven-Åke Nilsson)
6. HUN    (Tibor Decreceni, Imre Géra, József Pe-    2:14:18.8
          terman, András Takács)
7. SWI    (Gilbert Bischoff, Bruno Hubschmid, Ro-    2:14:33.6
          land Schaer, Ulrich Sutter)
8. ITA    (Osvaldo Castellan, Pasqualino Moretti,    2:14:36.2
          Francesco Moser, Giovanni Tonoli)
DISQ (Drugs): HOL (Fedor den Hertog, Hennie Kuiper, Cees Priem,
    Aad van den Hoek) 2:12:27.1

The Dutch team was disqualified after it was determined
that one of their members, Aad van den Hoek, had taken
Coramine, a drug which was permitted by the International Cyclists' Union but forbidden by the International
Olympic Committee. It was decided that the Belgian
team would not be awarded bronze medals because its
members had not been tested for drugs.

**1976 Montreal** T: 28, N: 28, D: 7.18.
*100 KM*
1. SOV    (Anatoly Chukanov, Valery Chaplygin,    2:08:53.
          Vladimir Kaminsky, Aavo Pikkuus)

2. POL    (Tadeusz Mytnik, Mieczyslaw Nowicki,    2:09:13.
          Stanislaw Szozda, Ryszard Szurkowski)
3. DEN    (Verner Blaudzun, Gert Frank, Jörgen    2:12:20.
          Hansen, Törgen Lund)
4. GER    (Hans-Peter Jakst, Olaf Paltian, Friedrich    2:12:35.
          von Löffelholz, Peter Weibel)
5. CZE    (Petr Buchaček, Petr Matoušek, Milan    2:12:56.
          Puzrla, Vladimir Vondraček)
6. GBR    (Paul Carbutt, Philip Griffiths, Dudley    2:13:10.
          Hayton, William Nickson)
7. SWE    (Tord Filipsson, Bernt Johansson, Sven-    2:13:13.
          Åke Nilsson, Tommy Prim)
8. NOR    (Stein Brathen, Geir Digerud, Arne    2:13:17.
          Klavenes, Magne Orre)

**1980 Moscow** T: 23, N: 23, D: 7.20.
*101 KM*
1. SOV    (Yuri Kashirin, Oleg Logvin, Sergei    2:01:21.7
          Shelpakov, Anatoly Yarkin)
2. GDR    (Falk Boden, Bernd Drogan, Olaf Ludwig,    2:02:53.2
          Hans-Joachim Hartnick)
3. CZE    (Michal Klasa, Vlastibor Konečný, Alipi    2:02:53.9
          Kostadinov, Jiří Škoda)
4. POL    (Stefan Ciekanski, Jan Jankiewicz,    2:04:13.8
          Czeslaw Lang, Witold Plutecki)
5. ITA    (Mauro De Pellegrin, Gianni Giacomini,    2:04:36.2
          Ivano Maffei, Alberto Minetti)
6. BUL    (Borislav Assenov, Venelin Houbenov,    2:05:55.2
          Yordan Penchev, Nencho Staikov)
7. FIN    (Harry Hannus, Kari Puisto, Patrick    2:05:58.2
          Wackstrom, Sixten Wackstrom)
8. YUG    (Bruno Bilic, Vinko Poloncic, Bojan    2:07:12.0
          Ropret, Bojan Udović)

**1984 Los Angeles** T: 26, N: 26, D: 8.5.
*100 KM*
1. ITA    (Marcello Bartalini, Marco Giovannetti,    1:58.28
          Eros Poli, Claudio Vandelli)
2. SWI    (Alfred Achermann, Richard Trinkler,    2:02:38
          Laurent Vial, Benno Wiss)
3. USA    (Ronald Kiefel, Roy Knickman, Davis    2:02:46
          Phinney, Andrew Weaver)
4. HOL    (Johan Alberts, Erik Breukink, Martinus    2:02:57
          Ducrot, Gert Jakobs)
5. SWE    (Bengt Asplund, Per Christiansson, Mag-    2:04:46
          nus Knutsson, Håkan Larsson)
6. FRA    (Jean François Bernard, Philippe    2:05:07
          Bouvatier, Thierry Marie, Denis Prlizzari)
7. DEN    (John Carlsen, Kim Jolin Eriksen, Lars    2:05:31
          Erik Jensen, Sören Liholt)
8. GBR    (Steve Poulter, Keith Reynolds, Peter    2:05:51
          Sanders, Darryl Webster)

The Soviet Union surely would have been the gold
medal favorite had their team not been prevented by
their government from competing. The U.S.S.R. had
won the last three Olympic team time trials as well as
the 1983 world championship. However, as it turned

out, they would have been hard-pressed to defeat the amazing Italians who, equipped with revolutionary spokeless carbon fiber disc wheels, completed the course in the fastest time ever recorded, despite losing 20 seconds while changing a wheel. Their winning margin of 4 minutes 10 seconds was unheard of at international-level competition.

The site of the race was one of the dullest venues in Olympic history—a 15½ mile concrete stretch of the Artesia Freeway between the Harbor Freeway and the Santa Ana Freeway. During the medal ceremony, the winning teams enjoyed the rare privilege of seeing their national flags raised in front of the Regal Plastic Company and a freeway exit sign for Avalon Blvd.

**1988 Seoul** T: 31, N: 31, D: 9.18.

| | | | COMBINED TIME |
|---|---|---|---|
| 1. | GDR | (Uwe Ampler, Mario Kummer, Maik Landsmann, Jan Schur) | 1:57:47.7 |
| 2. | POL | (Joachim Halupczok, Zenon Jaskula, Marek Leśniewski, Andrzej Sypytkowski) | 1:57:54.2 |
| 3. | SWE | (Björn Johansson, Jan Karlsson, Michel Lafis, Anders Jarl) | 1:59:47.3 |
| 4. | FRA | (Laurent Bezault, Eric Heulot, Pascal Lance, Thierry Laurent) | 1:59:49.8 |
| 5. | ITA | (Roberto Maggioni, Eros Poli, Mario Scirea, Flavio Vanzella) | 1:59:58.3 |
| 6. | GER | (Ernst Christl, Bernd Gröne, Rajmund Lehnert, Remig Stumpf) | 2:00:06.3 |
| 7. | SOV | (Vasily Zhdanov, Viktor Klimov, Asyat Saitov, Igor Sumnikov) | 2:00:27.0 |
| 8. | CZE | (Vladimír Hruza, Vladimír Kinst, Milan Křen, Jozef Regec) | 2:00:57.1 |

# Discontinued Events
## ONE-LAP RACE

**1896 Athens** C: 8, N: 5, D: 4.11.
*(333.33 Meters)*
1. Paul Masson           FRA   24.0
2. Stamatios Nikolopoulos   GRE   26.0
3. Adolf Schmal          AUT   26.0
4. E. Battel             GBR   26.2
5. Theodor Flameng       GER   27.0
5. F. Keeping            GBR   27.0
5. Theodor Leupold       GER   27.0
8. Joseph Rosemeyer      GER   27.2

Nikolopoulos was awarded second place after defeating Schmal in a race-off 25.4 to 26.6.

**1900–1904** not held

**1906 Athens** C: 24, N: 9, D: 4.23.
*(333.33 Meters)*
1. Francesco Verri       ITA   22.8
2. H. Crowther           GBR   23.2
3. Menjou                FRA   23.2
4. Emile Demangel        FRA   23.2
5. Eugène Debougnie      BEL   23.6
6. F. Della Ferrera      ITA   23.8
7. A. Verdesopoulos      GRE   23.8
8. H.C. Bouffler (GBR), Bruno Götze (GER), Max Götze (GER), John Matthews (GBR) 24.2

Crowther was awarded second place after winning a race-off. His time was 22.8, while Menjou clocked 23.2 and Demangel 23.6.

**1908 London** C: 46, N: 9, D: 7.15.
*(603.49 Meters)*
1. Victor Johnson        GBR   51.2
2. Emile Demangel        FRA   —
3. Karl Neumer           GER   —
4. Daniel Flynn          GBR   —

# 5000-METER TRACK RACE

**1906 Athens** C: 26, N: 9, D: 4.23.
1. Francesco Verri       ITA   7:28.6
2. H. Crowther           GBR   —
3. Fernand Vast          FRA   —
AC: Emile Demangel (FRA), Max Götze (GER)

**1908 London** C: 42, N: 8, D: 7.18.
1. Benjamin Jones        GBR   8:36.2
2. Maurice Schilles      FRA   —
3. André Auffray         FRA   —
4. E. Maréchal           FRA   —
5. Charles Kingsbury     GBR   —
6. Johannes van Spengen  HOL   —
7. Gerard Bosch van Drakestein  HOL   —

In the final of the 1000-meter sprint, Schilles beat Jones by inches. However, the race was declared void because the time limit was exceeded. Two days later in the 5000 meters it was Jones who held off Schilles' finishing sprint to win, by 6 inches.

# 10 KM TRACK RACE

**1896 Athens** C: 6, N: 4, D: 4.11.
1. Paul Masson           FRA   17:54.2
2. Léon Flameng          FRA   17:54.8
3. Adolf Schmal          AUT   —
4. Joseph Rosemeyer      GER   —
DNF: Georgios Kolettis (GRE), Aristidis Konstantinidis (GRE)

## 20 KM TRACK RACE

**1906 Athens** C: 24, N: 9, D: 4.23.
1. William Pett          GBR    29:00.0
2. Maurice Bardonneau    FRA    29:30.0
3. Fernand Vast          FRA    29:32.0
4. Hans Holly            AUT    —
5. Eduard Dannenberg     GER    —
AC: Ad. Böhm (GER), Edmond Luguet (FRA)

**1908 London** C: 44, N: 11, D: 7.14.
1. Charles Kingsbury     GBR    34:13.6
2. Benjamin Jones        GBR    —
3. Joseph Werbrouck      BEL    —
4. Louis Weintz          USA    —

Kingsbury, of Portsmouth, won by 3 inches.

## 50 KM TRACK RACE

**1920 Antwerp** C: 31, N: 10, D: 8.12.
1. Henry George          BEL    1:16:43.2
2. Cyril Alden           GBR    —
3. Piet Ikelaar          HOL    —
4. Ruggero Ferrario      ITA    —
5. Herbert McDonald      CAN    —
6. Franco Giorgetti      ITA    —
7. William Smith         SAF    —

Eyewitnesses said that Ikelaar actually finished second. The Jury of Appeal eventually agreed, but refused to reverse the judges' verdict, since it had already been announced.

**1924 Paris** C: 36, N: 16, D: 7.27.
1. Jacobus Willems       HOL    1:18:24.0
2. Cyril Alden           GBR    —
3. Frank Wyld            GBR    —
4. Angelo De Martino     ITA    —
5. Józef Lange           POL    —
6. Alfredo Dinale        ITA    —

## 100 KM TRACK RACE

**1896 Athens** C; 9, N: 5, D: 4.8.
1. Léon Flameng          FRA    3:08:19.2
2. Georgios Kolettis     GRE    —

The race required 300 circuits of the track. Once, when Kolettis' bike needed repair, Flameng stopped and waited for him. Flameng fell towards the end of the race, but still won by six or seven laps. He raced with a French flag tied around his leg.

**1908 London** C: 43, N: 11, D: 7.16.
1. Charles Bartlett      GBR    2:41:48.6
2. Charles Denny         GBR    —
3. Octave Lapize         FRA    —
4. William Pett          GBR    —
5. P. Texier             FRA    —
6. Walter Andrews        CAN    —

7. D.C. Robertson        GBR    —
8. Sydney Bailey         GBR    —

This was considered the most important cycling contest of the 1908 Olympics, and there were so many entrants that qualifying heats had to be run to cut down the field. In the second of these heats, a bad accident occurred when Harry Venn, a walking official, walked right onto the track and collided with Coeckelberg of Belgium. Coeckelberg fell to the ground and was cut on the thigh and head, but he managed to finish the race, qualifying for the final as a consequence of his having led much of the way. In the final, with more than two and a half hours gone and only one lap of the track remaining, the race had come down to Octave Lapize of France and three representatives of Great Britain, Charles Denny, Charles Bartlett, and William Pett. The four were moving around at a crawl when Bartlett suddenly darted to the inside, took the lead, and sprinted home to win by almost a length.

## 12-HOUR RACE

**1896 Athens** C: 7, N: 4, D: 4.13.

|                      |     | KM      |
| -------------------- | --- | ------- |
| 1. Adolf Schmal      | AUT | 295.3   |
| 2. F. Keeping        | GBR | 294.946 |

DNF: Georgios Paraskevopoulos (GRE), Konstantinos Konstantinou (GRE), Loverdos (GRE), Tryfiatis (GRE), Josef Welzenbacher (GER)

## 2000-METER TANDEM

**1906 Athens** T: 6, N: 4, D: 4.23.
1. GBR   (John Matthews, Arthur Rushen)          2:15.0
2. GER   (Max Götze, Bruno Götze)                —
3. GER   (Eduard Dannenberg, Otto Küpferling)    —

**1908 London** T: 17, N: 7, D: 7.15.
1. FRA   (Maurice Schilles, André Auffray)       3:07.6
2. GBR   (Frederick Hamlin, H. Thomas Johnson)   —
3. GBR   (Colin Brooks, Walter Isaacs)           —

Schilles and Auffray had never ridden together before the first round of this contest.

**1912** not held

**1920 Antwerp** T: 10, N: 6, D: 8.12.
1. GBR   (Harry Ryan, Thomas Lance)              2:49.4
2. SAF   (James Walker, William Smith)           —
3. HOL   (Frans de Vreng, Piet Ikelaar)          —
4. GBR   (William Steward, Cyril Alden)          —

**1924 Paris** T: 5, N: 5, D: 7.27.
1. FRA   (Lucien Choury, Jean Cugnot)            12.6 (last 200 meters)
2. DEN   (Willy Falck Hansen, Edmund Hansen)     —
3. HOL   (Gerard Bosch van Drakestein, Maurice Peeters)   —

**1928 Amsterdam** T: 7, N: 7, D: 8.7.
1. HOL   (Bernhard Leene, Daniel van Dijk)   11.8
2. GBR   (John Sibbit, Ernest Henry Chambers)   —
3. GER   (Karl Köther, Hans Bernhardt)
4. ITA   (Francesco Malatesta, Adolf Corsi)

**1932 Los Angeles** T: 5, N: 5, D: 8.3.

|  |  | 1ST RACE | 2ND RACE |
|---|---|---|---|
| 1. | FRA (Maurice Perrin, Louis Chaillot) | 12.3 | 12.0 |
| 2. | GBR (Ernest Henry Chambers, Stanley Chambers) | | — |
| 3. | DEN (Willy Gervin, Harald Christensen) | | |
| 4. | HOL (Bernhard Leene, Jacobus van Egmond) | | |

**1936 Berlin** T: 11, N: 11, D: 8.8.

|  |  | 1ST RACE | 2ND RACE |
|---|---|---|---|
| 1. | GER (Ernst Ihbe, Carl Lorenz) | 11.0 | 11.0 |
| 2. | HOL (Bernhard Leene, Hendrik Ooms) | — | — |
| 3. | FRA (Pierre Georget, Georges Maton) | | |
| 4. | ITA (Carlo Legutti, Bruno Loatti) | | |

5. BEL (François Cools, Roger Pirotte), DEN (Heino Dissing, Bjorn Stieler), GBR (Ernest Chambers, John Sibbit), USA (William Logan, Albert Sellinger)

**1948 London** T: 10, N: 10, D: 8.11.

|  |  | 1ST RACE | 2ND RACE | 3RD RACE |
|---|---|---|---|---|
| 1. | ITA (Ferdinando Teruzzi, Renato Perona) | — | 11.3 | 11.6 |
| 2. | GBR (Reginald Harris, Alan Bannister) | 11.1 | — | — |
| 3. | FRA (René Faye, Georges Dron) | | | |
| 4. | SWI (Jean Roth, Max Aeberli) | | | |

5. BEL (Louis van Schill, R. de Pauw), DEN (Hans Andersen, Evan Klamer), HOL (N. Buchly, M. van Gelder), USA (Marvin Thompson, Alfred Stiller)

In a thrilling finish, held in the dark, Teruzzi and Perona won the tie-breaker by a mere six inches.

**1952 Helsinki** T: 14, N: 14, D: 7.31.
1. AUS   (Lionel Cox, Russell Mockridge)   11.0
2. SAF   (Raymond Robinson, Thomas Shardelow)   —
3. ITA   (Antonio Maspes, Cesare Pinarello)
4. FRA   (Franck Le Normand, Robert Vidal)
5. DEN (Jens Eriksen, Olaf Holmstrup), GBR (Leslie Wilson, Alan Bannister), HUN (István Schillerwein, Imre Furmen), NZE (Colin Dickinson, Clarence Simpson)

**1956 Melbourne** T: 10, N: 10, D: 6.12.
1. AUS   (Ian Browne, Anthony Marchant)   10.8
2. CZE   (Ladislav Fouček, Václav Machek)   —
3. ITA   (Giuseppe Ogna, Cesare Pinarello)
4. GBR   (Peter Brotherton, Eric Thompson)
5. FRA (Robert Vidal, André Gruchet), NZE (Richard Johnston, Warren Johnston), SAF (Thomas Shardelow, Raymond Robinson), USA (James Rossi, Donald Ferguson)

Browne and Marchant were surprise winners. They finished last in their first-round heat and lost the repêchage to Czechoslovakia. However, in another repêchage, the Germans and Soviets crashed, leaving the Soviet riders unable to restart. In need of opponents for the German pair, the officials turned to the already-eliminated Australians and Americans. Browne and Marchant won the race, scored two more unexpected victories in the quarterfinals and semifinals, and then upset Fouček and Machek in the final.

**1960 Rome** T: 12, N: 12, D: 8.27.

|  |  | 1ST RACE | 2ND RACE |
|---|---|---|---|
| 1. | ITA (Giuseppe Beghetto, Sergio Bianchetto) | 10.7 | 10.8 |
| 2. | GDR (Jürgen Simon, Lothar Stäber) | — | — |
| 3. | SOV (Boris Vasilyev, Vladimir Leonov) | | |
| 4. | HOL (Marinus Paul, Melis Gerritsen) | | |

5. CZE (Juraj Miklusica, Dusan Skvarenina), FRA (Roland Surrugue, Michael Scob), GBR (David Handley, Eric Thompson), USA (Jack Hartman, David Sharp)

**1964 Tokyo** T: 13, N: 13, D: 10.20.

|  |  | 1ST RACE | 2ND RACE | 3RD RACE |
|---|---|---|---|---|
| 1. | ITA (Angelo Damiano, Sergio Bianchetto) | — | 10.85 | 10.75 |
| 2. | SOV (Imant Bodnieks, Viktor Logunov) | 10.80 | — | — |
| 3. | GER (Willi Fuggerer, Klaus Kobusch) | | | |
| 4. | HOL (Arie de Graaf, Peiter van der Touw) | | | |

5. AUS (Ian Browne, Daryl Perkins), CZE (Karel Paar, Karel Stark), DEN (Niels Fredborg, Per Jorgensen), HUN (Richárd Bicskey, Ferenc Habony)

**1968 Mexico City** T: 14, N: 14, D: 10.21.

|  |  | 1ST RACE | 2ND RACE |
|---|---|---|---|
| 1. | FRA (Daniel Morelon, Pierre Trentin) | 10.03 | 9.83 |
| 2. | HOL (Johannes Jansen, Leijn Loevesijn) | — | — |
| 3. | BEL (Daniel Goens, Robert van Lancker) | | |
| 4. | ITA (Walter Gorini, Luigi Borghetti) | | |

5. CZE (Ivan Kucirek, Milos Jelinek), GDR (Werner Otto, Jürgen Geschke), GER (Klaus Kobusch, Martin Stenzel), SOV (Igor Tselovalnikov, Imant Bodnieks)

**1972 Munich** T: 14, N: 14, D: 9.3.

|  |  | 1st RACE | 2ND RACE | 3RD RACE |
|---|---|---|---|---|
| 1. | SOV (Vladimir Semenets, Igor Tselovalnikov) | — | 10.52 | 10.60 |
| 2. | GDR (Jürgen Geschke, Werner Otto) | 10.68 | — | — |
| 3. | POL (Andrzej Bek, Benedykt Kocot) | | | |
| 4. | FRA (Daniel Morelon, Pierre Trentin) | | | |

5. BEL (Manu Snellinx, Noel Scetaert), CZE (Ivan Kucirek, Vladimir Popelka), GER (Jürgen Barth, Rainer Müller), HOL (Klaas Balk, Peter van Doorn)

# WOMEN

## 1000-METER SPRINT (SCRATCH)

**1896–1984** not held

**1988 Seoul** C: 12, N: 12, D: 9.24. WR: 11.245 (Connie Paraskevin-Young)

|   |   |   | 1ST RACE | 2ND RACE | 3RD RACE |
|---|---|---|---|---|---|
| 1. | Erika Salumäe | SOV | — | 12.00 | 12.58 |
| 2. | Christa Luding-Rothenburger | GDR | 11.68 | — | — |
| 3. | Connie Young | USA | | | |
| 4. | Isabelle Gautheron | FRA | | | |
| 5. | Julie Speight | AUS | | | |
| 6. | Zhou Suying | CHN | | | |
| 7. | Louise Jones | GBR | | | |
| 8. | Yang Hsiu-Chen | TAI | | | |

In 1984 Christa Rothenburger of Dresden won a gold medal in the 500-meter speed skating event in Sarajevo. In 1988, in Calgary, she missed another gold in the 500 by two one-hundredths of a second, but came back three days later to win the 1000-meter event. Eight years earlier, her coach, Ernst Luding, had persuaded her to take up cycling in the off-season. When she saw her first match sprint race she was terrified. "I was convinced that as soon as I tried to ride I would undoubtedly topple right over." Rothenburger learned quickly. At the 1986 world championships, her first international competition, she upset Estonian Erika Salumäe for the gold medal. Although Salumäe turned the tables in 1987, Rothenburger, who married Luding after Calgary, was on target to become the first person to win medals in the Winter and Summer Olympics in the same year.

In Seoul Luding-Rothenburger ensured her place in sports history by defeating Gautheron in the semifinals. She won the first race of the final and it looked like she might match Eddie Eagan's feat of winning Olympic championships in both winter and summer sports. But Salumäe outmaneuvered her twice in a row and Luding-Rothenburger ended up instead like Jacob Tullin: gold in winter, silver in summer.

## 4000-METER INDIVIDUAL PURSUIT

This event will be held for the first time in 1992.

## ROAD RACE

**1896–1980** not held

**1984 Los Angeles-Mission Viejo** C: 45, N; 16, D: 7.29.
**79.2 KM**
1. Connie Carpenter-Phinney　USA　2:11:14
2. Rebecca Twigg　USA　2:11:14

3. Sandra Schumacher　GER　2:11.14
4. Unni Larsen　NOR　2:11.14
5. Maria Canins　ITA　2:11:14
6. Jeannie Longo　FRA　2:12:35
7. Helle Sörensen　DEN　2:13:28
8. Ute Enzenauer　GER　2:13:28

At the age of 14, Connie Carpenter had competed at the 1972 Winter Olympics in Sapporo, finishing seventh in the 1500-meter speed skating event. An ankle injury forced her to switch to cycling four years later. She gave up the sport for rowing, but returned to the track in 1981, dominating U.S. women's cycling until the arrival of another early achiever, Rebecca Twigg of Seattle, Wash. Twigg's early achievements were not athletic, but academic. After completing 8th grade, the 14-year-old Twigg skipped four years of secondary schooling and went straight to the University of Washington, where she studied biology.

In 1982, when she was 19, Twigg beat Carpenter to become the world pursuit champion. She did not defend her championship, preferring to concentrate on road racing, since that would be the only women's cycling event contested at the Los Angeles Olympics. In her absence, Carpenter took the world pursuit title despite competing less than two months after breaking her arm.

In the Olympic road race, six women broke away at the mid-point. With 800 meters to go, Jeannie Longo clashed wheels with Maria Canins, causing her rear derailleur to break and her chain to come off. The remaining five prepared for the final sprint. Canins took off first, 500 meters from the finish. Schumacher, a 17-year-old surprise, was the next to make her move. With 200 meters to go it was the turn of Carpenter and Twigg. Twigg seemed to have a decisive lead at the 100-meter mark and Carpenter thought she had lost the gold as late as the 50-meter mark. But she sped on, caught Twigg a mere three meters from the finish line and, using a technique which she had practiced every day for a month, she threw her bike forward and won by less than half a wheel.

Carpenter's husband, Davis Phinney, who had taught her the bike-throw move, also competed at the 1984 Olympics, finishing fifth in the men's road race and earning a bronze medal in the team time trial.

**1988 Seoul** C: 53, N: 23, D: 9.26.
**82 KM**
1. Monique Knol　HOL　2:00:52
2. Jutta Niehaus　GER　2:00:52
3. Laima Zilporite　SOV　2:00:52
4. Genevieve Brunet　CAN　2:00:52
5. Valentina Evpak　SOV　2:00:52
6. Maria Blower　GBR　2:00:52
7. Marie Höljer　SWE　2:00:52
8. Inga Benedict　USA　2:00:52

Until the very end, this was a dull race inspired by a dull course. The only attempt at a break came from Inga

Benedict with about 5 kilometers to go. But she was hauled in by the heavy favorite, Jeannie Longo, who took the pack with her. Longo, still recovering from a hip fracture and bruise, eventually finished twenty-first. As they neared the finish line, 45 of the 53 starters were still in a pack. With 400 meters to go, 24-year-old substitute teacher Monique Knol, as she put it, "saw a little hole—*schwoook*—I went away and that was it. I sprinted by myself."

# EQUESTRIAN

Three-Day Event, Individual
Three-Day Event, Team
Jumping (Prix des Nations), Individual
Jumping (Prix des Nations), Team
Dressage, Individual
Dressage, Team
Discontinued Events

## THREE-DAY EVENT, INDIVIDUAL

The three-day event consists of three parts: dressage, endurance, and show jumping. The dressage and jumping portions follow the same basic rules and scoring as the regular dressage and jumping events. The endurance phase is a long-distance obstacle run broken into four sections: two "road and tracks," one "steeplechase," and one "cross-country." Penalty points are assessed for falls and overtime, while bonus points can be accumulated by completing any of the four sections of the endurance run under the set time limit.

**1896—1908** not held

**1912 Stockholm** C: 27, N: 7, D: 7.17.

|  |  | HORSE | PTS. |
|---|---|---|---|
| 1. Axel Nordlander | SWE | Lady Artist | 46.59 |
| 2. Friedrich von Rochow | GER | Idealist | 46.42 |
| 3. Jean Cariou | FRA | Cocotte | 46.32 |
| 4. Nils Adlercreutz | SWE | Atout | 46.31 |
| 5. Ernst Casparsson | SWE | Irmelin | 46.16 |
| 5. Rudolf Graf von Schaesberg-Tannheim | GER | Grundsee | 46.16 |
| 7. Eduard von Lütcken | GER | Blue Boy | 45.90 |
| 8. John Montgomery | USA | Deceive | 45.88 |

**1920 Antwerp** C: 25, N: 8, D: 9.10.

|  |  | HORSE | PTS. |
|---|---|---|---|
| 1. Helmer Mörner | SWE | Germania | 1775.00 |
| 2. Åge Lundström | SWE | Ysra | 1738.75 |
| 3. Ettore Caffaratti | ITA | Caniche | 1733.75 |
| 4. Roger Moeremans d'Emaus | BEL | Sweet Girl | 1652.50 |
| 5. Garibaldi Spighi | ITA | Otello | 1647.50 |
| 6. Harry Chamberlin | USA | Nigra | 1568.75 |
| 7. William West | USA | Black Boy | 1558.75 |
| 8. Georg von Braun | SWE | Diana | 1543.75 |

The competition consisted of jumping, a 20-kilometer course, and a 50-kilometer course, but no dressage.

**1924 Paris** C: 44, N: 13, D: 7, 26.

|  |  | HORSE | DRESSAGE | ENDURANCE | JUMPING | TOTAL PTS. |
|---|---|---|---|---|---|---|
| 1. Adolph van der Voort van Zijp | HOL | Silver Piece | 174.0 | 1402.0 | 400.0 | 1976.0 |
| 2. Frode Kirkebjerg | DEN | Meteor | 164.0 | 1409.5 | 280.0 | 1853.5 |
| 3. Sloan Doak | USA | Pathfinder | 156.0 | 1369.5 | 320.0 | 1845.5 |
| 4. Charles Pahud de Mortanges | HOL | Johnny Walker | 174.0 | 1334.0 | 320.0 | 1828.0 |
| 5. Claës König | SWE | Bojar | 166.0 | 1284.0 | 280.0 | 1730.0 |
| 6. Beaudouin de Brabandère | BEL | Modestie | 138.0 | 1190.5 | 400.0 | 1728.5 |
| 6. Edward de Fonblanque | GBR | Copper | 133.0 | 1275.5 | 320.0 | 1728.5 |
| 8. Frank Carr | USA | Proctor | 154.0 | 1333.0 | 240.0 | 1727.0 |

**1928 Amsterdam** C: 46, N: 17, D: 8.11.

|  |  | HORSE | DRESSAGE | ENDURANCE | JUMPING | TOTAL PTS. |
|---|---|---|---|---|---|---|
| 1. Charles Pahud de Mortanges | HOL | Marcroix | 237.82 | 1432.0 | 300.0 | 1969.82 |
| 2. Gerard de Kruyff | HOL | Va-t-en | 251.26 | 1416.0 | 300.0 | 1967.26 |
| 3. Bruno Neumann | GER | Ilja | 208.42 | 1436.0 | 300.0 | 1944.42 |
| 4. Adolph van der Voort van Zijp | HOL | Silver Piece | 224.60 | 1404.0 | 300.0 | 1928.60 |
| 5. Hans Olof von Essen | FIN | El Kaid | 180.64 | 1444.0 | 300.0 | 1924.64 |
| 6. Bjart Ording | NOR | And Over | 200.98 | 1412.0 | 300.0 | 1912.98 |
| 7. Nils Kettner | SWE | Caesar | 197.66 | 1404.0 | 300.0 | 1901.66 |
| 8. Arthur Quist | NOR | Hidalgo | 221.14 | 1404.0 | 270.0 | 1895.14 |

**1932 Los Angeles** C: 14, N: 5, D: 8.13.

|  |  | HORSE | DRESSAGE | ENDURANCE | JUMPING | TOTAL PTS. |
|---|---|---|---|---|---|---|
| 1. Charles Pahud de Mortanges | HOL | Marcroix | 311.833 | − 58.0 | −40.00 | 1813.83 |
| 2. Earl Thomson | USA | Jenny Camp | 300.000 | − 29.0 | −60.00 | 1811.00 |
| 3. Clarence von Rosen | SWE | Sunnyside Maid | 310.666 | − 58.5 | −42.75 | 1809.42 |
| 4. Harry Chamberlin | USA | Pleasant Smiles | 340.333 | −192.5 | −60.00 | 1687.83 |
| 5. Ernst Hallberg | SWE | Marokan | 290.333 | −171.0 | −40.00 | 1679.33 |
| 6. Karel Johan Schummelketel | HOL | Duiveltje | 267.500 | −195.0 | −58.00 | 1614.00 |
| 7. Morishige Yamamoto | JPN | Kingo | 257.333 | −207.5 | −40.25 | 1609.58 |
| 8. Edwin Argo | USA | Honolulu Tomboy | 333.000 | −392.5 | − 0.75 | 1539.25 |

Lieutenant Pahud de Mortanges completed his Olympic career with four gold medals and one silver.

**1936 Berlin** C: 50, N: 19, D: 8.16.

|  |  | HORSE | DRESSAGE | ENDURANCE | JUMPING | TOTAL PTS. |
|---|---|---|---|---|---|---|
| 1. Ludwig Stubbendorff | GER | Nurmi | − 96.7 | +69 | −10 | − 37.7 |
| 2. Earl Thomson | USA | Jenny Camp | −127.9 | +38 | −10 | − 99.9 |
| 3. Hans Mathiesen-Lunding | DEN | Jason | −134.2 | +42 | −10 | −102.2 |
| 4. Vincens Grandjean | DEN | Grey Friar | −115.9 | +11 | 0 | −104.9 |
| 5. Agoston Endrödy | HUN | Pandur | −134.7 | +39 | −10 | −105.7 |
| 6. Rudolf Lippert | GER | Fasan | −118.6 | +27 | −20 | −111.6 |
| 7. Alec Scott | GBR | Bob Clive | −152.3 | +45 | −10 | −117.3 |
| 8. Mario Mylius | SWI | Saphir | −122.0 | +57 | −20 | −145.0 |

The course was so difficult that three horses met their deaths and only 27 of the 50 entrants finished the competition.

**1948 London** C: 45, N: 16, D: 8.10.

| | | | HORSE | DRESSAGE | ENDURANCE | JUMPING | TOTAL PTS. |
|---|---|---|---|---|---|---|---|
| 1. | Bernard Chevallier | FRA | Aiglonne | −104 | +108 | 0 | + 4 |
| 2. | Frank Henry | USA | Swing Low | −117 | + 96 | 0 | −21 |
| 3. | Robert Selfelt | SWE | Claque | −109 | + 84 | 0 | −25 |
| 4. | Charles Anderson | USA | Reno Palisade | −111 | + 96 | −11.5 | −25.5 |
| 5. | Joaquin Nogueras Marquez | SPA | Epsom | −128 | + 87 | 0 | −41 |
| 6. | Erik Carlsen | DEN | Ezja | −113 | + 69 | 0 | −44 |
| 7. | Aecio Morrot Coelho | BRA | Guapo | −114 | + 72 | −10 | −52 |
| 8. | Fernando Marques Caveleiro | POR | Satari | −135 | + 90 | −10 | −55 |
| 8. | Fabio Mangilli | ITA | Guerriero da Capestrano | − 85 | + 72 | −42 | −55 |

**1952 Helsinki** C: 59, N: 21, D: 8.2.

| | | | HORSE | DRESSAGE | ENDURANCE | JUMPING | TOTAL PTS. |
|---|---|---|---|---|---|---|---|
| 1. | Hans von Blixen-Finecke, Jr. | SWE | Jubal | −123.33 | +105 | −10 | −28.33 |
| 2. | Guy Lefrant | FRA | Verdun | −119.50 | + 75 | −10 | −54.50 |
| 3. | Wilhelm Büsing | GER | Hutbertus | −103.50 | + 48 | 0 | −55.50 |
| 4. | Pedro Mercado | ARG | Mandinga | −130.80 | + 78 | −10 | −62.80 |
| 5. | Klaus Wagner | GER | Dachs | −109.66 | + 54 | −10 | −65.66 |
| 6. | Piero D'Inzeo | ITA | Pagoro | −118.80 | + 52 | 0 | −66.80 |
| 7. | Albert Hill | GBR | Stella | −126.33 | + 69 | −10 | −67.33 |
| 8. | Olof Stahre | SWE | Komet | −108.66 | + 81 | −41.75 | −69.41 |

Blixen-Finecke's father won a gold medal in the 1912 dressage.

**1956 Stockholm** C: 57, N: 19, D: 6.14.

| | | | HORSE | DRESSAGE | ENDURANCE | JUMPING | TOTAL PTS. |
|---|---|---|---|---|---|---|---|
| 1. | Petrus Kastenman | SWE | Iluster | −116.40 | +69.87 | −20 | − 66.53 |
| 2. | August Lütke-Westhues | GER | Trux von Kamax | −129.60 | +64.73 | −20 | − 84.87 |
| 3. | Francis Weldon | GBR | Kilbarry | −103.20 | +37.72 | −20 | − 85.48 |
| 4. | Lev Baklychkine | SOV | Guimnast | −119.20 | +42.55 | −20 | − 96.65 |
| 5. | Genko Rashkov | BUL | Euphoria | −146.00 | +44.77 | −10 | −111.23 |
| 6. | A. Laurence Rook | GBR | Wild Venture | −101.60 | − 4.29 | −13.75 | −119.64 |
| 7. | Giancarlo Gutierrez | ITA | Wiston | −138.80 | +12.37 | −10 | −136.43 |
| 8. | Juan Martín Merbilháa | ARG | Gitana I | −150.00 | +23.54 | −10 | −136.46 |

**1960 Rome** C: 73, N: 19, D: 9.10.

| | | | HORSE | DRESSAGE | ENDURANCE | JUMPING | TOTAL PTS. |
|---|---|---|---|---|---|---|---|
| 1. | Lawrence Morgan | AUS | Salad Days | −106.00 | +128.4 | −15.25 | + 7.15 |
| 2. | Neale Lavis | AUS | Mirrabooka | −124.50 | +108.0 | 0 | −16.50 |
| 3. | Anton Bühler | SWI | Gay Spark | − 89.01 | + 50.8 | −13 | −51.21 |
| 4. | Michael Bullen | GBR | Cottage Romance | −129.00 | + 66.4 | 0 | −62.60 |
| 5. | Saibattal Mursalimov | SOV | Satrap | − 79.00 | + 46.0 | −30.75 | −63.75 |
| 6. | Jack Le Goff | FRA | Image | −108.51 | + 55.6 | −20 | −72.91 |
| 7. | Lev Baklychkine | SOV | Bazis | −103.50 | + 58.4 | −20.25 | −85.35 |
| 8. | Marian Babirecki | POL | Volt | −127.00 | + 61.6 | −20 | −85.40 |

The endurance course was unnecessarily dangerous, and two horses were killed. The Italian organizers seemed unprepared for such disasters. The Danish horse Rolf II had to wait two and a half hours for the arrival of a veterinarian, and the Romanian horse Mures II, driven across the finish line despite a fatal injury, lay dead for hours before he was finally removed. Only 35 of the 73 entrants completed the competition.

**1964 Tokyo** C: 48, N: 12, D: 10.19.

| | | | HORSE | DRESSAGE | ENDURANCE | JUMPING | TOTAL PTS. |
|---|---|---|---|---|---|---|---|
| 1. | Mauro Checcoli | ITA | Surbean | −54.00 | +118.4 | 0 | +64.40 |
| 2. | Carlos Moratorio | ARG | Chalan | −42.00 | + 98.4 | 0 | +56.40 |
| 3. | Fritz Ligges | GER | Donkosak | −32.00 | + 91.2 | −10 | +49.20 |
| 4. | Michael Page | USA | Grasshopper | −43.00 | + 90.4 | 0 | +47.40 |
| 5. | Anthony Cameron | IRL | Black Salmon | −70.67 | +117.2 | 0 | +46.53 |
| 6. | Horst Karsten | GER | Condora | −49.00 | + 95.6 | −10 | +36.60 |
| 7. | J. William Roycroft | AUS | Eldorado | −65.00 | + 97.2 | 0 | +32.20 |
| 8. | Richard Meade | GBR | Barberry | −52.67 | +118.4 | −36 | +29.73 |

Mauro Checcoli, a 21-year-old student from Bologna, won the gold medal, but it was the 33rd-place finisher who made equestrian history. Helen Dupont of the United States became the first woman to compete in the Olympic three-day event.

**1968 Mexico City** C: 49, N: 13, D: 10.21.

| | | | HORSE | DRESSAGE | ENDURANCE | JUMPING | TOTAL PTS |
|---|---|---|---|---|---|---|---|
| 1. | Jean-Jacques Guyon | FRA | Pitou | − 73.01 | +44.4 | −10.25 | −38.86 |
| 2. | Derek Allhusen | GBR | Lochinvar | − 85.01 | +44.4 | 0 | −41.61 |
| 3. | Michael Page | USA | Foster | −107.51 | +59.2 | − 4 | −52.31 |
| 4. | Richard Meade | GBR | Cornishman V | − 97.01 | +54.8 | −22.25 | −64.46 |
| 5. | Reuben Jones | GBR | The Poacher | − 68.51 | + 4.4 | − 5.75 | −69.86 |
| 6. | James Wofford | USA | Kilkenny | −101.51 | +71.2 | −43.75 | −74.06 |
| 7. | Juliet Jobling-Purser | IRL | Jonny | − 72.51 | + 5.6 | − 1 | −79.11 |
| 8. | Wayne Roycroft | AUS | Zhivago | −103.50 | +21.2 | −12.75 | −95.05 |

Two more horses were killed during the endurance competition. This time they died of exhaustion.

**1972 Munich** C: 73, N: 19, D: 9.1.

| | | | HORSE | DRESSAGE | ENDURANCE | JUMPING | TOTAL PTS. |
|---|---|---|---|---|---|---|---|
| 1. | Richard Meade | GBR | Laurieston | −50.6 | +108.4 | 0 | −57.73 |
| 2. | Alessandro Argenton | ITA | Woodland | 48.6 | + 92.0 | 0 | −43.33 |
| 3. | Jan Jönsson | SWE | Sarajevo | −50.3 | + 90.0 | 0 | −39.67 |
| 4. | Mary Gordon-Watson | GBR | Cornishman V | −51.3 | + 81.8 | 0 | −30.27 |
| 5. | Kevin Freeman | USA | Good Mixture | −51.3 | + 91.2 | −10 | −29.87 |
| 6. | J. William Roycroft | AUS | Warrathoola | −36.0 | + 65.6 | 0 | −29.60 |
| 7. | Richard Sands | AUS | Depeche | −64.3 | + 99.2 | −10 | −24.87 |
| 8. | Bruce Davidson | USA | Plain Sailing | −40.3 | + 74.8 | −10 | −24.47 |

**1976 Montreal** C: 49, N: 13, D: 7.25.

| | | | HORSE | DRESSAGE | ENDURANCE | JUMPING | TOTAL PTS. |
|---|---|---|---|---|---|---|---|
| 1. | Edmund Coffin | USA | Bally-Cor | − 64.59 | − 50.4 | 0 | −114.99 |
| 2. | J. Michael Plumb | USA | Better & Better | − 66.25 | − 49.6 | −10 | −125.85 |
| 3. | Karl Schultz | GER | Madrigal | − 46.25 | − 63.2 | −20 | −129.45 |
| 4. | Richard Meade | GBR | Jacob Jones | − 73.75 | − 57.6 | −10 | −141.35 |
| 5. | Wayne Roycroft | AUS | Laurenson | − 80.84 | − 97.2 | 0 | −178.04 |
| 6. | Gerard Sinnott | IRL | Croghan | −101.25 | − 77.6 | 0 | −178.85 |
| 7. | Jean Valat | FRA | Vampire | − 92.50 | − 95.2 | 0 | −187.70 |
| 8. | Yuri Salnikov | SOV | Rumpel | − 86.66 | −102.8 | 0 | −189.46 |

**1980 Moscow** C: 28, N: 7, D: 7.27.

| | | HORSE | DRESSAGE | ENDURANCE | JUMPING | TOTAL PTS. |
|---|---|---|---|---|---|---|
| 1. Euro Federico Roman | ITA | Rossinan | −54.4 | − 49.2 | − 5 | −108.6 |
| 2. Aleksandr Blinov | SOV | Galzun | −64.4 | − 56.4 | 0 | −120.8 |
| 3. Yuri Salnikov | SOV | Pintset | −53.0 | − 93.6 | − 5 | −151.6 |
| 4. Valery Volkov | SOV | Tskheti | −54.0 | −125.6 | − 5 | −184.6 |
| 5. Tzvetan Donchev | BUL | Medisson | −66.4 | −114.4 | − 5 | −185.8 |
| 6. Miroslaw Sziapka | POL | Erywan | −52.4 | −184.4 | − 5 | −241.8 |
| 7. Anna Casagrande | ITA | Daleye | −61.2 | −190.0 | −15 | −266.2 |
| 8. Mauro Roman | ITA | Dourakine 4 | −63.4 | −218.0 | 0 | −281.4 |

The equestrian events were badly hit by the boycott, and an alternative competition was held in August at Fontainebleau, France, with 42 riders representing 14 nations. The winner was Nils Haagensen of Denmark, with Americans James Wofford and Torrance Watkins finishing second and third.

**1984 Los Angeles-Arcadia** C: 48, N: 15, D: 8.3.

| | | HORSE | DRESSAGE | ENDURANCE | JUMPING | TOTAL |
|---|---|---|---|---|---|---|
| 1. Mark Todd | NZE | Charisma | −51.6 | .0 | 0 | −51.6 |
| 2. Karen Stives | USA | Ben Arthur | −49.2 | .0 | −5 | −54.2 |
| 3. Virginia Holgate | GBR | Priceless | −56.4 | − .4 | 0 | −56.8 |
| 4. Torrance Watkins Fleischmann | USA | Finvarra | −57.6 | − 2.8 | 0 | −60.4 |
| 5. Pascal Morvillers | FRA | Gulliver "B" | −52.6 | −10.4 | 0 | −63.0 |
| 6. Lucinda Green | GBR | Regal Realm | −63.8 | .0 | 0 | −63.8 |
| 7. Marina Sciocchetti | ITA | Master Hunt | −67.0 | .0 | 0 | −67.0 |
| 8. Mauro Checcoli | ITA | Spey Cast Boy | −60.4 | − 1.6 | −5 | −67.0 |

Thirty-three-year-old Karen Stives, the final rider of the competition, entered the arena knowing that her ride would decide both the individual and team gold medals. If she cleared all 12 obstacles without a fault, she would come away with both golds. If she dislodged the rail of one fence, she would lose the individual gold to Mark Todd, but she would still secure first place for the U.S. team. If she knocked down two fences the team gold would be won by Great Britain. As the capacity crowd watched nervously, Stives successfully guided Ben Arthur over the first ten obstacles. But then, at the next to last obstacle—a triple jump—the horse nicked the top of the middle fence, sending the pole to the ground. Stives and Ben Arthur recovered to complete the course without incident.

Mark Todd was a 28-year-old dairy farmer who sold most of his herd to finance his Olympic quest.

**1988 Seoul** C: 50, N: 16, D: 9.22.

| | | HORSE | DRESSAGE | ENDURANCE | JUMPING | GRAND TOTAL |
|---|---|---|---|---|---|---|
| 1. Mark Todd | NZE | Charisma | −37.6 | .0 | −5 | −42.6 |
| 2. Ian Stark | GBR | Sir Wattie | −50.0 | −2.8 | 0 | −52.8 |
| 3. Virginia Leng (Holgate) | GBR | Master Craftsman | −43.2 | −8.8 | −10 | −62.0 |
| 4. Claus Erhorn | GER | Justyn Tyme | −39.6 | −16.0 | −6.75 | −62.35 |
| 5. Judith "Tinks" Pottinger | NZE | Volunteer | −65.8 | .0 | 0 | −65.8 |
| 6. Matthias Baumann | GER | Shamrock | −50.6 | −13.2 | −5 | −68.8 |
| 7. Jean Teulère | FRA | Mohican V | −57.6 | −6.4 | −5 | −69.0 |
| 8. Andrew Hoy | AUS | Kiwi | −57.0 | −32.0 | 0 | −89.0 |

Todd and Charisma led the field in both the dressage and endurance stages, then knocked over just one fence to become only the second repeat winners of the three-day event.

## THREE-DAY EVENT, TEAM

According to current rules, each team has four members, but the scores of only the top three finishers are counted.

**1896–1908** not held

**1912 Stockholm** T: 7, N: 7, D: 7.17.

|  | | HORSE | | TOTAL PTS. |
|---|---|---|---|---|
| 1. | SWE | | | 139.06 |
| | Axel Nordlander | Lady Artist | 46.59 | |
| | Nils Adlercreutz | Atout | 46.31 | |
| | Ernst Casparsson | Irmelin | 46.16 | |
| 2. | GER | | | 138.48 |
| | Friedrich von Rochow | Idealist | 46.42 | |
| | Rudolf Graf von Schaesberg-Tannheim | Grundsee | 46.16 | |
| | Eduard von Lütcken | Blue Boy | 45.90 | |
| 3. | USA | | | 137.33 |
| | Benjamin Lear | Poppy | 45.91 | |
| | John Montgomery | Deceive | 45.88 | |
| | Guy Henry | Chiswell | 45.54 | |
| 4. | FRA | | | 136.77 |
| | Jean Cariou | Cocotte | 46.32 | |
| | Bernard Meyer | Allons-y | 45.30 | |
| | Seigner | Dignité | 45.15 | |

**1920 Antwerp** T: 6, N: 6, D: 9.10.

|  | | HORSE | | TOTAL PTS. |
|---|---|---|---|---|
| 1. | SWE | | | 5057.50 |
| | Hellmer Mörner | Germania | 1775.00 | |
| | Åge Lundström | Yrsa | 1738.75 | |
| | Georg von Braun | Diana | 1543.75 | |
| 2. | ITA | | | 4735.00 |
| | Ettore Caffaratti | Caniche | 1733.75 | |
| | Garibaldi Spighi | Otello | 1647.50 | |
| | Giulio Cacciandra | Facetto | 1353.75 | |
| 3. | BEL | | | 4560.00 |
| | Roger Moeremans d'Emaus | Sweet Girl | 1652.50 | |
| | Oswald Lints | Martha | 1515.00 | |
| | Jules Bonvalet | Weppelghem | 1392.50 | |
| 4. | USA | | | 4477.50 |
| | Harry Chamberlin | Nigra | 1568.75 | |
| | William West | Black Boy | 1558.75 | |
| | John Barry | Raven | 1350.00 | |

**1924 Paris** T: 10, N: 10, D: 7.26.

|  | | HORSE | | TOTAL PTS. |
|---|---|---|---|---|
| 1. | HOL | | | 5297.5 |
| | Adolph van der Voort van Zijp | Silver Piece | 1976.0 | |

(continued right column)

|  | | HORSE | | TOTAL PTS. |
|---|---|---|---|---|
| | Charles Pahud de Mortanges | Johnny Walker | 1828.0 | |
| | Gerard de Kruyff | Addio | 1493.5 | |
| 2. | SWE | | | 4743.5 |
| | Claës König | Bojar | 1730.0 | |
| | Carl Torsten Sylvan | Amita | 1678.0 | |
| | Gustaf Hagelin | Varius | 1335.5 | |
| 3. | ITA | | | 4512.5 |
| | Alberto Lombardi | Pimplo | 1572.0 | |
| | Alessandro Alvisi | Capiligio | 1536.0 | |
| | Emanuele di Pralormo | Mount Felix | 1404.5 | |
| 4. | SWI | | | 4338.5 |
| | Hans Bühler | Mikosch | 1477.5 | |
| | Charles Stoffel | Kreuzritter | 1466.0 | |
| | Werner Fehr | Prahihans | 1395.0 | |
| 5. | BEL | | | 4233.5 |
| | Beaudouin de Brabandère | Modestie | 1728.5 | |
| | Jules Bonvalet | Weppelghem | 1428.0 | |
| | Joseph Fallon | Le Divorce | 1077.0 | |
| 6. | GBR | | | 4064.5 |
| | Edward de Fonblanque | Copper | 1728.5 | |
| | Keith Hervey | Wild Gal | 1354.0 | |
| | Albert Frederick Tod | White Surrey | 982.0 | |
| 7. | POL | | | 3571.5 |
| | Karol Rómmel | Krechowiak | 1648.5 | |
| | Kazimierz Szosland | Helusia | 961.5 | |
| | Kazimierz Rostowo-Suski | Lady | 958.5 | |

**1928 Amsterdam** T: 14, N: 14, D: 8.11.

|  | | HORSE | | TOTAL PTS. |
|---|---|---|---|---|
| 1. | HOL | | | 5865.68 |
| | Charles Pahud de Mortanges | Marcroix | 1969.82 | |
| | Gerard de Kruyff | Va-t-en | 1967.26 | |
| | Adolph van der Voort van Zijp | Silver Piece | 1928.60 | |
| 2. | NOR | | | 5395.68 |
| | Bjart Ording | And Over | 1912.98 | |
| | Arthur Quist | Hidalgo | 1895.14 | |
| | Eugen Johansen | Baby | 1587.56 | |
| 3. | POL | | | 5067.92 |
| | Michal Antoniewicz | Moja Mita | 1822.50 | |
| | Józef Trenkwald | Lwi Pazur | 1645.20 | |
| | Karol Rómmel | Doneuse | 1600.22 | |

**1932 Los Angeles** T: 4, N: 4, D: 8.13.

|  | | HORSE | | TOTAL PTS. |
|---|---|---|---|---|
| 1. | USA | | | 5038.083 |
| | Earl Thomson | Jenny Champ | 1811.000 | |
| | Harry Chamberlin | Plesant Smiles | 1687.833 | |
| | Edwin Argo | Honolulu Tomboy | 1539.250 | |
| 2. | HOL | | | 4689.083 |
| | Charles Pahud de Mortanges | Marcroix | 1813.833 | |
| | Karel Johan Schummelketel | Duiveltje | 1614.500 | |

| | HORSE | TOTAL PTS. |
|---|---|---|
| Aernout van Lennep | Henk | 1260.750 |

**1936 Berlin** T: 14, N: 14, D: 8.16.

| | HORSE | TOTAL PTS. |
|---|---|---|
| 1. GER | | − 676.65 |
| Ludwig Stubbendorff | Nurmi | − 37.70 |
| Rudolf Lippert | Fasan | − 111.60 |
| Konrad Freiherr von Wangenheim | Kurfürst | − 527.35 |
| 2. POL | | − 991.70 |
| Henryk Rojcewicz | Arlekin III | − 253.00 |
| Zdzislaw Kawecki | Bambino | − 300.70 |
| Seweryn Kulesza | Tosca | − 438.00 |
| 3. GBR | | − 9195.50 |
| Alec Scott | Bob Clive | − 117.30 |
| Edward Howard-Vyse | Blue Steel | − 324.00 |
| Richard Fanshawe | Bowie Knife | − 8754.20 |
| 4. CZE | | −18952.70 |
| Václav Procházka | Harlekyn | − 324.30 |
| Josef Dobes | Leskov | − 497.70 |
| Otomar Bureš | Mirko | −18130.70 |

Lieutenant Konrad Freiherr von Wangenheim was one of the German heroes of the Berlin Games. During the steeplechase portion of the endurance run, his horse, Kurfürst, stumbled at the fourth obstacle, a hurdle and pond, throwing the 26-year-old von Wangenheim to the ground and breaking his collarbone. Knowing that the German team would be disqualified if he failed to finish, von Wangenheim remounted and negotiated the remaining 32 obstacles without a fault. But the jumping competition still remained. The next day von Wangenheim appeared in the stadium with his arm in a sling. Just before he mounted Kurfürst, the sling was removed and his arm was tightly bound. However, at one of the early obstacles, a double jump, Kurfürst rushed ahead and von Wangenheim was forced to pull the reins with both hands. The horse reared up, fell backward, and landed on von Wangenheim, who managed to crawl out from underneath. Kurfürst lay still and was thought to be dead, but suddenly jumped back up. Von Wangenheim remounted and again completed the course without another fault. The stadium crowd of 100,000 gave von Wangenheim a prolonged standing ovation, as Germany won the gold medal.

The unusually enormous number of penalty points accumulated by Lieutenant Bureš of Czechoslovakia were a result of his taking 2 hours 46 minutes and 36 seconds to complete the eight-kilometer cross-country course, for which the time limit was 17 minutes 46 seconds.

**1948 London** T: 14, N: 14, D: 8.12.

| | HORSE | TOTAL PTS. |
|---|---|---|
| 1. USA | | −161.50 |
| Frank Henry | Swing Low | − 21.00 |

| | | | |
|---|---|---|---|
| Charles Anderson | Reno Palisade | − 26.50 | |
| Earl Thomson | Reno Rhythm | −114.00 | |
| 2. SWE | | | −165.00 |
| Robert Selfelt | Claque | − 25.00 | |
| Olof Stahre | Komet | − 70.00 | |
| Sigurd Svensson | Dust | − 70.00 | |
| 3. MEX | | | −305.25 |
| Humberto Mariles Cortés | Parral | − 61.75 | |
| Raúl Campero | Tarahumara | −120.50 | |
| Joaquin Solano Chagoya | Malinche | −123.00 | |
| 4. SWI | | | −404.50 |
| Alfred Blaser | Mahmud | − 59.25 | |
| Anton Bühler | Amour Amour | − 95.00 | |
| Pierre Musy | Französin | −250.25 | |
| 5. SPA | | | −422.50 |
| Joaquin Nogueras Marquez | Epsom | − 41.00 | |
| Fernando Gazapo de Sarraga | Vivian | −179.25 | |
| Santiago Martinez Larraz | Fogoso | −202.25 | |

**1952 Helsinki** T: 19, N: 19, D: 8.2.

| | HORSE | TOTAL PTS. |
|---|---|---|
| 1. SWE | | −221.94 |
| Hans von Blixen-Finecke, Jr. | Jubal | − 28.33 |
| Olof Stahre | Komet | − 69.41 |
| Karl Folke Frölén | Fair | −124.20 |
| 2. GER | | −235.49 |
| Wilhelm Büsing | Hubertus | − 55.50 |
| Klaus Wagner | Dachs | − 65.66 |
| Otto Rothe | Trux von Kamax | −114.33 |
| 3. USA | | −587.16 |
| Charles Hough | Cassivellannus | − 70.66 |
| Walter Staley | Craigwood Park | −168.50 |
| John Wofford | Benny Grimes | −348.00 |
| 4. POR | | −618.00 |
| Fernando Marques Cavaleiro | Caudel | −183.00 |
| Antonio Pereira de Almeida | Florentina | −216.20 |
| Joaquim Miguel Duarte Silva | Faial | −218.80 |
| 5. DEN | | −828.86 |
| Hans Anderson | Tom | −222.20 |
| Otto Acthon | Sirdar | −267.66 |
| Aage Rybaeck-Nielsen | Sahara | −339.00 |
| 6. IRL | | −953.52 |
| Henry Freeman-Jackson | Cuchulain | −268.66 |
| Ian Dudgeon | Hope | −269.20 |
| Mark Darley | Emily Little | −415.66 |

**1956 Stockholm** T: 19, N: 19, D: 6.14.

| | HORSE | TOTAL PTS. |
|---|---|---|
| 1. GBR | | − 355.48 |
| Frank Weldon | Kilbarry | − 85.48 |
| A. Laurence Rook | Wild Venture | −119.64 |
| Albert Hill | Countryman III | −150.36 |
| 2. GER | | − 475.91 |
| August Lütke-Westhues | Trux von Kamax | − 84.87 |
| Otto Rothe | Sissi | −158.04 |
| Klaus Wagner | PrinzeB | −233.00 |
| 3. CAN | | − 572.72 |
| John Rumble | Cilroy | −162.53 |
| James Elder | Colleen | −193.69 |
| Brian Herbinson | Tara | −216.50 |
| 4. AUS | | − 619.98 |
| Brian Crago | Radar | −147.42 |
| Wyatt Thompson | Brown Sugar | −155.06 |
| Ernest Barker | Dandy | −317.50 |
| 5. ITA | | − 691.14 |
| Giancarlo Gutierrez | Wiston | −136.43 |
| Adriano Capuzzo | Tuft of Heather | −139.41 |
| Giuseppe Molinari | Uccello | −415.30 |
| 6. ARG | | − 724.18 |
| Juan Martín Merbilháa | Gitana I | −136.46 |
| Eduardo Cano | Why | −242.01 |
| Carlos de la Serna | Fanion | −345.71 |
| 7 SOV | | −1112.33 |
| Lev Baklychkine | Guimnast | − 96.65 |
| Nikolai Chelenkov | Satrap | −297.68 |
| Valerian Kouibychev | Perekop | −718.00 |
| 8. SWI | | −1360.90 |
| Emil-Otto Gmür | Romeo | −378.51 |
| Roland Perret | Erlfried | −405.18 |
| Samuel Koechlin | Goya | −577.21 |

**1960 Rome** T: 18, N: 18, D: 9.10.

| | HORSE | TOTAL PTS. |
|---|---|---|
| 1. AUS | | −128.18 |
| Lawrence Morgan | Salad Days | + 7.15 |
| Neale Lavis | Mirrabooka | − 16.50 |
| J. William Roycroft | Our Solo | −118.83 |
| 2. SWI | | −386.02 |
| Anton Bühler | Gay Spark | − 51.21 |
| Hans Schwarzenbach | Burn Trout | −131.45 |
| Rudolf Günthardt | Atbara | −203.36 |
| 3. FRA | | −515.71 |
| Jack Le Goff | Image | − 72.91 |
| Guy Lefrant | Nicias | −208.50 |
| Jean Raymond Le Roy | Gardem | −234.30 |
| 4. GBR | | −516.21 |
| Michael Bullen | Cottage Romance | − 62.60 |
| Albert Hill | Wild Venture | −215.60 |
| Frank Weldon | Samuel Johnson | −238.01 |

| | | TOTAL PTS. |
|---|---|---|
| 5. ITA | | −528.21 |
| Lucio Tasca | Rahin | −125.80 |
| Ludovico Nava | Arcidosso | −161.91 |
| Giovanni Grignolo | Court Hill | −240.50 |
| 6. IRL | | −674.00 |
| Edward Harty | Harlequin | −112.30 |
| Anthony Cameron | Sonnet | −251.55 |
| Ian Dudgeon | Corrigneagh | −310.15 |

Suffering from a concussion and a broken collarbone as a result of a fall during the endurance test, 45-year-old Bill Roycroft insisted on leaving his hospital bed to compete in the jumping test, thus ensuring that the gold medal would go to Australia. Over the next sixteen years, three of Roycroft's sons represented Australia in the Olympics. He himself competed four more times.

**1964 Tokyo** T: 12, N: 12, D:10.19.

| | HORSE | TOTAL PTS. |
|---|---|---|
| 1. ITA | | + 85.80 |
| Mauro Checcoli | Surbean | + 64.40 |
| Paolo Angioni | King | + 17.87 |
| Giuseppe Ravano | Royal Love | + 3.53 |
| 2. USA | | + 65.86 |
| Michael Page | Grasshopper | + 47.40 |
| Kevin Freeman | Gallopade | + 17.13 |
| J. Michael Plumb | Bold Minstrel | + 1.33 |
| 3. GER/GDR | | + 56.73 |
| Fritz Ligges | Donkosak | + 49.20 |
| Horst Karsten | Condora | + 36.60 |
| Gerhard Schulz | Balza X | − 29.07 |
| 4. IRL | | + 42.86 |
| Anthony Cameron | Black Salmon | + 46.53 |
| Thomas Brennan | Kilkenny | + 1.13 |
| John Harty | San Michele | − 4.80 |
| 5. SOV | | − 19.63 |
| German Gazyumov | Gran | + 23.47 |
| Boris Konkov | Rumb | − 10.97 |
| Pavel Deyev | Satrap | − 32.13 |
| 6. ARG | | − 34.80 |
| Carlos Moratorio | Chalan | + 56.40 |
| Elvio Flores | Legitima | − 2.73 |
| Juan Gesualdi | Morrina | − 88.47 |
| 7. AUS | | − 67.27 |
| J. William Roycroft | Eldorado | + 32.20 |
| Brien Cobcroft | Stony Crossing | + 8.40 |
| John Kelly | Brigalow | −107.87 |
| 8. FRA | | −133.87 |
| Jack Le Goff | Leopard | − 37.87 |
| J. De Croutte de St. Martin | Mon Clos | − 38.47 |
| Hughes Landon | Laurier | − 57.53 |

**1968 Mexico City** T: 12, N: 12, D: 10.21.

| | HORSE | TOTAL PTS. |
|---|---|---|
| 1. GBR | | −175.93 |
| Derek Allhusen | Lochinvar | − 41.61 |

|  | HORSE |  | TOTAL PTS. |
|---|---|---|---|
| Richard Meade | Cornishman V | − 64.46 | |
| Reuben Jones | The Poacher | − 69.86 | |
| 2. USA | | | −245.87 |
| Michael Page | Foster | − 52.31 | |
| James Wofford | Kilkenny | − 74.06 | |
| J. Michael Plumb | Plain Sailing | −119.50 | |
| 3. AUS | | | −331.26 |
| Wayne Roycroft | Zhivago | − 94.95 | |
| Brien Cobcroft | Depeche | −108.76 | |
| J. William Roycroft | Warrathoola | −127.55 | |
| 4. FRA | | | −505.83 |
| Jean-Jacques Guyon | Pitou | − 38.86 | |
| André Le Goupil | Olivette B | −107.26 | |
| Jean Sarrazin | Joburg | −359.71 | |
| 5. GER | | | −518.22 |
| Horst Karsten | Adagio | −102.96 | |
| Jochen Mehrdorf | Lapiz Lazuli | −199.41 | |
| Klaus Wagner | Abdulla | −215.85 | |
| 6. MEX | | | −631.56 |
| Ernesto Del Castillo | Coficioso | −170.60 | |
| Ramon Mejia | Centinela | −182.90 | |
| Evaristo Avalos | Ludmilla II | −278.06 | |
| 7. GDR | | | −690.72 |
| Karl-Heinz Fuhrmann | Saturn | −218.25 | |
| Uwe Plank | Kranich | −231.01 | |
| Helmut Hartmann | Ingwer | −241.46 | |
| 8. CAN | | | −787.68 |
| Robin Hahn | Taffy | − 95.41 | |
| Norman Elder | Questionnaire | −332.46 | |
| Barry Sonshine | Durlas Eile | −359.81 | |

Australia's bronze medalist team included the father-son combination of Bill and Wayne Roycroft. The Roycrofts repeated their performance in 1976, when father Bill was 61 years old. Two more of Bill Roycroft's sons competed in the Olympics: Clarke in 1972 and Barry in 1976 and 1988. Wayne's wife, Vicki, took part in 1984 and 1988.

**1972 Munich** T: 18, N: 18, D: 9.1.

|  | HORSE |  | TOTAL PTS. |
|---|---|---|---|
| 1. GBR | | | + 95.53 |
| Richard Meade | Laurieston | + 57.73 | |
| Mary Gordon-Watson | Cornishman V | + 30.27 | |
| Bridget Parker | Cornish Gold | + 7.53 | |
| 2. USA | | | + 10.81 |
| Kevin Freeman | Good Mixture | + 29.87 | |
| Bruce Davidson | Plain Sailing | + 24.47 | |
| J. Michael Plumb | Free and Easy | − 43.53 | |
| 3. GER | | | − 18.00 |
| Harry Klugmann | Christopher Rob | + 8.00 | |
| Ludwig Goessing | Chikago | − 0.40 | |
| Karl Schultz | Pisco | − 25.60 | |
| 4. AUS | | | − 27.86 |
| J. William Roycroft | Warrathoola | + 29.60 | |
| Richard Sands | Depeche | + 24.87 | |
| Brian Schrapel | Wakool | − 82.33 | |

| 5. GDR | | | −127.93 |
|---|---|---|---|
| Rudolf Beerbohm | Ingolf | + 3.80 | |
| Jens Niehls | Big-Ben | − 60.00 | |
| Joachim Brohmann | Uranio | − 71.73 | |
| 6. SWI | | | −156.43 |
| Paul Hürlimann | Grand Times | − 11.03 | |
| Anton Bühler | Wukari | − 19.87 | |
| Alfred Schwarzenbach | Big Boy | −125.53 | |
| 7. SOV | | | −190.06 |
| Sergei Mukhin | Reisfeder | − 0.13 | |
| Valentin Gorelkin | Rok | − 34.93 | |
| Vladimir Lanugin | Zimar | −155.00 | |
| 8. ITA | | | −203.58 |
| Alessandro Argenton | Woodland | − 43.33 | |
| Dino Costantini | Lord Jim | − 98.18 | |
| Mario Turner | Forgotten Fred | −148.73 | |

**1976 Montreal** T: 12, N: 12, D: 7.25.

|  | HORSE |  | TOTAL PTS. |
|---|---|---|---|
| 1. USA | | | −441.00 |
| Edmund Coffin | Bally-Cor | −114.99 | |
| J. Michael Plumb | Better & Better | −125.85 | |
| Bruce Davidson | Irish-Cap | −200.16 | |
| 2. GER | | | −584.60 |
| Karl Schultz | Madrigal | −129.45 | |
| Herbert Blöcker | Albrant | −213.15 | |
| Helmut Rethemeier | Pauline | −242.00 | |
| 3. AUS | | | −599.54 |
| Wayne Roycroft | Laurenson | −178.04 | |
| Mervyn Bennett | Regal Reign | −206.04 | |
| J. William Roycroft | Version | −215.46 | |
| 4. ITA | | | −682.24 |
| Euro Federico Roman | Shamrock | −194.14 | |
| Mario Turner | Tempest Blisland | −213.19 | |
| Alessandro Argenton | Woodland | −274.91 | |
| 5. SOV | | | −721.55 |
| Yuri Salnikov | Rumpel | −189.46 | |
| Valery Dvorianinov | Zeila | −218.25 | |
| Viktor Kalinin | Araks | −313.84 | |
| 6. CAN | | | −808.81 |
| Juliet Graham | Sumatra | −202.69 | |
| Cathy Wedge | City Fella | −286.76 | |
| Robin Hahn | L'Esprit | −319.36 | |

**1980 Moscow** T: 7, N: 7, D: 7.27.

|  | HORSE |  | TOTAL PTS. |
|---|---|---|---|
| 1. SOV | | | − 457.00 |
| Aleksandr Blinov | Galzun | −120.80 | |
| Yuri Salnikov | Pintset | −151.60 | |
| Valery Volkov | Tskheti | −184.60 | |
| 2. ITA | | | − 656.20 |
| Euro Federico Roman | Rossinan | −108.60 | |
| Anna Casagrande | Daleye | −266.20 | |
| Mauro Roman | Dourakine 4 | −281.40 | |
| 3. MEX | | | −1172.85 |
| Manuel Mendivil Yocupicio | Remember | −319.75 | |

| David Barcena Rios | Bombon | −362.50 | |
| José Luis Perez Soto | Quelite | −490.60 | |
| 4. HUN | | | −1603.40 |
| László Cseresnyes | Fapipa | −436.20 | |
| István Grozner | Biboros | −498.60 | |
| Zoltán Horvath | Lamour | −668.60 | |

The substitute three-day event, held in August at Fountainbleau, was won by France, with West Germany second and Australia third.

**1984 Los Angeles-Arcadia** T: 11, N: 11, D: 8.3.

| | HORSE | | TOTAL PTS. |
| --- | --- | --- | --- |
| 1. USA | | | −186.00 |
| Karen Stives | Ben Arthur | − 54.20 | |
| Torrance Watkins Fleischmann | Finvarra | − 60.40 | |
| J. Michael Plumb | Blue Stone | − 71.40 | |
| 2. GBR | | | −189.20 |
| Virginia Holgate | Priceless | − 56.80 | |
| Lucinda Green | Regal Realm | − 63.80 | |
| Ian Stark | Oxford Blue | − 68.60 | |
| 3. GER | | | −234.00 |
| Dietmar Hogrefe | Foliant | − 74.40 | |
| Bettina Overesch | Peacetime | − 79.60 | |
| Claus Erhorn | Fair Lady | − 80.00 | |
| 4. FRA | | | −236.00 |
| Pascal Morvillers | Gulliver "B" | − 63.00 | |
| Marie Christine Duroy | Harley | − 85.40 | |
| Armand Bigot | Jacquou Du Bois | − 87.60 | |
| 5. AUS | | | −258.40 |
| Andrew Hoy | Davey | − 80.00 | |
| Mervyn Bennett | Regal Reign | − 87.40 | |
| Vicki Roycroft | Looking Ahead | − 91.00 | |
| 6. NZE | | | −280.00 |
| Mark Todd | Charisma | − 51.60 | |
| Mary Hamilton | Whist | − 98.00 | |
| Andrew Nicholson | Kahlua | −130.40 | |
| 7. ITA | | | −280.70 |
| Mauro Checcoli | Spey Cast Boy | 67.00 | |
| Marina Sciocchetti | Master Hunt | − 67.00 | |
| Bartolo Ambrosione | Brick | −146.70 | |
| 8. SWE | | | −339.85 |
| Jan Jonsson | Isolde | − 86.40 | |
| Göran Breisner | Bobalong | − 99.65 | |
| Christian Persson | Joel | −153.80 | |

**1988 Seoul** T: 10, N: 10, D: 9.22.

| | HORSE | | TOTAL PTS. |
| --- | --- | --- | --- |
| 1. GER | | | −225.95 |
| Claus Erhorn | Justyn Thyme | −62.35 | |
| Matthias Baumann | Shamrock | −68.80 | |
| Thies Kaspareit | Sherry | −94.80 | |
| 2. GBR | | | −256.80 |
| Ian Stark | Sir Wattie | −52.80 | |
| Virginia Leng | Master Craftsman | −62.00 | |
| Karen Straker | Get Smart | −142.00 | |

| 3. NZE | | | −271.20 |
| --- | --- | --- | --- |
| Mark Todd | Charisma | −42.60 | |
| Judith "Tinks" Pottinger | Volunteer | −65.80 | |
| Andrew Bennie | Grayshott | −162.80 | |
| 4. POL | | | −389.60 |
| Boguslaw Jarecki | Niewiaza | −111.40 | |
| Krzystof Rogowski | Alkierz | −114.80 | |
| Jerzy Rafalak | Dzwinograd | −163.40 | |
| 5. AUS | | | −457.60 |
| Andrew Hoy | Kiwi | −89.00 | |
| Scott Keach | Trade Commissioner | −176.60 | |
| David Green | Shannagh | −192.00 | |
| 6. FRA | | | −498.80 |
| Jean Teulère | Mohican V | −69.00 | |
| Vincent Berthet | Jet Crub | −202.20 | |
| Pascal Morvillers | Frangin III | −227.60 | |
| 7. KOR | | | −740.15 |
| Choi Myung-jin | Snuffler | −130.55 | |
| Park Dong-joo | Aqaba Legend | −227.00 | |
| Park So-woon | Moisson d'Avril | −382.60 | |

## JUMPING (PRIX DES NATIONS), INDIVIDUAL

Each horse and rider jumps two rounds. Fault points are assessed if an obstacle is knocked down, if the horse balks at an obstacle, and if the time limit is exceeded. In case of a tie, a jump-off is held. If the jump-off results in a tie, the fastest finisher is declared the winner.

**1896** not held

**1900 Paris** C: 45, N: 5, D: 5.29.

| | | HORSE | |
| --- | --- | --- | --- |
| 1. Aimé Haegeman | BEL | Benton II | 2:16.0 |
| 2. Georges van de Poele | BEL | Windsor Squire | 2:17.6 |
| 3. M. de Champsavin | FRA | Terpsichore | 2:26.0 |

**1904–1908** not held

**1912 Stockholm** C: 31, N: 8, D: 7.16.

| | | HORSE | FAULTS | JUMP-OFF |
| --- | --- | --- | --- | --- |
| 1. Jean Cariou | FRA | Mignon | 4 | 5 |
| 2. Rabod Wilhelm von Kröcher | GER | Dohna | 4 | 7 |
| 3. Emanuel de Blommaert de Soye | BEL | Clonmore | 5 | |
| 4. Herbert Scott | GBR | Shamrock | 6 | |
| 5. Sigismund Freyer | GER | Ultimus | 7 | |
| 6. Wilhelm Graf von Hohenau | GER | Pretty Girl | 9 | |
| 6. Nils Adlercreutz | SWE | Ilex | 9 | |
| 6. Ernst Casparsson | SWE | Kiriki | 9 | |

**1920 Antwerp** C: 25, N: 6, D: 7.16.

| | | HORSE | FAULTS |
|---|---|---|---|
| 1. Tommaso Lequio | ITA | Trebecco | 2 |
| 2. Alessandro Valerio | ITA | Cento | 3 |
| 3. Carl-Gustaf Lewenhaupt | SWE | Mon Coeur | 4 |
| 4. Paul Michelet | NOR | Raon | 5 |
| 5. Ferdinand de la Serna | BEL | Arsinoe | 6 |
| 5. Lars von Stockenström | SWE | Reward | 6 |
| 7. Henry Allen | USA | Don | 7 |
| 7. Santorre de Santa Rosa | ITA | Neruccio | 7 |
| 7. Roger Moeremans d'Emaus | BEL | Sweet Girl | 7 |

**1924 Paris** C: 43, N: 11, D: 7.27.

| | | HORSE | FAULTS | |
|---|---|---|---|---|
| 1. Alphonse Gemuseus | SWI | Lucette | 6 | |
| 2. Tommaso Lequio | ITA | Trebecco | 8.75 | |
| 3. Adam Królikiewicz | POL | Picador | 10 | |
| 4. Philip Bowden-Smith | GBR | Billy Boy | 10.5 | |
| 5. Antonio Borges d'Almeida | POR | Reginald | 12 | 2:28.8 |
| 6. Åke Thelning | SWE | Loke | 12 | 2:30.4 |
| 7. Axel Ståhle | SWE | Cecil | 12.25 | |
| 8. Nicolas Leroy | BEL | Vif Argent | 14.75 | |

**1928 Amsterdam** C: 46, N: 16, D: 8.12.

| | | HORSE | FAULTS | 1ST JUMP-OFF | 2ND JUMP-OFF | |
|---|---|---|---|---|---|---|
| 1. František Ventura | CZE | Eliot | 0 | 0 | 0 | |
| 2. Pierre Bertran de Balanda | FRA | Papillon | 0 | 0 | 2 | |
| 3. Charley Kuhn | SWI | Pepita | 0 | 0 | 4 | |
| 4. Kazimierz Gzowski | POL | Mylord | 0 | 2 | | 1:33.0 |
| 5. José Navarro Morenés | SPA | Zapatazo | 0 | 2 | | 1:36.0 |
| 6. Karl Hansen | SWE | Gerold | 0 | 2 | | 1:39.0 |
| 7. K. Fourquet | ITA | Joe Aleshire | 0 | DISQ. | | |
| 8. Alphonse Gemuseus | SWI | Lucette | 2 | | | |

**1932 Los Angeles** C: 11, N: 4, D: 8.14.

| | | HORSE | FAULTS |
|---|---|---|---|
| 1. Takeichi Nishi | JPN | Uranus | 8 |
| 2. Harry Chamberlin | USA | Show Girl | 12 |
| 3. Clarence von Rosen, Jr. | SWE | Empire | 16 |
| 4. William Bradford | USA | Joe Aleshire | 24 |
| 5. Ernst Hallberg | SWE | Kornett | 50.5 |

Takeichi Nishi was a lieutenant in the Japanese army when he won his gold medal. Promoted to colonel toward the end of World War II, he was made commander of a tank battalion on Iwo Jima. During the fierce fighting on that island, some of the U.S. officers learned that Nishi was on the island and hoped to meet him. They never got a chance. Nishi, who had many American friends, including Will Rogers, Mary Pickford, and Douglas Fairbanks, refused to surrender and instead joined a mass Japanese suicide.

**1936 Berlin** C: 54, N: 18, D: 8.16.

| | | HORSE | FAULTS | JUMP-OFF | |
|---|---|---|---|---|---|
| 1. Kurt Hasse | GER | Tora | 4 | 4 | 59.2 |
| 2. Henri Rang | ROM | Delfis | 4 | 4 | 1:12.8 |
| 3. József Platthy | HUN | Sello | 8 | 0 | 1:02.6 |
| 4. Georges van der Meersch | BEL | Ibrahim | 8 | 0 | 1:09.0 |
| 5. Carl Raguse | USA | Dakota | 8 | 4 | |
| 6. José Beltrão | POR | Biscuit | 12 | | |
| 6. Xavier Bizard | FRA | Bagatelle | 12 | | |
| 6. Johan Jacob Greter | HOL | Ernica | 12 | | |
| 6. Maurice Gudin de Vallerin | FRA | Ecuyère | 12 | | |
| 6. Cevat Koula | TUR | Sapkin | 12 | | |

**1948 London** C: 44, N: 15, D: 8.14.

|  |  | HORSE | FAULTS | JUMP-OFF | |
|---|---|---|---|---|---|
| 1. Humberto Mariles Cortés | MEX | Arete | 6.25 | | |
| 2. Rubén Uriza | MEX | Harvey | 8 | 0 | |
| 3. Jean François d'Orgeix | FRA | Sucre de Pomme | 8 | 4 | 38.9 |
| 4. Franklin Wing | USA | Democrat | 8 | 4 | 40.1 |
| 5. Jaime Garcia Cruz | SPA | Bizarro | 12 | | |
| 5. Eric Sörensen | SWE | Blatunga | 12 | | |
| 7. M. Fresson | FRA | Decametre | 16 | | |
| 7. Harry Llewellyn | GBR | Foxhunter | 16 | | |
| 7. Henry Nicoll | GBR | Kilgeddin | 16 | | |

General Mariles won the title in dramatic fashion. The last rider to enter the arena, he needed to incur fewer than eight faults to win the gold medal. This he did, clearing every obstacle but the water jump and losing 2¼ points for being eight seconds overtime. On the night of August 14, 1964, the 51-year-old Mariles was driving home from a party in his honor in Mexico City when another motorist attempted to force him off the road. At the next traffic light Mariles pulled out a gun and shot the man. He was sent to prison, but later released by presidential pardon. In 1972 he was arrested in Paris for drug-smuggling, but died in prison before coming to trial.

**1952 Helsinki** C: 51, N: 20, D: 8.3.

|  |  | HORSE | FAULTS | JUMP-OFF | |
|---|---|---|---|---|---|
| 1. Pierre Jonquères d'Oriola | FRA | Ali Baba | 8 | 0 | |
| 2. Oscar Cristi | CHI | Bambi | 8 | 4 | |
| 3. Fritz Thiedemann | GER | Meteor | 8 | 8 | 38.5 |
| 4. Eloi Massey Oliveira de Menezes | BRA | Bigua | 8 | 8 | 45.0 |
| 5. Wilfred White | GBR | Nizefella | 8 | 12 | |
| 6. Humberto Mariles Cortés | MEX | Petrolero | 8.75 | | |
| 7. Cesar Mendoza | CHI | Pillan | 12 | | 3:08.8 |
| 8. Argentino Molinuevo | ARG | Discutido | 12 | | 3:13.0 |

**1956 Stockholm** C: 66, N: 24, D: 6.16.

|  |  | HORSE | FAULTS |
|---|---|---|---|
| 1. Hans-Günter Winkler | GER | Halla | 4 |
| 2. Raimondo D'Inzeo | ITA | Merano | 8 |
| 3. Piero D'Inzeo | ITA | Uruguay | 11 |
| 4. Fritz Thiedemann | GER | Meteor | 12 |
| 4. Wilfred White | GBR | Nizefella | 12 |
| 6. Pierre Jonquères d'Oriola | FRA | Voulette | 15 |
| 7. Henrique Callado | POR | Martingil | 16 |
| 8. Carlos Delía | ARG | Discutido | 19 |

**1960 Rome** C: 60, N: 23, D: 9.7.

|  |  | HORSE | FAULTS |
|---|---|---|---|
| 1. Raimondo D'Inzeo | ITA | Posillipo | 12 |
| 2. Piero D'Inzeo | ITA | The Rock | 16 |
| 3. David Broome | GBR | Sunslave | 23 |
| 4. George Morris | USA | Simjon | 24 |
| 5. Hans-Günter Winkler | GER | Halla | 25 |
| 6. Fritz Thiedemann | GER | Meteor | 25.5 |

| | | HORSE | FAULTS |
|---|---|---|---|
| 7. Naldo Dasso | ARG | Final | 28 |
| 7. Bernard de Fombelle | FRA | Buffalo | 28 |
| 7. Hugh Wiley | USA | Master William | 28 |

**1964 Tokyo** C: 46, N: 17, D: 10.24.

| | | HORSE | FAULTS | JUMP-OFF |
|---|---|---|---|---|
| 1. Pierre Jonquères d'Oriola | FRA | Lutteur | 9 | |
| 2. Hermann Schridde | GER | Dozent | 13.75 | |
| 3. Peter Robeson | GBR | Firecrest | 16 | 0 |
| 4. Thomas Fahey | AUS | Bonvale | 16 | 8 |
| 5. Joaquim Miguel Duarte Silva | POR | Jeune France | 20 | |
| 5. Nelson Pessoa Filho | BRA | Huipil | 20 | |
| 7. Frank Chapot | USA | San Lucas | 20.5 | |
| 8. Kurt Jarasinski | GER | Torro | 22.25 | |

**1968 Mexico City** C: 41, N: 15, D: 10.23.

| | | HORSE | FAULTS | JUMP-OFF | |
|---|---|---|---|---|---|
| 1. William Steinkraus | USA | Snowbound | 4 | | |
| 2. Marion Coakes | GBR | Stroller | 8 | | |
| 3. David Broome | GBR | Mister Softee | 12 | 0 | 35.3 |
| 4. Frank Chapot | USA | San Lucas | 12 | 0 | 36.8 |
| 5. Hans-Günter Winkler | GER | Enigk | 12 | 0 | 37.5 |
| 6. James Elder | CAN | The Immigrant | 12 | 0 | 39.2 |
| 7. Monika Bachmann | SWI | Erbach | 16 | | |
| 7. Piero D'Inzeo | ITA | Fidux | 16 | | |
| 7. Argentino Molinuevo | ARG | Don Gustavo | 16 | | |
| 7. Alwin Schockemöhle | GER | Donal Rex | 16 | | |

**1972 Munich** C: 56, N: 22, D: 9.3.

| | | HORSE | FAULTS | JUMP-OFF |
|---|---|---|---|---|
| 1. Graziano Mancinelli | ITA | Ambassador | 8 | 0 |
| 2. Ann Moore | GBR | Psalm | 8 | 3 |
| 3. Neal Shapiro | USA | Sloopy | 8 | 8 |
| 4. James Day | CAN | Steelmaster | 8.75 | |
| 4. Hugo Simon | AUT | Lavendel | 8.75 | |
| 4. Hartwig Steenken | GER | Simona | 8.75 | |
| 7. Jean-Marcel Rozier | FRA | Sans Souci | 12 | |
| 8. Alfonso Segovia | SPA | Tic Tac | 16 | |
| 8. Fritz Ligges | GER | Robin | 16 | |

For a long time Mancinelli was a rider for the Milan horse-dealing company of Fratelli Rivolta. Consequently he was considered a professional, and many observers were surprised when he was included as a member of the Italian team in Tokyo in 1964. Banned from the team the day before the competition was to begin, he was reinstated at the last minute. The ruling turned in his favor when it was revealed that he was the adopted son of one of the Rivolta brothers—part of the family and therefore not a professional. Eight years later in Munich, Mancinelli rode a perfect round in the jump-off to earn the individual gold medal.

**1976 Montreal** C: 48, N: 20, D: 7.27.

| | | | HORSE | FAULTS | JUMP-OFF |
|---|---|---|---|---|---|
| 1. | Alwin Schockemöhle | GER | Warwick Rex | 0 | |
| 2. | Michel Vaillancourt | CAN | Branch County | 12 | 4 |
| 3. | François Mathy | BEL | Gai Luron | 12 | 8 |
| 4. | Debbie Johnsey | GBR | Moxy | 12 | 15.25 |
| 5. | Frank Chapot | USA | Viscount | 16 | |
| 5. | Guy Creighton | AUS | Mr. Dennis | 16 | |
| 5. | Marcel Rozier | FRA | Bayard de Maupas | 16 | |
| 5. | Hugo Simon | AUT | Lavendel | 16 | |

A 39-year-old factory owner, Alwin Schockemöhle was the first rider to complete the Olympic competition without a fault since František Ventura in 1928.

**1980 Moscow** C: 14, N: 7, D: 8.3.

| | | | HORSE | FAULTS | JUMP-OFF | |
|---|---|---|---|---|---|---|
| 1. | Jan Kowalczyk | POL | Artemor | 8 | | |
| 2. | Nikolai Korolkov | SOV | Espadron | 9.5 | | |
| 3. | Joaquin Perez Heras | MEX | Alymony | 12 | 4 | 43.23 |
| 4. | Oswaldo Mendez Herbruger | GUA | Pampa | 12 | 4 | 43.50 |
| 5. | Viktor Poganovsky | SOV | Topky | 15.5 | | |
| 6. | Wieslaw Hartman | POL | Norton | 16 | | |
| 7. | Barnabas Hevesi | HUN | Bohem | 24 | | |
| 8. | Marian Kozicki | POL | Bremen | 24.5 | | |

The Rotterdam Show Jumping Festival for Olympic boycotters was won by Hugo Simon of Austria, with John Whitaker of Great Britain second and Melanie Smith of the United States third.

**1984 Los Angeles-Arcadia** C: 51, N: 21, D: 8.12.

| | | | HORSE | FAULTS | JUMP-OFF |
|---|---|---|---|---|---|
| 1. | Joe Fargis | USA | Touch of Class | 4 | 0 |
| 2. | Conrad Homfeld | USA | Abdullah | 4 | 8 |
| 3. | Heidi Robbiani | SWI | Jessica V | 8 | 0 |
| 4. | Mario Deslauriers | CAN | Aramis | 8 | 4 |
| 5. | Bruno Candrian | SWI | Slygof | 8 | 8 |
| 6. | Luis Alvarez Cervera | SPA | Jexico De Park | 8.5 | |
| 7. | Frédéric Cottier | FRA | Flambeau C | 12 | |
| 7. | Paul Schockemöhle | GER | Deister | 12 | |
| 7. | Melanie Smith | USA | Calypso | 12 | |

Joe Fargis and Conrad Homfeld were companions and business partners who owned a breeding stable in Petersburg, Virginia. Fargis would have won the gold medal without a jump-off had not he and Touch of Class knocked down the final rail in the second round. This was their only fault in six rounds of Olympic competition.

**1988 Seoul** C: 74, N: 24, D: 10.2.

| | | | HORSE | FAULTS | JUMP-OFF | |
|---|---|---|---|---|---|---|
| 1. | Pierre Durand | FRA | Jappeloup de Luze | 1.25 | | |
| 2. | Greg Best | USA | Gem Twist | 4 | 4 | 45.70 |

| | | HORSE | FAULTS | JUMP-OFF | |
|---|---|---|---|---|---|
| 3. Karsten Huck | GER | Nepomuk | 4 | 4 | 54.75 |
| 4. David Broome | GBR | Countryman | 8 | | |
| 4. Anne Kursinski | USA | Starman | 8 | | |
| 6. Jaime Azcarraga | MEX | Chin Chin | 8 | | |
| 7. Joe Fargis (USA)—Mill Pearl, | | | 12 | | |

Marcus Fuchs (SWI)—Shandor
II, Thomas Fuchs (SWI)—Diners
Dollar Girl, Jos Lansink (HOL)—
Felix, Nicholas Skelton (GBR)—
Apollo, Franke Sloothaak
(GER)—Walzerkönig, Johannes
Tops (HOL)—Doreen

In 1984, France lost its chance for bronze in the team jumping competition when Pierre Durand fell. Four years later in Seoul, Durand, a 33-year-old bankruptcy administrator from Libourne, near Bordeaux, was given a chance to redeem himself. If he could ride a clear round, the bronze would go to the French. If he made even one mistake, the Canadians would take part in the medal ceremony. This time the team of Durand and Jappeloup de Luze was faultless. Four days later, in the individual final, it was Karsten Huck who needed a perfect round to win. But he and Nepomuk knocked down the next-to-last fence and the victory went to Durand.

# JUMPING (PRIX DES NATIONS), TEAM

**1896–1908** not held

**1912 Stockholm** T: 6, N: 6, D: 7.17.

| | HORSE | FAULTS | TOTAL PTS. |
|---|---|---|---|
| 1. SWE | | | 25 |
| Carl-Gustaf Lewenhaupt | Medusa | 2 | |
| Gustaf Kilman | Gatan | 10 | |
| Hans von Rosen | Lord Iron | 13 | |
| 2. FRA | | | 32 |
| Michel d'Astafort | Amazone | 5 | |
| Jean Cariou | Mignon | 8 | |
| Bernard Meyer | Allons-y | 19 | |
| 3. GER | | | 40 |
| Sigismund Freyer | Ultimus | 9 | |
| Wilhelm Graf von Hohenau | Pretty Girl | 13 | |
| Ernst-Hubertus Deloch | Hubertus | 18 | |
| 4. USA | | | 43 |
| John Montgomery | Deceive | 10 | |
| Guy Henry | Chiswell | 16 | |
| Benjamin Lear | Poppy | 17 | |
| 5. RUS | | | 50 |
| Aleksandr Rodzianko | Eros | 14 | |
| Michel Plechkov | Yvette | 18 | |
| Alexis Selikhov | Tugela | 18 | |
| 6. BEL | | | 60 |
| Emanuel de Blommaert de Soye | Clonmore | 2 | |
| Gaston de Trannoy | Capricieux | 28 | |
| Paul Convert | La Sioute | 30 | |

**1920 Antwerp** T: 5, N: 5, D: 9.12.

| | HORSE | FAULTS | TOTAL PTS. |
|---|---|---|---|
| 1. SWE | | | 14.00 |
| Claes König | Tresor | 2 | |
| Daniel Norling | Eros II | 6 | |
| Hans von Rosen | Poor Boy | 6 | |
| 2. BEL | | | 16.25 |
| Henri Laame | Biscuit | 2.75 | |
| André Coumans | Lisette | 5.25 | |
| Herman de Gaiffier d'Herstroy | Miss | 8.25 | |
| 3. ITA | | | 18.75 |
| Ettore Caffaratti | Tradittore | 1.50 | |
| Alessandro Alvisi | Raggio di Sole | 6.25 | |
| Giulio Cacciandra | Fortunello | 11 | |
| 4. FRA | | | 34.75 |
| Auguste de Laissardière | Othello | 7.50 | |
| Henri Horment | Dignité | 13.25 | |
| Théophile Carbon | Incas | 14 | |
| 5. USA | | | 42.00 |
| Harry Chamberlin | Nigra | 9 | |
| Karl Greenwald | Moses | 12 | |
| Vincent Erwin | Joffre | 21 | |

**1924 Paris** T: 11, N: 11, D: 7.27.

| | HORSE | FAULTS | TOTAL PTS. |
|---|---|---|---|
| 1. SWE | | | 42.25 |
| Åke Thelning | Loke | 12.00 | |
| Axel Ståhle | Cecil | 12.25 | |
| Åge Lundström | Anvers | 18.00 | |
| 2. SWI | | | 50.00 |
| Alphonse Gemuseus | Lucette | 6.00 | |
| Werner Stüber | Girandole | 20.00 | |
| Hans Bühler | Sailor Boy | 24.00 | |
| 3. POR | | | 53.00 |
| Antonio Borges d'Almeida | Reginald | 12.00 | |
| Helder de Souza Martins | Avro | 19.00 | |
| José Mousinho d'Albuquerque | Hetrugo | 22.00 | |
| 4. BEL | | | 57.00 |
| Nicolas Leroy | Vif Argent | 14.75 | |

| | | |
|---|---|---|
| Jacques Misonne | Torino | 19.50 |
| Gaston Mesmaekers | As de Pique | 22.75 |
| 5. ITA | | 57.50 |
| Tommaso Lequio di Assaba | Trebecco | 8.75 |
| Leone Valle | Struffo | 20.00 |
| Alessandro Alvisi | Grey Fox | 28.75 |
| 6. POL | | 58.50 |
| Adam Królikiewicz | Picador | 10.00 |
| Karol Rómmel | Faworyt | 18.00 |
| Zdzislaw Dziadulski | Zefer | 30.50 |
| 7. GBR | | 65.75 |
| Philip Bowden-Smith | Billy Boy | 10.50 |
| Capel Brunker | — | 25.50 |
| Geoffrey Brooke | — | 29.75 |
| 8. SPA | | 73.75 |
| José Alvarez de las Asturias y Bohorques (de los Trujillos) | — | 18.00 |
| N. Martinez Hombre | — | 22.00 |
| José Navarro Morenes | — | 33.75 |

**1928 Amsterdam** T: 15, N: 15, D: 8.12.

| | HORSE | FAULTS | TOTAL PTS. |
|---|---|---|---|
| 1. SPA | | | 4 |
| José Navarro Morenes | Zapatazo | 0 | |
| José Alvarez de las Asturias y Bohorques (de los Trujillos) | Zalamero | 2 | |
| Julio Garcia Fernandez | Revistada | 2 | |
| 2. POL | | | 8 |
| Kazimierz Gzowski | Mylord | 0 | |
| Kazimierz Szosland | Ali | 2 | |
| Michal Antoniewicz | Readgleadt | 6 | |
| 3. SWE | | | 10 |
| Karl Hansen | Gerold | 0 | |
| Carl Björnstierna | Kornett | 2 | |
| Ernst Hallberg | Loke | 8 | |
| 4. FRA | | | 12 |
| Pierre Bertran de Balanda | Papillon | 0 | |
| G. J. Couderc de Fonlongue | Vangerville | 4 | |
| Pierre Clavé | Le Trouvere | 8 | |
| 4. ITA | | | 12 |
| Francesco Forquet | Capineca | 0 | |
| Alessandro Bettoni-Cazzago | Aladino | 6 | |
| Tommaso Lequio di Assaba | Trebecco | 6 | |
| 4. POR | | | 12 |
| Luiz Ivens Ferraz | Marco Visconti | 4 | |
| Henrique de Sousa Martins | Avro | 4 | |
| José Mousinho d'Albuquerque | Hebraico | 4 | |
| 7. GER | | | 14 |
| Eduard Krüger | Donauwelle | 2 | |
| Richard Sahla | Correggio | 4 | |

| | | |
|---|---|---|
| Carl Friedrich Freiherr von Langen-Parow | Falkner | 8 |
| 8. SWI | | 18 |
| Charles Kuhn | Pepita | 0 |
| Alphonse Gemuseus | Lucette | 2 |
| Pierre de Muralt | Notas | 16 |

**1932 Los Angeles** T: 3, N: 3, D: 8.14.

No nation completed the course with three riders.

**1936 Berlin:** T: 18, N: 18, D: 8.16.

| | HORSE | FAULTS | TOTAL PTS. |
|---|---|---|---|
| 1. GER | | | 44.00 |
| Kurt Hasse | Tora | 4.00 | |
| Marten von Barnekow | Nordland | 20.00 | |
| Heinz Brandt | Alchimist | 20.00 | |
| 2. HOL | | | 51.50 |
| Johan Jacob Greter | Ernica | 12.00 | |
| Jan Adrianus de Bruine | Trixie | 15.00 | |
| Henri Louis van Schaik | Santa Bell | 24.50 | |
| 3. POR | | | 56.00 |
| José Beltrão | Biscuit | 12.00 | |
| Luis Marquéz do Funchal | Merle Blanc | 20.00 | |
| Luis Mena e Silva | Faussette | 24.00 | |
| 4. USA | | | 72.50 |
| Carl Raguse | Dakota | 8.00 | |
| William Bradford | Don | 27.00 | |
| Cornelius Jadwin | Ugly | 37.50 | |
| 5. SWI | | | 74.50 |
| Arnold Mettler | Durmitor | 15.00 | |
| Jürg Fehr | Corona | 29.00 | |
| Max Iklé | Exile | 30.50 | |
| 6. JPN | | | 75.00 |
| Manabu Iwahashi | Falaise | 15.25 | |
| Takeichi Nishi | Uranus | 20.75 | |
| Hirotsugu Inanami | Asafuji | 39.00 | |
| 7. FRA | | | 75.25 |
| Xavier Bizard | Bagatelle | 12.00 | |
| Maurice Gudin de Vallerin | Ecuyère | 12.00 | |
| Jean de Tillière | Adriano | 51.25 | |

**1948 London** T: 14, N: 14; D: 8.14.

| | HORSE | FAULTS | TOTAL PTS. |
|---|---|---|---|
| 1. MEX | | | 34.25 |
| Humberto Mariles Cortés | Arete | 6.25 | |
| Rubén Uriza | Harvey | 8.00 | |
| Alberto Valdes | Chihuchoc | 20.00 | |
| 2. SPA | | | 56.50 |
| Jaime Garcia Cruz | Bizarro | 12.00 | |
| José Navarro Morenes | Quorum | 20.00 | |
| Marcelino Gavilán y Ponce de Leon | Forajido | 24.50 | |
| 3. GBR | | | 67.00 |
| Harry Llewellyn | Foxhunter | 16.00 | |
| Henry Nicoll | Kilgeddin | 16.00 | |
| Arthur Carr | Monty | 35.00 | |

The course was so difficult that only three of the 14 teams managed to finish intact.

**1952 Helsinki** T: 15, N: 15, D: 8.3.

|  | HORSE | FAULTS | TOTAL PTS. |
|---|---|---|---|
| 1. GBR |  |  | 40.75 |
| Wilfred White | Nizefella | 8.00 |  |
| Douglas Stewart | Aherlow | 16.00 |  |
| Harry Llewellyn | Foxhunter | 16.75 |  |
| 2. CHI |  |  | 45.75 |
| Oscar Cristi | Bambi | 8.00 |  |
| Cesar Mendoza | Pillan | 12.00 |  |
| Ricardo Echeverria | Lindo Peal | 25.75 |  |
| 3. USA |  |  | 52.25 |
| William Steinkraus | Hollandia | 13.25 |  |
| Arthur John McCashin | Miss Budweiser | 16.00 |  |
| John Russell | Democrat | 23.00 |  |
| 4. BRA |  |  | 56.50 |
| Eloi Massey Oliveira de Menezes | Bigua | 8.00 |  |
| Renyldo Guimaraes Ferreira | Bibelot | 20.50 |  |
| Alvaro Dias de Toledo | Eldorado | 28.00 |  |
| 5. FRA |  |  | 59.00 |
| Pierre Jonquères d'Oriola | Ali Baba | 8.00 |  |
| Bertran Pernot du Breuil | Tourbillon | 20.00 |  |
| Jean-François d'Orgeix | Arlequin D. | 31.00 |  |
| 6. GER |  |  | 60.00 |
| Fritz Thiedemann | Meteor | 8.00 |  |
| Georg Höltig | Fink | 20.00 |  |
| Hans-Hermann Evèrs | Baden | 32.00 |  |
| 7. ARG |  |  | 60.75 |
| Sergio Dellacha | Santa Fe | 12.00 |  |
| Argentino Molinuevo | Discutido | 12.00 |  |
| Julio Sagastra | Don Juan | 36.75 |  |
| 8. POR |  |  | 64.00 |
| João Craveiro Lopes | Raso | 20.00 |  |
| Henrique Alves Calado | Caramulo | 20.00 |  |
| José Alves Carvalhosa | Mondina | 24.00 |  |

**1956 Stockholm** T: 20, N: 20, 6.15, 6.16.

|  | HORSE | FAULTS | TOTAL PTS. |
|---|---|---|---|
| 1. GER |  |  | 40.00 |
| Hans-Günter Winkler | Halla | 4.00 |  |
| Fritz Thiedemann | Meteor | 12.00 |  |
| Alfons Lütke-Westhues | Ala | 24.00 |  |
| 2. ITA |  |  | 66.00 |
| Raimondo D'Inzeo | Merano | 8.00 |  |
| Piero D'Inzeo | Uruguay | 11.00 |  |
| Salvatore Oppes | Pagoro | 47.00 |  |
| 3. GBR |  |  | 69.00 |
| Wilfred White | Nizefella | 12.00 |  |
| Patricia Smythe | Flanagan | 21.00 |  |
| Peter Robeson | Scorchin | 36.00 |  |
| 4. ARG |  |  | 99.50 |
| Carlos Delía | Discutido | 19.00 |  |
| Pedro Mayorga | Coriolano | 32.00 |  |
| Naldo Dasso | Ramito | 48.50 |  |

| 5. USA |  |  | 104.50 |
|---|---|---|---|
| Hugh Wiley | Trail Guide | 24.00 |  |
| William Steinkraus | Night Owl | 28.00 |  |
| Frank Chapot | Belair | 52.25 |  |
| 6. SPA |  |  | 117.25 |
| Carlos López Quesada | Tapatio | 27.75 |  |
| Francisco Goyoaga | Fahnénkönig | 28.00 |  |
| Carlos Figueroa Castillejo | Gracieux | 61.50 |  |
| 7. IRL |  |  | 131.25 |
| Kevin Barry | Ballyneety | 35.00 |  |
| William Ringrose | Liffey Vale | 44.00 |  |
| Patrick Kiernan | Ballynonty | 52.25 |  |
| 8. FRA |  |  | 154.50 |
| Pierre Jonquères d'Oriola | Voulette | 15.00 |  |
| Bernard Jevardat de Fombelle | Doria | 52.75 |  |
| Georges Calmon | Virtuoso | 86.75 |  |

**1960 Rome** T: 18, N: 18, 9.11.

|  | HORSE | FAULTS | TOTAL PTS. |
|---|---|---|---|
| 1. GER |  |  | 46.50 |
| Hans-Günter Winkler | Halla | 13.25 |  |
| Fritz Thiedemann | Meteor | 16.00 |  |
| Alwin Schockemöhle | Ferdl | 17.25 |  |
| 2. USA |  |  | 66.00 |
| Frank Chapot | Trail Guide | 20.00 |  |
| William Steinkraus | Ksar d'Esprit | 21.50 |  |
| George Morris | Sinjon | 24.50 |  |
| 3. ITA |  |  | 80.50 |
| Raimondo D'Inzeo | Posillipo | 8.00 |  |
| Piero D'Inzeo | The Rock | 32.00 |  |
| Antonio Oppes | The Scholar | 40.50 |  |
| 4. UAR |  |  | 135.50 |
| Gamal Harres | Nefertiti | 24.00 |  |
| Mohammed Zaki | Artos | 48.00 |  |
| Alwi Gazi | Mabrouk | 63.50 |  |
| 5. FRA |  |  | 168.75 |
| Bernard Jevardat de Fombelle | Buffalo | 32.50 |  |
| Max Fresson | Grand Veneur | 50.25 |  |
| Pierre Jonquères d'Oriola | Eclaire au Chocolat | 86.00 |  |
| 6. ROM |  |  | 175.00 |
| Vasile Pinciu | Barsan | 41.50 |  |
| Virgil Barbuceanu | Robot | 57.75 |  |
| Gheorghe Langa | Rubin | 75.75 |  |

**1964 Tokyo** T: 14, N: 14, D: 10.24.

|  | HORSE | FAULTS | TOTAL PTS. |
|---|---|---|---|
| 1. GER |  |  | 68.50 |
| Hermann Schridde | Dozent | 13.75 |  |
| Kurt Jarasinski | Torro | 22.25 |  |
| Hans-Günter Winkler | Fidelitas | 32.50 |  |
| 2. FRA |  |  | 77.75 |
| Pierre Jonquères d'Oriola | Lutteur | 9.00 |  |
| Janou Lefebvre | Kenavo D | 32.00 |  |
| Guy Lefrant | Monsieur de Littry | 36.75 |  |

| 3. ITA | | | 88.50 |
|---|---|---|---|
| Piero D'Inzeo | Sunbeam | 24.50 | |
| Raimondo D'Inzeo | Posillipo | 28.00 | |
| Graziano Mancinelli | Rockette | 36.00 | |
| 4. GBR | | | 97.25 |
| Peter Robeson | Firecrest | 16.00 | |
| David Broome | Jacopo | 37.00 | |
| William Barker | North Flight | 44.25 | |
| 5. ARG | | | 101.00 |
| Jorge Canaves | Confinado | 29.50 | |
| Hugo Arrambide | Chimbote | 34.25 | |
| Carlos Delia | Popin | 37.25 | |
| 6. USA | | | 107.00 |
| Frank Chapot | San Lucas | 20.50 | |
| Kathryn Kusner | Untouchable | 29.75 | |
| Mary Mairs | Tomboy | 56.75 | |
| 7. AUS | | | 109.00 |
| Thomas John Fahey | Bonvale | 16.00 | |
| Bridget Anne MacIntyre | Coronation | 39.50 | |
| Kevin Ashley Bacon | Ocean Foam | 53.50 | |
| 8. SPA | | | 118.75 |
| Fernando Goyoaga | Kif-Kif B. | 35.00 | |
| Enrique Martinez de Vallejo | Eolo IV | 40.00 | |
| A. Queipo de Llano | Infernal | 43.75 | |

**1968 Mexico City** T: 15, N: 15, D: 10.27.

| | HORSE | FAULTS | TOTAL PTS. |
|---|---|---|---|
| 1. CAN | | | 102.75 |
| James Elder | The Immigrant | 27.25 | |
| James Day | Canadian Club | 36.00 | |
| Thomas Gayford | Big Dee | 39.50 | |
| 2. FRA | | | 110.50 |
| Janou Lefebvre | Rocket | 29.75 | |
| Marcel Rozier | Quo vadis | 33.50 | |
| Pierre Jonquères d'Oriola | Nagir | 47.25 | |
| 3. GER | | | 117.25 |
| Alwin Schockemöhle | Donald Rex | 18.75 | |
| Hans-Günter Winkler | Enigk | 28.25 | |
| Hermann Schridde | Dozent | 70.25 | |
| 4. USA | | | 117.50 |
| Frank Chapot | San Lucas | 25.00 | |
| Kathryn Kusner | Untouchable | 44.50 | |
| Mary Chapot | White Lightning | 48.00 | |
| 5. ITA | | | 129.25 |
| Raimondo D'Inzeo | Bellevue | 24.25 | |
| Piero D'Inzeo | Fidux | 47.50 | |
| Graziano Mancinelli | Donerailo | 57.50 | |
| 6. SWI | | | 136.75 |
| Paul Weier | Satan | 36.75 | |
| Monica Bachmann | Erbach | 49.50 | |
| Arthur Blickenstorfer | Marianka | 50.50 | |
| 7. BRA | | | 138.00 |
| Nelson Pessoa | Pass-Op | 38.75 | |
| Lucia Faria | Rush du Camp | 44.75 | |
| José Reynoso | Cantal | 54.50 | |
| 8. GBR | | | 159.50 |
| David Broome | Mr. Softee | 20.00 | |
| R. Harvey Smith | Madison Time | 45.00 | |
| Marion Coakes | Stroller | 94.50 | |

**1972 Munich** T: 17, N: 17, D: 9.11.

| | HORSE | FAULTS | TOTAL PTS. |
|---|---|---|---|
| 1. GER | | | 32.00 |
| Fritz Ligges | Robin | 8.00 | |
| Gerhard Wiltfang | Askan | 12.00 | |
| Hartwig Steenken | Simona | 12.00 | |
| Hans-Günter Winkler | Torphy | 16.00 | |
| 2. USA | | | 32.25 |
| William Steinkraus | Main Spring | 4.00 | |
| Neal Shapiro | Sloopy | 8.25 | |
| Kathryn Kusner | Fleet Apple | 32.00 | |
| Frank Chapot | White Lightning | 36.00 | |
| 3. ITA | | | 48.00 |
| Vittorio Orlandi | Fulmer Feather | 8.00 | |
| Raimondo D'Inzeo | Fiorello II | 12.00 | |
| Graziano Mancinelli | Ambassador | 28.00 | |
| Piero D'Inzeo | Easter Light | 135.25 | |
| 4. GBR | | | 51.00 |
| Michael Saywell | Hideaway | 16.00 | |
| R. Harvey Smith | Summertime | 20.00 | |
| David Broome | Manhaton VI | 20.00 | |
| Ann Moore | Psalm | 32.00 | |
| 5. SWI | | | 61.25 |
| Monica Weier | Erbach | 17.75 | |
| Paul Weier | Wulf | 20.00 | |
| Max Hauri | Haiti | 23.50 | |
| Hermann von Siebenthal | Royal Havana | 135.25 | |
| 6. CAN | | | 64.00 |
| James Elder | Houdini | 8.00 | |
| James Day | Happy Fellow | 24.00 | |
| Terrance Millar | Le Dauphin | 35.00 | |
| Ian Miller | Shoeman | 44.00 | |
| 7. SPA | | | 66.00 |
| Alfonso Segovia | Tic Tac | 19.00 | |
| Enrique Martinez Vallejo | Val de Loire | 19.00 | |
| Luis Alvarez Cervera | Acorn | 28.00 | |
| Duque de Aveyro | Sunday Beau | 115.25 | |
| 8. ARG | | | 121.00 |
| Hugo Arrambide | Camalote | 27.00 | |
| Roberto Tagle | Simple | 40.00 | |
| Jorge Llambi | Okey Amigo | 48.00 | |
| Argentino Molinuevo | Abracadabra | 135.25 | |

Beginning in 1972, team totals were determined by adding the three best scores for each round rather than the three best scores for both rounds combined.

**1976 Montreal** T: 14, N: 14, D: 8.1.

| | HORSE | FAULTS | TOTAL PTS. |
|---|---|---|---|
| 1. FRA | | | 40.00 |
| Hubert Parot | Rivage | 12.00 | |
| Marcel Rozier | Bayard de Maupas | 12.00 | |
| Marc Roguet | Belle de Mars | 24.00 | |
| Michel Roche | Un Espoir | 32.00 | |
| 2. GER | | | 44.00 |
| Alwin Schockemöhle | Warwik Rex | 12.00 | |
| Hans-Günter Winkler | Torphy | 16.00 | |

|  | HORSE | FAULTS | TOTAL PTS. |
|---|---|---|---|
| Sönke Sönksen | Kwepe | 20.00 | |
| Paul Schockemöhle | Agent | 24.00 | |
| 3. BEL | | | 63.00 |
| Eric Wauters | Gute Sitte | 15.00 | |
| François Mathy | Gai Luron | 20.00 | |
| Edgar Gupper | Le Champion | 28.00 | |
| Stanny van Paeschen | Porsche | 36.00 | |
| 4. USA | | | 64.00 |
| Frank Chapot | Viscount | 16.00 | |
| Robert Ridland | South Side | 20.00 | |
| William Brown | Sandsablaze | 28.00 | |
| Michael Matz | Grande | 40.00 | |
| 5. CAN | | | 64.50 |
| James Day | Sympatico | 20.00 | |
| Michel Vaillancourt | Branch County | 20.50 | |
| Ian Millar | Countdown | 27.50 | |
| James Elder | Raffles II | 36.00 | |
| 6. SPA | | | 71.00 |
| Luis Alvarez-Cervera | Acorne | 16.00 | |
| Alfonso Segovia | Val de Loire | 23.00 | |
| José Rosillo | Agamenon | 36.00 | |
| Eduardo Amoros | Limited Edition | 39.00 | |
| 7. GBR | | | 76.00 |
| Debbie Johnsey | Moxy | 24.00 | |
| Roland Fernyhough | Bouncer | 31.00 | |
| Peter Robeson | Law Court | 32.00 | |
| Graham Fletcher | Hideaway | 36.00 | |
| 8. MEX | | | 76.25 |
| Fernando Hernandez | Fascination | 24.00 | |
| Fernando Senderos | Jet Run | 24.00 | |
| Luis Razo | Pueblo | 28.50 | |
| Carlos Aguirre | Consejero | 38.25 | |

**1980 Moscow** T: 6, N: 6, D: 7.29.

|  | HORSE | FAULTS | TOTAL PTS. |
|---|---|---|---|
| 1. SOV | | | 20.25 |
| Vyacheslav Chukanov | Gepatit | 4.00 | |
| Viktor Poganovsky | Topky | 8.25 | |
| Viktor Asmaev | Reis | 11.25 | |
| Nikolai Korolkov | Espadron | 12.00 | |
| 2. POL | | | 56.00 |
| Jan Kowalczyk | Artemor | 12.00 | |
| Wieslaw Hartman | Norton | 24.00 | |
| Marian Kozicki | Bremen | 37.50 | |
| Janusz Bobik | Szampan | 40.00 | |
| 3. MEX | | | 59.75 |
| Joaquin Perez Heras | Alymony | 12.00 | |
| Alberto Valdes Lacarra | Lady Mirka | 20.75 | |
| Gerardo Tazzer Valencia | Caribe | 31.75 | |
| Jesus Gomez Portugal | Massacre | 35.25 | |
| 4. HUN | | | 124.00 |
| Barnabás Hevesy | Bohem | 28.00 | |
| Ferenc Krucsó | Vadrozsa | 32.00 | |
| József Varró | Gambrinusz | 97.75 | |
| András Balogi | Artemis | 101.75 | |

| 5. ROM | | | 150.50 |
|---|---|---|---|
| Alexandru Bozan | Prejmer | 43.75 | |
| Dania Popescu | Sonor | 53.00 | |
| Dumitru Velea | Fudul | 73.75 | |
| Ion Popa | Licurici | 95.50 | |
| 6. BUL | | | 159.50 |
| Nikola Dimitrov | Vals | 46.75 | |
| Dimitar Ghenov | Makbet | 56.00 | |
| Boris Pavlov | Monblan | 60.75 | |
| Hristo Katchov | Povdo | 73.00 | |

The surprise winners of the Rotterdam Show Jumping Festival were the Canadians. Great Britain was second and Austria was third.

**1984 Los Angeles-Arcadia** T: 15, N: 15, D: 8.7.

|  | HORSE | FAULTS | TOTAL PTS. |
|---|---|---|---|
| 1. USA | | | 12.00 |
| Joe Fargis | Touch of Class | 0.00 | |
| Conrad Homfeld | Abdullah | 8.00 | |
| Leslie Burr | Albany | 12.00 | |
| Melanie Smith | Calypso | with. | |
| 2. GBR | | | 36.75 |
| Michael Whitaker | Overton Amanda | 8.00 | |
| John Whitaker | Ryans Son | 20.75 | |
| Steven Smith | Shining Example | 27.00 | |
| Timothy Grubb | Linky | 28.25 | |
| 3. GER | | | 39.25 |
| Paul Schockemöhle | Deister | 8.00 | |
| Peter Luther | Livius | 12.00 | |
| Franke Sloothaak | Farmer | 19.25 | |
| Fritz Ligges | Ramzes | 29.00 | |
| 4. CAN | | | 40.00 |
| Ian Millar | Big Ben | 12.00 | |
| Hugh Graham | Elrond | 16.00 | |
| James Elder | Shawline | 20.00 | |
| Mario Deslauriers | Aramis | 24.50 | |
| 5. SWI | | | 41.00 |
| Heidi Robbiani | Jessica V | 5.00 | |
| Bruno Candrian | Slygof | 12.00 | |
| Philippe Guerdat | Pybalia | 32.00 | |
| Willi Melliger | Van Gogh | 32.00 | |
| 6. FRA | | | 49.75 |
| Philippe Rozier | Jiva | 20.00 | |
| Frédéric Cottier | Flambeau C | 20.00 | |
| Eric Navet | J'T'Adore | 21.75 | |
| Pierre Durand | Jappeloup de Luze | elim. | |
| 7. SPA | | | 52.00 |
| Alberto Honrubia | Kaoua | 8.00 | |
| Luis Alvarez Cervera | Jexico De Park | 11.00 | |
| Rutherford Latham | Idaho E | 33.00 | |
| Luis Astolfi | Feinschnitt "Z" | 56.50 | |
| 8. ITA | | | 75.25 |
| Giorgio Nuti | Impedoumi | 16.00 | |
| Filippo Moyersoen | Adam II | 16.00 | |
| Graziano Mancinelli | Ideal De La Haye | 20.00 | |
| Bruno Scolari | Joyau D'Or | 39.25 | |

**1988 Seoul** T: 16, N: 16, D: 9.28.

| | HORSE | FAULTS | TOTAL PTS. |
|---|---|---|---|
| 1. GER | | | −17.25 |
| Ludger Beerbaum | The Freak | −4.25 | |
| Wolfgang Brinkmann | Pedro | −10.00 | |
| Dirk Hafemeister | Orchidee | −12.00 | |
| Franke Sloothaak | Walzerkönig | with. | |
| 2. USA | | | −20.50 |
| Joe Fargis | Mill Pearl | −4.25 | |
| Greg Best | Gem Twist | −8.00 | |
| Lisa Jacquin | For the Moment | −8.25 | |
| Anne Kursinski | Starman | −16.00 | |
| 3. FRA | | | −27.50 |
| Pierre Durand | Jappeloup de Luze | −5.00 | |
| Michel Robert | Pequignet La Fayette | −10.00 | |
| Frédéric Cottier | Flambeau | −16.00 | |
| Hubert Bourdy | Morgat | −16.50 | |
| 4. CAN | | | −28.75 |
| Ian Millar | Big Ben | −8.00 | |
| Mario Deslaurlers | Box Car Willie | −12.00 | |
| Lisa Carlsen | Kahlua | −16.00 | |
| Laura Tidball-Balisky | Lavendel | −22.75 | |
| 5. HOL | | | −32.25 |
| Wout-Jan van der Schans | Treffer | −8.25 | |
| Robbertus Ehrens | Sunrise | −12.00 | |
| Johannes Tops | Doreen | −16.00 | |
| Jos Lansink | Felix | −20.00 | |
| 6. GBR | | | −40.00 |
| Nicholas Skelton | Apollo | −12.00 | |
| David Broome | Countryman | −16.00 | |
| Malcolm Pyrah | Anglezarke | −16.00 | |
| Joseph Turi | Vital | −20.00 | |
| 7. SWI | | | −44.25 |
| Markus Fuchs | Shandor II | −12.00 | |
| Thomas Fuchs | Diners Dollar Girl | −12.25 | |
| Philippe Guerdat | Lanciano II | −20.00 | |
| Walter Gabáthuier | Jogger | 36.25 | |
| 8. BRA | | | −75.00 |
| Christina Johannpeter | Société | −25.50 | |
| André Johannpeter | Heartbreaker | −27.50 | |
| Vitor Teixeira | Going | −30.50 | |
| Paulo Stewart | Platon | −42.00 | |
| 8. SPA | | | −75.00 |
| Alfredo Fernández Duran | Kaoua | −21.00 | |
| Pedro Sanchez Aleman | Nuit Des Tourell | −28.25 | |
| Juan Garcia Trevijano | Tirol | −32.75 | |
| Luis Alvarez Cervera | Mirage Mexicain | −45.00 | |

## DRESSAGE, INDIVIDUAL

The dressage competition requires the rider to put the horse through a series of movements which display the degree of communication and cooperation between human and animal. Points are awarded for the proper execution of each movement.

**1896–1908** not held

**1912 Stockholm** C: 21, N: 8, D: 7.15.

| | | | HORSE | PTS. |
|---|---|---|---|---|
| 1. Carl Bonde | | SWE | Emperor | 15 |
| 2. Gustaf-Adolf Boltenstern, Sr. | | SWE | Neptun | 21 |
| 3. Hans von Blixen-Finecke, Sr. | | SWE | Maggie | 32 |
| 4. Friedrich von Oesterley | | GER | Condor | 36 |
| 5. Carl Rosenblad | | SWE | Miss Hastings | 43 |
| 6. Oskar af Ström | | SWE | Irish Lass | 47 |
| 7. Felix Burkner | | GER | King | 51 |
| 8. Carl Kruckenberg | | SWE | Kartusch | 51 |

**1920 Antwerp** C: 17, N: 5, D: 9.9.

| | | | HORSE | PTS. |
|---|---|---|---|---|
| 1. Janne Lundblad | | SWE | Uno | 27.937 |
| 2. Bertil Sandström | | SWE | Sabel | 26.312 |
| — Gustaf-Adolf Boltenstern, Sr. | | SWE | Iron | 26.187 |
| 3. Hans von Rosen | | SWE | Running Sister | 25.125 |
| 4. Wilhelm von Essen | | SWE | Nomeg | 24.875 |
| 5. Hédoin de Maillé | | FRA | Cheribiribi | 23.937 |
| 6. Michel Artola | | FRA | Plumard | 23.437 |
| 7. Gaston de Trannoy | | BEL | Bouton d'Or | 23.125 |
| 8. Jens Falkenberg | | NOR | Gjördis | 22.375 |

Colonel Boltenstern, on Iron, finished in third place, but was disqualified for practicing in the ring before the competition began.

**1924 Paris** C: 24, N: 9, D: 7.25.

| | | | HORSE | PTS. |
|---|---|---|---|---|
| 1. Ernst Linder | | SWE | Piccolomini | 276.4 |
| 2. Bertil Sandström | | SWE | Sabel | 275.8 |
| 3. Xavier Lesage | | FRA | Plumard | 265.8 |
| 4. Wilhelm von Essen | | SWE | Zobel | 260.0 |
| 5. Victor Ankarcrona | | SWE | Corona | 256.5 |
| 6. Emanuel Thiel | | CZE | Ex | 256.2 |
| 7. R. Wallon | | FRA | Magister | 243.2 |
| 7. H. von der Weid | | SWI | Uhlard | 243.2 |

**1928 Amsterdam** C: 29, N: 12, D: 8.11.

| | | | HORSE | PTS. |
|---|---|---|---|---|
| 1. Carl Friedrich Freiherr von Langen-Parow | | GER | Draufgänger | 237.42 |
| 2. Charles Marion | | FRA | Linon | 231.00 |
| 3. Ragnar Ohlson | | SWE | Gunstling | 229.78 |
| 4. Janne Lundblad | | SWE | Blackmar | 226.70 |
| 5. Emanuel Thiel | | CZE | Loki | 225.96 |
| 6. Hermann Linkenbach | | GER | Gimpel | 224.26 |
| 7. L.E.R. Wallon | | FRA | Clough-banck | 224.08 |
| 8. Jan van Reede | | HOL | Hans | 220.70 |

**1932 Los Angeles** C: 10, N: 4, D: 8.10.

| | | | HORSE | POINTS | ORDINALS |
|---|---|---|---|---|---|
| 1. Xavier Lesage | | FRA | Taine | 343.75 | 6 |
| 2. Charles Marion | | FRA | Linon | 305.42 | 14 |
| 3. Hiram Tuttle | | USA | Olympic | 300.50 | 14 |
| 4. Thomas Byström | | SWE | Guliver | 293.50 | 16 |
| 5. André Jousseaume | | FRA | Sorelta | 290.42 | 17 |

| | | HORSE | POINTS | ORDI-NALS |
|---|---|---|---|---|
| 6. Isaac Kitts | USA | American Lady | 282.08 | 17 |
| 7. Alvin Moore | USA | Water Pat | 276.33 | 20 |
| 8. Gustaf-Adolf Boltenstern, Jr. | SWE | Ingo | 277.83 | 21 |

Bertil Sandström of Sweden came in second but was relegated to last place for encouraging his horse, Kreta, by making clicking noises. He claimed that the noises were actually made by a creaking saddle, but the Jury of Appeal was not convinced. Moore was awarded seventh place, ahead of Boltenstern, because places were determined not by total points but by the rankings of the judges, using a system of ordinals such as is used in figure skating.

**1936 Berlin** C: 29, N: 11, D: 8.13.

| | | HORSE | PTS. |
|---|---|---|---|
| 1. Heinz Pollay | GER | Kronos | 1760.0 |
| 2. Friedrich Gerhard | GER | Absinth | 1745.5 |
| 3. Alois Podhajsky | AUT | Nero | 1721.5 |
| 4. Gregor Adlercreutz | SWE | Teresina | 1675.0 |
| 5. André Jousseaume | FRA | Favorite | 1642.5 |
| 6. Gérard de Ballore | FRA | Debaucheur | 1634.0 |
| 7. Peder Jensen | DEN | His Ex | 1596.0 |
| 8. Pierre Versteegh | HOL | Ad Astra | 1579.0 |

**1948 London** C: 19, N: 9, D: 8.9.

| | | HORSE | PTS. |
|---|---|---|---|
| 1. Hans Moser | SWI | Hummer | 492.5 |
| 2. André Jousseaume | FRA | Harpagon | 480.0 |
| 3. Gustaf-Adolf Boltenstern, Jr. | SWE | Trumf | 477.5 |
| 4. Robert Borg | USA | Klingson | 473.5 |
| 5. Henri Saint Cyr | SWE | Djimm | 444.5 |
| — Gehnäll Persson | SWE | — | 444.0 |
| 6. Jean Saint Fort Paillard | FRA | Sous les Ceps | 439.5 |
| 7. Alois Podhajsky | AUT | Teja | 437.5 |
| 8. Earl Thomson | USA | Pancraft | 421.0 |

The absurdity of the rules governing Olympic dressage reached its pinnacle in 1948, when sixth-place finisher Gehnäll Persson was disqualified when it was discovered that he was only a noncommissioned officer and thus ineligible to compete.

**1952 Helsinki** C: 27, N: 10, D: 7.29.

| | | HORSE | PTS. |
|---|---|---|---|
| 1. Henri Saint Cyr | SWE | Master Rufus | 561.0 |
| 2. Lis Hartel | DEN | Jubilee | 541.5 |
| 3. André Jousseaume | FRA | Harpagon | 541.0 |
| 4. Gustaf-Adolf Boltenstern, Jr. | SWE | Krest | 531.0 |
| 5. Gottfried Trachsel | SWI | Kursus | 531.0 |
| 6. Henri Chammartin | SWI | Wohler | 529.5 |
| 7. Gustav Fischer | SWI | Soliman | 518.5 |
| 7. Heinz Pollay | GER | Adular | 518.5 |

Between 1948 and 1952 dressage competition underwent a radical change. Not only were noncommissioned officers allowed to enter in 1952, so were other enlisted men. And not only were enlisted men allowed to enter, so were men

who were civilians. And not only were men who were civilians allowed to enter, but for the first time in Olympic equestrian history, four women were allowed to compete against men. One of those women was Lis Hartel of Denmark. In 1944 Lis Hartel, a 23-year-old pregnant mother, was one of Denmark's leading riders. Then, one morning in September, she awoke with a headache and a strange stiffness in her neck. A few days later paralysis began spreading throughout her body—she had become a victim of polio. But Lis Hartel was determined to regain her health. First she learned to lift her arm, then she regained the use of her thigh muscles. Then she gave birth to a healthy daughter. Soon she was crawling, and eight months after the attack, she was able to walk a bit by using crutches. Her friends hailed her recovery, but she was not finished. She insisted on mounting a horse. Reactivating the muscles necessary to keep from falling was so exhausting that she had to rest for two weeks before she tried a second time. Slowly but surely, Lis Hartel improved until, three years after her polio attack, she was able to compete in the Scandinavian riding championship, finishing second in the women's dressage. She remained paralyzed below the knees, but learned to do without those muscles. In 1952 she was chosen to represent Denmark in the Olympics, and she responded by earning the silver medal, even though she had to be helped on and off her horse. When gold medalist Henri Saint Cyr helped her up onto the victory platform for the medal presentation, it was one of the most emotional moments in Olympic history. Four years later, in Stockholm, she won another silver medal.

**1956 Stockholm** C: 36, N: 17, D: 6.16.

| | | HORSE | PTS. |
|---|---|---|---|
| 1. Henri Saint Cyr | SWE | Juli | 860 |
| 2. Lis Hartel | DEN | Jubilee | 850 |
| 3. Liselott Linsenhoff | GER | Adular | 832 |
| 4. Gehnäll Persson | SWE | Knaust | 821 |
| 5. André Jousseaume | FRA | Harpagon | 814 |
| 6. Gottfried Trachsel | SWI | Kursus | 807 |
| 7. Gustaf-Adolf Bolterstern, Jr. | SWE | Krest | 794 |
| 8. Henri Chammartin | SWI | Woehler | 789 |

The judging caused something of a scandal. The German judge, General Berger, ranked the three German riders first, second, and third and the Swedish judge, General Colliander, ranked the three Swedish riders first, second, and third. First-place finisher Henri Saint Cyr completed his harvest of four gold medals. The fifth-place finisher, 61-year-old André Jousseaume, was competing in his fifth Olympics. Between 1932 and 1952 he won two gold medals, two silver, and one bronze.

**1960 Rome** C: 17, N: 10, D: 9.6.

| | | HORSE | PTS. |
|---|---|---|---|
| 1. Sergei Filatov | SOV | Absent | 2144 |
| 2. Gustav Fischer | SWI | Wald | 2087 |
| 3. Josef Neckermann | GER | Asbach | 2082 |
| 4. Henri Saint Cyr | SWE | L'Etoile | 2064 |

| | | | |
|---|---|---|---|
| 5. Ivan Kalita | SOV | Korbey | 2007 |
| 6. Patricia Galvin | USA | Rath Patrick | 995 |
| 7. Rosemarie Springer | GER | Doublette | 985 |
| 8. Henri Chammartin | SWI | Wolfdietrich | 978 |

Finishing in 16th place was Kroum Lekarski of Bulgaria, whose first Olympic appearance has been in the three-day event in 1924.

**1964 Tokyo** C: 22, N: 9, D:10.23.

| | | HORSE | PTS. |
|---|---|---|---|
| 1. Henri Chammartin | SWI | Woermann | 1504 |
| 2. Harry Boldt | GER | Remus | 1503 |
| 3. Sergei Filatov | SOV | Absent | 1486 |
| 4. Gustav Fischer | SWI | Wald | 1485 |
| 5. Josef Neckermann | GER | Antoinette | 1429 |
| 6. Reiner Klimke | GER | Dux | 1404 |
| 7. Marianne Gossweiler | SWI | Stephan | 802 |
| 8. Patricia Galvin de la Tour d'Auvergne | USA | Rath Patrick | 783 |

**1968 Mexico City** C: 26, N: 9, D: 10.25.

| | | HORSE | PTS. |
|---|---|---|---|
| 1. Ivan Kizimov | SOV | Ikhor | 1572 |
| 2. Josef Neckermann | GER | Mariano | 1546 |
| 3. Reiner Klimke | GER | Dux | 1537 |
| 4. Ivan Kalita | SOV | Absent | 1519 |
| 5. Horst Köhler | GDR | Neuschnee | 1475 |
| 6. Yelena Petushkova | SOV | Pepei | 1471 |
| 7. Gustav Fischer | SWI | Wald | 1465 |
| 8. Liselott Linsenhoff | GER | Piaff | 855 |

**1972 Munich** C: 33, N: 13, D: 9.7.

| | | HORSE | PTS. |
|---|---|---|---|
| 1. Liselott Linsenhoff | GER | Piaff | 1229 |
| 2. Yelena Petushkova | SOV | Pepel | 1185 |
| 3. Josef Neckermann | GER | Venetia | 1177 |
| 4. Ivan Kizimov | SOV | Ikhor | 1159 |
| 5. Ulla Håkansson | SWE | Ajax | 1126 |
| 6. Ivan Kalita | SOV | Tarif | 1130 |
| 7. Karin Schlueter | GER | Liostroa | 1110 |
| 8. Maud Von Rosen | SWE | Lucky Boy | 1088 |

Twenty-one of the 33 riders were women, including Liselott Linsenhoff, the first female individual gold medalist. Second-place finisher Petushkova was a professor of biology at the University of Moscow and was, for some time, married to high-jumper Valery Brumel.

**1976 Montreal** C: 27, N: 11, D: 7.30.

| | | HORSE | PTS. |
|---|---|---|---|
| 1. Christine Stückelberger | SWI | Granat | 1486 |
| 2. Harry Boldt | GER | Woycek | 1435 |
| 3. Reiner Klimke | GER | Mehmed | 1395 |
| 4. Gabriela Grillo | GER | Ultimo | 1257 |
| 5. Dorothy Morkis | USA | Monaco | 1249 |
| 6. Viktor Ugryumov | SOV | Said | 1247 |
| 7. Christilot Boylen | CAN | Gaspano | 1217 |
| 8. Ulla Petersen | DEN | Chigwell | 1192 |

**1980 Moscow** C: 14, N: 6, D: 8.1.

| | | HORSE | PTS. |
|---|---|---|---|
| 1. Elisabeth Theurer | AUT | Mon Cherie | 1370 |
| 2. Yuri Kovshov | SOV | Igrok | 1300 |
| 3. Viktor Ugryumov | SOV | Shkval | 1234 |
| 4. Vera Misevich | SOV | Plot | 1231 |
| 5. Kyra Kyrklund | FIN | Piccolo | 1121 |
| 6. Anghelache Donescu | ROM | Dor | 960 |
| 7. Georgi Gadzhev | BUL | Vnimatelen | 881 |
| 8. Svetoslav Ivanov | BUL | Aleko | 850 |

Theurer was the only leading dressage rider to enter the Olympics. All the rest took part in the Dressage Festival the following week, which was won by Christine Stückelberger.

**1984 Los Angeles-Arcadia** C: 43, N: 18, D: 8.10.

| | | HORSE | PTS. |
|---|---|---|---|
| 1. Reiner Klimke | GER | Ahlerich | 1504 |
| 2. Anne Grethe Jensen | DEN | Marzog | 1442 |
| 3. Otto Hofer | SWI | Limandus | 1364 |
| 4. Ingamay Bylund | SWE | Aleks | 1332 |
| 5. Herbert Krug | GER | Muscadeur | 1323 |
| 6. Christopher Bartle | GBR | Wily Trout | 1279 |
| 6. Uwe Sauer | GER | Montevideo | 1279 |
| 8. Annemarie Sanders-Keyzer | HOL | Amon | 1271 |

Dr. Reiner Klimke, a 48-year-old lawyer from Münster, won his first individual gold medal to bring his Olympic total to 5 golds and 2 bronzes. In 1988, he won another gold in the team competition.

**1988 Seoul** C: 55, N: 18, D: 9.27.

| | | HORSE | PTS. |
|---|---|---|---|
| 1. Nicole Uphoff | GER | Rembrandt | 1521 |
| 2. Margit Otto-Crépin | FRA | Corlandus | 1462 |
| 3. Christine Stückelberger | SWI | Gauguin De Lully | 1417 |
| 4. Cynthia Ishoy | CAN | Dynasty | 1401 |
| 5. Kyra Kyrklund | FIN | Matador | 1393 |
| 6. Monica Theodorescu | GER | Ganimedes | 1385 |
| 7. Otto Hofer | SWI | Andiamo | 1383 |
| 8. Ann-Kathrin Linsenhoff | GER | Courage | 1374 |

This was the first time all three medals were won by women.

# DRESSAGE, TEAM

**1896–1924** not held

**1928 Amsterdam** T: 8, N: 8, D: 8.11.

| | HORSE | | TOTAL PTS. |
|---|---|---|---|
| 1. GER | | | 669.72 |
| Carl Friedrich Freiherr von Langen-Parow | Draufgänger | 237.42 | |
| Hermann Linkenbach | Gimpel | 224.26 | |
| Eugen Freiherr von Lotzbeck | Caracalla | 208.04 | |

|  | HORSE | | TOTAL PTS. |
|---|---|---|---|
| 2. SWE | | | 650.86 |
| Ragnar Ohlson | Gunstling | 229.78 | |
| Janne Lundblad | Blackmar | 226.70 | |
| Carl Bonde | Ingo | 194.38 | |
| 3. HOL | | | 642.96 |
| Jan van Reede | Hans | 220.70 | |
| Pierre Versteegh | His Excellence | 216.44 | |
| Gérard Le Heux | Valerine | 205.82 | |
| 4. FRA | | | 642.18 |
| Charles Marion | Linon | 231.00 | |
| Robert Wallon | Cloughbank | 224.08 | |
| Pierre Danloux | Rempart | 187.10 | |
| 5. CZE | | | 637.94 |
| Emanuel Thiel | Loki | 225.96 | |
| Otto Schöniger | Ex | 210.28 | |
| Jaroslav Hauf | Elegant | 201.70 | |
| 6. AUT | | | 600.40 |
| Arthur von Pongracz | Turridu | 204.28 | |
| Wilhelm Jaich | Graf | 204.16 | |
| Gustav Grachegg | Daniel | 191.96 | |
| 7. SWI | | | 569.08 |
| A. Mercier | Queen-Mary | 203.34 | |
| Otto Frank | Solon | 190.62 | |
| Werner Stuber | Ulhard | 175.12 | |
| 8. BEL | | | 499.70 |
| Oscar Lints | Rira-t-elle | 185.86 | |
| Henri Laame | Belga | 167.70 | |
| R.G.G. Delrue | Dreypuss | 146.14 | |

**1932 Los Angeles** T: 3, N: 3, D: 8.10.

|  | HORSE | | TOTAL PTS. |
|---|---|---|---|
| 1. FRA | | | 2818.75 |
| Xavier Lesage | Taine | 1031.25 | |
| Charles Marion | Linon | 916.25 | |
| André Jousseaume | Sorelta | 871.25 | |
| 2. SWE | | | 2678.00 |
| Bertil Sandström | Kreta | 964.00 | |
| Thomas Byström | Gulliver | 880.50 | |
| Gustaf-Adolf Boltenstern, Jr. | Ingo | 833.50 | |
| 3. USA | | | 2576.75 |
| Hiram Tuttle | Olympic | 901.50 | |
| Isaac Kitts | American Lady | 846.25 | |
| Alvin Moore | Water Pat | 829.00 | |

**1936 Berlin** T: 9, N: 9, D: 8.13.

|  | HORSE | | TOTAL PTS. |
|---|---|---|---|
| 1. GER | | | 5074.0 |
| Heinz Pollay | Kronos | 1760.0 | |
| Friedrich Gerhard | Absinth | 1745.5 | |
| Hermann von Oppeln-Bronikowski | Gimpel | 1568.5 | |
| 2. FRA | | | 4846.0 |
| André Jousseaume | Favorite | 1642.5 | |
| Gerard de Ballore | Debaucheur | 1634.0 | |
| Daniel Gillois | Nicolas | 1569.5 | |

| 3. SWE | | | 4660.5 |
|---|---|---|---|
| Gregor Adlercreutz | Teresina | 1675.0 | |
| Sven Colliander | Kal | 1530.5 | |
| Folke Sandström | Pergoia | 1455.0 | |
| 4. AUT | | | 4627.5 |
| Alois Podhajsky | Nero | 1721.5 | |
| Albert Dolleschall | Infant | 1476.0 | |
| Arthur von Pongracz | Georgine | 1430.0 | |
| 5. HOL | | | 4382.0 |
| Pierre Versteegh | Ad Astra | 1579.0 | |
| Gérard Le Heux | Zonnetje | 1422.0 | |
| Daniel Camerling-Helmolt | Wodan | 1381.0 | |
| 6. HUN | | | 4090.0 |
| Gusztáv von Pados | Ficsur | 1424.0 | |
| László von Magasházy | Tucsok | 1415.5 | |
| Pál Kerméry | Csintaian | 1250.5 | |
| 7. NOR | | | 4050.5 |
| Arthur Qvist | Jaspis | 1438.0 | |
| Eugene Johansen | Sorte Mand | 1388.0 | |
| Bjorn Bjornseth | Invictus | 1224.5 | |
| 8. CZE | | | 4026.0 |
| Frantisek Jandl | Nestor | 1453.0 | |
| Matej Pechmann | Ideal | 1319.0 | |
| Otto Schöniger | Helios | 1254.0 | |

The oldest competitor at the Berlin Olympics was 72-year-old General Arthur von Pongracz, of Austria's fourth-place team. Von Pongracz made his Olympic debut in Paris in 1924, when he was a mere youngster of 60.

**1948 London** T: 5, N: 5, D: 8.9.

|  | HORSE | | TOTAL PTS. |
|---|---|---|---|
| — SWE | | | 1366.0 |
| Gustav-Adolf Boltenstern, Jr. | Trumf | 477.5 | |
| Henri Saint Cyr | Djimm | 444.5 | |
| Gehnäll Persson | — | 444.0 | |
| 1. FRA | | | 1269.0 |
| André Jousseaume | Harpagon | 480.0 | |
| Jean Saint Fort Paillard | Sous les Ceps | 439.5 | |
| Maurice Buret | Saint Ouen | 349.5 | |
| 2. USA | | | 1256.0 |
| Robert Borg | Klingson | 473.5 | |
| Earl Thomson | Pancraft | 421.0 | |
| Frank Henry | Reno Overdo | 361.5 | |
| 3. POR | | | 1182.0 |
| Fernando Pais da Silva | Matamas | 411.0 | |
| Franciso Valadas | Feitico | 405.0 | |
| Luiz Mena e Silva | Fascinante | 366.0 | |
| 4. ARG | | | 1005.5 |
| Justo Iturralde | Pajarito | 397.0 | |
| Humberto Terzano | Bienvenido | 327.0 | |
| Oscar Goulu | Grillo | 281.5 | |

The first-place Swedish team was disqualified when it was learned that Persson, who had been entered as an officer, was actually only a noncommissioned officer.

**1952 Helsinki** T: 8, N: 8, D: 7.29.

| | HORSE | | TOTAL PTS. |
|---|---|---|---|
| 1. SWE | | | 1597.5 |
| Henri Saint Cyr | Master Rufus | 561.0 | |
| Gustaf-Adolf Boltenstern, Jr. | Krest | 531.0 | |
| Gehnäll Persson | Knaust | 505.5 | |
| 2. SWI | | | 1579.0 |
| Gottfried Trachsel | Krusus | 531.0 | |
| Henri Chammartin | Wohler | 529.5 | |
| Gustav Fischer | Solimon | 518.5 | |
| 3. GER | | | 1501.0 |
| Heinz Pollay | Adular | 518.5 | |
| Ida von Nagel | Afrika | 503.0 | |
| Fritz Thiedemann | Chronist | 479.5 | |
| 4. FRA | | | 1423.5 |
| André Jousseaume | Harpagon | 541.0 | |
| Jean Pelterln de Saint André | Vol au vent | 479.0 | |
| Jean Saint Ford Paillard | Tapir | 403.5 | |
| 5. CHI | | | 1340.5 |
| José Larrain | Rey de Oros | 473.5 | |
| Hector Clavel | Frontalera | 452.0 | |
| Ernesto Silva | Viareggio | 415.0 | |
| 6. USA | | | 1253.5 |
| Robert Borg | Bill Biddle | 492.0 | |
| Marjorie Haines | The Flying Dutchman | 446.0 | |
| Hartmann Pauly | Reno Overde | 315.5 | |
| 7. SOV | | | 1205.5 |
| Vladimir Raspopov | Imeninnik | 433.5 | |
| Vassily Tihonov | Pevec | 395.0 | |
| Nikolai Sitko | Cesar | 377.0 | |
| 8. POR | | | 1196.5 |
| Antonio Reymão Nogueira | Napeiro | 428.4 | |
| Francisco Valadas Júnior | Feitico | 422.0 | |
| Fernando Silva Paes | Matamas | 346.0 | |

**1956 Stockholm** T: 8, N: 8, D: 6.16.

| | HORSE | | TOTAL PTS. |
|---|---|---|---|
| 1. SWE | | | 2475.0 |
| Henri Saint Cyr | Juli | 860.0 | |
| Gehnäll Persson | Knaust | 821.0 | |
| Gustaf-Adolf Boltenstern, Jr. | Krest | 794.0 | |
| 2. GER | | | 2346.0 |
| Liselott Linsenhoff | Adular | 832.0 | |
| Hannelore Weygand | Perkunos | 785.0 | |
| Anneliese Küppers | Afrika | 729.0 | |
| 3. SWI | | | 2346.0 |
| Gottfried Trachsel | Kursus | 807.0 | |
| Henri Chammartin | Wohler | 789.0 | |
| Gustav Fischer | Vasello | 750.0 | |
| 4. SOV | | | 2170.0 |
| Sergei Filatov | Ingas | 744.0 | |
| Aleksandr Vtorov | Reportoir | 726.0 | |
| Nikolai Sitko | Skatschek | 700.0 | |
| 5. DEN | | | 2167.0 |
| Lis Hartel | Jubilee | 850.0 | |

| | | | |
|---|---|---|---|
| Hermann Zobel | Monty | 673.0 | |
| Inger Lemvigh-Müller | Bel Ami | 644.0 | |
| 6. FRA | | | 2016.0 |
| André Jousseaume | Harpagon | 814.0 | |
| Jean-Albert Brau | Vol d'Amour | 648.0 | |
| Jean Salmon | Kipling | 554.0 | |
| 7. NOR | | | 1912.5 |
| Else Christophersen | Diva | 739.0 | |
| Anne Lise Kielland | Clary | 601.5 | |
| Bodil Russ | Corona | 572.0 | |
| 8. ROM | | | 1862.0 |
| Gheorghe Teodorescu | Palatin | 721.0 | |
| Nicolae Mihalcea | Mihnea | 625.0 | |
| Niculae Marcoci | Corvin | 516.0 | |

**1960** not held

**1964 Tokyo** T: 6, N: 6, D: 10.23.

| | HORSE | | TOTAL PTS. |
|---|---|---|---|
| 1. GER | | | 2558.0 |
| Harry Boldt | Remus | 889.0 | |
| Reiner Klimke | Dux | 837.0 | |
| Josef Neckermann | Antoinette | 832.0 | |
| 2. SWI | | | 2526.0 |
| Henri Chammartin | Wormann | 870.0 | |
| Gustav Fischer | Wald | 854.0 | |
| Marianne Gussweiler | Stepan | 802.0 | |
| 3. SOV | | | 2311.0 |
| Sergei Filatov | Absent | 847.0 | |
| Ivan Kizimov | Ikhor | 758.0 | |
| Ivan Kalita | Moar | 706.0 | |
| 4. USA | | | 2130.0 |
| Patricia Galvin de la Tour d'Auvergne | Rath Patrick | 783.0 | |
| Anne Newberry | Forstrat | 707.0 | |
| Karen McIntosh | Malteser | 640.0 | |
| 5. SWE | | | 2068.0 |
| William Hamilton | Delicado | 777.0 | |
| Hans Wikne | Gaspari | 753.0 | |
| Bengt Ljungquist | Karat | 538.0 | |
| 6. JPN | | | 1779.5 |
| Kikuko Inoue | Katsunobori | 648.0 | |
| Nagahira Okabe | Seiha | 589.5 | |
| Yoritsune Matsudaira | Hamachidori | 542.0 | |

**1968 Mexico City** T. 8, N. 8, D: 10.24.

| | HORSE | | TOTAL PTS. |
|---|---|---|---|
| 1. GER | | | 2699 |
| Josef Neckermann | Mariano | 948 | |
| Reiner Klimke | Dux | 896 | |
| Liselott Linsenhoff | Piaff | 855 | |
| 2. SOV | | | 2657 |
| Ivan Kizimov | Ikhor | 908 | |
| Ivan Kalita | Absent | 879 | |
| Yelena Petushkova | Pepel | 870 | |
| 3. SWI | | | 2547 |
| Gustav Fischer | Wald | 866 | |

|  | HORSE |  | TOTAL PTS. |
|---|---|---|---|
| Henri Chammartin | Wolfdietrich | 845 |  |
| Marianne Gossweiler | Stephan | 836 |  |
| 4. GDR |  |  | 2357 |
| Horst Köhler | Neuschnee | 875 |  |
| Gerhard Brockmüller | Tristah | 789 |  |
| Wolfgang Müller | Marios | 693 |  |
| 5. GBR |  |  | 2332 |
| Domini Lawrence | San Fernando | 793 |  |
| H. Lorna Johnstone | El Guapo | 777 |  |
| Johanna Hall | Conversano Caprice | 762 |  |
| 6. CHI |  |  | 2015 |
| Guillermo Squella | Colchaguino | 693 |  |
| Antonio Piraino | Ciclon | 672 |  |
| Patricio Escudero | Prete | 650 |  |
| 7. CAN |  |  | 2012 |
| Inez Fischer-Credo | Marius | 732 |  |
| Christilot Hanson | Bonheur | 677 |  |
| Zoltan Sztehlo | Virtuose | 603 |  |
| 8. USA |  |  | 1919 |
| Kyra Downton | Cadet | 657 |  |
| Edith Master | Helios | 646 |  |
| Donnan Plumb | Attache | 616 |  |

**1972 Munich** T: 10, N: 10, D: 9.7.

|  | HORSE |  | TOTAL PTS. |
|---|---|---|---|
| 1. SOV |  |  | 5095 |
| Yelena Petushkova | Pepel | 1747 |  |
| Ivan Kizimov | Ikhor | 1701 |  |
| Ivan Kalita | Tarif | 1647 |  |
| 2. GER |  |  | 5083 |
| Liselott Linsenhoff | Piaff | 1763 |  |
| Josef Neckermann | Venetia | 1706 |  |
| Karin Schlüter | Lisotro | 1614 |  |
| 3. SWE |  |  | 4849 |
| Ulla Håkansson | Ajax | 1649 |  |
| Ninna Swaab | Casanova | 1622 |  |
| Maud Von Rosen | Lucky Boy | 1578 |  |
| 4. DEN |  |  | 4606 |
| Aksel Mikkelsen | Talisman | 1597 |  |
| Ulla Petersen | Chigwell | 1534 |  |
| Charlotte Ingemann | Souliman | 1475 |  |
| 5. GDR |  |  | 4552 |
| Gerhard Brockmüller | Marios | 1545 |  |
| Wolfgang Müller | Semafor | 1521 |  |
| Horst Köhler | Imanuel | 1486 |  |
| 6. CAN |  |  | 4418 |
| Christilot Hanson | Armagnac III | 1615 |  |
| Cynthia Neal | Bonne Annee | 1424 |  |
| Lorraine Stubbs | Venezuela | 1379 |  |
| 7. SWI |  |  | 4383 |
| Christine Stückelberger | Granat | 1528 |  |
| Hermann Duer | Sod | 1466 |  |
| Marita Aeschbacher | Charlamp | 1389 |  |
| 8. HOL |  |  | 4309 |
| Annie van Doorne | Pericles | 1480 |  |
| Friederie Benedictus | Turista | 1420 |  |
| John Swaab | Maharadscha | 1409 |  |

At age 46, Maud Von Rosen of the Swedish team became the oldest female medalist in Olympic history.

**1976 Montreal** T: 8, N: 8, D: 7.29.

|  | HORSE |  | TOTAL PTS. |
|---|---|---|---|
| 1. GER |  |  | 5155 |
| Harry Boldt | Woycey | 1863 |  |
| Reiner Klimke | Mehmed | 1751 |  |
| Gabriela Grillo | Ultimo | 1541 |  |
| 2. SWI |  |  | 4684 |
| Christine Stückelberger | Granat | 1869 |  |
| Ulrich Lehmann | Widin | 1425 |  |
| Doris Ramseier | Roch | 1390 |  |
| 3. USA |  |  | 4647 |
| Hilda Gurney | Keen | 1607 |  |
| Dorothy Morkis | Monaco | 1559 |  |
| Edith Master | Dahlwitz | 1481 |  |
| 4. SOV |  |  | 4542 |
| Viktor Ugryumov | Said | 1597 |  |
| Ivan Kalita | Tarif | 1520 |  |
| Ivan Kizimov | Rebus | 1425 |  |
| 5. CAN |  |  | 4538 |
| Christilot Boylen | Gaspano | 1590 |  |
| Lorraine Stubbs | True North | 1549 |  |
| Barbara Stracey | Jungherr II | 1399 |  |
| 6. DEN |  |  | 4448 |
| Ulla Petersen | Chigwell | 1552 |  |
| Tonny Jensen | Fox | 1521 |  |
| Niels Haagensen | Lowenstern | 1375 |  |
| 7. HOL |  |  | 4380 |
| Jo Rutten | Banjo | 1533 |  |
| Louky Van Olphen | Aleric | 1449 |  |
| Marjolyn Greeve | Lucky Boy | 1398 |  |
| 8. GBR |  |  | 4076 |
| Sarah Whitmore | Junker | 1375 |  |
| Jennie Loriston Clarke | Kadett | 1375 |  |
| Diana Mason | Special Ed | 1326 |  |

**1980 Moscow** T: 4, N: 4, D: 7.31.

|  | HORSE |  | TOTAL PTS. |
|---|---|---|---|
| 1. SOV |  |  | 4383 |
| Yuri Kovshov | Igrok | 1588 |  |
| Viktor Ugryumov | Shkval | 1541 |  |
| Vera Misevich | Plot | 1254 |  |
| 2. BUL |  |  | 3580 |
| Peter Mandazhiev | Stchibor | 1244 |  |
| Svetoslav Ivanov | Aleko | 1190 |  |
| Georgi Gadjev | Vnimatelen | 1146 |  |
| 3. ROM |  |  | 3346 |
| Anghelache Donescu | Dor | 1255 |  |
| Dumitru Veliku | Decebal | 1076 |  |
| Petre Rosca | Derbist | 1015 |  |
| 4. POL |  |  | 2945 |
| Józef Zagor | Hellios | 1061 |  |
| Elżbieta Morciniec | Sum | 954 |  |
| Wanda Wąsowska | Damask | 930 |  |

The Goodwood Dressage Festival, held as an alternative to the Olympics, was won by West Germany, with Switzerland second and Denmark third.

**1984 Los Angeles-Arcadia** T: 12, N: 12, D: 8.9.

| | HORSE | | TOTAL PTS. |
|---|---|---|---|
| 1. GER | | | 4955 |
| Reiner Klimke | Ahlerich | 1797 | |
| Uwe Sauer | Montevideo | 1582 | |
| Herbert Krug | Muscadeur | 1576 | |
| 2. SWI | | | 4673 |
| Otto Hofer | Limandus | 1609 | |
| Christine Stückelberger | Tansanit | 1606 | |
| Amy-Cathérine de Bary | Aintree | 1458 | |
| 3. SWE | | | 4630 |
| Ulla Håkanson | Flamingo | 1589 | |
| Ingamay Bylund | Aleks | 1582 | |
| Louise Nathhorst | Inferno | 1459 | |
| 4. HOL | | | 4586 |
| Annemarie Sanders-Keyzer | Amon | 1591 | |
| Tineke Bartels de Vrie | Duco | 1539 | |
| Jo Rutten | Ampere | 1456 | |
| 5. DEN | | | 4574 |
| Anne Grethe Jensen | Marzog | 1701 | |
| Torben Ulsö Olsen | Patricia | 1496 | |
| Marie-Louise Castenskiöld | Stradivarius | 1377 | |
| 6. USA | | | 4559 |
| Hilda Gurney | Keen | 1530 | |
| Sandy Pflueger-Clarke | Marco Polo | 1516 | |
| Robert Dover | Romantico | 1513 | |
| 7. CAN | | | 4503 |
| Christilot Boylen | Anklang | 1540 | |
| Bonny Chesson | Satchmo | 1496 | |
| Eva-Maria Pracht | Little Joe | 1467 | |
| 8. GBR | | | 4463 |
| Christopher Bartle | Wily Trout | 1547 | |
| Jane Bartle Wilson | Pinocchio | 1489 | |
| Jennie Loriston-Clarke | Prince Consort | 1427 | |

**1988 Seoul** T: 12, N: 12, D: 9.25.

| | HORSE | | TOTAL PTS. |
|---|---|---|---|
| 1. GER | | | 4302 |
| Nicole Uphoff | Rembrandt | 1458 | |
| Monica Theodorescu | Ganimedes | 1433 | |
| Ann-Kathrin Linsenhoff | Courage | 1411 | |
| 2. SWI | | | 4164 |
| Christine Stückelberger | Gauguin De Lully | 1430 | |
| Otto Hofer | Andiamo | 1392 | |
| Daniel Ramseier | Random | 1342 | |
| 3. CAN | | | 3969 |
| Cynthia Ishoy | Dynasty | 1363 | |
| Ashley Nicoll | Reipo | 1308 | |
| Gina Smith | Malte | 1298 | |
| 4. SOV | | | 3926 |
| Nina Menkova | Dixon | 1395 | |

| | | | |
|---|---|---|---|
| Olga Klimkova | Buket | 1272 | |
| Yuri Kovshov | Barin | 1259 | |
| 5. HOL | | | 3903 |
| Ellen Bontje | Petit Prince | 1312 | |
| Annemarie Sanders-Keyzer | Amon | 1303 | |
| Tineke Bartels | Olympic | 1288 | |
| 6. FIN | | | 3883 |
| Kyra Kyrklund | Matador | 1416 | |
| Tuulikki Sohlberg | Pakistan | 1242 | |
| Jennifer Eriksson | My Way | 1225 | |
| 6. USA | | | 3883 |
| Robert Dover | Federleicht | 1327 | |
| Jessica Ransehousen | Orpheus | 1308 | |
| Belinda Baudin | Christopher | 1248 | |
| 8. FRA | | | 3832 |
| Margit Otto-Crépin | Corlandus | 1455 | |
| Dominique D'Esme | Hopal Fleury Hn | 1219 | |
| Philippe Limousin | Iris de la Fosse | 1158 | |

# Discontinued Events

## HIGH JUMP

**1900 Paris** C: 18, N: 5, D: 6.2.

| | | | HORSE | M |
|---|---|---|---|---|
| 1. | Dominique Maximien Gardéres | FRA | Canela | 1.85 |
| 1. | Gian Giorgio Trissino | ITA | Oreste | 1.85 |
| 3. | Georges van de Poele | BEL | Ludlow | 1.70 |
| 4. | Gian Giorgio Trissino | ITA | Melopo | 1.70 |

The current record for the equestrian high jump is 2.47 meters, set in 1949 by Alberto Larraguibel of Chile on Huaso.

## LONG JUMP

**1900 Paris** C: 17, N: 5, D: 5.31.

| | | | HORSE | M |
|---|---|---|---|---|
| 1. | Constant van Langhendonck | BEL | Extra Dry | 6.10 |
| 2. | Gian Giorgio Trissino | ITA | Oreste | 5.70 |
| 3. | de Bellegarde | FRA | Tolla | 5.30 |
| 4. | Prince Napoléon Murat | FRA | Bayard | — |

The current record for the equestrian long jump is 8.40 meters, set in 1975 by André Ferreira of South Africa on Something.

## FIGURE RIDING

**1920 Antwerp** C: 17, N: 3, D: 9.11.

| | | | PTS. |
|---|---|---|---|
| 1. | Bouckaert | BEL | 30.5 |
| 2. | Fiel | FRA | 29.5 |
| 3. | Finet | BEL | 29.0 |
| 4. | van Ranst | BEL | — |
| 5. | van Schauwbroeck | BEL | — |
| 6. | van Cauwenberg | BEL | — |

## TEAMS

1. BEL  (Bouckaert, Finet, van Ranst)
2. FRA  (Fiel, Salins, Cauchy)
3. SWE  (Carl Green, Oskar Nilsson, Anders Märtensson)

This event was open only to soldiers below the rank of noncommissioned officer.

# FENCING

| MEN | WOMEN |
|---|---|
| Foil, Individual | Foil, Individual |
| Foil, Team | Foil, Team |
| Épée, Individual | |
| Épée, Team | |
| Sabre, Individual | |
| Sabre, Team | |
| Discontinued Events | |

## MEN

The three swords used in fencing competitions are the foil, the épée, and the sabre.

The *foil* has a flexible rectangular blade and a blunt point. Touches must be made with the point on the trunk of the body, between the collar and the hipbones.

The *épée* has a rigid triangular blade with a point that is covered by a cone with barbed points. Touches may be made on any part of the body.

The *sabre* is a flexible triangular blade with a blunt point. Both the point and the cutting edges can be used to score touches, which must be made on the body, above the waist.

Fencing tournaments are run on a round-robin basis. For the first round, the fencers are divided into pools. The leaders of each pool advance to the next round. When sixteen fencers remain, a double elimination tournament is held. Until 1984 the six survivors then moved on to the final pool. The last two fencers to be eliminated from the double eliminations were awarded joint seventh place. Ties for medal-winning positions were decided by *barrage*, or fence-offs. Ties for other places were decided by comparing the differential between touches (or hits) given and received. If a tie still existed, it was won by the fencer who had received the fewest touches.

In 1984 the individual fencing competitions were reorganized. The final group of sixteen now engage in a direct elimination with *répechage* to decide the final eight who then compete in a direct elimination rather than a round-robin pool.

## FOIL, INDIVIDUAL

**1896 Athens** C: 8, N: 2, D: 4.7.

| | | | W | L | TG | TR |
|---|---|---|---|---|---|---|
| 1. | Eugene-Henri Gravelotte | FRA | 4 | 0 | 12 | 7 |
| 2. | Henri Callot | FRA | 3 | 1 | 11 | 7 |
| 3. | Perikles Pierrakos-Mavromichalis | GRE | 2 | 1 | 7 | 4 |
| 3. | Athanasios Vouros | GRE | 2 | 1 | 5 | 4 |

| | | | | | |
|---|---|---|---|---|---|
| 5. | de Laborde | FRA | 1 | 2 | 5 | 7 |
| 5. | Konstantinos Komnios-Milliotis | GRE | 1 | 2 | 5 | 4 |
| 7. | Georgios Balakakis | GRE | 0 | 3 | 3 | 9 |
| 7. | Ioannis Poulos | GRE | 0 | 3 | 3 | 9 |

Gravelotte defeated Callot 3–2 in the final.

**1900 Paris** C: 54, N: 3, D: 5.21.

| | | | W | L |
|---|---|---|---|---|
| 1. | Emile Coste | FRA | 6 | 1 |
| 2. | Henri Masson | FRA | 5 | 2 |
| 3. | Marcel Jacques Boulenger | FRA | 4 | 3 |
| 4. | Debax | FRA | 4 | 3 |
| 5. | Pierre d'Hugues | FRA | 3 | 4 |
| 6. | Senat | FRA | 3 | 4 |
| 7. | Georges Dillon-Cavanagh | FRA | 2 | 5 |
| 8. | Rudolf Brosch | AUT | 1 | 6 |

**1904 St. Louis** C: 9, N: 3, D: 9.7.

| | | | W | L |
|---|---|---|---|---|
| 1. | Ramón Fonst | CUB | 3 | 0 |
| 2. | Albertson Van Zo Post | USA | 2 | 1 |
| 3. | Charles Tatham | USA | 1 | 2 |
| 4. | Gustav Casmir | GER | 0 | 3 |

**1906 Athens** C: 37, N: 12, D: 4.28.

| | | |
|---|---|---|
| 1. | Georges Dillon-Cavanagh | FRA |
| 2. | Gustav Casmir | GER |
| 3. | Pierre d'Hugues | FRA |
| 4. | Martin Harden | AUT |
| 5. | S. Okker | HOL |
| 6. | Federico Cesarano | ITA |

**1908** not held

**1912 Stockholm** C: 104, N: 16, D: 7.8.

| | | | W | L | TG | TR |
|---|---|---|---|---|---|---|
| 1. | Nedo Nadi | ITA | 7 | 0 | 35 | 8 |
| 2. | Pietro Speciale | ITA | 5 | 2 | 29 | 24 |
| 3. | Richard Verderber | AUT | 4 | 3 | 27 | 25 |
| 4. | László Berti | HUN | 4 | 3 | 23 | 25 |
| 5. | Edoardo Alajmo | ITA | 4 | 3 | 27 | 26 |
| 6. | Edgar Seligman | GBR | 3 | 4 | 23 | 29 |
| 7. | Béla Bekessy | HUN | 1 | 6 | 20 | 34 |
| 8. | Robert Montgomerie | GBR | 0 | 7 | 22 | 35 |

Nadi was a mere 18 years old when he won his first Olympic gold medal. The French team boycotted the competition after their proposal to include the upper arm as an attackable surface was rejected.

**1920 Antwerp** C: 64, N: 8, D: 8.23.

| | | W | L | TR |
|---|---|---|---|---|
| 1. Nedo Nadi | ITA | 10 | 1 | |
| 2. Philippe Cattiau | FRA | 9 | 2 | 14 |
| 3. Roger Ducret | FRA | 9 | 2 | 19 |
| 4. André Labatut | FRA | 7 | 4 | |
| 5. Aldo Nadi | ITA | 6 | 5 | 19 |
| 6. Fernand de Montigny | BEL | 6 | 5 | 27 |
| 7. — | | — | | |
| 8. Ivan Osiier | DEN | | | |

Nadi's performance at Antwerp was nothing short of spectacular, as he won an unprecedented and unequaled five gold medals. Not only did he win both the individual foil and sabre, but he was also the leader of the winning Italian teams in the foil, épée, and sabre.

**1924 Paris** C: 49, N: 17, D: 7.4.

| | | W | L | TG | TR |
|---|---|---|---|---|---|
| 1. Roger Ducret | FRA | 6 | 0 | 30 | 14 |
| 2. Philippe Cattiau | FRA | 5 | 1 | 29 | 11 |
| 3. Maurice van Damme | BEL | 4 | 2 | 23 | 16 |
| 4. Jacques Coutrot | FRA | 3 | 3 | 18 | 25 |
| 5. Roberto Larraz | ARG | 2 | 4 | 21 | 25 |
| 6. Ivan Osiier | DEN | 1 | 5 | 14 | 27 |
| 7. Balthazar de Beuckelaer | BEL | 0 | 6 | 13 | 30 |

DNS: Edgar Seligman (GBR)

In the absence of the Italians, who had withdrawn following an incident during the team foil, the individual competition was dominated by the French. Particularly formidable was Philippe Cattiau, who whipped through the tournament with an outstanding record of 23 wins and one loss and 119 touches given, as opposed to only 54 received. Unfortunately, his only loss was in the final pool to 26-year-old Roger Ducret, who beat Cattiau five touches to four to win the gold medal. Ducret had suffered six defeats (against 13 wins) on his way to the final.

**1928 Amsterdam** C: 54, N: 23, D: 8.1.

| | | | | | | BARRAGE | | | |
|---|---|---|---|---|---|---|---|---|---|
| | | W | L | TG | TR | W | L | TG | TR |
| 1. Lucien Gaudin | FRA | 9 | 2 | 49 | 24 | 2 | 0 | 10 | 5 |
| 2. Erwin Casmir | GER | 9 | 2 | 49 | 33 | 1 | 1 | 6 | 8 |
| 3. Giulio Gaudini | ITA | 9 | 2 | 53 | 34 | 0 | 2 | 7 | 10 |
| 4. Oreste Puliti | ITA | 8 | 3 | 51 | 27 | | | | |
| 5. Philippe Cattiau | FRA | 7 | 4 | 43 | 32 | | | | |
| 6. Raymond Bru | BEL | 7 | 4 | 42 | 41 | | | | |
| 7. Ugo Pignotti | ITA | 4 | 7 | 40 | 48 | | | | |
| 8. Fritz August Gazzera | GER | 4 | 7 | 37 | 49 | | | | |

Lucien Gaudin and Oreste Puliti entered the finals undefeated, but Puliti lost to Gaudin, Erwin Casmir, and Raymond Bru. In the final Casmir beat Gaudin 5–4, but in the barrage Gauden was the victor, 5–1. Gaudin was 41 years old.

**1932 Los Angeles** C: 26, N: 12, D: 8.5.

| | | W | L | TG | TR |
|---|---|---|---|---|---|
| 1. Gustavo Marzi | ITA | 9 | 0 | 45 | 17 |
| 2. Joseph Levis | USA | 6 | 3 | 38 | 35 |
| 3. Giulio Gaudini | ITA | 5 | 4 | 34 | 27 |
| 4. Gioacchino Guaragna | ITA | 5 | 4 | 37 | 33 |
| 5. Erwin Casmir | GER | 5 | 4 | 36 | 34 |
| 6. John Emrys Lloyd | GBR | 5 | 4 | 36 | 34 |
| 7. Roberto Larraz | ARG | 3 | 6 | 33 | 31 |
| 8. René Bougnol | FRA | 3 | 6 | 28 | 41 |

Twenty-three-year-old Gustavo Marzi completed the tournament with a record of 21–2.

**1936 Berlin** C: 62, N: 22, D: 8.6.

| | | W | L | TG | TR |
|---|---|---|---|---|---|
| 1. Giulio Gaudini | ITA | 7 | 0 | 35 | 20 |
| 2. Edward Gardère | FRA | 6 | 1 | 33 | 25 |
| 3. Giorgio Bocchino | ITA | 4 | 3 | 28 | 22 |
| 4. Erwin Casmir | GER | 4 | 3 | 31 | 29 |
| 5. Gioacchino Guaragna | ITA | 3 | 4 | 30 | 28 |
| 6. Raymond Bru | BEL | 3 | 4 | 25 | 31 |
| 7. André Gardère | FRA | 1 | 6 | 23 | 32 |
| 8. Georges de Bourguignon | BEL | 0 | 7 | 17 | 35 |

Between 1928 and 1936 the 6-foot 6-inch Gaudini won three gold medals, four silver, and two bronze. The 1936 foil was his only individual gold.

**1948 London** C: 63, N: 25, D: 8.4.

| | | W | L | TG | TR |
|---|---|---|---|---|---|
| 1. Jehan Buhan | FRA | 7 | 0 | 35 | 14 |
| 2. Christian d'Oriola | FRA | 5 | 2 | 29 | 18 |
| 3. Lajos Maszlay | HUN | 4 | 3 | 25 | 22 |
| 4. John Emrys Lloyd | GBR | 4 | 3 | 23 | 29 |
| 5. René Bougnol | FRA | 3 | 4 | 28 | 26 |
| 6. Manlio Di Rosa | ITA | 3 | 4 | 22 | 27 |
| 7. Paul Valcke | BEL | 1 | 6 | 23 | 31 |
| 8. Ivan Ruben | DEN | 1 | 6 | 15 | 33 |

The 36-year-old Buhan had gone to London to compete in the épée and was only entered in the foil at the last minute. Runner-up d'Oriola had surprised the fencing world in 1947 by winning the world championship in Lisbon at the tender age of 18. Buhan finished the tournament with a record of 24–1.

**1952 Helsinki** C: 61, N: 25, D: 7.24.

| | | W | L | TG | TR |
|---|---|---|---|---|---|
| 1. Christian d'Oriola | FRA | 8 | 0 | 40 | 12 |
| 2. Edoardo Mangiarotti | ITA | 6 | 2 | | 21 |
| 3. Manlio Di Rosa | ITA | 5 | 3 | | 22 |
| 4. Jacques Lataste | FRA | 4 | 4 | | 31 |
| 5. Jehan Buhan | FRA | 4 | 4 | 29 | 33 |
| 6. Mahmoud Younes | EGY | 4 | 4 | 27 | 33 |
| 7. Salah Dessouki | EGY | 2 | 6 | | 35 |
| 8. Giancarlo Bergamini | ITA | 2 | 6 | | 36 |

All three medalists were left-handed.

**1956 Melbourne** C: 32, N: 14, D: 11.26.

| | | | | | BARRAGE | | | |
|---|---|---|---|---|---|---|---|---|
| | | W | L | TG | TR | W | L | TG | TR |
| 1. Christian d'Oriola | FRA | 6 | 1 | 33 | 17 | | | | |
| 2. Giancarlo Bergamini | ITA | 5 | 2 | 33 | 26 | 1 | 0 | 5 | 4 |
| 3. Antonio Spallino | ITA | 5 | 2 | 30 | 21 | 0 | 1 | 4 | 5 |
| 4. Allan Jay | GBR | 4 | 3 | 29 | 26 | | | | |
| 5. József Gyuricza | HUN | 3 | 4 | 21 | 25 | | | | |
| 6. Claude Netter | FRA | 3 | 4 | 19 | 30 | | | | |
| 7. Mark Midler | SOV | 2 | 5 | 19 | 30 | | | | |
| 8. Raymond Paul | GBR | 0 | 7 | 15 | 35 | | | | |

D'Oriola was a 27-year-old law student when he became the first man since Nedo Nadi to win two individual foil gold medals. D'Oriola, a native of Perpignan, had some trouble adapting to the new electric foil, but he solved it quite well in time for the Melbourne Olympics.

**1960 Rome** C: 78, N: 31, D: 8.30.

| | | | | | | BARRAGE | | | |
|---|---|---|---|---|---|---|---|---|---|
| | | W | L | TG | TR | W | L | TG | TR |
| 1. Viktor Zhdanovich | SOV | 7 | 0 | 35 | 20 | | | | |
| 2. Yuri Sissikin | SOV | 4 | 2 | 27 | 21 | | | | |
| 3. Albert Axelrod | USA | 3 | 3 | 23 | 24 | 2 | 0 | 10 | 7 |
| 4. Witold Woyda | POL | 3 | 3 | 24 | 23 | 1 | 1 | 9 | 7 |
| 5. Mark Midler | SOV | 3 | 4 | 28 | 25 | 0 | 2 | 5 | 10 |
| 6. Roger Closset | FRA | 2 | 2 | 14 | 16 | | | | |
| 7. Henry Hoskyns | GBR | 2 | 5 | 21 | 33 | | | | |
| 8. Christian d'Oriola | FRA | 1 | 6 | 22 | 32 | | | | |

A 22-year-old student-teacher from Leningrad, Zhdanovich was the first Soviet fencer to win a gold medal. As such, he became a hero and was known in the newspapers as "Viktor the Victor."

**1964 Tokyo** C: 55, N: 21, D: 10.14.

| | | W | L | TG | TR |
|---|---|---|---|---|---|
| 1. Egon Franke | POL | 3 | 0 | 15 | 9 |
| 2. Jean-Claude Magnan | FRA | 2 | 2 | 14 | 10 |
| 3. Daniel Revenu | FRA | 1 | 3 | 12 | 11 |
| 4. Roland Losert | AUT | 0 | 3 | 4 | 15 |
| 5. Jenö Kamuti | HUN | | | | |
| 6. Tim Gressheim | GER | | | | |
| 7. Henry Hoskyns | GBR | | | | |
| 7. Sándor Szabó | HUN | | | | |

Egon Franke, a 29-year-old technical administrator from the small town of Gliwice, was an unexpected and popular winner.

**1968 Mexico City** C: 64, N: 25, D: 10.16.

| | | | | | | BARRAGE | | | |
|---|---|---|---|---|---|---|---|---|---|
| | | W | L | TG | TR | W | L | TG | TR |
| 1. Ionel Drimbă | ROM | 4 | 1 | 22 | 15 | | | | |
| 2. Jenö Kamuti | HUN | 3 | 2 | 19 | 14 | 1 | 0 | 5 | 4 |
| 3. Daniel Revenu | FRA | 3 | 2 | 22 | 17 | 0 | 1 | 4 | 5 |
| 4. Christian Noël | FRA | 2 | 3 | 14 | 18 | | | | |
| 5. Jean-Claude Magnan | FRA | 2 | 3 | 18 | 22 | | | | |
| 6. Mihai Tiu | ROM | 1 | 4 | 14 | 23 | | | | |
| 7. Tanase Muresan | ROM | | | | | | | | |
| 7. German Sveshnikov | SOV | | | | | | | | |

Ion Drimbă, a 26-year-old physical training instructor, went through the tournament with a record of 19–2. Two years later he defected to the West and retired from competition.

**1972 Munich** C: 58, N: 26, D: 8.30.

| | | W | L | TG | TR |
|---|---|---|---|---|---|
| 1. Witold Woyda | POL | 5 | 0 | 25 | 7 |
| 2. Jenö Kamuti | HUN | 4 | 1 | 23 | 19 |
| 3. Christian Noël | FRA | 2 | 3 | 17 | 18 |
| 4. Mihai Tiu | ROM | 2 | 3 | 17 | 20 |
| 5. Vladimir Denissov | SOV | 2 | 3 | 17 | 21 |
| 6. Marek Dabrowski | POL | 0 | 5 | 10 | 25 |

Thirty-three-year-old Witold Woyda qualified for the final with a modest record of 14–6, but then he completely dominated his last five opponents to take the gold medal.

**1976 Montreal** C: 56, N: 23, D: 7.21.

| | | | | | | BARRAGE | | | |
|---|---|---|---|---|---|---|---|---|---|
| | | W | L | TG | TR | W | L | TG | TR |
| 1. Fabio Dal Zotto | ITA | 4 | 1 | 24 | 15 | 1 | 0 | 5 | 1 |
| 2. Aleksandr Romankov | SOV | 4 | 1 | 21 | 13 | 0 | 1 | 1 | 5 |
| 3. Bernard Talvard | FRA | 3 | 2 | 19 | 21 | | | | |
| 4. Vassily Stankovich | SOV | 2 | 3 | 19 | 18 | | | | |
| 5. Frédéric Piotruszka | FRA | 2 | 3 | 13 | 19 | | | | |
| 6. Gregory Benkö | AUS | 0 | 5 | 15 | 25 | | | | |
| 7. Vladimir Denissov | SOV | | | | | | | | |
| 7. Christian Noël | FRA | | | | | | | | |

Dal Zotto, a student from Venice, celebrated his 19th birthday three days before the competition began.

**1980 Moscow** C: 37, N: 16, D: 7.23.

| | | | | | | BARRAGE | | | |
|---|---|---|---|---|---|---|---|---|---|
| | | W | L | TG | TR | W | L | TG | TR |
| 1. Vladimir Smirnov | SOV | 4 | 1 | 24 | 16 | 1 | 1 | 9 | 5 |
| 2. Pascal Jolyot | FRA | 4 | 1 | 24 | 17 | 1 | 1 | 5 | 5 |
| 3. Aleksandr Romankov | SOV | 4 | 1 | 22 | 15 | 1 | 1 | 5 | 9 |
| 4. Sabiryhan Ruziev | SOV | 2 | 3 | 20 | 19 | | | | |
| 5. Lech Koziejowski | POL | 1 | 4 | 15 | 21 | | | | |
| 6. Petru Koki | ROM | 0 | 5 | 8 | 25 | | | | |
| 7. Frédéric Pietruszka | FRA | | | | | | | | |
| 7. István Szelei | HUN | | | | | | | | |

Two years after winning the Olympic gold medal, Smirnov was defending his world championship in Rome when the foil of his opponent, Matthias Behr of West Germany, snapped and pierced Smirnov's mask, penetrated his eyeball and entered his brain. The 28-year-old Soviet fencer died nine days later.

**1984 Los Angeles-Long Beach** C: 58, N: 26, D: 8.2.

| | |
|---|---|
| 1. Mauro Numa | ITA |
| 2. Matthias Behr | GER |
| 3. Stefano Cerioni | ITA |

4. Frédéric Pietruszka  FRA
5. Andrea Borella  ITA
6. Mathias Gey  GER
7. Philippe Omnes  FRA
8. Thierry Soumagne  BEL
   Final: Numa 10–9 Behr
   3rd Place: Cerioni 10–5 Pietruszka

Mauro Numa may have won the gold medal, but his victory did not come easily. In his quarterfinal bout with Philippe Omnes, Numa trailed 6–8 with one minute left and then scored four straight touches in 49 seconds to win 10–8. In his semifinal match, he trailed Stefano Cerioni 1–6 before coming from behind to win 11–9. In the final against Matthias Behr, Numa was behind 3–7 with one minute to go. Again he scored four straight touches. Then Behr moved ahead 8–7. Numa was back with two quick scores. However, with two seconds remaining, Behr evened the count, sending the contest into sudden-death overtime. Within seconds Numa finally secured the win. Among the boycott missing was five-time world champion Aleksandr Romankov, who had won the last two world championships.

**1988 Seoul** C: 68, N: 29, D: 9.21.
1. Stefano Cerioni  ITA
2. Udo Wagner  GDR
3. Aleksandr Romankov  SOV
4. Ulrich Schreck  GER
5. Zsolt Érsek  HUN
6. Mauro Numa  ITA
7. Jens Howe  GDR
8. Mathias Gey  GER
   Final: Cerioni 10-7 Wagner
   3rd Place: Romankov 10-8 Schreck

Cerioni's victory capped a successful comeback following a 15-month suspension. During the 1986 world championships, the volatile Spanish-born fencer had offended tournament officials by screaming wildly and making obscene gestures.

# FOIL, TEAM

Current rules allow each team to have five members, four of whom take part in each contest. Each contest consists of 16 matches, with each member of a team fencing against each other member of the opposing team. Ties are decided by total touches. Very often a contest will end as soon as one team has clinched the victory.

**1896–1900** not held

**1904 St. Louis** T: 2, N: 2, D: 9.8.

|  |  | WON |
|---|---|---|
| 1. CUB/USA | (Ramón Fonst—CUB, Manuel Diaz—CUB, Albertson Van Zo Post—USA) | 7 |
| 2. USA | (Charles Tatham, Fitzhugh Townsend, Arthur Fox) | 2 |

**1906–1912** not held

**1920 Antwerp** T: 8, N: 8, D: 8.23.

|  |  | WON | LOST | MATCHES W | L |
|---|---|---|---|---|---|
| 1. ITA | (Baldo Baldi, Tommaso Constantino, Aldo Nadi, Nedo Nadi, Abelardo Olivier, Oreste Puliti, Pietro Speciale, Rodolfo Terlizzi) | 4 | 0 | 50 | 14 |
| 2. FRA | (Lionel Bony de Castellane, Gaston Amson, Philippe Cattiau, Roger Ducret, André Labatut, Georges Trombert, Marcel Perrot, Lucien Gaudin) | 3 | 1 | 44 | 18 |
| 3. USA | (Henry Breckinridge, Francis Honeycutt, Arthur Lyon, Harold Rayner, Robert Sears) | 2 | 2 | 22 | 42 |
| 4. DEN | (Ivan Osiier, Georg Hegner, Ejnar Levison, Poul Rasmussen, Kay Schröder) | 1 | 3 | 25 | 37 |
| 5. GBR | (Edgar Seligman, R.M.P. Willoughby, Philip Doyne, Robert Montgomerie, H. Evan James, Cecil Kershaw) | 0 | 4 | 17 | 47 |
| 6. BEL | (Marcel Beeve, Charles Crahay, Cuypers, Fernand de Montigny, de Schepper, Robert Hennet, Leon Tom, Pape) |  |  |  |  |
| 7. HOL |  |  |  |  |  |
| 8. CZE |  |  |  |  |  |

**1924 Paris** T: 12, N: 12, D: 6.30.

|  |  | WON | LOST | MATCHES W | L |
|---|---|---|---|---|---|
| 1. FRA | (Lucien Gaudin, Philippe Cattiau, Jacques Coutrot, Roger Ducret, Henri Jobier, André Labatut, Guy de Luget, Joseph Peroteaux) | 3 | 0 | 31 | 6 |
| 2. BEL | (Désiré Beaurain, Charles Crahay, Fernand de Montigny, Maurice van Damme, Marcel Bérré, Albert de Roocker) | 2 | 1 | 12 | 20 |
| 3. HUN | (László Berti, Sándor Posta, Zoltán Schenker, Ödön Tersztyánszky, István Licteneckert) | 1 | 2 | 9 | 23 |
| 4. ITA | (Oreste Puliti, Giorgio Pessina, Valentino Argento, Giorgio Chiavacci, Giulio Gaudini, Aldo Boni, Luigi Cuomo, Dante Carniel) | 0 | 3 | 1 | 4 |

FENCING,  MEN  /  299

5. ARG   (F. C. Bollini, Carmelo Ca-
          met, H. A. Casco, C. Guer-
          rico, Roberto Larraz, Luis
          Lucchetti, A. Santamarina,
          J. N. Sosa)

When the French and Italian teams met in the final pool at
the Vélodrome d'Hiver, it was assumed that the winner
would go on to take the gold medal. France took a 3–1
lead. In the fifth assault, Lucien Gaudin and Aldo Boni
were tied at four touches each when the jury awarded a decisive fifth touch to Gaudin. Boni was incensed and launched
a verbal attack against Kovács, the Hungarian judge.
Kovács approached the Jury of Appeal and demanded an
apology, whereupon Boni denied everything. Kovács
then produced a witness, the Italian-born Hungarian fencing master Italo Santelli, who reluctantly supported
Kovács' allegations of abusive language. The Italian team
withdrew in protest, and their remaining matches were
declared forfeited. Lost in the excitement was a brilliant
performance by Gaudin, who scored 22 victories without a
defeat and recorded 110 touches while receiving only 21.

However, the affair was not over. Back in Italy, the
Italian foil team issued a statement which accused
Santelli of testifying against them because he feared the
Italians would defeat the Hungarian team, which he had
coached. When he heard about this insult, Santelli, who
was over 60 years old, challenged Adolfo Contronei, the
Italian captain, to a real duel. Government permission
was obtained to fight the duel, but before the two men
could meet, Santelli's 27-year-old son, Giorgio, invoked
the *code duello* and demanded that he fight in his father's
place. In the small town of Abazzia near the Hungarian
border, Giorgio and Contronei met and fought with
heavy sabres. After two minutes the younger Santelli
slashed Contronei deeply on the side of the head, drawing blood. Doctors rushed in and halted the duel. Gior-

gio Santelli later moved to the United States, where he
became the coach of the U.S. team. He taught fencing to
8,000 people and spent over 100,000 hours with a sword
in his hand, but he never again engaged in a real duel.

**1928 Amsterdam** T: 16, N: 16, D: 7.30.

| | | | WON | LOST | MATCHES W | L |
|---|---|---|---|---|---|---|
| 1. | ITA | (Ugo Pignotti, Oreste Puliti, Giulio Gaudini, Giorgio Pessina, Giorgio Chiavac-ci, Gioacchino Guaragna) | 3 | 0 | 34 | 14 |
| 2. | FRA | (Lucien Gaudin, Philippe Cattiau, Roger Ducret, An-dré Labatut, Raymond Flacher, André Gaboriaud) | 2 | 1 | 23 | 25 |
| 3. | ARG | (Roberto Larraz, Raúl An-ganuzzi, Luis Lucchetti, Hector Lucchetti, Carmelo Camet) | 1 | 2 | 23 | 25 |
| 4. | BEL | (Max Janlet, Pierre Pecher, Raymond Bru, Albert de Roocker, Jean Verbrug-ghe, Charles Crahay) | 0 | 3 | 16 | 32 |
| 5. | HUN | (Ödön Tersztyánszky, György Rozgonyi, György Piller, József Rády, Gusz-táv Kálniczky, Péter Toth) | | | | |
| 5. | USA | (George Calnan, René Peroy, Joseph Levis, Har-old Rayner, Henry Breckin-ridge, Dernell Every) | | | | |

In Amsterdam the Italians gained their revenge against
the French with a 10–6 victory. The Italian team was led
by Chiavacci, who finished the tournament with 22 wins
and two losses, and Gaudini, who was 30–2, including
four straight victories against the French.

**1932 Los Angeles** T: 6, N: 6, D: 8.1.

| | | | WON | LOST | MATCHES W | L | BARRAGE WON | LOST | MATCHES W | L |
|---|---|---|---|---|---|---|---|---|---|---|
| 1. | FRA | (Philippe Cattiau, Edward Gardère, René Lemoine, René Bondoux, Jean Piot, René Bougnol) | 2 | 1 | 26 | 22 | 2 | 0 | 19 | 13 |
| 2. | ITA | (Giulio Gaudini, Gustavo Marzi, Ugo Pignotti, Giorgio Pessina, Gioacchino Guaranga, Rodolfo Terlizzi) | 2 | 1 | 31 | 17 | 1 | 1 | 17 | 9 |
| 3. | USA | (George Calnan, Joseph Le-vis, Hugh Allesandroni, Dernell Every, Richard Steere, Frank Righeimer) | 2 | 1 | 22 | 26 | 0 | 2 | 6 | 20 |
| 4. | DEN | (Axel Bloch, Erik Kofoed-Hansen, Aage Leidersdorff, Ivan Osiier) | 0 | 3 | 17 | 31 | | | | |

Italy and France tied in the barrage, 8–8, but France was awarded the victory on fewer touches received, 58–62.

**1936 Berlin** T: 18, N: 18, D: 8.4.

| | | WON | LOST | MATCHES W | L |
|---|---|---|---|---|---|
| 1. ITA | (Giulio Gaudini, Gioacchino Guaranga, Gustavo Marzi, Giorgio Bocchino, Manlio Di Rosa, Ciro Verratti) | 3 | 0 | 38 | 7 |
| 2. FRA | (Jacques Coutrot, André Gardère, René Lemoine, René Bougnol, Edward Gardère, René Bondoux) | 2 | 1 | 27 | 18 |
| 3. GER | (Siegfried Lerdon, August Heim, Julius Eisenecker, Erwin Casmir, Stefan Rosenbauer, Otto Adam) | 1 | 2 | 13 | 33 |
| 4. AUT | (Hans Lion, Roman Fischer, Hans Schönbaumsfeld, Ernst Baylon, Josef Losert, Karl Sudrich) | 0 | 3 | 13 | 33 |
| 5. BEL | (Georges de Bourguignon, André van de Werve de Vorselaer, Henri Paternoster, Raymond Bru, Heremans, Paul Valcke) | | | | |
| 5. USA | (Joseph Levis, Hugh Alessandroni, John Potter, John Hurd, Warren Dow, William Pecora) | | | | |
| 7. ARG | (Roberto Larraz, Hector Luchetti, Gorordo Palacios, Luis Luccheti, Valenzuela, M. Torrente) | | | | |
| 7. HUN | (Jószef Hatszeghy Hatz, Lajos Maszlay, Aladár Gerevich, Béla Bay, Ottó Hatszeghy Hatz, Antal Zirczy) | | | | |

France was the slight favorite, but the Italians breezed through the tournament with 104 wins and 19 losses. Verratti was 23–1 and Marzi 18–1. The deciding match with France was halted when Italy achieved an unbeatable 9–4 advantage.

**1948 London** T: 16, N: 16, D: 7.31.

| | | WON | LOST | MATCHES W | L |
|---|---|---|---|---|---|
| 1. FRA | (André Bonin, René Bougnol, Jehan Buhan, Jacques Lataste, Christian d'Oriola, Adrian Rommel) | 3 | 0 | 28 | 18 |
| 2. ITA | (Renzo Nostini, Manlio Di Rosa, Edoardo Mangiarotti, Giuliano Nostini, Giorgio Pellini, Saverio Ragno) | 2 | 1 | 28 | 15 |

| | | WON | LOST | MATCHES W | L |
|---|---|---|---|---|---|
| 3. BEL | (Georges de Bourguignon, Henry Paternoster, Edouard Yves, Raymond Bru, André van de Werwe de Vorsslaer, Paul Valcke) | 1 | 2 | 19 | 27 |
| 4. USA | (Daniel Bukantz, Dean Cetrulo, Dernell Every, Silvio Giolito, Nathaniel Lubell, Austin Prokop) | 0 | 3 | 14 | 29 |
| 5. ARG | (José Rodriguez, Fulvio Galami, M. Torrente, Felix Galimi) | | | | |
| 5. EGY | (Osman Abdel-Hafiz, Salah Dessouki, Mahmoud Younes, Mohamed Zulficar, Hassan Hosni Tewfik, M. Adbine) | | | | |
| 5. GBR | (René Paul, A.R. Smith, Harry Cooke, John Emrys Lloyd, P. Turquet, Ulrich Wendon) | | | | |
| 5. HUN | (Béla Bay, Aladár Gerevich, Jószef Hatszeghy Hatz, Lajos Maszlay, Pál Dunay, Endre Palócz) | | | | |

An incident marred the semifinal round. Dissatisfied with a call by the president of the judges, the Argentine team gave three cheers for their opponents, the Belgians, and withdrew in protest. A more pleasant kind of event took place in the semifinal match between Great Britain and the United States. Harry Cooke of Britain was trailing Dean Cetrulo 3–4, when the two men collided. Cooke's mask smashed into his face, cutting his nose. The American team immediately administered first aid to their opponent. After a rest Cooke returned to action and rallied to win 5–4. In the deciding match, France took a 6–3 lead over Italy, but the Italians came from behind to win five of the last seven fights. However, France won anyway on fewer touches received, 60–62.

**1952 Helsinki** T: 15, N: 15, D: 7.22.

| | | WON | LOST | MATCHES W | L |
|---|---|---|---|---|---|
| 1. FRA | (Jehan Buhan, Christian d'Oriola, Adrian Rommel, Claude Netter, Jacques Noël, Jacques Lataste) | 3 | 0 | 35 | 11 |
| 2. ITA | (Giancarlo Bergamini, Antonio Spallino, Manlio Di Rosa, Giorgio Pellini, Renzo Nostini, Edoardo Mangiarotti) | 2 | 1 | 34 | 12 |
| 3. HUN | (Endre Tilli, Aladár Gúrevich, Endre Palócz, Lajos | 1 | 2 | 16 | 31 |

Maszlay, Tibor Berczelly, József Sákovics)

| | | | | | |
|---|---|---|---|---|---|
| 4. | EGY | (Salah Dessouki, Mohamed Ali Riad, Osman Abdel-Hafiz, Mahmoud Younes, Mohamed Zulficar, Hassan Hosni Tawfik) | 0 | 3 | 8 | 39 |
| 5. | ARG | (Fulvio Galimi, José Rodriguez, Eduardo Sastre, Felix Galimi, Santiago Massini) | | | | |
| 5. | BEL | (Pierre van Houdt, André Verhalle, Alex Bourgeois, Paul Valcke, Edouard Yves, Gustave Balister) | | | | |

As usual, France and Italy dominated all other countries, entering their final showdown with match records of 54–9 and 55–6, respectively. Christian d'Oriola was the star of the tournament, winning ten matches without a loss. In the deciding confrontation he swept all four Italians by the scores of 5–0, 5–0, 5–1, and 5–2, leading the French team to an 8–6 victory.

### 1956 Melbourne T: 9, N: 9, D: 11.23.

| | | | MATCHES | | | |
|---|---|---|---|---|---|---|
| | | | WON | LOST | W | L |
| 1. | ITA | (Edoardo Mangiarotti, Giancarlo Bergamini, Antonio Spallino, Luigi Carpaneda, Manlio Di Rosa, Vittorio Lucarelli) | 3 | 0 | 26 | 22 |
| 2. | FRA | (Christian d'Oriola, Bernard Baudoux, Claude Netter, Jacques Lataste, Roger Closset, René Coicaud) | 2 | 1 | 28 | 20 |
| 3. | HUN | (József Gyuricza, József Sákovics, Mihály Fülöp, Endre Tilli, Lajos Somodi, Sr., József Marosi) | 1 | 2 | 22 | 24 |
| 4. | USA | (Albert Axelrod, Daniel Bukantz, Harold Goldsmith, Byron Kreiger, Nathaniel Lubell, Sewall Shurtz) | 0 | 3 | 18 | 28 |
| 5. | GBR | (René Paul, Henry Hoskyns, Raymond Paul, Allan Jay, Arnold Ralph Cooperman) | | | | |
| 5. | SOV | (Yuri Roudov, Yuri Ossipov, Mark Midler, Aleksandr Ovsiankine, Viktor Zhdanovich, Yuri Ivanov) | | | | |

Once again the championship was between France and Italy, and once again d'Oriola swept the Italians, receiving only seven hits in four assaults. This time, though, Italy's team was better balanced. Going into the last

bout, Italy led 8–7, but because the touches were even at 57, whoever won the last bout, which matched Spallino and Netter, would win the gold medal. Netter took an early lead, but Spallino came from behind to tie 4–4 and then win the championship for Italy on the final touch.

### 1960 Rome T: 16, N: 16, D: 9.2.
1. SOV (Viktor Zhdanovich, Mark Midler, Yuri Sissikin, German Sveshnikov, Yuri Rudov)
2. ITA (Alberto Pellegrino, Luigi Carpaneda, Mario Curletto, Aldo Aureggio, Edoardo Mangiarotti)
3. GER (Jürgen Brecht, Tim Gerresheim, Eberhard Mehl, Jürgen Theuerkauff)
4. HUN (Ferenc Czvikovsky, Jenö Kamuti, Mihály Fülöp, László Kamuti, József Gyuricza, József Sákovics)
5. FRA (Jacky Courtillat, Jean-Claude Magnan, Guy Barrabino, Claude Netter, Christian d'Oriola)
5. GBR (Henry Hoskyns, Allan Jay, Arnold Ralph Cooperman, Angus McKenzie, Raymond Paul)
5. POL (Egon Franke, Ryszard Parulski, Janusz Różycki, Ryszard Kunze, Witold Woyda)
5. USA (Gene Glazer, Harold Goldsmith, Joseph Paletta, Albert Axelrod, Daniel Bukantz)

Final: SOV 9–4 ITA
3rd Place: Ger 9–5 HUN

The Soviet Union became the first team since 1904 to break the Franco-Italian monopoly of the team foil event. In the final, Zhdanovich and Midler provided seven of nine Soviet wins.

### 1964 Tokyo T: 16, N: 16, D: 10.16.
1. SOV (German Sveshnikov, Yuri Sissikin, Mark Midler, Viktor Zhdanovich, Yuri Scharov)
2. POL (Zbigniew Skrudlik, Witold Wyoda, Egon Franke, Ryszard Parulski, Janusz Rózycki)
3. FRA (Daniel Revenu, Jacky Courtillat, Pierre Rodocanachi, Christian Nöel, Jean-Claude Magnan)
4. JPN (Kazuhiko Tabuchi, Fujio Shimizu, Kazuo Mano, Heizaburo Okawa, Sosuke Toda)
5. GER (Jürgen Brecht, Dieter Wellmann, Eberhard Mehl, Tim Gerresheim, Jürgen Theuerkauff)
6. ROM (Tănase Mureşan, Ionel Drimbă, Iuliu Falb, Stefan Haukler, Atila Csipler)
7. HUN (Jenö Kamuti, László Kamuti, József Gyuricza, Sándor Szabó, Béla Gyarmati)
7. ITA (Gianguido Milanesi, Pasquale La Ragione, Arcangelo Pinelli, Nicola Granieri)

Final: SOV 9–7 POL
3rd Place: FRA 9–4 JPN
5th Place: GER 8(60)–8(57)ROM

**1968 Mexico City** T: 17, N: 17, D: 10.19.
1. FRA (Daniel Revenu, Gilles Berolatti, Christian Nöel, Jean-Claude Magnan, Jacques Dimont)
2. SOV (German Sveshnikov, Yuri Scharov, Vassily Stankovich, Viktor Putiatin, Yuri Sissikin)
3. POL (Witold Woyda, Ryszard Parulski, Egon Franke, Zbigniew Skrudlik, Adam Lisewski)
4. ROM (Ionel Drimbǎ, Mihai Tiu, Ştefan Haukler, Tǎnase Mureşan, Iuliu Falb)
5. HUN (Sándor Szabó, Jenö Kamuti, László Kamuti, Gábor Füredi, Attila May)
6. GER (Jürgen Theuerkauff, Friedrich Wessel, Tim Gerresheim, Jürgen Brecht, Dieter Wellmann)
7. ITA (Pasquale La Ragione, Alfredo Del Francia, Nicola Granieri, Archangelo Pinelli, Michelle Maffei)
7. JPN (Masaya Fukuda, Heizaburo Ohkawa, Fujio Shimizu, Kazuhiko Wakasugi, Kazuo Mano)
   Final: FRA 9–6 SOV
   3rd Place: POL 9–3 ROM
   5th Place: HUN 9–4 GER

**1972 Munich** T: 13, N: 13, D: 9.2.
1. POL (Lech Koziejowski, Witold Woyda, Marek Dabrowski, Jerzy Kaczmarek, Arkadiusz Godel)
2. SOV (Vassily Stankovich, Viktor Poutiatin, Leonid Romanov, Anatoly Kotescev, Vladimir Denissov)
3. FRA (Daniel Revenu, Bernard Talvard, Gilles Berolatti, Jean-Claude Magnan, Christian Nöel)
4. HUN (Sándor Szabó, Csaba Fenyvesi, László Kamuti, István Marton, Jenö Kamuti)
5. GER (Klaus Reichert, Friedrich Wessel, Harald Hein, Dieter Wellmann, Erk Sens-Gorius)
6. JPN (Shiro Maruyama, Masaya Fukuda, Hiroshi Nakajima, Kiyoshi Uehara, Ichiro Serizawa)
7. CUB (Evelio Gonzalez, Eduardo Jhons, Jesus Gil, Enrique Salvat, Jorge Garbey)
7. ROM (Iuliu Falb, Ştefan Haukler, Mihai Tiu, Tǎnase Mureşan, Aurel Stefan)
   Final: POL 9–5 SOV
   3rd Place: FRA 9–7 HUN
   5th Place: GER 9–7 JPN

Poland secured the gold medal despite an early loss to Germany. In the same round, the U.S.S.R. was defeated by Japan. The match for first place was highlighted by Woyda's sweep of the four Soviet fencers. The French had been the favorites, but they lost in the semifinals, 9–6, to the Soviet Union.

**1976 Montreal** T: 14, N: 14, D: 7.24.
1. GER (Harald Hein, Thomas Bach, Erk Sens-Gorius, Klaus Reichert, Matthias Behr)
2. ITA (Fabio Dal Zotto, Attilio Calatroni, Carlo Montano, Stefano Simoncelli, Giovan Battista Coletti)
3. FRA (Daniel Revenu, Christian Nöel, Didier Flament, Bernard Talvard, Frédéric Pietruszka)
4. SOV (Sabirzhan Ruziev, Aleksandr Romankov, Vladimir Denissov, Vassily Stankovich)

5. POL (Leszek Martewicz, Lech Koziejowski, Ziemowit Wojciechowski, Arkadiusz Godel, Marek Dabrowski)
6. GBR (Geoffrey Grimmett, Barry Paul, Robert Bruniges, Graham Paul, Nicholas Bell)
7. HUN (József Komatits, Csaba Fenyvesi, Lajos Somodi, Jr., Jenö Kamuti, Sándor Erdös)
7. USA (Martin Lang, Edward Ballinger, Edward Wright, Edward Donofrio, Brooke Mackler)
   Final: GER 9–6 ITA
   3rd Place: FRA 9–4 SOV
   5th Place: POL 9–1 GBR

**1980 Moscow** T: 9, N: 9, D: 7.26.
1. FRA (Didier Flament, Pascal Jolyot, Frédéric Pietruszka, Philippe Bonnin, Bruno Boscherie)
2. SOV (Aleksandr Romankov, Vladimir Smirnov, Ashot Karagyan, Vladimir Lapitsky, Sabirzhan Ruziev)
3. POL (Boguslaw Zych, Adam Robak, Marian Sypniewski, Lech Koziejowski)
4. GDR (Siegmar Gutzeit, Hartmuth Behrens, Adrian Germanus, Klaus Kotzmann, Klaus Haertter)
5. ROM (Petru Kuki, Mihai Tiu, Sorin Roca, Tudor Petrus)
6. HUN (István Szelei, Ernö Kolczonay, András Papp, László Demény, Jenö Pap)
7. CUB (Efigenio Favier, Guillermo Betancourt, Heriberto Gonzalez, Pedro Hernandez)
8. GBR (John Llewellyn, Steven Paul, Robert Bruniges, Pierre Harper, Neal Mallett)
   Final: FRA 8(68)–8(60)SOV
   3rd Place: POL 9–5 GDR
   5th Place: ROM 9–7 HUN

In the semifinals, Soviet world champion Vladimir Lapitsky was accidentally run through the chest when his Polish opponent's foil broke his leather protective clothing. The sword severed a blood vessel but missed his heart. France's victory marked their 13th team foil medal in 14 Olympics.

**1984 Los Angeles-Long Beach** T: 14, N: 14, D: 8.7.
1. ITA (Mauro Numa, Andrea Borella, Stefano Cerioni, Angelo Scuri, Andrea Cipressa)
2. GER (Matthias Behr, Mathias Gey, Harald Hein, Frank Beck, Klaus Reichert)
3. FRA (Philippe Omnes, Patrick Groc, Frédéric Pietruszka, Pascal Jolyot, Marc Cerboni)
4. AUT (Joachim Wendt, Dieter Kotlowski, Georg Somloi, Robert Blaschka, Georg Loisel)
5. USA (Michael Marx, Gregory Massialas, Peter Lewison, Mark Smith, Michael McCahey)
6. GBR (William Gosbee, Pierre Harper, Nicholas Bell, Robert Bruniges, Graham Paul)
7. CHN (Chu Shisheng, Cui Yining, Yu Yifeng, Wang Wei, Zhang Jian)
8. BEL (Thierry Soumagne, Peter Joos, Stefan Joos, Stephane Ganeff)
   Final: ITA 8–7 GER
   3rd Place: FRA 9–3 AUT
   5th Place: USA 9–6 GBR
   7th Place: CHN 9–0 BEL (forfeit)

**1988 Seoul** T: 16, N: 16, D: 9.27.
1. SOV (Vladimir Aptsiauri, Anvar Ibragimov, Boris Koretsky, Ilgar Mamedov, Aleksandr Romankov)
2. GER (Matthias Behr, Thomas Endres, Mathias Gey, Ulrich Schreck, Thorsten Weidner)
3. HUN (István Busa, Zsolt Érsek, Róbert Gátai, Pál Szekeres, István Szelei)
4. GDR (Aris Enkelmann, Adrian Germanus, Jens Gusek, Jens Howe, Udo Wagner)
5. POL (Leszek Bandach, Waldemar Ciesielczyk, Piotr Kielpikowski, Marian Sypniewski, Boguslaw Zych)
6. FRA (Laurent Bel, Patrick Groc, Youssef Hocine, Patrice Lhotellier, Philippe Omnes)
7. ITA (Andrea Borella, Stefano Cerioni, Federico Cervi, Andrea Cipressa, Mauro Numa)
8. CHN (Lao Shaopei, Liu Yunhong, Ye Chong, Zhang Zhicheng)
Final: SOV 9–5 GER
3rd Place: HUN 9–5 GDR
5th Place: POL 8(60)–8(53) FRA
7th Place: ITA 9–4 CHN

The underdog Soviet team received its stiffest challenge from the Hungarians in the semifinals. Both sides won eight matches, but the U.S.S.R. won on touches, 57–51.

## ÉPÉE, INDIVIDUAL

**1896** not held

**1900 Paris** C: 101, N: 4, D: 6.14.
1. Ramón Fonst        CUB
2. Louis Perrée        FRA
3. Léon Sée            FRA
4. Georges de la Falaise  FRA
5. Camet               FRA
6. Edmond Wallace      FRA
7. Gaston Alibert      FRA
8. Leon Thiebaut       FRA

Ramón Fonst was only 16 years old when he won the Olympic championship. His teacher, Albert Ayot, won the competition for masters.

**1904 St. Louis** C: 5, N: 3, D: 9.7.
1. Ramón Fonst         CUB
2. Charles Tatham      USA
3. Albertson Van Zo Post  USA
4. Gustav Casmir       GER
5. Fitzhugh Townsend   USA

Not only did Fonst achieve a rare double victory in winning both the foil and épée, but he is also the only repeat winner in the individual épée.

**1906 Athens** C: 29, N: 10, D: 4.28.
1. Georges de la Falaise      FRA
2. Georges Dillon-Cavanagh    FRA
3. Alexander van Blijenburgh  HOL
4. Raphael Vigeveno           HOL
5. Emil Schön                 GER
6. Maurits Jacob van Löben Sels  HOL

**1908 London** C: 84, N: 13, D: 7.24

| | | W | L | T | BARRAGE W | L |
|---|---|---|---|---|---|---|
| 1. Gaston Alibert | FRA | 5 | 0 | 2 | | |
| 2. Alexandre Lippmann | FRA | 4 | 2 | 1 | 2 | 0 |
| 3. Eugène Olivier | FRA | 4 | 3 | 0 | 1 | 1 |
| 4. Robert Montgomerie | GBR | 4 | 1 | 2 | 0 | 2 |
| 5. Paul Anspach | BEL | 2 | 5 | 0 | | |
| 5. Cecil Haig | GBR | 2 | 5 | 0 | | |
| 5. Alfred Joan Labouchère | HOL | 2 | 3 | 2 | | |
| 8. Martin Holt | GBR | 1 | 5 | 1 | | |

Gaston Alibert completed the tournament with 21 wins, no losses, and two double hits, or ties. Two other contestants worth noting were Alfred Labouchère, who attracted quite a bit of attention because he was 6 feet 9 inches tall and Ivan Osiier, a 19-year-old from Denmark. Osiier ultimately competed in seven Olympics, making his first and final appearances in London—40 years apart. Along the way he qualified for nine finals, achieving his greatest success in 1912, when he won the individual épée silver medal. His wife, Ellen, was the first woman Olympic fencing champion.

**1912 Stockholm** C: 112, N: 16, D: 7.13.

| | | W | L | T |
|---|---|---|---|---|
| 1. Paul Anspach | BEL | 6 | 1 | 0 |
| 2. Ivan Osiier | DEN | 5 | 2 | 0 |
| 3. Philippe Le Hardy de Beaulieu | BEL | 4 | 2 | 1 |
| 4. Victor Boin | BEL | 4 | 2 | 1 |
| 5. Einar Sörensen | SWE | 3 | 4 | 0 |
| 6. Edgar Seligman | GBR | 2 | 4 | 1 |
| 7. Léon Tom | BEL | 1 | 6 | 0 |
| 8. Martin Holt | GBR | 0 | 4 | 3 |

The Italian Fencing Federation proposed that the length of the épée blade be extended to 94 cm. When this was rejected, the Italians refused to participate. Between 1908 and 1920 Paul Anspach won a total of four medals: two gold, one silver, and one bronze.

**1920 Antwerp** C: 46, N: 12, D: 8.23.

| | | WON |
|---|---|---|
| 1. Armand Massard | FRA | 9 |
| 2. Alexandre Lippman | FRA | 7 |
| 3. Gustave Buchard | FRA | 6 |
| 4. Ernest Gevers | BEL | 6 |
| 5. E. Moreau | FRA | 5 |
| 6. Antonio Mascarenhas de Menezes | POR | 5 |
| 7. — | — | — |
| 8. S. Casanova | FRA | — |

**1924 Paris** C: 67, N: 18, D: 7.11.

| | | WON | LOST | 1st BARRAGE W | 1st BARRAGE L | 2nd BARRAGE W | 2nd BARRAGE L |
|---|---|---|---|---|---|---|---|
| 1. Charles Delporte | BEL | 8 | 3 | | | | |
| 2. Roger Ducret | FRA | 7 | 4 | 2 | 1 | 1 | 0 |
| 3. Nils Hellsten | SWE | 7 | 4 | 2 | 1 | 0 | 1 |
| 4. Emile Cornereau | FRA | 7 | 4 | 1 | 2 | 1 | 0 |
| 5. Armand Massard | FRA | 7 | 4 | 1 | 2 | 0 | 1 |
| 6. Virgilio Mantegazza | ITA | 6 | 5 | | | | |
| 7. Gustave Buchard | FRA | 5 | 6 | | | | |
| 7. Léon Tom | BEL | 5 | 6 | | | | |

**1928 Amsterdam** C: 59, N: 22, D: 8.7.

| | | W | L | T | TG | TR | EXTRA FINAL W | EXTRA FINAL L | EXTRA FINAL T | EXTRA FINAL TG | EXTRA FINAL TR |
|---|---|---|---|---|---|---|---|---|---|---|---|
| 1. Lucien Gaudin | FRA | 8 | 0 | 1 | 18 | 5 | 2 | 0 | 20 | 12 | |
| 2. Georges Buchard | FRA | 7 | 2 | 0 | 15 | 8 | 1 | 1 | 19 | 21 | |
| 3. George Calnan | USA | 6 | 3 | 0 | 14 | 9 | 1 | 1 | 21 | 19 | |
| 4. Léon Tom | BEL | 6 | 2 | 1 | 15 | 9 | 0 | 2 | 12 | 20 | |
| 5. Nils Hellsten | SWE | 5 | 4 | 0 | 12 | 13 | | | | | |
| 6. Charles Delporte | BEL | 4 | 5 | 0 | 11 | 13 | | | | | |
| 7. Charles Debeur | BEL | 3 | 6 | 0 | 10 | 15 | | | | | |
| 8. S. Cicurel | EGY | 3 | 6 | 0 | 10 | 15 | | | | | |

Gaudin's record for the tournament was an impressive 34 wins and five losses, as he became the only fencer besides Ramón Fonst to win both the foil and épée.

**1932 Los Angeles** C: 28, N: 12, D: 8.9.

| | | W | L | T | TG | TR |
|---|---|---|---|---|---|---|
| 1. Giancarlo Cornaggia-Medici | ITA | 8 | 1 | 2 | 31 | 18 |
| 2. Georges Buchard | FRA | 8 | 3 | 0 | 27 | 17 |
| 3. Carlo Agostoni | ITA | 7 | 3 | 1 | 30 | 17 |
| 4. Saverio Ragno | ITA | 7 | 4 | 0 | 27 | 20 |
| 5. Bernard Schmetz | FRA | 7 | 4 | 0 | 26 | 22 |
| 6. Philippe Cattiau | FRA | 6 | 5 | 0 | 23 | 22 |
| 7. George Calnan | USA | 6 | 5 | 0 | 22 | 22 |
| 8. Balthazar de Beuckelaer | BEL | 4 | 7 | 0 | 19 | 25 |

**1936 Berlin** C: 68, N: 26, D: 8.11.

| | | W | L | T | TG | TR |
|---|---|---|---|---|---|---|
| 1. Franco Riccardi | ITA | 5 | 1 | 3 | 25 | 18 |
| 2. Saverio Ragno | ITA | 6 | 3 | 0 | 24 | 15 |
| 3. Giancarlo Cornaggia-Medici | ITA | 6 | 3 | 0 | 22 | 16 |
| 4. Hans Drakenberg | SWE | 4 | 3 | 2 | 20 | 20 |
| 5. Charles Debeur | BEL | 4 | 4 | 1 | 21 | 21 |
| 6. Henrique da Silveira | POR | 4 | 5 | 0 | 18 | 19 |
| 7. Raymond Stasse | BEL | 3 | 4 | 2 | 21 | 21 |
| 8. Ian Campbell-Gray | GBR | 3 | 4 | 2 | 18 | 24 |

Riccardi's total record was 24 wins, three losses, and four ties. In the quarterfinal pool, defending champion Cornaggia-Medici demonstrated his acute awareness of distance. Perplexed by the call of two straight double hits, he insisted that his opponent's blade was the wrong length. Measurements showed that it was in fact a half-inch too long.

**1948 London** C: 66, N: 25, D: 8.9.

| | | W | L | TG | TR | BARRAGE TG | BARRAGE TR |
|---|---|---|---|---|---|---|---|
| 1. Luigi Cantone | ITA | 7 | 2 | 24 | 15 | | |
| 2. Oswald Zappelli | SWI | 5 | 4 | 20 | 17 | 3 | 0 |
| 3. Edoardo Mangiarotti | ITA | 5 | 4 | 20 | 17 | 0 | 3 |
| 4. Henri Guérin | FRA | 5 | 4 | 20 | 19 | | |
| 5. Jean Radoux | BEL | 5 | 4 | 19 | 20 | | |
| 6. Henri Lepage | FRA | 4 | 5 | 19 | 20 | | |
| 7. Carlo Agostoni | ITA | 4 | 5 | 22 | 21 | | |
| 8. Emile Gretsch | LUX | 3 | 6 | 16 | 22 | | |

Thirty-one-year-old Luigi Cantone was allowed to compete at the last minute after Dario Mangiarotti injured his foot and had to withdraw. In the final pool, which took five and a half hours, Cantone lost his first two bouts to Carlo Agostoni and Edoardo Mangiarotti. Then he won seven straight to take first place without a barrage.

**1952 Helsinki** C: 76, N: 29, D: 7.28.

| | | W | L | TR |
|---|---|---|---|---|
| 1. Edoardo Mangiarotti | ITA | 7 | 2 | 12 |
| 2. Dario Mangiarotti | ITA | 6 | 3 | 16 |
| 3. Oswald Zappelli | SWI | 6 | 3 | 18 |
| 4. Léon Buck | LUX | 6 | 3 | 19 |
| 5. József Sákovics | HUN | 5 | 4 | 17 |
| 6. Carlo Pavesi | ITA | 4 | 5 | 21 |
| 7. Per Carleson | SWE | 3 | 6 | 20 |
| 8. Carl Forsell | SWE | 3 | 6 | 23 |

Milanese fencing master Giuseppe Mangiarotti began giving his sons lessons when they turned eight years old. Although both were right-handed, Giuseppe converted the younger boy, Edoardo, into a left-hander because he considered it an advantage in competition. When he was 11, Edoardo won the Italian junior foil title. But Giuseppe had been Italian professional épée champion 17 times, so when Edoardo turned 15 his father started training him with that weapon. At age 17, Edoardo was a member of the Italian épée team that won the gold medal at Berlin. By 1960 Edoardo had won 13 Olympic medals: four gold and one silver in team épée, one gold and two bronze in individual épée, one gold and three silver in team foil, and one silver in individual foil. His older brother, Dario, gained one gold and two silver.

**1956 Melbourne** C: 40, N: 17, D: 11.30.

|   |   |   |   |   |   |   | 1st BARRAGE | | | | 2nd BARRAGE | | | |
|---|---|---|---|---|---|---|---|---|---|---|---|---|---|---|
|   |   |   | W | L | TG | TR | W | L | TG | TR | W | L | TG | TR |
| 1. | Carlo Pavesi | ITA | 5 | 2 | 29 | 20 | 1 | 1 | 9 | 7 | 2 | 0 | 10 | 5 |
| 2. | Giuseppe Delfino | ITA | 5 | 2 | 30 | 27 | 1 | 1 | 7 | 7 | 1 | 1 | 10 | 8 |
| 3. | Edoardo Mangiarotti | ITA | 5 | 2 | 30 | 17 | 1 | 1 | 7 | 9 | 0 | 2 | 3 | 10 |
| 4. | Richard Pew | USA | 4 | 3 | 25 | 28 |   |   |   |   |   |   |   |   |
| 5. | Lajos Balthazár | HUN | 4 | 3 | 30 | 29 |   |   |   |   |   |   |   |   |
| 6. | René Queyroux | FRA | 3 | 4 | 29 | 25 |   |   |   |   |   |   |   |   |
| 7. | Per Carleson | SWE | 2 | 5 | 22 | 29 |   |   |   |   |   |   |   |   |
| 8. | Rolf Wiik | FIN | 0 | 7 | 15 | 35 |   |   |   |   |   |   |   |   |

Giuseppe Delfino came within one touch of winning the gold, but lost 5–4 to Richard Pew and was forced into the barrage.

**1960 Rome** C: 79, N: 32, D: 9.6.

|   |   |   |   |   |   |   | BARRAGE | |
|---|---|---|---|---|---|---|---|---|
|   |   |   | W | L | TG | TR | TG | TR |
| 1. | Giuseppe Delfino | ITA | 5 | 2 | 39 | 32 | 5 | 2 |
| 2. | Allan Jay | GBR | 5 | 2 | 39 | 23 | 2 | 5 |
| 3. | Bruno Habãrovs | SOV | 4 | 3 | 32 | 23 | 8 | 7 |
| 4. | József Sákovics | HUN | 4 | 3 | 30 | 31 | 7 | 8 |
| 5. | Roger Achten | BEL | 3 | 4 | 31 | 30 |   |   |
| 6. | Yves Dreyfus | FRA | 3 | 4 | 30 | 30 |   |   |
| 7. | Armand Mouyal | FRA | 3 | 4 | 25 | 30 |   |   |
| 8. | Giovanni Breda | ITA | 1 | 6 | 19 | 34 |   |   |

The 38-year-old Delfino utilized a rather unusual style to achieve his long-awaited gold medal. Rather than waste his energy going for a five-touch victory, he would content himself with a tie until time ran out. Then he would concentrate on, and usually win, the single sudden-death over-time hit. This tactic defeated Allan Jay in the final pool to force the barrage.

**1964 Tokyo** C: 65, N: 25, D: 10.19.

|   |   |   |   |   |   |   | BARRAGE | | | |
|---|---|---|---|---|---|---|---|---|---|---|
|   |   |   | W | L | TG | TR | W | L | TG | TR |
| 1. | Grigory Kriss | SOV | 2 | 1 | 12 | 11 | 1 | 0 | 5 | 2 |
| 2. | Henry Hoskyns | GBR | 2 | 1 | 15 | 12 | 0 | 1 | 2 | 5 |
| 3. | Guram Kostava | SOV | 1 | 2 | 12 | 12 | 1 | 0 | 5 | 0 |
| 4. | Gianluigi Saccaro | ITA | 1 | 2 | 10 | 14 | 0 | 1 | 0 | 5 |
| 5. | Bogdan Gonsior | POL |   |   |   |   |   |   |   |   |
| 6. | Claude Bourquard | FRA |   |   |   |   |   |   |   |   |
| 7. | Orvar Lindwall | SWE |   |   |   |   |   |   |   |   |
| 8. | Franz Rompza | GER |   |   |   |   |   |   |   |   |

In the final pool Kriss, a 23-year-old soldier from Kiev, defeated Hoskyns in a bout that saw four straight double (or simultaneous) hits. Hoskyns was a 33-year-old Somerset fruit farmer.

**1968 Mexico City** C; 73, N: 28, D: 10.22.

|   |   |   |   |   |   |   | BARRAGE | | | |
|---|---|---|---|---|---|---|---|---|---|---|
|   |   |   | W | L | TG | TR | W | L | T | TG | TR |
| 1. | Gyözö Kulcsár | HUN | 4 | 1 | 24 | 14 | 2 | 0 | 0 | 10 | 5 |
| 2. | Grigory Kriss | SOV | 4 | 1 | 25 | 19 | 0 | 1 | 1 | 8 | 10 |

| 3. | Gianluigi Saccaro | ITA | 4 | 1 | 21 | 19 | 0 | 1 | 1 | 7 | 10 |
| 4. | Viktor Modzalevsky | SOV | 2 | 3 | 20 | 23 |   |   |   |   |   |
| 5. | Herbert Polzhuber | AUT | 1 | 4 | 17 | 24 |   |   |   |   |   |
| 6. | Jean-Pierre Allemand | FRA | 0 | 5 | 17 | 25 |   |   |   |   |   |
| 7. | Peter Loetscher | SWI |   |   |   |   |   |   |   |   |   |
| 7. | Henryk Nielaba | POL |   |   |   |   |   |   |   |   |   |

The hero of Hungary's team épée victory four years earlier in Tokyo, Kulcsár completed the 1968 individual tournament with 17 wins and only one loss.

**1972 Munich** C: 72, N: 28, D: 9.6.

|   |   |   | W | I | TG | TR |
|---|---|---|---|---|---|---|
| 1. | Csaba Fenyvesi | HUN | 4 | 1 | 25 | 10 |
| 2. | Jacques la Degaillerie | FRA | 3 | 2 | 23 | 19 |
| 3. | Gyözö Kulcsár | HUN | 3 | 2 | 20 | 19 |
| 4. | Anton Alex Pongratz | ROM | 2 | 3 | 19 | 20 |
| 5. | Rolf Edling | SWE | 1 | 4 | 15 | 22 |
| 6. | Jacques Brodin | FRA | 0 | 5 | 13 | 25 |

Two of the three medals went to fencers from Budapest. Csaba Fenyvesi was a 29-year-old physician, Gyözö Kulcsár a 31-year-old engineer.

**1976 Montreal** C: 64, N: 25, D: 7.23.

|   |   |   |   |   |   |   | BARRAGE | | | |
|---|---|---|---|---|---|---|---|---|---|---|
|   |   |   | W | L | TG | TR | W | L | TG | TR |
| 1. | Alexander Pusch | GER | 3 | 2 | 22 | 18 | 2 | 0 | 10 | 7 |
| 2. | Jürgen Hehn | GER | 3 | 2 | 18 | 20 | 1 | 1 | 9 | 7 |
| 3. | Gyözö Kulcsár | HUN | 3 | 2 | 22 | 19 | 0 | 2 | 5 | 10 |
| 4. | Istvan Osztrics | HUN | 2 | 3 | 18 | 19 |   |   |   |   |
| 5. | Jerzy Janikowski | POL | 2 | 3 | 20 | 21 |   |   |   |   |
| 6. | Rolf Edling | SWE | 2 | 3 | 18 | 21 |   |   |   |   |
| 7. | Csaba Fenyvesi | HUN |   |   |   |   |   |   |   |   |
| 7. | Göran Floodström | SWE |   |   |   |   |   |   |   |   |

In the barrage Pusch defeated Hehn, 5–4, in a seesaw battle, and then scored the last two touches to beat Kulcsár 5–3. Pusch was only 21 years old.

**1980 Moscow** C: 42, N: 16, D: 7.28.

| | | W | L | TG | TR |
|---|---|---|---|---|---|
| 1. Johan Harmenberg | SWE | 4 | 1 | 22 | 21 |
| 2. Ernö Kolczonay | HUN | 3 | 2 | 23 | 19 |
| 3. Philippe Riboud | FRA | 3 | 2 | 20 | 17 |
| 4. Rolf Edling | SWE | 3 | 2 | 18 | 16 |
| 5. Aleksandr Mozhaev | SOV | 1 | 4 | 18 | 22 |
| 6. Ioan Popa | ROM | 1 | 4 | 18 | 24 |
| 7. Jaroslav Jurka | CZE | | | | |
| 7. Boris Lukomsky | SOV | | | | |

**1984 Los Angeles-Long Beach** C: 63, N: 26, D: 8.8.
1. Philippe Boisse      FRA
2. Björne Väggö      SWE
3. Philippe Riboud      FRA
4. Stefano Bellone      ITA
5. Michael Poffet      SWI
6. Elmar Borrmann      GER
7. Alexander Pusch      GER
8. Volker Fischer      GER
   Final: Boisse 10–5 Väggö
   3rd Place: Riboud 10–7 Bellone

Björne Väggö, ranked only 44th in the world, registered four straight upsets to qualify for the gold medal match, defeating world cup champion Olivier Lenglet, world cup runner-up Angelo Mazzoni, world champion Elmar Borrmann and World University Games champion Stefano Bellone. In the final, however, he was no match for 29-year-old Paris radiologist Philippe Boisse, who had survived a tight 12–11 semifinal bout against teammate Philippe Riboud, with whom he fenced twice a week.

**1988 Seoul** C: 79, N: 32, D: 9.24.
1. Arnd Schmitt      GER
2. Philippe Riboud      FRA
3. Andrei Shuvalov      SOV
4. Sandro Cuomo      ITA
5. Torsten Kühnemund      GDR
6. Jerri Bergström      SWE
7. Martin Brill      NZE
8. Vladimir Reznichenko      SOV
   Final: Schmitt 10–9 Riboud
   3rd Place: Shuvalov 10–8 Cuomo

Andrei Shuvalov compiled a record of 16 wins and only one loss before being tipped 10-9 in the semifinals by 23-year-old dental student Arnd Schmitt. In the final, Schmitt defeated two-time world champion Philippe Riboud by the same score.

# ÉPÉE, TEAM

**1896–1904** not held

**1906 Athens** T: 6, N: 6, D 4.28.
1. FRA      (Pierre d'Hugues, Georges Dillon-Cavanaugh, Mohr, Georges de la Falaise)

2. GBR      (William Desborough, Cosmo Duff-Gordon, Charles Robinson, Edgar Seligman)
3. BEL      (Constant Cloquet, Fernand de Montigny, Edmond Crahay, Philippe Le Hardy de Beaulieu)

In the first round Germany was due to meet Great Britain. However, a misunderstanding of the schedule found the Germans asleep at their hotel at the time the match was to start. Quickly roused, the Germans rushed to the fencing grounds and were easily beaten, 9–2. The final resulted in a tie. The rematch was held immediately; France won, 9–6.

**1908 London** T: 9, N: 9, D: 7.23.
1. FRA      (Gaston Alibert, Bernard Gravier, Alexandre Lippmann, Eugène Olivier, Henri-Georges Berger, Charles Collignon, Jean Stern)
2. GBR      (Edward Amphlett, C. Leaf Daniell, Cecil Haig, Robert Montgomerie, Martin Holt, Edgar Seligman)
3. BEL      (Paul Anspach, Fernand Bosmans, Fernand de Montigny, François Rom, Victor Willems, Désiré Beaurain, Ferdinand Feyerick)
4. ITA      (Marcello Bertinetti, Giuseppe Mangiarotti, Riccardo Nowak, Abelardo Olivier)
   Final: FRA 9–7 BEL
   Pool for 2nd: GBR 9–8 DEN; GBR 9–5 BEL

**1912 Stockholm** T: 11, N: 11, D: 7.10.

| | | W | L | TR |
|---|---|---|---|---|
| 1. BEL | (Paul Anspach, Henri Anspach, Robert Hennet, Fernand de Montigny, Jacques Ochs, François Rom, Gaston Salmon, Victor Willems) | 3 | 0 | |
| 2. GBR | (Edgar Seligman, Edward Amphlett, Robert Montgomerie, John Blake, Percival Davson, Arthur Everitt, Sydney Martineau, Martin Holt) | 1 | 2 | 28 |
| 3. HOL | (Adrianus de Jong, Willem Hubert van Blijenburgh, Jetze Doorman, Leonardus Salomonson, George van Rossem) | 1 | 2 | 30 |
| 4. SWE | (Einar Sörensen, Gustaf Lindblom, Pontus von Rosen, Louis Sparre, Georg Branting) | 1 | 2 | 32 |

**1920 Antwerp** T: 11, N: 11, D: 8.23.

| | | MATCHES | | | |
|---|---|---|---|---|---|
| | | WON | LOST | W | L |
| 1. ITA | (Nedo Nadi, Aldo Nadi, Abelardo Olivier, Tullio Bozza, Giovanni Canova, Andrea Marrazi, Dino Urbani, Antonio Allocchio, Tommaso Constantino, Paolo Thaon di Revel) | 5 | 0 | 40 | 23 |
| 2. BEL | (Ernest Gevers, Paul Anspach, Felix Goblet d'Alviella, Victor Boin, Joseph de Craecker, Léon Tom, | 4 | 1 | 39 | 34 |

3. FRA   (Maurice de Wée, Philippe Le Hardy de Beaulieu)

| | | | WON | LOST | W | L |
|---|---|---|---|---|---|---|
| 3. | FRA | (Maurice de Wée, Philippe Le Hardy de Beaulieu, Armand Massard, Alexandre Lippmann, Gustave Buchard, Georges Trombert, S. Casanova, Gaston Amson, E. Moreau) | 3 | 2 | 40 | 30 |
| 4. | POR | (Antonio Mascarenhas de Menezes, Jorge Paiva, Rui Mayer, João Sassetti, Henrique da Silveira, Frederico Paredes, Manuel Queiroz) | 2 | 3 | 30 | 35 |
| 5. | SWI | (Henri Jacquet, Léopold Montagnier, Franz Wilhelm, Frédéric Fitting, Eugène Empeyta, Louis de Tribolet, John Laurent Albaret, Edouard Fitting) | 1 | 4 | 33 | 41 |
| 6. | USA | (William Russell, Ray Dutcher, Henry Breckinridge, Arthur Lyon, Robert Sears, Harold Rayner) | 0 | 5 | 19 | 38 |

Two competitors worth noting were Nedo Nadi of Italy and Victor Boin of Belgium. Nadi, who won five gold medals in foil and sabre, was not as well known as an épéeist. His father, Beppe, considered the épée to be an "undisciplined" weapon and forbade the use of it in his *salle*. So Nedo would sneak out to enjoy the taboo sword. His insubordination paid off with a team épée gold medal in 1920. Boin's silver medal as part of the Belgian team was his third Olympic medal. His first two, however were earned not in fencing but in water polo: a silver in 1908 and a bronze in 1912. Boin also enjoyed swimming, skating, flying, ice hockey, and motorcycle racing. He was founder of the International Association of Sports Journalists and President of the Belgian Olympic Committee.

**1924 Paris** T: 16, N: 16, D: 7.9.

| | | | WON | LOST | W | L |
|---|---|---|---|---|---|---|
| 1. | FRA | (Lucien Gaudin, Georges Buchard, Roger Ducret, André Labatut, Lionel Liottel, Alexandre Lippmann, Georges Tainturier) | 3 | 0 | 29 | 16 |
| 2. | BEL | (Paul Anspach, Joseph de Craecker, Charles Delporte, Fernand de Montigny, Ernest Gevers, Léon Tom) | 2 | 1 | 24 | 22 |
| 3. | ITA | (Giulio Basletta, Marcello Bertinetti, Giovanni Canova, Vincenzo Cuccia, Virgilio Mantegazza, Oreste Moricca) | 1 | 2 | 21 | 26 |
| 4. | POR | (Antonio Mascarenhas de Menezes, Jorge Paiva, Paulo d'Eca Leal, Rui Mayer, Henrique da Silveira, Mário de Noronha, Frederico Paredes, Antonio Pinto Leite) | 0 | 3. | 18 | 28 |
| 5. | SPA | (J. Delgado, F. De Pomes-Soler, Diez de Rivera, F. Garcia-Bilbao, D. Garcia-Montoro, J. Lopez-Lara-Mallor, C. Miguel de los Reyes, M. Zabalza de la Fuente) | | | | |
| 5. | USA | (Henry Breckinridge, George Breed, George Calnan, Arthur Lyon, Allen Millner, William Russell, Leon Shore, Donald Waldhaus) | | | | |

**1928 Amsterdam** T: 18, N: 18, D: 8.5.

| | | | WON | LOST | W | L |
|---|---|---|---|---|---|---|
| 1. | ITA | (Carlo Agostoni, Marcello Bertinetti, Giancarlo Cornaggia Medici, Renzo Minoli, Giulio Basletta, Franco Riccardi) | 3 | 0 | 28 | 19 |
| 2. | FRA | (Armand Massard, Georges Buchard, Gaston Amson, Emile Cornic, Bernard Schmetz, René Barbier) | 2 | 1 | 24 | 22 |
| 3. | POR | (Paulo d'Eca Leal, Mário de Noronha, Jorge Paiva, João Sassetti, Frederico Paredes, Henrique de Silveira) | 1 | 2 | 21 | 26 |
| 4. | BEL | (Emile Barbier, Balthazar de Beuckalaer, Charles Dulporte, Charles Debeur, Léon Tom, Georges Dambois) | 0 | 3 | 20 | 26 |
| 5. | CZE | (M. G. Harden, J. Jungmann, F. Kriz, J. Tille, M. Beznoska, J. Cernohorsky) | | | | |
| 5. | HOL | (L. Kuypers, Adrianus de Jong, H. J. M. Wijnoldy Daniels, W. Driebergen, Alfred Joan Labouchère, Jr., K. J. van den Brandeler) | | | | |
| 5. | SPA | (J. M. de Tejada, D. Garcia Montoro, D. Diez de Rivera, F. de Pomes Soler, F. Gonzalez Badia) | | | | |
| 5. | USA | (Arthur Lyon, George Calnan, Allen Milner, Harold Rayner, Henry Breckinridge, Edward Barnett) | | | | |

**1932 Los Angeles** T: 7, N: 7, D: 8.7.

| | | WON | LOST | MATCHES W | L |
|---|---|---|---|---|---|
| 1. FRA | (Philippe Cattiau, Georges Buchard, Bernard Schmetz, Jean Piot, Fernand Jourdant, Georges Tainturier) | 3 | 0 | 30.5 | 17.5 |
| 2. ITA | (Carlo Agostoni, Giancarlo Cornaggia-Medici, Renzo Minoli, Franco Riccardi, Saverio Ragno) | 2 | 1 | 27.5 | 20.5 |
| 3. USA | (George Calnan, Gustave Heiss, Frank Righeimer, Tracy Jaeckel, Curtis Shears, Miguel de Capriles) | 1 | 2 | 20.5 | 22.5 |
| 4. BEL | (Raoul Hankart, André Poplimont, Max Janlet, Balthazar de Beuckelaer, Albert Mund) | 0 | 3 | 12.5 | 30.5 |

**1936 Berlin** T: 21, N: 21, D: 8.8.

| | | WON | LOST | MATCHES W | L |
|---|---|---|---|---|---|
| 1. ITA | (Saverio Ragno, Alfredo Pezzana, Giancarlo Cornaggia-Medici, Edoardo Mangiarotti, Franco Riccardi, Giancarlo Brusati) | 3 | 0 | 26 | 41 |
| 2. SWE | (Hans Granfelt, Sven Thofelt, Gösta Almgren, Gustaf Dyrssen, Hans Drakenberg, Birger Cederin) | 2 | 1 | 21 | 22 |
| 3. FRA | (Michel Pécheux, Bernard Schmetz, Georges Buchard, Henri Dulieux, Paul Wormser, Philippe Cattiau) | 1 | 2 | 21 | 23 |
| 4. GER | (Siegfried Lerdon, Joseph Uhlmann, Hans Esser, Eugen Geiwitz, Ernst Röthig, Otto Schröder) | 0 | 3 | 11 | 23 |
| 5. BEL | (Raymond Stasse, T'Sas, Charles Debeur, de Monceau, Plumier, Heim) | | | | |
| 5. POL | (Jerzy Staszewicz, Teodor Zaczyk, Rajmund Karwicki, Roman Kantor, Kazimierz Szempliński, Antoni Franz) | | | | |
| 5. POR | (Henrique de Silveira, Paulo d'Eca Leal, Antonio Mascarenhas de Menezes, Sasseti, Carinhas) | | | | |
| 5. USA | (Frank Righeimer, Thomas Sands, Tracy Jaeckel, Gustave Heiss, Miguel de Capriles, Andrew Boyd) | | | | |

**1948 London** T: 21, N: 21, D: 8.6.

| | | WON | LOST | MATCHES W | L |
|---|---|---|---|---|---|
| 1. FRA | (Henri Guérin, Henri Lepage, Marcel Desprets, Michel Pécheux, Edouard Artigas, Maurice Huet) | 3 | 0 | 31 | 10 |
| 2. ITA | (Luigi Cantone, Antonio Mandruzzato, Dario Mangiarotti, Edoardo Mangiarotti, Fiorenzo Marini, Carlo Agostoni) | 2 | 1 | 25 | 21 |
| 3. SWE | (Per Carleson, Frank Cervell, Carl Forssel, Bengt Ljungquist, Sven Thofelt, H. Arne Tollbom) | 1 | 2 | 18 | 26 |
| 4. DEN | (Mogens Lüchow, Erik Andersen, Ib Benjamin Nielsen, René Dybkaer, Jacob Lyng, Kenneth Flindt) | 0 | 3 | 12 | 29 |
| 5. BEL | (Raymond Stasse, L. Hauben, Raymond Bru, Jean Radoux, R. Henkart, Charles Debeur) | | | | |
| 5. HUN | (Imre Hennyey, Pál Dunay, Béla Rerrich, Béla Mikla, Lajos Balthazár, Béla Bay) | | | | |
| 5. LUX | (Fernand Leischen, Paul Anen, Emile Gretsch, G. Lamesch, E. Putz) | | | | |
| 5. SWI | (F. Thiebaud, R. Lips, Jean Hauert, Oswald Zappelli, Otto Rufenacht, M. Chamay) | | | | |

France qualified for the final pool despite being upset 10–5 in the semifinal pool by Belgium. The French team was led by Michel Pécheux, a last-minute addition, who was 11–0 in the final pool and 23–3 total.

**1952 Helsinki** T: 19, N: 19, D: 7.26.

| | | WON | LOST | MATCHES W | L |
|---|---|---|---|---|---|
| 1. ITA | (Dario Mangiarotti, Edoardo Mangiarotti, Franco Bertinetti, Carlo Pavesi, Giuseppe Delfino, Roberto Battaglia) | 3 | 0 | 32 | 11 |
| 2. SWE | (Bengt Ljundquist, Berndt-Otto Rehbinder, Sven Fahlman, Per Carleson, Carl Forssell, Lennart Magnusson) | 2 | 1 | 26 | 17 |
| 3. SWI | (Otto Rüfenacht, Paul Meister, Oswald Zappelli, Paul Barth, Willy Fitting, Mario Valota) | 1 | 2 | 18 | 24 |
| 4. LUX | (Emile Gretsch, Fernand Leischen, Paul Anen, Léon Buck) | 0 | 3 | 9 | 33 |

5. DEN  (Raimondo Carnera, Erik Swane-Lund, René Dybkaer, Mogens Lüchow, Ib Benjamin Nielsen, Jacob Lyng)

5. HUN  (Lajos Balthazár, Barnabás Berzsenyi, Béla Rerrich, József Sákovics, Imre Hennyey)

The 1952 Olympics saw the downfall of defending champion France, eliminated in the second round after losses to Luxemburg and Hungary. Italy defeated Sweden 8–5 in the deciding match, despite the efforts of Bengt Ljundquist who beat all four Italians.

**1956 Melbourne** T: 11, N: 11, D: 11.28.

|  |  | WON | LOST | W | L |
|---|---|---|---|---|---|
| 1. ITA | (Giuseppe Delfino, Alberto Pellegrino, Edoardo Mangiarotti, Carlo Pavesi, Giorgio Anglesio, Franco Bortinetti) | 3 | 0 | 34 | 10 |
| 2. HUN | (József Sákovics, Béla Rerrich, Lajos Balthazár, Ambrus Nagy, József Marosi, Barnabás Berzsenyi) | 2 | 1 | 22 | 22 |
| 3. FRA | (Armand Mouyal, Claude Nigon, Daniel Dagallier, Yves Dreyfus, René Queyroux) | 1 | 2 | 17 | 27 |
| 4. GBR | (René Paul, Michael Howard, Henry William Hoskyns, Allen Jay) | 0 | 3 | 15 | 29 |
| 5. BEL | (François Dehez, Roger Achten, Ghislain Delaunois, Marcel Vanderauwera, Jacques Debeur) |  |  |  |  |
| 5. SOV | (Arnold Chernushevich, Valentin Chernikov, Lev Saitchouk, Revas Tsirekidze, Iosas Oudras) |  |  |  |  |

**1960 Rome** T: 21, N: 21, D: 9.9.
1. ITA  (Giuseppe Delfino, Alberto Pellegrino, Carlo Pavesi, Edoardo Mangiarotti, Fiorenzo Marini, Gianluigi Saccaro)
2. GBR  (Allan Jay, Michael Howard, John Pelling, Henry William Hoskyns, Raymond Harrison, Michael Alexander)
3. SOV  (Guram Kostava, Bruno Habărovs, Arnold Chernushevich, Valentin Chernikov, Aleksandr Pavlovsky)
4. HUN  (József Marosi, Tamás Gábor, István Kausz, József Sákovics, Árpád Bárány)
5. GER  (Paul Gnaier, Fritz Zimmerman, Dieter Fänger, Georg Neuber, Helmut Anschütz, Walter Kostner)
5. LUX  (Roger Theisen, Edouard Schmit, Robert Schiel, Rodolphe Kugeler, Edmond Gutenkauff)

5. SWE  (Hans Lagerwall, Göran Abrahamsson, Ling Vannerus, Berndt Rehbinder, Carl-Wilhem Engdahl, Orvar Lindwall)
5. SWI  (Hans Baessler, Amez Droz, Paul Meister, Charles Ribordy, Claudio Polledri, Michel Steininger)
Final: ITA 9–5 GBR
3rd Place: SOV 9–5 HUN

The Italian squad included the last three individual épée champions: Mangiarotti (1952), Pavesi (1956), and Delfino (1960), as well as 21-year-old Gianluigi Saccaro, who fenced with a patch over his injured right eye. In Italy's semifinal match against the U.S.S.R., the usually subdued Delfino found himself trailing Chernikov 4–1 with 13 seconds left. He then scored three hits in 12 seconds to force an overtime bout, which he also won.

**1964 Tokyo** T: 18, N: 18, D: 10.21.
1. HUN  (Győző Kulcsár, Zoltán Nemere, Támás Gábor, István Kausz, Árpád Bárány)
2. ITA  (Gianluigi Saccaro, Giovanni Battista Breda, Gianfranco Paolucci, Giuseppe Delfino, Alberto Pellegrino)
3. FRA  (Claude Brodin, Yves Dreyfus, Claude Bourquard, Jack Guittet, Jacques Brodin)
4. SWE  (Ivar Genesjö, Orvar Lindwall, Hans Lagerwall, Göran Abrahamsson, Carl-Wilhem Engdahl)
5. POL  (Henryk Nielaba, Mikolaj Pomarnacki, Bogdan Gonsior, Bogdan Andrzejewski, Jerzy Pawlowski)
6. GER  (Franz Rompza, Max Geuter, Volkmar Würtz, Paul Gnaier, Haakon Stein)
7. SOV  (Bruno Khabarov, Guram Kostava, Yurl Smoliakov, Grigory Kriss, Aleksei Nikanchikov)
7. SWI  (Claudio Polledri, Paul Meister, Walter Bar, Jean Gontier, Michel Steininger)
Final: HUN 8–3 ITA
3rd Place: FRA 8(64)–8(59) SWE
5th Place: POL 8(66)–8(62) GER

Hungary broke the 44-year Italian–French domination of team épée, as Győző Kulcsár won all 20 of his bouts.

**1968 Mexico City** T: 20, N: 20, D: 10.25.
1. HUN  (Csaba Fenyvesi, Zoltán Nemere, Pál Schmitt, Győző Kulcsár, Pál Nagy)
2. SOV  (Grigory Kriss, Yosif Vitebsky, Aleksei Nikanchikov, Yuri Smollakov, Viktor Modzelevsky)
3. POL  (Bohdan Andrzejewski, Michal Butkiewicz, Bohdan Gonsior, Henryk Nielaba, Kazimierz Barburski)
4. GER  (Dieter Jung, Franz Rompza, Fritz Zimmerman, Max Geuter, Paul Gnaier)
5. GDR  (Bernd Uhlig, Klaus Dumke, Harry Fiedler, Hans-Peter Schulze)
6. ITA  (Gianfranco Paolucci, Claudio Francesconi, Giovanni Battista Breda, Gianluigi Saccaro, Antonio Albanese)
7. FRA  (François Jeanne, Claude Bourquard, Yves Boissier, Jacques Ladegaillerie, Jean-Pierre Allemand)
7. GBR  (Nicholas Halstead, Owen Bourne, Henry Hoskyns, Ralph Johnson, Peter Jacobs)
Final: HUN 7–4 SOV
3rd Place: POL 9–6 GER
5th Place: GDR 9–6 ITA

For the first time in 56 years, Italy failed to finish among the top three.

**1972 Munich** T: 20, N: 20, D: 9.9.
1. HUN (Istvan Osztrics, Sándor Erdös, Csaba Fenyvesi, Pál Schmitt, Gyözö Kulcsár)
2. SWI (Peter Löetscher, Christian Kauter, Guy Evéquoz, Daniel Giger, François Suchanecki)
3. SOV (Georgy Zajitsky, Grigory Kriss, Viktor Modzelevsky, Igor Valetov, Sergei Paramonov)
4. FRA (François Jeanne, Jacques Brodin, Pierre Marchand, Jean-Pierre Allemand, Jacques La Degaillerie)
5. ROM (Constantin Dutu, Costică Bărăgan, Anton Alex Pongratz, Alexandru Istrate, Nicolae Iorgu)
6. POL (Bohdan Andrzejewski, Jerzy Janikowski, Henryk Nielaba, Kazimierz Barburski, Bohdan Gonsior)
7. NOR (Jan Von Koss, Jeppe Normann, Ole Morch, Claus Morch)
7. SWE (Hans Wieselgren, Carl Von Essen, Orvar Joensson, Rolf Edling, Per Sundberg)
   Final: HUN 8–4 SWI
   3rd Place: SOV 9–4 FRA
   5th Place: ROM 9–3 POL

**1976 Montreal** T: 19, N: 19, D: 7.29.
1. SWE (Hans Jacobson, Orvar Jonsson, Carl Von Essen, Leif Högström, Göran Flodström, Rolf Edling)
2. GER (Alexander Pusch, Jürgen Hehn, Hanns Jana, Reinhold Behr, Volker Fischer)
3. SWI (Jean-Blaise Evéquoz, Michel Poffet, Daniel Giger, Christian Kauter, François Suchanecki)
4. HUN (Csaba Fenyvesi, Sándor Erdös, István Osztrics, Pál Schmitt, Gyözö Kulcsár)
5. SOV (Aleksandr Aboushahmetov, Viktor Modzelevsky, Vassilly Stankovich, Aleksandr Bykov, Boris Loukomski)
6. ROM (Ioan Popa, Anton Pongratz, Nicolae Iorgu, Paul Szabo)
7. ITA (John Pezza, Nicola Granieri, Fabio Dal Zotto, Marcello Bertinetti, Giovan Battista Coletti)
7. NOR (Nils Koppang, Jeppe Normann, Kjell Moe, Baard Vonen, Ole Moerch)
   Final: SWE 8–5 GER
   3rd Place: SWI 9–3 HUN
   5th Place: SOV 9–2 ROM

The world champion Swedish team received a setback in the first bout of the final match, when Göran Flodström was knocked out. Carl Von Essen was brought in as a replacement and won two crucial bouts, including one against Alexander Pusch, which took place while Flodström was being carried out on a stretcher.

**1980 Moscow** T: 11, N: 11, D: 7.31.
1. FRA (Philippe Riboud, Patrick Picot, Hubert Gardas, Michel Salesse, Philippe Boisse)
2. POL (Piotr Jablkowski, Andrzej Lis, Mariusz Strzalka, Ludomir Chronowski, Leszek Swornowski)

3. SOV (Boris Lukomsky, Aleksandr Abushakhmetov, Vladimir Smirnov, Ashot Karagan, Aleksandr Mozhaev)
4. ROM (Ioan Popa, Octavian Zidaru, Anton Pongratz, Costica Baragan, Petru Kuki)
5. SWE (Johan Harmenberg, Rolf Edling, Leif Högström, Göran Malkar, Hans Jacobsen)
6. CZE (Jaroslav Jurka, Jaromír Holub, Jiři Douba, Jiři Adam, Oldřich Kubišta)
7. GBR (Steven Paul, John Llewellyn, Neal Mallett, Robert Bruniges)
8. HUN (Ernö Kolczonay, István Osztrics, Laszlo Petö, Jenö Pap, Péter Takács)
   Final: FRA 8–4 POL
   3rd Place: SOV 9–5 ROM
   5th Place: SWE 9–2 CZE
   7th Place: GBR 16–0 HUN (forfeit)

Led by Philippe Riboud's 16–2 effort, France pulled off a major upset and won the team épée gold medal for the first time in 32 years.

**1984 Los Angeles-Long Beach** T: 16, N: 16, D: 8.11.
1. GER (Elmar Borrmann, Volker Fischer, Gerhard Heer, Rafael Nickel, Alexander Pusch)
2. FRA (Philippe Boisse, Jean-Michael Henry, Olivier Lenglet, Philippe Riboud, Michel Salesse)
3. ITA (Stefano Bellone, Sandro Cuomo, Cosimo Ferro, Roberto Manzi, Angelo Mazzoni)
4. CAN (Jacques Cardyn, Jean-Marc Chouinard, Alain Cote, Michel Dessureault, Daniel Perreault)
5. SWE (Jerri Bergström, Greger Forslöw, Kent Hjerpe, Jonas Rosén, Björne Väggö)
6. CHN (Cui Yining, Pang Jin, Zhao Lizhong, Zong Xiangqing)
7. KOR (Bong-Man Kim, Sung-Moon Kim, Il-Hee Lee, Kyung-Seung Min, Nam-Jin Yoon)
8. GBR (William Johnson, John Llewellyn, Neal Mallett, Steven Paul, Jonathan Stanbury)
   Final: GER 8–5 FRA
   3rd Place: ITA 8–2 CAN
   5th Place: SWE 8–6 CHN
   7th Place: KOR 8(69)–8(62) GBR

**1988 Seoul** T: 18, N: 18, D: 9.30.
1. FRA (Frédéric Delpla, Jean-Michel Henry, Olivier Lenglet, Philippe Riboud, Eric Srecki)
2. GER (Elmar Borrmann, Volker Fischer, Thomas Gerull, Alexander Pusch, Arnd Schmitt)
3. SOV (Andrei Shuvalov, Pavel Kolobkov, Vladimir Reznichenko, Mikhail Tyshko, Igor Tikhomirov)
4. ITA (Stefano Bellone, Andrea Bermond Das Ambrois, Sandro Cuomo, Angelo Mazzoni, Stefano Pantano)
5. SWI (Patrice Gaille, André Kuhn, Zsolt Madarasz, Gérald Pfefferle, Michel Poffet)
6. HUN (Laszlo Fabian, Ferenc Hegëdus, Ernö Kolczonay, Szabolcs Pásztor, Zoltán Székely)
7. KOR (Cho Hee-jae, Lee Il-hee, Lee Sang-ki, Yang Dal-sik, Yoon Nam-jin)
8. SWE (Johan Bergdahl, Jerri Bergström, Otto Drakenberg, Ulf Sandegren, Peter Vánky)
   Final: FRA 8-3 GER

3rd Place: SOV 8(65)–8(63) ITA
5th Place: SWI 8–4 HUN
7th Place: KOR 8(64)–8(60) SWE

In a rematch of the 1984 final, France was led by Lenglet (4–0) and Henry (3–0).

## SABRE, INDIVIDUAL

**1896 Athens** C: 5, N: 3, D: 4.9.

| | | W | L | TG | TR |
|---|---|---|---|---|---|
| 1. Ioannis Georgiadis | GRE | 4 | 0 | 12 | 6 |
| 2. Telemachos Karakalos | GRE | 3 | 1 | 11 | 5 |
| 3. Holger Nielsen | DEN | 2 | 2 | 10 | 9 |
| 4. Adolf Schmal | AUT | 1 | 3 | 7 | 11 |
| 5. Georgios Iatridis | GRE | 0 | 4 | 3 | 12 |

**1900 Paris** C: 32, N: 10, D: 6.25.

| 1. Georges de la Falaise | FRA |
|---|---|
| 2. Léon Thiébaut | FRA |
| 3. Siegfried Flesch | AUT |
| 4. Ámon von Gregurich | HUN |
| 5. Gyula von Iványi | HUN |
| 6. de Boissière | FRA |
| 7. Heinrich Terner | AUT |
| 8. Camillo Müller | AUT |

**1904 St. Louis** C: 5, N: 2, D: 9.8.

| | | | | | BARRAGE | |
|---|---|---|---|---|---|---|
| | | W | L | TG | W | L |
| 1. Manuel Diaz | CUB | 3 | 0 | 21 | | |
| 2. William Grebe | USA | 2 | 1 | 20 | 1 | 0 |
| 3. Albertson Van Zo Post | USA | 2 | 1 | 18 | 0 | 1 |
| 4. Theodore Carstens | USA | 1 | 2 | | | |
| 5. Arthur Fox | USA | 0 | 4 | | | |

**1906 Athens** C: 29, N: 8, D: 4.28.

| 1. Ioannis Georgiadis | GRE |
|---|---|
| 2. Gustav Casmir | GER |
| 3. Federico Cesarano | ITA |
| 4. Georges de la Falaise | FRA |
| 5. Ervin Mészáros | HUN |
| 6. Jenö Apáthy | HUN |

**1908 London** C: 76, N: 11, D: 7.24.

| | | | | | BARRAGE | |
|---|---|---|---|---|---|---|
| | | W | L | T | W | L |
| 1. Jenö Fuchs | HUN | 6 | 0 | 1 | 1 | 0 |
| 2. Béla Zulavszky | HUN | 6 | 1 | 0 | 0 | 1 |
| 3. Vilém Goppold von Lobsdorf | BOH | 4 | 2 | 1 | | |
| 4. Jenö Szántay | HUN | 3 | 3 | 1 | | |
| 5. Péter Tóth | HUN | 3 | 4 | 0 | | |
| 6. Lajos Werkner | HUN | 2 | 5 | 0 | | |
| 7. Jetze Doorman | HOL | 1 | 5 | 1 | | |
| 7. Georges de la Falaise | FRA | 1 | 6 | 0 | | |

Dr. Jenö Fuchs, the winner of four sabre gold medals in 1908 and 1912, recorded 22 wins, two losses, and one draw in the individual competition. Fuchs was also active in rowing and bobsledding.

**1912 Stockholm** C: 40, N: 9, D: 8.23.

| | | W | L | TG | TR |
|---|---|---|---|---|---|
| 1. Jenö Fuchs | HUN | 6 | 1 | 18 | 10 |
| 2. Béla Békéssy | HUN | 5 | 2 | 17 | 11 |
| 3. Ervin Mészáros | HUN | 5 | 2 | 17 | 12 |
| 4. Zoltán Schenker | HUN | 4 | 3 | 17 | 13 |
| 5. Nedo Nadi | ITA | 4 | 3 | 16 | 17 |
| 6. Péter Tóth | HUN | 2 | 5 | 12 | 17 |
| 7. Lajos Werkner | HUN | 1 | 6 | 13 | 19 |
| 8. Dezsö Földes | HUN | 1 | 6 | 9 | 20 |

**1920 Antwerp** C: 40, N: 9, D: 8.23.

| | | W | L | TR |
|---|---|---|---|---|
| 1. Nedo Nadi | ITA | 11 | 0 | |
| 2. Aldo Nadi | ITA | 9 | 2 | |
| 3. Adrianus de Jong | HOL | 7 | 4 | |
| 4. Oreste Puliti | ITA | 6 | 5 | 19 |
| 5. Jan van der Wiel | HOL | 6 | 5 | 22 |
| 6. Robert Hennet | BEL | 5 | 6 | 24 |
| 6. Léon Tom | BEL | 5 | 6 | 24 |
| 6. Henri Wijnoldij-Daniels | HOL | 5 | 6 | 24 |

The only break in Hungary's incredible 56-year domination of individual sabre occurred in 1920. Having been on the losing side of World War I, Hungary was not invited to the Antwerp Olympics.

**1924 Paris** C: 47, N: 15, D: 7.18.

| | | | | | | BARRAGE | | | |
|---|---|---|---|---|---|---|---|---|---|
| | | W | L | TG | TR | W | L | TG | TR |
| 1. Sándor Posta | HUN | 5 | 2 | 26 | 20 | 2 | 0 | 8 | 1 |
| 2. Roger Ducret | FRA | 5 | 2 | 22 | 18 | 1 | 1 | 4 | 7 |
| 3. János Garay | HUN | 5 | 2 | 23 | 20 | 0 | 2 | 4 | 8 |
| 4. Zóltan Schenker | HUN | 4 | 3 | 24 | 21 | 1 | 0 | 4 | 3 |
| 5. Adrianus de Jong | HOL | 4 | 3 | 24 | 21 | 0 | 1 | 3 | 4 |
| 6. Ivan Osiier | DEN | 2 | 5 | 15 | 24 | 1 | 0 | 4 | 2 |
| 7. G. J. Conraux | FRA | 2 | 5 | 23 | 22 | 0 | 1 | 2 | 4 |
| 8. H. A. Casco | ARG | 1 | 6 | 16 | 27 | | | | |

The Italians, led by Oreste Puliti, had already defeated the Hungarians to win the team sabre title, and another showdown seemed certain in the individual championship as four Italians and three Hungarians were among the twelve who qualified for the final round. The final matches began with the Official Jury of Appeal ordering the four Italians—Puliti, Bertinetti, Bini, and Sarrocchi—to fight off against each other. As expected, Puliti beat the other three with ease. But the judges were not satisfied. Led by Kovács, the Hungarian judge, they maintained that the other three had thrown their matches against Puliti in order to increase his chances for a gold medal.

Outraged by these accusations, Puliti threatened to cane Judge Kovács. Puliti was disqualified, and Bertinetti, Bini, and Sarrocchi walked out in protest. Two days later Puliti and Kovács ran into each other at a music hall and renewed their argument. When Kovács haughtily told Puliti that he couldn't understand the furious fencer because he didn't speak Italian, Puliti hit the Hungarian in the face and said that Kovács surely couldn't fail to understand that. The two men were pulled apart, but further words were exchanged and a formal duel was proposed.

Four months later Puliti and Kovács met again, at Nagykanizsa on the Yugoslav-Hungarian border. This time they were accompanied by seconds, swords, and spectators. After slashing away at each other for an hour, the two were finally separated by spectators, who had become concerned about the wounds which both men had received. Their honor restored, Puliti and Kovács shook hands and made up.

As for the Olympic competition, it was won by Sándor Posta in a three-way fence-off against fellow Hungarian János Garay and the French champion Roger Ducret, who left the 1924 Olympics with three gold medals and two silver.

**1928 Amsterdam** C: 44, N: 17, D: 8.11.

| | | W | L | TG | TR | BARRAGE TG | BARRAGE TR |
|---|---|---|---|---|---|---|---|
| 1. Ödön Tersztyánszky | HUN | 9 | 2 | 51 | 33 | 5 | 2 |
| 2. Attila Petschauer | HUN | 9 | 2 | 52 | 28 | 2 | 5 |
| 3. Bino Bini | ITA | 8 | 3 | 49 | 32 | | |
| 4. Gustavo Marzi | ITA | 8 | 3 | 49 | 34 | | |
| 5. Sándor Gombos | HUN | 8 | 3 | 49 | 38 | | |
| 6. Erwin Casmir | GER | 6 | 5 | 44 | 32 | | |
| 7. Arturo De Vecchi | ITA | 5 | 6 | 44 | 36 | | |
| 8. Roger Ducret | FRA | 5 | 6 | 42 | 47 | | |

Lieutenant Colonel Tersztyánszky died in an auto accident outside Budapest ten months after winning his gold medal. He was 40 years old.

**1932 Los Angeles** C: 25, N: 12, D: 8.13.

| | | W | L | TG | TR |
|---|---|---|---|---|---|
| 1. György Piller (Jekelfalussy) | HUN | 8 | 1 | 42 | 19 |
| 2. Giulio Gaudini | ITA | 7 | 2 | 39 | 28 |
| 3. Endre Kabos | HUN | 5 | 4 | 36 | 29 |
| 4. Erwin Casmir | GER | 5 | 4 | 32 | 30 |
| 5. Attila Petschauer | HUN | 5 | 4 | 37 | 32 |
| 6. John Huffman | USA | 5 | 4 | 38 | 35 |
| 7. Ivan Osiier | DEN | 4 | 5 | 32 | 35 |
| 8. Arturo De Vecchi | ITA | 3 | 6 | 27 | 36 |

Colonel Piller completed the tournament with a record of 19–2.

**1936 Berlin** C: 71, N: 26, D: 8.15.

| | | W | L | TG | TR |
|---|---|---|---|---|---|
| 1. Endre Kabos | HUN | 7 | 1 | 37 | 20 |
| 2. Gustavo Marzi | ITA | 6 | 2 | 35 | 22 |
| 3. Aladár Gerevich | HUN | 6 | 2 | 37 | 26 |
| 4. László Rajcsányi | HUN | 5 | 3 | 34 | 25 |
| 5. Vincenzo Pinton | ITA | 5 | 3 | 32 | 28 |
| 6. Giulio Gaudini | ITA | 3 | 5 | 27 | 28 |
| 7. Antoni Sobik | POL | 2 | 6 | 22 | 34 |
| 8. Josef Losert | AUT | 2 | 6 | 20 | 36 |

As a student, Kabos received a fencing outfit as a birthday gift from his godfather. He hid it in his wardrobe, but his friends came across it and teased him. The next day

he enrolled in a fencing club to spite them. At the Berlin Olympics Kabos compiled a record of 24–1 to win the gold medal. Kabos was killed during World War II when the Budapest Margaret Bridge blew up, the day before his 38th birthday.

**1948 London** C: 60, N: 24, D: 8.13.

| | | W | L | TG | TR |
|---|---|---|---|---|---|
| 1. Aladár Gerevich | HUN | 7 | 0 | 35 | 18 |
| 2. Vincenzo Pinton | ITA | 5 | 2 | 32 | 23 |
| 3. Pál Kovács | HUN | 5 | 2 | 33 | 24 |
| 4. Jacques Lefèvre | FRA | 4 | 3 | 27 | 26 |
| 5. George Worth | USA | 2 | 5 | 26 | 27 |
| 6. Gastone Darè | ITA | 2 | 5 | 25 | 30 |
| 7. Tibor Nyilas | USA | 2 | 5 | 20 | 31 |
| 8. Antonio Oliva Haro | MEX | 1 | 6 | 15 | 34 |

Aladár Gerevich competed in six Olympics between 1932 and 1960 (when he was 50 years old). He won seven gold medals, one silver, and two bronze. In winning his only individual gold medal Gerevich scored 19 victories against only one defeat.

**1952 Helsinki** C: 66, N: 26, D: 8.1.

| | | W | L | TR |
|---|---|---|---|---|
| 1. Pál Kovács | HUN | 8 | 0 | 19 |
| 2. Aladár Gerevich | HUN | 7 | 1 | 16 |
| 3. Tibor Berczelly | HUN | 5 | 3 | 22 |
| 4. Gastone Darè | ITA | 5 | 3 | 27 |
| 5. Werner Plattner | AUT | 4 | 4 | 34 |
| 6. Jacques Lefèvre | FRA | 3 | 5 | 25 |
| 7. Vincenzo Pinton | ITA | 2 | 6 | 32 |
| 8. Heinz Lechner | AUT | 2 | 6 | 35 |

Kovács was the third straight Hungarian to win the sabre gold after winning the bronze in the previous Olympics. Kovács was 40 years old and had first won the world sabre championship fifteen years earlier. In the final pool he needed one last victory to clinch the gold medal. Trailing Pinton 4–2, he scored three hits in the final minute to secure the championship with an undefeated record of 19–0. A mechanic, Kovács ultimately earned six Olympic gold medals.

**1956 Melbourne** C: 35, N: 17, D: 12.5.

| | | W | L | TG | TR | BARRAGE TG | BARRAGE TR |
|---|---|---|---|---|---|---|---|
| 1. Rudolf Kárpáti | HUN | 6 | 1 | 32 | 19 | | |
| 2. Jerzy Pawlowski | POL | 5 | 2 | 30 | 22 | | |
| 3. Lev Kuznyetsov | SOV | 4 | 3 | 29 | 24 | 5 | 2 |
| 4. Jacques Lefèvre | FRA | 4 | 3 | 27 | 25 | 2 | 5 |
| 5. Aladár Gerevich | HUN | 3 | 4 | 30 | 31 | | |
| 6. Wojciech Zablocki | POL | 2 | 5 | 17 | 29 | | |
| 7. Pál Kovács | HUN | 2 | 5 | 25 | 30 | | |
| 8. Luigi Narduzzi | ITA | 2 | 5 | 21 | 31 | | |

The 36-year-old Kárpáti, eventual winner of six Olympic gold medals, earned his first individual championship by putting together 18 victories against only one loss (to Pawlowski). Kárpáti believed that his love of music contributed to his skills as a fencer, since both are based on rhythm and timing.

**1960 Rome** C: 70, N: 29, D: 9.8.

|   |   |   | W | L | TG | TR | BARRAGE W | L | TG | TR |
|---|---|---|---|---|----|----|-----------|---|----|----|
| 1. | Rudolf Kárpáti | HUN | 5 | 2 | 31 | 25 | | | | |
| 2. | Zoltán Horváth | HUN | 4 | 3 | 29 | 26 | 2 | 1 | 14 | 8 |
| 3. | Wladimiro Calarese | ITA | 4 | 3 | 31 | 29 | 2 | 1 | 13 | 12 |
| 4. | Claude Arabo | FRA | 4 | 3 | 31 | 29 | 2 | 1 | 11 | 12 |
| 5. | Wojciech Zablocki | POL | 4 | 3 | 27 | 26 | 0 | 3 | 9 | 15 |
| 6. | Jerzy Pawlowski | POL | 3 | 4 | 28 | 28 | | | | |
| 7. | David Tyshler | SOV | 2 | 5 | 24 | 29 | | | | |
| 8. | Yakov Rylsky | SOV | 2 | 5 | 21 | 32 | | | | |

Following the quarterfinal round, the French team lodged a protest against Kárpáti, claiming the defending champion had purposely lost to Rohonyi of Romania in order to ensure that he, instead of Lefèvre of France, would advance to the next round. The protest was overruled. In the semifinals Kárpáti's loss to Arabo allowed the Frenchman to qualify for the final without a barrage. This time no protest was filed.

**1964 Tokyo** C: 52, N: 21, D: 10.20.

|   |   |   | W | L | TG | TR | BARRAGE TG | TR |
|---|---|---|---|---|----|----|------------|-----|
| 1. | Tibor Pézsa | HUN | 2 | 1 | 13 | 13 | 5 | 2 |
| 2. | Claude Arabo | FRA | 2 | 1 | 14 | 9 | 2 | 5 |
| 3. | Umar Mavlikhanov | SOV | 1 | 2 | 9 | 13 | 5 | 3 |
| 4. | Yakov Rylsky | SOV | 1 | 2 | 11 | 12 | 3 | 5 |
| 5. | Emil Ochyra | POL | | | | | | |
| 6. | Marcel Parent | FRA | | | | | | |
| 7. | Walter Köstner | GER | | | | | | |
| 8. | Dieter Wellmann | GER | | | | | | |

Pézsa won despite a relatively unimpressive overall record of 12 wins and seven losses.

**1968 Mexico City** C: 40, N: 16, D: 10.17.

|   |   |   | W | L | TG | TR | BARRAGE TG | TR |
|---|---|---|---|---|----|----|------------|-----|
| 1. | Jerzy Pawlowski | POL | 4 | 1 | 22 | 18 | 5 | 4 |
| 2. | Mark Rakita | SOV | 4 | 1 | 24 | 16 | 4 | 5 |
| 3. | Tibor Pézsa | HUN | 3 | 2 | 20 | 16 | | |
| 4. | Vladimir Nazlymov | SOV | 3 | 2 | 21 | 17 | | |
| 5. | Rolando Rigoli | ITA | 1 | 4 | 11 | 21 | | |
| 6. | József Nowara | POL | 0 | 5 | 15 | 25 | | |
| 7. | Umar Mavlikhanov | SOV | | | | | | |
| 8. | Serge Panizza | FRA | | | | | | |

In June, Pawlowski, a 35-year-old major in the Polish Army, received his master's degree in law, having written his dissertation on "A Critique of Hayek's Neo-Liberal Conception of Liberty and Law." In the final pool Pawlowski defeated world champion Mark Rakita 5–4. Then he beat him again by the same score in the barrage, to achieve a final win-loss total of 16-2. Pawlowski became interested in fencing at age 16 when he saw films of the 1948 London Olympics. He was world sabre champion

three times (in 1957, 1965, 1966) and runner-up four times. In his military pursuits, Pawlowski was considered a protégé of General Wojciech Jaruzelski, who later became Premier of Poland. In 1981 Pawlowski was asked by the Polish government to become a spy. When he refused, he was charged with *being* a spy and sentenced to twenty-five years in prison. His name was also removed from all Polish books about the Olympics.

**1972 Munich** C: 54, N: 23, D: 8.31.

|   |   |   | W | L | TG | TR |
|---|---|---|---|---|----|----|
| 1. | Viktor Sidiak | SOV | 4 | 1 | 23 | 15 |
| 2. | Péter Maróth | HUN | 3 | 2 | 21 | 20 |
| 3. | Vladimir Nazlymov | SOV | 3 | 2 | 21 | 21 |
| 4. | Michele Maffei | ITA | 3 | 2 | 20 | 21 |
| 5. | Regis Bonissent | FRA | 1 | 4 | 19 | 22 |
| 6. | Tamás Kovács | HUN | 1 | 4 | 17 | 22 |

Maffei, Kovács, and Sidiak each entered the final pool with records of 17–3, but Sidiak, emitting a growl each time he scored a hit, prevailed.

**1976 Montreal** C: 46, N: 18, D: 7.22.

|   |   |   | W | L | TG | TR |
|---|---|---|---|---|----|----|
| 1. | Viktor Krovopuskov | SOV | 5 | 0 | 25 | 14 |
| 2. | Vladimir Nazlymov | SOV | 4 | 1 | 23 | 18 |
| 3. | Viktor Sidiak | SOV | 3 | 2 | 22 | 20 |
| 4. | Ioan Pop | ROM | 2 | 3 | 22 | 20 |
| 5. | Mario Montano | ITA | 1 | 4 | 10 | 21 |
| 6. | Michele Maffei | ITA | 0 | 5 | 13 | 25 |
| 7. | Francisco de La Torre | CUB | | | | |
| 7. | Imre Gedövári | HUN | | | | |

**1980 Moscow** C: 30, N: 12, D: 7.25.

|   |   |   | W | L | TG | TR | BARRAGE TG | TR |
|---|---|---|---|---|----|----|------------|-----|
| 1. | Viktor Krovopuskov | SOV | 4 | 1 | 24 | 17 | 5 | 3 |
| 2. | Mikhail Burtsev | SOV | 4 | 1 | 23 | 18 | 3 | 5 |
| 3. | Imre Gedovari | HUN | 3 | 2 | 23 | 21 | | |
| 4. | Vassil Etropolski | BUL | 2 | 3 | 17 | 23 | | |
| 5. | Hristo Etropolski | BUL | 1 | 4 | 10 | 21 | | |
| 6. | Michele Maffei | ITA | 1 | 4 | 15 | 21 | | |
| 7. | Ferdinando Meglio | ITA | | | | | | |
| 7. | Vladimir Nazlymov | SOV | | | | | | |

Burtsev beat Krovopuskov in the final pool, 5–4, but Krovopuskov turned the tables in the barrage to become the third repeat winner in individual sabre.

**1984 Los Angeles-Long Beach** C: 33, N: 14, D: 8.4.
1. Jean François Lamour FRA
2. Marco Marin ITA
3. Peter Westbrook USA
4. Hervé Granger Veyron FRA
5. Pierre Guichot FRA
6. Marin Mustaţă ROM
7. Giovanni Scalzo ITA
8. Ioan Pop ROM
Final: Lamour 12–11 Marin
3rd Place: Westbrook 10–5 Granger-Veyron

The sabre competition was severely depleted by the Soviet-bloc boycott. However, Lamour's performance was nonetheless impressive, as he won all 19 of his bouts.

**1988 Seoul** C: 40, N: 18, D: 9.23.
1. Jean François Lamour    FRA
2. Janusz Olech    POL
3. Giovanni Scalzo    ITA
4. Philippe Delrieu    FRA
5. György Nébald    HUN
6. Georgy Pogosov    SOV
7. Felix Becker    GER
8. Jürgen Nolte    GER
    Final: Lamour 10–4 Olech
    3rd Place: Scalzo 10–2 Delrieu

When Lamour first competed in the Olympics in 1980, he was the only member of the 16-man French squad to go home without a medal. He finished twenty-first. When he was crowned Olympic champion in 1984, many French fencing aficionados scorned his victory over a boycott-depleted field and spoke of him winning a medal not of gold, but of chocolate. Lamour silenced his critics by winning the 1987 world championships and then repeating his Olympic triumph in Seoul.

## SABRE, TEAM

**1896–1904** not held

**1906 Athens** T: 4, N: 4, D: 4.28.
1. GER    (Gustav Casmir, Jacob Erckrath de Bary, August Petri, Emil Schön)
2. GRE    (Jean Georgiadis, Menelaos Sakorraphos, Ch. Zorbas, Triantaphylos Kordogiannis)
3. HOL    (James van Carnbee, Johannes Osten, George van Rossem, Maurits van Löben Sels)
4. HUN    (Péter Tóth, Jëno Apáthy, Ervin Mészáros, Bela Nagy)

**1908 London** T: 8, N: 8, D: 7.23.
1. HUN    (Jëno Fuchs, Oszkár Gerde, Péter Tóth, Lajos Werkner, Dezsö Földes)
2. ITA    (Riccardo Nowak, Alessandro Pirzio-Biroli, Abelardo Olivier, Marcello Bertinetti, Sante Ceccherini)
3. BOH    (Vilém Goppold von Lobsdorf, Jaroslav Tuček, Vlastimil Lada-Sázavsky, Otakar Lada, Bedřich Schejbal)
4. FRA    (Georges de la Falaise, B. de Lesseps, Marc Perrodon, Jean Joseph Renaud)
    Final: HUN 9–7 BOH

Péter Tóth of the Hungarian team became involved in a fight with a fellow student at age 15 and was challenged to a duel. After consultation with their classmates, the boys decided to postpone the duel until after final examinations. In the meantime Tóth enrolled in a fencing school and became so proficient that when final exams were over his opponent decided to drop the matter. Eleven years later Tóth won the first of his team sabre gold medals. Dr. Dezsö Földes, another member of the Hungarian team, emigrated to the United States in 1912 and set up a clinic for the poor in Cleveland.

In 1908, second place was contested by a pool of those teams which had lost to Hungary. Bohemia refused to take part, so Italy defeated Germany for second place.

**1912 Stockholm** T: 11, N: 11, D: 7.15.
1. HUN    (Jenö Fuchs, László Berti, Ervin Mészáros, Dezsö Földes, Oszkàr Gerde, Zoltán Schenker, Péter Tóth, Lajos Werkner)
2. AUT    (Richard Verderber, Otto Herschmann, Rudolf Cvetko, Friedrich Golling, Andreas Suttner, Albert Bogen, Reinhold Trampler)
3. HOL    (Willem van Blijenburgh, George van Rossem, Adrianus de Jong, Jetze Doorman, Dirk Scalongne, Hendrik de Iongh)
4. BOH    (Vilém Goppold von Lobsdorf, Otakar Svorcik, Josef Javurek, František Kříž, Zdeněk Bárta, Josef Pfeiffer, Bedřich Schejbal, Josef Čipera)
5. BEL, GBR, GER, RUS

**1920 Antwerp** T: 8, N: 8, D: 8.23.

| | | | | MATCHES | |
|---|---|---|---|---|---|
| | | WON | LOST | W | L |
| 1. ITA | (Nedo Nadi, Aldo Nadi, Oreste Puliti, Baldo Baldi, Francesco Gargano, Giorgio Santelli, Dino Urbani) | 6 | 0 | 76 | 20 |
| 2. FRA | (Georges Trombert, J. Margraff, Marc Perrodon, Henri de Saint Germain, Jean Lacroix, Mondielli) | 5 | 1 | 54 | 42 |
| 3. HOL | (Jan van der Wiel, Adrianus de Jong, Jetze Doorman, William van Blijenburgh, Louis Delaunoy, Salomon Zeidenrust, Henri Wijnoldij-Daniels) | 4 | 2 | 51 | 45 |
| 4. BEL | (Robert Hennet, Pierre Calle, Alexis Simonson, Léon Tom, Robert Feyerick, Charles Delporte, Harry Dombeeck) | 3 | 3 | 47 | 47 |
| 5. USA | (Edwin Fulinwidder, Arthur Lyon, Joseph Brooks Parker, John Dimond, Frederick Cunningham, Claiborne Walker, C. Bradford Fraley, Roscoe Bowman) | 2 | 4 | 37 | 59 |
| 6. DEN | (Ivan Osiier, Poul Rasmussen, Ejnar Levison, Aage Berntsen, William Bonde) | 1 | 5 | 39 | 55 |
| 7. CZE | | 0 | 2 | 9 | 23 |
| 7. GBR | (Alfred Ridley-Martin, William Marsh, W. Hammond, Cecil Kershaw, Ronald Campbell, Robin Daglish, Herbert Huntington) | 0 | 4 | 21 | 43 |

**1924 Paris** T: 14, N: 14, D: 7.15.

| | | | | MATCHES | |
|---|---|---|---|---|---|
| | | WON | LOST | W | L |
| 1. ITA | (Renato Anselmi, Guido Balzarini, Marcello Berti-netti, Bino Bini, Vincenzo Cuccia, Oreste Moricca, Oreste Puliti, Giulio Sarroc-chi) | 3 | 0 | 28 | 20 |
| 2. HUN | (László Berti, János Garay, Sándor Pósta, Jozsef Rády, Zoltán Schenker, Laszlo Széchy, Ödön Tersztyánszky, Jenö Uhlyá-rik) | 2 | 1 | 33 | 15 |
| 3. HOL | (Adrianus de Jong, Jetze Doorman, Hendrik Scher-penhuizen, Jan van der Wiel, Maarten van Dulm, Henri Wijnoldij-Daniels) | 1 | 2 | 18 | 30 |
| 4. CZE | (František Dvořák, Alexan-der Bárta, Josef Jung-mann, Luděk Oppl, Otakar Švorčik) | 0 | 3 | 17 | 31 |
| 5. ARG | (C. F. Camet, H. A. Casco, C. Guerrico, C. Merlo, P. Nazar-Anchorena, A. Ponce-Costa, R. Sola, S. Torres Blanco) | | | | |
| 5. FRA | (G. J. Conraux, De Saint Germain, J. F. Jannekeyn, L. Lifschitz, J. A. Margraff, M. M. J. Perrodon, M. M. Taillandier, G. O. E. Trombert) | | | | |

The crucial match between Italy and Hungary ended in an 8–8 tie, but Italy won by four touches, 46 to 50. Puliti was the star of the tournament, winning 26 of 28 bouts and scoring 110 touches while receiving only 39.

**1928 Amsterdam** T: 12, N: 12, D: 8.9.

| | | | | MATCHES | |
|---|---|---|---|---|---|
| | | WON | LOST | W | L |
| 1. HUN | (Ödön Tersztyánszky, Sán-dor Gombos, Attila Pet-schauèr, János Garay, Jó-zsef Rády, Gyula Glykais) | 2 | 0 | 23 | 9 |
| 2. ITA | (Bino Bini, Renato Ansel-mi, Gustavo Marzi, Oreste Puliti, Emilio Salafia, Giulio Sarrocchi) | 1 | 1 | 21 | 11 |
| 3. POL | (Adam Papée, Tadeusz Friedrich, Kazimierz Las-kowski, Wladyslaw Segda, Aleksander Malecki, Jerzy Zabielski) | 1 | 1 | 11 | 21 |

| 4. GER | (Erwin Casmir, Heinrich Moos, Hans Halberstadt, Hans Thomson) | 0 | 2 | 9 | 23 |
|---|---|---|---|---|---|
| 5. FRA | (R. G. Fristeau, Roger Ducret, Jean Lacroix, M. M. Taillandier, J. Piot, P. A. V. Oziol de Pignol) | | | | |
| 5. HOL | (C. W. Ekkart, H. G. Ha-gens, Maarten van Dulm, Jan van der Wiel, Adrianus de Jong, Henri Wijnoldij-Daniels) | | | | |
| 7. BEL | (J. Stordeur, M. Cuypers, J. Kesteloot, E. Yves, G. Kaanen) | | | | |
| 7. TUR | (T. Mouhiddin, E. Fouad, D. Nami, E. Enver) | | | | |

Hungary defeated Italy 9–7 in the decisive match. The Hungarian team was led by the high-strung 23-year-old Attila Petschauer of Budapest, who won all 20 of his bouts. While fighting in the Ukraine in 1943, Petschauer was tortured to death by anti-Semitic Hungarian army officers.

**1932 Los Angeles** T: 6, N: 6, D: 8.11.

| | | | | MATCHES | |
|---|---|---|---|---|---|
| | | WON | LOST | W | L |
| 1. HUN | (György Piller, Endre Ka-bos, Attila Petschauer, Ernö Nagy, Gyula Glykais, Aladár Gerevich) | 3 | 0 | 31 | 6 |
| 2. ITA | (Renato Anselmi, Arturo De Vecchi, Emilio Salafia, Ugo Pignotti, Gustavo Marzi, Giulio Guadini) | 2 | 1 | 20 | 14 |
| 3. POL | (Adam Papée, Tadeusz Friedrich, Wladyslaw Seg-da, Leszek Lubicz-Nyzz, Wladyslaw Doborowolski, Marian Šuski) | 1 | 2 | 10 | 26 |
| 4. USA | (Peter Bruder, John Huff-man, Norman Armitage, Nikolas Muray, Harold van Buskirk, Ralph Faulkner) | 0 | 3 | 16 | 30 |

Hungary won 56 bouts and lost only nine.

**1936 Berlin** T: 21, N: 21, D: 8.13.

| | | | | MATCHES | |
|---|---|---|---|---|---|
| | | WON | LOST | W | L |
| 1. HUN | (Tibor Berczelly, László Rajcsányi, Pál Kovács, Aladár Gerevich, Imre Rajczy, Endre Kabos) | 3 | 0 | 32 | 10 |
| 2. ITA | (Vincenzo Pinton, Giulio Gaudini, Aldo Masciotta, Gustavo Marzi, Aldo Mon-tano, Athos Tanzini) | 2 | 1 | 25 | 17 |

|  |  | WON | LOST | MATCHES | |
|---|---|---|---|---|---|
|  |  |  |  | W | L |
| 3. GER | (Richard Wahl, Julius Eisenecker, Erwin Casmir, August Heim, Hans Esser, Hans Jörger) | 1 | 2 | 14 | 25 |
| 4. POL | (Antoni Sobik, Wladyslaw Sagda, Wladyslaw Dobrowolski, Adam Papée, Marian Suski, Teodor Zaczyk) | 0 | 3 | 10 | 29 |
| 5. AUT | (Josef Losert, Hugo Weczerek, Karl Sudrich, Hubert Loisel, Karl Hanisch, Karl Kaschka) |  |  |  |  |
| 5. FRA | (Marcel Faure, Maurice Gramain, Edward Gardere, Jean Piot, Roger Barisien, André Gardere) |  |  |  |  |
| 5. HOL | (Ate Faber, Antonius Montfoort, Franciscus Mosman, Franciscus van Wieringen, Jacob Schriever) |  |  |  |  |
| 5. USA | (Peter Bruder, Miguel de Capriles, Bela de Nagy, John Huffman, Samuel Stewart, Norman Armitage) |  |  |  |  |

The Hungarians won their first seven matches by scores of 13–3 or better, and then defeated Italy 9–6 to win the gold medal. Their final bout total was 106 wins and 16 losses. Leading Hungarian scorers were Berczelly (24–3), Kovács (21–2), Rajcsányi (20–4) and Gerevich (17–2).

**1948 London** T: 17, N: 17, D: 8.11.

|  |  | WON | LOST | MATCHES | |
|---|---|---|---|---|---|
|  |  |  |  | W | L |
| 1. HUN | (Tibor Berczelly, Rudolf Kárpáti, Aladár Gerevich, Pál Kovács, László Rajcsányi, Bertalan Papp) | 3 | 0 | 29 | 13 |
| 2. ITA | (Gastone Darè, Carlo Turcato, Vincenzo Pinton, Mauro Racca, Aldo Montano, Renzo Nostini) | 2 | 1 | 24 | 24 |
| 3. USA | (Norman Armitage, George Worth, Tibor Nyilas, Dean Cetrulo, Miguel de Capriles, James Flynn) | 1 | 2 | 24 | 23 |
| 4. BEL | (Robert Bayot, Georges de Bourguignon, Ferdinand Jassogne, Eugène Laermans, Marcel Nys, Edouard Yves) | 0 | 3 | 12 | 29 |
| 5. ARG | (M. Aguero, José Luis D'Andrea Mohr, Edgardo Pomini, J. Cermesoni, F. Huergo, Daniel Sande) |  |  |  |  |

| 5. FRA | (Jean-François Tournon, J. Parent, M. Gramain, Jacques Lefèvre, Jean Levavasseur, G. Leveque) |
| 5. HOL | (H. Ter Weer, A. Hoevers, W. Van den Berg, F. Mosman, L. Kuijpers) |
| 5. POL | (Antoni Sobik, Boleslaw Banas, Teodor Zaczyk, Jerzy Wójcik, Jan Nawrocki) |

Berczelly had a 15–2 record, including four straight victories in the final 10–6 defeat of Italy. Hungary's total for the tournament was 65 wins and 20 losses.

**1952 Helsinki** T: 19, N: 19, D: 7.30.

|  |  | WON | LOST | MATCHES | |
|---|---|---|---|---|---|
|  |  |  |  | W | L |
| 1. HUN | (Bertalan Papp, László Rajcsányi, Rudolf Kárpáti, Aladár Gerevich, Pál Kovács, Tibor Berczelly) | 3 | 0 | 34 | 13 |
| 2. ITA | (Vincenzo Pintoh, Mauro Racca, Roberto Ferrari, Gastone Darè, Renzo Nostini, Giorgio Pellini) | 2 | 1 | 32 | 15 |
| 3. FRA | (Jacques Lefèvre, Jean Laroyenne, Maurice Piot, Jean Levavasseur, Bernard Morel, Jean-François Tournon) | 1 | 2 | 14 | 32 |
| 4. USA | (Norman Armitage, Miguel de Capriles, Tibor Nyilas, Alex Treves, George Worth, Allan Kwartler) | 0 | 3 | 13 | 33 |
| 5. AUT | (Werner Plattner, Heinz Putzl, Hubert Loisel, Heinz Lechner, Paul Kerb) |  |  |  |  |
| 5. BEL | (Marcel van der Auwera, Gustave Balister, François Heyvaert, Robert Bayot, Georges de Bourguignon, Edouard Yves) |  |  |  |  |
| 5. GBR | (Roger Tredgold, Olgierd Porebski, Robert Andersson, William Beatley, Ulrich Luke Wendon) |  |  |  |  |
| 5. POL | (Jerzy Twardokens, Leszek Suski, Jerzy Pawlowski, Wojciech Zablocki, Zygmunt Pawlas) |  |  |  |  |

Great tension built up in the final contest as Hungary's string of 35 victories and four Olympic gold medals appeared in jeopardy when Italy took a 7–5 lead. Then Berczelly beat Nostini 5–0 and Kárpáti beat Ferrari 5–0 to even the match at 7–7. Gerevich, who had lost his other three bouts against the Italians, recovered to defeat Enzo Pinton 5–3 and give Hungary an insurmountable lead of 8–7, with a 14-touch advantage. Hungary's tournament totals were 111 wins and 25 losses.

**1956 Melbourne** T: 8, N: 8, D: 12.3.

| | WON | LOST | MATCHES | |
|---|---|---|---|---|
| | | | W | L |
| 1. HUN (Attila Keresztes, Pál Kovács, Rudolf Kárpáti, Aladár Gerevich, Jenö Hámori, Dániel Magay) | 3 | 0 | 30 | 15 |
| 2. POL (Jerzy Pawlowski, Wojciech Zablocki, Marek Kuszewski, Zygmunt Pawlas, Ryszard Zub, Andrzej Piatkowski) | 2 | 1 | 23 | 22 |
| 3. SOV (Lev Kuznyetsov, Yakov Rylsky, Yevgeny Cherepovsky, David Tyschler, Leonid Bogdanov) | 1 | 2 | 22 | 25 |
| 4. FRA (Claude Gamot, Jacques Lefèvre, Bernard Morel, Jacques Roulot) | 0 | 3 | 17 | 30 |
| 5. ITA (Roberto Ferrari, Domenico Pace, Mario Ravagnan, Giuseppe Comini, Luigi Narduzzi, Gastone Daré) | | | | |

By 1956 the sabre contests were the only ones which were not using electronic scoring. Tensions were high during the match between Hungary and the U.S.S.R., since the Soviets had just invaded Hungary. The Hungarians were victorious, 9–7. After the Olympics Keresztes, Hámori, and Magay defected to the West. Keresztes and Hámori fenced for the United States in the 1964 Olympics.

**1960 Rome** T: 16, N: 16, D: 9.10.
1. HUN (Zoltán Horváth, Rudolf Kárpáti, Tamás Mendelényi, Pál Kovács, Gábor Delneky, Aladár Gerevich)
2. POL (Andrzej Piatkowski, Emil Ochyra, Wojciech Zablocki, Jerzy Pawlowski, Ryszard Zub, Marek Kuszewski)
3. ITA (Wladimiro Calarese, Gianpaolo Calanchini, Pierluigi Chicca, Mario Ravagnan, Roberto Ferrari)
4. USA (Allan Kwartler, George Worth, Michael D'Asaro, Alfonso Morales, Tibor Nyilas, R. Richard Dyer)
5. FRA (Marcel Parent, Claude Gamot, Jacques Lefèvre, Jacques Roulot, Claude Arabo)
5. GER (Dieter Lohr, Jürgen Theuerkauff, Wilfried Wohler, Peter von Krockov, Walter Köstner)
5. ROM (Dimitri Mustaţă, Cornel Pelmus, Ion Szanto, Ladislau Rohonyi, Eméric Arus)
5. SOV (Yevgeny Cherepovsky, Umar Mavlikhanov, Nugzar Asatiani, David Tyschler, Yakov Rylsky)
Final: HUN 9–7 POL
3rd Place: ITA 9–6 USA

In the match for first place, Poland took a 3–0 lead. Then Hungary won five in a row, but Poland came back to tie it, 6–6. Finally Kárpáti beat Pawlowski 5–3 to secure the

gold medal. Gerevich, 50 years old, won his sixth straight team sabre gold medal.

### HUNGARY'S TEAM SABRE WINNING STREAK

| | | |
|---|---|---|
| 1924 | 1948 | 1960 |
| 14 HOL 2 | 9 EGY 3 | 9 BEL 3 |
| 11 CZE 5 | 15 ARG 1 | |
| | 12 POL 3 | 9 ROM 3 |
| 1928 | 10 USA 6 | 9 ITA 6 |
| 14 USA 2 | 9 BEL 1 | 9 POL 7 |
| 13 GBR 3 | 10 ITA 6 | |
| 12 GER 4 | | 1964 |
| 12 FRA 4 | 1952 | 9 ARG 2 |
| 14 POL 2 | 15 POR 1 | 9 ROM 0 |
| 9 ITA 7 | 15 SAA 1 | |
| 11 DEN 1 | 9 DEN 0 | |
| | 13 FRA 3 | |
| 1932 | 13 BEL 3 | |
| 14 MEX 2 | 12 AUT 4 | |
| 13 USA 3 | 13 FRA 3 | |
| 9 ITA 2 | 13 USA 3 | |
| 9 POL 1 | 8 ITA 7 | |
| 1936 | 1956 | |
| 16 DEN 0 | 9 USA 1 | |
| 14 URU 2 | 12 FRA 4 | |
| 15 GER 1 | 9 SOV 7 | |
| 15 HOL 1 | 9 POL 4 | |
| 14 USA 2 | | |
| 13 GER 3 | | |
| 10 POL 1 | | |
| 9 ITA 6 | | |

**1964 Tokyo** T: 13, N: 13, D: 10.23.
1. SOV (Yakov Rylsky, Nugzar Asatiani, Mark Rakita, Umar Mavlikhanov, Boris Melnikov)
2. ITA (Wladimiro Calarese, Cesare Salvadori, Gianpaolo Calanchini, Pierluigi Chicca, Mario Ravagnan)
3. POL (Emil Ochyra, Jerzy Pawlowski, Ryszard Zub, Andrzej Piatkowski, Wojciech Zablocki)
4. FRA (Jean Ramez, Jacques Lefèvre, Claude Arabo, Marcel Parent, Robert Fraisse)
5. HUN (Péter Bakonyi, Miklós Meszéna, Attila Kovács, Zoltan Horvath, Tibor Pézsa)
6. GER (Dieter Wellmann, Klaus Allissat, Walter Köstner, Jürgen Theuerkauff, Percy Borucki)
7. ROM (Attila Csipler, Octavian Vintila, Tanase Muresan, Ionel Drimba)
7. USA (Alfonso Morales, Robert Blum, Eugene [Jenö] Hamori, Attila Keresztes, Thomas Orley)
Final: SOV 9–6 ITA
3rd Place: POL 8(60)–8(59) FRA
5th Place: HUN 9–3 GER

In the semifinals Hungary's winning streak was finally stopped at 46 when they were upset by Italy, 9–7. It was

Italy that had handed the Hungarians their last defeat 40 years earlier in Paris.

**1968 Mexico City** T: 12, N: 12, D: 10.21.
1. SOV (Vladimir Nazlymov, Eduard Vinokurov, Viktor Sidiak, Mark Rakita, Umar Mavlikhanov)
2. ITA (Wladimiro Calarese, Cesare Salvadori, Michele Maffei, Pierluigi Chicca, Rolando Rigoli)
3. HUN (Tamás Kóvács, Miklós Meszéna, Janos Kalmar, Péter Bakonyi, Tibor Pézsa)
4. FRA (Marcel Parent, Claude Arabo, Bernard Vallée, Serge Panizza, Jean Ramez)
5. POL (Jerzy Pawlowski, Józef Nowara, Franciszek Sobczak, Zygmunt Kawecki, Emil Ochyra)
6. USA (Alex Orban, Alfonso Morales, Anthony Keane, Robert Blum, Thomas Balla)
7. GBR (Alexander Leckie, Rodney Craig, David Acfield, Richard Oldcorn)
7. GER (Percy Borucki, Walter Köstner, Paul Wischeidt, Klaus Allisat, Volker Duschner)
   Final: SOV 9–7 ITA
   3rd Place: HUN 9–5 FRA
   5th Place: POL 9–5 USA

**1972: Munich** T: 13, N: 13, D: 9.4.
1. ITA (Michele Maffei, Mario Aldo Montano, Cesare Salvadori, Mario Tullio Montano, Rolando Rigoli)
2. SOV (Mark Rakita, Eduard Vinokurov, Viktor Bajenov, Victor Sidiak, Vladimir Nazlymov)
3. HUN (Pál Gerevich, Támás Kovács, Péter Marót, Tibor Pézsa, Péter Bakonyi)
4. ROM (Dan Irimiciuc, Iosif Budahazi, Gheorghe Culcea, Constantin Nicolae, Octavian Vintila)
5. POL (Józef Nowara, Krzysztof Grzegorek, Zygmunt Kawecki, Jerzy Pawlowski, Janusz Majewski)
6. CUB (Hilario Hipolito, Guzman Salazar, Francisco de la Torre, Manuel Ortiz, Manuel Suarez)
7. FRA (Regis Bonnissent, Bernard Dumont, Bernard Vallee, Philippe Bena, Serge Panizza)
7. GER (Walter Convents, Volker Duschner, Knut Höhne, Dieter Wellmann, Paul Wischeidt)
   Final: ITA 9–5 SOV
   3rd Place: HUN 8–7 ROM
   5th Place: POL 9–5 CUB

Maffei defeated all four Soviet fencers in the final, but it was Aldo Montano who won the decisive bout with Vinokurov, 5–1. Montano had previously been warned by the officials not to remove his mask before a decision had been announced. When he scored the winning hit the 205-pound Montano leaped up and down while his team manager and his cousin (and teammate), Tullio Montano, desperately held on to his helmet until the official call was made.

**1976 Montreal** T: 13, N: 13, D: 7.27.
1. SOV (Edouard Vinokurov, Viktor Krovopuskov, Mikhail Burtsev, Viktor Sidiak, Vladimir Nazlymov)
2. ITA (Mario Aldo Montano, Michele Maffei, Angelo Arcidiacono, Tommaso Montano, Mario Tullio Montano)

3. ROM (Dan Irimiciuc, Ioan Pop, Marin Mustaţă, Corneliu Marin, Alexandru Nilca)
4. HUN (Péter Marót, Tamás Kovács, Imre Gedóvari, Ferenc Hammang, Csaba Körmöczi)
5. CUB (Manuel Ortiz, Francisco de La Torre, Guzman Salazar, Ramon Hernandez, Lazaro Mora)
6. POL (Leszek Jablonowski, Sylwester Królikowski, Jacek Bierkowski, Józef Nowara)
7. USA (Paul Apostol, Peter Westbrook, Stephen Kaplan, Thomas Losonczy, Alex Orban)
7. FRA (Philippe Bena, Regis Bonnissent, Bernard Dumont, Didier Flament, Patrick Quivrin)
   Final: SOV 9–4 ITA
   3rd Place: ROM 9–4 HUN
   5th Place: CUB 9–6 POL

**1980 Moscow** T: 8, N: 8, D: 7.29.
1. SOV (Mikhail Burtsev, Viktor Krovopuskov, Viktor Sidiak, Vladimir Nazlymov, Nikolai Alyokhin)
2. ITA (Michele Maffei, Mario Aldo Montano, Marco Romano, Ferdinando Meglio)
3. HUN (Imre Gedövari, Rudolf Nebald, Pál Gerevich, Ferenc Hammang, György Nebald)
4. POL (Tadeusz Pigula, Leszek Jablonowski, Jacek Bierkowski, Andrzej Kostrzewa)
5. ROM (Ioan Pop, Marin Mustaţă, Corneliu Marin, Ion Pantelimonescu, Alexandru Nilca)
6. GDR (Rüdiger Müller, Hendrik Jung, Peter Ulbrich, Frank-Eberhard Höltje, Gerd May)
7. CUB (Manuel Ortiz, Jesus Ortiz, Jose Laverdecia, Guzman Salazar)
8. BUL (Hristo Etropolski, Nikolai Marincheshki, Vassil Etropolski, Georgi Chomakov, Marin Ivanov)
   Final: SOV 9–2 ITA
   3rd Place: HUN 9–6 POL
   5th Place: ROM 9–6 GDR

**1984 Los Angeles-Long Beach** T: 8, N: 8, D: 8.9.
1. ITA (Marco Marin, Gianfranco Dalla Barba, Giovanni Scalzo, Ferdinando Meglio, Angelo Arcidiacono)
2. FRA (Jean François Lamour, Pierre Guichot, Hervé Granger Veyron, Philippe Delrieu, Franck Ducheix)
3. ROM (Marin Mustaţă, Ioan Pop, Alexandru Chiculita, Corneliu Marin, Vilmos Szabo)
4. GER (Dieter Schneider, Jürgen Nolte, Freddy Scholz, Jörg Stratmann, Jörg Volkmann)
5. CHN (Wang Ruiji, Chen Jinchu, Yang Shisheng, Liu Guozhen, Liu Yunhong)
6. USA (Peter Westbrook, Steve Mormando, Phillip Reilly, Joel Glucksman, Michael Lofton)
   Final: ITA 9–3 FRA
   3rd Place: ROM 8–7 GER
   5th Place: CHN 9–7 USA

**1988 Seoul** T: 11, N: 11, D: 9.29.
1. HUN (Imre Bujdosó, László Csongrádi, Imre Gedövári, György Nébald, Bence Szabó)
2. SOV (Andrei Alshan, Mikhail Burtsev, Sergei Koryazhkin, Sergei Mindirgasov, Georgy Pogosov)

3. ITA (Massimo Cavaliere, Gianfranco Dalla Barba, Marco Marin, Ferdinando Meglio, Giovanni Scalzo)
4. FRA (Philippe Delrieu, Franck Ducheix, Hervé Granger Veyron, Pierre Guichot, Jean François Lamour)
5. POL (Marek Gniewkowski, Robert Kościelniakowski, Andrzej Kostrzewa, Janusz Olech, Tadeusz Pigula)
6. GER (Felix Becker, Jörg Kempenich, Jürgen Nolte, Dieter Schneider, Stephan Thoennessen)
7. USA (Robert Cottingham, Paul Friedberg, Michael Lofton, George Mormando, Peter Westbrook)
8. BUL (Hristo Etropolski, Vassil Etropolski, Nikolai Marincheshki, Nikolai Mateev, Georgi Chomakov)
Final: HUN 8(67)–8(64) SOV
3rd Place: ITA 8(64)–8(63) FRA
5th Place: POL 9–4 GER

The glory years of Hungarian team sabre ended in 1964 and the mantle passed to the Soviets who have, since then, qualified for every Olympic final except the boycotted Games of Los Angeles. Prior to the 1988 Olympics, the Soviets had won three straight world championships. In Seoul the Hungarians survived with a 3-touch victory over Poland in the quarterfinals. The U.S.S.R. took a 7-3 lead in the final, but Hungary fought back with four victories in a row and went on to win another 3-touch squeaker.

If the Hungarian triumph was a throwback to the 1950s, what happened in the bronze medal match brought back memories of the 1920s. Trailing 2-6, the French team protested the officiating. A violent argument ensued and the French stalked off the piste, threatening to withdraw. After 30 minutes they were lured back. They rallied to tie the Italians 8-8, but lost by 1 touch.

# Discontinued Events
## MASTERS FOIL FENCING

**1896 Athens** C: 2, N: 2, D: 4.7.

| | | TG | TR |
|---|---|---|---|
| 1. Leon Pyrgos | GRE | 3 | 1 |
| 2. Jean Perronnet | FRA | 1 | 3 |

Pyrgos, although a professional, was the first Greek winner of the modern Olympic Games.

**1900 Paris** C: 64, N: 7, D: 5.22.

| | | W | L | W | L |
|---|---|---|---|---|---|
| | | | | BARRAGE | |
| 1. Lucien Mérignac | FRA | 6 | 1 | 1 | 0 |
| 2. Alphonse Kirchhoffer | FRA | 6 | 1 | 0 | 1 |
| 3. Jean-Baptiste Mimiague | FRA | 4 | 3 | 1 | 0 |
| 4. Antonio Conte | ITA | 4 | 3 | 0 | 1 |
| 5. Jules Rossignol | FRA | 3 | 4 | | |
| 6. Leopold Ramus | FRA | 2 | 5 | | |

| 7. Italo Santelli | ITA | 0 | 7 |
|---|---|---|---|
| 8. Adolphe Rouleau | FRA | 3 | 4 |

Rouleau was placed last in the final pool because he withdrew from his bout with Mimiague "under the pretext of a sore thumb."

## MASTERS ÉPÉE FENCING

**1900 Paris** C: 54, N: 3?, D: 6.14.
1. Albert Ayat — FRA
2. Emile Bougnol — FRA
3. Henri Laurent — FRA
4. Hippolyte-Jacques Hyvernaud — FRA
5. Damotte — FRA
6. Brassart — FRA
7. Lezard — FRA
8. Jourdan — FRA

**1904** not held

**1906 Athens** C: 3, N: 3, D: 4.28.
1. Cyrille Verbrugge — BEL
2. Mario Gubiani — ITA
3. Ioannis Raïssis — GRE

## ÉPÉE FOR AMATEURS AND MASTERS

**1900 Paris** C: 8, N: 2, D: 6.15.
1. Albert Ayat — FRA
2. Ramón Fonst — CUB
3. Léon Sée — FRA
4. Georges de la Falaise — FRA
5. Emile Bougnol — FRA
5. Hippolyte-Jacques Hyvernaud — FRA
5. Henri Laurent — FRA
5. Louis Perrée — FRA

This event brought together the first four finishers in the amateur and masters tournaments. Ayat won without receiving a hit and was awarded a prize of 3000 francs.

## MASTERS SABRE FENCING

**1900 Paris** C: 44, N: 10, D: 6.27.

| | | W | L |
|---|---|---|---|
| 1. Antonio Conte | ITA | 7 | 0 |
| 2. Italo Santelli | ITA | 6 | 1 |
| 3. Milan Neralić | AUT | 4 | 3 |
| 4. François Delibes | BEL | 3 | 4 |
| 5. Michaux | RUS/FRA | 3 | 4 |
| 6. Xavier Anchetti | FRA | 2 | 5 |
| 7. Zachavrot | RUS | 2 | 5 |
| 8. Hebrant | BEL | 1 | 6 |

**1904** not held

**1906 Athens** C: 5, N: 5, D: 4.28.
1. Cyrille Verbrugge    BEL
2. Ioannis Raïssis      GRE
3. Gadini               ITA

## THREE-CORNERED SABRE

**1906 Athens** C: 22, N: 6, D: 4.28.
1. Gustav Casmir        GER
2. George van Rossem    HOL
3. Péter Tóth           HUN
4. Emil Schön           GER
5. Jëno Apáthy          HUN
6. Ernst Königsgarten   AUT

## SINGLE STICKS

**1904 St. Louis** C: 3, N: 1, D: 9.10.

|                        |     | TG |
|------------------------|-----|----|
| 1. Albertson Van Zo Post | USA | 11 |
| 2. William Scott O'Connor | USA | 8 |
| 3. William Grebe       | USA | 2 |

# _WOMEN_

## FOIL, INDIVIDUAL

**1896–1920** not held

**1924 Paris** C: 25, N: 9, D: 7.4.

|                    |     | W | L | TG | TR |
|--------------------|-----|---|---|----|----|
| 1. Ellen Osiier    | DEN | 5 | 0 | 25 | 14 |
| 2. Gladys Davis    | GBR | 4 | 1 | 23 | 16 |
| 3. Grete Heckscher | DEN | 3 | 2 | 22 | 16 |
| 4. Muriel Freeman  | GBR | 2 | 3 | 17 | 20 |
| 5. Yutha Barding   | DEN | 1 | 4 | 20 | 22 |
| 6. Gizella Tary    | HUN | 0 | 5 | 6  | 25 |

The first female Olympic fencing champion was 33-year-old Ellen Ottilia Osiier, who won all 16 of her bouts. She scored 80 touches and received only 34.

**1928 Amsterdam** C: 27, N: 11, D: 8.1.

|                    |     | W | L | TG | TR |
|--------------------|-----|---|---|----|----|
| 1. Helene Mayer    | GER | 7 | 0 | 35 | 9  |
| 2. Muriel Freeman  | GBR | 6 | 1 | 32 | 19 |
| 3. Olga Oelkers    | GER | 4 | 3 | 25 | 27 |
| 4. Erna Sondheim   | GER | 3 | 4 | 22 | 29 |
| 5. Gladys Daniell  | GBR | 2 | 5 | 23 | 27 |
| 6. Jenny Addams    | BEL | 2 | 5 | 23 | 30 |
| 6. Margit Dany     | HUN | 2 | 5 | 23 | 30 |
| 8. Johanna de Boer | HOL | 2 | 5 | 23 | 33 |

A German Jew, 17-year-old Helene Mayer swept through the tournament with surprising ease, winning 18 bouts and losing two.

**1932 Los Angeles** C: 17, N: 11, D: 8.3.

|                       |     | W | L | TG | TR | BARRAGE TG | BARRAGE TR |
|-----------------------|-----|---|---|----|----|----|----|
| 1. Ellen Preis        | AUT | 8 | 1 | 44 | 27 | 5 | 3 |
| 2. J. Heather Guinness | GBR | 8 | 1 | 43 | 19 | 3 | 5 |
| 3. Erna Bogáthy Bogen | HUN | 7 | 2 | 38 | 30 |   |   |
| 4. Jenny Addams       | BEL | 6 | 3 | 37 | 29 |   |   |
| 5. Helene Mayer       | GER | 5 | 4 | 38 | 27 |   |   |
| 6. Johanna de Boer    | HOL | 5 | 4 | 30 | 35 |   |   |
| 7. Gerda Munck        | DEN | 2 | 7 | 29 | 39 |   |   |
| 8. Marion Lloyd       | USA | 2 | 7 | 26 | 42 |   |   |
| 8. Grete Olsen        | DEN | 2 | 7 | 31 | 42 |   |   |

Preis won by defeating Guinness 5–3 in both the final pool and the barrage. During the barrage, Heather Guinness pointed out to the officials two touches against her which the officials had failed to acknowledge. This act of fair play proved to be the margin of victory. Preis eventually competed in five Olympics. Bronze medalist Erna Bogen was the daughter of Albert Bogen, who won a silver medal in team sabre in 1912. She later married seven-time sabre gold medalist Aladár Gerevich. Their son, Pál, earned two bronze medals in team sabre in 1972 and 1980.

**1936 Berlin** C: 41, N: 17, D: 8.5.

|                          |     | W | L | TG | TR |
|--------------------------|-----|---|---|----|----|
| 1. Ilona Schacherer-Elek | HUN | 6 | 1 | 33 | 17 |
| 2. Helene Mayer          | GER | 5 | 2 | 33 | 19 |
| 3. Ellen Preis           | AUT | 5 | 2 | 32 | 20 |
| 4. Hedwig Hass           | GER | 5 | 2 | 30 | 23 |
| 5. Karen Lachmann        | DEN | 3 | 4 | 23 | 24 |
| 6. Jenny Addams          | BEL | 2 | 5 | 18 | 28 |
| 7. Ilona Vargha          | HUN | 2 | 5 | 17 | 31 |
| 8. Grasser               | AUT | 0 | 7 | 11 | 35 |

In 1932 Helene Mayer left her family behind in Königstein, Germany, and moved to the United States, where she taught German at Mills College in Oakland, California. Under pressure from the U.S., the Nazis invited her back to compete in the Olympics. The Nazis rationalized their leniency toward her by stating that although she was Jewish, she had two "Aryan" grandparents. Also competing at Berlin were the defending Olympic champion, Ellen Preis and the European champion, Ilona Schacherer, later Elek, who was also Jewish. In the final pool, Schacherer-Elek defeated Mayer 5–4 and Preis 5–3, losing only to Hedwig Hass. On the victory platform Helene Mayer pleased the large German crowd by giving a "Heil Hitler" salute.

**1948 London** C: 39, N: 15, D: 8.2.

|                       |     | W | L | TG | TR |
|-----------------------|-----|---|---|----|----|
| 1. Ilona Elek         | HUN | 6 | 1 | 31 | 15 |
| 2. Karen Lachmann     | DEN | 5 | 2 | 24 | 11 |
| 3. Ellen Müller-Preis | AUT | 5 | 2 | 24 | 16 |
| 4. Maria Cerra        | USA | 5 | 2 | 23 | 16 |
| 5. Fritzi Filz        | AUT | 4 | 3 | 20 | 21 |
| 6. Margit Elek        | HUN | 1 | 6 | 10 | 26 |

| | | | | | |
|---|---|---|---|---|---|
| 7. Velleda Cessari | ITA | 1 | 6 | 15 | 27 |
| 8. Mary Glen Haig | GBR | 1 | 6 | 10 | 27 |

Ilona Elek's retention of her Olympic title after a 12-year interlude was a tremendous achievement in itself. But the manner in which she won added to the drama. In her next-to-last bout she trailed Maria Cerra 2–0 before scoring four straight hits. Then, with the winner earning the gold medal, she defeated Karen Lachmann 4–2 as well.

**1952 Helsinki** C: 37, N: 15, D: 7.27.

| | | | | | BARRAGE | | |
|---|---|---|---|---|---|---|---|
| | | W | L | TR | W | L | TG | TR |
| 1. Irene Camber | ITA | 5 | 2 | 22 | 1 | 0 | 4 | 3 |
| 2. Ilona Elek | HUN | 5 | 2 | 21 | 0 | 1 | 3 | 4 |
| 3. Karen Lachmann | DEN | 4 | 3 | 22 | 3 | 0 | 12 | 4 |
| 4. Janice Lee York | USA | 4 | 3 | 25 | 2 | 1 | 8 | 7 |
| 5. Maxine Mitchell | USA | 4 | 3 | 23 | 1 | 2 | 9 | 8 |
| 6. Renée Garilhe | FRA | 4 | 3 | 24 | 0 | 3 | 2 | 12 |
| 7. Lylian Lecomte-Guyonneau | FRA | 1 | 6 | 30 | | | | |
| 8. Magdolna Kovács-Nyári | HUN | 1 | 6 | 32 | | | | |

The 45-year-old Elek appeared well on her way to her third gold medal when she won her first 20 bouts, including five in the final pool. But then she lost to Mitchell and then to Camber, 4–3. Forced into a barrage, she was again defeated by Camber, 4–3.

**1956 Melbourne** C: 23, N: 11, D: 11.29.

| | | | | | | BARRAGE | |
|---|---|---|---|---|---|---|---|
| | | W | L | TG | TR | TG | TR |
| 1. Gillian Sheen | GBR | 6 | 1 | 26 | 20 | 4 | 2 |
| 2. Olga Orban | ROM | 6 | 1 | 27 | 17 | 2 | 4 |
| 3. Renée Garilhe | FRA | 5 | 2 | 26 | 14 | | |
| 4. Janice Lee Romary (York) | USA | 4 | 3 | 23 | 21 | | |
| 5. Kate Delbarre | FRA | 3 | 4 | 20 | 25 | | |
| 6. Karen Lachmann | DEN | 2 | 5 | 17 | 20 | | |
| 7. Ellen Müller-Preis | AUT | 1 | 6 | 20 | 25 | | |
| 8. Bruna Colombetti | ITA | 1 | 6 | 14 | 27 | | |

Sheen, a 28-year-old London dental surgeon, barely qualified for the final by winning a barrage to finish fourth in her semifinal pool. She lost 4–2 to Orban, but won the rest of her bouts to force a barrage. This time she defeated the Romanian, 4–2.

**1960 Rome** C: 56, N: 24, D: 9.1.

| | | | | | | BARRAGE | | |
|---|---|---|---|---|---|---|---|---|
| | | W | L | TG | TR | TG | TR | W | L |
| 1. Heidi Schmid | GER | 6 | 1 | 26 | 13 | | | | |
| 2. Valentina Rastvorova | SOV | 5 | 2 | 24 | 12 | | | | |
| 3. Maria Vicol | ROM | 4 | 3 | 23 | 18 | 2 | 0 | 8 | 5 |
| 4. Galina Gorokhova | SOV | 4 | 3 | 22 | 19 | 1 | 1 | 7 | 6 |
| 5. Olga Szabó-Orban | ROM | 4 | 3 | 20 | 20 | 0 | 2 | 4 | 8 |
| 6. Elżbieta Pawlas | POL | 2 | 5 | 14 | 24 | | | | |
| 7. Maria del Pilar Roldan | MEX | 2 | 5 | 13 | 25 | | | | |
| 8. Waltraut Ebert | AUT | 1 | 6 | 14 | 27 | | | | |

Heidi Schmid was a left-handed 21-year-old music teacher from Augsburg. She scored 18 wins against only two losses, one of which occurred after she had clinched the championship.

**1964 Tokyo** C: 39, N: 17, D: 10.15.

| | | | | | | BARRAGE | | | |
|---|---|---|---|---|---|---|---|---|---|
| | | W | L | TG | TR | W | L | TG | TR |
| 1. Ildikó Ujlaki-Rejtö | HUN | 2 | 1 | 10 | 5 | 2 | 0 | 8 | 1 |
| 2. Helga Mees | GER | 2 | 1 | 8 | 9 | 1 | 1 | 4 | 6 |
| 3. Antonella Ragno | ITA | 2 | 1 | 9 | 7 | 0 | 2 | 3 | 8 |
| 4. Galina Gorokhova | SOV | 0 | 3 | 6 | 12 | | | | |
| 5. Katalin Juhász | HUN | | | | | | | | |
| 6. Giovanna Masciotta | ITA | | | | | | | | |
| 7. Bruna Colombetti | ITA | | | | | | | | |
| 7. Catherine Rousselet | FRA | | | | | | | | |

Ildikó Ujlaki-Rejtö was born deaf on May 11, 1937. When she began fencing at age 14 her coaches communicated their instructions on pieces of paper. A factory worker, she faced Helga Mees, a 27-year-old secretary from Saarbrücken, for the championship. Mees had already beaten Ujlaki-Rejtö twice, in the first round and in the final round, but in the barrage the Hungarian won, 4–0.

**1968 Mexico City** C: 38, N: 16, D: 10.20.

| | | | | | |
|---|---|---|---|---|---|
| | | W | L | TG | TR |
| 1. Yelena Novikova | SOV | 4 | 1 | 19 | 11 |
| 2. Maria del Pilar Roldan | MEX | 3 | 2 | 17 | 14 |
| 3. Ildikó Ujlaki-Rejtö | HUN | 3 | 2 | 14 | 16 |
| 4. Brigitte Gapais | FRA | 2 | 3 | 15 | 15 |
| 5. Kerstin Palm | SWE | 2 | 3 | 17 | 17 |
| 6. Galina Gorokhova | SOV | 1 | 4 | 10 | 19 |
| 7. Giovanna Masciotta | ITA | | | | |
| 7. Heidi Schmid | GER | | | | |

Novikova, a tall 21-year-old student teacher, compiled a record of 15 wins and two losses. Silver medalist Roldan, a mother of two, came out of retirement to compete in the Olympics before a hometown crowd.

**1972 Munich** C: 44, N: 20, D: 9.3.

| | | | | | |
|---|---|---|---|---|---|
| | | W | L | TG | TR |
| 1. Antonella Ragno-Lonzi | ITA | 4 | 1 | 19 | 13 |
| 2. Ildikó Bóbis | HUN | 3 | 2 | 17 | 14 |
| 3. Galina Gorokhova | SOV | 3 | 2 | 16 | 14 |
| 4. Marie-Chantal Demaille | FRA | 3 | 2 | 14 | 16 |
| 5. Yelena Belova (Novikova) | SOV | 2 | 3 | 15 | 13 |
| 6. Kerstin Palm | SWE | 0 | 5 | 9 | 20 |

**1976 Montreal** C: 48, N: 20, D: 7.24.

| | | | | | | BARRAGE | |
|---|---|---|---|---|---|---|---|
| | | W | L | TG | TR | TG | TR |
| 1. Ildikó Schwarczenberger | HUN | 4 | 1 | 21 | 15 | 5 | 4 |
| 2. Maria Consolata Collino | ITA | 4 | 1 | 24 | 12 | 4 | 5 |
| 3. Yelena Belova (Novikova) | SOV | 3 | 2 | 21 | 19 | | |
| 4. Brigitte Dumont-Gapais | FRA | 2 | 3 | 17 | 17 | | |
| 5. Cornelia Hanisch | GER | 1 | 4 | 13 | 22 | | |
| 6. Ildikó Bóbis | HUN | 1 | 4 | 13 | 24 | | |
| 7. Valentina Sidorova | SOV | | | | | | |
| 7. Ecaterina Stahl (Jencic) | ROM | | | | | | |

The reigning world champion, Ecaterina Stahl, ran up a 15–2 record before being eliminated in the prefinal round by Ildikó Schwarczenberger. The final pool turned into an exciting three-way affair. Collino defeated Schwarczenberger 5–1, which appeared to end the Hungarian's chance for a gold medal. Then Yelena Belova beat Collino on the last hit to put Schwarczenberger back into a tie for first place. In her final match, Belova faced Ildikó Bóbis, who had lost all of her other final pool matches. A win would put her into a triple barrage. However, Bóbis summoned all her skill and defeated Belova 5–4. Inspired by her teammate's effort, Schwarczenberger won the final hit against Collino to take the championship.

**1980 Moscow** C: 33, N: 14, D: 7.24.

| | | W | L | TG | TR |
|---|---|---|---|---|---|
| 1. Pascale Trinquet | FRA | 4 | 1 | 21 | 16 |
| 2. Magda Maros | HUN | 3 | 2 | 23 | 17 |
| 3. Barbara Wysoczańska | POL | 3 | 2 | 19 | 18 |
| 4. Ecaterina Stahl (Jencic) | ROM | 2 | 3 | 19 | 21 |
| 5. Brigitte Gaudin (Latrille) | FRA | 2 | 3 | 20 | 22 |
| 6. Dorina Vaccaroni | ITA | 1 | 4 | 14 | 22 |
| 7. Katarina Loksova | CZE | | | | |
| 7. Delfina Skapska | POL | | | | |

**1984 Los Angeles-Long Beach** C: 42, N: 18, D: 8.3.
1. Luan Jujie          CHN
2. Cornelia Hanisch     GER
3. Dorina Vaccaroni     ITA
4. Elisabeta Guzganu    ROM
5. Véronique Brouquier  FRA
6. Laurence Modaine     FRA
7. Sabine Bischoff      GER
8. Brigitte Gaudin      FRA
   Final: Luan 8–3 Hanisch
   3rd Place: Vaccaroni 8–5 Guzganu

Luan, a 25-year-old from Nanjing, finished the tournament with a record of 17 wins and 2 losses. Hanisch had entered the final at 16–1.

**1988 Seoul** C: 45, N: 19, D: 9.22.
1. GER   Anja Fichtel
2. GER   Sabine Bau
3. GER   Zita Funkenhauser
4. HUN   Zsuzsanna Jánosi
5. SOV   Tatyana Sadovskaya
6. HUN   Gertrúd Stefanek
7. CHN   Sun Hongyun
8. SOV   Yelena Glikina
   Final: Fichtel 8-5 Bau
   3rd Place: Funkenhauser 8-7 Jánosi

The final was a rematch of the 1986 world championship, in which then-18-year-old Fichtel defeated Bau 8–3. Kerstin Palm of Sweden, who finished twenty-ninth, became the first woman in any sport to compete in seven Olympics. Her first appearance was in 1964.

## FOIL, TEAM

**1896–1956** not held

**1960 Rome** T: 12, N: 12, D: 9.3.
1. SOV   (Tatyana Petrenko, Valentina Rastvorova, Lyudmila Schishova, Valentina Prudskova, Aleksandra Zabelina, Galine Gorokhova)
2. HUN   (Györgyi Szekely, Ildikó Ujlaki-Reijtö, Magdolna Kovács-Nyári, Katalin Juhász, Lidia Dömölky)
3. ITA   (Irene Camber, Velleda Cesari, Antonella Ragno, Bruna Colombetti, Claudia Pasini)
4. GER   (Heidi Schmid, Helga Mees, Helga Stroh, Helmi Höhle, Gudrun Theuerkauff, Rosemarie Weiss)
5. FRA   (Monique Leroux, Regine Veronnet, Françoise Mailliard, Renée Garilhe, Kate Delbarre)
5. HOL   (Nina Kleyweg, Daniel Van Rossem, Helena Kokkes, Elisa Botbjil)
5. POL   (Elżbieta Pawlas, Silwia Julito, Barbara Orzechowska, Genowefa Migas, Wanda Kaczmarczyk)
5. ROM   (Ecaterina Lazar, Eugenia Mateianu, Olga Szabó-Orban, Maria Vicol)
   Final: SOV 9–3 HUN
   3rd Place: ITA 9–2 GER

The Soviets received their only scare in the quarterfinals, when they had to rally from a 3–8 deficit to defeat France by two touches. Their final win-loss total was 48–21.

**1964 Tokyo** T: 10, N: 10, D: 10.17.
1. HUN   (Ildikó Ujlaki-Rejtö, Katalin Juhász-Nagy, Lidia Sákovics-Dömölky, Judit Mendelényi-Ágoston, Paula Földessy Marosi)
2. SOV   (Galina Gorokhova, Valentina Prudskova, Tatyana Samusenko, Lyudmila Schishova, Valentina Rastvorova)
3. GER   (Heidi Schmid, Helga Mees, Rosemarie Scherberger, Gudrun Theuerkauff)
4. ITA   (Antonella Ragno, Giovanna Masciotta, Irene Camber, Natalina Sanguineti, Bruna Colombetti)
5. ROM   (Olga Szabó-Orban, Ileana Gyulai, Ana Dersidan, Maria Vicol, Ecaterina Jencic)
6. FRA   (Catherine Rousselet, Marie-Chantal Depetris, Brigitte Gapais, Annick Level, Colette Revenu)
   Final: HUN 9–7 SOV
   3rd Place: GER 9–5 ITA
   5th Place: ROM 9–6 FRA

**1968 Mexico City** T: 10, N: 10, D: 10.24.
1. SOV   (Aleksandra Zabelina, Yelena Novikova, Galina Gorokhova, Tatyana Samusenko, Svetlana Tširkova)
2. HUN   (Ildikó Bóbis, Lidia Sákovics, Ildikó Ujlaki-Rejtö, Mária Gulácsy, Paula Földessy-Marosi)
3. ROM   (Ecaterina Stahl [Jencic], Ileana Drimbă, Olga Szabó-Orban, Maria Vicol, Ana Ene-Dersidan)
4. FRA   (Cathérine Ceretti, Brigitte Gapais, Marie-Chantal Depetris, Claudette Herbster, Annick Level)
5. GER   (Heidi Schmid, Helga Koch, Gudrun Theuerkauff, Monika Pulch, Helga Volz-Mees)
6. ITA   (Antonella Ragno, Giulia Lorenzoni, Giovanna Masciotta, Bruna Colombetti, Silvana Sconciafurno)

Final: SOV 9–3 HUN
3rd Place: ROM 8(47)–8(45)FRA
5th Place: GER 8–7 ITA

**1972 Munich** T: 11, N: 11, D: 9.8.
1. SOV  (Yelana Belova [Novikova], Alexandra Zabelina, Tatyana Semusenko, Galina Gorokhova, Svetlana Tširkova)
2. HUN  (Ildikó Ságiné-Rejtö [Ujlaki-Rejtö], Ildikó Schwarczenberger [Tordasi], Ildikó Matuscakné-Ronay, Maria Szolnoki, Ildikó Bóbis)
3. ROM  (Ileana Gyulai, Ana Pascu, Ecaterina Stahl [Jencic], Olga Szabó-Orban)
4. ITA  (Antonella Ragno-Lonzi, Giulia Lorenzoni, Reka Der Cipriani, Maria Consolata Collino, Giuseppina Bersani)
5. GER  (Gudrun Theuerkauff, Irmela Broniecki, Karin Giesselmann, Monika Pulch, Erika Bethmann)
6. FRA  (Marie-Chantal Demaille, Catherine Ceretti, Claudie Josland, Brigitte Dumont-Gapais)
7. POL  (Halina Balon, Krystyna Urbánska-Machnicka, Jolanta Bebel-Rzymowska, Kamila Skladanowska, Elžbieta Franke)
7. USA  (Ruth White, Natalia Clovis, Tanya Adamovich, Harriet King, Ann O'Donnell)
Final: SOV 9–5 HUN
3rd Place: ROM 9–7 ITA
5th Place: GER 8–7 FRA

The Soviet team compiled a record of 52 wins and 20 losses. They were led by Belova (17–3) and Zabelina (14–4).

**1976 Montreal** T: 13, N: 13, D: 7.28.
1. SOV  (Yelana Belova [Novikova], Olga Kniazeva, Valentina Sidorova, Nailia Guiliazova, Valentina Nikonova)
2. FRA  (Brigitte Latrille, Brigitte Dumont-Gapais, Christine Muzio, Véronique Trinquet, Claudie Josland)
3. HUN  (Ildikó Schwarczenberger [Tordasi], Edit Kovács, Magda Maros, Ildikó Ságiné-Rejtö [Ujlaki-Rejtö], Ildikó Bóbis)
4. GER  (Karin Rutz, Cornelia Hanisch, Ute Kircheis, Brigitte Oertel, Jutta Höhne)
5. ITA  (Maria Consolata Collino, Giulia Lorenzoni, Dorlana Piglipooo, Susanna Batazzi, Carola Mangiarotti)
6. POL  (Jolanta Bebel-Rzymowska, Barbara Wysoczańska, Kamilla Mazurowska-Skladanowska, Krystyna Urbańska-Machnicka, Grażyna Staszak-Makowska)
7. GBR  (Wendy Ager, Susan Wrigglesworth, Hilary Cawthorne, Clare Halsted, Susan Green)
7. ROM  (Ileana Jenei, Marcela Moldovan, Ecaterina Stahl [Jencic], Ana Pascu, Magdalena Bartos)
Final: SOV 9–2 FRA
3rd Place: HUN 9–4 GER
5th Place: ITA 9–7 POL

The U.S.S.R. won almost without competition, with 50 wins and only 13 losses. Belova was 13–0 and Kniazeva 11–2. The final victory came on Belova's 29th birthday.

**1980 Moscow** T: 9, N: 9, D: 7.27.
1. FRA  (Brigitte Gaudin [Latrille], Pascale Trinquet, Isabelle Boeri-Begard, Véronique Brouquier, Christine Muzio)

2. SOV  (Valentina Sidorova, Nailia Guiliazova, Yelena Belova [Novikova], Irina Ushakova, Larisa Tsagaraeva)
3. HUN  (Ildikó Schwarczenberger [Tordasi], Magda Maros, Gertrud Stefanek, Zsuzsa Szöcz, Edit Kovács)
4. POL  (Delfina Skapska, Agnieszka Dubrawska, Jolanta Królikowska, Barbara Wysoczańska, Kamila Mazurowska-Skladanowska)
5. ITA  (Dorina Vaccaroni, Anna Rita Sparaciari, Susanna Batazzi, Carola Mangiarotti, Clara Mochi)
6. CUB  (Margarita Rodriguez Vargas, Marlene Font Kindelan, Maria Garcia Pascau, Clara Alfonso Freire, Mercedes del Risco Randich)
7. GBR  (Susan Wrigglesworth, Ann Brannon, Wendy Grant, Linda Martin, Hilary Cawthorne)
8. GDR  (Mandy Niklaus, Gabriele Janke, Sabine Hertrampf, Beate Schubert, Marion Schulze)
Final: FRA 9–6 SOV
3rd Place: HUN 9–7 POL
5th Place: ITA 9–6 CUB

**1984 Los Angeles-Long Beach** T: 10, N: 10, D: 8.7.
1. GER  (Christiane Weber, Cornelia Hanisch, Sabine Bischoff, Zita Funkenhauser, Ute Wessel)
2. ROM  (Aurora Dan, Koszto Veber, Rozalia Oros, Marcela Zsak, Elisabeta Guzganu)
3. FRA  (Laurence Modaine, Pascale Trinquet-Hachin, Brigitte Gaudin [Latrille], Véronique Brouquier, Anne Meygret)
4. ITA  (Dorina Vaccaroni, Clara Mochi, Margherita Zalaffi, Lucia Traversa, Carola Cicconetti)
5. CHN  (Luan Jujio, Zhu Qingyuan, Li Huahua, Wu Qiuhua)
6. USA  (Vincent Bradford, Sharon Monplaisir, Susan Badders, Debra Waples, Jana Angelakis)
7. GBR  (Ann Brannon, Linda Martin, Fiona McIntosh, Elizabeth Thurley, Katie Arup)
8. JPN  (Mieko Miyahara, Azusa Oikawa, Miyuki Maekawa, Tomoko Oka)
Final: GER 9–5 ROM
3rd Place: FRA 9–7 ITA
5th Place: CHN 9–5 USA

The decisive contest was the semifinal matchup between West Germany and Italy. Both sides registered eight wins, but in the final bout, Zita Funkenhauser managed three hits in her loss to Lucia Traversa, giving the West Germans a one touch advantage.

**1988 Seoul** T: 12, N: 12, D: 9.28.
1. GER  (Sabine Bau, Anja Fichtel, Zita Funkenhauser, Anette Klug, Christiane Weber)
2. ITA  (Francesca Bortolozzi, Annapia Gandolfi, Lucia Traversa, Dorina Vaccaroni, Margherita Zalaffi)
3. HUN  (Zsuzsanna Jánosi, Edit Kovács, Gertrúd Stefanek, Zsuzsa Szöcs, Katalin Tuschák)
4. SOV  (Yelena Glikina, Yelena Grishina, Tatyana Sadovskaya, Marina Soboleva, Olga Voshchakina)
5. CHN  (Li Huahua, Luan Jujie, Sun Hongyun, Xiao Aihua, Zhu Qingyuan)
6. USA  (Caitlin Bilodeau, Elaine Cheris, Sharon Monplaisir, Mary O'Neill)

7. FRA   (Brigitte Gaudin, Gisèle Meygret, Laurence Modaine, Nathalie Pallet, Isabelle Spennato)

8. KOR   (Kim Jin-soon, Shin Sung-ja, Tak Jung-im, Yoon Jung-sook)

Final: GER 9–4 ITA
3rd Place: HUN 9–2 SOV
5th Place: CHN 8(61)–8(60) USA
7th Place: FRA 9–4 KOR

The West Germans whipped their five opponents, registering 45 wins against only 15 losses. Weber was 14–1 and Fichtel 12–2.

# FIELD HOCKEY

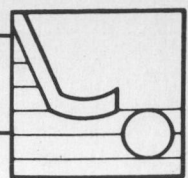

## MEN

A field hockey match is divided into two 35-minute halves. In the event of a draw, two 10-minute extra periods are played. A continued draw is decided by "sudden death."

**1896–1908** not held

**1908 London** T: 6, N: 3, D: 10.31.

| | | | W | L | T | PF | PA |
|---|---|---|---|---|---|---|---|
| 1. | GBR | England (H.I. Wood, Harold Scott Freeman, L. C. Baillon, John Robinson, Edgar Page, Alan Noble, Percy Rees, Gerald Logan, Stanley Shoveller, Reginald Pridmore, Eric Green) | 3 | 0 | 0 | 24 | 3 |
| 2. | IRL | Ireland (E. P. C. Holmes, Henry Brown, Walter Peterson, William Graham, Walter Campbell, Henry Murphy, C. F. Power, G. S. Gregg, Eric Allman-Smith, Frank Robinson, Robert Kennedy, W. G. McCormick) | 1 | 1 | 0 | 4 | 9 |
| 3. | GBR | Scotland (John Burt, Hugh Neilson, Colin Foulkes, Hew Fraser, Alexander Burt, Andrew Dennistoun, Norman Stevenson, Ivan Laing, John Harper-Orr, Hugh Walker, William Orchardson) | 1 | 1 | 0 | 5 | 6 |
| 3. | GBR | Wales (Bruce Turnbull, E. W. G. Richards, Llewollyn Evans, C. W. Shephard, R. Lyne, F. Connah, F. Gordon Phillips, A. A. Law, P. B. Turnbull, J. Ralph Williams, W. J. Pallott) | 0 | 1 | 0 | 1 | 3 |

Final: ENG 8–1 IRL

**1912** not held

**1920 Antwerp** T: 4, N: 4, 9.5.

| | | | W | L | T | PF | PA |
|---|---|---|---|---|---|---|---|
| 1. | GBR | (Harry Haslam, John Bennett, Charles Atkin, Harold Cooke, Eric Crockford, Cyril Wilkinson, William Smith, George McGrath, John McBryan, Stanley Shoveller, Rex Crummack, Arthur Leighton, H. K. Cassels, Colin Campbell, Charles Marcom) | 3 | 0 | 0 | 17 | 2 |
| 2. | DEN | (Andreas Rasmussen, Hans Christian Herlak, Frans Faber, Erik Husted, Henning Holst, Hans Jörgen Hansen, Hans Adolf Bjerrum, Thorvald Eigenbrod, Svend Blach, Steen Due, Ejvind Blach) | 2 | 1 | 0 | 15 | 8 |
| 3. | BEL | (Charles Delelienne, Maurice van den Bemden, Raoul Daufresne de la Chevalerie, René Strauwen, Fernand de Montigny, Adolphe Goemaere, Pierre Chibert, Andre Becquet, Raymond Keppens, Pierre Valcke, Jean van Nerom, Robert Gevers, Louis Diercxens) | 1 | 2 | 0 | 6 | 19 |
| 4. | FRA | (Paul Haranger, Robert Lelong, Pierre Estrabant, Georges Breuille, Jacques Morise, Edmond Loriol, Désiré Guard, Roland Bedel, André Bounal, Gaston Rogot, Pierre Rollin) | 0 | 3 | 0 | 3 | 12 |

**1924** not held

**1928 Amsterdam** T: 9, N: 9, D: 5.26.

| | | | W | L | T | PF | PA |
|---|---|---|---|---|---|---|---|
| 1. | IND | (Richard Allen, Leslie Hammond, Michael Rocque, Sayed Yusuf, Broome Eric Pinniger, Rex Norris, Ernest Goodsir-Cullen, Frederic Seaman, Dhyan Chand, George Marthins, Maurice Gateley, Jaipal Singh, Shaukat Ali, Feroze Khan) | 5 | 0 | 0 | 29 | 0 |
| 2. | HOL | (Adrian Katte, Reindert de Waal, Albert Tresling, Jan Ankerman, Emile Duson, Johannes Brand, August Kop, Gerrit Jannink, Paulus van de Rovaert, Robert van der Veen, Hendrik Visser t'Hooft) | 3 | 1 | 0 | 8 | 5 |
| 3. | GER | (Georg Brunner, Heinz Wöltje, Werner Proft, Erich Zander, Theodor Haag, Werner Freyberg, Herbert Kemmer, Herbert Hobein, Bruno Boche, Herbert Müller, Friedrich Horn, Erwin Franzkowiak, Hans Haussmann, Karl-Heinz Irmer, Aribert Heymann, Kurt Haverbeck, Rolf Wollner, Gerd Strantzen, Heinz Förstendorf) | 3 | 1 | 0 | 11 | 3 |

| | | W | L | T | PF | PA |
|---|---|---|---|---|---|---|
| 4. BEL | (Etienne Soubre, Johnny van der Straeten, Corneille Wellens Lambert Adelot, Claude Baudoux, Adolphe Goemaere, André Seeldrayers, Charles Delheid, Louis Diercxens, Yvon Baudoux, Charles Koning, Freddy Cattoir, Louis de Deken, Emile Vercken, Auguste Goditiabois, Georges Grosjean, René Mallieux) | 3 | 2 | 0 | 8 | 12 |

Final: IND 3–0 HOL
3rd Place: GER 3–0 BEL

The first Indian hockey clubs were formed in Calcutta in 1885. In 1926 India played its initial international matches against New Zealand. But it was the 1928 Olympics in Amsterdam that established India as the world's number-one power in field hockey. Led by 22-year-old Dhyan Chand, an army captain from Uttar Pradesh, the Indians whipped through the tournament without giving up a single goal. Chand eventually won three Olympic gold medals and later became coach of the Indian national team.

**1932 Los Angeles** T: 3, N: 3, D: 8.11.

| | | W | L | T | PF | PA |
|---|---|---|---|---|---|---|
| 1. IND | (Richard Allen, Arthur Hind, Carlyle Tapsell, Leslie Hammond, Masud Minhas, Broome Eric Pinniger, Lal Shah Bokhari, Richard Carr, Gurmit Singh Kullar, Dhyan Chand, Roop Singh, Sayed Mohammed Jaffar) | 2 | 0 | 0 | 35 | 2 |
| 2. JPN | (Shumkichi Hamada, Akio Sohda, Sadayoshi Kobayashi, Katsumi Shibata, Yoshio Sakai, Eiichi Nakamura, Haruhiko Kon, Hiroshi Nagata, Kenichi Konishi, Toshio Usami, Junzo Inohara) | 1 | 1 | 0 | 10 | 13 |
| 3. USA | (Harold Brewster, Samuel Ewing, Leonard O'Brien, Henry Greer, James Gentle, Horace Disston, Lawrence Knapp, Charles Shaeffer, Amos Deacon, William Boddington, David McMullin, Frederick Wolters) | 0 | 2 | 0 | 3 | 33 |

Interest in hockey spread rapidly throughout India following the Olympic triumph of 1928. When it came time to raise money to send a team to the Los Angeles Olympics, a journalist representing the Indian Hockey Federation approached Mahatma Gandhi and asked him to issue an appeal to the masses. Gandhi's only reply was, "What's hockey?" Nevertheless, an Indian team did make it to Los Angeles, paying its way by playing exhibition matches in Europe on the way home. The Indians had no problems with the competition, defeating Japan, 11–1, and the United States, 24–1. In the latter game, which had the highest score ever achieved in an international match, Roop Singh scored twelve goals and Dhyan Chand seven.

**1936 Berlin** T: 11, N: 11, D: 8.15.

| | | W | L | T | PF | PA |
|---|---|---|---|---|---|---|
| 1. IND | (Richard Allen, Carlyle Tapsell, Mohammed Hussain, Baboo Narsoo Nimal, Ernest John Goodsir-Cullen, Joseph Galibardy, Shabban Shahabud Din, Dara Singh, Dhyan Chand, Roop Singh, Sayed Mohammed Jaffar, Cyril Michie, Paul Peter Fernandes, Joseph Phillip, Garewal Gurcharan Singh, Ahsan Mohomed Khan, Ahmed Sher Khan, Lionel Emmett, Mirza Nasirud-Din Masood) | 5 | 0 | 0 | 38 | 1 |
| 2. GER | (Karl Dröse, Herbert Kemmer, Erich Zander, Alfred Gerdes, Erwin Keller, Heinrich Schmalix, Harald Huffmann, Werner Hamel, Kurt Weiss, Hans Scherbart, Fritz Messner, Tito Warnholtz, Detlef Okrent, Hermann Auf der Heide, Heinrich Peter, Carl Menke, Heinz Raack, Paul Mehlitz, Ludwig Beisiegel, Karl Ruck, Erich Cuntz, Werner Kubitzki) | 3 | 1 | 0 | 14 | 9 |
| 3. HOL | (Jan de Looper, Reindert de Waal, Max Westerkamp, Hendrik de Looper, Rudolf van der Haar, Antoine van Lierop, Pieter Gunning, Henri Schnitger, Ernst Willem van den Berg, Agathon de Roos, René Sparenberg, Carl Haybroek) | 3 | 1 | 1 | 13 | 10 |
| 4. FRA | (Raymond Tixier, Guy Chevalier, Paul Imbault, Claude Graveraux, Félix Grimonprez, François Verger, Paul Sartorius, Anatole Vologe, Joseph Goubert, Claude Soulé, Claude Roques, Etienne Guibal, Michel Verkindere, Marcel Lachmann, Guy Hénon, Emmanuel Gonat, Jean Rouget, Charles Imbault, Robert Rousse) | 2 | 3 | 0 | 7 | 19 |

Final: IND 8–1 GER
3rd Place: HOL 4–3 FRA

As a British colony, India was forced to march behind the flag of Great Britain. But in the dressing room before their final match against Germany, the Indian team saluted the tricolor flag of the Indian National Congress. The Germans fought hard and trailed only 1–0 at halftime. But the Indians wore them down after the break, winning 8–1, with Dhyan Chand scoring six goals while playing barefoot.

**1948 London** T: 13, N: 13, D: 8.13.

| | | W | L | T | PF | PA |
|---|---|---|---|---|---|---|
| 1. | IND (Leo Pinto, Trilochan Singh, Randhir Singh Gentle, Keshava Datt, Amir Kumar, Maxie Vaz, Kishan Lal, Kunwar Digvijay Singh, Grahanandan Singh, Patrick Jansen, Lawrie Fernandes, Ranganandhan Francis, Akhtar Hussain, Leslie Claudius, Jaswant Rajput, Reginald Rodrigues, Latifur Rehman, Balbir Singh, Walter D'Souza, Gerry Glacken) | 5 | 0 | 0 | 25 | 2 |
| 2. | GBR (David Brodie, George Sime, William Lindsay, Michael Walford, Frank Reynolds, Robin Lindsay, John Peake, Neil White, Robert Adlard, Norman Borrett, William Griffiths, Ronald Davies) | 3 | 1 | 1 | 21 | 4 |
| 3. | HOL (Antonius Richter, Henri Derckx, Johan Drijver, Jenne Langhout, Hermanus Loggere, Edouard Tiel, Willem van Heel, Andries Boerstra, Pieter Bromberg, Jan Kruize, Rius Esser, Henricus Bouwman) | 4 | 2 | 1 | 17 | 11 |
| 4. | PAK (M. Anwar Beg Moghal, Mohamad Niaz Khan, Mohamad Abdul Razzao, Hamid Ullah Khan Burki, Abdul Ghafoor Khan, Shah-Rukh Shahzada, Ahmed Masud, M. Shaikh, Iqtidar Ali Shah Dara, Abdul Aziz, Rhamat Ullah Shaikh, Sayed Mohamed Saleem, S. Khurrum, Mohamed Khawaja Taki, Mukhtar Bhatti, Abdul Hamid, M. D'Mello, Abdul Qayyum Khan, Azziz-ur-Rahman Khan, Mohmood Ul Hassan) | 4 | 2 | 1 | 25 | 7 |

Final: IND 4–0 GBR
3rd Place: HOL 1–1 PAK
3rd Place Replay: HOL 4–1 PAK

Ever since India first appeared on the international field hockey scene, Great Britain had studiously avoided playing the Indian team, apparently afraid of the embarrassment of losing to one of its colonies. However in 1948 India gained not only its independence from Britain, but also a chance to face its former mentor in what had now become the Indian national sport. The match for first place turned out to be no contest, as Great Britain, which had advanced to the final without giving up a goal, was itself shut out, 4–0.

**1952 Helsinki** T: 12, N: 12, D: 7.24.

| | | W | L | T | PF | PA |
|---|---|---|---|---|---|---|
| 1. | IND (Ranganandhan Francis, Dharam Singh, Randhir Singh Gentle, Leslie Claudius, Keshava Datt, Govind Perumal, Raghbir Lal, Kunwar Digvijay Singh, Balbir Singh, Udham Singh, Muniswarmy Rajgopal, Chinadorai Deshmutu, Meldric St. Clair Daluz, Grahanandan Singh) | 3 | 0 | 0 | 13 | 2 |
| 2. | HOL (Laurentz Mulder, Henri Derckx, Johan Drijver, Julius Ancion, Hermanus Loggere, Edouard Tiel, Willem van Heel, Rius Esser, Jan Hendrik Kruize, Andries Boerstra, Leonard Wery, Andries Dirk) | 2 | 1 | 0 | 3 | 6 |
| 3. | GBR (Graham Dadds, Roger Midgley, Denys Carnill, John Cockett, Dennis Eagan, Anthony Robinson, Anthony Nunn, Robin Fletcher, Richard Norris, John Conroy, John Taylor, Derek Day, Neil Nugent) | 2 | 1 | 0 | 4 | 4 |
| 4. | PAK (Abdul Waheed Qazl, Mohamad Niaz Khan, Asghar Ali Khan, Jack Britto, Manzoor Hussain Atif, Habib Ali Kiddi, Mahmudal Hassan, Abdul Hamid, Abdul Aziz Mallick, Habibur Rehman, Latifur Rehman, Abdul Latif Mir, Safdor Bahul, Mohamad Rafique Khan, Fazar Ur Rehman, Abdul Qayyum Khan, Azmat) | 1 | 2 | 0 | 7 | 3 |

Final: IND 6–1 HOL
3rd Place: GBR 2–1 PAK

**Nine of India's 13 goals were scored by Balbir Singh, a police inspector from Punjab**

**1956 Melbourne** T: 12, N: 12, D: 12.6.

| | | W | L | T | PF | PA |
|---|---|---|---|---|---|---|
| 1. | IND (Shankar Laxman, Bakshish Singh, Randhir Singh Gentle, Leslie Claudius, Amir Kumar, Govind Perumal, Raghbir Lal, Gurdev Singh, Balbir Singh, Udham Singh, Raghbir Singh Bhola, Charles Stephen, Ranganandhan Francis, Balkrishnan Singh, Amit Singh Bakshi, Hari Pal Kaushik, Hardyal Singh) | 5 | 0 | 0 | 38 | 0 |
| 2. | PAK (Zakir Hussain, Munir Ahmad Dar, Manzoor Hussain Atif, Ghulam Rasul, Anwar Ahmad Khan, Hussain Mussarat, Noor Alam, Abdul Hamid, Habibur | 3 | 1 | 1 | 10 | 4 |

3. GER (Alfred Lücker, Helmut Nonn, Günther Brennecke, Werner Delmes, Eberhard Ferstl, Hugo Dollheiser, Heinz Radzikowski, Wolfgang Nonn, Hugo Budinger, Werner Rosenbaum, Günther Ullerich) 2 1 2 8 6

4. GBR (David Archer, John Strover, Denys Carnill, John Cockett, Francis Davis, Anthony Robinson, Frederick Hugh Scott, Neil Forster, David Thomas, John Conroy, Michael Doughty, Stephan Johnson, Colin Dale, Geoffrey Cutter) 2 2 2 9 10

5. AUS (Louis Hailey, Alan Barblett, Desmond Spackman, Kevin Carton, Keith Leeson, Dennis Kemp, Raymond Whiteside, Ian Dick, Melville Pearce, Eric Pearce, Gordon Pearce, Maurice Foley) 2 2 0 6 5

6. NZE (David Goldsmith, Brian Johnston, Reginald Johansson, John Tynan, Murray Loudon, John Abrams, Archie Currie, Noel Hobson, Guy McGregor, Bruce Turner, Ivan Armstrong, Phillip Bygrave, William Schaefer) 1 2 0 8 10

Final: IND 1–0 PAK
3rd Place: GER 3–1 GBR

India began confidently with victories of 14–0 over Afghanistan and 16–0 over the United States. However they barely got by a roughhouse German team, 1–0, in the semifinal, and they won the final by the same score on a short corner hit by Gentle midway through the second half.

**1960 Rome** T: 16, N: 16, D: 9.9.

| | | W | L | T | PF | PA |
|---|---|---|---|---|---|---|
| 1. PAK | (Abdul Rashid, Bashir Ahmad, Manzoor Hussain Atif, Ghulam Rasul, Anwar Ahmad Khan, Habib Ali Kiddi, Noor Alam, Abdul Hamid, Abdul Waheed, Nasir Ahmad, Mutih Ullah, Mushtaq Ahmad, Munir Ahmad Dar, Khurshid Aslam) | 6 | 0 | 0 | 25 | 1 |
| 2. IND | (Shankar Laxman, Prithipal Singh, Jaman Lal Sharma, Leslie Claudius, Joseph Antic, Mohinder Lal, Joginder Singh, John Peter, Jaswant Singh, Udham Singh, Raghbir Singh Bhola, Charanjit Singh, Govind Sawant) | 5 | 1 | 0 | 19 | 2 |

3. SPA (Pedro Amat Fontanals, Francisco Caballer Soteras, Juan Angel Calzado de Castro, José Colomer Rivas, Carlos Del Coso Iglesias, José Antonio Dinares Massagué, Eduardo Dualde Santos de Lamadrid, Joaquin Dualde Santos de Lamadrid, Rafael Egusquiza Basterra, Ignacio Macaya Santos de Lamadrid, Pedro Murúa Leguizamon, Pedro Roig Junyent, Luis Maria Usoz Quintana, Narciso Ventalló Surralles) 4 1 1 11 4

4. GBR (Harold Cahill, John Neill, Denys Carnill, Charles Jones, Howard Davis, Neil Livingstone, Ian Taylor, John Hindle, Stuart Mayes, Frederick Scott, Derek Miller, Peter Croft, John Bell, Griffiths Saunders, Patrick Austen) 3 2 1 7 5

5. NZE (William Schaefer, John Abrams, Ian Kerr, Bruce Turner, John Cullen, John Ross Gillespie, Anthony Hayde, Guy McGregor, Noel Hobson, Mervyn McKinnon, Phillip Bygrave, James Barclay, Kelvin Percy, Murray Mathieson) 4 3 1 10 9

6. AUS (Louis Hailey, William Spackman, Mervyn Crossman, John McBryde, Kevin Carton, Julian Pearce, Gordon Pearce, Michael Craig, Raymond Evans, Eric Pearce, Donald Currie, Phillip Pritchard, Graham Wood, Errol Bill, Barry Malcolm) 4 3 2 16 10

7. GER (Wolfgang End, Helmut Nonn, Günther Ullerich, Dieter Krause, Werner Delmes, Eberhard Ferstl, Klaus Woller, Keller, Hugo Budinger, Norbert Schuler, Herbert Winters, Christian Buchting, Willi Brendel, Klaus Greinert) 2 3 0 11 4

7. KEN (George Saudi, Anthony Vaz, Sohal Avtar Singh, Jagnandan Singh, Deol Surjeet Singh, Silvester Fernandes, Edgar Fernandes, Hilary Fernandes, Panaser Surjeet Singh, Sandhu Pritan Singh, John Simonian, Gurarian Kirpal Singh, Egbert Fernandes, Aloysius Mendonca, Krishan Aggarwal, Sehmi Cursarah Singh) 2 2 2 11 5

Final: PAK 1–0 IND
3rd Place: SPA 2–1 GBR

<table>
<tr><td colspan="9"></td></tr>
</table>

| INDIA'S FIELD HOCKEY WINNING STREAK | | | | | | | | |
|---|---|---|---|---|---|---|---|---|
| **1928** | | | **1948** | | | **1960** | | |
| IND | 6–0 | AUS | IND | 8–0 | AUS | IND | 10–0 | DEN |
| IND | 9–0 | BEL | IND | 9–1 | ARG | IND | 4–1 | HOL |
| IND | 5–0 | DEN | IND | 2–0 | SPA | IND | 3–0 | NZE |
| IND | 5–0 | SWI | IND | 2–1 | HOL | IND | 1–0 | AUS |
| IND | 3–0 | HOL | IND | 4–0 | GBR | IND | 1–0 | GER |
| | | | | | | | | |
| **1932** | | | **1952** | | | | | |
| IND | 11–1 | JPN | IND | 4–0 | AUS | | | |
| IND | 24–1 | USA | IND | 3–1 | GBR | | | |
| | | | IND | 6–1 | HOL | | | |
| | | | | | | | | |
| **1936** | | | **1956** | | | | | |
| IND | 4–0 | HUN | IND | 14–0 | AFG | | | |
| IND | 7–0 | USA | IND | 16–0 | USA | | | |
| IND | 9–0 | JPN | IND | 6–0 | SIN | | | |
| IND | 10–0 | FRA | IND | 1–0 | GER | | | |
| IND | 8–1 | GER | IND | 1–0 | PAK | | | |

The early rounds saw some surprising incidents. In the quarterfinal contest between Germany and Pakistan, the score was tied 1–1 with only a few minutes to play. A penalty was called against Ullerich of Germany for illegally blocking a shot with his hand. The referee, Asselmann of Belgium, ordered a bully, or face-off. When a bully is called, two players, one from each team, touch sticks three times and then go after the ball. Ullerich bullied off for the Germans, but only touched sticks twice. The referee caught him and ordered the bully repeated. Again Ullerich struck before the third touch. This time the referee awarded a goal to Pakistan, a goal which gave Pakistan a 2–1 victory. The next day a consolation match was held between France and Belgium. With the score 0–0 and the French attacking, an Italian traffic policeman, on duty just outside the field, blew his whistle. The Belgians thought it was an umpire's whistle and stopped playing, whereupon the French team knocked the ball into the net for what proved to be the only goal of the game. Meanwhile India was forced into double overtime in the quarterfinals before they were able to defeat Australia, 1–0. But that was nothing compared to the Great Britain-Kenya match that followed. That contest went into six overtimes before Saunders of Great Britain scored to give the British a 2–1 victory after 127 minutes of play.

The semifinals were tense affairs, with both Pakistan and India scoring early and holding on for 1–0 wins over Spain and Great Britain, respectively. Entering the final, India had a cumulative Olympic record of 30 wins and no losses, their teams having scored 197 goals while allowing only eight. Unintimidated, the Pakistanis at-

tacked aggressively from the beginning. After 12 minutes Nasir Ahmad of Pakistan pushed a goal into the corner of the net. Despite vigorous play on both sides, that was the only score of the match. The Pakistanis were ecstatic, and most observers were thrilled to have seen such a hard-fought match. But back in India the loss to Pakistan was considered a national tragedy, and plans were immediately made to regain the Olympic title in Tokyo in 1964.

**1964 Tokyo** T: 15, N: 15, D: 10.23.

| | | | W | L | T | PF | PA |
|---|---|---|---|---|---|---|---|
| 1. | IND | (Shankar Laxman, Prithipal Singh, Dharam Singh, Mohinder Lal, Charanjit Singh, Gurbux Singh, Joginder Singh, John Peter, Harbinder Singh, Hari Pal Kaushik, Darshan Singh, Jagjit Singh, Bandu Patil, Udham Singh, Ali Sayeed) | 7 | 0 | 2 | 22 | 5 |
| 2. | PAK | (Abdul Hamid, Munir Ahmad Dar, Manzoor Hussain Atif, Saeed Anwar, Anwar Ahmad Khan, Muhammad Rashid, Khalid Mahmood, Zaka-ud-Din, Muhammad Afzal Manna, Mohammad Asad Malik, Mutih Ullah, Tariq Niazi, Zafar Hayat, Khurshid Azam, Khizar Nawaz, Tariq Aziz) | 7 | 1 | 0 | 20 | 4 |
| 3. | AUS | (Paul Dearing, Donald McWatters, Brian Glencross, John McBryde, Julian Pearce, Graham Wood, Robin Hodder, Raymond Evans, Eric Pearce, Patrick Nilan, Donald Smart, Antony Waters, Mervyn Crossman, Desmond Piper) | 5 | 3 | 0 | 20 | 10 |
| 4. | SPA | (Carlos Del Coso Iglesias, José Colomer Rivas, Julio Solaun Garteizgogeascoa, Juan Angel Calzado de Castro, José Antonio Dinares Massagué, Narciso Ventalló Surralles, Ignacio Macaya Santos de Lamadrid, Jaime Amat Fontanais, Eduardo Dualde Santos de Lamadrid, Jorge Vidal Mitjans, Jaime Echevarria Arteche, Luis Maria Usoz Quintana, Pedro Amat Fontanais, Francisco Amat Fontanais) | 4 | 2 | 3 | 18 | 9 |
| 5. | GDR | (Rainer Stephan, Axel Thieme, Klaus Vetter, Horst Brennecke, Klaus Bahner, Horst Dahmlos, Reiner Hanschke, Rolf Westphal, Lothar Lippert, Dieter Ehrlich, Adolf Krause, Karl-Heinz Freiberger) | 4 | 0 | 5 | 17 | 5 |

| | | | W | L | T | PF | PA |
|---|---|---|---|---|---|---|---|
| 6. | KEN | (John Simonian, Anthony Querobino Vaz, Avtar Singh Sohal, Surjeet Singh Panesar, Silvester Fernandes, Leo Fernandes, Edgar Simon Fernandes, Egbert Carmo Fernandes, Amar Singh Mangat, Aloysius Mendonca, Saude André George, Krishan Kumar Aggarwal, Tejparkash Singh Brar, Reynold D'Souza, Santokh Singh Matharu) | 4 | 3 | 1 | 10 | 13 |
| 7. | HOL | (Joost Boks, Jacob Leemhius, Jan Van Gooswilligen, Johan Fokker, Franciscus Fiolet, Theodorus Terlingen, Th. J. M. V. Van Vroonhoven, Arie Leendert de Keyzer, Guillaum Zweerts, Jacob Voigt, Nicolaas Spits, Jan Veentjer, John Elffers, Leendert Krol, Jan Van Hooft, Johan Mijnarends, Eric van Rossem, C. V. Coster Van Voorhout) | 4 | 3 | 1 | 21 | 7 |
| 7. | JPN | (Hiroshi Miwa, Tsuneya Yuzaki, Akio Takashima, Katsuhiro Yuzaki, Tetsuya Wakabayashi, Toshihiko Yamaoka, Kenji Takizawa, Shigeo Kadku, Hiroshi Tanaka, Michio Okabe, Seiji Kihara, Junichi Yamaguchi, Kunio Iwahashi) | 3 | 4 | 0 | 7 | 11 |

Final: IND 1–0 PAK
3rd Place: AUS 3–2 SPA
5th Place: GDR 3–0 KEN

India struggled through to the final, surviving 1–1 ties with Germany and Spain. Pakistan, on the other hand, won seven straight matches. However, in the deciding contest, with five minutes gone in the second half, Munir Ahmad Dar of Pakistan was penalized for stopping a shot with his foot. Mohinder Lal converted the penalty shot for the only goal of the game.

**1968 Mexico City** T: 16, N: 16, D: 10.26.

| | | | W | L | T | PF | PA |
|---|---|---|---|---|---|---|---|
| 1. | PAK | (Zakir Hussain, Tanvir Ahmad Dar, Tariq Aziz, Saeed Anwar, Riaz Ahmed, Guirez Akhtar, Khalid Mahmood Hussain, Mohammad Ashfaq, Abdul Rashid, Mohammad Asad Malik, Jahangir Ahmad Butt, Riaz Ud Din, Tariq Niazi) | 9 | 0 | 0 | 26 | 5 |
| 2. | AUS | (Paul Dearing, James Mason, Brian Glencross, Gordon Pearce, Julian Pearce, Robert Haigh, Donald Martin, Raymond Evans, Ronald Riley, Patrick Nilan, Donald Smart, Desmond | 5 | 3 | 1 | 15 | 8 |

| | | | W | L | T | PF | PA |
|---|---|---|---|---|---|---|---|
| | | Piper, Eric Pearce, Frederick Quinn) | | | | | |
| 3. | IND | (Rajendra Absolem Christy, Gurbux Singh, Prithipal Singh, Balbir Singh II, Ajitpal Singh, Krishna Murtay Perumal, Balbir Singh III, Balbir Singh I, Harbinder Singh, Inamur Rehman, Inder Singh, Munir Sait, Harmik Singh, Jagjit Singh, John Peter, Tarsem Singh, Gurbaksh Singh) | 7 | 2 | 0 | 23 | 7 |
| 4. | GER | (Wolfgang Rott, Günter Krauss, Utz Aichinger, Dirk Michel, Klaus Greinert, Ulrich Vos, Michael Krause, Norbert Schuler, Fritz Schmidt, Carsten Keller, Ulrich Sloma, Wolfgang Müller, Eckart Suhl, Friedrich-Wilhelm Josten, Jürgen Wein, Detlef Kittstein, Wolfgang Baumgart, Hermann End) | 5 | 3 | 1 | 16 | 8 |
| 5. | HOL | (Joost Boks, Theodorus Terlingen, Heiko Locker van Staveren, Charles de Lanoy Meijer, Johan Fokker, John Elffers, Frans Spits, Otto Boudewijn ter Haar, Charles Thole, Petrus Weemers, Arie de Keyzer, Aernout Brederode, Ewaldus Kist, Sebo Onno Ebbens, Theo van Vroonhoven, Gerardus Hijikema, Edo Buma) | 6 | 3 | 0 | 15 | 12 |
| 6. | SPA | (Carlos Del Coso Iglesias, Antonio Nogues, Julio Solaun Garteizgogeascoa, Francisco Fábregas, José Antonio Dinares Massagué, Juan Amat, Juan Quintana, José Salles, Francisco Amat Fontanais, Pedro Amat Fontanais, Agustin Masana, José Colomer Rivas, Jorge Fábregas, Narciso Ventalló Surralles, Rafael Camina, Jorge Vidal Mitjans, Juan José Alvear Calleja) | 3 | 3 | 3 | 9 | 7 |
| 7. | NZE | (Ross McPherson, Roger Capey, Alan Patterson, Keith Thomson, Selwyn Maister, John Anslow, Bruce Judge, John Christensen, Alan McIntyre, Barry Maister, Jan Borren, Edwin Salmon, John Hicks) | 3 | 1 | 4 | 9 | 7 |
| 8. | KEN | (John Simonian, Kirpal Bhardwaj, Avtar Singh Sohal, Harvinder Marwa, Surjeet Singh Panesar, Silvester Fernandes, Leo Fernandes, Santokh Singh Matharu, Davinder Deegan, Hilary Fernandes, Aloysius Men- | 4 | 3 | 1 | 12 | 8 |

donca, Mohamed Malik, Egbert Fernandes, Reynold Pereira)

Final: PAK 2–1 AUS
3rd Place: IND 2–1 GER
5th Place: HOL 1–0 SPA
7th Place: NZE 2–0 KEN

With the score tied 0–0 after 55 minutes in a preliminary match between India and Japan, a penalty stroke was awarded to India. The Japanese were so upset that they laid down their sticks and walked off the field, forfeiting the game. Earlier, India had lost to New Zealand, 2–1—the first time that India had given up more than one goal in an Olympic match. They lost their semifinal match to Australia by the same score. In the final, the winning goal was scored by Mohammad Asad Malik after 56 minutes of play.

**1972 Munich** T: 16, N: 16, D: 9.10.

| | | | W | L | T | PF | PA |
|---|---|---|---|---|---|---|---|
| 1. | GER | (Wolfgang Rott, Michael Peter, Dieter Freise, Michael Krause, Eduard Thelen, Horst Dröse, Carsten Keller, Ulrich Klaes, Wolfgang Baumgart, Uli Vos, Peter Trump, Peter Kraus, Werner Kaessmann, Wolfgang Strödter, Detlef Kittstein, Rainer Seifert, Eckart Suhl, Fritz Schmidt) | 8 | 1 | 0 | 21 | 5 |
| 2. | PAK | (Saleem Sherwani, Akhtarul Islam, Munawaruz Zaman, Saeed Anwar, Rasool Akhtar, Fazalur Rehman, Mudassar Asghar, Islahud Din, Abdul Rashid, Mohammad Asad Malik, Mohammad Shahnaz, Riaz Ahmed, Iftikhar Ahmed, Muhammad Zahid, Jahangir Ahmad Butt) | 6 | 2 | 1 | 19 | 7 |
| 3. | IND | (Manuel Frederick, Mukhbaln Singh, Michael Kindo, Krishna Murtay Perumal, Ajitpal Singh, Harmik Singh, Ganesh Mollerapoovayya, Harbinder Singh, Kulwant Singh, Ashok Kumar, Harcharan Singh, Govin Bilimogaputtaswamy, Virinder Singh, Cornelius Charles) | 6 | 1 | 2 | 27 | 11 |
| 4. | HOL | (Andre Bolhuis, Thijs Kaanders, Coen Kranenberg, Thies Kruize, Maarten Sikking, Frans Spits, Nico Spits, Bart Taminiau, Charles Thole, Piet Weemers, Jeroen Zweerts, Wouter Leefers, Flip van Lidth de Jeude, Paul Litjens, Marinus Dijkerman, Irving van Nes) | 5 | 3 | 1 | 21 | 14 |
| 5. | AUS | (Brian Glencross, Robert Haigh, Richard Charlesworth, Paul Dearing, Thomas Colder, James Mason, Terry McAskell, Patrick Nilan, Desmond Piper, Ronald Riley, Donald Smart, Gregory Browning, Robert Andrew, Graham Reid, Ronald Wilson, Wayne Hammond) | | | | | |
| 6. | GBR | (Austin Savage, Paul Svehlik, Tony Ekins, Keith Sinclair, Bernard Cotton, Rui Saldanha, Richard Oliver, Michael Crowe, Michael Corby, Peter Marsh, John French, Dennis Hay, Terry Gregg, Peter Mills, Sheik M. Ahmad, Graham Evans, Christopher Langhorne) | 5 | 3 | 1 | 18 | 12 |
| 7. | SPA | (Alberto Carera, Jorge Fábregas, Francisco Seguar, Juan Amat, Francisco Fábregas, José Salles, José Alustiza, José Borrell, Francisco Amat, Ramon Quintana, Juan Arbos, Jaime Arbos, Jaime Amat, Juan Quintana, Luis Towse, Jorge Camina, Antonio Nogues, Agustin Churruca) | 3 | 2 | 4 | 11 | 11 |
| 8. | MAL | (Khairuddin Bin Zainal, A. Francis Belavantheran, Sri Shanmuganathan, Poh Meng Phang, Wong Choon Hin, S. Dalasingam, Sion Ming Yang, Franco Louis D'Cruz, K. Mahendran, Singh Harnahal, R. Pathmarajah, Mohinder Razali Yeop Omar, Sayed Samàt, Sulaiman Saibot, Brian Santa Maria) | 4 | 4 | 1 | 11 | 11 |

Final: GER 1–0 PAK
3rd Place: IND 2–1 HOL
5th Place: AUS 2–1 GBR
7th Place: SPA 2–1 MAL

The final was a bitter and violent contest, with Michael Krause of Germany scoring the only goal of the game with ten minutes to play. The Pakistani team and their supporters in the stands were so angry at the officiating that they stormed the judges' table and poured water on Réné Frank, President of the International Hockey Federation. At the medal ceremony, several of the Pakistani players refused to face the German flag during the playing of the German national anthem. All 11 Pakistani finalists were banned for life by the International Olympic Committee, but reinstated in time for the 1976 Olympics.

**1976 Montreal** T: 11, N: 11, D: 7.30.

| | | | W | L | T | PF | PA |
|---|---|---|---|---|---|---|---|
| 1. | NZE | (Paul Ackerley, Jeff Archibald, Thur Borren, Alan Chesney, John Christensen, Greg Dayman, Tony Ineson, Alan McIntyre, Barry Maister, Selwyn Mais- | 3 | 1 | 2 | 9 | 9 |

|   |   | W | L | T | PF | PA |
|---|---|---|---|---|---|---|
| | ter, Trevor Manning, Arthur Parkin, Mohan Patel, Ramesh Patel) | | | | | |
| 2. AUS | (Robert Haigh, Richard Charlesworth, David Bell, Gregory Browning, Ian Cooke, Barry Dancer, Douglas Golder, Wayne Hammond, James Irvine, Malcolm Poole, Robert Proctor, Graham Reid, Ronald Riley, Trevor Smith, Terry Walsh) | 4 | 3 | 0 | 16 | 8 |
| 3. PAK | (Saleem Sherwani, Manzoor Hassan, Munawaruz Zaman, Saleem Nazim, Rasool Akhtar, Iftikhar Syed, Islah Islahuddin, Manzoor Hussain, Abdul Rashid, Shanaz Sheikh, Samiulah Khan, Qamar Zia, Arshad Mahmood, Arshad Ali Chaudry, Mudassar Asghar, Haneef Khan) | 4 | 1 | 1 | 20 | 11 |
| 4. HOL | (Maarten Sikking, Andre Bolhuis, Tim Steens, Geert van Eijk, Theodoor Doyer, Coen Kranenburg, Rob Toft, Wouter Leefers, Hans Jorritsma, Hans Kruize, Jan Albers, Paul Litjens, Imbert Jebbink, Ron Steens, Bart Taminiau, Wouter Kan) | 5 | 2 | 0 | 14 | 8 |
| 5. GER | (Wolfgang Rott, Klaus Ludwiczak, Michael Peter, Dieter Freise, Fritz Schmidt, Michael Krause, Horst Dröse, Werner Kaessmann, Uli Vos, Peter Caninenberg, Peter Trump, Hans Montag, Wolfgang Strödter, Heiner Dopp, Rainer Seifert, Ralf Lauruschkat) | 3 | 2 | 1 | 22 | 13 |
| 6. SPA | (Luis Alberto Carrera, Juan Amat, Jaime Arbos, Juan Arbos, Ricardo Cabot, Juan Colomer, Francisco Codina, Agustin Churruca, Francisco Fábregas, Jorge Fábregas, Agustin Masana, Juan Pellon, Ramon Quintana, José Salles, Francisco Segura, Luis Alberto Twose) | 2 | 2 | 2 | 12 | 17 |
| 7. IND | (Ajitpal Singh, Vaduvelu Phillips, Baldev Singh, Ashok Diwan, Bilimogga Govinda, Ashok Singh, Varinder Singh, Harcharan Singh, Mohinder Singh, Aslam Sher Khan, Syed Ali, Birbhadur Chattri, Chand Singh, Ajit Singh, Surjit Singh, Vasudevan Baskaran) | 4 | 3 | 0 | 16 | 12 |
| 8. MAL | (Khaliuddin Zainal, Azraai Md. Zain, Srishan Janath Nagana- | 2 | 5 | 0 | 4 | 11 |

thy, Francis Anthonysamy, Kok Ming Lam, Mohindar Singh Amar, Choon Hin Wong, Balasingam Singaram, Palanisamy Nallasamy, Rama Krishnan Rengasamy, Medhendran Murugesan, Singh Avtar Gill, Antony Cruz, Fook Loke Poon, Pathmarajah Ramalingam, Soon Kooi Ow)

Final: NZE 1–0 AUS
3rd Place: PAK 3–2 HOL
5th Place: GER 9–1 SPA
7th Place: IND 2–0 MAL

New Zealand didn't exactly overwhelm their opposition; in fact, they didn't even outscore them. But they scored when it counted, including a penalty shot by Tony Ineson early in the second half that gave them a 1–0 victory over Australia in the final.

**1980 Moscow** T: 6, N: 6, D: 7.26.

|   |   | W | L | T | PF | PA |
|---|---|---|---|---|---|---|
| 1. IND | (Allan Schofield, Chettri Bir Bhadur, Dung Dung Sylvanus, Rajinder Singh, Davinder Singh, Gurmail Singh, Ravinder Pal Singh, Vasudevan Baskaran, Somaya Maneypanda, Maharaj Krishon Kaushik, Charanjit Kumar, Mervyn Fernandis, Amarjit Rana Singh, Mohamed Shahid, Zafar Iqbal, Surinder Singh) | 4 | 0 | 2 | 43 | 9 |
| 2. SPA | (José Garcia, Juan Amat, Santiago Malgósa, Rafael Garralda, Francisco Fábregas, Juan Luis Coghen, Ricardo Cabot, Jaimes Arbos, Carlos Roca, Juan Pellon, Miguel de Paz, Miguel Chavez, Juan Arbos, Javier Cabot, Paulino Monsalve, Jaime Zumalacarregui) | 4 | 1 | 1 | 36 | 7 |
| 3. SOV | (Vladimir Pleshakov, Vyacheslav Lampeev, Leonid Pavlovsky, Sos Airapetyan, Farit Zigangirov, Valery Belyakov, Sergei Klevtsov, Oleg Zagoroonev, Aleksandr Gusev, Sergei Pleshakov, Mikhail Nichepurenko, Minneula Azizov, Aleksandr Sytchev, Aleksandr Myasnikov, Viktor Deputatov, Aleksandr Goncharov) | 4 | 2 | 0 | 32 | 12 |
| 4. POL | (Zygfryd Józefiak, Andrzej Mikina, Krystian Bąk, Wlodzimierz Stanislawski, Leszek Hensler, Jan Sitek, Jerzy Wybieralski, Leszek Tórz, Zbigniew Rachwalski, Henryk Horwat, An- | 2 | 3 | 1 | 20 | 17 |

drzej Myśliwiec, Leszek Andrze-
jczak, Jan Mielniczak, Mariusz
Kubiak, Adan Dolatowski, Krysz-
tof Glodowski)

| | | | W | L | T | PF | PA |
|---|---|---|---|---|---|---|---|
| 5. | CUB | (Angel Mora Parra, Severo Frometa Conte, Bernabe Izquier-do Martinez, Edgardo Vazquez Marquez, Hector Pedroso Gar-cia, Manuel Varela Perez, Raul Garcia Cabrera, Jorge Mico Gu-tierrez, Rudolfo Delgado Or-bañez, Lazaro Hernandez Ran-gel, Juan Blanco Peñalver, Juan Caballero Perez, Roberto Ra-mirez Hernandez, Angel Fon-tane Escobar, Ricardo Campos Hernandez, Juan Rios Alvarez) | 2 | 4 | 0 | 11 | 43 |
| 6. | TAN | (Leopold Gracias, Benedict Mendes, Soter Da Silva, Abra-ham Sykes, Yusuf Manwar, Jaypal Singh, Mohamed Manji, Rajabu Rajab, Jasbir Virdee, Islam Islam, Stephen D'Silva, Frederick Furtado, Taherali Has-sanali, Anoop Mukundan, Pat-rick Toto, Julius Peter) | 0 | 6 | 0 | 4 | 58 |

Final: IND 4–3 SPA
3rd Place: SOV 2–1 POL
5th Place: CUB 4–1 TAN

The 1980 field hockey tournament was decimated by the boycott. Of the 11 teams that competed in Montreal in 1976, only Spain and India were represented in Moscow. Cuba and Tanzania were added to fill the field even though they had little experience with the sport. It was like old times for India, trouncing Tanzania 18–0 and Cuba 13–0. However, they had a tougher match with Poland, salvaging a 2–2 tie when Mervyn Fernandis scored a goal with five seconds to play. India also scraped through with a 2–2 tie against Spain. The two teams met again in the final. India took a 3–0 lead and held on to win, 4–3, despite the fact that Juan Amat of Spain scored three goals in twelve minutes.

### 1984 Los Angeles-Monterey Park T: 12, N: 12, D: 8.11.

| | | | W | L | T | PF | PA |
|---|---|---|---|---|---|---|---|
| 1. | PAK | (G. Moinuddin, Qasim Zia, Nasir Ali, Abdul Rashid, Ayaz Mah-mood, Naeem Akhtar, Kaleemul-lah, Manzoor Hussain, Hasan Sardar, Hanir Khan, Khalid Ha-meed, Shahid Ali Khan, Tauqeer Dar, Ishtiaq Ahmed, Salleem Sherwani, Mushtaq Ahmad) | 4 | 0 | 3 | 19 | 8 |
| 2. | GER | (Christian Bassemir, Tobias Frank, Horst-Ulrich Hänel, Car-sten Fischer, Karl-Joachim Hür-ter, Eckhard Schmidt-Opper, Reinhard Krull, Michael Peter, Stefan Blöcher, Andreas Keller, Thomas Reck, Markku Slawyk, Thomas Gunst, Heiner Dopp, Volker Fried, Dirk Brinkmann) | 4 | 2 | 1 | 14 | 6 |
| 3. | GBR | (Ian Taylor, Stephan Martin, Paul Barber, Robert Cattrall, Jonathon Potter, Richard Dodds, William McConnell, Nor-man "Billy" Hughes, David Westcott, Richard Leman, Ste-phen Batchelor, Sean Kerly, James Duthie, Kulbir Bhaura, Mark Precious) | 5 | 1 | 1 | 13 | 8 |
| 4. | AUS | (Richard Charlesworth, James Irvine, Colin Batch, David Bell, Adrian Berce, Grant Boyce, Craig Davies, Peter Haselhurst, Treva King, Terry Leece, Grant Mitton, Michael Nobbs, Nigel Patmore, Trevor Smith, Neil Snowden, Terry Walsh) | 5 | 2 | 0 | 19 | 8 |
| 5. | IND | (Romeo James, Manohar Topno, Vineet Kumar Sharma, Somaya Maneypandomuttana, Joaquimmartin Carvaho, Rajin-der Singh, Charanjit Kumar, Mer-vyn Fernandis, Hardeep Singh, Mohamed Shahid, Zafar Iqbal, Nila Komol Singh, Iqbaljit Growal, Ravinder Pal Singh, Marcellusmark Gomes, Jala-ludin Syed) | 5 | 1 | 1 | 20 | 11 |
| 6. | HOL | (Petrus Hermans, Arno den Har-tog, Cees Jan Diepeveen, Henricus Pierik, Theodoor Doy-er, Thomas van't Hek, Peter van Asbeck, Willem van Asbeck, Hans Kruize, Ties Kruize, Ron-aldus Steens, Jan Hidde Kruize, Alexander Bos, Roderik Bouwman, René Klaassen, Maarten van Grimbergen) | 4 | 2 | 1 | 18 | 14 |
| 7. | NZE | (Jeffrey Archibald, Husmukh Bhikha, Christopher Brown, George Carnoutsos, Peter Daji, Laurence Gallen, Stuart Grim-shaw, Trevor Laurence, Grant McLeod, Brent Miskimmin, Pe-ter Miskimmin, Arthur Parkin, Ramesh Patel, Robin Wilson, Maurice Marquet, Graham Sligo) | 2 | 3 | 2 | 11 | 11 |
| 8. | SPA | (José Agut, Javier Cabot, Juan Arbos, Andres Gomez, Juan Carlos Peon, Jaime Arbos, Ri-cardo Cabot, Juan Malgosa, Carlos Roca, Mariano Bordas, Ignacio Cobos, Jorge Oliva, Mi-guel Depaz, Ignacio Escude, Santiago Malgosa) | 2 | 5 | 0 | 11 | 13 |

Final: PAK 2–1 GER
3rd Place: GBR 3–2 AUS
5th Place: IND 5–2 HOL
7th Place: NZE 1–0 SPA

Australia, unbeaten in two years and the winner of five straight international tournaments, seemed well on their way to their first Olympic championship when they were beaten 1–0 by a rough Pakistani team in a stunning semi-final upset.

"PAKISTAN AVENGES MUNICH" read a banner hoisted in the stands as play began in the final match, a reference to the ugly 1972 final between Pakistan and West Germany. This time, in the blistering heat at East Los Angeles College, it was the Asian champions who prevailed. For the first time in Olympic history, the gold medal was decided in overtime, as Kaleemullah scored his only goal of the tournament in the twelfth minute.

In the bronze medal match, the demoralized Australians were upset again, this time by a surprising British team which had qualified for the Olympic tournament only as a result of the Soviet withdrawal.

**1988 Seoul** T: 12, N: 12, D: 10.1.

|  |  | W | L | T | PF | PA |
|---|---|---|---|---|---|---|
| 1. GBR | (Ian Taylor, Veryan Pappin, David Faulkner, Paul Barber, Stephen Martin, Jon Potter, Richard Dodds, Martyn Grimley, Stephen Batchelor, Richard Leman, James Kirkwood, Kulbir Bhaura, Sean Kerly, Robert Clift, Imran Sherwani, Russell Garcia) | 5 | 1 | 1 | 18 | 8 |
| 2. GER | (Christian Schliemann, Tobias Frank, Horst-Ulrich Hänel, Carsten Fischer, Andreas Mollandin, Ekkhard Schmidt-Opper, Dirk Brinkmann, Heiner Dopp, Stefan Blöcher, Andreas Keller, Thomas Reck, Thomas Brinkmann, Hanns-Henning Fastrich, Michael Hilgers, Volker Fried, Michael Metz) | 5 | 1 | 1 | 16 | 7 |
| 3. HOL | (Prank Leistra, Marc Benninga, Cees Jan Diepeveen, Maurits Crucq, Rene Klaassen, Hendrik Jan Kooijman, Marc Delissen, Jacques Brinkman, Gerrit Jan Schlatmann, Tim Steens, Floris Jan Bove Lander, Patrick Faber, Ronald Jansen, Jan Hidde Kruize, Erik Parlevliet, Taco van den Honert) | 4 | 2 | 1 | 15 | 9 |
| 4. AUS | (Craig Davies, Colin Batch, John Bestall, Warren Birmingham, Richard Charlesworth, Andrew Deane, Michael York, Mark Hager, Jay Stacy, Neil Hawgood, Peter Noel, Graham Reid, Roger Smith, Neil Snowden, David Wansbrough, Ken Wark) | 5 | 2 | 0 | 22 | 8 |
| 5. PAK | (Mansoor Ahmed, Nasir Ali, Qazi Mohib-Ur-Rehman, Aamir-Zafar, Ishtiaq Ahmed, Naeem Akhtar, Qamar Ibrahim, Shahbaz Ahmed, Tariq Shaiikh, Zahid Sharif, Khalid Hamid, Khalid Bashir, Naeem Amjad, Tahir Zaman, Musaddiz Hussain) | 5 | 2 | 0 | 18 | 9 |
| 6. IND | (Rawat Rajinder Singh, Pargat Singh, Ashok Kumar, Mohinder-Pal Singh, Somaya Maneypandemuttana, Vivek Singh, Sujit Kumar, Subramani Baladadalaiash, Mohammad Shahid, Sebastian Jude Felix, Balwinder Singh, Mervyn Fernandis, Thoiba Singh, Gundeep Kumar, Jagbir Singh, Patterson Markphilip) | 3 | 3 | 1 | 16 | 15 |
| 7. SOV | (Vladimir Pleshakov, Viktor Deputatov, Igor Yulchiev, Sos Airapetyan, Vladimir Antakov, Vyacheslav Chechenov, Igor Atanov, Sergei Chakvorostov, Sergei Pleshakov, Mikhail Nichepurenko, Aleksandr Domashev, Igor Davydov, Aleksandr Myasnikov, Yevgeny Nechayev, Mikhail Bukatin) | 3 | 3 | 1 | 9 | 12 |
| 8. ARG | (Otto Schmitt, Alejandro Siri, Miguel Altube, Marcelo Mascheroni, Marcelo Garraffo, Edgardo Pailos, Alejandro Doherty, Aldo Ayala, Carlos Geneyro, Gabriel Minadeo, Alejandro Verga, Fernando Ferrara, Emanuel Roggero, Franco Nicola, Martin Sordelli, Mariano Silva) | 2 | 5 | 0 | 15 | 22 |

Final: GBR 3–1 GER
3rd Place: HOL 2–1 AUS
5th Place: PAK 2–1 IND
7th Place: SOV 4–1 ARG

As in 1984, the favored Australians swept through the preliminary round undefeated, only to be beaten in the semifinals. This time Great Britain spoiled the Australians' tournament when Sean Kerly broke a 2–2 tie with 1:22 to play. In the final, Britain faced West Germany, who had defeated them 2–1 in the preliminary round. But the Germans were frustrated by Britain's superb defensive play. Imran Sherwani, a newsagent from Stoke-on-Trent, scored two of Great Britain's three goals.

# WOMEN

**1896–1976** not held

**1980 Moscow** T: 6, N: 6, D: 7.31.

| | | W | L | T | PF | PA |
|---|---|---|---|---|---|---|
| 1. ZIM | (Sarah English, Ann Mary Grant, Brenda Phillips, Patricia McKillop, Sonia Robertson, Patricia Davies, Maureen George, Linda Watson, Susan Huggett, Gillian Cowley, Elizabeth Chase, Sandra Chick, Helen Volk, Christine Prinsloo, Arlene Boxhall, Anthea Stewart) | 3 | 0 | 2 | 13 | 4 |
| 2. CZE | (Jarmila Kralicková, Berta Hruba, Iveta Sranková, Lenka Vymazalová, Jirina Krizová, Jirina Kadlecová, Jirina Čermaková, Marta Urbanová, Kveta Petricková, Marie Sykorová, Ida Hubacková, Milada Blazková, Jana Lahodová, Alena Kyselicová, Jirina Hajková, Viera Podhanyiová) | 3 | 1 | 1 | 10 | 5 |
| 3. SOV | (Galina Inzhuvatova, Nelli Gorbatkova, Valentina Zazdravnykh, Nadezhda Ovechkina, Natella Krasnikova, Natalya Bykova, Lidlya Glubokova, Galina Vyuzhanina, Natalya Buzunova, Lyailya Akhmerova, Nadezhda Filippova, Yelena Gureva, Tatyana Yembakhtova, Tatyana Shvyganova, Alina Kham, Lyudmila Frolova) | 3 | 2 | 0 | 11 | 5 |
| 4. IND | (Margaret Toscano, Sudha Chaudhry, Gangotri Bhandari, Rekha Mundphan, Rupa Kumari Saini, Varsha Soni, Eliza Nelson, Prem Maya Sonir, Naazleen Madraswalla, Selma D'Silva, Lorraine Fernandes, Harpreet Gill, Balwinder Kaur Bhatia, Geeta Sareen, Nisha Sharma, Hutoxi Bagli) | 2 | 2 | 1 | 9 | 6 |
| 5. AUT | (Patricia Lorenz, Sabine Blemenschütz, Elisabeth Pistauer, Andrea Kozma, Brigitta Pecanka, Brigette Kindler, Friederike Stern, Regina Lorenz, Eleonore Pecanka, Ilse Stipanovsky, Andrea Porsch, Erika Csar, Dorit Ganster, Ulrike Kleinhansl, Eva Cambal, Jana Cejpek) | 2 | 3 | 0 | 6 | 11 |
| 6. POL | (Malgorzata Gajewska, Bogumila Pajor, Jolanta Sekulak, Jo- | 0 | 5 | 0 | 0 | 18 |

lanta Błędowska, Lucyna Matuszna, Danuta Stanislawska, Wieslawa Rylko, Lidia Zgajewska, Maria Kornek, Malgorzata Lipska, Halina Koldras, Lucyna Siejka, Dorota Bielska, Dorota Załęczna, Michalina Plekaniec, Jadwiga Koldras)

When five of the six nations scheduled to compete in the inaugural women's field hockey tournament withdrew as part of the Jimmy Carter boycott, it set the stage for a true Cinderella story. As white-ruled Rhodesia, Zimbabwe had been banned from the Olympics, but when the black majority took power, the ban was lifted. Desperate to fill the field, the Soviet Union and the International Olympic Committee contacted Zimbabwe five weeks before the start of the Games and offered to subsidize the sending of a team, the members of which were not selected until the weekend before the Olympics opened. Ironically, the team that represented Zimbabwe was all white. They were held to ties by Czechoslovakia and India, but they were the only team to avoid defeat. A 4–1 victory over Austria assured them of gold medals.

**1984 Los Angeles-Monterey Park** T: 6, N: 6, D: 8.10.

| | | W | L | T | PF | PA |
|---|---|---|---|---|---|---|
| 1. HOL | (Bernadette de Beus, Alette Pos, Margriet Zegers, Laurien Willemse, Marjolein Eysvogel, Josephine Boekhorst, Carina Benninga, Alexandra le Poole, Francisca Hillen, Marieke van Doorn, Sophie von Weiler, Aletta van Manen, Irene Hendriks, Elisabeth Sevens, Martine Ohr, Anneloes Nieuwenhuizen) | 4 | 0 | 1 | 14 | 6 |
| 2. GER | (Ursula Thielemann, Elke Drüll, Beate Deininger, Christina Moser, Hella Roth, Dagmar Breiken, Birgit Hagen, Birgit Hahn, Gabriele Appel, Andrea Lietz-Weiermann, Corinna Lingnau, Martina Koch, Gabriela Schley, Patricia Ott, Susanne Schmid, Sigrid Landgraf) | 2 | 1 | 2 | 9 | 9 |
| 3. USA | (Gwen Cheeseman, Beth Anders, Kathleen McGahey, Anita Miller, Regina Buggy, Christine Larson-Mason, Beth Beglin, Marcella Place, Julie Staver, Diane Moyer, Sheryl Johnson, Charlene Morett, Karen Shelton, Brenda Stauffler, Leslie Milne, Judy Strong) | 2 | 2 | 1 | 9 | 7 |
| 4. AUS | (Kym Ireland, Liane Tooth, Pamela Glossop, Susan Watkins, | 2 | 2 | 1 | 9 | 7 |

| | | W | L | T | PF | PA |
|---|---|---|---|---|---|---|
| | Lorraine Hillas, Robyn Leggatt, Sandra Pisani, Penny Gray, Robyn Holmes, Sharon Buchanan, Marian Aylmore, Colleen Pearce, Loretta Dorman, Julene Sunderland, Trisha Heberle, Evelyn Botfield) | | | | | |
| 5. CAN | (Laurie Lambert, Sharon Creelman, Jean Major, Laura Branchaud, Lynne Beecroft, Shelley Andrews, Darlene Stoyka, Phyllis Ellis, Karen Hewlett, Diane Virjee, Terry Wheatley, Lisa Bauer, Sheila Forshaw, Sharon Bayes, Zoe Mackinnon, Nancy Charlton) | 2 | 2 | 1 | 9 | 11 |
| 6. NZE | (Lesley Murdoch, Barbara Tilden, Mary Clinton, Susan McLeish, Isobel Thomson, Sandra Mackie, Jillian Smith, Jane Goulding, Robyn Blackman, Jan Martin, Harina Kohere, Jennifer McDonald, Shirley Haig, Catherine Thompson, Lesley Elliott, Christine Arthur) | 0 | 5 | 0 | 2 | 12 |

The Australian women entered the final match of the round-robin tournament with a clear understanding of what they needed to accomplish. If they could beat the heavily favored Dutch team by two goals, they would earn gold medals. If they won by one goal or tied, they would finish second. If they lost by one goal they would win bronze medals, and if they lost by three goals, they would finish out of the money. The Dutch won 2–0, which meant that Australia and the U.S. completed the tournament with identical records. Although the Australians had defeated the Americans 3–1, tournament rules stated that the bronze medals would be decided by a penalty stroke shoot-off, which took place 15 minutes after the last match. The U.S. won easily, 10–5.

**1988 Seoul** T: 8, N: 8, D: 9.30.

| | | W | L | T | PF | PA |
|---|---|---|---|---|---|---|
| 1. AUS | (Kathleen Partridge, Elspeth Clement, Liane Tooth, Loretta Dorman, Lorraine Hillas, Michelle Capes, Sandra Pisani, Deborah Bowman, Lee Capes, Kim Small, Sally Carbon, Jacqueline Pereira, Tracey Belbin, Rechelle Hawkes, Sharon Patmore, Maree Fish) | 3 | 0 | 2 | 12 | 8 |
| 2. KOR | (Kim Mi-sun, Han Ok-kyung, Chang Eun-jung, Han Keum-sil, Choi Choon-ok, Kim Soon-duk, Chung Sang-hyun, Jin Won-sim, Hwang Keum-sook, Cho Ki-hyang, Seo Kwang-mi, Park | 3 | 1 | 1 | 13 | 9 |

| | | W | L | T | PF | PA |
|---|---|---|---|---|---|---|
| | Soon-ja, Kim Young-sook, Seo Hyo-sun, Lim Kye-sook, Chung Eun-kyung) | | | | | |
| 3. HOL | (Bernadette DeBeus, Yvonne Buter, Willemien Aardenburg, Laurien Willemse, Marjolein Bolhuis, Lisanne Lejeune, Carina Benninga, Annemieke Fokke, Ingrid Wolff, Marieke van Doorn, Sophie von Weiler, Aletta van Manen, Noor Holsboer, Helen van der Ben, Martine Ohr, Anneloes Nieuwenhuizen) | 4 | 1 | 0 | 14 | 6 |
| 4. GBR | (Gill Atkins, Wendy Banks, Gill Brown, Karen Brown, Mary Nevill, Julie Cook, Vickey Dixon, Wendy Fraser, Barbara Hambly, Caroline Jordan, Violet McBride, Moira Macleod, Caroline Brewer, Jane Sixsmith, Kate Parker, Alison Ramsay) | 1 | 3 | 1 | 5 | 11 |
| 5. GER | (Susanne Schmid, Carola Hoffmann, Heike Gehrmann, Dagmar Bremer, Gabriele Uhlenbruck, Viola Grahl, Bettina Blumenbeg, Gaby Appel, Martina Hallmen, Christine Ferneck, Silke Wehrmeister, Caren Jungjohann, Eva Hegener, Susi Wolls Chlager, Gabriela Schowe) | 3 | 2 | 0 | 9 | 9 |
| 6. CAN | (Sharon Bayes, Wendy Baker, Deb Covey, Lisa Lyn, Laura Branchaud, Sandra Levy, Kathryn Johnson, Shona Schleppe, Michelle Conn, Liz Czenczek, Sheila Forshaw, Nancy Charlton, Sara Ballantyne, Sharon Creelman) | 1 | 3 | 1 | 8 | 11 |
| 7. ARG | (Laura Mulhall, Cecilia Colombo, Marisa López, Alejandra Tucat, Victoria Carbo, Fabiana Ricchezza, Gabriela Liz, Gabriela Sánchez, Moira Brinnand, Marcela Hussey, Alejandra Palma, Veronica Bengochea, Alina Vergara, Gabriela Pazos, Andrea Fioroni) | 2 | 3 | 0 | 6 | 7 |
| 8. USA | (Patricia Shea, Yolanda Hightower, Mary Koboldt, Marcia Pankratz, Cheryl Van Kuren, Diane Bracalente, Elizabeth Beglin, Marcell Von Schottenstein, Sandra Vander-Heyden, Tracey Fuchs, Sheryl Johnson, Sandra Costigan, Christy Morgan, Barbara Marois, Megan Donnelly, Donna Lee) | 0 | 4 | 1 | 6 | 12 |

Final: AUS 2–0 KOR
3rd Place: HOL 3–1 GBR

5th Place: GER 4–2 CAN
7th Place: ARG 3–1 USA

When Australia defeated the Netherlands 3–2 in the semifinals, it marked the first time in 8 years that the Dutch had failed to reach the final of an international tournament. Australia and South Korea played an exciting 5–5 draw to close the preliminary round. Australia tightened its defense for the final and successfully choked off the fast-paced offense of the Korean "Red Bees." Five minutes into the second half, Australian captain Debbie Bowman scored on a penalty stroke. Lee Capes added an insurance goal in the 58th minute.

# FOOTBALL (SOCCER)

Olympic soccer matches consist of two 45-minute halves.

**1896** not held

**1900 Paris** T: 3, N: 3, D: 9.23.

| | | | W | L | PF | PA |
|---|---|---|---|---|---|---|
| 1. GBR | (Upton Park Football Club—J. H. Jones, Claude Buckenham, Grosling, A. Chalk, T. E. Burridge, W. Quash, R. R. Turner Spackman, J. Nicholas, J. Zealley, Haslam) | | 1 | 0 | 4 | 0 |
| 2. FRA | (Union des sociétés françaises de sports athlétiques—Huteau, Bach, Pierre Allemane, Gaillard, Jean Bloch, Macaire, Fraysse, Garnier, Lambert, Grandjean, Fernand Canelle, Duparc, Peltier) | | 1 | 1 | 7 | 8 |
| 3. BEL | (Marcel Leboutte, R. Kelcom, Ernest Moreau, Alphonse Renier, Georges Pelgrims, C. van Hoorden, E. Neefs, Erich Thornton, Albert Delbecque, H. Spaunoghe, van Heuckelum, Londot) | | 0 | 1 | 4 | 7 |

**1904 St. Louis** T: 3, N: 2, D: 11.25.

| | | W | L | T | PF | PA |
|---|---|---|---|---|---|---|
| 1. CAN | (Galt Football Club—Ernest Linton, George Ducker, John Gourley, John Fraser, Albert Johnson, Robert Lane, Tom Taylor, Frederick Steep, Alexander Hall, Gordon McDonald, William Twaits) | 2 | 0 | 0 | 11 | 0 |
| 2. USA | (Christian Brothers College—Louis Menges, Joseph Lydon, Thomas January, John January, Charles January, Peter Ratican, Warren Brittingham, Alexander Cudmore, Charles Bartliff, Oscar Brockmeyer, Raymond Lawler) | 1 | 1 | 1 | 2 | 7 |
| 3. USA | (St. Rose School—Frank Frost, George Cooke, Henry Jameson, Joseph Brady, Martin Dooling, Dierkes, Cormic Cosgrove, O'Connell, Claude Jameson, Harry Tate, Thomas Cooke, Johnson) | 0 | 2 | 1 | 0 | 6 |

The St. Rose team managed to put one ball into the net. Unfortunately, it was into the goal they were defending.

**1906 Athens** T: 4, N: 2, D: 4.24.

| | | | W | L | PF | PA |
|---|---|---|---|---|---|---|
| 1. DEN | (Viggo Andersen, Peter Petersen, Charles Buchwald, Parmo Ferslew, Stefan Rasmussen, Aage Andersen, Oscar Nielsen-Nörland, Carl Frederick Petersen, Holger Fredriksen, August Lindgreen, Henry Rambusch, Hjalmar Heerup, Axel Hansen) | | 2 | 0 | 14 | 1 |
| 2. INT | Smyrna (Edwin Charnaud, Zareck Couyoumdzian, Edouard Giraud, Jacques Giraud, Henri Joly, Percy de la Fontaine, Donald Whittal, Albert Whittal, Godfrey Whittal, Herbert Whittal, Edward Whittal) | | 1 | 1 | 13 | 5 |
| 3. GRE | Thessaloniki Music Club (Georgios Vaporis, Nicolaos Pindos, A. Tegon, Nicolaos Pentzikis, Ioannis Kyrou, Georgis Sotiriadis, V. Zarkadis, Dimitrios Michitsopoulos, A. Karangonidis, Ioannis · Saridakis, Ioannis Abbot) | | 0 | 2 | 0 | 17 |

The Athens team was supposed to play off for second place, but refused on the grounds that they had already beaten Thessaloniki. The team from Smyrna was an international one.

**1908 London** T: 6, N: 5, D: 10.24.

| | | | W | L | PF | PA |
|---|---|---|---|---|---|---|
| 1. GBR | (Harold Bailey, William Corbett, Herbert Smith, Kenneth Hunt, Frederick Chapman, Robert Hawkes, Arthur Berry, Vivian Woodward, Hubert Stapley, Claude Purnell, Harold Hardman) | | 3 | 0 | 8 | 11 |
| 2. DEN | (Ludvig Drescher, Charles Buchwald, Harald Hansen, Harald Bohr, Kristian Middelboe, Nils Middelboe, Oscar Nielsen-Nörland, August Lindgreen, Sophus Nielsen, Vilhelm Wolffhagen, Björn Rasmussen, Marius Andersen, Johannes Gandil) | | 2 | 1 | 26 | 3 |
| 3. HOL | (Reinier Beeuwkes, Karel Heijting, Lou Otten, Johan Sol, Johannes de Korver, Emil Mundt, Jan Welcker, Edu Snethlage, Gerard Reeman, Jan Thomée, Georges de Bruyn Kops, Johan Kok) | | 1 | 1 | 2 | 4 |
| 4. SWE | (Oskar Bengtsson, Ake Fjästad, Teodor Malm, Sven Olsson, Hans Lindman, Olof Olsson, Sune Almkvist, Gustaf Bergström, Sven Ohis- | | 0 | 2 | 1 | 14 |

son, Karl Ansén, Nils Andersson, Valter Lidén, Arvid Fagrell, Karl Gustafsson)
Final: GBR 2–0 DEN
3rd Place: HOL 2–0 SWE

France entered two teams, both of which were thrashed by Denmark. In the 17–1 defeat of the French "B" team, Sophus Nielsen of Denmark scored 10 goals.

**1912 Stockholm:** T: 11, N: 11, D: 7.5.

| | | | W | L | PF | PA |
|---|---|---|---|---|---|---|
| 1. | GBR | (Ronald Brebner, Thomas Burn, Arthur Knight, Douglas McWhirter, Horace Littlewort, James Dines, Arthur Berry, Vivian Woodward, Harold Walden, Gordon Hoare, Ivan Sharpe, Edward Hanney, Gordon Wright, Harold Stamper) | 3 | 0 | 13 | 5 |
| 2. | DEN | (Sophus Hansen, Nils Middleboe, Harald Hansen, Charles Buchwald, Emil Jörgensen, Poul Berth, Oscar Nielsen-Nörland, Axel Thufason, Anton Olsen, Sophus Nielsen, Vilhelm Wolffhagen, Hjalmar Christoffersen, Aksel Petersen, Ivar Seidelin-Nielsen, Poul Nielsen) | 2 | 1 | 13 | 5 |
| 3. | HOL | (Marius Jan Göbel, David Wijnveldt, Piet Bouman, Gerardus Fortgens, Constant Feith, Nicolaas de Wolf, Dirk Lotsy, Johannes Boutmy, Jan van Breda Kolff, Huug de Groot, Caesar ten Cate, Jan van der Sluis, Jan Vos, Nicolaas Bouvy, Johannes de Korver) | 3 | 1 | 17 | 7 |
| 4. | FIN | (August Syrjäläinen, Jalmari Holopainen, Gösta Löfgren, Knut Lund, Eino Soinio, Viljo Lietola, Lauri Tanner, Bror Wiberg, Jarl Öhman, Artturi Nyyssönen, Algot Niska, Ragnar Wickström, Kaarlo Soinio) | 2 | 2 | 5 | 16 |
| 5. | HUN | (Gáspár Borbás, Imre Schlosser, Mihály Pataky, Sándor Bodnár, Béla Sebestyén, Antal Vágó, Jenö Károly, Gyula Biró, Imre Payer, Gyula Rumbold, László Domonkos) | 2 | 1 | 6 | 8 |
| 6. | AUT | (Müller, Neubauer, Studnicka, Merz, Hussack, Cimera, Braunsteiner, Brandstetter, Graubard Kurpiel, Noll) | 3 | 2 | 11 | 8 |
| 7. | GER | (Julius Hirsch, E. Kipp, Willi Worpitzky, Adolf Jäger, Karl Wegele, Hermann Bosch, Max Breunig, Georg Krogmann, Ernst Hollstein, Helmut Röpnack, Albert Weber, Gottfried Fuchs) | 1 | 2 | 18 | 8 |
| 7. | ITA | (Dino Mariani, Celeste Sardi, Felice Berardo, Franco Bontadini, Enea Zuffi, Pietro Leone, Giuseppe Milano, Carlo Demarchi, Renzo | 1 | 2 | 4 | 8 |

Devecchi, Angelo Binaschi, Pierino Campelli)
Final: GBR 4–2 DEN
3rd Place: HOL 9–0 FIN

Great Britain was leading 2–1 when Buchwald of Denmark was injured and had to be helped from the field. Denmark was forced to continue with only ten players, and Britain quickly capitalized by scoring two goals in three minutes. The Danes then adjusted to playing shorthanded, but it was too late and they lost, 4–2. In a consolation match against Russia, Gottfried Fuchs of Germany scored ten goals to match Nielsen's feat of four years earlier.

**1920 Antwerp** T: 14, N: 14, D: 9.5.

| | | | W | L | PF | PA |
|---|---|---|---|---|---|---|
| 1. | BEL | (Jan de Bie, Armand Swartenbroeks, Oscar Verbeeck, Joseph Musch, Emile Hanse, André Fierens, Louis van Hege, Henri Larnoe, Mathieu Bragard, Robert Coppée, Désiré Bastin, Félix Balyu, Fernand Nisot, Georges Hebdin) | 3 | 0 | 8 | 1 |
| 2. | SPA | (Ricardo Zamora, Pedro Vallana, Mariano Arrate, José Samitier, José Maria Belaustequigoita, Agustin Sancho, Ramón Equiazábal, Félix Sesúmaga, Patricio Arabolaza, Rafael Moreno, Domingo Acedo, Juan Artola, Francisco Pagazaurtundúa, Louis Otero, Joaquin Vázquez, Ramón Moncho Gil, Sabino Bilbao, Silverio Izaguirre) | 4 | 1 | 9 | 5 |
| 3. | HOL | (Robert McNeill, Henri Dénis, Bernard Verweij, Leonard Bosschart, Frederik Kuipers, Hermanus Steeman, Oscar van Rappard, Jan van Dort, Bernardus Groosjohan, Herman van Heijden, Jacob Bulder, Johannes de Natris, Evert Bulder, Adrianus Bieshaar) | 2 | 2 | 9 | 10 |
| 4. | ITA | (Piero Campelli, Giovanni Giacone, Antonio Bruna, Renzo de Vecchi, Virginio Rosetta, Calo di Nardo, Ettore Reinaudi, Mario Meneghetti, Giuseppe Parodi, Luigi Burlando, Rinaldo Roggero, Giustiniano Barucco, Pio Ferraris, Giuseppe Forlivesi, Cesare Lovati, Celeste Sardi, Adolfo Baloncieri, Emilio Badini, Guglielmo Brezzi, Emilio Santamaria Aristodemo, Alevildo de Marchi) | 2 | 2 | 6 | 7 |
| 5. | NOR | (Rolf Aas, Arne Andersen, Gunnar Andersen, Otto Aulie, Einar Gundersen, Asbjorn Halvorsen, Johnny Helgesen, Per Holm, John Johnson, Ellef Mohn, Michael Paulson, Per Skou, Rolf Thorstvedt, Sig- | 1 | 2 | 4 | 7 |

| | | W | L | PF | PA |
|---|---|---|---|---|---|
| | urd Wathne, Einar Wilhelms, Adolf Wold) | | | | |
| 5. SWE | (Rune Bergström, Albin Dahl, Karl Gustafsson, Fritjof Hillén, Herbert Karlsson, Waldus Lund, Bertil Nordenskjöld, Albert Olsson, Mauritz Sandberg, Ragnar Wicksell, Robert Zander, Albert Öjermark) | 1 | 2 | 14 | 7 |

2nd Place: SPA 3-1 HOL

The final matched the home team, Belgium, against the Czechoslovakians, who had outscored their opponents 15–1, on their way to the final. A partisan crowd of 40,000 watched with pleasure as Belgium took a 2–0 lead. But after several controversial calls, the Czech team had had enough and walked off the field en masse in protest. This threw the tournament into chaos. With Czechoslovakia disqualified, a playoff for second place was ordered. But France, which had lost to Czechoslovakia in the semifinals, refused to participate since many of the leading French players had already gone home. Eventually Spain defeated Sweden and Italy to qualify for the second-place match against Holland.

**1924 Paris** T: 22, N: 22, D: 6.9.

| | | W | L | T | PF | PA |
|---|---|---|---|---|---|---|
| 1. URU | (Andrés Mazali, José Nasazzi, Pedro Arispe, José Leandro Andrade, José Vidal, Alfredo Ghierra, Santos Urdinarán, Hector Scarone, Pedro Petrone, Pedro Céa, Angel Romano, Umberto Tomasina, José Naya, Alfredo Zibechi, Antonio Urdinaran) | 5 | 0 | 0 | 20 | 2 |
| 2. SWI | (Hans Pulver, Adolphe Reymond, Rudolf Ramseyer, August Oberhauser, Paul Schmiedlin, Aron Pollitz, Karl Ehrenbolger, Robert Pache, Walter Dietrich, Max Abegglen, Paul Fässler, Felix Bédouret, Adolphe Mengotti, Paul Sturzenegger, Edmond Kramer) | 4 | 1 | 1 | 15 | 6 |
| 3. SWE | (Sigfrid Lindberg, Axel Alfredsson, Fritjof Hillén, Gunnar Holmberg, Sven Friberg, Harry Sundberg, Evert Lundqvist, Sven Rydell, Per Kaufeldt, Tore Keller, Rudolf Kock, Gustaf Carlson, Charles Brommesson, Thorsten Svensson, Albin Dahl, Konrad Hirsch, Sven Lindqvist, Sten Mellgren) | 3 | 1 | 1 | 18 | 5 |
| 4. HOL | (Gejus van der Meulen, Henri Dénis, Hendrik Vermetten, Albert Oosthoek, Gerardus Krom, Gerardus Horstén, Johannes de Natris, Gerrit Visser, André Lefèvre, Ocker Formenoy, Marinus Sigmond, Bernard Verweij, Johannes Tetzner, Evert van Linge, Klaas Jan Breeuwer, Bernardus Groosjohan, Cornelius Pijl, Albert Snouck-Hurgronje, Johannes ter Beek) | 2 | 2 | 1 | 11 | 7 |
| 5. EGY | (Abaza Sayed Fahmy, Abdel Hamid Moharren, Abdel Kader Mohammed, El Hassany Aly-Fahmy, Mohammed El Mahdwy, Fouad Mahmoud, Iaghen Ibrahim, Hamdy Abdel-Salam Hegozi Hussein, Henein Rizkalla, Housny Khalil, Ismail El Sayed, Ismail Mahmoud, Mansour Ahmed, Marey Mahmoud, Moktar Mahmoud, Osman Gamil, Riad Aly, Mohammed Rouston, Salim Ahmed, Shawky Riad, Taha Kamel) | 1 | 1 | 0 | 3 | 5 |
| 5. FRA | (Bard, Batmale, Baumann, Bonnardel, Bover, Canthelou, Chayrigues, Chessneau, Cottenet, Crut, Devaquez, Domergue, Dufour, Dubly, Gravier, Gross, Huot, Isbecque, Jourda, Parachini, Renier) | 1 | 1 | 0 | 8 | 5 |
| 5. IRL | (Tom Aungier, Billy Cowzer, W. Ernest Crawford, Charlie Dowdall, Robert Duncan, Jimmy Dykes, John Farrell, Jimmy Ghent, Dennis Hannon, Tommy Healy, Frank Heaney, Joe Kendrick, Bertie Kerr, Pat Lee, Jack McCarthy, Alec McKay, Tom Muldoon, Tom Murphy, Jim Murray, Paddy O'Reilly, Sam Robinson, Bob Thomas) | 1 | 1 | 0 | 2 | 2 |
| 5. ITA | (Aliberti, Ardizone, Baldi, Baloncieri, Barbieri, Antonio Bruna, Luigi Burlando, Calvi, Giampiero Combi, Conti, Della-Valle, De Pra, Renzo de Vecchi, Fayenz, Antonio Janni, Virginio Levratto, Mario Magnozzi, Martin, Monti, Virginio Rosetta, Rosso) | 2 | 1 | 0 | 4 | 2 |

Final: URU 3–0 SWI
3rd Place: SWE 1–1 HOL
SWE 3–1 HOL

The tournament opened with an upset as Italy defeated one of the favorites, Spain, 1–0, on a goal that was actually kicked through the net by the Spanish captain, Vallana. The Uruguayan team caught the fancy of the crowd with its 2–1 come-from-behind win over Holland in the semifinals. Holland lodged a protest, but it was denied. Then, when a Dutch referee was assigned to the final, it was Uruguay's turn to protest. Their protest was accepted, and the Dutch official was replaced by a Frenchman. The stadium was packed with 60,000 people for the final match and another 5000 were left outside, causing a crush that led to several injuries. The Swiss struggled vigorously but were unable to stop the Uruguayans, who led 1–0 at the break before winning 3–0.

**1928 Amsterdam** T: 17, N: 17, D: 6.13.

| | | W | L | T | PF | PA |
|---|---|---|---|---|---|---|
| 1. URU | (Andres Mazáli, José Nasazzi, Pedro Arispe, José Leandro Andrade, Lorenzo Fernández, Juan Piriz, Alvaro Gestido, Santos Urdináran, Hector Castro, Pedro Petrone, Pedro Céa, Antonio Campolo, Adhemar Canavesi, Juan Arremón, René Borjas, Hector Scarone, Roberto Figueroa) | 4 | 0 | 1 | 12 | 5 |
| 2. ARG | (Angelo Bosio, Fernando Paternoster, Ludovico Bidoglio, Juan Evaristo, Luis Monti, Segundo Medici, Raimundo Orsi, Enrique Gainzarain, Manuel Ferreyra, Domingo Tarascuni, Adolfo Carricaborry, Feliciano Angel Perducca, Octavio Diaz, Roberto Cherro, Rudolfo Orlandini, Saúl Calandra) | 3 | 1 | 1 | 25 | 8 |
| 3. ITA | (Giampiero Combi, Delfo Bellini, Umberto Caligaris, Alfredo Pitto, Fulvio Bernardini, Pietro Genovesi, Adolfo Baloncieri, Elvio Banchero, Angelo Schiavio, Mario Magnozzi, Virgilio Levratto, Giovanni Deprà, Virginio Rosetta, Silvio Pietroboni, Antonio Janni, Enrico Rivolta, Gino Rosselli) | 3 | 1 | 1 | 25 | 11 |
| 4. EGY | (Abdelhamid Hamdi, Sayed Fahmy Abaza, Mohammed Ahmad Shemais, Gaber Yacout El-Soury, Fahmy El-Hassani, Abdelhalim Younis Hassan, Elsaid Ismail Mohamed Hooda, Aly Mohamed Riad, Mohmoud Ismail Mohamed Hooda, Moosa Hassan Moussa El-Ezam, Mohamed Gamil El-Zobeir, Mohamed Aly Rostam, Ahmed Mohamed Salem, Mohamed Ezz Eldin Gamal, Mahmoud Mokhtar Refaee, Ahmed Mahmoud Soliman) | 2 | 2 | 0 | 12 | 19 |
| 5. BEL | (Jean de Bie, S.J.M. Verhulst, H.V.B. Bierna, Georges Despae, Louis Versyp, H.C. Ditz- | 1 | 1 | 0 | 5 | 4 |

ler, H.M.J. de Deken, August Ruyssevelt, Jean Diddens, Jacques Moeschal, Raymond Braine, Gerard de Vos, Pierre Braine, B. Voorhoof, Florimond van Halme, Gustave Boesman, Jules Lavigne, Nicolaas Hoydonckx, Jean Caudron)

| | | | | | |
|---|---|---|---|---|---|
| 5. POR | (A. Fernandes Roquette, C. Alves Jr., J. Gomes Vieira, R. Soares Figueiredo, A. Silva, C. Matos Rodrigues, W. Motta Fonseca, J.M. Soares Louro, V. Marcolino da Silva, A. Martins, J.M. Martins, C. Santos Nunes, O. Maia Vasques de Carvalho, A.J. João, A. Ramos, J. Conçalves Tavares, R. Ornellas, J. Santos, L. dos Santos) | 1 | 1 | 0 | 3 | 3 |
| 5. SPA | (J. M. Yermo Solaegui, M. Marculeta Barberia, L. Regueiro Pagola, J. Quinococes Lopez, J. M. Jauregui Lagunas, L. Iruretagoyena Ayestaran, A. Mariscal Ibeuba, T. Arizcorreta Sein, F. Gamborena Hernandorona, A. Labarta Rey, P. Vallana Jeanaguenat, C. Errasti Suinaga, D. de Zaldua Anabitarte, J. Legarreta Abaitua, A. Gonzales de Audicana Inchaurraga, M. Sagarzazu Martinez, I. Alcorta y Hermoso, J. Errazquin Aurnas, J. Izaguirre Goena, A. Villaverde Llanos, F. Bienzobas Ocariz, R. Bilbar, Echevarria) | 1 | 1 | 1 | 9 | 9 |

Final: URU 1–1 ARG
URU 2–1 ARG
3rd Place: ITA 11–3 EGY

The first final ended in a draw and had to be replayed.

**1932 Los Angeles** not held

**1936 Berlin** T: 16, N: 16, D: 8.15.

| | | W | L | PF | PA |
|---|---|---|---|---|---|
| 1. ITA | (Bruno Venturini, Alfredo Foni, Pietro Rava, Giuseppe Baldo, Achille Piccini, Ugo Locatelli, Annibale Frossi, Libero Marchini, Sergio Bertoni, Carlo Biagi, Francesco Gabriotti, Luigi Scarabello, Giulio Cappelli, Alfonso Negro) | 4 | 0 | 13 | 2 |
| 2. AUT | (Eduard Kainberger, Ernst Künz, Martin Kargl, Anton Krenn, Karl Wahlmüller, Max Hofmeister, Walter Werginz, Adolf Laudon, Klement Steinmetz, Karl Kainberger, Franz Fuchsberger, Franz Mandi, Josef Kitzmüller) | 2 | 1 | 7 | 4 |

|  |  | W | L | PF | PA |
|---|---|---|---|---|---|
| 3. NOR | (Henry Johansen, Nils Eriksen, Öivind Holmsen, Fritjof Ulleberg, Jörgen Juve, Rolf Holmberg, Magdalon Monsen, Reidar Kvammen, Alf Martinsen, Odd Frantzen, Arne Brustad, Fredrik Horn, Sverre Hansen, Magnar Isaksen) | 3 | 1 | 10 | 4 |
| 4. POL | (Spirydion Albanski, Wladyslaw Szczepaniak, Antoni Galecki, Wilhelm Góra, Franciszek Cebulak, Ewald Dytko, Walerian Kisielinski, Michal Matyas, Teodor Peterek, Hubert God, Gerhard Wdarz, Henryk Martyna, Józef Kotlarczyk, Jan Wasiewicz, Ryszard Piec, Walenty Musielak, Fryc Scherfke) | 2 | 2 | 11 | 10 |
| 5. GBR | (Hadyn Hill, Guy Holmes, Robert Fulton, John Gardiner, Bernard Joy, Daniel Pettit, James Crawford, Joseph Kyle, John Dodds, Maurice Edelston, Lester Finch) | 1 | 1 | 6 | 5 |
| 5. GER | (Hans Jakob, Reinhold Münzenberg, Heinz Ditgens, Rudolf Gramlich, Ludwig Goldbrunner, Robert Bernard, Ernst Lehner, Otto Siffling, August Lenz, Adolf Urban, Wilhelm Simetsreiter) | 1 | 1 | 9 | 2 |
| 5. JPN | (Rihei Sano, Sekiji Suzuki, Teizo Takeuchi, Matoo Tatsuhara, Oita, Yoshuku Kin, Matsunaga Ukon, Taigo Kawamoto, Takeshi Kamo, Shogo Kamo, Koichi Teneda) | 1 | 1 | 3 | 10 |
| 5. PER | (Juan Valdivieso, Arturo Fernandez, Victor Lavalle, Carlos Tovar, Segundo Castillo, Orestes Jordan, Adelfo Magallanes, Jorge Alcade, Teodoro Fernandez, Alejandro Villanueva, José Morales) | 1 | 0 | 7 | 3 |

Final: ITA 2–1 AUT
3rd Place: NOR 3–2 POL

The status of Olympic soccer, already weakened by the introduction of the World Cup in 1930 and the exclusion of the sport from the 1932 Olympic Games, received another blow when the 1936 tournament was marred by unruly incidents. First came the match between Italy and the United States, in which two Americans were injured. When the German referee, Weingartner, ordered Achille Piccini of Italy to leave the game, he refused to go. Several Italian players surrounded Weingartner, pinned his arms to his sides, and covered his mouth with their hands. The game continued with Piccini still in the lineup, and Italy won 1–0.

This unfortunate affair was nothing compared to what took place five days later, during the quarterfinal contest between Peru and Austria. Austria led 2–0 at the interval, but Peru tied the game with two goals in the last 15 minutes. A 15-minute overtime period was then played without further scoring, so a second overtime was ordered. By this time the small but vocal group of Peruvian spectators had become frantic with emotion. What followed depends on which continent is telling the story. Evidently, the Peruvian fans rushed onto the field while the game was still in progress and actually attacked one of the Austrian players. The Peruvian team took advantage of the chaos to score two quick goals and win the game, 4–2. Austria protested immediately, and a Jury of Appeal, composed of five European men, ordered the match replayed two days later. The jury also decreed that the game be played behind locked doors with no spectators allowed. The Peruvians refused to show up, and the entire Peruvian Olympic contingent withdrew from the games, as did the Colombians, who supported their South American neighbors. Back in Lima, Peruvian demonstrators threw stones at the German consulate, while Peru's president, Oscar Benavides, denounced "the crafty Berlin decision." When German diplomats appealed to Benavides and pointed out that the decision had been made not by Germans but by officials of F.I.F.A., the international football federation, the president changed his position and blamed the demonstrations on Communists.

Meanwhile, back in Berlin, a bitterly contested final was fought out between Italy and Austria. The first 45-minute half ended without a score. Midway in the second half, Annibale Frossi, Italy's right wing, scored the first goal of the game. Eleven minutes later Karl Kainberger, Austria's inside left, tied the score and the match went into overtime. A quick goal by Frossi proved decisive, and Italy won the gold medal, 2–1.

**1948 London:** T: 18, N: 18, D: 8.13.

|  |  | W | L | PF | PA |
|---|---|---|---|---|---|
| 1. SWE | (Torsten Lindberg, Knut Nordahl, Erik Nilsson, Birger Rosengren, Bertil Nordahl, Sune Andersson, Kjell Rosén, Gunnar Gren, Gunnar Nordahl, Henry Carlsson, Nils Liedholm, Börje Leander) | 4 | 0 | 22 | 3 |
| 2. YUG | (Ljubomir Lovrič, Miroslav Brozovič, Branislav Stanovič, Zlatko Čajkovski, Miodrag Jovanovič, Zvonko Cimermančič, Rajko Mitić, Stjepan Bobek, Željko Čajkovski, Bernard Vukas, Franjo Šoštarič, Prvoslav Mihajlovič, Fränjo Wolfl, Kosta Tomaševič) | 3 | 1 | 13 | 6 |
| 3. DEN | (Ejgil Nielsen, Viggo Jensen, Knud Börge Overgaard, Axel Pilmark, Dion Örnvoid, Ivan Jensen, Johannes Plöger, Knud Lundberg, Carl Aage Praest, John Hansen, Jörgen Sörensen, Holger Seebach, Karl Aage Hansen) | 3 | 1 | 15 | 11 |
| 4. GBR | (Ronald Simpson, C. R. "Jack" Neale, Andrew Carmichael, J. Robert Hardisty, Eric Lee, Eric Fright, J. | 2 | 2 | 9 | 11 |

Alan Boyd, A. Aitken, Harry McIlvenny, J. Rawlings, William Amor, Kevin McAlinden, G. T. Manning, James McColl, Douglas McBain, Frank Donovan, Thomas Hopper, Denis Kelleher, Frederick Peter Kippax)

5. FRA (G. Rouxel, R. Krug, B. Bienvenu, R. Persillon, M. Colau, G. Robert, J. Heckel, J. Strappe, R. Hebinger, J. Paluch, R. Courbin) — 1 1 2 2

5. ITA (G. Casari, G. Giovannini, A. Stellin, T. Maestrelli, M. Neri, G. Mari, E. Cavigioli, A. Turconi, F. Pernigo, V. Cassani, E. Caprile) — 1 1 12 5

5. KOR (Hong Duk-yung, Pak Kyoo-chung, Pak Dai-chong, Choi Soon-gon, Kim Kyoo-whan, Min B.D., Woo Zung-whan, Bai C., Chung Nam-sik, Kim Yong-sik, Chung Kook-chin) — 1 1 5 13

5. TUR (C. Arman, M. Alyuz, V. Tosuncuk, N. Ozkaya, B. Eken, H. Saygin, F. Kircan, E. Keskin, G. Kilic, K. Andonyadis, S. Gulesin) — 1 1 5 3

Final: SWE 3–1 YUG
3rd Place: DEN 5 3 GBR

By 1948 the best players of Western Europe and South America were turning professional, and Olympic soccer began to be dominated by the state-sponsored "amateur" teams of Eastern Europe. Sweden was the last non-Communist team to win an unboycotted Olympic football tournament. Their team included three brothers, Gunnar, Bertil, and Knut Nordahl, as well as three firemen, including Gunnar Nordahl.

**1952 Helsinki** T: 25, N: 25, D: 8.2.

| | | | W | L | T | PF | PA |
|---|---|---|---|---|---|---|---|
| 1. | HUN | (Gyula Grosics, Jenö Buzánszky, Mihály Lantos, József Bozsik, Gyula Lóránt, József Zakariás, Nándor Hidegkuti, Sándor Kocsis, Péter Palotás, Ferenc Puskás, Zoltán Czibor, Jenö Dalnoki, Imre Kovács, László Budai II, Lajos Csordás) | 5 | 0 | 0 | 20 | 2 |
| 2. | YUG | (Vladimir Beara, Branislav Stankovič, Tomislav Crnkovič, Zlatko Čajkovski, Ivan Horvat, Vujadin Boškov, Tihomir Ognjanov, Rajko Mitič, Bernard Vukas, Stjepan Bobek, Branko Zebec) | 4 | 1 | 1 | 26 | 13 |
| 3. | SWE | (Karl Svensson, Lennart Samuelsson, Erik Nilsson, Olof Ahlund, Bengt Gustavsson, Gösta Lindh, Sylve Bengtsson, Gösta Löfgren, Ingvar Rydell, Yngve Brodd, Gösta Sandberg, Holger Hansson) | 3 | 1 | 0 | 9 | 8 |

4. GER (Rudolf Schönbeck, Hans Eberle, Herbert Jäger, Kurt Sommerlatt, Herbert Schäfer, Alfred Post, Ludwig Hinterstocker, Georg Stollenwerk, Hans Zeitler, Willi Schröder, Kurt Ehrmann, Erich Gleixner, Matthias Mauritz, Karl Klug) — 2 2 0 8 8

5. AUT (Fritz Nikolai, Walter Kollmann, Anton Krammar, Anton Wolf, Josef Walter, Robert Fendler, Hermann Hochleitner, Franz Feldinger, Erich Stumpf, Herbert Grohs, Otto Gollnhuber) — 1 1 0 5 6

5. BRA (Carlos Martins Cavalheiro, Mauro Torres Homen Rodrigues, Waldir Villas Boas, Zozimo Alves Calanzan, Adesio Alves Machado, Edison Campos Martins, Larry Pinto de Faria, Milton Pessanha, Edvaldo Neto, Humberto Barbosa Tozzi, Jansen Moreira) — 2 1 0 9 6

5. DEN (Jorgen Johansen, Poul Erik Petersen, Svend Nielsen, Erik Terkelsen, Poul Andersen, Steen Blicher, Jorgen Hansen, Poul Eyvind Petersen, Jens Hansen, Knud Lundberg, Holger Seebach) — 2 1 0 7 6

5. TUR (Erdoğan Arkin, Necdet Sentürk, Ridvan Bolatli, Mustafa Ertan, Basri Dirimilili, Ercüment Güder, Vasif Çetinel, Tekin Bilge, Yalçin Çaka, Muzaffer Tokac, Macit Gürdal) — 1 1 0 3 8

Final: HUN 2–0 YUG
3rd Place: SWE 2–0 GER

**1956 Melbourne** T: 11, N: 11, D: 12.8.

| | | | W | L | T | PF | PA |
|---|---|---|---|---|---|---|---|
| 1. | SOV | (Lev Yashin, Anatoly Bashashkin, Mikhail Ogognikov, Boris Kuznyetsov, Igor Netto, Anatoly Maslyonkin, Boris Tatushin, Anatoly Issayev, Nikita Simonyan, Sergei Salnikov, Anatoly Ilyun, Nikolai Tichenko, Aleksei Paramonov, Eduard Streltsov, Valentin Ivanov, Vladimir Ryjkin, Yosif Betsa, Boris Rasinsky) | 4 | 0 | 1 | 9 | 2 |
| 2. | YUG | (Petar Radenkovič, Mladen Koščak, Nikola Radovič, Ivan Šantek, Ljubisa Spajič, Dobroslav Krstič, Dragoslav Šekularac, Zlatko Papec, Sava Antič, Todor Veselinovič, Muhamed Mujič, Blagoje Vidinic, Ibrahim Biogradič, Luka Lipošinovič) | 2 | 1 | 0 | 13 | 3 |

| | | W | L | T | PF | PA |
|---|---|---|---|---|---|---|
| 3. BUL | (Yosif Yosilov, Kiril Rakarov, Nikola Kovatschev, Stefan Stefanov, Manol Manolov, Gavril Stojanov, Dimiter Milanov, Georgy Dimitrov, Panayot Panayotov, Ivan Kolev, Todor Diyev, Georgy Naydenov, Miltscho Goranov, Krum Yanev) | 2 | 1 | 0 | 10 | 3 |
| 4. IND | (Narayan Subramaniam, Syed Khaja Aziz, Shaikh Abdul Lateef, Mohamed Kempiah, Noor Muhamed, Ahmed Husain, Mohamed Kannayan, Neville Stephen D'Souza, Krishna Chandra Pal, Nikhil Kumar Nunday, Krishna Swamy Kittu, T. Abdul Rahaman, Muhamed Abdus Salam, Pradip Kuma Banerjee, Tulsidas Balaram, Peter Ramaswamy Thangaraj, Samar Banerjee) | 1 | 2 | 0 | 10 | 3 |
| 5. AUS | (Ronald Lord, Robert Bignell, John Pettigrew, George Arthur, William Sander, Bruce Morrow, Francis Loughran, Jack Lennard, Graham McMillan, Edward Smith, Alwyn Warren) | 1 | 1 | 0 | 4 | 4 |
| 5. GBR | (Harry Sharratt, Donald Stoker, Leslie Thomas Farrer, Lawrence Topp, Stanley Prince, Herbert Dodkins, James Lewis, John Hardisty, John Laybourne, George Bromilow, Charles Twissell) | 1 | 1 | 0 | 10 | 6 |

Final: SOV 1–0 YUG
3rd Place: BUL 3–0 IND

The winning goal was headed in early in the second half by Anatoly Ilyun. The Soviet victory was preserved when a goal by Yugoslavia's Zlatko Papec was disallowed because of an offside infraction.

**1960 Rome** T: 16, N: 16, D: 9.10.

| | | W | L | T | PF | PA |
|---|---|---|---|---|---|---|
| 1. YUG | (Blagoje Vidinič, Novak Roganovič, Fahrudin Jusufi, Zeljko Perušič, Vladimir Durkovič, Ante Žanetič, Andrija Ankovič, Zeljko Matuš, Milan Galič, Tomislav Knez, Borivoje Kostič, Milutin Soskič, Velimir Sombolac, Aleksandar Kozlina, Silvester Takač, Dusan Maravič) | 3 | 0 | 2 | 17 | 7 |
| 2. DEN | (Henry From, Poul Andersen, Poul Jensen, Bent Hansen, Hans Nielsen, Flemming Nielsen, Poul Pedersen, Tommy Troelsen, Harald Nielsen, Hen- | 4 | 1 | 0 | 11 | 7 |

ning Enoksen, Jörn Sörensen, John Danielsen)

| | | W | L | T | PF | PA |
|---|---|---|---|---|---|---|
| 3. HUN | (Gábor Török, Zoltán Dudás, Jenö Dalnoki, Ernö Solymosi, Pál Várhidi, Ferenc Kovács, Imre Sátori, János Göröcs, Flórián Albert, Pál Orosz, János Dunai, Lajos Faragó, Dezsö Novák, Oszkár Vilezzsál, Gyula Rákosi, László Pál, Tibor Pál) | 4 | 1 | 0 | 17 | 6 |
| 4. ITA | (Luciano Alfieri, Tarcisio Burgnich, Mario Trebbi, Paride Tumburus, Sandro Salvadore, Giovanni Trappatoni, Giancarlo Cella, Giovanni Rivera, Ugo Tomeazzi, Giacomo Bulgarelli, Giorgio Rossano, Orazio Rancati, Giorgio Ferrini, Giovanni Fanello, Gilberto Noletti, Luciano Magistrelli) | 2 | 1 | 2 | 11 | 7 |

Final: YUG 3–1 DEN
3rd Place: HUN 2–1 ITA

Three-time runner-up Yugoslavia shocked Denmark when their captain, Milan Galič, scored a goal from 30 meters out in the first minute of play. Ten minutes later, Zeljko Matuš made it 2–0 and it looked like a rout might be in the making. However, late in the first half, Galič was ejected for insulting a referee, and Yugoslavia played the rest of the game with only ten players. Nevertheless, they held on to their lead and prevailed 3–1. It is worth noting that Yugoslavia tied with Bulgaria in their preliminary pool and qualified for the semifinals only because they won a coin toss.

**1964 Tokyo** T: 14, N: 14, D: 10.23.

| | | W | L | T | PF | PA |
|---|---|---|---|---|---|---|
| 1. HUN | (Antal Szentmihályi, Dezsö Novák, Kálman Ihász, Gusztáv Szepesi, Árpád Orban, Ferenc Nógrádi, János Farkas, Tibor Csernai, Ferenc Bene, Imre Komora, Sándor Katona, József Gelei, Károly Polotai, Zoltán Varga) | 5 | 0 | 0 | 22 | 6 |
| 2. CZE | (František Schmucker, Anton Urban, Karel Zdenek Pičman, Josef Vojta, Vladimir Weiss, Jan Geleta, Jan Brumovsky, Ivan Mráz, Karel Lichtnégl, Vojtech Masny, František Valošek, Anton Svajlen, Karel Knesl, Stefan Matlak, Karel Nepomucky, František Knebort, Ludevit Cvetler) | 5 | 1 | 0 | 19 | 5 |
| 3. GDR | (Hans Jürgen Heinsch, Peter Rock, Manfred Geisler, Herbert Pankau, Manfred Walter, Gerhard Körner, Hermann Stöcker, Otto Frässdorf, Henning Fren- | 4 | 1 | 1 | 12 | 4 |

zel, Jürgen Nöldner, Eberhard Vogel, Horst Weigang, Klaus Urbanczyk, Bernd Bauchspiess, Klaus-Dieter Seehaus, Werner Unger, Wolfgang Barthels, Klaus Lisiewicz, Dieter Engelhardt)

| | | W | L | T | PF | PA |
|---|---|---|---|---|---|---|
| 4. | UAR (Reda Ahmed, Yaken Zaki, Amin Elisnawi, Mohamed Kotb, Raafat Attia, Mohamed Abdelat Elsherbini, Seddik Mohamed, Ibrahim Riad, Mohamed Badawi, Nabil Nosseir, K. Aly Etman, F. Aly Korshed, Darwish Amin, Rifaat Elfanagili, Ahmed Moust Gad, Kalil Shahin, Mahmoud Hassan, Taha Ismail, Farouk Mahmoud) | 2 | 3 | 1 | 18 | 16 |
| 5. | GHA (Dodoo-Ankrah, Samuel Okai, Emmanuel Oblitey, Sam Acquah, Addo-Odametey, Emmanuel Nkansah, Gyau Agyemang, Wilberforce Mfum, Edward Aggrey Fynn, Edward Acquah, Kofi Pare) | 1 | 1 | 1 | 5 | 8 |
| 5. | JPN (Kenzo Yokoyama, Hiroshi Katayama, Yoshitada Yamaguchi, Ryozo Suzuki, Aritatsu Ogi, Mitsuo Kamata, Saburo Kawabuchi, Shigeo Yaegashi, Kunishige Kamamoto, Teruki Miyamoto, Masashi Watanabe) | 1 | 2 | 0 | 5 | 9 |
| 5. | ROM (Ilie Datcu, Ilie Greavu, Bujdr Halmageanu, Emil Petru, Ion Nunweiller, Niculae Georgescu, Ion Pircalab, Gheorge Constantin, Ion Ionescu, Dan Coe, Carol Creinicheanu) | 2 | 1 | 0 | 5 | 4 |
| 5. | YUG (Ivan Curkovic, Hirsad Fazlagic, Svetozar Vujovic, Rudolf Belin, Milan Cop, Jovan Miladinovic, Spasoje Samardzic, Slaven Zambata, Ivan Osin, Lazar Radovic, Dragan Dzajic) | 1 | 2 | 0 | 8 | 8 |

Final: HUN 2–1 CZE
3rd Place: GDR 3–1 UAR

Most of the fireworks took place before the tournament even started. Beginning in 1952, so many nations began applying to compete in the Olympics that pre-Olympic soccer tournaments had to be held to decide the 16 Olympic teams. On May 24, 1964, one such qualifying match took place in Lima between Peru and Argentina. Argentina led 1–0, but with two minutes to play Peru scored to tie the game. However the Uruguayan referee, Angel Eduardo Payos, nullified the goal because of rough play by the Peruvians. While the crowd of 45,000 booed its disapproval, two spectators leaped onto the field and attacked the referee. They were quickly arrested, which angered the crowd even more. Then Payos ordered the game suspended, claiming, with obvious justification, that police protection on the field was inadequate. The incensed crowd surged onto the field while the police hustled Payos and the players to safety. Some spectators began breaking windows and before long mounted police appeared and began herding the rioters toward the exits, many of which were, unfortunately, locked. Tear-gas grenades were fired by the police, while the Peruvian soccer fans responded by throwing stones and bottles and setting part of the stadium on fire. The fighting spilled into the streets of Lima, and before the night was out, 328 people had been killed and over 500 injured. Most of those killed had been trampled to death, but at least four persons were shot by police bullets. The Peruvian government declared a national "state of siege" and suspended the constitution. Meanwhile, demonstrators marched to the National Palace demanding an end to police brutality and the declaration of a tie in the match with Argentina. Neither demand was met. Argentina, by the way, went to Tokyo but lost both of their games.

When the Olympic tournament finally commenced, two of the 16 qualifying teams were missing. North Korea dropped out after some of its track and swimming athletes were suspended for competing in the unsanctioned Games of the New Emerging Forces (GANEFO) in Jakarta. Italy, the only Western European team to qualify for the Tokyo tournament, withdrew following accusations that several of its players were actually professionals. This charge was fairly hard to deny considering that three members of the Italian Olympic team were also members of the Inter-Milan team, which was the reigning European Cup champion. In fact, Sandro Mazzola scored two of the goals that defeated Real Madrid in the Cup final.

The Olympic tournament itself was not very impressive, particularly after all that had preceded it. However, the final between Hungary and Czechoslovakia was an exciting match. Hungary's first goal, scored at the beginning of the second half, was actually put through the net by Josef Vojta of Czechoslovakia, who inadvertently deflected a Hungarian pass past his own goalie. Thirteen minutes later, Hungarian center forward Ferenc Bene outran the Czech defense and blasted in a second goal, which proved to be decisive.

**1968 Mexico City** T: 16, N: 16, D: 10.26.

| | | W | L | T | PF | PA |
|---|---|---|---|---|---|---|
| 1. | HUN (Károly Fatér, Dezsö Novák, Lajos Dunai, Miklós Páncsics, Iván Menczel, Lajos Szüca, Laszló Fazekas, Antal Dunai, László Nagy, Ernö Noskó, István Juhász, Lajos Kocsis, Istvan Básti, László Keglovich, István Sárközi) | 5 | 0 | 1 | 18 | 3 |

| | | W | L | T | PF | PA |
|---|---|---|---|---|---|---|
| 2. BUL | (Stoyan Yordanov, Atanas Gerov, Georgi Hristakiev, Milko Gaidarski, Kiril Ivkov, Ivailo Georgiev, Tsvetan Veselinov, Yevgeny Yanchovski, Peter Zhekov, Atanas Hristov, Asparuh Nikodimov, Kiril Stankov, Todor Krustev, Mihail Gionin, Yancho Dimitrov, Georgi Tsetkov, Ivan Zafirov, Georgi Vasilev) | 3 | 1 | 2 | 16 | 10 |
| 3. JPN | (Kenzo Yokoyama, Hiroshi Katayama, Yoshitada Yamaguchi, Mitsuo Kamata, Takaji Mori, Aritatsu Ogi, Teruki Miyamoto, Masashi Watanabe, Kunishige Kamamoto, Ikuo Matsumoto, Ryuichi Sugiyama, Masakatsu Miyamoto, Yasuyuki Kuwahara, Shigeo Yaegashi) | 3 | 3 | 0 | 10 | 9 |
| 4. MEX | (Javier Vargas, Juan Mañuel Alejándrez, Héctor Sanabria, Mario Pérez, Luis Regueiro, Luis Estrada, Vicente Pereda, Cesáreo Victorino, Javier Sánchez Galindo, Ignacio Basaguren, Albino Morales, Humberto Medina, Héctor Pulido, Elias Muñoz, Fernando Bustos) | 3 | 3 | 0 | 10 | 9 |
| 5. FRA | (Jean Lempereur, Freddy Zix, Michel Verhoeve, Gilbert Plante, Jean-Michel Larque, Jean Louis Hodoul, Daniel Perrigaud, Daniel Hortaville, Marc Case, Gerard Hallet, Henri Ribul) | 2 | 2 | 0 | 9 | 8 |
| 5. GUA | (Alberto Lopez, Llijon Leon, Roberto Camposeco, Hugo Montoya, Armando Melgar, Jorge Roldan, Hugo Torres, Carlos Valdez, Hugo Pena, David Stokes, Julio Garcia) | 2 | 2 | 0 | 6 | 4 |
| 5. ISR | (Haim Levin, Menacham Bello, Zvi Rosen, Shaia Shwager, Shmuel Rosenthal, Rachamim Talbi, Giora Shpigal, Jehoshua Faygenbaum, Mordechai Shpiegler, Itzhak Druker, George Borba) | 2 | 1 | 1 | 9 | 7 |
| 5. SPA | (Pedro Mora, Gregorio Benito, Francisco Espildora, Miguel Ochoa, Isidro Sala, Juan Asensi, Rafael Jean, Juan Fernandez, José Garzon, José Grande, Fernando Ortuno) | 2 | 1 | 1 | 4 | 2 |

Final: HUN 4–1 BUL
3rd Place: JPN 2–0 MEX

Morocco qualified for the final tournament, but refused to participate against Israel. They were replaced by Ghana. The Ghana-Israel game, won by Israel 5–3, disintegrated into brawling, which continued back at the Olympic Village. A match between Czechoslovakia and Guatemala was also disrupted by fighting. The final pitted defending champion Hungary against Bulgaria, which qualified only after their tied quarterfinal game with Israel was decided by the toss of a coin. Bulgaria scored first on a header by Dimitrov, but four minutes before the end of the first half, Menczel of Hungary evened the score. A minute later Dunai of Hungary put in another goal. At this point the situation deteriorated drastically. Referee Diego De Leo, an Italian-born naturalized Mexican, ejected Dimitrov for rough play. Seconds later another Bulgarian, Kiril Ivkov, was thrown out. An angry teammate, Atanas Hristov, kicked the ball toward the referee, and he too was ejected. The Mexican crowd was none too pleased with the actions of Mr. De Leo. Having already disrupted the third-place game by throwing cushions onto the field, they used the same tactic to show their disapproval and cause delay in the final. The ejections effectively ended the contest, as Bulgaria was forced to play the second half with only eight players. Juhász of Hungary was eventually banished as well, but the Hungarians still outnumbered the Bulgarians 10–8 and won easily, 4–1.

**1972 Munich** T: 16, N: 16, D: 9.10.

| | | W | L | T | PF | PA |
|---|---|---|---|---|---|---|
| 1. POL | (Hubert Kostka, Zbigniew Gut, Jerzy Gorgon, Zygmunt Anczok, Leslaw Cmikiewicz, Zygmunt Maszczyk, Jerzy Kraska, Kazimierz Deyna, Zygfryd Szoltysik, Wlodzimierz Lubanski, Robert Gadocha, Ryszard Szymczak, Antoni Szymanowski, Marian Ostafinski, Grzegorz Lato, Joachim Marx, Kazimierz Kmiecik) | 6 | 0 | 1 | 21 | 5 |
| 2. HUN | (István Géczi, Péter Vépi, Miklós Páncsics, Péter Juhász, Lajos Szücs, Mihály Kozma, Antal Dunai, Lajos Kü, Béla Váradi, Ede Dunai, László Bálint, Lajos Kocsis, Kálmán Tóth, Jozsef Kovács, László Branikovits, Csaba Vidáts, Ádám Rothermel) | 5 | 1 | 1 | 18 | 5 |
| 3. GDR | (Jürgen Croy, Manfred Zapf, Konrad Weise, Bernd Bransch, Jürgen Pommerenke, Jürgen Sparwasser, Hans-Jürgen Kreische, Joachim Streich, Wolfgang Seguin, Peter Ducke, Frank Ganzera, Lothar Kurbjuweit, Eberhard Vogel, Ralf Schulenberg, Reinhard Häfner, Harald Irmscher, Siegmar Wätzlich) | 4 | 2 | 1 | 23 | 9 |

3. SOV (Oleg Blochin, Murtaz Hurcilava, Yuri Istomin, Vladimir Kaplichnyi, Viktor Kolotov, Yevgeny Lovchev, Sergei Olshansky, Yevgeny Rudakov, Vyacheslav Semenov, Gennady Yevrushikhin, Oganes Zanazanian, Andrei Yakubik, Arkady Andriasian) 5 1 1 17 6

5. DEN (Mogens Therkilosen, Flemming Ahlberg, Svend Andersen, Per Rontved, Jorgen Rasmussen, Jack Hansen, Kresten Nygaard, Allan Simonsen, Max Rasmussen, Arvo Heino Hansen, Keld Bak, Leif Prinzlau, Hans Ewald Hansen) 3 2 1 11 10

5. GER (Hans Jürgen Bradler, Heiner Baltes, Reiner Hollmann, Egon Schmitt, Friedhelm Häbermann, Jürgen Kalb, Hermann Bitz, Ulrich Hoeness, Ottmar Hitzfeld, Bernd Nickel, Klaus Wunder, Ronald Worm, Rudi Seliger) 3 2 1 17 8

5. MEX (Jesus Rico, José Luis Trejo, Juan Alvarez, Enrique Martin Del Campo, Alejandro Hernandez, Fernando Blanco, Manuel Manzo, Daniel Razo, Leonardo Cuellar, Horacio Sanchez, Alejandro Peña, Alfredo Hernandez) 2 3 1 4 14

5. MOR (Mohamed Hazzaz, Mohamed Elfilali, Boujamaa Benkhrif, Abdallah Tazi, Ahmed Faras, Mohamed Merzaq, Ahmed Belkorchi, Larbi Ihardane, Khalifa Elbakhti, Abdelali Zahraoui, Mustapha Yaghcha, Ghazouani Mouhoub, Ahmed Najah, Atati Zouita Mohamed, Abdelfattah Jafri) 1 4 1 7 14

Final: POL 2–1 HUN
3rd Place: GDR 2–2 SOV

Hungary entered the final having lost only one of their last 21 Olympic matches going back to 1960. The game was played in torrential rain and near gale-force wind. Hungary led 1–0 at the interval, but when the teams switched sides for the second half Poland took advantage of having the wind at their backs and scored two goals to gain the victory.

**1976 Montreal** T: 13, N: 13, D: 7.31.

|  | W | L | T | PF | PA |
|---|---|---|---|---|---|
| 1. GDR (Jürgen Croy, Gerd Weber, Hans-Jürgen Dörner, Konrad Weise, Lothar Kurbjuwelt, Reinhard Lauck, Gert Heidler, Reinhard Häfner, Hans-Jürgen Riediger, Bernd Bransch, Martin Hoffman, Gerd Kische, Wolfram Löwe, Hartmut Schade, Dieter Riedel, Hans-Ullrich Grapenthin, Wilfried Gröbner) | 4 | 0 | 1 | 10 | 2 |
| 2. POL (Jan Tomaszewski, Antoni Szymanowski, Jerzy Gorgoń, Wojciech Rudy, Wladyslaw Zmuda, Zygmunt Maszczyk, Grzegorz Lato, Henryk Kasperczak, Kazimierz Deyna, Andrzej Szarmach, Kazimierz Kmiecik, Piotr Mowlik, Henryk Wawrowski, Henryk Wieczorek, Leslaw Ćmikiewicz, Jan Beniger, Roman Ogaza) | 3 | 1 | 1 | 11 | 5 |
| 3. SOV (Vladimir Astapovsky, Anatoly Konkov, Viktor Matvienko, Mikhail Fomenko, Stefan Reshko, Vladimir Troshkin, David Kiplani, Vladimir Onishenko, Victor Kolotov, Vladimir Veremeev, Oleg Blochin, Leonid Buriak, Vladimir Feodorov, Aleksandr Minaev, Viktor Zviagintsev, Leonid Nazarenko, Aleksandr Prokhorov) | 4 | 1 | 0 | 10 | 4 |
| 4. BRA (Carlos Gallo, Rosemiro Corrêa do Souza, Roberto Franquoira, Edino Nazareth Filho, Léo Lins Gama, Alberto Marquoo, Mario Emiliano, João Batista da Silva, Eudes Medeiros, Erivelto Martins, João dos Santos, Mauro de Campos, Julio da Silva Gurjol, Francisco Fraga da Silva, Jarbas Tomazoli Nunes, Edval da Costa, José Pessanha) | 2 | 2 | 1 | 6 | 6 |
| 5. FRA (Jean-Claude Larrieu, Henri Orlandini, Patrick Battiston, Claude Chazottes, Francis Meynieu, Michel Pottier, Alexandre Strassievitch, Henri Zambelli, Michel Couge, Jean Fernandez, Michel Platini, Francisco Rubio, Loic Amisse, Bruno Baronchelli, Eric Pecout, Olivier Rouyer, Jean Marc Schaer) | 2 | 2 | 1 | 9 | 7 |
| 5. IRN (Mansour Rashidi, Hassan Nazari, Andranik Eskandarian, Bijan Zolfagharnasab, Parviz Qelichkhani, Ali Parvin, Nasrollah Abdollahi, Nasser Nouraii, Hassan Rowshan, Ali-reza Khorshidi, Hassan Nayebagha, Gholam Mazloomi, Hessem Mirfakhali, Ghafoor Jahani, Ali-Reza Azizi, Nasser Hejazi) | 1 | 2 | 0 | 4 | 5 |
| 5. ISR (Itzhak Vissoker, Abrahm Lev, Yaron Oz, Haim Bar, Moshe | 0 | 1 | 3 | 4 | 7 |

| | W | L | T | PF | PA |
|---|---|---|---|---|---|

Shani, Itzak Peretz, Itzhak Shum, Elimeleh Leventhal, Rifaat Tourk, Gideon Damti, Josef Sorynow, Meir Nimni, Oded Nachness, Avraham Cohen, Joshua Gal, Ehud Ben-Tovim, Alon Ben-Dor)

| | | W | L | T | PF | PA |
|---|---|---|---|---|---|---|
| 5. PRK | (In-Chol Jin, Gwangsok Kim, Il-Nam Kim, Myong-Song Kim, Jong-U Ma, Jong-Hun Pak, Se-Uk An, Song-Nam Hong, Jong-Sok Cha, Sung-Gyu Kim, Song-Guk Yang, Gil-Wan An, Hi-Yon Li, Dong-Chan Myong, Kyong-Won Pak) | 1 | 2 | 0 | 3 | 9 |

Final: GDR 3–1 POL
3rd Place: SOV 2–0 BRA

Again the Olympic soccer final was played in heavy rain, and again it was dominated by the professional amateurs of Eastern Europe, including ten members of Poland's 1974 World Cup team. In the final match, East Germany scored two goals in the first 15 minutes and scored again with six minutes to play to secure the gold medal.

**1980 Moscow** T: 16, N: 16, D: 8.2.

| | | W | L | T | PF | PA |
|---|---|---|---|---|---|---|
| 1. CZE | (Stanislav Seman, Luděk Macela, Josef Mazura, Libor Radimec, Zdeněk Rygel, Petr Němec, Ladislav Vizek, Jan Berger, Jindřich Svoboda, Lubos Pokluda, Werner Lička, Rostislav Václavíček, Jaroslav Netolicka, Oldřich Rott, František Štambacher, František Kunzo) | 4 | 0 | 2 | 10 | 1 |
| 2. GDR | (Bodo Rudwaleit, Artur Ullrich, Lothar Hause, Frank Uhlig, Frank Baum, Rüdiger Schnuphase, Frank Terletzki, Wolfgang Steinbach, Jürgen Bähringer, Werner Peter, Dieter Kühn, Norbert Trieloff, Matthias Liebers, Bernd Jakubowski, Wolf-Rüdiger Netz, Matthias Müller) | 4 | 1 | 1 | 12 | 2 |
| 3. SOV | (Rinat Dasaev, Tengiz Sulakvelidze, Aleksandr Chivadze, Vagiz Khidiyatullin, Oleg Romantsev, Sergei Shavlo, Sergei Andreev, Vladimir Bessonov, Yuri Gavrilov, Fyodor Cherenkov, Valery Gazzaev, Vladimir Pilguj, Sergei Baltacha, Sergei Nikulin, Khoren Oganesyan, Aleksandr Prokopenko) | 5 | 1 | 0 | 10 | 3 |
| 4. YUG | (Dragan Pantelić, Nikica Cukrov, Ivan Gudelj, Milos Hrstic, | 3 | 2 | 1 | 9 | 7 |

Milan Jovin, Nikica Klincarski, Miso Krsticević, Dzevad Secerbegović, Vladimir Matijević, Dušan Pestić, Tomislav Ivković, Boro Primorać, Srebrenko Repcić, Milos Sestić, Zlatko Vujović, Zoran Vujović)

| | | W | L | T | PF | PA |
|---|---|---|---|---|---|---|
| 5. ALG | (Mourad Ahara, Mahmoud Guendouz, Bouzid Mahiduz, Chaabane Merzekane, Mohamed Kheddis, Rabah Madjer, Ali Fergani, Tadj Bensaoula, Lakhdar Belloumi, Salah Assad, Mohamed Rahmani, Salah Larbes, Djamel Menad, Abderrahmane Derquaz, Hocine Yahi, Mohamed Quamar Ghrib) | 1 | 2 | 1 | 4 | 4 |
| 5. CUB | (Jose Reinoso, Miguel Lopez, Raimundo Frometa, Luis Sánchez, Luis Dreke, Roberto Espinosa, Andres Roldan, Amado Povea, Dagoberto Lara, Ramon Núñez, Calixto Martinez, Roberto Pereira, Jorge Masso, Fermin Madera, Carlos Loredo, Luis Hernandez) | 2 | 2 | 0 | 3 | 12 |
| 5. IRQ | (Abdul Fatah Jassim, Adnan Derchal Hutar, Jamal Ali Hamza, Saad Jassih Mohammed, Hassan Farhan Hassoun, Alaa Ahmed Khdhayir, Adil Khohayrr Hafidh, Falah Hassan Jasim, Hadi Ahmed Basheer, Hussain Saeed Muhammed, Thamir Assoufi Elias, Ibrahim Ali Kadhum, Wathiq Aswad Muhyi, Nazar Asmraf Salman, Ali Kadhum Nasir, Kadom Shibib Abdulsada) | 1 | 1 | 2 | 4 | 5 |
| 5. KUW | (Ahmad Altarabulsi, Najeem Hubarak, Mahboub Hubarak, Jamal Alqabendi, Waleed Almubarak, Saed Alhouti, Fathi Marzouq, Jasem Sultan, Mujayed Alhaddad, Hamad Bohamad, Yousef Alsuwayed, Ahmad Hasan, Humoud Alshemmari, Sami Alhashash, Faisal Aldaakhil, Abdulnabi Alkhadi) | 1 | 1 | 2 | 4 | 5 |

Final: CZE 1–0 GDR
3rd Place: SOV 2–0 YUG

Seven of the 16 qualifying teams withdrew as part of the anti-Soviet boycott and were replaced by lesser teams. The only goal of the final was scored by a substitute, Jindřich Svoboda, who entered the game with 19 minutes to play and put in a header six minutes later. For the third straight time, the Olympic final was played in a rainstorm.

**1984 Los Angeles-Pasadena** T: 16, N: 16, D: 8.11.

| | | W | L | T | PP | PA |
|---|---|---|---|---|---|---|
| 1. | FRA (Albert Rust, William Ayache, Michel Bibard, Dominique Bijotat, François Brisson, Patrick Cubaynes, Patrice Garande, Philippe Jeannol, Guy Lacombe, Jean-Claude Lemoult, Jean-Philippe Rohr, Didier Sénac, Jean-Christoph Thouvenel, José Touré, Daniel Xuereb, Jean-Louis Zanon) | 4 | 0 | 2 | 13 | 6 |
| 2. | BRA (Gilmar Rinaldi, Ronaldo Silva, Jorge Luiz Brum, Mauro Galvao, Ademir Rock Kaeser, Andre Luiz Ferreira, Paulo Santos, Carlos Verri, João Leiehardt Neto, Augilmar Ollveira, Silvio Paiva, Luiz Carlos Winck, Davi Cortez Silva, Antonio José Gil, Francisco Vidal, Milton Cruz) | 5 | 1 | 0 | 9 | 5 |
| 3. | YUG (Ivan Pudar, Vlado Capljić, Mirsad Baljić, Srecko Kataneć, Marko Elsner, Ljubomir Radanović, Admir Smajić, Nenad Gracan, Milko Djurovski, Mehmed Bazdarević, Borislav Cvetković, Tomislav Ivković, Jovica Nikolić, Stjepan Deverić, Branko Miljus, Dragan Stojković, Mitar Mrkela) | 5 | 1 | 0 | 16 | 10 |
| 4. | ITA (Franco Tancredi, Riccardo Ferri, Fllippo Galli, Sebastiano Nela, Roberto Tricella, Pietro Vierchowod, Salvatore Bagni, Franco Baresi, Sergio Battistini, Antonio Sabato, Beniamino Vignola, Walter Zenga, Pietro Fanna, Daniele Massaro, Massimo Briaschi, Maurizio Iorio, Aldo Serena) | 3 | 3 | 0 | 5 | 5 |
| 5. | CAN (Tino Lettleri, Bob Lenarduzzi, Bruce Wilson, Terry Moore, Ian Bridge, Randy Ragan, David Norman, Gerry Gray, Ken Garraway, Dale Mitchell, Mike Sweeney, Igor Vrablic, Paul James, John Catliff) | 1 | 2 | 1 | 5 | 4 |
| 5. | CHI (Edwardo Fournier, Daniel Ahumada, Luis Mosquera, Alex Martinez, Leonel Contreras, Alejandro Hisis, Alfredo Núñez, Jaime Vera, Fernando Santis, Sergio Marchant, Juvenal Olmos, Carlos Ramos, Jaime Baeza, Marco Figueroa) | 1 | 1 | 2 | 2 | 2 |
| 5. | EGY (Adel Elmaamour, Ali El Sayed Gadallah, Rabie Yassen, Mahmoud Saleh, Ibrahim Youssif, Yehia Sedky, Mostafa Ismail, Shawki Gharib, Magdy Abdelghani, Mahmoud Elkhatib, Emad Soleman, Taher Abouzied, Badreldin Hamed, Mohamad Helmy, Omar Elzeer, Alaa Morsy, Nagy Salem) | | | | | |
| 5. | GER (Bernd Franke, Manfred Bockenfeld, Roland Dickgiesser, Dieter Bast, Bernd Wehmeyer, Guido Buchwald, Jürgen Groh, Rudolf Bommer, Dieter Schatzschneider, Andreas Brehme, Frank Mill, Alfred Schoen, Peter Lux, Uwe Rahn, Christian Schreier) | 2 | 2 | 0 | 10 | 6 |

Final: FRA 2–0 BRA
3rd Place: YUG 2–1 ITA

For the first time, professional football players were allowed to take part in an Olympic tournament. In the case of European and South American teams, only those professionals who had not yet competed in World Cup competition were considered eligible. This, plus the absence of all of the 1980 medalists, due to the Soviet-bloc boycott, led to a lively and wide-open competition.

The final, played before a crowd of 101,799, was won by the French on two second-half goals, a header by François Brisson, ten minutes into the half and a follow shot by Daniel Xuereb less than eight minutes later.

**1988 Seoul** T: 16, N: 16, D: 10.1.

| | | W | L | T | PF | PA |
|---|---|---|---|---|---|---|
| 1. | SOV (Dmitri Kharin, Gela Ketashvili, Igor Skliarov, Aleksei Cherednik, Arvidas Janonis, Yevgeny Kuznetsov, Igor Ponomarev, Aleksandr Borodyuk, Igor Dobrovolsky, Vladimir Lyuty, Yevgeny Yarovenko, Sergei Fokin, Vladimir Tatarchuk, Aleksei Prudnikov, Viktor Losev, Sergei Gorlukovich, Yuri Savichev, Arminas Narbekovas) | 5 | 0 | 1 | 14 | 6 |
| 2. | BRA (Claudio Taffarel, Jorge Campos, João Santos, Ricardo Raimundo, Ademir Kaefer, Iomar Nascimento, Geovani Silva, Edmar Santos, Hamilton Souza, Romario Farias, José Araujo, Andre Cruz, Luiz Winck, Aloisio Alves, Milton Souza, José Ferreira, Sergio Luiz, Jorge Silva, José Oliveira) | 5 | 1 | 0 | 12 | 4 |
| 3. | GER (Oliver Reck, Michael Schulz, Armin Görtz, Wolfgang Funkel, Thomas Hörster, Olaf Janssen, Rudi Bommer, Holger Fach, Jürgen Klinsmann, Wolfram Wuttke, Frank Mill, Uwe Kamps, | 4 | 2 | 0 | 16 | 4 |

| | | W | L | T | PF | PA |
|---|---|---|---|---|---|---|
| | Roland Grahammer, Thomas Hässler, Christian Schreier, Fritz Walter, Ralf Sievers, Gerhard Kleppinger, Karlheinz Riedle) | | | | | |
| 4. ITA | (Stefano Tacconi, Roberto Cravero, Andrea Carnevale, Luigi De Agostini, Ciro Ferrara, Mauro Tassotti, Angelo Colombo, Luca Pellegrini, Massimo Brambati, Stefano Carobbi, Massimo Crippa, Giuliano Giuliani, Antonio Virdis, Ruggiero Rizzitelli, Roberto Galla, Giuseppe Iachini, Stefano Desideri, Massimo Mauro, Alberigo Evani) | 3 | 3 | 0 | 11 | 13 |
| 5. ARG | (Luis Alberto Islas, Ruben José Aguero, Mauro Gabriel Aires, Carlos-Alejandr Alfaro Moreno, Claudio-Martin Cabrera, Jorge Alberto Comas, Hernan Edgardo Diaz, Nestor-Ariel Fabbri, Daniel Anibal Hernandez, Nestor Gabriel Lorenzo, Fabian Oscar Candelarich, Mario Bruno Lucca, Carlos Alberto Mayor, Pedro Damian Monzon, Hugo Leonardo Perez, Alejandro Ruidiaz, Alejandro Marcelo Russo, Dario Andres Siviski) | 1 | 2 | 1 | 4 | 5 |
| 5. AUS | (Jeffrey Olver, Gary Van Egmond, Graham Jennings, Charlie Yankos, Robert Dunn, Paul Wade, Frank Farina, Mike Petersen, Graham Arnold, John Kosmina, Oscar Crino, Alan Davidson, Andrew Koczka, Vlado Bozinoski, Robert Slater, David Mitchell, Scott Ollerenshaw, Michael Gibson) | 2 | 2 | 0 | 2 | 6 |
| 5. SWE | (Sven Andersson, Sulo Vattovaara, Peter Lönn, Göran Arnberg, Roland Nilsson, Jonas Thern, Leif Engqvist, Michael Andersson, Joakim Nilsson, Anders Limpár, Håkan Lindman, Bengt Nilsson, Martin Dahlin, Hans Eskilsson, Jan Hellström, Roger Ljung, Lars Eriksson, Ola Svensson, Anders Palmer, Stefan Rehn) | 2 | 1 | 1 | 7 | 5 |
| 5. ZAM | (David Chabala, Peter Mwanza, Edmon Mumba, Samuel Chomba, James Chitalu, Derby Makinka, Johnson Bwalya, Charles Musonda, Beston Chambeshi, Webster Chikabala, Lucky Msiska, Kalusha Bwalya, Manfred Chabinga, Ashols Melu, Richard Mwanza, Pearson Mwanza, Wisdom Mumba Chansa, Stone Nyirenda, Eston Mulenga) | 2 | 1 | 1 | 10 | 6 |

Final: SOV 2–1 BRA
3rd Place: GER 3–0 ITA

The highlight of the preliminary round was the shocking 4–0 trouncing of Italy by unheralded Zambia.

Both Brazil and the Soviet Union advanced to the final with come-from-behind overtime victories. The Soviets scored two goals in extra time to beat Italy, while the Brazilians defeated West Germany in a penalty kick shoot-out. Brazil's Romario Farias, the leading scorer in the tournament with seven, scored the first goal of the final in the 30th minute. Eleven minutes into the second half, Igor Dobrovolsky evened the match with a penalty kick. The decisive goal—the result of a fast-breaking counterattack—was struck in the 14th minute of overtime by substitute Yuri Savichev of Moscow.

# GYMNASTICS

MEN
All-Around
Horizontal Bar
Parallel Bars
Long Horse Vault
Side Horse (Pommeled Horse)

Rings
Floor Exercises
Team Combined Exercises
Discontinued Events

## MEN

Gymnastics competitions are divided into three parts. On the first two days, all gymnasts perform compulsory and optional exercises on all apparatuses. Their scores are then used to determine the winners of the team event. The 36 gymnasts who achieve the highest combined individual scores then move on to the individual All-Around finals, in which they once again compete on each apparatus. According to current rules only three gymnasts from each nation may compete in the individual All-Around finals. The top eight scorers on each apparatus, based on combined scores from the team and All-Around finals, then move on to the apparatus finals. Prior to 1984, only six gymnasts participated in the finals of each apparatus. The 1984 rules also limited the number of gymnasts from each nation to two for each apparatus. Current rules also impose a minimum age limit in the gymnastics competitions. Both men and women must turn 15 within the calendar year of the Games.

## ALL-AROUND

| | |
|---|---|
| HB = | Horizontal bar |
| PB = | Parallel bars |
| LHV = | Long horse vault |
| SH = | Side horse (pommeled horse) |
| R = | Rings |
| FE = | Floor exercises |
| SHV = | Side horse vault |
| CLSV = | Combined long and side horse vaults |
| 100 = | 100-yard run |
| SP = | Shot put |
| LJ = | Long jump |
| RC = | Rope climb |
| CLHJ = | Combined long and high jump |
| PV = | Pole vault |
| H = | Heaving a 50 kg stone |

**1896** not held

**1900 Paris** C: 134, N: 6?, D: 7.30.
*Events: HB, PB, LHV, SH, R, FE, LJ, RC, CLHJ, PV, H*

|  |  |  | PTS. |
|--|--|--|------|
| 1. | Gustave Sandras | FRA | 302 |
| 2. | Nöel Bas | FRA | 295 |
| 3. | Lucien Démanet | FRA | 293 |
| 4. | Pierre Payssé | FRA | 290 |
| 4. | Jules Rolland | FRA | 290 |
| 6. | Gustave Fabry | FRA | 283 |
| 7. | J. Martinez | FRA/ALG | 277 |
| 8. | Marcel Lalu | FRA | 275 |
| 8. | Mauvezain | FRA | 275 |

**1904 St. Louis** C: 119, N: 4, D: 7.2.

|  |  |  |  |  |  | FT.-IN. | | TIME | TOTAL |
|--|--|--|--|--|--|---------|-|------|-------|
|  |  |  | PB | HB | CLSV | LJ | SP | 100 | PTS. |
| 1. | Julius Lenhart | AUT | 14.40 | 14.60 | 14.00 | 18-0 | 28-6 | 12.0 | 69.80 |
| 2. | Wilhelm Weber | GER | 14.17 | 13.93 | 13.50 | 18-1 | 30-1 | 12.0 | 69.10 |
| 3. | Adolf Spinnler | SWI | 14.53 | 14.53 | 14.43 | 16-2¼ | 29-7 | 12.4 | 67.99 |
| 4. | Ernest Mohr | GER | 12.90 | 13.00 | 13.00 | 18-8¼ | 30-0 | 11.4 | 67.90 |
| 5. | Otto Wiegand | GER | 14.20 | 13.12 | 13.50 | 17-6 | 30-4¾ | 12.0 | 67.82 |
| 6. | Otto Steffen | USA | 12.80 | 14.10 | 12.63 | 18-1 | 30-9½ | 12.0 | 67.03 |
| 7. | Hugo Peitsch | GER | 14.03 | 14.30 | 13.23 | 16-10¾ | 27-4¾ | 12.0 | 66.66 |
| 8. | John Bissinger | USA | 13.10 | 12.37 | 12.10 | 18-4¾ | 32-9½ | 11.4 | 66.57 |

**1906 Athens** C: 37, N: 8, D: 5.1.
*Events: HB, PB, LHV, R, CLHJ*

|  |  |  | PTS. |
|--|--|--|------|
| 1. | Pierre Payssé | FRA | 97 |
| 2. | Alberto Braglia | ITA | 95 |
| 3. | Georges Charmoille | FRA | 94 |
| 4. | Carl Ohms | GER | 93 |
| 5. | Vitaliano Masotti | ITA | 92 |
| 6. | Pissié | FRA | 91 |

7. Nicolaos Aliprantis (GRE), Bélà Erody (HUN), Mario Gubiani (ITA), B. Hunzatko (BOH), Joseph Krämer (GER), D. Lavielle (FRA), Carl Schwartz (GER), Wilhelm Weber (GER)—90

**1906 Athens** C: 17, N: 6, D: 5.1.
*Events: HB, PB, LHV, SH, R, CLHJ*

|  |  |  | PTS. |
|--|--|--|------|
| 1. | Pierre Payssé | FRA | 116 |
| 2. | Alberto Braglia | ITA | 115 |
| 3. | Georges Charmoille | FRA | 113 |
| 4. | Carl Ohms | GER | 112 |
| 5. | Vitaliano Masotti | ITA | 111 |
| 6. | Béla Erody | HUN | 110 |
| 6. | Mario Gubiani | ITA | 110 |
| 6. | Pissié | FRA | 110 |
| 6. | Wilhelm Weber | GER | 110 |

This event combined the results of the five apparatuses in the previous event with the results of one more apparatus: the side or pommeled horse.

**1908 London** C: 97, N: 12, D: 7.15.
*Events: HB, PB, SH, R, RC*

|  |  |  | PTS. |
|--|--|--|------|
| 1. | Alberto Braglia | ITA | 317.0 |
| 2. | S.W. Tysal | GBR | 312.0 |
| 3. | Louis Ségura | FRA | 297.0 |
| 4. | Curt Steuernagel | GER | 273.5 |
| 5. | Friedrich Wolf | GER | 267.0 |
| 6. | Samuel Hodgetts | GBR | 266.0 |
| 7. | Marcel Lalu | FRA | 258.75 |
| 8. | R. Diaz | FRA | 258.5 |

**1912 Stockholm** C: 44, N: 9, D: 7.12.

|  |  |  | HB | PB | R | SH | TOTAL PTS. |
|--|--|--|----|----|---|----|------------|
| 1. | Alberto Braglia | ITA | 32.75 | 34.75 | 31.75 | 35.75 | 135.0 |
| 2. | Louis Ségura | FRA | 30.0 | 35.75 | 32.25 | 34.5 | 132.5 |
| 3. | Adolfo Tunesi | ITA | 30.25 | 35.0 | 30.5 | 35.75 | 131.5 |
| 4. | Guido Boni | ITA | 29.75 | 35.25 | 28.25 | 34.75 | 128.0 |
| 4. | Giorgio Zampori | ITA | 29.0 | 35.0 | 30.75 | 33.25 | 128.0 |
| 6. | Pietro Bianchi | ITA | 29.5 | 33.75 | 30.75 | 33.75 | 127.75 |
| 7. | Marcel Lalu | FRA | 29.25 | 35.5 | 30.5 | 31.75 | 127.0 |
| 7. | Marco Torrès | FRA | 30.25 | 35.0 | 31.0 | 30.75 | 127.0 |

**1920 Antwerp** C: 44, N: 9, D: 8.29.
**Events: HB, PB, SH, R**

|   |   |   | PTS. |
|---|---|---|---|
| 1. | Giorgio Zampori | ITA | 88.35 |
| 2. | Marco Torrès | FRA | 87.62 |
| 3. | Jean Gounot | FRA | 87.45 |
| 4. | Félicien Kempeneers | BEL | 86.25 |
| 5. | Georges Thurnherr | FRA | 86.00 |
| 6. | Laurent Grech | FRA | 85.65 |
| 7. | Luigi Maiocco | ITA | 85.38 |
| 8. | Luigi Costigliolo | ITA | 84.90 |

**1924 Paris** C: 72, N: 9, D: 7.20.

|   |   |   | HB | | PB | | LHV | | SH | | R | | SHV | | RC | | TOTAL PTS. |
|---|---|---|---|---|---|---|---|---|---|---|---|---|---|---|---|---|---|
| 1. | Leon Štukelj | YUG | 19.73 | (1) | 20.40 | (20) | 9.91 | (4) | 19.37 | (10) | 21.33 | (4) | 9.60 | (17) | 10.0 | (10) | 110.340 |
| 2. | Robert Pražák | CZE | 18.73 | (9) | 21.26 | (2) | 9.73 | (9) | 18.97 | (13) | 21.483 | (2) | 9.80 | (8) | 10.0 | (13) | 110.323 |
| 3. | Bedřich Supčík | CZE | 17.86 | (16) | 21.26 | (8) | 9.33 | (15) | 17.53 | (24) | 21.12 | (5) | 9.83 | (6) | 10.0 | (1) | 106.930 |
| 4. | Ferdinando Mandrini | ITA | 18.12 | (14) | 20.21 | (24) | 9.75 | (7) | 16.06 | (30) | 20.943 | (8) | 8.73 | (21) | 10.0 | (18) | 105.583 |
| 5. | Miroslav Klinger | CZE | 16.47 | (26) | 21.13 | (10) | 9.75 | (7) | 19.67 | (7) | 20.73 | (11) | 9.75 | (12) | 8.0 | (21) | 105.500 |
| 6. | Ladislav Vácha | CZE | 14.70 | (39) | 21.31 | (6) | 9.70 | (10) | 18.33 | (17) | 21.43 | (3) | 9.83 | (6) | 10.0 | (4) | 105.300 |
| 7. | August Güttinger | SWI | 18.886 | (8) | 21.63 | (1) | 9.08 | (17) | 19.60 | (8) | 17.57 | (37) | 8.41 | (29) | 10.0 | (3) | 105.176 |
| 8. | Jean Gounot | FRA | 19.043 | (6) | 20.15 | (25) | 9.00 | (18) | 17.30 | (27) | 19.73 | (19) | 9.93 | (2) | 10.0 | (6) | 105.153 |

Štukelj, a lawyer from Novo Mesto, eventually won three gold medals, one silver, and two bronze in his Olympic career, including a silver in the rings in 1936, when he was 37 years old.

**1928 Amsterdam** C: 88, N: 11, D: 8.10.

|   |   |   | HB | | PB | | LHV | | SH | | R | | TOTAL PTS. |
|---|---|---|---|---|---|---|---|---|---|---|---|---|---|
| 1. | Georges Miez | SWI | 57.5 | (1) | 49.75 | (30) | 28.25 | (4) | 57.75 | (2) | 54.25 | (8) | 247.500 |
| 2. | Hermann Hänggi | SWI | 56.5 | (4) | 54.25 | (3) | 27.125 | (18) | 59.25 | (1) | 49.5 | (36) | 246.625 |
| 3. | Leon Štukelj | YUG | 53.75 | (21) | 53.5 | (7) | 26.625 | (28) | 53.25 | (12) | 57.75 | (1) | 244.875 |
| 4. | Romeo Neri | ITA | 57.0 | (2) | 53.0 | (12) | 27.25 | (16) | 51.5 | (19) | 56.0 | (4) | 244.750 |
| 5. | Josip Primožič | YUG | 56.0 | (6) | 55.5 | (2) | 28.25 | (4) | 51.75 | (18) | 52.5 | (18) | 244.000 |
| 6. | Mauri Nybert-Noroma | FIN | 54.0 | (16) | 53.5 | (7) | 26.75 | (26) | 54.5 | (7) | 55.0 | (5) | 243.750 |
| 6. | Heikki Savolainen | FIN | 54.5 | (13) | 51.75 | (17) | 27.25 | (16) | 56.5 | (3) | 53.75 | (12) | 243.750 |
| 8. | Eugen Mack | SWI | 56.75 | (3) | 51.0 | (21) | 28.75 | (1) | 54.25 | (9) | 52.50 | (18) | 243.250 |

At the Amsterdam Games, 23-year-old Georges Miez won three gold medals and one silver. Between 1924 and 1936 his Olympic total was four gold, three silver, and one bronze.

**1932 Los Angeles** C: 24, N: 5, D: 8.12.

|   |   |   | HB | | PB | | LHV | | SH | | R | | TOTAL PTS. |
|---|---|---|---|---|---|---|---|---|---|---|---|---|---|
| 1. | Romeo Neri | ITA | 28.9 | (2) | 28.1 | (3) | 27.525 | (3) | 28.0 | (4) | 28.0 | (3) | 140.625 |
| 2. | István Pelle | HUN | 29.15 | (1) | 27.9 | (6) | 24.675 | (9) | 24.85 | (11) | 28.35 | (1) | 134.925 |
| 3. | Heikki Savolainen | FIN | 27.25 | (7) | 28.4 | (1) | 22.925 | (15) | 28.35 | (3) | 27.65 | (5) | 134.575 |
| 4. | Mario Lertora | ITA | 28.2 | (3) | 27.25 | (8) | 27.25 | (4) | 23.35 | (14) | 28.35 | (1) | 134.400 |
| 5. | Savino Guglielmetti | ITA | 28.2 | (3) | 28.4 | (1) | 28.325 | (1) | 22.6 | (16) | 26.85 | (6) | 134.375 |
| 6. | Frank Haubold | USA | 26.9 | (10) | 28.0 | (4) | 25.725 | (7) | 28.45 | (1) | 23.45 | (16) | 132.525 |
| 7. | Oreste Capuzzo | ITA | 27.5 | (6) | 27.3 | (7) | 23.7 | (10) | 26.15 | (9) | 27.8 | (4) | 132.450 |
| 8. | Frederick Meyer | USA | 27.1 | (9) | 26.45 | (14) | 27.55 | (2) | 28.4 | (2) | 22.15 | (19) | 131.650 |

## 1936 Berlin C: 111, N: 14, D: 8.11.

| | | HB | | PB | | LHV | | SH | | R | | FE | | TOTAL PTS. |
|---|---|---|---|---|---|---|---|---|---|---|---|---|---|---|
| 1. Alfred Schwarzmann | GER | 19.23 | (3) | 18.967 | (3) | 19.2 | (1) | 19.0 | (7) | 18.534 | (4) | 18.166 | (10) | 113.100 |
| 2. Eugen Mack | SWI | 18.9 | (9) | 18.834 | (5) | 18.967 | (2) | 19.167 | (2) | 18.0 | (13) | 18.466 | (3) | 112.334 |
| 3. Konrad Frey | GER | 19.267 | (2) | 19.067 | (1) | 17.666 | (20) | 19.333 | (1) | 17.733 | (18) | 18.466 | (3) | 111.532 |
| 4. Alois Hudec | CZE | 18.834 | (10) | 18.966 | (4) | 17.867 | (18) | 17.966 | (26) | 19.433 | (1) | 18.133 | (11) | 111.199 |
| 5. Martti Uosikkinen | FIN | 19.0 | (7) | 18.433 | (11) | 18.3 | (6) | 19.066 | (4) | 17.634 | (22) | 18.267 | (8) | 110.700 |
| 5. Michael Reusch | SWI | 18.566 | (18) | 19.034 | (2) | 18.266 | (7) | 19.0 | (7) | 18.434 | (6) | 17.400 | (22) | 110.700 |
| 7. Matthias Volz | GER | 18.8 | (11) | 17.033 | (38) | 18.467 | (3) | 18.766 | (10) | 18.667 | (3) | 18.366 | (5) | 110.099 |
| 8. Willi Stadel | GER | 18.7 | (14) | 18.133 | (18) | 18.033 | (14) | 18.887 | (9) | 16.966 | (36) | 18.3 | (6) | 108.999 |

## 1948 London C: 123, N: 16, D: 8.13.

| | | HB | | PB | | LHV | | SH | | R | | FE | | TOTAL PTS. |
|---|---|---|---|---|---|---|---|---|---|---|---|---|---|---|
| 1. Veikko Huhtanen | FIN | 39.2 | (3) | 39.3 | (2) | 38.4 | (6) | 38.7 | (1) | 37.8 | (11) | 36.3 | (34) | 229.7 |
| 2. Walter Lehmann | SWI | 39.4 | (12) | 39.0 | (5) | 38.1 | (8) | 37.6 | (11) | 38.4 | (4) | 36.5 | (29) | 229.0 |
| 3. Paavo Aaltonen | FIN | 38.4 | (12) | 38.8 | (7) | 39.1 | (1) | 38.7 | (1) | 37.3 | (17) | 36.5 | (29) | 228.8 |
| 4. Josef Stalder | SWI | 39.7 | (1) | 39.1 | (3) | 36.9 | (33) | 37.7 | (8) | 38.3 | (5) | 37.0 | (16) | 228.7 |
| 5. Christian Kipfer | SWE | 38.6 | (9) | 39.1 | (3) | 37.9 | (14) | 37.2 | (14) | 37.8 | (11) | 36.5 | (29) | 227.1 |
| 6. Emil Studer | SWI | 38.8 | (4) | 37.8 | (21) | 38.0 | (10) | 37.7 | (8) | 38.3 | (5) | 36.0 | (41) | 226.6 |
| 7. Zdenek Ružicka | CZE | 37.9 | (17) | 38.8 | (7) | 36.6 | (46) | 36.3 | (30) | 38.5 | (3) | 38.1 | (3) | 226.2 |
| 8. Kalevi Laitinen | FIN | 38.1 | (14) | 38.1 | (16) | 38.0 | (10) | 36.9 | (19) | 37.4 | (16) | 37.15 | (13) | 225.65 |

## 1952 Helsinki C: 185, N: 29, D: 7.21.

| | | HB | | PB | | LHV | | SH | | R | | FE | | TOTAL PTS. |
|---|---|---|---|---|---|---|---|---|---|---|---|---|---|---|
| 1. Viktor Chukarin | SOV | 19.4 | (5) | 19.6 | (2) | 19.2 | (1) | 19.5 | (1) | 19.55 | (2) | 18.45 | (29) | 115.7 |
| 2. Grant Shaginyan | SOV | 19.05 | (14) | 19.35 | (4) | 18.5 | (35) | 19.4 | (2) | 19.75 | (1) | 18.90 | (8) | 114.95 |
| 3. Josef Stalder | SWI | 19.5 | (2) | 19.5 | (3) | 18.8 | (13) | 19.2 | (5) | 19.1 | (11) | 18.65 | (19) | 114.75 |
| 4. Valentin Muratov | SOV | 19.2 | (9) | 19.25 | (9) | 18.7 | (19) | 18.3 | (32) | 19.35 | (5) | 18.85 | (11) | 113.65 |
| 5. Hans Eugster | SWI | 19.15 | (11) | 19.65 | (1) | 18.95 | (5) | 18.55 | (25) | 19.4 | (3) | 17.7 | (66) | 113.40 |
| 6. Vladimir Belyakov | SOV | 18.8 | (23) | 19.25 | (8) | 18.5 | (35) | 19.1 | (7) | 18.95 | (14) | 18.75 | (14) | 113.35 |
| 6. Yevgeny Korolkov | SOV | 18.8 | (23) | 19.3 | (5) | 18.4 | (44) | 19.4 | (2) | 19.15 | (7) | 18.3 | (35) | 113.35 |
| 8. Jean Tschabold | SWI | 19.35 | (6) | 19.3 | (5) | 18.7 | (19) | 19.05 | (8) | 18.75 | (23) | 18.15 | (41) | 113.30 |

Chukarin, a Ukrainian who had spent four years in a concentration camp during World War II, earned six medals at Helsinki—four gold and two silver.

## 1956 Melbourne C: 63, N: 18, D: 12.6.

| | | HB | | PB | | LHV | | SH | | R | | FE | | TOTAL PTS. |
|---|---|---|---|---|---|---|---|---|---|---|---|---|---|---|
| 1. Viktor Chukarin | SOV | 19.25 | (4) | 19.2 | (1) | 18.6 | (7) | 19.1 | (3) | 19.0 | (7) | 19.1 | (2) | 114.25 |
| 2. Takashi Ono | JPN | 19.6 | (1) | 19.1 | (1) | 18.5 | (16) | 19.2 | (2) | 19.05 | (5) | 18.75 | (8) | 114.20 |
| 3. Yuri Titov | SOV | 19.4 | (2) | 18.85 | (8) | 18.75 | (3) | 19.0 | (5) | 18.85 | (10) | 18.95 | (5) | 113.80 |
| 4. Masao Takemoto | JPN | 19.3 | (3) | 19.1 | (3) | 18.65 | (6) | 18.9 | (7) | 19.1 | (3) | 18.5 | (16) | 113.55 |
| 5. Valentin Muratov | SOV | 18.6 | (25) | 18.7 | (16) | 18.85 | (1) | 18.8 | (9) | 19.15 | (2) | 19.2 | (1) | 113.30 |
| 6. Helmut Bantz | GER | 19.15 | (6) | 18.8 | (6) | 18.85 | (1) | 18.75 | (12) | 18.6 | (18) | 18.75 | (8) | 112.90 |
| 7. Albert Azaryan | SOV | 18.95 | (8) | 19.0 | (5) | 18.55 | (11) | 18.75 | (12) | 19.35 | (1) | 17.95 | (40) | 112.55 |
| 8. Boris Shakhlin | SOV | 18.75 | (13) | 18.85 | (8) | 18.7 | (4) | 19.25 | (1) | 18.7 | (15) | 18.25 | (28) | 112.50 |

Chukarin, by then a 35-year-old teacher, added to his medal collection three gold, one silver, and one bronze at Melbourne, for a remarkable total of 11 Olympic medals.

**1960 Rome** C: 130, N: 23, D: 9.7.

|  |  | HB |  | PB |  | LHV |  | SH |  | R |  | FE |  | TOTAL PTS. |
|---|---|---|---|---|---|---|---|---|---|---|---|---|---|---|
| 1. Boris Shakhlin | SOV | 19.55 | (2) | 19.4 | (1) | 19.2 | (3) | 19.35 | (1) | 19.5 | (2) | 18.95 | (7) | 115.95 |
| 2. Takashi Ono | JPN | 19.6 | (1) | 19.4 | (1) | 19.3 | (1) | 19.15 | (4) | 19.45 | (3) | 19.0 | (4) | 115.9 |
| 3. Yuri Titov | SOV | 19.5 | (4) | 19.2 | (6) | 19.0 | (5) | 19.2 | (3) | 19.45 | (3) | 19.25 | (2) | 115.6 |
| 4. Shuji Tsurumi | JPN | 19.25 | (8) | 19.15 | (8) | 19.0 | (5) | 19.1 | (6) | 19.2 | (9) | 18.85 | (13) | 114.55 |
| 5. Yukio Endo | JPN | 19.45 | (6) | 19.2 | (6) | 19.05 | (4) | 18.85 | (10) | 19.0 | (12) | 18.9 | (10) | 114.45 |
| 5. Masao Takemoto | JPN | 19.55 | (2) | 19.25 | (4) | 19.0 | (5) | 18.6 | (26) | 19.25 | (8) | 18.8 | (14) | 114.45 |
| 7. Nobuyuki Aihara | JPN | 19.0 | (13) | 19.25 | (4) | 18.85 | (9) | 18.6 | (26) | 19.4 | (5) | 19.3 | (1) | 114.4 |
| 8. Miroslav Cerar | YUG | 19.5 | (4) | 19.15 | (8) | 18.75 | (13) | 19.05 | (7) | 19.05 | (11) | 18.75 | (17) | 114.25 |

Boris Shakhlin, a Ukrainian from the small town of Ishin, won four gold medals, two silver, and one bronze at the Rome Games to add to the two gold medals he had won at Melbourne four years earlier.

**1964 Tokyo** C: 130, N: 30, D: 10.20.

|  |  | HB |  | PB |  | LHV |  | SH |  | R |  | FE |  | TOTAL PTS. |
|---|---|---|---|---|---|---|---|---|---|---|---|---|---|---|
| 1. Yukio Endo | JPN | 19.4 | (3) | 19.55 | (1) | 19.4 | (3) | 18.7 | (16) | 19.5 | (1) | 19.4 | (1) | 115.95 |
| 2. Viktor Lisitsky | SOV | 19.25 | (6) | 19.5 | (2) | 19.5 | (1) | 18.75 | (13) | 19.1 | (9) | 19.3 | (2) | 115.4 |
| 2. Boris Shakhlin | SOV | 19.55 | (1) | 19.25 | (9) | 19.35 | (4) | 18.9 | (7) | 19.4 | (4) | 18.95 | (14) | 115.4 |
| 2. Shuji Tsurumi | JPN | 18.9 | (21) | 19.5 | (2) | 19.3 | (6) | 19.25 | (3) | 19.35 | (5) | 19.1 | (9) | 115.4 |
| 5. Franco Menichelli | ITA | 19.25 | (6) | 19.3 | (6) | 19.05 | (24) | 18.8 | (10) | 19.45 | (2) | 19.3 | (2) | 115.15 |
| 6. Haruhiro Yamashita | JPN | 19.25 | (6) | 19.3 | (6) | 19.5 | (1) | 19.15 | (4) | 18.75 | (21) | 19.15 | (7) | 115.1 |
| 7. Miroslav Cerar | YUG | 19.3 | (5) | 19.5 | (2) | 19.1 | (19) | 19.45 | (1) | 19.05 | (12) | 18.65 | (30) | 115.05 |
| 8. Takuji Hayata | JPN | 19.1 | (12) | 19.15 | (10) | 19.15 | (16) | 18.9 | (7) | 19.45 | (2) | 19.15 | (7) | 114.9 |

**1968 Mexico City** C: 117, N: 28, D: 10.24.

|  |  | HB |  | PB |  | LHV |  | SH |  | R |  | FE |  | TOTAL PTS. |
|---|---|---|---|---|---|---|---|---|---|---|---|---|---|---|
| 1. Sawao Kato | JPN | 19.45 | (3) | 19.35 | (3) | 18.9 | (5) | 19.0 | (8) | 19.55 | (1) | 19.65 | (1) | 115.9 |
| 2. Mikhail Voronin | SOV | 19.5 | (1) | 19.45 | (2) | 19.0 | (2) | 19.2 | (2) | 19.45 | (3) | 19.25 | (4) | 115.85 |
| 3. Akinori Nakayama | JPN | 19.5 | (1) | 19.55 | (1) | 18.85 | (7) | 18.85 | (12) | 19.5 | (2) | 19.4 | (2) | 115.65 |
| 4. Eizo Kenmotsu | JPN | 19.05 | (5) | 19.25 | (5) | 18.95 | (4) | 19.1 | (4) | 19.0 | (7) | 19.25 | (4) | 114.9 |
| 5. Takeshi Kato | JPN | 19.1 | (11) | 19.3 | (4) | 19.05 | (1) | 18.65 | (21) | 19.4 | (4) | 19.35 | (3) | 114.85 |
| 6. Sergei Diomidov | SOV | 19.3 | (6) | 18.9 | (23) | 18.9 | (5) | 19.0 | (8) | 19.05 | (6) | 18.95 | (9) | 114.1 |
| 7. Vladimir Klimenko | SOV | 19.1 | (11) | 19.25 | (5) | 18.85 | (7) | 19.1 | (4) | 18.9 | (9) | 18.75 | (13) | 113.95 |
| 8. Yukio Endo | JPN | 19.25 | (7) | 19.15 | (9) | 19.0 | (2) | 18.4 | (26) | 18.95 | (8) | 18.80 | (11) | 113.55 |

**1972 Munich** C: 113, N: 26, D: 8.30.

|  |  | HB |  | PB |  | LHV |  | SH |  | R |  | FE |  | TOTAL PTS. |
|---|---|---|---|---|---|---|---|---|---|---|---|---|---|---|
| 1. Sawao Kato | JPN | 19.525 | (2) | 19.275 | (1) | 19.0 | (2) | 18.9 | (3) | 19.15 | (4) | 18.8 | (6) | 114.650 |
| 2. Eizo Kenmotsu | JPN | 19.3 | (3) | 19.1 | (4) | 19.0 | (2) | 19.15 | (1) | 19.05 | (5) | 18.975 | (3) | 114.575 |
| 3. Akinori Nakayama | JPN | 19.275 | (4) | 19.275 | (1) | 18.75 | (7) | 18.75 | (7) | 19.25 | (1) | 19.025 | (1) | 114.325 |
| 4. Nikolai Andrianov | SOV | 19.25 | (5) | 18.925 | (6) | 19.35 | (1) | 18.7 | (8) | 19.0 | (6) | 18.975 | (3) | 114.200 |
| 5. Shigeru Kasamatsu | JPN | 19.25 | (5) | 18.825 | (10) | 18.625 | (10) | 19.075 | (2) | 18.9 | (7) | 19.025 | (1) | 113.700 |
| 6. Viktor Klimenko | SOV | 18.755 | (18) | 19.275 | (1) | 18.8 | (6) | 18.875 | (4) | 18.7 | (13) | 18.675 | (9) | 113.075 |
| 6. Klaus Köste | GDR | 18.975 | (11) | 19.1 | (4) | 18.875 | (4) | 18.4 | (17) | 18.85 | (9) | 18.875 | (5) | 113.075 |
| 8. Mitsuo Tsukahara | JPN | 19.675 | (1) | 18.625 | (15) | 18.35 | (22) | 18.15 | (20) | 19.225 | (2) | 18.75 | (8) | 112.775 |

The 5-foot 3-inch, 125-pound Kato became the third repeat winner of the men's All-Around championship, joining Alberto Braglia of Italy (1908 and 1912) and Viktor Chukarin of the Soviet Union (1952 and 1956).

**1976 Montreal** C: 90, N: 20, D: 7.21.

| | | HB | | PB | | LHV | | SH | | R | | FE | | TOTAL PTS. |
|---|---|---|---|---|---|---|---|---|---|---|---|---|---|---|
| 1. Nikolai Andrianov | SOV | 19.3 | (4) | 19.4 | (2) | 19.475 | (1) | 19.425 | (3) | 19.6 | (1) | 19.45 | (1) | 116.65 |
| 2. Sawao Kato | JPN | 19.5 | (2) | 19.475 | (1) | 19.1 | (8) | 19.3 | (5) | 19.075 | (6) | 19.2 | (3) | 115.65 |
| 3. Mitsuo Tsukahara | JPN | 19.525 | (1) | 19.375 | (3) | 19.45 | (2) | 19.2 | (7) | 19.0 | (9) | 19.025 | (7) | 115.575 |
| 4. Aleksandr Dityatin | SOV | 19.0 | (11) | 19.05 | (5) | 19.275 | (6) | 19.35 | (4) | 19.5 | (2) | 19.35 | (2) | 115.525 |
| 5. Hiroshi Kajiyama | JPN | 19.225 | (7) | 19.325 | (4) | 19.325 | (5) | 19.275 | (6) | 19.2 | (3) | 19.075 | (6) | 115.425 |
| 6. Andrzej Szajna | POL | 19.1 | (9) | 19.05 | (5) | 19.35 | (4) | 18.95 | (10) | 19.075 | (6) | 19.1 | (5) | 114.625 |
| 7. Michael Nikolay | GDR | 19.2 | (8) | 18.725 | (12) | 18.725 | (21) | 19.575 | (2) | 18.8 | (16) | 18.575 | (16) | 113.6 |
| 8. Imre Molnár | HUN | 18.875 | (16) | 18.875 | (9) | 19.375 | (3) | 19.2 | (7) | 18.7 | (19) | 18.55 | (17) | 113.575 |

The 5-foot 5½-inch Andrianov, who had collected a complete set of medals in 1972, added seven more in Montreal—four gold, two silver, and one bronze.

**1980 Moscow** C: 65, N: 14, D: 7.24.

| | | HB | | PB | | LHV | | SH | | R | | FE | | TOTAL PTS. |
|---|---|---|---|---|---|---|---|---|---|---|---|---|---|---|
| 1. Aleksandr Dityatin | SOV | 19.8 | (2) | 19.7 | (2) | 19.875 | (1) | 19.8 | (3) | 19.875 | (1) | 19.6 | (3) | 118.65 |
| 2. Nikolai Andrianov | SOV | 19.725 | (3) | 19.6 | (4) | 19.8 | (2) | 19.7 | (4) | 19.725 | (3) | 19.675 | (1) | 118.225 |
| 3. Stoyan Deltchev | BUL | 19.825 | (1) | 19.675 | (3) | 19.725 | (5) | 19.65 | (6) | 19.775 | (2) | 19.35 | (6) | 118.0 |
| 4. Aleksandr Tkachyov | SOV | 19.525 | (4) | 19.775 | (1) | 19.75 | (4) | 19.675 | (5) | 19.675 | (6) | 19.3 | (8) | 117.7 |
| 5. Roland Brückner | GDR | 19.075 | (17) | 19.45 | (5) | 19.775 | (3) | 19.625 | (7) | 19.725 | (3) | 19.65 | (2) | 117.3 |
| 6. Michael Nikolay | GDR | 19.475 | (6) | 19.35 | (7) | 19.575 | (11) | 19.875 | (2) | 19.525 | (8) | 18.95 | (13) | 116.75 |
| 7. Lutz Hoffmann | GDR | 19.4 | (9) | 19.05 | (11) | 19.7 | (6) | 19.125 | (14) | 19.425 | (10) | 19.325 | (7) | 116.025 |
| 8. Jiři Tabák | CZE | 19.225 | (11) | 18.975 | (15) | 19.675 | (7) | 18.675 | (22) | 19.6 | (7) | 19.525 | (4) | 115.675 |

Handsome Aleksandr Dityatin became the first person to win eight medals in one Olympic celebration. He gained three gold, four silver, and one bronze. Dityatin also became the first male gymnast to receive a ten in an Olympic competition, with his longhorse vault. Four more tens were awarded in rapid succession to Stoyan Deltchev on the rings, Aleksandr Tkachyov on the horizontal bar, and Zoltán Magyar and Michael Nikolay on the side horse. Meanwhile, Nikolai Andrianov added two gold, two silver, and one bronze to his collection for a grand career total of 15 Olympics medals—seven gold, five silver, and three bronze.

**1984 Los Angeles** C: 71, N: 19, D: 8.2.

| | | HB | | PB | | LHV | | SH | | R | | FE | | TOTAL PTS. |
|---|---|---|---|---|---|---|---|---|---|---|---|---|---|---|
| 1. Koji Gushiken | JPN | 19.9 | (3) | 19.8 | (3) | 19.875 | (1) | 19.525 | (10) | 19.85 | (2) | 19.75 | (3) | 118.7 |
| 2. Peter Vidmar | USA | 19.95 | (2) | 19.8 | (3) | 19.725 | (4) | 19.85 | (2) | 19.75 | (4) | 19.6 | (8) | 118.675 |
| 3. Li Ning | CHN | 19.6 | (9) | 19.675 | (7) | 19.775 | (3) | 19.9 | (1) | 19.8 | (3) | 19.825 | (1) | 118.575 |
| 4. Tong Fei | CHN | 19.975 | (1) | 19.625 | (8) | 19.725 | (4) | 19.75 | (4) | 19.75 | (4) | 19.725 | (5) | 118.55 |
| 5. Mitchell Gaylord | USA | 19.625 | (8) | 19.85 | (1) | 19.825 | (2) | 19.775 | (3) | 19.875 | (1) | 19.575 | (9) | 118.525 |
| 6. Bart Conner | USA | 19.8 | (4) | 19.8 | (3) | 19.625 | (10) | 19.675 | (5) | 19.675 | (9) | 19.775 | (2) | 118.35 |
| 7. Xu Zhiqiang | CHN | 19.6 | (9) | 19.775 | (6) | 19.725 | (4) | 19.65 | (6) | 19.725 | (6) | 19.75 | (3) | 118.225 |
| 8. Nobuyuki Kajitani | JPN | 19.225 | (22) | 19.825 | (2) | 19.7 | (7) | 19.625 | (7) | 19.7 | (7) | 19.3 | (17) | 117.375 |

Twenty-seven-year-old Koji Gushiken, placed only fifth after the preliminaries, came from behind to edge Peter Vidmar in the closest Olympic all-around competition in sixty years. "I'm neither a Christian nor a Buddhist," Gushiken later said, reflecting on the medal ceremony, "and suddenly I felt the existence of God. It was clear-cut and exceedingly beautiful."

Among the boycott missing was world champion and pre-boycott favorite Dimitri Bilozerchev of the U.S.S.R.

**1988 Seoul** C: 89, N: 23, D: 9.22.

|  |  | HB | PB | LHV | SH | R | FE | TOTAL PTS. |
|---|---|---|---|---|---|---|---|---|
| 1. Vladimir Artemov | SOV | 19.95 (1) | 19.975 (1) | 19.775 (2) | 19.775 (8) | 19.8 (4) | 19.85 (1) | 119.125 |
| 2. Valery Lyukin | SOV | 19.925 (2) | 19.9 (2) | 19.7 (3) | 19.875 (2) | 19.875 (2) | 19.8 (4) | 119.025 |
| 3. Dmitri Bilozerchev | SOV | 19.575(13) | 19.9 (2) | 19.8 (1) | 19.95 (1) | 19.975 (1) | 19.775 (5) | 118.975 |
| 4. Sven Tippelt | GDR | 19.4 (23) | 19.65 (7) | 19.675 (4) | 19.8 (5) | 19.875 (2) | 19.6 (14) | 118.0 |
| 5. Marius Gherman | ROM | 19.75 (5) | 19.65 (7) | 19.55 (10) | 19.7 (10) | 19.525(17) | 19.65 (12) | 117.825 |
| 6. Kalofer Hristozov | BUL | 19.55 (14) | 19.725 (5) | 19.3 (24) | 19.675(13) | 19.8 (4) | 19.7 (8) | 117.75 |
| 6. Wang Chongsheng | CHN | 19.775 (4) | 19.5 (24) | 19.65 (5) | 19.7 (10) | 19.625(14) | 19.5 (21) | 117.75 |
| 8. György Guczoghy | HUN | 19.425(19) | 19.625(12) | 19.525(13) | 19.8 (5) | 19.775 (7) | 19.525(19) | 117.675 |
| 8. Yukio Iketani | JPN | 19.625(10) | 19.65 (7) | 19.475(14) | 19.55 (18) | 19.525(17) | 19.85 (1) | 117.675 |

Dmitri Bilozerchev caused a sensation in 1983 when he became world champion at the tender age of 16. The following year he was kept out of the Olympics by the Soviet boycott, but he did win the Friendship Games for athletes from boycotting nations. In 1985 he won the European Championships and seemed on target to defend his world title when his career was suddenly derailed. Bilozerchev, on leave from training camp, drank too much champagne and, only ten days after receiving his driver's license, borrowed his father's car and went driving in a rainstorm. On the slippery Moscow streets he lost control and wrapped the car around a pole. His left leg was shattered into more than 40 pieces. He was injured so badly that amputation was seriously considered.

Abandoned by the Soviet sports community, Bilozerchev was determined to regain his world-class form. Unfortunately he renewed his training too early. Overcompensating for his still tender left leg, he injured his *right* leg and required surgery on his ankle in December 1986. Despite these setbacks, Bilozerchev managed to return to competition in time to win the 1987 world championship. Still only 21 years old, he was installed as the favorite for the 1988 Olympics. Bilozerchev performed brilliantly in Seoul. But at Olympic-level gymnastics it is necessary to make no mistakes. Bilozerchev made a big one. While performing on the horizontal bar, normally his best apparatus, he veered off center on a one-armed giant swing, lost his momentum, and landed on the bar. The resulting half-point penalty cost him the gold medal.

Ready to take advantage of Bilozerchev's lapse was teammate Vladimir Artemov. Back home in the Soviet Union Artemov was known as "The Permanent Runner-Up" and "Always Second." Indeed he had made a career of finishing second: at the 1984 Friendship Games, the 1985 world championships, and the 1986 Goodwill Games. He had placed third at the 1987 World Championships. In Seoul, however, Artemov was not to be denied.

Bilozerchev went on to win two gold medals in the apparatus finals. But in August 1989, he and teammate Vladimir Gogoladze were expelled from the Soviet team for going on a two-day drinking binge and for having "a corrupting influence on other members of the team."

# HORIZONTAL BAR

**1896 Athens** C: 15, N: 4, D: 4.9.
1. Hermann Weingärtner GER
2. Alfred Flatow GER
3. — —
4. Conrad Böcker GER
5. Karl Schumann GER

**1900** not held

**1904 St. Louis** C: 9, N: 1, D: 10.28.

|  |  | PTS. |
|---|---|---|
| 1. Anton Heida | USA | 40 |
| 1. Edward Hennig | USA | 40 |
| 3. George Eyser | USA | 39 |

**1908–1920** not held

**1924 Paris** C: 72, N: 9, D: 7.20.

|  |  | PTS. |
|---|---|---|
| 1. Leon Štukelj | YUG | 19.73 |
| 2. Jean Gutweniger | SWI | 19.236 |
| 3. André Higelin | FRA | 19.163 |
| 4. Antoine Rebetez | SWI | 19.053 |
| 4. Georges Miez | SWI | 19.053 |
| 6. Jean Gounot | FRA | 19.043 |
| 7. François Gangloff | FRA | 18.933 |
| 8. August Güttinger | SWI | 18.886 |

**1928 Amsterdam** C: 86, N: 11, D: 8.10.

|  |  | PTS. |
|---|---|---|
| 1. Georges Miez | SWI | 19.17 |
| 2. Romeo Neri | ITA | 19.00 |
| 3. Eugen Mack | SWI | 18.92 |
| 4. Hermann Hänggi | SWI | 18.83 |
| 4. Vittorio Lucchetti | ITA | 18.83 |
| 6. Josip Primožič | YUG | 18.67 |
| 7. Hans Grieder | SWI | 18.58 |
| 7. August Güttinger | FRA | 18.58 |

**1932 Los Angeles** C: 12, N: 6, D: 8.11.

| | | PTS. |
|---|---|---|
| 1. Dallas Bixler | USA | 18.33 |
| 2. Heikki Savolainen | FIN | 18.07 |
| 3. Einari Teräsvirta | FIN | 18.07 |
| 4. Veikko Pakarinen | FIN | 17.27 |
| 4. István Pelle | HUN | 17.27 |
| 6. Michael Schuler | USA | 15.57 |
| 7. Miklós Péter | HUN | 15.13 |
| 8. Mahito Haga | JPN | 12.47 |

Savolainen and Teräsvirta tied for second. While the judges discussed a method for deciding which one should get the silver medal, the two Finns talked it out and agreed that Savolainen should receive the silver and Teräsvirta the bronze. The judges abided by their decision.

**1936 Berlin** C: 111, N: 14, D: 8.11.

| | | PTS. |
|---|---|---|
| 1. Aleksanteri Saarvala | FIN | 19.367 |
| 2. Konrad Frey | GER | 19.267 |
| 3. Alfred Schwarzmann | GER | 19.233 |
| 4. Innozenz Stangl | GER | 19.167 |
| 4. Heikki Savolainen | FIN | 19.133 |
| 6. Veikko Pakarinen | FIN | 19.067 |
| 7. Martti Uosikkinen | FIN | 19.00 |
| 8. Walter Steffens | GER | 18.966 |

**1948 London** C: 123, N: 16, D: 8.13.

| | | PTS. |
|---|---|---|
| 1. Josef Stalder | SWI | 19.85 |
| 2. Walter Lehmann | SWI | 19.70 |
| 3. Veikko Huhtanen | FIN | 19.60 |
| 4. Raymond Dot | FRA | 19.40 |
| 4. Aleksanteri Saarvala | FIN | 19.40 |
| 4. Lajos Sántha | HUN | 19.40 |
| 4. Emil Studer | SWI | 19.40 |
| 8. Einari Teräsvirta | FIN | 19.35 |

**1952 Helsinki** C: 185, N: 29, D: 7.21.

| | | PTS. |
|---|---|---|
| 1. Jack Günthard | SWI | 19.55 |
| 2. Alfred Schwarzmann | GER | 19.50 |
| 2. Josef Stalder | SWI | 19.50 |
| 4. Heikki Savolainen | FIN | 19.45 |
| 5. Viktor Chukarin | SOV | 19.40 |
| 6. Jean Tschabold | SWI | 19.35 |
| 7. Helmut Bantz | GER | 19.25 |
| 7. Melchior Thalmann | SWI | 19.25 |

**1956 Melbourne** C: 63, N: 18, D: 12.6.

| | | PTS. |
|---|---|---|
| 1. Takashi Ono | JPN | 19.60 |
| 2. Yuri Titov | SOV | 19.40 |
| 3. Masao Takemoto | JPN | 19.30 |
| 4. Pavel Stolbov | SOV | 19.25 |
| 4. Viktor Chukarin | SOV | 19.25 |
| 6. Helmut Bantz | GER | 19.15 |
| 7. John Beckner | USA | 19.00 |
| 8. Albert Azaryan | SOV | 18.95 |

**1960 Rome** C: 130, N: 28, D: 9.10.

| | | PTS. |
|---|---|---|
| 1. Takashi Ono | JPN | 19.60 |
| 2. Masao Takemoto | JPN | 19.525 |
| 3. Boris Shakhlin | SOV | 19.475 |
| 4. Yukio Endo | JPN | 19.425 |
| 5. Miroslav Cerar | YUG | 19.40 |
| 5. Yuri Titov | SOV | 19.40 |

**1964 Tokyo** C: 130, N: 24, D: 10.23.

| | | PTS. |
|---|---|---|
| 1. Boris Shakhlin | SOV | 19.625 |
| 2. Yuri Titov | SOV | 19.550 |
| 3. Miroslav Cerar | YUG | 19.50 |
| 4. Viktor Lisitsky | SOV | 19.325 |
| 5. Yukio Endo | JPN | 19.050 |
| 6. Takashi Ono | JPN | 19.00 |

**1968 Mexico City** C: 115, N: 27, D: 10.26.

| | | PTS. |
|---|---|---|
| 1. Akinori Nakayarna | JPN | 19.55 |
| 1. Mikhail Voronin | SOV | 19.55 |
| 3. Eizo Kenmotsu | JPN | 19.375 |
| 4. Klaus Köste | GDR | 19.225 |
| 5. Sergei Diomidov | SOV | 19.15 |
| 6. Yukio Endo | JPN | 19.025 |

**1972 Munich** C: 113, N: 26, D: 9.1.

| | | PTS. |
|---|---|---|
| 1. Mitsuo Tsukahara | JPN | 19.725 |
| 2. Sawao Kato | JPN | 19.525 |
| 3. Shigeru Kasamatsu | JPN | 19.45 |
| 4. Eizo Kenmotsu | JPN | 19.35 |
| 5. Akinori Nakayama | JPN | 19.225 |
| 6. Nikolai Andrianov | SOV | 19.10 |

**1976 Montreal** C: 90, N: 20, D: 7.23.

| | | PTS. |
|---|---|---|
| 1. Mitsuo Tsukahara | JPN | 19.675 |
| 2. Eizo Kenmotsu | JPN | 19.50 |
| 3. Henry Boërio | FRA | 19.475 |
| 3. Eberhard Gienger | GER | 19.475 |
| 5. Gennadi Kryssin | SOV | 19.25 |
| 6. Ferenc Donáth | HUN | 19.20 |

**1980 Moscow** C: 65, N: 14, D: 7.25.

| | | PTS. |
|---|---|---|
| 1. Stoyan Deltchev | BUL | 19.825 |
| 2. Alexandr Dityatin | SOV | 19.75 |
| 3. Nikolai Andrianov | SOV | 19.675 |
| 4. Ralf-Peter Hemmann | GDR | 19.525 |
| 4. Michael Nikolay | GDR | 19.525 |
| 6. Sergio Suarez Aime | CUB | 19.45 |

**1984 Los Angeles** C: 71, N: 19, D: 8.4.

| | | PTS. |
|---|---|---|
| 1. Shinji Morisue | JPN | 20.00 |
| 2. Tong Fei | CHN | 19.975 |
| 3. Koji Gushiken | JPN | 19.95 |

4. Timothy Daggett    USA    19.85
4. Lou Yun            CHN    19.85
4. Peter Vidmar       USA    19.85
7. Marco Piatti       SWI    19.80
8. Daniel Wunderlin   SWI    19.675

**1988 Seoul** C: 89, N: 23, D: 9.24.

|    |                    |       | PTS.   |
|----|--------------------|-------|--------|
| 1. | Vladimir Artemov   | SOV   | 19.90  |
| 1. | Valery Lyukin      | SOV   | 19.90  |
| 3. | Holger Behrendt    | GDR   | 19.80  |
| 3. | Marius Gherman     | ROM   | 19.80  |
| 5. | Wang Chongsheng    | CHN   | 19.775 |
| 6. | Xu Zhiqiang        | CHN   | 19.70  |
| 7. | Curtis Hibbert     | CAN   | 19.675 |
| 8. | Andreas Wecker     | GDR   | 19.50  |

# PARALLEL BARS

**1896 Athens** C: 18, N: 4, D: 4.10.

1. Alfred Flatow          GER
2. Louis Zutter           SWI
3. Hermann Weingärtner    GER

One of Germany's first gold-medal winners, Alfred Flatow perished in a Nazi concentration camp in 1945.

**1900** not held

**1904 St. Louis** C: ?, N: 1, D: 10.28.

|    |              |      | PTS. |
|----|--------------|------|------|
| 1. | George Eyser | USA  | 44   |
| 2. | Anton Heida  | USA  | 43   |
| 3. | John Duha    | USA  | 40   |

Eyser's gymnastic feats were all the more impressive considering that one of his legs was made of wood. He also won a gold in the long horse vault, two silver in the pommeled horse and combined competition, and a bronze in the horizontal bar.

**1908–1920** not held

**1924 Paris** C: 72, N: 9, D: 7.20.

|    |                  |      | PTS.  |
|----|------------------|------|-------|
| 1. | August Güttinger | SWI  | 21.63 |
| 2. | Robert Pražak    | CZE  | 21.61 |
| 3. | Giorgio Zampori  | ITA  | 21.45 |
| 4. | Josef Wilhelm    | SWI  | 21.40 |
| 5. | Mario Lertora    | ITA  | 21.33 |
| 6. | Ladislav Vácha   | CZE  | 21.31 |
| 7. | J. Kos           | CZE  | 21.28 |
| 8. | Jean Gutweniger  | SWI  | 21.26 |

**1928 Amsterdam** C: 85, N: 11, D: 8.10.

|    |                      |      | PTS.  |
|----|----------------------|------|-------|
| 1. | Ladislav Vácha       | CZE  | 18.83 |
| 2. | Josip Primožič       | YUG  | 18.50 |
| 3. | Hermann Hänggi       | SWI  | 18.08 |
| 4. | Jan Gajdoš           | CZE  | 17.92 |
| 4. | André Lemoine        | FRA  | 17.92 |
| 4. | Bedrich Supčik       | CZE  | 17.92 |
| 7. | Mario Lertora (ITA), Mauri Nyberg-Noroma (FIN), Leon Štukelj (YUG), Melchior Wetzel (SWI) | | 17.83 |

**1932 Los Angeles** C: 15, N: 6, D: 8.12.

|    |                     |      | PTS.  |
|----|---------------------|------|-------|
| 1. | Romeo Neri          | ITA  | 18.97 |
| 2. | István Pelle        | HUN  | 18.60 |
| 3. | Heikki Savolainen   | FIN  | 18.27 |
| 4. | Mauri Nyberg-Noroma | FIN  | 17.80 |
| 5. | Mario Lertora       | ITA  | 17.53 |
| 6. | Alfred Jochim       | USA  | 17.47 |
| 7. | József Hegedüs      | HUN  | 17.30 |
| 7. | Miklós Péter        | HUN  | 17.30 |

**1936 Berlin** C: 111, N: 14, D: 8.11.

|    |                       |      | PTS.   |
|----|-----------------------|------|--------|
| 1. | Konrad Frey           | GER  | 19.067 |
| 2. | Michael Reusch        | SWI  | 19.034 |
| 3. | Alfred Schwarzmann    | GER  | 18.967 |
| 4. | Alois Hudec           | CZE  | 18.966 |
| 5. | Eugen Mack            | SWI  | 18.834 |
| 6. | Walter Bach           | SWI  | 18.733 |
| 7. | Heikki Savolainen     | FIN  | 18.633 |
| 8. | Eduard "Edi" Steinemann | SWI | 18.500 |

**1948 London** C: 123, N: 16, D: 8.13.

|    |                    |      | PTS.  |
|----|--------------------|------|-------|
| 1. | Michael Reusch     | SWI  | 19.75 |
| 2. | Veikko Huhtanen    | FIN  | 19.65 |
| 3. | Christian Kipfer   | SWI  | 19.55 |
| 3. | Josef Stalder      | SWI  | 19.55 |
| 5. | Walter Lehmann     | SWI  | 19.50 |
| 6. | Heikki Savolainen  | FIN  | 19.45 |
| 7. | Paavo Aaltonen     | FIN  | 19.40 |
| 7. | Zdenek Ružička     | CZE  | 19.40 |

**1952 Helsinki** C: 185, N: 29, D: 7.21.

|    |                   |      | PTS.  |
|----|-------------------|------|-------|
| 1. | Hans Eugster      | SWI  | 19.65 |
| 2. | Viktor Chukarin   | SOV  | 19.60 |
| 3. | Josef Stalder     | SWI  | 19.50 |
| 4. | Grant Schaginyan  | SOV  | 19.35 |
| 5. | Ferdinand Daniš   | CZE  | 19.30 |
| 5. | Yevgeny Korolkov  | SOV  | 19.30 |
| 5. | Jean Tschalbold   | SWI  | 19.30 |
| 8. | Vladimir Belyakov | SOV  | 19.25 |
| 8. | Valentin Muratov  | SOV  | 19.25 |

**1956 Melbourne** C: 63, N: 18, D: 12.6.

|   |   |   | PTS. |
|---|---|---|---|
| 1. | Viktor Chukarin | SOV | 19.20 |
| 2. | Masami Kubota | JPN | 19.15 |
| 3. | Takashi Ono | JPN | 19.10 |
| 3. | Masao Takemoto | JPN | 19.10 |
| 5. | Albert Azaryan | SOV | 19.00 |
| 6. | Nobuyuki Aihara | JPN | 18.90 |
| 6. | Bengt Lindfors | FIN | 18.90 |
| 8. | Onni Lappalainen (FIN), Olavi Leimuvirta (FIN), Shinsaku Tsukawai (JPN) | | 18.85 |

**1960 Rome** C: 130, N: 28, D: 9.10.

|   |   |   | PTS. |
|---|---|---|---|
| 1. | Boris Shakhlin | SOV | 19.40 |
| 2. | Giovanni Carminucci | ITA | 19.375 |
| 3. | Takashi Ono | JPN | 19.35 |
| 4. | Nobuyuki Aihara | JPN | 19.275 |
| 5. | Yuri Titov | SOV | 19.20 |
| 6. | Masao Takemoto | JPN | 19.125 |

**1964 Tokyo** C: 130, N: 29, D: 10.23.

|   |   |   | PTS. |
|---|---|---|---|
| 1. | Yukio Endo | JPN | 19.675 |
| 2. | Shuji Tsurumi | JPN | 19.45 |
| 3. | Franco Menichelli | ITA | 19.35 |
| 4. | Sergei Diomidov | SOV | 19.225 |
| 5. | Viktor Lisitsky | SOV | 19.20 |
| 6. | Miroslav Cerar | YUG | 18.45 |

**1968 Mexico City** C: 117, N: 28, D: 10.26.

|   |   |   | PTS. |
|---|---|---|---|
| 1. | Akinori Nakayama | JPN | 19.475 |
| 2. | Mikhail Voronin | SOV | 19.425 |
| 3. | Vladimir Klimenko | SOV | 19.225 |
| 4. | Takeshi Kato | JPN | 19.20 |
| 5. | Eizo Kenmotsu | JPN | 19.175 |
| 6. | Václav Kubička | CZE | 18.95 |

**1972 Munich** C: 113, N: 26, D: 9.1.

|   |   |   | PTS. |
|---|---|---|---|
| 1. | Sawao Kato | JPN | 19.475 |
| 2. | Shigeru Kasamatsu | JPN | 19.375 |
| 3. | Eizo Kenmotsu | JPN | 19.25 |
| 4. | Viktor Klimenko | SOV | 19.125 |
| 5. | Akinori Nakayama | JPN | 18.875 |
| 6. | Nikolai Andrianov | SOV | 17.975 |

**1976 Montreal** C: 90, N: 20, D: 7.23.

|   |   |   | PTS. |
|---|---|---|---|
| 1. | Sawao Kato | JPN | 19.675 |
| 2. | Nikolai Andrianov | SOV | 19.50 |
| 3. | Mitsuo Tsukahara | JPN | 19.475 |
| 4. | Bernd Jäger | GDR | 19.20 |
| 5. | Miloslav Netušil | CZE | 19.125 |
| 6. | Andrzej Szajna | POL | 18.95 |

**1980 Moscow** C: 65, N: 14, D: 7.25.

|   |   |   | PTS. |
|---|---|---|---|
| 1. | Aleksandr Tkachyov | SOV | 19.775 |
| 2. | Aleksandr Dityatin | SOV | 19.75 |
| 3. | Roland Brückner | GDR | 19.65 |
| 4. | Michael Nikolay | GDR | 19.60 |
| 5. | Stoyan Deltchev | BUL | 19.575 |
| 6. | Roberto Leon Richards-Aguiar | CUB | 19.50 |

**1984 Los Angeles** C: 71, N: 19, D: 8.4.

|   |   |   | PTS. |
|---|---|---|---|
| 1. | Bart Conner | USA | 19.95 |
| 2. | Nobuyuki Kajitani | JPN | 19.925 |
| 3. | Mitchell Gaylord | USA | 19.85 |
| 4. | Tong Fei | CHN | 19.825 |
| 5. | Koji Gushiken | JPN | 19.80 |
| 6. | Li Ning | CHN | 19.775 |
| 7. | Jürgen Geiger | GER | 19.60 |
| 7. | Daniel Winkler | GER | 19.60 |

**1988 Seoul** C: 89, N: 23, D: 9.24.

|   |   |   | PTS. |
|---|---|---|---|
| 1. | Vladimir Artemov | SOV | 19.925 |
| 2. | Valery Lyukin | SOV | 19.90 |
| 3. | Sven Tippelt | GDR | 19.75 |
| 4. | Kalofer Hristozov | BUL | 19.725 |
| 5. | Marius Gherman | ROM | 19.70 |
| 6. | Curtis Hibbert | CAN | 19.675 |
| 7. | Sylvio Kroll | GDR | 19.625 |
| 8. | Boris Preti | ITA | 19.60 |

# LONG HORSE VAULT

**1896 Athens** C: 15, N: 4, D: 4.9.
1. Karl Schumann   GER
2. Louis Zutter   SWI
3. Hermann Weingärtner   GER

**1900** not held

**1904 St. Louis** C: ?, N: 1, D: 10.28.

|   |   |   | PTS. |
|---|---|---|---|
| 1. | George Eyser | USA | 36 |
| 1. | Anton Heida | USA | 36 |
| 3. | William Merz | USA | 31 |

**1908–1920** not held

**1924 Paris** C: 70, N: 9, D: 7.20.

|   |   |   | PTS. |
|---|---|---|---|
| 1. | Frank Kriz | USA | 9.98 |
| 2. | Jan Koutny | CZE | 9.97 |
| 3. | Bohumil Mořkovsky | CZE | 9.93 |
| 4. | Leon Štukelj | YUG | 9.91 |
| 5. | Max Wandrer | USA | 9.85 |
| 6. | Ivan Porenta | YUG | 9.76 |
| 7. | Miroslav Klinger | CZE | 9.75 |
| 7. | Ferdinando Mandrini | ITA | 9.75 |

**1928 Amsterdam** C: 85, N: 11, D: 8.10.

| | | PTS. |
|---|---|---|
| 1. Eugen Mack | SWI | 9.58 |
| 2. Emanuel Löffler | CZE | 9.50 |
| 3. Stane Derganc | YUG | 9.46 |
| 4. Georges Miez | SWI | 9.42 |
| 4. Josip Primožič | YUG | 9.42 |
| 6. Georges Leroux | FRA | 9.33 |
| 7. August Güttinger | SWI | 9.28 |
| 7. Ivan Porenta | YUG | 9.28 |
| 7. Herman Witzig | USA | 9.28 |

**1932 Los Angeles** C: 10, N: 4, D: 8.10.

| | | PTS. |
|---|---|---|
| 1. Savino Guglielmetti | ITA | 18.03 |
| 2. Alfred Jochim | USA | 17.77 |
| 3. Edward Carmichael | USA | 17.53 |
| 4. Einari Teräsvirta | FIN | 17.53 |
| 5. Marcel Gleyre | USA | 17.46 |
| 6. István Pelle | HUN | 17.13 |
| 7. Miklós Péter | HUN | 16.97 |
| 8. Mario Lertora | ITA | 16.40 |

**1936 Berlin** C: 110, N: 14, D: 8.11.

| | | PTS. |
|---|---|---|
| 1. Alfred Schwarzmann | GER | 19.20 |
| 2. Eugen Mack | SWI | 18.967 |
| 3. Matthias Volz | GER | 18.467 |
| 4. Walter Bach | SWI | 18.40 |
| 5. Walter Beck | SWI | 18.367 |
| 6. Martti Uosikkinen | FIN | 18.30 |
| 7. Michael Reusch | SWI | 18.266 |
| 8. Georges Miez | SWI | 18.234 |
| 8. Josef Walter | SWI | 18.234 |

**1948 London** C: 123, N: 16, D: 8.13.

| | | PTS. |
|---|---|---|
| 1. Paavo Aaltonen | FIN | 19.55 |
| 2. Olavi Hove | FIN | 19.50 |
| 3. János Mogyorósi-Klencs | HUN | 19.25 |
| 3. Ferenc Pataki | HUN | 19.25 |
| 3. Leo Sotornik | CZE | 19.25 |
| 6. Veikko Huhtanen | FIN | 19.20 |
| 7. Einari Teräsvirta | FIN | 19.15 |
| 8. Walter Lehmann | SWI | 19.05 |
| 8. Sulo Salmi | FIN | 19.05 |

**1952 Helsinki** C: 185, N: 29, D: 7.21.

| | | PTS. |
|---|---|---|
| 1. Viktor Chukarin | SOV | 19.20 |
| 2. Masao Takemoto | JPN | 19.15 |
| 3. Takashi Ono | JPN | 19.10 |
| 3. Tadao Uesako | JPN | 19.10 |
| 5. Hans Eugster | SWI | 18.95 |
| 5. Theo Wied | GER | 18.95 |
| 7. Yosef Berdiyev | SOV | 18.90 |
| 7. Ernst Fivian | SWI | 18.90 |

**1956 Melbourne** C: 63, N: 18, D: 12.6.

| | | PTS. |
|---|---|---|
| 1. Helmut Bantz | GER | 18.85 |
| 1. Valentin Muratov | SOV | 18.85 |
| 3. Yuri Titov | SOV | 18.75 |
| 4. Boris Shakhlin | SOV | 18.70 |
| 4. Theo Wied | GER | 18.70 |
| 6. Masao Takemoto | JPN | 18.65 |
| 7. John Beckner (USA), | | |
| Jakob Kiefer (GER), | | |
| Robert Klein (GER), | | |
| Viktor Chukarin (SOV) | | 18.60 |

**1960 Rome** C: 130, N: 28, D: 9.10.

| | | PTS. |
|---|---|---|
| 1. Takashi Ono | JPN | 19.35 |
| 1. Boris Shakhlin | SOV | 19.35 |
| 3. Vladimir Portnoi | SOV | 19.225 |
| 4. Yuri Titov | SOV | 19.20 |
| 5. Yukio Endo | JPN | 19.175 |
| 6. Shuji Tsurumi | JPN | 19.15 |

**1964 Tokyo** C: 130, N: 29, D: 10.23.

| | | PTS. |
|---|---|---|
| 1. Haruhiro Yamashita | JPN | 19.60 |
| 2. Viktor Lisitsky | SOV | 19.325 |
| 3. Hannu Rantakari | FIN | 19.30 |
| 4. Shuji Tsurumi | JPN | 19.225 |
| 5. Boris Shakhlin | SOV | 19.20 |
| 6. Yukio Endo | JPN | 19.075 |

Yamashita executed a handspring in a piked position, a vault that became known as a "yamashita." One of the judges, Dr. Widmer of Switzerland, was so impressed that he gave Yamashita a ten—the highest mark possible.

**1968 Mexico City** C: 110, N: 20, D: 10.26.

| | | PTS. |
|---|---|---|
| 1. Mikhail Voronin | SOV | 19.00 |
| 2. Yukio Endo | JPN | 18.95 |
| 3. Sergei Diomidov | SOV | 18.925 |
| 4. Takeshi Kato | JPN | 18.775 |
| 5. Akinori Nakayama | JPN | 18.725 |
| 6. Eizo Kenmotsu | JPN | 18.65 |

**1972 Munich** C: 113, N: 26, D: 9.1.

| | | PTS. |
|---|---|---|
| 1. Klaus Köste | GDR | 18.85 |
| 2. Viktor Klimenko | SOV | 18.825 |
| 3. Nikolai Andrianov | SOV | 18.80 |
| 4. Sawao Kato | JPN | 18.55 |
| 4. Eizo Kenmotsu | JPN | 18.55 |
| 6. Peter Rohner | SWI | 18.525 |

Performing a yamashita and a forward somersault, the 5-foot 4½-inch Köste won East Germany's first gold medal in men's gymnastics.

**1976 Montreal** C: 90, N: 20, D: 7.23.

|  |  |  | PTS. |
|---|---|---|---|
| 1. | Nikolai Andrianov | SOV | 19.45 |
| 2. | Mitsuo Tsukahara | JPN | 19.375 |
| 3. | Hiroshi Kajiyama | JPN | 19.275 |
| 4. | Dănut Grecu | ROM | 19.20 |
| 5. | Zoltán Magyar | HUN | 19.15 |
| 5. | Imre Molnár | HUN | 19.15 |

**1980 Moscow** C: 65, N: 14, D: 7.25.

|  |  |  | PTS. |
|---|---|---|---|
| 1. | Nikolai Andrianov | SOV | 19.825 |
| 2. | Aleksandr Dityatin | SOV | 19.80 |
| 3. | Roland Brückner | GDR | 19.775 |
| 4. | Ralf-Peter Hemmann | GDR | 19.75 |
| 5. | Stoyan Deltchev | BUL | 19.70 |
| 6. | Jiři Tabák | CZE | 19.525 |

**1984 Los Angeles** C: 71, N: 19, D: 8.4.

| 1. | Lou Yun | CHN | 19.95 |
|---|---|---|---|
| 2. | Mitchell Gaylord | USA | 19.825 |
| 2. | Koji Gushiken | JPN | 19.825 |
| 2. | Li Ning | CHN | 19.825 |
| 2. | Shinji Morisue | JPN | 19.825 |
| 6. | James Hartung | USA | 19.80 |
| 7. | Warren Long | CAN | 19.70 |
| 8. | Daniel Wunderlin | SWI | 19.625 |

**1988 Seoul** C: 89, N: 23, D: 9.24.

|  |  |  | PTS. |
|---|---|---|---|
| 1. | Lou Yun | CHN | 19.875 |
| 2. | Sylvio Kroll | GDR | 19.862 |
| 3. | Park Jong-hoon | KOR | 19.775 |
| 4. | Dian Kolev | BUL | 19.737 |
| 5. | Holger Behrendt | GDR | 19.65 |
| 6. | Sergei Kharkov | SOV | 19.60 |
| 7. | Yukio Iketani | JPN | 19.525 |
| 8. | Vladimir Gogoladze | SOV | 19.512 |

# SIDE HORSE (POMMELED HORSE)

**1896 Athens** C: 15, N: 4, D: 4.9.

| 1. | Louis Zutter | SWI |
|---|---|---|
| 2. | Hermann Weingärtner | GER |

**1900** not held

**1904 St. Louis** C: 9, N: 1, D: 10.28.

|  |  |  | PTS. |
|---|---|---|---|
| 1. | Anton Heida | USA | 42 |
| 2. | George Eyser | USA | 33 |
| 3. | William Merz | USA | 29 |

**1908–1920** not held

**1924 Paris** C: 70, N: 9, D: 7.20.

|  |  |  | PTS. |
|---|---|---|---|
| 1. | Josef Wilhelm | SWI | 21.23 |
| 2. | Jean Gutweniger | SWI | 21.13 |

| 3. | Antoine Rebetez | SWI | 20.73 |
|---|---|---|---|
| 4. | Carl Widmer | SWI | 20.50 |
| 5. | Giuseppe Paris | ITA | 20.10 |
| 6. | Stane Derganc | YUG | 19.93 |
| 7. | Miroslav Klinger | CZE | 19.67 |
| 8. | August Güttinger | SWI | 19.60 |

**1928 Amsterdam** C: 87, N: 11, D: 8.10.

|  |  |  | PTS. |
|---|---|---|---|
| 1. | Hermann Hänggi | SWI | 19.75 |
| 2. | Georges Miez | SWI | 19.25 |
| 3. | Heikki Savolainen | FIN | 18.83 |
| 4. | Eduard "Edi" Steinemann | SWI | 18.67 |
| 5. | August Güttinger | SWI | 18.58 |
| 6. | Georges Leroux | FRA | 18.25 |
| 7. | Mauri Nyberg-Noroma | FIN | 18.17 |
| 7. | Melchior Wetzel | SWI | 18.17 |

**1932 Los Angeles** C: 10, N: 5, D: 8.11.

|  |  |  | PTS. |
|---|---|---|---|
| 1. | István Pelle | HUN | 19.07 |
| 2. | Omero Bonoli | ITA | 18.87 |
| 3. | Frank Haubold | USA | 18.57 |
| 4. | Frank Cumiskey | USA | 18.23 |
| 5. | Péter Boros | HUN | 17.57 |
| 6. | Alfred Jochim | USA | 17.07 |
| 7. | Heikki Savolainen | FIN | 17.00 |
| 8. | Veikko Pakarinen | FIN | 16.63 |

**1936 Berlin** C: 110, N: 14, D: 8.11.

|  |  |  | PTS. |
|---|---|---|---|
| 1. | Konrad Frey | GER | 19.333 |
| 2. | Eugen Mack | SWI | 19.167 |
| 3. | Albert Bachmann | SWI | 19.067 |
| 4. | Martti Uosikkinen | FIN | 19.066 |
| 5. | Walter Steffens | GER | 19.033 |
| 5. | Walter Bach | SWI | 19.033 |
| 7. | Michael Reusch | SWI | 19.00 |
| 7. | Alfred Schwarzmann | GER | 19.00 |

**1948 London** C: 123, N: 16, D: 8.13.

|  |  |  | PTS. |
|---|---|---|---|
| 1. | Paavo Aaltonen | FIN | 19.35 |
| 1. | Veikko Huhtanen | FIN | 19.35 |
| 1. | Heikki Savolainen | FIN | 19.35 |
| 4. | Luigi Zanetti | ITA | 19.15 |
| 5. | Guido Figone | ITA | 19.10 |
| 6. | Frank Cumiskey | USA | 18.95 |
| 7. | Michael Reusch | SWI | 18.90 |
| 8. | Aleksanteri Saarvala | FIN | 18.85 |
| 8. | Josef Stalder | SWI | 18.85 |
| 8. | Emil Studer | SWI | 18.85 |

Between 1928 and 1952 Heikki Savolainen of Joensuu won two gold medals, one silver, and six bronze. When he received his last medal, as a member of the third-place Finnish team in Helsinki, Savolainen was 44 years old.

**1952 Helsinki** C: 185, N: 29, D: 7.21.

|  |  |  | PTS. |
|---|---|---|---|
| 1. | Viktor Chukarin | SOV | 19.50 |
| 2. | Evgeny Korolkov | SOV | 19.40 |
| 2. | Grant Shaginyan | SOV | 19.40 |
| 4. | Mikhail Perelman | SOV | 19.30 |
| 5. | Josef Stalder | SWI | 19.20 |
| 6. | Hans Sauter | AUT | 19.15 |
| 7. | Vladimir Belyakov | SOV | 19.10 |
| 8. | Jean Tschabold | SWI | 19.05 |

**1956 Melbourne** C: 63, N: 18, D: 12.6.

|  |  |  | PTS. |
|---|---|---|---|
| 1. | Boris Shakhlin | SOV | 19.25 |
| 2. | Takashi Ono | JPN | 19.20 |
| 3. | Viktor Chukarin | SOV | 19.10 |
| 4. | Josef Škvor | CZE | 19.05 |
| 5. | Yuri Titov | SOV | 19.00 |
| 6. | Jaroslav Bim | CZE | 18.95 |
| 7. | Pavel Stolbov | SOV | 18.90 |
| 7. | Masao Takemoto | JPN | 18.90 |

**1960 Rome** C: 130, N: 28, D: 9.10.

|  |  |  | PTS. |
|---|---|---|---|
| 1. | Eugen Ekman | FIN | 19.375 |
| 1. | Boris Shakhlin | SOV | 19.375 |
| 3. | Shuji Tsurumi | JPN | 19.15 |
| 4. | Takashi Mitsukuri | JPN | 19.125 |
| 5. | Yuri Titov | SOV | 18.95 |
| 6. | Takashi Ono | JPN | 18.525 |

**1964 Tokyo** C: 130, N: 29, D: 10.22.

|  |  |  | PTS. |
|---|---|---|---|
| 1. | Miroslav Cerar | YUG | 19.525 |
| 2. | Shuji Tsurumi | JPN | 19.325 |
| 3. | Yuri Tsapenko | SOV | 19.20 |
| 4. | Haruhiro Yamashita | JPN | 19.075 |
| 5. | Harald Wigaard | NOR | 18.925 |
| 6. | Takashi Mitsukuri | JPN | 18.65 |

**1968 Mexico City** C: 114, N: 27, D: 10.26.

|  |  |  | PTS. |
|---|---|---|---|
| 1. | Miroslav Cerar | YUG | 19.325 |
| 2. | Olli Eino Laiho | FIN | 19.225 |
| 3. | Mikhail Voronin | SOV | 19.20 |
| 4. | Wilhelm Kubica | POL | 19.15 |
| 5. | Eizo Kenmotsu | JPN | 19.05 |
| 6. | Viktor Klimenko | SOV | 18.95 |

**1972 Munich** C: 113, N: 26, D: 9.1.

|  |  |  | PTS. |
|---|---|---|---|
| 1. | Viktor Klimenko | SOV | 19.125 |
| 2. | Sawao Kato | JPN | 19.00 |
| 3. | Eizo Kenmotsu | JPN | 18.95 |
| 4. | Shigeru Kasamatsu | JPN | 18.925 |
| 5. | Mikhail Voronin | SOV | 18.875 |
| 6. | Wilhelm Kubica | POL | 18.75 |

**1976 Montreal** C: 90, N: 20, D: 7.23.

|  |  |  | PTS. |
|---|---|---|---|
| 1. | Zoltán Magyar | HUN | 19.70 |
| 2. | Eizo Kenmotsu | JPN | 19.575 |
| 3. | Nikolai Andrianov | SOV | 19.525 |
| 3. | Michael Nikolay | GDR | 19.525 |
| 5. | Sawao Kato | JPN | 19.40 |
| 6. | Aleksandr Dityatin | SOV | 19.35 |

**1980 Moscow** C: 65, N: 14, D: 7.25.

|  |  |  | PTS. |
|---|---|---|---|
| 1. | Zoltán Magyar | HUN | 19.925 |
| 2. | Aleksandr Dityatin | SOV | 19.80 |
| 3. | Michael Nikolay | GDR | 19.775 |
| 4. | Roland Brückner | GDR | 19.725 |
| 5. | Aleksandr Tkachyov | SOV | 19.475 |
| 6. | Ferenc Donáth | HUN | 19.40 |

**1984 Los Angeles** C: 71, N: 19, D: 8.4.

|  |  |  | PTS |
|---|---|---|---|
| 1. | Li Ning | CHN | 19.95 |
| 1. | Peter Vidmar | USA | 19.95 |
| 3. | Timothy Daggett | USA | 19.825 |
| 4. | Tong Fei | CHN | 19.75 |
| 5. | Jean-Luc Cairon | FRA | 19.70 |
| 6. | Nobuyuki Kajitani | JPN | 19.625 |
| 7. | Benno Gross | GER | 19.525 |
| 8. | Josef Zellweger | SWI | 19.50 |

**1988 Seoul** C: 89, N: 23, D: 9.24.

|  |  |  | PTS. |
|---|---|---|---|
| 1. | Dmitri Bilozerchev | SOV | 19.95 |
| 1. | Zsolt Borkai | HUN | 19.95 |
| 1. | Lubomir Geraskov | BUL | 19.95 |
| 4. | Koichi Mizushima | JPN | 19.90 |
| 5. | Valery Lyukin | SOV | 19.875 |
| 6. | Daisuke Nishikawa | JPN | 19.85 |
| 7. | Sven Tippelt | GDR | 19.80 |
| 8. | Sylvio Kroll | GDR | 19.775 |

## RINGS

**1896 Athens** C: 8, N: 3, D: 4.9.
1. Ioannis Mitropoulos  GRE
2. Hermann Weingärtner  GER
3. Petros Persakis  GRE
4. —  —
5. Karl Schumann  GER

**1900** not held

**1904 St. Louis** C: 10, N: 1, D: 10.28.

|  |  |  | PTS. |
|---|---|---|---|
| 1. | Hermann Glass | USA | 45 |
| 2. | William Merz | USA | 35 |
| 3. | Emil Voigt | USA | 32 |

**1908–1920** not held

**1924 Paris** C: 70, N: 9, D: 7.20.

| | | PTS. |
|---|---|---|
| 1. Francesco Martino | ITA | 21.553 |
| 2. Robert Pražak | CZE | 21.483 |
| 3. Ladislav Vácha | CZE | 21.43 |
| 4. Leon Štukelj | YUG | 21.33 |
| 5. Bedřich Supčik | CZE | 21.12 |
| 6. Bohumil Mořkovsky | CZE | 21.083 |
| 7. Jan Koutny | CZE | 21.053 |
| 8. Ferdinando Mandrini | ITA | 20.943 |

**1928 Amsterdam** C: 87, N: 11, D: 8.10.

| | | PTS. |
|---|---|---|
| 1. Leon Štukelj | YUG | 19.25 |
| 2. Ladislav Vácha | CZE | 19.17 |
| 3. Emanuel Löffler | CZE | 18.83 |
| 4. Romeo Neri | ITA | 18.67 |
| 5. Mauri Nyberg-Noroma | FIN | 18.33 |
| 6. Bedřich Supčik | CZE | 18.25 |
| 7. Paul Krempel | USA | 18.17 |
| 8. Jan Gajdoš | CZE | 18.08 |
| 8. Georges Miez | SWI | 18.08 |
| 8. Armand Solbach | FRA | 18.08 |

**1932 Los Angeles** C: 14, N: 6, D: 8.12.

| | | PTS. |
|---|---|---|
| 1. George Gulack | USA | 18.97 |
| 2. William Denton | USA | 18.60 |
| 3. Giovanni Lattuada | ITA | 18.50 |
| 4. Richard Bishop | USA | 18.47 |
| 5. Oreste Capuzzo | ITA | 18.27 |
| 6. Franco Tognini | ITA | 18.03 |
| 7. Heikki Savolainen | FIN | 17.70 |
| 8. Toshihiko Sasano | JPN | 17.47 |

**1936 Berlin** C: 111, N: 14, D: 8.11.

| | | PTS. |
|---|---|---|
| 1. Alois Hudec | CZE | 19.433 |
| 2. Leon Štukelj | YUG | 18.867 |
| 3. Matthias Volz | GER | 18.667 |
| 4. Alfred Schwarzmann | GER | 18.534 |
| 5. Franz Beckert | GER | 18.533 |
| 6. Michael Reusch | SWI | 18.434 |
| 7. Jaroslav Kollinger | CZE | 18.433 |
| 8. Heikki Savolainen | FIN | 18.40 |

**1948 London** C: 123, N: 16, D: 8.13.

| | | PTS. |
|---|---|---|
| 1. Karl Frei | SWI | 19.80 |
| 2. Michael Reusch | SWI | 19.55 |
| 3. Zdenek Ružička | CZE | 19.25 |
| 3. Walter Lehmann | SWI | 19.20 |
| 5. Josef Stalder | SWI | 19.15 |
| 5. Emil Studer | SWI | 19.15 |
| 7. Vladimir Karas | CZE | 19.10 |
| 8. Heikki Savolainen | FIN | 19.05 |

**1952 Helsinki** C: 185, N: 29, D: 7.21.

| | | PTS. |
|---|---|---|
| 1. Grant Shaginyan | SOV | 19.75 |
| 2. Viktor Chukarin | SOV | 19.55 |
| 3. Hans Eugster | SWI | 19.40 |
| 3. Dimitri Leonkin | SOV | 19.40 |
| 5. Valentin Muratov | SOV | 19.35 |
| 6. Masao Takemoto | JPN | 19.20 |
| 7. Attia Ali Alizaky (EGY), | | 19.15 |
| Ferenc Kemény (HUN), | | |
| Yevgeny Korolkov (SOV), | | |
| Berndt Lindfors (FIN) | | |

**1956 Melbourne** C: 63, N: 18, D: 12.6.

| | | PTS. |
|---|---|---|
| 1. Albert Azaryan | SOV | 19.35 |
| 2. Valentin Muratov | SOV | 19.15 |
| 3. Masami Kubota | JPN | 19.10 |
| 3. Masao Takemoto | JPN | 19.10 |
| 5. Nobuyuki Aihara | JPN | 19.05 |
| 5. Takashi Ono | JPN | 19.05 |
| 7. Viktor Chukarin | SOV | 19.00 |
| 7. Shinsaku Tsukawaki | JPN | 19.00 |

**1960 Rome** C: 130, N: 28, D: 9.10.

| | | PTS. |
|---|---|---|
| 1. Albert Azaryan | SOV | 19.725 |
| 2. Boris Shakhlin | SOV | 19.50 |
| 3. Velik Kapsazov | BUL | 19.425 |
| 3. Takashi Ono | JPN | 19.425 |
| 5. Nobuyuki Aihara | JPN | 19.40 |
| 6. Yuri Titov | SOV | 19.275 |

**1964 Tokyo** C: 130, N: 29, D: 10.22.

| | | PTS. |
|---|---|---|
| 1. Takuji Haytta | JPN | 19.475 |
| 2. Franco Menichelli | ITA | 19.425 |
| 3. Boris Shakhlin | SOV | 19.40 |
| 4. Viktor Leontyev | SOV | 19.35 |
| 5. Shuji Tsurumi | JPN | 19.275 |
| 6. Yukio Endo | JPN | 19.25 |

**1968 Mexico City** C: 117, N: 28, D: 10.26.

| | | PTS. |
|---|---|---|
| 1. Akinori Nakayama | JPN | 19.45 |
| 2. Mikhail Voronin | SOV | 19.325 |
| 3. Sawao Kato | JPN | 19.225 |
| 4. Mitsuo Tsukahara | JPN | 19.125 |
| 5. Takeshi Kato | JPN | 19.05 |
| 6. Sergei Diomidov | SOV | 18.975 |

**1972 Munich** C: 113, N: 26, D: 9.1.

| | | PTS. |
|---|---|---|
| 1. Akinori Nakayama | JPN | 19.35 |
| 2. Mikhail Voronin | SOV | 19.275 |
| 3. Mitsuo Tsukahara | JPN | 19.225 |
| 4. Sawao Kato | JPN | 19.15 |
| 5. Eizo Kenmotsu | JPN | 18.95 |
| 5. Klaus Köste | GDR | 18.95 |

**1976 Montreal** C: 90, N: 20, D: 7.23.

| | | PTS. |
|---|---|---|
| 1. Nikolai Andrianov | SOV | 19.65 |
| 2. Aleksandr Dityatin | SOV | 19.55 |
| 3. Dănuț Grecu | ROM | 19.50 |
| 4. Ferenc Dónath | HUN | 19.20 |
| 5. Eizo Kenmotsu | JPN | 19.175 |
| 6. Sawao Kato | JPN | 19.125 |

**1980 Moscow** C: 65, N: 14, D: 7.25.

| | | PTS. |
|---|---|---|
| 1. Aleksandr Dityatin | SOV | 19.875 |
| 2. Aleksandr Tkachyov | SOV | 19.725 |
| 3. Jiří Tabak | CZE | 19.60 |
| 4. Roland Brückner | GDR | 19.575 |
| 5. Stoyan Deltchev | BUL | 19.475 |
| 6. Dănuț Grecu | ROM | 10.85 |

**1984 Los Angeles** C: 71, N: 19, D: 8.4.

| | | PTS. |
|---|---|---|
| 1. Koji Gushiken | JPN | 19.85 |
| 1. Li Ning | CHN | 19.85 |
| 3. Mitchell Gaylord | USA | 19.825 |
| 4. Tong Fei | CHN | 19.75 |
| 4. Peter Vidmar | USA | 19.75 |
| 6. Kyoji Yamawaki | JPN | 19.725 |
| 7. Emilian Nicula | ROM | 19.50 |
| 8. Josef Zellweger | SWI | 19.375 |

**1988 Seoul** C: 89, N: 23, D: 9.24.

| | | PTS. |
|---|---|---|
| 1. Holger Behrendt | GDR | 19.925 |
| 1. Dmitri Bilozerchev | SOV | 19.925 |
| 3. Sven Tippelt | GDR | 19.875 |
| 4. Kalofer Hristozov | BUL | 19.825 |
| 4. Valery Lyukin | SOV | 19.825 |
| 6. Juri Chechi | ITA | 19.80 |
| 7. Lou Yun | CHN | 19.80 |
| 8. György Guczoghy | HUN | 19.70 |

# FLOOR EXERCISES

**1896–1928** not held

**1932 Los Angeles** C: 25, N: 6, D: 8.8.

| | | PTS. |
|---|---|---|
| 1. István Pelle | HUN | 9.60 |
| 2. Georges Miez | SWI | 9.47 |
| 3. Mario Lertora | ITA | 9.23 |
| 4. Frank Haubold | USA | 9.00 |
| 4. Romeo Neri | ITA | 9.00 |
| 6. Heikki Savolainen | FIN | 8.97 |
| 7. Alfred Jochim | USA | 8.80 |
| 7. Martti Uosikkinen | FIN | 8.80 |

**1936 Berlin** C: 110, N: 14, D: 8.11.

| | | PTS. |
|---|---|---|
| 1. Georges Miez | SWI | 18.666 |
| 2. Josef Walter | SWI | 18.50 |
| 3. Konrad Frey | GER | 18.466 |
| 3. Eugen Mack | SWI | 18.466 |
| 5. Matthias Volz | GER | 18.366 |
| 6. Willi Stadel | GER | 18.30 |
| 6. Walter Steffens | GER | 18.30 |
| 8. Martti Uosikkinen | FIN | 18.267 |

**1948 London** C: 123, N: 16, D: 8.13.

| | | PTS. |
|---|---|---|
| 1. Ferenc Pataki | HUN | 19.35 |
| 2. János Mogyorósi-Klencs | HUN | 19.20 |
| 3. Zdenek Ružička | CZE | 19.05 |
| 4. Raymond Dot | FRA | 18.90 |
| 5. Elkana Grönne | DEN | 18.825 |
| 6. Pavel Benetka | CZE | 18.80 |
| 6. Leo Sotornik | CZE | 18.80 |
| 8. Vladimir Karas | CZE | 18.10 |

As a teenager in Budapest, Ferenc Pataki wanted to become an actor. His first role was a walk-on part in which he performed some acrobatic moves. His skill was immediately noticed and he was rerouted into gymnastics.

**1952 Helsinki** C: 185, N: 29, D: 7.21.

| | | PTS. |
|---|---|---|
| 1. K. William Thoresson | SWE | 19.25 |
| 2. Jerzy Jokiel | POL | 19.15 |
| 2. Tadao Uesako | JPN | 19.15 |
| 4. Takashi Ono | JPN | 19.05 |
| 5. Onni Lappalainen | FIN | 19.00 |
| 6. Kalevi Laitinen | FIN | 18.95 |
| 6. Anders Lindh | SWE | 18.95 |
| 8. Ferdinand Daniš | CZE | 18.90 |
| 8. Robert Stout | USA | 18.90 |

**1956 Melbourne** C: 63, N: 18, D: 12.6.

| | | PTS. |
|---|---|---|
| 1. Valentin Muratov | SOV | 19.20 |
| 2. Nobuyuki Aihara | JPN | 19.10 |
| 2. Viktor Chukarin | SOV | 19.10 |
| 2. K. William Thoresson | SWE | 19.10 |
| 5. Yuri Titov | SOV | 18.95 |
| 6. Ferdinand Daniš | CZE | 18.80 |
| 6. Mintscho Todorov | BUL | 18.80 |
| 8. Helmut Bantz | GER | 18.75 |
| 8. Takashi Ono | JPN | 18.75 |

**1960 Rome** C: 130, N: 28, D: 9.10.

| | | PTS. |
|---|---|---|
| 1. Nobuyuki Aihara | JPN | 19.45 |
| 2. Yuri Titov | SOV | 19.325 |
| 3. Franco Menichelli | ITA | 19.275 |
| 4. Takashi Mitsukuri | JPN | 19.20 |
| 4. Takashi Ono | JPN | 19.20 |
| 6. Jaroslav Šťastny | CZE | 19.05 |

**1964 Tokyo** C: 130, N: 29, D: 10.22.

| | | PTS. |
|---|---|---|
| 1. Franco Menichelli | ITA | 19.45 |
| 2. Yukio Endo | JPN | 19.35 |
| 2. Viktor Lisitsky | SOV | 19.35 |
| 4. Viktor Leontyev | SOV | 19.20 |
| 5. Takashi Mitsukuri | JPN | 19.10 |
| 6. Yuri Tsapenko | SOV | 18.85 |

**1968 Mexico City** C: 117, N: 28, D: 10.26.

| | | PTS. |
|---|---|---|
| 1. Sawao Kato | JPN | 19.475 |
| 2. Akinori Nakayama | JPN | 19.40 |
| 3. Takeshi Kato | JPN | 19.275 |
| 4. Mitsuo Tsukuhara | JPN | 19.05 |
| 5. Valery Karassev | SOV | 18.95 |
| 6. Eizo Kenmotsu | JPN | 18.925 |

**1972 Munich** C: 113, N: 26, D: 9.1.

| | | PTS. |
|---|---|---|
| 1. Nikolai Andrianov | SOV | 19.175 |
| 2. Akinori Nakayama | JPN | 19.125 |
| 3. Shigeru Kasamatsu | JPN | 19.025 |
| 4. Eizo Kenmotsu | JPN | 18.925 |
| 5. Klaus Köste | GDR | 18.825 |
| 6. Sawao Kato | JPN | 18.75 |

**1976 Montreal** C: 90, N: 20, D: 7.23.

| | | PTS. |
|---|---|---|
| 1. Nikolai Andrianov | SOV | 19.45 |
| 2. Vladimir Marchenko | SOV | 19.425 |
| 3. Peter Kormann | USA | 19.30 |
| 4. Roland Brückner | GDR | 19.275 |
| 5. Sawao Kato | JPN | 19.25 |
| 6. Eizo Kenmotsu | JPN | 19.10 |

**1980 Moscow** C: 65, N: 14, D: 7.25.

| | | PTS. |
|---|---|---|
| 1. Roland Brückner | GDR | 19.75 |
| 2. Nikolai Andrianov | SOV | 19.725 |
| 3. Aleksandr Dityatin | SOV | 19.70 |
| 4. Jiři Tabák | CZE | 19.675 |
| 5. Péter Kovács | HUN | 19.425 |
| 6. Lutz Hoffmann | GDR | 18.725 |

**1984 Los Angeles** C: 71, N: 19, D: 8.4.

| | | PTS. |
|---|---|---|
| 1. Li Ning | CHN | 19.925 |
| 2. Lou Yun | CHN | 19.775 |
| 3. Koji Sotomura | JPN | 19.70 |
| 3. Philippe Vatuone | FRA | 19.70 |
| 5. Bart Conner | USA | 19.675 |
| 6. Valentin Pintea | ROM | 19.60 |
| 7. Peter Vidmar | USA | 19.55 |
| 8. Koji Gushiken | JPN | 19.45 |

Li Ning, a good-natured crowd-pleaser, went home with more medals than any other athlete at the Los Angeles Olympics: 3 gold, 2 silver and 1 bronze.

**1988 Seoul** C: 89, N: 23, D: 9.24.

| | | PTS. |
|---|---|---|
| 1. Sergei Kharkov | SOV | 19.925 |
| 2. Vladimir Artemov | SOV | 19.90 |
| 3. Yukio Iketani | JPN | 19.85 |
| 3. Lou Yun | CHN | 19.85 |
| 5. Li Ning | CHN | 19.80 |
| 6. Boris Preti | ITA | 19.775 |
| 7. Kalofer Hristozov | BUL | 19.75 |
| 8. Curtis Hibbert | CAN | 19.525 |

## TEAM COMBINED EXERCISES

According to current rules, each nation's final score is determined by combining the scores of the top five performers on each apparatus.

**1896–1900** not held

**1904 St. Louis** T: 13, N: 1, D: 7.2.

| | TOTAL PTS. |
|---|---|
| 1. Turngemeinde Philadelphia | 374.43 |
| Julius Lenhart 69.80 (1), Philipp Kassel 64.56 (11), Anton Heida 62.72 (17), Max Hess 59.29 (31), Ernst Reckeweg 56.15 (46), John Grieb 55.21 (50) | |
| 2. New York Turnverein | 356.37 |
| Otto Steffen 67.03 (6), John Bissinger 66.57 (7), Emil Beyer 59.70 (30), Max Wolf 57.85 (33), Julian Schmitz 54.58 (56), Arthur Rosenkampf 48.34 (87) | |
| 3. Central Turnverein Chicago | 349.69 |
| George Mayer 61.66 (21), John Duha 61.02 (24), Edward Siegler 59.03 (32), Philipp Schuster 55.44 (49), Robert Mayack 54.53 (57), Charles Krause 53.01 (66) | |
| 4. Concordia Turnverein St. Louis | 344.01 |
| William Merz 65.25 (10), Georges Stapf 61.97 (20), John Dellert 57.41 (35), Emil Voigt 54.33 (59), George Eyser 52.10 (70), Hy. Meyland 48.52 (86) | |
| 5. South St. Louis Turnverein | 338.65 |
| Charles Umbs 63.39 (16), Andy Neu 61.21 (23), William Tritschler 54.73 (54), Christian Deubler 54.63 (55), Edward Tritschler 53.16 (65), John Leichinger 50.00 (81) | |
| 6. Norwegischer Turnverein Brooklyn | 334.00 |
| Ragnar Berg 60.24 (28), Charles Sörum 57.40 (36), Oliver Olsen 57.27 (38), Harry Hansen 55.00 (51), Oluf Landnes 53.64 (72), Bergin Nilsen 50.45 (80) | |

**1906 Athens** T: 6, N: 5, D: 4.22.

| | TOTAL PTS. |
|---|---|
| 1. NOR (Carl Albert Andersen, Oskar Bye, Conrad Carlsrud, Harald Anders Eriksen, Osvald Falch, Christian Fjeringen, Yngvar Fredriksen, Karl Johan Haagensen, Harald Halvorsen, Petter Hol, Andreas Hagelund, Eugen | 19.00 |

Ingebretsen, Matthias Jespersen, Fin Münster, Fridtjof Olsen, Carl Alfred Pedersen, Rasmus Pettersen, Thorleif Pettersen, Thorleif Rehn, Johan Stumpf)

2. DEN (Carl Andersen, Halvor Birch, H. Bukdahl, Kaj Gnudtzmann, Knud Holm, Erik Klem, Harald Klem, R. Kraft, Edvard Larsen, J. Lorentzen, Robert Madsen, Carl Manicus-Hansen, Oluf Olsen, Christian Petersen, Hans Pedersen, Niels Petersen, Viktor Rasmussen, Marius Skram-Jensen, Marius Thuesen) — 18.00

3. ITA Pistoia (Manlio Pastorini, Spartaco Nerozzi, Federico Bertinotti, Vitaliano Masotti, Raffaello Gianoni, Quintilio Mazzoncini, Azeglio Innocenti, Filiberto Innocenti, Ciro Civinini, Maurizio Masetti) — 16.71

4. ITA Roma (Cesare Tifi, Dante Aloisi, Enrico Brignoli, Pierino Caccialupi, Guido Colavini, Romeo Gianotti, Mario Gubiani, Venceslao Rossi, Romolo Tuzzi, Amadeo Zinzi) — 16.60

5. GER (O. Franko, Cassius Hermes, Fritz Hofmann, Julius Keyl, Bruno Mahler, Carl Ohms, Wilhelm Weber, Otto Wiegand) — 16.25

6. HUN (Béla Dáner, Arpád Erdös, Béla Erödl, Frigyes Gráf, Gyula Kakas, Nándor Kovács, Kálmán Szabó, Vilmos Szücs) — 14.45

**1908 London** T: 8, N: 8, D: 7.18.

| | | TOTAL PTS. |
|---|---|---|
| 1. SWE | (Gösta Åsbrink, Per Bertilsson, Andreas Cervin, Hjalmar Cedercrona, Rudolf Degermark, Carl Folcker, Sven Forssman, Erik Granfelt, Carl Hårleman, Nils Hellsten, Gunnar Höjer, Arvid Holmberg, Carl Holmberg, Osvald Holmberg, Hugo Jahnke, John Jarlén, Harald Johnsson, Rolf Johnsson, Nils Kantzow, Sven Landberg, Olle Lanner, Axel Jung, Osvald Moberg, Carl Martin Norberg, Erik Norberg, Thor Norborg, Axel Norling, Daniel Norling, Gösta Olsson, Leonard Peterson, Sven Rosen, Gustav Rosenqvist, Axel Sjöblom, Birger Sörvik, Haakon Sorvik, Karl Johan Svensson [Sarland], Gustaf Vinqvist, Nils Widforss) | 438 |
| 2. NOR | (Arthur Amundsen, Carl Albert Andersen, Otto Authen, Hermann Bohne, Trygve Böysen, Oscar Bye, Conrad Carlsrud, Sverre Gröner, Harald Halvorsen, Harald Hansen, Petter Hol, Eugen Ingebretsen, Ole Iversen, Mathias Jespersen, Sigge Johannesen, Nicolai Kiör, Karl Klaeth, Thor Larsen, Rolf Lefdahl, Hans Lem, Anders Moen, Frithjof Olsen, Carl Alfred Pedersen, Paul Pedersen, John Skrataas, Harald Smedvik, Sigvard Sivertsen, Andreas Strand, Olaf Syvertsen, Thomas Thorstensen) | 425 |
| 3. FIN | (Eino Forsström, Otto Granström, Johan Kemp, Jivari Kyykoski, Heikki Lehmusto, John Lindroth, Yrjö Linko, Edvard Linna, Matti Markanen, Kaarlo Mikkolainen, Veli Nieminen, | 405 |

Kaarlo Kustaa Paasia, Arvi Pohjanpää, Aarne Pohjonen, Eino Railio, Heikki Riipinen, Arno Saarinen, Einari Verner Sahlstein, Arne Salovaara, Kaarlo Sandelin, Elias Sipilä, Viktor Smeds, Kaarlo Soinio, Kurt Enoch Stenberg, Väinö Tiiri, Magnus Wegelius)

4. DEN (Carl Andersen, Hans Bredmose, Jens Chiewitz, Arvor Hansen, Christian Hansen, Ingvardt Hansen, Einar Hermann, Knud Holm, Paul Holm, O. Husted-Nielsen, Charles Jensen, Gorm Jensen, Hendrik Johansen, Harald Klem, Robert Madsen, Viggo Meulengracht-Madsen, Lucas Nielsen, Oluf Olsen, Niels Petersen, Nicolaj Philipsen, Heini Rasmussen, Victor Rasmussen, Marius Thuesen, Niels Turin-Nielsen) — 378

5. FRA (L. Bogart, A. Borizée, H. de Breyne, N. Constant, C. A. Courtois, L. Delattre, A. Delecluse, L. Delecluse, G. Demarle, J. Derov, C. Desmarcheliers, Charles Desmarcheliers, E. Dharaney, G. Donnet, E. Duhamel, A. Duponcheel, P. Durin, A. Eggremont, G. Guiot, L. Henneboiq, H. Hubert, D. Hudels, E. Labitte, L. Lestienne, R. Lis, V. Magnier, G. Nys, J. Parent, L. Pappe, V. Polidori, G. Pottier, A. Pinoy, L. Sandray, E. Schmoll, E. Steffe, E. Vercruysse, H. Vergin, E. Vicogne, J. Walmée, G. Warlouzer) — 319

6. ITA (Alfredo Accorsi, Nemo Agodi, Umberto Agliorini, Adriano Andreani, Vincenzo Blo, Flaminio Bottoni, Bruto Buozzi, Giovanni Bonati, Pietro Borsetti, Adamo Borzani, Gastone Calabresi, Carlo Celada, Tito Collevati, Antonio Cotechini, Guido Cristofori, Stanislao Dichiara, Giovanni Gasperini, A. Marchi, Carlo Marchiandi, Ettore Massari, Roberto Nardini, Gaetano Preti, Decio Pavani, Gino Ravenna, Massimo Ridolfi, Gustavo Taddia, Giannetto Termanini, Ugo Savonuzzi, Gioacchino Vaccari) — 316

7. HOL (C.L.J. Becker, M. Biel, J. de Boer, R.J.C. Blom, J. Bolt, E. Brouwer, C. van Daalen, J.H. Flemer, G.C. Gookol, J. Gondeket, D. Janssen, J.J. Kiefl, S. Kongin, H. N. van Leeuwen, A. Mok, A. d'Oliviera, J.J. Posthumus, J.H.A.G. Schmitt, J. Slier, J. Stikkelman, H.J.F. Thyssen, G.J. Wesling) — 297

8. GBR (P.A. Baker, W.F. Barrett, R. Bonney, J.H. Catley, M. Clay, E. Clough, J. Cotterell, W. Cowy, G.C. Cullen, F. Denby, Herbert Drury, W. Fitt, H. Gill, A.S. Harley, A.E. Hawkins, W.O. Hoare, J.A. Horridge, H.J. Huskinson, J.W. Jones, E. Justice, N.J. Keighley, R. Laycock, R. McGaw, J. McPhail, W. Manning, W.G. Merrifield, C.J. Oldaker, G. Parrott, E. Parsons, E.F. Richardson, J. Robertson, George Ross, D. Scott, J. F. Simpson, W.R. Skeeles, J. Speight, H. Stell, C.V. Suderman, William Tilt, Charles Vigurs, H. Waterman, E. Walton, E.A. Watkins, John Whitaker, F. Whitehead) — 196

**1912 Stockholm** T: 5, N: 5, D: 7.11.

|  |  | TOTAL PTS. |
|---|---|---|
| 1. ITA | (Guido Boni, Giuseppe Domenichelli, Luciano Savorini, Guido Romano, Angelo Zorzi, Giorgio Zampori, Giovanni Mangiante, Lorenzo Mangiante, Adolfo Tunesi, Pietro Bianchi, Paolo Salvi, Alberto Braglia, Alfredo Gollini, Serafino Mazzarocchi, Francesco Loi, Carlo Fregosi) | 265.75 |
| 2. HUN | (Lajos Aradi-Kmetykó, József Berkes-Bittenbinder, Imre Erdödy, Samu Fóti, Imre Gellért, Gyözö Halmos-Haberfeld, Ottó Helmich, István Herczeg, József Keresztessy, János Korponai-Krizmanich, Elemér Pászty, Árpád Pétery, Jenö Réti-Rittich, Ferenc Szücs, Ödön Téry, Géza Tuli) | 227.25 |
| 3. GBR | (Albert Betts, Harry Dickason, Samuel Hodgetts, Alfred Messenger, Edward Pepper, Charles Vigurs, Samuel Walker, John Whitaker, Sidney Cross, Bernard Franklin, Edward Potts, Reginald Potts, George Ross, Henry Oberholzer, Charles Simmons, Arthur Southern, Ronald McLean, Charles Luck, Herbert Drury, William McKune, William Titt, William Cowhig, Leonard Hanson) | 184.50 |
| 4. LUX | (Nicolas Adam, Charles Behm, André Bordang, Jean-Pierre Frantzen, François Hentges, Pierre Hentges, Michal Hemmerling, Jean-Baptiste Horn, Nicolas Kanivé, Emile Knepper, Nicolas Kummer, Marcel Langsam, Emile Lanners, Jean-Pierre Thommes, François Wagner, Antoine Wehrer, Ferdinand Wirtz, Joseph Zuang, Maurice Palgen) | 179.75 |
| 5. GER | (Walter Engelmann, Adolf Seebass, Alfred Staats, Hans Roth, Arno Glockauer, Alexander Sperling, Kurt Reichenbach, Rudolf Körner, Erwin Buder, Wilhelm Brülle, Heinrich Pahner, Johannes Reuschle, Walter Jesinghaus, Eberhard Sorge, Karl Richter, Erich Worm, Karl Jordan, Hans Werner) | 162.00 |

**1920 Antwerp** T: 5, N: 5, D: 8.29.

|  |  | TOTAL PTS. |
|---|---|---|
| 1. ITA | (Arnaldo Andreoli, Pietro Bianchi, Ettore Bellotto, Luigi Cambiaso, Luigi Contessi, Carlo Costigliolo, Luigi Costigliolo, Fernando Bonatti, Giuseppe Domenichelli, Roberto Ferrari, Carlo Fregosi, Romualdo Ghiglione, Ambrogio Levati, Francesco Loi, Vittorio Lucchetti, Luigi Maiocco, Ferdinando Mandrini, Giovanni Mangiante, Lorenzo Mangiante, Antonio Marovelli, Michele Mastromarino, Giuseppe Paris, Manlio Pastorini, Ezio Roselli, Paolo Salvi, Giovanni Battista Tubino, Giorgio Zampori, Angelo Zorzi) | 359.855 |
| 2. BEL | (Eugenius Auwerkerken, Théophile Bauer, François Claessens, Auguste Cootmans, Frans Gibens, Jean van Guysse, Albert Haepers, Dominique Jacobs, Félicien Kempeneers, Jules Labéeu, Hubert Lafortune, Auguste Landrieu, Charles Lannie, Constant Loriot, Alphonse van Mele, Ferdinand Minnaert, Nicolas Maerloos, Louis Stoop, François Verboven, Jean Verboven, Julien Verdonck, Joseph Verstraeten, Georges Vivex, Jules Julianus Wagemans) | 346.785 |
| 3. FRA | (Emile Bouchès, Paul Joseph Durin, Paulin Alexandre Lemaire, Georges Berger, Léon Delsarte, Georges Duvant, Louis Kempe, Lucien Démanet, Auguste Hoël, René Boulanger, Fernand Fauconnier, Albert Hersoy, Georges Lagouge, Ernest Lepinasse, Jules Pirard, Julien Wartelle, Paul Wartelle, Emile Martel, Georges Thurnherr, Alfred Buyenne, Eugène Pollet, Eugène Cordonnier, Arthur Hermann, André Higelin) | 340.100 |
| 4. CZE | (Josef Bochniček, Ladislav Bubeniček, Josef Czada, Stanislav Indruch, Miroslav Klinger, Josef Maly, Zdenek Opočensky, Josef Pagáč, František Pecháček, Robert Pražak, Josef Stolař, Svatopluk Svoboda, Ladislav Vácha, František Vaneček, Jaroslav Velda, Václav Virt) | 305.255 |
| 3. GBR | (S. Andrew, Albert Betts, A.G. Cocksedge, William Cotterill, William Cowhig, Sidney Cross, H.S. Dawswell, J.E. Dingley, S. Domville, H.W. Doncaster, R.E. Edgecombe, W. Edwards, H.J. Finchett, Bernard Wallis Franklin, J. Harris, Samuel Hodgetts, J. Cotterill, Stanley Leigh, G. Masters, Ronald McLean, O. Morris, E.P. Ness, A.E. Page, A.O. Pinner, E. Pugh, H.W. Taylor, J.A. Walker, R.H. Zandell) | 290.215 |

**1924 Paris** T: 9, N: 9, D: 7.20.

|  |  | TOTAL PTS. |
|---|---|---|
| 1. ITA | (Fernando Mandrini 105.583 [4], Mario Letora 103.619 [10], Vittorio Lucchetti 102.803 [12], Francesco Martino 101.529 [16], Luigi Cambiaso 101.320 [17], Giuseppe Paris 101.169 [18], Giorgio Zampori 96.549 [26], Luigi Maiocco 92.486 [33]) | 839.058 |
| 2. FRA | (Jean Gounot 105.153 [8], Léon Delsarte 104.739 [9], Albert Séquin 102.326 [15], Eugène Cordonnier 99.906 [21], François Gangloff 98.796 [23], Arthur Hermann 95.716 [27], André Higelin 92.133 [34], Joseph Huber 88.119 [39]) | 820.528 |
| 3. SWI | (August Güttinger 105.176 [7], Jean Gutweniger 102.342 [14], Hans Grieder 99.646 [22], Georges Miez 98.796 [24], Josef Wilhelm 97.096 [25], Otto Pfister 95.746 [28], Carl Widmer 94.936 [32], Antoine Rebetez 89.583 [38]) | 816.661 |

4. YUG (Leon Štukelj 110.340 [1], Ivan Porenta 100.172 [20], Stane Zilič 95.523 [29], Stane Derganc 95.293 [30], Miha Osvald 91.066 [36], Slavko Hlastan 81.248 [44], Rastko Poljšak 77.665 [45], Josip Primožič 77.393 [47])   762.101

5. USA (Frank Kriz 100.293 [19], Alfred Jochim 95.090 [31], John Pearson 89.852 [37], Frank Safanda 86.953 [41], Curtis Rottman 82.946 [42], Rudolph Novak 77.593 [46], Max Wandrer 76.320 [48], John Mais 72.770 [53])   715.117

6. GBR (Stanley Leigh 91.266 [35], H. Brown 87.059 [40], H.J. Finchett 81.710 [43], F. Hawkins 73.796 [49], T. Hopkins 72.350 [54], E. Leigh 69.200 [55], S. Humphreys 64.656 [64], A. Spencer 64.253 [65])   637.790

7. FIN (Jaakko Kunnas 73.473 [51], Otto Suhonen 72.843 [52], Akseli Roine 66.503 [56], Aarne Roine 65.46 [59], Mikko Hamalainen 65.23, Karonen 65.18 [63], Evert Kerttula 62.863 [66], Edward "Eetu" Kostamo 50.443 [70])   521.998

8. LUX (C. Quaino 73.569 [50], T. Jeitz 65.98 [57], E. Munhofen 65.556 [58], M. Erang 65.356 [60], A. Neumann 65.196 [62], J. Palzer 61.563 [67], P. Tolar 58.713 [68], M. Weishaupt 58.596 [69])   514.529

**1928 Amsterdam** T: 11, N: 11, D: 8.10.

|  | | TOTAL PTS. |
|---|---|---|
| 1. SWI | (Georges Miez 247.500 [1], Hermann Hänggi 246.625 [2], Eugen Mack 243.625 [8], Melchior Wetzel 240.875 [12], Eduard "Edi" Steinemann 237.875 [15], August Güttinger 237.750 [16], Hans Grieder 234.125 [18], Otto Pfister 230.875 [24]) | 1718.625 |
| 2. CZE | (Ladislav Vácha 242.875 [9], Emanuel Löffler 242.500 [10], Jan Gajdoš 240.625 [13], Josef Effenberger 208.875 [14], Bedřich Šupčík 233.250 [20], Václav Vesely 227.625 [28], Jan Koutny 225.250 [31], Ladislav Tikal 217.750 [37]) | 1712.25 |
| 3. YUG | (Leon Štukelj 244.875 [3], Josip Primožič 244.000 [5], Anton Malej 228.875 [25], Eduard Antonijevič 228.000 [26], Boris Gregorka 221.000 [33], Ivan Porenta 220.250 [34], Stane Derganc 211.875 [43], Dragutin Ciotti 210.000 [45]) | 1648.75 |
| 4. FRA | (Armand Solbach 241.625 [11], Georges Leroux 235.750 [17], André Lemoine 232.000 [22], Jean Larrouy 226.500 [29], E. Schmitt 219.125 [35], Jean Gounot 216.750 [39], A. Chatelain 202.375 [54], Alfred Kraus 100.25 [DNF]) | 1620.75 |
| 5. FIN | (Heikki Savolainen 243.750 [6], Mauri Nyberg 243.750 [6], Martti Uosikkinen 231.875 [23], Jaakko Kunnas 217.500 [38], U.K. Korhonen 209.875 [46], Rafael Ylönen | 1609.25 |

188.750 [61], Kaiku Kinos 185.375 [62], Birger Stenman 179.750 [66])

6. ITA (Romeo Neri 244.750 [4], Mario Lertora 233.375 [19], Vittorio Lucchetti 228.000 [26], Fernando Mandrini 226.250 [30], Giuseppe Lupi 224.000 [32], Mario Tambini 212.500 [41], Giuseppe Paris 203.250 [53], Ezio Roselli 192.625 [58])   1599.125

7. USA (Alfred Jochim 218.250 [36], Glenn Berry 212.750 [40], Frank Kriz 211.625 [44], Frank Haubold 209.375 [47], Harold Newhart 209.375 [47], John Pearson 208.75 [50], Herman Witzig 206.250 [51], Paul Krempel 203.625 [52])   1519.125

8. HOL (E.H. Melkman 199.500 [56], P.J. van Dam 199.375 [59], M. Jacobs 199.000 [60], I. Wijnschenk 182.625 [64], W.B. Pouw 182.125 [65], K. Boot 169.000 [71], J.F. van d. Vinden 169.000 [71], H.G. Licher 143.500 [85])   1364.875

**1932 Los Angeles** T: 5, N: 5, D: 8.10.

|  | | TOTAL PTS. |
|---|---|---|
| 1. ITA | (Romeo Neri 140.625 [1], Mario Lertora 134.400 [4], Savino Guglielmetti 134.375 [5], Oreste Capuzzo 132.450 [7]) | 541.850 |
| 2. USA | (Frank Haubold 132.525 [6], Frederick Meyer 131.650 [8], Alfred Jochim 129.075 [11], Frank Cumiskey 129.025 [12]) | 522.275 |
| 3. FIN | (Heikki Savolainen 134.575 [3], Mauri Nyberg-Noroma 129.800 [10], Veikko Pakarinen 122.700 [14], Einari Teräsvirta 122.700 [14]) | 509.995 |
| 4. HUN | (István Pelle 134.925 [2], Miklós Péter 119.200 [17], Péter Boros 105.775 [20], József Hegedüs 105.750 [21]) | 465.650 |
| 5. JPN | (Toshihiko Sasano 108.475 [19], Shigeo Honma 103.100 [22], Takashi Kondo 101.925 [23], Yoshitaki Takeda 88.500 [24]) | 402.000 |

**1936 Berlin** T: 14, N: 14, D: 8.11.

|  | | TOTAL PTS. |
|---|---|---|
| 1. GER | (Alfred Schwarzmann 113.100 [1], Konrad Frey 111.532 [3], Matthias Volz 110.099 [7], Willi Stadel 108.999 [8], Franz Beckert 107.200 [15], Walter Steffens 106.500 [17]) | 657.430 |
| 2. SWI | (Eugen Mack 112.334 [2], Michael Reusch 110.700 [5], Eduard "Edi" Steinemann 108.633 [10], Walter Bach 108.299 [11], Albert Bachmann 107.502 [13], Georges Miez 107.334 [14]) | 654.802 |
| 3. FIN | (Martti Uosikkinen 110.700 [5], Heikki Savolainen 108.766 [9], Mauri Nyberg-Noroma 106.801 [16], Aleksanteri Saarvala 105.235 [19], Esa Seeste 103.934 [24], Veikko Pakarinen 103.032 [28]) | 638.468 |
| 4. CZE | (Alois Hudec 111.199 [4], Jaroslav Kollinger 104.733 [23], Jan Sládek 103.399 [26], Jan | 625.763 |

|  | | TOTAL PTS. |
|---|---|---|

Gajdoš 103.065 [27], Vratislav Petraček 101.966 [34], Jindřich Tintera 101.401 [38])

5. ITA (Savino Guglielmetti 107.699 [12], Oreste Capuzzo 102.500 [30], Egidio Armelloni 101.601 [36], Danilo Fioravanti 101.467 [37], Franco Tognini 101.266 [39], Nicolo Tronci 100.600 [41]) — 615.133

6. YUG (Konrad Gralc 103.632 [25], Josip Primožič 102.367 [31], Leon Štukelj 102.300 [32], Miroslav Forte 99.200 [46], Jože Vadnov 95.934 [56], Janoz Pristov 94.933 [61]) — 598.366

7. HUN (István Pelle 105.566 [18], Lajos Tóth 101.867 [35], Miklós Péter 99.034 [47], Gábor Kecskeméti 97.766 [51], István Sárkány 94.565 [64], Jósef Sarlós 93.132 [71]) — 591.930

8. FRA (Walter 98.933 [49], Armand Solbach 97.633 [52], Lucien Masset 97.233 [53], Herold 96.168 [55], Antoine Schildwein 95.633 [59], Rousseau 94.666 [62]) — 580.266

**1948 London** T: 16, N: 16, D: 8.13.

|  | | TOTAL PTS. |
|---|---|---|

1. FIN (Veikko Huhtanen 229.70 [1], Paavo Aaltonen 228.80 [3], Kalevi Laitinen 225.65 [8], Olavi Rove 225.20 [10], Einari Teräsvirta 225.00 [12], Heikki Savolainen 223.95 [14]) — 1358.30

2. SWI (Walter Lehmann 229.00 [2], Josef Stalder 228.70 [4], Christian Kipfer 227.10 [5], Emil Studer 226.60 [6], Robert Lucy 223.30 [15], Michael Reusch 222.00 [18]) — 1356.70

3. HUN (Lajos Tóth 225.20 [10], Lajos Sántha 224.30 [13], László Baranyai 222.40 [16], Ferenc Pataki 221.30 [19], János Mogyorósi-Klencs 218.95 [27], Ferenc Varköi 218.70 [29]) — 1330.85

4. FRA (Raymond Dot 220.80 [20], Michel Mathiot 220.40 [22], Lucien Masset 219.95 [24], André Weingand 219.80 [25], Antoine Schlindwein 216.50 [34], Alphonse Anger 216.40 [35]) — 1313.85

5. ITA (Guido Figone 225.30 [9], Luigi Zanetti 219.00 [26], Savino Guglielmetti 217.20 [32], Domenico Grosso 214.10 [40], Quinto Vadi 214.00 [42], Danilo Fioravanti 210.70 [51]) — 1300.30

6. CZE (Zdenek Ružička 226.20 [7], Pavel Benetka 220.30 [23], Miroslav Málek 212.90 [47], Vladimir Karas 212.20 [48], Leo Sotornik 210.80 [50], František Wirth 209.70 [52]) — 1292.10

7. USA (Edward Scrobe 213.90 [44], Vincent D'Autorio 211.30 [49], William Roetzheim 209.10 [53], Joseph Kotys 208.50 [55], Frank Cumiskey 205.15 [62], Raymond Sorensen 204.55 [63]) — 1252.50

8. DEN (Paul Jessen 214.30 [38], Tage Gronne 213.50 [45], Freddy Jensen 208.35 [56], Arnold Thomsen 206.25 [58], Wilhelm Moller 201.75 [68], Poul Jensen 201.25 [70]) — 1245.40

**1952 Helsinki** T: 29, N: 29, D: 7.21.

|  | | TOTAL PTS. |
|---|---|---|

1. SOV (Viktor Chukarin 115.70 [1], Grant Shaginyan 114.95 [2], Valentin Muratov 113.65 [4], Yevgeny Korolkov 113.35 [6], Vladimir Belyakov 113.35 [6], Yosif Berdiyev 113.10 [10], Mikhail Perelman 112.50 [11], Dimitri Leonkin 103.75 [78]) — 574.40

2. SWI (Josef Stalder 114.75 [3], Hans Eugster 113.40 [5], Jean Tschabold 113.30 [8], Jack Günthard 111.60 [17], Melchior Thalmann 110.75 [25], Ernst Gebendinger 109.75 [39], Hans Schwarzentruber 108.40 [52], Ernst Fivian 107.95 [55]) — 567.50

3. FIN (Onni Lappalainen 111.85 [14], Berndt Lindfors 111.45 [19], Paavo Aaltonen 111.40 [20], Kaino Lempinen 110.60 [28], Heikki Savolainen 110.45 [29], Kalevi Laitinen 110.10 [35], Kalevi Viskari 109.80 [38], Olavi Rove 109.45 [42]) — 564.20

4. GER Helmut Bantz 113.25 [9], Adalbert Dickhut 110.85 [24], Theo Wied 110.70 [26], Alfred Schwarzmann 110.65 [27], Hans Pfann 110.20 [33], Erich Wied 109.70 [40], Friedel Overwien 108.65 [48], Jakob Kiefer 91.70 [150]) — 561.20

5. JPN (Takashi Ono 112.20 [12], Tadao Uesako 111.65 [15], Masao Takemoto 111.65 [15], Akitomo Kaneko 111.30 [21], Tetsumi Nabeya 110.10 [35]) — 556.90

6. HUN (Lajos Santha 111.50 [18], Ferenc Pataki 110.90 [23], József Fekete 108.90 [46], Karoly Kocsis 108.65 [48], Ferenc Kemény 108.40 [52], Sándor Rétl 107.75 [57], Lajos Tóth 107.45 [58], János Mogyorósi-Klencs 106.80 [61]) — 555.80

7. CZE (Ferdinand Daniš 112.00 [13], Zdenek Ružička 110.40 [30], J. Svoboda 110.05 [37], Lee Sotornik 109.50 [41], Josef Škvor 109.10 [44], J. Mikulec 108.95 [45], Vladimir Kejř 108.15 [54], M. Kolejka 106.70 [63]) — 555.55

8. USA (Edward Scrobe 110.40 [30], Robert Stout 110.15 [34], William Roetzheim 107.05 [59], Donald Holder 103.50 [80], John Beckner 103.40 [81], Charles Simms 102.40 [89], Walter Blattmann 102.35 [90], Vincent D'Antorio 101.20 [100]) — 543.15

**1956 Melbourne** T: 7, N: 7, D: 12.6.

|  | | TOTAL PTS. |
|---|---|---|

1. SOV (Viktor Chukarin 114.25 [1], Yuri Titov 113.80 [3], Valentin Muratov 113.30 [5], Albert Azaryan 112.55 [7], Boris Shakhlin 112.50 [8], Pavel Stolbov 111.75 [14]) — 568.25

2. JPN (Takashi Ono 114.20 [2], Masao Takemoto 113.55 [4], Masami Kubota 112.50 [8], Nobuyuki Aihara 112.45 [10], Shinsaku — 566.40

Tsukawaki 112.20 [12], Akira Kono 111.55 [16])

3. FIN (Kalevi Suoniemi 112.35 [11], Berndt Lindfors 111.60 [15], Martti Mansikka 110.60 [20], Onni Lappalainen 110.45 [22], Olavi Leimuvirta 109.35 [27], Raimo Heinonen 108.10 [37])  555.95

4. CZE (Ferdinand Daniš 111.90 [13], Josef Škvor 110.85 [18], Vladimir Kejř 110.30 [23], Zdenek Ružička 109.65 [26], Jaroslav Mikoška 109.35 [27], Jaroslav Bim 108.25 [26])  554.10

5. GER (Helmut Bantz 112.90 [6], Robert Klein 110.60 [20], Theo Wied 109.90 [25], Hans Pfann 109.15 [29], Erich Wied 107.50 [29], Jakob Kiefer 107.45 [42])  552.45

6. USA (John Beckner 111.00 [17], Jose Armando Vega 108.45 [31], Charles Simms 108.40 [32], Richard Beckner 108.30 [35], Abraham Grossfeld 107.75 [39], William Tom 107.35 [43])  547.50

7. AUS (Brian Blackburn 91.40 [58], Graham Bond 96.40 [54], David Gourlay 95.90 [55], John Lees 93.05 [56], Alexander Punton 85.75 [59], Bruce Sharp 92.95 [57])  477.15

**1960 Rome** T: 20, N: 20, D: 9.7.

| | | TOTAL PTS. |
|---|---|---|
| 1. JPN | (Takashi Ono 115.90 [2], Shuji Tsurumi 114.55 [4], Yukio Endo 114.45 [5], Masao Takemoto 114.45 [5], Nobuyuki Aihara 114.40 [7], Takashi Mitsukuri 114.10 [9]) | 575.20 |
| 2. SOV | (Boris Shakhlin 115.95 [1], Yuri Titov 115.60 [3], Albert Azaryan 113.35 [11], Vladimir Portnoi 113.30 [12], Nikolai Miligulo 113.05 [13], Valery Kerdemelidi 111.95 [17]) | 572.70 |
| 3. ITA | (Franco Menichelli 113.80 [10], Giovanni Carminucci 112.30 [14], Angelo Vicardi 110.90 [24], Pasquale Carminucci 110.40 [31], Orlando Polmonari 109.95 [38], Gianfranco Marzolla 109.05 [50]) | 559.05 |
| 4. CZE | (Ferdinand Daniš 112.10 [15], Jaroslav Štastny 111.50 [18], Jaroslav Bim 111.00 [23], Pavol Gajdoš 110.60 [28], Josef Trmal 110.25 [33], Ladislav Pazdera 108.85 [54]) | 557.15 |
| 5. USA | (Larry Banner 111.05 [21], John Beckner 110.85 [25], Donald Tonry 110.75 [27], Abraham Grossfeld 110.05 [36], Fred Orlofsky 109.45 [44], Garland O'Quinn 109.00 [53]) | 555.20 |
| 6. FIN | (Otto Kestola 112.00 [16], Eugen Ekman 110.45 [30], Olavi Leimuvirta 110.25 [33], Kauko Heikkinen 109.85 [40], Raimo Heinonen 109.60 [42], Sakkari Olkkonnen 109.40 [45]) | 554.45 |
| 7. GDR/ GER | (Günter Lyhs 110.80 [26], Siegfried Fülle 110.60 [28], Erwin Koppe 109.05 [50], Günter Nachtigall 108.75 [59], Karlheinz | 553.35 |

Friedrich 108.00 [67], Philipp Fürst 106.65 [76])

8. SWI (Ernst Fivian 111.05 [21], Max Benker 110.00 [37], Fritz Feuz 109.85 [40], André Brullmann 109.15 [47], Hans Schwarzentruber 109.15 [47], Edy Thomi 108.35 [63])  551.45

Masao Takemoto, a member of the Japanese team, had won a total of two silver medals and three bronze in 1952 and 1956, but he didn't win a gold medal until 1960, when he was 40 years old. He is the oldest gymnast in Olympic history to win a gold medal. In 1960 he also gained another silver medal on the horizontal bar.

**1964 Tokyo** T: 18, N: 18, D: 10.20.

| | | TOTAL PTS. |
|---|---|---|
| 1. JPN | (Yukio Endo 115.95 [1], Shuji Tsurumi 115.40 [2], Haruhiro Yamashita 115.10 [6], Takuji Hayata 114.90 [8], Takashi Mitsukuri 114.80 [9], Takashi Ono 114.40 [11]) | 577.95 |
| 2. SOV | (Boris Shakhlin 115.40 [2], Viktor Lisitsky 115.40 [2], Viktor Leontyev 114.50 [10], Yuri Tsapenko 114.40 [11], Yuri Titov 114.35 [13], Sergei Diomidov 114.20 [14]) | 575.45 |
| 3. GER/ GDR | (Siegfried Fülle 114.10 [15], Klaus Köste 112.75 [18], Erwin Koppe 112.45 [19], Peter Weber 112.35 [21], Philipp Fürst 112.35 [24], Günter Lyhs 111.70 [29]) | 565.10 |
| 4. ITA | (Franco Menichelli 115.15 [5], Luigi Cimnaghi 112.35 [21], Giovanni Carminucci 111.80 [27], Pasquale Carminucci 110.70 [42], Angelo Vicardi 109.40 [63], Bruno Franceschetti 108.70 [75]) | 560.90 |
| 5. POL | (Mikolaj Kubica 113.20 [16], Aleksander Rokosa 111.95 [25], Wilhelm Kubica 111.10 [35], Alfred Kucharczyk 111.05 [37], Jan Jankowicz 110.60 [45], Andrzej Konopka 108.70 [75]) | 559.50 |
| 6. CZE | (Bohumil Mudřik 111.50 [30], Ladislav Pazdera 110.70 [42], Václav Kubička 110.65 [44], Přemysl Krbec 110.60 [45], Karel Klečka 110.35 [52], Pavel Gajdoš 101.75 [106]) | 558.15 |
| 7. USA | (Makoto Sakamoto 112.40 [20], Russell Mitchell 111.20 [32], Ronald Barak 110.95 [39], Larry Banner 110.05 [55], Gregor Weiss 109.90 [59], Arthur Shurlock 109.10 [68]) | 556.95 |
| 8. FIN | (Eino Laiho 111.85 [26], Eugen Ekman 111.15 [34], Raimo Heinonen 110.95 [39], Hannu Rantakara 110.50 [48], Otto Kestola 109.95 [58], Kauko Heikkinen 109.35 [64]) | 556.20 |

**1968 Mexico City** T: 16, N: 16, D: 10.24.

| | | TOTAL PTS. |
|---|---|---|
| 1. JPN | (Sawao Kato 115.90 [1], Akinori Nakayama 115.65 [3], Eizo Kenmotsu 114.90 [4], | 575.90 |

|  |  |  | TOTAL PTS. |
|---|---|---|---|
|  | Takeshi Kato 114.85 [5], Yukio Endo 113.55 [8], Misuo Tsukahara 111.50 [18]) |  |  |
| 2. | SOV | (Mikhail Voronin 115.85 [2], Sergei Diomidov 114.10 [6], Viktor Klimenko 113.95 [7], Valery Karassev 113.25 [10], Viktor Lisitsky 112.60 [14], Valery Ilyinykh 111.90 [15]) | 571.10 |
| 3. | GDR | (Matthias Brehme 112.85 [12], Klaus Köste 111.85 [16], Siegfried Fülle 111.10 [21], Peter Weber 110.15 [26], Gerhard Dietrich 109.70 [34], Günter Beier 108.20 [51]) | 557.15 |
| 4. | CZE | (Václav Kubička 111.30 [19], Jiři Fejtek 111.20 [20], František Bocko 111.00 [22], Bohumil Mudřík 109.95 [28], Miloslav Netusil 109.40 [37], Václav Skoumal 109.30 [38]) | 557.10 |
| 5. | POL | (Wilhelm Kubica 113.15 [11], Mikolaj Kubica 112.80 [13], Sylwester Kubica 109.80 [31], Andrzej Gonera 109.25 [39], Aleksander Rokosa 108.85 [44], Jerzy Kruza 108.15 [53]) | 555.40 |
| 6. | YUG | (Miroslav Cerar 113.30 [9], Janez Brodnik 110.75 [23], Milenko Kersnič 109.85 [30], Milko Vratič 108.90 [42], Damir Anić 105.80 [75], Martin Šrot 104.80 [84]) | 550.75 |
| 7. | USA | (David Thor 110.60 [24], Fred Roethlisberger 109.70 [34], Stephen Hug 109.60 [36], Stephen Cohen 108.75 [46], Sidney Freudenstein 108.00 [57], Kanati Allen 105.45 [80]) | 548.90 |
| 8. | GER | (Heinz Häussler 108.80 [45], Helmut Tepasse 108.35 [50], Heiko Reinemer 108.20 [51], Hermann Hopfner 108.10 [55], Erich Hess 107.75 [60]) | 548.35 |

**1972 Munich** T: 16, N: 16, D: 8.29.

|  |  |  | TOTAL PTS. |
|---|---|---|---|
| 1. | JPN | (Sawao Kato 115.10 [1], Eizo Kenmotsu 114.75 [2], Shigeru Kasamatsu 114.40 [3], Akinori Nakayama 114.25 [4], Mitsuo Tsukahara 112.25 [11], Teruichi Okamura 111.20 [14]) | 571.25 |
| 2. | SOV | (Nikolai Andrianov 113.80 [5], Mikhail Voronin 112.95 [7], Viktor Klimenko 112.65 [8], Edvard Mikhaelian 112.50 [9], Aleksandr Maleev 110.70 [18], Vladimir Shukin 110.20 [20]) | 564.05 |
| 3. | GDR | (Klaus Köste 113.25 [6], Matthias Brehme 112.45 [10], Wolfgang Thüne 112.15 [12], Wolfgang Klotz 111.05 [16], Reinhard Rychly 109.95 [21], Jürgen Paeke 109.35 [28]) | 559.70 |
| 4. | POL | (Mikolaj Kubica 111.25 [13], Andrzej Szajna 111.15 [15], Sylwester Kubica 110.75 [16], Wilhelm Kubica 109.90 [22], Mieczyslaw Strzalka 106.45 [47], Jerzy Kruza 106.35 [49]) | 551.70 |
| 5. | GER | (Eberhard Gienger 109.75 [23], Walter Mössinger 109.70 [24], Günter Spies 108.70 | 546.40 |

|  |  |  | TOTAL PTS. |
|---|---|---|---|
|  | [30], Bernd Effing 107.75 [37], Reinhard Ritter 106.80 [43], Heinz Häussler 106.25 [51]) |  |  |
| 6. | PRK | (Li Song-sob 110.75 [16], Kim Song-yu 109.45 [25], Kim Song-il 108.25 [32], Shin Heung-do 107.75 [37], Ho Yun-hang 106.45 [47], Jo Jong-ryol 106.15 [53]) | 545.05 |
| 7. | ROM | (Petre Mihaiuc 109.30 [29], Dănut Grecu 108.10 [33], Gheorghe Paunescu 107.25 [41], Mircea Gheorghiu 105.00 [62], Nicolae Oprescu 104.60 [66], Constantin Petrescu 103.70 [73]) | 538.90 |
| 8. | HUN | (Imre Molnár 110.55 [19], Zoltán Magyar 108.70 [30], István Kiss 106.65 [45], Béla Herczeg 105.60 [56], Antal Kisteleki 105.30 [61], István Bérczi 104.95 [63]) | 538.60 |

**1976 Montreal** T: 12, N: 12, D: 7.20.

|  |  |  | TOTAL PTS. |
|---|---|---|---|
| 1. | JPN | (Sawao Kato 115.90 [2], Mitsuo Tsukahara 115.75 [3], Hiroshi Kajiyama 115.25 [5], Eizo Kenmotsu 115.15 [6], Hisato Igarashi 113.55 [15], Shun Fujimoto 84.55 [89]) | 576.85 |
| 2. | SOV | (Nikolai Andrianov 116.50 [1], Aleksandr Dityatin 115.15 [6], Gennady Kryssin 114.25 [8], Vladimir Marchenko 113.85 [11], Vladimir Tikhonov 112.15 [23]) | 576.45 |
| 3. | GDR | (Lutz Mack 113.00 [17], Bernd Jäger 112.95 [18], Michael Nikolay 112.90 [19], Roland Brückner 112.00 [24], Wolfgang Klotz 111.95 [25], Rainer Hanschke 111.50 [28]) | 564.65 |
| 4. | HUN | (Zoltán Magyar 114.25 [8], Imre Molnár 113.65 [13], Ferenc Donáth 113.60 [14], Béla Laufer 111.60 [26], Árpád Farkas 109.65 [40], Imre Bánrévi 109.15 [48]) | 564.45 |
| 5. | GER | (Eberhard Gienger 113.30 [16], Volker Rohrwick 112.20 [22], Edgar Jorek 111.25 [29], Werner Steinmetz 110.30 [34], Reinhard Dietze 108.80 [53], Reinhard Ritter 107.75 [61]) | 557.40 |
| 6. | ROM | Dănut Grecu 114.10 [10], Nicolae Oprescu 110.30 [34], Sorin Cepoi 109.95 [36], Ionel Checiches 109.85 [37], Mihai Bors 109.75 [38], Stefan Gall 109.15 [48]) | 557.30 |
| 7. | USA | (Wayne Young 111.55 [27], Kurt Thomas 111.05 [30], Peter Kormann 110.75 [31], Thomas Beach 110.55 [32], Marshall Avener 109.45 [43], Bart Conner 109.35 [46]) | 556.10 |
| 8. | SWI | (Robert Bretscher 112.35 [21], Ueli Bachmann 109.60 [41], Philippe Gaille 109.40 [44], Bernhard Locher 108.30 [55], Peter Rohner 108.25 [56], Armin Vock 81.45 [90]) | 550.60 |

The entire team competition came down to the horizontal bar routine of the Japanese star Mitsuo Tsukahara. A score above 9.5 would give Japan first place, while a score below 9.5 would turn over the gold medal to the U.S.S.R. Tsukahara came through in superb fashion and earned a 9.9 to ensure the fifth straight Japanese team victory.

Another hero of the Japanese gymnastics team was Shun Fujimoto. Fujimoto broke his leg at the knee while finishing his floor exercises routine. Not wanting to cause concern among his coaches or fellow team members during the tense competition with the Soviets, Fujimoto kept his injury to himself and went ahead with his side horse performance, earning a 9.5. Next up were the rings. Fujimoto completed a successful routine (9.7) and then faced a difficult moment—the dismount. Landing on his feet, he compounded his injury by dislocating his knee. The pain was intense: "My whole blood was boiling at my stomach." Fujimoto finally submitted himself to medical inspection and was convinced to withdraw from the remainder of the competition. Asked years later if he would have gone ahead on the rings if he had known how much pain he would experience, Fujimoto replied without hesitation: "No."

**1980 Moscow** T: 9, N: 9, D: 7.22.

| | | | TOTAL PTS. |
|---|---|---|---|
| 1. | SOV | (Aleksandr Dityatin 118.40 [1], Nikolai Andrianov 118.15 [2], Eduard Azaryan 117.40 [4], Aleksandr Tkachyov 117.40 [4], Bogdan Makuts 116.95 [6], Vladimir Markelov 116.40 [9]) | 598.60 |
| 2. | GDR | (Roland Brückner 116.90 [7], Michael Nikolay 116.50 [8], Lutz Hoffmann 115.75 [13], Ralf-Peter Hemmann 115.70 [14], Andreas Bronst 114.85 [15], Lutz Mack 114.00 [20]) | 581.15 |
| 3. | HUN | (Ferenc Donáth 115.90 [11], Zoltán Magyar 115.85 [12], Péter Kovács 114.70 [18], György Guczoghy 113.85 [21], István Vamos 113.10 [27], Zoltán Kelemen 112.70 [33]) | 575.00 |
| 4. | ROM | (Danut Grecu 114.85 [15], Kurt Sziller 114.00 [17], Aurelian Georgeneu 113.75 [22], Sorin Cepoi 113.55 [25], Nicolae Oprescu 112.95 [28], Romulus Bucurciu 112.75 [32]) | 572.30 |
| 5. | BUL | (Stoyan Delchev 117.50 [3], Dancho Yordanov 113.75 [22], Plamen Petkov 113.50 [26], Roumen Petkov 112.50 [34], Ognyan Bangiev 112.05 [39], Yanko Radanchev 111.60 [42]) | 571.55 |
| 6. | CZE | (Jiří Tabák 115.95 [10], Rudolf Babiak 114.10 [19], Dan Zoulík 113.70 [24], Miroslav Kučeřík 112.10 [38], Jan Migdau 111.95 [40], Jozef Konečný 111.35 [43]) | 569.80 |
| 7. | CUB | (Sergio Suarez Aime 112.50 [34], Roberto Leon Richards-Aguiar 112.45 [36], Miguel Arroyo 112.15 [37], Enrique Bravo 111.75 [41], Mario Castro 111.15 [46], Jorge Roche 83.40 [65]) | 563.20 |
| 8. | FRA | (Michel Boutard 112.95 [28], Willi Moy 112.85 [30], Henry Boerio 111.35 [43], Joel Suty 111.25 [45], Yves Boquel 108.65 [59], Marc Touchais 108.10 [62]) | 559.20 |

**1984 Los Angeles** T: 9, N: 9, D: 7.31.

| | | | TOTAL PTS. |
|---|---|---|---|
| 1. | USA | Peter Vidmar 118.55 [1], Bart Conner 118.30 [4], Mitchell Gaylord 118.15 [6], Timothy Daggett 117.85 [8], James Hartung 117.75 [9], Scott Johnson 116.60 [16] | 591.40 |
| 2. | CHN | Li Ning 118.45 [2], Tong Fei 118.40 [3], Xu Zhiqiang 118.15 [6], Lou Yun 117.65 [10], Li Xiaoping 116.85 [12], Li Yuejiu 116.70 [15] | 590.80 |
| 3. | JPN | Koji Gushiken 118.20 [5], Nobuyuki Kajitani 116.95 [11], Noritoshi Hirata 116.80 [13], Shinji Morisue 116.60 [16], Koji Sotomura 116.05 [25], Kyoji Yamawaki 115.65 [29] | 586.70 |
| 4. | GER | Jürgen Geiger 116.75 [14], Daniel Winkler 116.40 [18], Andreas Japtok 116.20 [21], Benno Gross 116.05 [25], Volker Rohrwick 115.45 [32], Bernhard Simmelbauer 115.25 [36] | 582.10 |
| 5 | SWI | Josef Zellweger 116.40 [18], Markus Lehmann 116.30 [20], Daniel Wunderlin 116.10 [22], Marco Piatti 115.95 [27], Bruno Cavelti 114.60 [43], Urs Meister 113.25 [59] | 579.95 |
| 6. | FRA | Jean-Luc Cairon 116.10 [22], Joël Suty 115.50 [31], Philippe Vatuone 115.45 [32], Laurent Barbieri 115.30 [34], Jacques Def 114.85 [41], Michel Boutard 113.25 [59] | 578.25 |
| 7. | CAN | Philippe Chartrand 115.75 [28], Brad Peters 115.15 [37], Warren Long 115.05 [38], Daniel Gaudet 114.60 [43], Frank Nutzenberger 114.30 [49], Allan Reddon 114.05 [51] | 577.15 |
| 8. | KOR | Chang Tae-eun 115.30 [34], Han Chung-sik 115.05 [38], Lee Jeoung-sik 114.70 [42], Ju Young-sam 113.95 [52], Nam Seoung-gu 113.75 [56], Chae Kwang-suk 113.50 [57] | 574.95 |

Competing at Pauley Pavilion on the campus of UCLA, the home arena for three of the six Americans (Vidmar, Gaylord and Daggett), the U.S. team scored an emotional upset victory over the world champion Chinese.

**1988 Seoul** T: 12, N: 12, D: 9.20.

| | | | TOTAL PTS. |
|---|---|---|---|
| 1. | SOV | (Vladimir Artemov 118.95 [1], Valery Lyukin 118.85 [2], Dmitri Bilozerchev 118.45 [3], Sergei Kharkov 118.40 [4], Vladimir Gogoladze 117.70 [6], Vladimir Novikov 117.50 [11]) | 593.35 |
| 2. | GDR | (Sylvio Kroll 117.85 [5], Sven Tippelt 117.60 [9], Ralf Büchner 117.20 [15], Holger Behrendt 116.95 [19], Ulf Hoffman 116.40 [29], Andreas Wecker 116.30 [30]) | 588.45 |

| | | TOTAL PTS. |
|---|---|---|
| 3. JPN | (Yukio Iketani 117.65 [8], Koichi Mizushima 117.45 [12], Daisuke Nishikawa 117.25 [13], Toshiharu Sato 116.65 [26], Hiroyuki Konishi 115.80 [37], Takahiro Yamada 115.40 [43]) | 585.60 |
| 4. CHN | (Wang Chongsheng 117.20 [15], Lou Yun 117.10 [17], Xu Zhiqiang 117.00 [18], Li Chunyang 116.15 [32], Guo Linxian 115.35 [45], Li Ning 114.95 [50]) | 585.25 |
| 5. BUL | (Kalofer Hristozov 117.70 [6], Lubomir Geraskov 116.75 [21], Dimitar Taskov 116.75 [21], Dian Kolev 116.30 [30], Stoycho Gotchev 115.95 [36], Petar Georgiev 115.60 [39]) | 585.10 |
| 6. HUN | (György Guczoghy 117.25 [13], Csaba Fajkusz 116.75 [21], Zsolt Horváth 115.50 [41], Zsolt Borkai 115.40 [43], Jenö Paprika 114.70 [55], Balázs Tóth 77.05 [89]) | 582.30 |
| 7. ROM | (Marius Gherman 117.55 [10], Marius Eugen Toba 116.75 [21], Nicolae Bejenaru 115.30 [46], Adrian Sandu 115.15 [48], Marian Rizan 114.85 [51], Valentin Pintea 105.55 [87]) | 581.70 |
| 8. ITA | (Boris Preti 116.90 [20], Juri Chechi 116.55 [27], Paolo Bucci 115.70 [38], Riccardo Trapella 114.75 [53], Gabriele Sala 114.25 [61], Vittorio Allievi 112.65 [78]) | 579.00 |

# Discontinued Events

## COMBINED COMPETITION (3 EVENTS)

**1904 St. Louis** C: 119, N: 3, D: 7.2.

Events: PB, HB, CLSV

| | | PTS. |
|---|---|---|
| 1. Adolf Spinnler | SWI | 43.49 |
| 2. Julius Lenhart | AUT | 43.00 |
| 3. Wilhelm Weber | GER | 41.60 |
| 4. Hugo Peitsch | GER | 41.56 |
| 5. Otto Wiegand | GER | 40.82 |
| 6. Otto Steffen | USA | 39.53 |

## COMBINED COMPETITION (4 EVENTS)

**1904 St. Louis** C: 10, N: 1, D: 10.29.

Events: PB, HB, SH, LHV

| | | PTS. |
|---|---|---|
| 1. Anton Heida | USA | 161 |
| 2. George Eyser | USA | 152 |
| 3. William Merz | USA | 135 |

| 4. John Duha | USA | — |
|---|---|---|
| 5. Edward Hennig | USA | — |

# ROPE CLIMBING

**1896 Athens** C: 5, N: 4, D: 4.10.
| 1. Nikolaos Andriakopoulos | GRE | 23.4 |
|---|---|---|
| 2. Thomas Xenakis | GRE | — |
| 3. Fritz Hofmann | GER | DNF |
| 4. Viggo Jensen | DEN | DNF |
| 5. Launceston Elliot | GBR | DNF |

**1904 St. Louis** C: ?, N: 1, D: 10.28.
| 1. George Eyser | USA | 7.0 |
|---|---|---|
| 2. Charles Krause | USA | 7.8 |
| 3. Emil Voigt | USA | 9.8 |

**1906 Athens** C: 17, N: 4, D: 4.25.
| 1. Georgios Aliprantis | GRE | 11.4 |
|---|---|---|
| 2. Béla Erody | HUN | 13.8 |
| 3. Konstantinos Kozanitas | GRE | 13.8 |
| 4. G. Georgantopoulos | ITA | 14.0 |
| 5. Nicolaos Aliprantis | GRE | 14.2 |
| 6. K. Pantzopoulos | GRE | 14.8 |
| 7. G. Koemzopoulos | GRE | 15.2 |
| 8. P. Pavlides | GRE | 15.6 |

**1908–1920** not held

**1924 Paris** C: 70, N: 9, D: 7.20.
| 1. Bedřich Supčik | CZE | 7.2 |
|---|---|---|
| 2. Albert Séguin | FRA | 7.4 |
| 3. August Güttinger | SWI | 7.8 |
| 3. Ladislav Vácha | CZE | 7.8 |
| 5. Stane Žilič | YUG | 8.0 |
| 6. Jean Gounot | FRA | 8.4 |
| 6. Arthur Hermann | FRA | 8.4 |
| 6. Frank Kriz | USA | 8.4 |
| 6. Ivan Porenta | YUG | 8.4 |

Supčik was Czechoslovakia's first Olympic champion.

**1928** not held

**1932 Los Angeles** C: 5, N: 2, D: 8.10.
| 1. Raymond Bass | USA | 6.7 |
|---|---|---|
| 2. William Galbraith | USA | 6.8 |
| 3. Thomas Connelly | USA | 7.0 |
| 4. Miklós Péter | HUN | 11.5 |
| 5. Péter Boros | HUN | 11.6 |

# CLUB SWINGING

**1904 St. Louis** C: 9, N: 1, D: 10.28.

| | | PTS. |
|---|---|---|
| 1. Edward Hennig | USA | 13.0 |
| 2. Emil Voigt | USA | 9.0 |
| 3. Ralph Wilson | USA | 5.0 |

Hennig remained active in club swinging and won the American championship as late as 1951, when he was 71 years old.

**1906–1928** not held

**1932 Los Angeles** C: 4, N: 2, D: 8.9.

| | | PTS. |
|---|---|---|
| 1. George Roth | USA | 8.97 |
| 2. Philip Erenberg | USA | 8.90 |
| 3. William Kuhlmeier | USA | 8.63 |
| 4. Francisco Alvarez | MEX | 8.47 |

Unemployed and nearly starving in the midst of the Great Depression, Roth, who once went 15 days without eating, would go to the Olympic Village each day, collect some food, and sneak it home to his wife and baby girl in East Hollywood. He competed with one of his daughter's booties stuffed inside his own shoe for good luck. After receiving his gold medal before 60,000 cheering spectators, Roth walked out of the stadium and hitchhiked home.

# SIDEHORSE VAULT

**1924 Paris** C: 70, N: 9, D: 7.20.

| | | PTS. |
|---|---|---|
| 1. Albert Séguin | FRA | 10.00 |
| 2. François Gangloff | FRA | 9.93 |
| 3. Jean Gounot | FRA | 9.90 |
| 4. Slavko Hlastan | YUG | 9.86 |
| 5. Stane Derganc | YUG | 9.85 |
| 6. Bedřich Supčik | CZE | 9.83 |
| 6. Ladislav Vácha | CZE | 9.83 |
| 8. Eugene Cordonnier (FRA), M. Erang (LUX), Frank Kriz (USA), Robert Pražak (CZE) | | 9.80 |

# TUMBLING

**1932 Los Angeles** C: 4, N: 2, D: 8.10.

| | | PTS. |
|---|---|---|
| 1. Rowland Wolfe | USA | 18.90 |
| 2. Edward Gross | USA | 18.67 |
| 3. William Hermann | USA | 18.37 |
| 4. István Pelle | HUN | 15.43 |

# PARALLEL BARS—TEAM

**1896 Athens** T: 3, N: 2, D: 4.9.

1. GER (Conrad Böcker, Alfred Flatow, Gustav Felix Flatow, Georg Hilmar, Fritz Manteuffel, Karl Neukirch, Richard Röstel, Gustav Schuft, Karl Schumann, Hermann Weingärtner)

2. GRE (Panhellenic Club of Athens—Sotirios Athanasopoulos, Nicolaos Andriakopoulos, Petros Persakis, Thomas Yenakis)

3. GRE (National Gymnastic Club of Athens—Ioannis Chrysaphis, Ioannis Mitropoulos, Dimitrios Loundras, Philippos Karvelas)

# HORIZONTAL BAR—TEAM

**1896 Athens** T: 1, N: 1, D: 4.9.

1. GER (Conrad Böcker, Alfred Flatow, Gustav Felix Flatow, Georg Hilmar, Fritz Manteuffel, Karl Neukirch, Richard Röstel, Gustav Schuft, Karl Schumann, Hermann Weingärtner)

# FREE EXERCISES AND APPARATUS—TEAM

**1912 Stockholm** T: 5, N: 5, D: 7.10.

| | | TOTAL PTS. |
|---|---|---|
| 1. NOR | (Isak Abrahamsen, Hans Beyer, Hartmann Björnson, Alfred Engelsen, Sigurd Jörgensen, Bjarne Johnsen, Knud Knudsen, Alf Lie, Rolf Lie, Tor Lund, Petter Martinsen, Per Mathiesen, Jacob Opdahl, Nils Opdahl, Bjarne Pettersen, Frithjof Saelen, Öistein Schirmer, Georg Selenius, Sigvard Sivertsen, Robert Sjursen, Einar Ström, Gabriel Thorstensen, Thomas Torstensen, Nils Voss) | 114.25 |
| 2. FIN | (Kaarlo Ekholm, Eino Forsström, Ero Hyvarinen, Mikko Hyvärinen, Ilmari Keinänen, Hjalmari Kivenheimo, Karl Fredrick Lund, Arvid Nydman, Eino Saastamoinen, Aarne Salovaara, Heikki Sammallahti, Hannes Sirola, Klaus Uno Suomela, Lauri Tanner, Väino Tiiri, Kaarlo Vähämäki, Kaarlo Vaasama, Tauno Ilmoniemi, Aarne Pelkonen, Ilmari Pernaja) | 109.25 |
| 3. DEN | (Aksel Andersen, Hjalmar Andersen, Halvor Birch, Herman Grimmelmann, Aage Hansen, Arvor Hansen, Christian Hansen, Charles Jensen, Poul Jörgensen, Hjalmar Johansen, Poul Krebs, Viggo Madsen, Lucas Nielsen, Richard Nordström, Oluf Olsen, Steen Olsen, Carl Pedersen, Christian Petersen, Niels Petersen, Christian Svendsen) | 106.25 |
| 4. GER | (Walter Engelmann, Adolf Seebass, Alfred Staats, Hans Roth, Arno Glockauer, Alexander Sperling, Kurt Reichenbach, Rudolf Körner, Erwin Buder, Wilhelm Brülle, Heinrich Pahner, Johannes Reuschle, Walter Jesinghaus, Eberhard Sorge, Karl Richter, Erich Worm, Karl Jordan, Hans Werner) | 84.25 |

|  | | TOTAL PTS. |
|---|---|---|
| 5. LUX | (Nicolas Adam, Charles Behm, André Bordang, Jean-Pierre Frantzen, François Hentges, Pierre Hentges, Michel Hemmerling, Jean-Baptiste Horn, Nicolas Kanivé, Emile Knepper, Nicolas Kummer, Marcel Langsam, Emile Lanners, Jean-Pierre Thommes, François Wagner, Antoine Wehrer, Ferdinand Wirtz, Joseph Zuang, Maurice Palgen) | 81.50 |

## SWEDISH SYSTEM—TEAM

**1912 Stockholm** T: 3, N: 3, D: 7.8.

|  | | TOTAL PTS. |
|---|---|---|
| 1. SWE | (Per Daniel Bertilsson, Carl-Ehrenfried Carlberg, Nils Daniel Gränfelt, Curt Hartzell, Osward Holmberg, Anders Hylander, Axel Janse, Anders Boo Kullberg, Sven Landberg, Per Nilsson, Benkt Rudolf Norelius, Axel Norling, Sven Rosén, Nils Silfverskiöld, Carl Silfverstrand, John Sörensson, Yngve Stiernspetz, Carl Erik Svensson, Karl Johan Svensson [Sarland], Knut Torell, Edvard Wennerholm, Claës Wersäll, David Wiman, Daniel Norling) | 937.46 |
| 2. DEN | (Sören Christensen, Ingvald Eriksen, Georg Falche, Thorkild Garp, Hans Trier Hansen, Johannes Hansen, Rasmus Hansen, Jens Kristian Jensen, Sören Alfred Jensen, Valdemar Jensen, Karl Kirk, Jens Kirkegaard, Olav Kjems, Carl Otto Larsen, Jens Peter Laursen, Marius Lefevre, Poul Sörensen Mark, Ejnar Olsen, Hans Pedersen, Hans Ejlert Pedersen, Aksel Sörensen, Martin Hansen Thau, Sören Thorborg, Kristen Möller Vadgaard, Peder Villemoes, Johannes Larsen Vinther, Olaf Pedersen, Peder Larsen Pedersen) | 898.84 |
| 3. NOR | (Arthur Amundsen, Jorgen Andersen, Trygve Boyesen, Georg Brustad, Conrad Christensen, Oscar Engelstad, Marius Eriksen, Axel Henry Hansen, Petter Hol, Eugen Ingebretsen, Olof Ingebretsen, Olof Jacobsen, Erling Jensen, Thor Jensen, Fritjof Olsen, Oscar Olstad, Edvin Paulsen, Carl Alfred Pedersen, Rolf Roback, Sigurd Smebye, Thorleif Thorkildsen, Paul Pedersen) | 857.21 |

# GYMNASTICS

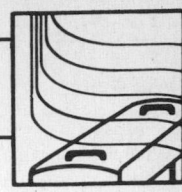

**WOMEN**
All-Around
Side Horse Vault
Asymmetrical (Uneven) Bars
Balance Beam

Floor Exercises
Team Combined Exercises
Rhythmic All-Around
Discontinued Event

# WOMEN

## ALL-AROUND

HV = Horse vault
AB = Asymmetrical (uneven) bars
BB = Balance beam
FE = Floor exercises

**1896–1948** not held

**1952 Helsinki** C. 134, N. 18, D: 7.23.

| | | | HV | | AB | | BB | | FE | | TOTAL PTS. |
|---|---|---|---|---|---|---|---|---|---|---|---|
| 1. | Maria Gorokhovskaya | SOV | 19.19 | (2) | 19.26 | (2) | 19.13 | (2) | 19.20 | (2) | 76.78 |
| 2. | Nina Bocharova | SOV | 19.03 | (6) | 18.99 | (4) | 19.22 | (1) | 18.70 | (10) | 75.94 |
| 3. | Margit Korondi | HUN | 18.40 | (22) | 19.40 | (1) | 19.02 | (3) | 19.00 | (3) | 75.82 |
| 4. | Galina Minaicheva | SOV | 19.16 | (3) | 18.89 | (8) | 18.66 | (10) | 18.96 | (6) | 75.67 |
| 5. | Galina Urbanovich | SOV | 19.10 | (5) | 18.62 | (12) | 18.93 | (5) | 18.99 | (4) | 75.64 |
| 6. | Ágnes Keleti | HUN | 18.10 | (41) | 19.16 | (3) | 18.96 | (4) | 19.36 | (1) | 75.58 |
| 7. | Pelageya Danilova | SOV | 19.02 | (12) | 18.00 | (7) | 18.76 | (9) | 18.60 | (11) | 75.03 |
| 8. | Galina Shamrai | SOV | 18.93 | (7) | 18.39 | (23) | 18.79 | (8) | 18.86 | (8) | 74.97 |

**1956 Melbourne** C. 65, N. 15, D. 12.5.

| | | | HV | | AB | | BB | | FE | | TOTAL PTS. |
|---|---|---|---|---|---|---|---|---|---|---|---|
| 1. | Larissa Latynina | SOV | 18.833 | (1) | 18.833 | (2) | 18.533 | (4) | 18.733 | (1) | 74.933 |
| 2. | Ágnes Keleti | HUN | 18.133 | (23) | 18.966 | (1) | 18.80 | (1) | 18.733 | (1) | 74.633 |
| 3. | Sofia Muratova | SOV | 18.666 | (5) | 18.80 | (3) | 18.433 | (10) | 18.566 | (4) | 74.466 |
| 4. | Elena Leuştean | ROM | 18.633 | (6) | 18.533 | (10) | 18.50 | (6) | 18.70 | (3) | 74.366 |
| 4. | Olga Tass | HUN | 18.733 | (3) | 18.633 | (6) | 18.466 | (7) | 18.533 | (7) | 74.366 |
| 6. | Tamara Manina | SOV | 18.80 | (2) | 18.333 | (16) | 18.633 | (2) | 18.466 | (9) | 74.233 |
| 7. | Eva Bosáková | CZE | 18.166 | (22) | 18.733 | (4) | 18.633 | (2) | 18.566 | (4) | 74.10 |
| 8. | Helena Rakoczy | POL | 18.50 | (7) | 18.70 | (5) | 18.133 | (16) | 18.366 | (14) | 73.70 |

The 1956 competition was dominated by 35-year-old Ágnes Keleti and 21-year-old Larissa Latynina. Keleti captured gold medals on three of the four apparatuses, but a lapse on the vault lost her the All-Around title to Latynina, a Ukrainian from Kherson. In 1952 and 1956 Keleti won a total of ten Olympic medals: five gold, three silver, and two bronze. After the games she decided not to return to Hungary. Instead she stayed in Australia and eventually settled in Israel.

**1960 Rome** C: 124, N: 27, D: 9.8.

| | | HV | | AB | | BB | | FE | | TOTAL PTS. |
|---|---|---|---|---|---|---|---|---|---|---|
| 1. Larissa Latynina | SOV | 18.966 | (3) | 19.433 | (2) | 19.066 | (3) | 19.566 | (1) | 77.031 |
| 2. Sofia Muratova | SOV | 19.032 | (2) | 19.299 | (3) | 19.132 | (2) | 19.233 | (4) | 76.696 |
| 3. Polina Astakhova | SOV | 18.766 | (4) | 19.633 | (1) | 18.233 | (28) | 19.532 | (2) | 76.164 |
| 4. Margarita Nikolayeva | SOV | 19.10 | (1) | 18.799 | (20) | 18.966 | (4) | 18.966 | (15) | 75.831 |
| 5. Sonia Iovan | ROM | 18.732 | (6) | 19.266 | (4) | 18.60 | (11) | 19.199 | (5) | 75.797 |
| 6. Keiko Ikeda (Tanaka) | JPN | 18.432 | (18) | 19.266 | (4) | 18.932 | (5) | 19.066 | (12) | 75.696 |
| 7. Lidiya Ivanova | SOV | 18.566 | (8) | 19.053 | (7) | 18.699 | (8) | 19.133 | (7) | 75.431 |
| 8. Vera Čáslavská | CZE | 18.699 | (7) | 18.733 | (21) | 18.766 | (6) | 19.10 | (9) | 75.298 |

**1964 Tokyo** C: 86, N: 24, D: 10.21.

| | | HV | | AB | | BB | | FE | | TOTAL PTS. |
|---|---|---|---|---|---|---|---|---|---|---|
| 1. Vera Čáslavská | CZE | 19.50 | (1) | 19.432 | (1) | 19.366 | (1) | 19.266 | (3) | 77.564 |
| 2. Larissa Latynina | SOV | 19.166 | (5) | 19.133 | (4) | 19.233 | (3) | 19.466 | (1) | 76.998 |
| 3. Polina Astakhova | SOV | 19.032 | (7) | 19.333 | (2) | 19.20 | (5) | 19.40 | (2) | 76.965 |
| 4. Birgit Radochla | GDR | 19.366 | (2) | 18.933 | (13) | 18.933 | (9) | 19.199 | (5) | 76.431 |
| 5. Hana Ružičková | CZE | 18.866 | (18) | 19.033 | (7) | 19.232 | (4) | 18.966 | (10) | 76.097 |
| 6. Keiko Ikeda (Tanaka) | JPN | 18.999 | (9) | 18.766 | (16) | 19.166 | (6) | 19.10 | (7) | 76.031 |
| 7. Toshiko Aihara (Shirasu) | JPN | 19.233 | (3) | 19.099 | (5) | 18.599 | (29) | 19.066 | (8) | 75.997 |
| 8. Yelena Volchetskaya | SOV | 19.233 | (3) | 18.633 | (24) | 18.966 | (7) | 18.933 | (13) | 75.765 |

Latynina collected six more Olympic medals to bring her career total to an unprecedented 18: nine gold, five silver, and four bronze. But in Tokyo she lost the All-Around title to a new star, Vera Čáslavská, a 22-year-old secretary from Prague.

**1968 Mexico City** C: 101, N: 24, D: 10.23.

| | | HV | | AB | | BB | | FE | | TOTAL PTS. |
|---|---|---|---|---|---|---|---|---|---|---|
| 1. Vera Čáslavská | CZE | 19.75 | (1) | 19.50 | (1) | 19.45 | (2) | 19.55 | (2) | 78.25 |
| 2. Zinaida Voronina | SOV | 19.40 | (5) | 19.25 | (4) | 18.80 | (15) | 19.40 | (4) | 76.85 |
| 3. Natalya Kuchinskaya | SOV | 19.45 | (3) | 18.10 | (37) | 19.60 | (15) | 19.60 | (1) | 76.75 |
| 4. Larissa Petrik | SOV | 19.20 | (8) | 18.95 | (11) | 19.00 | (5) | 19.55 | (2) | 76.70 |
| 4. Erika Zuchold | GDR | 19.65 | (2) | 19.05 | (6) | 19.00 | (5) | 19.00 | (8) | 76.70 |
| 6. Karin Janz | GDR | 19.20 | (8) | 19.30 | (2) | 19.05 | (4) | 19.00 | (8) | 76.55 |
| 7. Olga Karasseva | SOV | 19.15 | (10) | 19.00 | (7) | 18.70 | (18) | 19.15 | (5) | 76.00 |
| 7. Bohumila Řimnácová | CZE | 18.70 | (24) | 19.30 | (2) | 18.85 | (10) | 19.15 | (5) | 76.00 |

The undisputed heroine of the Mexico City Olympics was defending All-Around champion Vera Čáslavská. In April 1968, Čáslavská had signed the "Manifesto of 2000 Words," which rejected Soviet involvement in Czechoslovakia. On August 21, she was at a training camp in Moravia when Soviet tanks rolled into Prague. Warned by friends that she was in danger of arrest, Čáslavská fled to the small town of Šumperk in the Jeseníky Mountains. With the Olympics only two months away, Čáslavská was in hiding, keeping in shape by swinging from tree limbs and practicing her floor exercise in a meadow. After three weeks, the government consented to let her join the rest of the Czechoslovak team in Mexico.

After one of Čáslavská's performances on the balance beam received a 9.6, the audience spent ten minutes booing, howling, and chanting "Ver-a, Ver-a," until finally her mark was upped to 9.8. The last performer in the final event, Čáslavská thrilled her admirers by performing her floor exercise to the tune of "The Mexican Hat Dance." She eventually earned four gold medals and two silver to add to the three gold and two silver she had won four years earlier in Tokyo. In the floor exercises she shared first place with Larissa Petrik of the Soviet Union, which meant that the two women stood together on the top platform at the medal ceremony and listened first to Czechoslovakia's national anthem and then to the U.S.S.R.'s. Political observers noted that Čáslavská bowed her head and turned away during the playing of the Soviet anthem. Twenty-four hours later Čáslavská topped off her week by marrying Czechoslovak 1500-meter champion Josef Odlozil. After a civil ceremony at the Czechoslovakian ambassador's house, the happy couple pushed their way through a mob of 10,000 people to get to the altar of the Roman Catholic church in Xocalo

Square. After the fall of the Communist government in 1989, Čáslavská was appointed president of Czechoslovakia's national Olympic committee.

**1972 Munich** C: 118, N: 23, D: 10.30.

| | | HV | | AB | | BB | | FE | | TOTAL PTS. |
|---|---|---|---|---|---|---|---|---|---|---|
| 1. Lyudmila Tourischeva | SOV | 19.30 | (1) | 19.275 | (3) | 18.80 | (5) | 19.65 | (1) | 77.025 |
| 2. Karin Janz | GDR | 19.275 | (2) | 19.475 | (1) | 18.825 | (4) | 19.30 | (3) | 76.875 |
| 3. Tamara Lazakovitch | SOV | 19.00 | (6) | 19.225 | (4) | 19.325 | (1) | 19.30 | (3) | 76.85 |
| 4. Erika Zuchold | GDR | 19.275 | (2) | 19.30 | (2) | 18.80 | (5) | 19.075 | (6) | 76.45 |
| 5. Liubov Burda | SOV | 19.075 | (5) | 18.875 | (8) | 18.675 | (8) | 19.15 | (5) | 75.775 |
| 6. Angelika Hellmann | GDR | 18.925 | (7) | 19.15 | (5) | 18.425 | (14) | 19.05 | (7) | 75.55 |
| 7. Olga Korbut | SOV | 19.175 | (4) | 17.15 | (35) | 19.30 | (2) | 19.475 | (2) | 75.10 |
| 8. Elvira Saadi | SOV | 18.80 | (9) | 18.70 | (15) | 18.625 | (10) | 18.95 | (9) | 75.075 |

Vera Čáslavská had played a major role in popularizing women's gymnastics, but the real turning point came at the 1972 Munich Olympics. The All-Around championship was won by 19-year-old world champion Lyudmila Tourischeva, and the silver medal went to Karin Janz of Berlin, who also took first place on the horse vault and the uneven parallel bars. But it was neither of these capable young women who focused the attention of the world on gymnastics. Instead it was the seventh-place finisher, a 4-foot 11-inch, 85-pound 17-year-old from Grodno in Byelorussia—Olga Korbut.

Korbut was trained by the eccentric Renald Knysh, who kept a card file on all the young married couples in Grodno, particularly those whom he thought might produce future gymnasts. Olga qualified for the Olympics as an alternate and was allowed to compete only after a teammate was injured. During the team competition she caught the public's eye with a spectacular routine on the uneven parallel bars. By the end of the day it looked as if Olga had a good chance of pulling an upset and depriving Tourischeva of the All-Around championship. But the next day disaster struck. The crowd watched in silence as she started her performance on the uneven bars. She scuffed her feet on the mat as she mounted, then slipped off the bars during a later move; finally, she missed a simple kip to remount. The judges gave her a 7.5, and she was effectively eliminated from the race for All-Around champion. She returned to her seat to weep with disappointment.

Twenty hours later Olga Korbut was back in the arena to compete for the championships on the four individual apparatuses. With hundreds of millions of people all over the world watching, Olga regained her form, finished second to Karin Janz on the uneven parallel bars, and won the gold medal for both the balance beam and the floor exercises. Even in the United States, with its widespread antipathy to the U.S.S.R, little Olga Korbut's dramatic cycle of success, failure, and success captured the national imagination. Korbut never did beat Tourischeva, though, and it must have been confusing, at the very least, to the Soviet champion to realize that no matter how successful she was, she could never achieve the popularity of Olga Korbut.

**1976 Montreal** C: 86, N: 18, D: 7.19.

| | | HV | | AB | | BB | | FE | | TOTAL PTS. |
|---|---|---|---|---|---|---|---|---|---|---|
| 1. Nadia Comaneci | ROM | 19.625 | (4) | 20.00 | (1) | 19.95 | (1) | 19.70 | (3) | 79.275 |
| 2. Nelli Kim | SOV | 19.85 | (1) | 19.725 | (2) | 19.30 | (5) | 19.80 | (2) | 78.675 |
| 3. Lyudmila Tourischeva | SOV | 19.75 | (2) | 19.575 | (9) | 19.475 | (3) | 19.825 | (1) | 78.625 |
| 4. Teodora Ungureanu | ROM | 19.425 | (7) | 19.80 | (2) | 19.70 | (2) | 19.45 | (5) | 78.375 |
| 5. Olga Korbut | SOV | 19.525 | (6) | 19.80 | (2) | 19.325 | (4) | 19.375 | (6) | 78.025 |
| 6. Gitta Escher | GDR | 19.65 | (3) | 19.625 | (8) | 19.125 | (7) | 19.35 | (8) | 77.75 |
| 7. Márta Egervári | HUN | 19.60 | (5) | 19.775 | (4) | 18.725 | (10) | 19.225 | (9) | 77.325 |
| 8. Marion Kische | GDR | 19.325 | (10) | 19.70 | (6) | 18.55 | (14) | 19.375 | (6) | 76.95 |

Soviet women's gymnastics went through a period of turmoil and crisis between 1972 and 1976. When a Soviet team made an exhibition tour of the United States, the leader of the group was Lyudmila Tourischeva and the highlighted performer was their up-and-coming star Nelli Kim. But Americans showed little interest in Tourischeva and Kim; instead they turned out by the thousands to see Olga Korbut, the Munchkin of Munich.

It didn't take long for Olga to realize that huge profits were being made on her popularity, and she became more demanding of rewards for herself. When she insisted on going shopping for gifts for her family, Soviet officials were forced to allow it.

Back home, however, where heroes were measured by the number of medals they won and by their willingness to follow orders and be team players, Olga Korbut had become a thorn in the side of the Soviet bureaucracy. The situation was also hard on Tourischeva, who had always toed the party line and yet was forced to play second fiddle to an inferior gymnast. In his book *The Big Red Machine,* Yuri Brodkin tells of the shock and betrayal experienced by Tourischeva when, two days before the opening of the Montreal Olympics, the Soviet Training Council decided to remove her from her role of team captain and give the designation to Olga Korbut instead.

However the real threat to the competitive success of the Soviet team came not from internal dissension, but from a 4-foot 11-inch Romanian named Nadia Comaneci. Born in Onesti, Moldavia, Nadia had been trained as a gymnast since the age of 6. In 1975 she dethroned five-time European champion Tourischeva. At Montreal she was considered a slight favorite to take the All-Around championship even though she was only 14 years old. During the team competition she made Olympic history by receiving the first perfect scores of ten for her performances on the uneven bars and the balance beam. Before the Olympics were over, Nadia had been awarded seven 10s, while Nelli Kim had earned two perfect scores for her vault and floor exercise. Despite their superb performances, Korbut and Tourischeva were left with tears of disappointment. Tourischeva, in fact, won four medals, to bring her Olympic totals to four gold, two silver, and three bronze.

Nadia Comaneci didn't have the charisma of Olga Korbut, but she was an incredible athlete who was absolutely unafraid of dangerous moves and seemingly oblivious to the millions of people watching her. The most difficult part of the Olympics for Nadia were the obligatory press conferences. Many journalists seemed to forget her age. When one asked what her greatest wish was, she replied, "I want to go home." When another asked if she had plans for retirement, Nadia reminded him, "I'm only 14."

In an attempt to lessen the dominance of the nations strongest in gymnastics, a ruling had been passed prior to the Olympics that only three gymnasts from each country could compete in the final round of 36. The absurdity of this decision was shown when Elvira Saadi, who had achieved the seventh highest score during the individual competitions, was eliminated because she was the fourth-best Soviet performer, while Monique Bolleboom of Holland was allowed to continue even though she ranked 62nd out of 86. Not surprisingly, Bolleboom finished last in the final round.

**1980 Moscow** C: 62, N: 16, D: 7.24.

| | | HV | | AB | | BB | | FE | | TOTAL PTS. |
|---|---|---|---|---|---|---|---|---|---|---|
| 1. Yelena Davydova | SOV | 19.80 | (1) | 19.80 | (3) | 19.70 | (5) | 19.85 | (3) | 79.15 |
| 2. Nadia Comaneci | ROM | 19.675 | (4) | 19.725 | (6) | 19.80 | (1) | 19.875 | (1) | 79.075 |
| 2. Maxi Gnauck | GDR | 19.625 | (5) | 19.925 | (1) | 19.65 | (6) | 19.875 | (1) | 79.075 |
| 4. Natalya Shaposhnikova | SOV | 19.80 | (1) | 19.775 | (4) | 19.775 | (3) | 19.675 | (6) | 79.025 |
| 5. Nelli Kim | SOV | 19.525 | (10) | 19.725 | (6) | 19.80 | (1) | 19.375 | (13) | 78.425 |
| 6. Emilia Eberle | ROM | 19.40 | (14) | 19.85 | (2) | 19.30 | (11) | 19.85 | (3) | 78.40 |
| 7. Rodica Dunka | ROM | 19.60 | (6) | 19.35 | (14) | 19.75 | (4) | 19.65 | (7) | 78.35 |
| 8. Steffi Kräker | GDR | 19.725 | (3) | 19.775 | (4) | 19.175 | (12) | 19.525 | (10) | 78.20 |

The favorite in 1980 was defending world champion Yelena Mukhina of the U.S.S.R. However, sixteen days before the opening of the Moscow Olympics, Mukhina was practicing her floor exercise when she missed a one-and-a-half-turn salto with a 540-degree twist and broke her spine. Mukhina was paralyzed from the neck down. She was unable even to speak for six months.

In Mukhina's absence the contest for All-Around champion came down to the final apparatus. If Nadia Comaneci could score 9.95 on the balance beam, she would win outright. If she scored 9.9 she would share the gold medal with a surprising 18-year-old: 4-foot 10-inch Yelena Davydova. Since Nadia had previously been awarded a 9.9 and a 10 on the balance beam, it was quite possible that she could earn the higher mark. With the arena in complete silence, she went through her routine magnificently with only the slightest flaw following a forward flip with a half-twist. It seemed as if she had made it. But her score was not forthcoming. For 28 minutes the judges argued. Finally Nadia's score was flashed on the computer: 9.85, thanks to 9.8s awarded by the judges from Poland and the U.S.S.R. The next day Nadia took first place in the beam and the floor exercise events, giving her an Olympic total of five gold medals, three silver, and one bronze. Nineteen-eighty marked the first time that Soviet gymnasts failed to earn at least two of the medals in the All-Around event.

On the night of November 27, 1989, Nadia Comaneci, the youngest-ever recipient of the Hero of Socialist Labor Award, defected from Romania, slipping across the border to Hungary on foot. After contacting the U.S. embassy in Vienna, she made her way to America accompanied by Romanian émigré Constantin Panait, a Florida roofer. Her long-time fans in the West were thrilled by Comaneci's escape to freedom, but her relationship with her public quickly soured when it was revealed that she planned to live with Panait, even though he was married and the father of four children. Comaneci and Panait were soon separated, and she claimed he had held her hostage for three months. Eventually she settled in Canada.

**1984 Los Angeles** C: 65, N: 16, D: 8.3.

|  |  | HV |  | AB |  | BB |  | FE |  | TOTAL PTS. |
|---|---|---|---|---|---|---|---|---|---|---|
| 1. | Mary Lou Retton | USA | 19.95 | (1) | 19.7 | (4) | 19.6 | (3) | 19.925 | (1) | 79.175 |
| 2. | Ecaterina Szabó | ROM | 19.85 | (2) | 19.5 | (8) | 19.85 | (1) | 19.925 | (1) | 79.125 |
| 3. | Simona Pauca | ROM | 19.625 | (6) | 19.575 | (6) | 19.85 | (1) | 19.625 | (5) | 78.675 |
| 4. | Julianne McNamara | USA | 19.725 | (3) | 19.95 | (1) | 19.075 | (13) | 19.65 | (4) | 78.4 |
| 5. | Laura Cutina | ROM | 19.7 | (4) | 19.725 | (3) | 19.125 | (11) | 19.75 | (3) | 78.3 |
| 6. | Ma Yanhong | CHN | 19.3 | (15) | 19.95 | (1) | 19.55 | (4) | 19.05 | (13) | 77.85 |
| 7. | Zhou Ping | CHN | 19.525 | (7) | 19.4 | (9) | 19.175 | (10) | 19.375 | (8) | 77.775 |
| 8. | Chen Yongyan | CHN | 19.525 | (7) | 19.275 | (11) | 19.5 | (5) | 19.425 | (7) | 77.725 |

Ever since Olga Korbut had melted American hearts in 1972, U.S. sports fans had wondered when a home-grown female gymnastics star would emerge. Considering that no American woman had ever won an individual Olympics gymnastics medal, the prospects did not look bright. However, the Soviet boycott of 1984 opened the door—and in walked a 16-year-old from Fairmont, West Virginia, named Mary Lou Retton. At 4 feet 8¾ inches and weighing 94 pounds, the powerful Italian-American represented a new breed of female gymnast—more muscular and athletic.

Retton had never taken part in a major international tournament before the Olympics, having missed the 1983 world championships because of a wrist injury. She almost missed the Olympics as well when she suffered a knee injury less than six weeks before the Games began. Torn cartilage removed during arthroscopic surgery saved the day.

In Los Angeles the battle for the all-around gold medal developed into a tight contest between Retton and the Romanian champion Kati Szabó. With two rotations to go, Szabó led by .15 of a point. But Retton rose to the occasion, earning 10s for the floor exercise and the vault, and ensuring her place in sports history books, as well as in the pantheon of U.S. cultural heroes. Aspiring gymnasts should take heart from the story of Retton's first competition when she was still a little girl. Like so many little girls around the world, Mary Lou watched Nadia Comaneci score her history-making 10s in 1976. Retton noticed that the scoreboard, unprepared for Comaneci's perfection, had registered "1.0" rather than "10.0." After performing on the first apparatus in her first meet (the uneven bars), 8-year-old Mary Lou Retton jumped with joy when the scoreboard flashed "1.0." Alas, it really was a 1.0. However, she refused to give up on gymnastics until her 1.0s turned to genuine 10.0s.

**1988 Seoul** C: 90, N: 23, D: 9.23.

|  |  | HV |  | AB |  | BB |  | FE |  | TOTAL PTS. |
|---|---|---|---|---|---|---|---|---|---|---|
| 1. | Yelena Shushunova | SOV | 20.0 | (1) | 19.862 | (4) | 19.85 | (1) | 19.95 | (1) | 79.662 |
| 2. | Daniela Silivas | ROM | 19.85 | (3) | 20.0 | (1) | 19.837 | (2) | 19.95 | (1) | 79.637 |
| 3. | Svetlana Boginskaya | SOV | 19.887 | (2) | 19.862 | (4) | 19.837 | (2) | 19.812 | (4) | 79.4 |
| 4. | Gabriela Potorac | ROM | 19.607 | (7) | 19.737 | (7) | 19.937 | (2) | 19.775 | (7) | 79.037 |
| 5. | Natalya Lashchenova | SOV | 19.725 | (5) | 19.662 | (14) | 19.687 | (6) | 19.8 | (5) | 78.875 |
| 6. | Aurelia Dobre | ROM | 19.612 | (11) | 19.762 | (6) | 19.787 | (5) | 19.65 | (14) | 78.812 |
| 7. | Dörte Thümmler | GDR | 19.7 | (6) | 19.925 | (2) | 19.325 | (19) | 19.85 | (3) | 78.8 |
| 8. | Dagmar Kersten | GDR | 19.8 | (4) | 19.887 | (3) | 19.325 | (19) | 19.762 | (9) | 78.775 |

With two apparatuses left in the final, Silivas led Shushunova by the slim margin of .025 of a point. The deficiencies in gymnastics judging quickly became apparent. Shushunova performed a flawless floor exercise and was awarded a perfect 10.0. Silivas followed her onto the mat and gave an even better performance. But because Shushunova had already received the highest possible score, Silivas had to settle for a tie despite her superiority. This meant that the competition came down to the final apparatus: the vault. Silivas hopped slightly on landing. Although Soviet judge Nelli Kim gave her a scandalously low 9.8, Silivas' total score was 9.95. Still, this left the door open for Shushunova. Like Mary Lou Retton four years earlier, if she could achieve a 10.0, she would win the All-Around title. Shushunova's vault, a full-twisting Yurchenko, was high and perfect and the gold was hers. However, like Los Angeles silver-medalist Kati Szabó, Silivas came back two days later to win three of the four apparatus finals, while Shushunova, like Retton, won none.

# SIDE HORSE VAULT

**1896–1948** not held

**1952 Helsinki** C: 134, N: 18, D: 7.23.

| | | PTS. |
|---|---|---|
| 1. Yekaterina Kalinchuk | SOV | 19.20 |
| 2. Maria Gorokhovskaya | SOV | 19.19 |
| 3. Galina Minaicheva | SOV | 19.16 |
| 4. Medeya Dschugeli | SOV | 19.13 |
| 5. Galina Urbanovich | SOV | 19.10 |
| 6. Nina Bocharova | SOV | 19.03 |
| 7. Karin Lindberg | SWE | 18.79 |
| 7. Helena Rakoczy | POL | 18.79 |

**1956 Melbourne** C: 65, N: 15, D: 12.5.

| | | PTS. |
|---|---|---|
| 1. Larissa Latynina | SOV | 18.833 |
| 2. Tamara Manina | SOV | 18.80 |
| 3. Ann-Sofi Colling-Pettersson | SWE | 18.733 |
| 3. Olga Tass | HUN | 18.733 |
| 5. Sofia Muratova | SOV | 18.666 |
| 6. Elena Leuştean | ROM | 18.633 |
| 7. Natalia Kot | POL | 18.50 |
| 7. Helena Rakoczy | POL | 18.50 |

**1960 Rome** C: 124, N: 27, D: 9.9.

| | | PTS. |
|---|---|---|
| 1. Margarita Nikolayeva | SOV | 19.316 |
| 2. Sofia Muratova | SOV | 19.049 |
| 3. Larissa Latynina | SOV | 19.016 |
| 4. Adolfina Tačová | CZE | 18.783 |
| 5. Sonia Iovan | ROM | 18.766 |
| 6. Polina Astakhova | SOV | 18.716 |

**1964 Tokyo** C: 82, N: 23, D: 10.22.

| | | PTS. |
|---|---|---|
| 1. Vera Čáslavská | CZE | 19.483 |
| 2. Larissa Latynina | SOV | 19.283 |
| 2. Birgit Radochla | GDR | 19.283 |
| 4. Toshiko Aihara (Shirasu) | JPN | 19.282 |
| 5. Yelena Volchetskaya | SOV | 19.149 |
| 6. Ute Starke | GDR | 19.116 |

**1968 Mexico City** C: 101, N: 24, D: 10.25.

| | | PTS. |
|---|---|---|
| 1. Vera Čáslavská | CZE | 19.775 |
| 2. Erika Zuchold | GDR | 19.625 |
| 3. Zinaida Voronina | SOV | 19.50 |
| 4. Maria Krajčiróvá | CZE | 19.475 |
| 5. Natalya Kutschinskaya | SOV | 19.375 |
| 6. Miroslava Skleničková | CZE | 19.325 |

**1972 Munich** C: 118, N: 23, D: 8.31.

| | | PTS. |
|---|---|---|
| 1. Karin Janz | GDR | 19.525 |
| 2. Erika Zuchold | GDR | 19.275 |
| 3. Lyudmila Tourischeva | SOV | 19.25 |
| 4. Lyubov Burda | SOV | 19.225 |
| 5. Olga Korbut | SOV | 19.175 |
| 6. Tamara Lazakovitch | SOV | 19.05 |

**1976 Montreal** C: 86, N: 18, D: 7.22.

| | | PTS. |
|---|---|---|
| 1. Nelli Kim | SOV | 19.80 |
| 2. Carola Dombeck | GDR | 19.65 |
| 2. Lyudmila Tourischeva | SOV | 19.65 |
| 4. Nadia Comaneci | ROM | 19.625 |
| 5. Gitta Escher | GDR | 19.55 |
| 6. Márta Egervári | HUN | 19.45 |

**1980 Moscow** C: 62, N: 16, D: 7.25.

| | | PTS. |
|---|---|---|
| 1. Natalya Shaposhnikova | SOV | 19.725 |
| 2. Steffi Kräker | GDR | 19.675 |
| 3. Melita Rühn | ROM | 19.65 |
| 4. Yelena Davydova | SOV | 19.575 |
| 5. Nadia Comaneci | ROM | 19.35 |
| 6. Maxi Gnauck | GDR | 19.30 |

**1984 Los Angeles** C: 65, N: 16, D: 8.5.

| | | PTS. |
|---|---|---|
| 1. Ecaterina Szabó | ROM | 19.875 |
| 2. Mary Lou Retton | USA | 19.85 |
| 3. Lavinia Agache | ROM | 19.75 |
| 4. Tracee Talavera | USA | 19.70 |
| 5. Zhou Ping | CHN | 19.50 |
| 6. Kelly Brown | CAN | 19.425 |
| 6. Brigitta Lehmann | GER | 19.425 |
| 8. Chen Yongyan | CHN | 19.30 |

Two nights after finishing second to Mary Lou Retton in the all-around competition, Kati Szabó reestablished her dominance by winning three of the four apparatus finals. Szabó went home with 4 gold medals and 1 silver, a better haul than even Carl Lewis.

**1988 Seoul** C: 90, N: 23, D: 9.25.

| | | PTS. |
|---|---|---|
| 1. Svetlana Boginskaya | SOV | 19.905 |
| 2. Gabriela Potorac | ROM | 19.83 |
| 3. Daniela Silivas | ROM | 19.818 |
| 4. Boriana Stoyanova | BUL | 19.78 |
| 5. Brandy Johnson | USA | 19.774 |
| 6. Dagmar Kersten | GDR | 19.756 |
| 7. Wang Xiaoyan | CHN | 19.73 |
| 8. Yelena Shushunova | SOV | 19.712 |

Shushunova, who had dominated the event for three years, led after the preliminaries with a score of 10.0. However she muffed both vaults in the final, finishing her second attempt by landing on her knees.

## ASYMMETRICAL (UNEVEN) BARS

**1896–1948** not held

**1952 Helsinki** C: 134, N: 18, D: 7.23.

| | | PTS. |
|---|---|---|
| 1. Margit Korondi | HUN | 19.40 |
| 2. Maria Gorokhovskaya | SOV | 19.26 |
| 3. Ágnes Keleti | HUN | 19.16 |

| | | | |
|---|---|---|---|
| 4. | Nina Bocharova | SOV | 18.99 |
| 4. | Pelageya Danilova | SOV | 18.99 |
| 6. | Edit Perényi-Weckinger | HUN | 18.96 |
| 7. | Galina Shamrai | SOV | 18.93 |
| 8. | Galina Minaicheva | SOV | 18.89 |

**1956 Melbourne** C: 65, N: 15, D: 12.5.

| | | | PTS. |
|---|---|---|---|
| 1. | Ágnes Keleti | HUN | 18.966 |
| 2. | Larissa Latynina | SOV | 18.833 |
| 3. | Sofia Muratova | SOV | 18.80 |
| 4. | Eva Bosáková | CZE | 18.733 |
| 5. | Helena Rakoczy | POL | 18.70 |
| 6. | Aliz Kertész | HUN | 18.633 |
| 6. | Olga Tass | HUN | 18.633 |
| 8. | Natalia Kot | POL | 18.60 |

**1960 Rome** C: 124, N: 27, D: 9.9.

| | | | PTS. |
|---|---|---|---|
| 1. | Polina Astakhova | SOV | 19.616 |
| 2. | Larissa Latynina | SOV | 19.416 |
| 3. | Tamara Lyukhina | SOV | 19.399 |
| 4. | Sofia Muratova | SOV | 19.382 |
| 5. | Keiko Ikeda (Tanaka) | JPN | 19.333 |
| 6. | Sonia Iovan | ROM | 19.099 |

The audience was so upset by the low scoring of Ikeda's final routine that they booed for ten minutes until Astakhova stepped up for her turn.

**1964 Tokyo** C: 82, N: 23, D: 10.22.

| | | | PTS. |
|---|---|---|---|
| 1. | Polina Astakhova | SOV | 19.332 |
| 2. | Katalin Makray | HUN | 19.216 |
| 3. | Larissa Latynina | SOV | 19.199 |
| 4. | Toshiko Aihara (Shirasu) | JPN | 18.782 |
| 5. | Vera Čáslavská | CZE | 18.416 |
| 6. | Tamara Zamotailova (Lyukhina) | SOV | 17.833 |

**1968 Mexico City** C: 101, N: 24, D: 10.25

| | | | PTS. |
|---|---|---|---|
| 1. | Vera Čáslavská | CZE | 19.65 |
| 2. | Karin Janz | GDR | 19.50 |
| 3. | Zinaida Voronina | SOV | 19.425 |
| 4. | Bohumila Řimnácová | CZE | 19.35 |
| 5. | Erika Zuchold | GDR | 19.325 |
| 6. | Miroslava Skleničková | CZE | 18.20 |

**1972 Munich** C: 118, N: 23, D: 8.31.

| | | | PTS. |
|---|---|---|---|
| 1. | Karin Janz | GDR | 19.675 |
| 2. | Olga Korbut | SOV | 19.45 |
| 2. | Erika Zuchold | GDR | 19.45 |
| 4. | Lyudmila Tourischeva | SOV | 19.425 |
| 5. | Ilona Békési | HUN | 19.275 |
| 6. | Angelika Hellmann | GDR | 19.20 |

**1976 Montreal** C: 86, N: 18, D: 7.22.

| | | | PTS. |
|---|---|---|---|
| 1. | Nadia Comaneci | ROM | 20.00 |
| 2. | Teodora Ungureanu | ROM | 19.80 |
| 3. | Márta Egervári | HUN | 19.775 |
| 4. | Marion Kische | GDR | 19.75 |
| 5. | Olga Korbut | SOV | 19.30 |
| 6. | Nelli Kim | SOV | 19.225 |

**1980 Moscow** C: 62, N: 16, D: 7.25.

| | | | PTS. |
|---|---|---|---|
| 1. | Maxi Gnauck | GDR | 19.875 |
| 2. | Emilia Eberle | ROM | 19.85 |
| 3. | Maria Filatova | SOV | 19.775 |
| 3. | Steffi Kräker | GDR | 19.775 |
| 3. | Melita Rühn | ROM | 19.775 |
| 6. | Nelli Kim | SOV | 19.725 |

**1984 Los Angeles** C: 65, N: 16, D: 8.5.

| | | | PTS. |
|---|---|---|---|
| 1. | Ma Yanhong | CHN | 19.95 |
| 1. | Julianne McNamara | USA | 19.95 |
| 3. | Mary Lou Retton | USA | 19.80 |
| 4. | Miháela Stanulet | ROM | 19.65 |
| 5. | Romi Kessler | SWI | 19.425 |
| 6. | Zhou Ping | CHN | 19.35 |
| 7. | Noriko Mochizuki | JPN | 19.325 |
| 8. | Lavinia Agache | ROM | 19.15 |

**1988 Seoul** C: 90, N: 23, D: 9.25.

| | | | PTS. |
|---|---|---|---|
| 1. | Daniela Silivas | ROM | 20.00 |
| 2. | Dagmar Kersten | GDR | 19.987 |
| 3. | Yelena Shushunova | SOV | 19.962 |
| 4. | Dörte Thümmler | GDR | 19.90 |
| 5. | Svetlana Boginskaya | SOV | 19.899 |
| 6. | Iveta Poloková | CZE | 19.837 |
| 7. | Aurelia Dobre | ROM | 19.824 |
| 8. | Phoebe Mills | USA | 19.787 |

# BALANCE BEAM

**1896–1948** not held

**1952 Helsinki** C: 134, N: 18, D: 7.23.

| | | | PTS. |
|---|---|---|---|
| 1. | Nina Bocharova | SOV | 19.22 |
| 2. | Maria Gorokhovskaya | SOV | 19.13 |
| 3. | Margit Korondi | HUN | 19.02 |
| 4. | Ágnes Keleti | HUN | 18.96 |
| 5. | Galina Urbanovich | SOV | 18.93 |
| 6. | Tsvetana Stancheva | BUL | 18.86 |
| 6. | Olga Tass | HUN | 18.86 |
| 8. | Galina Shamrai | SOV | 18.79 |

**1956 Melbourne** C: 65, N: 15, D: 12.5.

|    |                    |     | PTS.   |
|----|--------------------|-----|--------|
| 1. | Ágnes Keleti       | HUN | 18.80  |
| 2. | Eva Bosáková       | CZE | 18.633 |
| 2. | Tamara Manina      | SOV | 18.633 |
| 4. | Larissa Latynina   | SOV | 18.533 |
| 4. | Anna Marejkova     | CZE | 18.533 |
| 6. | Elena Leuştean     | ROM | 18.50  |
| 7. | Margit Korondi     | HUN | 18.466 |
| 7. | Olga Tass          | HUN | 18.466 |
| 7. | Lyudmila Yegorova  | SOV | 18.466 |

**1960 Rome** C: 124, N: 27, D: 9.9.

|    |                       |     | PTS.   |
|----|-----------------------|-----|--------|
| 1. | Eva Bosáková          | CZE | 19.283 |
| 2. | Larissa Latynina      | SOV | 19.233 |
| 3. | Sofia Muratova        | SOV | 19.232 |
| 4. | Margarita Nikolayeva  | SOV | 19.183 |
| 5. | Keiko Ikeda (Tanaka)  | JPN | 19.132 |
| 6. | Vera Čáslavská        | CZE | 19.083 |

**1964 Tokyo** C: 83, N: 24, D: 10.23.

|    |                       |     | PTS.   |
|----|-----------------------|-----|--------|
| 1. | Vera Čáslavská        | CZE | 19.449 |
| 2. | Tamara Manina         | SOV | 19.399 |
| 3. | Larissa Latynina      | SOV | 19.382 |
| 4. | Polina Astakhova      | SOV | 19.366 |
| 5. | Hana Ružčková         | CZE | 19.349 |
| 6. | Keiko Ikeda (Tanaka)  | JPN | 19.216 |

**1968 Mexico City** C: 101, N: 24, D: 10.25.

|    |                     |     | PTS.   |
|----|---------------------|-----|--------|
| 1. | Natalya Kuchinskaya | SOV | 19.65  |
| 2. | Vera Čáslavská      | CZE | 19.575 |
| 3. | Larissa Petrik      | SOV | 19.25  |
| 4. | Karin Janz          | GDR | 19.225 |
| 4. | Linda Metheny       | USA | 19.225 |
| 6. | Erika Zuchold       | GDR | 19.15  |

**1972 Munich** c: 118, N: 23, D: 8.31.

|    |                     |     | PTS.   |
|----|---------------------|-----|--------|
| 1. | Olga Korbut         | SOV | 19.40  |
| 2. | Tamara Lazakovitch  | SOV | 19.375 |
| 3. | Karin Janz          | GDR | 18.975 |
| 4. | Mónika Császár      | HUN | 18.925 |
| 5. | Lyudmila Touricheva | SOV | 18.80  |
| 6. | Erika Zuchold       | GDR | 18.70  |

**1976 Montreal** C: 86, N: 18, D: 7.22.

|    |                      |     | PTS.   |
|----|----------------------|-----|--------|
| 1. | Nadia Comaneci       | ROM | 19.95  |
| 2. | Olga Korbut          | SOV | 19.725 |
| 3. | Teodora Ungureanu    | ROM | 19.70  |
| 4. | Lyudmila Tourischeva | SOV | 19.475 |
| 5. | Angelika Hellmann    | GDR | 19.45  |
| 6. | Gitta Escher         | GDR | 19.275 |

**1980 Moscow** C: 62, N: 16, D: 7.25.

|    |                        |     | PTS.   |
|----|------------------------|-----|--------|
| 1. | Nadia Comaneci         | ROM | 19.80  |
| 2. | Yelena Davydova        | SOV | 19.75  |
| 3. | Natalya Shaposhnikova  | SOV | 19.725 |
| 4. | Maxi Gnauck            | GDR | 19.70  |
| 5. | Radka Zemanová         | CZE | 19.65  |
| 6. | Emilia Eberle          | ROM | 19.40  |

**1984 Los Angeles** C: 65, N: 16, D: 8.5.

|    |                  |     | PTS.   |
|----|------------------|-----|--------|
| 1. | Simona Pauca     | ROM | 19.80  |
| 1. | Ecaterina Szabó  | ROM | 19.80  |
| 3. | Kathy Johnson    | USA | 19.65  |
| 4. | Mary Lou Retton  | USA | 19.55  |
| 5. | Ma Yanhong       | CHN | 19.45  |
| 6. | Romi Kessler     | SWI | 19.35  |
| 7. | Chen Yongyan     | CHN | 19.20  |
| 7. | Anja Wilhelm     | GER | 19.20  |

**1988 Seoul** C: 90, N: 23, D: 9.25.

|    |                        |     | PTS.   |
|----|------------------------|-----|--------|
| 1. | Daniela Silivas        | ROM | 19.924 |
| 2. | Yelena Shushunova      | SOV | 19.875 |
| 3. | Phoebe Mills           | USA | 19.837 |
| 3. | Gabriela Potorac       | ROM | 19.837 |
| 5. | Svetlana Boginskaya    | SOV | 19.787 |
| 6. | Diana Doudeva          | BUL | 19.724 |
| 7. | Kelly Garrison-Steves  | USA | 19.649 |
| 8. | Ulrike Klotz           | GDR | 18.125 |

Phoebe Mills of Northfield, Illinois, became the first female gymnast from the U.S. to win an individual medal at an unboycotted Olympics.

# FLOOR EXERCISES

**1896–1948** not held

**1952 Helsinki** C: 134, N: 18, D: 7.23.

|    |                     |     | PTS.  |
|----|---------------------|-----|-------|
| 1. | Ágnes Keleti        | HUN | 19.36 |
| 2. | Maria Gorokhovskaya | SOV | 19.20 |
| 3. | Margit Korondi      | HUN | 19.00 |
| 4. | Erzsébet Gulyás     | HUN | 18.99 |
| 4. | Galina Urbanovich   | SOV | 18.99 |
| 6. | Galina Minaicheva   | SOV | 18.96 |
| 7. | Olga Tass           | HUN | 18.89 |
| 8. | Galina Shamrai      | SOV | 18.86 |

**1956 Melbourne** C: 65, N: 15, D: 12.5.

|    |                   |     | PTS.   |
|----|-------------------|-----|--------|
| 1. | Ágnes Keleti      | HUN | 18.733 |
| 1. | Larissa Latynina  | SOV | 18.733 |
| 3. | Elena Leuştean    | ROM | 18.70  |
| 4. | Eva Bosáková      | CZE | 18.566 |
| 4. | Sofia Muratova    | SOV | 18.566 |
| 4. | Keiko Tanaka      | JPN | 18.566 |

7. Olga Tass          HUN   18.533
8. Doris Hedberg      SWE   18.50

**1960 Rome** C: 124, N: 27, D: 9.9.

|  | | PTS. |
|---|---|---|
| 1. Larissa Latynina | SOV | 19.583 |
| 2. Polina Astakhova | SOV | 19.532 |
| 3. Tamara Lyukhina | SOV | 19.449 |
| 4. Eva Bosáková | CZE | 19.383 |
| 5. Sofia Muratova | SOV | 19.349 |
| 6. Sonia Iovan | ROM | 19.232 |

**1964 Tokyo** C: 83, N: 24, D: 23.10.

|  | | PTS. |
|---|---|---|
| 1. Larissa Latynina | SOV | 19.599 |
| 2. Polina Astakhova | SOV | 19.50 |
| 3. Anikó Jánosi-Ducza | HUN | 19.30 |
| 4. Birgit Radochla | GDR | 19.299 |
| 5. Ingrid Föst | GDR | 19.266 |
| 6. Vera Čáslavská | CZE | 19.099 |

**1968 Mexico City** C: 101, N: 24, D: 10.20.

|  | | PTS. |
|---|---|---|
| 1. Vera Čáslavská | CZE | 19.675 |
| 1. Larissa Petrik | SOV | 19.675 |
| 3. Natalya Kuchinskaya | SOV | 19.65 |
| 4. Zinaida Voronina | SOV | 19.55 |
| 5. Olga Karasseva | SOV | 19.325 |
| 5. Bohumila Řimnácová | CZE | 19.325 |

**1972 Munich** C: 118, N: 23, D: 10.25.

|  | | PTS. |
|---|---|---|
| 1. Olga Korbut | SOV | 19.575 |
| 2. Lyudmila Tourischeva | SOV | 19.55 |
| 3. Tamara Lazakovitch | SOV | 19.45 |
| 4. Karin Janz | GDR | 19.40 |
| 5. Lyubov Burda | SOV | 19.10 |
| 5. Angelika Hellmann | GDR | 19.10 |

**1976 Montreal** C: 86, N: 18, D: 7.22.

|  | | PTS. |
|---|---|---|
| 1. Nelli Kim | SOV | 19.85 |
| 2. Lyudmila Tourischeva | SOV | 19.825 |
| 3. Nadia Comaneci | ROM | 19.75 |
| 4. Anna Pohludková | CZE | 19.575 |
| 5. Marion Kische | GDR | 19.475 |
| 6. Gitta Escher | GDR | 19.45 |

**1980 Moscow** C: 62, N: 16, D: 7.25.

|  | | PTS. |
|---|---|---|
| 1. Nadia Comaneci | ROM | 19.875 |
| 1. Nelli Kim | SOV | 19.875 |
| 3. Maxi Gnauck | GDR | 19.825 |
| 3. Natalya Shaposhnikova | SOV | 19.825 |
| 5. Emilia Eberle | ROM | 19.75 |
| 6. Jana Labáková | CZE | 19.725 |

**1984 Los Angeles** C: 65, N: 16, D: 8.5.

|  | | PTS. |
|---|---|---|
| 1. Ecaterina Szabó | ROM | 19.975 |
| 2. Julianne McNamara | USA | 19.95 |
| 3. Mary Lou Retton | USA | 19.775 |
| 4. Zhou Qiurui | CHN | 19.625 |
| 5. Romi Kessler | SWI | 19.575 |
| 6. Ma Yanhong | CHN | 19.45 |
| 7. Maiko Morio | JPN | 19.375 |
| 8. Laura Cutina | ROM | 19.15 |

When Ecaterina Szabó stepped up for her final Olympic routine, a power outage plunged the arena into darkness. When the lights were restored 8 minutes later, the scoreboard showed that Szabó's closest rival, Julianne McNamara, had been awarded a 10 for her performance. This meant that Szabó would need a 10 as well to assure herself of sole possession of first place. Unfazed by the delay or the pressure, she earned her 10 and, with it, her fourth gold medal.

**1988 Seoul** C: 90, N: 23, D: 9.25.

|  | | PTS. |
|---|---|---|
| 1. Daniela Silivas | ROM | 19.937 |
| 2. Svetlana Boginskaya | SOV | 19.887 |
| 3. Diana Doudeva | BUL | 19.85 |
| 4. Deliana Vodenicharova | BUL | 19.837 |
| 5. Beáta Storczer | HUN | 19.675 |
| 6. Phoebe Mills | USA | 19.662 |
| 7. Yelena Shushunova | SOV | 19.575 |
| 8. Dörte Thümmler | GDR | 19.525 |

Silivas returned home from Seoul with three gold medals and two silver. Doudeva became the first Bulgarian woman to win an Olympic gymnastics medal.

## TEAM COMBINED EXERCISES

According to current rules, each nation's final score is determined by combining the scores of the top five performers on each apparatus.

**1896–1924** not held

**1928 Amsterdam** T: 5, N: 5, D: 8.10.

| | | TOTAL PTS. |
|---|---|---|
| 1. HOL | (Petronella van Randwijk, Jacomina van den Berg, Annie Polak, Helena Nordheim, Alida van den Bos, Hendrika van Rumt, Anna van der Vegt, Elka de Levie, Jacoba Cornelia Stelma, Estella Agsteribbe, Petronella Burgerhof, Jud Simons) | 316.75 |
| 2. ITA | (Bianca Ambrosetti, Lavinia Gianoni, Luigina Perversi, Diana Pizzavini, Luigina Giavotti, Anna Tanzini, Carolina Tronconi, Ines Vercesi, Rita Vittadini, Virginia Giorgi, Germana Malabarba, Clara Marangoni) | 289.00 |

| | | | TOTAL PTS. |
|---|---|---|---|
| 3. | GBR | (Margaret Hartley, E. Carrie Pickles, Annie Broadbent, Amy Jagger, Ada Smith, Lucy Desmond, Doris Woods, Jessie Kite, Queenie Judd, Midge Moreman, Ethel Seymour, Hilda Smith) | 258.25 |
| 4. | HUN | (Mária Hámos, Aranka Hennyei, Anna Kael, Margit Pályi, Erzsébet Rudas, Nandorné Szeiler, Ilona Szöllösi, Judit Tóth, Rudolfné Herpich, Irén Hennyey, Margit Kövessy, Irén Rudas) | 256.50 |
| 5. | FRA | (Honorine Delescluse, Louise Delescluse, R. Oger, Georgette Meulebrouck, Mathilde Bataille, Galuelle Dhont, Valentine Héméryck, Jeanne Vanoverloop, Paulette Houteer, Berthe Verstraete, Genevieve Vankiersbilck, Antonie Straeteman) | 247.50 |

**1932** not held

**1936 Berlin** T: 8, N: 8, D: 8.12.

| | | | TOTAL PTS. |
|---|---|---|---|
| 1. | GER | (Trudi Meyer 67.55 [1], Erna Bürger 67.45 [2], Käthe Sohnemann 67.05 [3], Isolde Frölian 65.75 [8], Anita Bärwirth 65.45 [9], Paula Pöhlsen 65.00 [12], Friedel Iby 63.75 [17], Julie Schmitt 62.10 [27]) | 506.50 |
| 2. | CZE | (Vlasta Foltová 66.45 [5], Vlasta Dekanová 65.95 [6], Zdenka Veřmiřovska 65.90 [7], Matylda Pálfyová 64.10 [16], Anna Hřebřinová 62.70 [21], Božena Dobešová 62.65 [22], Marie Vetrovská 60.25 [28], Marie Bajerová 59.35 [45]) | 503.60 |
| 3. | HUN | (Margit Csillik 65.30 [11], Judit Tóth 64.70 [13], Margit Sándor-Nagy 64.55 [15], Gabriella Mészáros 63.05 [19], Eszter Voit 62.90 [20], Olga Törös 61.90 [30], Ilona Madary 61.25 [33], Margit Kalocsai 59.85 [41]) | 499.00 |
| 4. | YUG | (Dušica Radivojević 62.30 [25], Lidica Rupnik 62.25 [26], Marta Pustišek 62.00 [28], Olga Rajkovič 62.00 [28], Drogana Djordjevič 61.20 [34], Angelina Kopurenko 60.75 [35], Katarina Hribar 60.60 [36], Maja Veršec 58.65 [46]) | 485.60 |
| 5. | USA | (Consetta Caruccio 66.85 [4], Jennie Caputo 65.45 [9], Irma Haubold 62.45 [23], Margaret Duff 60.50 [37], Ada Lunardoni 60.25 [38], Adelaide Meyer 56.55 [50], Mary Wright 55.10 [54], Marie Kibler 5.75 [injured]) | 471.60 |
| 6. | POL | (Klara Sierońska 64.65 [14], Marta Majowska 63.15 [18], Matylda Osadnik 62.45 [23], Wislawa Noskiewicz 61.40 [32], Janina Skirlińska 60.20 [40], Alina Cichecka 59.70 [44], Julia Wojciechowska 57.87 [47], Stefania Krupowa 56.95 [49]) | 470.30 |
| 7. | ITA | (Ebore Canella 61.75 [31], Clara Bimbocci 59.75 [42], Elda Cividino 59.75 [42], Carmela Toso 57.60 [48], Pina Cipriotto 55.35 [52], Anny Avanzini 55.20 [53], Vittoria Avanzini 54.75 [55], Gianna Guaita 51.40 [59]) | 442.05 |
| 8. | GBR | (Mary Heaton 56.15 [51], Mary Kelly 53.70 [56], Lillian Ridgewell 53.00 [57], Doris Blake 52.45 [58], Brenda Crowe 49.00 [60], Clarice Hanson 49.00 [60], Marion Wharton 46.95 [62], Edna Gross 43.84 [63]) | 408.30 |

**1948 London** T: 11, N: 11, D: 8.14.

| | | | TOTAL PTS. |
|---|---|---|---|
| 1. | CZE | (Zdenka Honsová 54.85 [1], Miloslava Misáková 53.40 [4], Vera Ružičkova 53.00 [7], Božena Srncová 52.95 [8], Milena Mullerová 52.50 [10], Zdenka Veřmiřovská 50.00 [23], Olga Silhanová 49.95 [24], Marie Kovářová 49.60 [26]) | 445.45 |
| 2. | HUN | (Edit Perényi-Weckinger 54.25 [2], Mária Kova 53.40 [4], Irén Kárpáti-Karcsics 53.26 [6], Erzébet Gulyás-Köteles 52.25 [12], Erzsébet Balázs 52.10 [13], Olga Tass 51.45 [15], Anna Fehér 49.15 [28], Margit Sandor-Nagy 39.10 [74]) | 440.55 |
| 3. | USA | (Helen Schifano 51.70 [14], Clara Schroth 51.05 [17], Meta Elste 50.90 [18], Marian Barone 50.30 [19], Ladislava Bakanic 50.10 [20], Consetta Lenz [Caruccio] 49.10 [29], Anita Simonis 47.80 [39], Dorothy Dalton 47.65 [41]) | 422.63 |
| 4. | SWE | (Karin Lindberg 52.70 [9], Kerstin Bohman 51.40 [16], Ingrid Sandahl 51.00 [18], Göta Pettersson 50.10 [21], Gunnel Johansson 49.10 [29], Märta Andersson 49.05 [30], E. Ingrid Andersson 47.10 [47], Stina Haage 39.10 [74]) | 417.95 |
| 5. | HOL | (Jacoba Tonneman 52.50 [10], Helena Gerrietsen 49.50 [27], Jacoba Wijnands 47.25 [44], Johanna Ros 45.75 [54], Anna van Geene 45.45 [57], Klassje Post 44.80 [62], Geertruida Heil-Bonnet 42.55 [67], Barendina Meijer-Haantjes 38.30 [78]) | 408.35 |
| 6. | AUT | (Gertrude Fesl 51.05 [17], Gretchen Hehenberger 50.00 [23], Gertrude Kolar 48.65 [36], Edeltraud Schramm 45.10 [60], Erika Enzenhofer 38.95 [76]) | 405.45 |
| 7. | YUG | (V. Gerbeč 49.00 [34], D. Djordjevič 47.60 [42], R. Vojsk 47.20 [45], D. Djipalovič 47.15 [46], Tanja Žutič 45.25 [58], D. Basletič 42.70 [66], Z. Mijatovič 40.35 [72], N. Cerne 24.70 [88]) | 397.90 |
| 8. | ITA | (L. Micheli 53.65 [3], E. Santoni 47.55 [43], Licia Macchini 46.30 [52], V. Nuti 45.75 [54], L. Torriani 45.10 [60], Renata Bianchi 43.25 [65], N. Jcardi 40.70 [70], L. Pezzoni 28.20 [85]) | 394.20 |

In gymnastics, as in other sports in which scoring is dependent on subjective judging, controversies and partisan decisions are commonplace. But a special level of incompetence was displayed by one of the judges in the 1948 women's gymnastics competition when, scoring on a scale of one through ten, she awarded one gymnast a 13.1. The major benefactors of the strange scoring standards of 1948 were the Czechoslovakians, who won the gold medal under dramatic circumstances. Shortly after the Czech team arrived in London, one of its members, 22-year-old Eliska Misáková, was taken ill and confined to an iron lung. The day of her team's appearance at the Olympics, she died of infantile paralysis. The Czech team, which included her older sister, Miloslava, went ahead with its performance and was awarded first place. When the Czech flag was raised for the medal ceremony, it was bordered with a black ribbon. After the Olympics, Marie Provaznikova, the leader of the Czech women's team and the president of the Women's Technical Commission, refused to return to Czechoslovakia because "there is no freedom of speech, of the press or of assembly." She was the first Olympic participant to defect, although hardly the last.

**1952 Helsinki** T: 18, N: 18, D: 7.24.

|  |  | TOTAL PTS. |
|---|---|---|
| 1. SOV | (Maria Gorokhovskaya 76.78 [1], Nina Bocharova 75.94 [2], Galina Minaicheva 75.67 [4], Galina Urbanovich 75.64 [5], Pelageya Danilova 75.03 [7], Galina Schamrai 74.97 [8], Yekaterina Kalinchuk 73.91 [13]) | 527.03 |
| 2. HUN | (Margit Korondi 75.82 [3], Agnes Keleti 75.58 [6], Edit Perényi-Weckinger 74.77 [10], Olga Tass 74.71 [11], Erzsébet Gulyás 74.61 [12], Mária Zalai-Kövi 73.87 [15], Andrea Bodó 71.67 [28], Irén Daruházi-Karcscics 70.87 [40]) | 520.96 |
| 3. CZE | (Eva Vechtová 73.87 [14], Alena Chadimová 72.25 [20], Jana Rabasová 72.13 [21], Božena Srncová 72.08 [22], Hana Bobková 71.52 [31], Matylda Šinová 71.47 [33], Vera Vančurová 71.38 [34], Alena Reichová 70.40 [47]) | 503.32 |
| 4. SWE | (Karin Lindberg 73.13 [17], Gun Röring 72.07 [23], Evy Berggren 71.07 [36], Göta Pettersson 70.97 [37], Ann-Sofi Colling-Pettersson 70.71 [44], Ingrid Sandahl 69.68 [57], Hjördis Nordin 69.28 [65], Vanja Blomberg 67.84 [83]) | 501.00 |
| 5. GER | (Irma Walther 71.95 [24], Hanna Grages 71.77 [26], Elisabeth Ostermeier 70.91 [38], Wolfgard Voss 70.00 [53], Inge Sedlmaier 69.83 [54], Lydia Zeitlhofer 69.57 [60], Brigitte Kiesier 67.98 [80], Hilde Koop 63.40 [118]) | 495.20 |
| 6. ITA | (Lidia Pitteri 71.60 [30], Miranda Cicognani 71.50 [32], Licia Macchini 71.24 [35], Liliana Scaricabarozzi 70.81 [41], Grazia Bozzo 70.77 [42], Luciana Reali 70.62 [45], Elisabetta Durelli 70.39 [48], Renata Bianchi 69.76 [55]) | 494.74 |
| 7. BUL | (Tsvetana Stancheva 73.67 [16], Ivanka Doldzheva 72.81 [18], Saltirka Turpova 72.30 [19], Vasilka Stancheva 71.64 [29], Raina Grigorova 70.18 [49], Yordanka Yovkova | 493.77 |

66.37 [98], Stoyanka Angelova 64.85 [110], Penka Prisadashka 62.91 [122])

| 8. POL | (Stefania Świerzy 71.68 [27], Stefania Reindlowa 70.91 [38], Helena Rakoczy 70.74 [43], Zofia Kowalczyk 69.20 [67], Honorata Marcińczak 68.85 [69], Barbara Wilk-Slizowska 68.14 [76], Dorota Horzonek 67.57 [86], Ursula Lukomska 62.90 [123]) | 483.72 |
|---|---|---|

**1956 Melbourne** T: 9, N: 9, D: 12.7.

|  |  | TOTAL PTS. |
|---|---|---|
| 1. SOV | (Larissa Latynina 74.933 [1], Sofia Muratova 74.466 [3], Tamara Manina 74.233 [6], Lyudmila Yegorova 73.533 [10], Polina Astakhova 72.700 [17], Lidiya Kalinina 72.033 [21]) | 444.800 |
| 2. HUN | (Ágnes Keleti 74.633 [2], Olga Tass 74.366 [4], Margit Korondi 73.333 [12], Andrea Bodó 72.900 [14], Erzsébet Gulyás-Köteles 72.200 [18], Aliz Kertész 63.400 [61]) | 443.500 |
| 3. ROM | (Elena Leuştean 74.366 [4], Sonia Iovan 72.900 [14], Georgeta Hurmuzachi 72.733 [16], Emilia Vătăşoiu 72.100 [20], Elena Margarit 72.033 [21], Elena Săcalici 71.433 [30]) | 438.200 |
| 4. POL | (Helena Rakoczy 73.700 [8], Natalia Kot 73.633 [9], Danuta Nowak-Stachow 71.800 [25], Dorota Jokiel 71.000 [27], Barbara Slizowska 70.533 [45], Lidia Szczerbińska 70.300 [47]) | 436.500 |
| 5. CZE | (Eva Bosáková [Vechtova] 74.100 [7], Hana Marejková 73.500 [11], Matylda Šinová 71.800 [25], Vera Drazdikova 71.333 [32], Alena Reichová 70.866 [39], Miroslava Brdičková 70.833 [40]) | 435.356 |
| 6. JPN | (Keiko Tanaka 73.100 [13], Mitsuka Ikeda 71.900 [23], Kazuko Sogabe 71.833 [24], Shizuko Sakashita 71.500 [29], Kyoko Kubota 71.133 [34], Suzuko Seki 71.000 [36]) | 433.653 |
| 7. ITA | (Miranda Cicognani 71.600 [28], Luciana Reali 70.933 [37], Rosella Cicognani 70.766 [42], Elisa Calsi 70.733 [43], Elena Lagorara 70.700 [44], Luciana Lagorara 69.700 [50]) | 428.654 |
| 8. SWE | (Ann-Sofi Colling-Pettersson 71.40 [31], Eva Rönström 70.933 [37], Doris Hedberg 70.466 [46], Karin Lindberg 70.033 [48], Evy Berggren 69.966 [49], Maude Karlén 68.80 [53]) | 428.600 |

**1960 Rome** T: 17, N: 17, D: 9.8.

|  |  | TOTAL PTS |
|---|---|---|
| 1. SOV | (Larissa Latynina 77.031 [1], Sofia Muratova 76.696 [2], Polina Astakhova 76.164 [3], Margarita Nikolayeva 75.831 [4], Lidiya Ivanova [Kalinina] 75.431 [7], Tamara Lyukhina 66.664 [89]) | 382.320 |
| 2. CZE | (Vera Čáslavská 75.298 [8], Eva Bosáková [Vechtova] 75.197 [10], Ludmila Svédová | 373.323 |

TOTAL PTS

74.565 [13], Adolfina Tačová 74.564 [14], Matylda Matoušková [Sinova] 73.265 [26], Hana Ruzickova 72.732 [33])

3. ROM (Sonia Iovan 75.797 [5], Elena Leuştean 372.053 74.865 [11], Emilia Liţă 74.264 [16], Atanasia Ionescu 73.564 [21], Uta Poreceanu 73.197 [27], Elena Niculescu 70.563 [67])

4. JPN (Keiko Ikeda [Tanaka] 75.696 [6], Kiyoko Ono 371.422 75.398 [15], Kimiko Tsukada 73.398 [22], Toshiko Shirasu 73.298 [24], Ginko Abukawa 72.311 [43], Kazuko Sogabe 17.598 [56])

5. POL (Natalia Kot 74.864 [12], Danuta Stachow 368.620 73.930 [17], Barbara Eustachiewicz 73.298 [24], Eryka Madra 72.764 [32], Gizela Niedurna 72.647 [37], Brygida Dziuba 71.898 [52])

6. GDR (Ingrid Föst 75.265 [9], Roselore Sonntag 367.754 72.964 [29], Ute Starke 72.798 [31], Gretel Schiener 72.697 [34], Renate Schneider 72.029 [48], Karin Boldermann 71.298 [59])

7. HUN (Judit Füle 73.831 [19], Anikó Jánosi-Ducza 367.054 73.398 [22], Klára Förstner 72.697 [34], Katalin Müller 72.530 [38], Olga Tass 72.397 [40], Mária Bencsik 72.030 [46])

8. BUL (Raina Grigorova 73.898 [18], Ivanka 364.920 Doldzheva 72.332 [42], Saltirka Turpova 72.064 [45], Tsvetana Rangelova 71.996 [49], Elisaveta Mileva 71.964 [50], Stanka Pavlova 71.697 [54])

**1964 Tokyo** T: 10, N: 10, D: 10.21.

TOTAL PTS.

1. SOV (Larissa Latynina 76.998 [2], Polina Astakhova 280.890 76.965 [3], Yelena Volchetskaya 75.765 [8], Tamara Zamotailova [Lyukhina] 75.398 [13], Tamara Manina 75.397 [14], Lyudmila Gromova 74.398 [30])

2. CZE (Vera Čáslavská 77.564 [1], Hana Ružičková 379.989 76.097 [5], Jaroslava Sedlačková 75.598 [11], Adolfina Tkačiková [Tačová] 75.331 [19], Mária Krajčirová 74.898 [21], Jana Posnerová 74.765 [23])

3. JPN (Keiko Ikeda [Tanaka] 76.031 [6], Toshiko 377.889 Aihara [Shirasu] 75.997 [7], Kiyoko Ono 75.665 [9], Taniko Nakamura 75.198 [19], Ginko Chiba [Abukawa] 74.665 [24], Hiroko Tsuji 74.597 [25])

4. GER/ (Birgit Radochla 76.431 [4], Ute Starke 75.632 376.038
GDR [10], Ingrid Föst 75.465 [12], Karin Mannewitz 74.363 [31], Christel Felgner 74.014 [35], Barbara Stolz 73.430 [44])

5. HUN (Anikó Janosi-Ducza 75.33 [16], Katalin 375.455 Makray 75.330 [18], Mária Tressel 74.932 [21], Gyöngyi Kovacs-Mák 74.597 [26], Katalin Müller 74.565 [27], Márta Erdösi-Talnai 74.231 [32])

6. ROM (Sonia Iovan 75.397 [14], Elena Popescu- 371.984 Leuştean 75.130 [20], Elena Ceampelea 73.831 [37], Atanasia Ionescu 73.698 [41], Emilia Liţă 72.995 [48], Cristina Doboşan 72.497 [54])

7. POL (Gerda Brylka 74.563 [28], Malgorzata Wilczek 371.287 74.563 [28], Elzbieta Apostolska 73.831 [37], Dorota Miller 73.465 [43], Gizela Niedurny 72.365 [56], Barbara Eustachiewicz 72.197 [58])

8. SWE (Anna Marie Lundquist 73.798 [39], Laila 367.888 Egman 73.764 [40], Ewa Rydell 73.599 [42], Ulla Lindstrom 72.898 [50], Anne-Marie Lambert 72.796 [52], Gercla Lindahl 72.763 [53])

**1968 Mexico City** T: 14, N: 14, D: 10.23.

TOTAL PTS.

1. SOV (Zinaida Voronina 76.85 [2], Natalya 382.85 Kuchinskaya 76.75 [3], Larissa Petrik 76.70 [4], Olga Karasseva 76.00 [4], Lyudmila Tourischeva 74.50 [24], Lyubov Burda 74.20 [25])

2. CZE (Vera Čáslavská 78.25 [1], Bohumila 382.20 Řimnácová 76.00 [7], Miroslava Skleničková 75.85 [9], Máriana Krajčirová 75.85 [9], Hana Lišková 75.65 [11], Jana Kubičkova [Posnerová] 75.05 [15])

3. GDR (Erika Zuchold 76.70 [4], Karin Janz 76.55 [6], 379.10 Maritta Bauerschmidt 75.45 [12], Ute Starke 74.65 [22], Marianne Noack 74.10 [27], Magdalena Schmidt 73.95 [29])

4. JPN (Kazue Hanyu 75.30 [13], Miyuki Matsuhisa 375.45 74.90 [17], Taniko Mitsukuri 74.85 [18], Chieko Oda 74.80 [19], Mitsuko Kandori 74.65 [22], Kayoko Hashiguchi 73.15 [33])

5. HUN (Ágnes Bánfai 75.10 [14], Anikó Jánosi-Ducza 369.80 74.80 [19], Katalin Schmitt-Makray 74.15 [26], Márta Erdösi-Tolnai 72.45 [35], Katalin Száll-Müller 72.15 [37], Ilona Békési 71.85 [38])

6. USA (Cathy Rigby 74.95 [16], Linda Metheny 74.00 369.75 [28], Joyce Tanac 73.65 [30], Kathy Gleason 73.60 [31], Colleen Mulvihill 73.05 [34], Wendy Cluff 71.80 [39])

7. FRA (Evelyne Letourneur 74.80 [19], Jacqueline 361.75 Brisepierre 72.45 [35], Mireille Cayre 71.75 [40], Françoise Nourry 70.75 [46], Dominique Lauvard 70.15 [57], Nicole Bourdiau 69.05 [69])

8. BUL (Maria Karashka 73.30 [32], Vania Marinova 355.10 71.30 [44], Veselina Pasheva 70.45 [51], Neli Stoyanova 70.45 [51], Raina Atanasova 69.60 [65])

**1972 Munich** T: 19, N: 19, D: 9.28.

TOTAL PTS.

1. SOV (Lyudmila Tourischeva 76.85 [1], Olga Korbut 380.50 76.70 [3], Tamara Lazakovitch 76.40 [4],

Lyubov Burda 75.35 [6], Elvira Saadi 74.65 [8], Antonina Koshel 73.00 [20])

2. GDR (Karin Janz 76.85 [1], Erika Zuchold 76.00 [5], Angelika Hellmann 75.30 [7], Irene Abel 73.75 [13], Christine Schmitt 73.70 [14], Richarda Schmeisser 73.20 [17])  376.55

3. HUN (Ilona Békési 74.40 [9], Mónika Császár 73.85 [12], Krisztina Medveczky 73.60 [15], Anikó Kéry 73.40 [16], Márta Kelemen 73.00 [20], Zsuzsanna Nagy 71.45 [41])  368.25

4. USA (Cathy Rigby 74.25 [10], Kimberly Chace 73.05 [18], Roxanne Pierce 72.55 [25], Linda Metheny 72.50 [26], Joan Moore 72.50 [26], Nancy Thies 71.95 [35])  365.90

5. CZE (Mariana Némethová [Krajčirová] 74.00 [11], Zdena Dornáková 72.90 [23], Sona Brázdová 72.80 [24], Zdena Bujnáčková 72.50 [26], Hana Lišková 72.05 [33], Marcela Váchová 71.95 [35])  365.00

6. ROM (Elena Ceampelea 73.05 [18], Alina Goreac 72.25 [30], Anca Grigoraş 72.10 [31], Elisabeta Turcu 71.20 [44], Paula Ion 71.10 [46], Marcela Păunescu 70.50 [55])  360.70

7. JPN (Miyuki Matsuhisa 72.50 [26], Takato Hasegawa 72.00 [34], Eiko Hirashima 71.95 [35], Kayoko Saka 71.80 [40], Kazue Hanyu 71.30 [43], Toshiko Miyamoto 70.000 [60])  359.75

8. GER (Uta Schorn 72.10 [31], Jutta Oltersdorf 71.95 [35], Andrea Niederheide 71.10 [46], Angelika Kern 70.95 [48], Ulrike Weyh 70.85 [50], Ingrid Santer 68.85 [76])  357.95

**1976 Montreal** T: 12, N: 12, D: 7.19.

TOTAL PTS.

1. SOV (Nelli Kim 78.25 [2], Lyudmila Tourischeva 78.25 [2], Olga Korbut 77.95 [5], Elvira Saadi 77.45 [7], Maria Filatova 77.05 [9], Svetlana Grozdova 77.05 [9]  466.00

2. ROM (Nadia Comaneci 79.05 [1], Teodora Ungureanu 78.05 [4], Mariana Constantin 76.75 [14], Anca Grigoraş 76.70 [15], Gabriela Trusca 76.10 [18], Georgeta Gabor 75.70 [21])  462.35

3. GDR (Gitta Escher 77.60 [6], Marion Kische 77.20 [8], Kerstin Gerschau 77.00 [12], Angelika Hellmann 76.90 [13], Steffi Kräker 75.70 [21], Carola Dombeck 74.90 [33])  459.30

4. HUN (Márta Egervári 77.05 [9], Kriszta Medveczky 76.15 [17], Margit Tóth 76.05 [19], Éva Óvári 75.40 [25], Mária Lövei 75.15 [20], Márta Kelemen 74.65 [34])  454.45

5. CZE (Anna Pohludková 76.40 [16], Ingrid Holkovičova 75.60 [23], Jana Knopová 75.10 [28], Eva Porádková 75.05 [29], Drahomira Smolíková 75.05 [29], Alena Černáková 74.55 [40])  451.75

6. USA (Kimberly Chace 75.45 [24], Debra Willcox 75.05 [29], Leslie Wolfsberger 74.65 [34],  448.20

Colleen Casey 74.50 [41], Carrie Englert 74.40 [42], Doris Howard 74.15 [46])

7. GER (Andrea Bieger 75.95 [20], Petra Kurbjuweit 74.60 [36], Jutta Oltersdorf 74.60 [36], Traudi Schubert 73.60 [55], Uta Schorn 73.55 [56], Beate Renschler 73.25 [59])  445.55

8. JPN (Satoko Okazaki 75.30 [26], Miyuki Hironaki 75.00 [32], Nobue Yamazaki 73.85 [50], Chieko Kikkawa 73.65 [53], Sakiko Nozawa 73.45 [57], Kyoko Mano 72.80 [65])  444.05

**1980 Moscow** T: 8, N: 8, D: 7.23.

TOTAL PTS.

1. SOV (Natalya Shaposhnikova 79.15 [2], Yelena Davydova 79.00 [5], Nelli Kim 78.95 [6], Maria Filatova 78.80 [7], Stella Zakharova 78.75 [8], Yelena Naimuschina 78.40 [12])  394.90

2. ROM (Emilia Eberle 79.10 [3], Nadia Comaneci 79.05 [4], Rodica Dunka 78.50 [10], Melita Rühn 78.30 [13], Cristina Elena Grigoraş 78.00 [15], Dumitrita Turner 77.25 [22])  393.50

3. GDR (Maxi Gnauck 79.35 [1], Katharina Rensch 78.55 [9], Steffi Kräker 78.50 [10], Birgit Süss 77.90 [17], Silvia Hindorff 77.35 [21], Karola Sube 77.20 [23])  392.55

4. CZE (Eva Marečková 78.05 [14], Jana Labáková 77.85 [18], Katarina Šarišská 77.55 [19], Dana Brydlová 77.05 [20], Anita Sauerová 76.05 [33], Radke Zemanova 76.05 [33])  388.80

5. HUN (Erika Csányi 77.50 [29], Erika Flander 77.20 [23], Márta Egervári 76.50 [27], Lenke Almási 76.25 [29], Éva Óvári 76.25 [29], Erzsébet Hanti 75.35 [37])  384.30

6. BUL (Silvia Topalova 77.20 [23], Galina Marinova 76.50 [27], Krassimira Toneva 76.25 [29], Kamelia Eftimova 75.60 [35], Dimitrinka Filipova 75.50 [36], Antoaneta Rahneva 74.35 [41])  382.10

7. POL (Lucja Matraszek-Chydzińska 76.15 [32], Malgorzata Majza 75.20 [38], Anita Jokiel 74.95 [39], Wleslawa Zelaskowska 74.30 [42], Agata Jaroszek 73.65 [43], Katarzyna Snopko 73.45 [45])  376.25

8. PRK (Choe Jong-sil 74.85 [40], Sin Myong-ok 72.50 [45], Kang Myong-suk 72.35 [48], Kim Chun-son 71.40 [52], Choe Myong-hui 71.20 [54], Lo Ok-sil 70.50 [59])  364.05

**1984 Los Angeles** T: 16, N: 16, D: 8.1.

TOTAL PTS.

1. ROM (Ecaterina Szabó 78.12 [2], Laura Cutina 78.40 [3], Simona Pauca 78.05 [7], Cristina Grigoraş 77.90 [8], Mihaela Stanulet 77.70 [10], Lavinia Agache 77.60 [11])  392.02

2. USA (Mary Lou Retton 79.05 [1], Julianne McNamara 78.40 [3], Kathy Johnson 78.10 [6], Michelle Dusserre 77.55 [12], Tracee Talavera 77.10 [16], Pamela Bileck 76.80 [17])  391.20

|   |   |   | TOTAL PTS. |
|---|---|---|---|
| 3. | CHN | (Ma Yanhong 78.20 [5], Wu Jiani 77.75 [9], Chen Yongyan 77.35 [13], Zhou Ping 77.35 [13], Zhou Qiurui 76.50 [19], Huang Qun 76.30 [21]) | 388.60 |
| 4. | GER | (Elke Heine 76.55 [18], Anja Wilhelm 76.45 [20], Astrid Beckers 75.25 [29], Angela Golz 74.85 [31], Brigitta Lehmann 74.85 [31], Heike Schwarm 74.85 [31]) | 379.15 |
| 5. | CAN | (Andrea Thomas 75.85 [23], Bonnie Wittmeier 75.85 [23], Anita Botnen 75.55 [27], Gigi Zosa 75.40 [28], Jessica Tudos 74.75 [36], Kelly Brown 73.50 [50]) | 378.90 |
| 6. | JPN | (Maiko Morio 75.90 [22], Noriko Mochizuki 75.70 [26], Tokie Kawase 74.85 [31], Chihiro Oyagi 74.85 [31], Ayami Yukimori 73.90 [45], Sae Watanabe 73.75 [47]) | 376.75 |
| 7. | GBR | (Natalie Davies 75.05 [30], Amanda Harrison 74.55 [38], Kathleen Williams 74.45 [39], Hayley Price 74.05 [43], Lisa Young 74.05 [43], Sally Larner 73.60 [48]) | 373.85 |
| 8. | SWI | (Romi Kessler 77.35 [13], Susi Latanzio 74.40 [41], Natalie Seiler 74.15 [42], Monika Beer 73.20 [51], Bettina Ernst 73.20 [51], Marisa Jervella 72.55 [58]) | 373.50 |

As the winners of eight consecutive Olympic titles, the Soviet women's team would have been the overwhelming favorites in Los Angeles had they not been prevented from competing by their government's boycott.

**1988 Seoul** T: 12, N: 12, D: 9.21.

|   |   |   | TOTAL PTS. |
|---|---|---|---|
| 1. | SOV | (Yelena Shushunova 79.675 [1], Svetlana Boginskaya 79.40 [3], Natalya Lashchenova 78.90 [5], Svetlana Baitova 78.425 [13], Yelena Shevchenko 78.35 [14], Olga Strazheva 68.175 [85]) | 395.475 |
| 2. | ROM | (Daniela Silivas 79.575 [2], Gabriela Potorac 78.925 [4], Celestina Popa 78.575 [10], Eugenia Golea 77.875 [18], Camelia Voinea 77.775 [22]) | 394.125 |
| 3. | GDR | (Dagmar Kersten 78.65 [8], Dörte Thümmler 78.55 [11], Ulrike Klotz 78.275 [16], Gabriele Fähnrich 77.625 [25], Betti Schieferdecker 77.45 [30], Martina Jentsch 38.25 [87]) | 390.875 |
| 4. | USA | (Phoebe Mills 78.675 [6], Brandy Johnson 78.55 [11], Kelly Garrison-Steves 77.825 [21], Theresa Spivey 77.45 [30], Chelle Stack 77.40 [32], Melissa Marlowe 76.85 [46]) | 390.575 |
| 5. | BUL | (Diana Doudeva 78.65 [8], Deliana Vodenicharova 78.325 [15], Boriana Stoyanova 77.95 [17], Ivelina Raikova 77.85 [20], Maria Kartalova 77.25 [35], Khrabrina Khrabova 76.025 [62]) | 390.550 |
| 6. | CHN | (Chen Cuiting 77.875 [18], Fan Di 77.475 [28], Wang Wenjing 77.40 [32], Wang Huiying 77.35 | 388.400 |
|   |   | [34], Ma Ying 77.025 [41], Wang Xiaoyan 76.925 [44]) |  |
| 7. | CZE | (Iveta Poloková 77.65 [23], Hana Říčná 77.175 [38], Alena Dřevjaná 76.975 [43], Ivona Krmelová 76.725 [49], Martina Velisková 76.60 [52]) | 386.150 |
| 8. | HUN | (Eszter Óváry 77.50 [26], Andrea Ladányi 77.25 [35], Beáta Storczer 77.25 [35], Zsuzsanna Csisztu 76.775 [47], Zsuzsanna Miskó 76.275 [56], Ágnes Miskó 38.15 [88]) | 385.625 |

The Soviet women overcame the embarrassment of losing the 1987 world championships to the Romanians by easily continuing their Olympic undefeated streak.

Although the race for gold and silver was uneventful, controversy emerged in the battle for bronze when the East Germans found themselves facing unexpectedly stiff challenges from the U.S. and Bulgaria. The problem arose during the compulsory round while the American women were performing on the uneven bars. It was the responsibility of the U.S. alternate, Rhonda Faehn, to remove the springboard that competing gymnasts used to mount the bars. After Kelly Garrison-Steves had mounted, Faehn took hold of the springboard. But instead of climbing down from the podium, the competition platform, to the bench, she withdrew to the edge of the podium and watched Garrison-Steves go through her routine.

Ellen Berger, the East German president of the technical committee of the International Gymnastics Federation, immediately pointed out that Faehn's presence on the podium was an infraction of the rules and imposed a penalty of five tenths of a point. To apply this rarely enforced rule was petty, but technically correct. Unfortunately, as it turned out, the deduction cost the U.S. the bronze medal—they lost it to the East Germans by three tenths of a point.

U.S. coach Béla Karolyi was furious. He referred to Berger as a "cow" and called the ruling against the U.S. "a Communist plot."

International politics undoubtedly influenced the controversial decision; however, the ruling probably involved another factor of a more personal nature. Four years earlier at the Los Angeles Olympics, Béla Karolyi had jumped the press barricade to embrace his pupil, Mary Lou Retton. Ellen Berger, who was the head of the technical committee at that meet as well, reminded Karolyi that he was not a member of the U.S. coaching squad and was not allowed to be on the competition floor. She warned U.S. team officials that if Karolyi appeared on the floor again, she would enforce the rules and deduct three-tenths of a point from Retton's score. When U.S. head coach Don Peters told Karolyi of Berger's threat, he replied, "She doesn't have the guts to do it here with 10,000 screaming Americans."

Karolyi, who had been observed practicing his jump over the barricade the night before the competition, hopped over again on the night after he had been warned, when Retton completed the vault that won her the All-Around gold medal. Karolyi was right about Berger: she didn't penalize Retton three-tenths of a point, a penalty that would have cost her the gold medal, not in front of 10,000 screaming Americans. But four years later, Berger got her revenge on Karolyi and six young women were the victims.

## RHYTHMIC ALL-AROUND

**1896–1980** not held

**1984 Los Angeles** C: 33, N: 20, D: 8.11.

| | | HOOP | | BALL | | CLUBS | | RIBBON | | TOTAL PTS. |
|---|---|---|---|---|---|---|---|---|---|---|
| 1. Lori Fung | CAN | 14.525 | (3) | 14.425 | (4) | 14.6 | (2) | 14.4 | (2) | 57.95 |
| 2. Doina Staiculescu | ROM | 14.55 | (1) | 14.7 | (1) | 14.725 | (1) | 13.925 | (9) | 57.90 |
| 3. Regina Weber | GER | 14.55 | (1) | 14.425 | (4) | 14.35 | (5) | 14.375 | (3) | 57.70 |
| 4. Alina Dragan | ROM | 14.475 | (4) | 14.5 | (2) | 14.525 | (3) | 13.875 | (11) | 57.375 |
| 5. Milena Reljin | YUG | 14.175 | (10) | 14.375 | (6) | 14.275 | (7) | 14.425 | (1) | 57.25 |
| 6. Marta Canton | SPA | 14.275 | (7) | 14.2 | (9) | 14.35 | (5) | 14.125 | (4) | 56.95 |
| 7. Giulia Staccioli | ITA | 14.45 | (5) | 14.25 | (8) | 14.25 | (8) | 13.825 | (14) | 56.775 |
| 8. Hiroko Yamasaki | JPN | 14.3 | (6) | 14.35 | (7) | 14.175 | (10) | 13.85 | (12) | 56.075 |

There were few winners at the 1984 Olympics more unexpected than 21-year-old Lori Fung of Vancouver, Canada. Even with the absence of the boycotting nations, in particular the Bulgarians, Fung was a rank outsider, having finished 23rd at the 1983 world championships. However, in the interim, she had studied hard in Romania with gold medal favorite Doina Staiculescu. In Los Angeles, while others were dropping their balls, or having their ribbons disrupted by unpredictable currents from the air conditioning system, or suffering the exposure of their bra straps (an automatic deduction), Fung performed smoothly and went home with the gold medal.

**1988 Seoul** C: 35, N: 21, D: 9.30.

| | | HOOP | | ROPE | | CLUBS | | RIBBON | | TOTAL PTS. |
|---|---|---|---|---|---|---|---|---|---|---|
| 1. Marina Lobach | SOV | 15.0 | (1) | 15.0 | (1) | 15.0 | (1) | 15.0 | (1) | 60.00 |
| 2. Adriana Dunavska | BUL | 15.0 | (1) | 15.0 | (1) | 14.95 | (2) | 15.0 | (1) | 59.95 |
| 3. Aleksandra Timoshenko | SOV | 15.0 | (1) | 15.0 | (1) | 14.875 | (3) | 15.0 | (1) | 59.875 |
| 4. Bianka Panova | BUL | 15.0 | (1) | 15.0 | (1) | 14.775 | (4) | 14.95 | (4) | 59.725 |
| 5. Maria Isabel Lloret | SPA | 14.725 | (5) | 14.75 | (5) | 14.7 | (6) | 14.725 | (6) | 58.90 |
| 6. Andrea Sinkó | HUN | 14.65 | (7) | 14.75 | (5) | 14.725 | (5) | 14.65 | (8) | 58.775 |
| 7. Teresa Folga | POL | 14.55 | (10) | 14.675 | (9) | 14.6 | (13) | 14.8 | (5) | 58.625 |
| 8. Diana Schmiemann | GER | 14.6 | (8) | 14.65 | (11) | 14.7 | (6) | 14.65 | (8) | 58.60 |

Lobach, who had never before placed higher than fourth in a major international competition, was awarded a perfect score for each of her four routines in both the preliminary and the final. Nevertheless, she almost lost the gold medal when she came within one second of exceeding the time limit during her clubs performance. Fortunately, her pianist, Anatoly Vekshin, began playing faster at the end of the routine and Lobach finished just as the gong sounded.

Seventh-place finisher Teresa Folga of Kraków won the Miss Olympic Village beauty contest. In the words of the *Korea Herald*, Folga "outshined other contestants with her beautiful hair, slim and attractive body and eloquent conversation skills." She had been voted a similar prize by journalists attending the 1987 rhythmic world championships.

# *Discontinued Event*

## TEAM EXERCISE WITH PORTABLE APPARATUS

**1952 Helsinki** T: 16, N: 16, D: 7.24.

| | | | TOTAL PTS. |
|---|---|---|---|
| 1. | SWE | (Karin Lindberg, Gun Röring, Evy Berggren, Göta Pettersson, Ann-Sofi Colling-Pettersson, Ingrid Sandahl, Hjördis Nordin, Vanja Blomberg) | 74.20 |
| 2. | SOV | (Maria Gorokhovskaya, Nina Bocharova, Galina Minaicheva, Galina Urbanovich, Pelageya Danilova, Galina Schamrai, Medeya Dschugeli, Yekaterina Kalinchuk) | 73.00 |
| 3. | HUN | (Margit Korondi, Ágnes Keleti, Edit Perényi-Weckinger, Olga Tass, Erzsébet Gulyás, Mária Zalai-Kövi, Andrea Bodó, Irén Daruházi-Karcscics) | 71.60 |
| 4. | GER | (Irma Walther, Hanna Grages, Elisabeth Ostermeier, Wolfgard Voss, Inge Sedelmeier, Lydia Zeitlhofer, Brigitte Kiesler, Hilde Koop) | 71.20 |
| 5. | FIN | (Raili Tuominen, Vappu Salonen, Arja Lehtinen, Raili Hoviniemi, Pirkko Vilppunen, Maila Nisula, Pirkko Pyykönen, Raija Simola) | 70.60 |
| 6. | CZE | (Eva Vechtová, Alena Chadimová, Jana Rabasová, Božena Srncová, Hana Bobková, Matylda Šinová, Vera Vančurová, Alena Reichová) | 70.00 |
| 6. | HOL | (Helena Gerrietsen, Huiberdina Krul van der Nolk van Gogh, Johanna Cox-Ladru, Catharina Selbach, Jacoba Kampen, Johanna Ros, Bertha Selbach, Anna Simon) | 70.00 |
| 8. | YUG | (Sonja Rožman, Tanja Žutić, Anka Drinic, Nada Spasic, Milica Rožman, Ada Smolnikar, Marija Ivandekič, Tereza Kočiš) | 69.20 |

**1956 Melbourne** T: 9, N: 9, D: 12.7.

| | | | TOTAL PTS. |
|---|---|---|---|
| 1. | HUN | (Ágnes Keleti, Margit Korondi, Olga Tass, Andrea Bodó, Aliz Kertész, Erzsébet Gulyás-Köteles) | 75.20 |
| 2. | SWE | (Ann-Sofi Colling-Pettersson, Karin Lindberg, Eva Rönström, Evy Berggren, Doris Hedberg, Maude Karlén) | 74.20 |
| 3. | POL | (Helena Rakoczy, Natalia Kot, Dorota Jokiel, Danuta Nowak-Stachow, Barbara Ślizowska, Lidia Szczerbińska) | 74.00 |
| 3. | SOV | (Tamara Manina, Larissa Latynina, Sofia Muratova, Lidiya Kalinina, Polina Astakhova, Lyudmila Yegorova) | 74.00 |
| 5. | ROM | (Georgeta Hurmuzachi, Sonia Iovan, Elena Leuştean, Elena Margarit, Elena Săcălici, Emilia Vătăşoiu) | 73.40 |
| 6. | JPN | (Mitsuka Ikeda, Keiko Tanaka, Kazuko Sogabe, Kyoko Kubota, Suzuko Seki, Shizuko Sakashita) | 73.20 |
| 7. | CZE | (Eva Bosáková, [Vechtová], Hana Marejková, Matylda Šinová, Vera Drazdiková, Alena Reichová, Miraslava Brdičková) | 73.00 |
| 8. | ITA | (Miranda Cicognani, Luciana Reali, Rosella Cicognani, Elisa Calsi, Elena Lagorara, Luciana Lagorara) | 72.80 |

# TEAM HANDBALL

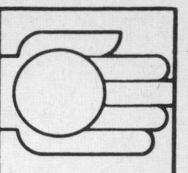

## MEN

Team handball is an exciting sport that deserves greater popularity. It is basically a combination of soccer and basketball. The ball is moved down the field as in basketball, but instead of being shot through a hoop it is thrown past a goalkeeper and into a net. There are two 30-minute halves.

**1896–1932** not held

**1936 Berlin** T: 6, N: 6, D: 8.14.

| | | W | L | PF | PA |
|---|---|---|---|---|---|
| 1. GER | (Heinz Körvers, Arthur Knautz, Willy Bandholz, Hans Keiter, Wilhelm Brinkmann, Georg Dascher, Erich Hermann, Hans Theilig, Helmut Berthold, Alfred Klingler, Fritz Fromm, Carl Kreutzberg, Heinrich Keimig, Wilhelm Müller, Kurt Dossin, Rudolf Stahl, Hermann Hansen, Fritz Spengler, Edgar Reinhardt, Günther Ortmann, Wilhelm Baumann, Helmuth Braselmann) | 5 | 0 | 96 | 19 |
| 2. AUT | (Alois Schnabel, Franz Bartl, Johann Tauscher, Otto Licha, Emil Juracka, Leopold Wohlrab, Jaroslav Volak, Alfred Schmalzer, Ludwig Schubert, Ferdinand Kiefler, Anton Perwein, Fritz Maurer, Franz Brunner, Fritz Wurmböck, Siegfried Purner, Hans Zehetner, Hans Houschka, Franz Bistricky, Franz Berghammer, Walter Reisp, Josef Krejci, Siegfried Powolny) | 4 | 1 | 60 | 29 |
| 3. SWI | (Willy Gysi, Robert Studer, Erich Schmill, Rolf Faes, Erland Herkenrath, Burkhard Gantenbein, Werner Meyer, Max Streib, Georg Mischon, Ernst Hufschmid, Eugen Seiterle, Edy Schmid, Max Blösch, Werner Scheurmann, Willy Schäfer, Willy Hufschmid, Rudolf Wirz) | 2 | 3 | 33 | 52 |
| 4. HUN | (Antal Ujváry, János Koppány, István Serényi, Lajos Kutasi, Frigyes Rakosi, Lörinc Galgóczy, Ferenc Cziráki, Gyula Takács, Miklós Fodor, Endre Salgó, Sándor Cséffai, Tibor Máté, Antal Benda, Imre Páli, Ferenc Velkei, Sándor Szomori) | 1 | 4 | 25 | 64 |
| 5. ROM | (Stefan Zoller, Carol Haffer, Ludovic Haffer, Bruno Holtzträger, Stefan Höchsmann, Robert Speck, Georg Herzog, Frederic Halmen, Wilhelm Kirschner, Wilhelm Heidel, Günther Schörsten, Peter Fesci, Ion Zikeli, Wilhelm Zaharias, Hertog Hermanstädter) | | | | |
| 6. USA | (Henry Oehler, Charles Dauner, Alfred Roseco, Herbert Carl Oehmichen, Edmund Schallenberg, William Ahlemeyer, Gerald Yantz, Joe Kaylor, Willy Renz, Walter Bowden, Fred Leinweber, Edward John Hagen, Otto Oehler, Philip Schupp) | 0 | 3 | 6 | 46 |

Final: GER 10–6 AUT
3rd Place: SWI 10–5 HUN
5th Place: ROM 10–3 USA

Field handball was invented in Germany, so when the Germans were given the opportunity to add one sport to the 1936 Olympics, they chose handball. In 1936 the game was played outdoors with 11 men on a side. Not surprisingly, Germany dominated the tournament, defeating the United States 29–1, Hungary 22–0 and 19–6, and Switzerland 16–6. Austria put up the best fight, trailing only 8–6 with five minutes to play.

**1948–1968** not held

**1972 Munich** T: 16, N: 16, D: 9.11.

| | | W | L | T | PF | PA |
|---|---|---|---|---|---|---|
| 1. YUG | (Abaz Arslanagić, Zoran Živković, Miroslav Pribanić, Hrvoje Horvat, Djoko Lavrnić, Zdravko Miljak, Slobodan Mišković, Branislav Pokrajać, Nebojša Popović, Milan Lazarević, Milorad Karalić, Albin Vidović, Zdenko Zorbo, Petar Fajdrić) | 7 | 0 | 0 | 140 | 105 |
| 2. CZE | (Ivan Satrapa, Vladimir Jarý, Jiři Kavan, Vladimir Haber, Jindřich Krepindl, Ladislav Beneš, Vincent Lafko, František Bruna, Petr Pospišil, Jaroslav Konecny, Pavel Mikes, Jaroslav Škarvan, František Králik, Andrej Lubósik, Zdenek Skara, Arnošt Limčik) | 3 | 3 | 1 | 114 | 99 |
| 3. ROM | (Cornel Penu, Gavril Kicsid, Valentin Samungi, Ştefan Birtalan, Cristian Gatu, Roland Gunesch, Simion Schöbel, Gheorghe Gruia, Constantin | 6 | 1 | 0 | 111 | 92 |

Tudosie, Alexandru Dincă, Werner Stöckl, Dan Marin, Ghiță Licu, Radu Voina, Adrias Cosma)

| | | W | L | T | PF | PA |
|---|---|---|---|---|---|---|
| 4. | GDR (Reiner Frieske, Peter Randt, Klaus Langhoff, Reiner Ganschow, Wolfgang Lakenmacher, Rainer Würdig, Jürgen Hildebrandt, Udo Röhrig, Wolfgang Böhme, Harry Zörnack, Josef Rose, Siegfried Voigt, Klaus Weiss, Rainer Zimmerman, Horst Jankhöfer, Peter Larisch) | 5 | 2 | 0 | 103 | 85 |
| 5. | SOV (Nikolai Semenov, Mikhail Ischenko, Aleksandr Panov, Vladimir Maksimov, Valentin Kulev, Vassily Ilyin, Anatoly Shevchenko, Yuri Klimov, Mikhail Lutsenko, Aleksandr Rezanov, Valery Gassi, Albert Oganezov, Yuri Lagutin, Ivan Ussatiy, Yan Vilson) | 3 | 1 | 3 | 91 | 84 |
| 6. | GER (Klaus Kater, Uwe Rathjen, Herwig Ahrendsen, Wolfgang Braun, Peter Bucher, Diethard Finkelmann, Klaus Lange, Herbert Lübking, Heiner Möller, Hans-Peter Neuhaus, Herbert Rogge, Herbert Wehnert, Hans-Jürgen Bode, Jochen Feldhoff, Josef Karrer, Klaus Westebbe) | 2 | 4 | 1 | 98 | 106 |
| 7. | SWE (Sten Olsson, Frank Ström, Björn Andersson, Dan Eriksson, Lennart Eriksson, Johan Fischerström, Benny Johansson, Jan Jonsson, Michael Koch, Thomas Persson, Goeran Hard, Af Segerstad, Bertil Söderberg) | 2 | 2 | 3 | 93 | 92 |
| 8. | HUN (József Horváth, Sándor Kaló, Károly Vass, István Varga, István Szabó, István Marosi, Sándor Vass, Lajos Simó, János Adorján, Sándor Takács, János Stiller, László Szabó) | 2 | 5 | 0 | 126 | 119 |

Final: YUG 21–16 CZE
3rd Place: ROM 19–16 GDR
5th Place: SOV 17–16 GER
7th Place: SWE 19–18 HUN

With the Olympics back in Germany, team handball was returned to the schedule, but this time there were seven men on a side and the matches were played indoors. The decisive match was the second-round contest between Yugoslavia and world champion Romania. With 15 minutes to play, Milan Lazarević scored to give Yugoslavia a 10–9 lead. Four minutes later Djoko Lavrnić scored again, and Yugoslavia had the first two-goal lead of the game. They built their lead to 14–11 and survived two late goals to win, 14–13. The final against Czechoslovakia was anticlimatic; Yugoslavia led 12–5 at halftime and 18–8 with 13 minutes to play.

**1976 Montreal** T: 11, N: 11, D: 7.28.

| | | W | L | T | PF | PA |
|---|---|---|---|---|---|---|
| 1. | SOV (Mikhail Ishchenko, Anatoly Fedyukin, Vladimir Maximov, Sergei Kushniryuk, Vassily Ilyin, Vladimir Kravzov, Yuri Klimov, Yuri Lagutin, Aleksandr Anpilogov, Yevgeny Chernyshov, Valery Gassiy, Anatoly Tomin, Yuri Kidyaev, Aleksandr Rezanov) | 5 | 1 | 0 | 130 | 92 |
| 2. | ROM (Cornel Penu, Gavril Kicsid, Cristian Gatu, Cezar Draganita, Radu Voina, Roland Gunesch, Alexandru Folker, Ştefan Birtalan, Adrian Cosma, Constantin Tudosie, Nicolae Munteanu, Werner Stöckl, Mircea Grabovschi, Ghiță Licu) | 3 | 1 | 1 | 106 | 90 |
| 3. | POL (Andrzej Szymczak, Piotr Cieśla, Zdzislaw Antczak, Zygfryd Kuchta, Jerzy Klempel, Janusz Brzozowski, Ryszard Przbysz, Jerzy Melcer, Andrzej Sokolowski, Jan Gmyrek, Henryk Rozmiarek, Alfred Kaluźiński, Wlodzimierz Zieliński, Mieczyslaw Wojczak) | 4 | 1 | 0 | 101 | 89 |
| 4. | GER (Manfred Hofmann, Jürgen Hahn, Günter Böttcher, Kurt Klühspies, Peter Kleibrink, Walter Oepen, Horst Spengler, Gerd Becker, Bernhard Busch, Joachim Deckarm, Rudolf Rauer, Arno Ehret, Heiner Brand, Peter Jaschke) | 4 | 2 | 0 | 115 | 97 |
| 5. | YUG (Abaz Arslanagić, Vlado Bojović, Ždravko Radjennović, Milorad Karalić, Radisav Pavicević, Žvonimir Serdarusić, Hrvoje Horvat, Branislav Pokrajać, Radivoj Krivokapić, Predrag Timko, Ždravko Miljak, Ždenko Žorko, Nebojsa Popović, Željko Nims) | 5 | 1 | 0 | 131 | 112 |
| 6. | HUN (Béla Bartalos, Ferenc Buday, Péter Kovács, István Varga, Mihály Süvöltös, István Szilágyi, József Kenyeres, László Janovszki, Károly Vass, Ernö Gubányi, Zsolt Kontra, Gábor Veröci) | 2 | 3 | 0 | 111 | 103 |
| 7. | CZE (Jan Packa, František Sulc, Ivan Satrapa, Vladimir Jary, Jiři Kavan, Stefan Katusak, Vladimir Haber, Jindrich Krepindl, Jiři Hanzl, Jaroslav Papiernik, Jozef Dobrotka, Bohumil Cepak, Jiři Liska, Pavel Mikes) | 2 | 2 | 1 | 110 | 103 |

| | | W | L | T | PF | PA |
|---|---|---|---|---|---|---|
| 8. DEN | (Kay Jorgensen, Palle Jensen, Anders Dahl-Nielsen, Lars Bock, Jorgen Frandsen, Claus From, Thomas Pazyj, Bent Larsen, Soren Andersen, Morten Christensen, Henrik Jacobsgaard, Johnny Pechnik, Thor Munkager, Jesper Petersen) | 2 | 4 | 0 | 113 | 127 |

Final: SOV 19–15 ROM
3rd Place: POL 21–18 GER
5th Place: YUG 21–19 HUN
7th Place: CZE 25–21 DEN

Again Romania entered the Olympics as defending world champions and again they were unable to win the tournament. They survived the preliminary pool undefeated to qualify for the final. The other pool was won by the Soviet Union despite a 20–18 loss to Yugoslavia, which was unlucky to finish fifth considering they lost only one match—to West Germany, 18–17. The U.S.S.R. took control of the final early, led 10–6 at halftime, and was never behind.

**1980 Moscow** T: 12, N: 12, D: 7.30.

| | | W | L | T | PF | PA |
|---|---|---|---|---|---|---|
| 1. GDR | (Siegfried Voigt, Günter Dreibrodt, Peter Rost, Klaus Gruner, Hans-Georg Beyer, Dietmar Schmidt, Hartmut Krüger, Lothar Döring, Ernst Gerlach, Frank-Michael Wahl, Ingolf Wiegert, Wieland Schmidt, Rainer Höft, Hans-Georg Jaunich) | 5 | 0 | 1 | 131 | 114 |
| 2. SOV | (Mikhail Ishchenko, Viktor Makhorin, Sergei Kushniryuk, Aleksandr Karshakevich, Vladimir Kravzov, Vladimir Belov, Anatoly Fedyukin, Aleksandr Anpilogov, Yevgeny Chernyshov, Aleksei Zhuk, Nikolai Tomin, Yuri Kidyaev, Vladimir Repiev, Voldemaras Novickis) | 4 | 2 | 0 | 156 | 98 |
| 3. ROM | (Nicolae Munteanu, Marian Dumitru, Iosif Boros, Maricel Voinea, Vasile Stinga, Radu Voina, Cezar Draganita, Cornel Durau, Ştefan Birtalan, Alexandru Folker, Neculai Vasilca, Lucian Vasilache, Adrian Cosma, Claudiu Eugen Ionescu) | 5 | 1 | 0 | 139 | 106 |
| 4. HUN | (Béla Bartalos, László Szabó, Péter Kovács, Sándor Vass, János Fodor, István Szilágyi, József Kenyeres, László Jánovszki, Ambrus Lele, Ernö Gubányi, Zsolt Kontra, Alpár Jegenyés, Árpád Pál, Miklós Kovácsics) | 3 | 1 | 2 | 114 | 108 |

| | | W | L | T | PF | PA |
|---|---|---|---|---|---|---|
| 5. SPA | (José Pagoaga, Juan Cabanas, Juan Maria Albisu, Vicente Calabuig, Juan de la Puente, Leon Lopez, José Novoa, Juan Uria, Agustin Milian, Francisco Lopez, Eugenio Serrano, Gregorio Lopez, Juan de Miguel, Juan Munoz) | 3 | 2 | 1 | 126 | 129 |
| 6. YUG | (Zlatan Arnautović, Momir Rnić, Enver Koso, Drago Jovović, Stjepan Obran, Jasmin Mrkonja, Peter Mahne, Pavle Jurina, Goran Nerić, Jovica Cvetković, Velibor Nenadić, Adnan Dizdar, Mile Isaković, Jovica Elezović) | 4 | 2 | 0 | 156 | 116 |
| 7. POL | (Andrzej Kącki, Zbigniew Gawlik, Piotr Czaczka, Marek Panas, Jerzy Klempel, Janusz Brzozowski, Zbigniew Tluczyński, Grzegorz Kosma, Daniel Waszkiewicz, Ryszard Jedliński, Henryk Rozmiarek, Alfred Kaluziński, Jerzy Garpiel, Mieczyslaw Wojczak) | 3 | 2 | 1 | 146 | 119 |
| 8. SWI | (Edi Wickli, Ernst Zuellig, Robert Jehle, Roland Brand, Max Schaer, Peter Haag, Walter Müller, Rudolf Weber, Hans Huber, Konrad Affolter, Hanspeter Lutz, Ugo Jametti, Peter Jehle, Martin Ott) | 2 | 4 | 0 | 132 | 121 |

Final: GDR 23–22 SOV
3rd Place: ROM 20–18 HUN
5th Place: SPA 24–23 YUG
7th Place: POL 23–22 SWI

The final was a particularly exciting match, as neither team ever led by more than two goals. As the clock ran down, East Germany led 20–19, but Aleksandr Anpilogov of the U.S.S.R. made a penalty shot with 22 seconds to play and the game went into overtime. Anpilogov also scored the first goal of the ten-minute extra period, but the Soviet Union was held scoreless for the next eight and a half minutes while the Germans took a 23–21 lead. Anpilogov scored the final goal of the game with 51 seconds left to play. East Germany's last point was put in by 23-year-old Hans-Georg Beyer, whose older brother, Udo, was winning the bronze medal in the shot put at the exact same time. Two days later, their sister, Gisela, finished fourth in the discus. Last-place finisher Kuwait had a tough tournament, including losses of 44–10 to Yugoslavia and 38–11 to the U.S.S.R.

**1984 Los Angeles-Fullerton, Inglewood** T: 12, N: 12, D: 8.11.

| | | W | L | T | PF | PA |
|---|---|---|---|---|---|---|
| 1. YUG | (Zlatan Arnautović, Momir Rnić, Veselin Vuković, Milan Kalina, Jovica Elezović, Zdravko Zovko, Branko Strbać, Pavle Jurina, Veselin Vujović, Slobodan | 5 | 0 | 1 | 141 | 93 |

| | W | L | T | PF | PA |
|---|---|---|---|---|---|
| Kuzmanovski, Mirko Basić, Dragan Mladenović, Zdravko Radjenović, Mile Isaković) | | | | | |
| 2. GER (Andreas Thiel, Arnulf Meffle, Rüdiger Neitzel, Martin Schwalb, Dirk Rauin, Michael Paul, Thomas Happe, Erhard Wunderlich, Thomas Springel, Klaus Wöller, Jochen Fraatz, Siegfried Roch, Ulrich Roth, Uwe Schwenker, Michael Roth) | 5 | 1 | 0 | 131 | 113 |
| 3. ROM (Nicolae Munteanu, Marian Dumitru, Iosif Boroş, Maricel Voinea, Vasile Stîngă, George Dogarescu, Gheorghe Covaciu, Cornel Durău, Alexandru Fölker, Neculai Vasilca, Alexandru Buligan, Vasile Oprea, Mircea Bedivan, Adrian Simion) | 5 | 1 | 0 | 143 | 110 |
| 4. DEN (Mogens Jeppesen, Jens Erik Roepstorff, Anders Dahl-Nielsen, Erik Veje Rasmussen, Keld Nielsen, Klaus Sletting Jensen, Morten Stig Christensen, Carsten Haurum, Hans Henrik Hattesen, Jörgen Gluver, Peter Michael Fenger, Poul Sörensen, Michael Strom, Per Skaarup) | 4 | 2 | 0 | 134 | 122 |
| 5. SWE (Claes Hellgren, Per Öberg, Danny Augustsson, Göran Bengtsson, Christer Magnusson, Per Carlén, Pär Jilsén, Lennarth Ebbinge, Björn Jilsén, Mats Lindau, Sten Sjögren, Rolf Hertzberg, Peter Olofsson, Mats Olsson) | 4 | 2 | 0 | 145 | 134 |
| 6. ICE (Einar Thorvardson, Thorglis Mathiesen, Thorbergur Adalsteinsson, Bjarni Gudmundsson, Jakob Sigurdsson, Sigurdur Gunnarsson, Atli Hilmarsson, Gudmundur Gudmundsson, Kristjan Arason, Thörbjorn Jensson, Jens Einarsson, Sigurdur Sveinsson, Brynjar Kvaran, Alfred Gislason, J. Steinar Birgisson) | 3 | 2 | 1 | 126 | 122 |
| 7. SWI (Martin Ott, Martin Glaser, Jürgen Baetschmann, Peter Weber, Max Schaer, Heinz Karrer, Roland Gassmann, René Barth, Norwin Platzer, Peter Hürlimann, Uwe Mall, Peter Jehle, Max Delhees, Markus Braun) | 3 | 3 | 0 | 101 | 119 |
| 8. SPA (Pedro Garcia, Juan Javier Cabanas, Juan Munoz, Javier Reino, Juan de la Puente, Cecilio Alonso, Juan Novoa, Juan Uria, Julian Ruiz, Eugenio | 2 | 4 | 0 | 122 | 124 |

Serrano, Lorenzo Rico, Rafael Lopez, Jaime Puig, Juan de Miguel)

Final: YUG 18–17 GER
3rd Place: ROM 23–19 DEN
5th Place: SWE 26–24 ICE
7th Place: SWI 18–17 SPA

West Germany was admitted to the Olympic tournament only after four of the qualifying teams withdrew as part of the Soviet-bloc boycott. Yet the Germans were able to complete their preliminary pool undefeated and advance to the final. There they met the Yugoslavs, who had survived an early 22–22 tie against Iceland and then beaten Romania 19–18 in a crucial matchup of the pre-Olympic favorites. The West Germans never held a lead after the first 12 minutes of the final, but they still clung to a 15–15 tie with 6 minutes remaining. Then Yugoslavia scored three unanswered goals and held on to win 18–17. Yugoslav coach Branislav Pokrajać was one of the players on the 1972 team which won Yugoslavia's other Olympic championship.

**1988 Seoul** T: 12, N: 12, D: 10.1.

| | W | L | T | PF | PA |
|---|---|---|---|---|---|
| 1. SOV (Andrei Lavrov, Aleksandr Tuchkin, Aleksandr Rymanov, Aleksandr Karshakevich, Yuri Nesterov, Georgy Sviridenko, Andrei Tyumentšev, Mikhail Vasilyev, Yuri Shevtsov, Vyacheslav Atavin, Valdemar Novitsky, Igor Chumak, Konstantin Sharovarov) | 6 | 0 | 0 | 162 | 107 |
| 2. KOR (Yoon Tae-il, Kim Jae-hwan, Sin Young-suk, Park Do-hun, Park Young-dae, Koh Suk-chang, Roh Hyun-suk, Oh Young-ki, Choi Suk-jae, Kang Jae-won, Lee Sang-hyo, Lim Jin-suk) | 4 | 2 | 0 | 152 | 149 |
| 3. YUG (Momir Rnić, Žlatko Saracevic, Iztok Puč, Goran Perkovać, Irfan Smajlagić, Žlatko Portner, Veselin Vujović, Jozef Holpert, Mirko Basić, Alvaro Nacinović, Slobodan Kuzmanovski, Ermin Velić) | 4 | 1 | 1 | 143 | 132 |
| 4. HUN (László Hoffmann, József Bordás, Péter Kovács, Mihály Kovács, János Fodor, László Marosi, Mihály Iváncsik, Jacob Sibalin, László Szabó, Géza Tóth, Ottó Csicsai, Imre Bíró, János Gyurka, Tibor Oross) | 3 | 3 | 0 | 125 | 120 |
| 5. SWE (Mats Olsson, Peder Järphag, Magnus Wislander, Johan Eklund, Ola Lindgren, Per Carlen, Erik Hajas, Per Carlsson, Björn Jilsén, Pär Jilsén, | 4 | 2 | 0 | 133 | 109 |

Sten Sjögren, Mats Fransson, Staffan Olsson, Claes Hellgren)

| 6. | CZE | (Michal Barda, Josef Škandík, Miroslav Bajgar, Libor Sovadina, Jiří Kotrč, Milan Brestovanský, Milan Folta, František Štika, Tomáš Bártek, Zdeněk Vaněk, Petr Baumruk, Karel Jindřichovský, Jan Novák, Peter Mesiarik) | 3 | 3 | 0 | 127 | 130 |
| 7. | GDR | (Peter Hofmann, Stephan Hauck, Peter Pysall, Frank-Michael Wahl, Holger Winselmann, Bernd Metzke, Andreas Neitzel, Rüdiger Borchardt, Jens Fiedler, Mike Fuhrig, Matthias Hahn, Wieland Schmidt, Holger Schneider) | 4 | 2 | 0 | 140 | 129 |
| 8. | ICE | (Einar Porvardarson, Thorgilsóttar Mathiesen, Jakob Sigurdsson, Bjarki Sigurdsson, Karl Thráinsson, Sigurdur Gunnarsson, Alfred Gíslason, Gudmundur Gudmundsson, Páll Ólafsson, Kristján Arason, Geir Sveinsson, Brynjar Kvaran, Sigurdur Sveinsson, Atli Hilmarsson, Gudmundur Hrafnkelsson) | 2 | 3 | 1 | 125 | 133 |

Final: SOV 32–25 KOR
3rd Place: YUG 27–23 HUN
5th Place: SWE 27–18 CZE
7th Place: GDR 31–29 ICE

The Soviet team, whose players averaged almost 6 feet 4 inches, swept through the tournament. Their closest match was a 22–18 victory over Sweden.

# WOMEN

Women's handball consists of two 25-minute halves; as in men's handball, there are seven players on a team.

**1896–1972** not held

**1976 Montreal** T: 6, N: 6, D: 7.28.

| | | | W | L | T | PF | PA |
|---|---|---|---|---|---|---|---|
| 1. | SOV | (Natalya Sherstyuk, Rafiga Shabanova, Lyubov Berezhnaya, Zinaida Turchina, Tatyana Makarez, Maria Litoshenko, Lyudmila Bobrus, Tatyana Gluschenko, Lyudmila Shubina, Galina Zakharova, Aldona Česaityte, Nina Lobova, Lyudmila Pantchuk, Larissa Karlova) | 5 | 0 | 0 | 92 | 40 |
| 2. | GDR | (Hannelore Zober, Gabriele Badorek, Evelyn Matz, Roswitha Krause, Christina Rost, Petra Uhlig, Christina Voss, Liane Michaelis, Silvia Siefert, Marion Tietz, Kristina Richter, Eva Paskuy, Waltraud Kretzschmar, Hannelore Burosch) | 3 | 1 | 1 | 89 | 47 |
| 3. | HUN | (Ágota Bujdosó, Márta Magyeri, Borbála Tóth-Harsányi, Katalin Laki, Amália Sterbinszky, Ilona Nagy, Klára Csík, Rozália Lelkes, Mária Vadász, Erzsébet Németh, Éva Angyal, Mária Berzsenyi, Marianna Nagy, Zsuzsanna Kezi) | 3 | 1 | 1 | 85 | 55 |
| 4. | ROM | (Elisabeta Ionescu, Rozalia Sos, Simona Arghir, Georgeta Lacusta, Doina Furcoiu, Niculina Sasu, Cristina Petrovici, Constantina Pitigoi, Doina Cojocaru, Magdalena Miklos, Marla Bosi, Viorica Doina Ionica, Maria Lackovics, Juliana Hobincu) | 2 | 3 | 0 | 73 | 83 |
| 5. | JPN | (Shoko Wada, Hiroko Kosahara, Natsue Shimada, Terumi Kurata, Mikiko Kato, Hitomi Matsushita, Emiko Yamashita, Kuriko Komori, Eiko Kawada, Mihoko Hozumi, Nanami Kino, Tokuko Kubo) | 1 | 4 | 0 | 72 | 115 |
| 6. | CAN | (Danielle Chenard, Louise Hurtubise, Denise Lemaire, Francine Boulay-Parizeau, Joanes Rail, Nicole Genier, Lucie Balthazar, Hélène Tetreault, Manon Charette, Monique Prud'-Homme, Louise Beaumont, Mariette Houle, Nicole Robert, Johanne Valois) | 0 | 5 | 0 | 35 | 106 |

**1980 Moscow** T: 6, N: 6, D: 7.29.

| | | | W | L | T | PF | PA |
|---|---|---|---|---|---|---|---|
| 1. | SOV | (Natalya Timoshkina, Larissa Karlova, Irina Palchikova, Zinaida Turchina, Tatyana Kochergina [Makarez], Lyudmila Poradnik [Bobrus], Larissa Savkina, Aldona Nenėnienė [Česaityte], Yulia Safina, Olga Zubareva, Valentina Lutaeva, Lyubov Odinokova [Berezhnaya], Sigita Strečen) | 5 | 0 | 0 | 99 | 52 |
| 2. | YUG | (Ana Titlić, Slavica Jeremić, Zorica Vojinovic, Radmila Drljaca, Katica Iles, Mirjana Ognjenović, Svetlana Anastasovski, Rada Savić, Svetlana Kitić, Mirjana Djurica, Biserka Višnjić, Vesna Radović, Jasna Merdan, Vesna Milosević) | 3 | 1 | 1 | 107 | 67 |

|   |   | W | L | T | PF | PA |
|---|---|---|---|---|----|----|
| 3. | GDR (Hannelore Zober, Katrin Krüger, Evelyn Matz, Roswitha Krause, Christina Rost, Petra Uhlig, Claudia Wunderlich, Sabine Röther, Kornelia Kunisch, Marion Tietz, Kristina Richter, Waltraud Kretzschmar, Birgit Heinecke, Renate Rudolph) | 3 | 1 | 1 | 91 | 58 |
| 4. | HUN (Mária Berzsenyi, Erzsébet Csajbok [Németh], Rozália Lelkes, Éva Csulik, Amália Sterbinszky, Klára Csik, Marianna Nagy, Ilona Mihályka, Mária Vadász, Erzsébet Balogh, Eva Angyal, Györgyi Ori, Piroska Budai, Klára Bonyhádi) | 1 | 3 | 1 | 65 | 74 |
| 5. | CZE (Mária Končeková, Elena Boledovičová, Daniela Nováková, Katerina Lamrichová, Alena Horalová, Jolana Nemethová, Viola Pavlasová, Piroska Polačekova, Jana Kutková, Věra Datinská, Milena Foltýnová, Elena Brezanyová, Petra Kominková) | 1 | 3 | 1 | 65 | 78 |
| 6. | CON (Madeleine Mitsotso, Pascaline Bobeka, Angelik Abebame, Nicole Oba, Henriette Koula, Solange Koulinka, Isabelle Azanga, Micheline Okemba, Viviane Okoula, Germaine Djimbi, Yolande Kada-Gango, Lopez-Pemba, Julienne Malaki, Yvonne Makouala) | 0 | 5 | 0 | 46 | 159 |

The U.S.S.R. faced its only threat against Hungary when they led 12–11 with just five minutes to play. The Soviets then scored four straight goals and won, 16–12. Roswitha Krause of the bronze-medal-winning East German team had won a silver medal in the freestyle swimming relay 12 years earlier in Mexico City.

**1984 Los Angeles-Fullerton** T: 6, N: 6, D: 8.9.

|   |   | W | L | T | PF | PA |
|---|---|---|---|---|----|----|
| 1. | YUG (Jasna Ptujeć, Mirjana Ognjenović, Zorica Pavicević, Ljubinka Janković, Svetlana Anastasovski, Svetlana Dasić-Kitić, Emilija Ercić, Alenka Cuderman, Svetlana Mugosa, Mirjana Djurica, Biserka Višnjić, Slavica Djukić, Jasna Kolar-Merdan, Ljijana Mugosa, Dragica Djurić) | 5 | 0 | 0 | 143 | 102 |
| 2. | KOR (Son Mi-na, Kim Kyung-soon, Lee Soon-ei, Jeong Hyoi-soon, Kim Mi-sook, Han Hwa-soon, Kim Ok-hwa, Kim Choon-yei, Jeung Soon-bok, Yoon Byung- | 3 | 1 | 1 | 125 | 119 |

soon, Lee Young-ja, Sung Kyung-hwa, Youn Soo-kyung)

|   |   | W | L | T | PF | PA |
|---|---|---|---|---|----|----|
| 3. | CHN (Wu Xingjiang, He Jianping, Zhu Juefeng, Zhang Weihong, Gao Xiumin, Wang Linwei, Liu Liping, Zhang Peijun, Sun Xiulan, Liu Yumei, Li Lan, Wang Mingxing, Chen Zhen) | 2 | 2 | 1 | 112 | 115 |
| 4. | GER (Elke Blumauer, Maike Becker, Corinna Kunze, Silvia Schmitt, Roswitha Mroczynski, Sabine Erbs, Dagmar Stelberg, Kerstin Jönsson, Astrid Hühn, Petra Platen, Claudia Sturm, Sabrina Koschella, Vanadis Putzke) | 2 | 3 | 0 | 91 | 100 |
| 4. | USA (Pamela Boyd, Carol Lindsey, Reita Clanton, Sherry Winn, Theresa Contos, Carmen Forest, Sandra De La Riva, Janice Trombly, Mary Phyllis Dwight, Cynthia Stinger, Melinda Hale, Leora "Sam" Jones, Penelope Stone) | 2 | 3 | 0 | 114 | 123 |
| 6. | AUT (Ulrike Huber, Ulrike Popp, Martina Neubauer, Karin Prokop, Susanne Unger, Milena Gschiessl-Foltýnová, Maria Sykora, Silvia Steinbauer, Karin Hillinger, Elisabeth Zehetner, Gabriele Gebauer, Vesna Radović, Teresa Zielewicz, Gudrun Neunteufel, Monika Unger) | 0 | 5 | 0 | 91 | 117 |

Yugoslavia was seriously challenged only in their opening match when they defeated West Germany 20–19 after Mirjana Djurica converted a penalty with 1:06 to play. During the Yugoslavs' 33–20 drubbing of the U.S., 27-year-old Jasna Kolar-Merdan scored an Olympic record 17 goals.

**1988 Seoul-Suwon** T: 8, N: 8, D: 9.29.

|   |   | W | L | T | PF | PA |
|---|---|---|---|---|----|----|
| 1. | KOR (Song Ji-hyun, Han Hyun-sook, Kim Choon-rye, Kim Myung-soon, Lee Ki-soon, Kim Hyun-mee, Kim Mi-sook, Suk Min-hee, Son Mi-na, Lim Mi-kyung, Kim Kyung-soon, Sung Kyung-hwa) | 4 | 1 | 0 | 120 | 106 |
| 2. | NOR (Vibeke Johnsen, Cathrine Svendsen, Heidi Sundal, Hanne Hegh, Susann Goksor, Hanne Hogness, Karin Singstao, Trine Haltvik, Berit Digre, Ingrid Steen, Karin Pettersen, Annette Skottvoll, Kristin Midthun, Marte Eliasson, Kjerstin Andersen) | 3 | 1 | 1 | 115 | 91 |
| 3. | SOV (Natalya Mitryuk, Larissa Karlova, Svetlana Mankova, Zinaida Turchina, Olga Semenova, Marina Bazanova, Na- | 3 | 1 | 1 | 112 | 85 |

talya Morskova, Tatyana Gorb, Yevgenia Tovstogan, Natalya Rusnachenko, Yelena Nemashkalo, Tatyana Dzhandzhgava, Natalya Anissimova, Yelina Guseva, Natalya Lapitskaya)

| | | | | | | |
|---|---|---|---|---|---|---|
| 4. YUG | (Mirjana Krstić, Slavica Rincić, Dragana Pesić, Svetlana Obucina, Zita Galić, Ljubinka Janković, Svetlana Micić, Ljijana Marković, Mirjana Djurica, Natasa Kolega, Slavica Djukić, Ljijana Mugosa, Svetlana Mugosa, Deanka Stojanović, Dragica Djurić) | 2 | 3 | 0 | 88 | 96 |
| 5. CZE | (Anna Hradská, Irena Tomašovičová, Daniela Trandžíková, Marie Šmídová, Gabriela Sabadošová, Julia Kolečániová, Zuzana Budayová, Alena Damitšová, Petra Lupačová, Mária Ďurišinová, Monika Hejtmánková, Lenka Pospíšilová, Jana Stašová, Bozena Mazgutova, Marta Pösová) | 4 | 1 | 0 | 141 | 102 |
| 6. CHN | (Zhang Hong, He Jianping, Zhang Weihong, Wang Mingxing, Chen Zhen, Li Lirong, Li Jie, Sun Xiulan, Xue Jinhua, Dai Jianfen, Wang Tao, Lu Guanghong) | 2 | 3 | 0 | 128 | 106 |
| 7. USA | (Kathy Callaghan, Amy Gamble, Margaret Gallagher, Sherry Winn, Karyn Palgut, Portia Lack, Sandra De La Riva, Kim Clarke, Cynthia Stinger, Angie Raynor, Leora Jones, Carol Peterka, Penelope Stone, Laura Coenen) | 1 | 4 | 0 | 104 | 123 |
| 8. IVC | (Elisabeth Kouassi, Wandou Guehi, Koko Elleingand, Emilie Djoman, Zomou Awa, Alimata Douamba, Mahoula Kramo, Clementinea Ble, Adjoua Ndri, Doumbia Bah, Julienne Vodoungbo, Hortense Konan, Gouna Irie, Brigitte Guigui) | 0 | 5 | 0 | 65 | 164 |

The Korean women, who had finished eleventh at the 1986 world championships, clinched their gold medal with a stunning, emotion-charged 21–19 upset of the U.S.S.R.

# ARCHERY

109. Q.F. Newall, winner of the 1908 women's archery competition.

# BASKETBALL

110

110. The greatest basketball team in Olympic history: the 1960 U.S. team. Ten of its members went on to successful careers in professional basketball.

111. Uljana Semjonova guards 6-foot 3-inch Lucy Harris (with ball) in 1976.

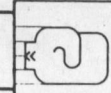

112

112. In 1964 South Korean flyweight Choh Dong-kih staged a 51-minute sitdown strike after being disqualified for holding his head too low.

113. Disqualified in his first fight in the 1964 Olympics, Spanish featherweight Valentin Loren takes out his frustration on the Hungarian referee.

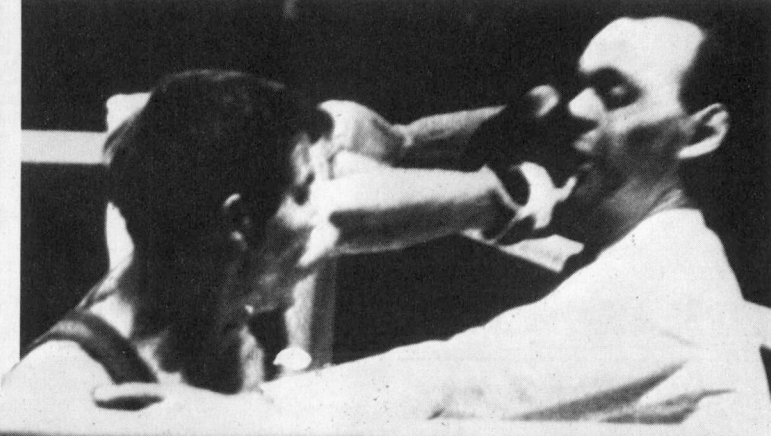

114. In 1988 bantamweight Byun Jong-il beat his countryman's sitdown record by 16 minutes.

115. Supporters of Uruguayan featherweight Basilio Alves storm the table of the Jury of Appeal following Alves' 1948 loss to American Eddie Johnson.

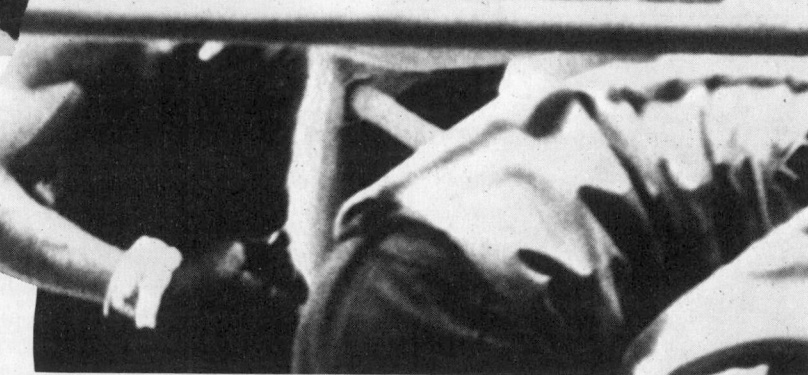

113

114

115

# BOXING

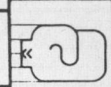

116

117

116. At 37, 1908 Featherweight champion Richard Gunn was the oldest boxing gold medalist in Olympic history.

117. László Papp, the first boxer to win three Olympic gold medals. He was Middleweight champion in 1948 and Light Middleweight champion in 1952 and 1956.

118. Roy Jones, referee Aldo Leoni and Park Si-hun react with shock at the announcement of the decision in the final of the 1988 Light Middleweight division.

# BOXING

119. *"Unroasted human beef of Old England": Harry Mallin, the 1920 and 1924 Middleweight gold medalist.*

120. *Outspoken Chris Finnegan, on his way to victory in the 1968 Middleweight division. His biggest challenge was producing a urine sample for the post-fight drug test.*

119

120

, U. S.

121

122

121. Eddie Eagan won the Light Heavyweight gold medal in 1920. Twelve years later, as a member of the winning four-man bobsled team, he became the only person to earn gold medals in both the Summer and Winter Games.

122. Cassius Clay, later Muhammed Ali (center), flanked by fellow 1960 gold medalists Edward Crook and Wilbert McClure.

# CANOEING

123. The exotic sport of slalom, or white water, canoeing was included in the 1972 Olympics and dominated by the East Germans, who had constructed an exact copy of the West German course that was used for the Olympics.

123

124

125

*124. Viktor Kapitonov (left) edges Livio Trapé at the finish line of the 1960 road race, only to discover that he still has one more 14½-kilometer lap to go. Twenty-four minutes later, Kapitonov defeated Trapé again.*

*125. Connie Carpenter-Phinney (foreground) edges ahead of Rebecca Twigg in the last second of the 1984 women's road race.*

*126. In 1968 the four Pettersson brothers of Sweden joined forces to win silver medals in the cycling team time trial.*

126

# EQUESTRIAN

127. A leading German hero of the 1936 Berlin Olympics, Konrad von Wangenheim broke his collarbone during the steeplechase portion of the equestrian three-day event. The next day he was thrown from his horse a second time but completed the competition, enabling the German team to win the gold medal.

128. In 1952 Lis Hartel of Denmark won a silver medal in the individual dressage event only eight years after being stricken with polio. Paralyzed below the knees, she had to be helped on and off her horse.

127

128

129

130

129. Nedo Nadi won gold
medals in five of the six fencing
events of 1920.

130. Aladar Gerevich (left) won
seven gold medals, one silver,
and two bronze between 1932
and 1960 (when he was 50
years old). Pál Kovács (right)
earned six gold medals and
one bronze between 1936 and
1960.

131. The award ceremony for
the 1936 women's foil:
(left to right) Ellen Preis (bronze),
Ilona Elek (gold), and German
Jew Helene Mayer (silver).

131

# GYMNASTICS

132. Lyudmila Tourisheva won the 1972 All-Around championship, but received little attention from the Western press, which was more interested in her less accomplished but more charismatic teammate . . .

133. . . . Olga Korbut, the Munchkin of Munich.

134. Nadia Comaneci, a veteran of 18 at the Moscow Olympics in 1980.

# JUDO

135

*135. Yasuhiro Yamashita prepares to throw Hitoshi Saito in the 1984 All Japan Judo Championship. Three and a half months later, they both won gold medals at the Los Angeles Olympics.*

# ROWING

136. Jack Kelly, father of Princess Grace of Monaco, won three rowing gold medals in 1920 and 1924.

# SHOOTING

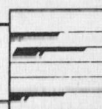

137. Károly Takács was a champion shooter when his right hand, his pistol hand, was shattered by a grenade. Ten years later, in 1948, Takács won his first Olympic gold medal—using his left hand.

138. Gerald Ouellette shot 60 straight bull's-eyes to win the 1956 smallbore rifle (prone) event.

137

138

# JUDO

| MEN | WOMEN |
|---|---|
| Extra-Lightweight | Extra-Lightweight |
| Half-Lightweight | Half-Lightweight |
| Lightweight | Lightweight |
| Half-Middleweight | Half-Middleweight |
| Middleweight | Middleweight |
| Half-Heavyweight | Half-Heavyweight |
| Heavyweight | Heavyweight |
| Discontinued Event | |

## JUDO TERMS

### Scoring

| | |
|---|---|
| Ippon | Full Point |
| Waza-ari | Almost ippon |
| Yuko | Almost waza-ari |
| Koka | Almost yuko |

### Penalties

| | |
|---|---|
| Hansokumake (= ippon) | Disqualification |
| Keikoku (= waza-ari) | Warning |
| Chui (= yuko) | Caution |
| Shido (= koka) | Note |

### Throws

| | |
|---|---|
| Harai goshi | Sweeping hip throw |
| O-soto-gari | Major outer reaping throw |
| O-uchi-gari | Major inner reaping throw |
| Seoi-nage | Over-the-shoulder throw |
| Tai-otoshi | Body drop |
| Uchi-mata | Inner thigh throw |

### Holds

| | |
|---|---|
| Kami-shio-gatame | Upper four quarters hold |
| Kesa-gatame | Scarf hold |
| Kuzure-kami-shiho-gatame | Variant on upper four quarters hold |
| Yoko-shiho-gatame | Side four quarters hold |

### Other Terms

| | |
|---|---|
| Awasewaza | Ippon by two waza-ari |
| Katsu | A system of resuscitation |
| Kinsa | Slight superiority or close decision |
| Shime-waza | Strangulation or choking techniques |
| Yusei-gachi | Win by superiority scores or officials' decision |

A judo match is won by a score of "ippon" which ends the match. A match which goes to full term without an ippon is decided by lesser scores. In the case of a tie, the majority decision of the referee and the two judges awards the match to the competitor who has displayed superiority.

Ippon can be scored by a clean, forceful throw; by holding the opponent mainly on his back for 30 seconds, under control, but not necessarily immobile; or by submission to a strangle, a choke or a lock applied against the elbow. Waza-ari is scored by a throw not quite good enough for ippon or by a 25-second hold-down. Yuko and koka can be scored for inferior throws or by 20- and 10-second hold-downs respectively. A second waza-ari in a match counts as ippon, but any amount of yukos is inferior to one waza-ari and any amount of kokas is inferior to one yuko.

In 1964 preliminary matches lasted ten minutes and final matches 15 minutes. In 1972 and 1976, the matches were six and ten minutes, and in 1980 and 1984 five and seven minutes. In 1988, all matches lasted five minutes.

# MEN

## EXTRA-LIGHTWEIGHT
### (60 kg—132.25 lbs)

**1896–1976** not held

**1980 Moscow** C: 29, N: 29, D: 8.1.

| | | | FINAL MATCH | |
|---|---|---|---|---|
| 1. | Thierry Rey | FRA | Koka | 7:00 |
| 2. | Rafael Rodriguez Carbenell | CUB | | |
| 3. | Aramby Emizh | SOV | | |
| 3. | Tibor Kincses | HUN | | |
| 5. | John Holliday | GBR | | |
| 5. | Pavel Petrikov | CZE | | |
| 7. | Samir Elnajjar | SYR | | |
| 7. | Reino Fagerlund | FIN | | |

**1984 Los Angeles** C: 27, N: 27, D: 8.4.

FINAL MATCH

1. Shinji Hosokawa — JPN — Yoko-shiho-gatame — 1:09
2. Kim Jae-yup — KOR
3. Neil Eckersley — GBR
3. Edward Liddie — USA
5. Guy Delvingt — FRA
5. Felice Mariani — ITA

**1988 Seoul** C: 37, N: 37, D: 9.25.

FINAL MATCH

1. Kim Jae-yup — KOR — Shido — 5:00
2. Kevin Asano — USA
3. Shinji Hosokawa — JPN
3. Amiran Totikashvili — SOV
5. Patrick Roux — FRA
5. Sheu Tsay-chwan — TAI

To qualify for the Olympic Games, Kim needed to lose 13 pounds in 20 days. He did this by limiting himself to one meal a day: a bowl of porridge with raw fish slices.

Kim, who was recovering from an injury to his backbone, had actually lost the Korean Olympic trials to Yun Hyun. However, the Korea Judo Association chose Kim as its representative anyway. After his victory in Seoul, Kim told the press, "I apologize to Yun and his mother. My gold medal is won together by them and me." In honor of his Olympic championship, Kim (unlike Yun and his mother) was rewarded with a lifetime pension of $16,600 a year by Korea's National Sports Promotion Foundation.

# HALF-LIGHTWEIGHT
## (65 kg—143 lbs)

**1896-1976** not held

**1980 Moscow** C: 29, N: 29, D: 7.01.

FINAL MATCH

1. Nikolai Solodukhin — SOV — Koka/shido — 7:00
2. Tsendying Damdin — MON
3. Iliyan Nedkov — BUL
3. Janusz Pawlowski — POL
5. Yves Delvingt — FRA
5. Torsten Reissmann — GDR
7. Wolfgang Biedron — SWE
7. Jaroslav Kriz — CZE

**1984 Los Angeles** C: 34, N: 34, D: 8.5.

FINAL MATCH

1. Yoshiyuki Matsuoka — JPN — Seoi-nage — 7:00
2. Hwang Jung-oh — KOR
3. Marc Alexandre — FRA
3. Josef Reiter — AUT
5. Stephen Gawthorpe — GBR
5. Sandro Rosati — ITA

**1988 Seoul** C: 42, N: 42, D: 9.26.

FINAL MATCH

1. Lee Kyung-keun — KOR — Yusei-gachi — 5:00
2. Janusz Pawlowski — POL
3. Bruno Carabetta — FRA
3. Yosuke Yamamoto — JPN
5. Tamás Bujkó — HUN
5. Brent Cooper — NZE

Like all members of the Korean judo team, Lee's training included periodic midnight visits to a cemetery, where he was forced to sit alone for an hour before being returned to his dormitory to watch videotapes of his potential opponents. Lee's path to the gold medal included a controversial semifinal split decision over Bruno Carabetta.

# LIGHTWEIGHT
## (71 kg—156.5 lbs)

**1896-1960** not held

**1964 Tokyo** C: 25, N: 18, D: 10.20
*(68 kg—150 lbs)*

FINAL MATCH

1. Takehide Nakatani — JPN — Awasewaza — 1:15
2. Eric Hänni — SWI
3. Aron Bogoljubov — SOV
3. Oleg Stepanov — SOV
5. Won Ku Chang (TAI), Paul Maruyama (USA), Park Chung-sam (KOR), Gerhard Zotter (AUT)

**1968** not held

**1972 Munich** C: 29, N: 29, D: 9.4.
*(63 kg—139 lbs)*

FINAL MATCH

1. Takao Kawaguchi — JPN — Kami-shiho-gatame — 0:39
3. Kim Yong-ik — PRK
3. Jean-Jacques Mounier — FRA
5. Wolfram Koppen — GER
5. Hector Rodriguez Torres — CUB
7. Chi-Hsiang Cheng — TAI
7. Ferenc Szabó — HUN
DISQ (Drugs): Bakhaavaa Buidaa (MON)

Buidaa lost a silver medal when he became the first person in judo history to fail a drug test.

**1976 Montreal** C: 32, N: 32, D: 7.26.
*(63 kg—139 lbs)*

FINAL MATCH

1. Hector Rodriguez Torres — CUB — Uchi-mata — 10:00
2. Chang Eun-kyung — KOR
3. Felice Mariani — ITA
3. József Tuncsik — HUN
5. Erich Pointner — AUT
5. Marian Standowicz — POL
7. Brad Farrow — CAN
7. José Pinto Gomes — POR

Surprisingly, two-time world champion Yoshiharu Minami was eliminated in his first match by Yves Delvingt of France. The final was a rugged contest, which was interrupted at one point to allow Rodriguez's ribs to be wrapped up by a doctor. Rodriguez told reporters that he began practicing judo to protect himself from his six older brothers.

**1980 Moscow** C: 30, N: 30, D: 7.30.

|  |  |  | FINAL MATCH |  |
|---|---|---|---|---|
| 1. | Ezio Gamba | ITA | Yushi-gachi | 7:00 |
| 2. | Neil Adams | GBR |  |  |
| 3. | Ravdan Davaadalai | MON |  |  |
| 3. | Karl-Heinz Lehmann | GDR |  |  |
| 5. | Edward Alksnin | POL |  |  |
| 5. | Christian Dyot | FRA |  |  |
| 7. | Kim Byong-gun | PRK |  |  |
| 7. | Michael Picken | AUS |  |  |

European champion Neil Adams needed less than four minutes to defeat his first three opponents, but in the final he lost a unanimous decision to his 21-year-old nemesis, Ezio Gamba.

**1984 Los Angeles** C: 30, N: 30, D: 8.6.

|  |  |  | FINAL MATCH |  |
|---|---|---|---|---|
| 1. | Ahn Byeong-keun | KOR | Seoi-nage | 7:00 |
| 2. | Ezio Gamba | ITA |  |  |
| 3. | Kerrith Brown | GBR |  |  |
| 3. | Luis Onmura | BRA |  |  |
| 5. | Glenn Beauchamp | CAN |  |  |
| 5. | Hidetoshi Nakanishi | JPN |  |  |

Defending Olympic champion Ezio Gamba needed only 4 minutes and 1 second to demolish his first four opponents, but he ran out of steam in the final and was beaten by Ahn Byeong-keun. Earlier, Ahn had defeated world champion Hidetoshi Nakanishi, who had suffered a broken rib in his opening match.

**1988 Seoul** C: 41, N: 41, D: 9.27.

|  |  |  | FINAL MATCH |  |
|---|---|---|---|---|
| 1. | Marc Alexandre | FRA | Koka | 5:00 |
| 2. | Sven Loll | GDR |  |  |
| 3. | Michael Swain | USA |  |  |
| 3. | Georgy Tenadze | SOV |  |  |
| 5. | Bertalan Hajtós | HUN |  |  |
| 5. | Steffen Stranz | GER |  |  |

Alexandre scored by knocking down Loll at 3:55 with a well-timed foot hook. Initially Kerrith Brown of Great Britain was awarded a bronze medal by virtue of his repêchage victory over world champion Michael Swain. However, he tested positive for Furosemide, a proscribed diuretic. When asked how he felt about backing into a bronze medal, Swain was philosophical. "I didn't want to win it this way," he said, "but I can always lie to my grandchildren."

# HALF-MIDDLEWEIGHT
## (78 kg—172 lbs)

**1896–1968** not held

**1972 Munich** C: 29, N: 29, D: 9.3.
**(70 kg—154 lbs)**

|  |  |  | FINAL MATCH |  |
|---|---|---|---|---|
| 1. | Toyokazu Nomura | JPN | Seoi-nage | 0:27 |
| 2. | Antoni Zajkowski | POL |  |  |
| 3. | Dietmar Hötger | GDR |  |  |
| 3. | Anatoli Novikov | SOV |  |  |
| 5. | Engelbert Doerbandt | GER |  |  |
| 5. | Antal Hetényi | HUN |  |  |
| 7. | Wang Jong-she | TAI |  |  |
| 7. | Reto Zinsli | SWI |  |  |

Nomura disposed of his five opponents in a total of ten minutes and 49 seconds.

**1976 Montreal** C: 29, N; 29, D: 7.29.
**(70 kg—154 lbs)**

|  |  |  | FINAL MATCH |  |
|---|---|---|---|---|
| 1. | Vladimir Nevzorov | SOV | Tai-otoshi | 10.00 |
| 2. | Koji Kuramoto | JPN |  |  |
| 3. | Marian Talaj | POL |  |  |
| 3. | Patrick Vial | FRA |  |  |
| 5. | Lee Chang-sun | KOR |  |  |
| 5. | Vaccinuf Morrison | GBR |  |  |
| 7. | Juan Carlos Rodriguez | SPA |  |  |
| 7. | John Van Hoek | AUS |  |  |

**1980 Moscow** C: 29, N: 29, D: 7.29.

|  |  |  | FINAL MATCH |  |
|---|---|---|---|---|
| 1. | Shota Khabareli | SOV | Yuko | 7:00 |
| 2. | Juan Ferrer La Hera | CUB |  |  |
| 3. | Harald Heinke | GDR |  |  |
| 3. | Bernard Tchoullouyan | FRA |  |  |
| 5. | Mircea Fratica | ROM |  |  |
| 5. | Ignacio Sanz Paz | SPA |  |  |
| 7. | Georgi Petrov | BUL |  |  |
| 7. | Slavko Sikiric | YUG |  |  |

**1984 Los Angeles** C: 38, N: 38, D: 8.7.

|  |  |  | FINAL MATCH |  |
|---|---|---|---|---|
| 1. | Frank Wieneke | GER | Seoi-nage | 4:04 |
| 2. | Neil Adams | GBR |  |  |
| 3. | Mircea Fratiçã | ROM |  |  |
| 3. | Michel Nowak | FRA |  |  |
| 5. | Filip Lesčak | YUG |  |  |
| 5. | Hiromitsu Takano | JPN |  |  |

Wieneke's sudden victory over Adams was a shocking upset. At the 3:50 mark, Adams glanced at the clock and thought, "Three minutes to go and you're Olympic champion." Wieneke launched a weak right-handed attack, which Adams easily repelled. But then Wieneke noticed Adams relax momentarily, so he quickly executed a left shoulder throw. The former world champion was down on the mat and the contest was over. It was the first time in his entire career that Adams had lost a match by ippon.

**1988 Seoul** C: 41, N: 41, D: 9.28.

| | | FINAL MATCH | |
|---|---|---|---|
| 1. Waldemar Legień | POL | Seoi-nage | 4:44 |
| 2. Frank Wieneke | GER | | |
| 3. Torsten Bréchôt | GDR | | |
| 3. Bashir Varayev | SOV | | |
| 5. Kevin Doherty | CAN | | |
| 5. Pascal Tayot | FRA | | |

Wieneke was defeated by the same shoulder throw that he had used to win four years earlier.

## MIDDLEWEIGHT
(86 kg—189.5 lbs)

**1896–1960** not held

**1964 Tokyo** C: 25, N: 20, D: 10.21.
*(80 kg—176 lbs)*

| | | FINAL MATCH | |
|---|---|---|---|
| 1. Isao Okano | JPN | Yoko-shiho-gatame | 1:36 |
| 2. Wolfgang Hofmann | GER | | |
| 3. James Bregman | USA | | |
| 3. Kim Eui-tae | KOR | | |
| 5. Lionel Grossain (FRA), Rodolf Perez (ARG), Lhoffei Shiozawa (BRA), Petrus Snijders (HOL) | | | |

In the quarterfinal match between Okano and Grossain, both the referee and Okano failed to notice that Grossain had been rendered unconscious by a Shime-waza. When the Japanese coach called their attention to the Frenchman's condition, Okano revived his opponent through the use of Katsu.

**1968** not held

**1972 Munich** C: 35, N: 35, D: 9.2.
*(80 kg—176 lbs)*

| | | FINAL MATCH | |
|---|---|---|---|
| 1. Shinobu Sekine | JPN | Yushi-gachi | 10:00 |
| 2. Oh Seung-lip | KOR | | |
| 3. Jean-Paul Coché | FRA | | |
| 3. Brian Jacks | GBR | | |
| 5. Guram Gogalauri | SOV | | |
| 5. Lutz Lischka | AUT | | |
| 7. Gerd Egger | GER | | |
| 7. Petr Jaekl | CZE | | |

Sekine, the All-Japan open category champion, actually lost to Oh in the preliminary pool. But he was able to fight his way into the final through repêchage, or second-

chance matches, and won by a split decision, to the great relief of all the Japanese who were present.

**1976 Montreal** C: 32, N:32, D: 7.28.
*(80 kg—176 lbs)*

| | | FINAL MATCH | |
|---|---|---|---|
| 1. Isamu Sonoda | JPN | O-uchi-gari | 10:00 |
| 2. Valery Dvoinikov | SOV | | |
| 3. Slavko Obadov | YUG | | |
| 3. Park Young-chul | KOR | | |
| 5. José Luis Frutos | SPA | | |
| 5. Fred Marhenke | GER | | |
| 7. Paul Buganey | AUS | | |
| 7. Suheyl Yesilnur | TUR | | |

Policeman Isamu Sonoda upset three-time world champion Shozo Fujii in the All-Japan championships, which served as Japan's Olympic qualifying tournament.

**1980 Moscow** C: 27, N: 27, D: 7.28.

| | | FINAL MATCH | |
|---|---|---|---|
| 1. Jürg Röthlisberger | SWI | Yuko | 7:00 |
| 2. Isaac Azcuy Oliva | CUB | | |
| 3. Aleksandr Jatskevitš | SOV | | |
| 3. Detlef Ultsch | GDR | | |
| 5. Walter Carmona | BRA | | |
| 5. Bertil Ström | SWE | | |
| 7. Peter Donnelly | GBR | | |
| 7. Henri-Richard Lobe | CAM | | |

**1984 Los Angeles** C: 29, N: 29, D: 8.8.

| | | FINAL MATCH | |
|---|---|---|---|
| 1. Peter Seisenbacher | AUT | Uchi-mata | 2:26 |
| 2. Robert Berland | USA | | |
| 3. Walter Carmona | BRA | | |
| 3. Seiki Nose | JPN | | |
| 5. Fabien Canu | FRA | | |
| 5. Densign White | GBR | | |

Seisenbacher, the first Austrian ever to win a major judo championship, dispatched his five opponents in an elapsed time of 11 minutes and 5 seconds.

**1988 Seoul** C: 36, N: 36, D: 9.29.

| | | FINAL MATCH | |
|---|---|---|---|
| 1. Peter Seisenbacher | AUT | Yusei-gachi | 5:00 |
| 2. Vladimir Shestakov | SOV | | |
| 3. Akinobu Osako | JPN | | |
| 3. Ben Spijkers | HOL | | |
| 5. Fabien Canu | FRA | | |
| 5. Densign White | GBR | | |

At age 28, Seisenbacher became the first judoka in Olympic history to retain his title.

## HALF-HEAVYWEIGHT
(95 kg—209 lbs)

**1896–1968** not held

**1972 Munich** C: 30, N: 30, D: 9.1.
*(93 kg—205 lbs)*

| | | FINAL MATCH | |
|---|---|---|---|
| 1. Shota Chochoshvili | SOV | Yushi-gachi | 10:00 |
| 2. David Starbrook | GBR | | |
| 3. Paul Barth | GER | | |
| 3. Chiaki Ishii | BRA | | |
| 5. Helmut Howiller | GDR | | |
| 5. James Wooley | USA | | |
| 7. Pierre Albertini | FRA | | |
| 7. Terry Farnsworth | CAN | | |

Two-time world champion Fumio Sasahara of Hokkaido, Japan, was unexpectedly thrown and defeated by 22-year-old Shota Chochoshvili of Tbilissi, Georgia. Chochoshvili then lost a split decision to Dave Starbrook, the operator of a newspaper, tobacco, and sweet shop in Hackney. The two met again in the finals, and this time Chochoshvili prevailed with a unanimous decision.

**1976 Montreal** C: 35, N: 35, D: 7.27.
*(93 kg—205 lbs)*

| | | FINAL MATCH | |
|---|---|---|---|
| 1. Kazuhiro Ninomiya | JPN | Keikoku | 10:00 |
| 2. Ramaz Harshiladze | SOV | | |
| 3. Jürg Röthlisberger | SWI | | |
| 3. David Starbrook | GBR | | |
| 5. Jeaki Cho | KOR | | |
| 5. Dietmar Lorenz | GDR | | |
| 7. An Ung-nam | PRK | | |
| 7. Abdoulaye Djiba | SEN | | |

Ninomiya, who won three of his four preliminary fights in one minute or less, had to lose over 25 pounds to make the weight limit.

**1980 Moscow** C: 23, N: 23, D: 7.27.

| | | FINAL MATCH | |
|---|---|---|---|
| 1. Robert Van de Walle | BEL | Koka | 7:00 |
| 2. Tengiz Khubuluri | SOV | | |
| 3. Dietmar Lorenz | GDR | | |
| 3. Henk Numan | HOL | | |
| 5. István Szepesi | HUN | | |
| 5. R. José Tornes Bastardo | CUB | | |
| 7. Daniel Radu | ROM | | |
| 7. Jean-Luc Rouge | FRA | | |

**1984 Los Angeles** C: 22, N: 22, D: 8.9.

| | | FINAL MATCH | |
|---|---|---|---|
| 1. Ha Hyoung-zoo | KOR | Yusei-gachi | 7:00 |
| 2. Douglas Vieira | BRA | | |
| 3. Bjarni Fridriksson | ICE | | |
| 3. Günter Neureuther | GER | | |
| 5. Yuri Fazi | ITA | | |
| 5. Joe Meli | CAN | | |

**1988 Seoul** C: 21, N: 21, D: 9.30.

| | | FINAL MATCH | |
|---|---|---|---|
| 1. Aurelio Miguel | BRA | Chui | 5:00 |
| 2. Marc Meiling | GER | | |
| 3. Dennis Stewart | GBR | | |
| 3. Robert Van de Walle | BEL | | |
| 5. Jacek Beutler | POL | | |
| 5. Jiří Sosna | CZE | | |

Incredibly, Miguel won all five of his matches without scoring a single point. He gained two victories by judges' decision and three, including the final, when his opponents were penalized for excessive passivity. Nineteen-eighty Olympic champion Robert Van de Walle earned a bronze in 1988 at the age of 34.

# HEAVYWEIGHT
## (Over 95 kg—209 lbs)

**1896–1960** not held

**1964 Tokyo** C: 15, N: 13, D: 10.22.
*(Over 80 kg—176 lbs)*

| | | FINAL MATCH | |
|---|---|---|---|
| 1. Isao Inokuma | JPN | Kinsa | 15.00 |
| 2. Alfred Douglas Rogers | CAN | | |
| 3. Anzor Kiknadze | SOV | | |
| 3. Parnaoz Chikviladze | SOV | | |
| 5. Kim Jong-dal | KOR | | |

Inokuma and Rogers were used to practicing together in Japan, so the final was a relatively quiet affair. The lightest entrant in the heavyweight division, Inokuma weighed only 192 pounds, compared to Rogers' 260 pounds.

**1968** not held

**1972 Munich** C: 21, N: 21, D: 8.31.
*(Over 93 kg—205 lbs)*

| | | FINAL MATCH | |
|---|---|---|---|
| 1. Willem Ruska | HOL | Harai-goshi | 1:43 |
| 2. Klaus Glahn | GER | | |
| 3. Motoki Nishimura | JPN | | |
| 3. Givi Onashvili | SOV | | |
| 5. Jean-Claude Brondani | FRA | | |
| 5. Douglas Nelson | USA | | |
| 7. Tijive Bankassou | HOL | | |
| 7. M'Bagnik Mebodj | SEN | | |

**1976 Montreal** C: 20, N: 20, D: 7.26.
*(Over 93 kg—205 lbs)*

| | | FINAL MATCH | |
|---|---|---|---|
| 1. Sergei Novikov | SOV | O-soto-gari | 1:19 |
| 2. Günther Neureuther | GER | | |
| 3. Allen Coage | USA | | |
| 3. Sumio Endo | JPN | | |
| 5. Gunsem Jalaa | MON | | |
| 5. Keith Remfry | GBR | | |
| 7. Abdoulaye Kote | SEN | | |
| 7. Radomir Kovačević | YUG | | |

A most unusual sight was the repêchage match between 5-foot 6½-inch, 259-pound Sumio Endo and 7-foot 0-

inch, 350-pound Jong-Gil Pak of North Korea. Endo, the defending world champion, was the victor.

**1980 Moscow** C: 18, N: 18, D: 7.27.

| | | FINAL MATCH |
|---|---|---|
| 1. Angelo Parisi | FRA | Ippon 6:14 |
| 2. Dimitur Zapryanov | BUL | |
| 3. Radomir Kovačević | YUG | |
| 3. Vladimir Kocman | CZE | |
| 5. Kim Myong-gyu | PRK | |
| 5. Paul Radburn | GBR | |
| 7. Wojciech Reszko | POL | |

Born in Italy, Parisi was a former member of the British team who married a Frenchwoman and changed citizenship.

**1984 Los Angeles** C: 16, N: 16, D: 8.10.

| | | FINAL MATCH |
|---|---|---|
| 1. Hitoshi Saito | JPN | Shido 7:00 |
| 2. Angelo Parisi | FRA | |
| 3. Mark Berger | CAN | |
| 3. Cho Yong-chul | KOR | |
| 5. Radomir Kovačević | YUG | |
| 5. Doug Nelson | USA | |

The 320-pound Saito made quick work of his first three opponents. Mark Berger lasted 17 seconds, Isidore Silas 29 seconds, and Radomir Kovačević 44 seconds. In the final, Parisi held firm, so firm in fact that he was penalized for inactivity, which cost him the match.

**1988 Seoul** C: 26, N: 26, D: 10.1.

| | | FINAL MATCH |
|---|---|---|
| 1. Hitoshi Saito | JPN | Keikoku 5:00 |
| 2. Henry Stöhr | GDR | |
| 3. Cho Yong-chul | KOR | |
| 3. Grigory Verichev | SOV | |
| 5. István Dubovsky | HUN | |
| 5. Dimitar Zaprianov | BUL | |

Saito, down to a trim 315 pounds, won his second Olympic championship by incurring only two warnings for inactivity to Stöhr's three.

# Discontinued Event
## OPEN

**1964 Tokyo** C: 9, N: 9, D: 10.23.

| | | FINAL MATCH |
|---|---|---|
| 1. Antonius Geesink | HOL | Kesa-gatame 9:22 |
| 2. Akio Kaminaga | JPN | |
| 3. Theodore Boronovskis | AUS | |
| 3. Klaus Glahn | GER | |

Geesink's victory was a shocking blow to the Japanese, even though he was two-time world champion and the clear favorite. In 1961 the 6-foot 6-inch, 267-pound judo instructor from Utrecht had become the first non-Japanese to win a world championship. Geesink had won his semifinal fight with Boronovskis in only 12 seconds. Although he failed to gain the gold medal, Kaminaga set an Olympic speed record in the repêchage round when he threw Thomas Ong of the Philippines in four seconds.

**1968** not held

**1972 Munich** C: 29, N: 29, D: 9.9.

| | | FINAL MATCH |
|---|---|---|
| 1. Willem Ruska | HOL | Yoko-shiho-gatame 3:58 |
| 2. Vitali Kusnezov | SOV | |
| 3. Jean-Claude Brondani | FRA | |
| 3. Angelo Parisi | GBR | |
| 5. Klaus Glahn | GER | |
| 5. Alfred Douglas Rogers | CAN | |
| 7. Tijini Benkassow | MOR | |
| 7. Chiaki Ishii | BRA | |

Having previously swept to victory in the heavyweight class, Ruska became the only person ever to win two Olympic gold medals in judo. In the open division, Ruska lost an early unanimous decision to Kusnezov, but was able to pin him when they met again in the final.

**1976 Montreal** C: 30, N: 30, D: 7.31.

| | | FINAL MATCH |
|---|---|---|
| 1. Haruki Uemura | JPN | Kuzure-kami-shiho-gatame 7:28 |
| 2. Keith Remfry | GBR | |
| 3. Jeaki Cho | KOR | |
| 3. Shota Chochoshvili | SOV | |
| 5. Jorge Portelli | ARG | |
| 5. Jean-Luc Rouge | FRA | |
| 7. Gunther Neureuther | GER | |
| 7. Pak Jong-gil | PRK | |

**1980 Moscow** C: 21, N: 21, D: 8.2.

| | | FINAL MATCH |
|---|---|---|
| 1. Dietmar Lorenz | GDR | Yushi-gachi 7:00 |
| 2. Angelo Parisi | FRA | |
| 3. Arthur Mapp | GBR | |
| 3. András Ozsvár | HUN | |
| 5. Sergei Novikov | SOV | |
| 5. Dambajan Tsend-Auish | MON | |
| 7. Pavelj Dragoi | ROM | |

Lorenz, a car mechanic and army officer, had the rare distinction of being a sixth Dan red-and-white belt judoka. At 5 feet 11 inches, he was also the shortest entrant in the open category.

**1984 Los Angeles** C: 15, N: 15, D: 8.11.

|  |  |  | FINAL MATCH |  |
|---|---|---|---|---|
| 1. Yasuhiro Yamashita | JPN | Yoko-shiho-gatame | 1:05 |
| 2. Mohamed Ali Rashwan | EGY |  |  |
| 3. Mihai Cioc | ROM |  |  |
| 3. Arthur Schnabel | GER |  |  |
| 5. Laurent del Colombo | FRA |  |  |
| 5. Xu Guoqing | CHN |  |  |

In October of 1977, Yasuhiro Yamashita lost by decision in the final of the Japanese Student Championships. Furious with himself for not fighting "like a warrior," he vowed never to allow such a lapse to occur again. In the next seven years Yamashita would suffer not a single loss, including 194 matches at national and international-level competition. All but five of his victories were by ippon. Included in that unbeaten string were four world championship titles. But one goal, his greatest goal, had eluded him—an Olympic gold medal.

When Japan joined the U.S.-led boycott of the 1980 Moscow Olympics, Yamashita appeared on national television pleading, with tears in his eyes, for a reversal of that decision. A week later Yamashita was held to a draw by Sumio Endo, who fell on top of Yamashita's left leg, breaking his ankle.

By the time 1984 rolled around, all this was forgotten and Yamashita seemed as sure a bet for a gold medal as anyone in Los Angeles. But in his second match, a victory over Arthur Schnabel, Yamashita tore a muscle in his right calf, causing him great pain and forcing him to walk with a limp. His next opponent, Laurent del Colombo, attacked Yamashita's right leg and scored a throw. Ten seconds later Laurent was flat on his back with the 5-foot 11-inch, 280-pound Yamashita on top of him. The match was quickly over.

In the final, Yamashita, described by one disgruntled opponent as "a refrigerator with a head on top," faced Mohamed Ali Rashwan, a 28-year-old building contractor from Alexandria. Yamashita scored a quick and easy victory, and was immediately overcome by his emotions. So sore was his leg that Rashwan had to help him onto the top step at the medal ceremony.

Afterwards, Rashwan told reporters, "I did not attack his right side because this is against my principles. I would not want to win this way." Rashwan was applauded for his good sportsmanship and news of his deed spread far and wide. On September 26, 1985, Rashwan was awarded the Fair Play Trophy by the International Committee for Fair Play. However, this inspiring tale of the true Olympic spirit has an odd twist to it. Videotapes of the Olympic final clearly show that Rashwan *did* try to attack Yamashita's injured leg. In fact, it was his first move, a mere ten seconds after the match began.

# WOMEN
## EXTRA-LIGHTWEIGHT
(48 kg—106 lbs)

This event will be held for the first time in 1992.

## HALF-LIGHTWEIGHT
(52 kg—114.61 lbs)

This event will be held for the first time in 1992.

## LIGHTWEIGHT
(56 kg—123 lbs)

This event will be held for the first time in 1992.

## HALF-MIDDLEWEIGHT
(61 kg—134.5 lbs)

This event will be held for the first time in 1992.

## MIDDLEWEIGHT
(66 kg—145.5 lbs)

This event will be held for the first time in 1992.

## HALF-HEAVYWEIGHT
(72 kg—158.5 lbs)

This event will be held for the first time in 1992.

## HEAVYWEIGHT
(Over 72 kg—158.5 lbs)

This event will be held for the first time in 1992.

# MODERN PENTATHLON

Individual
Team

The basic premise behind the modern pentathlon is that a soldier is ordered to deliver a message. He starts out on the back of an unfamiliar horse, but is forced to dismount and fight a duel with swords. He escapes, but is trapped and has to shoot his way out with a pistol. Then he swims across a river, and finally he finishes his assignment by running 4000 meters through the woods.

Between 1912 and 1952 the scoring was based on an athlete's placing in each of the five events. Since 1956, the modern pentathlon has been scored like the decathlon, with a set of charts assigning a point total to each performance.

## INDIVIDUAL

**1896–1908** not held

**1912 Stockholm** C: 32, N: 10, D: 7.12.

| | | | SHOOTING | SWIMMING | FENCING | RIDING | RUNNING | TOTAL |
|---|---|---|---|---|---|---|---|---|
| 1. | Gösta Lilliehöök | SWE | 3 | 10 | 5 | 4 | 5 | 27 |
| 2. | Gösta Åsbrink | SWE | 1 | 4 | 15 | 7 | 1 | 28 |
| 3. | Georg de Laval | SWE | 2 | 3 | 10 | 3 | 12 | 30 |
| 4. | Åke Grönhagen | SWE | 18 | 5 | 1 | 1 | 10 | 35 |
| 5. | George Patton | USA | 21 | 7 | 4 | 6 | 3 | 41 |
| 6. | Sidney Stranne | SWE | 11 | 9 | 3 | 8 | 11 | 42 |
| 7. | Karl Mannström | SWE | 14 | 14 | 16 | 2 | 9 | 55 |
| 8. | Edmund Bernhardt | AUT | 26 | 2 | 6 | 12 | 14 | 60 |

The fifth-place finisher was a 26-year-old army lieutenant, George S. Patton, Jr. who later went on to considerable fame as a general during World War II. Ironically, Patton might have won the event had he not been such a poor marksman, placing a mediocre 21st in a field of 32 in the shooting competition. Patton claimed that he was penalized for missing the target completely when in fact the bullet had gone through a previously-made hole. If he had been been able to prove his case, he would have won the gold medal. However, there is no evidence at all to support his contention.

If Lilliehöök had taken five more seconds to finish the 4000-meter cross-country run, he would have lost the gold medal.

**1920 Antwerp** C: 22, N: 8, D: 8.27.

| | | | SHOOTING | SWIMMING | FENCING | RIDING | RUNNING | TOTAL |
|---|---|---|---|---|---|---|---|---|
| 1. | Gustaf Dyrssen | SWE | 6 | 2 | 2 | 6 | 2 | 18 |
| 2. | Erik de Laval | SWE | 1 | 13 | 5 | 1 | 3 | 23 |
| 3. | Gösta Runö | SWE | 4 | 1 | 16 | 5 | 1 | 27 |

| | | SHOOTING | SWIMMING | FENCING | RIDING | RUNNING | TOTAL |
|---|---|---|---|---|---|---|---|
| 4. Bengt Uggla | SWE | 13 | 5 | 10 | 13 | 5 | 46 |
| 5. Marius Erik Christensen | DEN | 12 | 7 | 3 | 7 | 18 | 47 |
| 6. Harold Rayner | USA | 5 | 12 | 13 | 14 | 4 | 48 |
| 7. Hagelberg | FIN | 10 | 3 | 21 | 9 | 8 | 51 |
| 8. Robert Sears | USA | 3 | 8 | 9 | 11 | 20 | 51 |

**1924 Paris** C: 38, N: 11, D: 7.17.

| | | SHOOTING | SWIMMING | FENCING | RIDING | RUNNING | TOTAL |
|---|---|---|---|---|---|---|---|
| 1. Bo Lindman | SWE | 9 | 1 | 3 | 4 | 1 | 18 |
| 2. Gustaf Dyrssen | SWE | 20 | 4 | 1 | 3 | 11.5 | 39.5 |
| 3. Bertil Uggla | SWE | 7 | 21 | 5 | 5 | 7 | 45 |
| 4. Ivan Duranthon | FRA | 4 | 18 | 17.5 | 11 | 4 | 54.5 |
| 5. Harry Avellan | FIN | 17 | 6 | 17.5 | 1 | 14 | 55.5 |
| 6. Helge Jensen | DEN | 2 | 19 | 11.5 | 9.5 | 19 | 61 |
| 7. George Vokins | GBR | 24 | 11 | 10 | 8 | 11.5 | 64.5 |
| 8. C. Tonnet | HOL | 22 | 12 | 13.5 | 16 | 2 | 65.5 |

**1928 Amsterdam** C: 37, N: 14, D: 8.4.

| | | SHOOTING | SWIMMING | FENCING | RUNNING | RIDING | TOTAL |
|---|---|---|---|---|---|---|---|
| 1. Sven Thofelt | SWE | 6 | 2 | 4 | 21 | 14 | 47 |
| 2. Bo Lindman | SWE | 15 | 5 | 22 | 3 | 5 | 50 |
| 3. Helmuth Kahl | GER | 10 | 9 | 2 | 19 | 12 | 52 |
| 4. Ingvar Berg | SWE | 3 | 11 | 36 | 7 | 1 | 58 |
| 5. Heinz Hax | GER | 1 | 15 | 21 | 20 | 2 | 59 |
| 6. David Torquand-Young | GBR | 24 | 7 | 15 | 9 | 10 | 65 |
| 7. Hermann Hölter | GER | 16 | 8 | 11 | 21 | 13 | 69 |
| 7. C. Tonnet | HOL | 8 | 24 | 27 | 6 | 4 | 69 |

**1932 Los Angeles** C: 25, N: 10, D: 8.6.

| | | RIDING | FENCING | SHOOTING | SWIMMING | RUNNING | TOTAL |
|---|---|---|---|---|---|---|---|
| 1. Johan Oxenstierna | SWE | 4 | 14 | 2 | 5 | 7 | 32 |
| 2. Bo Lindman | SWE | 1 | 2.5 | 19 | 9 | 4 | 35.5 |
| 3. Richard Mayo | USA | 2 | 4.5 | 1 | 14 | 17 | 38.5 |
| 4. Sven Thofelt | SWE | 15 | 1 | 9 | 1 | 13 | 39 |
| 5. Willy Remer | GER | 12 | 10 | 4 | 13 | 8 | 47 |
| 6. Conrad Miersch | GER | 10 | 10 | 5 | 17 | 6 | 48 |
| 7. Elemér Somfay | HUN | 20 | 4.5 | 6 | 12 | 10 | 52.5 |
| 8. Digby Legard | GBR | 6 | 18 | 10 | 18 | 1 | 53 |

After taking a few practice shots in the woods just before the competition was to begin, Oxenstierna was confronted by an angry policeman who threatened to arrest him. Since the competition was about to begin, the police officer agreed to wait. He watched Oxenstierna shoot, realized he was not a criminal, and let him go.

**1936 Berlin** C: 42, N: 16, D: 8.6.

| | | RIDING | FENCING | SHOOTING | SWIMMING | RUNNING | TOTAL |
|---|---|---|---|---|---|---|---|
| 1. Gotthardt Handrick | GER | 2.5 | 2 | 4 | 9 | 14 | 31.5 |
| 2. Charles Leonard | USA | 15 | 10 | 1 | 6 | 7.5 | 39.5 |
| 3. Silvano Abba | ITA | 1 | 15.5 | 10 | 14 | 5 | 45.5 |
| 4. Sven Thofelt | SWE | 8.5 | 5.5 | 6 | 3 | 24 | 47 |
| 5. Nándor Orbán | HUN | 4 | 12.5 | 21 | 2 | 16 | 55.5 |
| 6. Hermann Lemp | GER | 31 | 3.5 | 11 | 1 | 21 | 67.5 |

| 7. Alfred Starbird | USA | 8.5 | 8.5 | 23 | 20 | 7.5 | 67.5 |
| 8. Rezsö Bartha | HUN | 27 | 12.5 | 3 | 12 | 22 | 76.5 |

In the pistol-shooting portion of the competition, Lieutenant Charles Leonard of St. Petersburg, Florida, became the first person in the history of the event to achieve a perfect score of 200.

**1948 London** C: 45, N: 16, D: 8.4.

| | | RIDING | FENCING | SHOOTING | SWIMMING | RUNNING | TOTAL |
|---|---|---|---|---|---|---|---|
| 1. William "Willie" Grut | SWE | 1 | 1 | 5 | 1 | 8 | 16 |
| 2. George Moore | USA | 2 | 3 | 21 | 17 | 4 | 47 |
| 3. Gösta Gärdin | SWE | 6 | 17 | 10 | 11 | 5 | 49 |
| 4. Lauri Vilkko | FIN | 17 | 38 | 4 | 3 | 2 | 64 |
| 5. Olavi Larkas | FIN | 26 | 3 | 7 | 19 | 16 | 71 |
| 6. Bruno Riem | SWI | 19 | 9 | 1 | 36 | 9 | 74 |
| 7. F. Hegner | SWI | 24 | 13 | 3 | 7 | 29 | 79 |
| 8. Richard Gruenther | USA | 13 | 12 | 14 | 24 | 19 | 81 |

Captain William Grut, a 33-year-old artillery officer, accomplished the most decisive victory in the history of the modern pentathlon, finishing first in three of the five events.

**1952 Helsinki** C: 51, N: 19, D: 7.25.

| | | RIDING | FENCING | SHOOTING | SWIMMING | RUNNING | TOTAL |
|---|---|---|---|---|---|---|---|
| 1. Lars Hall | SWE | 1 | 7 | 16 | 1 | 8 | 32 |
| 2. Gábor Benedek | HUN | 8 | 2 | 9 | 18 | 2 | 39 |
| 3. István Szondy | HUN | 3 | 4 | 12 | 5 | 17 | 41 |
| 4. Igor Novikov | SOV | 24 | 13 | 4 | 4 | 10 | 55 |
| 5. Frederick Denman | USA | 9 | 11 | 6 | 17 | 19 | 62 |
| 5. Olavi Mannonen | FIN | 2 | 37 | 10 | 9 | 4 | 62 |
| 7. Lauri Vilkko | FIN | 1 | 8 | 38 | 11 | 5 | 63 |
| 8. W. Thad McArthur | USA | 29 | 3 | 23 | 12 | 1 | 68 |

Twenty-five-year-old Lars Hall was the first nonmilitary winner of the modern pentathlon. A carpenter from Gothenburg, Hall had two lucky breaks. The horse that he drew for the equestrian competition was discovered to be lame. The horse that he was assigned as a substitute turned out to be the best horse in Finland, and Hall's only challenge was to keep from falling off as the horse raced through the course. Two days later, Hall arrived 20 minutes late for the pistol-shooting, but was saved from disqualification due to a Soviet protest that was still being sorted out.

**1956 Melbourne** C: 40, N: 16, D: 11.28.

| | | RIDING | FENCING | SHOOTING | SWIMMING | RUNNING | TOTAL |
|---|---|---|---|---|---|---|---|
| 1. Lars Hall | SWE | 1035 (4) | 889 (4) | 720(24) | 1030 (2) | 1159(12) | 4833 |
| 2. Olavi Mannonen | FIN | 997.5 (5) | 815 (8) | 880 (5) | 920(15) | 1162 (7) | 4774 |
| 3. Väinö Korhonen | FIN | 885 (9) | 963 (2) | 880 (5) | 905(16) | 1117(12) | 4750 |
| 4. Igor Novikov | SOV | 802.5(14) | 815 (8) | 920 (2) | 935 (6) | 1192 (4) | 4714 |
| 5. George Lambert | USA | 1070 (1) | 667(17) | 900 (4) | 975 (7) | 1081(15) | 4693 |
| 6. Gábor Benedek | HUN | 860 (11) | 889 (4) | 920 (2) | 855(18) | 1126(10) | 4650 |
| 7. William André | USA | 887.5 (5) | 889 (4) | 860 (8) | 870(17) | 1123(11) | 4629 |
| 8. Aleksandr Tarassov | SOV | 810 (13) | 778(10) | 880 (5) | 825(21) | 1186 (5) | 4479 |

**1960 Rome** C: 60, N: 23, D: 8.31.

| | | | RIDING | FENCING | SHOOTING | SWIMMING | RUNNING | TOTAL |
|---|---|---|---|---|---|---|---|---|
| 1. | Férenc Németh | HUN | 1009(31) | 977 (2) | 880(10) | 990 (6) | 1168 (7) | 5024 |
| 2. | Imre Nagy | HUN | 1048(19) | 1000 (1) | 840(23) | 935(18) | 1165 (8) | 4988 |
| 3. | Robert Beck | USA | 1039(24) | 977 (2) | 940 (3) | 1010 (4) | 1015(24) | 4981 |
| 4. | András Balczó | HUN | 1037(20) | 885 (6) | 760(36) | 1075 (1) | 1216 (2) | 4973 |
| 5. | Igor Novikov | SOV | 982(33) | 839 (9) | 860(15)* | 1035 (2) | 1246 (1) | 4962 |
| 6. | Nikolai Tatarinov | SOV | 1138 (5) | 747(19) | 820(27) | 885(28) | 1168 (6) | 4758 |
| 7. | Stanislaw Przybylski | POL | 1111(13) | 747(20) | 860(16) | 815(39) | 1198 (3) | 4731 |
| 8. | Jack Daniels | USA | 1024(27) | 793(12) | 900 (6) | 1015 (3) | 985(26) | 4717 |

**1964 Tokyo** C: 37, N: 15, D: 10.15.

| | | | RIDING | FENCING | SHOOTING | SWIMMING | RUNNING | TOTAL |
|---|---|---|---|---|---|---|---|---|
| 1. | Ferenc Török | HUN | 1070(15) | 1000 (1) | 960(10) | 960(23) | 1126 (5) | 5116 |
| 2. | Igor Novikov | SOV | 1040(26) | 856 (5) | 1020 (3) | 1055 (5) | 1096 (6) | 5067 |
| 3. | Albert Mokeyev | SOV | 970(33) | 748(15) | 1060 (1) | 1045 (7) | 1216 (1) | 5039 |
| 4. | Peter Macken | AUS | 1070(19) | 640(21) | 1020 (4) | 1035 (8) | 1132 (3) | 4897 |
| 5. | Viktor Mineyev | SOV | 1040(24) | 820 (9) | 960(13) | 1050 (6) | 1024(15) | 4894 |
| 6. | James Moore | USA | 1070(16) | 676(20) | 960(12) | 990(15) | 1195 (2) | 4891 |
| 7. | Imre Nagy | HUN | 1040(30) | 892 (2) | 960 (9) | 940(28) | 1042(11) | 4874 |
| 8. | Bo-Herman Jansson | SWE | 1100 (3) | 748(16) | 780(28) | 1075 (1) | 1057(10) | 4760 |

**1968 Mexico City** C: 48, N: 18, D: 10.17.

| | | | RIDING | FENCING | SHOOTING | SWIMMING | RUNNING | TOTAL |
|---|---|---|---|---|---|---|---|---|
| 1. | Björn Ferm | SWE | 1100 (5) | 885 (8) | 934(11) | 1075 (2) | 970 (5) | 4964 |
| 2. | András Balczó | HUN | 1010(22) | 931 (6) | 934(12) | 1054 (5) | 1024 (2) | 4953 |
| 3. | Pavel Lednev | SOV | 1070 (8) | 839(15) | 934 (9) | 1060 (4) | 892(16) | 4795 |
| 4. | Karl-Heinz Kutschke | GDR | 1070(10) | 632(41) | 846(26) | 1126 (1) | 1090 (1) | 4764 |
| 5. | Boris Onischenko | SOV | 995(28) | 885 (8) | 912(15) | 1054 (5) | 910(13) | 4756 |
| 5. | Raoul Gueguen | FRA | 1040(14) | 954 (5) | 912(13) | 1000(10) | 850(20) | 4756 |
| 7. | István Moná | HUN | 1010(20) | 1040 (2) | 868(22) | 943(23) | 847(22) | 4714 |
| 8. | Jeremy Fox | GBR | 1010(21) | 862(12) | 890(18) | 1006 (9) | 895(15) | 4663 |

DISQ (Drugs): Hans-Gunnar Liljenvall (SWE) 4664

Ferm, a 24-year-old economics student, kept busy during the 12-hour fencing competition by reading detective stories. When it came down to the final cross-country run, he needed to beat 14 minutes 30 seconds to win the gold medal. Ferm struggled through the unfamiliar rarefied air and crossed the finish line with only four seconds to spare. An ugly incident had marred the riding event. Hans-Jürgen Todt of West Germany drew a beautiful but stubborn horse named Ranchero, which balked three times at one of the obstacles. After completing the course, Todt, disconsolate at seeing his years of training gone to waste because of bad luck, attacked the horse and had to be pulled away by his teammates.

**1972 Munich** C: 59, N: 21, D: 8.31.

| | | | RIDING | FENCING | SHOOTING | SWIMMING | RUNNING | TOTAL |
|---|---|---|---|---|---|---|---|---|
| 1. | András Balczó | HUN | 1060(17) | 1057 (2) | 956(12) | 1060(25) | 1279 (3) | 5412 |
| 2. | Boris Onischenko | SOV | 945(42) | 1076 (1) | 1066 (2) | 1128(11) | 1120(21) | 5335 |
| 3. | Pavel Lednev | SOV | 1060(14) | 1019 (3) | 1022 (4) | 1092(18) | 1135(14) | 5328 |
| 4. | Jeremy Fox | GBR | 1100 (2) | 1019 (3) | 868(22) | 1024(32) | 1300 (1) | 5311 |
| 5. | Vladimir Shmelev | SOV | 920(47) | 962 (7) | 1022 (5) | 1176 (6) | 1222 (6) | 5302 |
| 6. | Björn Ferm | SWE | 1100 (4) | 943(10) | 978 (7) | 1112(13) | 1150(10) | 5283 |

| | | | | | | |
|---|---|---|---|---|---|---|
| 7. Heiner Thade | GER | 1065(12) | 962 (7) | 956(13) | 1012(37) | 1150 (9) | 5145 |
| 8. Risto Hurme | FIN | 950(40) | 981 (5) | 1044 (3) | 1068(24) | 1051(33) | 5094 |

Five-time world champion András Balczó finally won an Olympic individual gold medal at the age of 34. Tied for third place after four events, Balczó, a typewriter mechanic, set off on the cross-country course at a terrific pace and staggered home a winner. Quite an uproar developed when it was discovered through drug tests that 14 pentathletes had taken the tranquilizers Valium and Librium before going out on the shooting range. These drugs were banned by the International Modern Pentathlon Union, but were considered acceptable by the International Olympic Committee. For this reason no disqualifications were made.

**1976 Montreal** C: 47, N: 15, D: 7.22.

| | | RIDING | FENCING | SHOOTING | SWIMMING | RUNNING | TOTAL |
|---|---|---|---|---|---|---|---|
| 1. Janusz Pyciak-Peciak | POL | 1066(23) | 928 (5) | 1044 (3) | 1164(17) | 1318 (3) | 5520 |
| 2. Pavel Lednev | SOV | 1032(32) | 1096 (1) | 1022 (6) | 1092(30) | 1243(10) | 5485 |
| 3. Jan Bártu | CZE | 1100 (1) | 976 (3) | 1044 (5) | 1184(13) | 1162(22) | 5466 |
| 4. Daniele Masala | ITA | 1090(14) | 832(13) | 1066 (2) | 1244 (2) | 1201(17) | 5433 |
| 5. Adrian Parker | GBR | 1100 (1) | 712(30) | 868(29) | 1240 (7) | 1378 (1) | 5298 |
| 6. John Fitzgerald | USA | 1036(25) | 952 (4) | 1000 (9) | 1232 (8) | 1066(42) | 5286 |
| 7. Jorn Steffensen | DEN | 1100 (1) | 856 (9) | 1044 (4) | 1068(38) | 1213(14) | 5281 |
| 8. Boris Mosolov | SOV | 1036(25) | 856 (9) | 934(20) | 1212 (9) | 1162(22) | 5200 |

Pyciak-Peciak was only in fifth place after four events, but he ran a strong 4000 meters and finished with 12 seconds to spare in 12:29.70.

**1980 Moscow** C: 43, N: 19, D: 7.24.

| | | RIDING | FENCING | SHOOTING | SWIMMING | RUNNING | TOTAL |
|---|---|---|---|---|---|---|---|
| 1. Anatoly Starostin | SOV | 1068(13) | 1000 (4) | 1110 (2) | 1216(10) | 1174 (8) | 5568 |
| 2. Tamás Szombathelyi | HUN | 1100 (2) | 1026 (2) | 1088 (3) | 1144(24) | 1144(11) | 5502 |
| 3. Pavel Lednev | SOV | 1026(21) | 1026 (2) | 1022(15) | 1104(31) | 1204 (4) | 5382 |
| 4. Svante Rasmuson | SWE | 936(40) | 922 (7) | 1000(17) | 1332 (2) | 1183 (6) | 5373 |
| 5. Tibor Maracskó | HUN | 980(32) | 964 (6) | 956(27) | 1208(12) | 1171 (9) | 5279 |
| 6. Janusz Pyciak-Peciak | POL | 1070(12) | 844(13) | 978(25) | 1172(14) | 1204 (5) | 5268 |
| 7. Lennart Pettersson | SWE | 1050(18) | 922 (7) | 1088 (6) | 1156(19) | 1027(32) | 5243 |
| 8. Milan Kadlec | CZE | 1084 (8) | 792(20) | 1000 (4) | 1000(04) | 1177 (7) | 5220 |

Following his victory at the 1986 world championships, Starostin was one of 15 pentathletes who failed a doping test for sedatives and were banned from competition for 30 months.

**1984 Los Angeles-Irvine** C: 52, N: 18, D: 8.1.

| | | RIDING | FENCING | SWIMMING | SHOOTING | RUNNING | TOTAL |
|---|---|---|---|---|---|---|---|
| 1. Daniele Masala | ITA | 1100 (1) | 956 (4) | 1300 (8) | 978(10) | 1135(20) | 5469 |
| 2. Svante Rasmuson | SWE | 1070(13) | 1022 (2) | 1304 (4) | 912(24) | 1148(16) | 5456 |
| 3. Carlo Massullo | ITA | 1100 (2) | 758(27) | 1220(20) | 1066 (2) | 1262 (2) | 5406 |
| 4. Richard Phelps | GBR | 1100 (3) | 912 (5) | 1304 (5) | 780(43) | 1295 (1) | 5391 |
| 5. Michael Storm | USA | 1040(23) | 868(12) | 1288 (9) | 1088 (1) | 1041(30) | 5325 |
| 6. Paul Four | FRA | 1040(20) | 978 (3) | 1204(21) | 1066 (2) | 999(35) | 5287 |
| 7. Ivar Sisniega | MEX | 1070 (9) | 912 (5) | 1320 (2) | 780(43) | 1200 (7) | 5282 |
| 8. Jorge Quesada | SPA | 1060(16) | 890 (9) | 1172(25) | 1000 (8) | 1159(14) | 5281 |

The 1984 Olympics saw two important changes in the organization of the modern pentathlon competition. First, the event was compressed into four days instead of five. In order to discourage the pentathletes from taking sedatives and beta-blockers to steady their nerves before shooting, the shooting portion of the competition was moved to the morning of the final day, five hours before the cross country run.

The second change was instituted to create a more dramatic finish. Instead of starting the runners in random order, the leader after four events, in this case Daniele Masala, started first. The other runners were given a handicap time depending on how many points behind they were, with 3 points equalling one second. Thus Svante Rasmuson had to wait 8⅔ seconds before he started and Paul Four 15⅓ seconds. By the time Carlo Massullo hit the course in fifth place, Masala had been running 1 minute 10⅔ seconds. The new method meant that even though the scoring was the same, the first person across the finish line was actually the winner.

The finish was indeed a dramatic one. Rasmuson caught Masala with 100 meters to go and appeared headed for victory. But 20 meters from the finish, the exhausted Swedish medical student stumbled on the soft dirt after rounding the final sharp left turn. Rasmuson staggered into a potted plant which was being used to brighten up the course boundary, and Masala ran by to take the gold medal.

"Have you ever been so tired you can't even control your body?" Rasmuson asked later. Then he added, "I hate soft dirt."

**1988 Seoul** C: 65, N: 26, D: 9.22.

| | | RIDING | FENCING | SWIMMING | SHOOTING | RUNNING | TOTAL |
|---|---|---|---|---|---|---|---|
| 1. János Martinek | HUN | 1066 (6) | 990 (2) | 1264(15) | 868(45) | 1216 (6) | 5404 |
| 2. Carlo Massullo | ITA | 1010(19) | 881(13) | 1204(32) | 1044 (8) | 1240 (4) | 5379 |
| 3. Vakhtang Yagorashvili | SOV | 980(24) | 915 (8) | 1344 (2) | 978(16) | 1150(19) | 5367 |
| 4. Attila Mizsér | HUN | 1010(20) | 847(18) | 1196(33) | 934(26) | 1294 (1) | 5281 |
| 5. Christophe Ruer | FRA | 968(28) | 779(30) | 1348 (1) | 934(29) | 1213 (7) | 5242 |
| 6. Richard Phelps | GBR | 964(29) | 898(11) | 1304 (8) | 868(47) | 1195(11) | 5229 |
| 7. László Fábián | HUN | 876(47) | 1051 (1) | 1304 (8) | 802(53) | 1168(17) | 5201 |
| 8. Joël Bouzou | FRA | 1004(22) | 983 (3) | 1172(37) | 868(46) | 1171(16) | 5198 |

In 1988, thanks to improved drug-testing procedures, the competition was able to revert to its traditional five-day format. Martinek began the cross-country course 9⅔ seconds after Yagorashvili, passed him at the halfway mark and pulled away to a convincing victory, finishing 9 seconds ahead of Massullo.

# TEAM

**1896–1948** not held

**1952 Helsinki** T: 15, N: 15, D: 7.25.

| | | RIDING | FENCING | SHOOTING | SWIMMING | RUNNING | TOTAL |
|---|---|---|---|---|---|---|---|
| 1. HUN | Gábor Benedek<br>István Szondy<br>Aladár Kovácsi | 21 (2) | 16 (1) | 45 (4) | 46 (5) | 38 (3) | 166 |

| | | | | | | | |
|---|---|---|---|---|---|---|---|
| 2. SWE | Lars Hall | | | | | | |
| | Torsten Lindqvist | 18 (1) | 16 (1) | 68 (8) | 29 (2) | 51 (6) | 182 |
| | Claes Egnell | | | | | | |
| 3. FIN | Olavi Mannonen | | | | | | |
| | Lauri Vilkko | 38 (4) | 90(10) | 30 (1) | 27 (1) | 28 (1) | 213 |
| | Olavi Rokka | | | | | | |
| 4. USA | Frederick Denman | | | | | | |
| | W. Thad McArthur | 27 (3) | 50 (5) | 41 (2) | 49 (6) | 48 (4) | 215 |
| | Guy Troy | | | | | | |
| 5. SOV | Igor Novikov | | | | | | |
| | Pavel Rakityansky | 76 (6) | 69 (6) | 81(11) | 37 (4) | 30 (2) | 293 |
| | Aleksandr Dehayev | | | | | | |
| 6. BRA | Eduardo Leal Medeiros | | | | | | |
| | Aloysio Alves Borges | 94(11) | 42 (3) | 70 (9) | 34 (3) | 73 (9) | 313 |
| | Eric Tinoco Marques | | | | | | |
| 7. CHI | Nilo Floody Buxton | | | | | | |
| | Hernán Fuentes Besoain | 77 (7) | 42 (3) | 42 (3) | 90(11) | 81(11) | 336 |
| | Luis Carmona Barrales | | | | | | |
| 8. ARG | Luis Riera | | | | | | |
| | Carlos Velazquez | 53(15) | 98(12) | 52 (5) | 75 (9) | 77(10) | 355 |
| | Jorge Caceres Monie | | | | | | |

**1956 Melbourne** T: 12, N: 12, D: 11.28.

| | | RIDING | FENCING | SHOOTING | SWIMMING | RUNNING | TOTAL |
|---|---|---|---|---|---|---|---|
| 1. SOV | Igor Novikov | | | | | | |
| | Aleksandr Tarassov | 2457.5 (3) | 2194 (2) | 2850 (1) | 2880 (1) | 3579 (1) | 13690.5 |
| | Ivan Deryugin | | | | | | |
| 2. USA | George Lambert | | | | | | |
| | William André | 3020 (1) | 2008 (4) | 2560 (2) | 2780 (2) | 3114 (5) | 13482 |
| | Jack Daniels | | | | | | |
| 3. FIN | Olavi Mannonen | | | | | | |
| | Väinö Korhonen | 2512.5 (2) | 2008 (4) | 2520 (4) | 2755 (3) | 3390 (3) | 13185.5 |
| | Berndt Katter | | | | | | |
| 4. HUN | Gábor Benedek | | | | | | |
| | János Bódy | 1727.5 (4) | 2566 (1) | 2460 (5) | 2660 (4) | 3141 (4) | 12554.5 |
| | Antal Moldrich | | | | | | |
| 5. MEX | José Pérez Mier | | | | | | |
| | Antonio Almada Félix | 1700 (5) | 2008 (4) | 2560 (2) | 2640 (5) | 2073 (8) | 10981 |
| | David Romero Vargas | | | | | | |
| 6. ROM | Cornel Vena | | | | | | |
| | Dumitru Tintea | 1160 (8) | 2194 (2) | 2160 (6) | 2195 (8) | 2904 (6) | 10613 |
| | Victor Teodorescu | | | | | | |
| 7. GBR | Donald Cobley | | | | | | |
| | Thomas Hudson | 335 (11) | 1574 (7) | 1340 (8) | 2560 (6) | 3417 (2) | 9226 |
| | George Norman | | | | | | |
| 8. AUS | Neville Sayers | | | | | | |
| | Sven Coomer | 1060 (9) | 1264 (8) | 2040 (7) | 2220 (7) | 2241 (7) | 8825 |
| | George Nicoll | | | | | | |

**1960 Rome** T: 17, N: 17, D: 8.31.

| | | RIDING | FENCING | SHOOTING | SWIMMING | RUNNING | TOTAL |
|---|---|---|---|---|---|---|---|
| 1. HUN | Ferenc Németh | | | | | | |
| | Imre Nagy | 3094 (5) | 2740 (1) | 2480 (6) | 3000 (1) | 3549 (2) | 14863 |
| | András Balczó | | | | | | |
| 2. SOV | Igor Novikov | | | | | | |
| | Nikolai Tatarinov | 3087 (6) | 2326 (5) | 2460 (7) | 2845 (4) | 3591 (1) | 14309 |
| | Hanno Selg | | | | | | |

| | | RIDING | FENCING | SHOOTING | SWIMMING | RUNNING | TOTAL |
|---|---|---|---|---|---|---|---|
| 3. USA | Robert Beck<br>Jack Daniels<br>George Lambert | 3228 (4) | 2402 (3) | 2580 (2) | 3000 (2) | 2982 (7) | 14192 |
| 4. FIN | Kurt Lindeman<br>Berndt Katter<br>Eero Lohi | 2929(13) | 2480 (2) | 2580 (3) | 2705 (7) | 3171 (5) | 13865 |
| 5. POL | Stanislaw Przybylski<br>Kazimierz Paszkiewicz<br>Kazimierz Mazur | 3315 (3) | 1804(11) | 2660 (1) | 2535(12) | 3432 (3) | 13746 |
| 6. SWE | Per-Erik Ritzén<br>Sture Ericson<br>Björn Thofelt | 3078 (8) | 2352 (4) | 2360 (9) | 2585(11) | 2841(10) | 13216 |
| 7. GBR | Patrick Harvey<br>Donald Cobley<br>Peter Little | 3060 (9) | 1700(15) | 2400 (8) | 2670 (8) | 3273 (4) | 13103 |
| 8. MEX | Antonio Almada Félix<br>Sergio Escobedo<br>José Pérez Mier | 3393 (1) | 2184 (6) | 2540 (4) | 2625 (9) | 2103(16) | 12845 |

**1964 Tokyo** T: 11, N: 11, D: 10.15.

| | | RIDING | FENCING | SHOOTING | SWIMMING | RUNNING | TOTAL |
|---|---|---|---|---|---|---|---|
| 1. SOV | Igor Novikov<br>Albert Mokeyev<br>Viktor Mineyev | 3050(11) | 2385 (3) | 3040 (1) | 3150 (2) | 3336 (1) | 14961 |
| 2. USA | James Moore<br>David Kirkwood<br>Paul Pesthy | 3240 (3) | 2262 (4) | 2640 (5) | 2915 (6) | 3132 (3) | 14189 |
| 3. HUN | Ferenc Törk<br>Imre Nagy<br>Otto Török | 3150 (8) | 2590 (1) | 2380 (9) | 2885 (7) | 3168 (2) | 14173 |
| 4. SWE | Bo-Herman Jansson<br>Rolf Junefelt<br>Hans-Gunnar Liljenwall | 3240 (4) | 2057 (6) | 2460 (8) | 3200 (1) | 3099 (4) | 14056 |
| 5. AUS | Peter Macken<br>Donald McMiken<br>Duncan Page | 3210 (5) | 1770 (7) | 2880 (2) | 2990 (4) | 2853 (6) | 13703 |
| 6. GER | Wolfgang Gödicke<br>Uwe Adler<br>Elmar Frings | 3130 (9) | 1729 (8) | 2800 (4) | 2955 (5) | 2985 (5) | 13599 |
| 7. FIN | Jorma Hotanen<br>Keijo Vanhala<br>Kari Kaaja | 3120(10) | 2221 (5) | 2560 (6) | 2885 (8) | 2754 (9) | 13540 |
| 8. JPN | Yoshihide Fukutome<br>Shigeaki Uchino<br>Shigeki Mino | 3210 (6) | 1524(10) | 2860 (3) | 2865 (9) | 2943 (6) | 13402 |

**1968 Mexico City** T: 15, N: 15, D: 10.17.

| | | RIDING | FENCING | SHOOTING | SWIMMING | RUNNING | TOTAL |
|---|---|---|---|---|---|---|---|
| 1. HUN | András Balczó<br>István Móna<br>Ferenc Török | 2940 (5) | 3130 (1) | 2714 (1) | 2877 (6) | 2664 (4) | 14325 |
| 2. SOV | Pavel Lednev<br>Boris Onischenko<br>Stasys Saparnis | 3135 (1) | 2558 (2) | 2648 (5) | 3141 (1) | 2766 (2) | 14248 |
| 3. FRA | Raoul Gueguen<br>Lucien Guiguet<br>Jean-Pierre Giudicelli | 2855 (8) | 2168(11) | 2626 (6) | 2931 (4) | 2709 (3) | 13289 |

| | | RIDING | FENCING | SHOOTING | SWIMMING | RUNNING | TOTAL |
|---|---|---|---|---|---|---|---|
| 4. USA | James Moore<br>Robert Beck<br>M. Thomas Lough | 3030 (2) | 2324 (7) | 2670 (4) | 2844 (7) | 2412 (9) | 13280 |
| 5. FIN | Seppo Aho<br>Martti Ketelä<br>Jorma Hotanen | 2890 (6) | 2558 (2) | 2384(13) | 2799 (8) | 2607 (5) | 13238 |
| 6. GDR | Karl-Heinz Kutschke<br>Jörg Tscherner<br>Wolfgang Lüderitz | 2485(12) | 2194(10) | 2626 (6) | 3093 (2) | 2769 (1) | 13167 |
| 7. JPN | Toshio Fukui<br>Yuso Makihira<br>Katsuaki Tashiro | 2980 (4) | 2428 (5) | 2428 (9) | 2796 (9) | 2451 (6) | 13083 |
| 8. GBR | Jeremy Fox<br>Barry Lillywhite<br>Robert Phelps | 2790 (9) | 2324 (9) | 2670 (2) | 2952 (3) | 2157(11) | 12893 |

DISQ (Drugs): SWE (Björn Ferm, Hans-Gunnar Liljenvall, Hans Jacobson) 14188

The Swedish team finished third with 14,188 points, but was disqualified when one of its members, Hans-Gunnar Liljenvall, failed the drug test for alcohol. It was a common practice for pentathletes to steady their nerves with a bit of alcohol before the shooting contest, but Liljenvall, who finished eighth individually, was found to have a blood alcohol concentration well above the acceptable limit, despite the fact that he claimed he had only drunk two beers.

**1972 Munich** T: 19, N: 19, D: 8.31.

| | | RIDING | FENCING | SHOOTING | SWIMMING | RUNNING | TOTAL |
|---|---|---|---|---|---|---|---|
| 1. SOV | Boris Onischenko<br>Pavel Lednev<br>Vladimir Shmelev | 2925(13) | 3060 (1) | 3110 (1) | 3396 (2) | 3477 (2) | 15968 |
| 2. HUN | András Balczó<br>Zsigmond Villányi<br>Pál Bakó | 2975(10) | 2820 (2) | 2736 (2) | 3280 (5) | 3537 (1) | 15348 |
| 3. FIN | Risto Hurme<br>Veikko Salminen<br>Martti Ketelä | 3010 (6) | 2580 (4) | 2670 (3) | 3300 (3) | 3252 (9) | 14812 |
| 4. USA | Charles Richards<br>John Fitzgerald<br>Scott Taylor | 3115 (3) | 2280(10) | 2450(10) | 3564 (1) | 3393 (5) | 14802 |
| 5. SWE | Björn Ferm<br>Bo-Herman Jansson<br>Hans-Gunnar Liljenvall | 3125 (2) | 2640 (3) | 2428(11) | 3236 (7) | 3279 (8) | 14708 |
| 6. GER | Heiner Thade<br>Walter Esser<br>Hole Rössler | 3010 (7) | 2520 (7) | 2626 (4) | 3232 (8) | 3294 (7) | 14682 |
| 7. FRA | Michel Gueguen<br>Jean-Pierre Giudicelli<br>Raoul Gueguen | 2990 (8) | 2320 (9) | 2538 (8) | 3252 (6) | 3459 (3) | 14559 |
| 8. POL | Ryszard Wach<br>Janusz Pyciak-Peciak<br>Stanislaw Skwira | 2955(11) | 2420 (8) | 2362(13) | 3296 (4) | 3252(10) | 14285 |

**1976 Montreal** T: 14, N: 14, D: 7.22.

| | | RIDING | FENCING | SHOOTING | SWIMMING | RUNNING | TOTAL |
|---|---|---|---|---|---|---|---|
| 1. GBR | Adrian Parker<br>Robert Nightingale<br>Jeremy Fox | 3212 (3) | 2256 (8) | 2648 (8) | 3492 (5) | 3951 (1) | 15559 |

| | | | RIDING | FENCING | SHOOTING | SWIMMING | RUNNING | TOTAL |
|---|---|---|---|---|---|---|---|---|
| 2. | CZE | Jan Bártu<br>Bohumil Starnovsky<br>Jiři Adam | 2962(10) | 2783 (1) | 3000 (1) | 3400 (8) | 3306(12) | 15451 |
| 3. | HUN | Tamás Kancsal<br>Tibor Maracskó<br>Szvetiszláv Sasics | 2772(12) | 2773 (2) | 2758 (5) | 3528 (4) | 3564 (5) | 15395 |
| 4. | POL | Janusz Pyciak-Peciak<br>Krzysztof Trybusiewicz<br>Zbigniew Pacelt | 3170 (6) | 2132(11) | 2912 (3) | 3544 (3) | 3585 (2) | 15343 |
| 5. | USA | John Fitzgerald<br>Michael Burley<br>Robert Nieman | 3140 (7) | 2535 (4) | 2296(12) | 3768 (1) | 3546 (7) | 15285 |
| 6. | ITA | Daniele Masala<br>Pier Paolo Cristofori<br>Mario Medda | 3194 (4) | 2256 (8) | 2670 (6) | 3428 (7) | 3483 (8) | 15031 |
| 7. | FIN | Risto Hurme<br>Jussi Pelli<br>Heikki Hulkkonen | 2794(11) | 2597 (3) | 2802 (4) | 3228(10) | 3579 (3) | 15000 |
| 8. | SWE | Hans Lager<br>Bengt Lager<br>Gunnar Jacobson | 3268 (1) | 2318 (7) | 2340(11) | 3468 (6) | 3552 (6) | 14946 |

In 1976 the noble sport of modern pentathlon was wracked by controversy. First of all, Captain Orben Greenwald, a member of the U.S. team, was prevented from competing when his team manager, Lieutenant-Colonel Donald Johnson of the U.S. Modern Pentathlon Training Center, courtmartialed him for insubordination. Although the charge was thrown out as soon as an investigation was begun, Greenwald was refused accreditation when he arrived in Montreal.

The real shock came on the second day of competition, during the fencing tournament. The favored Soviet team was fencing against the team from Great Britain, when the British pentathletes noticed something odd about the defending silver medalist, Army Major Boris Onischenko. In his fight against Adrian Parker, the automatic light registered a hit for the Ukrainian even though he didn't appear to have touched his opponent. Veteran Jeremy Fox was next to be drawn against Onischenko. When he too lost a hit without being touched, it became obvious that something was wrong with Onischenko's épée. The weapon was taken away to be examined by the Jury of Appeal. Onischenko continued with a different sword, but an hour or so later the news came that he had been disqualified.

Evidently Onischenko, desperate for victory in his final international competition, had wired his sword with a well-hidden push-button circuit breaker which enabled him to register a hit whenever he wanted. It is unknown how long Onischenko had been using this trick, but his fencing scores, which were already high, had showed a marked upward surge beginning in 1970. He was spirited away from the Olympic Village almost immediately and was never seen outside the U.S.S.R. again.

Onischenko's disqualification eliminated the Soviets from the team competition, leaving an open field. After four events the British team was in fifth place, 547 points behind Czechoslovakia. But running was their specialty, and Parker, the first runner of the day, inspired the others to victory by completing the 4000-meter course in 12 minutes 9 seconds, the fastest time ever recorded in Olympic competition. Strong performances by Nightingale and Fox assured Britain of the unexpected victory.

**1980 Moscow** T: 12, N: 12, D: 7.24.

| | | | RIDING | FENCING | SHOOTING | SWIMMING | RUNNING | TOTAL |
|---|---|---|---|---|---|---|---|---|
| 1. | SOV | Anatoly Starostin<br>Pavel Lednev<br>Yevgeny Lipeev | 3194 (2) | 2896 (2) | 2956(7) | 3552 (4) | 3528 (1) | 16126 |
| 2. | HUN | Tamás Szombathelyi<br>Tibor Maracskó<br>László Horváth | 3088 (5) | 3042 (1) | 3000(6) | 3428 (9) | 3354 (4) | 15912 |
| 3. | SWE | Svante Rasmuson<br>Lennart Pettersson<br>George Horvath | 3022 (8) | 2714 (3) | 3220(1) | 3640 (1) | 3249 (7) | 15845 |

| | | RIDING | FENCING | SWIMMING | SHOOTING | RUNNING | TOTAL |
|---|---|---|---|---|---|---|---|
| 4. POL | Janusz Pyciak-Peciak<br>Jan Olesiński<br>Marek Bajan | 3208 (1) | 2506 (5) | 2846(8) | 3576 (3) | 3498 (2) | 15634 |
| 5. FRA | Paul Four<br>Joel Bouzou<br>Alani Cortes | 3070 (6) | 2600 (4) | 3088(3) | 3464 (8) | 3123(10) | 15345 |
| 6. CZE | Milan Kadlec<br>Jan Bártu<br>Bohumil Starnovsky | 3154 (3) | 2298 (8) | 3044(5) | 3504 (5) | 3339 (6) | 15339 |
| 7. FIN | Heikki Hulkkonen<br>Jussi Pelli<br>Pekka Santanen | 2851(11) | 2480 (6) | 3132(2) | 3384(10) | 3240 (8) | 15087 |
| 8. GBR | Robert Nightingale<br>Peter Whiteside<br>Nigel Clark | 2946(10) | 2246(10) | 2824(9) | 3584 (2) | 3462 (3) | 15062 |

**1984 Los Angeles-Irvine** T: 17, N: 17, D: 8.1.

| | | RIDING | FENCING | SWIMMING | SHOOTING | RUNNING | TOTAL |
|---|---|---|---|---|---|---|---|
| 1. ITA | Daniele Masala<br>Carlo Massullo<br>Pierpaolo Cristofori | 3240 (1) | 2560 (4) | 3716 (4) | 2912 (4) | 3632(1) | 16066 |
| 2. USA | Michael Storm<br>Robert Gregory Losey<br>Dean Glenesk | 3188 (2) | 2604 (3) | 3700 (6) | 2802 (7) | 3274(8) | 15568 |
| 3. FRA | Paul Four<br>Didier Boube<br>Joel Bouzou | 2994 (9) | 2626 (2) | 3484(11) | 3044 (1) | 3417(7) | 15565 |
| 4. SWI | Andy Jung<br>Peter Steinmann<br>Peter Minder | 3090 (5) | 2516 (5) | 3564(10) | 2956 (2) | 3217(9) | 15343 |
| 5. MEX | Ivar Sisniega<br>Alejandro Yrizar<br>Marcelo Hoyo | 3056 (7) | 2450 (7) | 3704 (5) | 2648 (9) | 3425(6) | 15283 |
| 6. GER | Achim Bellmann<br>Michael Rehbein<br>Christian Sandow | 3058 (6) | 2494 (6) | 3736 (3) | 2296(14) | 3444(5) | 15028 |
| 7. GBR | Richard Phelps<br>Michael Mumford<br>Stephen Sowerby | 2605(15) | 2362 (9) | 3764 (2) | 2626(10) | 3537(2) | 14894 |
| 8. SPA | Jorge Quesada<br>Eduardo Burguete<br>Federico Galera | 3106 (4) | 2208(11) | 3568 (9) | 2516(12) | 3493(4) | 14891 |

**1988 Seoul** T: 19, N: 19, D: 9.22.

| | | RIDING | FENCING | SWIMMING | SHOOTING | RUNNING | TOTAL |
|---|---|---|---|---|---|---|---|
| 1. HUN | János Martinek<br>Attila Mizsér<br>László Fábián | 2952 (5) | 2888 (1) | 3764 (4) | 2604(14) | 3678 (1) | 15886 |
| 2. ITA | Carlo Massullo<br>Daniele Masala<br>Gianluca Tiberti | 2998 (3) | 2392 (8) | 3732 (8) | 3110 (1) | 3339 (7) | 15571 |
| 3. GBR | Richard Phelps<br>Dominic Mahony<br>Graham Brookhouse | 2986 (4) | 2439 (7) | 3764 (4) | 2604(14) | 3483 (3) | 15276 |
| 4. FRA | Christophe Ruer<br>Joël Bouzou<br>Bruno Genard | 2884 (6) | 2473 (6) | 3780 (3) | 2714(11) | 3417 (4) | 15268 |

|  |  |  | RIDING | FENCING | SWIMMING | SHOOTING | RUNNING | TOTAL |
|---|---|---|---|---|---|---|---|---|
| 5. | SOV | Vakhtang Yagorashvili<br>German Yuferov<br>Anatoly Avdeev | 2376(14) | 2735 (2) | 3992 (1) | 2802 (7) | 3309 (8) | 15214 |
| 6. | CZE | Milan Kadlec<br>Tomáš Fleissner<br>Jiří Prokopius | 3050 (2) | 2361 (9) | 3508(14) | 2758 (9) | 3366 (6) | 15043 |
| 7. | SWI | Peter Steinmann<br>Andy Jung<br>Peter Burger | 2832 (8) | 2541 (5) | 3616(13) | 2472(17) | 3402 (5) | 14863 |
| 8. | MEX | Ivar Sisniega<br>Alejandro Yrizar<br>Marcelo Hoyo | 2730(11) | 2361 (9) | 3648(11) | 2560(16) | 3486 (2) | 14785 |

# ROWING

| MEN | WOMEN |
|---|---|
| Single Sculls | Single Sculls |
| Double Sculls | Double Sculls |
| Quadruple Sculls | Quadruple Sculls |
| Pair-Oared Shell Without Coxswain | Pair-Oared Shell Without Coxswain |
| Pair-Oared Shell With Coxswain | Four-Oared Shell Without Coxswain |
| Four-Oared Shell Without Coxswain | Eight-Oared Shell With Coxswain |
| Four-Oared Shell With Coxswain | Discontinued Events |
| Eight-Oared Shell With Coxswain | |
| Discontinued Events | |

## MEN

Since 1964 rowing contests have begun with qualifying tests. The eight fastest qualifiers advance directly to the semifinals, while the rest take part in a *repêchage*, or second-chance round (repêchage being the French word for "fishing again"). The four fastest participants in the repêchage races join the semifinals. The top six semifinalists take part in the final, while the other six take part in a *"petit-final,"* to determine 7th through 12th places.

Men's races are rowed on a 2000-meter course, women's on a 1000-meter course, no matter what the event.

## SINGLE SCULLS

**1896** not held

**1900 Paris** C: 10, N: 2, D: 8.26.
1. Henri Barrelet          FRA    7:35.6
2. André Gaudin            FRA    7:41.6
3. George Saint Ashe       GBR    8:15.6
4. Robert d'Heilly         FRA    8:16.0
DNF: Louis Prével (FRA)

**1904 St. Louis** C: 4, N: 1, D: 7.30.
1. Frank Greer             USA    10:08.5
2. James Juvenal           USA    —
3. Constance Titus         USA    —
4. Dave Dulfield           USA    —

**1906** not held

**1908 London** C: 9, N: 6, D: 7.31.
1. Harry Blackstaffe       GBR    9:26.0
2. Alexander McCulloch     GBR    —
3. Bernhard von Gaza       GER    —
3. Károly Levitzky         HUN    —

The 40-year-old Blackstaffe was twice the age of McCulloch, his opponent in the final. Yet he was able to finish more strongly and win by one and a quarter lengths.

**1912 Stockholm** C: 13, N: 11, D: 7.19.
1. William Kinnear         GBR    7:47.6
2. Polydore Veirman        BEL    7:56.0
3. Everard Butler          CAN    —
3. Mikhail Kusik           RUS    —

**1920 Antwerp** C: 10, N: 10, D: 8.29.
1. John Kelly, Sr.                USA    7:35.0
2. Jack Beresford                 GBR    7:36.0
3. D. Clarence Hadfield d'Arcy    NZE    7:48.0
4. Frits Evert Eyken              HOL    —

Philadelphia bricklayer Jack Kelly, who once won 126 straight races, was barred from competing in London's famous Diamond Sculls race at Henley because the Vesper Boat Club, of which he was a member, had been accused of professionalism three years earlier. Kelly got his revenge a few weeks later in the Olympics, when he defeated the Diamond Sculls winner, Jack Beresford, in the final. The two men were so exhausted after the race that they were unable to shake hands. Nevertheless, Kelly managed to recover sufficiently to win a second gold medal in the double sculls 30 minutes later. Kelly had two illustrious offspring. His son John, Jr., who competed in four Olympics himself, brought his father great joy when he won the Diamond Sculls at Henley in 1947 and 1949. His daughter was Grace Kelly, the famous film actress who later became Princess of Monaco.

**1924 Paris** C: 8, N: 8, D: 7.17.
1. Jack Beresford          GBR    7:49.2
2. William Garrett Gilmore USA    7:54.0
3. Josef Schneider         SWI    8:01.1
DNF: Arthur Bull (AUS)

In 1924 the system of repêchage was introduced, in which the second-place finishers in the preliminary heats are allowed a row-off for a place in the final. This was a break for Beresford, who lost to Gilmore in the opening round. Qualifying through the repêchage, Beresford turned the tables on Gilmore in the final and won by two and a half lengths. Despite his defeat, Gilmore had fond memories of the race. "During the last 200 meters," he later wrote, "when the sun seemed to get hotter with every stroke and I was making a supreme effort to grasp victory, a kindly breeze swept across the Seine, carrying a strong but pleasant scent from a perfumery which was not within sight. It was truly so strong that it first gagged me, but in a moment I was rowing on as if in a flowing river of the perfume itself."

**1928 Amsterdam** C: 15, N: 15, D: 8.10.
1. Henry Pearce          AUS     7:11.0
2. Kenneth Myers         USA     7:20.8
3. Theodore Collet       GBR     7:29.8
4. Lambertus Gunther     HOL     7:31.6
5. Joseph Wright         CAN
6. Josef Straka          CZE
7. Edouard Candeveau     SWI
8. V. Savrin             FRA

"Bobby" Pearce, a third-generation sculling champion from Sydney, faced an unexpected challenge in the middle of the final when a family of ducks passed single-file in front of his boat. Pearce let them pass and then sculled to a popular five-length victory. He had hoped that his Olympic win would allow him to row in the Diamond Sculls at Henley, but he was refused admission because he was a carpenter. Back in Sydney he was unable to find work due to the Depression. When Lord Dewar, the Canadian whisky manufacturer, learned of Pearce's plight, he offered him a job as a salesman. Ironically, this new position made Pearce eligible for Henley, since he was no longer a laborer. In 1931 he went to London and won the Diamond Sculls by six lengths. Although he moved to Hamilton, Ontario, in Canada, Pearce represented Australia again in 1932 and won a second gold medal.

**1932 Los Angeles** C: 5, N: 5, D: 8.13.
1. Henry Pearce          AUS     7:44.4
2. William Miller        USA     7:45.2
3. Guillermo Douglas     URU     8:13.6
4. Leslie Southwood      GBR     8:33.6

**1936 Berlin** C: 20, N: 20, D: 8.14.
1. Gustav Schäfer        GER     8:21.5
2. Josef Hasenöhrl       AUT     8:25.8
3. Daniel Barrow         USA     8:28.0
4. Charles Campbell      CAN     8:35.0
5. Ernst Rufli           SWI     8:38.9
6. Pascual José Giorgio  ARG     8:57.5

7. Roger Verey           POL
7. Humphry Lloyd Warren  GBR

**1948 London** C: 14, N: 14, D: 8.9.
1. Mervyn Wood           AUS     7:24.4
2. Eduardo Risso         URU     7:38.2
3. Romolo Catasta        ITA     7:51.4
4. Tranquilo Cappozzi    ARG
4. John Kelly, Jr.       USA
4. Jean Sepheriades      FRA
7. Anthony Rowe          GBR

The unusually handsome Wood was dubbed "The Cary Grant of Scullers" by U.S. journalists.

**1952 Helsinki** C: 18, N: 18, D: 7.23.
1. Yuri Tyukalov         SOV     8:12.8
2. Mervyn Wood           AUS     8:14.5
3. Teodor Kocerka        POL     8:19.4
4. J. Anthony Fox        GBR     8:22.5
5. Ian Stephen           SAF     8:31.4

**1956 Melbourne** C: 12, N: 12, D: 11.27.
1. Vyacheslav Ivanov     SOV     8:02.5
2. Stuart Mackenzie      AUS     8:07.7
3. John Kelly, Jr.       USA     8:11.8
4. Teodor Kocerka        POL     8:12.9

Mackenzie, who made his living as a chicken-sexer, seemed to have the race well in hand, but Ivanov made a sensational spurt with 200 meters to go and won going away. Eighteen-year-old Ivanov was so thrilled when he was presented with the gold medal that he jumped up and down with joy—and dropped the medal into Lake Wendouree. He immediately dived to the bottom of the water, but came back up empty-handed. After the games were over he was given a replacement medal by the I.O.C. He earned two more gold medals in 1960 and 1964. In 1959 Mackenzie became the first person to win both single and double sculls at Henley.

**1960 Rome** C: 13, N: 13, D: 9.3.
1. Vyacheslav Ivanov     SOV     7:13.96
2. Achim Hill            GDR     7:20.21
3. Teodor Kocerka        POL     7:21.26
4. James Hill            NZE     7:23.98
5. Harry Parker          USA     7:29.26
6. Savino Rebek          ITA     7:31.09

**1964 Tokyo** C: 13, N: 13, D: 10.15.
1. Vyacheslav Ivanov     SOV     8:22.51
2. Achim Hill            GDR     8:26.24
3. Gottfried Kottmann    SWI     8:29.68
4. Alberto Demiddi       ARG     8:31.51
5. Murray Watkinson      NZE     8:35.57
6. Donald Spero          USA     8:37.53
7. Robert Groen          HOL
8. Leif Gotfredsen       CAN

Ivanov staged another one of his famous finishing bursts, gaining 11 seconds on Hill in the last 500 meters. Actually he made such a tremendous effort that he blacked out before the finish line. In his book, *Winds of Olympic Lakes,* Ivanov wrote, "I don't remember how long it was before consciousness gradually returned. . . . I mustered the last ounce of my strength, raised my head and couldn't believe it: there was clear water ahead of me and nobody in front of me in those last 50 meters to the finish. I wondered whether it was a case of delirium and that I was having hallucinations. . . . I managed to find an extra bit of strength, picked up the oars and crossed the line first."

**1968 Mexico City** C: 17, N: 17, D: 10.19.
1. Henri Jan Wienese      HOL    7:47.80
2. Jochen Meissner        GER    7:52.00
3. Alberto Demiddi        ARG    7:57.19
4. John Van Blom          USA    8:00.51
5. Achim Hill             GDR    8:06.09
6. Kenneth Dwan           GBR    8:13.76
7. Zdzsislaw Bromek       POL
8. Niels Secher           DEN

**1972 Munich** C: 18, N: 18, D: 9.2.
1. Yuri Malishev          SOV    7:10.12
2. Alberto Demiddi        ARG    7:11.53
3. Wolfgang Güldenpfennig GDR    7:14.45
4. Udo Hild               GER    7:20.81
5. James Dietz            USA    7:24.81
6. Melchior Bürgin        SWI    7:31.99
7. John Drea              IRL
8. Yordan Vulchev         BUL

**1976 Montreal** C: 15, N: 15, D: 7.25.
1. Pertti Karppinen       FIN    7:29.03
2. Peter Michael Kolbe    GER    7:31.67
3. Joachim Dreifke        GDR    7:38.03
4. Sean Drea              IRL    7:42.50
5. Nikolai Dovgan         SOV    7:57.39
6. Ricardo Ibarra         ARG    8:03.05
7. James Dietz            USA
8. Edward Hale            AUS

Karppinen, a 6-foot 7-inch fireman from Parsio, won Finland's first rowing gold medal by coming from behind to upset world champion Kolbe and co-favorite Dreifke.

**1980 Moscow** C: 14, N: 14, D: 7.27.
1. Pertti Karppinen       FIN    7:09.61
2. Vassily Yakusha        SOV    7:11.66
3. Peter Kersten          GDR    7:14.88
4. Vladek Lacina          CZE    7:17.57
5. Hans Svensson          SWE    7:19.38
6. Hugh Matheson          GBR    7:20.28
7. Bernard Destraz        SWI
8. Konstantinos Kontomanolis GRE

**1984 Los Angeles-Lake Casitas** C: 16, N: 16, D: 8.5.
1. Pertti Karppinen       FIN    7:00.24
2. Peter Michael Kolbe    GER    7:02.19
3. Robert Mills           CAN    7:10.38
4. John Biglow            USA    7:12.00
5. Ricardo Ibarra         ARG    7:14.59
6. Konstantinos Kontomanolis GRE 7:17.03
7. Gary Reid              NZE
8. Raimund Haberl         AUT

Kolbe, now a ball-bearing salesman in Norway and the winner of four world championships, took the early lead. But Karppinen, as usual, came from behind, caught Kolbe after 1750 meters and then powered ahead in the last 25 meters to match Vyacheslav Ivanov's record of three single sculls gold medals.

**1988 Seoul** C: 22, N: 22, D: 9.24.
1. Thomas Lange           GDR    6:49.86
2. Peter Michael Kolbe    GER    6:54.77
3. Eric Verdonk           NZE    6:58.66
4. Hamish McGlashan       AUS    7:01.43
5. Kajetan Broniewski     POL    7:03.67
6. Andrew Sudduth         USA    7:11.45
7. Pertti Karpinnen       FIN
8. Jüri Jaanson           SOV

Lange, a 24-year-old medical student from Halle, was the defending world champion. He overhauled Kolbe at 1300 meters and pulled away to win by a wide margin. Kolbe earned his third silver medal at age 35.

## DOUBLE SCULLS

**1896–1900** not held

**1904 St. Louis** T: 3, N: 1, D: 7.30.
1. USA (Atalanta Boat Club, New York—John     10.03.2
   Mulcahy, William Varley)
2. USA (Ravenswood Boat Club, Long Island—John  —
   Hoben, James McLoughlin)
3. USA (Independent Rowing Club, New Orleans—  —
   John Wells, Joseph Ravanack)

**1906–1912** not held

**1920 Antwerp** T: 5, N: 5, D: 8.29.
1. USA (John Kelly, Sr., Paul Costello)        7:09.0
2. ITA (Erminio Dones, Pietro Annoni)          7:19.0
3. FRA (Alfred Plé, Gaston Giran)              7:21.0

**1924 Paris** T: 5, N: 5, D: 7.17.
1. USA (Paul Costello, John Kelly, Sr.)              6:34.0
2. FRA (Marc Detton, Jean-Pierre Stock)             6:38.0
3. SWI (Rudolf Bosshard, Heinrich Thoma)             —
4. BRA (Edumundo Castello-Branco, Carlos Castello-Branco)  —

**1928 Amsterdam** T: 10, N: 10, D: 7.17.
1. USA    (Paul Costello, Charles McIlvaine)       6:41.4
2. CAN    (Joseph Wright, Jack Guest)              6:51.0
3. AUT    (Leo Losert, Viktor Flessl)              6:48.8
4. GER    (Horst Hoeck, Gerhard Voigt)             6:48.2
5. HOL    (Henrl Cox, Constant Pieterse)           6:52.8
6. SWI    (Rudolf Bosshard, Maurice Rieder)        6:53.4

Costello won his third straight double sculls gold medal with relative ease. He and McIlvaine were never seriously challenged and won the final against Wright and Guest by five lengths.

**1932 Los Angeles** T: 5, N: 5, D: 8.13.
1. USA    (Kenneth Myers, William Garrett Gilmore) 7:17.4
2. GER    (Herbert Buhtz, Gerhard Boetzelen)       7:22.8
3. CAN    (Charles Pratt, Noël de Mille)           7:27.6
4. ITA    (Orfeo Paroli, Mario Moretti)            7:49.2

Veteran Olympians Myers and Gilmore were 36 and 37 years old, respectively.

**1936 Berlin** T: 12, N: 12, D: 8.14.
1. GBR    (Jack Beresford, Leslie Southwood)       7:20.8
2. GER    (Willy Kaidel, Joachim Pirsch)           7:26.2
3. POL    (Roger Verey, Jersy Ustupski)            7:36.2
4. FRA    (André Giriat, Robert Jacquet)           7:42.3
5. USA    (John Houser, William Dugan)             7:44.8
6. AUS    (William Dixon, Herbert Turner)          7:45.1

Beresford and Southwood were beaten by Kaidel and Pirsch in the first round, but qualified for the final through repêchage. The Germans led from the start, but the British pair caught them at 1800 meters, rowed neck and neck for 100 meters, and then pulled away to win by two and a half lengths. The 37-year-old Beresford was competing in his fifth Olympic Games. Each time he won a medal: in 1920 a silver in the single sculls; in 1924 a gold in the same event; in 1928 a silver in the eights; in 1932 a gold in the coxswainless fours; and finally, in 1936, this third gold, in the double sculls. Considering that he and Southwood won the Double Sculls Challenge Cup at Henley in 1939, it is quite possible that Beresford would have won a sixth medal had not World War II intervened.

**1948 London** T: 15, N: 15, D: 8.9.
1. GBR    (Richard Burnell, Bertram Bushnell)      6:51.3
2. DEN    (Ebbe Parsner, Aage Larsen)              6.55.3
3. URU    (William Jones, Juan Rodriguez)          7:12.4

**1952 Helsinki** T: 16, N: 16, D: 7.23.
1. ARG    (Tranquilo Cappozzo, Eduardo Guerrero)   7:32.2
2. SOV    (Georgi Zhilin, Igor Yemchuk)            7:38.3
3. URU    (Miguel Seijas, Juan Rodriguez)          7:43.7
4. FRA    (Jacques Maillet, Achille Giovannoni)    7:46.8
5. CZE    (Antonín Malinković, Jiři Vykoukal)      7:53.8
6. AUS    (John Rogers, Murray Riley), BEL (Robert George, Joseph Van Stichel), ITA (Silvio Bergamini, Lodovico Sommaruga)

**1956 Melbourne** T: 8, N: 8, D: 11.27.
1. SOV    (Aleksandr Berkutov, Yuri Tyukalov)      7:24.0
2. USA    (Bernard Paul Costello, James Gardiner)  7:32.2
3. AUS    (Murray Riley, Mervyn Wood)              7:37.4
4. GER    (Thomas Schneider, Kurt Hipper)          7:41.7

**1960 Rome** T: 16, N: 16, D: 9.3.
1. CZE    (Václav Kozák, Pavel Schmidt)            6:47.50
2. SOV    (Aleksandr Berkutov, Yuri Tyukalov)      6:50.49
3. SWI    (Ernst Hürlimann, Rolf Larcher)          6:50.59
4. FRA    (René Duhamel, Bernard Monnereau)        6:52.22
5. HOL    (Peter Bakker, Jacobus Rentmeester)      6:53.86
6. BEL    (Gérard Higny, Jean Lemaire)             6:56:40

Václav Kozák was a 23-year-old noncommissioned officer. His partner was 30-year-old Pavel Schmidt, a psychiatrist from Bratislava.

**1964 Tokyo** T: 13, N: 13, D: 10.15.
1. SOV    (Oleg Tyurin, Boris Dubrovsky)           7:10.66
2. USA    (Seymour Cromwell, James Storm)          7:13.16
3. CZE    (Vladimir Andrs, Pavel Hofmann)          7:14.23
4. SWI    (Melchior Bürgin, Martin Studach)        7:24.97
5. GER    (Helmut Lebert, Josef Steffes-Mies)      7:30.03
6. FRA    (René Duhamel, Bernard Monnereau)        7:41.80
7. GBR    (Michael Clay, Peter Webb)
8. HOL    (Max Alwin, Peter Bots)

**1968 Mexico City** T: 13, N: 13, D: 10.19.
1. SOV    (Anatoly Sass, Aleksandr Timoshinin)     6:51.82
2. HOL    (Leendert Frans van Dis, Henricus Droog) 6:52.80
3. USA    (William Maher, John Nunn)               6:54.21
4. BUL    (Atanas Schelev, Yordan Valtschev)       6:58.48
5. GDR    (Hans-Ulrich Schmied, Manfred Haake)     7:04.92
6. GER    (Wolfgang Glock, Udo Hild)               7:12.20
7. BRA    (Harri Klein, Edgard Gijsen)
8. ROM    (Alexandru Aposteanu, Octavian Pavelescu)

**1972 Munich** T: 18, N: 18, D: 9.2.
1. SOV    (Aleksandr Timoshinin, Gennady Korshikov) 7:01.77
2. NOR    (Frank Hansen, Svein Thögersen)          7:02.58
3. GDR    (Joachim Böhmer, Hans-Ulrich Schmied)    7:05.55
4. DEN    (Niels Secher, Jörgen Engelbrecht)       7:14.19
5. GBR    (Timothy Crooks, Patrick Delafield)      7:16.29
6. CZE    (Josef Straka, Vladek Lacina)            7:17.60
7. HOL    (Jan Bruyn, Paul Veenemans)
8. SWI    (Hans Ruckstuhl, Ulrich Isler)

Timoshinin and Korshikov took the lead shortly before the halfway mark and held on to win in the closest double sculls finish in Olympic history.

**1976 Montreal** T: 13, N: 13, D: 7.25.
1. NOR    (Frank Hansen, Alf Hansen)               7:13.20
2. GBR    (Chris Baillieu, Michael Hart)           7:15.26
3. GDR    (Hans-Ulrich Schmied, Jürgen Bertow)     7:17.45
4. SOV    (Yevgeny Barbakov, Gennady Korshikov)    7:18.87
5. GER    (Peter Becker, Gerhard Kroschewski)      7:22.15
6. FRA    (Jean-Noël Ribot, Jean-Michel Izart)     7:50.18
7. ITA    (Umberto Ragazzi, Silvio Ferrini)
8. USA    (William Belden, Lawrence Klecatsky)

Two years after Frank Hansen won the silver medal in the double sculls at the Munich Olympics, he asked his younger brother, Alf, to become his new partner. Together they took first place at the 1975 world championships and then went on to win the Olympics the following year. Frank, 30, was an electrician; Alf, 28, worked for the telephone company.

**1980 Moscow** T: 9, N: 9, D: 7.27.

| | | | |
|---|---|---|---|
| 1. | GDR | (Joachim Dreifke, Klaus Kröppelien) | 6:24.33 |
| 2. | YUG | (Zoran Pancic, Milorad Stanulov) | 6:26.34 |
| 3. | CZE | (Zdeněk Pecka, Václav Vochoska) | 6:29.07 |
| 4. | GBR | (Tim Clark, Chris Baillieu) | 6:31.13 |
| 5. | SOV | (Aleksandr Fomchenko, Yevgeny Duleyev) | 6:35.34 |
| 6. | POL | (Wieslaw Kujda, Piotr Tobolski) | 6:39.66 |
| 7. | SPA | (José Ramon Oyarzabal, José Luis Corta) | |
| 8. | FRA | (Marc Boudoux, Didier Gallet) | |

**1984 Los Angeles-Lake Casitas** T: 11, N: 11, D: 8.5.

| | | | |
|---|---|---|---|
| 1. | USA | (Bradley Lewis, Paul Enquist) | 6:36.87 |
| 2. | BEL | (Pierre-Marie Deloof, Dirk Crois) | 6:38.19 |
| 3. | YUG | (Zoran Pančič, Milorad Stanulov) | 6:39.59 |
| 4. | GER | (Andreas Schmelz, Georg Agrikola) | 6:40.41 |
| 5. | ITA | (Francesco Esposito, Ruggero Verroca) | 6:44.29 |
| 6. | CAN | (Tim Storm, Peter MacGowan) | 6:46.68 |
| 7. | AUT | (Wilfried Auerbach, Thomas Linemayr) | |
| 8. | FIN | (Reina Karppinen, Aarne Lindroos) | |

Starting in last place, Lewis and Enquist passed Deloof and Crois 300 meters from the finish and pulled away for a clear victory.

**1988 Seoul** C: 17, N: 17, D: 9.24.

| | | | |
|---|---|---|---|
| 1. | HOL | (Ronald Florijn, Nicolaas Rienks) | 6:21.13 |
| 2. | SWI | (Beat Schwerzmann, Ueli Bodenmann) | 6:22.59 |
| 3. | SOV | (Aleksandr Marchenko, Vassily Yakusha) | 6:22.87 |
| 4. | GER | (Christian Handle, Ralf Thienel) | 6:24.97 |
| 5. | GDR | (Uwe Mund, Uwe Heppner) | 6:26.20 |
| 6. | DEN | (Per Henrik Stisen Rasmussen, Bjarne Eltang) | 6:26.98 |
| 7. | SPA | (José Manuel Bermudez, Manuel Vera) | |
| 8. | BUL | (Vassil Radev, Danail Yordanov) | |

Florijn and Rienks fashioned a startling upset by rowing a powerful middle 1000 meters and then holding off the equally surprising Swiss.

# QUADRUPLE SCULLS

**1896–1972** not held

**1976 Montreal** T: 11, N: 11, D: 7.25.

| | | | |
|---|---|---|---|
| 1. | GDR | (Wolfgang Güldenpfennig, Rüdiger Reiche, Karl-Heinz Bussert, Michael Wolfgramm) | 6:18.65 |
| 2. | SOV | (Yevgeny Duleev, Yuri Yakomov, Aivars Lazdenieks, Vytautas Butkus) | 6:19.89 |
| 3. | CZE | (Jaroslav Helebrand, Václav Vochoska, Zdeněk Pecka, Vladek Lacina) | 6:21.77 |
| 4. | GER | (Norbert Kothe, Helmut Krause, Michael Gentsch, Helmut Wolber) | 6:24.81 |

| | | | |
|---|---|---|---|
| 5. | BUL | (Yordan Vulchev, Mincho Nikolov, Hristo Zhelev, Eftim Gerzilov) | 6:32.04 |
| 6. | USA | (Peter Cortes, Kenneth Foote, Neil Halleen, John van Blom) | 6:34.33 |
| 7. | FRA | (Roland Weill, Roland Thibaul, Patrick Morineau, Charles Imbert) | |
| 8. | SWI | (Hans Ruckstuhl, Denis Oswald, Jürg Weitnauer, Reto Wyss) | |

Martin Winter of the East German team had to undergo an emergency appendectomy and was replaced at the last minute by Bussert. The sudden change caused the team some problems in the opening round, and they lost to the U.S.S.R. But by the final they were all straightened out and won a hard-fought race. Winter finally won his gold medal in 1980.

**1980 Moscow** T: 12, N: 12, D: 7.27.

| | | | |
|---|---|---|---|
| 1. | GDR | (Frank Dundr, Karsten Bunk, Uwe Heppner, Martin Winter) | 5:49.81 |
| 2. | SOV | (Yuri Shapochka, Yevgeny Barbakov, Valery Kleshnev, Nikolai Dovgan) | 5:51.47 |
| 3. | BUL | (Mincho Nikolov, Lubomir Petrov, Ivo Roussev, Dogdan Dobrov) | 5:52.38 |
| 4. | FRA | (Christian Marquis, Jean Raymond Peltier, Charles Imbert, Roland Weill) | 5:53.45 |
| 5. | SPA | (Juan Solano, Jesus Gonzalez, Manuel Vera, Julio Oliver) | 6:01.19 |
| 6. | YUG | (Milan Arezina, Darko Zibar, Dragan Obradović, Nikola Stefanović) | 6:10.70 |
| 7. | POL | (Andrzej Skowroński, Zbigniew Andruszkiewicz, Ryszard Burak, Stanislaw Wierzbicki) | |
| 8. | HOL | (Victor Schheffers, Jeroen Vervoort, Rob Robbers, Ronald Vervoort) | |

**1984 Los Angeles-Lake Casitas** T: 10, N: 10, D: 8.5.

| | | | |
|---|---|---|---|
| 1. | GER | (Albert Hedderich, Raimund Hörmann, Dieter Wiedenmann, Michael Dürsch) | 5:57.55 |
| 2. | AUS | (Paul Reedy, Gary Gullock, Timothy McLaren, Anthony Lovrich) | 5:57.98 |
| 3. | CAN | (Doug Hamilton, Mike Hughes, Phil Monckton, Bruce Ford) | 5:59.07 |
| 4. | ITA | (Piero Poli, Renato Gaeta, Antonio Dell'Aquila, Stefano Lari) | 6:00.94 |
| 5. | FRA | (Marc Boudoux, Serge Fornara, Pascal Body, Pascal Dubosquelle) | 6:01.35 |
| 6. | SPA | (Luis Oliver, Jesus Gonzalez, Manuel Vera, Julio Oliver) | 6:04.99 |
| 7. | USA | (Curtis Fleming, Gregg Montesi, Ridgely Johnson, Bruce Beall) | |
| 8. | NOR | (Pal Sandli, Espen Thorsen, Vetle Vinje, Ivan Enstad) | |

Six weeks before the 1980 Olympics, the West German crew, prevented by the anti-Soviet boycott from taking part in the Games themselves, defeated the East German crew that went on to win in Moscow. The West Germans, a pipefitter, a butcher, a bank clerk and a machinist, stayed together for four more years and, in Los Angeles in 1984, staged a furious come-from-behind sprint to defeat the Australians in a photo-finish.

**1988 Seoul** T: 13, N: 13, D: 9.25.
| | | | |
|---|---|---|---|
| 1. | ITA | (Piero Poli, Gianluca Farina, Davide Tizzano, Agostino Abbagnale) | 5:53.37 |
| 2. | NOR | (Lars Bjonness, Vetle Vinje, Rolf Bernt Thorsen, Alf Hansen) | 5:55.08 |
| 3. | GDR | (Steffen Bogs, Steffen Zühlke, Heiko Habermann, Jens Köppen) | 5:56.13 |
| 4. | SOV | (Pavel Krupko, Aleksandr Zaskalko, Sergei Kiniakin, Yuri Zelikovich) | 5:57.18 |
| 5. | AUS | (Richard Powell, Brenton Terrell, Paul Reedy, Peter Antonie) | 5:59.15 |
| 6. | GER | (Christoph Galandi, Oliver Grüner, Georg Agrikola, Andreas Reinke) | 5:59.59 |
| 7. | POL | (Slawomir Cieślakowski, Andrzej Krzepiński, Miroslaw Mruk, Tomasz Świątek) | |
| 8. | HOL | (Robbert Bakker, Hans Kelderman, Juergen Nelis, Hermanus Van der Eerenbeemt) | |

Alf Hansen, the Norwegian stroke, had won gold in the double sculls in 1976. He added a silver in the quadruple twelve years later at age 40. During the celebration by the Italians, team member Davide Tizzano was thrown into the water and lost his gold medal in the muddy bottom of the Han River. A Korean diver, working as a security guard at the regatta course, retrieved it after a 50-minute search.

# PAIR-OARED SHELL WITHOUT COXSWAIN

**1896–1900** not held

**1904 St. Louis** T: 3, N: 1, D: 7.30.
| | | | |
|---|---|---|---|
| 1. | USA | (Seawanhaka Boat Club, Brooklyn, New York—Robert Farnam, Joseph Ryan) | 10:57.0 |
| 2. | USA | (Atalanta Boat Club, New York—John Mulcahy, William Varley) | — |
| 3. | USA | (Western Rowing Club, St. Louis, Missouri—John Joachim, Joseph Buerger) | — |

**1906** not held

**1908 London** T: 4, N: 3, D: 7.31.
| | | | |
|---|---|---|---|
| 1. | GBR | (Leander Club I—John Fenning, Gordon Thomson) | 9:41.0 |
| 2. | GBR | (Leander Club II—George Fairbairn, Philip Verdon) | — |

**1912–1920** not held

**1924 Paris** T: 3, N: 3, D: 7.17.
| | | | |
|---|---|---|---|
| 1. | HOL | (Antonie Beijnen, Wilhelm Rösingh) | 8:19.4 |
| 2. | FRA | (Maurice Bouton, Georges Piot) | 8:21.6 |
| DNS: | GBR | (Gordon Killick, C.T. Southgate) | |

**1928 Amsterdam** T:8, N: 8, D: 8.10.
| | | | |
|---|---|---|---|
| 1. | GER | (Bruno Müller, Kurt Moschter) | 7:06.4 |
| 2. | GBR | (Terence O'Brien, R. Archibald Nisbet) | 7:08.6 |
| 3. | USA | (Paul McDowell, John Schmitt) | 7:20.4 |
| 4. | ITA | (Romeo Sisti, Nino Bolzoni) | 7:24.4 |
| 5. | SWI | (Alois Reinhard, Wilhelm Müller) | 7:29.1 |
| 6. | HOL | (C.A. van Wankum, Hendrik van Suylekom) | 7:30.2 |

**1932 Los Angeles** T: 6, N: 6, D: 8.13.
| | | | |
|---|---|---|---|
| 1. | GBR | (Hugh Arthur Edwards, Lewis Clive) | 8:00.0 |
| 2. | NZE | (Cyril Stiles, Frederick Thompson) | 8:02.4 |
| 3. | POL | (Henryk Budziński, Janusz Mikolajczak) | 8:08.2 |
| 4. | HOL | (Godfried Röel, Pieter Roelofsen) | 8:08.4 |
| 5. | FRA | (Fernand Vandernotte, Marcel Vandernotte) | |

**1936 Berlin** T: 13, N: 13, D: 8.14.
| | | | |
|---|---|---|---|
| 1. | GER | (Willi Eichhorn, Hugo Strauss) | 8:16.1 |
| 2. | DEN | (Richard Olsen, Harry Larsen) | 8:19.2 |
| 3. | ARG | (Horacio Podestá, Julio Curatella) | 8:23.0 |
| 4. | HUN | (Károly Györy, Tibor Mamusich) | 8:25.7 |
| 5. | SWI | (Wilhelm Klopfer, Karl Müller) | 8:33.0 |
| 6. | POL | (Ryszard Borzuchowski, Edward Kobyliński) | 8:41.9 |

**1948 London** T: 12, N: 12, D: 8.6.
| | | | |
|---|---|---|---|
| 1. | GBR | (John Wilson, William Laurie) | 7:21.1 |
| 2. | SWI | (Hans Kalt, Josef Kalt) | 7:23.9 |
| 3. | ITA | (Felice Fanetti, Bruno Boni) | 7:31.5 |

Wilson and Laurie were best friends who joined the Colonial Service and were sent to the Sudan. Returning to London on leave in 1938, they entered the Henley Regatta and took first place. Then they went back to the Sudan and didn't touch an oar for ten years. In May 1948 they returned to Britain on another leave and decided to take up rowing again. After six weeks' training they entered the Henley Regatta and won again. This gained them an invitation to represent Great Britain at the Olympics, and they were granted six months' leave to prepare. Rowing on their favorite course at Henley, "the Desert Rats," as they were known, took the lead after 1150 meters and fought off a late challenge from the Kalt brothers to secure the gold medal.

**1952 Helsinki** T: 16, N: 16, D: 7.23.
| | | | |
|---|---|---|---|
| 1. | USA | (Charles Logg, Thomas Price) | 8:20.7 |
| 2. | BEL | (Michel Knuysen, Robert Baetens) | 8:23.5 |
| 3. | SWI | (Kurt Schmid, Hans Kalt) | 8:32.7 |
| 4. | GBR | (David Callender, Christopher Davidge) | 8:37.4 |
| 5. | FRA | (Jean-Pierre Souche, René Guissart) | 8:48.8 |

Logg and Price, of Rutgers University, were the Cinderella pair of 1952. Neither man had sat in a pair-oared shell until two months before the Olympics, and the 19-year-old Price had only started rowing in January.

**1956 Melbourne** T: 9, N: 9, D: 11.27.
| | | | |
|---|---|---|---|
| 1. | USA | (James Fifer, Duvall Hecht) | 7:55.4 |
| 2. | SOV | (Igor Buldakov, Viktor Ivanov) | 8:03.9 |
| 3. | AUT | (Alfred Sageder, Josef Kloimstein) | 8.11.8 |
| 4. | AUS | (Peter Adrian Raper, Maurice Grace) | 8:22.2 |

**1960 Rome** T: 18, N: 18, D: 9.3.
1. SOV (Valentin Boreyko, Oleg Golovanov) 7:02.01
2. AUT (Alfred Sageder, Josef Kloimstein) 7:03.69
3. FIN (Veli Lehtelä, Toimi Pitkänen) 7:03.80
4. GDR (Jochen Neuling, Heinz Weigel) 7:08.81
5. USA (Ted Frost, Robert Rogers) 7:17.08
6. YUG (Nikola Čupin, Antun Ivankovic) 7:20.91

**1964 Tokyo** T: 14, N: 14, D: 10.15.
1. CAN (George Hungerford, Roger Jackson) 7:32.94
2. HOL (Steven Blaisse, Ernst Venemans) 7:33.40
3. GER (Michael Schwan, Wolfgang Hottenrott) 7:38.63
4. GBR (James Lee Nicholson, Stewart Farquharson) 7:42.00
5. DEN (Peter Fich Christiansen, Hans Jórgen Boye) 7:48.13
6. FIN (Toimi Pitkänen, Veli Lehtelä) 8:05.74
7. SWI (Peter Bolliger, Nicolas Gobet)
8. POL (Czeslaw Nawrot, Alfons Ślusarski)

Sent to Tokyo as reserves for the Canadian eights team, Hungerford and Jackson were allowed to enter the coxless pairs as compensation. Given only six weeks to get used to each other, they had their first race together ever in the opening round of the Olympics. To compound their problems, Hungerford had not yet recovered from an attack of mononucleosis. In the final they stroked to a one-and-a-half-length lead at the 1500-meter mark and hung on desperately to win Canada's only victory of the 1964 Olympics. Hungerford and Jackson were considered such long shots that no Canadian journalists were present for their race. The two young men celebrated their victory by drinking seven Cokes each. The shell that they used had been loaned to them by the University of Washington; it was the same shell that had been used by Fifer and Hecht when they won the gold medal in 1956.

**1968 Mexico City** T: 18, N: 18, D: 10.19.
1. GDR (Jörg Lucke, Hans-Jürgen Bothe) 7:26.56
2. USA (Lawrence Hough, Philip "Tony" Johnson) 7:26.71
3. DEN (Peter Christiansen, Ib Ivan Larsen) 7:31.84
4. AUT (Dieter Ebner, Dieter Losert) 7:41.80
5. SWI (Fred Rüssli, Werner Zwimpfer) 7:46.79
6. HOL (Roelof Luynenburg, Rudolf Stokvis) —
7. AUS (David Ramage, Paul Guest)
8. POL (Alfons Ślusarski, Jerzy Broniec)

An exciting nip-and-tuck battle saw the favored team of Hough and Johnson take the lead with 500 meters to go, only to have Lucke and Bothe pass them in the last ten meters and win by a mere four feet.

**1972 Munich** T: 20, N: 20, D: 9.2.
1. GDR (Siegfried Brietzke, Wolfgang Mager) 6:53.16
2. SWI (Heinrich Fischer, Alfred Bachmann) 6:57.06
3. HOL (Roelof Luynenburg, Rudolf Stokvis) 6:58.70
4. CZE (Lubomir Zapletal, Petr Lakomy) 6:58.77
5. POL (Alfons Ślusarski, Jerzy Broniec) 7:02.74
6. ROM (Ilie Oantă, Dumitru Grumezescu) 7:42.90
7. GER (Erwin Haas, Lutz Ulbricht)
8. SOV (Vladimir Poliakov, Nikolai Vasiliev)

In 1968 a comedian named Heinz Quermann appealed over radio and TV for tall young people in East Germany to register with the rowing section of the Leipzig Sports Club. Among the respondents were two 16-year-olds, Siegfried Brietzke and Wolfgang Mager. When they began to achieve competitive success they became known as the "Quermann pair."

**1976 Montreal** T: 15, N: 15, D: 7.25.
1. GDR (Jörg Landvoigt, Bernd Landvoigt) 7:23.31
2. USA (Calvin Coffey, Michael Staines) 7:26.73
3. GER (Peter Vanroye, Thomas Strauss) 7:30.03
4. YUG (Žlatko Celent, Duško Mrduljas) 7:34.17
5. BUL (Valentin Stoev, Georgi Georgiev) 7:37.42
6. CZE (Miroslav Knapek, Vojtech Časka) 7:51.06
7. SOV (Gennady Kinko, Tiit Khelmyia)
8. FIN (Leo Ahonen, Kari Hanska)

The Landvoigt twins were 25-year-old steelworkers from Potsdam. The U.S. team, besides being the only American rowers to win medals at Montreal, were also noteworthy for their unusual combination of names—Coffey and Staines.

**1980 Moscow** T: 15, N: 15, D: 7.27.
1. GDR (Bernd Landvoigt, Jörg Landvoigt) 6:48.01
2. SOV (Yuri Pimenov, Nikolai Pimenov) 6:50.50
3. GBR (Charles Wiggin, Malcolm Carmichael) 6:51.47
4. ROM (Constantin Postoiu, Valer Toma) 6:53.49
5. CZE (Miroslav Vrastil, Miroslav Knapek) 7:01.54
6. SWE (Anders Larson, Anders Wilgotson) 7:02.52
7. IRL (Pat Gannon, William Ryan)
8. FRA (Jean-Claude Roussel, Dominique Lecointe)

The medal ceremony presented a bizarre sight, as the gold-medal-winning Landvoigt twins stood beside the silver-medal-winning Pimenov twins.

**1984 Los Angeles-Lake Casitas** T: 14, N: 14, D: 8.5.
1. ROM (Petru Iosub, Valer Toma) 6:45.39
2. SPA (Fernando Climent, Luis Lasurtegui) 6:48.47
3. NOR (Hans Magnus Grepperud, Sverre Loken) 6:51.81
4. GER (Thomas Möllenkamp, Axel Wöstmann) 6:52.53
5. ITA (Marco Romano, Pasquale Aiese) 6:55.88
6. USA (David De Ruff, John Strotbeck) 6:58.46
7. HOL (Sjoerd Hoekstra, Joost Adoma)
8. BRA (Ronaldo Carvalho, Ricardo Carvalho)

**1988 Seoul** T: 18, N: 18, D: 9.24.
1. GBR (Andrew Holmes, Steven Redgrave) 6:36.84
2. ROM (Dragos Neagu, Danut Dobre) 6:38.06
3. YUG (Bojan Presern, Sadik Mujkić) 6:41.01
4. BEL (Alain Lewuillon, Wim Van Belleghem) 6:45.47
5. GDR (Carl Ertel, Uwe Gasch) 6:48.86
6. SOV (Igor Zuborenko, Yalery Vyrvich) 6:51.11
7. GER (Frank Dietrich, Michael Twittmann)
8. FRA (Lavrent Lacasa, Alex Perahia)

Holmes and Redgrave had already earned gold medals in the coxed fours in 1984. In Seoul they led from start to finish to win the coxless pairs. Twenty-three hours later they placed third in the coxed pairs.

# PAIR-OARED SHELL WITH COXSWAIN

**1896** not held

**1900 Paris** T: 6, N: 3, D: 8.26.
1. HOL (Minerva, Amsterdam—François Antoine Brandt, Roelof Klein, Hermanus Brockmann)   7:34.2
2. FRA (Société Nautique de la Marne—Louis Martinet, Waleff, coxswain unknown)   7:34.4
3. FRA (Rowing Club Castillon—Carlos Deltour, Antoine Védrenne, Paoli)   7:57.2
4. FRA (Cercle Nautique de Reims—Mathieu, Ferlin, coxswain unknown)   8:01.0

Brockmann was coxswain for the Dutch crew in the opening heat, which they lost to the Société Nautique de la Marne. It was decided that Brockmann was too heavy, so he was replaced in the final by a small French boy whose name is unknown. This boy, who was under 10 years old and may have been as young as 7, is presumed to be the youngest competitor in Olympic history.

**1904** not held

**1906 Athens** T: 8, N: 5, D: 4.26.
*(1000 Meters)*
1. ITA (Bucintoro, Venice—Enrico Bruna, Emilio Fontanella, Giorgio Cesana)   4:23.0
2. ITA (Barion, Bari—Luigi Diana, Francesco Civera, Emilio Cesarana)   4:30.0
3. FRA (Société Nautique de la Basse Seine, Paris—Gaston Delaplane, Charles Delaporte, Marcel Frebourg)   —
4. FRA (Société Nautique de Bayonne—Adolphe Bernard, Joseph Halcet, Jean-Baptiste Mathieu)   —
5. BEL (Club Nautique—Max Orban, Remy Orban, Th. Psiliakos)

**1906 Athens** T: 7, N: 5, D: 4.26.
*(1609 Meters)*
1. ITA (Bucintoro, Venice—Enrico Bruna, Emilio Fontanella, Giorgio Cesana)   7:32.4
2. BEL (Société Nautique de Gand—Max Orban, Remy Orban, Th. Psiliakos)   8:00.0
3. FRA (Société Nautique de Bayonne—Adolphe Bernard, Joseph Halcet, Jean-Baptiste Mathieu)   8:08.6
4. DEN (Hannibal Ostergaard, Henning Rasmussen, Axel Steinthal)

Psiliakos was a young Greek who offered to cox for the Belgian pair.

**1908–1912** not held

**1920 Antwerp** T: 4, N: 4, D: 8.29.
1. ITA (Ercole Olgeni, Giovanni Scatturin, Guido De Filip)   7:56.0
2. FRA (Gabriel Poix, Maurice Bouton, Ernest Barberolle)   7:57.0
3. SWI (Edouard Candeveau, Alfred Felber, Paul Piaget)   —

**1924 Paris** T: 5, N: 5, D: 7.17.
1. SWI (Edouard Candeveau, Alfred Felber, Emile Lachapelle)   8:39.0
2. ITA (Ercole Olgeni, Giovanni Scatturin, Gino Sopracordevole)   8:39.1
3. USA (Leon Butler, Harold Wilson, Edward Jennings)   —
4. FRA (Eugène Constant, Raymond Talleux, Marcel Lepan)   —

The final was, by all accounts, a thrilling race, and was won by the Swiss by only two feet.

**1928 Amsterdam** T: 6, N: 6, D: 8.10.
1. SWI (Hans Schöchlin, Karl Schöchlin, Hans Bourquin)   7:42.6
2. FRA (Armand Marcelle, Edouard Marcelle, Henri Préaux)   7:48.4
3. BEL (Léon Flament, François de Coninck, Georges Anthony)
4. ITA (R. Vestrini, P.L. Vestrini, C. Milani)

**1932 Los Angeles** T: 4, N: 4, D: 8.13.
1. USA (Joseph Schauers, Charles Kieffer, Edward Jennings)   8:25.8
2. POL (Jerzy Braun, Janusz Ślązak, Jerzy Skolimowski)   8:31.2
3. FRA (Anselme Brusa, André Giriat, Pierre Brunet)   8:41.2
4. BRA (José Ramalho, Estevam Strata, Francisco Bricio)   8:53.2

**1936 Berlin** T: 12, N: 12, D: 8.14.
1. GER (Gerhard Gustmann, Herbert Adamski, Dieter Arend)   8:36.9
2. ITA (Almiro Bergamo, Guido Santin, Luciano Negrini)   8:49.7
3. FRA (Georges Tapie, Marceau Fourcade, Noël Vandernotte)   8:54.0
4. DEN (Raymond Larsen, Carl Berner, Aage Jensen)   8:55.8
5. SWI (Georges Gschwind, Hans Appenzeller, Rolf Spring)   9:10.9
6. YUG (Ivo Fabris, Elko Mrduljaš, Line Ljubičič)   9:19.4

**1948 London** T: 9, N: 9, D: 8.9.
1. DEN (Finn Pedersen, Tage Henriksen, Carl-Ebbe Andersen)   8:00.5
2. ITA (Giovanni Steffe, Aldo Tarlao, Alberto Radi)   8:12.2
3. HUN (Antal Szendey, Béla Zsitnik, Róbert Zimonyi)   8:25.2
4. FRA (Ampelio Sartor, Aristide Sartor, R. Crezen)
4. YUG (V. Ristic, M. Horvatin, D. Djordjevič)

**1952 Helsinki** T: 15, N: 15, D: 7.23.
1. FRA (Raymond Salles, Gaston Mercier, Bernard Malivoire) — 8:28.6
2. GER (Heinz-Joachim Manchen, Helmut Heinhold, Helmut Noll) — 8:32.1
3. DEN (Svend Pedersen, Poul Svendsen, Jörgen Frandsen) — 8:34.9
4. ITA (Giuseppe Ramani, Aldo Tarlao, Luciano Marion) — 8:38.4
5. FIN (Veijo Mikkolainen, Toimi Pitkänen, Erkki Lyijynen) — 8:40.8

**1956 Melbourne** T: 8, N: 8, D: 11.27.
1. USA (Arthur Ayrault, Conn Findlay, A. Kurt Seiffert) — 8:26.1
2. GER (Karl-Heinrich von Groddeck, Horst Arndt, Rainer Borkowsky) — 8:29.2
3. SOV (Igor Yemtschuk, Georgy Schilin, Vladimir Petrov) — 8:31.0
4. POL (Henryk Jagodziński, Zbigniew Szwarcer, Berthold Mainka) — 8:31.5

**1960 Rome** T: 18, N: 18, D: 9.3.
1. GER (Bernhard Knubel, Heinz Renneberg, Klaus Zerta) — 7:29.14
2. SOV (Antanas Bogdanavičius, Zigmas Jukna, Igor Rudakov) — 7:30.17
3. USA (Richard Draeger, Conn Findlay, H. Kent Mitchell) — 7:34.58
4. DEN (Jens Behrendt Jensen, Knud Nielsen, Sven Lysholt Hansen) — 7:39.20
5. ITA (Giancarlo Piretta, Renzo Ostino, Vincenzo Bruno) — 7:40.92
6. ROM (Stefan Kureska, Gheorghe Riffelt, Mircea Roger) — 7:49.57

**1964 Tokyo** T: 16, N: 16, D: 15.
1. USA (Edward Ferry, Conn Findlay, H. Kent Mitchell) — 8:21.23
2. FRA (Jacques Morel, Georges Morel, Jean-Claude Darouy) — 8:23.15
3. HOL (Jan Bos, Herman Rouwé, Frederik Hartsuiker) — 8:23.42
4. SOV (Nikolai Safronov, Leonid Rakovschik, Igor Rudakov) — 8:24.85
5. CZE (Václav Chalupa, Jiři Palko, Zdenek Mejstřik) — 8:36.21
6. POL (Kazimierz Maskręcki, Marian Siejkowski, Stanislaw Kozera) — 8:40.00
7. GDR (Günter Bergau, Peter Gorny, Karl-Heinz Danielowski)
8. AUT (Alfred Sageder, Josef Kloimstein, Peter Salzbacher)

**1968 Mexico City** T: 18, N: 18, D: 10.19.
1. ITA (Primo Baran, Renzo Sambo, Bruno Cipolla) — 8:04.81
2. HOL (Herman Suselbeek, Hadriaan van Nes, Roderick Rijnders) — 8:06.80
3. DEN (Jörn Krab, Harry Jörgensen, Preben Krab) — 8:08.07
4. GDR (Helmut Wollmann, Wolfgang Gunkel, Klaus-Dieter Neubert) — 8:08.22

5. USA (William Hobbs, Richard Edmunds, Stewart MacDonald) — 8:12.60
6. GER (Bernhard Hiesinger, Rolf Hartung, Lutz Benter) — 8:41.51
7. SWI (Urs Frankhauser, Urs Bitterli, Beat Wirz)
8. BUL (Georgi Atanasov, Georgi Nikolov, Veselin Staevski)

**1972 Munich** T: 21, N: 21, D: 9.2.
1. GDR (Wolfgang Gunkel, Jörg Lucke, Klaus-Dieter Neubert) — 7:17.25
2. CZE (Oldřich Svojanovský, Pavel Svojanovský, Vladimir Petřiček) — 7:19.57
3. ROM (Ştefan Tudor, Petre Ceapura, Ladislau Lovrenski) — 7:21.36
4. GER (Heinz Mussmann, Bernd Krause, Stefan Kuhnke) — 7:21.52
5. SOV (Vladimir Eshinov, Nikolai Ivanov, Yuri Lorenson) — 7:24.44
6. POL (Wojclech Repsz, Wieslaw Dlugosz, Jacek Rylski) — 7:28.92
7. NOR (Rolf Andreassen, Arne Bergodd, Thor Egil Olsen)
8. GBR (David Maxwell, Michael Hart, Alan Inns)

**1976 Montreal** T: 17, N: 17, D: 7.25.
1. GDR (Harald Jährling, Friedrich-Wilhelm Ulrich, Georg Spohr) — 7:58.99
2. SOV (Dmitri Bekhterev, Yuri Shurkalov, Yuri Lorenson) — 8:01.82
3. CZE (Oldřich Svojanovský, Pavel Svojanovský, Ludvik Vebr) — 8:03.82
4. BUL (Rumen Hristov, Tsvetan Petkov, Tosho Kishev) — 8:11.27
5. ITA (Primo Baran, Annibale Venier, Franco Venturnin) — 8:15.97
6. POL (Ryszard Stadniuk, Grzegorz Stellak, Ryszard Kubiak) — 8:23.02
7. GBR (Neil Christie, James Macleod, David Webb)
8. GER (Winfried Ringwald, Klaus Jaeger, Holger Hocke)

**1980 Moscow** T: 11, N: 11, D: 7.20.
1. GDR (Harald Jährling, Friedrich-Wilhelm Ulrich, Georg Spohr) — 7:02.54
2. SOV (Viktor Pereverzev, Gennady Kryuchkin, Aleksandr Lukyanov) — 7:03.35
3. YUG (Dusko Mrduljas, Zlatko Celent, Josip Reic) — 7:04.92
4. ROM (Petre Ceapura, Gabriel Bularda, Ladislau Lovrenski) — 7:07.17
5. BUL (Tsvetan Petkov, Rumen Hristov, Tosho Kishev) — 7:09.21
6. CZE (Josef Plaminek, Milan Škopek, Oldřich Hejdušek) — 7:09.41
7. ITA (Antonio Dell'Aquila, Giuseppe Abbagnale, Giuseppe Di Capua)
8. FRA (Serge Fornara, Herve Bourqvel, Jean-Pierre Huguet-Balenx)

**1984 Los Angeles-Lake Casitas** T: 12, N: 12, D: 8.5.
1. ITA (Carmine Abbagnale, Giuseppe Abbagnale, Giuseppe Di Capua) 7:05.99
2. ROM (Dimitrie Popescu, Vasile Tomoiaga, Dumitru Raducanu) 7:11.21
3. USA (Kevin Still, Robert Espeseth, Douglas Herland) 7:12.81
4. BRA (Valter Hime Soares, Angelo Rosio Neto, Nilton Silva Alonco) 7:17.07
5. CAN (Harold Backer, Tony Zasada, Ian Barkley) 7:18.98
6. GER (Hermann Gress, Dieter Göpfert, Rudolf Ziegler) 7:25.16
7. YUG (Dario Vidosević, Zlatko Celent, Mirko Ivancić)
8. GBR (Adrian Genziani, William Lang, Alan Inns)

The coxswain for the bronze-medal-winning U.S. team was 32-year-old Doug Herland, who stood 4 feet 9 inches tall and weighed 103 pounds. Herland was born with broken hips, broken ribs and a broken collarbone as a result of osteogenesis imperfecta—brittle bone disease. He broke bones twice a year for the first eight years of his life. Herland discovered rowing at Pacific Lutheran U. in Tacoma, Washington, where he earned a degree in social psychology. He went on to a career in social work, counseling handicapped and mentally retarded children, and establishing a rowing team for the disabled in Michigan.

The coxswain for the 11th place Belgian pair was the youngest competitor at the 1984 Olympics, 12-year-old Philippe Cuelenaere.

**1988 Seoul** T: 14, N: 14, D: 9.25.
1. ITA (Carmine Abbagnale, Giuseppe Abbagnale, Giuseppe Di Capua) 6:58.79
2. GDR (Mario Streit, Detlef Kirchhoff, René Rensch) 7:00.63
3. GBR (Andrew Holmes, Steven Redgrave, Patrick Sweeney) 7:01.95
4. ROM (Dimitrie Popescu, Vasile Tomoiaga, Ladislau Lovrensky) 7:02.60
5. BUL (Emil Groitzov, Atanas Andreev, Stefan Stoykov) 7:03.04
6. SOV (Andrei Korikov, Roman Kazantsev, Andrei Lipsky) 7:06.07
7. CZE (Jan Kabrhel, Jiří Ptak, Milan Škopek)
8. YUG (Roman Ambrozić, Milan Jansa, Saso Mirjanić)

The Abbagnale brothers of Pompeii parlayed a furious start into their second Olympic championship. Their younger brother, Agostino, a member of the Italian quadruple sculls team, also went home with a gold medal.

# FOUR-OARED SHELL WITHOUT COXSWAIN

**1896-1900** not held

**1904 St. Louis** T: 3, N: 1, D: 7.30.
1. USA (Century Boat Club, St. Louis—George Dietz, August Erker, Albert Nasse, Arthur Stockhoff) 9:05.8

2. USA (Mound City Rowing Club, St. Louis—Charles Aman, Michael Begley, Martin Fromanack, Frederick Suerig) —
3. USA (Western Rowing Club, St. Louis—Gustav Voerg, John Freitag, Louis Helm, Frank Dummerth) —

**1906** not held

**1908 London** T: 4, N: 3, D: 7.31.
1. GBR (Magdalen College B.C., Oxford—C. Robert Cudmore, James Gillan, Duncan McKinnon, John Somers-Smith) 8:34.0
2. GBR (Leander Club—Philip Filleul, Harold Barker, John Fenning, Gordon Thomson) —

**1912–1920** not held

**1924 Paris** T: 4, N: 4, D: 7.17.
1. GBR (Charles Eley, James MacNabb, Robert Morrison, Terrence Sanders) 7:08.6
2. CAN (Colin Finlayson, Archibald Black, George Mackay, William Wood) 7:18.0
3. SWI (Emile Albrecht, Alfred Probst, Eugen Sigg-Bächthold, Hans Walter) —
4. FRA (Théo Cremnitz, Jean Camuset, Henri Bonzano, Albert Bonzano) —

**1928 Amsterdam** T: 6, N: 6, D: 8.10.
1. GBR (John Lander, Michael Warriner, Richard Beesly, Edward Vaughan Bevan) 6:36.0
2. USA (Charles Karle, William Miller, George Heales, Ernest Bayer) 6:37.0
3. ITA (Cesare Rossi, Pietro Freschi, Umberto Bonadè, Paolo Gennari) 6:37.6
4. GER (Henry Zänker, Wolfgang Goedecke, Günther Roll, Werner Zschieke) DNS

The semifinal race between Great Britain and Germany saw a dramatic finish. The Germans led by half a length with 50 meters to go, when Zschieke, their stroke, suddenly collapsed and fell forward on his oars. His teammates stopped rowing and watched the British crew shoot past to victory. In the final, the British team, which was from Trinity College, Cambridge, trailed the U.S. crew for almost the entire race, caught them with 20 yards to go and spurted ahead to a half-length win.

**1932 Los Angeles** T: 5, N: 5, D: 8.13.
1. GBR (John Badcock, Hugh Edwards, Jack Beresford, Rowland George) 6:58.2
2. GER (Karl Aletter, Ernst Gaber, Walter Flinsch, Hans Maier) 7:03.0
3. ITA (Antonio Ghiardello, Francesco Cossu, Giliante D'Este, Antonio Provenzani) 7:04.0

4. USA (John McCosker, George Mattson, Thomas 7:14.2
Pierie, Edgar Johnson)

**1936 Berlin** T: 9, N: 9, D: 8.14.
1. GER (Rudolf Eckstein, Anton Rom, Martin Karl, 7:01.8
Wilhelm Menne)
2. GBR (Thomas Bristow, Alan Barrett, Peter Jackson, 7:06.5
John Duncan Sturrock)
3. SWI (Hermann Betschart, Hans Homberger, Alex 7:10.6
Homberger, Karl Schmid)
4. ITA (Antonio Ghiardello, Luigi Luscardo, Aldo 7:12.4
Pellizzoni, Francesco Pittaluga)
5. AUT (Rudolf Höpfler, Camillo Winkler, Wilhelm 7:20.5
Pichler, Johann Binder)
6. DEN (Knud Olsen, Keld Karise, Björn Dröyer, Boye 7:26.3
Emil Jensen)

**1948 London** T: 10, N: 10, D: 8.9.
1. ITA (Giuseppe Moioli, Elio Morille, Giovanni Inver- 6:39.0
nizzi, Franco Faggi)
2. DEN (Helge Halkjaer, Aksel Bonde Hansen, Helge 6:43.5
Schröder, Ib Storm Larsen)
3. USA (Frederick John Kingsbury, Stuart Griffing, 6:47.7
Gregory Gates, Robert Perew)
4. GBR (Peter Kirkpatrick, H. Rushmere, T. Christie, —
Anthony Butcher)
5. HOL (H. Van Suylokom, S. Haarsma, J. Dekker, J —
Van den Berg)
6. SAF (E. Ramsay, A. Ikin, D. Mayberry, C. Kietzman) —

**1952 Helsinki** T: 17, N: 17, D: 7.23.
1. YUG (Duje Bonačič, Velimir Valenta, Mate Tro- 7:16.0
janović, Petar Šegvič)
2. FRA (Pierre Blondiaux, Jacques Guissart, Marc 7:18.9
Bouissou, Roger Gautier)
3. FIN (Veikko Lommi, Kauko Wahlsten, Oiva Lommi, 7:23.3
Lauri Nevalainen)
4. GBR (Harry Almond, John Jones, James Crowden, 7:25.2
George Cadbury)
5. POL (Edward Schwarzer, Zbigniew Schwarzer, 7:26.2
Henryk Jagodziński, Zbigniew Żarnowiecki)

**1956 Melbourne** T: 12, N: 12, D: 11.27.
1. CAN (Archibald McKinnon, Lorne Loomer, Walter 7:08.8
D'Hondt, Donald Arnold)
2. USA (John Welchli, John McKinlay, Arthur McKin- 7:18.4
lay, James McIntosh)
3. FRA (René Guissart, Yves Delacour, Gaston 7:20.9
Mercier, Guy Guillabert)
4. ITA (Giuseppe Moioli, Attilio Cantoni, Giovanni 7:22.5
Zucchi, Abbondio Marcelli)

The Canadian crew consisted of four small-town boys
from the University of British Columbia, three of whom
had only been rowing for a year. In the final they were so
nervous that they almost missed the water with their first
stroke and were left behind. However, they were able to
catch up by the halfway mark and pull away to a five-
length victory. The four Canadians returned to the Olympics four years later in Rome and won silver medals as
part of the eights crew.

**1960 Rome** T: 16, N: 16, D: 9.3.
1. USA (Arthur Ayrault, Ted Nash, John Sayre, Richard 6:26.26
Wailes)
2. ITA (Tullio Baraglia, Renato Bosatta, Giancarlo 6:28.78
Crosta, Giuseppe Galante)
3. SOV (Igor Akhremchik, Yuri Bachurov, Valentin 6:29.62
Morkoykin, Anatoly Tarabrin)
4. CZE (Jindřich Blažek, Miroslav Jiska, René Libal, 6:34.30
Jaroslav Starosta)
5. GBR (J. Michael Beresford, Christopher Davidge, 6:36.18
Colin Porter, John Vigurs)
6. SWI (Paul Kölliker, Gottfried Kottmann, Kurt 6:38.81
Schmid, Rolf Streuli)

**1964 Tokyo** T: 14, N: 14, D: 10.15.
1. DEN (John Hansen, Björn Haslöv, Erik Petersen, 6:59.30
Kurt Helmudt)
2. GBR (John Michael Russell, Hugh Arthur Wardell- 7:00.47
Yerburgh, William Barry, John James)
3. USA (Geoffrey Picard, Richard Lyon, Theodore 7:01.37
Mittet, Theodore Nash)
4. HOL (Sjoerd Wartena, Jaap Enters, Herman 7:09.98
Boelen, Spike Castelein)
5. ITA (Romano Sgheiz, Fulvio Balatti, Giovanni 7:10.05
Zucchi, Luciano Sgheiz)
6. GER (Günter Schrörs, Horst Effertz, Albrecht Müller, 7:10.33
Manfred Misselhorn)
7. SOV (Tselestinas Yutsis, Eugenius Levitskas, Ionas
Mateyunas, Pavilas Liutkaitis)
8. AUT (Dieter Ebner, Horst Kuttelwascher, Dieter Losert, Manfred Kraushar)

**1968 Mexico City** T: 11, N: 11, D: 10.19.
1. GDR (Frank Forberger, Dieter Grahn, Frank Rüle, 6:39.18
Dieter Schubert)
2. HUN (Zoltán Melis, György Sarlós, József Csermely, 6:41.64
Antal Melis)
3. ITA (Renato Bosatta, Tullio Baraglia, Pier Angelo 6:44.01
Conti Manzini, Abramo Albini)
4. SWI (Roland Altenburger, Nicolas Noël Gobet, 6:45.78
Franz Rentsch, Alfred Meister)
5. USA (Peter Raymond, Raymond Wright, Charles 6:47.70
Hamlin, Lawrence Terry)
6. GER (Thomas Hitzbleck, Manfred Weinreich, Volk- 7:08.22
hart Buchter, Jochen Heck)
7. ROM (Pavel Cichi, Dumitru Ivanov, Emanoil Stratan,
Anton Chirlacopschi)
8. MEX (Roberto Retolaza, Arcadio Padilla, Jesus
Toscano, David Trejo)

**1972 Munich** T: 20, N: 20, D: 9.2.

1. GDR (Frank Forberger, Frank Rüle, Dieter Grahn, Dieter Schubert) 6:24.27
2. NZE (Dick Tonks, Dudley Storey, Ross Collinge, Noel Mills) 6:25.64
3. GER (Joachim Ehrig, Peter Funnekötter, Franz Held, Wolfgang Plottke) 6:28.41
4. SOV (Anatoly Tkachuk, Igor Kashurov, Aleksandr Motin, Vitaly Sapronov) 6:31.92
5. ROM (Emeric Tusa, Adalbert Agh, Mihai Naumencu, Francisc Papp) 6:35.60
6. DEN (Willy Poulsen, Peter Fich Christiansen, Egon Peterson, Rolf Andersen) 6:37.28
7. GBR (Frederick Smallbone, Leonard Robertson, James Clark, Mason William) 
8. BUL (Biser Boyadzhiev, Borislav Vasilev, Nikolai Kolev, Metodi Halvadzhiiski) 

Forberger, Rüle, Grahn, and Schubert had been rowing together for 11 years. In winning their second Olympic title, the Dresden four completed six years of unbeaten rowing in which they also won two world championships and two European championships. The lead changed hands six times in their exciting final race with the crew from New Zealand.

**1976 Montreal** T: 15, N: 15, D: 7.25.

1. GDR (Siegfried Brietzke, Andreas Decker, Stefan Semmler, Wolfgang Mager) 6:37.42
2. NOR (Ole Nafstad, Arne Bergodd, Finn Tveter, Rolf Andreassen) 6:41.22
3. SOV (Raul Arnemann, Nikolai Kuznetsov, Valery Dolinin, Anushavan Gasan-Dzhalalov) 6:42.52
4. NZE (Bob Murphy, Grant McAuley, Des Lock, David Lindstrom) 6:43.23
5. CAN (Brian Dick, Philip Monckton, Andrew van Ruyven, Ian Gordon) 6:46.11
6. GER (Bernhard Foelkel, Klaus Roloff, Wolfgang Horak, Johann Gabriel Konertz) 6:47.44
7. BUL (Dimiter Vulov, Dimiter Yanakiev, Todor Mrunkov, Rumen Hristov) 
8. USA (Tony Brooks, James Moroney, Gary Piantedosi, Hugh Stevenson) 

**1980 Moscow** T: 11, N: 11, D: 7.27.

1. GDR (Jürgen Thiele, Andreas Decker, Stefan Semmler, Siegfried Brietzke) 6:08.17
2. SOV (Aleksei Kamkin, Valery Dolinin, Aleksandr Kulagin, Vitaly Yeliseyev) 6:11.81
3. GBR (John Beattie, Ian McNuff, David Townsend, Martin Cross) 6:16.58
4. CZE (Vojtěch Caska, Jiři Prudil, Josef Neštický, Lubomir Zapletal) 6:18.63
5. ROM (Daniel Voiculescu, Carolică Ilies, Petru Iosub, Nicolae Simion) 6:19.45
6. SWI (Jürg Weitnauer, Bruno Saile, Hans-Konrad Trümpler, Stefan Netzle) 6:26.46
7. FRA (Jean-Pierre Bremer, Nicolas Lourdaux, Bernard Bruand, Dominique Basset) 

8. POL (Miroslaw Jarzembowski, Mariusz Trzciński, Henryk Trzciński, Marek Niedzialkowski) 

Siegfried Brietzke became the fourth of five rowers to win gold medals in three different Olympics, joining company with Paul Costello, Jack Beresford, and Vyacheslav Ivanov. In 1980 the East Germans dominated rowing so thoroughly that they won 11 of 14 finals. Every one of their 54 oarsmen and women went home with a medal.

**1984 Los Angeles-Lake Casitas** T: 10, N: 10, D: 8.5.

1. NZE (Leslie O'Connell, Shane O'Brien, Conrad Robertson, Keith Trask) 6:03.48
2. USA (David Clark, Jonathan Smith, Philip Stekl, Alan Forney) 6:06.10
3. DEN (Michael Jessen, Lars Nielsen, Per Rasmussen, Erik Christiansen) 6:07.72
4. GER (Norbert Kesslau, Volker Grabow, Jörg Puttlitz, Guido Grabow) 6:09.27
5. SWI (Bruno Saile, Jürg Weitnauer, Hans-Konrad Trümpler, Stefan Netzle) 6:09.50
6. SWE (Anders Wilgotson, Hans Svensson, Lars-Ake Lindqvist, Anders Larson) 6:11.71
7. CAN (Tim Turner, Ted Gibson, David Johnson, Stephen Beatty) 
8. AUS (David Doyle, James Lowe, Duncan Fisher, John Bentley) 

**1988 Seoul** T: 15, N: 15, D: 9.25.

1. GDR (Roland Schröder, Thomas Greiner, Ralf Brudel, Olaf Förster) 6:03.11
2. USA (Raoul Rodriguez, Thomas Bohrer, David Krmpotich, Richard Kennelly) 6:05.53
3. GER (Norbert Kesslau, Volker Grabow, Jörg Puttlitz, Guido Grabow) 6:06.22
4. GBR (Mark Buckingham, Stephen Peel, Simon Berrisford, Peter Mulkerrins) 6:06.74
5. ITA (Sergio Caropreso, Carlo Gaddi, Pasquale Marigliano, Valter Molea) 6:09.55
6. SOV (Ivan Vysotsky, Sergei Smirnov, Yuri Pimenov, Nikolai Pimenov) 11:03.77
7. NZE (Campbell Clayton-Greene, Geoffrey Cotter, William Coventry, Neil Gibson) 
8. FRA (Pascal Bahuaud, Dominique Lecointe, Jean Jacques Martigne, Olivier Pons) 

The unusual time registered by the Soviet team was a result of one of their seats breaking in the middle of the race.

# FOUR-OARED SHELL WITH COXSWAIN

**1896** not held

**1900 Paris** T: 8, N: 4, D: 8.26, 8.29.
*First Final*

1. FRA (Cercle de l'Aviron de Roubaix—Emile Delchambre, Jean Cau, Henri Bouchaert, Henri Hazebrouck, Charlot) 7:11.0

2. FRA (Union Nautique de Lyon—Charles Perrin, 7:18.0
Daniel Soubeyran, Emile Wegelin, Georges
Lumpp, coxswain unknown)

3. GER (R.C. Favorite Harmonia, Hamburg—Hugo 7:18.2
Rüster, Wilhelm Carstens, Julius Körner, Adolf
Möller, Gustav Moths, Max Ammermann)

**Second Final**

1. GER (Germania Rowing Club, Hamburg—Oscar 5:59.0
Gossler, Walther Katzenstein, Waldemar
Tietgens, Gustav Gossler, Carl Gossler)

2. HOL (Minerva Amsterdam—Gerhard Lotsy, 6:33.0
Coenraad Hiebendaal, Paulus Jan Lotsy, Johannes Terwogt, Hermanus Brockmann)

3. GER (Ludwigshafener R.V.—Carl Lehle, Ernst 6:35.0
Feller, Hermann Wilker, Otto Fickeisen, Franz
Kröwerath)

Incompetence on the part of regatta officials resulted in the unusual development of two separate finals in the 1900 Olympics in this event. At first it was declared that the winners of three heats would qualify for the final as would the second-place finisher in heat 3, which included four of the eight entrants. When it was discovered that the losers in heats 2 and 3 had recorded faster times than the winner of heat 1, the officials announced that an extra qualifying heat would have to be run. However, they were unable to notify all of the crews, so the extra heat was cancelled. It was then decided that the three heat winners would be joined in the final by the three fastest losers. But since the course was laid out for only four boats, the heat winners protested and refused to participate in the final. So the first final was run off with only Roubaix of the original qualifiers in the water. The result was obviously ridiculous, so a second final was announced for the three heat winners. Participants in both finals were awarded prizes.

**1904** not held

**1906 Athens** T: 8, N: 4, D: 4.24.

1. ITA (Bucintoro, Venice—Enrico Bruna, Emilio Fon- 0:10.0
tanella, Riccardo Jandinoni, Giorgio Cesana,
Giuseppe Poli)

2. FRA (Société Nautique de la Basse Seine, Paris— —
Gaston Delaplane, Charles Delaporte, Léon
Delignières, Paul Echard, Marcel Frebourg)

3. FRA (Société Nautique de Bayonne—Adolphe Ber- —
nard, Joseph Halcet, Jean-Baptiste Laporte,
Pierre Sourbe, Jean-Baptiste Mathieu)

4. DEN Knud Bay, Emanuel Saugmann, Frederick —
Bielefeldt, Henning Rasmussen, Hannibal
Ostergaard

5. GRE (N. Viaguinis, J. Kountouris, P. Nomikos, G. —
Tsakonas, Ch. Brisimitzakis)

6. GRE (N. Zamanos, G. Georgitseas, N. Bertos, P. —
Saousopoulos, D. Rediadis)

7. TUR (D. Whittal, N. Petroppulos, P. Pavlidis, J. —
Gounaris, N. Mardelis)

DNF: GRE (Ch. Liambeis, Ch. Rangos, M. Sakorrafos, G.
Bouboulis, K. Athanasiadis)

**1908** not held

**1912 Stockholm** T: 11, N: 9, D: 7.19.

1. GER (Ludwigshafener R.V.—Albert Arnheiter, Otto 6:59.4
Fickeisen, Rudolf Fickeisen, Hermann Wilker,
Otto Maier)

2. GBR (Thames R.C.—Julius Beresford, Charles Ver- —
non, Charles Rought, Bruce Logan, Geoffrey
Carr)

3. DEN (Polytehnic Roklub—Erik Bisgaard, Rasmus —
Peter Frandsen, Magnus Simonsen, Poul
Thymann, Eigil Clemmensen)

3. NOR (Christiana Roklub—Henry Larsen, Matias —
Torstensen, Theodor Klem, Håkon Tönsager,
Ejnar Tönsager)

**1920 Antwerp** T: 9, N: 9, D: 8.29.

1. SWI (Willy Brüderlin, Max Rudolf, Paul Rudolf, Hans 6:54.0
Walter, Paul Staub)

2. USA (Kenneth Myers, Carl Otto Klose, Franz 6:58.0
Federschmidt, Erich Federschmidt, Sherman
Clark)

3. NOR (Birger Var, Theodor Klem, Henry Larsen, Per 7:02.0
Gulbrandsen, Thoralf Hagen)

**1924 Paris** T: 10, N: 10, D: 7.17.

1. SWI (Emile Albrecht, Alfred Probst, Eugen Sigg- 7:18.4
Bächthold, Hans Walter, Emile Lachapelle)

2. FRA (Eugène Constant, Louis Gressier, Georges 7:21.6
Lecointe, Raymond Talleux, Marcel Lepan)

3. USA (Robert Gerhardt, Sidney Jelinek, Edward 7:23.0
Mitchell, Henry Welsford, John Kennedy)

4. ITA (Renato Berninzone, Marcello Casanova, Gastone Cerato, Jean Cipollina, Massimo
Ballestrero)

DNF: HOL (Johannes Brandsma, Jacob Brandsma, Dirk Fortuin,
Jean van Silfhout, Louis Dekker)

**1928 Amsterdam** T: 11, N: 11, D: 8.10.

1. ITA (Valerio Peratin, Giliante D'Este, Nicolo Vittori, 6:47.8
Giovanni Delise, Renato Petronio)

2. SWI (Ernst Haas, Joseph Meyer, Otto Bucher, Karl 7:03.4
Schwoglor, Fritz Bösch)

3. POL (Franciszek Bronikowski, Edmund Jankowski, 7:12.8
Leon Birkholc, Bernard Ormanowski, Bdeslaw
Drewek)

4. GER (Karl Golzo, Hans Nickel, Karl Hoffmann, 7:26.4
Werner Kleine, Alfred Krohn)

5. BEL (Maurice Delplanck, Théo Warnbeke, Al- 7:30.2
phonse Dewette, Charles van Son, Jean
Bauwens)

**1932 Los Angeles** T: 7, N: 7, D: 8.13.

1. GER (Hans Eller, Horst Hoeck, Walter Meyer, Joa- 7:19.0
chim Spremberg, Karl-Heinz Neumann)

2. ITA (Bruno Vattovaz, Giovanni Plazzer, Riccardo 7:19.2
Divora, Bruno Parovel, Giovanni Scherl)

3. POL (Jerzy Braun, Janusz Ślązak, Stanislaw Urban, 7:26.8
Edward Kobyliński, Jerzy Skolimowski)

4. NZE (Noel Pope, Somers Cox, Charles Saunders, 7:32.6
John Solomon, Delmont Gullery)

A spectacular finish saw the Germans win by a mere one foot.

**1936 Berlin** T: 16, N: 16, D: 8.14.
1. GER (Hans Maier, Walter Volle, Ernst Gaber, Paul Söllner, Fritz Bauer) 7:16.2
2. SWI (Hermann Betschart, Hans Homberger, Alex Homberger, Karl Schmid, Rolf Spring) 7:24.3
3. FRA (Fernand Vandernotte, Marcel Vandernotte, Marcel Cosmat, Marcel Chauvigné, Noël Vandernotte) 7:33.3
4. HOL (Martinus Schoorl, Hotse Sjoerd Bartlema, John Regout, Simon de Wit, Gerard Hallie) 7:34.7
5. HUN (Miklós Mihók, Vilmos Éden, Ákos Inotay, Alajos Szilassy-Szymiczek, László Molnár) 7:35.6
6. DEN (Hans Mikkelsen, Ibsen Sörensen, Flemming Jensen, Svend Aage Sörensen, Aage Jensen) 7:40.4

Coxswain for the French bronze medalists was 12-year-old Noël Vandernotte, whose father, Fernand, and uncle, Marcel, were also members of the crew.

**1948 London** T: 16, N: 16, D: 8.9.
1. USA (Warren Westlund, Robert Martin, Robert Will, Gordon Giovanelli, Allen Morgan) 6:50.3
2. SWI (Rudolf Reichling, Erich Schriever, Emile Knecht, Pierre Stebler, André Moccand) 6:53.3
3. DEN (Erik Larsen, Börge Nielsen, Henry Larsen, Harry Knudsen, Jörgen Ib Olsen) 6:58.6
4. FRA (J. Pieddeloup, R. Lotti, G. Maquat, Jean-Pierre Souche, M. Boigegrain); HUN (Miklós Zágon, Lajos Nagy, B. Nyilasi, Tibor Nádas, Róbert Zimonyi); ITA (R. Polloni, F. Gotti, R. Macario, R. Cerutti, Dominico Cambieri)

**1952 Helsinki** T: 17, N: 17, D: 7.23.
1. CZE (Karel Mejta, Jiři Havlis, Jan Jindra, Stanislav Lusk, Miroslav Koranda) 7:33.4
2. SWI (Enrico Bianchi, Karl Weidmann, Heinrich Scheller, Emile Ess, Walter Leiser) 7:36.5
3. USA (Carl Lovested, Alvin Ulbrickson, Richard Wahlström, Matthew Leanderson, Albert Rossi) 7:37.0
4. GBR (Roderick MacMillan, Graham Fisk, Laurence Guest, Peter de Giles, Paul Massey) 7:41.2
5. FIN (Kurt Grönholm, Paul Stråhlman, Birger Karlsson, Karl-Erik Johansson, Antero Tukiainen) 7:43.8

**1956 Melbourne** T: 10, N: 10, D: 11.27.
1. ITA (Alberto Winkler, Romano Sgheiz, Angelo Vanzin, Franco Trincavelli, Ivo Stefanoni) 7:19.4
2. SWE (Olof Larsson, Gösta Eriksson, Ivar Aronsson, Sven Ever Gunnarsson, Bertil Göransson) 7:22.4
3. FIN (Kauko Hänninen, Reino Poutanen, Veli Lehtelä, Toimi Pitkänen, Matti Niemi) 7:30.9
4. AUS (Gordon Cowey, Kevin McMahon, Reginald Libbis, Ian Allen, John Jenkinson) 7:31.1

**1960 Rome** T: 21, N: 21, D: 9.3.
1. GER (Gerd Cintl, Horst Effertz, Klaus Rieckemann, Jürgen Litz, Michael Obst) 6:39.12
2. FRA (Robert Dumontois, Claude Martin, Jacques Morel, Guy Nosbaum, Jean-Claude Klein) 6:41.62
3. ITA (Fulvio Balatti, Romano Sgheiz, Franco Trincavelli, Giovanni Zucchi, Ivo Stefanoni) 6:43.72
4. SOV (Oleg Aleksandrov, Igor Khokhlov, Boris Fyodorov, Valentin Zanin, Igor Rudakov) 6:45.67
5. AUS (Graeme Allen, Maxwell Annett, John Hudson, Roland Waddington, Lionel Robberds) 6:45.80
6. HUN (Tibor Bedekovics, Csaba Kovács, László Munteán, Pál Wágner, Gyula Lengyel) 6:51.65

**1964 Tokyo** T: 16, N: 16, D: 10.15.
1. GER (Peter Neusel, Bernhard Britting, Joachim Werner, Egbert Hirschfelder, Jürgen Oelke) 7:00.44
2. ITA (Renato Bosatta, Emilio Trivini, Giuseppe Galante, Franco De Pedrina, Giovanni Spinola) 7:02.84
3. HOL (Alex Mullink, Jan van de Graaf, Frederick van de Graaf, Robert van de Graaf, Marius Klumperbeek) 7:06.46
4. FRA (Yves Fraisse, Claude Pache, Gérard Jacquesson, Michel Dumas, Jean Claude Darouy) 7:13.92
5. SOV (Anatoly Tkatchuk, Vitaly Kurdchenko, Boris Kuzmin, Anatoly Luzgin, Vladimir Yevseyev) 7:16.05
6. POL (Szczepan Grajczyk, Marian Leszczyński, Ryszard Lubicki, Andrzej Nowaczyk, Jerzy Pawlowski) 7:28.15
7. USA (Paul Gunderson, Harry Pollock, Thomas Pollock, James Tew, Edward Washburn)
8. NZE (Darien Boswell, Alistair Dryden, Peter Masfen, Robert Page, Dudley Storey)

**1968 Mexico City** T: 13, N: 13, D: 10.19.
1. NZE (Richard Joyce, Dudley Storey, Ross Hounsell Collinge, Warren Cole, Simon Dickie) 6:45.62
2. GDR (Peter Kremtz, Roland Göhler, Manfred Gelpke, Klaus Jakob, Dieter Semetzky) 6:48.20
3. SWI (Denis Oswald, Hugo Waser, Peter Bolliger, Jakob Grob, Gottlieb Fröhlich) 6:49.04
4. ITA (Romano Sgheiz, Emilio Trivini, Giuseppe Galante, Luciano Sgheiz, Mariano Gottifredi) 6:49.54
5. USA (Luther Jones, William Purdy, Anthony Martin, Aspinwall Gardner Cadwalader, John Hartigan) 6:51.41
6. SOV (Anatoly Mentyrev, Nikolai Surov, Aleksei Mischin, Arkady Kudinov, Viktor Mikheyev) 7:00.00
7. ROM (Reinhold Batschi, Petre Ceapura, Stefan Tudor, Francisco Papp, Ladislau Lovrensky)
8. ARG (Hugo Aberastegui, Jose Robledo, Juan Gomez, Guillermo Segurado, Rolando Locatelli)

The winning New Zealand crew had never competed together before the Olympics.

**1972 Munich** T: 14, N: 14, D; 9.2.
1. GER   (Peter Berger, Hans-Johann Färber, Gerhard   6:31.85
Auer, Alois Bierl, Uwe Benter)
2. GDR   (Dietrich Zander, Reinhard Gust, Eckhard   6:33.30
Martens, Rolf Jobst, Klaus-Dieter Ludwig)
3. CZE   (Otakar Mareček, Karel Neffe, Vladimir Jánoš,   6:35.64
František Provaznik, Vladimir Petřiček)
4. SOV   (Vladimir Sterlik, Vladimir Soloviev, Aleksandr   6:37.71
Lyubaturov, Yuri Shamaev, Igor Rudakov)
5. USA   (David Sawyer, Charles Ruthford, Chad Ru-   6:41.86
dolph, Michael Vespoli, Stewart MacDonald)
6. NZE   (Warren Cole, Chris Nilsson, John Clark, David   6:42.55
Linstrom, Peter Lindsay)
7. HOL   (Wim Grothuis, Evert Kroes, Jan Woudenberg,
Johan ter Haar, Cornelis de Korver)
8. SWI   (Hanspeter Leuthi, Urs Frankhauser, Franz
Rentsch, Denis Oswald, Rolf Stadelmann)

**1976 Montreal** T: 14, N: 14, D: 7.25.
1. SOV   (Vladimir Eshinov, Nikolai Ivanov, Mikhail   6:40.22
Kuznetsov, Aleksandr Klepikov, Aleksandr
Lukianov)
2. GDR   (Andreas Schulz, Rüdiger Kunze, Walter   6:42.70
Diessner, Ullrich Diessner, Johannes Thomas)
3. GER   (Hans-Johann Färber, Ralph Kubail, Siegfried   6:46.96
Fricke, Peter Niehusen, Hartmut Wenzel)
4. CZE   (Otakar Mareček, Karel Neffe, Milan   6:50.15
Suchopar, Vladimir Jánoš, Vladimir Petřiček)
5. BUL   (Luchezar Boichev, Nasko Minchev, Ivan   6:52.88
Botev, Kiril Kirchev, Nenko Dobrev)
6. NZE   (Viv Haar, Danny Keane, Tim Logan, Ian   7:00.17
Boserio, David Simmons)
7. IRL   (Michael Ryan, James Muldoon, Willyam
Ryan, Christy O'Brien, Liam Redmond)
8. POL   (Jerzy Broniec, Adam Tomasiak, Jerzy
Ulczyński, Ryszard Burak, Wlodzimierz
Chmielewski)

**1980 Moscow** T: 12, N: 12, D: 7.27.
1. GDR   (Dieter Wendisch, Ullrich Diessner, Walter   6:14.51
Diessner, Gottfried Döhn, Andreas Gregor)
2. SOV   (Artūrs Garonskis, Dimants Krišjanis, Dzintars   6:19.05
Krišjanis, Žoržs Tikmers, Juris Bērziņs)
3. POL   (Grzegorz Stellak, Adam Tomasiak, Grzegorz   6:22.52
Nowak, Ryszard Stadniuk, Ryszard Kubiak)
4. SPA   (Manuel Bermudez, Isidro Martin, Salvador   6:26.23
Verges, Luis Marie Lasurtegui, Javier Sabria)
5. BUL   (Hristo Aleksandrov, Vilhem Germanov,   6:28.13
Georgi Petkov, Stoyan Stoyanov, Nenko
Dobrev)
6. SWI   (Daniel Homberger, Peter Rahn, Roland   6:30.26
Stocker, Peter Stocker, Karl Graf)
7. GBR   (Leonard Robertson, Gordon Rankine, Colin
Seymour, John Roberts, Alan Inns)
8. BRA   (Laildo Machado, Wandir Kuntze, Walter
Soares, Henrique Johann, Manoel Novo)

**1984 Los Angeles-Lake Casitas** T: 8, N: 8, D: 8.5.
1. GBR   (Martin Cross, Richard Budgett, Andrew   6:18.64
Holmes, Steven Redgrave, Adrian Ellison)

2. USA   (Thomas Kiefer, Gregory Springer, Michael   6:20.28
Bach, Edward Ives, John Stillings)
3. NZE   (Kevin Lawton, Donald Symon, Barrie Mab-   6:23.68
bott, Ross Tong, Brett Hollister)
4. ITA   (Giovanni Sergi Sergas, Giovanni Suarez,   6:26.44
Gino Iseppi, Giuseppe Carando, Siro Meli)
5. CAN   (David Ross, Tim Christian, Richard Doey,   6:28.78
Nick Toulmin, Paul Tessier)
6. GER   (Heribert Karches, Georg Konermann, Wolf-   6:34.23
ram Theim, Wolfgang Maennig, Manfred Klein)
7. BRA   (Andre Berezln, Luiz Santos, Denis Marinho,
Laildo Machado, Manoel Novo)
8. JPN   (Satoru Miyoshi, Tadashi Abe, Shunsuke
Kawamoto, Hideaki Maeguchi, Akihiro Koike)

**1988 Seoul** T: 14, N: 14, D: 9.24.
1. GDR   (Frank Klawonn, Bernd Eichwurzel, Bernd   6:10.74
Niesecke, Karsten Schmeling, Hendrik Reiher)
2. ROM   (Dimitrie Popescu, Ioan Snep, Valentin Robu,   6:13.58
Vasile Tomoiaga, Ladislau Lovrensky)
3. NZE   (George Keys, Ina Wright, Gregory Johnston,   6:15.78
Christopher White, Andrew Bird)
4. GBR   (Adam Clift, John Maxey, John Garrett, Martin   6:18.08
Cross, Vaughan Thomas)
5. USA   (John Terwilliger, Christopher Huntington,   6:18.47
Tom Darling, John Walters, Mark Zembsch)
6. YUG   (Sead Marušić, Lazo Pivač, Zlatko Celent,   6:23.28
Vladimir Banjanac, Dario Varga)
7. GER   (Roland Baar, Wolfgang Klapheck, Christoph
Korte, Andreas Lütkefeis, Martin Ruppel)
8. CZE   (Milan Doleček, Oldřich Hejdušek, Petr Hlídek,
Dušan Macháček, Michal Subrt)

# EIGHT-OARED SHELL
# WITH COXSWAIN

**1896** not held

**1900 Paris** T: 4, N: 4, D: 8.26.
1. USA   (Vesper Boat Club, Philadelphia—Louis Abell,   6.09.8
Harry Debaecke, William Carr, John Exley,
John Geiger, Edward Hedley, James Juvenal,
Roscoe Lockwood, Edward Marsh)
2. BEL   (Royal Club Nautique de Gand—Marcel van   6:13.8
Crombrugghe, Maurice Hemelsoet, Oscar de
Cock, Maurice Verdonck, Prospère Brugge-
man, Oscar de Somville, Frank Odberg, Jules
de Bisschop, Alfred Vanlandeghem)
3. HOL   (Minerva, Amsterdam—Walter Thijssen,   6:23.0
Ruurd Leegstra, Johannes van Dijk, Henricus
Tromp, Hendrik Offerhaus, Roelof Klein, Fran-
çois Brandt, Walter Middleberg, Hermanus
Brockmann)
4. GER   (Germania, Hamburg—Oscar Gossler,   6:33.0
Walther Katzenstein, Ernst Ascan Jencquel,
Theodor Alphons Lauezzari, Waldemar
Tietgens, Arthur Warncke, Edgar Katzenstein,
Gustav Gossler, Alexander Gleichmann von
Oven)

**1904 St. Louis** T: 2, N: 2, D: 7.30.
1. USA    (Vesper Boat Club, Philadelphia—Louis Abell,    7:50.0
          Joseph Dempsey, Michael Gleason, Frank
          Schell, James Flanigan, Charles Armstrong,
          Harry Lott, Frederick Cresser, John Exley)
2. CAN    (Argonaut Rowing Club, Toronto—Joseph    —
          Wright, Donald MacKenzie, William Wads-
          worth, George Strange, Phil Boyd, George
          Reiffenstein, W. Rice, A.B. Bailey, Thomas
          Loudon)

**1906** not held

**1908 London** T: 6, N: 5, D: 7.31.
1. GBR    (Leander Club—Albert Gladstone, Frederick    7:52.0
          Kelly, Banner Johnstone, Guy Nickalls,
          Charles Burnell, Ronald Sanderson, Raymond
          Etherington-Smith, Henry Bucknall, Gilchrist
          MacLagan)
2. BEL    (Royal Club Nautique de Gand—Oscar    —
          Taelman, Marcel Morimont, Rémy Orban,
          Georges Mijs, François Vergucht, Polydore
          Veirman, Oscar de Somville, Rodolphe Poma,
          Alfred Vanlandeghem)
3. CAN    (Argonaut Rowing Club, Toronto—Irvine Rob-    —
          ertson, George Wright, Julius Thomson, Walter
          Lewis, Gordon Bruce Balfour, Becher Gale,
          Charles Riddy, Geoffrey Taylor, Douglas
          Kertland)
3. GBR    (Cambridge University Boating Club—Fred-    —
          erick Jerwood, Eric Powell, Guy Carver, Ed-
          ward Williams, Henry Goldsmith, Harold
          Kitching, John Burn, Douglas Stuart, Richard
          Boyle)

**1912 Stockholm** T: 11, N: 7, D: 7.19.
1. GBR    (Leander Club—Edgar Burgess, Sidney    6:15.0
          Swann, Leslie Wormald, Ewart Horsfall, Angus
          James Gillan, Arthur Garton, Alister Kirby,
          Philip Fleming, Henry Wells)
2. GBR    (New College, Oxford—William Fison, William    6:19.0
          Parker, Thomas Gillespie, Beaufort Burdekin,
          Frederick Pitman, Arthur Wiggins, Charles
          Littlejohn, Robert Bourne, John Walker)
3. GER    (Berliner Ruder-Gesellschaft—Otto Liebing,
          Max Bröske, Max Vetter, Willi Bartholomä, Fritz
          Bartholomä, Werner Dehn, Rudolf Reichelt,
          Hans Mathiä, Kurt Runge)

**1920 Antwerp** T: 8, N: 8, D: 8.30.
1. USA    (Virgil Jacomini, Edwin Graves, William Jor-    6:02.6
          dan, Edward Moore, Allen Sanborn, Donald
          Johnston, Vincent Gallagher, Clyde King,
          Sherman Clark)
2. GBR    (Ewart Horsfall, Guy Nickalls, Richard Lucas,    6:05.0
          Walter James, John Campbell, Sebastian Earl,
          Ralph Shove, Sidney Swann, Robin John-
          stone)

3. NOR    (Theodor Nag, Conrad Olsen, Adolf Nilsen,    6:36.0
          Håkon Ellingsen, Thore Michelsen, Arne
          Mortensen, Karl Nag, Tollef Tollefsen, Thoralf
          Hagen)
4. FRA    (Albert Diebold, Charles Hahn, Frédéric Gross-    6:42.6
          mann, Robert Fleig, Henri Barbenès, Frédéric
          Fleig, Charles Schlewer, Emile Ruhlmann,
          Emile Barberolle)

The winning crew represented the U.S. Naval Academy.
Regatta officials first awarded the bronze medals to the
Swiss team because they had recorded the third fastest
time in the preliminary heats when they lost to Great
Britain. But after a protest, it was decided that the semifinal losers, Norway and France, should row off for third
place; however, this race was never held. Most Olympic
historians credit Norway with third place, since their
semifinal time was faster than that of France.

**1924 Paris** T: 10, N: 10, D: 7.17.
1. USA    (Leonard Carpenter, Howard Kingsbury, Dan-    6:33.4
          iel Lindley, John Miller, James Rockefeller,
          Frederick Sheffield, Benjamin Spock, Alfred
          Wilson, Laurence Stoddard)
2. CAN    (Arthur Bell, Robert Hunter, William Langford,    6:49.0
          Harold Little, John Smith, Warren Snyder,
          Norman Taylor, William Wallace, Ivor Camp-
          bell)
3. ITA    (Antonio Cattalinich, Francesco Cattalinich,
          Simeon Cattalinch, Giuseppe Crivelli, Latino
          Galasso, Pietro Ivanov, Bruno Sorich, Carlo
          Toniatti, Vittorio Gliubich)
4. GBR    (R. Bare, C.G.Chandler, H.B. Debenham, H.W.
          Dulley, S. Ian Fairbairn, A.F. Long, H.L.
          Morphy, C.H. Rew, J.S. Godwin)

Bill Havens was a member of the Yale University team
that won the right to represent the United States. However, he chose not to make the trip to Paris because his
wife was expecting their first child. That child, a boy
named Frank, was born five days after the closing of the
1924 Olympics. Twenty-eight years later, the Havens family finally got their Olympic gold medal when Frank won
the 10,000 meters Canadian canoeing singles event in
Helsinki.

One Yale crew member who did compete in 1924 and
win was a gangly 6-foot 4-inch junior named Ben Spock.
After graduating from medical school, Spock became a pe-
diatrician. In 1945 he finished writing a book called *The
Common Sense Book of Baby and Child Care,* which eventually sold over 25 million copies and gained its author international fame as "Dr. Spock, the baby expert." In 1972
he was the presidential candidate of the People's Party.

**1928 Amsterdam** T: 11, N: 11, D: 8.10.
1. USA    (Marvin Stalder, John Brinck, Francis Freder-    6:03.2
          ick, William Thompson, William Dally, James
          Workman, Hubert Caldwell, Peter Donlon,
          Donald Blessing)

2. GBR (James Hamilton, Guy Nickalls, John 6:05.6
Badcock, Donald Gollan, Harold Lane, Gordon Killick, Jack Beresford, Harold West, Arthur Sulley)

3. CAN (Frederick Hedges, Frank Fiddes, John Hand, Herbert Richardson, Jack Murdock, Athol Meech, Edgar Norris, William Ross, John Donnelly)

4. POL (Otto Gordzialkowski, Stanislaw Urban, Andrzej Soltan, Marian Wodziański, Janusz Ślązak, Waclaw Michalski, Jósef Laszewski, Henryk Niezabitowski, Jerzy Skolimowski)

5. GER (Karl Aletter, Ernst Gaber, Willi Reichert, Erwin Hoffstätter, Hermann Herbold, Gustav Maier, Robert Huber, Hans Maier, Fritz Bauer)

6. ITA (Medardo Lamberti, Arturo Moroni, Vittore Stocchi, Guglielmo Carubbi, Amilcare Canevari, Medardo Galli, Giulio Lamberti, Benedetto Borella, Angelo Polledri)

The United States was represented by the crew from the University of California at Berkeley. *New York Times* correspondent Wythe Williams described the work of coxswain Don Blessing as "one of the greatest performances of demonical howling ever heard on a terrestrial planet. . . . He gave the impression of a terrier suddenly gone mad. But such language and what a vocabulary! . . . One closed his eyes and waited for the crack of a cruel whip across the backs of the galley slaves." After they had won the Olympic championship, the galley slaves, following custom, grabbed their tormentor and threw him into the middle of Sloten Canal.

**1932 Los Angeles** T: 8, N: 8, D: 8.13.

1. USA (Edwin Salisbury, James Blair, Duncan Gregg, 6:37.6
David Dunlap, Burton Jastram, Charles Chandler, Harold Tower, Winslow Hall, Norris Graham)

2. ITA (Vittorio Cioni, Mario Ballori, Renato Bracci, 6:37.8
Dino Barsotti, Roberto Vestrini, Guglielmo Del Bimbo, Enrico Garzelli, Renato Barbieri, Cesare Milani)

3. CAN (Earl Eastwood, Joseph Harris, Stanley 6:40.4
Stanyar, Harry Fry, Cedric Liddell, William Thoburn, Donald Boal, Albert Taylor, George MacDonald)

4. GBR (Lewis Luxton, Donald McCowen, Harold 6:40.8
Rickett, Charles Sergel, William Sambell, Thomas Askwith, Kenneth Payne, David Haig-Thomas, John Ranking)

The U.S. team from the University of California and the Italian team from the University of Pisa staged a dramatic battle, which the Californians won by a foot with their very last stroke.

**1936 Berlin** T: 14, N: 14, D: 8.14.

1. USA (Herbert Morris, Charles Day, Gordon Adam, 6:25.4
John White, James McMillin, George Hunt, Joseph Rantz, Donald Hume, Robert Moch)

2. ITA (Guglielmo Del Bimbo, Dino Barsotti, Oreste 6:26.0
Grossi, Enzo Bartolini, Mario Checcacci, Dante Secchi, Ottorino Quaglierini, Enrico Garzelli, Cesare Milani)

3. GER (Alfred Rieck, Helmut Radach, Hans Kuschke, 6:26.4
Heinz Kaufmann, Gerd Völs, Werner Löckle, Hans-Joachim Hannemann, Herbert Schmidt, Wilhelm Mahlow)

4. GBR (Annesley Kingsford, Thomas Askwith, 6:30.1
McAlister Pender Lonnon, Desmond Kingsford, John Cherry, John Couchman, Hugh Mason, William Laurie, John Duckworth)

5. HUN (Pál Domonkos, Sándor Korompay, Hugo 6:30.3
Ballya, Imre Kapossy, Antal Szendey, Gábor Alapy, Frigyes Hollósi-Jung, László Szabó, Ervin Kereszthy)

6. SWI (Werner Schweizer, Fritz Feldmann, Rudolf 6:35.8
Homberger, Oskar Neuenschwander, Hermann Betschart, Hans Homberger, Alex Homberger, Karl Schmid, Rolf Spring)

An exciting blanket finish was won by the crew of the University of Washington, which moved up from fifth place at the halfway mark.

**1948 London** T: 12, N: 12, D: 8.9.
***(Ca. 1900 Meters)***

1. USA (Ian Turner, David Turner, James Hardy, 5:56.7
George Ahlgren, Lloyd Butler, David Brown, Justus Smith, John Stack, Ralph Purchase)

2. GBR (Christopher Barton, Maurice Lapage, Guy 6:06.9
Richardson, E. Paul Bircher, Paul Massey, C. Brian Lloyd, David Meyrick, Andrew Mellows, Jack Dearlove)

3. NOR (Kristoffer Lepsöe, Torstein Kråkenes, Hans 6:10.3
Egil Hansen, Halfdan Gran Olsen, Harald Kråkenes, Leif Naess, Thor Pedersen, Carl Henrik Monssen, Sigurd Monssen)

The victorious University of California at Berkeley crew had barely qualified for the Olympics, winning the U.S. tryouts by a mere one-tenth second over the University of Washington. But when they got to London they discovered that their most difficult challenge was behind them, as they won all three of their races by at least ten seconds.

**1952 Helsinki** T: 14, N: 14, D: 7.23.

1. USA (Franklin Shakespeare, William Fields, James 6:25.9
Dunbar, Richard Murphy, Robert Detweiler, Henry Proctor, Wayne Frye, Edward Stevens, Charles Manring)

2. SOV (Yevgeny Brago, Vladimir Rodimushkin, Alek- 6:31.2
sei Komarov, Igor Borisov, Slava Amiragov, Leonid Gissen, Yevgeny Samsonov, Vladimir Krukov, Igor Polyakov)

3. AUS (Robert Tinning, Ernest Chapman, Nimrood 6:33.1
Greenwood, Mervyn Finlay, Edward Pain, Phillip Cayzer, Thomas Chessel, David Anderson, Geoffrey Williamson)

4. GBR  (David Macklin, Alastair MacLeod, Nicholas  6:34.8
Clack, Roger Sharpley, Edward Worlidge,
Charles Lloyd, William Windham, David
Jennens, John Hinde)

5. GER  (Anton Reinartz, Michael Reinartz, Roland  6:42.8
Freiloff, Heinz Zünkler, Peter Betz, Stefan
Reinartz, Hans Betz, Toni Siebenhaar, Her-
mann Zander)

The winning crew was from the U.S. Naval Academy.

**1956 Melbourne** T: 10, N: 10, D: 11.27.
1. USA  (Thomas Charlton, David Wight, John Cooke,  6:35.2
Donald Beer, Caldwell Esselstyn, Charles
Grimes, Richard Wailes, Robert Morey, William
Becklean)

2. CAN  (Philip Kueber, Richard McClure, Robert Wil-  6:37.1
son, David Helliwell, Donald Pretty, William
McKerlich, Douglas McDonald, Lawrence
West, Carlton Ogawa)

3. AUS  (Michael Aikman, David Boykett, Angus Ben-  6:39.2
field, James Howden, Garth Manton, Walter
Howell, Adrian Monger, Bryan Doyle, Harold
Hewitt)

4. SWE  (Olof Larsson, Lennart Andersson, Kjell  6:48.1
Hansson, Rune Ivar Andersson, Sture Lennart
Hanson, Gösta Eriksson, Ivar Aronsson, Sven
Gunnarsson, Bertil Göransson)

The United States, represented by the Yale crew, finished third to Australia and Canada in the opening
round, but qualified for the semifinal through repêchage.
No Olympic eights had ever been won by a team that
lost its opening race, but the Yale crew broke this tradition to give the United States its eighth straight win in
the event.

**1960 Rome** T: 14, N: 14, D: 9.3.
1. GER  (Klaus Bittner, Karl-Heinz Hopp, Hans Lenk,  5:57.18
Manfred Ruiffs, Frank Schepke, Kraft
Schepke, Walter Schröder, Karl-Heinrich von
Groddeck, Willi Padge)

2. CAN  (Donald Arnold, Walter D'Hondt, Nelson Kuhn,  6:01.52
John Lecky, Lorne Loomer, Archibald Mc-
Kinnon, William McKerlich, Glen Mervyn,
Sohen Biln)

3. CZE  (Bohumil Janoušek, Jan Jindra, Jiří Lundak,  6:04.84
Stanislav Lusk, Václav Pavkovič, Ludek
Pojezny, Jan Švéda, Josef Ventus, Miroslav
Koniček)

4. FRA  (Christian Puibaraud, Jean Bellet, Emile Clerc,  6:06.57
Jean Ledoux, Gaston Mercier, Bernard
Meynadier, Joseph Moroni, Michel Viaud,
Alain Bouffard)

5. USA  (Joseph Baldwin, Peter Bos, Mark Moore,  6:08.06
Lyman Perry, Warren Sweetser, Gayle Thomp-
son, Robert Wilson, Howard Winfree, William
Long)

6. ITA  (Paolo Amorini, Vasco Cantarello, Giancarlo  6:12.73
Casalini, Luigi Prato, Vincenzo Prina,
Mazzareno Simonato, Luigi Spozio, Armido
Torri, Giuseppe Pira)

The U.S. winning streak was finally broken by a combined crew from Ratzeburg and Ditmarsia Kiel rowing
clubs. The Germans led from the start and were never
headed.

**1964 Tokyo** T: 14, N: 14, D: 10.15.
1. USA  (Joseph Amlong, Thomas Amlong, Harold  6:18.23
Budd, Emory Clark, Stanley Cwiklinski, Hugh
Foley, William Knecht, William Stowe, Robert
Zimonyi)

2. GER  (Klaus Aeffke, Klaus Bittner, Karl-Heinrich von  6:23.29
Groddeck, Hans-Jürgen Wallbrecht, Klaus
Behrens, Jürgen Schröder, Jürgen
Plagemann, Horst Meyer, Thomas Ahrens)

3. CZE  (Petr Čermák, Jiří Lundak, Jan Mrvik, Julius  6:25.11
Toček, Josef Ventus, Ludek Pojezny, Bohumil
Janoušek, Richard Novy, Miroslav Koniček)

4. YUG  (Boris Klavora, Jadran Barut, Joža Berc,  6:27.15
Vjekoslav Skalak, Marko Mandič, Alojz Colja,
Pavajo Martič, Lucijan Kelva, Zdenko Balaš)

5. SOV  (Juozas Jagelavičius, Yuri Suslin, Piatras  6:30.69
Karla, Vytautas Briedis, Vladimir Sterlik,
Zigmas Jukna, Antanas Bogdanavičius,
Rischard Voitkevich, Yuri Lorentson)

6. ITA  (Dario Giani, Sergio Tagliapetra, Gianpietro  6:42.78
Gilardi, Francesco Glorioso, Pietro Polti, Giu-
seppe Schiavon, Orlando Savarin, Sereno
Brunello, Ivo Stefanoni)

7. FRA  (André Fevret, Pierre Maddaloni, André Sloth,
Joseph Moroni, Robert Dumontois, Jean Pierre
Grimaud, Bernard Meynadier, Michel Viaud,
Alain Bouffard)

8. AUS  (David Ramage, David Boykett, Terence
Davies, Robert Lachel, Paul Guest, Martin
Tomanovits, Brian Vear, Graeme McCall,
Kevin Wickham)

The Vesper Club of Philadelphia, the first noncollegiate
eight to represent the United States in 60 years, scored a
one-and-a-quarter-length upset victory over the crew
from Ratzeburg, Germany. The Vesper coxswain was
Bob Zimonyi, a 46-year-old accountant who had defected after being a member of the 1956 Hungarian
squad. Zimonyi's first Olympic appearance had been in
the coxed fours of 1948.

**1968 Mexico City** T: 12, N: 12, D: 10.19.
1. GER  (Horst Meyer, Dirk Schreyer, Rüdiger Henning,  6:07.00
Wolfgang Hottenrott, Lutz Ulbricht, Egbert
Hirschfelder, Jörg Siebert, Nikolaus "Nico" Ott,
Günther Tiersch)

2. AUS  (Alfred Duval, Michael Morgan, Joseph Fazio,  6:07.98
Peter Dickson, David Dougals, John Ranch,
Gary Pearce, Robert Shirlaw, Alan Grover)

3. SOV (Zigmas Jukna, Antanas Bogdanavičius, 6:09.11
Vladimir Sterlik, Juozas Jagelavičius, Alek-
sandr Martyschkin, Vytautas Briedis, Valentin
Kravchuk, Viktor Suslin, Yuri Lorentson)

4. NZE (Alan Webster, Wybo Veldman, Alistair Dry- 6:10.43
den, John Hunter, Mark Brownlee, John Gib-
bons, Thomas Just, Gilbert Cawood, Robert
Page)

5. CZE (Vladimir Jánoš, Zdeněk Kuba, Oldřich Svo- 6:12:17
janovský, Karel Kolesa; Pavel Svojanovský,
Jan Walisch, Otakar Mareček, Petr Čermák,
Jiři Pták)

6. USA (Stephen Brooks, Curtis Canning, Andrew 6:14.34
Larkin, Scott Steketee, Franklin Hobbs,
Jacques Fiechter, Cleve Livingston, David
Higgins, Paul Hoffman)

7. GDR (Günter Bergau, Klaus-Dieter Bähr, Claus
Wilke, Peter Gorny, Reinhard Zerfowski, Peter
Hein, Manfred Schneider, Peter Prompe, Karl-
Heinz Danielowski)

8. HOL (Maarten Kloosterman, Pieter Bon, Eric
Nieche, Jaap Reesink, Gerard Van Enst, Jan
Steinhauser, Izak Wesdrop, Jan Van Laar-
hoven, Arthur Koning)

The victorious Ratzeburg crew used a shell that was 75
pounds lighter than the shells of the other teams.

**1972 Munich** T: 15, N: 15, D: 9.2.

1. NZE (Tony Hurt, Wybo Veldman, Dick Joyce, John 6:08.94
Hunter, Lindsay Wilson, Athol Earl, Trevor
Coker, Gary Robertson, Simon Dickie)

2. USA (Lawrence Terry, Fritz Hobbs, Peter Raymond, 6:11.61
Timothy Mickelson, Eugene Clapp, William
Hobbs, Cleve Livingston, Michael Livingston,
Paul Hoffman)

3. GDR (Hans-Joachim Borzym, Jörg Landvoigt, Ha- 6:11.67
rold Dimke, Manfred Schneider, Hartmut
Schreiber, Manfred Schmorde, Bernd
Landvolgt, Helnrlch Mederow, Dletmar
Schwarz)

4. SOV (Aleksandr Riazankin, Viktor Dementiev, Ser- 6:14.48
gei Koliaskin, Aleksandr Shitov, Valery
Bissarnov, Boris Vorobiev, Vladmir Savelov,
Aleksandr Martishkin, Viktor Mikheev)

5. GER (Reinhard Wendemuth, Frithjof Henckel, Nor- 6:14.91
bert Kindlmann, Wolfgang Hottenrott, Hans-
Ulrich Buchholz, Günter Petermann, Bernd
Truschinski, Winfried Ringwald, Manfred
Klein)

6: POL (Jerzy Ulczyński, Marian Siejkowski, Krzysztof 6:29.35
Marek, Jan Mlodzikowski, Grzegorz Stellak,
Marian Drążdżewski, Ryszard Gilo, Slawomir
Maciejowski, Ryszard Kubiak)

7. HUN (Zoltán Melis, András Pályi, Antal Gelley, Béla
Zsitnik, László Romvári, Péter Kokas, Imre
Dávid, Ágoston Bányai, Robert Oelschleger)

8. AUS (John Clark, Michael Morgan, Bryan Curtin,
Richard Curtin, Robert Paver, Kerry Jelbart,
Gary Pearce, Malcolm Shaw, Alan Grover)

The New Zealand team raised the $45,000 needed to sup-
port their training and trip to Munich by holding a series of
bingo games, as well as a raffle for a "dream kitchen."

**1976 Montreal** T: 13, N: 13, D: 7.25.

1. GDR (Bernd Baumgart, Gottfried Döhn, Werner 5:58.29
Klatt, Hans-Joachim Lück, Dieter Wendisch,
Roland Kostulski, Ulrich Karnatz, Karl-Heinz
Prudöhl, Karl Heinz Danielowski)

2. GBR (Richard Lester, John Yallop, Timothy Crooks, 6:00.82
Hugh Matheson, David Maxwell, James Clark,
Fred Smallbone, Leonard Robertson, Patrick
Sweeney)

3. NZE (Ivan Sutherland, Trevor Coker, Peter Dignan, 6:03.51
Lindsay Wilson, Athol Earl, Dave Rodger, Alex
Mclean, Tony Hurt, Simon Dickie)

4. GER (Reinhard Wendemuth, Bernd Truschinski, 6:06.15
Frank Schütze, Frithjof Henckel, Wolfram
Thiem, Volker Sauer, Otmar Kaufhold, Wolf-
Dieter Oschlies, Helmut Latz)

5. AUS (Islay Lee, Ian Clubb, Timothy Conrad, Robert 6:09.75
Paver, Gary Eubergang, Athol MacDonald,
Peter Shakespear, Brian Richardson, Stuart
Carter)

6. CZE (Pavel Konvička, Vaclav Mls, Josef Plaminek, 6:14.29
Josef Pokorny, Karel Mejta, Josef Nesticky,
Lubomir Zapletal, Miroslav Vrastil, Jiři Pták)

7. SOV (Aleksandr Shitov, Antanas Chikotas, Vassily
Potapov, Aleksandr Plyushkin, Anatoly
Nomtyrov, Igor Konnov, Anatoly Ivanov,
Vladimir Vasilyev, Vladimir Zharov)

8. CAN (Edgar Smith, Dirk Gidney, George Tintor,
James Henniger, Patrick Croskerry, Melvin La
Forme, Ronald Burak, Alexander Manson,
Robert Choquette)

The East German team included a butcher, a plumber, a
gardener, a mechanic, and a student.

**1980 Moscow** T: 9, N: 9, D: 7.27.

1. GDR (Bernd Krauss, Hans-Peter Koppe, Ulrich 5:49.05
Kons, Jörg Friedrich, Jens Doberschütz, Ul-
rich Karnatz, Uwe Dühring, Bernd Höing,
Klaus-Dieter Ludwig)

2. GBR (Duncan McDougall, Allan Whitwell, Henry 5:51.92
Clay, Chris Mahoney, Andrew Justice, John
Pritchard, Malcolm McGowan, Richard Stan-
hope, Colin Moynihan)

3. SOV (Viktor Kokoshin, Andrei Tishchenko, Jonas 5:52.66
Pinskus, Jonas Normantas, Andrei Lugin,
Aleksandr Mantsevich, Igor Maistrenko,
Grigory Dmitrienko, Aleksandr Tkachenko)

4. CZE (Pavel Pevný, Lubomir Janko, Ctirad 5:53.75
Jungmann, Karel Neffe, Karel Mejta, Dušan
Vičik, Milan Doleček, Milan Kyselý, Jiři Pták)

5. AUS (Islay Lee, Stephen Handley, William 5:56.74
Dankbaar, Andrew Withers, Timothy Wil-
loughby, James Lowe, Timothy Young, Brian
Richardson, David England)

6. BUL (Dimitur Yanakiev, Todor Mrunkov, Bozhidar 6:04.05
Rogelov, Ivan Botev, Yani Ignatóv, Mikhail
Petrov, Petur Patzev, Vesselin Shterev,
Ventzislav Kunchev)

7. HUN (Ferenc Kiss, Péter Tóvári, Róbert Sass, Attila
Strochmayer, András Kormos, Zoltán Sztár-
csevics, Kálmán Toronyi, László Kiss, Miklós
Bálint)

8. CUB (Wenceslao Borroto, Ismael Same, Juan Alfonso, Juan Bueno, Francisco Mora, Her-
menegildo Palacio, Jorge Alvarez, Antonio
Riano, Enrique Carrillo)

**1984 Los Angeles-Lake Casitas** T: 7, N: 7, D: 8.5.

1. CAN (Patrick Turner, Kevin Neufeld, Mark Evans, 5:41.32
Grant Main, Paul Steele, J. Michael Evans,
Dean Crawford, Blair Horn, Brian McMahon)

2. USA (Walter Lubsen, Andrew Sudduth, John 5:41.74
Terwilliger, Christopher Penny, Thomas Dar-
ling, Earl Borchelt, Charles Clapp, Bruce
Ibbetson, Robert Jaugstetter)

3. AUS (Craig Muller, Clyde Hefer, Sam Patten, Timo- 5:43.40
thy Willoughby, Ian Edmunds, James Bat-
tersby, Ion Popa, Steve Evans, Gavin
Thredgold)

4. NZE (Nigel Atherfold, David Rodger, Roger White- 5:44.14
Parsons, George Keys, Gregory Johnston,
Christopher White, Andrew Stevenson, Mi-
chael Stanley, Andrew Hay)

5. GBR (Duncan McDougall, Christopher Mahoney, 5:47.01
Salih Hassan, Clive Roberts, Adam Clift, John
Pritchard, Malcolm McGowan, Allan Whitwell,
Colin Moynihan)

6. FRA (Alain Duprat, Dominique Lecointe, Thierry 5:49.52
Louvet, Patrick Vibert-Vichet, Jacques Tabor-
ski, Jean-Jacques Martigne, Olivier Pons,
Bernard Chevalier, Jean-Pierre Huguet-
Balent)

7. CHI (Mario Castro, Carlos Neyra, Zibor Llanos, 6:07:03
Giorgio Vallebuona, Alejandro Rojas, Victor
Contreras, Rodolfo Pereira, Marcelo Rojas,
Rodrigo Abasolo)

A bizarre incident enlivened the eights competition. One
hundred meters after the start of the repêchage, the oar-
lock gate of the number 6 rower on the French crew
broke and he lost his oar. This was not unusual in itself,
but upon examination it was discovered that the gate had
been intentionally filed down so that it would snap under
pressure. A similar act of sabotage had occurred two
weeks earlier at the junior championships in Sweden.
That time the victims had been a U.S. women's crew. In
Los Angeles, the French were allowed to participate in
the final along with the six qualifiers. Thus all seven of
the original entrants went on to the final despite having
to endure two preliminary races and a repêchage.

The final had been expected to be a hot contest among
New Zealand, the U.S. and Australia. But the Canadians
led from start to finish, holding off a late sprint by the

Americans. At the 1984 Olympics, each of the eight
men's rowing titles was won by a different nation.

**1988 Seoul** T: 10, N: 10, D: 9.25.

1. GER (Thomas Möllenkamp, Matthias Mellinghaus, 5:46.05
Eckhardt Schultz, Ansgar Wessling, Armin
Eichholz, Thomas Domian, Wolfgang Maen-
nig, Bahne Rabe, Manfred Klein)

2. SOV (Veniamin But, Nikolai Komarov, Vassily 5:48.01
Tikhanov, Aleksandr Dumchev, Pavel Gurkov-
sky, Viktor Diduk, Viktor Omelyanovich, Andrei
Vassilyev, Aleksandr Lukyanov)

3. USA (Mike Teti, John Smith, Ted Patton, John 5:48.26
Rusher, Peter Nordell, Jeff McLaughlin, Doug
Burden, John Pescatore, Seth Bauer)

4. GBR (Richard Stanhope, Anton Obholzer, Peter 5:51.59
Beaumont, Gavin Stewart, Terence Dillon,
Salih Hassan, Stephen Turner, Nicholas Bur-
fitt, Simon Jeffries)

5. AUS (James Galloway, Hamish McGlashan, An- 5:53.73
drew Cooper, Michael Mckay, Mark Doyle,
James Tomkins, Ion Popa, Stephen Evans,
Dale Caterson)

6. CAN (Don Telfer, Kevin Neufeld, Jason Dorland, 5:54.26
Andrew Crosby, Paul Steele, Gerald Main,
Jamie Schaffer, John Wallace, Robert Mc-
Mahon)

7. ITA (Antonio Baldacci, Ettore Bulgarelli, Piero
Carletto, Giuseppe Di Palo, Renato Gaeta,
Dino Lucchetta, Giovanni Suarez, Annibale
Venier, Franco Zucchi)

8. BUL (Roumen Alexiev, Emil Bondev, Yuri
Dyulgurov, Ivo Gulov, Dimitar Kambursky,
Ventzislav Kanchev, Ivan Stanev, Dimitar
Tonchev, Nikola Zlatanov)

# Discontinued Events

## SIX-MAN NAVAL ROWING BOATS

**1906 Athens** T: 4, N: 2, D: 4.24
*(2000 Meters)*

1. ITA (Varese) 10:45.0
2. GRE (Spetzia) —
3. GRE (Hydra) —
4. GRE (Psara) —

## SIXTEEN-MAN NAVAL ROWING BOATS

**1906 Athens** T: 5, N: 2, D: 4.24.
*(3000 Meters)*

1. GRE (Poros) 16:35.0
2. GRE (Hydra) 17:09.6
3. ITA (Varese) —

4. GRE (Psara) —
5. GRE (Spetzia) —

## COXED FOURS INRIGGERS

**1912 Stockholm** T: 6, N: 4, D: 7.18.
1. DEN (Ejlert Allert, Jörgen Hansen, Carl Möller, Carl Petersen, Poul Hartmann) 7:47.0
2. SWE (Ture Rosvall, William Bruhn-Möller, Conrad Brunkman, Herman Dahlbäck, Wilhelm Wilkens) 7:56.2
3. NOR (Claus Hoyer, Reidar Holter, Magnus Herseth, Frithjof Olstad, Olaf Bjornstad) —

# WOMEN

All women's races are rowed on a 1000-meter course.

## SINGLE SCULLS

**1896–1972** not held

**1976 Montreal** C: 11, N: 11, D: 7.24.
1. Christine Scheiblich GDR 4:05.56
2. Joan Lind USA 4:06.21
3. Elena Antonova SOV 4:10.24
4. Rositsa Spasova BUL 4:10.86
5. Ingrid Munneke HOL 4:18.71
6. Mariann Ambrus HUN 4:22.59
7. Annick Anthoine FRA
8. Christel Agrikola GER

**1980 Moscow** C: 11, N: 11, D: 7.26.
1. Sanda Toma ROM 3:40.69
2. Antonina Makhina SOV 3:41.65
3. Martina Schröter GDR 3:43.54
4. Rositsa Spasova BUL 3:47.22
5. Beryl Mitchell GBR 3:49.71
6. Beata Dziadura POL 3:51.45
7. Frances Cryan IRL
8. Mariann Ambrus HUN

**1984 Los Angeles-Lake Casitas** C: 16, N: 16, D: 8.4.
1. Valeria Račilă ROM 3:40.68
2. Charlotte Geer USA 3:43.89
3. Ann Haesebrouck BEL 3:45.72
4. Andrea Schreiner CAN 3:45.97
5. Lise Marianne Justesen DEN 3:47.79
6. Beryl Mitchell GBR 3:51.20
7. Stephanie Foster NZE
8. Jos Compaan HOL

**1988 Seoul** C: 13, N: 13, D: 9.25.
1. GDR Jutta Behrendt 7:47.19
2. USA Anne Marden 7:50.28

3. BUL Magdalena Georgieva 7:53.65
4. HOL Harriet van Ettekoven 7:57.29
5. ROM Marioara Popescu 7:59.44
6. DEN Inger Pors 7:59.77
7. GRE Antonia Zweir
8. SOV Natalya Kvasha

Defending world champion Magdalena Georgieva pushed to a 2.86-second lead at the 1500-meter mark, but then blew up and faded to third, leaving the victory to 1986 world champion Jutta Behrendt of Berlin.

## DOUBLE SCULLS

**1896–1972** not held

**1976 Montreal** T: 10, N: 10, D: 7.24.
1. BUL (Svetla Otsetova, Zdravka Yordanova) 3:44.36
2. GDR (Sabine Jahn, Petra Boesler) 3:47.86
3. SOV (Leonora Kaminskaitė, Genovaitė Ramoš-klenė) 3:49.93
4. NOR (Solfrid Johansen, Ingunn Brechan) 3:52.18
5. USA (Jan Palchikoff, Diane Braceland) 3:58.25
6. CAN (Cheryl Howard, Beverley Cameron) 4:06.23
7. HOL (Andrea Vissers, Hellie Klaasee)
8. CZE (Miluse Neffova, Zuzana Prokesova)

**1980 Moscow** T: 7, N: 7, D: 7.26.
1. SOV (Yelena Khloptseva, Larissa Popova) 3:16.27
2. GDR (Cornelia Linse, Heidi Westphal) 3:17.63
3. ROM (Olga Homeghi, Valeria Răcilă-Roşca) 3:18.91
4. BUL (Svetla Otsetova, Zdravka Yordanova) 3:23.14
5. POL (Hanna Jarkiewicz, Janina Klucznik) 3:27.25
6. HUN (Ilona Bata, Klara Pétervári-Langhoffer) 3:35.70

**1984 Los Angeles-Lake Casitas** T: 8, N: 8, D: 8.4.
1. ROM (Marioara Popescu, Elisabeta Oleniuc) 3:26.75
2. HOL (Greet Hellemans, Nicolette Hellemans) 3:29.13
3. CAN (Daniele Laumann, Silken Laumann) 3:29.82
4. SWE (Carina Gustavsson, Marie Carlsson) 3:30.79
5. NOR (Haldis Lenes, Solfrid Johansen) 3:32.09
6. USA (Cathleen Thaxton, Julia Geer) 3:32.33
7. AUT (Ingeborg Niedermayer, Vera Sommerbauer)
8. GBR (Nonie Ray, Sally Bloomfield)

**1988 Seoul** T: 10, N: 10, D: 9.24.
1. GDR (Birgit Peter, Martina Schröter) 7:00.48
2. ROM (Elisabeta Lipa, Veronica Cogeanu) 7:04.36
3. BUL (Violeta Ninova, Stefka Madina) 7:06.03
4. SOV (Marina Zhukova, Maria Omelyanovich) 7:12.67
5. CHN (Guo Mei, Cao Mianying) 7:18.69
6. USA (Monica Havelka, Cathy Tippett) 7:21.28
7. CAN (Silken Laumann, Kay Worthington)
8. SWE (Maria Brandin, Carina Gustafsson)

## QUADRUPLE SCULLS

**1896–1984** not held

**1988 Seoul** T: 10, N: 10, D: 9.25.
1. GDR (Kerstin Förster, Kristina Mundt, Beate 6:21.06
   Schramm, Jana Sorgers)
2. SOV (Irina Kalimbet, Svetlana Mazy, Inna Frolova, 6:23.47
   Antonina Dumcheva)
3. ROM (Anişoara Balan, Anişoara Minea, Veronica 6:23.81
   Cogeanu, Elisabeta Lipa)
4. BUL (Pavlina Hristova, Galia Anohrieva, Iskra 6:24.10
   Velinova, Krassimira Tocheva)
5. CZE (Hana Krejčová, Ĺubica Kurhajcová, Blanka 6:41.86
   Mikysková, Irena Soukupová)
6. BEL (Marie-Anne Vandermoere, Ann Haesebrouck, 6:43.79
   Lucia Focque, Annelies Bredael)
7. HOL (Jos Compaan, Marjan Pentenga, Nicolette
   Wessel, Marijke Zeekant)
8. HUN (Erika Bertényi, Ildikó Cserey, Anikó Kapócs,
   Katalin Sarlós)

## PAIR-OARED SHELL WITHOUT COXSWAIN

**1896–1972** not held

**1976 Montreal** T: 11, N: 11, D: 7.24.
1. BUL (Siika Kelbecheva, Stoyanka Grouicheva) 4:01.22
2. GDR (Angelika Noack, Sabine Dähne) 4:01.64
3. GER (Edith Eckbauer, Thea Einöder) 4:02.35
4. SOV (Natalya Gorodilova, Anna Karnaushenko) 4:03.27
5. CAN (Tricia Smith, Elisabeth Craig) 4:08.09
6. ROM (Marlena Predescu, Marinela Maxim) 4:15:44
7. USA (Susan Morgan, Laura Staines)
8. POL (Anna Karbowiak, Malgorzata Kowalska)

**1980 Moscow** T: 6, N: 6, D: 7.26.
1. GDR (Ute Steindorf, Cornelia Klier) 3:30.49
2. POL (Malgorzata Dlużewska, Czeslawa Kościań- 3:30.95
   ska)
3. BUL (Siika Barboulova [Kelbecheva], Stoyanka 3:32.39
   Kourbatova [Grouicheval])
4. ROM (Florica Dospinescu, Elena Oprea) 3:35.14
5. SOV (Larissa Zavarzina, Galina Stepanova) 4:12.53

Despite the fact that there were only six entrants, regatta officials insisted that two elimination heats and a repêchage be run in order to trim the field in the final to five.

**1984 Los Angeles-Lake Casitas** T: 6, N: 6, D: 8.4.
1. ROM (Rodica Arba [Puscatu], Elena Horvat) 3:32.60
2. CAN (Elizabeth Craig, Tricia Smith) 3:36.06
3. GER (Ellen Becker, Iris Völkner) 3:40.50
4. HOL (Harriet van Ettekoven, Lynda Cornet) 3:44.01
5. USA (Barbara Kirch, Chari Towne) 3:44.35
6. GBR (Katerine Panter, Ruth Howe) 3:48.53

**1988 Seoul** T: 10, N: 10, D: 9.24.
1. ROM (Rodica Arba [Puscatu], Olga Homeghi) 7:28.13
2. BUL (Radka Stoyanova, Lalka Berberova) 7:31.95

3. NZE (Nicola Payne, Lynley Hannen) 7:35.68
4. GDR (Kerstin Spittler, Katrin Schröder) 7:40.47
5. SOV (Sarmite Stone, Marina Smorodina) 7:53.19
6. USA (Barbara Kirch, Mara Keggi) 7:56.27
7. CAN (Jennifer-Kirsten Barnes, Sarah Ann Ogilvie)
8. GBR (Alison Bonner, Kim Thomas)

Arba and Homeghi were the overwhelming favorites, having won 40 straight races since 1986, including two world championships. In addition, they both had extensive Olympic experience. Arba, besides being the defending champion in the pairs, had won a bronze medal in the eights in 1980. Homeghi too took home a bronze in 1980 and a gold in 1984; hers were in the double sculls and coxed fours. In Seoul they were unchallenged in the pairs. Twenty-four hours later they both added silvers to their medal haul as part of the Romanian eights crew.

## FOUR-OARED SHELL WITHOUT COXSWAIN

This event will be held for the first time in 1992.

## EIGHT-OARED SHELL WITH COXSWAIN

**1896–1972** not held

**1976 Montreal** T: 8, N: 8, D: 7.24.
1. GDR (Viola Goretzki, Christiane Knetsch, Ilona 3:33.32
   Richter, Brigitte Ahrenholz, Monika Kallies,
   Henrietta Ebert, Helma Lehmann, Irina Müller,
   Marina Wilke)
2. SOV (Lyubov Talalayeva, Nadezhda Roshchina, 3:36.17
   Klavdiya Koženkova, Elena Zubko, Olga
   Kolkova, Nelli Tarakanova, Nadezhda Rozgon,
   Olga Guzenko, Olga Pugovskaya)
3. USA (Jacqueli Zoch, Anita DeFrantz, Carie Graves, 3:38.68
   Marion Greig, Anne Warner, Peggy McCarthy,
   Carol Brown, Gail Ricketson, Lynn Silliman)
4. CAN (Carol Eastmore, Rhonda Ross, Nancy Hig- 3:39.52
   gins, Mazina DeLure, Susan Antoft, Wendy
   Pullan, Christine Neuland, Gail Cort, Illoana
   Smith)
5. GER (Waltraud Roick, Erika Endriss, Monika 3:41.06
   Zipplies, Birgit Kiesow, Hiltrud Gürtler, Isolde
   Eisele, Marianne Weber, Eva Dick, Ingrid
   Huhn-Wagner)
6. ROM (Elena Oprea, Florica Petcu, Filigonia Tol, 3:44.79
   Aurelia Marinescu, Georgeta Militaru, Iuliana
   Munteanu, Elena Avram, Marioara Constantin,
   Aneta Matei)
7. POL (Anna Brandysiewicz, Boguslawa Kozlowska,
   Barbara Wenta-Wojciechowska, Danuta
   Konkalec, Róża Data, Mieczyslawa Franczyk,
   Maria Stadnicka, Aleksandra Kaczyńska,
   Dorota Zdanowska)

8. HOL    (Karin Abma, Joke Dierdorf, Barbara Dejong, Annette Schortingshuis, Marleen Van Ry, Maria Kusters, Liesbeth Pascal, Loes Schutte, Evelien Koogie)

In 1986, Anita DeFrantz of the 1976 third-place U.S. team became the first black woman to be selected for membership on the International Olympic Committee.

**1980 Moscow** T: 6, N: 6, D: 7.26.
1. GDR    (Martina Boesler, Kersten Neisser, Christiane    3:03.32
Köpke [Knetsch], Birgit Schütz, Gabriele Kühn [Lohs], Ilona Richter, Marita Sandig, Karin Metze, Marina Wilke)
2. SOV    (Olga Pivovarova, Nina Umanets, Nadezhda    3:04.29
Prishchepa, Valentina Zhulina, Tatyana Stetsenko, Yelena Tereshina, Nina Preobrazhenskaya, Mariya Pazyun, Nina Frolova)
3. ROM    (Angelica Aposteanu, Marlena Zagoni, Rodica    3:05.63
Frintu, Florica Bucur, Rodica Puscatu, Ana Iliuta, Maria Constantinescu, Elena Bondar, Elena Dobritoiu)
4. BUL    (Daniela Stavreva, Stefka Koleva, Todorka    3:10.03
Vassileva, Snezhka Hristeva, Roumiana Kostova, Veneta Karamandtzoukova, Mariana Mincheva, Valentina Aleksandrova, Stanka Georgieva)
5. GBR    (Gillian Hodges, Joanna Toch, Penelope    3:13.85
Sweet, Lin Clark, Elizabeth Paton, Rosemary Clugston, Nicola Boyes, Beverley Jones, Pauline Wright)

**1984 Los Angeles-Lake Casitas** T: 6, N: 6, D: 8.4.
1. USA    (Shyril O'Steen, Harriet Metcalf, Carol Bower,    2:59.80
Carie Graves, Jeanne Flanagan, Kristine Norelius, Kristen Thorsness, Kathryn Keeler, Betsy Beard)
2. ROM    (Doina Balan, Marioara Trasca, Aurora Plesca,    3:00.87
Aneta Mihaly, Adriana Chelariu, Mihaela Armasescu, Camelia Diaconescu, Lucia Sauca, Viorica Ioja)
3. HOL    (Nicolette Hellemans, Lynda Cornet, Harriet    3:02.92
van Ettekoven, Greet Hellemans, Marieke van Drogenbroek, Anne Marie Quist, Catharina Neelissen, Willemien Vaandrager, Martha Laurijsen)
4. CAN    (Christine Clarke, Lisa Robertson, Kathey    3:03.64
Lichty, Carol Colgan, Cathy Lund, Kay Worthington, Gail Cort, Joan Gillingham, Lesleh Anderson-Herweck)
5. GBR    (Alexa Forbes, Katharine McNicol, Kathryn    3:04.51
Holroyd, Belinda Holmes, Sarah Hunter-Jones, Astrid Ayling, Ann Callaway, Gillian Hodges, Susan Bailey)
6. GER    (Elke Riesenkönig, Claudia Hornung, Iris    3:09.92
Völkner, Ellen Becker, Sabine Hinkelmann, Heike Neu, Kerstin Rehders, Angelika Beblo, Heidrun Barth)

**1988 Seoul** T: 7, N: 7, D: 9.25.
1. GDR    (Annegret Strauch, Judith Zeidler, Kathrin    6:15.17
Haacker, Ute Wild, Anja Kluge, Beatrix Schröer, Ramona Balthasar, Uta Stange, Daniela Neunast)
2. ROM    (Doina Balan, Marioara Trasca, Veronica    6:17.44
Necula, Herta Anitas, Adriana Bazon, Mihaela Armasescu, Rodica Arba, Olga Homeghi, Ecaterina Oancia)
3. CHN    (Zhou Xiuhua, Zhang Yali, He Yanwen, Han    6:21.83
Yaqin, Zhang Xianghua, Zhou Shouying, Yang Xiao, Hu Yadong, Li Ronghua)
4. SOV    (Margarita Teselko, Marina Znak, Nadezhda    6:22.35
Sugako, Sandra Brazauskaitė, Yelena Pukhayeva, Sariya Zakirova, Natalya Fedorenko, Lidiya Averyanova, Aouchra Gudeliunaitė)
5. BUL    (Teodora Zareva, Violeta Zareva, Neviana    6:25.02
Ivanova, Olia Stoichkova, Todorka Vassileva, Rita Todorova, Mariana Stoyanova, Daniela Oronova, Greta Georgieva)
6. USA    (Juliet Thompson, Christine Campbell, Abigail    6:26.66
Peck, Margaret Mallery, Susan Broome, Stephanie Maxwell, Anna Seaton, Alison Townley, Elizabeth Beard)

# Discontinued Events

## QUADRUPLE SCULLS WITH COXSWAIN

**1976 Montreal** T: 9, N: 9, D: 7.19.
1. GDR    (Anke Borchmann, Jutta Lau, Viola Poley,    3:29.99
Roswietha Zöbelt, Liane Weigelt)
2. SOV    (Anna Kondrachina, Mira Bryunina, Larissa    3:32.49
Aleksandrova, Galina Ermolaeva, Nadezhda Chemysheva)
3. ROM    (Ioana Tudoran, Maria Micsa, Felicia    3:32.76
Afrasiloaia, Elisabeta Lazar, Elena Giurca)
4. BUL    (Iskra Velinova, Verka Aleksieva, Troyanka    3:34.13
Vasileva, Svetla Gincheva, Stanka Georgieva)
5. CZE    (Anna Marešová, Marie Bartaková, Jarmila    3:42.53
Patková, Hana Kavková, Alena Svobodová)
6. DEN    (Kirsten Thomsen, Else Maersk-Kristensen,    3:46.99
Judith Andersen, Karen Nielsen, Kirsten Plum-Jensen)
7. USA    (Karen McCloskey, Lisa Hansen, Elizabet Hills, Claudia Schneider, Irene Moreno)
8. HUN    (Ilona Bata, Kamilla Kosztolányi, Valéria Gyimesi, Ágnes Szijj, Erzsébet Nagy)

**1980 Moscow** T: 7, N: 7, D: 7.26.
1. GDR (Sybille Reinhardt, Jutta Ploch, Jutta Lau,   3:15.32
Roswietha Zobelt, Liane Buhr [Weigelt])
2. SOV (Antonina Pustovit, Yelena Matievskaya, Olga   3:15.73
Vasilchenko, Nadezhda Lyubimova, Nina
Cheremisina)
3. BUL (Mariana Serbezova, Roumeliana Boneva, Do-   3:16.10
lores Nakova, Ani Bakova, Stanka Georgieva)
4. ROM (Marta Macoviciuc, Aneta Mihaly, Sofia   3:16.82
Banovici, Mariana Zaharia, Elena Giurca)
5. POL (Boguslawa Tomasiak, Mariola Abrahamczyk,   3:20.95
Maria Kobylińska, Aleksandra Kaczyńska, Ma-
ria Dzieża)
6. HOL (Ineke Donkervoort, Lily Meeuwisse, Greet   3:22.64
Hellemans, Jos Compaan, Monique Pronk)

**1984 Los Angeles-Lake Casitas** T: 7, N: 7, D: 8.4.
1. ROM (Maricica Taran, Anişoara Sorohan, Ioana   3:14.11
Badea, Sofia Corban, Ecaterina Oancia)
2. USA (Anne Marden, Lisa Rohde, Joan Lind, Virginia   3:15.57
Gilder, Kelly Rickon)
3. DEN (Hanne Eriksen, Birgitte Hanel, Charlotte   3:16.02
Koefoed, Bodil Steen Rasmussen, Jette Hejli
Sörensen)
4. GER (Anne Dickmann, Regina Kleine-Kuhlmann,   3:16.81
Ute Kumitz, Sabine Reuter, Kathrien Plück-
hahn)
5. FRA (Evelyne Imbert, Lydie Dubedat, Christine   3:17.87
Gosse, Helene Ledoux, Patricia Couturier)
6. ITA (Raffaella Memo, Alessandra Borio, Donata   3:21.48
Minorati, Antonella Corazza, Roberta Del
Core)

# FOUR-OARED SHELL
# WITH COXSWAIN

**1976 Montreal** T: 8, N: 8, D: 7.24.
1. GDR (Karin Metze, Bianka Schwede, Gabriele Lohs,   3:45.08
Andrea Kurth, Sabine Hess)
2. BUL (Ginka Gyurova, Liliana Vaseva, Reni   3:48.24
Yordanova, Mariika Modeva, Kapka Geor-
gieva)
3. SOV (Nadezhda Sevostyanova, Lyudmila Krokhina,   3:49.38
Galina Mishenina, Anna Pasokha, Lidiya
Krylova)
4. ROM (Elena Oprea, Florica Petcu, Filigonia Tol,   3:51.17
Aurelia Marinescu, Aneta Matei)
5. HOL (Liesbeth Vosmaer-De Bruin, Hette Borrias,   3:54.36
Myrian van Rooyen, Ans Gravesteyn, Monique
Pronk)
6. USA (Pamela Behrens, Catherine Menges, Nancy   3:56.50
Storrs, Julia Geer, Mary Kellogg)
7. CAN (Linda Schaumleffel, Dolores Young, Monica
Draeger, Joy Fera, Barbara Mutch)

8. GBR (Gillian Webb, Pauline Bird, Clare Grove,
Diana Bishop, Pauline Wright)

**1980 Moscow** T: 6, N: 6, D: 7.26.
1. GDR (Ramona Kapheim, Silvia Fröhlich, Angelika   3:19.27
Noack, Romy Saalfeld, Kirsten Wenzel)
2. BUL (Ginka Gyurova, Mariika Modeva, Rita   3:20.75
Todorova, Iskra Velinova, Nadezhda Filipova)
3. SOV (Mariya Fadeyeva, Galina Sovetnikova, Marina   3:20.92
Studneva, Svetlana Semyonova, Nina Chere-
misina)
4. ROM (Georgeta Masca Militaru, Florica Szilaghy,   3:22.08
Maria Tănasa, Valeria Cătescu, Aneta Matei)
5. AUS (Anne Chirnside, Verna Westwood, Pamela   3:26.37
Westendorf, Sally Harding, Susanne Palfrey-
man)

**1984 Los Angeles-Lake Casitas** T: 9, N: 9, D: 8.4.
1. ROM (Florica Lavric, Maria Fricioiu, Chira Apostol,   3:19.30
Olga Bularda [Homeghi], Viorica Ioja)
2. CAN (Marilyn Brain, Angie Schneider, Barbara   3:21.55
Armbrust, Jane Tregunno, Lesley Thompson)
3. AUS (Robyn Grey-Gardner, Karen Brancourt, Su-   3:23.29
san Chapman, Margot Foster, Susan Lee)
4. USA (Abigail Peck, Patricia Spratlen, Janet Harville,   3:23.58
Elizabeth Miles, Valerie McClain-Ward)
5. HOL (Marieke van Drogenbroek, Anne Marie Quist,   3:23.97
Catharina Neelissen, Willemien Vaandrager,
Martha Laurijsen)
6. GER (Heiko Neu, Sabine Hinkelmann, Kerstin   3:29.03
Rehders, Angelika Beblo, Heidrun Barth)
7. GBR (Teresa Millar, Jean Genchl, Joanna Toch,
Kathryn Ball, Kathryn Talbot)
8. CHN (Huang Meixia, Yang Xiao, Shi Meiping, Chen
Changfeng, Zhang Liming)

**1988 Seoul** T: 10, N: 10, D: 9.24.
1. GDR (Martina Walther, Gerlinde Doberschütz,   6:56.00
Carola Hornig, Birte Siech, Sylvia Rose)
2. CHN (Zhang Xianghua, Hu Yadong, Yang Xiao,   6:58.78
Zhou Shouying, Li Ronghua)
3. ROM (Marioara Trasca, Veronica Necula, Herta   7:01.13
Anitas, Doina Balan, Ecaterina Oancia)
4. BUL (Teodora Zareva, Violeta Zareva, Miglena   7:02.27
Mihaleva, Svetla Durchova, Greta Georgieva)
5. USA (Jennifer Corbet, Sarah Gengler, Elizabeth   7:09.12
Bradley, Cynthia Eckert, Kimberly Santiago)
6. GBR (Fiona Johnston, Katherine Grose, Joanne   7:10.80
Gough, Susan Smith, Alison Norrish)
7. CAN (Heather Clarke, Tricia Smith, Lesley Thompson, E. Jane Tregunno, Jennifer Walinga)
8. POL (Grażyna Blad, Elżbieta Jankowska, Zyta
Jarka, Elwira Lorenz, Czeslawa Szczepińska)

# SHOITNG

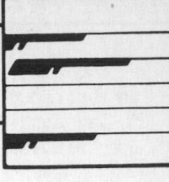

**MEN**
Rapid-Fire Pistol
Free Pistol
Air Pistol
Small-Bore Rifle, Prone
Small-Bore Rifle, Three Positions
Air Rifle
Moving Target
Discontinued Events

**WOMEN**
Sport Pistol
Air Pistol
Small Bore Rifle, Three Positions
Air Rifle

**MIXED**
Trap Shooting
Skeet Shooting

## MEN

International shooting competitions have employed a wide variety of tie-breaking rules, including shoot-offs (designated by slash lines in the following charts) and by the positions of the bullets on the target. Current practice in case of ties is to award the victory to whichever shooter recorded the highest score in the final series. Ties after the final are decided by shootout.

Every few years someone conquers a target and achieves a perfect score. At this point the officials of the International Shooting Union alter the target by decreasing the size of the bull's-eye and the rings. It is for this reason that the world records for various events sometimes go down instead of up.

Sexual integration of Olympic shooting began in 1968. In 1984, however, some of the events were divided into separate men's and women's competitions.

Another major change was instituted in 1988. For the first time, a final round was created in which the leading scorers from the preliminary round shoot off against each other while standing on the firing line at the same time. Scores in the final are added to the preliminary scores to determine the winner.

## RAPID-FIRE PISTOL

Since 1948 the rapid-fire pistol event has consisted of two 30-shot courses at five silhouettes 25 meters away. The shooter, using a .22 caliber pistol, has eight seconds to fire at each of the five targets. Then the targets reappear and he has six seconds to fire. Finally he must attempt shots at each of the targets within four seconds. This set of 15 shots is repeated four times. In the final, two sets of five shots are taken with a four-second time limit.

**1896 Athens** C: 4, N: 3, D: 4.11.

|  |  | PTS. |
|---|---|---|
| 1. Ioannis Phrangoudis | GRE | 344 |

| 2. Georgios Orphanidis | GRE | 249 |
|---|---|---|
| 3. Holger Nielsen | DEN | — |
| DNF: Sidney Merlin (GBR) | | |

**1900 Paris** C: ?, N: ?, D: 8.4.

|  |  | PTS. |
|---|---|---|
| 1. Maurice Larrouy | FRA | 58 |
| 2. Léon Moreaux | FRA | 57 |
| 3. Eugène Balme | FRA | 57 |
| 4. Paul Moreau | FRA | 57 |
| 5. Paul Probst | SWI | 57 |
| 6. Joseph Labbé | FRA | 57 |

**1904** not held

**1906 Athens** C: 28, N: 8, D: 4.26.

|  |  | PTS. |
|---|---|---|
| 1. Maurice Lecoq | FRA | 258 |
| 2. Léon Moreaux | FRA | 249 |
| 3. Aristides Rangavis | GRE | 244 |
| 4. Louis Richardet | SWI | 241 |
| 5. Johan Hübner von Holst | SWE | 239 |
| 6. Cesare Liverziani | ITA | 238 |
| 7. Hermann Martin | FRA | 236 |
| 8. Thephtsakis | GRE | 235 |

**1908 London** C: 43, N: 7, D: 7.11.

|  |  | PTS. |
|---|---|---|
| 1. Paul van Asbroeck | BEL | 490 |
| 2. Réginald Storms | BEL | 487 |
| 3. James Gorman | USA | 485 |
| 4. Charles Axtell | USA | 480 |
| 5. J.A. Wallingford | GBR | 467 |
| 6. A. Barbillat | FRA | 466 |
| 7. W. Ellicott | GBR | 458 |
| 8. Ira Calkins | USA | 457 |

**1912 Stockholm** C: 42, N: 10, D: 6.29.

|  |  | PTS. |
|---|---|---|
| 1. Alfred Lane | USA | 287 |
| 2. Paul Palén | SWE | 286 |
| 3. Johan Hübner von Holst | SWE | 283 |
| 3. John Dietz | USA | 283 |

| | | PTS. |
|---|---|---|
| 5. Curt Törnmark | SWE | 280 |
| 6. Eric Carlberg | SWE | 278 |
| 7. Georg de Laval | SWE | 277 |
| 8. Walter Winans | USA | 276 |

**1920 Antwerp** C: 38, N: 14, D: 8.3.

| | | PTS. |
|---|---|---|
| 1. Guilherme Paraense | BRA | 274 |
| 2. Raymond Bracken | USA | 272 |
| 3. Fritz Zulauf | SWI | 269 |

**1924 Paris** C: 55, N: 17, D: 6.28.

| | | PTS. |
|---|---|---|
| 1. Henry Bailey | USA | 18 |
| 2. Wilhelm Carlberg | SWE | 18 |
| 3. Lennart Hannelius | FIN | 18 |
| 4. Lorenzo Amaya | ARG | 18 |
| 5. M. Osinaldi | ARG | 18 |
| 6. A. de Castelbajac | FRA | 18 |
| 7. Unio Sarlin | FIN | 18 |
| 8. Einar Liberg | NOR | 18 |

The 1924 match consisted of three series of six shots at six silhouettes in ten seconds. Eight of the 55 competitors achieved perfect scores and, according to the rules of the day, shot off another round of six shots, but this time within eight seconds. All eight shooters had perfect scores, so a second shoot-off string was ordered. This time three of the shooters missed. The third round saw Osinaldi fall by the wayside, the fourth round Amaya, and the fifth round Hannelius. Bailey and Carlberg had now each hit 48 straight targets. A sixth shoot-off was called, and again the two men had perfect scores. Bailey, a 31-year-old gunnery sergeant in the U.S. Marine Corps, fired first in the seventh shoot-off. After calling for the silhouettes, he attempted to fire his first shot. But his .22 autoloader malfunctioned and the cartridge stuck in the breech. Rather than give up, Bailey coolly pulled the spent case out with his fingers, closed the breech, and got off five shots in what remained of his eight seconds. All five shots hit their targets. Carlberg, who had already won three gold medals, three silver, and one bronze since the 1906 games, was either unnerved or gracious, for he missed two of his next six shots and Bailey won the match.

**1928** not held

**1932 Los Angeles** C: 18, N: 7, D: 8.12.

| | | PTS. |
|---|---|---|
| 1. Renzo Morigi | ITA | 36 |
| 2. Heinz Hax | GER | 36 |
| 3. Domenico Matteucci | ITA | 36 |
| 4. Walter Boninsegni | ITA | 35 |
| 4. José Gonzalez Delgado | SPA | 35 |
| 4. Arturo Villanueva | MEX | 35 |

The first three series of six shots were shot at eight seconds each. Those with perfect scores took another six

shots in six seconds. The eleven survivors shot again at four seconds. Six men were still perfect and shot another round in three seconds. Boninsegni, Delgado, and Villanueva each missed once, leaving Hax, Morigi, and Matteucci still in the contest. The next round required shooting six shots at six turning silhouettes in two seconds. Major Morigi amazed the crowd, which consisted mostly of Los Angeles policemen, by hitting all six targets, the last one after it had already started to turn away.

**1936 Berlin** C: 53, N: 22, D: 8.7.

| | | PTS. |
|---|---|---|
| 1. Cornelius van Oyen | GER | 30/6 |
| 2. Heinz Hax | GER | 30/5 |
| 3. Torsten Ullman | SWE | 30/4/4 |
| 4. Angelos Papadimas | GRE | 30/4/1 |
| 5. Helge Meuller | SWE | 30/3 |
| 6. Walter Boninsegni | ITA | 29/6/3 |
| 7. Kazimierz Suchorzewski | POL | 29/6/1 |
| 8. Haralds Marwe | LAT | 29/3 |

**1948 London** C: 59, N: 22, D: 8.4. WR: 570 (Carlos Enrique Diaz Sáenz Valiente)

| | | PTS. | |
|---|---|---|---|
| 1. Károly Takács | HUN | 580 | WR |
| 2. Carlos Enrique Diaz Sáenz Valiente | ARG | 571 | |
| 3. Sven Lundqvist | SWE | 569 | |
| 4. Torsten Ullman | SWE | 564 | |
| 5. Leonard Ravilo | FIN | 563/36 | |
| 6. Väinö Heusala | FIN | 563/34 | |
| 7. Lajos Borzsonyi | HUN | 562 | |
| 8. Buhring Anderson | NOR | 559 | |

Károly Takács was a member of the Hungarian world champion pistol shooting team in 1938 when, while serving as a sergeant in the army, a grenade exploded in his right hand—his pistol hand—and shattered it completely. Undaunted, Takács taught himself to shoot with his left hand, and ten years later, at the age of 38, he won an Olympic gold medal.

**1952 Helsinki** C: 53, N: 28, D: 7.28. WR: 582 (Huelet Benner)

| | | PTS. |
|---|---|---|
| 1. Károly Takács | HUN | 579 |
| 2. Szilárd Kun | HUN | 578 |
| 3. Gheorghe Lichiardopol | ROM | 578 |
| 4. Carlos Enrique Diaz Sáenz Valiente | ARG | 577 |
| 5. Pentti Linnosvuo | FIN | 577 |
| 6. Panait Calcai | ROM | 575 |
| 7. William McMillan | USA | 575 |
| 8. Vassily Frolov | SOV | 573 |

**1956 Melbourne** C: 35, N: 22, D: 12.5. WR: 589 (Carlos Enrique Diaz Sáenz Valiente)

| | | PTS. | |
|---|---|---|---|
| 1. Stefan Petrescu | ROM | 587 | OR |
| 2. Yevgeny Cherkassov | SOV | 585 | |
| 3. Gheorghe Lichiardopol | ROM | 581 | |
| 4. Pentti Linnosvuo | FIN | 581 | |

| | | | |
|---|---|---|---|
| 5. Oscar Cervo | ARG | 580 | |
| 6. Szilárd Kun | HUN | 578 | |
| 7. Kalle Sievänen | FIN | 576 | |
| 8. Károly Takács | HUN | 575 | |

**1960 Rome** C: 57, N: 35, D: 9.9. WR: 592 (Aleksandr Kropotin, Aleksandr Zabelin)

| | | PTS. | |
|---|---|---|---|
| 1. William McMillan | USA | 587/147 | EOR |
| 2. Pentti Linnosvuo | FIN | 587/139 | EOR |
| 3. Aleksandr Zabelin | SOV | 587/135 | EOR |
| 4. Hansrüdi Schneider | SWI | 586 | |
| 5. Stefan Petrescu | ROM | 585 | |
| 6. Gavril Maghiar | ROM | 583 | |
| 7. Czeslaw Zajac | POL | 582 | |
| 8. Jiři Hrnecek | CZE | 582 | |

**1964 Tokyo** C: 53, N:34, D: 10.19. WR: 595 (Aleksandr Kropotin)

| | | PTS. | |
|---|---|---|---|
| 1. Pentti Linnosvuo | FIN | 592 | OR |
| 2. Ion Tripşa | ROM | 591 | |
| 3. Lubomir Nacovsky | CZE | 590 | |
| 4. Hans Albrecht | SWI | 590 | |
| 5. Szilárd Kun | HUN | 589 | |
| 6. Marcel Roşca | ROM | 588 | |
| 7. Igor Bakalov | SOV | 588 | |
| 8. Kanji Kubo | JPN | 587 | |

Pentti Linnosvuo became only the second shooter to win gold medals in both the rapid-fire and free pistol events. Alfred Lane won both in the same year (1912), while Linnosvuo's victories were eight years apart.

Two different participants in this event were inspired to defect following the Games. First Bela Gabor, who finished 23rd, sought asylum at the West German Embassy rather than return to his native Hungary. Then 53rd place finisher Ma Chin-shan, a retired army officer from Taiwan, took refuge in the Ginza office of the General Council of Chinese Merchants of Tokyo, requesting that he be allowed to return to mainland China to live with his parents whom he had not seen since World War II. To this day, Ma remains the only Olympic athlete to defect *to* a Communist country.

**1968 Mexico City** C: 56, N: 34, D: 10.23. WR: 596 (Virgil Atanasiu)

| | | PTS. | |
|---|---|---|---|
| 1. Józef Zapedzki | POL | 593 | OR |
| 2. Marcel Roşca | ROM | 591/147 | |
| 3. Renart Suleimanov | SOV | 591/146/148 | |
| 4. Christian Düring | GDR | 591/146/147 | |
| 5. Erich Masurat | GER | 590 | |
| 6. Gerhard Dommrich | GDR | 589 | |
| 7. Lubomir Nacovsky | CZE | 588 | |
| 8. Giovanni Liverzani | ITA | 588 | |

**1972 Munich** C: 62, N: 38, D: 9.1. WR: 598 (Giovanni Liverzani)

| | | PTS. | |
|---|---|---|---|
| 1. Józef Zapedzki | POL | 595 | OR |
| 2. Ladislav Falta | CZE | 594 | |

| | | | |
|---|---|---|---|
| 3. Victor Torshin | SOV | 593 | |
| 4. Paul Buser | SWI | 592 | |
| 5. Jaime Gonzalez | SPA | 592 | |
| 6. Giovanni Liverzani | ITA | 591 | |
| 7. Dencho Denev | BUL | 590 | |
| 8. Gerhard Petritsch | AUT | 590 | |

The 43-year-old Zapedzki was a major in the Polish army when he won his second gold medal. After the competition he visited nearby Dachau and laid a wreath at the grave of his father, who had been killed by the Nazis thirty years earlier.

**1976 Montreal** C: 48, N: 30, D: 7.23. WR: 598 (Giovanni Liverzani)

| | | PTS. | |
|---|---|---|---|
| 1. Norbert Klaar | GDR | 597 | OR |
| 2. Jürgen Wiefel | GDR | 596 | |
| 3. Roberto Ferraris | ITA | 595 | |
| 4. Afanasy Kuzmin | SOV | 595 | |
| 5. Corneliu Ion | ROM | 595 | |
| 6. Erwin Glock | GER | 594 | |
| 7. Gerhard Petritsch | AUT | 594 | |
| 8. Marin Stan | ROM | 594 | |

Bill McMillan of the United States, competing in his sixth Olympics, scored only one point below his gold-medal-winning performance of 1960. However the quality of marksmanship had improved so much in 16 years that he was able to finish in only a tie for 16th place in 1976. The winner, Norbert Klaar, was a 26-year-old car mechanic from the small industrial town of Wittenberge on the river Elbe. He shot a perfect 300 in the second course.

**1980 Moscow** C: 40, N: 26, D: 7.25. WR: 598 (Giovanni Liverzani, Corneliu Ion)

| | | PTS. | |
|---|---|---|---|
| 1. Corneliu Ion | ROM | 596/148/147/148 | |
| 2. Jürgen Wiefel | GDR | 596/148/147/147 | |
| 3. Gerhard Petritsch | AUT | 596/146 | |
| 4. Vladas Turla | SOV | 595 | |
| 5. Roberto Ferraris | ITA | 595 | |
| 6. Afanasy Kuzmin | SOV | 595 | |
| 7. Marin Stan | ROM | 595 | |
| 8. Rafael Rodriguez | CUB | 594 | |

**1984 Los Angeles-Chino** C: 55, N: 31, D: 8.2. WR: 599 (Igor Puzyrev)

| | | PTS. | |
|---|---|---|---|
| 1. Takeo Kamachi | JPN | 595 | |
| 2. Corneliu Ion | ROM | 593 | |
| 3. Rauno Bies | FIN | 591/146 | |
| 4. Delival Nobre | BRA | 591/141 | |
| 5. Choong-Yull Yang | KOR | 590 | |
| 6. Alfred Radke | GER | 590 | |
| 7. Park Jong-gil | KOR | 590 | |
| 8. Bernardo Tobar | COL | 590 | |

Competing in his fourth Olympics, Takeo Kamachi finally won a medal at the age of 48.

**1988 Seoul** C: 32, N: 23, D: 9.23. WR: 599 (Igor Puzyrev) 697 (Ralf Schumann)

| | | PTS. | |
|---|---|---|---|
| 1. Afanasi Kuzmin | SOV | 698 | WR |
| 2. Ralf Schumann | GDR | 696 | |
| 3. Zoltán Kovács | HUN | 693 | |
| 4. Alberto Sevieri | ITA | 693 | |
| 5. Adam Kaczmarek | POL | 691 | |
| 6. Bernardo Tovar | COL | 690 | |
| 7. John McNally | USA | 690 | |
| 8. Dirk Köhler | GER | 689 | |

When he was 22 years old, Afanasi Kuzmin had a dream that he had won an Olympic gold medal. As a result, he kept going in the sport until his dream came true, 19 years later. Kuzmin shot a 598 in the qualifying round to lead by 1 point, then achieved a perfect score in the final.

## FREE PISTOL

The free pistol event is a leisurely affair in which the shooter has two and a half hours in which to fire 60 shots at a target 50 meters (55 yards) away. The 10-ring, or bull's-eye, of the target is only two inches in diameter. The final consists of 10 shots with 75 seconds for each shot.

**1896 Athens** C: 5, N: 3, D: 4.11.

| | | PTS. |
|---|---|---|
| 1. Sumner Paine | USA | 442 |
| 2. Holger Nielsen | DEN | 285 |
| 3. Ioannis Phrangoudis | GRE | — |
| 4. Leonidas Morakis | GRE | — |
| 5. Georgios Orphanidis | GRE | — |

Sumner Paine was working in Paris when his brother John showed up as part of the Boston Athletic Association team that was on its way to the Olympic Games. John convinced his brother to join him, so the two, not knowing the events or conditions, loaded up with eight guns and 3500 rounds of ammunition (they used only 96) and took the next train to Athens.

**1900 Paris** C: 20, N: 4, D: 8.1.

| | | PTS. |
|---|---|---|
| 1. Conrad Karl Röderer | SWI | 503 |
| 2. Achille Paroche | FRA | 466 |
| 3. Konrad Stäheli | SWI | 453 |
| 4. Louis Richardet | SWI | 448 |
| 5. Louis Duffoy | FRA | 442 |
| 6. G. van Haan | HOL | 437 |
| 7. Friedrich Luthi | SWI | 435 |
| 7. Léon Moreau | FRA | 435 |

**1904** not held

**1906 Athens** C: 21, N: 8, D: 4.23.

| | | PTS. |
|---|---|---|
| 1. Georgios Orphanidis | GRE | 221 |
| 2. Jean Fouconnier | FRA | 219 |
| 3. Aristides Rangavis | GRE | 218 |
| 4. Konrad Stäheli | SWI | 206 |
| 5. Konstantinos Skarlotos | GRE | 206 |
| 6. Maurice Lecoq | FRA | 205 |
| 7. Ludwig Ternajgo | AUT | 199 |
| 8. Cesare Liverziani | ITA | 199 |

**1908** not held

**1912 Stockholm** C: 54, N: 12, D: 7.2.

| | | PTS. |
|---|---|---|
| 1. Alfred Lane | USA | 499 |
| 2. Peter Dolfen | USA | 474 |
| 3. Charles Stewart | GBR | 470 |
| 4. Georg de Laval | SWE | 470 |
| 5. Erik Boström | SWE | 468 |
| 6. Horatio Poulter | GBR | 461 |
| 7. Henry Sears | USA | 459 |
| 8. Nikolai Panin (Kolomenkin) | RUS | 457 |

Alfred Lane of New York City was only 20 years old when he went to Stockholm and won three gold medals. Eight years later in Antwerp he added two more gold medals and one bronze. Eighth-place finisher Kolomenkin, a ten-time Russian pistol champion, was also a well-known figure skater who had won a gold medal in the special figures event of 1908.

**1920 Antwerp** C: 36, N: 13, D: 8.2.

| | | PTS. |
|---|---|---|
| 1. Karl Frederick | USA | 496 |
| 2. Afranio da Costa | BRA | 489 |
| 3. Alfred Lane | USA | 481 |
| 4. Lauritz Larsen | DEN | 475 |
| 5. Niels Larsen | DEN | 470 |
| 6. Anders Wilhelm Andersson | SWE | 467 |
| 7. Paul van Asbroek | BEL | 466 |
| 8. Casimir Reuterskiöld | SWE | 464 |
| 8. Iason Sappas | GRE | 464 |

Da Costa used a new Colt .22 that had been loaned to the Brazilian team by the U.S. team, and ammunition given to him by Alfred Lane.

**1924–1932** not held

**1936 Berlin** C: 43, N: 19, D: 8.7. WR: 547 (Torsten Ullman)

| | | PTS. | |
|---|---|---|---|
| 1. Torsten Ullman | SWE | 559 | WR |
| 2. Erich Krempel | GER | 544 | |
| 3. Charles des Jammonières | FRA | 540 | |

| | | |
|---|---|---|
| 4. Marcel Bonin | FRA | 538 |
| 5. Tapio Vartiovaara | FIN | 537 |
| 6. Elliott Jones | USA | 536 |
| 7. Georges Stathis | GRE | 532 |
| 8. Aatto Nuora | FIN | 532 |

Earlier in the day Ullman had won a bronze medal in the rapid-fire pistol event.

**1948 London** C: 50, N: 22, D: 8.2. WR: 559 (Torsten Ullman)

| | | PTS. |
|---|---|---|
| 1. Edwin Vasquez Cam | PER | 545 |
| 2. Rudolf Schnyder | SWI | 539/60/21 |
| 3. Torsten Ullman | SWE | 539/60/16 |
| 4. Huelet Benner | USA | 539/58 |
| 5. Beat Rhyner | SWI | 536 |
| 6. Angel León de Gozalo | SPA | 534 |
| 7. Ambrus Balogh | HUN | 532 |
| 8. M. LaFortune | BEL | 530 |

Vasquez is the only Peruvian ever to win an Olympic gold medal.

**1952 Helsinki** C: 48, N: 28, D: 7.25. WR: 559 (Torsten Ullman)

| | | PTS. | |
|---|---|---|---|
| 1. Huelet Benner | USA | 553 | OR |
| 2. Angel León de Gozalo | SPA | 550 | |
| 3. Ambrus Balogh | HUN | 549 | |
| 4. Konstantin Martazov | SOV | 546 | |
| 5. Lev Vainshtein | SOV | 546 | |
| 6. Torsten Ullman | SWE | 543 | |
| 7. Klaus Lahti | FIN | 541 | |
| 8. Beat Rhyner | SWI | 539 | |

**1956 Melbourne** C: 33, N: 22, D: 11.30. WR: 566 (Anton Yasinsky)

| | | PTS. | |
|---|---|---|---|
| 1. Pentti Linnosvuo | FIN | 556/26 | OR |
| 2. Makhmud Umarov | SOV | 556/24 | OR |
| 3. Offutt Pinion | USA | 551 | |
| 4. Choji Hosaka | JPN | 550/24 | |
| 5. Anton Yasinsky | SOV | 550/20 | |
| 6. Torsten Ullman | SWE | 610 | |
| 7. Åke Lindblom | SWE | 542 | |
| 8. Leonard Tolhurst | AUS | 541 | |

**1960 Rome** C: 67, N: 40, D: 9.6. WR: 566 (Anton Yasinsky)

| | | PTS. | |
|---|---|---|---|
| 1. Aleksei Gustchin | SOV | 560 | OR |
| 2. Makhmud Umarov | SOV | 552/26 | |
| 3. Yoshihisa Yoshikawa | JPN | 552/20 | |
| 4. Torsten Ullman | SWE | 550 | |
| 5. Stanislaw Romik | POL | 548 | |
| 6. Alfred Späni | SWI | 546 | |
| 7. Vladimir Kudrna | CZE | 545 | |
| 8. Horst Kadner | GDR | 544 | |

Fourth-place finisher Ullman was now 52 years old.

**1964 Tokyo** C: 52, N: 42, D: 10.18. WR: 566 (Anton Yasinsky)

| | | PTS. | |
|---|---|---|---|
| 1. Väinö Markkanen | FIN | 560 | EOR |
| 2. Franklin Green | USA | 557 | |
| 3. Yoshihisa Yoshikawa | JPN | 554/26 | |
| 4. Johann Garreis | GDR | 554/24 | |
| 5. Anthony Chivers | GBR | 552 | |
| 6. Antonio Vita Segura | PER | 550 | |
| 7. Leif Larsson | SWE | 549 | |
| 8. Thomas Smith | USA | 548 | |

**1968 Mexico City** C: 69, N: 42, D: 10.18. WR: 566 (Anton Yasinsky)

| | | PTS. | |
|---|---|---|---|
| 1. Grigory Kossykh | SOV | 562/30 | OR |
| 2. Heinz Mertel | GER | 562/26 | OR |
| 3. Harald Vollmar | GDR | 560 | |
| 4. Arnold Vitarbo | USA | 559 | |
| 5. Pawel Malek | POL | 556 | |
| 6. Helmut Artelt | GDR | 555 | |
| 7. Nelson Onate | CUB | 555 | |
| 8. Neagu Bratu | ROM | 554 | |

**1972 Munich** C: 59, N: 37, D: 8.28. WR: 572 (Grigory Kossykh)

| | | PTS. | |
|---|---|---|---|
| 1. Ragnar Skanåker | SWE | 567 | OR |
| 2. Dan Iuga | ROM | 562 | |
| 3. Rudolf Dollinger | AUT | 560 | |
| 4. Rajmund Stachurski | POL | 559 | |
| 5. Harald Vollmar | GDR | 558 | |
| 6. Hynek Hromada | CZE | 556 | |
| 7. Kornel Marosvari | HUN | 555 | |
| 8. Grigory Kossykh | SOV | 555 | |

**1976 Montreal** C: 47, N: 32, D: 7.18. WR: 572 (Grigory Kossykh, Harald Vollmar)

| | | PTS. | |
|---|---|---|---|
| 1. Uwe Potteck | GDR | 573 | WR |
| 2. Harald Vollmar | GDR | 567 | |
| 3. Rudolf Dollinger | AUT | 562 | |
| 4. Heinz Mertel | GER | 560 | |
| 5. Ragnar Skanåker | SWE | 560 | |
| 6. Vincenzo Tondo | ITA | 559 | |
| 7. Grigory Kossykh | SOV | 559 | |
| 8. Dencho Denev | BUL | 557 | |

**1980 Moscow** C: 33, N: 19, D: 7.20. WR: 577 (Moritz Minder, Paavo Palokangas)

| | | PTS. | |
|---|---|---|---|
| 1. Aleksandr Melentev | SOV | 581 | WR |
| 2. Harald Vollmar | GDR | 568 | |
| 3. Ljubcho Diakov | BUL | 565 | |
| 4. Soh Gil-san | PRK | 565 | |
| 5. Seppo Saarenpää | FIN | 565 | |
| 6. Sergei Pyzhianov | SOV | 564 | |
| 7. Ragnar Skanåker | SWE | 563 | |
| 8. Paavo Palokangas | FIN | 561 | |

**1984 Los Angeles-Chino** C: 56, N: 38, D: 7.29. WR: 581
(Alexandr Melentev)

| | | PTS. |
|---|---|---|
| 1. Xu Haifeng | CHN | 566 |
| 2. Ragnar Skanåker | SWE | 565 |
| 3. Wang Yifu | CHN | 564 |
| 4. Jürgen Hartmann | GER | 560 |
| 5. Vincenzo Tondo | ITA | 560 |
| 6. Philippe Cola | FRA | 559 |
| 7. Hector De Lima Carrillo | VEN | 558 |
| 8. Paavo Palokangas | FIN | 558 |

To Xu Haifeng, a former "barefoot doctor" and chemical fertilizer salesman, went the honor of not only being the first gold-medal winner of the 1984 Olympics, but also of becoming the first representative of China to win an Olympic medal. He defeated 50-year-old Ragnar Skanåker, who added a silver medal to the gold he had won twelve years earlier.

**1988 Seoul** C: 43, N: 31, D: 9.18. WR: 581 (Aleksandr Melentev)
666 (Igor Basinsky)

| | | PTS. |
|---|---|---|
| 1. Sorin Babii | ROM | 660 |
| 2. Ragnar Skanåaker | SWE | 657 |
| 3. Igor Basinsky | SOV | 657 |
| 4. Taniou Kiriakov | BUL | 656 |
| 5. Gernot Eder | GDR | 654 |
| 6. Gyula Karácsony | HUN | 654 |
| 7. Arndt Kaspar | GER | 651 |
| 8. Wang Yifu | CHN | 651 |

Babii trailed Basinsky by 4 points following the preliminary round, with 54-year-old Skanåaker another 2 points back in fourth place. Basinsky seemed rattled in the final and scored only 87 points to Babii's 94 and Skanåaker's 93. Skanåaker was more than twice as old as the other top five finishers.

# AIR PISTOL

Competition in the qualification round consists of 60 shots at a distance of 10 meters with a time limit of 2 hours and 15 minutes. The top eight shooters take part in a 10-shot final series.

**1896-1984** not held

**1988 Seoul** C: 44, N: 29, D: 9.24. WR: 590 (Vladas Turla, Igor Basinsky) 692.3 (Igor Basinsky)

| | | PTS. |
|---|---|---|
| 1. Tanue Kiriakov | BUL | 687.9 |
| 2. Erich Buljung | USA | 687.9 |
| 3. Xu Haifeng | CHN | 684.5 |
| 4. Sorin Babii | ROM | 683.3 |
| 5. Igor Basinsky | SOV | 683.2 |
| 6. Miroslav Ružička | CZE | 681.4 |
| 7. Jerzy Pietrzak | POL | 678.3 |
| 8. Boris Kokorev | SOV | 677.3 |

U.S. Army shooting instructor Erich Buljung equaled the 60-shot world record in the preliminary round. In the 10-shot final, however, his 5-point lead gradually evaporated until Kiriakov trailed by only 0.7 points after nine shots. On the final shot Kiriakov outscored Buljung 9.8 to 9.1 to finish in a tie. The Bulgarian was awarded the gold medal on the basis of his higher point total in the final round.

# SMALL-BORE RIFLE, PRONE

The small-bore rifle, prone match is shot at a distance of 50 meters with a .22 rimfire rifle. Originally the 10-ring bull's-eye was .89 inches in diameter. When high scores became too common, it was scaled down in 1958 to .487 inches. The shooter must keep his wrist at least six inches above the ground. He is given one hour and 45 minutes in which to take 60 shots and is also allowed 15 sighting shots, which can only be taken between the strings of ten record shots. The final consists of 10 shots with a time limit of 45 seconds per shot.

**1896–1906** not held

**1908 London** C: 19, N: 5, D: 7.11.

| | | PTS. |
|---|---|---|
| 1. A.A. Carnell | GBR | 387 |
| 2. Harry Humby | GBR | 386 |
| 3. George Barnes | GBR | 385 |
| 4. M.K. Matthews | GBR | 384 |
| 5. Edward Amoore | GBR | 383 |
| 6. William Pimm | GBR | 379 |
| 7. A.E. Taylor | GBR | 376 |
| 8. H.I. Hawkins | GBR | 374 |

**1912 Stockholm** C: 41, N: 9, D: 7.4.

| | | PTS. |
|---|---|---|
| 1. Frederick Hird | USA | 194 |
| 2. William Milne | GBR | 193 |
| 3. Harry Burt | GBR | 192 |
| 4. Edward Lessimore | GBR | 192 |
| 5. Francis Kemp | GBR | 190 |
| 6. Robert Murray | GBR | 190 |
| 7. William Leushner | USA | 189 |
| 8. Erik Bostrom | SWE | 189 |

**1920** not held

**1924 Paris** C: 66, N: 19, D: 6.23.

| | | PTS. |
|---|---|---|
| 1. Pierre Coquelin de Lisle | FRA | 398 |
| 2. Marcus Dinwiddie | USA | 396 |
| 3. Josias Hartmann | SWI | 394 |
| 4. Erik Saetter-Lassen | DEN | 393 |
| 4. Anders Peter Nielsen | DEN | 393 |
| 4. Johannes Theslöf | FIN | 393 |
| 7. Viktor Knutsson | SWE | 392 |
| 7. Jakob Reich | SWI | 392 |

Silver medalist Marcus Dinwiddie was a 17-year-old schoolboy from Washington, D.C. His record score of 396 out of 400 held up for most of the match, until the 23-year-old Coquelin de Lisle hit a sensational set of 100, 100, 99, and 99.

**1928** not held

**1932 Los Angeles** C: 26, N: 9, D: 8.13.

| | | PTS. | |
|---|---|---|---|
| 1. Bertil Rönnmark | SWE | 294/296 | |
| 2. Gustavo Huet | MEX | 294/290 | |
| 3. Zoltán Hradetzky-Soós | HUN | 293 | |
| 4. Mario Zorzi | ITA | 293 | |
| 5. Gustaf Andersson | SWE | 292 | |
| 5. William Harding | USA | 292 | |
| 5. Karl Larsson | SWE | 292 | |
| 5. Francisco Real | POR | 292 | |

Antonius Limberkovits of Hungary fired one bull's-eye which he had unfortunately aimed at the wrong target. He called out his mistake to the officials, who ruled the shot a complete miss. Had he not made this error and had he not been so honest, Lemberkovits would have won the gold medal.

**1936 Berlin** C: 66, N: 25, D: 8.8.

| | | PTS. | |
|---|---|---|---|
| 1. Willy Högeberg | NOR | 300 | WR |
| 2. Ralph Berzsenyi | HUN | 296 | |
| 3. Wladyslaw Karaś | POL | 296 | |
| 4. Martin Gison | PHI | 296 | |
| 5. José Trindade Mello | BRA | 296 | |
| 6. Jacques Mazoyer | FRA | 296 | |
| 7. Gustavo Huet | MEX | 296 | |
| 8. Bertil Rönnmark | SWE | 295 | |

The 30-year-old Rögeberg fired the first perfect score ever recorded in international competition. Fourth-place finisher Gison was captured by the Japanese during World War II and forced to take part in the infamous Bataan death march. He survived and was able to compete in the 1948 Olympics in London.

**1948 London** C: 71, N: 26, D: 8.3.

| | | PTS. | |
|---|---|---|---|
| 1. Arthur Cook | USA | 599/43 | WR |
| 2. Walter Tomsen | USA | 599/42 | WR |
| 3. Jonas Jonsson | SWE | 597/44 | |
| 4. Halvor Kongsjorden | NOR | 597/39 | |
| 5. Thore Skredegaard | NOR | 597/39 | |
| 6. Enrique Baldwin Ponte | PER | 596/39 | |
| 7. J. Ravila | FIN | 596/39 | |
| 8. Willy Rögeberg | NOR | 596/37 | |

Cook and Tomsen each missed the 10-ring only once in 60 shots, but Cook was awarded first place because he had fired one shot more than Tomsen within the 3/8-inch inner bull's-eye.

**1952 Helsinki** C: 58, N: 32, D: 7.29. WR: 400 (T. Manttari)

| | | PTS. | |
|---|---|---|---|
| 1. Iosif Sìrbu | ROM | 400/33 | EWR |
| 2. Boris Andreyev | SOV | 400/28 | EWR |
| 3. Arthur Jackson | USA | 399/28 | |
| 4. Gilmour Boa | CAN | 399/28 | |
| 5. Erich Spörer | GER | 399/25 | |
| 6. Otto Horber | SWI | 398/29 | |
| 7. Veikko Leskinen | FIN | 398/28 | |
| 8. Severino Moreira | BRA | 398/22 | |

Sìrbu was Romania's first Olympic champion.

**1956 Melbourne** C: 44, N: 25, D: 12.5. WR: 598 (Gilmour Boa)

| | | PTS. |
|---|---|---|
| 1. Gerald Ouellette | CAN | 600 |
| 2. Vassily Borissov | SOV | 599 |
| 3. Gilmour Boa | CAN | 598 |
| 4. Otakar Horínek | CZE | 598 |
| 5. Iosif Sârbu | ROM | 598 |
| 6. Sándor Krebs | HUN | 598 |
| 7. Erling Kongshaug | NOR | 598 |
| 8. Severino Moreira | BRA | 597 |

After he had done poorly in the three-position small-bore event, Ouellette and his teammate Gilmour Boa decided that they should both use Boa's rifle for the prone competition, even though this meant that they both had to shoot within the same two-and-a-half-hour time limit. Boa went first and, coached by Ouellette, matched his world record of 598. Then, with half the time remaining, it was Ouellette's turn. Coached by Boa, who encouraged the Windsor, Ontario, tool designer to take two breaks to ease the pressure, Ouellette shot 60 straight bull's-eyes for a perfect score. Unfortunately, his score was not accepted as a world record because the Australian officials had set the targets one and a half meters too close. Ouellette's second appearance in the Olympics didn't come until 12 years later, when he finished sixth in the three-position event in Mexico City.

**1960 Rome** C: 85, N: 46, D: 9.10. WR: 595 (János Holup)

| | | PTS. |
|---|---|---|
| 1. Peter Kohnke | GER | 590 |
| 2. James Hill | USA | 589 |
| 3. Enrico Forcella Pelliccioni | VEN | 587 |
| 4. Vassily Borissov | SOV | 586 |
| 5. Arthur Skinner | GBR | 586 |
| 6. Yukio Inokuma | JPN | 586 |
| 7. Daniel Puckel | USA | 585 |
| 8. Marcel Koen | BUL | 585 |

Eighteen-year-old Peter Kohnke of Bremervorde was the youngest of the 85 entrants in the prone event.

**1964 Tokyo** C: 73, N: 43, D: 10.16. WR: 595 (János Holup, Rudolf Bortz)

| | | PTS. | |
|---|---|---|---|
| 1. László Hammerl | HUN | 597 | WR |
| 2. Lones Wigger | USA | 597 | WR |

| | | PTS. | |
|---|---|---|---|
| 3. Tommy Pool | USA | 596 | |
| 4. Gilmour Boa | CAN | 595 | |
| 5. Nicolae Rotaru | ROM | 595 | |
| 6. Akihiro Rinzaki | JPN | 594 | |
| 7. Karl Wenk | GER | 594 | |
| 8. Traian Cogut | ROM | 593 | |

László Hammerl was a 22-year-old medical student from Budapest. He was awarded the victory on the basis of a tie-breaking rule which stated that whoever had the highest score in the final string of ten shots was the winner.

**1968 Mexico City** C: 86, N: 45, D: 10.19. WR: 598 (David Boyd, Alfons Meyer)

| | | PTS. | |
|---|---|---|---|
| 1. Jan Kurka | CZE | 598 | EWR |
| 2. László Hammerl | HUN | 598 | EWR |
| 3. Ian Ballinger | NZE | 597 | |
| 4. Nicolae Rotaru | ROM | 597 | |
| 5. John Palin | GBR | 596 | |
| 6. Jean Loret | FRA | 596 | |
| 7. Bjorn Bakken | NOR | 595 | |
| 8. Gary Anderson | USA | 595 | |

This time Hammerl lost the gold medal because of the same tie-breaking rule from which he had benefitted four years earlier. Eulalia Rolińska of Poland and Gladys de Seminario of Peru had the distinction of being the first women to compete in Olympic shooting. They finished 22nd and 31st, respectively.

**1972 Munich** C: 101, N: 59, D: 8.28. WR: 598 (David Boyd, Alfons Meyer, Jan Kurka, László Hammerl, Peter Gorewski, Wolfram Waibel, Manfred Fiess, Esa Kervinen)

| | | PTS. | |
|---|---|---|---|
| 1. Li Ho-jun | PRK | 599 | WR |
| 2. Victor Auer | USA | 598 | |
| 3. Nicolae Rotaru | ROM | 598 | |
| 4. Giuseppe de Chirico | ITA | 597 | |
| 5. Jiři Vogler | CZE | 597 | |
| 6. Jaime Santiago | PUR | 597 | |
| 7. Lones Wigger | USA | 597 | |
| 8. László Hammerl | HUN | 597 | |

After his victory, Li was asked by reporters to what he attributed his brilliant performance. He replied, "I thought I was shooting at my enemies. Our Prime Minister, Kim-Il Sung, told us prior to our departure to shoot as if we were fighting our enemies. And that's exactly what I did." This attitude was considered to be unsportsmanlike, and so a second press conference was called at which Li claimed he had been misquoted. Second-place finisher Vic Auer was a North Hollywood TV scriptwriter who had written for *Death Valley Days*, *Gunsmoke*, and *Bonanza*.

**1976 Montreal** C: 76, N: 49, D: 7.19. WR: 599 (Li Ho-jun, Karel Bulan, Mircea Ilca)

| | | PTS. | |
|---|---|---|---|
| 1. Karlheinz Smieszek | GER | 599 | EWR |
| 2. Ulrich Lind | GER | 597 | |
| 3. Gennady Lushchikov | SOV | 595 | |
| 4. Anton Müller | SWI | 595 | |
| 5. Walter Frescura | ITA | 594 | |
| 6. Arne Sörensen | CAN | 593 | |
| 7. Henning Clausen | DEN | 593 | |
| 8. Desanka Pesut | YUG | 592 | |

Smieszek, a 27-year-old insurance agent, was a surprise winner who had never before won a major shooting title.

**1980 Moscow** C: 56, N: 33, D: 7.21. WR: 599 (Li Ho-jun, Karel Bulan, Mircea Ilca, Karlheinz Smieszek, Alistair Allan, Lones Wigger)

| | | PTS. | |
|---|---|---|---|
| 1. Károly Varga | HUN | 599 | EWR |
| 2. Hellfried Heilfort | GDR | 599 | EWR |
| 3. Petur Zapianov | BUL | 598 | |
| 4. Krzysztof Stefaniak | POL | 598 | |
| 5. Timo Hagmaan | FIN | 597 | |
| 6. Aleksandr Mastianin | SOV | 597 | |
| 7. Nonka Matova | BUL | 597 | |
| 8. Walter Frescura | ITA | 597 | |

Varga broke his shooting hand playing soccer two days before the competition and had to wear a bandage while he shot. After winning the gold medal he explained that the injury had actually helped him, because it forced him to squeeze the trigger more delicately.

**1984 Los Angeles-Chino** C: 71, N: 46, D: 7.30. WR: 600 (Alister Allan, Ernest VandeZande, Edward Etzel, Donald Durbin)

| | | PTS. | |
|---|---|---|---|
| 1. Edward Etzel | USA | 599 | EOR |
| 2. Michel Bury | FRA | 596 | |
| 3. Michael Sullivan | GBR | 596 | |
| 4. Alister Allan | GBR | 595 | |
| 5. Francesco Nanni | SMR | 594 | |
| 6. Hans Strand | SWE | 594 | |
| 7. John Duus | NOR | 594 | |
| 8. Ulrich Lind | GER | 593 | |

Ed Etzel of Morgantown, West Virginia, completed his 60 shots in only 40 minutes and was the first of the 71 shooters to finish. Francesco Manni's fifth place finish made him the most successful Olympic athlete ever from the tiny nation of San Marino (pop. 22,000).

**1988 Seoul** C: 55, N: 33, D: 9.19. WR: 600 (thirteen shooters) 704.9 (Petr Kůrka)

| | | PTS. |
|---|---|---|
| 1. Miroslav Varga | CZE | 703.9 |
| 2. Cha Young-chul | KOR | 702.8 |

| | | | |
|---|---|---|---|
| 3. Attila Záhonyi | HUN | 701.9 |
| 4. Pavel Soukeník | CZE | 701.2 |
| 5. Alister Allan | GBR | 700.9 |
| 6. Xu Xiaoguang | CHN | 700.6 |
| 7. Bernd Rücker | GER | 700.5 |
| 8. Michael Ashcroft | CAN | 698.5 |

Varga required only 28 minutes to achieve a perfect score of 600 in the qualifying round. His speed turned out to be well advised, as a thunderstorm swept in a few minutes later, darkening the sky and impairing the vision of the remaining shooters. In the final, Cha drew within 0.2 points with two shots remaining, but Varga shot a pair of 10.6s to hold him off. Cha's closing in on Varga caused great excitement among the Korean spectators, who clapped and cheered after each of Cha's shots even though other shooters were still firing. This was an unprecedented breach of etiquette on the part of the crowd.

## SMALL-BORE RIFLE, THREE POSITIONS

In the small-bore rifle, three-position event, each entrant shoots 40 shots prone, 40 kneeling, and 40 standing, with a .22 rifle at a target 50 meters away. The target is the same as that used in the prone event. In the final the top eight qualifiers take ten shots in the standing position.

**1896–1948** not held

**1952 Helsinki** C: 44, N: 25, D: 7.29. WR: 1167 (K. Steigelmann)

| | | PRONE | | KNEELING | | STANDING | TOTAL PTS. |
|---|---|---|---|---|---|---|---|
| 1. Erling Kongshaug | NOR | 397 | | 387 | | 380 | 1164/53 |
| 2. Vilho Ylönen | FIN | 397 | | 394 | WR | 373 | 1164/53 |
| 3. Boris Andreyev | SOV | 400 | WR | 387 | | 376 | 1163 |
| 4. Ernst Huber | SWI | 397 | | 390 | | 375 | 1162 |
| 5. Pyotr Avilov | SOV | 395 | | 385 | | 382 | 1162 |
| 6. Iosif Sârbu | ROM | 400 | WR | 383 | | 378 | 1161 |
| 7. Uno Berg | SWE | 396 | | 388 | | 374 | 1158 |
| 8. Veikko Leskinen | FIN | 398 | | 390 | | 369 | 1157 |

**1956 Melbourne** C: 44, N: 28, D: 12.4. WR: 1176 (Ole Jensen)

| | | PRONE | | KNEELING | STANDING | TOTAL PTS. | |
|---|---|---|---|---|---|---|---|
| 1. Anatoly Bogdanov | SOV | 396 | | 392 | 384 | 1172 | OR |
| 2. Otakar Hořinek | CZE | 393 | | 395 | 384 | 1172 | OR |
| 3. Nils Johan Sundberg | SWE | 397 | | 396 | 374 | 1167 | |
| 4. Vassily Borrisov | SOV | 395 | | 391 | 377 | 1163 | |
| 5. Vilho Ylönen | FIN | 394 | | 386 | 381 | 1161 | |
| 6. Gilmour Boa | CAN | 400 | WR | 391 | 368 | 1159 | |
| 7. Iosif Sârbu | ROM | 397 | | 392 | 368 | 1157 | |
| 8. Anders Kvissberg | SWE | 394 | | 389 | 373 | 1156 | |

**1960 Rome** C: 75, N: 40, D: 9.8. WR: 1149 (Klaus Zähringer)

| | | PRONE | KNEELING | STANDING | TOTAL PTS. | |
|---|---|---|---|---|---|---|
| 1. Viktor Shamburkin | SOV | 394 | 386 | 369 | 1149 | EWR |
| 2. Marat Niyasov | SOV | 384 | 388 | 373 | 1145 | |
| 3. Klaus Zähringer | GER | 394 | 381 | 364 | 1139 | |
| 4. Dušan Houdek | CZE | 387 | 386 | 366 | 1139 | |
| 5. Jerzy Nowicki | POL | 394 | 378 | 365 | 1137 | |
| 6. Esa Kervinen | FIN | 392 | 381 | 364 | 1137 | |
| 7. Daniel Puckel | USA | 390 | 385 | 361 | 1137 | |
| 8. János Holup | HUN | 394 | 384 | 356 | 1134 | |

**1964 Tokyo** C: 75, N: 40, D: 9.8. WR: 1157 (Gary Anderson)

| | | PRONE | KNEELING | STANDING | TOTAL PTS. | |
|---|---|---|---|---|---|---|
| 1. Lones Wigger | USA | 398 | 394 | 372 | 1164 | WR |
| 2. Velichko Velichkov | BUL | 396 | 384 | 372 | 1152 | |
| 3. László Hammerl | HUN | 397 | 387 | 367 | 1151 | |
| 4. Harry Köcher | GDR | 394 | 389 | 365 | 1148 | |
| 5. Jerzy Nowicki | POL | 396 | 389 | 362 | 1147 | |
| 6. Tommy Pool | USA | 393 | 392 | 362 | 1147 | |
| 7. Ion Olarescu | ROM | 393 | 391 | 360 | 1144 | |
| 8. Kurt Müller | SWI | 390 | 386 | 367 | 1143 | |

U.S. Army Captain Lones Wigger of Carter, Montana, had never shot before a large crowd before. Teammate Gary Anderson advised him not to be afraid of the crowd but to feel a part of it. Wigger set a world record in the prone event, but lost on a tie-breaker. Four days later he set another world record in the three-position event, but this time he finished 12 points ahead of his nearest competitor. Eight years later, at the Munich Olympics, Wigger won another gold medal in the 300-meter free rifle event.

**1968 Mexico City** C: 62, N: 35, D: 10.21. WR: 1165 (Gary Anderson)

| | | PRONE | STANDING | KNEELING | | TOTAL PTS. |
|---|---|---|---|---|---|---|
| 1. Bernd Klingner | GER | 394 | 367 | 396 | WR | 1157 |
| 2. John Writer | USA | 395 | 370 | 391 | | 1156 |
| 3. Viktor Parkhimovich | SOV | 395 | 366 | 393 | | 1154 |
| 4. John Foster | USA | 394 | 369 | 390 | | 1153 |
| 5. José Gonzales | MEX | 397 | 376 | 379 | | 1152 |
| 6. Gerald Ouellette | CAN | 396 | 364 | 391 | | 1151 |
| 7. Peter Kohnke | GER | 395 | 368 | 388 | | 1151 |
| 8. Kurt Müller | SWI | 390 | 373 | 388 | | 1151 |

**1972 Munich** C: 69, N: 41, D: 8.30. WR: 1165 (Gary Anderson, Oleg Lapkin)

| | | PRONE | STANDING | | KNEELING | TOTAL PTS. | |
|---|---|---|---|---|---|---|---|
| 1. John Writer | USA | 395 | 381 | WR | 390 | 1166 | WR |
| 2. Lanny Bassham | USA | 390 | 375 | | 392 | 1157 | |
| 3. Werner Lippoldt | GDR | 393 | 372 | | 388 | 1153 | |
| 4. Petr Kovařik | CZE | 397 | 368 | | 388 | 1153 | |
| 5. Vladimir Agishev | SOV | 392 | 369 | | 391 | 1152 | |
| 6. Andrzej Sieledcow | POL | 395 | 369 | | 387 | 1151 | |
| 7. Gottfried Kustermann | GER | 397 | 364 | | 388 | 1149 | |
| 8. Nicolae Rotaru | ROM | 397 | 361 | | 390 | 1148 | |

**1976 Montreal** C: 57, N: 35, D: 7.21. WR: 1167 (Lones Wigger) |

| | | PRONE | STANDING | KNEELING | TOTAL PTS. |
|---|---|---|---|---|---|
| 1. Lanny Bassham | USA | 397 | 373 | 392 | 1162 |
| 2. Margaret Murdock | USA | 398 | 376 | 388 | 1162 |
| 3. Werner Seibold | GER | 397 | 377 | 386 | 1160 |
| 4. Srecko Pejović | YUG | 391 | 379 | 386 | 1156 |
| 5. Sven Johansson | SWE | 394 | 367 | 391 | 1152 |
| 6. Li Ho-jun | PRK | 390 | 373 | 389 | 1152 |
| 7. Zdravko Milutinović | YUG | 394 | 394 | 389 | 1152 |
| 8. Aleksandr Mitrofanov | SOV | 394 | 369 | 388 | 1151 |

After finishing second in 1972, Lanny Bassham, a soldier from Fort Worth, Texas, became convinced that his technical skill had to be supplemented by mental training. He went to the Montreal Olympics as the favorite. His U.S. teammate was Margaret Murdock, a 33-year-old nurse from Topeka, Kansas. In 1970 Murdock had won the standing event at the world championships while she was four months' pregnant. At the 1976 Olympics, Bassham and Murdock finished in a tie at 1162. Bassham was awarded the gold medal because he had scored three 100s to Murdock's two. Bassham felt that the tie-breaker was a silly rule, and at the medal ceremony he pulled Murdock up to the first-place platform and they stood together for the playing of the U.S. national anthem. Murdock was probably less upset about the tie-breaking rule, since it was the same rule that had allowed her to gain a place on the U.S. team when she and John Writer finished with the same scores at the U.S. tryouts. Bassham later started a mental management business to help people become better shooters and make more money. Murdock was the first woman to win an Olympic shooting medal.

**1980 Moscow** C: 39, N: 21, D: 7.23. WR: 1172 (Nonka Matova) |

| | | PRONE | STANDING | KNEELING | TOTAL PTS. | |
|---|---|---|---|---|---|---|
| 1. Viktor Vlasov | SOV | 398 | 378 | 397 | 1173 | WR |
| 2. Bernd Hartstein | GDR | 399 | 374 | 393 | 1166 | |
| 3. Sven Johansson | SWE | 398 | 379 | 388 | 1165 | |
| 4. Mauri Röppänen | FIN | 397 | 379 | 388 | 1164 | |
| 4. Aleksandr Mitrofanov | SOV | 397 | 378 | 389 | 1164 | |
| 6. Nonka Matova | BUL | 396 | 377 | 390 | 1163 | |
| 7. Hellfried Heilfort | GDR | 394 | 378 | 390 | 1162 | |
| 8. Eugeniusz Pędzisz | POL | 397 | 368 | 391 | 1156 | |

**1984 Los Angeles-Chino** C: 51, N: 29, D: 8.1. WR: 1173 (Viktor Vlasov, Vladimir Lvov) |

| | | PRONE | STANDING | KNEELING | TOTAL PTS. | |
|---|---|---|---|---|---|---|
| 1. Malcolm Cooper | GBR | 397 | 381 | 395 | 1173 | EWR |
| 2. Daniel Nipkow | SWI | 396 | 381 | 386 | 1163 | |
| 3. Alister Allan | GBR | 392 | 378 | 392 | 1162 | |
| 4. Kurt Hillenbrand | GER | 396 | 369 | 389 | 1154 | |
| 5. Bo Arne Lilja | DEN | 394 | 375 | 384 | 1153 | |
| 6. Glenn Dubis | USA | 396 | 368 | 387 | 1151 | |
| 7. Jean Pierre Amat | FRA | 393 | 375 | 382 | 1150 | |
| 7. Peter Heinz | GER | 394 | 375 | 381 | 1150 | |

**1988 Seoul** C: 47, N: 25, D: 9.22. WR: 1183 (Petr Kůrka) 1283.4 (Petr Kůrka)

| | | PRONE | STANDING | KNEELING | FINAL | TOTAL PTS. |
|---|---|---|---|---|---|---|
| 1. Malcolm Cooper | GBR | 400 EWR | 387 | 393 | 99.3 | 1279.3 |
| 2. Alister Allan | GBR | 399 | 386 | 396 | 94.6 | 1275.6 |
| 3. Kirill Ivanov | SOV | 399 | 382 | 392 | 102.0 | 1275.0 |
| 4. Klavs Jorn Christensen | DEN | 399 | 387 | 391 | 96.6 | 1273.6 |
| 5. Glenn Dubis | USA | 400 EWR | 386 | 388 | 99.5 | 1273.5 |
| 6. Grachya Petikyan | SOV | 394 | 387 | 392 | 99.2 | 1272.2 |
| 7. Harald Stenvaag | NOR | 395 | 389 | 389 | 98.7 | 1271.7 |
| 8. Goran Maksimović | YUG | 399 | 383 | 391 | 98.5 | 1271.5 |

One week before the competition began, a clumsy technician from the BBC knocked over Cooper's rifle and cracked the stock. Fortunately the defending Olympic champion was able to repair it with the help of a Soviet gunsmith.

## AIR RIFLE

In the qualifying round 60 shots are taken at a distance of 10 meters. The center ring is 1 millimeter across. The final consists of 10 shots with a 75-second time limit per shot.

**1896–1980** not held

**1984 Los Angeles-Chino** C: 52, N: 35, D: 8.3. WR: 590 (Harald Stenvaag)

| | | PTS. |
|---|---|---|
| 1. Philippe Heberle | FRA | 589 |
| 2. Andreas Kronthaler | AUT | 587 |
| 3. Barry Dagger | GBR | 587 |
| 4. Nicolas Berthelot | FRA | 585 |
| 5. Peter Heinz | GER | 583 |
| 5. John Rost | USA | 583 |
| 7. Harald Stenvaag | NOR | 582 |
| 7. Itzchak Yonassi | ISR | 582 |

Defending world champion Philippe Heberle, a 21-year-old fire fighter from Belfort, was also two-time cross-bow world champion.

**1988 Seoul** C: 46, N: 29, D: 9.20. WR: 597 (Sergei Martinov) 699.1 (Tapio Saeynevirta)

| | | PTS. |
|---|---|---|
| 1. Goran Maksimović | YUG | 695.6 |
| 2. Nicolas Berthelot | FRA | 694.2 |
| 3. Johann Riederer | GER | 694.0 |
| 4. Robert Foth | USA | 692.5 |
| 5. Harald Stenvaag | NOR | 692.0 |
| 6. Attila Záhonyi | HUN | 691.4 |
| 7. An Byung-kyun | KOR | 690.7 |
| 8. Andreas Wolfram | GDR | 689.8 |

## MOVING TARGET

Between 1972 and 1988 the moving target or running boar event consisted of 60 shots at 50 meters. The target, a life-size reproduction of a wild boar with a two-inch 10-ring, crossed a ten-meter gap. The boar did 30 fast runs at two and a half seconds and 30 slow runs at five seconds. In 1988 the four best shooters in the qualification round took 10 more shots in the final at fast-run speed. This is the only event in which telescopic sights are allowed. Also, unlike other shooting events, ties in the qualifying round are decided by the number of 10s shot. In 1992 the moving target event will be shot with an air rifle at 10 meters.

**1896** not held

**1900 Paris** C: ?, N: 3, D: 7.17.

| | | PTS. |
|---|---|---|
| 1. Louis Debray | FRA | 20 |
| 2. P. Nivet | FRA | 20 |
| 3. Comte de Lambert | FRA | 19 |
| 4. Gabriel Veyre | FRA | 19 |
| 5. de Schlumberger | FRA | 19 |
| 6. Paul Desart | FRA | 19 |

**1904–1968** not held

**1972 Munich** C: 28, N: 16, D: 9.1. WR: 566 (Göete Gåård)

| | | PTS. | |
|---|---|---|---|
| 1. Lakov Zhelezniak | SOV | 569 | WR |
| 2. Helmut Bellingrodt | COL | 565 | |
| 3. John Kynoch | GBR | 562 | |
| 4. Valery Postoianov | SOV | 560 | |
| 5. Christoph-Michael Zeisner | GER | 554 | |
| 6. Göete Gåård | SWE | 553 | |
| 7. Günther Danne | GER | 551 | |
| 8. Karl-Axel Karlsson | SWE | 551 | |

**1976 Montreal** C: 27, N: 16, D: 7.23. WR: 577 (Helmut Bellingrodt, Valery Postoianov)

| | | PTS. | |
|---|---|---|---|
| 1. Aleksandr Gazov | SOV | 579 | WR |
| 2. Aleksandr Kedyarov | SOV | 576 | |
| 3. Jerzy Greszkiewicz | POL | 571 | |
| 4. Thomas Pfeffer | GDR | 571 | |
| 5. Wolfgang Hamberger | GER | 567 | |
| 6. Helmut Bellingrodt | COL | 567 | |
| 7. Karl Karlsson | SWE | 565 | |
| 8. Louis Theimer | USA | 564 | |

**1980 Moscow** C: 19, N: 11, D: 7.24. WR: 581 (Thomas Pfeffer)

| | | PTS. | |
|---|---|---|---|
| 1. Igor Sokolov | SOV | 589 | WR |
| 2. Thomas Pfeffer | GDR | 589 | |
| 3. Aleksandr Gazov | SOV | 587 | |
| 4. András Doleschall | HUN | 584 | |
| 5. Tibor Bodnár | HUN | 584 | |
| 6. Jorma Lievonen | FIN | 584 | |
| 7. Giovanni Mezzani | ITA | 582 | |
| 8. Hans-Jürgen Helbig | GDR | 579 | |

**1984 Los Angeles-Chino** C: 23, N: 15, D: 7.31. WR: 595 (Igor Sokolov)

| | | PTS. |
|---|---|---|
| 1. Li Yuwei | CHN | 587 |
| 2. Helmut Bellingrodt | COL | 584 |
| 3. Huang Shiping | CHN | 581 |
| 4. Uwe Schröder | GER | 581 |
| 5. David Lee | CAN | 580 |
| 6. Kenneth Skoglund | NOR | 576 |
| 7. Jorma Lievonen | FIN | 576 |
| 8. Ezio Cini | ITA | 576 |

**1988 Seoul** C: 23, N: 16, D: 9.23. WR:596 (Nikolai Lapin) 691 (Sergei Lusov, Nikolai Lapin)

| | | PTS. |
|---|---|---|
| 1. Tor Heiestad | NOR | 689 |
| 2. Huang Shiping | CHN | 687 |
| 3. Gennady Avramenko | SOV | 686 |
| 4. Ján Kermiet | CZE | 679 |
| 5. András Doleschall | HUN | 588 |
| 6. Attila Solti | HUN | 588 |
| 7. Thomas Pfeffer | GDR | 587 |
| 8. Christian Stützinger | GER | 586 |

Heiestad was a 26-year-old farm mechanic from Oslo.

# Discontinued Events
## RAPID-FIRE PISTOL TEAMS

**1920 Antwerp** T: 8, N: 8, D: 8.3.
*(30 Meters)*

| | | TOTAL PTS. |
|---|---|---|
| 1. USA | (Louis Harant, Alfred Lane, Karl Frederick, James Snook, Michael Kelly) | 1310 |
| 2. GRE | (Alexandros Theophilakis, Ioannis Theophilakis, Georgios Moraitinis, Alexandros Vrasivanopoulos, Iason Sappas) | 1285 |
| 3. SWI | (Fritz Zulauf, Joseph Jehle, Gustave Amoudruz, Hans Egli, Domenico Giambonini) | 1270 |
| 4. BRA | (Afranio Da Costa, Sebastião Wolf, Dario Barbosa, Fernando Soledade, Guilherme Paraense) | 1261 |

| | | |
|---|---|---|
| 5. FRA | (Joseph Pecchia, Maujean, Léon Johnson, Emile Boitout, André Regaud) | 1239 |
| 6. SPA | (José Bento Lopez, Luis Calvet Sandoz, Antônio Bonilla Sanmartin, Antônio Vasquez de Aldana, José Maria Trepat Miro) | 1224 |
| 7. BEL | (Paul van Asbroek, Norbert van Molle, Philippe Cammaerts, Robert Andrieux, Bastin, de Coster) | 1221 |
| 8. POR | (Herminio Rebelo, Antônio Dos Santos, Antônio Soares Ferreira Damiao, Antônio da Silva Martins, Dario Cannas) | 1184 |

## FREE PISTOL TEAMS

**1920 Antwerp** T: 12, N: 12, D: 8.2.
*(50 Meters)*

| | | TOTAL PTS. |
|---|---|---|
| 1. USA | (Karl Frederick, Alfred Lane, James Snook, Michael Kelly, Raymond Bracken) | 2372 |
| 2. SWE | (Anders Wilhelm Andersson, Casimir Reuterskiöld, Gunnar Gabrielsson, Sigvard Hultcrantz, Anders Johnson) | 2289 |
| 3. BRA | (Afranio da Costa, Guilherme Paraense, Sebastião Wolf, Dario Barbosa, Fernando Soledade) | 2264 |
| 4. GRE | (Alexandros Theophilakis, Ioannis Theophilakis, Georgios Moraitinis, Alexandros Vrosivanopoulos, Iason Sappas) | 2240 |
| 5. BEL | (Paul van Asbroek, Conrad Adrianono, Arthur Balbaert, Joseph Haesaerts, François Heyens) | 2229 |
| 6. FRA | (Joseph Pecchia, Maujean, Léon Johnson, Emile Boitout, André Regaud) | 2225 |
| 7. ITA | (Riccardo Ticchi, Alfredo Galli, Roberto Preda, Giancarlo Boriani, Raffaele Frasca) | 2224 |
| 8. DEN | (Jens Andersen, Niels Larsen, Lars Jörgen Madsen, Carl Pedersen, Otto Plantener) | 2159 |

Dr. James H. Snook of the gold-medal-winning U.S. team gained national notoriety in June of 1929 after he was arrested for first-degree murder. Snook, then a 48-year-old professor of veterinary medicine at Ohio State University, confessed to killing his 25-year-old mistress, Theora Hix, by beating her with a hammer following an overly violent sexual act. He was put to death in an electric chair eight months later.

## MILITARY REVOLVER

**1896 Athens** C: 16, N: 3, D: 4.10.
*(25 Meters)*

| | | PTS. |
|---|---|---|
| 1. John Paine | USA | 442 |
| 2. Sumner Paine | USA | 380 |
| 3. Nikolaos Dorakis | GRE | 205 |
| 4. Ioannis Phrangoudis | GRE | — |
| 5. Holger Nielsen | DEN | — |

The Paine brothers set a precedent for family involvement in the Olympics by taking first and second.

**1900–1904** not held

**1906 Athens** C: 31, N: 9, D: 4.24.
*(20 Meters)*

| | | PTS. |
|---|---|---|
| 1. Louis Richardet | SWI | 253 |
| 2. Alexandros Theophilakis | GRE | 250 |
| 3. Georgios Skotadis | GRE | 240 |
| 4. Konrad Stäheli | SWI | 240 |
| 5. Léon Moreaux | FRA | 239 |
| 6. Ludwig Ternajgo | AUT | 235 |
| 7. M. Triantaphilades | GRE | 235 |
| 8. Anastasios Metaxas | GRE | 233 |

**1906 Athens** C: 31, N: 9, D: 4.23.
*(20 Meters—Model 1873–74)*

| | | PTS. |
|---|---|---|
| 1. Jean Fouconnier | FRA | 219 |
| 2. Raoul de Boigne | FRA | 216 |
| 3. Hermann Martin | FRA | 215 |
| 4. Maurice Lecoq | FRA | 211 |
| 5. Ludwig Ternajgo | AUT | 208 |
| 6. Aristides Rangavis | GRE | 201 |
| 7. Louis Richardet | SWI | 199 |
| 8. A. Hronis | GRE | 198 |

This contest required the use of a Gras-type revolver first made in France in 1873.

# MILITARY REVOLVER TEAMS

**1900 Paris** T: 4, N: 4, D: 8.1.
*(50 Meters)*

| | | TOTAL PTS. |
|---|---|---|
| 1. SWI | (Conrad Karl Röderer, Konrad Stäheli, Louis Richardet, Friedrich Lüthi, Paul Probst) | 2271 |
| 2. FRA | (Achille Paroche, Louis Duffoy, Léon Moreaux, Trinité, Maurice Lecoq) | 2203 |
| 3. HOL | (G. van Haan, Henrik Sillem, Antonius Bouwens, Solko van den Bergh, Anthony Sweus) | 1876 |
| 4. BEL | (Rooman, Théves, Victor Robert, Eichorn, Lebègue) | 1823 |

**1904–1906** not held

**1908 London** T: 7, N: 7, D: 7.11.
*(50 Yards)*

| | | TOTAL PTS. |
|---|---|---|
| 1. USA | (James Gorman, Ira Calkins, John Dietz, Charles Axtell) | 1914 |
| 2. BEL | (Paul van Asbroek, Réginald Storms, Charles Paumier du Verger, René Englebert) | 1863 |
| 3. GBR | (J.A. Wallingford, Geoffrey Coles, Henry Lynch-Staunton, W. Ellicott) | 1817 |

| | | |
|---|---|---|
| 4. FRA | (A. Barbillat, André Regaud, Léon Moreaux, Jean Depassis) | 1750 |
| 5. SWE | (Wilhelm Carlberg, Eric Carlberg, Johan Hübner von Holst, Frans Albert Schartau) | 1732 |
| 6. HOL | (J. van der Kop, G.A. van den Bergh, Jan Johannes de Blécourt, Petrus ten Bruggencate) | 1632 |
| 7. GRE | (Frangiskos Mavromatis, Alexandros Theophilakis, Ioannis Theophilakis, Georgios Orphanidis) | 1576 |

**1912 Stockholm** T: 7, N: 7, D: 6.29.
*(30 Meters)*

| | | TOTAL PTS. |
|---|---|---|
| 1. SWE | (Wilhelm Carlberg, Eric Carlberg, Johan Hübner von Holst, Paul Palén) | 1145 |
| 2. RUS | (Amos de Kasch, Nikolai de Melnitsky, Pavel de Voyloshnikov, Georgi de Panteleymonov) | 1091/118 |
| 3. GBR | (Hugh Durant, Albert Kempster, Charles Stewart, Horatio Poulter) | 1107/117 |
| 4. USA | (Alfred Lane, Reginald Sayre, Walter Winans, John Dietz) | 1097/117 |
| 5. GRE | (Konstantinos Skarlatos, Ioannis Theophilakis, Frangiskos Mavromatis, Georgios Petropoulos) | 1057 |
| 6. FRA | (Edmond Sandoz, Charles de Jaubert, Marquis de Crequi-Montfort, Maurice Faure) | 1041 |
| 7. GER | (Bernhard Wandollek, Gerhard Bock, Georg Meyer, Heinrich Hoffmann) | 890 |

**1912 Stockholm** T: 5, N: 5, D: 7.2.
*(50 Meters)*

| | | TOTAL PTS. |
|---|---|---|
| 1. USA | (Alfred Lane, Henry Sears, Peter Dolfen, John Dietz) | 1916 |
| 2. SWE | (Georg de Laval, Eric Carlberg, Wilhelm Carlberg, Erik Boström) | 1849 |
| 3. GBR | (Horatio Poulter, Hugh Durant, Albert Kempster, Charles Stewart) | 1804 |
| 4. RUS | (Nikolai Panin [Kolomenkin], Grigory de Schesterikov, Pavel de Voyloshnikov, Nikolai de Melnitsky) | 1801 |
| 5. GRE | (Frangiskos Mavromatis, Ioannis Theophilakis, Konstantinos Skarlatos, Alexandros Theophilakis) | 1731 |

# DUELING PISTOL

**1906 Athens** C: 24, N: 7, D: 4.24.
*(20 Meters)*

| | | PTS. |
|---|---|---|
| 1. Léon Moreaux | FRA | 242 |
| 2. Cesare Liverziani | ITA | 233 |
| 3. Maurice Lecoq | FRA | 231 |
| 4. Konstantinos Skarlatos | GRE | 221 |
| 5. Ludwig Ternajgo | AUT | 218 |
| 6. Frangiskos Mavromatis | GRE | 214 |

**1906 Athens** C: 22, N: 7, D: 4.25.
*(25 Meters)*

|  |  | BULL'S-EYE/PTS. |
|---|---|---|
| 1. Konstantinos Skarlatos | GRE | 29/133 |
| 2. Johann Hubner von Holst | SWE | 27/115 |
| 3. Wilhelm Carlberg | SWE | 26/115 |
| 4. Gerald Merlin | GBR | 26/103 |
| 5. Sándor Török | HUN | 25/104 |
| 6. Léon Moreaux | FRA | 23/104 |
| 7. Sidney Merlin | GBR | 23/103 |
| 7. Ludwig Ternajgo | AUT | 23/103 |

# FREE RIFLE

**1896 Athens** C: 42, N: 7, D: 4.9.
*(200 Meters)*

|  |  | PTS. |
|---|---|---|
| 1. Pantelis Karasevdas | GRE | 2320 |
| 2. Paulos Pavlidis | GRE | 1978 |
| 3. Nikolaos Trikoupes | GRE | 1713 |
| 4. Anastasios Metaxas | GRE | 1701 |
| 5. Georgios Orphanidis | GRE | 1698 |
| 6. Viggo Jensen | DEN | 1640 |
| 7. Georgios Diamantis | GRE | 1456 |
| 8. A. Baumann | SWI | 1294 |

**1900–1904** not held

**1906 Athens** C: 25, N: 5, D: 4.28.
*(300 Meters, Any Position)*

|  |  | PTS. |
|---|---|---|
| 1. Marcel Meyer de Stadelhofen | SWI | 243 |
| 2. Konrad Stäheli | SWI | 238 |
| 3. Léon Moreaux | FRA | 234 |
| 4. Gudbrand Skatteboe | NOR | 230 |
| 5. Albert Helgerud | NOR | 230 |
| 6. Julius Braathe | NOR | 224 |
| 7. Raoul de Boigne | FRA | 224 |
| 8. Jean Fouconnier | FRA | 223 |

**1908 London** C: 49, N: 8, D: 7.11.
*(1000 Yards)*

|  |  | PTS. |
|---|---|---|
| 1. Joshua "Jerry" Millner | GBR | 98 |
| 2. Kellogg Kennon Casey | USA | 93 |
| 3. Maurice Blood | GBR | 92 |
| 4. Richard Barnett | GBR | 92 |
| 5. Ted Ranken | GBR | 92 |
| 6. T. Caldwell | GBR | 91 |
| 7. John Sellars | GBR | 91 |
| 8. S.H. Kerr | CAN | 91 |

The target for this long-range event was six feet by ten feet, with a 36-inch bull's-eye. Colonel Millner was well over 60 years old.

# FREE RIFLE TEAMS

**1906 Athens** T: 4, N: 4, D: 4.28.
*(300 Meters)*

|  |  | TOTAL PTS. |
|---|---|---|
| 1. SWI | (Konrad Stäheli, Jean Reich, Louis Richardet, Marcel Meyer de Stadelhofen, Alfred Grutter) | 4617 |
| 2. NOR | (Gudbrand Skatteboe, Albert Helgerud, Julius Braathe, Johann Möller, O. Holm) | 4534 |
| 3. FRA | (Jean Fouconnier, Léon Moreaux, Maurice Faure, Raoul de Boigne, Maurice Lecoq) | 4511 |

**1908 London** T: 9, N: 9, D: 7.11.
*(300 Meters)*

|  |  | TOTAL PTS. |
|---|---|---|
| 1. NOR | (Albert Helgerud, Ole Saether, Gudbrand Skatteboe, Olaf Saether, Einar Liberg, Julius Braathe) | 5055 |
| 2. SWE | (G. Adolf Jonsson, P. Olof Avidsson, Axel Jansson, Gustav Adolf Sjöberg, Claes Rundberg, Janne Gustafsson) | 4711 |
| 3. FRA | (Léon Johnson, Eugène Balme, André Parmentier, Albert Courquin, Maurice Lecoq, Raoul de Boigne) | 4652 |
| 4. DEN | (Niels Andersen, Lars Jörgen Madsen, Ole Olsen, Kristian Christensen, Christian Petersen, Hans Kristian Schultz) | 4543 |
| 5. BEL | (Charles Paumier du Verger, Paul van Asbroek, Ernest Ista, Henri Sauveur, Joseph Geens, Edouard Poty) | 4509 |
| 6. GBR | (J.A. Wallingford, H.I. Hawkins, C.W. Churcher, T.W. Raddall, J. Bostock, R.H. Brown) | 4355 |
| 7. HOL | (G.A. van den Bergh, C. Brosch, C. van Altenburg, A.W.J. de Gee, Uilke Vuurman, P.J. Druyaard) | 4130 |
| 8. FIN | (Frans Nassling, Gustaf Nyman, Heikki Huttunen, Voitto Kolko, Emil Nassling, Huvi Tulskunen) | 3962 |

**1912 Stockholm** T: 7, N: 7, D: 7.4.
*(300 Meters)*

|  |  | TOTAL PTS. |
|---|---|---|
| 1. SWE | (Mauritz Eriksson, C. Hugo Johansson, Erik Blomqvist, Carl Björkman, Bernhard Larsson, G. Adolf Jonsson) | 5655 |
| 2. NOR | (Gudbrand Skatteboe, Ole Saether, Östen Östensen, Albert Helgerud, Olaf Saether, Einar Liberg) | 5605 |
| 3. DEN | (Ole Olsen, Lars Jörgen Madsen, Niels Larsen, Lauritz Larsen, Niels Andersen, Jens Madsen Haislund) | 5529 |
| 4. FRA | (Paul Colas, Louis Percy, Léon Johnson, Pierre Gentil, Raoul de Boigne, Auguste Marion) | 5471 |
| 5. FIN | (Voitto Kolho, Heikki Huttunen, Gustaf Richard Nyman, Emil Holm, Huvi Tuiskunen, Vilho Vauhkonen) | 5323 |

| | | TOTAL PTS. |
|---|---|---|
| 6. SAF | (George Harvey, Robert Bodley, Robert Patterson, Andrew Smith, Ernest Keeley, George Whelan) | 4897 |
| 7. RUS | Paul de Waldaine, Theothan de Lebedoff, Alexander de Tillo, Constantin de Kalinine, Dimitri de Kouskoff, Paul de Lesche) | 4892 |

**1920 Antwerp** T: 14, N: 14, D: 7.31.
*(300 Meters)*

| | | TOTAL PTS. |
|---|---|---|
| 1. USA | (Morris Fisher, Carl Osburn, Dennis Fenton, Lloyd Spooner, Willis Lee) | 4876 |
| 2. NOR | (Östen Östensen, Otto Olsen, Olaf Sletten, Gudbrand Skatteboe, Albert Helgerud) | 4748 |
| 3. SWI | (Fritz Kuchen, Gustave Amoudruz, Schneeberger, Fahrner, Siegenthaler) | 4698 |
| 4. FIN | (Voitto Kolho, Kalle Lappalainen, Veli Nieminen, Magnus Wegelius, Vilho Vauhkonen) | 4668 |
| 5. DEN | (Niels Larsen, Peter Petersen, Niels Laursen, Anton Andersen, Lars Jörgen Madsen) | 4644 |
| 6. SWE | (Mauritz Eriksson, Carl Hugo Johansson, Erik Blomqvist, Viktor Knutsson, Leon Lagerlöf) | 4591 |
| 7. FRA | (Achille Paroche, Paul Colas, André Parmentier, Albert Regnier, Emile Rumeau) | 4487 |
| 8. HOL | (G.A. van den Bergh, A.H. Bouwens, H.M. Bouwens, C.M. van Dalen, P.J. Brussard) | 4383 |

**1924 Paris** T: 18, N: 18, D: 6.27.
*(400 + 600 + 800 Meters)*

| | | TOTAL PTS. |
|---|---|---|
| 1. USA | (Morris Fisher, Walter Stokes, Joseph Crockett, Chan Coulter, Sidney Hinds) | 676 |
| 2. FRA | (Emile Rumeau, Albert Courquin, Pierre Hardy, Georges Roes, Paul Colas) | 646 |

| | | |
|---|---|---|
| 3. HAI | (Ludovic Augustin, Astrel Rolland, Ludovic Valborge, Destin Destine, Eloi Metullus) | 646 |
| 4. SWI | (Jakob Reich, Arnold Rösli, Willy Schnyder, C. Stucheli, Albert Tröndle) | 635 |
| 5. FIN | (Aarne Valkama, Vilho Nieminen, Voitto Kolho, Heikki Huttunen, Johannes Theslöf) | 628 |
| 6. DEN | (Niels Larsen, Lars Jörgen Madsen, Anders Nielsen, Erik Saetter-Lassen, Peter Geltzer) | 626 |
| 7. SWE | (Carl Hugo Johansson, Ivar Wester, Mauritz Eriksson, Olle Ericsson, Gustaf Anderson) | 623 |
| 8. NOR | (Ludvig Larsen, Olaf Johansson, Willy Rogeberg, Halvard Angaard, Otto Olsen) | 594 |

France defeated Haiti in the shoot-off for second place. Lieutenant Sidney Hinds shot a perfect 50 for the U.S. team, a performance that was all the more remarkable considering that he was accidentally shot in the foot in the middle of the competition, when the Belgian rifleman beside him knocked his rifle to the ground in the midst of an argument with an official.

## FREE RIFLE, THREE POSITIONS

This event required 120 shots from 300 meters at a 39-inch target with a bull's-eye less than four inches in diameter. In other words, it was like shooting a bullet through an apple three football fields away.

**1896 Athens** C: 20, N: 3, D: 4.12.

| | | TOTAL PTS. |
|---|---|---|
| 1. Georgios Orphanidis | GRE | 1583 |
| 2. Ioannis Phrangoudis | GRE | 1312 |
| 3. Viggo Jensen | DEN | 1305 |
| 4. Anastasios Metaxas | GRE | 1102 |
| 5. Pantelis Karasevdas | GRE | 1039 |

**1900–1904** not held

**1906 Athens** C: 20, N: 4, D: 4.28. WR: 1004 (Charles Paumier de Verger)

| | | PRONE | KNEELING | STANDING | TOTAL PTS. |
|---|---|---|---|---|---|
| 1. Gudbrand Skatteboe | NOR | 339 | 310 | 324 | 973 |
| 2. Konrad Stäheli | SWI | 328 | 340 | 278 | 946 |
| 3. Jean Reich | SWI | 327 | 320 | 289 | 936 |
| 4. Louis Richardet | SWI | 332 | 338 | 265 | 935 |
| 5. Léon Moreaux | FRA | 322 | 317 | 293 | 932 |
| 6. Marcel Meyer de Stadelhofen | SWI | 306 | 324 | 296 | 926 |
| 7. Julius Braathe | NOR | 319 | 292 | 310 | 921 |
| 8. Maurice Lecoq | FRA | 309 | 305 | 300 | 914 |

**1908 London** C: 51, N: 10, D: 7.11. WR: 1004 (Charles Paumier de Verger)

| | | PRONE | KNEELING | STANDING | TOTAL PTS. |
|---|---|---|---|---|---|
| 1. Albert Helgerud | NOR | 340 | 292 | 277 | 909 |
| 2. Harry Simon | USA | 365 | 294 | 228 | 887 |

| | | | | | |
|---|---|---|---|---|---|
| 3. Ole Saether | NOR | 327 | 284 | 272 | 883 |
| 4. Gustav Adolf Sjöberg | SWE | 338 | 285 | 251 | 874 |
| 5. Janne Gustafsson | SWE | 324 | 283 | 265 | 872 |
| 6. Julius Braathe | NOR | 303 | 291 | 257 | 851 |
| 7. Axel Jansson | SWE | 312 | 296 | 235 | 843 |
| 8. Léon Johnson | FRA | 303 | 282 | 250 | 835 |

**1912 Stockholm** C: 84, N: 9, D: 7.2. WR: 1078 (Konrad Stäheli) |

| | | PRONE | KNEELING | STANDING | TOTAL PTS. |
|---|---|---|---|---|---|
| 1. Paul Colas | FRA | 362 | 342 | 283 | 987 |
| 2. Lars Jörgen Madsen | DEN | 330 | 333 | 318 | 981 |
| 3. Niels Larsen | DEN | 355 | 334 | 318 | 962 |
| 4. Carl Hugo Johansson | SWE | 341 | 326 | 292 | 959 |
| 5. Gudbrand Skatteboe | NOR | 343 | 308 | 305 | 956 |
| 6. Bernhard Larsson | SWE | 341 | 339 | 274 | 954 |
| 7. Albert Helgerud | NOR | 354 | 317 | 281 | 952 |
| 8. Tonnes Björkman | SWE | 340 | 322 | 285 | 947 |

**1920 Antwerp** C: 70, N: 14, D: 7.31. WR: 1078 (Konrad Stäheli) |

| | | PRONE | KNEELING | STANDING | TOTAL PTS. |
|---|---|---|---|---|---|
| 1. Morris Fisher | USA | 347 | 361 | 288 | 996 |
| 2. Niels Larsen | DEN | 328 | 341 | 320 | 989 |
| 3. Östen Östensen | NOR | 347 | 324 | 309 | 980 |
| 4. Carl Osburn | USA | 353 | 347 | 280 | 980 |
| 5. Gudbrand Skatteboe | NOR | 361 | 330 | 204 | 975 |
| 5. Lloyd Spooner | USA | 341 | 328 | 306 | 975 |
| 7. Mauritz Erikooon | SWE | — | — | — | 974 |
| 7. Voitto Kolho | FIN | 357 | 316 | 301 | 974 |

Sergeant Morris Fisher, who played the violin for relaxation, found himself too nervous to take the first shot in the standing position. After 20 minutes of standing at the firing line, aiming but not taking a shot, his coach ordered him to shoot even if he missed the target. Fisher shot wide but within the scoring rings, and then went on to win the match.

**1924 Paris** C: 73, N: 19, D: 6.27.
*(600 Meters)*

| | | PTS. |
|---|---|---|
| 1. Morris Fisher | USA | 95 |
| 2. Carl Osburn | USA | 95 |
| 3. Niels Larsen | DEN | 93 |
| 4. Walter Stokes | USA | 92 |
| 5. Ludovic Augustin | HAI | 91 |
| 6. Albert Courquin | FRA | 90 |
| 6. Ludovic Valborge | HAI | 90 |
| 8. Carl Hugo Johansson | SWE | 88 |

Fisher earned two gold medals in 1924 to go with the three he had won in 1920.

**1928–1936** not held

**1948 London** C: 46, N: 13, D: 8.6. WR: 1124 (E. Kivistik)

| | | PRONE | KNEELING | STANDING | TOTAL PTS. |
|---|---|---|---|---|---|
| 1. Emil Grünig | SWI | 390 | 375 | 355 | 1120 |
| 2. Pauli Janhonen | FIN | 387 | 376 | 351 | 1114 |
| 3. Willy Rögeberg | NOR | 382 | 373 | 357 | 1112 |
| 4. Kurt Johansson | SWE | 383 | 374 | 347 | 1104 |
| 5. Kullervo Leskinen | FIN | 389 | 368 | 346. | 1103 |
| 6. Olavi Elo | FIN | 379 | 359 | 357 | 1095 |
| 7. Halvor Kongsjorden | NOR | 384 | 373 | 336 | 1093 |
| 8. Holger Erbén | SWE | 380 | 367 | 344 | 1091 |

**1952 Helsinki** C: 32, N: 18, D: 7.27. WR: 1124 (E. Kivistik)

| | | PRONE | KNEELING | | STANDING | TOTAL PTS. | |
|---|---|---|---|---|---|---|---|
| 1. Anatoly Bogdanov | SOV | 388 | 376 | | 359 | 1123 | OR |
| 2. Robert Bürchler | SWI | 389 | 381 | WR | 350 | 1120 | |
| 3. Lev Vainshtein | SOV | 378 | 376 | | 355 | 1109 | |
| 4. August Hollenstein | SWI | 384 | 370 | | 354 | 1108 | |
| 5. Vilho Ylönen | FIN | 379 | 377 | | 351 | 1107 | |
| 6. Robert Sandager | USA | 384 | 371 | | 349 | 1104 | |
| 7. Holger Erbén | SWE | 347 | 376 | | 379 | 1102 | |
| 8. Walther Fröstell | SWE | 335 | 375 | | 389 | 1099 | |

**1956 Melbourne** C: 20, N: 14, D: 12.1. WR: 1143 (Anatoly Bogdanov)

| | | PRONE | | KNEELING | STANDING | TOTAL PTS | |
|---|---|---|---|---|---|---|---|
| 1. Vassily Borissov | SOV | 396 | WR | 383 | 359 | 1138 | OR |
| 2. Allan Erdman | SOV | 392 | | 385 | 360 | 1137 | |
| 3. Vilho Ylönen | FIN | 387 | | 382 | 359 | 1128 | |
| 4. Jorma Taitto | FIN | 392 | | 379 | 349 | 1120 | |
| 5. Constantin Antonescu | ROM | 386 | | 374 | 341 | 1101 | |
| 6. Nils Johan Sundberg | SWE | 384 | | 367 | 343 | 1094 | |
| 7. Anders Kvissberg | SWE | 389 | | 362 | 342 | 1093 | |
| 8. James Smith | USA | 381 | | 368 | 333 | 1082 | |

**1960 Rome** C: 39, N: 22, D: 9.5. WR: 1145 (Anatoly Bogdanov)

| | | PRONE | KNEELING | STANDING | TOTAL PTS. |
|---|---|---|---|---|---|
| 1. Hubert Hammerer | AUT | 390 | 379 | 360 | 1129 |
| 2. Hans Spillman | SWI | 397 | 377 | 353 | 1127 |
| 3. Vassily Borissov | SOV | 383 | 381 | 363 | 1127 |
| 4. Vilho Ylönen | FIN | 389 | 381 | 356 | 1126 |
| 5. Moissey Itkis | SOV | 380 | 379 | 365 | 1124 |
| 6. Vladimir Stiborik | CZE | 383 | 380 | 360 | 1123 |
| 7. John Foster | USA | 380 | 384 | 357 | 1121 |
| 8. Sandor Krebs | HUN | 386 | 373 | 359 | 1118 |

**1964 Tokyo** C: 30, N: 18, D: 10.15. WR: 1150 (August Hollenstein)

| | | PRONE | KNEELING | STANDING | TOTAL PTS. | |
|---|---|---|---|---|---|---|
| 1. Gary Anderson | USA | 382 | 384 | 377 | 1153 | WR |
| 2. Shota Kveliashvili | SOV | 389 | 389 | 366 | 1144 | |
| 3. Martin Gunnarsson | USA | 389 | 380 | 367 | 1136 | |
| 4. Aleksandr Gerasimenok | SOV | 396 | 376 | 363 | 1135 | |
| 5. August Hollenstein | SWI | 382 | 381 | 372 | 1135 | |
| 6. Esa Kervinen | FIN | 392 | 383 | 358 | 1133 | |
| 7. Kurt Müller | SWI | 392 | 385 | 354 | 1121 | |
| 8. Harry Köcher | GDR | 392 | 378 | 360 | 1130 | |

Gary Anderson was a theological student from Axtell, Nebraska.

**1968 Mexico City** C: 30, N: 16, D: 10.23. WR: 1156 (Gary Anderson)

| | | PRONE | | KNEELING | STANDING | TOTAL PTS. | |
|---|---|---|---|---|---|---|---|
| 1. Gary Anderson | USA | 394 | | 389 | 374 | 1157 | WR |
| 2. Vladimir Kornev | SOV | 398 | WR | 384 | 369 | 1151 | |
| 3. Kurt Müller | SWI | 395 | | 379 | 374 | 1148 | |
| 4. Shota Kveliashvili | SOV | 394 | | 383 | 365 | 1142 | |
| 5. Erwin Vogt | SWI | 398 | WR | 384 | 358 | 1140 | |
| 6. Hartmut Sommer | GER | 389 | | 384 | 358 | 1140 | |
| 7. John Foster | USA | 386 | | 386 | 368 | 1140 | |
| 8. Péter Sándor | HUN | 394 | | 376 | 368 | 1138 | |

Anderson, by now a 29-year-old army lieutenant and Presbyterian minister, told reporters that he intended to keep up his involvement in shooting "because I think it's important for a minister to be actively involved in what people are doing." He later became executive director of the National Rifle Association.

**1972 Munich** C: 33, N: 20, D: 9.2. WR: 1157 (Gary Anderson)

| | | PRONE | KNEELING | STANDING | | TOTAL PTS. |
|---|---|---|---|---|---|---|
| 1. Lones Wigger | USA | 394 | 382 | 379 | WR | 1155 |
| 2. Boris Melnik | SOV | 394 | 387 | 374 | | 1155 |
| 3. Lajos Papp | HUN | 394 | 391 | 304 | | 1140 |
| 4. Uto Wunderlich | GDR | 393 | 388 | 368 | | 1149 |
| 5. Karel Bulan | CZE | 394 | 382 | 370 | | 1146 |
| 6. Jaakko Minkkinen | FIN | 396 | 386 | 364 | | 1146 |
| 7. Lanny Bassham | USA | 389 | 387 | 368 | | 1144 |
| 8. Valentin Kornev | SOV | 391 | 387 | 365 | | 1143 |

# INDIVIDUAL MILITARY RIFLE

**1900 Paris** C: 30, N: 6, D: 8.5.
*(300 Meters, Three Positions)*

| | | PRONE | KNEELING | STANDING | TOTAL PTS |
|---|---|---|---|---|---|
| 1. Emil Kellenberger | SWI | 324 | 314 | 292 | 930 |
| 2. Anders Peter Nielsen | DEN | 330 | 314 | 277 | 921 |
| 3. Paul van Asbroek | BEL | 329 | 289 | 299 | 917 |
| 3. Ole Östmo | NOR | 312 | 308 | 297 | 917 |
| 5. Lars Jörgen Madsen | DEN | 301 | 299 | 305 | 905 |
| 6. Charles Paumier du Verger | BEL | 302 | 297 | 298 | 897 |
| 7. Achille Paroche | FRA | 332 | 287 | 268 | 887 |
| 8. Franz Böckli | SWI | 289 | 300 | 294 | 883 |

*(300 Meters, Standing)*

| | | PTS. |
|---|---|---|
| 1. Lars Jörgen Madsen | DEN | 305 |
| 2. Ole Östmo | NOR | 299 |
| 3. Charles Paumier du Verger | BEL | 298 |
| 4. Paul van Asbroek | BEL | 297 |
| 5. Franz Böckli | SWI | 294 |
| 6. Emil Kellenberger | SWI | 292 |
| 7. Jules Bury | BEL | 282 |
| 7. Alfred Grütter | SWI | 282 |

**(300 Meters, Kneeling)**

| | | PTS. |
|---|---|---|
| 1. Konrad Stäheli | SWI | 324 |
| 2. Emil Kellenberger | SWI | 314 |
| 2. Anders Peter Nielsen | DEN | 314 |
| 4. Paul van Asbroek | BEL | 308 |
| 5. Maximilaan Ravenswaaij | HOL | 306 |
| 6. Uilke Vuurman | HOL | 303 |
| 7. Franz Böckli | SWI | 300 |
| 8. Lars Jörgen Madsen | DEN | 299 |

**(300 Meters, Prone)**

| | | PTS. |
|---|---|---|
| 1. Achille Paroche | FRA | 332 |
| 2. Anders Peter Nielsen | DEN | 330 |
| 3. Ole Östmo | NOR | 329 |
| 4. Léon Moreaux | FRA | 325 |
| 5. Emil Kellenberger | SWI | 324 |
| 6. Henrik Sillem | HOL | 317 |
| 7. Auguste Cavadini | FRA | 316 |
| 8. Paul van Asbroek | BEL | 312 |
| 8. Uilke Vuurman | HOL | 312 |

**1904** not held

**1906 Athens** C: 31, N: 8, D: 4.24.
**(200 Meters, Standing or Kneeling)**

| | | PTS. |
|---|---|---|
| 1. Léon Moreaux | FRA | 187 |
| 1. Louis Richardet | SWI | 187 |
| 3. Jean Reich | SWI | 183 |
| 4. Johann Möller | NOR | 175 |
| 5. Maurice Faure | FRA | 173 |
| 6. Gerald Merlin | GBR | 169 |
| 7. Sidney Merlin | GBR | 166 |
| 8. Georgios Orphanidis | GRE | 165 |

**1906 Athens** C: 46, N: 11, D: 4.23.
**(300 Meters, Standing or Kneeling)**

| | | PTS. |
|---|---|---|
| 1. Louis Richardet | SWI | 238 |
| 2. Jean Reich | SWI | 234 |
| 3. Raoul de Boigne | FRA | 232 |
| 4. Léon Moreaux | FRA | 231 |
| 5. Maurice Lecoq | FRA | 224 |
| 6. Julius Braathe | NOR | 223 |
| 7. Marcel Meyer de Stadelhofen | SWI | 222 |
| 8. Gudbrand Skatteboe | NOR | 221 |

**1908** not held

**1912 Stockholm** C: 91, N: 12, D: 7.1.
**(300 Meters)**

| | | PTS. |
|---|---|---|
| 1. Sándor Prokopp | HUN | 97 |
| 2. Carl Osburn | USA | 95 |
| 3. Embret Skogen | NOR | 95 |
| 4. Nicolaos Levidis | GRE | 95 |
| 5. Nils Romander | SWE | 94 |

| | | |
|---|---|---|
| 6. Arthur Fulton | GBR | 92 |
| 7. Rezsö Velez | HUN | 92 |
| 8. Carl Flodström | SWE | 91 |

**1912 Stockholm** C: 85, N: 12, D: 7.1.
**(600 Meters, Any Position)**

| | | PTS. |
|---|---|---|
| 1. Paul Colas | FRA | 94 |
| 2. Carl Osburn | USA | 94 |
| 3. John Jackson | USA | 93 |
| 4. Allan Briggs | USA | 93 |
| 5. Philip Plater | GBR | 90 |
| 6. Verner Jernström | SWE | 88 |
| 7. Harcourt Ommundsen | GBR | 88 |
| 8. Charles Burdette | USA | 87 |

**1920 Antwerp** T: 49, N: 12, D: 7.29–30.
**(300 Meters, Prone)**

| | | PTS. |
|---|---|---|
| 1. Otto Olsen | NOR | 60 |
| 2. Léon Johnson | FRA | 59/58 |
| 3. Fritz Kuchen | SWI | 59/57 |
| 4. Vilho Vauhkonen | FIN | 59/56 |
| 5. Achille Paroche | FRA | 59/56 |
| 6. Erik Blomqvist | SWE | 58 |
| 6. Mauritz Eriksson | SWE | 58 |
| 6. Albert Helgerud | NOR | 58 |
| 6. Carl Hugo Johansson | SWE | 58 |
| 6. Olaf Sletten | NOR | 58 |
| 6. Lloyd Spooner | USA | 58 |

**1920 Antwerp** C: 48, N: 12, D: 7.29–30.
**(300 Meters, Standing)**

| | | PTS. |
|---|---|---|
| 1. Carl Osburn | USA | 56 |
| 2. Lars Jörgen Madsen | DEN | 55 |
| 3. Lawrence Nuesslein | USA | 54/56 |
| 4. Erik Saetter-Lassen | DEN | 54/52 |
| 5. Joseph Janssens | BEL | 54/47 |
| 6. Riccardo Ticchi | ITA | 54/44 |
| 7. Anders Peter Nielsen | DEN | 53 |
| 7. Anders Martinus Petersen | DEN | 53 |
| 7. Lloyd Spooner | USA | 53 |

**1920 Antwerp** C: 46, N: 11, D: 7.29–30.
**(600 Meters, Prone)**

| | | PTS. |
|---|---|---|
| 1. Carl Hugo Johansson | SWE | 59/58 |
| 2. Mauritz Eriksson | SWE | 59/56/6 |
| 3. Lloyd Spooner | USA | 59/56/5 |
| 4. Ioannis Theophilakis | GRE | 59/55 |
| 5. Erik Blomqvist | SWE | 58 |
| 5. Joseph Jackson | USA | 58 |
| 5. Olaf Sletten | NOR | 58 |
| 8. Poul Gerlow | DEN | 57 |
| 8. Joseph Lawless | USA | 57 |
| 8. Erik Ohlsson | SWE | 57 |

# MILITARY RIFLE TEAMS

### 1900 Paris T: 6, N: 6, D: 8.5.
*(300 Meters)*

| | | | TOTAL PTS. |
|---|---|---|---|
| 1. | SWI | (Emil Kellenberger, Franz Böckli, Konrad Stäheli, Louis Richardet, Alfred Grütter) | 4399 |
| 2. | NOR | (Ole Östmo, Hellmer Hermandsen, Tom Seeberg, Ole Saether, Olaf Frydenlund) | 4290 |
| 3. | FRA | (Achille Paroche, Léon Moreaux, Auguste Cavadini, Maurice Lecoq, René Thomas) | 4278 |
| 4. | DEN | (Anders Peter Nielsen, Lars Jörgen Madsen, Viggo Jensen, Laurids Worslund Jensen-Kjaer, Axel Kristensen) | 4265 |
| 5. | HOL | (Maximiliaan Ravenswaaij, Uilke Vuurman, Henrik Sillem, Antonlus Bouwens, Solko van den Bergh) | 4221 |
| 6. | BEL | (Paul van Asbroek, Charles Paumier du Verger, Jules Bury, Edouard Myin, Joseph Baras) | 4166 |

### 1904–1906 not held

### 1908 London T: 8, N: 8, D: 7.11.
*(200 + 500 + 600 + 800 + 900 + 1000 Yards)*

| | | | TOTAL PTS. |
|---|---|---|---|
| 1. | USA | (William Leushner, William Martin, C.B. Winder, Kellogg Kennon Casey, Albert Eastman, Charles Benedict) | 2531 |
| 2. | GBR | (Harcourt Ommundsen, Fleetwood Varley, Arthur Fulton, Philip Richardson, W.G. Padgett, J.E. Martin) | 2497 |
| 3. | CAN | (William Smith, Charles Crowe, B.M. Williams, D. McInnis, William Eastcott, S.H. Kerr) | 2439 |
| 4. | FRA | (Raoul de Boigne, Albert Courquin, Eugène Balme, Daniel Merillon, Léon Hecht, André Parmentier) | 2227 |
| 5. | SWE | (Claes Rundberg, O. Jörgensen, Janne Gustafson, Per Olof Arvidsson, Axel Jansson, Gustaf Adolf Jonsson) | 2213 |
| 6. | NOR | (Ole Saether, Einar Liberg, Gudbrand Skatteboe, Albert Helgerud, Mathias Glomnes, Jörgen Bruu) | 2192 |
| 7. | GRE | (Ioannis Theophilakis, Frangiskos Mavromatis, Alexandros Theophilakis, Georgios Orphanidis, Mathias Triantaphilades, D. Rediadis) | 1999 |
| 8. | DEN | (Niels Andersen, Kristian Christensen, L.P.M. Jensen, Niels Larsen, H. Jensen, Ole Olsen) | 1909 |

The Russians had sent word that they were going to enter a team, but when they finally arrived the competition was long over. It turned out that Russia was still operating on the Julian calendar, whereas the rest of the world was using the Gregorian calendar; the two calendars were 12 days apart.

### 1912 Stockholm T: 10, N: 10, D: 6.29.
*(200 + 400 + 500 + 600 Meters)*

| | | | TOTAL PTS. |
|---|---|---|---|
| 1. | USA | (Charles Burdette, Allan Briggs, Harry Adams, John Jackson, Carl Osburn, Warren Sprout) | 1687 |
| 2. | GBR | (Harcourt Ommundsen, Henry Burr, Edward Skilton, James Reid, Edward Parnell, Arthur Fulton) | 1602 |
| 3. | SWE | (Mauritz Eriksson, Verner Jernström, Carl Björkman, Tönnes Björkman, Bernhard Larsson, Carl Hugo Johansson) | 1570 |
| 4. | SAF | (George Harvey, Robert Bodley, Andrew Smith, Ernest Keeley, Charles Jeffreys, Robert Patterson) | |
| 5. | FRA | (Louis Percy, Paul Colas, Raoul de Boigne, Pierre Gentil, Léon Johnson, Maxime Lardin) | 1515 |
| 6. | NOR | (O. Christian Degnes, Arne Sunde, O.A. Jensen, Hans Nordvik, Olav Husby, Mathias Glomnes) | 1473 |
| 7. | GRE | (Frangiskos Mavromatis, Alexandros Theophilakis, S. Theophilakis, Nicolaos Levidis, Iakovos Theophilas, Spiridon Mostras) | 1445 |
| 8. | DEN | (Niels Andersen, Lars Jörgen Madsen, Rasmus Friis, Hans Schultz, Niels Larsen, Jens Hajslund) | 1419 |

### 1920 Antwerp T: 15, N: 15, D: 7.29.
*(300 Meters, Standing)*

| | | | TOTAL PTS. |
|---|---|---|---|
| 1. | DEN | (Lars Jörgen Madsen, Niels Larsen, Anders Petersen, Erik Saetter-Lassen, Anders Nielsen) | 266 |
| 2. | USA | (Carl Osburn, Lawrence Nuesslein, Lloyd Spooner, Willis Lee, Thomas Brown) | 255 |
| 3. | SWE | (Olle Ericsson, Carl Hugo Johansson, Leonard Lagerlöf, Walfrid Hellman, Mauritz Eriksson) | 255 |
| 4. | ITA | (Riccardo Ticchi, Camillo Isnardi, Luigi Favretti, Giancarlo Boriani, Sem De Ranieri) | 251 |
| 5. | FRA | (Léon Johnson, Achille Paroche, Emile Rumeau, André Parmentier, Georges Roe) | 249 |
| 6. | NOR | (Östen Östensen, Otto Olsen, Olaf Sletten, Albert Helgerud, Gudbrand Skatteboe) | 242 |
| 7. | FIN | (Voitto Kolho, Kalle Lapalainen, Vilho Vauhkonen, Karl Magnus Wegelius, Nestori Tolvonen) | 235 |
| 8. | SWI | (Fritz Kuchen, Albert Tröndle, Arnold Rösli, Walter Lienhard, Caspar Widner) | 234 |

### 1920 Antwerp T: 15, N: 15, D: 7.29.
*(300 Meters, Prone)*

| | | | TOTAL PTS. |
|---|---|---|---|
| 1. | USA | (Carl Osburn, Joseph Jackson, Lloyd Spooner, Morris Fisher, Willis Lee) | 289 |
| 2. | FRA | (Léon Johnson, Achille Paroche, Emile Rumeau, André Parmentier, Georges Roe) | 283 |

3. FIN (Voitto Kolho, Kalle Lappalainen, Heikki Veli Nieminen, Vilho Vauhkonen, Karl Magnus Wegelius) — TOTAL PTS. 281

4. SWI (Fritz Kuchen, Albert Tröndle, Arnold Rösli, Walter Lienhard, Caspar Widmer) — 281

5. SWE (Mauritz Eriksson, Erik Blomqvist, Carl Hugo Johansson, Thure Holmberg, Verner Jernström) — 281

6. NOR (Östen Östensen, Otto Olsen, Olaf Stetten, Albert Helgerud, Jacob Onsrud) — 280

7. SPA (José Bento Lopez, Antônio Bonilla Sanmartin, Domingo Somoza, Luis Calvet Sandoz, Antônio Moreira Montero) — 278

8. SAF (Robert Bodley, David Smith, Paxton, Frederick Morgan) — 276

**1920 Antwerp** T: 14, N: 14, D: 7.29–30, 8.2.
*(600 Meters, Prone)*

| | | TOTAL PTS. |
|---|---|---|
| 1. USA | (Dennis Fenton, Ollie Schriver, Willis Lee, Lloyd Spooner, Joseph Jackson) | 287/283/284 |
| 2. SAF | (David Smith, Robert Bodley, Ferdinand Buchanan, George Harvey, Frederick Morgan) | 287/283/279 |
| 3. SWE | (Carl Hugo Johansson, Mauritz Eriksson, Erik Blomqvist, Erik Ohlsson, Gustaf Adolf Jonsson) | 287/275 |
| 4. NOR | (Otto Olsen, Östen Östensen, Albert Helgerud, Olaf Sletten, Jacob Onsrud) | 282 |
| 5. FRA | (Léon Johnson, Achille Paroche, Emile Rumeau, André Parmentier, Georges Roe) | 280 |
| 6. SWI | (Fritz Kuchen, Albert Tröndle, Arnold Rösli, Walter Lienhard, Caspar Widmer) | 279 |
| 7. GRE | (Andreas Vichos, Ioannis Theophilakis, Alexandros Theophilakis, Konstantinos Kephalas, Vassilios Xylinakis, Emmanuel Peristerakis) | 270 |
| 8. FIN | Voitto Kolho, Kalle Lapalainen, Heikki Veli Nieminen, Vilho Vauhkonen, Karl Magnus Wegelius) | 268 |

**1920 Antwerp** T: 14, N: 14, D: 7.29.
*(300 + 600 Meters, Prone)*

| | | TOTAL PTS. |
|---|---|---|
| 1. USA | (Joseph Jackson, Willis Lee, Ollie Schriver, Carl Osburn, Lloyd Spooner) | 573 |
| 2. NOR | (Otto Olsen, Albert Helgerud, Olaf Sletten, Östen Östensen, Jacob Onsrud) | 565 |
| 3. SWI | (Schneeberger, Joseph Jehle, Weibel, Fritz Kuchen, E. Addor) | 563/280 |
| 4. FRA | (Léon Johnson, Achille Paroche, Emile Rumeau, André Parmentier, Georges Roe) | 563/276 |

5. SAF (David Smith, Robert Bodley, Ferdinand Buchanan, George Harvey, Frederick Morgan) — 560

6. SWE (Erik Blomqvist, Carl Hugo Johansson, Gustaf Adolf Jonsson, Mauritz Eriksson, Bror Andreasson) — 558

7. GRE (Andreas Vichos, Ioannis Theophilakis, Konstantinos Kephalas, Vassilios Xylinakis, Emmanuel Peristerakis) — 553

8. CZE (Rudolf Jelen, Josef Sucharda, Vaclav Hindl, Josef Linert, Antonin Brych) — 536

# SMALL-BORE RIFLE

**1908 London** C: 22, N: 5, D: 7.11.
*(25 Yards, Moving Target)*

| | | | PTS. |
|---|---|---|---|
| 1. | J.F. Fleming | GBR | 24 |
| 2. | M.K. Matthews | GBR | 24 |
| 3. | W.B. Marsden | GBR | 24 |
| 4. | Edward Newitt | GBR | 24 |
| 5. | Philip Plater | GBR | 22 |
| 6. | William Pimm | GBR | 21 |
| 7. | William Milne | GBR | 21 |
| 8. | Otto von Rosen | SWE | 18 |

*(25 Yards, Disappearing Target)*

| | | | PTS. |
|---|---|---|---|
| 1. | William Styles | GBR | 45 |
| 2. | H.I. Hawkins | GBR | 45 |
| 3. | Edward Amoore | GBR | 45 |
| 4. | William Milne | GBR | 45 |
| 5. | John Milne | GBR | 45 |
| 6. | A.W. Wilde | GBR | 45 |
| 7. | Wilhelm Carlberg | SWE | 45 |
| 8. | Harry Humby | GBR | 45 |

**1912 Stockholm** C: 36, N: 8, D. 7.5.
*(25 Meters, Disappearing Target)*

| | | | PTS. |
|---|---|---|---|
| 1. | Wilhelm Carlberg | SWE | 242 |
| 2. | Johan Hübner von Holst | SWE | 233 |
| 3. | Gustaf Ericsson | SWE | 231 |
| 4. | Joseph Pepé | GBR | 231 |
| 5. | Robert Cook Murray | GBR | 228 |
| 6. | Axel Gyllenkrok | SWE | 227 |
| 7. | William Pimm | GBR | 225 |
| 8. | Frederick Hird | USA | 221 |

**1920 Antwerp** C: 50, N: 10, D: 8.2.
*(50 Meters, Standing)*

| | | | PTS. |
|---|---|---|---|
| 1. | Lawrence Nuesslein | USA | 391 |
| 2. | Arthur Rothrock | USA | 386 |
| 3. | Dennis Fenton | USA | 385 |

# MINIATURE RIFLE TEAMS

**1908 London** T: 3, N: 3, D: 7.11.
*(50 + 100 Yards)*

| | | | TOTAL PTS. |
|---|---|---|---|
| 1. | GBR | (M.K. Matthews, Harry Humby, William Pimm, Edward Amoore) | 771 |
| 2. | SWE | (Wilhelm Carlberg, Eric Carlberg, Johan Hübner von Holst, Frans Albert Schartau) | 737 |
| 3. | FRA | (Paul Colas, André Regaud, Léon Lecuyer, Henri Bonnéfoy) | 710 |

**1912 Stockholm** T: 4, N: 4, D: 7.5.
*(25 Meters)*

| | | | TOTAL PTS. |
|---|---|---|---|
| 1. | SWE | (Johan Hübner von Holst, Eric Carlberg, Wilhelm Carlberg, Gustaf Boivie) | 925 |
| 2. | GBR | (William Pimm, Joseph Pepé, William Milne, William Styles) | 917 |
| 3. | USA | (Frederick Hird, Warren Sprout, Neil McDonnell, William Leushner) | 881 |
| 4. | GRE | (Ioannis Theophilakis, Frangiskos Mavromatis, Nicolaos Levidis, Iakovos Theophilas) | 716 |

**1912 Stockholm** T: 6, N: 6, D: 7.3.
*(50 Meters)*

| | | | TOTAL PTS. |
|---|---|---|---|
| 1. | GBR | (William Pimm, Edward Lessimore, Joseph Pepé, Robert Cook Murray) | 762 |
| 2. | SWE | (Arthur Nordenswan, Eric Carlberg, Ruben Örtegren, Wilhelm Carlberg) | 748 |
| 3. | USA | (Warren Sprout, William Leushner, Frederick Hird, Carl Osburn) | 744 |
| 4. | FRA | (Léon Johnson, Pierre Gentil, André Regaud, Maxime Lardin) | 714 |
| 5. | DEN | (Paul Gerlow, Lars Jörgen Madsen, Frants Nielsen, Hans Petter Denver) | 708 |
| 5. | GRE | (Ioannis Theophilakis, Iakovos Theophilas, Frangiskos Mavromatis, Nicolaos Levidis) | 708 |

**1920 Antwerp** T: 10, N: 10, D: 8.2.
*(50 Meters)*

| | | | TOTAL PTS. |
|---|---|---|---|
| 1. | USA | (Lawrence Nuesslein, Arthur Rothrock, Dennis Fenton, Willis Lee, Ollie Schriver) | 1899 |
| 2. | SWE | (Sigge Hultcrantz, Erik Ohlsson, J. Leon Lagerlöf, Ragnar Stare, Olle Ericsson) | 1873 |
| 3. | NOR | (Anton Olsen, Albert Helgerud, Sigvart Johansen, Olaf Saether, Östen Östensen) | 1866 |
| 4. | DEN | (Lars Jörgen Madsen, Erik Saetter-Lassen, Anders Nielsen, O. Wegener, Christian Möller) | 1862 |
| 5. | FRA | (Léon Johnson, Achille Paroche, Emile Rumeau, André Parmentier, Georges Roes) | 1847 |

| | | | |
|---|---|---|---|
| 6. | BEL | (Paul van Asbroek, Norbert van Molle, Phillippe Cammaerts, Victor Robert, Louis Andrieu) | 1785 |
| 7. | ITA | (Alfredo Galli, Raffaele Frasca, Peppy Campus, Franco Micheli, Riccardo Ticchi) | 1777 |
| 8. | SAF | (Lishman, Frederick Morgan, George Harvey, Robert Bodley, Paxton) | 1755 |

# RUNNING DEER SHOOTING, SINGLE SHOT

**1908 London** C: 15, N: 4, D: 7.11.

| | | | PTS. |
|---|---|---|---|
| 1. | Oscar Swahn | SWE | 25 |
| 2. | Ted Ranken | GBR | 24 |
| 3. | Alexander Rogers | GBR | 24 |
| 4. | Maurice Blood | GBR | 23 |
| 5. | Albert Joseph Kempster | GBR | 22 |
| 6. | W.R. Lane-Joynt | GBR | 21 |
| 7. | Walter Winans | USA | 21 |
| 8. | James Cowan | GBR | 21 |

In 1908, Oscar Swahn was already 60 years old when he won his *first* Olympic gold medal, taking a total of two gold and one bronze. In 1912 he won one gold and one bronze, and in Antwerp, in 1920, at the age of 72, he won his first silver medal as part of the Swedish double-shot running deer team. He died in 1927.

**1912 Stockholm** C: 34, N: 7, D: 7.1.

| | | | PTS. |
|---|---|---|---|
| 1. | Alfred Swahn | SWE | 41/20 |
| 2. | Åke Lundeberg | SWE | 41/17 |
| 3. | Nestori Toivonen | FIN | 41/11 |
| 4. | Karl Larsson | SWE | 39 |
| 5. | Oscar Swahn | SWE | 39 |
| 6. | Sven Arvid Lindskog | SWE | 39 |
| 7. | Heinrich Elbogen | AUI | 38 |
| 8. | Adolf Ture Cederström | SWE | 37 |

Although Oscar Swahn was able to finish only fifth in Stockholm, his 32-year-old son Alfred earned the gold medal after a three-way shoot-off. Alfred's Olympic career was even more successful than his father's. Between 1908 and 1924 he won nine medals—three gold, three silver, and three bronze.

**1920 Antwerp** C: 22, N: 4, D: 7.27.

| | | | PTS. |
|---|---|---|---|
| 1. | Otto Olsen | NOR | 43 |
| 2. | Alfred Swahn | SWE | 41/20 |
| 3. | Harald Natvig | NOR | 41/19 |
| 4. | — | FIN | 40 |
| 4. | — | FIN | 40 |
| 6. | Lawrence Nuesslein | USA | 38 |

**1924 Paris** C: 32, N: 8, D: 7.3.

|  |  |  | PTS. |
|---|---|---|---|
| 1. | John Boles | USA | 40 |
| 2. | Cyril Mackworth-Praed | GBR | 39 |
| 3. | Otto Olsen | NOR | 39 |
| 4. | Otto Hultberg | SWE | 39 |
| 5. | Martti Liuttula | FIN | 37 |
| 6. | Alfred Swahn | SWE | 37 |
| 7. | Einar Liberg | NOR | 36 |
| 8. | Harold Natvig | NOR | 36 |

## TEAM RUNNING DEER SHOOTING, SINGLE-SHOT

**1908 London** T: 2, N: 2, D: 7.11.

|  |  |  | TOTAL PTS. |
|---|---|---|---|
| 1. | SWE | (Alfred Swahn, Arvid Knöppel, Oscar Swahn, Ernst Rosell) | 86 |
| 2. | GBR | (Charles Nix, W.R. Lane-Joynt, W. Ellicott, Ted Ranken) | 85 |

**1912 Stockholm** T: 5, N: 5, D: 7.4.

|  |  |  | TOTAL PTS. |
|---|---|---|---|
| 1. | SWE | (Alfred Swahn, Oscar Swahn, Åke Lundeberg, Per Olof Arvidsson) | 151 |
| 2. | USA | (W. Neil McDonell, Walter Winans, William Leushner, William Libbey) | 132 |
| 3. | FIN | (Axel Fredrik Londen, Nestori Toivonen, Toivo Väänänen, Ernst Rosenqvist) | 123 |
| 4. | AUT | (Adolf Michel, Eberhard Steinböck, Peter Paternelli, Heinrich Ellbogen) | 115 |
| 4. | RUS | (Harry Blau, Basil de Skrotsky, Dmitri de Barkov, Aleksandr de Dobryansky) | 108 |

**1920 Antwerp** T: 4, N: 4, D: 7.26.

|  |  |  | TOTAL PTS. |
|---|---|---|---|
| 1. | NOR | (Harald Natvig, Otto Olsen, Ole Andreas Lilloe-Olsen, Einar Liberg, Hans Nordvik) | 178 |
| 2. | FIN | (Robert Tikkanen, Nestori Toivonen, Karl Magnus Wegelius, Kalle Lapalainen, Yrjö Kolho) | 159 |
| 3. | USA | (Thomas Brown, Lawrence Nuesslein, Lloyd Spooner, Carl Osburn, Willis Lee) | 158 |
| 4. | SWE | (Per Kinde, Karl Larsson, Bengt Lagercrantz, Alfred Swahn, Oscar Swahn) | 153 |

**1924 Paris** T: 6, N: 6, D: 7.3.

|  |  |  | TOTAL PTS. |
|---|---|---|---|
| 1. | NOR | (Ole Andreas Lilloe-Olsen, Einar Liberg, Harald Natvig, Otto Olsen) | 160 |

**2.** SWE (Alfred Swahn, Fredrik Landelius, Otto Hultberg, G. Mauritz Johansson) **154**

**3.** USA (John Boles, Walter Stokes, Chan Coulter, Dennis Fenton) **148**

**4.** GBR (Cyril Mackworth-Praed, Alexander Rogers, John Faunthorpe, John O'Leary) **136**

**5.** FIN (Karl Magnus Wegelius, Martti Liuttula, Jalo Urho Autonen, Robert Tikkanen) **130**

**6.** HUN (Gusztáv Szomjas, Rezsö Velez, Elemér Takács, László Szomjas) **97**

## RUNNING DEER SHOOTING, DOUBLE-SHOT

**1908 London** C: 15, N: 4, D: 7.11.

|  |  |  | PTS. |
|---|---|---|---|
| 1. | Walter Winans | USA | 46/44 |
| 2. | Ted Ranken | GBR | 46/41 |
| 3. | Oscar Swahn | SWE | 38 |
| 4. | Maurice Blood | GBR | 34 |
| 5. | Albert Kempster | GBR | 34 |
| 6. | W. Ellicott | GBR | 33 |
| 7. | Alexander Rogers | GBR | 33 |
| 8. | Ernst Rosell | SWE | 33 |

**1912 Stockholm** C: 20, N: 6, D: 7.3.

|  |  |  | PTS. |
|---|---|---|---|
| 1. | Åke Lundeberg | SWE | 79 |
| 2. | Edvard Benedicks | SWE | 74 |
| 3. | Oscar Swahn | SWE | 72 |
| 4. | Alfred Swahn | SWE | 68 |
| 5. | Per Olof Arvidsson | SWE | 68 |
| 6. | Sven Arvid Lindskog | SWE | 67 |
| 7. | Erik Sökjer-Petersén | SWE | 65 |
| 8. | E.W. Lindewald | SWE | 64 |

**1920 Antwerp** C: 23, N: 4, D: 7.27.

|  |  |  | PTS. |
|---|---|---|---|
| 1. | Ole Andreas Lilloe-Olsen | NOR | 82 |
| 2. | Fredrik Landelius | SWE | 77 |
| 3. | Einar Liberg | NOR | 71 |

**1924 Paris** C: 31, N: 8, D: 7.3.

|  |  |  | PTS. |
|---|---|---|---|
| 1. | Ole Andreas Lilloe-Olsen | NOR | 76 |
| 2. | Cyril Mackworth-Praed | GBR | 72 |
| 3. | Alfred Swahn | SWE | 72 |
| 4. | Fredrik Landelius | SWE | 70 |
| 5. | Einar Liberg | NOR | 70 |
| 6. | Robert Tikkanen | FIN | 69 |
| 7. | John Boles | USA | 64 |
| 8. | Karl Magnus Wegelius | FIN | 64 |

# TEAM RUNNING DEER SHOOTING, DOUBLE-SHOT

**1920 Antwerp** T: 4, N: 4, D: 7.26.

| | | | TOTAL PTS. |
|---|---|---|---|
| 1. | NOR | (Ole Andreas Lilloe-Olsen, Thorstein Johansen, Harald Natvig, Hans Nordvik, Einar Liberg) | 343 |
| 2. | SWE | (Alfred Swahn, Oscar Swahn, Fredrik Landelius, Bengt Lagercrantz, Edvard Benedicks) | 336 |
| 3. | FIN | (Robert Tikkanen, Nestori Toivonen, Karl Magnus Wegelius, Vilho Vauhkonen, Yrjö Kolho) | 285 |
| 4. | USA | (Thomas Brown, Willis Lee, Lawrence Nuesslein, Carl Osburn, Lloyd Spooner) | 282 |

**1924 Paris** T: 6, N: 6, D. 7.3.

| | | | TOTAL PTS. |
|---|---|---|---|
| 1. | GBR | (Cyril Mackworth-Praed, Allen Whitty, Herbert Perry, Philip Neame) | 263 |
| 2. | NOR | (Ole Andreas Lilloe-Olsen, Otto Olsen, Harald Natvig, Einar Liberg) | 262 |
| 3. | SWE | (Alfred Swahn, G. Mauritz Johansson, Fredrik Landelius, Axel Ekblom) | 250 |
| 4. | FIN | (Karl Magnus Wegelius, Jalo Urho Autonen, Martti Liuttula, Robert Tikkanen) | 239 |
| 5. | USA | (Chan Coulter, Walter Stokes, John Boles, Dennis Fenton) | 233 |
| 6. | CZE | (Miloslav Hlaváč, Josef Sucharda, Rudolf Jelen, Josef Hosa) | 204 |

# RUNNING DEER SHOOTING, SINGLE- AND DOUBLE-SHOT

**1952 Helsinki** C: 14, N: 7, D: 7.29. WR: 398 (Rolf Bergersen)

| | | | PTS. | |
|---|---|---|---|---|
| 1. | John Larsen | NOR | 413 | WR |
| 2. | Per Olof Sköldberg | SWE | 409 | |
| 3. | Tauno Mäki | FIN | 407 | |
| 4. | Rolf Bergersen | NOR | 399 | |
| 5. | B. Thorleif Kockgård | SWE | 397 | |
| 6. | Yrjö Miettinen | FIN | 392 | |
| 7. | Petr Nikolayev | SOV | 385 | |
| 8. | Vladimir Sevryugin | SOV | 383 | |

**1956 Melbourne** C: 11, N: 6, D: 12.4.

| | | | PTS. | |
|---|---|---|---|---|
| 1. | Vitaly Romanenko | SOV | 441 | OR |
| 2. | Per Olof Sköldberg | SWE | 432 | |
| 3. | Vladimir Sevryugin | SOV | 429 | |
| 4. | Miklós Kovács | HUN | 417 | |
| 5. | Miklós Kocsis | HUN | 416 | |
| 6. | Rolf Bergersen | NOR | 409 | |
| 7. | Benkt Austrin | SWE | 405 | |
| 8. | John Larsen | NOR | 390 | |

# TRAP (CLAY PIGEON) SHOOTING TEAMS

**1908 London** T: 4, N: 3, D: 7.11.

| | | | TOTAL PTS. |
|---|---|---|---|
| 1. | GBR | (Alexander Maunder, J.F. Pike, Charles Palmer, J.M. Postans, F.W. Moore, P. Easte) | 407 |
| 2. | CAN | (Walter Ewing, George Beattie, A.W. Westover, Mylie Fletcher, George Vivian, D. McMackon) | 405 |
| 3. | GBR | (George Whitaker, G.H. Skinner, John Butt, W.B. Morris, H.P. Creasey, R. Hutton) | 372 |
| 4. | HOL | (J.W. Wilson, I. Von Voorst, C. Viroly, E. Von Voorst, De Pallandt, R. de Favauge) | 174 |

**1912 Stockholm** T: 6, N: 6, D: 7.1.

| | | | TOTAL PTS. |
|---|---|---|---|
| 1. | USA | (Charles Billings, Ralph Spotts, John Hendrickson, James Graham, Edward Gleason, Frank Hall) | 532 |
| 2. | GBR | (John Butt, William Grosvenor, Harry Robinson Humby, Alexander Maunder, Charles Palmer, George Whitaker) | 511 |
| 3. | GER | (Erich Graf von Bernstorff, Freiherr von Zeidlitz und Leipe, Horst Goeldel, Albert Preuss, Erland Koch, Alfred Goeldel) | 510 |
| 4. | SWE | (Carl Wollert, Alfred Swahn, Johann Ekman, Hjalmar Frisell, Åke Lundeberg, Victor Wallenberg) | 243 |
| 5. | FIN | (Edvard Bacher, Karl Fazer, Robert Huber, Gustaf Adolf Schnitt, Emil Johannes Collan, Axel Fredrik Londen) | 233 |
| 6. | FRA | (Henri de Castex, Marquis de Crequi-Monfort, Edouard Creuzè de Lesser, André Fleury, Charles Jaubert, René Texier) | 90 |

**1920 Antwerp** T: 8, N: 8, D: 7.22.

| | | | TOTAL PTS. |
|---|---|---|---|
| 1. | USA | (Mark Arie, Frank Troeh, Frank Wright, Jay Clark, Horace Bonser, Forest McNeir) | 547 |
| 2. | BEL | (Albert Bosquet, Joseph Cogels, Emile Dupont, Henri Quersin, Louis van Tilt, Edouard Fesinger) | 503 |
| 3. | SWE | (Erik Lundqvist, Per Kinde, Fredrik Landelius, Alfred Swahn, Karl Richter, Erik Sökjer-Petersén) | 500 |
| 4. | GBR | (Harry Humby, William Grosvenor, W. Ellicot, George Whitaker, Ernest Pocock, Charles Palmer) | 488 |
| 5. | CAN | (George Beattie, Samuel Vance, William McLaren, Robert Montgomery, William Hamilton, Arue Oliver) | 474 |
| 6. | HOL | (R. de Favauge, Gerard van der Vliet, M. Pieter Waller, Emile Jurgens, F. Jurgens, Eduardus van Voorst tot Voorst) | 222 |

| | | TOTAL PTS. |
|---|---|---|
| 7. FRA | (André Fleury, Marcel Lafite, Henri de Castox, Augustin Berjat, René Texier, J. de Lareinty-Tholozau) | 210 |
| 7. NOR | (Oluf Kjör, Nordal Lunde, Harald Natvig, Thorstein Johansen, Hans Nordvik, Ole Andreas Lilloe-Olsen) | 210 |

**1924 Paris** T: 12, N: 12, D: 7.7.

| | | TOTAL PTS. |
|---|---|---|
| 1. USA | (Frank Hughes, Samuel Sharman, William Silkworth, Fred Etchen) | 363 |
| 2. CAN | (George Beattie, James Montgomery, Samuel Vance, John Black, Samuel Newton, William Barnes) | 360 |
| 3. FIN | (Konrad Huber, Robert Huber, Werner Ekman, Robert Tikkanen) | 360 |
| 4. SWE | (Erik Lundqvist, Fredrik Landelius, Alfred Swahn, Magnus Hallman) | 354 |
| 5. BEL | (Albert Bosquet, Louis d'Heur, Emile Dupont, Jacques Mouton) | 354 |
| 6. AUT | (Heinrich Bartosch, August Baumgartner, Hans Schödl, Erich Zoigner) | 347 |
| 7. NOR | (Ole Andreas Lilloe-Olsen, O. Wessmann-Kjaer, E. Holmsen, M. Stenersen) | 336 |
| 8. GBR | (John O'Leary, Enoch Jenkins, H.V. Larsen, Cyril Mackworth-Praed) | 328 |

## LIVE PIGEON SHOOTING

**1900 Paris** C: 4, N: 4, D: 6.27.

| | | BIRDS KILLED |
|---|---|---|
| 1. Léon de Lunden | BEL | 21 |
| 2. Maurice Faure | FRA | 20 |
| 3. Donald Mackintosh | AUS | 18 |
| 3. Crittenden Robinson | USA | 18 |

This disgusting event marked the only time in Olympic history when animals were killed on purpose.

# WOMEN

## SPORT PISTOL

The sport pistol competition is fired at a distance of 25 meters. The qualifying round is divided into two 30-shot stages: precision and rapid-fire. Six minutes are allowed for the precision stage. In the rapid-fire stage shots are taken at a turning target. The bull's-eye in the precision stage is 5 centimeters across. The rapid-fire target is 100 centimeters by 15 centimeters (about 4 by 6 inches). The final consists of 10 rapid-fire shots.

**1896–1980** not held

**1984 Los Angeles-Chino** C: 30, N: 21, D: 7.29. WR: 592 (G. Korsun)

| | | PTS. |
|---|---|---|
| 1. Linda Thom | CAN | 585/198 |
| 2. Ruby Fox | USA | 585/197 |
| 3. Patricia Dench | AUS | 583/196 |
| 4. Liu Haiying | CHN | 583/195 |
| 5. Kristina Fries | SWE | 581 |
| 6. Wen Zhifang | CHN | 578 |
| 7. Debora Srour | BRA | 578 |
| 8. Maria Macovei | ROM | 577 |

Linda Thom was a 40-year-old chef and caterer from Ottawa.

**1988 Seoul** C: 35, N: 24, D: 9.19. WR: 595 (Nino Salukvadze) 695 (Nino Salukvadze)

| | | PTS. |
|---|---|---|
| 1. Nino Salukvadze | SOV | 690 |
| 2. Tomoko Hasegawa | JPN | 686 |
| 3. Jasna Šekarić | YUG | 686 |
| 4. Lieselotte Breker | GER | 685 |
| 5. Ágnes Ferencz | HUN | 685 |
| 6. Kristina Fries | SWE | 685 |
| 7. Evelyne Manchon | FRA | 684 |
| 8. Marina Dobrancheva | SOV | 682 |

Nineteen-year-old Nino Salukvadze of Soviet Georgia also won a silver medal in the air pistol event.

## AIR PISTOL

Forty shots are taken from a distance of 10 meters with a time limit of 90 minutes. The top eight qualifiers take part in a 10-shot final with 75 seconds per shot.

**1896–1984** not held

**1988 Seoul** C: 37, N: 26, D: 9.21. WR: 389 (Marina Dobrancheva) 489 (Jasna Šekarić)

| | | PTS. | |
|---|---|---|---|
| 1. Jasna Šekarić | YUG | 489.5 | WR |
| 2. Nino Salukvadze | SOV | 487.9 | |
| 3. Marina Dobrancheva | SOV | 485.2 | |
| 4. Anne Goffin | BEL | 480.2 | |
| 5. Anke Völker | GDR | 479.3 | |
| 6. Liu Haiying | CHN | 476.9 | |
| 7. Lieselotte Breker | GER | 476.0 | |
| 8. Christine Strahalm | AUT | 472.6 | |

Salukvadke, who had won the sport pistol championship 2 days earlier, set a world record of 390 in the preliminary round. However, this left her only one point up on defending world champion Jasna Šekarić, who outshot her on seven of the first eight shots of the final to set a world record of her own. The battle for the bronze medal looked like it would be a tight contest between Breker and Dobrancheva. However, when the final began, Breker failed to get off her first shot before the time limit elapsed. She was forced to take a zero for the shot, which put her out of the running.

## SMALL-BORE RIFLE, THREE POSITIONS

The rules are the same as for the men's competition with the exception that 20 shots, rather than 40, are taken at each position.

**1896–1980** not held

**1984 Los Angeles-Chino** C: 27, N: 17, D: 8.2. WR: 592 (Marlies Helbig)

| | | PRONE | STAND-ING | KNEEL-ING | TOTAL |
|---|---|---|---|---|---|
| 1. Wu Xiaoxuan | CHN | 197 | 187 | 197 | 581 |
| 2. Ulrike Holmer | GER | 197 | 191 | 190 | 578 |
| 3. Wanda Jewell | USA | 194 | 189 | 195 | 578 |
| 4. Gloria Parmentier | USA | 199 | 187 | 190 | 576 |
| 5. Anne Grethe Jeppesen | NOR | 196 | 190 | 188 | 574 |
| 6. Jin Dongxiang | CHN | 193 | 183 | 195 | 571 |
| 7. Biserka Vrbek | YUG | 196 | 181 | 192 | 569 |
| 8. Mirjana Jovović | YUG | 196 | 182 | 191 | 569 |

Wu, who also won a bronze medal in the air rifle event, told reporters the secret of her success at the Olympics: "I just concentrated on the music of our national anthem and shot."

**1988 Seoul** C: 37, N: 21, D: 9.21. WR: 592 (Marlis Helbig, Anna Malukhina) 691.6 (Vessela Letcheva)

| | | PRONE | STAND-ING | KNEEL-ING | FINAL | TOTAL |
|---|---|---|---|---|---|---|
| 1. Sylvia Sperber | GER | 200 | 193 | 197 | 95.6 | 685.6 |
| 2. Vessela Letcheva | BUL | 199 | 192 | 192 | 100.2 | 683.2 |
| 3. Valentina Cherkasova | SOV | 198 | 193 | 195 | 95.4 | 681.4 |
| 4. Katja Klepp | GDR | 199 | 187 | 198 | 96.5 | 680.5 |
| 5. Sharon Bowes | CAN | 196 | 194 | 194 | 96.5 | 680.5 |
| 6. Anna Malukhina | SOV | 198 | 191 | 196 | 93.4 | 678.4 |
| 7. Launi Meili | USA | 197 | 190 | 195 | 94.5 | 676.5 |
| 8. Anita Karlsson | SWE | 198 | 193 | 192 | 93.4 | 676.4 |

After finishing eleventh in the air rifle event in 1984, Sylvia Sperber retired from the sport even though she was only 19 years old. She returned to competition three years later. In 1988 she equaled the world record in the air rifle, took a silver in that event at Seoul, and then, three days later, earned a gold in the three-position competition.

## AIR RIFLE

The shooters have 90 minutes to fire 40 shots at a target 10 meters away. The bull's-eye is 1 millimeter in diameter. The eight finalists take 10 more shots with a time limit of 75 seconds per shot.

**1896–1980** not held

**1984 Los Angeles-Chino** C: 33, N: 20, D: 7.31. WR: 395 (Anna Malukhina, Marlies Helbig)

| | | PTS. |
|---|---|---|
| 1. Pat Spurgin | USA | 393 |
| 2. Edith Gufler | ITA | 391 |
| 3. Wu Xiaoxuan | CHN | 389 |
| 4. Sharon Bowes | CAN | 388 |
| 5. Yvette Courault | FRA | 386 |
| 6. Gisela Sailer | GER | 385 |
| 7. Siri Landsem | NOR | 384 |
| 8. Sirpa Ylonen | FIN | 383 |

Just before the competition began, a friend gave Pat Spurgin the following advice: "Just be like a duck." After winning the gold medal, the surprisingly poised 18-year-old from Billings, Montana, explained that to be like a duck meant, "Sit still on the surface, but paddle like hell underneath."

**1988 Seoul** C: 45, N: 29, D: 9.18. WR: 399 (Vessela Letcheva, Éva Joó, Sylvia Sperber) 504.0 (Vessela Letcheva)

| | | PTS. |
|---|---|---|
| 1. Irina Shilova | SOV | 498.5 |
| 2. Sylvia Sperber | GER | 497.5 |
| 3. Anna Malukhina | SOV | 495.8 |
| 4. Zhang Qiuping | CHN | 494.7 |
| 5. Pirjo Peltola | FIN | 493.6 |
| 6. Launi Meili | USA | 493.3 |
| 7. Sharon Bowes | CAN | 493.1 |
| 8. Gabriele Bühlmann | SWI | 493.0 |

The favorite in this event, the first to be decided at the Seoul Olympics, was world champion, world record holder, and two-time Female Shooter of the Year, Vessela Letcheva of Bulgaria. Letcheva was the focus of heavy media attention in South Korea, where she was considered unusually beautiful. Unnerved by the pressure of celebrity, she finished in a tie for seventeenth place. A few minutes later, a Korean shooting official found Letcheva wailing and beating her head against a restroom wall. Three days later she came from behind to earn a silver medal in the three-position event.

# *MIXED*

## TRAP SHOOTING

In the trap or clay pigeon event, clay saucers four and a third inches in diameter are flung into the air at various angles. The shooter is allowed two shots with a shotgun at each saucer (or bird). According to current rules, after 150 targets, the top 24 shooters advance to a semifinal round and fire at 50 more targets. The 6 best semifinalists shoot 25 targets in the final.

**1896** not held

**1900 Paris** C: 51, N: 4, D: 7.15.

| | | | PTS. |
|---|---|---|---|
| 1. | Roger de Barbarin | FRA | 17 |
| 2. | René Guyot | FRA | 17 |
| 3. | Justinien de Clary | FRA | 17 |
| 4. | Cesar Bettex | FRA | 16 |
| 5. | Hilaret | FRA | 15 |
| 6. | Edouard Geynet | FRA | 13 |
| 7. | Merlin | GBR | 12 |
| 8. | De Schonen | ? | 12 |

**1904 St. Louis** not held

**1906 Athens** C: 12, N: 4, D: 4.26.
*Single Shot*

| | | | PTS. |
|---|---|---|---|
| 1. | Gerald Merlin | GBR | 24 |
| 2. | Ioannis Peridis | GRE | 24 |
| 3. | Sidney Merlin | GBR | 23 |
| 4. | Maurice Faure | FRA | 22 |
| 5. | Thanopoulos | GRE | 16 |
| 6. | I. Delpopoulos | GRE | 14 |
| 7. | Sándor Török | HUN | 12 |
| 8. | D. P. Petropoulos | GRE | 7 |

**1906 Athens** C: 10, N: 4, D: 4.26.
*Double Shot*

| | | | PTS. |
|---|---|---|---|
| 1. | Sidney Merlin | GBR | 15 |
| 2. | Anastasios Metaxas | GRE | 13 |
| 3. | Gerald Merlin | GBR | 12 |
| 4. | Ioannis Theophilakis | GRE | 11 |
| 5. | Maurice Faure | FRA | 9 |
| 6. | Jean Fouconnier | FRA | 8 |
| 6. | K. Tanopoulos | GRE | 8 |
| 6. | Sándor Török | HUN | 8 |

**1908 London** C: 61, N: 8, D: 8.11.

| | | | PTS. |
|---|---|---|---|
| 1. | Walter Ewing | CAN | 72 |
| 2. | George Beattie | CAN | 60 |
| 3. | Alexander Maunder | GBR | 57 |
| 3. | Anastasios Metaxas | GRE | 57 |
| 5. | Charles Palmer | GBR | 55 |
| 5. | A.W. Westover | CAN | 55 |
| 7. | Mylie Fletcher | CAN | 53 |
| 7. | R. Hutton | GBR/IRL | 53 |
| 7. | J.W. Wilson | HOL | 53 |

**1912 Stockholm** C: 61, N: 11, D: 7.2.

| | | | PTS. |
|---|---|---|---|
| 1. | James Graham | USA | 96 |
| 2. | Alfred Göldel | GER | 94 |
| 3. | Harry Blau | RUS | 91 |
| 4. | Harry Humby | GBR | 88 |
| 4. | Anastasios Metaxas | GRE | 88 |
| 4. | Albert Preuss | GER | 88 |
| 4. | Gustaf Adolf Schnitt | FIN | 88 |
| 4. | Freiherr von Zeidlitz und Leipe | GER | 88 |

**1920 Antwerp** C: 53, N: 9, D: 7.24.

| | | | PTS. |
|---|---|---|---|
| 1. | Mark Arie | USA | 95 |
| 2. | Frank Troeh | USA | 93 |
| 3. | Frank Wright | USA | 87 |
| 4. | Frederick Plum | USA | 87 |
| 5. | Horace Bonser | USA | 87 |
| 6. | Robert Montgomery | CAN | 86 |
| 7. | Nordal Lunde | NOR | 85 |
| 7. | Henri Quevsin | BEL | 85 |

**1924 Paris** C: 44, N: 14, D: 7.8.

| | | | PTS. | |
|---|---|---|---|---|
| 1. | Gyula Halasy | HUN | 98/8 | OR |
| 2. | Konrad Huber | FIN | 98/7 | OR |
| 3. | Frank Hughes | USA | 97 | |
| 4. | James Montgomery | CAN | 97 | |
| 5. | Louis d'Heur | BEL | 96/8 | |
| 6. | George Beattie | CAN | 96/7 | |
| 6. | Samuel Sharman | USA | 96/7 | |
| 6. | Samuel Vance | CAN | 96/7 | |

**1928–1948** not held

**1952 Helsinki** C: 40, N: 22, D: 7.26.

| | | | PTS. |
|---|---|---|---|
| 1. | George Généreux | CAN | 192 |
| 2. | Knut Holmqvist | SWE | 191 |
| 3. | Hans Liljedahl | SWE | 190 |
| 4. | František Čapek | CZE | 188 |
| 5. | Konrad Huber | FIN | 188 |
| 6. | Ioannis Koutsis | GRE | 187 |
| 7. | Galliano Rossini | ITA | 187 |
| 8. | Italo Bellini | ITA | 186 |

George Généreux, of Saskatoon, Saskatchewan, was only 17 years old when he won the Olympic championship. Holmqvist needed to score a perfect 25 on his last round to tie Généreux, but he missed his next to last shot.

**1956 Melbourne** C: 32, N: 18, D: 12.1.

| | | | PTS. | |
|---|---|---|---|---|
| 1. | Galliano Rossini | ITA | 195 | OR |
| 2. | Adam Smelczyński | POL | 190 | |
| 3. | Alessandro Ciceri | ITA | 188/24 | |
| 4. | Nikolai Mogilevsky | SOV | 188/23 | |
| 5. | Yuri Nikandrov | SOV | 188/22 | |
| 6. | František Čapek | CZE | 187 | |

SHOOTING, MIXED / 471

7. Knut Holmqvist      SWE   178
8. Hans Liljedahl      SWE   177

**1960 Rome** C: 51, N: 28, D: 10.1.

|   | | | PTS. |
|---|---|---|---|
| 1. | Ion Dumitrescu | ROM | 192 |
| 2. | Galliano Rossini | ITA | 191 |
| 3. | Sergei Kalinin | SOV | 190 |
| 4. | James Clark | USA | 188 |
| 5. | Hans Aasnes | NOR | 185 |
| 5. | Joseph Wheater | GBR | 185 |
| 7. | Adam Smelczyński | POL | 184 |
| 8. | Claude Foussier | FRA | 183 |
| 8. | Karni Singh | IND | 183 |

**1964 Tokyo** C: 51, N: 28, D: 10.17.

|   | | | PTS. | |
|---|---|---|---|---|
| 1. | Ennio Mattarelli | ITA | 198 | OR |
| 2. | Pavel Senitšev | SOV | 194/25 | |
| 3. | William Morris | USA | 194/24 | |
| 4. | Galliano Rossini | ITA | 194/23 | |
| 5. | Ion Dumitrescu | ROM | 193 | |
| 5. | Mario Lira | CHI | 193 | |
| 7. | John Braithwaite | GBR | 192 | |
| 8. | Joachim Marscheider | GDR | 191 | |

**1968 Mexico City** C: 59, N: 34, D: 10.19. WR: 198 (Ennio Mattarelli)

|   | | | PTS. | |
|---|---|---|---|---|
| 1. | John Braithwaite | GBR | 198 | EWR |
| 2. | Thomas Garrigus | USA | 196/25/25 | |
| 3. | Kurt Czekalla | GDR | 196/25/23 | |
| 4. | Pavel Senitšev | SOV | 196/22 | |
| 5. | Pierre Candelo | FRA | 195 | |
| 6. | Adam Smelczyński | POL | 195 | |
| 7. | Aleksandr Alipov | SOV | 195 | |
| 8. | John Primrose | CAN | 194 | |

The 43-year-old Braithwaite missed two of his first 13 shots, but then hit the last 187 in a row. A veterinary surgeon from Preston, near Liverpool, Braithwaite took up clay pigeon shooting because he could no longer stand to shoot real birds and animals and see them suffer.

**1972 Munich** C: 57, N: 33, D: 8.29. WR: 198 (Ennio Mattarelli, John Braithwaite, Silvano Basagni)

|   | | | PTS. | |
|---|---|---|---|---|
| 1. | Angelo Scalzone | ITA | 199 | WR |
| 2. | Michel Carrega | FRA | 198 | |
| 3. | Silvano Basagni | ITA | 195 | |
| 4. | Burckhardt Hoppe | GDR | 193 | |
| 5. | Johnny Påhlsson | SWE | 193 | |
| 6. | James Poindexter | USA | 192 | |
| 7. | John Primrose | CAN | 192 | |
| 8. | Marcos Olsen | BRA | 191 | |

**1976 Montreal** C: 44, N: 29, D: 7.20. WR: 199 (Angelo Scalzone, Michel Carrega)

|   | | | PTS. |
|---|---|---|---|
| 1. | Donald Haldeman | USA | 190 |
| 2. | Armando Silva Marques | POR | 189 |
| 3. | Ubaldesco Baldi | ITA | 189 |
| 4. | Burckhardt Hoppe | GDR | 186 |
| 5. | Aleksandr Androshkin | SOV | 185 |
| 6. | Adam Smelczyński | POL | 183 |
| 7. | John Primrose | CAN | 183 |
| 8. | Bernard Blondeau | FRA | 182 |

The low scores were due to poor weather conditions. In a sport where contestants are known to calm their nerves with alcohol or tranquilizers, it came as a shock when 65-year-old Paul Cerutti of Monaco was disqualified after it was found that he had been taking amphetamines. The stimulants did him little good anyway. He finished 43rd out of a field of 44.

**1980 Moscow** C: 34, N: 22, D: 7.22. WR: 199 (Angelo Scalzone, Michel Carrega)

|   | | | PTS. |
|---|---|---|---|
| 1. | Luciano Giovannetti | ITA | 198 |
| 2. | Rustam Yambulatov | SOV | 196/24/25 |
| 3. | Jörg Damme | GDR | 196/24/24 |
| 4. | Josef Hojny | CZE | 196/23 |
| 5. | Eladio Vallduvi | SPA | 195 |
| 6. | Aleksandr Asanov | SOV | 195 |
| 7. | Silvano Basagni | ITA | 194 |
| 8. | Burckhardt Hoppe | GDR | 192 |

The 34-year-old Giovannetti celebrated his victory by tossing his cap into the air and shooting a hole through it.

**1984 Los Angeles-Chino** C: 70, N: 42, D: 7.31. WR: 200 (Daniel Carlisle)

|   | | | PTS. |
|---|---|---|---|
| 1. | Luciano Giovannetti | ITA | 192/24 |
| 2. | Francisco Boza | PER | 192/23 |
| 3. | Daniel Carlisle | USA | 192/22 |
| 4. | Timo Nieminen | FIN | 191 |
| 5. | Michel Carrega | FRA | 190 |
| 6. | Eli Ellis | AUS | 190 |
| 7. | Terry Rumbel | AUS | 189 |
| 8. | Johnny Pahlsson | SWE | 189 |

Giovannetti, a gun-shop owner from Pistoia, finished strongly to become the first repeat winner in Olympic trap shooting. On May 22, 1990, bronze medalist Dan Carlisle broke an obscure world record by shooting down 3,172 clay targets in one hour.

**1988 Seoul** C: 49, N: 28, D: 9.20. WR: 200 (Daniel Carlisle) 224 (Miroslav Bednařík)

|   | | | PTS. |
|---|---|---|---|
| 1. | Dmitri Monakov | SOV | 222/8 |
| 2. | Miroslav Bednařík | CZE | 222/7 |
| 3. | Franz Peeters | BEL | 219/16 |
| 4. | Francisco Boza | PER | 219/15 |

|   |   |   | PTS. |
|---|---|---|------|
| 5. | Bean van Limbeek | HOL | 219/7 |
| 6. | Kazumi Watanabe | JPN | 216 |
| 7. | Urmas Saaliste | SOV | 194 |
| 8. | Arimatti Nummela | FIN | 194 |

Monakov, the defending world champion, and Bednařík, the 1986 world champion, both completed the semifinals with a score of 197 and then shot perfect rounds in the final. This necessitated a sudden death shoot-off. But first Monakov and Bednařík had to wait for the three-way shoot-off for third place. When their turn came, Monakov and Bednařík both hit their first seven shots, but the Czechoslovak missed his eighth bird, and when Monakov made his, the contest was over. Less than a year later, Bednařík was killed in a motorcycle accident. He was 24 years old.

## SKEET SHOOTING

Skeet shooting is similar to trap shooting in that the shooter, using a shotgun, fires at a flung four-and-a-third-inch clay saucer. However, in the skeet match, the shooter moves around to eight different stations and is sometimes thrown two "birds" at a time. The birds may be thrown up to three seconds after they are called. Whereas trap birds are sent out from ground level, in skeet they are released from two towers, one high, one low.

**1896–1964** not held

**1968 Mexico City** C: 52, N: 30, D: 10.22. WR: 198 (J. Faber, Konrad Wirnhier)

|   |   |   | PTS. |   |
|---|---|---|------|---|
| 1. | Yevgeny Petrov | SOV | 198/25 | EWR |
| 2. | Romano Garagnani | ITA | 198/24/25 | EWR |
| 3. | Konrad Wirnhier | GER | 198/24/23 | EWR |
| 4. | Yuri Tsuranov | SOV | 196 | |
| 5. | Pedro Gianella | PER | 194 | |
| 6. | Nicolas Atalah | CHI | 194 | |
| 7. | Jorge Jottar | CHI | 194 | |
| 8. | Panagiotis Xanthakos | GRE | 194 | |

**1972 Munich** C: 63, N: 37, D: 9.2. WR: 200 (Yevgeny Petrov, Yuri Tsuranov)

|   |   |   | PTS. |
|---|---|---|------|
| 1. | Konrad Wirnhier | GER | 195/25 |
| 2. | Yevgeny Petrov | SOV | 195/24 |
| 3. | Michael Buchheim | GDR | 195/23 |
| 4. | Joe Neville | GBR | 194 |
| 5. | Roberto Castrillo Garcia | CUB | 194 |
| 6. | Klaus Reschke | GDR | 193 |
| 7. | Elie Penot | FRA | 193 |
| 8. | Paschalis Georgiou | GRE | 192 |

World champion Yuri Tsuranov of the U.S.S.R. was so upset by a judge's call against him that he walked off the field. The jury decided to penalize him three birds for

leaving, but permitted him to continue the round. He ended up three points shy of a tie for first place and finished ninth instead.

**1976 Montreal** C: 68, N: 41, D: 7.24. WR: 200 (Yevgeny Petrov, Yuri Tsuranov, Jariel Zhgentii, Hans Kjeld Rasmussen, Wieslaw Gawlikowski)

|   |   |   | PTS. |   |
|---|---|---|------|---|
| 1. | Josef Panaček | CZE | 198 | EOR |
| 2. | Eric Swinkels | HOL | 198 | EOR |
| 3. | Wieslaw Gawlikowski | POL | 196 | |
| 4. | Klaus Reschke | GDR | 196 | |
| 5. | Franz Schitzhofer | AUT | 195 | |
| 6. | Edgardo Zachrisson | GUA | 194 | |
| 7. | Juan Avalos | SPA | 194 | |
| 8. | Jean Petitpied | FRA | 194 | |

**1980 Moscow** C: 46, N: 25, D: 7.26. WR: 199 (Joseph Clemmons)

|   |   |   | PTS. |
|---|---|---|------|
| 1. | Hans Kjeld Rasmussen | DEN | 196/25/25 |
| 2. | Lars-Göran Carlsson | SWE | 196/25/24 |
| 3. | Roberto Castrillo Garcia | CUB | 196/25/23 |
| 4. | Pavel Pulda | CZE | 196/24 |
| 5. | Celso Giardini | ITA | 196/24 |
| 6. | Guillermo Torres | CUB | 195 |
| 7. | Francisco Perez | SPA | 195 |
| 8. | Ari Westergard | FIN | 195 |

Because too many perfect scores had been achieved, the rules were changed to make the match speedier and more difficult.

**1984 Los Angeles-Chino** C: 69, N: 41, D: 8.4. WR: 200 (Matthew Dryke, Jan Hula)

|   |   |   | PTS. |   |
|---|---|---|------|---|
| 1. | Matthew Dryke | USA | 198 | EOR |
| 2. | Ole Riber Rasmussen | DEN | 196/25 | |
| 3. | Luca Scribani Rossi | ITA | 196/23 | |
| 4. | Johannes Pierik | HOL | 194 | |
| 5. | Anders Berglind | SWE | 194 | |
| 6. | Norbert Hofmann | GER | 194 | |
| 7. | Jorge Molina | COL | 194 | |
| 8. | Ian Hale | AUS | 193 | |

As a teenager, Matt Dryke performed as a trick shooter, shooting through washers and shooting speed skeet while riding a unicycle. Although he never gave up trick and fancy shooting, he also became involved in competitive shooting, entering the Olympics as the world record holder and prohibitive favorite. Spurred on by an enthusiastic crowd which unnerved other competitors, Dryke did not disappoint his supporters. In 1989 Dryke received a two-year suspension when he tested positive for cocaine.

**1988 Seoul** C: 52, N: 31, D: 9.24. WR: 200 (Matthew Dryke, Jan Hula, Ole Riber Rasmussen) 224 (Matthew Dryke, Luca Scribani Rossi, Ole Riber Rasmussen)

|   |   |   | PTS. |
|---|---|---|------|
| 1. | Axel Wegner | GDR | 222 |
| 2. | Alfonso de Iruarrizaga | CHI | 221 |

3. Jorge Guardiola     SPA    220
4. Daniel Carlisle       USA    220
5. Zhang Weigang     CHN    219
6. Jürgen Raabe       GDR    219
7. Luca Scribani Rossi   ITA     196
8. Firmo Emilio Roberti   ARG   196

Guardiola was awarded the bronze medal by virtue of his higher score over Carlisle in the final (24–23).

# SWIMMING

MEN | 200-Meter Individual Medley
50-Meter Freestyle | 400-Meter Individual Medley
100-Meter Freestyle | 4 × 100-Meter Freestyle Relay
200-Meter Freestyle | 4 × 200-Meter Freestyle Relay
400-Meter Freestyle | 4 × 100-Meter Medley Relay
1500-Meter Freestyle | Springboard Diving
100-Meter Backstroke | Platform Diving
200-Meter Backstroke | Water Polo
100-Meter Breaststroke | Discontinued Events
200-Meter Breaststroke |
100-Meter Butterfly |
200-Meter Butterfly |

## MEN

### 50-METER FREESTYLE

**1896–1900** not held

**1904 St. Louis** C: 9, N: 2, D: 9.6.
**(50 Yards—45.72 Meters)**

| | | | SWIM-OFF |
|---|---|---|---|
| 1. Zoltán Halmay | HUN | 28.2 | 28.0 |
| 2. J. Scott Leary | USA | 28.2 | 28.6 |
| 3. Charles Daniels | USA | — | |
| 4. David Gaul | USA | — | |
| 5. Leo Goodwin | USA | — | |
| 6. Raymond Thorne | USA | — | |

Halmay defeated Leary by a foot. However, the U.S. judge declared that Leary had won. A brawl broke out and went on for some time. Finally it was decided to call the race a dead heat and to have the two men swim again. After two false starts, Halmay was off quickly and won easily.

**1906–1984** not held

**1988 Seoul** C: 71, N: 44, D: 9.24. WR: 22.23 (Thomas Jager)
| 1. Matthew Biondi | USA | 22.14 | WR |
|---|---|---|---|
| 2. Thomas Jager | USA | 22.36 | |
| 3. Gennady Prigoda | SOV | 22.71 | |
| 4. Dano Halsall | SWI | 22.83 | |
| 5. Stefan Volery | SWI | 22.84 | |
| 6. Vladimir Tkashenko | SOV | 22.88 | |
| 7. Frank Henter | GER | 23.03 | |
| 8. Andrew Baildon | AUS | 23.15 | |

Prior to the Olympics, friendly rivals Tom Jager and Matt Biondi had faced each other 14 times at 50 meters. Jager, a psychology graduate from U.C.L.A., had won 10 of those confrontations, including the ones at the 1986 world championships and the 1988 Olympic trials. In fact, Biondi hadn't beaten Jager in two years. However, Biondi entered the final on a roll. Although his personal best in competition was a 22.33 set in 1986, he had beaten that time 50 times at the U.S. Olympic training camp. And in Seoul he had already won five medals, including three gold. In the final, Biondi was able to keep up with Jager's typically fast start and then power his way to the finish in world record time.

Peter Williams, a South African competing in the United States for the University of Indiana, was not allowed to take part in the Games. In April, Williams had clocked a 22.18 in a time trial without competitors. His time was not allowed as a world record, not because it was achieved outside of competition, but because Williams was a citizen of South Africa. Steve Crocker also did not compete, due to the rule limiting each nation to two entrants. Crocker's time of 22.65 at the U.S. trials, had he been given the opportunity to repeat it in Seoul, would have been good enough for the bronze medal. On the other hand, so would Dano Halsall's Olympic preliminary time of 22.61 or Gennady Prigoda's of 22.57.

### 100-METER FREESTYLE

**1896 Athens** C: 10, N: 4, D: 4.11.
| 1. Alfréd Hajós | HUN | 1:22.2 | OR |
|---|---|---|---|
| 2. Otto Herschmann | AUT | 1:22.8 | |

The first Olympic swimming contests were held outdoors in open water, in and around the Bay of Zea at Phaleron, near Piraeus, and were watched by 40,000 people on the shore. The weather had turned unusually cold, and on the morning of the competition the temperature in the water dropped to 55 degrees Fahrenheit (13 degrees Centigrade). The eventual winner of two of the three races, the 100 meters and the 1200 meters, was Alfréd Hajós, an 18-year-old from Budapest. Hajós recalled the experience of climbing into the water from the boat that had carried the 13 swimmers to the starting point: "The icy water almost cut into our stomachs. Until 70 meters it was a neck-and-neck race, but then I got my second wind and won the competition. My time wasn't anything to brag about."

Hajós was 13 years old when he felt compelled to become a good swimmer after his father drowned in the Danube River. In 1895 he won the 100-meter title at the unofficial European championships in Vienna. In 1902 he was a member of the first Hungarian national football team. Hajós went on to become a successful architect, winning a prize in the architectural division of the Olympic Art Contest in 1924. He was born Alfréd Guttmann, but, following the fashion among Eastern European Jews of the time, he competed under a pseudonym. Later he legally changed his name to Hajós.

**1900** not held

**1904 St. Louis** C: 8 or 9, N: 2, D: 9.5.
**(100 yards)**
| | | |
|---|---|---|
| 1. Zoltán Halmay | HUN | 1:02.8 |
| 2. Charles Daniels | USA | — |
| 3. J. Scott Leary | USA | — |
| 4. Francis Gailey | USA | — |
| 5. David Hammond | USA | — |
| 6. Leo Goodwin | USA | — |

Including the Intercalated Games of 1906, in which he won one gold medal and one silver, Halmay earned a total of nine Olympic medals: three gold, five silver, and one bronze.

**1906 Athens** C: 9, N: 5, D: 4.24. WR: 1:05.8 (Zoltán Halmay)
| | | |
|---|---|---|
| 1. Charles Daniels | USA | 1:13.4 |
| 2. Zoltán Halmay | HUN | 1:14.2 |
| 3. Cecil Healy | AUS | — |
| 4. Paul Radmilovic | GBR | — |
| 5. John Derbyshire | GBR | — |
| 6. Hjalmar Johansson | SWE | — |

**1908 London** C: 34, N: 12, D: 7.20. WR: 1:05.8 (Zoltán Halmay)
| | | |
|---|---|---|
| 1. Charles Daniels | USA | 1:05.6 WR |
| 2. Zoltán Halmay | HUN | 1:06.2 |
| 3. Harald Julin | SWE | 1:08.0 |
| 4. Leslie Rich | USA | — |

In 1908, 24-year-old Charles Daniels of New York City closed out his Olympic career, having won five gold medals, one silver, and two bronze, including the Intercalated Games of 1906.

**1912 Stockholm** C: 34, N: 12, D: 7.10. WR: 1:02.4 (Kurt Bretting)
| | | |
|---|---|---|
| 1. Duke Paoa Kahanamoku | USA | 1:03.4 |
| 2. Cecil Healy | AUS | 1:04.6 |
| 3. Kenneth Huszagh | USA | 1:05.6 |
| 4. Kurt Bretting | GER | 1:05.8 |
| 5. Walter Ramme | GER | 1:06.4 |
DNS: William Longworth (AUS)

Duke Paoa Kahinu Makoe Hulikohoa Kahanamoku was born on August 24, 1890, in the palace of Princess Ruth in Honolulu. At the time of his birth, Queen Victoria's son, the Duke of Edinburgh, was visiting Hawaii, so Kahanamoku's father named his own new son Duke in honor of the occasion. In Stockholm Kahanamoku impressed the European spectators with his powerful, smooth stroking, and quickly became one of the most popular figures at the Games. His first-round time of 1:02.6 was more than two seconds faster than any of the other swimmers. He won his second round heat in a leisurely 1:03.8, the fastest time of the round. Because of a misunderstanding, the three U.S. representatives, Kahanamoku, Kenneth Huszagh, and Perry McGillivray, failed to show up for the semifinals on Sunday evening July 7. Holding the final without them seemed absurd, so the three were allowed to take part in an extra heat on Tuesday, with the stipulation that to qualify for the final the winner would have to beat the time of William Longworth, who had finished third in the first heat in 1:06.2. If this happened, then the second-place finisher in the special heat would also advance to the final. Not wanting to take any chances, Duke Kahanamoku equaled Kurt Bretting's world record of 1:02.4, allowing Huszagh to qualify as well. In the final, the following day, Kahanamoku took the time to look back and survey the field at the halfway mark. Noting that he had a comfortable lead, he eased up a bit and still won by two yards.

**1920 Antwerp** C: 33, N: 15, D: 8.24/8.29. WR: 1:01.4 (Duke Paoa Kahanamoku)
**First Final**
| | | |
|---|---|---|
| 1. Duke Paoa Kahanamoku | USA | 1:00.4 WR |
| 2. Pua Kela Kealoha | USA | 1:02.2 |
| 3. William Harris | USA | 1:03.2 |
| 4. Norman Ross | USA | 1:03.8 |
| 5. William Herald | AUS | — |
| 6. George Vernot | CAN | — |
**Second Final**
| | | |
|---|---|---|
| 1. Duke Paoa Kahanamoku | USA | 1:01.4 |
| 2. Pua Kela Kealoha | USA | 1:02.6 |
| 3. William Harris | USA | 1:03.0 |
| 4. William Herald | AUS | 1:03.8 |
| 5. George Vernot | CAN | — |
DNS: Norman Ross (USA)

Kahanamoku equaled his own world record of 1:01.4 in the semifinals, and then set a new record of 1:00.4 in the final, to celebrate his 30th birthday. However, Herald claimed that he had been fouled by Ross, so the race was ordered reswum. The order of the finish was exactly the same the second time, except that Ross, who had won the 1500-meter championship the day after the first 100-meter final, didn't take part.

Kahanamoku eventually competed in four Olympics,

winning three gold medals and two silver. Later he appeared in several Hollywood films, usually as a Hawaiian king. He also played a major role in introducing the sport of surfing around the world.

**1924 Paris** C: 30, N: 15, D: 7.20. WR: 57.4 (Johnny Weissmuller)

| | | | |
|---|---|---|---|
| 1. Johnny Weissmuller | USA | 59.0 | OR |
| 2. Duke Paoa Kahanamoku | USA | 1:01.4 | |
| 3. Samuel Kahanamoku | USA | 1:01.8 | |
| 4. Arne Borg | SWE | 1:02.0 | |
| 5. Katsuo Takaishi | JPN | 1:03.0 | |
| 6. Orvar Trolle (SWE) | | | |

Johnny Weissmuller was born to German Swabian parents in what is now Romania on June 2, 1904. His family emigrated to the United States in 1908. His father worked as a coal miner before moving to Chicago, where he died of tuberculosis before his son had started on the path to fame and fortune. On July 9, 1922, Johnny made swimming history by becoming the first person to swim 100 meters in less than one minute. On February 17, 1924, he lowered his time from 58.6 to 57.4, establishing a world record that would last for ten years. At the start of the 100-meter final at the Paris Olympics, Weissmuller found himself with 34-year-old defending champion Duke Kahanamoku on one side of him and Duke's 19-year-old brother, Sam, on the other side. Weissmuller was worried that the two Hawaiians had planned to swim a team race against him, but as they stood above the water Duke turned to him and said, "Johnny, good luck. The most important thing in this race is to get the American flag up there three times. Let's do it." And they did, with Weissmuller starting quickly and winning easily. That day he also won a gold medal in the 4 × 200-meter relay and a bronze medal in water polo. Two days earlier he had won the 400-meter freestyle. Johnny Weissmuller was one of the most popular participants at the 1924 Olympics, delighting the tough Parisian crowd not only with his superb swimming, but also with a comedy diving act, which he put on several times between races with his partner, Stubby Kruger. After Weissmuller's 100 meters victory, the crowd of 7000 stood and called for him for two or three minutes, until it was announced that he would appear again later in the afternoon.

**1928 Amsterdam** C: 30, N: 17, D: 8.11. WR: 57.4 (Johnny Weissmuller)

| | | | |
|---|---|---|---|
| 1. Johnny Weissmuller | USA | 58.6 | OR |
| 2. István Bárány | HUN | 59.8 | |
| 3. Katsuo Takaishi | JPN | 1:00.0 | |
| 4. George Kojac | USA | 1:00.8 | |
| 5. Walter Laufer | USA | 1:01.0 | |
| 6. Walter Spence | CAN | 1:01.4 | |
| 7. Alberto Zorilla | ARG | 1:01.6 | |

Coming out of the midrace turn in the 100 meters final at Amsterdam, Weissmuller inadvertently gulped a mouthful of water and almost blacked out. He lost two yards, but regained his composure and went on to win the fourth of his five Olympic gold medals. A couple of years later Weissmuller was training for the 1932 Olympics, when he got an offer of $500 a week to work for the BVD Underwear Company, advertising swimsuits. Out in Hollywood one of his BVD photos was noticed, and he was invited to try out for the part of Tarzan. Needless to say, he got the part, and in 1932 Weissmuller made his film debut in *Tarzan, the Ape Man.* The first of four Olympic medalists to play the part of Tarzan in the movies (the others being Buster Crabbe, Herman Brix, and Glenn Morris), Weissmuller acted in 11 more Tarzan films in the next 16 years. Another activity he engaged in more than once was getting married, which he did five times.

In 1959 Johnny Weissmuller was taking part in a celebrity golf tournament in Havana during a period in which Fidel Castro's guerrilla troops were doing battle with the soldiers of the Batista government. Weissmuller was on his way to the golf course with some friends and a couple of bodyguards, when rebel soldiers suddenly appeared out of the bushes and surrounded their car. The guerrillas disarmed the guards and pointed their rifles at the decadent Yankee imperialists. But Weissmuller had the proper solution to an otherwise difficult situation. Slowly raising himself to his full height, he beat his chest with his fists and let out an enormous yell. After a moment of stunned silence, the revolutionaries broke into smiles of delight and began calling out, "Tarzan! Tarzan! *Bienvenido!* Welcome to Cuba!" Dropping their weapons, they crowded around Johnny, shaking his hand and asking for his autograph. After a few minutes Weissmuller and his party were not only not kidnapped, but they were actually given a rebel escort to the golf course.

**1932 Los Angeles** C: 22, N: 10, D: 8.7. WR: 57.4 (Johnny Weissmuller)

| | | |
|---|---|---|
| 1. Yasuji Miyazaki | JPN | 58.2 |
| 2. Tatsugo Kawaishi | JPN | 58.6 |
| 3. Albert Schwartz | USA | 58.8 |
| 4. Manuella Kalili | USA | 59.2 |
| 5. Zenjiro Takahashi | JPN | 59.2 |
| 6. Ramond Thompson | USA | 59.5 |

The 1932 men's swimming contests were highlighted by the fantastic performances of the Japanese, who stunned the Americans by winning the relay and by taking first and second in four of the five individual events. The first of these victories was recorded by 15-year-old Yasuji Miyazaki, who brought his schoolbooks with him to Los Angeles so that he wouldn't fall too far behind in his studies. Miyazaki had set an Olympic record of 58.0 in the semifinals.

**1936 Berlin** C: 45, N: 23, D: 8.9. WR: 56.4 (Peter Fick)

| | | |
|---|---|---|
| 1. Ferenc Csík | HUN | 57.6 |
| 2. Masanori Yusa | JPN | 57.9 |
| 3. Shigeo Arai | JPN | 58.0 |
| 4. Masaharu Taguchi | JPN | 58.1 |

| 5. | Helmut Fischer | GER | 59.3 |
| 6. | Peter Fick | USA | 59.7 |
| 7. | Arthur Lindegren | USA | 59.9 |

Between 1912 and 1944 there were only three world record holders for the 100-meter freestyle: Duke Kahanamoku (1912–1922), Johnny Weissmuller (1922–1934), and Peter Fick (1934–1944). After the first round it appeared that the final would be a contest between Fick and the three Japanese, Taguchi recording the fastest time of 57.5 (an Olympic record), followed by Fick's 57.6. The semifinals were won by Taguchi and Yusa in 57.9 and 57.5 respectively, with Fick looking unusually off form. However the final provided a major upset. While the Japanese and Americans raced against each other, a 22-year-old Hungarian medical student named Ferenc Csík sneaked up in the outside lane to win the race in his fastest time ever. Although there was no question of who had finished first, there was a good deal of controversy regarding the remaining places. Photos of the finish led observers to believe that the actual order was 2—Taguchi, 3—Yusa, 4—Fick, 5—Arai, 6—Fischer, 7—Lindegren.

Dr. Csík died in an air raid in 1945 while administering first aid to a wounded man.

**1948 London** C: 41, N: 20, D: 7.31. WR: 55.4 (Alan Ford)

| 1. | Walter Ris | USA | 57.3 | OR |
| 2. | Alan Ford | USA | 57.8 | |
| 3. | Géza Kádas | HUN | 58.1 | |
| 4. | Keith Carter | USA | 58.3 | |
| 4. | Alexandre Jany | FRA | 58.3 | |
| 6 | Per-Olof Olsson | SWE | 59.3 | |
| 7. | Zoltán Szilárd | HUN | 59.6 | |
| 8. | Taha El Gamal | EGY | 1:00.5 | |

Alex Jany led the 50-meter turn, but he was passed in the next 25 meters by Ford, Kádas, and Ris. In the last ten meters Wally Ris of Iowa surged past the others to take first place.

**1952 Helsinki** C: 61, N: 33, D: 7.27. WR: 55.4 (Alan Ford)

| 1. | Clarke Scholes | USA | 57.4 |
| 2. | Hiroshi Suzuki | JPN | 57.4 |
| 3. | Göran Larsson | SWE | 58.2 |
| 4. | Toru Goto | JPN | 58.5 |
| 5. | Géza Kádas | HUN | 58.6 |
| 6. | Rex Aubrey | AUS | 58.7 |
| 7. | Aldo Eminente | FRA | 58.7 |
| 8. | Ronald Gora | USA | 58.8 |

Scholes set an Olympic record of 57.1 in his preliminary heat.

**1956 Melbourne** C: 34, N: 19, D: 11.30. WR: 54.8 (Richard Cleveland)

| 1. | Jon Henricks | AUS | 55.4 | OR |
| 2. | John Devitt | AUS | 55.8 | |
| 3. | Gary Chapman | AUS | 56.7 | |
| 4. | Logan Reid Patterson | USA | 57.2 | |

| 5. | Richard Hanley | USA | 57.6 |
| 6. | William Woolsey | USA | 57.6 |
| 7. | Atsushi Tani | JPN | 58.0 |
| 8. | Aldo Eminente | FRA | 58.1 |

Jon Henricks was the first favorite to win the 100-meter freestyle since Johnny Weissmuller. His victory in the final was his 56th straight win at that distance over a three-year period. When asked the secret of his success, Henricks, who was as feisty as his good friend and fellow Olympic champion Dawn Fraser, once replied, "You see that goddamn pool there—well, if you want to get to the top of it, dive in and start swimming. You do that for three, four or five years, and every time you stop swimming your coach bawls you out. . . . You get a crazy ear disease from these tropical waters, but you've still got to keep on swimming. You get your head shaved to make you look like a zombie so that you will cut down water resistance, and you shave your legs for the same reason. You get invitations to a party and you write back regretting you are unable to attend owing to a prior engagement. That's a lie, of course, the only prior engagement is at the pool, going up and down, up and down, then up and down again. You finish going up and down and it's time to do some weightlifting—or maybe go to sleep while your coach goes out playing golf or fishing."

**1960 Rome** C: 51, N: 34, D: 8.26. WR: 54.6 (John Devitt)

| 1. | John Devitt | AUS | 55.2 | OR |
| 2. | Lance Larson | USA | 55.2 | OR |
| 3. | Manuel Dos Santos | BRA | 55.4 | |
| 4. | R. Bruce Hunter | USA | 55.6 | |
| 5. | Gyula Dobai | HUN | 56.3 | |
| 6. | Richard Pound | CAN | 56.3 | |
| 7. | Aubrey Burer | SAF | 56.3 | |
| 8. | Per-Ola Lindberg | SWE | 57.1 | |

Two leading contenders were absent from the final. An appendectomy just prior to the U.S. trials prevented Jeff Farrell from qualifying as one of the three American representatives, and defending champion Jon Henricks was eliminated in the semifinals as a result of intestinal problems developed on the way from Australia to Rome.

Dos Santos led the final at the turn, but Larson and Devitt passed him at 70 meters and finished in a near dead heat. Devitt congratulated Larson and left the pool in disappointment. Confusion developed, however, when the judges met to discuss their verdict. Of the three judges assigned the task of determining who had finished first, two voted for Devitt and one for Larson. However the second-place judges also voted 2-1 for Devitt. In other words, of the six judges involved, three thought Devitt had won and three thought Larson had won. When the electronic timers were consulted, it turned out that Larson had registered 55.1 seconds and Devitt 55.2. The unofficial paper tapes at the end of the pool also showed Larson winning—by four inches. Despite this evidence, the chief judge, who did not have any say in the matter according to the official rules, ordered Larson's time changed to 55.2 and gave the decision to Devitt. Four years of protests failed to change the result.

**1964 Tokyo** C: 66, N: 33, D: 10.12. WR: 52.9 (Alain Gottvalles)

| | | | |
|---|---|---|---|
| 1. Donald Schollander | USA | 53.4 | OR |
| 2. Robert McGregor | GBR | 53.5 | |
| 3. Hans-Joachim Klein | GER | 54.0 | |
| 4. Gary Ilman | USA | 54.0 | |
| 5. Alain Gottvalles | FRA | 54.2 | |
| 6. Michael Austin | USA | 54.5 | |
| 7. Gyula Dobai | HUN | 54.9 | |
| 8. Uwe Jacobsen | GER | 56.1 | |

The fastest times of the qualifying rounds, 54.0 and 53.9, were recorded by Gary Ilman, with Don Schollander close behind at 54.3 and 54.0. In the final, however, Ilman ran into a wave just after the turn and momentarily lost his concentration. Schollander finished strongly, passed McGregor in the last five meters, and won by about six inches. Schollander, who was born in Charlotte, North Carolina, and raised in Lake Oswego, Oregon, was trained by George Haines in Santa Clara, California. Before the Tokyo Games were over, the 18-year-old Schollander had become the first swimmer to win four gold medals at one Olympics.

A minor controversy developed over the awarding of the bronze medal. The judges were split as to whether Ilman or Klein had finished third. Both were clocked in the same time. The Japanese had thoughtfully provided electronic timers for the swimming events and, even though they were not used officially, they were consulted by the judges. It turned out that Ilman and Klein had stopped the clock at the exact same hundredth of a second, but that Klein had finished one one-thousandth of a second sooner. After 35 minutes of consultation, the judges decided that even if the electronic timing was unofficial, it had provided sufficient cause to award third place to Klein.

**1968 Mexico City** C: 64, N: 35, D: 10.19. WR: 52.6 (Kenneth Walsh, Zachary Zorn)

| | | | |
|---|---|---|---|
| 1. Michael Wenden | AUS | 52.2 | WR |
| 2. Kenneth Walsh | USA | 52.8 | |
| 3. Mark Spitz | USA | 53.0 | |
| 4. Robert McGregor | GBR | 53.5 | |
| 5. Leonid Ilyichev | SOV | 53.8 | |
| 6. Georgi Kulikov | SOV | 53.8 | |
| 7. Luis Nicolao | ARG | 53.9 | |
| 8. Zachary Zorn | USA | 53.9 | |

Zac Zorn had equaled Ken Walsh's world record at the U.S. Olympic trials, and the Americans went to Mexico City as heavy favorites. But they hadn't counted on 18-year-old Michael Wenden of Liverpool, New South Wales. Wenden's heat time of 53.6 was seven-tenths of a second faster than anyone else's, and his semifinal time of 52.9 was a half-second better than the rest. In the final, Zac Zorn, weakened by a week-long illness, went all-out

for the first 50 meters and reached the turn almost a full body length ahead of the other swimmers. But he had exhausted himself, and eventually faded to last place. Wenden, on the other hand, swam the race of his life to score the most decisive 100-meter victory in 40 years.

**1972 Munich** C: 48, N: 30, D: 9.3. WR: 51.47 (Mark Spitz)

| | | | |
|---|---|---|---|
| 1. Mark Spitz | USA | 51.22 | WR |
| 2. Jerry Heidenreich | USA | 51.65 | |
| 3. Vladimir Bure | SOV | 51.77 | |
| 4. John Murphy | USA | 52.08 | |
| 5. Michael Wenden | AUS | 52.41 | |
| 6. Igor Grivennikov | SOV | 52.44 | |
| 7. Michel Rousseau | FRA | 52.90 | |
| 8. Klaus Steinbach | GER | 52.92 | |

Mark Spitz had three goals at the Munich Games. The first was to prove himself better than Don Schollander by becoming the first swimmer to win five gold medals in one Olympics. The second was to become the first athlete in any sport to win six gold medals in one Olympics. The third goal was to go one better and win seven gold medals. It was this final goal that Mark Spitz was having doubts about on September 1. He had already won five gold medals. A sixth gold medal seemed assured, since the final race of the Olympics, the medley relay, looked to be a certain U.S. victory. But about the 100-meter freestyle, Spitz was not so certain. Jerry Heidenreich had been swimming very well lately and had to be considered a serious threat. Spitz's father, Arnold, had constantly stressed to his son from an early age the motto "Swimming isn't everything, winning is." For Mark Spitz, it would have been better to enter four events and win all four than to enter seven events and win only six.

When he heard rumors that Spitz was thinking of withdrawing from the 100 freestyle, Spitz's coach, Sherm Chavoor, who was in Munich as the coach of the U.S. women's team, rushed over to see his student. Chavoor successfully convinced Spitz that he would be perceived as "chicken" if he avoided a confrontation with Heidenreich. Finding this an unacceptable option, Spitz decided against withdrawing.

The heats were swum on the morning of September 2, and the semifinals seven hours later. In both races Spitz held back and finished behind defending champion Michael Wenden and slower than Jerry Heidenreich. In the final the following night, Spitz surprised Heidenreich when he departed from his usual tactics by going out at full speed rather than saving his strength for the second lap, as he usually did. Spitz reached the turn with a clear lead. With 15 yards to go, Spitz suddenly lost his rhythm, but he pulled himself together and reached the wall a half-stroke ahead of the onrushing Heidenreich.

**1976 Montreal** C: 41, N: 28, D: 7.25. WR: 50.59 (Jim Montgomery)

| | | | |
|---|---|---|---|
| 1. Jim Montgomery | USA | 49.99 | WR |
| 2. Jim Babashoff | USA | 50.81 | |

| | | | |
|---|---|---|---|
| 3. Peter Nocke | GER | 51.31 | |
| 4. Klaus Steinbach | GER | 51.68 | |
| 5. Marcello Guarducci | ITA | 51.70 | |
| 6. Joe Bottom | USA | 51.79 | |
| 7. Vladimir Bure | SOV | 52.03 | |
| 8. Andrei Krylov | SOV | 52.15 | |

Montgomery won his semifinal heat in 50.39 to break his own world record. In the final he not only set another record, but he also became the first person to break the 50-second barrier for 100 meters. Three weeks later in Philadelphia, Jonty Skinner brought the record down to 49.44. Skinner was not allowed to compete in the Olympics because he was from South Africa. He later became a coach at the University of Alabama.

**1980 Moscow** C: 39, N: 27, D: 7.27. WR: 49.44 (Jonty Skinner)

| | | | |
|---|---|---|---|
| 1. Jörg Woithe | GDR | 50.40 | |
| 2. Per Holmertz | SWE | 50.91 | |
| 3. Per Johansson | SWE | 51.29 | |
| 4. Sergei Kopliakov | SOV | 51.34 | |
| 5. Raffaele Franceschi | ITA | 51.69 | |
| 6. Sergei Krasyuk | SOV | 51.80 | |
| 7. René Ecuyer | FRA | 52.01 | |
| 8. Graeme Brewer | AUS | 52.22 | |

Woithe recorded his best time ever, 50.21, in the semifinals. Three days after the boycotted Olympic final, the U.S. Outdoor National was won in 50.19 by Rowdy Gaines, who had twice clocked 49.61. Chris Cavanaugh was second in 50.26.

**1984 Los Angeles** C: 68, N: 44, D: 7.31. WR: 49.36 (Ambrose "Rowdy" Gaines)

| | | | |
|---|---|---|---|
| 1. Ambrose "Rowdy" Gaines | USA | 49.80 | OR |
| 2. Mark Stockwell | AUS | 50.24 | |
| 3. Per Johansson | SWE | 50.31 | |
| 4. Michael Heath | USA | 50.41 | |
| 5. Dano Halsall | SWI | 50.50 | |
| 6. Stephan Caron | FRA | 50.70 | |
| 6. Alberto Mestre Sosa | VEN | 50.70 | |
| 8. Dirk Korthals | GER | 50.93 | |

In 1980, Rowdy Gaines, then at the peak of his career, had been expected to win four gold medals. His dreams of triumph and glory were shattered by the U.S. boycott. He decided to stick it out until 1984 and qualified for the 100-meter freestyle by finishing second to Mike Heath at the U.S. trials. This time Gaines felt much less confident of victory. He even prepared a loser's speech in which he would graciously praise those swimmers who had beaten him. In the afternoon, between the qualifying heats and the final, a nervous Gaines tried to relax by watching "The Newlywed Game" and Woody Woodpecker cartoons on television. Only a talk with fellow swimmer Tracy Caulkins calmed him down temporarily.

But standing on the starting block before the race, Gaines, who, at 25, was older than 66 of his 67 rivals in Los Angeles, was trembling like a leaf. However, he still had the presence of mind to recall some important advice from his coach, Richard Quick. Quick had noticed that the starter for the men's swimming events, Frank Silvestri of Panama, was very quick to pull the trigger, so quick in fact that the U.S. team had protested against him at the 1983 Pan-American Games.

With this in mind, Gaines was ready for Silvestri and was first off the blocks, while leading contenders Mark Stockwell and Mike Heath were left behind. Gaines maintained his lead for the entire race, earning the first of his three gold medals.

**1988 Seoul** C: 77, N: 51, D: 9.22. WR: 48.42 (Matthew Biondi)

| | | | |
|---|---|---|---|
| 1. Matthew Biondi | USA | 48.63 | OR |
| 2. Christopher Jacobs | USA | 49.08 | |
| 3. Stephan Caron | FRA | 49.62 | |
| 4. Gennady Prigoda | SOV | 49.75 | |
| 5. Yuri Bashkatov | SOV | 50.08 | |
| 6. Andrew Baildon | AUS | 50.23 | |
| 7. Per Johansson | SWE | 50.35 | |
| 8. Tommy Werner | SWE | 50.54 | |

Six-foot-six-inch Matt Biondi had already recorded the 10 fastest 100-meter times in history, so his victory in Seoul was not surprising. Still, it was his first gold medal in an individual event and made up for his disappointment in losing the 100-meter butterfly by one one-hundredth of a second. When he climbed out of the Olympic pool after his victory, Biondi fulfilled a commercial contract by announcing to the TV cameras, "I'm going to Disneyland." And then, "I'm going to Disney World." The I.O.C. ordered NBC-TV to destroy the tape of Biondi's statement, which they did quickly. Silver medalist Chris Jacobs was a former cocaine and alcohol addict who gave up drugs and drink two years before the Games.

## 200-METER FREESTYLE

**1896** not held

**1900 Paris** C: 26, N: 9, D: 8.12. WR(220 yards): 2:38.2 (Frederick Lane)

**(220 Yards)**

| | | | |
|---|---|---|---|
| 1. Frederick Lane | AUS | 2:25.2 | OR |
| 2. Zoltán Halmay | HUN | 2:31.4 | |
| 3. Karl Ruberl | AUT | 2:32.0 | |
| 4. Richard Cranshaw | GBR | 2:45.6 | |
| 5. Maurice Hochepied | FRA | 2:53.0 | |
| 6. Stapleton | GBR | 2:55.0 | |

The unusually fast times were due to the fact that the 1900 swimming races were held in the River Seine and swum *with* the current. In honor of his victories in Paris, Lane was awarded a 50-pound bronze statue of a horse and an equally large bronze of Jean François Millet's *The Gleaners*.

**1904 St. Louis** C: 4, N: 2, D: 9.6 WR(220 yards): 2:28.6 (Frederick Lane)

**(220 Yards)**
| | | |
|---|---|---|
| 1. Charles Daniels | USA | 2:44.2 |
| 2. Francis Gailey | USA | 2:46.0 |
| 3. Emil Rausch | GER | 2:56.0 |
| 4. Edgar Adams | USA | — |

**1906–1964** not held

**1968 Mexico City** C: 57, N: 27, D: 10.24. WR: 1:54.3 (Donald Schollander)
| | | | |
|---|---|---|---|
| 1. Michael Wenden | AUS | 1:55.2 | OR |
| 2. Donald Schollander | USA | 1:55.8 | |
| 3. John Nelson | USA | 1:58.1 | |
| 4. Ralph Hutton | CAN | 1:58.6 | |
| 5. Alain Mosconi | FRA | 1:59.1 | |
| 6. Robert Windle | AUS | 2:00.9 | |
| 7. Semyon Belits-Geiman | SOV | 2:01.5 | |

DNS: Stephen Rerych (USA)

Michael Wenden won his second gold medal, while Don Schollander added a silver to his five golds. Afterward Schollander announced his retirement, telling reporters, "I'm finished with water—in fact I may not take a bath or a shower for another two years."

**1972 Munich** C: 46, N: 31, D: 8.29. WR: 1:53.5 (Mark Spitz)
| | | | |
|---|---|---|---|
| 1. Mark Spitz | USA | 1:52.78 | WR |
| 2. Steven Genter | USA | 1:53.73 | |
| 3. Werner Lampe | GER | 1:53.99 | |
| 4. Michael Wenden | AUS | 1:54.40 | |
| 5. Frederick Tyler | USA | 1:54.96 | |
| 6. Klaus Steinbach | GER | 1:55.65 | |
| 7. Vladimir Bure | SOV | 1:57.24 | |
| 8. Ralph Hutton | CAN | 1:57.56 | |

Spitz trailed Genter with 50 meters to go, but came from behind to win his third gold medal in two days. Genter's performance was remarkable for the fact that he underwent surgery in Munich for a partially collapsed lung and had been released from the hospital only the day before the race. On the victory platform Spitz waved his shoes at the crowd and the cameras. Called before an I.O.C. committee, he successfully convinced them that he had been motivated by exuberance rather than commercialism.

**1976 Montreal** C: 55, N: 33, D: 7.19. WR: 1:50.32 (Bruce Furniss)
| | | | |
|---|---|---|---|
| 1. Bruce Furniss | USA | 1:50.29 | WR |
| 2. John Naber | USA | 1:50.50 | |
| 3. Jim Montgomery | USA | 1:50.58 | |
| 4. Andrei Krylov | SOV | 1:50.73 | |
| 5. Klaus Steinbach | GER | 1:51.09 | |
| 6. Peter Nocke | GER | 1:51.71 | |
| 7. Gordon Downie | GBR | 1:52.78 | |
| 8. Andrei Bogdanov | SOV | 1:53.33 | |

Furniss moved ahead in the last 50 meters to edge Naber, who had won the 100-meter backstroke an hour earlier.

**1980 Moscow** C: 42, N: 25, D: 7.21. WR: 1:49.16 (Ambrose "Rowdy" Gaines)
| | | | |
|---|---|---|---|
| 1. Sergei Kopliakov | SOV | 1:49.81 | OR |
| 2. Andrei Krylov | SOV | 1:50.76 | |
| 3. Graeme Brewer | AUS | 1:51.60 | |
| 4. Jörg Woithe | GDR | 1:51.86 | |
| 5. Ron McKeon | AUS | 1:52.60 | |
| 6. Paolo Revelli | ITA | 1:52.76 | |
| 7. Thomas Lejdström | SWE | 1:52.94 | |
| 8. Fabrizio Rampazzo | ITA | 1:53.25 | |

On August 1, the U.S. Outdoor National was won by Rowdy Gaines in 1:50.02.

**1984 Los Angeles** C: 56, N: 36, D: 7.29. WR: 1:47.55 (Michael Gross)
| | | | |
|---|---|---|---|
| 1. Michael Gross | GER | 1:47.44 | WR |
| 2. Michael Heath | USA | 1:49.10 | |
| 3. Thomas Fahrner | GER | 1:49.69 | |
| 4. Jeffrey Float | USA | 1:50.18 | |
| 5. Alberto Mestre Sosa | VEN | 1:50.23 | |
| 6. Frank Drost | HOL | 1:51.62 | |
| 7. Marco Dell 'Uomo | ITA | 1:52.20 | |
| 8. Peter Dale | AUS | 1:53.84 | |

Standing 6 feet 7 inches and with a "wingspan" of 6 feet 11 inches, Michael Gross of Offenbach gained the nickname "The Albatross." In the 200-meter freestyle, Gross overwhelmed his opposition, winning by two bodylengths (two very long bodylengths) and becoming the first West German ever to win an Olympic swimming title.

**1988 Seoul** C: 63, N: 41, D: 9.19. WR: 1:47.44 (Michael Gross)
| | | | |
|---|---|---|---|
| 1. Duncan Armstrong | AUS | 1:47.25 | WR |
| 2. Anders Holmertz | SWE | 1:47.89 | |
| 3. Matthew Biondi | USA | 1:47.99 | |
| 4. Artur Wojdat | POL | 1:48.40 | |
| 5. Michael Gross | GER | 1:48.59 | |
| 6. Steffen Zesner | GDR | 1:48.77 | |
| 7. Troy Dalbey | USA | 1:48.86 | |
| 8. Thomas Fahrner | GER | 1:49.19 | |

A talent-rich field lined up for the final. Michael Gross was the world record holder at 200 meters, the defending Olympic champion, and the two-time defending world champion. Matt Biondi, the world record holder in the 100-meter freestyle, had clocked the fastest non-Gross time of the year. Artur Wojdat, the world record holder in the 400-meter freestyle, had registered the best time of the preliminaries: 1:48.02. Anders Holmertz, although barely qualifying for the Olympic final, had swum the fastest time of 1987 in winning the European championship.

Few people paid any attention to Duncan Armstrong of Brisbane. More should have, though—his qualifying time of 1:48.66 bettered his two-year-old pre-Olympic best by 1.3 seconds. Armstrong, who was ranked forty-sixth in the world at the time, appeared to be peaking at the right time.

Armstrong was coached by Lawrie Laurence, who had

coached Jon Sieben to an upset victory over Michael Gross in the 200-meter butterfly at the 1984 Olympics. Following the preliminaries of the Seoul 200-meter freestyle, Lawrence devised a special strategy for Armstrong in the final. He was assigned to lane 6 (as Sieben had been four years earlier) with Biondi beside him in lane 5. Because Biondi could be counted on to lead for the first 150 meters, Lawrence advised Armstrong to conserve energy by swimming as close to Biondi's lane as possible, drafting in the wake of the powerful American. Armstrong followed the strategy to perfection. Placed third at the final turn, he passed Holmertz and then slingshotted away from Biondi with 25 meters to go. His time of 1:47.25 ended Michael Gross' 5-year reign as world record holder.

## 400-METER FREESTYLE

**1896 Athens** C: 3, N: 2, D: 4.11.
**(500 Meters)**
| | | |
|---|---|---|
| 1. Paul Neumann | AUT | 8:12.6 |
| 2. Antonios Pepanos | GRE | 9:57.6 |
| 3. Eustathios Choraphas | GRE | |

**1900** not held

**1904 St. Louis** C: 4, N: 2, D: 9.7. WR(440 yards): 5:22.2
**(440 Yards)**
| | | |
|---|---|---|
| 1. Charles Daniels | USA | 6:16.2 |
| 2. Francis Gailey | USA | 6:22.0 |
| 3. Otto Wahle | AUT | 6:39.0 |
| 4. Leo Goodwin | USA | — |

**1906 Athens** C: 12, N: 5, D: 4.26. WR(440 yards): 5:19.0
| | | |
|---|---|---|
| 1. Otto Scheff | AUT | 6:23.8 |
| 2. Henry Taylor | GBR | 6:24.4 |
| 3. John Arthur Jarvis | GBR | 6:27.2 |
| 4. Alajos Bruckner | HUN | — |
| 5. Paul Radmilovic | GBR | — |
| 6. Cecil Healy | AUS | — |

**1908 London** C: 25, N: 10, D: 7.16. WR(440 yards): 5:19.0
| | | |
|---|---|---|
| 1. Henry Taylor | GBR | 5:36.8 |
| 2. Francis Beaurepaire | AUS | 5:44.2 |
| 3. Otto Scheff | AUT | 5:46.0 |
| 4. William Foster | GBR | — |

Henry Taylor of Oldham, Lancashire, won the first of his three gold medals at the London Games. Including the Intercalated Games of 1906 and the Olympics of 1912 and 1920, Taylor earned a total of four gold medals, one silver, and three bronze. This race also marked the first appearance of "Frank" Beaurepaire, who was still winning Olympic medals in 1924 at the age of 33. Beaurepaire missed the 1912 Olympics when he was suspended for professionalism. His crime? As part of his job as a physical education teacher, he lectured on swimming and lifesaving.

**1912 Stockholm** C: 26, N: 13, D: 7.14. WR: 5:23.0 (Frank Beaurepaire)
| | | |
|---|---|---|
| 1. George Hodgson | CAN | 5:24.4 |
| 2. John Hatfield | GBR | 5:25.8 |
| 3. Harold Hardwick | AUS | 5:31.2 |
| 4. Cecil Healy | AUS | 5:37.8 |
| 5. Béla Las-Torres | HUN | 5:42.0 |

Hodgson had won the 1500 meters four days earlier.

**1920 Antwerp** C: 20, N: 11, D: 8.28. WR: 5:14.6 (Norman Ross)
| | | |
|---|---|---|
| 1. Norman Ross | USA | 5:26.8 |
| 2. Ludy Langer | USA | 5:29.0 |
| 3. George Vernot | CAN | 5:29.6 |
| 4. Fred Kahele | USA | — |

DNF: Francis Beaurepaire (AUS), William Harris (USA)

Twenty-four-year-old Norman Ross also won gold medals in the 1500-meter freestyle and in the 4 × 200-meter relay. He later achieved success as a radio music announcer.

**1924 Paris** C: 23, N: 13, D: 7.18. WR: 4:54.7 (Arne Borg)
| | | | |
|---|---|---|---|
| 1. Johnny Weissmuller | USA | 5:04.2 | OR |
| 2. Arne Borg | SWE | 5:05.6 | |
| 3. Andrew "Boy" Charlton | AUS | 5:06.6 | |
| 4. Åke Borg | SWE | 5:26.0 | |
| 5. John Hatfield | GBR | 5:32.0 | |
| 6. Lester Smith (USA) | | | |

This was a thrilling race in which no more than five feet separated Weissmuller and Borg at any time. At 100 meters, Borg led by six inches. At the halfway mark, it was Weissmuller by nine inches, and at 300 meters, Borg touched first by three inches. Weissmuller finally drew away 20 meters from the finish and won by four feet.

Arne and Åke Borg were twin brothers.

**1928 Amsterdam** C: 26, N: 17, D: 8.9. WR: 4:50.3 (Arne Borg)
| | | | |
|---|---|---|---|
| 1. Alberto Zorilla | ARG | 5:01.6 | OR |
| 2. Andrew "Boy" Charlton | AUS | 5:03.6 | |
| 3. Arne Borg | SWE | 5:04.6 | |
| 4. Clarence "Buster" Crabbe | USA | 5:05.4 | |
| 5. Austin Clapp | USA | 5:16.0 | |
| 6. Raymond Ruddy | USA | 5:25.0 | |

Charlton and Borg were so intent on their personal duel that they failed to notice Zorilla creep up in the outside lane and move ahead in the last 50 meters.

**1932 Los Angeles** C: 19, N: 10, D: 8.10. WR: 4:47.0 (Jean Taris)
| | | | |
|---|---|---|---|
| 1. Clarence "Buster" Crabbe | USA | 4:48.4 | OR |
| 2. Jean Taris | FRA | 4:48.5 | |
| 3. Tsutomu Oyokota | JPN | 4:52.3 | |
| 4. Takashi Yokoyama | JPN | 4:52.5 | |
| 5. Noboru Sugimoto | JPN | 4:56.1 | |
| 6. Andrew "Boy" Charlton | AUS | 4:58.6 | |

Takashi Yokoyama set Olympic records of 4:53.2 and 4:51.4 in the opening round and the semifinals, but the final turned out to be a duel between world record holder Jean Taris and local favorite Buster Crabbe. Taris sprinted to an early lead and reached the halfway mark two lengths ahead. By 300 meters, Crabbe had cut the gap to one length. He continued to edge closer, finally drawing even 25 meters from the finish. The excitement was so great that swimmers and ushers rushed over from all parts of the stadium, while Johnny Weissmuller, sitting in the front row, leaped a fence to get a closer view of the finish. Crabbe touched the wall inches ahead of Taris. "That one-tenth of a second changed my life," Crabbe later recalled. "It was then that [the Hollywood producers] discovered latent histrionic abilities in me." Crabbe went on to great fame as an actor; he was best known for his roles as Tarzan, Buck Rogers, and Flash Gordon. He died on April 23, 1983, at the age of 75.

**1936 Berlin** C: 34, N: 16, D: 8.12. WR: 4:38.7 (Jack Medica)
1. Jack Medica       USA   4:44.5   OR
2. Shumpei Uto       JPN   4:45.6
3. Shozo Makino      JPN   4:48.1
4. Ralph Flanagan    USA   4:52.7
5. Hiroshi Negami    JPN   4:53.6
6. Jean Taris        FRA   4:53.8
7. Robert Leivers    GBR   5:00.9

Jack Medica of Seattle staged a thrilling last-lap spurt to overtake Uto ten meters from the finish.

**1948 London** C: 41, N: 21, D: 8.4. WR: 4:35.2 (Alexandre Jany)
1. William Smith     USA   4:41.0   OR
2. James McLane      USA   4:43.4
3. John Marshall     AUS   4:47.4
4. Géza Kádas        HUN   4:49.4
5. György Mitró      HUN   4:49.9
6. Alexandre Jany    FRA   4:51.4
7. Jack Hale         GBR   4:55.9
8. Alfredo Yantorno  ARG   4:58.7

Bill Smith had been stricken with typhoid when he was six years old, and took up swimming to rebuild his body.

**1952 Helsinki** C: 51, N: 29, D: 7.30. WR: 4:26.9 (John Marshall)
1. Jean Boiteux          FRA   4:30.7   OR
2. Ford Konno            USA   4:31.3
3. Per-Olof Östrand      SWE   4:35.2
4. Peter Duncan          SAF   4:37.9
5. John Wardrop          GBR   4:39.9
6. Wayne Moore           USA   4:40.1
7. James McLane          USA   4:40.3
8. Hironashin Furuhashi  JPN   4:42.1

Boiteux held off a late challenge from Ford Konno to win a surprise gold medal. As soon as he touched the wall, an older Frenchman in a beret rushed forward, leaped fully clothed into the water, and embraced the new champion. Reporters gathered around to find out who he was. "Coach?" "Manager?" they asked in various languages. Beaming with pride and overcome with emotion, the man in the beret held his arms up and uttered one word: "Papa!"

**1956 Melbourne** C: 32, N: 19, D: 12.4. WR: 4:26.7 (Ford Konno)
1. Murray Rose         AUS   4:27.3   OR
2. Tsuyoshi Yamanaka   JPN   4:30.4
3. George Breen        USA   4:32.5
4. Kevin O'Halloran    AUS   4:32.9
5. Hans Zierold        GDR   4:34.6
6. Garry Winram        AUS   4:34.9
7. Koji Nonoshita      JPN   4:38.2
8. Angelo Romani       ITA   4:41.7

Murray Rose was a 17-year-old vegetarian who became known as "The Seaweed Streak." Since his diet could not be provided for in the Olympic Village, Rose's parents moved him out and took care of his nutrition. His three gold medals at the Melbourne Games made a lot of Australians think twice about their diet.

**1960 Rome** C: 40, N: 25, D: 8.31. WR(440 yards): 4:15.9 (Jon Konrads)
1. Murray Rose         AUS   4:18.3   OR
2. Tsuyoshi Yamanaka   JPN   4:21.4
3. Jon Konrads         AUS   4:21.8
4. Ian Black           GBR   4:21.8
5. Alan Somers         USA   4:22.0
6. Murray McLachlan    SAF   4:26.3
7. Eugene Lenz         USA   4:26.8
8. Makoto Fukui        JPN   4:29.6

By 1960, both Murray Rose and Tsuyoshi Yamanaka had moved to Los Angeles and become students at the University of Southern California. In Rome, Alan Somers set an Olympic record of 4:19.2 in the qualifying round, but was unable to reproduce his time in the final. Although four years had passed since the last Olympics, Rose and Yamanaka repeated their one-two finish, with the exact same distance separating them.

**1964 Tokyo** C: 49, N: 27, D: 10.15. WR: 4:12.7 (Donald Schollander)
1. Donald Schollander      USA   4:12.2   WR
2. Frank Wiegand           GDR   4:14.9
3. Allan Wood              AUS   4:15.1
4. Roy Saari               USA   4:16.7
5. John Nelson             USA   4:16.9
6. Tsuyoshi Yamanaka       JPN   4:19.1
7. Russell Phegan          AUS   4:20.2
8. Semyon Belits-Geiman    SOV   4:21.4

Schollander swam the last 100 meters in 1:01.7 to win his third gold medal.

**1968 Mexico City** C: 37, N: 20, D: 10.23. WR: 4:06.5 (Ralph Hutton)
1. Michael Burton     USA   4:09.0   OR
2. Ralph Hutton       CAN   4:11.7
3. Alain Mosconi      FRA   4:13.3
4. Gregory Brough     AUS   4:15.9
5. Graham White       AUS   4:16.7
6. John Nelson        USA   4:17.2

7. Hans-Joachim Fassnacht   GER   4:18.1
8. Brent Berk                USA   4:26.0

The day before the qualifying heats, Mike Burton woke up feeling nauseated; later he fainted in an elevator in the Olympic Village. The next day he "took it easy" and qualified in 4:19.3. He took charge of the final before the halfway mark and won going away, covering the last 100 meters in 1:01.6.

**1972 Munich** C: 43, N: 28, D: 9.1. WR: 4:00.11 (Kurt Krumpholz)

| | | | |
|---|---|---|---|
| — Rick DeMont | USA | 4:00.26 | |
| 1. Bradford Cooper | AUS | 4:00.27 | OR |
| 2. Steven Genter | USA | 4:01.94 | |
| 3. Tom McBreen | USA | 4:02.64 | |
| 4. Graham Windeatt | AUS | 4:02.93 | |
| 5. Brian Brinkley | GBR | 4:06.69 | |
| 6. Bengt Gingsjö | SWE | 4:06.75 | |
| 7. Werner Lampe | GER | 4:06.97 | |

Rick DeMont was a 16-year-old from San Rafael, California. Allergic to wheat and fur, he had been taking medication for asthma since he was four years old. When DeMont qualified for the U.S. Olympic team, he was asked to fill out a standard medical form in which he listed all medications that he took. The team physicians of most other nations took this information from their athletes, found out the component parts of the various drugs from the *Physician's Desk Reference (PDR)* or similar works, and compared them to the list of banned drugs issued by the I.O.C. for the 1972 Olympics. If any forbidden drugs were being used, the physicians came up with acceptable substitutes for their athletes. Unfortunately the U.S. team physicians were not so well organized. Evidently they never even looked at the forms. Instead, they just told the athletes not to take any drugs within 48 hours of competing without first clearing it with a doctor.

The night before the 400 meters competition, Rick DeMont woke up wheezing between 1 a.m. and 2 a.m., and took a tablet of Marax, unaware that it contained the banned drug ephedrine. At 8 a.m. he took another tablet. He swam his heat at about noon and qualified easily. Since his prescription said to take one tablet every six hours, he might have taken one more dose of Marax later in the day. The final began at 6:40 p.m. DeMont started slowly, saving his strength. In last place after 100 meters and sixth after 200, he picked up speed in the second half of the race. Swimming the last 100 meters in 58.22 seconds, he defeated Cooper by one-hundredth of a second, the smallest margin possible. After the race, DeMont, along with the other two medalists, was taken away for dope testing. At the awards ceremony there was no indication of any problem.

Two days later, on Sunday, DeMont, who was the world record holder at 1500 meters, took part in the preliminary round of that event, qualifying without being pressed. The next morning, however, he was informed that he had failed the drug test after the 400 meters and therefore would not be allowed to take part in the final of the 1500 meters. A distraught DeMont watched from the stands.

Over the next couple of days, hearings were held, affidavits were filed, and confusion reigned. At one point, DeMont's pharmacist in California received a call from a U.S. doctor in Munich asking him, among other things, what Marax contained. Apparently, not one U.S. team physician had bothered to take a copy of the *PDR* to Germany. The I.O.C. ordered DeMont disqualified and issued a stern reprimand to the U.S. officials in charge. Put on the defensive, team physicians tried to blame the swimming coaches, DeMont's family doctor, even the teenager himself. Yet DeMont had made no attempt to hide the fact that he took Marax. He didn't even know it was forbidden. When team officials had entered his room at the Olympic Village on Sunday to confiscate his drugs, the bottle of Marax was sitting in plain view.

By 1976 U.S. swim officials had learned their lesson. Before the Montreal Olympics, the 51 members of the U.S. team were questioned carefully about their medications, and it was learned that 16 of them were unknowingly using banned drugs. Substitutes were found for those 16, but all of this was far too late to help Rick DeMont, who had become the first American since Jim Thorpe to be forced to return his gold medal.

**1976 Montreal** C: 47, N: 29, D: 7.22. WR: 3:53.08 (Brian Goodell)

| | | | |
|---|---|---|---|
| 1. Brian Goodell | USA | 3:51.03 | WR |
| 2. Tim Shaw | USA | 3:52.54 | |
| 3. Vladimir Raskatov | SOV | 3:55.76 | |
| 4. Djan Madruga Garrido | BRA | 3:57.18 | |
| 5. Stephen Holland | AUS | 3:57.59 | |
| 6. Sándor Nagy | HUN | 3:57.81 | |
| 7. Vladimir Mikheev | SOV | 4:00.79 | |
| 8. Stephen Badger | CAN | 4:02.83 | |

Brian Goodell had already won the 1500 meters gold medal two days earlier. United States dominance in the 400-meter freestyle was so great that Vladimir Raskatov's pre-Olympic European record of 3:58.02 would not have qualified him for the final at the U.S. trials. Silver medalist Tim Shaw also won a silver medal in water polo in 1984.

**1980 Moscow** C: 28, N: 16, D: 7.24. WR: 3:50.49 (Peter Szmidt)

| | | | |
|---|---|---|---|
| 1. Vladimir Salnikov | SOV | 3:51.31 | OR |
| 2. Andrei Krylov | SOV | 3:53.24 | |
| 3. Ivar Stukolkin | SOV | 3:53.95 | |
| 4. Djan Madruga Garrido | BRA | 3:54.15 | |
| 5. Daniel Machek | CZE | 3:55.66 | |
| 6. Sándor Nagy | HUN | 3:56.83 | |
| 7. Max Metzker | AUS | 3:56.87 | |
| 8. Ronald McKeon | AUS | 3:57.00 | |

Twenty-year-old Vladimir Salnikov of Leningrad was one of several Soviet swimmers who had been training in the United States when President Jimmy Carter made his first speech threatening a boycott of the Moscow Olympics unless Soviet troops pulled out of Afghanistan. However, Soviet coach Sergei Vaitsekhovsky was quick to thank American swimmers and coaches for the subsequent Soviet successes at the Olympics. "The Americans," he explained, "surprised us by not keeping any of their training secrets from us, which means there must still be some decent people left in the world."

Peter Szmidt of Canada set a world record of 3:50.49 in the 400 meters just before the Moscow Games began. At the U.S. Outdoor National on July 31, Mike Bruner finished first in 3:52.19, followed by Brian Goodell in 3:52.99.

**1984 Los Angeles** C: 36, N: 25, D: 8.2. WR: 3:48.32 (Vladimir Salnikov)

| | | | |
|---|---|---|---|
| 1. George DiCarlo | USA | 3:51.23 | OR |
| 2. John Mykkanen | USA | 3:51.49 | |
| 3. Justin Lemberg | AUS | 3:51.79 | |
| 4. Stefan Pfeiffer | GER | 3:52.91 | |
| 5. Franck Iacono | FRA | 3:54.58 | |
| 6. Darjan Petric | YUG | 3:54.88 | |
| 7. Marco Dell'Uomo | ITA | 3:55.44 | |
| 8. Ronald McKeon | AUS | 3:55.48 | |

In the absence of world record holder and defending Olympic champion Vladimir Salnikov, the gold medal was won by 21-year-old George DiCarlo who led from the start and held on to break Salnikov's Olympic record. But the real stir in the 400-meter freestyle came a few minutes later. For the 1984 Games a consolation final had been added to determine places 9 through 16. It was here that Thomas Fahrner of West Germany saw a chance to redeem himself for the blunder he had committed in the preliminary round. Hoping to qualify just fast enough to gain an outside lane for the final, Fahrner took it easy and found himself shut out completely with only the ninth fastest qualifying time. In the consolation race, Fahrner gave it everything he had, bettering his personal best by almost two seconds and breaking DiCarlo's short-lived Olympic record with a time of 3:50.91.

**1988 Seoul** C: 49, N: 33., D: 9.23. WR: 3:47.38 (Artur Wojdat)

| | | | |
|---|---|---|---|
| 1. Uwe Dassler | GDR | 3:46.95 | WR |
| 2. Duncan Armstrong | AUS | 3:47.15 | |
| 3. Artur Wojdat | POL | 3:47.34 | |
| 4. Matthew Cetlinski | USA | 3:48.09 | |
| 5. Mariusz Podkościelny | POL | 3:48.59 | |
| 6. Stefan Pfeiffer | GER | 3:49.96 | |
| 7. Kevin Boyd | GBR | 3:50.16 | |
| 8. Anders Holmertz | SWE | 3:51.04 | |

All eight finalists had to break Thomas Fahrner's Olympic record just to qualify for the final. Holmertz took the early lead with Cetlinski and Wojdat close behind, Dassler in fourth, and Armstrong last. There were no changes in position for the first 200 meters. At 225 me-ters Cetlinski passed Holmertz and stayed in front until the 350 mark. Then he was caught by Wojdat, who sprinted home to break his own world record. Wojdat finished third. He was no match for the incredible closing rushes of Dassler and Armstrong who swam the last 100 meters in 55.55 and 55.02, respectively. Dassler beat Armstrong by 1 foot with Wojdat another foot behind. Dassler improved his personal record by 2 seconds; Armstrong bettered his pre-Olympic best by 5 seconds.

# 1500-METER FREESTYLE

**1896 Athens** C: 9, N: 4, D: 4.11.
*(1200 Meters)*

| | | |
|---|---|---|
| 1. Alfréd Hajós | HUN | 18:22.2 |
| 2. Ioannis Andreou | GRE | 21:03.4 |
| 3. Eustathios Choraphas | GRE | — |

The competitors had to battle not only each other, but also horribly cold weather and 12-foot waves. Alfréd Hajós, the eventual winner, gave the following graphic description of the race:

"Three small boats took us out to the open sea, which was quite rough. My body had been smeared with a half-inch-thick layer of grease, for I was more cunning after the 100 meters event, and tried to protect myself against the cold. We jumped into the water at the start of a pistol, and from that point on the boats left the competitors to the mercy of the waves, rushing back to the finish line, to inform the jury of the successful start.

"I must say that I shivered from the thought of what would happen if I got a cramp from the cold water. My will to live completely overcame my desire to win. I cut through the water with a powerful determination and only became calm when the boats came back in my direction, and began to fish out the numbed competitors who were giving up the struggle. At that time I was already at the mouth of the bay. The roar of the crowd increased . . . I won ahead of the others with a big lead."

**1900 Paris** C: 16, N: 6, D: 8.12.
*(1000 Meters)*

| | | |
|---|---|---|
| 1. John Arthur Jarvis | GBR | 13:40.2 |
| 2. Otto Wahle | AUT | 14:53.6 |
| 3. Zoltán Halmay | HUN | 15:16.4 |
| 4. Max Hainle | GER | 15:22.6 |
| 5. Louis Martin | FRA | 16:34.4 |
| 6. Leuillieux | FRA | 16:53.2 |

**1904 St. Louis** C: 7, N: 4, D: 9.6. WR: 24:36.2
*(1 Mile—1609.34 Meters)*

| | | |
|---|---|---|
| 1. Emil Rausch | GER | 27:18.2 |
| 2. Géza Kiss | HUN | 28:28.2 |
| 3. Francis Gailey | USA | 28:54.0 |
| 4. Otto Wahle | AUT | — |

DNF: Edgar Adams (USA), Louis deBreda Handley (USA), John Meyers (USA)

**1906 Athens** C: 24, N: 10, D: 4.24.
*(1 Mile—1609.34 Meters)*

| | | | |
|---|---|---|---|
| 1. | Henry Taylor | GBR | 28:28.0 |
| 2. | John Arthur Jarvis | GBR | 30:07.6 |
| 3. | Otto Scheff | AUT | 30:53.4 |
| 4. | Max Pape | GER | 32:34.6 |
| 5. | Emil Rausch | GER | 32:40.6 |
| 6. | Ernst Bahnmeyer | GER | 33:29.4 |
| 7. | Oskar Schiele | GER | 33:52.4 |
| 8. | Leopold Mayer | AUT | 34:41.0 |

**1908 London** C: 19, N: 8, D: 7.25.

| | | | | |
|---|---|---|---|---|
| 1. | Henry Taylor | GBR | 22:48.4 | WR |
| 2. | Thomas Battersby | GBR | 22:51.2 | |
| 3. | Francis Beaurepaire | AUS | 22:56.2 | |

DNF: Otto Scheff (AUT)

Battersby led from the start and wasn't overtaken by Taylor until less than 200 meters remained. Taylor's time was the first internationally acknowledged world record for the 1500-meter freestyle. An English swimmer with the unusually appropriate name of L. Moist was eliminated in the semifinals.

**1912 Stockholm** C: 19, N: 11, D: 7.10. WR: 22:48.4 (Henry Taylor)

| | | | | |
|---|---|---|---|---|
| 1. | George Hodgson | CAN | 22:00.0 | WR |
| 2. | John Hatfield | GBR | 22:39.0 | |
| 3. | Harold Hardwick | AUS | 23:15.4 | |

DNF: Malcolm Champion (NZF), Béla Las-Torres (HUN)

Until the 1984 Games, George Hodgson of Montreal was the only Canadian to win an Olympic swimming championship. In the first round he set a world record of 22:23.0. He bettered this time in the final, setting a 1000-meter world record of 14:37.0 on the way. After completing 1500 meters, he continued on to swim the mile, setting three world records in one race. Four days later, he also won the 400-meter race. His 1500-meter record lasted for 11 years.

**1920 Antwerp** C: 24, N: 13, D: 8.25. WR: 22:00.0 (George Hodgson)

| | | | |
|---|---|---|---|
| 1. | Norman Ross | USA | 22:23.2 |
| 2. | George Vernot | CAN | 22:36.4 |
| 3. | Francis Beaurepaire | AUS | 23:04.0 |
| 4. | Fred Kahele | USA | — |
| 5. | Eugene Bolden | USA | — |
| 6. | Harold Annison | GBR | — |

**1924 Paris** C: 22, N: 12, D: 7.15. WR: 21:15.0 (Arne Borg)

| | | | | |
|---|---|---|---|---|
| 1. | Andrew "Boy" Charlton | AUS | 20:06.6 | WR |
| 2. | Arne Borg | SWE | 20:41.4 | |
| 3. | Francis Beaurepaire | AUS | 21:48.4 | |
| 4. | John Hatfield | GBR | 21:55.6 | |
| 5. | Katsuo Takaishi | JPN | 22:10.4 | |
| 6. | Åke Borg (SWE) | | | |

Raised in the slums on the outskirts of Sydney, Boy Charlton was adopted by Tom Adrian, who also became his coach and trainer. At the age of 16, Charlton, along

with Adrian, was on his way to the Paris Olympics on a steamer with the rest of the Australian team. Unfortunately, Adrian suffered a nervous breakdown and threw himself overboard. He was fished out safely, but he was never the same again, and there was great apprehension that Charlton's performance would be adversely affected. Instead, the teenager seemed more determined than ever, winning his preliminary heat in 21:20.8. Arne Borg, "The Swedish Sturgeon," came right back in the next heat to break his own world record in a time of 21:11.4. However, in the final, it was Charlton who prevailed, bettering Borg's two-day-old record by over a minute.

**1928 Amsterdam** C: 19, N: 13, D: 8.6. WR: 19:07.2 (Arne Borg)

| | | | | |
|---|---|---|---|---|
| 1. | Arne Borg | SWE | 19:51.8 | OR |
| 2. | Andrew "Boy" Charlton | AUS | 20:02.6 | |
| 3. | Clarence "Buster" Crabbe | USA | 20:28.8 | |
| 4. | Raymond Ruddy | USA | 21:05.0 | |
| 5. | Alberto Zorilla | ARG | 21:23.8 | |
| 6. | Garnet Ault | CAN | 21:46.0 | |

Arne Borg led from start to finish to win his only Olympic gold medal. Borg was an extremely popular athlete in Sweden and abroad. Once he was called up for military service, but ignored the notice in order to take a tour of Spain. Imprisoned upon his return to Sweden, he received so many gifts of food and wine during his incarceration that he gained 17 pounds before he was finally released. Between 1921 and 1929, Borg set 32 world records at distances from 300 yards to one mile. His 1500 meters world record of 19:07.2, set in Bologna on September 2, 1927, remained unbroken for almost 11 years. He set the record despite having just lost four teeth in a water polo match against France.

**1932 Los Angeles** C: 15, N: 8, D: 8.13. WR: 19.07.2 (Arne Borg)

| | | | | |
|---|---|---|---|---|
| 1. | Kusuo Kitamura | JPN | 19:12.4 | OR |
| 2. | Shozo Makino | JPN | 19:14.1 | |
| 3. | James Cristy | USA | 19:39.5 | |
| 4. | Noël Philip Ryan | AUS | 19:45.1 | |
| 5. | Clarence "Buster" Crabbe | USA | 20:02.7 | |
| 6. | Jean Taris | FRA | 20:09.7 | |

Fourteen-year-old Kusuo Kitamura pulled away from his 17-year-old teammate, Shozo Makino, in the final 300 meters. Kitamura, the youngest male ever to win an Olympic swimming gold medal, grew up to become the Japanese representative to the International Labor Organization.

**1936 Berlin** C: 21, N: 10, D: 8.15. WR: 19:07.2 (Arne Borg)

| | | | |
|---|---|---|---|
| 1. | Noboru Terada | JPN | 19:13.7 |
| 2. | Jack Medica | USA | 19:34.0 |
| 3. | Shumpei Uto | JPN | 19:34.5 |
| 4. | Sunao Ishiharada | JPN | 19:48.5 |
| 5. | Ralph Flanagan | USA | 19:54.8 |
| 6. | Robert Leivers | GBR | 19:57.4 |
| 7. | Heinz Arendt | GER | 19:59.0 |

Terada took the lead at the gun and drew away slowly but steadily to win by 25 meters.

**1948 London** C: 39, N: 21, D: 8.7. WR: 18:58.8 (Tomikatsu Amano)
1. James McLane      USA  19:18.5
2. John Marshall     AUS  19:31.3
3. György Mitró      HUN  19:43.2
4. György Csordás    HUN  19:54.2
5. Marjan Stipetič   YUG  20:10.7
6. Forbes Norris     USA  20:18.8
7. Donald Bland      GBR  20:19.8
8. William Heusner   USA  20:45.4

**1952 Helsinki** C: 37, N: 22, D: 8.2. WR: 18:19.0 (Hironashin Furuhashi)
1. Ford Konno        USA  18:30.3  OR
2. Shiro Hashizume   JPN  18:41.4
3. Tetsuo Okamoto    BRA  18:51.3
4. James McLane      USA  18:51.5
5. Joseph Bernardo   FRA  18:59.1
6. Yasuo Kitamura    JPN  19:00.4
7. Peter Duncan      SAF  19:12.1
8. John Marshall     AUS  19:53.4

Ford Konno of Hawaii caught up with Hashizume after 1200 meters and pulled away to a decisive victory, covering the last 100 meters in 1:11.7.

**1956 Melbourne** C: 20, N: 11, D: 12.7. WR: 17:59.5 (Murray Rose)
1. Murray Rose       AUS  17:58.9
2. Tsuyoshi Yamanaka JPN  18:00.3
3. George Breen      USA  18:08.2
4. Murray Garretty   AUS  18:26.5
5. William Slater    CAN  18:38.1
6. Jean Boiteux      FRA  18:38.3
6. Yukiyoshi Aoki    JPN  18:38.3
8. Garry Winram      AUS  19:06.2

George Breen set a world record of 17:52.9 in the third heat of the qualifying round. After 800 meters in the final, he, Rose, and Yamanaka were neck and neck. Then Rose began to surge ahead. He had built up a six-meter lead with only 100 meters to go, when Yamanaka began to sprint. He drew to within a yard of Rose, while the Australian crowd screamed at their young hero until he was finally alerted to the danger behind him. One last push earned Rose his third gold medal.

**1960 Rome** C: 30, N: 19, D: 9.3. WR: 17:11.0 (Jon Konrads)
1. Jon Konrads       AUS  17:19.6  OR
2. Murray Rose       AUS  17:21.7
3. George Breen      USA  17:30.6
4. Tsuyoshi Yamanaka JPN  17:34.7
5. József Katona     HUN  17:43.7
6. Murray McLachlan  SAF  17:44.9
7. Alan Somers       USA  18:02.8
8. Richard Campion   GBR  18:22.7

Latvian-born Jon Konrads, a survivor of childhood polio, swam stroke for stroke with George Breen for 1050 meters before drawing away.

**1964 Tokyo** C: 31, N: 21, D: 10.17. WR: 16:58.7 (Roy Saari)
1. Robert Windle     AUS  17:01.7  OR
2. John Nelson       USA  17:03.0
3. Allan Wood        AUS  17:07.7
4. William Farley    USA  17:18.2
5. Russell Phegan    AUS  17:22.4
6. Sueaki Sasaki     JPN  17:25.3
7. Roy Saari         USA  17:29.2
8. József Katona     HUN  17:30.8

Noticeably absent was Murray Rose, who had been refused a place on the Australian team because he wouldn't return home for the Australian National Championships in February, unaware that they also served as Olympic tryouts. Rose presented his own version of a tryout on August 2, when he set a world record of 17:01.8. This embarrassed the officials of the Australian Swimming Union, but they refused to make an exception to the rules they had laid down.

**1968 Mexico City** C: 21, N: 16, D: 10.26. WR: 16:08.5 (Michael Burton)
1. Michael Burton    USA  16:38.9  OR
2. John Kinsella     USA  16:57.3
3. Gregory Brough    AUS  17:04.7
4. Graham White      AUS  17:08.0
5. Ralph Hutton      CAN  17:15.6
6. Guillermo Echevarria MEX 17:36.4
7. Juan Alanis       MEX  17:46.6
8. John Nelson       USA  18:05.1

**1972 Munich** C: 42, N: 30, D: 9.4. WR: 15:52.91 (Rick DeMont)
1. Michael Burton    USA  15:52.58  WR
2. Graham Windeatt   AUS  15:58.48
3. Douglas Northway  USA  16:09.25
4. Bengt Gingsjö     SWE  16:16.01
5. Graham White      AUS  16:17.22
6. Mark Treffers     NZE  16:18.84
7. Bradford Cooper   AUS  16:30.49
8. Guillermo Garcia  MEX  16:36.03

Burton led for the first 600 meters, then Windeatt took over. By the 1200-meter mark, Burton was back in the lead for good, and dipped just below Rick DeMont's world record to win the third gold medal of his career.

**1976 Montreal** C: 31, N: 20, D: 7.20. WR: 15:06.66 (Brian Goodell)
1. Brian Goodell     USA  15:02.40  WR
2. Bobby Hackett     USA  15:03.91
3. Stephen Holland   AUS  15:04.66
4. Djan Madruga Garrido BRA 15:19.84
5. Vladimir Salnikov SOV  15:29.45
6. Max Metzker       AUS  15:31.53
7. Paul Hartloff     USA  15:32.08
8. Zoltán Wladár     HUN  15:45.97

The 1976 1500 meters final quickly resolved into a three-man race, with all three medalists ultimately breaking the world record. Bobby Hackett of Yonkers, New York, took the early lead and held it for 950 meters, at which point he was passed by Steve Holland. Holland was still in front after 1300 meters, but then Brian Goodell of Mission Viejo, California, stormed past both Hackett and Holland, taking the lead 150 meters from the finish and pulling away with a time of 57.73 seconds over the last 100 meters.

**1980 Moscow** C: 18, N: 11, D: 7.22. WR: 15:02.40 (Brian Goodell)
1. Vladimir Salnikov      SOV   14:58.27   WR
2. Aleksandr Chaev        SOV   15:14.30
3. Max Metzker            AUS   15:14.49
4. Rainer Strohbach       GDR   15:15.29
5. Borut Petric           YUG   15:21.78
6. Rafael Escalas         SPA   15:21.88
7. Zoltán Wladár          HUN   15:26.70
8. Eduard Petrov          SOV   15:28.24

Vladimir Salnikov won three gold medals at the 1980 Olympics, but the big one was in the 1500 meters. In the final, on July 22, Salnikov became the first swimmer to break the 15-minute barrier, a feat that had been eagerly anticipated since Brian Goodell came within two and a half seconds at the previous Olympics.

**1984 Los Angeles** C: 27, N: 19, D: 8.4. WR: 14:54.76 (Vladimir Salnikov)
1. Michael O'Brien        USA   15:05.20
2. George DiCarlo         USA   15:10.59
3. Stefan Pfeiffer        GER   15:12.11
4. Rainer Henkel          GER   15:20.03
5. Franck Iacono          FRA   15:26.96
6. Stefano Grandi         ITA   15:28.58
7. David Shemilt          CAN   15:31.28
8. Wayne Shillington      AUS   15:38.18

Mike O'Brien, a 6-foot 6-inch 18-year-old, took the lead from DiCarlo after 600 meters and pulled away for an unchallenged victory. At the Friendship Games in Moscow three weeks later, Vladimir Salnikov took first place with a time of 15:03.51.

**1988 Seoul** C: 35, N: 22, D: 9.25. WR: 14:54.76 (Vladimir Salnikov)
1. Vladimir Salnikov      SOV   15:00.40
2. Stefan Pfeiffer        GER   15:02.69
3. Uwe Dassler            GDR   15:06.15
4. Matthew Cetlinski      USA   15:14.76
5. Mariusz Podkościelny   POL   15:14.76
6. Rainer Henkel          GER   15:18.19
7. Kevin Boyd             GBR   15:21.16
8. Darjan Petric          YUG   15:37.12

Between 1977 and 1986 Vladimir Salnikov won 61 consecutive finals at 1500 meters. He broke the 15-minute mark four times. No one else did it even once. Then, at the 1986 world championships, Salnikov finished fourth.

The following year, at the European championships, he failed to qualify for the final. It appeared that he was over the hill and ready for retirement. But Salnikov refused to give up. Trained by his wife, Marina, he mounted a comeback aimed at regaining his Olympic title in Seoul. The coaches of the Soviet team were dubious and refused to select him as a member of the national team. However, the Soviet Minister of Sport intervened and announced that if Vladimir Salnikov thought he deserved to represent the U.S.S.R. in the 1988 Olympics, then the coaches must find a place for him. Still, Salnikov was not considered a serious medal contender. *Time* magazine summed up the consensus: "Salnikov's long day as the world's freestyle champion has passed. He can expect nothing more in Seoul than to see the last of his records fall in front of him."

But in the preliminary round, Salnikov served notice that he was still a threat. His qualifying time of 15:07.83 was second only to that of Matt Cetlinski. In the final, Cetlinski, in lane 4, took the early lead. Salnikov, beside him in lane 5, stayed close behind him in second place. Then, after 675 meters, Salnikov surged ahead, extending his lead steadily until the final 100 meters when Stefan Pfeiffer managed to close the gap somewhat. Salnikov became only the third swimmer to win Olympic gold medals eight years apart. The others were Duke Kahanamoku and Dawn Fraser. At 28, Salnikov was also the oldest Olympic swimming champion in 56 years.

At 11:30 that night, after all the photos and interviews and ceremonies and congratulations were over, Vladimir Salnikov walked into the cafeteria at the athletes' village, hoping to grab a late snack. There were about 250 or 300 athletes and coaches in the room, representing a wide variety of nations and sports. As word spread that Salnikov had entered, the athletes and coaches spontaneously stopped eating, rose, and gave him a standing ovation.

## 100-METER BACKSTROKE

**1896–1900** not held

**1904 St. Louis** C: 6, N: 2, D: 9.6.
*(100 Yards)*
1. Walter Brack           GER   1:16.8
2. Georg Hoffmann         GER   —
3. Georg Zacharias        GER   —
4. William Orthwein       USA   —
AC: David Hammond (USA), Edwin Swatek (USA)

**1906** not held

**1908 London** C: 21, N: 11, D: 7.17. WR: 1:25.0
1. Arno Bieberstein       GER   1:24.6   WR
2. Ludvig Dam             DEN   1:26.6
3. Herbert Haresnape      GBR   1:27.0
4. Gustav Aurisch         GER   —

**1912 Stockholm** C: 18, N: 7, D: 7.14. WR: 1:15.6 (Otto Fahr)
1. Harry Hebner        USA    1:21.2
2. Otto Fahr           GER    1:22.4
3. Paul Kellner        GER    1:24.0
4. András Baronyi      HUN    1:25.2
5. Otto Gross          GER    1:25.8

Hebner set an Olympic record of 1:20.8 in the semifinals.

**1920 Antwerp** C: 12, N: 6, D: 8.23. WR: 1:15.6 (Otto Fahr)
1. Warren Paoa Kealoha   USA    1:15.2
2. Ray Kegeris           USA    1:16.2
3. Gérard Blitz          BEL    1:19.0
4. Percy McGillivray     USA    1:19.4
5. Harold Kruger         USA    —
6. Gaspard Lemaire       BEL    —

Seventeen-year-old Warren Kealoha set a world record of 1:14.8 in the preliminary round.

**1924 Paris** C: 20, N: 11, D: 7.8. WR: 1:12.4 (Warren Kealoha)
1. Warren Paoa Kealoha   USA    1:13.2   OR
2. Paul Wyatt            USA    1:15.4
3. Károly Bartha         HUN    1:17.8
4. Gérard Blitz          BEL    1:19.6
5. Austin Rawlinson      GBR    1:20.0
6. Giyo Saito (JPN)

**1928 Amsterdam** C: 19, N: 12, D: 8.9. WR: 1:09.0 (George Kojac)
1. George Kojac      USA    1:08.2   WR
2. Walter Laufer     USA    1:10.0
3. Paul Wyatt        USA    1:12.0
4. Toshio Irie       JPN    1:13.6
5. Ernst Küppers     GER    1:13.8
6. John Besford      GBR    1:15.4

**1932 Los Angeles** C: 16, N: 9, D: 8.12. WR: 1:08.2 (George Kojac)
1. Masaji Kiyokawa    JPN    1:08.6
2. Toshio Irie        JPN    1:09.8
3. Kentaro Kawatsu    JPN    1:10.0
4. Robert Zehr        USA    1:10.9
5. Ernst Küppers      GER    1:11.3
6. Robert Kerber      USA    1:12.8

**1936 Berlin** C: 30, N: 17, D: 8.14. WR: 1:04.8 (Adolf Kiefer)
1. Adolf Kiefer        USA    1:05.9   OR
2. Albert Vandeweghe   USA    1:07.7
3. Masaji Kiyokawa     JPN    1:08.4
4. Taylor Drysdale     USA    1:09.4
5. Kiichi Yoshida      JPN    1:09.7
6. Yasuhiko Kojima     JPN    1:10.4
7. Percival Oliver     AUS    1:10.7

**1948 London** C: 39, N: 24, D: 8.6. WR: 1:04.0 (Allen Stack)
1. Allen Stack           USA    1:06.4
2. Robert Cowell         USA    1:06.5
3. Georges Vallerey      FRA    1:07.8
4. Mario Chaves          ARG    1:09.0
5. Clemente Mejia Avila  MEX    1:09.0

6. Johannes Wild      SAF    1:09.1
7. John Brockway      GBR    1:09.2
8. Albert Kinnear     GBR    1:09.6

**1952 Helsinki** C: 38, N: 25, D: 8.1. WR: 1:03.6 (Allen Stack)
1. Yoshinobu Oyakawa   USA    1:05.4   OR
2. Gilbert Bozon       FRA    1:06.2
3. Jack Taylor         USA    1:06.4
4. Allen Stack         USA    1:07.6
5. Pedro Galvao        ARG    1:07.7
6. Robert Wardrop      GBR    1:07.8
7. Boris Škanata       YUG    1:08.1
8. Nicolaas Meiring    SAF    1:08.3

**1956 Melbourne** C: 25, N: 14, D: 12.6. WR: 1:02.1 (Gilbert Bozon)
1. David Theile         AUS    1:02.2   OR
2. John Monckton        AUS    1:03.2
3. Frank McKinney       USA    1:04.5
4. Robert Christophe    FRA    1:04.9
5. John Hayres          AUS    1:05.0
6. Graham Sykes         GBR    1:05.6
7. Albert Wiggins       USA    1:05.8
8. Yoshinobu Oyakawa    USA    1:06.9

**1960 Rome** C: 37, N: 27, D: 8.31. WR(110 yards): 1:01.5 (John Monckton)
1. David Theile         AUS    1:01.9   OR
2. Frank McKinney       USA    1:02.1
3. Robert Bennett       USA    1:02.3
4. Robert Christophe    FRA    1:03.2
5. Leonid Barbier       SOV    1:03.5
6. Wolfgang Wagner      GDR    1:03.5
7. John Monckton        AUS    1:04.1
8. Veiko Siymar         SOV    1:04.6

After the 1956 Olympics, David Theile of Brisbane dropped out of swimming for two years so that he could concentrate on his medical studies. Yet he was able to come back better than ever to defend his championship. John Monckton was even with Theile at 50 meters but misjudged the turn and hit the wall with his head.

**1964** not held

**1968 Mexico City** C: 37, N: 26, D: 10.22. WR: 58.4 (Roland Matthes)
1. Roland Matthes       GDR    58.7   OR
2. Charles Hickcox      USA    1:00.2
3. Ronald Mills         USA    1:00.5
4. Larry Barbiere       USA    1:01.1
5. James Shaw           CAN    1:01.4
6. Bob Schoutsen        HOL    1:01.8
7. Reinhard Blechert    GER    1:01.9
8. Franco Del Campo     ITA    1:02.0

Roland Matthes of Erfurt, Thuringia, was 16 years old when he set his first backstroke world record on September 11, 1967. In the next six years he would break records in the 100-meter and 200-meter backstroke 16 times. He also won four Olympic gold medals, two silver, and two bronze. In 1978 Matthes married Olympic champion Kornelia Ender. Their first child, Francesca, was born later that year, the product of parents who, between them, had earned eight gold medals, six silver medals, and two bronze. The couple was later divorced.

**1972 Munich** C: 39, N: 27, D: 8.29. WR: 56.3 (Roland Matthes)
1. Roland Matthes    GDR    56.58    OR
2. Michael Stamm     USA    57.70
3. John Murphy       USA    58.35
4. Mitchell Ivey     USA    58.48
5. Igor Grivennikov  SOV    59.50
6. Lutz Wanja        GDR    59.80
7. Jürgen Krüger     GDR    59.93
8. Tadashi Honda     JPN    1:00.41

**1976 Montreal** C: 41, N: 29, D: 7.19. WR: 56.30 (Roland Matthes)
1. John Naber        USA    55.49    WR
2. Peter Rocca       USA    56.34
3. Roland Matthes    GDR    57.22
4. Carlos Berrocal   PUR    57.28
5. Lutz Wanja        GDR    57.49
6. Bob Jackson       USA    57.69
7. Mark Kerry        AUS    57.94
8. Mark Tonelli      AUS    58.42

When John Naber was 9 years old he visited Olympia, in Greece, and told his parents that someday he would become an Olympic champion. Eleven years later, now 6 feet 6 inches tall and 195 pounds, Naber fulfilled his vow. In 1974 he had ended Roland Matthes' seven-year winning streak. Matthes was still the holder of the world record, but an appendectomy six weeks before the 1976 Olympics hurt his chances for defending his title. Naber set a world record of 56.19 in the semifinals and then set another one 24 hours later to win the first of his four gold medals.

**1980 Moscow** C: 33, N: 23, D: 7.21. WR: 55.49 (John Naber)
1. Bengt Baron       SWE    56.33
2. Viktor Kuznetsov  SOV    56.99
3. Vladimir Dolgov   SOV    57.63
4. Miloslav Rolko    CZE    57.74
5. Sándor Wladár     HUN    57.84
6. Fred Eefling      HOL    57.95
7. Mark Tonelli      AUS    57.98
8. Gary Abraham      GBR    58.38

The victory of 18-year-old Bengt Baron of Finspang, Sweden, was so unexpected that even he was stunned. "I just can't understand how I did it," he told reporters afterward. His pre-Olympic best had been 57.77. Silver medalist Viktor Kuznetsov served a suspension after testing positive for steroids in 1978. Ten days after the Olympic final, the U.S. Outdoor National championship was won by Peter Rocca in a time of 56.64, with Bob Jackson second at 56.78.

**1984 Los Angeles** C: 45, N: 31, D: 8.3. WR: 55.19 (Richard Carey)
1. Richard Carey     USA    55.79
2. David Wilson      USA    56.35
3. Mike West         CAN    56.49
4. Gary Hurring      NZE    56.90
5. Mark Kerry        AUS    57.18
6. Bengt Baron       SWE    57.34
7. Sandy Goss        CAN    57.46
8. Hans Kroes        HOL    58.07

Rick Carey won the second of his three gold medals. This time he pleased his critics by smiling and celebrating his victory despite his disappointment at not setting a world record. Three weeks later, the Friendship Games were won by Vladimir Shemetov in a time of 55.88.

**1988 Seoul** C: 52, N: 38, D: 9.24. WR: 54.91 (David Berkoff)
1. Daichi Suzuki     JPN    55.05
2. David Berkoff     USA    55.18
3. Igor Poliansky    SOV    55.20
4. Sergei Zabolotnov SOV    55.37
5. Mark Tewksbury    CAN    56.09
6. Frank Baltrusch   GDR    56.10
7. Frank Hoffmeister GER    56.19
8. Sean Murphy       CAN    56.32

On March 15, 1988, Rick Carey's 4½-year-old world record finally fell to Igor Poliansky, who swam 55.17 in Tallinn, Estonia. Poliansky dropped the record to 55.16 the following night and then to 55.00 four months later in Moscow. But on August 13, David Berkoff, competing in the U.S. Olympic trials, broke Poliansky's record twice: 54.95 in the prelims and 54.91 in the final. Berkoff, a Harvard senior from Willow Grove, Pennsylvania, caused a sensation with his submarine start. Using a dolphin kick borrowed from the butterfly stroke, Berkoff swam 32 kicks underwater, exploding to the surface after 35 meters. Berkoff was not the first to use the technique, but he was the first world-class backstroker to stay under for so long.

In the preliminaries at Seoul, Berkoff swam a 54.51 to set the sixth world record in less than six and a half months. In the final, however, Berkoff got off to a slow start. After 30 meters, Berkoff, Suzuki, and Poliansky were all still underwater. When Berkoff popped up last, 5 meters later, he was in first place, but not by nearly the margin he had expected. Suzuki, who had been practicing the submerged start daily for seven years (three years longer than Berkoff) caught Berkoff with 10 meters to go and won by about 10 inches. Suzuki had placed eleventh at the 1984 Olympics and competed only once a year at the international level. He appeared truly stunned by his victory. After the medal ceremony he told reporters, "I did not expect to win the gold medal. I can't believe it's true, yet I find myself in this interview."

The F.I.N.A. banned the submarine start immediately after the Seoul Olympics, ruling that any backstroker still underwater after 10 meters would be disqualified. This ruling was later amended to 15 meters.

# 200-METER BACKSTROKE

**1896** not held

**1900 Paris** C: 36, N: 5, D: 8.12.
1. Ernst Hoppenberg    GER    2:47.0
2. Karl Ruberl    AUT    2:56.0
3. Johannes Drost    HOL    3:01.0
4. Johannes Bleomen    HOL    3:02.2
5. Thomas Burgess    FRA    3:12.6
6. de Romand    FRA    3:38.0

**1904–1960** not held

**1964 Tokyo** C: 34, N: 21, D: 10.13. WR: 2:10.9 (Thomas Stock)
1. Jed Graef    USA    2:10.3    WR
2. Gary Dilley    USA    2:10.5
3. Robert Bennett    USA    2:13.1
4. Shigeo Fukushima    JPN    2:13.2
5. Ernst-Joachim Küppers    GER    2:15.7
6. Viktor Mazanov    SOV    2:15.9
7. Ralph Hutton    CAN    2:15.9
8. Peter Reynolds    AUS    2:16.6

**1968 Mexico City** C: 30, N: 21, D: 10.25. WR: 2:07.5 (Roland Matthes)
1. Roland Matthes    GDR    2:09.6    OR
2. Mitchell Ivey    USA    2:10.6
3. Jack Horsley    USA    2:10.9
4. Gary Hall    USA    2:12.6
5. Santiago Esteva    SPA    2:12.9
6. Leonid Dobrosskokin    SOV    2:15.4
7. Joachim Rother    GDR    2:15.8
8. Franco Del Campo    ITA    2:16.5

**1972 Munich** C: 36, N: 25, D: 9.2. WR: 2:02.8 (Roland Matthes)
1. Roland Matthes    GDR    2:02.82    EWR
2. Michael Stamm    USA    2:04.09
3. Mitchell Ivey    USA    2:04.33
4. Bradford Cooper    AUS    2:06.59
5. Alexander "Tim" McKee    USA    2:07.29
6. Lothar Noack    GDR    2:08.67
7. Zoltán Verrasztó    HUN    2:10.09
8. Jean-Paul Berjeaud    FRA    2:11.77

**1976 Montreal** C: 33, N: 23, D: 7.24. WR: 2:00.64 (John Naber)
1. John Naber    USA    1:59.19    WR
2. Peter Rocca    USA    2:00.55
3. Dan Harrigan    USA    2:01.35
4. Mark Tonelli    AUS    2:03.17
5. Mark Kerry    AUS    2:04.07
6. Miloslav Rolko    CZE    2:05.81
7. Robert Rudolf    HUN    2:07.30
8. Zoltán Verrasztó    HUN    2:08.23

With this race, John Naber won his fourth gold medal and became the first backstroker to break the two-minute barrier for 200 meters.

**1980 Moscow** C: 25, N: 16, D: 7.26. WR: 1:59.19 (John Naber)
1. Sándor Wladár    HUN    2:01.93
2. Zoltán Verrasztó    HUN    2:02.40
3. Mark Kerry    AUS    2:03.14
4. Vladimir Shemetov    SOV    2:03.48
5. Fred Eefting    HOL    2:03.92
6. Michael Söderlund    SWE    2:04.10
7. Douglas Campbell    GBR    2:04.23
8. Paul Moorfoot    AUS    2:06.15

Three days after the Moscow final, Steve Barnicoat won the U.S. Outdoor National in 2:01.06. Second place went to Peter Rocca in 2:01.34.

**1984 Los Angeles** C: 34, N: 25, D: 7.31. WR: 1:58.86 (Richard Carey)
1. Richard Carey    USA    2:00.23
2. Frédéric Delcourt    FRA    2:01.75
3. Cameron Henning    CAN    2:02.37
4. Ricardo Prado    BRA    2:03.05
5. Gary Hurring    NZE    2:03.10
6. Nicolai Klapkarek    GER    2:03.95
7. Ricardo Aldabe    SPA    2:04.53
8. David Orbell    AUS    2:04.61

After setting an Olympic record of 1:58.99 in the prelims, Rick Carey of Mt. Kisco, New York, an extremely self-critical perfectionist, assumed that he would be able to break his own world record in the final. He won the race, but fell far short of the record. Afterwards he expressed nothing but disappointment, anger and dejection. He ignored the cheers of the crowd and the congratulations of his opponents. At the medal ceremony he hung his head and again ignored the audience, pausing only once on the way out to kiss his mother. This behavior led to such a torrent of harsh criticism from the U.S. press that Carey felt compelled to issue a formal apology which concluded, "I found it very difficult to smile when my performance didn't live up to my expectations. By not breaking the world record I felt I had not only let myself down, but also the crowd. . . . But, please, don't get the impression that I didn't appreciate winning. What everyone saw was purely an emotional reaction—or over-reaction—to Rick Carey's imperfection." Ironically, at the Friendship Games in Moscow three weeks later, Carey's world record was broken by Sergei Zabolotnov in a time of 1:58.41.

**1988 Seoul** C: 44, N: 32, D: 9.22. WR: 1:58.14 (Igor Poliansky)
1. Igor Poliansky    SOV    1:59.37
2. Frank Baltrusch    GDR    1:59.60
3. Paul Kingsman    NZE    2:00.48
4. Sergei Zabolotnov    SOV    2:00.52
5. Dirk Richter    GDR    2:01.67
6. Jens-Peter Berndt    GER    2:01.84
7. Daniel Veatch    USA    2:02.26
8. Rogerio Romero    BRA    2:02.28

Poliansky hailed from Novosibirsk in western Siberia where his mother was a librarian and his father worked in a meat factory. He had dominated this event since 1985, losing only once to Zabolotnov at the 1987 European championships. In Seoul, Polyansky, Zabolotnov, and Baltrusch swam first, second, and third for the first 150 meters. Then Zabolotnov faded and Baltrusch came on with a rush, but Polyansky held on for the victory.

## 100-METER BREASTSTROKE

The most rigidly defined of swimming strokes, the breaststroke requires swimmers to follow several rules:

1. All leg and arm movements must be made simultaneously. Alternating movements are not allowed.

2. Both shoulders must be kept in line with the water.

3. The hands must be pushed forward together and from the breast, and must be brought back on or under the surface of the water.

4. Only the backward and out frog-leg kick is allowed.

5. At turns and at the finish, both hands must touch the wall simultaneously.

6. Except for the start and the first stroke and kick after each turn, a part of the head must be kept above the surface of the water.

The breaststroke has always been the most controversial stroke because of ongoing arguments as to what constitutes legal or illegal technique. In the early 1930s some U.S. swimmers discovered a "loophole" in the rules then in force and began bringing their arms back *above* the surface of the water, which saved precious time and energy. In 1952, this new technique, known as the butterfly, was officially recognized as the fourth Olympic swimming style and given its own set of competitions, separate from the breaststroke.

Classical breaststroke enthusiasts, rid at last of the upstart butterfly stroke, were not allowed even a moment to breathe a sigh of relief, thanks to the Japanese, who discovered another loophole—underwater swimming. Swimming *below* the surface of the water turned out to be faster than swimming on the surface, so in 1956 underwater swimming was banned from breaststroke competitions.

**1896–1964** not held

**1968 Mexico City** C: 39, N: 24, D: 10.19. WR: 1:06.2 (Nikolai Pankin)

| | | | |
|---|---|---|---|
| 1. Donald McKenzie | USA | 1:07.7 | OR |
| 2. Vladimir Kosinsky | SOV | 1:08.0 | |
| 3. Nikolai Pankin | SOV | 1:08.0 | |
| 4. José Sylvio Fiolo | BRA | 1:08.1 | |
| 5. Yevgeny Mikhailov | SOV | 1:08.4 | |
| 6. Ian O'Brien | AUS | 1:08.6 | |
| 7. Alberto Forelli | ARG | 1:08.7 | |
| 8. Egon Henninger | GDR | 1:09.7 | |

**1972 Munich** C: 44, N: 31, D: 8.30. WR: 1:05.8 (Nikolai Pankin)

| | | | |
|---|---|---|---|
| 1. Nobutaka Taguchi | JPN | 1:04.94 | WR |
| 2. Thomas Bruce | USA | 1:05.43 | |
| 3. John Hencken | USA | 1:05.61 | |
| 4. Mark Chatfield | USA | 1:06.01 | |
| 5. Walter Kusch | GER | 1:06.23 | |
| 6. José Sylvio Fiolo | BRA | 1:06.24 | |
| 7. Nikolai Pankin | SOV | 1:06.36 | |
| 8. David Wilkie | GBR | 1:06.52 | |

In the first semifinal John Hencken set a world record of 1:05.68. Less than ten minutes later, Nobutaka Taguchi broke that record with a time of 1:05.13 in the second semifinal. The following evening, in the final, Taguchi overtook Tom Bruce in the last 25 meters and set yet another world record.

**1976 Montreal** C: 32, N: 22, D: 7.20. WR: 1:03.88 (John Hencken)

| | | | |
|---|---|---|---|
| 1. John Hencken | USA | 1:03.11 | WR |
| 2. David Wilkie | GBR | 1:03.43 | |
| 3. Arvydas Juozaitis | SOV | 1:04.23 | |
| 4. Graham Smith | CAN | 1:04.26 | |
| 5. Giorgio Lalle | ITA | 1:04.37 | |
| 6. Walter Kusch | GER | 1:04.38 | |
| 7. Duncan Goodhew | GBR | 1:04.66 | |
| 8. Chris Woo | USA | 1:05.13 | |

John Hencken, a 22-year-old graduate of Stanford University with a degree in electrical engineering, equaled his own world record of 1:03.88 in the preliminary round, and broke it with a time of 1:03.62 in the semifinals. Hardpressed by David Wilkie in the final, he set another record of 1:03.11.

**1980 Moscow** C: 26, N: 20, D: 7.22. WR: 1:02.86 (Gerald Mörken)

| | | |
|---|---|---|
| 1. Duncan Goodhew | GBR | 1:03.44 |
| 2. Arsen Miskarov | SOV | 1:03.82 |
| 3. Peter Evans | AUS | 1:03.96 |
| 4. Aleksandr Fedorovsky | SOV | 1:04.00 |
| 5. János Dzvonyár | HUN | 1:04.67 |
| 6. Lindsay Spencer | AUS | 1:05.04 |
| 7. Pablo Restrepo | COL | 1:05.91 |

DISQ: Albán Vermes (HUN)

Jeered at by his schoolmates as an adolescent because an accident had left him bald, and also because he was dyslexic, Duncan Goodhew vowed that he would become an Olympic champion. Although his stepfather, a retired air vice-marshal, refused to attend the Games because his government opposed British participation, Goodhew's mother was in the audience to watch her son's dream come true. Despite all the noise in the stadium, Goodhew "seemed to hear her voice above all the others."

At the U.S. Outdoor National a week later, Steve Lundquist clocked 1:02.88 and Bill Barrett 1:02.93. The world record of 1:02.86 had been set by Gerald Mörken of West Germany in 1977.

**1984 Los Angeles** C: 52, N: 37, D: 7.29. WR: 1:02.13 (John Moffet)

| 1. Steve Lundquist | USA | 1:01.65 | WR |
|---|---|---|---|
| 2. Victor Davis | CAN | 1:01.99 | |
| 3. Peter Evans | AUS | 1:02.97 | |
| 4. Adrian Moorhouse | GBR | 1:03.25 | |
| 5. John Moffet | USA | 1:03.29 | |
| 6. Brett Stocks | AUS | 1:03.49 | |
| 7. Gerald Mörken | GER | 1:03.95 | |
| 8. Raffaele Avagnano | ITA | 1:04.11 | |

At the U.S. Olympic trials on June 25, John Moffet had defeated Steve Lundquist for the first time, and taken away his world record for good measure. Competing in the Olympics five weeks later, Moffet led all qualifiers with an Olympic record of 1:02.16. Unfortunately, pushing off the wall at the 50-meter turn, Moffet badly tore a muscle in his right thigh. As the seriousness of his injury became apparent, doctors injected his leg with xylocaine and taped his thigh. But his chances for Olympic victory were fading fast. In the ready room before the final, Moffet took Lundquist aside and said, "If something goes haywire with my leg, win the gold for the U.S.A." Lundquist did just that, fighting off a determined challenge from Victor Davis and regaining his world record.

**1988 Seoul** C: 61, N: 45, D: 9.19. WR: 1:01.65 (Steve Lundquist)

| 1. Adrian Moorhouse | GBR | 1:02.04 |
|---|---|---|
| 2. Károly Güttler | HUN | 1:02.05 |
| 3. Dmitri Volkov | SOV | 1:02.20 |
| 4. Victor Davis | CAN | 1:02.38 |
| 5. Tamás Debnár | HUN | 1:02.50 |
| 6. Richard Schroeder | USA | 1:02.55 |
| 7. Gianni Minervini | ITA | 1:02.93 |
| 8. Christian Poswiat | GDR | 1:03.43 |

When he was 12 years old, Adrian Moorhouse of Bingley, Yorkshire, watched on television as David Wilkie won a gold medal in the 200-meter breaststroke. Moorhouse thought to himself, "I want one of those."

Eight years later at the Los Angeles Olympics swimming aficionados thought that he had a very good chance of winning "one of those" in the 100-meter event. However, he finished a disappointing fourth and went home to England without a medal. While he was still in Los Angeles he received a telegram from his former Sunday school teacher, Geoff Carter. It read, "Very bad luck, all proud of you. There will be a next time." Moorhouse kept the telegram and four years later took it with him to Seoul. This time he entered the competition as the clear favorite, having recorded the fastest time in the world in 1986, 1987, and pre-Olympic 1988.

In the preliminaries, Moorhouse was the fastest qualifier, with a time of 1:02.19. In the final, Dmitri Volkov turned first, with Moorhouse 1.3 seconds back in sixth place. Moorhouse expected Volkov to die by the 75-meter mark. When he didn't, Moorhouse realized for the first time that "maybe the Olympics mean something to him too." In fact, Volkov was, in his own words,

"washed out" by the 75-meter mark, but he managed to stay in front for another 15 meters.

When Moorhouse reached the finish, he wasn't sure whether he had beaten Volkov for the gold. He hadn't even noticed Károly Güttler two lanes away. When he looked back at the scoreboard, Moorhouse discovered that he had edged out Güttler by only one one-hundredth of a second. As elated as he was, Moorhouse cringed with guilt for having "stolen" the gold from Güttler. Actually, the Hungarian, who was not considered a medal contender, was ecstatic at having earned an unexpected silver.

After the medal ceremony, Moorhouse tucked the four-year-old telegram from his Sunday school teacher into the box that contained his gold medal.

## 200-METER BREASTSTROKE

**1896–1906** not held

**1908 London** C: 27, N: 10, D: 7.18.

| 1. Frederick Holman | GBR | 3:09.2 | WR |
|---|---|---|---|
| 2. William Robinson | GBR | 3:12.8 | |
| 3. Pontus Hanson | SWE | 3:14.6 | |
| 4. Ödön Toldi | HUN | 3:15.2 | |

Twenty-five meters from the finish, the 25-year-old Holman overtook Robinson, who was 38 years old.

**1912 Stockholm** C: 24, N: 11, D: 7.10. WR: 3:00.8 (Felicien Coubert)

| 1. Walter Bathe | GER | 3:01.8 | OR |
|---|---|---|---|
| 2. Wilhelm Lützow | GER | 3:05.0 | |
| 3. Kurt Mahlisch | GER | 3:08.0 | |
| 4. Percy Courtman | GBR | 3:08.8 | |
| DNF: Thor Henning (SWE) | | | |

**1920 Antwerp** C: 24, N: 12, D: 8.29. WR: 2:56.6 (Percy Courtman)

| 1. Håkan Malmroth | SWE | 3:04.4 |
|---|---|---|
| 2. Thor Henning | SWE | 3:09.2 |
| 3. Arvo Aaltonen | FIN | 3:12.2 |
| 4. Jack Howell | USA | — |
| 5. Ivan Stedman | AUS | — |
| DNF: Per Cederblom (SWE) | | |

**1924 Paris** C: 28, N: 16, D: 7.17. WR: 2:50.4 (Erich Rademacher)

| 1. Robert Skelton | USA | 2:56.6 |
|---|---|---|
| 2. Joseph de Combe | BEL | 2:59.2 |
| 3. William Kirschbaum | USA | 3:01.0 |
| 4. Bengt Linders | SWE | 3:02.2 |
| 5. Robert Wyss | SWI | 3:05.6 |
| 6. Thor Henning (SWE) | | |

Skelton set an Olympic record of 2:56.0 in the opening round.

**1928 Amsterdam** C: 21, N: 13, D: 8.8. WR: 2:48.0 (Erich Rademacher)

| 1. Yoshiyuki Tsuruta | JPN | 2:48.8 | OR |
|---|---|---|---|
| 2. Erich Rademacher | GER | 2:50.6 | |

3. Teofilo Yldefonzo     PHI   2:56.4
4. Erwin Sietas          GER   2:56.6
5. Eric Harling          SWE   2:56.8
6. Walter Spence         CAN   2:57.2

**1932 Los Angeles** C: 18, N: 11, D: 8:13. WR: 2:44.0 (Leonard Spence)
1. Yoshiyuki Tsuruta     JPN   2:45.4
2. Reizo Koike           JPN   2:46.6
3. Teofilo Yldefonzo     PHI   2:47.1
4. Erwin Sietas          GER   2:48.0
5. Jikirum Adjaluddin    PHI   2:49.2
6. Shigeo Nakagawa       JPN   2:52.8

Koike defeated Tsuruta 2:44.9 to 2:45.4 in the first semifinal. The defending champion repeated his time exactly in the final, but this time it was good enough to win.

**1936 Berlin** C: 25, N: 11, D: 8.15. WR: 2:37.2 (Jack Kasley)
1. Tetsuo Hamuro         JPN   2:41.5   OR
2. Erwin Sietas          GER   2:42.9
3. Reizo Koike           JPN   2:44.2
4. John Herbert Higgins  USA   2:45.2
5. Saburo Ito            JPN   2:47.6
6. Joachim Balke         GER   2:47.8
7. Teofilo Yldefonzo     PHI   2:51.1

**1948 London** C: 32, N: 20, D: 8.7. WR: 2:30.0 (Joseph Verdeur)
1. Joseph Verdeur        USA   2:39.3   OR
2. Keith Carter          USA   2:40.2
3. Robert Sohl           USA   2:43.9
4. John Davies           AUS   2:43.7
5. Anton "Tone" Cerer    YUG   2:46.1
6. Willy Otto Jordan     BRA   2:46.4
7. A. Kandil             EGY   2:47.5
8. Bjorn Bonte           HOL   2:47.6

The first seven finishers all used the butterfly stroke. The judges awarded Bob Sohl the bronze medal even though his official time was slower than that of Davies.

**1952 Helsinki** C: 40, N: 27, D: 8.2. WR: 2:27.3 (Herbert Klein)
1. John Davies           AUS   2:34.4   OR
2. Bowen Stassforth      USA   2:34.7
3. Herbert Klein         GER   2:35.9
4. Nobuyasu Hirayama     JPN   2:37.4
5. Takayoshi Kajikawa    JPN   2:38.6
6. Jiro Nagasawa         JPN   2:39.1
7. Maurice Lusien        FRA   2:39.8
8. Ludevit Komadel       CZE   2:40.1

**1956 Melbourne** C: 21, N: 17, D: 12.6. WR: 2:31.0 (Masaru Furukawa)
1. Masaru Furukawa       JPN   2:34.7   OR
2. Masahiro Yoshimura    JPN   2:36.7
3. Charis Yunichev       SOV   2:36.8
4. Terry Gathercole      AUS   2:38.7
5. Igor Zasseda          SOV   2:39.0
6. Knud Gleie            DEN   2:40.0
7. Manuel Sanguily       CUB   2:42.0
DISQ: Hughes Broussard (FRA)

For the first time, the butterfly stroke and the breaststroke were separated into two different events. Differences in interpretation of what was a breaststroke and what wasn't led to six disqualifications. The most controversial was the ousting of Herbert Klein of Germany, who won the second heat. He was accused of using a scissors kick and of dipping his right shoulder. Furukawa was one of the least visible Olympic champions, since his unusual technique kept him underwater 75 percent of the time.

**1960 Rome** C: 42, N: 30, D: 8.30. WR: 2:36.5 (Terry Gathercole)
1. William Mulliken      USA   2:37.4
2. Yoshihiko Osaki       JPN   2:38.0
3. Wieger Mensonides     HOL   2:39.7
4. Egon Henninger        GDR   2:40.1
5. Roberto Lazzari       ITA   2:40.1
6. Terry Gathercole      AUS   2:40.2
7. Andrzej Klopotowski   POL   2:41.2
8. Paul Halt             USA   2:41.4

The slower times in 1960 were the result of the banning of underwater swimming in 1957, five months after Masaru Furukawa's Olympic victory. Bill Mulliken's win was considered a major upset, since his pre-Olympic best had been 2:40.9. In the semifinals he set an Olympic record of 2:37.2.

**1964 Tokyo** C: 33, N: 20, D: 10.15. WR: 2:28.2 (Chester Jastremski)
1. Ian O'Brien          AUS   2:27.8   WR
2. Georgy Prokopenko    SOV   2:28.2
3. Chester Jastremski   USA   2:29.6
4. Aleksandr Tutakayev  SOV   2:31.0
5. Egon Henninger       GDR   2:31.1
6. Osamu Tsurumine      JPN   2:33.6
7. Wayne Anderson       USA   2:35.0
8. Vladimir Kosinsky    SOV   2:38.1

Seventeen-year-old Ian O'Brien didn't catch Prokopenko until five meters from the finish.

**1968 Mexico City** C: 36, N: 23, D: 10.22. WR: 2:27.4 (Vladimir Kosinsky)
1. Felipe Múñoz         MEX   2:28.7
2. Vladimir Kosinsky    SOV   2:29.2
3. Brian Job            USA   2:29.9
4. Nikolai Pankin       SOV   2:30.3
5. Yevgeny Mikhailov    SOV   2:32.8
6. Egon Henninger       GDR   2:33.2
7. Philip Long          USA   2:33.6
8. Osamu Tsurumine      JPN   2:34.9

The 1968 Olympics was ten days old and the host country had yet to win a gold medal when 17-year-old Felipe "Pepe" Múñoz stood at the edge of the pool before the start of the final of the 200-meter breaststroke. He was also known as "Tibio" (lukewarm) because his father was from Aguascalientes (hot waters) and his mother from Río Frío (cold river). Múñoz was not the favorite, that role falling to world record holder Vladimir Kosinsky, but there was hope that the Mexican would gain a medal, and since he *had* registered the fastest time of the heats (2:31.1), maybe, just maybe, a miracle might happen.

At the halfway mark Múñoz was in fourth place behind Kosinsky, Henninger, and Job. But then, in the most dramatic fashion possible, Múñoz began to gain on the leaders. Coming off the final turn, with 50 meters to go, he was only inches behind Kosinsky. The excitement in the stadium reached a fever pitch as 8000 cheering Mexicans voiced the hopes of the hundreds of thousands more who were watching on television. Twenty-five meters from the finish Múñoz caught Kosinsky, and in the last few meters he moved ahead, touching the wall a half-second ahead of the Soviet champion. Before he could make a move of his own, Múñoz was hoisted out of the pool and carried, dripping wet and in tears, around the arena. His American coach, Ron Johnson, was thrown into the pool despite the fact that his broken hand was encased in plaster.

**1972 Munich** C: 40, N: 27, D: 9.2. WR: 2:22.79 (John Hencken)

| | | | |
|---|---|---|---|
| 1. John Hencken | USA | 2:21.55 | WR |
| 2. David Wilkie | GBR | 2:23.67 | |
| 3. Nobutaka Taguchi | JPN | 2:23.88 | |
| 4. Richard Colella | USA | 2:24.28 | |
| 5. Felipe Muñoz | MEX | 2:26.44 | |
| 6. Walter Kusch | GER | 2:26.55 | |
| 7. Igor Cherdakov | SOV | 2:27.15 | |
| 8. Klaus Katzur | GDR | 2:27.44 | |

Hencken's superiority was never in doubt, as he led from start to finish.

**1976 Montreal** C: 26, N: 18, D: 7.24. WR: 2:18.21 (John Hencken)

| | | | |
|---|---|---|---|
| 1. David Wilkie | GBR | 2:15.11 | WR |
| 2. John Hencken | USA | 2:17.26 | |
| 3. Richard Colella | USA | 2:19.20 | |
| 4. Graham Smith | CAN | 2:19.42 | |
| 5. Charles Keating | USA | 2:20.79 | |
| 6. Arvydas Juozaitis | SOV | 2:21.87 | |
| 7. Nikolai Pankin | SOV | 2:22.21 | |
| 8. Walter Kusch | GER | 2:22.36 | |

In 1976, 12 of the 13 men's swimming events were won by swimmers from the United States. The only exception was the 200-meter breaststroke. In that race, David Wilkie of Scotland became the first British male to win an Olympic swimming title in 68 years.

**1980 Moscow** C: 19, N: 14, D: 7.26. WR: 2:15.11 (David Wilkie)

| | | |
|---|---|---|
| 1. Robertas Zhulpa | SOV | 2:15.85 |
| 2. Albán Vermes | HUN | 2:16.93 |
| 3. Arsen Miskarov | SOV | 2:17.28 |
| 4. Gennady Utenkov | SOV | 2:19.64 |
| 5. Lindsay Spencer | AUS | 2:19.68 |
| 6. Duncan Goodhew | GBR | 2:20.92 |
| 7. Peter Berggren | SWE | 2:21.65 |
| 8. Jörg Walter | GDR | 2:22.39 |

**1984 Los Angeles** C: 47, N: 35, D: 8.2. WR: 2:14.58 (Victor Davis)

| | | | |
|---|---|---|---|
| 1. Victor Davis | CAN | 2:13.34 | WR |
| 2. Glenn Beringen | AUS | 2:15.79 | |
| 3. Etienne Dagon | SWI | 2:17.41 | |
| 4. Richard Schroeder | USA | 2:18.03 | |
| 5. Ken Fitzpatrick | CAN | 2:18.86 | |
| 6. Pablo Restrepo | COL | 2:18.96 | |
| 7. Alexandre Yokochi | POR | 2:20.69 | |

DISQ: Marco Del Prete (ITA)

World-record holder Victor Davis took command before the 50-meter turn, kept a clear lead throughout the race, and then poured it on in the final 50 meters to set another world record and win by the largest margin in an Olympic breaststroke final in 60 years. Victor Davis died on Nov. 13, 1989, after being struck by a car following an altercation outside a bar. He was 25 years old. His ashes were scattered at sea along with a quart of water from lane 5 of the University of Southern California pool, where he had won his Olympic gold medal.

**1988 Seoul** C: 54, N: 40, D: 9.23. WR: 2:13.34 (Victor Davis)

| | | |
|---|---|---|
| 1. József Szabó | HUN | 2:13.52 |
| 2. Nick Gillingham | GBR | 2:14.12 |
| 3. Sergio Lopez | SPA | 2:15.21 |
| 4. Mike Barrowman | USA | 2:15.45 |
| 5. Valery Lozik | SOV | 2:16.16 |
| 6. Vadim Alexeev | SOV | 2:16.70 |
| 7. Jonathan Cleveland | CAN | 2:17.10 |
| 8. Péter Szabó | HUN | 2:17.12 |

The two Szabós (not related) and Barrowman all practiced the new "wave-action" breaststroke taught by Hungarian coach József Nagy.

## 100-METER BUTTERFLY

As in the breaststroke, butterfly swimmers must keep their shoulders in line with the surface of the water, they must move their arms and legs simultaneously, and they must not swim underwater, except for the first stroke after the start and after each turn. Unlike the breaststroke, butterfly rules allow swimmers to bring back their arms over the water and to kick their legs and feet up and down.

**1896–1964** not held

**1968 Mexico City** C: 47, N: 23, D: 10.21. WR: 55.6 (Mark Spitz)

| | | | |
|---|---|---|---|
| 1. Douglas Russell | USA | 55.9 | OR |
| 2. Mark Spitz | USA | 56.4 | |
| 3. Ross Wales | USA | 57.2 | |
| 4. Vladimir Nemshilov | SOV | 58.1 | |
| 5. Satoshi Maruya | JPN | 58.6 | |
| 6. Yuri Suzdaltsev | SOV | 58.8 | |
| 7. Lutz Stoklasa | GER | 58.9 | |
| 8. Robert Cusack | AUS | 59.8 | |

Mark Spitz and Doug Russell had raced against each other many times in the 100-meter butterfly, and the result was always the same: Russell would take the early lead and then Spitz would finish strongly to win. In Mexico City, though, the two Californians separately and secretly decided to reverse their tactics. This allowed Russell to come from behind and defeat Spitz for the first time.

**1972 Munich** C: 39, N: 26, D: 8.31. WR: 54.56 (Mark Spitz)
1. Mark Spitz            USA   54.27   WR
2. Bruce Robertson       CAN   55.56
3. Jerry Heidenreich     USA   55.74
4. Roland Matthes        GDR   55.87
5. David Edgar           USA   56.11
6. Byron MacDonald       CAN   57.27
7. Hartmut Flöckner      GDR   57.40
8. Neil Rogers           AUS   57.90

Spitz won his fourth gold medal of the Munich Games.

**1976 Montreal** C: 43, N: 29, D: 7.21. WR: 54.27 (Mark Spitz)
1. Matt Vogel            USA   54.35
2. Joe Bottom            USA   54.50
3. Gary Hall             USA   54.65
4. Roger Pyttel          GDR   55.09
5. Roland Matthes        GDR   55.11
6. Clay Evans            CAN   55.81
7. Hideaki Hara          JPN   56.34
8. Neil Rogers           AUS   56.57

**1980 Moscow** C: 34, N: 29, D: 7.23. WR: 54.15 (Pär Arvidsson)
1. Pär Arvidsson         SWE   54.92
2. Roger Pyttel          GDR   54.94
3. David Lopez           SPA   55.13
4. Kees Vervoorn         HOL   55.25
5. Yevgeny Seredin       SOV   55.35
6. Gary Abraham          GBR   55.42
7. Xavier Savin          FRA   55.66
8. Alexei Markovsky      SOV   55.70

On August 2, William Paulus won the U.S. Outdoor National championship in 54.34. Second was Matt Gribble in 54.51. On July 22, in Canada, West Germany's Michael Gross recorded a 54.69.

**1984 Los Angeles** C: 53, N: 39, D: 7.30. WR: 53:38 (P. Pablo Morales)
1. Michael Gross         GER   53.08   WR
2. P. Pablo Morales      USA   53.23
3. Glenn Buchanan        AUS   53.85
4. Rafael Vidal Castro   VEN   54.27
5. Andrew Jameson        GBR   54.28
6. Anthony Mosse         NZE   54.93
7. Andreas Behrend       GER   54.95
8. Bengt Baron           SWE   55.14

In a race that was so fast that the top six finishers all set national records, Michael Gross rocketed past Pablo Morales ten meters from the finish to win his second gold medal and set his second world record of the 1984 Olympics.

**1988 Seoul** C: 51, N: 36, D: 9.21. WR: 52.84 (P. Pablo Morales)
1. Anthony Nesty         SUR   53.00   OR
2. Matthew Biondi        USA   53.01
3. Andy Jameson          GBR   53.30
4. Jonathan Sieben       AUS   53.33
5. Michael Gross         GER   53.44
6. Jay Mortenson         USA   54.07
7. Thomas Ponting        CAN   54.09
8. Vadym Yaroshchuk      SOV   54.60

Favorite Matt Biondi led from the start. Ten meters from the finish, he was still in first place by 2 feet. But as he neared the touch pad, he was caught between strokes and elected to kick in the last few feet instead of taking an extra stroke. However, he was farther away than he thought and his miscalculation allowed 20-year-old Anthony Nesty of Surinam to slip by and win by less than an inch.

The top five finishers all set personal records. Nesty had placed fifth at the 1986 world championships and had the fourth best time of 1987. Still, his victory was a shocker. Surinam, a small tropical nation (population: 380,000) on the east coast of South America, had never before produced an Olympic medalist. Surinam had only one Olympic-size pool, so Nesty, who was born in Trinidad, had gone to live and train in the United States and to study at the University of Florida.

Nesty, a retiring sort, returned to Surinam a hero. After leaving the airport, his motorcade was stopped by a crowd of people in Onverwacht who insisted on giving him $3000. The government chipped in with a larger sum. In addition, the local stadium was renamed for him and a stamp was issued in his honor, as were gold and silver commemorative coins. Anthony Nesty was also the first black swimmer to win an Olympic medal.

As for Biondi, he was left to ponder his narrow loss. After the race he mused, "One one-hundredth of a second—what if I had grown my fingernails longer?" Biondi successfully channeled his anger and disappointment and went on to win five gold medals.

## 200-METER BUTTERFLY

**1896–1952** not held

**1956 Melbourne** C: 19, N: 14, D: 12.1. WR: 2:16.7 (William Yorzyk)
1. William Yorzyk        USA   2:19.3   OR
2. Takashi Ishimoto      JPN   2:23.8
3. György Tumpek         HUN   2:23.9
4. Jack Nelson           USA   2:26.6
5. John Marshall         AUS   2:27.2
6. Eulalio Rios Aleman   MEX   2:27.3
7. Brian Wilkinson       AUS   2:29.7
8. Alexandru Popescu     ROM   2:31.0

**1960 Rome** C: 34, N: 23, D: 9.2. WR: 2:13.2 (Michael Troy)
1. Michael Troy          USA   2:12.8   WR
2. Neville Hayes         AUS   2:14.6
3. J. David Gillanders   USA   2:15.3
4. Federico Dennerlein   ITA   2:16.0
5. Haruo Yoshimuta       JPN   2:18.3
6. Kevin Berry           AUS   2:18.5
7. Valentin Kuzmin       SOV   2:18.9
8. Kenzo Izutsu          JPN   2:19.4

**1964 Tokyo** C: 32, N: 19, D: 10.18. WR: 2:06.9 (Kevin Berry)
1. Kevin Berry           AUS   2:06.6   WR
2. Carl Robie            USA   2:07.5
3. Fred Schmidt          USA   2:09.3
4. Philip Riker          USA   2:11.0
5. Valentin Kuzmin       SOV   2:11.3
6. Yoshinori Kadonaga    JPN   2:12.6
7. Brett Hill            AUS   2:12.8
8. Daniel Sherry         CAN   2:14.6

**1968 Mexico City** C: 29, N: 18, D: 10.24. WR: 2:05.7 (Mark Spitz)
1. Carl Robie            USA   2:08.7
2. Martin Woodroffe      GBR   2:09.0
3. John Ferris           USA   2:09.3
4. Valentin Kuzmin       SOV   2:10.6
5. Peter Feil            SWE   2:10.9
6. Folkert Meeuw         GER   2:11.5
7. Victor Sharygin       SOV   2:11.9
8. Mark Spitz            USA   2:13.5

Having won five gold medals at the 1967 Pan-American Games, Mark Spitz brashly predicted that he would win six golds at the 1968 Olympics in Mexico City. Instead, he fell far short of his expectations. He did gain two gold medals, but they were in relays rather than individual events. After finishing third in the 100-meter freestyle, he placed second in his specialty, the 100-meter butterfly, thus losing his place on the medley relay team to the winner, Douglas Russell. Spitz's last appearance of the 1968 Olympics was in the 200-meter butterfly, in which he was the world record holder. Along with John Ferris, Spitz managed to lead the qualifiers in 2:10.6. But in the final it was clear that his confidence had been shattered. Exhausted by a long week of races, he was never in contention and finished far back in last place.

Carl Robie, on the other hand, was in tip-top shape. Four years earlier he had been the favorite, but was upset by Kevin Berry. In Mexico City, with the attention on Spitz, Robie was able to relax and hold off a late challenge from Martin Woodroffe to gain the victory.

**1972 Munich** C: 29, N: 20, D: 8.28. WR: 2:01.53 (Mark Spitz)
1. Mark Spitz            USA   2:00.70   WR
2. Gary Hall             USA   2:02.86
3. Robin Backhaus        USA   2:03.23
4. Jorgé Delgado         ECU   2:04.60
5. Hans Fassnacht        GER   2:04.69
6. András Hargitay       HUN   2:04.69

7. Hartmut Flöckner      GDR   2:05.34
8. Folkert Meeuw         GER   2:05.57

It seemed only fitting that Mark Spitz's first race of the 1972 Olympics should be the same one as his last race at the 1968 Games—the 200-meter butterfly. Here was a chance for Spitz to redeem himself immediately for his disappointing performances four years earlier. Not surprisingly Spitz was more than a bit nervous as he stood on the starting block before the final, but once he was in the water his victory was never in doubt. Afterward he leaped out of the water with his arms held high. The four-year psychological burden had been lifted, and Mark Spitz was on his way to becoming the first person in history to win seven gold medals in one Olympics.

**1976 Montreal** C: 38, N: 25, D: 7.18 WR: 1:59.63 (Roger Pyttel)
1. Mike Bruner           USA   1:59.23   WR
2. Steven Gregg          USA   1:59.54
3. Bill Forrester        USA   1:59.96
4. Roger Pyttel          GDR   2:00.02
5. Michael Kraus         GER   2:00.46
6. Brian Brinkley        GBR   2:01.49
7. Jorgé Delgado         ECU   2:01.95
8. Aleksandr Manachinsky SOV   2:04.61

**1980 Moscow** C: 25, N: 19, D: 7.20. WR: 1:59.23 (Mike Bruner)
1. Sergei Fesenko        SOV   1:59:76
2. Philip Hubble         GBR   2:01.20
3. Roger Pyttel          GDR   2:01.39
4. Peter Morris          GBR   2:02.27
5. Mikhail Gorelik       SOV   2:02.44
6. Kees Vervoorn         HOL   2:02.52
7. Pär Arvidsson         SWE   2:02.61
8. Stephen Poulter       GBR   2:02.93

This was one event in which the boycotting Americans were sorely missed. In 1972 and 1976 U.S. swimmers had swept all three medals, and they probably could have done it again in 1980. At the U.S. Outdoor National on July 30, Craig Beardsley of Harrington Park, New Jersey, set a world record of 1:58.21 in his qualifying heat. He won the final in 1:58.46, followed by Mike Bruner in 1:59.13 and Bill Forrester in 1:59.40. Eighth-place finisher Steve Gregg clocked 2:00.98—faster than the silver medal winner in Moscow ten days earlier.

**1984 Los Angeles** C: 35, N: 28, D: 8.3. WR: 1:57.05 (Michael Gross)
1. Jon Sieben            AUS   1:57.04   WR
2. Michael Gross         GER   1:57.40
3. Rafael Vidal Castro   VEN   1:57.51
4. P. Pablo Morales      USA   1:57.75
5. Anthony Mosse         NZE   1:58.75
6. Thomas Ponting        CAN   1:59.37
7. Peter Ward            CAN   2:00.39
8. Patrick Kennedy       USA   2:01.03

With two gold medals already under his belt, Michael Gross entered his best event, the 200-meter butterfly, as the clear favorite. He expected stiff challenges from Pablo Morales and Rafael Vidal and that's exactly what he got. But over in lane 6, something completely unexpected happened. Seventeen-year-old Jon Sieben, from the Brisbane suburb of Coorparoo, seventh at the halfway mark and fourth with 50 meters to go, shot past the favorites to out-touch Gross and gain the victory, the world record, and one of the most surprising upsets in Olympic swimming history. Sieben's time of 1:57.04 was over four seconds faster than his pre-Olympic best of 2:01.17.

The rabidly pro-U.S. crowd gave Sieben a standing ovation, and the outcome was so delightful that the defeated favorites expressed pleasure more than disappointment. Gross, who had refused to appear before reporters following his two gold-medal races, and whose disdain for pomp and press had earned him the nickname "The American" in West Germany, sat beside Sieben after the 200 butterfly preferring to praise the young Australian rather than talk about himself.

**1988 Seoul** C: 40, N: 29, D: 9.24. WR: 1:56.24 (Michael Gross)
| | | | |
|---|---|---|---|
| 1. Michael Gross | GER | 1:56.94 | OR |
| 2. Benny Nielsen | DEN | 1:58.24 | |
| 3. Anthony Mosse | NZE | 1:58.28 | |
| 4. Thomas Ponting | CAN | 1:58.91 | |
| 5. Melvin Stewart | USA | 1:59.19 | |
| 6. David Wilson | AUS | 1:59.20 | |
| 7. Jon Kelly | CAN | 1:59.48 | |
| 8. Anthony Nesty | SUR | 2:00.80 | |

Michael Gross had dominated this event since 1981, winning two world championships, four European championships, and setting four world records. The only stain on his record was his unexpected loss to Jon Sieben at the 1984 Olympics. In Seoul, Gross placed fifth in the two events he had won in Los Angeles: the 200-meter freestyle and the 100-meter butterfly. But in the 200 fly, he lived up to the expectations, leading from start to finish and winning by a body length.

# 200-METER INDIVIDUAL MEDLEY

In individual medley races the order of strokes is butterfly, backstroke, breaststroke, and freestyle.

**1896–1964** not held

**1968 Mexico City** C: 46, N: 27, D: 10.20. WR: 2.10.6 (Charles Hickcox)
| | | | |
|---|---|---|---|
| 1. Charles Hickcox | USA | 2:12.0 | OR |
| 2. Gregory Buckingham | USA | 2:13.0 | |
| 3. John Ferris | USA | 2:13.3 | |
| 4. Juan Bello | PER | 2:13.7 | |
| 5. George Smith | CAN | 2:15.9 | |
| 6. John Gilchrist | CAN | 2:16.6 | |
| 7. Michael Holthaus | GER | 2:16.8 | |
| 8. Péter Lázár | HUN | 2:18.3 | |

Hickcox won the first of his three gold medals.

**1972 Munich** C: 39, N: 26, D: 9.3. WR: 2:09.3 (Gunnar Larsson, Gary Hall)
| | | | |
|---|---|---|---|
| 1. Gunnar Larsson | SWE | 2:07.17 | WR |
| 2. Alexander "Tim" McKee | USA | 2:08.37 | |
| 3. Steven Furniss | USA | 2:08.45 | |
| 4. Gary Hall | USA | 2:08.49 | |
| 5. András Hargitay | HUN | 2:09.66 | |
| 6. Mikhail Suharev | SOV | 2:11.78 | |
| 7. Juan Bello | PER | 2:11.87 | |
| 8. Hans Ljungberg | SWE | 2:13.56 | |

Larsson and McKee duplicated their one-two finish in the 400-meter individual medley, as the first four finishers all broke the world record.

**1976–1980** not held

**1984 Los Angeles** C: 45, N: 34, D: 8.4. WR: 2.02.45 (Alex Baumann)
| | | | |
|---|---|---|---|
| 1. Alex Baumann | CAN | 2:01.42 | WR |
| 2. Pedro Pablo Morales | USA | 2:03.05 | |
| 3. Neil Cochran | GBR | 2:04.38 | |
| 4. Robin Brew | GBR | 2:04.52 | |
| 5. Steve Lundquist | USA | 2:04.91 | |
| 6. Andrew Phillips | JAM | 2:05.60 | |
| 7. Nicolai Klapkarek | GER | 2:05.88 | |
| 8. Ralf Diegel | GER | 2:06.66 | |

Baumann won his second gold medal of the Los Angeles Games, setting a world record, as he had in the 400 individual medley five days earlier. The victor at the Friendship Games, with a time of 2:02.51, was Jens-Peter Berndt of East Germany, who defected to the U.S. less than five months later and competed for West Germany in 1988.

**1988 Seoul** C: 56, N: 35, D: 9.25. WR: 2:00.56 (Tamás Darnyi)
| | | | |
|---|---|---|---|
| 1. Tamás Darnyi | HUN | 2:00.17 | WR |
| 2. Patrick Kühl | GDR | 2:01.61 | |
| 3. Vadym Yaroshchuk | SOV | 2:02.40 | |
| 4. Mikhail Zubkov | SOV | 2:02.92 | |
| 5. Peter Bermel | GER | 2:03.81 | |
| 6. Robert Bruce | AUS | 2:04.34 | |
| 7. Raik Hannermann | GDR | 2:04.82 | |
| 8. Gary Anderson | CAN | 2:06.35 | |

When Tamás Darnyi was 15 years old, he lost the vision in his left eye after being hit by a snowball during some horseplay. He underwent four operations to repair a detached retina. Although the surgery did not restore his sight, it did give him sensitivity to light. Beginning in 1985 Darnyi won every major title in both individual medal events. In Seoul, the 21-year-old Budapest native was in third place after 150 meters. Then, as expected, he pulled away with a 27.73 freestyle leg to win his second gold medal and set his second world record.

# 400-METER INDIVIDUAL MEDLEY

**1896–1960** not held

**1964 Tokyo** C: 30, N; 18, D: 10.14. WR: 4:48.6 (Richard Roth)
1. Richard Roth        USA    4:45.4    WR
2. Roy Saari           USA    4:47.1
3. Gerhard Hetz        GER    4:51.0
4. Carl Robie          USA    4:51.4
5. John Gilchrist      CAN    4:57.6
6. Johannes Jiskoot    HOL    5:01.9
7. György Kosztolánczy HUN    5:01.9
8. Terry Buck          AUS    5:03.0

Three days before the competition, world record holder Dick Roth was stricken with an acute attack of appendicitis. Japanese doctors recommended an immediate operation, but Roth refused. Since he also refused to take drugs, they packed him in ice instead. Willing the pain to subside temporarily, the 17-year-old Californian took the lead 70 meters from the finish and won the final in world record time.

**1968 Mexico City** C: 35, N: 22, D: 10.23. WR: 4:39.0 (Charles Hickcox)
1. Charles Hickcox      USA    4:48.4
2. Gary Hall            USA    4:48.7
3. Michael Holthaus     GER    4:51.4
4. Gregory Buckingham   USA    4:51.4
5. John Gilchrist       CAN    4:56.7
6. Reinhard Merkel      GER    4:59.8
7. Andrei Dunaev        SOV    5:00.3
8. Rafael Hernandez     MEX    5:04.3

Hickcox and Hall swam side by side, almost neck and neck for the entire race.

**1972 Munich** C: 32, N: 24, D: 8.30. WR: 4:30.81 (Gary Hall)
1. Gunnar Larsson           SWE    4:31.98    OR
2. Alexander "Tim" McKee    USA    4:31.98    OR
3. András Hargitay          HUN    4:32.70
4. Steven Furniss           USA    4:35.44
5. Gary Hall                USA    4:37.38
6. Bengt Gingsjö            SWE    4:37.96
7. Graham Windeatt          AUS    4:40.39
8. Wolfram Sperling         GDR    4:40.66

Both Larsson and McKee were credited with the Olympic record, but Larsson was declared the winner by two one-thousandths of a second, 4:31.981 to 4:31.983. Bronze medalist András Hargitay had almost drowned in the Danube River at the age of nine. "After that," he recalled, "my mother ordered me to learn how to swim, and this is what's come of it."

**1976 Montreal** C: 31, N: 22, D: 7.25. WR: 4:26.00 (Zóltan Verrasztó)
1. Rod Strachan            USA    4:23.68    WR
2. Alexander "Tim" McKee   USA    4:24.62
3. Andrei Smirnov          SOV    4:26.90
4. András Hargitay         HUN    4:27.13
5. Graham Smith            CAN    4:28.64
6. Steven Furniss          USA    4:29.23
7. Andrew Ritchie          CAN    4:29.87
8. Hans-Joachim Geisler    GER    4:34.95

**1980 Moscow** C: 23, N: 17, D: 7.27. WR: 4:20.05 (Jesse Vassallo)
1. Aleksandr Sidorenko     SOV    4:22.89    OR
2. Sergei Fesenko          SOV    4:23.43
3. Zoltán Verrasztó        HUN    4:24.24
4. András Hargitay         HUN    4:24.48
5. Djan Madruga Garrido    BRA    4:26.81
6. Miloslav Rolko          CZE    4:26.99
7. Leszek Górski           POL    4:28.89
8. Daniel Machek           CZE    4:29.86

Three days after the Olympic final, the U.S. Outdoor National was won by world record holder Jesse Vassallo in 4:21.51.

**1984 Los Angeles** C: 23, N: 19, D: 7.30. WR: 4:17.53 (Alex Baumann)
1. Alex Baumann          CAN    4:17.41    WR
2. Ricardo Prado         BRA    4:18.45
3. Robert Woodhouse      AUS    4:20.50
4. Jesus Vassallo        USA    4:21.46
5. Maurizio Divano       ITA    4:22.76
6. Jeffrey Kostoff       USA    4:23.28
7. Stephen Poulter       GBR    4:25.80
8. Giovanni Franceschi   ITA    4:26.05

Born in Prague, 4-year-old Alex Baumann was in New Zealand with his family when Soviet tanks rolled into Czechoslovakia in 1968. Baumann's parents refused to return to their homeland, eventually settling instead in Sudbury, Ontario. Proud to be a Canadian, Baumann appeared at the Olympics sporting a maple-leaf tattoo (and a diamond-stud earring)—and earned Canada's first swimming gold medal since 1912. Baumann was unable to meet with reporters after the race because he required almost two hours to produce a urine sample for the drug-testing. In the middle of his third beer, medical officials discovered that he was under age and forced him to switch to soft drinks.

In Moscow three weeks later, Jens-Peter Berndt of East Germany clocked 4:18.29 to win at the Friendship Games.

**1988 Seoul** C: 34, N: 24, D: 9.21. WR: 4:15.42 (Tamás Darnyi)
1. Tamás Darnyi          HUN    4:14.75    WR
2. David Wharton         USA    4:17.36
3. Stefano Battistelli   ITA    4:18.01
4. József Szabó          HUN    4:18.15
5. Patrick Kühl          GDR    4:18.44
6. Jens-Peter Berndt     GER    4:21.71
7. Luca Sacchi           ITA    4:23.23
8. Peter Bermel          GER    4:24.02

This race was billed as a showdown between world record holder Tamás Darnyi, who was blind in one eye, and former world record holder David Wharton, who was born severely hearing-impaired. However, Darnyi built such a large lead during the backstroke leg that the second half of the contest was anticlimactic.

# 4 × 100-METER FREESTYLE RELAY

**1896–1960** not held

**1964 Tokyo** T: 13, N: 13, D: 10.14. WR: 3:36. 1 (USA—Clark, McDonough, Ilman, Townsend)

1. USA (Stephen Clark, Michael Austin, 3:32.2 WR
Gary Ilman, Donald Schollander)
2. GER/GDR (Horst Löffler, Frank Wiegand, 3:37.2
Uwe Jacobsen, Hans-Joachim Klein)
3. AUS (David Dickson, Peter Doak, John 3:39.1
Ryan, Robert Windle)
4. JPN (Kunihiro Iwasaki, Tadaharu Goto, 3:40.5
Tatsuo Fujimoto, Yukiaki Okabe)
5. SWE (Bengt-Olof Nordvall, E. Lester 3:40.7
Eriksson, Jan Lundin, Per-Ola Lindberg)
6. SOV (Viktor Mazanov, Vladimir 3:42.1
Schuvalov, Viktor Semchenkov, Yuri Sumtsov)
7. GBR (Robert Lord, John Martin-Dye, 3:42.6
Peter Kendrew, Robert McGregor)

DISQ. FRA (Alain Gottvalles, Gerard Gropaiz, Pierre Canavese, Jean Curtillet)

Steve Clark had failed to qualify for the U.S. team in any individual events, but he made up for it by winning three gold medals in the relays. His lead-off leg in the 4 × 100-meter freestyle relay equaled Alain Gottvalles' 100-meter world record of 52.9 seconds and also earned him the right to swim the freestyle leg of the medley relay.

**1968 Mexico City** T: 16, N: 16, D: 10.17. WR: 3:32.5 (USA—Zorn, Rerych, Walsh, Schollander)

1. USA (Zachary Zorn, Stephen Rerych, Mark 3:31.7 WR
Spitz, Kenneth Walsh)
2. SOV (Semyon Belits-Geiman, Viktor Mazanov, 3:34.2
Georgi Kulikov, Leonid Ilyichev)
3. AUS (Gregory Rogers, Robert Windle, Robert 3:34.7
Cusack, Michael Wenden)
4. GBR (Mike Turner, David Hombrow, Robert 3:38.4
McGregor, Anthony Jarvis)
5. GDR (Frank Wiegand, Udo Poser, Horst- 3:38.8
Günther Gregor, Lothar Gericke)
6. GER (Wolfgang Kremer, Olaf von Schilling, 3:39.0
Peter Schorning, Hans Fassnacht)
7. CAN (Glen Finch, George Smith, Ralph Hut- 3:39.2
ton, John Gilchrist)
8. JPN (Kunihiro Iwasaki, Masayuki Ohsawa, 3:41.5
Satoru Nakano, Teruhiko Kitani)

**1972 Munich** T: 13, N: 13, D: 8.28. WR: 3:28.8 (USA, Los Angeles Swim Club—Havens, Weston, Frawley, Heckl)

1. USA (David Edgar, John Murphy, Jerry 3:26.42 WR
Heidenreich, Mark Spitz)
2. SOV (Vladimir Bure, Viktor Mazanov, Viktor 3:29.72
Aboimov, Igor Grivennikov)
3. GDR (Roland Matthes, Wilfried Hartung, Pe- 3:32.42
ter Bruch, Lutz Unger)

4. BRA (Ruy Aquino Oliveira, Paulo Zanetti, 3:33.14
Paulo Becskehazy, José Diaz-Aranha)
5. CAN (Bruce Robertson, Brian Phillips, Timo- 3:33.20
thy Bach, Robert Kasting)
6. GER (Klaus Steinbach, Werner Lampe, 3:33.90
Rainer Jacob, Hans Fassnacht)
7. FRA (Gilles Vigne, Alain Mosconi, Alain 3:34.13
Hermitte, Michel Rousseau)
8. SPA (Jorge Comas, Antonio Culebras, En- 3:38.21
rique Melo, José Pujol)

The U.S. "reserve" team of Dave Fairbank, Gary Conelly, Jerry Heidenreich, and Dave Edgar clocked 3:28.84 in the qualifying round to equal the world record. Six hours later, in the final, Fairbank and Conelly were replaced by John Murphy and Mark Spitz, and a new world record was set. It was Spitz's second gold medal of the evening.

**1976–1980** not held

**1984 Los Angeles** T: 23, N: 23, D: 8.2. WR: 3:19.26 (USA— Cavanaugh, Leamy, McCagg, Gaines)

1. USA (Christopher Cavanaugh, Michael 3:19.03 WR
Heath, Matthew Biondi, Ambrose "Rowdy" Gaines)
2. AUS (Gregory Fasala, Neil Brooks, Michael 3:19.68
Delany, Mark Stockwell)
3. SWE (Thomas Lejdström, Bengt Baron, 3:22.69
Mikael Orn, Per Johansson)
4. GER (Dirk Korthals, Andreas Schmidt, Alex- 3:22.98
ander Schowtka, Michael Gross)
5. GBR (David Lowe, Roland Lee, Paul Easter, 3:23.61
Richard Burrell)
6. FRA (Stephan Caron, Laurent Neuville, 3:24.63
Dominique Bataille, Bruno Lesaffre)
7. CAN (David Churchill, Blair Hicken, Alex 3:24.70
Baumann, Donald "Sandy" Goss)
8. ITA (Marcello Guarducci, Marco Colombo, 3:24.97
Motello Savino, Fabrizio Rampazzo)

**1988 Seoul** T: 22, N: 22, D: 9.23. WR: 3:17.08 (USA—McCadam, Heath, Wallace, Biondi)

1. USA (Christopher Jacobs, Troy Dalbey, 3:16.53 WR
Thomas Jager, Matthew Biondi)
2. SOV (Gennady Prigoda, Yuri Bashkatov, 3:18.33
Nikolai Yevseyev, Vladimir Tkachenko)
3. GDR (Dirk Richter, Thomas Flemming, Lars 3:19.82
Hinneburg, Steffen Zesner)
4. FRA (Stephan Caron, Christophe Kalfayan, 3:20.02
Laurent Neuville, Bruno Gutzeit)
5. SWE (Per Johansson, Tommy Werner, 3:21.07
Joakim Holmquist, Göran Titus)
6. GER (Michael Gross, Thomas Fahrner, Björn 3:21.65
Zikarsky, Peter Sitt)
7. GBR (Mike Fibbens, Mark Foster, Roland 3:21.71
Lee, Andy Jameson)
8. ITA (Roberto Gleria, Giorgio Lamberti, 3:22.93
Fabrizio Rampazzo, Andrea Ceccarini)

As usual, the U.S. won this event with a world record. This time the U.S.S.R., by placing their fastest swimmers first, managed to keep pace with the Americans for 300 meters. But as soon as anchor Matt Biondi hit the water the race ceased to be close. Biondi, already credited with the seven fastest relay splits in history, swam a 47.81 to earn the third of his five gold medals.

# 4 × 200-METER FREESTYLE RELAY

**1896–1904** not held

**1906 Athens** T: 6, N: 6, D: 4.26.
*(4 × 250 Meters)*
1. HUN   (József Ónody, Henrik Hajós, Geza Kiss,   16:52.4
         Zoltán Halmay)
2. GER   (Ernst Bahnmeyer, Oskar Schiele, Emil   17:16.2
         Rausch, Max Pape)
3. GBR   (William Henry, John Derbyshire, Henry Taylor,   —
         John Arthur Jarvis)
4. USA   (Frank Bornamann, Joseph Spencer, Maquard   —
         Schwartz, Charles Daniels)
5. SWE   (Harald Julin, Robert Andersson, Charles   —
         Norelius, Hjalmar Johansson)
DNF: AUT (Edmund Bernhardt, Leopold Mayer, Simon Orlik, Otto
         Scheff)

Forty-seven-year-old William Henry of the British team is the oldest person ever to have won a swimming medal.

**1908 London** T: 6, N: 6, D: 7.24.
1. GBR   (John        Derbyshire,   Paul   10:55.6   WR
         Radmilovic, William Foster, Henry
         Taylor)
2. HUN   (József Munk, Imre Zachár, Béla   10:59.0
         Las-Torres, Zoltán Halmay)
3. USA   (Harry Hebner, Leo Goodwin,   11:02.8
         Charles Daniels, Leslie Rich)
4. AUS/NZE (Francis Beaurepaire, Fred Spring-   —
         field, Reginald Baker, Theodore
         Tartakover)

The Hungarians seemed to have the race well in hand, when Halmay suddenly began to lose consciousness during the last 50 meters. He struggled to the finish line, but had to be hauled from the pool before he drowned.

**1912 Stockholm** T: 5, N: 5, D: 7.15.
1. AUS/NZE (Cecil Healy, Malcolm Champion,   10:11.6   WR
         Leslie Boardman, Harold Hard-
         wick)
2. USA   (Kenneth Huszagh, Harry Hebner,   10:20.0
         Perry McGillivray, Duke Paoa Ka-
         hanamoku)
3. GBR   (William Foster, Thomas Batters-   10:28.2
         by, John Hatfield, Henry Taylor)
4. GER   (Oskar Schiele, Georg Kunisch,   10:37.0
         Kurt Bretting, Max Ritter)

**1920 Antwerp** T: 7, N: 7, D: 8.29.
1. USA   (Perry McGillivray, Pua Kela Kealoha,   10:04.4   WR
         Norman Ross, Duke Paoa Kahana-
         moku)
2. AUS   (Henry Hay, William Herald, Ivan Sted-   10:25.4
         man, Francis Beaurepaire)
3. GBR   (Leslie Savage, Edward Percival Peter,   10:37.2
         Henry Taylor, Harold Annison)
4. SWE   (Robert Andersson, Frans Moller, Orvar   —
         Trolle, Arne Borg)
5. ITA   (Mario Massa, Agostino Frassinetti, An-   —
         tonio Quarantotto, Gilio Bisagno)

**1924 Paris** T: 13, N: 13, D: 7.20.
1. USA   (Wallace O'Connor, Harry Glancy,   9:53.4   WR
         Ralph Breyer, Johnny Weiss-
         muller)
2. AUS   (Maurice Christie, Ernest Henry,   10:02.2
         Francis Beaurepaire, Andrew
         "Boy" Charlton)
3. SWE   (Georg Werner, Orvar Trolle, Åke   10:06.8
         Borg, Arne Borg)
4. JPN   (Torahiko Miyahata, Katsuo Takai-   10:15.2
         shi, Kazuo Noda, Kazuo Onoda)
5. GBR   (John Thomson, Albert Dicken,   10:29.4
         Harold Annison, Edward Percival
         Peter)
6. FRA   (Guy Middleton, Henri Padou,   —
         Edouard    Vanzeveren,    Emile
         Zeibig)

**1928 Amsterdam** T: 13, N: 13, D: 8.11.
1. USA   (Austin Clapp, Walter Laufer,   9:36.2   WR
         George Kojac, Johnny Weiss-
         muller)
2. JPN   (Hiroshi Yoneyama, Nobuo Arai,   9.41.4
         Tokuhei Sada, Katsuo Takaishi)
3. CAN   (F. Munro Bourne, James Thomp-   9:47.8
         son, Garnet Ault, Walter Spence)
4. HUN   (András Wanié, Rezsö Wanié,   9:57.0
         Géza Sziagritz-Tarródy, István
         Bárány)
5. SWE   (Aulo Gustafsson, Sven Petters-   10:01.8
         son, Eskil Lundahl, Arne Borg)
6. GBR   (Reginald Sutton, Joseph White-   10:15.8
         side, Edward Percival Peter, Al-
         bert Dicken)
7. SPA   (J. Gonzalez Espuglas, E. Artal   —
         Garriga, R. Artigas Rigual, F. Se-
         gala Torres)

Johnny Weissmuller completed his Olympic career by winning his fifth gold medal.

**1932 Los Angeles** T: 7, N: 7, D: 8.9. WR: 9:36.2 (USA—Clapp, Laufer, Kojac, Weissmuller)
1. JPN   (Yasuji Miyazaki, Masanori Yusa,   8:58.4   WR
         Takashi Yokoyama, Hisakichi To-
         yoda)

2. USA    (Frank Booth, George Fissler,   9:10.5
Marola Kalili, Manuella Kalili)

3. HUN    (András Wanié, László Szabados,   9:31.4
András Székely, István Bárány)

4. CAN    (George Larson, George Burrows,   9:36.3
Walter Spence, F. Munro Bourne)

5. GBR    (Joseph Whiteside, Robert Lei-   9:45.8
vers, Mostyn French-Williams,
Reginald Sutton)

6. ARG    (Carlos Kennedy, Leopoldo Ta-   10:13.1
hier, Roberto Peper, Alfredo
Rocca)

7. BRA    (Manoel Lourenço Silva, Isaac   10:36.5
Dos Santos Moraes, Manoel
Rocha Villar, Benevenuto Martins
Nunes)

**1936 Berlin** T: 18, N: 18, D: 8.11. WR: 8:52.2 (JPN—Yusa,
Makino, Isharada, Negami)

1. JPN    (Masanori Yusa, Shigeo Sugiura, Masa-   8:51.5   WR
haru Taguchi, Shigeo Arai)

2. USA    (Ralph Flanagan, John Macionis, Paul   9:03.0
Wolf, Jack Medica)

3. HUN    (Árpád Lengyel, Oszkár Abay-Nemes,   9:12.3
Ödön Gróf, Ferenc Csík)

4. FRA    (Alfred Nakache, Christian Talli, René   9:18.2
Cavalero, Jean Taris)

5. GER    (Werner Plath, Wolfgang Heimlich, Her-   9:19.0
mann Heibel, Helmut Fischer)

6. GBR    (Mostyn French-Williams, Romana Gabri-   9:21.5
elson, Robert Leivers, Norman Wain-
wright)

7. CAN    (F. Munro Bourne, Hamerton, Robert   9:27.5
Hooper, Robert Pirie)

8. SWE    (Björn Borg, Sten Olov Bolldén, Sven   9:37.5
Petterson, Gunnar Werner)

**1948 London** T: 14, N: 14, D: 8.3. WR: 8:51.5 (JPN—Yusa,
Sugiura, Taguchi, Arai)

1. USA    (Walter Ris, James McLane, Wallace   8:46.0   WR
Wolf, William Smith)

2. HUN    (Elemér Szathmáry, György Mitró, Imre   8:48.4
Nyéki, Géza Kádas)

3. FRA    (Joseph Bernardo, Henri Padou, René   9:08.0
Cornu, Alexandre Jany)

4. SWE    (Martin Lundén, Per-Olof Östrand, Olle   9:09.1
Johansson, Per-Olof Olsson)

5. YUG    (Vanja Illič, Čiril Pelhan, Ivan Puhar,   9:14.0
Branko Vidovič)

6. ARG    (Horatio White, José Duranona, Juan   9:19.2
Garay, Alfredo Yantorno)

7. MEX    (Ramon Bravo Prieto, Angel Maldonado   9:20.2
Campos, Apolonio Diaz Castillo, Alberto
Isaac Ahumada)

8. BRA    Sergio Alencar Rodrigues, Willy Jordan,   9:31.0
Rof Kestener Egon, Aram Boghossian)

**1952 Helsinki** T: 17, N: 17, D: 7.29, WR: 8:29.4 (USA, Yale
University—Moore, McLane, Sheff, Thoman)

1. USA    (Wayne Moore, William Woolsey, Ford   8:31.1   OR
Konno, James McLane)

2. JPN    (Hiroshi Suzuki, Yoshihiro Hamaguchi,   8:33.5
Toru Goto, Teijiro Tanikawa)

3. FRA    (Joseph Bernardo, Aldo Eminente, Alex-   8:45.9
andre Jany, Jean Boiteux)

4. SWE    (Lars Svanteson, Göran Larsson, Per-   8:46.8
Olof Östrand, Olle Johansson)

5. HUN    (László Gyöngyösi, György Csordás,   8:52.6
Géza Kádas, Imre Nyéki)

6. GBR    (Frank Botham, Ronald Burns, Thomas   8:52.9
Welsh, John Wardrop)

7. SAF    (Graham Johnston, Dennis Ford, John   8:55.1
Durr, Peter Duncan)

8. ARG    (Federico Zwanck, Marcelo Trabucco,   8:56.9
Pedro Galvao, Severo Yantorno)

Knowing that they would lose under normal circumstances, the Japanese reversed the usual order of their
swimmers, putting the fastest man first and the slowest
last. They did build up a big lead, but Ford Konno closed
the gap and Jimmy McLane pulled away in the final 100
meters.

**1956 Melbourne** T: 11, N: 11, D: 12.3. WR: 8:24.5 (SOV—Nikitin,
Strushanov, Nikolayev, Sorokin)

1. AUS    (Kevin O'Halloran, John Devitt, Murray   8:23.6   WR
Rose, Jon Henricks)

2. USA    (Richard Hanley, George Breen, Wil-   8:31.5
liam Woolsey, Ford Konno)

3. SOV    (Vitaly Sorokin, Vladimir Strushanov,   8:34.7
Gennady Nikolayev, Boris Nikitin)

4. JPN    (Manabu Koga, Atsushi Tani, Koji   8:36.6
Nonoshita, Tsuyoshi Yamanaka)

5. GER/GDR    (Hans Köhler, Hans-Joachim Reich,   8:43.4
Hans Zierold, Horst Bleeker)

6. GBR    (Kenneth Williams, Ronald Roberts,   8:45.2
Neil McKechnie, John Wardrop)

7. ITA    (Federico Dennerlein, Paolo Galletti,   8:46.2
Guido Elmi, Anthony Romani)

8. SAF    (William Steuart, A. Briscoe, Dennis   8:49.5
Ford, Peter Duncan)

**1960 Rome** T: 15, N: 15, D: 9.1. WR(880 yards): 8:16.6 (AUS—
Henricks, Dickson, Konrads, Rose)

1. USA    (George Harrison, Richard Blick, Mi-   8:10.2   WR
chael Troy, F. Jeffrey Farrell)

2. JPN    (Makoto Fukui, Hiroshi Ishii, Tsuyoshi   8:13.2
Yamanaka, Tatsuo Fujimoto)

3. AUS    (David Dickson, John Devitt, Murray   8:13.8
Rose, Jon Konrads)

4. GBR    (Hamilton Milton, Jon Martin-Dye, Rich-   8:28.1
ard Campion, Ian Black)

5. FIN    (Ilkka Suvanto, Kari Haavisto, Stig-   8:29.7
Olof Grenner, Harri Käyhko)

6. SWE    (Sven-Göran Johansson, Lars-Erik   8:31.0
Bengtsson, Bengt Nordvall, Per-Ola
Lindberg)

7. GER/GDR   (Frank Wiegand, Gerhard Hetz, Hans   8:31.8
             Zierold, Hans Klein)

8. SOV       (Igor Lushkovski, Gennady Nikolayev,   8:32.2
             Vitaly Sorokin, Boris Nikitin)

**1964 Tokyo** T: 15, N: 15, D: 10.18. WR: 8:01.8 (USA—Mettler, Wall, Lyons, Schollander)

1. USA      (Stephen Clark, Roy Saari, Gary Ilman,   7:52.1   WR
            Donald Schollander)

2. GDR/GER  (Horst-Günther Gregor, Gerhard Hetz,   7:59.3
            Frank Wiegand, Hans-Joachim Klein)

3. JPN      (Makoto Fukui, Kunihiro Iwasaki,   8:03.8
            Toshio Shoji, Yukiaki Okabe)

4. AUS      (David Dickson, Allan Wood, Peter   8:05.5
            Doak, Robert Windle)

5. SWE     (Mats Svensson, E. Lester Eriksson,   8:08.0
            Hans Rosendahl, Jan Lundin)

6. FRA     (Jean-Pascal Curtillet, Pierre Cana-   8:08.7
            vese, Francis Luyce, Alain Gottvalles)

7. SOV      (Semyon Belits-Geiman, Vladimir Bere-   8:15.1
            zin, Aleksandr Paramonov, Yevgeny
            Novikov)

8. ITA      (Sergio De Gregorio, Bruno Bianchi,   8:18.1
            Giovanni Orlando, Pietro Bascaini)

With this race Steve Clark earned his third gold medal, and Don Schollander became the first swimmer in Olympic history to win four gold medals in one Olympics.

**1968 Mexico City** T: 16, N: 16, D: 10.21 WR: 7:52.1 (USA—Clark, Saari, Ilman, Schollander; USA, Santa Clara Swim Club—Ilman, Spitz, Wall, Schollander)

1. USA      (John Nelson, Stephen Rerych, Mark Spitz,   7:52.33
            Donald Schollander)

2. AUS      (Gregory Rogers, Graham White, Robert   7:53.77
            Windle, Michael Wenden)

3. SOV      (Vladimir Bure, Semyon Belits-Geiman, Georgi   8:01.66
            Kulikov, Leonid Ilyichev)

4. CAN      (George Smith, Ronald Jacks, John Gilchrist,   8:03.22
            Ralph Hutton)

5. FRA      (Michel Rousseau, Gerard Letast, Francis   8:03.77
            Luyce, Alain Mosconi)

6. GER     (Hans Fassnacht, Olaf von Schilling, Volkert   8:04.33
            Meeuw, Wolfgang Kremer)

7. GDR     (Frank Wiegand, Horst-Günter Gregor, Alfred   8:06.00
            Müller, Jochen Herbst)

8. SWE     (Hans Ljungberg, Karl Larson, Sven Ferm, Erik   8:12.11
            Eriksson)

**1972 Munich** T: 14, N: 14, D: 8.31. WR: 7:43.3 (USA—Spitz, Heidenreich, Tyler, McBreen)

1. USA      (John Kinsella, Frederick Tyler, Steven   7:35.78   WR
            Genter, Mark Spitz)

2. GER     (Klaus Steinbach, Werner Lampe,   7:41.69
            Hans-Günter Vosseler, Hans-Joachim
            Fassnacht)

3. SOV      (Igor Grivennikov, Viktor Mazanov,   7:45.76
            Georgi Kulikov, Vladimir Bure)

4. SWE     (Bengt Gingsjö, Hans Ljungberg,   7:47.37
            Anders Bellbring, Gunnar Larsson)

5. AUS      (Michael Wenden, Graham Windeatt,   7:48.66
            Robert Nay, Bradford Cooper)

6. GDR     (Wilfried Hartung, Peter Bruch, Udo   7:49.11
            Poser, Lutz Unger)

7. CAN      (Bruce Robertson, Brian Phillips, Ian   7:53.61
            MacKenzie, Ralph Hutton)

8. GBR     (Brian Brinkley, John Mills, Michael   7:55.59
            Bailey, Colin Cunningham)

One hour after winning the 100-meter butterfly, Mark Spitz was back in the water to swim the anchor leg for the 4 × 200-meter freestyle relay team. Steve Genter's third leg of 1:52.72 gave the U.S. a big lead. Spitz took over from there to gain his fifth gold medal and fifth world record in four days.

**1976 Montreal** T: 18, N: 18, D: 7.21. WR: 7:30.54 (USA, Long Beach Swim Club—Favero, Shaw, S. Furniss, B. Furniss)

1. USA      (Mike Bruner, Bruce Furniss, John   7:23.22   WR
            Naber, Jim Montgomery)

2. SOV      (Vladimir Raskatov, Andrei Bogdanov,   7:27.97
            Sergei Kopliakov, Andrei Krylov)

3. GBR     (Alan McClatchey, David Dunne, Gor-   7:32.11
            don Downie, Brian Brinkley)

4. GER     (Klaus Steinbach, Peter Nocke, Werner   7:32.27
            Lampe, Hans-Joachim Geisler)

5. GDR     (Roger Pyttel, Wilfried Hartung, Rainer   7:38.92
            Strohbach, Frank Pfütze)

6. HOL      (Abdul Ressand, René van der Kuil,   7:42.56
            André in Het Veld, Henk Elzerman)

7. SWE     (Pär Arvidsson, Peter Petterson,   7:42.84
            Anders Bellbring, Bengt Gingsjö)

8. ITA      (Marcello Guarducci, Roberto   7:43.39
            Pangaro, Paolo Barelli, Paolo Revelli)

The U.S. team of Doug Northway, Tim Shaw, Mike Bruner, and Bruce Furniss set a world record of 7:30.33 in the qualifying round. That night, Northway and Shaw were replaced by John Naber and Jim Montgomery, and another world record was set.

**1980 Moscow** T: 13, N: 13, D: 7.23. WR: 7:20.82 (USA—B. Furniss, Forrester, Hackett, Gaines)

1. SOV      (Sergei Kopliakov, Vladimir Salnikov, Ivar Stu-   7:23.50
            kolkin, Andrei Krylov)

2. GDR     (Frank Pfütze, Jörg Woithe, Detlev Grabs,   7:28.60
            Rainer Strohbach)

3. BRA      (Jorge Lutz Fernandes, Marcus Laborne   7:29.30
            Mattioli, Cyro Marques, Djan Madruga
            Garrido)

4. SWE     (Michael Söderlund, Pelle Wikström, Per-Alvar   7:30.10
            Magnusson, Thomas Lejdström)

5. ITA      (Paolo Revelli, Raffaele Franceschi, Andrea   7:30.37
            Ceccarini, Fabrizio Rampazzo)

6. GBR     (Douglas Campbell, Philip Hubble, Martin   7:30.81
            Smith, Andrew Astbury)

7. AUS      (Graeme Brewer, Mark Tonelli, Mark Kerry,   7:30.82
            Ron McKeon)

8. FRA      (Fabien Noel, Mark Lazzaro, Dominique Petit,   7:36.08
            Paskal Laget)

**1984 Los Angeles** T: 14, N: 14, D: 7.30. WR: 7:20.40 (GER—Fahrner, Schmidt, Schwotka, Gross)

| | | | |
|---|---|---|---|
| 1. | USA | (Michael Heath, David Larson, Jeffrey Float, L. Bruce Hayes) | 7:15.69 WR |
| 2. | GER | (Thomas Fahrner, Dirk Korthals, Alexander Schowtka, Michael Gross) | 7:15.73 |
| 3. | GBR | (Neil Cochran, Paul Easter, Paul Howe, Andrew Astbury) | 7:24.78 |
| 4. | AUS | (Peter Dale, Justin Lemberg, Ronald McKeon, Graeme Brewer) | 7:25.63 |
| 5. | CAN | (Donald "Sandy" Goss, Wayne Kelly, Peter Szmidt, Alex Baumann) | 7:26.51 |
| 6. | SWE | (Michael Söderlund, Tommy Wermer, Anders Holmertz, Thomas Lejdström) | 7:26.53 |
| 7. | HOL | (Hans Kroes, Peter Drost, Edsard Schlingemann, Frank Drost) | 7:26.72 |
| 8. | FRA | (Stephan Caron, Dominique Bataille, Michel Pou, Pierre Andraca) | 7:30.16 |

The 1984 gold medal for prescience goes to sportswriter Craig Neff of *Sports Illustrated* who predicted in the magazine's souvenir program: "In what should be a heartstopping 4 × 200 free relay, the West Germans will likely lose their world record and the gold medal to the U.S.—but just barely."

The world record went quickly in the qualifying round when the U.S. "B" team of Geoffrey Gaberino, David Larson, Bruce Hayes and Richard Saeger swam a 7.18.87. In the final, Gaberino and Saeger were replaced by Mike Heath and Jeff Float. Normally the U.S. coaches would have had Heath swim the anchor leg, since he was the fastest man on the team. But the presence of Michael Gross as the West German anchor called for a change of strategy. It was decided to swim Heath first and build up as big a lead as possible before Gross hit the water. The unenviable task of fighting off the brilliant German swimmer was given to 21-year-old Bruce Hayes, an experienced anchor man. This was the only event for which Hayes had qualified, so much of his training concentrated on practicing his finishing touch.

Swimming the third leg for the U.S. was Jeff Float, who had lost 80% of his hearing in his right ear and 60% in his left ear when he contracted viral meningitis at the age of 13 months. So great was the roar of the crowd during the final as Float lengthened the U.S. lead against Alexander Schowtka that, for the first time in his life, he heard the crowd cheering him on. When Float touched the wall at the end of his leg, he handed over to Hayes a three-yard lead. But Gross went out so powerfully that he caught Hayes after only 50 meters, and passed him after 100. Hayes was shocked that Gross had appeared by his side so quickly, but he didn't panic. Instead he kept the pressure on. Gross came out of the final turn with a two-foot lead, but then Hayes began gaining on the world record holder. As they reached for the wall it was impossible to to tell who had won. All eyes turned to the scoreboard. Almost immediately, the number "1"

appeared next to "USA," setting off a wildly emotional celebration.

Michael Gross, whose 1:46.89 split was the fastest ever recorded, was, as always, as gracious in defeat as in victory. "I just ran out of gas," he said. "That was a really hot race. It was an honorable defeat."

**1988 Seoul** T: 16, N: 16, D: 9.21. WR: 7:13.10 (GER—Sitt, Henkel, Fahrner, Gross)

| | | | |
|---|---|---|---|
| 1. | USA | (Troy Dalbey, Matthew Cetlinski, Douglas Gjertsen, Matthew Biondi) | 7:12.51 WR |
| 2. | GDR | (Uwe Dassler, Sven Lodziewski, Thomas Flemming, Steffen Zesner) | 7:13.68 |
| 3. | GER | (Erik Hochstein, Thomas Fahrner, Rainer Henkel, Michael Gross) | 7:14.35 |
| 4. | AUS | (Thomas Stachewicz, Ian Brown, Jason Plummer, Duncan Armstrong) | 7:15.23 |
| 5. | ITA | (Roberto Gleria, Giorgio Lamberti, Massimo Trevisan, Valerio Giambalvo) | 7:16.00 |
| 6. | SWE | (Anders Holmertz, Tommy Werner, Michael Söderlund, Christer Wallin) | 7:19.10 |
| 7. | FRA | (Michel Pou, Franck Iacono, Olivier Fougeroud, Ludovic Depickere) | 7:24.69 |
| 8. | CAN | (Turlough O'Hare, Donald "Sandy" Goss, Donald Haddow, Gary Vandermeulen) | 7:24.91 |

The United States entered this race in the unaccustomed role of underdog to the world record-holding West Germans and the world champion East Germans. Anders Holmertz put Sweden in the lead after the first leg. At the halfway mark, Italy was in front, thanks to a powerful swim by Giorgio Lamberti. At that point East Germany was in second place, West Germany in fourth, and the U.S. in fifth. Thomas Flemming gave the GDR a bodylength lead over the U.S. with one lap to go. Then Matt Biondi took over. Two hours earlier he had missed a gold medal in the 100-meter butterfly by one one-hundredth of a second and now he was tired of losing. He passed Steffen Zesner after 75 meters, recorded the fastest relay split in history (1:46.44), and won by a bodylength.

The following night, U.S. team member Troy Dalbey caused a scandal when he stole a 65-pound decorative lion's mask from a hotel bar. He was arrested along with teammate Doug Gjertsen, but both swimmers were subsequently released after they apologized to the Korean people.

# 4 × 100-METER MEDLEY RELAY

In medley relays, the order of strokes is backstroke, breaststroke, butterfly, and freestyle.

**1896–1956** not held

**1960 Rome** T: 18, N: 18, D: 9.1. WR: 4:09.2 (USA, Indianapolis Athletic Club—McKinney, Jastremski, Troy, Sintz)

1. USA    (Frank McKinney, Paul Hait, Lance Larson, F. Jeffrey Farrell)    4:05.4    WR
2. AUS    (David Theile, Terry Gathercole, Neville Hayes, Geoffrey Shipton)    4:12.0
3. JPN    (Kazuo Tomita, ʻKoichi Hirakida, Yoshihiko Osaki, Keigo Shimizu)    4:12.2
4. CAN    (Robert Wheaton, Steve Rabinovitch, Cameron Grout, Richard Pound)    4:16.8
5. SOV    (Leonid Barbier, Leonid Kolesnikov, Grigory Kiselyov, Igor Lushkovski)    4:16.8
6. ITA    (Guiseppe Avellone, Roberto Lazzari, Federico Dennerlein, Bruno Bianchi)    4:17.2
7. GBR    (Graham Sykes, Christopher Walkden, Ian Black, Stanley Clarke)    4:17.6
8. HOL    (Johannes Jiskoot, Wieger Mensonides, Gerrit Korteweg, Ronald Kroon)    4:18.2

The U.S. "reserve" team of Bob Bennett, Paul Hait, Dave Gillanders, and Steve Clark set a world record of 4:08.2 in the qualifying round. Only Hait also took part in the final, in which a new U.S. team set another world record.

**1964 Tokyo** T: 14, N: 14, D: 10.16. WR: 4:00.1 (USA—McGeagh, Craig, Richardson, Clark)

1. USA    (Harold Thompson Mann, William Craig, Fred Schmidt, Stephen Clark)    3:58.4    WR
2. GDR/GER    (Ernst-Joachim Küppers, Egon Henninger, Horst-Günther Gregor, Hans-Joachim Klein)    4:01.6
3. AUS    (Peter Reynolds, Ian O'Brien, Kevin Berry, David Dickson)    4:02.3
4. SOV    (Viktor Mazanov, Georgy Prokopenko, Valentin Kuzmin, Vladimir Schuvalov)    4:04.2
5. JPN    (Shigeo Fukushima, Kenji Ishikawa, Isao Nakajima, Yukiaki Okabe)    4:06.6
6. HUN    (József Csikány, Ferenc Lenkei, József Gurrich, Gyula Dobai)    4:08.5
7. ITA    (Chiaffredo Rora, Gian Corrado Gross, Giampiero Fossati, Pietro Boscaini)    4:10.3
8. GBR    (Geoffrey Thwaites, Neil Nicholson, Brian Jenkins, Robert McGregor)    4:11.4

Backstroker Thompson Mann led off for the United States with a world record of 59.6, the first time that the one minute barrier had ever been broken for the 100-meter backstroke. The German and Soviet teams caught up by the halfway mark, but Fred Schmidt put the victory away for the United States with a 56.8 butterfly leg, and Steve Clark sealed it with a 52.4 anchor.

**1968 Mexico City** T: 18, N: 18, D: 10.26. WR: 3:56.5 (GDR—Matthes, Henninger, Gregor, Wiegand)

1. USA    (Charles Hickcox, Donald McKenzie, Douglas Russell, Kenneth Walsh)    3:54.9    WR
2. GDR    (Roland Matthes, Egon Henninger, Horst-Günther Gregor, Frank Wiegand)    3:57.5

3. SOV    (Yuri Gromak, Vladimir Kossinsky, Vladimir Nemshilov, Leonid Ilyichev)    4:00.7
4. AUS    (Karl Byrom, Ian O'Brien, Robert Cusack, Michael Wenden)    4:00.8
5. JPN    (Yasuo Tanaka, Nobutaka Taguchi, Satoshi Maruya, Kunihiro Iwasaki)    4:01.8
6. GER    (Reinhard Blechert, Gregor Betz, Lutz Stoklasa, Wolfgang Kremer)    4:05.4
7. CAN    (James Shaw, William Mahony, Toomas Arusoo, John Gilchrist)    4:07.3
8. SPA    (Santiago Esteva, José Duran, Arturo Lang, José Chicoy)    4;08.8

Roland Matthes opened with a backstroke world record of 58.0, but Doug Russell's butterfly leg put the United States in the lead to stay.

**1972 Munich** T: 17, N: 17, D: 9.4. WR: 3:50.4 (USA—Campbell, Dahlberg, Spitz, Heidenreich)

1. USA    (Michael Stamm, Thomas Bruce, Mark Spitz, Jerry Heidenreich)    3:48.16    WR
2. GDR    (Roland Matthes, Klaus Katzur, Hartmut Flöckner, Lutz Unger)    3:52.12
3. CAN    (Eric Fish, William Mahony, Bruce Robertson, Robert Kasting)    3:52.26
4. SOV    (Igor Grivennikov, Nikolai Pankin, Viktor Sharygin, Vladimir Bure)    3:53.26
5. BRA    (Romulo Duncan Arantes, José Sylvio Fiolo, Sergio Waismann, José Roberto Diñiz-Aranha)    3:57.89
6. JPN    (Tadashi Honda, Nobutaka Taguchi, Yasuhiro Komazaki, Jiro Sasaki)    3:58.23
7. GBR    (Colin Cunningham, David Wilkie, John Mills, Malcolm Windeatt)    3:58.82
8. HUN    (László Cseh, Sándor Szabó, István Szentirmay, Attila Császári)    3:59.07

Once again, Roland Matthes opened with a world record performance, but then the Americans took over, as Mark Spitz, swimming the butterfly leg, won his seventh gold medal.

**1976 Montreal** T: 14, N: 14, D: 7.22. WR: 3:48.16 (USA—Stamm, Bruce, Spitz, Heidenreich)

1. USA    (John Naber, John Hencken, Matt Vogel, Jim Montgomery)    3:42.22    WR
2. CAN    (Stephen Pickell, Graham Smith, Clay Evans, Gary MacDonald)    3:45.94
3. GER    (Klaus Steinbach, Walter Kusch, Michael Kraus, Peter Nocke)    3:47.29
4. GBR    (James Carter, David Wilkie, John Mills, Brian Brinkley)    3:49.56
5. SOV    (Igor Omelchenko, Arvydas Juozaitis, Yevgeny Seredin, Andrei Krylov)    3:49.90
6. AUS    (Mark Kerry, Paul Jarvie, Neil Rogers, Peter Coughlan)    3:51.54
7. ITA    (Enrico Bisso, Giorgio Lalle, Paolo Barelli, Marcello Guarducci)    3:52.92
8. JPN    (Tadashi Honda, Nobutaka Taguchi, Hideaki Hara, Tsuyoshi Yanagidate)    3:54.74

In the qualifying round, Americans Peter Rocca, Chris Woo, Joe Bottom, and Jack Babashoff set a world record of 3:47.28. The 1976 U.S. team was so strong that they were able to field a completely different foursome in the final and set yet another world record.

**1980 Moscow** T: 11, N: 11, D: 7.24. WR: 3:42.22 (USA—Naber, Hencken, Vogel, Montgomery)
1. AUS  (Mark Kerry, Peter Evans, Mark Tonelli, Neil  3:45.70
         Brooks)
2. SOV  (Viktor Kuznetsov, Arsen Miskarov, Yevgeny  3:45.92
         Seredin, Sergei Kopliakov)
3. GBR  (Gary Abraham, Duncan Goodhew, David  3:47.71
         Lowe, Martin Smith)
4. GDR  (Dietmar Göhring, Jörg Walter, Roger Pyttel,  3:48.25
         Jörg Woithe)
5. FRA  (Frédéric Delcourt, Olivier Borios, Xavier  3:49.19
         Savin, René Ecuyer)
6. HUN  (Sándor Wladár, Janos Dzvonyar, Zoltán  3:50.29
         Verrasztó, Gábor Mészáros)
7. HOL  (Fred Eefting, Albert Boonstra, Kees Vervoorn,  3:51.81
         Cees Jan Winkel)
8. BRA  (Romulo Duncan Arantes, Serglo Pinto  3:53.23
         Ribeiro, Claudo Mamede Kestener, Jorge Luiz
         Fernandes)

Australian anchorman Neil Brooks swam a stirring 49.86 to overtake 200-meter freestyle gold medalist Sergei Kopliakov and give Australia an upset victory.

**1984 Los Angeles** T: 21, N: 21, D: 8.4. WR: 3:40.42 (USA—Carey, Lundquist, Gribble, Gaines)
1. USA  (Richard Carey, Steve Lundquist, P.  3:39.30  WR
         Pablo Morales, Ambrose "Rowdy"
         Gaines)
2. CAN  (Mike West, Victor Davis, Thomas  3:43.23
         Ponting, Donald "Sandy" Goss)
3. AUS  (Mark Kerry, Peter Evans, Glenn Bu-  3:43.25
         chanan, Mark Stockwell)
4. GER  (Stefan Peter, Gerald Mörken, Michael  3:44.26
         Gross, Dirk Korthals)
5. SWE  (Bengt Baron, Peter Berggren, Thomas  3:47.13
         Lejdström, Per Johansson)
6. GBR  (Neil Harper, Adrian Moorhouse, An-  3:47.39
         drew Jameson, Richard Burrell)
7. SWI  (Patrick Ferland, Etienne Dagon,  3:47.93
         Theophile David, Dano Halsall)
DISQ: JPN (Daichi Suzuki, Shigehiro Takahashi, Taihei Saka, Hiroshi Sakamoto)

Rick Carey opened with an Olympic backstroke record of 55.41 and the rest of the race was never close.

**1988 Seoul** T: 25, N: 25, D: 9.25. WR: 3:38.28 (USA—Carey, Moffet, Morales, Biondi)
1. USA  (David Berkoff, Richard Schroeder,  3:36.93  WR
         Matthew Biondi, Christopher Jacobs)
2. CAN  (Mark Tewksbury, Victor Davis,  3:39.28
         Thomas Ponting, Donald "Sandy"
         Goss)

3. SOV  (Igor Poliansky, Dmitri Volkov, Vadim  3:39.96
         Yaroshchuk, Gennady Prigoda)
4. GER  (Frank Hoffmeister, Alexander Mayer,  3:42.98
         Michael Gross, Björn Zikarsky)
5. JPN  (Daichi Suzuki, Hironobu Nagahata,  3:44.36
         Hiroshi Miura, Shigeo Ogata)
6. AUS  (Carl Wilson, Ian Mcadam, Jonathan  3:45.85
         Sieben, Andrew Baildon)
7. HOL  (Hans Kroes, Ronald Dekker, Frank  3:46.85
         Drost, Patrick Dybiona)
DISQ: GBR (Neil Harper, Adrian Moorhouse, Andrew Jameson, Mark Foster)

David Berkoff opened with a sizzling 54.56 backstroke leg and the U.S. never looked back. Matt Biondi left Seoul with five gold medals, one silver, and one bronze. The West German team celebrated the end of the meet by walking to the blocks dressed in lederhosen. At the 1986 world championships they had appeared in togas made of bedsheets.

## SPRINGBOARD DIVING

This event is performed from a springboard three meters (9 feet 10 inches) above the water. Olympic competitions begin with a preliminary round. The top twelve divers then advance to the final, which consists of 11 dives—five required and six voluntary. The judges' scores are multiplied by a coefficient that is determined by the degree of difficulty of the attempted dive.

**1896–1906** not held

**1908 London** C: 23, N: 8, D: 7.18.

|   |   |   | PTS. |
|---|---|---|---|
| 1. | Albert Zürner | GER | 85.5 |
| 2. | Kurt Behrens | GER | 85.3 |
| 3. | George Gaidzik | USA | 80.8 |
| 3. | Gottlob Walz | GER | 80.8 |

**1912 Stockholm** C: 18, N: 7, D: 7.9

|   |   |   | PTS. |
|---|---|---|---|
| 1. | Paul Günther | GER | 79.23 |
| 2. | Hans Luber | GER | 76.78 |
| 3. | Kurt Behrens | GER | 73.73 |
| 4. | Albert Zürner | GER | 73.33 |
| 5. | Robert Zimmerman | CAN | 72.54 |
| 6. | Herbert Pott | GBR | 71.45 |
| 7. | John Jansson | SWE | 69.64 |
| 8. | George Gaidzik | USA | 68.01 |

**1920 Antwerp** C: 14, N: 9, D: 8.27.

|   |   |   | PTS. |
|---|---|---|---|
| 1. | Louis Kuehn | USA | 675.4 |
| 2. | Clarence Pinkston | USA | 655.3 |
| 3. | Louis Balbach | USA | 649.5 |
| 4. | Gustaf Blomgren | SWE | 587.5 |
| 5. | Gunnar Ekstrand | SWE | 559.25 |
| 6. | John Jansson | SWE | 544.75 |

**1924 Paris** C: 17, N: 9, D: 7.17.

| | | PTS. |
|---|---|---|
| 1. Albert White | USA | 696.4 |
| 2. Ulise "Pete" Desjardins | USA | 693.2 |
| 3. Clarence Pinkston | USA | 653.0 |
| 4. Edmund Lindmark | SWE | 599.1 |
| 5. Richmond Eve | AUS | 564.3 |
| 6. Adolf Hellqvist | SWE | 544.9 |
| 7. Kurt Sjöberg | SWE | 538.3 |
| 8. H. Hemsing | HOL | 490.8 |

**1928 Amsterdam** C: 24, N: 15, D: 8.8.

| | | PTS. |
|---|---|---|
| 1. Ulise "Pete" Desjardins | USA | 185.04 |
| 2. Michael Galitzen (Mickey Riley) | USA | 174.06 |
| 3. Farid Simaika | EGY | 172.46 |
| 4. Harold Smith | USA | 168.96 |
| 5. Arthur Mund | GER | 154.72 |
| 6. Ewald Riebschläger | GER | 153.86 |
| 7. Heinz Plumanns | GER | 150.18 |
| 8. Alfred Phillips | CAN | 149.48 |

Born in Canada, and raised from the age of 10 in Miami Beach, 5-foot 3-inch Pete Desjardins was the first male diver in Olympic history to win both the springboard and platform events. A graduate of Stanford University, he later turned professional and was billed as "The Little Bronze Statue from the Land of Real Estate, Grapefruits and Alligators."

**1932 Los Angeles** C: 13, N: 7, D: 8.8.

| | | PTS. |
|---|---|---|
| 1. Michael Galitzen (Mickey Riley) | USA | 161.38 |
| 2. Harold Smith | USA | 158.54 |
| 3. Richard Degener | USA | 151.82 |
| 4. Alfred Phillips | CAN | 134.64 |
| 5. Leo Esser | GER | 134.30 |
| 6. Kazuo Kobayashi | JPN | 133.76 |
| 7. Emile Poussard | FRA | 128.66 |
| 8. Tetsutaro Namae | JPN | 125.18 |

**1936 Berlin** C: 24, N: 15, D: 8.11.

| | | PTS. |
|---|---|---|
| 1. Richard Degener | USA | 163.57 |
| 2. Marshall Wayne | USA | 159.56 |
| 3. Albert Greene | USA | 146.29 |
| 4. Tsuneo Shibahara | JPN | 144.92 |
| 5. Erhard Weiss | GER | 141.24 |
| 6. Leo Esser | GER | 137.99 |
| 7. Winfried Marauhn | GER | 134.61 |
| 8. Tomio Koyanagi | JPN | 133.07 |

Degener's margin of victory was provided by an almost perfect full twist with a one and a half somersault. He was awarded a score of 19.55. Wayne attempted the same dive but earned only 15.54 points.

**1948 London** C: 26, N: 15, D: 8.3.

| | | PTS. |
|---|---|---|
| 1. Bruce Harlan | USA | 163.64 |
| 2. Miller Anderson | USA | 157.29 |
| 3. Samuel Lee | USA | 145.52 |
| 4. Joaquin Capilla Pérez | MEX | 141.79 |
| 5. Raymond Mulinghausen | FRA | 126.55 |
| 6. Svante Johansson | SWE | 120.20 |
| 7. Kamal Hassan | EGY | 119.90 |
| 8. Thomas Christiansen | DEN | 114.59 |

**1952 Helsinki** C: 36, N: 20, D: 7.28.

| | | PTS. |
|---|---|---|
| 1. David Browning | USA | 205.29 |
| 2. Miller Anderson | USA | 199.84 |
| 3. Robert Clotworthy | USA | 184.92 |
| 4. Joaquin Capilla Pérez | MEX | 178.33 |
| 5. Roman Brener | SOV | 165.63 |
| 6. Milton Busin | BRA | 155.91 |
| 7. Tony Turner | GBR | 151.90 |
| 8. Aleksei Zigalov | SOV | 151.31 |

The divers were somewhat distracted by the presence of too many people near the board, including a photographer in a frogman outfit who actually stationed himself *in* the pool.

**1956 Melbourne** C: 24, N: 19, D: 8.29.

| | | PTS. |
|---|---|---|
| 1. Robert Clotworthy | USA | 159.56 |
| 2. Donald Harper | USA | 156.23 |
| 3. Joaquin Capilla Pérez | MEX | 150.69 |
| 4. Glen Whitten | USA | 148.55 |
| 5. Gennady Udalov | SOV | 140.64 |
| 6. Roman Brener | SOV | 139.14 |
| 7. Gunther Mund | CHI | 137.53 |
| 8. József Gerlach | HUN | 136.08 |

**1960 Rome** C: 32, N: 19, D: 8.29.

| | | PTS. |
|---|---|---|
| 1. Gary Tobian | USA | 170.00 |
| 2. Samuel Hall | USA | 167.08 |
| 3. Juan Botella | MEX | 162.30 |
| 4. Alvaro Gaxiola | MEX | 150.42 |
| 5. Ernest Meissner | CAN | 144.07 |
| 6. Lamberto Mari | ITA | 143.97 |
| 7. Toshio Yamano | JPN | 140.46 |
| 8. Hans-Dieter Pophal | GDR | 133.95 |

After the preliminary round, one judge, a Soviet woman, was replaced for being overly nationalistic in her scoring. Silver medalist Sam Hall gained dubious international fame in December, 1986, when he was arrested as a free-lance spy in Nicaragua. Hall, who once served in the Ohio House of Representatives, described himself as a "self-employed military advisor and counterterrorist." He was subsequently released by the Nicaraguan government, who declared him a victim of mental illness.

**1964 Tokyo** C: 27, N: 16, D: 10.14.

|   |   |   | PTS. |
|---|---|---|------|
| 1. | Kenneth Sitzberger | USA | 159.90 |
| 2. | Francis Gorman | USA | 157.63 |
| 3. | Larry Andreasen | USA | 143.77 |
| 4. | Hans-Dieter Pophal | GDR | 142.58 |
| 5. | Göran Lundqvist | SWE | 138.65 |
| 6. | Boris Polulyakh | SOV | 138.64 |
| 7. | Mikhail Safonov | SOV | 134.00 |
| 8. | Vladimir Vasin | SOV | 133.48 |

Navy Lieutenant Frank Gorman actually outscored Ken Sitzberger on nine of his ten dives. But he missed badly with his ninth round back, two-and-a-half somersault tuck, and lost 11.20 points. In 1988, toward the end of the Seoul Olympics, 1964 bronze medalist Larry Andreasen, then 42 years old, dived 160 feet from the center of the Gerald Desmond Bridge in Long Beach, California. Andreasen was under the mistaken impression that he was breaking the record for the highest dive. In fact, the record was 174 feet 8 inches. He survived the dive uninjured, but was arrested.

**1968 Mexico City** C: 28, N: 16, D: 10.20.

|   |   |   | PTS. |
|---|---|---|------|
| 1. | Bernard Wrightson | USA | 170.15 |
| 2. | Klaus Dibiasi | ITA | 159.74 |
| 3. | James Henry | USA | 158.09 |
| 4. | Luis Niño de Rivera | MEX | 155.71 |
| 5. | Franco Giorgio Cagnotto | ITA | 155.70 |
| 6. | Keith Russell | USA | 151.75 |
| 7. | Tord Anderson | SWE | 151.50 |
| 8. | Donald Wagstaff | AUS | 150.18 |

Bernie Wrightson moved up from third place to first with his last three dives.

**1972 Munich** C: 32, N: 16, D: 8.30.

|   |   |   | PTS. |
|---|---|---|------|
| 1. | Vladimir Vasin | SOV | 594.09 |
| 2. | Franco Giorgio Cagnotto | ITA | 591.63 |
| 3. | Craig Lincoln | USA | 577.29 |
| 4. | Klaus Dibiasi | ITA | 559.05 |
| 5. | Michael Finneran | USA | 557.34 |
| 6. | Vyacheslav Strahov | SOV | 556.20 |
| 7. | Falk Hoffmann | GDR | 544.95 |
| 8. | Norbert Huda | GER | 524.16 |

The U.S. string of eleven straight springboard victories was finally broken. The next to last dive was the decisive one. Cagnotto missed and was awarded only 48.72 points, while Vasin recorded 75.60 points, the highest score of the competition.

**1976 Montreal** C: 30, N: 16, D: 7.22.

|   |   |   | PTS. |
|---|---|---|------|
| 1. | Philip Boggs | USA | 619.05 |
| 2. | Franco Giorgio Cagnotto | ITA | 570.48 |
| 3. | Aleksandr Kosenkov | SOV | 567.24 |

|   |   |   |   |
|---|---|---|---|
| 4. | Falk Hoffmann | GDR | 553.53 |
| 5. | Robert Cragg | USA | 548.19 |
| 6. | Gregory Louganis | USA | 528.96 |
| 7. | Carlos Giron | MEX | 523.59 |
| 8. | Klaus Dibiasi | ITA | 516.18 |

**1980 Moscow** C: 24, N: 16, D: 7.23.

|   |   |   | PTS. |
|---|---|---|------|
| 1. | Aleksandr Portnov | SOV | 905.025 |
| 2. | Carlos Giron | MEX | 892.140 |
| 3. | Franco Giorgio Cagnotto | ITA | 871.500 |
| 4. | Falk Hoffmann | GDR | 858.510 |
| 5. | Aleksandr Kosenkov | SOV | 855.120 |
| 6. | Christopher Snode | GBR | 844.470 |
| 7. | Vyacheslav Troshin | SOV | 820.050 |
| 8. | Ricardo Camacho | SPA | 749.340 |

Aleksandr Portnov's victory was clouded by controversy. Distracted by the noise of the crowd watching the final of the men's 100-meter butterfly, Portnov turned a two and a half backward somersault into a belly flop. He immediately protested and was awarded a re-dive, which he hit beautifully. Giron, Cagnotto, and Hoffman objected, claiming that they had been subjected to similar distractions. Hoffman was particularly annoyed, since his later claim that one of his dives had been disrupted by a photographer's flash was denied. The medal ceremony was delayed for two days until a final decision was announced by the International Amateur Swimming Federation (F.I.N.A). In Mexico City demonstrations were held outside the Soviet embassy to protest the ruling.

**1984 Los Angeles** C: 30, N: 19, D: 8.8.

|   |   |   |   |
|---|---|---|---|
| 1. | Gregory Louganis | USA | 754.41 |
| 2. | Tan Liangde | CHN | 662.31 |
| 3. | Ronald Merriott | USA | 661.32 |
| 4. | Li Hongping | CHN | 646.35 |
| 5. | Christopher Snode | GBR | 609.51 |
| 6. | Piero Italiani | ITA | 578.94 |
| 7. | Albin Killat | GER | 569.52 |
| 8. | Stephen Foley | AUS | 561.93 |

Of Samoan and northern European ancestry, Greg Louganis was given up for adoption by his 15-year-old parents. Like so many future Olympic champions, Louganis suffered through a difficult childhood. Taunted by his classmates in El Cajon, California, he was called "retarded" because he was dyslexic, and "nigger" because he had dark skin. He began smoking cigarettes when he was 8 years old. When he turned 13, his adoptive parents found illegal drugs in his room and turned him over to the authorities. As a teenager he depended so heavily on alcohol that he considered himself an alcoholic. But Louganis survived these hard times by escaping into the world of diving. He was so good that he qualified for the Montreal Olympics at the age of 16. He finished sixth in the springboard event and second in the platform. Favored to win two gold medals at the 1980 Olympics, he was shut out by the U.S. boycott, but accomplished the feat instead at the 1982 world championships. In 1984 he performed brilliantly despite the heavy pressure of being the overwhelming favorite. His winning margin of over 94 points was unprecedented in Olympic history.

**1988 Seoul** C: 35, N: 23, D: 9.20.

| | | PTS. |
|---|---|---|
| 1. Gregory Louganis | USA | 730.80 |
| 2. Tan Liangde | CHN | 704.88 |
| 3. Li Deliang | CHN | 665.28 |
| 4. Albin Killat | GER | 661.47 |
| 5. Mark Bradshaw | USA | 642.99 |
| 6. Jorge Mondragon | MEX | 616.02 |
| 7. Jesús Mena | MEX | 598.77 |
| 8. Edwin Jongejans | HOL | 588.33 |

Greg Louganis won 19 consecutive international springboard competitions between 1982 and 1987. Then, in 1988, he was beaten twice by Tan Liangde, who had been studying videotapes of Louganis for 6 years. In Seoul, Louganis was leading the preliminary round when he stepped onto the board for his ninth dive, a reverse two and a half somersault in the pike position. The defending Olympic champion leapt into the air, but failed to push out far enough. When he came down, he hit his head on the board and fell clumsily into the water. It was not Louganis' first confrontation with diving danger. Once, in 1976, he hit the bottom of the platform and ended up with two black eyes and a bloody nose. In 1979 in Tbilisi in Soviet Georgia he hit the top of the platform and was knocked unconscious. He had to be rescued from the pool. He woke up 20 minutes later surrounded by doctors. In 1981 he broke his collarbone when he hit the bottom of a pool. In 1984 he became disoriented during a platform dive in New Zealand and landed on his back. In 1987, at the U.S. Indoor Championship, in an incident eerily similar to the one in Seoul, he came within an inch or two of hitting the springboard on a reverse one and a half in the layout position.

In Seoul, Louganis climbed out of the pool unassisted. Four temporary sutures were applied to his head and, incredibly, 35 minutes later he was back on the board ready for his next dive: another reverse somersault. He scored 87.12 points, the highest score by any diver in the preliminaries. After qualifying for the final with his last dive, he was taken to the hospital where the sutures were replaced by five mattress stitches and a waterproof patch.

The next day, despite great pressure from Tan, Louganis hit all 11 of his dives—including the one he had botched in the preliminaries—and earned his third gold medal.

## PLATFORM DIVING

This event is staged from a rigid platform ten meters (32 feet 9¾ inches) above the water. The finalists perform four compulsory dives and six voluntary dives.

**1896–1900** not held

**1904 St. Louis** C: 5, N: 2, D: 9.7.

| | | PTS. |
|---|---|---|
| 1. George Sheldon | USA | 12.66 |
| 2. Georg Hoffmann | GER | 11.66 |
| 3. Alfred Braunschweiger | GER | 11.33 |
| 3. Frank Kehoe | USA | 11.33 |
| 5. Otto Hooff | GER | — |

The German team protested Sheldon's victory, but their protest was rejected by James Sullivan, the U.S. official in charge. Kehoe and Braunschweiger tied, and a dive-off was ordered. Braunschweiger refused to take part, so Kehoe was awarded third place. Most Olympic historians credit Braunschweiger with a share of third anyway. Apparently the Americans and Germans disagreed as to what constituted a proper dive. The Americans felt that the manner in which a diver hit the water was important, while the Germans, who attempted more difficult dives but tended to land on their stomachs and chests, contended that landings didn't matter.

**1906 Athens** C: 24, N: 8, D: 4.26.

| | | PTS. |
|---|---|---|
| 1. Gottlob Walz | GER | 156.0 |
| 2. Georg Hoffmann | GER | 150.2 |
| 3. Otto Satzinger | AUT | 147.4 |
| 4. Albert Zürner | GER | 144.6 |
| 5. G. Melville Clark | GBR | 144.0 |
| 6. Hjalmar Johansson | SWE | 143.4 |
| 7. Robert Andersson | SWE | 142.2 |
| 8. Fritz Nicolai | GER | 138.0 |

**1908 London** C: 23, N: 6, D: 7.24.

| | | PTS. |
|---|---|---|
| 1. Hjalmar Johansson | SWE | 83.75 |
| 2. Karl Malmström | SWE | 78.73 |
| 3. Arvid Spångberg | SWE | 74.00 |
| 4. Robert Andersson | SWE | 68.30 |
| 5. George Gaidzik | USA | 56.30 |

**1912 Stockholm** D: 21, N: 6, D: 7.15.

| | | PTS. | ORDINALS |
|---|---|---|---|
| 1. Erik Adlerz | SWE | 73.94 | 7 |
| 2. Albert Zürner | GER | 72.60 | 10 |
| 3. Gustaf Blomgren | SWE | 69.56 | 16 |
| 4. Hjalmar Johansson | SWE | 67.80 | 22 |
| 5. George Yvon | GBR | 67.66 | 22 |
| 6. Harald Arbin | SWE | 62.62 | 31 |
| 7. Albin Carlsson | SWE | 63.16 | 32 |
| 8. Toivo Aro | FIN | 57.05 | 40 |

**1920 Antwerp** C: 15, N: 7, D: 8.29.

| | | PTS. |
|---|---|---|
| 1. Clarence Pinkston | USA | 100.67 |
| 2. Erik Adlerz | SWE | 99.08 |
| 3. Harry Prieste | USA | 93.73 |
| 4. Gustaf Blomgren | SWE | 90.78 |

| 5. Yngve Johnson | SWE | 88.36 |
| 6. Louis Balbach | USA | 84.80 |

**1924 Paris** C: 20, N: 10, D: 7.20.

|  |  | PTS. |
|---|---|---|
| 1. Albert White | USA | 97.46 |
| 2. David Fall | USA | 97.30 |
| 3. Clarence Pinkston | USA | 94.60 |
| 4. Erik Adlerz | SWE | 93.78 |
| 5. Eugène Lenormand | FRA | 87.54 |
| 6. Helge Öberg | SWE | 85.80 |
| 7. S. Sorensen | DEN | 80.92 |
| 8. Adolf Hellqvist | SWE | 80.64 |

**1928 Amsterdam** C: 24, N: 12, D: 8.11.

|  |  | PTS. | ORDINALS |
|---|---|---|---|
| 1. Ulise "Pete" Desjardins | USA | 98.74 | 6 |
| 2. Farid Simaika | EGY | 99.58 | 9 |
| 3. Michael Galitzen (Mickey Riley) | USA | 92.34 | 15 |
| 4. Walter Colbath | USA | 87.78 | 21 |
| 5. Ewald Riebschläger | GER | 82.44 | 27 |
| 6. Karl Schumm | GER | 80.54 | 28 |
| 7. Alfred Phillips | CAN | 77.26 | 35 |
| 8. A. Reginald Knight | GBR | 72.22 | 41 |

Simaika was originally announced as the winner, and the Egyptian national anthem was played. Then it was declared that a mistake had been made, that ordinals (place-figures), not total points, determined the winner. Consequently, Desjardins was given his second gold medal.

**1932 Los Angeles** C: 8, N: 5, D: 8.13.

|  |  | PTS. |
|---|---|---|
| 1. Harold Smith | USA | 124.80 |
| 2. Michael Galitzen (Mickey Riley) | USA | 124.28 |
| 3. Frank Kurtz | USA | 121.98 |
| 4. Josef Staudinger | AUT | 103.44 |
| 5. Carlos Curiel | MEX | 83.82 |
| 6. Jesús Flores Albo | MEX | 77.94 |
| 7. Alfred Phillips | CAN | 77.10 |
| 8. Hidekatsu Ishida | JPN | 75.92 |

**1936 Berlin** C: 26, N: 15, D: 8.15.

|  |  | PTS. |
|---|---|---|
| 1. Marshall Wayne | USA | 113.58 |
| 2. Elbert Root | USA | 110.60 |
| 3. Hermann Stork | GER | 110.31 |
| 4. Erhard Weiss | GER | 110.15 |
| 5. Frank Kurtz | USA | 108.61 |
| 6. Tsuneo Shibahara | JPN | 107.40 |
| 7. Siegfried Viebahn | GER | 105.00 |
| 8. Tomio Koyanagi | JPN | 94.54 |

**1948 London** C: 25, N: 15, D: 8.5.

|  |  | PTS. |
|---|---|---|
| 1. Samuel Lee | USA | 130.05 |
| 2. Bruce Harlan | USA | 122.30 |
| 3. Joaquin Capilla Pérez | MEX | 113.52 |

| 4. Lennart Brunnhage | SWE | 108.62 |
| 5. Peter Heatly | GBR | 105.29 |
| 6. Thomas Christiansen | DEN | 105.22 |
| 7. Raymond Mulinghausen | FRA | 103.01 |
| 8. George Athans | CAN | 100.91 |

Sammy Lee was a 28-year-old Korean-American army doctor. For his last dive he chose a forward three and a half somersault. Once, when performing a similar dive, he had mistaken the sky for the water and pulled out too soon. Now with the Olympic title on the line, he was afraid he would repeat the mistake. "I dove, hit the water, felt numb and tingling and decided: 'I did a belly flop.'" When he popped out of the water he discovered that, far from belly-flopping, his dive had been rated almost perfect. "I just walked on water out of that pool," he later recalled.

**1952 Helsinki** C: 31, N: 17, D: 8.1.

|  |  | PTS. |
|---|---|---|
| 1. Samuel Lee | USA | 156.28 |
| 2. Joaquin Capilla Pérez | MEX | 145.21 |
| 3. Gunther Haase | GER | 141.31 |
| 4. John McCormack | USA | 138.74 |
| 5. Alberto Capilla Pérez | MEX | 136.44 |
| 6. Rodolfo Perea | MEX | 128.28 |
| 7. Aleksandr Bakatin | SOV | 126.86 |
| 8. Roman Brener | SOV | 126.31 |

Sammy Lee celebrated his 32nd birthday by winning his second gold medal.

**1956 Melbourne** C: 22, N: 10, D: 12.6.

|  |  | PTS. |
|---|---|---|
| 1. Joaquin Capilla Pérez | MEX | 152.44 |
| 2. Gary Tobian | USA | 152.41 |
| 3. Richard Connor | USA | 149.79 |
| 4. József Gerlach | HUN | 149.25 |
| 5. Roman Brener | SOV | 142.95 |
| 6. William Farrell | USA | 139.12 |
| 7. Ferenc Siák | HUN | 138.83 |
| 8. Mikhail Chachba | SOV | 134.51 |

Third in 1948 and second in 1952, Capilla completed his set of platform diving medals by executing a superb forward one and a half somersault with a double twist on his final dive. The highest-scored dive of the competition, it gave Capilla a 0.03 point edge over Tobian. The U.S. team lodged a protest against the Soviet and Hungarian judges, but F.I.N.A. Secretary Bertil Sallfors rejected the complaint, explaining, "There can be no protests against the judges." Soviet judge Eva Bozd-Morskaya had given Gary Tobian an average score of 6.35, while his average overall score had been 7.3. On the other hand, she had scored Mikhail Chachba 7.38, while *his* overall average had been 6.37. This incident led to a change in the rules which allowed individual judges to be eliminated because of incompetence.

**1960 Rome** C: 28, N: 18, D: 9.2.

|  |  | PTS. |
|---|---|---|
| 1. Robert Webster | USA | 165.56 |
| 2. Gary Tobian | USA | 165.25 |
| 3. Brian Phelps | GBR | 157.13 |
| 4. Roberto Madrigal Garcia | MEX | 152.86 |
| 5. Rolf Sperling | GDR | 151.83 |
| 6. Gennady Galkin | SOV | 141.69 |
| 7. Fritz Enskat | GER | 138.86 |
| 8. Anatoly Sysoev | SOV | 135.59 |

Webster moved from third place to first with his last three dives.

**1964 Tokyo** C: 30, N: 16, D: 10.18.

|  |  | PTS. |
|---|---|---|
| 1. Robert Webster | USA | 148.58 |
| 2. Klaus Dibiasi | ITA | 147.54 |
| 3. Thomas Gompf | USA | 146.57 |
| 4. Roberto Madrigal Garcia | MEX | 144.27 |
| 5. Viktor Palagin | SOV | 143.77 |
| 6. Brian Phelps | GBR | 143.18 |
| 7. Rolf Sperling | GDR | 142.24 |
| 8. Toshio Otsubo | JPN | 142.05 |

This time Webster was only in sixth place with three dives to go, but still managed to withstand the pressure and successfully defend his championship.

**1968 Mexico City** C: 35, N: 17, D: 10.26.

|  |  | PTS. |
|---|---|---|
| 1. Klaus Dibiasi | ITA | 164.18 |
| 2. Alvaro Gaxiola | MEX | 154.49 |
| 3. Edwin Young | USA | 153.93 |
| 4. Keith Russell | USA | 152.34 |
| 5. José Robinson | MEX | 143.62 |
| 6. Lothar Matthes | GDR | 141.75 |
| 7. Luis Niño de Rivera | MEX | 141.16 |
| 8. Franco Giorgio Cagnotto | ITA | 138.89 |

Coached by his father, Carlo, who had finished tenth in the 1936 Olympics, Klaus Dibiasi of Bolzano practiced between 130 and 150 dives a day, six days a week. In Mexico City, Dibiasi began his amazing Olympic winning streak by becoming the first Italian ever to win a gold medal in a swimming or diving event.

**1972 Munich** C: 35, N: 18, D: 9.4.

|  |  | PTS. |
|---|---|---|
| 1. Klaus Dibiasi | ITA | 504.12 |
| 2. Richard Rydze | USA | 480.75 |
| 3. Franco Giorgio Cagnotto | ITA | 475.83 |
| 4. Lothar Matthes | GDR | 465.75 |
| 5. David Ambartsumyan | SOV | 463.56 |
| 6. Richard Early | USA | 462.45 |
| 7. Vladimir Kapirulin | SOV | 459.21 |
| 8. Carlos Giron | MEX | 442.41 |

**1976 Montreal** C: 25, N: 14 D: 7.27.

|  |  | PTS. |
|---|---|---|
| 1. Klaus Dibiasi | ITA | 600.51 |
| 2. Gregory Louganis | USA | 576.99 |
| 3. Vladimir Aleynik | SOV | 548.61 |
| 4. Kent Vosler | USA | 544.14 |
| 5. Patrick Moore | USA | 538.17 |
| 6. Falk Hoffmann | GDR | 531.60 |
| 7. David Ambartsumyan | SOV | 516.21 |
| 8. Carlos Giron | MEX | 513.93 |

Seventeen-year-old Soviet diver Sergei Nemtsanov finished a disappointing ninth, and then caused something of a sensation when he disappeared mysteriously from the Olympic Village. Soviet officials charged that he had been abducted. When he showed up again, the Western press claimed that Nemtsanov had left the Village voluntarily, but that the Soviets had tracked him down and hauled him back against his will.

**1980 Moscow** C: 23, N: 14, D: 7.28.

|  |  | PTS. |
|---|---|---|
| 1. Falk Hoffmann | GDR | 835.650 |
| 2. Vladimir Aleynik | SOV | 819.705 |
| 3. David Ambartsumyan | SOV | 817.440 |
| 4. Carlos Giron | MEX | 809.805 |
| 5. Dieter Waskow | GDR | 802.800 |
| 6. Thomas Knuths | GDR | 783.975 |
| 7. Sergei Nemtsanov | SOV | 775.860 |
| 8. Niki Sajkovic | AUT | 725.145 |

**1984 Los Angeles** C: 26, N: 18, D: 8.12.

|  |  | PTS. |
|---|---|---|
| 1. Gregory Louganis | USA | 710.91 |
| 2. Bruce Kimball | USA | 643.50 |
| 3. Li Kongzheng | CHN | 638.28 |
| 4. Tong Hui | CHN | 604.77 |
| 5. Albin Killat | GER | 551.97 |
| 6. Dieter Dörr | GER | 536.07 |
| 7. Christopher Snode | GBR | 524.40 |
| 8. David Bedard | CAN | 518.13 |

As Greg Louganis stood 33 feet above the water, preparing for his final dive, he told himself, "No matter what I do, my mother is still going to love me." He then executed a near-perfect reverse tuck to become the first platform diver to score over 700 points and the first male since 1928 to win both the springboard and platform competitions.

Bruce Kimball overtook Li Kongzheng with his final dive to win the silver medal. In 1981 Kimball was struck head-on by a drunken driver. Every bone in his face was broken, his skull was fractured, his left leg broken, the ligaments in his knee torn, his liver was lacerated, and his spleen had to be removed. When he returned to diving nine months later, he earned the nickname "The Comeback Kid." On August 1, 1988, two weeks before the U.S. Olympic diving trials, Kimball, himself drunk, plowed into a crowd of teenagers while driving 75 miles per hour, killing two boys and injuring four others. Despite the tragedy, Kimball took part in the trials but failed to make the team. He subsequently pleaded guilty to vehicular manslaughter and was sentenced to 17 years in prison.

**1988 Seoul** C: 26, N: 15, D: 9.27.

|   |   |   | PTS. |
|---|---|---|---|
| 1. | Gregory Louganis | USA | 638.61 |
| 2. | Xiong Ni | CHN | 637.47 |
| 3. | Jesús Mena | MEX | 594.39 |
| 4. | Georgy Chogovadze | SOV | 585.96 |
| 5. | Jan Hempel | GDR | 583.77 |
| 6. | Li Kongzheng | CHN | 543.81 |
| 7. | Steffen Haage | GDR | 541.02 |
| 8. | Vladimir Timoshinin | SOV | 534.66 |

Greg Louganis, hoping to become the first male diver to win both the springboard and platform events twice in a row, found himself in an unusually close battle with 14-year-old Xiong Ni. The difference in their scores was never more than 10 points. With one dive remaining, Xiong led by exactly three points. His final dive was a brilliantly executed inward three and a half somersault in the tuck position. With a degree of difficulty of 3.2, it earned him 82.56 points. This meant that Louganis needed to score 85.56 points on *his* last dive, a reverse three and a half somersault in the tuck position, also known as the "Dive of Death" because it had proved fatal to two divers. Louganis performed it beautifully, although his entry was less than perfect. However, the high degree of difficulty, 3.4, allowed him to score 86.70 points and squeeze out a narrow, highly emotional victory. And just how young was Xiong Ni? After one dive he came out of the water with blood on his face. At first it was thought that he had injured himself. But it turned out that all he had suffered was a broken pimple.

# WATER POLO

Water polo is played with seven men on a team. Between 1960 and 1980, matches consisted of four five-minute quarters. In 1984 the quarters were extended to seven minutes.

**1896** not held

**1900 Paris** T: 7, N: 3, D: 8.12.

|   |   |   | W | L | PF | PA |
|---|---|---|---|---|---|---|
| 1. | GBR | (Osborne Swimming Club, Manchester—Arthur Robertson, Thomas Coe, Eric Robinson, Peter Kemp, George Wilkinson, John Henry Derbyshire, William Lister) | 3 | 0 | 29 | 3 |
| 2. | BEL | (Swimming et Water Polo Club, Brussels—Albert Michant, Fernand Fayaerts, Henri Cohen, Victor de Behr, Oscar Grégoire, Victor Sonnemans, Jean de Backer) | 2 | 1 | 9 | 8 |

|   |   |   | W | L | PF | PA |
|---|---|---|---|---|---|---|
| 3. | FRA | (Libellule de Paris—Henri Peslier, Thomas Burgess, Decuyper, Pesloy, Paul Vasseur, Devenot, Louis Laufray) | 0 | 1 | 1 | 10 |
| 4. | FRA | (Pupilles de Neptune de Lille—Louis Martin, Coulon, Fardelle, Favier, Leriche, Charles Treffel, Désiré Merchez) | 0 | 1 | 1 | 5 |

Final GBR 7–2 BEL

A complete record of all the games played in this tournament is not available.

**1904 St. Louis** T: 3, N: 1, D: 9.6.

|   |   |   | W | L | PF | PA |
|---|---|---|---|---|---|---|
| 1. | USA | (New York Athletic Club—David Bratton, George Van Cleef, Leo Goodwin, Louis Handley, David Hesser, Joseph Ruddy, James Steen) | 2 | 0 | 11 | 0 |
| 2. | USA | (Chicago Athletic Club—Rex Breach, Jerome Steever, Edwin Swatek, Charles Healy, Frank Kehoe, David Hammond, William Tuttle) | 0 | 1 | 0 | 6 |
| 3. | USA | (Missouri Athletic Club—John Meyers, Manfred Toeppen, Gwynne Evans, Amadee Reyburn, Fred Schreiner, Agustus Goessling, William Orthwein) | 0 | 1 | 0 | 5 |

The Missouri team refused to play for second place, so the Chicago team was awarded the silver medal by forfeit. Originally, a German team had also been entered, but when the Germans discovered that what the Americans called "water polo" was actually a strange sport called "softball water polo," they withdrew. The Americans used a deflated ball, and goals only counted if a player held the ball in the opposing goal.

**1906** not held

**1908 London** T: 4, N: 4, D: 7.22.

|   |   |   | W | L | PF | PA |
|---|---|---|---|---|---|---|
| 1. | GBR | (Charles Smith, George Nevinson, George Cornet, Thomas Thould, George Wilkinson, Paul Radmilovic, Charles Forsyth) | 1 | 0 | 9 | 2 |
| 2. | BEL | (Albert Michant, Herman Meyboom, Victor Boin, Joseph Pletincx, Fernand Feyaerts, Oscar Grégoire, Herman Donners) | 2 | 1 | 18 | 14 |
| 3. | SWE | (Torsten Kumfeldt, Axel Runström, Harald Julin, Pontus Hanson, Gunnar Wennerström, Robert Andersson, Erik Bergvall) | 0 | 1 | 4 | 8 |
| 4. | HOL | (Johan Rühl, Johan Cortlever, Jan Hulswit, Eduard Meijer, Karel Meijer, Pieter Ooms, Bouke Benehga) | 0 | 1 | 1 | 8 |

Final: GBR 9–2 BEL

Paul Radmilovic of the British team eventually took part in five Olympics as a swimmer and water polo player, and also competed in the 1906 Intercalated Games.

**1912 Stockholm** T: 6, N: 6, D: 7.13.

| | | W | L | PF | PA |
|---|---|---|---|---|---|
| 1. GBR | (Charles Smith, George Cornet, Charles Bugbee, Arthur Hill, George Wilkinson, Paul Radmilovic, Isaac Bentham) | 3 | 0 | 21 | 8 |
| 2. SWE | (Torsten Kumfeldt, Harald Julin, Max Gumpel, Pontus Hanson, Vilhelm Anderson, Robert Andersson, Erik Bergqvist) | 3 | 1 | 22 | 11 |
| 3. BEL | (Albert Durant, Herman Donners, Victor Boin, Joseph Pletincx, Oscar Grégoire, Herman Meyboom, Félicien Courbet, Jean Hoffman, Pierre Nijs) | 3 | 2 | 22 | 21 |
| 4. AUT | (Rudolf Buchfelder, Richard Manuel, Walter Schachtitz, Otto Scheff, Josef Wagner, Ernst Kovács, Hermann Buchfelder) | 1 | 3 | 10 | 25 |
| 5. HUN | (Sándor Ádám, László Beleznai, Tibor Fazekas, Jenö Hégner Tóth, Károly Rémi, János Wenk, Imre Zachár) | 0 | 2 | 9 | 11 |
| 6. FRA | (Gustave Prouvost, Gaston Vanlaere, Georges Rigal, Paul Louis Beulque, Jean Rodier, Jean Thorailler, Henri Decotu, Paul Vasseur) | 0 | 2 | 3 | 11 |

Final: GBR 8–0 AUT

**Great Britain's closest call was a 7–5 overtime victory over Belgium.**

**1920 Antwerp** T: 12, N: 12, D: 8.28.

| | | W | L | T | PF | PA |
|---|---|---|---|---|---|---|
| 1. GBR/IRL | (Charles Smith, Noel Purcell, Christopher Jones, Charles Bugbee, William Dean, Paul Radmilovic, William Peacock) | 3 | 0 | 0 | 19 | 4 |
| 2. BEL | (Albert Durant, Paul Gailly, Pierre Nijs, Joseph Pletincx, Maurice Blitz, René Bauwens, Gérard Blitz, Pierre Dewin) | 4 | 1 | 0 | 27 | 9 |
| 3. SWE | (Theodor Nauman, Pontus Hanson, Max Gumpel, Vilhelm Anderson, Nils Backlund, Robert Andersson, Erik Andersson, Harald Julin, Erik Bergqvist) | 4 | 1 | 0 | 36 | 11 |
| 4. USA | (Preston Steiger, Sophus Jensen, Michael McDermott, Clement Browne, Herbert Vollmer, Harry Hebner, James Cardson, William Vosburgh, G. Albert Taylor, Duke Paoa Kahanamoku, Perry McGillivray) | 2 | 3 | 0 | 18 | 19 |

| | | W | L | T | PF | PA |
|---|---|---|---|---|---|---|
| 5. HOL | (Karel Struys, Carl Kratz, Karel Meijer, Johan Cortlever, Piet Hein Plantinga, Gérard Bohlander, Jean van Silfhout) | 1 | 2 | 0 | 8 | 12 |
| 6. BRA | — | 1 | 1 | 1 | 9 | 9 |
| 7. SPA | (Manuel Armanque, Balcells, Ramon Berdemás, Jaime Fontanet, Francisco Gilbert, Luis Gilbert, Enrique Granados, Rosich, Alfonso Tusell, Antônio Vilacoro) | 1 | 2 | 1 | 3 | 15 |
| 8. GRE | — | 1 | 1 | 0 | 6 | 8 |

Final: GBR 3–2 BEL

The victory of the team from the United Kingdom was not a popular one. After the final match Belgian spectators attacked the British and Irish players, who had to be taken away under the protection of armed guards.

**1924 Paris** T: 13, N: 13, D: 7.20.

| | | W | L | PF | PA |
|---|---|---|---|---|---|
| 1. FRA | (Paul Dujardin, Noël Delberghe, Georges Rigal, Henri Padou, Robert Desmettre, Albert Mayaud, Albert Delborgies) | 4 | 0 | 16 | 6 |
| 2. BEL | (Albert Durant, Joseph Pletincx, Pierre Dewin, Gerard Blitz, Joseph Cludts, Georges Fleurix, Paul Gailly, Jules Thiry, Pierre Vermetten, Joseph de Combe, Maurice Blitz) | 4 | 1 | 18 | 10 |
| 3. USA | (Frederick Lauer, Oliver Horn, Clarence Mitchell, George Schroth, Herbert Vollmer, Johnny Weissmuller, Arthur Austin, John Norton, Wallace O'Connor) | 3 | 2 | 13 | 11 |
| 4. SWE | (Theodor Nauman, Gösta Persson, Vilhelm Anderson, Martin Norberg, Erik Andersson, Nils Backlund, Cletus Anderson, Hilmer Wictorin) | 3 | 3 | 27 | 12 |
| 5. HUN | (István Barta, Tibor Fazekas, Márton Homonnai, Alajos Keserü, Lajos Homonnai, János Wenk, Ferenc Keserü, József Vértesy) | 2 | 2 | 17 | 17 |
| 6. CZE | (Václav Ankrt, František Franěk, František Kúrka, Hugo Klempfner, Josef Tomášek, Jiři Reitman, Béla Nemenyi, Jan Hora, František Vacin, Jaroslav Hummelhans) | 2 | 2 | 11 | 15 |
| 7. HOL | (Gérard Bohlander, Frdereick Bohlander, W. Bokhoven, Jan den Boer, Jacques Köhler, Karel Struys, Antoine van Senus) | 1 | 2 | 12 | 10 |

Final: FRA 3–0 BEL

The French victory over Belgium came as a great surprise. The Parisian crowd was so excited that, after the playing of the "Marseillaise," they demanded that the Belgian national anthem be played as well. Belgium's loss dropped them into a playoff pool for second place. After defeating Sweden 4–2, they beat the United States,

2–1. However, the Americans lodged a protest, which was allowed. The match was replayed, and the Belgians won again, 2–1.

**1928 Amsterdam** T: 14, N: 14, D: 8.11.

| | | W | L | PF | PA |
|---|---|---|---|---|---|
| 1. GER | (Erich Rademacher, Otto Cordes, Emil Benecke, Fritz Gunst, Joachim Rademacher, Karl Bähre, Max Amann, Johannes Blank) | 3 | 0 | 18 | 10 |
| 2. HUN | (István Barta, Sándor Ivády, Alajos Keserü, Márton Homonnai, Ferenc Keserü, József Vértesy, Olivér Halassy) | 3 | 1 | 26 | 8 |
| 3. FRA | (Paul Dujardin, Jules Keignaert, Henri Padou, Emile Bulteel, Achille Tribouillet, Henri Cuvelier, Albert Vandeplancke, Ernest Rogez, Albert Thévenon) | 5 | 1 | 41 | 7 |
| 4. GBR | (Edward Temme, Paul Radmilovic, Edward Percival Peters, Nicholas Beaman, Jack Budd, Leslie Ablett, Richard Hodgson, John Hatfield, William Quick, W.G. Freeguard) | 2 | 2 | 15 | 21 |
| 5. BEL | (J. Brandeleer, Rene Bouwens, J. Malissart, Gerard Blitz, Pierre Coppieters, L. van Gheem, Henri de Pauw, F. Visser, A. Mélardy) | 1 | 1 | 14 | 6 |
| 5. HOL | (Abraham van Olst, Jean van Silfhout, Antoine van Senus, Jacques Köhler, Kees Leenheer, Jan Scholte, Ko Köhler) | 1 | 1 | 14 | 6 |

Final: GER 5–2 HUN

Germany defeated Hungary in overtime after the regulation periods ended in a 2–2 tie.

**1932 Los Angeles** T: 5, N: 5, D: 8.13.

| | | W | L | T | PF | PA |
|---|---|---|---|---|---|---|
| 1. HUN | (György Bródy, Sándor Ivády, Márton Homonnai, Olivér Halassy, József Vertesy, Janös Németh, Ferenc Keserü, Alajos Keserü, István Barta, Miklós Sárkány) | 3 | 0 | 0 | 30 | 2 |
| 2. GER | (Erich Rademacher, Fritz Gunst, Otto Cordes, Emil Benecke, Joachim Rademacher, Heiko Schwartz, Hans Schulze, Hans Eckstein) | 2 | 1 | 1 | 23 | 13 |
| 3. USA | (Herbert Wildman, F. Calvert Strong, Charles Finn, C. Harold McAllister, Philip Daubenspeck, Austin Clapp, Wallace O'Connor) | 2 | 1 | 1 | 20 | 12 |
| 4. JPN | (Takashige Matsumoto, Akira Fujita, Shuji Doi, Iwao Tokito, Yasutaro Sakagami, Takaji Takebayashi, Tosuke Sawami, Seibei Kimura) | 0 | 3 | 0 | 0 | 37 |

The team from Brazil, having lost 7–3 to Germany, gave a cheer for their conquerors, climbed out of the pool, and physically attacked the Hungarian referee, Béla Komjadi. They didn't let up until the police arrived. Needless to say, the entire Brazilian team was suspended and their remaining games were forfeited.

**1936 Berlin** T: 16, N: 16, D: 8.15.

| | | W | L | T | PF | PA |
|---|---|---|---|---|---|---|
| 1. HUN | (György Bródy, Kálmán Hazai, Márton Homonnai, Olivér Halassy, Jenö Brandi, Janös Németh, Mihály Bozsi, György Kutasi, Miklós Sárkány, Sándor Tarics, István Molnár) | 8 | 0 | 1 | 57 | 5 |
| 2. GER | (Paul Klingenburg, Bernhard Baier, Gustav Schürger, Fritz Gunst, Josef Hauser, Hans Schneider, Hans Schulze, Fritz Stölze, Heinrich Krug, Alfred Kienzle, Helmuth Schwenn) | 8 | 0 | 1 | 56 | 10 |
| 3. BEL | (Henri Disy, Joseph de Combe, Henri Stoelen, Fernand Isselé, Albert Castelyns, Gérard Blitz, Pierre Coppieters, Henri de Pauw, Edmond Michiels) | 4 | 3 | 2 | 17 | 17 |
| 4. FRA | (Georges Delporte, Paul Lambert, Maurice Lefebvre, Henri Padou, Roger Vandecastelle, André Busch, René Joder) | 4 | 5 | 0 | 21 | 37 |
| 5. HOL | (Johannes van Woerkom, Jean van Oostrom Soede, Rudolf den Hamer, Gerard Regter, Hans Maier, Cornelius van Aelst, Alexander Franken, Herman Veenstra, Jan van Hateren) | 3 | 1 | 5 | 23 | 28 |
| 6. AUT | (Franz Wenninger, Karl Seitz, Karl Steinbach, Sebastian Ploner, Franz Schönfels, Alfred Lergetporer, Wilhelm Hawlik, Erwin Blasl, Otto Muller, Anton Kunz, Peter Reidl) | 5 | 3 | 1 | 31 | 18 |
| 7. SWE | (Åke Nauman, Bertil Berg, Tore Ljungqvist, Gösta Persson, Erik Holm, Georg Svensson [Sollermark], Göte Andersson, Tore Lindzén, Runar Sandström) | 3 | 6 | 0 | 29 | 18 |
| 8. GBR | (Alfred North, David Grogan, William Martin, Robert Mitchell, Leslie Ablett, David McGregor, Ernest Blake) | 2 | 4 | 3 | 28 | 46 |

Hungary and Germany tied 2–2, but Hungary was awarded first place on the basis of a greater goal differential.

Olivér Halassy played on three Hungarian Olympic water polo teams, despite the fact that one of his legs had been amputated below the knee following an accident when he was 11. On September 10, 1946, at the age of 37, Halassy was murdered while walking down the street in Budapest.

**1948 London** T: 18, N: 18, D: 8.7.

| | | W | L | T | PF | PA |
|---|---|---|---|---|---|---|
| 1. | ITA (Pasquale Buonocore, Emilio Bulgarelli, Cesare Rubini, Geminio Ognio, Ermenegildo Arena, Aldo Ghira, Gianfranco Pandolfini, Mario Maioni, Tullio Pandolfini) | 8 | 0 | 2 | 47 | 24 |
| 2. | HUN (Endre Györffi, Miklós Holop, Dezsö Gyarmati, Károly Szittya, Oszkár Csuvik, István Szivós, Dezsö Lemhényi, László Jeney, Deszö Fábián, Jenö Brandi) | 6 | 3 | 1 | 45 | 27 |
| 3. | HOL (Johannes Rohner, Cornelis Korevaar, Cornelius Braasem, Hans Stam, Albert Ruimschotel, Rudolph van Feggelen, Fritz Smol, Pieter Salomons, Hendrikus Keetelaar) | 6 | 1 | 3 | 65 | 23 |
| 4. | BEL (Théo-Léo de Smet, Georges Leenheere, Emile d'Hooge, Paul Rigaumont, Fernand Isselé, Willy Simons, Alphonse Martin) | 2 | 2 | 6 | 32 | 25 |
| 5. | SWE (Rune Öberg, Erik Holm, Rolf Julin, Roland Spángberg, Arne Jutner, Olle Johansson, Åke Julin, Folke Eriksson, Knut Gadd, Olle Ohlsson) | 6 | 3 | 1 | 31 | 14 |
| 6. | FRA (François Debonnet, Maurice Lefebvre, Robert Le Bras, Marco Diener, Robert Himgi, Roger Dewasch, Jacques Berthe, Raymond Massol, Jacques Viaene, Emile Bermyn, Marcel Spilliaert) | 4 | 2 | 4 | 32 | 24 |
| 7. | EGY (Ahmed Nessim, Taha El Gamal, M. Kadry, M. Haraga, H. Said, Abdel Aziz Mohammed Khalifa, S. Gharbo, M. Hemmat) | 1 | 4 | 5 | 26 | 35 |
| 8. | SPA (Juan Serra Liobet, José Pujol Coma, Carlos Falp Mont, Carlos Marti Arenas, Francisco Castillo Caupana, Augustin Mestres Ribas, Valintin Sabate Mas, Francisco Sabate Figa) | 2 | 8 | 0 | 26 | 33 |

**1952 Helsinki** T: 21, N: 21, D: 8.2.

| | | W | L | T | PF | PA |
|---|---|---|---|---|---|---|
| 1. | HUN (László Jeney, György Vízvári, Dezsö Gyarmati, Kálmán Markovits, Antal Bolvári, István Szivós, György Kárpáti, Róbert Antal, Dezsö Fábián, Károly Szittya, Dezsö Lemhényi, István Hasznos, Miklós Martin) | 7 | 0 | 3 | 60 | 21 |
| 2. | YUG (Zdravko Kovačić, Veljko Bakašun, Ivo Štakula, Ivo Kurtini, Boško Vuksanović, Zdravko Ježic, Lovro Radonjić, Marko Brainović, Vlado Ivković) | 7 | 0 | 3 | 46 | 16 |
| 3. | ITA (Raffaello Gambino, Vincenzo Polito, Cesare Rubini, Carlo Peretti, Ermenegildo Arena, Maurizio Mannelli, Renato De Sanzuane, Renato Traiola, Geminio Ognio, Salvatore Gionta, Lucio Ceccarini) | 8 | 2 | 0 | 53 | 29 |
| 4. | USA (Harry Bisbey, James Norris, Edward Jaworski, Norman Lake, William Kooistra, Peter Stange, Norman Dornblaser, John Spargo, Robert Hughes, Maroni Burns) | 5 | 6 | 0 | 43 | 41 |
| 5. | HOL (Marcus van Gelder, Gerrit Bijsma, Cornelis Korevaar, Cornelius Braasem, Frits Smol, Rudolph van Geggelen, Johannes Cabout) | 7 | 2 | 1 | 45 | 22 |
| 6. | BEL (Théo-Léo de Smet, Alphonse Martin, Joseph Smits, André Laurent, Marcel Heyninck, Roland Sierens, Johan van den Steen, François Maesschalck, Georges Leenheere, Joseph Reynders) | 6 | 3 | 1 | 37 | 35 |
| 7. | SOV (Boris Goikhman, Yevgeny Semenov, Yuri Teplov, Lev Kokorin, Valentin Prokopov, Aleksandr Liferenko, Pyotr Mshvenieradze, Yuri Schlyapin, Vitaly Ushakov) | 4 | 4 | 2 | 43 | 34 |
| 8. | SPA (Leandro Ribera, Ricardo Conde, José Bazán, Roberto Queralt, Antônio Subirana, Augustin Mestres Ribas, José Abellan, Francisco Castillo Caupano) | 3 | 7 | 0 | 33 | 41 |

Holland defeated Yugoslavia 3–2 in a game of the semifinal round. However the Yugoslavs protested two decisions of the referee, and the match was ordered replayed. This time Yugoslavia won, 2–1, and advanced to the final round, in which they tied Hungary, 2–2, but lost because of a lower goal differential. One of the Hungarian players was Dezsö Gyarmati, who eventually won medals in five different Olympics (1948–1964.) His wife, Éva Székely, was a breaststroker who won a gold medal in 1952 and a silver in 1956.

**1956 Melbourne** T: 10, N: 10, D: 12.7.

| | | W | L | T | PF | PA |
|---|---|---|---|---|---|---|
| 1. | HUN (Ottó Boros, István Hevesi, Dezsö Gyarmati, Kálmán Markovits, Antal Bolvári, Mihály Mayer, György Kárpáti, László Jeney, István Szivós, Tivadar Kanizsa, Ervin Zádor) | 7 | 0 | 0 | 32 | 6 |
| 2. | YUG (Zdravko Kovačić, Ivo Cipci, | 6 | 1 | 1 | 28 | 13 |

Hrvoje Kačič. Marjan Žurej,
Zdravko Ježić, Lovro Radonjič,
Tomislav Franjkovič, Vladimir
Ivkovič)

3. SOV (Boris Goikhman, Viktor Age- 5 3 0 23 20
yev, Yuri Schlyapin, Vyacheslav
Kurennoi, Pyotr Breus, Pyotr
Mshvenieradze, Nodar Gyak-
haria, Mikhail Ryschak, Valentin
Prokopov, Boris Markarov)

4. ITA (Enzo Cavazzoni, Cesare Ru- 4 3 0 21 16
bini, Angelo Marciani, Paolo
Pucci, Federico Dennerlein, Giuseppe D'Altrui, Alfonso Buono-
core, Cosimo Antonelli, Luigi
Mannelli, Maurizio D'Achille)

5. USA (Robert Horn, William Ross, Rob- 2 5 1 18 25
ert Frojen, Wallace Wolf, Ronald
Severa, James Gaughran, William Kooistra, Kenneth Hahn,
Robert Hughes, Sam Kooistra)

6. GER (Karl Neuse, Alfred Obscherni- 1 5 1 18 25
kat, Wilfried Bode, Hans-
Joachim Schneider, Wilhelm
Sturm, Hans-Günther Hilker,
Friedhelm Osselmann, Emil
Bildstein, Erich Pennekamp,
Hans Werner Seher)

7. GBR (Arthur Grady, Gerald Worcell, 3 2 0 25 20
John, Jack Jones, Peter Pass,
Ronald Turner, Terence Miller,
E. Clifford Spooner, John Fergu-
son, Robert Knights)

8. ROM (Alexandru Marinescu, Zoltan 3 3 0 30 17
Hospodar, Aurel Zahan, Gavril
Nagy, Francisc Simon, Ivan Bor-
di, Alexandru Szabo, Alexandru
Badita, Iosif Deutsch)

On November 4, 1956, 200,000 Soviet troops invaded
Hungary to put down a major revolt against Communist
rule. The bitter feelings between the Hungarians and Soviets carried over into the Olympics, which were held less
than three weeks later. Hostilities culminated in the water polo match between the two countries on December
6. The game quickly turned into a brawl and was halted
by the referee before completion, with Hungary leading
4–0. Hungary was credited with a victory; however the
police had to be called in to prevent a riot, as the 5500
spectators wanted to punish the Soviets further. Half of
the Hungarian Olympic delegation refused to return to
Hungary.

**1960 Rome** T: 16, N: 16, D: 9.3.

|   |   |   | W | L | T | PF | PA |
|---|---|---|---|---|---|----|----|
| 1. | ITA | (Dante Rossi, Giuseppe D'Altrui, Eraldo Pizzo, Gianni Lonzi, Franco Lavoratori, Rosario Parmegiani, Danio Bardi, | 8 | 0 | 1 | 37 | 15 |

Brunello Spinelli, Salvatore
Gionta, Amadeo Ambron, Giancarlo Guerrini)

2. SOV (Leri Gogoladze, Givi Chikva- 6 2 1 35 26
naya, Vyacheslav Kurennoi,
Anatoly Kartashov, Yuri Grigo-
rovsky, Pyotr Mshvenieradze,
Vladimir Semyonov, Boris Goikhman, Yevgeny Salzyn, Viktor
Ageyev, Vladimir Novikov)

3. HUN (Ottó Boros, István Hevesi, 5 2 2 45 22
Mihály Mayer, Dezsö Gyarmati,
Tivadar Kanizsa, Zoltán Dömö-
tör, László Felkai, László Jeney,
András Katona, Kálmán Mark-
ovits, Péter Rusorán, György
Kárpáti, János Konrád, András
Bodnár)

4. YUG (Milan Muškatirović, Hrvoje 7 2 0 31 15
Kačić, Zlatko Šimenc, Zdravko
Ježić, Marijan Žužej, Ante
Nardeli, Mirko Sandič, Božidar
Stanišić. Dragoljub Siljak)

5. ROM (Mircea Stefănescu, Alexandru 4 3 2 34 26
Bădită, Aurel Zahan, Gavrila
Blajek, Alexandru Szabo, Anatol
Grintescu, Stefan Kroner)

6. GER (Hans Hoffmeister, Hans- 4 5 0 42 48
Joachim Schneider, Hans Scho-
pers, Bernd Strasser, Lajos
Nagy, Friedhelm Osselmann,
Dieter Seiz, Emil Bildstein,
Jürgen Honig)

7. USA Robert Horn, Marvin Burns, Ron- 4 5 0 42 48
ald Severa, Ronald Crawford,
Fred Tisue, Wallace Wolf, Robert Volmer, Gordon Hall,
Charles Bittick, Charles McIlroy)

8. HOL (Lambertus Kniest, Harry 1 7 1 32 38
Lamme, Frederik van der Zwan,
Harro Ran. Abraham Leenard.
Henri Vriend, Alfred van Dorp,
Johannes Muller, Hendrik
Hermsen)

**1964 Tokyo** T: 13, N: 13, D: 10.18.

|   |   |   | W | L | T | PF | PA |
|---|---|---|---|---|---|----|----|
| 1. | HUN | (Miklos Ambrus, László Felkai, János Konrád, Zoltán Dömötör, Tivadar Kanizsa, Péter Rusorán, György Kárpáti, Ottó Boros, Mihály Mayer, Dénes Pócsik, András Bodnár, Deszö Gyarmati) | 6 | 0 | 2 | 43 | 17 |
| 2. | YUG | (Milan Muškatirović, Ivo Trumbić, Vinko Rosić, Zlatko Šimenc, Bozidar Stanišić, Ante Nardeli, Zoran Janković, Mirko Sandić, Ozren Bonačič, Frane Nonkovič, Karlo Stipanić) | 7 | 0 | 2 | 42 | 16 |

| | | W | L | T | PF | PA |
|---|---|---|---|---|---|---|
| 3. | SOV (Igor Grabovsky, Vladimir Kuznyetsov, Boris Grishin, Boris Popov, Nikolai Kalashnikov, Zenon Bortkevich, Nikolai Kuzynetsov, Viktor Ageyev, Leonid Osipov, Vladimir Semyonov, Eduard Yegorov) | 5 | 2 | 1 | 20 | 13 |
| 4. | ITA (Dante Rossi, Giuseppe D'Altrui, Eraldo Pizzo, Gianni Lonzi, Franco Lavoratori, Rosario Parmegiani, Mario Cevasco, Eugenio Merello, Alberto Spinola, Danio Bardi, Giancarlo Guerrini, Federico Dennerlein) | 4 | 4 | 0 | 17 | 19 |
| 5. | ROM (Mircea Ştefănescu, Anatol Grintescu, Alexandru Szabo, Ştefan Kroner, Nicolae Firoiu, Gruia Novac, Cornel Mărculescu, Emil Muresan, Aurel Zahan, Iosif Kulineac) | 4 | 3 | 1 | 36 | 28 |
| 6. | GDR (Peter Schmidt, Hubert Höhne, Siegfried Ballerstedt, Edgar Thiele, Klaus Schulze, Jürgen Thiel, Klaus Schlenkrich, Heinz Mäder, Dieter Vohs, Jürgen Kluge, Heinz Wittig) | 3 | 5 | 0 | 26 | 26 |
| 7. | BEL (Hendrik Hermsen, Abraham Leenards, Willem van Springelen, Gerardus Wormgoor, Alfred van Dorp, Henri Vriend, Nicolaas van der Voet, Willem Vriend, Johan Muller, Jan Bultman, Lambertus Kniest) | 2 | 6 | 0 | 28 | 43 |
| 8. | HOL (Bruno de Hesselle, Frank Dosterlinck, Roger de Wilde, Jacques Caufrier, Andre Laurent, Karel de Vis, Jose de Vis, Jose Dumont, Johan van den Steen, Leon Pickers, Joseph Stappers) | 4 | 5 | 0 | 37 | 47 |

Thirty-seven-year-old Dezsö Gyarmati brought his medal total to three gold, one silver, and one bronze. The Hungarians' narrow victory was the result of a 4–4 tie with Yugoslavia, in which they scored their final goal with only 25 seconds to play. After that they won because of a greater goal differential in the final round. A minor controversy developed when Hungary and Italy complained that the shallow pool (5 feet 10 inches deep) allowed the taller Yugoslav players to stand with their heads above the water.

### 1968 Mexico City T: 15, N: 15, D: 10.26.

| | | W | L | T | PF | PA |
|---|---|---|---|---|---|---|
| 1. | YUG (Karlo Stipanić, Ivo Trumbić, Ozren Bonačić, Uroš Marović, Ronald Lopatny, Zoran Janković, Miroslav Poljak, Dejan Dabović, Djordje Perišić, Mirko Sandić, Zdravko Hebel) | 7 | 1 | 1 | 86 | 35 |
| 2. | SOV (Vadim Gulyayev, Givi Chikvanaya, Boris Grishin, Aleksandr Dolgushin, Aleksei Barkalov, Yuri Grigorovsky, Vladimir Semyonov, Aleksandr Shidlovsky, Vyacheslav Skok, Leonid Osipov, Oleg Bovin) | 6 | 2 | 0 | 62 | 36 |
| 3. | HUN Endre Molnár, Mihály Mayer, Istvan Szivós, János Konrád, László Felkai, Ferenc Konrád, Dénes Pócsik, András Bodnár, Zoltán Dömötör, János Steinmetz) | 6 | 2 | 0 | 54 | 26 |
| 4. | ITA (Alberto Alberani Samaritani, Eraldo Pizzo, Mario Cevasco, Gianni Lonzi, Enzo Barlocco, Franco Lavoratori, Gianni De Magistris, Alessandro Ghibellini, Giancarlo Guerrini, Paolo Ferrando, Eugenio Merello) | 6 | 2 | 1 | 57 | 38 |
| 5. | USA (Anton Van Dorp, David Ashleigh, Russell Webb, Ronald Crawford, Stanley Cole, Bruce Bradley, L. Dean Willeford, Barry Weitzenberg, Gary Sheerer, John Parker, Steven Barnett) | 5 | 2 | 1 | 49 | 43 |
| 6. | GDR (Hans-Georg Fehn, Klaus Schlenkrich, Jürgen Thiel, Siegfried Ballerstedt, Peter Rund, Jürgen Schüler, Jürgen Kluge, Veit Herrmanns, Manfred Herzog, Hans-Ulrich Lange, Peter Schmidt) | 6 | 2 | 1 | 78 | 30 |
| 7. | HOL (Feike de Vries, Hans Wouda, Louis Geutjes, Johannes Hoogveld, Alfred van Dorp, Hans Parrell, Nicolaas van der Voet, Ad Moolhuijzen, Bart Bonger, Andreas Hermsen, Evert Kroon) | 5 | 3 | 1 | 53 | 39 |
| 8. | CUB (Oscar Periche, Waldimiro Arcos, Miguel Garcia, Rolando Valdes, Ruben Junco, Guillermo Martinez, Ibrahim Rodriguez, Osvaldo Garcia, Roberto Rodriguez, Guillermo Canete, Jesús Perez) | 3 | 4 | 1 | 38 | 51 |

In the final match, Yugoslavia defeated the U.S.S.R. 13–11 in overtime, despite seven goals by Aleksei Barkalov, including two in the last 35 seconds of regulation. Australia had been accepted as one of the 16 teams to take part in the tournament. However, the Australian Olympic Committee considered it a waste of money to send their team to Mexico City. The players paid their own way, but were not allowed to compete.

**1972 Munich** T: 16, N: 16, D: 9.4.

| | | | W | L | T | PF | PA |
|---|---|---|---|---|---|---|---|
| 1. | SOV | (Vadim Gulyaev, Anatoly Akimov, Aleksandr Dreval, Aleksandr Dolgushin, Vladimir Shmudski, Aleksandr Kabanov, Aleksei Barkalov, Aleksandr Shidlovski, Nikolai Melnikov, Leonid Osipov, Vyacheslav Sobchenko) | 7 | 0 | 2 | 52 | 25 |
| 2. | HUN | (Endre Molnár, András Bodnár, István Görgényi, Zoltán Kásás, Tamás Faragó, László Sárosi, István Szivós, István Magas, Dénes Pócsik, Ferenc Konrád, Tibor Cservenyák) | 6 | 0 | 3 | 45 | 24 |
| 3. | USA | (James Slatton, Stanley Cole, Russell Webb, Barry Weitzenberg, Gary Sheerer, Bruce Bradley, Peter Asch, James Ferguson, Steven Barnett, John Parker, Eric Lindroth) | 7 | 1 | 2 | 55 | 41 |
| 4. | GER | (Gerd Olbert, Hermann Haverkamp, Peter Teicher, Kurt Küpper, Günter Wolf, Ingulf Nossek, Ludger Weeke, Kurt Schuhmann, Jürgen Stiefel, Hans Georg Simon, Hans Hoffmeister) | 2 | 2 | 5 | 36 | 31 |
| 5. | YUG | (Karlo Stipanić, Ratko Rudić, Ozron Bonačić, Uroo Marović, Ronald Lopatny, Zoran Jankovic, Sinisa Belamarić, Dušan Antunović, Djordje Perišić, Mirko Sandić, Milos Marković) | 5 | 4 | 1 | 55 | 48 |
| 6. | ITA | (Alberto Alberani, Eraldo Pizzo, Roldano Simeoni, Mario Cevasco, Allessandro Ghibellini, Gianni De Magistris, Guglielmo Marsili, Silvio Baracchini, Franco Lavoratori, Sante Marsili, Ferdinando Lignano) | 3 | 4 | 2 | 48 | 42 |
| 7. | HOL | (Evert Kroon, Hans Wouda, Jan Evert Veer, Hans Hoogveld, Wim Hermsen, Hans Parrel, Ton Schmidt, Mart Bras, Tony Buunk, Gyze Stroboer, Wim van der Schilde) | 6 | 1 | 2 | 43 | 31 |
| 8. | ROM | (Serban Huber, Bogdan Mihailescu, Gheorghe Zamfirescu, Gruia Novac, Dinu Popescu, Claudiu Rusu, Iosif Kuliniac, Cornel Rusu, Viorel Rus, Radu Lazar, Corneliu Fratila) | 5 | 4 | 1 | 62 | 45 |

The tournament included a bloody match between Yugoslavia and Cuba, and a contest between Hungary and Italy in which eight players were suspended within one 38-second span.

**1976 Montreal** T: 12, N: 12, D: 7.27.

| | | | W | L | T | PF | PA |
|---|---|---|---|---|---|---|---|
| 1. | HUN | (Endre Molnár, István Szivós Jr., Tamás Faragó, László Sárosi, György Horkai, Gábor Csapó, Attila Sudár, György Kenéz, György Gerendás, Ferenc Konrád, Tibor Cservenyák) | 7 | 0 | 1 | 45 | 32 |
| 2. | ITA | (Alberto Alberani, Roldano Simeoni, Silvio Baracchini, Sante Marsili, Marcello Del Duca, Gianni De Magistris, Alessandro Ghibellini, Luigi Castagnola, Riccardo De Magistris, Vincenzo D'Angelo, Umberto Panerai) | 4 | 1 | 3 | 47 | 33 |
| 3. | HOL | (Evert Kroon, Nicolaas Landeweerd, Jan Evert Veer, Hans van Zeeland, Ton Buunk, Piet de Zwarte, Hans Smits, Rik Toonen, Gyze Stroboer, Andy Hoepelman, Alex Boegschoten) | 5 | 1 | 2 | 32 | 27 |
| 4. | ROM | Florin Slavei, Corneliu Rusu, Gheorghe Zamfirescu, Adrian Nastasiu, Dinu Popescu, Claudiu Rusu, Ilie Slavei, Liviu Raducanu, Viorel Rus, Adrian Schervan, Doru Spinu) | 2 | 2 | 4 | 44 | 39 |
| 5. | YUG | (Milos Marković, Ozren Bonačić, Uros Marović, Predrag Manojlović, Djuro Savinović, Damir Polić, Sinisa Belamarić, Dušan Antunović, Dejan Dabović, Boško Lozica, Zoran Kačić) | 1 | 2 | 5 | 46 | 34 |
| 6. | GER | (Günter Kilian, Ludger Weeke, Hans-Georg Simon, Jürgen Stiefel, Roland Freund, Wolfgang Mechler, Martin Jellinghaus, Werner Obschernikat, Horst Kilian, Peter Röhle, Günter Wolf) | 2 | 5 | 1 | 24 | 28 |
| 7. | CUB | (Oscar Periche, Osvaldo García, Ramón Peña, Lázaro Costa, David Rodriguez, Nelson Dominguez Avila, Jorge Rizo, Eugenio Almeneiro, Jesus Perez, Gerardo Rodriguez, Oriel Dominguez Avila) | 5 | 1 | 2 | 66 | 31 |
| 8. | SOV | (Anatoly Klebanov, Sergei Kotenko, Aleksandr Dreval, Aleksandr Dolgushin, Vitaly Romanchuk, Aleksandr Kabanov, Aleksei Barkalov, Nikolai Melnikov, Nugzar Mshvenieradze, Vladimir Iselidze, Aleksandr Zakharov) | 4 | 2 | 2 | 47 | 28 |

The Soviet team was so humiliated by their failure to qualify for the final round of six that they tried to withdraw from the losers' round for seventh to 12th places, claiming that five of their players were too ill to compete. After forfeiting one game against Cuba, F.I.N.A. officials convinced them to continue with the tournament.

**1980 Moscow** T: 12, N: 12, D: 7.29.

| | | | W | L | T | PF | PA |
|---|---|---|---|---|---|---|---|
| 1. | SOV | (Yevgeny Sharonov, Sergei Kotenko, Vladimir Akimov, Yevgeny Grishin, Mait Riisman, Aleksandr Kabanov, Aleksei Barkalov, Erkin Shagaev, Georgy Mshvenieradze, Mikhail Ivanov, Vyacheslav Sobchenko) | 8 | 0 | 0 | 58 | 31 |
| 2. | YUG | (Luka Vezilić, Zoran Gopcević, Damir Polić, Ratko Rudić, Zoran Mustur, Zoran Roje, Milivoj Bebić, Slobodan Trifunović, Boško Lozica, Predrag Manojlović, Milorad Krivokapić) | 5 | 1 | 2 | 58 | 42 |
| 3. | HUN | (Andre Molnár, István Szivós Jr., Attila Sudár, György Gerendás, György Horkai, Gábor Csapó, István Kiss, István Udvardi, László Kuncz, Tamás Faragó, Károly Hauszler) | 5 | 2 | 1 | 51 | 44 |
| 4. | SPA | (Manuel Delgado, Gaspar Ventura, Antonio Esteller, Federico Sabria, Manuel Estiarte, Pedro Robert, Jorge Alonso, José Alcázar, Antonio Aguilar, Jorge Carmona, Salvador Franch) | 4 | 4 | 0 | 43 | 42 |
| 5. | CUB | (Oscar Periche Cordet, Orlando Cowley del Barrio, Barbaro Diaz Cervantes, Lazaro Costa Mendez, Pedro Rodriguez Rodriguez, Nelson Dominguez Avila, Jorge Rizo Perera, Arturo Ramos Hernandez, Calos Benitez Suarez, Gerardo Rodriguez Peñalver, Oriel Dominguez Avila) | 2 | 3 | 3 | 50 | 49 |
| 6. | HOL | (Wouly de Bie, Nicolaas Landeweerd, Jan Evert Veer, Hans van Zeeland, Ton Buunk, Erik Noordergraaf, Stan van Belkum, Adrianus van Mil, Dick Nieuwenhuizen, Jan Jaap Korevaar, Rudolf Misdorp) | 2 | 5 | 1 | 42 | 48 |
| 7. | AUS | (Michael Turner, David Neesham, Robert Bryant, Peter Montgomery, Julian Muspratt, Andrew Kerr, Anthony Folson, Charles Turner, Martin Callaghan, Randall Goff, Andrew Steward) | 5 | 2 | 1 | 45 | 39 |
| 8. | ITA | (Alberto Alberani, Roldano Simeoni, Alfio Misaggi, Sante Marsili, Massimo Fondelli, Gianni De Magistris, Antonello Steardo, Paolo Ragosa, Romeo | 4 | 3 | 1 | 40 | 35 |

Collina, D'Angelo Vincenzo, Umberto Panerai)

The U.S.S.R. clinched first place with a tension-packed 8–7 victory over Yugoslavia. Between 1928 and 1980, Hungarian water polo teams won medals in twelve consecutive Olympics.

**1984 Los Angeles** T: 12, N: 12, D: 8.10.

| | | | W | L | T | PF | PA |
|---|---|---|---|---|---|---|---|
| 1. | YUG | (Milorad Krivokapić, Deni Lusić, Zoran Petrović, Bozo Vuletić, Veselin Djuho, Zoran Roje, Milivoj Bebić, Perica Bukić, Goran Sukno, Tomislav Paskvalin, Igor Milanović, Dragan Andrić) | 6 | 0 | 1 | 72 | 44 |
| 2. | USA | (Craig Wilson, Kevin Robertson, Gary Figueroa, Peter Campbell, Douglas Burke, Joseph Vargas, Jon Svendsen, John Siman, Andrew McDonald, Terry Schroeder, Jody Campbell, Timothy Shaw) | 6 | 0 | 1 | 65 | 43 |
| 3. | GER | (Peter Röhle, Thomas Loebb, Frank Otto, Rainer Hoppe, Armando Fernandez, Thomas Huber, Jürgen Schröder, Rainer Osselmann, Hagen Stamm, Roland Freund, Dirk Theismann, Santiago Chalmovsky, Werner Obschernikat) | 4 | 2 | 1 | 74 | 46 |
| 4. | SPA | (Leandro Ribera, José Morillo, Felix Fernandez, Alberto Canal, Manuel Estiarte, Pedro Robert, Rafael Aguilar, Jorge Signes, Antonio Aguilar, Jorge Carmona, Jorge Sans, Jorge Neira) | 3 | 2 | 2 | 73 | 67 |
| 5. | AUS | (Michael Turner, Richard Pengelley, Robert Bryant, Peter Montgomery, Russell Sherwell, Andrew Kerr, Raymond Mayers, Charles Turner, Martin Callaghan, Christopher Wybrow, Russell Basser, Julian Muspratt, Glenn Townsend) | 2 | 3 | 2 | 58 | 58 |
| 6. | HOL | (Woulie de Bie, Nicolaas Landeweerd, Erik Noordegraff, Ed van Es, Ton Buunk, Dick Nieuwenhuizen, Stan van Belkum, Adrianus van Mil, Johan Aantjes, Anton Heiden, Remco Pielstroom, Roald van Noort, Ruud Misdorp) | 2 | 5 | 0 | 45 | 65 |
| 7. | ITA | (Roberto Gandolfi, Alfio Misaggi, Andrea Pisano, Antonello Steardo, Mario Fiorillo, Gianni De Magistris, Marco Galli, Marco D'Altrui, Marco Baldineti, Vicenzo D'Angelo, Romeo Col- | 4 | 1 | 2 | 75 | 52 |

lina, Stefano Postiglione, Umberto Panerai)

| | | | | W | L | T | PF | PA |
|---|---|---|---|---|---|---|---|---|

8. GRE (Ioannis Vossos, Spyros Capralos, Sotirios Stathakis, Andreas Gounas, Kiriakos Giannopoulos, Aristidis Kefalogiannis, Anastasios Papanastasiou, Dimitrios Seletopoulos, Antonios Aronis, Markellos Sitarenios, George Mavrotas, Xenofon Moudatsios, Stavros Giannopoulos) — 3 2 2 66 65

Trailing 5–2 with less than three minutes remaining in the third quarter of their final match against the U.S., Yugoslavia patiently rallied to tie the game 5–5 with three minutes left in the final period. Tenacious defense allowed the relatively inexperienced Yugoslavians to hold on until the end. The two teams finished with identical records but Yugoslavia won the tournament as a result of a greater goal differential in the medal round.

**1988 Seoul** T: 12, N: 12, D: 10.1.

| | | W | L | T | PF | PA |
|---|---|---|---|---|---|---|
| 1. YUG | (Aleksandar Šoštar, Deni Lušić, Dubravko Šimenc, Perica Bukić, Veselin Djuho, Dragan Andrić, Mirko Vičević, Igor Gočanin, Mislav Bezmalinović, Tomislav Paškvalin, Igor Milanović, Goran Radjenović, Renco Posinković) | 6 | 1 | 0 | 83 | 55 |
| 2. USA | (Craig Wilson, Kevin Robertson, James Bergeson, George Campbell, Douglas Kimball, Edward Klass, Alan Mouchawar, Jeffrey Campbell, Gregory Boyer, Terry Schroeder, Jody Campbell, Christopher Duplanty, Michael Evans) | 5 | 2 | 0 | 71 | 56 |
| 3. SOV | (Yevgeny Sharonov, Nurlan Mendygaliev, Yevgeny Grishin, Aleksandr Kolotov, Sergei Naumov, Viktor Berenduga, Sergei Kotenko, Dmitri Apanasenko, Georgy Mshvenieradze, Mikhail Ivanov, Sergei Markoch, Nikolai Smirnov, Mikhail Giorgadze) | 4 | 2 | 1 | 84 | 51 |
| 4. GER | (Peter Röhle, Dirk Jacoby, Frank Otto, Uwe Sterzik, Armando Fernandez, Andreas Ehrl, Ingo Borgmann, Rainer Osselmann, Hagen Stamm, Thomas Huber, Dirk Theismann, René Reimann, Werner Obschernikat) | 5 | 2 | 0 | 83 | 65 |
| 5. HUN | (Péter Kuna, Gábor Bujka, Gábor Schmiedt, Zsolt Petőváry, István Pintér, Tibor Keszthelyi, Balázs Vincze, Zoltán Mohi, Tibor Pardi, László Tóth, András Gyöngyösi, Zoltán Kósz, Imre Tóth) | | | | | |
| 6. SPA | (Jesús Rollan, Miguel Chillida, Marco Antonio Gonzalez, Miguel Perez, Manuel Estiarte, Pere Robert, Jorge Paya, Jose Antonio Rodriguez, Jorge Sans, Salvador Gomez, Mariano Moya, Jorge Neira, Pedro Garcia) | 4 | 2 | 1 | 66 | 55 |
| 7. ITA | (Paolo Trapanese, Alfio Misaggi, Andrea Pisano, Antonello Steardo, Alessandro Campagna, Paolo Caldarella, Mario Fiorillo, Francesco Porzio, Stefano Postiglione, Riccardo Empestini, Massimiliano Ferretti, Marco D'Altrui, Gianni Averaimo) | 3 | 2 | 2 | 66 | 53 |
| 8. AUS | (Glenn Townsend, Richard Pengelley, Christopher Harrison, Troy Stockwell, Andrew Wightman, Andrew Kerr, Raymond Mayers, Geoffrey Clark, John Fox, Christopher Wybrow, Simon Asher, Andrew Taylor, Donald Cameron) | 3 | 4 | 0 | 53 | 59 |

Final: YUG 9–7 USA (overtime)
3rd Place: SOV 14–13 GER

Yugoslavia and the United States played each other eight times in the two and a half months before the Olympics; the U.S. won five matches, Yugoslavia three. They met again to open the preliminary round in Seoul. The U.S. won again, this time 7–6 on a goal by Jim Bergeson with 5 seconds to play.

Ten days later, the American and Yugoslavian teams, both of which returned five players from their 1984 Olympic squads, matched up yet again in a replay of the Los Angeles final. In fact, as the championship game developed, there were certain eerie and, for the U.S., unfortunate similarities between the two contests. Just as they had four years earlier, the U.S. team took a 5–2 lead in the third quarter. Then, just as it had four years earlier, the U.S. play became tentative and the Yugoslavians fought back to tie the score 5–5. This time they also took the lead 6–5, although the U.S. scored one more goal to break a 10-minute drought with 2:12 to play. The game ended 6–6.

Following the rather unsatisfactory conclusion of the 1984 Olympics, in which the gold medal was determined by goal differential, the F.I.N.A. decided to change the rules to allow six-minute overtime periods in the medal round. In fact, the 1986 world championship was decided when Yugoslavia's Igor Milanović defeated the U.S.S.R. by scoring a goal with three-tenths of a second remaining in the *fourth* overtime period.

In Seoul no such marathon was needed. Yugoslavia scored three unanswered goals in the first 3:35 of overtime and held on for a 9-7 victory. The Yugoslavian players *averaged* 6 feet 6 inches tall.

# Discontinued Events

## 100-METER FREESTYLE FOR SAILORS

**1896 Athens** C: 3, N: 1, D: 4.11.
1. Ioannis Malokinis      GRE   2:20.4
2. Spiridon Chasapis    GRE    —
3. Dimitrios Drivas       GRE    —

This rather specialized event was limited to members of the Greek navy.

## 880-YARD FREESTYLE

**1904 St. Louis** C: 6, N: 4, D: 9.7.
1. Emil Rausch       GER    13:11.4
2. Francis Gailey     USA   13.23.4
3. Géza Kiss           HUN    —
4. Edgar Adams       USA    —
AC: Jamison Handy (USA), Otto Wahle (AUT)

## 4000-METER FREESTYLE

**1900 Paris** C: 29, N: 7, D: 8.19.
1. John Arthur Jarvis    GBR      58:24.0
2. Zoltán Halmay         HUN    1:08:55.4
3. Louis Martin            FRA    1:13:08.4
4. Thomas Burgess       FRA    1:15:07.6
5. Eduard Meijer          HOL    1:16:37.2
6. Fabio Mainoni          ITA    1:18:25.4

## 400-METER BREASTSTROKE

**1904 St. Louis** C: 4, N: 2, D: 9.7.
*(440 Yards—402.33 Meters)*
1. Georg Zacharias    GER    7:23.6
2. Walter Brack         GER    —
3. Jamison Handy      USA    —
4. Jörg Hoffmann       GER    —

**1906–1908** not held

**1912 Stockholm** C: 17, N: 10, D: 7.12.
1. Walter Bathe       GER    6:29.6   OR
2. Thor Henning       SWE    6:35.6
3. Percy Courtman     GBR    6:36.4
4. Kurt Malisch        GER    6:37.0
DNF: Willy Lützow (GER)

The appropriately named Walter Bathe won without being seriously threatened.

**1920 Antwerp** C: 18, N: 10, D: 8.25.
1. Håkan Malmroth       SWE    6:31.8
2. Thor Henning          SWE    6:45.2
3. Arvo Aaltonen         FIN     6:48.0
4. Jack Howell           USA    6:51.0
5. Per Cederblom         SWE    —
6. Michael McDermott     USA    —

## 200-METER TEAM SWIMMING

**1900 Paris** T: 4, N: 2, D: 8.12.
1. GER   (1—Ernst Hoppenberg 2:35.0, 2—Max Hainle   32
         2:36.0, 4—Max Schöne, 6—Julius Frey, 19—
         Herbert von Petersdorff)
2. FRA   (Tritons Lillois—Maurice Hochepied, Verbecke,   51
         Cadet, Bertrand, Victor Hochepied)
3. FRA   (Pupilles de Neptune, Lille—G. Leuillieux, Louis   61
         Martin, Houben, Tartara, Désiré Merchez)
4. FRA   (Libellule de Paris—members unknown)   65

This was not a relay, but a team race in which 20 men were entered. Each team was assigned points according to the places in which its individual members finished. Von Petersdorff did not actually take part and so was awarded a tie for last place. A British team had also been entered, but was misinformed as to the starting time and arrived after the race was over.

## 4 × 50-YARD FREESTYLE RELAY

**1904 St. Louis** T: 4, N: 1, D: 9.7.
1. USA   (New York Athletic Club # 1—Joseph Ruddy,   2:04.6
         Leo Goodwin, Louis Handle, Charles Daniels)
2. USA   (Chicago Athletic Club—David Hammond, Wil-   —
         liam Tuttle, Hugo Goetz, Raymond Thorne)
3. USA   (Missouri Athletic Club—Amadee Reyburn,   —
         Gwynne Evans, Marquard Schwartz, William
         Orthwein)
4. USA   (New York Athletic Club #2—Edgar Adams,   —
         David Bratton, George Van Cleaf, David
         Hesser)

A German team lined up to start the race, but the Americans objected, claiming that the race was for clubs only and that the German swimmers were not all from the same club. Not surprisingly, the U.S. officials in charge ruled in favor of the Americans.

## OBSTACLE RACE

**1900 Paris** C: 12, N: 5, D: 8.12.
1. Frederick Lane     AUS    2:38.4
2. Otto Wahle         AUT    2:40.0
3. Peter Kemp         GBR    2:47.4
4. Karl Ruberl         AUT    2:51.2

| | | |
|---|---|---|
| 5. Stapleton | GBR | 2:55.0 |
| 6. William Henry | GBR | 2:58.0 |

This quaint event required the participants to struggle past three sets of obstacles. First they had to climb over a pole, then they had to scramble over a row of boats, and finally they had to swim *under* another row of boats. Some sources state that the contestants swam through barrels rather than over and under boats. Frederick Lane was probably better known for his victory in the unimpeded 200-meter freestyle.

## UNDERWATER SWIMMING

**1900 Paris** C: 10, N: 4, D: 8.12.

| | | M | TIME | PTS. |
|---|---|---|---|---|
| 1. Charles de Vendeville | FRA | 60 | 1:08.4 | 188.4 |
| 2. A. Six | FRA | 60 | 1:05.4 | 185.4 |
| 3. Peder Lykkeberg | DEN | 28.50 | 1:30.0 | 147.0 |
| 4. de Romand | FRA | 47.50 | 50.2 | 145.0 |
| 5. Tisserand | FRA | 30.75 | 48.0 | 109.5 |
| 6. Hans Aniol | GER | 36.95 | 30.0 | 103.9 |

Two points were awarded for each meter swum and one point for each second that the swimmer was able to stay under water.

## PLUNGE FOR DISTANCE

**1904 St. Louis** C: 5, N: 1, D: 0.6.

| | | M | FT.-IN. |
|---|---|---|---|
| 1. William Dickey | USA | 19.05 | 62-6 |
| 2. Edgar Adams | USA | 17.53 | 57-6 |
| 3. Leo Goodwin | USA | 17.37 | 57-0 |
| 4. Newman Samuels | USA | 16.76 | 55-0 |
| 5. Charles Pyrah | USA | 14.02 | 46-0 |

In the plunge for distance, the contestants began with a standing dive, then remained motionless for 60 seconds or until their heads broke the surface of the water, whichever came first. Then the length of their dives was measured. Charles Pyrah held the U.S. record at 63 feet, but was "completely out of form" according to the local newspapers. It was most unfortunate that the great British plungers John Arthur Jarvis and W. Taylor did not make the trip to St. Louis. Jarvis won the 1904 Amateur Swimming Association plunging championship with a plunge of 75 feet 4 inches, while Taylor was the national record holder at 78 feet 9 inches. In 1930 Arthur Beaumont plunged 85 feet 10 inches. The A.S.A. championship was discontinued after 1946.

## PLAIN HIGH DIVING

The plain high dive was just that—nothing fancy, no twists or somersaults.

**1912 Stockholm** C: 30, N: 8, D: 7.11.

| | | POINTS | ORDINALS |
|---|---|---|---|
| 1. Erik Adlerz | SWE | 40.0 | 7 |
| 2. Hjalmar Johansson | SWE | 39.3 | 12 |
| 3. John Jansson | SWE | 39.1 | 12 |
| 4. Viktor Crondahl | SWE | 37.1 | 22 |
| 5. Tovio Aro | FIN | 36.5 | 26 |
| 6. Axel Runström | SWE | 36.0 | 26 |
| 7. Ernst Brandsten | SWE | 36.2 | 28 |

DNF Paul Günther (GER)

**1920 Antwerp** C: 22, N: 11, D: 8.25.

| | | POINTS | ORDINALS |
|---|---|---|---|
| 1. Arvid Wallman | SWE | 183.5 | 7 |
| 2. Nils Skoglund | SWE | 183.0 | 8 |
| 3. John Jansson | SWE | 176.0 | 16 |
| 4. Erik Adlerz | SWE | 173.0 | 19 |
| 5. Yrjö Valkama | FIN | 167.5 | 23 |
| 6. Herold Jansson | DEN | 159.0 | 27 |
| 7. Fernand Sauvage | BEL | — | 34 |
| 8. Adolpho Wellish | BRA | — | 37 |

Silver medalist Nils Skoglund was 13 years old.

**1924 Paris** C: 25, N: 10, D: 7.15.

| | | TIME | ORDINALS |
|---|---|---|---|
| 1. Richmond Eve | AUS | 160.0 | 13.5 |
| 2. John Jansson | SWE | 157.0 | 14.5 |
| 3. Harold Clarke | GBR | 158.0 | 15.5 |
| 4. Ben Trash | USA | 145.0 | 23.5 |
| 5. Raymond Vincent | FRA | 144.0 | 26.5 |
| 6. Peter Desjardins | USA | 141.0 | 28 |
| 7. A. Reginald Knight | GBR | 137.0 | 31 |
| 8. Arvid Wallman | SWE | 136.0 | 31 |

# SWIMMING

## 141

139. Duke Kahanamoku, winner of the 1912 and 1920 100-meter freestyle. He also finished second in 1924 at the age of 33.

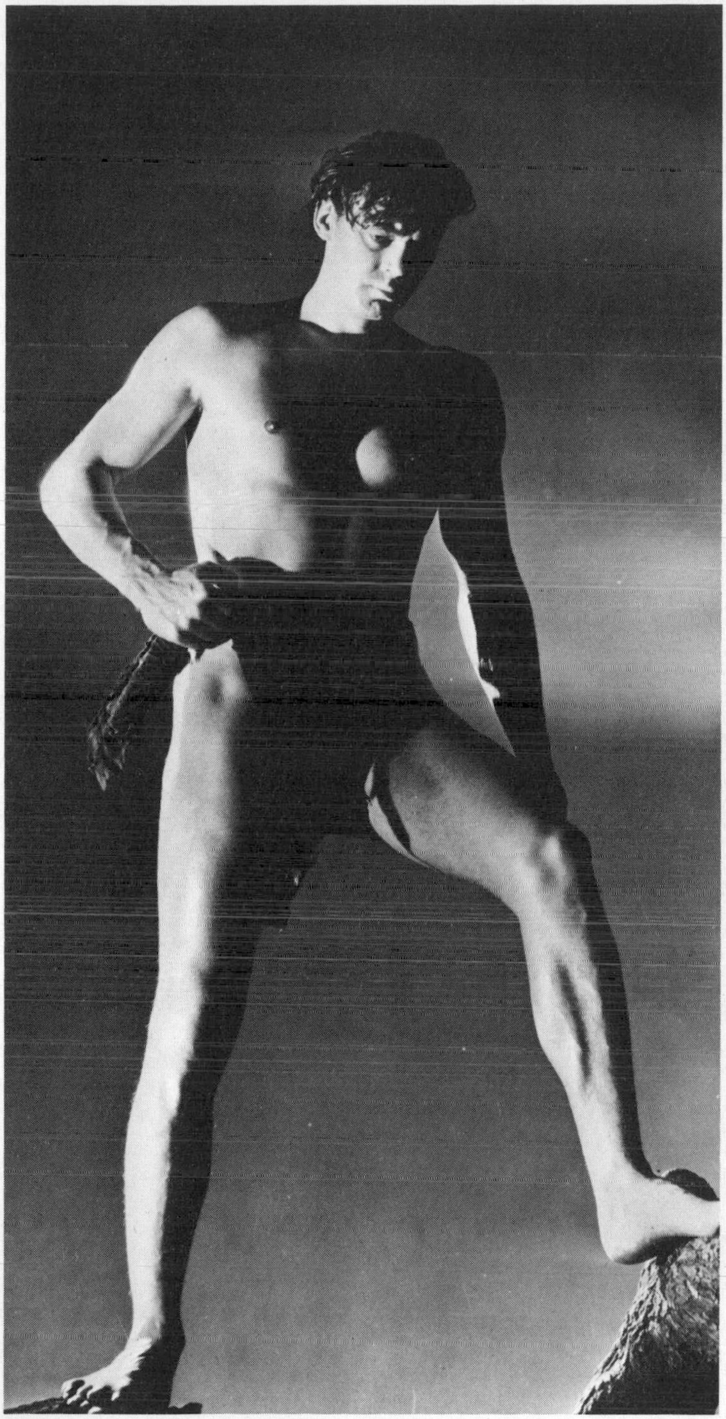

140. Johnny Weissmuller won five gold medals in 1924 and 1928 and then gained international fame as Tarzan.

141. Buster Crabbe came from behind to win the 1932 400-meter freestyle by one tenth of a second, in a thrilling finish. He attracted the attention of Hollywood producers, who later cast him as Tarzan, Buck Rogers, and Flash Gordon.

140

# SWIMMING

142

142. In 1964 Don Schollander became the first swimmer to earn four gold medals at one Olympics.

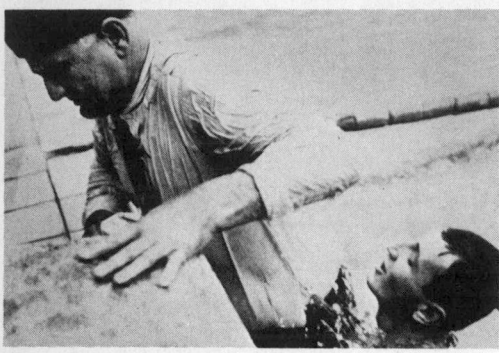

143

143. Jean Boiteux, winner of the 1952 400-meter freestyle, helps his proud father out of the pool after the latter leaped in to congratulate his son.

144

144. Mocked by his schoolmates because an accident left him bald and because he was dyslexic, Duncan Goodhew fought back by winning a gold medal in the 1980 100-meter breaststroke.

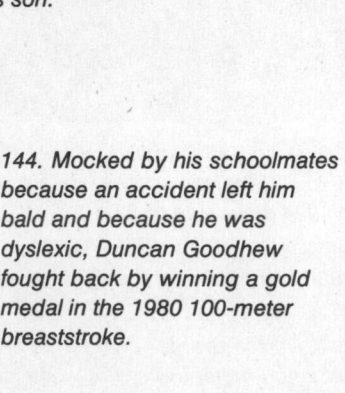

145

145. Alfréd Hajós survived 55-degree Fahrenheit water and 12-foot waves to win the 1200-meter freestyle in 1896. He later recalled, "My will to live completely overcame my desire to win."

146. After earning a gold medal in the 1984 4 x 200-meter freestyle relay, hearing-impaired swimmer Jeff Float uses sign language to say "I love you" to the crowd.

147. In 1988, Greg Louganis became the first male diver to win both the springboard and platform events in consecutive Olympics.

146

147

148

148. Klaus Dibiasi won an unprecedented three consecutive gold medals in the platform diving competitions of 1968, 1972, and 1976. He also earned a silver medal in 1964.

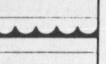

149

150

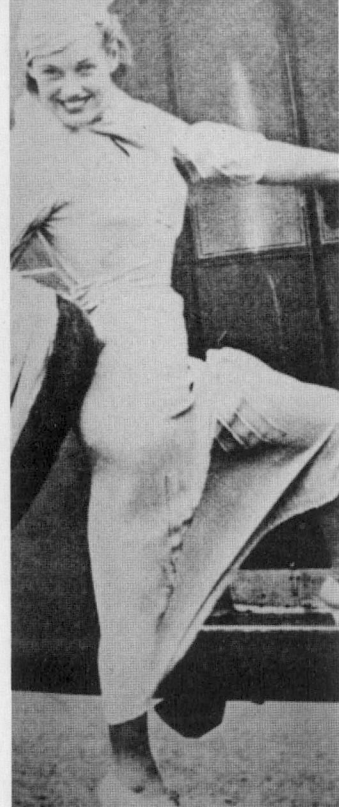

149. *Little Francesca Matthes, with her parents, Kornelia Ender and Roland Matthes, who between them won 16 swimming medals in 1968, 1972, and 1976. The couple later divorced.*

150. *Controversial Dawn Fraser won a total of four gold medals and four silver medals in 1956, 1960, and 1964.*

151. *Eleanor Holm won the 100-meter backstroke in 1932 and was on her way to defend her title in Berlin in 1936 when she was derailed by a major scandal.*

152. *Fourteen-year-old Krisztina Egerszegi won the 1988 200-meter backstroke to become the youngest swimming champion in Olympic history.*

151

152

153

153. *A thrilling moment in the 1988 solo synchronized swimming competition.*

154. *In 1952 and 1956 Pat McCormick swept both the springboard and platform diving competitions.*

154

155. Charlotte Cooper became the first female Olympic champion when she won the tennis tournament in Paris in 1900.

# WEIGHTLIFTING

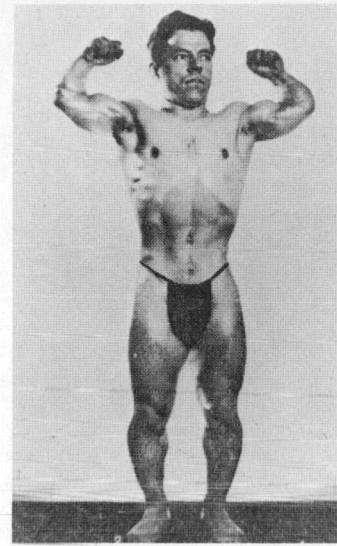

156

157

158

156. The arms of 4-foot 10-Inch Joe Di Pietro were so short that he could barely raise the bar above his head. Yet he was still able to win the 1948 Bantamweight gold medal.

157. Weightlifters Chen Weiqiang (left) and Tsai Wen-Lee become the first athletes from China and Taiwan to share an Olympic medal platform after taking the gold and bronze medals, respectively, in the 60 kg category in 1984.

158. The Turkish government paid the Bulgarian government over $1,000,000 to allow Featherweight weightlifter Naim Suleymanoğlü to compete for Turkey in 1988.

159. The 1936 Middleweight lifting champion, Khadr Sayed El Touni *(center), lifted 15 pounds more than the Light Heavyweight winner.*

159

160. Tommy Kono won three Olympic medals in three different weight categories in 1952, 1956, and 1960. His mental control led one rival to comment, "When Kono looks at me from the wings, he works on me like a python on a rabbit."

161. The 1948 Light Heavyweight silver medalist, Harold Sakata, gained greater fame as the evil Oddjob in the James Bond film Goldfinger.

160

161

# WEIGHTLIFTING

162. Launceston Elliot, winner of the one-hand lift in 1896.

163. Vassily Alexeyev, Super Heavyweight weightlifting champion in 1972 and 1976, keeping in shape during the off-season.

162

163

# WRESTLING

164

165

166

164. Thirty-nine-year-old Wilfried Dietrich (bottom) throwing 412-pound Chris Taylor during the 1972 Super Heavyweight freestyle wrestling tournament.

165. Anders Ahlgren and Ivar Böhling wrestled for nine hours in the final of the 1912 Greco-Roman Light Heavyweight division before officials declared a draw.

166. Carl Westergren won three Greco-Roman wrestling gold medals in three different weight divisions: Middleweight in 1920, Light Heavyweight in 1924, and Heavyweight in 1932 (at the age of 36).

167. Middleweight Greco-Roman wrestler Mikhail Mamiashvili finds himself in a tight squeeze in his 1988 final match against Tibor Komáromi. Mamiashvili emerged victorious.

168. Jeff Blatnick drops to his knees and gives thanks after winning a gold medal in the Super Heavyweight division of the 1984 Greco-Roman wrestling competition. Two years earlier, suffering from cancer, Blatnick had undergone extensive radiation treatment following the removal of his spleen and appendix.

167

# DISCONTINUED SPORTS

169

170

169. *George Lyon, winner of the 1904 golf event, keeping his ball on the eye.*

170. *Tough pulling in the 1906 tug of war.*

# TEAM SPORTS

171. *An unusual play from the 1948 football (soccer) tournament. Henry Carlsson of Sweden scores a goal against Denmark which is caught by his teammate Gunnar Nordahl, who had dashed into the opposing goal to avoid an offside call.*

171

172

173

172. *The famous 1964 Japanese women's volleyball team in action.*

173. *A typical scene from a team handball match.*

# SWIMMING

**WOMEN**

| | | |
|---|---|---|
| 50-Meter Freestyle | 100-Meter Breaststroke | 4 × 100-Meter Freestyle Relay |
| 100-Meter Freestyle | 200-Meter Breaststroke | 4 × 100-Meter Medley Relay |
| 200-Meter Freestyle | 100-Meter Butterfly | Synchronized Swimming: Solo |
| 400-Meter Freestyle | 200-Meter Butterfly | Synchronized Swimming: Duet |
| 800-Meter Freestyle | 200-Meter Individual Medley | Springboard Diving |
| 100-Meter Backstroke | 400-Meter Individual Medley | Platform Diving |
| 200-Meter Backstroke | | |

## WOMEN

### 50-METER FREESTYLE

**1896–1984** not held

**1988 Seoul** C: 50, N: 33, D: 9.25. WR: 24.98 (Yang Wenyi)
1. Kristin Otto        GDR   25.49   OR
2. Yang Wenyi        CHN   25.64
3. Katrin Meissner     GDR   25.71
3. Jill Sterkel         USA   25.71
5. Leigh Ann Fetter    USA   25.78
6. Tamara Costache   ROM   25.80
7. Catherine Plewinski   FRA   25.90
8. Karen Van Wirdum   AUS   26.01

At the 1982 world championships, 6-foot 1-inch Kristin Otto of Leipzig won three gold medals. At the 1986 world championships she won four gold medals and at the 1987 European championships she won five. Incredibly, Otto was able to improve on her record by earning an unprecedented six golds in Seoul. Her final victory, and the one that was least expected, came in the 50-meter freestyle. Otto, who had been expected to win three to five gold medals four years earlier, until East Germany announced its boycott of the Los Angeles Games, was unanimously voted the outstanding competitor of the 1988 Olympics by an I.O.C. panel.

Jill Sterkel, who tied for third place, became the first female swimmer to win medals 12 years apart. In 1976 she had earned a gold as a member of the U.S. freestyle relay team.

### 100-METER FREESTYLE

**1896–1908** not held

**1912 Stockholm** C: 27, N: 8, D: 7.2. WR: 1:20.6 (Daisy Curwen)
1. Fanny Durack            AUS   1:22.2
2. Wilhelmina Wylie      AUS   1:25.4
3. Jennie Fletcher        GBR   1:27.0
4. Margarete "Grete" Rosenberg   GER   1:27.4
5. Annie Speirs                GBR   1:27.4
DNS: Daisy Curwen (GBR)

Fanny Durack's biggest struggle came before the Olympics. The men who were in charge of naming the Australian team thought it an absurd waste of time and money to send women to Stockholm. Fanny convinced them to give her a tryout, but the men were not impressed by what they saw. Eventually she built up enough support to allow her to go. In the fourth heat of the second round, Durack swam a 1:19.8 to break Daisy Curwen's world record. In the semifinals she defeated Curwen, who then went straight to the hospital for an emergency appendectomy. Durack led the final from start to finish and won easily. At one time Fanny Durack held every world record in women's swimming, from 50 yards to one mile.

**1920 Antwerp** C: 16, N: 8, D: 8.25. WR: 1:16.2 (Fanny Durack)
1. Ethelda Bleibtrey    USA   1:13.6   WR
2. Irene Guest           USA   1:17.0
3. Frances Schroth     USA   1:17.2
4. Constance Jeans    GBR   1:22.8
5. Violet Walrond      NZE   —
6. Jane Gylling         SWE   —
7. Charlotte Boyle      USA   —

Bleibtrey broke the world record in the third heat with a time of 1:14.4, then broke the record again in winning the final. Eventually she won all three swimming events for women at Antwerp.

**1924 Paris** C: 16, N: 7, D: 7.20. WR: 1:12.8 (Gertrude Ederle)
1. Ethel Lackie          USA   1:12.4
2. Mariechen Wehselau   USA   1:12.8
3. Gertrude Ederle      USA   1:14.2
4. Constance Jeans      GBR   1:15.4
5. Irene Tanner         GBR   1:20.8
6. Maria Vierdag (HOL)

The U.S. sweep was particularly impressive considering the absurd restrictions imposed on the female swimmers by the U.S. Olympic Committee. American officials, concerned about protecting their teenaged swimmers from the immoral temptations of Paris, housed the young ladies way outside the city and forced them to spend five to six hours a day traveling to and from the Olympic pool. In the first heat, Mariechen Wehselau of Honolulu set a world record of 1:12.2. Lackie and Ederle won the next two heats in 1:12.8 and 1:12.6. In the final race, Wehselau held a two-yard lead at the 50-meter turn, with Ederle second and Lackie third. But 17-year-old Ethel Lackie of Chicago put on a fantastic spurt in the last 25 meters to edge Wehselau for first place.

Two years later Gertrude Ederle, the 19-year-old daughter of a New York City butcher, carved herself a permanent place in the history books with a swimming feat that shocked the world. Just after seven a.m. on the morning of August 6, 1926, she set off from France in an attempt to become the first woman to swim the English Channel. That day, the London *Daily News* ran an editorial which haughtily announced, "Even the most uncompromising champion of the rights and capacities of women must admit that in contests of physical skill, speed and endurance they must remain forever the weaker sex." Such overblown male chauvinism was buried in an avalanche of feminist joy when Ederle reached the English coast at Kingsdown in a time of 14 hours 31 minutes—almost two hours faster than the *men's* record for the Channel swim.

Ederle returned home to a tickertape parade attended by an estimated 2,000,000 people. A slew of personal appearances followed, but this period involved a series of setbacks. By 1933 she had suffered a nervous breakdown, become deaf as a result of her Channel swim, and received a serious back injury that forced her to wear a cast for four and a half years. Not one to wallow in self-pity, Ederle went right ahead with her life and eventually began teaching swimming to deaf children.

**1928 Amsterdam** C: 24, N: 11, D: 8.11. WR: 1:10.0 (Ethel Lackie)

| | | | |
|---|---|---|---|
| 1. Albina Osipowich | USA | 1:11.0 | OR |
| 2. Eleanor Garatti | USA | 1:11.4 | |
| 3. Margaret Joyce Cooper | GBR | 1:13.6 | |
| 4. Joan McDowall | GBR | 1:13.6 | |
| 5. Susan Laird | USA | 1:14.6 | |
| 6. Charlotte Lehmann | GER | 1:15.2 | |

**1932 Los Angeles** C: 20, N: 10, D: 8.8. WR: 1:06.6 (Helene Madison)

| | | | |
|---|---|---|---|
| 1. Helene Madison | USA | 1:06.8 | OR |
| 2. Willemijntje den Ouden | HOL | 1:07.8 | |
| 3. Eleanor Saville (Garatti) | USA | 1:09.3 | |
| 4. Josephine McKim | USA | 1:09.3 | |
| 5. Neville Bult | AUS | 1:09.9 | |
| 6. Jennie Maakal | SAF | 1:10.8 | |

If ever there was a sure bet for a gold medal, it was 5-foot 10½-inch, 154-pound Helene Madison, a 19-year-old from Seattle, Washington, who was invariably referred to by the press as "shapely." During a 16½-month period in 1930–31, Madison broke all 16 world records for the distances between 100 yards and 1 mile. However, the results of the semifinals in Los Angeles raised serious doubts as to whether she could actually win the final. The first semifinal was won by 14-year-old Willy den Ouden in the surprisingly fast time of 1:07.6. In the second semi, Helene Madison went all out for the first 50 meters and then huffed home to win in 1:09.9, a time that would have placed her only fifth in the first semi. The American coaches advised Madison to change her tactics and save herself for the second half of the final race. This proved to be advice well worth taking, as Madison forged to a full-length lead between 50 and 75 meters before bumping into the lane divider. A final burst of speed provided her with a comfortable margin of victory.

Joyce Cooper of Great Britain was most unlucky to be drawn in the first semifinal. Her times of 1:09.0 and 1:09.2 would have been good enough for third place in the final.

After the Olympics it appeared that Helene Madison was headed for a very glamorous life, but things didn't work out that way. In 1933 she played a minor role in the film *The Warrior's Husband*. Then she tried to earn a living as a nightclub entertainer, a swimming instructor, and a department store clerk. In 1935 she became a probationary nurse at a Seattle hospital, but she failed to earn a registered nurse's certificate. She was also frustrated in her personal life. Married and divorced three times, she was living alone with her Siamese cat when she died of cancer in 1970 at the age of 56.

**1936 Berlin** C: 33, N: 14, D: 8.10. WR: 1:04.6 (Willemijntje den Ouden)

| | | | |
|---|---|---|---|
| 1. Hendrika "Rie" Mastenbroek | HOL | 1:05.9 | OR |
| 2. Jeannette Campbell | ARG | 1:06.4 | |
| 3. Gisela Arendt | GER | 1:06.6 | |
| 4. Willemijntje den Ouden | HOL | 1:07.6 | |
| 5. Catherina Wagner | HOL | 1:08.1 | |
| 6. Olive McKean | USA | 1:08.4 | |
| 7. Katherine Rawls | USA | 1:08.7 | |

Six months before the Berlin Games, Willy den Ouden swam a phenomenal 1:04.6, setting a world record that would last for 20 years. But in the preliminary rounds of the Olympics, it was her 17-year-old teammate, Rie Mastenbroek, who recorded the fastest times. In the final Mastenbroek was fifth at the 50-meter turn and was still behind Arendt and Campbell (whose parents were Scottish) with only ten meters to go. But her furious finishing strokes gave her a dramatic victory. Over the next five days Mastenbroek won two more gold medals and one silver medal.

**1948 London** C: 34, N: 14, D: 8.2. WR: 1:04.6 (Willemijntje den Ouden)

| | | |
|---|---|---|
| 1. Greta Andersen | DEN | 1:06.3 |
| 2. Ann Curtis | USA | 1:06.5 |
| 3. Marie-Louise Vaessen | HOL | 1:07.6 |
| 4. Karen-Margrete Harup | DEN | 1:08.1 |
| 5. Ingegärd Fredin | SWE | 1:08.4 |
| 6. Irma Schumacher | HOL | 1:08.4 |
| 7. Elisabeth Ahlgren | SWE | 1:08.8 |
| 8. Fritze Carstensen | DEN | 1:09.1 |

Greta Andersen later became a professional and swam the English Channel six times, culminating in an England-to-France record of 13 hours 14 minutes, which she set in 1964 at the age of 36.

**1952 Helsinki** C: 41, N: 19, D: 7.28. WR: 1:04.6 (Willemijntje den Ouden)
1. Katalin Szöke          HUN    1:06.8
2. Johanna Termeulen      HOL    1:07.0
3. Judit Temes            HUN    1:07.1
4. Joan Harrison          SAF    1:07.1
5. Joan Alderson          USA    1:07.1
6. Irma Heijting-Schuhmacher HOL 1:07.3
7. Marilee Stepan         USA    1:08.0
8. Angela Barnwell        GBR    1:08.6

The 1952 100-meter freestyle race saw a thrilling finish in which the lead changed hands three times in the last ten meters and the first six women finished within two feet of each other. Judit Temes, who had set an Olympic record of 1:05.5 in the first round, pushed to the front after 90 meters, but then Joan Harrison moved ahead. The South African swimmer had the unfortunate experience of finishing out of the medals despite the fact that she appeared to be in first place with only five meters to go. The eventual winner, 16-year-old Katalin Szöke, had been well-known in Hungary for quite some time. Her mother had introduced her to swimming when she was only six months old, and she became known as "Kati, the World's First Waterproof Baby." She was able to stay afloat unaided before she was two years old. Szöke's husband, Kalman Markovits, was a member of Hungary's gold medal water polo team in 1952 and 1956.

**1956 Melbourne** C: 35, N: 16, D: 12.1 WR: 1:02.4 (Lorraine Crapp)
1. Dawn Fraser        AUS    1:02.0   WR
2. Lorraine Crapp     AUS    1:02.3
3. Faith Leech        AUS    1:05.1
4. Joan Rosazza       USA    1:05.2
5. Virginia Grant     CAN    1:05.4
6. Shelley Mann       USA    1:05.6
7. Marrion Roe        NZE    1:05.6
8. Natalie Myburgh    SAF    1:05.8

Dawn Fraser was the youngest of eight children born to working-class parents in Balmain, an industrial suburb of Sydney. On February 21, 1956, Fraser broke Willy den Ouden's 20-year-old world record and upset Lorraine Crapp to win the Australian championship in a time of 1:04.5. Dawn was not that impressed by her feat and told reporters that she could do a lot better. At the time some people may have considered Fraser to be excessively cocky, but it turned out that she was absolutely right. In fact, the quality of women's freestyle swimming was going through a period of rapid change. In the next eight months the 100 meters record was lowered five more times, twice by Cockie Gastelaars of the Netherlands,

once more by Dawn Fraser, and, finally, twice in the month of October by Lorraine Crapp.

With Gastelaars out of the Games because of the Dutch Olympic boycott, there was no question that the battle for the gold medal would be between Crapp and Fraser. In the first heat of the first round, Crapp swam a 1:03.4 to lower the Olympic record by over two seconds. In the fifth heat Fraser lowered it further with a 1:02.4. The two Australian teenagers then won their semifinal races, Fraser in 1:03.0 and Crapp in 1:03.1. The day before the women's final, the Australian men had scored a sweep in the 100-meter freestyle, and with Faith Leech recording the third fastest time in each of the first two rounds, it looked as if the Australian women might match the accomplishments of their male counterparts.

The night before the race Dawn Fraser went to bed early, prayed for the strength to win, and then thought through the race, particularly the turn, before she finally dropped off to sleep. Before long she was stricken by a nightmare, which she later described quite graphically in her autobiography, *Below the Surface*. "The gun went off," she began, "but I had honey on my feet and it was hard to pull them away from the starting block. I finally fought free and dived high. . . . It seemed a long time before I hit the water, and the water wasn't water; it was spaghetti. I fought with it and kept going up and down in the one place, like a yo-yo. The spaghetti strands tangled and tied my feet, and I was swimming with my arms alone. Of course I fouled up the turn and took a few mouthfuls, and I woke up gasping and fighting in a sea of spaghetti."

She must have been somewhat relieved the next day to discover that the pool was in fact filled with water, although she was still incredibly nervous, since she had never before swum in an international meet. Fraser and Crapp pulled away from the others after only 25 meters. Fraser completed the turn first, but Crapp caught up with her with 25 meters to go; the two reached the finish without knowing which one had won. They were so far ahead of the others that they were able to turn around and watch their teammate, Faith Leech, win the battle for third place. After her victory was announced, Dawn Fraser borrowed a ladder from a TV crew and climbed into the stands to share tears of joy with her parents, and to savor a moment which they had all dedicated to Dawn's dead brother, Don, who had introduced her to swimming when she was a child. Starting with that day in Melbourne, Dawn Fraser was the world record holder at 100 meters for the next 15 years.

**1960 Rome** C: 32, N: 19, D: 8.29. WR(110 yards). 1:00.2 (Dawn Fraser)
1. Dawn Fraser            AUS    1:01.2   OR
2. S. Christine Von Saltza USA   1:02.8
3. Natalie Steward        GBR    1:03.1
4. Carolyn Wood           USA    1:03.4
5. Csilla Dobai-Madarász  HUN    1:03.6

| | | | |
|---|---|---|---|
| 6. Erica Terpstra | HOL | 1:04.3 | |
| 7. Cockie Gastelaars | HOL | 1:04.7 | |
| 8. Marie Stewart | CAN | 1:05.5 | |

Undefeated at 100 meters since the last Olympics, Dawn Fraser made news by becoming the first woman to defend an Olympic swimming title. But she made bigger news the following day with her defiance of Australian officials. Thinking she had the day off, she had stayed up late, celebrating. In the morning a routine meeting of the Australian women's swim team turned into a violent argument, which didn't end until Fraser had smacked teammate Jan Andrew in the face with a pillow. Fraser spent the rest of the morning shopping for a wedding dress (which she didn't use) and sightseeing in Rome. She returned to the Olympic Village in time for lunch and had just finished a big plate of spaghetti when Roger Pegram, the manager of the Australian swimming team, approached her and ordered her to get dressed so that she could swim the butterfly leg of the medley relay qualifying heat. Stating that she was stuffed and unprepared, Fraser refused to swim and returned to her room for a nap. Eventually Alva Colquhoun volunteered to take her place, but for the remainder of their stay in Rome, the Australian women punished Fraser by "sending her to Coventry." In others words, they refused to speak a single word to her or to each other as long as Fraser was in the room.

**1964 Tokyo** C: 44, N: 22, D: 10.13. WR: 58.9 (Dawn Fraser)

| | | | |
|---|---|---|---|
| 1. Dawn Fraser | AUS | 59.5 | OR |
| 2. Sharon Stouder | USA | 59.9 | |
| 3. Kathleen Ellis | USA | 1:00.8 | |
| 4. Erica Terpstra | HOL | 1:01.8 | |
| 5. Marion Lay | CAN | 1:02.2 | |
| 6. Csilla Dobai-Madarász | HUN | 1:02.4 | |
| 7. Ann Hagberg | SWE | 1:02.5 | |
| 8. Lynette Bell | AUS | 1:02.7 | |

On October 27, 1962, Dawn Fraser, swimming in Melbourne, became the first woman to break the one-minute barrier for 100 meters when she covered the longer distance of 110 yards in 59.9 seconds. By February 29, 1964, she had cut her time down to 58.9, and it was almost eight years before anyone would do better. But in March, tragedy struck. She was driving home from a football social with three passengers, her mother, her sister, and a friend, when her car skidded and crashed into a parked truck. Her mother was killed, her sister was knocked unconscious, and Dawn herself spent six weeks with her neck in plaster because of a chipped vertebra.

Seven months later Dawn Fraser was, remarkably, back in form for the Olympics. By this time she was 27 years old, an old-timer by swimming standards who was known to her teammates as "Granny." She had by no means lost her rebellious spirit, however. Ordered by team officials to skip the opening-day ceremonies, she sneaked in anyway and enjoyed the parade and festivi-

ties. She tied her own Olympic record of 1:00.6 (set in the 1960 relay) in the first round and then swam a 59.9 in the semifinals. Entering the final she was sure that her only serious challenger would be 15-year-old Sharon Stouder of Glendora, California. Fraser took the lead immediately, but Stouder swam a tremendous race and caught her at the 70-meter mark. Fraser was not to be denied, though, and she called on an extra reserve of strength to pull away once again. Stouder's time of 59.9 made her the first woman other than Dawn Fraser to break one minute. Later Fraser committed the final indiscretion of her career, when she led a middle-of-the-night raid to steal a "souvenir" flag from the Emperor's palace. She was arrested, but the charges were dropped and the Emperor gave her the flags as a gift. However, the Australian Swimming Union slapped her with a ten-year suspension which was lifted after four years. The escapade in no way detracted from her status as a national heroine, since most Australians were less interested in her out-of-the-pool antics than they were in the fact that she had become the first Olympic swimmer of either sex to win the same event three times. In 1990, Fraser was elected to the parliament of New South Wales.

**1968 Mexico City** C: 57, N: 27, D: 10.19. WR: 58.9 (Dawn Fraser)

| | | | |
|---|---|---|---|
| 1. Jan Henne | USA | 1:00.0 | |
| 2. Susan Pedersen | USA | 1:00.3 | |
| 3. Linda Gustavson | USA | 1:00.3 | |
| 4. Marion Lay | CAN | 1:00.5 | |
| 5. Martina Grunert | GDR | 1:01.0 | |
| 6. Alexandra Jackson | GBR | 1:01.0 | |
| 7. Mirjana Segrt | YUG | 1:01.5 | |
| 8. Judit Turóczy | HUN | 1:01.6 | |

**1972 Munich** C: 46, N: 23, D: 8.29. WR: 58.5 (Shane Gould)

| | | | |
|---|---|---|---|
| 1. Sandra Neilson | USA | 58.59 | OR |
| 2. Shirley Babashoff | USA | 59.02 | |
| 3. Shane Gould | AUS | 59.06 | |
| 4. Gabriele Wetzko | GDR | 59.21 | |
| 5. Heidemarie Reineck | GER | 59.73 | |
| 6. Andrea Eife | GDR | 59.91 | |
| 7. Magdolna Patoh | HUN | 1:00.02 | |
| 8. Enith Brigitha | HOL | 1:00.09 | |

Following the Australian sweeps of 1956, the number of entrants per nation per event was reduced from three to two. This restriction was dropped after 1960, then reinstated after the U.S. sweeps of 1968. It was dropped again in 1976, but reinstated once more in 1984 as a result of the East German sweeps of 1976 and 1980. In 1972 the Australian favorite, Shane Gould, lost her first freestyle race in two years when she was beaten by two Southern California high school students, Sandy Neilson and Shirley Babashoff. Neilson led all the way, but Babashoff had to come from seventh place at the turn to nip Gould for the silver. The one-two victory gave confidence to the U.S. swimmers, who had been wearing T-shirts that read, "All that glitters is not Gould."

**1976 Montreal** C: 45, N: 25, D: 7.19. WR: 55.73 (Kornelia Ender)

| | | | |
|---|---|---|---|
| 1. Kornelia Ender | GDR | 55.65 | WR |
| 2. Petra Priemer | GDR | 56.49 | |
| 3. Enith Brigitha | HOL | 56.65 | |
| 4. Kim Peyton | USA | 56.81 | |
| 5. Shirley Babashoff | USA | 56.95 | |
| 6. Claudia Hempel | GDR | 56.99 | |
| 7. Jill Sterkel | USA | 57.06 | |
| 8. Jutta Weber | GER | 57.26 | |

At Munich in 1972, the East German women swimmers failed to win a single gold medal, yet four years later in Montreal they were able to finish first in 11 of 13 events. This extraordinary transformation actually began at the 1973 world swimming championships in Belgrade, Yugoslavia, where the East German women appeared wearing the latest model of their skin-tight, semi-see-through Lycra suits. Some people began to raise a protest, until it was revealed that the suits had actually been invented and manufactured in *West* Germany. By 1976 the Americans in particular were also accusing the East German women of appearing too muscular and masculine, of being shot up with anabolic steroids, and of being "all work and no play" types, who would be unable ever to bear children.

Although there is little doubt that experiments with steroids and other drugs were being carried out, the primary reason for East Germany's success was the enormous emphasis that country placed on legitimate sports science. While U.S. and Soviet scientists were busy conquering space and designing weapons systems, the East Germans were studying athletes—taking blood tests and muscle biopsies, checking oxygen levels, and testing for nutritional needs. The scandalous "Belgrade suits" of 1973 soon became commonplace throughout the world. Likewise, the East Germans were years ahead in studies of such things as lactic acid buildup during training. When the East German coaches heard the accusations that their young swimmers were too muscular and that they were using steriods, the East Germans responded that the muscles were a result of a concentrated weightlifting program, and that if America's women swimmers didn't start lifting weights seriously, they would never catch up.

At the age of 13, Kornelia Ender of Bitterfeld won three silver medals at the 1972 Olympics. The following year, in East Berlin, she broke Shane Gould's world record in the 100-meter freestyle. In the three years preceding the 1976 Olympics, Ender broke the world record for that event nine times. Two months before the Montreal Games, the 5-foot 10-inch, 154-pound Ender announced her engagement to backstroker Roland Matthes. She set her tenth 100 meters world record in the Olympic final, her second gold medal of the Games. After the Olympics were over Kornelia Ender was reunited with her grandmother, who had left East Germany in 1961 and moved to Kansas.

**1980 Moscow** C: 30, N: 22, D: 7.21. WR: 55.41 (Barbara Krause)

| | | | |
|---|---|---|---|
| 1. Barbara Krause | GDR | 54.79 | WR |
| 2. Caren Metschuck | GDR | 55.16 | |
| 3. Ines Diers | GDR | 55.65 | |
| 4. Olga Klevakina | SOV | 57.40 | |
| 5. Cornelia van Bentum | HOL | 57.63 | |
| 6. Natalya Strunnikova | SOV | 57.83 | |
| 7. Guylaine Berger | FRA | 57.88 | |
| 8. Agneta Eriksson | SWE | 57.90 | |

In 1980 the East German women duplicated their 1976 feat of winning 11 of 13 events. But this time, with the U.S. and Canada out of the Games, they were able to take 15 other medals as well, which meant that they *averaged* two out of three medals per event.

Like Kornelia Ender, Barbara Krause was introduced to swimming as therapy for orthopedic problems. One of East Germany's leading swimmers in 1976, she was forced to sit out the Montreal Games because of illness. As she followed the competition from her sickbed, she made the decision to continue swimming for four more years so that she could take part in the 1980 Olympics. With only 30 starters in the 100-meter freestyle, the smallest field since 1932, it was decided to skip the semifinals and simply allow the swimmers with the eight fastest times in the heats to qualify directly for the final, a practice which has since been institutionalized. Barbara Krause won the third heat in 54.98 to lower her own world record and to become the first woman to break the 55-second barrier. In the final she was hard-pressed by her East German teammates, but she led all the way and set yet another world record.

**1984 Los Angeles** C: 45, N: 30, D: 7.29. WR: 54.79 (Barbara Krause)

| | | |
|---|---|---|
| 1. Nancy Hogshead | USA | 55.92 |
| 1. Carrie Steinseifer | USA | 55.92 |
| 3. Annemarie Verstappen | HOL | 56.08 |
| 4. Cornelia van Bentum | HOL | 56.43 |
| 5. Michele Pearson | AUS | 56.83 |
| 6. June Croft | GBR | 56.90 |
| 7. Susanne Schuster | GER | 57.11 |
| 8. Angela Russel | AUS | 58.09 |

In 1972, when Gunnar Larsson and Tim McKee were both timed at 4:31.98 in the final of the men's 400-meter individual medley, the timing was taken to thousandths of a second and Larsson was declared the winner. Because of possible technical problems, it was decided that hundredths of a second would have to do in the future. So, in 1984, when Hogshead and Steinseifer registered the same time in the 100-meter freestyle, a dead-heat was declared and each was awarded a gold medal, the first double gold medal in Olympic swimming history. Nancy Hogshead eventually left Los Angeles with three gold medals and one silver. Conspicuously missing from the competition were Kristin Otto and Birgit Meineke of East Germany, who had clocked

55.75 and 55.79 respectively at the Friendship Games on August 19.

**1988 Seoul** C: 57, N: 35, D: 9.19. WR: 54.73 (Kristin Otto)

| | | |
|---|---|---|
| 1. Kristin Otto | GDR | 54.93 |
| 2. Zhuang Yong | CHN | 55.47 |
| 3. Catherine Plewinski | FRA | 55.49 |
| 4. Manuela Stellmach | GDR | 55.52 |
| 5. Silvia Poll | CRC | 55.90 |
| 6. Karin Brienesse | HOL | 56.15 |
| 7. Dara Torres | USA | 56.25 |
| 8. Cornelia van Bentum | HOL | 56.54 |

Twenty-two-year-old Kristin Otto won the first of her six gold medals.

## 200-METER FREESTYLE

**1896–1964** not held

**1968 Mexico City** C: 39, N: 23, D: 10.22. WR: 2:06.7 (Deborah Meyer)

| | | | |
|---|---|---|---|
| 1. Deborah Meyer | USA | 2:10.5 | OR |
| 2. Jan Henne | USA | 2:11.0 | |
| 3. Jane Barkman | USA | 2:11.2 | |
| 4. Gabriele Wetzko | GDR | 2:12.3 | |
| 5. Mirjana Segrt | YUG | 2:13.3 | |
| 6. Claude Mandonnaud | FRA | 2:14.9 | |
| 7. Lynette Bell | AUS | 2:15.1 | |
| 8. Olga Kozicova | CZE | 2:16.0 | |

This was Debbie Meyer's second gold medal of the 1968 Olympics.

**1972 Munich** C: 33, N: 17, D: 9.1. WR: 2:05.21 (Shirley Babashoff)

| | | | |
|---|---|---|---|
| 1. Shane Gould | AUS | 2:03.56 | WR |
| 2. Shirley Babashoff | USA | 2:04.33 | |
| 3. Keena Rothhammer | USA | 2:04.92 | |
| 4. Ann Marshall | USA | 2:05.45 | |
| 5. Andrea Eife | GDR | 2:06.27 | |
| 6. Hansje Bunschoten | HOL | 2:08.40 | |
| 7. Anke Rijnders | HOL | 2:09.41 | |
| 8. Karin Tuelling | GDR | 2:11.70 | |

Between July 1971 and January 1972, Shane Gould set world records in all five internationally recognized freestyle distances: the 100, 200, 400, 800, and 1500 meters. In the 1972 Olympics, the 15-year-old phenomenon swam 12 races in eight days, logging 4200 meters of competitive swimming. In the 200 meters final Gould built up a large lead in the first 100 meters. World record holder Shirley Babashoff almost cut the gap in half, but could get no further. Shane Gould closed out the Munich Olympics with three gold medals, one silver, and one bronze. A year later, tired of the sacrifices required of a cham-

pion swimmer, Gould announced her retirement at the age of 16.

**1976 Montreal** C: 40, N: 22, D: 7.22. WR: 1:59.78 (Kornelia Ender)

| | | | |
|---|---|---|---|
| 1. Kornelia Ender | GDR | 1:59.26 | WR |
| 2. Shirley Babashoff | USA | 2:01.22 | |
| 3. Enith Brigitha | HOL | 2:01.40 | |
| 4. Annelies Maas | HOL | 2:02.56 | |
| 5. Gail Amundrud | CAN | 2:03.32 | |
| 6. Jennifer Hooker | USA | 2:04.20 | |
| 7. Claudia Hempel | GDR | 2:04.61 | |
| 8. Irina Vlasova | SOV | 2:05.63 | |

Kornelia Ender equaled her own world record to win the 100-meter butterfly, then returned to face Shirley Babashoff in the very next race, the 200-meter freestyle. Babashoff had defeated Ender in the 200 at the 1975 world championships, but Ender had chopped almost three seconds off her time in the following year. Babashoff took the early lead and held it for the first 100 meters, but Ender moved ahead over the next length of the pool and won going away to earn her second gold medal in 27 minutes. She thus became the first female swimmer to win four gold medals at one Olympics.

**1980 Moscow** C: 22, N: 14, D: 7.24. WR: 1:58.23 (Cynthia Woodhead)

| | | | |
|---|---|---|---|
| 1. Barbara Krause | GDR | 1:58.33 | OR |
| 2. Ines Diers | GDR | 1:59.64 | |
| 3. Carmela Schmidt | GDR | 2:01.44 | |
| 4. Olga Klevakina | SOV | 2:02.29 | |
| 5. Reggie De Jong | HOL | 2:02.76 | |
| 6. June Croft | GBR | 2:03.15 | |
| 7. Natalya Strunnikova | SOV | 2:03.74 | |
| 8. Irina Aksyonova | SOV | 2:04.00 | |

Krause staged a phenomenal comeback to win her second gold medal. Trailing Ines Diers by over a second after 150 meters, she swam the last 50 meters in 28.47 to win by a comfortable margin. Eight days later, world record holder Cynthia Woodhead won the U.S. Outdoor National championship in 1:59.44.

**1984 Los Angeles** C: 36, N: 25, D: 7.30. WR: 1:57.75 (Kristin Otto)

| | | |
|---|---|---|
| 1. Mary Wayte | USA | 1:59.23 |
| 2. Cynthia Woodhead | USA | 1:59.50 |
| 3. Annemarie Verstappen | HOL | 1:59.69 |
| 4. Michele Pearson | AUS | 1:59.79 |
| 5. Cornelia van Bentum | HOL | 2:00.59 |
| 6. June Croft | GBR | 2:00.64 |
| 7. Ina Beyermann | GER | 2:01.89 |
| 8. Anna McVann | AUS | 2:02.87 |

On May 23, at the East German trials, Kristin Otto had set a world record of 1:57.75. She was followed by Birgit Meineke in 1:58.75.

**1988 Seoul** C: 44, N: 29, D: 9.21. WR: 1:57.55 (Heike Friedrich)

| | | | |
|---|---|---|---|
| 1. Heike Friedrich | GDR | 1:57.65 | OR |
| 2. Silvia Poll | CRC | 1:58.67 | |
| 3. Manuela Stellmach | GDR | 1:59.01 | |
| 4. Mary Wayte | USA | 1:59.04 | |
| 5. Natalia Trefilova | SOV | 1:59.24 | |
| 6. Mitzi Kremer | USA | 2:00.23 | |
| 7. Stephanie Ortwig | GER | 2:00.73 | |
| 8. Cecile Prunier | FRA | 2:02.88 | |

The prohibitive favorite, world champion and world record holder Heike Friedrich, let Wayte and Kremer set the pace for the first half of the race, then stormed ahead for an easy bodylength victory over Silvia Poll, Costa Rica's first Olympic medalist. The 6-foot 3½-inch, blonde-haired Poll was the daughter of German-born parents who had moved to Costa Rica from Nicaragua when she was 8 years old.

## 400-METER FREESTYLE

**1896–1912** not held

**1920 Antwerp** C: 16, N: 7, D: 8.28. WR (300 meters): 4:43.6
**(300 Meters)**

| | | | |
|---|---|---|---|
| 1. Ethelda Bleibtrey | USA | 4:34.0 | WR |
| 2. Margaret Woodbridge | USA | 4:42.8 | |
| 3. Frances Schroth | USA | 4:52.0 | |
| 4. Constance Jeans | GBR | 4:52.4 | |
| 5. Eleanor Uhl | USA | — | |
| 6. Jane Gylling | SWE | — | |

**1924 Paris** C: 18, N: 8, D: 7.15. WR: 5:53.2 (Gertrude Ederle)

| | | | |
|---|---|---|---|
| 1. Martha Norelius | USA | 6:02.2 | OR |
| 2. Helen Wainwright | USA | 6:03.8 | |
| 3. Gertrude Ederle | USA | 6:04.8 | |
| 4. Doris Molesworth | GBR | 6:25.4 | |
| DNF: Gwitha Shand (NZE) | | | |
| 6. Irene Tanner (GBR) | | | |

Fifteen-year-old, Stockholm-born Martha Norelius pulled away from Wainwright and Ederle in the final 15 meters. In the 1924 Olympics five swimmers took part in each final, while sixth place was awarded to the nonfinalist who recorded the fastest time in the semifinals.

**1928 Amsterdam** C: 14, N: 9, D: 8.6. WR: 5:49.6 (Martha Norelius)

| | | | |
|---|---|---|---|
| 1. Martha Norelius | USA | 5:42.8 | WR |
| 2. Maria Braun | HOL | 5:57.8 | |
| 3. Josephine McKim | USA | 6:00.2 | |
| 4. Sarah Stewart | GBR | 6:07.0 | |
| 5. Frederica van der Goes | SAF | 6:07.2 | |
| 6. Irene Tanner | GBR | 6:11.6 | |

Norelius swam a 5:45.4 opening heat to break her own world record and defended her title by winning the final easily, again in world record time. Norelius dominated

women's swimming from 1922 to 1929. She later married Canada's 1928 double sculls silver medalist, Joe Wright.

**1932 Los Angeles** C: 14, N: 9, D: 8.13. WR: 5:31.0 (Helene Madison)

| | | | |
|---|---|---|---|
| 1. Helene Madison | USA | 5:28.5 | WR |
| 2. Lenore Kight | USA | 5:28.6 | |
| 3. Jennie Maakal | SAF | 5:47.3 | |
| 4. Margaret Joyce Cooper | GBR | 5:49.7 | |
| 5. Yvonne Godard | FRA | 5:54.4 | |
| 6. Norene Forbes | USA | 6:06.0 | |

Helene Madison and Lenore Kight pulled away from the others immediately and went through most of the race with Madison one foot ahead. Kight moved into the lead at 325 meters, but Madison drew even at the final turn. In the end, Madison was able to touch the last wall inches ahead of Kight and thus win her third gold medal.

**1936 Berlin** C: 20, N: 10, D: 8.15. WR: 5:16.0 (Willemijntje den Ouden)

| | | | |
|---|---|---|---|
| 1. Hendrika "Rie" Mastenbroek | HOL | 5:26.4 | OR |
| 2. Ragnhild Hveger | DEN | 5:27.5 | |
| 3. Lenore Wingard (Kight) | USA | 5:29.0 | |
| 4. Mary Lou Petty | USA | 5:32.2 | |
| 5. Piedade Coutinho Azevedo | BRA | 5:35.2 | |
| 6. Kazue Koijma | JPN | 5:43.1 | |
| 7. Grete Frederiksen | DEN | 5:45.0 | |
| 8. Catharine Wagner | HOL | 5:46.0 | |

Fifteen-year-old Ragnhild Hveger led throughout the race, but Rie Mastenbroek fought back in the final 25 meters to gain a one-meter victory and win her third gold medal. Between 1936 and 1942 Hveger broke 42 individual world records. From 1938 until 1953 she was the official world record holder in the 200, 400, 800, and 1500 meters. She retired in 1945, but came back in 1952 to finish fifth in the 400 in the Helsinki Olympics at the age of 31. Rie Mastenbroek, who won three gold medals and one silver, had a most difficult post-Olympic life. After a disastrous first marriage ended, she worked 14 hours a day as a cleaning woman to support her children. In 1972 she told *Sports Illustrated,* "I am forgotten. No one remembers who I was. . . . Sometimes I think, 'Oh, dear, oh, dear, how good I must have been, how really *good*!' "

**1948 London** C: 19, N: 11, D: 8.7. WR: 5:00.1 (Ragnhild Hveger)

| | | | |
|---|---|---|---|
| 1. Ann Curtis | USA | 5:17.8 | OR |
| 2. Karen-Margrete Harup | DEN | 5:21.2 | |
| 3. Catherine Gibson | GBR | 5:22.5 | |
| 4. Fernande Caroen | BEL | 5:25.3 | |
| 5. Brenda Helser | USA | 5:26.0 | |
| 6. Piedade Silva Tavares | BRA | 5:29.4 | |
| 7. Fritze Carstensen | DEN | 5:29.4 | |
| 8. Nancy Lees | USA | 5:32.9 | |

**1952 Helsinki** C: 34, N: 17, D: 8.2. WR: 5:00.1 (Ragnhild Hveger)
1. Valéria Gyenge     HUN   5:12.1   OR
2. Éva Novák     HUN   5:13.7
3. Evelyn Kawamoto     USA   5:14.6
4. Carolyn Green     USA   5:16.5
5. Ragnhild Andersen-Hveger     DEN   5:16.9
6. Éva Székely     HUN   5:17.9
7. Anna Maria Schultz     ARG   5:24.0
8. Greta Andersen     DEN   5:27.0

Ragnhild Hveger's 1940 world record was still in the books when, as Ragnhild Andersen-Hveger, she prepared for the start of the 1952 Olympic 400 meters final, the same event in which she had won a silver medal 16 years earlier. In Helsinki she led for the first 275 meters, but couldn't keep up the pace.

**1956 Melbourne** C: 26, N: 13, D: 12.7. WR: 4:47.2 (Lorraine Crapp)
1. Lorraine Crapp     AUS   4:54.6   OR
2. Dawn Fraser     AUS   5:02.5
3. Sylvia Ruuska     USA   5:07.1
4. Marley Shriver     USA   5:12.9
5. Rypszima Székely     HUN   5:14.2
6. Sandra Morgan     AUS   5:14.3
7. Héda Frost     FRA   5:15.4
8. Valéria Gyenge     HUN   5:21.0

On August 25, 1956, 17-year-old Lorraine Crapp became the first woman to swim 400 meters in less than five minutes when she broke Ragnhild Hveger's 16-year-old world record with a time of 4:50.8. In that same race she also bettered the world records for 200 meters, 220 yards, and 440 yards. Two and a half months later at the Olympics, Dawn Fraser kept up with her teammate for 100 meters, but then Crapp drew clear to win by almost eight seconds.

**1960 Rome** C: 22, N: 13, D: 9.1. WR: 4:44.5 (S. Christine Von Saltza)
1. S. Christine Von Saltza     USA   4:50.6   OR
2. Jane Cederqvist     SWE   4:53.9
3. Catharina Lagerberg     HOL   4:56.9
4. Ilsa Konrads     AUS   4:57.9
5. Dawn Fraser     AUS   4:58.5
6. Nancy Rae     GBR   4:59.7
7. Cornelia Schimmel     HOL   5:02.3
8. Bibbi Segerstrom     SWE   5:02.4

Sixteen-year-old Chris Von Saltza moved quickly into the lead, built up a five-second gap after 300 meters, and was too far ahead to be affected by the late surge of Jane Cederqvist. Von Saltza had won the first of her three gold medals. Third- and fourth-place finishers Lagerberg and Konrads were the world record holders at 800 meters and 1500 meters, respectively, neither of which was an Olympic distance at the time.

**1964 Tokyo** C: 30, N: 16, D: 10.18. WR: 4:39.5 (Marilyn Ramenofsky)
1. Virginia Duenkel     USA   4:43.3   OR
2. Marilyn Ramenofsky     USA   4:44.6
3. Terri Stickles     USA   4:47.2
4. Dawn Fraser     AUS   4:47.6
5. Jane Hughes     CAN   4:50.9
6. Elizabeth Long     GBR   4:52.0
7. Kim Herford     AUS   4:52.9
8. Gun Lilja     SWE   4:53.0

Seventeen-year-old Ginny Duenkel of West Orange, New Jersey, also won a bronze medal in the 100-meter backstroke. In the 400-meter freestyle she took the lead after 175 meters and pulled away, slowly but steadily.

**1968 Mexico City** C: 30, N: 17, D: 10.20. WR: 4:24.5 (Debbie Meyer)
1. Debbie Meyer     USA   4:31.8   OR
2. Linda Gustavson     USA   4:35.5
3. Karen Moras     AUS   4:37.0
4. Pamela Kruse     USA   4:37.2
5. Gabriele Wetzko     GDR   4:40.2
6. Marla Teresa Ramirez     MEX   4:42.2
7. Angela Coughlan     CAN   4:51.9
8. Ingrid Morris     SWE   4:53.8

At the U.S. Olympic trials, 16-year-old Debbie Meyer set world records in the 200, 400, and 800. The rarefied air of Mexico City prevented her from duplicating that feat, but she did win all three races, starting with the 400 meters.

**1972 Munich** C: 29, N: 17, D: 8.30. WR: 4:21.2 (Shane Gould)
1. Shane Gould     AUS   4:19.44   WR
2. Novella Calligaris     ITA   4:22.44
3. Gudrun Wagner     GDR   4:23.11
4. Shirley Babashoff     USA   4:23.59
5. Jenny Wylie     USA   4:24.07
6. Keena Rothhammer     USA   4:24.22
7. Hansje Bunschoten     HOL   4:29.70
8. Anke Rijnders     HOL   4:31.51

Shane Gould came back from her loss in the 100 meters the previous day to win her second gold medal.

**1976 Montreal** C: 34, N: 22, D: 7.20. WR: 4:11.69 (Barbara Krause)
1. Petra Thümer     GDR   4:09.89   WR
2. Shirley Babashoff     USA   4:10.46
3. Shannon Smith     CAN   4:14.60
4. Rebecca Perrott     NZE   4:14.76
5. Kathy Heddy     USA   4:15.50
6. Brenda Borgh     USA   4:17.43
7. Annelies Maas     HOL   4:17.44
8. Sabine Kahle     GDR   4:20.42

On June 3, 1976, Barbara Krause broke Shirley Babashoff's world record by over three seconds. However, two weeks later she suffered an attack of angina and had to be dropped from the East German squad. Fifteen-year-old Petra Thümer, who had finished second to Krause in the East German championships, rose to the occasion at the Olympics. She built up most of her lead during the second 100 meters and then fought off Babashoff's attempts to close the gap. Thümer's time would have won her a silver medal in the 1968 *men's* 400-meter race and a gold in 1964.

**1980 Moscow** C: 19, N: 12, D: 7.22. WR: 4:06.28 (Tracey Wickham)
| | | | | |
|---|---|---|---|---|
| 1. Ines Diers | GDR | 4:08.76 | OR |
| 2. Petra Schneider | GDR | 4:09.16 | |
| 3. Carmela Schmidt | GDR | 4:10.86 | |
| 4. Michelle Ford | AUS | 4:11.65 | |
| 5. Irina Aksyonova | SOV | 4:14.40 | |
| 6. Annelies Maas | HOL | 4:15.79 | |
| 7. Reggie de Jong | HOL | 4:15.95 | |
| 8. Olga Klevakina | SOV | 4:19.18 | |

This was one race that was definitely affected by the anti-Soviet boycott. Missing was world record holder Tracey Wickham of Australia as well as Kim Linehan and Cynthia "Sippy" Woodhead of the United States, who clocked 4:07.77 and 4:08.17, respectively, at the U.S. national championships on July 31. In their absence, the East Germans had a field day. Petra Schneider led for over 300 meters, but 16-year-old Ines Diers finished strongly to win. Before the Moscow Games were over Diers had won five medals: two gold, two silver and one bronze.

**1984 Los Angeles** C: 25, N: 17, D: 7.31. WR: 4:06.28 (Tracey Wickham)
| | | | | |
|---|---|---|---|---|
| 1. Tiffany Cohen | USA | 4:07.10 | OR |
| 2. Sarah Hardcastle | GBR | 4:10.27 | |
| 3. June Croft | GBR | 4:11.49 | |
| 4. Kimberly Linehan | USA | 4:12.26 | |
| 5. Anna McVann | AUS | 4:13.95 | |
| 6. Jolande van der Meer | HOL | 4:16.05 | |
| 7. Birgit Kowalczik | GER | 4:16.33 | |
| 8. Julie Daigneault | CAN | 4:16.41 | |

Eighteen-year-old Tiffany Cohen led from start to finish and won by five meters, registering the fastest women's 400-meter time since Tracey Wickham set her world record in 1978. The Friendship Games event in Moscow three weeks later was won by East Germany's Astrid Strauss with a time of 4:07.66.

**1988 Seoul** C: 30, N: 21, D: 9.22. WR: 4:05.45 (Janet Evans)
| | | | | |
|---|---|---|---|---|
| 1. Janet Evans | USA | 4:03.85 | WR |
| 2. Heike Friedrich | GDR | 4:05.94 | |
| 3. Anke Möhring | GDR | 4:06.62 | |
| 4. Tami Bruce | USA | 4:08.16 | |
| 5. Janelle Esford | AUS | 4:10.64 | |
| 6. Isabelle Arnould | BEL | 4:11.73 | |
| 7. Stephanie Ortwig | GER | 4:13.05 | |
| 8. Natalya Trefilova | SOV | 4:13.92 | |

When Heike Friedrich was only 15 years old, she won five gold medals at the 1985 European championships. The following year she added four golds at the world championships. By the time of the 1988 Olympics, she was still undefeated in major international competition, having won 13 consecutive finals. She added a fourteenth victory in Seoul when she finished first in the 200-meter freestyle. But the following night she finally met her match in Janet Evans, a 17-year-old student at appropriately named El Dorado High School in Placentia, California.

Despite her small size and unorthodox windmill stroke, Evans was a natural-born swimmer. She was swimming laps at the age of two, literally before she was out of diapers. By the time she was 3 years old she had already mastered the butterfly and breaststroke. During her early years of competition other swimmers snickered and laughed at her diminutive stature, but the laughter stopped in 1987 when, at the age of 15, the 95-pound Evans broke the world record at 800 meters and 1500 meters, the 1500 record having stood the onslaught of larger swimmers for over seven and a half years and the 800 for almost nine. On December 20, 1987, she eclipsed Tracey Wickham's nine-year-old record at 400 meters.

In the Olympic final Evans took the early lead, but Friedrich and East German teammate Anke Möhring, both strong finishers, stayed right by her shoulder. Friedrich, who had planned to win the race with a world record of 4:05, pushed the pace in the third 100, leaving Möhring behind. But Evans refused to be passed. However, with 100 meters to go, her lead was down to 1 foot. Then, surprisingly, it was Evans who pulled away in the final two laps by swimming the second half of the race faster than she had the first half. It was the first "negative split" of her career and it earned her the second of her three gold medals.

# 800-METER FREESTYLE

**1896–1964** not held

**1968 Mexico City** C: 26, N: 16, D: 10.24. WR: 9.10.4 (Deborah Meyer)
| | | | | |
|---|---|---|---|---|
| 1. Deborah Meyer | USA | 9:24.0 | OR |
| 2. Pamela Kruse | USA | 9:35.7 | |
| 3. Maria Teresa Ramirez | MEX | 9:38.5 | |
| 4. Karen Moras | AUS | 9:38.6 | |
| 5. Patricia Caretto | USA | 9:51.3 | |
| 6. Angela Coughlan | CAN | 9:56.4 | |
| 7. Denise Langford | AUS | 9:56.7 | |
| 8. Laura Vaca | MEX | 10.02.5 | |

Debbie Meyer was never really challenged as she became the first swimmer to win three individual gold medals in one Olympics. The only excitement of the race came when 15-year-old Maria Teresa Ramirez came from behind to nip Karen Moras for the bronze medal, bringing joy to the Mexican crowd.

**1972 Munich** C: 36, N: 19, D: 9.3. WR: 8:53.83 (Jo Harshberger)
| | | | |
|---|---|---|---|
| 1. Keena Rothhammer | USA | 8:53.68 | WR |
| 2. Shane Gould | AUS | 8:56.39 | |
| 3. Novella Calligaris | ITA | 8:57.46 | |
| 4. Ann Simmons | USA | 8:57.62 | |
| 5. Gudrun Wegner | GDR | 8:58.89 | |
| 6. Jo Harshberger | USA | 9:01.21 | |
| 7. Hansje Bunschoten | HOL | 9:16.69 | |
| 8. Narelle Moras | AUS | 9:19.06 | |

Calligaris led for 500 meters, but then Rothhammer, fourth at the halfway mark, took the lead and pulled away.

**1976 Montreal** C: 19, N: 11, D: 7.25. WR: 8:39.63 (Shirley Babashoff)
| | | | |
|---|---|---|---|
| 1. Petra Thümer | GDR | 8:37.14 | WR |
| 2. Shirley Babashoff | USA | 8:37.59 | |
| 3. Wendy Weinberg | USA | 8:42.60 | |
| 4. Rosemary Milgate | AUS | 8:47.21 | |
| 5. Nicole Kramer | USA | 8:47.33 | |
| 6. Shannon Smith | CAN | 8:48.15 | |
| 7. Regina Jäger | GDR | 8:50.40 | |
| 8. Jennifer Turrall | AUS | 8:52.88 | |

On June 4, 1976, Petra Thümer set a world record of 8:40.68, but 17 days later Shirley Babashoff bettered that time by a second. This was Babashoff's last chance for an individual gold medal so she withdrew from the 400-meter individual medley in order to save her strength for her long-distance showdown with Thümer, who had beaten her at 400 meters five days earlier. Shannon Smith led for 300 meters, but then Thümer took over. Babashoff trailed right behind her, but every time she drew closer, Thümer would draw away again. In the end Thümer had her second world record and Babashoff had her sixth Olympic silver medal.

**1980 Moscow** C: 14, N: 9, D: 7.27. WR: 8:24.62 (Tracey Wickham)
| | | | |
|---|---|---|---|
| 1. Michelle Ford | AUS | 8:28.90 | OR |
| 2. Ines Diers | GDR | 8:32.55 | |
| 3. Heike Dähne | GDR | 8:33.48 | |
| 4. Irina Aksyonova | SOV | 8:38.05 | |
| 5. Oxana Komissarova | SOV | 8:42.04 | |
| 6. Pascale Verbauwen | BEL | 8:44.84 | |
| 7. Ines Geissler | GDR | 8:45.28 | |
| 8. Yelena Ivanova | SOV | 8:46.45 | |

Eighteen-year-old Michelle Ford took the lead after 250 meters and pulled away to break the East German gold medal monopoly. Missing were world record holder Tracey Wickham of Australia and U.S. champion Kim Linehan whose best time was 8:24.70 and who clocked an 8:27.86 two days after the Olympic final.

**1984 Los Angeles** C: 20, N: 14, D: 8.3. WR: 8:24.62 (Tracey Wickham)
| | | | |
|---|---|---|---|
| 1. Tiffany Cohen | USA | 8:24.95 | OR |
| 2. Michele Richardson | USA | 8:30.73 | |
| 3. Sarah Hardcastle | GBR | 8:32.60 | |
| 4. Anna McVann | AUS | 8:37.94 | |
| 5. Carla Lasi | ITA | 8:42.45 | |
| 6. Jolande van der Meer | HOL | 8:42.86 | |
| 7. Monica Olmi | ITA | 8:47.32 | |
| 8. Karen Ward | CAN | 8:48.12 | |

Challenged only by the memory of Tracey Wickham's six-year-old world record, Tiffany Cohen added the 800 gold to the one she had won in the 400 three days earlier.

**1988 Seoul** C: 27, N: 19, D: 9.24. WR: 8:17.12 (Janet Evans)
| | | | |
|---|---|---|---|
| 1. Janet Evans | USA | 8:20.20 | OR |
| 2. Astrid Strauss | GDR | 8:22.09 | |
| 3. Julie McDonald | AUS | 8:22.93 | |
| 4. Anke Möhring | GDR | 8:23.09 | |
| 5. Tami Bruce | USA | 8:30.86 | |
| 6. Janelle Elford | AUS | 8:30.94 | |
| 7. Isabelle Arnould | BEL | 8:37.47 | |
| 8. Antoaneta Strumenlieva | BUL | 8.41.05 | |

As they stood on the blocks waiting for the start of the final, Janet Evans and her East German rivals presented an odd sight. Astrid Strauss measured 6 feet 1½ inches and weighed 181 pounds. Teammate Anke Möhring was 5 feet 11¼ inches and 152 pounds. Between them stood the favorite, Evans, 5 feet 5¼ inches and a mere 101 pounds. Her main challengers were thought to be Möhring, the former world record holder, and Julie McDonald, the fastest qualifier and the last person to beat Evans, a year earlier in Brisbane. However, it was Strauss who gave Evans the best run for her money, improving her personal best by 4.43 seconds. But even she was 10 feet behind at the finish, as Janet Evans won the last of her three gold medals.

## 100-METER BACKSTROKE

**1896–1920** not held

**1924 Paris** C: 10, N: 5, D: 7.20. WR: 1:22.4 (Sybil Bauer)
| | | | |
|---|---|---|---|
| 1. Sybil Bauer | USA | 1:23.2 | OR |
| 2. Phyllis Harding | GBR | 1:27.4 | |
| 3. Aileen Riggin | USA | 1:28.2 | |
| 4. Florence Chambers | USA | 1:30.8 | |
| 5. Jarmila Müllerová | CZE | 1:31.2 | |
| 6. Ellen King (GBR) | | | |

Sybil Bauer of Chicago was the world record holder in all women's backstroke events when she completely outclassed her opposition at the Paris Olympics. She was still undefeated when she died of intestinal cancer on January 31, 1927, at the age of 23. Bronze medalist Aileen Riggin became the first person to win medals in both swimming and diving.

**1928 Amsterdam** C: 12, N: 7, D: 8.11 WR: 1:22.0 (Willy van den Turk)

| | | |
|---|---|---|
| 1. Maria Braun | HOL | 1:22.0 |
| 2. Ellen King | GBR | 1:22.2 |
| 3. Margaret Joyce Cooper | GBR | 1:22.8 |
| 4. Marion Gilman | USA | 1:24.2 |
| 5. Eleanor Holm | USA | 1:24.4 |
| 5. Lisa Lindstrom | USA | 1:24.4 |
| 7. E.P. Stockley | NZE | 1:25.8 |

Ellen King of Scotland equaled the world record in the first heat. In the second heat, 17-year-old local favorite Maria Braun broke the world record with a time of 1:21.6.

**1932 Los Angeles** C: 12, N. 7, D: 8.11. WR: 1:18.2 (Eleanor Holm)

| | | |
|---|---|---|
| 1. Eleanor Holm | USA | 1:19.4 |
| 2. Philomena "Bonny" Mealing | AUS | 1:21.3 |
| 3. Elizabeth Valerie Davies | GBR | 1:22.5 |
| 4. Phyllis Harding | GBR | 1:22.6 |
| 5. Joan McSheehy | USA | 1:23.2 |
| 6. Margaret Joyce Cooper | GBR | 1:23.4 |

DNS: Maria Philipsen-Braun (HOL)

Eighteen-year-old Eleanor Holm, the daughter of a Brooklyn fire captain, inched ahead after 25 meters, held off the challenge of Bonny Mealing, and pulled away in the last 25 meters. Holm had set an Olympic record of 1:18.3 in her qualifying heat.

**1936 Berlin** C: 21, N: 12, D: 8.13. WR: 1:15.8 (Hendrika "Rie" Mastenbroek)

| | | |
|---|---|---|
| 1. Dina "Nida" Senff | HOL | 1:18.9 |
| 2. Hendrika "Rie" Mastenbroek | HOL | 1:19.2 |
| 3. Alice Bridges | USA | 1:19.4 |
| 4. Edith Motridge | USA | 1:19.6 |
| 5. Tove Bruunström | DEN | 1:20.4 |
| 6. Lorna Frampton | GBR | 1:20.6 |
| 7. Phyllis Harding | GBR | 1:21.5 |

Life had been very full for Eleanor Holm between Olympics. While in Hollywood she had met singer and orchestra leader Art Jarrett, who was a fellow alumnus of Erasmus Hall High School back in Brooklyn. Five months later, on September 2, 1933, they were married in Beverly Hills. For the next three years Holm led a very active social life and joined her husband singing in nightclubs. But she always kept in shape. In 1935 she set a world record for the 100-meter backstroke, and in 1936 she also broke the record for 200 meters. On February 27, 1936, her 100-meter record was broken by Rie Mastenbroek. However, when Eleanor Holm boarded the S.S. *Manhattan* on July 15 for the nine-day voyage to Germany, along with about 350 other members of the U.S. Olympic team, she was still the favorite to defend her championship, and there was little hint of the outrageous scandal that was about to bring an abrupt end to her amateur career.

Now on her way to her third Olympics, married and

used to a flashy and independent life-style, Eleanor did not take too well to the third-class accommodations and strict regulations that had been arranged by the American Olympic Committee. She felt more comfortable in the first-class section, which happened to be where the American officials were staying, as well as the press. On Friday, July 17, Mr. Maybaum of the United States Lines, which owned the S.S. *Manhattan,* invited Eleanor to attend a party he was throwing that night in the A-deck bar and lounge. She was the only team member invited. Quick to accept, she stayed up until six a.m., matching drinks with the sportswriters. She had to be helped back to her cabin.

The next day there was much joking and wisecracking among the non-Olympic first-class passengers about the "training techniques" of the U.S. team. Embarrassed U.S. Olympic officials issued Holm a warning, but she was defiant and continued to drink in public off and on for the next few days. When advised by friends to moderate her behavior, she reminded them that she was "free, white, and 22."

On July 23, while the ship made a prolonged stopover in Cherbourg, France, with the passengers confined to ship, Holm attended an afternoon and evening champagne party. At about ten-thirty p.m. the official team chaperone, Ada Taylor Sackett, discovered Eleanor staggering along the deck, accompanied by a young man. After returning to her cabin, which she shared with two other swimmers, Holm stuck her head out the porthole and began shouting obscenities. Her roommates, Olive McKean and Mary Lou Petty, pulled her back inside and convinced her to go to sleep. At midnight Mrs. Sackett returned with the team doctor, J. Hubert Lawson, and the ship's doctor. Dr. Lawson found Holm "in a deep slumber which approached a state of coma." His diagnosis: "Acute alcoholism." The physical examination failed to awaken her. Members of the American Olympic Committee met to discuss the charges against Holm, which also included shooting craps. (She never denied the charges and later boasted that she had won "a couple hundred dollars" just before the final party.)

At six a.m. team manager Herbert Holm (no relation) woke Eleanor and informed her that the American Olympic Committee had voted to remove her from the team. She went to the stateroom of Avery Brundage, president of the A.O.C., and pleaded her case through a crack in the door. It was to no avail. More than half of the U.S. team members signed a petition asking for Eleanor's reinstatement and the press split was about the same.

The news of Eleanor Holm's expulsion caused a sensation when the S.S. *Manhattan* docked in Hamburg, particularly when word began to spread about the details of the case. When her final appeal was denied, Holm lashed back at the American officials, pointing out that they had held cocktail parties every night and that they had ignored the athletes. Joseph Goebbels' Nazi propaganda periodical, *Der Angriff,* took the side of the A.O.C., editorializing, "She probably didn't believe they could disqualify her, but she thought wrong. It wasn't herself who mattered. It was the others—and discipline. For that no sacrifice is too great, no matter how many tears are shed."

Eleanor Holm didn't get to participate in the 1936 Olympics, but that didn't prevent her from having a good time in Berlin. The Nazis quickly forgave her lack of discipline and entertained her as a special visitor. "I had such fun!" she told *Sports Illustrated* 36 years later. "I enjoyed the parties, the *Heil Hitlers,* the uniforms, the flags. . . . Göring was fun. He had a good personality. So did the one with the club foot [Goebbels]. Göring gave me a sterling-silver swastika. I had a mold made of it and I put a diamond Star of David in the middle." Holm issued a public challenge to whoever won the Olympic championship to face her in a swim-off, but when the day came for the final of the women's 100-meter backstroke, Eleanor Holm, who hadn't been beaten in seven years, was sitting in the stands instead of swimming in the pool.

As it happened, the competition, although it did not get as much press attention as all that had preceded it, was not without its own element of sensation. Sixteen-year-old Nida Senff surprised the experts by recording the fastest preliminary times, 1:16.6. and 1:17.1. In the final she was away quickly and had opened up a two-meter lead by the halfway mark. But she missed touching the wall and had to go back. This dropped her to sixth place out of seven, but she sped on, regained the lead with 20 meters to go, and won with a very little bit to spare. She might have lost anyway had not world record holder Rie Mastenbroek become entangled in the lane ropes. Of the four events which Mastenbroek entered in 1936, this was the only one she didn't win.

As for Eleanor Holm, she became more popular than ever. In 1938 she divorced Art Jarrett and also acted in her only film, co-starring as Jane in *Tarzan's Revenge* with 1936 decathlon champion Glenn Morris. The following year she married impresario Billy Rose. The pair divorced in 1954 following a spicy case, which became known as "The War of the Roses" and which was filled with titillating accusations of sexual "misbehavior" on both sides. She later became an interior decorator and retired to Miami Beach.

**1948 London** C: 24, N: 16, D: 8.5. WR: 1:10.9 (Cor Kint)

| | | | |
|---|---|---|---|
| 1. Karen-Margrete Harup | DEN | 1:14.4 | OR |
| 2. Suzanne Zimmerman | USA | 1:16.0 | |
| 3. Judith Davies | AUS | 1:16.7 | |
| 4. Ilona Novák | HUN | 1:18.4 | |
| 5. Hendrika van der Horst | HOL | 1:18.8 | |
| 6. Dirkje van Ekris | HOL | 1:18.9 | |
| 7. Muriel Mellon | USA | 1:19.0 | |
| 8. Greta Galliard | HOL | 1:19.1 | |

Eliminated in the semifinals was French swimmer and journalist Monique Berlioux who later became Director of the International Olympic Committee.

**1952 Helsinki** C: 20, N: 14, D: 7.31. WR: 1:10.9 (Cor Kint)

| | | |
|---|---|---|
| 1. Joan Harrison | SAF | 1:14.3 |
| 2. Geertje Wielema | HOL | 1:14.5 |
| 3. Jean Stewart | NZE | 1:15.8 |
| 4. Johanna de Korte | HOL | 1:15.8 |
| 5. Barbara Stark | USA | 1:16.2 |
| 6. Gertrud Herrbruck | GER | 1:18.0 |
| 7. Margaret McDowall | GBR | 1:18.4 |
| DISQ: Hendrika van der Horst (HOL) | | |

Joan Harrison's upset victory was so unexpected that Alex Bulley, the South African team manager, fainted from excitement when he realized she had won.

**1956 Melbourne** C: 23, N: 14, D: 12.5. WR: 1:10.9 (Cor Kint)

| | | | |
|---|---|---|---|
| 1. Judith Grinham | GBR | 1:12.9 | OR |
| 2. Carin Cone | USA | 1:12.9 | |
| 3. Margaret Edwards | GBR | 1:13.1 | |
| 4. Helga Schmidt | GER | 1:13.4 | |
| 5. Maureen Murphy | USA | 1:14.1 | |
| 6. Julie Hoyle | GBR | 1:14.3 | |
| 7. Sara Barber | CAN | 1:14.3 | |
| 8. Gerganyia Beckitt | AUS | 1:14.7 | |

**1960 Rome** C: 30, N: 19, D: 9.3. WR: 1:09.2 (Lynn Burke)

| | | | |
|---|---|---|---|
| 1. Lynn Burke | USA | 1:09.3 | OR |
| 2. Natalie Steward | GBR | 1:10.8 | |
| 3. Satoko Tanaka | JPN | 1:11.4 | |
| 4. Laura Ranwell | SAF | 1:11.4 | |
| 5. Rosy Piacentini | FRA | 1:11.4 | |
| 6. Sylvia Lewis | GBR | 1:11.8 | |
| 7. Maria van Velsen | HOL | 1:12.1 | |
| 8. Nadine Delache | FRA | 1:12.4 | |

**1964 Tokyo** C: 31, N: 17, D: 10.14. WR: 1:08.3 (Virginia Duenkel)

| | | | |
|---|---|---|---|
| 1. Cathy Ferguson | USA | 1:07.7 | WR |
| 2. Christine Caron | FRA | 1:07.9 | |
| 3. Virginia Duenkel | USA | 1:08.0 | |
| 4. Satoko Tanaka | JPN | 1:08.6 | |
| 5. Nina Harmar | USA | 1:09.4 | |
| 6. Linda Ludgrove | GBR | 1:09.5 | |
| 7. Eileen Weir | CAN | 1:09.8 | |
| 8. Jill Norfolk | GBR | 1:11.2 | |

The 1964 final matched six past and present world record holders at various backstroke distances: Caron, Duenkel, Tanaka, Ferguson, Ludgrove, and Norfolk. Sixteen-year-old Kiki Caron had set a 100 meters world record of 1:08.6 on June 14, but that was broken by Ginny Duenkel on September 28. In the Olympic final, however, it was 16-year-old 200 meters record holder Cathy Ferguson who edged ahead just before the finish to gain her second world record and her first gold medal.

**1968 Mexico City** C: 40, N: 23, D: 10.23. WR: 1:06.4 (Karen Muir)

| | | | |
|---|---|---|---|
| 1. Kaye Hall | USA | 1:06.2 | WR |
| 2. Elaine Tanner | CAN | 1:06.7 | |
| 3. Jane Swagerty | USA | 1:08.1 | |
| 4. Kendis Moore | USA | 1:08.3 | |
| 5. Andrea Gyarmati | HUN | 1:09.1 | |
| 6. Lynette Watson | AUS | 1:09.1 | |
| 7. Sylvie Canet | FRA | 1:09.3 | |
| 8. Glenda Stirling | NZE | 1:10.6 | |

Sixteen-year-old world record holder Karen Muir was excluded from Olympic competition because she was from South Africa, which has been banned from the Olympics since 1964 because of its government's racial policies. In Muir's absence, the favorite was 17-year-old Elaine Tanner of Vancouver, who had the fastest times of the qualifying rounds, setting Olympic records of 1:07.6 and 1:07.4 in the heats and semifinals. But as Canada's main gold medal hope, she carried a heavy burden. "Usually, before a race," she explained afterward, "you're concentrating on strategy, the other swimmers, the race. But at Mexico all I could think about was the twenty million people who were expecting me to win." Another finalist was 17-year-old Kaye Hall of Tacoma, Washington, who had been beaten by Tanner several times and as recently as the semifinals the previous day. Tanner and Hall swam neck and neck for 50 meters. but Hall surged ahead at the turn, and even though Tanner produced her best time ever, she couldn't catch the inspired American teenager.

**1972 Munich** C: 37, N: 21, D: 9.2. WR: 1:05.6 (Karen Muir)

| | | | |
|---|---|---|---|
| 1. Melissa Belote | USA | 1:05.78 | OR |
| 2. Andrea Gyarmati | HUN | 1:06:26 | |
| 3. Susie Atwood | USA | 1:06.34 | |
| 4. Karen Moe | USA | 1:06.69 | |
| 5. Wendy Cook | CAN | 1:06.70 | |
| 6. Enith Brigitha | HOL | 1:06.82 | |
| 7. Christine Herbst | GDR | 1:07.27 | |
| 8. Silke Pielen | GER | 1:07.36 | |

This was the first of Melissa Belote's three gold medals. She had orginally turned to the backstroke because it was the only stroke that kept the chlorine out of her eyes. Belote attributed her fine performance in Munich to the fact that she felt relaxed and unpressured since she was not expected to win.

**1976 Montreal** C: 34, N: 21, D: 7.21. WR: 1:01.51 (Ulrike Richter)

| | | | |
|---|---|---|---|
| 1. Ulrike Richter | GDR | 1:01.83 | OR |
| 2. Birgit Treiber | GDR | 1:03.41 | |
| 3. Nancy Garapick | CAN | 1:03.71 | |
| 4. Wendy Hogg-Cook | CAN | 1:03.93 | |
| 5. Cheryl Gibson | CAN | 1:05.16 | |
| 6. Nadejda Stavko | SOV | 1:05.19 | |
| 7. Antje Stille | GDR | 1:05.30 | |
| 8. Diane Edelijn | HOL | 1:05.53 | |

The order of finish for the first four places was exactly the same as it had been a year earlier at the 1975 world championships in Cali, Colombia. Seventeen-year-old Ulrike Richter had broken the 100 meters world record nine times in the three years preceding the Montreal Olympics.

**1980 Moscow** C: 26, N: 18, D: 7.23. WR: 1:01.51 (Ulrike Richter)

| | | | |
|---|---|---|---|
| 1. Rica Reinisch | GDR | 1:00.86 | WR |
| 2. Ina Kleber | GDR | 1:02.07 | |
| 3. Petra Riedel | GDR | 1:02.64 | |
| 4. Carmen Bunaciu | ROM | 1:03.81 | |
| 5. Carine Verbauwen | BEL | 1:03.82 | |
| 6. Larissa Gorchakova | SOV | 1:03.87 | |
| 7. Monique Bosga | HOL | 1:04.47 | |
| 8. Manuela Carosi | ITA | 1:05.10 | |

Fifteen-year-old Rica Reinisch had quite a successful week at the Moscow Olympics. First she equaled Ulrike Richter's four-year-old 100-meter backstroke world record of 1:01.51 while swimming the opening leg for East Germany's victorious medley relay team. Two days later she broke Richter's record by clocking 1:01.50 in her elimination heat. In the final, 24 hours later, Reinisch took the lead early on the way to her third world record. Four days later, in the 200-meter backstroke final, she earned her third gold medal and her fourth world record.

**1984 Los Angeles** C: 31, N: 21, D: 7.31. WR: 1:00.86 (Rica Reinisch)

| | | |
|---|---|---|
| 1. Theresa Andrews | USA | 1:02.55 |
| 2. Betsy Mitchell | USA | 1:02.63 |
| 3. Jolanda de Rover | HOL | 1:02.91 |
| 4. Carmen Bunaciu | ROM | 1:03.21 |
| 5. Aneta Patrascoiu | ROM | 1:03.29 |
| 6. Svenja Schlicht | GER | 1:03.46 |
| 7. Beverley Rose | GBR | 1:04.16 |
| 8. Carmel Clark | NZE | 1:04.47 |

On August 24, at the Friendship Games in Moscow, East Germany's Ina Kleber set a world record of 1:00.59. At the East German Olympic trials, Kristin Otto had clocked her best time of the year, 1:01.13.

**1988 Seoul** C: 41, N: 30, D: 9.22. WR: 1:00.59 (Ina Kleber)

| | | |
|---|---|---|
| 1. Kristin Otto | GDR | 1:00.89 |
| 2. Krisztina Egerszegi | HUN | 1:01.56 |
| 3. Cornelia Sirch | GDR | 1:01.57 |
| 4. Betsy Mitchell | USA | 1:02.71 |
| 5. Beth Barr | USA | 1:02.78 |
| 6. Silvia Poll | CRC | 1:03.34 |
| 7. Nicole Livingstone | AUS | 1:04.15 |
| 8. Marion Aizpors | GER | 1:04.19 |

Kristin Otto won the second of her six gold medals and, an hour later, earned her third in the 4 × 100-meter freestyle relay. One curiosity of note occurred among the lower-ranked swimmers. Olympic rules provided for a "B" final to be swum by the ninth through sixteenth fastest qualifiers. Manuela Carosi of Italy and Karen Lord of Australia tied for sixteenth place and were forced to swim off for the final spot in the "B" final. Again they finished in a dead heat and had to return to the water for a second swimoff. They were exactly even at 50 meters, but Carosi finally won, 1:04.62 to 1:04.75. To her credit, Carosi finished third in the "B" final, her fourth race of the day, with her best time yet: 1:03.80.

# 200-METER BACKSTROKE

**1896–1964** not held

**1968 Mexico City** C: 30, N: 19, D: 10.25. WR: 2:23.8 (Karen Muir)
1. Lillian "Pokey" Watson   USA   2:24.8   OR
2. Elaine Tanner   CAN   2:27.4
3. Kaye Hall   USA   2:28.9
4. Lynette Watson   AUS   2:29.5
5. Wendy Burrell   GBR   2:32.3
6. Zdenka Gasparac   YUG   2:33.5
7. Maria Corominas   SPA   2:33.9
8. Bendicte Duprez   FRA   2:36.6

**1972 Munich** C: 37, N: 20, D: 9.4. WR: 2:20.64 (Melissa Belote)
1. Melissa Belote   USA   2:19.19   WR
2. Susie Atwood   USA   2:20.38
3. Donna Gurr   CAN   2:23.22
4. Annegret Kober   GER   2:23.35
5. Christine Herbst   GDR   2:23.44
6. Enith Brigitha   HOL   2:23.70
7. Deborah Palmer   AUS   2:24.65
8. Leslie Cliff   CAN   2:25.80

Melissa Belote swam a 2:20.58 in the heats to break her own world record. She broke it again in the final eight hours later to win her third gold medal in three days.

**1976 Montreal** C: 31, N: 18, D: 7.25. WR: 2:12.47 (Birgit Treiber)
1. Ulrike Richter   GDR   2:13.43   OR
2. Birgit Treiber   GDR   2:14.97
3. Nancy Garapick   CAN   2:15.60
4. Nadejda Stavko   SOV   2:16.28
5. Melissa Belote   USA   2:17.27
6. Antje Stille   GDR   2:17.55
7. Klavdia Studennikova   SOV   2:17.74
8. Wendy Hogg-Cook   CAN   2:17.95

The 200-meter backstroke had seen five different world record holders in the two and a half years prior to the Montreal Olympics: Belote, Richter, Garapick, Treiber, and Stille. All five started in the Olympic final. As it turned out, there was little drama; Ulrike Richter led from start to finish to gain her third gold medal.

**1980 Moscow** C: 21, N: 13, D: 7.27. WR: 2:11.95 (Linda Jezek)
1. Rica Reinisch   GDR   2:11.77   WR
2. Cornelia Polit   GDR   2:13.75
3. Birgit Treiber   GDR   2:14.14
4. Carmen Bunaciu   ROM   2:15.20
5. Yolande van der Straeten   BEL   2:15.58
6. Carine Verbauwen   BEL   2:16.66
7. Lisa Forrest   AUS   2:16.75
8. Larissa Gorchakova   SOV   2:17.72

Reinisch improved her personal best from 2:15.59 in only eight weeks.

**1984 Los Angeles** C: 27, N: 18, D: 8.4. WR: 2:09.91 (Cornelia Sirch)
1. Jolanda de Rover   HOL   2:12.38
2. Amy White   USA   2:13.04
3. Aneta Patrascoiu   ROM   2:13.29
4. Georgina Parkes   AUS   2:14.37
5. Tori Trees   USA   2:15.73
6. Svenja Schlicht   GER   2:15.93
7. Carmen Bunaciu   ROM   2:16.15
8. Carmel Clark   NZE   2:17.89

At the Friendship Games, three weeks after the Olympics, Kathrin Zimmermann of East Germany recorded a time of 2:12.56.

**1988 Seoul** C: 32, N: 23, D: 9.25. WR: 2:08.60 (Betsy Mitchell)
1. Krisztina Egerszegi   HUN   2:09.29   OR
2. Kathrin Zimmerman   GDR   2:10.61
3. Cornelia Sirch   GDR   2:11.45
4. Cynthia "Beth" Barr   USA   2:12.39
5. Nicole Livingstone   AUS   2:13.43
6. Andrea Hayes   USA   2:15.02
7. Jolanda de Rover   HOL   2:15.17
8. Svenja Schlicht   GER   2:15.94

Two-time world champion Cornelia Sirch led the qualifying round with an Olympic record of 2:10.46. But 14-year-old Krisztina Egerszegi, emboldened by her silver medal in the 100-meter backstroke, felt for the first time that she was capable of beating the East Germans. This despite the fact that, at 99 pounds, the Budapest native was 42 pounds lighter than any of her opponents in the final. Sirch took the early lead with Egerszegi right beside her. After the turn at 100 meters, Egerszegi suddenly sprinted ahead and continued to pull away for the remainder of the race. Discouraged, Sirch was also passed by teammate Kathrin Zimmerman, who had to beat her four-year-old personal best to do it. Krisztina Egerszegi is the youngest person ever to win a gold medal in swimming.

# 100-METER BREASTSTROKE

**1896–1964** not held

**1968 Mexico City** C: 33, N: 20, D: 10.19. WR: 1:14.2 (Catie Ball)
1. Djurdjica Bjedov   YUG   1:15.8   OR
2. Galina Prozumenshikova   SOV   1:15.9
3. Sharon Wichman   USA   1:16.1
4. Uta Frommater   GER   1:16.2
5. Catie Ball   USA   1:16.7
6. Kyoe Nakagawa   JPN   1:17.0
7. Svetlana Babanina   SOV   1:17.2
8. Ana Norbis   URU   1:17.3

Catie Ball of Jacksonville, Florida, set her fifth 100-meter breaststroke world record seven weeks before the opening of the 1968 Olympics. But in Mexico City she succumbed to a viral infection and lost ten pounds. She competed anyway, but could finish only fifth. Twenty-one-year-old Djurdjica Bjedov is the only Yugoslav ever to have won an Olympic swimming championship. Previous to the Olympics her main claim to fame had been finishing third in a 200-meter heat at the 1966 European championships.

**1972 Munich** C: 40, N: 23, D: 9.2. WR: 1:14.2 (Catie Ball)

| | | | |
|---|---|---|---|
| 1. Catherine Carr | USA | 1:13.58 | WR |
| 2. Galina Stepanova (Prozumenshikova) | SOV | 1:14.99 | |
| 3. Beverley Whitfield | AUS | 1:15.73 | |
| 4. Ágnes Kiss-Kaczander | HUN | 1:16.26 | |
| 5. Judy Melick | USA | 1:17.16 | |
| 6. Verena Eberle | GER | 1:17.16 | |
| 7. Britt-Marie Smedh | SWE | 1:17.19 | |
| 8. Dorothy Harrison | GBR | 1:17.49 | |

**1976 Montreal** C: 38, N: 23, D: 7.24. WR: 1:11.93 (Carola Nitschke)

| | | |
|---|---|---|
| 1. Hannelore Anke | GDR | 1:11.16 |
| 2. Lyubov Rusanova | SOV | 1:13.04 |
| 3. Marina Koshevaia | SOV | 1:13.30 |
| 4. Carola Nitschke | GDR | 1:13.33 |
| 5. Gabriele Askamp | GER | 1:14.15 |
| 6. Marina Iurchenia | SOV | 1:14.17 |
| 7. Margaret Kelly | GBR | 1:14.20 |
| 8. Karla Linke | GDR | 1:14.21 |

In the fifth heat of the opening round, 18-year-old Hannelore Anke of Aue set a new world record of 1:11.11. Nine hours later in the semifinals, she lowered the record to 1:10.86. In the final, two nights later, Anke's slowest performance of the Games was good enough for an easy gold medal.

**1980 Moscow** C: 25, N: 19, D: 7.26. WR: 1:10.20 (Ute Geweniger)

| | | |
|---|---|---|
| 1. Ute Geweniger | GDR | 1:10.22 |
| 2. Elvira Vasilkova | SOV | 1:10.41 |
| 3. Susanne Nielsson | DEN | 1:11.16 |
| 4. Margaret Kelly | GBR | 1:11.48 |
| 5. Eva-Marie Håkansson | SWE | 1:11.72 |
| 6. Susannah Brownsdon | GBR | 1:12.11 |
| 7. Lina Kačiušytė | SOV | 1:12.21 |
| 8. Monica Bonon | ITA | 1:12.51 |

Sixteen-year-old Ute Geweniger clocked a 1:10.11 in the fourth heat to break her own world record. In the final she was only fifth at the turn. Three days later, Tracy Caulkins set a U.S. record of 1:10.40.

**1984 Los Angeles** C: 30, N: 21, D: 8.2. WR: 1:08.51 (Ute Geweniger)

| | | | |
|---|---|---|---|
| 1. Petra van Staveren | HOL | 1:09.88 | OR |
| 2. Anne Ottenbrite | CAN | 1:10.69 | |
| 3. Cathérine Poirot | FRA | 1:10.70 | |
| 4. Tracy Caulkins | USA | 1:10.88 | |
| 5. Eva-Marie Håkansson | SWE | 1:11.14 | |
| 6. Hiroko Nagasaki | JPN | 1:11.33 | |

| | | |
|---|---|---|
| 7. Susan Rapp | USA | 1:11.45 |
| 8. Jean Hill | GBR | 1:11.82 |

Three weeks after the Olympic final, 15-year-old Sylvia Gerasch of East Germany set a world record of 1:08.29 at the Friendship Games. Second place went to fellow East German Ute Geweniger in 1:08.59, and third to Larissa Belokon of the Soviet Union in 1:09.63.

**1988 Seoul** C: 42, N: 27, D: 9.23. WR: 1:07.91 (Silke Hörner)

| | | | |
|---|---|---|---|
| 1. Tania Dangalakova (Bogomilova) | BUL | 1:07.95 | OR |
| 2. Antoaneta Frenkeva | BUL | 1:08.74 | |
| 3. Silke Hörner | GDR | 1:08.83 | |
| 4. Allison Higson | CAN | 1:08.86 | |
| 5. Yelena Volkova | SOV | 1:09.24 | |
| 6. Tracey McFarlane | USA | 1:09.60 | |
| 7. Huang Xiaomin | CHN | 1:10.53 | |
| 8. Annett Rex | GDR | 1:10.67 | |

In 1987 Tania Dangalakova, the reigning European champion in the 200-meter breaststroke, made a move not uncommon among 23-year-old female swimmers: she put aside her competitive career to have a baby. But the following year she did something highly unusual: she staged a successful comeback. In the preliminary round she set an Olympic record of 1:08.35. This time was matched two heats later by the overwhelming favorite, Silke Hörner. Hörner, the world record holder at 100 meters, had won the 200-meter gold medal with a world record two days earlier. In the 100-meter final Hörner swam the first 50 meters in 31.58, faster than world record pace. Dangalakova was right behind her. Prior to her pregnancy, Dangalakova had had a reputation for swimming a fast first half and then dying badly for the remainder of the race. In fact that is exactly what she did in the 200-meter final. This time, however, it was Hörner who struggled to the finish line while Dangalakova took the lead at 80 meters and went on to become Bulgaria's first Olympic swimming champion. She was so overcome by emotion after her victory that she collapsed in tears and was unable to speak to the press.

## 200-METER BREASTSTROKE

**1896–1920** not held

**1924** C: 15, N: 8, D: 7.18. WR: 3:20.4 (Irene Gilbert)

| | | | |
|---|---|---|---|
| 1. Lucy Morton | GBR | 3:33.2 | OR |
| 2. Agnes Geraghty | USA | 3:34.0 | |
| 3. Gladys Carson | GBR | 3:35.4 | |
| 4. Vivan Pettersson | SWE | 3:37.6 | |
| 5. Irene Gilbert | GBR | 3:38.0 | |
| 6. Laury Koster | LUX | 3:39.2 | |
| 7. Hjördis Töpel | SWE | 3:47.6 | |

The first qualifying heat was won by Marie Baron of Holland in 3:22.6, with Agnes Geraghty second in 3:27.6. Baron was disqualified, however, for making a faulty turn. Geraghty led the final for 150 meters, but she couldn't withstand the surprising closing rush of 26-year-old Lucy Morton.

**1928 Amsterdam** C: 21, N: 12, D: 8.9. WR: 3:11.2 (Lotte Mühe)

| | | |
|---|---|---|
| 1. Hildegard Schrader | GER | 3:12.6 |
| 2. Mietje "Marie" Baron | HOL | 3:15.2 |
| 3. Lotte Mühe | GER | 3:17.6 |
| 4. Else Jacobsen | DEN | 3:19.0 |
| 5. Margaret Hoffman | USA | 3:19.2 |
| 6. Brita Hazelius | SWE | 3:23.0 |

Lotte Mühe broke Marie Baron's world record on July 15, but three weeks later in Amsterdam it was her teammate, 18-year-old Hilde Schrader, who was in control. Her opening heat time of 3:11.6 bettered the Olympic record by 16 seconds. In the semifinals Schrader equaled Mühe's world record. The final was her slowest race, but with good reason: the straps of her bathing suit broke. She was able to finish, but after the race she had to stay in the water until her suit could be fixed.

**1932 Los Angeles** C: 11, N: 7, D: 8.9. WR: 3:03.4 (Else Jacobsen)

| | | |
|---|---|---|
| 1. Clare Dennis | AUS | 3:06.3 OR |
| 2. Hideko Maehata | JPN | 3:06.4 |
| 3. Else Jacobsen | DEN | 3:07.1 |
| 4. Margery Hinton | GBR | 3:11.7 |
| 5. Margaret Hoffman | USA | 3:11.8 |
| 6. Anne Govednik | USA | 3:16.0 |
| 7. Jane Cadwell | USA | 3:18.2 |

Mere inches separated Dennis and Jacobsen for the first 175 meters. Jacobsen wilted slightly at the end, enabling the fast-finishing Maehata to beat her by a foot for second place.

**1936 Berlin** C: 23, N: 12, D: 8.11. WR: 3:00.4 (Hideko Maehata)

| | | |
|---|---|---|
| 1. Hideko Maehata | JPN | 3:03.6 |
| 2. Martha Geneger | GER | 3:04.2 |
| 3. Inge Sörensen | DEN | 3:07.8 |
| 4. Johanna "Hanni" Hölzner | GER | 3:09.5 |
| 5. Johanna Waalberg | HOL | 3:09.5 |
| 6. Doris Storey | GBR | 3:09.7 |
| 7. Jeannette Kastein | HOL | 3:12.8 |

The year 1936 saw the first Olympic appearance of the controversial butterfly stroke, in which the swimmer recovers her arms above the water rather than under. The first woman to try the stroke in the Olympics was Lenk of Brazil who was eliminated in the semifinals. Silver medalist Martha Geneger was 14 years old, while bronze medalist Inge Sörensen was only 12 years and 24 days old. By contrast, Hideko Maehata, who set an Olympic record of 3:01.9 in her preliminary heat, was an elderly 22.

**1948 London** C: 22, N: 14, D: 8.3. WR: 2:49.2 (Petronella van Vliet)

| | | |
|---|---|---|
| 1. Petronella van Vliet | HOL | 2:57.2 |
| 2. Beatrice Lyons | AUS | 2:57.7 |
| 3. Éva Novák | HUN | 3:00.2 |
| 4. Éva Székely | HUN | 3:02.5 |
| 5. Adriana de Groot | HOL | 3:06.2 |
| 6. Elizabeth Church | GBR | 3:06.1 |
| 7. A.J. Hom | HOL | 3:07.5 |
| 8. Jytte Hansen | DEN | 3:08.1 |

De Groot was awarded fifth place despite the fact that her official time was slower than that of Church.

**1952 Helsinki** C: 34, N: 19, D: 7.29. WR: 2:48.5 (Éva Novák)

| | | |
|---|---|---|
| 1. Éva Székely | HUN | 2:51.7 OR |
| 2. Éva Novák | HUN | 2:54.4 |
| 3. Helen "Elenor" Gordon | GBR | 2:57.6 |
| 4. Klára Killermann | HUN | 2:57.6 |
| 5. Jytte Hansen | DEN | 2:57.8 |
| 6. Maria Gavrisch | SOV | 2:58.9 |
| 7. Ulla-Britt Eklund | SWE | 3:01.8 |
| 8. Petronella Garritsen | HOL | 3:02.1 |

Like 100-meter freestyle winner Katalin Szöke, 25-year-old Éva Székely was married to a member of the 1952 champion Hungarian water polo team. Husband Dezsö Gyarmati also won water polo gold medals in 1956 and 1964. Székely was the first female butterfuly stroker to win a gold medal. Following the 1952 Olympics, the breaststroke and butterfly were separated into two different events.

**1956 Melbourne** C: 14, N: 10, D: 11.30. WR: 2:46.4 (Adelaide den Haan)

| | | |
|---|---|---|
| 1. Ursula Happe | GER | 2:53.1 OR |
| 2. Éva Székely | HUN | 2:54.8 |
| 3. Eva-Maria ten Elsen | GDR | 2:55.1 |
| 4. Vinka Jeričević | YUG | 2:55.8 |
| 5. Klára Killermann | HUN | 2:56.1 |
| 6. Helen "Elenor" Gordon | GBR | 2:56.1 |
| 7. Mary Sears | USA | 2:57.2 |
| 8. Christine Gosden | GBR | 2:59.2 |

World record holder Ada den Haan was unable to compete because the Netherlands withdrew from the 1956 Games to protest the Soviet invasion of Hungary.

**1960 Rome** C: 29, N: 19, D: 9.27. WR: 2:50.2 (Wiltrud Urselmann)

| | | |
|---|---|---|
| 1. Anita Lonsbrough | GBR | 2:49.5 WR |
| 2. Wiltrud Urselmann | GER | 2:50.0 |
| 3. Barbara Göbel | GDR | 2:53.6 |
| 4. Adelaide den Haan | HOL | 2:54.4 |
| 5. Margareta Kok | HOL | 2:54.6 |
| 6. Anne Warner | USA | 2:55.4 |
| 7. Patty Kempner | USA | 2:55.5 |
| 8. Dorrit Kristensen | DEN | 2:55.7 |

In 1957 underwater stroking was banned from breaststroke competitions, which explains why the world record was slower in 1960 than it was in 1956. Nineteen-year-old Anita Lonsbrough, a clerk for the Huddersfield Corporation in Yorkshire, faced a problem not uncommon to amateur athletes in Great Britain. Far from being appreciative of the free publicity that her swimming exploits brought them, her employers actually docked her wages whenever she took time off for training. Her victory in Rome was the result of iron nerves and perfect tactics. She trailed Urselmann by two seconds at the halfway mark, then she gradually closed the gap, catching the tiring German with 25 meters to go. Urselmann surprised Lonsbrough with a final spurt, but Lonsbrough, who had calmly varnished her nails while waiting for the race to start, held on for the victory.

**1964 Tokyo** C: 26, N: 15, D: 10.12. WR: 2:45.4 (Galina Prozumenshikova)

| | | | |
|---|---|---|---|
| 1. Galina Prozumenshikova | SOV | 2:46.4 | OR |
| 2. Claudia Kolb | USA | 2:47.6 | |
| 3. Svetlana Babanina | SOV | 2:48.6 | |
| 4. Stella Mitchell | GBR | 2:49.0 | |
| 5. Jill Slattery | GBR | 2:49.6 | |
| 6. Bärbel Grimmer | GDR | 2:51.0 | |
| 7. Klena Bimolt | HOL | 2:51.3 | |
| 8. Ursula Küper | GDR | 2:53.9 | |

Prozumenshikova, a 15-year-old schoolgirl from Sevastopol, let Babanina set the pace for 100 meters and then surged ahead to win the U.S.S.R.'s first gold medal in swimming.

**1968 Mexico City** C: 21, N: 20, D: 10.23. WR: 2:38.5 (Catie Ball)

| | | | |
|---|---|---|---|
| 1. Sharon Wichman | USA | 2:44.4 | OR |
| 2. Djurdjica Bjedov | YUG | 2:46.4 | |
| 3. Galina Prozumenshikova | SOV | 2:47.0 | |
| 4. Alla Grebennikova | SOV | 2:47.1 | |
| 5. Cathy Jamison | USA | 2:48.4 | |
| 6. Svetlana Babanina | SOV | 2:48.4 | |
| 7. Chieno Shibata | JPN | 2:51.5 | |
| 8. Ana Norbis | URU | 2:51.9 | |

Prozumenshikova was leading after 175 meters when she suddenly ran out of energy and barely hung on for third place. She had to be administered oxygen as soon as the race was over. Sharon Wichman's victory meant that the gold medals in the first ten Olympic women's 200-meter breaststroke competitions had been won by swimmers from eight different nations.

**1972 Munich** C: 39, N: 22, D: 8.29. WR: 2:38.5 (Catie Ball)

| | | | |
|---|---|---|---|
| 1. Beverley Whitfield | AUS | 2:41.71 | OR |
| 2. Dana Schoenfield | USA | 2:42.05 | |
| 3. Galina Stepanova (Prozumenshikova) | SOV | 2:42.36 | |
| 4. Claudia Clevenger | USA | 2:42.88 | |
| 5. Petra Nows | GER | 2:43.41 | |
| 6. Ágnes Kiss-Kaczander | HUN | 2:43.41 | |
| 7. Lyudmila Porubaiko | SOV | 2:44.48 | |
| 8. Éva Kiss | HUN | 2:45.12 | |

As usual, Galina Prozumenshikova took the early lead and eventually opened a four-meter gap. But just as she had done four years earlier, the Soviet swimmer, now Galina Stepanova, "died" in the final 50 meters and faded to third place. Meanwhile, 18-year-old Beverley Whitfield, in last place after 50 meters and fourth place after 150 meters, sprinted home to pass Stepanova and

stave off a final challenge from Schoenfield. As she climbed out of the pool, Whitfield called out to her teammates, "For once I kept my cool. This is the greatest feeling in the world."

**1976 Montreal** C: 38, N: 21, D: 7.21. WR: 2:34.99 (Karla Linke)

| | | | |
|---|---|---|---|
| 1. Marina Koshevaia | SOV | 2:33.35 | WR |
| 2. Marina Yurchenya | SOV | 2:36.08 | |
| 3. Lyubov Rusanova | SOV | 2:36.22 | |
| 4. Hannelore Anke | GDR | 2:36.49 | |
| 5. Karla Linke | GDR | 2:36.97 | |
| 6. Carola Nitschke | GDR | 2:38.27 | |
| 7. Margaret Kelly | GBR | 2:38.37 | |
| 8. Deborah Rudd | GBR | 2:39.01 | |

Koshevaia moved up from fifth to first during the third 50 meters and then pulled away to the most decisive women's breaststroke victory in Olympic history.

**1980 Moscow** C: 25, N: 19, D: 7.23. WR: 2:28.36 (Lina Kačiušytė)

| | | | |
|---|---|---|---|
| 1. Lina Kačiušytė | SOV | 2:29.54 | OR |
| 2. Svetlana Varganova | SOV | 2:29.61 | |
| 3. Yulia Bogdanova | SOV | 2:32.39 | |
| 4. Susanne Nielsson | DEN | 2:32.75 | |
| 5. Irena Fleissnerová | CZE | 2:33.23 | |
| 6. Ute Geweniger | GDR | 2:34.34 | |
| 7. Bettina Löbel | GDR | 2:34.51 | |
| 8. Sylvia Rinka | GDR | 2:35.38 | |

Svetlana Varganova led for almost the entire race while Lithuanian Lina Kačiušytė improved from last place at 50 meters to fourth place at the halfway mark and second place two and a half seconds behind Varganova, with 50 meters to go. An impressive finishing spurt earned 17-year-old Kačiušytė the gold medal.

**1984 Los Angeles** C: 23, N: 16, D: 7.30. WR: 2:28.36 (Lina Kačiušytė)

| | | |
|---|---|---|
| 1. Anne Ottenbrite | CAN | 2:30.38 |
| 2. Susan Rapp | USA | 2:31.15 |
| 3. Ingrid Lempereur | BEL | 2:31.40 |
| 4. Hiroko Nagasaki | JPN | 2:32.93 |
| 5. Sharon Kellett | AUS | 2.33.60 |
| 6. Ute Hasse | GER | 2:33.82 |
| 7. Susannah Brownsdon | GBR | 2:35.07 |
| 8. Kimberly Rhodenbaugh | USA | 2:35.51 |

The term "accident-prone" was meant for people like Anne Ottenbrite of Whitby, Ontario. Fortunately for Ottenbrite, all of her accidents had been relatively minor. Having previously survived bloody encounters with a plateglass window and a potato processor, on May 21st she dislocated her right kneecap while showing off a new pair of shoes. Unable to take part in the Canadian trials, she was placed on the team anyway. During her brief stay in Los Angeles before the Olympics began, Ottenbrite suffered a whiplash injury to her neck when the van in which she was travelling crashed into the back of another car. Relaxing back at the Olympic Village, she strained a thigh muscle while playing a video game.

Despite all of these mishaps, the 18-year-old Ottenbrite moved ahead of Hiroko Nagasaki after the mid-way point of the Olympic final and held off the closing rushes of Rapp and Lempereur to win a gold medal. Ottenbrite's victory was a mild surprise, but the real shocker was the performance of 15-year-old Ingrid Lempereur, who bettered her pre-Olympic personal best by 6.36 seconds.

At the Friendship Games on August 20th, Larissa Belokon finished first in 2:29.13 and Sylvia Gerasch second in 2:29.62.

**1988 Seoul** C: 43, N: 27, D: 9.21. WR: 2:27.27 (Allison Higson)
| 1. | Silke Hörner | GDR | 2:26.71 | WR |
|---|---|---|---|---|
| 2. | Huang Xiaomin | CHN | 2:27.49 | |
| 3. | Antoaneta Frenkeva | BUL | 2:28.34 | |
| 4. | Tania Dangalakova (Bogomilova) | BUL | 2:28.43 | |
| 5. | Yulia Bogacheva | SOV | 2:28.54 | |
| 6. | Ingrid Lempereur | BEL | 2:29.42 | |
| 7. | Allison Higson | CAN | 2:29.60 | |
| 8. | Manuela Dalla Valle | ITA | 2:29.86 | |

Hörner, whose hobby was collecting palm trees in her Leipzig apartment, took the lead from Dangalakova in the third quarter of the race and recaptured the world record she had lost to Higson four months earlier. It was Hörner's third world record at 200 meters.

## 100-METER BUTTERFLY

**1896–1952** not held

**1956 Melbourne** C: 12, N: 8, D: 12.5. WR: 1:10.5 (Aartje Voorbij)
| 1. | Shelly Mann | USA | 1:11.0 | OR |
|---|---|---|---|---|
| 2. | Nancy Ramey | USA | 1:11.9 | |
| 3. | Mary Sears | USA | 1:14.4 | |
| 4. | Mária Littomeritzky | HUN | 1:14.9 | |
| 5. | Beverly Bainbridge | AUS | 1:15.2 | |
| 6. | Jutta Langenau | GDR | 1:17.4 | |
| 7. | Elizabeth Whittall | CAN | 1:17.9 | |
| 8. | Sara Barber | CAN | 1:18.4 | |

With world record holder Atie Voorbij absent because of the Dutch boycott, the inaugural women's butterfly event was swept by the Americans. Crippled by polio at the age of six, Shelly Mann began swimming to regain strength in her arms and legs.

**1960 Rome** C: 25, N: 16, D: 8.30. WR: 1:09.1 (Nancy Ramey)
| 1. | Carolyn Schuler | USA | 1:09.5 | OR |
|---|---|---|---|---|
| 2. | Marianne Heemskerk | HOL | 1:10.4 | |
| 3. | Janice Andrew | AUS | 1:12.2 | |
| 4. | Sheila Watt | GBR | 1:13.3 | |
| 5. | Aartje Voorbij | HOL | 1:13.3 | |
| 6. | Zinaida Belovetskaya | SOV | 1:13.3 | |
| 7. | Kristina Larsson | SWE | 1:13.6 | |
| DNF: Carolyn Wood (USA) | | | | |

Fourteen-year old Carolyn Wood had beaten Carolyn Schuler at the U.S. trials. A close second after 70 meters

of the Olympic final, Wood swallowed too much water, became confused, and stopped swimming.

**1964 Tokyo** C: 31, N: 16, D: 10.16 WR (110 yards): 1:05 1 (Ada Kok)
| 1. | Sharon Stouder | USA | 1:04.7 | WR |
|---|---|---|---|---|
| 2. | Ada Kok | HOL | 1:05.6 | |
| 3. | Kathleen Ellis | USA | 1:06.0 | |
| 4. | Ella Pyrhönen | FIN | 1:07.3 | |
| 5. | Donna De Varona | USA | 1:08.0 | |
| 6. | Heike Hustede | GER | 1:08.5 | |
| 7. | Eiko Takahashi | JPN | 1:09.1 | |
| 8. | Mary Stewart | CAN | 1:10.0 | |

**1968 Mexico City** C: 28, N: 21, D: 10.21. WR: 1:04.5 (Ada Kok)
| 1. | Lynette McClements | AUS | 1:05.5 |
|---|---|---|---|
| 2. | Ellie Daniel | USA | 1:05.8 |
| 3. | Susan Shields | USA | 1:06.2 |
| 4. | Ada Kok | HOL | 1:06.2 |
| 5. | Andréa Gyarmati | HUN | 1:06.8 |
| 6. | Heike Hustede | GER | 1:06.9 |
| 7. | Toni Hewitt | USA | 1:07.5 |
| 8. | Helga Lindner | GDR | 1:07.6 |

Lynn McClements was a 17-year-old typist from Perth.

**1972 Munich** C: 30, N: 21, D: 9.1. WR: 1:03.9 (Mayumi Aoki)
| 1. | Mayumi Aoki | JPN | 1:03.34 | WR |
|---|---|---|---|---|
| 2. | Roswitha Beier | GDR | 1:03.61 | |
| 3. | Andréa Gyarmati | HUN | 1:03.73 | |
| 4. | Deena Deardurff | USA | 1:03.95 | |
| 5. | Dana Shrader | USA | 1:03.98 | |
| 6. | Ellie Daniel | USA | 1:04.08 | |
| 7. | Gudrun Beckmann | GER | 1:04.15 | |
| 8. | Noriko Asano | JPN | 1:04.25 | |

Aoki was only in seventh place at the midrace turn. Bronze medalist Andréa Gyarmati was the daughter of 1952 breaststroke gold medalist Éva Székely and Dezső Gyarmati, who won three gold medals in water polo.

**1976 Montreal** C: 39, N: 26, D: 7.2. WR: 1:00.13 (Kornelia Ender)
| 1. | Kornelia Ender | GDR | 1:00.13 | EWR |
|---|---|---|---|---|
| 2. | Andrea Pollack | GDR | 1:00.98 | |
| 3. | Wendy Boglioli | USA | 1:01.17 | |
| 4. | Camille Wright | USA | 1:01.41 | |
| 5. | Rosemarie Gabriel (Kother) | GDR | 1:01.56 | |
| 6. | Wendy Quirk | CAN | 1:01.75 | |
| 7. | Lelei Fonoimoana | USA | 1:01.95 | |
| 8. | Tamara Shelofastova | SOV | 1:02.74 | |

At 7:48 p.m. on July 22, 1976, Kornelia Ender won the 100-meter butterfly final in world record time. At 8:03 she descended from the victory platform and went to the dressing room. At 8:08 she returned to the pool for the final of the 200-meter freestyle. At 8:13 she was racing through the water again, and by 8:15 she had won her second gold medal in 27 minutes.

**1980 Moscow** C: 24, N: 18, D: 7.24. WR: 59.26 (Mary T. Meagher)

| | | |
|---|---|---|
| 1. Caren Metschuck | GDR | 1:00.42 |
| 2. Andrea Pollack | GDR | 1:00.90 |
| 3. Christiane Knacke | GDR | 1:01.44 |
| 4. Ann Osgerby | GBR | 1:02.21 |
| 5. Lisa Curry | AUS | 1:02.40 |
| 6. Agneta Mårtensson | SWE | 1:02.61 |
| 7. Maria del Milagro Paris | CRC | 1:02.89 |
| 8. Janet Osgerby | GBR | 1:02.90 |

The British representatives, Ann and Janet Osgerby, were 17-year-old twins from Chorley, Lancashire. Ann was 20 minutes older and 0.69 seconds faster. Missing from the competition due to the anti-Soviet boycott were world record holder Mary T. Meagher and Tracy Caulkins, who clocked 59.41 and 1:00.75, respectively, at the U.S. Outdoor National on August 2.

**1984 Los Angeles** C: 35, N: 23, D: 8.2. WR: 57.93 (Mary T. Meagher)

| | | |
|---|---|---|
| 1. Mary T. Meagher | USA | 59.26 |
| 2. Jenna Johnson | USA | 1:00.19 |
| 3. Karin Seick | GER | 1:01.36 |
| 4. Annemarie Verstappen | HOL | 1:01.56 |
| 5. Michelle MacPherson | CAN | 1:01.58 |
| 6. Janet Tibbits | AUS | 1:01.78 |
| 7. Cornelia van Bentum | HOL | 1:01.94 |
| 8. Ina Beyermann | GER | 1:02.11 |

In 1980, 15-year-old Mary T. Meagher of Louisville, Kentucky, was the world record holder in both butterfly events and the favorite to win two gold medals in Moscow until the anti-Soviet boycott forced her to stay home. The following year she lowered her world record by a phenomenal 1.33 seconds. She never approached that time again, but neither did anyone else. In Los Angeles in 1984, Meagher set an Olympic record of 59.05 in the preliminaries and then overcame a fast start by teammate Jenna Johnson to win the first of her three gold medals.

**1988 Seoul** C: 40, N: 28, D: 9.23. WR: 57.93 (Mary T. Meagher)

| | | | |
|---|---|---|---|
| 1. Kristin Otto | GDR | 59.00 | OR |
| 2. Birte Weigang | GDR | 59.45 | |
| 3. Qian Hong | CHN | 59.52 | |
| 4. Catherine Plewinski | FRA | 59.58 | |
| 5. Janel Jorgensen | USA | 1:00.48 | |
| 6. Cornelia van Bentum | HOL | 1:00.62 | |
| 7. Mary T. Meagher | USA | 1:00.97 | |
| 8. Wang Xiachong | CHN | 1:01.15 | |

Kristin Otto won her fourth gold medal of the Seoul Games. Birte Weigang is the daughter of Horst Weigang, who won a bronze medal as the goalkeeper for East Germany's 1964 football team.

## 200-METER BUTTERFLY

**1896-1964** not held

**1968 Mexico City** C: 21, N: 16, D: 10.24. WR(220 yards): 2:21.0 (Ada Kok)

| | | | |
|---|---|---|---|
| 1. Ada Kok | HOL | 2:24.7 | OR |
| 2. Helga Lindner | GDR | 2:24.8 | |
| 3. Ellie Daniel | USA | 2:25.9 | |
| 4. Toni Hewitt | USA | 2:26.2 | |
| 5. Heike Hustede | GER | 2:27.9 | |
| 6. Diane Giebel | USA | 2:31.7 | |
| 7. Margaret Auton | GBR | 2:33.2 | |
| 8. Yasuko Fujii | JPN | 2:34.3 | |

Six-foot, 183-pound Ada Kok, "The Gentle Giant," had experienced nothing but disappointment in the Olympics. Because of her world records and her general domination of international competitions, she had been expected to win gold medals, but in Tokyo she had to settle for two silver medals in the 100-meter butterfly and the medley relay. Four years later, in Mexico City, Kok was part of the Dutch medley relay team that finished seventh. Then, in the 100-meter butterfly, she finished a disappointing fourth. This left her one last chance for an Olympic victory—the 200-meter butterfly. Her chances seemed slim after her previous defeats, but she recorded the fastest time of the eliminations. In the final she was third at the final turn behind Heike Hustede and Helga Lindner, but Kok's powerful finish gave her a popular and well-deserved victory.

**1972 Munich** C: 24, N: 17, D: 9.4. WR: 2:16.62 (Karen Moe)

| | | | |
|---|---|---|---|
| 1. Karen Moe | USA | 2:15.57 | WR |
| 2. Lynn Colella | USA | 2:16.34 | |
| 3. Ellie Daniel | USA | 2:16.74 | |
| 4. Rosemarie Kother | GDR | 2:17.11 | |
| 5. Noriko Asano | JPN | 2:19.50 | |
| 6. Helga Lindner | GDR | 2:20.47 | |
| 7. Gail Neall | AUS | 2:21.88 | |
| 8. Mayumi Aoki | JPN | 2:22.84 | |

Karen Moe let Daniel and Kother set the pace for 150 meters and then took the lead after the final turn.

**1976 Montreal** C: 32, N: 19, D: 7.19. WR: 2:11.22 (Rosemarie Gabriel [Kother])

| | | | |
|---|---|---|---|
| 1. Andrea Pollack | GDR | 2:11.41 | OR |
| 2. Ulrike Tauber | GDR | 2:12.50 | |
| 3. Rosemarie Gabriel (Kother) | GDR | 2:12.86 | |
| 4. Karen Thornton (Moe) | USA | 2:12.90 | |
| 5. Wendy Quirk | CAN | 2:13.68 | |
| 6. Cheryl Gibson | CAN | 2:13.91 | |
| 7. Tamara Shelofastova | SOV | 2:14.26 | |
| 8. Natalia Popova | SOV | 2:14.50 | |

**1980 Moscow** C: 21, N: 14, D: 7.21. WR: 2:07.01 (Mary T. Meagher)

| | | | |
|---|---|---|---|
| 1. Ines Geissler | GDR | 2:10.44 | OR |
| 2. Sybille Schönrock | GDR | 2:10.45 | |
| 3. Michelle Ford | AUS | 2:11.66 | |
| 4. Andrea Pollack | GDR | 2:12.13 | |
| 5. Dorota Brzozowska | POL | 2:14.12 | |
| 6. Ann Osgerby | GBR | 2:14.83 | |

7. Agneta Martensson    SWE    2:15.22
8. Alla Grishchenkova    SOV    2:15.70

Geissler led at 50 meters and 100 meters, while Schönrock was first to touch at 150. In the end, the 17-year-old Geissler reached the wall in time to win the closest of victories. However neither woman's time came close to the performance of 15-year-old Mary T. Meagher of Cincinnati, who set a world record of 2:06.37 at the U.S. Outdoor National nine days after the Olympic final.

**1984 Los Angeles** C: 29, N: 18, D: 8.4. WR: 2:05.96 (Mary T. Meagher)

| | | | |
|---|---|---|---|
| 1. Mary T. Meagher | USA | 2:06.90 | OR |
| 2. Karen Phillips | AUS | 2:10.56 | |
| 3. Ina Beyermann | GER | 2:11.91 | |
| 4. Nancy Hogshead | USA | 2:11.98 | |
| 5. Samantha Purvis | GBR | 2:12.33 | |
| 6. Naoko Kume | JPN | 2:12.57 | |
| 7. Sonja Hausladen | AUT | 2:15.38 | |
| 8. Cornelia van Bentum | HOL | 2:17.39 | |

Mary T. Meagher led from start to finish and won by seven meters. Her time of 2:06.90 was her fastest since her 1981 world record and gave her the seven fastest times ever. Silver medalist Karen Phillips bettered her pre-Olympic best time by four seconds. First place at the Friendship Games on August 26 went to 1980 Olympic champion Ines Geissler with a time of 2:09.96.

**1988 Seoul** C: 28, N: 21, D: 9.25. WR: 2:05.96 (Mary T. Meagher)

| | | |
|---|---|---|
| 1. Kathleen Nord | GDR | 2:09.51 |
| 2. Birte Weigang | GDR | 2:09.91 |
| 3. Mary T. Meagher | USA | 2:10.80 |
| 4. Stela Pura | ROM | 2:11.28 |
| 5. Trina Radke | USA | 2:11.55 |
| 6. Kiyomi Takahashi | JPN | 2:11.62 |
| 7. Wang Xiaohong | CHN | 2:12.34 |
| 8. Cornelia van Bentum | HOL | 2:13.17 |

Mary T. Meagher entered the Olympics as the defending champion, the holder of the 11 fastest times in history and the fastest time of the year (2:09.13 at the U.S. trials). But, like most of the U.S. swimmers in 1988, she was unable to match her trials time and suffered only her third 200-meter butterfly loss in nine years. Twenty-two-year-old Kathleen Nord of Magdeburg overcame teammate Birte Weigang in the last 50 meters to earn the victory.

# 200-METER INDIVIDUAL MEDLEY

In individual medley races the order of strokes is butterfly, backstroke, breaststroke, and freestyle.

**1896–1964** not held

**1968 Mexico City** C: 39, N: 26, D: 10.20. WR: 2:23.5 (Claudia Kolb)

| | | | |
|---|---|---|---|
| 1. Claudia Kolb | USA | 2:24.7 | OR |
| 2. Susan Pedersen | USA | 2:28.8 | |
| 3. Jan Henne | USA | 2:31.4 | |
| 4. Sabine Steinbach | GDR | 2:31.4 | |
| 5. Yoshimi Nishigawa | JPN | 2:33.7 | |
| 6. Marianne Seydel | GDR | 2:33.7 | |
| 7. Larissa Zakharova | SOV | 2:37.0 | |

DISQ: Shelagh Ratcliffe (GBR)

When she was 14 years old, Claudia Kolb of Santa Clara, California, earned a surprise silver medal in the 200-meter breaststroke. Four years later she overwhelmed her opposition to win both the 200-meter and 400-meter individual medleys.

**1972 Munich** C: 44, N: 26, D: 8.28. WR: 2:23.5 (Claudia Kolb)

| | | | |
|---|---|---|---|
| 1. Shane Gould | AUS | 2:23.07 | WR |
| 2. Kornelia Ender | GDR | 2:23.59 | |
| 3. Lynn Vidali | USA | 2:24.06 | |
| 4. Jennifer Bartz | USA | 2:24.55 | |
| 5. Leslie Cliff | CAN | 2:24.83 | |
| 6. Evelyn Stolze | GDR | 2:25.90 | |
| 7. Yoshimi Nishigawa | JPN | 2:26.35 | |
| 8. Carolyn Woods | USA | 2:27.42 | |

Lynn Vidali led by over a second after 150 meters, but Shane Gould used her freestyle strength to catch her 20 meters later and win the first of her three gold medals. In second place was 13-year-old Kornelia Ender, who won the first of her eight Olympic medals.

**1976–1980** not held

**1984 Los Angeles** C: 27, N: 21, D: 8.3. WR: 2:11.73 (Ute Geweniger)

| | | | |
|---|---|---|---|
| 1. Tracy Caulkins | USA | 2:12.64 | OR |
| 2. Nancy Hogshead | USA | 2:15.17 | |
| 3. Michele Pearson | AUS | 2:15.92 | |
| 4. Lisa Curry | AUS | 2:16.75 | |
| 5. Christiane Pielke | GER | 2:17.82 | |
| 6. Manuela Dalla Valle | ITA | 2:18.60 | |
| 7. Petra Zindler | GER | 2:19.86 | |
| 8. Katrine Bomstad | NOR | 2:20.48 | |

Tracy Caulkins won the second of her three gold medals. Three weeks later, the Friendship Games competition was won by world record holder Ute Geweniger in 2:11.79. In second place with a time of 2:14.56 was Yelena Dendeberova of the Soviet Union.

**1988 Seoul** C: 36, N: 24, D: 9.24. WR: 2:11.73 (Ute Geweniger)

| | | | |
|---|---|---|---|
| 1. Daniela Hunger | GDR | 2:12.59 | OR |
| 2. Yelena Dendeberova | SOV | 2:13.31 | |
| 3. Noemi Lung | ROM | 2:14.85 | |
| 4. Jodie Clayworthy | AUS | 2:16.31 | |
| 5. Marianne Muis | HOL | 2:16.40 | |
| 6. Aneta Patrascoiu | ROM | 2:16.70 | |
| 7. Lin Li | CHN | 2:17.42 | |
| 8. Whitney Hedgepeth | USA | 2:17.99 | |

Sixteen-year-old Daniela Hunger of Berlin overcame Dendeberova in the final 50 meters.

## 400-METER INDIVIDUAL MEDLEY

**1896–1960** not held

**1964 Tokyo** C: 22, N: 12, D: 10.17. WR: 5:14.9 (Donna De Varona)
| | | | |
|---|---|---|---|
| 1. Donna De Varona | USA | 5:18.7 | OR |
| 2. Sharon Finneran | USA | 5:24.1 | |
| 3. Martha Randall | USA | 5:24.2 | |
| 4. Veronika Holletz | GDR | 5:25.6 | |
| 5. Linda McGill | AUS | 5:28.4 | |
| 6. Elisabeth Heukels | HOL | 5:30.3 | |
| 7. Anita Lonsbrough | GBR | 5:30.5 | |
| 8. Márta Egerváry | HUN | 5:38.4 | |

Donna De Varona was a popular and much-photographed winner. She later became a television sports commentator as well as an activist for women in sports.

**1968 Mexico City** C: 28, N: 19, D: 10.25. WR: 5:04.7 (Claudia Kolb)
| | | | |
|---|---|---|---|
| 1. Claudia Kolb | USA | 5:08.5 | OR |
| 2. Lynn Vidali | USA | 5:22.2 | |
| 3. Sabine Steinbach | GDR | 5:25.3 | |
| 4. Susan Pedersen | USA | 5:25.8 | |
| 5. Shelagh Ratcliffe | GBR | 5:30.5 | |
| 6. Marianne Seydel | GDR | 5:32.0 | |
| 7. Tui Shipston | NZE | 5:34.6 | |
| 8. Laura Vaca | MEX | 5:35.7 | |

Claudia Kolb won by 20 meters, the most decisive women's swimming victory in 40 years.

**1972 Munich** C: 38, N: 26, D: 8.31. WR: 5:04.7 (Claudia Kolb)
| | | | |
|---|---|---|---|
| 1. Gail Neall | AUS | 5:02.97 | WR |
| 2. Leslie Cliff | CAN | 5:03.57 | |
| 3. Novella Calligaris | ITA | 5:03.99 | |
| 4. Jennifer Bartz | USA | 5:05.56 | |
| 5. Evelyn Stolze | GDR | 5:06.80 | |
| 6. Mary Montgomery | USA | 5:09.98 | |
| 7. Lynn Vidali | USA | 5:13.06 | |
| 8. Nina Petrova | SOV | 5:15.68 | |

Gail Neall, from the Sydney suburb of Gordon, led from start to finish and broke Claudia Kolb's four-year-old world record.

**1976 Montreal** C: 20, N: 11, D: 7.24. WR: 4:48.79 (Birgit Treiber)
| | | | |
|---|---|---|---|
| 1. Ulrike Tauber | GDR | 4:42.77 | WR |
| 2. Cheryl Gibson | CAN | 4:48.10 | |
| 3. Becky Smith | CAN | 4:50.48 | |
| 4. Birgit Treiber | GDR | 4:52.40 | |
| 5. Sabine Kahle | GDR | 4:53.50 | |
| 6. Donnalee Wennerstrom | USA | 4:55.34 | |
| 7. Joann Baker | CAN | 5:00.19 | |
| 8. Monique Rodahl | NZE | 5:00.21 | |

For the fourth straight time the 400-meter individual medley was led start to finish, as 18-year-old Ulrike Tauber of Karl-Marx Stadt bettered the world record by a phenomenal 6.02 seconds.

**1980 Moscow** C: 16, N: 11, D: 7.26. WR: 4:38.44 (Petra Schneider)
| | | | |
|---|---|---|---|
| 1. Petra Schneider | GDR | 4:36.29 | WR |
| 2. Sharron Davies | GBR | 4:46.83 | |
| 3. Agnieszka Czopek | POL | 4:48.17 | |
| 4. Grit Slaby | GDR | 4:48.54 | |
| 5. Ulrike Tauber | GDR | 4:49.18 | |
| 6. Sonya Dangalakova | BUL | 4:49.25 | |
| 7. Olga Klevakina | SOV | 4:50.91 | |
| 8. Magdalena Bialas | POL | 4:53.30 | |

Once again the 400-meter individual medley was completely dominated by one swimmer. This time it was an easy win and new world record for 17-year-old Petra Schneider, who had been trained in part by her older teammate Ulrike Tauber. In the United States on July 30, Tracy Caulkins clocked 4:40.61 at the Outdoor National to bolster her position as second fastest female medley swimmer in the world.

**1984 Los Angeles** C: 18, N: 13, D: 7.29. WR: 4:36.10 (Petra Schneider)
| | | |
|---|---|---|
| 1. Tracy Caulkins | USA | 4:39.24 |
| 2. Suzanne Landells | AUS | 4:48.30 |
| 3. Petra Zindler | GER | 4:48.57 |
| 4. Susan Heon | USA | 4:49.41 |
| 5. Nathalie Gingras | CAN | 4:50.55 |
| 6. Donna McGinnis | CAN | 4:50.65 |
| 7. Gaynor Stanley | GBR | 4:52.83 |
| 8. Katrine Bomstad | NOR | 4:53.28 |

Since 1978 Tracy Caulkins of Nashville, Tennessee, had set five world records, over 60 U.S. records and had won 48 U.S. national titles, twelve more than any other swimmer. All that was missing from her sterling career was an Olympic championship. That void was filled when she led the 400-meter individual medley from start to finish, winning by almost 15 meters.

**1988 Seoul** C: 30, N: 22, D: 9.19. WR: 4:36.10 (Petra Schneider)
| | | |
|---|---|---|
| 1. Janet Evans | USA | 4:37.76 |
| 2. Noemi Lung | ROM | 4:39.46 |
| 3. Daniela Hunger | GDR | 4:39.76 |
| 4. Yelena Dendeberova | SOV | 4:40.44 |
| 5. Kathleen Nord | GDR | 4:41.64 |
| 6. Jodie Clayworthy | AUS | 4:45.86 |
| 7. Lin Li | CHN | 4:47.05 |
| 8. Donna Procter | AUS | 4:47.51 |

Janet Evans took command on the backstroke leg and won the first of her three gold medals.

## 4 × 100-METER FREESTYLE RELAY

**1896–1908** not held

**1912 Stockholm** T: 4, N; 4, D: 7.15.
1. GBR (Bella Moore, Jennie Fletcher, Annie Speirs, Irene Steer) — 5:52.8 WR
2. GER (Wally Dressel, Louise Otto, Hermine Stindt, Margarete Rosenberg) — 6:04.6
3. AUT (Margarete Adler, Klara Milch, Josephine Sticker, Berta Zahourek) — 6:17.0
4. SWE (Greta Johansson, Karin Lundgren, Sonja Johnsson, Vera Thulin) — —

**1920 Antwerp** T: 3, N: 3, D: 8.29.
1. USA (Margaret Woodbridge, Frances Schroth, Irene Guest, Ethelda Bleibtrey) — 5:11.6 WR
2. GBR (Hilda James, Constance Mabel Jeans, Charlotte Radcliffe, Grace McKenzie) — 5:40.6
3. SWE (Aina Berg, Emy Machnow, Karin Nilsson, Jane Gylling) — 5:43.6

**1924 Paris** T: 6, N: 6, D: 7.18.
1. USA (Gertrude Ederle, Euphrasia Donnelly, Ethel Lackie, Mariechen Wehselau) — 4:58.8 WR
2. GBR (Florence Barker, Grace McKenzie, Irene Vera Tanner, Constance Mabel Jeans) — 5:17.0
3. SWE (Aina Berg, Wivan Pettersson, Gulli Everlund, Hjördis Töpel) — 5:35.6
4. DEN (Vibeke Möller, Hedevig Rasmussen, Karen Maud Rasmussen, Agnete Olsen) — 5:42.4
5. FRA (Ernestine Lebrun, Gilberte Mortier, Bibienne Pellegry, Marguerite Protin) — 5:43.4
6. HOL (Mietje Baron, Alida Bolten, Geertruida Klapwijk, Maria Vierdag) — 5:45.8

**1928 Amsterdam** T: 7, N: 7, D: 8.9.
1. USA (Adelaide Lambert, Eleanor Garatti, Albina Osipowich, Martha Norelius) — 4:47.0 WR
2. GBR (Margaret Joyce Cooper, Sarah Stewart, Irene Vera Tanner, Ellen King) — 5:02.8
3. SAF (Kathleen Russell, Rhoda Rennie, Marie Bedford, Frederica van der Goes) — 5:13.4
4. GER (Charlotte Lehmann, Reni Erkens-Küpper, Hertha Wunder, Irmintraut Schneider) — 5:14.4
5. FRA (Bibienne Pellegry, A. Dupire, Marguerite Ledoux, Claire Horrent) — 5.32.0
DISQ: HOL (E.A.G. Smits, G.C. Baumeister, Maria Vierdag, Maria Braun)

**1932 Los Angeles** T: 5, N: 5, D: 8.12. WR: 4:47.6 (USA—Lambert, Garatti, Osipowich, Norelius)
1. USA (Josephine McKim, Helen Johns, Eleanor Saville [Garatti], Helene Madison) — 4:38.0 WR

2. HOL (Maria Vierdag, Maria Oversloot, Cornelia Laddé, Willemijntje den Ouden) — 4:47.5
3. GBR (Elizabeth Valerie Davies, Helen Varcoe, Margaret Joyce Cooper, Edna Hughes) — 4:52.4
4. CAN (Irene Pirie, Irene Mullen, Ruth Kerr, Betty Edwards) — 5:05.7
5. JPN (Kazue Kojima, Hatsuko Morioka, Misao Yokota, Yukie Arata) — 5:06.7

**1936 Berlin** T: 9, N: 9, D: 8.14. WR: 4:32.8 (HOL—Selbach, Mastenbroek, Wagner, den Ouden)
1. HOL (Johanna Selbach, Catherina Wagner, Willemijntje den Ouden, Hendrika "Rie" Mastenbroek) — 4:36.0 OR
2. GER (Ruth Halbsguth, Leni Lohmar, Ingeborg Schmitz, Gisela Arendt) — 4:36.8
3. USA (Katherine Rawls, Bernice Lapp, Mavis Freeman, Olive McKean) — 4:40.2
4. HUN (Ilona Ács, Ágnes Bíró, Véra Harsányi, Magdolna Lenkei) — 4:48.0
4. CAN (Mary McConkey, Irene Milton-Pirie, Margaret Stone, Phyllis Dewar) — 4:48.0
6. GBR (Margaret Jeffery, Zilpha Grant, Edna Hughes, Olive Wadham) — 4:51.0
7. DEN (Ragnhild Hveger, Bruunstrom, Eva Svendsen, Eva Arendt) — 4:51.4

Germany led for 200 meters before den Ouden gave Holland the lead. The race was still in doubt with 20 meters to go, at which point Mastenbroek sprinted to victory.

**1948 London** T: 11, N: 11, D: 8.6. WR: 4:27.6 (DEN—Arndt, Kraft, Ove-Peterson, Hveger)
1. USA (Marie Corridon, Thelma Kalama, Brenda Helser, Ann Curtis) — 4:29.2 OR
2. DEN (Eva Riise, Karen-Margrete Harup, Greta Andersen, Fritze Carstensen) — 4:29.6
3. HOL (Irma Schumacher, Margot Marsman, Marie-Louise Vaessen, Johanna Termeulen) — 4:31.6
4. GBR (Patricia Nielsen, Margaret Wellington, Lillian Preece, Catherine Gibson) — 4:34.7
5. HUN (Mária Littomeritzky, Judit Temes, Ilona Novák, Éva Székely) — 4:44.8
6. BRA (Eleonora Schmitt, Maria Leão da Costa, Talita de Alencar Rodrigues, Piedade Silva Tavares) — 4:49.1
7. FRA (Josette Arene, Gisele Vallerey, Colette Thomas, Ginette Jany) — 4:49.8
DISQ: SWE (Gisela Thidholm, Elisabeth Ahlgren, Marianne Lundquist, Ingegard Fredin)

Ann Curtis swam a spectacular anchor leg to give the United States a come-from-behind victory over Denmark. She was timed in 1:04.4, which unofficially bettered Willy den Ouden's 12-year-old world record for the 100 meters. However, marks set during relays do not qualify for world records unless they are accomplished on the first leg.

**1952 Helsinki** T: 13, N: 13, D: 8.1. WR: 4:27.2 (HUN—Littomeritzky, Novák, Székely, Szöke)

1. HUN    (Ilona Novák, Judit Temes, Éva Novák    4:24.4    WR
           Katalin Szöke)
2. HOL    (Marie-Louise Linssen [Vaessen], Koosje    4:29.0
           van Voorn, Johanna Termeulen, Irma
           Heijting-Schuhmacher)
3. USA    (Jacqueline La Vine, Marilee Stepan,    4:30.1
           Joan Alderson, Evelyn Kawamoto)
4. DEN    (Rita Larsen, Mette Ove-Peterson, Greta    4:36.2
           Andersen, Ragnhild Andersen-Hveger)
5. GBR    (Phyllis Linton, Jean Botham, Angela    4:37.8
           Barnwell, Lillian Preece)
6. SWE    (Marianne Lundquist, Anita Andersson,    4:39.0
           Maud Berglund, Ingegärd Fredin)
7. GER    (Elisabeth Rechlin, Vera Schäferkordt,    4:40.3
           Kati Jansen, Gisela Jacobs [Arendt])
8. FRA    (Gaby Tanguy, Maryse Morandini,    4:44.1
           Ginette Jany, Josette Arene)

Temes, Novák, and Szöke swam legs of 1:05.8, 1:05.1, and 1:05.7, respectively, each of which was a full second faster than Szöke's time when she won the 100-meter freestyle final four days earlier.

**1956 Melbourne** T: 10, N: 10, D: 12.6 WR: 4:19.7 (AUS—Crapp, Fraser, Leech, Gibson)

1. AUS    (Dawn Fraser, Faith Leech, Sandra Mor-    4:17.1    WR
           gan, Lorraine Crapp)
2. USA    (Sylvia Ruuska, Shelly Mann, Nancy    4:19.2
           Simons, Joan Rosazza)
3. SAF    (Jeanette Myburgh, Susan Roberts, Nata-    4:25.7
           lie Myburgh, Moira Abernathy)
4. GER    Ingrid Künzel, Hertha Hasse, Käthi    4:26.1
           Jansen, Birgit Klomp)
5. CAN    (Helen Stewart, Gladys Priestley, Sara    4:28.3
           Barber, Virginia Grant)
6. SWE    (Anita Hellström, Birgitta Wängberg,    4:30.0
           Anna Larsson, Kate Jobson)
7. HUN    (Maria Littomeritzky, Katalin Szöke, Judit    4:31.1
           Temes, Valéria Gyenge)
8. GBR    (Frances Hogben, Judith Grinham, Mar-    4:35.8
           garet Girvan, Fearne Ewart)

Lorraine's Crapp's anchor leg of 1:03.1 sealed the victory.

**1960 Rome** T: 12, N: 12, D: 9.3. WR (440 yards): 4:16.2 (AUS—Fraser, Colquhoun, Konrads, Crapp)

1. USA    (Joan Spillane, Shirley Stobs, Carolyn    4:08.9    WR
           Wood, S. Christine Von Saltza)
2. AUS    (Dawn Fraser, Ilsa Konrads, Lorraine    4:11.3
           Crapp, Alva Colquhoun)
3. GDR/   (Christel Steffin, Heidi Pechstein, Gisela    4:19.7
   GER    Weiss, Ursula Brunner)
4. HUN    (Anna Temesvári, Mária Frank, Kátalin    4:21.2
           Boros, Csilla Dobai-Madarász)
5. GBR    (Natalie Steward, Beryl Noakes, Judy    4:24.6
           Samuel, Christine Harris)

6. SWE    (Inger Thorngren, Karin Larsson, Kristina    4:25.1
           Larsson, Birte Segerström)
7. ITA    (Paola Saini, Annamaria Cecchi, Ro-    4:26.8
           sanna Contardo, Maria Christina Pacifici)
8. SOV    (Irina Liakhovskaia, Ulvi Voog, Galina    4:29.0
           Sosnova, Marina Shamal)

In 1956 Lorraine Crapp had been one of Australia's heroines, winning two gold medals and one silver. But in 1960 she had other things on her mind. The night before the Australian team left for Rome she had secretly married Bill Thurlow, one of the doctors associated with the Australian swimmers. Thurlow traveled to Rome on his own and rented an apartment. After the lights were put out at the Olympic Village, Crapp would sneak out and spend the night with her husband. When Australian officials became suspicious of her early morning absences, Crapp admitted her deception. Unfortunately, the officials overreacted. Instead of simply giving her permission to sleep outside the Village as many other married athletes did, they punished her by restricting her movements and keeping watch on her. Demoralized, Crapp swam a lackluster third leg in the freestyle relay, losing a crucial five yards and 2.7 seconds to Carolyn Wood.

**1964 Tokyo** T: 10, N: 10, D: 10.15. WR: 4:07.6 (USA—Allsup, Stickles, Seidel, Bricker)

1. USA    (Sharon Stouder, Donna De    4:03.8    WR
           Varona, Lillian "Pokey" Watson,
           Kathleen Ellis)
2. AUS    (Robyn Thorn, Janice Murphy,    4:06.9
           Lynette Bell, Dawn Fraser)
3. HOL    (Paulina van der Wildt, Catharina    4:12.0
           Beumer, Wilhelmina van Weer-
           denburg, Erica Terpstra)
4. HUN    (Judit Turóczy, Éva Erdélyi,    4:12.1
           Katalin Takács, Csilla Dobai-
           Madarász)
5. SWE    (Ann-Charlott Lilja, Katrin Anders-    4:14.0
           son, Ulla Jäfvert, Ann-Christine
           Hagberg)
6. GDR/GER    (Martina Grunert, Traudi Beierlein,    4:15.0
           Rita Schumacher, Heidi Pech-
           stein)
7. CAN    (Mary Stewart, Patricia Thomp-    4:15.9
           son, Helen Kennedy, Marion Lay)
8. ITA    (Paola Saini, Maria Christina Pa-    4:17.2
           cifici, Mara Sacchi, Daniela
           Beneck)

**1968 Mexico City** T: 15, N: 15, D: 10.26. WR: 4:01.1 (USA, Santa Clara Swim Club—Gustavson, Watson, Carpinelli, Henne)

1. USA    (Jane Barkman, Linda Gustavson, Susan    4:02.5    OR
           Pedersen, Jan Henne)
2. GDR    (Gabriele Wetzko, Roswitha Krause, Uta    4:05.7
           Schmuck, Martina Grunert)
3. CAN    (Angela Coughlan, Marilyn Corson,    4:07.2
           Elaine Tanner, Marion Lay)
4. AUS    (Janet Steinbeck, Susan Eddy, Lynette    4:08.7
           Watson, Lynette Bell)

5. HUN (Edit Kovács, Magdolna Patoh, Andréa 4:11.0
Gyarmati, Judit Turóczy)

6. JPN (Shigeko Kawanishi, Yoshimi Nishigawa, 4:13.6
Yasuko Fujii, Miwako Kobayashi)

7. GBR (Shelagh Ratcliffe, Fiona Kellock, Susan 4:18.0
Williams, Alexandra Jackson)

DISQ: FRA (Marie Kersaudy, Simone Hanner, Daniele Dorleans,
Claude Mandonnaud)

**1972 Munich** T: 16, N: 16, D: 8.30. WR: 3:58.11 (USA—Peyton,
Neilson, Barkman, Babashoff)

1. USA (Sandra Neilson, Jennifer Kemp, Jane 3:55.19 WR
Barkman, Shirley Babashoff)

2. GDR (Gabriele Wetzko, Andrea Eife, Elke 3:55.55
Sehmisch, Kornelia Ender)

3. GER (Jutta Weber, Heidemarie Reineck, Gu- 3:57.93
drun Beckmann, Angela Steinbach)

4. HUN (Andréa Gyarmati, Judit Turóczy, Edit 4:00.39
Kovács, Magdolna Patoh)

5. HOL (Enith Brigitha, Anke Rijnders, Hansje 4.01.49
Bunschoten, Josien Elzerman)

6. SWE (Anita Zarnowiecki, Eva Andersson, 4:02.69
Diana Olsson, Irwi Johansson)

7. CAN (Wendy Cook, Judy Wright, Mary-Beth 4:03.83
Rondeau, Leslie Cliff)

8. AUS (Deborah Palmer, Leanne Francis, 4:04.82
Sharon Booth, Shane Gould)

Until August 18, 1972, no women's relay team had broken
the four-minute barrier. On that day Neilson, Barkman,
Babashoff, and Kim Peyton of the United States recorded a
time of 3:58.11. Twelve days later, in the qualifying heats of
the Olympics, the East Germans tied that mark. That evening, in the final, the record took another battering. Sandy
Neilson took a quarter-second lead over Gabriele Wetzko, and the remaining American swimmers held on with
great determination, withstanding a continuous challenge
from the East Germans that lasted until the final touch.

**1976 Montreal** T: 14, N: 14, D: 7.25. WR: 3:48.80 (GDR, Sports
Club Dynamo—Krause, Seltman, Gabriel, Pollack)

1. USA (Kim Peyton, Wendy Boglioli, Jill 3:44.82 WR
Sterkel, Shirley Babashoff)

2. GDR (Kornelia Ender, Petra Priemer, Andrea 3:45.50
Pollack, Claudia Hempel)

3. CAN (Gail Amundrud, Barbara Clark, Becky 3:48.81
Smith, Anne Jardin)

4. HOL (Ineke Ran, Linda Faber, Annelies 3:51.67
Maas, Enith Brigitha)

5. SOV (Lyubov Kobzova, Irina Vlasova, Ma- 3:52.69
rina Kliuchnikova, Larissa Tsareva)

6. FRA (Guylaine Berger, Sylvie Le Noach, 3:56.73
Caroline Carpentier, Chantal Schertz)

7. SWE (Pia Martensson, Ylva Persson, Diana 3:57.25
Olsson, Ida Hansson)

8. GER (Jutta Weber, Marion Platten, Regina 3:58.33
Nissen, Beate Jasch)

The freestyle relay was the last women's swimming event
of the Montreal Olympics. In the first 12 events, the East

Germans had won 11 gold medals, the Soviet Union had
won one, and the United States had won none. With 100-
meter gold medalist Kornelia Ender swimming the first
leg, East Germany took a 1.16-second lead. East Germany's second swimmer was 100-meter silver medalist Petra Priemer. But Wendy Boglioli swam a 55.81 leg to draw
the United States 0.35 seconds closer. Jill Sterkel followed
with a blistering 55.78, passing Andrea Pollack and giving
the United States a lead of 0.40 seconds. Shirley Babashoff's 56.28 assured the United States of a gold medal at
last. Babashoff finished her Olympic career with two gold
medals, both in the freestyle relay, and six silver medals.

**1980 Moscow** T: 9, N: 9, D: 7.27. WR: 3:43.43 (USA—Caulkins,
Elkins, Sterkel, Woodhead)

1. GDR (Barbara Krause, Caren Metschuck Ines 3:42.71 WR
Diers, Sarina Hülsenbeck)

2. SWE (Carina Ljungdahl, Tina Gustafsson, Agneta 3:48.93
Mårtensson, Agneta Friksson)

3. HOL (Cornelia van Bentum, Wilma van Velsen, 3:49.51
Reggie de Jong, Annelies Maas)

4. GBR (Sharron Davies, Kaye Lovatt, Jacquelene 3:51.71
Willmott, June Croft)

5. AUS (Lisa Curry, Karen van de Graaf, Rosemary 3:54.16
Brown, Michelle Pearson)

6. MEX (Isabel Reuss, Dagmar Erdman, Teresa 3:55.41
Rivera, Helen Plaschinski)

7. BUL (Dobrinka Mincheva, Roumiana Nikolova, Ani 3:56.34
Kostova, Sonya Dingalakova)

8. SPA (Natalia Mas, Margarita Armengol, Laura 3:58.73
Flaque, Gloria Casado)

Although there were only nine teams, two qualifying
heats were held to determine which eight teams would
advance to the final. In the second heat the Soviet Union
was disqualified for an improper changeover, which
made it much easier to decide who the finalists would be.
The East Germans won easily. If the United States had
entered a team they probably would have finished second, based on times from the same period.

**1984 Los Angeles** T: 12, N: 12, D: 7.31. WR: 3:42.71 (GDR—
Krause, Metschuck, Diers, Hülsenbeck)

1. USA (Jenna Johnson, Carrie Steinseifer, Dara 3:43.43
Torres, Nancy Hogshead)

2. HOL (Annemarie Verstappen, Elles Voskes, Desi 3:44.40
Reijers, Cornelia van Bentum)

3. GER (Iris Zscherpe, Susanne Schuster, Christiane 3:45.56
Pielke, Karin Seick)

4. AUS (Michele Pearson, Angela Russel, Anna 3:47.79
McVann, Lisa Curry)

5. CAN (Pamela Rai, Carol Klimpel, Cheryl McArton, 3:49.50
Jane Kerr)

6. GBR (June Croft, Nicola Fibbens, Debra Gore, 3:50.12
Annabelle Cripps)

7. SWE (Maria Kardum, Agneta Eriksson, Petra Hilder, 3:51.24
Karin Furuhed)

8. FRA (Caroline Amoric, Sophie Kamoun, Veronique 3:52.15
Jardin, Laurence Bensimon)

Three weeks after the Olympics final, the East German Friendship Games team of Kristin Otto, Karen König, Heike Friedrich and Birgit Meineke set a world record of 3:42.41. The Soviet team was second in 3:44.31.

**1988 Seoul** T: 15, N: 15, D: 9.22. WR: 3:40.57 (GDR—Otto, Stellmach, Schulze, Friedrich)
1. GDR (Kristin Otto, Katrin Meissner, Daniela Hunger, Manuela Stellmach) 3:40.63 OR
2. HOL (Marianne Muis, Mildred Muis, Cornelia van Bentum, Karin Brienesse) 3:43.39
3. USA (Mary Wayte, Mitzi Kremer, Laura Walker, Dara Torres) 3:44.25
4. CHN (Xia Fujie, Yang Wenyi, Lou Yaping, Zhuang Yong) 3:44.69
5. SOV (Yelena Dendeberova, Svetlana Issakova, Natalya Trefilova, Svetlana Kopchikova) 3:44.99
6. CAN (Kathy Bald, Patricia Noall, Andrea Nugent, Jane Kerr) 3:46.75
7. GER (Stephanie Ortwig, Marion Aizpors, Christiane Pielke, Karin Seick) 3:46.90
8. DEN (Gitta Jensen, Pia Sorensen, Mette Jacobsen, Annette Moldrup Jorgensen) 3:49.25

# 4 × 100-METER MEDLEY RELAY

In medley relays the order of strokes is backstroke, breaststroke, butterfly, and freestyle.

**1896–1956** not held

**1960 Rome** T: 13, N: 13, D: 9.2. WR: 4:44.6 (USA—Cone, Bancroft, Collins, Von Saltza)
1. USA (Lynn Burke, Patty Kempner, Carolyn Schuler, S. Christine Von Saltza) 4:41.1 WR
2. AUS (Marilyn Wilson, Rosemary Lassig, Janice Andrew, Dawn Fraser) 4:45.9
3. GDR/GER (Ingrid Schmidt, Ursula Küper, Bärbel Fuhrmann, Ursel Brunner) 4:47.6
4. HOL (Maria van Velsen, Adelaide den Haan, Marianne Heemskerk, Erica Terpstra) 4:47.6
5. GBR (Sylvia Lewis, Anita Lonsbrough, Sheila Watt, Natalie Steward) 4:47.6
6. HUN (Magdolna Dávid, Klara Bartos-Killermann, Márta Egerváry, Csilla Dobai-Madarász) 4:53.7
7. JPN (Satoko Tanaka, Yoshiko Takamatsu, Shizue Miyabe, Yoshiko Sato) 4:56.4
8. SOV (Larissa Viktorova, Lyudmila Korobova, Zinaida Belovskaya, Marina Shamal) 4:58.1

U.S. leadoff swimmer Lynn Burke finished her leg in 1:09.0 to break the 100-meter backstroke world record for the fourth time in seven weeks. The race was no contest after that, with the United States winning by seven meters. Burke and Von Saltza were best friends who trained together and lived together in the home of Von Saltza's parents in Saratoga, California. They were both coached by George Haines. They dieted together, cut their hair the same way, and, in Rome, they won gold medals together. Von Saltza went home with three and Burke with two.

**1964 Tokyo** T: 9, N: 9, D: 10.18. WR: 4:34.6 (USA—Ferguson, Goyette, Ellis, Randall)
1. USA (Cathy Ferguson, Cynthia Goyette, Sharon Stouder, Kathleen Ellis) 4:33.9 WR
2. HOL (Kornelia Winkel, Klena Bimolt, Ada Kok, Erica Terpstra) 4:37.0
3. SOV (Tatyana Savelyeva, Svetlana Babanina, Tatyana Devyatova, Natalya Ustinova) 4:39.2
4. JPN (Satoko Tanaka, Noriko Yamamoto, Eiko Takahashi, Michiko Kihara) 4:42.0
5. GBR (Jill Norfolk, Stella Mitchell, Mary Anne Cotterill, Elizabeth Long) 4:45.8
6. CAN (Eileen Weir, Marion Lay, Mary Stewart, Helen Kennedy) 4:49.9
DISQ: GDR/GER (Ingrid Schmidt, Bärbel Grimmer, Heike Hustede, Martina Grunert), HUN (Mária Balla, Zsuzsa Kovacs, Márta Egerváry, Csilla Dobai-Madarász)

Cathy Ferguson gave the United States the lead after the first leg, but Svetlana Babanina, swimming two seconds faster than the official world record, touched first at 200 meters. Sharon Stouder then pulled away by a commanding margin, which Kathy Ellis added to. Stouder finished the Olympics with three gold medals and one silver, Ellis with two gold and two bronze.

**1968 Mexico** T: 16, N: 16, D: 10.17. WR: 4:28.1 (USA—Hall, Ball, Daniel, Pedersen)
1. USA (Kaye Hall, Catie Ball, Ellie Daniel, Susan Pedersen) 4:28.3 OR
2. AUS (Lynette Watson, Lynette McClements, Judy Playfair, Janet Steinbeck) 4:30.0
3. GER (Angelika Kraus, Uta Frommater, Heike Hustede, Heidemarie Reineck) 4:36.4
4. SOV (Tinatin Lekveishvili, Alla Grebennikova, Tatyana Devyatova, Lidia Grebets) 4:37.0
5. GDR (Martina Grunert, Eva Wittke, Helga Lindner, Uta Schmuck) 4:38.0
6. GBR (Wendy Burrell, Dorothy Harrison, Margaret Auton, Alexandra Jackson) 4:38.3
7. HOL (Jacobje Buter, Klena Bimolt, Ada Kok, Petronella Bos) 4:38.7
8. HUN (Mária Lantos, Edit Kovács, Andréa Gyarmati, Judit Turóczy) 4:42.9

The United States led Australia by 0.7 seconds at 100 meters, 0.3 at 200, and 0.5 at 300 before Susan Pedersen pulled away from Janet Steinbeck for the victory.

**1972 Munich** T: 16, N: 16, D: 8.30. WR: 4:25.34 (USA—Atwood, Vidali, Daniel, Barkman).

| | | | |
|---|---|---|---|
| 1. | USA | (Melissa Belote, Catherine Carr, Deena Deardurff, Sandra Neilson) | 4:20.75 WR |
| 2. | GDR | (Christine Herbst, Renate Vogel, Roswitha Beier, Kornelia Ender) | 4:24.91 |
| 3. | GER | (Silke Pielen, Verena Eberle, Gudrun Beckmann, Heidemarie Reineck) | 4:26.46 |
| 4. | SOV | (Tinatin Lekveishvili, Galina Stepanova [Prozumenshikova], Irina Ustimenko, Tatyana Zolotnickaia) | 4:27.81 |
| 5. | HOL | (Enith Brigitha, Alie te Riet, Anke Rijnders, Hansje Bunschoten) | 4:29.99 |
| 6. | JPN | (Suzuko Matsumura, Yoko Yamamoto, Mayumi Aoki, Yoshimi Nishigawa) | 4:31.56 |
| 7. | CAN | (Wendy Cook, Sylvia Dockerill, Marylin Corson, Leslie Cliff) | 4:31.56 |
| 8. | SWE | (Diana Olsson, Britt-Marie Smedh, Eva Wikner, Anita Zarnowiecki) | 4:32.61 |

**1976 Montreal** T: 17, N: 17, D: 7.18. WR: 4:13.41 (GDR, Sports Club Dynamo—Seltman Nitschke, Pollack, Krause).

| | | | |
|---|---|---|---|
| 1. | GDR | (Ulrike Richter, Hannelore Anke, Andrea Pollack, Kornelia Ender) | 4.07.95 WR |
| 2. | USA | (Linda Jezek, Lauri Siering, Camille Wright, Shirley Babashoff) | 4:14.55 |
| 3. | CAN | (Wendy Hogg, Robin Corsiglia, Susan Sloan, Anne Jardin) | 4:15.22 |
| 4. | SOV | (Nadezhda Stavko, Marina Iurchenia, Tamara Shelofastova, Larissa Tsareva) | 4:16.05 |
| 5. | HOL | (Diane Edelijn, Wijda Mazereeuw, Jose Damen, Enith Brigitha) | 4:19.03 |
| 6. | GBR | (Joy Beasley, Margaret Kelly, Susan Jenner, Deborah Hill) | 4:23.25 |
| 7. | JPN | (Yoshimi Nishigawa, Toshiko Haruoka, Yasue Hatsuda, Sachiko Yamazaki) | 4:23.47 |
| 8. | AUS | (Michelle Devries, Judith Hudson, Linda Hanel, Jenny Tate) | 4:25.91 |

The first women's swimming event to be decided in 1976, the medley relay was won with an awesome display by the East German swimmers. Richter, Anke, Pollack, and Ender each recorded the fastest time for her leg.

**1980 Moscow** T: 10, N: 10, D: 7.20. WR: 4:07.95 (GDR—Richter, Anke, Pollack, Ender).

| | | | |
|---|---|---|---|
| 1. | GDR | (Rica Reinisch, Ute Geweniger, Andrea Pollack, Caren Metschuck) | 4:06.67 WR |
| 2. | GBR | (Helen Jameson, Margaret Kelly, Ann Osgerby, June Croft) | 4:12.24 |
| 3. | SOV | (Yelena Kruglova, Elvira Vasilkova, Alla Grishchenkova, Natalya Strunnikova) | 4:13.61 |
| 4. | SWE | (Annika Uvehall, Eva-Marie Håkansson, Agneta Mårtensson, Tina Gustafson) | 4:16.91 |
| 5. | ITA | (Laura Foralosso, Sabrina Seminatore, Cinzia Savi-Scarponi, Monica Vallarin) | 4:19.05 |
| 6. | AUS | (Lisa Forrest, Lisa Curry, Karen Van De Graaf, Rosemary Brown) | 4:19.90 |

| | | | |
|---|---|---|---|
| 7. | ROM | (Carmen Bunaciu, Brigitte Press, Mariana Parachiv, Irinel Panulescu) | 4:21.27 |
| 8. | BUL | (Sonya Dangalakova, Tania Bogomilova, Ani Moneva, Dobrinka Mincheva) | 4:22.38 |

Rica Reinisch opened with a world-record-equaling backstroke leg and Ute Geweniger followed with 100 meters of breaststroking that bettered the official world record. Pollack and Metschuck recorded the fastest times of their respective legs, and the East Germans were on their way again.

**1984 Los Angeles** T: 13, N: 13, D: 8.3. WR: 4:05.79 (GDR—Kleber, Geweniger, Geissler, Meineke).

| | | | |
|---|---|---|---|
| 1. | USA | (Theresa Andrews, Tracy Caulkins, Mary T. Meagher, Nancy Hogshead) | 4:08.34 |
| 2. | GER | (Svenja Schlicht, Ute Hasse, Ina Beyermann, Karin Seick) | 4:11.97 |
| 3. | CAN | (Reema Abdo, Anne Ottenbrite, Michelle MacPherson, Pamela Rai) | 4:12.98 |
| 4 | GBR | (Beverley Rose, Jean Hill, Nicola Fibbens, June Croft) | 4:14.05 |
| 5. | ITA | (Manuela Carosi, Manuela Dalla Valle, Roberta Lanzarotti, Silvia Persi) | 4:17.40 |
| 6. | SWI | (Eva Gysling, Patricia Brülhart, Carole Brook, Marie-Thérèse Armentero) | 4:19.02 |

DISQ: JPN (Naomi Sekido, Hiroko Nagasaki, Naoko Kume, Kaori Yanase)

DISQ: SWE (Anna-Karin Eriksson, Eva-Marie Håkansson, Agneta Eriksson, Maria Kardum)

U.S. team members Caulkins, Meagher and Hogshead each won three gold medals in Los Angeles. Their main competition in the medley relay had been expected to come from the Dutch team, which was disqualified for jumping too soon during an exchange in the preliminary round. Three weeks after the Olympic final, the East German Friendship Games team of Ina Kleber, Sylvia Gerasch, Ines Geissler and Birgit Meineke set a world record of 4:03.69. The Soviets were second in 4:08.13.

**1988 Seoul** T: 18, N: 18, D: 9.24. WR: 4:03.69 (GDR—Kleber, Gerasch, Geissler, Meineke).

| | | | |
|---|---|---|---|
| 1. | GDR | (Kristin Otto, Silke Hörner, Birte Weigang, Katrin Meissner) | 4:03.74 OR |
| 2. | USA | (Beth Barr, Tracey McFarlane, Janel Jorgensen, Mary Wayte) | 4:07.90 |
| 3. | CAN | (Lori Melien, Allison Higson, Jane Kerr, Andrea Nugent) | 4:10.49 |
| 4. | AUS | (Nicole Livingstone, Lara Hooiveld, Fiona Alessandri, Karen Van Wirdum) | 4:11.57 |
| 5. | HOL | (Jolanda de Rover, Linda Moes, Cornelia van Bentum, Karin Brienesse) | 4:12.19 |
| 6. | BUL | (Bistra Gospodinova, Tania Dangalakova [Bogomilova], Neviana Miteva, Natacha Hristova) | 4:12.36 |
| 7. | GER | (Svenja Schlicht, Britta Dahm, Gabi Rehaa, Marion Aizpors) | 4:12.89 |
| 8. | ITA | (Lorenza Vigarani, Manuela Dalla Valle, Ilaria Tocchini, Silvia Persi) | 4:13.85 |

# SYNCHRONIZED SWIMMING: SOLO

Current rules permit each nation three entrants, but only one swimmer per nation is allowed to advance to the final.

**1896–1980** not held

**1984 Los Angeles** C: 17, N: 17, D: 8.12.
1. Tracie Ruiz          USA   198.467
2. Carolyn Waldo        CAN   195.300
3. Miwako Motoyoshi     JPN   187.050
4. Marijke Engelen      HOL   182.632
5. Gudrun Hänisch       GER   182.017
6. Caroline Holmyard    GBR   182.000
7. Muriel Hermine       FRA   180.534
8. Karin Singer         SWI   178.383

This event, which was added to the Olympic program only two months before the Games began, was won by 21-year-old world champion Tracie Ruiz of Bothell, Washington, whose father was Hawaiian and mother a Norwegian-German mixture. Her Latin surname came from her stepfather.

**1988 Seoul** C: 46, N: 18, D: 9.30.
1. Carolyn Waldo        CAN   200.150
2. Tracie Ruiz-Conforto USA   197.633
3. Mikako Kotani        JPN   191.850
4. Muriel Hermine       FRA   190.100
5. Karin Singer         SWI   185.600
6. Nicola Shearn        GBR   181.933
7. Khristina Falasinidi SOV   180.650
8. Gerlind Scheller     GER   175.983

Carolyn Waldo of Beaconville, Quebec, used the compulsory figures to build an insurmountable lead over Ruiz-Conforto, who had defeated Waldo in a pre-Olympic competition in Seoul in June.

# SYNCHRONIZED SWIMMING: DUET

**1896–1980** not held

**1984 Los Angeles** T: 18, N: 18, D: 8.9.
1. Candy Costie, Tracie Ruiz              USA   195.584
2. Sharon Hambrook, Kelly Kryczka         CAN   194.234
3. Saeko Simura, Miwako Motoyoshi         JPN   187.992
4. Caroline Holmyard, Carolyn Wilson      GBR   184.050
5. Edith Boss, Karin Singer               SWI   180.109
6. Catrien Eijken, Marijke Engelen        HOL   179.058
7. Pascale Besson, Muriel Hermine         FRA   176.709
8. Claudia Novelo, Pilar Ramirez          MEX   176.409

**1988 Seoul** T: 15, N: 15, D: 10.1.
1. Michelle Cameron, Carolyn Waldo        CAN   197.317
2. Sarah Josephson, Karen Josephson       USA   197.284
3. Miyako Tanaka, Mikako Kotani           JPN   190.159
4. Karine Schuler, Anne Capron            FRA   184.792

5. Edith Boss, Karin Singer               SWI   183.950
6. Maria Cherniaeva, Tatyana Titova       SOV   182.667
7. Nicola Shearn, Lian Goodwin            GBR   179.075
8. Lourdes Candini, Sonia Cardenas        MEX   176.833

Cameron and Waldo achieved a narrow victory, thanks to a superb performance in the compulsory figures and patriotic judging on the part of Canadian judge Joyce Corner. During the freestyle routine, Corner was the only one of seven judges to give Cameron and Waldo a higher mark than the Josephson twins. Had she not done so, their final placings would have been reversed.

# SPRINGBOARD DIVING

This event is performed from a springboard three meters above the water. In women's competition each finalist makes five compulsory dives and five voluntary dives chosen from approved groups. Each type of dive is assigned a certain degree of difficulty, such as 1.8 or 2.5. Each judge's score is multiplied by the degree of difficulty to determine a total score.

**1896–1912** not held

**1920 Antwerp** C; 4, N: 1, D: 8.29.

|   |   |   | PTS. | ORDINALS |
|---|---|---|---|---|
| 1. | Aileen Riggin | USA | 539.9 | 9 |
| 2. | Helen Wainwright | USA | 534.8 | 9 |
| 3. | Thelma Payne | USA | 534.1 | 12 |
| 4. | Aileen Allen | USA | 489.9 | 20 |

Tiny Aileen Riggin of Newport, Rhode Island, was only 14 years old when she won her Olympic gold medal. At 4 feet 7 inches and 65 pounds, she was the smallest athlete at the 1920 Olympics. In 1922 she was the subject of the first underwater and slow-motion swimming films. She returned to the Olympics in 1924 and won a silver medal for springboard diving and a bronze in the 100-meter backstroke. Later she turned professional, played the part of a slave dancer in the 1933 film *Roman Scandals,* and starred in Billy Rose's first Aquacade. She also became one of America's first women sportswriters and, at the age of 82, she set nine national age-group swim records.

**1924 Paris** C: 17, N: 7, D: 7.18.

|   |   |   | PTS. | ORDINALS |
|---|---|---|---|---|
| 1. | Elizabeth Becker | USA | 474.5 | 8 |
| 2. | Aileen Riggin | USA | 460.4 | 12 |
| 3. | Caroline Fletcher | USA | 436.4 | 16 |
| 4. | Eva Ollivier | SWE | 412.6 | 20 |
| 5. | Signe Johanson | SWE | 412.6 | 21 |
| 6. | Klara Bornett | AUT | 370.2 | 28 |

**1928 Amsterdam** C: 10, N; 4, D: 8.9.

|   |   |   | PTS. | ORDINALS |
|---|---|---|---|---|
| 1. | Helen Meany | USA | 78.62 | 6 |
| 2. | Dorothy Poynton | USA | 75.62 | 13 |

3. Georgia Coleman     USA   73.38   14
4. Ilse Meudtner       GER   67.42   22
5. Margret Borgs       GER   65.16   26
6. Lini Söhnchen       GER   63.28   34
7. G. Klapwijk         HOL   60.98   35
8. A.I.M. van Leeuwen  HOL   59.82   35

**1932 Los Angeles** C: 8, N: 6, D: 8.10.

|   |   |   | PTS. |
|---|---|---|---|
| 1. | Georgia Coleman | USA | 87.52 |
| 2. | Katherine Rawls | USA | 82.56 |
| 3. | Jane Fauntz | USA | 82.12 |
| 4. | Olga Jordan | GER | 77.60 |
| 5. | Doris Ogilvie | CAN | 77.00 |
| 6. | Magdalene Epply | AUT | 63.70 |
| 7. | Etsuo Kamakura | JPN | 60.78 |
| 8 | Ingrid Larsen | DEN | 57.26 |

Georgia Coleman, the first woman to do a two and a half forward somersault, completed her Olympic career with four medals: one gold, two silver, and one bronze. She died in 1941 at the age of 29. In 1932 the system of ordinals (place-figures) was dropped and total points became the determining factor in deciding places.

**1936 Berlin** C: 16, N: 9, D: 8.12.

|   |   |   | PTS |
|---|---|---|---|
| 1. | Marjorie Gestring | USA | 89.27 |
| 2. | Katherine Rawls | USA | 88.35 |
| 3. | Dorothy Poynton Hill | USA | 82.36 |
| 4. | Gerda Daumerlang | GER | 78.27 |
| 5. | Olga Jentsch-Jordan | GER | 77.98 |
| 6. | Masayo Osawa | JPN | 73.94 |
| 7. | Suse Heinze | GER | 71.49 |
| 8. | Fusako Kono | JPN | 70.27 |

Gold medalist Marjorie Gestring of Los Angeles was only 13 years and 9 months old. She remains the youngest person in Olympic history to win an individual gold medal in any sport. Katy Rawls repeated her silver medal and, two days later, added a bronze medal as a member of the U.S. freestyle relay team.

**1948 London** C: 16, N: 8, D: 8.3.

|   |   |   | PTS. |
|---|---|---|---|
| 1. | Victoria Draves | USA | 108.74 |
| 2. | Zoe Ann Olsen | USA | 108.23 |
| 3. | Patricia Elsener | USA | 101.30 |
| 4. | Nicole Pellissard | FRA | 100.38 |
| 5. | Gudrun Grömer | AUT | 93.30 |
| 6. | Edna Child | GBR | 91.63 |
| 7. | Madeleine Moreau | FRA | 89.43 |
| 8. | J. Heck | HOL | 87.61 |

Vicki Draves had a Filipino father and an English mother, but she was born and raised in San Francisco. She did not begin diving until she was 16 years old. Silver medalist Zoe Ann Olsen married baseball star Jackie Jensen before the next Olympics.

**1952 Helsinki** C: 15, N: 7, D: 7.30.

|   |   |   | PTS. |
|---|---|---|---|
| 1. | Patricia McCormick | USA | 147.30 |
| 2. | Madeleine Moreau | FRA | 139.34 |
| 3. | Zoe Ann Jensen-Olsen | USA | 127.57 |
| 4. | Ninel Krutova | SOV | 116.86 |
| 5. | Charmian Welsh | GBR | 116.38 |
| 6. | Lyubov Shigalova | SOV | 113.83 |
| 7. | Nicole Pellissard | FRA | 111.98 |
| 8. | Phyllis Long | GBR | 108.82 |

Pat McCormick of Long Beach, California, won the first of her four gold medals. Mady Moreau became the first non-American woman to win a springboard medal after six straight U.S. sweeps.

**1956 Melbourne** C: 17, N: 8, D: 12.4.

|   |   |   | PTS. |
|---|---|---|---|
| 1. | Patricia McCormick | USA | 142.36 |
| 2. | Jeanne Stunyo | USA | 125.89 |
| 3. | Irene MacDonald | CAN | 121.40 |
| 4. | Barbara Gilders | USA | 120.76 |
| 5. | Valentina Chumicheva | SOV | 118.50 |
| 6. | Phyllis Long | GBR | 107.61 |
| 7. | Nicole Darrigrand (Pellissard) | FRA | 106.32 |
| 8. | Kanoko Tsutani | JPN | 103.12 |

Eight months before the Melbourne Olympics, Pat McCormick gave birth to a baby boy. She had continued training throughout her pregnancy and swam a half-mile a day up until two days before childbirth. In 1956 she repeated her double gold medal performance of 1952.

**1960 Rome** C; 16, N: 10, D: 8.27.

|   |   |   | PTS. |
|---|---|---|---|
| 1. | Ingrid Krämer | GDR | 155.81 |
| 2. | Paula Jean Pope (Myers) | USA | 141.24 |
| 3. | Elizabeth Ferris | GBR | 139.09 |
| 4. | Mary "Patsy" Willard | USA | 137.82 |
| 5. | Ninel Krutova | SOV | 136.11 |
| 6. | Irene MacDonald | CAN | 134.69 |
| 7. | Phyllis Long | GBR | 129.63 |
| 8. | Dorothea DuPon | HOL | 123.35 |

The U.S. string of eight consecutive springboard victories was finally broken by 17-year-old Ingrid Krämer of Dresden. The Rome Games were the fourth straight Olympics at which both diving events were won by the same woman.

**1964 Tokyo** C: 21, N: 9, D: 10.12.

|   |   |   | PTS. |
|---|---|---|---|
| 1. | Ingrid Engel-Krämer | GDR | 145.00 |
| 2. | Jeanne Collier | USA | 138.36 |
| 3. | Mary "Patsy" Willard | USA | 138.18 |
| 4. | Sue Gossick | USA | 129.70 |
| 5. | Tamara Fyedosova | SOV | 126.33 |
| 6. | Yelena Anokhina | SOV | 125.60 |
| 7. | Kanoko Mabuchi | JPN | 125.28 |
| 8. | Angelika Hilbert | GER | 123.27 |

Ingrid Engel-Krämer took over the lead from Patsy Willard on her seventh dive and went on to win her third gold medal.

**1968 Mexico City** C: 22, N: 15, D: 10.18

| | | PTS. |
|---|---|---|
| 1. Sue Gossick | USA | 150.77 |
| 2. Tamara Pogoscheva (Fyedosova) | SOV | 145.30 |
| 3. Keala O'Sullivan | USA | 145.23 |
| 4. Maxine "Micki" King | USA | 137.38 |
| 5. Ingrid Gulbin (Engel-Krämer) | GDR | 135.82 |
| 6. Vyera Baklanova | SOV | 132.31 |
| 7. Beverly Boys | CAN | 130.31 |
| 8. Elena Anokhina | SOV | 129.17 |

Twenty-year-old Sue Gossick of Tarzana, California, didn't move into the lead until the ninth round. Pogoscheva, leading after seven dives, missed her eighth dive badly, but earned the highest score of the competition with her final attempt, to jump back from fourth place to second. In fifth place was the one and only Ingrid Krämer, competing in her third Olympics, each under a different name.

**1972 Munich** C: 30, N: 18, D: 8.28

| | | PTS. |
|---|---|---|
| 1. Maxine "Micki" King | USA | 450.03 |
| 2. Ulrika Knape | SWE | 434.19 |
| 3. Marina Janicke | GDR | 430.92 |
| 4. Janet Ely | USA | 420.99 |
| 5. Beverly Boys | CAN | 418.89 |
| 6. Agneta Henriksson | SWE | 417.48 |
| 7. Cynthia Potter | USA | 413.58 |
| 8. Elzbieta Wierniuk | POL | 408.36 |

In Mexico City Micki King of Pontiac, Michigan, had been in first place after eight dives. But during her ninth dive, a reverse one and a half layout, she hit the board and broke her left forearm. She completed her final dive, but dropped to fourth place. Four years later in Munich, King, now a 28-year-old air force captain, took the lead from Ulrika Knape with her eighth dive and this time steered clear of the diving board to win the gold medal. Her final dive, a reverse one and a half somersault with one and a half twists, was the same dive she had attempted four years earlier with a broken arm. After her victory she had to submit to a drug test. However it took King two hours to produce a urine sample. By that time everyone but the doctors had gone home, so she returned alone to the Olympic Village and had a chocolate drink. Three Australian weightlifters told her "a gold medalist shouldn't be drinking chocolate" and shared with her a bottle of wine.

**1976 Montreal** C: 27, N: 15, D: 7.20.

| | | PTS. |
|---|---|---|
| 1. Jennifer Chandler | USA | 506.19 |
| 2. Christa Köhler | GDR | 469.41 |
| 3. Cynthia Potter | USA | 466.83 |

| 4. Heidi Ramlow | GDR | 462.15 |
|---|---|---|
| 5. Karin Guthke | GDR | 459.81 |
| 6. Olga Dmitrieva | SOV | 432.24 |
| 7. Irina Kalinina | SOV | 417.99 |
| 8. Barbara Nejman | USA | 365.07 |

**1980 Moscow** C: 24, N: 13, D: 7.21.

| | | PTS. |
|---|---|---|
| 1. Irina Kalinina | SOV | 725.910 |
| 2. Martina Proeber | GDR | 698.895 |
| 3. Karin Guthke | GDR | 685.245 |
| 4. Zhanna Tsirulnikova | SOV | 673.665 |
| 5. Martina Jäschke | GDR | 668.115 |
| 6. Valerie McFarlane | AUS | 651.045 |
| 7. Irina Sidorova | SOV | 650.265 |
| 8. Lourdes Gonzalez | CUB | 640.005 |

**1984 Los Angeles** C: 24, N: 18, D: 8.6.

| | | PTS. |
|---|---|---|
| 1. Sylvie Bernier | CAN | 530.70 |
| 2. Kelly McCormick | USA | 527.46 |
| 3. Christina Seufert | USA | 517.62 |
| 4. Li Yihua | CHN | 506.52 |
| 5. Li Qiaoxian | CHN | 487.68 |
| 6. Elsa Tenorio | MEX | 463.56 |
| 7. Lesley Smith | ZIM | 451.89 |
| 8. Debbie Fuller | CAN | 450.99 |

The women's springboard event had been billed as a showdown between the Americans and the Chinese, but a consistent performance by 20-year-old Sylvie Bernier of Ste. Foy, Quebec, gave her the victory. Bernier, who had a history of caving in in pressure situations, solved her problem by completely ignoring the standings throughout the competition. She even drowned out the public-address announcer by listening to the soundtrack from the movie "Flashdance" between dives. It wasn't until she had completed her final dive that her coach informed her the gold medal would be hers unless Kelly McCormick, daughter of four-time Olympic champion Pat McCormick, scored over 70 points on her last dive. McCormick's dive was an excellent one, but earned her only 67.20 points.

**1988 Seoul** C: 27, N: 19, D: 9.25.

| | | PTS. |
|---|---|---|
| 1. Gao Min | CHN | 580.23 |
| 2. Li Qing | CHN | 534.33 |
| 3. Kelly McCormick | USA | 533.19 |
| 4. Irina Lashko | SOV | 526.65 |
| 5. Marina Babkova | SOV | 506.43 |
| 6. Wendy Lucero | USA | 498.81 |
| 7. Brita Baldus | GDR | 479.19 |
| 8. Daphne Jongehans | HOL | 465.45 |

In 1988, world champion Gao Min of Zigong in Sichuan Province became the first female diver to score over 600 points in a springboard competition. In Seoul, the 18-year-old Gao took the lead with her sixth dive, finished with the three highest scores of the day, and achieved the most decisive women's diving victory since Pat McCormick's in 1956.

## PLATFORM DIVING

This event is performed from a static board ten meters above the water. Each finalist attempts four compulsory dives and four voluntary dives.

**1896–1908** not held

**1912 Stockholm** C: 14, N; 3, D: 7.13.

| | | PTS. | ORDINALS |
|---|---|---|---|
| 1. Greta Johansson | SWE | 39.9 | 5 |
| 2. Lisa Regnell | SWE | 36.0 | 11 |
| 3. Isabelle White | GBR | 34.0 | 17 |
| 4. Elsa Regnell | SWE | 33.2 | 20 |
| 5. Ellen Eklund | SWE | 31.9 | 22 |
| 6. Elsa Andersson | SWE | 31.3 | 25 |
| 7. Selma Andersson | SWE | 27.3 | 36 |
| 8. Thora Larsson | SWE | 26.8 | 39 |

Seventeen-year-old Greta Johansson was the unanimous choice of the five judges.

**1920 Antwerp** C: 15, N: 7, D: 8.28.

| | | PTS. | ORDINALS |
|---|---|---|---|
| 1. Stefani Fryland-Clausen | DEN | 34.6 | 6 |
| 2. Eileen Armstrong | GBR | 33.3 | 10 |
| 2. Eva Ollivier | SWE | 33.3 | 11 |
| 4. Isabelle White | GBR | 31.7 | — |
| 5. Aileen Riggin | USA | 31.4 | — |
| 6. Betty Grimes | USA | 26.7 | — |

**1924 Paris** C: 11, N: 6, D: 7.20.

| | | PTS. | ORDINALS |
|---|---|---|---|
| 1. Caroline Smith | USA | 33.2 | 10.5 |
| 2. Elizabeth Becker | USA | 33.4 | 11 |
| 3. Hjördis Töpel | SWE | 32.8 | 15.5 |
| 4. Edith Bechmann-Nielsen | DEN | 31.6 | 17.5 |
| 5. Helen Meany | USA | 29.0 | 22 |
| 6. Isabelle White | GBR | 28.0 | 28.5 |

National prejudice reared its ugly head in the judging of the women's high dive. The Danish judge gave first place to Bechmann-Nielsen of Denmark. The Swedish judge voted for Töpel of Sweden, and the American judge registered a three-way tie for first among the three Americans. The British judge voted for Smith and the French judge for Becker.

**1928 Amsterdam** C: 17, N; 8, D: 8.11.

| | | PTS. | ORDINALS |
|---|---|---|---|
| 1. Elizabeth Becker Pinkston | USA | 31.6 | 9 |
| 2. Georgia Coleman | USA | 30.6 | 10.5 |
| 3. Lala Sjöquist | SWE | 29.2 | 13.5 |
| 4. Mietje Baron | HOL | 27.2 | 21 |
| 5. Greta Onnela | FIN | 26.0 | 25 |
| 6. Hanni Rehborn | GER | 25.6 | 26 |

Elizabeth Becker Pinkston balanced her 1924 springboard gold with first place in the platform diving four years later. Between Olympics she had married Clarence Pinkston, whom she had met when both were members of the 1924 U.S. diving team in Paris.

**1932 Los Angeles** C: 7, N: 5, D: 8.12.

| | | PTS. |
|---|---|---|
| 1. Dorothy Poynton | USA | 40.26 |
| 2. Georgia Coleman | USA | 35.56 |
| 3. Marion Roper | USA | 35.22 |
| 4. Lala Sjöquist | SWE | 34.52 |
| 5. Ingrid Larsen | DEN | 31.96 |
| 6. Etsuko Kamakuru | JPN | 31.36 |
| 7. Magdalene Epply | AUS | 26.76 |

**1936 Berlin** C: 22, N: 10, D: 8.13.

| | | PTS. |
|---|---|---|
| 1. Dorothy Poynton Hill | USA | 33.93 |
| 2. Velma Dunn | USA | 33.63 |
| 3. Käthe Köhler | GER | 33.43 |
| 4. Reiko Osawa | JPN | 32.53 |
| 5. Cornelia Gilissen | USA | 30.47 |
| 6. Fusako Kono | JPN | 30.24 |
| 7. Jean Gilbert | GBR | 30.16 |
| 8. Anne Ehseheidt | GBR | 29.90 |

Stylish Dorothy Poynton Hill, competing in her third Olympics at the age of 21, gained her fourth medal. She won two gold medals in the platform and a silver and bronze in the springboard.

**1948 London** C: 15, N: 9, D: 8.6.

| | | PTS. |
|---|---|---|
| 1. Victoria Draves | USA | 68.87 |
| 2. Patricia Elsener | USA | 66.28 |
| 3. Birte Christoffersen | DEN | 66.04 |
| 4. Ali Staudinger | AUT | 64.59 |
| 5. Juno Stover | USA | 62.63 |
| 6. Nicole Pellissard | FRA | 61.07 |
| 7. Eva Peterson | SWE | 60.86 |
| 8. Inge Beeken-Gregersen | DEN | 59.54 |

Vicki Draves became the first female diver to win two gold medals in one Olympics.

**1952 Helsinki** C: 15, N: 8, D: 8.2

| | | PTS. |
|---|---|---|
| 1. Patricia McCormick | USA | 79.37 |
| 2. Paula Jean Myers | USA | 71.63 |
| 3. Juno Irwin (Stover) | USA | 70.49 |
| 4. Nicole Pellisard | FRA | 66.89 |
| 5. Phyllis Long | GBR | 63.19 |
| 6. Tatyana Vereina | SOV | 61.09 |
| 7. Diana Spencer | GBR | 60.76 |
| 8. Eugenia Bogdanovskaya | SOV | 57.50 |

This was the second of Pat McCormick's four gold medals. Bronze medalist Juno Irwin was three and a half months' pregnant with her second child.

**1956 Melbourne** C: 18, N: 10, D: 12.7.

|  |  | PTS. |
|---|---|---|
| 1. Patricia McCormick | USA | 84.85 |
| 2. Juno Irwin (Stover) | USA | 81.64 |
| 3. Paula Jean Myers | USA | 81.58 |
| 4. Nicole Darrigrand (Pellissard) | FRA | 78.80 |
| 5. Tatyana Karakashyants-Vereina | SOV | 76.95 |
| 6. Lyubov Shigalova | SOV | 76.40 |
| 7. Phyllis Long | GBR | 76.15 |
| 8. Birte Hansson | SWE | 75.21 |

Pat McCormick moved ahead of Juno Irwin after the sixth of seven dives to win her fourth gold medal. McCormick was a 26-year-old mother of one, Irwin a 28-year-old mother of three.

**1960 Rome** C: 18, N: 12, D: 8.30.

|  |  | PTS. |
|---|---|---|
| 1. Ingrid Krämer | GDR | 91.28 |
| 2. Paula Jean Pope (Myers) | USA | 88.94 |
| 3. Ninel Krutova | SOV | 86.99 |
| 4. Juno Irwin (Stover) | USA | 83.59 |
| 5. Raisa Gorokhovskaya | SOV | 83.03 |
| 6. Norma Thomas | GBR | 82.21 |
| 7. Nicole Darrigrand (Pellissard) | FRA | 81.18 |
| 8. Phyllis Long | GBR | 80.98 |

Krämer clinched her diving double with a final one and a half forward somersault with a double twist that turned out to be the highest-scoring dive of the competition. Paula Jean Pope, a 25-year-old mother of two, won her third straight platform medal.

**1964 Tokyo** C: 24, N: 11, D: 10.15.

|  |  | PTS. |
|---|---|---|
| 1. Lesley Bush | USA | 99.80 |
| 2. Ingrid Engel-Krämer | GDR | 98.45 |
| 3. Galina Alekseyeva | SOV | 97.60 |
| 4. Linda Cooper | USA | 96.30 |
| 5. Christine Lanzke | GDR | 92.92 |
| 6. Ingeborg Pertmayr | AUT | 92.70 |
| 7. Natalya Kuznetsova | SOV | 90.91 |
| 8. Barbara Talmage | USA | 89.60 |

Seventeen-year-old Lesley Bush of Princeton, New Jersey, took the lead after the first dive and was never headed. Asked afterward how she felt when she realized she was in first place and might upset Ingrid Krämer's attempt to match Pat McCormick's four gold medals, Bush replied, "It was sort of scary, but gee, gosh, it was great."

**1968 Mexico City** C: 24, N: 15, D: 10.23.

|  |  | PTS. |
|---|---|---|
| 1. Milena Duchková | CZE | 109.59 |
| 2. Natalya Lobanova (Kuznetsova) | SOV | 105.14 |
| 3. Ann Peterson | USA | 101.11 |
| 4. Beverly Boys | CAN | 97.97 |
| 5. Boguslawa Pietkiewicz | POL | 95.28 |
| 6. Regina Krause | GER | 93.08 |

| 6. Keiko Ohsaki | JPN | 93.08 |
|---|---|---|
| 8. Nancy Robertson | CAN | 90.66 |

Duchková overcame Lobanova with her last two dives, much to the delight of the crowd, which favored the 16-year-old Czechoslovakian because she was small and because her nation was occupied by Soviet troops.

**1972 Munich** C: 27, N: 17, D: 9.2.

|  |  | PTS. |
|---|---|---|
| 1. Ulrika Knape | SWE | 390.00 |
| 2. Milena Duchková | CZE | 370.92 |
| 3. Marina Janicke | GDR | 360.54 |
| 4. Janet Ely | USA | 352.68 |
| 5. Maxine "Micki" King | USA | 346.38 |
| 6. Sylvia Fiedler | GDR | 341.67 |
| 7. Nancy Robertson | CAN | 334.02 |
| 8. Ingeborg Pertmayr | AUT | 321.03 |

Knape took the lead from Duchková after the sixth of eight dives and then earned the gold medal with a final dive that received the highest score of the competition.

**1976 Montreal** C: 25, N: 12, D: 7.25.

|  |  | PTS. |
|---|---|---|
| 1. Elena Vaytsekhovskaya | SOV | 406.59 |
| 2. Ulrika Knape | SWE | 402.60 |
| 3. Deborah Wilson | USA | 401.00 |
| 4. Irina Kalinina | SOV | 398.67 |
| 5. Cindy Shatto | CAN | 389.50 |
| 6. Teri York | CAN | 378.39 |
| 7. Melissa Briley | USA | 376.86 |
| 8. Heidi Ramlow | GDR | 365.64 |

Eighteen-year-old Ukrainian Elena Vaytsekhovskaya jumped from fifth place to first with her fifth dive, a superbly executed backward two and a half somersault, piked.

**1980 Moscow** C: 17, N: 11, D: 7.26.

|  |  | PTS. |
|---|---|---|
| 1. Martina Jäschke | GDR | 596.250 |
| 2. Servard Emirzyan | SOV | 576.465 |
| 3. Liana Tsotadze | SOV | 575.925 |
| 4. Ramona Wenzel | GDR | 542.070 |
| 5. Yelena Matyushenko | SOV | 540.180 |
| 6. Elsa Tenorio | MEX | 539.445 |
| 7. Valerie McFarlane | AUS | 499.785 |
| 8. Ildikó Kelemen | HUN | 476.535 |

In fourth place after the preliminaries, Jäschke swept into first place on the fifth dive of the final round.

**1984 Los Angeles** C: 21, N: 14, D: 8.10.

|  |  | PTS. |
|---|---|---|
| 1. Zhou Jihong | CHN | 435.51 |
| 2. Michele Mitchell | USA | 431.19 |
| 3. Wendy Wyland | USA | 422.07 |
| 4. Chen Xiaoxia | CHN | 419.76 |
| 5. Valerie Beddoe | AUS | 388.56 |
| 6. Debbie Fuller | CAN | 371.49 |

| 7. Elsa Tenorio | MEX | 360.45 |
| 8. Guadalupe Canseco | MEX | 352.89 |

At five-feet, one-inch and weighing 92 pounds, 19-year-old Zhou Jihong of Hubei Province was unusually small for a diver. She also differed from her competitors in the choice of music she listened to on her headphones between dives. While the others received inspiration from upbeat popular songs, Zhou relaxed with piano concertos. This tactic seemed to help her avoid the last-minute choking for which Chinese divers had become famous.

**1988 Seoul** C: 20, N: 14, D: 9.18.

| | | PTS. |
|---|---|---|
| 1. Xu Yanmei | CHN | 445.20 |
| 2. Michele Mitchell | USA | 436.95 |
| 3. Wendy Lian Williams | USA | 400.44 |
| 4. Angela Stasiulevich | SOV | 386.22 |
| 5. Chen Xiaodan | CHN | 384.15 |
| 6. Yelena Miroshina | SOV | 381.93 |

| 7. Kamilla Gamme | NOR | 366.45 |
| 8. Silke Abicht | GDR | 350.61 |

After seven dives, the 17-year-old favorite, Xu Yanmei, led Michele Mitchell by only .27 of a point. For her final dive, Xu earned mostly 8s for a back 2½ pike for a total of 68.73 points. Mitchell, next to dive, missed slightly on the entry of her forward 3½ tuck and was awarded 7.5s for 60.75 points. The last diver was 14-year-old Chen Xiaodan, who had led the preliminary round, but who now stood firmly in third place, a formidable 83.82 points away from a gold medal. But Chen had scored 81.18 on her last dive and decided to forego caution and instead try "to win the whole meet." However, she went way too far over on a back 3½ tuck and almost landed on her stomach. Scores ranging from 1.5 to 3.0 left her with 22.77 points and fifth place. The ecstatic beneficiary of Chen's mistake was Wendy Lian Williams. Williams had been in last place after three dives and only fifth place after seven.

# TABLE TENNIS

In table tennis, the entrants are divided into round-robin groups. The top two players or teams in each group advance to an elimination tournament. In women's doubles, the top four teams in the two round-robin groups advance to the quarterfinals.

# MEN
## SINGLES

**1896–1984** not held

**1988 Seoul** C: 64, N: 35, D: 10.1.

| | | | MATCHES | | GAMES | |
|---|---|---|---|---|---|---|
| | | | W | L | W | L |
| 1. | KOR | Yoo Nam-kyu | 11 | 0 | 33 | 3 |
| 2. | KOR | Kim Ki-taik | 10 | 1 | 31 | 12 |
| 3. | SWE | Erik Lindh | 10 | 1 | 30 | 12 |
| 4. | HUN | Tibor Klampár | 8 | 3 | 26 | 17 |
| 5. | CHN | Jiang Jialiang | 10 | 1 | 31 | 6 |
| 6. | CHN | Chen Longcan | 8 | 3 | 27 | 12 |
| 7. | SWE | Jörgen Persson | 8 | 3 | 28 | 14 |
| 8. | SWE | Jan-Ove Waldner | 8 | 3 | 26 | 13 |

Final: Yoo—Kim 17–21, 21–19, 21–11, 23–21
3rd Place: Lindh—Klampár 14–21, 21–17, 21–17, 21–16
5th Place: Jiang—Chen 21–12, 21–16, 21–17
7th Place: Persson—Waldner 21–15, 21–16, 21–17

The inaugural men's table tennis tournament was highlighted by the shocking upsets of all five of the top-seeded players, none of whom advanced to the semifinals. In the round of 16, number four ranked Andrzej Grubba of Poland was beaten by the fifth seed, Jörgen Persson, who was in turn eliminated in the quarterfinals by Asian Games champion Yoo Nam-kyu. The quarterfinals also saw the defeat of number two seed Jan-Ove Waldner and number three Chen Longcan, who lost five-game cliffhangers to underdogs Kim Ki-taik and Tibor Klampár. But the biggest stunner was the demise of two-time world champion Jiang Jialiang. Jiang, a national hero of movie-star proportions, was beaten in four games by tenth-ranked Erik Lindh. In the semifinals, Yoo and Kim, responding to a wildly enthusiastic crowd, pre-vailed in straight games to set up a much-appreciated all-Korean final.

## DOUBLES

**1896–1984** not held

**1988 Seoul** T: 32, N: 23, D: 9.30.

| | | | MATCHES | | GAMES | |
|---|---|---|---|---|---|---|
| | | | W | L | W | L |
| 1. | CHN | (Chen Longcan, Wei Qingguang) | 10 | 0 | 20 | 3 |
| 2. | YUG | (Ilja Lupulesku, Zoran Primorać) | 8 | 2 | 17 | 8 |
| 3. | KOR | (Ahn Jae-hyung, Yoo Nam-kyu) | 9 | 1 | 18 | 3 |
| 4. | KOR | (Kim Ki-taik, Kim Wan) | 7 | 3 | 16 | 7 |
| 5. | CHN | (Jiang Jialiang, Xu Zengcai) | 9 | 1 | 18 | 5 |
| 6. | POL | (Andrzej Grubba, Leszek Kucharski) | 7 | 3 | 15 | 7 |
| 7. | SWE | (Erik Lindh, Jörgen Persson) | 7 | 3 | 14 | 6 |
| 8. | SWE | (Mikael Appelgren, Jan-Ove Waldner) | 6 | 4 | 14 | 10 |

Final: Chen/Wei—Lupulesku/Primorać 20–22, 21–8, 21–9
3rd Place: Ahn/Yoo—Kim/Kim 21–13, 21–16
5th Place: Jiang/Xu—Grubba/Kucharski 21–7, 21–12
7th Place: Lindh/Persson—Appelgren/Waldner 21–10, 21–14

The final match was a replay of the 1987 world championship final. The result was also the same, with Chen and Wei defeating Lupulesku and Primorać two games to one.

# WOMEN
## SINGLES

**1896–1984** not held

**1988 Seoul** C: 48, N: 28, D: 10.1.

| | | | MATCHES | | GAMES | |
|---|---|---|---|---|---|---|
| | | | W | L | W | L |
| 1. | CHN | Chen Jing | 9 | 0 | 27 | 2 |
| 2. | CHN | Li Huifen | 8 | 1 | 26 | 4 |
| 3. | CHN | Jiao Zhimin | 8 | 1 | 24 | 9 |
| 4. | CZE | Marie Hrachová | 6 | 3 | 20 | 12 |
| 5. | SOV | Flyura Bulatova | 8 | 1 | 24 | 8 |

| | | | | | | |
|---|---|---|---|---|---|---|
| 6. | SOV | Valentina Popova | 6 | 3 | 18 | 9 |
| 7. | HOL | Bettine Vriesekoop | 7 | 2 | 21 | 9 |
| 8. | KOR | Hong Cha-ok | 5 | 4 | 16 | 15 |

Final: Chen—Li 21–17, 21–16, 21–23, 15–21, 21–15
3rd Place: Jiao—Hrachová 21–18, 21–19, 21–17
5th Place: Bulatova—Popova 21–16, 21–11, 22–20
7th Place: Vriesekoop—Hong 21–19, 21–16, 25–23

The table tennis world was shocked and somewhat suspicious when Chinese officials announced that their Olympic team would include secondary stars Li Huifen and Chen Jing instead of the number one ranked player in the world, He Zhili, and number three ranked Dai Lili. It was rumored that He was being punished for refusing to throw matches to other Chinese players during the 1987 world championship, which she won. Chen's coach, Xi Enting, summed up the Olympic prospects of his 21-year-old protégé by saying, "I think there are two possible outcomes: one is that she [Chen] will become famous overnight and the other is that she will yield to the pressure, perform poorly and receive a lasting blow to her confidence."

As it turned out, Chen and Li crushed their opposition. Chen advanced to the final without losing a single game, while Li lost only one. Meanwhile, rumors spread in the Korean press that Li had won her semifinal contest over top seed Jiao Zhimin because Jiao had been ordered to throw the match. Jiao was hounded by the Korean media wherever she went because of interest in her "politically incorrect" romance with South Korean doubles champion Ahn Jae-hyung.

Despite the circus and scandal surrounding the women's singles tournament, the final was an exciting, hard-fought battle, won three games to two by Chen, who thus escaped "a lasting blow to her confidence."

## DOUBLES

**1896–1984** not held

**1988 Seoul** T: 15, N: 15, D: 9.30.

| | | | MATCHES | | GAMES | |
|---|---|---|---|---|---|---|
| | | | W | L | W | L |
| 1. | KOR | (Hyun Jung-hwa, Yang Young-ja) | 10 | 0 | 20 | 2 |
| 2. | CHN | (Chen Jing, Jiao Zhimin) | 8 | 1 | 17 | 4 |
| 3. | YUG | (Jasna Fazlić, Gordana Perkucin) | 7 | 3 | 15 | 7 |
| 4. | JPN | (Mika Hoshino, Kiyomi Ishida) | 4 | 5 | 10 | 11 |
| 5. | CZE | (Marie Hrachová, Renata Kasalová) | 7 | 2 | 14 | 7 |
| 6. | SOV | (Flyura Bulatova, Yelena Kovtun) | 6 | 4 | 13 | 10 |
| 7. | HOL | (Mirjam Kloppenburg, Bettine Vriesekoop) | 5 | 4 | 10 | 11 |
| 8. | HUN | (Csilla Bátorfi, Edit Urbán) | 4 | 6 | 11 | 14 |

Final: Hyun/Yang—Chen/Jiao 21-19, 16-21, 21-10
3rd Place: Fazlić/Perkucin—Hoshino/Ishida 21–14, 11-21, 21–16
5th Place: Hracová/Kasalová—Bulatova/Kovtun 21–10, 8–21, 21–19
7th Place: Kloppenburg/Vriesekoop—Bátorfi/Urbán 21–18, 21–23, 21–17

Hyun and Yang took an 11–2 lead in the decisive third game of the final, which they went on to win 21–10.

# TENNIS

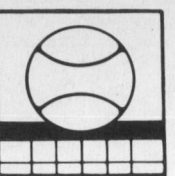

| MEN | WOMEN | Discontinued Event |
|---|---|---|
| Singles | Singles | |
| Doubles | Doubles | |

# MEN

## SINGLES

**1896 Athens** C: 13, N: 7, D: 4.11.
1. John Pius Boland          GBR/IRL
2. Dionysios Kasdaglis      EGY
3. Momcsilló Topavicza      HUN
3. K. Paspatis              GRE
5. A. Akratopoulos          GRE
5. E. Rallis                GRE
   Final: Boland—Kasdaglis, 6–3, 6–1

Boland was a student at Oxford when he learned about the revival of the Olympic Games from a fellow student, S. Manaos of Greece. Boland traveled to Athens as a spectator but Manaos, who was by then the secretary of the Organizing Committee, arranged to have Boland entered in the tennis competition. Later in life Boland became a renowned barrister, politician, author, and ardent proponent of Irish independence.

**1900 Paris** C: 13, N: 3, D: 7.11.
1. Hugh "Laurie" Doherty    GBR
2. Harold Mahony            GBR/IRL
3. Reginald Doherty         GBR
3. A.B.J. Norris            GBR
   Final: H. Doherty—Mahony, 6–4, 6–2, 6–3

The Doherty brothers were scheduled to play one another in the semifinals, but refused to do so in a "minor" tournament. Reginald stepped aside and agreed to let his younger brother advance to the final. Between them, Reggie and Laurie won 9 Wimbledon Singles championships between 1897 and 1906.

**1904 St. Louis** C: 27, N: 1, D: 9.3.
1. Beals Wright             USA
2. Robert LeRoy             USA
3. Alonzo Bell             USA
3. Edgar Leonard            USA
5. W.E. Blatherwick (USA), Charles Cresson (USA), John Neely (USA), Semp Russ (USA).
   Final: Wright—LeRoy, 6–4, 6–4

**1906 Athens** C: 18, N: 6, D: 4.23.
1. Max Decugis              FRA
2. Maurice Germot           FRA
3. Zdenek "Jánsky" Žemla    BOH
   Final: Decugis—Germot, 6–1, 7–9, 6–1, 6–1

**1908 London** C: 31, N: 9, D: 7.15.
1. Josiah Ritchie           GBR
2. Otto Froitzheim          GER
3. Wilberforce Vaughan Eaves GBR
4. Ivie Richardson          SAF
5. C.R. Brown (CAN), George Caridia (GBR), Charles Dixon (GBR), Maurice Germot (FRA)
   Final: Ritchie—Froitzheim, 7–5, 6–3, 6–4
   3rd Place: Eaves—Richardson, 6–2, 6–2, 6–3

**1908 London** C: 7, N: 2, D: 5.14.
*Indoor Courts*
1. Arthur Gore              GBR
2. George Caridia           GBR
3. Josiah Ritchie           GBR
4. Wilberforce Vaughan Eaves GBR
   Final: Gore—Caridia, 6–3, 7–5, 6–4

**1912 Stockholm** C: 49, N: 12, D: 7.5.
1. Charles Winslow          SAF
2. Harold Kitson            SAF
3. Oscar Kreuzer            GER
4. Ladislav "Rázny" Žemla   BOH
5. Louis Heyden (GER), Otto von Müller (GER), Ludwig Salm (AUT), Arthur Zborzil (AUT)
   Final: Winslow—Kitson, 7–5, 4–6, 10–8, 8–6
   3rd Place: Kreuzer—Žemla-Rázny, 6–2, 3–6, 6–3, 6–1

The level of competition at the 1912 Olympics was somewhat disappointing, due to the fact that the Swedish organizers scheduled the tournament at the same time as the Wimbledon championships.

**1912 Stockholm** C: 22, N: 6, D: 5.12.
*Indoor Courts*
1. André Gobert             FRA
2. Charles Dixon            GBR
3. Anthony Wilding          NZE
4. F. Gordon Lowe           GBR
5. George Caridia           GBR
5. Gunnar Setterwall        SWE
   Final: Gobert—Dixon, 8–6, 6–4, 6–4
   3rd Place: Wilding—Lowe, 4–6, 6–2, 7–5, 6–0

**1920 Antwerp** C: 41, N: 14, D: 8.23.
1. Louis Raymond            SAF
2. Ichiya Kumagae           JPN

3. Charles Winslow     SAF
4. Oswald Noel Turnbull     GBR
     Final: Raymond—Kumagae, 5–7, 6–4, 7–5, 6–4
     3rd Place: Winslow—Turnbull WO

The second round included one marathon match between Gordon Lowe of Great Britain and Zerlendi of Greece, which lasted for almost six hours over a two-day period. At one point, the ballboys, bored by the prolonged cautious rallying, left the court and went to lunch, forcing Lowe and Zerlindi to suspend play. Eventually Lowe won, 14–12, 6–8, 5–7, 6–4, 6–4. Lowe was subsequently eliminated in the fourth round after another five-set battle against Winslow. Raymond almost didn't make it into the final, having survived his semifinal match with Turnbull 2–6, 1–6, 6–2, 6–2, 6–1.

**1924 Paris** C: 82, N: 27, D: 7.20.
1. Vincent Richards     USA
2. Henri Cochet     FRA
3. Umberto Luigi de Morpurgo     ITA
4. Jean Borotra     FRA
5. T. Harada (JPN), S. Jacob (IND), René Lacoste (FRA), R. Norris Williams (USA)
     Final: Richards—Cochet, 6–4, 6–4, 5–7, 4–6, 6–2
     3rd Place: de Morpurgo—Borotra, 1–6, 6–1, 8–6, 4–6, 7–5

**1928–1984** not held

**1988 Seoul** C: 64, N: 32, D: 9.30.
1. Miloslav Mečíř     CZE
2. Tim Mayotte     USA
3. Stefan Edberg     SWE
3. Brad Gilbert     USA
5. Paolo Canè (ITA), Martin Jaite (ARG), Michiel Schapers (HOL), Carl-Uwe Steeb (GER)
     Final: Mečíř—Mayotte, 3–6, 6–2, 6–4, 6–2

The critical match of the tournament took place in the semifinals when Wimbledon champion Stefan Edberg faced Slovak Miloslav Mečíř. Edberg, who had won the 1984 Olympic demonstration tournament, had defeated Mečíř in the Wimbledon semifinals in July 4–6, 2–6, 6–4, 6–3, 6–4. But in Seoul it was Mečíř who came from behind to win 3–6, 6–0, 1–6, 6–4, 6–2. Tim Mayotte advanced to the final by losing only one set in five matches, but was no match for Mečíř's hypnotic precision stroking.

# DOUBLES

**1896 Athens** T: 6, N: 5, D: 4.11.
1. IRL/GER    (John Pius Boland, Fritz Traun)
2. EGY/GRE    (Dionysios Kasdaglis, Demetrios Petrokokkinos)
3. AUS/GBR    (Edwin Flack, George Robertson)
     Final: Boland/Traun—Kasdaglis/Petrokokkinos, 5–7, 6–4, 6–1

Boland entered the tournament at the last minute, when Traun's partner fell ill. When the Union Jack was run up the pole to honor Boland's half of the victory, he objected vehemently, pointing out that the Irish had a flag of their own. The officials apologized and agreed to have an Irish flag prepared.

At the closing ceremony, Britain's George Robertson greatly pleased the crowd by reading an ode which he had written in ancient Greek in Pindaric meter to honor the Olympic Games.

**1900 Paris** T: 8, N: 3, D: 7.11.
1. GBR    (Reginald Doherty, Hugh "Laurie" Doherty)
2. USA/FRA    (Basil Spalding de Garmendia, Max Decugis)
3. FRA    (André Prévost, G. de la Chapelle)
3. IRL/GBR    (Harold Mahony, A.B.J. Norris)
     Final: Doherty/Doherty—de Garmendia/Decugis, 6–1, 6–1, 6–0

**1904 St. Louis** T: 15, N: 2, D: 9.3.
1. USA    (Edgar Leonard, Beals Wright)
2. USA    (Alonzo Bell, Robert LeRoy)
3. USA    (Joseph Wear, Allen West)
3. USA    (Clarence Gamble, Arthur Wear)
5. Frank Wheaton, Hunter (USA), Charles Cresson, Semp Russ (USA), Ralph McKittrick, Dwight Davis (USA), Hugh McKittrick Jones, Harold Kauffman (USA)
     Final: Leonard/Wright—Bell/LeRoy, 6–4, 6–4, 6–2

**1906 Athens** T: 7, N: 5, D: 4.25.
1. FRA    (Max Decugis, Maurice Germot)
2. GRE    (Xenophon Kasdaglis, Ioannis Ballis)
3. BOH    (Zdenek "Jánsky" Žemla, Ladislav "Rázny" Žemla)
4. GRE    (T. Simiriotis, N. Zariphis)
     Final: Decugis/Germot—Kasdaglis/Ballis, 6–4, 6–2, 6–1
     3rd Place: Z. Žemla/L. Žemla—Simiriotis/Zariphis, 6–2, 6–3

**1908 London** T: 12, N: 7, D. 7.15.
1. GBR    (George Hillyard, Reginald Doherty)
2. GBR/IRL    (Josiah Ritchie, James Parke)
3. GBR    (Charles Cazalet, Charles Dixon)
4. FRA    (Max Decugis, Maurice Germot)
5. GBR    (Walter Crawley, Kenneth Powell)
5. SAF    (R. Gauntlett, Harald Kitson)
     Final: Hillyard/Doherty—Ritchie/Parke, 9–7, 7–5, 9–7

Hillyard was 44 years old at the time of his Olympic victory.

**1908 London** T: 5, N: 2, D: 5.14.
*Indoor Courts*
1. GBR    (Arthur Gore, Herbert Roper Barrett)
2. GBR    (George Simond, George Caridia)
3. SWE    (Gunnar Setterwall, Wollmar Boström)
4. GBR    (Josiah Ritchie, Lionel Escombe)
     Final: Gore/Barrett—Simond/Caridia, 6–2, 2–6, 6–3, 6–3
     3rd Place: Setterwall/Boström—Ritchie/Escombe, 4–6, 6–3, 1–6, 6–0, 6–3

**1912 Stockholm** T: 21, N: 10, D: 7.4.
1. SAF    (Charles Winslow, Harold Kitson)
2. AUT    (Felix Pipes, Arthur Zborzil)
3. FRA    (Albert Canet, Marc Mény de Marangue)
4. BOH    (Ladislav "Rázny" Žemla, Jiří Just)
5. Michel Soumarokoff, Alexandr Alenitzyn (RUS), Wollmar Bolström, Curt Benckert (SWE), Charles Wennergren, Carl Olof Nylén (SWE), Robert Spiess, Louis Heyden (GER)
     Final: Winslow/Kitson—Pipes/Zborzil, 4–6, 6–1, 6–2, 6–2
     3rd Place: Canet/Mény—L. Žemla/Just, 13–11, 6–3, 8–6

**1912 Stockholm** T: 8, N: 3, D: 5.12.
*Indoor Courts*
1. FRA    (André Gobert, Maurice Germot)
2. SWE    (Gunnar Setterwall, Carl Kempe)
3. GBR    (Charles Percy Dixon, Arthur Ernest Beamish)
4. GBR    (Arthur Gore, Herbert Roper Barrett)
   Final: Gobert/Germot—Setterwall/Kempe, 6–4, 12–14, 6–2, 6–4
   3rd Place: Dixon/Beamish—Gore/Barrett, 6–2, 0–6, 10–8, 2–6, 6–3

**1920 Antwerp** T: 22, N:12, D: 8.23.
1. GBR    (Oswald Noel Turnbull, Max Woosnam)
2. JPN    (Ichiya Kumagae, Seiichiro Kashio)
3. FRA    (Max Decugis, Pierre Albarran)
4. FRA    (François Blanchy, Jacques Brugnon)
5. Jack Nielsen, Conrad Langaard (NOR), Norton, Louis Raymond (SAF), Dodd, Blackburn (SAF), Balbil, Colombo (ITA)
   Final: Turnbull/Woosnam—Kamagae/Kashio, 6–2, 5–7, 7–5, 7–5
   3rd Place: Decugis/Albarran—Blanchy/Brugnon, WO

**1924 Paris** T: 39, N: 24, D: 7.21.
1. USA    (Vincent Richards, Frank Hunter)
2. FRA    (Jacques Brugnon, Henri Cochet)
3. FRA    (Jean Borotra, René Lacoste)
4. SAF    (John Condon, Ivie John Richardson)
5. Henning Müller, Charles Wennergren (SWE), R. Norris Williams, W. Washburn (USA), José Alonso, Manuel Alonso-Areyzaga (SPA), S. Hadi, D. Rutnam (IND)
   Final: Richards/Hunter—Brugnon/Cochet, 4–6, 6–2, 6–3, 2–6, 6–3
   3rd Place: Borotra/Lacoste—Condon/Richardson, 6–3, 10–8, 6–3

Richards and Hunter, the reigning champions of Wimbledon, won an arduous five–set semifinal match against Borotra and Lacoste, 6–2, 6–3, 0–6, 5–7, 6–3. They won the final by taking four of the last five games.

**1928–1984** not held

**1988 Seoul** T: 31, N: 31, D: 10.1.
1. USA    (Ken Flach, Robert Seguso)
2. SPA    (Emilio Sanchez, Sergio Casal)
3. CZE    (Miloslav Mečíř, Milan Srejber)
3. SWE    (Stefan Edberg, Anders Järryd)
5. Darren Cahill, John Fitzgerald (AUS), Morten Christensen, Michael Tauson (DEN), Guy Forget, Henri Leconte (FRA), Slobodom Živojinović, Goran Ivanišević (YUG)
   Final: Flach/Seguso—Sanchez/Casal, 6–3, 6–4, 6–7 (5–7), 6–7 (1–7), 9–7

Flach and Seguso led two sets to zero and 5-3 in the third set tiebreaker. But Sanchez and Casal pulled out the next 4 points to take the set, then won another tiebreaker in the fourth set. In the fifth set the Americans led 5–4 with Flach serving. But the gritty Spaniards fought back again, breaking service and moving ahead 6–5. Flach and Seguso fell behind 15–30, but came back to win the game, break Casal's serve, and move up 7–6. Again San-chez and Casal broke Flach's serve to tie the match. Then Sanchez lost his service and, finally, Seguso served out the game at love and the match was over after 3 hours and 42 minutes.

# WOMEN
## SINGLES

**1896** not held

**1900 Paris** C: 6, N: 4, D: 7.11.
1. Charlotte Cooper       GBR
2. Hélène Prévost         FRA
3. Marion Jones           USA
4. Hedwig Rosenbaum       BOH
   Final: Cooper—Prévost, 6–1, 6–4

Charlotte "Chattie" Cooper had already won three of her five Wimbledon titles when she traveled to Paris for the Olympics. She was the first female champion of the modern Games.

**1904 St. Louis** not held

**1906 Athens** C: 5, N: 1, D: 4.24.
1. Esmee Simiriotou       GRE
2. Sophia Marinou         GRE
3. Euphrosine Paspati     GRE
   Final: Simiriotou—Marinou, 2–6, 6–3, 6–3

**1908 London** C: 5, N: 1, D: 7.15.
1. Dorothea Chambers      GBR
2. Dorothy Boothby        GBR
3. Joan Winch             GBR
   Final: Chambers—Boothby, 6-1, 7-5

Due to numerous withdrawals, only four matches were contested, and Chambers won three of them. Boothby advanced to the final without playing a single game. Between 1903 and 1914 Chambers won 7 Wimbledon singles titles.

**1908 London** C: 7, N: 2, D: 5.14.
*Indoor Courts*
1. Gwendoline Eastlake-Smith   GBR
2. Angela Greene               GBR
3. Märtha Adlerstråhle         SWE
4. Elsa Wallenberg             SWE
   Final: Eastlake-Smith—Greene, 6–2, 4–6, 6–0
   3rd Place: Alderstråhle—Wallenberg, 1–6, 6–3, 6–2

**1912 Stockholm** C: 8, N: 4, D: 7.4.
1. Marguerite Broquedis    FRA
2. Dora Köring             GER
3. Molla Bjurstedt         NOR
4. Edit Arnheim            SWE

Final: Broquedis—Köring, 4–6, 6–3, 6–4
3rd Place: Bjurstedt—Arnheim, 6–2, 6–2

**1912 Stockholm** C: 8, N: 3, D: 5.11.
*Indoor Courts*
1. Edith Hannam                        GBR
2. Thora Gerda Sophy Castenschiold     DEN
3. Mabel Parton                        GBR
4. Sigrid Fick                         SWE
    Final: Hannam—Castenschiold, 6–4, 6–3
    3rd Place: Parton—Fick, 6–3, 6–3

According to the Official Report of the 1912 Games, in the third-place match, "the difficult screws of [Mrs. Parton] were altogether too much for the Swedish representative."

**1920 Antwerp** C: 18, N: 7, D: 8.23.
1. Suzanne Lenglen                     FRA
2. E. Dorothy Holman                   GBR
3. Kathleen "Kitty" McKane             GBR
4. Sigfrid Fick                        SWE
5. Elisabeth d'Ayen (FRA), Lily von Essen (SWE)
    Final: Lenglen—Holman, 6–3, 6–0
    3rd Place: McKane—Fick, 6–2, 6–0

Defending Wimbledon champion Suzanne Lenglen was one of the greatest women tennis players of all time. In the ten sets that it took her to win the Olympic singles title, she lost only four games.

**1924 Paris** C: 31, N: 14, D: 7.20.
1. Helen Wills                         USA
2. Julie "Didi" Vlasto                 FRA
3. Kathleen "Kitty" McKane             GBR
4. Germaine Golding                    FRA
5. E. "Lili" d'Alvarez (SPA), Marion Jessup (USA), Molla Bjurstedt-Mallory (NOR), Dorothy Shepherd-Barron (GBR)
    Final: Wills—Vlasto, 6–2, 6–2
    3rd Place: McKane—Golding, 5–7, 6–3, 6–0

In the semifinals McKane won her first set against Vlasto, 6–0, and was leading the second set 3–0 when a disruption occurred which turned the contest around. The match on the center court having just concluded, the Parisian crowd moved over to court number 3 to watch McKane and Vlasto. The umpire, Louis Raymond of South Africa, was calling the score in English and continued to do so, despite increasingly agitated requests from the audience that the score be announced in French. After things settled down, McKane had lost her touch and Vlasto was able to win 13 of the next 16 games to gain a 0–6, 7–5, 6–1 victory. However Vlasto was no match for the 18-year-old sensation Helen Wills, who succeeded Suzanne Lenglen as the queen of tennis.

**1928–1984** not held

**1988 Seoul** C: 48, N: 26, D: 10.1.
1. Stefanie Graf                       GER
2. Gabriela Sabatini                   ARG

3. Zina Garrison                       USA
3. Manuela Maleeva                     BUL
5. Rafaella Reggi (ITA), Larissa Savchenko (SOV), Pam Shriver (USA), Natalya Zvereva (SOV)
    Final: Graf—Sabatini, 6–3, 6–3

In 1984 Steffi Graf, then 15 years old, won the Olympic demonstration tournament despite being its youngest entrant. By 1987 she was ranked number one in the world, and in 1988 she won the Australian Open, the French Open, Wimbledon, and, less than a week before the Olympics, the U.S. Open to become only the fifth player in history to win tennis' Grand Slam. She arrived in Seoul with a 5-month, 35-match winning streak. Her most difficult challenge came in the quarterfinals when she trailed Larissa Savchenko 3–1 in the third set. Graf then won five straight games to close out the match. In the final she faced Gabriela Sabatini, the only player to beat her in 1988. But this time Graf kept Sabatini on the defensive and won in straight sets.

# DOUBLES

**1896–1912** not held

**1920 Antwerp** T: 9, N: 5, D: 8.23.
1. GBR    (Winifred Margaret McNair, Kathleen "Kitty" McKane)
2. GBR    (Geraldine Beamish, E. Dorothy Holman)
3. FRA    (Suzanne Lenglen, Elisabeth d'Ayen)
4. BEL    (Marie Storms, Fernande Arendt)
    Final: McNair/McKane—Beamish/Holman, 8–6, 6–4
    3rd Place: Lenglen/d'Ayen—Storms/Arendt, WO

**1924 Paris** T: 11, N: 8, D: 7.19.
1. USA    (Hazel Wightman, Helen Wills)
2. GBR    (P. Edith Covell, Kathleen "Kitty" McKane)
3. GBR    (Dorothy Shepherd-Barron, Evelyn Colyer)
4. FRA    (Marguerite Billout, Yvonne Bourgeois)
5. SWE    (Sigrid Fick, Lily von Essen)
    Final: Wightman/Wills—Covell/McKane, 7–5, 8–6
    3rd Place: Shepherd-Barron/Colyer—Billout/Bourgeois, 6–1, 6–2

**1928–1984** not held

**1988 Seoul** T: 14, N: 14, D: 9.30.
1. USA    (Pam Shriver, Zina Garrison)
2. CZE    (Jana Novotná, Helena Suková)
3. AUS    (Elizabeth Smylie, Wendy Turnbull)
3. GER    (Stefanie Graf, Claudia Kohde-Kilsch)
5. Carling Bassett-Seguso/Jill Hetherington (CAN), Natmali Tauziat/Isabe Demongeot (FRA), Etsuko Inoue/Kumiko Okamoto (JPN), Larissa Savchenko/Natalya Zvereva (SOV)
    Final: Shriver/Garrison—Novotná/Suková, 4–6, 6–2, 10–8

With Garrison serving at 9-8 in the final set, she and Shriver lost 5 match points, including two double faults. Finally, on the sixth try, the Americans won when Novotná hit long on a service return.

# Discontinued Event

## MIXED DOUBLES

**1900 Paris** T: 6, N: 4, D: 7.11.
1. GBR        (Charlotte Cooper, Reginald Doherty)
2. FRA/IRL    (Hélène Prévost, Harold Mahony)
3. BOH/GBR   (Hedwig Rosenbaum, Archibald Walden)
3. USA/GBR   (Marion Jones, Hugh "Laurie" Doherty)
      Final: Cooper/R. Doherty—Prévost/Mahony, 6–2, 6–4

**1904 St. Louis** not held

**1906 Athens** T: 4, N: 2, D: 4.26.
1. FRA   (Marie Decugis, Max Decugis)
2. GRE   (Sophia Marinou, Georgios Simiriotis)
3. GRE   (Aspasia Matsa, Xenophon Kasdaglis)
      Final: Decugis/Decugis—Marinou/Simiriotis, 6–1, 6–2

**1908 London** not held

**1912 Stockholm** T: 6, N: 4, D: 7.5.
1. GER   (Dora Köring, Heinrich Schomburgk)
2. SWE   (Sigrid Fick, Gunnar Setterwall)
3. FRA   (Marguerite Broquedis, Albert Canet)
      Final: Köring/Schomburgk—Fick/Setterwall, 6–4, 6–0

Shortly after the final match began, Mrs. Fick inadvertently smashed her partner in the face rather severely. In the words of the Official Report for 1912: "This little accident seemed to put Setterwall off his game, for his play fell off tremendously. . . ."

**1912 Stockholm** T: 8, N: 3, D: 5.12.
*Indoor Courts*
1. GBR   (Edith Hannam, Charles Percy Dixon)
2. GBR   (Helen Aitchison, Herbert Roper Barrett)
3. SWE   (Sigrid Fick, Gunnar Setterwall)
4. SWE   (Margareta Cederschiöld, Carl Kempe)
      Final: Hannam/Dixon—Aitchison/Barrett, 4–6, 6–3, 6–2
      3rd Place: Fick/Setterwall—Cederschiöld/Kempe WO

**1920 Antwerp** T: 16, N: 7, D: 8.23.
1. FRA   (Suzanne Lenglen, Max Decugis)
2. GBR   (Kathleen "Kitty" McKane, Max Woosnam)
3. CZE   (Milada Skrbková, Ladislav "Rázny" Žemla)
4. DEN   (Amory Folmer-Hansen, Erik Tegner)
5. Chaudoir, Lammens (BEL), Marie Storms, Halot (BEL)
      Final: Lenglen/Decugis—McKane/Woosnam, 6–4, 6–2
      3rd Place: Skrbková/L. Žemla—Folmer-Hansen/Tegner, 8–6, 6–4

**1924 Paris** T: 21, N: 14, D: 7.21.
1. USA   (Hazel Wightman, R. Norris Williams)
2. USA   (Marion Jessup, Vincent Richards)
3. HOL   (Cornelia Bouman, Hendrik Timmer)
4. GBR   (Kathleen "Kitty" McKane, John Gilbert)
5. P. Covell, Godfree (GBR), Sigrid Fick, Henning Müller (SWE), M. Wallis, E. McCrea (IRL)
      Final: Wightman/Williams—Jessup/Richards, 6–2, 6–3
      3rd Place: Bouman/Timmer—McKane/Gilbert, WO

# VOLLEYBALL

## MEN

Volleyball matches are decided on the basis of the best three out of five sets. A team wins a set when it scores 15 points, provided the margin is two or more points. Points can only be scored by the serving team. If the defensive team wins a rally, it gains the serve.

**1896–1960** not held

**1964 Tokyo** T: 10, N: 10, D: 10.23.

| | | | MATCHES | | SETS | | | |
|---|---|---|---|---|---|---|---|---|
| | | | W | L | W | L | PF | PA |
| 1. | SOV | (Ivan Bugjenkov, Nikolai Burobin, Yuri Chesnokov, Vascha Kacharava, Valery Kalatschikhin, Vitaly Kovalenko, Stanislav Ljugailo, Georgy Mondzolovoky, Yuri Poyarkov, Eduard Sibiryakov, Yuri Vengerovsky, Dmitri Voskoboynikov) | 8 | 1 | 25 | 5 | 415 | 279 |
| 2. | CZE | (Milan Čuda, Bohumil Golián, Zdenek Humhal, Petr Kop, Josef Labuda, Josef Musil, Karel Paulus, Boris Perušič, Pavel Schenk, Václav Šmidl, Josef Šorm, Ladislav Toman) | 8 | 1 | 26 | 10 | 486 | 399 |
| 3. | JPN | (Yutaka Demachi, Tsutomu Koyama, Sadatoshi Sugahara, Naohiro Ikeda, Yasutaka Sato, Toshiaki Kosedo, Tokihiko Higuchi, Masayuki Minami, Takeshi Tokutomi, Teruhisa Moriyama, Yuzo Nakamura, Katsutoshi Nekoda) | 7 | 2 | 22 | 12 | 475 | 372 |
| 4. | ROM | (Gheorghe Fieraru, Horatiu Nicolau, Aurel Drăgan, Iuliu Szöcs, William Schreiber, Mihai Grigorovici, Davila Plocon, Nicolae Bărbută, Eduard Derzsi, Mihai Chezan, Constantin Ganciu, Mihai Coste) | 6 | 3 | 19 | 15 | 432 | 394 |
| 5. | BUL | (Dimiter Karov, Yvan Gochev, Georgi Konstantinov, Petko Panteleev, Peter Kruchmarov, Simeon Srandev, Lachezar Stoyanov, Boris Gyuderov, Kiril Ivanov, Slavcho Slavov, Georgi Spasov, Angel Koritarov) | 5 | 4 | 20 | 16 | 464 | 429 |
| 6. | HUN | (Béla Czafik, Vilmos Iváncsó, Csaba Lantos, Gábor Bodò, István Molnár, Otto Prouza, Ferenc Tüske, Tibor Flórián, László Gálos, Antal Kangyerka, Mihály Tatár, Ferenc Jánosi) | 4 | 5 | 18 | 18 | 449 | 474 |
| 7. | BRA | (Joao Claudio Franca, Jose Schwart da Costa, H. Leao de Oliveira, Newdon Emanuel de Victor, Carlos Albano Feitosa, Marco Antonio Volpi, Carlos Arthur Nuzman, J. de Oliveira Ramalho, Decio Viotti de Azevedo, V.M. Barcellos Borges) | 3 | 6 | 13 | 23 | 410 | 474 |
| 8. | HOL | (Jacob Korsloot, Jurjaan Kodlen, Johannes Tinkhof, Jan Martinus Oosterbaan, Robert Groenhuijzen, Pieter Swieter, Johan van Wijnen, Jacques de Vink, Dingeman van der Stoep, Jacques Ewalds, Johannes van der Hoek, Franklin Constandse) | 2 | 7 | 11 | 24 | 378 | 482 |

The U.S.S.R. was awarded first place on the basis of a better ratio of points for and points against. The Soviets lost to Japan, but won their crucial match against Czechoslovakia, 15–9, 15–8, 5–15, 10–15, 15–7.

**1968 Mexico City** T: 10, N: 10, D: 10.26.

| | | | MATCHES | | SETS | | | |
|---|---|---|---|---|---|---|---|---|
| | | | W | L | W | L | PF | PA |
| 1. | SOV | (Eduard Sibiryakov, Valery Kravchenko, Vladimir Belyayev, Yevgeny Lapinsky, Oleg Antropov, Vasilijus Matuse- | 8 | 1 | 26 | 8 | 464 | 326 |

|  | | W | L | W | L | PF | PA |
|---|---|---|---|---|---|---|---|
| | vas, Viktor Mikhalchuk, Vladimir Ivanov, Ivan Bugjenkov, Georgy Mondzolevsky) | | | | | | |
| 2. JPN | (Masayuki Minami, Katsutoshi Nekoda, Mamoru Shiragami, Isao Koizumi, Yasuaki Mitsumori, Jungo Morita, Tadayoshi Yokota, Seiji Oko, Tetsuo Sato, Kenji Shimaoka, Kenji Kimura) | 7 | 2 | 24 | 6 | 430 | 253 |
| 3. CZE | (Antonin Procházka, Jiři Svoboda, Lubomir Zajiček, Josef Musil, Josef Smolka, Vladimir Petlak, Petr Kop, František Sokol, Bohumil Golián, Zdenek Groessl, Pavel Schenk, Drahomir Koudelka) | 7 | 2 | 22 | 15 | 454 | 412 |
| 4. GDR | (Horst Peter, Eckhardt Tielscher, Siegfried Schneider, Manfred Heine, Rainer Tscharke, Eckehard Pietzsch, Arnold Schulz, Rudi Schumann, Jürgen Kessel, Walter Toussaint, Jürgen Freiwald, Wolfgang Webner) | 6 | 3 | 22 | 12 | 449 | 373 |
| 5. POL | (Stanislaw Zduńczyk, Aleksander Skiba, Jerzy Szymczyk, Edward Skorek, Zbigniew Jasiukiewicz, Tadeusz Siwek, Zdzislaw Ambroziak, Stanislaw Gościniak, Romuald Paszkiewicz, Hubert Wagner, Wojciech Rutkowski, Zbigniew Zarzycki) | 6 | 3 | 18 | 11 | 370 | 280 |
| 6. BUL | (Alexander Trenev, Dimiter Zlatanov, Gramen Prinov, Peter Krutschmarov, Alexander Aleksandrov, Zdravko Simeonov, Milio Milev, Dimiter Karov, Kiri Slavov, Dinio Atanasov, Angel Koritarov, Stoyan Stoev) | 4 | 5 | 16 | 17 | 379 | 385 |
| 7. USA | (Daniel Patterson, Pedro Velasco, John Henn, Robert May, Larry Rundle, David Bright, Smitty Duke, John Alstrom, Jon Stanley, Thomas Haine, Rudy Suwara, Winthrop Davenport) | 4 | 5 | 15 | 18 | 382 | 414 |
| 8. BEL | (Jozef Mol, Pul Mesdagh, Fernand Walder, William Bossaerts, Bernard Vailant, Roger Maes, Ronald Vandewal, Hugo Huybrechts, Roger Vandergoten, Benno Saelens, Berto Poosen, Leo Dierckx) | 2 | 7 | 6 | 24 | 239 | 417 |

The Soviet team was upset by the United States in their opening contest. Shaken out of their complacency, they went on to win the rest of their matches easily, with only a brief five-set scare from the East Germans. They beat Japan 4–15, 15–13, 15–9, 15–13, in the decisive match.

**1972 Munich** T: 12, N: 12, D: 9.9.

|  | | MATCHES | | SETS | | | |
|---|---|---|---|---|---|---|---|
| | | W | L | W | L | PF | PA |
| 1. JPN | (Kenji Kimura, Yoshihide Fukao, Jungo Morita, Seiji Oko, Tadayoshi Yokota, Katsutoshi Nekoda, Yasuhiro Noguchi, Kenji Shimaoka, Yuzo Nakamura, Tetsuo Nishimoto, Masayuki Minami, Tetsuo Sato) | 7 | 0 | 21 | 3 | 348 | 192 |
| 2. GDR | (Siegfried Schneider, Arnold Schulz, Wolfgang Webner, Eckehard Pietzsch, Rudi Schumann, Wolfgang Weise, Horst Hagen, Horst Peter, Wolfgang Löwe, Rainer Tscharke, Wolfgang Maibohm, Jürgen Maune) | 5 | 2 | 16 | 8 | 295 | 256 |
| 3. SOV | (Victor Borsch, Vyacheslav Domani, Vladimir Patkin, Leonid Zaiko, Yuri Starunski, Aleksandr Saprykine, Vladimir Kondra, Efim Chulak, Vladimir Poutiatov, Valery Kravchenko, Yevgeny Lapinsky, Yuri Poyarkov) | 6 | 1 | 19 | 6 | 340 | 296 |
| 4. BUL | (Dimiter Karov, Brunko Iliev, Alexander Trenev, Ivan Ivanov, Dimiter Zlatanov, Zdravko Simeonov, Tsano Tsanov, Kiril Slavov, Emil Vulchev, Emile Trenev, Luchezar Stoyanov, Ivan Dimitrov) | 4 | 3 | 15 | 14 | 386 | 347 |
| 5. ROM | (Gabriel Udisteanu, Gyula Bartha, Corneliu Oros, Laurentiu Dumănoiu, William Schreiber, Marian | 4 | 3 | 9 | 15 | 300 | 286 |

Stamate, Mircea Codoi, Romeo Enescu, Cristian Ion, Stelian Moculescu, Viorel Bălas)

6. CZE (Drahomir Koudelka, Vladimir Petlak, Stefan Pipa, Pavel Schenk, Zdenek Groessl, Jaroslav Stanco, Miroslav Nekola, Milan Vapenka, Lubomir Zajiček, Jaroslav Penč, Milan Reznicek, Jaroslav Tomas)  4  3  15  9  321  274

7. KOR (Jin Jun-tak, Kim Chung-han, Lee Yong-kwan, Kim Kun-bong, Lee Sun-koo, Choi Jong-ok, Park Kee-won, Kim Kyui-hwan, Chung Dong-kee, Kang Man-soo)  3  4  10  13  284  270

8. BRA (Joao Jens, Delano Couto, Jorge Franco, Antonio Moreno, Luiz Eymard, Zech Coelho, Joco Marcelino, Mario Procopio, Paulo de Freitas, Decio Cattaruzzi, Alexandre Abeid, Celso Kalache)  2  5  12  16  316  373

Final: JPN—GDR 11–15, 15–2, 15–10, 15–10
3rd Place: SOV—BUL 15–11, 15–8, 15–13
5th Place: ROM—CZE 8–15, 15–7, 15–10, 16–14
7th Place: KOR—BRA 18–16, 15–7, 15–5

**1976 Montreal** T: 9, N: 9, D: 7.30.

| | | MATCHES | | SETS | | | |
|---|---|---|---|---|---|---|---|
| | | W | L | W | L | PF | PA |
| 1. | POL (Wlodzimierz Stefański, Bronislaw Bebel, Lech Lasko, Edward Skorek, Tomasz Wójtowicz, Wieslaw Gawlowski, Mieczyslaw Rybaczewski, Zbigniew Lubiejewski, Ryszard Bosek, Wlodzimierz Sadalski, Zbigniew Zarzycki, Marek Karbarz) | 6 | 0 | 18 | 9 | 377 | 293 |
| 2. | SOV (Anatoly Polishuk, Vyacheslav Zaitsev, Efim Chulak, Vladimir Dorohov, Aleksandr Ermilov, Pavels Selivanovs, Oleg Moliboga, Vladimir Kondra, Yuris Starunski, Vladimir Chernyshev, Vladimir Ulanov, Aleksandr Savin, Yuri Chesnokov, Vladimir Patkin) | 4 | 1 | 14 | 3 | 247 | 162 |
| 3. | CUB (Leonel Marshall, Victoriano Sarmientos, Ernesto Martinez, Victor Garcia, Carlosy Salas, Raul Virches, Jesus Savigne, Lorenzo Martinez, Diego Lapera, Antonio Rodriguez, Alfredo Figueredo, Jorge Perez) | 4 | 2 | 14 | 7 | 280 | 212 |
| 4. | JPN (Takashi Maruyama, Katsutoshi Nekoda, Katsumi Oda, Tetsuo Nishimoto, Yasunori Yasuda, Yoshihide Fukao, Shoichi Yanagimoto, Mikiyasu Tanaka, Tadayoshi Yokota, Seiji Oko, Kenji Shimaoka, Tetsuo Sato) | 2 | 3 | 8 | 8 | 157 | 204 |
| 5. | CZE (Miroslav Nekola, Jaroslav Penč, Stefan Pipa, Vladimir Petlak, Josef Mikunda, Jaroslav Stanco, Vlastimil Lenert, Milan Šlambor, Pavel Rerabek, Josef Vondrka, Drahomir Koudelka, Jaroslav Tomaš) | 4 | 2 | 14 | 7 | 282 | 234 |
| 6. | KOR (Kim Kon bong, Cho Jas-back, Lee Yong-kwan, Park Ki-won, Chong Moon-kyong, Lee Sun-koo, Lee Choun pyo, Lee In, Kim Choong-han, Lee Jong-won, Kang Man-soo, Lim Ho-dam) | 2 | 4 | 10 | 14 | 245 | 295 |
| 7. | BRA (Paulo de Freitas, Sergio Danilas, Alexandre Abeid, Eloi Neto, Antonio Mereno, Berhard Rajzman, William da Silva, Celso Alexandre Kalche, José Guimaraes, Jean Luc Rosat, Fernando de Avila, Paulo Petterle) | 2 | 3 | 8 | 11 | 216 | 228 |
| 8. | ITA (Andrea Nannini, Paolo Montorsi, Stefano Sibani, Giorgio Goldoni, Francesco Dall Olio, Fabrizio Nassi, Rodolfo Giovenzana, Andrea Nencini, Mario Mattioli, Giovanni Lanfranco, Erasmo Salemme, Marco Negri) | 0 | 5 | 2 | 15 | 125 | 148 |

Final: POL—SOV 11–15, 15–13, 12–15, 19–17, 15–7
3rd Place: CUB—JPN 15–8, 15–9, 15–8
5th Place: CZE—KOR 15–9, 10–15, 15–2, 15–9
7th Place: BRA—ITA 15–8, 15–6, 15–8

The U.S.S.R. and Poland reached the final match by completely different routes. The Soviet team, whose members averaged 6 feet 4¼ inches, swept through its four preliminary matches without losing a single set. Poland, on the other hand, was extended to five sets in three of their five victories, including a tense 13–15, 10–15, 15–6, 15–9, 20–18 win over Cuba. The Poles, however, were well prepared for such marathons—their daily training regimen required each player to jump 392 times over a four-and-a-half-foot barrier while wearing 20- to 30-pound weights on his legs and body. The turning point in the two-and-a-half-hour final came in the fourth set, with the Soviet Union leading two sets to one and 15–14—one point short of the gold medal. With the contest in the balance, 6-foot 7-inch Tomasz Wójtowicz smashed a long spike from behind the ten-foot line that saved the day. Eighteen serves later the Poles won the set, 19–17.

**1980 Moscow** T: 10, N: 10, D: 8.1.

| | | MATCHES | | SETS | | | |
|---|---|---|---|---|---|---|---|
| | | W | L | W | L | PF | PA |
| 1. SOV | (Yuri Panchenko, Vyacheslav Zaitsev, Aleksandr Savin, Vladimir Dorokhov, Aleksandr Yermilov, Pavels Selivanovs, Oleg Moliboga, Vladimir Kondra, Vladimir Chernyshev, Fyodor Lashchenov, Valery Krivov, Viljar Loor) | 6 | 0 | 18 | 2 | 297 | 190 |
| 2. BUL | (Stoyan Gounchev, Hristo Stoyanov, Dimiter Zlatanov, Dimitar Dimitrov, Petko Petkov, Mitko Todorov, Kaspar Simeonov, Emil Vulchev, Hristo Iliev, Yordan Angelov, Tsano Tsanov, Stefan Dimitrov) | 4 | 2 | 13 | 8 | 263 | 241 |
| 3. ROM | (Corneliu Oros, Laurentiu Dumanoiu, Dan Girleanu, Nicu Stoian, Sorin Macavei, Constantin Sterea, Neculae Vasile Pop, Gunter Enescu, Valter-Korneliu Chifu, Marius Chata-Chitiga) | 4 | 2 | 13 | 9 | 290 | 230 |
| 4. POL | (Robert Malinowski, Maciej Jarosz, Wieslaw Czaja, Lech Lasko, Tomasz Wójtowicz, Wieslaw Gawlowski, Wojciech Drzyzga, Boguslaw Kanicki, Ryszard Bosek, Wlodzimierz Nalazek, Leszek Molenda) | 3 | 3 | 12 | 11 | 303 | 271 |
| 5. BRA | (Joao Granjeiro, Mario | 4 | 2 | 15 | 10 | 328 | 288 |

Xando Oliveira Neto, Antonio Gueiros, José Montanaro, Antonio Moreno, Renan Dal Zotto, William da Silva, Amauri Ribeiro, Bernardo Rocha Rezende, Jean Luc Rosat, Deraldo Wanderley, Berhard Rajzman)

| 6. YUG | (Vladimir Bogoevski, Vladimir Trifunović, Aleksandar Tacevski, Ždravko Kuljić, Goran Srbinovski, Ivica Jelić, Boro Jović, Radovan Malević, Miodrag Mitić, Ljubomir Travica, Mladen Kasić, Slobodan Lozancić) | 3 | 3 | 13 | 13 | 310 | 302 |
| 7. CUB | (Diego Lapera, Victor Garcia, Luis Oviedo, Ernesto Martinez, Ricardo Leyva, Jorge Garbey, Raul Vilches, Carlos Salas, Antonio Perez, Leonel Marshall, Carlos Ruiz, José David) | 2 | 4 | 11 | 13 | 298 | 280 |
| 8. CZE | (Igor Prielozny, Pavel Valach, Vlado Sirvon, Jan Repak, Josef Novotny, Jaroslav Smid, Vlastimil Lenert, Nicu Stoian, Jan Cifra, Pavel Rerabek, Josef Pick, Cyril Krejci) | 1 | 5 | 7 | 17 | 253 | 335 |

Final: SOV—BUL 15–7, 15–13, 14–16, 15–11
3rd Place: ROM—POL 15–10, 9–15, 15–13, 15–9
5th Place: BRA—YUG 14–16, 15–9, 8–15, 15–10, 15–8
7th Place: CUB—CZE 14–16, 15–7, 15–10, 15–6

The team from Libya had a particularly difficult tournament, losing all five matches and all 15 sets, and scoring only 30 points while giving up 225.

**1984 Los Angeles-Long Beach** T: 10, N: 10, D: 8.11.

| | | MATCHES | | SETS | | | |
|---|---|---|---|---|---|---|---|
| | | W | L | W | L | PF | PA |
| 1. USA | (Dusty Dvorak, David Saunders, Stephen Salmons, Paul Sunderland, Rich Duwelius, Stephen Timmons, Craig Buck, Marc Waldie, Chris Marlowe, Aldis Berzins, Pat Powers, Charles "Karch" Kiraly) | 5 | 1 | 15 | 4 | 258 | 159 |
| 2. BRA | (Bernardo Rezende, Mario Xando Oliveira Neto, Antonio Ribeiro, José Montanaro, Ruy Campos Nascimento, | 4 | 2 | 13 | 8 | 267 | 214 |

Ranan Dal Zotto, William da Silva, Amauri Ribeiro, Marcus Freire, Domingos Lampariello Neto, Bernard Rajzman, Fernando D'Avila)

| | | W | L | W | L | PF | PA |
|---|---|---|---|---|---|---|---|
| 3. ITA | (Marco Negri, Pier Paolo Lucchetta, Gian Carlo Dametto, Franco Bertoli, Francesco Dall'Olio, Piero Rebaudengo, Giovanni Errichiello, Guido De Luigi, Fabio Vullo, Giovanni Lanfranco, Paolo Vecchi, Andrea Lucchetta) | 4 | 2 | 15 | 7 | 280 | 231 |
| 4. CAN | (Glenn Hoag, Terry Danyluk, John Barrett, Dave Jones, Paul Gratton, Al Coulter, Tom Jones, Don Saxton, Randy Wagner, Alex Ketyzynski, Rick Bacon, Garth Pischke) | 3 | 3 | 10 | 9 | 221 | 212 |
| 5. KOR | (Lee Jong-kyung, Kang Doo-tae, Chang Yoon-chang, Lee Yong-sun, Lee Bum-joo, Yang Jin-wung, Moon Yong-kwan, Yoo Joong-tak, Kim Ho-chul, No Jin-su, Kang Man-soo, Chung Euy-tak) | 5 | 1 | 15 | 8 | 312 | 253 |
| 6. ARG | (Daniel Castellani, Esteban Martinez, Carlos Wagenpfeil, Alejandro Diz, Hugo Conte, Waldo Kantor, Raul Quiroga, Jon Uriarte, Alcides Cuminetti, Leonardo Wiernes) | 2 | 4 | 11 | 13 | 282 | 307 |
| 7. JPN | (Koshi Sobu, Eiji Shimomura, Kazuya Mitake, Eizaburo Mitsuhashi, Hiroaki Okuno, Yasushi Furukawa, Shuji Yamada, Mikiyasu Tanaka, Kimio Sugimoto, Minoru Iwata, Akihiro Iwashima, Shunichi Kawai) | 4 | 2 | 13 | 8 | 271 | 245 |
| 8. CHN | (Yan Jianming, Song Jinwei, Yu Juemin, Zhai Jixin, Zhang Yousheng, Yang Liqun, Cao Ping, Shen Keqin, Zuo Yue, Xiao Jinsong, Zhao Duo, Liu Changcheng) | 1 | 5 | 4 | 15 | 200 | 261 |

Final: USA—BRA 15–6, 15–6, 15–7
3rd Place: ITA–CAN 15–11, 15–12, 15–8
5th Place: KOR–ARG 15–13, 9–15, 15–9, 15–7
7th Place: JPN–CHN 16–14, 15–9, 15–6

Considering that volleyball was invented in the United States (by William G. Morgan in Holyoke, Massachusetts, in 1895), the U.S. had been remarkably unsuccessful in international competition, qualifying for the Olympics only once since it became an official sport in 1964. However, the long drought ended in 1984. The U.S. team went to Los Angeles with a 24-match winning streak, including four straight victories over the world champion Soviet team, all of which took place in the U.S.S.R. The streak was ended in the fourth match of the tournament when an inspired Brazilian team beat the Americans 15–12, 15–11, 15–2. But five nights later, in the final, the U.S. turned the tables on the Brazilians, overwhelming them in straight sets.

**1988 Seoul** T: 12, N: 12, D: 10.2.

| | | MATCHES | | SETS | | | |
|---|---|---|---|---|---|---|---|
| | | W | L | W | L | PF | PA |
| 1. USA | (Troy Tanner, David Saunders, Jon Root, Robert Ctvrtlik, Robert Partie, Stephen Timmons, Craig Buck, Scott Fortune, Ricci Luyties, Jeffery Stork, Eric Sato, Charles "Karch" Kiraly) | 7 | 0 | 21 | 4 | 366 | 211 |
| 2. SOV | (Yuri Panchenko, Andrei Kuznetsov, Vyacheslav Zaitsev, Igor Runov, Vladimir Shkurikhin, Yevgony Krasilnikov, Raimonds Vilde, Valery Losev, Yuri Sapega, Aleksandr Sorokolet, Yaroslav Antonov, Yuri Cherednik) | 5 | 2 | 18 | 7 | 332 | 282 |
| 3. ARG | (Claudio Zulianello, Daniel Castellani, Eduardo Martinez, Alejandro Diz, Daniel Colla, Carlos Weber, Hugo Conte, Waldo Kantor, Raul Quiroga, Jon Uriarte, Esteban De Palma, Juan Carlos Cuminetti) | 4 | 3 | 14 | 12 | 325 | 317 |
| 4. BRA | (Mauricio Lima, Wagner Rocha, Paulo Roese, José Montanaro, Paulo da Silva, Renan Dal Zotto, William da Silva, Amauri Ribeiro, Antonio Gouveia, Domingos Lampariello Neto, Leonidio De Pra Filho, André Ferreira) | 4 | 3 | 16 | 13 | 374 | 342 |
| 5. HOL | (Martin Teffer, Pieter-Jan Leeuwerink, Ronald Boudrie, Jan-Marcus Posthuma, Ronald Zoodsma, Ronald Zwerver, Avital | 5 | 2 | 16 | 9 | 314 | 272 |

| | | W | L | W | L | PF | PA |
|---|---|---|---|---|---|---|---|
| | Selinger, Edwin Benne, Teunis Buys, Peter Blange, Marco Brouwers, Karl Grabert) | | | | | | |
| 6. BUL | (Kostadin Mitev, Petyo Draguiev, Borislav Kyossev, Ljubomir Ganev, Ilian Kaziiski, Dimo Tonev, Petko Petkov, Plamen Hristov, Sava Kovachev, Nayden Naydenov, Milcho Milanov, Tzvetan Florov) | 3 | 4 | 10 | 12 | 259 | 270 |
| 7. SWE | (Urban Lennartsson, Jannis Kalmazidis, Jan Hedengård Karlsson, Tomas Hoszek, Anders Lundmark, Per-Anders Sääf, Bengt Gustafson, Håakan Björne, Lars Nilsson, Peter Tholse, Patrik Johansson) | 3 | 4 | 14 | 16 | 350 | 388 |
| 8. FRA | (Philippe Blain, Hervé Mazzon, Eric N'Gapeth, Eric Bouvier, Christophe Meneau, Jean-Marc Jurkovitz, Laurent Tillie, Olivier Rossard, Patrick Duflos, Alain Fabiani, Philippe-Marie Salvan) | 3 | 4 | 12 | 13 | 312 | 300 |

Final: USA—SOV 13–15, 15–10, 15–4, 15–8
3rd Place: ARG—BRA 15–10, 15–17, 15–8, 12–15, 15–9
5th Place: HOL—BUL 15–6, 15–8, 15–10
7th Place: SWE—FRA 12–15, 15–5, 8–15, 15–12, 15–12

The U.S. team faced a stiff challenge from Argentina in the preliminary round, losing the first two sets before coming from behind to win the last three, exactly as they had in the 1987 Pan Am Games. In the final, the Americans confronted their number one rivals—and drinking buddies—the team from the U.S.S.R. The two teams had already played nine matches in 1988 with the U.S. winning seven. In the Olympic final, the Americans, all of whom grew up in Southern California, wore down the Soviets in the first two sets, then overwhelmed them in the last two.

The bronze medal match between Argentina and Brazil was an epic struggle that lasted 3 hours and 10 minutes. The starting lineup for the Dutch team, which placed fifth, *averaged* 6 feet 7⅔ inches.

# WOMEN

**1896–1960** not held

**1964 Tokyo** T: 6, N: 6, D: 10.23.

| | | MATCHES | | SETS | | | |
|---|---|---|---|---|---|---|---|
| | | W | L | W | L | PF | PA |
| 1. JPN | (Masae Kasai, Emiko Miyamoto, Kinuko Tanida, Yuriko Handa, Yoshiko Matsumura, Sata Isobe, Katsumi Matsumura, Yoko Shinozaki, Setsuko Sasaki, Yuko Fujimoto, Masako Kondo, Ayano Shibuki) | 5 | 0 | 15 | 1 | 238 | 93 |
| 2. SOV | (Nelly Abramova, Astra Biltauere, Lyudmila Buldakova, Lyudmila Gureyeva, Valentina Kamenek, Marita Katusheva, Ninel Lukanina, Valentina Mishak, Tatyana Roschina, Inna Ryskal, Antonina Ryschova, Tamara Tikhonina) | 4 | 1 | 12 | 3 | 212 | 97 |
| 3. POL | (Krystyna Czajkowska, Maria Golimowska, Krystyna Jakubowska, Danuta Kordaczuk-Wagner, Krystyna Krupa, Józefa Ledwig, Jadwiga Marko, Jadwiga Rutkowska, Maria Śliwka, Zofia Szczęśniewska) | 3 | 2 | 10 | 6 | 180 | 162 |
| 4. ROM | (Ana Mocan, Cornelia Lăzeanu, Natalia Todorovschi, Doina Ivănescu, Doina Popescu, Sonia Colceru, Lia Vanea, Alexandrina Chezan, Ileana Enculescu, Elisabeta Goloşie, Marina Stanca, Doina Coste) | 2 | 3 | 6 | 9 | 140 | 172 |
| 5. USA | (Jean Gaertner, Gail O'Rourke, Linda Murphy, Lou Galloway, Verneda Thomas, Mary Perry, Mary Peppler, Nancy Owen, Patricia Bright, Jane Ward, Sharon Peterson, Barbara Harwerth) | 1 | 4 | 3 | 12 | 98 | 213 |
| 6. KOR | (Suh Choon-kang, Moon Kyung-sook, Ryoo Choonja, Kim Kil-ja, Oh Soonok, Chung Jong-uen, Choi Don-hi, Hong Namsun, Oh Chung-ja, Yoon Jung-sook, Kwak Ryongja, Lee Keun-soo) | 0 | 5 | 0 | 15 | 94 | 225 |

Ten of the 12 members of the Japanese team came from the Nichibo spinning mill in Kaizuku, near Osaka. Their coach, the notorious Hirofumi Daimatsu, was the manager of the office supplies procurement department at the mill. Daimatsu was famous for his draconian methods: hitting the young women on the head, kicking them on their hips, insulting them, goading them, making them practice a minimum of six hours a day, seven days a week, 51 weeks a year. He was the first coach to introduce the rolling receive, in which a player dives to the ground, hits the ball, rolls over, and returns quickly to her feet.

Japanese sports fans looked forward with great anticipation to the Olympic volleyball tournament. Their great hopes almost met with disaster when the North Korean team withdrew over a political dispute, leaving the competition one team short of the six required to conduct an official tournament. The Japanese solved the problem by giving the South Korean Olympic Committee team 1,000,000 yen to send a team. The Japanese were never seriously challenged. The only time they lost a set (15–13, to Poland) was because Daimatsu pulled some of his better players when he saw that the Soviet coach was watching. The final Japanese victory over the U.S.S.R. gained an 80 percent audience rating on Japanese television.

After the game, the team captain, 31-year-old Masae Kasai, was invited to the official residence of Japan's prime minister, Eisaku Sato. She confessed to Sato that she wanted to marry, but that her rigorous training schedule had prevented her from meeting any men. Sato promised to help her and subsequently introduced Kasai to Kazuo Nakamura, whom she later married. As for Daimatsu, he quit coaching and joined an advertising agency. In 1968 he was elected to the House of Councilors, the upper house of the Japanese Parliament. He served until 1974 and died of a heart attack in 1978.

**1968 Mexico City** T: 8, N: 8, D: 10.26.

| | | MATCHES | | SETS | | | |
|---|---|---|---|---|---|---|---|
| | | W | l | W | L | PF | PA |
| 1. | SOV | 7 | 0 | 21 | 3 | 333 | 194 |

(Lyudmila Buldakova, Lyudmila Mikhailovskaya, Vera Lantratova, Vera Galushka, Tatyana Sarycheva, Tatyana Ponyayeva, Nina Smoleeva, Inna Ryskal, Galina Leontieva, Roza Salikhova, Valentina Vinogradova)

| | | | | | | | |
|---|---|---|---|---|---|---|---|
| 2. | JPN | 6 | 1 | 19 | 3 | 318 | 147 |

(Setsuko Yoshika, Suzue Takayama, Toyoko Iwahara, Yukiyo Kojima, Sachiko Fukunaka, Kunie Shishikura, Setsuko Inoue, Sumie Oinuma, Keiko Hama)

| | | | | | | | |
|---|---|---|---|---|---|---|---|
| 3. | POL | 5 | 2 | 15 | 11 | 324 | 304 |

(Krystyna Czajkowska, Józefa Ledwig, Elżbieta Porzec, Wanda Wiecha, Zofia Szczęśniewska, Krystyna Jakubowska, Lidia Żmuda-Chmielnicka, Barbara Niemczyk, Halina Aszkielowicz, Krystyna Krupa, Jadwiga Marko-Książek, Krystyna Ostromęcka)

| | | | | | | | |
|---|---|---|---|---|---|---|---|
| 4. | PER | 3 | 4 | 12 | 15 | 306 | 327 |

(Esperanza Jimenez, Teresa Nuñez, Irma Cordero, Olga Asato, Aida Reyna, Alicia Sanchez, Luisa Fuentes, Ana Maria Ramirez, Norma Velarde)

| | | | | | | | |
|---|---|---|---|---|---|---|---|
| 5. | KOR | 3 | 4 | 11 | 14 | 276 | 305 |

(Moon Kuyong-sook, Park Kum-sook, Suh Hee-sook, Lee Eun-ok, Hwang Kyu-ok, Lee Hyang-seem, Yang Jin-soo, Kim Young-ja, Kim Oe-sun, An Kyoung-Ja)

| | | | | | | | |
|---|---|---|---|---|---|---|---|
| 6. | CZE | 3 | 4 | 11 | 15 | 307 | 307 |

(Pavlina Šteffková, Elena Poláková, Karla Šašková, Jitka Senečká, Vera Strunčová, Vera Hrabáková, Julia Bendeová, Anna Mifková, Irena Tichá, Hana Vlašaková, Eva Siroká, Hilda Mazurová)

| | | | | | | | |
|---|---|---|---|---|---|---|---|
| 7. | MEX | 1 | 6 | 7 | 18 | 215 | 228 |

(Isabel Nogueira, Carolina Mendoza, Rogelia Romo, Yolanda Reynoso, Carmen Rodriguez, Gloria Inzua, Alicia Cardenas, Gloria Casales, Patricia Nava, Trinidad Macias, Blanca Garcia, Eloisa Cabada)

| | | | | | | | |
|---|---|---|---|---|---|---|---|
| 8. | USA | 0 | 7 | 4 | 21 | 196 | 353 |

(Jane Ward, Nancy Owen, Fanny Hopeau, Barbara Perry, Ninja Jorgensen, Miki McFadden, Sharon Peterson, Patti Bright, Laurie Lewis, Marilyn McReavy, Mary Perry, Kathryn Heck)

The crucial match between the Japanese and the Soviets was won by the U.S.S.R., 15–10, 16–14, 3–15, 15–9. After his team had been booed during its game against Czechoslovakia, the Soviet coach was asked if his players had been affected by the crowd's hostility. He replied, "If my athletes cannot stand such distractions, they are not professionals and should be left home." Reminded that the Olympics were for amateurs only, the embarrassed coach claimed he had been misquoted.

**1972 Munich** T: 8, N: 8, D: 9.7.

| | | | MATCHES | | SETS | | | |
|---|---|---|---|---|---|---|---|---|
| | | | W | L | W | L | PF | PA |
| 1. | SOV | (Inna Ryskal, Vera Douiounova, Tatiana Tretiakova, Nina Smoleeva, Roza Salikhova, Lyudmila Buldakova, Tatiana Gonobobeleva, Lyubov Turina, Galina Leontieva, Tatyana Sarycheva) | 5 | 0 | 15 | 5 | 270 | 206 |
| 2. | JPN | (Sumie Oinuma, Noriko Yamashita, Seiko Shimakage, Makiko Furukawa, Takako Iida, Katsumi Matsumura, Michiko Shiokawa, Takako Shirai, Mariko Okamoto, Keiko Hama, Yaeko Yamazaki, Toyoko Iwahara) | 4 | 1 | 14 | 3 | 244 | 131 |
| 3. | PRK | (Ri Chun-ok, Kim Myong-suk, Kim Zung-bok, Kang Ok-sun, Kim Yeunja, Hwang He-suk, Jang Ok-rim, Paek Myong-suk, Ryom Chun-ja, Kim Su-dae, Jong Ok-jin) | 3 | 2 | 10 | 6 | 211 | 154 |
| 4. | KOR | (Kim Young-ja, Lee In-sook, Lee Soon-bok, Jo Hea-chung, Yu Kyung-hwa, Kim Eun-hee, Lee Jung-ja, Yu Jung-hyae, Yoon Young-nae) | 2 | 3 | 7 | 9 | 169 | 189 |
| 5. | HUN | (Éva Szalay Sebök, Judit Gerhard Kiss, Emerencia Király Siry, Ilona Buzek Maklári, Judit Hazsik Fekete, Ágnes Torma, Mária Gál, Katalin Schadek Eichler, Judit Blauman Schlégl, Emöke Énekes, Zsuzsanna Török Bokros) | 3 | 2 | 10 | 10 | 256 | 252 |
| 6. | CUB | (Mercedes Perez, Ana Diaz, Margarita Mayeta, Mercedes Pomares, Nurys Sebey, Claritza Herrera, Miriam Herrera, Mercedes Roca, Claudina Villaurrutia) | 2 | 3 | 8 | 10 | 181 | 252 |
| 7. | CZE | (Irena Svobodova, Ludmila Vinduskova, Jana Semecka, Dorota Jelinkova, Anna Mifkova, Marie Vapenkova, Elena Moskalova, Hilda Mazurova, Maria Malisova, Hana Vlasakova) | 1 | 4 | 6 | 12 | 191 | 241 |
| 8. | GER | (Ingrid Lorenz, Annedore Richter, Ursel Westphal, Birgit Pörner, Margret Stender, Annette Ellerbracke, Rike Ruschenburg, Marianne Lepa, Traute Schäfer, Erika Heucke, Regina Pütz) | 0 | 5 | 0 | 15 | 131 | 228 |

Final: SOV—JPN 15–11, 4–15, 15–11, 9–15, 15–11
3rd Place: PRK—KOR 15–7, 15–9, 15–9
5th Place: HUN—CUB 13–15, 16–14, 14–16, 15–5, 15–11
7th Place: CZE—GER 15–13, 15–4, 16–14

The final was so closely fought that at one point in the fourth set there were 24 service changes in a row without a single point being scored. During the tournament, a German woman named Ingeborg Schell filed a civil suit against the Japanese coach, Joji Kojima, for using "inhuman methods for making his team fit."

**1976 Montreal** T: 8, N: 8, D: 7.30.

| | | | MATCHES | | SETS | | | |
|---|---|---|---|---|---|---|---|---|
| | | | W | L | W | L | PF | PA |
| 1. | JPN | (Takako Iida, Mariko Okamoto, Echiko Maeda, Noriko Matsuda, Takako Shirai, Kiyomi Kato, Yuko Arakida, Katsuko Kanesaka, Mariko Yoshida, Shoko Takayanagi, Hiromi Yano, Juri Yokoyama) | 5 | 0 | 15 | 0 | 225 | 84 |
| 2. | SOV | (Anna Rostova, Lyudmila Shetinina, Lilia Osadchaya, Natalya Kushnir, Olga Kozakova, Nina Smoleeva, Lyubov Rudovskaya, Larissa Bergen, Inna Ryskal, Lyudmila Chernysheva, Zoya Iusova, Nina Muradian) | 4 | 1 | 12 | 7 | 248 | 211 |
| 3. | KOR | (Lee Soon-bok, Yu Jung-hye, Byon Kyung-ja, Lee Soo-nok, Baik Myung-sun, Chang Hee-sook, Ma Kum-ja, Yun Young-nae, Yu Kyung-hwa, Park Mi-kum, Jung Soo-nok, Jo Hea-jung) | 3 | 2 | 10 | 11 | 260 | 259 |
| 4. | HUN | (Zsuzsanna Szloboda, Gyöngyi Bardi, Éva Biszku, Zsuzsanna Biszku, Lucia Bánhegyi, Gabriella Feketé Csapó, Ágnes Hubai Gajdos, Judit Blauman Schlégl, Ágnes | 2 | 3 | 7 | 11 | 192 | 234 |

Torma, Katalin Schadek Eichler, Emerencia Király Siry, Eva Szalay Sebök)

| | | | | | | |
|---|---|---|---|---|---|---|
| 5. CUB | (Mercedes Perez Hernandez, Imilsis Tellez Quesada, Ana Diaz Martinez, Mercedes Pomares Primelles, Lucila Urgelles Savon, Mercedes Roca, Miriam Herrera, Claudina Villaurrutia, Melanea Tartabull, Nelly Barnet Wilson, Ana Maria Garcia Crespo, Evelina Borroto) | 3 | 2 | 12 | 9 | 267 250 |
| 6. GDR | (Karla Roffeis, Johanna Strotzer, Cornelia Rickert, Christine Walther, Ingrid Mierzwiak, Helga Offen, Barbara Czekalla, Jutta Balster, Anke Westendorf, Hannelore Meincke, Monika Meissner, Gudrun Gärtner) | 1 | 4 | 8 | 14 | 237 286 |
| 7. PER | (Mercedes Gonzales, Maria Cardenas, Teresa Núñez, Irma Cordero, Ana Cecilia Carrillo, Luisa Merea, Della Cordova, Silvia Quevedo, Luisa Fuentes, Maria Del Risco, Maria Cervera, Maria Ostolaza) | 2 | 3 | 9 | 12 | 239 250 |
| 8. CAN | (Carole Bishop, Barbara Dalton, Kathy Girvan, Patty Olson, Regyna Armonas, Anne Ireland, Mary Dempster, Claire Lloyd, Betty Baxter, Connie Lebrun, Debbie Hoopa, Audrey Vandorvelden) | 0 | 5 | 6 | 15 | 198 292 |

Final. JPN—SOV 15-7, 15-8, 15-2
3rd Place: KOR—HUN 12-15, 15-12, 15-10, 15-6
5th Place: CUB—GDR 15-12, 15-12, 15-8
7th Place: PER—CAN 15-9, 12-15, 15-4, 15-7

The Japanese team dominated the tournament so completely that only once did an opponent (South Korea) reach double figures in a single set.

**1980 Moscow** T: 8, N: 8, D: 7.29.

| | | MATCHES | | SETS | | | |
|---|---|---|---|---|---|---|---|
| | | W | L | W | L | PF | PA |
| 1. SOV | (Nadezhda Radzevich, Natalya Razumova, Olga Solovova, Yelena Akhaminova, Larissa Pavlova, Yelena Andreyuk, Irina Makagonova, Lyubov Kozyreva, Svetlana Nikishina, Lyudmila Chernysheva, Svetlana Badulina, Lidiya Loginova) | 5 | 0 | 15 | 3 | 254 | 172 |
| 2. GDR | (Ute Kostrzewa, Andrea Heim, Annette Schultz, Christine Mummhardt, Heike Lehmann, Barbara Czekalla, Karla Roffeis, Martina Schmidt, Anke Westendorf, Karin Püschel, Brigitte Fetzer, Katharina Bullin) | 3 | 2 | 11 | 11 | 277 | 271 |
| 3. BUL | (Tania Dimitrova, Valentina Ilieva, Galina Stancheva, Silva Petrunova, Anka Hristolova, Verka Borisova, Margarita Gherasimova, Roumiana Kaicheva, Maya Georgieva, Tania Gogova, Tzvetana Bozhurina, Rossitza Dimitrova) | 3 | 2 | 12 | 9 | 257 | 225 |
| 4. HUN | (Julianna Simon Szalonna, Éva Szalay Sebök, Gyöngyi Gerevich [Bardi], Ágnes Balajczá Juhász, Lucia Banhegyi Rado, Gabriella Feketé Csapó, Emöke Szegedi Varghá, Emerencia Király Siry, Ágnes Torma, Erzsébet Vargá Palinkás, Gabriella Lengyel, Bernadett Köszegi) | 2 | 3 | 10 | 12 | 234 | 279 |
| 5. CUB | (Mercedes Perez Hernandez, Imilsis Tellez Quesada, Ana Diaz Martinez, Mercedes Pomares Primelles, Mavis Guilarte Fernandez, Erenia Diaz Ioca, Maura Alfonso Drake, Josefina Capote Travieso, Nelly Barnet Wilson, Ana Maria Garcia Crespo, Lucila Urgelles Savon) | 3 | 2 | 10 | 7 | 219 | 166 |
| 6. PER | (Carmen Pimentel, Gaby Cardenas, Raquel Chumpitaz, Ana Cecilia Carrillo, Maria Del Risco, Cecilia Tait, Silvia Leon, Aurora Heredia, Gina Torrealva, Natalia Malaga) | 1 | 4 | 7 | 12 | 189 | 257 |
| 7. BRA | (Denise Porto Mattioli, Ivonette das Neves, Lenice Peluso Oliveira, Regina Vilela Santos, | 1 | 4 | 7 | 12 | 210 | 248 |

| | W | L | W | L | PF | PA |
|---|---|---|---|---|---|---|

Fernanda Emerick Silva, Paula Rodrigues Mello, Maria Isabel Alencar, Eliana Maria Aleixo, Maria Castanheira, Jacqueline Cruz Silva, Vera Helena Mossa, Rita Cassia Teixeira)

| | W | L | W | L | PF | PA |
|---|---|---|---|---|---|---|
| 8. ROM (Mariana Ionescu, Gabriela Coman, Dorina Savoiu, Victoria Georgescu, Ileana Dobroschi, Victoria Banciu, Irina Petculet, Orina Georgescu, Iuliana Enescu, Ioana Liteanu, Corina Crivat, Elena Piron) | 2 | 3 | 7 | 13 | 221 | 243 |

Final: SOV—GDR 15–12, 11–15, 15–13, 15–7
3rd Place: BUL—HUN 15–5, 13–15, 6–15, 15–4, 15–8
5th Place: CUB—PER 15–9, 15–7, 12–15, 15–5
7th Place: BRA—ROM 15–8, 15–12, 15–12

### 1984 Los Angeles-Long Beach T: 8, N: 8, D: 8.7.

| | | MATCHES | | SETS | | | |
|---|---|---|---|---|---|---|---|
| | | W | L | W | L | PF | PA |
| 1. CHN | (Lang Ping, Liang Yan, Zhu Ling, Hou Yuzhu, Yang Xilan, Jiang Ying, Li Yanjun, Yang Xiaojun, Zheng Meizhu, Zhang Rongfang) | 4 | 1 | 13 | 3 | 234 | 148 |
| 2. USA | (Paula Weishoff, Susan Woodstra, Rita Crockett, Laurie Flachmeier, Carolyn Becker, Flora Hyman, Rose Magers, Julie Vollertsen, Debbie Green, Kimberly Ruddins, Jeanne Beauprey, Linda Chisholm) | 4 | 1 | 12 | 6 | 239 | 218 |
| 3. JPN | (Yumi Egami, Kimie Morita, Yoko Mitsuya, Miyoko Hirose, Kyoko Ishida, Yoko Kagabu, Norie Hiro, Kayoko Sugiyama, Sachiko Otani, Keiko Miyajima, Emiko Odaka, Kumi Nakada) | 4 | 1 | 12 | 5 | 222 | 154 |
| 4. PER | (Carmen Pimentel, Rosa Garcia, Isabel Heredia, Gabriela Perez Del Solar, Cecilia Del Risco, Cecilia Tait, Luisa Cervera, Denisse Fajardo, Miriam Gallardo, Gina Torrealva, Natalia Malaga) | 2 | 3 | 7 | 11 | 192 | 229 |
| 5. KOR | (Lee Eun-kyung, Lee | 3 | 2 | 12 | 7 | 240 | 194 |

Un-yim, Lee Young-sun, Kim Jeong-sun, Han Kyung-ae, Lee Myung-hee, Kim Ok-soon, Park Mi-hee, Lim Hae-suk)

| | | W | L | W | L | PF | PA |
|---|---|---|---|---|---|---|---|
| 6. GER | (Ruth Holzhausen, Gudrun Witte, Beate Bühler, Regina Vossen, Sigrid Terstegge, Andrea Sauvigny, Renate Riek, Marina Staden, Almut Kemperdick, Terry Place-Brandel, Ute Hankers) | 2 | 3 | 6 | 9 | 160 | 184 |
| 7. BRA | (Vera Leme, Fernanda Da Silva, Monica Da Silva, Maria Salgado, Heloisa Roese, Regina Pereira Uchoa, Jacqueline Silva, Ana Maria Richa, Sandra Lima, Eliani Miranda Da Costa, Luiza Pinheiro Machado, Ana Margarida Alvares) | 1 | 4 | 6 | 12 | 212 | 236 |
| 8. CAN | (Diane Ratnik, Suzi Smith, Tracy Mills, Joyce Gamborg, Audrey Vandervelden, Monica Hitchcock, Karen Fraser, Rachel Beliveau, Lise Martin, Caroline Cote, Barb Broen, Josee Lebel) | 0 | 5 | 0 | 15 | 88 | 225 |

Final: CHN—USA 16–14, 15–3, 15–9
3rd Place: JPN—PER 13–15, 15–4, 15–7, 15–10
5th Place: KOR—GER 15–10, 15–10, 15–2
7th Place: BRA—CAN 15–9, 15–3, 15–8

The Chinese had defeated the U.S. in seven of eight pre-Olympic matches, but when the two teams faced each other for the first time in Los Angeles, in a preliminary match, the more experienced Americans came out on top 15–13, 7–15, 16–14, 15–12. Four nights later they met again to decide the championship. As the Chinese team entered the arena, their star spiker, Lang Ping, noticed a television screen displaying a freeze-frame of the U.S. coach and three of his players wearing gold medals around their necks. Lang stopped, pointed out the image to her teammates and said, "Let's pluck the medals from their necks." The Chinese team then put on a brilliant, almost flawless performance to defeat the U.S. in straight sets.

### 1988 Seoul T: 8, N: 8, D: 9.29.

| | | MATCHES | | SETS | | | |
|---|---|---|---|---|---|---|---|
| | | W | L | W | L | PF | PA |
| 1. SOV | (Valentina Ogienko, Yelena Volkova, Irina Smirnova, Tatyana Sidorenko, Irina Parkhomchuk, Olga Shkurnova, | 4 | 1 | 14 | 5 | 268 | 190 |

| | | Players | W | L | | | | |
|---|---|---|---|---|---|---|---|---|
| 2. | PER | (Cenaida Uribe, Rosa García, Gabriela Perez Del Solar, Isabel Heredia, Cecilia Tait, Luisa Cervera, Denisse Fajardo, Alejandra De La Guerra, Gina Torrealva, Natalia Malaga) | 4 | 1 | 14 | 9 | 303 | 269 |
| 3. | CHN | (Li Guojun, Hou Yuzhu, Yang Xilan, Su Huijuan, Jiyang Ying, Cui Yongmei, Yang Xiaojun, Zheng Meizhu, Wu Dan, Li Yueming) | 3 | 2 | 11 | 7 | 217 | 202 |
| 4. | JPN | (Yumi Maruyama, Kayoko Sugiyama, Reiko Takizawa, Miyako Yamashita, Akemi Sugiyama, Ichiko Sato, Norie Hiro, Kumi Nakada, Motoko Obayashi, Yukiko Takahashi, Sachico Fujita, Noriyuki Muneuchi) | 2 | 3 | 10 | 12 | 256 | 265 |
| 5. | GDR | (Steffi Schmidt, Susanne Lahme, Monika Beu, Ariane Radfan, Kathrin Langschwager, Maike Arlt, Brit Wiedemann, Ute Steppin, Grit Jensen, Dörte Stüdemann, Heike Jensen, Ute Langenau) | 3 | 2 | 10 | 9 | 238 | 246 |
| 6. | BRA | (Kerly Santos, Ana Beatriz Moser, Vera Mossa, Eliani Costa, Ana Maria Richa, Maria Trade, Ana Claudia Ramos, Marcia Cunha, Ana Lucia Barros, Sandra Suruagy, Fernanda Venturini, Cimone Storm) | 1 | 4 | 7 | 14 | 235 | 276 |
| 7. | USA | (Melissa McLinden, Angela Rock, Elizabeth Masakayan, Kimberly Oden, Kimberly Ruddins, Caren Kemner, Tammy Webb, Deitre Collins, Laurel Kessel, Prikeba Phipps, Liane Sato, Jayne McHugh) | 2 | 3 | 9 | 13 | 257 | 263 |
| 8. | KOR | (Park Mi-hee, Kim Kyung-hee, Kim Kui-soon, Lim Hye-sook, Yoo Young-mi, Nam Soon-ok, Yoon Chung-hye, Park Bok-rye, Kim Yoon-hye, Ji Kyung-hee) | 1 | 4 | 8 | 13 | 224 | 277 |

Final: SOV—PER 10–15, 12–15, 15–13, 15–7, 17–15
3rd Place: CHN—JPN 15–13, 15–6, 15–6
5th Place: GDR—BRA 15–9, 15–4, 11–15, 15–11
7th Place: USA—KOR 15–4, 12–15, 13–15, 15–9, 15–8

In 1948 Edwin Vasquez Cam of Peru won a gold medal in free pistol shooting. In the forty years that followed, no Peruvian was able to earn another Olympic title. But in 1988 the Peruvian people caught gold medal fever, pinning their hopes on their popular women's volleyball team. The team members were so well known that they were referred to always by their first names: Rosa, Gina, Natalia, Denisse, 6 foot 4½ inch Gabriela, and the media favorite, Cecelia.

With Cuba boycotted out of the Games, Peru's leading rivals were Japan, which had never finished out of the medals; the Soviet Union, which had never placed worse than second; and China, which had won each year's major tournament from 1981 through 1986 before faltering in 1987. So important was women's volleyball in China that when a new coach had to be chosen, the four leading contenders debated on national television.

In the very first match of the tournament, Japan defeated the U.S.S.R. in five sets, the final set going to 19–17. Prior to 1988 the Soviets had lost only two of 27 Olympic contests—both to Japan. Three days later, Peru, trailing China 9–14 in the fifth set, scored 7 straight points to win the match. In their next match the Peruvians spotted the U.S. two sets, then came roaring back for another five-set victory. In the first semifinal, the U.S.S.R. obliterated the Chinese 15–0, 15–9, 15–2. The second semi saw Peru take the first two sets from Japan 15–9, 15–6, then lose the next two 6–15, 10–15, before sealing the victory 15–13.

The final took place at 6.30 a.m., Peru time, with almost the entire nation glued to the nearest television set. The Peruvian women won the first two sets 15–10, 15–12, and led the third 12–6. At this point, with most of the 6500 spectators cheering wildly for Peru, the Soviet coach, Nicolai Karpol, called timeout and made three substitutions. When play resumed, the momentum had shifted. The Soviets outscored the Peruvians 9–1 to win the set. They then took the next set 15–7 and led 6–0 in the fifth set. But Peru would not give in. They fought back to tie the score at 7. The U.S.S.R. moved ahead again, 10–7. Again Peru came from behind to tie. They even took the lead at 15–14. Both sides fought off match points. Finally, the Soviets won 17–15. .The Soviet women were so drained, physically and emotionally, that medical personnel had to be rushed onto the court to revive them for the medal ceremony.

Four of the six Soviet starters, as well as coach Karpol, were members of the Uralochka factory team of Sverdlovsk.

# WEIGHTLIFTING

| Flyweight | Light Heavyweight |
|---|---|
| Bantamweight | Middle Heavyweight |
| Featherweight | 100 Kg |
| Lightweight | Heavyweight |
| Middleweight | Super Heavyweight—Unlimited Weight |

Each contestant is allowed three attempts at each type of lift. The *snatch* is performed by lifting the bar from the floor to overhead in one movement and holding it there for two seconds. The *clean and jerk,* or *jerk,* is a two-part lift. First the weight is brought up to the shoulders and then, using the combined strength of arms and legs, it is raised overhead. The *press,* which was discontinued following the 1972 Olympics, required the lifter to bring the bar to his shoulders, wait two seconds for the judges' approval, and then lift the bar overhead using only the arms. When a tie occurs, the man with the lower bodyweight is declared the winner. If a lifter completes a successful lift within 10 kilograms of the world record, he is allowed a fourth attempt, which does not count as part of the competition but can count as a world record.

## FLYWEIGHT

(52 kg—114.61 lbs)

**1896–1968** not held

**1972 Munich** C: 17, N: 13, D: 8.31. WR: 342.5 kg (Sándor Holczreiter)

|  |  |  | PRESS |  | SNATCH |  | JERK |  | TOTAL KG |
|---|---|---|---|---|---|---|---|---|---|
| 1. | Zygmunt Smalcerz | POL | 112.5 | OR | 100.0 |  | 125.0 |  | 337.5 |
| 2. | Lajos Szücs | HUN | 107.5 |  | 95.0 |  | 127.5 |  | 330.0 |
| 3. | Sándor Holczreiter | HUN | 112.5 | OR | 92.5 |  | 122.5 |  | 327.5 |
| 4. | Tetsuhide Sasaki | JPN | 105.0 |  | 97.5 |  | 120.0 |  | 322.5 |
| 5. | Gyi Aung | MYA | 95.0 |  | 105.0 | WR | 120.0 |  | 320.0 |
| 6. | Pak Dong-geun | PRK | 97.5 |  | 90.0 |  | 130.0 | OR | 317.5 |
| 7. | Chaiya Sukchinda | THA | 100.0 |  | 92.5 |  | 120.0 |  | 312.5 |
| 8. | Ion Hortopan | ROM | 97.5 |  | 95.0 |  | 117.5 |  | 310.0 |

Charlie Depthios of Indonesia took an extra lift at the end of the competition and set a world jerk record of 132.5 kg.

**1976 Montreal** C: 23, N: 18, D: 7.18. WR: 242.5 kg (Aleksandr Voronin)

|  |  |  | SNATCH | JERK |  | TOTAL KG |  |
|---|---|---|---|---|---|---|---|
| 1. | Aleksandr Voronin | SOV | 105.0 | 137.5 | OR | 242.5 | EWR |
| 2. | György Köszegi | HUN | 107.5 | 130.0 |  | 237.5 |  |
| 3. | Mohammad Nassiri | IRN | 100.0 | 135.0 |  | 235.0 |  |
| 4. | Masatomo Takeuchi | JPN | 105.0 | 127.5 |  | 232.5 |  |
| 5. | Francisco Casamayor | CUB | 100.0 | 127.5 |  | 227.5 |  |
| 6. | Stefan Leletko | POL | 95.0 | 125.0 |  | 220.0 |  |

|   |   | SNATCH | JERK | TOTAL KG |
|---|---|---|---|---|
| 7. Boleslav Pachol | CZE | 95.0 | 122.5 | 217.5 |
| 8. Daniel Nuñez Aguiar | CUB | 92.5 | 122.5 | 215.0 |

At 4 feet 8¼ inches, Voronin, an electrician from Kerekoo, was the shortest man in the competition. Taking an extra lift after winning the gold medal, he set a world jerk record of 141 kg.

**1980 Moscow** C: 18, N: 15, D: 7.20. WR: 247.5 kg (Aleksandr Voronin)

|   |   | SNATCH |   | JERK |   | TOTAL KG |   |
|---|---|---|---|---|---|---|---|
| 1. Kanybek Osmanoliev | SOV | 107.5 |   | 137.5 | EOR | 245.0 | OR |
| 2. Ho Bong-choi | PRK | 110.0 | OR | 135.0 |   | 245.0 |   |
| 3. Han Gyong-si | PRK | 110.0 | OR | 135.0 |   | 245.0 |   |
| 4. Béla Oláh | HUN | 110.0 | OR | 135.0 |   | 245.0 |   |
| 5. Stefan Leletko | POL | 105.0 |   | 135.0 |   | 240.0 |   |
| 6. Ferenc Hornyák | HUN | 107.5 |   | 130.0 |   | 237.5 |   |
| 7. Francisco Casamayor | CUB | 102.5 |   | 130.0 |   | 232.5 |   |
| 8. Adjya Jugdernamjil | MON | 97.5 |   | 117.5 |   | 215.0 |   |

This unusually close contest was won by Osmanoliev as a result of his lower bodyweight. Han and Oláh had registered the same bodyweight, but Han was awarded third place when the two lifters were reweighed *after* the competition and Han was 3½ ounces lighter. Han set a world snatch record of 113 kg on his fourth attempt.

**1984 Los Angeles-Westchester** C: 20, N: 15, D: 7.29. WR: 262.5 kg (Neno Terziiski)

|   |   | SNATCH | JERK | TOTAL KG |
|---|---|---|---|---|
| 1. Zeng Guoqiang | CHN | 105.0 | 130.0 | 235.0 |
| 2. Zhou Peishun | CHN | 107.5 | 127.5 | 235.0 |
| 3. Kazushito Manabe | JPN | 102.5 | 130.0 | 232.5 |
| 4. Hidemi Miyashita | JPN | 107.5 | 122.5 | 230.0 |
| 5. Maman Suryaman | INA | 102.5 | 125.0 | 227.5 |
| 6. Bang Hyo-mun | KOR | 100.0 | 125.0 | 225.0 |
| 7. José Diaz Lopez | PAN | 95.0 | 125.0 | 220.0 |
| 8. Levent Erdogan | TUR | 95.0 | 120.0 | 215.0 |

DISQ (Drugs): Mahmood Tarha (LEB) 230.0

No sport was as hard-hit by the 1984 Soviet-bloc boycott as weightlifting. Missing from the competition in the ten weight categories were all ten of the defending world champions, 29 of the 30 medalists at the last world championships, and 94 of the top 100 ranked lifters.

Zeng was awarded first place because he weighed 3½ ounces less than Zhou. Tarha, in fourth place, was disqualified because he tested positive for anabolic steroids. At the Friendship Games, held in Varna, Bulgaria, for weightlifters from boycotting nations, the gold medal went to world record holder Neno Terziiski of Bulgaria with a total of 252.5 kg.

**1988 Seoul** C: 24, N: 18, D: 9.18. WR: 267.5 kg (He Zhuoqiang)

|   |   | SNATCH |   | JERK |   | TOTAL KG |   |
|---|---|---|---|---|---|---|---|
| 1. Sevdalin Marinov | BUL | 120.0 | WR | 150.0 | OR | 270.0 | WR |
| 2. Chun Byung-kwan | KOR | 112.5 |   | 147.5 |   | 260.0 |   |

|    |                    |     | SNATCH | JERK  | TOTAL KG |
|----|--------------------|-----|--------|-------|----------|
| 3. | He Zhuoqiang       | CHN | 112.5  | 145.0 | 257.5    |
| 4. | Zhang Shoulie      | CHN | 115.0  | 142.5 | 257.5    |
| 5. | Jacek Gutowski     | POL | 112.5  | 135.0 | 247.5    |
| 6. | Traian Ciharean    | ROM | 110.0  | 130.0 | 240.0    |
| 7. | Béla Oláh          | HUN | 107.5  | 130.0 | 237.5    |
| 8. | Kazushito Manabe   | JPN | 105.0  | 125.0 | 230.0    |

Despite He Zhuoqiang's having set a world record 3 months before the Olympics, Marinov had dominated the division since 1985, when he won the world championship at age 17.

## BANTAMWEIGHT
### (56 kg—123 lbs)

**1896–1936** not held

**1948 London** C: 19, N: 14, D: 8.9. WR: 300 kg (Joseph Di Pietro)

|    |                 |     | PRESS |    | SNATCH |    | JERK  |    | TOTAL KG |    |
|----|-----------------|-----|-------|----|--------|----|-------|----|----------|----|
| 1. | Joseph Di Pietro| USA | 105.0 | OR | 90.0   |    | 112.5 |    | 307.5    | WR |
| 2. | Julian Creus    | GBR | 82.5  |    | 95.0   | OR | 120.0 |    | 297.5    |    |
| 3. | Richard Tom     | USA | 87.5  |    | 90.0   |    | 117.5 |    | 295.0    |    |
| 4. | Lee Kyu-hyuk    | KOR | 77.5  |    | 92.5   |    | 120.0 |    | 290.0    |    |
| 5. | Mahmoud Namjou  | IRN | 82.5  |    | 82.5   |    | 122.5 | OR | 287.5    |    |
| 6. | Marcel Thévenet | FRA | 90.0  |    | 80.0   |    | 110.0 |    | 280.0    |    |
| 7. | Rosaire Smith   | CAN | 82.5  |    | 85.0   |    | 110.0 |    | 277.5    |    |
| 8. | Maurice Crow    | NZE | 77.5  |    | 85.0   |    | 110.0 |    | 272.5    |    |

Joe Di Pietro's height was variously reported as 4 feet 8 inches or 4 feet 10 inches. Whichever figure is correct, his arms were so short that he was barely able to raise the bar above his head.

**1952 Helsinki** C: 19, N: 18, D: 7.25. WR: 317.5 kg (Mahmoud Namjou)

|    |                       |     | PRESS | SNATCH |    | JERK  |    | TOTAL KG |    |
|----|-----------------------|-----|-------|--------|----|-------|----|----------|----|
| 1. | Ivan Udodov           | SOV | 90.0  | 97.5   | OR | 127.5 | OR | 315.0    | OR |
| 2. | Mahmoud Namjou        | IRN | 90.0  | 95.0   |    | 122.5 |    | 307.5    |    |
| 3. | Ali Mirzal            | IRN | 95.0  | 92.5   |    | 112.5 |    | 300.0    |    |
| 4. | Kim Hae-nam           | KOR | 80.0  | 95.0   |    | 120.0 |    | 295.0    |    |
| 5. | Kamal Mahmoud Mahgoub | EGY | 75.0  | 95.0   |    | 122.5 |    | 292.5    |    |
| 6. | Pedro Landero         | PHI | 90.0  | 87.5   |    | 115.0 |    | 292.5    |    |
| 7. | Maurice Megennis      | GBR | 82.5  | 85.0   |    | 112.5 |    | 280.0    |    |
| 8. | Lon Mohamed Noor      | SIN | 77.5  | 85.0   |    | 112.5 |    | 275.0    |    |

**1956 Melbourne** C: 16, N: 13, D: 11.23. WR: 335 kg (Vladimir Stogov)

|    |                  |     | PRESS |     | SNATCH |    | JERK  |    | TOTAL KG |    |
|----|------------------|-----|-------|-----|--------|----|-------|----|----------|----|
| 1. | Charles Vinci    | USA | 105.0 | EOR | 105.0  | OR | 132.5 |    | 342.5    | WR |
| 2. | Vladimir Stogov  | SOV | 105.0 | EOR | 105.0  | OR | 127.5 |    | 337.5    |    |
| 3. | Mahmoud Namjou   | IRN | 100.0 |     | 102.5  |    | 130.0 |    | 332.5    |    |
| 4. | Yu In-ho         | KOR | 90.0  |     | 95.0   |    | 135.0 | OR | 320.0    |    |
| 5. | Kim Hae-nam      | KOR | 85.0  |     | 95.0   |    | 127.5 |    | 307.5    |    |
| 6. | Yoshio Nanbu     | JPN | 87.5  |     | 97.5   |    | 120.0 |    | 305.0    |    |
| 7. | Reginald Gaffley | SAF | 97.5  |     | 90.0   |    | 117.5 |    | 305.0    |    |
| 8. | Yukio Furuyama   | JPN | 90.0  |     | 87.5   |    | 125.0 |    | 302.5    |    |

As weigh-in time approached, the 4-foot 10-inch Vinci was one and a half pounds overweight. After an hour of running and sweating he was still seven ounces over the limit with 15 minutes to go. Fortunately, a severe last-minute haircut did the trick, and Vinci went on to win the gold medal.

**1960 Rome** C: 22, N: 18, D: 9.7. WR: 345 kg (Vladimir Stogov)

|  |  | PRESS |  | SNATCH |  | JERK |  | TOTAL KG |  |
|---|---|---|---|---|---|---|---|---|---|
| 1. Charles Vinci | USA | 105.0 | EOR | 107.5 | EWR | 132.5 |  | 345.0 | EWR |
| 2. Yoshinobu Miyake | JPN | 97.5 |  | 105.0 |  | 135.0 | EOR | 337.5 |  |
| 3. Esmaiil Elmkhan | IRN | 97.5 |  | 100.0 |  | 132.5 |  | 330.0 |  |
| 4. Shigeo Kogure | JPN | 90.0 |  | 102.5 |  | 130.0 |  | 322.5 |  |
| 5. Marian Jankowski | POL | 92.5 |  | 100.0 |  | 130.0 |  | 322.5 |  |
| 6. Imre Földi | HUN | 100.0 |  | 90.0 |  | 130.0 |  | 320.0 |  |
| 7. Yu In-ho | KOR | 90.0 |  | 95.0 |  | 130.0 |  | 315.0 |  |
| 8. Husain Hasan | IRQ | 87.5 |  | 100.0 |  | 125.0 |  | 312.5 |  |

**1964 Tokyo** C: 24, N: 18, D: 10.11. WR: 352.5 kg (Yoshinobu Miyake)

|  |  | PRESS |  | SNATCH |  | JERK |  | TOTAL KG |  |
|---|---|---|---|---|---|---|---|---|---|
| 1. Aleksei Vakhonin | SOV | 110.0 |  | 105.0 |  | 142.5 | OR | 357.5 | WR |
| 2. Imre Földi | HUN | 115.0 | OR | 102.5 |  | 137.5 |  | 355.0 |  |
| 3. Shiro Ichinoseki | JPN | 100.0 |  | 110.0 | OR | 137.5 |  | 347.5 |  |
| 4. Henryk Trebicki | POL | 105.0 |  | 102.5 |  | 135.0 |  | 342.5 |  |
| 5. Yang Mu-shin | KOR | 97.5 |  | 107.5 |  | 135.0 |  | 340.0 |  |
| 6. Yukio Furuyama | JPN | 105.0 |  | 100.0 |  | 130.0 |  | 335.0 |  |
| 7. Yu In-ho | KOR | 97.5 |  | 100.0 |  | 137.5 |  | 335.0 |  |
| 8. Martin Dias | GUY | 100.0 |  | 102.5 |  | 132.5 |  | 335.0 |  |

Vakhonin, a 4-foot 10¾ inch, 29-year-old coal miner, set a world record in the jerk that was not allowed because he was, by then, overweight. The lift did count as an *Olympic* record, however. The same treatment was given to Ichinoseki's snatch record. Földi, who had sweated down from a featherweight, was handicapped in the snatch because one of his fingers was missing and another was paralyzed. Vakhonin disappeared from international competition prior to the 1968 Olympics after being accused of "conduct unbecoming a Master of Sport."

**1968 Mexico City** C: 20, N: 19, D: 10.13. WR: 367.5 kg (Gennady Chetin)

|  |  | PRESS |  | SNATCH | JERK |  | TOTAL KG |  |
|---|---|---|---|---|---|---|---|---|
| 1. Mohammad Nassiri | IRN | 112.5 |  | 105.0 | 150.0 | WR | 367.5 | EWR |
| 2. Imre Földi | HUN | 122.5 | OR | 105.0 | 140.0 |  | 367.5 | EWR |
| 3. Henryk Trebicki | POL | 115.0 |  | 107.5 | 135.0 |  | 357.5 |  |
| 4. Gennady Chetin | SOV | 110.0 |  | 102.5 | 140.0 |  | 352.5 |  |
| 5. Shiro Ichinoseki | JPN | 110.0 |  | 107.5 | 132.5 |  | 350.0 |  |
| 6. Fernando Baez Cruz | PUR | 120.0 |  | 92.5 | 132.5 |  | 345.0 |  |
| 7. Atanas Kirov | BUL | 105.0 |  | 100.0 | 130.0 |  | 335.0 |  |
| 8. Chaiya Sukchinda | TAI | 100.0 |  | 105.0 | 125.0 |  | 330.0 |  |

Nassiri was awarded first place because his bodyweight was ten ounces less than Földi's.

**1972 Munich** C: 24, N: 20, D: 8.28. WR: 375 kg (Gennady Chetin)

|   |   |   | PRESS |   | SNATCH | JERK | TOTAL KG |   |
|---|---|---|---|---|---|---|---|---|
| 1. | Imre Földi | HUN | 127.5 | OR | 107.5 | 142.5 | 377.5 | WR |
| 2. | Mohammad Nassiri | IRN | 127.5 | OR | 100.0 | 142.5 | 370.0 |   |
| 3. | Gennady Chetin | SOV | 120.0 |   | 107.5 | 140.0 | 367.5 |   |
| 4. | Henryk Trebicki | POL | 122.5 |   | 107.5 | 135.0 | 365.0 |   |
| 5. | Atanas Kirov | BUL | 117.5 |   | 105.0 | 140.0 | 362.5 |   |
| 6. | George Vasiliades | AUS | 115.0 |   | 102.5 | 137.5 | 355.0 |   |
| 7. | Hiroshi Ono | JPN | 115.0 |   | 105.0 | 135.0 | 355.0 |   |
| 8. | Georgi Todorov | BUL | 110.0 |   | 100.0 | 140.0 | 350.0 |   |

Tenth-place finisher Koji Miki of Japan set an Olympic snatch record of 112.5 kg and then broke the world record with an extra lift of 114 kg. Polish-born Zeev Friedman, who finished twelfth, was one of the 11 Israelis who were murdered at the Games by Palestinian terrorists.

**1976 Montreal** C: 24, N: 19, D: 7.19. WR: 260 kg (Atanas Kirov)

|   |   |   | SNATCH |   | JERK | TOTAL KG |   |
|---|---|---|---|---|---|---|---|
| 1. | Norair Nurikian | BUL | 117.5 | OR | 145.0 | 262.5 | WR |
| 2. | Grzegorz Cziura | POL | 115.0 |   | 137.5 | 252.5 |   |
| 3. | Kenkichi Ando | JPN | 107.5 |   | 142.5 | 250.0 |   |
| 4. | Leszek Skorupa | POL | 112.5 |   | 137.5 | 250.0 |   |
| 5. | Imre Földi | HUN | 105.0 |   | 140.0 | 245.0 |   |
| 6. | Bernhard Backfisch | GER | 105.0 |   | 137.5 | 242.5 |   |
| 7. | Carlos Lastre | CUB | 105.0 |   | 135.0 | 240.0 |   |
| 8. | Fazlollah Dehkhoda | IRN | 105.0 |   | 135.0 | 240.0 |   |

Imre Földi became the only weightlifter to take part in five Olympics.

**1980 Moscow** C: 21, N: 17, D: 7.21. WR: 272.5 kg (Daniel Núñez Aguiar)

|   |   |   | SNATCH |   | JERK |   | TOTAL KG |   |
|---|---|---|---|---|---|---|---|---|
| 1. | Daniel Núñez Aguiar | CUB | 125.0 | WR | 150.0 |   | 275.0 | WR |
| 2. | Yurik Sarkisian | SOV | 112.5 |   | 157.5 | WR | 270.0 |   |
| 3. | Tadeusz Dembończyk | POL | 120.0 |   | 145.0 |   | 265.0 |   |
| 4. | Andreas Letz | GDR | 115.0 |   | 150.0 |   | 265.0 |   |
| 5. | Yang Eui-yong | PRK | 112.5 |   | 150.0 |   | 265.0 |   |
| 6. | Imre Stefanovics | HUN | 115.0 |   | 145.0 |   | 260.0 |   |
| 7. | Gheorghe Maftei | ROM | 105.0 |   | 142.5 |   | 247.5 |   |
| 8. | Pavel Petre | ROM | 105.0 |   | 140.0 |   | 245.0 |   |

Dembończyk was awarded the bronze medal as a result of a post-competition weigh-in.

**1984 Los Angeles-Westchester** C: 20, N: 18, D: 7.30. WR: 300 kg (Naim Suleymanoğlü)

|   |   |   | SNATCH |   | JERK | TOTAL KG |
|---|---|---|---|---|---|---|
| 1. | Wu Shude | CHN | 120.0 |   | 147.5 | 267.5 |
| 2. | Lai Runming | CHN | 125.0 | EOR | 140.0 | 265.0 |
| 3. | Masahiro Kotaka | JPN | 112.5 |   | 140.0 | 252.5 |
| 4. | Takashi Ichiba | JPN | 110.0 |   | 140.0 | 250.0 |
| 5. | Kim Chil-bong | KOR | 105.0 |   | 140.0 | 245.0 |
| 6. | Dionisio Muñoz | SPA | 110.0 |   | 132.5 | 242.5 |
| 7. | Arvo Ojalehto | FIN | 105.0 |   | 137.5 | 242.5 |
| 8. | Albert Hood | USA | 112.5 |   | 130.0 | 242.5 |

One of the most popular weightlifters at the Los Angeles Olympics was fourth place finisher Takashi Ichiba who entertained the audience by performing a back flip *before* each lift.

Few boycotting athletes in 1984 were more missed than world record holder Naim Suleymanoğlü, the 16-year-old boy wonder from Bulgaria. At the Friendship Games in September, Suleymanoğlü defeated Oksen Mirzoian of the U.S.S.R. 297.5 kg to 295.0 kg. In 1986 Suleymanoğlü, a member of Bulgaria's Turkish minority, defected after a competition in Melbourne, Australia, and moved to Turkey.

**1988 Seoul** C: 23, N: 17, D: 9.19. WR: 300 kg (Naim Suleymanoğlü)

| | | SNATCH | | JERK | | TOTAL KG | |
|---|---|---|---|---|---|---|---|
| 1. Oksen Mirzoyan | SOV | 127.5 | OR | 165.0 | OR | 292.5 | OR |
| 2. He Yingqiang | CHN | 125.0 | | 162.5 | | 287.5 | |
| 3. Liu Shoubin | CHN | 127.5 | OR | 140.0 | | 267.5 | |
| 4. Dirdja Wihardja | INA | 112.5 | | 142.5 | | 255.0 | |
| 5. Takashi Ichiba | JPN | 107.5 | | 145.0 | | 252.5 | |
| 6. Kim Kwi-shik | KOR | 110.0 | | 142.5 | | 252.5 | |
| 7. Joaquin Valle | SPA | 112.5 | | 135.0 | | 247.5 | |
| 8. Giovanni Scarantino | ITA | 110.0 | | 135.0 | | 245.0 | |

DISQ (Drugs): Mitko Grablev (BUL) 297.5

# FEATHERWEIGHT
## (60 kg—132 lbs)

**1896–1912** not held

**1920 Antwerp** C: 14, N: 11, D: 8.28.

| | | PRESS | SNATCH | JERK | TOTAL KG |
|---|---|---|---|---|---|
| 1. François de Haes | BEL | 60.0 | 65.0 | 95.0 | 220.0 |
| 2. Alfred Schmidt | EST | 55.0 | 65.0 | 90.0 | 210.0 |
| 3. Eugène Ryther | SWI | 55.0 | 65.0 | 90.0 | 210.0 |
| 4. Luigi Gatti | ITA | 50.0 | 55.0 | 90.0 | 195.0 |
| 5. Ludvik Wágner | CZE | 50.0 | 65.0 | 80.0 | 195.0 |
| 6. Gustav Eriksson | SWE | 47.5 | 65.0 | 80.0 | 192.5 |
| 7. L. de Haes | BEL | 45.0 | 60.0 | 85.0 | 190.0 |
| 7. Karl Koiv | EST | 45.0 | 60.0 | 85.0 | 190.0 |

Schmidt was awarded second place after jerking 92.5 kg in a lift-off against Ryther.

**1924 Paris** C: 21, N: 11, D: 7.21.

| | | ONE-HAND SNATCH | | ONE-HAND JERK | | PRESS | | TWO-HAND SNATCH | | TWO-HAND JERK | | TOTAL KG |
|---|---|---|---|---|---|---|---|---|---|---|---|---|
| 1. Pierino Gabetti | ITA | 65.0 | OR | 77.5 | | 72.5 | | 82.5 | OR | 105.0 | OR | 402.5 |
| 2. Andreas Stadler | AUT | 65.0 | OR | 75.0 | | 65.0 | | 75.0 | | 105.0 | OR | 385.0 |
| 3. Arthur Reinmann | SWI | 57.5 | | 70.0 | | 80.0 | OR | 75.0 | | 100.0 | | 382.5 |
| 4. Maurice Martin | FRA | 60.0 | | 62.5 | | 75.0 | | 82.5 | OR | 100.0 | | 380.0 |
| 5. Wilhelm Rosinek | AUT | 57.5 | | 75.0 | | 67.5 | | 70.0 | | 105.0 | OR | 375.0 |
| 6. Gustav Ernesaks | EST | 60.0 | | 80.0 | OR | 67.5 | | 72.5 | | 92.5 | | 372.5 |
| 7. Alfred Baxter | GBR | 55.0 | | 65.0 | | 70.0 | | 75.0 | | 105.0 | OR | 370.0 |
| 8. E. Juillerat | SWI | 55.0 | | 70.0 | | 67.5 | | 75.0 | | 100.0 | | 367.5 |

M.H. Djemal Bey of Turkey, who finished 14th, was only 13 years old.

**1928 Amsterdam** C: 22, N: 13, D: 7.29.

|   |   |   | PRESS |   | SNATCH |   | JERK |   | TOTAL KG |   |
|---|---|---|---|---|---|---|---|---|---|---|
| 1. | Franz Andrysek | AUT | 77.5 | | 90.0 | OR | 120.0 | OR | 287.5 | OR |
| 2. | Pierino Gabetti | ITA | 80.0 | | 90.0 | OR | 112.5 | | 282.5 | |
| 3. | Hans Wölpert | GER | 92.5 | WR | 82.5 | | 107.5 | | 282.5 | |
| 4. | Giuseppe Conca | ITA | 92.5 | WR | 80.0 | | 105.0 | | 277.5 | |
| 5. | Arthur Reinmann | SWI | 82.5 | | 82.5 | | 110.0 | | 275.0 | |
| 6. | Andreas Stadler | AUT | 72.5 | | 80.0 | | 115.0 | | 267.5 | |
| 7. | H. Baudrand | FRA | 77.5 | | 80.0 | | 107.5 | | 265.0 | |
| 8. | M.H. Djemal Bey | TUR | 85.0 | | 75.0 | | 102.5 | | 262.5 | |
| 8. | Josef Vacek | CZE | 80.0 | | 82.5 | | 100.0 | | 262.5 | |
| 8. | F. Vitasek | CZE | 80.0 | | 82.5 | | 100.0 | | 262.5 | |

**1932 Los Angeles** C: 6, N: 4, D: 7.31.

|   |   |   | PRESS | SNATCH | JERK | TOTAL KG |   |
|---|---|---|---|---|---|---|---|
| 1. | Raymond Suvigny | FRA | 82.5 | 87.5 | 117.5 | 287.5 | EOR |
| 2. | Hans Wölpert | GER | 85.0 | 87.5 | 110.0 | 282.5 | |
| 3. | Anthony Terlazzo | USA | 82.5 | 85.0 | 112.5 | 280.0 | |
| 4. | Helmut Schäfer | GER | 77.5 | 77.5 | 112.5 | 267.5 | |
| 5. | Attilio Bescapè | ITA | 82.5 | 77.5 | 102.5 | 262.5 | |
| 6. | Richard Bachtell | USA | 70.0 | 80.0 | 102.5 | 252.5 | |

An eating binge on the way to Los Angeles forced Suvigny to lose ten pounds in one week in order to make the weight limit.

**1936 Berlin** C: 21, N: 13, D: 8.2. WR: 297.5 kg (Max Walther)

|   |   |   | PRESS |   | SNATCH |   | JERK |   | TOTAL KG |   |
|---|---|---|---|---|---|---|---|---|---|---|
| 1. | Anthony Terlazzo | USA | 92.5 | EOR | 97.5 | OR | 122.5 | | 312.5 | WR |
| 2. | Saleh Mohammed Soliman | EGY | 85.0 | | 95.0 | | 125.0 | OR | 305.0 | |
| 3. | Ibrahim Hassan Shams | EGY | 80.0 | | 95.0 | | 125.0 | OR | 300.0 | |
| 4. | Anton Richter | AUT | 80.0 | | 97.5 | OR | 120.0 | | 297.5 | |
| 5. | Georg Liebsch | GER | 92.5 | OR | 90.0 | | 107.5 | | 290.0 | |
| 6. | Attilo Bescapè | ITA | 87.5 | | 90.0 | | 110.0 | | 287.5 | |
| 7. | John Terry | USA | 75.0 | | 92.5 | | 120.0 | | 287.5 | |
| 8. | Max Walther | GER | 75.0 | | 90.0 | | 115.0 | | 280.0 | |

**1948 London** C: 23, N: 18, D: 8.9. WR: 320 kg (Arvid Anderson)

|   |   |   | PRESS |   | SNATCH |   | JERK |   | TOTAL KG |   |
|---|---|---|---|---|---|---|---|---|---|---|
| 1. | Mahmoud Fayad | EGY | 92.5 | | 105.0 | WR | 135.0 | WR | 332.5 | WR |
| 2. | Rodney Wilkes | TRI | 97.5 | | 97.5 | | 122.5 | | 317.5 | |
| 3. | Jaafar Salmasi | IRN | 100.0 | OR | 97.5 | | 115.0 | | 312.5 | |
| 4. | Nam Su-il | KOR | 92.5 | | 92.5 | | 122.5 | | 307.5 | |
| 5. | Rodrigo Del Rosario | PHI | 97.5 | | 92.5 | | 117.5 | | 307.5 | |
| 6. | Kotaro Ishikawa | USA | 92.5 | | 95.0 | | 120.0 | | 307.5 | |
| 7. | Johan Runge | DEN | 95.0 | | 90.0 | | 120.0 | | 305.0 | |
| 8. | Max Heral | FRA | 85.0 | | 95.0 | | 120.0 | | 300.0 | |

**1952 Helsinki** C: 22, N: 21, D: 7.25. WR: 332.5 kg (Mahmoud Fayad)

|   |   |   | PRESS | SNATCH |   | JERK |   | TOTAL KG |   |
|---|---|---|---|---|---|---|---|---|---|
| 1. | Rafael Chimishkyan | SOV | 97.5 | 105.0 | EOR | 135.0 | EOR | 337.5 | WR |
| 2. | Nikolai Saksonov | SOV | 95.0 | 105.0 | | 132.5 | | 332.5 | |

| | | PRESS | | SNATCH | JERK | TOTAL KG |
|---|---|---|---|---|---|---|
| 3. Rodney Wilkes | TRI | 100.0 | | 100.0 | 122.5 | 322.5 |
| 4. Rodrigo Del Rosario | PHI | 105.0 | OR | 92.5 | 120.0 | 317.5 |
| 5. Said Khalifa Gouda | EGY | 85.0 | | 102.5 | 125.0 | 312.5 |
| 6. Chay Weng Yew | SIN | 87.5 | | 97.5 | 127.5 | 312.5 |
| 7. Balint Nagy | HUN | 85.0 | | 97.5 | 125.0 | 307.5 |
| 8. Mohsen Tabatabaii | IRN | 90.0 | | 97.5 | 120.0 | 307.5 |

**1956 Melbourne** C: 21, N: 19, D: 11.23. WR: 350 kg (Rafael Chimishkyan)

| | | PRESS | | SNATCH | | JERK | | TOTAL KG | |
|---|---|---|---|---|---|---|---|---|---|
| 1. Isaac Berger | USA | 107.5 | | 107.5 | OR | 137.5 | OR | 352.5 | WR |
| 2. Yevgeny Minayev | SOV | 115.0 | WR | 100.0 | | 127.5 | | 342.5 | |
| 3. Marian Zieliński | POL | 105.0 | | 102.5 | | 127.5 | | 335.0 | |
| 4. Rodney Wilkes | TRI | 100.0 | | 105.0 | | 125.0 | | 330.0 | |
| 5. Hiroyoshi Shiratori | JPN | 97.5 | | 100.0 | | 127.5 | | 325.0 | |
| 6 Georg Miske | GDR | 100.0 | | 95.0 | | 125.0 | | 320.0 | |
| 7. Tan Ser Cher | SIN | 92.5 | | 92.5 | | 130.0 | | 315.0 | |
| 8. Lee Kyung-sob | KOR | 90.0 | | 95.0 | | 132.5 | | 312.5 | |

Ike Berger was an Israeli-born teenager from Brooklyn.

**1960 Rome** C: 28, N: 25, D: 9.7. WR: 372.5 kg (Isaac Berger)

| | | PRESS | | SNATCH | | JERK | | TOTAL KG | |
|---|---|---|---|---|---|---|---|---|---|
| 1. Yevgeny Minayev | SOV | 120.0 | EWR | 110.0 | OR | 142.5 | OR | 372.5 | EWR |
| 2. Isaac Berger | USA | 117.5 | | 105.0 | | 140.0 | | 362.5 | |
| 3. Sebastiano Mannironi | ITA | 107.5 | | 110.0 | | 135.0 | | 352.5 | |
| 4. Kim Hae-nam | KOR | 105.0 | | 105.0 | | 135.0 | | 345.0 | |
| 5. Yukio Furuyama | JPN | 107.5 | | 102.5 | | 135.0 | | 345.0 | |
| 6. Hosni Abbas | UAR | 102.5 | | 95.0 | | 140.0 | | 337.5 | |
| 7. Tun Kywe | MYA | 100.0 | | 100.0 | | 127.5 | | 327.5 | |
| 8. Alberto Nogar | PHI | 97.5 | | 100.0 | | 127.5 | | 325.0 | |

The competition took ten hours and didn't end until four a.m., when Berger twice failed to jerk 152.5 kg. Minayev had lost to Berger six straight times prior to the Olympics. In Rome, he made all nine of his lifts.

**1964 Tokyo** C: 22, N: 20, D: 10.12. WR: 387.5 kg (Yoshinobu Miyake)

| | | PRESS | | SNATCH | | JERK | | TOTAL KG | |
|---|---|---|---|---|---|---|---|---|---|
| 1. Yoshinobu Miyake | JPN | 122.5 | OR | 122.5 | OR | 152.5 | WR | 397.5 | WR |
| 2. Isaac Berger | USA | 122.5 | OR | 107.5 | | 152.5 | WR | 382.5 | |
| 3. Mieczyslaw Nowak | POL | 112.5 | | 115.0 | | 150.0 | | 377.5 | |
| 4. Hiroshi Fukuda | JPN | 120.0 | | 115.0 | | 140.0 | | 375.0 | |
| 5. Sebastiano Mannironi | ITA | 112.5 | | 112.5 | | 145.0 | | 370.0 | |
| 6. Kim Hae-nam | KOR | 115.0 | | 112.5 | | 140.0 | | 367.5 | |
| 7. Rudolf Kozlowski | POL | 110.0 | | 107.5 | | 140.0 | | 357.5 | |
| 8. Hosni Abbas | UAR | 105.0 | | 100.0 | | 137.5 | | 342.5 | |

Yoshinobu Miyake, who had won the Bantamweight silver medal in 1960, was a 24-year-old lieutenant in the National Self-Defense Force. Only 5 feet tall, he came from a poor family in Miyagi prefecture in northern Japan. His parents sold some pigs to raise the money to see their son compete in the Olympics.

**1968 Mexico City** C: 28, N: 22, D: 10.14. WR: 397.5 kg
(Yoshinobu Miyake)

| | | PRESS | | SNATCH | JERK | | TOTAL KG | |
|---|---|---|---|---|---|---|---|---|
| 1. Yoshinobu Miyake | JPN | 122.5 | EOR | 117.5 | 152.5 | EWR | 392.5 | |
| 2. Dito Shanidze | SOV | 120.0 | | 117.5 | 150.0 | | 387.5 | |
| 3. Yoshiyuki Miyake | JPN | 122.5 | EOR | 115.0 | 147.5 | | 385.0 | |
| 4. Jan Wojnowski | POL | 117.5 | | 115.0 | 150.0 | | 382.5 | |
| 5. Mieczyslaw Nowak | POL | 117.5 | | 110.0 | 147.5 | | 375.0 | |
| 6. Nasrollah Dehnavi | IRN | 117.5 | | 107.5 | 140.0 | | 365.0 | |
| 7. Young Moo-shin | KOR | 110.0 | | 115.0 | 140.0 | | 365.0 | |
| 8. Manuel Mateos | MEX | 120.0 | | 100.0 | 140.0 | | 360.0 | |

Yoshiyuki Miyake was six years younger than his brother Yoshinobu.

**1972 Munich** C: 13, N; 11, D: 8.29. WR: 402.5 kg (Dito Shanidze)

| | | PRESS | | SNATCH | JERK | | TOTAL KG | |
|---|---|---|---|---|---|---|---|---|
| 1. Norair Nurikian | BUL | 127.5 | OR | 117.5 | 157.5 | WR | 402.5 | EWR |
| 2. Dito Shanidze | SOV | 127.5 | OR | 120.0 | 152.5 | | 400.0 | |
| 3. János Benedek | HUN | 125.0 | | 120.0 | 145.0 | | 390.0 | |
| 4. Yoshinobu Miyake | JPN | 120.0 | | 120.0 | 145.0 | | 385.0 | |
| 5. Kurt Pittner | AUT | 125.0 | | 112.5 | 145.0 | | 382.5 | |
| 6. Rolando Chang | CUB | 120.0 | | 115.0 | 142.5 | | 377.5 | |
| 7. Mieczyslaw Nowak | POL | 120.0 | | 110.0 | 145.0 | | 375.0 | |
| 8. Peppino Tanti | ITA | 120.0 | | 107.5 | 140.0 | | 367.5 | |

This division saw the rare appearance of an athlete from Albania. Ymez Pampuri broke the Olympic record in the press and actually led the competition after the first round due to his lower bodyweight. However he could do no better than 12th and tenth in the snatch and jerk, respectively, and wound up in ninth place.

**1976 Montreal** C: 17, N: 13, D: 7.20. WR: 285 kg (Georgi Todorov)

| | | SNATCH | | JERK | | TOTAL KG | |
|---|---|---|---|---|---|---|---|
| 1. Nikolai Kolesnikov | SOV | 125.0 | OR | 160.0 | OR | 285.0 | EWR |
| 2. Georgi Todorov | BUL | 122.5 | | 157.5 | | 280.0 | |
| 3. Kazumasa Hirai | JPN | 125.0 | OR | 150.0 | | 275.0 | |
| 4. Takashi Saito | JPN | 110.0 | | 152.5 | | 262.5 | |
| 5. Edward Weitz | ISR | 110.0 | | 152.5 | | 262.5 | |
| 6. Davoud Maleki | IRN | 115.0 | | 145.0 | | 260.0 | |
| 7. Pedro Fuentes | CUB | 112.5 | | 145.0 | | 257.5 | |
| 8. Om Jong-guk | PRK | 110.0 | | 145.0 | | 255.0 | |

Kolesnikov set a jerk world record of 161.5 kg on his fourth attempt.

**1980 Moscow** C: 18, N: 14, D: 7.22. WR: 297.5 kg (Viktor Mazin)

| | | SNATCH | | JERK | | TOTAL KG | |
|---|---|---|---|---|---|---|---|
| 1. Viktor Mazin | SOV | 130.0 | OR | 160.0 | EOR | 290.0 | OR |
| 2. Stefan Dimitrov | BUL | 127.5 | | 160.0 | EOR | 287.5 | |
| 3. Marek Seweryn | POL | 127.5 | | 155.0 | | 282.5 | |
| 4. Antoni Pawlak | POL | 120.0 | | 150.0 | | 275.0 | |
| 5. Julio Loscos | CUB | 125.0 | | 150.0 | | 275.0 | |
| 6. František Nedved | CZE | 122.5 | | 150.0 | | 272.5 | |

| | | SNATCH | JERK | TOTAL KG |
|---|---|---|---|---|
| 7. Victor Perez | CUB | 117.5 | 152.5 | 270.0 |
| 8. Gelu Radu | ROM | 115.0 | 150.0 | 265.0 |

**1984 Los Angeles-Westchester** C: 21, N: 17, D: 7.31. WR: 315 kg (Stefan Topurov)

| | | SNATCH | JERK | TOTAL KG |
|---|---|---|---|---|
| 1. Chen Weiqiang | CHN | 125.0 | 157.5 | 282.5 |
| 2. Gelu Radu | ROM | 125.0 | 155.0 | 280.0 |
| 3. Tsai Wen-Yee | TAI | 125.0 | 147.5 | 272.5 |
| 4. Kaoru Wabiko | JPN | 120.0 | 150.0 | 270.0 |
| 5. Yosuke Muraki | JPN | 120.0 | 147.5 | 267.5 |
| 6. Lee Myeong-su | KOR | 117.5 | 150.0 | 267.5 |
| 7. Sorie Enda Nasution | INA | 115.0 | 152.5 | 267.5 |
| 8. Uolevi Kahelin | FIN | 112.5 | 155.0 | 267.5 |

Silver medalist Gelu Radu was the only medalist at the 1983 world championships to take part in the 1984 Olympics. The medal ceremony for this event held a special drama as it marked the first time that the platform was shared by athletes from China and Taiwan. Chen and Tsai shook hands and spoke kindly of each other.

At the Friendship Games in Varna, Bulgaria, in September, Stefan Topurov of Bulgaria broke his own world record with a combined lift of 322.5 kg. He was followed by two Soviet lifters, Yurik Sarkisian at 315 kg and Anton Kodzhabashev at 295 kg. At the 1983 world championships, Topurov had jerked 180 kg to become the first person in history to lift three times his own bodyweight.

**1988 Seoul** C: 17, N: 14, D: 9.20. WR: 335 kg (Naim Suleymanoğlü)

| | | SNATCH | | JERK | | TOTAL KG | |
|---|---|---|---|---|---|---|---|
| 1. Naim Suleymanoğlü | TUR | 152.5 | WR | 190.0 | WR | 342.5 | WR |
| 2. Stefan Topurov | BUL | 137.5 | | 175.0 | | 312.5 | |
| 3. Ye Huanming | CHN | 127.5 | | 160.0 | | 287.5 | |
| 4. Min Joon-ki | KOR | 125.0 | | 155.0 | | 280.0 | |
| 5. Yosuke Muraki | JPN | 127.5 | | 150.0 | | 277.5 | |
| 6. Giannis Sidriopoulos | GRE | 120.0 | | 145.0 | | 265.0 | |
| 7. Kazushige Oguri | JPN | 117.5 | | 142.5 | | 260.0 | |
| 8. Tolentino Murillo | COL | 120.0 | | 140.0 | | 260.0 | |

He was born Naim Suleimanov in the small mountain village of Ptichar in the region of Bulgaria with the highest concentration of ethnic Turks. His father, a miner, was 5 feet tall. His mother, who worked in a hot house, was 4 feet 7½ inches. Naim himself topped out just shy of 5 feet. Short though he may have been, he was also strong. In a nation where weightlifters are heroes, he was quickly discovered by Bulgarian sports officials.

He first competed internationally in a junior championship and, at the age of 14, came within 5½ pounds of breaking the *adult* world record for combined lifts. At 15 he set his first world record and at 16 he became the second lifter to clean and jerk three times his bodyweight. In recognition of his achievements, the Bulgarian government gave Suleimanov his own apartment and a monthly stipend. However, in 1984, at the same time that he was being well treated, the government also began a crack down on the Turkish minority. In December, Suleimanov returned from a training camp to his parents' hometown of Momchilgrad (they had moved there when he was 3) to discover that a major demonstration by Turks had been violently suppressed by Bulgarian authorities. The anti-Turkish campaign intensified. Mosques were closed, Moslem holidays and burials were banned, and the use of the Turkish language was outlawed, as was the wearing of Turkish clothes. Violators were imprisoned and even executed.

In 1985, Suleimanov attended a ten-day training camp in Melbourne, Australia. There he was approached by Bulgarian defectors of Turkish descent who offered to help him defect. The 18-year-old declined, but told them that if the Bulgarian government changed his name to a non-Islamic one, as they had done to other Turks, he would reconsider. When he returned to Bulgaria his passport was confiscated and he was issued a new one bearing the name Naum Shalamanov. During a tournament in Vienna, he told reporters that he was unhappy with his new name. The Bulgarian government forced him to recant on national television.

In December 1986, Suleimanov, by now a two-time world champion, returned to Melbourne for the World Cup competition. When the tournament was over, he joined the rest of the Bulgarian team for a banquet at the Leonda restaurant in the Melbourne suburb of Haw-

thorn. At one point he excused himself to go to the men's room—and never returned. After hiding out for four days, he presented himself to the Turkish consulate and asked for asylum. He was flown to London where he was met by a private jet belonging to Turkey's prime minister, Turgut Ozal. Upon arrival at the airport in Turkey, Suleimanov kissed the tarmac and became an instant national hero.

Olympic rules state that if an athlete changes nationality, he must wait three years to take part in international competition unless he receives a waiver from the country he has left. The Bulgarian government granted this waiver in 1988 after receiving over $1,000,000 from the Turkish government, as well as an assurance from Suleimanov (who by now had assumed the Turkish equivalent of his original name—Naim Suleymanoğlu) that he would suspend his public criticisms of their policies.

In Seoul, Suleymanoğlu lived up to all expectations. He broke the snatch world record with his second lift, then broke it again with his third. He repeated his double world record in the clean and jerk. His combined total was larger than that of the winner in the lightweight division and his best lifts in both the snatch and jerk were greater than those of Paul Anderson when he won the heavyweight division in 1956. At that time, Anderson weighed 303 pounds. Suleymanoğlu in 1988 weighed 132.

## LIGHTWEIGHT
### (67.5 kg—148.75 lbs)

**1896–1912** not held

**1920 Antwerp** C: 12, N: 10, D: 8.28.

| | | | ONE-HAND SNATCH | ONE-HAND JERK | TWO-HAND JERK | TOTAL KG |
|---|---|---|---|---|---|---|
| 1. | Alfred Neuland | EST | 72.5 | 75.0 | 110.0 | 257.5 |
| 2. | Louis Williquet | BEL | 60.0 | 75.0 | 105.0 | 240.0 |
| 3. | Florimond Rooms | BEL | 55.0 | 70.0 | 105.0 | 230.0 |
| 4. | Giulio Monti | ITA | 55.0 | 70.0 | 105.0 | 230.0 |
| 5. | Fernand Arnout | FRA | 60.0 | 60.0 | 100.0 | 220.0 |
| 5. | Martin Olofsson | SWE | 55.0 | 70.0 | 95.0 | 220.0 |
| 7. | Vaquette | FRA | 55.0 | 65.0 | 95.0 | 215.0 |
| 8. | Johny Grun | LUX | 52.5 | 67.5 | 90.0 | 210.0 |
| 8. | W. Nimwegen | HOL | 55.0 | 65.0 | 90.0 | 210.0 |

**1924 Paris** C: 22, N: 12, D: 7.22.

| | | | ONE-HAND SNATCH | ONE-HAND JERK | TWO-HAND PRESS | TWO-HAND SNATCH | TWO-HAND JERK | TOTAL KG |
|---|---|---|---|---|---|---|---|---|
| 1. | Edmond Décottignies | FRA | 70.0 | 92.5 | 77.5 | 85.0 | 115.0 OR | 440.0 |
| 2. | Anton Zwerina | AUT | 75.0 OR | 80.0 | 77.5 | 82.5 | 112.5 | 427.5 |
| 3. | Bohumil Durdis | CZE | 70.0 | 82.5 | 72.5 | 90.0 | 110.0 | 425.0 |
| 4. | Leopold Treffny | AUT | 65.0 | 85.0 | 77.5 | 85.0 | 112.5 | 425.0 |
| 5. | Joseph Jaquenoud | SWI | 65.0 | 85.0 | 77.5 | 85.0 | 105.0 | 417.5 |
| 6. | Eduard Vanaaseme | EST | 65.0 | 77.5 | 85.0 | 80.0 | 107.5 | 415.0 |

| | | ONE-HAND SNATCH | ONE-HAND JERK | | TWO-HAND PRESS | TWO-HAND SNATCH | TWO-HAND JERK | TOTAL KG |
|---|---|---|---|---|---|---|---|---|
| 7. August Scheffer | HOL | 62.5 | 80.0 | | 80.0 | 82.5 | 110.0 | 415.0 |
| 8. F. Bichsel | SWI | 70.0 | 95.0 | WR | 65.0 | 75.0 | 105.0 | 410.0 |

**1928 Amsterdam** C: 18, N: 12, D: 7.29. WR: 325 kg (Kurt Helbig)

| | | PRESS | | SNATCH | | JERK | | TOTAL KG |
|---|---|---|---|---|---|---|---|---|
| 1. Hans Haas | GER | 90.0 | OR | 97.5 | | 135.0 | OR | 322.5 |
| 1. Kurt Helbig | AUT | 85.0 | | 102.5 | OR | 135.0 | OR | 322.5 |
| 3. Fernand Arnout | FRA | 85.0 | | 97.5 | | 120.0 | | 302.5 |
| 4. Albert Aeschmann | SWI | 87.5 | | 90.0 | | 120.0 | | 297.5 |
| 5. Willi Reinfrank | GER | 85.0 | | 90.0 | | 120.0 | | 295.0 |
| 6. Jules Meese | FRA | 90.0 | OR | 87.5 | | 115.0 | | 292.5 |
| 7. Anton Hangel | AUT | 77.5 | | 90.0 | | 120.0 | | 287.5 |
| 8. Gastone Pierini | ITA | 90.0 | OR | 82.5 | | 110.0 | | 282.5 |

**1932 Los Angeles** C: 6, N: 4, D: 7.31. WR: 325 kg (Kurt Helbig)

| | | PRESS | | SNATCH | | JERK | TOTAL KG | |
|---|---|---|---|---|---|---|---|---|
| 1. René Duverger | FRA | 97.5 | OR | 102.5 | EOR | 125.0 | 325.0 | EWR |
| 2. Hans Haas | AUT | 82.5 | | 100.0 | EOR | 125.0 | 307.5 | |
| 3. Gastone Pierini | ITA | 92.5 | | 90.0 | | 120.0 | 302.5 | |
| 4. Pierino Gabetti | ITA | 85.0 | | 95.0 | | 120.0 | 300.0 | |
| 5. Arnie Sundberg | USA | 77.5 | | 90.0 | | 117.5 | 285.0 | |
| 6. Walter Zagurski | USA | 82.5 | | 90.0 | | 112.5 | 285.0 | |

**1936 Berlin** C: 16, N: 12, D: 8.2. WR: 337.5 kg (Anwar Mohammed Mesbah)

| | | PRESS | | SNATCH | | JERK | | TOTAL KG | |
|---|---|---|---|---|---|---|---|---|---|
| 1. Robert Fein | AUT | 105.0 | OR | 100.0 | | 137.5 | | 342.5 | WR |
| 1. Anwar Mohammed Mesbah | EGY | 92.5 | | 105.0 | OR | 145.0 | OR | 342.5 | WR |
| 3. Karl Jansen | GER | 95.0 | | 100.0 | | 132.5 | | 327.5 | |
| 4. Karl Schwitalle | GER | 95.0 | | 100.0 | | 127.5 | | 322.5 | |
| 5. John Terpak | USA | 97.5 | | 100.0 | | 125.0 | | 322.5 | |
| 6. El Sayed Ibrahim Masoud | EGY | 90.0 | | 100.0 | | 132.5 | | 322.5 | |
| 7. René Duverger | FRA | 97.5 | | 95.0 | | 125.0 | | 317.5 | |
| 8. Robert Mitchell | USA | 85.0 | | 97.5 | | 130.0 | | 312.5 | |

Originally Mesbah was awarded sole possession of first place because he had weighed three and a half ounces less than Fein at the precompetition weigh-in. The Austrians lodged a protest, which was upheld, and both men received gold medals.

**1948 London** C: 22, N: 17, D: 8.10. WR: 367.5 kg (Stanley Stanczyk)

| | | PRESS | | SNATCH | | JERK | | TOTAL KG | |
|---|---|---|---|---|---|---|---|---|---|
| 1. Ibrahim Hassanien Shams | EGY | 97.5 | | 115.0 | OR | 147.5 | OR | 360.0 | OR |
| 2. Attia Hamouda | EGY | 105.0 | | 110.0 | | 145.0 | | 360.0 | OR |
| 3. James Halliday | GBR | 90.0 | | 110.0 | | 140.0 | | 340.0 | |
| 4. John Terpak | USA | 102.5 | | 102.5 | | 135.0 | | 340.0 | |
| 5. John Stuart | CAN | 107.5 | OR | 100.0 | | 125.0 | | 332.5 | |
| 6. Kim Suk-young | KOR | 95.0 | | 100.0 | | 135.0 | | 330.0 | |
| 7. La See-yun | KOR | 90.0 | | 100.0 | | 125.0 | | 330.0 | |
| 8. Joseph Pittman | USA | 100.0 | | 95.0 | | 127.5 | | 322.5 | |

Shams won a dramatic confrontation with his teammate Hamouda. After Shams missed a jerk of 145 kg,

Hamouda successfully lifted the same weight on his final attempt. This forced Shams, who had set the world jerk record nine years earlier, to add 2.5 kg to the bar if he hoped to tie Hamouda and win as a result of his lower bodyweight. With the audience in complete silence, Shams approached the bar twice and then turned away. The third time, he seized the bar quickly and, in a flash, had it up to his shoulders and over his head for the victory. Shams' 1939 snatch of 116.5 kg stood as a world record until the 1952 Olympics. His 153.5 kg jerk of the same year was still on the books in 1957.

**1952 Helsinki** C: 24, N: 22, D: 7.26. WR: 367.5 kg (Stanley Stanczyk)

|   |   |   | PRESS | SNATCH | | JERK | TOTAL KG | |
|---|---|---|---|---|---|---|---|---|
| 1. | Tamio "Tommy" Kono | USA | 105.0 | 117.5 | WR | 140.0 | 362.5 | OR |
| 2. | Yevgeny Lopatin | SOV | 100.0 | 107.5 | | 142.5 | 350.0 | |
| 3. | Verne Barberis | AUS | 105.0 | 105.0 | | 140.0 | 350.0 | |
| 4. | Kim Chang-hee | KOR | 100.0 | 105.0 | | 140.0 | 345.0 | |
| 5. | Hassan Ferdows | IRN | 102.5 | 107.5 | | 135.0 | 345.0 | |
| 6. | Abd El Khadr El Touni | EGY | 105.0 | 107.5 | | 130.0 | 342.5 | |
| 7. | Johan Runge | DEN | 105.0 | 97.5 | | 127.5 | 330.0 | |
| 8. | Ging Hwie Thio | INA | 105.0 | 92.5 | | 130.0 | 327.5 | |

Tommy Kono was a sickly child who suffered from asthma. His parents tried the usual traditional Japanese cures, such as bear kidneys, burned birds, and powdered snakes. "I used to wish with all my might for good health," he said. During World War II he and his family were forced to leave their home in Sacramento, California, and move to the Tule Lake detention camp for Japanese-Americans. It was there that 14-year-old Tommy was introduced to weightlifting. He caught on quickly and began what was to become an amazing career, which included two Olympic gold medals and one silver, and 21 world records set in four different divisions. His ability to move up and down in weight division without losing strength allowed him to fill in wherever the U.S. team needed him; thus each of his three Olympic medals was won in a different category. He accomplished this by following an unusual system of dieting. If he needed to add weight, he would eat six or seven meals a day. If he needed to shed a few pounds, he would restrict himself to "only" three meals a day. In 1954 Kono won the Mr. World contest, and in 1955 and 1957 he was chosen Mr. Universe. He balanced his muscle-man image by washing and ironing his own clothes and doing his own cooking and cleaning. Yet another talent of Tommy Kono was his mental control—always an important factor in weightlifting. One of his many victims was Fyodor Bogdanovsky who always lost to Kono, often performing well below his capabilities. Bogdanovsky once said, "When Kono looks at me from the wings, he works on me like a python on a rabbit."

**1956 Melbourne** C: 18, N: 17, D: 11.24. WR: 382.5 kg (Nicolai Kostilev)

|  |  |  | PRESS |  | SNATCH |  | JERK |  | TOTAL KG |  |
|---|---|---|---|---|---|---|---|---|---|---|
| 1. | Igor Rybak | SOV | 110.0 |  | 120.0 | OR | 150.0 | OR | 380.0 | OR |
| 2. | Rafael Khabutdinov | SOV | 125.0 | OR | 110.0 |  | 137.5 |  | 372.5 |  |
| 3. | Kim Chang-hee | KOR | 107.5 |  | 112.5 |  | 150.0 | OR | 370.0 |  |
| 4. | Kenji Onuma | JPN | 110.0 |  | 110.0 |  | 147.5 |  | 367.5 |  |
| 5. | Henrik Tamraz | IRN | 115.0 |  | 105.0 |  | 145.0 |  | 365.0 |  |
| 6. | Jan Czepulkowski | POL | 120.0 |  | 105.0 |  | 135.0 |  | 360.0 |  |
| 7. | Ivam Abadzhiev | BUL | 102.5 |  | 117.5 |  | 137.5 | . | 357.5 |  |
| 8. | Nil Tun Maung | MYA | 110.0 |  | 105.0 |  | 137.5 |  | 352.5 |  |

**1960 Rome** C: 33, N: 29, D: 9.8. WR: 390 kg (Viktor Bushuyev)

|  |  |  | PRESS |  | SNATCH |  | JERK |  | TOTAL KG |  |
|---|---|---|---|---|---|---|---|---|---|---|
| 1. | Viktor Bushuyev | SOV | 125.0 | EOR | 122.5 | OR | 150.0 |  | 397.5 | WR |
| 2. | Tan Howe Liang | SIN | 115.0 |  | 110.0 |  | 155.0 | OR | 380.0 |  |
| 3. | Abdul Wahid Aziz | IRQ | 117.5 |  | 115.0 |  | 147.5 |  | 380.0 |  |
| 4. | Marian Zieliński | POL | 115.0 |  | 110.0 |  | 150.0 |  | 375.0 |  |
| 5. | Waldemar Baszanowski | POL | 105.0 |  | 117.5 |  | 147.5 |  | 380.0 |  |
| 6. | Mihály Huszka | HUN | 110.0 |  | 107.5 |  | 147.5 |  | 365.0 |  |
| 7. | Werner Dittrich | GDR | 107.5 |  | 115.0 |  | 140.0 |  | 362.5 |  |
| 7. | Zdenek Otáhal | CZE | 115.0 |  | 107.5 |  | 140.0 |  | 362.5 |  |

Tan Howe Liang is the only athlete from Singapore to have won an Olympic medal.

**1964 Tokyo** C: 20, N: 18, D: 10.13. WR: 430 kg (Waldemar Baszanowski)

|  |  |  | PRESS |  | SNATCH |  | JERK |  | TOTAL KG |  |
|---|---|---|---|---|---|---|---|---|---|---|
| 1. | Waldemar Baszanowski | POL | 132.5 |  | 135.0 | OR | 165.0 | OR | 432.5 | WR |
| 2. | Vladimir Kaplunov | SOV | 140.0 | EWR | 127.5 |  | 165.0 |  | 432.5 | WR |
| 3. | Marian Zieliński | POL | 140.0 | EWR | 120.0 |  | 160.0 |  | 420.0 |  |
| 4. | Anthony Garcy | USA | 127.5 |  | 125.0 |  | 160.0 |  | 412.5 |  |
| 5. | Zdenek Otáhal | CZE | 130.0 |  | 117.5 |  | 152.5 |  | 400.0 |  |
| 6. | Hiroshi Yamazaki | JPN | 120.0 |  | 120.0 |  | 157.5 |  | 397.5 |  |
| 7. | Parviz Jalayer | IRN | 120.0 |  | 120.0 |  | 155.0 |  | 395.0 |  |
| 8. | Alfred Kornprobst | GER | 122.5 |  | 112.5 |  | 150.0 |  | 385.0 |  |

One of the greatest weightlifters of all time, Waldemar Baszanowski defeated Vladimir Kaplunov because he was ten and a half ounces lighter than his rival. Nine months later, at the European championships in Sofia, Bulgaria, the men tied again, and again Baszanowski was awarded first place as a result of his lower bodyweight.

**1968 Mexico City** C: 20, N: 17, D: 10.15. WR: 440 kg (Waldemar Baszanowski)

|  |  |  | PRESS |  | SNATCH |  | JERK |  | TOTAL KG |  |
|---|---|---|---|---|---|---|---|---|---|---|
| 1. | Waldemar Baszanowski | POL | 135.0 |  | 135.0 | EOR | 167.5 | OR | 437.5 | OR |
| 2. | Parviz Jalayer | IRN | 125.0 |  | 132.5 |  | 165.0 |  | 422.5 |  |
| 3. | Marian Zieliński | POL | 135.0 |  | 125.0 |  | 160.0 |  | 420.0 |  |
| 4. | Nobuyuki Hatta | JPN | 135.0 |  | 127.5 |  | 155.0 |  | 417.5 |  |
| 5. | Won Shin-hee | KOR | 127.5 |  | 125.0 |  | 162.5 |  | 415.0 |  |
| 6. | János Bagócs | HUN | 132.5 |  | 122.5 |  | 157.5 |  | 412.5 |  |
| 7. | Takeo Kimura | JPN | 125.0 |  | 120.0 |  | 160.0 |  | 405.0 |  |
| 8. | Kostadin Tilev | BUL | 132.5 |  | 115.0 |  | 150.0 |  | 397.5 |  |

**1972 Munich** C: 22, N: 20, D: 8.30. WR: 450 kg (Waldemar Baszanowski)

| | | PRESS | | SNATCH | | JERK | | TOTAL KG | |
|---|---|---|---|---|---|---|---|---|---|
| 1. Mukharby Kirzhinov | SOV | 147.5 | | 135.0 | EOR | 177.5 | WR | 460.0 | WR |
| 2. Mladen Kuchev | BUL | 157.5 | WR | 125.0 | | 167.5 | | 450.0 | |
| 3. Zbigniew Kaczmarek | POL | 145.0 | | 125.0 | | 167.5 | | 437.5 | |
| 4. Waldemar Baszanowski | POL | 142.5 | | 130.0 | | 162.5 | | 435.0 | |
| 5. Nasrollah Dehnavi | IRN | 150.0 | | 125.0 | | 160.0 | | 435.0 | |
| 6. Jenö Ambrózi | HUN | 142.5 | | 120.0 | | 165.0 | | 427.5 | |
| 7. Won Shin-hee | KOR | 132.5 | | 130.0 | | 165.0 | | 427.5 | |
| 8. Masao Kato | JPN | 140.0 | | 120.0 | | 165.0 | | 425.0 | |

**1976 Montreal** C: 23, N: 19, D: 7.21. WR: 312.5 kg (Mukharbi Kirzhinov)

| | | SNATCH | | JERK | TOTAL KG | |
|---|---|---|---|---|---|---|
| 1. Pyotr Korol | SOV | 135.0 | EOR | 170.0 | 305.0 | OR |
| 2. Daniel Senet | FRA | 135.0 | EOR | 165.0 | 300.0 | |
| 3. Kazimierz Czarnecki | POL | 130.0 | | 165.0 | 295.0 | |
| 4. Gunter Ambrass | GDR | 125.0 | | 170.0 | 295.0 | |
| 5. Yatsuo Shimaya | JPN | 127.5 | | 165.0 | 292.5 | |
| 6. Roberto Urrutia | CUB | 130.0 | | 162.5 | 292.5 | |
| 7. Werner Schraut | GER | 127.5 | | 162.5 | 290.0 | |
| 8. Roland Chavigny | FRA | 130.0 | | 155.0 | 285.0 | |

DISQ (Drugs): Zbigniew Kaczmarek (POL) 307.5

Kaczmarek finished first but was subsequently disqualified after a test revealed that he had taken prohibited drugs.

**1980 Moscow** C: 20, N: 16, D: 7.23. WR: 337.5 kg (Yanko Roussev)

| | | SNATCH | | JERK | | TOTAL KG | |
|---|---|---|---|---|---|---|---|
| 1. Yanko Roussev | BUL | 147.5 | OR | 195.0 | WR | 342.5 | WR |
| 2. Joachim Kunz | GDR | 145.0 | | 190.0 | | 335.0 | |
| 3. Mincho Pachov | BUL | 142.5 | | 182.5 | | 325.0 | |
| 4. Daniel Senet | FRA | 147.5 | OR | 175.0 | | 322.5 | |
| 5. Gunter Ambrass | GDR | 140.0 | | 180.0 | | 320.0 | |
| 6. Zbigniew Kaczmarek | POL | 140.0 | | 177.5 | | 317.5 | |
| 7. Raul Gonzalez | CUB | 145.0 | | 172.5 | | 317.5 | |
| 8. Virgel Dociu | ROM | 140.0 | | 170.0 | | 310.0 | |

**1984 Los Angeles-Westchester** C: 19, N: 17, D: 8.1. WR: 352.5 kg (Andreas Behm)

| | | SNATCH | JERK | TOTAL KG |
|---|---|---|---|---|
| 1. Yao Jingyuan | CHN | 142.5 | 177.5 | 320.0 |
| 2. Andrei Socaci | ROM | 142.5 | 170.0 | 312.5 |
| 2. Jouni Grönman | FIN | 140.0 | 172.5 | 312.5 |
| 4. Dean Willey | GBR | 140.0 | 170.0 | 310.0 |
| 5. Choji Taira | JPN | 132.5 | 172.5 | 305.0 |
| 6. Yasushige Sasaki | JPN | 140.0 | 162.5 | 302.5 |
| 7. Basil Stellios | AUS | 137.5 | 165.0 | 302.5 |
| 8. Ma Jianping | CHN | 130.0 | 167.5 | 297.5 |

First place at the Friendship Games went to 1980 Olympic champion Yanko Roussev with a combined total of 337.5 kg. Second was his Bulgarian teammate Alexandr Varbanov at 335 kg.

**1988 Seoul** C: 29, N: 25, D: 9.21. WR: 355 kg (Mikhail Petrov)

|    |                           |     | SNATCH |    | JERK  | TOTAL KG |
|----|---------------------------|-----|--------|----|-------|----------|
| 1. | Joachim Kunz              | GDR | 150.0  |    | 190.0 | 340.0    |
| 2. | Israil Militosyan         | SOV | 155.0  | OR | 182.5 | 337.5    |
| 3. | Li Jinhe                  | CHN | 147.5  |    | 177.5 | 325.0    |
| 4. | Marek Seweryn             | POL | 145.0  |    | 172.5 | 317.5    |
| 5. | Ergun Batmaz              | TUR | 145.0  |    | 172.5 | 317.5    |
| 6. | Xiao Minglin              | CHN | 132.5  |    | 172.5 | 305.0    |
| 7. | István Kerek              | HUN | 132.5  |    | 170.0 | 302.5    |
| 8. | Christos Constandinidis   | GRE | 137.5  |    | 162.5 | 300.0    |

DISQ (Drugs): Angel Guenchev (BUL) 362.5

Bulgaria entered the 1988 Olympic weightlifting tournament expecting to win four or five gold medals and an equal number of silver medals. At first things appeared to be going well: Sevdalin Marinov won the flyweight division, Mitko Grablev won the bantamweight division, Stefan Topurov took second in the featherweight division, Angel Guenchev won the lightweight division, and Borislav Gidikov won the middleweight division. Then disaster struck: Grablev was disqualified when he tested positive for a diuretic used as a masking agent for steroids. Two days later Guenchev was disqualified for the same reason. Clearly the Bulgarians had underestimated the sophistication of the Olympic drug-testing equipment. After the announcement of the results of Guenchev's drug test, the Bulgarian Weightlifting Federation withdrew the rest of their team from competition.

With Guenchev disqualified, the gold medal was awarded to 29-year-old Joachim Kunz, who had not won a major championship in four years.

# MIDDLEWEIGHT
## (75 kg—165 lbs)

**1896–1912** not held

**1920 Antwerp** C: 10, N: 7, D: 8.28.

|    |                    |     | ONE-HAND SNATCH | ONE-HAND JERK | TWO-HAND JERK | TOTAL KG |
|----|--------------------|-----|-----------------|---------------|---------------|----------|
| 1. | Henri Gance        | FRA | 65.0            | 75.0          | 105.0         | 245.0    |
| 2. | Pietro Bianchi     | ITA | 60.0            | 70.0          | 107.5         | 237.5    |
| 2. | Albert Pettersson  | SWE | 55.0            | 75.0          | 107.5         | 237.5    |
| 4. | M. Ringelberg      | HOL | 55.0            | 65.0          | 105.0         | 225.0    |
| 5. | Paul Ledran        | FRA | 55.0            | 65.0          | 100.0         | 220.0    |
| 6. | Christian Jensen   | DEN | 55.0            | 60.0          | 100.0         | 215.0    |
| 7. | Marchand           | BEL | 55.0            | 55.0          | 95.0          | 205.0    |
| 8. | P.L. Belmer        | HOL | 0.0             | 65.0          | 100.0         | 165.0    |

Both Bianchi and Pettersson hoisted 107.5 kg in a lift-off, using a two-handed jerk. They then drew lots to determine who would be awarded the silver medal rather than bronze. Bianchi won.

**1924 Paris** C: 25, N: 13, D: 7.22.

| | | ONE-HAND SNATCH | | ONE-HAND JERK | | TWO-HAND PRESS | | TWO-HAND SNATCH | TWO-HAND JERK | | TOTAL KG |
|---|---|---|---|---|---|---|---|---|---|---|---|
| 1. Carlo Galimberti | ITA | 77.5 | | 95.0 | OR | 97.5 | WR | 95.0 | 127.5 | WR | 492.5 |
| 2. Alfred Neuland | EST | 82.5 | WR | 90.0 | | 77.5 | | 90.0 | 115.0 | | 455.0 |
| 3. Jaan Kikkas | EST | 70.0 | | 87.5 | | 80.0 | | 85.0 | 127.5 | WR | 450.0 |
| 4. Hamed Samy | EGY | 72.5 | | 77.5 | | 97.5 | WR | 85.0 | 115.0 | | 447.5 |
| 5. Albert Aeschmann | SWI | 67.5 | | 87.5 | | 82.5 | | 87.5 | 117.5 | | 442.5 |
| 6. Roger François | FRA | 72.0 | | 80.0 | | 87.5 | | 87.5 | 117.5 | | 442.5 |
| 7. Rupert Eidler | AUT | 65.0 | | 90.0 | | 82.5 | | 85.0 | 115.0 | | 437.5 |
| 8. Pierre Vibert | FRA | 72.5 | | 75.0 | | 80.0 | | 85.0 | 115.0 | | 432.5 |

**1928 Amsterdam** C: 23, N: 15, D: 7.29. WR: 320 kg (Carlo Galimberti)

| | | PRESS | | SNATCH | | JERK | | TOTAL KG | |
|---|---|---|---|---|---|---|---|---|---|
| 1. Roger François | FRA | 102.5 | | 102.5 | | 130.0 | | 335.0 | WR |
| 2. Carlo Galimberti | ITA | 105.0 | WR | 97.5 | | 130.0 | | 332.5 | |
| 3. August Scheffer | HOL | 97.5 | | 105.0 | OR | 125.0 | | 327.5 | |
| 4. Franz Zinner | GER | 87.5 | | 100.0 | | 135.0 | OR | 322.5 | |
| 5. Gaston Le Pût | FRA | 92.5 | | 95.0 | | 125.0 | | 312.5 | |
| 6. Wilhelm Hofmann | GER | 90.0 | | 95.0 | | 120.0 | | 305.0 | |
| 7. Houssein Mouktah | EGY | 95.0 | | 92.5 | | 120.0 | | 302.5 | |
| 8. Jan van Rompey | BEL | 92.5 | | 85.0 | | 115.0 | | 292.5 | |

**1932 Los Angeles** C: 7, N: 6, D: 7.31. WR: 342.5 kg (Rudolf Ismayr)

| | | PRESS | SNATCH | | JERK | | TOTAL KG | |
|---|---|---|---|---|---|---|---|---|
| 1. Rudolf Ismayr | GER | 102.5 | 110.0 | OR | 132.5 | | 345.0 | WR |
| 2. Carlo Galimberti | ITA | 102.5 | 105.0 | | 132.5 | | 340.0 | |
| 3. Karl Hipfinger | AUT | 90.0 | 107.5 | | 140.0 | OR | 337.5 | |
| 4. Roger François | FRA | 102.5 | 102.5 | | 130.0 | | 335.0 | |
| 5. Stanley Kratkowski | USA | 82.5 | 102.5 | | 120.0 | | 305.0 | |
| 6. Julio Juaneda | ARG | 75.0 | 90.0 | | 120.0 | | 285.0 | |
| 7. Sam Termine | USA | 87.5 | 105.0 | | 0.0 | | 192.5 | |

**1936 Berlin** C: 16, N: 12, D: 8.5. WR: 385 kg (Khadr Sayed El Touni)

| | | PRESS | | SNATCH | | JERK | | TOTAL KG | |
|---|---|---|---|---|---|---|---|---|---|
| 1. Khadr Sayed El Touni | EGY | 117.5 | WR | 120.0 | WR | 150.0 | OR | 387.5 | WR |
| 2. Rudolf Ismayr | GER | 107.5 | | 102.5 | | 142.5 | | 352.5 | |
| 3. Adolf Wagner | GER | 97.5 | | 112.5 | | 142.5 | | 352.5 | |
| 4. Anton Hangel | AUT | 95.0 | | 110.0 | | 137.5 | | 342.5 | |
| 5. Stanley Kratkowski | USA | 95.0 | | 107.5 | | 135.0 | | 337.5 | |
| 6. Hans Valla | AUT | 102.5 | | 102.5 | | 130.0 | | 335.0 | |
| 7. Carlo Galimberti | ITA | 100.0 | | 102.5 | | 130.0 | | 332.5 | |
| 8. Pierre Alleene | FRA | 90.0 | | 105.0 | | 135.0 | | 330.0 | |

Twenty-one-year-old Khadr Sayed El Touni was one of the sensations of the 1936 Olympics. Not only did he outclass his opponents in the Middleweight division, but he actually lifted 15 kilograms more than the winner of the Light Heavyweight division. El Touni died of electrocution in 1956 while making a home repair.

**1948 London** C: 24, N: 18, D: 8.10. WR: 405 kg (Stanley Stanczyk)

|  |  | PRESS |  | SNATCH |  | JERK |  | TOTAL KG |  |
|---|---|---|---|---|---|---|---|---|---|
| 1. Frank Spellman | USA | 117.5 |  | 120.0 |  | 152.5 |  | 390.0 | OR |
| 2. Peter George | USA | 105.0 |  | 122.5 | OR | 155.0 | OR | 382.5 |  |
| 3. Kim Sung-jip | KOR | 122.5 | OR | 112.5 |  | 145.0 |  | 380.0 |  |
| 4. Khadr Sayed El Touni | EGY | 120.0 |  | 117.5 |  | 142.5 |  | 380.0 |  |
| 5. Gérard Gratton | CAN | 112.5 |  | 107.5 |  | 140.0 |  | 360.0 |  |
| 6. Pierre Bouladoux | FRA | 102.5 |  | 110.0 |  | 142.5 |  | 355.0 |  |
| 7. Orlando Garrido Luloaga | CUB | 112.5 |  | 107.5 |  | 135.0 |  | 355.0 |  |
| 8. G. William Watson | GBR | 100.0 |  | 110.0 |  | 140.0 |  | 350.0 |  |

Peter George's only chance to win the gold medal was to clean and jerk 165 kg—11 kilograms more than Stanley Stanczyk's world record. After pacing back and forth for twelve tense minutes, the 19-year-old George rubbed his hands with a block of chalk. Suddenly he crushed the chalk to dust and approached the bar. With great deliberation and concentration, he took hold of the weight, prepared his body, and hoisted the bar to his shoulders. The audience burst into applause, but quieted down quickly as George prepared for the second part of the lift. He pushed the bar overhead, but staggered and dropped it and had to settle for second place. Kim Sung-jip was Korea's first Olympic medalist.

**1952 Helsinki** C: 21, N: 20, D: 7.26. WR: 405 kg (Stanley Stanczyk)

|  |  | PRESS |  | SNATCH |  | JERK |  | TOTAL KG |  |
|---|---|---|---|---|---|---|---|---|---|
| 1. Peter George | USA | 115.0 |  | 127.5 | OR | 157.5 | OR | 400.0 | OR |
| 2. Gérard Gratton | CAN | 122.5 | EOR | 112.5 |  | 155.0 |  | 390.0 |  |
| 3. Kim Sung-jip | KOR | 122.5 | EOR | 112.5 |  | 147.5 |  | 382.5 |  |
| 4. Ismail Ragab | EGY | 115.0 |  | 117.5 |  | 150.0 |  | 382.5 |  |
| 5. Moustafa Laham | LEB | 115.0 |  | 112.5 |  | 142.5 |  | 370.0 |  |
| 6. Åke Hedberg | SWE | 102.5 |  | 105.0 |  | 150.0 |  | 357.5 |  |
| 7. Angel Sposato | ARG | 107.5 |  | 110.0 |  | 140.0 |  | 357.5 |  |
| 8. Jalal Mansouri | IRN | 110.0 |  | 107.5 |  | 140.0 |  | 357.5 |  |

**1956 Melbourne** C: 16, N: 15, D: 11.24. WR: 415 kg (Fyodor Bogdanovsky)

|  |  | PRESS |  | SNATCH |  | JERK |  | TOTAL KG |  |
|---|---|---|---|---|---|---|---|---|---|
| 1. Fyodor Bogdanovsky | SOV | 132.5 | OR | 122.5 |  | 165.0 | OR | 420.0 | WR |
| 2. Peter George | USA | 122.5 |  | 127.5 | EOR | 162.5 |  | 412.5 |  |
| 3. Ermanno Pignatti | ITA | 117.5 |  | 117.5 |  | 147.5 |  | 302.5 |  |
| 4. Jan Bochenek | POL | 120.0 |  | 112.5 |  | 150.0 |  | 382.5 |  |
| 5. Kim Sung-jip | KOR | 125.0 |  | 110.0 |  | 145.0 |  | 380.0 |  |
| 6. Krzysztof Beck | POL | 122.5 |  | 112.5 |  | 145.0 |  | 380.0 |  |
| 7. Ebrahim Peyravi | IRN | 107.5 |  | 117.5 |  | 147.5 |  | 372.5 |  |
| 8. Adrien Gilbert | CAN | 112.5 |  | 115.0 |  | 142.5 |  | 370.0 |  |

History repeated itself when defending champion Peter George, now a dentist in the U.S. Army, needed a world-record jerk to take first place. He attempted 170 kg, but couldn't make the weight. Nonetheless, his record of one gold and two silver medals is most impressive.

**1960 Rome** C: 27, N: 20, D: 9.8. WR: 430 kg (Tamio "Tommy" Kono)

| | | PRESS | | SNATCH | | JERK | | TOTAL KG | |
|---|---|---|---|---|---|---|---|---|---|
| 1. Aleksandr Kurynov | SOV | 135.0 | | 132.5 | OR | 170.0 | WR | 437.5 | WR |
| 2. Tamio "Tommy" Kono | USA | 140.0 | OR | 127.5 | | 160.0 | | 427.5 | |
| 3. Gyözö Veres | HUN | 130.0 | | 120.0 | | 155.0 | | 405.0 | |
| 4. Marcel Paterni | FRA | 127.5 | | 120.0 | | 152.5 | | 400.0 | |
| 5. Krzysztof Beck | POL | 135.0 | | 117.5 | | 147.5 | | 400.0 | |
| 6. Mohammad Amitehrani | IRN | 117.5 | | 120.0 | | 155.0 | | 392.5 | |
| 7. Koh Yung-chang | KOR | 115.0 | | 120.0 | | 150.0 | | 385.0 | |
| 8. Roland Lortz | GER | 115.0 | | 112.5 | | 155.0 | | 382.5 | |

Tommy Kono, having already won gold medals as a Lightweight in 1952 and as a Light Heavyweight in 1956, decided to compete in the Middleweight division in 1960 because he had heard that Kurynov was "a very tough opponent." He heard right. The 26-year-old Soviet aviation engineer pulled off the victory and topped it with a world-record clean and jerk on his final attempt.

**1964 Tokyo** C: 19, N: 17, D: 10.14. WR: 445 kg (Viktor Kurentsov)

| | | PRESS | | SNATCH | | JERK | | TOTAL KG | |
|---|---|---|---|---|---|---|---|---|---|
| 1. Hans Zdražila | CZE | 130.0 | | 137.5 | OR | 177.5 | WR | 445.0 | EWR |
| 2. Viktor Kurentsov | SOV | 135.0 | | 130.0 | | 175.0 | | 440.0 | |
| 3. Masashi Ouchi | JPN | 140.0 | EOR | 135.0 | | 162.5 | | 437.5 | |
| 4. Lee Jong-sup | KOR | 130.0 | | 127.5 | | 175.0 | | 432.5 | |
| 5. Sadahiro Miwa | JPN | 120.0 | | 132.5 | | 170.0 | | 422.5 | |
| 6. Mihály Huszka | HUN | 135.0 | | 125.0 | | 160.0 | | 420.0 | |
| 7. Rolf Maier | FRA | 130.0 | | 122.5 | | 165.0 | | 417.5 | |
| 8. Veliko Konarov | BUL | 130.0 | | 130.0 | | 155.0 | | 415.0 | |

**1968 Mexico City** C: 20, N: 17, D: 10.16. WR: 482.5 kg (Viktor Kurentsov)

| | | PRESS | | SNATCH | | JERK | | TOTAL KG | |
|---|---|---|---|---|---|---|---|---|---|
| 1. Viktor Kurentsov | SOV | 152.5 | OR | 135.0 | | 187.5 | WR | 475.0 | OR |
| 2. Masashi Ouchi | JPN | 140.0 | | 140.0 | OR | 175.0 | | 455.0 | |
| 3. Károly Bakos | HUN | 137.5 | | 132.5 | | 170.0 | | 440.0 | |
| 4. Russell Knipp | USA | 147.5 | | 122.5 | | 167.5 | | 437.5 | |
| 5. Lee Chun-sik | KOR | 140.0 | | 132.5 | | 165.0 | | 437.5 | |
| 6. Werner Dittrich | GDR | 140.0 | | 130.0 | | 165.0 | | 435.0 | |
| 7. Miroslav Kolarik | CZE | 140.0 | | 127.5 | | 162.5 | | 430.0 | |
| 8. Frederick Lowe | USA | 132.5 | | 127.5 | | 170.0 | | 430.0 | |

In 1964 Kurentsov had entered the Olympics as the holder of the world record. However, in Tokyo he suffered an attack of nervousness and completed only four of his nine lifts. Four years later, at the next Olympics, he was a new man. Between lifts he calmly lay on a bed backstage reading Tolstoi. His winning margin was the largest in the Middleweight division since El Touni's great performance in 1936.

**1972 Munich** C: 26, N: 22, D: 8.31. WR: 482.5 (Viktor Kurentsov)

| | | PRESS | SNATCH | JERK | TOTAL KG | |
|---|---|---|---|---|---|---|
| 1. Yordan Bikov | BUL | 160.0 | 140.0 | 185.0 | 485.0 | WR |
| 2. Mohamed Trabulsi | LEB | 160.0 | 140.0 | 172.5 | 472.5 | |

| | | PRESS | SNATCH | | JERK | TOTAL KG |
|---|---|---|---|---|---|---|
| 3. Anselmo Silvino | ITA | 155.0 | 140.0 | | 175.0 | 470.0 |
| 4. Ondrej Hekel | CZE | 150.0 | 142.5 | EOR | 170.0 | 462.5 |
| 5. Franklin Zielecke | GDR | 150.0 | 140.0 | | 170.0 | 460.0 |
| 6. Gábor Szarvas | HUN | 150.0 | 135.0 | | 175.0 | 460.0 |
| 7. András Stark | HUN | 152.5 | 137.5 | | 170.0 | 460.0 |
| 8. Russell Knipp | USA | 160.0 | 127.5 | | 170.0 | 457.5 |

Vladimir Kanygin of the U.S.S.R. set an Olympic record in the press of 165 kg, but he failed at all three attempts at the snatch and was disqualified.

**1976 Montreal** C: 17, N: 14, D: 7.22. WR: 345 kg (Yordan Mitkov)

| | | SNATCH | | JERK | | TOTAL KG | |
|---|---|---|---|---|---|---|---|
| 1. Yordan Mitkov | BUL | 145.0 | OR | 190.0 | OR | 335.0 | OR |
| 2. Vartan Militosyan | SOV | 145.0 | OR | 185.0 | | 330.0 | |
| 3. Peter Wenzel | GDR | 145.0 | OR | 182.5 | | 327.5 | |
| 4. Wolfgang Hübner | GDR | 142.5 | | 177.5 | | 320.0 | |
| 5. Arvo Ala-Pöntiö | FIN | 137.5 | | 177.5 | | 315.0 | |
| 6. András Stark | HUN | 140.0 | | 175.0 | | 315.0 | |
| 7. Ondrej Hekel | CZE | 140.0 | | 172.5 | | 312.5 | |
| 8. Daniel Zayas | CUB | 140.0 | | 170.0 | | 310.0 | |

DISQ (Drugs): Dragomir Ciorosian (ROM) 320.0

Fifth-place finisher Ciorosian was disqualified for drug use.

**1980 Moscow** C: 16, N: 14, D: 7.24. WR: 355 kg (Assen Zlatev)

| | | SNATCH | | JERK | | TOTAL KG | |
|---|---|---|---|---|---|---|---|
| 1. Assen Zlatev | BUL | 160.0 | OR | 200.0 | OR | 360.0 | WR |
| 2. Aleksandr Pervy | SOV | 157.5 | | 200.0 | OR | 357.5 | |
| 3. Nedelcho Kolev | BUL | 157.5 | | 187.5 | | 345.0 | |
| 4. Julio Echenique Gonzalez | CUB | 145.0 | | 182.5 | | 327.5 | |
| 5. Dragomir Ciorosian | ROM | 140.0 | | 182.5 | | 322.5 | |
| 6. Tapio Kinnunen | FIN | 142.5 | | 177.5 | | 320.0 | |
| 7. Bertil Sollevi | SWE | 137.5 | | 172.5 | | 310.0 | |
| 8. Newton Burrowes | GBR | 130.0 | | 172.5 | | 302.5 | |

After the formal competition was over, Zlatev jerked 205.5 kg for a new world record.

**1984 Los Angeles-Westchester** C: 21, N: 17, D: 8.2. WR: 370.0 kg (Alexandr Varbanov)

| | | SNATCH | JERK | TOTAL KG |
|---|---|---|---|---|
| 1. Karl-Heinz Radschinsky | GER | 150.0 | 190.0 | 340.0 |
| 2. Jacques Demers | CAN | 147.5 | 187.5 | 335.0 |
| 3. Dragomir Cioroslan | ROM | 147.5 | 185.0 | 332.5 |
| 4. David Morgan | GBR | 145.0 | 185.0 | 330.0 |
| 5. Li Shunzhu | CHN | 147.5 | 175.0 | 322.5 |
| 6. Mohammed Yaseen Mohammed | IRQ | 140.0 | 180.0 | 320.0 |
| 7. Antonio Pignone | AUS | 147.5 | 170.0 | 317.5 |
| 8. Park Chun-jong | KOR | 137.5 | 175.0 | 312.5 |

In 1983 Demers was arrested for smuggling steroid tablets into Canada, although his trial was delayed until after the Olympics. Demers qualified for the Canadian team again in 1988, but was dropped before the Games when he tested positive for steroids despite having injected someone else's clean urine into his bladder. In 1985 Radschinsky was arrested in West Germany for possessing steroids with intent to sell.

At the Friendship Games in September, Zdravko Stoichkov of Bulgaria set a world record of 377.5 kg. In second place was Vladimir Kuznetsov of the U.S.S.R. at 362.5 kg.

**1988 Seoul** C: 25, N: 20, D: 9.22. WR: 380 kg (Aleksandr Varbanov)

| | | SNATCH | | JERK | | TOTAL KG | |
|---|---|---|---|---|---|---|---|
| 1. Borislav Gidikov | BUL | 167.5 | OR | 207.5 | OR | 375.0 | OR |
| 2. Ingo Steinhöfel | GDR | 165.0 | | 195.0 | | 360.0 | |
| 3. Aleksandr Varbanov | BUL | 157.5 | | 200.0 | | 357.5 | |
| 4. Cai Yanshu | CHN | 157.5 | | 190.0 | | 347.5 | |
| 5. Andrei Socaci | ROM | 152.5 | | 195.0 | | 347.5 | |
| 6. Waldemar Kosiński | POL | 152.5 | | 180.0 | | 332.5 | |
| 7. Dean Willey | GBR | 152.5 | | 180.0 | | 332.5 | |
| 8. Roberto Urrutia | USA | 150.0 | | 177.5 | | 327.5 | |
| DISQ (Drugs): Kalman Csengeri (HUN) 350.0 | | | | | | | |

# LIGHT HEAVYWEIGHT
## (82.5 kg—181.5 lbs)

**1896–1912** not held

**1920 Antwerp** C: 11, N: 8, D: 8.28.

| | | ONE-HAND SNATCH | ONE-HAND JERK | TWO-HAND JERK | TOTAL KG |
|---|---|---|---|---|---|
| 1. Ernest Cadine | FRA | 70.0 | 90.0 | 135.0 | 295.0 |
| 2. Fritz Hünenberger | SWI | 75.0 | 90.0 | 112.5 | 277.5 |
| 3. Erik Pettersson | SWE | 62.5 | 92.5 | 112.5 | 267.5 |
| 4. Erik Carlsson | SWE | 67.5 | 75.0 | 120.0 | 262.5 |
| 5. Maurice Davéne | FRA | 65.0 | 70.0 | 115.0 | 250.0 |
| 6. Gino Mattiello | ITA | 60.0 | 70.0 | 105.0 | 235.0 |
| 7. I. Welter | HOL | 65.0 | 70.0 | 95.0 | 230.0 |
| 8. Jaroslav Dvorak | CZE | 55.0 | 65.0 | 107.0 | 227.5 |
| 8. Lionel van de Roye | BEL | 57.5 | 65.0 | 105.0 | 227.5 |

**1924 Paris** C: 20, N: 12, D: 7.23.

| | | ONE-HAND SNATCH | ONE-HAND JERK | | TWO-HAND PRESS | TWO-HAND SNATCH | TWO-HAND JERK | | TOTAL KG |
|---|---|---|---|---|---|---|---|---|---|
| 1. Charles Rigoulot | FRA | 87.5 OR | 92.5 | | 85.0 | 102.5 | 135.0 | EOR | 502.5 |
| 2. Fritz Hünenberger | SWI | 80.0 | 107.5 | WR | 80.0 | 97.5 | 125.0 | | 490.0 |
| 3. Leopold Friedrich | AUT | 75.0 | 95.0 | | 95.0 | 95.0 | 130.0 | | 490.0 |
| 4. Karl Freiberger | AUT | 75.0 | 95.0 | | 92.5 | 95.0 | 130.0 | | 487.5 |
| 5. Carlos Bergara | ARG | 80.0 | 85.0 | | 92.5 | 97.5 | 127.5 | | 482.5 |
| 6. Mario Giambelli | ITA | 77.5 | 95.0 | | 82.5 | 95.0 | 130.0 | | 480.0 |
| 7. A. Schärer | SWI | 75.0 | 85.0 | | 100.0 | 95.0 | 120.0 | | 475.0 |
| 8. Jaroslav Skobla | CZE | 70.0 | 95.0 | | 92.5 | 85.0 | 127.5 | | 470.0 |

**1928 Amsterdam** C: 15, N: 10, D: 7.29. WR: 350 kg (Jakob Vogt)

| | | PRESS | | SNATCH | | JERK | | TOTAL KG | |
|---|---|---|---|---|---|---|---|---|---|
| 1. El Sayed Mohammed Nosseir | EGY | 100.0 | EOR | 112.5 | OR | 142.5 | WR | 355.0 | WR |
| 2. Louis Hostin | FRA | 100.0 | EOR | 110.0 | | 142.5 | WR | 352.5 | |
| 3. Johannes Verheijen | HOL | 95.0 | | 105.0 | | 137.5 | | 337.5 | |

|   |   | PRESS |   | SNATCH |   | JERK | TOTAL KG |   |
|---|---|---|---|---|---|---|---|---|
| 4. Václav Pšenička | CZE | 100.0 | EOR | 105.0 |   | 130.0 | 335.0 |   |
| 4. Jakob Vogt | GER | 100.0 | EOR | 105.0 |   | 130.0 | 335.0 |   |
| 6. Karl Freiberger | AUT | 95.0 |   | 95.0 |   | 132.5 | 322.5 |   |
| 7. Karl Bierwirth | GER | 95.0 |   | 95.0 |   | 125.0 | 315.0 |   |
| 7. Pierre Vibert | FRA | 95.0 |   | 95.0 |   | 125.0 | 315.0 |   |
| 7. Josef Zemann | AUT | 75.0 |   | 105.0 |   | 135.0 | 315.0 |   |

El Sayed Nosseir caused quite a sensation with his prelift ritual of raising his arms and head to the sky and calling out for Allah's assistance. A minor incident occurred during the award ceremony when the band struck up the Austrian national anthem by mistake instead of the French "Marseillaise." There were chuckles throughout the crowd, but the French were not amused.

**1932 Los Angeles** C: 4, N: 3, D: 7.31. WR: 365 kg (Jakob Vogt)

|   |   | PRESS |   | SNATCH |   | JERK |   | TOTAL KG |   |
|---|---|---|---|---|---|---|---|---|---|
| 1. Louis Hostin | FRA | 102.5 | OR | 112.5 | EOR | 150.0 | OR | 365.0 | EWR |
| 2. Svend Olsen | DEN | 102.5 | OR | 107.5 |   | 150.0 | OR | 360.0 |   |
| 3. Henry Duey | USA | 92.5 |   | 105.0 |   | 132.5 |   | 330.0 |   |
| 4. William Good | USA | 95.0 |   | 97.5 |   | 130.0 |   | 322.5 |   |

Hostin was so confident of victory that he traded jokes with the referee while he was lifting.

**1936 Berlin** C: 14, N: 9, D: 8.3. WR: 375 kg (Fritz Haller)

|   |   | PRESS |   | SNATCH |   | JERK |   | TOTAL KG |   |
|---|---|---|---|---|---|---|---|---|---|
| 1. Louis Hostin | FRA | 110.0 | OR | 117.5 | OR | 145.0 |   | 372.5 | OR |
| 2. Eugen Deutsch | GER | 105.0 |   | 110.0 |   | 150.0 | OR | 365.0 |   |
| 3. Ibrahim Wasif | EGY | 100.0 |   | 110.0 |   | 150.0 | OR | 360.0 |   |
| 4. Helmut Opschruf | GER | 97.5 |   | 110.0 |   | 147.5 |   | 355.0 |   |
| 5. Nicolas Scheitler | LUX | 105.0 |   | 105.0 |   | 140.0 |   | 350.0 |   |
| 6. Fritz Haller | AUT | 97.5 |   | 110.0 |   | 142.5 |   | 350.0 |   |
| 7. William Good | USA | 100.0 |   | 105.0 |   | 145.0 |   | 350.0 |   |
| 8. Mohammed Ahmed Geissa | EGY | 95.0 |   | 110.0 |   | 142.5 |   | 347.5 |   |

Eugen Deutsch was originally disqualified for missing all three of his snatch attempts. An hour later the Jury of Appeal validated one of his snatches, giving him the silver medal and causing resentment among many non-German observers. Matters were made worse when, at the medal ceremony, the Turkish flag was raised instead of the French flag and the national anthem of Egypt was played instead of the "Marseillaise."

**1948 London** C: 16, N: 13, D: 8.11. WR: 425 kg (Grigory Novack)

|   |   | PRESS |   | SNATCH |   | JERK |   | TOTAL KG |   |
|---|---|---|---|---|---|---|---|---|---|
| 1. Stanley Stanczyk | USA | 130.0 | OR | 130.0 | OR | 157.5 | OR | 417.5 | OR |
| 2. Harold Sakata | USA | 110.0 |   | 117.5 |   | 152.5 |   | 380.0 |   |
| 3. Gösta Magnusson | SWE | 110.0 |   | 120.0 |   | 145.0 |   | 375.0 |   |
| 4. Jean Debuf | FRA | 107.5 |   | 112.5 |   | 150.0 |   | 370.0 |   |
| 5. Osvaldo Forte | ARG | 105.0 |   | 115.0 |   | 147.5 |   | 367.5 |   |
| 6. James Varaleau | CAN | 112.5 |   | 112.5 |   | 140.0 |   | 365.0 |   |
| 7. Juhani Vellamo | FIN | 100.0 |   | 115.0 |   | 140.0 |   | 355.0 |   |
| 8. Rassoul Raiisi | IRN | 110.0 |   | 110.0 |   | 135.0 |   | 355.0 |   |

Stanczyk made a great impression on the audience, not only because of his superior lifting, but because of his outstanding sportsmanship. With his third snatch he attempted a new world record of 132.5 kg. He successfully hoisted the weight and the judges signaled a fair lift. However Stanczyk shook his head and tapped his leg to indicate that his knee had scraped the floor, thus invalidating his lift. Despite this miss, his eventual winning margin of 37.5 kg. was the largest in any division in Olympic history.

Stanley Stanczyk was a well-known figure in weightlifting circles, but the man who really achieved fame was silver medalist Harold Sakata. After completing a successful career as a professional wrestler (using the name Tosh Togo), Sakata became an actor. He eventually reached international stardom in the role of Oddjob in the James Bond film *Goldfinger*.

**1952 Helsinki** C: 22, N: 19, D: 7.27. WR: 425 kg (Grigory Novack)

| | | PRESS | SNATCH | JERK | | TOTAL KG | |
|---|---|---|---|---|---|---|---|
| 1. Trofim Lomakin | SOV | 125.0 | 127.5 | 165.0 | OR | 417.5 | EOR |
| 2. Stanley Stanczyk | USA | 127.5 | 127.5 | 160.0 | | 415.0 | |
| 3. Arkady Vorobyev | SOV | 120.0 | 127.5 | 160.0 | | 407.5 | |
| 4. Mohammad Hassan Rahnavardi | IRN | 120.0 | 122.5 | 160.0 | | 402.5 | |
| 5. Jean Debuf | FRA | 117.5 | 122.5 | 160.0 | | 400.0 | |
| 6. Issy Bloomberg | SAF | 127.5 | 115.0 | 150.0 | | 392.5 | |
| 7. Osvaldo Forte | ARG | 112.5 | 115.0 | 155.0 | | 382.5 | |
| 8. Clyde Emrich | USA | 120.0 | 115.0 | 145.0 | | 380.0 | |

The 1952 Light Heavyweight competition was an excellent three-way contest which unfortunately got caught up in the Cold War. The United States fired the first salvo when they lodged a protest after American Clyde Emrich had a press of 120 kg disallowed. After much fussing and arguing by U.S. officials, Emrich went ahead and made the weight at his next attempt. Then Stanczyk was given credit for a press of 127.5 kg and the Soviets claimed that he had leaned back too far for a legal press. The judges voted 2–1 in Stanczyk's favor. When Vorobyev lost consciousness during his last press attempt, the Americans accused the Russians of drugging their lifters. At the end of the press, Stanczyk led Lomakin by 2.5 kg. Lomakin and Vorobyev both snatched 127.5 kg at their first attempt, while Stanczyk achieved the weight only at his last try. However, both Soviet lifters failed twice at 132.5 kg. So, with only the jerk left, Stanczyk still led Lomakin by 2.5 kg. All three leaders successfully jerked 160 kg. Both Stanczyk and Lomakin missed at 165 kg, but Lomakin had one more attempt left to him. This time he made the weight and moved into first place.

Then came Vorobyev's turn. He decided to go for broke and called for 170 kg—a world record. Vorobyev approached the bar, took hold of it, raised it a couple inches and dropped it again. An argument immediately broke out as to whether his action should be counted as an official attempt. Vorobyev shut out the commotion and prepared himself for another try. When he turned again to the bar, silence returned. He heaved the weight onto his chest and thrust it into the air at arm's length. "Although my muscles strained to the very limit," Vorobyev later wrote, "my heart was singing. I had done it! I had won!" The audience roared with excitement. But then Vorobyev staggered and dropped the bar just as the referee called out, "Release." One judge ruled that it had been a valid lift, but the other two rejected it. Forty minutes of arguing ensued, until finally the results were announced: Lomakin first, Stanczyk second, Vorobyev third.

Vorobyev returned to the dressing room in a deep depression and began slowly to undress. Suddenly his coach burst into the room and told him that he had been awarded one more attempt. But Vorobyev was unprepared. He needed more time to compose himself and warm up, but the officials had already started the clock. Forced to hurry back to the platform, he was unable to handle the weight a second time and fell backward, with the bar pinning him to the floor. The Soviets continued to argue that Vorobyev had been forced to hold his previous lift for more than two seconds, but the results were allowed to stand.

**1956 Melbourne** C: 10, N: 9, D: 11.26. WR: 435 kg (Tamio "Tommy" Kono)

| | | | PRESS | | SNATCH | | JERK | | TOTAL KG | |
|---|---|---|---|---|---|---|---|---|---|---|
| 1. | Tamio "Tommy" Kono | USA | 140.0 | OR | 132.5 | OR | 175.0 | WR | 447.5 | WR |
| 2. | Vassili Stepanov | SOV | 135.0 | | 130.0 | | 162.5 | | 427.5 | |
| 3. | James George | USA | 120.0 | | 130.0 | | 167.5 | | 417.5 | |
| 4. | Jalal Mansouri | IRN | 132.5 | | 122.5 | | 162.5 | | 417.5 | |
| 5. | Philip Caira | GBR | 127.5 | | 122.5 | | 155.0 | | 405.0 | |
| 6. | Václav Pšenička | CZE | 125.0 | | 120.0 | | 155.0 | | 400.0 | |
| 7. | Marcel Paterni | FRA | 132.5 | | 115.0 | | 147.5 | | 395.0 | |
| 8. | John Powell | AUS | 120.0 | | 117.5 | | 145.0 | | 382.5 | |

James George used a fourth lift to set a snatch world record of 137.5 kg.

**1960 Rome** C: 24, N: 21, D: 9.9. WR: 457.5 kg (Rudolf Plukfelder)

| | | | PRESS | SNATCH | | JERK | | TOTAL KG |
|---|---|---|---|---|---|---|---|---|
| 1. | Ireneusz Paliński | POL | 130.0 | 132.5 | EOR | 180.0 | WR | 442.5 |
| 2. | James George | USA | 132.5 | 132.5 | EOR | 165.0 | | 430.0 |
| 3. | Jan Bochenek | POL | 130.0 | 120.0 | | 170.0 | | 420.0 |
| 4. | Géza Tóth | HUN | 125.0 | 125.0 | | 167.5 | | 417.5 |
| 5. | Jouni Kailajärvi | FIN | 130.0 | 125.0 | | 162.5 | | 417.5 |
| 6. | Peter Tachev | BUL | 130.0 | 125.0 | | 160.0 | | 415.0 |
| 7. | Minoru Kubota | JPN | 125.0 | 120.0 | | 155.0 | | 400.0 |
| 8. | Willy Claes | BEL | 125.0 | 112.5 | | 155.0 | | 392.5 |

**1964 Tokyo** C: 24, N: 21, D: 10.16. WR: 477.5 kg (Gyözö Veres)

| | | | PRESS | | SNATCH | | JERK | | TOTAL KG | |
|---|---|---|---|---|---|---|---|---|---|---|
| 1. | Rudolf Plukfelder | SOV | 150.0 | | 142.5 | OR | 182.5 | | 475.0 | OR |
| 2. | Géza Tóth | HUN | 145.0 | | 137.5 | | 185.0 | OR | 467.5 | |
| 3. | Gyözö Veres | HUN | 155.0 | OR | 135.0 | | 177.5 | | 467.5 | |
| 4. | Jerzy Kaczkowski | POL | 145.0 | | 135.0 | | 167.5 | | 455.0 | |
| 5. | Gary Cleveland | USA | 152.5 | | 135.0 | | 167.5 | | 455.0 | |

|   |   | PRESS | SNATCH | JERK | TOTAL KG |
|---|---|---|---|---|---|
| 7. Kaarlo Kangasniemi | FIN | 150.0 | 135.0 | 165.0 | 450.0 |
| 8. Karl Arnold | GDR | 140.0 | 132.5 | 167.5 | 435.0 |

**1968 Mexico City** C: 26, N: 22, D: 10.17. WR: 485 kg (Vladimir Belyayev)

|   |   | PRESS | SNATCH | | JERK | | TOTAL KG | |
|---|---|---|---|---|---|---|---|---|
| 1. Boris Selitsky | SOV | 150.0 | 147.5 | OR | 187.5 | OR | 485.0 | EWR |
| 2. Vladimir Belyayev | SOV | 152.5 | 147.5 | OR | 185.0 | | 485.0 | EWR |
| 3. Norbert Ozimek | POL | 150.0 | 140.0 | | 182.5 | | 472.5 | |
| 4. Gyözö Veres | HUN | 150.0 | 140.0 | | 182.5 | | 472.5 | |
| 5. Karl Arnold | GDR | 155.0 | 137.5 | | 175.0 | | 467.5 | |
| 6. Hans Zdražila | CZE | 135.0 | 147.5 | OR | 180.0 | | 462.5 | |
| 7. Jouni Kailajärvi | FIN | 140.0 | 130.0 | | 175.0 | | 445.0 | |
| 8. Lee Jong-sup | KOR | 135.0 | 130.0 | | 175.0 | | 440.0 | |

**1972 Munich** C: 24, N: 21, D: 9.2. WR: 527.5 kg (Valery Shary)

|   |   | PRESS | | SNATCH | | JERK | | TOTAL KG | |
|---|---|---|---|---|---|---|---|---|---|
| 1. Leif Jenssen | NOR | 172.5 | OR | 150.0 | OR | 185.0 | | 507.5 | OR |
| 2. Norbert Ozimek | POL | 165.0 | | 145.0 | | 187.5 | | 497.5 | |
| 3. György Horváth | HUN | 160.0 | | 142.5 | | 192.5 | OR | 495.0 | |
| 4. Bernhard Radtke | GDR | 162.5 | | 145.0 | | 185.0 | | 492.5 | |
| 5. Christos Iakovou | GRE | 170.0 | | 137.5 | | 182.5 | | 490.0 | |
| 6. Kaarlo Kangasniemi | FIN | 150.0 | | 145.0 | | 185.0 | | 480.0 | |
| 7. Rolf Milser | GER | 165.0 | | 132.5 | | 180.0 | | 477.5 | |
| 8. Juhani Avellan | FIN | 140.0 | | 145.0 | | 182.5 | | 467.5 | |

The two Soviet representatives, world champion Boris Pavlov and world record holder Valery Shary, were so intent on beating each other that they started pressing at too high a weight. Both men missed all three attempts and were disqualified. Representing Israel was 28-year-old David Berger, originally of Shaker Heights, Ohio. The next day, Berger was one of the 11 Israelis who were killed by terrorists.

**1976 Montreal** C: 17, N: 14, D: 7.24. WR: 372.5 kg (Trendafil Stoichev)

|   |   | SNATCH | | JERK | | TOTAL KG | |
|---|---|---|---|---|---|---|---|
| 1. Valery Shary | SOV | 162.5 | OR | 202.5 | OR | 365.0 | OR |
| 2. Trendafil Stoichev | BUL | 162.5 | OR | 197.5 | | 360.0 | |
| 3. Péter Baczako | HUN | 157.5 | | 187.5 | | 345.0 | |
| 4. Nicolaos Iliadis | GRE | 150.0 | | 190.0 | | 340.0 | |
| 5. Juhani Avellan | FIN | 145.0 | | 185.0 | | 330.0 | |
| 6. Stefan Jacobsson | SWE | 147.5 | | 170.0 | | 317.5 | |
| 7. Sueo Fujishiro | JPN | 140.0 | | 175.0 | | 315.0 | |
| 8. Gerd Kennel | GER | 135.0 | | 177.5 | | 312.5 | |

DISQ (Drugs): Blagoi Blagoev (BUL) 362.5

**1980 Moscow** C: 19, N: 17, D: 7.26. WR: 390 kg (Yurik Vardanyan)

|   |   | SNATCH | | JERK | | TOTAL KG | |
|---|---|---|---|---|---|---|---|
| 1. Yurik Vardanyan | SOV | 177.5 | WR | 222.5 | WR | 400.0 | WR |
| 2. Blagoi Blagoev | BUL | 175.0 | | 197.5 | | 372.5 | |
| 3. Dušan Poliačik | CZE | 160.0 | | 207.5 | | 367.5 | |
| 4. Jan Lisowski | POL | 150.0 | | 205.0 | | 355.0 | |
| 5. Krassimir Drăndarov | BUL | 155.0 | | 200.0 | | 355.0 | |
| 6. Pawel Rabczewski | POL | 155.0 | | 195.0 | | 350.0 | |

|  |  | SNATCH | JERK | TOTAL KG |
|---|---|---|---|---|
| 7. Detlef Blasche | GDR | 152.5 | 192.5 | 345.0 |
| 8. Juhani Avellan | FIN | 150.0 | 182.5 | 332.5 |

Vardanyan's total would have earned him a gold medal in either of the next two higher weight classes.

**1984 Los Angeles-Westchester** C: 19, N: 16, D: 8.4. WR: 400 kg (Yurik Vardanyan)

|  |  | SNATCH | JERK | TOTAL KG |
|---|---|---|---|---|
| 1. Petre Becheru | ROM | 155.0 | 200.0 | 355.0 |
| 2. Robert Kabbas | AUS | 150.0 | 192.5 | 342.5 |
| 3. Ryoji Isaoka | JPN | 150.0 | 190.0 | 340.0 |
| 4. Newton Burrowes | GBR | 147.5 | 180.0 | 327.5 |
| 5. Ebraheem Elbakh | EGY | 145.0 | 177.5 | 322.5 |
| 6. Lee Kang-seong | KOR | 140.0 | 182.5 | 322.5 |
| 7. Yvan Darsigny | CAN | 142.5 | 180.0 | 322.5 |
| 8. Allister Nalder | NZE | 142.5 | 175.0 | 317.5 |

On September 15, at the Friendship Games, Yurik Vardanyan broke his own 4-year-old world record with combined lifts of 405 kg. Second place went to Asen Zlatev of Bulgaria with 380 kg and third to László Király of Hungary with 370 kg.

**1988 Seoul** C: 22, N: 20, D: 9.24. WR: 405 kg (Yurik Vardanyan)

|  |  | SNATCH | JERK | TOTAL KG |
|---|---|---|---|---|
| 1. Israil Arsamakov | SOV | 167.5 | 210.0 | 377.5 |
| 2. István Messzi | HUN | 170.0 | 200.0 | 370.0 |
| 3. Lee Hyung-kun | KOR | 160.0 | 207.5 | 367.5 |
| 4. David Morgan | GBR | 165.0 | 200.0 | 365.0 |
| 5. Krzystzof Siemion | POL | 162.5 | 195.0 | 357.5 |
| 6. Ryoji Isaoka | JPN | 155.0 | 195.0 | 350.0 |
| 7. Fausto Tosi | ITA | 155.0 | 185.0 | 340.0 |
| 8. Ali Eroğlü | TUR | 145.0 | 185.0 | 330.0 |

# MIDDLE HEAVYWEIGHT
(90 kg—198.25 lbs)

**1896–1948** not held

**1952 Helsinki** C: 20, N: 20, D: 7.27. WR: 427.5 kg (Norbert Schemansky)

|  |  | PRESS |  | SNATCH |  | JERK |  | TOTAL KG |  |
|---|---|---|---|---|---|---|---|---|---|
| 1. Norbert Schemansky | USA | 127.5 |  | 140.0 | WR | 177.5 | WR | 445.0 | WR |
| 2. Grigory Novak | SOV | 140.0 | OR | 125.0 |  | 145.0 |  | 410.0 |  |
| 3. Lennox Kilgour | TRI | 125.0 |  | 120.0 |  | 157.5 |  | 402.5 |  |
| 4. Mohammed Ibrahim Saleh | EGY | 110.0 |  | 125.0 |  | 162.5 |  | 397.5 |  |
| 5. Firouz Pejhan | IRN | 112.5 |  | 120.0 |  | 155.0 |  | 387.5 |  |
| 6. Kenneth McDonald | AUS | 107.5 |  | 125.0 |  | 152.5 |  | 385.0 |  |
| 7. Francisco Rensonnet | ARG | 107.5 |  | 112.5 |  | 150.0 |  | 370.0 |  |
| 8. Theunis Jonck | SAF | 112.5 |  | 110.0 |  | 145.0 |  | 367.5 |  |

The 5-foot 3½-inch, 195-pound Novak was hampered by a leg injury, but it is very doubtful that he could have beaten Detroit's Norbert Schemansky, who upped his own world record by 38½ pounds. Schemansky eventually became the only weightlifter to win four Olympic medals—including a bronze in the Heavyweight division in 1964 at the age of 40.

**1956 Melbourne** C: 15, N: 14, D: 11.26. WR: 460 kg (Arkady Vorobyov)

| | | PRESS | | SNATCH | JERK | | TOTAL KG | |
|---|---|---|---|---|---|---|---|---|
| 1. Arkady Vorobyov | SOV | 147.5 | WR | 137.5 | 177.5 | EOR | 462.5 | WR |
| 2. David Sheppard | USA | 140.0 | | 137.5 | 165.0 | | 442.5 | |
| 3. Jean Debuf | FRA | 130.0 | | 127.5 | 167.5 | | 425.0 | |
| 4. Mohammad Hassan Rahnavardi | IRN | 140.0 | | 127.5 | 157.5 | | 425.0 | |
| 5. Ivan Veselinov | BUL | 132.5 | | 120.0 | 155.0 | | 407.5 | |
| 6. Tan Kim Bee | MAL | 117.5 | | 122.5 | 155.0 | | 395.0 | |
| 7. Lennox Kilgour | TRI | 127.5 | | 117.5 | 145.0 | | 390.0 | |
| 8. Leonard Treganowan | AUS | 122.5 | | 117.5 | 150.0 | | 390.0 | |

A former deep-sea diver, Vorobyov made up for his disappointment in the controversial 1952 Light Heavyweight competition. He later became a doctor, wrote several textbooks on weightlifting, and served as coach of the Soviet team.

**1960 Rome** C: 20, N: 17, D: 9.9. WR: 470 kg (Arkady Vorobyov)

| | | PRESS | | SNATCH | | JERK | | TOTAL KG | |
|---|---|---|---|---|---|---|---|---|---|
| 1. Arkady Vorobyov | SOV | 152.5 | | 142.5 | OR | 177.5 | EOR | 472.5 | WR |
| 2. Trofim Lomakin | SOV | 157.5 | WR | 130.0 | | 170.0 | | 457.5 | |
| 3. Louis Martin | GBR | 137.5 | | 137.5 | | 170.0 | | 445.0 | |
| 4. John Pulskamp | USA | 140.0 | | 125.0 | | 167.5 | | 432.5 | |
| 5. François Vincent | FRA | 130.0 | | 132.5 | | 160.0 | | 422.5 | |
| 6. Vladimir Savov | BUL | 110.0 | | 137.5 | | 165.0 | | 412.5 | |
| 7. Czeslaw Bialas | POL | 130.0 | | 122.5 | | 157.5 | | 410.0 | |
| 8. Leonardo Masu | ITA | 135.0 | | 117.5 | | 155.0 | | 407.5 | |

**1964 Tokyo** C: 19, N: 18, D: 10.17. WR: 480 kg (Louis Martin)

| | | PRESS | | SNATCH | | JERK | | TOTAL KG | |
|---|---|---|---|---|---|---|---|---|---|
| 1. Vladimir Golovanov | SOV | 165.0 | OR | 142.5 | EOR | 180.0 | | 487.5 | WR |
| 2. Louis Martin | GBR | 155.0 | | 140.0 | | 180.0 | | 475.0 | |
| 3. Ireneusz Paliński | POL | 150.0 | | 135.0 | | 182.5 | OR | 467.5 | |
| 4. William March | USA | 155.0 | | 135.0 | | 177.5 | | 467.5 | |
| 5. Lazăr Baroga | ROM | 145.0 | | 135.0 | | 180.0 | | 460.0 | |
| 6. Árpád Nemessányi | HUN | 140.0 | | 142.5 | EOR | 177.5 | | 460.0 | |
| 7. Jouni Kailajärvi | FIN | 145.0 | | 127.5 | | 180.0 | | 452.5 | |
| 8. Peter Tachev | BUL | 145.0 | | 130.0 | | 170.0 | | 445.0 | |

**1968 Mexico City** C: 29, N: 22, D: 10.18. Wr: 522.5 kg (Kaarlo Kangasniemi)

| | | PRESS | | SNATCH | | JERK | | TOTAL KG | |
|---|---|---|---|---|---|---|---|---|---|
| 1. Kaarlo Kangasniemi | FIN | 172.5 | OR | 157.5 | WR | 187.5 | | 517.5 | OR |
| 2. Jaan Talts | SOV | 160.0 | | 150.0 | | 197.5 | WR | 507.5 | |
| 3. Marêk Gołąb | POL | 165.0 | | 145.0 | | 185.0 | | 495.0 | |
| 4. Bo Johansson | SWE | 165.0 | | 145.0 | | 182.5 | | 492.5 | |
| 5. Jaakko Kailajärvi | FIN | 145.0 | | 150.0 | | 190.0 | | 485.0 | |
| 6. Árpád Nemessányi | HUN | 150.0 | | 145.0 | | 187.5 | | 482.5 | |
| 7. Philip Grippaldi | USA | 155.0 | | 137.5 | | 185.0 | | 477.5 | |
| 8. Viteslav Orszag | CZE | 157.5 | | 130.0 | | 175.0 | | 462.5 | |

**1972 Munich** C: 23, N: 15, D: 9.3. WR: 562.5 kg (David Rigert)

|   |   | PRESS | SNATCH | JERK |   | TOTAL KG |   |
|---|---|---|---|---|---|---|---|
| 1. Andon Nikolov | BUL | 180.0 | 155.0 | 190.0 | | 525.0 | OR |
| 2. Atanas Shopov | BUL | 180.0 | 145.0 | 192.5 | | 517.5 | |
| 3. Hans Bettembourg | SWE | 182.5 | 145.0 | 185.0 | | 512.5 | |
| 4. Philip Grippaldi | USA | 170.0 | 140.0 | 195.0 | | 505.0 | |
| 5. Patrick Holbrook | USA | 162.5 | 145.0 | 197.5 | EOR | 505.0 | |
| 6. Nicolo Ciancio | AUS | 170.0 | 145.0 | 190.0 | | 505.0 | |
| 7. Juan Curbelo | CUB | 172.5 | 140.0 | 182.5 | | 495.0 | |
| 8. Jaakko Kailajärvi | FIN | 150.0 | 150.0 | 187.5 | | 487.5 | |

The clear favorite, world record holder David Rigert of Chakhti, set an Olympic record in the press of 187.5 kg. However, he failed at all three of his attempts to snatch 160 kg, despite the fact that he held the world record of 167.5 kg. Rigert was so upset that he literally pulled his hair out and banged his head against a wall. He was finally restrained by his colleagues, but the next day he threw another fit and had to be sent home. Gold-medal-winner Andon Nikolov was a former trouble-maker who was introduced to weightlifting in reform school.

**1976 Montreal** C: 19, N: 16, D: 7.25. WR: 400 kg (David Rigert)

|   |   | SNATCH |   | JERK |   | TOTAL KG |   |
|---|---|---|---|---|---|---|---|
| 1. David Rigert | SOV | 170.0 | OR | 212.5 | OR | 382.5 | OR |
| 2. Lee James | USA | 165.0 | | 197.5 | | 362.5 | |
| 3. Atanas Shopov | BUL | 155.0 | | 205.0 | | 360.0 | |
| 4. György Rehus | HUN | 157.5 | | 192.5 | | 350.0 | |
| 5. Peter Petzold | GDR | 152.5 | | 192.5 | | 345.0 | |
| 6. Alberto Blanco | CUB | 152.5 | | 192.5 | | 345.0 | |
| 7. Yvon Coussin | FRA | 152.5 | | 180.0 | | 332.5 | |
| 8. Gudmundur Sigurdsson | ICE | 145.0 | | 187.5 | | 332.5 | |

DISQ (Drugs): Philip Grippaldi (USA) 355.0

Rigert, the heaviest man to snatch twice his bodyweight, had no reason to lose any hair this time in Montreal, as his excellent lifting gave him a comfortable victory.

**1980 Moscow** C: 18, N: 16, D: 7.27. WR: 400 kg (David Rigert)

|   |   | SNATCH |   | JERK | TOTAL KG |
|---|---|---|---|---|---|
| 1. Péter Baczakó | HUN | 170.0 | EOR | 207.5 | 377.5 |
| 2. Roumen Aleksandrov | BUL | 170.0 | EOR | 205.0 | 375.0 |
| 3. Frank Mantek | GDR | 165.0 | | 205.0 | 370.0 |
| 4. Dalibor Rehak | CZE | 165.0 | | 200.0 | 365.0 |
| 5. Witold Walo | POL | 160.0 | | 200.0 | 360.0 |
| 6. Lubomír Sršeň | CZE | 160.0 | | 207.5 | 357.5 |
| 7. Vasile Groapă | ROM | 160.0 | | 195.0 | 355.0 |
| 8. Nicolaos Iliadis | GRE | 150.0 | | 195.0 | 345.0 |

David Rigert reverted to his form of eight years earlier when he started snatching at 170 kg, failed at all three attempts, and was eliminated.

**1984 Los Angeles-Westchester** C: 26, N: 21, D: 8.5. WR: 420 kg
(Blagoi Blagoev)

|  |  |  | SNATCH |  | JERK |  | TOTAL KG |  |
|---|---|---|---|---|---|---|---|---|
| 1. | Nicu Vlad | ROM | 172.5 | OR | 220.0 | OR | 392.5 | OR |
| 2. | Dumitru Petre | ROM | 165.0 |  | 195.0 |  | 360.0 |  |
| 3. | David Mercer | GBR | 157.5 |  | 195.0 |  | 352.5 |  |
| 4. | Peter Immesberger | GER | 155.0 |  | 195.0 |  | 350.0 |  |
| 5. | Hwang Woo-won | KOR | 152.5 |  | 197.5 |  | 350.0 |  |
| 6. | Nikos Iliadis | GRE | 155.0 |  | 195.0 |  | 350.0 |  |
| 7. | Henri Junch Hoeg | DEN | 152.5 |  | 195.0 |  | 347.5 |  |
| 8. | José Garces | MEX | 150.0 |  | 192.5 |  | 342.5 |  |

Handsome Nicu Vlad was known in Romania as "The Apollo of the Barbells." At the Friendship Games in Varna on September 16, Viktor Solodov set a world record of 422.5 kg. In second place at 400 kg., was Blagoi Blagoev, the man whose record Solodov broke.

**1988 Seoul** C: 29, N: 23, D: 9.25. WR: 422.5 kg (Viktor Solodov)

|  |  |  | SNATCH |  | JERK |  | TOTAL KG |  |
|---|---|---|---|---|---|---|---|---|
| 1. | Anatoly Khrapaty | SOV | 187.5 | OR | 225.0 | OR | 412.5 | OR |
| 2. | Nail Mukhamedyarov | SOV | 177.5 |  | 222.5 |  | 400.0 |  |
| 3. | Slawomir Zawada | POL | 180.0 |  | 220.0 |  | 400.0 |  |
| 4. | Andrzej Piotrowski | POL | 165.0 |  | 200.0 |  | 365.0 |  |
| 5. | Attila Buda | HUN | 175.0 |  | 185.0 |  | 360.0 |  |
| 6. | David Mercer | GBR | 157.5 |  | 200.0 |  | 357.5 |  |
| 7. | Roland Feldhoffer | GER | 150.0 |  | 200.0 |  | 350.0 |  |
| 8. | Keith Boxell | GBR | 157.5 |  | 192.5 |  | 350.0 |  |

# 100 KG
## (220.25 lbs)

**1896–1976** not held

**1980 Moscow** C: 17, N: 13, D: 7.28. WR: 402.5 kg (David Rigert)

|  |  |  | SNATCH |  | JERK |  | TOTAL KG |  |
|---|---|---|---|---|---|---|---|---|
| 1. | Ota Zaremba | CZE | 180.0 | OR | 215.0 |  | 395.0 | OR |
| 2. | Igor Nikitin | SOV | 177.5 |  | 215.0 |  | 392.5 |  |
| 3. | Alberto Blanco Fernandez | CUB | 172.5 |  | 212.5 |  | 385.0 |  |
| 4. | Michael Hennig | GDR | 165.0 |  | 217.5 | OR | 382.5 |  |
| 5. | János Sólyomvári | HUN | 175.0 |  | 205.0 |  | 380.0 |  |
| 6. | Manfred Funke | GDR | 170.0 |  | 207.5 |  | 377.5 |  |
| 7. | Anton Baraniak | CZE | 165.0 |  | 210.0 |  | 375.0 |  |
| 8. | László Varga | HUN | 172.5 |  | 195.0 |  | 367.5 |  |

**1984 Los Angeles-Westchester** C: 16, N: 14, D: 8.6. WR: 440 kg
(Yuri Zakharevich)

|  |  |  | SNATCH | JERK |  | TOTAL KG |
|---|---|---|---|---|---|---|
| 1. | Rolf Milser | GER | 167.5 | 217.5 | EOR | 385.0 |
| 2. | Vasile Groapă | ROM | 165.0 | 217.5 | EOR | 382.5 |
| 3. | Pekka Niemi | FIN | 160.0 | 207.5 |  | 367.5 |
| 4. | Kevin Roy | CAN | 160.0 | 197.5 |  | 357.5 |
| 5. | Ken Clark | USA | 155.0 | 197.5 |  | 352.5 |
| 6. | Franz Langthaler | AUT | 162.5 | 187.5 |  | 350.0 |
| 7. | Rich Shanko | USA | 155.0 | 195.0 |  | 350.0 |
| 8. | Jean-Marie Kretz | FRA | 150.0 | 192.5 |  | 342.5 |

International weightlifting competitions are separated into two sessions. In the afternoon the less-distinguished lifters take part in the "B" session and in the evening the leading contenders lift in the "A" session. The top lifter in the 100 kg. division "B" session was 31-year-old Pekka Niemi. Since no "B" lifter had ever won a medal in an international meet, Niemi skipped the evening session and went instead to the Los Angeles Coliseum to watch the track and field events. Niemi was playing with an Electronic Messaging System computer terminal in the press section when a German TV reporter said, "Let's see what you did." Niemi pushed some buttons and on the screen appeared the news that he had finished third. Meanwhile, back at the weightlifting venue at Loyola Marymount University, the medal ceremony was being delayed while officials unsuccessfully searched for Niemi or anyone else from the Finnish delegation. Finally they went ahead with the presentation with the bronze medal platform empty. When Niemi called home to share the good news, he learned that his family had learned of his good fortune on Finnish television before he himself had found out in Los Angeles. The next day Niemi received his medal at a special ceremony, after which he patiently signed 200 autographs.

Six weeks later at the Friendship Games Pavel Kuznetsov of the Soviet Union won first place with a lift total of 427.5 kg. Second was Andor Szanyi of Hungary at 390 kg.

**1988 Seoul** C: 21, N: 17, D: 9.26. WR: 440 kg (Yuri Zakharevich)

|   |   |   | SNATCH |   | JERK |   | TOTAL KG |   |
|---|---|---|---|---|---|---|---|---|
| 1. | Pavel Kuznetsov | SOV | 190.0 | OR | 235.0 | OR | 425.0 | OR |
| 2. | Nicu Vlad | ROM | 185.0 |   | 217.5 |   | 402.5 |   |
| 3. | Peter Immesberger | GER | 175.0 |   | 220.0 |   | 395.0 |   |
| 4. | János Bökfi | HUN | 180.0 |   | 212.5 |   | 392.5 |   |
| 5. | Francis Tournefier | FRA | 170.0 |   | 215.0 |   | 385.0 |   |
| 6. | Denis Garon | CAN | 160.0 |   | 222.5 |   | 382.5 |   |
| 7. | Hwang Woo-won | KOR | 162.5 |   | 220.0 |   | 382.5 |   |
| 8. | Franz Langthaler | AUT | 172.5 |   | 205.0 |   | 377.5 |   |

DISQ (Drugs): Andor Szanyi (HUN) 407.5

# HEAVYWEIGHT
## (110 kg—242.5 lbs)

**1896–1968** not held

**1972 Munich** C: 26, N: 19, D: 9.22. WR: 590 kg (Valery Yakubovsky)

|   |   |   | PRESS |   | SNATCH | JERK | TOTAL KG |   |
|---|---|---|---|---|---|---|---|---|
| 1. | Jaan Talts | SOV | 210.0 | OR | 165.0 | 205.0 | 580.0 | OR |
| 2. | Aleksandr Kraichev | BUL | 197.5 |   | 162.5 | 202.5 | 562.5 |   |
| 3. | Stefan Grützner | GDR | 185.0 |   | 162.5 | 207.5 | 555.0 |   |
| 4. | Helmut Losch | GDR | 190.0 |   | 152.5 | 205.0 | 547.5 |   |
| 5. | Roberto Vezzani | ITA | 192.5 |   | 147.5 | 205.0 | 545.0 |   |
| 6. | János Hanzlik | HUN | 190.0 |   | 157.5 | 195.0 | 542.5 |   |
| 7. | Kauko Kangasniemi | FIN | 175.0 |   | 165.0 | 197.5 | 537.5 |   |
| 8. | Rainer Dörrzapf | GER | 170.0 |   | 165.0 | 187.5 | 522.5 |   |

**1976 Montreal** C: 22, N: 18, D: 7.26. WR: 417.5 kg (Valentin Hristov)

| | | SNATCH | | JERK | | TOTAL KG |
|---|---|---|---|---|---|---|
| 1. Yuri Zaitsev | SOV | 165.0 | | 220.0 | OR | 385.0 |
| 2. Krustiu Semerdzhiev | BUL | 170.0 | OR | 215.0 | | 385.0 |
| 3. Tadeusz Rutkowski | POL | 167.5 | | 210.0 | | 377.5 |
| 4. Pierre Gourrier | FRA | 157.5 | | 215.0 | | 372.5 |
| 5. Jürgen Ciezki | GDR | 162.5 | | 210.0 | | 372.5 |
| 6. Javier Gonzalez | CUB | 160.0 | | 205.0 | | 365.0 |
| 7. Leif Nilsson | SWE | 157.5 | | 207.5 | | 365.0 |
| 8. Rudolf Strejcek | CZE | 162.5 | | 200.0 | | 362.5 |

DISQ (Drugs): Valentin Hristov (BUL) 400.0, Mark Cameron (USA) 375.0

**1980 Moscow** C: 13, N: 13, D: 7.29. WR: 420 kg (Leonid Taranenko)

| | | SNATCH | | JERK | | TOTAL KG | |
|---|---|---|---|---|---|---|---|
| 1. Leonid Taranenko | SOV | 182.5 | | 240.0 | WR | 422.5 | WR |
| 2. Valentin Hristov | BUL | 185.0 | OR | 220.0 | | 405.0 | |
| 3. György Szalai | HUN | 172.5 | | 217.5 | | 390.0 | |
| 4. Leif Nilsson | SWE | 167.5 | | 212.5 | | 380.0 | |
| 5. Vinzenz Hortnagl | AUT | 170.0 | | 202.5 | | 372.5 | |
| 6. Stefan Tasnadi | ROM | 165.0 | | 195.0 | | 360.0 | |
| 7. Donald Mitchell | AUS | 162.5 | | 190.0 | | 352.5 | |
| 8. Dimitrios Zarzavatsidis | GRE | 155.0 | | 192.5 | | 347.5 | |

**1984 Los Angeles-Westchester** C: 15, N: 12, D: 8.7. WR: 440 kg. (Vyacheslav Klokov)

| | | SNATCH | JERK | TOTAL KG |
|---|---|---|---|---|
| 1. Norberto Oberburger | ITA | 175.0 | 215.0 | 390.0 |
| 2. Stefan Tasnadi | ROM | 167.5 | 212.5 | 380.0 |
| 3. Guy Carlton | USA | 167.5 | 210.0 | 377.5 |
| 4. Frank Seipelt | GER | 160.0 | 207.5 | 367.5 |
| 5. Albert Squires | CAN | 165.0 | 200.0 | 365.0 |
| 6. Richard Eaton | USA | 152.5 | 200.0 | 352.5 |
| 7. Ioannis Gerontas | GRE | 152.5 | 197.5 | 350.0 |
| 8. Olaf Peters | GER | 157.5 | 190.0 | 347.5 |

DISQ (Drugs): Göran Pettersson (SWE) 360.0

On September 17, 1980, Olympic champion Leonid Taranenko lifted a world record 442.5 kg. to win at the Friendship Games. Second was Soviet teammate Yuri Zakharevich with 427.5 kg., and third Yanko Georgiev of Bulgaria with 412.5 kg.

**1988 Seoul** C: 20, N: 15, D: 9.27. WR: 452.5 kg (Yuri Zakharevich)

| | | SNATCH | | JERK | | TOTAL KG | |
|---|---|---|---|---|---|---|---|
| 1. Yuri Zakharevich | SOV | 210.0 | WR | 245.0 | WR | 455.0 | WR |
| 2. József Jacsó | HUN | 190.0 | | 237.5 | | 427.5 | |
| 3. Ronny Weller | GDR | 190.0 | | 235.0 | | 425.0 | |
| 4. Michael Schubert | GDR | 190.0 | | 235.0 | | 425.0 | |
| 5. Aleksandr Popov | SOV | 187.5 | | 232.5 | | 420.0 | |
| 6. Norberto Oberburger | ITA | 187.5 | | 227.5 | | 415.0 | |
| 7. Stanislaw Malysa | POL | 180.0 | | 215.0 | | 395.0 | |
| 8. Frank Seipelt | GER | 170.0 | | 217.5 | | 387.5 | |

In 1983 Yuri Zakharevich dislocated his left elbow while attempting a snatch world record. Doctors rebuilt his elbow using synthetic tendons. He returned to competition in 1984 and won the next four European championships as well as the next three world championships. In Seoul he broke the snatch world record twice as well as the record for combined total.

## SUPER HEAVYWEIGHT—UNLIMITED WEIGHT
### (Heavyweight 1896-1968)

**1896 Athens** C: 4, N: 3?, D: 4.7.
*One-Hand Lift*

| | | KG |
|---|---|---|
| 1. Launceston Elliot | GBR | 71.0 |
| 2. Viggo Jensen | DEN | 57.2 |
| 3. Alexandros Nikolopoulos | GRE | — |

**1896 Athens** C: 6, N: 5, D: 4.7.
*Two-Hand Lift*

| | | KG |
|---|---|---|
| 1. Viggo Jensen | DEN | 111.5 |
| 2. Launceston Elliot | GBR | 111.5 |
| 3. Alexandros Nikolopoulos | GRE | 90.0 |
| 3. Karl Schumann | GER | 90.0 |
| 3. Momcsilló Topavicza | HUN | 90.0 |
| 3. Sotirios Versis | GRE | 90.0 |

The first instance of an Olympic judging controversy occurred in the two-handed lift. Jensen and Elliot tied at 111.5 kg, but the Dane was awarded first place as a result of his better style, Elliot having moved one foot while lifting. Jensen was quite a versatile athlete. In addition to winning the weightlifting competition, he also finished second in the free pistol, third in the military rifle, and fourth in the rope climb.

**1900 Paris** not held

**1904 St. Louis** C: 4, N: 2, D: 9.3.
*Two-Hand Lift*

| | | KG |
|---|---|---|
| 1. Perikles Kakousis | GRE | 111.70 |
| 2. Oscar Osthoff | USA | 84.37 |
| 3. Frank Kungler | USA | 79.61 |
| 4. Oscar Olson | USA | 67.81 |

**1904 St. Louis** C: 3, N: 1, D: 9.3.
*All-Around Dumbbell Contest*

| | | |
|---|---|---|
| 1. Oscar Osthoff | USA | 48 points |
| 2. Frederick Winters | USA | 45 points |
| 3. Frank Kungler | USA | 10 points |

The all-around dumbbell contest, won by Oscar Osthoff of Milwaukee, consisted of nine different types of lifts as well as an optional section.

**1906 Athens** C: 12, N: 7, D: 4.27.
*One-Hand Lift*

| | | KG |
|---|---|---|
| 1. Josef Steinbach | AUT | 76.55 |
| 2. Tullio Camilotti | ITA | 73.75 |
| 3. Heinrich Schneidereit | GER | 70.75 |
| 4. Alexandre Maspoli | FRA | 70.75 |
| 5. Carl Svensson | SWE | 65.45 |
| 6. Heinrich Rondi | GER | 65.45 |
| 6. Ioannis Varanakis | GRE | 65.45 |
| 8. Marcel Dubois | BEL | 60.40 |

A successful lift was not recorded unless the weight was lifted with *each* hand.

**1906 Athens** C: 10, N: 6, D: 4.27.
*Two-Hand Lift*

| | | KG |
|---|---|---|
| 1. Dimitrios Tofalos | GRE | 142.5 |
| 2. Josef Steinbach | AUT | 136.5 |
| 3. Alexandre Maspoli | FRA | 129.5 |
| 3. Heinrich Rondi | GER | 129.5 |
| 3. Heinrich Schneidereit | GER | 129.5 |
| 6. Perikles Kakousis | GRE | 121.5 |
| 7. Tullio Camilotti | ITA | 108.5 |
| 7. Stephanos Christopoulos | GRE | 108.5 |
| 7. Marcel Dubois | BEL | 108.5 |
| 7. Ioannis Varanakis | GRE | 108.5 |

Josef Steinbach caused a stir when he objected to the rule in the two-hand lift which required that the bar be raised straight to the shoulders before being brought overhead. Steinbach wanted to use the continental style, which allowed him to rest the weight at his waist before moving it to his shoulders. After Tofalos had won the competition and the jury had departed, Steinbach walked back to the bar and, using the forbidden style, lifted it easily over his head. The sportsmanlike Greek crowd, unaware of the rules, thought that Steinbach had been cheated of victory.

Tofalos, the son of a count, had been run over by a wagon as a young boy. His upper arm was crushed and doctors wanted to amputate it, but Tofalos' father wouldn't allow it. Dimitrios recovered the use of his arm even though it was two and a half inches shorter than his uninjured arm. After winning at the Olympics, Tofalos turned professional and eventually went to America, where he entered vaudeville and became a wrestler. In a match against world champion Frank Gotch, Tofalos got caught in one of Gotch's famous toe-holds, but refused to submit. His stubbornness cost him six months in the hospital with a dislocated hip. Tofalos became a U.S. citizen in 1921 and remained a popular figure in professional wrestling and physical culture circles for the rest of his life.

**1908–1912** not held

**1920 Antwerp** C: 10, N: 8, D: 8.28.

|   |   | PRESS | SNATCH | JERK | TOTAL KG |
|---|---|---|---|---|---|
| 1. Filippo Bottino | ITA | 70.0 | 75.0 | 120.0 | 265.0 |
| 2. Joseph Alzin | LUX | 65.0 | 75.0 | 120.0 | 260.0 |
| 3. Louis Bernot | FRA | 65.0 | 75.0 | 115.0 | 255.0 |
| 4. Erik Juul Jensen | DEN | 60.0 | 75.0 | 115.0 | 250.0 |
| 5. Joseph Duchâteau | FRA | 65.0 | 72.5 | 110.0 | 247.5 |
| 6. Richard Brunn | SWE | 60.0 | 70.0 | 115.0 | 245.0 |

**1924 Paris** C: 19, N: 12, D: 7.24.

|   |   | ONE-HAND SNATCH | ONE-HAND JERK | PRESS | TWO-HAND SNATCH | TWO-HAND JERK | TOTAL KG |
|---|---|---|---|---|---|---|---|
| 1. Giuseppe Tonani | ITA | 80.0 | 95.0 | 112.5 | 100.0 | 130.0 | 517.5 |
| 2. Franz Aigner | AUT | 80.0 | 97.5 OR | 112.5 | 95.0 | 130.0 | 515.0 |
| 3. Harald Tammer | EST | 75.0 | 95.0 | 90.0 | 97.5 | 140.0 OR | 497.5 |
| 4. Louis Dannoux | FRA | 80.0 | 95.0 | 87.5 | 100.0 | 135.0 | 497.5 |
| 5. Karlis Leilands | LAT | 77.5 | 87.5 | 100.0 | 100.0 | 132.5 | 497.5 |
| 6. Filippo Bottino | ITA | 77.5 | 85.0 | 110.0 | 97.5 | 125.0 | 495.0 |
| 7. Kaljo-Feliks Raag | EST | 80.0 | 92.5 | 90.0 | 97.5 | 130.0 | 490.0 |
| 8. Claudius Dutrieve | FRA | 75.0 | 82.5 | 90.0 | 100.0 OR | 120.0 | 467.5 |

Places three through five were determined by a two-hand jerk lift-off.

**1928 Amsterdam** C: 17, N: 11, D: 7.29.

|   |   | PRESS | SNATCH | JERK | TOTAL KG |
|---|---|---|---|---|---|
| 1. Josef Strassberger | GER | 122.5 OR | 107.5 | 142.5 | 372.5 WR |
| 2. Arnold Luhäär | EST | 100.0 | 110.0 OR | 150.0 OR | 360.0 |
| 3. Jaroslav Skobla | CZE | 100.0 | 107.5 | 150.0 OR | 357.5 |
| 4. Karlis Leilands | LAT | 110.0 | 105.0 | 140.0 | 355.0 |
| 5. Josef Leppelt | AUT | 105.0 | 110.0 OR | 140.0 | 355.0 |
| 5. Rudolf Schilberg | AUT | 115.0 | 105.0 | 135.0 | 355.0 |
| 7. Giuseppe Tonani | ITA | 117.5 | 97.5 | 137.5 | 352.5 |
| 8. Hermann Volz | GER | 97.5 | 110.0 | 132.5 | 340.0 |

**1932 Los Angeles** C: 6, N: 4, D: 7.30. WR: 400 kg (El Sayed Mohammed Nosseir)

|   |   | PRESS | SNATCH | JERK | TOTAL KG |
|---|---|---|---|---|---|
| 1. Jaroslav Skobla | CZE | 112.5 | 115.0 | 152.5 OR | 380.0 OR |
| 2. Václav Pšenička | CZE | 112.5 | 117.5 OR | 147.5 | 377.5 |
| 3. Josef Strassberger | GER | 125.0 OR | 110.0 | 142.5 | 377.5 |
| 4. Marcel Dumoulin | FRA | 95.0 | 107.5 | 140.0 | 342.5 |
| 5. Albert Manger | USA | 100.0 | 92.5 | 122.5 | 315.0 |
| 6. Howard Turbyfill | USA | 77.5 | 95.0 | 132.5 | 305.0 |

Twenty-four years later, Skobla's son Jiři won the bronze medal in the shot put at Melbourne.

**1936 Berlin** C: 13, N: 9, D: 8.5. WR: 407.5 kg (Václav Pšenička)

|   |   | PRESS | SNATCH | JERK | TOTAL KG |
|---|---|---|---|---|---|
| 1. Josef Manger | GER | 132.5 OR | 122.5 | 155.0 | 410.0 WR |
| 2. Václav Pšenička | CZE | 122.5 | 125.0 | 155.0 | 402.5 |
| 3. Arnold Luhäär | EST | 115.0 | 120.0 | 165.0 OR | 400.0 |
| 4. Ronald Walker | GBR | 110.0 | 127.5 OR | 160.0 | 397.5 |

| | | PRESS | SNATCH | JERK | TOTAL KG |
|---|---|---|---|---|---|
| 5. Hussein Mokhtar | EGY | 112.5 | 122.5 | 160.0 | 395.0 |
| 6. Josef Zemann | AUT | 110.0 | 122.5 | 155.0 | 387.5 |
| 7. Paul Wahl | GER | 115.0 | 110.0 | 150.0 | 375.0 |
| 8. Rudolf Shilberg | AUT | 125.0 | 107.5 | 140.0 | 372.5 |

**1948 London** C: 16, N: 14, D: 8.11. WR: 455 kg (John Davis)

| | | PRESS | | SNATCH | | JERK | | TOTAL KG | |
|---|---|---|---|---|---|---|---|---|---|
| 1. John Davis | USA | 137.5 | OR | 137.5 | OR | 177.5 | WR | 452.5 | OR |
| 2. Norbert Schemansky | USA | 122.5 | | 132.5 | | 170.0 | | 425.0 | |
| 3. Abraham Charité | HOL | 127.5 | | 125.0 | | 160.0 | | 412.5 | |
| 4. Alfred Knight | GBR | 117.5 | | 117.5 | | 155.0 | | 390.0 | |
| 5. Hanafi Mustafa | EGY | 120.0 | | 115.0 | | 150.0 | | 385.0 | |
| 6. Niels Petersen | DEN | 115.0 | | 112.5 | | 155.0 | | 382.5 | |
| 7. Robert Allart | BEL | 122.5 | | 110.0 | | 145.0 | | 377.5 | |
| 8. Pieter Taljaard | SAF | 117.5 | | 112.5 | | 145.0 | | 375.0 | |

With his fourth attempt, Davis set a snatch world record of 142.5 kg.

**1952 Helsinki** C: 13, N: 11, D: 7.27. WR: 482.5 kg (John Davis)

| | | PRESS | | SNATCH | | JERK | TOTAL KG | |
|---|---|---|---|---|---|---|---|---|
| 1. John Davis | USA | 150.0 | OR | 145.0 | OR | 165.0 | 460.0 | OR |
| 2. James Bradford | USA | 140.0 | | 132.5 | | 165.0 | 437.5 | |
| 3. Humberto Selvetti | ARG | 150.0 | OR | 120.0 | | 162.5 | 432.5 | |
| 4. Heinz Schattner | GER | 130.0 | | 130.0 | | 162.5 | 422.5 | |
| 5. William David Daillie | CAN | 145.0 | | 122.5 | | 152.5 | 420.0 | |
| 6. Norberto Ferreira | ARG | 140.0 | | 115.0 | | 155.0 | 410.0 | |
| 7. D. Harold Cleghorn | NZE | 130.0 | | 117.5 | | 152.5 | 400.0 | |
| 8. Franz Hölbl | AUT | 115.0 | | 117.5 | | 155.0 | 387.5 | |

John Davis of Brooklyn was never bested in Olympic competition in either the press, the snatch, or the jerk, and was undefeated in all competitions between 1938 and 1953. Fourth-place finisher Schattner was a circus performer. He began his act by hoisting a weightlifting bar attached to two enormous globes. Once they were above his head, the globes opened to reveal his wife and son.

**1956 Melbourne** C: 9, N: 9, D: 11.26. WR: 519.5 kg (Paul Anderson)

| | | PRESS | SNATCH | | JERK | | TOTAL KG | |
|---|---|---|---|---|---|---|---|---|
| 1. Paul Anderson | USA | 167.5 | 145.0 | EOR | 187.5 | OR | 500.0 | OR |
| 2. Humberto Selvetti | ARG | 175.0 | OR | 145.0 | EOR | 180.0 | 500.0 | OR |
| 3. Alberto Pigaiani | ITA | 150.0 | 130.0 | | 172.5 | | 452.5 | |
| 4. Firouz Pejhan | IRN | 147.5 | 132.5 | | 170.0 | | 450.0 | |
| 5. Eino Mäkinen | FIN | 127.5 | 137.5 | | 167.5 | | 432.5 | |
| 6. William David Baillie | CAN | 147.5 | 122.5 | | 162.5 | | 432.5 | |
| 7. Franz Hölbl | AUT | 142.5 | 125.0 | | 157.5 | | 425.0 | |
| 8. Richard Jones | NZE | 125.0 | 122.5 | | 150.0 | | 397.5 | |

What had been expected to be an easy victory for Paul Anderson of Toccoa, Georgia, developed instead into a dramatic showdown between Anderson, who had developed a strep throat, and 1952's bronze medalist, Humberto Selvetti of Argentina. Selvetti surprised the audience by taking the lead in the press with a lift of 175 kg, after Anderson had missed twice at 172.5 kg. When it came time for the jerk, Selvetti was still ahead by 7.5 kg. Anderson watched as Selvetti successfully jerked 170 kg and 180 kg before missing at 185. Anderson, deciding to go straight for the victory, called for 187.5 kg for his first attempt. He failed. He tried it a second time, but missed again. Now he was down to one last lift that would determine if he would finish first or last. Straining heroically, Anderson balanced the weight above his head and finished the competition with a weight total of 500 kg, exactly the same as that of Humberto Selvetti. Paul Anderson was a huge man who weighed in at 303¼ pounds (137.9 kg) after losing 60 pounds to get in shape for the Olympics. Ironically though, he won his gold medal because his bodyweight was actually *less* than that of Selvetti, who was a mammoth 316½ pounds (143.5 kg). Anderson was a devout Christian who opened his home to delinquent and orphaned children.

**1960 Rome** C: 18, N: 15, D: 9.10. WR: 533 kg (Paul Anderson)

| | | PRESS | | SNATCH | | JERK | | TOTAL KG | |
|---|---|---|---|---|---|---|---|---|---|
| 1. Yuri Vlasov | SOV | 180.0 | OR | 155.0 | OR | 202.5 | WR | 537.5 | WR |
| 2. James Bradford | USA | 180.0 | OR | 150.0 | | 182.5 | | 512.5 | |
| 3. Norbert Schemansky | USA | 170.0 | | 150.0 | | 180.0 | | 500.0 | |
| 4. Mohamed Mahmoud Ibrahim | UAR | 140.0 | | 137.5 | | 177.5 | | 455.0 | |
| 5. Eino Mäkinen | FIN | 140.0 | | 142.5 | | 172.5 | | 455.0 | |
| 6. William David Baillie | CAN | 147.5 | | 132.5 | | 170.0 | | 450.0 | |
| 7. Alberto Pigaiani | ITA | 152.5 | | 127.5 | | 170.0 | | 450.0 | |
| 8. Václav Syrový | CZE | 145.0 | | 125.0 | | 172.5 | | 435.0 | |

Although Vlasov's main opponents were the two veterans Bradford and Schemansky, most of the audience was aware of a third, invisible opponent—Paul Anderson, who had turned professional, but whose world record was still on the books. Vlasov assured himself the gold medal and an Olympic record with his first jerk of 185 kg. He followed with a 195, then stunned the crowd by jerking 202.5 kg and setting two world records (jerk and total lifts) with one lift. After his Olympic victory, Vlasov quit lifting and turned to his great love—writing poetry. But he had trouble selling his work. He was also cast in the role of Pierre Bezukhov in the Soviet epic film *War and Peace*. However, at the last minute director Sergei Bondarchuk took the role for himself. Unable to support himself as a creative artist, Vlasov returned to weightlifting and began preparations for the Tokyo Olympics.

**1964 Tokyo** C: 21, N: 18, D: 10.18. WR: 580 kg (Yuri Vlasov)

| | | PRESS | | SNATCH | | JERK | | TOTAL KG | |
|---|---|---|---|---|---|---|---|---|---|
| 1. Leonid Zhabotinsky | SOV | 187.5 | | 167.5 | OR | 217.5 | WR | 572.5 | OR |
| 2. Yuri Vlasov | SOV | 197.5 | WR | 162.5 | | 210.0 | | 570.0 | |
| 3. Norbert Schemansky | USA | 180.0 | | 165.0 | | 192.5 | | 537.5 | |
| 4. Gary Gubner | USA | 175.0 | | 150.0 | | 187.5 | | 512.5 | |
| 5. Károly Ecser | HUN | 175.0 | | 147.5 | | 185.0 | | 507.5 | |
| 6. Mohamed Mahmoud Ibrahim | UAR | 162.5 | | 145.0 | | 187.5 | | 495.0 | |
| 7. Ivan Veselinov | BUL | 165.0 | | 135.0 | | 190.0 | | 490.0 | |
| 8. Hwang Ho-dong | KOR | 162.5 | | 135.0 | | 185.0 | | 482.5 | |

Zhabotinsky, a 341-pound Ukrainian, scored a major upset when he came from behind to defeat teammate Yuri Vlasov by breaking Vlasov's world jerk record on his final attempt. A half hour earlier, Zhabotinsky had lulled Vlasov into a false sense of security by going up to him and conceding defeat. When Vlasov realized that he had been made the victim of a dishonest trick, he was furious. "I was choked with tears," he later wrote. "I flung the silver medal through the window. . . . I had always revered the purity, the impartiality of contests of strength. That night, I understood that there is a kind of strength that has nothing to do with justice."

In 1989, Vlasov, by then an outspoken critic of the Soviet sports system, with its emphasis on victory at any cost, was elected to the Council of People's Deputies. On May 30 of that year, he stunned the Communist government when he attacked the K.G.B. in a speech that was broadcast live throughout the nation.

**1968 Mexico City** C. 17, N: 14, D: 10.19. WR: 590 kg (Leonid Zhabotinsky)

|   |   |   | PRESS |   | SNATCH |   | JERK | TOTAL KG |   |
|---|---|---|---|---|---|---|---|---|---|
| 1. | Leonid Zhabotinsky | SOV | 200.0 | OR | 170.0 | OR | 202.5 | 572.5 | EOR |
| 2. | Serge Reding | BEL | 195.0 | | 147.5 | | 212.5 | 555.0 | |
| 3. | Joseph Dube | USA | 200.0 | OR | 145.0 | | 210.0 | 555.0 | |
| 4. | Manfred Rieger | GDR | 175.0 | | 155.0 | | 202.5 | 532.5 | |
| 5. | Rudolf Mang | GER | 177.5 | | 152.5 | | 195.0 | 525.0 | |
| 6. | Mauno Lindroos | FIN | 157.5 | | 145.0 | | 192.5 | 495.0 | |
| 7. | Kalevi Lahdenranta | FIN | 160.0 | | 147.5 | | 185.0 | 492.5 | |
| 8. | Donald Oliver | NZE | 147.5 | | 142.5 | | 200.0 | 490.0 | |

Zhabotinsky, now up to 359 pounds, reveled in his role of "World's Strongest Man." At the opening ceremony in Mexico City he astonished the crowd by carrying the huge Soviet flag one-handed. In the competition, he was so sure of victory that he passed his last two attempts in the jerk, upsetting the audience, which had hoped to see him try for a world record.

**1972 Munich** C: 13, N: 11, D: 9.6. WR: 645kg (Vassily Alexeyev)

|   |   |   | PRESS |   | SNATCH |   | JERK |   | TOTAL KG |   |
|---|---|---|---|---|---|---|---|---|---|---|
| 1. | Vassily Alexeyev | SOV | 235.0 | OR | 175.0 | OR | 230.0 | OR | 640.0 | OR |
| 2. | Rudolf Mang | GER | 225.0 | | 170.0 | | 215.0 | | 610.0 | |
| 3. | Gerd Bonk | GDR | 200.0 | | 155.0 | | 217.5 | | 572.5 | |
| 4. | Jouko Leppä | FIN | 205.0 | | 157.5 | | 210.0 | | 572.5 | |
| 5. | Manfred Rieger | GDR | 190.0 | | 162.5 | | 205.0 | | 557.5 | |
| 6. | Petr Pavlasek | CZE | 192.5 | | 165.0 | | 200.0 | | 557.5 | |
| 7. | Kalevi Lahdenranta | FIN | 190.0 | | 165.0 | | 200.0 | | 555.0 | |
| 8. | Fernando Bernal | CUB | 190.0 | | 147.5 | | 207.5 | | 545.0 | |

Vassily Alexeyev came to international attention on January 24, 1970, when he broke the world record for the press, the jerk, and the three-lift total. On March 18 of the same year, he became the first person to lift a combined total of 600 kg. Six months later, while competing in Columbus, Ohio, he broke the 500-pound barrier for the jerk. Since Alexeyev only operated on the metric system, he was somewhat confused when his successful lift brought him so much attention. At Munich, the 30-year-old champion checked in at 337 pounds. The competition was no competition as Alexeyev racked up a convincing 30 kg winning margin. Married in 1962 to a woman named Olympiada, Alexeyev was spotted in Munich having a breakfast of 26 fried eggs and a steak.

**1976 Montreal** C: 11, N: 8, D: 7.27. WR: 442.5 kg (Vassily Alexeyev)

|   |   |   | SNATCH |   | JERK |   | TOTAL KG |
|---|---|---|--------|---|------|---|----------|
| 1. | Vassily Alexeyev | SOV | 185.0 | OR | 255.0 | WR | 440.0 |
| 2. | Gerd Bonk | GDR | 170.0 | | 235.0 | | 405.0 |
| 3. | Helmut Losch | GDR | 165.0 | | 222.5 | | 387.5 |
| 4. | Jan Nagy | CZE | 160.0 | | 227.5 | | 387.5 |
| 5. | Bruce Wilhelm | USA | 172.5 | | 215.0 | | 387.5 |
| 6. | Gerardo Fernandez | CUB | 165.0 | | 200.0 | | 365.0 |
| 7. | Robert Edmond | AUS | 157.5 | | 190.0 | | 347.5 |
| 8. | Jan-Olof Nolsjo | SWE | 152.5 | | 185.0 | | 337.5 |

DISQ (Drugs): Petř Pavlašek (CZE) 387.5

Once again, Alexeyev, now 34 years old and over 345 pounds, was unchallenged. Between 1970 and 1977 he set 80 world records, a number that is particularly significant when one considers that he allegedly received from the Soviet government a prize of $700 to $1500 every time he broke a world record. He was unbeaten from 1970 until 1978.

Sixth-place finisher Petř Pavlašek was disqualified when he registered a positive result on a urine test for drugs.

**1980 Moscow** C: 12, N: 8, D: 7.30. WR: 445kg (Vassily Alexeyev)

|   |   |   | SNATCH |   | JERK | TOTAL KG |   |
|---|---|---|--------|---|------|----------|---|
| 1. | Sultan Rakhmanov | SOV | 195.0 | OR | 245.0 | 440.0 | EOR |
| 2. | Jürgen Heuser | GDR | 182.5 | | 227.5 | 410.0 | |
| 3. | Tadeusz Rutkowski | POL | 180.0 | | 227.5 | 407.5 | |
| 4. | Rudolf Strejček | CZE | 182.5 | | 220.0 | 402.5 | |
| 5. | Bohuslav Braum | CZE | 180.0 | | 217.5 | 397.5 | |
| 6. | Francisco Mendez Polo | CUB | 175.0 | | 220.0 | 395.0 | |
| 7. | Robert Skolimowski | POL | 175.0 | | 210.0 | 385.0 | |
| 8. | Talal Najjar | SYR | 157.5 | | 205.0 | 362.5 | |

Competing for the first time since he was injured during the 1978 world championship, Alexeyev failed three times to snatch 180 kg and was eliminated. Thirty-year-old Sultan Rakhmanov, whose mother was Ukrainian ansd whose father was an Uzbek, made six perfect lifts to score a decisive victory.

**1984 Los Angeles-Westchester** C: 9, N: 7, D: 8.8. WR: 465 kg (Aleksandr Gunyashev)

|   |   |   | SNATCH | JERK | TOTAL KG |
|---|---|---|--------|------|----------|
| 1. | Dean Lukin | AUS | 172.5 | 240.0 | 412.5 |
| 2. | Mario Martinez | USA | 185.0 | 225.0 | 410.0 |
| 3. | Manfred Nerlinger | GER | 177.5 | 220.0 | 397.5 |
| 4. | Ioannis Tsintsaris | GRE | 162.5 | 185.0 | 347.5 |

| | | SNATCH | JERK | TOTAL KG |
|---|---|---|---|---|
| 5. Bartholomew Oluoma | NGR | 150.0 | 187.5 | 337.5 |
| 6. Mosad Mosbah | EGY | 150.0 | 180.0 | 330.0 |
| DISQ (Drugs): Stefan Laggner (AUT) 385.0 | | | | |

Dean Lukin was a 305-pound millionaire tuna fisherman from Port Lincoln, South Australia.

**1988 Seoul** C: 17, N: 13, D: 9.29. WR: 472.5 kg (Aleksandr Kurlovich)

| | | SNATCH | | JERK | TOTAL KG | |
|---|---|---|---|---|---|---|
| 1. Aleksandr Kurlovich | SOV | 212.5 | OR | 250.0 | 462.5 | OR |
| 2. Manfred Nerlinger | GER | 190.0 | | 240.0 | 430.0 | |
| 3. Martin Zawieja | GER | 182.5 | | 232.5 | 415.0 | |
| 4. Mario Martinez | USA | 175.0 | | 232.5 | 407.5 | |
| 5. Petr Hudeček | CZE | 175.0 | | 225.0 | 400.0 | |
| 6. Reda El Batoty | EGY | 175.0 | | 217.5 | 392.5 | |
| 7. Charles Garzarella | AUS | 162.5 | | 207.5 | 370.0 | |
| 8. Paulos Saltsidis | GRE | 160.0 | | 207.5 | 367.5 | |

In December 1984, Aleksandr Kurlovich was arrested by customs officials in Montreal and charged with importing anabolic steroids with intent to sell. He pleaded guilty and paid a fine of $450. The U.S.S.R. Weightlifting Federation banned him from competition for two years. In 1987 he returned to win the world championship. His two leading challengers at the Olympics, Antonio Krastev of Bulgaria and fellow Soviet Leonid Taranenko, withdrew from the competition, presumably because of fear of exposure as a result of improved drug testing techniques.

Although he failed to make a single successful lift, Jiří Zubrický of Czechoslovakia set a record anyway: at 365½ pounds (164.95 kg), he was the heaviest weightlifter ever to take part in the Olympics.

# FREESTYLE WRESTLING

| | |
|---|---|
| Light Flyweight | Welterweight |
| Flyweight | Middleweight |
| Bantamweight | Light Heavyweight |
| Featherweight | Heavyweight |
| Lightweight | Super Heavyweight |

International amateur wrestling follows a complicated system of scoring. Beginning in 1984, matches of two three-minute rounds replaced matches of three three-minute rounds. As a match progresses, contestants score points as a result of successful holds, positions of advantage, and near-throws. A match is terminated as a result of a fall or if one wrestler achieves a 12-point lead. If the six-minute mark is reached without a fall or 12-point lead, the wrestler with the most points is declared the winner. Through 1984, in case of a tie, the victory was awarded to the contestant who achieved the highest-scoring move or who scored the last point. In 1988, a sudden death overtime period was introduced. Each man is then assigned a certain number of points for the match according to the following chart. Until 1984, scoring was done with negative or "bad" points rather than positive points.

| | |
|---|---|
| 4 | win by fall |
| 4 | win by 12 or more points |
| 4 | win by passivity—winner uncautioned |
| 3.5 | win by 8–11 points |
| 3 | win by less than 8 points |
| 3 | win by passivity—winner cautioned once |
| 2 | win by passivity—winner cautioned twice |
| 1 | lose by less than 8 points |
| 0.5 | lose by 8–11 points |
| 0 | lose by 12 or more points |
| 0 | withdrawal due to injury |
| 0 | lose by passivity |
| 0 | lose by fall |
| 0 | lose by disqualification (the most common cause being passivity or lack of aggressiveness) |

Participants in each weight class are divided by lot into two pools. A wrestler is eliminated from competition by two defeats. When all but three wrestlers in a group have been eliminated, the survivors engage in a round robin to determine first, second, and third. The winners of the two pools meet for the championship. The runners-up meet for third and fourth place and the third place fin-ishers in each pool meet to decide fifth and sixth place. In 1988, a "B" final was instituted to determine seventh place. Before 1984, tournaments were organized differently, using final round-robin rounds instead of single matches for first, third and fifth places.

## LIGHT FLYWEIGHT
### (48 kg—106 lbs)

**1896–1900** not held

**1904 St. Louis** C: 4, N: 1, D: 10.15.
1. Robert Curry          USA
2. John Hein             USA
3. Gustav Thiefenthaler  USA

Curry, of New York City, threw Thiefenthaler in 4:05 and Hein in 2:38.

**1906–1968** not held

**1972 Munich** C: 14, N: 14, D: 8.31.

| | | ROUND ELIMINATED | BAD PTS. | FINAL ROUND |
|---|---|---|---|---|
| 1. Roman Dmitriev | SOV | — | 2 | 4 |
| 2. Ognyan Nikolov | BUL | — | 5 | 4 |
| 3. Ebrahim Javadi | IRN | — | 3.5 | 4 |
| 4. Sefer Baygin | TUR | 4 | 6.5 | |
| 5. Ion Arapu | ROM | 4 | 7 | |
| 6. Masahiko Umeda | JPN | 4 | 8 | |
| 7. Sergio Gonzalez | USA | 3 | 6 | |
| 7. Jürgen Möbius | GDR | 3 | 6 | |

Dmitriev grew up grazing reindeer in Yakutia.

**1976 Montreal** C: 18, N: 18, D: 7.31.

| | | ROUND ELIMINATED | BAD PTS. | FINAL ROUND |
|---|---|---|---|---|
| 1. Hasan Isaev | BUL | — | 4 | 3 |
| 2. Roman Dmitriev | SOV | — | 1 | 5 |
| 3. Akira Kudo | JPN | — | 0 | 8 |
| 4. Gombo Khishigbaatar | MON | 5 | 6 | |

| | | | | |
|---|---|---|---|---|
| 5. Kim Hwa-kyung | KOR | 5 | 6 | |
| 6. Li Yong-nam | PRK | 5 | 8 | |
| 7. Kuddusi Ozdemir | TUR | 4 | 7 | |
| 8. Willi Heckmann | GER | 4 | 8 | |

Dmitriev actually defeated two-time world champion Isaev, but lost four points as the result of a double disqualification against Kudo.

**1980 Moscow** C: 14, N: 14, D: 7.29.

| | | ROUND ELIMINATED | BAD PTS. | FINAL ROUND |
|---|---|---|---|---|
| 1. Claudio Pollio | ITA | — | 5.5 | 3 |
| 2. Jang Se-hong | PRK | — | 5 | 4 |
| 3. Sergei Kornilaev | SOV | — | 1 | 5 |
| 4. Jan Falandys | POL | 5 | 6.5 | |
| 5. Mahabir Singh | IND | 5 | 9 | |
| 6. László Biró | HUN | 4 | 9 | |
| 7. Roumen Yordanov | BUL | 3 | 6 | |
| 8. Gheorghe Rasovan | ROM | 3 | 7 | |

Pollio lost to Kornilaev, but won the gold medal anyway after the Soviet wrestler was thrown in the final match by Jang Se-hong, who had been disqualified in his match against Pollio.

**1984 Los Angeles-Anaheim** C: 7, N: 7, D: 8.9.

| | | FINAL MATCH | |
|---|---|---|---|
| 1. Robert Weaver | USA | Fall | 2:58 |
| 2. Takashi Irie | JPN | | |
| 3. Son Gab-do | KOR | 13-7 | 6:00 |
| 4. Gao Wenhe | CHN | | |
| 5. Reiner Heugabel | GER | Passivity | 5:21 |
| 6. Kent Andersson | SWE | | |
| 7. Sunil Dutt | IND | | |

Freestyle Wrestling was hard hit by the Soviet-bloc boycott. Twenty-three of the 30 medalists at the 1983 world championships were from boycotting nations, including nine of the ten gold medal winners. The light flyweight division was so depleted that there were only seven entrants—the smallest wrestling competition since 1932. Bobby Weaver, who had finished second at the 1979 world championships and fifth in 1983, needed a total of only 8 minutes and 26 seconds to dispose of his three opponents.

**1988 Seoul** C: 19, N: 19, D: 9.29.

| | | FINAL MATCH | |
|---|---|---|---|
| 1. Takashi Kobayashi | JPN | 16-4 | 6:00 |
| 2. Ivan Tzonov | BUL | | |
| 3. Sergei Karamchakov | SOV | 3-1 | 6:00 |
| 4. Tim Vanni | USA | | |
| 5. Reiner Heugabel | GER | Passivity | 4:27 |
| 6. Ilyas Sukruoğlü | TUR | | |
| 7. Volker Anger | GDR | Forfeit | |
| 8. Naser Zeinalnis | IRN | | |

Two-time defending world champion Li Jae-sik missed the competition because of North Korea's boycott. Lee Sang-ho of South Korea had finished second to Li at the 1987 world championships, but at the Olympics Lee suffered a broken arm in the first minute of his opening match against Takashi Kobayashi. Thereafter, Kobayashi dominated the tournament except for a close call against Ilyas Sukruoğlü. Sukruoğlü led 5–3 with 10 seconds remaining when Kobayashi scored on a 3-point move to win 6–5 and advance to the final.

# FLYWEIGHT
**(52 kg—114 ½ lbs)**

**1896–1900** not held

**1904 St. Louis** C: 3, N: 1, D: 10.15.
***(52.16 kg–115 lbs)***
1. George Mehnert  USA
2. Gustav Bauer  USA
3. William Nelson  USA

**1906–1936** not held

**1948 London** C: 11, N: 11, D: 7.31.

| | | ROUND ELIMINATED | BAD PTS. | FINAL ROUND |
|---|---|---|---|---|
| 1. Lennart Viitala | FIN | — | 2 | 2 |
| 2. Halit Balamir | TUR | — | 4 | 2 |
| 3. Thure Johansson | SWE | — | 5 | 6 |
| 4. Rassoul Raiisi | IRN | 4 | 6 | |
| 5. Pierre Baudric | FRA | 4 | 7 | |
| 6. Kha-Shaba Jadav | IND | 3 | 5 | |
| 7. William Jernigan | USA | 3 | 7 | |

**1952 Helsinki** C: 16, N: 16, D: 7.23.

| | | ROUND ELIMINATED | BAD PTS. | FINAL ROUND |
|---|---|---|---|---|
| 1. Hasan Gemici | TUR | — | 4 | 3 |
| 2. Yushu Kitano | JPN | — | 4 | 4 |
| 3. Mahmoud Mollaghasemi | IRN | — | 3 | 4 |
| 4. Georgy Sayadov | SOV | 6 | 0 | |
| 5. Heinrich Weber | GER | 4 | 6 | |
| 6. Louis Baise | SAF | 4 | 7 | |
| 7. Giordano Degiorgi | ITA | 3 | 5 | |
| 7. Robert Peery | USA | 3 | 5 | |

**1956 Melbourne** C: 11, N: 11, D: 12.1.

| | | ROUND ELIMINATED | BAD PTS. | FINAL ROUND |
|---|---|---|---|---|
| 1. Mirian Tsalkalamanidze | SOV | — | 5 | 3 |
| 2. Mohammad Ali Khojastepour | IRN | — | 3 | 3 |
| 3. Hüseyin Akbaş | TUR | — | 2 | 4 |
| 4. Tadashi Asai | JPN | 4 | 7 | |
| 5. Richard Delgado | USA | 3 | 6 | |
| 5. André Zoete | FRA | 3 | 6 | |
| 7. Abdul Aziz | PAK | 3 | 7 | |
| 7. Baban Daware | IND | 3 | 7 | |

Tsalkalamanidze gained the gold medal by throwing Khojastépour after four minutes.

**1960 Rome** C: 17, N: 17, D: 9.6.

| | | ROUND ELIMI-NATED | BAD PTS. | FINAL ROUND |
|---|---|---|---|---|
| 1. Ahmet Bilek | TUR | — | 5 | 2 |
| 2. Masayuki Matsubara | JPN | — | 4 | 4 |
| 3. Mohammad Ebrahim Seifpour | IRN | — | 3 | 6 |
| 4. Paul Neff | GER | 6 | 9 | |
| 5. Elliott Gray Simons | USA | 5 | 8 | |
| 6. Ali Aliyev | SOV | 5 | 8 | |
| 7. Nikola Dimitrov | BUL | 4 | 7 | |
| 8. André Zoete | FRA | 4 | 8 | |

**1964 Tokyo** C: 22, N: 22, D: 10.14.

| | | ROUND ELIMINATED | BAD PTS. | FINAL ROUND |
|---|---|---|---|---|
| 1. Yoshikatsu Yoshida | JPN | — | 2 | 1 |
| 2. Chang Chang-sun | KOR | — | 3 | 3 |
| 3. Ali Akbar Heidari | IRN | 5 | 6 | |
| 4. Ali Aliyev | SOV | 5 | 7 | |
| 4. Cemal Yanilmaz | TUR | 5 | 7 | |
| 4. André Zoete | FRA | 5 | 7 | |
| 7. Elliott Gray Simons | USA | 4 | 6 | |
| 8. Muhammed Niaz | PAK | 4 | 7 | |

**1968 Mexico City** C: 23, N: 23, D: 10.20.

| | | ROUND ELIMINATED | BAD PTS. | FINAL ROUND |
|---|---|---|---|---|
| 1. Shigeo Nakata | JPN | — | 3.5 | 1 |
| 2. Richard Sanders | USA | — | 0 | 4 |
| 3. Surenjav Sukhbaatar | MON | — | 5 | 7 |
| 4. Nazar Albaryan | SOV | 5 | 6.5 | |
| 5. Vincenzo Grassi | ITA | 5 | 6.5 | |
| 6. Sudesh Kumar | IND | 5 | 7.5 | |
| 7. Mohammad Ghorbani | IRN | 5 | 8 | |
| 7. Paul Neff | GER | 5 | 8 | |

**1972 Munich** C: 24, N: 24, D: 8.31.

| | | ROUND ELIMINATED | BAD PTS. | FINAL ROUND |
|---|---|---|---|---|
| 1. Kiyomi Kato | JPN | — | 1.5 | 2 |
| 2. Arsen Alkhverdiev | SOV | — | 5.5 | 5 |
| 3. Kim Gwong-hyong | PRK | — | 5.5 | 5 |
| 4. Sudesh Sudeshkumar | IND | 6 | 7 | |
| 5. Petru Ciarnău | ROM | 6 | 7.5 | |
| 6. Gordon Bertie | CAN | 5 | 7.5 | |
| 7. Henrik Gál | HUN | 4 | 7 | |
| 7. John Kinsella | AUS | 4 | 7 | |

**1976 Montreal** C: 19, N: 19, D: 7.31.

| | | ROUND ELIMINATED | BAD PTS. | FINAL ROUND |
|---|---|---|---|---|
| 1. Yuji Takada | JPN | — | 0 | 0.5 |
| 2. Aleksandr Ivanov | SOV | — | 1.5 | 3.5 |
| 3. Jeon Hae-sup | KOR | — | 2 | 8 |
| 4. Henrik Gál | HUN | 5 | 7 | |

| 5. Nermedin Selimov | BUL | 5 | 8.5 |
|---|---|---|---|
| 6. Wladyslaw Stecyk | POL | 5 | 9 |
| 7. Li Bong-sun | PRK | 4 | 7 |
| 8. Eloy Abreu | CUB | 4 | 9 |

Two-time world champion Yuji Takada of Gunma overwhelmed the field, pinning six of his seven opponents, five of them in less than two minutes. He also outpointed Ivanov 20–11.

**1980 Moscow** C: 16, N: 16, D: 7.30.

| | | ROUND ELIMINATED | BAD PTS. | FINAL ROUND |
|---|---|---|---|---|
| 1. Anatoly Beloglazov | SOV | — | 1.5 | 0 |
| 2. Wladyslaw Stecyk | POL | — | 4 | 5 |
| 3. Nermedin Selimov | BUL | — | 4.5 | 7 |
| 4. Lajos Szabó | HUN | 6 | 9 | |
| 5. Jang Dok-ryong | PRK | 4 | 6.5 | |
| 6. Nanzadying Burgedaa | MON | 4 | 7 | |
| 7. Koce Efremov | YUG | 4 | 8 | |
| 8. Hartmut Reich | GDR | 3 | 6.5 | |

After winning his first two matches on decisions, Anatoly Beloglazov needed only 4:54 to dispose of his last four opponents. Twenty-four hours and 48 minutes after Beloglazov won the Flyweight gold medal, his twin brother, Sergei, won the Bantamweight tournament.

**1984 Los Angeles-Anaheim** C: 17, N: 17, D: 8.10.

| | | FINAL MATCH | |
|---|---|---|---|
| 1. Šaban Trstena | YUG | Injury | |
| 2. Kim Jong-kyu | KOR | | |
| 3. Yuji Takada | JPN | 12–0 | 4:34 |
| 4. Ray Takahashi | CAN | | |
| 5. Aslan Seyhanli | TUR | 14–5 | 6:00 |
| 6. Mahavir Singh | IND | | |
| 7. Fritz Niebler | GER | | |
| 8. Liang Dejin | CHN | | |

Kim tore a muscle in his left shoulder during his match with Fritz Niebler of West Germany and was unable to take part in the final. The crucial match for 19-year-old Šaban Trstena of Scopia, Macedonia, was an 8–8 decision over 1976 Olympic champion Yuji Takada.

**1988 Seoul** C: 31, N: 31, D: 9.30.

| | | FINAL MATCH | |
|---|---|---|---|
| 1. Mitsuru Sato | JPN | 13–2 | 6:00 |
| 2. Šaban Trstena | YUG | | |
| 3. Vladimir Toguzov | SOV | 14–1 | 6:00 |
| 4. László Bíró | HUN | | |
| 5. Aslan Seyhanli | TUR | 5–4 | 6:00 |
| 6. Kim Jong-ho | KOR | | |
| 7. Tserenbatar Enebayar | MON | Injury | |
| 8. Valentin Yordanov | BUL | | |

Sato threw his first five opponents and then outpointed Kim 15–0 in 4:02 to advance to the final. The favorite had been three-time world champion Valentin Yordanov, who competed under the government-imposed surname Dimitrov. Yordanov won his first three matches, then lost 11–5 to Trstena and 14–1 to Toguzov before withdrawing from the "B" final because of injury.

# BANTAMWEIGHT
(57 kg—125½ lbs)

**1896-1900** not held

**1904 St. Louis** C: 7, N: 1, D: 10.15.
*(56.70 kg—125 lbs)*
1. Isidor Niflot        USA
2. August Wester      USA
3. Z.B. Strebler        USA

Niflot won the championship by throwing Wester in 1:58.

**1906** not held

**1908 London** C: 13, N: 3, D: 7.20.
*(54 kg—119 lbs)*
1. George Mehnert    USA
2. William Press       GBR
3. Aubert Côté         CAN
4. F. Tomkins          GBR
5. F. Davis (GBR), B. Sansom (GBR), G.J. Saunders (GBR)

Mehnert, a 26-year-old from Newark, New Jersey, had won the Flyweight championship in St. Louis four years earlier.

**1912–1920** not held

**1924 Paris** C: 12, N: 8, D: 7.14.
*(56 kg—123½ lbs)*
1. Kustaa Pihlajamäki    FIN
2. Kaarlo Mäkinen        FIN
3. Bryant Hines          USA
4. Gaston Ducayla        FRA
5. Ragnar Larsson        SWE
5. H.F. Sansum           GBR

Pihlajamäki won the first of his three Olympic medals (two gold, one silver). His younger brother, Hermanni, also won a gold and a bronze in freestyle wrestling.

**1928 Amsterdam** C: 8, N: 8, D: 8.1.
*(56 kg—123½ lbs)*
1. Kaarlo Mäkinen      FIN
2. Edmond Spapen       BEL
3. James Trifunov       CAN
4. H.E. Sansum         GBR
5. Robert Hewitt        USA
6. A. Piguet            SWI

**1932 Los Angeles** C: 8, N: 8, D: 8.3.
*(56 kg—123½ lbs)*
1. Robert Pearce      USA
2. Ödön Zombori       HUN
3. Aatos Jaskari       FIN

4. Joseph Reid        GBR
5. Julien Depuichaffray  FRA
6. Georgios Zervinis    GRE

**1936 Berlin** C: 14, N: 14, D: 8.5.
*(56 kg—123½ lbs)*

| | | ROUND ELIMINATED | BAD PTS. | FINAL ROUND |
|---|---|---|---|---|
| 1. Ödön Zombori | HUN | — | 4 | 0 |
| 2. Ross Flood | USA | — | 2 | 3 |
| 3. Johannes Herbert | GER | 5 | 5 | |
| 4. Herman Tuvesson | SWE | 5 | 6 | |
| 5. Aatos Jaskari | FIN | 4 | 7 | |
| 6. Ahmet Çakiryildiz | TUR | 4 | 7 | |
| 7. Marcello Nizzola | ITA | 3 | 5 | |
| 8. Cesar Gaudard | SWI | 3 | 6 | |
| 8. Auguste Laporte | BEL | 3 | 6 | |

**1948 London** C: 15, N: 15, D: 7.31.

| | | ROUND ELIMINATED | BAD PTS. | FINAL ROUND |
|---|---|---|---|---|
| 1. Nasuh Akar | TUR | — | 2 | 0 |
| 2. Gerald Leeman | USA | — | 3 | 3 |
| 3. Charles Kouyos | FRA | 5 | 7 | |
| 4. Joseph Trimpont | BEL | 5 | 7 | |
| 5. Lajos Bencze | HUN | 4 | 5 | |
| 5. Raymond Cazaux | GBR | 4 | 5 | |
| 5. Sayad Hafez | EGY | 4 | 5 | |
| 5. Erik Persson | SWE | 4 | 5 | |

**1952 Helsinki** C: 20, N: 20, D: 7.23.

| | | ROUND ELIMINATED | BAD PTS. | FINAL ROUND |
|---|---|---|---|---|
| 1. Shohachi Ishii | JPN | — | 4 | 2 |
| 2. Rashid Mamedbekov | SOV | — | 3 | 4 |
| 3. Kha-Shaba Jadav | IND | — | 4 | 6 |
| 4. Edvin Westerby | SWE | 5 | 7 | |
| 5. Cemil Saribacak | TUR | 4 | 5 | |
| 6. Lajos Bencze | HUN | 4 | 5 | |
| 7. Ferdinand Schmitz | GER | 4 | 6 | |
| 8. Eigil Johanson | DEN | 3 | 5 | |
| 8. Mehdi Yaghoubi | IRN | 3 | 5 | |

A talented judoka, Ishii was forced to give up judo when U.S. occupation forces banned the sport after World War II. Ishii switched to wrestling and won Japan's first post-war gold medal.

**1956 Melbourne** C: 14, N: 14, D: 12.1.

| | | ROUND ELIMINATED | BAD PTS. | FINAL ROUND |
|---|---|---|---|---|
| 1. Mustafa Dağistanli | TUR | — | 4 | 1 |
| 2. Mehdi Yaghoubi | IRN | — | 4 | 2 |
| 3. Mikhail Chakhov | SOV | 5 | 6 | |
| 4. Lee Sang-kyoon | KOR | 5 | 7 | |
| 5. Minoru Iizuka | JPN | 4 | 5 | |
| 6. Alfred Kämmerer | GDR | 3 | 5 | |
| 7. Din Zahur | PAK | 3 | 6 | |
| 8. Adolfo Diaz | ARG | 3 | 7 | |
| 8. Tarakeshwar Pandey | IND | 3 | 7 | |

**1960 Rome** C: 19, N: 19, D: 9.6.

| | | ROUND ELIMINATED | BAD PTS. | FINAL ROUND |
|---|---|---|---|---|
| 1. Terrence McCann | USA | — | 5 | 2 |
| 2. Nezhdet Zalev | BUL | — | 2 | 4 |
| 3. Tadeusz Trojanowski | POL | — | 4 | 6 |
| 4. Tadashi Asai | JPN | 5 | 6 | |
| 5. Tanuo Jaskari | FIN | 5 | 7 | |
| 6. Mikhail Chakhov | SOV | 5 | 8 | |
| 7. Mehdi Yaghoubi | IRN | 4 | 6 | |
| 8. Luigi Chinazzo | ITA | 4 | 8 | |

**1964 Tokyo** C: 20, N: 20, D: 10.14.

| | | ROUND ELIMINATED | BAD PTS. | FINAL ROUND |
|---|---|---|---|---|
| 1. Yojiro Uetake | JPN | — | 3 | 2 |
| 2. Hüseyin Akbaş | TUR | — | 5 | 4 |
| 3. Aydyn Ibragimov | SOV | — | 3 | 6 |
| 4. David Auble | USA | 5 | 6 | |
| 5. Choi Young-kil | KOR | 5 | 7 | |
| 6. Bishamber Singh | IND | 5 | 8 | |
| 7. János Varga | HUN | 4 | 7 | |
| 8. Abdollah Khodabande | IRN | 3 | 6 | |

**1968 Mexico City** C: 21, N: 21, D: 10.20.

| | | ROUND ELIMINATED | BAD PTS. |
|---|---|---|---|
| 1. Yojiro Uetake | JPN | — | 5.5 |
| 2. Donald Behm | USA | 7 | 6.5 |
| 3. Abutaleb Talebi | IRN | 7 | 7.5 |
| 4. Ali Aliyev | SOV | 7 | 8.5 |
| 5. Ivan Shavov | BUL | 6 | 7.5 |
| 6. Zbigniew Żedzicki | POL | 5 | 8 |
| 7. Bishamber Singh | IND | 5 | 8.5 |
| 8. Sukhbaatar Bazaryn | MON | 4 | 7 |

**1972 Munich** C: 28, N: 28, D: 8.31.

| | | ROUND ELIMINATED | BAD PTS. | FINAL ROUND |
|---|---|---|---|---|
| 1. Hideaki Yanagida | JPN | — | 4 | 1 |
| 2. Richard Sanders | USA | — | 4 | 3 |
| 3. László Klinga | HUN | 7 | 8.5 | |
| 4. Prem Premnath | IND | 7 | 9 | |
| 5. Ivan Shavov | BUL | 6 | 7 | |
| 6. Horst Mayer | GDR | 6 | 7.5 | |
| 7. Ramezan Kheder | IRN | 6 | 8 | |
| 8. Jorge Ramos | CUB | 5 | 6 | |

Silver medalist Richard Sanders, a bartender from Portland, Oregon, had long hair, a beard, and a mustache, and wore a bead necklace. Seven weeks after the Olympics, Sanders was killed in an automobile accident while touring in Europe. He was 23 years old.

**1976 Montreal** C: 21, N: 21, D: 7.31.

| | | ROUND ELIMINATED | BAD PTS. | FINAL ROUND |
|---|---|---|---|---|
| 1. Vladimir Umin | SOV | — | 7 | 2 |
| 2. Hans-Dieter Brüchert | GDR | — | 3.5 | 4 |
| 3. Masao Arai | JPN | — | 4.5 | 6 |
| 4. Miho Doukov | BUL | 6 | 8 | |
| 5. Ramezan Kheder | IRN | 6 | 8 | |
| 6. Migd Khoilogdorj | MON | 6 | 8 | |
| 7. George Chatziioannidis | GRE | 5 | 8.5 | |
| 8. Zbigniew Żedzicki | POL | 4 | 6 | |

**1980 Moscow** C: 16, N: 16, D: 7.31.

| | | ROUND ELIMINATED | BAD PTS. | FINAL ROUND |
|---|---|---|---|---|
| 1. Sergei Beloglazov | SOV | — | 0 | 0 |
| 2. Li Ho-pyong | PRK | — | 6 | 5 |
| 3. Dugarsuren Ouinbold | MON | — | 2 | 7 |
| 4. Ivan Tzochev | BUL | 5 | 7 | |
| 5. Aurel Neagu | ROM | 4 | 6 | |
| 6. Wieslaw Kończak | POL | 4 | 7 | |
| 7. Karim Salman Muhsin | IRQ | 4 | 8 | |
| 8. Sándor Németh | HUN | 4 | 9 | |

Sergei Beloglazov, the twin brother of Flyweight winner Anatoly Beloglazov, threw five of his six opponents and defeated Ouinbold by disqualification, after leading in points 15–0. He outpointed his six victims, 58–3.

**1984 Los Angeles-Anaheim** C: 16, N: 16, D: 8.11.

| | | FINAL MATCH | |
|---|---|---|---|
| 1. Hideaki Tomiyama | JPN | 8–3 | 6:00 |
| 2. Barry Davis | USA | | |
| 3. Kim Eui-kon | KOR | 7–4 | 6:00 |
| 4. Orlando Caceres | PUR | | |
| 5. Rohtas Singh | IND | 3–2 | 6:00 |
| 6. Zoran Sorov | YUG | | |
| 7. Guanbunima | CHN | | |
| 8. Ibrahim Akgun | TUR | | |

With his 85-year-old grandfather in the audience for good luck, and with defending Olympic and world champion Sergei Beloglazov prevented from competing because of the Soviet-bloc boycott, two-time world champion Hideaki Tomiyama outclassed the field.

**1988 Seoul** C: 25, N: 25, D: 10.1.

| | | FINAL MATCH | |
|---|---|---|---|
| 1. Sergei Beloglazov | SOV | 5–1 | 6:00 |
| 2. Askari Mohammadian | IRN | | |
| 3. Noh Kyung-sun | KOR | 9–8 | 9:00 |
| 4. Ahmet Ak | TUR | | |
| 5. Valentin Ivanov | BUL | 5–3 | 6:00 |
| 6. Béla Nagy | HUN | | |
| 7. Haltma Battul | MON | 3–1 | 6:00 |
| 8. Ryo Kanehama | JPN | | |

Six-time world champion Sergei Beloglazov regained his Olympic title without being seriously challenged.

# FEATHERWEIGHT
(62 kg—136½ lbs)

**1896–1900** not held

**1904 St. Louis** C: 9, N: 1, D: 10.15.
*(61.23 kg—135 lbs)*
1. Benjamin Bradshaw   USA
2. Theodore McLear   USA
3. Charles Clapper   USA

**1906** not held

**1908 London** C: 12, N: 2, D: 7.22.
*(60.3 kg—132½ lbs)*
1. George Dole   USA
2. James Slim   GBR
3. William McKie   GBR
4. W. Tagg   GBR
5. A.J. Goddard (GBR), J.A. Webster (GBR), J.G. White (GBR)

Dole, a 5-foot 3½-inch student from Yale, was the only non-British wrestler in the Featherweight division.

**1912** not held

**1920 Antwerp** C: 11, N: 6, D: 8.21.
*(60 kg—132 lbs)*
1. Charles Ackerly   USA
2. Samuel Gerson   USA
3. P.W. Bernard   GBR
4. D.R. Shindes   IND

Ackerly, former captain of the Cornell University team, and Gerson, former captain of the University of Pennsylvania team, had each defeated the other once in collegiate competition, but Ackerly won the tie-breaker across the seas in Antwerp. Thirty-two years later Gerson organized the U.S. Olympians, an alumni association for former members of U.S. Olympic teams.

**1924 Paris** C: 17, N: 12, D: 7.14.
*(61 kg  134½ lbs)*
1. Robin Reed   USA
2. Chester Newton   USA
3. Katsutoshi Naito   JPN
4. Sigfrid Hansson   SWE
5. Clifford Chilcott   CAN
6. Edvard Huupponen   FIN

Reed and Newton were longtime rivals from Portland, Oregon. One of the greatest U.S. wrestlers ever, Reed eventually retired undefeated.

**1928 Amsterdam** C: 9, N: 9, D: 8.1.
*(61 kg—134½ lbs)*
1. Allie Morrison   USA
2. Kustaa Pihlajamäki   FIN
3. Hans Minder   SWI
4. René Rottenfluc   FRA

**1932 Los Angeles** C: 10, N: 10, D: 8.3.
*(61 kg—134½ lbs)*
1. Hermanni Pihlajamäki   FIN
2. Edgar Nemir   USA
3. Einar Karlsson   SWE

4. Joseph Taylor   GBR
5. Ioannis Farmakidis   GRE
6. Jean Chasson   FRA

**1936 Berlin** C: 15, N: 15, D: 8.4.
*(61 kg—134½ lbs)*

| | | ROUND ELIMINATED | BAD PTS. |
|---|---|---|---|
| 1. Kustaa Pihlajamäki | FIN | — | 1 |
| 2. Francis Millard | USA | 6 | 5 |
| 3. Gösta Jönsson | SWE | 6 | 5 |
| 4. John Vernon Pettigrew | CAN | 5 | 7 |
| 5. Ferenc Tóth | HUN | 4 | 6 |
| 6. Mitsuzo Mizutani | JPN | 4 | 7 |
| 7. Marco Gavelli | ITA | 3 | 5 |
| 8. Yasar Erkan (TUR), Nevil Hall (SAF), Norman Morrell (GBR) | | 3 | 7 |

**1948 London** C: 17, N: 17, D: 7.31.
*(63 kg—139 lbs)*

| | | ROUND ELIMINATED | BAD PTS. | FINAL ROUND |
|---|---|---|---|---|
| 1. Gazanfer Bilge | TUR | — | 0 | 1 |
| 2. Ivar Sjölin | SWE | — | 2 | 3 |
| 3. Adolf Müller | SWI | 6 | 5 | |
| 4. Paavo Hietala | FIN | 5 | 6 | |
| 4. Ferenc Tóth | HUN | 5 | 6 | |
| 6. Harold "Hal" Moore | USA | 4 | 5 | |
| 7. Antoine Raeymaeckers | BEL | 4 | 6 | |
| 8. I. Abdel Hamid | EGY | 4 | 7 | |
| 8. Arnold Parsons | GBR | 4 | 7 | |

Bilge was rewarded by the Turkish government with a house and 20,000 liras ($7,142). This made him ineligible for the 1952 Olympics, but he was able to parlay his rewards into a fortune as a bus mogul. In 1963 Bilge was imprisoned after he shot Adil Atan, a business rival who had won a bronze medal as a Light Heavyweight wrestler in 1952.

**1952 Helsinki** C: 21, N: 21, D: 7.23.
*(63 kg—139 lbs)*

| | | ROUND ELIMINATED | BAD PTS. | FINAL ROUND |
|---|---|---|---|---|
| 1. Bayram Şit | TUR | — | 2 | 1 |
| 2. Nasser Givéchi | IRN | — | 4 | 4 |
| 3. Josiah Henson | USA | — | 5 | 6 |
| 4. K.D. Mangave | IND | 5 | 6 | |
| 5. Risaburo Tominaga | JPN | 5 | 7 | |
| 6. Rauno Mäkinen | FIN | 4 | 5 | |
| 7. Albert Bernard | CAN | 4 | 6 | |
| 7. Abdel Essawi | EGY | 4 | 6 | |

**1956 Melbourne** C: 13, N: 13, D: 12.1.
*(63 kg—139 lbs)*

| | | ROUND ELIMINATED | BAD PTS. | FINAL ROUND |
|---|---|---|---|---|
| 1. Shozo Sasahara | JPN | — | 4 | 1 |
| 2. Joseph Mewis | BEL | — | 3 | 4 |
| 3. Erkki Penttilä | FIN | — | 4 | 6 |

| | | ROUND ELIMINATED | BAD PTS. | FINAL ROUND |
|---|---|---|---|---|
| 4. Myron Roderick | USA | 4 | 5 | |
| 5. Bayram Şit | TUR | 4 | 5 | |
| 6. Nasser Givéchi | IRN | 4 | 7 | |
| 6. Linar Salimulin | SOV | 4 | 7 | |
| 8. Ram Sarup | IND | 3 | 6 | |

**1960 Rome** C: 25, N: 25, D: 9.6.
*(63 kg—139 lbs)*

| | | ROUND ELIMINATED | BAD PTS. | FINAL ROUND |
|---|---|---|---|---|
| 1. Mustafa Dağistanli | TUR | — | 4 | 1 |
| 2. Stancho Kolev | BUL | — | 3 | 3 |
| 3. Vladimir Rubashvili | SOV | 6 | 7 | |
| 4. Tamiji Sato | JPN | 6 | 7 | |
| 5. Joseph Mewis | BEL | 5 | 8 | |
| 6. Mohamed Akhtar | PAK | 5 | 9 | |
| 7. Abraham Geldenhuys | SAF | 4 | 6 | |
| 8. Azohadi Khaden | IRN | 4 | 9 | |

**1964 Tokyo** C: 21, N: 21, D: 10.14.
*(63 kg—139 lbs)*

| | | ROUND ELIMINATED | BAD PTS. | FINAL ROUND |
|---|---|---|---|---|
| 1. Osamu Watanabe | JPN | — | 2 | 2 |
| 2. Stancho Kolev | BUL | — | 5 | 5 |
| 3. Nodar Khokhashvili | SOV | — | 5 | 5 |
| 4. Robert "Bobby" Douglas | USA | 5 | 6 | |
| 5. Mohammed Ebrahimi | AFG | 5 | 7 | |
| 6. Mohammad Ebrahim Seifpour | IRN | 5 | 8 | |
| 7. Rainer Schilling | GER | 4 | 6 | |
| 8. Mario Tovar Gonzalez | MEX | 4 | 7 | |

Watanabe's 1–0 win over Khokhashvili was his 186th consecutive victory. He didn't give up a single point in any of his six Olympic matches. Kolev was awarded the silver medal because he weighed less than Khokhashvili.

**1968 Mexico City** C: 23, N: 23, D: 10.20.
*(63 kg—139 lbs)*

| | | ROUND ELIMINATED | BAD PTS. | FINAL ROUND |
|---|---|---|---|---|
| 1. Masaaki Kaneko | JPN | — | 1.5 | 3.5 |
| 2. Enyu Todorov | BUL | — | 2 | 4.5 |
| 3. Shamseddin Seyyedabbasi | IRN | — | 2.5 | 5 |
| 4. Nicolaos Karypidis | GRE | 5 | 6.5 | |
| 5. Petre Coman | ROM | 5 | 8 | |
| 6. Yeikan Tedeyev | SOV | 4 | 6 | |
| 7. Vehbi Akdag | TUR | 4 | 6.5 | |
| 7. Ismail Al Karaghouli | IRQ | 4 | 6.5 | |

**1972 Munich** C: 26, N: 26, D: 8.31.

| | | ROUND ELIMINATED | BAD PTS. | FINAL ROUND |
|---|---|---|---|---|
| 1. Zagalav Abdulbekov | SOV | — | 3.5 | 2 |
| 2. Vehbi Akdag | TUR | — | 5.5 | 5 |

| | | ROUND ELIMINATED | BAD PTS. | FINAL ROUND |
|---|---|---|---|---|
| 3. Ivan Krustev | BUL | — | 5 | 5 |
| 4. Kiroshi Abe | JPN | 6 | 6 | |
| 5. Shamseddin Seyyedabbasi | IRN | 5 | 5.5 | |
| 6. Petre Coman | ROM | 5 | 6 | |
| 7. Joseph Burge House | GUA | 5 | 7 | |
| 8. Gerhard Weisenberg | GER | 4 | 8 | |

**1976 Montreal** C: 17, N: 17, D: 7.31.

| | | ROUND ELIMINATED | BAD PTS. | FINAL ROUND |
|---|---|---|---|---|
| 1. Yang Jung-mo | KOR | — | 1 | 3 |
| 2. Zeveg Oidov | MON | — | 3 | 4 |
| 3. Gene Davis | USA | — | 8 | 5 |
| 4. Mohsen Farahvashi | IRN | 6 | 10 | |
| 5. Ivan Yankov | BUL | 5 | 8 | |
| 6. Sergei Timofeev | SOV | 4 | 7 | |
| 7. Kenkichi Maekawa | JPN | 4 | 8 | |
| 8. Helmut Strumpf | GDR | 4 | 9 | |

Yang Jung-mo was South Korea's first Olympic gold medal winner.

**1980 Moscow** C: 13, N: 13, D: 7.29.

| | | ROUND ELIMINATED | BAD PTS. | FINAL ROUND |
|---|---|---|---|---|
| 1. Magomedgasan Abushev | SOV | — | 2.5 | 1.5 |
| 2. Miho Doukov | BUL | — | 5.5 | 3 |
| 3. Georges Hadjiioannidis | GRE | — | 5 | 7.5 |
| 4. Raul Cascaret Fonseca | CUB | 5 | 6.5 | |
| 5. Aurel Suteu | ROM | 5 | 8.5 | |
| 6. Ulzibayar Nasanjargal | MON | 4 | 6 | |
| 7. Brian Aspen | GBR | 3 | 6.5 | |
| 8. Zoltán Szalontai | HUN | 3 | 7.5 | |

**1984 Los Angeles-Anaheim** C: 16, N: 16, D: 8.9.

| | | FINAL MATCH | |
|---|---|---|---|
| 1. Randy Lewis | USA | 24–11 | 4:52 |
| 2. Kosei Akaishi | JPN | | |
| 3. Lee Jung-keun | KOR | 11–6 | 6:00 |
| 4. Cris Brown | AUS | | |
| 5. Martin Herbster | GER | 11–4 | 6:00 |
| 6. Antonio La Bruna | ITA | | |
| 7. Selman Kaygusuz | TUR | | |
| 8. Gerard Santoro | FRA | | |

Randy Lewis of Rapid City, South Dakota, had a much more difficult time getting into the Olympics than he did once he got there. In 1980 Lewis made the U.S. team, but the boycott prevented him from competing. In 1984, at the U.S. Olympic trials, Lewis defeated world championship silver medalist Lee Roy Smith. But Smith filed a protest which was upheld and a re-wrestle was ordered. When Smith emerged victorious, Lewis, supported by U.S. coach Dan Gable, filed a protest of his own. An arbitrator ordered that the final 50 seconds of the original match be re-wrestled. This time Lewis won. The next day, only two days before the Los Angeles opening ceremonies, Lewis defeated Rick Delegatta to finally secure his participation in the Olympics.

Lewis outscored his first four opponents 52–4 to advance to the final, where he overwhelmed Akaishi in the first two minutes of the second period.

**1988 Seoul** C: 28, N: 28, D: 9.29.

| | | | FINAL MATCH | |
|---|---|---|---|---|
| 1. | John Smith | USA | 4–0 | 6:00 |
| 2. | Stepan Sarkisyan | SOV | | |
| 3. | Simeon Shterev | BUL | 5–2 | 6:00 |
| 4. | Akbar Fallah | IRN | | |
| 5. | Jörg Helmdach | GER | 5–4 | 6:00 |
| 6. | Avirmed Enhe | MON | | |
| 7. | Giovanni Schillaci | ITA | 5–0 | 6:00 |
| 8. | Gary Bohay | CAN | | |

John Smith, the 1987 world champion, qualified for the U.S. Olympic team by twice defeating Randy Lewis, the same man who had prevented John's older brother, Lee Roy, from qualifying in 1984. In Seoul, Smith suffered a fractured nose in his second match with Simeon Shterev. He also wrestled with an abscessed left ear, which had to be drained daily. In the final, Smith demoralized Sarkisyan early in the first round by slipping free of the Armenian's best leghold.

# LIGHTWEIGHT
## (60 kg—149 ½ lbs)

**1896–1900** not held

**1904 St. Louis** C: 10, N: 1, D: 10.15.
*(65.77 kg—145 lbs)*
1. Otto Roehm          USA
2. Rudolph Tesing      USA
3. Albert Zirkel       USA
4. William Hennessy    USA

**1906** not held

**1908 London** C: 11, N: 2, D: 7.24.
*(66.6 kg—147 lbs)*
1. George de Relwyskow    GBR
2. William Wood           GBR
3. Albert Gingell         GBR
4. George MacKenzie       GBR
5. John Krug              USA

Relwyskow had already won a silver medal in the Middleweight division when he took first place against the lightweights.

**1912** not held

**1920 Antwerp** C: 11, N: 6, D: 8.21.
*(67.5 kg—149 lbs)*
1. Kaarlo "Kalle" Anttila   FIN
2. Gottfrid Svensson        SWE

3. Peter Wright        GBR
4. Auguste Thijs       BEL

**1924 Paris** C: 16, N: 10, D: 7.14.
*(66 kg—145½ lbs)*
1. Russell Vis          USA
2. Volmari Vikström     FIN
3. Arvo Haavisto        FIN
4. G. Gardiner          GBR
5. W. J. Montgomery     CAN
5. Emile Pouvroux       FRA

**1928 Amsterdam** C: 11, N: 11, D: 8.1.
*(66 kg—145½ lbs)*
1. Osvald Käpp               EST
2. Charles Pacôme            FRA
3. Eino Leino                FIN
4. Birger Nilsen             NOR
5. Carlo Tesdorf Jörgensen   DEN
6. Clarence Berryman         USA

**1932 Los Angeles** C: 8, N: 8, D: 8.3.
*(66 kg—145½ lbs)*
1. Charles Pacôme        FRA
2. Károly Kárpáti        HUN
3. Gustaf Klarén         SWE
4. Melvin Clodfelter     USA
5. Kustaa Pihlajamäki    FIN

In the 1928 final, Pacôme, a law student, had lost a controversial decision to Osvald Käpp. Four years later in Los Angeles, the two met again in the first round. This time Pacôme won on points. Three more victories later, he was awarded the gold medal.

**1936 Berlin** C: 17, N: 17, D: 8.4.
*(66 kg—145½ lbs)*

| | | | ROUND ELIMINATED | BAD PTS | FINAL ROUND |
|---|---|---|---|---|---|
| 1. | Károly Kárpáti | HUN | — | 3 | 1 |
| 2. | Wolfgang Ehrl | GER | — | 4 | 2 |
| 3. | Hermanni Pihlajamäki | FIN | | 4 | 0 |
| 4. | Charles Delporte | FRA | 5 | 6 | |
| 5. | Harley De Witt Strong | USA | 4 | 5 | |
| 6. | Paride Romagnoli | ITA | 4 | 7 | |
| 7. | Eiichi Kazama | JPN | 4 | 5 | |
| 8. | Adalbert Toots | EST | 4 | 7 | |

**1948 London** C: 18, N: 18, D: 7.31.
*(67 kg—147½ lbs)*

| | | | ROUND ELIMINATED | BAD PTS. |
|---|---|---|---|---|
| 1. | Celal Atik | TUR | — | 1 |
| 2. | Gösta Frändfors | SWE | 6 | 6 |
| 3. | Hermann Baumann | SWI | 6 | 8 |
| 4. | Garibaldo Nizzola | ITA | 6 | 10 |
| 5. | William Koll | USA | 4 | 6 |
| 6. | Kim Suk-young | KOR | 4 | 7 |
| 6. | Sulo Leppänen | FIN | 4 | 7 |
| 8. | László Bakos | HUN | 3 | 5 |

Atik won five of his six bouts by falls and defeated Leppänen on points.

**1952 Helsinki** C: 23, N: 23, D: 7.23.
*(67 kg—147½ lbs)*

| | | ROUND ELIMINATED | BAD PTS. | FINAL ROUND |
|---|---|---|---|---|
| 1. Olle Anderberg | SWE | — | 1 | 2 |
| 2. Jay Thomas Evans | USA | — | 2 | 4 |
| 3. Jahanbakte Towfigh | IRN | — | 4 | 6 |
| 4. Aram Yaltyryan | SOV | 5 | 7 | |
| 5. Risto Talosela | FIN | 5 | 7 | |
| 6. Heinrich Nettesheim | GER | 4 | 6 | |
| 6. Takeo Shimotori | JPN | 4 | 6 | |
| 8. Jan Cools | BEL | 4 | 7 | |
| 8. Godfey Pienaar | SAF | 4 | 7 | |

**1956 Melbourne** C: 19, N: 19, D: 12.1.
*(67 kg—147½ lbs)*

| | | ROUND ELIMINATED | BAD PTS. |
|---|---|---|---|
| 1. Emamali Habibi | IRN | — | 4 |
| 2. Shigeru Kasahara | JPN | 5 | 6 |
| 3. Alimbeg Bestayev | SOV | 6 | 6 |
| 4. Gyula Tóth | HUN | 5 | 5 |
| 5. Jay Thomas Evans | USA | 4 | 5 |
| 5. Garibaldo Nizzola | ITA | 4 | 5 |
| 7. Mario Tovar González | MEX | 4 | 7 |
| 8. Muhammad Ashraf | PAK | 4 | 7 |

**1960 Rome** C: 24, N: 24, D: 9.6.
*(67 kg—147½ lbs)*

| | | ROUND ELIMINATED | BAD PTS. | FINAL ROUND |
|---|---|---|---|---|
| 1. Shelby Wilson | USA | — | 5 | 1 |
| 2. Vladimir Sinyavsky | SOV | — | 5 | 3 |
| 3. Enyu Dimov | BUL | 6 | 6 | |
| 4. Bong Chang-won | KOR | 6 | 8 | |
| 4. Mostafa Tajik | IRN | 6 | 8 | |
| 6. Garibaldo Nizzola | ITA | 5 | 7 | |
| 7. Martti Peltoniemi | FIN | 5 | 8 | |
| 8. Kazuo Abe | JPN | 4 | 8 | |
| 8. Raymond Lougheed | CAN | 4 | 8 | |
| 8. Hayrullah Sahin | TUR | 4 | 8 | |

Shelby Wilson of Ponca City, Oklahoma, won the gold medal without registering a single fall.

**1964 Tokyo** C: 22, N: 22, D: 10.14.
*(70 kg—154½ lbs)*

| | | ROUND ELIMINATED | BAD PTS. | FINAL ROUND |
|---|---|---|---|---|
| 1. Enyu Vulchev (Dimov) | BUL | — | 5 | 1 |
| 2. Klaus-Jürgen Rost | GER | — | 5 | 3 |
| 3. Iwao Horiuchi | JPN | 5 | 6 | |
| 4. Mahmut Atalay | TUR | 5 | 6 | |
| 5. Abdollah Movahhed | IRN | 5 | 7 | |
| 6. Zarbeg Beriashvili | SOV | 4 | 6 | |
| 6. Chung Dong-goo | KOR | 4 | 6 | |
| 6. Gregory Ruth | USA | 4 | 6 | |

**1968 Mexico City** C: 26, N: 26, D: 10.20.
*(70 kg—154½ lbs)*

| | | ROUND ELIMINATED | BAD PTS. | FINAL ROUND |
|---|---|---|---|---|
| 1. Abdollah Movahhed | IRN | — | 4 | 1 |
| 2. Enyu Vulchev (Dimov) | BUL | — | 4 | 3 |
| 3. Sereeter Danzandarjaa | MON | 6 | 7.5 | |
| 4. Wayne Wells | USA | 6 | 8 | |
| 5. Zarbeg Beriashvili | SOV | 5 | 6 | |
| 6. Udey Chand | IND | 5 | 6 | |
| 7. Iwao Horivchi | JPN | 5 | 8 | |
| 8. Klaus-Jürgen Rost | GER | 5 | 9.5 | |

**1972 Munich** C: 25, N: 25, D: 8.31.

| | | ROUND ELIMINATED | BAD PTS. | FINAL ROUND |
|---|---|---|---|---|
| 1. Dan Gable | USA | — | 1.5 | 2 |
| 2. Kikuo Wada | JPN | — | 4.5 | 3 |
| 3. Ruslan Ashuraliev | SOV | — | 4.5 | 6 |
| 4. Tsedendamba Natsagdorj | MON | 5 | 6 | |
| 5. Ali Sahin | TUR | 5 | 6 | |
| 6. Udo Schröder | GDR | 5 | 8 | |
| 7. Wlodzimierz Cieślak | POL | 5 | 8.5 | |
| 8. József Rusznyák | HUN | 4 | 7 | |

Twenty-three-year-old Dan Gable of Waterloo, Iowa, trained seven hours a day, every day, for three years prior to the Munich Olympics. Between 1963 and 1973 he compiled a record of 299 wins, 6 loses and 3 draws. In 1984 he served as the coach of the U.S. Olympic freestyle wrestling team.

**1976 Montreal** C: 24, N: 24, D: 7.31.

| | | ROUND ELIMINATED | BAD PTS. | FINAL ROUND |
|---|---|---|---|---|
| 1. Pavel Pinigin | SOV | — | 6 | 3.5 |
| 2. Lloyd Keaser | USA | — | 1 | 3.5 |
| 3. Yasaburo Sugawara | JPN | — | 6 | 5 |
| 4. Doncho Zhekov | BUL | 6 | 8.5 | |
| 5. José Ramos | CUB | 5 | 7 | |
| 6. Tsedendamba Natsagdorj | MON | 5 | 7 | |
| 7. Rami Miron | ISR | 5 | 9 | |
| 8. Eberhard Probst | GDR | 4 | 6.5 | |

Pinigin outpointed Keaser 12–1 in the final match.

**1980 Moscow** C: 18, N: 18, D: 7.29.

| | | ROUND ELIMINATED | BAD PTS. | FINAL ROUND |
|---|---|---|---|---|
| 1. Saipulla Absaidov | SOV | — | 1 | 1 |
| 2. Ivan Yankov | BUL | — | 5 | 4 |
| 3. Saban Sejdi | YUG | — | 2 | 7 |
| 4. Jagmander Singh | IND | 5 | 6 | |
| 5. Eberhard Probst | GDR | 5 | 7.5 | |
| 6. Octavian Dusa | ROM | 4 | 7 | |
| 7. Ali Hussain Faris | IRQ | 4 | 8 | |
| 8. Pekka Rauhala | FIN | 4 | 9.5 | |

Absaidov outscored his five opponents 59–1, with only Yankov lasting the full nine minutes.

**1984 Los Angeles-Anaheim** C: 22, N: 22, D: 8.11.

| | | FINAL MATCH | |
|---|---|---|---|
| 1. You In-tak | KOR | 5–5 | 6:00 |
| 2. Andrew Rein | USA | | |
| 3. Jukka Rauhala | FIN | Injury | 3:02 |
| 4. Masakazu Kamimura | JPN | | |
| 5. Zsigmond Kelevitz | AUS | 11–3 | 6:00 |
| 6. Fevzi Seker | TUR | | |
| 7. Erwin Knosp | GER | | |
| 8. René Neyer | SWI | | |

You scored an early 3-point arm throw which eventually gave him the victory. In the second period he suffered a lower back spasm requiring two injury time-outs. He had to be helped onto the victory podium and supported by security personnel during the playing of the Korean national anthem.

**1988 Seoul** C: 30, N: 30, D: 10.1.

| | | FINAL MATCH | |
|---|---|---|---|
| 1. Arsen Fadzayev | SOV | 6–0 | 6:00 |
| 2. Park Jang-soon | KOR | | |
| 3. Nate Carr | USA | 5–1 | 6:00 |
| 4. Kosei Akaishi | JPN | | |
| 5. David McKay | CAN | 4–1 | 6:00 |
| 6. Jukka Rauhala | FIN | | |
| 7. Alexander Leipold | GER | 14–10 | 6:00 |
| 8. Angel Yasenov | BUL | | |

Fadzayev, undefeated in international competition and a four-time world champion, overwhelmed each of his six opponents. Park qualified for the final by gaining a controversial 3–2 victory over Carr, which led to the suspension of the officials in charge of the match.

# WELTERWEIGHT

(74 kg—163 lbs)

**1896–1900** not held

**1904 St. Louis** C: 10, N: 1, D: 10.15.
*(71.67 kg—158 lbs)*
1. Charles Erickson    USA
2. William Beckmann    USA
3. Jerry Winholtz    USA
4. William Hennessy    USA
5. Otto Roehm    USA

Erickson was a member of the Norwegian Turnverein of Brooklyn.

**1906–1920** not held

**1924 Paris** C: 13, N: 7, D: 7.14.
*(72 kg—158½ lbs)*
1. Hermann Gehri    SWI

2. Eino Leino    FIN
3. Otto Müller    SWI
4. Guy Lookabough    USA
5. William Johnson    USA

**1928 Amsterdam** C: 11, N: 11, D: 8.1.
*(72 kg—158½ lbs)*
1. Arvo Haavisto    FIN
2. Lloyd Appelton    USA
3. Maurice Letchford    CAN
4. Jean Jourlin    FRA
5. T. Harry Morris    AUS

**1932 Los Angeles** C: 9, N: 9, D: 8.3.
*(72 kg—158½ lbs)*
1. Jack Van Bebber    USA
2. Daniel MacDonald    CAN
3. Eino Leino    FIN
4. Jean Földeak    GER
5. Gyula Zombori    HUN

**1936 Berlin** C: 16, N: 16, D: 8.4.
*(72 kg—158½ lbs)*

| | | ROUND ELIMINATED | BAD PTS. | FINAL ROUND |
|---|---|---|---|---|
| 1. Frank Lewis | USA | — | 3 | 3 |
| 2. Ture Andersson | SWE | — | 4 | 3 |
| 3. Joseph Schleimer | CAN | — | 3 | 6 |
| 4. Jean Jourlin | FRA | 5 | 5 | |
| 5. Willy Angst | SWI | 5 | 7 | |
| 6. Josef Paar | GER | 4 | 5 | |
| 7. Julien Beke | BEL | 3 | 6 | |
| 7. Huseyin Erçetin | TUR | 3 | 6 | |
| 7. John O'Hara | AUS | 3 | 6 | |

Frank Lewis of Cushing, Oklahoma, was awarded first place even though he was thrown by Andersson in the fourth round.

**1948 London** C: 16, N: 16, D: 7.31.
*(73 kg—161 lbs)*

| | | ROUND ELIMINATED | BAD PTS. | FINAL ROUND |
|---|---|---|---|---|
| 1. Yaşar Doğu | TUR | — | 0 | 1 |
| 2. Richard Garrard | AUS | — | 2 | 5 |
| 3. Leland Merrill | USA | — | 3 | 4 |
| 4. Jean-Baptiste Leclerc | FRA | 4 | 6 | |
| 5. Kálmán Sóvári | HUN | 4 | 7 | |
| 6. Frans Westergren | SWE | 3 | 5 | |
| 7. Willy Angst | SWI | 3 | 6 | |
| 7. Harry Peace | CAN | 3 | 6 | |
| 7. Whang Byung-kwan | KOR | 3 | 6 | |
| 7. Abbas Zandi | IRN | 3 | 6 | |

**1952 Helsinki** C: 20, N: 20, D: 7.23.
*(73 kg—161 lbs)*

| | | ROUND ELIMINATED | BAD PTS. | FINAL ROUND |
|---|---|---|---|---|
| 1. William Smith | USA | — | 2 | 4 |
| 2. Per Berlin | SWE | — | 3 | 4 |

| | | ROUND ELIMI- NATED | BAD PTS. | FINAL ROUND |
|---|---|---|---|---|
| 3. Abdullah Modjtabavi | IRN | — | 4 | 4 |
| 4. Alberto Longarela | ARG | 4 | 5 | |
| 5. Mohamed Hassan Moussa | EGY | 4 | 6 | |
| 5. Ladislav Sekal | CZE | 4 | 6 | |
| 5. Tsuguo Yamazaki | JPN | 4 | 6 | |
| 8. Aleksanteri Keisala | FIN | 4 | 7 | |

Twenty-three-year-old Bill Smith of Cedar Falls, Iowa, was so surprised by his victory that at the medal ceremony he mounted the third-place stand instead of the winner's pedestal.

**1956 Melbourne** C: 15, N: 15, D: 12.1.
*(73 kg—161 lbs)*

| | | ROUND ELIMINATED | BAD PTS. | FINAL ROUND |
|---|---|---|---|---|
| 1. Mitsuo Ikeda | JPN | — | 3 | 2 |
| 2. Ibrahim Zengin | TUR | — | 4 | 3 |
| 3. Vakhtang Balavadze | SOV | — | 4 | 6 |
| 4. Per Berlin | SWE | 4 | 5 | |
| 4. Nabi Sorouri | IRN | 4 | 5 | |
| 4. Coenraad de Villiers | SAF | 4 | 5 | |
| 7. Mitious Petkov | BUL | 4 | 6 | |
| 8. Ernest Fischer | USA | 3 | 7 | |
| 8. Alfred Tischendorf | GDR | 3 | 7 | |

**1960 Rome** C: 23, N: 23, D: 9.6.
*(73 kg—161 lbs)*

| | | ROUND ELIMINATED | BAD PTS. | FINAL ROUND |
|---|---|---|---|---|
| 1. Douglas Blubaugh | USA | — | 0 | 1 |
| 2. Ismail Ogan | TUR | — | 4 | 4 |
| 3. Muhammed Bashir | PAK | — | 5 | 7 |
| 4. Gaetano De Vescovi | ITA | 5 | 7 | |
| 4. Emamali Habibi | IRN | 5 | 7 | |
| 4. Yutaka Kaneko | JPN | 5 | 7 | |
| 7. Coenraad de Villiers | SAF | 4 | 7 | |
| 8. Åxe Carlsson | SWE | 4 | 8 | |

Doug Blubaugh of Ponca City, Oklahoma, qualified for the U.S. team by beating his former Oklahoma State teammate Phil Kinyon, after four scoreless draws. In fact, Blubaugh and Kinyon had drawn ten straight matches before Blubaugh finally won a decision. In Rome he tore through the opposition, winning five of his seven bouts by throws and one by default. Only Ogan lasted the full 12 minutes.

**1964 Tokyo** C: 22, N: 22, D: 10.14.
*(78 kg—172 lbs)*

| | | ROUND ELIMI- NATED | BAD PTS. | FINAL ROUND |
|---|---|---|---|---|
| 1. Ismail Ogan | TUR | — | 4 | 4 |
| 2. Guliko Sagaradze | SOV | — | 4 | 4 |
| 3. Mohammad Ali Sanatkaran | IRN | — | 4 | 4 |
| 4. Petko Dermendzhiev | BUL | 5 | 8 | |
| 5. Yasuo Watanabe | JPN | 4 | 6 | |
| 6. Philip Oberlander | CAN | 4 | 6 | |
| 7. Muhammad Afzal | PAK | 4 | 7 | |
| 8. Madho Singh | IND | 4 | 8 | |

Ogan was awarded first place because he weighed 2 kg (4.4 lbs) less than Sagaradze. Sanatkaran was relegated to third place because his two draws came in the final round.

**1968 Mexico City** C: 19, N: 19, D: 10.20.
*(78 kg—172 lbs)*

| | | ROUND ELIMI- NATED | BAD PTS. | FINAL ROUND |
|---|---|---|---|---|
| 1. Mahmut Atalay | TUR | — | 4.5 | 1 |
| 2. Daniel Robin | FRA | — | 5 | 3 |
| 3. Dagvasuren Purev | MON | 5 | 6 | |
| 4. Ali Mohammad Momeni | IRN | 5 | 6.5 | |
| 5. Tatsuo Sasaki | JPN | 5 | 6.5 | |
| 6. Yuri Schakmuradov | SOV | 5 | 8 | |
| 7. Stephen Combs | USA | 5 | 8 | |
| 7. Angel Sotirov | BUL | 5 | 8 | |

In 1968, Daniel Robin won silver medals in both the freestyle and Greco-Roman competitions.

**1972 Munich** C: 25, N: 25, D: 8.31.

| | | ROUND ELIMINATED | BAD PTS. | FINAL ROUND |
|---|---|---|---|---|
| 1. Wayne Wells | USA | — | 2 | 2 |
| 2. Jan Karlsson | SWE | — | 4 | 4 |
| 3. Adolf Seger | GER | — | 5 | 6 |
| 4. Yancho Pavlov | BUL | 6 | 7.5 | |
| 5. Mansour Barzegar | IRN | 5 | 7 | |
| 5. Wolfgang Nitschke | GDR | 5 | 7 | |
| 5. Daniel Robin | FRA | 5 | 7 | |
| 8. Miklós Urbanovics | HUN | 4 | 6.5 | |

Wells was a lawyer from Norman, Oklahoma.

**1976 Montreal** C: 21, N: 21, D: 7.31.

| | | ROUND ELIMINATED | BAD PTS. | FINAL ROUND |
|---|---|---|---|---|
| 1. Jiichiro Date | JPN | — | 0 | 1 |
| 2. Mansour Barzegar | IRN | — | 2 | 5 |
| 3. Stanley Dziedzic | USA | — | 2 | 6 |
| 4. Ruslan Ashuraliev | SOV | 5 | 7.5 | |
| 5. Marin Pircalabu | ROM | 5 | 9 | |
| 6. Fred Hempel | GDR | 5 | 10 | |
| 7. Jarmo Overmark | FIN | 4 | 7 | |
| 8. Kiro Ristov | YUG | 4 | 8 | |

Date threw six of his seven opponents and outpointed Dziedzic 10–5.

**1980 Moscow** C: 18, N: 18, D: 7.30.

| | | ROUND ELIMINATED | BAD PTS. | FINAL ROUND |
|---|---|---|---|---|
| 1. Valentin Angelov | BUL | — | 2 | 2 |
| 2. Jamtsying Davaajav | MON | — | 6 | 4 |
| 3. Dan Karabin | CZE | — | 7.5 | 6 |
| 4. Pavel Pinigin | SOV | 6 | 8.5 | |
| 5. Ryszard Ścigalski | POL | 5 | 7 | |
| 6. Rajander Singh | IND | 4 | 7 | |
| 7. István Fehér | HUN | 4 | 9 | |
| 8. Riccardo Niccolini | ITA | 4 | 9 | |

Angelov earned his gold medal by gaining five victories in one day. The big surprise was his win against Pinigin. Pinigin took Angelov to the mat twice in the first minute, but the Bulgarian came back to register a fall after 1:59. In the final match Angelov won on points, 6–5, over Davaajav.

**1984 Los Angeles-Anaheim** C: 22, N: 22, D: 8.10.

| | | FINAL MATCH | |
|---|---|---|---|
| 1. David Schultz | USA | 4–1 | 6:00 |
| 2. Martin Knosp | GER | | |
| 3. Šaban Sejdi | YUG | 5–1 | 6:00 |
| 4. Rajender Singh | IND | | |
| 5. Naomi Higuchi | JPN | 7–3 | 6:00 |
| 6. Han Myung-woo | KOR | | |
| 7. Marc Mongeon | CAN | | |
| 8. Pekka Rauhala | FIN | | |

The only defending world champion free style wrestler to take part in the 1984 Olympics, Dave Schultz, won one match by a fall and his other five by a combined score of 42–2. Twenty-four hours after Schultz was awarded his gold medal, his younger brother, Mark, won the middleweight division.

**1988 Seoul** C: 30, N: 30, D: 9.30.

| | | FINAL MATCH | |
|---|---|---|---|
| 1. Kenneth Monday | USA | 5–2 | 6:42 |
| 2. Adlan Varayev | SOV | | |
| 3. Rakhmad Sofiadi | BUL | 8–3 | 6:00 |
| 4. Lodoy Bayar | MON | | |
| 5. Pekka Rauhala | FIN | Injury | 3:00 |
| 6. Ayatollah Vagozari | IRN | | |
| 7. Yoon Kyung-jae | KOR | Injury | |
| 8. Uwe Westendorf | GDR | | |

Kenny Monday of Tulsa, Oklahoma, qualified for the final by pinning one opponent and outscoring six others 34–2. For the gold medal, he faced defending world champion Adlan Varayev who had beaten him in two of their three previous meetings. Neither man scored for over 4 minutes. Then, with 1:45 remaining, Monday took a 1–0 lead with a single-leg pick. Forty-five seconds later Varayev scored with a double-leg takedown to move ahead 2–1. With 17 seconds left, Monday evened the match with a crotch lift reversal. Forty seconds into the sudden death overtime, Monday caught the tiring Varayev in a bodylock, lifted him into the air, and slammed him to the mat for a 3-point takedown.

# MIDDLEWEIGHT
## (82 kg—181 lbs)

**1896–1906** not held

**1908 London** C: 12, N: 3, D: 7.21.
*(73 kg—161 lbs)*
1. Stanley Bacon     GBR
2. George de Relwyskow     GBR
3. Frederick Beck     GBR
4. Carl Georg Anderson     SWE
5. Edgar Bacon (GBR), Aubrey Coleman (GBR)

**1912** not held

**1920 Antwerp** C: 16, N: 9, D: 8.21.
*(75 kg—165½ lbs)*
1. Eino Leino     FIN
2. Väinö Penttala     FIN
3. Charles Johnson     USA
4. Angus Frantz     USA

**1924 Paris** C: 14, N: 9, D: 7.14.
*(79 kg—174 lbs)*
1. Fritz Hagmann     SWI
2. Pierre Ollivier     BEL
3. Viho Pekkala     FIN
4. J. Pentillä     FIN
5. Robert Christoffersen     DEN
5. Noel Rhys     GBR

**1928 Amsterdam** C: 9, N: 9, D: 8.1.
*(79 kg—174 lbs)*
1. Ernst Kyburz     SWI
2. Donald Stockton     CAN
3. Samuel Rabin     GBR
4. Ralph Hammond     USA
4. A. Praeg     SAF

**1932 Los Angeles** C: 7, N: 7, D: 8.3.
*(79 kg—174 lbs)*
1. Ivar Johansson     SWE
2. Kyösti Luukko     FIN
3. József Tunyogi     HUN
4. Robert Hess     USA
5. Sumiyuki Kotani     JPN
6. Emile Poilvé     FRA

This was the first of Johansson's three Olympic medals. Four days later he won the Greco-Roman Welterweight division and four *years* later, in Berlin, he was victorious as a Greco-Roman middleweight.

**1936 Berlin** C: 15, N: 15, D: 8.4.
*(79 kg—174 lbs)*

| | | ROUND ELIMINATED | BAD PTS. | FINAL ROUND |
|---|---|---|---|---|
| 1. Emile Poilvé | FRA | — | 1 | 0 |
| 2. Richard Voliva | USA | — | 3 | 3 |
| 3. Ahmet Kireçci | TUR | 5 | 6 | |
| 4. Ernst Krebs | SWI | 5 | 7 | |
| 5. Jaroslav Sysel | CZE | 4 | 6 | |
| 6. Kyösti Luukko | FIN | 4 | 7 | |
| 7. Ercole Gallegati | ITA | 3 | 5 | |
| 8. János Riheczky | HUN | 3 | 5 | |

Poilvé registered five throws in six matches, as well as a second-round decision over Luukko.

**1948 London** C: 16, N: 16, D: 7.31.
*(79 kg—174 lbs)*

| | | ROUND ELIMINATED | BAD PTS. | FINAL ROUND |
|---|---|---|---|---|
| 1. Glen Brand | USA | — | 2 | 0 |
| 2. Adil Candemir | TUR | — | 4 | 3 |
| 3. Erik Lindén | SWE | 5 | 5 | |
| 4. Carel Reitz | SAF | 4 | 5 | |
| 5. Paavo Sepponen | FIN | 4 | 5 | |
| 6. André Brunaud | FRA | 4 | 7 | |
| 7. Maurice Vachon | CAN | 3 | 5 | |
| 8. Bruce Arthur | AUS | 3 | 6 | |

Twenty-four-year-old Glen Brand of Clarion, Iowa, was awarded first place after he threw Candemir in the fourth round and then decisioned Linden in Round 5.

**1952 Helsinki** C: 17, N: 17, D: 7.23.
*(79 kg—174 lbs)*

| | | ROUND ELIMINATED | BAD PTS. | FINAL ROUND |
|---|---|---|---|---|
| 1. David Tsimakuridze | SOV | — | 4 | 2 |
| 2. Gholam Reza Takhti | IRN | — | 2 | 3 |
| 3. György Gurics | HUN | — | 5 | 6 |
| 4. Gustav Gocke | GER | 5 | 6 | |
| 5. Haydar Zafer | TUR | 4 | 5 | |
| 6. Leon Genuth | ARG | 4 | 7 | |
| 6. Carel Reitz | SAF | 4 | 7 | |
| 8. Bengt Lindblad | SWE | 3 | 5 | |

**1956 Melbourne** C: 15, N: 15, D: 12.1.
*(79 kg—174 lbs)*

| | | ROUND ELIMINATED | BAD PTS. | FINAL ROUND |
|---|---|---|---|---|
| 1. Nikola Stanchev | BUL | — | 4 | 1 |
| 2. Daniel Hodge | USA | — | 4 | 3 |
| 3. Georgy Skhirtladze | SOV | — | 4 | 6 |
| 4. Ismet Atli | TUR | 5 | 5 | |
| 5. Kazuo Katsuramoto | JPN | 4 | 6 | |
| 5. Johann Sterr | GER | 4 | 6 | |
| 7. Bengt Lindblad | SWE | 3 | 7 | |
| 7. Abbas Zandi | IRN | 3 | 7 | |

Stanchev was the first Bulgarian to win an Olympic gold medal.

**1960 Rome** C: 19, N: 19, D: 9.6.
*(79 kg—174 lbs)*

| | | ROUND ELIMINATED | BAD PTS. |
|---|---|---|---|
| 1. Hasan Güngör | TUR | — | 4 |
| 2. Georgy Skhirtladze | SOV | 5 | 6 |
| 3. Hans Yngve Antonsson | SWE | 5 | 6 |
| 4. Edward De Witt | USA | 5 | 7 |
| 5. Prodan Gardzhev | BUL | 4 | 6 |
| 5. Géza Hollósi | HUN | 4 | 6 |
| 5. Madho Singh | IND | 4 | 6 |
| 8. Takashi Nagai | JPN | 4 | 7 |

**1964 Tokyo** C: 16, N: 16, D: 10.14.
*(87 kg—192 lbs)*

| | | ROUND ELIMINATED | BAD PTS. | FINAL ROUND |
|---|---|---|---|---|
| 1. Prodan Gardzhev | BUL | — | 5 | 2 |
| 2. Hasan Güngör | TUR | — | 5 | 2 |
| 3. Daniel Brand | USA | 5 | 6 | |
| 4. Mansour Mehdizadeh | IRN | 5 | 6 | |
| 5. Géza Hollósi | HUN | 4 | 6 | |
| 5. Tatsuo Sasaki | JPN | 4 | 6 | |
| 7. Günther Bauch | GDR | 4 | 9 | |
| 7. Faiz Muhammad | PAK | 4 | 9 | |

Güngör was deprived of a second gold medal because he outweighed Gardzhev by 1 kg (2.2 lbs).

**1968 Mexico City** C: 22, N: 22, D: 10.20.
*(87 kg—192 lbs)*

| | | ROUND ELIMINATED | BAD PTS. |
|---|---|---|---|
| 1. Boris Gurevich | SOV | — | 4.5 |
| 2. Munkbat Jigjid | MON | 7 | 6.5 |
| 3. Prodan Gardzhev | BUL | 7 | 7.5 |
| 4. Thomas Peckham | USA | 7 | 8 |
| 5. Hüseyin Gürsoy | TUR | 6 | 7 |
| 6. Peter Döring | GDR | 4 | 6 |
| 7. Ronald Grinstead | GBR | 4 | 8 |
| 8. Shigeru Endo | JPN | 4 | 8.5 |

Gurevitch finished the tournament with draws against Jigjid and Gardzhev.

**1972 Munich** C: 24, N: 24, D: 8.31.

| | | ROUND ELIMINATED | BAD PTS. |
|---|---|---|---|
| 1. Levan Tediashvili | SOV | — | 4.5 |
| 2. John Peterson | USA | 6 | 6 |
| 3. Vasile Iorga | ROM | 6 | 7 |
| 4. Horst Stottmeister | GDR | 6 | 7 |
| 5. Tatsuo Sasaki | JPN | 5 | 6 |
| 6. Peter Neumair | GER | 5 | 7 |
| 7. Kurt Elmgren | SWE | 4 | 6 |
| 8. Jan Wypiórczyk | POL | 4 | 7 |

**1976 Montreal** C: 18, N: 18, D: 7.31.

| | | ROUND ELIMINATED | BAD PTS. | FINAL ROUND |
|---|---|---|---|---|
| 1. John Peterson | USA | — | 2 | 0.5 |
| 2. Viktor Novoyilov | SOV | — | 5.5 | 5 |
| 3. Adolf Seger | GER | — | 6.5 | 6.5 |
| 4. Mehmet Uzun | TUR | 6 | 7.5 | |
| 5. Ismail Abilov | BUL | 5 | 7.5 | |
| 6. Henryk Mazur | POL | 4 | 6 | |
| 7. István Kovács | HUN | 4 | 6 | |
| 8. Masaru Motegi | JPN | 4 | 8 | |

In 1972 John Peterson of Comstock, Wisconsin, won a silver medal, while his brother, Ben, a light heavyweight, won a gold. Four years later in Montreal they reversed medals.

**1980 Moscow** C: 14, N: 14, D: 7.31.

| | | ROUND ELIMINATED | BAD PTS. | FINAL ROUND |
|---|---|---|---|---|
| 1. Ismail Abilov | BUL | — | 1 | 1 |
| 2. Magomedhan Aratsilov | SOV | — | 3 | 3 |
| 3. István Kovács | HUN | — | 4 | 8 |
| 4. Henryk Mazur | POL | 5 | 8.5 | |
| 5. Abdula Memedi | YUG | 4 | 7 | |
| 6. Zevegying Duvchin | MON | 4 | 8 | |
| 7. Gunter Busarello | AUT | 3 | 7 | |
| 8. Mohammad Eloulabi | SYR | 3 | 7.5 | |

Abilov outpointed his five opponents 50–5. Only Aratsilov lasted nine minutes, losing a fifth-round 8–4 decision to the 29-year-old Bulgarian champion.

**1984 Los Angeles-Anaheim** C: 16, N: 16, D: 8.11.

| | | FINAL MATCH | |
|---|---|---|---|
| 1. Mark Schultz | USA | 13–0 | 1:59 |
| 2. Hideyuki Nagashima | JPN | | |
| 3. Chris Rinke | CAN | 5–2 | 6:00 |
| 4. Reiner Trik | GER | | |
| 5. Kim Tae-woo | KOR | 10–3 | 6:00 |
| 6. Kenneth Reinsfield | NZE | | |
| 7. Iraklis Deskoulidis | GRE | | |
| 8. Luciano Ortelli | ITA | | |

With all of the top four 82 kg wrestlers boycotted out of the Olympics, the favorites' role fell to Resit Karabacek of Turkey and Mark Schultz, younger brother of 74 kg champion Dave Schultz. As it happened, Karabacek and Schultz met in the first round. Only 30 seconds into the match Karabacek, who had never before been pinned, was thrown by a single leg counter and the match was over. As Karabacek writhed in agony, having suffered a fractured left elbow, Schultz happily paraded around the mat, showing no interest in his opponent's condition. After escorting Karabacek to the hospital, Turkish officials filed a protest, claiming that Schultz had used an illegal hold. Their protest was upheld and Karabacek, who was unable to continue, was declared the winner by disqualification. However, because the protest was filed more than 30 minutes after the match ended, Schultz was

not disqualified from the tournament. An extra judge was assigned to scrutinize the Schultz brothers during the remainder of the competition. Mark Schultz then put together four straight victories to match his brother's gold medal.

**1988 Seoul** C: 29, N: 29, D: 10.1.

| | | FINAL MATCH | |
|---|---|---|---|
| 1. Han Myung-woo | KOR | 4–0 | 6:00 |
| 2. Necmi Gencalp | TUR | | |
| 3. Josef Lohyňa | CZE | Passivity | 7:54 |
| 4. Aleksandr Tambovtsev | SOV | | |
| 5. Puntsag Suhbat | MON | Injury | |
| 6. Mark Schultz | USA | | |
| 7. Atsushi Ito | JPN | 5–4 | 6:29 |
| 8. Hans Gstöttner | GDR | | |

# LIGHT HEAVYWEIGHT
## (90 kg—198 ½ lbs)

**1896–1912** not held

**1920 Antwerp** C: 13, N: 8, D: 8.21.
*(80 kg—186½ lbs)*
1. Anders Larsson    SWE
2. Charles Courant    SWI
3. Walter Maurer    USA
4. John Redman    USA

**1924 Paris** C: 16, N: 10, D: 7.14.
*(87 kg—192 lbs)*
1. John Spellman    USA
2. Rudolf Svensson    SWE
3. Charles Courant    SWI
4. Carl Westergren    SWE
5. W.G. Wilson    GBR
6. George Rumple    CAN

**1928 Amsterdam** C: 7, N: 7, D: 8.1.
*(87 kg—192 lbs)*
1. Thure Sjöstedt    SWE
2. Arnold Bögli    SWI
3. Henri Lefèbre    FRA
4. Heywood Edwards    USA
5. Jacques van Assche    BEL

**1932 Los Angeles** C: 4, N: 4, D: 8.3.
*(87 kg—192 lbs)*
1. Peter Mehringer    USA
2. Thure Sjöstedt    SWE
3. Eddie Scarf    AUS
4. H. Madison    CAN

Pete Mehringer of Kinsley, Kansas, first learned how to wrestle from a correspondence course. After the Olympics, he played professional football and worked as a stuntman in Hollywood. His credits included *Knute Rockne, All-American*.

**1936 Berlin** C: 12, N: 12, D: 8.4.
*(87 kg—192 lbs)*

| | | ROUND ELIMINATED | BAD PTS. | FINAL ROUND |
|---|---|---|---|---|
| 1. Knut Fridell | SWE | — | 2 | 1 |
| 2. August Neo | EST | — | 5 | 4 |
| 3. Erich Siebert | GER | — | 5 | 6 |
| 4. Paul Dätwyler | SWI | 4 | 6 | |
| 5. Ray Clemons | USA | 4 | 7 | |
| 6. Eddie Scarf | AUS | 3 | 5 | |
| 7. Hubert Prokop | CZE | 3 | 7 | |
| 8. Ede Virág-Ébner | HUN | 3 | 7 | |

**1948 London** C: 15, N: 15, D: 7.31.
*(87 kg—192 lbs)*

| | | ROUND ELIMINATED | BAD PTS. | FINAL ROUND |
|---|---|---|---|---|
| 1. Henry Wittenberg | USA | — | 1 | 2 |
| 2. Fritz Stöckli | SWI | — | 1 | 3 |
| 3. Bengt Fahlkvist | SWE | — | 2 | 4 |
| 4. Muharrem Candaş | TUR | 5 | 7 | |
| 4. Fernand Payette | CAN | 5 | 7 | |
| 6. Patrick Morton | SAF | 3 | 5 | |
| 7. Spyros Deftreraios | GRE | 3 | 6 | |
| 7. John Sullivan | GBR | 3 | 6 | |
| 7. Oscar Verona | ITA | 3 | 6 | |

Each of the three matches of the final round was an epic struggle and each was decided by a split decision of the judges. Wittenberg was a 29-year-old New York policeman.

**1952 Helsinki** C: 13, N: 13, D: 7.23.
*(87 kg—192 lbs)*

| | | ROUND ELIMINATED | BAD PTS. | FINAL ROUND |
|---|---|---|---|---|
| 1. Wiking Palm | SWE | — | 4 | 2 |
| 2. Henry Wittenberg | USA | — | 4 | 3 |
| 3. Adil Atan | TUR | — | 6 | 5 |
| 4. Avgust Englas | SOV | 5 | 7 | |
| 5. Abass Zandi | IRN | 4 | 5 | |
| 6. Jacob Theron | SAF | 3 | 5 | |
| 7. Max Leichter | GER | 3 | 7 | |

**1956 Melbourne** C: 12, N: 12, D: 12.1.
*(87 kg—192 lbs)*

| | | ROUND ELIMINATED | BAD PTS. | FINAL ROUND |
|---|---|---|---|---|
| 1. Gholam Reza Takhti | IRN | — | 0 | 2 |
| 2. Boris Kulayev | SOV | — | 2 | 4 |
| 3. Peter Blair | USA | — | 4 | 6 |
| 4. Gerald Martina | IRL | 4 | 6 | |
| 5. Adil Atan | TUR | 4 | 7 | |
| 5. Kevin Coote | AUS | 4 | 7 | |
| 7. Mitsuhiro Ohira | JPN | 3 | 7 | |
| 7. Wiking Palm | SWE | 3 | 7 | |
| 7. Jacob Theron | SAF | 3 | 7 | |

**1960 Rome** C: 19, N: 19, D: 9.6.
*(87 kg—192 lbs)*

| | | ROUND ELIMINATED | BAD PTS. | FINAL ROUND |
|---|---|---|---|---|
| 1. İsmet Atli | TUR | — | 5 | 1 |
| 2. Gholam Reza Takhti | IRN | — | 0 | 3 |
| 3. Anatoly Albul | SOV | 5 | 6 | |
| 4. Wiking Palm | SWE | 5 | 6 | |
| 5. Daniel Brand | USA | 5 | 7 | |
| 6. Hermanus van Zyl | SAF | 5 | 9 | |
| 7. Singh Sajjan | IND | 4 | 8 | |
| 8. Kazuo Abe | JPN | 4 | 9 | |
| 8. György Gurics | HUN | 4 | 9 | |

Takhti pinned his first five opponents before losing on points to Atli. Albul was awarded the bronze medal over Palm on the basis of lower bodyweight.

**1964 Tokyo** C: 16, N: 16, D: 10.14.
*(97 kg—214 lbs)*

| | | ROUND ELIMINATED | BAD PTS. | FINAL ROUND |
|---|---|---|---|---|
| 1. Aleksandr Medved | SOV | — | 3 | 2 |
| 2. Ahmet Ayik | TUR | — | 5 | 4 |
| 3. Said Mustafov | BUL | — | 5 | 6 |
| 4. Gholam Reza Takhti | IRN | 5 | 6 | |
| 5. Peter Jutzeler | SWI | 5 | 9 | |
| 6. Gerald Conine | USA | 4 | 6 | |
| 7. Heinz Kiehl | GER | 4 | 7 | |
| 8. Imre Vigh | HUN | 3 | 6 | |

Medved secured the first of his three gold medals by pinning Mustafov in the final bout after only 39 seconds.

**1968 Mexico City** C: 16, N: 16, D: 10.20.
*(97 kg—214 lbs)*

| | | ROUND ELIMINATED | BAD PTS. | FINAL ROUND |
|---|---|---|---|---|
| 1. Ahmet Ayik | TUR | — | 4 | 2 |
| 2. Schota Lomidze | SOV | — | 5 | 3 |
| 3. József Csatári | HUN | — | 5 | 7 |
| 4. Said Mustafov | BUL | 5 | 6.5 | |
| 5. Khorloo Baianmunkh | MON | 5 | 8.5 | |
| 6. Jess Lewis | USA | 4 | 6 | |
| 7. Ryszard Dlugosz | POL | 4 | 7 | |
| 8. Gerd Bachmann | GDR | 3 | 6 | |

**1972 Munich** C: 23, N: 23, D: 8.31.

| | | ROUND ELIMINATED | BAD PTS. | FINAL ROUND |
|---|---|---|---|---|
| 1. Benjamin Peterson | USA | — | 4 | 2 |
| 2. Gennady Strakhov | SOV | — | 4 | 2 |
| 3. Károly Bajkó | HUN | 6 | 6.5 | |
| 4. Russi Petrov | BUL | 6 | 8.5 | |
| 5. Reza Khorrami | IRN | 5 | 7 | |
| 5. Barbaro Morgan | CUB | 5 | 7 | |
| 7. Günter Spindler | GDR | 5 | 8 | |
| 8. Gueclue Mehmet | TUR | 4 | 8 | |

Ben Peterson, whose brother, John, won a silver medal in the Middleweight division, picked up a surprise gold medal by pinning world champion Roussi Petrov after 2:41 of his final bout.

**1976 Montreal** C: 21, N: 21, D: 7.31.

| | | ROUND ELIMINATED | BAD PTS. | FINAL ROUND |
|---|---|---|---|---|
| 1. Levan Tediashvili | SOV | — | 1 | 2 |
| 2. Benjamin Peterson | USA | — | 3.5 | 4 |
| 3. Stelica Morcov | ROM | — | 7 | 6 |
| 4. Horst Stottmeister | GDR | 6 | 7.5 | |
| 5. Terry Paice | CAN | 5 | 7 | |
| 6. Pawel Kurczewski | POL | 5 | 8.5 | |
| 7. Frank Andersson | SWE | 5 | 8.5 | |
| 8. Barbaro Morgan | CUB | 4 | 7.5 | |

One of the greatest amateur wrestlers of all time, Levan "Teddy" Tediashvili had not lost a match since 1971. At the Munich Olympics he had defeated John Peterson to win the Middleweight division. Four years later Tediashvili moved up to Light Heavyweight and outpointed John's brother, Ben, 11–5 for a second gold medal. Tediashvili, a law student and vineyard worker, was a brash performer who was known to wink at pretty women in the crowd just before pinning his opponents. In 1988, Tediashvili played the part of bandit folk-hero Gogi Kenkeshvili in the film *Khareba and Gogi*.

**1980 Moscow** C: 15, N: 15, D: 7.20.

| | | ROUND ELIMI- NATED | BAD PTS. | FINAL ROUND |
|---|---|---|---|---|
| 1. Sanasar Oganesyan | SOV | — | 2 | 1.5 |
| 2. Uwe Neupert | GDR | — | 4.5 | 4 |
| 3. Aleksander Cichoń | POL | — | 0.5 | 6.5 |
| 4. Ivan Ginov | BUL | 5 | 7 | |
| 5. Dashdorj Tserentogtokh | MON | 5 | 8.5 | |
| 6. Christophe Andanson | FRA | 4 | 7 | |
| 7. Ion Ivanov | ROM | 4 | 7.5 | |
| 8. Mick Pikos | AUS | 4 | 8 | |

**1984 Los Angeles-Anaheim** C: 16, N: 16, D: 8.9.

| | | FINAL MATCH | |
|---|---|---|---|
| 1. Ed Banach | USA | 15–3 | 4:02 |
| 2. Akira Ota | JPN | | |
| 3. Noel Loban | GBR | 5–1 | 6:00 |
| 4. Clark Davis | CAN | | |
| 5. Macauley Appah | NGR | Injury | |
| 6. Ismail Temiz | TUR | | |
| 7. Majeed Abdul | PAK | | |
| 8. Michele Azzola | ITA | | |

On the way to the final, Ed Banach defeated his first three opponents by a combined score of 37–4, and then threw Majeed Abdul of Pakistan in 48 seconds. Ed was the twin brother of Lou Banach, who won the heavyweight division two nights later.

**1988 Seoul** C: 28, N: 28, D: 9.29.

| | | FINAL MATCH | |
|---|---|---|---|
| 1. Makharbek Khadartsev | SOV | 16–0 | 3:27 |
| 2. Akira Ota | JPN | | |
| 3. Kim Tae-woo | KOR | 1–0 | 6:00 |
| 4. Gábor Tóth | HUN | | |
| 5. James Scherr | USA | 3–1 | 6:00 |
| 6. Rumen Alabakov | BUL | | |
| 7. Iraklis Deskoulidis | GRE | 4–2 | 6:00 |
| 8. Zeveg Duvchin | MON | | |

Two-time world champion Makharbek Khadartsev pinned four of his seven opponents and outpointed two more in less than 3½ minutes. Only Edwin Lins of Austria lasted the full 6 minutes and even he lost 10–1. Khadartsev, like 68-kilogram champion Arsen Fadzayev, grew up in the North Ossetian region of the U.S.S.R.

# HEAVYWEIGHT
## (100 kg—220 lbs)

**1896–1968** not held

**1972 Munich** C: 17, N: 17, D: 8.31.

| | | ROUND ELIMINATED | BAD PTS. | FINAL ROUND |
|---|---|---|---|---|
| 1. Ivan Yarygin | SOV | — | 0 | 0 |
| 2. Khorloo Baianmunkh | MON | — | 1 | 5 |
| 3. József Csatári | HUN | — | 2 | 7 |
| 4. Vasil Todorov | BUL | 5 | 7.5 | |
| 5. Enache Panait | ROM | 5 | 9 | |
| 6. Ryszard Dlugosz | POL | 4 | 7 | |
| 7. Abolfazl Anvari | IRN | 4 | 9 | |
| 8. Julio Tamussin | ITA | 3 | 6.5 | |

In an inspired performance, 23-year-old Ivan Yarygin pinned all seven of his opponents. Only Baianmunkh was able to last more than three minutes with the Soviet strongman. Yarygin spent a total of only 17 minutes and eight seconds on the mat in his seven matches.

**1976 Montreal** C: 15, N: 15, D: 7.31.

| | | ROUND ELIMINATED | BAD PTS. | FINAL ROUND |
|---|---|---|---|---|
| 1. Ivan Yarygin | SOV | — | 2 | 1.5 |
| 2. Russell Hellickson | USA | — | 3.5 | 4 |
| 3. Dimo Kostov | BUL | — | 4.5 | 6.5 |
| 4. Petr Drozda | CZE | 5 | 8 | |
| 5. Khorloo Baianmunkh | MON | 4 | 5.5 | |
| 6. Kazuo Shimizu | JPN | 4 | 8 | |
| 7. Hans Stratz | GER | 3 | 7 | |
| 8. Daniel Vernik | ARG | 3 | 8 | |

In 1974 Yarygin was beaten in the European championships by Harald Büttner of East Germany. He was immediately removed from the Soviet team and replaced by veteran Vladimir Gulyutkin, who proceeded to win the 1974 world championship. But at the 1975 world championships, Büttner pinned Gulyutkin in 57 seconds and Yarygin was brought back after a year's absence from international competition. At the 1976 European championships, held in Leningrad three months before the Olympics, Yarygin was back to his old ways, overpowering each of his opponents. In Montreal, Yarygin faced Büttner in the very first round and defeated him 13–5. Yarygin's fifth and final victory was his most difficult, a 19–13 verdict over Russ Hellickson of Oregon, Wisconsin, who had moved up from Light Heavyweight to Heavyweight after losing five straight matches to Levan Tediashvili.

**1980 Moscow** C: 15, N: 15, D: 7.30.

| | | ROUND ELIMINATED | BAD PTS. | FINAL ROUND |
|---|---|---|---|---|
| 1. Ilya Mate | SOV | — | 2 | 1 |
| 2. Slavcho Chervenkov | BUL | — | 3 | 3.5 |
| 3. Július Strnisko | CZE | — | 4 | 7.5 |
| 4. Harald Büttner | GDR | 5 | 6.5 | |
| 5. Tomasz Busse | POL | 5 | 7 | |
| 6. Vasile Puşcaşu | ROM | 4 | 6 | |
| 7. Barbaro Morgan | CUB | 3 | 7.5 | |
| 8. Khorloo Baianmunkh | MON | 3 | 8 | |

**1984 Los Angeles-Anaheim** C: 11, N: 11, D: 8.11.

| | | FINAL MATCH | |
|---|---|---|---|
| 1. Lou Banach | USA | Fall | 1:01 |
| 2. Joseph Atiyeh | SYR | | |
| 3. Vasile Puşcaşu | ROM | 4–3 | 6:00 |
| 4. Hayri Sezgin | TUR | | |
| 5. Tamon Honda | JPN | Injury | |
| 6. Georgios Pikilidis | GRE | | |
| 7. Kartar Singh Dhillon | IND | | |
| 8. Wayne Brightwell | CAN | | |

Lou Banach, twin brother of light-heavyweight gold medalist Ed Banach, pinned four of his five opponents, all within two minutes. Only Wayne Brightwell lasted the full six minutes. Joseph Atiyeh, a student at Louisiana State University, was the first representative of Syria ever to win an Olympic medal.

**1988 Seoul** C: 22, N: 22, D: 9.30.

| | | FINAL MATCH | |
|---|---|---|---|
| 1. Vasile Puşcaşu | ROM | 1–0 | 6:00 |
| 2. Leri Khabelov | SOV | | |
| 3. William Scherr | USA | Fall | 3:31 |
| 4. Uwe Neupert | GDR | | |
| 5. Georgi Karaduchev | BUL | Fall | 1:32 |
| 6. Bold Javhlantugs | MON | | |
| 7. Noel Loban | GBR | Injury | |
| 8. Joe Byung-eun | KOR | | |

Puşcaşu, competing in his third Olympics at the age of 32, upset two-time world champion Khabelov by engineering a single-leg takedown with 19 seconds left in regulation time.

# SUPER HEAVYWEIGHT
## (Heavyweight 1904—1968)

A maximum weight limit—286 lbs.—was imposed for the first time at the 1988 Olympics.

**1896–1900** not held

**1904 St. Louis** T: 5, N: 1, D: 10.15.
1. Bernhuff Hansen    USA
2. Frank Kungler    USA
3. Fred Warmbold    USA

Hansen, a representative of the Norwegian Turnverein of Brooklyn, needed only 7:30 to pin his three opponents. In 1904 anyone over 158 pounds was considered a heavyweight. Currently, a 158-pound wrestler would compete in the Welterweight division.

**1906** not held

**1908 London** C: 11, N: 3, D: 7.23.
1. George Con O'Kelly    GBR/IRL
2. Jacob Gundersen    NOR
3. Edmond Barrett    GBR/IRL
4. E.E. Nixon    GBR
5. L. Bruce    GBR

Shortly before the Olympic Games, Barrett had defeated O'Kelly for the British Heavyweight championship. But at the Olympics the 221-pound O'Kelly came up against Barrett in the third round and pinned him after 2:14. Gundersen put up a tougher battle, and it took O'Kelly 17:02 to keep him on the mat for the required two falls.

**1912** not held

**1920 Antwerp** C: 8, N: 5, D: 8.21.
1. Robert Roth    SWI
2. Nathan Pendleton    USA
3. Frederick Meyer    USA
3. Ernst Nilsson    SWE

**1924 Paris** C: 12, N: 6, D: 7.14.
1. Harry Steel    USA
2. Henri Wernli    SWI
3. Andrew McDonald    GBR
4. Ernst Nilsson    SWE
5. Johan Richthoff    SWE
6. Edmond Dame    FRA

**1928 Amsterdam** C: 7, N: 7, D: 8.1.
1. Johan Richthoff    SWE
2. Aukusti Sihvola    FIN
3. Edmond Dame    FRA
4. Edward George    USA
5. Henri Wernli    SWI

Edward "Don" George later became a professional wrestling champion.

**1932 Los Angeles** C: 3, N: 3, D: 8.3.

| | | BAD PTS. |
|---|---|---|
| 1. Johan Richthoff | SWE | 2 |
| 2. John Riley | USA | 3 |
| 3. Nikolaus Hirschl | AUT | 6 |

Richthoff was 34 years old when he successfully defended his Olympic title.

**1936 Berlin** C: 11, N: 11, D: 8.4.

| | | ROUND ELIMINATED | BAD PTS. |
|---|---|---|---|
| 1. Kristjan Palusalu | EST | — | 2 |
| 2. Josef Klapuch | CZE | 4 | 4 |
| 3. Hjalmar Nyström | FIN | 5 | 5 |
| 4. Nils Åkerlindh | SWE | 4 | 4 |
| 5. Robert Herland | FRA | 4 | 6 |
| 6. Werner Bürki | SWI | 4 | 7 |
| 7. Georg Gehring | GER | 3 | 5 |
| 8. George Chiga | CAN | 3 | 6 |

The 27-year-old Palusalu, one of the quiet heroes of the Berlin Games, achieved a rare double by winning the Heavyweight title in both freestyle and Greco-Roman.

**1948 London** C: 9, N: 9, D. 7.31.

| | | ROUND ELIMINATED | BAD PTS. | FINAL ROUND |
|---|---|---|---|---|
| 1. Gyula Bóbis | HUN | — | 2 | 0 |
| 2. Bertil Antonsson | SWE | — | 3 | 2 |
| 3. Joseph Armstrong | AUS | — | 4 | 6 |
| 4. Sadik Esen | TUR | 4 | 7 | |
| 5. Josef Ružička | CZE | 3 | 5 | |
| 5. Abolghasem Sakhdari | IRN | 3 | 5 | |
| 7. Richard Hutton | USA | 3 | 6 | |

Bóbis began wrestling as a flyweight and kept moving up in division as he grew, until, at the age of 38, he won the Olympic gold medal as a heavyweight.

**1952 Helsinki** C: 13, N: 13, D: 7.23.

| | | ROUND ELIMINATED | BAD PTS. | FINAL ROUND |
|---|---|---|---|---|
| 1. Arsen Mekokishvili | SOV | — | 2 | 2 |
| 2. Bertil Antonsson | SWE | — | 2 | 3 |
| 3. Kenneth Richmond | GBR | — | 4 | 6 |
| 4. Irfan Atan | TUR | 4 | 5 | |
| 5. William Kerslake | USA | 4 | 6 | |
| 6. Taisto Kangasniemi | FIN | 4 | 6 | |
| 7. Natale Vecchi | ITA | 4 | 7 | |
| 7. Willi Waltner | GER | 4 | 7 | |

When Ken Richmond entered the ring he was one of the most recognized men in the world, even though no one knew his name. Richmond's muscular body was famous because he was the one who struck the gong at the beginning of J. Arthur Rank films. Richmond almost pinned Mekokishvili in the second minute of their third-round bout, but the 256-pound Georgian broke loose and regained the offensive to win a split decision. The following day Mekokishvili won another split decision from Bertil Antonsson to secure the gold medal.

**1956 Melbourne** C: 11, N: 11, D: 12.1.

| | | ROUND ELIMINATED | BAD PTS. | FINAL ROUND |
|---|---|---|---|---|
| 1. Hamit Kaplan | TUR | — | 1 | 2 |
| 2. Yusein Mehmedov | BUL | — | 3 | 3 |
| 3. Taisto Kangasniemi | FIN | — | 3 | 6 |
| 4. Ray Mitchell | AUS | 4 | 7 | |
| 4. Kenneth Richmond | GBR | 4 | 7 | |
| 6. Ivan Vykhristyuk | SOV | 3 | 5 | |
| 7. William Kerslake | USA | 3 | 6 | |

**1960 Rome** C: 17, N: 17, D: 9.6.

| | | ROUND ELIMINATED | BAD PTS. | FINAL ROUND |
|---|---|---|---|---|
| 1. Wilfried Dietrich | GER | — | 1 | 2 |
| 2. Hamit Kaplan | TUR | — | 5 | 4 |
| 3. Savkus Dzarassov | SOV | — | 2 | 6 |
| 4. Pietro Marascalchi | ITA | 5 | 8 | |
| 5. Lyutvi Ahmedov | BUL | 4 | 6 | |
| 5. János Reznák | HUN | 4 | 6 | |
| 7. Bertil Antonsson | SWE | 4 | 7 | |
| 8. William Kerslake | USA | 4 | 8 | |

Dietrich won Greco-Roman silver medals in 1956 and 1960, but his only gold came in freestyle wrestling, after he held defending champion Hamit Kaplan to a draw in the final match.

**1964 Tokyo** C: 13, N: 13, D: 10.14.

| | | ROUND ELIMINATED | BAD PTS. | FINAL ROUND AND 3RD PLACE |
|---|---|---|---|---|
| 1. Aleksandr Ivanitsky | SOV | — | 2 | 2 |
| 2. Lyutvi Ahmedov | BUL | — | 3 | 2 |
| 3. Hamit Kaplan | TUR | 4 | 7 | 2 |
| 4. Bohumil Kubat | CZE | 4 | 7 | 2 |
| 5. Denis McNamara | GBR | 4 | 7 | 8 |
| 6. Ştefan Ştîngu | ROM | 4 | 8 | |
| 7. Wilfried Dietrich | GER | 3 | 8 | |
| 7. Larry Kristoff | USA | 3 | 6 | |
| 7. Masanori Saito | JPN | 3 | 6 | |

Thirty-one-year-old Hamit Kaplan of Amasya, Anatolia, completed his set of Olympic medals by winning the bronze.

**1968 Mexico City** C: 15, N: 15, D: 10.20.

| | | ROUND ELIMINATED | BAD PTS. | FINAL ROUND |
|---|---|---|---|---|
| 1. Aleksandr Medved | SOV | — | 1 | 1 |
| 2. Osman Duraliev | BUL | — | 4 | 3 |
| 3. Wilfried Dietrich | GER | — | 5 | 8 |
| 4. Ştefan Ştîngu | ROM | 5 | 6 | |
| 5. Larry Kristoff | USA | 4 | 6 | |
| 6. Abolfazl Anvari | IRN | 4 | 9 | |
| 7. Erdeneotchir Elziisaihan | MON | 4 | 9 | |
| 8. Raymond Uytterheaghe | FRA | 3 | 9 | |

Dietrich won his fifth Olympic medal (one gold, two silver, two bronze) at the age of 35.

**1972 Munich** C: 13, N: 13, D: 8.31.

| | | ROUND ELIMINATED | BAD PTS. | FINAL ROUND |
|---|---|---|---|---|
| 1. Aleksandr Medved | SOV | — | 2 | 1 |
| 2. Osman Duraliev | BUL | — | 4 | 3 |
| 3. Chris Taylor | USA | 5 | 6 | |
| 4. Eskandar Filabi | IRN | 5 | 8.5 | |
| 5. Wilfried Dietrich | GER | 4 | 6 | |
| 6. Peter Germer | GDR | 4 | 8 | |
| 7. Ştefan Ştîngu | ROM | 4 | 8.5 | |
| 8. Stanislaw Makowiecki | POL | 3 | 7.5 | |

The biggest confrontation of the 1972 tournament came in the very first round, when two-time Olympic champion Aleksandr Medved of Minsk met 6-foot 5-inch, 412-pound Chris Taylor of Dowagiac, Michigan. Medved had beaten Taylor three times, but this time they fought to a standoff. The 231-pound Ukrainian was awarded a controversial decision when the Turkish referee, Umit Demirag, penalized Taylor for passivity. This evident injustice led to Demirag's dismissal as an Olympic referee, although the judgment against Taylor was allowed to stand. Both Medved and Taylor won the rest of their bouts. Medved became the only freestyle wrestler to win gold medals at three different Olympics.

A nasty incident took place in the third-round match between Giyasettin Yilmaz of Turkey and Bulgarian veteran Osman Duraliev. The two men collided in the third minute, and Yilmaz came away with a bleeding nose. Enraged, he refused to go to his corner and was disqualified. Then he went berserk, shouting at the referee, chasing Duraliev, and tearing apart his own dressing room. Yilmaz was finally subdued by 1968 Light Heavyweight gold medalist Ahmet Ayik.

**1976 Montreal** C: 15, N: 15, D: 7.31.

| | | ROUND ELIMINATED | BAD PTS. | FINAL ROUND |
|---|---|---|---|---|
| 1. Soslan Andiev | SOV | — | 2 | 1 |
| 2. József Balla | HUN | — | 7 | 5 |
| 3. Ladislau Simon | ROM | — | 6 | 6 |
| 4. Roland Gehrke | GDR | 6 | 8 | |
| 5. Nikola Dinev | BUL | 5 | 6 | |
| 6. Yorihide Isogai | JPN | 4 | 7 | |
| 7. Eskandar Filabi | IRN | 4 | 8 | |
| 8. Mamadou Sakho | SEN | 4 | 8.5 | |

**1980 Moscow** C: 12, N: 12, D: 7.31.

| | | ROUND ELIMINATED | BAD PTS. | FINAL ROUND |
|---|---|---|---|---|
| 1. Soslan Andiev | SOV | — | 1 | 1 |
| 2. József Balla | HUN | — | 5 | 5 |
| 3. Adam Sandurski | POL | — | 0 | 6 |
| 4. Roland Gehrke | GDR | 4 | 7 | |
| 5. Andrei Ianko | ROM | 4 | 8 | |
| 6. Mamadou Sakho | SEN | 4 | 8.5 | |

| 7. Petur Ivanov | BUL | 3 | 7 |
|---|---|---|---|
| 8. Arturo Diaz | CUB | 3 | 8 |

Seven-foot, 297-pound Adam Sandurski demolished his first four opponents in 9:50 but then lost on points, 6–3, to defending champion Soslan Andiev of Ordzhenikidze, Georgia.

**1984 Los Angeles-Anaheim** C: 8, N: 8, D: 8.10.

| | | FINAL MATCH | |
|---|---|---|---|
| 1. Bruce Baumgartner | USA | 10–2 | 6:00 |
| 2. Bob Molle | CAN | | |
| 3. Ayhan Taskin | TUR | Fall | 1:44 |
| 4. Hassan El Hadad | EGY | | |
| 5. Mamadou Sakho | SEN | Injury | |
| 6. Vasile Andrei | ROM | | |
| 7. Koichi Ishimori | JPN | | |
| 8. Panayotis Pikilidis | GRE | | |

An amiable 264-pounder, Bruce Baumgartner of Haledon, New Jersey, was not seriously challenged in his three matches.

In a sport where competitors frequently have to go to great lengths to stay below the weight limit for their division, it is sometimes forgotten that super-heavyweights have to make a minimum weight. Harouna Niang of Mauritania had the unfortunate experience of travelling ten thousand miles to the Olympics and then being disqualified and prevented from competing because he weighed in at only 216 pounds.

**1988 Seoul** C: 14, N: 14, D: 10.1.

| | | FINAL MATCH | |
|---|---|---|---|
| 1. David Gobezhishvili | SOV | 3–1 | 6:00 |
| 2. Bruce Baumgartner | USA | | |
| 3. Andreas Schröder | GDR | Passivity | 4:21 |
| 4. László Klauz | HUN | | |
| 5. Atanas Atanassov | BUL | 8–3 | 6:00 |
| 6. Daniel Payne | CAN | | |
| 7. Adam Sandurski | POL | 7–5 | 6:00 |
| 8. Ralf Bremmer | GER | | |

David Gobezhishvili was world champion in 1985, but the following year Bruce Baumgartner defeated him three times. Stung by these losses, Soviet wrestling officials removed Gobezhishvili from the national team and replaced him with Aslan Khardartsev, who went on to win the 1987 world championship and the 1988 European championship. However, Gobezhishvili was allowed to represent the U.S.S.R. in the 1988 World Cup, where he defeated Baumgartner. Soviet coach Ivan Yarygin decided to let Gobezhishvili and Khardartsev wrestle without a time limit to determine who would go to the Olympics. Gobezhishvili finally won after almost a half hour. In Seoul, Gobezhishvili, who grew up in the tiny mountain village of Khuruti, in Soviet Georgia, scored his first point against Baumgartner only 17 seconds into the final match. He added two more points in the second period before giving up a single point with 10 seconds left.

# GRECO-ROMAN WRESTLING

| Light Flyweight | Middleweight |
|---|---|
| Flyweight | Light Heavyweight |
| Bantamweight | Heavyweight |
| Featherweight | Super Heavyweight |
| Lightweight | Discontinued Event |
| Welterweight | |

In Greco-Roman wrestling the use of the legs is prohibited, and no holds may be made below the hips. The system of scoring is the same as in freestyle wrestling.

## LIGHT FLYWEIGHT

### (48 kg—106 lbs)

**1896–1968** not held

**1972 Munich** C: 20, N: 20, D: 9.10.

| | | | ROUND ELIMINATED | DAD PTS. | FINAL ROUND |
|---|---|---|---|---|---|
| 1. | Gheorghe Berceanu | ROM | — | 1 | 1 |
| 2. | Rahim Aliabadi | IRN | — | 5 | 3 |
| 3. | Stefan Angelov | BUL | — | 3.5 | 8 |
| 4. | Raimo Hirvonen | FIN | 5 | 6 | |
| 5. | Kazuharu Ishida | JPN | 5 | 7 | |
| 6. | Lorenzo Calafiore | ITA | 5 | 8 | |
| 7. | Bernd Drechsel | GDR | 4 | 7 | |
| 8. | Günter Maas | GER | 3 | 6.5 | |

**1976 Montreal** C: 15, N: 15, D: 7.24.

| | | | ROUND ELIMINATED | BAD PTS. | FINAL ROUND |
|---|---|---|---|---|---|
| 1. | Alexei Shumakov | SOV | — | 0 | 2 |
| 2. | Gheorghe Berceanu | ROM | — | 2 | 4 |
| 3. | Stefan Angelov | BUL | — | 3 | 6 |
| 4. | Yoshite Moriwaki | JPN | 5 | 8 | |
| 5. | Dietmar Hinz | GDR | 4 | 6 | |
| 6. | Mitchell Kawasaki | CAN | 4 | 7 | |
| 7. | Salin Bora | TUR | 4 | 7 | |
| 8. | Michael Farina | USA | 3 | 8 | |
| 8. | Rashid Mohammadzadé | IRN | 3 | 8 | |

In the final round Shumakov outpointed Angelov 5–4 and Berceanu 10–6.

**1980 Moscow** C: 10, N: 10, D: 7.22.

| | | | ROUND ELIMINATED | BAD PTS. | FINAL ROUND |
|---|---|---|---|---|---|
| 1. | Zaksylik Ushkempirov | SOV | — | 3.5 | 1.5 |
| 2. | Constantin Alexandru | ROM | — | 6 | 4 |
| 3. | Ferenc Seres | HUN | — | 7 | 6.5 |
| 4. | Pavel Hristov | BUL | 5 | 7.5 | |
| 5. | Reijo Haaparanta | FIN | 4 | 9 | |
| 6. | Alfredo Olvera | MEX | 3 | 7.5 | |
| 7 | Vincenzo Maenza | ITA | 2 | 6.5 | |
| 8. | Roman Klerpacz | POL | 2 | 7 | |

**1984 Los Angeles-Anaheim** C: 12, N: 12, D: 8.1.

| | | | FINAL MATCH | |
|---|---|---|---|---|
| 1. | Vincenzo Maenza | ITA | 12–0 | 1:59 |
| 2. | Markus Scherer | GER | | |
| 3. | Ikuzo Saito | JPN | 7–5 | 6:00 |
| 4. | Salih Bora | TUR | | |
| 5. | Kent Andersson | SWE | 10–3 | 6:00 |
| 6. | Jun Dae-je | KOR | | |
| 7. | Li Haisheng | CHN | | |
| 8. | Lars Ronningen | NOR | | |

Twenty-two-year-old Vincenzo Maenza of Faenza outscored his four opponents 31–0.

**1988 Seoul** C: 15, N: 15, D: 9.20.

| | | | FINAL MATCH | |
|---|---|---|---|---|
| 1. | Vincenzo Maenza | ITA | 3–0 | 6:00 |
| 2. | Andrzej Glab | POL | | |
| 3. | Bratan Tzenov | BUL | Passivity | 7:28 |
| 4. | Magyatdin Allakhverdyev | SOV | | |
| 5. | Khaled Alfaraj | SYR | 16–6 | 6:00 |
| 6. | Markus Scherer | GER | | |
| 7. | Yang Zhizong | CHN | Injury | |
| 8. | Kwon Duk-yong | KOR | | |

Maenza proved that his 1984 victory over a boycott-depleted field was no fluke by earning an emotional repeat victory in Seoul. He reached the final by defeating Tzenov 4–3 after 42 seconds of sudden death overtime.

## FLYWEIGHT
### (52 kg—114½ lbs)

**1896–1936** not held

**1948 London** C: 13, N: 13, D: 8.6.

|  |  | ROUND ELIMINATED | BAD PTS. | FINAL ROUND |
|---|---|---|---|---|
| 1. Pietro Lombardi | ITA | — | 3 | 1 |
| 2. Kenan Olcay | TUR | — | 3 | 3 |
| 3. Reino Kangasmaki | FIN | 5 | 6 |  |
| 4. Malte Möller | SWE | 5 | 6 |  |
| 5. Gyula Szilágyi | HUN | 5 | 5 |  |
| 6. Fridtjof Clausen | NOR | 4 | 7 |  |
| 7. Mohamed Abd El Al | EGY | 3 | 6 |  |
| 7. M. Varela | ARG | 3 | 6 |  |

**1952 Helsinki** C: 17, N: 17, D: 7.27.

|  |  | ROUND ELIMINATED | BAD PTS. | FINAL ROUND |
|---|---|---|---|---|
| 1. Boris Gurevitch | SOV | — | 3 | 2 |
| 2. Ignazio Fabra | ITA | — | 3 | 4 |
| 3. Leo Honkala | FIN | — | 2 | 6 |
| 4. Heinrich Weber | GER | 4 | 5 |  |
| 5. Mahmoud Omar Fawzy | EGY | 4 | 6 |  |
| 5. Bengt Johansson | SWE | 4 | 6 |  |
| 7. Maurice Mewis | BEL | 4 | 7 |  |
| 7. Borivoje Vukov | YUG | 4 | 7 |  |

**1956 Melbourne** C: 11, N: 11, D: 12.6.

|  |  | ROUND ELIMINATED | BAD PTS. | FINAL ROUND |
|---|---|---|---|---|
| 1. Nikolai Solovyov | SOV | — | 4 | 3 |
| 2. Ignazio Fabra | ITA | — | 4 | 4 |
| 3. Durum Ali Egribaş | TUR | — | 4 | 4 |
| 4. Dumitru Pirvulescu | ROM | 4 | 7 |  |
| 5. István Baranya | HUN | 3 | 5 |  |
| 5. Borivoje Vukov | YUG | 3 | 5 |  |
| 7. Maurice Mewis | BEL | 3 | 6 |  |

**1960 Rome** C: 18, N: 18, D: 8.31.

|  |  | ROUND ELIMINATED | BAD PTS. |
|---|---|---|---|
| 1. Dumitru Pirvulescu | ROM | — | 5 |
| 2. Osman Sayed | UAR | 5 | 6 |
| 3. Mohammad Paziraii | IRN | 5 | 6 |
| 4. Takashi Hirata | JPN | 5 | 7 |
| 5. Ignazio Fabra | ITA | 5 | 8 |
| 5. Ivan Kochergin | SOV | 5 | 8 |
| 7. Borivoje Vukov | YUG | 4 | 6 |
| 8. Bengt Frandfors | SWE | 4 | 7 |

**1964 Tokyo** C: 18, N: 18, D: 10.19.

|  |  | ROUND ELIMINATED | BAD PTS. | FINAL ROUND |
|---|---|---|---|---|
| 1. Tsutomu Hanahara | JPN | — | 3 | 1 |
| 2. Angel Kerezov | BUL | — | 4 | 4 |
| 3. Dumitru Pirvulescu | ROM | — | 2 | 7 |
| 4. Ignazio Fabra | ITA | 4 | 6 |  |
| 4. Rolf Lacour | GER | 4 | 6 |  |
| 4. Maurice Mewis | BEL | 4 | 6 |  |
| 4. J. Richard Wilson | USA | 4 | 6 |  |
| 8. Burhan Bozkurt | TUR | 3 | 6 |  |
| 8. Vasilios Ganotis | GRE | 3 | 6 |  |
| 8. Shin Sang-shik | KOR | 3 | 6 |  |

**1968 Mexico City** C: 24, N: 24, D: 10.26.

|  |  | ROUND ELIMINATED | BAD PTS. |
|---|---|---|---|
| 1. Peter Kirov | BUL | — | 5 |
| 2. Vladimir Bakulin | SOV | 6 | 6 |
| 3. Miroslav Zeman | CZE | 6 | 8 |
| 4. Imre Alker | HUN | 6 | 8.5 |
| 5. Rolf Lacour | GER | 5 | 6 |
| 6. Jussi Vesterinen | FIN | 5 | 7.5 |
| 7. Enrique Jimenez | MEX | 4 | 6 |
| 8. Metin Cikmaz | TUR | 4 | 7 |
| 8. Shin Sang-shik | KOR | 4 | 7 |

**1972 Munich** C: 22, N: 22, D: 9.10.

|  |  | ROUND ELIMINATED | BAD PTS. | FINAL ROUND |
|---|---|---|---|---|
| 1. Peter Kirov | BUL | — | 2 | 4 |
| 2. Koichiro Hirayama | JPN | — | 3 | 5 |
| 3. Giuseppe Bognanni | ITA | — | 5 | 7 |
| 4. József Doncsecz | HUN | 5 | 8 |  |
| 4. Jan Michalik | POL | 5 | 8 |  |
| 4. Miroslav Zeman | CZE | 5 | 8 |  |
| 7. Vassilios Ganotis | GRE | 4 | 6 |  |
| 8. Jamsran Munkhotchir | MON | 4 | 8 |  |

**1976 Montreal** C: 17, N: 17, D: 7.24.

|  |  | ROUND ELIMINATED | BAD PTS. | FINAL ROUND |
|---|---|---|---|---|
| 1. Vitaly Konstantinov | SOV | — | 3 | 4 |
| 2. Nicu Ginga | ROM | — | 5.5 | 5 |
| 3. Koichiro Hirayama | JPN | — | 8 | 5 |
| 4. Rolf Krauss | GER | 5 | 8.5 |  |
| 5. Lajos Rácz | HUN | 4 | 6 |  |
| 6. Moradali Shirani | IRN | 4 | 7 |  |
| 7. Antonio Caltabiano | ITA | 4 | 7.5 |  |
| 8. Baek Seung-hyun | KOR | 4 | 9 |  |

**1980 Moscow** C: 10, N: 10, D: 7.23.

|  |  | ROUND ELIMINATED | BAD PTS. | FINAL ROUND |
|---|---|---|---|---|
| 1. Vakhtang Blagidze | SOV | — | 1 | 1 |
| 2. Lajos Rácz | HUN | — | 4 | 5 |
| 3. Mladen Mladenov | BUL | — | 5 | 6 |
| 4. Nicu Ginga | ROM | 4 | 8 |  |
| 5. Antonín Jelínek | CZE | 4 | 8 |  |
| 6. Stanislaw Wróblewski | POL | 3 | 7 |  |
| 7. Taisto Halonen | FIN | 2 | 7 |  |
| 8. Abdulnasser Eloulabi | SYR | 2 | 8 |  |

Blagidze defeated Rácz, 19–1, in the final match.

**1984 Los Angeles-Anaheim** C: 12, N: 12, D: 8.2.

| | | | FINAL MATCH | |
|---|---|---|---|---|
| 1. | Atsuji Miyahara | JPN | 9–4 | 6:00 |
| 2. | Daniel Aceves | MEX | | |
| 3. | Bang Dae-du | KOR | 13–1 | 3:46 |
| 4. | Hu Richa | CHN | | |
| 5. | Jon Ronningen | NOR | 14–0 | 2:54 |
| 6. | Taisto Halonen | FIN | | |
| 7. | Erol Kemah | TUR | | |
| 8. | Mihai Cismasu | ROM | | |

**1988 Seoul** C: 21, N: 21, D: 9.21.

| | | | FINAL MATCH | |
|---|---|---|---|---|
| 1. | Jon Ronningen | NOR | 12–7 | 6:00 |
| 2. | Atsuji Miyahara | JPN | | |
| 3. | Lee Jae-suk | KOR | 4–3 | 6:00 |
| 4. | Aleksandr Ignatenko | SOV | | |
| 5. | Roman Kierpacz | POL | Passivity | 3:29 |
| 6. | Tibor Jankovics | CZE | | |
| 7. | Hristo Fliev | BUL | 9–3 | 6:00 |
| 8. | Peter Stjernberg | SWE | | |

# BANTAMWEIGHT

## (57 kg—125½ lbs)

**1896–1920** not held

**1924 Paris** C: 25, N: 15, D: 7.10.
*(58 kg—128 lbs)*

1. Eduard Pütsep — EST
2. Anselm Ahlfors — FIN
3. Väinö Ikonen — FIN
4. Sigfrid Hansson — SWE
5. Adolf Herschmann — AUT
6. Ragnvald Olsen — NOR
7. József Tasnádi — HUN
8. Armand Magyar — HUN

**1928 Amsterdam** C: 19, N: 19, D: 8.5.
*(58 kg—128 lbs)*

1. Kurt Leucht — GER
2. Jindrich Maudr — CZE
3. Giovanni Gozzi — ITA
4. Oscar Lindelöf — SWE
5. Ödön Zombori — HUN
6. Eduard Pütsep — EST
7. Herman Andersen — DEN
8. Anselm Ahlfors — FIN

**1932 Los Angeles** C: 7, N: 7, D: 8.7.
*(56 kg—123½ lbs)*

1. Jakob Brendel — GER
2. Marcello Nizzola — ITA
3. Louis François — FRA
4. Herman Tuvesson — SWE

**1936 Berlin** C: 18, N: 18, D: 8.9.
*(56 kg—123½ lbs)*

| | | | ROUND ELIMINATED | BAD PTS. | FINAL ROUND |
|---|---|---|---|---|---|
| 1. | Márton Lörincz | HUN | — | 3 | 1 |
| 2. | Egon Svensson | SWE | — | 0 | 3 |
| 3. | Jakob Brendel | GER | 5 | 5 | |
| 4. | Väinö Perttunen | FIN | 5 | 5 | |
| 5. | Iosef Tözer | ROM | 5 | 6 | |
| 6. | Evald Sikk | EST | 4 | 5 | |
| 7. | Robert Voigt | DEN | 4 | 7 | |
| 8. | Dante Bertoli | ITA | 4 | 7 | |

**1948 London** C: 13, N: 13, D: 8.6.

| | | | ROUND ELIMINATED | BAD PTS. | FINAL ROUND |
|---|---|---|---|---|---|
| 1. | Kurt Pettersén | SWE | — | 4 | 1 |
| 2. | Ali Mahmoud Hassan | EGY | — | 2 | 3 |
| 3. | Halil Kaya | TUR | 5 | 6 | |
| 4. | Taisto Lempinen | FIN | 4 | 5 | |
| 5. | Elvidio Flamini | ARG | 4 | 6 | |
| 6. | Lajos Bencze | HUN | 3 | 5 | |
| 6. | Reidar Maerlie | NOR | 3 | 5 | |
| 8. | Nikolaos Biris | GRE | 3 | 0 | |

**1952 Helsinki** C: 17, N: 17, D: 7.27.

| | | | ROUND ELIMINATED | BAD PTS. | FINAL ROUND |
|---|---|---|---|---|---|
| 1. | Imre Hódos | HUN | — | 4 | 4 |
| 2. | Zakaria Chihab | LEB | — | 6 | 4 |
| 3. | Artem Teryan | SOV | — | 4 | 4 |
| 4. | Hubert Persson | SWE | 5 | 7 | |
| 5. | Reidar Maerlie | NOR | 4 | 5 | |
| 6. | Ferdinand Schmitz | GER | 4 | 6 | |
| 7. | Ion Popescu | ROM | 4 | 7 | |
| 8. | Pietro Lombardi | ITA | 3 | 5 | |

**1956 Melbourne** C: 28, N: 28, D: 8.31.

| | | | ROUND ELIMINATED | BAD PTS. | FINAL ROUND |
|---|---|---|---|---|---|
| 1. | Konstantin Vyrupayov | SOV | — | 4 | 4 |
| 2. | Edvin Westerby | SWE | — | 1 | 4 |
| 3. | Francisc Horvath | ROM | — | 4 | 4 |
| 4. | Imre Hódos | HUN | 4 | 5 | |
| 5. | Alfred Kämmerer | GER | 4 | 5 | |
| 6. | Dinko Petrov | BUL | 3 | 5 | |
| 7. | Adolfo Diaz | ARG | 3 | 6 | |

**1960 Rome** C: 28, N: 28, D: 8.31.

| | | | ROUND ELIMINATED | BAD PTS. | FINAL ROUND |
|---|---|---|---|---|---|
| 1. | Oleg Karavayev | SOV | — | 2 | 1 |
| 2. | Ion Cernea | ROM | — | 5 | 3 |
| 3. | Dinko Petrov | BUL | 5 | 6 | |
| 4. | Edvin Westerby | SWE | 5 | 6 | |
| 5. | Jiři Švec | CZE | 5 | 7 | |
| 5. | Yasar Ylmaz | TUR | 5 | 7 | |
| 7. | Masamitsu Ichiguchi | JPN | 5 | 8 | |
| 7. | Bernard Knitter | POL | 5 | 8 | |

**1964 Tokyo** C: 18, N: 18, D: 10.19.

| | | ROUND ELIMINATED | BAD PTS. |
|---|---|---|---|
| 1. Masamitsu Ichiguchi | JPN | — | 4 |
| 2. Vladlen Trostyansky | SOV | 5 | 6 |
| 3. Ion Cernea | ROM | 5 | 8 |
| 4. Jiři Švec | CZE | 5 | 8 |
| 5. Karmal Ali | UAR | 4 | 6 |
| 5. Tsviatko Pashkulev | BUL | 4 | 6 |
| 5. Fritz Stange | GER | 4 | 6 |
| 8. Unver Basergil | TUR | 4 | 7 |

**1968 Mexico City** C: 24, N: 24, D: 10.26.

| | | ROUND ELIMINATED | BAD PTS. | FINAL ROUND |
|---|---|---|---|---|
| 1. János Varga | HUN | — | 6 | — |
| 2. Ion Baciu | ROM | 6 | 7.5 | 4 |
| 3. Ivan Kochergin | SOV | 6 | 7.5 | 6.5 |
| 4. Othon Moschidis | GRE | 6 | 7.5 | 6.5 |
| 5. Koji Sakurama | JPN | 5 | 6.5 | |
| 6. Elsayad Ibrahim | UAR | 5 | 9 | |
| 6. Kaya Öczan | TUR | 5 | 9 | |
| 8. Risto Björlin | FIN | 4 | 6 | |

**1972 Munich** C: 30, N: 30, D: 9.10.

| | | ROUND ELIMINATED | BAD PTS. | FINAL ROUND |
|---|---|---|---|---|
| 1. Rustem Kazakov | SOV | — | 5 | 0 |
| 2. Hans-Jürgen Veil | GER | — | 4 | 4 |
| 3. Risto Björlin | FIN | 7 | 8 | |
| 4. János Varga | HUN | 7 | 9 | |
| 5. Hristo Traikov | BUL | 6 | 6 | |
| 6. Ion Baciu | ROM | 5 | 6 | |
| 7. Ikuei Yamamoto | JPN | 5 | 8.5 | |
| 8. Józef Lipień | POL | 4 | 8 | |

World champion Rustem Kazakov pinned local favorite Hans-Jürgen Veil in 2:58 to win the gold medal.

**1976 Montreal** C: 17, N: 17, D: 7.24.

| | | ROUND ELIMINATED | BAD PTS. | FINAL ROUND |
|---|---|---|---|---|
| 1. Pertti Ukkola | FIN | — | 4.5 | 2 |
| 2. Ivan Frgić | YUG | — | 6 | 3 |
| 3. Farhat Mustafin | SOV | — | 4.5 | 7 |
| 4. Yoshima Suga | JPN | 5 | 8 | |
| 5. Mihai Botila | ROM | 5 | 8 | |
| 6. Krasimir Stefanov | BUL | 4 | 6 | |
| 7. József Doncsecz | HUN | 4 | 7.5 | |
| 8. Josef Krysta | CZE | 4 | 8 | |

Ukkola earned his upset victory by barely outpointing Mustafin and Frgić with scores of 6–5 and 5–4.

**1980 Moscow** C: 13, N: 13, D: 7.24.

| | | ROUND ELIMINATED | BAD PTS. | FINAL ROUND |
|---|---|---|---|---|
| 1. Shamil Serikov | SOV | — | 1 | 1 |
| 2. Józef Lipień | POL | — | 6 | 7 |
| 3. Benni Ljungbeck | SWE | — | 5 | 8 |
| 4. Mihai Botila | ROM | 5 | 11.5 | |
| 5. Antonino Caltabiano | ITA | 4 | 7 | |
| 6. Josef Krysta | CZE | 4 | 7 | |
| 7. Gyula Molnár | HUN | 4 | 7 | |
| 8. Georgi Donev | BUL | 3 | 7 | |

Serikov outpointed Lipień 11–4 in the final match.

**1984 Los Angeles-Anaheim** C: 16, N: 16, D: 8.3.

| | | FINAL MATCH | |
|---|---|---|---|
| 1. Pasquale Passarelli | GER | 8–5 | 6:00 |
| 2. Masaki Eto | JPN | | |
| 3. Haralambos Holidis | GRE | 2–1 | 6:00 |
| 4. Nicolae Zamfir | ROM | | |
| 5. Frank Famiano | USA | Injury | |
| 6. Benni Ljungbeck | SWE | | |
| 7. Mehmets Erhat Karadag | TUR | | |
| 8. Park Byung-hyo | KOR | | |

Passarelli, a 27-year-old insurance agent, spent the last 96 seconds of his final match with world champion Eto in a back body arch to avoid being pinned.

**1988 Seoul** C: 21, N: 21, D: 9.22.

| | | FINAL MATCH | |
|---|---|---|---|
| 1. András Sike | HUN | Injury | 3:38 |
| 2. Stoyan Balov | BUL | | |
| 3. Haralambos Holidis | GRE | 6–1 | 6:00 |
| 4. Yang Changling | CHN | | |
| 5. Huh Byung-ho | KOR | Fall | 1:44 |
| 6. Ghazi Salah | IRQ | | |
| 7. Aleksandr Chestakov | SOV | Forfeit | |
| 8. Rifat Yildiz | GER | | |

# FEATHERWEIGHT
(62 kg—136½ lbs)

**1896–1908** not held

**1912 Stockholm** C: 38, N: 13, D: 7.12.
*(60 kg—132½ lbs)*
1. Kaarlo Koskelo FIN
2. Georg Gerstäcker GER
3. Otto Lasanen FIN
4. Kaarlo Leivonen FIN
5. Erik Öberg SWE

**1920 Antwerp** C: 21, N: 10, D: 8.26.
*(60 kg—132½ lbs)*
1. Oskar Friman FIN
2. Heikki Kähkönen FIN
3. Fritiof Svensson SWE
4. Alexandre Boumans BEL
5. Aage Tergersen DEN
6. Josef Beranek CZE

**1924 Paris** C: 27, N: 15, D: 7.10.
*(60 kg—132½ lbs)*
1. Kaarlo "Kalle" Anttila FIN
2. Aleksanteri Toivola FIN

3. Erik Malmberg    SWE
4. Arthur Nord    NOR
5. Fritiof Svensson    SWE
6. M. Capron    FRA
6. Ödön Radvány    HUN

Anttila was 36 years old when he won his second Olympic gold medal. In Antwerp in 1920 he had finished first in the freestyle Lightweight division.

**1928 Amsterdam** C: 20, N: 20, D: 8.5.
*(60 kg—132½ lbs)*
1. Voldemar Väli    EST
2. Erik Malmberg    SWE
3. Giacomo Quaglia    ITA
4. Károly Kárpáti    HUN
5. Ernst Steinig    GER
6. Aage Meier (DEN), Arakan Saim (TUR), Aleksanteri Toivola (FIN)

**1932 Los Angeles** C: 8, N: 8, D: 8.7.
*(61 kg—134½ lbs)*
1. Giovanni Gozzi    ITA
2. Wolfgang Ehrl    GER
3. Lauri Koskela    FIN
4. Jindřich Maudr    CZE
5. Kiyoshi Kase    JPN

**1936 Berlin** C: 19, N: 19, D: 8.9.
*(61 kg—104½ lbs)*

| | | ROUND ELIMINATED | BAD PTS. |
|---|---|---|---|
| 1. Yaşar Erkan | TUR | — | 4 |
| 2. Aarne Reini | FIN | 7 | 5 |
| 3. Einar Karlsson | SWE | 7 | 5 |
| 4. Sebastian Hering | GER | 5 | 5 |
| 5. Krishjanis Kundsinsh | LAT | 5 | 6 |
| 6. Valentino Borgia | ITA | 4 | 5 |
| 7. Henryk Ślązak | POL | 4 | 6 |
| 8. Gyula Móri | HUN | 4 | 6 |

**1948 London** C: 17, N: 17, D: 8.6.
*(61 kg—134½ lbs)*

| | | ROUND ELIMINATED | BAD PTS. | FINAL ROUND |
|---|---|---|---|---|
| 1. Mehmet Oktav | TUR | — | 3 | 0 |
| 2. Olle Anderberg | SWE | — | 3 | 3 |
| 3. Ferenc Tóth | HUN | 6 | 6 | |
| 4. Georg Weidner | AUT | 5 | 5 | |
| 5. Luigi Campanella | ITA | 5 | 6 | |
| 6. Sayed Kandil | EGY | 4 | 7 | |
| 6. Egil Solsvik | NOR | 4 | 7 | |
| 6. Safi Taha | LEB | 4 | 7 | |
| 6. Erkki Talosela | FIN | 4 | 7 | |

The decisive match took place in the third round, when Oktav threw Anderberg in 2:48.

**1952 Helsinki** C: 17, N: 17, D: 7.27.
*(61 kg—134½ lbs)*

| | | ROUND ELIMINATED | BAD PTS. | FINAL ROUND |
|---|---|---|---|---|
| 1. Yakov Punkin | SOV | — | 2 | 0 |
| 2. Imre Polyák | HUN | — | 3 | 4 |
| 3. Abdel Rashed | EGY | — | 5 | 6 |
| 4. Umberto Trippa | ITA | 4 | 5 | |
| 5. Bartholomäus Brötzner | AUT | 4 | 6 | |
| 6. Hasan Bozbey | TUR | 4 | 7 | |
| 7. Safi Taha | LEB | 3 | 3 | |
| 8. Ernest Gondzik | POL | 3 | 5 | |
| 8. Erkki Talosela | FIN | 3 | 5 | |

Punkin finished strongly, pinning Polyák in 1:26 and Rashad in 3:28.

**1956 Melbourne** C: 10, N: 10, D: 12.6.
*(61 kg—134½ lbs)*

| | | ROUND ELIMINATED | BAD PTS. | FINAL ROUND |
|---|---|---|---|---|
| 1. Rauno Mäkinen | FIN | — | 4 | 4 |
| 2. Imre Polyák | HUN | — | 3 | 4 |
| 3. Roman Dzneladze | SOV | — | 4 | 4 |
| 4. Muzahir Sille | TUR | 4 | 6 | |
| 5. Gunnar Håkansson | SWE | 3 | 5 | |
| 6. Umberto Trippa | ITA | 3 | 7 | |
| 7. Ion Popescu | ROM | 3 | 7 | |

Mäkinen was the son of 1928 freestyle Bantamweight winner Kaarlo Mäkinen.

**1960 Rome** C: 25, N: 25, D: 8.31.
*(61 kg—134½ lbs)*

| | | ROUND ELIMINATED | BAD PTS. | FINAL ROUND |
|---|---|---|---|---|
| 1. Müzahir Sille | TUR | — | 5 | 1 |
| 2. Imre Polyák | HUN | — | 3 | 3 |
| 3. Konstantin Vyrupayev | SOV | 6 | 6 | |
| 4. Umberto Trippa | ITA | 6 | 6 | |
| 5. Mihai Schultz | ROM | 6 | 8 | |
| 6. Saiid Ebrahimian | IRN | 5 | 7 | |
| 6. Vojtech Tulli | CZE | 5 | 7 | |
| 8. Lee Allen | USA | 4 | 7 | |

**1964 Tokyo** C: 27, N: 27, D: 10.19.
*(63 kg—139 lbs)*

| | | ROUND ELIMINATED | BAD PTS. | FINAL ROUND |
|---|---|---|---|---|
| 1. Imre Polyák | HUN | — | 1 | 2 |
| 2. Roman Rurua | SOV | — | 4 | 2 |
| 3. Branislav Martinović | YUG | 5 | 4 | |
| 4. Ronald Finley | USA | 5 | 6 | |
| 4. Mostafa Mansour | UAR | 5 | 6 | |
| 6. Joseph Mewis | BEL | 4 | 6 | |
| 6. Rassoul Mirmalek | IRN | 4 | 6 | |
| 6. Koji Sakurama | JPN | 4 | 6 | |

After finishing second three straight times, Polyák finally won an Olympic gold medal.

**1968 Mexico City** C: 23, N: 23, D: 10.26.
**(63 kg—139 lbs)**

| | | ROUND ELIMINATED | BAD PTS. | FINAL ROUND |
|---|---|---|---|---|
| 1. Roman Rurua | SOV | — | 2 | 2 |
| 2. Hideo Fujimoto | JPN | — | 5 | 2 |
| 3. Simeon Popescu | ROM | 6 | 6.5 | |
| 4. Dimiter Galinchev | BUL | 6 | 8 | |
| 5. Hizir Alakoc | TUR | 5 | 6 | |
| 6. Martti Laakso | FIN | 4 | 6 | |
| 7. James Hazewinkel | USA | 4 | 8.5 | |
| 8. Lothar Schneider | GDR | 4 | 9 | |

**1972 Munich** C: 19, N: 19, D: 9.10.

| | | ROUND ELIMINATED | BAD PTS. |
|---|---|---|---|
| 1. Georgi Markov | BUL | — | 3 |
| 2. Heinz-Helmut Wehling | GDR | 6 | 6.5 |
| 3. Kazimierz Lipień | POL | 6 | 6.5 |
| 4. Hideo Fujimoto | JPN | 6 | 7.5 |
| 5. Djemal Megrelishvili | SOV | 6 | 8 |
| 6. Ion Păun | ROM | 5 | 7.5 |
| 7. Martti Laakso | FIN | 5 | 8 |
| 7. Stylianos Mygiakis | GRE | 5 | 8 |

**1976 Montreal** C: 17, N: 17, D: 7.24.

| | | ROUND ELIMINATED | BAD PTS. | FINAL ROUND |
|---|---|---|---|---|
| 1. Kazimierz Lipień | POL | — | 3.5 | 3.5 |
| 2. Nelson Davidian | SOV | — | 4 | 4 |
| 3. László Réczi | HUN | — | 5.5 | 4.5 |
| 4. Teruhiko Miyahara | JPN | 7 | 8 | |
| 5. Ion Păun | ROM | 6 | 8 | |
| 6. Pekka Hjelt | FIN | 4 | 7 | |
| 7. Stylianos Mygiakis | GRE | 4 | 8.5 | |
| 8. Stoyan Lazarov | BUL | 3 | 7 | |

Kazimierz Lipień won the world championship in 1973 and 1974, but in 1975 he lost a controversial decision to Nelson Davidian. The two met again in the sixth round of the Olympics in Montreal, with Davidian gaining another controversial victory, 10–6. In that match, Viktor Igumenov, the Soviet coach, was ordered to leave the competition area after he illegally shouted instructions to Davidian. Igumenov continued to yell orders, but from a greater distance. Lipień salvaged the gold medal anyway by outpointing Réczi 13–4, the nine-point margin reducing Lipień's bad marks for the bout from 1 to 0.5. Lipień's twin brother, Jozef, won a Bantamweight silver medal in 1980. At the 1975 world championships, the Poles were accused of substituting Jozef for Kazimierz in one match. Their accusers should have known better, since Jozef always parted his hair on the left side, while Kazimierz parted his on the right. At the post-tournament press conference in Montreal, Kazimierz, a 27-year-old plumber, advised aspiring wrestlers to abstain from smoking and drinking. "And no women," added bronze medalist László Réczi. But Lipień dis-

agreed. "That is taking sacrifices too far," he said, "women are good to wrestle with, too."

**1980 Moscow** C: 11, N: 11, D: 7.22.

| | | ROUND ELIMINATED | BAD PTS. | FINAL ROUND |
|---|---|---|---|---|
| 1. Stylianos Mygiakis | GRE | — | 6 | 2 |
| 2. István Tóth | HUN | — | 3 | 4 |
| 3. Boris Kramorenko | SOV | 5 | 7 | |
| 4. Ivan Frgić | YUG | 5 | 7 | |
| 5. Panayot Kirov | BUL | 4 | 9 | |
| 6. Kazimierz Lipień | POL | 3 | 6 | |
| 7. Radwan Karout | SYR | 3 | 8 | |
| 8. Michal Vejsada | CZE | 3 | 8 | |

Mygiakis was the first "Greco" ever to win a Greco-Roman gold medal in the Olympics.

**1984 Los Angeles-Anaheim** C: 20, N: 20, D: 8.1.

| | | FINAL MATCH | |
|---|---|---|---|
| 1. Kim Weon-kee | KOR | 3–3 | 6:00 |
| 2. Kent-Olle Johansson | SWE | | |
| 3. Hugo Dietsche | SWI | 8–4 | 6:00 |
| 4. Abdurrahim Kuzu | USA | | |
| 5. Douglas Yeats | CAN | 15–3 | 4:41 |
| 6. Salem Bekhit | EGY | | |
| 7. Bernd Gabriel | GER | | |
| 8. Seiichi Osanai | JPN | | |

**1988 Seoul** C: 17, N: 17, D: 9.20.

| | | FINAL MATCH | |
|---|---|---|---|
| 1. Kamandar Madzhidov | SOV | 6–2 | 6:00 |
| 2. Zhivko Vangelov | BUL | | |
| 3. An Dae-hyun | KOR | Passivity | 3:15 |
| 4. Jenö Bódi | HUN | | |
| 5. Peter Behl | GER | 5–1 | 6:00 |
| 6. Isaac Anderson | USA | | |
| 7. Gilles Jalabert | FRA | Injury | |
| 8. Hugo Dietsche | SWI | | |

# LIGHTWEIGHT
## (68 kg—150 lbs)

**1896–1904** not held

**1906 Athens** C: 12, N: 7, D: 5.1.
**(75 kg–165½ lbs)**

1. Rudolf Watzl        AUT
2. Karl Karlsen        DEN
3. Ferenc Holuban      HUN
4. René Dobrinovitz    GRE
4. Karel Halik         BOH
4. Alexander Wendrinsky AUT

**1908 London** C: 25, N: 10, D: 7.25.
**(66.6 kg—147 lbs)**

1. Enrico Porro        ITA
2. Nikolai Orlov       RUS
3. Arvid Lindén        FIN

4. Gunnar Persson    SWE
5. Gustaf Malmström (SWE), József Maróthy (HUN), Anders Moller (DEN), Ödön Radvány (HUN)

Porro, a 23-year-old Milanese sailor, was unbeaten in international competition. He was awarded a decision over Orlov after 50 minutes of very little action.

**1912 Stockholm** C: 48, N: 13, D: 7.13.
*(67.5 kg—149 lbs)*
1. Eemil Wäre       FIN
2. Gustaf Malmström  SWE
3. Edvin Matiasson   SWE
4. Ödön Radvány      HUN
5. Johan Nilsson     SWE
5. Volmar Vikström   FIN

Wäre pinned all five of his opponents, completing his feat by defeating Malmström after an epic 60-minute struggle.

**1920 Antwerp** C: 22, N: 14, D: 8.26.
*(67.5 kg—149 lbs)*
1. Eemil Wäre         FIN
2. Taavi Tamminen     FIN
3. Frithjof Andersen  NOR
4. Frits Janssens     BEL

**1924 Paris** C: 28, N: 18, D: 7.10.
*(67.5 kg—149 lbs)*
1. Oskar Friman        FIN
2. Lajos Keresztes     HUN
3. Kalle Westerlund    FIN
4. Albert Kusnets      EST
5. František Kratochvil CZE
6. Charles Frisenfeldt (DEN), Arne Gaupseth (NOR), Mihály Matura (HUN)

In 1920 Friman won the Featherweight title. Four years later in Paris, at the age of 31, he gained his second gold medal.

**1928 Amsterdam** C: 19, N: 19, D: 8.5.
*(67.5 kg—149 lbs)*
1. Lajos Keresztes     HUN
2. Eduard Sperling     GER
3. Edvard Westerlund   FIN
4. Tayare Yalaz        TUR
5. Vladimir Vávra      CZE
6. Walter Massop       HOL
7. Ryszard Błażyca     POL
7. Frits Janssens      BEL

Keresztes turned to wrestling on the advice of a doctor who prescribed the sport as a cure for "prolonged neurosis."

**1932 Los Angeles** C: 6, N: 6, D: 8.7.
*(66 kg—145½ lbs)*
1. Erik Malmberg       SWE
2. Abraham Kurland     DEN

3. Eduard Sperling     GER
4. Aarne Reini         FIN

With this victory the 35-year-old Malmberg completed his set of Olympic medals, having previously earned a Featherweight bronze in 1924 and silver in 1928.

**1936 Berlin** C: 18, N: 18, D: 8.9.
*(66 kg—145½ lbs)*

|    |    | ROUND ELIMINATED | BAD PTS. | FINAL ROUND |
|----|----|------------------|----------|-------------|
| 1. Lauri Koskela | FIN | — | 2 | 2 |
| 2. Josef Herda | CZE | — | 3 | 3 |
| 3. Voldemar Väli | EST | — | 2 | 5 |
| 4. Herbert Olofsson | SWE | 5 | 5 | |
| 5. Alberto Molfino | ITA | 4 | 6 | |
| 6. Arild Dahl | NOR | 4 | 7 | |
| 7. Zbigniew Szajewski | POL | 4 | 7 | |
| 8. Dragomir Borlovan | ROM | 3 | 5 | |

**1948 London** C: 17, N: 17, D: 8.6.
*(67 kg—147½ lbs)*

|    |    | ROUND ELIMINATED | BAD PTS. | 3RD PLACE |
|----|----|------------------|----------|-----------|
| 1. Gustav Freij | SWE | — | 2 | |
| 2. Aage Eriksen | NOR | 5 | 5 | |
| 3. Károly Ferencz | HUN | 5 | 6 | 1 |
| 4. Charil Damage | LEB | 5 | 6 | 2 |
| 5. Johannes Munnikes | HOL | 4 | 6 | |
| 6. Georgios Petmezas | GRE | 4 | 7 | |
| 6. Ahmet Senol | TUR | 4 | 7 | |
| 6. Eino Virtanen | FIN | 4 | 7 | |

**1952 Helsinki** C: 19, N: 19, D: 7.27.
*(67 kg—147½ lbs)*

|    |    | ROUND ELIMINATED | BAD PTS. | FINAL ROUND |
|----|----|------------------|----------|-------------|
| 1. Schazam Salin | SOV | — | 3 | 1 |
| 2. Gustav Freij | SWE | — | 3 | 3 |
| 3. Mikuláš Athanasov | CZE | — | 5 | 6 |
| 4. Gyula Tarr | HUN | 5 | 6 | |
| 5. Franco Benedetti | ITA | 4 | 7 | |
| 5. Dumitru Cuc | ROM | 4 | 7 | |
| 5. Kalle Haapasalmi | FIN | 4 | 7 | |
| 8. Kamel Hussein | EGY | 3 | 5 | |
| 8. Erich Schmidt | SAA | 3 | 5 | |

**1956 Melbourne** C: 10, N: 10, D: 12.6.
*(67 kg—147½ lbs)*

|    |    | ROUND ELIMINATED | BAD PTS. | FINAL ROUND |
|----|----|------------------|----------|-------------|
| 1. Kyösti Lehtonen | FIN | — | 1 | 1 |
| 2. Riza Dogan | TUR | — | 6 | 3 |
| 3. Gyula Tóth | HUN | — | 2 | 6 |
| 4. Bartholomäus Brötzner | AUT | 4 | 8 | |
| 5. Dimiter Yanchev | BUL | 4 | 9 | |
| 6. Dumitru Gheorghe | ROM | 3 | 7 | |

**1960 Rome** C: 23, N: 23, D: 8.31.
*(67 kg—147½ lbs)*

| | | ROUND ELIMINATED | BAD PTS. | FINAL ROUND |
|---|---|---|---|---|
| 1. Avtandil Koridze | SOV | — | 5 | 1 |
| 2. Branislav Martinovič | YUG | — | 4 | 3 |
| 3. Gustav Freij | SWE | 5 | 6 | |
| 4. Karel Matoušek | CZE | 5 | 6 | |
| — Dimitro Stoyanov (Dimiter Yanchev) | BUL | 5 | 8 | |
| 5. Dumitru Gheorghe | ROM | 4 | 7 | |
| 5. Ernest Gondzik | POL | 4 | 7 | |
| 5. Adil Güngör | TUR | 4 | 7 | |
| 5. Mitsuharu Kitamura | JPN | 4 | 7 | |
| 5. Kyösti Lehtonen | FIN | 4 | 7 | |
| 5. Jacques Pourtau | FRA | 4 | 7 | |

Charges of "fix" were hurled following a fifth round bout between Koridze and Dimiter Yanchev of Bulgaria, then known as Dimitro Stoyanov. Koridze needed to score a fall to force a final showdown with Martinovič. Anything less—a draw or even a points victory—would give the gold medal to the Yugoslav. After 11 minutes of inactivity, with only one minute left before the end of the bout, Koridze spoke a few words to Stoyanov and then threw him to the ground and pinned him. The Yugoslavs immediately lodged a protest. Stoyanov, who had originally been awarded fifth place, was disqualified from the tournament, but Koridze was not punished and went on to defeat Martinovič and to win the gold medal.

**1964 Tokyo** C: 19, N: 19, D: 10.19.
*(70 kg—154½ lbs)*

| | | ROUND ELIMINATED | BAD PTS. | 2ND PLACE |
|---|---|---|---|---|
| 1. Kazim Ayvaz | TUR | — | 5 | |
| 2. Valeriu Bularcă | ROM | 5 | 6 | 3 |
| 3. David Gvantseladze | SOV | 5 | 6 | 4 |
| 4. Tokuaki Fujita | JPN | 5 | 6 | 5 |
| 5. Stevan Horvat | YUG | 5 | 7 | |
| 6. Eero Tapio | FIN | 5 | 8 | |
| 7. Bror Jonsson | SWE | 4 | 6 | |
| 8. Ivan Ivanov | BUL | 4 | 7 | |

**1968 Mexico City** C: 26, N: 26, D: 10.26.
*(70 kg—154½ lbs)*

| | | ROUND ELIMINATED | BAD PTS. | FINAL ROUND |
|---|---|---|---|---|
| 1. Munji Mumemura | JPN | — | 5 | 3.5 |
| 2. Stevan Horvat | YUG | — | 5 | 5 |
| 3. Petros Galaktopoulos | GRE | — | 5 | 5.5 |
| 4. Klaus Rost | GER | 6 | 8 | |
| 5. Eero Tapio | FIN | 5 | 7.5 | |
| 6. Werner Holzer | USA | 5 | 8 | |
| 6. Gennady Sapunov | SOV | 5 | 8 | |
| 8. Antal Steer | HUN | 4 | 6 | |

**1972 Munich** C: 23, N: 23, D: 9.10.

| | | ROUND ELIMINATED | BAD PTS. |
|---|---|---|---|
| 1. Shamil Khisamutdinov | SOV | — | 2.5 |
| 2. Stoyan Apostolov | BUL | 6 | 5 |
| 3. Gian-Matteo Ranzi | ITA | 6 | 6 |
| 4. Manfred Schöndorfer | GER | 6 | 7.5 |
| 5. Takashi Tanoue | JPN | 5 | 6 |
| 6. Seyit Hisirli | TUR | 4 | 6 |
| 6. Antal Steer | HUN | 4 | 6 |
| 8. Sreten Damjanovic | YUG | 4 | 7.5 |

**1976 Munich** C: 21, N: 21, D: 7.24.

| | | ROUND ELIMINATED | BAD PTS. | FINAL ROUND |
|---|---|---|---|---|
| 1. Suren Nalbandyan | SOV | — | 3 | 2 |
| 2. Ştefan Rusu | ROM | — | 3 | 3 |
| 3. Heinz-Helmut Wehling | GDR | — | 8 | 7 |
| 4. Lars-Erik Skiöld | SWE | 6 | 9.5 | |
| 5. Andrzej Supron | POL | 5 | 8 | |
| 6. Manfred Schöndorfer | GER | 5 | 9 | |
| 7. Erol Mutlu | TUR | 4 | 6 | |
| 8. Markku Yli-Isotalo | FIN | 4 | 7 | |

The 20-year-old Nalbandyan gained a crucial 5–3 victory over Rusu in the fourth round and then outpointed Supron 7–4 and Wehling 12–9. In 1984, Nalbandyan was sentenced to three years in a labor camp for selling black-market alcohol.

**1980 Moscow** C: 15, N: 15, D: 7.24.

| | | ROUND ELIMINATED | BAD PTS. | FINAL ROUND |
|---|---|---|---|---|
| 1. Ştefan Rusu | ROM | — | 4 | 2 |
| 2. Andrzej Supron | POL | — | 1 | 3 |
| 3. Lars-Erik Skiöld | SWE | — | 1 | 7 |
| 4. Suren Nalbandyan | SOV | 5 | 8 | |
| 5. Buyandelger Bold | MON | 5 | 9 | |
| 6. Ivan Atanassov | BUL | 4 | 8 | |
| 7. Reinhard Hartmann | AUT | 4 | 8 | |
| 8. Károly Gaál | HUN | 3 | 7 | |

The cast of characters was almost the same as it was four years earlier. Nalbandyan was the first of the four favorites to be eliminated when he and Rusu were charged with a double disqualification after 7:09 of their fifth-round match. In the final round-robin Rusu outpointed Supron 3–2 and Skiöld 5–1.

**1984 Los Angeles-Anaheim** C: 14, N: 14, D: 8.3.

| | | FINAL MATCH | |
|---|---|---|---|
| 1. Vlado Lisjak | YUG | Fall | 0:57 |
| 2. Tapio Sipilä | FIN | | |
| 3. James Martinez | USA | Fall | 0:25 |
| 4. Stefan Negrisan | ROM | | |
| 5. Deitmar Streitler | AUT | 8–4 | 6:00 |
| 6. Mohamed Mutei Alnakdali | SYR | | |
| 7. Shaban Ibrahim | EGY | | |
| 8. Sumer Kocak | TUR | | |

In a major upset, the defending world champion, Tapio Sipilä, was quickly thrown by a late substitute to the Yugoslav team, Vlado Lisjak, a 22-year-old truck driver from the village of Petrinja.

**1988 Seoul** C: 31, N: 31, D: 9.22.

|  |  |  | FINAL MATCH | |
|---|---|---|---|---|
| 1. Levon Dzhulfalakyan | SOV | 9–3 | 6:00 |
| 2. Kim Sung-moon | KOR | | |
| 3. Tapio Sipilä | FIN | 7–4 | 6:00 |
| 4. Petrica Carare | ROM | | |
| 5. Jerzy Kopański | POL | Passivity | 5:07 |
| 6. Yasuhiro Okubo | JPN | | |
| 7. Morten Brekke | NOR | 6–5 | 6:42 |
| 8. Attila Repka | HUN | | |

Dzhulfalakyan, a 24-year-old Armenian, faced his stiffest challenge from Carare, who forced him into overtime before succumbing.

# WELTERWEIGHT
(74 kg—163 lbs)

**1896–1928** not held

**1932 Los Angeles** C: 8, N: 8, D: 8.7.
*(72 kg-159 lbs)*
1. Ivar Johansson — SWE
2. Väinö Kajander-Kajukorpi — FIN
3. Ercole Gallegati — ITA
4. Osvald Käpp — EST
5. Börge Jensen — DEN

Ivar Johansson, a 29-year-old policeman from Norrköping, put on a remarkable performance from August 1 through August 7. First he won the freestyle Middleweight division with four bouts in three days. Then he spent the next 24 hours fasting and sweating in a sauna so that he could compete as a welterweight in the Greco-Roman competition. Eleven pounds lighter, he won four more matches and earned a second gold medal.

**1936 Berlin** C: 14, N: 14, D: 8.9.
*(72 kg—159 lbs)*

|  |  | ROUND ELIMINATED | BAD PTS. | FINAL ROUND |
|---|---|---|---|---|
| 1. Rudolf Svedberg | SWE | — | 2 | 2 |
| 2. Fritz Schäfer | GER | — | 1 | 2 |
| 3. Eino Virtanen | FIN | — | 4 | 6 |
| 4. Eduard Pütsep | EST | 5 | 6 | |
| 5. Nurettin Boytorun | TUR | 5 | 7 | |
| 5. Silvio Tozzi | ITA | 5 | 7 | |
| 7. Jean De Feu | BEL | 4 | 6 | |
| 7. Adolf Rieder | SWI | 4 | 6 | |

**1948 London** C: 16, N: 16, D: 8.6.
*(73 kg—160 lbs)*

|  |  | ROUND ELIMINATED | BAD PTS. | FINAL ROUND |
|---|---|---|---|---|
| 1. Gösta Andersson | SWE | — | 3 | 2 |
| 2. Miklós Szilvási | HUN | — | 3 | 3 |
| 3. Henrik Hansen | DEN | — | 4 | 6 |
| 4. René Chesneau | FRA | 4 | 7 | |
| 4. Veikko Männikö | FIN | 4 | 7 | |
| 4. Josef Schmidt | DEN | 4 | 7 | |
| 7. Bjorn Cook | NOR | 3 | 5 | |
| 8. Nicolaos Felgen | LUX | 3 | 6 | |
| 8. Luigi Rigamonti | ITA | 3 | 6 | |

**1952 Helsinki** C: 18, N: 18, D: 7.27.
*(73 kg—160 lbs)*

|  |  | ROUND ELIMINATED | BAD PTS. | FINAL ROUND |
|---|---|---|---|---|
| 1. Miklós Szilvási | HUN | — | 1 | 1 |
| 2. Gösta Andersson | SWE | — | 1 | 4 |
| 3. Khalil Taha | LEB | — | 5 | 6 |
| 4. Semen Marushkin | SOV | 4 | 6 | |
| 5. Marin Belusiça | ROM | 3 | 5 | |
| 5. René Chesneau | FRA | 3 | 5 | |
| 5. Osvaldo Riva | ITA | 3 | 5 | |
| 5. Ahmet Şenol | TUR | 3 | 5 | |

In 1946, while on duty as a policeman, Miklós Szilvási was accidentally shot in the left leg by a machine gun. His left foot was temporarily paralyzed. Through exercise and willpower, Szilvási regained the use of his foot and represented Hungary at the 1948 Olympics. He finished second, losing a decision to Gösta Andersson in the final match. Four years later the two met again for the championship, and this time Szilvási won a split decision.

**1956 Melbourne** C: 11, N: 11, D: 12.6.
*(73 kg—160 lbs)*

|  |  | ROUND ELIMINATED | BAD PTS. | FINAL ROUND |
|---|---|---|---|---|
| 1. Mithat Bayrak | TUR | — | 2 | 2 |
| 2. Vladimir Maneyev | SOV | — | 2 | 4 |
| 3. Per Berlin | SWE | — | 0 | 6 |
| 4. Veikko Rantanen | FIN | 3 | 5 | |
| 5. James Holt | USA | 3 | 6 | |
| 5. Siegfried Schäfer | GDR | 3 | 6 | |
| 7. Miklós Szilvási | HUN | 3 | 7 | |
| 8. Mitiou Petkov | ROM | 3 | 7 | |

**1960 Rome** C: 27, N: 27, D: 8.31.
*(73 kg—160 lbs)*

|  |  | ROUND ELIMINATED | BAD PTS. | FINAL ROUND |
|---|---|---|---|---|
| 1. Mithat Bayrak | TUR | — | 5 | 1 |
| 2. Günter Maritschnigg | GER | — | 5 | 5 |
| 3. René Schiermeyer | FRA | — | 5 | 6 |
| 4. Stevan Horvat | YUG | 6 | 6 | |
| 5. Grigory Gamarnik | SOV | 6 | 7 | |

| | | ROUND ELIMINATED | BAD PTS. | FINAL ROUND |
|---|---|---|---|---|
| 6. Matti Laakso | FIN | 5 | 7 | |
| 7. Antal Rizmayer | HUN | 5 | 8 | |
| 8. Hansjörg Hirschbuhl | SWI | 4 | 7 | |

**1964 Tokyo** C: 19, N: 19, D: 10.19.
*(78 kg—172 lbs)*

| | | ROUND ELIMINATED | BAD PTS. | FINAL ROUND |
|---|---|---|---|---|
| 1. Anatoly Kolesov | SOV | — | 7 | 5 |
| 2. Kiril Petkov | BUL | — | 7 | 6 |
| 3. Bertil Nyström | SWE | — | 7 | 6 |
| 4. Boleslaw Dubicki | POL | — | 7 | 7 |
| 5. Antal Rizmayer | HUN | 4 | 6 | |
| 5. Ion Tăranu | ROM | 4 | 6 | |
| 7. Russell Camilleri | USA | 4 | 7 | |
| 7. René Schiermeyer | FRA | 4 | 7 | |
| 7. Asghar Zowghian | IRN | 4 | 7 | |

Five of the last six matches ended in draws, which meant that Kolesov's victory by decision over Dubicki was the tie-breaker.

**1968 Mexico City** C: 22, N: 22, D: 10.26.
*(78 kg—172 lbs)*

| | | ROUND ELIMINATED | BAD PTS. | FINAL ROUND |
|---|---|---|---|---|
| 1. Rudolf Vesper | GDR | — | 4.5 | 3.5 |
| 2. Daniel Robin | FRA | — | 5 | 4 |
| 3. Károly Bajkó | HUN | — | 5.5 | 5.5 |
| 4. Metodi Zarev | BUL | 5 | 8 | |
| 5. Ion Tăranu | ROM | 5 | 9.5 | |
| 6. Jan-Ivar Karström | SWE | 4 | 6 | |
| 7. Harald Barlie | NOR | 4 | 7 | |
| 7. Franz Berger | AUT | 4 | 7 | |
| 7. Milovan Nenadic | YUG | 4 | 7 | |

**1972 Munich** C: 21, N: 21, D: 9.10.

| | | ROUND ELIMINATED | BAD PTS. | FINAL ROUND |
|---|---|---|---|---|
| 1. Vítězslav Mácha | CZE | — | 5.5 | 1 |
| 2. Petros Galaktopoulos | GRE | — | 3 | 3 |
| 3. Jan Karlsson | SWE | 5 | 6 | |
| 4. Ivan Kolev | BUL | 5 | 6.5 | |
| 5. Momir Kecman | YUG | 5 | 7.5 | |
| 6. Daniel Robin | FRA | 5 | 8 | |
| 7. Klaus-Jürgen Pohl | GDR | 5 | 8 | |
| 8. Werner Schröter | GER | 4 | 7.5 | |

Mácha lost his opening bout to Ivan Kolev, but then won five in a row to secure the gold medal. Married to Miss Bohemia of 1971, Mácha was technically a miner, although he actually spent six to seven hours a day training.

**1976 Montreal** C: 18, N: 18, D: 7.24.

| | | ROUND ELIMINATED | BAD PTS. | FINAL ROUND |
|---|---|---|---|---|
| 1. Anatoly Bykov | SOV | — | 1 | 1 |
| 2. Vítězslav Mácha | CZE | — | 1.5 | 3 |

| | | ROUND ELIMINATED | BAD PTS. | FINAL ROUND |
|---|---|---|---|---|
| 3. Karlheinz Helbing | GER | — | 6 | 8 |
| 4. Mikko Huhtala | FIN | 5 | 7.5 | |
| 5. Klaus-Dieter Göpfert | GDR | 5 | 10 | |
| 6. Gheorghe Ciobotaru | ROM | 4 | 7 | |
| 7. Jan Karlsson | SWE | 4 | 8 | |
| 8. Petros Galaktopoulos | GRE | 3 | 7 | |

Crucial matches took place in the fourth round when Bykov outpointed Ciobotaru 7–6 and Mácha edged Huhtala 4–3. In the fifth round Bykov was awarded a controversial victory by disqualification over Göpfert, with six seconds left and the score tied 5–5. Bykov's final win over Mácha was by a margin of 7–3.

**1980 Moscow** C: 14, N: 14, D: 7.23.

| | | ROUND ELIMINATED | BAD PTS. | FINAL ROUND |
|---|---|---|---|---|
| 1. Ferenc Kocsis | HUN | — | 1 | 2 |
| 2. Anatoly Bykov | SOV | — | 4 | 5 |
| 3. Mikko Huhtala | FIN | — | 5 | 7 |
| 4. Yanko Shopov | BUL | 5 | 7 | |
| 5. Lennart Lundell | SWE | 4 | 6 | |
| 6. Vítězslav Mácha | CZE | 4 | 8 | |
| 7. Gheorghe Minea | ROM | 4 | 8 | |
| 8. Jacques van Lancker | BEL | 3 | 7 | |

The final bout between Kocsis and Bykov ended with Bykov disqualified for inactivity after 7:21.

**1984 Los Angeles-Anaheim** C: 17, N: 17, D: 8.2.

| | | FINAL MATCH | |
|---|---|---|---|
| 1. Jouko Salomäki | FIN | 5–4 | 6:00 |
| 2. Roger Tallroth | SWE | | |
| 3. Ştefan Rusu | ROM | 6–1 | 6:00 |
| 4. Kim Young-nam | KOR | | |
| 5. Karolj Kasap | YUG | 6–3 | 6:00 |
| 6. Martial Mischler | FRA | | |
| 7. Christopher Catalfo | USA | | |
| 8. Mohamed Hamad | EGY | | |

Salomäki took a 5–0 lead and held on for the victory. Ştefan Rusu earned a bronze medal to go with the silver and gold he had won in the lightweight division in 1976 and 1980.

**1988 Seoul** C: 19, N: 19, D: 9.21.

| | | FINAL MATCH | |
|---|---|---|---|
| 1. Kim Young-nam | KOR | 2–1 | 6:00 |
| 2. Daulet Turlykhanov | SOV | | |
| 3. Józef Tracz | POL | 2–0 | 6:00 |
| 4. János Takács | HUN | | |
| 5. Martial Mischler | FRA | 4–1 | 6:00 |
| 6. Borislav Velichkov | BUL | | |
| 7. Roger Tallroth | SWE | 5–1 | 6:00 |
| 8. Hiromichi Ito | JPN | | |

Defending Olympic and world champion Jouko Salomäki was quickly eliminated by losing his first two bouts to Tallroth and Mischler. The final pitted Turlykhanov, a Soviet of Korean descent, against Kim, the 28-

year-old son of poor farmers in Hampyong in Cholla province. When Kim began wrestling, he practiced on the wooden floor of his high school gymnasium, which was sparsely covered with dried rice stalks because the school could not afford mats. Turlykhanov led 1–0 at the break. But 25 seconds into the second round, Kim rolled his opponent onto his back for a 2-point score, then repelled Turlykhanov's advances for the remainder of the match. Kim was South Korea's first gold-medal winner of the Seoul Olympics. His victory brought great joy to the entire nation and earned him an $800 monthly pension for the rest of his life.

# MIDDLEWEIGHT
(82 kg—181 lbs)

**1896–1904** not held

**1906 Athens** C: 16, N: 9, D: 5.1.
*(85 kg—187½ lbs)*
1. Verner Weckman      FIN
2. Rudolf Lindmayer    AUT
3. Robert Behrens      DEN
4. Wenzel Goldbach     AUT
5. Josef Vaclav Hradecky (BOH), Ettore Pomburi (ITA), Sauveur (BEL), Franz Šolar (AUT)

**1908 London** C: 21, N: 9, D: 7.25.
*(73 kg—161 lbs)*
1. Frithiof Mårtensson    SWE
2. Mauritz Andersson      SWE
3. Anders Andersen        DEN
4. Jóhannes Jósefsson     DEN/ICE
5. J. Belmer (HOL), Johannes Eriksen (DEN), Axel Frank (SWE), Axel Larson (DEN), Marcel Dubois (BEL)

The final between Mårtensson and Mauritz Andersson was postponed overnight due to a minor injury to Mårtensson. Jósefsson, an Icelandic nationalist forced to compete under the Danish flag, fractured his arm in the semifinals and had to forfeit the match for third place.

**1912 Stockholm** C: 38, N: 14, D: 7.13.
*(75 kg—165½ lbs)*
1. Claes Johanson     SWE
2. Martin Klein       RUS/EST
3. Alfred Asikainen   FIN
4. Karl Åberg         FIN
4. August Jokinen     FIN
6. Johannes Sint      HOL

The longest wrestling contest in Olympic history was the semifinal bout between Klein and Asikainen. The two men struggled on for hours under the hot sun, stopping every half hour for a brief refreshment break. Finally, after 11 hours, Klein, an Estonian competing for Czarist Russia, pinned his opponent. However, he was so ex-

hausted by his ordeal that he was unable to take part in the final. Johanson was awarded first place by default.

**1920 Antwerp** C: 22, N: 11, D: 8.26.
*(75 kg—165½ lbs)*
1. Carl Westergren      SWE
2. Artur Lindfors       FIN
3. Matti Perttilä       FIN
4. Johannes Eillebrecht HOL

The phenomenal Carl Westergren won the first of his three Olympic gold medals, each in a different division.

**1924 Paris** C: 27, N: 19, D: 7.10.
*(75 kg—165½ lbs)*
1. Edvard Westerlund        FIN
2. Artur Lindfors          FIN
3. Roman Steinberg         EST
4. Giuseppe Gorletti       ITA
5. Viktor Fischer          AUT
5. Nikola Grbič            YUG
7. Robert Christoffersen   DEN
7. Waclaw Okulicz-Kozaryn  POL

**1928 Amsterdam** C: 17, N: 17, D: 8.5.
*(75 kg—165½ lbs)*
1. Väinö Kokkinen      FIN
2. László Papp         HUN
3. Albert Kusnets      EST
4. Jóhannes Jacobsen   DEN
5. Jean Saenen         BEL
6. František Hála       CZE
7. Enrico Bonassin     ITA
7. Nurettin Boyturun   TUR

Kokkinen, a restaurant owner from Helsinki, pinned all five of his opponents.

**1932 Los Angeles** C: 4, N: 4, D: 8.7.
*(79 kg—174 lbs)*
1. Väinö Kokkinen   FIN
2. Jean Földeak     GER
3. Axel Cadier      SWE

**1936 Berlin** C: 16, N: 16, D: 8.9.
*(79 kg—174 lbs)*

|  |  | ROUND ELIMINATED | BAD PTS. | FINAL ROUND |
|---|---|---|---|---|
| 1. Ivar Johansson | SWE | — | 2 | 1 |
| 2. Ludwig Schweikert | GER | — | 3 | 2 |
| 3. József Palotás | HUN | — | 4 | 6 |
| 4. Väinö Kokkinen | FIN | 5 | 6 | |
| 5. Ibrahim Erabi | EGY | 4 | 6 | |
| 6. Ercole Gallegati | ITA | 4 | 6 | |
| 7. Francise Cocos | ROM | 4 | 6 | |
| 8. Koloman Kis | YUG | 3 | 6 | |
| 8. Johans Pointner | AUT | 3 | 6 | |
| 8. Josef Pribyl | CZE | 3 | 6 | |

**1948 London** C: 13, N: 13, D: 8.6.
*(79 kg—174 lbs)*

| | | ROUND ELIMINATED | BAD PTS. | FINAL ROUND |
|---|---|---|---|---|
| 1. | Axel Grönberg | SWE | — | 2 | 1 |
| 2. | Muhlis Tayfur | TUR | — | 4 | 3 |
| 3. | Ercole Gallegati | ITA | 5 | 5 | |
| 4. | Jean-Baptiste Benoy | BEL | 5 | 6 | |
| 5. | Kaare Larsen | NOR | 5 | 7 | |
| 6. | Juho Kinnunen | FIN | 4 | 5 | |
| 7. | Gyula Németi | HUN | 4 | 5 | |
| 8. | A. Vogel | AUT | 3 | 6 | |

**1952 Helsinki** C: 11, N: 11, D: 7.27.
*(79 kg—174 lbs)*

| | | ROUND ELIMINATED | BAD PTS. | FINAL ROUND |
|---|---|---|---|---|
| 1. | Axel Grönberg | SWE | — | 4 | 2 |
| 2. | Kalervo Rauhala | FIN | — | 3 | 4 |
| 3. | Nikolai Byelov | SOV | — | 3 | 6 |
| 4. | Gyula Németi | HUN | 4 | 5 | |
| 5. | Ali Özdemir | TUR | 3 | 5 | |
| 6. | Ercole Gallegati | ITA | 3 | 6 | |
| 7. | Gustav Gocke | GER | 3 | 7 | |

**1956 Melbourne** C: 10, N: 10, D: 12.6.
*(79 kg—174 lbs)*

| | | ROUND ELIMINATED | BAD PTS. | FINAL ROUND |
|---|---|---|---|---|
| 1. | Givy Kartoziya | SOV | — | 3 | 2 |
| 2. | Dimiter Dobrev | BUL | — | 4 | 4 |
| 3. | Karl-Axel Rune Jansson | SWE | — | 5 | 6 |
| 4. | Johann Sterr | GER | 4 | 6 | |
| 5. | György Gurics | HUN | 3 | 5 | |
| 6. | Viljo Punkari | FIN | 3 | 6 | |
| 7. | James Peckham | USA | 3 | 7 | |

**1960 Rome** C: 24, N: 24, D: 8.31.
*(79 kg—174 lbs)*

| | | ROUND ELIMINATED | BAD PTS. |
|---|---|---|---|
| 1. | Dimiter Dobrev | BUL | — | 4 |
| 2. | Lothar Metz | GDR | 6 | 6 |
| 3. | Ion Tăranu | ROM | 6 | 7 |
| 4. | Kazim Ayvaz | TUR | 6 | 7 |
| 5. | Boleslaw Dubicki | POL | 5 | 7 |
| 5. | Nikolai Chuchalov | SOV | 5 | 7 |
| 7. | Yacous Romanos | LEB | 4 | 7 |
| 8. | Russell Camilleri | USA | 4 | 7 |

**1964 Tokyo** C: 20, N: 20, D: 10.19.
*(87 kg—192 lbs)*

| | | ROUND ELIMINATED | BAD PTS. | 2ND PLACE |
|---|---|---|---|---|
| 1. | Branislav Simič | YUG | — | 4 | |
| 2. | Jiři Kormanik | CZE | 5 | 6 | 1 |
| 3. | Lothar Metz | GDR | 5 | 6 | 3 |
| 4. | Géza Hollósi | HUN | 5 | 7 | |

| 4. | Valentin Olenik | SOV | 5 | 7 |
|---|---|---|---|---|
| 6. | Kraliu Bimbalov | BUL | 5 | 8 |
| 7. | Richard Wayne Baughman | USA | 4 | 7 |
| 8. | Ismail Selekman | TUR | 4 | 7 |

Simič, competing in his third Olympics, managed to take first place without having to face either Kormanik or Metz.

**1968 Mexico City** C: 19, N: 19, D: 10.26.
*(87 kg—192 lbs)*

| | | ROUND ELIMINATED | BAD PTS. |
|---|---|---|---|
| 1. | Lothar Metz | GDR | — | 5 |
| 2. | Valentin Olenik | SOV | 6 | 6 |
| 3. | Branislav Simič | YUG | 6 | 6 |
| 4. | Nicolae Neguţ | ROM | 6 | 8.5 |
| 5. | Richard Wayne Baughman | USA | 5 | 8 |
| 5. | Peter Krumov | BUL | 5 | 8 |
| 7. | Czeslaw Kwinciński | POL | 4 | 7 |
| 8. | Häkon Overby | NOR | 4 | 7 |

**1972 Munich** C: 20, N: 20, D: 9.10.

| | | ROUND ELIMINATED | BAD PTS. | FINAL ROUND |
|---|---|---|---|---|
| 1. | Csaba Hegedüs | HUN | — | 3 | 2 |
| 2. | Anatoly Nazarenko | SOV | — | 4 | 3 |
| 3. | Milan Nenadič | YUG | — | 4 | 7 |
| 4. | Miroslav Janota | CZE | 5 | 7 | |
| 5. | Ion Gabor | ROM | 5 | 9 | |
| 6. | Frank Hartmann | GDR | 4 | 6 | |
| 7. | Ali Yagmur | TUR | 4 | 7 | |
| 8. | Kiril Dimitrov | BUL | 4 | 7.5 | |

Nazarenko, the 1970 world champion, and Hegedüs, the 1971 world champion, met in the very first round, with Hegedüs winning a decision. Neither man lost another bout for the rest of the tournament.

**1976 Montreal** C: 17, N: 17, D: 7.24.

| | | ROUND ELIMINATED | BAD PTS. | FINAL ROUND |
|---|---|---|---|---|
| 1. | Momir Petković | YUG | — | 4.5 | 2 |
| 2. | Vladimir Cheboksarov | SOV | — | 6 | 4 |
| 3. | Ivan Kolev | BUL | — | 7 | 6 |
| 4. | Leif Andersson | SWE | 6 | 8 | |
| 5. | Miroslav Janota | CZE | 5 | 8 | |
| 6. | Kazuhiro Takanishi | JPN | 5 | 8.5 | |
| 7. | Ion Enache | ROM | 4 | 7 | |
| 8. | Adam Ostrowski | POL | 4 | 7 | |

The crucial third-round contest between Petković and Cheboksarov ended in a 6–6 tie, but Petković was given the victory after complex tie-breaker rules were invoked.

**1980 Moscow** C: 12, N: 12, D: 7.24.

| | | ROUND ELIMINATED | BAD PTS. | FINAL ROUND |
|---|---|---|---|---|
| 1. | Gennady Korban | SOV | — | 1 | 2 |
| 2. | Jan Dolgowicz | POL | — | 7 | 3 |
| 3. | Pavel Pavlov | BUL | — | 1 | 7 |

4. Leif Andersson  SWE  4  8
5. Detlef Kühn  GDR  3  8
6. Mihály Toma  HUN  3  8
7. Mohammad Eloulabi  SYR  3  9
8. Miroslaw Janota  CZE  2  7

Korban defeated Dolgowicz, 11–4, and Pavlov, 13–7.

**1984 Los Angeles-Anaheim** C: 15, N: 15, D: 8.3.

|   |   |   | FINAL MATCH | |
|---|---|---|---|---|
| 1. Ion Draica | ROM | 4–3 | 6:00 |
| 2. Dimitrios Thanopoulos | GRE | | |
| 3. Sören Claesson | SWE | 5–2 | 6:00 |
| 4. Momir Petković | YUG | | |
| 5. Jarmo Övermark | FIN | 5–3 | 6:00 |
| 6. Mohamed El Ashram | EGY | | |
| 7. Louis Santerre | CAN | | |
| 8. Kim Sang-kyu | KOR | | |

**1988 Seoul** C: 21, N: 21, D: 9.22.

|   |   |   | FINAL MATCH | |
|---|---|---|---|---|
| 1. Mikhail Mamiashvili | SOV | 10–1 | 6:00 |
| 2. Tibor Komáromi | HUN | | |
| 3. Kim Sang-kyu | KOR | 6–5 | 6:00 |
| 4. Stig Arild Kleven | NOR | | |
| 5. Goran Kasum | YUG | Passivity | 4:26 |
| 6. Magnus Frodriksson | SWE | | |
| 7. John Morgan | USA | Forfeit | |
| 8. Bogdan Daras | POL | | |

Mamiashvili had already won three world championships at 74 kilograms when he moved up to challenge 82-kilogram world champion Komáromi in 1988. He defeated the Hungarian at the European championships in May and then again at the Olympics in Seoul.

# LIGHT HEAVYWEIGHT
(90 kg—198 ½ lbs)

**1896–1906** not held

**1908 London** C: 21, N: 0, D. 7.22.
*(93 kg—205 lbs)*
1. Verner Weckman  FIN
2. Yrjö Saarela  FIN
3. Carl Jensen  DEN
4. Hugó Payr  HUN
5. A. Banbrook (GBR), Marcel Dubois (BEL), Fritz Larsson (SWE), J. van Westerop (HOL)

In the final match, Weckman, who had won the Middleweight gold medal in 1906, scored the first fall in 4:22. But Saarela won the second one in 5:07. Weckman, a 25-year-old engineer, prevailed in the deciding confrontation, after 16:10. At the award ceremony the Finnish flag was not hoisted. In its place was a sign bearing the word "Finland." Rumors spread that the tyrannical Czarist Russian government had forbidden the use of the Finnish national flag. However, the Finnish colors were raised up the flagpole later in the day.

**1912 Stockholm** C: 29, N: 11, D: 7.14.
*(82.5 kg—182 lbs)*
1. —
2. Anders Ahlgren  SWE
2. Ivar Böhling  FIN
3. Béla Varga  HUN
4. August Rajala  FIN

Ahlgren fought his way to the final match by pinning six opponents, each within 35 minutes. But in Böhling he met his equal—literally. Ahlgren and Böhling struggled hour after hour without either man giving in, until finally, after nine hours, officials called the contest a draw. The rules of the Olympic competition stated that it was necessary for a first-place winner actually to defeat his adversary, so the officials decided to declare Ahlgren and Böhling co-winners of the second prize.

**1920 Antwerp** C: 18, N: 10, D: 8.26.
*(82 kg—182 lbs)*
1. Claes Johanson  SWE
2. Edil Rosenqvist  FIN
3. Johannes Eriksen  DEN
4. Johannes Sint  HOL

**1924 Paris** C: 22, N: 15, D: 7.10.
*(82.5 kg—182 lbs)*
1. Carl Westergren  SWE
2. Rudolf Svensson  SWE
3. Onni Pellinen  FIN
4. Ibrahim Moustafa  EGY
5. Emil Weckstén  FIN
6. Rudolf Loos (EST), A. Misset (HOL), Béla Varga (HUN)

Westergren had won the Middleweight title four years earlier in Antwerp.

**1928 Amsterdam** C: 17, N: 17, D: 8.5.
*(82.5 kg—182 lbs)*
1. Ibrahim Moustafa  EGY
2. Adolf Rieger  GER
3. Onni Pellinen  FIN
4. Nicolas Appelo  BEL
5. Ejnar Hansen  DEN
6. Imre Szalay  HUN

**1932 Los Angeles** C: 3, N: 3, D: 8.7.
*(87 kg—192 lbs)*

|   |   | BAD PTS. |
|---|---|---|
| 1. Rudolf Svensson | SWE | 1 |
| 2. Onni Pellinen | FIN | 3 |
| 3. Mario Gruppioni | ITA | 6 |

**1936 Berlin** C: 13, N: 13, D: 8.9.
*(87 kg—192 lbs)*

|   |   | ROUND ELIMINATED | BAD PTS. | FINAL ROUND |
|---|---|---|---|---|
| 1. Axel Cardier | SWE | — | 2 | 1 |
| 2. Edwins Bietags | LAT | — | 1 | 3 |

| | | ROUND ELIMI-NATED | BAD PTS. | FINAL ROUND |
|---|---|---|---|---|
| 3. August Neo | EST | 5 | 5 | |
| 4. Werner Seelenbinder | GER | 5 | 6 | |
| 5. Umberto Silvestri | ITA | 4 | 6 | |
| 6. Olaf Knutsen | NOR | 4 | 6 | |
| 7. Franz Foidl | AUT | 4 | 6 | |
| 8. Mustafa Avcioglu Cakmak | TUR | 3 | 5 | |

Seelenbinder was an anti-Nazi hero who was executed because of his opposition to Hitler.

**1948 London** C: 14, N: 14, D: 8.6.
*(87 kg—192 lbs)*

| | | ROUND ELIMI-NATED | BAD PTS. | FINAL ROUND |
|---|---|---|---|---|
| 1. Karl-Erik Nilsson | SWE | — | 2 | 1 |
| 2. Kaelpo Gröndahl | FIN | — | 1 | 3 |
| 3. Ibrahim Orabi | EGY | 5 | 6 | |
| 4. Gyula Kovács | HUN | 4 | 5 | |
| 5. Kenneth Richmond | GBR | 4 | 6 | |
| 6. Erling Lauridsen | DEN | 4 | 7 | |
| 7. Peter Enzinger | AUT | 3 | 6 | |
| 8. Mustafa Avcioglu Cakmak | TUR | 3 | 7 | |
| 8. Charles Istaz | BEL | 3 | 7 | |

An incident of sorts took place in the fifth round, when Nilsson threw Orabi over his head and the referee ruled it a fall. While the Egyptians protested, Orabi stretched out on the mat and refused to move. After 15 minutes Nilsson was called back from the dressing room and ordered to continue the match. Nilsson then scored another fall and the matter was settled.

**1952 Helsinki** C: 10, N: 10, D: 7.27.
*(87 kg—192 lbs)*

| | | ROUND ELIMINATED | BAD PTS. | FINAL ROUND |
|---|---|---|---|---|
| 1. Kaelpo Gröndahl | FIN | — | 2 | 2 |
| 2. Chalva Chikhladze | SOV | — | 4 | 3 |
| 3. Karl-Erik Nilsson | SWE | — | 5 | 6 |
| 4. Gyula Kovács | HUN | 4 | 5 | |
| 5. Ismet Atli | TUR | 3 | 6 | |
| 6. Umberto Silvestri | ITA | 3 | 7 | |
| 6. Michel Skaff | LEB | 3 | 7 | |

The final bout between Gröndahl and Chikhladze was dull and cautious and was won by Gröndahl on a split decision.

**1956 Melbourne** C: 10, N: 10, D: 12.6.
*(87 kg—192 lbs)*

| | | ROUND ELIMINATED | BAD PTS. | 2ND PLACE |
|---|---|---|---|---|
| 1. Valentin Nikolayev | SOV | — | 4 | |
| 2. Petko Sirakov | BUL | 4 | 5 | 1 |
| 3. Karl-Erik Nilsson | SWE | 4 | 5 | 3 |
| 4. Robert Steckle | CAN | 4 | 7 | |

| | | | | |
|---|---|---|---|---|
| 5. Dale Thomas | USA | 3 | 6 | |
| 5. Eugen Wiesberger | AUT | 3 | 6 | |
| 7. Veikko Lahti | FIN | 3 | 7 | |
| 8. Adil Atan | TUR | 3 | 7 | |

**1960 Rome** C: 17, N: 17, D: 8.31.
*(87 kg—192 lbs)*

| | | ROUND ELIMINATED | BAD PTS. | FINAL ROUND |
|---|---|---|---|---|
| 1. Tevfik Kiş | TUR | — | 6 | 2 |
| 2. Kralyu Bimbalov | BUL | — | 6 | 2 |
| 3. Givy Kartozlya | SOV | 6 | 8 | |
| 4. Péter Piti | HUN | 6 | 8 | |
| 5. Antero Vanhanen | FIN | 5 | 7 | |
| 6. José Panizo Rodriguez | SPA | 4 | 7 | |
| 7. Gheorghe Popovici | ROM | 4 | 8 | |
| 8. Eugen Wiesberger | AUT | 4 | 8 | |

Kis was awarded first place because he weighed less than Bimbalov.

**1964 Tokyo** C: 18, N: 18, D: 10.19.
*(97 kg—214 lbs)*

| | | ROUND ELIMINATED | BAD PTS. |
|---|---|---|---|
| 1. Boyan Radev | BUL | — | 2 |
| 2. Per Svensson | SWE | 5 | 6 |
| 3. Heinz Kiehl | GER | 5 | 6 |
| 4. Nicolae Martinescu | ROM | 5 | 8 |
| 5. Rostom Abashidze | SOV | 4 | 6 |
| 5. Ferenc Kiss | HUN | 4 | 6 |
| 5. Peter Jutzeler | SWI | 4 | 6 |
| 8. Eugen Wiesberger | AUT | 4 | 7 |

Radev breezed through the tournament, aided by the fact that he faced only one wrestler, Martinescu, who finished in the top eight.

**1968 Mexico City** C: 16, N: 16, D: 10.26.
*(97 kg—214 lbs)*

| | | ROUND ELIMINATED | BAD PTS. | FINAL ROUND |
|---|---|---|---|---|
| 1. Boyan Radev | BUL | — | 0.5 | 2.5 |
| 2. Nikolai Yakovenko | SOV | — | 1 | 3.5 |
| 3. Nicolae Martinescu | ROM | — | 4 | 7 |
| 4. Per Svensson | SWE | 4 | 6 | |
| 5. Tore Hem | NOR | 4 | 8 | |
| 6. Peter Jutzeler | SWI | 3 | 6 | |
| 6. Cay Malmberg | FIN | 3 | 6 | |
| 6. Waclaw Orlowski | POL | 3 | 6 | |

Radev and Yakovenko tied, but Radev threw Martinescu in 4:58 to win the gold medal.

**1972 Munich** C: 14, N: 14, D: 9.10.

| | | ROUND ELIMINATED | BAD PTS. | FINAL ROUND |
|---|---|---|---|---|
| 1. Valery Rezantsev | SOV | — | 2 | 2 |
| 2. Josip Čorak | YUG | — | 3 | 5 |
| 3. Czeslaw Kwienciński | POL | — | 5 | 5 |
| 4. József Percsi | HUN | 5 | 6.5 | |

| | | | ROUND ELIMINATED | BAD PTS. | FINAL ROUND |
|---|---|---|---|---|---|
| 5. | Håkon Överbye | NOR | | 5 | 9 |
| 6. | Nicolae Neguţ | ROM | | 4 | 8 |
| 7. | Kimiichi Tani | JPN | | 4 | 9 |
| 8. | Günter Kowalewski | GER | | 3 | 8 |

Rezantsev suffered a first-round draw with Neguţ and then won six straight bouts.

**1976 Montreal** C: 13, N: 13, D: 7.24.

| | | | ROUND ELIMINATED | BAD PTS. | FINAL ROUND |
|---|---|---|---|---|---|
| 1. | Valery Rezantsev | SOV | — | 2 | 2 |
| 2. | Stoyan Ivanov | BUL | — | 5 | 5 |
| 3. | Czeslaw Kwieciński | POL | — | 3 | 7 |
| 4. | Darko Nisavić | YUG | 5 | 9 | |
| 5. | Frank Andersson | SWE | 4 | 6 | |
| 6. | István Séllyei | HUN | 4 | 8 | |
| 7. | James Johnson | USA | 3 | 8 | |
| 7. | Sadao Sato | JPN | 3 | 8 | |

Valery Rezantsev dominated Light Heavyweight Greco-Roman wrestling in the 1970s. He went to Montreal as the defending Olympic champion and the five-time defending world champion. In his final bout he was held to a 6–6 tie by Ivanov, but a tie-breaker gave him the victory anyway.

**1980 Moscow** C: 15, N: 15, D: 7.22.

| | | | ROUND ELIMINATED | BAD PTS | FINAL ROUND |
|---|---|---|---|---|---|
| 1. | Norbert Növényi | HUN | — | 1 | 2 |
| 2. | Igor Kanygin | SOV | — | 6.5 | 5 |
| 3. | Petre Dicu | ROM | — | 6 | 7 |
| 4. | Frank Andersson | SWE | 5 | 7 | |
| 5. | Thomas Horschel | GDR | 4 | 8 | |
| 6. | José Poll Martinez | CUB | 4 | 8.5 | |
| 7. | Christophe Andanson | FRA | 3 | 6.5 | |
| 8. | Georgios Pozidis | GRE | 3 | 7 | |

Növényi scattered four opponents and then outpointed Kanygin 7–6 and Dicu 4–1.

**1984 Los Angeles-Anaheim** C: 13, N: 13, D: 8.1.

| | | | FINAL MATCH | |
|---|---|---|---|---|
| 1. | Steven Fraser | USA | 1–1 | 6:00 |
| 2. | Ilie Matei | ROM | | |
| 3. | Frank Andersson | SWE | 5–0 | 6:00 |
| 4. | Uwe Sachs | GER | | |
| 5. | Jean-François Court | FRA | 4–2 | 6:00 |
| 6. | Georgios Pozidis | GRE | | |
| 7. | Toni Hannula | FIN | | |
| 8. | Franz Marx | AUT | | |

Fraser, a deputy sheriff from Ann Arbor, Michigan, became the first U.S. Greco-Roman wrestler ever to win an Olympic medal. With less than 50 seconds remaining in the final, he trailed Matei 1–0. But then Fraser caught the Romanian in a front headlock. The roar of the crowd seemed to give Fraser an extra injection of strength and he scored a takedown to gain the final point of the match and thus the victory.

**1988 Seoul** C: 22, N: 22, D: 9.20.

| | | | FINAL MATCH | |
|---|---|---|---|---|
| 1. | Atanas Komchev | BUL | 4–0 | 6:00 |
| 2. | Harri Koskela | FIN | | |
| 3. | Vladimir Popov | SOV | Fall | 1:36 |
| 4. | Christer Gulldén | SWE | | |
| 5. | Andreas Steinbach | GER | Passivity | 4:43 |
| 6. | Franz Pitschmann | AUT | | |
| 7. | Olaf Koschnitzke | GDR | Forfeit | |
| 8. | Georgios Pikilidis | GRE | | |

# HEAVYWEIGHT
## (100 kg—220 lbs)

**1896—1968** not held

**1972 Munich** C: 15, N: 15, D: 9.10.

| | | | ROUND ELIMINATED | BAD PTS. | FINAL ROUND |
|---|---|---|---|---|---|
| 1. | Nicolae Martinescu | ROM | — | 5.5 | 0 |
| 2. | Nikolai Iakovenko | SOV | — | 1 | 4 |
| 3. | Ferenc Kiss | HUN | 5 | 6.5 | |
| 4. | Hristo Ignatov | BUL | 5 | 9 | |
| 5. | Fredi Albrecht | GDR | 4 | 7 | |
| 6. | Tore Hem | NOR | 4 | 8 | |
| 7. | Andrzej Skrzydlewski | POL | 4 | 8.5 | |
| 8. | Rudolf Luescher | SWI | 2 | 6 | |

**1976 Montreal** C: 13, N: 13, D: 7.24.

| | | | ROUND ELIMINATED | BAD PTS. | FINAL ROUND |
|---|---|---|---|---|---|
| 1. | Nikolai Balboshin | SOV | — | 0 | 0 |
| 2. | Kamen Goranov | BUL | — | 4 | 5 |
| 3. | Andrzej Skrzydlewski | POL | — | 3 | 7 |
| 4. | Brad Rheingans | USA | 4 | 6 | |
| 5. | Tore Hem | NOR | 4 | 7 | |
| 6. | Heinz Schäfer | GER | 4 | 8 | |
| 7. | József Farkas | HUN | 3 | 8 | |
| 7. | Nicolae Martinescu | ROM | 3 | 8 | |

Balboshin needed only 16 minutes and 48 seconds to win his five matches.

**1980 Moscow** C: 9, N: 9, D: 7.23.

| | | | ROUND ELIMINATED | BAD PTS. | FINAL ROUND |
|---|---|---|---|---|---|
| 1. | Georgi Raikov | BUL | — | 1 | 2 |
| 2. | Roman Bierla | POL | — | 1 | 4 |
| 3. | Vasile Andrei | ROM | 4 | 7 | |
| 4. | Refik Memisevic | YUG | 4 | 7 | |
| 5. | Georgios Pikilidis | GRE | 3 | 8 | |
| 6. | Oldřich Dvorak | CZE | 3 | 8 | |
| 7. | Nikolai Balboshin | SOV | 2 | 4 | |
| 8. | Svend Erik Studsgaard | DEN | 2 | 8 | |

Raikov defeated Birlea by disqualification after 7:52. Defending champion Nikolai Balboshin, injured during the second round, was forced to withdraw.

**1984 Los Angeles-Anaheim** C: 8, N: 8, D: 8.3.

|  |  |  | FINAL MATCH | |
|---|---|---|---|---|
| 1. | Vasile Andrei | ROM | 12–0 | 4:16 |
| 2. | Greg Gibson | USA | | |
| 3. | Jozef Tertelje | YUG | 3–0 | 6:00 |
| 4. | Georgios Pikilidis | GRE | | |
| 5. | Franz Pitschmann | AUT | 7–5 | 6:00 |
| 6. | Fritz Gerdsmeier | GER | | |
| 7. | Yoshiro Fujita | JPN | | |
| 7. | Karl-Johan Gustafsson | SWE | | |

Andrei defeated each of his four opponents in less than 4½ minutes.

**1988 Seoul** C: 18, N: 18, D: 9.21.

|  |  |  | FINAL MATCH | |
|---|---|---|---|---|
| 1. | Andrzej Wroński | POL | 3–1 | 6:00 |
| 2. | Gerhard Himmel | GER | | |
| 3. | Dennis Koslowski | USA | 6–0 | 6:00 |
| 4. | Ilia Georgiev | BUL | | |
| 5. | Jožef Tertelje | YUG | Injury | |
| 6. | Yoo Young-tai | KOR | | |
| 7. | Guram Gedekhauri | SOV | Injury | |
| 8. | Tamás Gáspár | HUN | | |

Andrzej Wroński was one of the most unexpected winners of the Seoul Olympics. Before 1988 he had never placed in the top eight of a major international competition. His most noteworthy accomplishment was finishing *third* in the 1987 Polish championships. Meanwhile, the Olympic field was filled with winners, most notably the defending Olympic champion, Vasile Andrei; the defending world champion, Guram Gedekhauri; the world championship runner-up, Dennis Koslowski; the 1986 world champion, Tamás Gáspár; the 1986 European champion, Jožef Tertelje; and the 1987 European champion, Ilia Georgiev. None of these worthies made it to the final. Gáspár was forced to withdraw after he was injured in his match with Gerhard Himmel, the bronze medalist at the 1988 European championship. The others proceeded to knock each other off. Andrei defeated Gedekhauri, as did Tertelje. Tertelje beat Andrei. Koslowski beat Tertelje. Gedekhauri beat Koslowski. Georgiev lost to both Gáspár and Himmel. Even Wroński lost once when he was pinned by Gedekhauri. In fact, he was the only wrestler at the 1988 Olympics to win a gold medal despite having lost a match.

What Wroński did do was to register three upset victories: 1–0 over Tertelje, 1–0 over Koslowski, and a passivity win over Andrei. In the final he scored all of his points when he lifted Himmel from a prone position and threw him to the mat.

# SUPER HEAVYWEIGHT
## (Heavyweight 1896–1968)

A maximum weight limit—286 lbs.—was imposed for the first time at the 1988 Olympics.

**1896 Athens** C: 5, N: 4, D: 4.11.

| 1. | Karl Schumann | GER | Fall |
|---|---|---|---|
| 2. | Georgios Tsitas | GRE | |
| 3. | Stephanos Christopoulos | GRE | |

Schumann also won the rope climb.

**1900–1904** not held

**1906 Athens** C: 10, N: 6, D: 5.1.

| 1. | Soren Marius Jensen | DEN |
|---|---|---|
| 2. | Henri Baur | AUT |
| 3. | Marcel Dubois | BEL |
| 4. | Stephanos Christopoulos | GRE |
| 4. | D. Psaltopoulos | GRE |

**1908 London** C: 7, N: 4, D: 7.24.

| 1. | Richárd Weisz | HUN |
|---|---|---|
| 2. | Aleksandr Petrov | RUS |
| 3. | Soren Marius Jensen | DEN |
| 4. | Hugó Payr | HUN |

**1912 Stockholm** C: 18, N: 9, D: 7.14.

| 1. | Yrjö Saarela | FIN |
|---|---|---|
| 2. | Johan Olin | FIN |
| 3. | Sören Marius Jensen | DEN |
| 4. | Jakob Neser | GER |
| 5. | Emil Backenius | FIN |
| 5. | Kaarlo "Kalle" Wiljamaa | FIN |

**1920 Antwerp** C: 22, N: 11, D: 8.26.

| 1. | Adolf Lindfors | FIN |
|---|---|---|
| 2. | Poul Hansen | DEN |
| 3. | Martti Nieminen | FIN |
| 4. | Alexander Weyand | USA |

**1924 Paris** C: 17, N: 10, D: 7.10.

| 1. | Henri Deglane | FRA |
|---|---|---|
| 2. | Edil Rosenqvist | FIN |
| 3. | Rajmund Badó | HUN |
| 4. | Emil Larsen | DEN |
| 5. | Harry Nilsson (SWE), Janis Pollis (LAT), L. Pothier (BEL) | |

One of the many incidents which plagued the judgeable sports at the Paris Olympics occurred in the second round of the Greco-Roman Heavyweight tournament. Local favorite Henri Deglane, age 22, was pitted against 39-year-old Claes Johansson, who had won the Middleweight title in 1912 and the Light Heavyweight title in 1920. After 20 minutes of fighting, Johansson was declared the winner on points. The French team protested the decision, and the Jury of Appeal ordered the two men to wrestle for six more minutes, after which Deglane was declared the victor. Johansson was so disgusted that he withdrew from the competition. Deglane went on to win four more decisions and the gold medal.

**1928 Amsterdam** C: 15, N: 15, D: 8.5.

| 1. | Rudolf Svensson | SWE |
|---|---|---|
| 2. | Hjalmar Eemil Nyström | FIN |

3. Georg Gehring     GER
4. Eugen Wiesberger     AUT
5. Josef Urban     CZE
6. Rajmund Badó     HUN
7. Aleardo Donati     ITA
7. Mehmed Çoban     TUR

**1932 Los Angeles** C: 5, N: 5, D: 8.7.
1. Carl Westergren     SWE
2. Josef Urban     CZE
3. Nikolaus Hirschi     AUT
4. Georg Gehring     GER
5. Aleardo Donati     ITA

Westergren, a bus driver from Malmo, compiled an outstanding record at the Olympics. Following in the footsteps of Claes Johansson, he won the Middleweight title in 1920 and the Light Heavyweight title in 1924. In 1928, as a light heavyweight, he was pinned in the first round by Onni Pellinen. However he returned to the Olympics in 1932 as a 36-year-old heavyweight and won a third gold medal.

**1936 Berlin** C: 12, N: 12, D: 8.9.

| | | ROUND ELIMINATED | BAD PTS. | FINAL ROUND |
|---|---|---|---|---|
| 1. | Kristjan Palusalu   EST | — | 3 | 1 |
| 2. | John Nyman   SWE | — | 3 | 3 |
| 3. | Kurt Hornfischer   GER | 5 | 5 | |
| 4. | Mehmet Çoban   TUR | 4 | 6 | |
| 5. | Hjalmar Femil Nyström   FIN | 4 | 6 | |
| 6. | Aleardo Donati   ITA | 4 | 7 | |
| 7. | Joseph Klapuch   CZE | 3 | 6 | |
| 8. | Alberto Swejnicks   LAT | 3 | 6 | |

**1948 London** C: 9, N: 9, D: 8.6.

| | | ROUND ELIMINATED | BAD PTS. | FINAL ROUND |
|---|---|---|---|---|
| 1. | Ahmet Kireçci   TUR | — | 1 | 1 |
| 2. | Tor Nilsson   SWE | — | 3 | 3 |
| 3. | Guido Fantoni   ITA | — | 1 | 6 |
| 4. | Taisto Kangasniemi   FIN | 3 | 5 | |
| 5. | József Tarányi   HUN | 3 | 6 | |
| 6. | Moritz Inderbitzin   SWI | 3 | 7 | |

Kirecci had received a bronze medal as a middleweight 12 years earlier in Berlin.

**1952 Helsinki** C: 10, N: 10, D: 7.27.

| | | ROUND ELIMINATED | BAD PTS. | FINAL ROUND |
|---|---|---|---|---|
| 1. | Johannes Kotkas   SOV | — | 0 | 0 |
| 2. | Josef Ružička   CZE | — | 3 | 3 |
| 3. | Tauno Kovanen   FIN | — | 6 | 6 |
| 4. | Willi Waltner   GER | 4 | 7 | |
| 5. | Alexandru Suli   ROM | 3 | 5 | |
| 6. | Bengt Fahlkvist   SWE | 3 | 6 | |
| 6. | Antoine Georgoulis   GRE | 3 | 6 | |
| 8. | Guido Fantoni   ITA | 3 | 7 | |

Kotkas, a 37-year-old Estonian from Tartu, pinned his four opponents in an elapsed time of 13 minutes 36 seconds.

**1956 Melbourne** C: 10, N: 10, D: 12.6.

| | | ROUND ELIMINATED | BAD PTS. | FINAL ROUND |
|---|---|---|---|---|
| 1. | Anatoly Parfenov   SOV | — | 4 | 2 |
| 2. | Wilfried Dietrich   GER | — | 5 | 4 |
| 3. | Adelmo Bulgarelli   ITA | — | 4 | 6 |
| 4. | Hamit Kaplan   TUR | 4 | 6 | |
| 5. | Bertil Antonsson   SWE | 4 | 7 | |
| 6. | Taisto Kangasniemi   FIN | 3 | 6 | |
| 7. | Yusein Mehmedov   BUL | 3 | 7 | |
| 7. | Antoine Georgoulis   GRE | 3 | 7 | |

Parfenov was one of the least overwhelming Olympic champions ever. He was originally declared the loser in his opening contest with Dietrich. However a protest by the Soviet team was upheld by the Jury of Appeal. In the second round Parfenov lost to Antonsson. Then he won a forfeit in the third round and received a bye in the fourth round. In the fifth round he gained his only undisputed victory, a decision over Bulgarelli. Fortunately for Parfenov, his two wins were enough to take first place.

**1960 Rome** C: 12, N: 12, D: 8.31.

| | | ROUND ELIMINATED | BAD PTS. | FINAL ROUND |
|---|---|---|---|---|
| 1. | Ivan Bogdan   SOV | — | 4 | 4 |
| 2. | Wilfried Dietrich   GER | — | 5 | 4 |
| 3. | Bohumil Kubát   CZE | — | 5 | 4 |
| 4. | István Kozma   HUN | 4 | 6 | |
| 5. | Lucjan Sosnowski   POL | 4 | 6 | |
| 6. | Radoslav Kasabov   BUL | 4 | 8 | |
| 7. | Adelmo Bulgarelli   ITA | 3 | 6 | |
| 8. | Sten Ragnar Svensson   SWE | 3 | 9 | |

Dietrich was awarded the silver medal because his bodyweight was less than that of Bohumil "Weeny" Kubát. In fact, it was 88 pounds less than Kubát's. Dietrich weighed 198 pounds, while Kubát weighed 286.

**1964 Tokyo** C: 11, N: 11, D: 10.19.

| | | ROUND ELIMINATED | BAD PTS. | FINAL ROUND |
|---|---|---|---|---|
| 1. | István Kozma   HUN | — | 1 | 2 |
| 2. | Anatoly Roshin   SOV | — | 3 | 2 |
| 3. | Wilfried Dietrich   GER | 5 | 7 | |
| 4. | Petr Kment   CZE | 5 | 8 | |
| 5. | Sten Ragnar Svensson   SWE | 4 | 6 | |
| 6. | Robert Pickens   USA | 3 | 7 | |
| 7. | Radoslav Kasabov   BUL | 3 | 8 | |
| 8. | Tsuneharu Sugiyama   JPN | 3 | 8 | |

Kozma weighed in at 320 pounds.

**1968 Mexico City** C: 15, N: 15, D: 10.26.

| | | ROUND ELIMI- NATED | BAD PTS. | FINAL ROUND |
|---|---|---|---|---|
| 1. István Kozma | HUN | — | 2.5 | 2.5 |
| 2. Anatoly Roshin | SOV | — | 3.5 | 2.5 |
| 3. Petr Kment | CZE | — | 5 | 8 |
| 4. Sten Ragnar Svensson | SWE | 5 | 7 | |
| 5. Constantin Buşiu | ROM | 4 | 7 | |
| 6. Stefan Petrov | BUL | 4 | 8 | |
| 7. Raymond Uytterheaeghe | FRA | 4 | 9 | |
| 8. Edward Wojda | POL | 4 | 9.5 | |

As in 1964, Kozma won the gold medal despite being held to a draw by Roshin. This time the huge Hungarian threw his other four opponents, two of them within 40 seconds. Kment was injured and forced to withdraw from his final two matches against Kozma and Roshin.

**1972 Munich** C: 13, N: 13, D: 9.10.

| | | ROUND ELIMINATED | BAD PTS. | FINAL ROUND |
|---|---|---|---|---|
| 1. Anatoly Roshin | SOV | — | 2 | 1 |
| 2. Aleksandr Tomov | BUL | — | 3 | 5 |
| 3. Victor Dolîpschi | ROM | — | 4 | 6 |
| 4. József Csatári | HUN | 4 | 8 | |
| 4. Wilfried Dietrich | GER | 4 | 8 | |
| 4. Istvan Semeredi | YUG | 4 | 8 | |
| 7. Petr Kment | CZE | 3 | 7 | |

Thirty-eight-year-old Wilfried Dietrich, attempting to win a medal in his fifth consecutive Olympics, was disqualified in his third-round match against Victor Dolîpschi. Dietrich was so upset by the decision that he withdrew from the competition even though he only had four negative points. Forty-year-old Anatoly Roshin was the oldest wrestler ever to win an Olympic medal.

**1976 Montreal** C: 12, N: 12, D: 7.24.

| | | ROUND ELIMINATED | BAD PTS. | FINAL ROUND |
|---|---|---|---|---|
| 1. Aleksandr Kolchinsky | SOV | — | 0 | 1 |
| 2. Aleksandr Tomov | BUL | — | 4 | 3 |
| 3. Roman Codreanu | ROM | — | 2 | 8 |
| 4. Henryk Tomanek | POL | 4 | 8 | |
| 5. William "Pete" Lee | USA | 4 | 8 | |
| 6. János Rovnyai | HUN | 3 | 8 | |
| 7. Einar Gundersen | NOR | 3 | 8 | |
| 7. Richard Wolff | GER | 3 | 8 | |

Three-time defending world champion Aleksandr Tomov had defeated Kolchinsky six straight times, culminating in the European championships three months before the Olympics. However in Montreal Tomov was upset in the first round when he was pinned in only 1:14 by 331-pound Pete Lee of Muncie, Indiana. Tomov recovered to win his next three matches and qualify for the final round-robin. In the meantime, Kolchinsky used up only six minutes and 38 seconds in finishing off his first four opponents. He followed this by outpointing Tomov 12–6 in his final bout.

**1980 Moscow** C: 10, N: 10, D: 7.24.

| | | ROUND ELIMINATED | BAD PTS. | FINAL ROUND |
|---|---|---|---|---|
| 1. Aleksandr Kolchinsky | SOV | — | 0 | 1 |
| 2. Aleksandr Tomov | BUL | — | 0 | 3 |
| 3. Hassan Bchara | LEB | — | 8 | 8 |
| 4. József Farkas | HUN | 4 | 10 | |
| 5. Prvoslav Ilić | YUG | 3 | 8 | |
| 6. Roman Codreanu | ROM | 3 | 8 | |
| 6. Arturo Diaz Mora | CUB | 3 | 8 | |
| 8. Marek Galinski | POL | 2 | 8 | |

The superiority of Kolchinsky and Tomov was shown by the fact that the other eight wrestlers all reached eight penalty points before the two champions had even received their first bad mark. Kolchinsky, the lightest man in the tournament at 220 pounds, defeated 375-pound Roman Codreanu in 7:50 in his opening bout. Then he disposed of his next four opponents in an elapsed time of 11:27. In the final contest Kolchinsky outpointed Tomov 4–2 to win his second straight gold medal.

**1984 Los Angeles-Anaheim** C: 8, N: 8, D: 8.2.

| | | FINAL MATCH | |
|---|---|---|---|
| 1. Jeffrey Blatnick | USA | 2–0 | 6:00 |
| 2. Refik Memiševic | YUG | Passivity | 4:16 |
| 3. Victor Dolîpschi | ROM | | |
| 4. Panayotis Pikilidis | GRE | 7–3 | 6:00 |
| 5. Hassan El Hadad | EGY | | |
| 6. Masaya Ando | JPN | | |
| 6. Antonio Lapenna | ITA | | |

DISQ (Drugs): Thomas Johansson (SWE)

In October of 1982, Jeff Blatnick of Niskayuna, New York, seemed a most unlikely candidate to win a gold medal in the Olympics. To begin with, no U.S. athlete in his sport, Greco-Roman wrestling, had *ever* won an Olympic medal in any division. And, although he had qualified for the 1980 team that was not allowed to go to Moscow, he was no longer considered number one in the nation. And then there was the matter of his health. In May he had noticed small lumps on his neck. In July he was diagnosed as suffering from Hodgkin's disease, a form of cancer. In August his spleen and appendix were removed and in October he began radiation therapy.

But Jeffrey Blatnick was no quitter. Inspired by the memory of his brother David, who had died in a motorcycle accident in 1977, Blatnick resumed training almost immediately, despite warnings from his doctors. At the 1984 U.S. Olympic trials, he won a controversial two-match victory over 390-pound favorite Pete Lee. Lee was disqualified for slapping in the first match and for inactivity in the second.

Blatnick entered the Olympic tournament as an underdog, but in his first bout he upset gold medal favorite Refik Memiševic, when the later was disqualified for passivity. However, in his second match, Blatnick was defeated 4–3 by Panayotis Pikilidis. It is unusual for a wrestler to qualify for the final after losing a match, particularly when his preliminary pool consists of only four men. But the next day, Memišević beat Pikilidis and Blatnick found himself one victory away from an Olympic championship. His opponent in the final would be Thomas Johansson who, at 275 pounds, outweighed Blatnick by over 35 pounds.

Just before he went out to wrestle Johansson, Blatnick saw his parents underneath the stands and approached them.

"It's so close, Jeff, so close," said his father, Carl. "The Swede is big, but you've come too far to let anything stop you now."

Then his mother, Angela, whispered to him, "For David, Jeffrey, for David."

The final match was close and hard-fought. After 4¾ minutes neither wrestler had scored a point, but Blatnick had been cautioned twice, Johansson only once. Then, with only 64 seconds left, Blatnick took Johansson to the mat for a score. With the screams of the crowd getting louder and louder, Blatnick scored again 38 seconds later.

The audience counted down the final seconds and when they reached zero, the arena was filled with emotional celebration. Blatnick fell to his knees, crossed himself, joined his hands in prayer and looked up, far beyond the ceiling. Then, for the first time since his older brother had died seven years earlier, Jeffrey Blatnick cried. And cried and cried and cried. And, judging from the mail he would subsequently receive, all over the world millions of people cried with him. But not all dramatic stories have clean, happy endings. In September of 1985, Blatnick's cancer returned. This time he required 28 sessions of chemotherapy to send it into remission.

As for Johansson, he tested positive for steroids and lost his medal. After serving an 18-month suspension, he won the 1986 world championship and finished third at the 1988 Olympics.

**1988 Seoul** C: 16, N: 16, D: 9.22.

|  |  |  | FINAL MATCH | |
|---|---|---|---|---|
| 1. Aleksandr Karelin | SOV | 5-3 | 6:00 |
| 2. Rangel Gerovski | BUL | | |
| 3. Thomas Johansson | SWE | Passivity | 5:04 |
| 4. Hassan Elhadad | EGY | | |
| 5. László Klauz | HUN | Passivity | 5:00 |
| 6. Kazuya Deguchi | JPN | | |
| 7. Roman Wroclawski | POL | Forfeit | |
| 8. Duane Koslowski | USA | | |

Twenty-one-year-old Aleksandr Karelin trailed 3–0 in the final, then came from behind for the victory. Gerovski was the only one of his five opponents to last the full 6 minutes.

# Discontinued Event
## OPEN

**1906 Athens** C: 2, N: 2, D: 5.1.
1. Soren Marius Jensen    DEN
2. Verner Weckman    FIN

# YACHTING

| MEN | WOMEN | MIXED |
|---|---|---|
| Boardsailing | Boardsailing | Star |
| Finn | Europe | Flying Dutchman |
| 470 | 470 | Tornado |
| | | Soling |
| | | Discontinued Events |

Each class in yachting runs seven races over a course usually marked by buoys. Since 1968 each yacht has been assessed minus points depending on its order of finish.

1st place: 0     5th place: 10
2nd place: 3     6th place: 11.7
3rd place: 5.7    7th place: 13
4th place: 8     add one point for each subsequent place

At the conclusion of the final race, each yacht is allowed to drop its worst score. The remaining minus points are added and the yacht with the lowest total wins.

# MEN

## BOARDSAILING

**1896–1980** not held

**1984 Los Angeles-Long Beach** C: 38, N: 38, D: 8.8.
*Windglider*

| | | | PTS. |
|---|---|---|---|
| 1. | Stephan van den Berg | HOL | 27.7 |
| 2. | Randall Scott Steele | USA | 46.0 |
| 3. | Bruce Kendall | NZE | 46.4 |
| 4. | Gildas Guillerot | FRA | 52.4 |
| 5. | Klaus Maran | ITA | 54.4 |
| 6. | Greg Hyde | AUS | 55.7 |
| 7. | Dirk Meyer | GER | 67.2 |
| 8. | Björn Eybl | AUT | 80.0 |

The inaugural boardsailing competition used the Windglider, a board 12 feet 9 inches long and 25½ inches wide which carried 70 square feet of sail.

**1988 Seoul-Pusan** C: 45, N: 45, D: 9.27.
*Division II*

| | | | PTS. |
|---|---|---|---|
| 1. | Bruce Kendall | NZE | 35.4 |
| 2. | Jan Boersma | NLA | 42.7 |
| 3. | Michael Gebhardt | USA | 48.0 |
| 4. | Bart Verschoor | HOL | 53.4 |
| 5. | Robert Nagy | FRA | 61.7 |
| 6. | Francesco Wirz | ITA | 63.0 |
| 7. | Jorge Garcia Velazco | ARG | 70.1 |
| 8. | Carlos Iniesta | SPA | 81.7 |

The Division II board chosen for the competition was a 12-foot-long, round-bottomed sailboard with a 73-square-foot sail. The boardsailors faced heavy winds which, on the fifth day, gusted up to 25 knots and stirred up waves of almost 2 meters. In that race, only 19 of the 43 starters completed the course. These conditions should have favored the heavier boardsailors. However, the winner, Bruce Kendall, weighed only 143 pounds. The 24-year-old Kendall did run into problems on land: listening to rock music on a Walkman while skateboarding, he fell off and badly grazed his hand. New Zealand team officials ordered him to stay off his skateboard until after the Olympics.

## FINN

The Finn class uses a centerboard dinghy and a one-man crew. Boats are assigned at random, although since 1976 a helmsman may provide his own sail and mast.

**1896–1912** not held

**1920 Antwerp** T: 2, N: 1, D: 7.10.
*12-Foot Dinghy*
1. HOL   (Johannes Hin, Franciscus Hin)
2. HOL   (Arnoud Eugéne van der Biesen, Petrus Beukers)

**1920 Antwerp** T: 1, N: 1, D: 7.10.
*18-Foot Dinghy*
1. GBR   (Francis Richards, T. Hedberg)

**1924 Paris** C: 17, N: 17, D: 7.13.

| | | | PTS. |
|---|---|---|---|
| 1. | Léon Huybrechts | BEL | 2 |
| 2. | Henrik Robert | NOR | 7 |
| 3. | Hans Dittmar | FIN | 8 |
| 4. | Santiago Amat Cansino | SPA | 8 |
| 5. | Johannes Hin | HOL | 10 |
| 6. | Clarence Hammar | SWE | 11 |

7. Gordon Fowler          GBR    12
8. F. Guilherme-Burnay    POR    15

The Official Report of 1924 attributes to Huybrechts a sixth sense that allowed him to anticipate changes in wind direction. Second, third, and fourth place were decided by an extra race.

**1928 Amsterdam** C: 23, N: 20, D: 8.9.

1. Sven Thorell                    SWE
2. Henrik Robert                   NOR
3. Bertil Broman                   FIN
4. Willem de Vries-Lentsch         HOL
5. Egon Beyn                       GER
6. Tito Nordio                     ITA
7. J.J. Andersen                   DEN
8. Harold Gaydon, Gordon Fowler    GBR

Thorell won four of eight races and also placed second twice.

**1932 Los Angeles** C: 11, N; 11, D: 8.12.

|   |   |   | PTS. |
|---|---|---|------|
| 1. | Jacques Lebrun | FRA | 87 |
| 2. | Adriaan Maas | HOL | 85 |
| 3. | Santiago Amat Cansino | SPA | 76 |
| 4. | Edgar Behr | GER | 74 |
| 5. | Reginald Dixon | CAN | 72 |
| 6. | Colin Ratsey | GBR | 69 |
| 7. | Charles Lyon | USA | 66 |
| 8. | Silvio Treleani | ITA | 62 |

**1936 Berlin–Kiel** C: 25, N: 25, D: 8.12.

|   |   |   | PTS. |
|---|---|---|------|
| 1. | Daniel Kagchelland | HOL | 163 |
| 2. | Werner Krogmann | GER | 150 |
| 3. | Peter Scott | GBR | 131 |
| 4. | Erich Wichmann-Harbeck | CHI | 130 |
| 5. | Giuseppe Fago | ITA | 115 |
| 6. | Jacques Lebrun | FRA | 109 |
| 7. | Tibor Heinrich | HUN | 102 |
| 8. | Willy Pieper | SWI | 99 |

**1948 London** C: 21, N: 21, D: 8.12.

|   |   |   | PTS. |
|---|---|---|------|
| 1. | Paul Elvström | DEN | 5543 |
| 2. | Ralph Evans | USA | 5408 |
| 3. | Jacobus de Jong | HOL | 5204 |
| 4. | Richard Sarby | SWE | 4603 |
| 5. | Paul McLaughlin | CAN | 4535 |
| 6. | Felix Sienra Castellanos | URU | 4079 |
| 7. | Jean-Jacques Herbulot | FRA | 4068 |
| 8. | R. Van der Haeghen | BEL | 3660 |

Twenty-year-old Paul Elvström began his Olympic career quietly, failing to finish the first day's race. After five races, the competition appeared to be a tight contest between Evans, McLaughlin, and Sarby. All the others were more than 800 points behind. Elvström was in eighth place. But on the sixth day the young Dane fin-ished first, 23 seconds ahead of Herbulot, and the extra 301 points that he gained propelled Elvström into third place, 564 points behind Evans. This meant that Evans could clinch the gold medal by finishing third on the final day. However he landed in fifth place, three minutes away from his goal, while Evström took first place again, three minutes and seven seconds ahead of de Jong; the 301-point bonus for winning provided the margin of victory in the final standings.

**1952 Helsinki** C: 28, N: 28, D: 7.28.

|   |   |   | PTS. |
|---|---|---|------|
| 1. | Paul Elvström | DEN | 8209 |
| 2. | Charles Currey | GBR | 5449 |
| 3. | Richard Sarby | SWE | 5051 |
| 4. | Jacobus de Jong | HOL | 5033 |
| 5. | Wolfgang Erndl | AUT | 4273 |
| 6. | Morits Skaugen | NOR | 4073 |
| 7. | Adelchi Pelaschiar | ITA | 4068 |
| 8. | Paul McLaughlin | CAN | 4033 |

Elvström won three of the first four races and gained so many points that he had earned the gold medal without having to race the last day. He entered anyway and won again. His other placings were a fifth, a third, and a fourth.

**1956 Melbourne** C: 20, N: 20, D: 12.5.

|   |   |   | PTS. |
|---|---|---|------|
| 1. | Paul Elvström | DEN | 7509 |
| 2. | André Nelis | BEL | 6254 |
| 3. | John Marvin | USA | 5953 |
| 4. | Jürgen Vogler | GER | 4199 |
| 5. | Richard Sarby | SWE | 3990 |
| 6. | Eric Bongers | SAF | 3912 |
| 7. | Adelchi Pelaschiar | ITA | 3409 |
| 8. | Bruce Kirby | CAN | 3213 |

Elvström finished first in the opening race, fell to eighth and 15th in the next two, and then won each of the last four races.

**1960 Rome-Naples** C: 35, N: 35, D: 9.7.

|   |   |   | PTS. |
|---|---|---|------|
| 1. | Paul Elvström | DEN | 8171 |
| 2. | Aleksandr Tsutselov | SOV | 6520 |
| 3. | André Nelis | BEL | 5934 |
| 4. | Ronald Jenyns | AUS | 5758 |
| 5. | Reinaldo Conrad | BRA | 5176 |
| 6. | Ralph Roberts | NZE | 5140 |
| 7. | Ian Bruce | CAN | 5133 |
| 8. | Kenneth Albury | BAH | 5092 |

Elvström, now 32 years old, chalked up three firsts, one second, and two fifths to clinch his fourth gold medal without having to enter the final race. This time Elvström, who was not in perfect health, declined to start.

**1964 Tokyo** C: 33, N: 33, D: 10.21.

|   | | | PTS. |
|---|---|---|---|
| 1. | Wilhelm Kuhweide | GER | 7638 |
| 2. | Peter Barrett | USA | 6373 |
| 3. | Henning Wind | DEN | 6190 |
| 4. | Peter Mander | NZE | 5684 |
| 5. | Hubert Raudaschl | AUT | 5405 |
| 6. | Colin Ryrie | AUS | 5273 |
| 7. | Joerg Bruder | BRA | 4956 |
| 8. | Panagiotis Kouligas | GRE | 4546 |

In 1964 East and West Germany entered a combined team. However, a dispute developed as to which side should be represented in the Finn class. At the last moment the International Yacht Racing Union interceded and authorized the West German helmsman, Willi Kuhweide. Kuhweide sailed well throughout the regatta and won the gold medal by placing second, first, fourth, sixth, fifth, third, and first.

**1968 Mexico City-Acapulco** C: 36, N: 36, D: 10.21.

|   | | | PTS. |
|---|---|---|---|
| 1. | Valentin Mankin | SOV | 11.7 |
| 2. | Hubert Raudaschl | AUT | 53.4 |
| 3. | Fabio Albarelli | ITA | 55.1 |
| 4. | Ronald Jenyns | AUS | 67.0 |
| 5. | Panagiotis Kouligas | GRE | 71.0 |
| 6. | Jan Winquist | FIN | 72.0 |
| 7. | Arne Akerson | SWI | 77.0 |
| 8. | Philippe Soria | FRA | 80.0 |

Mankin had a consistent series, placing third, fifth, first, first, second, second, and first.

**1972 Munich-Kiel** C: 35, N: 35, D: 9.8.

|   | | | PTS. |
|---|---|---|---|
| 1. | Serge Maury | FRA | 58.0 |
| 2. | Ilias Hatzipavlis | GRE | 71.0 |
| 3. | Victor Potapov | SOV | 74.7 |
| 4. | John Bertrand | AUS | 76.7 |
| 5. | Thomas Lundqvist | SWE | 81.0 |
| 6. | Kim Weber | FIN | 85.7 |
| 7. | Hans-Christian Schröder | GDR | 91.0 |
| 8. | György Fináczy | HUN | 94.0 |

**1976 Montreal-Kingston** C: 28, N: 28, D: 7.27.

|   | | | PTS. |
|---|---|---|---|
| 1. | Jochen Schümann | GDR | 35.4 |
| 2. | Andrei Balashov | SOV | 39.7 |
| 3. | John Bertrand | AUS | 46.4 |
| 4. | Claudio Biekarck | BRA | 54.7 |
| 5. | Kent Carlson | SWE | 66.4 |
| 6. | Anastassios Boudouris | GRE | 77.0 |
| 7. | David Howlett | GBR | 77.7 |
| 8. | Sanford Riley | CAN | 83.0 |

Schümann and Balashov entered the final race in a tie for first place. Schümann pulled away on the last day and finished 40 seconds ahead of his rival.

John Bertrand made sailing history in 1983 when he broke the 132-year-old U.S. monopoly of the America's Cup with his yacht, *Australia III*.

**1980 Moscow-Tallinn** C: 21, N: 21, D: 7.29.

|   | | | PTS. |
|---|---|---|---|
| 1. | Esko Rechardt | FIN | 36.7 |
| 2. | Wolfgang Mayrhofer | AUT | 46.7 |
| 3. | Andrei Balashov | SOV | 47.4 |
| 4. | Claudio Biekarck | BRA | 53.0 |
| 5. | Jochen Schümann | GDR | 54.4 |
| 6. | Kent Carlson | SWE | 63.7 |
| 7. | Ryszard Skarbiński | POL | 71.1 |
| 8. | Mark Neeleman | HOL | 76.0 |

**1984 Los Angeles-Long Beach** C: 28, N: 28, D: 8.8.

|   | | | PTS. |
|---|---|---|---|
| 1. | Russell Coutts | NZE | 34.7 |
| 2. | John Bertrand | USA | 37.0 |
| 3. | Terry Neilson | CAN | 37.7 |
| 4. | Joaquin Blanco | SPA | 60.7 |
| 5. | Wolfgang Gerz | GER | 66.1 |
| 6. | Chris Pratt | AUS | 68.0 |
| 7. | Michael Mcintyre | GBR | 70.7 |
| 8. | Jorge Zarif Neto | BRA | 78.7 |

The decisive moment in the Finn class competition came in the very first race when Bertrand, who finished first, was disqualified for touching Coutt's bow while attempting to port-tack. This provided Coutts with his eventual margin of victory. Coutts was almost disqualified himself at the final weigh-in when his clothing was found to be one pound overweight. However, a third weigh-in, for which Coutts carefully arranged each garment, found him just below the 20 kg maximum.

**1988 Seoul-Pusan** C: 33, N: 33, D: 9.27.

|   | | | PTS. |
|---|---|---|---|
| 1. | José Luis Doreste | SPA | 38.1 |
| 2. | Peter Holmberg | VIR | 40.4 |
| 3. | John Cutler | NZE | 45.0 |
| 4. | Stuart Childerley | GBR | 50.7 |
| 5. | Lasse Hjortnaes | DEN | 51.0 |
| 6. | Thomas Schmid | GER | 72.1 |
| 7. | Roy Heiner | HOL | 78.4 |
| 8. | Oleg Khopyorsky | SOV | 81.0 |

Doreste, whose younger brother, Luis, won a gold medal in the 470 class in 1984, survived a close and bitter contest that wasn't decided until the last race. Doreste, who was disqualified in the fourth race, accused his opponents of trying to win "in the jury room" rather than on the water. Peter Holmberg won the first-ever medal for the U.S. Virgin Islands and would have earned the gold had he not drifted a few feet over the line at the start of the fourth race.

In the fifth race, Lawrence Lemieux of Canada was in second place when he noticed Joseph Chan, the 470 crew from Singapore, struggling in the water 25 yards from his capsized boat. Chan had injured his back and was being swept away by the powerful currents. Lemieux turned around and saved Chan, who was too exhausted to heave himself into the Canadian's boat. The International Olympic Committee gave Lemieux a special award for his act of gallantry. Lemieux, baffled by the attention he received, reminded reporters of what might have happened if he had ignored Chan. "I'm not *that* intense," he said.

## 470

The 470 is a two-person fiberglass craft that is 470 centimeters long. Like the Flying Dutchman, it uses a centerboard dinghy and a trapeze. From 1976 through 1984 this event was open to competitors of both sexes. In 1988, the 470 class was divided into two separate competitions, one for men and one for women.

**1896–1972** not held

**1976 Montreal-Kingston** C: 28, N: 28, D: 7.27.

|  |  |  | PTS. |
|---|---|---|---|
| 1. | GER | (Frank Hübner, Harro Bode) | 42.4 |
| 2. | SPA | (Antonio Gorostegui, Pedro Millet) | 49.7 |
| 3. | AUS | (Ian Brown, Ian Ruff) | 57.0 |
| 4. | SOV | (Viktor Potapov, Aleksandr Potapov) | 57.0 |
| 5. | NZE | (Mark Paterson, Brett Bennett) | 59.7 |
| 6. | GBR | (Philip Crebbin, Derek Clark) | 69.4 |
| 7. | SWI | (Jean-Claude Vuithier, Laurent Quellet) | 71.7 |
| 8. | FRA | (Marc Laurent, Roger Surmin) | 79.4 |

**1980 Moscow-Tallinn** C: 14, N: 14, D: 7.29.

|  |  |  | PTS. |
|---|---|---|---|
| 1. | BRA | (Marcos Rizzo Soares, Eduardo Penido) | 36.4 |
| 2. | GDR | (Jörn Borowski, Egbert Swensson) | 38.7 |
| 3. | FIN | (Jouko Lindgren, Georg Tallberg) | 39.7 |
| 4. | HOL | (Henk Van Gent, Jan Van Den Hondel) | 49.4 |
| 5. | POL | (Leon Wrobel, Tomasz Stocki) | 53.0 |
| 6. | SPA | (Gustavo Doreste, Alfredo Rigau) | 54.1 |
| 7. | ITA | (Ernesto Treves, Silvio Necchi) | 57.7 |
| 8. | SWE | (Lars Bengtsson, Stefan Bengtsson) | 60.0 |

Gold medal winners Soares and Penido, wind surfers from Rio de Janeiro, were only 19 and 20 years old, respectively. Had Borowski and Swensson crossed the finish line two seconds sooner in the final race, they would have taken the championship away from the Brazilians. Barowski was the son of Paul Borowski, who won medals in the Dragon class in 1968 and 1972.

**1984 Los Angeles-Long Beach** T: 28, N: 28, D: 8.8.

|  |  |  | PTS. |
|---|---|---|---|
| 1. | SPA | (Luis Doreste, Roberto Molina) | 33.7 |
| 2. | USA | (Stephan Benjamin, Christopher Steinfeld) | 43.0 |
| 3. | FRA | (Thierry Peponnet, Luc Pillot) | 49.4 |
| 4. | GER | (Wolfgang Hunger, Joachim Hunger) | 50.1 |
| 5. | ITA | (Thomaso Chieffi, Enrico Chieffi) | 57.0 |
| 6. | FIN | (Peter von Koskull, Johan von Koskull) | 67.4 |
| 7. | GBR | (Catherine Foster, Peter Newlands) | 70.0 |
| 8. | ISR | (Shimshon Brokman, Eitan Friedlander) | 70.0 |

The unheralded Spanish duo, born in the Canary Islands and residents of Barcelona, earned their gold medals without having to take part in the final race.

**1988 Seoul-Pusan** C: 29, N: 29, D: 9.27.

|  |  |  | PTS. |
|---|---|---|---|
| 1. | FRA | (Thierry Peponnet, Luc Pillot) | 34.7 |
| 2. | SOV | (Tonu Tõniste, Toomas Tõniste) | 46.0 |
| 3. | USA | (John Shadden, Charlie McKee) | 51.0 |
| 4. | SPA | (Feranado Leon, Francisco Sánchez Luna) | 55.0 |
| 5. | GER | (Wolfgang Hunger, Joachim Hunger) | 58.7 |
| 6. | NZE | (Peter Evans, Simon Mander) | 62.7 |
| 7. | ITA | (Sandro Montefusco, Paolo Montefusco) | 68.7 |
| 8. | CAN | (Nigel Cochrane, Gordon McIlquham) | 71.7 |

The previously unknown Tõniste twins from Estonia won the fourth and fifth races and finished second in the sixth race to take the overall lead. All they had to do to win gold medals was place ahead of Peponnet and Pillot in the final race, which was sailed in near-gale conditions. The Tõnistes were in the lead with less than a lap to go when they suffered a severe capsize and were forced to retire.

# WOMEN
## BOARDSAILING

This event will be held for the first time in 1992.

## EUROPE

The Europe class is a single-handed dinghy, 11 feet long and weighing only 140 lbs. (63.5 kg).

This event will be held for the first time in 1992.

## 470

**1896–1984** not held

**1988 Seoul-Pusan** C: 21, N: 21, D: 9.27.

|  |  |  | PTS. |
|---|---|---|---|
| 1. | USA | (Allison Jolly, Lynne Jewell) | 26.7 |
| 2. | SWE | (Marit Söderström, Birgitta Bengtsson) | 40.0 |
| 3. | SOV | (Larissa Moskalenko, Irina Chunikhovskaya) | 45.4 |
| 4. | FIN | (Bettina Lemström, Annika Lemström) | 47.0 |
| 5. | GER | (Susanne Meyer, Katrin Adlkofer) | 56.4 |
| 6. | AUS | (Nicola Green, Karyn Davis) | 57.0 |
| 7. | GDR | (Susanne Theel, Silke Preuss) | 57.4 |
| 8. | FRA | (Florence Lebrun, Sophie Berge) | 81.7 |

The first women to take part in Olympic yachting were Dorothy Wright of Great Britain, who crewed for her husband in the uncontested 7-meter class in 1920, and

Virginia Hériot of France, who won a gold medal in the 8-meter class in 1928. The first woman to skipper an Olympic boat was Britain's Cathy Foster in the 1984 470 class.

Söderström and Jolly had faced each other six times in world championships prior to 1988, with Söderström winning four. However, Jolly's two victories came, significantly, in the Olympic years of 1980 and 1984. In the inaugural women-only competition in Seoul, Jolly and Jewell took two firsts, two seconds, and a third. But because they were disqualified in the fifth race for tacking too close, they needed to finish fourteenth or better in the final race to earn gold medals. Despite the treacherous weather conditions, this did not seem a difficult task. However, in the middle of the race they dropped off a large wave. As a result, the wire connecting the jib to the halyard broke and their jib sail sagged down the jib wire.

"There goes the gold," said Jolly, as they dropped back from fourth place to fifteenth. "We've got to fight!" answered Jewell, who, despite 30 knots of wind and 10-foot waves, spent the next 5 minutes repairing the jib with a small piece of spare twine. With the sail back in place, they managed to finish ninth.

# MIXED

## STAR

The Star class is a 6.9-meter- (22-foot 8-inch) long shallow monotype of American origin, with a 281-square-foot sail. It has a two-person crew.

**1896–1928** not held

**1932 Los Angeles** T: 7, N: 7, D: 8.12.

|   |   |   | PTS. |
|---|---|---|---|
| 1. | USA | (Gilbert Gray, Andrew Libano) | 46 |
| 2. | GBR | (Colin Ratsey, Peter Jaffe) | 35 |
| 3. | SWE | (Gunnar Asther, Daniel Sundén-Cullberg) | 28 |
| 4. | CAN | (Henry Wylie, Henry Simmonds) | 27 |
| 5. | FRA | (Jean-Jacques Herbulot, Jean Peytel) | 26 |
| 6. | HOL | (Jan Maas, Adriaan Maas) | 14 |
| 7. | SAF | (Arent Van Soelen, Cecil Goodricke) | 7 |

The *Jupiter,* skippered by 30-year-old Gilbert Gray of New Orleans, won five of the seven races.

**1936 Berlin-Kiel** T: 12, N: 12, D: 8.10.

|   |   |   | PTS. |
|---|---|---|---|
| 1. | GER | (Peter Bischoff, Hans-Joachim Weise) | 80 |
| 2. | SWE | (Arvid Laurin, Uno Wallentin) | 64 |
| 3. | HOL | (Willem de Vries-Lentsch, Adriaan Maas) | 63 |
| 4. | GBR | (Keith Grogono, William Welply) | 56 |
| 5. | USA | (William Waterhouse, Woodbridge Metcalf) | 51 |

|   |   |   | |
|---|---|---|---|
| 6. | NOR | (Öivind Christensen, Sigurd Herbern) | 44 |
| 7. | FRA | (Jean-Jacques Herbulot, de Montaut) | 41 |
| 8. | TUR | (Harun Ulman, Behzat Baydar) | 38 |

Bischoff matched Gray's feat of winning five of seven races. The Germans had clinched the gold medals after the sixth race, but raced the next day anyway and won again.

**1948 London** T: 17, N: 17, D: 8.12.

|   |   |   | PTS. |
|---|---|---|---|
| 1. | USA | (Hilary Smart, Paul Smart) | 5828 |
| 2. | CUB | (Carlos De Cárdenas Culmell, Carlos De Cárdenas, Jr.) | 4949 |
| 3. | HOL | (Adriaan Maas, Edward Stutterheim) | 4731 |
| 4. | GBR/BAH | (Durward Knowles, Sloan Farrington) | 4372 |
| 5. | ITA | (Agostino Straulino, Nicolo Rode) | 4370 |
| 6. | POR | (Joaquim De Mascarenhas Fiuza, Julio De Sousa Leite Gorinho) | 4292 |
| 7. | AUS | (Alexander Sturrock, Len Fenton) | 3828 |
| 8. | CAN | (Norman Gooderham, A. Gerald Fairhead) | 2635 |

Paul Smart was a 56-year-old lawyer from New York. His 23-year-old son, Hilary, was a student at Harvard.

**1952 Helsinki** T: 21, N: 21, D: 7.28.

|   |   |   | PTS. |
|---|---|---|---|
| 1. | ITA | (Agostino Straulino, Nicolo Rode) | 7635 |
| 2. | USA | (John Reid, John Price) | 7126 |
| 3. | POR | (Joaquim De Mascarenhas Fiuza, Francisco Rebelo De Andrade) | 4903 |
| 4. | CUB | (Carlos De Cárdenas Culmell, Carlos De Cárdenas, Jr.) | 4535 |
| 5. | BAH | (Durward Knowles, Sloan Farrington) | 4405 |
| 6. | FRA | (Edouard Chabert, Jean-Louis Dauris) | 3866 |
| 7. | SWE | (Bengt Melin, Björn Carlsson) | 3785 |
| 8. | HOL | (Adriaan Maas, Edward Stutterheim) | 3510 |

The Italians and the Americans engaged in a private battle, winning all seven races and generally leaving the others far behind. Straulino skippered the *Merope* to three firsts and four seconds. The U.S. pair placed first four times and third once, but also finished seventh in the second race and eighth on the final day.

**1956 Melbourne** T: 12, N: 12, D: 12.5.

|   |   |   | PTS. |
|---|---|---|---|
| 1. | USA | (Herbert Williams, Lawrence Low) | 5876 |
| 2. | ITA | (Agostino Straulino, Nicolo Rode) | 5649 |
| 3. | BAH | (Durward Knowles, Sloan Farrington) | 5223 |
| 4. | POR | (Duarte De Almeida Bello, José Bustorff Silva) | 3825 |
| 5. | FRA | (Philippe Chancerel, Michel Parent) | 3126 |
| 6. | CUB | (Carlos De Cárdenas Culmell, Jorge De Cárdenas) | 2714 |
| 7. | GBR | (Bruce Banks, Stanley Potter) | 2387 |
| 8. | SOV | (Timir Pinegin, Fyodor Shutkov) | 1778 |

Skippered by 48-year-old Sussex-born Herbert Williams of Evanston, Illinois, the *Kathleen* placed first, fifth, second, first, second, second, second.

**1960 Rome-Naples** T: 26, N: 26, D: 9.7.

| | | | PTS. |
|---|---|---|---|
| 1. | SOV | (Timir Pinegin, Fyodor Shutkov) | 7619 |
| 2. | POR | (José Quina, Mário Quina) | 6665 |
| 3. | USA | (William Parks, Robert Halperin) | 6269 |
| 4. | ITA | (Agostino Straulino, Carlo Rolandi) | 6047 |
| 5. | SWI | (Hans Bryner, Ulrich Bucher) | 5716 |
| 6. | BAH | (Durward Knowles, Sloan Farrington) | 5282 |
| 7. | GER | (Bruno Splieth, Eckart Wagner) | 4745 |
| 8. | YUG | (Mario Fafangel, Janko Kosmina) | 3977 |

This was the first Soviet victory in Olympic yachting, a sport which had previously been considered the domain of capitalists. Oddly enough, the Soviet craft, the *Tornado,* had been built in Old Greenwich, Connecticut.

**1964 Tokyo** T: 17, N: 17, D: 10.21.

| | | | PTS. |
|---|---|---|---|
| 1. | BAH | (Durward Knowles, C. Cecil Cooke) | 5664 |
| 2. | USA | (Richard Stearns, Lynn Williams) | 5585 |
| 3. | SWE | (Pelle Pettersson, Holger Sundström) | 5527 |
| 4 | FIN | (Peder Tallberg, Henrik Tallberg) | 5402 |
| 5. | SOV | (Timir Pinegin, Fyodor Shutkov) | 4305 |
| 6. | GER | (Bruno Splieth, Karsten Meyer) | 4175 |
| 7. | CAN | (David Miller, William West) | 3565 |
| 8. | POR | (Manuel Duarte, Pinto Fernando) | 3330 |

Forty-six-year-old Durward Knowles was competing in his fifth Olympics. If Stearns and Williams had finished six seconds faster in the last race, they would have won the gold medal.

**1968 Mexico City-Acapulco** T: 20, N. 20, D: 10.21.

| | | | PTS. |
|---|---|---|---|
| 1. | USA | (Lowell North, Peter Barrett) | 14.4 |
| 2. | NOR | (Peder Lunde, Per Olav Wiken) | 43.7 |
| 3. | ITA | (Franco Cavallo, Camilo Gargano) | 44.7 |
| 4. | DEN | (Paul Elvström, Poul Mik-Meyer) | 50.4 |
| 5. | BAH | (Durward Knowles, Percival Knowles) | 63.4 |
| 6. | AUS | (David Forbes, Richard Williamson) | 68.7 |
| 7. | BRA | (Erik Schmidt, Axel Schmidt) | 74.4 |
| 8. | SWI | (Edwin Bernet, Rolf Amrein) | 75.0 |

North and Barrett secured first place after six races, but won the seventh race anyway.

**1972 Munich-Kiel** T: 18, N: 18, D: 9.8.

| | | | PTS. |
|---|---|---|---|
| 1. | AUS | (David Forbes, John Anderson) | 28.1 |
| 2. | SWE | (Pelle Pettersson, Stellan Westerdahl) | 44.0 |
| 3. | GER | (Wilhelm Kuhweide, Karsten Meyer) | 44.4 |
| 4. | BRA | (Jorge Bruder, Jan Willem Aten) | 52.7 |
| 5. | ITA | (Flavio Scala, Mauro Testa) | 58.4 |
| 6. | POR | (Antonio Correia, Ulrich Anjos) | 68.4 |
| 7. | GBR | (Stuart Jardine, John Wastall) | 68.7 |
| 8. | HUN | (András Gosztonyi, György Holovits) | 74.0 |

The Australians were assured of first place after the sixth race.

**1976** not held

**1980 Moscow-Tallinn** T: 13, N: 13, D: 7.29.

| | | | PTS. |
|---|---|---|---|
| 1. | SOV | (Valentin Mankin, Aleksandr Muzõtšenko) | 24.7 |
| 2. | AUT | (Hubert Raudaschl, Karl Ferstl) | 31.7 |
| 3. | ITA | (Giorgio Gorla, Alfio Peraboni) | 36.1 |
| 4. | SWE | (Peter Sundelin, Håkan Lindström) | 44.7 |
| 5. | DEN | (Jens Håkon Christensen, Morten Nielsen) | 45.7 |
| 6. | HOL | (Boudewijn Binkhorst, Jacob Vandenberg) | 49.4 |
| 7. | SPA | (Antonio Gorostegui, José Maria Benavides) | 72.7 |
| 8. | GDR | (Wolf-Eberhard Richter, Olaf Engelhardt) | 83.7 |

Forty-one-year-old Valentin Mankin gained his third gold medal, having won the Finn class in 1968 and the Tempest in 1972. He also won a silver in the 1976 Tempest. The Austrians could have won with a fourth-place finish in the last race, but they could do no better than ninth. Most damaging to the Austrians was the third race, in which they were disqualified after finishing first.

**1984 Los Angeles-Long Beach** T: 19, N: 19, D: 8.8.

| | | | PTS. |
|---|---|---|---|
| 1. | USA | (William E. Buchan, Stephen Erickson) | 29.7 |
| 2. | GER | (Joachim Griese, Michael Marcour) | 41.4 |
| 3. | ITA | (Giorgio Gorla, Alfio Peraboni) | 43.5 |
| 4. | SWE | (Kent Carlson, Henrik Eyermann) | 43.7 |
| 5. | AUT | (Hubert Raudaschl, Karl Ferstl) | 53.4 |
| 6. | GRE | (Ilias Hatzipavlis, Leonidas Pelekanakis) | 67.0 |
| 7. | SPA | (Antonio Gorostegui, José Luis Doreste) | 74.0 |
| 8. | HOL | (Hans Binkhorst, Wilom van Walt Meijer) | 76.0 |

After six races, the gold medal was still up for grabs among the four leaders. Buchan, a 49-year-old building contractor from Seattle, Washington, got off to a poor start and he and Erickson found themselves discussing how to protect third place. But a sudden wind shift, coupled with a mistake by Gorla, who missed a mark and had to go around the buoy again, opened the way for the Americans, who shot through for their third victory of the regatta. As Buchan would later say, "In five minutes we went from nothing to silver to gold. I've been sailing these little suckers for 35 years, and I've never felt the speed I had. I still don't know how I did it." Buchan's son, Carl, won a gold medal in the Flying Dutchman class.

**1988 Seoul-Pusan** C: 21, N: 21, D: 9.27.

| | | | PTS. |
|---|---|---|---|
| 1. | GBR | (Michael McIntyre, Bryn Vaile) | 45.7 |
| 2. | USA | (Mark Reynolds, Hal Haenel) | 48.0 |
| 3. | BRA | (Torben Grael, Nelson Falcao) | 50.0 |
| 4. | SWE | (Mats Johansson, Mats Hansson) | 56.7 |
| 5. | ITA | (Giorgio Gorla, Alfio Peraboni) | 63.1 |
| 6. | CAN | (D. Ross MacDonald, D. Bruce MacDonald) | 63.7 |
| 7. | AUS | (Colin Beashel, Gregory Torpy) | 66.4 |
| 8. | SOV | (Viktor Solovyov, Aleksandr Zybin) | 68.4 |

McIntyre and Vaile were in fourth place after six races. To earn gold medals they needed to win the final race, with Reynolds and Haenel placing worse than fifth and Grael and Falcao worse than fourth. As it happened, the

Brazilians could manage only eighth place; the Americans suffered a broken mast and failed to finish. Meanwhile, McIntyre and Vaile successfully fought off a challenge from the Australian pair to win by 11 seconds. Regarding his upset victory, McIntyre, a car-phone sales manager from West Dean, near Salisbury, said, "In my wildest dreams I thought we could win, but not in any other state of mind."

The skipper of the 19th place Bahamian boat was 1964 Olympic champion Durwood Knowles, who, at age 70, was the third-oldest competitor in any sport in the history of the Olympics. He was also one of only three people to take part in eight Olympics.

# FLYING DUTCHMAN

The Flying Dutchman class uses a centerboard dinghy and a crew of two, one of whom is attached to the boat by a rope and a trapeze. This allows him to lean far outside the craft without falling overboard. The boat is 6.05 meters (19 feet 10 inches) long.

**1896–1956** not held

**1960 Rome-Naples** T: 31, N: 31, D: 9.7.

| | | | PTS. |
|---|---|---|---|
| 1. | NOR | (Peder Lunde, Jr., Björn Bergvall) | 6774 |
| 2. | DEN | (Hans Fogh, Ole Erik Petersen) | 5991 |
| 3. | GER | (Rolf Mulka, Ingo von Bredow, Achim Kadelbach) | 5882 |
| 4. | ZIM | (David Butler, Christopher Bevan) | 5792 |
| 5. | HOL | (Gijsbertus Verhagen, Gerardus Lautenschütz) | 5452 |
| 6. | SOV | (Aleksandr Shelkovnikov, Viktor Pilchin) | 5123 |
| 7. | GBR | (Slotty Dawes, James Ramus) | 4954 |
| 8. | NZE | (Murray Rae, Ronald Watson) | 4641 |

Eighteen-year-old Peder Lunde came from an illustrious sailing family. His grandfather Eugen won a gold medal in the six-meter class in 1924, and his father and mother Peder and Vibeke, won silver medals in the 5.5-meter class in 1952. Young Peder also gained a Star class silver medal in 1968.

**1964 Tokyo** T: 21, N: 21, D: 10.21.

| | | | PTS. |
|---|---|---|---|
| 1. | NZE | (Helmer Pedersen, Earle Wells) | 6255 |
| 2. | GBR | (Franklyn Musto, Arthur Morgan) | 5556 |
| 3. | USA | (Harry Melges, William Bentsen) | 5158 |
| 4. | DEN | (Ole Erik Petersen, Hans Fogh) | 4500 |
| 5. | SOV | (Aleksandr Shelkovnikov, Viktor Pilchin) | 4375 |
| 6. | HOL | (Gijsbertus Verhagen, Nicolaas de Jong) | 4214 |
| 7. | FRA | (Marcel-André Buffet, Alain-François Lehoerff) | 3864 |
| 8. | AUT | (Karl Geiger, Werner Fischer) | 3706 |

Pedersen and Wells got off to a slow start, placing 16th the first day and failing to finish the second race. After that they picked up three firsts, a third, and a fourth.

**1968 Mexico City-Acapulco** T: 30, N: 30, D: 10.21.

| | | | PTS. |
|---|---|---|---|
| 1. | GBR | (Rodney Pattison, Iain Macdonald-Smith) | 3.0 |
| 2. | GER | (Ullrich Libor, Peter Naumann) | 43.7 |
| 3. | BRA | (Reinaldo Conrad, Burkhard Cordes) | 48.4 |
| 4. | AUS | (Carl Ryves, James Sargeant) | 49.1 |
| 5. | NOR | (Björn Lofteröd, Odd Lofteröd) | 52.4 |
| 6. | FRA | (Bertrand Cheret, Bruno Trouble) | 68.0 |
| 7. | CAN | (Roger Green, Stewart Green) | 79.0 |
| 8. | NZE | (Geoffrey Smale, Ralph Roberts) | 84.0 |

Submarine lieutenant Rod Pattison and solicitor's clerk Iain Macdonald-Smith finished first in the opening race, but were disqualified for interference. Undeterred by what they considered an unjust decision, the two men guided their boat *Superdocious* to five straight victories. Sailing cautiously on the final day, they still placed second to win the competition by a wide margin.

**1972 Munich-Kiel** T: 29, N: 29, D: 9.8.

| | | | PTS. |
|---|---|---|---|
| 1. | GBR | (Rodney Pattisson, Christopher Davies) | 22.7 |
| 2. | FRA | (Yves Pajot, Marc Pajot) | 40.7 |
| 3. | GER | (Ullrich, Libor, Peter Naumann) | 51.1 |
| 4. | BRA | (Reinaldo Conrad, Burkhard Cordes) | 62.4 |
| 5. | YUG | (Anton Grego, Simo Nikolić) | 63.7 |
| 6. | SOV | (Vladimir Leontiev, Valery Zoubanov) | 67.7 |
| 7. | DEN | (Hans Fogh, Elrik Brock) | 74.4 |
| 8. | AUS | (Mark Bethwaite, Timothy Alexander) | 75.7 |

Pattisson and Davies won four of the first six races and didn't bother to start on the final day.

**1976 Montreal-Kingston** T: 20, N: 20, D: 7.27.

| | | | PTS. |
|---|---|---|---|
| 1. | GER | (Jörg Diesch, Eckart Diesch) | 34.7 |
| 2. | GBR | (Rodney Pattisson, Julian Brooke Houghton) | 51.7 |
| 3. | BRA | (Reinaldo Conrad, Peter Eicker) | 52.1 |
| 4. | CAN | (Hans Fogh, Evert Bastet) | 57.1 |
| 5. | SOV | (Vladimir Leontiev, Valery Zubanov) | 59.4 |
| 6. | USA | (Norman Freeman, John Mathias) | 65.7 |
| 7. | SPA | (Alesandro Abascal, José Benavides) | 66.0 |
| 8. | FRA | (Yves Pajot, Marc Pajot) | 72.0 |

For the third straight time, Rod Pattison was first across the finishing line in the opening race. However, he fell off badly in the last three races, placing 18th, 12th, and 11th. The Diesch brothers were ten points ahead after six races. On the way to the starting line for the final race they discovered that their centerboard was cracked. They returned to shore, obtained permission to replace the board, made the repair, and still arrived on time to compete. They placed fifth, good enough to take the gold medal.

**1980 Moscow-Tallinn** T: 15, N: 15, D: 7.29.

| | | | PTS. |
|---|---|---|---|
| 1. | SPA | (Alesandro Abascal, Miguel Noguer) | 19.0 |
| 2. | IRL | (David Wilkins, James Wilkinson) | 30.0 |
| 3. | HUN | (Szabolcs Detre, Zsolt Detre) | 45.7 |

| 4. | GDR | (Wolfgang Haase, Wolfgang Wenzel) | 51.4 |
| 5. | SOV | (Vladimir Leontyev, Valery Zubanov) | 51.7 |
| 6. | DEN | (Jörgen Böjsen Möller, Jacob Böjsen Möller) | 54.5 |
| 7. | HOL | (Jan Erik Vollebregt, Sjoerd Vollebregt) | 54.7 |
| 8. | BRA | (Reinaldo Conrad, Manfred Kaufmann) | 63.4 |

Helmsman Alesandro Abascal, a 28-year-old physicist, won without having to take part in the final race. He and medical student Miguel Noguer had three firsts, a second, and two fourths in the first six races.

**1984 Los Angeles-Long Beach** T: 17, N: 17, D: 8.8.

| | | | PTS. |
|---|---|---|---|
| 1. | USA | (Jonathan McKee, William Carl Buchan) | 19.7 |
| 2. | CAN | (Terry McLaughlin, Evert Bastet) | 22.7 |
| 3. | GBR | (Jonathan Richards, Peter Allam) | 48.7 |
| 4. | DEN | (Jörgen Bojsen-Möller, Jacob Bojsen-Möller) | 52.4 |
| 5. | GER | (Jörg Diesch, Eckart Diesch) | 56.7 |
| 6. | BRA | (Alan Adler, Marcus Tenke) | 61.7 |
| 7. | ITA | (Mario Celon, Claudio Celon) | 78.7 |
| 8. | ISR | (Yoel Sela, Eldad Amir) | 79.4 |

McLaughlin entered the last race with a three-point lead over McKee, after winning three of the first six races. But the intense jockeying for position found the Canadians over the line at the start, forcing them to go back and re-start. McKee and Buchan, son of Star class winner Bill Buchan, needed to finish two places ahead of McLaughlin and Bastet, which is exactly what they did, placing sixth to the Canadians' eighth.

**1988 Seoul-Pusan** C: 22, N: 22, D: 9.27.

| | | | PTS. |
|---|---|---|---|
| 1. | DEN | (Jörgen Bojsen-Möller, Christian Grönborg) | 31.4 |
| 2. | NOR | (Olepetter Pollen, Erik Bjorkum) | 37.4 |
| 3. | CAN | (Frank McLaughlin, John Millen) | 48.4 |
| 4. | ISR | (Yoel Sela, Eldad Amir) | 59.7 |
| 5. | NZE | (Murray Jones, Gregory Knowles) | 60.0 |
| 6. | GBR | (Roger Yeoman, Neal McDonald) | 72.7 |
| 7. | BRA | (Alan Adler, Marcus Tomke) | 78.4 |
| 8. | GER | (Albert Batzill, Peter Lang) | 79.0 |

The three medal-winning crews trained together in north Jutland, Denmark, an area chosen by Bojsen-Möller because the rough ocean conditions were similar to those in Pusan. The Danes clinched first place before the final race.

Sela and Amir almost became Israel's first Olympic medalists. Unfortunately for them, the second race fell on the Jewish high holiday of Yom Kippur. Israeli Olympic officials made it clear that any of their athletes who competed on Yom Kippur would be withdrawn from competition and sent home, a punishment which they did in fact mete out to the Israeli men's 470 crew. Sela and Amir would have won medals had they taken part in the second race and placed higher than eleventh, a result which they bettered in five of their six races.

# TORNADO

The Tornado is a two-man catamaran, the fastest of all Olympic classes. The vessel is 20 feet (6.1 meters) long and has a sail area of 235 square feet (21.85 square meters).

**1896–1972** not held

**1976 Montreal-Kingston** C: 14, N: 14, D: 7.28.

| | | | PTS. |
|---|---|---|---|
| 1. | GBR | (Reginald White, John Osborn) | 18.0 |
| 2. | USA | (David McFaull, Michael Rothwell) | 36.0 |
| 3. | GER | (Jörg Spengler, Jörg Schmall) | 37.7 |
| 4. | AUS | (Brian Lewis, Warren Rock) | 44.4 |
| 5. | SWE | (Peter Kolni, Jörgen Kolni) | 57.4 |
| 6. | SWI | (Walter Steiner, Albert Schiess) | 63.4 |
| 7. | CAN | (Larry Woods, Michael de le Roche) | 69.7 |
| 8. | ITA | (Franco Pivoli, Cesare Biagi) | 71.7 |

Forty-year-old Reg White and his 30-year-old brother-in-law, John Osborn, won four of the first six races; they were able to sit out the final day.

**1980 Moscow-Tallinn** C: 11, N: 11, D: 7.29.

| | | | PTS. |
|---|---|---|---|
| 1. | BRA | (Alexandre Welter, Lars Sigurd Björkström) | 21.4 |
| 2. | DEN | (Peter Due, Per Kjergard) | 30.4 |
| 3. | SWE | (Göran Marotröm, Jörgen Ragnarsson) | 33.7 |
| 4. | SOV | (Viktor Potapov, Aleksandr Zybin) | 35.1 |
| 5. | HOL | (Williem Van Walt Meijer, Govert Brasser) | 39.0 |
| 6. | FIN | (Pekka Narko, Juha Siira) | 47.7 |
| 7. | AUT | (Hubert Porkert, Hermann Kupfrler) | 67.7 |
| 8. | GDR | (Uwe Steingross, Jörg Schramme) | 82.0 |

**1984 Los Angeles-Long Beach** T: 20, N: 20, D: 8.8.

| | | | PTS. |
|---|---|---|---|
| 1. | NZE | (Rex Sellers, Christopher Timms) | 14.7 |
| 2. | USA | (Randy Smyth, Jay Glaser) | 37.0 |
| 3. | AUS | (Chris Cairns, John Anderson) | 50.4 |
| 4. | DEN | (Paul Elvström, Inge Trine Elvström) | 51.1 |
| 5. | BER | (Alan Burland, Christopher Nash) | 53.5 |
| 6. | GBR | (Robert White, David Campbell-James) | 53.7 |
| 7. | BRA | (Lars Grael, Glein Haynes) | 74.7 |
| 8. | FRA | (Yves Loday, Bernard Pichery) | 81.0 |

This was expected to be a dramatic showdown between Smyth and Cairns. Meanwhile, the sentimental favorite was four-time Finn class Olympic champion Paul Elvström, who came out of retirement to compete with his daughter, Trine. With all the attention focused on these three, Rex Sellers, a 33-year-old lobster fisherman, slipped through for a decisive victory. Sellers and Timms compiled a record of two firsts, three seconds and a third to clinch the gold medal after the sixth race. When asked if he would be back to take part in the final race anyway, Sellers replied, "If we're still standing after tonight's celebration." The New Zealand boat was not at the starting line the next day.

**1988 Seoul-Pusan** C: 23, N: 23, D: 9.27.

| | | | PTS. |
|---|---|---|---|
| 1. | FRA | (Jean-Yves Le Déroff, Nicolas Hénard) | 16.0 |
| 2. | NZE | (Rex Sellers, Christopher Timms) | 35.4 |
| 3. | BRA | (Lars Grael, Clinio Freitas) | 40.1 |
| 4. | AUT | (Norbert Petschel, Christian Claus) | 46.0 |
| 5. | ITA | (Giorgio Zuccoli, Luca Santella) | 60.1 |
| 6. | NOR | (Per Arne Nilsen, Carl Johannessen) | 67.7 |
| 7. | SOV | (Yuri Konovalov, Sergei Kravsov) | 70.0 |
| 8. | GBR | (Robert White, Jeremy Newman) | 70.1 |

Le Déroff and Hénard, sailing instructors from Brest, took three firsts and two seconds in the first five races, then sailed a cautious fifth to secure the gold medals without having to participate in the final race. In fifteenth place was Paul Elvström of Denmark, competing in his eighth Olympics at the age of 60.

# SOLING

The Soling is a three-man keelboat. It is 26 feet 11 inches (8.2 meters) long and weighs 2282 pounds (1035 kilograms).

**1896–1968** not held

**1972 Munich-Kiel** C: 26, N: 26, D: 9.8.

| | | | PTS. |
|---|---|---|---|
| 1. | USA | (Harry Melges, William Bentsen, William Allen) | 8.7 |
| 2. | SWE | (Stig Wennerström, Lennart Roslund, Bo Knape, Stefan Krook) | 31.7 |
| 3. | CAN | (David Miller, John Ekels, Paul Cote) | 47.1 |
| 4. | FRA | (Jean-Marie le Guillou, Bernard Drubay, Jean-Yves Pellerin) | 53.0 |
| 5. | GBR | (John Oakeley, Charles Reynolds, Barry Dunning) | 54.7 |
| 6. | BRA | (Axel Schmidt-Preben, Patrick Matte Mascarenhas, Erik Schmidt-Preben) | 64.7 |
| 7. | SOV | (Timir Pinegin, Valentin Zamotaikin, Rais Galimov) | 65.0 |
| 8. | POL | (Zygfryd Perlicki, Józef Blaszczyk, Stanislaw Stefański) | 75.0 |

The competition was limited to six races because of bad weather. Paul Elvström, attempting to become the first person in history to win gold medals at five different Olympics, became infuriated and disillusioned by a bumping incident with the French crew, packed up his boat and drove home in a huff after the fifth race, finishing 13th overall. Crown Prince Harald of Norway placed tenth. Less illustrious, but more successful, was helmsman Buddy Melges of Zelda, Wisconsin, who guided his boat to three firsts, a second, a third, and a fourth on his way to the gold medal.

**1976 Montreal-Kingston** C: 24, N: 24, D: 7.27.

| | | | PTS. |
|---|---|---|---|
| 1. | DEN | (Poul Jensen, Valdemar Bandolowski, Erik Hansen) | 46.7 |
| 2. | USA | (John Kolius, Walter Glasgow, Richard Hoepfner) | 47.4 |
| 3. | GDR | (Dieter Below, Michael Zachries, Olaf Engelhard) | 47.4 |
| 4. | SOV | (Boris Budnikov, Valentin Zamotaikin, Nikolai Poljakov) | 48.7 |
| 5. | HOL | (Geert Bakker, Harald de Vlaming, Pieter Keijzer) | 58.0 |
| 6. | GER | (Wilhelm Kuhweide, Karsten Meyer, Axel May) | 60.7 |
| 7. | FRA | (Patrick Haegeli, Patrick Oeuvrard, Bruno Trouble) | 64.0 |
| 8. | CAN | (Glen Dexter, Sandy Macmillan, Andreas Josenhans) | 68.7 |

The 1976 Soling regatta was so close that the Danish team didn't know they had won until they returned to their berth and saw a large crowd waiting for them. Had they finished seven seconds slower in the final race they would have had to settle for bronze medals instead of gold. Instead, they swept past the French boat before the finish line to place fifth, and the extra 1.7 points provided their margin of victory.

**1980 Moscow-Tallinn** C: 9, T: 9, D: 7.29.

| | | | PTS. |
|---|---|---|---|
| 1. | DEN | (Poul Jensen, Valdemar Bandolowski, Erik Hansen) | 23.0 |
| 2. | SOV | (Boris Budnikov, Aleksandr Budnikov, Nikolai Poljakov) | 30.4 |
| 3. | GRE | (Anastassios Boudouris, Anastassios Gavrilis, Aristidis Rapanakis) | 31.1 |
| 4. | GDR | (Dieter Below, Bernd Klenke, Michael Zachries) | 37.4 |
| 5. | HOL | (Geert Bakker, Steven Bakker, Dick Coster) | 45.0 |
| 6. | BRA | (Vicente D'Avila Brun, Gastao D'Avila Brun, Roberto Luiz Souza) | 47.1 |
| 7. | SWI | (Jean-François Corminboeuf, Roger-Claude Guignard, Robert Perret) | 71.7 |
| 8. | SWE | (Jan Andersson, Göran Andersson, Bertil Larsson) | 75.7 |

The three Danes defended their championship by winning the last two races, with the Soviet boat in second place both times.

**1984 Los Angeles-Long Beach** T: 22, N: 22, D: 8.8.

| | | | PTS. |
|---|---|---|---|
| 1. | USA | (Robert Haines, Edward Trevelyan, Roderick Davis) | 33.7 |
| 2. | BRA | (Torben Grael, Daniel Adler, Ronaldo Senfft) | 43.4 |
| 3. | CAN | (Hans Fogh, John Kerr, Steve Calder) | 49.7 |
| 4. | GBR | (Christopher Law, Edward Leask, Jeremy Richards) | 54.7 |
| 5. | NOR | (Dag Halfdan Usterud, Stein Lund Halvorsen, Börre Skui) | 57.7 |
| 6. | GRE | (Anastassios Boudouris, Dimitrios Deligiannis, George Spiridis) | 59.2 |

7. AUS   (Gary Sheard, Tim Dorning, Dean Gordon)   62.4
8. GER   (Wilhelm Kuhweide, Axel May, Eckhard Loll)   71.0

The U.S. team won without having to compete in the final race. Bronze medalist Hans Marius Fogh was competing in his sixth Olympics, having won a silver medal in 1960 while representing Denmark in the Flying Dutchman class.

**1988 Seoul-Pusan** C: 20, N: 20, D: 9.27.

|  |  | PTS. |
|---|---|---|
| 1. GDR | (Jochen Schümann, Thomas Flach, Bernd Jäkel) | 11.7 |
| 2. USA | (John Kostecki, William Baylis, Robert Billingham) | 14.0 |
| 3. DEN | (Jesper Bank, Jan Dupont Mathiasen, Steen Secher) | 52.7 |
| 4. GBR | (Lawrie Smith, Edward Leask, Jeremy Richards) | 67.1 |
| 5. BRA | (José Paulo Dias, José Augusto Dias, Christoph Bergman) | 67.4 |
| 6. FRA | (Michel Kermarec, Stanislas Dripaux, Xavier Phelippon) | 68.4 |
| 7. NZE | (Thomas Dodson, Simon Daubney, Aran Hansen) | 74.4 |
| 8. SWE | (Lennart Persson, Eje Öberg, Tony Wallin) | 77.7 |

This exciting competition pitted two-time world champion John Kostecki against 1976 Finn gold medalist Jochen Schümann. Earlier in the year, Schümann had defeated Kostecki at the European championships. In Seoul, both men took three firsts and two seconds. Schümann won because his sixth best finish was a third to Kostecki's fourth. In the final race, the East German had to place second. Schümann started poorly, but moved up from ninth place to second by the start of the final leg, then held his position to finish.

# *Discontinued Events*

## .5–TON CLASS

**1900 Paris-Meulan** C: 7, N: 1, D: 5.24

|  |  |  | PTS. | TIME |
|---|---|---|---|---|
| 1. | Texier | FRA | 18 | 20:40.38 |
| 2. | Pierre Gervais | FRA | 18 | 20:56.12 |
| 3. | Henri Monnot | FRA | 15 | |
| 4. | M. Monnot | FRA | 13 | |
| 5. | G. Semichon | FRA | 10 | |
| 6. | Jean d'Estournelles de Constant | FRA | 6 | |

## .5–1 TON CLASS

**1900 Paris-Meulan** T: 8, N: 3, D: 5.24.

|  |  |  | PTS. | TIME |
|---|---|---|---|---|
| 1. | GBR | (Lorne Currie, John Gretton, Linton Hope) | 17 | 6:42.01 |
| 2. | FRA | (Jacques Baudrier, Jean Lebret, Marcotte, R. William Martin, Jules Valton) | 17 | 6:44.21 |
| 3. | FRA | (E. Michelet, F. Michelet) | 17 | 6:49.37 |
| 4. | FRA | (J. de Chabannes la Palice) | 13 | |

## 1–2 TON CLASS

**1900 Paris-Meulan** T: 5, N: 3, D: 5.24.

|  |  |  | PTS. |
|---|---|---|---|
| 1. | SWI | (Hermann-Alexandre de Pourtalés) | 19 |
| 2. | FRA | (F. Vilamitjana) | 17 |
| 3. | FRA | (Jacques Baudrier) | 15 |

## 2–3 TON CLASS

**1900 Paris-Meulan** T: 4, N: 3, D: 5.25.

|  |  |  | PTS. |
|---|---|---|---|
| 1. | GBR | (William Exshaw) | 20 |
| 2. | FRA | (Susse) | 18 |
| 3. | FRA | (Auguste Donny) | 15 |
| 4 | GER | (Ferdinand Schlatter) | 15 |

## 3–10 TON CLASS

**1900 Paris-Meulan** T: 12, N: 3, D: 5.25.

|  |  |  | PTS. |
|---|---|---|---|
| 1. | FRA | (E. Michelet, F. Michelet) | 16 |
| 2. | FRA | (Maurice Gufflet) | 16 |
| 3. | HOL | (H. Smulders) | 15 |

## 10–20 TON CLASS

**1900 Paris-Le Havre** T: 6, N: 2, D: 8.6.

|  |  |  | PTS. |
|---|---|---|---|
| 1. | FRA | (Emile Billard, P. Perquer) | 29 |
| 2. | FRA | (Jean Decazes) | 24 |
| 3. | GBR | (Edward Hore) | 23 |
| 4. | FRA | (Cronier) | 20 |
| 5. | GBR | (S.M. Mellor) | 18 |
| 6. | FRA | (Jules Valton) | 17 |

## OPEN CLASS

**1900 Paris-Meulan** T: ?, N: ?, D: 5.20.

| 1. | GBR | (Lorne Currie, John Gretton, Linton Hope) | 5:56.17 |
|---|---|---|---|
| 2. | GER | (Martin Wiesner, Heinrich Peters, Ottokar Weise, George Naue, Arthur Bloomfield, Karl Maria Binder, Futchtegott Baumann) | 5:58:17 |
| 3. | FRA | (E. Michelet, F. Michelet) | 6:12:12 |
| 4. | FRA | (Emile Sacre) | 7:11:08 |
| 5. | FRA | (Jean d'Estournelles de Constant) | — |

DISQ: Texier (FRA), Louis-Auguste Dormeuil (FRA)

# 5.5-METER

**1952 Helsinki** T: 16, N: 16, D: 7.28.

| | | | PTS. |
|---|---|---|---|
| 1. | USA | (Britton Chance, Sumner White, Edgar White, Michael Schoettle) | 5751 |
| 2. | NOR | (Peder Lunde, Sr., Vibeke Lunde, Börre Falkum-Hansen) | 5325 |
| 3. | SWE | (Folke Wassén, Magnus Wassén, Carl Erik Ohlson) | 4554 |
| 4. | POR | (Duarte De Almeida Bello, Fernando Coelho Bello, Julio Sousa Leite Gorinho) | 4450 |
| 5. | ARG | (Rodolfo Vollenweider, Tomas Galfrascoli, Ludovico Kempter) | 3982 |
| 6. | GBR | (Robert Perry, John Dillon, Neil Cochran-Patrick) | 3727 |
| 7. | SAF | (Leslie Horsfield, Joseph Ellis-Brown, Eric Benningfield) | 3338 |
| 8. | FIN | (Hans Dittmar, Aarne Castrén, Johan Stadigh) | 3292 |

**1956 Melbourne** T: 10, N: 10, D: 12.5.

| | | | PTS. |
|---|---|---|---|
| 1. | SWE | (Lars Thörn, Hjalmar Karlsson, Sture Stork) | 5527 |
| 2. | GBR | (Robert Perry, Neil Cochran-Patrick, John Dillon, David Bowker) | 4050 |
| 3. | AUS | (Alexander Sturrock, Deveraux Mytton, Douglas Buxton) | 4022 |
| 4. | USA | (Ferdinand Schoettle, Victor Sheronas, John Bryant, Robert Stinson) | 3971 |
| 5. | NOR | (Peder Lunde, Sr., Odd Harsheim, Halfdan Ditlev-Simonsen, Jr.) | 3807 |
| 6. | FRA | (Albert Cadot, Jean-Jacques Herbulot, Dominque Perroud) | 1779 |
| 7. | ITA | (Massimo Oberti, Antonio Carattino, Carlo Spirito, Antonio Cosentino) | 1677 |
| 8. | SOV | (Konstantin Alexandrov, Konstantin Melgounov, Lev Alexeev) | 1598 |

**1960 Rome-Naples** T: 19, N: 19, D: 9.7.

| | | | PTS. |
|---|---|---|---|
| 1. | USA | (George O'Day, James Hunt, David Smith) | 6900 |
| 2. | DEN | (William Berntsen, Steen Christensen, Sören Hancke) | 5678 |
| 3. | SWI | (Henri Copponex, Pierre Girard, Manfred Metzger) | 5122 |
| 4. | ARG | (Roberto Sieburger, Enrique Sieburger, Carlos Sieburger) | 4402 |
| 5. | SWE | (Bengt Sjösten, Claes Turitz, Göran Witting) | 4277 |
| 6. | GBR | (Robin Aisher, George Nicholson, John Ruggles) | 3807 |
| 7. | NOR | (Finn Ferner, Odd Harsheim, Knut Wang) | 3765 |
| 8. | BAH | (Robert Symonette, Basil Kelly, George Roy Ramsey) | 3024 |

**1964 Tokyo** T: 15, N: 15, D: 10.21.

| | | | PTS. |
|---|---|---|---|
| 1. | AUS | (William Northram, James Sargeant, Peter O'Donnell) | 5981 |
| 2. | SWE | (Lars Thörn, Sture Stork, Ernst Arne Karlsson) | 5284 |
| 3. | USA | (John McNamara, Francis Scully, Joseph Batchelder) | 5106 |

| | | | |
|---|---|---|---|
| 4. | ITA | (Agostino Straulino, Bruno Petronio, Massimo Minervini) | 4738 |
| 5. | GER | (Fritz Kopperschmidt, Herbert Reich, Eckart Wagner, Uwe Mares) | 3057 |
| 6. | FIN | (Johann Gullichsen, K. Peter Frazer, Juhani Salovaara) | 3039 |
| 7. | CAN | (S.A. McDonald, J.D. Woodward, G. Bernard Skinner) | 2955 |
| 8. | NOR | (Crown Prince Harald, Eirik Johannessen, Stein Foyen) | 2860 |

Former racing-car driver Bill Northram was a 59-year-old grandfather of five when he skippered the yacht *Barrenjoey* to a gold medal.

**1968 Mexico City-Acapulco** T: 14, N: 14, D: 10.21.

| | | | PTS. |
|---|---|---|---|
| 1. | SWE | (Ulf Sundelin, Jörgen Sundelin, Peter Sundelin) | 8.0 |
| 2. | SWI | (Louis Noverraz, Bernhard Dunand, Marcel Stern) | 32.0 |
| 3. | GBR | (Robin Aisher, Adrian Jardine, Paul Anderson) | 39.8 |
| 4. | GER | (Rudolf Harmstorf, Karl-August Stolze, Harald Stein) | 47.4 |
| 5. | ITA | (Giuseppe Zucchinetti, Antonio Carattino, Domenico Carattino) | 51.1 |
| 6. | CAN | (Stanley Leibel, Ernest Weiss, Jack Hasen) | 68.0 |
| 7. | AUS | (William Solomons, James Hardy, Gilbert Kaufman) | 69.4 |
| 8. | USA | (Gardner Cox, Stephen Colgate, Stuart Walker) | 74.7 |

The Sundelin brothers, from the small resort town of Ektorp, won five of the seven races, finishing fourth and fifth in the other two. Silver medalist Louis Noverraz was 66 years old.

# 6-METER

**1908 London-Ryde** T: 5, N: 4, D: 7.29.
1. GBR  (Gilbert Laws, T.D. McMeekin, Charles Crichton)
2. BEL  (Léon Huybrechts, Louis Huybrechts, Henri Weewauters)
3. FRA  (Henri Arthus, Louis Potheau, P. Rabot)
4. GBR  (J.W. Leuchars, W. Leuchars, F.R. Smith)
5. SWE  (Karl Sjögren, Birger Gustafsson, Jonas Jonsson)

**1912 Stockholm-Nynas** T: 6, N: 5, D: 7.22.
1. FRA  (Amédée Thubé, Gaston Thubé, Jacques Thubé)
2. DEN  (Hans Meulengracht-Madsen, Steen Herschend, Sven Thomsen)
3. SWE  (Harald Sandberg, Erik Sandberg, Otto Aust)
4. SWE  (Olof Mark, Einar Hagberg, Jonas Jonsson)
5. FIN  (Ernst Estlander, Torsten Sandelin, Ragnar Stenbäck)
5. NOR  (Edvard Christansen, Hans Ferd. Christiansen, E. Kragh Christiansen)

**1920 Antwerp** T: 2, N: 2, D: 7.26.
1. NOR  (Andreas Brecke, Paal Kaasan, Ingolf Röd)
2. BEL  (Léon Huybrechts, John Klotz, Charles van den Bussche)

**1924 Paris-Le Havre** T: 9, N: 9, D: 7.26.

|  |  |  | PTS. |
|---|---|---|---|
| 1. | NOR | (Eugen Lunde, Christopher Dahl, Anders Lundgren) | 2 |
| 2. | DEN | (Wilhelm Vett, Knud Degn, Christian Nielsen) | 5 |
| 3. | HOL | (Johan Carp, Johannes Guépin, Jan Vreede) | 5 |
| 4. | SWE | (Nils Rinman, Olle Rinman, Magnus Hellström) | 12 |
| 5. | BEL | (Léon Huybrechts, John Klotz, Léopold Standaert) | 16 |
| 5. | FRA | (G. Herpin, H. Louit, Pierre Moussié) | 16 |

**1928 Amsterdam** T: 13, N: 13, D: 8.9.

| 1. | NOR | (Crown Prince Olav, Johan Anker, Erik Anker, Haakon Bryhn) |
|---|---|---|
| 2. | DEN | (Niels Otto Möller, Aage Höy-Petersen, Peter Schlütter, Svend Linck) |
| 3. | EST | (Nikolai Veksin, William von Wirén, Eberhard Vogdt, Andreas Fählmann, Georg Fählmann) |
| 4. | HOL | (Hendrik Pluijgers, Carl Huisken, Willem Schouten, Hendrik Fokker) |
| 5. | BEL | (Léon Huybrechts, Arthur Sneyers, Frits Mulder, Ludovic Franck, Willy van Rompaey) |
| 6. | USA | (Herman Whiton, Conway Olmstead, Willets Outerbridge, James Thompson, Frederick Morris) |
| 7. | SWE | (H. Hansson, G. Lindahl, Yngve Lindquist, Hakon Reuter) |
| 8. | FRA | — |

**1932 Los Angeles** T: 3, N: 3, D: 8.12.

|  |  |  | PTS |
|---|---|---|---|
| 1. | SWE | (Tore Holm, Martin Hindorff, Olle Åkerlund, Åke Bergqvist) | 18 |
| 2. | USA | (Frederick Conant, Robert Carlson, Temple Ashbrook, Charles Smith, Donald Douglas, Emmett Davis) | 12 |
| 3. | CAN | (Philip Rogers, Gerald Wilson, Gardner Boultbee, Kenneth Glass) | 4 |

The Swedes won all six races.

**1936 Berlin-Kiel** T: 12, N: 12, D: 8.10.

|  |  |  | PTS. |
|---|---|---|---|
| 1. | GBR | (Charles Leaf, Christopher Boardman, Miles Belville, Russell Harmer, Leonard Martin) | 67 |
| 2. | NOR | (Magnus Konow, Karsten Konow, Fredrik Meyer, Vadjuv Nyquist, Alf Tveten) | 66 |
| 3. | SWE | (Sven Salén, Dagmar Salén, Lennart Ekdahl, Martin Hindorff, Torsten Lord) | 62 |
| 4. | ARG | (Julio Sieburger, Claudio Bincaz, Germán Frers, Edlef Hosmann, Jorge Linck) | 52 |
| 5. | ITA | (Renato Cosentino, Giuliano Oberti, Massimo Oberti, Giovanni Stampa, Giuseppe Volpi) | 50 |
| 6. | GER | (Hans Lubinus, Dietrich Christensen, Kurt Frey, Theodor Thomsen, Haimar Wedemeyer) | 49 |
| 7. | FIN | (Curt Mattson, Yngve Pacius, Ragnar Stenbaeck, Holger Sumelius, Lars-Gunnar Winqvist) | 43 |
| 8. | HOL | (Johan Carp, Ansco Dokkum, Cornelis Jonker, Herman Looman, Ernst Moltzer) | 42 |

**1948 London** T: 11, N: 11, D: 8.12.

|  |  |  | PTS. |
|---|---|---|---|
| 1. | USA | (Herman Whiton, Alfred Loomis, James Weekes, James Smith, Michael Mooney) | 5472 |
| 2. | ARG | (Enrique Sieburger, Emilio Homps, Rufino Rodriguez de le Torre, Rodolfo Rivademar, Julio Sieburger) | 5120 |
| 3. | SWE | (Tore Holm, Torsten Lord, Martin Hindorff, Karl Ameln, Gösta Salén) | 4033 |
| 4. | NOR | (Magnus Konow, Anders Evensen, Lars Musaeus, Håkon Solem, Ragnar Hargreaves) | 3217 |
| 5. | GBR | (J.H. Hume, J.D.H. Hume, B.G. Hardie, H.G. Hardie, H. Hunter) | 2879 |
| 6. | BEL | (Ludovic Franck, Emile Hayoit, Willy Huybrechts, Henri van Riel, Willy van Rompaey) | 2752 |
| 7. | SWI | (Henri Copponex, P. Bonnet, R. Fehlmann, André Firmenich, E. Lachapelle, Louis Noverraz, Charles Stern, Marcel Stern) | 2594 |
| 8. | ITA | (Giovanni Reggio, Giorgio Audizio, R. Costentino, A. Croce, G. deLuca, Luigi Poggi, Enrico Poggi) | 2099 |

**1952 Helsinki** T: 11, N: 11, D: 7.28.

|  |  |  | PTS. |
|---|---|---|---|
| 1. | USA | (Herman Whiton, Eric Ridder, Julian Roosevelt, Everard Endt, Emelyn Whiton, John Morgan) | 4870 |
| 2. | NOR | (Finn Ferner, Johan Ferner, Erik Heiberg, Carl Mortensen, Tor Arneborg) | 4648 |
| 3. | FIN | (Ernst Westerlund, Paul Sjoberg, Ragnar Jansson, Adolf Konto, Rolf Turkka) | 3944 |
| 4. | SWE | (Sven Salén, Martin Hindorff, Torsten Lord, Jacob Lars Lundström, Karl Ameln) | 3773 |
| 5. | ARG | (Enrique Sieburger, Rufino Rodriguez de la Torre, Werner von Foerster, Horacio Monti, Hercules Morini) | 3393 |
| 6. | SWI | (Louis Noverraz, André Firmenich, Charles Stern, Marcel Stern, François Chapot) | 3020 |
| 7. | CAN | (Norman Gooderham, Kenneth Bradfield, William Copeland, William Macintosh, Donald Tytler) | 3013 |
| 8. | ITA | (Enrico Poggi, Antonio Cosentino, Pietro Reggio, Giusto Spigno, Andrea Ferrari) | 2500 |

Herman Whiton and the *Llanoria* repeated their 1948 triumph, winning the final race by 81 seconds. Finland's bronze-medal-winning yacht, *Ralia,* was the same boat that Sweden had used four years earlier to gain the bronze medal in London. The Swedes had named it *Ali Baba.*

# 6-METER, 1907 RATING

**1920 Antwerp** T: 4, N: 2, D: 7.10.

| 1. | BEL | (Emile Cornellie, Florimond Cornellie, Fréderic-Albert Bruynseels) |
|---|---|---|
| 2. | NOR | (Einar Torgersen, Leif Erichsen, Annan Knudsen) |
| 3. | NOR | (Henrik Agersborg, Tygve Pedersen, Einar Berntsen) |
| 4. | BEL | (Louis Depiere, Raymond Bauwens, Willy Valcke) |

# 6.5-METER

**1920 Antwerp** T: 2, N: 2, D: 7.10.
1. HOL  (Johan Carp, Petrus Wernink, Bernard Carp)
2. FRA  (Albert Weil, Félix Picon, Robert Monier)

# 7-METER

**1908 London-Ryde** T: 1, N: 1, D: 7.29.
1. GBR  (Charles Rivett-Carnac, Norman Bingley, Richard Dixon, Frances Clytie Rivett-Carnac)

**1920 Antwerp** T: 1, N: 1, D: 7.10.
1. GBR  (Cyril Wright, Dorothy Wright, R.H. Coleman, W.J. Maddison)

# 8-METER

**1908 London-Ryde** T: 5, N: 3, D: 7.29.
1. GBR  (Blair Cochrane, Arthur Wood, Hugh Sutton, John Rhodes, Charles Campbell)
2. SWE  (Carl Hellström, Edmund Thormählen, Eric Wellerus, Erik Sandberg, Harald Wallin)
3. GBR  (R. Himloke, Collingwood Hughes, Saint John Hughes, George Ratsey, William Ward)
4. NOR  (Johan Anker, Einar Hvoslef, Christian Jensen, Magnus Konow, Eilert Falch Lund)
5. SWE  (John Carlsson, Einar Hagberg, Hjalmar Lönroth, Karl Ljungberg, August Olsson)

**1912 Stockholm-Nynas** T: 7, N: 4, D: 7.22.
1. NOR  (Thoralf Glad, Thomas Valentin Aas, Andreas Brecke, Torleiv Corneliussen, Christian Jebe)
2. SWE  (Bengt Heyman, Emil Henriques, Herbert Westermark, Nils Westermark, Alvar Thiel)
3. FIN  (Bertil Tallberg, Gunnar Tallberg, Arthur Ahnger, Emil Lindh, Georg Westling)
4. FIN  (Gustaf Estlander, Curt Andstén, Jarl Andstén, Carl Girsén, Bertil Justén)
5. RUS  (Herman von Adlerberg, Johan Färber, W. Yilevich, E.A. Kuhn, V.P. Kusmichev)
5. SWE  (Fritz Sjöqvist, Johan Sjöqvist, Ragnar Gripe, Theodor Grönfors, Erik Hagström)

**1920 Antwerp** T: 3, N: 2, D: 7.10.
1. NOR  (Magnus Konow, Reidar Marthiniussen, Ragnar Vig, Thorleif Christoffersen)
2. NOR  (Jens Salvesen, Lauritz Schmidt, Fin Schiander, Nils Thomas, Ralph Tschudi)
3. BEL  (Albert Grisar, Willy de l'Arbre, Georges Hellebuyck, Léopold Standaert, Henri Weewauters)

**1924 Paris-Le Havre** T: 5, N: 5, D: 7.26.

|  |  |  | PTS. |
|---|---|---|---|
| 1. | NOR | (August Ringvold, Sr., Rick Bockelie, Harald Hagen, Ingar Nielsen, August Ringvold, Jr.) | 2 |
| 2. | GBR | (E.E. Jacob, Thomas Riggs, Walter Riggs, Ernest Roney, Gordon Fowler) | 5 |

| 3. | FRA | (Louis Bréguet, Pierre Ganthier, R. Girardet, A. Guerrier, G. Mollard) | 5 |
|---|---|---|---|
| 4. | BEL | (Fernand Carlier, Maurice Passelecq, Emmanuel Pauwels, Victor Vandersleyen, Paul van Halteren) | 8 |
| 5. | ARG | (Louis Domingo Aguirre, C.J. Guerrico, J.C. Milberg, B. Milhas, M.R. Uriburu) | — |

**1928 Amsterdam** T: 8, N: 8, D: 8.9.
1. FRA  (Donatien Bouché, André Lesauvage, Jean Lesieur, Virginie Hériot, Charles de la Sabliere, André Derrien)
2. HOL  (Lambertus Doedes, Maarten de Wit, Johannes van Hoolwerff, Gerardus de Vries Lentsch, Hendrik Kersken, Cornelis van Staveren)
3. SWE  (Johan Sandblom, Philip Sandblom, Carl Sandblom, Tore Holm, Clarence Hammar, Wilhelm Törsleff)
4. ITA  (Francesco Giovanelli, Guido Giovanelli, Marcantonio de Beaumont-Bonelli, Carlo Alberto d'Alberti, Edoardo Moscatelli, Mario Bruzzone)
4. NOR  (Jens Salvesen, Magnus Konow, W. Wilhelmsen, Bernhard Lund)
6. USA  (Owen Churchill, Benjamin Weston, Manfred Curry, Frank Hekma, Nicholas Barry Hekma)
7. GBR  (Kenneth Preston, Robert Steele, Joseph Compton, Beryl Preston, Francis Preston)
8. ARG  (Rodrigues de la Torre, Ortiz Sauze Aquirre, Gil Elizalde Iglesias, Peralta Ramos)

**1932 Los Angeles** T: 2, N: 2, D: 8.9.

|  |  |  | PTS. |
|---|---|---|---|
| 1. | USA | (Owen Churchill, John Biby, William Cooper, Carl Dorsey, Robert Sutton, Alan Morgan, Pierpont Davis, Alphonse Burnand, Thomas Webster, John Huettner, Richard Moore, Kenneth Carey) | 8 |
| 2. | CAN | (Ronald Maitland, Ernest Cribb, Harry Jones, Peter Gordon, Hubert Wallace, George Gyles) | 4 |

**1936 Berlin-Kiel** T: 12, N: 10, D: 8.10.

|  |  |  | PTS. |
|---|---|---|---|
| 1. | ITA | (Giovanni Reggio, Bruno Bianchi, Luigi De Manincor, Domenico Mordini, Luigi Poggi, Enrico Poggi) | 55 |
| 2. | NOR | (Olav Ditlev-Simonsen, John Ditlev-Simonsen, Hans Struknaes, Lauritz Schmidt, Nordahl Wallem, Jacob Tullin Thams) | 53 |
| 3. | GER | (Hans Howaldt, Alfried Krupp von Bohlen und Halbach, Felix Scheder-Bieschin, Eduard Mohr, Otto Wachs, Fritz Bischoff) | 53 |
| 4. | SWE | (Marcus Wallenberg, Tore Holm, Wilhelm Moberg, Detlow von Braun, Per Gedda, Bo Westerberg) | 51 |
| 5. | FIN | (Gunnar Grönblom, Sven Grönblum, Hilding Silander, Oscar Sumelius, Olof Wallin, Walter Kjellberg) | 37 |
| 6. | GBR | (Kenneth Preston, Beryl Preston, Francis Preston, Robert Steele, Joseph Compton, John Eddy) | 36 |
| 7. | ARG | (Rodriguez de la Torre, Ortiz Sauze Aguirre, Gil Elizalde, Iglesias, Peralta Ramos) | 25 |

8. DEN    (Niels Hansen, Hans Tholstrup, Otto Danielsen,    22
Carl Berntsen, Vagn Kastrup, Niels Schibbye)

The Germans led after six races, but finished only sixth on the final day. Norway was awarded second place after winning a sail-off against Germany two days later. Jacob Thams of the Norwegian crew had won the ski-jump in the first Winter Olympics at Chamonix in 1924.

## 8-METER, 1907 RATING

**1920 Antwerp** T: 2, N: 1, D: 7.10.
1. NOR    (August Ringvold, Sr., Thorleif Holbye, Tell Wagle, Kristoffer Olsen, A. Bruun Jacobsen)
2. NOR    (Niels Marius Nielsen, Johan Faye, Christian Dick, Sten Abel)

## 10-METER

**1912 Stockholm** T: 5, N: 3, D: 7.22.
1. SWE    (Carl Hellström, Erik Wallerius, Harald Wallerius, Humbert Lundén, Herman Nyberg, Harry Rosensvärd, Paul Isberg, Filip Ericsson)
2. FIN    (Harry Wahl, Waldemar Björkstèn, Jacob Carl Björnström, Bror Benediktus Brennar, Allan Franck, Erik Lindh, Aarne Pekkalainen)
3. RUS    (Ester Belvselsky, Ernest Brasche, A. Pusnitsky, Aleksandr Rodionov, Yossif Schomaker, Filipp Strauch, Karl Lindblom)
4. SWE    (Björn Bothén, Bo Bothén, Wilhelm Forsberg, Einar Lindén, Karl Lindholm, Erik Waller)

## 10-METER, 1907 RATING

**1920 Antwerp** T: 1, N: 1, D: 7.10.
1. NOR    (Erik Herseth, Sigurd Holter, Ingar Nielsen, Ole Sörensen, Gunnar Jamvold, Petter Jamvold, Claus Juell)

## 10-METER 1919 RATING

**1920 Antwerp** T: 1, N: 1, D: 7.10.
1. NOR    (Archer Arentz, Willy Gilbert, Robert Gjertsen, Arne Sejersted, Halfdan Schjött, Trygve Schjött, Otto Falkenberg)

## 12-METER

**1908 London-Firth of Clyde** T: 2, N: 1, D: 8.12.
1. GBR    (Thomas Glen-Coats, J.H. Downes, John Buchanan, J.C. Bunten, A.D. Downes, David Dunlop, John Mackenzie, Albert Martin, Gerald Tait, J.S. Aspin)
2. GBR    (Charles MacIver, J.G. Kenion, James Baxter, W.P. Davidson, J.F. Jellico, T.A.R. Littledale, C. MacLeod Robertson, J.F.D. Spence, J.M. Adam, C.R. MacIver)

**1912 Stockholm-Nynas** T: 3, N: 3, D: 7.21.
1. NOR    (Johan Anker, Alfred Larsen, Nils Bertelsen, Halfdan

Hansen, Magnus Konow, Petter Larsen, Eilert Falch Lund, Fritz Staib, Arnfinn Heje, Gustav Thaulow)
2. SWE    (Nils Persson, Hugo Clason, Richard Sällström, Nils Lamby, Kurt Gergström, Dick Bergström, Carl Lindqvist, Per Bergman, Sigurd Kander, Folke Johansson)
3. FIN    (Ernst Krogius, Max Alfthan, Erik Hartvall, Jarl Hulldén, Sigurd Juslen, Elno Sandelin, John Silén)

## 12-METER, 1907 RATING

**1920 Antwerp** T: 1, N: 1, D: 7.10.
1. NOR    (Henrik Östervold, Jan Östervold, Ole Östervold, Hans Naess, Lauritz Christiansen, Halvor Mögster, Rasmus Birkeland, Halvor Birkeland, Kristen Östervold)

## 12-METER, 1919 RATING

**1920 Antwerp** T: 1, N: 1, D: 7.10.
1. NOR    (Johan Friele, Olav Örvig, Arthur Allers, Christen Wiese, Martin Borthen, Egil Reimers, Kaspar Hassel, Thor Örvig, Erik Örvig)

## SHARPIE—12 SQUARE METERS

**1956 Melbourne** T: 13, N: 13, D: 12.5.

|    |     |                                    | PTS. |
|----|-----|------------------------------------|------|
| 1. | NZE | (Peter Mander, John Cropp)         | 6000 |
| 2. | AUS | (Roland Tasker, John Scott)        | 6086 |
| 3. | GBR | (Jasper Blackall, Terrence Smith)  | 4859 |
| 4. | ITA | (Mario Capio, Emilio Massino)      | 3928 |
| 5. | SAF | (John Sully, Alfred Evans)         | 2917 |
| 6. | GER | (Rolf Mulka, Ingo von Bredow)      | 2840 |
| 7. | SOV | (Boris Iliine, Aleksandr Chumakov) | 2479 |
| 8. | FRA | (Roger Tiriau, Claude Flahault)    | 2058 |

Tasker and Scott appeared to have won the final race and the gold medal, but a protest by the French led to their disqualification, leaving the Australians tied in points with New Zealand's Mander and Cropp. The New Zealand pair was awarded first place because they had won three races while the Australians had won only two.

## 30 SQUARE METERS

**1920 Antwerp** T: 1, N: 1, D: 7.10.
1. SWE    (Gösta Lundqvist, Rolf Steffenburg, Gösta Bengtsson, Axel Calvert)

## 40 SQUARE METERS

**1920 Antwerp** T: 2, N: 1, D: 7.10.
1. SWE    (Tore Holm, Yngve Holm, Axel Rydin, Georg Tengvall)
2. SWE    (Gustav Svensson, Ragnar Svensson, Per Almstedt, Erick Mellbin)

# SWALLOW

**1948 London** T: 14, N: 14, D: 8.12.

| | | | PTS. |
|---|---|---|---|
| 1. | GBR | (Stewart Morris, David Bond) | 5625 |
| 2. | POR | (Duarte De Almeida Bello, Fernando Pinto Coelho Bello) | 5579 |
| 3. | USA | (Lockwood Pirie, Owen Tory) | 4352 |
| 4. | SWE | (Stig Hedberg, Lars Matton) | 3342 |
| 5. | DEN | (Johan Rathje, Nolly Petersen) | 2935 |
| 6. | ITA | (Dario Salata, Achille Roncoroni) | 2893 |
| 7. | CAN | (John Robertson, Richard Townsend) | 2807 |
| 8. | NOR | (Övind Christensen, Knut Bengtson) | 2768 |

The Swallow class was the same size as the Star, but with a smaller sail area (200 square feet rather than 281). Morris and Bond came within 15 seconds of losing the gold medal in the final race.

# DRAGON

**1948 London** T: 12, N: 12, D: 8.12.

| | | | PTS. |
|---|---|---|---|
| 1. | NOR | (Thor Thorvaldsen, Sigve Lie, Håkon Barfod) | 4746 |
| 2. | SWE | (Folke Bohlin, Hugo Jonsson, Gösta Brodin) | 4621 |
| 3. | DEN | (William Berntsen, Ole Berntsen, Klaus Baess) | 4223 |
| 4. | GBR | (William Eriç Strain, G.H. Brown, J. Wallace) | 3943 |
| 5. | ITA | (Giuseppe Canessa, Bruno Bianchi, Luigi DeManincor) | 3366 |
| 6. | FIN | (Rainer Packalen, Niilo Orama, Aatos Hirvisalo) | 3057 |
| 7. | ARG | (Roberto Sieburger) | 2843 |
| 8. | HOL | (C. Jonker) | 2508 |

**1952 Helsinki** T: 17, N: 17, D: 7.28.

| | | | PTS. |
|---|---|---|---|
| 1. | NOR | (Thor Thorvaldsen, Sigve Lie, Håkon Barfod) | 6130 |
| 2. | SWE | (Per Gedda, Sidney Boldt-Christmas, Erland Almkvist) | 5556 |
| 3. | GER | (Theodor Thomsen, Erich Natusch, Georg Nowka) | 5352 |
| 4. | ARG | (Roberto Sieburger, Jorge Del Rio Salas, Horacio Campi) | 5339 |
| 5. | DEN | (Ole Bernsten, William Berntsen Aage Birch) | 4460 |
| 6. | HOL | (Willem van Duyl, Abraham Dudok van Heel, Michiel Dudok van Heel) | 4041 |
| 7. | BRA | (Wolfgang Richter, Peter Mangels, Francisco Felici Italo Osoldi) | 2884 |
| 8. | POR | (João Tito, Carlos Lourenco, Alberto Graca) | 2782 |

**1956 Melbourne** T: 16, N: 16, D: 12.5.

| | | | PTS. |
|---|---|---|---|
| 1. | SWE | (Folke Bohlin, Bengt Palmquist, Leif Wikström) | 5723 |
| 2. | DEN | (Ole Berntsen, Cyril Andresen, Christian von Bülow) | 5723 |
| 3. | GBR | (Graham Mann, Ronald Backus, Jonathan Janson) | 4547 |
| 4. | ARG | (Jorge Sales Chaves, Arnoldo Pekelharing, Boris Belada) | 4225 |
| 5. | AUS | (Graham Drane, Brian Carolan, James Carolane) | 3769 |

| | | | |
|---|---|---|---|
| 6. | ITA | (Sergio Sorrentino, Piero Gorgatto, Adelchi Pelaschiar) | 3404 |
| 7. | NOR | (Thor Thorvaldsen, Carl Svae, Björn Gulbrandsen) | 3253 |
| 8. | CAN | (David Howard, Herald Howard, Donald Tytler) | 3186 |

The Swedes came from behind to win the last two races and tie the Danes at 5723 points. Sweden was then awarded first place because they won three races to Denmark's one.

**1960 Rome-Naples** T: 27, N: 27, D: 9.7.

| | | | PTS. |
|---|---|---|---|
| 1. | GRE | (Crown Prince Constantin, Odysseus Eskitzoglou, Georgios Zaimis) | 6733 |
| 2. | ARG | (Jorge Salas Chaves, Hector Calegaris, Jorge Del Rio) | 5715 |
| 3. | ITA | (Antonio Cosentino, Antonio Ciciliano, Giulio De Stefano) | 5704 |
| 4. | NOR | (Öivind Christensen, Arild Amundsen, Carl Otto Svae) | 5403 |
| 5. | CAN | (Samuel McDonald, Lynn Watters, Gordon Norton) | 5177 |
| 6. | DEN | (Aage Birch, Paul Jörgensen, Niels Markussen) | 4715 |
| 7. | GBR | (Graham Mann, Jonathan Janson, Ian Hannay) | 4604 |
| 8. | GER | (Hans Ravenborg, Günther Benecke, Peter Rebien) | 4329 |

Twenty-year-old Crown Prince Constantin received the traditional victory dunking by being pushed into the water by his mother, Queen Frederika.

One member of the Philippine crew, which finished twenty-fourth, was Francisco Gonzalez, who gained dubious notoriety four years later when he shot the pilot of a commercial airplane in Northern California, causing the death of forty-four people, including himself. Gonzalez had taken out a $100,000 flight insurance policy before boarding the flight.

**1964 Tokyo** T: 23, N: 23, D: 10.21.

| | | | PTS. |
|---|---|---|---|
| 1. | DEN | (Ole Berntsen, Christian von Bülow, Ole Poulsen) | 5854 |
| 2. | GDR | (Peter Ahrendt, Ulrich Mense, Wilfried Lorenz) | 5826 |
| 3. | USA | (Lowell North, Charles Rogers, Richard Deaver) | 5523 |
| 4. | GBR | (Edwin Parry, Jeremy Harris, Peter Reade) | 5090 |
| 5. | BER | (Edmund Cooper, Eugene Simmons, Conrad Soares) | 5055 |
| 6. | ITA | (Sergio Sorrentino, Sergio Furlan, Annibale Pelaschiar) | 4636 |
| 7. | BAH | (Godfrey Kelly, Basil Kelly, Robert Eardley) | 4294 |
| 8. | GRE | (Odysseus Eskitzoglou, Georgios Zaimis, Themistoklis Magoulas) | 4188 |

The East Germans finished 16 seconds short of a gold medal in the final race.

**1968 Mexico City-Acapulco** T: 23, N: 23, D: 10.21.

| | | | PTS. |
|---|---|---|---|
| 1. | USA | (George Friedrichs, Barton Jahncke, Gerald Schreck) | 6.0 |

2. DEN (Aage Birch, Poul Höj Jensen, Niels Markussen) 26.4
3. GDR (Paul Barowski, Karl-Heinz Thun, Konrad Weichert) 32.7
4. CAN (Stephen Tupper, David Miller, Timothy Irwin) 64.1
5. AUS (John Cuneo, Thomas Anderson, John Ferguson) 65.0
6. SWE (Gunnar Broberg, Lennart Eisner, Sven Hanson) 71.4
7. GER (Klaus Oldendorff, Peter Stuicken, Axel May) 74.0
8. FRA (Michel Briand, Michel Alexandre, Pierre Blanchard) 81.4

The U.S. crew won four of the seven races and also finished second twice and sixth once.

**1972 Munich-Kiel** T: 23, N: 23, D: 9.8.

| | | PTS. |
|---|---|---|
| 1. AUS | (John Cuneo, Thomas Anderson, John Shaw) | 13.7 |
| 2. GDR | (Paul Borowski, Konrad Weichert, Karl Heinz Thun) | 41.7 |
| 3. USA | (Donald Cohan, Charles Horter, John Marshall) | 47.7 |
| 4. GER | (Franz Heilmeier, Richard Kuchler, Konrad Glas) | 47.7 |
| 5. NZE | (Ronald Watson, Noel Everett, Fraser Beer) | 51.0 |
| 6. SWE | (Jörgen Sundelin, Peter Sundelin, Ulf Sundelin) | 67.4 |
| 7. DEN | (Poul Höj Jensen, Frank Höj Jensen, Gunnar Dahlgaard) | 68.0 |
| 8. FIN | (Kurt Nyman, Göran Schauman, Aleksander Bielaczyc) | 68.7 |

Skippered by 44-year-old optician John Cuneo, the Australian yacht won the first three races of a competition that was cut short after six races due to inclement weather.

# TEMPEST

**1972 Munich-Kiel** T: 21, N: 21, D: 9.8.

| | | PTS. |
|---|---|---|
| 1. SOV | (Valentin Mankin, Vitaly Dyrdyra) | 28.1 |
| 2. GDR | (Alan Warren, David Hunt) | 34.4 |

3. USA (Glen Foster, Peter Dean) 47.7
4. SWE (John Albrechtson, Ingvar Hansson) 57.4
5. HOL (Bernard Staartjes, Kees Kuppershoek) 58.7
6. NOR (Peder Lunde, Jr., Aksel Gresvig) 70.0
7. BRA (Mario Buckup, Peter Ficker) 73.7
8. IRL (David Wilkins, Sean Whitaker) 74.7

**1976 Montreal-Kingston** T: 16, N: 16, D: 7.27.

| | | PTS. |
|---|---|---|
| 1. SWE | (John Albrechtson, Ingvar Hansson) | 14.0 |
| 2. SOV | (Valentin Mankin, Vladislav Akimenko) | 30.4 |
| 3. USA | (Dennis Conner, Conn Findlay) | 32.7 |
| 4. GER | (Uwe Mares, Wolf Stadler) | 42.1 |
| 5. ITA | (Giuseppe Milone, Roberto Mottola) | 55.4 |
| 6. DEN | (Claes Thunbo Christensen, Finn Thunbo Christensen) | 62.7 |
| 7. CAN | (Allan Leibel, Lorne Leibel) | 65.1 |
| 8. HOL | (Ben Staartjes, Ab Ekels) | 78.7 |

Funeral director Allen Warren and his partner, David Hunt, provided a light touch to the Kingston Regatta. Their six-year-old keelboat, *Gift 'Orse,* was damaged in transit and performed poorly at the Olympics. After the final race, Warren and Hunt took some acetone and a flare and set their boat on fire. "She went lame on us," said Warren, "so we decided the poor, old 'orse should be cremated." "My skipper has style," added Hunt, "but not that much. I tried to persuade him to burn with the ship, but he wouldn't agree."

Bronze medalist Conn Findlay also won two gold medals and one bronze medal in the coxed pair rowing events of 1956–1964. His skipper, Dennis Conner, won the America's Cup in 1980, lost it in 1983, won it back in 1987, and defended it in a catamaran in 1988.

# DISCONTINUED SPORTS

Cricket
Croquet
Golf
Jeu De Paume
Lacrosse
Motor Boating

Polo
Rackets
Roque
Rugby
Tug of War

## CRICKET

**1900 Paris** T: 2, N: 2, D: 8.20.
1. GBR   (C.B.K. Beachcroft, John Symes, Frederick Cuming, Montagu Toller, Alfred Bowerman, Alfred Powlesland, William Donne, Frederick Christian, George Buckley, Francis Burchell, Harry Corner, Arthur Birkett)
2. FRA   (T.H. Jordan, A.J. Schneidau, R. Horne, Henry Terry, F. Roques, W. Anderson, D. Robinson, W.T. Attrill, W. Browning, A. McEvoy, P.H. Tomalin, J. Braid)
   Final: GBR 262—104 FRA

## CROQUET

**1900 Paris** C: 20, N: 1, D: 7.
*Singles—1 Ball*

|   |   | PTS. |
|---|---|------|
| 1. Aumoitte | FRA | 45 |
| 2. John | FRA | 21 |

*Singles—2 Balls*
1. Waydelick   FRA
2. Vignerot   FRA
3. Sautereau   FRA

*Doubles*
1. FRA (John, Aumoitte)

## GOLF

**1900 Paris** C: 12, N: 3, D: 10.2.
*Men*

|   |   | SHOTS |
|---|---|-------|
| 1. Charles Sands | USA | 167 |
| 2. Walter Rutherford | GBR | 168 |
| 3. David Robertson | GBR | 175 |
| 4. Frederick Taylor | USA | 182 |
| 5. H.E. Daunt | FRA | 184 |
| 6. George Thorne | GBR | 185 |
| 7. W.B. Dove | GBR | 186 |
| 8. Albert Lambert | USA | 189 |

C: 10, N: 2, D: 10.3
*Women*

|   |   | PTS. |
|---|---|------|
| 1. Margaret Abbott | USA | 47 |
| 2. Pauline Whittier | USA | 49 |
| 3. Daria Pratt | USA | 53 |

| 4. Froment-Meurice | FRA | 56 |
| 5. Ridgeway | USA | 57 |
| 6. Fournier-Starlovèze | FRA | 58 |
| 7. Mary Abbott | USA | 65 |
| 7. Baronne Fain | FRA | 65 |

Margaret Abbott was the first U.S. woman to win an Olympic gold medal. A 5-foot 11-inch, 22-year-old Chicago socialite, she traveled to Paris in 1899 with her mother, literary editor and novelist Mary Ives Abbott, so that she could study art. Ten women took part in the final nine-hole round of the ladies' golf competition. Abbott later told relatives that she won the tournament "because all the French girls apparently misunderstood the nature of the game scheduled for that day and turned up to play in high heels and tight skirts." Two years later Margaret Abbott, by then a resident of New York City, married political satirist Finley Peter Dunne. She died in 1955, unaware that the tournament she had won was a part of the Olympics.

**1904 St. Louis** C: 75, N: 2, D: 9.24.
*Men*

|   |   | SHOTS |
|---|---|-------|
| 1. George Lyon | CAN | 3 and 2 |
| 2. H. Chandler Egan | USA | |
| 3. Burt McKinnie | USA | |
| 4. Francis Newton | USA | |
| 5. Harry Allen (USA), Albert Lambert (USA), Mason Phelps (USA), Daniel Sawyer (USA) | | |

George Lyon was an eccentric athlete who didn't pick up a golf club until he was 38 years old. Before that he had competed successfully in baseball, tennis, and cricket. Once he even set a Canadian record in the pole vault. Lyon was 46 when he traveled down from Toronto to take part in the Olympics. He caused quite a stir when he played in St. Louis because of his unorthodox swing. He wielded the club more like a cricket bat, provoking some newspapers to criticize his "coal-heaver's swing." On the course he was an endless source of cheerful energy, singing, telling jokes and even doing handstands. A 36-hole qualifying round reduced the field from 75 to 32. The survivors then engaged in a match play elimination tournament. In the semifinals Lyon, the only golfer who wasn't from the United States, defeated Francis Newton, the Pacific Coast champion, on the last of 36 holes. His final match was a surprise victory over the 23-year-old U.S. champion, Chandler Egan. Lyon was awarded a $1500 sterling silver trophy, which he accepted after walking down the path to the ceremony on his hands. In 1908 George Lyon traveled to England to compete in the London Olympics. However, an internal dispute among British golfers caused them to boycott the games, leaving Lyon as the only entrant. Offered the gold medal by default, he refused it. Lyon was still winning championships twenty years later and shot his age for 18 holes until he was 78 years old. He died the following year.

**1904 St. Louis** T: 3, N: 1, D: 9.17.
*Teams*

|  |  |  | SHOTS |
|---|---|---|---|
| 1. | USA | (Western Golf Association—H. Chandler Egan, Robert Hunter, Kenneth Edwards, Clement Smoot, Walter Egan, Ned Sawyer, Edward "Ned" Cummins, Mason Phelps, Nathaniel Moore, Warren Wood) | 1749 |
| 2. | USA | (Trans Mississippi Golf Association—Albert Lambert, Stewart Stickney, Bert McKinnie, William Stickney, Ralph McKittrick, Frederick Semple, Francis Newton, Harry Potter, John Cady, John Maxwell) | 1770 |
| 3. | USA | (United States Golf Association—Douglas Cadwalader, Allan Lard, Jesse Carleton, Simeon Price, Harold Weber, John Rahm, Arthur Hussey, Orus Jones, Harold Fraser, George Oliver) | 1839 |

# JEU DE PAUME

Jeu de Paume, also known as "court tennis," was the forerunner of modern-day tennis.

**1908 London** C: 11, N: 2, D: 5.28.

|  |  |  | SETS |
|---|---|---|---|
| 1. | Jay Gould | USA | 6–5, 6–4, 6–4 |
| 2. | Eustace Miles | GBR | |
| 3. | Neville Lytton | GBR | 6–2, 6–4, 6–4 |
| 4. | Arthur Page | GBR | |

# LACROSSE

**1904 St. Louis** T: 3, N: 2, D: 7.7.
1. CAN (Shamrock Lacrosse Team, Winnipeg, Manitoba—George Cloutier, George Cattanach, Benjamin Jamieson, Jack Flett, George Bretz, Eli Blanchard, Hilliard Laidlaw, H. Lyle, W. Brennaugh, L.H. Pentland, Sandy Cowan, William Laurie Burns, William Orris)
2. USA (St. Louis Amateur Athletic Association, St. Louis, Missouri—Hunter, Patrick Grogan, Passmore, Lehman, Hess, J.W. Dowling, A.H. Venn, Sullivan, Murphy, Gibson, Woods, Patridge, Young, Ross)
3. CAN (Mohawk Indians, Brantford, Ontario—Black Hawk, Black Eagle, Almighty Voice, Flat Iron, Spotted Tail, Half Moon, Lightfoot, Snake Eater, Red Jacket, Night Hawk, Rain in Face, Man Afraid Soap)
Final: Shamrock 6–1 St. Louis
Shamrock 8–2 St. Louis

**1908 London** T: 2, N: 2, D: 10.24.
1. CAN (Frank Dixon, George "Doc" Campbell, Angus Dillion, Richard Louis Duckett, George Rennie, Clarence McKerrow, Alexander Turnbull, Henry Hoobin, Ernest Hamilton, John Broderick, Thomas Gorman, Patrick 'Paddy' Brennan)
2. GBR (C.H. Scott, G. Mason, H.W. Ramsay, E.O. Dutton, J. Parker-Smith, Wilfred Johnson, Norman Whitley, Gerald Buckland, S. Hayes, G. Alexander, R.G. Martin, E.P. Jones)
Final: CAN 14–10 GBR

Good sportsmanship was the order of the day in the lacrosse competition. When Frank Dixon of Canada broke his stick, R.G. Martin of Great Britain offered to withdraw from the game until a new one could be found. The contest was tied at 9–9 when the Canadians scored five straight goals to clinch the victory.

# MOTOR BOATING

**1908 London** C: 14, N: 2, D: 8.28–29.
**Open Class, 40 Nautical Miles**
1. Émile Thubron    FRA    2:26:53
**8-Meter Class, 40 Nautical Miles**
1. Thomas Thornycroft, Bernard Redwood    GBR    2:28:26
**Under 60-Foot Class, 40 Nautical Miles**
1. Thomas Thornycroft, Bernard Redwood    GBR    2:28:58

# POLO

**1900 Paris** T: 4, N: 4, D: 6.2.
1. GBR/USA (Foxhunters Hurlingham—Alfred Rawlinson, Frank Mackey, Foxhall Keene, Dennis Daly, John George Beresford)
2. GBR/USA (Club Rugby—Walter McCreary, Frederick Freake, Walter Buckmaster, Joé de Madre)
3. FRA/GBR (Bagatelle Paris—Louis de Bisaccia, A. Fauquet Lemaitre, Jean Bounood, Maurice Raoul-Duval, Frédéric Agnew Gill, Robert Fournier-Sarloveze, Edouard Alphonse de Rothschild)
4. USA/MEX (Guillermo Hayden Wright, Eustaquio de Escandón, Pablo de Escandón, Manuel de Escandón, Marquis de Villavieja)
Final: Foxhunters 3–1 Club Rugby

**1904-1906** not held

**1908 London** T: 3, N: 1, D: 6.21.
1. GBR (Roehampton—Charles Miller, Patteson Nickalls, George Miller, Herbert Wilson)
2. GBR (Hurlingham—John Wodehouse, Walter Buckmaster, Frederick Freake, Walter Jones)
3. GBR (Ireland—Percy O'Reilly, Hardress Lloyd, John McCann, Anthony Rotherham)
Scores:    Roehampton 3–1 Hurlingham
Roehampton 5–1 Ireland

**1912** not held

**1920 Antwerp** T: 4, N: 4, D: 6.29.

| | | | W | L | PF | PA |
|---|---|---|---|---|---|---|
| 1. | GBR | (Teignmouth Melville, Frederick Barrett, John Wodehouse, Vivian Lockett) | 2 | 0 | 21 | 14 |
| 2. | SPA | (Leopoldo de la Maza, Justo San Miguel, Alvaro de Figueroa, Hernando Fitz-James) | 1 | 1 | 24 | 16 |
| 3. | USA | (Arthur Harris, Terry Allen, John Montgomery, Nelson Margetts) | 1 | 1 | 16 | 16 |
| 4. | BEL | (Alfred Grisar, Maurice Lysen, Clément van der Straeten, Gaston Peers de Nieuwburg) | 0 | 2 | 6 | 21 |

Final: GBR 13–11 SPA

**1924 Paris** T: 5, N: 5, D: 7.12.

| | | | W | L | PF | PA |
|---|---|---|---|---|---|---|
| 1. | ARG | (Arturo Kenny, Juan Nelson, Enrique Padilla, Juan Miles, Guillermo Brooke Naylor) | 4 | 0 | 46 | 14 |
| 2. | USA | (Elmer Boeseke, Thomas Hitchcock, Frederick Roe, Rodman Wanamaker) | 3 | 1 | 43 | 11 |
| 3. | GBR | (Frederick Guest, Frederick Barrett, Denis Bingham, Percival Wise) | 2 | 2 | 33 | 24 |
| 4. | SPA | (Leopoldo de la Maza, Justo San Miguel, Luis de Figueroa, Alvaro de Figueroa, Rafael Henestrosa, Hernando Stuart) | 1 | 3 | 22 | 42 |
| 5. | FRA | (Charles Prince de Polignac, Pierre de Jumilhac, Jules Macaire, Hubert de Monbrison, Jean Pastra) | 0 | 4 | 6 | 59 |

The decisive match was the one between Argentina and the United States. Juan Nelson was the hero of the game, scoring a goal in the closing seconds of the seventh and final chukker to give Argentina a surprise 6–5 victory.

**1928–1932** not held

**1936 Berlin** T: 5, N: 5, D: 7.8.

| | | | W | L | T | PF | PA |
|---|---|---|---|---|---|---|---|
| 1. | ARG | (Luis Duggan, Roberto Cavanagh, Andrès Gazzotti, Manuel Andrada) | 2 | 0 | 0 | 26 | 5 |
| 2. | GBR | (Bryan Fowler, W.N. Hinde, David Dawnay, Humphrey Guinness) | 1 | 1 | 0 | 13 | 22 |
| 3. | MEX | (Juan Garcia Zazueta, Antonio Nava Castillo, Julio Muller Luján, Aberto Ramos Sesma) | 1 | 2 | 0 | 32 | 30 |
| 4. | HUN | (Tivadar Dienes-Öhm, Imre Szentpály, Dezsö Kovács, István Bethlen, Kálmán Bartalis) | 1 | 1 | 1 | 26 | 30 |
| 5. | GER | (Heinrich Amsinck, Walter Bartram, Miles Reincke, Arthur Köser) | 0 | 1 | 1 | 14 | 24 |

Final: ARG 11–0 GBR
3rd Place: MEX 16–2 HUN

Hungary and Germany were so outclassed that they weren't even included in the competition for first or second place. Instead, the tournament was arranged so that they played for the right to play for the bronze medal against the loser among the other three teams. Over 45,000 people watched Argentina's final victory over Great Britain.

# RACKETS

**1908 London** C: 7, N: 1, D: 4.27.
*Men's Singles*
1. GBR   Evan Noel
2. GBR   Henry Leaf
3. GBR   John Jacob Astor
3. GBR   Henry Brougham
Final: Noel—Leaf WO

Leaf had to withdraw from the final because he had injured his hand in the doubles competition.

**1908 London** T: 3, N: 1, D: 4.27.
*Men's Doubles*
1. GBR   Vane Pennel/John Jacob Astor
2. GBR   Edward Bury/Cecil Browning
3. GBR   Evan Noel/Henry Leaf
Final: Pennel/Astor—Bury/Browning, 6–15, 15–7, 16–15, 15–6, 15–7

# ROQUE

**1904 St. Louis** C: 4, N: 1, D: 8.13.

| | | | W | L | PF | PA |
|---|---|---|---|---|---|---|
| 1. | Charles Jacobus | USA | 5 | 1 | 187 | 109 |
| 2. | Smith Streeter | USA | 4 | 2 | 156 | 142 |
| 3. | Charles Brown | USA | 2 | 4 | (109?) | 147 |
| 4. | William Chalfant | USA | 1 | 5 | 106 | 160 |

Roque is a variation of croquet, played on a hard-surfaced court with a raised border that can be used for bank shots. It is unknown how many points Brown scored in his loss to Chalfant.

# RUGBY

**1900 Paris** T: 3, N: 3, D: 10.28.

| | | | W | L | PF | PA |
|---|---|---|---|---|---|---|
| 1. | FRA | (Alexandre Pharamond, Frantz Reichel, Jean Collas, Albert Henriquez, Auguste Giroux, André Rischmann, Jean Binoche, A. Albert, Charles Gondouin, Lefebvre-Hubert, Sarrade, Wladimir Aitoff, Joseph Oliv- | 2 | 0 | 54 | 25 |

ier, G. Gautier, Victor Larchandat, J. Hervé, A. Roosevelt)

| | | | | | | |
|---|---|---|---|---|---|---|
| 2. | GER | (Hermann Kreuzer, Arnold Landvoigt, Heinrich Reitz, Jacob Herrmann, Erich Ludwig, Hugo Betting, August Schmierer, Fritz Müller, Adolf Stockhausen, Hans Latscha, Willy Hofmeister, Georg Wenderoth, Eduard Poppe, Richard Ludwig, Albert Arnheim) | 0 | 1 | 17 | 27 |
| 3. | GBR | (H.A. Loveitt, Raymond Whittindale, H.S. Nicol, Claudius Whittindale, L. Hood, J. Henry Birtles, J. Cantion, C.P. Deykin, J.G. Wallis, V. Smith, M.L. Logan, F.C. Bayliss, M.W. Talbot, Francis Wilson, Arthur Darby) | 0 | 1 | 8 | 27 |

**1908 London** T: 2, N: 2, D: 10.19.
1. AUS (Phillip Carmichael, Charles Russell, Daniel Carroll, John Hickey, Francis Bede-Smith, Christopher McKivatt, Arthur McCabe, Thomas Griffen, Jumbo Barnett, Patrick McCue, Sydney Middleton, Thomas Richards, Mannie McArthur, Charles McMurtrie, Robert Craig)
2. GBR (Edward Jackett, J.C. "Barney" Solomon, Bert Solomon, L.F. Dean, J.T. Jose, Thomas Wedge, James Davey, Richard Jackett, E.J. Jones, Arthur Wilson, Nicholas Tregurtha, A. Lawry, C.R. Marshall, A. Willcocks, J. Trevaskis)
Final: AUS 32–3 GBR

**1912** not held

**1920 Antwerp** T: 2, N: 2, D: 9.5.
1. USA (Daniel Carroll, Charles Doe, George Fish, James Fitzpatrick, Joseph Hunter, Morris Kirksey, Charles Mehan, John Muldoon, John O'Neil, John Patrick, Cornelius Righter, Rudolph Scholz, Charles Tilden, Heaton Wrenn, Robert Templeton)
2. FRA (André Chilo, Grenet, François Bordes, René Crabos, Edouard Bader, Thiercelin, Curtet, Forestier, Raymond Berrurier, Eugène Soulié, Labeyrie, Alfred Eluère, Robert Lavasseur, Constant Lamaignière, Robert Thierry)
Final: USA 8–0 FRA

The U.S. team included Morris Kirksey, who also won a silver medal in the 100-meter dash and a gold in the 4 × 100-meter relay, and Dink Templeton, who later became a famous track coach. Another American player was Daniel Carroll, who had been a member of the victorious Australian squad 12 years earlier.

**1924 Paris** T: 3, N: 3, D: 5.18.

| | | | W | L | PF | PA |
|---|---|---|---|---|---|---|
| 1. | USA | (Philip Clark, Norman Cleveland, Hugh Cunningham, Dudley De Groot, Robert Devereaux, George Dixon, Charles Doe, Linn Farrish, | 2 | 0 | 54 | 3 |

Edward Graff, Richard Hyland, Caesar Manelli, John O'Neil, John Patrick, William Rogers, Rudolph Scholz, Colby Slater, Norman Slater, Edward Turkington, Alan Valentine, Alan Williams)

| | | | | | | |
|---|---|---|---|---|---|---|
| 2. | FRA | (René Araou, Jean Bayard, Louis Beguet, André Béhotéguy, Alexandre Bioussa, Etienne Bonnes, René Bousquet, Aime Cassayet, Clément Dupont, Albert Dupouy, Jean Etchberry, Henri Galau, Gilbert Gerintes, Raoul Got, Adolphe Jauréguy, René Lasserre, Marcel-Frédéric Lubin-Lebrère, Etienne Piquirai, Jean Vaysse) | 1 | 1 | 61 | 20 |
| 3. | ROM | (Dumitru Armăsel, Eugen Sfetescu, Sorin Mihăilescu, Paul Nedelcovici, Teodor Marian, Mihail Vardala, Soare Sterian, Iosif Nemeş, Atanasie Tănăsescu, Dumitru Volvoreanu, Paul Vidraşcu, Nicolae Mărăscu, Mircea Sfetescu, Gheorghe Bentia, Teodor Florian, Ion Garlesteanu, Gheorge Sfetescu) | 0 | 2 | 3 | 98 |

Over 30,000 French spectators watched in horror as their team was thrashed by the upstart Americans. After two French players were injured, the U.S. team was booed and hissed for the remainder of the game. Fighting broke out in the stands, and Gideon Nelson, an art student from De Kalb, Illinois, was knocked unconscious after being hit in the face with a walking stick. At the awards ceremony "The Star-Spangled Banner" was drowned out by the booing of the crowd, and the U.S. team had to be escorted from the field under police protection.

# TUG OF WAR

In each contest, the first team to pull the other team six feet was declared the winner. If neither team succeeded in so doing in five minutes, the one which had pulled the furthest was given the victory.

**1900 Paris** T: 2, N: 3, D: 7.16.
1. SWE/DEN (Gustaf Söderström, Karl Staaf, August Nilsson, Eugen Schmidt, Edgar Aabye, Charles Winckler)
2. FRA (R. Basset, Jean Collas, Charles Gondouin, Joseph Roffo Farrade, Albert Henriquez de Zubiera)

The U.S. team was unable to take part because three of its six members were engaged in the final of the hammer throw. After the official competition, the American teams took part in a "friendly" tug, which broke up when American spectators rushed forward and joined in.

**1904 St. Louis** T: 6, N: 3, D: 9.1.
1. USA (Milwaukee Athletic Club—Oscar Olson, Sidney Johnson, Henry Seiling, Conrad Magnussen, Pat Flanagan)
2. USA (St. Louis Southwest Turnverein #1—Max Braun, William Seiling, Orin Upshaw, Charles Rose, August Rodenberg)
3. USA (St. Louis Southwest Turnverein #2—Charles Haberkorn, Frank Kungler, Charles Thias, Harry Jacobs, Oscar Friede)
4. USA (New York Athletic Club—Charles Dieges, Samuel Jones, Leon Feuerbach, Charles Chadwick, James Mitchel)
5. GRE (Pan-Hellenic Athletic Club—Nicolaos Georgantas, Perikles Kakousis, Demetri Demetracopoulos, Anastasios Georgopoulos, B. Metalos)
5. SAF (Boer Team—C. Walker, P. Hillense, J. Schutte, P. Lombard, P. Visser)

**1906 Athens** T: 4, N: 4, D: 4.30.
1. GER (Heinrich Schneidereit, Heinrich Rondi, Wilhelm Born, Willy Dörr, Karl Kaltenbach, Wilhelm Ritzenhof, Joseph Kramer, Julius Wagner)
2. GRE (Spyros Vellas, Panagiotis Triboulidis, Vasilios Psachos, Georgios Psachos, Konstantinos Lazaris, Spyros Lazaris, Georgios Papachristou, Antonios Tsitas)
3. SWE (Carl Svensson, Anton Gustafsson, Axel Norling, Claes Wersäll, Oswald Holmberg, Erik Granfeit, Gustaf Grönberger, Eric Lemming)
4. AUT (Josef Steinbach, Rudolf Arnold, Henri Baur, Wenzel Goldbach, Rudolf Watzl, Rudolf Lindmayer, Leopold Lahner, Franz Solar)

**1908 London** T: 5, N: 3, D: 7.18.
1. GBR (City Police—William Hirons, Frederick Goodfellow, Edmond Barrett, James Shephard, Frederick Humphreys, Edwin Mills, Albert Ireton, Frederick Merriman)
2. GBR (Liverpool Police—Patrick Philbin, James Clark, Thomas Butler, Alexander Kidd, George Smith, Thomas Swindlehurst, Daniel McLowry, William Greggan)
3. GBR (K. Division Metropolitan Police—Walter Tammas, Willy Slade, Alexander Munro, Ernest Ebbage, Thomas Homewood, Walter Chaffe, James Woodget, Joseph Dowler)

Surprising as it may seem, the friendly sport of tug of war touched off one of the biggest controversies of the 1908 Games. In the first round, the Liverpool Police pulled the U.S. team over the line in a matter of seconds. The Americans immediately protested that the Liverpudlians had used special illegal boots with steel cleats, spikes, and heels. The British maintained that they were wearing standard, run-of-the-mill police boots, and the protest was disallowed, whereupon the Americans withdrew from the remainder of the competition. After the tournament, the captain of the victorious London City Police team challenged the Americans to a pull in their stockinged feet, but there is no record of such a contest actually taking place.

**1912 Stockholm** T: 2, N: 2, D: 7.8.
1. SWE (Adolf Bergman, Arvid Andersson, Johan Edman, Erik Fredriksson, Carl Jonsson, Erik Larsson, August Gustafsson, Carl Lindström)
2. GBR (Alexander Munro, James Shepherd, John Sewell, Joseph Dowler, Edwin Mills, Frederick Humphreys, Mathias Hynes, Walter Chaffe)

**1920 Antwerp** T: 5, N: 5, D: 8.18.
1. GBR (George Canning, Frederick Holmes, Edwin Mills, James Shepherd, Harry Stiff, John Sewell, Frederick Humphreys, Ernest Thorn)
2. HOL (Wilhelmus Bekkers, Johannes Hangeveld, Sytse Jansma, Hendrikus Janssen, Antonius van Loon, Willem van Loon, Marinus van Rekum, Willem van Rekum)
3. BEL (Georges Bourguignon, Alphonse Ducatillon, R. Maertens, C. Piek, Henri Pintens, Charles van den Broeck, François van Hoorenbeek, Désiré Wuyts)

# WINTER
# GAMES

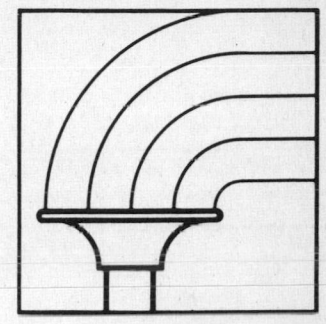

174

174. *The 1932 U.S. four-man bobsled team: (left to right) Jay O'Brien, Eddie Eagan, Clifford Gray, and Billy Fiske. Eight years later, only Eagan was still alive.*

176

175. *The 1980 U.S. ice hockey team celebrates its final victory over Finland.*

176. *Dick Button, men's figure skating champion of 1948 and 1952.*

175

177. Brian Boitano (right) consoles Brian Orser after defeating him in the figure skating competition of 1988.

178. Katarina Witt, who received 35,000 love letters following her victory in the 1984 women's figure skating competition. Four years later she became the event's first repeat champion since Sonja Henie.

177

178

# WINTER

179. Sonja Henie was only 23 years old when she earned her third consecutive figure skating gold medal.

180. Peggy Fleming won an overwhelming victory in the 1968 women's figure skating competition.

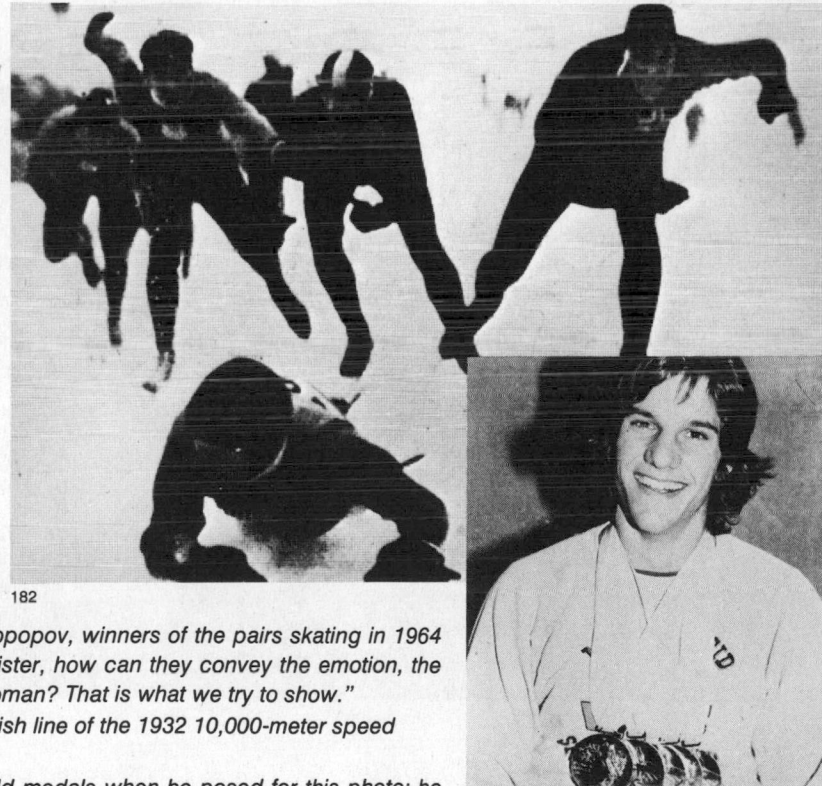

181. Lyudmila Belousova and Oleg Protopopov, winners of the pairs skating in 1964 and 1968. "These pairs of brother and sister, how can they convey the emotion, the love, that exists between a man and a woman? That is what we try to show."

182. Irving Jaffee stumbles across the finish line of the 1932 10,000-meter speed skating race.

183. Eric Heiden had won only three gold medals when he posed for this photo; he borrowed the other two. Later he won two more of his own.

## 183

184

185

184. Lydia Skoblikova won six speed skating gold medals in 1960 and 1964, more than any other athlete in the history of the Winter Olympics.

185. The 1952 giant slalom champion, Stein Eriksen, was the inspiration for the stereotype of the suave and handsome ski instructor.

186

186. Marja-Liisa Hämäläinen, winner of all three women's individual cross-country races at the 1984 Sarajevo Games tried to run away from the press after her victories. She was finally cornered and forced to submit to interviews.

187. In 1976 Rosi Mittermaier came within thirteen one-hundredths of a second of becoming the first woman to win all three alpine skiing events.

187

188. (Left to right) Seiji Aochi (bronze), Yukio Kasaya (gold), and Akitsugu Konno (silver), popular winners of the 1972 70-meter ski jump.

189. Winner of the 1980 slalom and giant slalom, Hanni Wenzel was the first-ever Olympic gold medalist from the tiny nation of Liechtenstein.

188

189

# THE MOMENT OF VICTORY

190

190. Torgny Mogren, 1988 4 x 100-kilometer nordic ski relay.

191. Uwe Dassler, 1988 400-meter freestyle swimming.

191

# FOUR HAPPY WINNERS

192. Gaston Alibert,
1908 epée fencing.

193. F. Morgan Taylor,
1924 400-meter hurdles.

192

193

194. Chuhei Nambu,
1932 triple jump.

195. Jacques Lebrun,
1932 Finn class
yachting.

194

195

# THREE BIGGEST GOLD MEDAL WINNERS

196. A rare photo of Paavo Nurmi smiling. Between 1920 and 1928 he won nine gold medals and three silver.

197. Between 1956 and 1964, gymnast Larissa Latynina won 18 medals (nine gold, five silver, and four bronze), more than any athlete in Olympic history.

198. In 1968 and 1972 Mark Spitz earned nine gold medals, one silver, and one bronze, including a record seven gold medals in 1972.

196

197

198

199

200

201

199. In 1964 Ewa Klobukowska won a bronze medal in the 100-meter dash and a gold in the 4 x 100-meter relay. Three years later she became the first athlete to fail a sex test.

200. Lance Larson, in Lane Four, appears to touch first at the finish of the 1960 100-meter freestyle. Yet John Devitt, in Lane Three, was awarded the gold medal.

201. Sixteen-year-old Rick DeMont (center) finished first in the 1972 400-meter freestyle, but was disqualified for taking an asthma drug he didn't know was on the prohibited list.

202. Lauri Lehtinen interfered with Ralph Hill during the homestretch of the 1932 5000-meter run. However, Hill declined to file a protest.

202

203

203. The romance of U.S. hammer thrower
Harold Connolly and Czechoslovakian discus
thrower Olga Fikotová caused an international
incident in 1956.

204. The Zátopeks, Dana and Emil, heroes of
the 1952 Helsinki Olympics.

# FIVE HEROES OF LESSER-KNOWN SPORTS

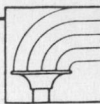

205

206

207

205. Gert Fredriksson won six canoeing gold medals between 1948 and 1960.

206. Dhyan Chand, star of the Indian field hockey team from 1928 to 1936, later became coach of the national team.

207. Lars Hall, the only repeat winner of the modern pentathlon (1952 and 1956).

208. Paul Elvström won four straight gold medals in the Finn class of the yachting competitions between 1948 and 1960.

209. Sixten Jernberg won nine medals (four gold, three silver, two bronze) in nordic skiing between 1956 and 1964.

208

209

# BIATHLON

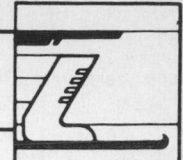

| MEN | WOMEN |
|---|---|
| 10 Kilometers | 7.5 Kilometers |
| 20 Kilometers | 15 Kilometers |
| 4 × 7.5-Kilometer Relay | 3 × 7.5-Kilometer Relay |

Biathlon is a combination of cross-country skiing and rifle shooting.

## MEN

### 10 KILOMETERS

Each contestant stops twice during the course, once to shoot five shots prone and once to shoot five shots standing. Each missed target is punished by forcing the skier to ski a 150-meter penalty loop.

**1924–1976** not held

**1980 Lake Placid** C: 50, N: 17, D: 2.19.

|  |  |  | MISSED TARGETS | TIME |
|---|---|---|---|---|
| 1. | Frank Ullrich | GDR | 2 | 32:10.69 |
| 2. | Vladimir Alikin | SOV | 0 | 32:53.10 |
| 3. | Anatoly Alyabyev | SOV | 1 | 33:09.16 |
| 4. | Klaus Siebert | GDR | 2 | 33:32.76 |
| 5. | Kjell Sobak | NOR | 1 | 33:34.64 |
| 6. | Peter Zelinka | CZE | 1 | 33:45.20 |
| 7. | Odd Lirhus | NOR | 2 | 34:10.39 |
| 8. | Peter Angerer | GER | 4 | 34:13.43 |

**1984 Sarajevo** C: 64, N: 26, D: 2.14.

|  |  |  | MISSED TARGETS | TIME |
|---|---|---|---|---|
| 1. | Eirik Kvalfoss | NOR | 2 | 30:53.8 |
| 2. | Peter Angerer | GER | 1 | 31:02.4 |
| 3. | Matthias Jacob | GDR | 0 | 31:10.5 |
| 4. | Kjell Söbak | NOR | 1 | 31:19.7 |
| 5. | Šalna Algimantas | SOV | 2 | 31:20.8 |
| 6. | Yvon Mougel | FRA | 2 | 31:32.9 |
| 7. | Frank-Peter Roetsch | GDR | 2 | 31:49.8 |
| 8. | Fritz Fischer | GER | 2 | 32:04.7 |

**1988 Calgary-Canmore** C: 72, N: 22, D: 2.23.

|  |  |  | MISSED TARGETS | TIME |
|---|---|---|---|---|
| 1. | Frank-Peter Roetsch | GDR | 1 | 25:08.1 |
| 2. | Valery Medvedtsev | SOV | 0 | 25:23.7 |
| 3. | Sergei Chepikov | SOV | 0 | 25:29.4 |
| 4. | Birk Anders | GDR | 2 | 25:51.8 |
| 5. | André Sehmisch | GDR | 2 | 25:52.3 |
| 6. | Frank Luck | GDR | 1 | 25:57.6 |
| 7. | Tapio Piipponen | FIN | 1 | 26:02.2 |
| 8. | Johann Passler | ITA | 2 | 26:07.7 |

Roetsch became the first biathlete to win both individual events.

### 20 KILOMETERS

Each skier stops four times—twice to take five shots prone and twice to take five shots standing. In 1960 and 1964 each missed target incurred a two-minute penalty. In 1968 the penalty was reduced to one minute.

**1924–1956** not held

**1960 Squaw Valley** C: 30, N: 9, D: 2.21.

|  |  |  | TIME | MISSED TARGETS | ADJUSTED TIME |
|---|---|---|---|---|---|
| 1. | Klas Lestander | SWE | 1:33:21.6 | 0 | 1:33:21.6 |
| 2. | Antti Tyrväinen | FIN | 1:29:57.7 | 2 | 1:35:57.7 |
| 3. | Aleksandr Privalov | SOV | 1:28:54.2 | 3 | 1:34:54.2 |
| 4. | Vladimir Melanin | SOV | 1:27:42.4 | 4 | 1:35:42.4 |
| 5. | Valentin Pshenitsin | SOV | 1:30:45.8 | 3 | 1:36:45.8 |
| 6. | Dmitri Sokolov | SOV | 1:28:16.7 | 5 | 1:38:16.7 |
| 7. | Ola Waerhang | NOR | 1:36:35.8 | 1 | 1:38:35.8 |
| 8. | Martti Meinila | FIN | 1:29:17.0 | 5 | 1:39:17.0 |

Lestander was only the 15th fastest skier of 30, but he was also the only one to hit all 20 targets. The fastest man was Victor Arbez of France, who clocked in at 1:25:58.4. However, he missed 18 of 20 targets and placed 25th. In fact, the entire four-man French team seemed ill-prepared for the shooting portion of the event: of 80 shots taken, they missed 68.

**1964 Innsbruck-Seefeld** C: 50, N: 14, D: 2.4.

|  |  |  | TIME | MISSED TARGETS | ADJUSTED TIME |
|---|---|---|---|---|---|
| 1. | Vladimir Melanin | SOV | 1:20:26.8 | 0 | 1:20:26.8 |
| 2. | Aleksandr Privalov | SOV | 1:23:42.5 | 0 | 1:23:42.5 |
| 3. | Olav Jordet | NOR | 1:22:38.8 | 1 | 1:24:38.8 |
| 4. | Ragnar Tveiten | NOR | 1:19:52.5 | 3 | 1:25:52.5 |
| 5. | Wilhelm György | ROM | 1:22:18.0 | 2 | 1:26:18.0 |
| 6. | József Rubiś | POL | 1:22:31.6 | 2 | 1:26:31.6 |
| 7. | Valentin Pshenitsin | SOV | 1:22:59.0 | 2 | 1:26:59.0 |
| 8. | Hannu Posti | FIN | 1:25:16.5 | 1 | 1:27:16.5 |

**1968 Grenoble-Autrans** C: 60, N: 18, D: 2.12.

| | | TIME | MISSED TARGETS | ADJUSTED TIME |
|---|---|---|---|---|
| 1. | Magnar Solberg | NOR | 1:13:45.9 | 0 | 1:13:45.9 |
| 2. | Aleksandr Tikhonov | SOV | 1:12:40.4 | 2 | 1:14:40.4 |
| 3. | Vladimir Goundartsev | SOV | 1:16:27.4 | 2 | 1:18:27.4 |
| 4. | Stanislaw Szczepaniak | POL | 1:17:56.8 | 1 | 1:18:56.8 |
| 5. | Arve Kinnari | FIN | 1:17:47.9 | 2 | 1:19:47.9 |
| 6. | Nikolai Pousanov | SOV | 1:17:14.5 | 3 | 1:20:14.5 |
| 7. | Victor Mamatov | SOV | 1:19:20.8 | 1 | 1:20:20.8 |
| 8. | Stanislaw Lukaszczyk | POL | 1:16:28.1 | 4 | 1:20:28.1 |

Magnar Solberg, a 31-year-old policeman, was practically unknown in the world of biathlon. He attained his victory by achieving a perfect shooting score—the first time he had ever accomplished such a feat. As photographers crowded around the surprised champion, he told them, "I am very happy, but too tired to smile."

**1972 Sapporo-Makomanai** C: 54, N: 14, D: 2.9.

| | | TIME | MISSED TARGETS | ADJUSTED TIME |
|---|---|---|---|---|
| 1. | Magnar Solberg | NOR | 1:13:55.50 | 2 | 1:15:55.50 |
| 2. | Hansjörg Knauthe | GDR | 1:15:07.60 | 1 | 1:16:07.60 |
| 3. | Lars-Göran Arwidson | SWE | 1:14:27.03 | 2 | 1:16:27.03 |
| 4. | Aleksandr Tikhonov | SOV | 1:12:48:65 | 4 | 1:16:48.65 |
| 5. | Yrjö Salpakari | FIN | 1:14:51.43 | 2 | 1:16:51.43 |
| 6. | Esko Saira | FIN | 1:12:34.80 | 5 | 1:17:34.80 |
| 7. | Victor Mamatov | SOV | 1:16:16.26 | 2 | 1:18:16.26 |
| 8. | Tor Svendsberget | NOR | 1:15:26.54 | 3 | 1:18:26.54 |

**1976 Innsbruck-Seefeld** C: 51, N: 19, D: 2.6.

| | | TIME | MISSED TARGETS | ADJUSTED TIME |
|---|---|---|---|---|
| 1. | Nikolai Kruglov | SOV | 1:12:12.26 | 2 | 1:14:12.26 |
| 2. | Heikki Ikola | FIN | 1:13:54.10 | 2 | 1:15:54.10 |
| 3. | Aleksandr Elizarov | SOV | 1:13:05.57 | 3 | 1:16:05.57 |
| 4. | Willy Bertin | ITA | 1:13:50.36 | 3 | 1:16:50.36 |
| 5. | Aleksandr Tikhonov | SOV | 1:10:18.33 | 7 | 1:17:18.33 |
| 6. | Esko Saira | FIN | 1:15:32.84 | 2 | 1:17:32.84 |
| 7. | Lino Jordan | ITA | 1:15:49.83 | 2 | 1:17:49.83 |
| 8. | Sune Adolfsson | SWE | 1:16:00.50 | 2 | 1:18:00.50 |

**1980 Lake Placid** C: 49, N: 18, D: 2.16.

| | | TIME | MISSED TARGETS | ADJUSTED TIME |
|---|---|---|---|---|
| 1. | Anatoly Alyabyev | SOV | 1:08:16.31 | 0 | 1:08:16.31 |
| 2. | Frank Ullrich | GDR | 1:05:27.29 | 3 | 1:08:27.79 |
| 3. | Eberhard Rösch | GDR | 1:09:11.73 | 2 | 1:11:11.73 |
| 4. | Svein Engen | NOR | 1:08:30.25 | 3 | 1:11:30.25 |
| 5. | Erkki Antila | FIN | 1:07:32.32 | 4 | 1:11:32.32 |
| 6. | Yvon Mougel | FRA | 1:08:33.60 | 3 | 1:11:33.60 |
| 7. | Vladimir Barnashov | SOV | 1:07:49.49 | 4 | 1:11:49.49 |
| 8. | Vladimir Alikin | SOV | 1:06:05.30 | 6 | 1:12:05.30 |

**1984 Sarajevo** C: 63, N: 25, D: 2.11.

| | | TIME | MISSED TARGETS | ADJUSTED TIME |
|---|---|---|---|---|
| 1. | Peter Angerer | GER | 1:09:52.7 | 2 | 1:11:52.7 |
| 2. | Frank-Peter Roetsch | GDR | 1:10:21.4 | 3 | 1:13:21.4 |
| 3. | Eirik Kvalfoss | NOR | 1:09:02.4 | 5 | 1:14:02.4 |
| 4. | Yvon Mougel | FRA | 1:10:53.1 | 4 | 1:14:53.1 |
| 5. | Frank Ullrich | GDR | 1:11:53.7 | 3 | 1:14:53.7 |
| 6. | Rolf Storsveen | NOR | 1:11:23.9 | 4 | 1:15:23.9 |
| 7. | Fritz Fischer | GER | 1:11:49.7 | 4 | 1:15:49.7 |
| 8. | Leif Andersson | SWE | 1:13:19.3 | 3 | 1:16:19.3 |

**1988 Calgary-Canmore** C: 71, N: 21, D: 2.20.

| | | TIME | MISSED TARGETS | ADJUSTED TIME |
|---|---|---|---|---|
| 1. | Frank-Peter Roetsch | GDR | 53:33.3 | 3 | 56:33.3 |
| 2. | Valery Medvedtsev | SOV | 54:54.6 | 2 | 56:54.6 |
| 3. | Johann Passler | ITA | 55:10.1 | 2 | 57:10.1 |
| 4. | Sergei Chepikov | SOV | 56:17.5 | 1 | 57:17.5 |
| 5. | Yuri Kashkarov | SOV | 55:43.1 | 2 | 57:43.1 |
| 6. | Eirik Kvalfoss | NOR | 54:54.6 | 3 | 57:54.6 |
| 7. | André Sehmisch | GDR | 55:11.4 | 3 | 58:11.4 |
| 8. | Tapio Piipponen | FIN | 55:18.3 | 3 | 58:18.3 |

# 4 × 7.5-KILOMETER RELAY

Each skier shoots twice and has eight shots to make five hits. For each miss he has to ski a penalty loop of 150 meters. Unlike the individual events, in which the competitors race against the clock, one after another, in the biathlon relay all teams start at the same time.

**1924–1964** not held

**1968 Grenoble-Autrans** T: 14, N: 14, D: 2.15.

| | | | MISSED TARGETS | TIME |
|---|---|---|---|---|
| 1. | SOV | (Aleksandr Tikhonov, Nikolai Pousanov, Victor Mamatov, Vladimir Goundartsev) | 2 | 2:13:02.4 |
| 2. | NOR | (Ola Waerhang, Olav Jordet, Magnar Solberg, Jon Istad) | 5 | 2:14:50.2 |
| 3. | SWE | (Lars-Göran Arwidson, Tore Eriksson, Olle Petrusson, Holmfrid Olsson) | 0 | 2:17:26.3 |
| 4. | POL | (Józef Rózak, Andrzej Fiedor, Stanislaw Lukaszczyk, Stanislaw Szczepaniak) | 4 | 2:20:19.6 |
| 5. | FIN | (Juhani Suutarinen, Heikki Floejt, Kalevi Vähäkylä, Arve Kinnari) | 5 | 2:20:41.8 |
| 6. | GDR | (Heinz Kluge, Hans-Gert Jahn, Horst Koschka, Dieter Speer) | 4 | 2:21:54.5 |
| 7. | ROM | (Gheorghe Cimpoia, Constant Carabela, Nicolae Barbarescu, Wilhelm Gyorgy) | 4 | 2:25:39.8 |
| 8. | USA | (Ralph Wakely, Edward Williams, William Spencer, John Ehrensbeck) | 8 | 2:28:35.5 |

**1972 Sapporo-Makomanai** T: 13, N: 13, D: 2.11.

| | | MISSED TARGETS | TIME |
|---|---|---|---|
| 1. SOV | (Aleksandr Tikhonov, Rinnat Safine, Ivan Biakov, Victor Mamatov) | 3 | 1:51:44.92 |
| 2. FIN | (Esko Saira, Juhani Suutarinen, Heikki Ikola, Mauri Röppänen) | 3 | 1:54:37.25 |
| 3. GDR | (Hansjörg Knauthe, Joachim Meischner, Dieter Speer, Horst Koschka) | 4 | 1:54:57.67 |
| 4. NOR | (Tor Svendsberget, Kåre Hovda, Ivar Nordkild, Magnar Solberg) | 7 | 1:56:24.41 |
| 5. SWE | (Lars-Göran Arwidson, Olle Petrusson, Torsten Wadman, Holmfrid Olsson) | 6 | 1:56:57.40 |
| 6. USA | (Peter Karns, Dexter Morse, Dennis Donahue, William Bowerman) | 1 | 1:57:24.32 |
| 7. POL | (Józef Różak, Józef Stopka, Andrzej Rapacz, Aleksander Klima) | 4 | 1:58:09.92 |
| 8. JPN | (Isao Ohno, Shozo Sasaki, Miki Shibuya, Kazuo Sasakubo) | 5 | 1:59:09.48 |

**1976 Innsbruck-Seefeld** T: 15, N: 15, D: 2.13.

| | | MISSED TARGETS | TIME |
|---|---|---|---|
| 1. SOV | (Aleksandr Elizarov, Ivan Biakov, Nikolai Kruglov, Aleksandr Tikhonov) | 0 | 1:57:55.64 |
| 2. FIN | (Henrik Flöjt, Esko Saira, Juhani Suutarinen, Heikki Ikola) | 2 | 2:01:45.58 |
| 3. GDR | (Karl-Heinz Menz, Frank Ullrich, Manfred Beer, Manfred Geyer) | 5 | 2:04:08.61 |
| 4. GER | (Heinrich Mehringer, Gerd Winkler, Josef Keck, Claus Gehrke) | 4 | 2:04:11.86 |
| 5. NOR | (Kjell Hovda, Terje Hanssen, Svein Engen, Tor Svendsberget) | 6 | 2:05:10.28 |
| 6. ITA | (Lino Jordan, Pierantonio Clementi, Luigi Weiss, Willy Bertin) | 3 | 2:06:16.55 |
| 7. FRA | (Rene Arpin, Yvon Mougel, Marius Falquy, Jean Claude Viry) | 5 | 2:07:34.42 |
| 8. SWE | (Mats-Åke Lantz, Torsten Wadman, Sune Adolfsson, Lars Göran Arwidson) | 8 | 2:08:46.90 |

**1980 Lake Placid** T: 15, N: 15, D: 2.22.

| | | MISSED TARGETS | TIME |
|---|---|---|---|
| 1. SOV | (Vladimir Alikin, Aleksandr Tikhonov, Vladimir Barnashov, Anatoly Alyabyev) | 0 | 1:34:03.27 |
| 2. GDR | (Mathias Jung, Klaus Siebert, Frank Ullrich, Eberhard Rösch) | 3 | 1:34:56.99 |
| 3. GER | (Franz Bernreiter, Hans Estner, Peter Angerer, Gerd Winkler) | 2 | 1:37:30.26 |
| 4. NOR | (Svein Engen, Kjell Sobak, Odd Lirhus, Sigleif Johansen) | 3 | 1:38:11.76 |
| 5. FRA | (Yvon Mougel, Denis Sandona, André Geourjon, Christian Poirot) | 0 | 1:38:23.36 |
| 6. AUT | (Rudolf Horn, Franz-Josef Weber, Josef Koll, Alfred Eder) | 4 | 1:38:32.02 |
| 7. FIN | (Keijo Kuntola, Erkki Antila, Kari Saarela, Raimo Seppanen) | 6 | 1:38:50.84 |
| 8. USA | (Martin Hagen, Lyle Nelson, Donald Nielsen, Peter Hoag) | 0 | 1:39:24.29 |

Thirty-three-year-old Aleksandr Tikhonov announced his retirement after winning his fourth straight biathlon relay gold medal.

**1984 Sarajevo** T: 17, N: 17, D: 2.17.

| | | MISSED TARGETS | TIME |
|---|---|---|---|
| 1. SOV | (Dmitri Vasilyev, Yuri Kachkarov, Šalna Algimantas, Sergei Buligin) | 2 | 1:38:51.7 |
| 2. NOR | (Odd Lirhus, Eirik Kvalfoss, Rolf Storsveen, Kjell Söbak) | 2 | 1:39:03.9 |
| 3. GER | (Ernst Reiter, Walter Pichler, Peter Angerer, Fritz Fischer) | 1 | 1:39:05.1 |
| 4. GDR | (Holger Wick, Frank-Peter Roetsch, Matthias Jacob, Frank Ullrich) | 1 | 1:40:04.7 |
| 5. ITA | (Adriano Darioli, Gottlieb Taschler Johann Passler, Andreas Zingerle) | 0 | 1:42:32.8 |
| 6. CZE | (Jaromir Šimůnek, Zdeněk Hák, Petr Zelinka, Jan Matouš) | 4 | 1:42:40.5 |
| 7. FIN | (Keijo Tiitola, Toivo Makikyro, Arto Jaaskelainen, Tapio Piipponen) | 2 | 1:43:16.0 |
| 8. AUT | (Rudolf Horn, Walter Hoerl, Franz Schuler, Alfred Eder) | 1 | 1:43:28.1 |

**1988 Calgary-Canmore** T: 16, N: 16, D: 2.26.

| | | MISSED TARGETS | TIME |
|---|---|---|---|
| 1. SOV | (Dmitri Vasilyev, Sergei Chepikov, Aleksandr Popov, Valery Medvedtsev) | 0 | 1:22:30.0 |

|  |  | MISSED TARGETS | TIME |
|---|---|---|---|
| 2. GER | (Ernst Reiter, Stefan Höck, Peter Angerer, Friedrich Fischer) | 0 | 1:23.37.4 |
| 3. ITA | (Werner Kiem, Gottlieb Taschler, Johann Passler, Andreas Zingerle) | 0 | 1:23.51.5 |
| 4. AUT | (Anton Lengauer-Stockner, Bruno Hofstätter, Franz Schuler, Alfred Eder) | 0 | 1:24.17.6 |
| 5. GDR | (Jürgen Wirth, Frank-Peter Roetsch, Matthias Jacob, André Sehmisch) | 3 | 1:24.28.4 |
| 6. NOR | (Geir Einang, Frode Loberg, Gisle Fenne, Eirik Kvalfoss) | 0 | 1:25.57.0 |
| 7. SWE | (Peter Sjödén, Mikael Löfgren, Roger Westling, Leif Andersson) | 3 | 1:29.11.9 |
| 8. BUL | (Vasil Bozhilov, Vladimir Velichkov, Krasimir Videnov, Hristo Vodenicharov) | 7 | 1:29.24.9 |

The East Germans took four of the top six places in the 10-kilometer individual event and thus were expected to give the Soviet team a stiff challenge. However, leadoff skier Jürgen Wirth, who had test-fired in windy conditions, failed to readjust the sight on his rifle when the wind died down and missed three of his first five shots, leaving East Germany in twelfth place with an insurmountable deficit of almost two minutes.

# WOMEN
## 7.5 KILOMETERS
This event will be held for the first time in 1992.

## 15 KILOMETERS
This event will be held for the first time in 1992.

## 3 × 7.5-KILOMETER RELAY
This event will be held for the first time in 1992.

# BOBSLED

Two-Man
Four-Man

The final time is the combined total of four separate runs, two on one day, two more on the next.

## TWO-MAN

**1924–1928** not held

**1932 Lake Placid** T: 12, N: 8, D: 2.10.
1. USA    (J. Hubert Stevens, Curtis Stevens)       8:14.74
2. SWI    (Reto Capadrutt, Oscar Geier)             8:16.28
3. USA    (John Heaton, Robert Minton)              8:29.15
4. ROM    (Papana Alexandru, Hubert Dumitru)        8:32.47
5. GER    (Hanns Kilian, Sebastian Huber)           8:35.36
6. ITA    (Teofilo Rossi di Montelera, Italo Casini) 8:36.33
7. GFR    (Werner Huth, Max Ludwig)                 8:45.05
8. ITA    (Agostini Lanfranchi, Gaetano Lanfranchi)  8:50.66

J. Hubert Stevens and his brother, Curtis, were local residents of Lake Placid. They trailed Capadrutt and Geier by 6.32 seconds after the first run, but registered the fastest times in each of the other three runs to overtake the Swiss team for the victory. The Stevens brothers, aged 41 and 33, attributed part of their success to the fact that they heated their runners with blowtorches for 25 minutes prior to hitting the snow, a tactic that is now highly illegal, but which was then considered unusual but acceptable.

**1936 Garmisch-Partenkirchen** T: 23, N: 13, D: 2.15.
1. USA    (Ivan Brown, Alan Washbond)               5:29.29
2. SWI    (Fritz Feierabend, Joseph Beerli)         5:30.64
3. USA    (Gilbert Colgate, Richard Lawrence)       5:33.96
4. GBR    (Frederick McEvoy, James Cardno)          5:40.25
5. GER    (Hanns Kilian, Hermann von Valta)         5:42.01
6. GER    (Fritz Grau, Albert Brehme)               5:44.71
7. SWI    (Reto Capadrutt, Charles Bouvier)         5:46.23
8. BEL    (Rene Lunden, Eric de Spoelberch)         5:46.28

Ivan Brown of Keene Valley, New York, was an especially superstitious competitor. One of his quirks was a need to find at least one hairpin on the ground every day. Fortunately he had been able to accomplish this feat for 24 consecutive days prior to the Olympics. Brown was also the only driver to compete without goggles; he claimed they dulled his eyesight and added wind resistance.

**1948 St. Moritz** T: 16, N: 9, D: 1.31.
1. SWI    (Felix Endrich, Friedrich Waller)         5:29.2
2. SWI    (Fritz Feierabend, Paul Hans Eberhard)    5:30.4
3. USA    (Frederick Fortune, Schuyler Carron)      5:35.3
4. BEL    (Max Houben, Jacques Mouvet)              5:37.5
5. GBR    (William Coles, Raymond Collings)         5:37.9

6. ITA    (Mario Vitali, Dario Poggi)               5:39.0
7. NOR    (Arne Holst, Ivar Johansen)               5:38.2
8. ITA    (Nino Bibbia, Ediberto Campadese)         5:38.6

In 1953 Felix Endrich won the two-man bobsled world championship at Garmisch-Partenkirchen. Less than a week later he was leading a four-man bob down the same course when his sled hurtled over the wall at "dead man's curve" and crashed into a tree. The 31-year-old Endrich was killed almost instantly.

**1952 Oslo** T: 18, N: 9, D. 2.15.
1. GER    (Andreas Ostler, Lorenz Nieberl)          5:24.54
2. USA    (Stanley Benham, Patrick Martin)          5:26.89
3. SWI    (Fritz Feierabend, Stephan Waser)         5:27.71
4. SWI    (Felix Endrich, Werner Spring)            5:29.15
5. FRA    (André Robin, Henri Rivière)              5:31.98
6. BEL    (Marcel Leclef, Albert Casteleyns)        5:32.51
7. USA    (Frederick Fortune, John Helmer)          5:33.82
8. SWE    (Olle Axelsson, Jan de Man Lapidoth)      5:35.77

Ostler and Nieberl recorded the best time on each of the four runs despite the fact that they were using a 16-year-old bobsled.

**1956 Cortina** T: 25, N: 14, D: 1.28.
1. ITA    (Lamberto Dalla Costa, Giacomo Conti)     5:30.14
2. ITA    (Eugenio Monti, Renzo Alverà)             5:31.45
3. SWI    (Max Angst, Harry Warburton)              5:37.46
4. SPA    (Alfonso de Portago, Vicente Sartorius y Cabeza de Vaca)   5:07.00
5. USA    (Waightman Washbond, Patrick Biesiadecki) 5:38.16
6. USA    (Arthur Tyler, Edgar Seymour)             5:40.08
7. SWI    (Franz Kapus, Heinrich Angst)             5:40.11
8. GER    (Andreas Ostler, Hans Hohenester)         5:40.13

Dalla Costa and Monti finished first and second respectively on each of the four runs. Dalla Costa was a 35-year-old jet pilot who had never raced anywhere but Cortina.

**1960** not held

**1964 Innsbruck-Igls** T: 19, N: 11, D: 2.1.
1. GBR    (Anthony Nash, Robin Dixon)               4:21.90
2. ITA    (Sergio Zardini, Romano Bonagura)         4:22.02
3. ITA    (Eugenio Monti, Sergio Siorpaes)          4:22.63
4. CAN    (Victor Emery, Peter Kirby)               4:23.49
5. USA    (Lawrence McKillip, James Ernest Lamy)    4:24.60
6. GER    (Franz Wörmann, Hubert Braun)             4:24.70
7. USA    (Charles McDonald, Charles Pandolph)      4:25.00
8. AUT    (Erwin Thaler, Josef Nairz)               4:25.51

**1968 Grenoble-Alpe d'Huez** T: 22, N: 11, D: 2.6.

| | | | |
|---|---|---|---|
| 1. | ITA | (Eugenio Monti, Luciano De Paolis) | 4:41.54 |
| 2. | GER | (Horst Floth, Pepi Bader) | 4:41.54 |
| 3. | ROM | (Ion Panţuru, Nicolae Neagoe) | 4:44.46 |
| 4. | AUT | (Erwin Thaler, Reinhold Durnthaler) | 4:45.13 |
| 5. | GBR | (Anthony Nash, Robin Dixon) | 4:45.16 |
| 6. | USA | (Paul Lamey, Robert Huscher) | 4:46.03 |
| 7. | GER | (Wolfgang Zimmerer, Peter Utzschneider) | 4:46.40 |
| 8. | AUT | (Max Kaltenberger, Fritz Dinkhauser) | 4:46.63 |

"Now I can retire a happy man," said Eugenio Monti after completing his 12-year quest for an Olympic gold medal. But his victory did not come easily. Trailing by one-tenth of a second after three runs, Monti drove his bob to a course record of 1:10.05, only to watch Floth race down in 1:10.15. This left the Italians and Germans in a tie for first place, and it was announced that both teams would be awarded gold medals. However, the judges later reversed their decision, invoking world bobsled rules. Sole possession of first place was given to the team that recorded the fastest single heat time—and 40-year-old Eugenio Monti had finally won his Olympic gold medal.

**1972 Sapporo-Taineyama** T: 21, N: 11, D: 2.5.

| | | | |
|---|---|---|---|
| 1. | GER | (Wolfgang Zimmerer, Peter Utzschneider) | 4:57.07 |
| 2. | GER | (Horst Floth, Pepi Bader) | 4:58.84 |
| 3. | SWI | (Jean Wicki, Edy Hubacher) | 4:59.33 |
| 4. | ITA | (Gianfranco Gaspari, Mario Armano) | 5:00.45 |
| 5. | ROM | (Ion Panţuru, Ion Zangor) | 5:00.53 |
| 6. | SWE | (Carl-Erik Eriksson, Jan Johansson) | 5:01.40 |
| 7. | SWI | (Hans Candrian, Heinz Schenker) | 5:01.44 |
| 8. | AUT | (Herbert Gruber, Josef Oberhauser) | 5:01.60 |

**1976 Innsbruck-Igls** T: 24, N: 13, D: 2.6.

| | | | |
|---|---|---|---|
| 1. | GDR | (Meinhard Nehmer, Bernhard Germeshausen) | 3:44.42 |
| 2. | GER | (Wolfgang Zimmerer, Manfred Schumann) | 3:44.99 |
| 3. | SWI | (Erich Schärer, Josef Benz) | 3:45.70 |
| 4. | AUT | (Fritz Sperling, Andreas Schwab) | 3:45.74 |
| 5. | GER | (Georg Heibl, Fritz Ohlwärter) | 3:46.13 |
| 6. | AUT | (Dieter Delle Karth, Franz Köfel) | 3:46.37 |
| 7. | GDR | (Horst Schönau, Raimund Bethge) | 3:46.97 |
| 8. | ITA | (Giorgio Alvera, Franco Perruquet) | 3:47.30 |

Nehmer and Germeshausen earned four Olympic medals each in 1976 and 1980, including three golds. A former javelin thrower, Nehmer was 35 years old when he earned his first medal.

**1980 Lake Placid** T: 20, N: 11, D: 2.16.

| | | | |
|---|---|---|---|
| 1. | SWI | (Erich Schärer, Josef Benz) | 4:09.36 |
| 2. | GDR | (Bernhard Germeshausen, Hans Jürgen Gerhardt) | 4:10.93 |
| 3. | GDR | (Meinhard Nehmer, Bogdan Musiol) | 4:11.08 |
| 4. | SWI | (Hans Hildebrand, Walter Rahm) | 4:11.32 |
| 5. | USA | (Howard Silher, Dick Nalley) | 4:11.73 |
| 6. | USA | (Brent Rushlaw, Joseph Tyler) | 4:12.12 |
| 7. | AUT | (Fritz Sperling, Kurt Oberhöller) | 4:13.58 |
| 8. | GER | (Peter Hell, Heinz Busche) | 4:13.74 |

**1984 Sarajevo** T: 28, N: 16, D: 2.11.

| | | | |
|---|---|---|---|
| 1. | GDR | (Wolfgang Hoppe, Dietmar Schauerhammer) | 3:25.56 |
| 2. | GDR | (Bernhard Lehmann, Bogdan Musiol) | 3:26.04 |
| 3. | SOV | (Zintis Ekmanis, Vladimir Alexandrov) | 3:26.16 |
| 4. | SOV | (Jānis Kipurs, Aiwar Šnepsts) | 3:26.42 |
| 5. | SWI | (Hans Hiltebrand, Meinrad Müller) | 3:26.76 |
| 6. | SWI | (Ralph Pichler, Rico Freiermuth) | 3:28.23 |
| 7. | ITA | (Guerrino Ghedina, Andrea Meneghin) | 3:29.09 |
| 8. | GER | (Anton Fischer, Hans Metzler) | 3:29.18 |

Fifty-three-year-old Carl-Erik Eriksson of Sweden became the first person to compete in six Winter Olympics. His best performance was a sixth-place finish in the 1972 two-man event. In 1984 he finished 19th in the two-man and 21st in the four-man.

**1988 Calgary** T: 41, N: 23, D: 2.22.

| | | | |
|---|---|---|---|
| 1. | SOV | (Jānis Kipurs, Vladimir Kozlov) | 3:53.48 |
| 2. | GDR | (Wolfgang Hoppe, Bogdan Musiol) | 3:54.19 |
| 3. | GDR | (Bernhard Lehmann, Mario Hoyer) | 3:54.64 |
| 4. | SWI | (Gustav Weder, Donat Acklin) | 3:56.06 |
| 5. | AUT | (Ingo Appelt, Harald Winkler) | 3:56.49 |
| 6. | SWI | (Hans Hiltebrand, André Kiser) | 3:56.52 |
| 7. | GER | (Anton Fischer, Christoph Langen) | 3:56.62 |
| 8. | AUT | (Peter Kienast, Christian Mark) | 3:56.91 |

Defending Olympic champion Wolfgang Hoppe registered the fastest time of the first run, but finished only eighth best in the second run. Hoppe complained bitterly of the poor racing conditions, comparing his slide down the dirt- and dust-covered track to "running on sandpaper." Hoppe, who was tied for second place after the first day, was not alone in his criticism. Six nations, including the first-place Soviet Union, filed a protest asking that the results of the first two runs be disallowed. The protest was denied and the next day the competition continued. However, the third run was finally canceled—after 28 sleds had already raced—because of excessive sand on the track due to warm weather and high winds.

The competition was resumed one day later. Hoppe clocked the fastest times in both the third and fourth runs, but the 1.21-second deficit he had incurred in the second run was too much to overcome. The upset victory went to Jānis Kipurs, a 30-year-old Latvian who had taken up bobsledding when he answered a newspaper ad in 1980.

Hoppe continued to fume about the racing conditions. Besides the failure to protect the run from poor weather, his main objection was that the field was too large. Because bobsled competitions do not allow the top 15 seeds to race first, as is done in alpine skiing, the course is often badly chewed up before one or more of the favorites gets to it. This was precisely what had happened to Hoppe in the second run.

Hoppe's criticisms were not completely unjustified. The 1988 competition did include some unusual entrants, several of whom came from countries with little or no snow. In fact, the snowless nations organized their own informal "Caribbean Cup." Among the warm-weather sledders were the four Tames Perea brothers, who represented Mexico, although they earned their living as waiters in Dallas, Texas; the popular Jamaican bobsled team, which helped finance its training by selling tee-shirts, sweatshirts, and a reggae record; 52-year-old Harvey Hook of the U.S. Virgin Islands; and John Foster, who had previously represented the Virgin Islands in yachting and did so again in 1988. The "Caribbean Cup" was won by New Zealand's Alexander Peterson and Peter Henry, who tied for twentieth place overall. The top finish by a team from a truly snow-free country was the twenty-ninth place earned by Bart Carpentier Alting and Bart Dreschsel of the Netherlands Antilles. Carpentier Alting, attempting a rare double, also finished thirty-sixth of thirty-eight in the one-man luge.

## FOUR-MAN

**1924 Chamonix** T: 9, N: 5, D: 2.3.

| | | | |
|---|---|---|---|
| 1. SWI | (Eduard Scherrer, Alfred Neveu, Alfred Schläppi, Heinrich Schläppi) | 5:45.54 |
| 2. GBR | (Ralph Broome, Thomas Arnold, Alexander Richardson, Rodney Soher) | 5:48.83 |
| 3. BEL | (Charles Mulder, René Mortiaux, Paul van den Broeck, Victor Verschueren, Henri Willems) | 6:02.29 |
| 4. FRA | (A. Berg, H. Aldebert, G. André, Jean de Suarez D'Aulan) | 6:22.95 |
| 5. GBR | (Gary Horton, Archibald Crabbe, Joe Fairlie, Cecil Pim) | 6:40.71 |
| 6. ITA | (Lodovico Obexer, Massimo Fink, Paolo Herbert, Giuseppe Steiner, Aloise Trenker) | 7:15.41 |

**1928 St. Moritz** T: 23, N: 14, D: 3.19.

| | | | |
|---|---|---|---|
| 1. USA | (William Fiske, Nion Tucker, Geoffrey Mason, Clifford Gray, Richard Parke) | 3:20.5 |
| 2. USA | (Jennison Heaton, David Granger, Lyman Hine, Thomas Doe, Jay O'Brien) | 3:21.0 |
| 3. GER | (Hanns Kilian, Valentin Krempel, Hans Hess, Sebastian Huber, Hans Nägle) | 3:21.9 |
| 4. ARG | (Arturo Gramajo R. Gonzales, M. de Maria, R. Iglesias, J. Nash) | 3:22.6 |
| 5. ARG | (Eduardo Hope, J. del Caril, H. Milberg, H. Iglesias, H. Gramajo) | 3:22.9 |
| 6. BEL | (Ernest Lambert, Marcel Sedille-Courbon, Léon Tom, Max Houben, Walter Ganshof van der Meersch) | 3:24.5 |
| 7. ROM | (G. Socolescu, J. Gavat, T. Nitescu, P. Ghitulescu, M. Socolescu) | 3:24.6 |
| 8. SWI | (C. Stoffel, R. Fonjallaz, H. Hohnes, E. Coppetti, L. Koch) | 3:25.7 |

The competition was limited to two runs due to heavy thawing.

**1932 Lake Placid** T: 7, N: 5, D: 2.15.

| | | | |
|---|---|---|---|
| 1. USA | (William Fiske, Edward Eagan, Clifford Gray, Jay O'Brien) | 7:53.68 |
| 2. USA | (Henry Homburger, Percy Bryant, F. Paul Stevens, Edmund Horton) | 7:55.70 |

| | | | |
|---|---|---|---|
| 3. GER | (Hanns Kilian, Max Ludwig, Hans Melhorn, Sebastian Huber) | 8:00.04 |
| 4. SWI | (Reto Capadrutt, Hans Eisenhut, Charles Jenny, Oscar Geier) | 8:12.18 |
| 5. ITA | (Teofilo Rossi Di Montelera, Agostino Lanfranchi, Gaetano Lanfranchi, Italo Casini) | 8:24.21 |
| 6. ROM | (Papana Alexandru, Ionescu Alexandru, Ulise Petrescu, Hubert Dumitru) | 8:24.22 |
| 7. GER | (Walther von Mumm, Hasso von Bismarck, Gerhard Hessert, Georg Gyssling) | 8:25.45 |

Eddie Eagan is the only person to have won a gold medal in both the Summer and Winter Olympics. Eagan came from a poor family in Denver, but made his way through Yale, Harvard Law School, and Oxford, became a successful lawyer, and married an automobile heiress. He lived his life according to the precepts of Frank Merriwell, the fictional hero of dime novels. In 1932 he wrote, "To this day I have never used tobacco, because Frank didn't. My first glass of wine, which I do not care for, was taken under social compulsion in Europe. Frank never drank." Back in 1920, Eddie Eagan won the Light Heavyweight boxing championship at the Antwerp Olympics. Later he won the U.S. amateur Heavyweight title and became the first American to win the amateur championship of Great Britain. In 1932 he showed up as a member of the four-man bob team led by boy wonder Billy Fiske, who had driven a U.S. team to victory at the 1928 Olympics when he was only 16 years old. The other members of the 1932 squad were St. Moritz veterans 48-year-old Jay O'Brien, who happened to be the head of the U.S. Olympic Bobsled Committee, and 40-year-old Clifford "Tippy" Gray, a songwriter who was actually a citizen of Great Britain. Their main rivals were the team driven by civil engineer Henry Homburger, which was known as the Saranac Lake Red Devils.

The weather was so poor during the Olympics that the four-man bob had to be delayed until after the official closing ceremony. The officials in charge of the bobsled competitions ordered that all four heats be run on February 14. But after the second round, Paul Stevens of the Red Devils protested the poor racing conditions and stalked off. Most of the competitors followed him, and the officials were forced to reschedule runs 3 and 4 the next day. Fiske's team recorded the fastest time for each of the first three runs. The Red Devils picked up 2.31 seconds on their final run, but it wasn't enough.

Fiske and his partners never raced together again. In fact, three of them died within a one-year period starting in 1940. Jay O'Brien died of a heart attack at the age of 57. Billy Fiske was the first American to join the British Royal Air Force in 1939; wounded over Germany the following year, he died in England when he was only 29 years old. Tippy Gray, whose 3000 songs included "Got a Date with an Angel" and "If You Were the Only Girl in the World," died in 1941. Gray was such a modest man that his children never even knew that he had won two Olympic gold medals until after he died.

**1936 Garmisch-Partenkirchen** T: 18, N: 10, D: 2.12.
1. SWI (Pierre Musy, Arnold Gartmann, Charles Bouvier, Joseph Beerli) 5:19.85
2. SWI (Reto Capadrutt, Hans Aichele, Fritz Feierabend, Hans Bütikofer) 5:22.73
3. GBR (Frederick McEvoy, James Cardno, Guy Dugdale, Charles Green) 5:23.41
4. USA (J. Hubert Stevens, Crawford Merkel, Robert Martin, John Shene) 5:24.13
5. BEL (Max Houben, Martial van Schelle, Louis de Ridder, Paul Graeffe) 5:28.92
6. USA (Francis Tyler, James Bickford, Richard Lawrence, Max Bly) 5:29.00
7. GER (Hanns Kilian, Sebastian Huber, Fritz Schwarz, Hermann von Valta) 5:29.07
8. BEL (Rene Lunden, Eric de Spoelberch, Philippe de Pret Roose, Gaston Braun) 5:29.82

Again the bobsled competition was disrupted by bad weather—this time heavy rain. The first day's two runs were dangerous and unpredictable, but the next day the course was fast and smooth. Musy, a 25-year-old Swiss Army lieutenant, was the son of a former president of Switzerland.

**1948 St. Moritz** T: 15, N: 9, D: 2.7.
1. USA (Francis Tyler, Patrick Martin, Edward Rimkus, William D'Amico) 5.20.1
2. BEL (Max Houben, Freddy Mansveld, Louis-Georges Niels, Jacques Mouvet) 5:21.3
3. USA (James Bickford, Thomas Hicks, Donald Dupree, William Dupree) 5:21.5
4. SWI (Fritz Feierabend, Friedrich Waller, Felix Endrich, Heinrich Angst) 5:22.1
5. NOR (Arne Holst, Ivar Johansen, Reidar Berg, Alf Large) 5:22.5
6. ITA (Nino Bibbia, Giancarlo Ronchetti, Edilberto Campadese, Luigi Cavalieri) 5:23.0
7. GBR (William Coles, William McLean, R.W. Pennington Collins, George Holliday) 5:23.9
8. SWI (Franz Kapus, Rolf Spring, B. Schilter, Paul Eberhard) 5:25.4

The competition was halted in the middle of the second round when a water pipe burst, flooding the bob run. The winning team from Lake Placid, New York, weighed a total of 898 pounds.

**1952 Oslo** T: 15, N: 9, D: 2.22.
1. GER (Andreas Ostler, Friedrich Kuhn, Lorenz Nieberl, Franz Kemser) 5:07.84
2. USA (Stanley Benham, Patrick Martin, Howard Crossett, James Atkinson) 5:10.48
3. SWI (Fritz Feierabend, Albert Madörin, André Filippini, Stephan Waser) 5:11.70
4. SWI (Felix Endrich, Fritz Stöckli, Franz Kapus, Werner Spring) 5:13.98
5. AUT (Karl Wagner, Franz Eckhart, Hermann Palka, Paul Aste) 5:14.74
6. SWE (Kjell Holmström, Felix Fernström, Nils Landgren, Jan de Man Lapidoth) 5:15.01

7. SWE (Gunnar Åhs, Börje Ekedahl, Lennart Sandin, Gunnar Garpö) 5:17.86
8. ARG (Carlos Tomasi, Roberto Bordeau, Hector Tomasi, Carlos Sareistian) 5:18.85

The four members of the winning German team weighed in at 1041½ pounds. At a meeting held prior to the Olympics, the International Bobsled and Tobogganing Federation passed a rule limiting future teams from weighing more than 880 pounds.

**1956 Cortina** T: 21, N: 13, D: 2.4.
1. SWI (Franz Kapus, Gottfried Diener, Robert Alt, Heinrich Angst) 5:10.44
2. ITA (Eugenio Monti, Ulrico Giardi, Renzo Alverà, Renato Mocellini) 5:12.10
3. USA (Arthur Tyler, William Dodge, Charles Butler, James Lamy) 5:12.39
4. SWI (Max Angst, Albert Gartmann, Harry Warburton, Rolf Gerber) 5:14.27
5. ITA (Dino DeMartin, Giovanni DeMartin, Giovanni Tabacchi, Carlo Da Pra) 5:14.66
6. GER (Hans Rösch, Martin Pössinger, Lorenz Nieberl, Silvester Wackerle, Sr.) 5:18.02
7. AUT (Loserth, Thurner, Schwarzböck, Dominik) 5:18.29
8. GER (Franz Schelle, Jakob Nirschel, Hans Henn, Edmund Koller) 5:18.50

Franz Kapus was 46 years old when he drove the Swiss team to victory by scoring the fastest times in all but the first run.

**1960** not held

**1964 Innsbruck-Igls** T: 18, N: 11, D: 2.7.
1. CAN (Victor Emery, Peter Kirby, Douglas Anakin, John Emery) 4:14.46
2. AUT (Erwin Thaler, Adolf Koxeder, Josef Nairz, Reinhold Durnthaler) 4:15.48
3. ITA (Eugenio Monti, Sergio Siorpaes, Benito Rigoni, Gildo Siorpaes) 4:15.60
4. ITA (Sergio Zardini, Romano Bonagura, Sergio Mocellini, Ferruccio Dalla Torre) 4:15.89
5. GER (Franz Schelle, Otto Göbl, Ludwig Siebert, Josef Sterff) 4:16.19
6. USA (William Hickey, Charles Pandolph, Reginald Benham, William Dundon) 4:17.23
7. AUT (Paul Aste, Hans Stoll, Herbert Gruber, Andreas Arnold) 4:17.73
8. SWI (Herbert Kiessel, Oskar Lory, Bernhard Wild, Hansrudi Beuggar) 4:18.12

The winning Canadian team was made up of four bachelors from Montreal. Canada had never before entered an Olympic bobsled competition.

**1968 Grenoble-Alpe d'Huez** T: 19, N: 11, D: 2.15.
1. ITA (Eugenio Monti, Luciano De Paolis, Roberto Zandonella, Mario Armano) 2:17.39
2. AUT (Erwin Thaler, Reinhold Durnthaler, Herbert Gruber, Josef Eder) 2:17.48

3. SWI   (Jean Wicki, Hans Candrian, Willi Hofmann,   2:18.04
Walter Graf)

4. ROM   (Ion Panțuru, Nicolae Neagoe, Petre Hristovici,   2:18.14
Gheorghe Maftei)

5. GER   (Horst Floth, Pepi Bader, Willi Schäfer, Frank   2:18.33
Lange)

6. ITA   (Gianfranco Gaspari, Leonardo Cavallini, Giu-   2:18.36
seppe Rescigno, Andrea Clemente)

7. FRA   (Francis Luiggi, Maurice Grether, Andre Patey,   2:18.84
Gerard Monrazel)

8. GBR   (Anthony Nash, Robin Dixon, Guy Renwick,   2:18.84
Robin Widdows)

The danger of a sudden thaw forced the officials to limit the contest to only two runs. Eugenio Monti won two silver medals in 1956, two bronze medals in 1964, and two gold medals in 1968.

**1972 Sapporo-Teineyama** T: 18, N: 10, D: 2.11.

1. SWI   (Jean Wicki, Edy Hubacher, Hans Leuteneg-   4:43.07
ger, Werner Carmichel)

2. ITA   (Nevio De Zordo, Gianni Bonichon, Adriano   4:43.83
Frassinelli, Corrado Dal Fabbro)

3. GER   (Wolfgang Zimmerer, Peter Utzschneider, Ste-   4:43.92
fan Gaisreiter, Walter Steinbauer)

4. SWI   (Hans Candrian, Heinz Schenker, Erwin Juon,   4:44.56
Gaudenz Beeli)

5. GER   (Horst Floth, Pepi Bader, Donat Ertel, Walter   4:45.09
Gilik)

6. AUT   (Herbert Gruber, Josef Oberhauser, Utz   4:45.77
Chwalla, Josef Eder)

7. AUT   (Werner Dellekarth, Fritz Sperling, Werner   4:46.66
Moser, Walter Dellekarth)

8. ITA   (Gianfranco Gaspari, Luciano De Paolis, Ro-   4:46.73
berto Zandonella, Mario Armano)

**1976 Innsbruck-Igls** T: 21, N: 12, D: 2.14.

1. GDR   (Meinhard Nehmer, Jochen Babock, Bernhard   3:40.43
Germeshausen, Bernhard Lehmann)

2. SWI   (Erich Schärer, Ulrich Bächli, Rudolf Marti,   3:40.89
Josef Benz)

3. GER   (Wolfgang Zimmerer, Peter Utzschneider,   3:41.37
Bodo Bittner, Manfred Schumann)

4. GDR   (Horst Schönau, Horst Bernhard, Harald   3:42.44
Seifert, Raimund Bethge)

5. GER   (Georg Heibl, Hans Morant, Siegfried Radant,   3:42.47
Fritz Ohlwärter)

6. AUT   (Werner Delle Karth, Andreas Schwab, Otto   3:43.21
Breg, Franz Köfel, Heinz Krenn)

7. AUT   (Fritz Sperling, Kurt Oberholler, Gerd   3:43.79
Zaunschirm, Dieter Gehmacher)

8. ROM   (Dragos Panaitescu, Paul Neagu, Costel   3:43.91
Ionescu, Gheorghe Lixandru)

**1980 Lake Placid** T: 17, N: 10, D: 2.24.

1. GDR   (Meinhard Nehmer, Bogdan Musiol, Bernhard   3:59.92
Germeshausen, Hans-Jürgen Gerhardt)

2. SWI   (Erich Schärer, Ulrich Bächli, Rudolf Marti,   4:00.87
Josef Benz)

3. GDR   (Horst Schönau, Ronald Wetzig, Detlef Richter,   4:00.97
Andreas Kirchner)

4. AUT   (Fritz Sperling, Heinrich Bergmüller, Franz   4:02.62
Rednak, Bernhard Purkrabek)

5. AUT   (Walter Delle Karth, Franz Paulweber, Gerd   4:02.95
Zaunschirm, Kurt Oberhöller)

6. SWI   (Hans Hiltebrand, Ulrich Schindler, Walter   4:03.69
Rahm, Armin Baumgartner)

7. GER   (Peter Hell, Hans Wagner, Heinz Busche,   4:04.40
Walter Barfuss)

8. ROM   (Dragos Panaitescu, Dorel Critudor, Sandu   4:04.68
Mitrofan, Gheorghe Lixandru)

**1984 Sarajevo** T: 24, N: 15, D: 2.18.

1. GDR   (Wolfgang Hoppe, Roland Wetzig, Dietmar   3:20.22
Schauerhammer, Andreas Kirchner)

2. GDR   (Bernhard Lehmann, Bogdan Musiol, Ingo   3:20.78
Voge, Eberhard Weise)

3. SWI   (Silvio Giobellina, Heinz Stettler, Urs Salz-   3:21.39
mann, Rico Freiermuth)

4. SWI   (Ekkehard Fasser, Hans Märchy, Kurt Poletti,   3:22.90
Rolf Strittmatter)

5. USA   (Jeff Jost, Joe Briski, Thomas Barnes, Hal   3:23.33
Hoye)

6. SOV   (Jānis Kipurs, Maris Poikans, Ivar Berzups,   3:23.51
Aiwar Šnepsts)

7. ROM   (Dorin Degan, Cornel Popescu, Georghe   3:23.76
Lixandru, Costel Petrariu)

8. ITA   (Guerrino Ghedina, Stefano Ticci, Paolo   3:23.77
Scaramuzza, Andrea Meneghin)

The top three teams finished 1, 2, 3, in each of the four runs.

**1988 Calgary** T: 26, N: 17, D: 2.28.

1. SWI   (Ekkehard Fasser, Kurt Meier, Marcel Fässler,   3:47.51
Werner Stocker)

2. GDR   (Wolfgang Hoppe, Dietmar Schauerhammer,   3:47.58
Bogdan Musiol, Ingo Voge)

3. SOV   (Jānis Kipurs, Guntis Osis, Juris Tone,   3:48.26
Vladimir Kozlov)

4. USA   (Brent Rushlaw, Hal Hoye, Michael Wasko,   3:48.28
William White)

5. SOV   (Maris Poikans, Olafs Klyavinch, Ivars   3:48.35
Bersups, Juris Judzerns)

6. AUT   (Peter Kienast, Franz Siegl, Christian Mark,   3:48.65
Kurt Teigl)

7. AUT   (Into Appelt, Josef Muigg, Gerhard Redl,   3:48.95
Harald Winkler)

8. GDR   (Detlef Richter, Bodo Ferl, Ludwig Jahn,   3:49.06
Alexander Szelig)

Third after two runs and second after three, 35-year-old Ekkehard Fasser eked out an upset victory in the final competition of his career. Fasser and his crew gained their advantage over Hoppe and the East Germans in the first 50 meters of the 1475-meter course, picking up a combined time of one sixteen-hundredth of a second over four runs.

# ICE HOCKEY

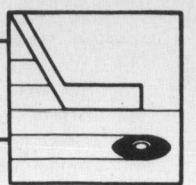

Ice hockey matches are divided into three 20-minute periods.

**1920 Antwerp** T: 7, N: 7, D: 4.30.

| | | | W | L | PF | PA |
|---|---|---|---|---|---|---|
| 1. CAN | (Robert Benson, Wally Byron, Frank Frederickson, Chris Fridfinnson, Michael Goodman, Haldor Halderson, Konrad Johannesson, Allan "Huck" Woodman) | | 3 | 0 | 29 | 1 |
| 2. USA | (Raymond Booney, Anthony Conroy, Herbert Drury, J. Edward Fitzgerald, George Geran, Frank Goheen, Joseph McCormick, Lawrence McCormick, Frank Synott, Leon Parker Tuck, Cyril Weidenborner) | | 3 | 1 | 52 | 2 |
| 3. CZE | (Adolf Dušek, Karel Hartman, Vilém Loos, Jan Peka, Karel Pešek, Josef Šroubek, Otakar Vindyš, Jan Palouš, Karel Wälver) | | 1 | 2 | 1 | 31 |
| 4. SWE | (Vilhelm Arwe, Erik Burman, Seth Howander, Georg Johansson, Einar Lindqvist, Einar Lundell, Anton Mattsson, Nils Molander, Sven Säfwenberg, Einar Svensson) | | 3 | 3 | 17 | 19 |

Canada scored victories of 15–0 over Czechoslovakia, 2–0 over the United States, and 12–1 over Sweden. According to the rules of the tournament, the three teams that lost to Canada then played off for second place. The United States beat Sweden, 7–0, and Czechoslovakia, 16–0. Then Czechoslovakia defeated Sweden, 1–0, to win the bronze medal, even though the Czechs had been outscored 1 to 31 in their three matches. Canada was represented by the Winnipeg Falcons, who had just defeated the University of Toronto for the Canadian championship. The invitation to the Olympics came at such short notice that the Falcons didn't have time to return home to Winnipeg. Funds had to be raised to buy the players new clothes for the overseas journey.

**1924 Chamonix** T: 8, N: 8, D: 2.8.

| | | | W | L | PF | PA |
|---|---|---|---|---|---|---|
| 1. CAN | (Jack Cameron, Ernest Collett, Albert McCaffery, Harold McMunn, Duncan Munro, W. Beattie Ramsay, Cyril Slater, Reginald Smith, Harry Watson) | | 5 | 0 | 110 | 3 |
| 2. USA | (Clarence Abel, Herbert Drury, Alphonse Lacroix, John Langley, John Lyons, Justin McCarthy, Willard Rice, Irving Small, Frank Synott) | | 4 | 1 | 73 | 6 |

| | | | W | L | PF | PA |
|---|---|---|---|---|---|---|
| 3. GBR | (William Anderson, Lorne Carr-Harris, Colin Carruthers, Eric Carruthers, Guy Clarkson, Ross Cuthbert, George Holmes, Hamilton Jukes, Edward Pitblado, Blane Sexton) | | 3 | 2 | 40 | 38 |
| 4. SWE | (Ruben Allinger, Vilhelm Arwe, Erik Burman, Birger Holmqvist, Gustaf Johansson, Hugo Johansson, Karl Josefson, Ernst Karlberg, Nils Molander, Einar Ohlsson) | | 2 | 3 | 21 | 49 |
| 5. CZE | (W. Stransky, J. Rezac, Otakar Vindyš, Vilém Loos, Josef Šroubek, J. Jirkovsky, J. Malecek, J. Fleischmann, M. Fleischmann, Jan Palouš, J. Krasl) | | 1 | 2 | 14 | 41 |
| 5. FRA | (B. Poule, P.E. Bouillon, L. Brasseur, A. Charlet, P. Charpentier, J. Chaudron, H. Couttet, R. Couvert, M. Del Valle, A. De Rauch, G.F. De Wilde, A. Hassler, C. Lavaivre, H. Levy-Grunwald, J. Nard, C. Payot, P. Payot, L. Quaglia, G. Simond) | | 1 | 2 | 9 | 42 |
| 7. BEL | (Victor Verschueren, Paul Van den Broeck, Henri Louette, Frederick Rudolph, Andre Poplimont, Gaston Van Volckxsom, Charles Van den Driessche, Louis de Ridder) | | 0 | 3 | 8 | 35 |
| 7. SWI | (B. Leuzinger, W. deSiebenthal, D. Unger, E. Mottier, R. Savoie, M. Jaccard, F. Auckenthaler, Ernest Jacquet, P. Muller, A. Verdeil, E. Filiol) | | 0 | 3 | 2 | 53 |

The Canadian team, the Toronto Granites, displayed extraordinary superiority. After defeating Czechoslovakia, 30–0, and Sweden, 22–0, they outscored Switzerland, 18–0 in the first period alone and then breezed to a 33–0 victory, before crushing Great Britain, 19–2. Meanwhile the U.S. team had beaten Belgium 19–0, France 22–0, Great Britain 11–0, and Sweden 20–0. The final match between Canada and the United States was a rough battle that saw Canada's Harry Watson knocked cold after only 20 seconds of play. Watson recovered, however, and, with blood in his eyes, scored the first two goals of the game. Canada led 2–1 after the first period and 5–1 after the second. A single third-period goal accounted for the final score of 6–1.

**1928 St. Moritz** T: 11, N: 11, D: 2.19.

| | | | W | L | T | PF | PA |
|---|---|---|---|---|---|---|---|
| 1. CAN | (Charles Delahay, Frank Fisher, Louis Hudson, Norbert Mueller, | | 3 | 0 | 0 | 38 | 0 |

Herbert Plaxton, Hugh Plaxton, Roger Plaxton, John Porter, Frank Sullivan, Joseph Sullivan, Ross Taylor, David Trottier)

| | | | W | L | T | PF | PA |
|---|---|---|---|---|---|---|---|
| 2. | SWE | (Carl Abrahamsson, Emil Bergman, Birger Holmqvist, Gustaf Johansson, Henry Johansson, Nils Johansson, Ernst Karlberg, Erik Larsson, Bertil Linde, Sigurd Öberg, Vilhelm Petersen, Kurt Sucksdorf) | 3 | 1 | 1 | 12 | 14 |
| 3. | SWI | (Gianni Andreossi, Murezzan Andreossi, Robert Breiter, Louis Dufour, Charles Fasel, Albert Geromini, Fritz Kraatz, Adolf Martignoni, Heinrich Meng, Anton Morosani, Luzius Rüedi, Richard Torriani) | 2 | 2 | 1 | 9 | 21 |
| 4. | GBR | (Blane Sexton, Eric Carruthers, Ross Cuthbert, F.M.G. Melland, Victor Tait, C.I. Wylde, Colin Carruthers, W.G. Speechley, H.G.E. Greenwood, William Brown, G.E.H. Rogers, B.H. Fawcett) | 2 | 4 | 0 | 11 | 27 |

Canada was represented by the 1926 Toronto University team, which had stayed together and, renamed the Toronto Graduates, had won the Canadian championships. They arrived in Switzerland ten days before the opening of the Games. When Olympic officials saw the Canadians practice they realized that the rest of the teams would be completely outclassed. Consequently, they devised an unusual organization for the tournament. Canada was advanced straight to the final round, while the other ten nations were divided into three pools. The winners of the three pools then joined Canada in the final round. This odd system turned out to be well justified, as Canada obliterated Sweden 11–0, Great Britain 14–0, and Switzerland 13–0.

### 1932 Lake Placid T: 4, N: 4, D: 2.13.

| | | | W | L | T | PF | PA |
|---|---|---|---|---|---|---|---|
| 1. | CAN | (William Cockburn, Clifford Crowley, Albert Duncanson, George Garbutt, Roy Hinkel, Victor Lundquist, Norman Malloy, Walter Monson, Kenneth Moore, N. Romeo Rivers, Harold Simpson, Hugh Sutherland, W. Stanley Wagner, J. Aliston Wise) | 5 | 0 | 1 | 32 | 4 |
| 2. | USA | (Osborn Anderson, John Bent, John Chase, John Cookman, Douglas Everett, Franklin Farrell, Joseph Fitzgerald, Edward Frazier, John Garrison, Gerard Hallock, Robert Livingston, Francis Nelson, Winthrop Palmer, Gordon Smith) | 4 | 1 | 1 | 27 | 5 |

| | | | W | L | I | PF | PA |
|---|---|---|---|---|---|---|---|
| 3. | GER | (Rudi Ball, Alfred Heinrich, Erich Herker, Gustav Jaenecke, Werner Korff, Walter Leinweber, Erich Römer, Marquardt Slevogt, Martin Schröttle, Georg Strobl) | 2 | 4 | 0 | 7 | 26 |
| 4. | POL | (Adam Kowalski, Aleksander Kowalski, Wlodzimierz Krygier, Albert Maurer, Roman Sabiński, Kazimierz Sokolowski, Jósef Stogowski, Witalis Ludwiczak, Czeslaw Marchewczyk, Kazimierz Materski) | 0 | 6 | 0 | 3 | 34 |

Because of the worldwide Depression, only four nations appeared for the Olympic hockey tournament. Consequently, it was decided that each team would play each other team twice. The Canadian team from Winnipeg won their first five matches, including a 2–1 victory over the United States. This meant that a win or a tie in the second match against the United States would assure Canada of first place. If the United States won, then a third match would be required. The United States took a 2–1 lead, but with 50 seconds to play, Rivers shot a bouncing puck into the net to tie the score. Three scoreless overtimes later, Canada was declared the tournament winner.

### 1936 Garmisch-Partenkirchen I: 15, N: 15, D: 2.16.

| | | | W | L | I | PF | PA |
|---|---|---|---|---|---|---|---|
| 1. | GBR | (Alexander Archer, James Borland, Edgar Bronchley, James Chappell, John Coward, Gordon Dailley, John Davey, Carl Erhardt, James Foster, John Kilpatrick, Archibald Stinchcombe, Robert Wyman) | 5 | 0 | 2 | 17 | 3 |
| 2. | CAN | (Maxwell Deacon, Hugh Farquharson, Kenneth Farmer, James Haggarty, Walter Kitchen, Raymond Milton, Francis Moore, Herman Murray, Arthur Nash, David Neville, Ralph St. Germain, Alexander Sinclair, William Thomson) | 7 | 1 | 0 | 54 | 7 |
| 3. | USA | (John Garrison, August Kammer, Philip LaBatte, John Lax, Thomas Moone, Eldrige Ross, Paul Rowe, Francis Shaugnessy, Gordon Smith, Francis Spain, Frank Stubbs) | 5 | 2 | 1 | 10 | 4 |
| 4. | CZE | (Josef Boháč, Alois Cetkovsky, Karel Hromádka, Drahos Jirotka, Zdenek Jirotka, Jan Košek, Oldřich Kučera, Josef Maleček, Jan Peka, Jaroslav Pusbauer, Jiři Tožička, Ladislav Troják, Walter Ullrich) | 5 | 3 | 0 | 16 | 16 |
| 5. | GER | (Wilhelm Egginger, Joachim Albrecht von Bethmann-Hollweg, Gustav Jaenecke, Phillip | 3 | 2 | 1 | 10 | 9 |

| | | W | L | T | PF | PA |
|---|---|---|---|---|---|---|
| | Schenk, Rudi Ball, Karl Kögel, Anton Wiedemann, Herbert Schibukat, Alois Kuhn, Werner George, Georg Strobl, Paul Trautmann) | | | | | |
| 5. SWE | (Hermann Carlsson, Sven Bergquist, Bertil Lundell, Holger Engberg, Torsten Jöhncke, Yngve Liljeberg, Bertil Norberg, Vilhelm Petersen, Åke Ericson, Stig Andersson, Lennart Hellman, Vilhelm Larsson, Ruben Carlsson) | 2 | 3 | 0 | 5 | 7 |
| 7. AUT | (Hermann Weiss, Hans Trauttenberg, Rudolf Vojta, Oskar Nowak, Friedrich Demmer, Franz Csöngei, Hans Tatzer, Willibald Stanek, Lambert Neumaier, Franz Schüssler, Emil Seidler, Josef Göbl) | 2 | 4 | 0 | 12 | 11 |
| 7. HUN | (István Csak, Ferenc Monostori, Miklós Barcza, László Róna, Frigyes Helmeczi, Sándor Magyar, András Gergely, László Gergely, Béla Háray, Zoltán Jeney, Sándor Miklós, Ferenc Szamosi, Mátyás Farkas) | 2 | 4 | 0 | 16 | 77 |

Germany's leading hockey player was Rudi Ball, a Jew who fled the country when the Nazis began their campaign of anti-Semitism. One month before the Games began, he returned to lead the German team after being invited back by the Nazi leadership. He was the only Jewish member of the German Winter Olympics team.

A major squabble developed over the eligibility of two British players, Alex Archer and goalie James Foster. Archer and Foster were Canadians who, along with 12 other players, had moved to England in 1935. The day before the Olympic tournament began, the International Ice Hockey Federation voted unanimously to ban the two players from competing in the Olympics. Two days later, however, Archer and Foster along with several other Canadian-born players, were on the ice playing in Great Britain's opening match against Sweden. Why they were allowed to play, and what happened in the interim, is still a subject of controversy. The British version is that the Canadians, proud to be members of the Commonwealth, graciously withdrew their objection to Foster and Archer playing for Great Britain. The American version is that the British simply ignored the rules and weren't punished. At any rate, Canada's Olympic undefeated streak was halted at 20 by Great Britain in the semifinal round, when Edgar Brenchley scored a goal in the 14th minute of the final period to give the British a 2–1 victory. Great Britain remained unbeaten by surviving a 0–0 triple overtime tie with the United States in their final match.

## 1948 St. Moritz T: 9, N: 9, D: 2.8.

| | | W | L | T | PF | PA |
|---|---|---|---|---|---|---|
| 1. CAN | (Murray Dowey, Bernard Dunster, Jean Orval Gravelle, Patrick Guzzo, Walter Halder, Thomas Hibbert, Henri-André Laperrière, John Lecompte, George Mara, Albert Renaud, Reginald Schroeter, Irving Taylor) | 7 | 0 | 1 | 69 | 5 |
| 2. CZE | (Vladimir Bouzek, Augustin Bubnik, Jaroslav Drobny, Přemysl Hajny, Zdenek Jarkovský, Stanislav Konopásek, Bohumil Modry, Miloslav Pokorny, Václav Rozinák, Moroslav Sláma, Karel Stibor, Vilibald Štovik, Ladislav Troják, Josef Trousilek, Oldřich Zábrodsky, Vladimir Zábrodský, Vladimir Kobranov) | 7 | 0 | 1 | 80 | 18 |
| 3. SWI | (Hans Bänninger, Alfred Bieler, Heinrich Boller, Ferdinand Cattini, Hans Cattini, Hans Dürst, Walter Dürst, Emil Handschin, Heini Lohrer, Werner Lohrer, Reto Perl, Gebhard Poltera, Ulrich Poltera, Beat Rüedi, Otto Schubiger, Richard Torriani, Hans Trepp) | 6 | 2 | 0 | 67 | 21 |
| —USA | (Robert Baker, Ruben Bjorkman, Robert Boeser, Bruce Cunliffe, John Garrity, Donald Geary, Goodwin Harding, Herbert Van Ingen, John Kirrane, Bruce Mather, Allan Opsahl, Fred Pearson, Stanton Priddy, Jack Riley, Ralph Warburton) | 5 | 3 | 0 | 86 | 33 |
| 4. SWE | (Stig Andersson, Åke Andersson, Stig Carlsson, Åke Ericson, Rolf Ericson, Svante Granlund, Arne Johansson, Rune Johansson, Gunnar Landelius, Klas Lindström, Lars Ljungman, Holger Nurmela, Bror Pettersson, Rolf Pettersson, Kurt Svanberg, Sven Thunman) | 4 | 4 | 0 | 55 | 28 |
| 5. GBR | (Leonhard Baker, Beryl Bailey, James Chappell, Gerry Davey, Fred Dunkelman, Arthur Green, Frank Green, Frank Jardine, John Murray, John Oxley, Stanley Simon, William Smith, Archibald Stinchecombe, Thomas Syme) | 3 | 5 | 0 | 39 | 47 |
| 6. POL | (Henryk Bromer, Mieczyslaw Burda, Stefan Csorich, Tadeusz Dolewski, Alfred Gansiniec, Thomas Jasiński, Mieczslaw Kasprzycki, Boleslaw Kolasa, Adam Kowalski, Eugeniusz | 2 | 6 | 0 | 20 | 97 |

Lewacki, Jan Maciejko, Czeslaw Marchewczyk, Mieczyslaw Palus, Henryk Przeździecki, Hilary Skarzyński, Maksymilian Wiecek, Ernest Ziaja)

| | | | | | | |
|---|---|---|---|---|---|---|
| 7. | AUT | (Albert Böhm, Franz Csöngei, Friedrich Demmer, Egon Engel, Walter Feistritzer, Gustav Gross, Adolf Hafner, Alfred Huber, Julius Juhn, Oskar Nowack, Jörg Reichel, Johann Schneider, Willibald Stanek, Herbert Ulrich, Fritz Walter, Helfried Winger, Rudolf Wurmbrandt) | 1 | 7 | 0 | 33 | 77 |
| 8. | ITA | (C. Apollonio, G. Bassi, M. Bedogni, L. Bestagini, C. Bulgheroni, I. Dionisi, A. Fabris, V. Fardella, A. Federici, U. Gerli, D. Innocenti, C. Mangini, D. Menardi, O. Rauth, F. Rossi, G. Zopegni) | 0 | 8 | 0 | 24 | 156 |

The controversy that engulfed the 1948 ice hockey tournament actually began a year earlier, when the International Ice Hockey Federation ruled that the Amateur Athletic Union was being replaced as the governing body for amateur ice hockey in the United States by the American Hockey Association (A.H.A.). Avery Brundage, chairman of the American Olympic Committee (A.O.C.), accused the A.H.A. of being under commercial sponsorship and refused to sanction its team. Consequently, two U.S. teams arrived in Switzerland prepared to play in the Olympic tournament. Two days before the opening ceremony, the executive committee of the International Olympic Committee (I.O.C.) voted to bar both U.S. teams from competition. However, the Swiss Olympic Committee, siding with the International Ice Hockey Federation, defied the International Olympic Committee and announced that the A.H.A. team would be allowed to play. The A.O.C. team got to take part in the opening-day parade, while the A.H.A. team watched from the stands. But after that, the A.O.C. team had nothing to do but enjoy their paid vacation.

Meanwhile, the A.H.A. players raked up a couple of amazing scores, beating Poland 23–4 and Italy 31–1. Their coach justified these thrashings because the rules stated that if two teams were tied at the end of the tournament, the one with the largest cumulative scoring margin would be declared the winner.

The I.O.C. disowned the ice hockey tournament, but later gave it official approval on the condition that the A.H.A. team not be included in the placings.

With one day left in the competition, three nations—Canada, Czechoslovakia, and Switzerland—all had a chance to finish in first place. In the morning Czechoslovakia defeated the United States, 4–3, which eliminated Switzerland's hopes of placing higher than second. The final match pitted Canada against the Swiss. Two days earlier the Czechs and the Canadians had played a 0–0 tie. Consequently, Canada needed to beat Switzerland by at least two goals to win the gold medal on the basis of the goal differential tie-breaker. About 5000 Swiss perched on mountain cliffs and watched the game, pelting officials with snowballs whenever they disagreed with a call. Their enthusiasm did little good, as the Canadian team tallied a goal in each period and won, 3–0. A final note about the Italian team: in addition to their 31–1 loss to the United States, they lost to Sweden 23–0, Canada 21–1, Czechoslovakia 22–3, and Switzerland 16–0.

**1952 Oslo** T: 9, N: 9, D: 2.24.

| | | | W | L | T | PF | PA |
|---|---|---|---|---|---|---|---|
| 1. | CAN | (George Abel, John Davies, William Dawe, Robert Dickson, Donald Gauf, William Gibson, Ralph Hansch, Robert Meyers, David Miller, Eric Paterson, Thomas Pollock, Allan Purvis, Gordon Robertson, Louis Secco, Francis Sullivan, Robert Watt) | 7 | 0 | 1 | 71 | 14 |
| 2. | USA | (Ruben Bjorkman, Leonard Ceglarski, Joseph Czarnota, Richard Desmond, Andre Gambucci, Clifford Harrison, Gerald Kilmartin, John Mulhern, John Noah, Arnold Oss, Robert Rompre, James Sedin, Allen Van, Donald Whiston, Kenneth Yackel) | 6 | 1 | 1 | 43 | 21 |
| 3. | SWE | (Göte Almqvist, Hans Andersson, Stig "Tvilling" Andersson, Åke Andersson, Lars Björn, Göte Blomqvist, Thord Flodqvist, Erik Johansson, Gösta Johansson, Rune Johansson, Sven Johansson, Åke Lassas, Holger Nurmela, Hans Öberg, Lars Pettersson, Lars Svensson, Sven Thunman) | 7 | 2 | 0 | 53 | 22 |
| 4. | CZE | (Slavomir Barton, Miloslav Blažek, Václav Bubnik, Vlastimil Bubnik, Miloslav Charouzd, Bronislav Danda, Karel Gut, Vlastimil Hajšman, Jan Lidral, Miroslav Nový, Miloslav Ošmera, Zdenek Pýcha, Miroslav Rejman, Jan Richter, Oldrich Sedlak, Jiri Sekyra, Josef Záhorsky) | 6 | 3 | 0 | 50 | 23 |
| 5. | SWI | (Gian Bazzi, Hans Bänninger, François Blank, Bixio Celio, Reto Delnon, Walter Dürst, Emil Golaz, Emil Handschin, Paul Hofer, Willy Pfister, Gebhard Poltera, Ulrich Poltera, Otto | 4 | 4 | 0 | 40 | 40 |

|  | | W | L | T | PF | PA |
|---|---|---|---|---|---|---|
| | Schläpfer, Otto Schubiger, Alfred Streun, Hans Trepp, Paul Wyss) | | | | | |
| 6. POL | (Michal Antuszewicz, Henryk Bromowicz, Kazimierz Chodakowski, Stefan Csorich, Rudolf Czech, Alfred Gansiniec, Jan Hampel, Marian Jezak, Eugeniusz Lewacki, Roman Pęczek, Hilary Skarzyński, Konstanty Świcarz, Stanislaw Szlendak, Zdzislaw Trojanowski, Adolf Wróbel, Alfred Wróbel) | 2 | 5 | 1 | 21 | 56 |
| 7. FIN | (Yrjo Hakala, Aarne Honkavaara, Erkki Hytonen, Pentti Isotalo, Matti Karumaa, Ossi Kauppi, Keijo Kuusela, Kauko Makinen, Pekka Myllyla, Christian Rapp, Esko Rehoma, Matti Rintakoski, Eero Saari, Eero Salisma, Lauri Silvan, Unto Vitala, Jukka Vuolio) | 2 | 6 | 0 | 21 | 60 |
| 8. GER | (Karl Bierschel, Markus Egen, Karl Enzler, Georg Guggemos, Alfred Hoffmann, Engelbert Holderied, Walter Kremershof, Ludwig Kuhn, Dieter Niess, Hans Georg Pescher, Fritz Poitsch, Herbert Schibukat, Xaver Unsinn, Heinz Wackers, Karl Wild) | 1 | 6 | 1 | 21 | 53 |

Canada, represented by the Edmonton Mercurys, won their first seven games. A final 3–3 tie with the United States gave them the championship. The Americans were just as thrilled by the outcome, since it meant they would finish second instead of fourth. The U.S. team was not popular with the spectators because of their rough style of play. In fact, three of the U.S. players, Czarnota, Yackel, and Gambucci, spent more time in the penalty box than the team totals of any of the other eight teams in the tournament.

Between 1920 and 1952, Canadian ice hockey teams compiled an extraordinary Olympic record of 37 wins, 1 loss, and 3 ties. In those 41 games they scored 403 goals while allowing only 34.

**1956 Cortina** T: 10, N: 10, D: 2.4.

|  | | W | L | T | PF | PA |
|---|---|---|---|---|---|---|
| 1. SOV | (Yevgeny Babich, Usevolod Bobrov, Nikolai Chlystov, Aleksei Guryshev, Yuri Krylov, Alfred Kuchevsky, Valentin Kusin, Grigory Mkrtchan, Viktor Nikiforov, Yuri Pantyuchov, Nikolai Puchkov, Viktor Shuvalov, Genrich Sidorenkov, Nikolai Sologubov, Ivan Tregubov, Dmitri Ukolov, Aleksandr Uvarov) | 7 | 0 | 0 | 40 | 9 |
| 2. USA | (Wendell Anderson, Wellington Burnett, Eugene Campbell, Gordon Christian, William Cleary, Richard Dougherty, Willard Ikola, John Matchefts, John Mayasich, Daniel McKinnon, Richard Meredith, Weldon Olson, John Petroske, Kenneth Purpur, Donald Rigazio, Richard Rodenheiser, Edward Sampson) | 5 | 2 | 0 | 33 | 16 |
| 3. CAN | (Denis Brodeur, Charles Brooker, William Colvin, Alfred Horne, Arthur Hurst, Byrle Klinck, Paul Knox, Kenneth Laufman, Howard Lee, James Logan, Floyd Martin, Jack McKenzie, Donald Rope, Georges Scholes, Gérald Théberge, Robert White, Keith Woodall) | 6 | 2 | 0 | 53 | 12 |
| 4. SWE | (Lars Björn, Sigurd Bröms, Stig Carlsson, Yngve Casslind, Sven Johansson, Vilgot Larsson, Åke Lassas, Lars-Erik Lundvall, Ove Malmberg, Nils Nilsson, Holger Nurmela, Hans Öberg, Ronald Pettersson, Lars Svensson, Hans Tvilling [Andersson], Stig "Tvilling" Andersson, Bertz Zetterberg) | 2 | 4 | 1 | 17 | 27 |
| 5. CZE | (Stanislav Bacilek, Stavomir Barton, Václav Bubnik, Vlastimil Bubnik, Jaromir Bünter, Otto Čimrman, Bronislav Danda, Karel Gut, Jan Jendek, Jan Kasper, Miroslav Kluc, Ždenek Návrat, Václav Pantuček, Bohumil Prošek, František Vaněk, Jan Vodička, Vladimir Zábrodsky) | 3 | 4 | 0 | 32 | 36 |
| 6. GER | (Paul Ambros, Martin Beck, Toni Biersack, Karl Bierschel, Markus Egen, Arthur Endress, Bruno Guttowski, Alfred Hoffmann, Hans Huber, Ulrich Jansen, Günther Jochems, Rainer Kossmann, Rudolf Pittrich, Hans Rampf, Kurt Sepp, Ernst Trautwein, Martin Zach) | 1 | 5 | 2 | 15 | 41 |
| 7. ITA | (Carmine Tucci, Carlo Montemurro, Aldo Federici, Mario Bedogni, Bernardo Tomei, Giovanni Furlani, Giampiero Branduardi, Aldo Maniacco, Ernesto Crotti, Giancarlo Agazzi, Gianfranco Darin, Rino Alberton, Giulio Oberhammer, Francesco Macchietto) | 3 | 1 | 2 | 26 | 14 |

8. POL (Janusz Zawadzki, Kazimierz Chodakowski, Stanislaw Olczyk, Mieczyslaw Chmura, Henryk Bromowicz, Józef Kurek, Zdzislaw Nowak, Szymon Janiczko, Adolf Wróbel, Kazimierz Bryniarski, Marian Herda, Hilary Skarżyński, Bronislaw Gosztyla, Rudolf Czech, Alfred Wróbel, Edward Kocząb, Wladyslaw Pabisz)   2 3 0 15 22

The Soviet team made a great impression, not only with their excellent play, but with their good sportsmanship and clean style as well.

**1960 Squaw Valley** T: 9, N: 9, D: 2.28.

|  | | W | L | T | PF | PA |
|---|---|---|---|---|---|---|
| 1. USA | (Roger Christian, William Christian, Robert Cleary, William Cleary, Eugene Grazia, Paul Johnson, John Kirrane, John Mayasich, Jack McCartan, Robert McVey, Richard Meredith, Weldon Olson, Edwyn Owen, Rodney Paavola, Lawrence Palmer, Richard Rodenheiser, Thomas Williams) | 7 | 0 | 0 | 48 | 17 |
| 2. CAN | (Robert Attersley, Maurice "Moo" Benoit, James Connelly, Jack Douglas, Fred Etcher, Robert Forhan, Donald Head, Harold Hurley, Kenneth Laufman, Floyd Martin, Robert McKnight, Clifford Pennington, Donald Rope, Robert Rousseau, George Samolenko, Harry Sinden, Darryl Sly) | 6 | 1 | 0 | 55 | 15 |
| 3. SOV | (Veniamin Aleksandrov, Aleksandr Alyimetov, Yuri Baulin, Mikhail Bychkov, Vladimir Grebennikov, Yevgeny Groshev, Viktor Yakushev, Yevgeny Yorkin, Nikolai Karpov, Alfred Kuchevsky, Konstantin Loktev, Stanislav Petuchov, Viktor Prjazhnikov, Nikolai Puchkov, Genrich Sidorenkov, Nikolai Sologubov, Yuri Tsitsinov) | 4 | 2 | 1 | 40 | 23 |
| 4. CZE | (Vlastimil Bubnik, Josef Černy, Bronislav Danda, Vladimir Dvořaček, Josef Golonka, Karel Gut, Jaroslav Jiřik, Jan Kasper, František Maslan, Vladimir Nadrchal, Vaclav Pantuček, Rudolf Potsch, Jan Starsi, František Tikal, František Vanek, Miroslav Vlach, Jaroslav Volf) | 3 | 4 | 0 | 44 | 31 |
| 5. SWE | (Anders Andersson, Lars Björn, Gert Blomé, Sigurd Bröms, Einar Granath, Sven Johansson, Bengt Lindqvist, Lars-Erik Lundvall, Nils Nilsson, Bert-Ola Nordlander, Carl-Göran Öberg, Ronald Pettersson, Ulf Sterner, Roland Stoltz, Hans Svedberg, Kjell Svensson, Sune Wretling) | 2 | 4 | 1 | 40 | 24 |
| 6. GER | (Paul Ambros, Georg Eberl, Markus Egen, Ernst Eggerbauer, Michael Hobelsberger, Hans Huber, Uli Jansen, Hans Rampf, Josef Reif, Otto Schneitberger, Siegfried Schubert, Horst Schuldes, Kurt Sepp, Ernst Trautwein, Xaver Unsinn, Leonhard Waitl, Horst Metzer) | 1 | 6 | 0 | 9 | 54 |
| 7. FIN | (Yrjo Hakala, Raimo Kilpiö, Kolso, Lampainen, Esko Luostarinen, Niemii, Nieminen, Kalevi Numminen, Heino Pulli, Rassa, Rastio, Jouni Seistamo, Sonio, Vainio, Juhani Wahlsten) | 3 | 2 | 1 | 63 | 23 |
| 8. JPN | (Akazawa, S. Honma, T. Honma, Inatsun, Inatsun, Irie, Iwaoka, Kakihara, Miyasaki, Murano, Ono, Segawa, Shimada, Takagi, Takeshima, Tenabu, Tomita, Yamada) | 2 | 3 | 1 | 34 | 68 |

When they first started playing together, the U.S. squad hardly seemed to be the "Team of Destiny" that they were to become. Before leaving for Squaw Valley, they played an 18-game training tour and compiled an unimpressive record of ten wins, four losses, and four ties. Not only did they lose to Michigan Tech and Denver University, but less than three weeks before the Olympics began, the U.S. team actually lost, 7–5, to the Warroad Lakers of Warroad, Minnesota. However their first Olympic match set the tone for the rest of the tournament. Trailing Czechoslovakia 4–3 after two periods, they scored four straight goals in the final period and won, 7–5. This was followed by three convincing victories over Australia (12–1), Sweden (6–3), and Germany (9–1).

On February 25 they faced the cofavorite Canadian team. Bob Cleary of Westwood, Massachusetts, took a pass from John Mayasich and scored the first goal after 12 minutes and 47 seconds. Paul Johnson, formerly of the University of Minnesota, scored an unassisted goal in the second period, and the United States held on to win, 2–1. The real star of the game was goalie Jack McCartan, who turned back 39 shots, including 20 in the second period alone.

Two days later the United States went up against the defending champions from the U.S.S.R. The Americans drew first blood after 4:04 of the first period, when Bill Cleary scored after taking a pass from his brother Bob. However the Soviets tied the score a minute later on a goal by Aleksandrov. At the 9:37 mark Bychkov struck from 15 feet in front of the cage and the U.S.S.R. led 2–1. Their lead held for the rest of the first period and most of the second until Billy Christian, with an assist from *his* brother, Roger, fired a shot past Puchkov, the Soviet goalie, to make the score 2–2. The two teams fought on even terms for the next 24 minutes. Then, with five minutes to play, the Christian brothers teamed up for another goal. From there on McCartan took over and heroically protected the U.S. goal, while the partisan overflow crowd screamed with joy. It was the first time that the United States had beaten the U.S.S.R. at ice hockey.

All that stood between the U.S. team and the Olympic championship was an eight a.m. game the next day against the same Czechoslovakian team that they had beaten to open the tournament. But the Americans were so emotionally spent that they were unable to sleep, and they arrived at the arena exhausted and tense. The Czechs wasted no time, scoring their first goal after only eight seconds. After two periods, Czechoslovakia led 4–3. During the break between periods, Nikolai Sologubov, the captain of the U.S.S.R. team, entered the U.S. dressing room to give the Americans a piece of advice. Since he didn't speak English, Sologubov pantomimed that the U.S. players should take some oxygen. A tank was obtained, and the revived Americans went back on the ice with visions of the gold medals that were almost within their grasp. After almost six scoreless minutes, the U.S. team went on a rampage, as the Clearys and Christians scored six straight goals to win 9–4. The very same team that had lost to the Warroad, Minnesota, Lakers had won the Olympic gold medal.

A few words about the 1960 Australian team: They lost all six of their matches, giving up 88 goals while scoring only ten. Even when things went right for the Australians they went wrong. Trailing in the first period of a consolation match against Finland, Cunningham scored Australia's only goal of the game. In his excited attempt to follow through the shot, Australian center Ivor Vesley went straight into the net, smashed his head on the iron crossbar, and had to be taken to the hospital. Finland won, 14–1.

**1964 Innsbruck** T: 16, N: 16, D: 2.8.

| | | | W | L | T | PF | PA |
|---|---|---|---|---|---|---|---|
| 1. | SOV | (Veniamin Aleksandrov, Aleksandr Alyimetov, Vitaly Davydov, Anatoly Firsov, Eduard Ivanov, Viktor Konovalenko, Viktor Kuzkin, Konstantin Loktev, Boris Mayorov, Yevgeny Mayorov, Stanislav Petuchov, Aleksandr Ragulin, Vyacheslav Starshinov, Leonid Volkov, Victor Yakushev, Boris Zaitsev) | 7 | 0 | 0 | 54 | 10 |
| 2. | SWE | (Anders Andersson, Gert Blomé, Lennart Häggroth, Lennart Johansson, Nils Johansson, Sven "Tumba" Johansson, Lars Lundvall, Eilert Määttä, Hans Mild, Nils Nilsson, Bert Nordlander, Carl Öberg, Uno Öhrlund, Ronald Pettersson, Ulf Sterner, Roland Stoltz, Kjell Svensson) | 5 | 2 | 0 | 47 | 16 |
| 3. | CZE | (Vlastimil Bubnik, Josef Černý, Jiří Dolana, Vladimir Dzurilla, Josef Golonka, František Gregor, Jiří Holik, Jaroslav Jiřik, Jan Klapáč, Vladimir Nadrchal, Rudolf Potsch, Stanislav Pryl, Ladislav Smid, Stanislav Sventek, František Tikal, Miroslav Vlach, Jaroslav Walter) | 5 | 2 | 0 | 38 | 19 |
| 4. | CAN | (Henry Akervall, Gary Begg, Roger Bourbonnais, Kenneth Broderick, Raymond Cadieux, Terrence Clancy, Brian Conacher, Paul Conlin, Gary Dineen, Robert Forhan, Larry Johnston, Seth Martin, John McKenzie, Terrence O'Malley, Rodney-Albert Seiling, George-Raymond Swarbrick) | 5 | 2 | 0 | 32 | 17 |
| 5. | USA | (David Brooks, Herbert Brooks, Roger Christian, William Christian, Paul Coppo, Daniel Dilworth, Dates Fryberger, Paul Johnson, Thomas Martin, James McCoy, Wayne Meredith, William Reichart, Donald Ross, Patrick Rupp, Gary Schmaltzbauer, James Westby, Thomas Yurkovich) | 2 | 5 | 0 | 29 | 33 |
| 6. | FIN | (Raimo Kilpiö, Juhani Lahtinen, Rauno Lehtiö, Esko Luostarinen, Ilka Mäsikämmen, Seppo Nikkilä, Kalevi Numminen, Lasse Oksanen, Jorma Peltonen, Heino Pulli, Matti Reunamäki, Jouni Seistamo, Jorma Suokko, Juhani Wahlsten, Jarmo Wasama) | 2 | 5 | 0 | 10 | 31 |
| 7. | GER | (Paul Ambros, Bernd Herzig, Michael Hobelsberger, Ernst Köpf, Albert Loibl, Josef Reif, Otto Schneitberger, Georg Scholz, Siegfried Schubert, Dieter Schwimmbeck, Ernst Trautwein, Leonhard Waitl, Helmut Zanghellini) | 2 | 5 | 0 | 13 | 49 |
| 8. | SWI | (Franz Berry, Roger Chappot, Rolf Diethelm, Elvin Friedrich, Gaston Furrer, Oskar Jenny, René Kiener, Pio Parolini, Kurt Pfammatter, Gerald Rigolet, Max Ruegg, Walter Salzmann, Herold Truffer, Peter Wespi, Otto Wittwer) | 0 | 7 | 0 | 9 | 57 |

The tournament was actually much closer than the standings make it appear. If Canada had been able to defeat the U.S.S.R. in their final match, they would have finished first instead of fourth. The Canadians did in fact take a 2–1 lead, but the well-balanced Soviet team tied the score with a goal by Starshinov at the end of the second period. The U.S.S.R. gained a 3–2 victory, thanks to an early third-period goal by Veniamin Aleksandrov.

**1968 Grenoble** T: 14, N: 14, D: 2.17.

| | | W | L | T | PF | PA |
|---|---|---|---|---|---|---|
| 1. SOV | (Viktor Konovalenko, Viktor Zinger, Viktor Blinov, Aleksandr Ragulin, Viktor Kuzkin, Oleg Zaitsev, Igor Romichevsky, Vitaly Davydov, Yevgeny Zymin, Vyacheslav Starshinov, Boris Mayorov, Viktor Polupanov, Anatoly Firsov, Yuri Moiseyev, Anatoly Ionov, Yevgeny Michakov, Veniamin Aleksandrov, Vladimir Vikulov) | 6 | 1 | 0 | 48 | 10 |
| 2. CZE | (Vladimir Dzurilla, Vladimir Nadrchal, Josef Horešovský, Karel Masopust, Jan Suchý, František Pospišil, Jan Hrhatý, Jiři Kochta, Jan Klapáč, Jiři Holik, František Sevčik, Jaroslav Jiřik, Josef Černý, Jan Havel, Petr Hejma, Václav Nedomanský, Jozef Golonka, Oldřich Machač, Petr Hejma) | 5 | 1 | 1 | 33 | 17 |
| 3. CAN | (Wayne Stephenson, Kenneth Broderick, Terrence O'Malley, Paul Conlin, John Barry MacKenzie, Brian Glennie, Marshall Johnstone, Francis Huck, Morris Mott, Raymond Cadieux, Gerry Pinder, Stephen Montoith, Dan O'Shea, Roger Bourbonnais, William McMillan, Ted Hargreaves, Gary Dineen, Herbert Pinder) | 5 | 2 | 0 | 28 | 15 |
| 4. SWE | (Leif Holmqvist, Hans Dahllöf, Lars-Erik Sjöberg, Arne Carlsson, Lennart Svedberg, Roland Stoltz, Nils Johansson, Björn Palmqvist, Folke Bengtsson, Carl-Göran Öberg, Håkan Wickberg, Tord Lundström, Henric Hedlund, Svante Granholm, Roger Olsson, Leif Henriksson, Lars-Göran Nilsson) | 4 | 2 | 1 | 23 | 18 |
| 5. FIN | (Urpo Ylönen, Pentti Koskela, Paavo Tirkonen, Juha Rantasila, Ilpa Koskela, Pekka Kuusisto, Lalli Partinen, Seppo Lindström, Matti Reunamäki, Juhani Wahlsten, Matti Keinonen, Lasse Oksanen, Jorma Peltonen, Esa Peltonen, Karl Johanson, Veli-Pekka Ketola, Matti Harju, Pekka Leimu) | 4 | 3 | 1 | 28 | 25 |
| 6. USA | (Herbert Brooks, John Cunniff, John Dale, Craig Falkman, Robert Paul Hurley, Thomas Hurley, Leonard Lilyholm, James Logue, John Morrison, Louis Nanne, Robert Paradise, Lawrence Pleau, Bruce Riutta, Donald Ross, Patrick Rupp, Larry Stordahl, Douglas Volmar, Patrick Loyne) | 2 | 4 | 1 | 23 | 28 |
| 7. GER | (Ernst Köpf, Bernd Kuhn, Lorenz Funk, Gustav Hanig, Horst Meindl, Heinz Weisenbach, Leonhard Waitl, Heinz Bader, Josef Schramm, Günther Knauss, Hans Schichtl, Josef Völk, Rudolf Thanner, Manfred Gmeiner, Peter Lax, Josef Reif, Alois Schloder) | 2 | 6 | 0 | 20 | 39 |
| 8. GDR | (Ullrich Noack, Bernd Karrenbauer, Hartmut Nickel, Helmut Novy, Wolfgang Plotka, Wilfried Sock, Dieter Pürschel, Klaus Hirche, Dieter Kratzsch, Dieter Voigt, Manfred Buder, Lothar Fuchs, Peter Prusa, Joachim Ziesche, Bernd Poindl, Dietmar Peters, Bernd Hiller, Rüdiger Noack) | 1 | 7 | 0 | 16 | 49 |

The final outcome of the 1968 competition was still in doubt with only two matches left to be played. The heavily favored Soviet team had received a shocking 5–4 defeat at the hands of Czechoslovakia, their first loss since 1963. This meant that the championship hinged on the games between Czechoslovakia and Sweden and the U.S.S.R. and Canada, all of whom had records of five wins and one loss. A Czech win conbined with a Soviet win would give the gold medal to Czechoslovakia. However, the overcautious Czechoslovakian players, physically and emotionally exhausted by their upset victory over the U.S.S.R. in their previous game, fell behind the determined Swedes 2–1 late in the second period. They managed to score one goal to tie in the seventh minute of the final period, but that was all. The game ended in a 2–2 draw, which ended Czechoslovakia's chances for first place. This left the Canada-U.S.S.R. match to decide the winner. Firsov scored first for the Soviets after 14:51. Michakov made it 2–0 after 12:44 of the second period. Three more Soviet goals in the final period settled the issue, 5–0 for the U.S.S.R.

**1972 Sapporo** T: 11, N: 11, D: 2.13.

| | | W | L | T | PF | PA |
|---|---|---|---|---|---|---|
| 1. SOV | (Vladislav Tretiak, Aleksandr Pachkov, Vitaly Davydov, Vladimir Lutchenko, Aleksandr Ragulin, Viktor Kuzkin, Gennady Tsygankov, Valery Vasilyev, Valery Kharlamov, Yuri Blinov, Vladimir Petrov, Anatoly Firsov, Aleksandr Maltsev, Vladimir Chadrin, Boris Mikhailov, Vladimir Vikulov, Aleksandr Yakushev) | 4 | 0 | 1 | 33 | 13 |
| 2. USA | (Michael Curran, Peter Sears, James McElmury, Thomas Mellor, Frank Sanders, Charles Brown, Richard McGlynn, Walter Olds, Kevin Ahearn, Stuart Irving, Mark Howe, Henry Boucha, Keith Christiansen, Robbie Ftorek, Ronald Naslund, Craig Sarner, Timothy Sheehy) | 4 | 2 | 0 | 23 | 18 |
| 3. CZE | (Vladimir Dzurilla, Jiři Holeček, František Pospišil, Karel Vohralik, Josef Horešovský, Oldřich Machač, Vladimir Bednář, Rudolf Tajcnár, Josef Černý, Jiři Holik, Bohuslav Šťastný, Richard Farda, Ivan Hlinka, Vaclav Nedomanský, Jiři Kochta, Vladimir Martinec, Eduard Novák, Jaroslav Holik) | 4 | 2 | 0 | 34 | 15 |
| 4. SWE | (Leif Holmqvist, Christer Abrahamsson, Thomas Abrahamsson, Lars-Erik Sjöberg, Kjell-Rune Milton, Stig Östling, Bert-Ola Nordlander, Kenneth Ekman, Tord Lundstrom, Lars-Göran Nilsson, Håkan Pettersson, Håkan Wickberg, Mats Åhlberg, Björn Palmqvist, Hans Hansson, Inge Hammarström, Hans Lindberg, Thomas Bergman, Stig-Göran Johansson, Mats Lindh) | 3 | 2 | 1 | 25 | 14 |
| 5. FIN | (Jorma Valtonen, Stig Wetzell, Ilpo Koskela, Seppo Lindström, Heikki Riihiranta, Heikki Järn, Juha Rantasila, Pekka Marjamäki, Jorma Vehmanen, Jorma Peltonen, Veli-Pekka Ketola, Matti Murto, Matti Keinonen, Harri Linnonmaa, Juhani Tamminen, Lasse Oksanen, Esa Peltonen, Jorma Peltonen, Seppo Repo, Lauri Mononen, Timo Turunen) | 3 | 3 | 0 | 27 | 25 |
| 6. POL | (Andrzej Tkacz, Walery Kosyl, Ludwik Czachowski, Stanislaw Fryźlewicz, Jerzy Potz, Marian Feter, Adam Kopczyński, Andrzej Szczepaniec, Feliks Góralczyk, Tadeusz Kacik, Krzysztof Bialynicki, Józef Slowakiewicz, Leszek Tokarz, Wieslaw Tkacz, Józef Batkiewicz, Tadeusz Oblój, Walenty Ziętara, Robert Góralczyck, Stefan Chowaniec) | 1 | 5 | 0 | 13 | 39 |
| 7. GER | (Anton Kehle, Rainer Makatsch, Otto Schneitberger, Josef Völk, Werner Modes, Paul Langner, Rudolf Thanner, Karl Egger, Rainer Phillip, Bernd Kuhn, Reinhold Bauer, Johann Eimannsberger, Lorenz Funk, Erich Kühnhackl, Alois Schloder, Anton Hofherr, Hans Rothkirch) | 3 | 2 | 0 | 22 | 14 |
| 8. NOR | (Kare Ostensen, Tore Walberg, Oyvind Berg, Jan Kinder, Svein Hansen, Terje Steen, Birger Jansen, Thor Martinsen, Tom Roymark, Thom Kristensen, Steinar Bjolbakk, Svein Hagensten, Roy Jansen, Bjorn Johansen, Morten Sethereng, Terje Thoen, Arne Mikkelsen) | 3 | 2 | 0 | 17 | 27 |

Again the championship was decided by the final match—this time between the U.S.S.R. and Czechoslovakia. The winner-take-all game turned out to be an anticlimax, as the Soviet team took a 4–0 lead in the second period and coasted to a 5–2 victory. The United States was awarded second place because they had beaten Czechoslovakia, 5–1. For the first time since the Winter Olympics began, Canada did not take part in the ice hockey tournament. The Canadians withdrew from international amateur competition in 1969 because they objected to facing the professional amateurs of the U.S.S.R. and other Communist countries.

**1976 Innsbruck** T: 12, N: 12, D: 2.14.

| | | W | L | PF | PA |
|---|---|---|---|---|---|
| 1. SOV | (Vladislav Tretiak, Aleksandr Sidelnikov, Boris Aleksandrov, Sergei Babinov, Aleksandr Gusiev, Valery Kharlamov, Aleksandr Yakushev, Viktor Zlukov, Sergei Kapustin, Vladimir Lutchenko, Yuri Lyapkin, Aleksandr Maltsev, Boris Mikhailov, Vladimir Petrov, Vladimir Chadrin, Viktor Szalimov, Gennady Tsygankov, Valery Vasilyev) | 5 | 0 | 40 | 11 |
| 2. CZE | (Jiři Holeček, Jiři Crha, Oldřich Machač, Milan Chalupa, František Pospišil, Miroslav Dvořák, Milan Kajkl, Jiři Bubla, Milan Nový, Vladimir Martinec, Jiři Novák, Bohuslav Šťastný, Jiri Holik, Ivan Hlinka, Eduard Novák, | 2 | 2 | 17 | 10 |

Jaroslav Pouzar, Bohuslav Eber-
mann, Josef Augusta)

3. GER (Erich Weishaupt, Anton Kehle, 2 3 21 24
Rudolf Thanner, Josef Völk, Udo
Kiessling, Stefan Metz, Klaus
Auhuber, Ignaz Berndaner,
Rainer Philipp, Lorenz Funk,
Wolfgang Boos, Ernst Köpf,
Ferenc Vozar, Walter Köberle,
Erich Kühnhackl, Alois Schlo-
der, Martin Hinterstocker, Franz
Reindl)

4. FIN (Matti Hagman, Reijo Laksola, 2 3 19 18
Antti Leppänen, Henry Leppä,
Seppo Lindström, Pekka Mar-
jamäki, Matti Murto, Timo Num-
melin, Esa Peltonen, Timo Saari,
Jorma Vehmanen, Urpo Ylönen,
Hannu Haapalainen, Seppo
Ahokainen, Tapio Koskinen,
Pertti Koivulahti, Hannu Ka-
panen, Matti Rautiainen)

5. USA (Steven Alley, Daniel Bolduc, 2 3 15 21
Blane Comstock, Robert Do-
bek, Robert Harris, Jeffrey Hy-
manson, Paul Jensen, Steven
Jensen, Richard Lamby, Robert
Lundeen, Robert Miller, Doug-
las Ross, Gary Ross, William
"Buzz" Schneider, Stephen
Sertich, John Taft, Theodore
Thorndike, James Warden)

6. POL (Stefan Chowaniec, Andrzej 0 4 9 37
Tkacz, Andrzej Iskrzycki, Marek
Marcińczak, Josef Matiewicz,
Tadeusz Obłój, Jerzy Potz,
Andrzej Słowakiewicz, Andrzej
Zabawa, Walenty Ziętara, Karol
Zurek, Walery Kosyl, Robert
Góralczyk, Kordian Jajszczok,
Wiesław Jobczyk, Leszek Kokos-
zka, Henryk Pytel, Mieczysław
Jaskierski, Marian Kajzerek)

7. ROM (Valerian Netedu, Vasile Morar, 4 1 23 15
Elöd Antal, Sandor Gall, George
Justinian, Ion Ionita, Desideriu
Varga, Doru Morosan, Doru Tu-
reanu, Dumitru Axinte, Eduard
Pana, Vasile Hutanu, Ion Gheor-
ghiu, Tibri Miclos, Alexandru Ha-
lauca, Marian Pisaru, Nicolae Vi-
san)

8. AUT (Daniel Gritsch, Franz Schil- 3 2 18 14
cher, Walter Schneider, Ger-
hard Hausner, Johann Schuller,
Michael Herzog, Günther Ober-
huber, Othmar Russ, Max
Moser, Rudolf Koenig, Josef
Ruschnig, Franz Voves, Josef
Schwitzer, Peter Cini, Josef

Kriechbaum, Alexander Sad-
jina, Herbert Poek, Herbert
Moertl)

The tournament was thrown into confusion when Czechoslovakia's captain, František Pospišil, was chosen for a
random drug test after a victory over Poland. The team
trainer immediately admitted that Pospišil had been
given codeine to combat a virus infection. The I.O.C.
expelled Pospišil and ordered the game against Poland
declared null and void. The final decision on the case was
actually delayed, so as not to spoil the drama of the
winner-take-all game between Czechoslovakia and the
U.S.S.R. In that match, the Czechs led 3–2 in the final
period. But with five minutes to play Aleksandr
Yakushev tied the score. Twenty-four seconds later Valery Kharlamov knocked the puck into the net again to
give the U.S.S.R. their fourth straight set of gold medals
in ice hockey.

**1980 Lake Placid** T: 12, N: 12, D: 2.24.

| | | | W | L | T | PF | PA |
|---|---|---|---|---|---|---|---|
| 1. | USA | (James Craig, Kenneth Morrow, Michael Ramsey, William Baker, John O'Callahan, Bob Suter, David Silk, Neal Broten, Mark Johnson, Steven Christoff, Mark Wells, Mark Pavelich, Eric Stro-bel, Michael Eruzione, David Christian, Robert McClanahan, William "Buzz" Schneider, Philip Verchota, John Harrington) | 6 | 0 | 1 | 33 | 15 |
| 2. | SOV | (Vladimir Myshkin, Vladislav Tre-tiak, Vyacheslav Fetisov, Vasily Pervukhin, Valery Vasilyev, Alek-sei Kasatonov, Sergei Starikov, Zinetula Bilyaletdinov, Vladimir Krutov, Aleksandr Maltsev, Yuri Lebedev, Boris Mikhailov, Vla-dimir Petrov, Valery Kharlamov, Helmuts Balderis, Viktor Zluktov, Aleksandr Golikov, Sergei Maka-rov, Vladimir Golikov, Aleksandr Skvortsov) | 6 | 1 | 0 | 63 | 17 |
| 3. | SWE | (Per-Eric "Pelle" Lindbergh, Wil-liam Löfqvist, Tomas Jonsson, Sture Andersson, Ulf Wein-stock, Jan Eriksson, Tommy Sa-muelsson, Mats Waltin, Thomas Eriksson, Per Lundqvist, Mats Åhlberg, Håkan Eriksson, Mats Näslund, Lennart Norberg, Bengt Lundholm, Leif Holm-gren, Dan Söderström, Harald Lückner, Lars Mohlin, Bo Berg-lund) | 4 | 1 | 2 | 31 | 19 |
| 4. | FIN | (Antero Kivelä, Jorma Valtonen, Seppo Suoraniemi, Olli Saari-nen, Hannu Haapalainen, Tapio | 3 | 3 | 1 | 31 | 25 |

|   |   |   | W | L | T | PF | PA |
|---|---|---|---|---|---|----|----|
| | Levo, Kari Eloranta, Lasse Lit-<br>ma, Esa Peltonen, Ismo Villa,<br>Mikko Leinonen, Markku Kiima-<br>lainen, Jari Kurri, Jukka Koski-<br>lahti, Hannu Koskinen, Reijo<br>Leppänen, Markku Hakulinen,<br>Jukka Porvari, Jarmo Mäkitalo,<br>Timo Susi) | | | | | | | |
| 5. | CZE | (Jiří Kralik, Karel Lang, Jan<br>Neliba, Vitezslav Duras, Milan<br>Chalupa, Arnold Kadleč, Miro-<br>slav Dvořak, František Kaberle,<br>Jiří Bubla, Milan Nový, Jiří No-<br>vák, Miroslav Frycer, Marian<br>Šťastný, Anton Šťastný, Vincent<br>Lukač, Karel Holy, Jaroslav Pou-<br>zar, Bohuslav Ebermann, Peter<br>Šťastný) | 4 | 2 | 0 | 40 | 17 |
| 6. | CAN | (Robert Dupuis, Paul Pageau,<br>Warren Anderson, J. Bradley<br>Pirie, Randall Gregg, Timothy<br>Watters, D. Joseph Grant, Don-<br>ald Spring, Terrence O'Malley,<br>Ronald Davidson, Glenn Ander-<br>son, Kevin Maxwell, James Nill,<br>John Devaney, Paul Maclean,<br>Daniel D'Alvise, Ken Berry, Da-<br>vid Hindmarch, Kevin Primeau,<br>Stelio Zupancich) | 3 | 3 | 0 | 29 | 18 |
| 7. | POL | (Henryk Wojtynek, Pawel Lu-<br>kaszka, Andrzej Ujwary, Henryk<br>Janiszewski, Henryk Gruth, An-<br>drzej Jańczy, Jerzy Potz, Lud-<br>wik Synowiec, Marek Marciń-<br>czak, Stefan Chowaniec, Wie-<br>slaw Jobczyk, Tadeusz Oblój,<br>Dariusz Sikora, Leszek Ko-<br>koszka, Andrzej Zabawa, Hen-<br>ryk Pytel, Stanislaw Klocek, Le-<br>szek Jachna, Bogdan Dziubiń-<br>ski, Andrzej Malysiak) | 2 | 3 | 0 | 15 | 23 |
| 7. | ROM | (Valerian Netedu, Gheorghe<br>Hutan, Mihail Popescu, Ion<br>Berdila, Sandor Gall, Elöd Antal,<br>Istvan Antal, Doru Morosan,<br>George Justinian, Doru Tur-<br>eanu, Dumitru Axinte, Marian<br>Costea, Constantin Nistor, Alex-<br>andru Halauca, Laszlo Solyom,<br>Bela Nagy, Traian Cazacu,<br>Adrian Olenici, Marian Pisaru,<br>Zoltan Nagy) | 1 | 3 | 1 | 13 | 29 |

Just as Canada dominated Olympic ice hockey from 1920 through 1952, so the Soviet Union has been in control since then. Between 1956 and 1984 the U.S.S.R. played 52 games, tallying 46 victories, four defeats, and two ties. In those 52 games they scored 366 goals while giving up only 98. The only nation to break the Soviet monopoly has been the United States, which won the ice hockey tournament the two times during that period that the Winter Olympics were held in the United States—in 1960 and 1980. The 1960 and 1980 U.S. squads were remarkably similar. Both were patchwork teams whose success was completely unexpected. Both teams put together a series of upsets and come-from-behind wins, culminating in a come-from-behind victory over the favored Soviet team followed by one final come-from-behind performance against a lesser opponent, who almost spoiled the whole drama.

But there *were* two important differences. The first was television. In 1960 appreciation of the thrilling victories of the U.S. team was limited mostly to sports fans. In 1980 the excitement of the tournament reached into almost every U.S. household and united the country in a remarkable manner. The other difference was the mood of the country. In 1960 most Americans were feeling prosperous and proud. The victory of the Olympic ice hockey team was basically perceived as a pleasant surprise. In 1980 the United States was in the midst of an identity crisis. It is difficult for most people in the world to understand that Americans, as a nation, could ever feel persecuted and mistreated, but that was the case in 1980. With hostages in Iran, Russians in Afghanistan, and inflation on the rise, it seemed that nothing was going right. When President Jimmy Carter ordered a boycott of the Summer Olympics, Americans were left with the Winter Olympics as their only vehicle for regaining a sense of pride in the world arena. The problem was that speed skater Eric Heiden was the only likely prospect for a gold medal that the U.S. had. Then, with theatrically perfect timing, the 20 young men who comprised the U.S. ice hockey team showed up to offer the ideal tonic to cure the American malaise.

Nine of the U.S. players were from the University of Minnesota, as was the coach, two-time Olympian Herb Brooks. Known as "The Khomeini of Ice Hockey," Brooks was a fanatic disciplinarian who told his young team (average age: 22), "Gentlemen, you don't have enough talent to win on talent alone." Instead they played 63 exhibition games, including a final match, three days before the Olympics opened, against the same U.S.S.R. team that had beaten the National Hockey League All-Stars. The U.S. Olympic team was crushed by the Soviets, 10–3. When the tournament began, the United States was seeded seventh out of 12 teams.

The teams were split into two round-robin divisions. The first- and second-place teams in each division would then advance to a final round-robin of four teams. Favored to advance from the division in which the United States had been placed were Czechoslovakia and Sweden, who happened to be the Americans' first two opponents. In the opening game between the United States and Sweden, the Swedes scored first and led 2–1 as the contest entered its final minute. In desperation, Brooks pulled goalie Jim Craig and put in an extra skater. The gamble paid off as Bill Baker slammed in a shot from 55 feet with 27 seconds left in the game, allowing the United States to escape with a tie. Next came the powerful Czech team. Again the United States gave up the first goal, this time after only 2:23 of the first period. However, the Americans had the game tied up 2–2 by the end of the period. Then, surprisingly, they forged ahead to a shocking 7–3 victory. By this time the U.S. ice hockey team had attracted the nation's attention. In their third game, they spotted Norway a 1–0 lead and then scored five goals in the last two periods to win 5–1. Their next match, against Romania, a 7–2 victory, was notable because it was the only one of seven games in which the Americans scored first. Against West Germany they fell behind 2–0 and then won 4–2.

This put the United States into the medal round along with Sweden, Finland, and the U.S.S.R. The 2–2 tie with Sweden was carried over as part of the final round-robin, as was the Soviets' 4–2 victory over Finland. At five p.m. on Friday, February 22, the U.S. team went out onto the ice to face the best ice hockey team in the world, professional or amateur. That morning Coach Brooks had given his team an uncharacteristic pep talk. "You're born to be a player," he said. "You're meant to be here. This moment is yours. You're meant to be here at this time." Not surprisingly, the U.S.S.R. scored the first goal, as Vladimir Krutov cut off a slap shot by Aleksei Kasatonov and deflected it into the net. Buzz Schneider evened the score five minutes later, but three and a half minutes after that Sergei Makorov put the Soviets ahead again. It looked like the period would end with the score 2–1, but Mark Johnson knocked in a blocked shot with one second left, to bring the United States even once more.

When the second period began, Vladislav Tretiak, considered by many to be the best goalie in the world, had been replaced by Vladimir Myshkin. The U.S.S.R. quickly moved back into the lead on a power-play goal by Aleksandr Maltsev at 2:18, and the period ended with the Soviets ahead 3–2. Amazed to find themselves only one goal behind with 20 minutes to play, the U.S. players sensed their destiny. After 8:39 of the third period Mark Johnson picked up the puck as it slipped away from a Soviet defender and shoveled it past Myshkin from five feet out. The United States was tied again. Less than one and a half minutes later, at the ten-minute mark, team captain Mike Eruzione, using a Soviet defender as a screen, fired off a 30-foot shot that went through Myshkin and into the net. The partisan crowd burst into wild cheering that continued for the rest of the game. For the final 10 minutes goalie Jim Craig (who recorded 39 saves in the game) and the rest of the U.S. team fought off a seemingly endless barrage of attacks by the Soviets. When the last seconds had finally ticked off, the emotional excitement that filled the arena was so great that even many of the Soviet players had to smile as they congratulated their American counterparts. Back in the dressing room, the U.S. team sang "God Bless America," even though they couldn't remember all the words. Meanwhile, Coach Brooks had locked himself in the men's room with his emotions. "Finally I snuck out into the hall," he said, "and the state troopers were all standing there crying."

But there was still one more game to be played. In fact, if the United States lost to Finland on February 24, they would only finish in third place, and the U.S.S.R. would win the tournament anyway. And the Finns were not prepared to roll over and concede defeat. They scored first and led 2–1 after two periods. But the Americans had come too far to lose it all in the final match. Dave Christian, whose father and uncle had been members of the 1960 U.S. squad, sent a pass to Phil Verchota, who sped down the left side of the ice and tied the score with a 15-foot shot at 2:25. At 6:05 Rob McClanahan put the United States in the lead with a stuff shot, and at 16:25 Mark Johnson scored an insurance goal. When the game ended three and a half minutes later, the score was 4–2. American TV viewers were treated to two more emotional moments. While the rest of the team jumped for joy and hugged each other, Jim Craig skated around the rink until he found in the crowd the one person with whom he most wanted to share this moment—his widowed father. Later, at the medal ceremony, Mike Eruzione took the stand as the captain of his team. But after the playing of "The Star-Spangled Banner," he called his teammates onto the platform to join him in accepting the cheers of the crowd.

**1984 Sarajevo** T: 12, N: 12, D: 2.19.

| | | W | L | T | PF | PA |
|---|---|---|---|---|---|---|
| 1. SOV | (Zinatula Bilyaletdinov, Sergei Chepelev, Nikolai Drozdetsky, Vyacheslav Fetisov, Aleksandr Gerasimov, Aleksei Kasatonov, Andrei Komutov, Vladimir Kovin, Aleksandr Kozhernikov, Vladimir Krutov, Igor Larionov, Sergei Makarov, Vladimir Myshkin, Vasily Pervukhin, Aleksandr Skvortsov, Sergei Starikov, Igor Stelnov, Vladislav Tretiak, Victor Tumenev, Michail Vasiliev) | 7 | 0 | 0 | 48 | 5 |
| 2. CZE | (Jaroslav Benák, Vladimir Caldr, František Cernik, Milan Chalupa, Miloslav Horava, Jiří Hrdina, Arnold Kadlec, Jaroslav Korbela, Jiří Králik, Vladimir Kynos, Jiří Lála, Igor Liba, Vincent Lukáč, Dušan Pašek, Pavel Richter, Darius Rusnák, Vladimir Růžička, Jaromir Sindel, Radoslav Svoboda, Eduard Uvíra) | 6 | 1 | 0 | 40 | 9 |
| 3. SWE | (Thomas Ahlen, Per-Erik Eklund, Thomas Eklund, Bo Ericsson, Lars Erikson, Peter Gra- | 4 | 2 | 1 | 36 | 17 |

din, Mats Hessel, Peter Michael Hjälm, Göran Lindblom, Tommy Mörth, Leif Nordin, Jens Öhling, Rolf-Lennart Riddervall, Thomas Rundquist, Tomas Sandström, Karl Södergren, Mats Thelin, Arne Thelvén, Göte Wälitalo, Mats Waltin)

| | | W | L | T | PF | PA |
|---|---|---|---|---|---|---|
| 4. | CAN | 4 | 3 | 0 | 24 | 16 |

(Warren Anderson, Robin Bartel, Russ Courtnall, Jean Daigneault, Kevin Dineen, Dave Donnelly, Bruce Driver, Darren Eliot, Pat Flatley, Dave Gagner, Mario Gosselin, Vaugh Karpan, Doug Lidster, Darren Lowe, Kirk Muller, James Patrick, Craig Redmond, Dave Tippett, Carey Wilson, Dan Wood)

| | | W | L | T | PF | PA |
|---|---|---|---|---|---|---|
| 5. | GER | 4 | 1 | 1 | 34 | 21 |

(Manfred Ahne, Ignaz Berndaner, Michael Betz, Bernhard Englbrecht, Karl Friesen, Dieter Hegen, Ulrich Hiemer, Ernst Höfner, Udo Kiessling, Harold Kreis, Marcus Kuhl, Erich Kühnhackl, Andreas Niederberger, Joachim Reil Franz Reindl, Roy Roedger, Peter Scharf, Helmut Steiger, Gerhard Truntschka, Manfred Wolf)

| | | W | L | T | PF | PA |
|---|---|---|---|---|---|---|
| 6. | FIN | 2 | 3 | 1 | 31 | 26 |

(Raimo Helminen, Risto Jalo, Arto Javanainen, Timo Jutila, Erkki Laine, Markus Lehto, Mika Lehto, Pertti Lehtonen, Jarmo Mäkitalo, Anssi Melametsä, Hannu Oksanen, Arto Ruotanen, Simo Saarinen, Ville Siren, Arto Sirviö, Perti Skriko, Raimo Summanen, Kari Takko, Juka Tammi, Harri Tuohimaa, Jorma Valtonen)

| | | W | L | T | PF | PA |
|---|---|---|---|---|---|---|
| 7. | USA | 2 | 2 | 2 | 23 | 21 |

(Marc Behrend, Barry Scott Bjugstad, Robert Brooke, Chris Chelios, Richard Costello, Mark Fusco, Scott Fusco, Steven Griffith, Paul Guay, Gary Haight, John Harrington, Tomas Hirsch, Al Iafrate, David A. Jensen, David H. Jensen, Kurt Kleinendorst, Mark Kumpel, Pat Lafontaine, Robert Mason, Corey Millen, Edward Olczyk, Gary Sampson, Tim Thomas, Philip Verchota)

| | | W | L | T | PF | PA |
|---|---|---|---|---|---|---|
| 8. | POL | 1 | 5 | 0 | 20 | 44 |

(Janusz Adamiec, Marek Cholewa, Andrzey Chowaniec, Jerzy Christ, Jozef Chrzastek, Czeslaw Drozd, Bogdan Gebczyk, Henrik Gruth, Andrzej Hachula, Andrezej Hanisz, Leszek Jachna, Wieslav Jobszyk, Stanislaw Klocek, Andrzey Nowak, Wlodzimierz Olszewski, Bogdan Pawlik, Jan Piecko, Henryk Pytel, Gabriel Samolej, Dariusz Sikora, Krystian Sikorski, Jan Stopczyk, Ludwik Synowiec, Robert Szopinski, Andrzej Ujwary, Andrzey Zabawa)

With the Winter Olympics once again being held outside the United States, the ice hockey tournament returned to normalcy. As usual, the Soviets overwhelmed every team they played. Even their final 2–0 victory over Czechoslovakia was never really in doubt. The U.S. team, seeded seventh, finished seventh.

**1988 Calgary** T: 12, N: 12, D: 2.28.

| | | W | L | T | PF |
|---|---|---|---|---|---|
| 1. | SOV | 7 | 1 | 0 | 45 |

(Ilya Byakin, Igor Stelnov, Vyacheslav Fetisov, Aleksei Gusarov, Aleksei Kasatonov, Sergei Starikov, Vyacheslav Bykov, Sergei Yashin, Valery Kamensky, Sergei Svetlov, Aleksandr Chernykh, Andrei Khomutov, Vladimir Krutov, Igor Larionov, Andrei Lomakin, Sergei Makarov, Aleksandr Mogilny, Anatoly Semenov, Aleksandr Kozhevnikov, Igor Kravchuk, Vitaly Samoylov, Sergei Mylnikov)

| | | W | L | T | PF |
|---|---|---|---|---|---|
| 2. | FIN | 5 | 2 | 1 | 34 |

(Timo Blomqvist, Kari Eloranta, Jyrki Lumme, Jukka Virtanen, Arto Ruotanen, Reijo Ruotsalainen, Simo Saarinen, Kai Suikkanen, Raimo Helminen, Iiro Järvi, Esa Keskinen, Erkki Lehtonen, Reijo Mikkolainen, Janne Ojanen, Timo Susi, Pekka Tuomisto, Teppo Numminen, Jari Torkki, Jukka Tammi, Jarmo Myllys)

| | | W | L | T | PF |
|---|---|---|---|---|---|
| 3. | SWE | 4 | 1 | 3 | 33 |

(Peter Andersson, Anders Eldebrink, Lars Ivarsson, Lars Karlsson, Mats Kihlström, Tommy Samuelsson, Mikael Andersson, Bo Berglund, Jonas Bergqvist, Peter Eriksson, Michael Hjälm, Mikael Johansson, Lars Molin, Lars-Gunnar Pettersson, Thomas Rundqvist, Ulf Sandström, Håkan Södergren, Jens Öhling, Thomas Eriksson, Thom Eklund, Peter Åslin, Anders Bergman, Peter Lindmark)

| | | W | L | T | PF |
|---|---|---|---|---|---|
| 4. | CAN | 5 | 2 | 1 | 31 |

(Chris Felix, Randy Gregg, Timothy Watters, Anthony Stiles, Trent Yawney, Zarley Zalapski,

Claude Vilgrain, Kenneth Berry, Serge Boisvert, Brian Bradley, Ken Yaremchuk, Marc Habscheid, Robert Joyce, Vaughn Karpan, Merlin Malinowski, Steven Tambellini, Wallace Schreriber, Gordon Sherven, Serge Roy, Jim Peplinski, Sean Burke, Andrew Moog)

| | | | | | | |
|---|---|---|---|---|---|---|
| 5. | GER | (Ron Fischer, Udo Kiessling, Horst-Peter Kretschmer, Dieter Medicus, Andreas Niederberger, Harold Kreis, Manfred Schuster, Manfred Wolf, Christian Brittig, Peter Draisaitl, Georg Franz, Dieter Hegen, Georg Holzmann, Peter Obresa, Roy Roedger, Peter Schiller, Helmut Steiger, Gerd Truntschka, Bernd Truntschka, Joachim Reil, Helmut de Raaf, Karl-Heinz Friesen, Josef Schlickenrieder) | 5 | 3 | 0 | 25 | 27 |
| 6. | CZE | (Jaroslav Benák, Mojmir Božik, Rudolf Suchánek, Miloslav Horava, Bedrich Ščerban, Antonin Stavjaňa, Jiří Sejba, Jiří Doležal, Oto Haščák, Jiří Hrdina, Rostislav Vlach, Jiří Lála, Igor Liba, Petr Vlk, David Volek, Dušan Pašek, Petr Rosol, Vladimír Růžička, Radim Raděvic, Eduard Uvíra, Dominik Hašek, Jaromir Šindel, Petr Bříza) | 4 | 4 | 0 | 33 | 28 |
| 7. | USA | (Greg Brown, Guy Gosselin, | 3 | 3 | 0 | 35 | 31 |

Peter Laviolette, Jeffrey Norton, Eric Weinrich, Dave Snuggerud, Allen Bourbeau, Kevin Stevens, John Donatelli, Scott Fusco, Tony Granato, Craig Janney, James Johannson, Scott Young, Stephen Leach, Bradley MacDonald, Cory Millen, Kevin Miller, Brian Leetch, Todd Okerlund, Michael Richter, Chris Terreri, John Blue)

| | | | | | | |
|---|---|---|---|---|---|---|
| 8. | SWI | (Patrice Brasey, André Künzi, Jakob Kölliker, Fausto Mazzoleni, Andreas Ritsch, Bruno Rogger, Philipp Neuenschwander, Gaëtan Boucher, Manuele Celio, Thomas Vrabec, Jörg Eberle, Felix Hollenstein, Peter Jaks, Roman Wäger, Markus Leuenberger, Fredy Lüthi, Gil Montandon, Peter Schlagenhauf, Urs Burkart, Andreas Zehnder, Thomas Mueller, Pietro Cunti, Olivier Anken, Richard Bucher, Renato Tosio) | 3 | 3 | 0 | 23 | 18 |

In the weeks leading up to the Calgary Olympics, the international press was filled with articles declaring the end of the Soviet ice hockey dynasty. Perhaps the team from the U.S.S.R. was still favored, but only by a slight margin. But once the tournament began, it was clear that nothing had changed. The Soviets cruised through the preliminary round, then crushed Canada 5–0 and Sweden 7–1. They did lose 2–1 to Finland in their final match, but by that time they had already clinched first place.

# LUGE (TOBOGGAN)

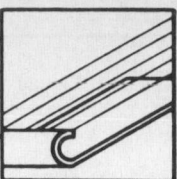

| MEN | WOMEN |
|---|---|
| Single | Single |
| Two-Seater | |
| Discontinued Event | |

Luge sleds are similar to toboggans. Participants, known as sliders, careen down the course feet first, guiding the luge with their legs and shoulders. Luge has the reputation of being one of the most dangerous sports in the Olympics. The two-seater event is decided on the basis of two runs, the singles on a total of four. All 63 medals awarded in luge since its permanent inclusion in the Olympic program in 1964 have been won by four nations: Germany, Austria, Italy, and the U.S.S.R.

## MEN
### SINGLE

**1924–1960** not held

**1964 Innsbruck-Igls** C: 36, N: 10, D: 2.1.
1. Thomas Köhler        GDR    3:26.77
2. Klaus Bonsack        GDR    3:27.04
3. Hans Plenk           GDR    3:30.15
4. Rolf Greger Ström    NOR    3:31.21
5. Josef Feistmantl     AUT    3:31.34
6. Mieczyslaw Pawelkiewicz  POL  3:33.02
7. Carlo Prinoth        ITA    3:33.49
8. Franz Tiefenbacher   AUT    3:33.86

Critics who had contended that luge was too dangerous a sport to be included in the Olympics gained sad support for their arguments when Polish-born British slider Kazimierz Kay-Skrzypeski was killed during a trial run on the Olympic course at Igls two weeks before the Games began. German sliders Josef Fleischmann and Josef Lenz were also severely injured in a separate accident.

**1968 Grenoble-Alpe d'Huez** C: 50, N: 15, D: 2.15.
1. Manfred Schmid       AUT    2:52.48
2. Thomas Köhler        GDR    2:52.66
3. Klaus Bonsack        GDR    2:53.33
4. Zbigniew Gawior      POL    2:53.51
5. Josef Feistmantl     AUT    2:53.57
6. Hans Plenk           GDR    2:53.67

7. Horst Hörnlein       GDR    2:54.10
8. Jerzy Wojnar         POL    2:54.62

After the East German women were disqualified for heating the runners on their sleds, the coaches of seven of the men's teams signed a petition saying they would all walk out if the East German men were allowed to continue in the contest, which still had one round to go. The International Luge Federation decided against suspending the East German men, but bad weather intervened and the competition was ended after three runs anyway.

**1972 Sapporo-Tineyama** C: 45, N: 13, D: 2.7.
1. Wolfgang Scheidel    GDR    3:27.58
2. Harald Ehrig         GDR    3:28.39
3. Wolfram Fiedler      GDR    3:28.73
4. Klaus Bonsack        GDR    3:29.16
5. Leonhard Nagenrauft  GER    3:29.67
6. Josef Fendt          GER    3:30.03
7. Manfred Schmid       AUT    3:30.05
8. Paul Hildgartner     ITA    3:30.55

**1976 Innsbruck-Igls** C: 43, N: 15, D: 2.7.
1. Dettlef Günther      GDR    3:27.688
2. Josef Fendt          GER    3:28.196
3. Hans Rinn            GDR    3:28.574
4. Hans-Heinrich Wickler  GDR  3:29.454
5. Manfred Schmid       AUT    3:29.511
6. Anton Winkler        GER    3:29.520
7. Reinhold Sulzbacher  AUT    3:30.398
8. Dainis Bremze        SOV    3:30.576

During the 1975 Olympic Test Competition on the same course that would be used for the Olympics, the East Germans had set up cameras and timers all along the run to help determine the fastest routes through each of the straightaways and curves.

**1980 Lake Placid** C: 30, N: 13, D: 2.16.
1. Bernhard Glass       GDR    2:54.796
2. Paul Hildgartner     ITA    2:55.372
3. Anton Winkler        GER    2:56.545
4. Dettlef Günther      GDR    2:57.163
5. Gerhard Sandbichler  AUT    2:57.451
6. Franz Wilhelmer      AUT    2:57.483
7. Gerd Böhmer          GER    2:57.769
8. Anton Wembacher      GER    2:58.012

After two runs Dettlef Günther seemed to be well on his way to a repeat victory. However, he crashed near the end of his third run and, although he was able to climb back aboard and finish, the three seconds he had lost effectively removed him from the competition for first place. This left Italy's Ernst Haspinger in the lead, with one run to go. Unfortunately, he fell victim to the same turn as Günther and lost nine seconds, which dropped him to 21st place.

**1984 Sarajevo** C: 32, N: 16, D: 2.12.
| | | | |
|---|---|---|---|
| 1. Paul Hildgartner | ITA | 3:04.258 |
| 2. Sergei Danilin | SOV | 3:04.962 |
| 3. Valery Dudin | SOV | 3:05.012 |
| 4. Michael Walter | GDR | 3:05.031 |
| 5. Torsten Görlitzer | GDR | 3:05.129 |
| 6. Ernst Haspinger | ITA | 3:05.327 |
| 7. Yuri Kharchenko | SOV | 3:05.548 |
| 8. Markus Prock | AUT | 3:05.839 |

Görlitzer led after the first two runs, but 31-year-old Paul Hildgartner of Kiens (Chienes) in the Südtyrol region of Italy recorded the fastest time in both of the final two runs. Hildgartner had previously won a gold medal in the 1972 two-seater event and a silver in the 1980 single competition.

**1988 Calgary** C: 38, N: 18, D: 2.15.
| | | | |
|---|---|---|---|
| 1. Jens Müller | GDR | 3:05.548 |
| 2. Georg Hackl | GER | 3:05.916 |
| 3. Yuri Kharchenko | SOV | 3:06.274 |
| 4. Thomas Jacob | GDR | 3:06.358 |
| 5. Michael Walter | GDR | 3:06.933 |
| 6. Sergei Danilin | SOV | 3:07.098 |
| 7. Johannes Schettel | GER | 3:07.371 |
| 8. Hansjörg Raffl | ITA | 3:07.525 |

Müller, second to Hackl at the European championship two weeks prior to the Olympics, won three of the four runs and was three one-thousandths of a second out of first in the other.

## TWO-SEATER

**1924–1960** not held

**1964 Innsbruck-Igls** T: 14, N: 8, D: 2.1.
| | | | |
|---|---|---|---|
| 1. AUT | (Josef Feistmantl, Manfred Stengl) | 1:41.62 |
| 2. AUT | (Reinhold Senn, Helmut Thaler) | 1:41.91 |
| 3. ITA | (Walter Aussendorfer, Sigisfredo Mair) | 1:42.87 |
| 4. DEN | (Walter Eggert, Helmut Vollprecht) | 1:43.08 |
| 5. ITA | (Giampaolo Ambrosi, Giovanni Graber) | 1:43.77 |
| 5. POL | (Lucjan Kudzia, Ryszard Pędrak) | 1:43.77 |
| 7. POL | (Edward Fender, Mieczyslaw Pawelkiewicz) | 1:45.13 |
| 8. CZE | (Jan Hamrik, Jiři Hujer) | 1:45.41 |

**1968 Grenoble-Alpe d'Huez** T: 14, N: 8, D: 2.18.
| | | | |
|---|---|---|---|
| 1. GDR | (Klaus Bonsack, Thomas Köhler) | 1:35.85 |
| 2. AUT | (Manfred Schmid, Ewald Walch) | 1:36.34 |
| 3. GER | (Wolfgang Winkler, Fritz Nachmann) | 1:37.29 |

| | | | |
|---|---|---|---|
| 4. GER | (Hans Plenk, Bernhard Aschauer) | 1:37.61 |
| 5. GDR | (Horst Hörnlein, Reinhard Bredow) | 1:37.81 |
| 6. POL | (Zbigniew Gawior, Ryszard Gawior) | 1:37.85 |
| 7. AUT | (Josef Feistmantl, Wilhelm Biechl) | 1:38.11 |
| 8. ITA | (Giovanni Graber, Enrico Graber) | 1:38.15 |

**1972 Sapporo-Teineyama** T: 20, N: 11, D: 2.10.
| | | | |
|---|---|---|---|
| 1. GDR | (Horst Hörnlein, Reinhard Bredow) | 1:28.35 |
| 1. ITA | (Paul Hildgartner, Walter Plaikner) | 1:28.35 |
| 3. GDR | (Klaus Bonsack, Wolfram Fiedler) | 1:29.16 |
| 4. JPN | (Satoru Arai, Masatoshi Kobayashi) | 1:29.63 |
| 5. GER | (Hans Brandner, Balthasar Schwarm) | 1:29.66 |
| 5. POL | (Miroslaw Więckowski, Wojciech Kubik) | 1:29.66 |
| 7. AUT | (Manfred Schmid, Ewald Walch) | 1:29.75 |
| 8. ITA | (Sigisfredo Mair, Ernst Mair) | 1:30.26 |

The results of the first run, which had been won by Hildgartner and Plaikner, were cancelled due to a malfunctioning starting gate. The Italians argued that the run should be counted, since all contestants had suffered equally. Their protest was denied. The tie which resulted from the two official runs caused a sticky problem. Finally the International Luge Federation, in consultation with I.O.C. president Avery Brundage, decided to award gold medals to both teams.

**1976 Innsbruck-Igls** T: 25, N: 15, D: 2.10.
| | | | |
|---|---|---|---|
| 1. GDR | (Hans Rinn, Norbert Hahn) | 1:25.604 |
| 2. GER | (Hans Brandner, Balthasar Schwarm) | 1:25.889 |
| 3. AUT | (Rudolf Schmid, Franz Schachner) | 1:25.919 |
| 4. GER | (Stefan Hölzlwimmer, Rudolf Grösswang) | 1:26.238 |
| 5. AUT | (Manfred Schmid, Reinhold Sulzbacher) | 1:26.424 |
| 6. CZE | (Jindřich Zeman, Vladimir Resl) | 1:26.826 |
| 7. ITA | (Karl Feichter, Ernst Haspinger) | 1:27.171 |
| 8. SOV | (Dainis Bremze, Aigars Krikis) | 1:27.407 |

**1980 Lake Placid** T: 19, N: 12: D: 2.19.
| | | | |
|---|---|---|---|
| 1. GDR | (Hans Rinn, Norbert Hahn) | 1:19.331 |
| 2. ITA | (Peter Gschnitzer, Karl Brunner) | 1:19.606 |
| 3. AUT | (Georg Fluckinger, Karl Schrott) | 1:19.795 |
| 4. GDR | (Bernd Hahn, Ulrich Hahn) | 1:19.914 |
| 5. ITA | (Hansjörg Raffl, Alfred Silulner) | 1:19.976 |
| 6. GER | (Anton Winkler, Anton Wembacher) | 1:20.012 |
| 7. GER | (Hans Brandner, Balthasar Schwarm) | 1:20.063 |
| 8. CZE | (Jindřich Zeman, Vladimir Resl) | 1:20.142 |

Hans Rinn and Norbert Hahn became the first repeat winners of an Olympic luge event. Norbert was no relation to Bernd and Ulrich Hahn, two brothers who finished fourth.

**1984 Sarajevo** T: 15, N: 9, D: 2.15.
| | | | |
|---|---|---|---|
| 1. GER | (Hans Stanggassinger, Franz Wembacher) | 1:23.620 |
| 2. SOV | (Yevgeny Belousov, Aleksandr Belyakov) | 1:23.660 |
| 3. GDR | (Jörg Hoffmann, Jochen Pietzsch) | 1:23.887 |
| 4. AUT | (Georg Fluckinger, Franz Wilhelmer) | 1:23.902 |
| 5. AUT | (Günther Lemmerer, Franz Lechleitner) | 1:24.133 |
| 6. ITA | (Hans-Jörg Raffl, Norbert Huber) | 1:24.353 |
| 7. SOV | (Yuris Eyssak, Eynar Veykcha) | 1:24.366 |
| 8. GER | (Thomas Schwab, Wolfgang Staudinger) | 1:24.634 |

Byelousov and Belyakov led after the first run and were on their way to the best time of the second run when they faltered just before the end, losing about one-sixth of a second in the last few meters. This gave Stanggassinger and Wembacher the victory by four one-hundredths of a second.

**1988 Calgary** T: 18, N: 11, D: 2.19.

| | | | |
|---|---|---|---|
| 1. | GDR | (Jörg Hoffmann, Jochen Pietzsch) | 1:31.940 |
| 2. | GDR | (Stefan Krausse, Jan Behrendt) | 1:32.039 |
| 3. | GER | (Thomas Schwab, Wolfgang Staudinger) | 1:32.274 |
| 4. | GER | (Stefan Ilsanker, Georg Hackl) | 1:32.298 |
| 5. | AUT | (Georg Fluckinger, Robert Manzenreiter) | 1:32.364 |
| 6. | SOV | (Vitaly Melnik, Dmitri Alexeev) | 1:32.459 |
| 7. | ITA | (Kurt Brugger, Wilfried Huber) | 1:32.553 |
| 7. | SOV | (Yevgeny Belousov, Aleksandr Belyakov) | 1:32.553 |

# Discontinued Event
## SKELETON (CRESTA RUN)

The skeleton is a heavy sled which is ridden head first in a prone position and steered by dragging one's feet and shifting one's weight. The event is held only when the Olympics are in St. Moritz.

**1928 St. Moritz** C: 10, N: 6, D: 2.17.

| | | | |
|---|---|---|---|
| 1. | Jennison Heaton | USA | 3:01.8 |
| 2. | John Heaton | USA | 3:02.8 |
| 3. | David Northesk | GBR | 3:05.1 |
| 4. | Agostino Lanfranchi | ITA | 3:08.7 |
| 5. | A. Berner | SWI | 3:08.8 |
| 6. | Franz Unterlechner | AUT | 3:13.5 |
| 7. | A. del Torso | ITA | 3:14.9 |
| 8. | L. Hasenknopf | AUT | 3:36.7 |

The Heaton brothers recorded the two fastest times in each of the three runs.

**1932–1936** not held

**1948 St. Moritz** C: 15, N: 6, D: 2.4.

| | | | |
|---|---|---|---|
| 1. | Nino Bibbia | ITA | 5:23.2 |
| 2. | John Heaton | USA | 5:24.6 |
| 3. | John Crammond | GBR | 5:25.1 |
| 4. | William Martin | USA | 5:28.0 |
| 5. | Gottfried Kägi | SWI | 5:29.9 |
| 6. | Richard Bott | GBR | 5:30.4 |
| 7. | J. S. Coats | GBR | 5:31.9 |
| 8. | Fairchilds MacCarthy | USA | 5:35.5 |

John Heaton of New Haven, Connecticut, had the rare experience of winning consecutive silver medals in the same event—20 years apart. The first time he was 19, the second time 39.

# WOMEN
## SINGLE

**1896–1960** not held

**1964 Innsbruck-Igls** C: 16, N: 6, D: 2.4.

| | | | |
|---|---|---|---|
| 1. | Ortrun Enderlein | GDR | 3:24.67 |
| 2. | Ilse Geisler | GDR | 3:27.42 |
| 3. | Helene Thurner | AUT | 3:29.06 |
| 4. | Irena Pawelczyk | POL | 3:30.52 |
| 5. | Barbara Gorgón-Flont | POL | 3:32.73 |
| 6. | Oldřiska Tylová | CZE | 3:32.76 |
| 7. | Friederike Matejka | AUT | 3:34.68 |
| 8. | Helena Macher | POL | 3:35.87 |

**1968 Grenoble-Alpe d'Huez** C: 26, N: 10, D: 2.15.

| | | | |
|---|---|---|---|
| 1. | Erica Lechner | ITA | 2:28.66 |
| 2. | Christa Schmuck | GER | 2:29.37 |
| 3. | Angelika Dünhaupt | GER | 2:29.56 |
| 4. | Helena Macher | POL | 2:30.05 |
| 5. | Jadwiga Damse | POL | 2:30.15 |
| 6. | Dana Beldová | CZE | 2:30.35 |
| 7. | Anna Mąka | POL | 2:30.40 |
| 8. | Ute Gaehler | GER | 2:30.42 |

DISQ: Ortrun Enderlein (GDR) 2:28.04, Anna-Maria Müller (GDR) 2:28.06, Angela Knösel (GDR) 2:28.93

The weather-shortened competition ended with defending champion Ortrun Enderlein in first place and East German teammates Anna-Maria Müller and Angela Knösel in second and fourth. However the East German women aroused suspicion by consistently showing up at the last minute and then disappearing as soon as they finished a run. Their toboggans were examined, and it was discovered that their runners had been illegally heated. The three East Germans were disqualified by unanimous vote of the Jury of Appeal. The East German Olympic Committee made a pathetic attempt to blame the affair on a "capitalist revanchist plot," but they failed to address the fact that the problem had been discovered by the Polish president of the Jury, Lucian Swiderski.

**1972 Sapporo-Teineyama** C: 22, N: 8, D: 2.7.

| | | | |
|---|---|---|---|
| 1. | Anna-Maria Müller | GDR | 2:59.18 |
| 2. | Ute Rührold | GDR | 2:59.49 |
| 3. | Margit Schumann | GDR | 2:59.54 |
| 4. | Elisabeth Demleitner | GER | 3:00.80 |
| 5. | Yuko Otaka | JPN | 3:00.98 |
| 6. | Halina Kanasz | POL | 3:02.33 |
| 6. | Wieslawa Martyka | POL | 3:02.33 |
| 8. | Sarah Felder | ITA | 3:02.90 |

After the 1968 scandal, I.O.C. president Avery Brundage had spoken with the disqualified East German women and encouraged them to win the medals next time around. Anna-Maria Müller took this advice to heart and did exactly that, winning an especially close battle with her two teenage teammates. Asked why she enjoyed such a dangerous sport, Müller replied, "I love this sport because it provides a harmonious counterbalance to my work as a pharmacist."

**1976 Innsbruck-Igls** C: 26, N: 12, D: 2.7.

| | | |
|---|---|---|
| 1. Margit Schumann | GDR | 2:50.621 |
| 2. Ute Rührold | GDR | 2:50.846 |
| 3. Elisabeth Demleitner | GER | 2:51.056 |
| 4. Eva-Maria Wernicke | GDR | 2:51.262 |
| 5. Antonia Mayr | AUT | 2:51.360 |
| 6. Margit Graf | AUT | 2:51.459 |
| 7. Monika Schefftschik | GER | 2:51.540 |
| 8. Angelika Schafferer | AUT | 2:52.322 |

Undefeated since the 1972 Olympics, Lieutenant Margit Schumann was only in fifth place after the first two runs, but recorded the best times on each of the last two runs to take the victory. The unusually attractive Ute Rührold won her second straight silver medal, even though she was only 21 years old.

**1980 Lake Placid** C: 18, N: 8, D: 2.16.

| | | |
|---|---|---|
| 1. Vera Zozulya | SOV | 2:36.537 |
| 2. Melitta Sollmann | GDR | 2:37.657 |
| 3. Ingrīda Amantova | SOV | 2:37.817 |
| 4. Elisabeth Demleitner | GER | 2:37.918 |
| 5. Ilona Brand | GDR | 2:38.115 |
| 6. Margit Schumann | GDR | 2:38.255 |
| 7. Angelika Schafferer | AUT | 2:38.935 |
| 8. Astra Ribena | SOV | 2:39.011 |

Latvian Vera Zozulya recorded the fastest time in each of the four runs to upset two-time world champion Melitta Sollmann.

**1984 Sarajevo** C: 27, N: 15, 2.12.

| | | |
|---|---|---|
| 1. Steffi Martin | GDR | 2:46.570 |
| 2. Bettina Schmidt | GDR | 2:46.873 |
| 3. Ute Weiss | GDR | 2:47.248 |
| 4. Ingrīda Amantova | SOV | 2:48.480 |
| 5. Vera Zozulya | SOV | 2:48.641 |
| 6. Marie Luise Rainer | ITA | 2:49.138 |
| 7. Annefried Goellner | AUT | 2:49.373 |
| 8. Andrea Hatle | GER | 2:49.491 |

World champion Steffi Martin recorded the fastest time in each of the four runs.

**1988 Calgary** C: 24, N: 14, D: 2.16.

| | | |
|---|---|---|
| 1. Steffi Walter [Martin] | GDR | 3:03.973 |
| 2. Ute Oberhoffner [Weiss] | GDR | 3:04.105 |
| 3. Cerstin Schmidt | GDR | 3:04.181 |
| 4. Veronika Bilgeri | GER | 3:05.670 |
| 5. Yulia Antipova | SOV | 3:05.787 |
| 6. Bonny Warner | USA | 3:06.056 |
| 7. Marie-Claude Doyon | CAN | 3:06.211 |
| 8. Nadezhda Danilina | SOV | 3:06.364 |

Defending champion Steffi Walter trailed teammate Ute Oberhoffner by thirty-eight thousandths of a second after two runs. The final two runs were delayed for one day because of heavy winds. When the competition resumed, Walter picked up one hundred eighty-one thousandths of a second on the third run, giving her the margin of victory. The East German women clocked the three fastest times for each of the four runs.

# FIGURE SKATING

MEN
WOMEN
Pairs
Ice Dance
Discontinued Event

According to current figure skating rules, each skater or pair appears twice, performing a two-minute short program with seven required moves (33⅓ percent of the total score), and a freestyle long program (66⅔ percent). Until 1992, singles skaters began by performing compulsory figures which accounted for 30 percent of the total score.

The nine judges assign each skater a score from 0 to 6 points, but more importantly, each judge ranks the skaters from best to worst. The numerical equivalents for each place (1 for first, 2 for second, etcetera) are called *ordinals*. If, at the end of the competition, one skater has received the first-place votes of a majority of the judges, then he or she is declared the winner. If no one has a majority, then the first-place votes are added to the second-place votes. If there is still no one with a majority of votes then the person with the lowest ordinal total is the winner. If a tie still exists, the skater with the most points is awarded the victory.

## MEN

**1908 London** C: 9, N: 5, D: 10.29.

| | | | ORDINALS | PTS. |
|---|---|---|---|---|
| 1. | Ulrich Salchow | SWE | 7 | 1886.5 |
| 2. | Richard Johansson | SWE | 10 | 1826.0 |
| 3. | Per Thorén | SWE | 14 | 1787.0 |
| 4. | John Keiller Greig | GBR | 19 | 1554.5 |
| 5. | B. March | GBR | 29 | 1160.0 |
| 6. | Irving Brokaw | USA | 30 | 1201.0 |
| 7. | Henri Torrome | ARG | 31 | 1144.5 |

Early in 1908 Salchow suffered his first defeat in six years, losing to Nicolai Panin (Kolomenkin) of Russia. At the London Olympics, the two met again. Salchow was given three first-place votes for his compulsory figures to Panin's two. Panin withdrew in protest, claiming that the judging was stacked against him. Salchow was the originator of the jump which now bears his name. To perform a Salchow, a skater must take off from the back

inside edge of one skate, make a complete turn in the air, and land on the back outside edge of the opposite skate.

**1920 Antwerp** C: 9, N: 9, D: 4.27.

| | | | ORDINALS | PTS. |
|---|---|---|---|---|
| 1. | Gillis Grafström | SWE | 7 | 2838.50 |
| 2. | Andreas Krogh | NOR | 18 | 2634.00 |
| 3. | Martin Stixrud | NOR | 24.5 | 2561.50 |
| 4. | Ulrich Salchow | SWE | 25.5 | 2572.50 |
| 5. | Sakari Ilmanen | FIN | 30 | 2458.00 |
| 6. | Nathaniel Niles | USA | 49 | 1976.25 |
| 7. | Basil Williams | GBR | 49.5 | — |
| 8. | Alfred Megroz | SWI | 52.5 | — |

All seven judges awarded first place to Grafström.

**1924 Chamonix** C: 11, N: 9, D: 1.30.

| | | | ORDINALS | PTS. |
|---|---|---|---|---|
| 1. | Gillis Grafström | SWE | 10 | 367.89 |
| 2. | Willy Böckl | AUT | 13 | 359.82 |
| 3. | Georges Gautschi | SWI | 23 | 319.07 |
| 4. | Josef Sliva | CZE | 28 | 310.77 |
| 5. | John Page | GBR | 36 | 295.36 |
| 6. | Nathaniel Niles | USA | 46 | 274.47 |
| 7. | Melville Rogers | CAN | 51 | 269.82 |
| 8. | Pierre Brunet | FRA | 54 | 268.61 |

The Czech judge ranked Sliva of Czechoslovakia first, the two Austrian judges voted for Böckl of Austria, and the other four judges, none of whom was Swedish, gave first place to Gillis Grafström.

**1928 St. Moritz** C: 17, N: 10, D: 2.17.

| | | | ORDINALS | PTS. |
|---|---|---|---|---|
| 1. | Gillis Grafström | SWE | 12 | 1630.75 |
| 2. | Willy Böckl | AUT | 13 | 1625.50 |
| 3. | Robert von Zeebroeck | BEL | 27 | 1542.75 |
| 4. | Karl Schäfer | AUT | 35 | 1463.75 |
| 5. | Josef Sliva | CZE | 36 | 1469.00 |
| 6. | Marcus Nikkanen | FIN | 46 | 1480.00 |
| 7. | Pierre Brunet | FRA | 50 | 1447.75 |
| 8. | Ludwig Wrede | AUT | 53 | 1368.75 |

The 34-year-old Grafström won his third straight gold medal despite suffering from a badly swollen knee. Grafström's smooth, orthodox, and perfectly executed routines appealed to the judges more than Böckl's more aggressive performance and von Zeebroeck's spectacular leaps and spins.

**1932 Lake Placid** C: 12, N: 8, D: 2.9.

| | | ORDINALS | PTS. |
|---|---|---|---|
| 1. Karl Schäfer | AUT | 9 | 2602.0 |
| 2. Gillis Grafström | SWE | 13 | 2514.5 |
| 3. Montgomery Wilson | CAN | 24 | 2448.3 |
| 4. Marcus Nikkanen | FIN | 28 | 2420.1 |
| 5. Ernst Baier | GER | 35 | 2334.8 |
| 6. Roger Turner | USA | 40 | 2297.6 |
| 7. James Madden | USA | 52 | 2049.6 |
| 8. Gail Borden II | USA | 54 | 2110.8 |

This competition marked a changing of the guard, as 38-year-old three-time Olympic champion Gillis Grafström lost to 22-year-old, soon-to-be two-time Olympic champion Karl Schäfer. Graström suffered a sudden mental lapse at the very beginning of his performance, evidently starting to trace a different figure than the one that was required. He recovered and skated smoothly thereafter, but he was penalized an average of almost eight points by each judge.

**1936 Garmisch-Partenkirchen** C: 25, N: 12, D: 2.14.

| | | ORDINALS | PTS. |
|---|---|---|---|
| 1. Karl Schäfer | AUT | 7 | 2959.0 |
| 2. Ernst Baier | GER | 24 | 2805.3 |
| 3. Felix Kaspar | AUT | 24 | 2801.0 |
| 4. Montgomery Wilson | CAN | 30 | 2671.5 |
| 5. Henry Graham Sharp | GBR | 34 | 2758.9 |
| 6. Jack Dunn | GBR | 42 | 2714.0 |
| 7. Marcus Nikkanen | FIN | 54 | 2664.7 |
| 8. Elemer Tardonfalvi | HUN | 56 | 2652.3 |

Schäfer was the unanimous choice of the seven judges. An extreme example of national prejudice by a judge was committed by Judge von Orbán of Hungary, who placed the two Hungarian skaters, Dénes Pataky and Elemer Tardonfalvi, second and third, while none of the other judges ranked them higher than seventh and eighth.

**1948 St. Moritz** C: 16, N: 10, D: 2.5.

| | | ORDINALS | PTS. |
|---|---|---|---|
| 1. Richard Button | USA | 10 | 191.177 |
| 2. Hans Gerschwiler | SWI | 23 | 181.122 |
| 3. Edi Rada | AUT | 33 | 178.133 |
| 4. John Lettengarver | USA | 36 | 176.400 |
| 5. Ede Király | HUN | 42 | 174.400 |
| 6. James Grogan | USA | 62 | 168.711 |
| 7. Henry Graham Sharp | GBR | 67 | 167.044 |
| 8. Hellmut May | AUT | 68 | 165.666 |

Two days before the free-skating portion of the competition, 18-year-old Dick Button, a Harvard freshman from Englewood, New Jersey, successfully completed a double axel for the first time. He was anxious to include this new move in his program but, as the leader going into the final round, he was hesitant to risk his position by trying a move with which he was not yet fully confident. In his book *Dick Button on Skates,* he recalled, "I disliked being so unprepared. But the cravenness of backing away from something because of the pressure of the Olympic games repulsed me and, once I had made up my mind, I could not divert the steps that culminated in the double axel." The jump went perfectly and Button was awarded first place by eight of the nine judges. Only the Swiss judge voted a first for Gerschwiler of Switzerland.

**1952 Oslo** C: 14, N: 11, D: 2.21.

| | | ORDINALS | PTS. |
|---|---|---|---|
| 1. Richard Button | USA | 9 | 1730.3 |
| 2. Helmut Seibt | AUT | 23 | 1621.3 |
| 3. James Grogan | USA | 24 | 1627.4 |
| 4. Hayes Alan Jenkins | USA | 40 | 1571.3 |
| 5. Peter Firstbrook | CAN | 43 | 1558.1 |
| 6. Carlo Fassi | ITA | 50 | 1528.4 |
| 7. Alain Giletti | FRA | 63 | 1469.1 |
| 8. Freimut Stein | GER | 72 | 1403.6 |

By 1952 Dick Button was a Harvard senior working on a thesis entitled "International Socialism and the Schumann Plan." Once again he had a new move to unveil at the Olympics—the triple loop, which required him to make three complete revolutions in the air and then come down smoothly. He could have played it safe, skipped the triple loop, and probably won anyway, but he felt that this would have been a form of failure. Button was very anxious, and his parents were so nervous that they couldn't sit together. In his autobiography, Button describes the triple loop: "I forgot in momentary panic which shoulder should go forward and which back. I was extraordinarily conscious of the judges, who looked so immobile at rinkside. But this was it. . . . The wind cut my eyes, and the coldness caused tears to stream down my checks. Up! Up! Height was vital. Round and around again in a spin which took only a fraction of a second to complete before it landed on a clean steady back edge. I pulled away breathless, excited and overjoyed, as applause rolled from the faraway stands like the rumbling of a distant pounding sea."

All nine judges placed Button first, far ahead of the other skaters. Dick Button turned professional a few months later and toured with the Ice Capades. Later he became a lawyer, an actor, a TV sports commentator, and an entrepreneur. The seventh-place finisher in 1952, Alain Giletti, was only 12 years old.

**1956 Cortina** C: 16, N: 11, D: 2.1.

| | | ORDINALS | PTS. |
|---|---|---|---|
| 1. Hayes Alan Jenkins | USA | 13 | 166.43 |
| 2. Ronald Robertson | USA | 16 | 165.79 |
| 3. David Jenkins | USA | 27 | 162.82 |
| 4. Alain Giletti | FRA | 37 | 159.63 |
| 5. Karol Divin | CZE | 49.5 | 154.25 |

|   |   | ORDINALS | PTS. |
|---|---|---|---|
| 6. Michael Booker | GBR | 53.5 | 154.26 |
| 7. Norbert Felsinger | AUT | 71 | 150.55 |
| 8. Charles Snelling | CAN | 67 | 150.42 |

The three Americans finished in the same order as they had in the 1955 world championships. Twenty-two-year-old Hayes Alan Jenkins of Colorado Springs, Colorado, had practiced 40 hours a week, 10 months a year, for nine years.

**1960 Squaw Valley** C: 19, N: 10, D: 2.26.

|   |   | ORDINALS | PTS. |
|---|---|---|---|
| 1. David Jenkins | USA | 10 | 1440.2 |
| 2. Karol Divin | CZE | 22 | 1414.3 |
| 3. Donald Jackson | CAN | 31 | 1401.0 |
| 4. Alain Giletti | FRA | 31 | 1399.2 |
| 5. Timothy Brown | USA | 43 | 1374.1 |
| 6. Alain Calmat | FRA | 54 | 1340.3 |
| 7. Robert Brewer | USA | 66 | 1320.3 |
| 8. Manfred Schnelldorfer | GER | 75 | 1303.3 |

David Jenkins, the younger brother of 1956 champion Hayes Alan Jenkins, trailed Karol Divin after the compulsory figures. However, his free-skating program won first-place votes from all nine judges, and he won eight of nine first places overall.

**1964 Innsbruck** C: 24, N: 11, D: 2.6.

|   |   | ORDINALS | PTS. |
|---|---|---|---|
| 1. Manfred Schnelldorfer | GER | 13 | 1916.9 |
| 2. Alain Calmat | FRA | 22 | 1876.5 |
| 3. Scott Allen | USA | 26 | 1873.6 |
| 4. Karol Divin | CZE | 32 | 1862.8 |
| 5. Emmerich Danzer | AUT | 42 | 1824.0 |
| 6. Thomas Litz | USA | 77 | 1764.7 |
| 7. Peter Jonas | AUT | 79 | 1752.0 |
| 8. Nobuo Sato | JPN | 88 | 1746.2 |

Manfred Schnelldorfer, a 20-year-old architecture student from Munich, was a former German roller skating champion. Two days shy of his 15th birthday, Scotty Allen of Smoke Rise, New Jersey, became the youngest person to win a medal in the Winter Olympics.

**1968 Grenoble** C: 28, N: 15, D: 2.16.

|   |   | ORDINALS | PTS. |
|---|---|---|---|
| 1. Wolfgang Schwarz | AUT | 13 | 1904.1 |
| 2. Timothy Wood | USA | 17 | 1891.6 |
| 3. Patrick Pera | FRA | 31 | 1864.5 |
| 4. Emmerich Danzer | AUT | 29 | 1873.0 |
| 5. Gary Visconti | USA | 52 | 1810.2 |
| 6. John "Misha" Petkevich | USA | 56 | 1806.2 |
| 7. Jay Humphry | CAN | 63 | 1795.0 |
| 8. Ondrej Nepela | CZE | 70 | 1772.8 |

Wolfgang Schwarz, who was famous for consistently finishing second behind fellow Austrian Emmerich Danzer, won the narrowest of victories over Tim Wood. If either the Canadian judge or the British judge had given one more point to Wood, he would have won. Instead, Schwarz earned five first place votes, while Wood was awarded only four. World champion Danzer had the best scores of the free-skating portion of the competition, but he was only fourth in the compulsories. He lost out on a bronze medal because of the placement rule, five to four, despite the fact that he had more points and fewer ordinals than Patrick Pera.

**1972 Sapporo** C: 17, N: 10, D: 2.11.

|   |   | ORDINALS | PTS. |
|---|---|---|---|
| 1. Ondrej Nepela | CZE | 9 | 2739.1 |
| 2. Sergei Chetveroukhin | SOV | 20 | 2672.4 |
| 3. Patrick Pera | FRA | 28 | 2653.1 |
| 4. Kenneth Shelley | USA | 43 | 2596.0 |
| 5. John "Misha" Petkevich | USA | 47 | 2591.5 |
| 6. Jan Hoffmann | GDR | 55 | 2567.6 |
| 7. Haig Oundjian | GBR | 65 | 2538.8 |
| 8. Vladimir Kovalev | SOV | 80 | 2521.6 |

Ondrej Nepela first competed in the Olympics in 1964, when he was 13 years old. That year he placed 22nd out of 24. In 1968 he moved up to eighth place, and in 1972, a seasoned veteran of 21, he was the unanimous choice of the judges, despite falling during a competition for the first time in four years. He had been attempting a triple-toe loop jump. Nepela died of throat cancer at the age of 38.

**1976 Innsbruck** C: 20, N: 13, D: 2.11.

|   |   | ORDINALS | PTS. |
|---|---|---|---|
| 1. John Curry | GBR | 11 | 192.74 |
| 2. Vladimir Kovalev | SOV | 28 | 187.64 |
| 3. Toller Cranston | CAN | 30 | 187.38 |
| 4. Jan Hoffman | GDR | 34 | 187.34 |
| 5. Sergei Volkov | SOV | 53 | 184.08 |
| 6. David Santee | USA | 49 | 184.28 |
| 7. Terry Kubicka | USA | 56 | 183.30 |
| 8. Yuri Ovchinnikov | SOV | 75 | 180.04 |

Birmingham-born John Curry had two major obstacles to overcome on his way to a gold medal. The first was a lack of proper training facilities in England. This he solved by moving to Colorado in 1973. His second obstacle was the fact that the Soviet and Eastern European judges did not approve of his style of skating, which they considered too feminine. Actually Curry, who believed that figure skating was an art as well as a sport, felt that his style was in the tradition of three-time gold medalist Gillis Grafström. For the Olympics, however, Curry supplemented his natural elegance with enough "masculine" jumps, so that even the Communist judges could find no fault with his performance. The Soviet judge gave first place to Kovalev and the Canadian judge gave first place to Cranston, but even they placed Curry second.

**1980 Lake Placid** C: 17, N: 10, D: 2.21.

|   |   | ORDINALS | PTS. |
|---|---|---|---|
| 1. Robin Cousins | GBR | 13 | 189.48 |
| 2. Jan Hoffman | GDR | 15 | 189.72 |

| 3. | Charles Tickner | USA | 28 | 187.06 |
|---|---|---|---|---|
| 4. | David Santee | USA | 34 | 185.52 |
| 5. | Scott Hamilton | USA | 45 | 181.78 |
| 6. | Igor Bobrin | SOV | 55 | 177.40 |
| 7. | Jean-Christophe Simond | FRA | 64 | 175.00 |
| 8. | Mitsuru Matsumura | JPN | 75 | 172.28 |

There were four favorites in the 1980 competition: world champion Vladimir Kovalev of the U.S.S.R., former world champions Charles Tickner and Jan Hoffman, and European champion Robin Cousins of Bristol, England. Hoffman was taking part in his fourth Olympics, having first competed in 1968 when he was 12 years old. Twenty-sixth in 1968, he moved up to sixth in 1972 and fourth in 1976. Cousins, like John Curry before him, trained in Colorado with Carlo and Christa Fassi, who had also coached Peggy Fleming and Dorothy Hamill. In Denver Cousins lived only a few blocks from Charles Tickner.

Kovalev dropped out after placing fifth in the compulsories. Hoffman was in first place, followed by Tickner, Santee, and Cousins. The next day Cousins skated a brilliant short program to move into second place. He made one slip at the beginning of his long program, but otherwise skated flawlessly. Six judges gave Cousins first place, while three voted for Hoffman. Actually Cousins' worst fall came at the awards ceremony, where, dazzled by the lights and the applause and the emotion, he stumbled while trying to negotiate the one and a half steps to the victory platform. In his book, *Skating for Gold,* Cousins recalls the raising of the British flag to honor his victory: "As it was slowly going up, I lost sight of [my parents] for a while. But when the Union Jack was finally above our heads, we were looking directly at each other. So I was able to know how they were feeling and they could see how I was feeling, but it is difficult to describe that to anyone else."

**1984 Sarajevo** C: 23, N: 14, D: 2.16.

| | | | ORDINALS |
|---|---|---|---|
| 1. | Scott Hamilton | USA | 3.4 |
| 2. | Brian Orser | CAN | 5.6 |
| 3. | Josef Sabovčik | CZE | 7.4 |
| 4. | Rudi Cerne | GER | 8.2 |
| 5. | Brian Boitano | USA | 11.0 |
| 6. | Jean-Christophe Simond | FRA | 11.8 |
| 7. | Aleksandr Fadeyev | SOV | 13.2 |
| 8. | Vladimir Kotin | SOV | 16.2 |

Scott Hamilton, the adopted son of two college professors in Bowling Green, Ohio, was considered a shoo-in to win at Sarajevo. Beginning in September 1980, the 5-foot 2½-inch, 108-pound Hamilton had won 16 straight tournaments including three world championships. But the pressure of great expectations got to him and the quality of his performance was below that of his usual brilliance. He finished second to Brian Orser in both the short and long programs. However, the big lead that Hamilton had built up during the compulsories, in which Orser placed seventh, carried him to the top platform at

the medal ceremony. Despite his own disappointment with his performance, Hamilton's good nature and dry wit made him a most popular winner.

**1988 Seoul** C: 28, N: 21, D: 2.20.

| | | | ORDINALS |
|---|---|---|---|
| 1. | Brian Boitano | USA | 3.0 |
| 2. | Brian Orser | CAN | 4.2 |
| 3. | Viktor Petrenko | SOV | 7.8 |
| 4. | Aleksandr Fadeyev | SOV | 8.2 |
| 5. | Grzegorz Filipowski | POL | 10.8 |
| 6. | Vladimir Kotin | SOV | 13.4 |
| 7. | Christopher Bowman | USA | 13.8 |
| 8. | Kurt Browning | CAN | 15.4 |

The North American media promoted this event as "The Battle of the Brians": Brian Orser of Penetanguishene, Ontario, and Brian Boitano of Sunnyvale, California. They had met 10 times in international competition, with Orser leading the series 7–3. However, by 1988 they were so evenly matched that it was impossible to choose a favorite. Over the years, Orser had developed a reputation as a nervous performer who stumbled at major championships. He placed second at the 1984 Olympics, second at the 1984 world championships, second at the 1985 world championships, and second again at the 1986 world championships. In 1987 he finally broke through his invisible barrier and won his first world title. Boitano, meanwhile, had been crowned world champion in 1986 before finishing second to Orser in 1987.

In Calgary, Orser placed first in the short program and trailed Boitano by a negligible margin going into the long program, which was worth 50 percent of the total score. Boitano skated first and gave a stunning performance, with only a barely perceptible bobble in a triple jump landing. In figure skating it is rare for a champion to do his best in a major competition because of the enormous pressure involved, but Boitano broke the rule. "I felt like angels were lifting and spinning me," he would later explain.

Despite Boitano's near-perfection, it was still possible for Orser, a superior artistic skater, to salvage the gold medal. But the pressure on Orser was even greater than that on Boitano. On top of the natural stress brought on by competing for an Olympic title, Orser carried with him the burden of being the host country's only gold medal hope. Ninety seconds into his routine, Orser nearly missed a triple flip jump, landing on two feet instead of one. Still, in the words of Dick Button, it was only "the slightest of slightest glitches," and not enough to settle the contest in Boitano's favor. But late in his routine, a fatigued Orser downgraded a triple axel to a double and his fate was sealed.

As it was, the judging could hardly have been closer. Four judges voted for Orser, three for Boitano, and two scored it a tie. In figure skating, each judge gives each competitor two scores—one for technical merit and one for artistic expression. In case of a tie, the skater with the higher technical score is given the edge. Both judges who had ranked the Brians evenly, had awarded Boitano higher marks for technical merit, so he ended up winning 5–4.

All of the hype about the "Battle of the Brians" aside, Boitano and Orser were actually good friends. At the medal ceremony, Boitano was plagued by contradictory emotions. "I almost felt guilty feeling great," he would later say. "I tried to hold it back, so me feeling great wouldn't make him feel worse."

The third-place winner, Viktor Petrenko, was the first Ukrainian to win a medal in an individual event at a Winter Olympics.

# WOMEN

**1908 London** C: 5, N: 3, D: 10.29.

| | | ORDINALS | PTS. |
|---|---|---|---|
| 1. Madge Syers | GBR | 5 | 1262.5 |
| 2. Elsa Rendschmidt | GER | 11 | 1055.0 |
| 3. Dorothy Greenhough-Smith | GBR | 15 | 960.5 |
| 4. Elna Montgomery | SWE | 21 | 851.5 |
| 5. Gwendolyn Lycett | GBR | 23 | 820.0 |

Madge Syers, who came out of retirement to compete in the Olympics, was the unanimous choice of the five judges.

**1920 Antwerp** C: 6, N: 4, D: 4.25.

| | | ORDINALS | PTS. |
|---|---|---|---|
| 1. Magda Julin | SWE | 12 | 913.50 |
| 2. Svea Norén | SWE | 12.5 | 887.75 |
| 3. Theresa Weld | USA | 15.5 | 898.00 |
| 4. Phyllis Johnson | GBR | 18.5 | 869.50 |
| 5. Margot Moe | NOR | 22.5 | 859.75 |
| 6. Ingrid Gulbrandsen | NOR | 24 | 847.50 |

Magda Julin won the closest of all Olympic figure skating contests despite the fact that she received no first-place votes. The British judge voted for Johnson, the Swedish judge for Norén, and the Norwegian judge placed Moe and Gulbrandsen first and second, even though the other judges put them last. The Belgian judge voted for Weld and the French judge declared a tie between Norén and Weld. Julin did receive three second-place votes and won according to the placings countback rule.

**1924 Chamonix** C: 8, N: 6, D: 1.29.

| | | ORDINALS | PTS. |
|---|---|---|---|
| 1. Herma Planck-Szabó | AUT | 7 | 299.17 |
| 2. Beatrix Loughran | USA | 14 | 279.85 |
| 3. Ethel Muckelt | GBR | 26 | 250.07 |
| 4. Theresa Blanchard-Weld | USA | 27 | 249.53 |
| 5. Andrée Joly | FRA | 38 | 231.92 |
| 6. Cecil Smith | CAN | 44 | 230.75 |

| | | | |
|---|---|---|---|
| 7. Kathleen Shaw | GBR | 46 | 221.00 |
| 8. Sonja Henie | NOR | 50 | 203.82 |

In retrospect, the 1924 competition was most notable for the appearance of the last-place finisher, 11-year-old Sonja Henie, who was to become the most famous figure skater of all time. In Chamonix, however, it was Herma Planck-Szabó who received the first-place votes of all seven judges.

**1928 St. Moritz** C: 20, N: 8, D: 2.18.

| | | ORDINALS | PTS. |
|---|---|---|---|
| 1. Sonja Henie | NOR | 8 | 2452.25 |
| 2. Fritzi Burger | AUT | 25 | 2248.50 |
| 3. Beatrix Loughran | USA | 28 | 2254.50 |
| 4. Maribel Vinson | USA | 32 | 2224.50 |
| 5. Cecil Smith | CAN | 32 | 2213.75 |
| 6. Constance Wilson | CAN | 35 | 2173.00 |
| 7. Melitta Brunner | AUT | 48 | 2087.50 |
| 8. Ilse Hornung | AUT | 54 | 2050.75 |

Sonja Henie was born in Oslo on April 8, 1912. Her father was a wealthy furrier, the owner of Norway's largest fur company, as well as the owner of Oslo's first automobile. Sonja gained valuable experience at the 1924 Olympics. Two years later she had improved enough to finish second at the world championships. In 1927 the world championships were held on Henie's home rink in Oslo. Henie won the title, but not without some controversy concerning the judging. There were five judges: one Austrian, one German, and three from Norway. The Austrian and the German both gave their first-place votes to Herma Planck-Szabó. However, all three Norwegian judges voted for Sonja Henie, giving her the championship. The ensuing uproar prompted the International Skating Union to institute a rule, still in existence, allowing only one judge per country in international meets. At the 1928 Olympics there was no such controversy, as Henie was awarded first place by six of the seven judges. Only the American judge voted for Beatrix Loughran, who had the unusual distinction of receiving one vote for each of the first seven places.

**1932 Lake Placid** C: 15, N: 7, D: 10.9.

| | | ORDINALS | PTS. |
|---|---|---|---|
| 1. Sonja Henie | NOR | 7 | 2302.5 |
| 2. Fritzi Burger | AUT | 18 | 2167.1 |
| 3. Maribel Vinson | USA | 23 | 2158.5 |
| 4. Constance Wilson-Samuel | CAN | 28 | 2131.9 |
| 5. Vivi-Anne Hultén | SWE | 29 | 2129.5 |
| 6. Yvonne de Ligne | BEL | 45 | 1942.5 |
| 7. Megan Taylor | GBR | 55 | 1911.8 |
| 8. Cecilia Colledge | GBR | 64 | 1851.6 |

Sonja Henie was the unanimous choice of the seven judges. Already Sonja Henie imitators were springing up, wherever figure skating was appreciated. Two 11-year-olds from Great Britain, Megan Taylor and Cecilia Colledge, placed seventh and eighth at Lake Placid.

**1936 Garmisch-Partenkirchen** C: 26, N: 13, D: 2.15.

| | | ORDINALS | PTS. |
|---|---|---|---|
| 1. Sonja Henie | NOR | 7.5 | 425.5 |
| 2. Cecilia Colledge | GBR | 13.5 | 418.1 |
| 3. Vivi-Anne Hultén | SWE | 28 | 394.7 |
| 4. Liselotte Landbeck | BEL | 32 | 393.3 |
| 5. Maribel Vinson | USA | 39 | 388.7 |
| 6. Hedy Stenuf | AUT | 40 | 387.6 |
| 7. Emmy Putzinger | AUT | 49 | 381.8 |
| 8. Viktoria Lindpaintner | GER | 51 | 381.4 |

By 1936 Sonja Henie was so popular that police had to be called out to control the crowds around her in places as far apart as New York City and Prague. She had announced that she would retire from competition following the 1936 world championships, to be held one week after the Olympics. She wanted to close out her amateur career with a third Olympic gold medal, so she felt great tension preceding the competition. When the scoring totals were posted for the compulsory figures, Henie was only 3.6 points ahead of Colledge. When Henie was told the results she tore the offending sheet of paper off the announcements board and ripped it to shreds, stating that it was a misrepresentation. Fifteen-year-old Cecilia Colledge was the second skater to perform her free-skating program. As she glided onto the ice she gave the Nazi salute, which pleased the crowd. Just as she prepared to begin her routine, it was discovered that someone had put on the wrong music, and she was forced to endure a delay while the proper record was found. Not surprisingly, Colledge almost fell during the first minute of her performance. But she recovered sufficiently to earn an average score of 5.7. Sonja Henie, the last of the 26 skaters, appeared nervous, but skated with great vigor and precision. An average score of 5.8 assured her of her third gold medal. A week later she won her tenth straight world championship, a feat surpassed only by Ulrich Salchow, who won 11 consecutive world titles from 1901 through 1911.

During her competitive career, Sonja Henie accumulated 1473 cups, medals, and trophies. After she turned professional her parents convinced Twentieth Century-Fox to put her in the movies. Henie's first film, *One in a Million,* was a big success, and nine more films followed. In 1937 she earned over $200,000. Her father died that year, but Sonja definitely inherited his business acumen. She made enough money to allow her to engage in an occasional indulgence. The only person she trusted to sharpen her skates was Eddie Pec. One time while Sonja was performing in Chicago, she needed her skates sharpened. So she called Eddie Pec in New York. Pec took the next train to Chicago, arriving the following day. He spent a couple minutes sharpening Henie's skates, then turned around and took the next train back to New York.

Sonja Henie became a U.S. citizen in 1941. After divorcing two Americans, the 44-year-old Henie married her childhood sweetheart, Norwegian shipowner Niels Onstad. Sonja Henie died of leukemia at the age of 57, while on an ambulance airplane flying her from Paris to Oslo. She was worth over $47 million at the time of her death.

Another future actress who took part in the 1936 figure skating competition was Vera Hruba of Czechoslovakia, who placed 17th. As Vera Hruba Ralston, she starred in numerous B pictures, including *The Lady and the Monster, Hoodlum Empire,* and *I, Jane Doe.* Her specialties were Westerns and pioneer films.

**1948 St. Moritz** C: 25, N: 10, D: 2.6.

| | | ORDINALS | PTS. |
|---|---|---|---|
| 1. Barbara Ann Scott | CAN | 11 | 163.077 |
| 2. Eva Pawlik | AUT | 24 | 157.588 |
| 3. Jeanette Altwegg | GBR | 28 | 156.166 |
| 4. Jirina Nekolová | CZE | 34 | 154.088 |
| 5. Alena Vrzánová | CZE | 44 | 153.044 |
| 6. Yvonne Sherman | USA | 62 | 149.833 |
| 7. Bridget Shirley Adams | GBR | 69 | 148.644 |
| 8. Gretchen Merrill | USA | 73 | 148.466 |

Barbara Ann Scott, the 19-year-old world champion from Ottawa, had put in 20,000 hours of practice prior to the Olympics. The day of the free-skating competition, the ice was badly chewed up by two hockey matches. Just before Scott went out to perform, one of the earlier skaters, Eileen Seigh of the United States, gave her a complete description of the location of all the ruts and clean spots all over the rink. Scott won seven of the nine first-place votes, with the Austrian judge voting for Pawlik and the British judge for Altwegg.

**1952 Oslo** C: 25, N: 12, D: 2.20.

| | | ORDINALS | PTS. |
|---|---|---|---|
| 1. Jeanette Altwegg | GBR | 14 | 1455.8 |
| 2. Tenley Albright | USA | 22 | 1432.2 |
| 3. Jacqueline du Bief | FRA | 24 | 1422.0 |
| 4. Sonya Klopfer | USA | 36 | 1391.7 |
| 5. Virginia Baxter | USA | 50 | 1369.9 |
| 6. Suzanne Morrow | CAN | 56 | 1344.0 |
| 7. Barbara Wyatt | GBR | 63 | 1335.4 |
| 8. Gundi Busch | GER | 75 | 1316.6 |

Jeanette Altwegg placed only fourth in free-skating. However she had built up such a large lead during the compulsory figures that she won anyway.

**1956 Cortina** C: 21, N: 11, D: 2.2.

| | | ORDINALS | PTS. |
|---|---|---|---|
| 1. Tenley Albright | USA | 12 | 169.67 |
| 2. Carol Heiss | USA | 21 | 168.02 |
| 3. Ingrid Wendl | AUT | 39 | 159.44 |
| 4. Yvonne Sugden de Monfort | GBR | 53 | 156.62 |
| 5. Hanna Eigel | AUT | 52 | 157.15 |
| 6. Carole Jane Pachl | CAN | 73 | 154.74 |
| 7. Hannerl Walter | AUT | 83.5 | 153.89 |
| 8. Catherine Machado | USA | 86.5 | 153.48 |

Tenley Albright, a surgeon's daughter from Newton Center, Massachusetts, had been stricken by nonparalytic polio at the age of 11. Less than two weeks before the Cortina Olympics, Tenley was practicing when she hit a rut. As she fell, her left skate hit her ankle joint, cut through three layers of her right boot, slashed a vein, and severely scraped the bone. Her father arrived two days later and patched her up. In the Olympic competition she skated well enough to earn the first-place votes of ten of the 11 judges. Back in the United States she entered Harvard Medical School and eventually became a surgeon herself.

**1960 Squaw Valley** C: 26, N: 13, D: 2.23.

| | | ORDINALS | PTS. |
|---|---|---|---|
| 1. Carol Heiss | USA | 9 | 1490.1 |
| 2. Sjoukje Dijkstra | HOL | 20 | 1424.8 |
| 3. Barbara Roles | USA | 26 | 1414.9 |
| 4. Jana Mrázková | CZE | 53 | 1338.7 |
| 5. Joan Haanappel | HOL | 52 | 1331.9 |
| 6. Laurence Owen | USA | 57 | 1343.0 |
| 7. Regine Heitzer | AUT | 58 | 1327.9 |
| 8. Anna Galmarini | ITA | 79 | 1295.0 |

In 1956, 16-year-old Carol Heiss of Ozone Park, Queens, traveled to Cortina with her mother, who was dying of cancer. She gained a silver medal at the Olympics, but two weeks later, she defeated Tenley Albright for the first time to win the world championship in Garmisch-Partenkirchen. In October her mother died, but Carol Heiss took a vow to win an Olympic gold medal in her honor. This she did with extraordinary ease in 1960, earning the first-place votes of all nine judges. After the Olympics, Heiss attempted a Hollywood career, but understandably lost interest after making one film: *Snow White and the Three Stooges*.

**1964 Innsbruck** C: 30, N: 14, D: 2.2.

| | | ORDINALS | PTS. |
|---|---|---|---|
| 1. Sjoukje Dijkstra | HOL | 9 | 2018.5 |
| 2. Regine Heitzer | AUT | 22 | 1945.5 |
| 3. Petra Burka | CAN | 25 | 1940.0 |
| 4. Nicole Hassler | FRA | 38 | 1887.7 |
| 5. Miwa Fukuhara | JPN | 50 | 1845.1 |
| 6. Peggy Fleming | USA | 59 | 1819.6 |
| 7. Christine Haigler | USA | 74 | 1803.8 |
| 8. Albertina Noyes | USA | 73 | 1798.9 |

Two-time world champion Sjoukje Dijkstra was the unanimous first-place choice of the nine judges. She was the third straight silver medalist to win a gold medal four years later.

**1968 Grenoble** C: 32, N: 15, D: 2.11.

| | | ORDINALS | PTS. |
|---|---|---|---|
| 1. Peggy Fleming | USA | 9 | 1970.5 |
| 2. Gabriele Seyfert | GDR | 18 | 1882.3 |
| 3. Hana Mašková | CZE | 31 | 1828.8 |
| 4. Albertina Noyes | USA | 40 | 1797.3 |
| 5. Beatrix Schuba | AUT | 51 | 1773.2 |
| 6. Zsuzsa Almássy | HUN | 57 | 1757.0 |

| 7. Karen Magnussen | CAN | 63 | 1759.4 |
| 8. Kumiko Ohkawa | JPN | 61 | 1763.6 |

Like Carol Heiss, Peggy Fleming came from a family which had sacrificed greatly to further her passion for figure skating. Peggy's father, who had moved the family from Cleveland to Pasadena, California, to Colorado Springs (and Carlo Fassi), died in 1966. Her mother designed and sewed all of Peggy's dresses. As a competition, the contest at Grenoble had little to offer. Fleming built up a huge lead after the compulsory figures and easily won all of the first-place votes. Likewise, Gaby Seyfert was awarded all of the second-place votes. Peggy Fleming was the only U.S. gold medal winner of the Grenoble Games.

**1972 Sapporo** C: 19, N: 14, D: 2.7.

| | | ORDINALS | PTS. |
|---|---|---|---|
| 1. Beatrix Schuba | AUT | 9 | 2751.5 |
| 2. Karen Magnussen | CAN | 23 | 2673.2 |
| 3. Janet Lynn | USA | 27 | 2663.1 |
| 4. Julie Holmes | USA | 39 | 2627.0 |
| 5. Zsuzsa Almássy | HUN | 47 | 2592.4 |
| 6. Sonja Morgenstern | GDR | 53 | 2579.4 |
| 7. Rita Trapanese | ITA | 55 | 2574.8 |
| 8. Christine Errath | GDR | 78 | 2489.3 |

World champion Trixi Schuba built up a large lead with her compulsory figures and coasted to victory with a seventh place in free-skating.

**1976 Innsbruck** C: 21, N: 15, D: 2.13.

| | | ORDINALS | PTS. |
|---|---|---|---|
| 1. Dorothy Hamill | USA | 9 | 193.80 |
| 2. Dianne de Leeuw | HOL | 20 | 190.24 |
| 3. Christine Errath | GDR | 28 | 188.16 |
| 4. Anett Pötzsch | GDR | 33 | 187.42 |
| 5. Isabel de Navarre | GER | 59 | 182.42 |
| 6. Wendy Burge | USA | 63 | 182.14 |
| 7. Susanna Driano | ITA | 63 | 181.62 |
| 8. Linda Fratianne | USA | 67 | 181.86 |

For the fifth straight time the women's figure skating was decided by unanimous decision. Hamill's victory was particularly exciting for her coach, Carlo Fassi, who achieved a unique double, having also coached the men's winner, John Curry.

**1980 Lake Placid** C: 22, N: 15, D: 2.23.

| | | ORDINALS | PTS. |
|---|---|---|---|
| 1. Anett Pötzsch | GDR | 11 | 189.00 |
| 2. Linda Fratianne | USA | 16 | 188.30 |
| 3. Dagmar Lurz | GER | 28 | 183.04 |
| 4. Denise Biellmann | SWI | 43 | 180.06 |
| 5. Lisa-Marie Allen | USA | 45 | 179.42 |
| 6. Emi Watanabe | JPN | 48 | 179.04 |
| 7. Claudia Kristofics-Binder | AUT | 60 | 176.88 |
| 8. Susanna Driano | ITA | 77 | 172.82 |

The closest Olympic women's figure skating competition in 60 years showcased the friendly rivalry between Linda Fratianne of Los Angeles and Anett Pötzsch of Karl-Marx Stadt. In 1977 Fratianne had won the world championship, but in 1978 she was defeated by Pötzsch. The following year, Linda won back the title, but at the Olympics, the pendulum swung Anett's way. Both 19-year-olds tried to increase their chances of victory by altering their appearance. Linda had cosmetic surgery to her nose, while Anett lost ten pounds. Both tried to appear brighter, livelier, sexier. In the end, it turned out that glamour was unimportant, as Pötzsch gained a solid lead in the compulsory figures and Fratianne was unable to close the gap. Denise Biellmann ranked first in free-skating, but her 12th place in the compulsories kept her out of the medals.

**1984 Sarajevo** C: 23, N: 16, D: 2.18.

|   |   |   | ORDINALS |
|---|---|---|---|
| 1. | Katarina Witt | GDR | 3.2 |
| 2. | Rosalyn Sumners | USA | 4.6 |
| 3. | Kira Ivanova | SOV | 9.2 |
| 4. | Tiffany Chin | USA | 11.0 |
| 5. | Anna Kondrashova | SOV | 11.8 |
| 6. | Elaine Zayak | USA | 14.2 |
| 7. | Manuela Ruben | GER | 15.0 |
| 8. | Yelena Vodorezova | SOV | 15.4 |

The 1984 Olympics pitted defending world champion Rosalynn Sumners against 1982 world champion Elaine Zayak and the beautiful up-and-coming East German, Katarina Witt. Zayak removed herself from the competition for the gold medal by placing 13th in the compulsories, which were won by Sumners, with Witt a strong third. Witt took a slight lead following the short program, and turned the free-skating into a head-to-head showdown. Witt, skating before Sumners, achieved high marks, but not high enough to put first place out of reach for Sumners. The Edmonds, Washington, native looked close to victory, but in the closing seconds of her routine, she let up slightly, turning a triple-toe loop into a double and a double axel into a single. This lapse probably also turned her gold medal into silver. After her Olympic victory, Katarina Witt received 35,000 love letters.

**1988 Calgary** C: 31, N: 23, D: 2.27.

|   |   |   | ORDINALS |
|---|---|---|---|
| 1. | Katarina Witt | GDR | 4.2 |
| 2. | Elizabeth Manley | CAN | 4.6 |
| 3. | Debra Thomas | USA | 6.0 |
| 4. | Jill Trenary | USA | 10.4 |
| 5. | Midori Ito | JPN | 10.6 |
| 6. | Claudia Leistner | GER | 13.2 |
| 7. | Kira Ivanova | SOV | 13.6 |
| 8. | Anna Kondrashova | SOV | 15.2 |

The 1988 competition turned out to be a classic matchup between defending Olympic and world champion Katarina Witt and the only person to beat her in five years,

the 1986 world champion, Stanford pre-medical student Debi Thomas. After the short program, Thomas held a slight lead over Witt, with local favorite Elizabeth Manley a distant third.

As it happened, both Witt and Thomas chose to perform their long program to Georges Bizet's *Carmen*. Witt, first on the ice, skated cautiously and tentatively. Having immersed herself in the character of Carmen, her artistic presentation was flawless, but because she took few risks, her marks for technical merit were unimpressive and she left the door open for Thomas to seize the gold medal. But Thomas was preceded by Elizabeth Manley. The 5-foot Canadian, who had a reputation for crumbling under pressure, brought down the house with a brilliant performance that would ultimately earn her an unexpected silver medal.

Thomas began her routine with a triple toe loop combination, but she underrotated the second jump and landed badly. Barely 20 seconds into her four-minute program, she gave up. "The whole reason I came here was to be great," she later explained, "and after that I couldn't be great." Thomas missed two more triples, once touching the ice with her hand to keep from falling. Despite her disappointing performance, Thomas made history by becoming the first black athlete to win a medal in the Winter Olympics. Witt, for her part, became the first repeat winner in singles figure skating since Sonja Henie.

# PAIRS

**1908 London** T: 3, N: 2, D: 10.29.

|   |   |   | ORDINALS | PTS. |
|---|---|---|---|---|
| 1. | Anna Hübler<br>Heinrich Burger | GER | 5 | 56.0 |
| 2. | Phyllis Johnson<br>James Johnson | GBR | 10 | 51.5 |
| 3. | Madge Syers<br>Edgar Syers | GBR | 13 | 48.0 |

**1920 Antwerp** T: 8, N: 6, D: 4.26.

|   |   |   | ORDINALS | PTS. |
|---|---|---|---|---|
| 1. | Ludovika Jakobsson<br>Walter Jakobsson | FIN | 7 | 80.75 |
| 2. | Alexia Bryn<br>Yngvar Bryn | NOR | 15.5 | 72.75 |
| 3. | Phyllis Johnson<br>Basil Williams | GBR | 25 | 66.25 |
| 4. | Theresa Weld<br>Nathaniel Niles | USA | 28.5 | 62.50 |
| 5. | Ethel Muckelt<br>Sydney Wallwork | GBR | 34 | 61.25 |
| 6. | Georgette Herbos<br>Georges Wagemans | BEL | 41.5 | 56.00 |
| 7. | Simone Sabouret<br>Charles Sabouret | FRA | 45.5 | — |
| 8. | Madeleine Macdonald Beaumont<br>Kenneth Macdonald Beaumont | GBR | 55 | — |

**1924 Chamonix** T: 9, N: 7, D: 1.31.

| | | ORDINALS | PTS. |
|---|---|---|---|
| 1. Helene Engelmann<br>Alfred Berger | AUT | 9 | 10.64 |
| 2. Ludovika Jakobsson<br>Walter Jakobsson | FIN | 18.5 | 10.25 |
| 3. Andrée Joly<br>Pierre Brunet | FRA | 22 | 9.89 |
| 4. Ethel Muckelt<br>John Page | GBR | 30.5 | 9.93 |
| 5. Georgette Herbos<br>Georges Wagemans | BEL | 37 | 8.82 |
| 6. Theresa Blanchard-Weld<br>Nathaniel Niles | USA | 39 | 9.07 |
| 7. Cecil Smith<br>Melville Rogers | CAN | 41.5 | 9.11 |
| 8. Mildred Richardson<br>Thomas Richardson | GBR | 57 | 7.68 |

**1928 St. Moritz** T: 13, N: 10, D: 2.19.

| | | ORDINALS | PTS. |
|---|---|---|---|
| 1. Andrée Joly<br>Pierre Brunet | FRA | 14 | 100.50 |
| 2. Lilly Scholz<br>Otto Kaiser | AUT | 17 | 99.25 |
| 3. Melitta Brunner<br>Ludwig Wrede | AUT | 29 | 93.25 |
| 4. Beatrix Loughran<br>Sherwin Badger | USA | 43 | 87.50 |
| 5. Ludovika Jakobsson<br>Walter Jakobsson | FIN | 51 | 84.00 |
| 6. Josy van Leberghe<br>Robert van Zeebroeck | BEL | 54 | 83.00 |
| 7. Ethel Muckelt<br>John Page | GBR | 61.5 | 79.00 |
| 8. Ilse Kishauer<br>Ernst Gaste | GER | 63 | 75.75 |

**1932 Lake Placid** T: 7, N: 4, D: 2.12.

| | | ORDINALS | PTS. |
|---|---|---|---|
| 1. Andrée Brunet (Joly)<br>Pierre Brunet | FRA | 12 | 76.7 |
| 2. Beatrix Loughran<br>Sherwin Badger | USA | 16 | 77.5 |
| 3. Emília Rotter<br>László Szollás | HUN | 20 | 76.4 |
| 4. Olga Orgonista<br>Sándor Szalay | HUN | 28 | 72.2 |
| 5. Constance Wilson-Samuel<br>Montgomery Wilson | CAN | 35 | 69.6 |
| 6. Frances Claudet<br>Chauney Bangs | CAN | 36 | 68.9 |
| 7. Gertrude Meredith<br>Joseph Savage | USA | 49 | 59.8 |

**1936 Garmisch-Partenkirchen** T: 18, N: 12, D: 2.13.

| | | ORDINALS | PTS. |
|---|---|---|---|
| 1. Maxi Herber<br>Ernst Baier | GER | 11 | 11.5 |
| 2. Ilse Pausin<br>Erik Pausin | AUT | 19.5 | 11.4 |
| 3. Emília Rotter<br>László Szollás | HUN | 32.5 | 10.8 |
| 4. Piroska Szekrényessy<br>Attila Szekrényessy | HUN | 38.5 | 10.6 |
| 5. Maribel Vinson<br>George Hill | USA | 46.5 | 10.4 |
| 6. Louise Bertram<br>Stewert Reburn | CAN | 68.5 | 9.8 |
| 7. Violet Cliff<br>Leslie Cliff | GBR | 56.5 | 10.1 |
| 8. Eva Prawitz<br>Otto Weiss | GER | 74.5 | 9.5 |

Thirty-year-old Berlin architect Ernst Baier and his 15-year-old protégée, Maxi Herber, were early exponents of "shadow skating," in which both skaters perform the exact same moves without touching. The judges seemed to have trouble with the Canadian pair, Bertram and Reburn, who received a wide variety of scores, ranging from third and fourth place from the Swedish and Norwegian judges to 13th and 14th from the Austrian and German judges.

**1948 St. Moritz** T: 15, N: 11, D: 2.7.

| | | ORDINALS | PTS. |
|---|---|---|---|
| 1. Micheline Lannoy<br>Pierre Baugniet | BEL | 17.5 | 11.227 |
| 2. Andrea Kékessy<br>Ede Király | HUN | 26 | 11.109 |
| 3. Suzanne Morrow<br>Wallace Diestelmeyer | CAN | 31 | 11.000 |
| 4. Yvonne Sherman<br>Robert Swenning | USA | 53 | 10.581 |
| 5. Winnifred Silverthorne<br>Dennis Silverthorne | GBR | 53 | 10.572 |
| 6. Karol Kennedy<br>Michael Kennedy | USA | 59.5 | 10.536 |
| 7. Marianna Nagy<br>László Nagy | HUN | 89 | 9.909 |
| 8. Jennifer Nicks<br>John Nicks | GBR | 98 | 9.700 |

**1952 Oslo** T: 13, N: 9, D: 2.22.

| | | ORDINALS | PTS. |
|---|---|---|---|
| 1. Ria Falk<br>Paul Falk | GER | 11.5 | 102.6 |
| 2. Karol Kennedy<br>Michael Kennedy | USA | 17.5 | 100.6 |
| 3. Marianna Nagy<br>László Nagy | HUN | 31 | 97.4 |
| 4. Jennifer Nicks<br>John Nicks | GBR | 39 | 95.4 |
| 5. Frances Dafoe<br>Norris Bowden | CAN | 48 | 94.4 |
| 6. Janet Gerhauser<br>John Nightingale | USA | 54 | 92.6 |

| | | | |
|---|---|---|---|
| 7. Silvia Grandjean<br>Michel Grandjean | SWI | 53 | 92.7 |
| 8. Ingeborg Minor<br>Hermann Braun | GER | 73.5 | 81.8 |

**1956 Cortina** T: 11, N: 7, D: 2.3.

| | | ORDINALS | PTS. |
|---|---|---|---|
| 1. Elisabeth Schwartz<br>Kurt Oppelt | AUT | 14 | 11.31 |
| 2. Frances Dafoe<br>Norris Bowden | CAN | 16 | 11.32 |
| 3. Marianna Nagy<br>László Nagy | HUN | 32 | 11.03 |
| 4. Marika Kilius<br>Franz Ningel | GER | 35.5 | 10.98 |
| 5. Carole Ormaca<br>Robin Greiner | USA | 56 | 10.71 |
| 6. Barbara Wagner<br>Robert Paul | CAN | 54.5 | 10.74 |
| 7. Lucille Ash<br>Sully Kothmann | USA | 59.5 | 10.63 |
| 8. Vera Suchanova<br>Zdenek Dolezal | CZE | 68.5 | 10.53 |

In this unusually close contest, both Schwarz and Oppelt and Dafoe and Bowden received four first-place votes, with the Hungarian judge voting for the Nagys. The Austrians won because they also received five second-place votes while the Canadians earned three seconds and two thirds. The decisive moment came when a tired Fran Dafoe lost her balance and faltered during a lift. The crowd, which had grumbled all along about the judging, became unruly when the popular German couple of 12-year-old Marika Kilius and 19-year-old Franz Ningel received scores only good enough for fourth place. Members of the audience pelted the judges and referee with oranges, and the ice had to be cleared three times before the competition could go on.

**1960 Squaw Valley** T: 13, N: 7, D: 2.19.

| | | ORDINALS | PTS. |
|---|---|---|---|
| 1. Barbara Wagner<br>Robert Paul | CAN | 7 | 80.4 |
| 2. Marika Kilius<br>Hans-Jürgen Bäumler | GER | 19 | 76.8 |
| 3. Nancy Ludington<br>Ronald Ludington | USA | 27.5 | 76.2 |
| 4. Maria Jelinek<br>Otto Jelinek | CAN | 26 | 75.9 |
| 5. Margret Göbl<br>Franz Ningel | GER | 36 | 72.5 |
| 6. Nina Zhuk<br>Stanislav Zhuk | SOV | 38 | 72.3 |
| 7. Rita Blumenberg<br>Werner Mensching | GER | 53 | 70.2 |
| 8. Diana Hinko<br>Heinz Dopfl | AUT | 54.5 | 69.8 |

Gold medal winner Bob Paul later gained further renown as a choreographer for Peggy Fleming, Dorothy Hamill, and Linda Fratianne, as well as for entertainers Donny and Marie Osmond.

**1964 Innsbruck** T: 17, N: 7, D: 1.29.

| | | ORDINALS | PTS. |
|---|---|---|---|
| 1. Lyudmila Belousova<br>Oleg Protopopov | SOV | 13 | 104.4 |
| 2. Marika Kilius<br>Hans-Jürgen Bäumler | GER | 15 | 103.6 |
| 3. Debbi Wilkes<br>Guy Revell | CAN | 35.5 | 98.5 |
| 4. Vivian Joseph<br>Ronald Joseph | USA | 35.5 | 98.2 |
| 5. Tatiana Zhuk<br>Aleksandr Gavrilov | SOV | 45 | 96.6 |
| 6. Gerda Johner<br>Rüdi Johner | SWI | 56 | 95.4 |
| 7. Judianne Fotheringill<br>Jerry Fotheringill | USA | 69.5 | 94.7 |
| 8. Cynthia Kauffman<br>Ronald Kauffman | USA | 74.0 | 92.8 |

Lyudmila Belousova and her husband, Oleg Protopopov, were awarded five first-place votes to four for Kilius and Bäumler. The Leningrad couple had finished ninth in 1960. In 1966 Kilius and Bäumler returned their silver medals following allegations that they had signed a professional contract before the start of the Innsbruck Games. They were officially rehabilitated by the I.O.C. in 1987.

**1968 Grenoble** T: 18, N: 8, D: 2.14.

| | | ORDINALS | PTS. |
|---|---|---|---|
| 1. Lyudmila Belousova<br>Oleg Protopopov | SOV | 10 | 315.2 |
| 2. Tatyana Zhuk<br>Aleksandr Gorelik | SOV | 17 | 312.3 |
| 3. Margot Glockshuber<br>Wolfgang Danne | GER | 30 | 304.4 |
| 4. Heidemarie Steiner<br>Heinz-Ulrich Walther | GDR | 37 | 303.1 |
| 5. Tamara Moskvina<br>Aleksei Michine | SOV | 44 | 300.3 |
| 6. Cynthia Kauffman<br>Ronald Kauffman | USA | 58 | 297.0 |
| 7. Sandi Sweitzer<br>Roy Wagelein | USA | 64.5 | 294.5 |
| 8. Gudrun Hauss<br>Walter Häfner | GER | 67 | 293.6 |

Belousova and Protopopov, now 32 and 35 years old, respectively, climaxed their spectacular amateur career with an elegant display that earned them a second Olympic championship. Protopopov told the press, "Art cannot be measured by points. We skate from the heart. To us it is spiritual beauty that matters. . . . These pairs of brother and sister, how can they convey the emotion, the love, that exists between a man and a woman? That is what we try to show."

**1972 Sapporo** T: 16, N: 9, D: 2.6.

| | | ORDINALS | PTS. |
|---|---|---|---|
| 1. Irina Rodnina<br>Aleksei Ulanov | SOV | 12 | 420.4 |
| 2. Lyudmila Smirnova<br>Andrei Suraikin | SOV | 15 | 419.4 |
| 3. Manuela Gross<br>Uwe Kagelmann | GDR | 29 | 411.8 |
| 4. Alicia "Jojo" Starbuck<br>Kenneth Shelley | USA | 35 | 406.8 |
| 5. Almut Lehmann<br>Herbert Wiesinger | GER | 52 | 399.8 |
| 6. Irina Chernieva<br>Vassily Blagov | SOV | 52 | 399.1 |
| 7. Melissa Militano<br>Mark Militano | USA | 65.5 | 393.0 |
| 8. Annette Kansy<br>Axel Salzmann | GDR | 68.0 | 392.6 |

At the 1969 European championships, Belousova and Protopopov were dethroned by Irina Rodnina (19) and Aleksei Ulanov (21). The younger couple, knowing they couldn't compete on the same terms with the elegant and sophisticated Olympic champions, had developed a new style, full of dazzling and complex leaps and stunts. Rodnina and Ulanov thrilled the audience and the judges in 1969 and continued undefeated for the next three years. However, as the Sapporo Olympics approached, the Soviet team was in great turmoil. Ulanov, tired of being spurned and mocked by Rodnina, had become romantically involved with Lyudmila Smirnova of the number-two U.S.S.R. team. The harmonious interaction between the partners of the two pairs was severely disrupted. Nevertheless, they finished first and second, with Rodnina leaving the ice in tears.

**1976 Innsbruck** T: 14, N: 9, D: 2.7.

| | | ORDINALS | PTS. |
|---|---|---|---|
| 1. Irina Rodnina<br>Aleksandr Zaitsev | SOV | 9 | 140.54 |
| 2. Romy Kermer<br>Rolf Oesterreich | GDR | 21 | 136.35 |
| 3. Manuela Gross<br>Uwe Kagelmann | GDR | 34 | 134.57 |
| 4. Irina Vorobieva<br>Aleksandr Vlasov | SOV | 35 | 134.52 |
| 5. Tai Babilonia<br>Randy Gardner | USA | 36 | 134.24 |
| 6. Kerstin Stolfig<br>Veit Kempe | GDR | 59 | 129.57 |
| 7. Karin Künzle<br>Christian Künzle | SWI | 64 | 128.97 |
| 8. Corinna Halke<br>Eberhard Rausch | GER | 72 | 127.37 |

Following the 1972 season, Aleksei Ulanov married Lyudmila Smirnova and a nationwide search was begun to find a new partner for Irina Rodnina. The winner was Aleksandr Zaitsev of Leningrad. Before long, the new pair had not only clicked as skaters, but they had also become wife and husband. Rodnina, still under the direction of the controversial Soviet trainer Stanislav Zhuk, continued her winning ways as if nothing had happened.

**1980 Lake Placid** T: 11, N: 7, D: 2.17.

| | | ORDINALS | PTS. |
|---|---|---|---|
| 1. Irina Rodnina<br>Aleksandr Zaitsev | SOV | 9 | 147.26 |
| 2. Marina Cherkosova<br>Sergei Shakrai | SOV | 19 | 143.80 |
| 3. Manuela Mager<br>Uwe Bewersdorff | GDR | 33 | 140.52 |
| 4. Marina Pestova<br>Stanislav Lednovich | SOV | 31 | 141.14 |
| 5. Caitlin Carruthers<br>Peter Carruthers | USA | 46 | 137.38 |
| 6. Sabine Baess<br>Tassilo Thierbach | GDR | 53 | 136.00 |
| 7. Sheryl Franks<br>Michael Botticelli | USA | 64 | 133.84 |
| 8. Christina Riegel<br>Andreas Nischwitz | GER | 71 | 129.36 |

In 1978 Irina Rodnina won her tenth straight world championship. She took off the following year to have a baby and, in her absence, the world title was won by two young people from Los Angeles, Tai Babilonia and Randy Gardner. Tai and Randy had been skating together for over eight years, since they were 10 and 12. The stage was set for a dramatic confrontation as Rodnina and Zaitsev attempted a comeback, while Tai and Randy tried to end the Soviet domination of pairs skating. Unfortunately, Randy Gardner suffered a groin injury prior to his arrival in Lake Placid. With a shot of lidocaine to kill the pain, Randy went out on the ice to warm up before the Olympic short program. But he fell four times, and the disappointed pair were forced to withdraw. Rodnina and Zaitsev skated flawlessly and, for the second straight time, won the first-place votes of all nine judges. Thus Rodnina matched the accomplishments of Sonja Henie by winning ten world championships and three Olympic gold medals.

**1984 Sarajevo** T: 15, N: 7, D: 2.12.

| | | ORDINALS |
|---|---|---|
| 1. Yelena Valova<br>Oleg Vasilyev | SOV | 1.4 |
| 2. Caitlin "Kitty" Carruthers<br>Peter Carruthers | USA | 2.8 |
| 3. Larissa Selezneva<br>Oleg Makarov | SOV | 3.8 |
| 4. Sabine Baess<br>Tassilo Thierbach | GDR | 5.6 |
| 5. Birgit Lorenz<br>Knut Schubert | GDR | 7.0 |

| 6. | Jill Watson<br>Burt Lancon | USA | 9.2 |
| 7. | Barbara Underhill<br>Paul Martini | CAN | 9.4 |
| 8. | Katerina Matousek<br>Lloyd Eisler | CAN | 11.6 |

Valova and Vasilyev were the unanimous choice of the nine judges. Peter and Kitty Carruthers were brother and sister, separately adopted by Charles and Maureen Carruthers of Burlington, Massachusetts.

**1988 Calgary** T: 15, N: 8, D: 2.16.

| | | | ORDINALS |
| --- | --- | --- | --- |
| 1. | Yekaterina Gordeyeva<br>Sergei Grinkov | SOV | 1.4 |
| 2. | Yelena Valova<br>Oleg Vasilyev | SOV | 2.8 |
| 3. | Jill Watson<br>Peter Oppegard | USA | 4.2 |
| 4. | Larissa Seleznova<br>Oleg Makarov | SOV | 6.4 |
| 5. | Gillian Wachsman<br>Todd Waggoner | USA | 6.6 |
| 6. | Denise Benning<br>Lyndon Johnston | CAN | 9.0 |
| 7. | Peggy Schwarz<br>Alexander König | GDR | 10.4 |
| 8. | Christine Hough<br>Doug Ladret | CAN | 11.2 |

The popular Katya Gordeyeva and her partner Sergei Grinkov were the only pair to complete their long program without a major error.

# ICE DANCE

Ice dance competitions consist of three parts. First the skaters perform three compulsory dances, which represent 30 percent of their final score. Then comes the original set pattern dance (20 percent) and finally the four-minute free dance, which accounts for 50 percent of the total.

**1924–1972** not held

**1976 Innsbruck** T: 18, N: 9, D: 2.9.

| | | | ORDINALS | PTS. |
| --- | --- | --- | --- | --- |
| 1. | Lyudmila Pakhomova<br>Aleksandr Gorshkov | SOV | 9 | 209.92 |
| 2. | Irina Moiseeva<br>Andrei Minenkov | SOV | 20 | 204.88 |
| 3. | Colleen O'Conner<br>James Millns | USA | 27 | 202.64 |
| 4. | Natalya Linichuk<br>Gennady Karponosov | SOV | 35 | 199.10 |
| 5. | Krisztina Regöczy<br>András Sallay | HUN | 48.5 | 195.92 |

| 6. | Matilde Ciccia<br>Lamberto Ceserani | ITA | 58.5 | 191.46 |
| 7. | Hilary Green<br>Glyn Watts | GBR | 57 | 191.40 |
| 8. | Janet Thompson<br>Warren Maxwell | GBR | 78 | 186.80 |

Five-time world champions Lyudmila Pakhomova and Aleksandr Gorshkov sat out the 1975 world championships while Gorshkov underwent an operation. He was completely recovered for the Olympics, and the husband-wife team from Moscow had little trouble captivating the judges and garnering all nine first-place votes.

**1980 Lake Placid** T: 12, N: 8, D: 2.19.

| | | | ORDINALS | PTS. |
| --- | --- | --- | --- | --- |
| 1. | Natalya Linichuk<br>Gennady Karponosov | SOV | 13 | 205.48 |
| 2. | Krisztina Regöczy<br>András Sallay | HUN | 14 | 204.52 |
| 3. | Irina Moiseeva<br>Andrei Minenkov | SOV | 27 | 201.86 |
| 4. | Liliana Rehakova<br>Stanislav Drastich | CZE | 39 | 198.02 |
| 5. | Jayne Torvill<br>Christopher Dean | GBR | 42 | 197.12 |
| 6. | Lorna Wighton<br>John Dowding | CAN | 54 | 193.80 |
| 7. | Judy Blumberg<br>Michael Seibert | USA | 66 | 190.30 |
| 8. | Natalia Bestemianova<br>Andrei Bukin | SOV | 75 | 188.38 |

The Soviet pair won a 5–4 decision over the Hungarians. The announcement of the results was greeted by catcalls and boos from the American audience, which preferred the lively, upbeat style of Regöczy and Sallay to the staid, traditional image of Linichuk and Karponosov.

**1984 Sarajevo** T: 19, N: 12, D: 2.14.

| | | | ORDINALS |
| --- | --- | --- | --- |
| 1. | Jayne Torvill<br>Christopher Dean | GBR | 2.0 |
| 2. | Natalya Bestemianova<br>Andrei Bukin | SOV | 4.0 |
| 3. | Marina Klimova<br>Sergei Ponomarenko | SOV | 7.0 |
| 4. | Judy Blumberg<br>Michael Seibert | USA | 7.0 |
| 5. | Carol Fox<br>Richard Dalley | USA | 10.6 |
| 6. | Karen Barber<br>Nicky Slater | GBR | 11.4 |
| 7. | Olga Volozhinskaya<br>Aleksandr Svinin | SOV | 14.6 |
| 8. | Tracy Wilson<br>Robert McCall | CAN | 15.4 |

The first time that the Nottingham City Council voted to grant £14,000 to Jayne Torvill and Christopher Dean to help them while they trained to become world champions, there were protests that the expenditure was a frivolous waste. Three world championships later, no one was complaining anymore as "T&D" had brought the town more glory than D.H. Lawrence, though not quite as much as Robin Hood.

Dean, a former police trainee, and Torvill, a former insurance clerk, brought to the discipline of ice-dancing a new level of greatness, which earned them the first perfect scores of 6.0 in the event's history. At Sarajevo they mesmerized the audience with their interpretation of Ravel's *Bolero,* receiving from the judges 12 6.0s out of 18 marks including across-the-board perfect scores for artistic impression.

**1988 Calgary** T: 20, N: 14, D: 2.23.

| | | ORDINALS |
|---|---|---|
| 1. Natalya Bestemianova<br>Andrei Boukin | SOV | 2.0 |
| 2. Marina Klimova<br>Sergei Ponomarenko | SOV | 4.0 |
| 3. Tracy Wilson<br>Robert McCall | CAN | 6.0 |
| 4. Natalya Annenko<br>Genrich Sretensky | SOV | 8.0 |
| 5. Kathrin Beck<br>Christoff Beck | AUT | 10.0 |
| 6. Suzanne Semanick<br>Scott Gregory | USA | 12.0 |
| 7. Klára Engi<br>Attila Tóth | HUN | 14.0 |
| 8. Isabelle Duchesnay<br>Paul Duchesnay | FRA | 16.0 |

As an athletic competition, the ice dancing tournament left much to be desired. The twenty teams were ranked in the same order in all three sections of the meet, except for the fifteenth- and fourteenth-placed pairs, who switched places after the compulsory dances.

## Discontinued Event
### SPECIAL FIGURES

**1908 London** C: 3, N: 2, D: 10.29.

| | | ORDINALS | PTS. |
|---|---|---|---|
| 1. Nikolai Panin (Kolomenkin) | RUS | 5 | 219 |
| 2. Arthur Cumming | GBR | 10 | 164 |
| 3. George Hall-Say | GBR | 15 | 104 |

The first Russian Olympic gold medal winner, 35-year-old Nikolai Kolomenkin, competed under a pseudonym, Nikolai Panin, a common practice among wealthy Russians for whom participation in sports was considered undignified. Four years later in Stockholm, Kolomenkin was a member of the Russian military revolver team, which finished in fourth place.

# SPEED SKATING

MEN
500 Meters
1000 Meters
1500 Meters
5000 Meters
10,000 Meters
Short Track: 1000 Meters
Short Track: 5000-Meter Relay
Discontinued Event

## MEN

### 500 METERS

In speed skating, the competitors skate against the clock, although they race in pairs.

**1924 Chamonix** C: 27, N: 10, D: 1.26. WR: 43.4 (Oscar Mathisen)

| | | |
|---|---|---|
| 1. Charles Jewtraw | USA | 44.0 |
| 2. Oskar Olsen | NOR | 44.2 |
| 3. Roald Larsen | NOR | 44.8 |
| 3. A. Clas Thunberg | FIN | 44.8 |
| 5. Asser Vallenius | FIN | 45.0 |
| 6. Axel Blomqvist | SWE | 45.2 |
| 7. Charles Gorman | CAN | 45.4 |
| 8. Joseph Moore | USA | 45.6 |
| 8. Harald Ström | NOR | 45.6 |

This was the first event to be decided in the first Olympic Winter Games. Figure skating and ice hockey competitions held prior to 1924 were incorporated in the regular Summer Games.

**1928 St. Moritz** C: 33, N: 14, D: 2.13. WR: 43.1 (Roald Larsen)

| | | | |
|---|---|---|---|
| 1. Bernt Evensen | NOR | 43.4 | OR |
| 1. A. Clas Thunberg | FIN | 43.4 | OR |
| 3. John O'Neil Farrell | USA | 43.6 | |
| 3. Jaako Friman | FIN | 43.6 | |
| 3. Roald Larsen | NOR | 43.6 | |
| 6. Håkon Pedersen | NOR | 43.8 | |
| 7. Charles Gorman | CAN | 43.9 | |
| 8. Bertel Backmann | FIN | 44.4 | |

**1932 Lake Placid** C: 16, N: 4, D: 2.4. WR: 42.6 (A. Clas Thunberg)

| | | | |
|---|---|---|---|
| 1. John Shea | USA | 43.4 | EOR |
| 2. Bernt Evensen | NOR | — | |
| 3. Alexander Hurd | CAN | — | |
| 4. Frank Stack | CAN | — | |
| 5. William Logan | CAN | — | |
| 6. John O'Neil Farrell | USA | — | |

In 1932 the speed skating competitions were held as actual races, with five or six men in a heat, rather than the usual way of two skaters at a time racing against the clock. This new method, known as the North American Rules, so outraged world record holder and five-time Olympic champion Clas Thunberg that he refused to participate. New York Governor Franklin D. Roosevelt officially opened the Third Olympic Winter Games on the morning of February 4. A local speed skater, 21-year-old Jack Shea, recited the Olympic oath on behalf of the 306 assembled athletes. A short time later the three qualifying heats were held for the 500 meters speed skating. Not surprisingly, five of six qualifiers were North Americans. Following the heats, the first period of the Canada–U.S.A. ice hockey game was played. Then came the 500 meters final. Shea tore into the lead and finished five yeards ahead of co-defending champion Bernt Evensen. Shea's victory was very popular, since he was a hometown boy from Lake Placid, as was 1924 winner Charles Jewtraw.

**1936 Garmisch-Partenkirchen** C: 36, N: 14, D: 2.11. WR: 42.4 (Allan Potts)

| | | | |
|---|---|---|---|
| 1. Ivar Ballangrud | NOR | 43.4 | EOR |
| 2. George Krog | NOR | 43.5 | |
| 3. Leo Freisinger | USA | 44.0 | |
| 4. Shozo Ishihara | JPN | 44.1 | |
| 5. Delbert Lamb | USA | 44.2 | |
| 6. Karl Leban | AUT | 44.8 | |
| 6. Allan Potts | USA | 44.8 | |
| 8. Antero Ojala | FIN | 44.9 | |
| 8. Jorma Ruissalo | FIN | 44.9 | |
| 8. Birger Vasenius | FIN | 44.9 | |

**1948 St. Moritz** C: 42, N: 15, D: 1.31. WR: 41.8 (Hans Engnestangen)

| | | | |
|---|---|---|---|
| 1. Finn Helgesen | NOR | 43.1 | OR |
| 2. Kenneth Bartholomew | USA | 43.2 | |
| 2. Thomas Byberg | NOR | 43.2 | |
| 2. Robert Fitzgerald | USA | 43.2 | |
| 5. Kenneth Henry | USA | 43.3 | |
| 6. Sverre Farstad | NOR | 43.6 | |
| 6. Torodd Hauer | NOR | 43.6 | |
| 6. Delbert Lamb | USA | 43.6 | |
| 6. Frank Stack | CAN | 43.6 | |

**1952 Oslo** C: 41, N: 14, D: 2.16. WR: 41.2 (Yuri Sergeev)

| | | |
|---|---|---|
| 1. Kenneth Henry | USA | 43.2 |
| 2. Donald McDermott | USA | 43.9 |
| 3. Gordon Audley | CAN | 44.0 |
| 3. Arne Johansen | NOR | 44.0 |
| 5. Finn Helgesen | NOR | 44.0 |
| 6. Hroar Elvenes | NOR | 44.1 |
| 6. Kiyotaka Takabayashi | JPN | 44.1 |
| 8. Gerardus Maarse | HOL | 44.2 |
| 8. Toivo Salonen | FIN | 44.2 |

The Norwegian Skating Union chose as one of their four entrants in this race Finn Hodt, who had served a sentence for collaborating with the Nazis, and who had gone so far as to fight for the Germans on the Eastern Front. One month before the Oslo Games, the Norwegian Olympic committee overruled the Skating Union, voting 25–2 to ban Hodt and all other collaborators from representing Norway in the Oslo Olympics.

**1956 Cortina** C: 47, N: 17, D: 1.28. WR: 40.2 (Yevgeny Grishin)

| | | | |
|---|---|---|---|
| 1. Yevgeny Grishin | SOV | 40.2 | EWR |
| 2. Rafael Gratch | SOV | 40.8 | |
| 3. Alv Gjestvang | NOR | 41.0 | |
| 4. Yuri Sergeev | SOV | 41.1 | |
| 5. Toivo Salonen | FIN | 41.7 | |
| 6. William Carow | USA | 41.8 | |
| 7. Malmsten Bengt | SWE | 41.9 | |
| 7. Colin Hickey | AUS | 41.9 | |

**1960 Squaw Valley** C: 46, N: 15, D: 2.24. WR: 40.2 (Yevgeny Grishin)

| | | | |
|---|---|---|---|
| 1. Yevgeny Grishin | SOV | 40.2 | EWR |
| 2. William Disney | USA | 40.3 | |
| 3. Rafael Gratch | SOV | 40.4 | |
| 4. Hans Wilhelmsson | SWE | 40.5 | |
| 5. Gennady Voronin | SOV | 40.7 | |
| 6. Alv Gjestvang | NOR | 40.8 | |
| 7. Richard "Terry" McDermott | USA | 40.9 | |
| 7. Toivo Salonen | FIN | 40.9 | |

Grishin's time was remarkable, considering that he stumbled and skidded in the homestretch, losing at least a second.

**1964 Innsbruck** C: 44, N: 19, D: 2.4. WR: 39.5 (Yevgeny Grishin)

| | | | |
|---|---|---|---|
| 1. Richard "Terry" McDermott | USA | 40.1 | OR |
| 2. Alv Gjestvang | NOR | 40.6 | |
| 2. Yevgeny Grishin | SOV | 40.6 | |
| 2. Vladimir Orlov | SOV | 40.6 | |
| 5. Keiichi Suzuki | JPN | 40.7 | |
| 6. Edward Rudolph | USA | 40.9 | |
| 7. Heike Hedlund | FIN | 41.0 | |
| 8. William Disney | USA | 41.1 | |
| 8. Villy Haugen | NOR | 41.1 | |

Terry McDermott, a 23-year-old barber from Essexville, Michigan, stunned the skating world with his surprise victory, the only U.S. gold medal of the 1964 Winter Games. McDermott used skates that he had borrowed from the U.S. coach, Leo Freisinger. He also got some help from Mrs. Freisinger. When Lydia Skoblikova won four speed skating gold medals in 1964, she wore a good-luck pin that had been given to her by Mrs. Freisinger. McDermott heard about this story and asked the coach's wife if he too could have such a pin. Freisinger gave McDermott her last pin, and he put it to good use. In 1968 Dianne Holum also received a Freisinger pin, although she didn't win her gold medal until 1972.

**1968 Grenoble** C: 48, N: 17, D; 2.14. WR: 39.2 (Erhard Keller)

| | | |
|---|---|---|
| 1. Erhard Keller | GER | 40.3 |
| 2. Richard "Terry" McDermott | USA | 40.5 |
| 2. Magne Thomassen | NOR | 40.5 |
| 4. Yevgeny Grishin | SOV | 40.6 |
| 5. Neil Blatchford | USA | 40.7 |
| 5. Arne Herjuaunet | NOR | 40.7 |
| 5. John Wurster | USA | 40.7 |
| 8. Seppo Hänninen | FIN | 40.8 |
| 8. Haakan Holmgren | SWE | 40.8 |
| 8. Keiichi Suzuki | JPN | 40.8 |

In 1968 McDermott had the misfortune of being drawn in the last of 24 pairs on ice that had been badly melted by the sun. Keller, a dental student from Munich, was a gracious winner. He said of McDermott, "What he did today was just sheer guts. If he had started in the earlier heats while the ice was still good, I'd have lost. It's as simple as that."

**1972 Sapporo** C: 37, N: 16, D: 2.5. WR: 38.0 (Leo Linkovesi)

| | | | |
|---|---|---|---|
| 1. Erhard Keller | GER | 39.44 | OR |
| 2. Hasse Börjes | SWE | 39.69 | |
| 3. Valery Muratov | SOV | 39.80 | |
| 4. Per Björang | NOR | 39.91 | |
| 5. Seppo Hänninen | FIN | 40.12 | |
| 6. Leo Linkovesi | FIN | 40.14 | |
| 7. Ove Konig | SWE | 40.25 | |
| 8. Masaki Suzuki | JPN | 40.35 | |

This was the only one of the 1972 men's skating races that wasn't won by Ard Schenk, who fell after four steps and finished 34th.

**1976 Innsbruck** C: 29, N: 15, D: 2.10. WR: 37.00 (Yevgeny Kulikov)

| | | | |
|---|---|---|---|
| 1. Yevgeny Kulikov | SOV | 39.17 | OR |
| 2. Valery Muratov | SOV | 39.25 | |
| 3. Daniel Immerfall | USA | 39.54 | |
| 4. Mats Wallberg | SWE | 39.56 | |
| 5. Peter Mueller | USA | 39.57 | |
| 6. Jan Bazen | HOL | 39.78 | |
| 6. Arnulf Sunde | NOR | 39.78 | |
| 8. Andrei Malikov | SOV | 39.85 | |

**1980 Lake Placid** C: 37, N: 18, D: 2.15. WR: 37.00 (Yevgeny Kulikov)

| | | | |
|---|---|---|---|
| 1. Eric Heiden | USA | 38.03 | OR |
| 2. Yevgeny Kulikov | SOV | 38.37 | |
| 3. Lieuwe de Boer | HOL | 38.48 | |

| 4. | Frode Rönning | NOR | 38.66 |
|---|---|---|---|
| 5. | Daniel Immerfall | USA | 38.69 |
| 6. | Jarle Pedersen | NOR | 38.83 |
| 7. | Anatoly Medennikov | SOV | 38.88 |
| 8. | Gaétan Boucher | CAN | 38.90 |

As a 17-year-old, Eric Heiden had competed in the 1976 Olympics in Innsbruck, finishing seventh in the 1500 and 19th in the 5000. Thus it came as quite a shock the following year when he seemingly appeared from nowhere to win the overall title at the 1977 world championships. His victory was so unexpected that even Heiden wondered if his performance might have been a fluke. It wasn't. He successfully defended his world title in 1978 and 1979, and became a national hero—not in his native country, the United States, but in Norway and the Netherlands, where speed skating is taken more seriously.

The 1980 Olympics began with Heiden the favorite in all five men's speed skating events. If there was one distance at which he was thought to be shaky, it was the 500. A week earlier Heiden had lost at 500 meters to teammate Tom Plant at the world speed skating sprint championship. At Lake Placid Heiden was paired against world record holder Yevgeny Kulikov. The two favorites were the first pair to skate. Kulikov was slightly ahead at 100 meters, but they raced neck and neck most of the way. Coming out of the last curve, Kulikov slipped slightly and Heiden, who had a 32-inch waist but 27-inch thighs, pulled ahead and won.

**1984 Sarajevo** C: 42, N: 20, D: 2.10. WR: 36.57 (Pavel Pegov)

| 1. | Sergei Fokichev | SOV | 38.19 |
|---|---|---|---|
| 2. | Yoshihiro Kitazawa | JPN | 38.30 |
| 3. | Gaétan Boucher | CAN | 38.39 |
| 4. | Dan Jansen | USA | 38.55 |
| 5. | K. Nick Thometz | USA | 38.56 |
| 6. | Vladimir Kozlov | SOV | 38.57 |
| 7. | Frode Rönning | NOR | 38.58 |
| 8. | Uwe-Jens Mey | GDR | 38.65 |

Fokichev's victory was a total surprise. He had not previously competed in a major international meet and was not even considered by pre-meet prognosticators.

**1988 Calgary** C: 37, N: 15, D: 2.14. WR: 36.55 (K. Nick Thometz)

| 1. | Uwe-Jens Mey | GDR | 36.45 | WR |
|---|---|---|---|---|
| 2. | Jan Ykema | HOL | 36.76 | |
| 3. | Akira Kuroiwa | JPN | 36.77 | |
| 4. | Sergei Fokichev | SOV | 36.82 | |
| 5. | Bae Ki-tae | KOR | 36.90 | |
| 6. | Igor Zhelezovsky | SOV | 36.94 | |
| 7. | Guy Thibault | CAN | 36.96 | |
| 8. | K. Nick Thometz | USA | 37.16 | |

One of the favorites was Dan Jansen of West Allis, Wisconsin, who won the World Sprint Championship held in his hometown one week before the Olympics. At 6:00 a.m. on the day of the 500-meter event, Jansen received a phone call informing him that his sister, Jane Beres, was about to succumb to the leukemia she had been fighting

for over a year. Dan spoke to her and although she could not respond, she indicated to him through another brother who was with her that she wanted Dan to remain in Calgary and compete. At noon, Dan Jansen learned that his sister had died less than three hours after he had spoken to her. At 5:00 p.m. he was on the ice, preparing for his race. After false starting, he took off quickly, but at the first turn he slipped and fell, just as he had at the World Cup meet on the same track two months earlier. Four days later, Jansen took part in the 1000-meter race but fell again.

# 1000 METERS

**1924–1972** not held

**1976 Innsbruck** C: 31, N: 16, 2.12. WR: 1:16.92 (Valery Muratov)

| 1. | Peter Mueller | USA | 1:19.32 |
|---|---|---|---|
| 2. | Jörn Didriksen | NOR | 1:20.45 |
| 3. | Valery Muratov | SOV | 1:20.57 |
| 4. | Aleksandr Safronov | SOV | 1:20.84 |
| 5. | Hans van Helden | HOL | 1:20.85 |
| 6. | Gaétan Boucher | CAN | 1:21.23 |
| 7. | Mats Wallberg | SWE | 1:21.27 |
| 8. | Pertti Niittylae | FIN | 1:21.43 |

**1980 Lake Placid** C: 41, N: 19, D: 2.19. WR: 1:13.60 (Eric Heiden)

| 1. | Eric Heiden | USA | 1:15.18 | OR |
|---|---|---|---|---|
| 2. | Gaétan Boucher | CAN | 1:16.68 | |
| 3. | Vladimir Lobanov | SOV | 1:16.91 | |
| 3. | Frode Rönning | NOR | 1:16.91 | |
| 5. | Peter Mueller | USA | 1:17.11 | |
| 6. | Bert de Jong | HOL | 1:17.29 | |
| 7. | Andreas Dietel | GDR | 1:17.71 | |
| 8. | Oloph Granath | SWE | 1:17.74 | |

Boucher had the good fortune to be skating first, paired against Eric Heiden. The silver medals in the three shortest races in 1980 were won by whoever was paired with Heiden.

**1984 Sarajevo** C: 43, N: 20, D: 2.14. WR: 1:12.58 (Pavel Pegov)

| 1. | Gaétan Boucher | CAN | 1:15.80 |
|---|---|---|---|
| 2. | Sergei Khlebnikov | SOV | 1:16.63 |
| 3. | Kai Arne Engelstad | NOR | 1:16.75 |
| 4. | K. Nick Thometz | USA | 1:16.85 |
| 5. | André Hoffmann | GDR | 1:17.33 |
| 6. | Viktor Chacherin | SOV | 1:17.42 |
| 7. | Andreas Dietel | GDR | 1:17.46 |
| 7. | Hilbert van der Duim | HOL | 1:17.46 |

**1988 Calgary** C: 40, N: 16, D: 2.18. WR: 1:12.58 (Pavel Pegov)

| 1. | Nikolai Gulyaev | SOV | 1:13.03 | OR |
|---|---|---|---|---|
| 2. | Uwe-Jens Mey | GDR | 1:13.11 | |
| 3. | Igor Zhelezovsky | SOV | 1:13.19 | |
| 4. | Eric Flaim | USA | 1:13.53 | |
| 5. | Gaétan Boucher | CAN | 1:13.77 | |
| 6. | Michael Hadschieff | AUT | 1:13.84 | |
| 7. | Guy Thibault | CAN | 1:14.16 | |
| 8. | Peter Adeberg | GDR | 1:14.19 | |

Two months before the Olympics, Gulyaev was caught passing a packet of anabolic steroids to a Norwegian skater. Gulyaev claimed that the packet had been given to him by a Soviet trainer and that he was unaware of its contents. The I.O.C. and the International Skating Union, although skeptical of his account, were unable to uncover evidence to disprove it. Two days before the Opening Ceremonies, Gulyaev was cleared to compete.

## 1500 METERS

**1924 Chamonix** C: 22, N: 9, D: 1.27. WR: 2:17.4 (Oscar Mathisen)
| | | |
|---|---|---|
| 1. A. Clas Thunberg | FIN | 2:20.8 |
| 2. Roald Larsen | NOR | 2:22.0 |
| 3. Sigurd Moen | NOR | 2:25.6 |
| 4. Julius Skutnabb | FIN | 2:26.6 |
| 5. Harald Ström | NOR | 2:29.0 |
| 6. Oskar Olsen | NOR | 2:29.2 |
| 7. Harry Kaskey | USA | 2:29.8 |
| 8. Charles Jewtraw | USA | 2:31.6 |
| 8. Joseph Moore | USA | 2:31.6 |

In 1924 30-year-old A. Clas Thunberg won three gold medals, one silver, and one bronze. Four years later he followed up with two more gold medals.

**1928 St. Moritz** C: 30, N: 14, D: 2.14. WR: 2:17.4 (Oscar Mathisen)
| | | |
|---|---|---|
| 1. A. Clas Thunberg | FIN | 2:21.1 |
| 2. Bernt Evensen | NOR | 2:21.9 |
| 3. Ivar Ballangrud | NOR | 2:22.6 |
| 4. Roald Larsen | NOR | 2:25.3 |
| 5. Edward Murphy | USA | 2:25.9 |
| 6. Valentine Bialas | USA | 2:26.3 |
| 7. Irving Jaffee | USA | 2:26.7 |
| 8. John Farrell | USA | 2:26.8 |

**1932 Lake Placid** C: 18, N: 6, D: 2.5. WR: 2:17.4 (Oscar Mathisen)
| | | |
|---|---|---|
| 1. John Shea | USA | 2:57.5 |
| 2. Alexander Hurd | CAN | — |
| 3. William Logan | CAN | — |
| 4. Frank Stack | CAN | — |
| 5. Raymond Murray | USA | — |
| 6. Herbert Taylor | USA | — |

American officials, having already irritated the foreign teams with their strange mass starts, left them completely exasperated with a ruling in the second heat. In the middle of the race the judges suddenly stopped the contest, accused the skaters of "loafing," and ordered the race rerun. In the final Taylor was leading, but he lost his balance coming out of the last turn and tumbled across the track into a snowbank. Shea found himself in first place and crossed the finish line eight yards ahead of Hurd.

**1936 Garmisch-Partenkirchen** C: 37, N: 15, D: 2.13. WR: 2:17.4 (Oscar Mathisen)
| | | | |
|---|---|---|---|
| 1. Charles Mathisen | NOR | 2:19.2 | OR |
| 2. Ivar Ballangrud | NOR | 2:20.2 | |
| 3. Birger Wasenius | FIN | 2:20.9 | |
| 4. Leo Freisinger | USA | 2:21.3 | |
| 5. Max Stiepl | AUT | 2:21.6 | |
| 6. Karl Wazulek | AUT | 2:22.2 | |
| 7. Harry Haraldsen | NOR | 2:22.4 | |
| 8. Hans Engnestangen | NOR | 2:23.0 | |

A brief note about the world record: Oscar Mathisen of Norway first broke the world record for the 1500 meters in 1908. By January 11, 1914 he had lowered his time to 2:19.4. One week later, in Davos, Switzerland, he skated a 2:17.4. This time remained a world record for 23 years, until Michael Staksrud, also skating at Davos, recorded a 2:14.9. Mathisen's performance was only bettered twice in the 38 years between 1914 and 1952.

**1948 St. Moritz** C: 45, N: 14, D: 2.2. WR: 2:13.8 (Hans Engnestangen)
| | | | |
|---|---|---|---|
| 1. Sverre Farstad | NOR | 2:17.6 | OR |
| 2. Åke Seyffarth | SWE | 2:18.1 | |
| 3. Odd Lundberg | NOR | 2:18.9 | |
| 4. Lauri Parkkinen | FIN | 2:19.6 | |
| 5. Gustav Harry Jansson | SWE | 2:20.0 | |
| 6. John Werket | USA | 2:20.2 | |
| 7. Kalevi Laitinen | FIN | 2:20.3 | |
| 8. Gothe Hedlund | SWE | 2:20.7 | |

Farstad was a 27-year-old cartoonist.

**1952 Oslo** C: 39, N: 13, D: 2.18. WR: 2:12.9 (Valentin Chaikin)
| | | |
|---|---|---|
| 1. Hjalmar Andersen | NOR | 2:20.4 |
| 2. Willem van der Voort | HOL | 2:20.6 |
| 3. Roald Aas | NOR | 2:21.6 |
| 4. Carl-Erik Asplund | SWE | 2:22.6 |
| 5. Cornelis "Kees" Broekman | HOL | 2:22.8 |
| 6. Lauri Parkkinen | FIN | 2:23.0 |
| 7. Kauko Salomaa | FIN | 2:23.3 |
| 8. Sigvard Ericsson | SWE | 2:23.4 |

**1956 Cortina** C: 54, N: 18, D: 1.30. WR: 2:09.1 (Yuri Mikhailov)
| | | | |
|---|---|---|---|
| 1. Yevgeny Grishin | SOV | 2:08.6 | WR |
| 1. Yuri Mikhailov | SOV | 2:08.6 | WR |
| 3. Toivo Salonen | FIN | 2:09.4 | |
| 4. Juhani Järvinen | FIN | 2:09.7 | |
| 5. Robert Merkulov | SOV | 2:10.3 | |
| 6. Sigvard Ericsson | SWE | 2:11.0 | |
| 7. Colin Hickey | AUT | 2:11.8 | |
| 8. Boris Shilkov | SOV | 2:11.9 | |

**1960 Squaw Valley** C: 48, N: 16, D: 2.26. WR: 2:06.3 (Juhani Järvinen)
| | | |
|---|---|---|
| 1. Roald Aas | NOR | 2:10.4 |
| 1. Yevgeny Grishin | SOV | 2:10.4 |

3. Boris Stenin          SOV   2:11.5
4. Jouko Jokinen         FIN   2:12.0
5. Per Olov Brogren      SWE   2:13.1
5. Juhani Järvinen       FIN   2:13.1
7. Toivo Salonen         FIN   2:13.2
8. André Kouprianoff     FRA   2:13.3

Grishin registered his second straight tie for first place at 1500 meters and collected his fourth Olympic gold medal. In 1952 he had also competed as a cyclist.

**1964 Innsbruck** C: 54, N: 21, D: 2.6. WR: 2:06.3 (Juhani Järvinen)
1. Ants Antson           SOV   2:10.3
2. Cornelis "Kees" Verkerk  HOL  2:10.6
3. Villy Haugen          NOR   2:11.2
4. Jouko Launonen        FIN   2:11.9
5. Lev Zaitsev           SOV   2:12.1
6. Ivar Eriksen          NOR   2:12.2
6. Edouard Matoussevich  SOV   2:12.2
8. Juhani Järvinen       FIN   2:12.4

**1968 Grenoble** C: 53, N: 18, D: 2.16. WR: 2:02.5 (Magne Thomassen)
1. Cornelis "Kees" Verkerk  HOL  2:03.4  OR
2. Ivar Eriksen          NOR   2:05.0
2. Adrianus "Ard" Schenk HOL   2:05.0
4. Magne Thomassen       NOR   2:05.1
5. Johnny Höglin         SWE   2:05.2
5. Björn Tveter          NOR   2:05.2
7. S. Erik Stiansen      NOR   2:05.5
8. Edouard Matoussevitch SOV   2:06.1

Kees Verkerk was a 25-year-old bartender from the village of Putteshoak who also played the trumpet on a Dutch television show.

**1972 Sapporo** C: 39, N: 16, D: 2.6. WR: 1:58.7 (Adrianus "Ard" Schenk)
1. Adrianus "Ard" Schenk HOL   2:02.96  OR
2. Roar Grönvold         NOR   2:04.26
3. Göran Claesson        SWE   2:05.89
4. Björn Tveter          NOR   2:05.94
5. Jan Dols              HOL   2:06.58
6. Valery Lavrouchkin    SOV   2:07.16
7. Daniel Carroll        USA   2:07.24
8. Cornelis "Kees" Verkerk  HOL  2:07.43

**1976 Innsbruck** C: 30, N: 19, D: 2.13. WR: 1:58.7 (Adrianus "Ard" Schenk)
1. Jan Egil Storholt     NOR   1:59.38  OR
2. Yuri Kondakov         SOV   1:59.97
3. Hans van Helden       HOL   2:00.87
4. Sergei Riabev         SOV   2:02.15
5. Daniel Carroll        USA   2:02.26
6. Piet Kleine           HOL   2:02.28
7. Eric Heiden           USA   2:02.40
8. Colin Coates          AUS   2:03.34

Storholt, an electrician from Trondheim, celebrated his 27th birthday the day he won the gold medal.

**1980 Lake Placid** C: 36, N: 16, D: 2.21. WR: 1:54.79 (Eric Heiden)
1. Eric Heiden           USA   1:55.44  OR
2. Kai Arne Stenshjemmet NOR   1:56.81
3. Terje Andersen        NOR   1:56.92
4. Andreas Dietel        GDR   1:57.14
5. Yuri Kondakov         SOV   1:57.36
6. Jan Egil Storholt     NOR   1:57.95
7. Tomas Gustafson       SWE   1:58.18
8. Vladimir Lobanov      SOV   1:59.38

Midway through his race against Stenshjemmet, Heiden almost fell when he hit a rut in the ice. But he was able to steady himself before he had lost more than a few hundredths of a second, and he went on to win his fourth gold medal.

**1984 Sarajevo** C: 40, N: 20, D: 2.16. WR: 1:54.26 (Igor Zhelezovsky)
1. Gaétan Boucher        CAN   1:58.36
2. Sergei Khlebnikov     SOV   1:58.83
3. Oleg Bozhyev          SOV   1:58.89
4. Hans van Helden       FRA   1:59.39
5. Andreas Ehrig         GDR   1:59.41
6. Andreas Dietel        GDR   1:59.73
7. Hilbert van der Duim  HOL   1:59.77
8. Viktor Chacherin      SOV   1:59.81

Boucher, a 25-year-old marketing student from St. Hubert, Quebec, left Sarajevo with two gold medals and one bronze. He had already won a silver in the 1000 meters in 1980.

**1988 Calgary** C: 40, N: 20, D: 2.20. WR: 1:52.50 (Igor Zhelezovsky)
1. André Hoffmann        GDR   1:52.06  WR
2. Eric Flaim            USA   1:52.12
3. Michael Hadschieff    AUT   1:52.31
4. Igor Zhelezovsky      SOV   1:52.63
5. Toru Aoyanagi         JPN   1:52.85
6. Aleksandr Klimov      SOV   1:52.97
7. Nikolai Gulyaev       SOV   1:53.04
8. Peter Adeberg         GDR   1:53.57

## 5000 METERS

**1924 Chamonix** C: 22, N: 10, D: 1.26. WR: 8:26.5 (Harald Ström)
1. A. Clas Thunberg      FIN   8:39.0
2. Julius Skutnabb       FIN   8:48.4
3. Roald Larsen          NOR   8:50.2
4. Sigurd Moen           NOR   8:51.0
5. Harald Ström          NOR   8:54.6
6. Valentine Bialas      USA   8:55.0
7. Edvin Paulsen         NOR   8:59.0
8. Richard Donovan       USA   9:05.3

Thunberg won the first of his five Olympic gold medals.

**1928 St. Moritz** C: 33, N: 14, D: 2.13. WR: 8:26.5 (Harald Ström)
1. Ivar Ballangrud        NOR    8:50.5
2. Julius Skutnabb        FIN    8:59.1
3. Bernt Evensen          NOR    9:01.1
4. Irving Jaffee          USA    9:01.3
5. Armand Carlsen         NOR    9:01.5
6. Valentine Bialas       USA    9:06.3
7. Michael Staksrud       NOR    9:07.3
8. Otto Polacsek          AUT    9:08.9

This was the first of Ballangrud's seven Olympic medals.

**1932 Lake Placid** C: 18, N: 6, D: 2.4. WR: 8:21.6 (Ivar Ballangrud)
1. Irving Jaffee          USA    9:40.8
2. Edward Murphy          USA    —
3. William Logan          CAN    —
4. Herbert Taylor         USA    —
5. Ivar Ballangrud        NOR    —
6. Bernt Evensen          NOR    —
7. Frank Stack            CAN    —
8. C. Harry Smyth         CAN    —

**1936 Garmisch–Partenkirchen** C: 37, N: 16, D: 2.12. WR: 8:17.2 (Ivar Ballangrud)
1. Ivar Ballangrud        NOR    8:19.6   OR
2. Birger Vasenius        FIN    8:23.3
3. Antero Ojala           FIN    8:30.1
4. Jan Langedijk          HOL    8:32.0
5. Max Stiepl             AUT    8:35.0
6. Ossi Blomqvist         FIN    8:36.6
7. Charles Mathisen       NOR    8:36.9
8. Karl Wazulek           AUT    8:38.4

**1948 St. Moritz** C: 40, N: 14, D: 2.1. WR: 8:13.7 (Åke Seyffarth)
1. Reidar Liaklev         NOR    8:29.4
2. Odd Lundberg           NOR    8:32.7
3. Göthe Hedlund          SWE    8:34.8
4. Gustav Jansson         SWE    8:34.9
5. Jan Langedijk          HOL    8:36.2
6. Cornelis "Kees" Broekman  HOL  8:37.3
7. Åke Seyffarth          SWE    8:37.9
8. Pentti Lammio          FIN    8:40.7

Åke Seyffarth, who had set the world record seven years earlier, lost precious seconds on the final lap when he brushed against a photographer who had jumped onto the ice to take a picture.

**1952 Oslo** C: 35, N: 13, D: 2.17. WR: 8:03.7 (Nikolai Mamonov)
1. Hjalmar Andersen       NOR    8:10.6   OR
2. Cornelis "Kees" Broekman  HOL  8:21.6
3. Sverre Haugli          NOR    8:22.4
4. Anton Huiskes          HOL    8:28.5
5. Willem van der Voort   HOL    8:30.6
6. Carl-Erik Asplund      SWE    8:30.7
7. Pentti Lammio          FIN    8:31.9
8. Arthur Mannsbarth      AUT    8:36.2

Spurred on by a standing ovation from the crowd of 24,000, 28-year-old truck driver Hjalmar Andersen achieved the largest winning margin in the history of the 5000 meters.

**1956 Cortina** C: 46, N: 17, D: 1.29. WR: 7:45.6 (Boris Shilkov)
1. Boris Shilkov          SOV    7:48.7   OR
2. Sigvard Ericsson       SWE    7:56.7
3. Oleg Goncharenko       SOV    7:57.5
4. Willem de Graaf        HOL    8:00.2
4. Cornelis "Kees" Broekman  HOL  8:00.2
6. Roald Aas             NOR    8:01.6
7. Olof Dahlberg          SWE    8:01.8
8. Knut Johannesen        NOR    8:02.3

**1960 Squaw Valley** C: 37, N: 15, D: 2.25. WR: 7:45.6 (Boris Shilkov)
1. Viktor Kosichkin       SOV    7:51.3
2. Knut Johannesen        NOR    8:00.8
3. Jan Pesman             HOL    8:05.1
4. Torstein Seiersten     NOR    8:05.3
5. Valery Kotov           SOV    8:05.4
6. Oleg Goncharenko       SOV    8:06.6
7. Ivar Nilsson           SWE    8:09.1
7. Keijo Tapiovaara       FIN    8:09.1

**1964 Innsbruck** C: 44, N: 19, D: 2.5. WR: 7:34.3 (Jonny Nilsson)
1. Knut Johannesen        NOR    7:38.4   OR
2. Per Ivar Moe           NOR    7:38.6
3. Fred Anton Maier       NOR    7:42.0
4. Victor Kosichkin       SOV    7:45.8
5. Herman Strutz          AUT    7:48.3
6. Jonny Nilsson          SWE    7:48.4
7. Ivar Nilsson           SWE    7:49.0
8. Rutgerus Liebrechts    HOL    7:50.9

Skating in the fifth pair, 19-year-old Per Ivar Moe recorded the second-fastest 5000 meters ever. Then he watched as Olympic veteran Knut Johannesen assaulted his time as part of the 14th pair. With five of 12½ laps to go, Johannesen was three seconds behind Moe's pace. But he caught up with two laps left and pushed for the finish with the crowd on its feet, rooting him on. Unfortunately, as he crossed the finish line, the clock stopped at 7:38.7—one-tenth of a second slower than Moe. But then the scoreboard was revised to match the official time—7:38.4—and Johannesen had won his second gold medal. Between 1956 and 1964 he won two gold, two silver, and one bronze.

**1968 Grenoble** C: 38, N: 17, D: 2.15. WR: 7:26.2. (Fred Anton Maier)
1. Fred Anton Maier       NOR    7:22.4   WR
2. Cornelis "Kees" Verkerk  HOL   7:23.2
3. Petrus Nottet          HOL    7:25.5
4. Per-Willy Guttormsen   NOR    7:27.8
5. Johnny Höglin          SWE    7:32.7
6. Örjan Sandler          SWE    7:32.8

7. Jonny Nilsson     SWE   7:32.9
8. Jan Bols          HOL   7:33.1

Verkerk broke Maier's world record by three seconds and then watched as the 29-year-old clerk won it back 20 minutes later.

**1972 Sapporo** C: 28, N: 14, D: 2.4. WR: 7:12.0 (Adrianus "Ard" Schenk)

1. Adrianus "Ard" Schenk   HOL   7:23.61
2. Roar Grönvold        NOR   7:28.18
3. Sten Stensen         NOR   7:33.39
4. Göran Claeson       SWE   7:36.17
5. Willy Olsen          NOR   7:36.47
6. Cornelis "Kees" Verkerk   HOL   7:39.17
7. Valery Lavrouchkin    SOV   7:39.26
8. Jan Bols           HOL   7:39.40

Schenk skated first, while it was snowing, but he still managed to outstrip the field.

**1976 Innsbruck** C: 31, N: 17, D: 2.11. WR: 7.07.82 (Hans van Helden)

1. Sten Stensen       NOR   7:24.48
2. Piet Kleine         HOL   7:26.47
3. Hans van Helden    HOL   7:26.54
4. Victor Varlamov     SOV   7:30.97
5. Klaus Wunderlich   GDR   7:33.82
6. Daniel Carroll       USA   7:36.46
7. Vladimir Ivanov     SOV   7:37.73
8. Örjan Sandler      SWE   7:39.69

**1980 Lake Placid** C: 29, N: 15, D: 2.16. WR: 6.56.9 (Kai Arne Stenshjemmet)

1. Eric Heiden           USA   7:02.29   OR
2. Kai Arne Stenshjemmet   NOR   7:03.28
3. Tom-Erik Oxholm     NOR   7:05.59
4. Hilbert van der Duim   HOL   7:07.97
5. Öyvind Tveter       NOR   7:08.36
6. Piet Kleine         HOL   7:08.96
7. Michael Woods      USA   7:10.39
8. Ulf Ekstrand       SWE   7:13.13

Stenshjemmet, skating two pairs after Eric Heiden, stayed ahead of his pace for ten and a half laps, but began his arm swinging too early and couldn't keep it up. It was Heiden's second gold medal.

**1984 Sarajevo** C: 42, N: 20, D: 2.12. WR: 6:54.66 (Aleksandr Baranov)

1. S. Tomas Gustafson   SWE   7:12.28
2. Igor Malkov         SOV   7:12.30
3. René Schöfisch      GDR   7:17.49
4. Andreas Ehrig       GDR   7:17.63
5. Oleg Bogzhyev      SOV   7:17.96
6. Pertti Niittylä       FIN   7:17.97
7. Bjorn Nyland       NOR   7:18.27
8. Werner Jaeger      AUT   7:18.61

Skating in the first pair, Gustafson, who had trained in Wisconsin with Diane Holum and Eric Heiden, came off the ice thinking his time would be good enough for fifth or sixth place. Three pairs later, Malkov, not realizing how close he was to Gustafson's time, faded in the last 400 meters and lost by one-fiftieth of a second.

**1988 Calgary** C: 38, N: 18, D: 2.17. WR: 6:43.59 (Geir Karlstad)

1. S. Tomas Gustafson   SWE   6:44.63   OR
2. Leo Visser          HOL   6:44.98
3. Gerard Kemkers     HOL   6:45.92
4. Eric Flaim          USA   6:47.09
5. Michael Hadschieff   AUT   6:48.72
6. David Silk           USA   6:49.95
7. Geir Karlstad       NOR   6:50.88
8. Roland Freier       GDR   6:51.42

Defending champion Tomas Gustafson, skating seven pairs after Leo Visser, was eight tenths of a second behind Visser's pace with 400 meters to go. The public-address announcer informed the audience that Gustafson was going for the silver or bronze medal. But the 28-year-old Swede, who had struggled through knee surgery, meningitis, and the death of his father since his last Olympic victory, had set his sights higher. "How do you describe happiness?" he said afterward. "I'd have to write a poem."

## 10,000 METERS

**1924 Chamonix** C: 16, N: 6, D: 1.27. WR: 17:22.6 (Oscar Mathisen)

1. Julius Skutnabb     FIN   18:04.8
2. A. Clas Thunberg   FIN   18:07.8
3. Roald Larsen       NOR   18:12.2
4. Fritjof Paulsen      NOR   18:13.0
5. Harald Ström       NOR   18:18.6
6. Sigurd Moen       NOR   18:19.0
7. Léon Quaglia       FRA   18:25.0
8. Valentine Bialas    USA   18:34.0

Skutnabb defeated Thunberg head-on, since they were paired together. This reversed the order of finish of the 5000, which had been held the previous day.

**1928 St. Moritz** C: 10, N: 6, D: 2.14. WR: 17:17.4 (Armand Carlsen)

1. Irving Jaffee       USA   18:36.5
2. Bernt Evensen     NOR   18.36.6
3. Otto Polacsek      AUT   20:00.9
4. Rudolf Riedl       AUT   20:21.5
5. Keistutis Bulota    LIT   20:22.2
6. Armand Carlsen    NOR   20:56.1
7. Valentine Bialas    USA   21:05.4

Officially, this race never took place. After seven of the ten entrants had completed their heats, the temperature rose suddenly, and the officials in charge ordered the day's times cancelled and the races rerun. By the time a final decision had been reached, the Norwegians, who had already made it clear that they considered Jaffee the champion, had gone home, so the contest was cancelled. As far as the skaters were concerned, the matter had been settled after the first heat, when Jaffee came from behind to nip Evensen just before the finish line. However sports historians generally consider the 1928 10,000 meters to have been a non-event.

**1932 Lake Placid** C: 18, N: 6, D: 2.8. WR: 17:17.4 (Armand Carlsen)

| | | | |
|---|---|---|---|
| 1. | Irving Jaffee | USA | 19:13.6 |
| 2. | Ivar Ballangrud | NOR | — |
| 3. | Frank Stack | CAN | — |
| 4. | Edwin Wedge | USA | — |
| 5. | Valentine Bialas | USA | — |
| 6. | Bernt Evensen | NOR | — |
| 7. | Alexander Hurd | CAN | — |
| 8. | Edward Schroeder | USA | — |

The turmoil that marred the 1932 speed skating competitions culminated in disputes that broke out during the heats of the 10,000 meters. For this contest the North Americans tacked on a rule which required each skater to do his share in setting the pace. After the first heat Alex Hurd, who won the race, as well as Edwin Wedge of the United States and Shozo Ishihara of Japan, were disqualified for not doing their share. In the second heat Frank Stack was disqualified for interference after a protest by Bernt Evensen. After much haggling and many threats it was decided to rerun the two races the following day. Ironically, the same eight men who had originally qualified for the final qualified again. The final race was slow and tactical, as all eight stayed in a bunch until the last lap. Jaffee won by five yards, but the finish was so close that only two yards separated Ballangrud in second place from Evensen in sixth. Bronze medalist Frank Stack was still competing in the Olympics in 1952 when, at the age of 46, he finished 12th in the 500 meters.

**1936 Garmisch-Partenkirchen** C: 30, N: 14, D: 2.14. WR: 17:17.4 (Armand Carlsen)

| | | | |
|---|---|---|---|
| 1. | Ivar Ballangrud | NOR | 17:24.3 OR |
| 2. | Birger Vasenius | FIN | 17:28.2 |
| 3. | Max Stiepl | AUT | 17:30.0 |
| 4. | Charles Mathisen | NOR | 17:41.2 |
| 5. | Ossi Blomqvist | FIN | 17:42.4 |
| 6. | Jan Langedijk | HOL | 17:43.7 |
| 7. | Antero Ojala | FIN | 17:46.6 |
| 8. | Edward Schroeder | USA | 17:52.0 |

Ballangrud and Vasenius, paired together, raced neck and neck for 4000 meters before the Norwegian began to pull away. Ballangrud completed his Olympic career with four gold medals, two silver, and one bronze.

**1948 St. Moritz** C: 27, N: 11, D: 2.3. WR: 17:05.5 (Charles Mathisen)

| | | | |
|---|---|---|---|
| 1. | Åke Seyffarth | SWE | 17:26.3 |
| 2. | Lauri Parkkinen | FIN | 17:36.0 |
| 3. | Pentti Lammio | FIN | 17:42.7 |
| 4. | Kornel Pajor | HUN | 17:45.6 |
| 5. | Cornelis "Kees" Broekman | HOL | 17:54.7 |
| 6. | Jan Langedijk | HOL | 17:55.3 |
| 7. | Odd Lundberg | NOR | 18:05.8 |
| 8. | Harry Jansson | SWE | 18:08.0 |

**1952 Oslo** C: 30, N: 12, D: 2.19. WR: 16.32.6 (Hjalmar Andersen)

| | | | |
|---|---|---|---|
| 1. | Hjalmar Andersen | NOR | 16:45.8 OR |
| 2. | Cornelis "Kees" Broekman | HOL | 17:10.6 |
| 3. | Carl-Erik Asplund | SWE | 17:16.6 |
| 4. | Pentti Lammio | FIN | 17:20.5 |
| 5. | Anton Huiskes | HOL | 17:25.5 |
| 6. | Sverre Haugli | NOR | 17:30.2 |
| 7. | Kazuhiko Sugawara | JPN | 17:34.0 |
| 8. | Lauri Parkkinen | FIN | 17:36.8 |

Hjalmar "Hjallis" Andersen's unusually large margin of victory, the most decisive in Olympic history, earned him his third gold medal in three days.

**1956 Cortina** C: 32, N: 15, D: 1.31. WR: 16:32.6 (Hjalmar Andersen)

| | | | |
|---|---|---|---|
| 1. | Sigvard Ericsson | SWE | 16:35.9 OR |
| 2. | Knut Johannesen | NOR | 16:36.9 |
| 3. | Oleg Goncharenko | SOV | 16:42.3 |
| 4. | Sverre Haugli | NOR | 16:48.7 |
| 5. | Cornelius "Kees" Broekman | HOL | 16:51.2 |
| 6. | Hjalmar Andersen | NOR | 16:52.6 |
| 7. | Boris Yakimov | SOV | 16:59.7 |
| 8. | Olof Dahlberg | SWE | 17:01.3 |

Skating three pairs after Johannesen, 25-year-old woodchopper Sigge Ericsson so exhausted himself keeping ahead of Johannesen's pace that he lost two seconds on the final lap. However he was able to hold on and win anyway.

**1960 Squaw Valley** C: 30, N: 15, D: 2.27. WR: 16:32.6 (Hjalmar Andersen)

| | | | |
|---|---|---|---|
| 1. | Knut Johannesen | NOR | 15:46.6 WR |
| 2. | Viktor Kosichkin | SOV | 15:49.2 |
| 3. | Kjell Bäckman | SWE | 16:14.2 |
| 4. | Ivar Nilsson | SWE | 16:26.0 |
| 5. | Terence Monaghan | GBR | 16:31.6 |
| 6. | Torstein Seiersten | NOR | 16:33.4 |
| 7. | Olof Dahlberg | SWE | 16:34.6 |
| 8. | Jouko Jarvinen | FIN | 16:35.4 |

Since February 10, 1952, the world record for 10,000 meters had been Hjallis Andersen's 16:32.6. But with the ice perfect and the weather sunny and calm, five different skaters bettered Andersen's mark. Skating in the second pair, Kjell Bäckman chopped over 18 seconds off the record with a 16:14.2. Two pairs later, Knut Johannesen, a 26-year-old carpenter, became the first person to break the 16-minute barrier with a phenomenal 15:46.6. Johannesen's world record lasted for three years, but it almost didn't survive the rest of the day. Two pairs after Johannesen came Viktor Kosichkin, who stayed ahead of Johannesen's place for 6400 meters and was still even after 7600 meters. After that, though, Kosichkin began to tire and crossed the finish line 2.6 seconds too late. He did, however, have the rare experience of breaking the world record by more than 43 seconds and earning only a silver medal.

**1964 Innsbruck** C: 33, N: 19, D: 2.7. WR: 15:33.0 (Jonny Nilsson)

| | | | |
|---|---|---|---|
| 1. Jonny Nilsson | SWE | 15:50.1 | |
| 2. Fred Anton Maier | NOR | 16:06.0 | |
| 3. Knut Johannesen | NOR | 16:06.3 | |
| 4. Rutgerus Liebrechts | HOL | 16:08.6 | |
| 5. Ants Antson | SOV | 16:08.7 | |
| 6. Victor Kosichkin | SOV | 16:19.3 | |
| 7. Gerhard Zimmermann | GER | 16:22.5 | |
| 8. Alfred Malkin | GBR | 16:35.2 | |

**1968 Grenoble** C: 28, N: 13, D: 2.17. WR: 15:20.3 (Fred Anton Maier)

| | | | |
|---|---|---|---|
| 1. Johnny Höglin | SWE | 15:23.6 | OR |
| 2. Fred Anton Maier | NOR | 15:23.9 | |
| 3. Örjan Sandler | SWE | 15:31.8 | |
| 4. Per-Willy Guttormsen | NOR | 15:32.6 | |
| 5. Cornelis "Kees" Verkerk | HOL | 15:33.9 | |
| 6. Jonny Nilsson | SWE | 15:39.6 | |
| 7. Magne Thomassen | NOR | 15:44.9 | |
| 8. Petrus Nottet | HOL | 15:54.7 | |

Höglin, who had never before gone faster than 15:40, was one of the surprise winners of the 1968 Winter Games. Maier had the advantage of skating first, but Höglin, in the seventh pair, moved ahead of Maier's pace with three of 25 laps to go.

**1972 Sapporo** C: 24, N: 14, D: 2.7. WR: 14:55.9 (Adrianus "Ard" Schenk)

| | | | |
|---|---|---|---|
| 1. Adrianus "Ard" Schenk | HOL | 15:01.35 | OR |
| 2. Cornelis "Kees" Verkerk | HOL | 15:04.70 | |
| 3. Sten Stensen | NOR | 15:07.08 | |
| 4. Jan Bols | HOL | 15:17.99 | |
| 5. Valery Lavrouchkin | SOV | 15:20.08 | |
| 6. Göran Claesson | SWE | 15:30.19 | |
| 7. Kimmo Koskinen | FIN | 15:38.87 | |
| 8. Gerhard Zimmermann | GER | 15:43.92 | |

Handsome Ard Schenk won his third gold medal to match the single Olympics record of Ivar Ballangrud and Hjalmar "Hjallis" Andersen. Two weeks later in Norway, Schenk became the first person in 60 years to sweep all four events at the world championships. The last person to achieve the feat had been Oscar Mathisen in 1912.

**1976 Innsbruck** C: 20, N: 13, D: 2.14. WR: 14:50.31 (Sten Stensen)

| | | | |
|---|---|---|---|
| 1. Piet Kleine | HOL | 14:50.59 | OR |
| 2. Sten Stensen | NOR | 14:53.30 | |
| 3. Hans van Helden | HOL | 15:02.02 | |
| 4. Victor Varlamov | SOV | 15:06.06 | |
| 5. Örjan Sandler | SWE | 15:16.21 | |
| 6. Colin Coates | AUS | 15:16.80 | |
| 7. Daniel Carroll | USA | 15:19.29 | |
| 8. Franz Krienbuhl | SWI | 15:36.43 | |

Stensen had set a world record of 14:50.31 three weeks earlier. In Innsbruck, skating sixth, he was able to do only 14:53.30. Two pairs later, Piet Kleine, a 6-foot 5-inch 24-year-old unemployed carpenter, attacked Stenson's pace in steady fashion. He moved ahead at the halfway mark and stayed at least two seconds faster for the last eight laps.

**1980 Lake Placid** C: 25, N: 12, D: 2.23. WR: 14:34.33 (Viktor Leskin)

| | | | |
|---|---|---|---|
| 1. Eric Heiden | USA | 14:28.13 | WR |
| 2. Piet Kleine | HOL | 14:36.03 | |
| 3. Tom-Erik Oxholm | NOR | 14:36.60 | |
| 4. Michael Woods | USA | 14:39.53 | |
| 5. Öyvind Tveter | NOR | 14:43.53 | |
| 6. Hilbert van der Duim | HOL | 14:47.58 | |
| 7. Viktor Leskin | SOV | 14:51.72 | |
| 8. Andreas Ehrig | GDR | 14:51.94 | |

Having already become the first male speed skater to win four gold medals in one Olympics, Eric Heiden took the night off before his final race to attend the United States-U.S.S.R. ice hockey match. The U.S. team included two friends of Heiden's from Madison, Wisconsin, Mark Johnson and Bobby Suter. Heiden was so excited by the U.S. victory—more excited than by his own accomplishments—that he had trouble falling asleep and ended up oversleeping in the morning. Snatching a few pieces of bread for breakfast, he rushed to the track and, skating in the second pair, calmly broke the world record by over six seconds. He had become the first person in Olympic history to win five individual gold medals at one games (three of Mark Spitz's seven gold medals had been in relay events). Repelled by the instant celebrity that followed his feats, Eric Heiden announced that he would retire at the end of the season. "Maybe if things had stayed the way they were," he told the press, "and I could still be obscure in an obscure sport, I might want to keep skating. I really liked it best when I was a nobody."

**1984 Sarajevo** C: 32, N: 17, D: 2.18. WR: 14:23.59 (S. Tomas Gustafson)

| | | | |
|---|---|---|---|
| 1. Igor Malkov | SOV | 14:39.90 | |
| 2. S. Tomas Gustafson | SWE | 14:39.95 | |
| 3. René Schöfisch | GDR | 14:46.91 | |
| 4. Geir Karlstad | NOR | 14:52.40 | |
| 5. Michael Hadschieff | AUT | 14:53.78 | |
| 6. Dmitri Bochkarov | SOV | 14:55.65 | |
| 7. Michael Woods | USA | 14:57.30 | |
| 8. Henry Nilsen | NOR | 14:57.81 | |

Six days after 19-year-old Igor Malkov narrowly missed beating Tomas Gustafson for the 5000-meter gold medal, he again found himself skating after the Swede. This time he paced himself well and finished strongly to win by one-twentieth of a second.

**1988 Calgary** C: 32, N: 19, D: 2.21. WR: 13:48.51 (Geir Karlstad)

| | | | |
|---|---|---|---|
| 1. S. Tomas Gustafson | SWE | 13:48.20 | WR |
| 2. Michael Hadschieff | AUT | 13:56.11 | |
| 3. Leo Visser | HOL | 14:00.55 | |
| 4. Eric Flaim | USA | 14:05.57 | |
| 5. Gerard Kemkers | HOL | 14:08.34 | |
| 6. Yuri Klyuyev | SOV | 14:09.68 | |
| 7. Roberto Sighel | ITA | 14:13.60 | |
| 8. Roland Freier | GDR | 14:19.60 | |

Tomas Gustafson brought his career Olympic medal total to three golds and one silver. Gerard Kemkers finished fifth despite falling in the fifth lap. Colin Coates of Australia, competing in his sixth Olympics, placed twenty-sixth, twenty years after his first appearance.

## SHORT TRACK: 1000 METERS

This event will be held for the first time in 1992.

## SHORT TRACK: 5000-METER RELAY

This event will be held for the first time in 1992.

## *Discontinued Event*
## FOUR RACES COMBINED EVENT

**1924 Chamonix** C: 22, N: 9, D: 1.27.

| | | PTS. |
|---|---|---|
| 1. A. Clas Thunberg | FIN | 5.5 |
| 2. Roald Larsen | NOR | 9.5 |
| 3. Julius Skutnabb | FIN | 11 |
| 4. Sigurd Moen | NOR | 17 |
| 4. Harald Ström | NOR | 17 |
| 6. León Quaglia | FRA | 25 |
| 7. Alberts Rumba | LAT | 27 |
| 8. Leon Jucewicz | POL | 32 |

The concept of an all-around champion has continued to be a matter of major importance in world championships, but was never included again in the Olympics.

# SPEED SKATING

WOMEN
500 Meters
1000 Meters
1500 Meters
3000 Meters
5000 Meters
Short Track: 500 Meters
Short Track: 3000-Meter Relay

## WOMEN

### 500 METERS

**1924–1956** not held

**1960 Squaw Valley** C: 23, N: 10, D: 2.20. WR: 45.6 (Tamara Rylova)

| | | |
|---|---|---|
| 1. Helga Haase | GDR | 45.9 |
| 2. Natalya Donchenko | SOV | 46.0 |
| 3. Jeanne Ashworth | USA | 46.1 |
| 4. Tamara Rylova | SOV | 46.2 |
| 5. Hatsue Takamizawa | JPN | 46.6 |
| 6. Klara Guseva | SOV | 46.8 |
| 6. Elwira Seroczyńska | POL | 46.8 |
| 8. Fumie Hama | JPN | 47.4 |

**1964 Innsbruck** C: 28, N: 14, D: 1.30. WR: 44.9 (Inga Voronina)

| | | | |
|---|---|---|---|
| 1. Lydia Skoblikova | SOV | 45.0 | OR |
| 2. Irina Yegorova | SOV | 45.4 | |
| 3. Tatyana Sidorova | SOV | 45.5 | |
| 4. Jeanne Ashworth | USA | 46.2 | |
| 4. Janice Smith | USA | 46.2 | |
| 6. Gunilla Jacobsson | SWE | 46.5 | |
| 7. Janice Lawler | USA | 46.6 | |
| 8. Helga Haase | GDR | 47.2 | |

On January 27, 1962, Inga Voronina of the U.S.S.R. set world records for the 500 meters and 1500 meters. The next day she broke the world record at 3000 meters. However, the following year it was another Soviet skater, Lydia Skoblikova, a teacher from Chelyabinsk, who won the gold medal for all four distances at the world championships in Karuizawa, Japan. Voronina, not fully recovered from a bad stomach ailment, failed to make the Soviet Olympic team in 1964. Skoblikova, on the other hand, entered the competition as the favorite in three of the four events. Only in the 500 meters, the first distance to be contested, was she expected to have a tough time. Yegorova opened the day with a 45.4. This held up as the best time until Skoblikova, skating in the 13th of 14 pairs, zipped past the finish line in 45.0. Before the week was out she had duplicated her world championship feat by sweeping all four women's events.

**1968 Grenoble** C: 28, N: 11, D: 2.9. WR: 44.7 (Tatyana Sidorova)

| | | |
|---|---|---|
| 1. Lyudmila Titova | SOV | 46.1 |
| 2. Jennifer Fish | USA | 46.3 |
| 2. Dianne Holum | USA | 46.3 |
| 2. Mary Meyers | USA | 46.3 |
| 5. Elisabeth van den Brom | HOL | 46.6 |
| 6. Kaija Mustonen | FIN | 46.7 |
| 6. Sigrid Sundby | NOR | 46.7 |
| 8. Kirsti Biermann | NOR | 46.8 |

On February 3, Tatyana Sidorova set a world record of 44.7, but six days later in Grenoble she could do no better than 46.9 and finished in a tie for ninth place. The unusual triple American tie for second place was accomplished by Mary Meyers of St. Paul, Minnesota (the day before her 22nd birthday), 16-year-old Dianne Holum of Northbrook, Illinois, and 18-year-old Jennifer Fish of Strongville, Ohio.

**1972 Sapporo** C: 29, N: 12, D: 2.10. WR: 42.5 (Anne Henning)

| | | | |
|---|---|---|---|
| 1. Anne Henning | USA | 43.33 | OR |
| 2. Vera Krasnova | SOV | 44.01 | |
| 3. Lyudmila Titova | SOV | 44.45 | |
| 4. Sheila Young | USA | 44.53 | |
| 5. Monika Pflug | GER | 44.75 | |
| 6. Atje Keulen-Deelstra | HOL | 44.89 | |
| 7. Kay Lunda | USA | 44.95 | |
| 8. Alla Boutova | SOV | 45.17 | |

Sixteen-year-old Anne Henning of Northbrook, Illinois, the world record holder and heavy favorite, was paired against Canada's Sylvia Burka, who had impaired vision in one eye. At the crossover Burka didn't see Henning and headed toward a collision. Rather than push her way past Burka, Henning stood up, let her pass, and then dug in faster than ever. Despite losing a full second because of the mishap (which caused Burka's disqualification), Henning still won the gold medal with a time of 43.70. The officials allowed her another run at the end of the competition and she improved to 43.33. Henning was undoubtedly aided by her superstitious mother, who watched the race while holding a clutch of good-luck charms, including a four-leaf clover, Japanese beads, a Christmas ornament, and two U.S. flags. Afterward Henning told reporters, "I just can't wait to be normal again. But, you know, I suppose people will never really let me be normal again, will they?"

**1976 Innsbruck** C: 27, N: 13, D: 2.6. WR: 40.91 (Sheila Young)
1. Sheila Young        USA   42.76  OR
2. Cathy Priestner     CAN   43.12
3. Tatyana Averina     SOV   43.17
4. Leah Poulos         USA   43.21
5. Vera Krasnova       SOV   43.23
6. Lyubov Sachikova    SOV   43.80
7. Makiko Nagaya       JPN   43.88
8. Paula Halonen       FIN   43.99

Sheila Young won a complete set of medals at the 1976 Games, the first U.S. athlete to win three medals at a single Winter Olympics.

**1980 Lake Placid** C: 31, N: 15, D: 2.15. WR: 40.68 (Sheila Young)
1. Karin Enke           GDR   41.78  OR
2. Leah Mueller (Poulos) USA  42.26
3. Natalya Petruseva    SOV   42.42
4. Ann-Sofie Järnström  SWE   42.47
5. Makiko Nagaya        JPN   42.70
6. Cornelia Jacob       GDR   42.98
7. Beth Heiden          USA   43.18
8. Tatiana Tarasova     SOV   43.26

Eighteen-year-old Karin Enke was practically unknown in speed skating circles until a week before the Olympics, when she won the world sprint championship in West Allis, Wisconsin, after qualifying for the East German team as an alternate. She showed that her victory was no fluke when she took the Olympic gold medal at Lake Placid.

**1984 Sarajevo** C: 33, N: 16, D: 2.10. WR: 39.67 (Christa Rothenburger)
1. Christa Rothenburger  GDR   41.02  OR
2. Karin Enke            GDR   41.28
3. Natalya Chive         SOV   41.50
4. Irina Kuleshova       SOV   41.70
5. Skadi Walter          GDR   42.16
6. Natalya Petruseva     SOV   42.19
7. Monika Holzner (Pflug) GER  42.40
8. Bonnie Blair          USA   42.53

Two years after earning her Olympic gold medal, Christa Rothenburger of Dresden won the women's match sprint title at the 1986 world cycling championships.

**1988 Calgary** C: 30, N: 15, D: 2.22. WR: 39.39 (Christa Rothenburger)
1. Bonnie Blair          USA   39.10  WR
2. Christa Rothenburger  GDR   39.12
3. Karin Kania (Enke)    GDR   39.24
4. Angela Stahnke        GDR   39.68

5. Seiko Hashimoto       JPN   39.74
6. Shelley Rhead         CAN   40.36
7. Monika Holzner-Gawenus (Pflug)  GER  40.53
8. Shoko Fusano          JPN   40.61

Defending champion Christa Rothenburger, skating in the second pair, blasted her own world record by a quarter of a second. Two pairs later, Bonnie Blair of Champaign, Illinois, who began skating at the age of 2, got off to the best start of her life, clocking 10.55 seconds for the first 100 meters to Rothenburger's 10.57. That difference of two one-hundredths of a second turned out to be Blair's final margin of victory.

## 1000 METERS

**1924–1956** not held

**1960 Squaw Valley** C: 22, N: 10, D: 2.22. WR: 1:33.4 (Tamara Rylova)
1. Klara Guseva          SOV   1:34.1
2. Helga Haase           GDR   1:34.3
3. Tamara Rylova         SOV   1:34.8
4. Lydia Skoblikova      SOV   1:35.3
5. Helena Pilejczyk      POL   1:35.8
5. Hatsue Takamizawa     JPN   1:35.8
7. Fumie Hama            JPN   1:36.1
8. Jeanne Ashworth       USA   1:36.5

Elwira Seroczyńska of Poland had the fastest time going into the final curve, but with 100 meters to go, one of her skates hit the dividing line, and she fell.

**1964 Innsbruck** C: 28, N: 13, D: 2.1. WR: 1:31.8 (Lydia Skoblikova)
1. Lydia Skoblikova      SOV   1:33.2  OR
2. Irina Yegorova        SOV   1:34.3
3. Kaija Mustonen        FIN   1:34.8
4. Helga Haase           GDR   1:35.7
5. Valentina Stenina     SOV   1:36.0
6. Gunilla Jacobsson     SWE   1:36.5
7. Janice Smith          USA   1:36.7
8. Kaija-Lisa Keskivitikka FIN 1:37.6

With this race Skoblikova became the first woman to win three gold medals at one Winter Olympics and the first person of either sex to win five Winter gold medals.

**1968 Grenoble** C: 29, N: 12, D: 2.11. WR: 1:31.8 (Lydia Skoblikova)
1. Carolina Geijssen     HOL   1:32.6  OR
2. Lyudmila Titova       SOV   1:32.9
3. Dianne Holum          USA   1:33.4
4. Kaija Mustonen        FIN   1:33.6
5. Irina Yegorova        SOV   1:34.4
6. Sigrid Sundby         NOR   1:34.5
7. Jeanne Ashworth       USA   1:34.7
8. Kaija-Lisa Keskivitikka FIN 1:34.8

Geijssen was a 21-year-old Amsterdam secretary who skated to work each day. She was the first Dutch skater to win an Olympic gold medal.

**1972 Sapporo** C: 33, N: 12, D: 2.11. WR: 1:27.3 (Anne Henning)
1. Monika Pflug          GER   1:31.40   OR
2. Atje Keulen-Deelstra  HOL   1:31.61
3. Anne Henning          USA   1:31.62
4. Lyudmila Titova       SOV   1:31.85
5. Nina Statkevitch      SOV   1:32.21
6. Dianne Holum          USA   1:32.41
7. Elly van den Brom     HOL   1:32.60
8. Sylvia Burka          CAN   1:32.95

Seventeen-year-old Monika Pflug was a surprise winner. A bookbinding apprentice from Munich, she false-started twice. Threatened with disqualification if she jumped the gun again, she started slowly, but was able to make up lost time after the first 200 meters.

**1976 Innsbruck** C: 27, N: 10, D: 2.7. WR: 1:23.46 (Tatyana Averina)
1. Tatyana Averina       SOV   1:28.43   OR
2. Leah Poulos           USA   1:28.57
3. Sheila Young          USA   1.29.14
4. Sylvia Burka          CAN   1:29.47
5. Monika Holzner (Pflug) GER  1:29.54
6. Cathy Priestner       CAN   1:29.66
7. Lyudmila Titova       SOV   1:30.06
8. Hoike Lange           GDR   1:30.55

**1980 Lake Placid** C: 37, N: 16, D: 2.17. WR: 1:23.46 (Tatyana Averina)
1. Natalya Petruseva     SOV   1:24.10   OR
2. Leah Mueller (Poulos) USA   1:25.41
3. Silvia Albrecht       GDR   1:26.46
4. Karin Enke            GDR   1:26.66
5. Beth Heiden           USA   1:27.01
6. Annie Borckink        HOL   1:27.24
7. Sylvia Burka          CAN   1:27.50
8. Ann-Sofie Järnström   SWE   1:28.10

Petruseva and Mueller were the second pair to skate. Mueller was ahead at 200 meters, but Petruseva took the lead and eventually pulled away to win by 40 feet. For Mueller, it was her third Olympic silver medal. A couple of weeks earlier, Petruseva had won the world sprint championship in Norway, but then had taken seven hours to produce a urine sample, leading to rumors that she had taken illegal drugs. Suspicions seemed confirmed when she finished only eighth in the 1500 meters, the opening Olympic event. But after taking the bronze medal in the 500 meters, she won the 1000 meters and passed the urine test for drugs without any problems. Part of the Soviet success in speed skating has to be due to the fact that, as of 1980, there were 1202 Olympic-size speed skating rinks in the U.S.S.R., whereas in the United States, a nation of comparable population, there were only two.

**1984 Sarajevo** C: 38, N: 17, D: 2.13. WR: 1:19.31 (Natalya Petruseva)
1. Karin Enke                      GDR   1:21.61   OR
2. Andrea Schöne (Mitscherlich)    GDR   1:22.83
3. Natalya Petruseva               SOV   1:23.21
4. Valentina Lalenkova             SOV   1:23.68
5. Christa Rothenburger            GDR   1:23.98
6. Yvonne van Gennip               HOL   1:25.36
7. Erwina Rys-Ferens               POL   1:25.81
8. Monika Holzner (Pflug)          GER   1:25.87

Enke, skating one pair after Schöne, won her second gold medal of the Sarajevo Games and her third overall.

**1988 Calgary** C: 27, N: 12, D: 2.22. WR: 1.18.11 (Karin Kania [Enke])
1. Christa Rothenburger   GDR   1:17.65   WR
2. Karin Kania (Enke)     GDR   1:17.70
3. Bonnie Blair           USA   1:18.31
4. Andrea Ehrig           GDR   1:19.32
   (Mitscherlich, Schöne)
5. Seiko Hashimoto        JPN   1:19.75
6. Angela Stahnke         GDR   1:20.05
7. Leslie Bader           USA   1:21.09
8. Katie Class            USA   1:21.10

Seven months after earning the gold medal at 1000 meters, Christa Rothenburger took a silver in the cycling sprint race in Seoul to become the only athlete in Olympic history to win medals in winter and summer in the same year.

## 1500 METERS

**1924–1956** not held

**1960 Squaw Valley** C: 23, N: 10, D: 2.21. WR: 2:25.5 (Khalida Schegoloeva)
1. Lydia Skoblikova      SOV   2:25.2   WR
2. Elwira Seroczyńska    POL   2:25.7
3. Helena Pilejczyk      POL   2:27.1
4. Klara Guseva          SOV   2:28.7
5. Valentina Stenina     SOV   2:29.2
6. Iris Sihvonen         FIN   2:29.7
7. Christina Scherling   SWE   2:31.5
8. Helga Haase           GDR   2:31.7

This was the first of Skoblikova's six career gold medals.

**1964 Innsbruck** C: 30, N: 14, D: 1.31. WR: 2:19.0 (Inga Voronina)
1. Lydia Skoblikova        SOV   2:22.6   OR
2. Kaija Mustonen          FIN   2:25.5
3. Berta Kolokoltseva      SOV   2:27.1
4. Kim Song-soon           PRK   2:27.7
5. Helga Haase             GDR   2:28.6
6. Christina Scherling     SWE   2:29.4
7. Valentina Stenina       SOV   2:29.9
8. Kaija-Lisa Keskivitikka FIN   2:30.0

**1968 Grenoble** C: 30, N: 13, D: 2.10. WR: 2:19.0 (Inga Artamonova [Voronina])

| | | | |
|---|---|---|---|
| 1. Kaija Mustonen | FIN | 2:22.4 | OR |
| 2. Carolina Geijssen | HOL | 2:22.7 | |
| 3. Christina Kaiser | HOL | 2:24.5 | |
| 4. Sigrid Sundby | NOR | 2:25.2 | |
| 5. Lasma Kaouniste | SOV | 2:25.4 | |
| 6. Kaija-Lisa Keskivitikka | FIN | 2:25.8 | |
| 7. Lyudmila Titova | SOV | 2:26.8 | |
| 8. Ruth Schleiermacher | GDR | 2:27.1 | |

Defending champion Lydia Skoblikova finished 11th, while future champion Dianne Holum was 13th.

**1972 Sapporo** C: 31, N: 12, D: 2.9. WR: 2:15.8 (Christina Baas-Kaiser)

| | | | |
|---|---|---|---|
| 1. Dianne Holum | USA | 2:20.85 | OR |
| 2. Christina Baas-Kaiser | HOL | 2:21.05 | |
| 3. Atje Keulen-Deelstra | HOL | 2:22.05 | |
| 4. Elisabeth van den Brom | HOL | 2:22.27 | |
| 5. Rosemarie Taupadel | GDR | 2:22.35 | |
| 6. Nina Statkevitch | SOV | 2:23.19 | |
| 7. Connie Carpenter | USA | 2:23.93 | |
| 8. Sigrid Sundby | NOR | 2:24.07 | |

As a 16-year-old in 1968, Dianne Holum had won a silver medal in the 500 meters and a bronze in the 1000. In 1972 she added a gold in the 1500 meters and a silver in the 3000. The success of the Dutch system of training was shown not only by the fact that Dutch skaters finished second, third, and fourth, but by the fact that Dianne Holum used a Dutch coach as well. The following year she took on a young pupil of her own—14-year-old Eric Heiden—and coached him all the way to the 1976 and 1980 Olympics.

**1976 Innsbruck** C: 26, N: 12, D: 2.5. WR: 2:09.90 (Tatyana Averina)

| | | | |
|---|---|---|---|
| 1. Galina Stepanskaya | SOV | 2:16.58 | OR |
| 2. Sheila Young | USA | 2:17.06 | |
| 3. Tatyana Averina | SOV | 2:17.96 | |
| 4. Lisbeth Korsmo | NOR | 2:18.99 | |
| 5. Karin Kessow | GDR | 2:19.05 | |
| 6. Leah Poulos | USA | 2:19.11 | |
| 7. Ines Bautzmann | GDR | 2:19.63 | |
| 8. Erwina Ryś | POL | 2:19.69 | |

**1980 Lake Placid** C: 31, N: 14, D: 2.14. WR: 2:07.18 (Halida Vorobieva)

| | | | |
|---|---|---|---|
| 1. Annie Borckink | HOL | 2:10.95 | OR |
| 2. Ria Visser | HOL | 2:12.35 | |
| 3. Sabine Becker | GDR | 2:12.38 | |
| 4. Bjorg Eva Jensen | NOR | 2:12.59 | |
| 5. Sylvia Filipsson | SWE | 2:12.84 | |
| 6. Andrea Mitscherlich | GDR | 2:13.05 | |
| 7. Beth Heiden | USA | 2:13.10 | |
| 8. Natalya Petruseva | SOV | 2:14.15 | |

Borckink, a 28-year-old nursing student, had never before finished in the top three in an international meet.

**1984 Sarajevo** C: 32, N: 15, D: 2.9. WR: 2:04.04 (Natalya Petruseva)

| | | | |
|---|---|---|---|
| 1. Karin Enke | GDR | 2:03.42 | WR |
| 2. Andrea Schöne (Mitscherlich) | GDR | 2:05.29 | |
| 3. Natalya Petruseva | SOV | 2:05.78 | |
| 4. Gabi Schönbrunn | GDR | 2:07.69 | |
| 5. Erwina Ryś-Ferens | POL | 2:08.08 | |
| 6. Valentina Lalenkova | SOV | 2:08.17 | |
| 7. Natalya Kurova | SOV | 2:08.41 | |
| 8. Björg Eva Jensen | NOR | 2:09.53 | |

A converted figure skater from Dresden, Karin Enke, the 1980 Olympic champion at 500 meters, had set a world record of 2:03.40 on December 8. However the International Skating Union refused to recognize her record because they had received insufficient advance notice of the meet in which she was competing. Determined to prove herself at the Olympics, Enke again broke Petruseva's world record, which had been set at high-altitude.

**1988 Calgary** C: 28, N: 13, D: 2.27. WR: 1:59.30 (Karin Kania [Enke])

| | | | |
|---|---|---|---|
| 1. Yvonne van Gennip | HOL | 2:00.68 | OR |
| 2. Karin Kania (Enke) | GDR | 2:00.82 | |
| 3. Andrea Ehrig (Mitscherlich, Schöne) | GDR | 2:01.49 | |
| 4. Bonnie Blair | USA | 2:04.02 | |
| 5. Yelena Lapuga | SOV | 2:04.24 | |
| 6. Seiko Hashimoto | JPN | 2:04.38 | |
| 7. Gunda Kleemann | GDR | 2:04.68 | |
| 7. Erwina Ryś-Ferens | POL | 2:04.68 | |

Van Gennip bettered her personal best by almost four seconds to earn the second of her three gold medals. At her post-race press conference van Gennip inadvertently caused a sensation. Asked to describe her feelings, she replied, "I am not emotional here, but in my bed, I am emotional." When reporters began to laugh, she made it clear that they had misinterpreted her words. Karin Kania's second-place finish gave her a career total of three gold medals, four silvers, and one bronze.

## 3000 METERS

**1924–1956** not held

**1960 Squaw Valley** C: 20, N: 10, D: 2.23. WR: 5:13.8 (Rimma Zukova)

| | | |
|---|---|---|
| 1. Lydia Skoblikova | SOV | 5:14.3 |
| 2. Valentina Stenina | SOV | 5:16.9 |
| 3. Eevi Huttunen | FIN | 5:21.0 |
| 4. Hatsue Takamizawa | JPN | 5:21.4 |
| 5. Christina Scherling | SWE | 5:25.5 |

6. Helena Pilejczyk      POL    5:26.2
7. Elwira Seroczyńska     POL    5:27.3
8. Jeanne Ashworth        USA    5:28.5

**1964 Innsbruck** C: 28, N: 13, D: 2.2. WR: 5:06.0 (Inga Voronina)
1. Lydia Skoblikova       SOV    5:14.9
2. Han Pil-hwa            PRK    5:18.5
2. Valentina Stenina      SOV    5:18.5
4. Klara Nesterova (Guseva)   SOV    5:22.5
5. Kaija Mustonen         FIN    5:24.3
6. Hatsue Nagakubo        JPN    5:25.4
7. Kim Song-soon          KOR    5:25.9
8. Doreen McCannel        CAN    5:26.4

With this race Lydia Skoblikova became the first person to win four gold medals in a single Winter Olympics and the first to win six gold medals all together. Further excitement was caused by the last skater, tiny Han Pil-hwa, a previously unknown North Korean who kept up Skoblikova's pace for four of the seven laps before falling back to a tie for second place.

**1968 Grenoble** C: 26, N: 12, D: 2.12. WR: 4:54.6 (Christina Kaiser)
1. Johanna Schut          HOL    4:56.2    OR
2. Kaija Mustonen         FIN    5:01.0
3. Christina Kaiser       HOL    5:01.3
4. Kaija-Lisa Keskivitikka   FIN    5:03.9
5. Wilhelmina Burgmeijer  HOL    5:05.1
6. Lydia Skoblikova       SOV    5:08.0
7. Christina Lindblom     SWE    5:00.0
8. Anna Sablina           SOV    5:12.5

**1972 Sapporo** C: 22, N: 10, D: 2.12. WR: 4:46.5 (Christina Baas-Kaiser)
1. Christina Baas-Kaiser  HOL    4:52.14   OR
2. Dianne Holum           USA    4:58.67
3. Atje Keulen-Deelstra   HOL    4:59.91
4. Sippie Tigelaar        HOL    5:01.67
5. Nina Statkevitch       SOV    5:01.79
6. Kapitolina Sereguina   SOV    5:01.88
7. Tuula Vilkas           FIN    5:05.92
8. Lyudmilla Savroulina   SOV    5:06.61

After the race, the two Dutch medalists, both of whom were 33 years old, were asked by a reporter if they were planning to retire. Baas-Kaiser replied, "What's the matter, don't we skate fast enough?"

**1976 Innsbruck** C: 26, N: 12, D: 2.8. WR: 4:44.69 (Tamara Kuznyetsova)
1. Tatyana Averina        SOV    4:45.19   OR
2. Andrea Mitscherlich    GDR    4:45.23
3. Lisbeth Korsmo         NOR    4:45.24
4. Karin Kessow           GDR    4:45.60
5. Ines Bautzmann         GDR    4:46.67
6. Sylvia Filipsson       SWE    4:48.15
7. Nancy Swider           USA    4:48.46
8. Sylvia Burka           CAN    4:49.04

If the top three skaters had actually been on the ice at the same time, only 16 inches would have separated them at the finish.

**1980 Lake Placid** C: 29, N: 14, D: 2.20. WR: 4:31.00 (Galina Stepanskaya)
1. Bjorg Eva Jensen       NOR    4:32.13   OR
2. Sabine Becker          GDR    4:32.79
3. Beth Heiden            USA    4:33.77
4. Andrea Mitscherlich    GDR    4:37.69
5. Erwina Ryś-Ferens      POL    4:37.89
6. Mary Docter            USA    4:39.29
7. Sylvia Filipsson       SWE    4:40.22
8. Natalya Petruseva      SOV    4:42.59

**1984 Sarajevo** C: 26, N: 14, D: 2.15. WR: 4:21.70 (Gabi Schönbrunn)
1. Andrea Schöne (Mitscherlich)   GDR    4:24.79   OR
2. Karin Enke             GDR    4:26.33
3. Gabi Schönbrunn        GDR    4:33.13
4. Olga Pleshkova         SOV    4:34.42
5. Yvonne van Gennip      HOL    4:34.80
6. Mary Docter            USA    4:36.25
7. Bjorg Eva Jensen       NOR    4:36.28
8. Valentina Lalenkova    SOV    4:37.36

Twenty-three-year-old Andrea Schöne of Dresden skated first and recorded a time that no one else could match.

**1988 Calgary** C: 29, N: 16, D: 2.23. WR: 4:16.76 (Gabi Zange [Schönbrunn])
1. Yvonne van Gennip      HOL    4:11.94   WR
2. Andrea Ehrig           GDR    4:12.09
   (Mitscherlich, Schöne)
3. Gabi Zange (Schönbrunn)   GDR    4:16.92
4. Karin Kania (Enke)     GDR    4:18.80
5. Erwina Ryś-Ferens      POL    4:22.59
6. Svetlana Boyko         SOV    4:22.00
7. Seiko Hashimoto        JPN    4:23.29
7. Yelena Lapuga          SOV    4:23.29

The first pair on the ice were East German veterans Karin Kania and defending champion Andrea Ehrig. Kania, overanxious to win a gold medal, went out too fast, suffered a muscle cramp, and became so exhausted that she barely finished the race. Ehrig, on the other hand, kept to a steady pace and ripped over 4½ seconds off teammate Gabi Zange's world record. But three pairs later, 23-year-old Yvonne van Gennip, trailing Ehrig's pace for 2600 meters, made up eight tenths of a second on the final lap to score an upset victory.

# 5000 METERS

**1924–1984** not held

**1988 Calgary** C: 25, N: 14, D: 2.28. WR: 7:20.36 (Yvonne van Gennip)

| | | | |
|---|---|---|---|
| 1. Yvonne van Gennip | HOL | 7:14.13 | WR |
| 2. Andrea Ehrig (Mitscherlich, Schöne) | GDR | 7:17.12 | |
| 3. Gabi Zange (Schönbrunn) | GDR | 7:21.61 | |
| 4. Svetlana Boyko | SOV | 7:28.39 | |
| 5. Yelena Lapuga | SOV | 7:28.65 | |
| 6. Seiko Hashimoto | JPN | 7:34.43 | |
| 7. Gunda Kleeman | GDR | 7:34.59 | |
| 8. Jasmin Krohn | SWE | 7:36.56 | |

Two months before the Olympics, Yvonne van Gennip was lying in a hospital bed recovering from surgery to her right foot, which had become infected after she cut it by tying her skate lace too tightly. After two weeks in the hospital, van Gennip's Olympic expectations had been reduced to a bronze medal or two. But when she arrived in Calgary, she discovered that she was well rested and in the best condition of her life. Inspired by Bonnie Blair's defeat of the supposedly unbeatable East Germans in the 500-meter race, van Gennip scored upset victories in both the 3000 and the 1500.

Andrea Ehrig, skating in the first pair of the 5000 meters, bettered van Gennip's world record by 3.24 seconds. Four pairs later, van Gennip fell behind Ehrig's pace but finished strongly to earn her third gold medal of the Calgary games. Ehrig, competing in her fourth Olympics and using her third name, brought her combined medal total to one gold, five silvers, and one bronze.

## SHORT TRACK: 500 METERS

This event will be held for the first time in 1992.

## SHORT TRACK: 3000-METER RELAY

This event will be held for the first time in 1992.

# ALPINE SKIING

MEN
Downhill
Slalom
Giant Slalom
Super Giant Slalom
Alpine Combined

## MEN

### DOWNHILL

The first downhill race was held in Crans-Montana, Switzerland, in 1911. It was organized by an Englishman, Arnold Lunn, who also invented the modern slalom in 1922 and was the main force in obtaining Olympic recognition for alpine skiing in 1936.

Of the 34 medals which have been awarded in the men's downhill race, 32 have gone to Western Europeans; of these, eleven went to Austria, ten to Switzerland and seven to France.

**1924–1936** not held

**1948 St. Moritz** C: 112, N: 25, D: 2.2.
1. Henri Oreiller       FRA    2:55.0
2. Franz Gabl           AUT    2:59.1
3. Karl Molitor         SWI    3:00.3
3. Rolf Olinger         SWI    3:00.3
5. Egon Schöpf          AUT    3:01.2
6. Silvio Alverà        ITA    3:02.4
6. Carlo Gartner        ITA    3:02.4
8. Fernand Grosjean     SWI    3:03.1

A member of the French underground during World War II, Henri Oreiller was a cocky, clowning fellow who warned the other skiers he was so confident of victory that they needn't bother racing against him. He careened down the two-mile course like an acrobat, flying over bumps without caution and then regaining his balance in midair.

**1952 Oslo-Norefjell** C: 81, N: 27, D: 2.16.
1. Zeno Colò            ITA    2:30.8
2. Othmar Schneider     AUT    2:32.0
3. Christian Pravda     AUT    2:32.4
4. Fredy Rubi           SWI    2:32.5
5. William Beck         USA    2:33.3
6. Stein Eriksen        NOR    2:33.8

7. Gunnar Hjeltnes      NOR    2:35.9
8. Carlo Gartner        ITA    2:36.5

Zeno Colò was a colorful 31-year-old restaurant owner from Tuscany, whose form on the slopes was almost as unorthodox as that of Oreiller.

**1956 Cortina** C: 75, N: 27, D: 2.3.
1. Anton Sailer         AUT    2:52.2
2. Raymond Fellay       SWI    2:55.7
3. Andreas Molterer     AUT    2:56.2
4. Roger Staub          SWI    2:57.1
5. Hans-Peter Lanig     GER    2:59.8
6. Gino Burrini         ITA    3:00.2
7. Kurt Hennrich        CZE    3:01.5
8. Charles Bozon        FRA    3:01.9

Toni Sailer had already won the giant slalom and the slalom and was confident of completing his alpine sweep, since he held the course record of 2:46.2 for the downhill. However, as he tightened the straps that tied his boots to his skis, one of the straps broke. "That had never happened to me before," he later wrote. "I had not even thought it possible that such straps could break and had therefore not taken along a spare." It was almost his turn to race. If he couldn't find a strap, he would have to withdraw. Unfortunately, the problem was so rare that none of the other skiers had brought along spare straps either. Then Hansl Senger, the trainer of the Italian team, walked by and noticed the Austrians in panic. Senger immediately took the straps from his own bindings and handed them to Sailer. Strong winds and a glassy course prevented 28 of the 75 starters from reaching the finish line, and sent eight men to the hospital. But Sailer was able to survive one near spill and complete the course three and a half seconds faster than anyone else.

After the victory ceremony, Sailer joined his parents and, holding his three gold medals in his hand, said, "It's a good thing there are three medals. One for you, Father, one for you, Mother. Then there is a third one for me." Sailer later became an actor and singer, and then went into business as a hotel owner and an investor in a textile company, before settling in as the operator of a children's ski school. He also coached the Austrian national team during the 1970s.

**1960 Squaw Valley** C: 63, N: 21, D: 2.22.

| | | |
|---|---|---|
| 1. Jean Vuarnet | FRA | 2:06.0 |
| 2. Hans-Peter Lanig | GER | 2:06.5 |
| 3. Guy Périllat | FRA | 2:06.9 |
| 4. Willy Forrer | SWI | 2:07.8 |
| 5. Roger Staub | SWI | 2:08.9 |
| 6. Bruno Alberti | ITA | 2:09.1 |
| 7. Karl Schranz | AUT | 2:09.2 |
| 8. Charles Bozon | FRA | 2:09.6 |

In 1960 the downhill race was postponed for three days because of heavy snow. Vuarnet was the first Olympic gold medalist to use metal skis and no wax.

**1964 Innsbruck** C: 84, N: 27, D: 1.30.

| | | |
|---|---|---|
| 1. Egon Zimmermann | AUT | 2:18.16 |
| 2. Léo Lacroix | FRA | 2:18.90 |
| 3. Wolfgang Bartels | GER | 2:19.48 |
| 4. Joos Minsch | SWI | 2:19.54 |
| 5. Ludwig Leitner | GER | 2:19.67 |
| 6. Guy Périllat | FRA | 2:19.79 |
| 7. Gerhard Nenning | AUT | 2:19.98 |
| 8. Willi Favre | SWI | 2:20.23 |

The downhill competition was held under a cloud of gloom following the death of 19-year-old Ross Milne of Australia, who was killed during a practice run on January 25 when he flew off the course and smashed into a tree. Twenty-four-year-old Egon Zimmermann was the third alpine gold medalist to come from Lech, a hamlet of less than 200 people which had been converted to a ski resort following World War II. Also from Lech were Orthmar Schneider, the 1952 slalom winner, and Trude Beiser, who won the women's downhill the same year.

**1968 Grenoble-Chamrousse** C: 86, N: 29, D: 2.9.

| | | |
|---|---|---|
| 1. Jean-Claude Killy | FRA | 1:59.85 |
| 2. Guy Périllat | FRA | 1:59.93 |
| 3. John-Daniel Dätwyler | SWI | 2:00.32 |
| 4. Heinrich Messner | AUT | 2:01.03 |
| 5. Karl Schranz | AUT | 2:01.89 |
| 6. Ivo Mahlknecht | ITA | 2:02.00 |
| 7. Gerhard Prinzing | GER | 2:02.10 |
| 8. Bernard Orcel | FRA | 2:02.22 |

Jean-Claude Killy grew up in the resort village of Val d'Isère in the French Savoy Alps. His love of danger worried his parents, but his father encouraged his sporting endeavors anyway. Killy dropped out of school at the age of 16 in order to join the French ski team, and soon became known for his fun-loving attitude. Once he entered a ski-jump competition in Wengen, Switzerland, and caused a sensation by dropping his pants after take-off and finishing his jump in longjohns. Apparently he dropped his pants in other places as well, since he also contracted VD in Sun Valley and was named in a paternity suit in Austria. He was declared innocent. While serving with the French Army in Algeria, Killy contracted amoebic parasitosis, but he regained his health sufficiently to qualify for the 1964 French Olympic team in all three alpine events. At Innsbruck he placed fifth in the giant slalom, but failed to finish the downhill and slalom. Killy started to pick up speed after the 1964 Olympics, however, and by 1967 he was on top of the world. During the 1966–67 season he won 12 of 16 World Cup meets, and the following summer he won a sports car race in Sicily. Despite some troubles at the start of the 1967–68 season, Killy went to the 1968 Olympics confident of victory.

There was certainly a lot of pressure on Killy to win in Grenoble. French fans were anxious for him to duplicate the 1952 triple-gold performance of Austria's Toni Sailer. In addition, a huge Jean-Claude Killy industry was waiting to spring into production if Killy won three gold medals. Ski-makers, boot-makers, binding-makers, glove-makers, and others were ready with fat contracts for Killy's product endorsements, which he had already been giving out as readily as he could within the restrictions set up by the International Ski Federation. But these restrictions weren't good enough for I.O.C. President Avery Brundage. Shortly before the games, Killy signed a contract with an Italian ski pole manufacturer. The International Ski Federation informed Killy that the contract violated the rules of amateurism, so Killy backed off, whereupon the ski pole manufacturer threatened to sue him. The French Ski Federation and the French Sports Ministry undertook hasty negotiations with the Italian ski pole manufacturer in an attempt to settle the issue before the Olympics. "Payments for damages"—sums never revealed—satisfied the Italians.

Brundage demanded that all trade names and trademarks be removed from the skis used by competitors in the 1968 Olympics. The International Ski Federation, the team managers, and the skiers themselves rejected the ban, claiming that the entire sport of alpine skiing was dependent on the financial support of ski-makers. On the eve of the Games an awkward compromise was reached whereby the skiers would be allowed to keep the trade names and trademarks on their skis, but their skis would be taken away from them before they could be photographed. The policemen in charge of this unpleasant task were particularly on edge when Jean-Claude Killy, the favorite, shot down the slopes as the 14th contestant in the opening alpine race—the downhill. Killy slashed across the finish line eight one-hundredths of a second faster than his teammate, yoga practitioner Guy Périllat. Immediately, Michel Arpin, Killy's friend and adviser, rushed out and embraced Killy, making sure that the photographers got a good view of the pouch on his back, which was emblazoned with the word "Dynamic," the brand of skis that Killy used, and his gloves, which bore the Dynamic trademark—two yellow bars. When a policeman, surrounded by a horde of photographers, confiscated Killy's skis, Michel Arpin took one of his own skis and planted it in the snow so that the two yellow bars on the tip were right next to Killy's head.

Eventually Killy gave up competitive skiing and traveled to the United States, where he signed commercial contracts with Chevrolet, United Air Lines, Bristol-Myers, *Ladies' Home Journal,* Head Skis, Lange boots, Mighty Mac sportswear, Wolverine gloves and after-ski boots, and numerous other companies. Killy later served as copresident of the organizing committee of the 1992 Albertville Olympics.

**1972 Sapporo-Eniwadake** C: 55, N: 20, D: 2.7.

| | | | |
|---|---|---|---|
| 1. | Bernhard Russi | SWI | 1:51.43 |
| 2. | Roland Collombin | SWI | 1:52.07 |
| 3. | Heinrich Messner | AUT | 1:52.40 |
| 4. | Andreas Sprecher | SWI | 1:53.11 |
| 5. | Erik Håker | NOR | 1:53.16 |
| 6. | Walter Tresch | SWI | 1:53.19 |
| 7. | Karl Cordin | AUT | 1:53.32 |
| 8. | Robert Cochran | USA | 1:53.39 |

Most people in the sports world breathed a sigh of relief when Avery Brundage announced that he would retire after the completion of the 1972 Olympics. But the 84-year-old Brundage decided to go out with a bang by staging one final attack against commercialism in alpine skiing. Although he considered at least 30 or 40 skiers to be in violation of the rules of amateurism, Brundage chose to concentrate his attack on Austrian hero Karl Schranz, who was reputedly earning at least $40,000 to $50,000 a year as a "tester and designer" for various ski product manufacturers. Schranz was not alone in receiving such income, but he had also committed the crime of being outspoken in his criticism of Brundage.

Karl Schranz was the son of a poor railway worker in St. Anton in the Arlberg Mountains. His father died of work-related tuberculosis at an early age. In 1962 Schranz won the world downhill and combined championships and in 1964 he earned a silver medal in the Olympic giant slalom. In 1968 he appeared to have won the Olympic slalom until his disqualification for missing a gate was announced. By 1972 he had won every honor that is offered in international alpine skiing—except an Olympic gold medal. The 33-year-old Schranz delayed his retirement in the hope of achieving that final goal. But three days before the opening of the Sapporo Games, Avery Brundage got his way, and the I.O.C. voted 28–14 to ban Schranz from participating in the Olympics. Austrian Olympic officials announced that their ski team would withdraw from the games, but the Austrian skiers decided to compete anyway. While Brundage accused the alpine skiers of being "trained seals of the merchandisers," Schranz told the press, "If Mr. Brundage had been poor, as I was, and as were many other athletes, I wonder if he wouldn't have a different attitude. . . . If we followed Mr. Brundage's recommendations to their true end, then the Olympics would be a competition only for the very rich. No man of ordinary means could ever afford to excel in his sport."

When Schranz returned to Vienna he was met by 100,000 Austrian supporters and treated to a tickertape parade. It was the largest demonstration in Austria since World War II. Because Brundage was an American (he was known in Austria as "the senile millionaire from Chicago"), the U.S. embassy in Vienna was subjected to bomb threats and protests. The hypocrisy of the I.O.C's decision against Schranz was shown by the fact that the eventual downhill gold medalist, Bernhard Russi, had allowed his photo and name to be used on matchboxes, car stickers, and newspaper advertisements as part of a large-scale pre-Olympic publicity campaign for a Swiss insurance company. Karl Schranz announced his retirement from competitive skiing as soon as the 1972 Olympics had ended. In 1988, the I.O.C. awarded Schranz a symbolic medal as a participant in the Sapporo Games.

**1976 Innsbruck** C: 74, N: 27, D: 2.5.

| | | | |
|---|---|---|---|
| 1. | Franz Klammer | AUT | 1:45.73 |
| 2. | Bernhard Russi | SWI | 1:46.06 |
| 3. | Herbert Plank | ITA | 1:46.59 |
| 4. | Philippe Roux | SWI | 1:46.69 |
| 5. | Ken Read | CAN | 1:46.83 |
| 6. | Andy Mill | USA | 1:47.06 |
| 7. | Walter Tresch | SWI | 1:47.29 |
| 8. | David Irwin | CAN | 1:47.41 |

In 1975 Franz Klammer of Mooswald in Carinthia won eight of nine World Cup downhill races. When the Olympics came to Innsbruck the following year there was great pressure on the 22-year-old Klammer as an Austrian favorite competing in Austria. Further pressure was exerted by defending champion Bernhard Russi, who sped down the 3145-meter (1.95 miles) Olympic hill in 1:46.06. The 15th starter of the day, Klammer fell one-fifth of a second off Russi's pace, but fought back wildly in the last 1000 meters to nip Russi by one-third of a second. Flushed with excitement, Klammer told reporters, "I thought I was going to crash all the way. . . . Now I've got everything. I don't need anything else."

**1980 Lake Placid** C: 47, N: 22, D: 2.14

| | | | |
|---|---|---|---|
| 1. | Leonhard Stock | AUT | 1:45.50 |
| 2. | Peter Wirnsberger | AUT | 1:46.12 |
| 3. | Steve Podborski | CAN | 1:46.62 |
| 4. | Peter Müller | SWI | 1:46.75 |
| 5. | Pete Patterson | USA | 1:47.04 |
| 6. | Herbert Plank | ITA | 1:47.13 |
| 7. | Werner Grissmann | AUT | 1:47.21 |
| 8. | Valery Tsyganov | SOV | 1:47.34 |

The Austrian alpine team was so strong that they had seven men ranked in the top 20 in the world. When it was decided to leave Franz Klammer behind, team manager Karl "Downhill Charlie" Kahr had to explain the decision on national television. Leonhard Stock, who had broken a collarbone in December, was chosen to go to Lake Placid as an alternate. But when he recorded the fastest time in two of the three pre-Olympic trial runs, Austrian alpine officials changed their minds and declared that Stock was now a starter, along with Harti

Weirather, but that the other three Austrians— Wirnsberger, Grissmann, and Sepp Walcher—would have to have a race-off for the final two spots. Walcher lost out. The four remaining Austrians all placed in the top nine, as Leonhard Stock went from being an alternate who had never won a World Cup race to being an Olympic champion in less than 30 hours. After the 1980 Olympics, he never won another race.

**1984 Sarajevo** C: 61, N: 25, D: 2.16.
1. William Johnson        USA    1:45.59
2. Peter Müller           SWI    1:45.86
3. Anton Steiner          AUT    1:45.95
4. Pirmin Zurbriggen      SWI    1:46.05
5. Helmut Höflehner       AUT    1:46.32
5. Urs Räber              SWI    1:46.32
7. Sepp Wildgruber        GER    1:46.53
8. Steve Podborski        CAN    1:46.59

When Bill Johnson was seventeen years old, he was caught red-handed trying to steal a car. The judge in charge of his case, upon learning that Johnson was an excellent skier, sent him not to prison, but to a ski academy. The judge's decision turned out to be a fine advertisement for creative sentencing. Not only did Johnson never steal another car, but his skiing led him all the way to the Olympics. Still, two months before the Sarajevo Games, Bill Johnson seemed an unlikely candidate to win a gold medal. No U.S. male skier had ever won an Olympic downhill medal. And there was nothing in the least bit impressive about Johnson's record on the World Cup circuit. But then, in mid-January, he won the prestigious Lauberhorn downhill at Wengen, Switzerland. A couple of undistinguished performances were followed by a fourth at Cortina and Johnson suddenly looked like a serious contender, particularly considering that the Olympic course on Mt. Bjelašnica was relatively free of turns—perfect for a "glider" like Bill Johnson, who was able to keep his tuck longer than other skiers. When he scored the best series of places during the five practice runs, Johnson actually found himself the betting favorite.

Not the modest type, Johnson agreed with the emerging consensus. "I don't even know why everyone else is here," he announced to reporters. "They should hand [the gold medal] to me. Everyone else can fight for second place."

Heavy snow and powerful winds caused the downhill to be postponed three times, but Johnson seemed unperturbed by the delays. "Everyone knows it's my kind of course," he said.

When the weather finally cleared on the mountain, Johnson made good on his boasts. When told afterwards that the beaten skiers of the "downhill mafia"—Austria and Switzerland, had grumbled that he had won because the course was an easy one, Johnson snapped, "If it's so easy, why didn't *they* win it?"

**1988 Calgary-Nakiska** C: 51, N: 18, D: 2.15.
1. Pirmin Zurbriggen      SWI    1:59.63
2. Peter Müller           SWI    2:00.14
3. Franck Piccard         FRA    2:01.24
4. Leonhard Stock         AUT    2:01.56
5. Gerhard Pfaffenbichler AUT    2:02.02
6. Markus Wasmeier        GER    2:02.03
7. Anton Steiner          AUT    2:02.19
8. Martin Bell            GBR    2:02.49

The two favorites in the 1988 downhill, Peter Müller and Pirmin Zurbriggen, were both Swiss and they had both won a world championship in the event (Müller in 1987, Zurbriggen in 1985). But there the similarities ended. Müller was a "flatlander" from the Zurich suburb of Adliswil; Zurbriggen was from the tiny village of Saas Almagell (population 300) in the Valais Alps. Müller, age 30, fit the stereotype of the wild, high-living alpine ski champion; Zurbriggen, age 25, was every Swiss parent's dream son, a homebody who helped his mother do the dishes, prayed three times a day, and made pilgrimages to Lourdes. Müller was a downhill specialist; Zurbriggen was an all-arounder entered in all five alpine events in Calgary. Zurbriggen was also the overall World Cup champion in 1984 and 1987 and runner-up to Marc Girardelli in 1985 and 1986.

Müller, who had a history of skiing well in North America, was the first skier down the course. The next six skiers failed to come within three seconds of Müller's time and it became clear that he had had a great run. By the time Zurbriggen, skiing 14th, started, Müller still led by 1.42 seconds. Zurbriggen had watched the first two turns of Müller's run and knew immediately that he would need the race of his life to beat him. He tried to avoid hearing Müller's final time, but heard it anyway, which increased his nervousness. Nevertheless, Zurbriggen exploded down the course with an aggressiveness that belied his gentle exterior and Müller was forced to settle for his second straight silver medal.

## SLALOM

Whereas the downhill requires pure speed, the slalom (or "special slalom") is more a test of control. Each skier is required to weave in and out of blue- and red-flagged double poles, or "gates." There are two runs on different courses. Times for the two runs are added to determine final places.

**1924–1936** not held

**1948 St. Moritz** C: 76, N: 22, D: 2.5.
1. Edi Reinalter          SWI    2:10.3
2. James Couttet          FRA    2:10.8
3. Henri Oreiller         FRA    2:12.8
4. Silvio Alverà          ITA    2:13.2
5. Olle Dahlman           SWE    2:13.6
6. Egon Schöpf            AUT    2:14.2

7. Jack Reddish      USA   2:15.5
8. Karl Molitor      SWI   2:16.2

Alverà led after the first run, followed by Couttet, Reinalter, and Oreiller. Reinalter's second run of 1:02.6 was a half second faster than the next best skier, Egon Schöpf.

**1952 Oslo** C: 86, N: 27, D: 2.19.
1. Othmar Schneider   AUT   2:00.0
2. Stein Eriksen      NOR   2:01.2
3. Guttorm Berge      NOR   2:01.7
4. Zeno Colò          ITA   2:01.8
5. Stig Sollander     SWE   2:02.6
6. James Couttet      FRA   2:02.8
7. Fredy Rubi         SWI   2:03.3
8. Per Rollum         NOR   2:04.5

The fastest time of the first run, 59.2, was first posted by Stein Eriksen, who had won the giant slalom four days earlier, and then equaled by Hans Senger of Austria. Downhill silver medalist Othmar Schneider was third in 59.5. The second run saw Senger fall, while Schneider's 1:00.5 was beaten only by Fredy Rubi's 59.7. Antoin Miliordos of Greece, disgusted by the fact that he fell 18 times, sat down and crossed the finish line backward. His time for one run was 26.9 seconds slower than Schneider's time for two runs.

**1956 Cortina** C: 89, N: 29, D: 1.31.
1. Anton Sailer           AUT   3:14.7
2. Chiharu Igaya          JPN   3:18.7
3. Stig Sollander         SWE   3:20.2
4. Joseph Brooks Dodge    USA   3:21.8
5. Georges Schneider      SWI   3:22.8
6. Gérard Pasquier        FRA   3:24.6
7. Charles Bozon          FRA   3:26.2
8. Bernard Perret         FRA   3:26.3

Sailer recorded the fastest times in both runs and won his second gold medal.

**1960 Squaw Valley** C: 63, N: 21, D: 2.24.
1. Ernst Hinterseer       AUT   2:08.9
2. Matthias Leitner       AUT   2:10.3
3. Charles Bozon          FRA   2:10.4
4. Ludwig Leitner         GER   2:10.5
5. Josef "Pepi" Stiegler  AUT   2:11.1
6. Guy Périllat           FRA   2:11.8
7. Hans-Peter Lanig       GER   2:14.3
8. Parlde Milianti        ITA   2:14.4

Eighteen-year-old Willi Bogner of Germany, whose father was the first designer of stretch pants, had the fastest time of the first run, 1:08.8. Hinterseer and Leitner, fifth and ninth after the first run, led the way on the second course in 58.2 and 59.2. Bogner, meanwhile, had fallen and was disqualified.

**1964 Innsbruck** C: 96, N: 28, D: 2.8.
1. Josef "Pepi" Stiegler  AUT   2:11.13
2. William Kidd           USA   2:11.27
3. James Heuga            USA   2:11.52
4. Michel Arpin           FRA   2:12.91
5. Ludwig Leitner         GER   2:12.94
6. Adolf Mathis           SWI   2:12.99
7. Gerhard Nenning        AUT   2:13.20
8. Wallace "Bud" Werner   USA   2:13.46

Pepi Stiegler, a 26-year-old photographer, had twice been removed from the Austrian team and replaced by Egon Zimmermann. Both times he was reinstated after public pressure. After the first run, Stiegler led by a second over Karl Schranz, who was followed by Heuga, Nenning, Mathis, and Kidd. Stiegler skied cautiously the second time around, registering the 8th best time, but his first-round performance turned out to be good enough to edge the Americans.

**1968 Grenoble-Chamrousse** C: 100, N: 33, D: 2.17.
1. Jean-Claude Killy       FRA   1:39.73
2. Herbert Huber           AUT   1:39.82
3. Alfred Matt             AUT   1:40.00
4. Dumeng Giovanoli        SWE   1:40.22
5. Vladimir Sabich         USA   1:40.49
6. Andrzej Bachleda        POL   1:40.61
7. James Heuga             USA   1:40.97
8. Alain Penz              FRA   1:41.14

With two gold medals down and one to go for Jean-Claude Killy, the slalom was held in bad weather, with fog, mist, and shadows prevailing. The skiers pleaded that the contest be postponed, but the officials in charge refused. Appropriately, the sun shown through only once—during Killy's first run, which was good enough to put him in first place. Killy was the first skier of the second round, so he was forced to wait anxiously as the others came down the hill. Häkon Mjön of Norway bettered Killy's time, but was disqualified for missing two gates. Then came the turn of Karl Schranz, the biggest threat to Killy's goal of a triple crown. But something curious happened as Schranz sped through the fog, something that has never been fully explained. As Schranz approached the 22nd gate, a mysterious figure in black crossed the course. Schranz skidded to a halt and, with three witnesses in tow, walked back to the starting point to ask for a rerun. Colonel Robert Readhead, the British referee, granted Schranz's request. This time Schranz achieved an almost perfect run, beat Killy's time, and was declared the unofficial winner. Schranz was allowed to enjoy the postrace press conference, while Killy sulked in the corner. But two hours later it was announced that Schranz had been disqualified for missing two gates just prior to his encounter with the mysterious interloper.

The Austrians were outraged. Schranz claimed that if he did miss a gate or two it was because he had already been distracted by the sight of someone on the course. His supporters contended that the mystery man had been a French policeman or soldier who had purposely interfered with Schranz in order to insure Killy's victory. The French, on the other hand, hinted that Schranz had made up the whole story after he had missed a gate. A final five-hour meeting of the Jury of Appeal ended with a 3–2 vote against Schranz, with two Frenchmen and a Swiss voting to give the gold medal to Killy, while Colonel Readhead and a Norwegian supported Schranz. Because of this incident, the 1968 Winter Olympics ended in a rather ugly mood, but back home in Val d'Isère Killy had no trouble putting it out of his mind. "The party went on for two and a half days," he later recalled, "and the whole time I never saw the sun once."

**1972 Sapporo-Teineyama** C: 72, N: 31, D: 2.13.
1. Francisco Fernandez Ochoa   SPA   1:49.27
2. Gustav Thöni                ITA   1:50.28
3. Roland Thöni                ITA   1:50.30
4. Henri Duvillard             FRA   1:50.45
5. Jean-Noël Augert            FRA   1:50.51
6. Eberhard Schmalzl           ITA   1:50.83
7. David Zwilling              AUT   1:51.97
8. Edmund Bruggmann            SWI   1:52.03

The biggest surprise of the 1972 Winter Games was the sensational victory of 21-year-old Paquito Ochoa of Spain, who had never before finished higher than sixth in an international meet. Not only was Ochoa's gold medal the first ever won by Spain in the Winter Olympics, but it was the first Spanish victory of any kind since the equestrian team jumping competition of 1928. Ochoa was so overcome by emotion that he was unable to speak to reporters except to say, "I can't believe it. It can't be true." An hour later, referring to Spain's leading matador, he said, "El Cordobés is a little man compared with me. I am the champion."

**1976 Innsbruck** C: 94, N: 31, D: 2.14.
1. Piero Gros              ITA   2:03.29
2. Gustav Thöni            ITA   2:03.73
3. Willy Frommelt          LIE   2:04.28
4. Walter Tresch           SWI   2:05.26
5. Christian Neureuther    GER   2:06.56
6. Wolfgang Junginger      GER   2:07.08
7. Alois Morgenstern       AUT   2:07.18
8. Peter Luscher           SWI   2:08.10

Fifth after the first run, Gros was "as sure as I could be that I could never beat Thöni. In my opinion at that time Gustavo had the gold medal in his pocket." But a superb second run, over a second faster than that of Thöni, his teammate and mentor, gave Gros the victory.

**1980 Lake Placid** C: 79, N: 28, D: 2.22.
1. Ingemar Stenmark    SWE   1:44.26
2. Phillip Mahre       USA   1:44.76
3. Jacques Lüthy       SWI   1:45.06
4. Hans Enn            AUT   1:45.12

5. Christian Neureuther   GER   1:45.14
6. Petar Popangelov       BUL   1:45.40
7. Anton Steiner          AUT   1:45.41
8. Gustav Thöni           ITA   1:45.99

Skiing with a three-inch metal plate and four screws in his left ankle joint, the result of a bad fall 11 months earlier, Phil Mahre of White Pass, Washington, whizzed down the first run in 53.31. Because he was the first skier to compete, there was no way to judge if this was a good time or a bad time. But by the time the 13th skier, favorite Ingemar Stenmark, had completed the course over a half second slower than Mahre, it was clear that the 22-year-old American would enter the second round in first place. However Stenmark, in fourth place, had come from behind three days earlier to win the giant slalom, and he was known for his lightning second runs. Sure enough, he tore down the course in 50.37, a time that no one could beat. Three skiers later, Phil Mahre, needing a 50.94 to win the gold medal, never gained his rhythm and could only manage 51.45. Ingemar Stenmark, the Silent Swede, had completed his slalom double, but was not impressed by his accomplishment. "History is not important," he said. "The important thing is that I am satisfied with myself." As for Phil Mahre, he was back on the slopes the next day—filming an American Express commercial.

**1984 Sarajevo** C: 101, N: 37, D: 2.19.
1. Phillip Mahre           USA   1:39.41
2. Steven Mahre           USA   1:39.62
3. Didier Bouvet          FRA   1:40.20
4. Jonas Nilsson          SWE   1:40.25
5. Oswald Tötsch          ITA   1:40.48
6. Petar Popangelov       BUL   1:40.68
7. Bojan Križaj           YUG   1:41.51
8. Lars-Göran Halvarsson  SWE   1:41.70

Of the seven World Cup slalom events held prior to the Olympics, six had been won by either Ingemar Stenmark or Marc Girardelli, neither of whom was allowed to take part in the Sarajevo Games. Stenmark's punishment was a result of his being a professional, a rather ludicrous charge considering the huge amounts of money being earned by numerous other skiers. Girardelli's problem was that he competed for Luxembourg even though he was an Austrian citizen.

With Stenmark and Girardelli gone, the natural favorites seemed to be three-time defending World Cup champion Phil Mahre and his twin brother Steve. But after a decade on the circuit, the Mahres seemed to have lost their competitive edge. They were already thinking ahead to their post-Olympic retirement. Phil was also concerned about his pregnant wife, Dolly, who was back in the United States with a due date of February 27. The 1983–84 season had been a disaster for the Mahres. Steve stood 45th in the World Cup standings, Phil 62nd. Even when things went right, they went wrong. On January 16,

Steve had won the slalom at Parpan, Switzerland, with Phil placing sixth. Then it was discovered that the twins had inadvertently switched their number bibs and both were disqualified. Girardelli was awarded the victory. The situation did not improve for the Mahres in Sarajevo. In the giant slalom, held five days before the slalom, Phil finished eighth and Steve seventeenth.

At a press conference, Phil tried to put things in perspective. "I'm pretty mellow about Sarajevo," he said. "I have nothing to prove, nothing to escape. I've enjoyed myself, and that's the essence of sport." Then he added, "I think it is unfortunate that all the emphasis is on coming here and winning medals. The problem with gold medals is that it sets you for life or it doesn't. Well, I'm set for life, so I don't care."

The U.S. press did not take kindly to Phil Mahre's relativist attitude. Referring to his eighth place giant slalom finish, Dan Barreiro of the *Dallas Morning News* ranted, "That's the good news. The bad news is Mahre gets another chance Sunday in the slalom. I hope he chokes again. Or that he doesn't even show up. Phil Mahre is America's best skier, but he could do us all a favor by getting out of town. Right now." Not to be outdone by his crosstown rival, Skip Bayless of the *Dallas Times Herald* referred to Phil as the "ugly American skier." "Perhaps Mahre never sat in front of a free-enterprise TV and got caught up in some Yank beating some communist at some foreign game."

The slalom course on Mt. Bjelašnica turned out to be a difficult one, as only 47 of the 101 starters managed to complete both runs. But while other skiers were literally falling by the wayside and Texas sportswriters were sniffing the odor of crow in their kitchens, the Mahre twins were back to their old form. At the end of the first run, Steve was in first place with a big lead of almost seven-tenths of a second, and Phil was in third. In second place was Jonas Nilsson, who was not considered a threat, due to his inexperience.

Phil Mahre executed an excellent second run and then immediately grabbed a walkie-talkie radio to pass on some final advice to the only person who stood between him and a gold medal—his brother Steve. Steve could have skied a safe race and still won. Instead he attacked the course, made too many mistakes, and had to settle for the silver medal.

For two brothers to win the gold and silver in the same event certainly makes for a fine day, but there was more good news for the Mahres. As they left the Olympic Village to attend the medal ceremony, Phil was informed that his wife had just given birth to their second child and first son. At a press conference after the ceremony, Phil was asked what part his wife had played in his career. He tried to answer, but was stopped by tears. Steve put his arm around his brother, who then recovered enough to say, "Heck, there she was, doing all the work while I was out there playing."

**1988 Calgary-Nakiska** C: 109, N: 37, D: 2.27.
1. Alberto Tomba      ITA   1:39.47
2. Frank Wörndl       GER   1:39.53
3. Paul Frommelt      LIE   1:39.84
4. Bernhard Gstrein   AUT   1:40.08
5. Ingemar Stenmark   SWE   1:40.22
6. Jonas Nilsson      SWE   1:40.23
7. Pirmin Zurbriggen  SWI   1:40.48
8. Oswald Tötsch      ITA   1:40.55

World champion Frank Wörndl recorded the fastest time of the first run, with Jonas Nilsson second and Alberto Tomba, who had won the giant slalom two days earlier, third. The winner of the second run was the legend: Ingemar Stenmark, but his eleventh place earlier in the day kept him out of the medals. Tomba, who had skied with relative caution in the first run, went all out to register the second fastest time of the second run. Then he watched as Wörndl suffered a momentary lapse of concentration in the middle of the course, allowing Tomba to gain the closest-ever victory in a men's alpine race.

## GIANT SLALOM

The giant slalom is similar to the slalom except the course is longer, the gates are farther apart, and the corners are not so sharp.

**1924–1948** not held

**1952 Oslo-Norefjell** C: 83, N: 26, D: 2.15.
1. Stein Eriksen        NOR   2:25.0
2. Christian Pravda     AUT   2:26.9
3. Toni Spiss           AUT   2:28.8
4. Zeno Colò            ITA   2:29.1
5. Georges Schneider    SWI   2:31.2
6. Joseph Brooks Dodge  USA   2:32.6
6. Stig Sollander       SWE   2:32.6
8. Bernhard Perren      SWI   2:33.1

Stein Eriksen was the first of only three skiers from outside of the Alps to win an Olympic men's alpine gold medal. He was also the first skiing superstar. He was handsome, stylish, and glamorous. At the Oslo Games he proved to be a modest winner, declaring, "I had a great advantage over most of the others because I knew the course by heart." In 1954 Eriksen won the world combined alpine championship. Immediately afterward, he became a ski school director at Boyne Mt., Michigan. He moved on to Heavenly Valley, California, in 1957, Aspen Highlands, Colorado, in 1959, Sugarbush, Vermont, in 1965, Snowmass, Colorado, in 1969, and Park City, Utah, in 1973. Everywhere he went Stein Eriksen became the inspiration for the stereotypical ski instructor of the 1950s and 1960s—rich, good-looking, an outdoorsman who made women melt, and, above all, an Olympic champion.

**1956 Cortina** C: 95, N: 29, D: 1.29.

1. Anton Sailer        AUT    3:00.1
2. Andreas Molterer    AUT    3:06.3
3. Walter Schuster     AUT    3:07.2
4. Adrien Duvillard    FRA    3:07.2
5. Charles Bozon       FRA    3:08.4
6. Ernst Hinterseer    AUT    3:08.5
7. Hans-Peter Lanig    GER    3:08.6
8. Sepp Behr           GER    3:11.4

The 1956 giant slalom was held on the "Ilio Colli" course at Cortina. Ilio Colli was a local skier who had crashed into a tree at 50 m.p.h. during a race. He broke his skull and died instantly. Each participant in the giant slalom was handed a souvenir picture of Colli. In his book *My Way to the Triple Olympic Victory,* Toni Sailer wrote, "It is a beautiful thought to name such a famous course . . . after a dead racer, even if it is not exactly encouraging for those starting to be handed such a death notice." When the sixth skier, Andreas "Anderl" Molterer, came down in 3:06.3, he was mobbed and congratulated. But Molterer waved everyone away, telling them, "Toni hasn't come yet." When Toni did come, he came really fast—in 3:00.1, over six seconds better than any of the other 94 skiers. In the next five days Sailer also won the slalom and the downhill.

**1960 Squaw Valley** C: 65, N: 21, D: 2.21.

1. Roger Staub            SWI    1:48.3
2. Josef "Pepi" Stiegler  AUT    1:48.7
3. Ernst Hinterseer       AUT    1:49.1
4. Thomas Corcoran        USA    1:49.7
5. Bruno Alberti          ITA    1:50.1
6. Guy Périllat           FRA    1:50.7
7. Karl Schranz           AUT    1:50.8
8. Paride Milianti        ITA    1:50.9

**1964 Innsbruck** C: 96, N: 29, D: 2.2.

1. François Bonlieu       FRA    1:46.71
2. Karl Schranz           AUT    1:47.09
3. Josef "Pepi" Stiegler  AUT    1:48.05
4. Willy Favre            SWI    1:48.69
5. Jean-Claude Killy      FRA    1:48.92
6. Gerhard Nenning        AUT    1:49.68
7. William Kidd           USA    1:49.97
8. Ludwig Leitner         GER    1:50.04

Mountain guide François Bonlieu engaged in a running battle with the French coaches and officials and refused to listen to their advice. His rebelliousness turned out to be wisdom, as he upset the Austrians on their own course.

**1968 Grenoble-Chamrousse** C: 99, N: 36, D: 2.12.

1. Jean-Claude Killy      FRA    3:29.28
2. Willy Favre            SWI    3:31.50
3. Heinrich Messner       AUT    3:31.83
4. Guy Périllat           FRA    3:32.06
5. William Kidd           USA    3:32.37

6. Karl Schranz           AUT    3:33.08
7. Dumeng Giovanoli       SWI    3:33.55
8. Gerhard Nenning        AUT    3:33.61

For the first time the giant slalom was decided by a combination of two runs on separate days, rather than by a single run. This was the second of Killy's three gold medals. He had the fastest time of the first run and extended his winning margin over the second run.

**1972 Sapporo-Teineyama** C: 73, N: 27, D: 2.10.

1. Gustav Thöni          ITA    3:09.62
2. Edmund Bruggmann      SWI    3:10.75
3. Werner Mattle         SWE    3:10.99
4. Alfred Hagn           GER    3:11.16
5. Jean-Noël Augert      FRA    3:11.84
6. Max Rieger            GER    3:11.96
7. David Zwilling        AUT    3:12.32
8. Reinhard Tritscher    AUT    3:12.42

Erik Håker of Norway had the fastest time of the first run, followed by Alfred Hagn and Gustav Thöni. When Håker opened the second run by falling and Hagn skied too cautiously, the way was open for the 20-year-old Thöni to become the first Italian to win an alpine gold medal since Zeno Colò won the downhill in 1952.

**1976 Innsbruck** C: 97, N: 32, N: 2.9.

1. Heini Hemmi           SWI    3:26.97
2. Ernst Good            SWI    3:27.17
3. Ingemar Stenmark      SWE    3:27.41
4. Gustav Thöni          ITA    3:27.67
5. Phillip Mahre         USA    3:28.20
6. Engelhard Pargätzi    SWI    3:28.76
7. Fausto Radici         ITA    3:30.09
8. Franco Bieler         ITA    3:30.24

Neither Hemmi nor Good had ever won a World Cup race. They had been placed third and second after the first run, behind Gustav Thöni. However, Thöni's second run was only the eighth best of the day, while Hemmi's and Good's were second and third best. Ingemar Stenmark, ninth after the first run, stormed back with the fastest second-round time to take the bronze medal and establish a pattern that was to make him extremely famous in the years to come.

**1980 Lake Placid** C: 78, N: 28, D: 2.19.

1. Ingemar Stenmark      SWE    2:40.74
2. Andreas Wenzel        LIE    2:41.49
3. Hans Enn              AUT    2:42.51
4. Bojan Križaj          YUG    2:42.53
5. Jacques Lüthy         SWI    2:42.75
6. Bruno Nöckler         ITA    2:42.95
7. Joel Gaspoz           SWI    2:43.05
8. Boris Strel           YUG    2:43.24

Born in the small village of Tarnaby in Swedish Lapland, about 100 miles south of the Arctic Circle, Ingemar Stenmark learned to ski at an early age because, "It was a thing I could do alone." When he was 10 years old he wrote a school essay on "How I See My Future." Stenmark wrote that he wanted to be a ski racer. When the teacher returned his paper she told him that his dream was "unrealistic . . . impossible to achieve." She was wrong. Ingemar Stenmark grew up to become the most successful ski racer in history. He was the overall World Cup leader three times and he won the slalom and giant slalom titles eight times each. When he retired in 1989, he had won a record 86 World Cup races. No other skier has won half that many.

On September 14, 1979, Stenmark, then 23 years old, was practicing his downhill technique in the Italian Alps when he lost control and tumbled violently down the hill for 200 meters. Lying unconscious on the snow, he began foaming at the mouth and experiencing spasms. He had suffered a major concussion. But five months later he was in top shape again for the Olympics, although he did skip the downhill race. As usual, Stenmark skied somewhat cautiously on his first run of the giant slalom, placing third behind Andreas Wenzel and Bojan Križaj. But on the second day Stenmark roared down the course almost a full second faster than anyone else. "I'm not disappointed," said silver medalist Wenzel. "I had an idea this would happen."

**1984 Sarajevo** C: 108, N: 38, D: 2.14.
1. Max Julen SWI 2:41.18
2. Jure Franko YUG 2:41.41
3. Andreas Wenzel LIE 2:41.75
4. Franz Gruber AUT 2:42.08
5. Boris Strel YUG 2:42.36
6. Hubert Strolz AUT 2:42.71
7. Alex Giorgi ITA 2:43.00
8. Phillip Mahre USA 2.43.25

Twenty-two-year-old Max Julen of Zermatt led after the first run and clocked the second fastest time of the second run to hold off the powerful finish of hometown favorite Jure Franko. Franko, the first Yugoslav to win a Winter Olympics medal, became a national hero, his performance touching off boisterous celebrations in Sarajevo.

**1988 Calgary-Nakiska** C: 117, N: 39, D: 2.25.
1. Alberto Tomba ITA 2:06.37
2. Hubert Strolz AUT 2:07.41
3. Pirmin Zurbriggen SWI 2:08.39
4. Ivano Camozzi ITA 2:08.77
5. Rudolf Nierlich AUT 2:08.92
6. Andreas Wenzel AUT 2:09.03
7. Helmut Mayer LIE 2:09.09
8. Frank Wörndl AUT 2:09.22

Alberto Tomba, the son of a wealthy textile merchant, didn't win his first World Cup race until November 27, 1987, but in the two and a half months before the Olympics he won seven slalom and giant slalom races. His

sudden success catapulted the raucous Italian from being an unknown into the role of favorite.

Tomba obliterated the field in the first run, registering a time 1.14 seconds faster than Hubert Strolz in second place. While waiting for the second run, Tomba impulsively walked up to a pay phone and placed a collect call to his startled family in Lazzaro di Savenna, a suburb of Bologna. Perhaps he just wanted to remind his father of the elder Tomba's promise to buy his son a Ferrari if he won a gold medal in Calgary.

Two other incidents occurred during the break between runs. Race officials disqualified the entire Canadian team for wearing ski suits that had not been submitted for safety inspection. Having punished the Canadians, they went down the line and eliminated the Bolivians, the Moroccans, the Lebanese, and the Taiwanese, as well. On a darker note, Austria's leading orthopedic surgeon, Jörg Oberhammer, collided with another skier, fell beneath a snow-grooming machine, and was killed instantly. This horrible incident was witnessed by Swiss skiers Pirmin Zurbriggen and Martin Hangl, who happened to be passing overhead in a chairlift. A shaken Zurbriggen still managed to capture the bronze medal, but Hangl collapsed near the starting gate and had to withdraw.

When the competition resumed, Strolz picked up one tenth of a second over Tomba, but it wasn't nearly enough to prevent the latter from qualifying for his Ferrari. "I want it red," he told reporters.

## SUPER GIANT SLALOM

The Super-G, first included in the World Cup in 1983, is an attempt to combine the speed of the downhill with the technical skills of the giant slalom.

**1024–1984** not held

**1988 Calgary-Nakiska** C: 94, N: 34, D: 2.21.
1. Franck Piccard FRA 1:39.66
2. Helmut Mayer AUT 1:40.96
3. Lars-Börje Eriksson SWE 1:41.08
4. Hubert Strolz AUT 1:41.11
5. Günther Mader AUT 1:41.96
5. Pirmin Zurbriggen SWI 1:41.96
7. Luc Alphand FRA 1:42.27
8. Leonhard Stock AUT 1:42.36

Franck Piccard, a 23-year-old from Albertville, the hub of the 1992 Winter Games, had never won a World Cup race. He had, however, picked up a bronze medal in the downhill six days before the Super-G. When he reached the end of the latter race, he felt he had blown it. "I was really angry with myself," he said. But one by one he watched the favorites fall or at least commit worse mistakes than he had, and before he knew it, he had earned France's first alpine gold in twenty years.

# ALPINE COMBINED

This event combines one downhill run and, the next day, two slalom runs.

**1924–1932** not held

**1936 Garmisch-Partenkirchen** C: 66, N: 21, D: 2.9.

|   |   |   | PTS. |
|---|---|---|------|
| 1. | Franz Pfnür | GER | 99.25 |
| 2. | Gustav Lantschner | GER | 96.26 |
| 3. | Emile Allais | FRA | 94.69 |
| 4. | Birger Ruud | NOR | 93.38 |
| 5. | Roman Wörndle | GER | 91.16 |
| 6. | Rudolf Cranz | GER | 91.03 |
| 7. | Giacinto Sertorelli | ITA | 90.39 |
| 8. | Alf Konningen | NOR | 90.06 |

Franz Pfnür, a 27-year-old woodcarver and cabinetmaker from Bavaria, was second to Birger Ruud in the downhill and first in both runs of the slalom. Silver medalist Gustav "Guzzi" Lantschner was described by Albion Ross of *The New York Times* as "a violent Nazi." Born and raised in Innsbruck, Austria, Lantschner moved to Germany and became a cameraman for the Nazi party. Resat Erces of Turkey showed great patience when he completed the downhill course in 22:44.4—18 minutes slower than Birger Ruud.

**1948 St. Moritz** C: 78, N: 24, D: 2.4.

|   |   |   | PTS. |
|---|---|---|------|
| 1. | Henri Oreiller | FRA | 3.27 |
| 2. | Karl Molitor | SWI | 6.44 |
| 3. | James Couttet | FRA | 6.95 |
| 4. | Edi Mall | AUT | 8.54 |
| 5. | Silvio Alverà | ITA | 8.71 |
| 6. | Hans Hansson | SWE | 9.31 |
| 7. | Vittorio Chierroni | ITA | 9.69 |
| 8. | Hans Nogler | AUT | 9.96 |

**1952–1984** not held

**1988 Calgary-Nakiska** C: 56, N: 20, D: 2.17.

|   |   |   | PTS. |
|---|---|---|------|
| 1. | Hubert Strolz | AUT | 36.55 |
| 2. | Bernhard Gstrein | AUT | 43.45 |
| 3. | Paul Accola | SWI | 48.24 |
| 4. | Luc Alphand | FRA | 57.73 |
| 5. | Peter Jurko | CZE | 58.56 |
| 6. | Jean-Luc Cretier | FRA | 62.98 |
| 7. | Markus Wasmeier | GER | 65.44 |
| 8. | Adrian Bíreš | CZE | 68.50 |

Pirmin Zurbriggen recorded the fastest time in the downhill and led by over two seconds after the first run of the slalom. He seemed well on his way to his second gold of the Calgary Games when he hooked a tip on the 39th of 57 gates on the second slalom run, ran right into the 40th gate, spun around, and landed on his back. Hubert Strolz, a 25-year-old policeman and a good friend of Zurbriggen's, was the immediate beneficiary of the Swiss star's mistake.

Paul Accola took the bronze despite placing only twenty-fourth in the downhill. He did record the best combined time in the slalom. Only 26 of the 56 starters completed all three runs.

# ALPINE SKIING

WOMEN
Downhill
Slalom
Giant Slalom
Super Giant Slalom
Alpine Combined

## WOMEN

### DOWNHILL

**1924–1936** not held

**1948 St. Moritz** C: 37, N: 11, D: 2.2.
1. Hedy Schlunegger    SWI    2:28.3
2. Trude Beiser    AUT    2:29.1
3. Resi Hammer    AUT    2:30.2
4. Celina Seghi    ITA    2:31.1
5. Lina Mittner    SWI    2:31.2
6. Suzanne Thiollière    FRA    2:31.4
7. Françoise Gignoux    FRA    2:32.4
7. Laila Schou-Nilsen    NOR    2:32.4

**1952 Oslo-Norefjell** C: 42, N: 13, D: 2.17.
1. Trude Jochum-Beiser    AUT    1:47.1
2. Annemarie Buchner    GER    1:48.0
3. Giuliana Minuzzo    ITA    1:49.0
4. Erika Mahringer    AUT    1:49.5
5. Dagmar Rom    AUT    1:49.8
6. Madeleine Berthod    SWI    1:50.7
7. Margit Hvammen    NOR    1:50.9
8. Joanne Hewson    CAN    1:51.3

**1956 Cortina** C: 47, N: 16, D: 2.1.
1. Madeleine Berthod    SWI    1:40.7
2. Frieda Dänzer    SWI    1:45.4
3. Lucile Wheeler    CAN    1:45.9
4. Giuliana Chenal-Minuzzo    ITA    1:47.0
4. Hilde Hofherr    AUT    1:47.3
6. Carla Marchelli    ITA    1:47.7
7. Dorothea Hochleitner    AUT    1:47.9
8. Josette Neviere    FRA    1:49.2

Madeleine Berthod, the favorite in the event, celebrated her 25th birthday the day she won the downhill gold medal. Her margin of victory was four times larger than any other winner's in this event.

**1960 Squaw Valley** C: 42, N: 14, D: 2.20.
1. Heidi Biebl    GER    1:37.6
2. Penelope Pitou    USA    1:38.6
3. Traudl Hecher    AUT    1:38.9
4. Pia Riva    ITA    1:39.9

5. Jerta Schir    ITA    1:40.5
6. Anneliese Meggl    GER    1:40.8
7. Sonja Peril    GER    1:41.0
8. Erika Netzer    AUT    1:41.1

As a first-year student in high school, Penny Pitou made the boys' varsity ski team and finished fifth in the New Hampshire state slalom championship before being banned from further competition by the local school board. At the age of 15 she qualified for the U.S. Olympic team, finishing 31st, 34th, and 34th. Four years later she was the favorite at Squaw Valley, but the pressure on her was great. "The predictions that I'm going to win make me nervous," she said. "America is putting its hopes on me and it's a terrible feeling. . . . I'd be much happier being a normal girl, sitting at home or going to school." A near-fall three gates from the finish cost her about two seconds and the gold medal. Later she was married for a few years to Austrian downhill gold medalist Egon Zimmermann. And later still she became New Hampshire's first female bank director.

**1964 Innsbruck** C: 43, N: 15, D: 2.6.
1. Christl Haas    AUT    1:55.39
2. Edith Zimmermann    AUT    1:56.42
3. Traudl Hecher    AUT    1:56.66
4. Heidi Biebl    GER    1:57.87
5. Barbara Henneberger    GER    1:58.03
6. Madeleine Bochatay    FRA    1:59.11
7. Nancy Greene    CAN    1:59.23
8. Christine Terraillon    FRA    1:59.66

When she was three years old, Christl Haas told her parents that she wanted to become a ski racer. Seventeen years later the 5-foot 10-inch Haas, skiing in the 13th position, had no trouble living up to her role of an Austrian favorite competing in Austria.

**1968 Grenoble-Chamrousse** C: 39, N: 14, D: 2.10.
1. Olga Pall    AUT    1:40.87
2. Isabelle Mir    FRA    1:41.33
3. Christl Haas    AUT    1:41.41
4. Brigitte Seiwald    AUT    1:41.82
5. Annie Famose    FRA    1:42.15
6. Felicity Field    GBR    1:42.79
7. Fernande Bochatay    SWI    1:42.87
8. Marielle Goitschel    FRA    1:42.95

The Austrians went 1, 3, 4 despite the absence of one of their leading performers: 1966 world champion Erica Schinegger. During routine medical testing prior to the Grenoble Games, doctors were surprised to discover that the saliva of the 20-year-old ski star contained only male hormones. Further examination revealed that Schinegger, who was raised as a girl, actually had male sex organs which had grown inside instead of outside. Schinegger eventually underwent corrective surgery, changed his name to Eric, married, became a father and, in 1988, handed over his world championship gold medal to second-place finisher Marielle Goitschel.

**1972 Sapporo-Eniwadake** C: 41, N: 13, D: 2.5.

| | | | |
|---|---|---|---|
| 1. | Marie-Theres Nadig | SWI | 1:36.68 |
| 2. | Annemarie Pröll | AUT | 1:37.00 |
| 3. | Susan Corrock | USA | 1:37.68 |
| 4. | Isabelle Mir | FRA | 1:38.62 |
| 5. | Rosi Speiser | GER | 1:39.10 |
| 6. | Rosi Mittermaier | GER | 1:39.32 |
| 7. | Bernadette Zurbriggen | SWI | 1:39.49 |
| 8. | Annie Famose | FRA | 1:39.70 |

The first noteworthy time was 1:38.62, registered by the eighth skier, Isabelle Mir. Next on the course was French heroine Annie Famose, who was having an exhausting time defending her eligibility from accusations of "commercialism" by the International Ski Federation. Famose finished in eighth place. The tenth skier, unheralded Susan Corrock of Ketchum, Idaho, surprised the experts by taking the lead in 1:37.68. Three skiers later came an even bigger surprise. Seventeen-year-old Marie-Theres Nadig of Flums, Switzerland, who had never won a World Cup race, beat Corrock's time by exactly one second. The 15th skier was the pre-Olympic favorite, 18-year-old Annemarie Pröll. The previous year she had become the youngest-ever overall winner of the World Cup. Pröll skied an excellent race, but finished one third of a second slower than Nadig. Disappointed and angry, she refused to attend the post-race press conference.

According to *Ski* magazine, after her victory Marie-Theres Nadig told the following story to her coach: "I was on the last flat stretch that leads into the steep wall before the finish, when I thought suddenly of a film [*The Love Bug*] I had seen last summer. It was about a funny little car that dreamed of racing in the Grand Prix. The little car was called Herbie. In each race it would start ahead of the other champions who would chase it. Suddenly I saw myself in the role of Herbie. I was being chased by hordes of other racers. A voice inside me said, 'Go, Herbie, go, go, go.' At each 'go,' I would lower my body still further to cut the wind resistance. In my whole life I never skied in such a low crouch. I could easily have fallen. But inside me, I always heard the voice crying out, 'Go, Herbie, go.' "

**1976 Innsbruck** C: 38, N: 15, D: 2.8.

| | | | |
|---|---|---|---|
| 1. | Rosi Mittermaier | GER | 1:46.16 |
| 2. | Brigitte Totschnigg | AUT | 1:46.68 |
| 3. | Cynthia Nelson | USA | 1:47.50 |
| 4. | Nicola-Andrea Spiess | AUT | 1:47.71 |
| 5. | Danielle Debernard | FRA | 1:48.48 |
| 6. | Jacqueline Rouvier | FRA | 1:48.58 |
| 7. | Bernadette Zurbriggen | SWI | 1:48.62 |
| 8. | Marlies Oberholzer | SWI | 1:48.68 |

Rosi Mittermaier had never before won a major downhill race, even though she was competing in her tenth World Cup season and her third Olympics.

**1980 Lake Placid** C: 28, N: 13, D: 2.17.

| | | | |
|---|---|---|---|
| 1. | Annemarie Moser-Pröll | AUT | 1:37.52 |
| 2. | Hanni Wenzel | LIE | 1:38.22 |
| 3. | Marie-Theres Nadig | SWI | 1:38.36 |
| 4. | Heidi Preuss | USA | 1:39.51 |
| 5. | Kathy Kreiner | CAN | 1:39.53 |
| 6. | Ingrid Eberle | AUT | 1:39.63 |
| 7. | Torill Fjeldstad | NOR | 1:39.69 |
| 7. | Cynthia Nelson | USA | 1:39.69 |

Winning two Olympic silver medals would probably be a dream come true for most skiers, but when Annemarie Pröll won two silvers at Sapporo in 1972, losing both times to Marie-Theres Nadig, she considered it a failure and a humiliation. She was back to her winning ways before long, but in March 1975, after marrying ski salesman Herbert Moser, she retired from competitive skiing and bypassed the 1976 Olympics. After her father died later that year, Annemarie Pröll returned to the circuit. By 1979 she had won six of the last nine annual World Cups and finished second twice. However, the 1980 season had seen her win only one downhill race to Nadig's six. Motivated by the only achievement that had eluded her, Moser-Pröll, the sixth skier, sped down the course on Whiteface Mountain in 1:37.52. Her time withstood the onslaughts of Nadig and Wenzel and earned her the final jewel in her champion's crown.

**1984 Sarajevo** C: 32, N: 13, D: 2.16.

| | | | |
|---|---|---|---|
| 1. | Michela Figini | SWI | 1:13.36 |
| 2. | Maria Walliser | SWI | 1:13.41 |
| 3. | Olga Charvátová | CZE | 1:13.53 |
| 4. | Ariane Ehrat | SWI | 1:13.95 |
| 5. | Jana Gantnerová | CZE | 1:14.14 |
| 6. | Marina Kiehl | GER | 1:14.30 |
| 6. | Gerry Sorensen | CAN | 1:14.30 |
| 8. | Lea Sölkner | AUT | 1:14.39 |

Michela Figini scored her first World Cup victory only two weeks before the Olympics. At Sarajevo she recorded the fastest time in three of the five practice runs and was leading the real race on February 15th when it was cancelled because of fog. The next day she confirmed her new consistency by becoming, at age 17, the youngest skier ever to win an Olympic gold medal.

**1988 Calgary-Nakiska** C: 35, N: 14, D: 2.19.

| | | |
|---|---|---|
| 1. Marina Kiehl | GER | 1:25.86 |
| 2. Brigitte Oertli | SWI | 1:26.61 |
| 3. Karen Percy | CAN | 1:26.62 |
| 4. Maria Walliser | SWI | 1:26.89 |
| 5. Laurie Graham | CAN | 1:26.99 |
| 6. Petra Kronberger | AUT | 1:27.03 |
| 7. Regine Mösenlechner | GER | 1:27.16 |
| 8. Elisabeth Kirchler | AUT | 1:27.19 |

Marina Kiehl, a 23-year-old millionaire's daughter from Munich, had a reputation for having a lofty and generally unpleasant personality. Her manager and her sponsors finally convinced her to control her sharp tongue and to make an effort to be friendly to those around her. Kiehl succeeded in making herself more likable, but her race results declined dramatically. Things got so bad that a popular German sports writer urged her, in print, to "go ahead and be rude again, because when you are bad you are better." When German Olympic officials threatened to drop her from the roster for the Super-G, her best event, Kiehl exploded at them, much to the relief of her fans. A deal was worked out: if Kiehl finished in the top six of the downhill, she could also take part in the Super-G. If she failed, she would be bumped from the starting lineup.

In seven years on the World Cup circuit, Kiehl had never won a downhill race. In Calgary she had a wild run, almost falling twice. "I was out of control up there," she explained afterward, "so I just let the skis go faster and faster." Because she had twice lost races to unheralded, late-starting skiers, Kiehl refused to celebrate her victory until the final Argentinian had skied off the course. Three days later Kiehl competed in the Super-G—and finished in a tie for twelfth place.

## SLALOM

**1924–1936** not held

**1948 St. Moritz** C: 28, N: 10, D: 2.5.

| | | |
|---|---|---|
| 1. Gretchen Fraser | USA | 1:57.2 |
| 2. Antoinette Meyer | SWI | 1:57.7 |
| 3. Erika Mahringer | AUT | 1:58.0 |
| 4. Georgette Miller-Thiollière | FRA | 1:58.8 |
| 5. Renée Clerc | SWI | 2:05.8 |
| 6. Anneliese Schuh-Proxauf | AUT | 2:06.7 |
| 7. Rese Hammerer | AUT | 2:08.6 |
| 8. Andrea Mead | USA | 2:08.8 |

Gretchen Fraser of Vancouver, Washington, had qualified for the U.S. team for the 1940 Olympics that were never held. Eight years later she was considered an unknown quantity. Skiing in the first position she clocked the fastest time of the first run—59.7. Erika Mahringer was one-tenth of a second behind her. As Fraser prepared to lead off the second round, a problem suddenly developed in the telephone timing system between the

top and the bottom of the hill. Despite a 17-minute delay at such a critical time, Fraser finished the second run in 57.5, a time beaten only by Antoinette Meyer (57.0.)

**1952 Oslo** C: 40, N: 14, D: 2.20.

| | | |
|---|---|---|
| 1. Andrea Mead Lawrence | USA | 2:10.6 |
| 2. Ossi Reichert | GER | 2:11.4 |
| 3. Annemarie Buchner | GER | 2:13.3 |
| 4. Celina Seghi | ITA | 2:13.8 |
| 5. Imogene Anna Opton | USA | 2:14.1 |
| 6. Madeleine Berthod | SWI | 2:14.9 |
| 7. Agnel Marysette | FRA | 2:15.6 |
| 8. Trude Jochum-Beiser | AUT | 2:15.9 |
| 8. Giuliana Minuzzo | ITA | 2:15.9 |

Nineteen-year-old Andrea Mead Lawrence of Rutland, Vermont, fell early in her first run, but got up, and showed her superiority by finishing the course with the fourth best time. She overhauled the leaders with a second run that was two seconds faster than anyone else's. Lawrence became the first American skier to win two gold medals. By the time of the opening of the 1956 Games, she had given birth to three children.

**1956 Cortina** C: 48, N: 16, D: 1.30.

| | | |
|---|---|---|
| 1. Renée Colliard | SWI | 1:52.3 |
| 2. Regina Schöpf | AUT | 1:55.4 |
| 3. Yevgenia Sidorova | SOV | 1:56.7 |
| 4. Giuliana Chenal-Minuzzo | ITA | 1:56.8 |
| 5. Josefine Frandl | AUT | 1:57.9 |
| 6. Inger Björnbakken | NOR | 1:58.0 |
| 6. Astrid Sandvik | NOR | 1:58.0 |
| 8. Josette Neviere | FRA | 1:58.3 |

Renée Colliard, a pharmacy student from Geneva, was making her first appearance as a member of the Swiss team. Racing in the number-one position, she registered the fastest time in each run.

**1960 Squaw Valley** C: 43, N: 14, D: 2.26.

| | | |
|---|---|---|
| 1. Anne Heggtveit | CAN | 1:49.6 |
| 2. Betsy Snite | USA | 1:52.9 |
| 3. Barbara Henneberger | GER | 1:56.6 |
| 4. Thérèse Leduc | FRA | 1:57.4 |
| 5. Hilde Hofherr | AUT | 1:58.0 |
| 5. Liselotte Michel | SWI | 1:58.0 |
| 7. Stalian Korzukhina | SOV | 1:58.4 |
| 8. Sonja Sperl | GER | 1:58.8 |

**1964 Innsbruck** C: 48, N: 16, D: 2.1.

| | | |
|---|---|---|
| 1. Christine Goitschel | FRA | 1:29.86 |
| 2. Marielle Goitschel | FRA | 1:30.77 |
| 3. Jean Saubert | USA | 1:31.36 |
| 4. Heidi Biebl | GER | 1:34.04 |
| 5. Edith Zimmermann | AUT | 1:34.27 |
| 6. Christl Haas | AUT | 1:35.11 |
| 7. Liv Jagge | NOR | 1:36.38 |
| 8. Patricia du Roy de Blicquy | BEL | 1:37.01 |

Christine and Marielle Goitschel, teenaged sisters from Val d'Isère, the home of Jean-Claude Killy, were the stars of the 1964 ski contests. Marielle, the favorite, had the fastest time of the first run, 43.09, with her older sister, Christine, in second place at 43.85. Christine prevailed in the second round, giving the Goitschels a one-two finish. That same day, back in France, their younger sister, Patricia, won a National Junior title.

**1968 Grenoble-Chamrousse** C: 49, N: 18, D: 2.13.
1. Marielle Goitschel      FRA    1:25.86
2. Nancy Greene            CAN    1:26.15
3. Annie Famose            FRA    1:27.89
4. Gina Hathorn            GBR    1:27.92
5. Isabelle Mir            FRA    1:28.22
6. Burgl Färbinger         GER    1:28.90
7. Glorianda Cipolla       ITA    1:29.74
8. Bernadette Rauter       AUT    1:30.44

Sixteen-year-old Judy Nagel of Enumclaw, Washington, was the surprise leader of the first run, but she fell at the beginning of her second run and, although she finished the course, was disqualified for missing a gate.

**1972 Sapporo-Teineyama** C: 42, N: 13, D: 2.11.
1. Barbara Cochran         USA    1:31.24
2. Danièlle Debernard      FRA    1:31.26
3. Florence Steurer        FRA    1:32.69
4. Judy Crawford           CAN    1:33.95
5. Annemarie Pröll         AUT    1:34.03
6. Pamela Behr             GER    1:34.27
7. Monika Kaserer          AUT    1:34.36
8. Patricia Boydstun       USA    1:35.59

Back home in Richmond, Vermont, Barbara Cochran's father had taught his talented children how to save a tenth of a second by setting their bodies in motion before pushing open the starting wand that sets off the timing mechanism. That one-tenth second turned out to be the difference betwen gold and silver for Barbara Cochran. Her time for the first run was three one-hundredths of a second faster than Danièlle Debernard. In the final run Debernard was able to pick up only one of the three-hundredths of a second. Only 19 of 42 starters made it through both runs without falling or missing a gate.

**1976 Innsbruck** C: 42, N: 14, D: 2.11.
1. Rosi Mittermaier        GER    1:30.54
2. Claudia Giordani        ITA    1:30.87
3. Hanni Wenzel            LIE    1:32.20
4. Danièlle Debernard      FRA    1:32.24
5. Pamela Behr             GER    1:32.31
6. Linda Cochran           USA    1:33.24
7. Christa Zechmeister     GER    1:33.72
8. Wanda Bieter            ITA    1:35.66

For the second straight time, 42 women started the Olympic slalom, but only 19 finished both courses without missing a gate. Rosi Mittermaier recorded the fastest time of the second run after trailing teammate Pamela

Behr by nine-hundredths of a second after the first run. Mittermaier had already won the downhill race three days earlier.

**1980 Lake Placid** C: 47, N: 21, D: 2.23.
1. Hanni Wenzel            LIE    1:25.09
2. Christa Kinshofer       GER    1:26.50
3. Erika Hess              SWI    1:27.89
4. Mariarosa Quario        ITA    1:27.92
5. Claudia Giordani        ITA    1:29.12
6. Nadezhda Patrakeeva     SOV    1:29.20
7. Daniela Zini            ITA    1:29.22
8. Christin Cooper         USA    1:29.28

German-born Hanni Wenzel moved to tiny Liechtenstein (population 25,000) when she was one year old. She was granted Liechtenstein citizenship after winning the slalom at the 1974 world championships in St. Moritz. Having already finished second in the downhill and first in the giant slalom at the 1980 Olympics, Wenzel breezed through the slalom, registering the best time in both the first and second runs. By earning two gold medals and one silver in one Olympics, she matched the 1976 feat of Rosi Mittermaier. Hanni's brother, Andreas, won the silver medal in the downhill, to give Liechtenstein four medals at the Lake Placid Games, one for every 6250 people. If the U.S. had won the same number of medals per capita it would have won 36,000 medals. Actually there were only 114 medals awarded.

**1984 Sarajevo** C: 45, N: 19, D: 2.17.
1. Paoletta Magoni         ITA    1:36.47
2. Perrine Pelen           FRA    1:37.38
3. Ursula Konzett          LIE    1:37.50
4. Roswitha Steiner        AUT    1:37.84
5. Erika Hess              SWI    1:37.91
6. Malgorzata Tlalka       POL    1:37.95
7. Maria Rosa Quario       ITA    1:37.99
8. Anni Kronbichler        AUT    1:38.05

The first run leader was unheralded Christelle Guignard of France, however she missed a turn on the top half of the second run and failed to finish. In fact, only 21 of the 45 starters completed both runs without missing a gate. The winner was 19-year-old Paoletta Magoni, a bricklayer's daughter from Selvino who had never before finished better than sixth in a World Cup race.

**1988 Calgary-Nakiska** C: 57, N: 25, D: 2.26.
1. Vreni Schneider              SWI    1:36.69
2. Mateja Svet                  YUG    1:38.37
3. Christa Kinshofer-Güthlein   GER    1:38.40
4. Roswitha Steiner             AUT    1:38.77
5. Blanca Fernández Ochoa       SPA    1:39.44
6. Ida Ladstätter               AUT    1:39.59
7. Paoletta Magoni Sforza       ITA    1:39.76
8. Dorota Tlalka-Mogore         FRA    1:39.86

Schneider, who had already won the giant slalom two days earlier, recorded the fastest time in both runs. Camilla Nilsson of Sweden trailed Schneider by only one one-hundredth of a second after the first run, but fell early in the second run and was eliminated.

# GIANT SLALOM

**1924–1948** not held

**1952 Oslo-Norefjell** C: 45, N: 15, D: 2.14.
1. Andrea Mead Lawrence   USA   2:06.8
2. Dagmar Rom   AUT   2:09.0
3. Annemarie Buchner   GER   2:10.0
4. Trude Klecker   AUT   2:11.4
5. Katy Rodolph   USA   2:11.7
6. Borghild Niskin   NOR   2:11.9
7. Celina Seghi   ITA   2:12.5
8. Ossi Reichert   GER   2:13.2

Silver medalist Dagmar Rom was a well-known Austrian film actress.

**1956 Cortina** C: 49, N: 16, D: 1.27.
1. Ossi Reichert   GER   1:56.5
2. Josefine Frandl   AUT   1:57.8
3. Dorothea Hochleitner   AUT   1:58.2
4. Madeleine Berthod   SWI   1:58.3
4. Andrea Mead Lawrence   USA   1:58.3
6. Lucile Wheeler   CAN   1:58.6
7. Borghild Niskin   NOR   1:59.0
8. Marysette Agnel   FRA   1:59.4

**1960 Squaw Valley** C: 44, N: 14, D: 2.23.
1. Yvonne Rüegg   SWI   1:39.9
2. Penelope Pitou   USA   1.40.0
3. Giuliana Chenal-Minuzzo   ITA   1:40.2
4. Betsy Snite   USA   1.40.4
5. Carla Marchelli   ITA   1:40.7
5. Anneliese Meggl   GER   1:40.7
7. Thérèse Leduc   FRA   1:40.8
8. Anne-Marie Leduc   FRA   1:41.5

**1964 Innsbruck** C: 46, N: 15, D: 2.3.
1. Marielle Goitschel   FRA   1:52.24
2. Christine Goitschel   FRA   1:53.11
2. Jean Saubert   USA   1.53.11
4. Christl Haas   AUT   1:53.86
5. Annie Famose   FRA   1:53.89
6. Edith Zimmermann   AUT   1:54.21
7. Barbara Henneberger   GER   1:54.26
8. Traudl Hecher   AUT   1:54.55

On February 1, Christine Goitschel had won the slalom with her younger sister, Marielle, second and Jean Saubert third. Christine was the first of the three to go down the course of the giant slalom two days later. Her time of 1:53.11 looked good. Three skiers later Jean Saubert clocked the exact same time despite the introduction of timing to the hundredth of a second. When Marielle Goitschel, the 14th skier, heard that Saubert

had equaled her sister's time, she attacked the course with extra determination and earned herself the gold medal.

After her victory, 18-year old Marielle announced to the press that she had just become engaged to a 20-year-old French skier by the name of Jean-Claude Killy, who had finished fifth in the giant slalom the day before. "I am happy and I am in love," she enthused. While the more gullible reporters scurried away to spread the exciting news around the world, Marielle and Christine sat back and enjoyed their little hoax. When the press caught up with Killy, he smiled and spilled out the truth. "The joke of a tomboy," he said. "Marielle talks too much." It says a lot about the fully justified self-confidence of the Goitschel sisters that they had actually planned their practical joke the night before the race, on the assumption that one of them would win the gold medal.

**1968 Grenoble-Chamrousse** C: 47, N: 18, D: 2.15.
1. Nancy Greene   CAN   1:51.97
2. Annie Famose   FRA   1:54.61
3. Fernande Bochatay   SWI   1:54.74
4. Florence Steurer   FRA   1:54.75
5. Olga Pall   AUT   1:55.61
6. Isabelle Mir   FRA   1:56.07
7. Marielle Goitschel   FRA   1:56.09
8. Divina Galica   GBR   1:56.58

In 1967 Nancy Greene of Rossland, British Columbia, won the inaugural World Cup despite missing three of the nine meets. The following year she participated in her third Olympics, finally winning a well-deserved gold medal.

**1972 Sapporo-Teineyama** C: 42, N: 13, D: 2.8.
1. Marie-Theres Nadig   SWI   1:29.90
2. Annemarie Pröll   AUT   1:30.75
3. Wiltrud Drexel   AUT   1:32.35
4. Laurie Kreiner   CAN   1:32.48
5. Rosl Speiser   GER   1:32.56
6. Florence Steurer   FRA   1:32.59
7. Divina Galica   GBR   1:32.72
8. Brit Lafforgue   FRA   1:32.80

Hoping to avenge her upset defeat at the hands of Marie-Theres Nadig in the downhill, Annemarie Pröll, the second skier, slammed down the course in 1:30.75. Her time held up until Nadig, in the tenth spot, clocked 1:29.90. Pröll, bearing the burden of being the favorite, was bitterly disappointed. "Two silver medals don't equal one gold medal," she said. Nadig attributed her victory to the fact that she was relaxed while Pröll had been under enormous pressure. After the Olympics, however, Nadig learned first hand what her rival had had to endure. "After Sapporo," Nadig later said, "people expected everything from me. They expected me to win all the time, and after a while I didn't know where I was."

**1976 Innsbruck** C: 45, N: 17, D: 2.13.

| | | |
|---|---|---|
| 1. Kathy Kreiner | CAN | 1:29.13 |
| 2. Rosi Mittermaier | GER | 1:29.25 |
| 3. Danièlle Debernard | FRA | 1:29.95 |
| 4. Lise-Marie Morerod | SWI | 1:30.40 |
| 5. Marie-Theres Nadig | SWI | 1:30.44 |
| 6. Monika Kaserer | AUT | 1:30.49 |
| 7. Wilma Gatta | ITA | 1:30.51 |
| 8. Evi Mittermaier | GER | 1:30.64 |

There was great excitement before the running of the giant slalom because everyone wanted to know if Rosi Mittermaier would become the first woman to sweep the three alpine races. They didn't have to wait long to find out. The first skier on the course, 18-year-old Kathy Kreiner of Timmins, Ontario, had an excellent run and flashed across the finish line in 1:29.13. Three skiers later it was Rosi Mittermaier's turn. A half-second ahead of Kreiner's pace at the halfway mark, Mittermaier lost precious fractions of a second when she approached one of the lower gates too directly. Her final time was one-eighth of a second slower than Kreiner's.

**1980 Lake Placid** C: 46, N: 21, D: 2.21.

| | | |
|---|---|---|
| 1. Hanni Wenzel | LIE | 2:41.66 |
| 2. Irene Epple | GER | 2:42.12 |
| 3. Perrine Pelen | FRA | 2:42.41 |
| 4. Fabienne Serrat | FRA | 2:42.42 |
| 5. Christa Kinshofer | GER | 2:42.63 |
| 6. Annemarie Moser-Pröll | AUT | 2:43.19 |
| 7. Christin Cooper | USA | 2:44.71 |
| 8. Maria Epple | GER | 2:45.56 |

For the first time, the women's giant slalom was held as a two-run competition. Wenzel had the fastest time of the first run and the third fastest of the second. She was Liechtenstein's first Olympic gold medal winner.

**1984 Sarajevo** C: 54, N: 21, D: 2.13.

| | | |
|---|---|---|
| 1. Debbie Armstrong | USA | 2:20.98 |
| 2. Christin Cooper | USA | 2:21.38 |
| 3. Perrine Pelen | FRA | 2:21.40 |
| 4. Tamara McKinney | USA | 2:21.83 |
| 5. Marina Kiehl | GER | 2:22.03 |
| 6. Blanca Fernández Ochoa | SPA | 2:22.14 |
| 7. Erika Hess | SWI | 2:22.51 |
| 8. Olga Charvátová | CZE | 2:22.57 |

With hundreds of sports journalists crowding around and pestering the world's leading skiers from the moment they arrived in Sarajevo, 20-year-old Debbie Armstrong of Seattle, Wash., was blessed with anonymity. The night before the giant slalom, she watched Peter and Kitty Carruthers win silver medals for pairs figure skating and then stayed up late indulging her addiction to peanut butter. The next day, relaxed and "having fun," she recorded the second fastest time of the first run, only one-tenth of a second behind teammate Christin Cooper. During the 2½ hour break before the final run, Armstrong, who had never won a World Cup race, was more than a little excited.

"I felt so good at the top," she would say afterwards. "I was so happy waiting for that second run. It was so much fun. I knew it was a good hill for me. I knew if I stayed relaxed the skiing would take care of itself. I didn't feel the pressure."

According to Cooper, who would hit the course immediately after Armstrong, "She was so hyped up, it was really funny. She kept coming up to me and bouncing all over me and telling me to have a good time. She would say, 'I'm just going to have fun out there, just have fun, have fun!' And when she was in the gate, I could hear her talking to herself. She was saying, 'Okay, De . . . have a good run, have a good run. Just have a good time.' And then she turned to me and said, 'You too, Coop. Have the run of your life.' " With that, Armstrong was out of the starting gate and down the slope. Her time was the fourth best of the second run, but when Cooper slipped at the fifth gate, losing valuable moments, the gold medal went to the ebullient Armstrong.

At the post-race press conference she was asked what she had sacrificed to become a champion skier. She replied, "Nothing. Skiing is my life. That's what I love to do." Then she added characteristically, "It's fun."

Armstrong, who finished 13th in the 1988 giant slalom, never won another international race.

**1988 Calgary-Nakiska** C: 64, N: 26, D: 2.24.

| | | |
|---|---|---|
| 1. Vreni Schneider | SWI | 2:06.49 |
| 2. Christa Kinshofer-Güthlein | GER | 2:07.42 |
| 3. Maria Walliser | SWI | 2:07.72 |
| 4. Mateja Svet | YUG | 2:07.80 |
| 5. Christine Meier | GER | 2:07.88 |
| 6. Ulrike Maier | AUT | 2:08.10 |
| 7. Anita Wachter | AUT | 2:08.38 |
| 8. Catherine Quittet | FRA | 2:08.84 |

The first-round leader was Spain's Blanca Fernández Ochoa. She was followed by 1980 silver medalist Christa Kinshofer-Güthlein, Anita Wachter, Christine Meier, and, in fifth place, the favorite, world champion and World Cup champion Vreni Schneider. Fernández Ochoa fell early in her second run. Schneider, on the other hand, registered the fastest time of the round to score one of her patented come-from-behind victories.

Only 29 of the 64 starters completed both runs. In 28th place was Seba Johnson of the U.S. Virgin Islands, the first black skier to take part in the Olympics and, at age 14, the youngest competitor at the Calgary Games.

## SUPER GIANT SLALOM

**1924–1984** not held

**1988 Calgary-Nakiska** C: 46, N: 20, D: 2.22.

| | | |
|---|---|---|
| 1. Sigrid Wolf | AUT | 1:19.03 |
| 2. Michela Figini | SWI | 1:20.03 |

| | | |
|---|---|---|
| 3. Karen Percy | CAN | 1:20.29 |
| 4. Regine Mösenlechner | GER | 1:20.33 |
| 5. Anita Wachter | AUT | 1:20.36 |
| 6. Maria Walliser | SWI | 1:20.48 |
| 7. Zoë Haas | SWI | 1:20.91 |
| 7. Micaela Marzola | ITA | 1:20.91 |

Five weeks before the Olympics, Sigrid Wolf won a Super-G race in Lech, Austria, but was disqualified for wearing a safety pin on her number bib to keep it from flapping in the wind. In Calgary, Wolf again raced with a safety pin—but this time it was attached to a necklace for good luck.

# ALPINE COMBINED

**1924–1932** not held

**1936 Garmisch-Partenkirchen** C: 37, N: 13, D: 2.8.

| | | PTS. |
|---|---|---|
| 1. Christl Cranz | GER | 97.06 |
| 2. Käthe Grasegger | GER | 95.26 |
| 3. Laila Schou Nilsen | NOR | 93.48 |
| 4. Erna Steuri | SWI | 92.36 |
| 5. Hadi Pfeiffer | GER | 91.85 |
| 6. Lisa Resch | GER | 88.74 |
| 7. Johanne Dybwad | NOR | 85.90 |
| 8. Jeanette Kessler | GBR | 83.97 |

Christl Cranz was only sixth in the downhill, but her times in the two slalom runs were so superior that she won anyway. Her first run was four seconds faster than her closest competitor and her second run was 7.2 seconds better than any of her rivals. Diana Gordon-Lennox, representing Canada, received an ovation because she skied both the downhill and slalom with one arm in a cast and using only one pole. She also wore a monocle while competing. Gordon-Lennox finished 29th.

**1948 St. Moritz** C: 28, N: 10, D: 2.4.

| | | PTS. |
|---|---|---|
| 1. Trude Beiser | AUT | 6.58 |
| 2. Gretchen Fraser | USA | 6.95 |
| 3. Erika Mahringer | AUT | 7.04 |
| 4. Celina Seghi | ITA | 7.46 |
| 5. Françoise Gignoux | FRA | 8.14 |
| 6. Rosmarie Bleuer | SWI | 8.80 |
| 7. Anneliese Schuh-Proxauf | AUT | 9.76 |
| 8. Hedy Schlunegger | SWI | 10.20 |

**1952–1984** not held

**1988 Calgary-Nakiska** C: 39, N: 14, D: 2.21.

| | | PTS. |
|---|---|---|
| 1. Anita Wachter | AUT | 29.25 |
| 2. Brigitte Oertli | SWI | 29.48 |
| 3. Maria Walliser | SWI | 51.28 |
| 4. Karen Percy | CAN | 54.47 |
| 5. Lenka Kebrlová | CZE | 60.87 |
| 6. Lucia Medzihradská | CZE | 63.56 |
| 7. Michelle McKendry | CAN | 64.85 |
| 8. Kerrin Lee | CAN | 65.20 |

Wachter's surprising third-place finish in the downhill run set her up as the overnight favorite. Oertli, the pre-Olympic favorite, picked up 2.26 seconds in the two slalom runs, but it wasn't enough to overcome her eleventh-place finish in the downhill.

# FREESTYLE SKIING

## MEN
### MOGULS

Moguls are snow bumps. A moguls competition consists of high-speed turns on a heavily moguled course. Skiers are judged on their speed as well as on their technique.

This event will be held for the first time in 1992.

## WOMEN
### MOGULS

This event will be held for the first time in 1992.

# NORDIC SKIING

**MEN**

15 Kilometers (Classical)
30 Kilometers (Classical)
50 Kilometers (Freestyle)
4 × 10-Kilometer Relay
2 × 15-Kilometer Combined Pursuit
Ski Jump, Normal Hill, Individual

Ski Jump, Large Hill, Individual
Ski Jump, Large Hill, Team
Nordic Combined, Individual
Nordic Combined, Team

## MEN

Cross-country, or *langlauf*, races are run against the
clock with the skiers leaving the starting line at 30-second
intervals. The only exceptions are the 4 × 10-kilometer
relay, in which the first runners for each team start together, and the second half of the combined pursuit.

Two skiing techniques are used in Nordic events. The
"classical" requires a diagonal stride; the "freestyle" has
no restrictions and employs the faster "skating" style.

## 15 KILOMETERS (CLASSICAL)

The 18- and 15-kilometer cross-country race has been
thoroughly dominated by four nations: Norway, Sweden,
Finland, and the U.S.S.R. These four nations have won
all 45 medals, and only five other countries have managed to finish in the top eight.

**1924 Chamonix** C: 41, N: 12, D: 2.2.
*18 Kilometers*
| | | | |
|---|---|---|---|
| 1. | Thorleif Haug | NOR | 1:14.31.0 |
| 2. | Johan Gröttumsbråten | NOR | 1:15.51.0 |
| 3. | Tapani Niku | FIN | 1:16.26.0 |
| 4. | Jon Maardalen | NOR | 1:16.56.0 |
| 5. | Einar Landvik | NOR | 1:17.27.0 |
| 6. | Per Erik Hedlund | SWE | 1:17.49.0 |
| 7. | Matti Raivio | FIN | 1:19.10.0 |
| 8. | Elis Sandin | SWE | 1:19.24.0 |

Thorleif Haug won the second of his three gold medals,
having won the 50-kilometer race three days earlier. The
Scandinavians took the first 11 places.

**1928 St. Moritz** C: 49, N: 15, D: 2.17.
*18 Kilometers*
| | | | |
|---|---|---|---|
| 1. | Johan Gröttumsbråten | NOR | 1:37.01.0 |
| 2. | Ole Hegge | NOR | 1:39.01.0 |
| 3. | Reidar Ödegaard | NOR | 1:40.11.0 |
| 4. | Veli Saarinen | FIN | 1:40.57.0 |
| 5. | Hagbart Haakonsen | NOR | 1:41.29.0 |
| 6. | Per Erik Hedlund | SWE | 1:41.51.0 |
| 7. | Lars Theodor Johnsson | SWE | 1:41.59.0 |
| 7. | Martti Lappalainen | FIN | 1:41.59.0 |

**1932 Lake Placid** C: 42, N: 11, D: 2.10.
*18 Kilometers*
| | | | |
|---|---|---|---|
| 1. | Sven Utterström | SWE | 1:23.07.0 |
| 2. | Axel Wikström | SWE | 1:25.07.0 |
| 3. | Veli Saarinen | FIN | 1:25.24.0 |
| 4. | Martti Lappalainen | FIN | 1:26.31.0 |
| 5. | Arne Rustadstuen | NOR | 1:27.06.0 |
| 6. | Johan Gröttumsbråten | NOR | 1:27.15.0 |
| 7. | Valmari Toikka | FIN | 1:27.51.0 |
| 8. | Ole Stenen | NOR | 1:28.05.0 |

Once again, Scandinavians took the first 11 places.

**1936 Garmisch–Partenkirchen** C: 75, N: 22, D: 2.12.
*18 Kilometers*
| | | | |
|---|---|---|---|
| 1. | Erik-August Larsson | SWE | 1:14.38.0 |
| 2. | Oddbjörn Hagen | NOR | 1:15.33.0 |
| 3. | Pekka Niemi | FIN | 1:16.59.0 |
| 4. | Martin Matsbo | SWE | 1:17.02.0 |
| 5. | Olaf Hoffsbakken | NOR | 1:17.37.0 |
| 6. | Arne Rustadstuen | NOR | 1:18.13.0 |
| 7. | Sulo Nurmela | FIN | 1:18.20.0 |
| 8. | Artur Häggblad | SWE | 1:18.55.0 |

**1948 St. Moritz** C: 84; N: 15, D: 1.31.
*18 Kilometers*
| | | | |
|---|---|---|---|
| 1. | Martin Lundström | SWE | 1:13.50.0 |
| 2. | Nils Östensson | SWE | 1:14.22.0 |
| 3. | Gunnar Eriksson | SWE | 1:16.06.0 |
| 4. | Heikki Hasu | FIN | 1:16.43.0 |
| 5. | Nils Karlsson | SWE | 1:16.54.0 |
| 6. | Sauli Rytky | FIN | 1:18.10.0 |
| 7. | August Kiuru | FIN | 1:18.25.0 |
| 8. | Teuvo Laukkanen | FIN | 1:18.51.0 |

**1952 Oslo** C: 80, N: 18, D: 2.18.
*18 Kilometers*
| | | | |
|---|---|---|---|
| 1. | Hallgeir Brenden | NOR | 1:01.34.0 |
| 2. | Tapio Mäkelä | FIN | 1:02.09.0 |
| 3. | Paavo Lonkila | FIN | 1:02.20.0 |
| 4. | Heikki Hasu | FIN | 1:02.24.0 |
| 5. | Nils Karlsson | SWE | 1:02.56.0 |
| 6. | Martin Stokken | NOR | 1:03.00.0 |
| 7. | Nils Täpp | SWE | 1:03.35.0 |
| 8. | Tauno Sipila | FIN | 1:03.40.0 |

In an amazing display of regional dominance, Finland, Norway, and Sweden claimed the first 17 places. Hallgeir Brenden, a 23-year-old lumberjack and farmer from the small town of Tyrsil, was also Norway's national steeplechase champion.

**1956 Cortina** C: 62, N: 20, D: 1.30.
| | | |
|---|---|---|
| 1. Hallgeir Brenden | NOR | 49:39.0 |
| 2. Sixten Jernberg | SWE | 50:14.0 |
| 3. Pavel Kolchin | SOV | 50:17.0 |
| 4. Veikko Hakulinen | FIN | 50:31.0 |
| 5. Håkon Brusveen | NOR | 50:36.0 |
| 6. Martin Stokken | NOR | 50:45.0 |
| 7. Nikolai Anikin | SOV | 50.58.0 |
| 8. Lennart Larsson | SWE | 51:03.0 |

Kolchin and Anikin were the first non-Scandinavians to crack the top eight in this event. This was also the first time that the race was conducted at 15 kilometers rather than 18.

**1960 Squaw Valley** C: 54, N: 19, D: 2.23.
| | | |
|---|---|---|
| 1. Håkon Brusveen | NOR | 51:55.5 |
| 2. Sixten Jernberg | SWE | 51:58.6 |
| 3. Veikko Hakulinen | FIN | 52:03.0 |
| 4. Einar Östby | NOR | 52:18.0 |
| 4. Gennady Vaganov | SOV | 52:18.0 |
| 6. Eero Mäntyranta | FIN | 52:40.6 |
| 7. Janne Stefansson | SWE | 52:41.0 |
| 8. Rolf Rämgård | SWE | 52:47.3 |

**1964 Innsbruck-Seefeld** C: 71, N: 24, D: 2.2.
| | | |
|---|---|---|
| 1. Eero Mäntyranta | FIN | 50:54.1 |
| 2. Harald Grönningen | NOR | 51:34.8 |
| 3. Sixten Jernberg | SWE | 51:42.2 |
| 4. Väinö Huhtala | FIN | 51:45.4 |
| 5. Janne Stefansson | SWE | 51:46.4 |
| 6. Pavel Kolchin | SOV | 51:52.0 |
| 7. Igor Voronchikin | SOV | 51:53.9 |
| 8. Magnar Lundemo | NOR | 51:55.2 |

Mäntyranta and Grönningen took the same places they had taken in the 30-kilometer race three days earlier. Mäntyranta made his living on skis as a border patrol officer, a common vocation for state-supported skiers.

**1968 Grenoble-Autrans** C: 75, N: 24, D: 2:10.
| | | |
|---|---|---|
| 1. Harald Grönningen | NOR | 47:54.2 |
| 2. Eero Mäntyranta | FIN | 47:56.1 |
| 3. Gunnar Larsson | SWE | 48:33.7 |
| 4. Kalevi Laurila | FIN | 48:37.6 |
| 5. Jan Halvarsson | SWE | 48:39.1 |
| 6. Bjarne Andersson | SWE | 48:41.1 |
| 7. Pål Tyldum | NOR | 48:42.0 |
| 8. Odd Martinsen | NOR | 48:59.3 |

A three-time silver medalist, Grönningen finally beat his friend and rival Mäntyranta.

**1972 Sapporo-Makomanai** C: 62, N: 19, D: 2.7.
| | | |
|---|---|---|
| 1. Sven-Ake Lundbäck | SWE | 45:28.24 |
| 2. Fedor Simashev | SOV | 46:00.84 |
| 3. Ivar Formo | NOR | 46:02.68 |
| 4. Juha Mieto | FIN | 46:02.74 |
| 5. Yuri Skobov | SOV | 46:04.59 |
| 6. Axel Lesser | GDR | 46:17.01 |
| 7. Walter Demel | GER | 46:17.36 |
| 8. Gunnar Larsson | SWE | 46:23.29 |

**1976 Innsbruck-Seefeld** C: 80, N: 25, D: 2.8.
| | | |
|---|---|---|
| 1. Nikolai Bazhukov | SOV | 43:58.47 |
| 2. Yevgeny Beliaev | SOV | 44:01.10 |
| 3. Arto Koivisto | FIN | 44:19.25 |
| 4. Ivan Garanin | SOV | 44:41.98 |
| 5. Ivar Formo | NOR | 45:29.11 |
| 6. William Koch | USA | 45:32.22 |
| 7. Georg Zipfel | GER | 45:38.10 |
| 8. Odd Martinsen | NOR | 45:41.33 |

**1980 Lake Placid** C: 63, N: 22, D: 2.17.
| | | |
|---|---|---|
| 1. Thomas Wassberg | SWE | 41:57.63 |
| 2. Juha Mieto | FIN | 41:57.64 |
| 3. Ove Aunli | NOR | 42:28.62 |
| 4. Nikolai Zimyatov | SOV | 42:33.96 |
| 5. Yevgeny Beliaev | SOV | 42:46.02 |
| 6. Józef Luszczek | POL | 42:59.03 |
| 7. Aleksandr Zavyalov | SOV | 43:00.81 |
| 8. Harri Kirvesniemi | FIN | 43:02.01 |

Six-foot 5-inch Juha Mieto could be forgiven if he cursed the invention of electronic timing. In 1972 he missed winning a bronze medal because a clock registered his time as six one-hundredths of a second slower than that of Ivar Formo. Eight years later in Lake Placid, Mieto was the 54th skier to start and he finished 36 seconds faster than any of the other 53. But then he watched anxiously as Thomas Wassberg strained toward the finish line and crossed in 41 minutes and 57.63 seconds—one one-hundredth of a second faster than Juha Mieto. This incident led the rulemakers to decree that henceforth all times in cross-country races would be rounded to the nearest tenth of a second.

**1984 Sarajevo** C: 91, N: 34, D: 2.13.
| | | |
|---|---|---|
| 1. Gunde Svan | SWE | 41:25.6 |
| 2. Aki Karvonen | FIN | 41:34.9 |
| 3. Harri Kirvesniemi | FIN | 41:45.6 |
| 4. Juha Mieto | FIN | 42:05.8 |
| 5. Vladimir Nikitin | SOV | 42:31.6 |
| 6. Nikolai Zimyatov | SOV | 42:34.5 |
| 7. Uwe Bellmann | GDR | 42:35.8 |
| 8. Tor Håkon Holte | NOR | 42:37.4 |
| DISQ: Ove Aunli (NOR) 42:31.6 | | |

At age 22, Gunde Svan became the youngest person ever to win an Olympic cross-country title. Ove Aunli, who finished in a tie for fifth place, was disqualified for using a skating step during the last 200 meters.

**1988 Calgary-Canmore** C: 90, N: 32, D: 2.19.
1. Mikhail Devyatyarov     SOV   41:18.9
2. Pål Gunnar Mikkelsplass NOR   41:33.4
3. Vladimir Smirnov        SOV   41:48.5
4. Oddvar Brå              NOR   42:17.3
5. Uwe Bellmann            GDR   42:17.8
6. Maurilio De Zolt        ITA   42:31.2
7. Vegard Ulvang           NOR   42:31.5
8. Harri Kirvesniemi       FIN   42:42.8

Devyatyarov attributed the success of the Soviet Nordic skiers at the Calgary Games to the fact that they trained on a course with the same profile as the one at Canmore and at the same altitude.

This race saw the unusual inclusion of an entrant from Fiji. Rusiate Rogoyawa learned to ski while studying electrical engineering in Oslo, Norway. He finished eighty-third.

# 30 KILOMETERS (CLASSICAL)

**1924–1952** not held

**1956 Cortina** C: 54, N: 18, D: 1.27.
1. Veikko Hakulinen    FIN   1:44:06.0
2. Sixten Jernberg     SWE   1:44:30.0
3. Pavel Kolchin       SOV   1:45:45.0
4. Anatoly Shelyukin   SOV   1:45:46.0
5. Vladimir Kuzin      SOV   1:46:09.0
6. Fedor Terentyev     SOV   1:46:43.0
7. Per-Erik Larsson    SWE   1:46:51.0
8. Lennart Larsson     SWE   1:46:56.0

**1960 Squaw Valley** C: 48, N: 17, D: 2.19.
1. Sixten Jernberg     SWE   1:51:03.9
2. Rolf Fämgård        SWE   1:51:16.9
3. Nikolai Anikin      SOV   1:52:28.2
4. Gennady Vaganov     SOV   1:52:49.2
5. Lennart Larsson     SWE   1:53:53.2
6. Veikko Hakulinen    FIN   1:54:02.0
7. Tolmo Alatalo       FIN   1:54:06.5
8. Aleksei Kuznyetsov  SOV   1:54:23.9

**1964 Innsbruck-Seefeld** C: 69, N: 22, D: 1.30.
1. Eero Mäntyranta     FIN   1:30:50.7
2. Harald Grönningen   NOR   1:32:02.3
3. Igor Voronchikin    SOV   1:32:15.8
4. Janne Stefansson    SWE   1:32:34.8
5. Sixten Jernberg     SOV   1:32:39.6
6. Kalevi Laurila      FIN   1:32:41.4
7. Assar Rönnlund      SWE   1:32:43.6
8. Einar Östby         NOR   1:32:54.6

**1968 Grenoble-Autrans** C: 66, N: 22, D: 2.6.
1. Franco Nones        ITA   1:35:39.2
2. Odd Martinsen       NOR   1:36:28.9
3. Eero Mäntyranta     FIN   1:36:55.3
4. Vladimir Voronkov   SOV   1:37:10.8
5. Giulio De Florian   ITA   1:37:12.9

6. Kalevi Laurila      FIN   1:37:29.8
7. Kalevi Oikarainen   FIN   1:37:34:4
8. Gunnar Larsson      SWE   1:37:48.1

Of the 51 men's cross-country events that have been held in the Olympics, 50 of them have been won by Sweden (18), Norway (11), the U.S.S.R. (11), and Finland (10). The only gold medalist from a non-nordic nation has been Franco Nones, a 27-year-old customs officer from the village of Catella di Fiemma in the Dolomite Mountains. It is true that Nones was trained in northern Sweden by a Swedish coach, but his victory was nonetheless a major surprise, particularly coming as it did in the first event of the 1968 Winter Games. It is also worth noting that of the 153 medals that have been awarded in men's cross-country skiing the Scandinavians and Soviets have won 144 of them.

**1972 Sapporo-Makomanai** C: 50, N: 19, D: 2.4.
1. Vyacheslav Vedenine  SOV   1:36:31.15
2. Pål Tyldum           NOR   1:37:25.30
3. Johs Harviken        NOR   1:37:32.44
4. Gunnar Larsson       SWE   1:37:33.72
5. Walter Demel         GER   1:37:45.33
6. Fedor Simashev       SOV   1:38:22.50
7. Alois Kälin          SWI   1:38:40.72
8. Gert-Dietmar Klause   GDR   1:39:15.54

The 5-foot 4¼-inch Vedenine was the first Soviet skier to win an individual Olympic gold medal.

**1976 Innsbruck-Seefeld** C: 09, N: 21, D: 2.5.
1. Sergei Saveliev      SOV   1:30:29.38
2. William Koch         USA   1:30:57.84
3. Ivan Garanin         SOV   1:31:09.29
4. Juha Mieto           FIN   1:31:20.39
5. Nikolai Bazhukov     SOV   1:31:33.14
6. Gert-Dietmar Klause  GDR   1:32:00.91
7. Albert Giger         SWI   1:32:17.71
8. Arto Koivisto        FIN   1:32:23.11

The only American ever to have won an Olympic nordic skiing medal, Bill Koch of Guilford, Vermont, responded to his sudden celebrity in a typically Vermont manner. When a reporter asked, "Have you lived in Vermont all your life?" Koch replied, "Not yet."

**1980 Lake Placid** C: 57, N: 20, D: 2.14.
1. Nikolai Zimyatov     SOV   1:27:02.80
2. Vassily Rochev       SOV   1:27:34.22
3. Ivan Lebanov         BUL   1:28:03.87
4. Thomas Wassberg      SWE   1:28:40.35
5. Jósef Luszczek       POL   1:29:03.64
6. Matti Pitkänen       FIN   1:29:35.03
7. Juha Mieto           FIN   1:29:45.08
8. Ove Aunli            NOR   1:29:54.02

Zimyatov won the first of his three gold medals at Lake Placid. Lebanov was the first Bulgarian to win a medal in the Winter Olympics.

**1984 Sarajevo** C: 72, N: 26, D: 2.10.

| | | |
|---|---|---|
| 1. Nikolai Zimyatov | SOV | 1:28:56.3 |
| 2. Aleksandr Zavialov | SOV | 1:29:23.3 |
| 3. Gunde Svan | SWE | 1:29:35.7 |
| 4. Vladimir Sakhnov | SOV | 1:30:30.4 |
| 5. Aki Karvonen | FIN | 1:30:59.7 |
| 6. Lars-Erik Eriksen | NOR | 1:31:24.8 |
| 7. Harri Kirvesniemi | FIN | 1:31:37.4 |
| 8. Juha Mieto | FIN | 1:31:48.3 |

Soviet army captain Nikolai Zimyatov struggled through blizzard conditions to win his fourth Olympic gold medal.

**1988 Calgary-Canmore** C: 90, N: 32, D: 2.15.

| | | |
|---|---|---|
| 1. Aleksei Prokurorov | SOV | 1:24:26.3 |
| 2. Vladimir Smirnov | SOV | 1:24:35.1 |
| 3. Vegard Ulvang | NOR | 1:25:11.6 |
| 4. Mikhail Devyatyarov | SOV | 1:25:31.3 |
| 5. Giorgio Vanzetta | ITA | 1:25:37.2 |
| 6. Pål Gunnar Mikkelsplass | NOR | 1:25:44.6 |
| 7. Gianfranco Polvara | ITA | 1:26:02.7 |
| 8. Marco Albarello | ITA | 1:26:09.1 |

# 50 KILOMETERS (FREESTYLE)

**1924 Chamonix** C: 33, N: 11, D: 1.30.

| | | |
|---|---|---|
| 1. Thorleif Haug | NOR | 3:44:32.0 |
| 2. Thoralf Strömstad | NOR | 3:46:23.0 |
| 3. Johan Gröttumsbråten | NOR | 3:47:46.0 |
| 4. Jon Maardalen | NOR | 3:49:48.0 |
| 5. Torkel Persson | SWE | 4:05:59.0 |
| 6. Ernst Alm | SWE | 4:06:31.0 |
| 7. Matti Raivio | FIN | 4:06.50.0 |
| 8. Oscar Lindberg | SWE | 4:07.44.0 |

**1928 St. Moritz** C: 41, N: 11, D: 2.14.

| | | |
|---|---|---|
| 1. Per Erik Hedlund | SWE | 4:52:03.0 |
| 2. Gustaf Jonsson | SWE | 5:05:30.0 |
| 3. Volger Andersson | SWE | 5:05.46.0 |
| 4. Olav Kjelbotn | NOR | 5:14:22.0 |
| 5. Ole Hegge | NOR | 5:17:58.0 |
| 6. Tauno Lappalainen | FIN | 5:18:33.0 |
| 7. Anders Strom | SWE | 5:21:54.0 |
| 8. Johan Stoa | NOR | 5:25:30.0 |

This race was accompanied by freakish weather. At the beginning of the race the temperature was near zero, however by the end it had risen to 77° Fahrenheit (25° Centigrade). Hedlund's phenomenal margin of victory is unequaled in Olympic history.

**1932 Lake Placid** C: 32, N: 9, D: 2.13.

| | | |
|---|---|---|
| 1. Veli Saarinen | FIN | 4:28:00.0 |
| 2. Väinö Likkanen | FIN | 4:28:20.0 |
| 3. Arne Rustadstuen | NOR | 4:31:53.0 |
| 4. Ole Hegge | NOR | 4:32:04.0 |
| 5. Sigurd Vestad | NOR | 4:32:40.0 |
| 6. Sven Utterström | SWE | 4:33:25.0 |
| 7. Tauno Lappalainen | FIN | 4:45:02.0 |
| 8. Karl Lindberg | SWE | 4:47.22.0 |

The 1932 race was held in a raging blizzard. The start was delayed three hours while contestants and officials argued about the course.

**1936 Garmisch-Partenkirchen** C: 36, N: 11, D: 2.15.

| | | |
|---|---|---|
| 1. Elis Wiklund | SWE | 3:30:11.0 |
| 2. Axel Wikström | SWE | 3:33:20.0 |
| 3. Nils-Joel Englund | SWE | 3:34:10.0 |
| 4. Hjalmar Bergström | SWE | 3:35:50.0 |
| 5. Klaes Karppinen | FIN | 3:39:33.0 |
| 6. Arne Tuft | NOR | 3:41:18.0 |
| 7. Frans Heikkinen | FIN | 3:42:44.0 |
| 8. Pekka Niemi | FIN | 3:44:14.0 |

**1948 St. Moritz** C: 28, N: 9, D: 2.6.

| | | |
|---|---|---|
| 1. Nils Karlsson | SWE | 3:47:48.0 |
| 2. Harald Eriksson | SWE | 3:52:20.0 |
| 3. Benjamin Vanninen | FIN | 3:57:28.0 |
| 4. Pekka Vanninen | FIN | 3:57:58.0 |
| 5. Anders Törnkvist | SWE | 3:58:20.0 |
| 6. Edi Schild | SWI | 4:05:37.0 |
| 7. Pekka Kuvaja | FIN | 4:10:02.0 |
| 8. Jaroslav Cardal | CZE | 4:14:34.0 |

**1952 Oslo** C: 36, N: 13, D: 2.20.

| | | |
|---|---|---|
| 1. Veikko Hakulinen | FIN | 3:33:33.0 |
| 2. Eero Kolehmainen | FIN | 3:38:11.0 |
| 3. Magnar Estenstad | NOR | 3:38:28.0 |
| 4. Olav Ökern | NOR | 3:38:45.0 |
| 5. Kalevi Mononen | FIN | 3:39:21.0 |
| 6. Nils Karlsson | SWE | 3:39:30.0 |
| 7. Edvin Landsem | NOR | 3:40:43.0 |
| 8. Harald Maartmann | NOR | 3:43:43.0 |

This was the first of woodchopper Veikko Hakulinen's seven Olympic medals.

**1956 Cortina** C: 33, N: 13, D: 2.2.

| | | |
|---|---|---|
| 1. Sixten Jernberg | SWE | 2:50:27.0 |
| 2. Veikko Hakulinen | FIN | 2:51:45.0 |
| 3. Fedor Terentyev | SOV | 2:53:32.0 |
| 4. Eero Kolehmainen | FIN | 2:56:17.0 |
| 5. Anatoly Shelyukin | SOV | 2:56:40.0 |
| 6. Pavel Kolchin | SOV | 2:58:00.0 |
| 7. Victor Baranov | SOV | 3:03:55.0 |
| 8. Antti Sivonen | FIN | 3:04:16.0 |

**1960 Squaw Valley** C: 31, N: 10, D: 2.27.

| | | |
|---|---|---|
| 1. Kalevi Hämäläinen | FIN | 2:59:06.3 |
| 2. Veikko Hakulinen | FIN | 2:59:26.7 |
| 3. Rolf Rämgård | SWE | 3:02:46.7 |
| 4. Lennart Larsson | SWE | 3:03:27.9 |
| 5. Sixten Jernberg | SWE | 3:05:18.0 |
| 6. Pentti Pelkonen | FIN | 3:05:24.5 |
| 7. Gennady Vaganov | SOV | 3:05:27.6 |
| 8. Veikko Rasanen | FIN | 3:06:04.4 |

Finland, Norway, Sweden, and the U.S.S.R. took the first 15 places.

**1964 Innsbruck–Seefeld** C: 41, N: 14, D: 2.5.
1. Sixten Jernberg       SWE   2:43:52.6
2. Assar Rönnlund        SWE   2:44:58.2
3. Arto Tiainen          FIN   2:45:30.4
4. Janne Stefansson      SWE   2:45:36.6
5. Sverre Steinsheim     NOR   2:45:47.2
6. Harald Grönningen     NOR   2:47:03.6
7. Einar Östby           NOR   2:47:20.6
8. Ole Ellefsaeter       NOR   2:47:45.8

In 1956 Sixten Jernberg had predicted that whoever started the course last in the 50-kilometer race would win. Instead Jernberg, who started next to last, was the winner. At Innsbruck in 1964 he was the next to last starter again, and again he finished in first place. Three days later he earned another gold medal by skiing the second leg on Sweden's relay team. He closed out his Olympic career two days after his 35th birthday, having won nine medals: four gold, three silver, and two bronze.

**1968 Grenoble–Autrans** C: 51, N: 17, D: 2.15.
1. Ole Ellefsaeter       NOR   2:28:45.8
2. Vyacheslav Vedenine   SOV   2:29:02.5
3. Josef Haas            SWI   2:29:14.8
4. Pål Tyldum            NOR   2:29:26.7
5. Melcher Risberg       SWE   2:29:37.0
6. Gunnar Larsson        SWE   2:29:37.2
7. Jan Halvarsson        SWE   2:30:05.9
8. Reidar Hjermstad      NOR   2:31:01.8

Ole Ellefsaeter, a forestry technician and pop singer, celebrated his 29th birthday by winning the 50-kilometer gold medal.

**1972 Sapporo–Makomanai** C: 40, N: 13, D: 2.10.
1. Pål Tyldum            NOR   2:43:14.75
2. Magne Myrmo           NOR   2:43:29.45
3. Vyacheslav Vedenine   SOV   2:44:00.19
4. Reidar Hjermstad      NOR   2:44:14.51
5. Walter Demel          GER   2:44:32.67
6. Werner Geeser         SWI   2:44:34.13
7. Lars-Arne Bolling     SWE   2:45:06.80
8. Fedor Simachev        SOV   2:45:08.93

Tyldum, the next to last starter, was only placed 18th after 15 kilometers, 78½ seconds behind the leader, Werner Geeser. By the 25-kilometer mark he had moved up to tenth place, but he was now 103½ seconds slower than Geeser. At 40 kilometers Geeser was still in first, but fading, while Tyldum had moved up to third, less than 26 seconds off Geeser's pace. While Geeser and Simachev tired dramatically in the last 10 kilometers, Tyldum plowed on to victory.

**1976 Innsbruck–Seefeld** C: 59, N: 15, D: 2.14.
1. Ivar Formo            NOR   2:37:30.05
2. Gert-Dietmar Klause   GDR   2:38:13.21
3. Benny Södergren       SWE   2:39:39.21
4. Ivan Garanin          SOV   2:40:38.94

5. Gerhard Grimmer       GDR   2:41:15.46
6. Per Knut Aaland       NOR   2:41:18.06
7. Pål Tyldum            NOR   2:42:21.86
8. Tommy Limby           SWE   2:42:43.58

**1980 Lake Placid** C: 51, N: 14, D: 2.23.
1. Nikolai Zimyatov      SOV   2:27:24.60
2. Juha Mieto            FIN   2:30:20.52
3. Alexandr Zavyalov     SOV   2:30:51.52
4. Lars Erik Eriksen     NOR   2:30:53.00
5. Sergei Saveliev       SOV   2:31:15.82
6. Yevgeny Beliaev       SOV   2:31:21.19
7. Oddvar Brå            NOR   2:31:46.83
8. Sven-Åke Lundbäck     SWE   2:31:59.65

Zimyatov won this third gold medal in ten days, having skied a total of 105 kilometers.

**1984 Sarajevo** C: 54, N: 21, D: 2.19.
1. Thomas Wassberg       SWE   2:15:55.8
2. Gunde Svan            SWE   2:16:00.7
3. Aki Karvonen          FIN   2:17:04.7
4. Harri Kirvesniemi     FIN   2:18:34.1
5. Jan Lindvall          NOR   2:19:27.1
6. Andreas Grünfelder    SWI   2:19:46.2
7. Aleksandr Zavyalov    SOV   2:20:27.6
8. Vladimir Sakhnov      SOV   2:20:53.7

**1988 Calgary–Canmore** C: 70, N: 23, D: 2.27.
1. Gunde Svan            SWE   2:04:30.9
2. Maurilio De Zolt      ITA   2:05:36.4
3. Andi Grünenfelder     SWI   2:06:01.9
4. Vegard Ulvang         NOR   2:06:32.3
5. Holger Bauroth        GDR   2:07:02.4
6. Jan Ottosson          SWE   2:07:34.8
7. Kari Ristanen         FIN   2:08:08.1
8. Uwe Bellmann          GDR   2:08:18.6

The 69th of 70 starters, Gunde Svan earned his second gold medal of the Calgary Games to match the two he won in Sarajevo in 1984. Silver medalist Maurilio De Zolt was 37 years old.

Roberto Alvarez of Mexico was the last of the 61 finishers in a time of 3:22:25.1—almost 52 minutes slower than the man in sixtieth place, Battulga Dambajamtsyn of Mongolia.

## 2 × 15-KILOMETER COMBINED PURSUIT

On the first day of the combined pursuit event, skiers race 15 kilometers, using the classical technique. On the second day, setting out from a staggered start based on the results of the previous day, they race another 15 kilometers freestyle.

This event will be held for the first time in 1992.

# 4 × 10-KILOMETER RELAY

In 1988 this was a freestyle event; however, in 1992 two skiers will use the classical technique and two will skate.

**1924–1932** not held

**1936 Garmisch-Partenkirchen** T: 16, N: 16, D: 2.10.
1. FIN (Sulo Nurmela, Klaes Karppinen, Matti Lähde, Kalle Jalkanen) 2:41:33.0
2. NOR (Oddbjörn Hagen, Olaf Hoffsbakken, Sverre Brodahl, Bjarne Iversen) 2:41:39.0
3. SWE (John Berger, Erik Larsson, Arthur Häggblad, Martin Matsbo) 2:43:03.0
4. ITA (Giulio Gerardi, Severino Menardi, Vincenzo Demetz, Giovanni Kasebacher) 2:50:05.0
5. CZE (Cyril Musil, Gustav Berauer, Lukas Mihalak, František Simunek) 2:51:56.0
6. GER (Friedel Däuber, Willi Bogner, Herbert Leupold, Anton Zeller) 2:54:54.0
7. POL (Michal Górski, Marian Woyna-Orlewicz, Stanislaw Karpiel, Bronislaw Czech) 2:58:50.0
8. AUT (Alfred Robner, Harald Bosio, Erich Gallwitz, Hans Baumann) 3:02:48.0

Kalle Jalkanen, the last Finnish skier, staged a spectacular come-from-behind victory. Trailing Bjarne Iversen of Norway by 82 seconds when he took over the baton, he caught him as they entered the ski stadium and won by only 20 yards.

**1948 St. Moritz** T: 11, N: 11, D: 2.3.
1. SWE (Nils Östensson, Nils Täpp, Gunnar Eriksson, Martin Lundström) 2:32:08.0
2. FIN (Lauri Silvennoinen, Teuvo Laukkanen, Sauli Rytky, August Kiuru) 2:41:06.0
3. NOR (Erling Evensen, Olaf Ökern, Reidar Nyborg, Olav Hagen) 2:44:33.0
4. AUT (Josl Gstrein, Josef Deutschmann, Engelbert Hundertpfund, Karl Rafreider) 2:47:18.0
5. SWI (Niklaus Stump, Robert Zurbriggen, Max Müller, Edi Schild) 2:48:07.0
6. ITA (Vincenzo Perruchon, Silvio Confortola, Rizzieri Rodighiero, Severino Compagnoni) 2:51:00.0
7. FRA (René Jeandel, Gerard Perrier, Marius Mora, Benoit Carrara) 2:51:53.0
8. CZE (Stefan Kovalcik, František Balvin, Jaroslav Zejicek, Jaroslav Cardal) 2:54:56.0

**1952 Oslo** T: 13, N: 13, D: 2.23.
1. FIN (Heikki Hasu, Paavo Lonkila, Urpo Korhonen, Tapio Mäkelä) 2:20:16.0
2. NOR (Magnar Estenstad, Mikal Kirkholt, Martin Stokken, Hallgeir Brenden) 2.23:13.0
3. SWE (Nils Täpp, Sigurd Andersson, Enar Josefsson, Martin Lundström) 2:24:13.0

4. FRA (Gerard Perrier, Benoit Carrara, Jean Mermet, René Mandrillon) 2:31:11.0
5. AUT (Hans Eder, Friedrich Krischan, Karl Rafreider, Josef Schneeberger) 2:34:36.0
6. ITA (Arrigo Delladio, Nino Anderlini, Frederico de Florian, Vincenzo Perruchon) 2:35:33.0
7. GER (Hubert Egger, Albert Mohr, Heinz Hauser, Rudi Kopp) 2:36:37.0
8. CZE (Vladimir Simunek, Stefan Kovalcik, Vlastimil Melich, Jaroslav Cardal) 2:37:12.0

**1956 Cortina** T: 14, N: 14, D: 2.4.
1. SOV (Fedor Terentyev, Pavel Kolchin, Nikolai Anikin, Vladimir Kuzin) 2:15:30.0
2. FIN (August Kiuru, Jormo Kortalainen, Arvo Viitanen, Veikko Hakulinen) 2:16:31.0
3. SWE (Lennart Larsson, Gunnar Samuelsson, Per-Erik Larsson, Sixten Jernberg) 2:17:42.0
4. NOR (Håkon Brusveen, Per Olsen, Marten Stokken, Hallgeir Brenden) 2:21:16.0
5. ITA (Pompeo Fattor, Ottavio Compagnoni, Innocenzo Chatrian, Frederico De Florian) 2:23:28.0
6. FRA (Victor Arbez, René Mandrillon, Benoit Carrara, Jean Mermet) 2:24:06.0
7. SWI (Werner Zwingli, Victor Kronig, Fritz Kocher, Marcel Huguenin) 2:24:30.0
8. CZE (Emil Okuliar, Vlastimil Melich, Josef Prokes, Ilja Matous) 2:24:54.0

The first two Soviet skiers, Terentyev and Kolchin, built up an insurmountable lead of two and three-quarter minutes.

**1960 Squaw Valley** T: 11, N: 11, D: 2.25.
1. FIN (Toimi Alatalo, Eero Mäntyranta, Väinö Huhtala, Veikko Hakulinen) 2:18:45.6
2. NOR (Harald Grönningen, Hallgeir Brenden, Einar Östby, Håkon Brusveen) 2:18:46.4
3. SOV (Anatoly Shelyukin, Gennady Vaganov, Aleksei Kuznetsov, Nikolai Anikin) 2:21:21.6
4. SWE (Lars Olsson, Janne Stefansson, Lennart Larsson, Sixten Jernberg) 2:21:31.8
5. ITA (Giulio De Florian, Giuseppe Steiner, Pompeo Fattor, Marcello De Dorigo) 2:22:32.5
6. POL (Andrzej Mateja, Józef Rysula, Józef Gut-Misiaga, Kazimierz Zelek) 2:26:25.3
7. FRA (Victor Arbez, René Mandrillon, Benoit Carrara, Jean Mermet) 2:26:30.8
8. SWI (Fritz Kocher, Marcel Huguenin, Lorenz Possa, Alphonse Baume) 2:29:36.8

Since the relay is the only skiing event in which the participants actually race against each other, it is also the only event which has the potential for a truly exciting finish. Such a finish occurred in 1960. Lars Olsson gave Sweden a seven-second lead at the end of the first leg, but the second Swedish skier, Janne Stefansson, was quickly overtaken by Brenden and Mäntyranta. At the halfway mark, Norway and Finland were tied. Then Norway's Einar Östby pulled away to a 20-second lead. Håkon Brusveen, winner of the 15-kilometer race two days earlier, took over the last leg for Norway, followed by six-time Olympic medalist, 35-year-old Veikko Hakulinen. After eight kilometers Hakulinen overhauled Brusveen, but the Norwegian pulled back into the lead. With 100 meters to go, Hakulinen began to pass Brusveen again. Edging ahead in the final strides, the great Finnish veteran managed to win by three feet. It was a fitting ending to Hakulinen's marvelous Olympic career, during which he earned three gold medals, each in a different event and each in a different Olympics, as well as three silver medals and one bronze.

**1964 Innsbruck-Seefeld** T: 15, N: 15, D: 2.8.
1. SWE (Karl Åke Asph, Sixten Jernberg, Janne Stefansson, Assar Rönnlund) 2:18:34.6
2. FIN (Väinö Huhtala, Arto Tialnen, Kalevi Laurila, Eero Mäntyranta) 2:18:42.4
3. SOV (Ivan Utrobin, Gennady Vaganov, Igor Voronchikin, Pavel Kolchin) 2:18:46.9
4. NOR (Magnar Lundemo, Erling Steineidet, Einar Östby, Harald Grönningen) 2:19:11.9
5. ITA (Giuseppe Steiner, Marcello De Dorlgo, Giulio De Florian, Franco Nones) 2:21:16.8
6. FRA (Victor Arbez, Felix Mathieu, Roger Pires, Paul Romand) 2:26:31.4
7. GDR/ (Heinz Seidel, Helmut Weidlich, Enno Röder, GER Walter Demel) 2:26:34.4
8. POL (Józef Gut-Misiaga, Tadeusz Jankowski, Edward Budny, Józef Rysyla) 2:27:27.0

Another thrilling finish, in which Väinö Huhtala gave Finland a 5.9-second lead after the first lap with the U.S.R. in second, Norway third, and Sweden fourth. By the halfway mark, Vaganov of the Soviet Union had moved into a 11.6-second lead over second-place Norway, with Italy in third, followed by Sweden and Finland. Pavel Kolchin took over the last leg for the Soviet Union, followed 13.4 seconds later by Grönningen of Norway, 31.5 seconds later by Assar Rönnlund of Sweden, and 32.3 seconds later by Eero Mäntyranta. Grönningen passed Kolchin to take the lead, but he exhausted himself by his effort and was passed shortly afterward by Mäntyranta, Rönnlund, and Kolchin. A few hundred meters short of the finish line Rönnlund summoned an extra reserve of energy, pushed ahead of Mäntyranta, and won by 7.8 seconds.

**1968 Grenoble-Autrans** T: 15, N: 15, D: 2.14.
1. NOR (Odd Martinsen, Pål Tyldum, Harald Grönningen, Ole Ellefsaeter) 2:08:33.5
2. SWE (Jan Halvarsson, Bjarne Andersson, Gunnar Larsson, Assar Rönnlund) 2:10:13.2
3. FIN (Kalevi Oikarainen, Hannu Taipale, Kalevi Laurila, Eero Mäntyranta) 2:10:56.7

4. SOV (Vladimir Voronkov, Anatoly Akentiev, Valery Tarakanov, Vyacheslav Vedenine) 2:10:57
5. SWI (Konrad Hischier, Josef Haas, Florian Koch, Alois Kälin) 2:15:32.4
6. ITA (Giulio De Florian, Franco Nones, Palmiro Serafini, Aldo Stella) 2:16:32.2
7. GDR (Gerhard Grimmer, Axel Lesser, Peter Thiel, Gert-Dietmar Klause) 2:19:22.8
8. GER (Helmut Gerlach, Walter Demel, Herbert Steinbeisser, Karl Buhl) 2:19:37.6

Eero Mäntyranta made up over 26 seconds on the final leg to nip Vedenine at the finish line for the bronze medal. This gave Mäntyranta an Olympic medal total of three gold, two silver, and two bronze.

**1972 Sapporo-Makomanai** T: 14, N: 14, D: 2.13.
1. SOV (Vladimir Voronkov, Yuri Skobov, Fedor Simachev, Vyacheslav Vedenine) 2:04:47.94
2. NOR (Oddvar Brå, Pål Tyldum, Ivar Formo, Johs Harviken) 2:04:57.06
3. SWI (Alfred Kälin, Albert Giger, Alois Kälin, Eduard Hauser) 2:07:00.06
4. SWE (Thomas Magnusson, Lars-Göran Åslund, Gunnar Larsson, Sven-Åke Lundbäck) 2:07:03.60
5. FIN (Hannu Taipale, Juha Mietö, Juhani Repo, Osmo Karjalainen) 2:07:50.19
6. GDR (Gerd Hessler, Axel Lesser, Gerhard Grimmer, Gert-Dietmar Klause) 2:10:03.73
7. GER (Franz Betz, Urban Hettich, Hartmut Dopp, Walter Demel) 2:10:42.85
8. CZE (Stanislav Henych, Jan Fajstavr, Jan Michalko, Jan Ilavsky) 2:11:27.55

Vedenine began the final leg 61½ seconds behind Johs Harviken, but he overtook the Norwegian one kilometer from the finish and won by over nine seconds.

**1976 Innsbruck-Seefeld** T: 16, N: 16, D: 2.12.
1. FIN (Matti Pitkänen, Juha Mieto, Pertti Teurajärvi, Arto Koivisto) 2:07:59.72
2. NOR (Pål Tyldum, Einar Sagstuen, Ivar Formo, Odd Martinsen) 2:09:58.36
3. SOV (Yevgeny Beliaev, Nikolai Bazhukov, Sergei Saveliev, Ivan Garanin) 2:10:51.46
4. SWE (Benny Söderg ren, Christer Johansson, Thomas Wassberg, Sven-Åke Lundbäck) 2:11:16.86
5. SWI (Franz Renggli, Edi Hauser, Heinz Gähler, Alfred Kälin) 2:11:28.53
6. USA (Douglas Peterson, Timothy Caldwell, William Koch, Ronny Yaeger) 2:11:41.35
7. ITA (Renzo Chiocchetti, Tonio Biondini, Ulrico Kostner, Giulio Capitanio) 2:12:07.12
8. AUT (Rudolf Horn, Reinhold Feichter, Werner Vogel, Herbert Wachter) 2:12:22.80

East Germany was in second place when their second skier, Axel Lesser, ran into a spectator, injured his knee, and had to abandon the race.

**980 Lake Placid** T: 10, N: 10, D: 2.20.

| | | | |
|---|---|---|---|
| . SOV | (Vassily Rochev, Nikolai Bazhukov, Yevgeny Beliaev, Nikolai Zimyatov) | 1:57:03.46 |
| 2. NOR | (Lars Erik Eriksen, Per Knut Aaland, Ove Aunli, Oddvar Brå) | 1:58:45.77 |
| 3. FIN | (Harri Kirvesniemi, Pertti Teurajärvi, Matti Pitkänen, Juha Mieto) | 2:00:00.18 |
| 4. GER | (Peter Zipfel, Wolfgang Müller, Dieter Notz, Jochen Behle) | 2:00:27.74 |
| 5. SWE | (Sven-Åke Lundbäck, Thomas Eriksson, Benny Kohlberg, Thomas Wassberg) | 2:00:42.71 |
| 6. ITA | (Maurilio De Zolt, Benedetto Carrara, Giulio Capitanio, Giorgio Vanzetta) | 2:01:09.93 |
| 7. SWI | (Hansüli Kreuzer, Konrad Hallenbarter, Edi Hauser, Gaudenz Ambühl) | 2:03:36.57 |
| 8. USA | (William Koch, Timothy Caldwell, James Galanes, Stanley Dunklee) | 2:04:12.17 |

**1984 Sarajevo** T: 17, N: 17, D: 2.16.

| | | | |
|---|---|---|---|
| 1. SWE | (Thomas Wassberg, Benny Kohlberg, Jan Ottoson, Gunde Svan) | 1:55:06.3 |
| 2. SOV | (Aleksandr Batiuk, Aleksandr Zavyalov, Vladimir Nikitin, Nikolai Zimyatov) | 1:55:16.5 |
| 3. FIN | (Kari Ristanen, Juha Mieto, Harri Kirvesniemi, Aki Karvonen) | 1:56:31.4 |
| 4. NOR | (Lars-Erik Eriksen, Jan Lindvall, Ove Aunli, Tor Håkon Holte) | 1:57:27.6 |
| 5. SWI | (Giachem Guidon, Konrad Hallenbarter, Joos Ambühl, Andreas Grünenfelder) | 1:58:06.0 |
| 6. GER | (Jochen Behle, Stefan Dotzler, Franz Schöbel, Peter Zipfel) | 1:59:30.2 |
| 7. ITA | (Maurilio De Zolt, Alfred Runggaldier, Giulio Capitanio, Giorgio Vanzetta) | 1:59:30.3 |
| 8. USA | (Dan Simoneau, Timothy Caldwell, James Galanes, William Koch) | 1:59:52.3 |

The anchor leg matched 15-kilometer gold medalist Gunde Svan against 30-kilometer gold medalist Nikolai Zimyatov. Zimyatov took off with a lead of a fraction of a second. Svan tracked him the whole way and then, as planned, launched his successful attack one kilometer from the finish.

**1988 Calgary-Canmore** T: 16, N: 16, D: 2.22.

| | | | |
|---|---|---|---|
| 1. SWE | (Jan Ottosson, Thomas Wassberg, Gunde Svan, Torgny Mogren) | 1:43:58.6 |
| 2. SOV | (Vladimir Smirnov, Vladimir Sakhnov, Mikhail Devyatyarov, Aleksei Prokurorov) | 1:44:11.3 |
| 3. CZE | (Radim Nyc, Vaclav Korunka, Pavel Benc, Ladislav Švanda) | 1:45:22.7 |
| 4. SWI | (Andi Grünenfelder, Jürg Capol, Giachem Guidon, Jeremias Wigger) | 1:46:16.3 |
| 5. ITA | (Silvano Barco, Albert Walder, Giorgio Vanzetta, Maurilio De Zolt) | 1:46:16.7 |
| 6. NOR | (Pål Gunnar Mikkelsplass, Oddvar Brå, Vegard Ulvang, Terje Langli) | 1:46:48.7 |
| 7. GER | (Walter Kuss, Georg Fischer, Jochen Behle, Herbert Fritzenwenger) | 1:48:05.0 |

| | | | |
|---|---|---|---|
| 8. FIN | (Jari Laukkanen, Harri Kirvesniemi, Jari Räsänen, Kari Ristanen) | 1:48:2... |

The U.S.S.R. and Sweden were virtually even at the halfway point. Midway through the third leg, Gunde Svan pulled away from Mikhail Devyatyarov, who then fell, trying to maintain contact. By the time he passed off to Torgny Mogren, Svan had given Sweden a 27-second lead. Aleksei Prokurorov cut the deficit to 7 seconds with 5 kilometers to go. But he, too, fell, and he was never able to pick up the challenge again.

# SKI JUMP, NORMAL HILL, INDIVIDUAL

The first ski-jumping contest was held in Trysil, Norway, in 1862. Jumps are scored according to two criteria: distance and style. Style points are determined by five judges. The highest and lowest scores are dropped and the points awarded by the remaining three judges are added together. Each contestant takes two jumps. In 1964 the ski jump was split into two events: the small hill, or 70-meter jump, and the big hill, or 90-meter jump. The hills vary in size from Olympics to Olympics and the events are now known as normal hill and large hill.

**1924–1960** not held

**1964 Innsbruck-Seefeld** C: 53, N: 15, D: 1.31.

| | | | FIRST JUMP (M) | SECOND JUMP (M) | TOTAL PTS. |
|---|---|---|---|---|---|
| 1. | Veikko Kankkonen | FIN | 80.0 | 79.0 | 229.9 |
| 2. | Toralf Engan | NOR | 79.0 | 79.0 | 226.3 |
| 3. | Targeir Brandtzäg | NOR | 79.0 | 78.0 | 222.9 |
| 4. | Josef Matous | CZE | 80.5 | 77.0 | 218.2 |
| 5. | Dieter Neuendorf | GDR | 78.5 | 77.0 | 214.7 |
| 6. | Helmut Recknagel | GDR | 77.0 | 75.5 | 210.4 |
| 7. | Kurt Elima | SWE | 76.0 | 75.0 | 208.9 |
| 8. | Hans Olav Sörensen | NOR | 76.0 | 74.5 | 208.6 |

In 1964 the competitors were allowed to use the best two of three jumps. This rule saved Kankkonen, whose mediocre first jump landed him in 29th place. However his second and third leaps were masterpieces.

**1968 Grenoble-Autrans** C: 58, N: 18, D: 2.11.

| | | | FIRST JUMP (M) | SECOND JUMP (M) | TOTAL PTS. |
|---|---|---|---|---|---|
| 1. | Jiři Raška | CZE | 79.0 | 72.5 | 216.5 |
| 2. | Reinhold Bachler | AUT | 77.5 | 76.0 | 214.2 |
| 3. | Baldur Preiml | AUT | 80.0 | 72.5 | 212.6 |
| 4. | Björn Wirkola | NOR | 76.5 | 72.5 | 212.0 |
| 5. | Topi Mattila | FIN | 78.0 | 72.5 | 211.9 |
| 6. | Anatoly Zheglanov | SOV | 79.5 | 74.5 | 211.5 |
| 7. | Dieter Neuendorf | GDR | 76.5 | 73.0 | 211.3 |
| 8. | Vladimir Beloussov | SOV | 73.5 | 73.0 | 207.5 |

**1972 Sapporo-Miyanomori** C: 56, N: 16, D: 2.6.

| | | FIRST JUMP (M) | SECOND JUMP (M) | TOTAL PTS. |
|---|---|---|---|---|
| 1. | Yukio Kasaya | JPN | 84.0 | 79.0 | 244.2 |
| 2. | Akitsugu Konno | JPN | 82.5 | 79.0 | 234.8 |
| 3. | Seiji Aochi | JPN | 83.5 | 77.5 | 229.5 |
| 4. | Ingolf Mork | NOR | 78.0 | 78.0 | 225.5 |
| 5. | Jiři Raška | CZE | 78.5 | 78.0 | 224.8 |
| 6. | Wojciech Fortuna | POL | 82.0 | 76.5 | 222.0 |
| 7. | Karel Kodejska | CZE | 80.0 | 75.5 | 220.2 |
| 7. | Gari Napalkov | SOV | 79.5 | 76.0 | 220.2 |

Before 1972 Japan had won a total of one medal in the Winter Olympics. Consequently, when 28-year-old Yukio Kasaya won three straight meets in Europe one month before the Sapporo Games, Japan's hopes for a gold medal in the first Winter Olympics to be held in Asia were concentrated on Kasaya. The excitement was particularly great because Kasaya was a hometown boy from Japan's northernmost island of Hokkaido, where the games were being held. Kasaya's teammates, Akitsugu Konno and Seiji Aochi, were also from Hokkaido. Scattered among the 100,000 people at the bottom of the jumping hill were old schoolmates of Kasaya's waving the flag of Yoichimachi High School, Kasaya's alma mater. Despite the enormous pressure, Kasaya produced the best jump of each round. While the nation rejoiced over the stunning Japanese sweep, Kasaya, who had made 10,000 jumps since he was 11 years old, reminded the press of his personal motto, "Challenge not your rivals, but yourself."

**1976 Innsbruck-Seefeld** C: 55, N: 15, D: 2.7.

| | | FIRST JUMP (M) | SECOND JUMP (M) | TOTAL PTS. |
|---|---|---|---|---|
| 1. | Hans-Georg Aschenbach | GDR | 84.5 | 82.0 | 252.0 |
| 2. | Jochen Danneberg | GDR | 83.5 | 82.5 | 246.2 |
| 3. | Karl Schnabl | AUT | 82.5 | 81.5 | 242.0 |
| 4. | Jaroslav Balcar | CZE | 81.0 | 81.5 | 239.6 |
| 5. | Ernst von Grüningen | SWI | 80.5 | 80.5 | 238.7 |
| 6. | Reinhold Bachler | AUT | 80.5 | 80.5 | 237.2 |
| 7. | Anton Innauer | AUT | 80.5 | 81.5 | 233.5 |
| 7. | Rudolf Wanner | AUT | 79.5 | 79.5 | 233.5 |

Aschenbach later admitted to having taken anabolic steroids for eight years. He described his victory in 1976 as his greatest moment in sports, but also his most anxious. "Those were the worst hours of my life. I had won at the Olympic Winter Games on the small tower. Then the doping control. My God, what I went through. Will they catch you? Or was the timing correct once again? Was everything for nothing? Will you be the one they place the blame on, the idiot that is the butt of laughter for everybody? Nobody can imagine what you go through. You even forget that you have won."

**1980 Lake Placid** C: 48, N: 16, D: 2.17.

| | | FIRST JUMP (M) | SECOND JUMP (M) | TOTAL PTS. |
|---|---|---|---|---|
| 1. | Anton Innauer | AUT | 89.0 | 90.0 | 266.3 |
| 2. | Manfred Deckert | GDR | 85.0 | 88.0 | 249.2 |
| 2. | Hirokazu Yagi | JPN | 87.0 | 83.5 | 249.2 |
| 4. | Masahiro Akimoto | JPN | 83.5 | 87.5 | 248.5 |
| 5. | Pentti Kokkonen | FIN | 86.0 | 83.5 | 247.6 |
| 6. | Hubert Neuper | AUT | 82.5 | 88.5 | 245.5 |
| 7. | Alfred Groyer | AUT | 85.5 | 83.5 | 245.3 |
| 8. | Jouko Törmänen | FIN | 83.0 | 85.5 | 243.5 |

Toni Innauer, a 21-year-old vegetarian, used his superb form to win by a huge margin.

**1984 Sarajevo** C: 58, N: 17, D: 2.12.

| | | FIRST JUMP (M) | SECOND JUMP (M) | TOTAL PTS. |
|---|---|---|---|---|
| 1. | Jens Weissflog | GDR | 90.0 | 87.0 | 215.2 |
| 2. | Matti Nykänen | FIN | 91.0 | 84.0 | 214.0 |
| 3. | Jari Puikkonen | FIN | 81.5 | 91.5 | 212.8 |
| 4. | Stefan Stannarius | GDR | 84.0 | 89.5 | 211.1 |
| 5. | Rolf Berg | NOR | 86.0 | 86.5 | 208.5 |
| 6. | Andreas Felder | AUT | 84.0 | 87.0 | 205.6 |
| 7. | Piotr Fijas | POL | 87.0 | 88.0 | 204.5 |
| 8. | Vegard Opaas | NOR | 86.0 | 87.0 | 203.8 |

Nineteen-year old World Cup leader Jens Weissflog overcame his rival Matti Nykänen with a solid, though unspectacular, second jump.

**1988 Calgary** C: 58, N: 19, D: 2.14.

| | | FIRST JUMP (M) | SECOND JUMP (M) | TOTAL PTS. |
|---|---|---|---|---|
| 1. | Matti Nykänen | FIN | 89.5 | 89.5 | 229.1 |
| 2. | Pavel Ploc | CZE | 84.5 | 87.0 | 212.1 |
| 3. | Jiři Malec | CZE | 88.0 | 85.5 | 211.8 |
| 4. | Miran Tepeš | YUG | 84.0 | 83.5 | 211.2 |
| 5. | Jiři Parma | CZE | 83.5 | 82.5 | 203.8 |
| 6. | Heinz Kuttin | AUT | 87.0 | 80.5 | 199.7 |
| 7. | Jari Puikkonen | FIN | 84.0 | 80.0 | 199.1 |
| 8. | Staffan Tällberg | SWE | 83.0 | 81.0 | 198.1 |

Matti Nykänen outclassed the opposition to win the first of his three Calgary gold medals. In last place was the popular English plasterer, Michael "Eddie the Eagle" Edwards, who scored less than half the points of any other jumper. Edwards once summed up the mental challenge of ski jumping with this description of his first encounter with the sport: "When I looked from the top of the jump, I was so frightened that my bum shriveled up like a prune."

# SKI JUMP, LARGE HILL, INDIVIDUAL

(1924–1956: Various Lengths; 1960–1964: 80 Meters; 1968–1988: 90 Meters; 1992: 120 Meters)

**1924 Chamonix** C: 27, N: 9, D: 2.4.

| | | FIRST JUMP (M) | SECOND JUMP (M) | TOTAL PTS. |
|---|---|---|---|---|
| 1. Jacob Tullin Thams | NOR | 49.0 | 49.0 | 18.960 |
| 2. Narve Bonna | NOR | 47.5 | 49.0 | 18.689 |
| 3. Anders Haugen | USA | 49.0 | 50.0 | 17.916 |
| 4. Thorleif Haug | NOR | 44.0 | 44.5 | 17.821 |
| 5. Einar Landvik | NOR | 42.0 | 44.5 | 17.521 |
| 6. Axel Nilsson | SWE | 42.5 | 44.0 | 17.146 |
| 7. Menotti Jacobsen | SWE | 43.0 | 42.0 | 17.083 |
| 8. Alexander Girardbille | SWI | 40.5 | 41.5 | 16.794 |

The final results of this event were not decided until 50 years after it took place. In 1924 it appeared that the great Thorleif Haug had finished third, thus winning two medals at one time: a bronze in the ski jump and a gold in the nordic combined, to go with the two gold medals he had already won in the 50-kilometer and 15-kilometer races. However, in 1974 Toralf Strömstad, who had earned a silver medal in the 1924 nordic combined, discovered an error in the computation of the scores. Haug, who had been dead for 40 years, was demoted to fourth place, while Norwegian-born Anders Haugen was moved up to third. Haugen, the only American ever to place in the top four in ski-jumping, was awarded his medal in a special ceremony in Oslo. He was 83 years old.

**1928 St. Moritz** C: 38, N: 13, D: 2:18.

| | | FIRST JUMP (M) | SECOND JUMP (M) | TOTAL PTS. |
|---|---|---|---|---|
| 1. Alf Andersen | NOR | 60.0 | 64.0 | 19.208 |
| 2. Sigmund Ruud | NOR | 57.5 | 62.5 | 18.542 |
| 3. Rudolf Burkert | CZE | 57.0 | 59.5 | 17.937 |
| 4. Axel Nilsson | SWE | 53.5 | 60.0 | 16.937 |
| 5. Sven Lundgren | SWE | 48.0 | 59.0 | 16.708 |
| 6. Rolf Monsen | USA | 53.0 | 59.5 | 16.687 |
| 7. Sepp Muhlbauer | SWI | 52.0 | 58.0 | 16.541 |
| 8. Ernst Feuz | SWI | 52.5 | 58.5 | 16.458 |

The longest jump of the day was recorded by defending champion Jacob Tullin Thams, who stretched out to 73 meters but fell badly when he reached the ground. The consequent loss in style points dropped him to 28th place.

**1932 Lake Placid** C: 34, N: 10, D: 2.12.

| | | FIRST JUMP (M) | SECOND JUMP (M) | TOTAL PTS. |
|---|---|---|---|---|
| 1. Birger Ruud | NOR | 66.5 | 69.0 | 228.1 |
| 2. Hans Beck | NOR | 71.5 | 63.5 | 227.0 |
| 3. Kaare Wahlberg | NOR | 62.5 | 64.0 | 219.5 |
| 4. Sven Eriksson | SWE | 65.5 | 64.0 | 218.9 |

| | | FIRST JUMP (M) | SECOND JUMP (M) | TOTAL PTS. |
|---|---|---|---|---|
| 5. Caspar Oimen | USA | 63.0 | 67.5 | 216.7 |
| 6. Fritz Kaufmann | SWI | 63.5 | 65.5 | 215.8 |
| 7. Sigmund Ruud | NOR | 63.0 | 62.5 | 215.1 |
| 8. Goro Adachi | JPN | 60.0 | 66.0 | 210.7 |

Hans Beck and the Ruud brothers were brought up together in the mining town of Kongsberg. Confusion concerning the scoring computations caused a four-hour delay in the announcement of the placings, and even then it was orginally stated that Beck had won.

**1936 Garmisch-Partenkirchen** C: 48, N: 14, D: 2.16.

| | | FIRST JUMP (M) | SECOND JUMP (M) | TOTAL PTS. |
|---|---|---|---|---|
| 1. Birger Ruud | NOR | 75.0 | 74.5 | 232.0 |
| 2. Sven Eriksson | SWE | 76.0 | 76.0 | 230.5 |
| 3. Reidar Andersen | NOR | 74.0 | 75.0 | 228.9 |
| 4. Kaare Wahlberg | NOR | 73.5 | 72.0 | 227.0 |
| 5. Stanislaw Marusarz | POL | 73.0 | 75.5 | 221.6 |
| 6. Lauri Valonen | FIN | 73.5 | 67.0 | 219.4 |
| 7. Masaji Iguro | JPN | 74.5 | 72.5 | 218.2 |
| 8. Arnold Kongsgaard | NOR | 74.5 | 72.5 | 217.7 |

**1948 St. Moritz** C: 49, N: 14, D: 2.7.

| | | FIRST JUMP (M) | SECOND JUMP (M) | TOTAL PTS. |
|---|---|---|---|---|
| 1. Petter Hugsted | NOR | 65.0 | 70.0 | 228.1 |
| 2. Birger Ruud | NOR | 64.0 | 67.0 | 226.6 |
| 3. Thorleif Schjelderup | NOR | 64.0 | 67.0 | 225.1 |
| 4. Matti Pietikainen | FIN | 69.5 | 69.0 | 224.6 |
| 5. Gordon Wren | USA | 68.0 | 68.5 | 222.8 |
| 6. Leo Laakso | FIN | 66.0 | 69.5 | 221.7 |
| 7. Asbjörn Ruud | NOR | 58.0 | 67.5 | 220.2 |
| 8. Aatto Pietikainen | FIN | 69.0 | 68.0 | 215.4 |

Two-time gold medalist Birger Ruud, now 36 years old, went to St. Moritz as a coach. But when he saw the poor weather the night before the competition, he decided to compete in place of the less experienced George Thrane. Ruud's confidence in himself paid off with a silver medal.

**1952 Oslo** C: 44, N: 13, D: 2.24.

| | | FIRST JUMP (M) | SECOND JUMP (M) | TOTAL PTS. |
|---|---|---|---|---|
| 1. Arnfinn Bergmann | NOR | 67.5 | 68.0 | 226.0 |
| 2. Torbjörn Falkanger | NOR | 68.0 | 64.0 | 221.5 |
| 3. Karl Holmström | SWE | 67.0 | 65.5 | 219.5 |
| 4. Toni Brutscher | GER | 66.5 | 62.5 | 216.5 |
| 4. Halvor Naes | NOR | 63.5 | 64.5 | 216.5 |
| 6. Arne Hoel | NOR | 66.5 | 63.5 | 215.5 |
| 7. Antti Hyvärinen | FIN | 66.5 | 61.5 | 213.5 |
| 8. Sepp Weiler | GER | 67.0 | 63.0 | 213.0 |

Between 1924 and 1952 Norway won 14 of the 18 medals awarded in the ski jumps. Since 1952, the Norwegians have earned only 6 of a possible 48 medals in individual events.

**1956 Cortina** C: 51, N: 16, D: 2.5.

| | | FIRST JUMP (M) | SECOND JUMP (M) | TOTAL PTS. |
|---|---|---|---|---|
| 1. | Antti Hyvärinen | FIN | 81.0 | 84.0 | 227.0 |
| 2. | Aulis Kallakorpi | FIN | 83.5 | 80.5 | 225.0 |
| 3. | Harry Glass | GDR | 83.5 | 80.5 | 224.5 |
| 4. | Max Bolkart | GER | 80.0 | 81.5 | 222.5 |
| 5. | Sven Pettersson | SWE | 81.0 | 81.5 | 220.0 |
| 6. | Andreas Däscher | SWI | 82.0 | 82.0 | 219.5 |
| 7. | Eino Kirjonen | FIN | 78.0 | 81.0 | 219.0 |
| 8. | Werner Lesser | GDR | 77.5 | 77.5 | 210.0 |

**1960 Squaw Valley** C: 45, N: 15, D: 2.28.

| | | FIRST JUMP (M) | SECOND JUMP (M) | TOTAL PTS. |
|---|---|---|---|---|
| 1. | Helmut Recknagel | GDR | 93.5 | 84.5 | 227.2 |
| 2. | Niilo Halonen | FIN | 92.5 | 83.5 | 222.6 |
| 3. | Otto Leodolter | AUT | 88.5 | 83.5 | 219.4 |
| 4. | Nikolai Kamensky | SOV | 90.5 | 79.0 | 216.9 |
| 5. | Thorbjörn Yggeseth | NOR | 88.5 | 82.5 | 216.1 |
| 6. | Max Bolkart | GER | 87.5 | 81.0 | 212.6 |
| 7. | Ansten Samuelstuen | USA | 90.0 | 79.0 | 211.5 |
| 8. | Juhani Karkinen | FIN | 87.5 | 82.0 | 211.4 |

**1964 Innsbruck** C: 52, N: 15, D: 2.9.

| | | FIRST JUMP (M) | SECOND JUMP (M) | TOTAL PTS. |
|---|---|---|---|---|
| 1. | Toralf Engan | NOR | 93.5 | 90.5 | 230.7 |
| 2. | Veikko Kankkonen | FIN | 95.5 | 90.5 | 228.9 |
| 3. | Torgeir Brandtzäg | NOR | 92.0 | 90.0 | 227.2 |
| 4. | Dieter Bokeloh | GDR | 92.0 | 83.5 | 214.6 |
| 5. | Kjell Sjöberg | SWE | 90.0 | 85.0 | 214.4 |
| 6. | Aleksandr Ivannikov | SOV | 90.0 | 83.5 | 213.3 |
| 7. | Helmut Recknagel | GDR | 89.0 | 86.5 | 212.8 |
| 8. | Dieter Neuendorf | GDR | 92.5 | 84.5 | 212.6 |

A second ski jump event was added in 1964 in order to give more competitors a chance to win medals in a sport where a sudden gust of wind or a split-second mistake can send the best jumper down to defeat. As it turned out, however, the same three men took the medals in both events. The 1964 competition was the only one in which the contestants were allowed to use the two best of three jumps.

**1968 Grenoble-St. Nizier** C: 58, N: 17, D: 2:18.

| | | FIRST JUMP (M) | SECOND JUMP (M) | TOTAL PTS. |
|---|---|---|---|---|
| 1. | Vladimir Beloussov | SOV | 101.5 | 98.5 | 231.3 |
| 2. | Jiři Raška | CZE | 101.0 | 98.0 | 229.4 |
| 3. | Lars Grini | NOR | 99.0 | 93.5 | 214.3 |
| 4. | Manfred Queck | GDR | 96.5 | 98.5 | 212.8 |
| 5. | Bent Tomtum | NOR | 98.5 | 95.0 | 212.2 |
| 6. | Reinhold Bachler | AUT | 98.5 | 95.0 | 210.7 |
| 7. | Wolfgang Stöhr | GDR | 96.5 | 92.5 | 205.9 |
| 8. | Anatoly Zheglanov | SOV | 99.0 | 92.0 | 205.7 |

**1972 Sapporo-Okurayama** C: 52, N: 15, D: 2.11.

| | | FIRST JUMP (M) | SECOND JUMP (M) | TOTAL PTS. |
|---|---|---|---|---|
| 1. | Wojciech Fortuna | POL | 111.0 | 87.5 | 219.9 |
| 2. | Walter Steiner | SWI | 94.0 | 103.0 | 219.8 |
| 3. | Rainer Schmidt | GDR | 98.5 | 101.0 | 219.3 |
| 4. | Tauno Käyhkö | FIN | 95.0 | 100.5 | 219.2 |
| 5. | Manfred Wolf | GDR | 107.0 | 89.5 | 215.1 |
| 6. | Gari Napalkov | SOV | 99.5 | 92.0 | 210.1 |
| 7. | Yukio Kasaya | JPN | 106.0 | 85.0 | 209.4 |
| 8. | Danilo Pudgar | YUG | 92.5 | 97.5 | 206.0 |

Fortuna's first jump was so spectacular that he was able to win the gold medal even though his second jump was only the 22nd best of the round.

**1976 Innsbruck** C: 54, N: 15, D: 2.15.

| | | FIRST JUMP (M) | SECOND JUMP (M) | TOTAL PTS. |
|---|---|---|---|---|
| 1. | Karl Schnabl | AUT | 97.5 | 97.0 | 234.8 |
| 2. | Anton Innauer | AUT | 102.5 | 91.0 | 232.9 |
| 3. | Henry Glass | GDR | 91.0 | 97.0 | 221.7 |
| 4. | Jochen Danneberg | GDR | 102.0 | 89.5 | 221.6 |
| 5. | Reinhold Bachler | AUT | 95.0 | 91.0 | 217.4 |
| 6. | Hans Wallner | AUT | 93.5 | 92.5 | 216.9 |
| 7. | Bernd Eckstein | GDR | 94.0 | 91.5 | 216.2 |
| 8. | Hans-Georg Aschenbach | GDR | 92.5 | 89.0 | 212.1 |

**1980 Lake Placid** C: 50, N: 16, D: 2.23.

| | | FIRST JUMP (M) | SECOND JUMP (M) | TOTAL PTS. |
|---|---|---|---|---|
| 1. | Jouko Törmänen | FIN | 114.5 | 117.0 | 271.0 |
| 2. | Hubert Neuper | AUT | 113.0 | 114.5 | 262.4 |
| 3. | Jari Puikkonen | FIN | 110.5 | 109.5 | 248.5 |
| 4. | Anton Innauer | AUT | 110.0 | 107.0 | 245.7 |
| 5. | Armin Kogler | AUT | 110.0 | 108.0 | 245.6 |
| 6. | Roger Ruud | NOR | 110.0 | 109.0 | 243.0 |
| 7. | Hansjörg Sumi | SWI | 117.0 | 110.0 | 242.7 |
| 8. | James Denney | USA | 109.0 | 104.0 | 239.1 |

**1984 Sarajevo** C: 53, N: 17, D: 2.18.

| | | FIRST JUMP (M) | SECOND JUMP (M) | TOTAL PTS. |
|---|---|---|---|---|
| 1. | Matti Nykänen | FIN | 116.0 | 111.0 | 231.2 |
| 2. | Jens Weissflog | GDR | 107.0 | 107.5 | 213.7 |
| 3. | Pavel Ploc | CZE | 103.5 | 109.0 | 202.9 |
| 4. | Jeffrey Hastings | USA | 102.5 | 107.0 | 201.2 |
| 5. | Jari Puikkonen | FIN | 103.5 | 102.0 | 196.6 |
| 6. | Armin Kogler | AUT | 106.0 | 99.5 | 195.6 |
| 7. | Andreas Bauer | GER | 105.0 | 100.5 | 194.6 |
| 8. | Vladimir Podzimek | CZE | 98.5 | 108.0 | 194.5 |

Notoriously ill-tempered Matti Nykänen of Jyväskla put together two near-perfect jumps to achieve the largest winning margin in Olympic jumping history.

**1988 Calgary** C: 55, N: 18, D: 2.23.

| | | FIRST JUMP (M) | SECOND JUMP (M) | TOTAL PTS. |
|---|---|---|---|---|
| 1. | Matti Nykänen | FIN | 118.5 | 107.0 | 224.0 |
| 2. | Erik Johnsen | NOR | 114.5 | 102.0 | 207.9 |
| 3. | Matjaž Debelak | YUG | 113.0 | 108.0 | 207.7 |
| 4. | Thomas Klauser | GER | 114.5 | 102.5 | 205.1 |
| 5. | Pavel Ploc | CZE | 114.5 | 102.5 | 204.1 |
| 6. | Andreas Felder | AUT | 113.5 | 103.0 | 203.9 |
| 7. | Horst Bulau | CAN | 112.5 | 99.5 | 197.6 |
| 8. | Staffan Tällberg | SWE | 110.0 | 102.0 | 196.6 |

In a competition that was postponed four times because of dangerous winds, Nykänen, mellowed somewhat by fatherhood, became the first ski jumper to win two gold medals in one Olympics.

## SKI JUMP, LARGE HILL, TEAM

Each team member takes two jumps.

**1924–1984** not held

**1988 Calgary** T: 11, N: 11, D: 2.24.

| | | | TOTAL PTS. |
|---|---|---|---|
| 1. | FIN | (Matti Nykänen 228.8, Ari-Pekka Nikkola 207.9, Jari Puikkonen 193.6, Tuomo Ylipulli 192.3) | 634.4 |
| 2. | YUG | (Matjaž Zupan 211.5, Matjaž Debelak 207.5, Primož Ulaga 207.1, Miran Tepeš 192.8) | 625.5 |
| 3. | NOR | (Erik Johnsen 218.7, Ole Gunnar Fidjestol 193.9, Ole Christian Eidhammer 177.2, Jon Inge Kjorum 128.4) | 596.1 |
| 4. | CZE | (Pavel Ploc 204.1, Jiří Malec 193.4, Jiří Parma 189.3, Ladislav Dluhoš 165.4) | 586.8 |
| 5. | AUT | (Günter Stranner 197.5, Heinz Kuttin 193.3, Ernst Vettori 186.0, Andreas Felder 176.3) | 577.6 |
| 6. | GER | (Thomas Klauser 197.6, Josef Heumann 180.9, Andreas Bauer 175.1, Peter Rohwein 174.3) | 559.0 |
| 7. | SWE | (Jan Boklöv 180.1, Staffan Tällberg 178.7, Anders Daun 174.2, Per-Inge Tällberg 161.5) | 539.7 |
| 8. | SWI | (Gérard Balanche 175.0, Christian Hauswirth 175.0, Fabrice Piazzini 166.2, Christoph Lehmann 156.7) | 516.1 |

Matti Nykänen won his third gold medal of the Calgary Games to give him a two-Olympics total of four golds and one silver.

## NORDIC COMBINED, INDIVIDUAL

**1924 Chamonix** C: 30, N: 9, D: 2.4.

| | | | 18 KM | SKI JUMP | TOTAL PTS. |
|---|---|---|---|---|---|
| 1. | Thorleif Haug | NOR | 1:14:31.0 | 17.821 | 18.906 |
| 2. | Thoralf Strömstad | NOR | 1:17:03.0 | 17.687 | 18.219 |
| 3. | Johan Gröttumsbråten | NOR | 1:15:51.0 | 16.333 | 17.854 |
| 4. | Harald Ökern | NOR | 1:20:30.0 | 17.395 | 17.260 |
| 5. | Axel Nilsson | SWE | 1:25:29.0 | 16.500 | 14.063 |
| 6. | Josef Adolf | CZE | 1:31:17.0 | 12.833 | 13.729 |
| 7. | Vincenz Buchberger | CZE | 1:32:32.0 | 16.250 | 13.625 |
| 8. | Menotti Jacobsson | SWE | 1:37:10.0 | 16.896 | 12.823 |

**1928 St. Moritz** C: 35, N: 14, D: 2.18.

| | | | 18 KM | SKI JUMP | TOTAL PTS. |
|---|---|---|---|---|---|
| 1. | Johan Gröttumsbråten | NOR | 1:37:01.0 | 15.667 | 17.833 |
| 2. | Hans Vinjarengen | NOR | 1:41:44.0 | 12.856 | 15.303 |
| 3. | John Snersrud | NOR | 1:50:51.0 | 16.917 | 15.021 |
| 4. | Paavo Nuotio | FIN | 1:48:46.0 | 15.729 | 14.927 |
| 5. | Esko Järvinen | FIN | 1:46:33.0 | 14.286 | 14.810 |
| 6. | Sven Eriksson | SWE | 1:52:20.0 | 16.312 | 14.593 |
| 7. | Ludwig Böck | GER | 1:48:56.0 | 11.812 | 13.260 |
| 8. | Ole Kolterrud | NOR | 1:50:17.0 | 13.500 | 13.146 |

**1932 Lake Placid** C: 33, N: 10, D: 2.11.

| | | | 18 KM | SKI JUMP | TOTAL PTS. |
|---|---|---|---|---|---|
| 1. | Johan Gröttumsbråten | NOR | 1:27:15.0 | 206.0 | 446.00 |
| 2. | Ole Stenen | NOR | 1:28:05.0 | 200.3 | 436.05 |
| 3. | Hans Vinjarengen | NOR | 1:32:40.0 | 221.6 | 434.60 |
| 4. | Sverre Kolterud | NOR | 1:34:36.0 | 214.7 | 418.70 |
| 5. | Sven Eriksson | SWE | 1:39:32.0 | 220.8 | 402.30 |
| 6. | Antonin Barton | CZE | 1:33:39.0 | 188.6 | 397.10 |
| 7. | Bronislaw Czech | POL | 1:36:37.0 | 197.0 | 392.00 |
| 8. | František Simunek | CZE | 1:39:58.0 | 196.8 | 375.30 |

Gröttumsbråten closed out his Olympic career with three gold medals, one silver, and one bronze.

**1936 Garmisch-Partenkirchen** C: 51, N: 16, D: 2.13.

| | | | 18 KM | SKI JUMP | TOTAL PTS. |
|---|---|---|---|---|---|
| 1. | Oddbjörn Hagen | NOR | 1:15:33.0 | 190.3 | 430.3 |
| 2. | Olaf Hoffsbakken | NOR | 1:17:37.0 | 192.0 | 419.8 |
| 3. | Sverre Brodahl | NOR | 1:18:01.0 | 182.6 | 408.1 |
| 4. | Lauri Valonen | FIN | 1:26:34.0 | 222.6 | 401.2 |
| 5. | František Simunek | CZE | 1:19:09.0 | 175.3 | 394.3 |
| 6. | Bernt Osterklöft | NOR | 1:21:37.0 | 188.7 | 393.8 |
| 7. | Stanislaw Marusarz | POL | 1:25:27.0 | 208.9 | 393.3 |
| 7. | Timo Murama | FIN | 1:24:52.0 | 205.8 | 393.3 |

**1948 St. Moritz** C: 39, N: 13, D: 2.1.

| | | | 18 KM | SKI JUMP | TOTAL PTS. |
|---|---|---|---|---|---|
| 1. | Heikki Hasu | FIN | 1:16:43.0 | 208.8 | 448.80 |
| 2. | Martti Huhtala | FIN | 1:19:28.0 | 209.5 | 433.65 |
| 3. | Sven Israelsson | SWE | 1:21:35.0 | 221.9 | 433.40 |
| 4. | Niklaus Stump | SWI | 1:21:44.0 | 213.0 | 421.50 |
| 5. | Olavi Sihvonen | FIN | 1:21:50.0 | 209.2 | 416.20 |
| 6. | Eilert Dahl | NOR | 1:22:12.0 | 208.8 | 414.30 |
| 7. | Pauli Salonen | FIN | 1:22:15.0 | 206.3 | 413.30 |
| 8. | Olav Dufseth | NOR | 1:22:26.0 | 201.1 | 412.60 |

**1952 Oslo** C: 25, N: 11, D: 2.18.

| | | | SKI JUMP | 18 KM | TOTAL PTS. |
|---|---|---|---|---|---|
| 1. | Simon Slåttvik | NOR | 223.5 | 1:05:40.0 | 451.621 |
| 2. | Heikki Hasu | FIN | 207.5 | 1:02:24.0 | 447.500 |
| 3. | Sverre Stenersen | NOR | 223.0 | 1:09:44.0 | 436.335 |
| 4. | Paavo Korhonen | FIN | 206.0 | 1:05:30.0 | 434.727 |
| 5. | Per Gjelten | NOR | 212.0 | 1:07:40.0 | 432.848 |
| 6. | Ottar Gjermundshaug | NOR | 206.0 | 1:06:13.0 | 432.121 |
| 7. | Aulis Sipponen | FIN | 198.5 | 1:06:03.0 | 425.227 |
| 8. | Eeti Nieminen | FIN | 206.0 | 1:08:24.0 | 424.181 |

February 18, 1952, was a great day in the history of Norwegian sports. Hjallis Andersen won the 1500-meter skating event, Hallgeir Brenden won the 18-kilometer cross-country race, and Simon Slåttvik won the nordic combined. People all over Oslo left their jobs and spilled into the streets to celebrate. *The New York Times* reported, with some annoyance, that at the Hotel Viking, where the press was staying, half of the waiters walked out, and "It took more than an hour to order food and another two hours to get it." The year 1952 was the first time that the jumping half of the nordic combined was held before the skiing.

**1956 Cortina** C: 36, N: 12, D: 1.31.

| | | | SKI JUMP | 15 KM | TOTAL PTS. |
|---|---|---|---|---|---|
| 1. | Sverre Stenersen | NOR | 215.0 | 56:18.0 | 455.000 |
| 2. | Bengt Eriksson | SWE | 214.0 | 1:00:36.0 | 437.400 |
| 3. | Franciszek Gąsienica-Groń | POL | 203.0 | 57:55.0 | 436.800 |
| 4. | Paavo Korhonen | FIN | 196.5 | 56:02.0 | 435.597 |
| 5. | Arne Barhaugen | NOR | 199.0 | 57:11.0 | 435.581 |
| 6. | Tormod Knutsen | NOR | 203.0 | 58:22.0 | 435.000 |
| 7. | Nikolai Gusakov | SOV | 200.0 | 58:17.0 | 432.300 |
| 8. | Alfredo Prucker | ITA | 201.0 | 58:52.0 | 431.100 |

**1960 Squaw Valley** C: 33, N: 13, D: 2.22.

| | | | SKI JUMP | 15 KM | TOTAL PTS. |
|---|---|---|---|---|---|
| 1. | Georg Thoma | GER | 221.5 | 59:23.8 | 457.952 |
| 2. | Tormod Knutsen | NOR | 217.0 | 59:31.0 | 453.000 |
| 3. | Nikolai Gusakov | SOV | 212.0 | 58:29.4 | 452.000 |
| 4. | Pekka Ristola | FIN | 214.0 | 59:32.8 | 449.871 |
| 5. | Dmitri Kochkin | SOV | 219.5 | 1:01:32.1 | 444.694 |
| 6. | Arne Larson | NOR | 215.0 | 1:01:10.1 | 444.613 |
| 7. | Sverre Stenersen | NOR | 205.5 | 1:00:24.0 | 438.081 |
| 8. | Lars Dahlqvist | SWE | 201.5 | 59:46.0 | 436.532 |

**1964 Innsbruck-Seefeld** C: 32, N: 11, D: 2.3.

| | | | SKI JUMP (70 M) | 15 KM | TOTAL PTS. |
|---|---|---|---|---|---|
| 1. | Tormod Knutsen | NOR | 238.9 | 50:58.6 | 469.28 |
| 2. | Nikolai Kiselev | SOV | 233.0 | 51:49.1 | 453.04 |
| 3. | Georg Thoma | GER | 241.1 | 52:31.2 | 452.88 |
| 4. | Nikolai Gusakov | SOV | 223.4 | 51:19.8 | 449.36 |
| 5. | Arne Larsen | NOR | 198.3 | 50:49.6 | 430.63 |
| 6. | Arne Barhaugen | NOR | 191.3 | 50:40.4 | 425.63 |

| 7. | Vyacheslav Driagin | SOV | 216.2 | 52:58.3 | 422.75 |
|---|---|---|---|---|---|
| 8. | Ezio Damolin | ITA | 198.1 | 51:42.3 | 419.54 |

**1968 Grenoble-Autrans** C: 41, N: 13, D: 2.11.

| | | | SKI JUMP (70 M) | 15 KM | TOTAL PTS. |
|---|---|---|---|---|---|
| 1. | Franz Keller | GER | 240.1 | 50:45.2 | 449.04 |
| 2. | Alois Kälin | SWI | 193.2 | 47:21.5 | 447.99 |
| 3. | Andreas Kunz | GDR | 216.9 | 49:19.8 | 444.10 |
| 4. | Tomáš Kučera | CZE | 217.4 | 50:07.7 | 434.14 |
| 5. | Ezio Damolin | ITA | 206.0 | 49:36.2 | 429.54 |
| 6. | Józef Gąsienica | POL | 217.7 | 50:34.5 | 428.78 |
| 7. | Robert Makara | SOV | 222.8 | 51:09.3 | 426.92 |
| 8. | Vyacheslav Driagin | SOV | 222.8 | 51:22.0 | 424.38 |

Had Kälin been able to finish the cross-country race 2.3 seconds sooner, he would have won the gold medal.

**1972 Sapporo-Miyanomori/Makomanai** C: 39, N: 14, D: 2.5.

| | | | SKI JUMP (70 M) | 15 KM | TOTAL PTS. |
|---|---|---|---|---|---|
| 1. | Ulrich Wehling | GDR | 200.9 | 49:15.3 | 413.340 |
| 2. | Rauno Miettinen | FIN | 210.0 | 51:08.2 | 405.505 |
| 3. | Karl-Heinz Luck | GDR | 170.8 | 48:24.0 | 398.800 |
| 4. | Erkki Kilpinen | FIN | 185.0 | 49:52.6 | 391.845 |
| 5. | Yuji Katsuro | JPN | 195.1 | 51:10.9 | 390.200 |
| 6. | Tomáš Kučera | CZE | 191.8 | 51:04.0 | 387.935 |
| 7. | Aleksandr Nossov | SOV | 201.3 | 52:00.7 | 387.700 |
| 8. | Kaare Olavberg | NOR | 180.4 | 50:08.9 | 384.800 |

Hideki Nakano of Japan had the unusual distinction of finishing first among the competitors in the nordic combined in the ski jump, but last in the 15-kilometer race. This left him in 13th place overall.

**1976 Innsbruck-Seefeld** C: 34, N: 14, D: 2.8.

| | | | SKI JUMP (70 M) | 15 KM | TOTAL PTS. |
|---|---|---|---|---|---|
| 1. | Ulrich Wehling | GDR | 225.5 | 50:28.95 | 423.39 |
| 2. | Urban Hettich | GER | 198.9 | 48:01.55 | 418.90 |
| 3. | Konrad Winkler | GDR | 213.9 | 49:51.11 | 417.47 |
| 4. | Rauno Miettinen | FIN | 219.9 | 51:12.21 | 411.30 |
| 5. | Claus Tuchscherer | GDR | 218.7 | 51:16.12 | 409.51 |
| 6. | Nikolai Nagovitzin | SOV | 196.1 | 49:05.97 | 406.44 |
| 7. | Valery Kapayev | SOV | 202.9 | 49:53.26 | 406.14 |
| 8. | Tom Sandberg | NOR | 195.7 | 49:09.34 | 405.53 |

**1980 Lake Placid** C: 31, N: 9, D: 2.18.

| | | | SKI JUMP (70 M) | 15 KM | TOTAL PTS. |
|---|---|---|---|---|---|
| 1. | Ulrich Wehling | GDR | 227.2 | 49:24.5 | 432.200 |
| 2. | Jouko Karjalainen | FIN | 209.5 | 47:44.5 | 429.500 |
| 3. | Konrad Winkler | GDR | 214.5 | 48:45.7 | 425.320 |
| 4. | Tom Sandberg | NOR | 203.7 | 48:19.4 | 418.465 |
| 5. | Uwe Dotzauer | GDR | 217.6 | 49:52.4 | 418.415 |
| 6. | Karl Lustenberger | SWI | 212.7 | 50:01.1 | 412.210 |
| 7. | Aleksandr Maiorov | SOV | 194.4 | 48:19.6 | 409.135 |
| 8. | Gunter Schmieder | GDR | 201.7 | 49:42.0 | 404.075 |

The 27-year-old Wehling became the first man to win three consecutive gold medals in the same individual Winter event.

**1984 Sarajevo** C: 28, N: 11, D: 2.12.

| | | | SKI JUMP (70 M) | 15 KM | TOTAL PTS. |
|---|---|---|---|---|---|
| 1. | Tom Sandberg | NOR | 214.7 | 47:52.7 | 422.595 |
| 2. | Jouko Karjalainen | FIN | 196.9 | 46:32.0 | 416.900 |
| 3. | Jukka Ylipulli | FIN | 208.3 | 48:28.5 | 410.825 |
| 4. | Rauno Miettinen | FIN | 205.5 | 49:02.2 | 402.970 |
| 5. | Thomas Müller | GER | 209.1 | 49:32.7 | 401.995 |
| 6. | Aleksandr Prosvirnin | SOV | 199.4 | 48:40.1 | 400.185 |
| 7. | Uwe Dotzauer | GDR | 199.5 | 48:56.8 | 397.780 |
| 8. | Hermann Weinbuch | GER | 201.6 | 49:13.4 | 397.390 |

**1988 Calgary-Canmore** C: 42, N: 13, D: 2.28.

| | | | SKI JUMP (70 M) | 15 KM | TOTAL PTS. |
|---|---|---|---|---|---|
| 1. | Hippolyt Kempf | SWI | 217.9 | 38:16.8 | 432.230 |
| 2. | Klaus Sulzenbacher | AUT | 228.5 | 39:46.5 | 429.375 |
| 3. | Allar Levandi | SOV | 216.6 | 39:12.4 | 422.590 |
| 4. | Uwe Prenzel | GDR | 207.6 | 38:18.8 | 421.630 |
| 5. | Andreas Schaad | SWI | 207.2 | 38:18.0 | 421.350 |
| 6. | Torbjorn Lokken | NOR | 199.4 | 37:39.0 | 419.400 |
| 7. | Miroslav Kopal | CZE | 208.7 | 38:48.0 | 418.800 |
| 8. | Marko Frank | GDR | 209.4 | 39:08.2 | 416.020 |

Nineteen eighty-eight marked the first time that Nordic Combined used the Gundersen Method, in which the starting order and intervals in the cross-country race are based on the results of the ski jump, with 9 points being equal to 1 minute. World Cup leader Klaus Sulzenbacher earned the right to start first, with Hippolyt Kempf in third place 1:10.7 behind. Kempf caught Sulzenbacher 2.3 kilometers from the finish and pulled away to win by 19 seconds.

Because of delays caused by poor weather, the ski jump and cross-country race were held on the same day.

## NORDIC COMBINED, TEAM

In this event each team member takes three jumps, although only the two best count in the scoring. The next day, a 3 × 10-kilometer relay is held; the starting order is based on the results of the ski jump. Each 12 points behind the leading team in the ski jump is equal to a 1-minute handicap at the start of the relay.

**1924–1984** not held

**1988 Calgary-Canmore** T: 11, N: 11, D: 2.23.

| | | | SKI JUMP (70 M) | 10 KM | TOTAL PTS. |
|---|---|---|---|---|---|
| 1. | GER | Hans-Peter Pohl | 204.7 | 27:26.7 | 792.08 |
| | | Hubert Schwarz | 227.2 | 27:45.7 | |
| | | Thomas Müller | 197.9 | 25:33.6 | |
| 2. | SWI | Andreas Schaad | 195.4 | 25:34.7 | 791.40 |
| | | Hippolyt Kempf | 199.8 | 25:12.9 | |
| | | Fredy Glanzmann | 176.2 | 25:09.8 | |
| 3. | AUT | Günther Csar | 193.7 | 26:39.7 | 785.90 |
| | | Hansjörg Aschenwald | 204.5 | 28:33.7 | |
| | | Klaus Sulzenbacher | 228.4 | 25:47.5 | |
| 4. | NOR | Hallstein Bogseth | 195.0 | 26:18.6 | 782.40 |
| | | Trond Arne Bredesen | 201.1 | 27:04.0 | |
| | | Torbjorn Lokken | 200.5 | 25:25.8 | |
| 5. | GDR | Thomas Prenzel | 183.9 | 26:23.9 | 764.38 |
| | | Marko Frank | 195.9 | 26:12.1 | |
| | | Uwe Prenzel | 191.8 | 25:37.5 | |
| 6. | CZE | Ladislav Patraš | 192.0 | 26:49.7 | 756.56 |
| | | Ján Klimko | 184.7 | 26:30.4 | |
| | | Miroslav Kopal | 196.8 | 25:42.0 | |
| 7. | FIN | Pasi Saapunki | 165.0 | 26:29.7 | 733.52 |
| | | Jouko Parviainen | 201.9 | 26:42.3 | |
| | | Jukka Ylipulli | 194.4 | 26:44.3 | |
| 8. | FRA | Jean Bohard | 178.0 | 27:04.9 | 715.40 |
| | | Xavier Girard | 187.2 | 26:43.2 | |
| | | Fabrice Guy | 175.8 | 25:57.3 | |

The West Germans led after the ski jump, with Austria second and Switzerland back in sixth place. Günther Csar, starting 16 seconds after Hans-Peter Pohl, gave Austria a 31-second lead after the first leg of the relay, but Hubert Schwarz put West Germany back in the lead to stay. The Swiss, starting with a handicap of 4 minutes 52 seconds, staged a dramatic come-from-behind effort, but fell 3.4 seconds short of victory. "It's a very thrilling, frustrating feeling," said Swiss anchorman Fredy Glanzmann, "to be so near to the leader where you can almost touch him, but you can't touch him because your legs won't let you."

# NORDIC SKIING

## WOMEN

Except for the combined pursuit, participants in the individual events start at 30-second intervals and race against the clock. In the relay all teams start at the same time.

## 5 KILOMETERS (CLASSICAL)

**1924–1960** not held

**1964 Innsbruck-Seefeld** C: 32, N: 14, D: 2.5.
1. Claudia Boyarskikh    SOV    17.50.5
2. Mirja Lehtonen    FIN    17.52.9
3. Alevtina Kolchina    SOV    18:08.4
4. Eudokia Mekshilo    SOV    18:16.7
5. Toini Pöysti    FIN    18:25.5
6. Toini Gustaffson    SWE    18.25.7
7. Barbro Martinsson    SWE    18:26.4
8. Eeva Ruoppa    FIN    18.29.8

In 1964 Claudia Boyarskikh, a 24-year-old teacher from Siberia, swept all three women's nordic events.

**1968 Grenoble-Autrans** C: 34, N: 12, D: 2.13.
1. Toini Gustafsson    SWE    16:45.2
2. Galina Kulakova    SOV    16:48.4
3. Alevtina Kolchina    SOV    16:51.6
4. Barbro Martinsson    SWE    16:52.9
5. Marjatta Kajosmaa    FIN    16:54.6
6. Rita Achkina    SOV    16.35.1
7. Inger Aufles    NOR    16:58.1
8. Senja Puoula    FIN    17:00.3

Toini Gustafsson was the last skier to leave the starting line. Kept informed of Kulakova's time at each kilometer, she knew exactly what time she had to beat. Four seconds off Kulakova's pace with only one kilometer to go, Gustafsson poured it on to win with three seconds to spare. A 26-year-old physical education teacher, Gustafsson also won the 10-kilometer contest and gained a silver medal in the relay after recording the fastest leg of the race.

**1972 Sapporo-Makomanai** C: 43, N: 12, D: 2.9.
1. Galina Kulakova    SOV    17:00.50
2. Marjatta Kajosmaa    FIN    17:05.50
3. Helena Šikolová    CZE    17:07.32
4. Alevtina Olunina    SOV    17:07.40
5. Hilkka Kuntola    FIN    17:11.67
6. Lyubov Moukhatcheva    SOV    17:12.08
7. Berit Mördre-Lammedal    NOR    17:16.79
8. Aslaug Dahl    NOR    17:17.49

Kulakova, a 29-year-old physical education teacher from Izhevsk, matched Claudia Boyarskikh's feat of capturing all three women's nordic gold medals.

**1976 Innsbruck-Seefeld** C: 44, N: 14, D: 2.9.
1. Helena Takalo    FIN    15:48.69
2. Raisa Smetanina    SOV    15:49.73
3. Nina Baldycheva    SOV    16:12.82
4. Hilkka Kuntola    FIN    16:17.74
5. Eva Olsson    SWE    16:27.15
6. Zinaida Amosova    SOV    16:33.78
7. Monika Debertshäuser    GDR    16:34.94
8. Grete Kummen    NOR    16:35.43
DISQ (Drugs): Galina Kulakova (SOV) 16:07.36

Defending champion Kulakova finished third, but was disqualified for having used a nasal spray which contained the banned drug ephedrine. She was, however, allowed to compete in the 10-kilometer race and the relay.

**1980 Lake Placid** C: 38, N: 12, D: 2.15.
1. Raisa Smetanina    SOV    15:06.92
2. Hilkka Riihivuori (Kuntola)    FIN    15:11.96
3. Kvĕtoslava Jeriová    CZE    15:23.44
4. Barbara Petzold    GDR    15:23.62
5. Nina Baldycheva    SOV    15:29.03
6. Galina Kulakova    SOV    15:29.58
7. Veronika Hesse    GDR    15:31.83
8. Helena Takalo    FIN    15:32.12

**1984 Sarajevo** C: 52, N: 14, D: 2.12.

| | | |
|---|---|---|
| 1. Marja-Liisa Hämäläinen | FIN | 17:04.0 |
| 2. Berit Aunli (Kvello) | NOR | 17:14.1 |
| 3. Květoslava Jeriová | CZE | 17:18.3 |
| 4. Lillemor Marie Risby (Johansson) | SWE | 17:26.3 |
| 5. Inger Nybråten | NOR | 17:28.2 |
| 6. Brit Pettersen | NOR | 17:33.6 |
| 7. Anne Jahren | NOR | 17:38.3 |
| 8. Ute Noack | GDR | 17:46.0 |

Hämäläinen won the second of her three gold medals.

**1988 Calgary-Canmore** C: 55, N: 17, D: 2.17.

| | | |
|---|---|---|
| 1. Marjo Matikainen | FIN | 15:04.0 |
| 2. Tamara Tikhonova | SOV | 15:05.3 |
| 3. Vida Vencienė | SOV | 15:11.1 |
| 4. Anne Jahren | NOR | 15:12.6 |
| 5. Marja-Liisa Kirvesniemi (Hämäläinen) | FIN | 15:16.7 |
| 6. Inger Helene Nybråten | NOR | 15:17.7 |
| 7. Marie-Helene Westin | SWE | 15:28.9 |
| 8. Svetlana Nageikina | SOV | 15:29.9 |

Matikainen moved ahead after four kilometers, then used every last ounce of energy to push herself across the finish line 1.3 seconds faster than Tikhonova's time, before collapsing.

# 10 KILOMETERS (CLASSICAL)

**1924–1948** not held

**1952 Oslo** C: 20, N: 8, D: 2.23.

| | | |
|---|---|---|
| 1. Lydia Wideman | FIN | 41:40.0 |
| 2. Mirja Hietamies | FIN | 42:39.0 |
| 3. Siira Rantanen | FIN | 42:50.0 |
| 4. Märta Norberg | SWE | 42:53.0 |
| 5. Sirkka Polkunen | FIN | 43:07.0 |
| 6. Rakel Wahl | NOR | 44:54.0 |
| 7. Marit Oiseth | NOR | 45:04.0 |
| 8. Margit Albrechtsson | SWE | 45:05.0 |

**1956 Cortina** C: 40, N: 11, D: 1:28.

| | | |
|---|---|---|
| 1. Lyubov Kosyreva | SOV | 38:11.0 |
| 2. Radya Eroshina | SOV | 38:16.0 |
| 3. Sonja Edström | SWE | 38:23.0 |
| 4. Alevtina Kolchina | SOV | 38:46.0 |
| 5. Siira Rantanen | FIN | 39:40.0 |
| 6. Mirja Hietamies | FIN | 40.18.0 |
| 7. Irma Johansson | SWE | 40:20.0 |
| 8. Sirkka Polkunen | FIN | 40:25.0 |

**1960 Squaw Valley** C: 24, N: 7, D: 2.20.

| | | |
|---|---|---|
| 1. Maria Gusakova | SOV | 39:46.6 |
| 2. Lyubov Baranova (Kosyreva) | SOV | 40:04.2 |
| 3. Radya Eroshina | SOV | 40:06.0 |
| 4. Alevtina Kolchina | SOV | 40:12.6 |
| 5. Sonja Ruthström (Edström) | SWE | 40:35.5 |
| 6. Toini Pöysti | FIN | 40:41.9 |
| 7. Barbro Martinsson | SWE | 41:06.2 |
| 8. Irma Johansson | SWE | 41:08.3 |

**1964 Innsbruck-Seefeld** C: 35, N: 13, D: 2.1.

| | | |
|---|---|---|
| 1. Claudia Boyarskikh | SOV | 40:24.3 |
| 2. Eudokia Mekshilo | SOV | 40:26.6 |
| 3. Maria Gusakova | SOV | 40:46.6 |
| 4. Britt Strandberg | SWE | 40:54.0 |
| 5. Toini Pöysti | FIN | 41:17.4 |
| 6. Senja Pusula | FIN | 41:17.8 |
| 7. Alevtina Kolchina | SOV | 41:26.2 |
| 8. Toini Gustafsson | SWE | 41:41.1 |

**1968 Grenoble-Autrans** C: 34, N: 11, D: 2.9.

| | | |
|---|---|---|
| 1. Toini Gustafsson | SWE | 36:46.5 |
| 2. Berit Mördre | NOR | 37:54.6 |
| 3. Inger Aufles | NOR | 37:59.9 |
| 4. Barbro Martinsson | SWE | 38:07.1 |
| 5. Marjatta Kajosmaa | FIN | 38:09.0 |
| 6. Galina Kulakova | SOV | 38:26.7 |
| 7. Alevtina Kolchina | SOV | 38:52.9 |
| 8. Babben Damon-Enger | NOR | 38:54.4 |

**1972 Sapporo-Makomanai** C: 42, N: 11, D: 2.6.

| | | |
|---|---|---|
| 1. Galina Kulakova | SOV | 34:17.82 |
| 2. Alevtina Olunina | SOV | 34:54.11 |
| 3. Marjatta Kajosmaa | FIN | 34:56.45 |
| 4. Lyubov Moukhatcheva | SOV | 34:58.56 |
| 5. Helena Takalo | FIN | 35:06.34 |
| 6. Aslaug Dahl | NOR | 35:18.84 |
| 7. Helena Šikolová | CZE | 35:29.33 |
| 8. Hilkka Kuntola | FIN | 35:36.71 |

**1976 Innsbruck-Seefeld** C: 44, N: 15, D: 2.10.

| | | |
|---|---|---|
| 1. Raisa Smetanina | SOV | 30:13.41 |
| 2. Helena Takalo | FIN | 30:14.28 |
| 3. Galina Kulakova | SOV | 30:38.61 |
| 4. Nina Baldycheva | SOV | 30:52.58 |
| 5. Eva Olsson | SWE | 31:08.72 |
| 6. Zinaida Amosova | SOV | 31:11.23 |
| 7. Barbara Petzold | GDR | 31:12.20 |
| 8. Veronika Schmidt | GDR | 31:12.33 |

**1980 Lake Placid** C: 38, N: 12, D: 2.18.

| | | |
|---|---|---|
| 1. Barbara Petzold | GDR | 30:31.54 |
| 2. Hilkka Riihivuori (Kuntola) | FIN | 30:35.05 |
| 3. Helena Takalo | FIN | 30:45.25 |
| 4. Raisa Smetanina | SOV | 30:54.48 |
| 5. Galina Kulakova | SOV | 30:58.46 |
| 6. Nina Balycheva | SOV | 31:22.93 |
| 7. Marlies Rostock | GDR | 31:28.79 |
| 8. Veronika Hesse (Schmidt) | GDR | 31:29.14 |

The East German propaganda apparatus broke down somewhat in the case of Barbara Petzold, who was described in half the press releases as a medical student and in the other half as a law student. Either way, she told the press that training and competing left her little time for her studies.

**1984 Sarajevo** C: 52, N: 15, D: 2.9.

| | | |
|---|---|---|
| 1. Marja-Liisa Hämäläinen | FIN | 31:44.2 |
| 2. Raisa Smetanina | SOV | 32:02.9 |

| | | |
|---|---|---|
| 3. Brit Pettersen | NOR | 32:12.7 |
| 4. Berit Aunli (Kvello) | NOR | 32:17.7 |
| 5. Anne Jahren | NOR | 32:26.2 |
| 6. Lillemor Marie Risby (Johansson) | SWE | 32:34.6 |
| 7. Marit Myrmael | NOR | 32:35.3 |
| 8. Julia Stepanova | SOV | 32:45.7 |

Hämäläinen, a 28-year-old physiotherapist from Simpele, near the Soviet border, gained revenge over Finnish journalists. "A hundred times they've written that I would never become anybody," she would say, "and I wanted to show people that I am somebody and that if I didn't do well, there was always a reason."

**1988 Calgary-Canmore** C: 52, N: 17, D: 2.14.

| | | |
|---|---|---|
| 1. Vida Vencienė | SOV | 30:08.3 |
| 2. Raisa Smetanina | SOV | 30:17.0 |
| 3. Marjo Matikainen | FIN | 30:20.5 |
| 4. Svetlana Nageikina | SOV | 30:26.5 |
| 5. Tamara Tikhonova | SOV | 30:38.9 |
| 6. Inger Helene Nybråten | NOR | 30:51.7 |
| 7. Pirkko Määttä | FIN | 30:52.4 |
| 8. Marie-Helene Westin | SWE | 30:53.5 |

## 20 KILOMETERS (FREESTYLE)

**1924–1980** not held

**1984 Sarajevo** C: 40, N: 13, D: 2.18.

| | | |
|---|---|---|
| 1. Marja-Liisa Hämäläinen | FIN | 1:01:45.0 |
| 2. Raisa Smetanina | SOV | 1:02:26.7 |
| 3. Anne Jahren | NOR | 1:03:13.6 |
| 4. Blanka Paulů | CZE | 1:03:16.9 |
| 5. Lillemor Marie Risby (Johansson) | SWE | 1:03:31.8 |
| 6. Brit Pettersen | NOR | 1:03:49.0 |
| 7. Lyubov Liadova | SOV | 1:03:53.3 |
| 8. Evi Kratzer | SWI | 1:03:56.4 |

After winning her third gold medal, Marja-Liisa Hämäläinen tried to avoid Finnish reporters by jumping over a fence and running away. Finally headed off and trapped, the farmer's daughter submitted to photographs and interviews. In addition to her three individual golds, she earned a bronze medal in the relay. Her fiancé, Harri Kirvesniemi, won two nordic bronze medals.

**1988 Calgary-Canmore** C: 55, N: 18, D: 2.25

| | | |
|---|---|---|
| 1. Tamara Tikhonova | SOV | 55:53.6 |
| 2. Anfisa Reztsova | SOV | 56:12.8 |
| 3. Raisa Smetanina | SOV | 57:22.1 |
| 4. Christina Gilli-Brügger | SWI | 57:37.4 |
| 5. Simone Opitz | GDR | 57:54.3 |
| 6. Manuela Di Centa Sioli | ITA | 57:55.2 |
| 7. Kerstin Moring | GDR | 58:17.2 |
| 8. Marianne Dahlmo | NOR | 58:31.1 |

DISQ: Nina Gavrylyuk SOV 58:26.9

Competing in her fourth Olympics, 35-year-old Raisa Smetanina became the first woman to win nine winter medals. Her final total: three gold, five silver, and one bronze. One of Smetanina's teammates, Nina Gavrylyuk, placed eighth, but was disqualified for wearing the logo of a shoe manufacturer on the front of her headband.

## 2 × 10-KILOMETER COMBINED PURSUIT

This event will be held for the first time in 1992.

## 4 × 5-KILOMETER RELAY

In 1988 this was a freestyle event, but in 1992 two skiers will use the classical technique and two will skate.

**1924–1952** not held

**1956 Cortina** T: 10, N: 10, D: 2.1.
*3 × 5-Kilometer*

| | | | |
|---|---|---|---|
| 1. | FIN | (Sirkka Polkunen, Mirja Hietamies, Siira Rantanen) | 1:09:01.0 |
| 2. | SOV | (Lyubov Kozyreva, Alevtina Kolchina, Radya Eroshina) | 1:09:28.0 |
| 3. | SWE | (Irma Johansson, Anna Lisa Eriksson, Sonja Edström) | 1:09:48.0 |
| 4. | NOR | (Kjelltrig Brusveen, Gina Regland, Rakel Wahl) | 1:10:50.0 |
| 5. | POL | (Maria Gąsienica-Bukowa, Józefa Pęksa, Zofia Krzeptowska) | 1:13:20.0 |
| 6. | CZE | (Eva Benešová, Libuse Patocková, Eva Lauermanová) | 1:14:19.0 |
| 7. | GDR/ GER | (Elfriede Uhlig, Else Ammann, Sonnhilde Hausschild) | 1:15:33.0 |
| 8. | ITA | (Fides Romanin, Rita Bottero, Ildegarda Taffra) | 1:16:11.0 |

Rantanen of Finland took off six seconds behind Eroshina, passed her, lost the lead, then passed her again to win by 100 yards.

**1960 Squaw Valley** T: 5, N: 5, D: 2.26.
*3 × 5-Kilometer*

| | | | |
|---|---|---|---|
| 1. | SWE | (Irma Johansson, Britt Strandberg, Sonja Ruthström [Edström]) | 1:04:21.4 |
| 2. | SOV | (Radya Eroshina, Maria Gusakova, Lyubov Baranova [Kozyreva]) | 1:05:02.6 |
| 3. | FIN | (Siira Rantanen, Eeva Ruoppa, Toini Pöysti) | 1:06:27.5 |
| 4. | POL | (Stefania Biegun, Helena Gąsienica-Daniel, Józefa Pęksa-Czerniawska) | 1:07:24.6 |
| 5. | GDR/ GER | (Rita Czech-Blasl, Renate Borges, Sonnhilde Kallus [Hausschild]) | 1:09:25.7 |

On the first leg, Radya Eroshina fell and broke one of her skis. She picked up a replacement, but lost over a minute, a delay which cost the U.S.S.R. the gold medal. The Soviets lodged a protest, claiming that Irma Johansson of Sweden had cut in front of Eroshina and caused her to fall. After viewing films of the race, the U.S.S.R. withdrew their protest.

**1964 Innsbruck-Seefeld** T: 8, N: 8, D: 2.7.
**3 × 5-Kilometer**
1. SOV (Alevtina Kolchina, Eudokia Mekshilo, Clau- 59:20.2
   dia Boyarskikh)
2. SWE (Barbro Martinsson, Brit Strandberg, Toini 1:01:27.0
   Gustafsson)
3. FIN (Senja Pusula, Toini Pöysti, Mirja Lehtonen) 1:02:45.1
4. GER (Christine Nestler, Rita Czech-Blasl, Renate 1:04:29.9
   Dannhauser)
5. BUL (Rosa Dimova, Nadezhda Vasileva, 1:06:40.4
   Krastana Stoeva)
6. CZE (Jarmila Skodová, Eva Brizová, Eva Pau- 1:08.42.8
   lusová)
7. POL (Teresa Trzebunia, Czeslawa Stopka, Ste- 1:08.55.4
   fania Biegun)
8. HUN (Éva Blazs, Mária Tarnai, Ference Hemrik) 1:10:16.3

**1968 Grenoble-Autrans** T: 8, N: 8, D: 2.16.
**3 × 5-Kilometer**
1. NOR (Inger Aufles, Babben Damon-Enger, Berit 57:30.0
   Mördre)
2. SWE (Britt Strandberg, Toini Gustafsson, Barbro 57:51.0
   Martinsson)
3. SOV (Alevtina Kolchina, Rita Achkina, Galina 58:13.6
   Kulakova)
4. FIN (Senja Pusula, Marjatta Olkkonen, Marjatta 58:45.1
   Kajosmaa)
5. POL (Weronika Budny, Józefa Pęksa- 59:04.7
   Czerniawska, Stefania Biegun)
6. GDR (Renate Köhler, Gudrun Schmidt, Christine 59:33.9
   Nestler)
7. GER (Michaela Endler, Barbara Barthel, Monika 1:01:49.3
   Mrklas)
8. BUL (Pandeva Velitska, Nadezhda Vasileva, 1:05:35.7
   Szvetana Sotirova)

**1972 Sapporo-Makomanai** T: 11, N: 11, D: 2.12.
**3 × 5-Kilometer**
1. SOV (Lyubov Moukhatcheva, Alevtina Olunina, 48:46.15
   Galina Kulakova)
2. FIN (Helena Takalo, Hilkka Kuntola, Marjatta 49:19.37
   Kajosmaa)
3. NOR (Inger Aufles, Aslaug Dahl, Berit Mördre- 49:51.49
   Lammedal)
4. GER (Monika Mrklas, Ingrid Rothfuss, Michaela 50:25.61
   Endler)
5. GDR (Gabriele Haupt, Renate Fischer, Anni 50:28.45
   Unger)
6. CZE (Alena Bartušová, Helena Šikolová, Milena 51:16.16
   Cillerová)
7. POL (Anna Duraj, Józefa Chromik, Weronika 51:49.13
   Budny)
8. SWE (Meeri Bodelid, Eva Ohlsson, Birgitta 51:51.84
   Lindqvist)

**1976 Innsbruck-Seefeld** T: 9, N: 9, D: 2.12.
1. SOV (Nina Baldycheva, Zinaida Amosova, Raisa 1:07:49.75
   Smetanina, Galina Kulakova)

2. FIN (Liisa Suihkonen, Marjatta Kajosmaa, Hilkka 1:08:36.57
   Kuntola, Helena Takalo)
3. GDR (Monika Debertshäuser, Sigrun Krause, Bar- 1:09:57.95
   bara Petzold, Veronika Schmidt)
4. SWE (Lena Carlzon, Görel Partapuoli, Marie Jo- 1:10:14.68
   hansson, Eva Olsson)
5. NOR (Berit Kvello, Marit Myrmael, Berit Jo- 1:11:09.08
   hannessen, Grete Kummen)
6. CZE (Hana Pasiárová, Gabriela Sekajová, Alena 1:11:27.83
   Bartošová, Blanka Paulů)
7. CAN (Shirley Firth, Joan Groothuysen, Susan 1:14:02.72
   Holloway, Sharon Firth)
8. POL (Anna Pawlusiak, Anna Gębala-Duraj, Maria 1:14:13.40
   Trebunia, Wladyslawa Majerczyk)

**1980 Lake Placid** T: 8, N: 8, D: 2.21.
1. GDR (Marlies Rostock, Carola Anding, Veronika 1:02:11.10
   Hesse [Schmidt], Barbara Petzold)
2. SOV (Nina Baldycheva, Nina Rocheva, Galina 1:03:18.30
   Kulakova, Raisa Smetanina)
3. NOR (Brit Pettersen, Anette Böe, Marit Myrmael, 1:04:13.50
   Berit Aunli [Kvello])
4. CZE (Dagmar Palecková, Gabriela Svobodová, 1:04:31.39
   Blanka Paulů, Květoslava Jeriová)
5. FIN (Marja Auroma, Marja-Liisa Hämäläinen, He- 1:04:41.28
   lena Takalo, Hilkka Riihivuori [Kuntola])
6. SWE (Lillemor Marie Johansson, Karin Lamberg, 1:05:16.32
   Eva Olsson, Lena Carlzon-Lundbäck)
7. USA (Alison Owen-Spencer, Beth Paxson, Leslie 1:06:55.41
   Bancroft, Margaret Spencer)
8. CAN (Angela Schmidt, Shirley Firth, Esther Miller, 1:07:45.75
   Joan Groothuysen)

The U.S.S.R.'s second-place finish gave Kulakova her
eighth Olympic medal—four gold, two silver, and two
bronze. Smetanina brought her total to five—three gold
and two silver.

**1984 Sarajevo** T: 12, N: 12, D: 2.15.
1. NOR (Inger Helene Nybråten, Anne Jahren, Brit 1:06:49.7
   Pettersen, Berit Aunli [Kvello])
2. CZE (Dagmar Švubová, Blanka Paulů, Gabriela 1:07:34.7
   Svobodová, Kvetoslava Jeriová)
3. FIN (Pirkko Määttä, Eija Hyytiäinen, Marjo 1:07:36.7
   Matikainen, Marja-Liisa Hämäläinen)
4. SOV (Julia Stepanova, Lyubov Liadova, 1:07:55.0
   Nadezhda Bourlakova, Raisa Smetanina)
5. SWE (Karin Lamberg, Doris Hugosson, Lillemor 1:09:30.0
   Marie Risby [Johansson], Ann Rosendahl)
6. SWI (Karin Thomas, Monika Germann, Christine 1:09:40.3
   Brügger, Evi Kratzer)
7. USA (Susan Long, Judy Rabinowitz, Lynn 1:10:48.4
   Spencer-Galanes, Patricia Ross)
8. GDR (Petra Voge, Petra Rohrmann, Carola 1:11:10.7
   Anding, Ute Noack)

The fastest time of the race, 16:12.6, was recorded by
Květa Jeriová who actually overcame triple gold-
medalist Marja-Liisa Hämäläinen on the anchor leg to
win the silver medal for Czechoslovakia.

**1988 Calgary-Canmore** T: 12, N: 12, D: 2.21.

1. SOV (Svetlana Nageikina, Nina Gavrylyuk, Tamara Tikhonova, Anfisa Reztsova) — 59:51.1

2. NOR (Trude Dybendahl, Marit Wold, Anne Jahren, Marianne Dahlmo) — 1:01:33.0

3. FIN (Pirkko Määttä, Marja-Liisa Kirvesniemi [Hämäläinen], Marjo Matikainen, Jaana Savolainen) — 1:01:53.8

4. SWI (Karin Thomas, Sandra Parpan, Evi Kratzer, Christina Gilli-Brügger) — 1:01:59.4

5. GDR (Kerstin Moring, Simone Opitz, Silke Braun, Simone Greiner-Petter) — 1:02.19.9

6. SWE (Lis Frost, Anna-Lena Fritzon, Karin Lamberg-Skog, Marie-Helene Westin) — 1:02:24.9

7. CZE (Lubomira Balazova, Viera Klimková, Ivana Radlova, Alžběta Havrančiková) — 1:03:37.1

8. USA (Dorcas Denhartog, Leslie Thompson, Nancy Fiddler, Leslie Krichko) — 1:04:08.8

In a move almost without precedent, the Sunday night television news in the U.S.S.R. was delayed two minutes to allow the broadcast of the end of this race.